CHILTON'S AUTO REPAIR MANUAL 1954-1963

...artment

...OMPANY

...ia

Copyri...   ...71   All Rights Reserved
Publish...   Ontario, Canada, by Thomas Nelson & Sons, Ltd.
ISBN 0...   Manufactured in the United States of America

TROUBLE CHECKS

Trouble Checks is an accumulation of test hints most useful to mechanics in car trouble-shooting. It is designed as a reminder of the most logical and frequent causes of trouble within the area being tested. The list is practical and has been gathered from years of mechanical experience. It is compiled by Chilton editors as a prompter and refresher for the mechanic with a problem.

BRAKES, HYDRAULIC ✓

POOR OR NO PEDAL

1. Worn or separated lining.
2. Broken shoe.
3. Leak or break in hydraulic lines.
4. Open residual pressure valve in master cylinder.
5. Leak in master cylinder.
6. Leak in wheel cylinder.
7. Air in system. (Indication of fluid loss).

Note: On some designs, (parking brake on rear wheels) air may enter the system via sluggish acting rear wheel cylinders or because there is no residual pressure in the system, if the parking brake is applied suddenly.

DRAGGING BRAKES

1. Shoes adjusted to high or binding.
2. Master cylinder relief port closed.
   A. No play in master cylinder push rod.
   B. Mineral oil in system swelling master cup.
   C. Master cylinder piston not returning all the way.

HARD PEDAL

1. Lining condition.
2. Eccentric shoe-to-drum relationship causing low lining contact area.
3. Brakes dragging, overheating.

SOFT OR SPONGY PEDAL

1. Air in the hydraulic system.
   A. Leaky wheel cylinders or lines.
   B. Incorrect type fluid (low boiling point).
2. Master cylinder primary cup leaking.
3. Poor lining to drum contact.
   A. Shoes not concentric with drum.
4. Drums that have been turned too thin permitting expansion under heat and pressure.

GRABBING AND UNEVEN

1. Foreign substance, (brake fluid, grease, oil, water, dust, etc.) on lining surface.
2. Obstructions, one or more, in brake lines.
3. Linings of different friction values being used on opposite wheels.
4. Lining length different on opposite wheels.
5. Loose or detached lining.
6. Gummy or stuck wheel cylinders.
7. Eccentric shoe-to-drum relationship on one or more wheels.
8. Worn or poorly adjusted wheel bearings.
9. Wheel cylinders of different diameters on opposite wheels.
10. Misaligned, warped or sticking shoe.
11. Incorrect wheel alignment.
12. Out of round drum.
13. Bent spindle.
14. Bent backing plate.

SQUEAL, GRUNT, CHATTER

1. Old, burnt or hardened and glazed lining.
2. Lining loose on shoes.
3. Lining not concentric with drum.
4. Drum out-of-round or bell-mouthed.
5. Shoe mounting loose at pivot or retaining points.
6. Wheel cylinder loose.
7. Loose or worn front suspension parts.
8. Wheel bearings worn or loose.
9. Backing plate loose.
10. Drum dampening spring weak or missing.
11. Hub-to-drum attachment loose.

SNAPPING OR CLICKING NOISE

1. Loose backing plates.
2. Shoes binding on pins or backing plates.
3. Loose or worn front suspension.
4. Cracked brake drum.
5. Tool marks left in a newly turned drum.

BRAKES, POWER ✓

To isolate trouble in the brake system of any power brake equipped car, it is necesary to determine whether the conventional system or the vacuum system is at fault.

It is obvious that some brake troubles such as, pulling to one side, brake squeal and chatter are elements of friction and unrelated to power assist; where-as application, release, hard pedal, etc. could be caused by the power brake mechanism.

VACUUM SYSTEM CHECK
Hard Pedal

With engine off, apply the service brakes enough times to completely exhaust the vacuum brake reserve tank. Then slightly depress the brake pedal while starting the engine. If the vacuum system is in good working order, the pedal will tend to apply itself. If the pedal does not tend to apply itself, check the vacuum supply at various points along the system from intake manifold to power brake cylinder. It requires 17-20 inches of vacuum to properly operate the power brake assist.

Check Valve Test

With engine off, wait about five minutes, then apply the brakes; there should be enough vacuum left in reserve to assist in three or four brake applications. If not, check for vacuum leaks and replace vacuum check valve.

Brake Drag Test

With both front wheels off the ground, check for free turning wheels. Then have someone spin the wheels and immediately start the engine, (with idle throttle and no pressure on the brake pedal). After the wheels stop turning, check for brake drag. If a drag is present now, with the engine running but not before the engine was started, rebuild or renew the power brake cylinder assembly.

TROUBLE CHECKS

Brake Fluid Loss with No Apparent Leak

Disconnect vacuum line from manifold to power brake cylinder, at the cylinder. Check for fluid dampness in this tube. If fluid is being drawn into the vacuum tube and is being burnt in the engine cylinders, the leak will not show up in the hydraulic system, the power brake cylinder must be rebuilt or replaced. Depending upon the degree of leak, the engine may have rough idle, it may smoke and in severe cases, may even smell like a castor oil lubricated race car.

SEVERE (TOUCHY) BRAKES

1. Reaction diaphragm leaking.
2. Sticky slide valve action.
3. Restricted or blocked atmospheric vent in vacuum piston assembly.
4. Rubber seals in power brake cylinder sticking.
5. Pedal linkage binding.

SLOW OR NO PEDAL RETURN

1. Binding pedal linkage.
2. Compensator port in power cylinder blocked.
3. Excessive seal friction in power cylinder.
4. Piston stroke interference in power cylinder.

5. Faulty residual check valve.
6. Sticky slide valve in power cylinder.
7. Broken power piston return spring.
8. Dry or damaged leather piston packing seal.

PEDAL VIBRATES (ON BELLOWS TYPE UNIT)

1. Free play incorrectly adjusted.
2. Power brake trigger out of adjustment or bent.
3. Master cylinder push rod out of adjustment.
4. Trigger damaged or bent.
5. Binding inside power cylinder unit.

CLUTCH ✓

SLIPPING

1. Worn or burnt clutch facings.
2. Facings saturated with oil.
3. Weak or broken pressure plate springs.
4. Pressure plate inproperly adjusted.
5. Binding of clutch release levers.
6. Release bearing binding on sleeve.
7. Binding of clutch hub on splined shaft.
8. Poor linkage adjustment (no pedal free play).

GRAB OR CHATTER

1. Worn or burnt clutch facings. mounts.
2. Glazed or oily clutch facings.
3. Warped or broken driven plate.
4. Loose hub springs or rivets.
5. Flattened facing cushion springs.
6. Warped or broken pressure plate.
7. Misalignment of clutch with flywheel and crankshaft.

DRAG, GEAR CLASH

1. Poor linkage adjustment—too much pedal free play.
2. Warped or bent driven plate.
3. Broken clutch facings.
4. Clutch shaft bent or out of true.
5. Gummy clutch facings.
6. Hub binds on splined shaft.
7. Pressure plate warped or levers out of adjustment.
8. Broken or loose engine mounts.
9. Release fork pivot or linkage worn.

10. Loose clutch housing-to-engine bolts.
11. Misalignment of clutch with flywheel and crankshaft.
12. Transmission oil incorrect or low level.

CLUTCH NOISES

Aside from linkage and spring noises, so called clutch noise is usually of a bearing nature and may not originate in the clutch itself. However, the following conditions are relative to the clutch or immediate vicinity.

Release Bearing

If the release bearing is at fault, the noise will occur at any time the bearing is active. This means that, (clutch linkage being correctly adjusted) the bearing noise will only be heard while the pedal is depressed far enough to cause release bearing-to-clutch finger contact. The sound, depending upon degree of failure, may run from a shrill screech to a grinding and scraping noise.

Pilot Bearing

The clutch shaft pilot bearing is

active, (as a rotating bearing) only while the crankshaft and clutch shaft are turning at different speeds or in opposite directions. Full clutch release is usually required to start the noise which is a high pitched squeal.

Clutch Shaft Rear Bearing (Front Trans. Bearing)

This bearing is active whenever the engine is running with the clutch engaged, (in or out of gear). The noise is more apparent in low and intermediate gear than in neutral or direct gear.

Miscellaneous Noises

1. Clutch jazz or rumble: caused by poor torque dampening at hub of driven clutch plate.
2. Rattle or jazz. Apparent during application and release: caused by worn or broken parts in either pressure plate assembly or driven plate; may also be worn splines on the clutch shaft.
3. Thumping noise when idleing: loose flywheel or crankshaft pulley. If the noise leaves when the clutch is released, the pressure, or cover plate may be loosely mounted to the flywheel. The crankshaft may even have excessive end play.

ELECTRICAL SYSTEM ✓

BATTERY NEEDS RECHARGING

The basic cause for a battery needing frequent charging is either a bad battery, it has too much work to do or is receiving insufficient charge from the electrical generating system. Battery tests are covered in the Unit Repair Section under "Engine Diagnosis, Professional Approach."

D.C. GENERATOR

Not Charging
1. Broken or loose fan belt.

2. Voltage regulator not working.
3. Open or short in charging circuit.
4. Brushes stuck, worn or oil coated.
5. Commutator worn or dirty.
6. Commutator mica high, needs undercutting.
7. Commutator shorted.
8. Solder melted and thrown from commutator segment connections.

TROUBLE CHECKS

9. Bad front or rear armature bearing.
10. Open or shorted field circuit.

Generator Noise
1. Drive belt glazed or partially broken.
2. Generator loosely mounted.
3. Broken or bent generator, fan or crankshaft pulley.
4. End plates loose or broken.
5. Generator fan rubbing the end plate.
6. Bent armature shaft.
7. Rough or dry bearings.
8. Armature rubbing the fields.
9. Armature out of round or rough.
10. Mica needs undercutting.
11. Brushes glazed or cocked.
12. Too much brush tension.

High Resistance in Charging Circuit

This is usually caused by loose or dirty connections, breaks in wiring or undersized wiring. Depending upon the part of the system in which high resistance occurs, the battery will receive insufficient charge or too much charge, high voltage, flaring and burnt out lamps, burned ignition points, etc.

If high resistance is present between the battery and regulator, the regulator maintains a constant voltage but the resistance reduces the current available to charge the battery. In this situation, the battery would be constantly undercharged.

Another area that is frequently at fault is that portion of the circuit that lies between the regulator base and the generator body. Approximately one ohm resistance in this part of the circuit will prevent the voltage regulator from working. This will cause the generator to produce uncontrolled charging. The result will probably be an overcharged bat-

tery, head light flare and burnt out electrical parts and accessories.

Excessive resistance can be quickly found by making a voltage drop test with a voltmeter, across the various parts of a circuit.

AC GENERATOR—ALTERNATOR

Low or No Charging
1. Blown fuse.
2. Broken or loose fan belt.
3. Voltage regulator not working.
4. Brushes sticking.
5. Slip ring dirty.
6. Open circuit.
7. Bad wiring connections.
8. Bad diode rectifier.
9. High resistance in charging circuit.
10. Voltage regulator needs adjusting.
11. Grounded stator.
12. May be open rectifiers (check all three phases).
13. If rectifiers are found blown or open, check capacitor.

Note: See "Alternating Current Generators", in the Unit Repair Section.

Noisy Unit
1. Damaged rotor bearings.
2. Poor alignment of unit.
3. Broken or loose belt.
4. Open diode rectifiers.

Regulator Points Burnt or Stuck
1. Regulator set too high.
2. Poor ground connections.
3. Shorted generator field.
4. Regulator air gap incorrect.

STARTER

Starter Won't Crank the Engine
1. Dead battery.
2. Open starter circuit, such as:
    A. Broken or loose battery cables.
    B. Inoperative starter motor solenoid.

C. Broken or loose wire from starter switch to solenoid.
    D. Poor solenoid or starter ground.
    E. Bad starter switch, (ignition, dash button or carburetor).
3. Defective starter internal circuit, such as:
    A. Dirty or burnt commutator.
    B. Stuck, worn or broken brushes.
    C. Open or shorted armature.
    D. Open or grounded fields.
4. Starter motor mechanical faults, such as:
    A. Jammed armature end bearings.
    B. Bad bearing allowing armature to rub fields.
    C. Bent shaft.
    D. Broken starter housing.
    E. Bad starter worm or drive mechanism.
    F. Bad starter drive or flywheel driven gear.
5. Engine hard or impossible to crank, such as:
    A. Hydrostatic lock, water in combustion chamber.
    B. Crankshaft seizing in bearings.
    C. Piston or ring seizing.
    D. Bent or broken connecting rod.
    E. Seizing of connecting rod bearing.
    F. Flywheel jammed or broken.
    G. In some remote cases, an incondescent particle in the combustion chamber of a hot engine will prevent starting. This condition acts like a low battery or ignition timing so far ahead that the engine kicks back; the piston refuses to pass over top center. A two or three minute wait is generally enough to cool the troubled spot and temporarily clear the fault.

Starter Spins Free, Won't Engage
1. Gummy or broken drive mechanism.

ENGINE COOLING SYSTEM—LIQUID ✔

The cooling system is a very critical area and one that is usually neglected until trouble arises. Trouble that originates in a faulty cooling system may manifest itself in many apparently unrelated ways. Poor gas mileage and early piston ring failure due to sludge is one example of too low engine operating temperature. Detonation, poor performance and complete engine failure may be the result of the other extreme; an overly hot engine. The important thing is to maintain an engine temperature peculiar to the manufacturer's intentions and design.

The following are some causes of abnormal temperatures:

ENGINE TEMPERATURE, TOO HIGH
1. Not enough coolant.
2. Loose or broken fan belt.
3. Clogged radiator.
4. Pugged or collapsed hoses, (check the bottom hose for collapse at high engine rpm.).
5. Fuel of improper grade.
6. Insufficient lubrication.
7. Poor or no water pump circulation.
8. Engine operating under abnormal load conditions.

9. Insufficient air circulation.
10. Rusted out water distributer tube; will cause hot spots and uneven engine cooling.

ENGINE TEMPERATURE—TOO LOW—SLOW WARM-UP
1. Thermostat holding open.
2. Manifold heat control valve stock open.
3. Temperature indicator or sending unit inoperative or out of calibration.

Note: All engines that indicate low temperature should have the engine coolant checked with a shop thermometer (while the engine is running) to verify the accuracy of the heat indicator.

TROUBLE CHECKS ✓✓

ENGINE ✓

Engine trouble can be separated into four general groups:
1. Won't start
2. Performs poorly
3. Improper lubrication
4. Noisy

WON'T START

Assuming the engine will crank, there are four reasons why an engine won't start. This group can be divided four ways:
1. **The combustion chamber is not receiving adequate spark.**
2. **The proper fuel-air mixture is not reaching the cylinders.**
3. **Poor compression.**
4. **Timing is incorrect.**

Some of the above reasons overlap in scope, however, a thorough probe into all four factors should uncover the specific fault.

Weak or No Spark To Combustion Chambers

1. Burnt or poorly gapped distributer points.
2. Short or open condenser.
3. Short or open coil.
4. Poor primary circuit from ignition switch to points in distributer.
5. Neutral safety switch bad or out of adjustment.
6. Low or dead battery.
7. On overdrive equipped cars, bad kick-down switch.
8. High starter draw.
9. Defective ignition switch.
10. High resistance anywhere in primary or secondary ignition circuit.
11. Moisture and dirt on distributer cap, ignition wires and plug porcelains.
12. Cracked distributer cap.
13. Broken rotor.
14. Reversed coil polarity.

Improper Fuel—Air Mixture To Cylinders

1. Fuel tank empty or line to fuel pump blocked or open. Many car fuel pumps are now equipped with a replaceable filter in the tank.
2. Fuel tank not vented to atmosphere.
3. Weak or completely bad fuel pump. (Make fuel pump volume and pressure test.)
4. Fuel stoppage at carburetor filter or float level valve.
5. Leaking carburetor float.
6. Poorly adjusted float level.
7. Air, (vacuum) leak at carburetor or intake manifold, (beware of faulty double action fuel pumps and vacuum operated accessories.

8. Poor compression, (low vacuum reading).
9. Inferior fuel.
10. Obstructed or dirty carburetor air cleaner.
11. Leaky manifold heat riser.
12. Automatic choke stuck or out of adjustment.

    Note: A choke thermostat spring that has fatigued needs replacement, not mere adjustment.
13. Engine valves not seating properly, burnt, sticky or out of adjustment.
14. Hydraulic valve lifter trouble (improper oil pressure, worn or stuck tappets).
15. Camshaft wear or breakage.
16. Valve timing incorrect.
17. Manifold heat control valve not working.
18. Vapor lock, under certain conditions.
19. Low engine operating temperature (below 170° F).
20. High engine operating temperature (above 190° F).

Poor Compression

1. Poorly seating exhaust or intake valves.
2. Worn or sludged-up rings.
3. Blown head gasket.
4. Valve timing incorrect.
5. Cracked or broken piston.
6. Beware of short connecting rods in cars equipped with dual engine options. However remote, it is mechanically possible to install the connecting rods of the shorter stroked engine into the bores and onto the crankshaft of the higher displacement engine. This error will shorten the piston stroke and result in low compression.

Timing Incorrect

1. Poorly gapped distributor points.
2. Distributer static timing incorrect.
3. Distributer governor advance, faulty.
4. Distributer, vacuum control, defective.
5. Distribution of secondary current to spark plugs, out of firing sequence.
6. Ignition timing not coincident with cylinder timing.
7. Valve timing incorrect.

PERFORMS POORLY

The purpose of this manual is to point out, in concise form, the best and quickest return route to factory performance standards. Special performance coverage is not possible here. The subject becoming controversial and too involved for general coverage.

1. Distributer trouble, points, condenser, timing, etc.
2. Weak coil.
3. Bad or incorrect spark plugs or wiring.
4. Carburetor out of adjustment or broken.
5. Leaky intake manifold or carburetor gasket.
6. Leaky vacuum operated units or accessories.
8. Poor fuel—compression ratio—timing balance.
9. Faulty fuel supply.
10. Poor compression, valves, rings, gasket, etc.
11. Exhaust back pressure—clogged muffler or tail pipe.
12. Clogged air filter or inlet.
13. Cooling system failure.
14. Leaky heat riser or stuck heat control valve.
15. Poor understanding as factory accepted standard.

IMPROPER LUBRICATION

1. Low oil level.
2. Very high oil level, (causing foaming).
3. Clogged oil pump screen.
4. Oil pump sucking air, loose pump mount inside crankcase.
5. Dirty oil.
6. Clogged or saturated oil filter.
7. Oil contamination, (such as water, acid, gum, abrasives, antifreeze, etc.
8. Improper viscosity or quality of oil.
9. By-pass valve stuck.

Note: All name brand oils are good and engine manufacturers recommendations should be followed. However, extreme service exposure may alter engine requirements, viz. More frequent oil changes, heavy duty oil, use of detergents, etc.

NOISE

As long as combustion and reciprocating engines are used to furnish power, a certain degree of noise will be present. The best we can do is maintain the noise level as established by the manufacturer as standard.

To catalogue all the causes of noise would require coverage larger than

one volume will permit. We therefore will limit our list to mechanical causes most common to the automotive gasoline engine.

1. **Valve Noise.**
   A. Sticky valves.
   B. Stuck hydraulic tappets.
   C. Dry hydraulic tappets.
   D. Bent valve stem.
   E. Warped valve head.
   F. Broken valve spring.
   G. Tappet out of adjustment.
   H. Rocker lever loose.
   I. Push rod bent or worn.
   J. Rocker shaft worn or loose.
   K. Valve or tappet guide worn.
2. **Piston Noise.**
   A. Collapsed or broken piston.
   B. Scored piston or cylinder wall.
   C. Broken piston rings.

F. Crankshaft end play, (noticeable when actuating clutch).
G. Crankshaft misalignment.

4. **Detonation.**
   Detonation is a spontaneous combustion within the cylinder. It
   D. Carbon on piston and cylinder head making physical contact.
   E. Top cylinder ridge striking top piston ring.
   F. Loose or broken piston pin.
3. **Crankshaft Bearing Noise.**
   A. Loose connecting rod bearing.
   B. Loose main bearing.
   C. Bent connecting rod, (sounds like bearing).
   D. Loose flywheel or converter, (sounds like bearing).
   E. Loose crankshaft damper or pulley, (sounds like bearing).

is caused by an imbalance of compression ratio, heat, fuel value, and timing. Detonation can be annoying, wasteful and very destructive to engine parts.

The following factors or combinations there-of should be checked as contributing elements.

A. Cooling system temperature.
B. Spark plug appearance.
C. Ignition timing index.
D. Fuel octane rating.
E. Incandescence within the combustion area caused by carbon particles, sharp edges, burnt spark plugs, etc.
F. Lean carburetor mixture.
G. Stuck manifold heat control valve.

FUEL SYSTEM ✓

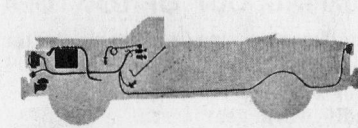

Because air is about a 15:1 factor in the gasoline-to-air importance ratio, it certainly justifies inclusion in fuel system checks.

LEAN MIXTURE OR NO GASOLINE

1. Accelerator discharge into the carburetor throat.
2. Pump discharge into the carburetor bowl.
3. Fuel filter at carburetor.
4. Fuel pump pressure, volume and vacuum gauge reading.
5. Condition of gas tank-to-pump line.

6. Freedom of stand pipe or tank filter.
7. Condition of tank (sludge, scale, etc.).
8. Tank adequately ventilated.
9. Dirt in carburetor.
10. Carburetor jet too small.
11. Carburetor metering rod too large.
12. Air leak at carburetor.
13. Air leak at intake manifold.

14. Low float adjustment.

RICH MIXTURE OR FLOODING

1. Loaded float.
2. Float level too high.
3. Vapor lock.
4. Air cleaner blocked.
5. Carburetor discharge jet too large.
6. Metering rod too small.
7. Choke sticking in closed position.
8. Carburetor needle valve not seating.
9. Fuel pump pressure too high.
10. Anti-perculator valve clogged.

INSTRUMENTS ✓

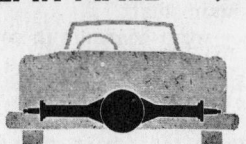

The testing of instruments entails the use of common sense and a system of elimination. The most reliable method of testing is by comparison of doubtful units with known serviceable units of the same type.

REAR AXLE ✓

See "Rear Axle" coverage in the "Unit Repair Section" of the manual.

AUTOMATIC TRANSMISSION ✓

For "Test Procedures," and other detailed information see Unit Repair Section, Transmission Group of the manual.

TROUBLE CHECKS ✔✔

STEERING AND GEOMETRY ✔

MANUAL STEERING ADJUSTMENT

1. Not adjusted to high spot.
2. Worn or bent steering linkage.
3. Worn worm bearings.
4. Worn sector shaft bearings.
5. Chipped worm or sector gear tooth surface. This can happen from the sudden impact of collision or a bad road bump. To find this condition, adjust the high spot adjustment too tight, then feel steering gear for roughness by turning steering wheel thru the entire turning radius. **Don't forget to return high spot adjustment to normal.**
6. Tire pressure to be equal and correct.
7. Wheel bearings and front suspension correct.

POWER STEERING ADJUSTMENT

See "Power Steering" in the "Unit Repair Section" of the manual.

GEOMETRY

See "Wheel Alignment" and "Suspension, Front Align" in the "Unit Repair Section" of the manual.

STANDARD TRANSMISSION ✔

JUMPING OUT OF HIGH GEAR

Misalignment of transmission case or clutch housing.
Worn pilot bearing in crankshaft.
Bent transmission shaft.
Worn high speed sliding gear.
Worn teeth in clutch shaft.
Insufficient spring tension on shifter rail plunger.
Bent or loose shifter fork.
End play in clutch shaft.
Gears not engaging completely.
Loose or worn bearings on clutch shaft or main shaft.

STICKING IN HIGH GEAR

Clutch not releasing fully.
Burred or battered teeth on clutch shaft.
Burred or battered transmission main shaft.
Frozen synchronizing clutch.
Stuck shifter rail plunger.
Gear shift lever twisting and binding shifter rail.
Battered teeth on high speed sliding gear or on sleeve.
Lack of lubrication.
Improper lubrication.
Corroded transmission parts.
Defective main shaft pilot bearing.

JUMPING OUT OF SECOND GEAR

Insufficient spring tension on shifter rail plunger.
Bent or loose shifter fork.
Gears not engaging completely.
End play in transmission main shaft.
Loose transmission gear bearing.
Defective main shaft pilot bearing.
Bent transmission shaft.
Worn teeth on second speed sliding gear or sleeve.
Loose or worn bearings on transmission main shaft.
End play in countershaft.

STICKING IN SECOND GEAR

Clutch not releasing fully.
Burred or battered teeth on sliding sleeve.
Burred or battered transmission main shaft.
Frozen synchronizing clutch.
Stuck shifter rail plunger.
Gear shift lever twisting and binding shifter rail.
Lack of lubrication.
Improper lubrication.
Corroded transmission parts.
Second speed transmission gear bearings locked will give same effect as gears stuck in second.

JUMPING OUT OF LOW GEAR

Insufficient spring tension on shifter rail plunger.
Bent or loose shifter fork.
Badly worn gear teeth.
Gears not engaging completely.
End play in transmission main shaft.
End play in countershaft.
Loose or worn bearings on transmission main shaft.
Loose or worn bearings in counter shaft.
Defective main shaft pilot bearing.

STICKING IN LOW GEAR

Clutch not releasing fully.
Burred or battered transmission main shaft.
Stuck shifter rail plunger.
Gear shift lever twisting and binding shifter rail.
Lack of lubrication.
Improper lubrication.
Corroded transmission parts.

JUMPING OUT OF REVERSE GEAR

Insufficient spring tension on shifter rail plunger.
Bent or loose shifter fork.
Badly worn gear teeth.
Gears not engaging completely.
End play in transmission main shaft.
Idler gear bushings loose or worn.
Loose or worn bearings on transmission main shaft.
Defective main shaft pilot bearing.

STICKING IN REVERSE GEAR

Clutch not releasing fully.
Burred or battered transmission main shaft.
Stuck shifter rail plunger.
Gear shift lever twisting and binding shifter rail.
Lack of lubrication.
Improper lubrication.
Corroded transmission parts.

FAILURE OF GEARS TO SYNCHRONIZE

Clutch not releasing fully.
Detent springs weak or broken.
Weak or broken springs under balls in sliding gear sleeve.
Scored or worn cones.
Improper lubrication.
Constant mesh gear not turning freely on transmission main shaft. Will synchronize in that gear only.
Binding pilot bearing in crankshaft.
Binding bearing on clutch shaft.
Binding countershaft.
Binding pilot bearing on mainshaft will synchronize in high gear only.

GEARS SPINNING WHEN SHIFTING INTO GEAR FROM NEUTRAL

Clutch not releasing fully.
Binding pilot bearing in crankshaft.

BUICK INDEX

AIR CONDITIONING
Service 1092

BRAKES, HYDRAULIC
Adjustments 938
Bleed brakes 941
Hand brake, adjust 21
Master cylinder, R & R 20
Master cylinder service 939
Parking brake 21
References 20

BRAKES, POWER
Power unit overhaul 954
Power unit R & R 20
Trouble shooting 954

CLUTCH
Clutch assembly, R & R 34
Clutch pedal, adjust 34

COOLING SYSTEM
Radiator core, R & R 23
Temperature gauge 19
Thermostat 23
Water manifolds 23
Water pump, R & R 23

ELECTRICAL SYSTEM
Battery 17
Chassis 16
Delcotron specifications 12
Distributor, R & R 16
Distributor specifications 12
Engine 16
Fuses and circuit breakers 11
Gauges 1024
Generator regulator
   specifications 12
Generator regulators 1026
Generator, R & R 17
Generator service 1026
Generator trouble shooting ... 1026
Horn buttons 31
Ignition firing order & timing ... 9
Ignition timing procedure 19
Ignition timing specifications ... 9
Instruments 19
Starter, R & R 17
Starter service 1046
Starter specifications 13
Starter systems 17

ENGINE ASSEMBLY
References 23
Cylinder head, R & R 25
Cylinder head nut tightening 12
Engine assembly, R & R 24
Engine diagnosis 1012
Engine firing order & timing 9
Engine lubrication 27
Engine marking code 10
Exhaust manifold, R & R 25
Exhaust system 22
Inlet manifold, R & R 25
Oil filter, R & R 27
Oil pan, R & R 27
Oil pressure specifications 14
Oil pump 27
Piston and rod, assemble 28
Piston specifications 13

ENGINE ASSEMBLY—continued
Quick reference specifications ... 9
Rear main bearing oil seal 28
Rocker arm lubrication 25
Rocker arms & shaft 25
Specifications, general, engine ... 14
Timing case cover & seal 26
Timing chain, R & R 26
Trouble shooting charts 1012
Tune-up procedures 16
Tune up specifications 10
Valve guide, R & R 25
Valve lifters, hydraulic, removal ... 26
Valve specifications 13
Valve clearance specifications ... 13
Valve timing specifications ... 10
Vibration damper, R & R 26

ENGINE LUBRICATION
Oil filter 27
Oil pan, R & R 27
Oil pump, R & R 27

EXHAUST SYSTEM
Exhaust pipe 22
Muffler 22
Tail pipe 22
Manifold 25

FUEL SYSTEM
Carburetors 972
Fuel gauge service 1024
Fuel pump pressure 10
Fuel pump service 1020
Fuel tank, R & R 22
Vacuum pump 22

INSTRUMENTS
Speedminder, R & R 19
Speedometer 19
Ammeter 19
Fuel gauge 19
Temperature gauge 19

RADIO, R & R
References 46

REAR AXLE AND SUSPENSION
Axle assembly, R & R 46
Axle shaft 918
Axle shaft oil seal 918
Coil spring, R & R 46
Pinion bearings 918
Ring gear & pinion 918
Trouble shooting 919

SPECIFICATIONS
Battery 13
Brake cylinder sizes 11
Capacities
   Axle, rear 15
   Cooling system 15
   Crankcase 15
   Fuel tank 15
   Transmission, automatic .. 15
   Transmission, manual 15
Chassis, general 11
Cylinder head tightening 12
Distributor 12
Engine, general 14
Engine tune-up 10

SPECIFICATIONS—continued
Fuses and circuit breakers 11
Generator regulators 12
Light bulbs 11
Main bearings 15
Model identification illustrations ... 8
Model year identification 10
Piston and pins 13
Quick reference specifications ... 9
Rod bearings 15
Starters 13
Torque wrench 14
Valves 13
Wheel alignment 15

STEERING, MECHANICAL
Adjust gear housing 1052
Gear assembly, R & R 32
Horn button, R & R 31
Steering wheel, R & R 31

STEERING, POWER
Power steering & pump 33
Pump assembly 1058
Unit overhaul 1058

SUSPENSION, FRONT
Alignment procedures 1082
Alignment specifications 15
Ball joints, R & R 30
Idler arm, R & R 33
King pins and bushings 1087
Knuckle supports 1087
Shock absorbers 1087
Support arms 1087
Suspension references 29

TORQUE TUBE
R & R Tube & Shatt 42

TRANSMISSION, AUTOMATIC
Dyna Flow—1954 706
   Linkage adjust 38
   R & R 39
Dyna Flow—1955-63 706
   Linkage adjust 41
   R & R 42
Triple turbine 722
   Linkage adjust 40
   R & R 40
References 38

TRANSMISSION, MANUAL SHIFT
References 35
Disassemble transmission 38
Shift control adjustments 35
Transmission, R & R 36

TROUBLE CHECKS
Procedures 1

TUNE-UP
Procedures 16
Specifications 10
Engine diagnosis 1012

UNIVERSAL JOINT AND DRIVE SHAFT
Disassemble U joint 43
U joint & drive shaft, R & R ... 44

BUICK

YEAR IDENTIFICATION

1954

1955

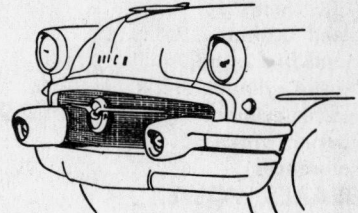

1956

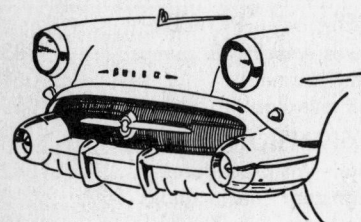

1957

1958

1959

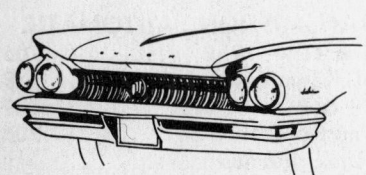

1960

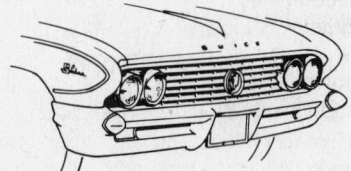

1961

1962

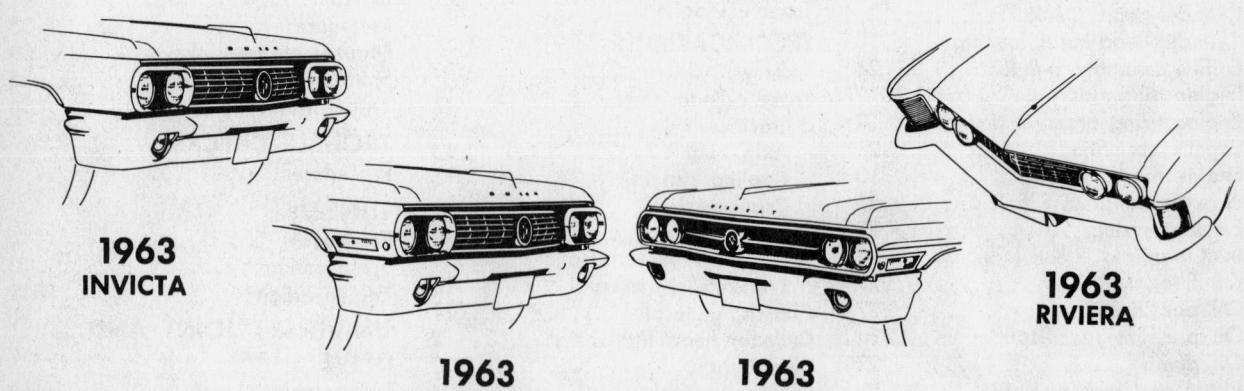

1963
INVICTA

1963
ELECTRA

1963
WILDCAT

1963
RIVIERA

QUICK WORKING SPECIFICATIONS

DISTRIBUTOR
Breaker Point Gap (In.)
1954-63 .... .015
Cam Angle (Degrees)
1954-56, all 29½
1957-63, all 30

SPARK PLUGS

Year	Type	Gap Inches
1954-55, all	44S	.032
1956-58, all	44	.032
1959-63, all	44S	.035

IGNITION TIMING
(Spark occurs before T.C.)
1954-58, all ....5 degrees
1959-63, Synchromesh ......5 degrees
1959-63, Auto trans. ....12 degrees

GENERATOR AND REGULATOR SPECIFICATIONS

YEAR AND SERIES	GENERATOR Field Current In Amperes 12 Volt	REGULATOR Cut-out Closing Voltage	Current Regulator Setting	Voltage Regulator Setting
1954-56 All V8	— 1.55	12.7	30	14.5±1.(A)
1957 All V8	— 1.74	12.8	35	14.5±1.(A)
1958-62 All V8	— 1.50	12.5	35	14.5±1.(A)

(A) Surrounding temperatures guide this adjustment. Higher temperatures require lower settings and lower temperatures permit higher settings, within limits.

VALVES
Operating Tappet Clearance
Hydraulic lifters have zero clearance.
1954-63, all—Hydraulic

WHEEL ALIGNMENT
Caster (Degrees)
1954, all ....½ N to ¾ P
1955, all ....¾ N to ½ P
1956, all ....1½ N to ½ P
1957, all ....1¾ N to ½ P
1958 ....¼ N to ¾ P
1959, Air ....2 N to 0
1959, Coil ....2½ N to ½ N
1960-61 ....1½ N to ½ N
1962-63 ....1½ N to ½ N

Camber (Degrees)
1954-56, all ....⅝ N to ⅞ P
1957-59, all ....½ N to 1 P
1959-61 ....0 to 1 P
1962-63 ....0 to ¾ P

Toe-in
1954-55 ....0 to 1/16
1956-58 ....1/16 to ⅛
1959-61 ....1/16 to 5/32
1962-63 ....3/16 to ¼

King Pin Inclination
1954-55 0
1956-61 7
1962-63 9

Wheel Pivot Ratio
When outer wheel is 20° inner wheel is:
1954 thru 1956 ....22½°
1957-58 ....Manual, 21°; Power, 22°
1959-61 ....Coil, 23; Air, 22
1962-63 ....22°

CAPACITIES
Engine Crankcase (Quarts)
(Add 1 qt. for new filter)
1954-56, all 6
1957-58, all 5
1959-63, all 4

Synchro Transmission (Pints)
1954-55, Ser. 40 ....1¾
1954-56, Ser. 50 ....2½
1956-61, all 2½
1962 ....Not Used
1963 ....2¼

Dynaflow Transmission (Pints)
1954-55, all Series 20
1956, all Series 21
1957, all 22
1958, variable pitch 24
1958-59, flight pitch 25
1959-63, twin turbine 24

Rear Axle (Pints)
1954-55 ....4½
1956-58 6
1959-63 ....6½

Gas Tank Capacity (Gallons)
1954-56, all 19
1957-63, all 20

Cooling Capacity (Quarts)
(Add 1¼ qts. for heater)
1954-55, all Ser. Synchromesh..16½
1954-55, all Ser. Dynaflow 18½
1956, all Series 17½
1957-63, all 16½

FIRING ORDER and TIMING

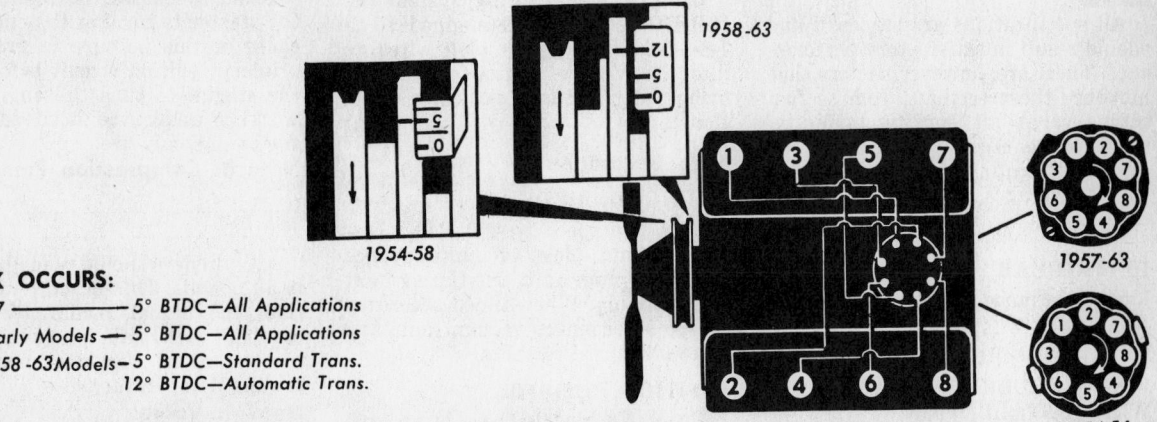

1958-63

1954-58

1957-63

1954-56

SPARK OCCURS:
1954-57 —————— *5° BTDC—All Applications*
1958 Early Models —— *5° BTDC—All Applications*
Late 1958 -63 Models— *5° BTDC—Standard Trans.*
12° BTDC—Automatic Trans.

NOTE:
THESE ARE APPROXIMATE SETTINGS. ENGINE DESIGN, ALTITUDE, TEMPERATURE, FUEL AND ENGINE CONDITION WILL ALL INFLUENCE TIMING THE DETERMINING FACTOR, LIMITING ADVANCE, WILL STILL BE THE "KNOCK POINT" OF THE INDIVIDUAL ENGINE.

BUICK

CAR SERIAL NUMBER LOCATION AND ENGINE IDENTIFICATION

CAR IDENTIFICATION —
ALL MODELS

Plate attached to left front door hinge post.

ENGINE IDENTIFICATION

ENGINE IDENTIFICATION IS MADE THROUGH THE ENGINE NUMBER.

BEGINNING 1954

The first digit of the car serial number indicates the series: 4-series

4400, 6-series 4600, 7-series 4700, 8-series 4800. Next is a letter, designating the year: "A"-1954, "B"-1955, "C"-1956, etc. The third prefix is a digit (1 thru 8). This digit identifies the location of manufacture. The remaining six digits constitute the individual car serial number.

TUNE-UP SPECIFICATIONS

Year Model	Spark Plugs		Distributor (Note 1)				Ignition Timing (Note 2)	Compression Pressure Cranking (Note 3)	Valves (Note 4)			Fuel Pump Pressure	Engine Idle Speed Neutral (Note 5)
									Tappet Clearance Hot		Timing		
	Type	Gap	Cam Angle	Point Gap	Arm Spring Tension				Inlet	Exhaust	Inlet Opens		
1954													
Series 40, V8	44-5	.032	29½	.015	19–23		5B	130	Zero	Zero	25B	5	450
Series 50, 60, 70, V8	44-5	.032	29½	.015	19–23		5B	150	Zero	Zero	25B	5	450
1955													
Series 40, V8	44-5	.032	29½	.015	19–23		5B	140	Zero	Zero	25B	5	450
Series 50, 60, V8	44-5	.032	29½	.015	19–23		5B	155	Zero	Zero	25B	5	450
Series 70, V8	44-5	.032	29½	.015	19–23		5B	155	Zero	Zero	28B	5	450
1956													
Series 40, V8	44	.032	29½	.015	19–23		5B	155	Zero	Zero	25B	6½	450
Series 50, 60, 70, V8	44	.032	29½	.015	19–23		5B	155	Zero	Zero	30B	6½	450
1957													
Series 40, W.O./D., V8	44	.032	30	.015	19–23		5B	140	Zero	Zero	25B	6½	485
Series 40, W./D., V8	44	.032	30	.015	19–23		5B	170	Zero	Zero	25B	6½	485
Series 50, 60, 70, V8	44	.032	30	.015	19–23		5B	185	Zero	Zero	34B	6½	485
1958													
Series 40, W.O./D., V8	44	.032	30	.015	19–23		5B	140	Zero	Zero	25B	5¾	485
Series 40, W./D., V8	44	.032	30	.015	19–23		5B	170	Zero	Zero	34B	5¾	485
Series 50, 60, 70, 700, V8	44	.032	30	.015	19–23		5B	185	Zero	Zero	34B	5¾	485
1959-61 Note 6													
Series 4400, W.O./D., V8	44S	.035	30	.015	19–23		5B	150	Zero	Zero	25B	5¾	485
Series 4400, W./D., V8	44S	.035	30	.015	19–23		12B	160	Zero	Zero	34B	5¾	485
Series 4600, 4700, 4800, V8	44S	.035	30	.015	19–23		12B	180	Zero	Zero	33B	5¾	485
1962													
Series 4400, 4600, 4800, V8	44S	.032	30	.015	19–23		12B	170	Zero	Zero	28B	5¾	485
1963													
Series 4400, V8	44S	.032	30	.015	19–23		12B	170	Zero	Zero	28B	5¾	485
Series 4600 & Wildcat V8	44S	.032	30	.015	19–23		12B	170	Zero	Zero	37B	5¾	485
Series 4700, V8	44S	.032	30	.015	19–23		12B	170	Zero	Zero	31B	5¾	485
Series 4800, V8	44S	.032	30	.015	19–23		12B	170	Zero	Zero	28B	5¾	485

NOTES FOR TUNE-UP SPECIFICATIONS TABLE

Notes:

All specifications are standard and should result in satisfactory performance. There are, however, factors that influence these settings, such as fuel octane value, air density, humidity, temperature, etc. Timing charts, like other specifications must be considered as averages, subject to modification.

DRIVE GEAR

1954-63—Pinned to distributor shaft.

Note 1:

FIRING ORDER AND SPARK PLUG WIRE INSTALLATION

All Buick V8 engine cylinders are numbered from front to back; left bank, 2-4-6-8; right bank, 1-3-5-7.

Using this numbering system the FIRING ORDER of V8 engine is: 1-2-7-8-4-5-6-3. The spark plug wires go into the V8 distributor cap in the firing order and in a clockwise direction.

Note 2: Ignition

TIMING PROCEDURE

Reduce idle speed to 400 RPM. Disconnect and plug vacuum advance line at Vacuum unit. Use timing light to set timing. When timed according to specs reconnect vacuum unit and reset idle speed to specs.

IGNITION RESISTOR

On all V8 models there is an ignition ballast resistor connected between the ignition switch and the coil. A contact finger in the starter solenoid by-passes the resistor when the starter is turning the engine. Because of this be sure to ground the primary ignition circuit before using the starter to turn the engine when working under the hood; otherwise the engine may fire.

Note 3: Compression Pressure

10.25:1 .... 180 lbs.
9.0 :1 .... 160 lbs.

All cylinders should read alike within 10 pounds. This is more important than the actual reading. Take the reading with: all plugs removed; throttle open; engine at normal operating temperature.

Note 4: Valves

Zero in the Tappet Clearance column indicates hydraulic lifters are standard equipment.

10

NOTES FOR TUNE-UP SPECIFICATIONS TABLE — continued

Note 5: Idle Speed

Idle speeds as shown are for engines in good condition and with the transmission in Neutral. The proper idle speed for an engine depends on its condition and also on whether or not it has a Dynaflow transmission.

Higher idling speeds are required for engines in poor condition and also for engines used with Dynaflow.

Note 6: Beginning 1959 Models

Cars equipped with the Triple-Turbine Transmission cannot be started by pushing. These transmissions do not have a rear pump. When towing be careful not to exceed 25 m.p.h. unless the drive shaft has been disconnected.

FUSES and CIRCUIT BREAKERS

CIRCUITS NOT CONNECTED TO THE FUSE BLOCK

Head, Tail, Instrument Panel, Head Indicator, Parking, License, Ignition:

1954-63 : 24 amp. Circut Breaker on Headlamp Switch.

Glove Compartment Light:

1954-58 in wire at light
.................AGA or AGC 2
1959-63 ....AGC 5

Cigar Lighter:

Thermal fuse (replaceable) is part of lighter socket.

Power Seats, Windows and Top:

Automatic reset circuit breaker on the left cowl panel. Plus another circuit breaker in each motor.

Radio:

Special 7.5 amp. fuse at end of "A" lead at the set.

Automatic Antenna:

AGA or AGC 15 fuse near the switch.

Air Conditioner Temperature Control:

AGA   fuse in wiring near control.

Tne Power Brake Vacuum Pump Used in 1954:

SFE 14 in the wiring near the fuse block.

FUSE BLOCK CONNECTIONS

THE FUSE BLOCK BEHIND THE LEFT SIDE OF THE INSTRUMENT PANEL CARRIES FUSES OF THE FOLLOWING VALUE TO PROTECT THE NAMED CIRCUITS.

Back-up and Brake-on Warning Light

1954-55 ....SFE 9
1956-58 ....AGC 10

Direction Signal and Stop Light

1954-56 ....SFE 9
1957-63 ....SFE 10

Note: Flasher is plugged in fuse block

Heater and Blowers

1954-55 ....SFE 9
1956-63 ....SFE 20

Dome Light, and Luggage Compartment

1954-63 ....SFE 2°

Clock

1954-56 ....AGA 2
1957-58 ....AGC 1
1959-63 ....AGC 2

Air Conditioner Clutch Control

1957-63 ....AGC 5

Speedometer Buzzer

1957-58 ....AGC 1
1959-63 ....AGC 5

LIGHT BULBS

(C.P. MEANS CANDLE POWER)

Telltale Lights for Headlight Beam, Direction Signals and Dynaflow Quadrant:

12 Volt, No. 53.
(One C.P. miniature bayonet base.)

Dash Lights for Instrument Cluster, Clock, Glove Compartment, Radio, Ignition Switch and Brake Warning:

12 Volt, No. 57.
(2 C.P. miniature bayonet base.)

License Plate Light and Map Light:

12 Volt, No. 67.
(3 C.P. single contact base or No. 90 —6 C.P. single contact base.)

Brake Warning Light:

12 Volt, No. 57.
(2 C.P. single contact base.)

Trunk Light:

12 Volt, No. 89.
(6 C.P. single contact base.)

GENERAL CHASSIS and BRAKE SPECIFICATIONS

Year and Model	Chassis			Brake Cylinder Bore		Wheel Cylinder Diameter (In.)	
	Overall Length in Inches	Tire Size		Master Cyl. (In.) Std.	Pow.	Front	Rear
1954 V8, 40 Series	206.3	7.60x15		1.0		1⅛	1.0
V8, 50 Series	216.8	8.00x15		1.0		1⅛	1.0
V8, 60 Series	206.3	7.60x15		1.0		1⅛	1.0
V8, 70 Series	216.8	8.00x15		1.0		1⅛	1.0
1955 V8, 40 Series	206.7	7.10x15		1.0		1⅛	1.0
V8, 50 Series	216.0	7.60x15		1.0		1⅛	1.0
V8, 60 Series	206.7	7.60x15		1.0		1⅛	1.0
V8, 70 Series	216.0	8.00x15		1.0		1⅛	1.0
1956 V8, 40 Series	205.1	7.10x15		17/32	21/32	1⅛	1.0
V8, 50 Series	213.6	7.60x15		17/32	21/32	1⅛	1.0
V8, 60 Series	205.1	7.60x15		17/32	21/32	1⅛	1.0
V8, 70 Series	213.6	8.00x15		17/32	21/32	1⅛	1.0
1957 V8, 40 Series	208.4	7.10x15		1.0	21/32	1⅛	1.0
V8, 50 Series	215.3	7.60x15		1.0	21/32	1⅛	1.0
V8, 60 Series	208.4	7.60x15		1.0	21/32	1⅛	1.0
V8, 70 Series	215.3	8.00x15		1.0	21/32	1⅛	1.0
1958 V8, 40 Series	211.8	7.10x15		1.0	21/32	1⅛	1.0
V8, 50 Series	219.1	7.60x15		1.0	21/32	1⅛	1.0
V8, 60 Series	211.8	7.60x15		1.0	21/32	1⅛	1.0
V8, 70 Series	219.1	8.00x15		1.0	21/32	1⅛	1.0
V8, 700 Series	227.1	8.00x15		1.0	21/32	1⅛	1.0
1959 V8, 4400, 4600	217.4	7.60x15		1.0	21/32	1⅛	1.0
V8, 4700	220.6	8.00x15		1.0	21/32	1⅛	1.0
V8, 4800	225.4	8.00x15		1.0	21/32	1⅛	1.0
1960 V8, 4400, 4600	217.9	7.60x15		1.0		1⅛	1.0
V8, 4700	221.2	8.00x15		1.0		1⅛	1.0
V8, 4800	225.9	8.00x15		1.0		1⅛	1.0
1961 V8, 4400, 4600	213.2	7.60x15		1.0		1⅛	1.0
V8, 4700	219.2	8.00x15		1.0		1⅛	1.0
1962 V8, 4400, 4600	214.1	7.60x15		1.0		1⅛	1.0
1963 V8, 4400, 4600, Wildcat	215.7	7.60x15		1.0		1⅛	1.0
V8, 4700	208.0	7.10x15		1.0		1⅛	1.0
V8, 4800	221.7	8.00x15		1.0		1⅛	1.0

BUICK

Dome Light:

12 Volt, No. 1004.
(15 C.P. double contact base.)

Front Combination Park and Signal Light, also Combination Tail and Stop Light:

12 Volt, No. 1034.
(4 & 32 C.P. double contact base.)

Rear Signal Light and Back-up Light:

12 Volt, No. 1073.
(32 C.P. single contact base.)
Note: Some early models used:
6 Volt, No. 1129.

Headlight (Twin Sealed Beam):

High Beam: 12 Volt, No. 4001.
(3.75 Watts Two contact base.)

Low and High Beam: 12 Volt, No. 4002.
(37.5-50 Watts. Three contact base.)
Note: The face of the lamp Glass has a "1" or "2" embossed on it to indicate bulb number. 1—No. 4001. 2—No. 4002.

Headlight (Single Sealed Beam):

12 Volt, No. 5400.
(50 & 40 C.P. three contact base.)

DELCO-REMY DISTRIBUTOR SPECIFICATIONS

Year	Delco-Remy No.	Rotation	Cam Angle (Deg.)	Breaker Point Gap Inch	Breaker Arm Spring Tension	Governor Control @ Dist. R.P.M.		Vac. Control Data		
						Adv. Starts	Full Adv.	Inches of Vacuum To Start Advance	Inches of Vacuum For Full Advance	Max. Adv. of Dist. in Degrees
1954-55	1110849	C	26-33*	.015	19-23 oz.	1° @ 375	12° @ 1750	6.5-8.5	12-14	9-10½
1956	1110861	C	26-33*	.015	19-23 oz.	1° @ 375	12° @ 1750	6.5-8.5	12-14	9-10½
1957	1110870	C	30	**	19-23 oz.	1° @ 475	13° @ 1875	6.5-8.5	12-14	9-10½
1958	1110870	C	30	**	19-23 oz.	1° @ 475	13° @ 1875	6.5-8.5	12-14	9-10½
	1110934	C	30	**	19-23 oz.	1° @ 475	12° @ 1875	6.5-8.5	12-14	9-10½
1959	1110936	C	30	**	19-23 oz.	1° @ 475	14° @ 1875	6.5-8.5	12-14	9-10½
1960 Le Sabre	1110963	C	30	**	19-23 oz.	1° @ 325	13° @ 1875	6.5-8.5	13-15	10-11
Invicta-Electra	1110961	C	30	**	19-23 oz.	1° @ 375	11° @ 1900	8 - 10	17-19	8-9
1961	1110961	C	30	.013-.019	19-23	1° @ 375	11° @ 1900	8-10	18	8-9
	1110962	C	30	.013-.019	19-23	1° @ 550	11° @ 1900	6.5-8.5	12	8-10
1962-63 ALL	1110993	C	30	.013-.019	19-23	1° @ 550	11° @ 1900	8-10	18	8-10

* Dwell Meter not recommended for setting Buick Points. ** Turn adjusting screw clockwise until engine becomes rough. Then reverse screw ½ turn.

GENERATOR and REGULATOR SPECIFICATIONS

YEAR	GENERATORS				REGULATORS					
	Field Current in Amperes		Brush Spring Tension		Cut-Out Relay		Current & Voltage Regulator Air Gaps	Current Regulator Setting	Voltage Regulator Setting	
	at 6 Volts	. at 12 Volts			Air Gap	Closing Voltage				
1954-56 All Series, V8	—	1.55	28		.020	12.7	.075	30	14.5	
1957 All Series, V8	—	1.74	29		.020	12.8	.075	35	14.5	
1958-62, Note: 1 All Series, V8	—	1.50	29		.020	12.5	Note: 2	35	14.5	
With Air Condition	—	2.76	29		.020	12.5		45	14.5	

Note 1: 1958-62 Generator and Regulator

The High Output Generator for 1958-62 uses a special double contact voltage control regulator. Never ground the field while regulator is connected to the field because this may cause damage to the voltage regulator contacts.

The regulator used with air-conditioned cars cannot be interchanged with that used on cars without air-conditioning.

Note 2: 1958-62 Current and Voltage Regulator

The double contact voltage regulator used starting in 1958; air gap—.067, upper contact point opening—.016, current regulator air gap—.075.

DELCOTRON AND A.C. REGULATOR SPECIFICATIONS

Delcotron Model Number	Ground Polarity	Field Current Draw (Amperes)	CURRENT OUTPUT			RUNNING VOLTAGE			REGULATOR		FIELD RELAY	
			Engine R.P.M.	Amperes	Volts	Engine R.P.M.	Amperes	Volts @ 125°	Model Number	Point Gap	Armature Air Gap	Closing Voltage
1963	1100623	Neg.	1.9 to 2.2	1100	17.0	14	6500	42	13.6-14.4	1119512	.015	6.5-8.5

CYLINDER HEAD NUT TIGHTENING SEQUENCE

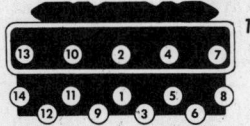

1954-61 all V-8 Tighten to 65-75 ft. lbs.

1962 -63 V-8 Tighten to 65-75 ft. lbs.

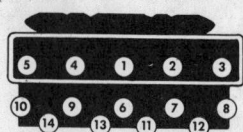

BATTERY and STARTER SPECIFICATIONS

YEAR	BATTERY				STARTERS						
					Lock Test			No-Load Test			
	Ampere Hour Capacity	Volts	Group Number	Terminal Grounded	Amps.	Volts	Torque	Amps.	Volts	R.P.M.	Brush Spring Tension
1954 All Series, V8	60	12	3EM/3EE	Neg.	460	5.2	11.	95	10.1	3,500	30
1955 All Series, V8	60	12	3KM/3EA	Neg.	470	5.4	10.5	95	10.1	3,500	37
1956 All Series, V8	62	12	3KM/3EA	Neg.	470	5.4	10.5	95	10.1	3,500	37
1957 All Series, V8	70	12	3KM/3EA	Neg.	330	3.5	Locked	100	10.6	5,100	35
1958-59 All Series, V8	70	12	3EM	Neg.	330	3.5	Locked	100	10.6	3600	35
1960-61 Le Sabre	70	12	3KMB	Neg.	330	3.5	Locked	100	10.6	3,600	35
Invicta, Electra	70	12	3KMB	Neg.	330	2.0	Locked	120	10.6	4,700	35
1962-63 All Series	70	12	3KMB	Neg.	330	2.0	Locked	120	10.6	4,700	35

VALVE SPECIFICATIONS

YEAR	Seat Angle	Intake Valve Lift Note: 1	Exhaust Valve Lift	Valve Spring Pressure Note: 2		Stem to Guide Clearance		Stem Diameter	Are Valve Guides Removable
				Outer	Inner	Inlet	Exhaust		
1954-55									
Series 40, V8	45	.358	.350	43@1.50	24@1.50	.0025	.0030	.3317	Yes
Series 50, 60, 70, V8	45	.378	.350	43@1.50	24@1.50	.0025	.0030	.3317	Yes
1956									
Series 40, V8	45	.358	.350	45@1.50	26@1.50	.0025	.0035	.3317	Yes
Series 50, 60, 70, V8	45	.378	.350	45@1.50	26@1.50	.0025	.0035	.3317	Yes
1957									
Series 40, 50, 60, 70, V8	45	.423	.423	42@1.50	25@1.62	.0025	.0035	.3317	Yes
1958									
Series 40, W./S., V8	45	.378	.378	92@1.15	62@1.24	.0025	.004	Note: 3	Yes
Series 40, W/D., V8	45	.423	.423	96@1.11	66@1.20	.0025	.004	Note: 3	Yes
Series 50, 60, 70, 700, V8	45	.423	.423	96@1.11	66@1.20	.0025	.004	Note: 3	Yes
1959-61									
4400 W./S., V8	45	.403	.403	96@1.16	76@1.25	Note: 4	.004	Note: 4	Yes
4400 W/D., V8	45	.443	.441	96@1.16'	76@1.25	Note: 4	.004	Note: 4	Yes
All other V8	45	.439	.441	96@1.16	76@1.25	Note: 4	.004	Note: 4	Yes
1962-63 All Series	45	.439	.441	96@1.16	76@1.25	Note: 4	.004	Note: 4	Yes

Note 1: Camshaft Sprocket Index Marks

1954-56, V8:
12 pins on chain between mark on camshaft sprocket and mark on crankshaft sprocket.
1957-63 V8:
Align marks on sprockets nearest each other and in line with the shaft centers.

Note 2: Valve Springs
1954-63—Intake and exhaust springs are the same.

Note 3: 1958 Stem Diameter
Intake—.372; exhaust—.371.
Note 4: 1959-63 Stem Diameter and Clearance
Inlet Diameter: Tapered Stem .3715 to .3730.

Inlet Clearance: Top—.002; Bottom—.0035.
Exhaust Diameter: Tapered Stem .3705 to .3720.

Abbreviations
W/S—With Synchromesh Transmission.
W/D—With Dynaflow Transmission.

PISTON AND PIN SPECIFICATIONS

Year and Model	PISTON				PISTON PIN			
	Skirt Clearance		Diameter	Bushing	FIT			Lock
	Min.	Max.			In Rod	In Piston		
1954-55—40	.0015	.0015	940	None	.0004	.0004		Bolt
1954-55—50, 60, 70	.0017	.0017	.940	None	.0004	.0004		Bolt
1956—All	.0017	.0017	.940	None	Press	.0004		In Rod
1957-58—All 1959—LaSabre	.0011	.0026	.9994-.9997	None	Press	.0007-.0015		In Rod
1959—Exc. LaSabre	.0013	.0028	.9994-.9997	None	Press	.0007-.0015		In Rod
1960-63—LaSabre	.0011	.0026	.9994-.9997	None	Press	0007-.0015		In Rod
1960-63—Exc. LaSabre	.0013	.0028	.9994-.9997	None	Press	.0007-.0015		In Rod

GENERAL ENGINE SPECIFICATIONS

Year Model Engine Type	Bore and Stroke	Number of Main Bearings	Type of Valve Lifter Used	Cubic Inch Displacement	AMA Horsepower	Advertised Horsepower at Stated RPM	Advertised Torque at Stated RPM	Compression Ratio	Oil Pressure At 35 MPH (Note 1)	Cam Shaft Drive
1954										
Series 40, W.O./D., V8	$3\frac{5}{8}$x$3\frac{13}{64}$	5	Hydraulic	264	42.05	143@4200	228@2400	7.2–1	35	Chain
Series 40, W./D., V8	$3\frac{5}{8}$x$3\frac{13}{64}$	5	Hydraulic	264	42.05	150@4200	240@2400	8.0–1	35	Chain
Series 60, W.O./D., V8	4x$3\frac{13}{64}$	5	Hydraulic	322	51.2	195@4100	302@2400	8.0–1	35	Chain
Series 60, W./D., V8	4x$3\frac{13}{64}$	5	Hydraulic	322	51.2	200@4100	309@2400	8.5–1	35	Chain
Series 50, W.O./D., V8	4x$3\frac{13}{64}$	5	Hydraulic	322	51.2	177@4100	295@2000	8.0–1	35	Chain
Series 50, W./D., V8	4x$3\frac{13}{64}$	5	Hydraulic	322	51.2	182@4100	300@2000	8.5–1	35	Chain
Series 70, V8	4x$3\frac{13}{64}$	5	Hydraulic	322	51.2	200@4100	309@2400	8.5–1	35	Chain
1955										
Series 40, W.O./D., V8	$3\frac{5}{8}$x$3\frac{13}{64}$	5	Hydraulic	264	42.05	NA	NA	7.5–1	35	Chain
Series 40, W./D., V8	$3\frac{5}{8}$x$3\frac{13}{64}$	5	Hydraulic	264	42.05	188@4800	256@2400	8.4–1	35	Chain
Series 50, 60, W.O./D., V8	4x$3\frac{13}{64}$	5	Hydraulic	322	51.2	NA	NA	8.4–1	35	Chain
Series 50, 60, W./D., V8	4x$3\frac{13}{64}$	5	Hydraulic	322	51.2	236@4600	330@3000	9.0–1	35	Chain
Series 70, V8	4x$3\frac{13}{64}$	5	Hydraulic	322	51.2	236@4600	330@3000	9.0–1	35	Chain
1956										
Series 40, W.O./D., V8	4x$3\frac{13}{64}$	5	Hydraulic	322	51.2	NA	NA	7.6–1	35	Chain
Series 40, W./D., V8	4x$3\frac{13}{64}$	5	Hydraulic	322	51.2	220@4400	319@2400	8.9–1	35	Chain
Series 50, 60, 70, V8	4x$3\frac{13}{64}$	5	Hydraulic	322	51.2	255@4400	341@3200	9.5–1	35	Chain
1957										
Series 40, W.O./D., V8	$4\frac{1}{8}$x$3\frac{25}{64}$	5	Hydraulic	364	54.4	NA	NA	8.0–1	40	Chain
Series 40, W./D., V8	$4\frac{1}{8}$x$3\frac{25}{64}$	5	Hydraulic	364	54.4	250@4600	300@2400	9.5–1	40	Chain
Series 50, 60, 70, V8	$4\frac{1}{8}$x$3\frac{25}{64}$	5	Hydraulic	364	54.4	300@4600	400@3200	10.0–1	40	Chain
1958										
Series 40, W.O./D., V8	$4\frac{1}{8}$x$3\frac{25}{64}$	5	Hydraulic	364	54.4	NA	NA	8.0–1	40	Chain
Series 40, W./D., V8	$4\frac{1}{8}$x$3\frac{25}{64}$	5	Hydraulic	364	54.4	250@4400	300@2400	9.5–1	40	Chain
Series 50, 60, 70, 700, V8	$4\frac{1}{8}$x$3\frac{25}{64}$	5	Hydraulic	364	54.4	300@4600	400@3200	10.0 1	40	Chain
1959-61										
Series 4400, W.O./D., V8	$4\frac{1}{8}$x$3\frac{13}{32}$	5	Hydraulic	364	54.4	210@4000	384@2400	8.5-1	40	Chain
Series 4400, W./D., V8	$4\frac{1}{8}$x$3\frac{13}{32}$	5	Hydraulic	364	54.4	250@4400	384@2400	10.5-1	40	Chain
Series 4600, 4700, 4800, V8	$4\frac{3}{16}$x$3\frac{41}{64}$	5	Hydraulic	401	56.1	325@4400	445@2800	10.5-1	40	Chain
1962										
All Series	$4\frac{3}{16}$x$3\frac{41}{64}$	5	Hydraulic	401	56.1	325@4400	445@2800	10.25:1	40	Chain
1963										
All Exc. Wildcat	$4\frac{3}{16}$x$3\frac{41}{64}$	5	Hydraulic	401	56.1	325@4400	445@2800	10.25:1	40	Chain
Wildcat	$4\frac{5}{16}$x$3\frac{41}{64}$	5	Hydraulic	425	59.5	,340@4400	465@2800	10.25:1	40	Chain

NOTES FOR GENERAL ENGINE SPECIFICATIONS

Note 1: Oil Flow

OIL FILTER TYPE

1954-63 ....Full flow

OIL PRESSURE GAUGE

Before 1960

The oil pressure gauge is of the pressure expansion type (not electrical). It is located in the instrument cluster and is connected to the engine oil system in the crankcase by a small diameter tube.

1957-58; To gain access to the gauge: Disconnect battery, remove upper instrument panel-center. Replacement of the tube will require dismounting the fuse block and removal of the glove box.

1959; To gain access to the gauge: Disconnect battery and remove lower left control housing. Replacement of the tube is simple and does not require the removal of other units as in the case of prior models.

Beginning 1960

An electrical sending unit and indicator light are used to show insufficient oil pressure.

ROCKER SHAFT OIL SUPPLY V8

1954-63, All V8: Oil from the pump enters the oil filter thru drilled passages in the crankcase. From the filter it goes to the main gallery which runs lengthwise of the engine below the camshaft. The camshaft front bearing journal meters oil flow from the main oil gallery to the lifter galleries in each bank. From the lifter oil gallery the oil flows thru drilled passages in the block and head to a counterbored recess surrounding the bolt which attaches the front rocker shaft bracket to the head. An oversized bolt hole thru the bracket carries the oil to the hollow rocker shafts from where it is distributed by the drilled rockers to the push rods and valve stems.

ENGINE TIGHTENING SPECIFICATIONS

Part	Location	Thread & Size	Torque Ft. lb.
Plug	Spark	14MM	22-28
Plug	Crank C. Drain	18MM	30-35
Bolt	Water Pump Cover	1/4-20	6-8
Bolt	Timing Chain Cover	5/16-18	20-25
Bolt	Engine Oil Pan	5/16-18	6-15
Bolt	Valve Lifter Cover	5/16-18	4-6 (in. lb)
Nut	Valve Rocker Cover	5/16-24	4-6 (in. lb)
Bolt	Intake Manifold	3/8-16	25-30

Part	Location	Thread & Size	Torque Ft. lb.
Bolt	Ex. Manifold	3/8-16	10-15
Bolt	Rocker Shaft Brkt.	3/8-16	30-35
Bolt	Water Manifold	3/8-16	25-30
Nut	Conn. Rod Cap	3/8-24	40-45
Bolt	Flywheel Mounting	7/16-20	50-60
Bolt	Cylinder Head	7/16-14	65-75
Bolt	Main Bearing Cap	1/2-13	110-120
Bolt	Harmonic Balancer	3/4-16	200-220

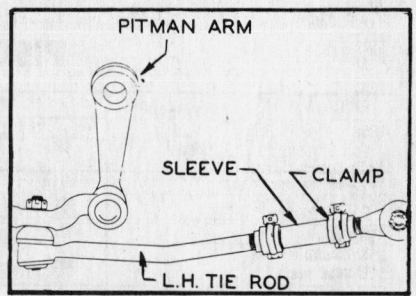

TIGHTEN ALL BALL STUD NUTS TO 55 FT. LBS. DO NOT BACK OFF TO INSERT COTTER PIN

CRANKSHAFT BEARING JOURNAL SIZES

YEAR	MAIN BEARING JOURNALS				CONNECTING ROD BEARING JOURNALS		
	Journal Diameter	Oil Clearance	End Play of Shaft	End Play Held By	Journal Diameter	Oil Clearance	End Play
1954-58 All V8	2.4985	.0015	.006	#5A	2.2495	.0012	.009
1959-61 Series 4400	2.4985	.0015	.006	#5	2.2495	.0012	.009
Series 4600, 4700, 4800	2.4985	.0015	.006	#3	2.2495	.0012	.009
1962-63 All V8	2.4985	.0015	.006	#3	2.2495	.0012	.009

Note A: 1959-63 Models

Series 4400: End Play is held by No. 5.

Series 4600, 4700, 4800: End Play is held by No. 3.

CAPACITIES

YEAR	Engine Crankcase Add 1 Qt. For New Filter	Transmissions Pints to Refill After Draining		Rear Axle Pints	Gasoline Tank Gallons	Cooling System Quarts Note (A)
		Manual	Automatic			
1954-55 Series 40, V8	6	1¾	20	4½	19	16½
Series 50, V8	6	2½	20	4½	19	16½
Series 70, V8	6	N.U.	20	4½	19	18½
1956 All Series V8	6	2½	21	6	19	17½
1957 All Series V8	5	2½	22	6	20	16½
1958 Series 40, V8, W./S.	5	2½	N.U.	6	20	16½
Series 40, 50, 60, W./V.P.	5	N.U.	24	6	20	16½
All Series, V8 W./F.P.	5	N.U.	25	6	20	16½
1959-61 Series 40, V8, W./S.	4	2½	N.U.	6½	20	16½
All Series, V8, W/Twin. T.	4	N.U.	24	6½	20	16½
1962 All Series	4	N.U.	24	6½	20	16½
1963 All Series	4	2¼	24	6½	20	16½

Note: (A)—Add 1½ qts. for heater.

FRONT WHEEL ALIGNMENT

YEAR	CASTER		CAMBER		Toe-In (Inches)	King-Pin Inclination (Degrees)	WHEEL PIVOT RATIO	
	Range (Degrees)	Pref. Setting	Range (Degrees)	Pref. Setting			Inner Wheel	Outer Wheel
1954 All Series	½N to ¾P		⅝N to ⅞P		0 to 1/16	0	22½	20
1955 All Series	¾N to ½P		⅝N to ⅞P		0 to 1/16	0	22½	20
1956 All Series	1½N to ½P		⅝N to ⅞P		1/16 to ⅛	7	22½	20
1957 All Series	1¾N to ½P		½N to 1P		1/16 to ⅛	7	21	20
1958 Coil Suspension	¼N to ¾P		½N to 1P		1/16 to ⅛	7	21	20
Air Suspension	¼N to ¾P		½N to 1P		1/16 to ⅛	7	22	20
1959 Coil Suspension	2½N to ½N	Equal	½N to 1P	½P	1/16 to 5/32	7	23	20
1959-61 Le Sabre-Invicta	2N to 0*	Equal	0 to 1P	½P	1/16 to 5/32	7	20	18
Electra	1½N to ½N	Equal	0 to 1P	½P	1/16 to 5/32	7	20	18
1962-63 All Series	1½N to ½N	1°N	0 to ¾P	⅜P	3/16 to ¼	9	22½	20

* Same as Electra when power steering is used.

TUNE-UP

ENGINE TUNE-UP AND DIAG-
NOSIS ARE SO CLOSELY RE-
LATED THAT ONE PROCEDURE
SHOULD SERVE BOTH
PURPOSES. A MORE PROFES-
SIONAL APPROACH IS CON-
TAINED IN THE "UNIT REPAIR"
SECTION UNDER "ENGINE
DIAGNOSIS."

Compression Check

1. Remove the plug wires.
2. Blow foreign matter from around the spark plugs with compressed air. Then loosen the plugs one turn.
3. Replace plug wies, start engine and snap throttle open for one or two seconds. (This should clear the engine of dislodged carbon particles.)
4. Stop engine and remove the plug wires and spark plugs.
5. Remove the air cleaner. Then block the carburetor throttle wide open.
6. Hook up a starter remote-control cable and switch. Then crank the engine through about four strokes for each cylinder while reading the compression pressure on a reliable cylinder compression gauge.
7. Record the maximum pressures of each cylinder. Variation between cylinders should not exceed 15 lb.

Note: A compression check should be the first step in the course of tune-up events. Only if compression is within limits, should tune-up be continued.

Spark Plugs

Use a good plug tester, if available, and service or renew the spark plugs. Detailed information on diagnosing spark plug troubles can be found in the Unit Repair section, under Tune-Up.

In spark plug installation, be sure of the following:
1. Use plugs of correct model, gapped properly.
2. Thoroughly clean the cylinder head and spark plug threads.
3. Carefully torque the spark plugs to 25-35 ft. lb.

Generator Drive Belt

Check the condition of the belt and adjust tension to ½" deflection when 15 pounds pressure is applied midway between the water pump and the generator pulley.

Battery

1. Check condition of battery.
2. Clean, lubricate and tighten cable connections both ends.

Other Electrical

1. Check Generator output.
2. Check Regulator.
3. Check Starter Motor current draw.
4. Check Ignition Coil output.
5. Check Ignition Wiring.
6. Test Primary Circuit resistance.
7. Test spark intensity at each plug wire.

Cooling System

1. Examine for coolant leaks, (engine, radiator, pump, heater and all hoses).
2. Look for coolant contamination, (rust, oil, etc.) in the radiator.
3. Recharge cooling system with anti-freeze or rust inhibitor.

Distributor

1. Replace and/or reset breaker points.
2. Lubricate distributor cam.
3. Lubricate distributor shaft bushing at the oil cup.
4. Check and adjust vacuum control.
5. Inspect and clean distributor rotor and cap.

Fuel System

1. Clean pump sediment bowl.
2. Check pump pressure and capacity, (fuel filter may be partially obstructed).
3. Clean carburetor bowl and adjust float.

Final Adjustments

1. Set ignition timing with a light.
2. Then road test the car and, if necessary, modify the prescribed setting within limits to accommodate the variables of engine and operating conditions and fuel anti-knock value.

   Note: This final timing adjustment is made in the shop but as a result of road test.
3. Check and adjust engine idle speed.
4. Adjust carburetor idle mixture.

ENGINE ELECTRICAL SYSTEM

DISTRIBUTOR REMOVAL

Disconnect the distributor primary wire from the coil and disconnect the pipe from the vacuum unit. Remove distributor cap by inserting a screwdriver in upper slotted end of cap latches, press down and turn ninety degrees.

Make a mark on the distributor body in line with the rotor. Match-mark position of vacuum unit to the engine.

Remove one bolt and clamp to release distributor and remove from crankcase.

INSTALLATION

If engine was inadvertently turned over while distributor was out proceed as follows:

Remove right rocker arm cover. Using a wrench on the crankshaft pulley bolt, turn the engine over until both valves for No. 1 cylinder (forward one of right bank) are closed. The timing mark on the crankshaft pulley should be aligned with the correct degree mark. No. 1 cylinder is now at firing point.

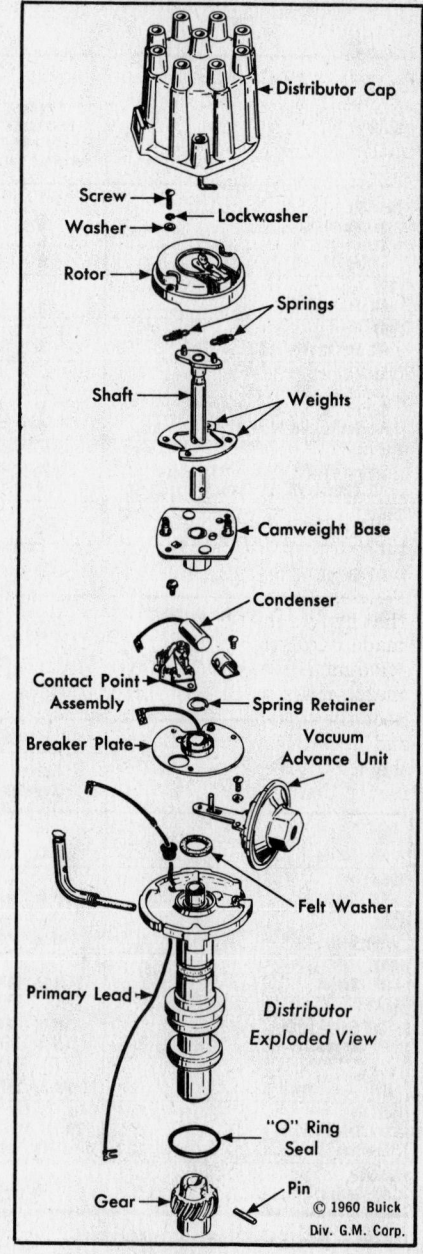

Distributor Cap

Screw — Lockwasher
Washer —
Rotor —
Springs
Shaft — Weights
Camweight Base
Condenser
Contact Point Assembly — Spring Retainer
Breaker Plate — Vacuum Advance Unit
Felt Washer
Primary Lead —
Distributor Exploded View
"O" Ring Seal
Gear — Pin

© 1960 Buick
Div. G.M. Corp.

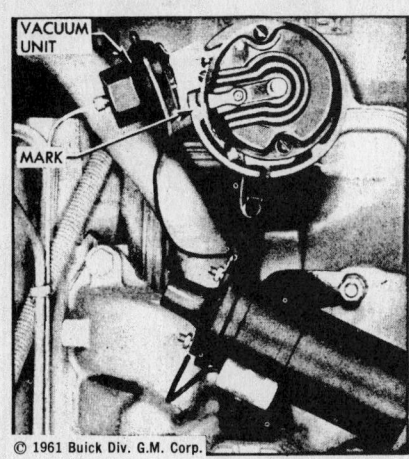

Installing distributor in engine

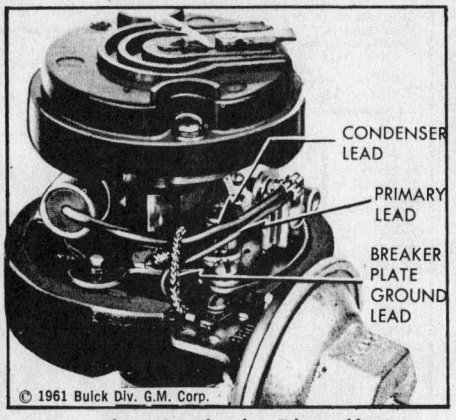

Locating Leads in Distributor

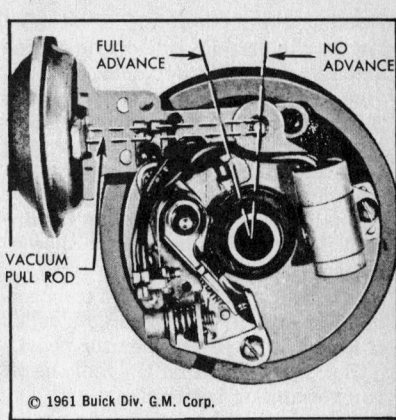

Vacuum Advance Mechanism

Install distributor in engine with rotor in position to fire No. 1 cylinder. The vacuum unit should align with the match-mark made when distributor was removed. Press down lightly on distributor if it does not seat correctly. Use starter to turn engine until the tang on the distributor shaft slips into the slot in the oil pump shaft. This will not disturb the relationship between the distributor and the camshaft as the drive gear engages before the tang. However, it will be necessary to return the engine to the No. 1 firing point and check that rotor is also at No. 1 firing point. Reconnect vacuum pipe and primary wire. Rotate the distributor body slightly until contacts just start to open. Install and tighten distributor clamp. Install distributor cap. Start engine and adjust cam dwell.

If the engine has not been disturbed since the distributor was removed proceed as follows:

Insert distributor into the block so that the rotor is pointing to the mark made on distributor housing and the vacuum advance is aligned with the match-mark made on the engine. Connect the vacuum pipe, primary wire, and install the distributor cap. Fill the oiler tube with light engine oil. Install distributor clamp. Check that

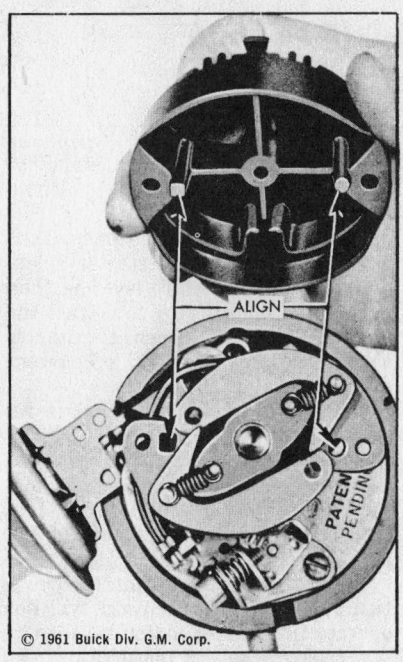

Removing and installing rotor

spark plug wires are correctly routed. Start engine and adjust cam dwell and then adjust ignition timing. Rotate distributor body counterclockwise to advance the timing.

GENERATOR AND REGULATOR

REFERENCES

GENERATOR REMOVAL AND INSTALLATION

Unfasten bolt holding tension bar to generator. Push generator in toward engine to release drive belt. Unfasten two generator mounting bolts to release generator from engine.

When reinstalling, adjust generator to tension bar nut so that it requires 10-20 ft. lbs. torque on a wrench applied to the generator pulley bolt to slip the pulley on the belt.

Before the engine is started, momentarily short from the "Bat" to the "Gen" terminals of the regulator with a screwdriver. This gives a momentary surge of current from the battery to the generator and so correctly polarizes the generator with respect to the battery.

Failure to so polarize the generator before starting the engine may severely damage the regulator since reversed polarity causes vibration, arcing and burning of the relay points.

A.C. GENERATOR ("Delcotron")
References

Beginning 1962 "Delcotron," the AC generator by Delco-Remy is used on Buick passenger cars. These units are furnished in two service types with companion voltage regulators. A three-unit regulator will be used with vehicles having a 42 or 52 ampere Delcotron. Vehicles such as police equipment, etc. will use a 62 ampere Delcotron and be furnished with a two-unit transistorized regulator.

Repair and test details on the Delcotron and it's regulators are covered in the Unit Repair Section of this manual, under "Alternating Current Generators.

BATTERY AND STARTER

REFERENCES

Detailed information on the battery and starter will be found in the Battery and Starter Specifications Table of this section.

A more general discussion of starters and their troubles can be found in the Unit Repair section under the heading Starters.

STARTER SYSTEM
1957-59

The Buick V8 starter motor is of the Solenoid-Relay type with over

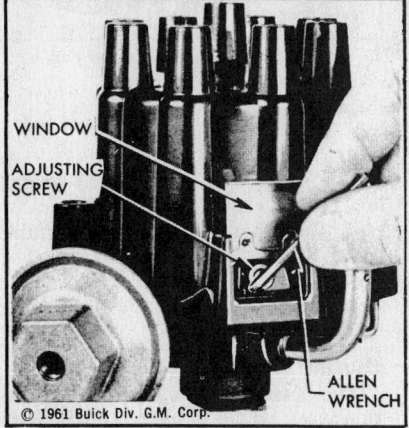

Adjusting contact point dwell angle

running clutch drive. It is situated low on the driver's side of the engine and removable by detaching the engine splash pan and two starter attaching bolts. **(CAUTION)** Disconnect the battery before attempting removal or any work on the starter or solenoid unit.

Dual exhaust equipped cars require that the left exhaust pipe be disconnected at the manifold.

The Buick starter system incorporates a switch at the carburetor which is actuated by the accelerator pedal.

Buick suggests that the radio be off when cranking the engine.

On cars with automatic transmissions, the control must be in P or N position so that Neutral safety switch is closed.

The sequence of events in the Buick starting process follows:

When the ignition switch is turned on and the accelerator pedal is depressed the throttle shaft closes the carburetor starter switch.

Current now flows thru the magnet windings of the solenoid switch relay, which is mounted on the left fender skirt, then thru the field windings of the generator and so to ground. The flow of current thru the windings of the solenoid switch relay causes the core to pull the relay armature against the relay contacts.

This results in a flow of current to the starter motor solenoid switch, which is mounted on the starter.

The current flows thru the "pull-in" and "hold-in" coils of the starter solenoid causing the shift lever to move the starter pinion into engagement with the flywheel ring gear. As this engagement takes place the starter solenoid switch contacts are closed which starts the starter motor turning and also cuts out the "pull-in" coil to save current.

When the engine starts operating the generator starts charging. The

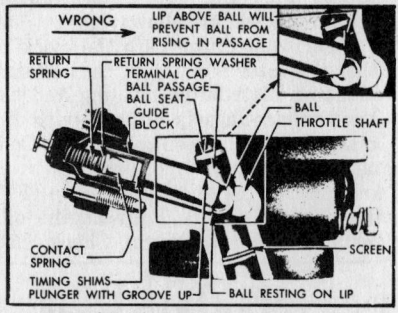

Typical cranking system circuit

resultant output of current stops the flow of current thru the solenoid switch relay on the left fender. The points of the relay then open, thus cutting current to the starter solenoid. The solenoid shift lever is then pulled upon by a spring to retract the starter pinion which opens the starter solenoid switch which cuts off current flow to the starter motor.

When the accelerator pedal is released after the engine is operating the carburetor starter switch opens and manifold vacuum proceeds to hold the carburetor starter switch contacts inoperative despite movement of the accelerator pedal.

While the engine is running operation of the accelerator pedal will not operate the starter motor because of two separate safety features.

1. Blocking effect of generator voltage on current flow in the starter solenoid relay.

2. Vacuum working on the carburetor starter switch holds the ball in the switch up above the switch plunger and out of contact with the throttle shaft.

Note: It is important that the carburetor starter switch contact should occur at the correct throttle opening. If insufficient, car will not start properly when cold. If too much, car may not start due to unloading of choke system.

Beginning 1960

Starting with 1960 production the starter circuit is completed by a spring loaded ignition switch. To activate the starter, the ignition key is turned to the extreme right. When the engine fires, release the ignition key.

Assembly of carburetor starter switch 1957-59

LOCATION OF HORN RELAY
Thru 1958

The horn relay is mounted on the left fender skirt below the generator regulator. In appearance it is similar to the Safety-Minder Buzzer. The buzzer has a resistor, one end of which is spot welded to the mounting bracket.

Starting 1959

The horn relay is a part of the junction block which is near the battery.

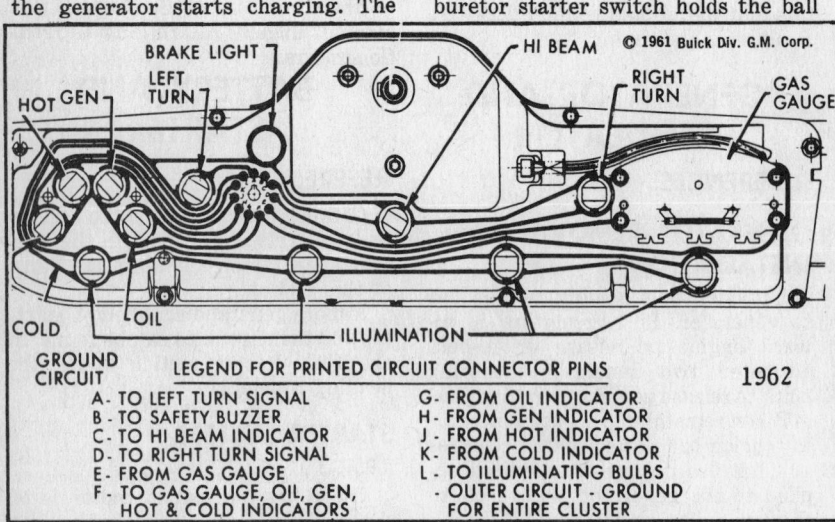

Instrument Cluster - Back Side

LEGEND FOR PRINTED CIRCUIT CONNECTOR PINS

A- TO LEFT TURN SIGNAL
B- TO SAFETY BUZZER
C- TO HI BEAM INDICATOR
D- TO RIGHT TURN SIGNAL
E- FROM GAS GAUGE
F- TO GAS GAUGE, OIL, GEN, HOT & COLD INDICATORS
G- FROM OIL INDICATOR
H- FROM GEN INDICATOR
J- FROM HOT INDICATOR
K- FROM COLD INDICATOR
L- TO ILLUMINATING BULBS
- OUTER CIRCUIT - GROUND FOR ENTIRE CLUSTER

1962

INSTRUMENTS

SPEEDOMETER HEAD R & R

This AC speedometer has a horizontal drum type head. It is painted, half red and half black, on the diagonal. As the car accelerates and the drum revolves, a red line moves laterally across the dial face.

1957-58 Models

To Remove and Replace: Disconnect battery, remove the upper Instrument Panel (top of dash). This will expose the back of the instrument cluster. Remove wires from instruments and tube from Oil Pressure Gauge, remove Thermo Gauge from cluster but let it hang free. Disconnect Speedometer cable and remove unit. Reinstall by reversing above procedure.

1959-63 Models

Speedometer head design has been changed from the horizontal drum type to the more conventional sweep hand indicator.

Remove instrument panel by:

1. Removing 4 screws from front edge of instrument panel cover.
2. Remove cover by lifting up and pulling it toward rear of car.
3. Lower left control plate and disconnect printed circut plug.
4. On cars with parking brake warning light, unplug light socket from cluster by reaching under the instrument panel.
5. Remove three nuts that attach cluster to instrument panel, lift cluster up and disconnect speedometer cable. Then remove instrument cluster assembly.
6. Disconnect speedometer or any other unit involved in repairs or replacement.
7. Install instrument cluster by reversing removal procedure.

Note:

The projection on the disconnect plug must be lined up with the keyway in the printed circut when assembling plug on connector pins.

SPEEDMINDER

1957-58

The unit is located on the left hand side, under the dash and requires removal of the fuse block to gain access.

This buzzer-warning device may be adjusted by the driver to sound at any speed between 20 and 110 M.P.H. It has a speed range lasting through 15 M.P.H.

1959-63

These models have the unit mounted under the dash, to the right of steering column. The buzzer circuit contains a 5 Amp. fuse that has a

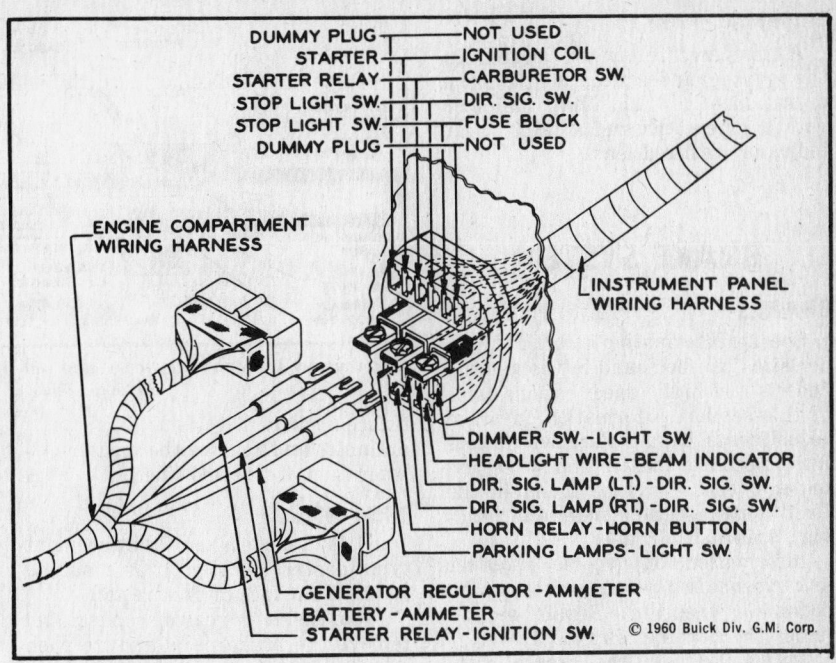

Engine compartment to instrument panel wiring harness connectors

dual purpose with the parking brake warning light. It is marked Bk and Bz on the fuse block.

1958 CHARGE INDICATOR (AMMETER)

Altho the indicator resembles a normal ammeter it is not an ammeter and the scale is not graduated in amperes. It does not show the amount of current flowing.

The current required to move the needle against the stop for both charge and discharge is ten amperes.

The instrument indicates charge when the battery is being charged, but does not indicate how much, except relatively.

Above 30 m.p.h., it should never show a discharge reading. If it does, the generator and regulator should be tested.

AMMETER REPLACEMENT

1957-58

Disconnect battery, remove upper instrument panel, center to gain access to Ammeter.

Beginning 1960

An indicator light is used to show when system is not charging.

FUEL GAUGE—DASH UNIT

1957-58

The electric fuel gauge may be reached by removing the upper instrument panel, center.

1959-63

Access to the gauge may be accomplished by removing the lower right control housing.

Information covering operation and troubles of the fuel gauge will be found in the Unit Repair section under the heading: Gages.

Detailed information on the carburetor and how to adjust it will be found in the Unit Repair section under the broad heading: Carburetors, and the specific heading of the make of carburetor being used on the engine being worked on. Carter, Holley, Rochester and Stromberg carburetors are covered.

Dash pot adjustment can be found under Automatic Transmission Linkage Adjustment of this car section.

TEMPERATURE GAUGE

1954-59

Buick uses an AC, sealed-in, vapor pressure type unit. It is **not** electrically operated. It consists of a gauge head, capillary tube and vapor bulb. Do not disturb the unity of this combination for any reason as pressure balance will be affected and the unit ruined.

To Remove and Replace 1954-59 Models

Disconnect battery, drain cooling system, remove upper instrument panel center. This will permit access for removal of gauge head from back of instrument cluster. Loosen and remove vapor plug from left rear cylinder head. Remove capilary tube from clip on engine side of dash and pull tube and bulb through dash to complete removal operation.

Reverse procedure for replacement.

BUICK

Beginning 1960

A temperature switch located in the right cylinder head controls the operation of a "Cold" heat indicator with a green lens and a "Hot" heat indicator with red lens.

BRAKE SYSTEM

BRAKES

Specific information on brake cylinder sizes can be found in the general chassis and brake specifications table of this section. Information on brake adjustments, band replacement, bleeding procedure, master and wheel cylinder overhaul can be found in the Unit Repair section under the heading: Brakes, Hydraulic.

Information on trouble shooting and overhauling power brakes can be found in the Unit Repair section under the heading: Brakes, Power.

Information on the grease seals which may need replacement can be found in the unit repair section. The front wheel grease seals under the head: Suspension, Front Repair. The rear wheel grease seals under the head: Axles, Rear.

BRAKE PEDAL CLEARANCE

Thru 1955 Models

Adjust master cylinder push rod so that there is 1/4 to 1/2 inch free play of the brake pedal, before the push rod contacts the piston in the master cylinder. This free play is measured at the pedal, not at the push rod.

1956 Models

No linkage adjustment is required.

1957-58 Models

Adjust the master cylinder and push rod so that there is from 1/16 to 1/8 inch free pedal play before the push rod contacts the piston in the master cylinder. The push rod adjustment is located well up under the dash above the steering column. It is a threaded rod with a jam nut to secure the adjustment.

REMOVE THE MASTER CYLINDER FROM THE CAR

Thru 1955 Models

Jack up the car sufficiently high so that the operator can work under it and support with stand jacks. Disconnect the master cylinder inner and outer push rods at the pedal adjusting nut. Disconnect the brake pipe from the master cylinder and tape the end of the pipe to prevent en-

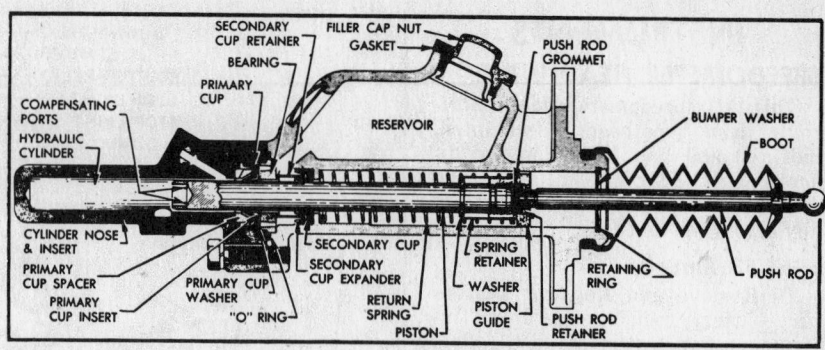

Displacement type master cylinder used with 1956 models only. The cylinder is mounted on the engine side of the toe-board.

trance of dirt.

Unbolt and remove the master cylinder from the frame side rail.

1956 Models

All 1956 models use a displacement type master cylinder. It is mounted on the front face of the firewall.

From inside the car disconnect and remove the brake pedal and its push rod. Remove the steering column rubber seal and pull the floor mat away from the toe pan and take off the toe pan. The master cylinder is connected to this toe pan.

Disconnect the stoplight wires and the lines to the master cylinder on the engine side. On the bench the toe pan can be taken from the master cylinder itself.

1957-58 Models

From under the dash remove the cotter pin and clevis pin from the brake push rod. This is located just in back of the dash above the steering column. Remove the rubber steering column filler plate from the toeboard at the steering column to give access to the two lower bracket bolts.

Over on the left remove the one cap screw which holds the wire junction block bracket to the parking brake bracket, and let the wire junction block fall down out of the way.

On the left pedal bracket at the upper forward corner, remove the nut and bolt which connect the pedal bracket to the master cylinder brace. Remove the bolt from the upper rear corner and push the brake pedal and bracket assembly up out of the way.

Still under the dash, remove the large hex nut from the front of the master cylinder.

On the engine side disconnect and cap the hydraulic brake line and remove the stop light wires. Remove the four cap screws which hold the master cylinder filler plate to the firewall and pull out the master cylinder and the mounting plate. On the bench, remove the three cap screws which hold the mounting plate to the master cylinder.

Note: Master cylinder head nut under the dash is rather difficult of access and it may help somewhat to take out the bolts which hold the ventilator frame into the firewall and remove the ventilator frame. It is possible, however, to remove the head nut without taking out the ventilator frame.

A special socket, can be used. Using this tool it is not necessary to remove the brake brackets. Simply remove the brake push rod. Cleanse and fit the special socket over the push rod to loosen the large head nut.

1959-63 Models

A head nut is not used. Disconnect clevis. Disconnect pipe. Remove four bolts to release master cylinder.

POWER BRAKE UNIT REMOVAL

Thru 1955

Remove cranking motor splash pan.

Disconnect pedal return spring, remove front clevis pin, remove pedal push rod and brake cylinder push rod together as a unit.

Disconnect the breather tube which is clamped to inlet tube on power-cylinder-air-cleaner cover.

Disconnect the pipe and hose that connects the vacuum check valve to power cylinder.

Disconnect the reservoir to hydraulic cylinder pipe. Allow reservoir and pipe to drain.

Disconnect brake fluid distributor to hydraulic cylinder pipe and allow to drain. Cover pipe ends to keep out dirt.

Remove nuts and lockwashers attaching power cylinder to its support and remove from car.

Reverse procedure to reinstall.

1956 Only

Disconnect brake pipe from master cylinder and tape end of pipe to prevent entrance of dirt.

Disconnect vacuum lines from power brake cylinder. Place drip pan under power cylinder reservoir and unbolt reservoir from unit.

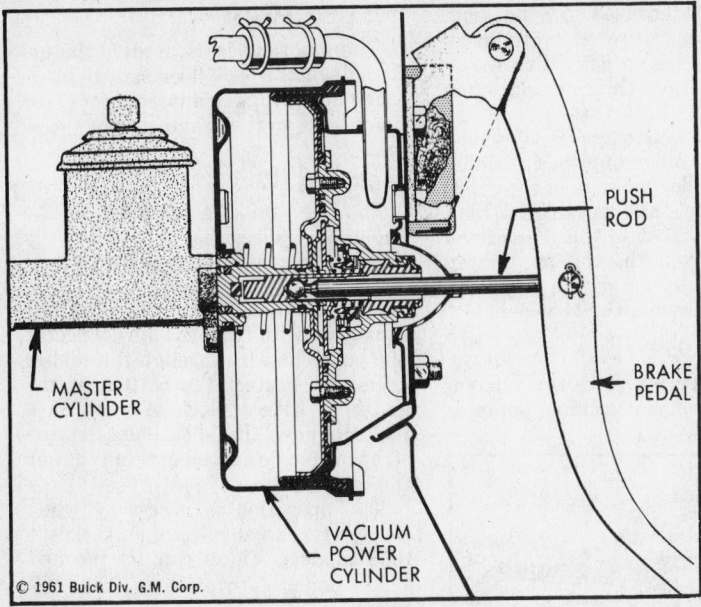

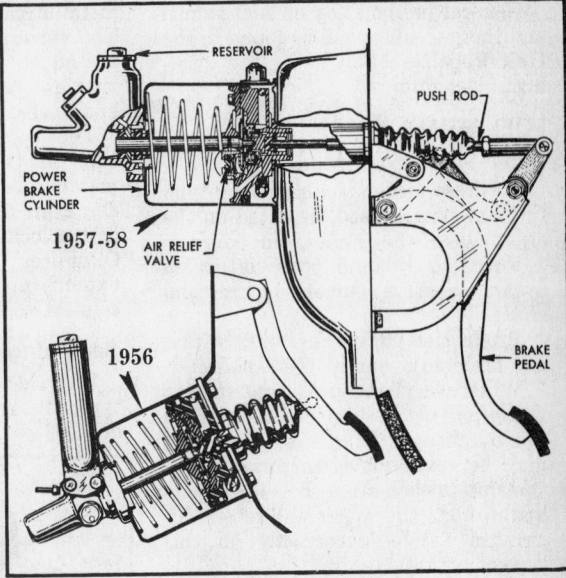

Power Brake and Pedal Mechanism

Power brake installation

Disconnect stoplight wires from switch.

Disconnect push rod from brake pedal and remove brake pedal.

Remove screws holding steering column jacket rubber seal and push seal up on jacket.

Pull floor mat away from toe pan and remove toe pan. The master cylinder is bolted to the toe pan. Remove three bolts to release assembly from toe pan.

Reverse procedure to install and then proceed to adjust the power brake pedal: Loosen nut on right side of pedal bracket.

Turn the eccentric pedal pivot bolt on left side of pedal to adjust pedal vertically until the pedal and push rod operate free of any bind.

(Feel for center location of push rod where it passes thru the air valve.)

Hold eccentric pivot bolt and tighten nut.

1957-58 Models

Disconnect battery ground strap.

Remove push rod clevis pin.

Lift brake pedal out of way and remove large nut holding brake unit to the cowl.

Disconnect stoplight wire at switch. Unfasten brake pipe at hydraulic cylinder and cap to keep out dirt.

Disconnect vacuum hoses at vacuum tee.

Unfasten bolts holding power brake unit to ventilation duct and remove unit from car.

Reverse procedure to reinstall. Do not use vacuum power when bleeding brake system.

Check that brake pedal returns completely when released slowly.

Using a foot rule, measure from left top side of pedal pad perpendicular to the toe pan. Distance should be 5¼-5¾ inches.

Loosen push rod locknut and turn push rod as necessary to adjust pedal height.

When vacuum system is working and pedal travels to within one inch of the floor with a hard feel, brake shoes need relining. If pedal has spongy feeling brake system needs bleeding.

1959-63 Models

Working from below, disconnect the brake pipe from the master cylinder. The stop-light switch has been moved to the front brake pipe distributor. Disconnect push rod from pedal. Roll back the carpet and remove four bolts holding the power brake unit to the toe-plate. Remove screws holding toe-plate to toe-pan. Remove the toe-plate. Disconnect vacuum hoses at the tee. Remove power brake unit.

REFILLING MASTER CYLINDERS

Thru 1955 Models

The master cylinder can be filled from the engine compartment. It is located behind the steering column. Where it is required that the hydraulic system be pressure bled it is advisable to attach the pressure bleeding device from underneath the car rather than to try to connect it up from the engine compartment.

Starting With 1956 Models

The master cylinder is located in the engine compartment and is filled from under the hood.

PARKING BRAKE LEVER

Starting with 1952 production the parking brake lever on Buick cars is a foot operated treadle.

To remove the treadle first disconnect the cable and then unbolt the treadle frame from its mounting under the dash.

This can be accomplished without particular difficulty since there is no great interference with the mounting studs.

PARKING BRAKE CABLE REPLACEMENT

To replace the parking brake cable disconnect the cable at the lever under the dash and also at the adjusting sheave under the car. Disconnect the clamp which holds the conduit assembly to the transmission and also the clamp which holds the conduit assembly to the dash.

The upper end of the cable is slid out into the engine compartment and then the cable is slid out through the bottom. Note carefully the position the cable occupies since it must be replaced through the same "path" that the old cable followed. The cable is not long enough to follow a new path.

FUEL SYSTEM

A chart covering causes of excess fuel consumption will be found in the Unit Repair section under the heading: Fuel Consumption Chart.

Data on capacity of the gas tank will be found in the Capacities table. Data on correct engine idle speed and fuel pump pressure will be found in the Tune-Up Specifications table. Both the above tables can be found at the start of their sections.

General information on fuel pumps and their troubles will be found in the Unit Repair section under the heading: Fuel Pumps.

FUEL PUMP

1954 Thru 1956 Models

On these models double acting type fuel pumps are used, mounted on the right side of the engine front cover.

Fuel and vacuum pump is driven by an eccentric attached to the camshaft.

Production engines are built with a gas filter adjacent to the carburetor.

When servicing the combination pump, do not fail to carefully mark the diaphragm flanges so that they may be reassembled in correct relationship to each other. It is possible to install both the upper and lower diaphragm flanges incorrectly on this type of pump.

Two types of kits are available for this combination pump; the diaphragm kit which consists of the diaphragms. valves and springs, and the overhaul kit which consists of links, levers and also the parts contained in the diaphragm kit.

Fuel pump pressure should be 5¾ lb. at any speed.

1957-63 Models

These models use a single fuel pump mounted on the right side of the engine front cover. Flexible type gas lines are used.

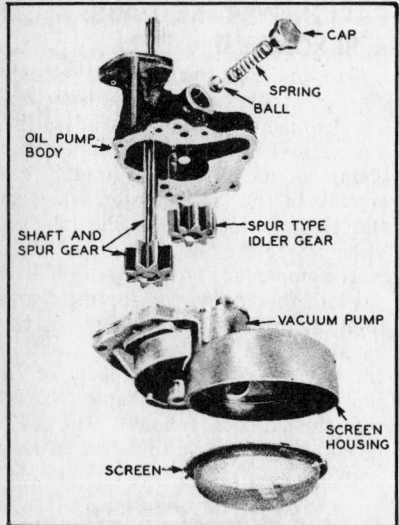

Combination Oil and vacuum pump—1957-58 production

VACUUM PUMP

1957-58

On 1957 and 1958 models the vacuum pump is an integral part of the oil pump. It is located in the crankcase. It is a vane type pump, consisting of a rotor and two spring loaded non-

metallic vanes encased in a housing. The vacuum pump rotor is driven by the oil pump driven gear thru a key that extends thru the common pump end cover.

The vacuum passage is a drilled hole in the oil pump body which matches a drilled passage in the cylinder crankcase that terminates in a fitting located just to the rear of the Oil Filter. From this fitting, tubing extends up the rear of the engine to connect to the windshield wiper.

Beginning 1959

Electric wipers replace the vacuum type, therefore, no vacuum pump is needed.

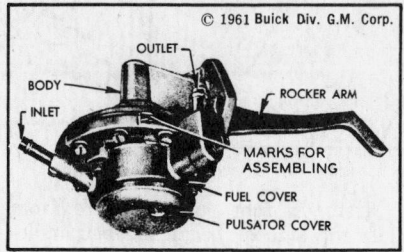

Location of pump parts

FUEL TANK

1954 Thru 1956 Models

On these models the fuel tank is held under the luggage compartment floor and is attached to the frame by two steel straps.

At the back of each steel strap is a T bolt or hook bolt which passes through a hole in the frame cross member and is secured by a nut and lock washer.

Since these bolts are exposed to weather at all times it is advisable to use a rust removing fluid on the bolts before attempting to turn the nuts off, particularly on cars which are over two years old.

Such rust destroying fluids will render it much simpler to remove the nut without possible risk to the steel straps.

Protect the bottom of the tank with a large piece of wood and support it on a jack before loosening the mounting straps.

On models which do not have a port over the gasoline gage lower the tank just sufficiently to permit removing the gasoline gage wire from the top of the tank before removing the tank from the vehicle.

The filler neck is connected to the tank by a rubber hose which is very similar to the radiator hose. Clamps which hold the hose to the filler neck and to the tank neck are the same as radiator hose clamps and radiator hose clamps can be used at this point.

1957-60 Models

The gas tank is secured to the underside of the back floor pan with two steel mounting straps connected by hook bolts to the frame at their back end.

Beginning 1961

The fuel tank is attached to the underbody directly, by two bolts through the rear flange and two nuts at the front flange.

In the trunk, disconnect the gas tank gage wire from the pin connector and push the wire through the rubber grommet. Protect the bottom of the gas tank with a block of wood on a jack. Remove the hook bolts, let the straps come down and carefully lower the tank.

This operation is necessary when replacing gas gauge-tank unit, except 1958 models. These can be reached from underneath without tank removal.

The gasoline connector line is flexible and can be disconnected either before or after the tank is lowered. To avoid the possibility of damaging the line disconnect it first. Be careful of the breather line which projects forward from the upper front edge of the tank.

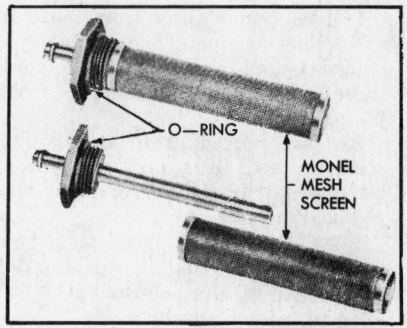

Fuel strainer—1957

EXHAUST SYSTEM

EXHAUST PIPE MUFFLER AND TAIL PIPE

Models With Crossover

On the V-8 models the exhaust crossover pipe is made in one piece where it connects to both of the exhaust manifolds. The split pipe connects from both exhaust manifolds to a common flange connection at the exhaust pipe. Gaskets used at these connections should be installed dry.

1958-63 MODELS WITH DUAL EXHAUST SYSTEM

1958 Models

The dual exhaust system is standard equipment on 70-700 series and optional on 40-50 and 60 series cars.

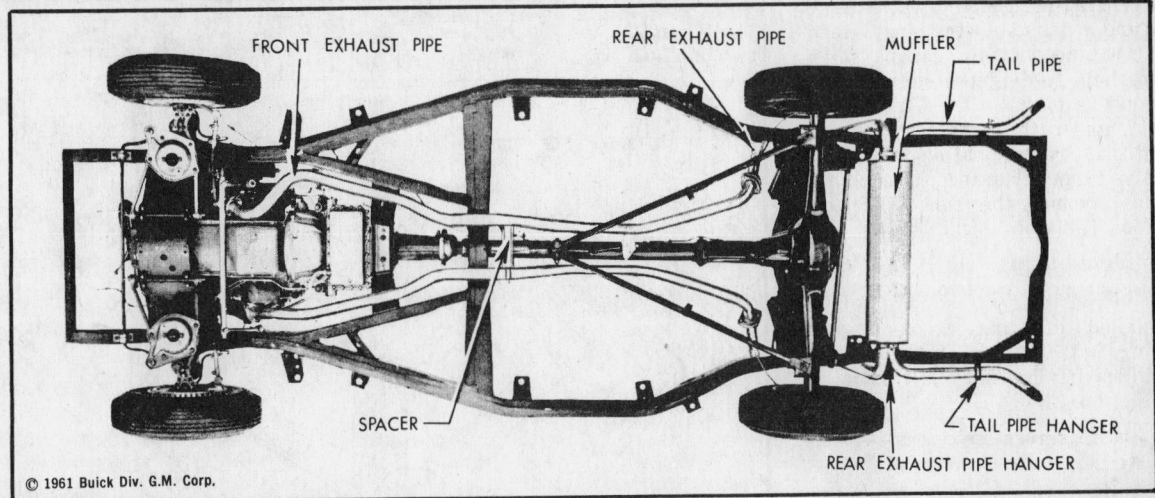

FRONT EXHAUST PIPE · REAR EXHAUST PIPE · MUFFLER · TAIL PIPE

SPACER · TAIL PIPE HANGER · REAR EXHAUST PIPE HANGER

© 1961 Buick Div. G.M. Corp.

Dual Exhaust

1959 Models

The dual exhaust system is standard equipment on series 4700-4800 cars and is optional on all series 4400-4600 cars.

The right exhaust manifold is the same on either single or dual exhaust pipe equipped cars. The left exhaust manifold, exhaust pipes, and the front and rear muffler assemblies are not interchangeable between single and dual exhaust cars.

The right manifold contains the manifold heat control valve. It also contains the carburetor choke heat stove, a tube type, mounted on the outside of the manifold. Heat is drawn from this point, (via insulated pipe) to the automatic choke housing.

Beginning 1960

The exhaust system has been changed. Both the single system, with crossover (Le Sabre and Invicta) and the dual system, (Electra) use a single muffler mounted crosswise of the chassis, just back of the rear axle.

COOLING SYSTEM

RADIATOR CORE REMOVAL

1954 Thru 1956 Models

To remove the radiator core, first remove the water pump. Disconnect the radiator hoses and then loosen the radiator attaching bolts, tilt the radiator slightly backwards and raise it up out of the car.

1957-63 Models

Remove the cap screws which hold the fan blades to the fan hub and then take off the blades and the spacer and pump pulley. Remove the top and bottom radiator hose and the two hoses which connect the dynaflow oil cooler to the radiator. Remove the bolts which hold the radiator core to the radiator cradle and lift the core straight up.

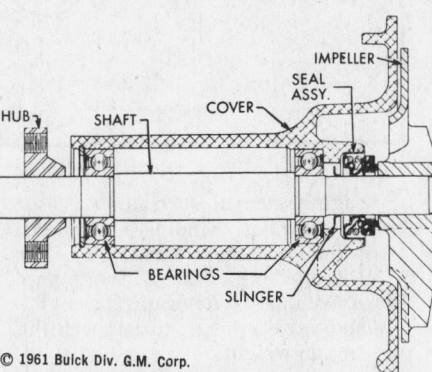

IMPELLER · SEAL ASSY. · COVER · HUB · SHAFT · BEARINGS · SLINGER

© 1961 Buick Div. G.M. Corp.

Water Pump Cover Assembly

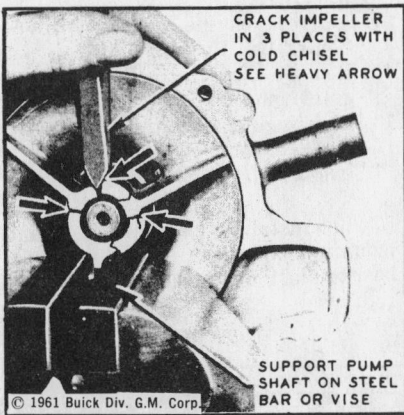

CRACK IMPELLER IN 3 PLACES WITH COLD CHISEL SEE HEAVY ARROW

SUPPORT PUMP SHAFT ON STEEL BAR OR VISE

© 1961 Buick Div. G.M. Corp.

Cracking Water Pump Impeller

WATER PUMP REMOVAL

It is possible to remove and replace the water pump on all Buick cars without disturbing the radiator core. This is accomplished by removing the fan belt, fan blades, and pulley, disconnect the hoses and remove the water pump attaching bolts.

On V-8 models, two sizes (3/8 and 5/16) of bolts are used in cover of the water pump. The larger size passes through the front cover into the cylinder block.

WATER MANIFOLDS

To remove the water manifold, detach the upper radiator hose and remove the two attaching bolts which hold the manifold to the front of each cylinder head. Lift the manifold straight up to free the neoprene seal in the water pump housing. **Caution:** On assembly use a NEW seal. Mounting gaskets may be coated with compound.

THERMOSTAT REMOVAL

The thermostat is contained in the water outlet elbow mounted on the front of the water manifold.

To replace the thermostat, disconnect the upper radiator hose, remove the radiator water outlet attaching bolts, lift off the outlet and take out the thermostat.

Caution:

In replacing a thermostat, avoid installing the unit backwards. It is possible, with dire results.

ENGINE

REFERENCES

In the specifications tables of this section there are listed all the available facts about the engines. Engine identification is covered near the beginning of this Buick Car Section, just prior to Tune-Up-Specifications.

Valves

Detailed information on the valves, the type of valve guide and the location of valve timing marks, can be found in the Valve Specifications Table of this section.

BUICK

A general discussion of valve clearance and a chart showing how to read pressure and vacuum gauges when using them to diagnose engine troubles will be found in the Unit Repair section under the heading: "Engine Diagnosis, Professional Approach."

Valve tappet clearance for each engine is given in the Tune-Up Specifications Table of Buick Tune-up section.

Bearings

Detailed information on engine bearings will be found in the Crankshaft Bearing Journal Sizes Table of this section.

V8 Engine Piston and Rod Installation

Pistons and Pins

Detailed information on pistons and piston pins, together with information on piston, rod and crankshaft relationship for assembly, will be found in the Piston and Pin Specifications Table of this section.

Engine crankcase capacities are listed in the Capacities Table of this Buick Car Section.

Approved torque wrench readings and head bolt tightening sequences are covered in the Torque Specifications Table of this section.

Information on the engine marking code will be found in the Engine Identification Table at the start of the Buick section.

ENGINE R & R

The reason for removal, degree of disassembly, and extent and type of shop equipment may all influence the following procedure.

1. Drain cooling system.
2. Scribe hinge outline on underside of hood. Remove hood attaching bolts and remove hood.
3. Disconnect battery cables.
4. Remove radiator and heater hoses.
5. Disconnect transmission oil cooler lines.
6. Remove attaching bolts and lift out radiator.
7. Disconnect exhaust pipe or pipes at the exhaust manifold/s.
8. Disconnect transmission control linkage.
9. Disconnect accelerator to carburetor linkage.
10. Disconnect all engine component wiring that would interfere with

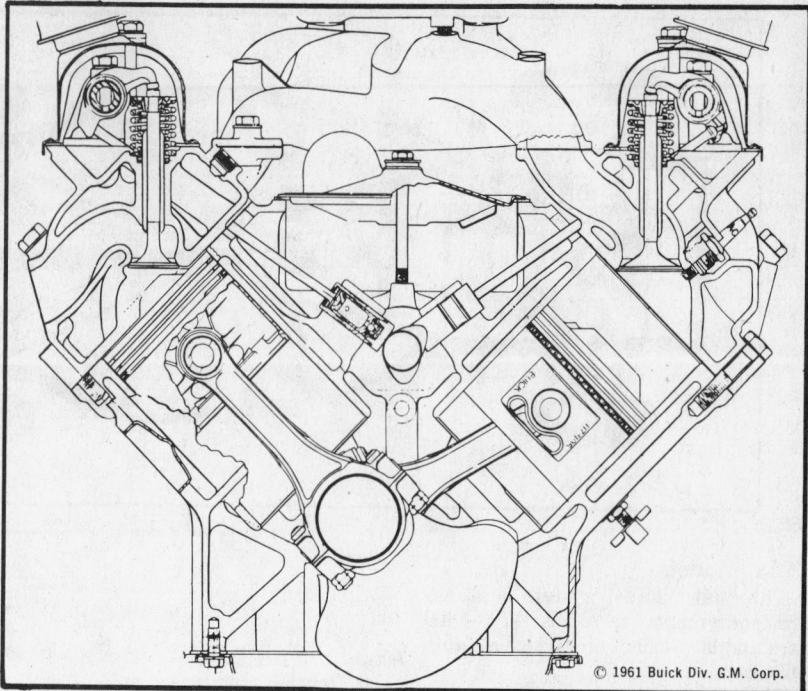

1958 thru 1963 V-8 engine

© 1961 Buick Div. G.M. Corp.

engine removal, such as, generator wires, gauge sending unit wires, primary ignition wires, etc.

11. Disconnect gas line at fuel pump.
12. Attach lifting device to the engine and raise enough to support the engine weight.
13. Remove bottom Bell Housing converter from drive plate (flywheel).
14. Separate engine from transmission at Bell Housing.
15. Remove engine attachment at engine mounts.
16. Lift engine foward and upward to clear engine compartment.
17. Install by reversing above procedure.

When installing an engine, the front mounting pad to frame bolts should be the last mounting bolts to be tightened.

Loosen the spark plug cover in order to free the valve cover

© 1959 Buick Div. G.M. Corp.

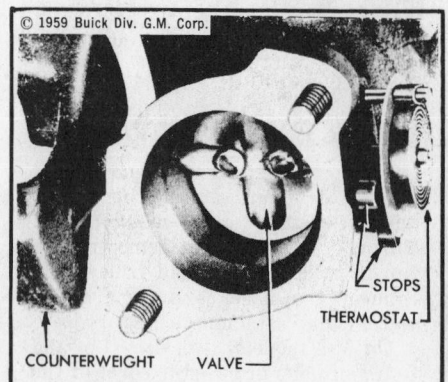

© 1959 Buick Div. G.M. Corp.

Heat damper located in left exhaust

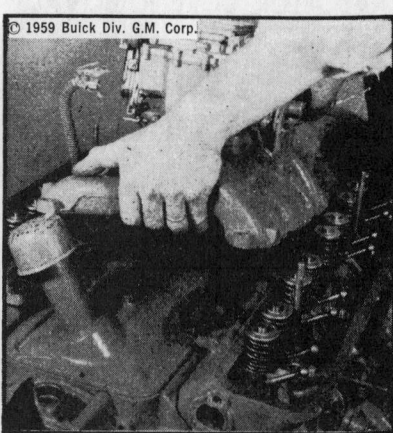

© 1959 Buick Div. G.M. Corp.

Remove carburetor and intake manifold as an assembly

ENGINE MANIFOLDS

V-8 Models

The inlet manifold may be removed from the center of the engine block without removing any other part of the engine.

Take off the air cleaner and disconnect the vacuum, gas and accelerator rods from the carburetor, unbolt and lift off the manifold.

On the V-8 models the exhaust manifolds on each side may be removed with some slight difficulty without taking off any other part of the engine unless the car is equipped with power steering in which case it will be necessary to either remove the power steering gear box or take off the cylinder head on the left bank in order to get at the manifold.

In either case whether or not the model is equipped with power steering the right exhaust manifold may be removed without taking off any other part of the engine.

On 1957-58 models remove the generator mounting bracket for access to the front manifold bolts.

CYLINDER HEAD

REMOVAL

Remove all carburetor and throttle linkage connections, the vacuum line to the distributor, and the lines to the fuel pump. Unbolt the inlet manifold from between the two blocks and lift it off the car.

Remove the rocker cover, then detach the exhaust manifold at the flange connection rather than at the head.

Note: The exhaust manifold can be disconnected from the head but this procedure takes somewhat longer than detaching it at the exhaust flange connection.

Remove the rocker cover and take off the rocker assemblies. Mark them carefully for reassembly.

Note: There are no oil lines connections to the rocker assemblies since oil is fed through the rocker front bracket.

Detach the front water manifold

© 1959 Buick Div. G.M. Corp.

Lift out push rods. Push rods can be installed either way. There is no top or bottom

from both cylinder heads, unbolt and lift off the head.

Caution: The cylinder heads are interchangeable right for left. However, if the head taken from the right bank is installed on the left bank it will be necessary to change the water outlet plugs, heater plugs, heat indicator plugs, etc.

VALVE SYSTEM

REMOVAL OF ROCKER SHAFTS AND PUSH RODS

To remove the rocker shafts; first remove the air cleaner, then the rocker cover and then take out the bolts which hold the rocker shaft backets to the cylinder head.

Carefully mark the rocker shaft so that it will be returned on the same cylinder head from which it was removed since these rocker shafts can be used on either cylinder head.

If they are placed on the wrong head the counter-bored bracket will not pass oil to the rocker shafts and they will very shortly wear out from lack of lubrication.

After the rocker shafts have been taken off, the push rods can be taken out of their bores without removing the cylinder head.

ROCKER SHAFT LUBRICATION

Oil is fed through the front rocker shaft bracket on both cylinder heads. The front bracket has an oversize bore which permits oil to pass around the outside of the bolt up to the hollowed out rocker shaft.

VALVE GUIDE REPLACEMENT

Remove the cylinder head and take out the valves and valve spring assemblies. Now measure very carefully the amount the valve guide protrudes from the cylinder head before driving it out so that the new guide can be driven down exactly that amount. Make up a stack of washers equivalent to the protrusion of the guide before removing the guide from the head.

When driving out the valve guides support the cylinder head as near to the valve guide as practical.

A pilot type driver should be used and the guide should be driven out from the bottom, or the guide may be pressed out if an arbor press is available.

Start the new guide into the top of the head and tap it gently to insure that it is starting straight. Once started straight, it can be driven into position very quickly.

When the new valve guide has been driven in the correct distance, enter a new valve into the guide to make sure that the valve will operate freely up and down. The slightest sign of binding in the new valve guide means that the guide itself has become riveted over or slightly warped in the driving process and will have to be reamed.

Buick valve guides should be finish reamed to size after installation. Use a reamer that will give the valve stem to guide clearance listed in the Valve Specifications Table at the start of this section.

Always reface the valve seat when new guides have been installed to be absolutely certain that the valve seat is concentric to the new guide.

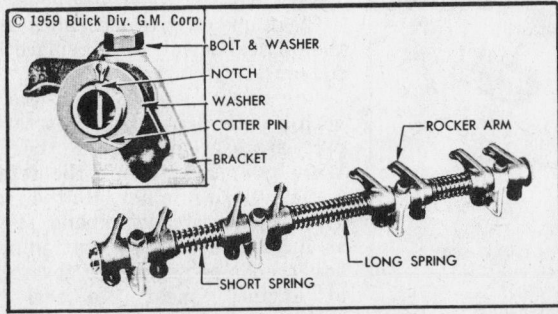

© 1959 Buick Div. G.M. Corp.

BOLT & WASHER
NOTCH
WASHER
COTTER PIN
BRACKET
ROCKER ARM
LONG SPRING
SHORT SPRING

Rocker arm and shaft assembly

DRIVE OLD GUIDE OUT FROM COMBUSTION CHAMBER SIDE

DRIVE NEW GUIDE IN FROM TOP SIDE OF HEAD

© 1961 Buick Div. G.M. Corp.

J 269
J 5240-1
J 5240-2
GUIDES
J 5251

Removing and installing valve guides

VALVE SPRINGS

To check the condition of the valve springs line up the inlet valve springs on a flat surface and, using a straight edge compare the height of the springs. If all of the springs are the same height as determined with the straight edge, it may be assumed safely that the springs are in good condition since it is very unlikely that all of the springs would collapse the same amount.

If one or more of the springs are lower than the rest it is advisable to secure at least one new spring and then compare the other springs with the new one for free length.

Replace all springs which do not come up to the standard set by the new one.

Repeat the operation on the exhaust valve springs.

⏱ CHILTON TIME-SAVER

The following is a method for replacing valve springs, oil seals or spring retainers without removing the cylinder head.

1. Entirely dismantle a spark plug and save the threaded shell.
2. To this shell, braze or weld an air chuck.
3. Remove the valve rocker cover. Remove the rocker arm from the affected valve.
4. Remove the spark plug from the affected cylinder.
5. Turn the crankshaft to bring the piston of this cylinder down, away from possible contact with the valve head. Sharply tap the valve retainer to loosen the valve lock.
6. Then turn the crankshaft to bring the piston in this cylinder to the

Exact Top of its Compression Stroke.

7. Screw in the chuck equipped spark plug shell.
8. Hook up an air hose to the chuck and turn on the pressure (about 200 lb).
9. With a strong and constant supply of air holding the valve closed, compress the valve spring and remove the lock and retainer.
10. Make the necessary replacements and reassemble.

<u>NOTE:</u> It is important that the operation be performed exactly as stated, in this order. The piston in the affected cylinder must be on exact top center to prevent air pressure from turning the crankshaft.

VALVE REMOVAL

Remove the air cleaner, the rocker cover, the rockers and the intake manifold. Disconnect the exhaust manifolds at their flanges, leaving the manifold attached to the heads.

From the right bank remove the generator mounting bracket, and from the left the power steering pump. Disconnect the heat indicator, remove fuel and vacuum lines. Remove the bolts which hold the water manifolds to the cylinder heads, unbolt and remove the cylinder heads. Take the heads to a bench and, using a C type or lever type valve spring compressor, compress the valve springs, remove the keeper, release the valve springs, and push the valves to the combustion chamber side of the head.

REMOVAL OF HYDRAULIC LIFTERS

To remove the lifters, remove the rocker cover and take off the rocker shaft assemblies and lift out the push rods. Then remove the intake manifold.

The valve chamber cover plate can then be removed giving access to the lifters.

The lifters are barrel type which will come right up out of their bores requiring no other tools than the fingers.

If more effort than can be given by the fingers is required it indicates that gum or other sticky substances present in the oil and is probably the cause of the failure of the lifter.

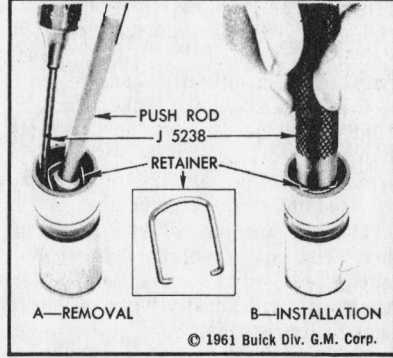

Removing and installing plunger retainer

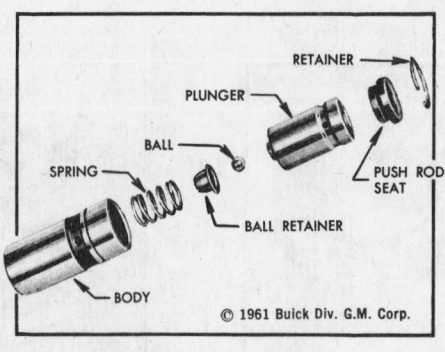

Hydraulic valve lifter parts

TIMING CASE COVER TIMING CHAIN

VIBRATION DAMPER REMOVAL

Remove the radiator core and take out the cap screws which hold the fan pulley to the vibration damper. Remove the large bolt from the center of the crankshaft and insert a bolt type puller into the holes which held the fan pulley. Pull off the vibration damper.

REPLACEMENT OF TIMING CHAIN AND FRONT OIL SEAL

All V-8 Engines Thru 1956

Drain cooling system and remove radiator core, shroud, fan belt, fan and pulley and vibration damper.

Remove all bolts holding timing gear cover and the water manifold to the engine block and cylinder heads. Do not remove the five small bolts holding the water pump to the water manifold.

Remove water-manifold-timing-chain-cover assembly, being careful not to tear the oil pan gasket.

Remove oil slinger from crankshaft and remove the bolt, lockwasher and plain washer holding fuel-pump-drive eccentric and camshaft sprocket to camshaft.

If there has been doubt about the valve timing, turn the crankshaft so that the camshaft sprocket keyway points down. The "O" marks on the two sprockets should be to the left of the engine and there should be twelve (12) pins of the timing chain between them, including teeth aligned with the marks.

Remove camshaft sprocket and timing chain.

End thrust of the camshaft is taken by a thrust plate fastened to the block behind the sprocket. End play of the camshaft is controlled by a spacer ring just behind the thrust plate and in front of the camshaft front bearing journal. The spacing ring provides end play of the camshaft of .004 to .008 when the camshaft sprocket is tightened into place.

Clean up the cover assembly and if the oil seal seems worn replace it as follows:

Remove the braided fabric packing with a screwdriver and then tap the pressed steel retainer out of the cover. Work new packing into the retainer and drive the retainer into the recess. The packing should expand slightly as it seats. Install so that joint between ends of packing is toward top of engine. Smear the seal with vaseline.

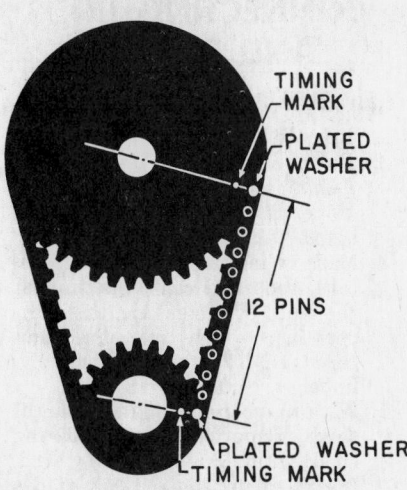

Timing chain and sprocket marks
V8 thru 1956

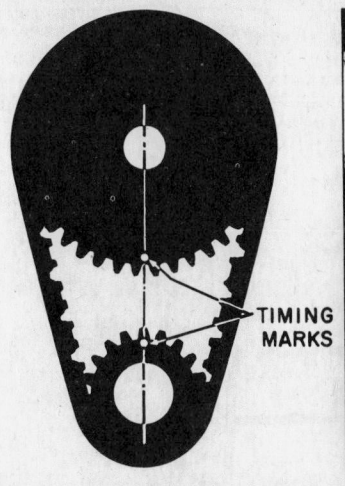

Timing chain and sprocket marks
V8 starting 1957

Oil filter installation

When ready to install the chain turn the crankshaft, if it has been turned since chain was removed, so that pistons No. 1 and No. 4 are on top dead center. Turn camshaft so that sprocket keyway points down.

Place chain and sprocket back in place so marks on sprockets are to left of engine and twelve link-pins apart.

Install fuel pump drive eccentric so that keyway fits over key in camshaft. Fasten all in place.

Install oil slinger on end of crankshaft with hollow side outward.

Reverse procedure to complete installation. Keep engine speed low for a short while after installation of oil seal.

All V-8 Engines Starting With 1957 Production

The procedure given for V8 engines thru 1956 applies as well to those starting with 1957 production except that the sprocket timing marks are changed.

The "O" marks starting with 1957 production are on the sprockets and should be set to be nearest each other and in line with the shaft centers.

The end play of the camshaft on these engines is taken by the hub of the camshaft sprocket. The distributor drive gear keeps the thrust rearward. The thrust plate and spacer ring have been eliminated.

ENGINE LUBRICATION

OIL PAN REMOVAL

V-8 Engines

The V-8 engine oil pan can be removed readily from underneath the car without any difficulty. It may be necessary in some cases however, to disconnect and lower the steering idler arm bracket and rotate the crankshaft somewhat in order to clear the counterbalances.

OIL PUMP REMOVAL

The oil pump, on all engines, is driven by a tongue at the bottom of the distributor shaft. The oil pump can be removed after the oil pan has been taken off. The vacuum pump, which is attached to the oil pump on 1957-58 models, is serviced only as an assembly. Check the oil pump driven gear and driving key before replacing the vacuum pump.

OIL FILTER

1954-57

Loosen container bolt and allow oil to drain out. Remove bolt to release container, element and old gasket. Clean container and gasket surfaces. Install new gasket and filter element in case. Tighten bolt. Check for leaks after engine has run for 5 minutes.

Beginning 1958

A screw-off-and-disposable element and can type filter is used. The filter should be changed at 4,000 miles or 6 month intervals, which ever comes first.

⏻ CHILTON TIME-SAVER

A few cases of difficulty in oil filter replacement have come to our attention. The trouble starts with oil filter elements being turned on too tightly. The unit may be too tight to remove by hand and it may collapse in the grip of a tool that applies enough squeeze to grip the element hard enough to turn it.

AN ALTERNATE METHOD OF REMOVAL:

1. Raise the car on a jack or hoist and place a drip pan under the filter.

2. With a 12 inch to 14 inch slender punch drive a hole in the element from one side to the other.

NOTE: Before punching the hole, consider the angle required for the punch to act as a lever, with the least interference.

3. With the drift all the way thru the filter and acting as a lever, turn the unit counterclockwise enough to break it loose.

4. Final loosening and removal can now be accomplished by hand.

TO REPLACE

1. Coat the gasket on the new filter with oil.

2. Place the new filter in position on the block.

3. Hand tighten until contact is made between the filter gasket and the adapter face.

4. Tighten by further turning the filter ½ turn.

5. Run the engine at fast idle and check for oil leaks.

6. Check the oil and bring crankcase to level if necessary.

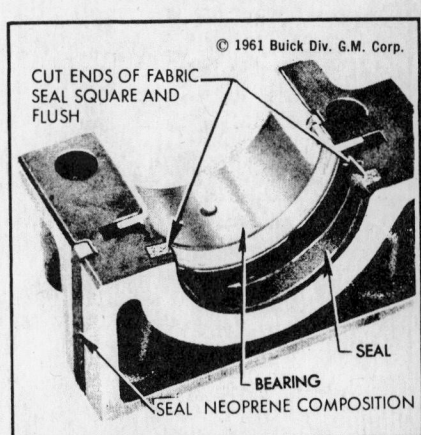

Rear main bearing cap

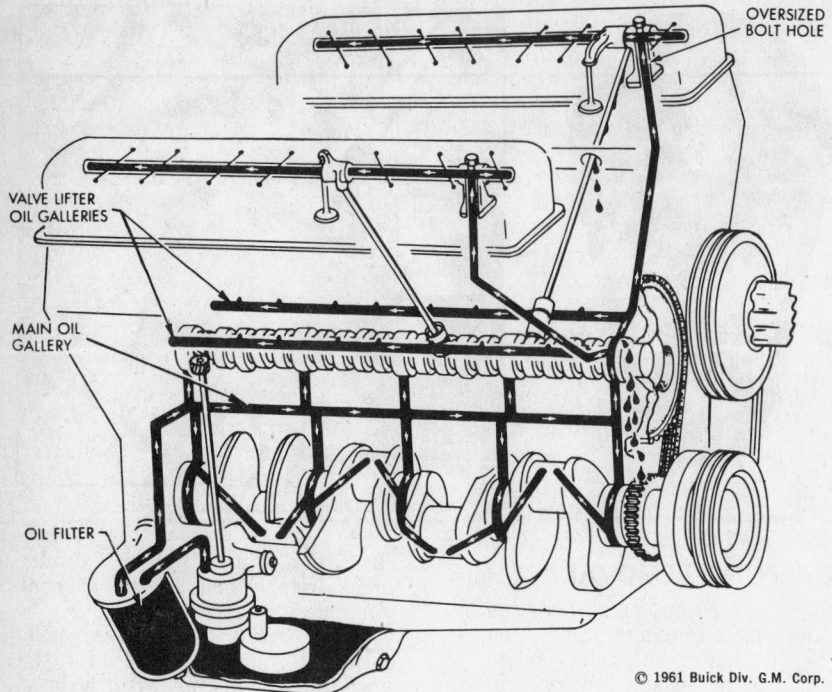

VALVE LIFTER
OIL GALLERIES

MAIN OIL
GALLERY

OIL FILTER

OVERSIZED
BOLT HOLE

© 1961 Buick Div. G.M. Corp.

Engine Lubrication, V-8

CONNECTING RODS AND PISTONS

REMOVE PISTON ASSEMBLIES

1. Remove cylinder heads.
2. Remove oil pan.
3. Examine cylinder bores for top ridge. If ridge exists, remove it before taking pistons out.
4. Mark cylinder numbers on all pistons, rods and caps. Starting at the front of the engine, the cylinders in the right bank are numbered 1-3-5-7; the left bank cylinders are numbered 2-4-6-8.
5. With number 4 crankpin straight down, remove cap and bearing shell from #1 connecting rod. Install connecting rod bolt guides to hold upper half of the bearing shell in place.
6. Push piston and rod assembly up out of the cylinder. Then remove bolt guides and reinstall cap and bearing shell on the rod.
7. Remove the remaining rod and piston assemblies in the same manner.
8. Carefully remove old rings with piston ring expander.
9. Carefully press out the old pin.

Note: Check the cylinder bores for out-of-round, taper or other damage. Any cylinders requiring attention may be bored or honed the same as any conventional cast iron cylinder block.

Fitting Rings and Pins

When new rings are installed without reboring the cylinders, cylinder wall glaze should be broken. This can be done by using the finest grade stones in a cylinder hone.

New piston rings must be checked for clearance in piston grooves and for cap in cylinder bores.

When fitting new rings to new pistons the side clearance for compression rings should be .003" to .005". Side clearance of the oil ring should be .0035" to .0095".

REAR MAIN BEARING OIL SEAL REPLACEMENT

Buick uses an oil slinger and groove, a braided fabric seal and two cork or neoprene strips to seal the rear main bearing. The braided fabric seal can be installed in the crankcase half (upper) only when crankshaft is removed; however, the seal can be replaced in the lower half whenever the lower half (cap) has been removed. To renew the seals in the cap proceed as follows:

Remove the old seals and clean up the the cap. Place new braided seal in groove with both ends projecting above parting surface of cap. Force seal into groove by rubbing down with a hammer handle or other smooth device until seal is seated in groove and ends project above the parting face of the cap not more than 1/16 inch. Using a razor blade, cut ends off flush with parting surface.

The cork seals on the sides are slightly longer than need be. Coat the groove on the sides of the cap with gasket cement. When the cement is tacky carefully work the cork into the grooves with a putty knife. Lightly compress the seals into the grooves with a vise for a few minutes while the cement sets.

Now cut the ends of the cork seals square and flush with the machined surface of the cap.

Grease the exposed surfaces of the cork with vaseline before reinstalling the cap in the engine. Caution: The engine must be operated at slow speed when first started after installation of new braided seals.

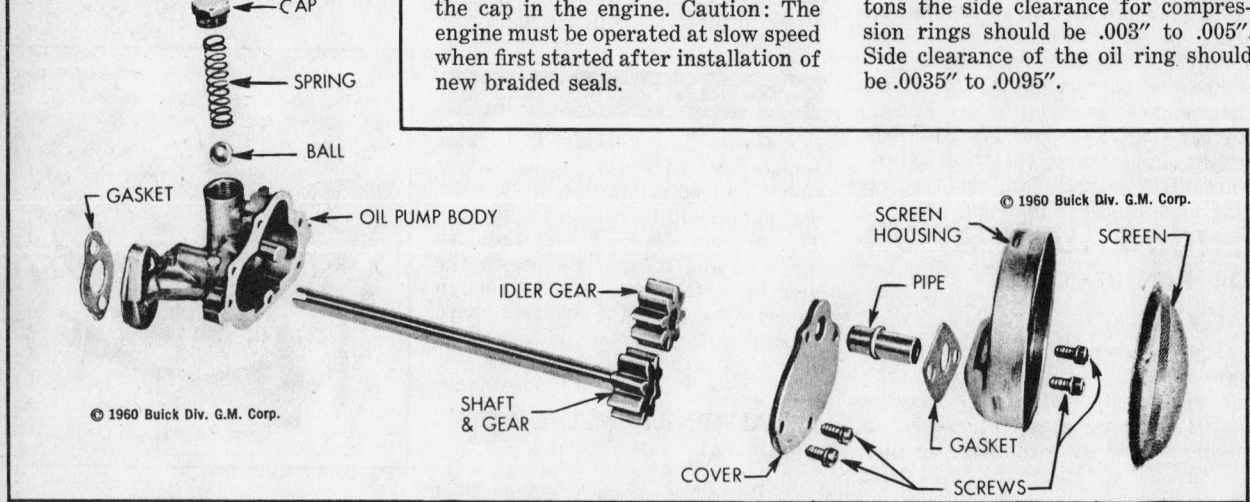

CAP

SPRING

BALL

GASKET

OIL PUMP BODY

IDLER GEAR

SHAFT & GEAR

COVER

SCREEN HOUSING

PIPE

SCREEN

GASKET

SCREWS

© 1960 Buick Div. G.M. Corp.

© 1960 Buick Div. G.M. Corp.

Oil Pump Assembly —1959-63

Check end gap of compression rings by placing them in the bore in which they will operate. Then push them to the bottom of the bore with a piston. Now measure the end gap in each ring. The end gap should be no less than .015".

If piston pin bosses are worn out of round or oversize, the piston and pin should be replaced. Oversize pins are not practical because the pin is a press fit in the connecting rod. Piston pins must fit the piston with an easy finger push at 70°F, (.0003" to .0005").

In assembling the piston to the connecting rod a press, is ideal. However, substitutes are available that will answer the purpose.

If the rod assembly is to go into the **left** bank, the **boss on the rod** and cap go toward the **rear** of the engine. If the rod assembly is to go into the **right** bank, the **boss on the rod** and cap go toward the **front** of the engine. In both cases the connecting rod bearing oil spurt holes point "UP".

Connecting Rod Bearings

1. Remove connecting rod cap with bearing shell. Wipe all oil from the bearing area.
2. Place a piece of Plastigage lengthwise along the bottom center of the lower bearing shell. Then install cap with bearing shell and torque the bolt nuts to 30-35 ft. lb. **Note:** Do not turn crankshaft.
3. Remove the cap and shell. The gauge material will be found flattened and adhering to either the bearing shell or the crankpin. **Do not remove it.**
4. Using the scale that comes with the gauge, measure the flattened gauge material at its widest point. The number within the graduation which comes closest to the width of the gauging material indicates the bearing to crankpin clearance in thousandths of an inch.

5. Desired clearance for a new bearing is .0002" to .0023". If the bearing has been in service, it is wise to install a new bearing if clearance exceeds .003".
6. If a new bearing is required, try a "standard," then each undersize bearing in turn until one is found that is within specifications.
7. With the proper bearing selected, clean off the gauging material, reinstall the bearing cap and torque to 40-45 ft. lb.
8. After the bearing cap has been torqued, it should be possible to move the connecting rod back and forth on the crankpin, the extent of end clearance.

INSTALL PISTON ASSEMBLIES

1. Carefully assemble the piston to the connecting rod, (press in the pin).
2. Remove piston and rod from the press. Rock the piston on the pin to be sure pin or piston boss was not damaged during the pressing operation.
3. Install ring expander in lower ring groove. Position the ends of the expander above the piston pin where groove is not slotted. The ends of the expander must butt together.
4. Install oil ring rails over expander with gaps "up" on same side of piston as oil spurt hole in connecting rod.
5. Install compression rings, (with a ring expander) in top and center groove.
6. Coat all bearing surfaces, rings and piston skirt with engine oil.
7. Position the crankpin of the cylinder being worked on, "Down."
8. Remove connecting rod bearing cap and with upper bearing shell correctly seated in the rod, install connecting rod bolt guides.
9. Make sure the gaps in the two oil ring rails are "UP" toward

the center of the engine. Make sure the gaps of the compression rings are **not** in line with each other or the oil ring rails. Be sure the ends of the oil ring spacer-expander are butted and not overlapped.
10. With a good ring compressor, install the piston and rod assembly into the cylinder bore and carefully TAP down until the rod bearing is solidly seated on the crankpin.
11. Remove the connecting rod bolt guides and install cap and lower bearing shell. Torque to 40-45 ft. lb.
12. Install other piston and rod assemblies in the same manner. When the assemblies are all installed, the oil spurt holes will be "UP". The rib on the edge of the rod cap will be on the same side as the conical boss on the connecting rod web. These marks will be toward the other connecting rod on the same crankpin.
13. Accumulated end clearance between rod bearings on any crankpin should be .005" to .012".
14. Install oil screen and oil pan.
15. Install cylinder heads.

After starting the engine, avoid high speeds but do not run on slow idle for a while. A better break-in speed is about 800-1,000 R.P.M. for the first hour.

FRONT SUSPENSION

REFERENCES

General instructions covering the front suspension and how to repair and adjust it, together with information on installation of front wheel bearings and grease seals, are given in the Unit Repair section under the heading: Suspension, Front Repair.

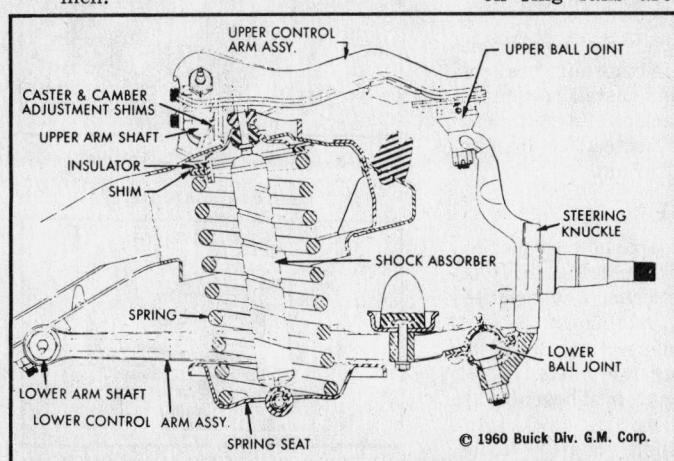

CASTER & CAMBER ADJUSTMENT SHIMS · UPPER ARM SHAFT · INSULATOR · SHIM · SPRING · LOWER ARM SHAFT · LOWER CONTROL ARM ASSY. · SPRING SEAT · UPPER CONTROL ARM ASSY. · UPPER BALL JOINT · STEERING KNUCKLE · SHOCK ABSORBER · LOWER BALL JOINT

© 1960 Buick Div. G.M. Corp.

Front suspension, 1958-60

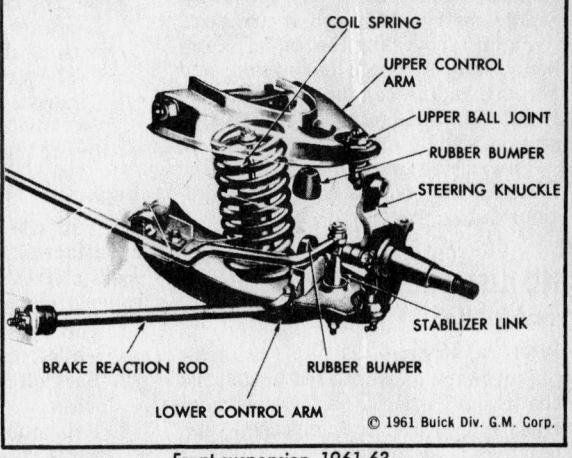

COIL SPRING · UPPER CONTROL ARM · UPPER BALL JOINT · RUBBER BUMPER · STEERING KNUCKLE · STABILIZER LINK · RUBBER BUMPER · BRAKE REACTION ROD · LOWER CONTROL ARM

© 1961 Buick Div. G.M. Corp.

Front suspension, 1961-63

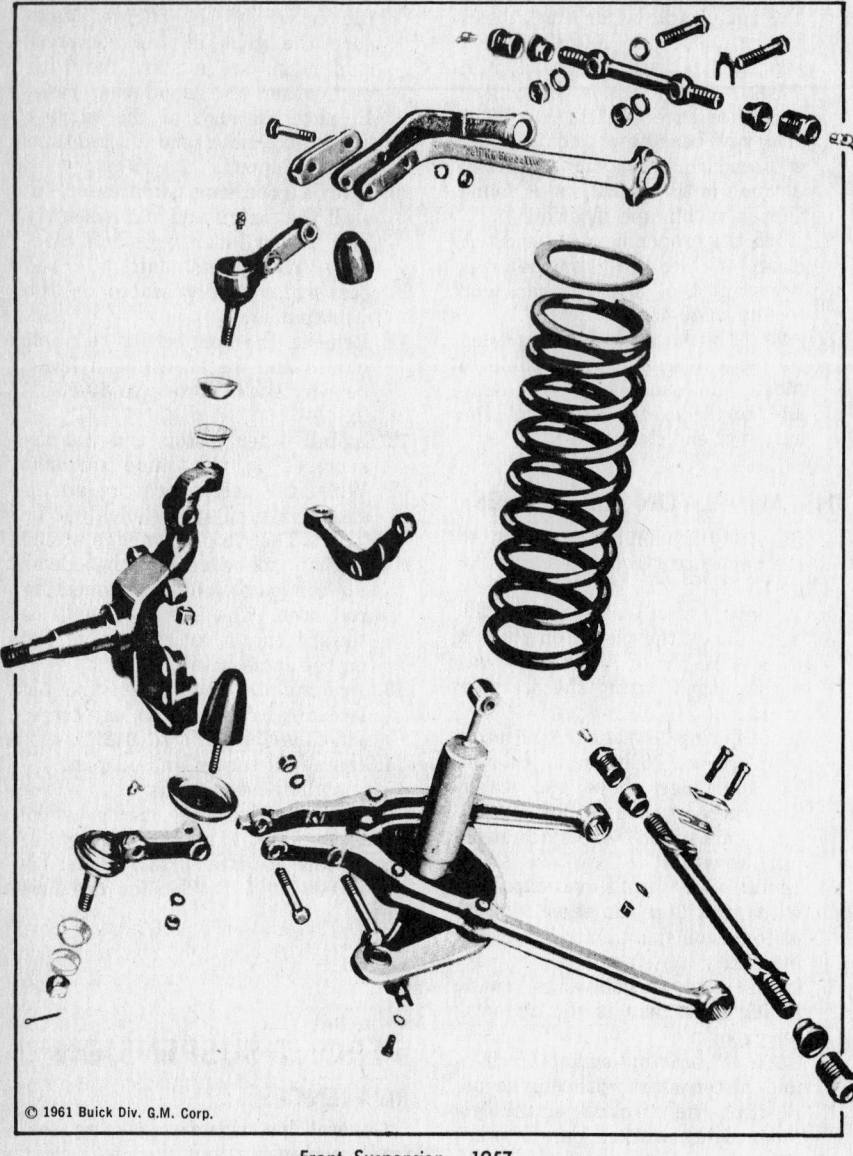

Front Suspension —1957

© 1961 Buick Div. G.M. Corp.

4. If either cotter pin hole in spindle lines up with nut castelations, back off the nut 1/12 turn and install cotter pin. Otherwise, back off the nut to the first position that will accept an horizontal or vertical cotter pin.
5. Install cotter pin and lock spindle nut into position.

BALL JOINT—UPPER

The upper ball joint is spring loaded in its socket. If the upper stud has any noticeable shake, or if it can be twisted in its socket with the fingers, the ball joint should be replaced.

Remove

1. Raise front of car. Remove wheel with hub and drum assembly.
2. Remove cotter pin from the nut on ball joint tapered stud. Loosen nut but do not remove.
3. Force of chassis spring will be in favor of disengaging tapered stud from steering knuckle. Rap knuckle sharply with a hammer in the area of the tapered stud to disengage stud from knuckle.
4. Support lower control arm with jack and remove nut from ball joint stud. Raise upper control arm and remove tapered stud from knuckle.
5. Using a wire, hold the brake backing plate and steering knuckle assembly out of the way and to prevent damage to the brake hose.
6. With an appropriate socket, remove the ball joint from the control arm.

Definitions of the points of steering geometry are covered in the Unit Repair section under the heading: Suspension—Front Alignment. This article also covers trouble shooting front end geometry and irregular tire wear.

Figures covering the caster, camber, toe-in, king pin inclination, and turning radius can be found in the Front Wheel Alignment Table of this section.

Tire size figures can be found in the General Chassis and Brake Specifications Table.

ADJUST FRONT WHEEL BEARINGS

Prior to 1961

Ball bearings were used to suspend the front wheels. Adjustment of freshly cleaned and repacked ball bearings is as follows:

1. Tighten spindle nut to 30 ft. lbs. and rotate the wheel to seat the bearings.
2. Back off spindle nut and retorque to 12½ ft. lbs.
3. If either cotter pin hole aligns with a slot in the nut, back off 1/12 turn and install cotter pin. Otherwise, back off nut until nearest hole and castelation line up. Insert the cotter pin.

Beginning 1961

Front wheels are now suspended upon tapered roller bearings. Adjustment of freshly cleaned and repacked roller bearings is as follows:

1. Torque spindle nut to 19 ft. lbs. while rotating the wheel.
2. Back off the nut until bearings are loose.
3. Retorque spindle nut to 11 ft. lbs. while rotating the wheel.

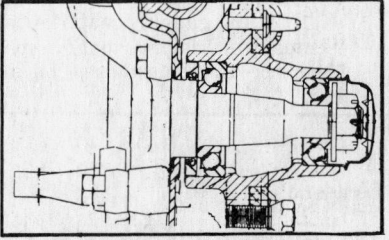

Front Wheel Bearings 1954-60

© 1961 Buick Div. G.M. Corp.

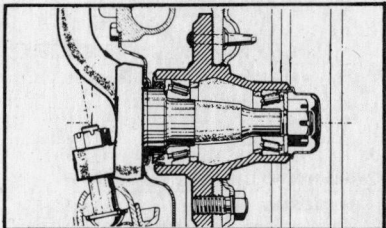

Front Wheel Bearings , 1961-63

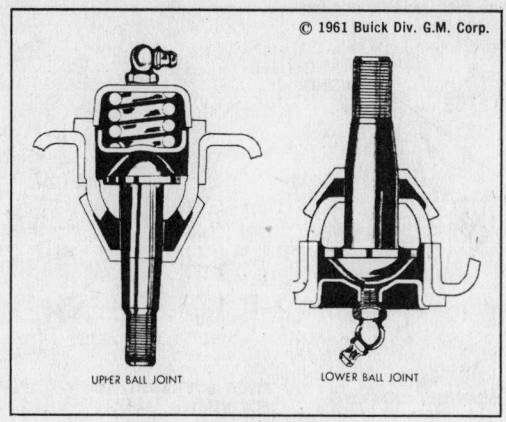

Upper and lower ball joints

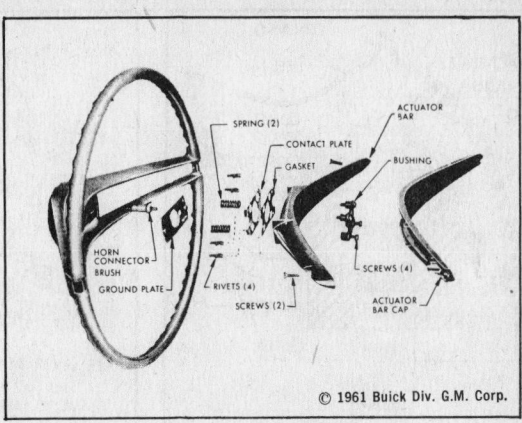

Steering Wheel Assembly

Install

1. Install new ball joint into control arm and tighten until hex section of ball joint seats firmly into arms.
2. Turn stud to align the cotter pin hole fore and aft and assemble rubber dust shield over stud.
3. Remove tie-back wire from steering knuckle and backing plate assembly and assemble tapered stud to knuckle. Install castellated nut, torque to 35-60 ft. lb. and install cotter pin.
4. Reinstall wheel with hub and drum.

Note: Upper and lower joints look alike but are not interchangeable. Upper joints are spring loaded. Lower joints depend on the force of the chassis spring to keep the ball loaded.

BALL JOINT—LOWER

Remove

1. Raise car and support under side rails.
2. Remove wheel and tire assembly.
3. Remove hub dust cap.
4. Remove hub and drum assembly.
5. Remove backing plate and brake assembly by removing the two backing plate attaching bolts and nuts and the brake anchor bolt.
6. Without detaching the brake hose, place the plate and brake assembly above the upper control arm.
7. Place a safety stand or jack under lower control arm as far out on the arm as possible. Do not allow the arm to rest upon the stand but about ½ inch below it.
8. Remove cotter pin and loosen, **(Don't remove)** ball joint attaching nut.
9. Rap steering knuckle to separate stud from knuckle.

10. Raise stand or jack against control arm, remove nut and raise steering knuckle off tapered stud.
11. Remove ball joint from lower control arm with appropriate socket.
12. Remove upper rubber bumper from frame to help in later installation of new ball joint.

Install

1. Start new ball joint into threads of lower control arm, then set up tight with appropriate socket. Point the 45 dgeree grease fitting toward the center-line of the car. Install grease shield.
2. Install steering knuckle over tapered ball joint stud.
3. Install stud nut and torque to 60-70 ft. lbs. Lock nut with cotter pin.
4. Reinstall rubber bumper into the frame.
5. Be certain that a new oil seal ring is installed over the knuckle spindle to seal backing plate. Torque for the ¾" bolt and nut is 60-75 ft. lbs. The 11/16" bolt and nut is 40-60 ft. lbs. and the anchor bolt torque is 130-150 ft. lbs.
6. Install hub and drum assembly and adjust the spindle nut as follows:
   a. Torque nut to 19 ft. lbs. while rotating the wheel.
   b. Back off the nut until bearings are loose.
   c. Retorque the nut to 11 ft. lbs. while rotating the wheel.
   d. If either cotter pin hole in spindle lines up with nut castelations, back off the nut ½ turn and install cotter pin. Otherwise, back off the nut to the first position that will accept a horizontal or vertical cotter pin.

   e. Install cotter pin and lock spindle nut into position.
7. Install wheel and tire assembly, then lower car to floor.

STEERING WHEEL AND HORN BUTTON

STEERING WHEEL REMOVAL

On all models of Buick the steering wheel can be removed readily after the horn button has been taken off. Be sure to disconnect wire at horn cable connector.

Caution: In all cases a steering wheel puller should be used to remove the steering wheel since prying or driving at the wheel will likely result in damage.

Before the steering wheel is removed mark it carefully so that it can be assembled readily in the same position from which it was removed.

On most models a blind spline is used to insure that the wheel will only go on in one direction.

HORN BUTTON REMOVAL
1954-57 Horn Button

Pry out the monogram, it is held by the prongs of a retaining spring, and unscrew and remove the horn sensitivity adjusting nut. Remove the contact plate, spring and insulators. Remove the steering wheel nut to release the operating ring, cushion, and contact spacer. When reassembling tighten the sensitivity adjusting nut until the horns start to blow then back nut off one-half turn.

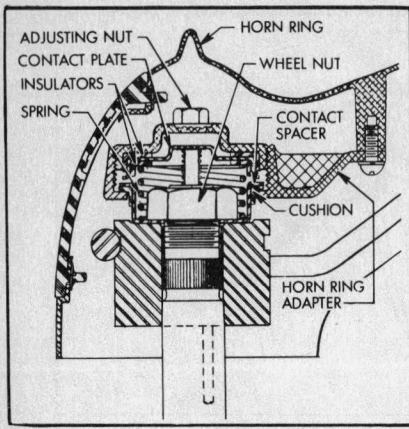

Horn ring contacts

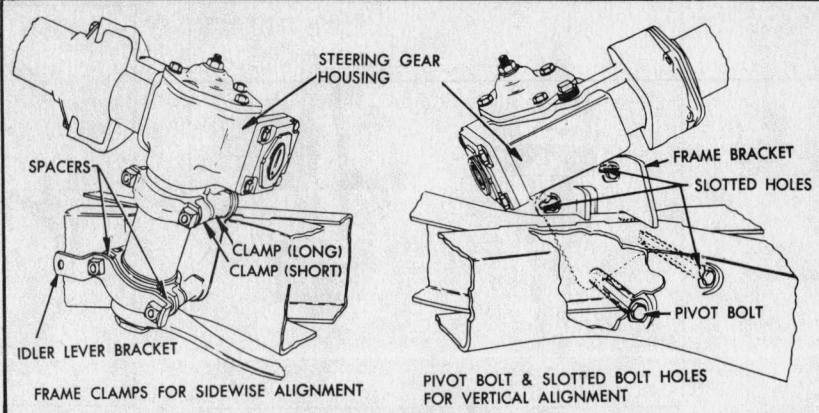

Steering gear alignment—1954-56

1958-63 Horn Button
Series 40 Standard

Cap with rubber retainer snaps over rim of contact cap. Use thin blade to pry cap out. Remove screws to release cap.

1958-63 Horn Button
All Others

The horn ring is held in place by three Phillips head screws which are located on the underside of the horn ring. Remove these screws, remove adjusting nut, contact plate, spring, and two insulators. Remove steering wheel nut and take off the horn ring.

Remove the lines from the carburetor and take off the air cleaner.

Disconnect the tie rod from the pitman arm.

Disconnect the shifter mechanism at the bottom of the steering gear.

Disconnect the brace at the dash panel and pull it to one side.

Remove the gear shift lever and the direction signal lever and also disconnect the directional signal wires from the switch on the dash panel.

Disconnect the steering gear mounting bolts at the frame, move the steering gear as far as possible to the rear, turn the unit over until the pitman arm is in the uppermost position, then raise the forward end of the steering gear assembly up between the engine and the fender and bring the assembly forward into the engine compartment to remove it.

Note: A great deal of time will be saved if two men remove the gear assembly, since this will make the job much easier and prevent scratching finished surfaces.

Note: The steering wheel is mounted on a serrated shaft and a suitable puller should be used to remove it.

The gear is replaced by reversing the removal procedure. Again two men should be used to reinstall the steering mechanism.

MANUAL STEERING GEAR

Manual Steering Gear

Instructions covering the overhaul of the steering gear will be found in the Unit Repair section under the heading: Manual Steering Gears.

REMOVAL

All Models Thru 1956

Disconnect all steering column wires, including the back-up switch, horn, turn signal and the Dynaflow neutral safety switch wire.

Remove the steering wheel.

Set the direction signal switch in the off position and remove the wires from the fuse block.

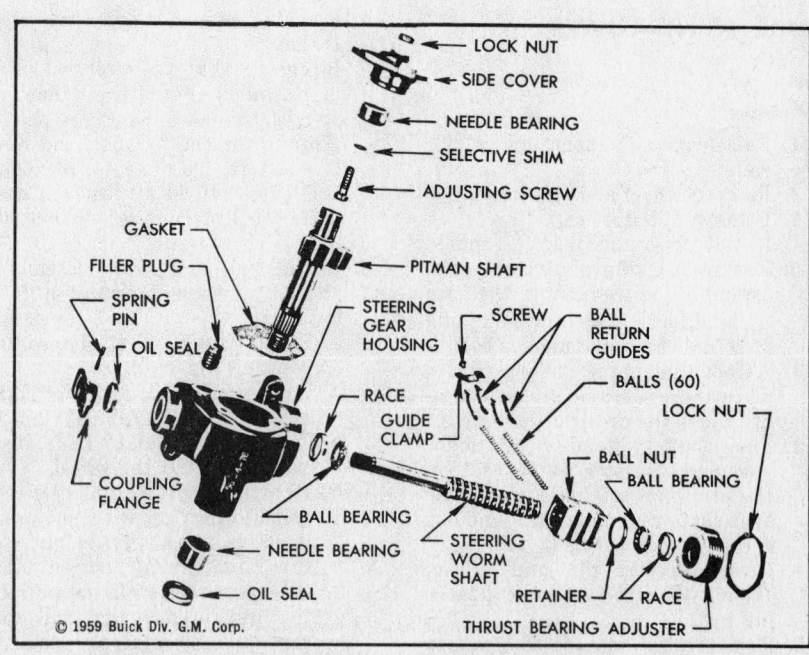

Manual steering gear disassembled—1957-63

All Models Starting 1957

The steering gear mechanism is in two pieces coupled together with a universal joint.

To remove the lower gear box, disconnect the universal joint and (on power steering) disconnect both hydraulic hoses. It is easier to disconnect them at the pump. Be sure to match mark the steering shaft flanges.

From under the car, disconnect the steering Pitman arm from the Pitman Shaft and remove the bolts at outside of left frame side rail which hold the gear housing to the frame and lower the gear assembly to the floor.

When reinstalling tighten Pitman Arm nut to 90-110 ft. lbs.

STEERING IDLER ARM

The idler arm bracket is held to the right frame side rail by two cap screws. Remove the cap screws and lower the tie rods. Unscrew the bracket from the bushing and then take the bushing out of the idler arm.

Bracket and bushing are usually replaced in sets.

POWER STEERING GEAR

Power Steering Gears

Trouble shooting and repair instructions covering power steering gears are given in the Unit Repair Section under the heading: Power Steering.

Replacement of Pitman Shaft Seals with Power Steering Gear Still in Place

Disconnect pitman arm from pitman shaft. Clean end of pitman shaft and housing. Tape the splines of the pitman shaft to keep them from cutting the seal. Use only one layer of tape. Too much tape will prevent passage of the seal. Using lock-ring pliers remove the seal retaining ring.

Start the engine and turn the steering wheel to the right so that the oil pressure in the housing will force the seals out. Catch the seal and the oil in a container. Turn off the engine when the two seals are out.

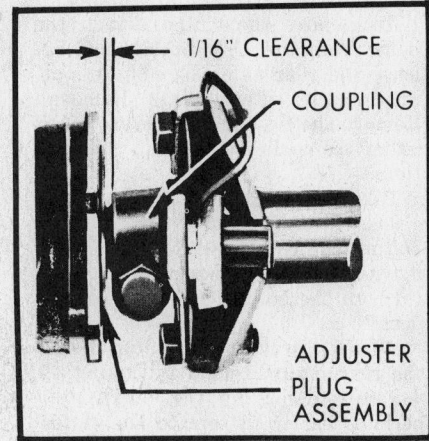

Correct Installation of Lower Coupling

This method of seal removal eliminates the possible scoring of the seal seats while attempting to pry them out.

Inspect the two old seals for damage to the rubber covering on the outside diameter. If it seems scored or scratched inspect the housing for burrs, etc. and remove them before installing the new seals.

Lubricate the two new seals with petroleum jelly. Put the one with a single lip in first, then put in a washer, drive seal in far enough to permit installation of double lip seal, washer and the seal retaining ring. The first seal is not supposed to bottom in its counterbore.

Fill reservoir to proper level, start engine, turn wheel to right and check for leaks.

Remove the tape and reinstall the pitman arm. Tighten nut to 90-110 ft. lbs.

REMOVAL OF POWER STEERING GEAR

Disconnect the hoses at the steering gear and elevate their ends above the pump to prevent oil from draining out of the pump.

Match-mark upper and lower steering shaft flanges to assure correct assembly. Then disconnect the flexible coupling.

Working under the car, remove pitman shaft nut and remove the pitman arm. Remove the four steering gear to frame bolts at outside of left frame rail. Remove steering gear.

Reverse procedure to install.

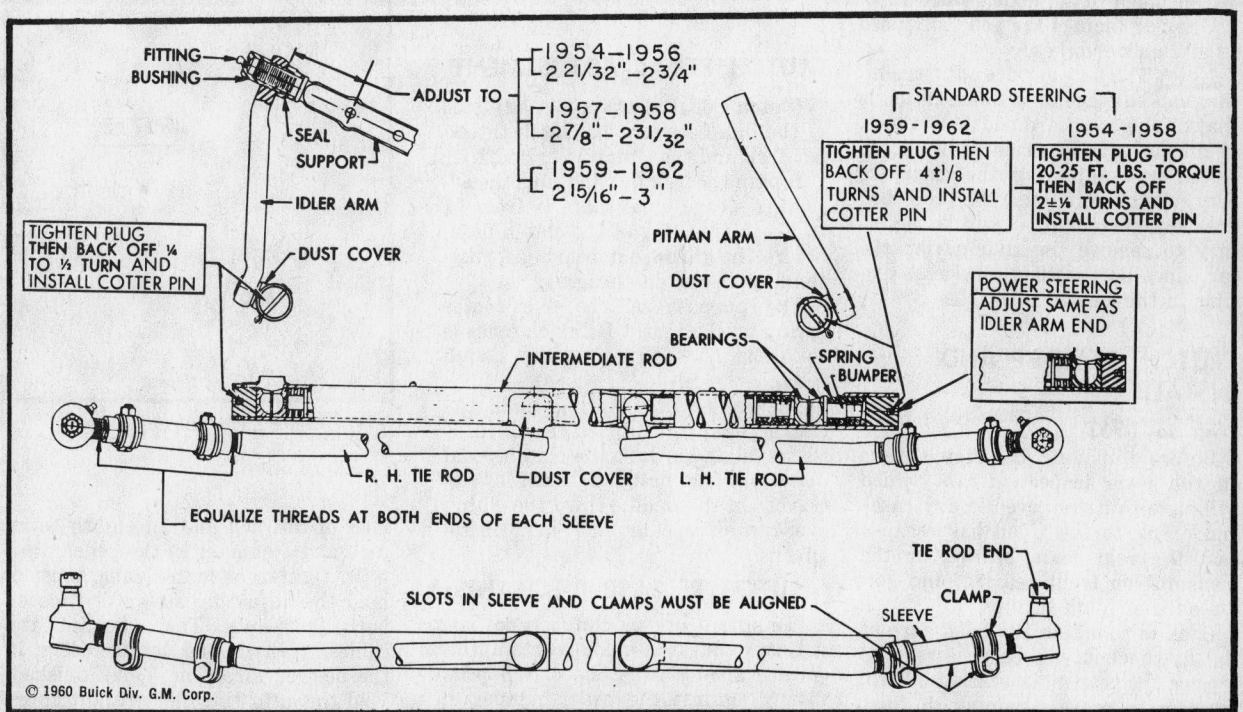

Typical Steering Linkage—1954-63

© 1960 Buick Div. G.M. Corp.

REMOVAL OF POWER STEERING GEAR PUMP

When removing the pump, use shipping plugs and caps to cover the hose connectors, unions, and hose ends to keep out dirt.

When pump is installed on mounting bracket, adjust drive belt tension by using a torque wrench applied to the pulley nut. With a new belt the tension should be set so that the pulley will slip in the belt when 40 to 45 ft. lbs. torque is applied to pulley nut. With a used belt the torque should be 30-35 ft. lbs.

1959-63 Rotary Valve Power Steering Gear and Pump

This gear responds faster, requires less manual effort and retains feel-of-the-road steering. Parking effort is about one half that of previous models.

Removal of rotary valve type power steering gear or pump involves the same procedure as prior models.

More detailed information on maintenance and overhaul procedure is covered in the Unit Repair Section, under Power Steering.

CLUTCH ASSEMBLY

1954-1960

Two types of clutches are used on Buick cars.

The series 40 and 50 use the diaphragm type clutch and series 60 and 70 use the coil spring type clutch.

The diaphragm type having been discontinued in all models since 1955.

Grooved facings are generally used on all Buick clutches.

<u>Note:</u> The only service adjustment that can be made on a Buick clutch is that of the toe board pedal clearance. If difficulty is experienced with the clutch and adjusting the clearance between the pedal and the toe board does not correct it, it will be necessary to remove the clutch from the car, since no practical service is possible in the car.

CLUTCH, REMOVE AND INSTALL

Prior to 1961

Before removing the clutch, take off the lower inspection pan (which will have to be removed in any case) and check to see if oil has escaped past the rear main bearing or the transmission front bearing, and gotten on the clutch facings.

If oil is found on the front face of the flywheel it will be necessary to replace the rear main bearing oil seal in order to prevent ruining the new clutch.

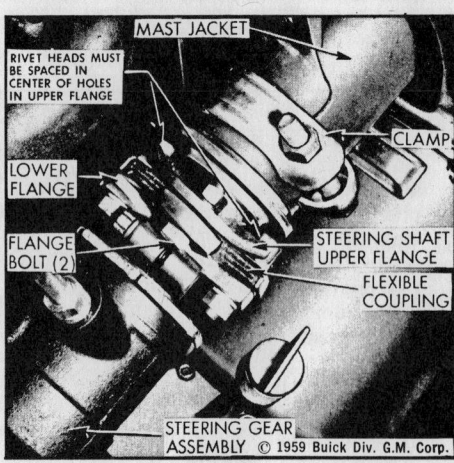

Steering gear flexible coupling

To remove the clutch detach the bolts from the U/joint ball and release the rear axle assembly as outlined under Rear Axle Removal. Remove the transmission as explained under transmission later in this section.

Take off the clutch throwout fork.

The clutch is then removed by unbolting the cover assembly from the flywheel and lowering the clutch through the bottom of the inspection port.

Where observation has shown that the rear main bearing is leaking oil and thus damaging the clutch it is perhaps easier to replace the clutch by removing the engine. In this way a new rear main bearing oil seal and a new clutch are installed at the same time. Install clutch by reversing above procedure.

CLUTCH PEDAL ADJUSTMENT

Clutch pedal clearance is adjusted at the link between the clutch throwout fork and the clutch idler shaft.

Loosen the lock nut and turn the adjusting sleeve until there is from 3/4 to 1 inch free play of the clutch pedal before the throw-out bearing strikes the fingers (or diaphragm).

The purpose of the over-center spring used on most Buick clutches is to assist in depressing the clutch pedal.

The over-center spring pulls the clutch pedal up the last one-third of its travel and it pulls the clutch pedal down on the first one-third of its travel. On the middle third the clutch over-center spring has very little effect.

CLUTCH RELEASE MECHANISM

To obtain proper clutch pedal lash adjustment, first make certain that return spring pulls the clutch pedal firmly against the pedal bumper up under the dash. If the pedal doesn't

contact the bumper, check the pedal and linkage for binding or lack of lubrication and also check the condition of the release yoke return spring (under the car at the clutch).

Before making any clutch linkage adjustment the equalizer must be in the correct position. This is done by inserting a one-quarter by two and a half inch bolt through the gauging hole in the equalizer from the bottom as it lines up with the two holes in the equalizer bracket. Held in this position, if the cable is too loose, pull slack out of the cable until holes do align. If the cable is too tight, tension must be loosened at the cable adjusting sleeve until one-quarter inch bolt will be held in the gauging holes.

Remove the clevis pin which holds the adjustable release rod to the clutch yoke. Loosen the jam nut and adjust the end until the cap clevis pin fits freely with the yoke held toward the rear. Now lengthen the rod by rotating it four complete turns. This provides the proper clearance between the clutch release bearing and the release levers. This will give a

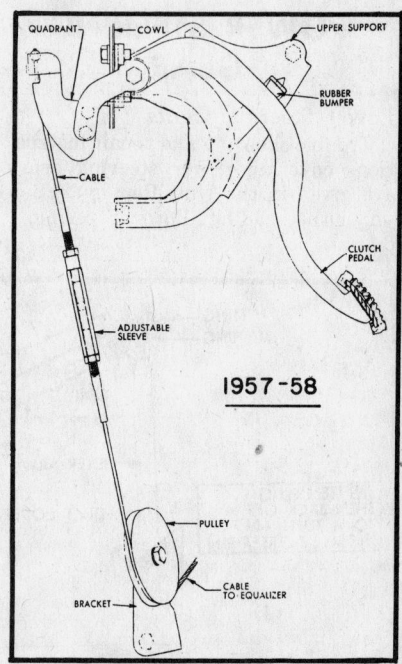

Clutch pedal lash adjustment

lash of an inch and an eighth to an inch and a quarter at the pedal.

To tighten or loosen cable tension, hold the adjusting sleeve and loosen both jam nuts. Then, holding the cables, turn the adjusting sleeve in the desired direction. When finished, hold the adjusting sleeve and tighten the jam nuts.

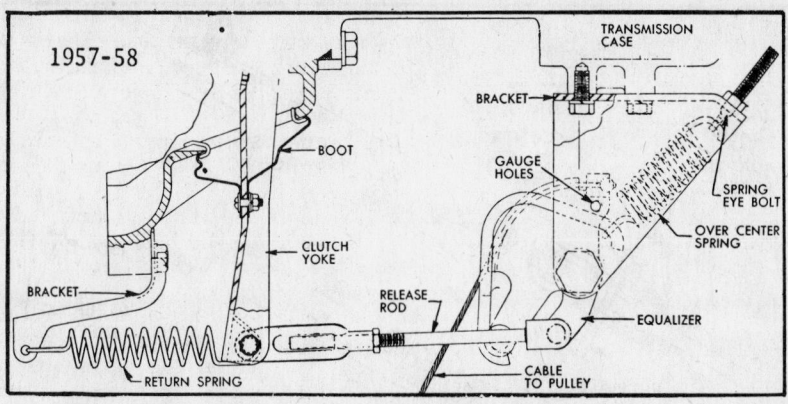

1957-58

Lower-Clutch release mechanism

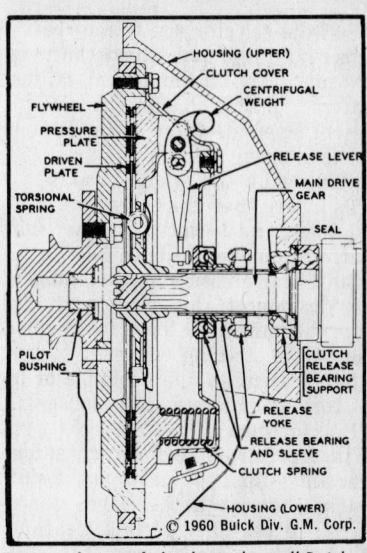

© 1960 Buick Div. G.M. Corp.

Sectional view of clutch used on all Buicks from 1956-60

STANDARD TRANSMISSION

REFERENCES

Transmission refill capacities will be found in the Capacities Table.

Trouble shooting and repair of overdrive units are covered in the Unit Repair section under the heading: Transmission—Overdrive.

SHIFT CONTROL ADJUSTMENT

Thru 1956

Before adjusting the transmission shifter mechanism make certain that the grommets are in good condition and that the linkage will shift freely back and forth. Replace any worn or loose grommet.

Note: In this text the term selector rod and selector will be used to designate the rod and mechanism which complete the cross shift. The term shift rod or shift lever will be used in reference to the rod which completes the longitudinal shift, that is, the shift from second to high or from low to reverse.

The selector rod or lever is then the mechanism which transfers from the low and reverse range to the high and second range. Make the adjustments in the following order: Shift the transmission to neutral and disconnect the selector rod from the selector control lever.

(Move the selector rod back and forth to make sure that the shaft in the transmission moves freely.) Any binding in this selector shaft may prevent the transmission from automatically moving across from the low to the second and high range.

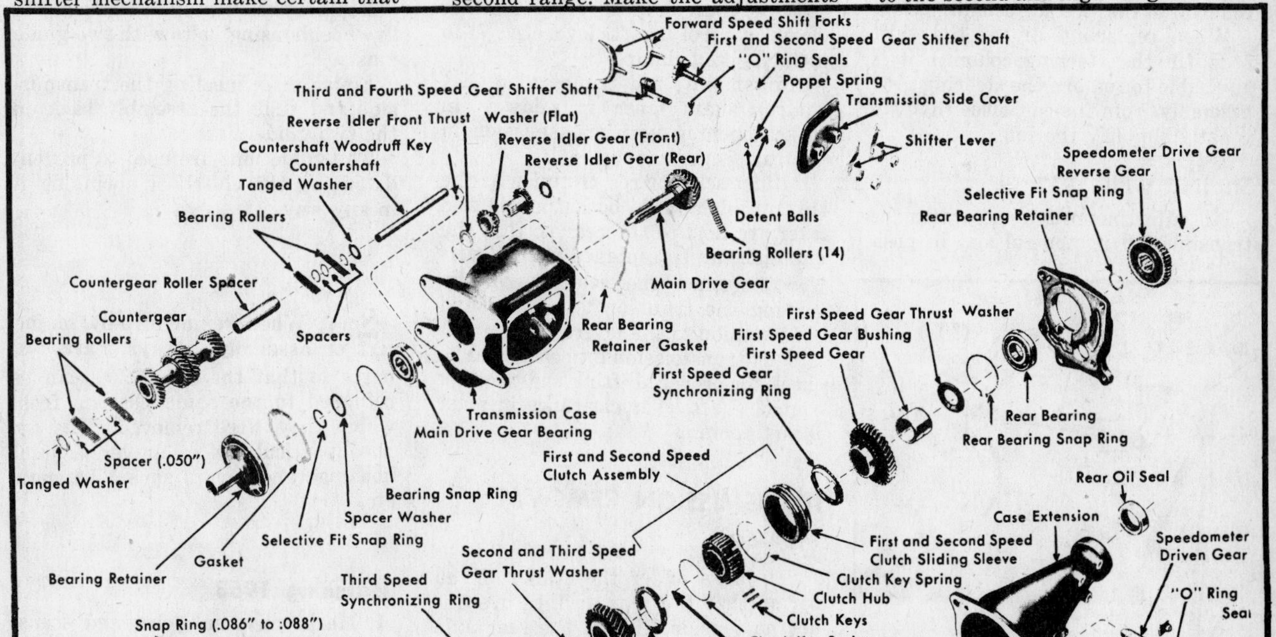

Four Speed Transmission—Exploded View

Pull the selector rod to the rear as far as it will go and adjust the trunnion until the trunnion pin is just centered in the hole in the selector control lever insulator at the bottom of the steering column.

Connect up the selector rod.

To insure that the gears enter into full mesh, adjustment of the shift control should be made as follows:

Shift transmission into second gear and disconnect the lower shift rod from the shift idler lever (at the bottom of the steering column).

Replace any of the bushings or insulators which are worn or loose.

Pull forward on the lower shift rod to insure full engagement in second gear and adjust the clevis on the shift rod so that when the clevis is connected to the idler lever a clearance of 1/8 inch exists between the shift control lever housing and the edge of the opening in the steering column jacket.

To check this, shift the transmission into high gear. A clearance of approximately 1/8 inch then exists between the control lever housing and the column jacket.

When these adjustments have been achieved reconnect the shift rods.

Replacement of selector rods control shaft and lower bearings requires removal of the steering column jacket.

When replacing any of the shift rods (in the steering column) it is advisable to remove the steering gear assembly from the car, since this will greatly simplify the job.

Starting with 1957

All adjustments are made with the transmission in neutral and in position for shifting into second or third gear.

Raise or lower jacket clamp until selector control lever pivot bushing clears control shaft lever by 7/16 inch. Tighten clamp.

Adjust shift rod trunnion so that control shaft lever is midway in jacket opening with transmission in neutral.

Adjust selector rod trunnion at the transmission while both the rod and lever are held to the rear so that the trunnion can be repinned to the lever. Now lengthen the selector rod by turning the trunnion two turns and pin trunnion to the lever.

Shift transmission into each gear to check for proper shifting and to check control shaft lever clearance in mast jacket opening.

TRANSMISSION REMOVAL
1954-60

Set jacks under the frame of the car so that the rear springs are under no tension. Unbolt the rear axle at the spring hangers and at the universal joint and slide it backward out of the way.

To do this it will be necessary to disconnect the brake lines, track bar, shock absorbers, etc.

Disconnect the shift mechanism rods and the speedometer cable.

Support the rear of the engine on a jack.

Remove the rear engine support

and note the number of shims on it so that they can be replaced the same way they were removed.

Replace the two top bell housing to flywheel housing bolts with two guide pins.

Finish disconnecting the transmission and slide the assembly back on the two guide pins.

The guide pins are used to prevent damaging the clutch or springing it in any way.

Note: When removing any major part or assembly, always mark the parts so that the assemblies can be returned to the same position from which they were removed. This applies particularly to universal joint housings and covers spring hangers, etc.

Beginning 1963

1. Mark universal joint and transmission shaft companion flange for proper indexing at time of installation. Remove two "U" bolts and disconnect driveshaft at the front joint. Slide the driveshaft rearward as far as possible and tie to one side.
2. Disconnect shift linkage from transmission by first removing equalizer spring. Slide shift equalizer to full left position to

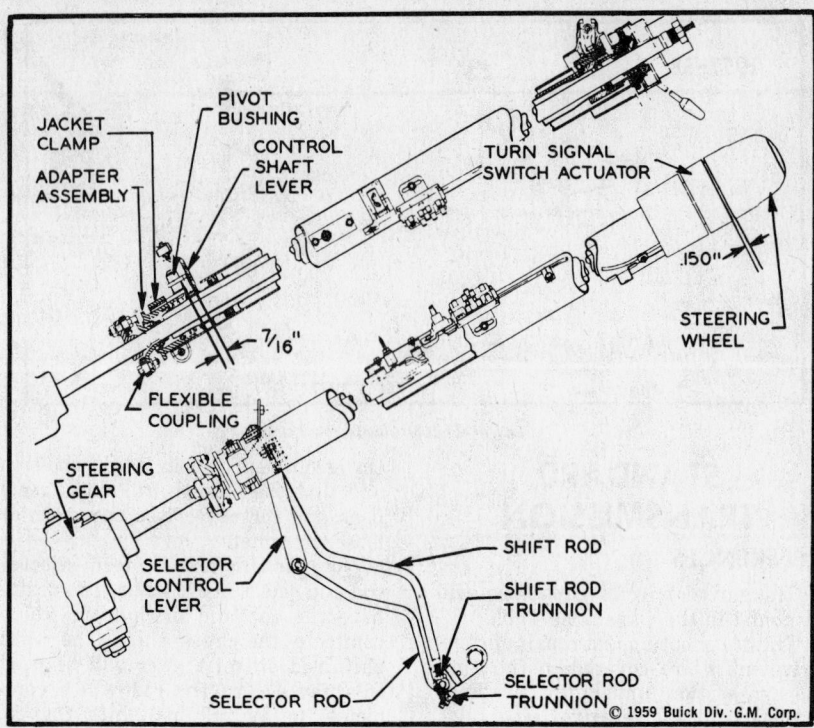

JACKET CLAMP · ADAPTER ASSEMBLY · PIVOT BUSHING · CONTROL SHAFT LEVER · TURN SIGNAL SWITCH ACTUATOR · STEERING WHEEL · .150" · 7/16" · FLEXIBLE COUPLING · STEERING GEAR · SELECTOR CONTROL LEVER · SHIFT ROD · SHIFT ROD TRUNNION · SELECTOR ROD · SELECTOR ROD TRUNNION © 1959 Buick Div. G.M. Corp.

Synchromesh transmission shift mechanism—1954-60 except 1954-55 series 40

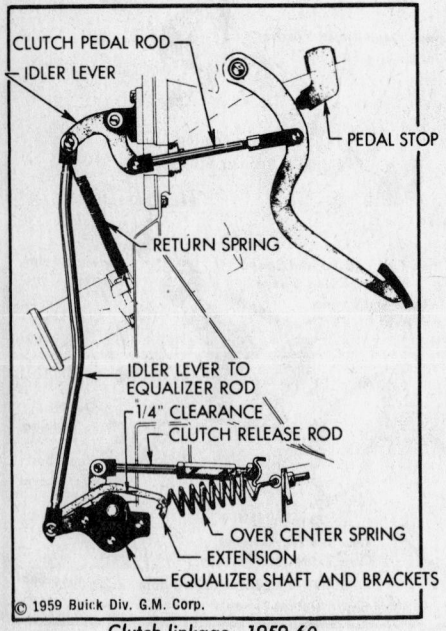

CLUTCH PEDAL ROD · IDLER LEVER · PEDAL STOP · RETURN SPRING · IDLER LEVER TO EQUALIZER ROD · 1/4" CLEARANCE · CLUTCH RELEASE ROD · OVER CENTER SPRING · EXTENSION · EQUALIZER SHAFT AND BRACKETS © 1959 Buick Div. G.M. Corp.

Clutch linkage—1959-60

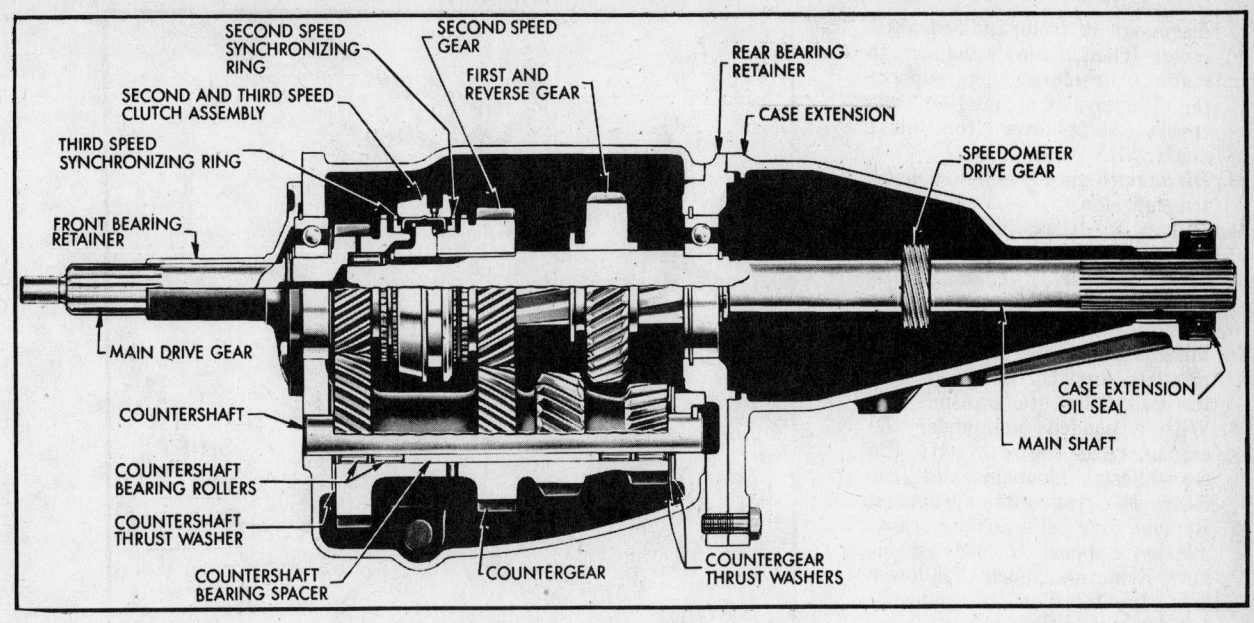

SECOND SPEED SYNCHRONIZING RING
SECOND AND THIRD SPEED CLUTCH ASSEMBLY
THIRD SPEED SYNCHRONIZING RING
SECOND SPEED GEAR
FIRST AND REVERSE GEAR
REAR BEARING RETAINER
CASE EXTENSION
SPEEDOMETER DRIVE GEAR
FRONT BEARING RETAINER
MAIN DRIVE GEAR
COUNTERSHAFT
COUNTERSHAFT BEARING ROLLERS
COUNTERSHAFT THRUST WASHER
COUNTERSHAFT BEARING SPACER
COUNTERGEAR
COUNTERGEAR THRUST WASHERS
CASE EXTENSION OIL SEAL
MAIN SHAFT

1963, 3-Speed Manual Transmission

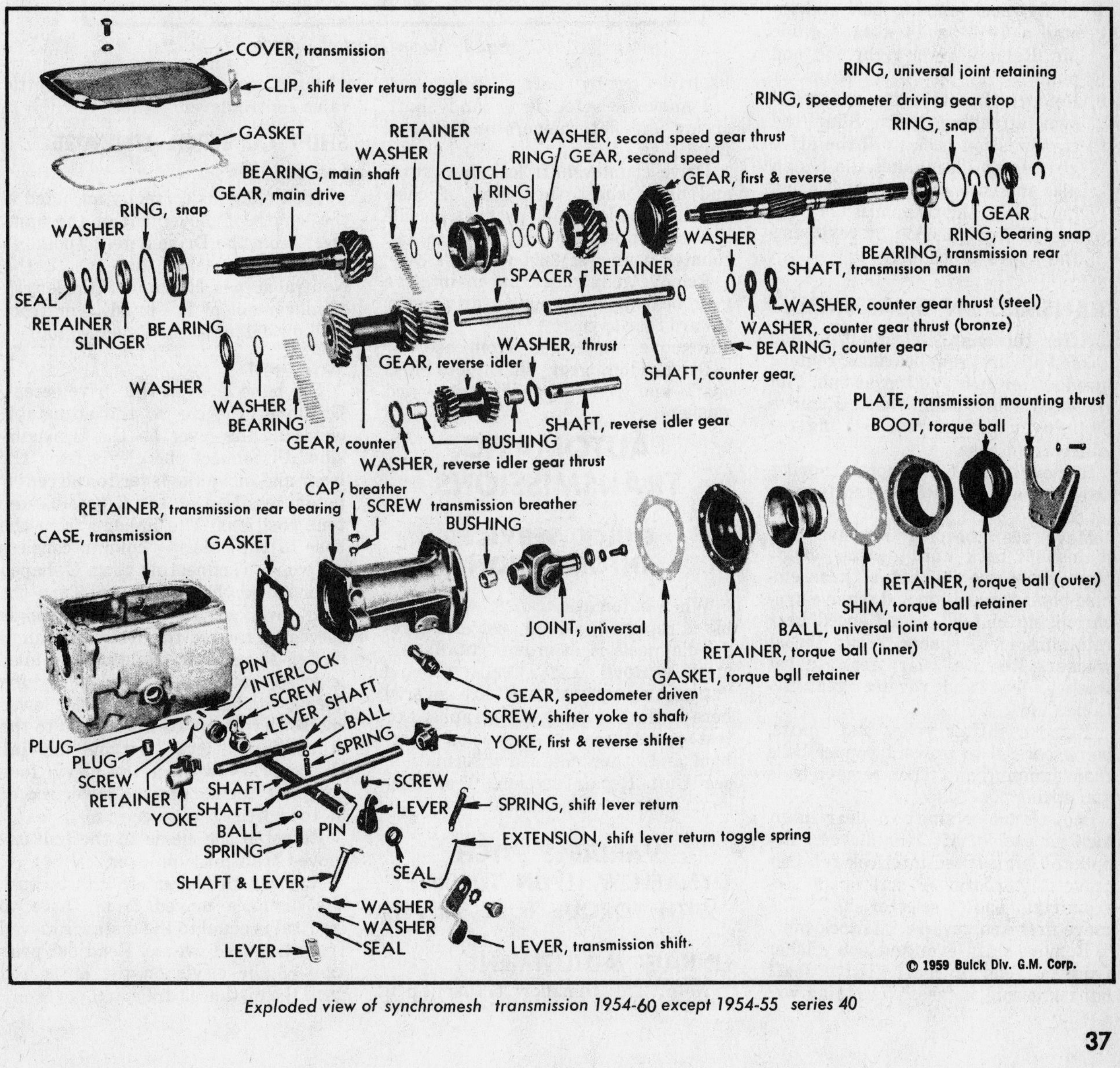

COVER, transmission
CLIP, shift lever return toggle spring
RING, universal joint retaining
RING, speedometer driving gear stop
RING, snap
GASKET
RETAINER WASHER
WASHER, second speed gear thrust
RING GEAR, second speed
GEAR, first & reverse
BEARING, main shaft
CLUTCH RING
GEAR, main drive
WASHER
GEAR
RING, snap
SHAFT, transmission main
RING, bearing snap
BEARING, transmission rear
WASHER
SEAL
RETAINER
SLINGER
BEARING
WASHER
SPACER
RETAINER
WASHER, counter gear thrust (steel)
WASHER, counter gear thrust (bronze)
BEARING, counter gear
WASHER, thrust
SHAFT, counter gear
GEAR, reverse idler
WASHER BEARING
SHAFT, reverse idler gear
GEAR, counter
BUSHING
WASHER, reverse idler gear thrust
PLATE, transmission mounting thrust
BOOT, torque ball
CAP, breather
SCREW transmission breather
BUSHING
RETAINER, transmission rear bearing
CASE, transmission
GASKET
JOINT, universal
RETAINER, torque ball (outer)
SHIM, torque ball retainer
BALL, universal joint torque
RETAINER, torque ball (inner)
GASKET, torque ball retainer
PIN INTERLOCK
SCREW
LEVER SHAFT
BALL
SPRING
GEAR, speedometer driven
SCREW, shifter yoke to shaft
YOKE, first & reverse shifter
PLUG
PLUG
SCREW
RETAINER
YOKE
SHAFT
SHAFT
BALL
SPRING
PIN
SHAFT & LEVER
SCREW
LEVER
SPRING, shift lever return
EXTENSION, shift lever return toggle spring
SEAL
WASHER
WASHER
LEVER
SEAL
LEVER, transmission shift

© 1959 Buick Div. G.M. Corp.

Exploded view of synchromesh transmission 1954-60 except 1954-55 series 40

disengage it from 2nd-3rd shift lever. Then slide equalizer to right to remove from support pin. Remove transmission 1st-reverse shift lever from shift shaft.

3. Disconnect speedometer cable at transmission.
4. Loosen all three exhaust pipe ball joints to permit transmission and rear of engine to be lowered.
5. Remove two bolts holding transmission mounting pad to transmission support. Leave mounting pad bolted to transmission.
6. With a padded jack under the engine, raise the unit until the transmission mounting pad just clears the transmission support.
7. Remove four bolts holding transmission support to body members. Remove support, then lower the jack to allow transmission to clear the underbody.
8. Remove upper left transmission to flywheel housing bolt and install a 7/16" x 14 x 4½" guide pin. Remove lower right bolt and pin.
9. Remove the other two transmission attaching bolts. Slide the transmission back until the drive gear shaft disengages the clutch disc and clears the flywheel housing. Lower the transmission.
10. Install transmission by reversing the above procedure.

TRANSMISSION DISASSEMBLY

After thoroughly cleaning outside to keep all dirt from bearings, remove speedometer gear and torque ball. Pull universal from main shaft. Remove retaining ring and rear bearing retainer from case.

Remove cover, toggle spring, spring extension and clip. Remove shift yoke set screw.

Move rear bearing retainer and mainshaft back until bearing clears case. Raise main shaft with assembled parts toward top and remove synchronizing clutch, second speed gear retaining ring, spacer, front thrust washer. Remove gear, rear thrust washer, first and reverse gear retainer and gear.

Remove shifter yokes and shafts, being careful to prevent poppet balls from jumping out. Then remove balls and springs.

Move selector shaft to clear interlock as each shaft is removed. Remove second and high speed interlock retainer shifter lever set screws and second from right end of selector shaft. Remove first and reverse interlock pin.

Remove shift lever and lock washer from left end of shaft. Drive shaft out right side of case. Welsh plug will

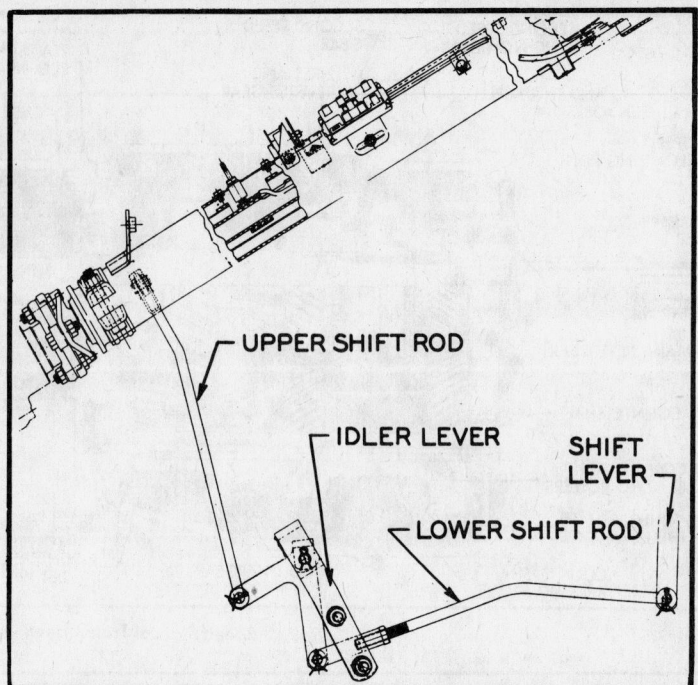

Fig. 1—Manual Control Linkage

be driven out by shaft.

Remove selector lever and shaft, spring and flat washers and oil seal from case.

Drive countershaft lock into shaft and drive shaft thru rear of case. Bearing loader will prevent needle bearings from dropping into case. Let counter gear rest on bottom of case.

Remove snap ring from main drive gear bearing and remove drive gear toward rear of case.

Remove counter gear from case.

Drive idler gear shaft lock into shaft and remove shaft, gear and washers.

AUTOMATIC TRANSMISSIONS

QUICK SERVICE INFORMATION

When automatic transmission trouble is reported, a road test and careful diagnosis is in order. "TRANSMISSION REMOVE AND REPLACE" and "LINKAGE ADJUSTMENTS" are covered here in the following paragraphs. For test procedures, transmission overhaul and other detailed information, see Unit Repair section, Transmission Group, of this manual.

VARIABLE PITCH DYNAFLOW (TWIN TURBINE WITH TORQUE TUBE DRIVE)

LINKAGE ADJUSTMENT

<u>Note:</u> The Dynaflow transmission does not use a governor nor a throttle valve control lever.

SHIFT CONTROL LINKAGE
See Fig. 1

The linkage is correctly adjusted if the length of movement of the hand lever from the Drive detent (point at which lever seems to seat) to the Neutral stop is the same as the length of movement of the hand lever from the Low detent to the Reverse stop.

To Adjust

Put hand lever at the Drive detent. Go under the car to the adjustable clevis at the lever on the transmission. Disconnect the clevis from the lever and move the lever to the center detent position of the 5 possible detent positions. The linkage from the base of the steering column consists of two rods connecting at an L shaped lever called the idler lever. Turn the idler lever so that the upper rod is forced up toward the steering column as far as possible. Holding the idler lever so that the upper rod is up, turn the clevis at the rear end of the lower rod so that it can be refastened to the transmission lever without moving the lever. Now turn the clevis four complete turns onto the lower rod so as to shorten the lower rod.

Refasten the clevis to the still unmoved transmission lever.

Recheck the hand lever to be sure the distance moved from Drive to Neutral is equal to the distance moved from Low to Reverse. Readjust position of the clevis on the lower rod until the distances are equal.

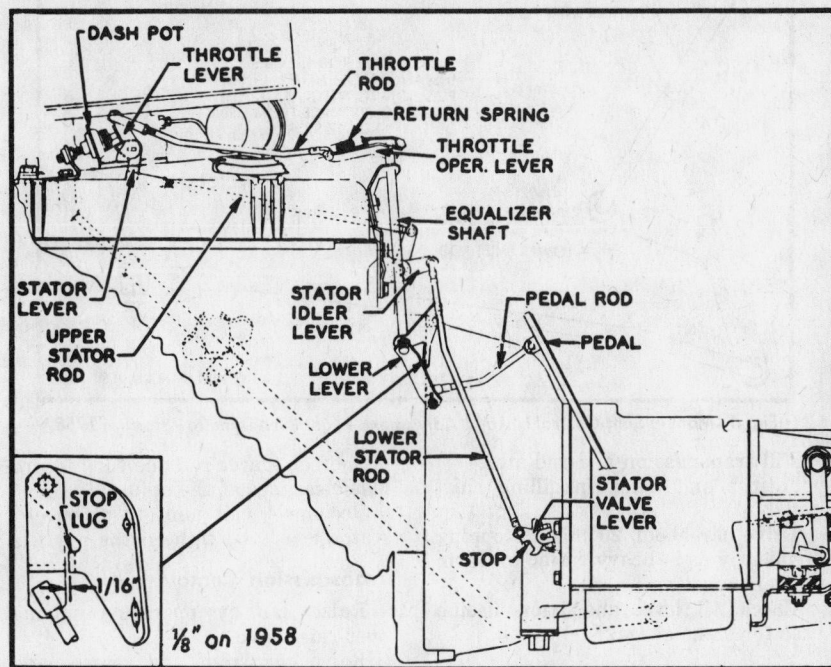

Fig. 2—Throttle and stator control linkage

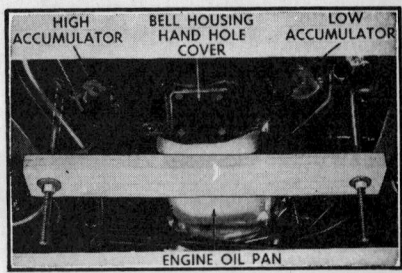

Fig. 3—Support Bar under engine

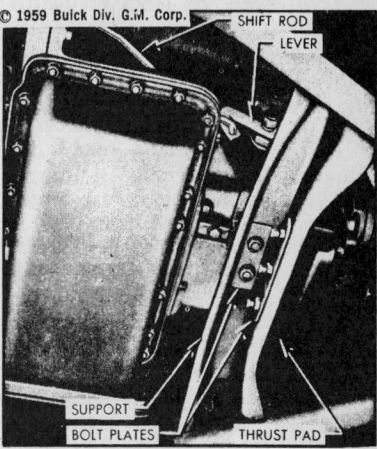

Fig. 4—Left rear view of Dynaflow

STATOR OPERATING LEVER

See Fig. 2

Check that when accelerator pedal is against the floor the throttle valve in the carburetor is wide open. Now holding the accelerator pedal against the floor, turn the adjusting screw at the stator operating lever on the equalizer shaft to remove all vertical play from the rod which runs from the operating lever to the stator valve lever on the high accumulator. Turn the screw back ½ turn to provide a slight clearance between the stator valve lever and its stop.

DASHPOT ADJUSTMENT

With engine at operating temperature and off fast idle and hand lever at Drive, hold the car with the brakes and run engine up to about 1500 RPM. Release the pedal quickly and note engine operation as the throttle closes.

If the engine stalls screw the dashpot forward. If it takes too long to idle down screw the dashpot back.

DYNAFLOW REMOVAL (TWIN TURBINE WITH TORQUE TUBE DRIVE)

See Figs. 3, 4, & 5

Drain cooling system and transmission oil pan. Hoist front and rear of car and support firmly at least two feet above the floor.

Disconnect drive shaft and torque

tube at the universal joint. This requires disconnection of rear springs.

Remove bell housing lower front pan and hand hole cover.

Loosen one flywheel drain plug to provide an air vent then remove other drain plug which is on side opposite and drain flywheel.

Disconnect hoses from oil cooler and disconnect rubber hose in oil filler line.

Disconnect transmission shift rod at both ends.

Disconnect speedometer cable at the rear bearing retainer.

Remove three nuts and plate that support transmission at rear bearing retainer. Remove shims between support and thrust pad. Save these shims.

Remove two bolts and plate which attach transmission mounting pad to the support.

Install engine support bar (or jack) under rear end of lower crankcase. Place left side hook over frame at rear of brake master cylinder.

Do not let hooks injure brake lines.

Place transmission jack or hoist in position and adjust it to support the transmission.

Tighten the nuts on the engine support bar (or raise the jack) to raise engine and transmission support. Thrust pad may now be removed from under the rear bearing retainer.

Mark in sequence (1, 2 and 3) with paint the positions of the bolts holding the converter to the flywheel so that marks show on:

The primary pump.
The primary pump cover.
The flywheel.

In order that these three units may be replaced in the same position. Otherwise the unit may have to be rebalanced. Early models employed 6 bolts, in which case mark all six.

Disconnect bell housing from the engine. Move exhaust pipe hanger forward to clear bolts on left side.

Move transmission rearward to disengage hub of converter pump from crankshaft. Lower transmission and remove to bench.

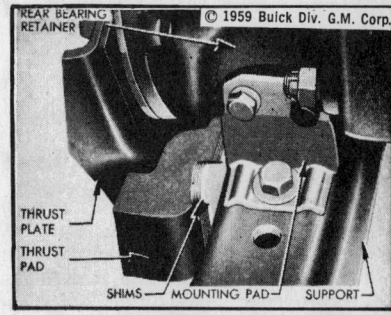

Fig. 5—Thrust Pad and Shim detail

INSTALLATION

Note: Lack of care in installing the Dynaflow to the flywheel and engine block will permit the unit to cock and result in compression of the converter and destruction of the front oil pump. Converter when mounted on input shaft must turn freely.

Turn flywheel so that the marks on the converter primary pump, pump cover and flywheel are aligned in the same order 1, 2 and 3 as when removed. This will assure that the drain plugs of the converter are opposite the holes in the flywheel, that the balance of the assembly is as it was and that the attaching bolt holes are aligned.

Adjust lifting equipment so that the bell housing seats squarely against the flywheel housing. Install the two housing dowl bolts and follow with remaining bolts. Install exhaust pipe hanger with the left hand bolts and crankcase ventilator pipe support with lower right hand bolt.

Tighten all the bolts gradually to 45-55 lbs torque leaving the lower right hand bolt till last for if it is tightened first the bell housing may be thrown out of alignment.

Attach thrust pad to thrust plate.

Raise transmission and install mounting pad.

Lower transmission until weight is carried by the mounting pad and support. Attach pad to support with bolt plate and two self locking nuts. Fig. 4.

Remove transmission lift and engine support bar.

With engine and transmission resting freely on their mountings install sufficient shims between the thrust pad and the transmission support to fill the space. Install bolt plate and three self locking nuts to attach thrust pad to support. Fig. 5.

Use the shank of an 11/32" drill to align bolt holes in flywheel and converter being sure the markings (1, 2, and 3) on each of the three units match those on the others. Install bolts and tighten evenly to 25-30 ft lbs. torque.

Tighten flywheel drain plugs and install bell housing cover and hand hole cover.

Connect hose from lower side of engine water pump to the lower connection of transmission oil cooler.

If car has heater connect hose from it to the upper connection on oil cooler.

Connect speedometer cable at rear bearing retainer.

Install shift rod at shift lever on transmission at rear bearing retainer.

Cement a new gasket in recess in front end of torque tube and make sure propeller shaft oil seals are installed on propeller shaft in the following order: Spring retainer, spring, seal cap, oil seal.

Bolt torque tube to torque ball.

Place oil filler pipe spring bracket over filler pipe and connect pipe to oil pan pipe, with both pipes contacting inside the rubber connector hose. Place spring bracket over front end of bell housing dowel bolt.

Being sure outside of transmission is free of oil lower car to floor.

Check that oil filler pipe is properly placed and not contacting floor of car. Tighten nut holding filler pipe bracket.

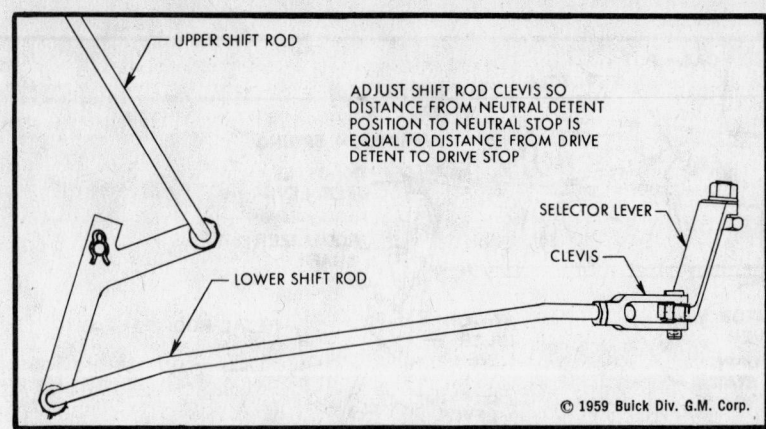

Fig. 6—Manual Shift Control Linkage Adjustment. Flight Pitch Dynaflow starting 1958

Fill transmission and radiator.

Adjust and finish installing shift rod.

Drive car about 20 miles stopping frequently as in heavy traffic to warm up transmission.

Check oil level and transmission case for signs of leakage.

FLIGHT PITCH (TRIPLE TURBINE)

1958 AND 1959 DYNAFLOW

Manual Linkage Adjustment

Move hand control lever to the "D" position. The lever will seem to seat. Move lever toward "Grade Retard" position and note how far it moves before it hits the stop. (Do not lift the lever.) Return the lever to Neutral and then move it toward Reverse. Note how far lever moves before it hits the stop. Fig. 6.

If the distance moved from "Drive" to the "Grade Retard" stop is the same as the distance moved from "Neutral" to the "Reverse" stop, the shift control linkage is correctly adjusted.

If the distances are not equal, return hand lever to Drive and working under the car at the rod and clevis attached to the transmission lever, disconnect the clevis from the lever and put the lever in the center position of the five available, which is "Drive."

Pull the rod rearward until it stops. Do not cause hand lever to move.

Adjust clevis so it can be refastened to the lever and fasten.

Stator Linkage

Disconnect upper stator rod ball joint from stator lever on carburetor. With engine at operating temperature and carburetor throttle at hot idle, adjust the upper stator rod so that the ball joint will just slip freely into carburetor stator lever with transmission stator lever and stator rod pushed rearward.

Shorten stator rod one turn to provide clearance at the stop.

Reconnect ball joint to carburetor stator lever and tighten the nut.

Transmission Removal

Raise car by operating manual over-ride valve.

Raise car front and rear, solidly supporting front suspension and rear of frame. Support axle housing with floor jack.

To prevent damage to air spring assemblies, carefully and slowly loosen air lines from rear air springs to allow springs to bleed air out. Remove plungers from air spring. Fig. 12.

Disconnect height control valve links at strut rods using 7/16" wrench.

Disconnect radius rod at axle end using 3/4" wrench and 9/16" deep socket.

Disconnect lower ends of rear shock absorbers using 5/8" wrench.

Disconnect parking brake cable at rear cable sheave and at bracket on torque tube. Disconnect brake hose from pipe at frame X member and remove yoke. Cover hose and pipe to prevent entrance of dirt.

To prevent strain on parts, disconnect exhaust pipe at manifold and loosen exhaust pipe to muffler joint.

Install 3" guide pins in alternate bolt holes in torque ball. Remove remaining two torque tube flange bolts using 9/16" socket.

Lower axle assembly and push back to clear torque ball.

Remove converter housing cover. Turn flywheel until one converter drain plug can be loosened to provide an air vent. Turn flywheel until opposite drain plug is down. Remove this plug and allow oil to drain from converter. Match mark converter cover to flywheel and converter pump.

Remove filler pipe from oil pan and allow oil to drain from transmission.

Remove converter to flywheel bolts using 1/2" socket.

Disconnect oil cooler pipes. Disconnect speedometer cable. Disconnect stator control rod at transmission lever. Disconnect lower shift rod at transmission lever and upper shift rod at idler lever. Leave lower rod, idler lever and bracket attached to crossmember.

Support transmission securely and use jack to safely support engine.

Remove two nuts and four bolts and nuts holding rubber mounts to support using 9/16" socket.

Raise engine and transmission just enough to relieve strain on support. Remove eight attaching bolts and nuts using 9/16" socket and remove transmission support. If shims are present, note number and location so they may be reinstalled in original position.

Lower transmission and engine sufficiently to remove six transmission case to crankcase bolts using 5/8" socket and extension.

With engine separately supported, move transmission to rear to disengage converter pump cover from crankshaft. Lower transmission and remove from under car.

NOTE: If transmission is to be placed on oily surface, remove mounts to prevent deterioration of rubber.

CAUTION: Do not tilt transmission forward as weight of converter may damage bushings in front planet carrier and oil rings on first turbine shaft.

Installation

Turn flywheel so that one hole for converter attaching bolt is straight up and wide flange is straight down. Be certain drive lugs on converter pump do not disengage from front pump gear.

Raise transmission into place with same equipment used for removal. Align converter attaching bolt holes with flywheel holes before moving transmission forward against crankcase. Align match marks.

Adjust lifting equipment so transmission meets crankcase squarely. Install converter housing to crankcase bolts, tightening evenly to 45-55 ft. lbs. torque.

Install three flywheel to converter bolts, tightening to 25-30 ft. lbs. torque.

Check converter drain plugs for tightness and install converter housing cover.

Raise transmission just enough to install transmission support, installing any shims in their original position. Tighten bolts to 25-30 ft. lbs. torque. Install two nuts and four bolts and nuts holding mounts to support. Tighten to 25-30 ft. lbs. torque.

NOTE: If transmission cannot be made to seat on support, the front engine mounts should be loosened and engine raised (by means of a pry bar) and pulled forward to remove bind from front mounts. If bind is allowed to remain, engine may set up vibration when running. Following installation of transmission, retighten motor mounts.

Remove engine support jack and transmission hoist.

Connect upper shift rod to idler lever and lower shift rod to transmission lever. Connect stator control rod to transmission lever. Connect speedometer cable.

Connect oil filler pipe to oil pan. Connect oil cooler pipes.

NOTE: Following installation, check to insure that pipes are not contacting transmission support, frame, front spring crossmember, body, etc.

With 3" guide pins in place, align and connect torque tube to torque ball, making certain that blank splines on propeller shaft line up with those in rear yoke of universal joint. Remove guide pins and install bolts.

Install parking brake cable. Connect brake hose to pipes and secure with yoke at frame X member. Bleed rear brakes and adjust parking brake cable.

Loosely connect radius rod and shock absorbers.

Connect air lines to rear air spring domes.

Insert plungers into air springs, and carefully pull down on height control valve arm to partially inflate air spring assembly and retain plunger.

Connect height control valve links to strut rod brackets.

Connect and tighten exhaust system. Be certain all pipes are centered in holes in frame and no bind exists.

Wipe all oil from outside of transmission and lower car so normal weight is on rear wheels. Tighten shock absorber bolts and radius rod bolts. Lower car to floor.

Pour four quarts of a good grade of Automatic Transmission Fluid into transmission. Raise rear wheels and with transmission in "Drive" "D" range and engine idling add eight more quarts. Place transmission selector lever in "N" Neutral and lower rear wheels to touch ground. Check oil level and add oil as necessary to bring to level on dipstick. Engine and transmission should be at operating temperature.

Check car for proper adjustment of linkage. Road test car thoroughly with frequent stops and starts as might be encountered in heavy traffic. A thorough warm-up is desired.

Place car on hoist and carefully examine transmission and all connections for leaks. Recheck oil level.

DYNAFLOW (TWIN TURBINE WITH OPEN DRIVESHAFT
Throttle Linkage, Adjust
1. Make sure that the accelerator pedal is free and in good condition; that it is securely mounted and that the floor mat is properly installed.
2. Move throttle lever to wide open position and make sure stator linkage does not interfere with throttle opening completely.
3. Disconnect throttle rod from throttle operating lever.
4. While a helper holds the accelerator pedal hard against the floor mat, hold throttle in wide open position. Hold rear end of throttle rod at hole in throttle operating lever. Rod end must be about 1/16" short of entering hole in lever. Adjust throttle rod to achieve this condition.
5. Connect and cotter pin the throttle rod to the operating lever.
6. Hold choke valve lightly closed and move lever to wide open position to check adjustment of choke unloader. If unloader doesn't operate properly, adjust according to specification charts in Unit Repair section, under "Carburetors."
7. Finally, check for smooth throttle operation. The ideal situation is to have freedom of operation with a full opening of the throttle valve just as the accelerator pedal strikes the floor mat.

Stator Linkage, Adjust
1. Move upper end of stator idler lever forward and hold against pressure of stator valve spring.
2. Move throttle lever to wide open position. Lever on the carburetor should contact stator lever just as throttle reaches wide open position.
3. Any clearance between throttle lever and stator lever must be eliminated by, shortening the upper stator rod at the turnbuckle.
4. If wide open throttle causes the stator idler lever upper end to bend farther forward, lengthen upper stator rod at turnbuckle.
5. Lock up turnbuckle.

Dash Pot, Adjust
1. With engine at operating temperature, transmission in "Drive," and brakes firmly applied, jab accelerator sharply and release.

SUPPORT

MOUNTING PAD

SUPPORT TO FRAME BOLTS (4 EACH SIDE)

SHIMS

Flight Pitch Dynaflow Mounting Detail. Starting 1958

2. If engine stalls from receleration surge, move dash pot toward lever until its function prevents engine stalling. If, on the other hand, too much time is required to fully reach a closed throttle position, move dash pot away from throttle lever.

3. If satisfactory results can not be obtained, renew the dashpot.

TRANSMISSION REMOVE (TWIN TURBINE, OPEN DRIVE)

1. Raise car from floor.
2. Disconnect exhaust pipes.
3. Remove converter housing cover.
4. Drain converter by alternate removal of converter plugs.
5. Remove filler pipe and drain the transmission.
6. Disconnect cooler pipes.
7. Remove three flywheel-to-converter bolts.
8. Disconnect speedometer cable, stator control rod at accumulator and lower shift rods at equalizer.
9. Disconnect equalizer bracket at accumulator bolts. Slide equalizer out of bushing in frame rail. Remove equalizer and bracket.
10. Disconnect drive shaft at rear universal joint. Support shaft up and out of the way to protect center universal joint.
11. Place transmission jack as necessary.
12. Remove two center bearing support-to-frame bolts and slide propeller shaft rearward until shaft is disengaged from transmission output shaft.
13. Remove bolts attaching mounting pad to rear bearing retainer.
14. Raise transmission jack slightly. Remove bolts holding support to frame rails. Remove support and pad as an assembly.

    Note: If shims are present note number and location so that they may be reinstalled in original position.

15. Place suitable jack under rear end of engine so that the engine can be safely supported while transmission is out.
16. Lower transmission just enough to reach converter housing bolts. With engine and transmission supported by separate jacks, disconnect converter housing from engine crankcase.
17. Move transmission rearward to disengage hub of converter pump cover from crankshaft. Lower transmission and remove it from under car.

TRANSMISSION INSTALL (TWIN TURBINE, OPEN DRIVE)

1. Install by reversing removal procedure.
2. Torque converter housing bolts to 45-55 ft. lbs.
3. Torque converter-to-flywheel bolts to 30 ft. lbs.
4. Torque mounting pad-to-rear bearing retainer bolts to 50-60 ft. lbs.

UNIVERSAL JOINTS AND DRIVE SHAFT

UNIVERSAL JOINT AND TORQUE BALL

All Models Thru 1956

The universal joint is splined to the rear end of the transmission mainshaft and is retained there by a heavy steel washer and bolt. The universal joint is entirely enclosed by the transmission rear bearing retainer and by the torque ball and retainers which are attached to the rear end of the transmission. The universal joint bearings are held by retainer rings to the universal joint cross. The rear yoke is splined internally and engages the propeller shaft. The outside diameter of the rear yoke is ground to provide a bearing for a bronze bushing in the torque ball. The torque ball is supported between an inner and outer retainer which is centrally located and bolted to the transmission rear bearing retainer. The retainers are copper plated and the mating surfaces of the torque ball are also plated to prevent scoring during break in. An oil seal is provided to prevent the transmission lubricant from escaping out of the torque ball.

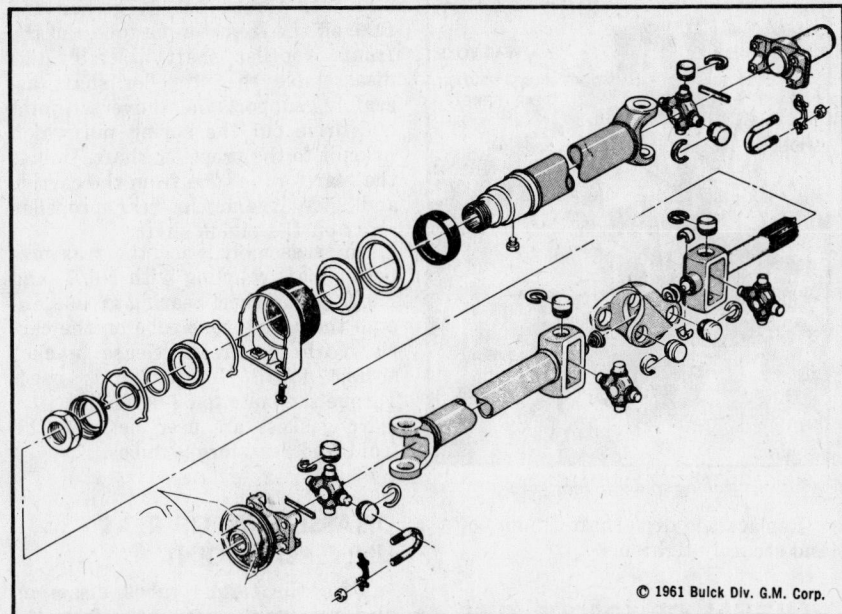

Propeller shaft—1961-63

© 1961 Buick Div. G.M. Corp.

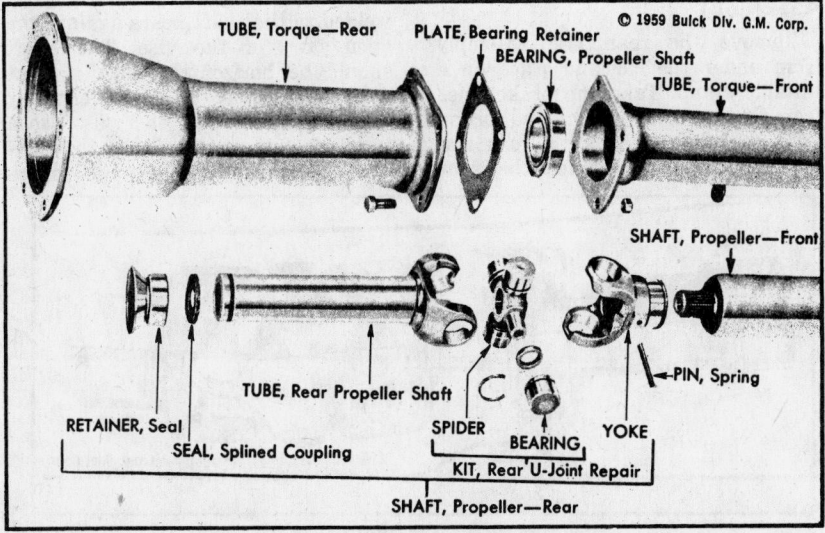

TUBE, Torque—Rear   PLATE, Bearing Retainer

© 1959 Buick Div. G.M. Corp.

BEARING, Propeller Shaft

TUBE, Torque—Front

SHAFT, Propeller—Front

TUBE, Rear Propeller Shaft

PIN, Spring

RETAINER, Seal

SEAL, Splined Coupling

SPIDER   BEARING   YOKE

KIT, Rear U-Joint Repair

SHAFT, Propeller—Rear

Propeller shaft—1957-60

To service the universal joint it is necessary to remove the rear axle assembly from under the vehicle.

Access to the bolt which holds the universal yoke to the mainshaft is through the universal joint itself. Simply hold it in a straight line and put the socket and the handle down through the universal joint to engage this nut.

Remove the retaining bolt and slide the complete universal joint off the back of the transmission mainshaft.

Take the universal joint to a bench and examine all bearings, yokes, cross, etc., for score, scratches or wear.

If necessary, disassemble the joint and replace any worn or damaged parts.

Reinstall the universal joint being careful not to include any dirt or grit

which may be dropping from the under side of the car.

Always install new oil seal in the torque ball when installing a new universal joint. In fact, it is a good practime to install a new oil seal at any time when the rear axle assembly is removed.

1957-60

The torque tube has an enlarged section at the rear which is bolted to the carrier behind the pinion bearings.

There are two propeller shafts and two universal joints.

The front propeller shaft has a splined stud at each end. The front splines slide in the front universal joint which is in the torque ball. The

rear splined end of the front propeller shaft is pinned in the rear universal joint.

The rear propeller shaft has internal splines at each end. The front splined end is welded onto the rear universal joint. The rear splined end slides over the splines of the differential drive pinion shaft. This connection must be packed with grease at assembly and lubricated every 1000 miles thru the plug in the torque tube to the fitting on the rear propeller shaft.

The rear universal joint is supported in the torque tube by a sealed ball bearing which requires no lubrication.

The torque ball has a bonded rubber compression ring which acts as a cushion between the ball and the outer retainer. It also acts as an oil tight seal.

The strut rods are bolted to the torque tube bracket thru rubber bushings.

A transmission oil seal is mounted in the rear flange of the torque ball. It bears against a sleeve pressed over the front splines of the front propeller shaft.

A differential gear grease seal is behind the drive pinion nut.

To service the front universal joint remove the rear axle assembly from underneath the vehicle as outlined for the earlier models.

The rear, or second universal joint, also requires that the rear axle be removed, but to service the rear joint it is necessary to disconnect the torque rods and disconnect the torque tube at the flange.

Beginning 1961

The propeller shaft consists of a two-piece open shaft with standard universal joints front and rear. A double constant velocity joint is used between the shafts with a center support bearing at rear of front shaft and splined front yoke at front of rear shaft.

DISASSEMBLY

Mark yokes to assure original position assembly and balance, and disassemble rear section first.

1. Remove snap rings from bearings.

2. Clamp rear shaft yoke in vise. Support shaft so link yoke is free to move vertically.

3. Using pipe coupling of about 1¼" I.D., apply force on link yoke around bearing. Drive down until about ¼" of bearing projects. **Caution:** Drive no farther than ball and socket will allow easily.

4. Rotate shaft 180° and repeat steps 2 and 3.

BUICK

5. Clamp ¼" projections in vise and remove bearings by driving link yokes upward.

6. Separate spider, shaft yoke and shaft from link yoke.

7. Remove shaft yoke bearings by clamping spider in vise, with jaws against spider journals.

8. With same tool drive yoke down until bearing is free of yoke.

9. Rotate shaft 180° and repeat steps 7 and 8.

10. Remove ball stud seal staking and pry out old seal.

11. Remove large washer, ball stud seats, small washer and spring.

12. Reassemble in reverse of above.

ADJUSTMENT OF UNIVERSAL JOINT AND TORQUE BALL ASSEMBLY

Careful adjustment is required of the universal joint torque ball since if the joint is made up too loosely it will most certainly leak oil and if it is made up too tightly it will score and eventually seize.

Shims are available for use at the flange between the inner and outer ball in the following thicknesses: .002, .004, .006, .009, .011, .013, .015.

Disconnect the flange from the front end of the driveshaft so that a wooden plug can be inserted into the torque ball. With the torque ball nicely lubricated and the bolts thoroughly tightened it should require a pull of 15 to 25 ft lbs. to move the ball around the circle.

If more pressure than this is required, unbolt the universal joint and use a thicker shim between the inner and outer shell at the flange.

If the joint is found to be too loose, remove the shims and install a thinner shim until it does require 15 to 25 ft lbs. torque to rotate the flange portion of the torque ball.

Installing spider in rear yoke

Replace the driveshaft flange bolts and securely tighten.

REMOVAL OF TORQUE TUBE AND PROPELLER SHAFT ASSEMBLY

Remove the rear axle assembly from under the car and place on a suitable stand. Take the brake lines from the rear axle housing and torque tube. Disconnect the strut rods and remove the bolts which hold the front

and rear torque tube together and take off the front torque tube and the front propeller shaft assembly. To disassemble the propeller shaft assembly, support the universal joint and drive out the spring pin which holds it to the propeller shaft. Unbolt the rear torque tube from the carrier and slide it and the rear propeller shaft off the pinion shaft.

On reassembly, pack the rear propeller shaft coupling with No. 1, and No. 0 grade wheel bearing grease. Install the rear torque tube on the carrier with the brake release bracket spring down. No gasket is used. Torque the bolts to 50-60 ft. lbs.

No gaskets are used between the front and rear torque tubes.

DISASSEMBLY OF REAR UNIVERSAL JOINT

With the torque tubes disassembled, remove the snap rings from the bearings. Lay the rear propeller shaft assembly on a vise so that the yoke welded to the shaft bears against the open jaws of the vise. The shaft should be horizontal and the front yoke must be free to move vertically between the jaws of the vise. Use a small piece of pipe or similar tool having a diameter large enough to en-

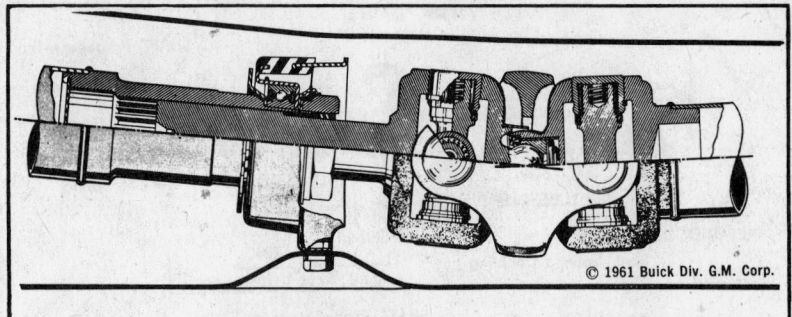

Constant velocity joint. 1961-63

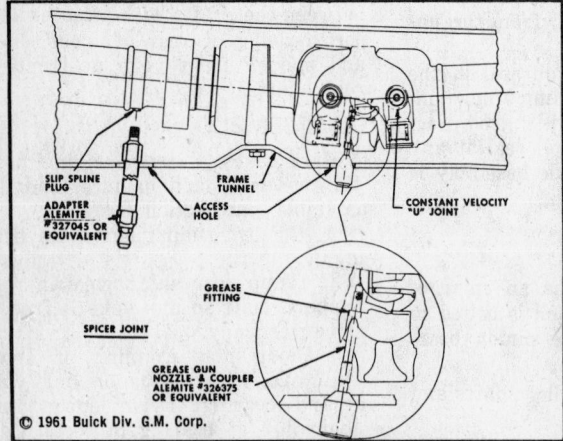

Propeller Shaft Slip Spline
and Constant Velocity Universal Joint
Lubrication Points (Spicer Joint)

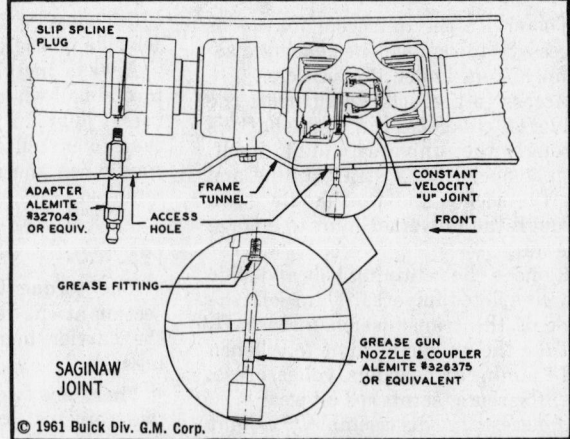

Propeller Shaft Slip Spline
and Constant Velocity Universal Joint
Lubrication Points (Saginaw Joint)

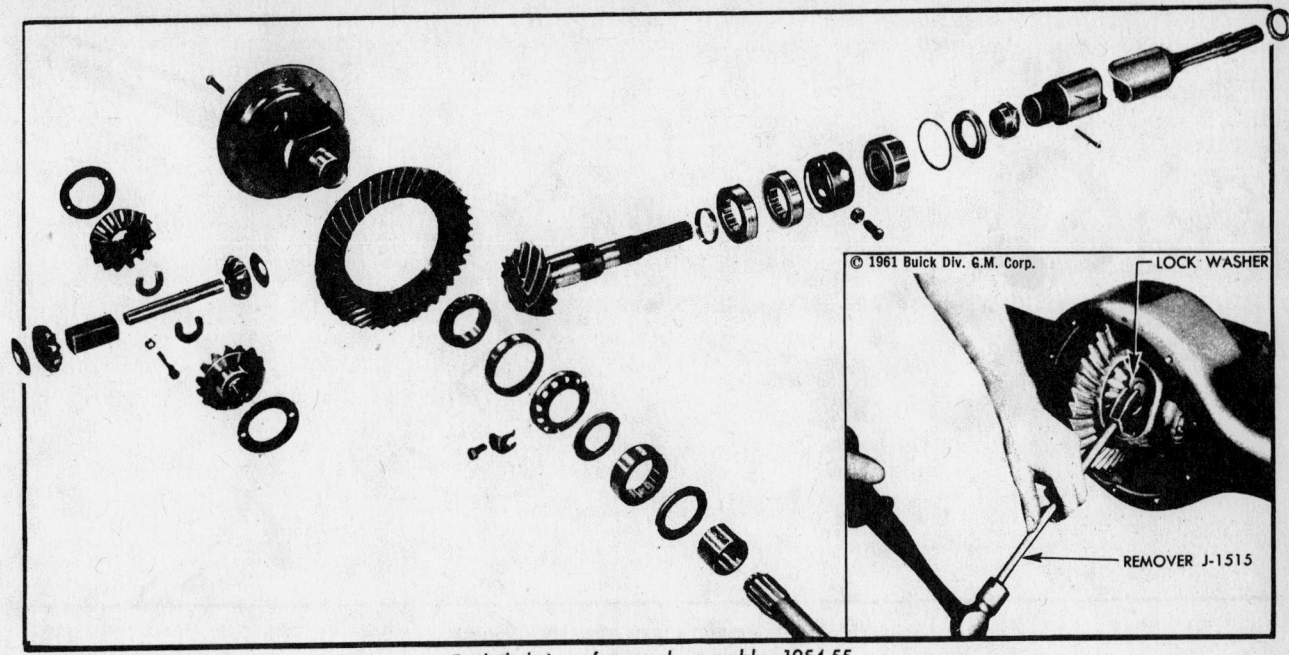

© 1961 Buick Div. G.M. Corp.

LOCK WASHER

REMOVER J-1515

Exploded view of rear axle assembly—1954-55

circle the bearing and apply force on the front yoke around the bearing. Drive the yoke down until the bearing projects far enough so that the snap ring groove is just visible. Rotate the shaft assembly 180 degrees and repeat to partially remove the opposite bearing. Place flat washers in the lower end of the bearing and again apply force around the bearing in which the washers were installed and which should completely remove the bearing from the yoke. Take the front yoke from the spider and drive out the remaining bearing with a brass drift.

On reassembly the nibs or bosses on the universal joint cross go toward the rear.

HOW TO CHECK FOR PROPELLER SHAFT VIBRATION

Objectionable vibration at 65 m.p.h. or higher can be due to an unbalanced propeller shaft. The condition can be due to a bent shaft or misaligned universal joints.

To check that propeller shaft is at fault note car speed in High gear at which vibration appears. Shift a synchromesh transmission into 2nd gear, or a Dynaflow into Low range. Drive car at same engine speed as before.

If vibration is the same whether in Direct drive or a lower gear, the propeller shaft is OK. If vibration disappears or lessens in lower gear the propeller shaft is out of balance.

Or try this procedure:

Jack up all wheels so car is relatively level. Have rear jack under center of differential housing.

Check runout of front and rear wheels. Should not exceed ⅛ inch at side of tire.

With transmission in High or Direct, run engine and note speeds at which vibration occurs.

Remove rear wheels and again note speed points of vibration. If vibration is gone the tire-wheel assemblies are out of balance.

Remove rear brake drums and again note speeds at which vibration occurs. If vibration is gone the brake drums are out of balance.

Put transmission in Neutral. With brake drums gone and transmission in Neutral, if vibration is gone the propeller shaft is out of balance. Continual vibration indicates an out-of-balance condition of the engine.

TORQUE TUBE OIL LEAKS

Oil coming from the joint between the torque tube and the differential carrier is due to a leaking seal: the front seal if the leaking is like transmission lubricant, the rear seal if it is like differential lubricant. In either case be sure to use a non-hardening sealing-compound on the O.D. of the new seal before installing it.

LUBRICATION OF SLIP SPLINES
Beginning 1961 Models

Lubrication of all Buick propeller shaft slip splines and Le Sabre, Invicta, and Electra constant velocity universal joint center ball is as follows:

All major lubrication equipment manufacturers now have available adapters to apply lubricant to the propeller shaft slip spline on all 1961-62 Buicks and the constant velocity universal joint center ball on the Le-Sabre, Invicta, and Electra. The constant velocity universal joint center ball should be lubricated at 5,000 mile intervals with multi-purpose grease EP#1 grade. No other lubricant is satisfactory for use at this point.

1. Rotate propeller shaft so fitting is visible through rear hole of frame tunnel.
2. Use special adapter held firmly against conical fitting to force multi-purpose grease EP#1 grade into center ball socket.

The propeller shaft slip spline on all models should be lubricated every 10,000 miles.

Le Sabre, Invicta, Electra Series:

1. Rotate propeller shaft so plug is accessible through forward hole in frame tunnel. Remove plug.
2. Install extended length fitting or adapter to fill cavity with multi-purpose grease EP#1 grade.
3. Reinstall plug.

Due to the position of the slip spline when the car is raised on some types of modern hoists, it is necessary to fill the slip spline lubricant cavity by forcing lubricant through the spline into the cavity. For this reason, either a fitting or an adapter is necessary in order to build up sufficient pressure to fill the slip spline cavity.

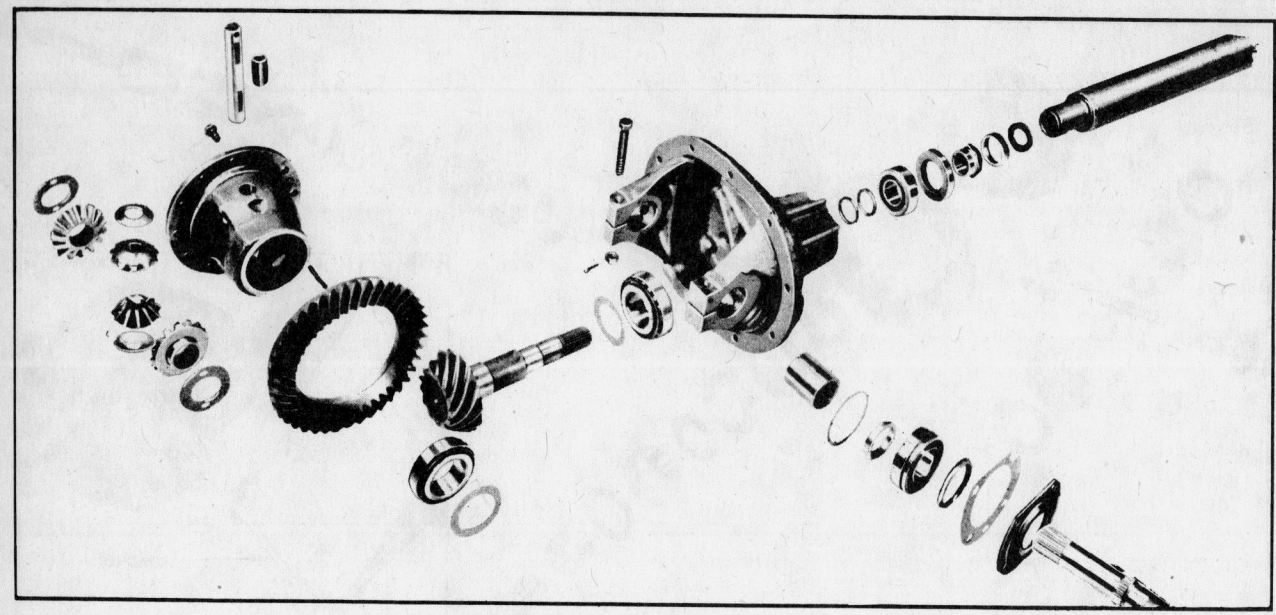

Exploded view of rear axle assembly—1956-60

REAR AXLE

TROUBLE SHOOTING AND ADJUSTMENT

General instructions covering the troubles of the rear axle and how to repair and adjust it, together with information on installation of rear axle bearings and grease seals, are given in the Unit Repair section under the heading: Axles, Rear.

Capacities of the rear axle are given in the Capacities Table of this section.

REMOVAL AND INSTALLATION OF REAR AXLE ASSEMBLY

Note: It is not necessary to remove the rear axle assembly for repair of a strut rod, an axle shaft, a wheel bearing, or a wheel bearing seal. If car has air suspension, exhaust all air before disconnecting a radius rod or the torque tube.

Place car stands solidly under frame so that rear end of car is high enough to work on. Place a floor jack under center of axle housing so it just supports the weight of the rear axle assembly.

Disconnect lower ends of rear springs. (On cars with air suspension, disconnect rear height control valve links. Pull valve levers down carefully to exhaust all air pressure from air spring units. Remove two bolts retaining plunger bearing plate to rear axle housing.)

Disconnect lower ends of rear shock absorbers; parking brake cable at rear cable sheave and at bracket on torque tube; brake hose from pipe at frame cross member (plug to save fluid and keep out dirt).

At the torque ball install two 3-inch guide pins and disconnect tube from ball.

Roll rear axle assembly from under the car.

When reinstalling, rotate a rear wheel to align the propeller shaft and universal joint blind splines. Tighten torque tube to torque ball bolts to 45-55 ft. lbs.

REAR COIL SPRING REMOVAL

Disconnect the shock absorber link and the torsion bar. Place a jack at the frame in front of the rear spring and jack up the frame.

Remove the bolt which holds the spring to the lower perch. NOTE: The left side of the car has a left thread bolt holding the spring, and the right side of the car has a right thread bolt holding the spring. Remove the upper and lower bolts and take out the coil spring. If necessary jack the car up a sufficient amount so it will come out readily.

Beginning 1961

A differential carrier, common to open driveshaft design, started with 1961-62 production.

For detailed information on removal and installation and other aspects of reconditioning, see "Unit Repair Section" under "Axles, Rear."

POSITIVE TRACTION DIFFERENTIAL

No special attention is required in this area, except with the lubricant used.

Under no circumstances use anything but special Buick Differential Lubricant: Spec. No. 723.

RADIO R & R

1961-63

1. Remove control knobs, felt washers, inner knobs and hex nuts from the radio unit.
2. Remove 4 retaining screws from console trim and remove the trim.
3. From within the ash tray, remove the 2 radio-to-instrument panel attaching bolts.
4. Pull radio out. Then disconnect speaker, antenna, battery and foot switch wires.
5. Install radio by reversing above procedure.

BUICK SPECIAL INDEX

Page

AIR CONDITIONING

Service 1092

BRAKES, HYDRAULIC

Adjustments 938
Bleed brakes 938
Brake references 54
Hand brake lever & cable 54
Master cylinder service 938

BRAKES, POWER

References 54
Power unit overhaul 954
Trouble shooting 954

COOLING SYSTEM

Thermostat 55
Water pump, R & R 56

CLUTCH

Clutch assembly, R & R 63
Clutch pedal, adjust 64

ELECTRICAL SYSTEM

Battery 54
Chassis 54
Delcotron references 52
Distributor, R & R 52
Distributor references 51
Distributor specifications 49
Engine 54
Engine firing order & timing 48
Fuses and circuit breakers 48
Gauges 1024
Generator R & R 52
Generator service 1026
Generator specifications 49
Generator trouble shooting chart 1026
Horn button 61
Ignition timing procedure 51
Instruments 54
Starter, R & R 54
Starter specifications 50
Starter systems 54

ENGINE ASSEMBLY

Cylinder head, R & R 57
Engine assembly, R & R 56
Engine diagnosis 1012
Exhaust manifold, R & R 55
Inlet manifold, R & R 55
Lubrication 59
Oil pan, R & R 59
Oil pump 59
Piston and rod, R & R 59
References 56
Rocker arms & shaft 57

ENGINE ASSEMBLY—continued

Timing case 57
Timing chain 57
Trouble shooting charts 1012
Tune-up specifications 49
Valve specifications 50

ENGINE LUBRICATION

Oil Filter 54
Oil pan, R & R 59
Oil pump 59

EXHAUST SYSTEM

Exhaust manifold 55
Intake manifold 55

FUEL SYSTEM

Carburetor adjustments 54
Carburetor specifications 972
Fuel gauge service 1020
Fuel pump pressure 49
Fuel pump 55
Fuel tank, R & R 55

INSTRUMENTS

Instrument cluster, R & R 54
Temperature Gauge 56
Oil Pressure Gauge 56
Speedometer 54

RADIO, R & R

References 68

REAR AXLE AND SUSPENSION

Axle assembly, R & R 68
Axle shaft 918
Axle shaft oil seal 918
Pinion bearings 918
Ring gear & pinion 918
Spring, rear R & R 68
Trouble shooting 919

SPECIFICATIONS

Battery 54
Brake cylinder sizes 51
Capacities 50
Chassis, general 51
Cylinder head tightening 50
Delcatron 49
Distributor 49
Engine, general 50
Engine identification 49
Engine, tune-up 49
Fuses and circuit breakers 48
Generator regulators 49

SPECIFICATIONS—continued

Ignition timing specifications 49
Light bulbs 48
Main bearings 50
Model identification 48
Piston & pins 49
Quick reference specifications . . . 48
Rod bearings 50
Starters 50
Tune-up 49
Valves 50
Wheel alignment 50

STEERING, MANUAL

Adjust gear housing 1052
Gear assembly, R & R 61
Horn button R & R 61
Steering wheel, R & R 61

STEERING, POWER

Power steering references 62
Pump assembly 1058
Trouble shooting 1081
Unit overhaul 1058

SUSPENSION, FRONT

Alignment procedures 1082
Alignment specifications 50
Ball joints, R & R 61
Coil springs 61
References 60

TRANSMISSION, AUTOMATIC

References 66
Disassembly of transmission 67
General information 728
Throttle linkage adjust 66
Transmission, R & R 67

TRANSMISSION, MANUAL

Shift controls 65
Transmission, R & R 67

TROUBLE CHECKS

Procedures 1

TUNE-UP

Procedures 51
Specifications 49
Engine diagnosis 1012

UNIVERSAL JOINT AND DRIVE LINES

U joint & drive line, R & R 67

BUICK SPECIAL

YEAR IDENTIFICATION

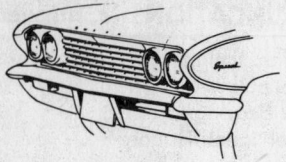

1961

1962

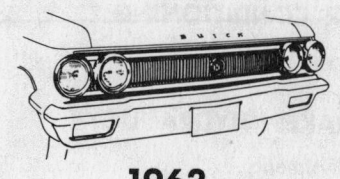

1963

QUICK WORKING SPECIFICATIONS

DISTRIBUTOR SPECIFICATIONS

Make ....Delco-Remy
Type of Advance
................Centrifugal & Vacuum
Point Gap ....016"
Point Spring Tension .... 19-23 oz.
Cam Dwell ....28°-32°

SPARK PLUGS

Year	Type	Gap
1961-63. V8	45-FFS	.035"
1962-63. V6	44S	.035"

IGNITION TIMING

(Spark occurs degrees before T.C.)
1961-63, All Std. Trans. ....5° B.T.C.
1961-63, all Auto. Trans. ..7½° B.T.C.

GENERATOR & REGULATOR

Year and Series	Generator Field Current In Amperes 12 Volt	Regulator Cut-Out Closing Voltage	Regulator Current Regulator Setting	Regulator Voltage Regulator Setting
1961-62	1.74	12.8	36	14.4

(A) Surrounding temperatures guide this adjustment, as much as 1 volt. Higher temperatures require lower settings and lower temperatures permit higher settings, within this limit.

DELCOTRON

For "Delcotron" specifications, see following pages.

COMPRESSION PRESSURE

Cranking ....160 PSI

CAPACITIES

Engine Crankcase (Qts.)
1961-63 4

Rear Axle (Pts.)
1961-63 2

Gasoline Tank (Gallons)
1961 14
1962-63 16

Transmission, Manual (Pts.)
1961-63 ....2¼

Transmission, Automatic (Pts.)
1961-63 Refill 12

Cooling System
1961-63 V8 Less Heater ....12 Qts.
1962-63 V6 Less Heater ......10½ Qts.

VALVES

Operating Tappet Clearance
1961-63—All ....Hydraulic ....Zero

Valve Timing (Inlet Opens)
1961-63 V8 ....29° BTC
1962-63 V6 ....18° BTC

BULB SPECIFICATIONS

Headlamps

	Candle Power	Number
Outer:		
High Beam 37½W		4002
Low Beam ....50 W		
Inner:		
High Beam 37½W		4001

Other Lamps

Headlamp Indicator 2		158
Parking & Front Turn ..4/32		1034
Tail, Stop & Rear Turn 4/32		1034
Turn Indicator 2		158
License Plate 3		67
Instrument 2		1816
Dome Light 15		211

CIRCUIT BREAKER

A 15 ampere circuit breaker is used to protect the headlamps and front parking lamps. It is mounted on light switch.

FUSES

Stop Lights, Directional Lights
& Indicator ....20 Amp.—1¼"
Panel Lights &
Rheostat .... 3 Amp.—1¼"
Wiper & Washer
Motor ....25 Amp.—1¼"
Tail, License &
Dome Lights ....9 Amp.—⅞"
Back Up Lights
(If Used) ....9 Amp.—⅞"
Heater Blower
(If Used) ....20 Amp.—1¼"

FIRING ORDER and TIMING

SPARK OCCURS:
1961-63, 5°—Idle (V-6 or V-8) Standard Trans.
7½°—Idle (V-6 or V-8) Automatic Trans.

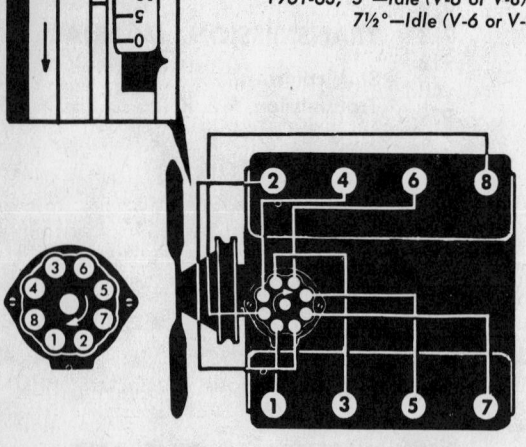

Buick Special V-8

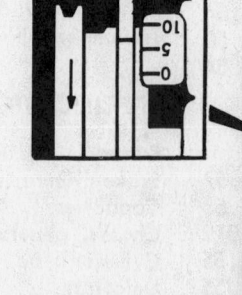

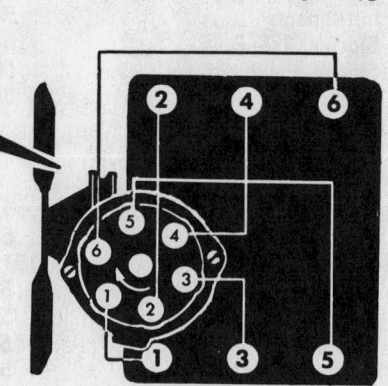

Buick Special V-6

NOTE:
THESE ARE APPROXIMATE SETTINGS. ENGINE DESIGN, ALTITUDE, TEMPERATURE, FUEL AND ENGINE CONDITION WILL ALL INFLUENCE TIMING. THE DETERMINING FACTOR, LIMITING ADVANCE, WILL STILL BE THE "KNOCK POINT" OF THE INDIVIDUAL ENGINE.

CAR SERIAL NUMBER LOCATION AND ENGINE IDENTIFICATION

ENGINE IDENTIFICATION IS MADE THROUGH THE ENGINE NUMBER.

The vehicle identification number is stamped on cowl to frame brace in engine compartment. The first digit of the number indicates the series ("0" for 4000 series, "1" for series 4100 and "3" for 4300 series, etc.). The next digit is a letter designating the year ("H" for 1961, "I" for 1962, etc.). The third prefix is a number in-

dicating the assembly plant at which the car was built (1 - Flint, 2 - South Gate). The remaining group of 6 digits is the individual car serial number. This number is also stamped on the crankcase just forward of the right cylinder head and constitutes the legal engine number. On this same crank-case surface (stamped upside down) when viewed from the front of the engine) is the engine production code number. On the V-6 engine, this num-

ber appears on the front of the crank-case below the left cylinder head gasket. This number, along with the vehicle identification number (car serial number) is used to identify the engine on product reports, etc. The production code number does not constitute a legal engine number for registration, titles, etc. A ¼" long dash (—) after the production code number indicates a .010" oversize cylinder bore engine.

TUNE UP SPECIFICATIONS

YEAR AND MODEL	SPARK PLUGS Type	Gap	DISTRIBUTOR Cam Angle	Point Gap	Arm Spring Tension (Ounce)	Ignition Timing	Compression Pressure Cranking	VALVES Tappet Clearance Intake	Exhaust	Timing Inlet Opens	Fuel Pump Pressure	Engine Idle Speed
1961 V8	45FFC	.035	30°	.016	19-23	5B	160	Zero	Zero	29B	4-5¼	525
1962 V8	45FFS	.035	30°	.016	19-23	7½B	160	Zero	Zero	29B	4-5¼	525
V6	44S	.035	30°	.016	19-23	7½B	160	Zero	Zero	18B	4-5¼	525
1963 V8-4100	45FFS	.035	30°	.016	19-23	5B	160	Zero	Zero	29B	4-5¼	525
V8-4300	44FFS	.035	30°	.016	19-23	7½B	160	Zero	Zero	29B	4-5¼	525
V6-4000	44S	.035	30°	.016	19-23	7½B	160	Zero	Zero	18B	4-5¼	525

Note:

All specifications are standard and should result in satisfactory performance. There are, however, factors that influence these settings, such as fuel octane value, air density, humidity, temperature, etc. Timing charts, like other specifications must be considered as averages, subject to modification.

DISTRIBUTOR SPECIFICATIONS

YEAR AND MODEL	Delco-Remy Part Number	Rotation	Cam Angle Degrees	BREAKER Point Opening (Inch)	Arm Spring (Ounce)	GOVERNOR CONTROL @ DIST. R.P.M. Advance Starts	Full Advance	VACUUM CONTROL DATA Inches of Vacuum To Start Advance	Inches of Vacuum For Full Advance	Max. Adv. of Dist. In Degrees
1961 V8	1115136	C	28-32	.016	19-23	1°@535	14@1850	6-8	14	14°
1962-63 V8-All	1110977	C	28-32	.016	19-23	1°@535	14@1850	6-8	14-16	14-18
V6-All	1110286	C	28-32	.016	19-23	1°@535	14@1850	6-8	14-16	14-18

GENERATOR AND REGULATOR SPECIFICATIONS

YEAR AND MODEL	GENERATORS Field Current Amperes At 12 Volts	Brush Spring Tension (Ounce)	REGULATORS Cut-Out Relay Air Gap	Closing Voltage	Current And Voltage Regulator Air Gaps	Current Regulator Setting Amps.	Voltage Regulator Setting
1961-62 All	1.74	28	.020"	12.8	.075"	31-36	14.4

DELCOTRON AND A.C. REGULATOR SPECIFICATIONS

Delcotron Model Number	Ground Polarity	Field Current Draw (Amperes)	CURRENT OUTPUT Engine R.P.M.	Amperes	Volts	RUNNING VOLTAGE Engine R.P.M.	Amperes	Volts @125°	REGULATOR Model Number	Point Gap	FIELD RELAY Armature Air Gap	Closing Voltage
1100622	Neg.	1.9 to 2.2	1100	12.	14	6500	42	13.5-14.3	1119506	.015	.015	6.5-8.5
1100633	Neg.	4.1 to 4.5	1100	24.	14	6500	62	13.3-13.9	1119506	.015	.015	6.5-8.5

PISTON AND PIN SPECIFICATIONS

YEAR AND MODEL	PISTON Skirt Clearance Top	Bottom	Diameter	Bushing	PISTON PIN FIT In Piston	In Rod	Lock
1961-63 V8	.0005-.0011	.0075-.0013	.8747-.8750	None	.00005-.0001	Press	In Rod
1962-63 V6	.0005-.0011	.0010-.0016	.8747-.8750	None	.00005-.0001	Press	In Rod

BUICK SPECIAL

BATTERY AND STARTER SPECIFICATIONS

YEAR AND MODEL	BATTERY				STARTERS						Brush Spring Tension
	Amp. Hour Capacity	Volts	Group Number	Terminal Grounded	LOCK TEST			NO-LOAD TEST			
					Amps.	Volts	Torque	Amps.	Volts	R.P.M.	
1961-62 All	40	12	M1	Neg.	300	4.0	N.A.	70	10.6	6750	35
1963 All											
6 cyl.—4000	40	12	17M2	Neg.	N.A.	N.A.	N.A.	70	10.6	6750	35
V-8—4100, 4300	61	12	25M	Neg.	N.A.	N.A.	N.A.	70	10.6	6750	35

CAPACITIES

YEAR AND MODEL	Engine Crankcase Add 1 Qt. For New Filter	Transmission Pints to Refill After Draining		Rear Axle Pints	Gasoline Tank Gallons	Cooling System Quarts
		Manual	Automatic			
1961 V8	4	2¼	12	2	14	12(A)
1962-63 V8	4	2¼	12	2	16	12(A)
V6	4	2¼	12	2	16	10½(A)

(A) ADD 1½ QUARTS FOR HEATER.

GENERAL ENGINE SPECIFICATIONS

YEAR AND MODEL	Bore And Stroke	Number of Main Bearings	Type of Valve Lifter	Cubic Inch Displacement	AMA Horsepower	Adv. Horsepower At Stated RPM	Adv. Torque At Stated RPM	Compression Ratio	Oil Pressure At 35 MPH	Camshaft Drive
1961 V8	3.5x2.8	5	Hydraulic	215	39.2	155@4400	220@2200	8.8-1	35	Chain
1962-63 V8 4100	3.5x2.8	5	Hydraulic	215	39.2	155@4600	220@2400	8.8-1	35	Chain
V8 4300	3.5x2.8	5	Hydraulic	215	39.2	200@5000	240@3200	10.25-1	35	Chain
V6 All	3.625x3.2	4	Hydraulic	198	31.54	135@4600	205@2400	8.8-1	35	Chain

CRANKSHAFT BEARING JOURNAL SIZES

YEAR AND MODEL	MAIN BEARING JOURNALS				CONNECTING ROD BEARING JOURNALS		
	Journal Diameter	Oil Clearance	End Play Of Shaft	End Play Held By	Journal Diameter	Oil Clearance	End Play
1961 V8	2.2992	.0005"-.0020"	.006	3	2.000"	.0005"-.002"	.006"-.014"
1962-63 V8	2.2992	.0005"-.0021"	.006	3	2.000"	.0002"-.0022"	.006"-.014"
V6	2.2992	.0005"-.0021"	.006	2	2.000"	.0002"-.0022"	.006"-.014"

VALVE SPECIFICATIONS

YEAR AND MODEL	Seat Angle	Intake Valve Lift	Exhaust Valve Lift	VALVE SPRING PRESSURE		STEM TO GUIDE CLEARANCE		Stem Diameter	Are Guides Removable
				Outer	Inner	Inlet	Exh.		
1961-62 All	45°	.383"	.383"	64@1⁴¹/₆₄	None	.001"-.003"	.001"-.003"	Note A	Yes B
1963 V8	45°	.383"	.383"	64@1⁴¹/₆₄	None	.001"-.003"	.001"-.003"	Note A	Yes
V6	45°	.385"	.385"	64@1⁴¹/₆₄	None	.001"-.003"	.001"-.003"	Note A	No

Note A: Exhaust—.3407" top; .3402" bottom.   Intake—.3412" top: .3407" bottom.   Note: B V6 Guides NOT replaceable.

FRONT WHEEL ALIGNMENT

YEAR AND MODEL	CASTER		CAMBER		Toe-In (Inches)	Kingpin Inclination (Degrees)	WHEEL PIVOT RATIO	
	Range (Degrees)	Pref. Setting	Range (Degrees)	Pref. Setting			Inner Wheel	Outer Wheel
1961 V8	1½N-2½N	2-N	¼N-1N	⅜-N	1/16"	7½	23⅔°	20°
1962-63 All	0-1°N	½N	⅜P-⅜N	0	⅛-³/₁₆	7½	23⅔	20°

CYLINDER HEAD NUT TIGHTENING SEQUENCE

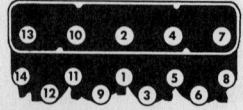
1961, V8, tighten to 50-55 ft. lbs.

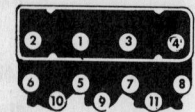
1962-63, V6, tighten to 65-70 ft. lbs.

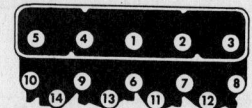
1962-63, V8, tighten to 50-55 ft. lbs.

GENERAL CHASSIS AND BRAKE SPECIFICATIONS

YEAR AND MODEL	CHASSIS		BRAKE CYLINDER BORE		
	Overall Length (Inches)	Tire Size	Master Cylinder (Inches)	Wheel Cylinder (Inches)	
				Front	Rear
1961-62 All	188.4	6.50x13	1.00	1.00	7/8
1963 All	192.1	650x13	1.00	1.00	7/8

TUNE-UP

ENGINE TUNE-UP AND DIAGNOSIS ARE SO CLOSELY RELATED THAT ONE PROCEDURE SHOULD SERVE BOTH PURPOSES

Compression Check

1. Remove the plug wires.
2. Blow foreign matter from around the spark plugs with compressed air. Then loosen the plugs one turn.
3. Replace plug wires, start engine and snap throttle open for one or two seconds. (This should clear the engine of dislodged carbon particles.)
4. Stop engine and remove the plug wires and spark plugs.
5. Remove the air cleaner. Then block the carburetor throttle wide open.
6. Hook up a starter remote-control cable and switch. Then crank the engine through about four strokes for each cylinder while reading the compression pressure on a reliable cylinder compression gauge.
7. Record the maximum pressures of each cylinder. Variation between cylinders should not exceed 15 lb.

Note: A compression check should be the first step in the course of tune-up events. Only if compression is within limits, should tune-up be continued.

Spark Plugs

Use a good plug tester, if available, and service or renew the spark plugs. Detailed information on diagnosing spark plug troubles can be found in the Unit Repair section, under Tune-Up.

In spark plug installation, be sure of the following:

1. Use plugs of correct model, gapped properly.
2. Thoroughly clean the cylinder head and spark plug threads.
3. Carefully torque the spark plugs to 15-20 ft. lbs. on the V-8, and 25-35 on the V-6.

Generator Drive Belt

Check the condition of the belt and adjust tension to 1/2" deflection when 15 pounds pressure is applied midway between the water pump and the generator pulley.

Battery

1. Check condition of battery.
2. Clean, lubricate and tighten cable connections both ends.

Other Electrical

1. Check Generator output.
2. Check Regulator.
3. Check Starter Motor current draw.
4. Check Ignition Coil output.
5. Check Ignition Wiring.
6. Test Primary Circuit resistance.
7. Test spark intensity at each plug wire.

Cooling System

1. Examine for coolant leaks, (engine, radiator, pump, heater and all hoses).
2. Look for coolant contamination, (rust, oil, etc.) in the radiator.
3. Recharge cooling system with anti-freeze or rust inhibitor.

Distributor

1. Replace and/or reset breaker points.
2. Lubricate distributor cam.
3. Lubricate distributor shaft bushing at the oil cup.
4. Check and adjust vacuum control.
5. Inspect and clean distributor rotor and cap.

Fuel System

1. Clean pump sediment bowl.
2. Check pump pressure and capacity, (fuel filter may be partially obstructed).
3. Clean carburetor bowl and adjust float.

Final Adjustments

1. Set ignition timing with a light.
2. Then road test the car and, if necessary, modify the prescribed setting within limits to accommodate the variables of engine and operating conditions and fuel anti-knock valve.

    Note: This final timing adjustment is made in the shop but as a result of road test.

3. Check and adjust engine idle speed.
4. Adjust carburetor idle mixture.

DISTRIBUTOR

REFERENCES

Detailed information on: distributor drive, direction of distributor rotation; cylinder numbering; firing order; point gap; cam dwell; timing mark location; spark plugs, spark advance; ignition resistor location, and idle speed; will be found in the Tune-up Specifications table of this section. Further information on trouble shooting, general tune-up procedures, how to replace ignition wires, how to choose the proper spark plug, adjust timing, will be found in the Unit Repair Section under the heading: Ignition-Distributors-Tune-up.

The distributor is located between the two cylinder banks, up front. The rotor turns in a clockwise direction, as viewed from the top.

Engine timing requirements are satisfied by the action of the breaker plate which is controlled by the effort of a vacuum diaphragm working against spring tension. The diaphragm moves the breaker plate in a counter-clockwise direction to advance the timing, and the springs move the plate in a clockwise direction to retard the timing. The degree of timing, within automatic control limits, is determined by the amount of vacuum applied to the spring loaded diaphragm and breaker plate.

Caution:

Design of the V6-90° engine requires a pecular form of distributor cam. The distributor may be serviced in the regular way and should cause no more problems than any other distributor, if the firing plan is thoroughly understood.

The distributor cam is not ground to standard 6 cylinder indexing intervals. This special form requires that the original pattern of spark plug wiring be used. The engine will not run in balance if #1 spark plug wire is inserted into #6 distributor cap tower, even though each wire in firing sequence is advanced to the next distributor tower. There is a difference between the firing intervals of each succeeding cylinder through the 720 degree engine cycle.

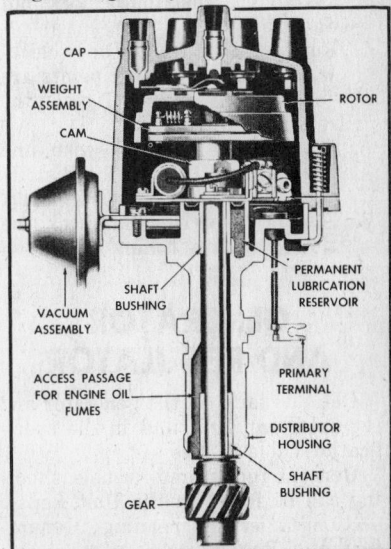

Distributor and Cap Assembly

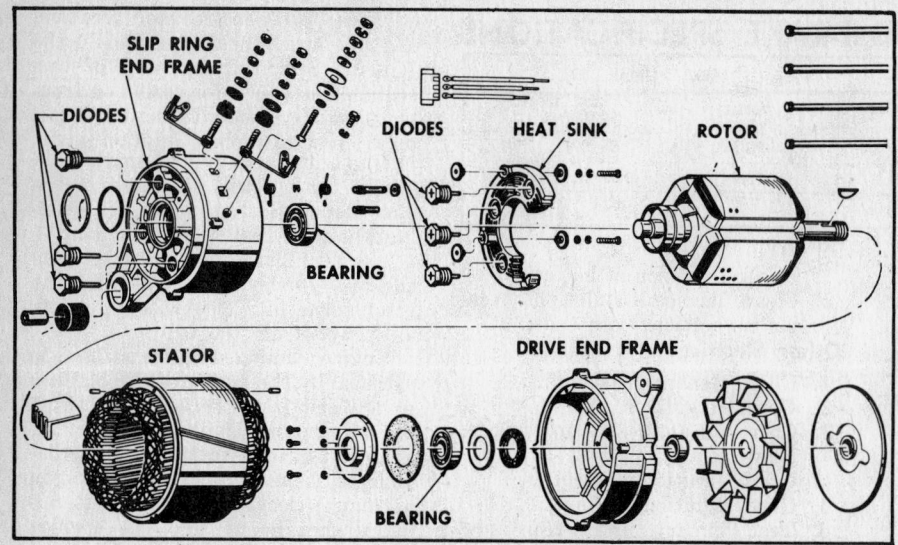

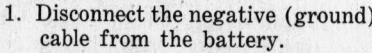

ADJUSTING SCREW
(TURN TO ADJUST SETTING)

Adjusting Voltage Regulator Setting

Exploded View of Alternating Current Generator

DISTRIBUTOR REMOVE

1. Remove distributor cap, primary wire and vacuum line at the distributor.
2. Scribe a mark on the distributor body, locating the position of the rotor and scribe another mark on the distributor body and engine block, showing the position of the body in the block.
3. Remove the hold-down screw and lift the distributor out of the block.

DISTRIBUTOR INSTALL

1. If engine has been disturbed, rotate the crankshaft to bring the piston of number one cylinder to the top of its compression stroke.
2. Position the distributor in the block with the rotor at #1 firing position. Make sure the oil pump intermediate drive shaft is properly seated in the oil pump.
3. Install the distributor lock but do not tighten.
4. Rotate the distributor body clockwise until the breaker points are just starting to open. Tighten the retaining screw.
5. Connect the primary wire and the vacuum line to the distributor, then install distributor cap.
6. Start the engine and check the timing with a timing light.

GENERATOR AND REGULATOR

Detailed facts on the generator and regulator can be found in the specification table in this section.

General repair and trouble shooting can be found in the Unit Repair section under the heading; Generators and Regulators.

GENERATOR REMOVE

1. Disconnect the negative (ground) cable from the battery.
2. Disconnect armature, field, and ground wires at the generator terminals.
3. Remove adjustment arm to generator bolt. Remove the two pivot bolts from the mounting bracket. Remove generator and belt.

GENERATOR INSTALL

1. Reverse the above procedure.
2. **Polarize the generator** by disconnecting the wire from the **field** terminal of the regulator and momentarily touch it to the **bat** terminal of the regulator. The quick surge of current will correctly polarize the generator.
3. Adjust fan belt tension so as to obtain ½" belt deflection when applying 15 lb. thumb pressure to the belt, midway between the generator and fan pulleys.

Caution: Do not use a "jumper" wire to polarize the generator. The regulator points may be burned if you do.

A.C. GENERATOR ("Delcotron")

Beginning with 1962, an alternating current generator is used on Buick Special. This change is to satisfy the increase in electrical loads imposed on the battery by modern conditions of traffic and driving patterns.

The DELCOTRON is covered in the Unit Repair section of this manual, under "Generators and Regulators."

Caution:

Since the Delcotron and regulator are designed for use on only one po-

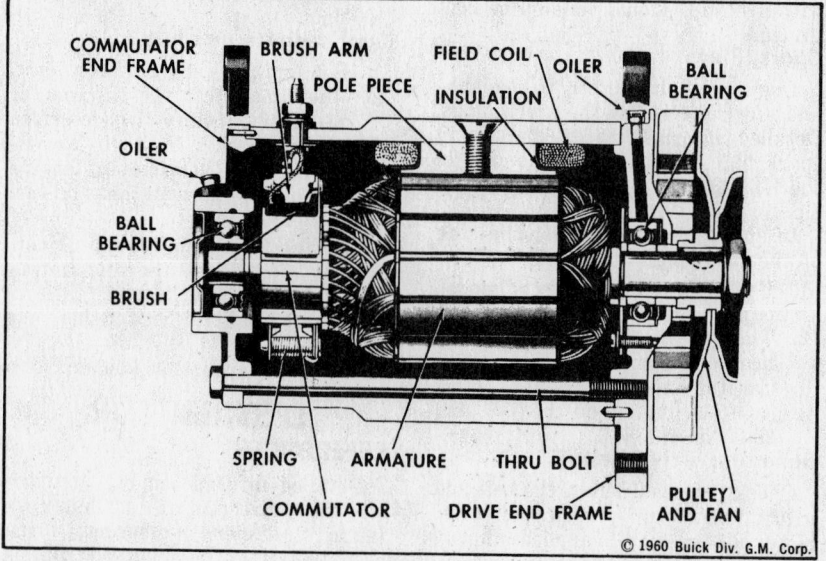

© 1960 Buick Div. G.M. Corp.

Generator

larity system, the following precautions must be observed:

1. The polarity of the battery, generator and regulator must be matched and considered before making any electrical connections in the system.
2. When connecting a booster battery, be sure to connect the negative battery terminals together and the postive battery terminals together.
3. When connecting a charger to the battery, connect the charger positive lead to the battery positive terminal. Connect the charger negative lead to the battery negative terminal.
4. Never operate the Delcotron on open circuit. Be sure that all connections in the circuit are clean and tight.
5. Do not short across or ground any of the terminals on the Delcotron regulator.
6. Do not attempt to polarize the Delcotron.
7. Do not use test lamps of more than 12 volts for checking diode continuity.

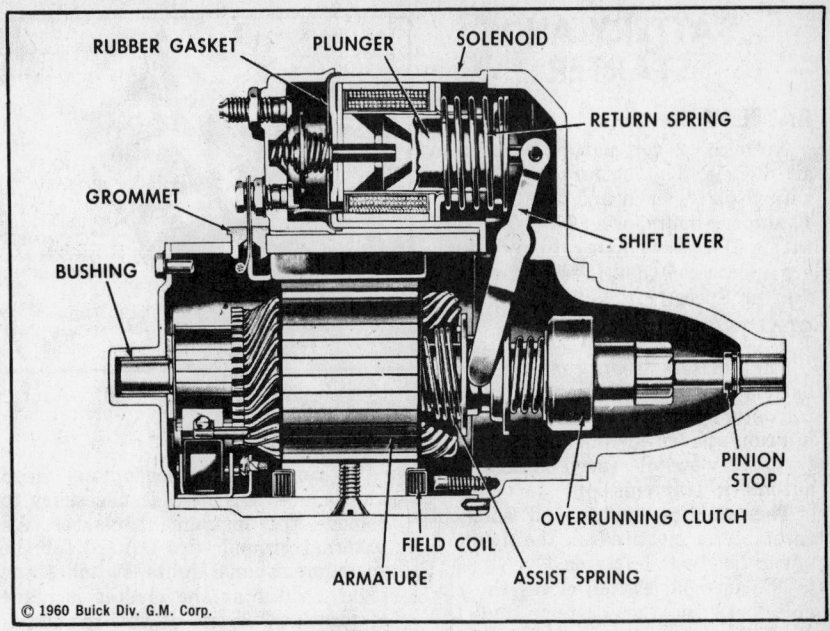

Starter Motor and Solenoid

8. Avoid long soldering times when replacing diodes or transistors. Prolonged heat is damaging to these units.

9. Disconnect the battery ground terminal when servicing any A.C. system. This will prevent the possibility of accidental reversing of polarity.

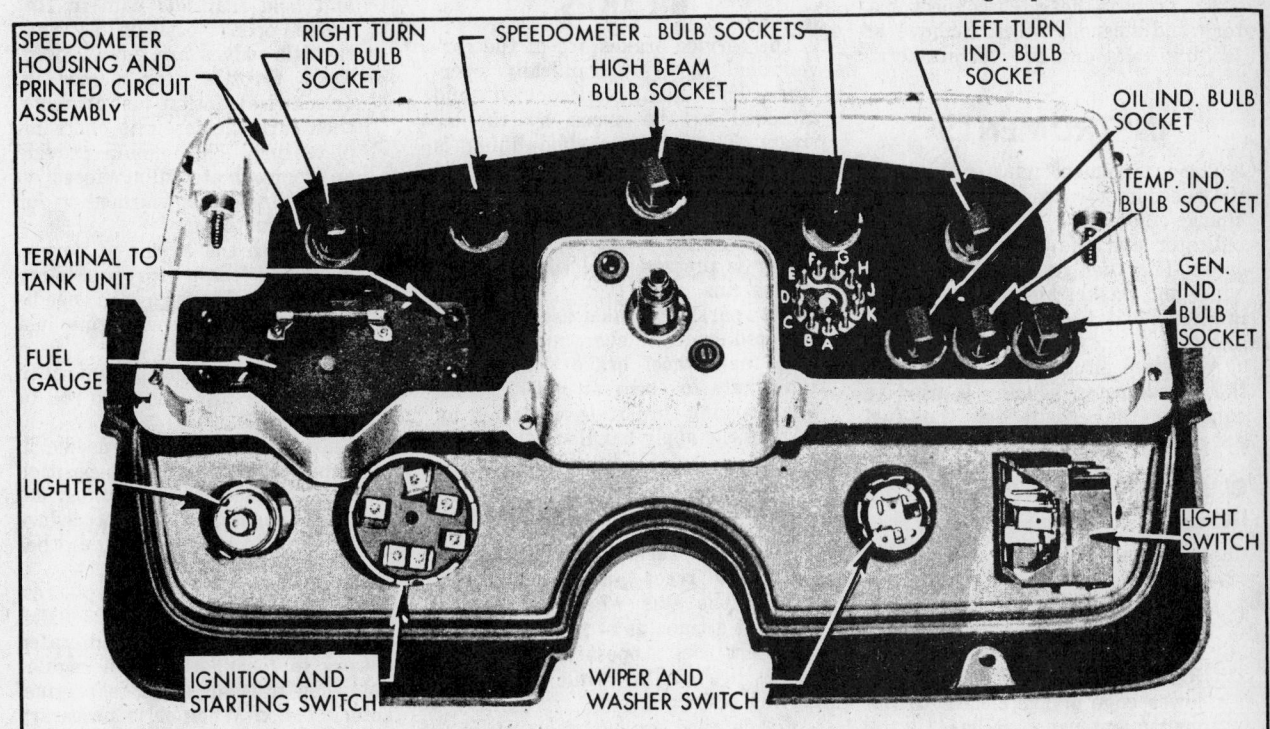

LEGEND FOR CONNECTOR PINS AND CORRESPONDING WIRE COLOR IN DISCONNECT PLUG

A. Gen. Indicator to Generator - Red
B. Temp. Indicator to Temperature and Ignition Switches - Yellow with Black Stripe
C. Oil Indicator to Oil Pressure Switch - Black with White Stripe
D. To Speedometer Lights - White
E. Ground - Black

F. To Left Turn Indicator - Dark Green
G. To High Beam Indicator - Gray
H. To Right Turn Indicator - Light Green
J. Battery to Fuel Gauge, Gen., Oil and Temp. Indicators - Yellow
K. Dash Unit Fuel Gauge to Tank Unit - Brown

© 1960 Buick Div. G.M. Corp.

Back of Cluster

BUICK SPECIAL

BATTERY AND STARTER

BATTERY

A Delco 12 volt battery is used in all models. The battery has 6 cells with 9 plates each and a capacity of 40 ampere-hours, or a 66 plate battery with a 61 ampere hour rating, depending upon car model. (See Battery and Starter Specs.)

STARTER

The starter circuit consists of the battery, battery cables, starting motor, starter motor solenoid switch, ignition-starter switch and the neutral safety switch, (used on cars with automatic transmission).

The starting motor and solenoid assembly is mounted on the flywheel upper housing, left side.

The solenoid switch closes the circuit between the battery and the starting motor. It also operates the shift lever that moves the drive pinion into mesh with the flywheel ring gear.

STARTER, R & R

No problem here. Disconnect battery and solenoid wires. Remove attaching bolts and lift out starter.

INSTRUMENTS

The instrument cluster includes the speedometer head, the generator charge indicator, the oil pressure indicator and the temperature indicator. The fuel gauge, light switch, wiper and washer switch, starter and ignition switch and the cigarette lighter.

A printed circuit which is part of the speedometer housing is used to complete the circuit for the fuel gauge and the lights in the cluster.

CLUSTER REMOVE AND INSTALL

1. Disconnect battery.
2. Remove cluster hood, then from under the panel, remove two attaching nuts from the studs that hold the cluster at each side.
3. Remove two screws that hold the lower edge of the cluster to the instrument panel tie bar.
4. Disconnect wiring harness connectors from headlight switch, windshield wiper switch, ignition switch, and cigar lighter.
5. Disconnect speedometer cable and printed circuit plug.
6. Remove cluster by pulling rearward and at the same time lifting up.
7. Install cluster by reversing above steps, then reconnect battery.

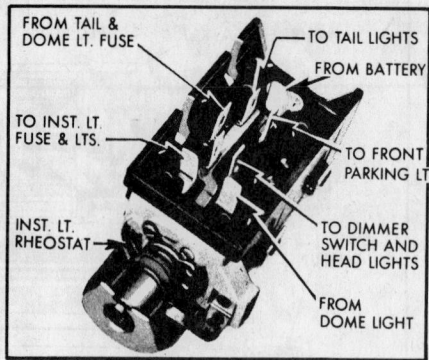

Back of Light Switch

SPEEDOMETER

To remove the speedometer head and printed circuit it is necessary to remove the instrument cluster. An external ground wire is used for the instrument panel lights, switches and cigar lighter as the cluster is made of plastic. One end of this ground is attached to a tab on the cigar lighter retainer. The other end is attached to the steering mast jacket support by a screw.

BRAKES

The service brakes are of the conventional type, hydraulically operated. The lining is molded and attached to the shoes by tubular rivets. The primary shoe lining is shorter than the secondary lining and is of different composition.

Brake drum lining-contact-surfaces are cast iron, however, the drum proper is pressed steel with integral cooling fins.

The parking brake uses a hand operated control lever, enclosed cables, rear wheel brake shoe levers and struts to the rear wheel shoes. The parking brake is released by turning the apply handle to the right.

Beginning 1963

Self adjusters have been added to the service brakes. The system is designed to react and progressively tighten the star wheel adjuster, a notch at a time, as required. The self adjusters only operate when the brakes are applied while the car is moving rearward.

For detailed service brake information, see "Brakes, Hydraulic" in the "Unit Repair Section."

POWER BRAKES

Starting with 1962 power brakes are optional on cars equipped with automatic transmission. This installation is similar to that of the large line of cars.

Repair methods can be found in Unit Repair Section.

FUEL SYSTEM

CARBURETOR

The carburetor is a Rochester two barrel down draft compact unit mounted centerally between the two cylinder heads.

A four barrel carburetor is standard on the Skylark and optional on the others.

Note: More detailed information including adjustments and specifications may be found in the "Unit Repair Section," under "Carburetors."

Idle and Choke Adjustments

Carburetor adjustments should not be attempted until it is known that all other items affecting engine performance are correct.

1. Adjust needle (idle mixture) valves all the way in, until they are just seated. Then back off one complete turn. This is a temporary setting.
2. Back off the throttle stop screw and hold fast idle cam in **Hot** (wide open) position so that throttle valves are fully closed.
3. Turn throttle stop screw **in**, (clockwise) until it just contacts, then turn the screw **in** one complete turn. This should provide an approximate idling speed so the engine can be warmed up for final adjustment.
4. Now, with the engine at normal operating temperature and idling at 525 RPM, turn the needle valve **"in"** until the engine just begins to lag.
5. Then turn the needle **out** until the engine just begins to roll or gallop.
6. Then, slowly turn the needle in again and hunt for the position that produces the smoothest engine idle. Repeat this procedure on the idle mixture of the other barrel.
7. Readjust the throttle stop screw to obtain a hot idle of 525 RPM.

The choke thermostat is calibrated to work in conjunction with regular fuel when it is adjusted to original factory index. When it is necessary to adjust the thermostat, loosen the cover attaching screws and move the cover one point at a time until the desired results are obtained.

Do not try to accommodate for old and heat fatigued thermostats by adjustment. Original physical properties of the thermostat change after long use. Unit replacement is necessary to again obtain correct calibration throughout the choke operating range. Renew old choke thermostats.

Throttle Linkage and Dash Pot Adjustments

The procedure for adjusting throttle linkage is identical on "Standard" or "Automatic" transmission cars. On automatic transmission cars, however, the linkage actuates other linkage connected to a valve in the transmission. Also, automatic transmission cars have a dash pot to prevent engine stalling from too-quick release of the accelerator pedal.

1. To adjust throttle linkage, make sure the accelerator pedal is free and in good linkage condition.
2. On automatic transmission equipped cars, see "Throttle Linkage Adjustment" of "Automatic Transmission," on the next few pages of this car section.
3. Disconnect rear end of throttle rod from throttle operating lever.
4. While a helper presses the accelerator firmly against the floor, hold throttle in wide open position. Hold rear end of throttle rod at hole in throttle operating lever. The rod end must be 1/16" short of entering the hole in the lever. Adjust throttle rod length to obtain this condition.
5. Connect throttle rod to operating lever and attach cotter pin.
6. Now, press accelerator to the floor and recheck throttle for wide open position.
7. Hold choke valve closed and move throttle lever to wide open position to check adjustment of choke unloader.
8. Finally check that there is a full opening of the throttle valve as the accelerator pedal just strikes the floor.
9. Now adjust the dash pot by turning the plunger until it just touches the throttle lever.
10. With the gear selector in "Drive" and the brakes firmly set, jab the accelerator and release it quickly. Note engine operation as the throttle closes.
11. If engine stalls due to too quick deceleration, move the dash pot plunger toward the throttle lever until the stalling is corrected. If too much time is required for throttle to close, move the plunger away from the throttle lever.
12. If correct control cannot be obtained, renew the dash pot.

FUEL PUMP

An AC Type HQ fuel pump is used. It is mounted on the right side of the timing chain cover in an inverted position. The pump lever works from the underside of a camshaft eccentric. It is of the single action diaphragm type and is equipped with a pulsation dampening chamber for stabilizing fuel flow.

FUEL FILTER

V-8 Engine

The fuel filter is of the glass bowl type and is located in the line between the fuel pump and the carburetor. The filter is mounted solidly in a steel line and requires no mounting bracket. The filtering element should be replaced every 5,000 miles. To clean the filter, remove the glass bowl and dump the contents. Soak the bowl in alcohol, inspect the filtering element and replace if necessary. Wipe the bowl clean and reinstall.

V-6 Engine

The V-6 engine gas filter is located in the carburetor fuel inlet. The element is sintered bronze and placed with the cupped end outward. The element is so spring loaded as to permit fuel to by-pass, in the event of element clogging.

The element should be removed and cleaned in a good solvent at 12,000 miles or 12 month periods.

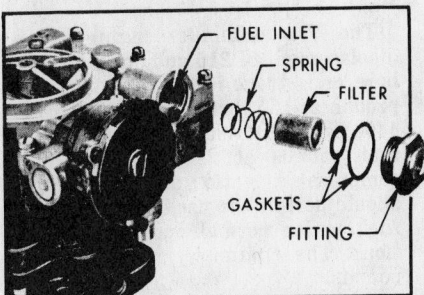

Fuel Filter

FUEL TANK

The fuel tank is attached by two strap type supports to the body under the trunk compartment.

The gas tank filler is soldered into an opening at the center of the left side of the tank. It is accessible through a door in the left rear quarter.

The stand pipe and fuel gauge sending unit are integral and require tank removal for replacement.

Tank Remove

1. Remove the gasoline by syphoning into a clean container.
2. Remove vent pipe.
3. Remove hoses and cups.
4. Disconnect the vent pipe from the breather pipe.
5. Disconnect gauge sending unit wire at the connector.
6. Disconnect support straps at their rear ends and lower the tank.

Tank Install

Install in reverse order of removal.

INTAKE MANIFOLD AND EXHAUST SYSTEM

INTAKE MANIFOLD

V-8 Engine

The temperature of the aluminum intake manifold is controlled by engine coolant. The coolant enters the two front corners of the manifold and flows through a jacket along the lower level then forward along the upper level to the engine thermostat. No exhaust manifold heat control valve is used.

Positive crankcase ventilation is furnished on cars manufactured for sale in areas subject to air pollution control.

V-6 Engine

Coolant flows into the cast iron intake manifold water passage from the forward port of the cylinder heads to the thermostat housing and thermostat by-pass. A nipple in the manifold permits connection of the heater hose nipple.

EXHAUST MANIFOLD

V-8 Engine

The right exhaust manifold contains the carburetor choke heat stove. This stove consists of an alloy steel heating tube mounted in a drilled hole in the manifold and a heating chamber on the outside of the manifold. Heated air is drawn from the heat stove through an insulated tube into the automatic choke housing.

V-6 Engine

The controlling source of exhaust heat is a heat control valve in the right exhaust manifold. This offset valve has a thermostat spring which tends to hold the valve closed under cold operating conditions.

This tension causes a pressure build up in the right exhaust manifold which forces exhaust through the cross-over passage under the carburetor to the left exhaust manifold and out the pipe and muffler.

All exhaust connections except at the muffler are of the ball joint type. There are no gaskets used in the exhaust system.

COOLING SYSTEM

The cooling system is pressurized to 15 lb. Coolant temperature is controlled by a 170° thermostat housed in the forward (outlet) end of the intake manifold. This pellet type thermostat controls circulation and temperature in the intake manifold as well as the engine proper. A 180° thermostat is available for use with non-volatile type, permanent antifreeze solutions.

BUICK SPECIAL

Caution:

Be sure the thermostat is not reversed in its installed position. The temperature sensitive side should extend toward the rear.

Special Note:

It is advisable to use a highly inhibited ethylene-gylcol anti-freeze type coolant in the Buick Special, both **winter** and **summer**. GM specification #1899M or its equivalent is recommended.

WATER PUMP

The water pump cover is die cast aluminum into which the water pump bearing outer race is shrunk fit. Therefore, the cover, shaft bearing and hub are not replaceable. The shaft seal and the impeller are the only replaceable parts.

Remove

1. Drain cooling system.
2. Loosen belt or belts, then remove fan blades and pulley or pulleys from hub on water pump shaft. Remove belt or belts.
3. Disconnect hose from water pump inlet and heater hose from nipple. Remove bolts then remove pump and gasket from the timing case cover.
4. Check pump shaft bearings for end play or roughness. If bearings are not serviceable, the assembly must be replaced.

Install

1. Install pump assembly with new gasket. Bolts and lock washers must be torqued evenly.
2. Connect radiator hose to pump inlet and heater hose to nipple. Fill cooling system and check all points of possible coolant leaks.
3. Install fan pulley or pulleys and fan blade. Install belt or belts and adjust for correct tension.

ENGINE TEMPERATURE AND OIL PRESSURE SENDING UNITS

Temp. Gauge

A temperature switch located in right front of the intake manifold controls the operation of the **"Temp"** indicator light located in the instrument cluster.

If the engine cooling system is not working properly and the coolant temperature reaches 248°, the **"Temp"** indicator light will burn in the instrument cluster.

Oil Pressure

The oil pressure sending unit is located in the oil pump cover and operates an indicator light in the instrument cluster.

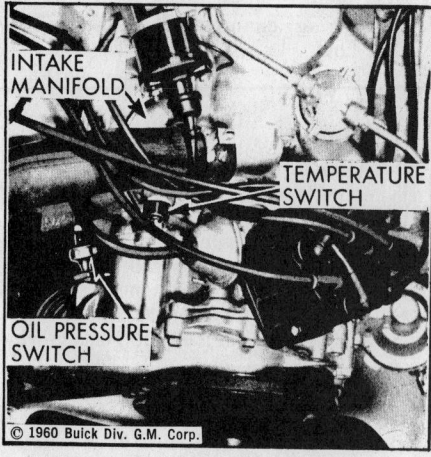

Oil Pressure and Temperature Sending Units

If engine oil pressure drops below a safe level during operation, the circuit is completed through the sending unit to ground. This will cause the **"Oil"** indicator light in the cluster to burn.

ENGINE

REFERENCES

The V-8 aluminum engine has a displacement of 215 cubic inches. The bore and stroke is 3.5″ x 2.8″ which produces 150 brake horsepower at 4400 RPM. Developed torque is 220 foot pounds at 2200 RPM with a compression ratio of 8.8:1. This should permit the use of regular type fuel, under normal operating conditions. The engine weighs about 318 pounds.

The concave domed pistons are aluminum alloy, anodized for long lasting surface finish. They operate within cast iron cylinder bores that are cast in the aluminum cylinder block. These sleeves are locked in place by grooves turned into their O.D.

Caution: To help prevent thread damage, all bolts used in aluminum must be free of grit and well lubricated before installation. This caution applies particularly to cylinder head and main bearing cap bolts.

"Special Thread Lubricant" is available for this purpose. Sealing compound is also available and should be used as a non-hardening sealer and lubricant to prevent coolant seepage at the cylinder head bolts.

A new V-6 engine is optional beginning with 1962. It is of cast iron with a bore and stroke of 3.625x3.2 inches and 198 cubic inch displacement. Compression ratio of 8.8 to 1 allows use of regular fuels.

Tune up and repair operations are, in general, similar to those of the 215 cu. in. V-8.

ENGINE REMOVE

1. Disconnect battery cables.
2. Drain cooling system and remove heater and radiator hoses.
3. Disconnect exhaust pipes at the manifolds.
4. Remove Hood assembly.
5. Remove radiator.
6. On standard transmission models, disconnect the clutch control linkage. On automatic transmission equipped cars disconnect the selector and throttle control linkage.

Buick Special V-8 Engine

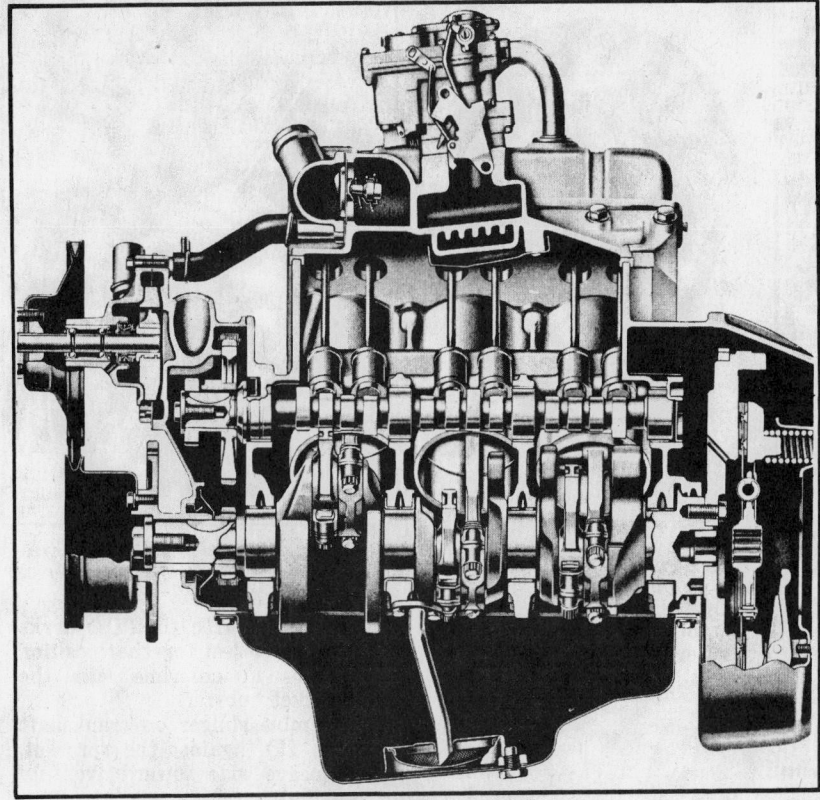

Buick Special V-6 Engine

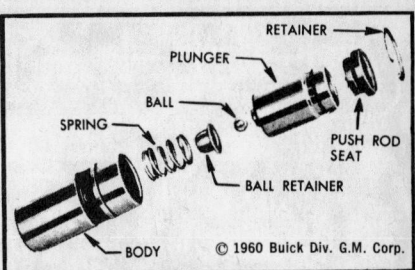

Valve Lifter

7. Disconnect the involved wiring such as; generator, starter, sending units, etc.
8. Disconnect fuel line at fuel pump.
9. Mark the front universal joint for reassembly, then disconnect the front joint by removing the "U"-bolts. Slide the front propeller shaft rearward as far as possible and tie to one side.
10. Disconnect both engine front mounts.
11. To afford clearance and prevent damage, remove the oil filter unit.
12. Attach lifting device to engine.
13. Lift engine weight, then disconnect rear engine mount at transmission.
14. Lift the engine further and move it forward to clear the engine compartment.
15. Then raise fully and remove from the car.

ENGINE INSTALL

Install the engine in the reverse order of removal.

CYLINDER HEADS

INTAKE MANIFOLD REMOVE

1. Drain cooling system.
2. Remove carburetor air cleaner. Disconnect all tubes and hoses from the carburetor. Disconnect and remove the coil.
3. Disconnect temperature indicator wire from sending unit.
4. Disconnect accelerator and transmission linkage at carburetor. Disconnect throttle return spring.
5. Slide front thermostat by-pass hose clamp back on the hose. Disconnect upper radiator hose at outlet.
6. Disconnect heater hose at the temperature control valve inlet. Force the end of the hose down to permit coolant to drain from intake manifold.
7. Remove 12 manifold-to-head attaching bolts.
8. Remove intake manifold and carburetor as an assembly by sliding rearward to disengage the thermostat by-pass hose from the water pump. Remove intake manifold gasket sound absorber.
9. On V-8 models be sure there is no coolant present. Then remove intake manifold gasket clamps and remove the gasket. Remove rubber gasket seal.

EXHAUST MANIFOLD REMOVE

1. Remove exhaust manifold-to-exhaust pipe attaching bolts.
2. On the right side, remove generator rear attaching bolt.
3. Unlock and remove exhaust manifold-to-cylinder head bolts. Remove the manifold.

ROCKER ARM REMOVE

1. Pull spark plug wire retainers from brackets on rocker arm cover. Disconnect plug wires at the spark plugs and tie back out of the way.
2. Remove four screws holding the rocker arm cover to the cylinder head. On the right side, remove vent pipe. Remove rocker arm cover and gasket.
3. Remove four rocker arm shaft bracket-to-cylinder head attaching bolts. Remove rocker arm and shaft assembly. (Vent pipe oil baffle is mounted under rear bolts on right rocker arm and shaft assembly.)
4. Remove the push rods.
5. If lifters are to be serviced, remove them. If not, protect them with clean cloth.

CYLINDER HEAD REMOVE

1. Remove cylinder head bolts, (fourteen).
2. Lift off cylinder head and gasket. Note: Valve grinding is handled in the conventional manner. Guides are replaceable in the V-8 only.

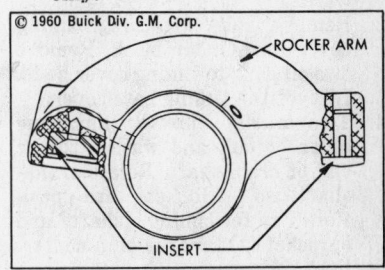

Rocker Arm Cut-Away

TIMING CASE

TIMING CHAIN

Remove

1. Drain cooling system.
2. Disconnect radiator and heater hoses at water pump and disconnect lower radiator hose at radiator. Remove attaching bolts and brackets and remove radiator.
3. Remove fan, fan pulleys and belt, or belts.
4. Remove crankshaft pulley.

Valve Train Arrangement

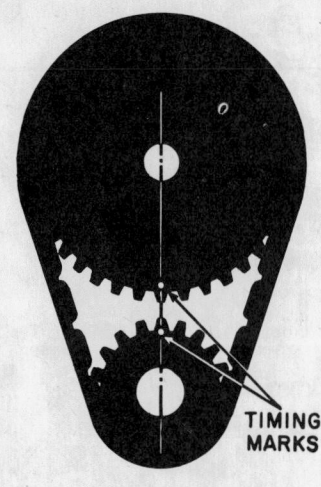

Valve Timing Plan

Fuel Pump and Distributor Drive

5. Remove harmonic balancer from crankshaft.
6. If car has power steering, remove the pump bracket bolts and move the steering pump out of the way.
7. Disconnect lines and remove the fuel pump.
8. Remove generator (without brackets).
9. Remove distributor cap and pull spark plug wire retainers off brackets on rocker arm cover. Swing distributor cap with wires out of the way. Disconnect distributor primary wire.
10. Remove distributor.
11. Loosen and slide front clamp on Thermostat by-pass hose rearward.
12. Remove bolts attaching timing cover to cylinder block. Remove two oil pans to timing cover bolts.
13. Lift off the timing case cover.
14. Temporarily install harmonic balancer bolt and washer to the end of crankshaft. Rotate crankshaft so sprockets are positioned as for timing, (shafts and sprocket "O" marks on a centerline). Now remove harmonic balancer bolt with a sharp rap on the wrench handle to prevent changing the position of the sprockets.
15. Remove front crankshaft oil slinger.
16. Remove bolt and special washer holding the camshaft distributor drive gear and fuel pump eccentric to the camshaft. Slide gear and eccentric off the shaft.
17. Use two large screwdrivers to alternately pry the camshaft sprocket then the crankshaft sprocket forward and off their respective shafts.

18. Thoroughly clean the sprockets, distributor drive gear, fuel pump eccentric and crankshaft oil slinger.

Install

1. Make sure, with sprockets temporarily installed, that #1 piston is at top dead center and the camshaft sprocket "O" mark straight down and on a centerline of both shafts.
2. Remove the camshaft sprocket and assemble the timing chain on both sprockets. Then slide the sprockets-and-chain assembly on

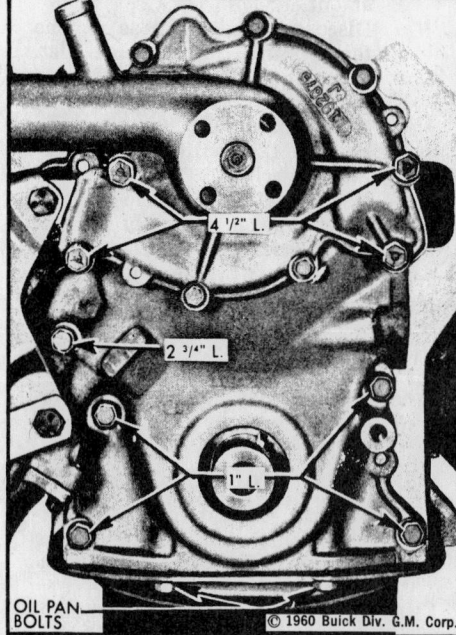

Timing Chain Cover Bolts

the shafts with the "O" marks in their closest together position and on a centerline with the sprocket hubs.
3. Assemble slinger on crankshaft with I.D. against the sprocket, (concave side toward front of engine).
4. Slide fuel pump eccentric on camshaft and Woodruff key with oil groove forward.
5. Install distributor drive gear.
6. Install drive gear and eccentric bolt and retaining washer. Torque to 40-45 ft. lb.
7. Reinstall timing case cover by reversing removal procedure, paying particular attention to the following points.
   A. Remove oil pump cover and pack space around the oil pump gears **completely full** of petroleum jelly. There must be no air space left inside the pump. Reinstall the pump cover using new gasket.
   B. The gasket surface of the block and timing chain cover must be clean and smooth. Use a new gasket correctly positioned.
   C. Install chain cover being certain the dowel pins engage the dowel pin holes before starting the attaching bolts.
   D. Lube the bolt threads before installation and install them according to the illustration.
   E. If the car has power steering, the front pump bracket should be installed at this time.
   F. Lube the O.D. of the harmonic balancer before installation to prevent damage to the seal when starting the engine.

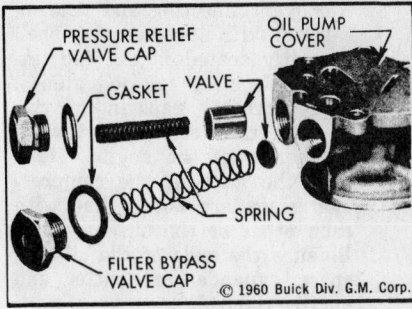

Pressure Relief and Filter By-Pass

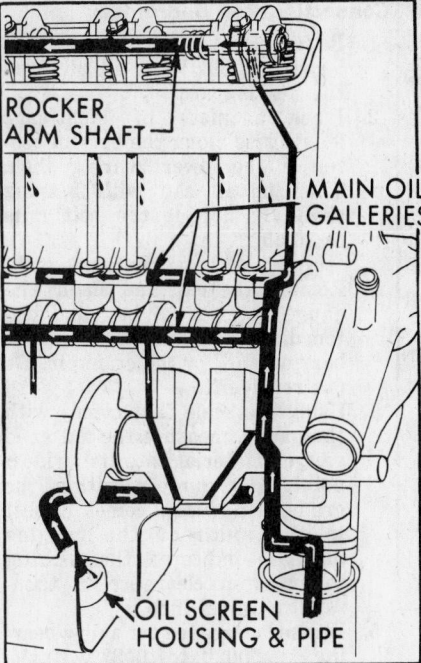

Engine Lubrication

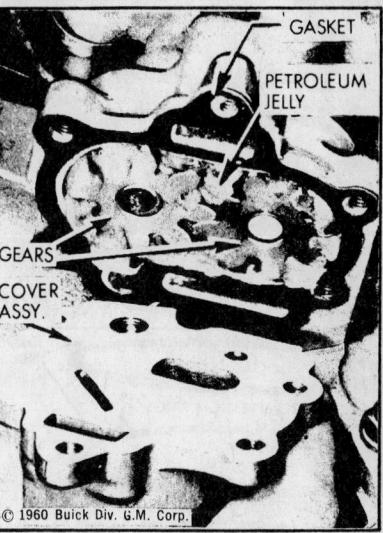

Prime the Pump with Petroleum Jelly

ENGINE LUBRICATION

The engine lubrication system is the force feed type, where oil is supplied under pressure to the crankshaft, connecting rods, camshaft bearings and valve lifters. Oil is supplied under controlled volume to the rocker arm bearings and push rods. All other moving engine parts are lubricated by gravity flow or splash.

OIL PUMP

The oil pump is located in the timing chain cover where it is connected by a drilled passage in the cylinder crankcase to an oil screen housing and stand pipe assembly.

Oil is drawn into the pump through the screen and pipe. Oil is discharged from the pump to the oil pump cover assembly. The cover assembly consists of an oil pressure relief valve, an oil filter by-pass valve and a nipple for installation of an oil filter. The oil pressure relief valve limits oil pressure to a maximum of 33 pounds per square inch. The oil filter by-pass valve opens if the filter becomes clogged to the extent that 4½ to 5 pounds pressure difference exists between the filter inlet and exhaust. This is a safeguard for oil passage to the main engine oil galleries in case of filter stoppage.

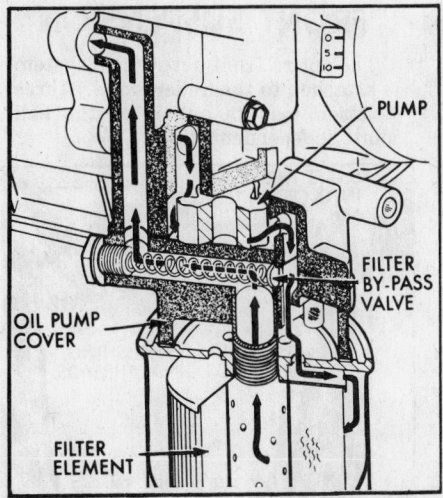

Oil Flow Through Filter

OIL FILTER

An A.C. oil filter is mounted on the oil pump at the right front corner of the engine. It requires no special tools and is completely disposable.

OIL PAN REMOVE AND INSTALL

1. Raise car and support on stands.
2. Drain engine oil.
3. Disconnect exhaust pipe at crossover.
4. If standard transmission equipped, loosen clutch equalizer-to-frame attaching bolts.
5. Remove steering idler arm bracket-to-suspension crossmember attaching bolts.
6. Support engine with a padded jack under the oil pan.
7. Remove bolts and nuts attaching engine mounts to mount brackets.
8. Raise engine and insert bolts through bracket bolt holes, then lower engine so mounts rest on bolts.
9. Remove flywheel housing bolts. Then remove housing.
10. Remove oil pan bolts and lower the oil pan enough to remove oil pump pipe and screen-to-cylinder block attaching bolts.
11. Rotate crankshaft to provide maximum clearance at the front end of oil pan. Move the front of the pan to the right and lower the pan through opening between crossmember and steering linkage intermediate shaft.
12. Install by reversing removal procedure.

CONNECTING RODS AND PISTONS

REMOVE PISTON ASSEMBLIES

1. Remove cylinder heads.
2. Remove oil pan.
3. Examine cylinder bores for top ridge. If ridge exists, remove it before taking pistons out.
4. Number all the pistons, connecting rods and caps. Starting at the front, the **right bank** is numbered 2-4-6-8. The **left bank** is numbered, 1-3-5-7.

With the V-6 engine the right bank is numbered 2-4-6. The left bank, 1-3-5, from the front.

5. With number 4 crankpin straight down, remove cap and bearing shell from #1 connecting rod. Install connecting rod bolt guides to hold upper half of the bearing shell in place.
6. Push piston and rod assembly up out of the cylinder. Then remove bolt guides and reinstall cap and bearing shell on the rod.
7. Remove the remaining rod and piston assemblies in the same manner.
8. Carefully remove old rings with piston ring expander.
9. Carefully press out the old pin.

Note: Check the cylinder bores for out-of-round, taper or other damage. Any cylinders requiring attention may be bored or honed the same as any conventional cast iron cylinder block.

Fitting Rings and Pins

When new rings are installed without reboring the cylinders, cylinder wall glaze should be broken. This can be done by using the finest grade stones in a cylinder hone.

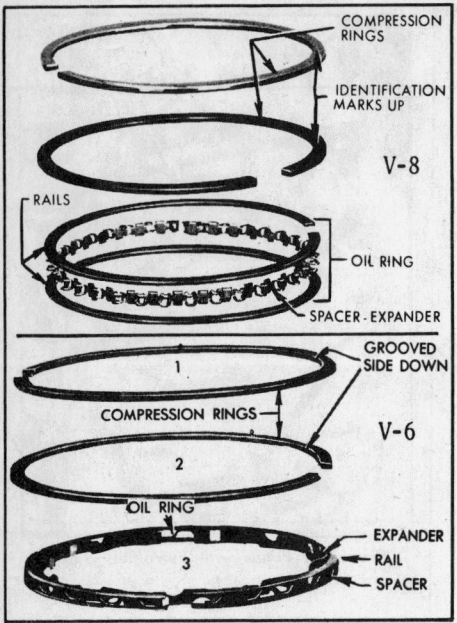

Piston Rings

New piston rings must be checked for clearance in piston grooves and for cap in cylinder bores.

When fitting new rings to new pistons the side clearance for compression rings should be .003″ to .005″. Side clearance of the oil ring should be .0035″ to .0095″.

Check end gap of compression rings by placing them in the bore in which they will operate. Then push them to the bottom of the bore with a piston. Now measure the end gap in each ring. The end gap should be no less than .015″.

If piston pin bosses are worn out of round or oversize, the piston and pin should be replaced. Oversize pins are not practical because the pin is a press fit in the connecting rod. Piston pins must fit the piston with an easy finger push at 70°F, (.0003″ to .0005″).

In assembling the piston to the connecting rod a press, (as illustrated) is ideal. However, substitutes are available that will answer the purpose.

If the rod assembly is to go into the **left** bank, the **boss on the rod** and cap go toward the **rear** of the engine. If the rod assembly is to go into the **right** bank, the **boss on the rod** and cap go toward the **front** of the engine. In both cases the connecting rod bearing oil spurt holes point "UP".

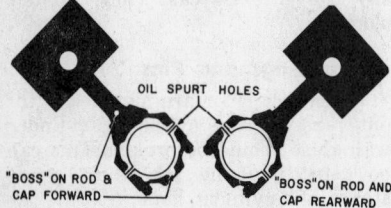

Piston and Rod Assembly

Connecting Rod Bearings

1. Remove connecting rod cap with bearing shell. Wipe all oil from the bearing area.
2. Place a piece of Plastigage lengthwise along the bottom center of the lower bearing shell. Then install cap with bearing shell and torque the bolt nuts to 30-35 ft. lb.
   Note: Do not turn crankshaft.
3. Remove the cap and shell. The gauge material will be found flattened and adhering to either the bearing shell or the crankpin. **Do not remove it.**
4. Using the scale that comes with the gauge, measure the flattened gauge material at its widest point. The number within the graduation which comes closest to the width of the gauging material indicates the bearing to crankpin clearance in thousandths of an inch.
5. Desired clearance for a new bearing is .0002″ to .0023″. If the bearing has been in service, it is wise to install a new bearing if clearance exceeds .003″.
6. If a new bearing is required, try a "standard," then each undersize bearing in turn until one is found that is within specifications.
7. With the proper bearing selected, clean off the gauging material, reinstall the bearing cap and torque to 40-45 ft. lb.
8. After the bearing cap has been torqued, it should be possible to move the connecting rod back and forth on the crankpin, the extent of end clearance.

INSTALL PISTON ASSEMBLIES

1. Carefully assemble the piston to the connecting rod, (press in the pin).
2. Remove piston and rod from the press. Rock the piston on the pin to be sure pin or piston boss was not damaged during the pressing operation.
3. Install ring expander in lower ring groove. Position the ends of the expander above the piston pin where groove is not slotted. The ends of the expander must butt together.
4. Install oil ring rails over expander with gaps "up" on same side of piston as oil spurt hole in connecting rod.
5. Install compression rings, (with a ring expander) in top and center groove.
6. Coat all bearing surfaces, rings and piston skirt with engine oil.
7. Position the crankpin of the cylinder being worked on, "Down."

8. Remove connecting rod bearing cap and with upper bearing shell correctly seated in the rod, install connecting rod bolt guides.
9. Make sure the gaps in the two oil ring rails are "UP" toward the center of the engine. Make sure the gaps of the compression rings are **not** in line with each other or the oil ring rails. Be sure the ends of the oil ring spacer-expander are butted and not overlapped.
10. With a good ring compressor, install the piston and rod assembly into the cylinder bore and carefully TAP down until the rod bearing is solidly seated on the crankpin.
11. Remove the connecting rod bolt guides and install cap and lower bearing shell. Torque to 30-35 ft. lb.
12. Install other piston and rod assemblies in the same manner. When the assemblies are all installed, the oil spurt holes will be "UP". The rib on the edge of the rod cap will be on the same side as the conical boss on the connecting rod web. These marks will be toward the other connecting rod on the same crankpin.
13. Accumulated end clearance between rod bearings on any crankpin should be .005″ to .012″.
14. Install oil screen and oil pan.
15. Install cylinder heads.
    Note: Before starting a new or reconditioned engine it is advisable to pack the oil pump with petroleum jelly to insure pump priming for immediate lubrication. See "Timing Case Install" in this section.
    After starting the engine, avoid high speeds but do not run on slow idle for a while. A better break-in speed is about 800-1,000 R.P.M. for the first hour.

FRONT SUSPENSION

The entire front suspension system is attached to the underbody by three isolation mounts and is of the ball joint, independent type.

Upper Control Arm Bushings

FRONT SPRINGS

Because of weight variations due to undercoating, optional equipment, etc. the spring dimensions given below are for the standard car only. Curb weight, (height) includes fuel, oil, coolant and a spare tire but no passengers.

Spring Remove

1. Raise front of car. Remove wheel with hub and drum.
2. Disconnect stabilizer bar and remove front shock absorber.
3. Disconnect lower control arm ball joint from steering knuckle.
4. Lower jack until spring is fully extended and remove coil spring.

Spring Install

1. Tape the insulator to top of spring. (Top of spring coil is flat.)
2. Position spring and insulator up in front suspension cross member. Rotate the spring to index the end of the bottom coil with the lower control arm spring seat.
3. Raise lower control arm to compress spring and allow assembly of ball joint to steering knuckle. Connect up ball joint.
4. Install shock absorber. Connect stabilizer link to lower control arms.

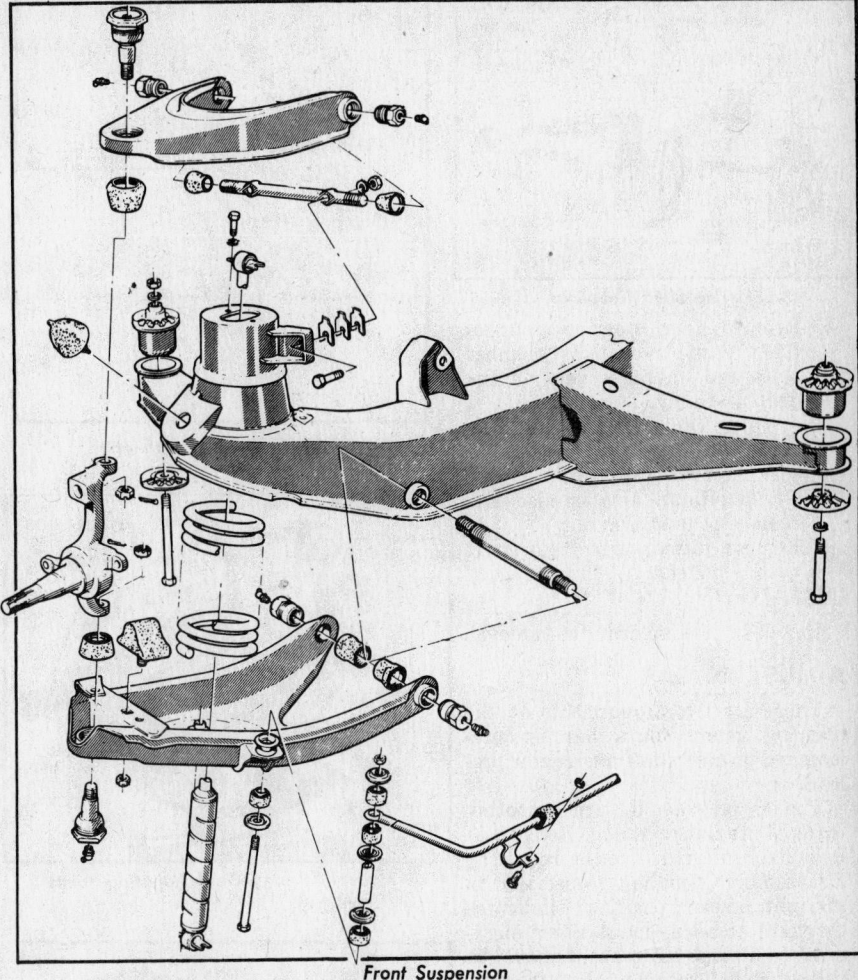

Front Suspension

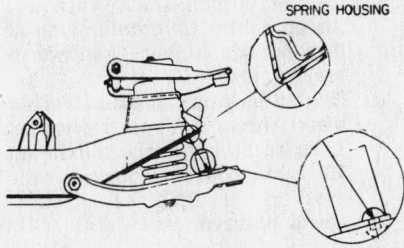

LOWEST POINT OF SPRING HOUSING

FRONT   IMMEDIATELY BEHIND FRONT RIVET OF COMPRESSION BUMPER

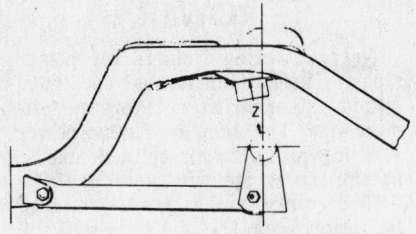

REAR COIL SPRING

© 1960 Buick Div. G.M. Corp.

MODEL	FRONT COIL Y ± 1/4			REAR COIL Z ± 3/8		
	CURB WEIGHT	NORMAL LOAD	NO. PASS.	CURB WEIGHT	NORMAL LOAD	NO. PASS.
4019	4.40	3.30	2	6.65	4.86	2
4035	4.40	3.30	2	5.94	4.54	2
4119	4.40	3.30	2	6.65	4.86	2
4135	4.40	3.30	2	5.94	4.54	2

CHASSIS TRIM DIMENSION 1961

Trim Height Chart

5. Reinstall wheel with hub and drum assembly. Adjust wheel bearings.

STEERING WHEEL AND HORN BUTTON

REMOVE

1. Unplug the horn ground (Tan) wire connector at mast jacket.
2. Remove steering hub emblem, on standard wheels remove cap by inserting screwdriver through hole in cap and loosening retaining screw. Unplug horn brush wire from cap.
3. Loosen steering wheel nut.
4. Apply steering wheel puller and pull wheel up to the nut. Now remove puller, nut and steering wheel.

INSTALL

Note: Location marks are provided on the steering wheel and shaft to simplify proper indexing at the time of installation.

1. Install wheel with the location mark aligned with that of the shaft.

2. Install the wheel nut and torque to 25 ft. lb.
3. On the standard wheel, plug horn wire terminals together and install the cap assembly on steering wheel hub. Tighten the retaining screw.
4. On the deluxe wheel, install emblem.
5. Plug horn wires together on mast jacket.

STEERING GEAR —MANUAL

REMOVE

Note: Due to compact conditions it is necessary to remove the assembly from the car to remove the pitman arm and nut from the pitman shaft.

1. Remove lower coupling clamp bolt and nut.
2. Loosen the mast jacket at the toe pan and the instrument panel. Pull the mast jacket up far enough to remove the worm shaft to steering gear coupling.
3. Jack up car and disconnect pitman arm from intermediate rod by unscrewing the end plugs.

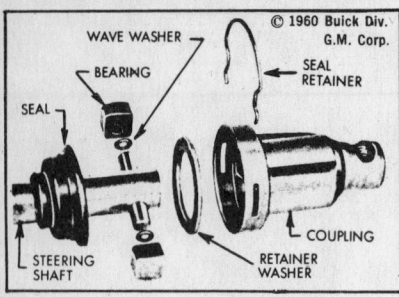

Steering Shaft Coupling

4. Remove four steering gear-to-front suspension cross member bolts and nuts and remove the gear assembly.

Note: Do not remove pitman arm from gear unless shaft or seal are to be removed.

5. Grasp pitman arm in vise and remove pitman arm nut.

6. Remove pitman arm from shaft with a puller.

INSTALL

Install in reverse order of removal.

ADJUST IN CAR

There are two adjustments on the steering gear: Worm bearing preload and pitman shaft overcenter preload.

The wheel should turn smoothly through its entire range. Roughness indicates internal trouble requiring disassembly. Binding (especially in straight ahead position) indicates too tight an adjustment. Steer alignment or linkage adjustment should be corrected before bear adjustment.

1. Be sure the steering gear-to-cross member bolts are torqued to 55 ft. lb.

2. Disconnect intermediate rod from pitman arm by unscrewing end plug until bearings will release ball socket.

3. Turn steering wheel slowly from one extreme to the other. **Never turn the wheel hard against the stopping point.**

4. Remove emblem or cap from steering wheel.

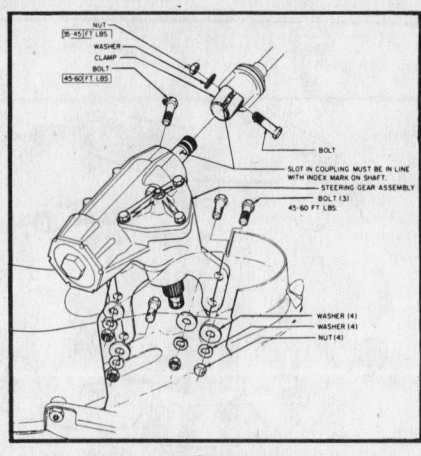

Manual Steering Gear Installation

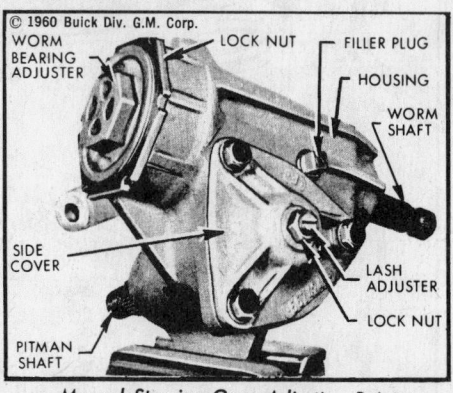

Manual Steering Gear Adjusting Points

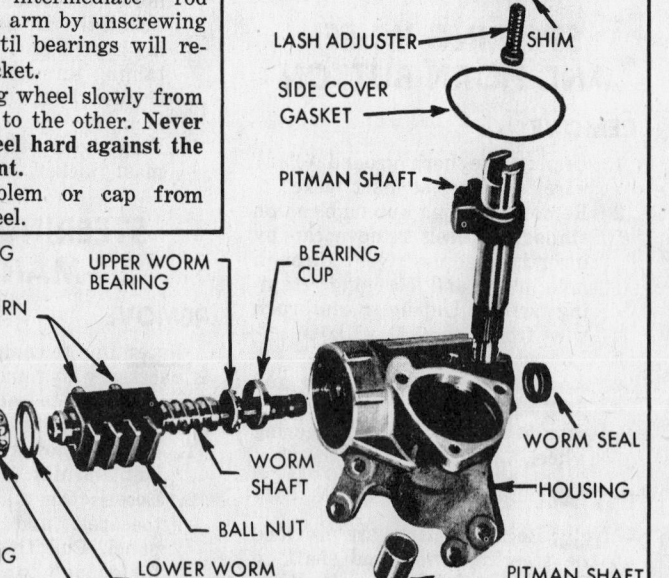

Manual Steering Gear—Exploded view

Worm Bearing Preload

5. Check worm bearing preload by turning the steering wheel gently in one direction until it stops. This positions the gear away from the "High Point" load.

6. Attach a 15/16" socket and "inch-pounds" torque wrench to the steering wheel nut. Turn the worm shaft with the wrench, through a one revolution range from either extreme. Torque required to keep the wheel moving through either one—revolution extreme should be 2-7 inch pounds.

7. Be sure the gear case side cover bolts are torqued to 30 ft. lb.

Straight Ahead Preload

8. Turn steering wheel from one extreme to the other while counting total turns. Then turn the wheel back exactly midway. This positions the steering gear on the "High Spot" or straight ahead position. A slight "drag" should exist at this point.

10. Check torque used to rotate the wheel through the "High Point" range. Torque should be 4 to 8 inch pounds **higher than worm bearing preload.** The total "overcenter" pull should not exceed 13 inch pounds.

11. Adjust pitman shaft overcenter preload by loosening lock nut and turning pitman shaft wash adjuster screw to obtain 4 to 8 inch pounds higher than worm bearing preload.

12. Tighten lock nut. Rotate steering wheel through it's entire range. Then recheck for the maximum 13 inch pounds torque while passing through the straight ahead position.

STEERING GEAR —POWER

Note: Steering linkage for power steering is the same as that used with manual steering except for the pitman arm. The arm used with power steering has a larger splined hole to fit the power steering gear shaft.

The rotary valve power steering is optional on the 4,000 and 4,100 series.

For more detailed information, see the Unit Repair Section, Steering—Power, Section 11.

PUMP

The Rotary Valve Power Steering Pump is mounted on the engine and belt driven from crankshaft pulley. The reservoir is integral with the pump housing.

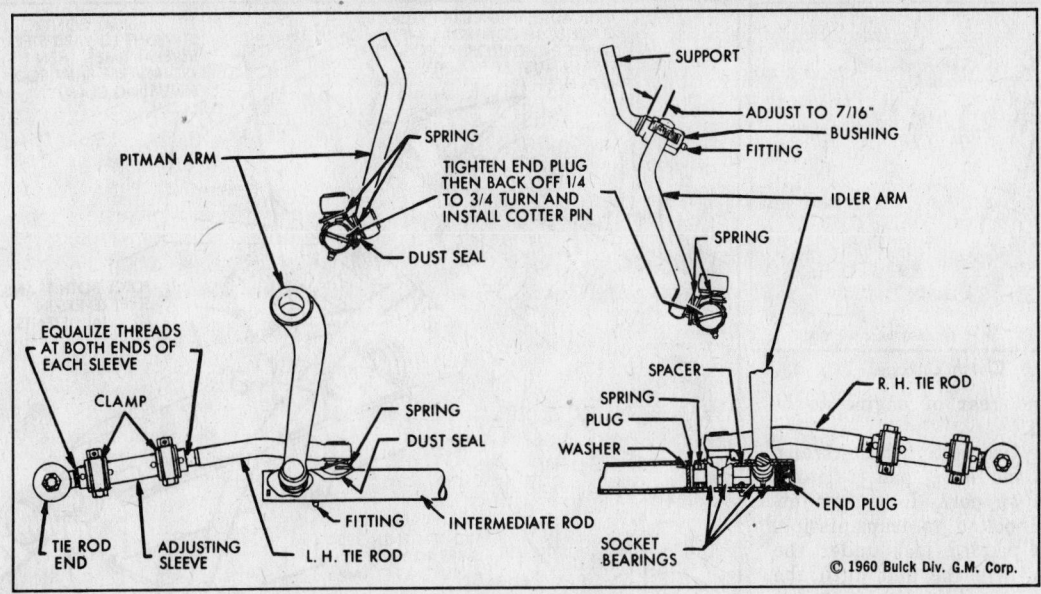

Manual and Power Steering Linkage

The pump housing encloses the flow control valve and the rotor assembly. The flow control valve and spring are retained in the pump housing by the pressure union. This permits servicing the flow control valve without removing the pump.

The rotor assembly consists of a drive shaft, a thrust plate, a rotor with ten vanes, a pump ring and a pressure plate. The shaft is held to the rotor by a retaining ring. Oil enters the rotor section of the housing through a reservoir hole in the housing.

CLUTCH

A single plate, 9½" dry disc clutch is used in cars with manual transmissions. The unit is conventional in design with coil springs and three release levers. The levers are counterbalanced and are not adjustable.

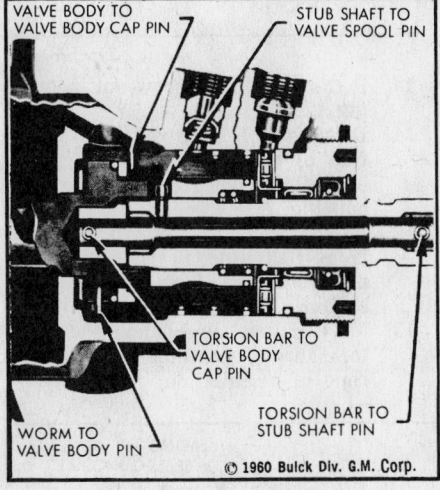

Attaching Pins for Valve Parts

CLUTCH REMOVE

1. Mark universal joint and transmission shaft companion flange for proper indexing at time of installation. Remove two "U" bolts and disconnect driveshaft at the front joint. Slide the driveshaft rearward as far as possible and tie to one side.
2. Disconnect shift linkage from transmission by first removing equalizer spring. Slide shift equalizer to full left position to disengage it from 2nd-3rd shift lever. Then slide equalizer to right to remove from support pin. Remove transmission 1st-reverse shift lever from shift shaft.
3. Disconnect speedometer cable at transmission.
4. Loosen all three exhaust pipe ball joints to permit transmis-

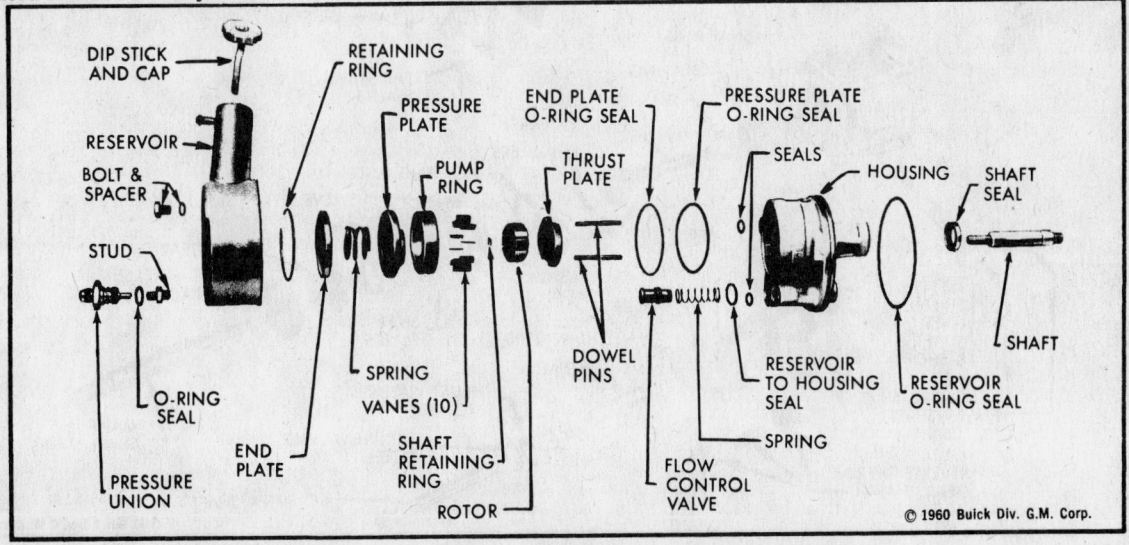

Power Steering Pump

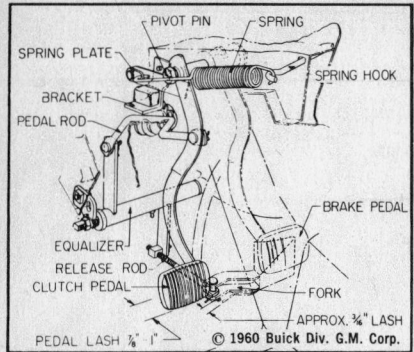

Clutch Linkage

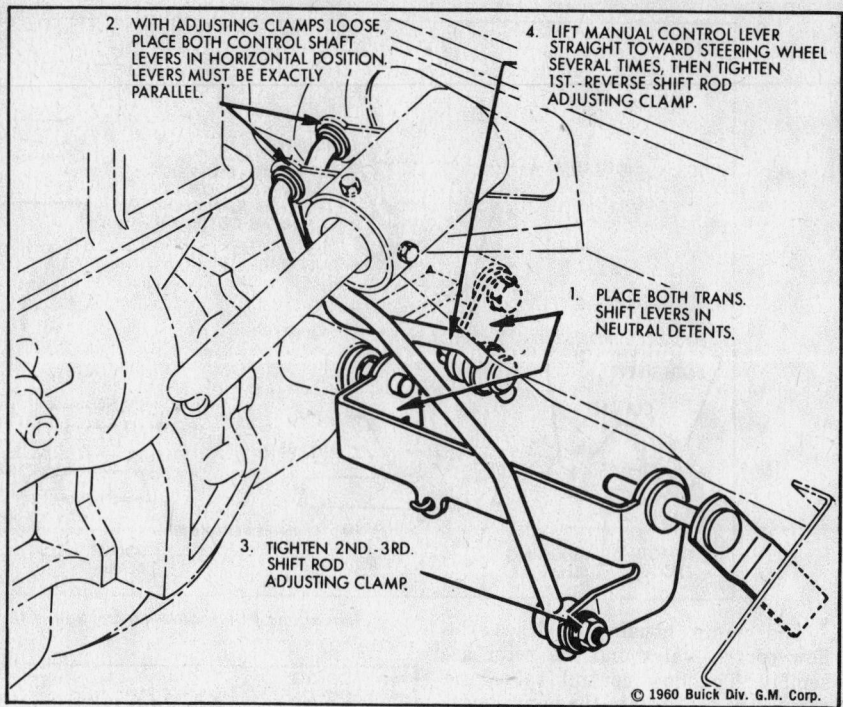

2. WITH ADJUSTING CLAMPS LOOSE, PLACE BOTH CONTROL SHAFT LEVERS IN HORIZONTAL POSITION. LEVERS MUST BE EXACTLY PARALLEL.

4. LIFT MANUAL CONTROL LEVER STRAIGHT TOWARD STEERING WHEEL SEVERAL TIMES, THEN TIGHTEN 1ST.-REVERSE SHIFT ROD ADJUSTING CLAMP.

1. PLACE BOTH TRANS. SHIFT LEVERS IN NEUTRAL DETENTS.

3. TIGHTEN 2ND.-3RD. SHIFT ROD ADJUSTING CLAMP.

© 1960 Buick Div. G.M. Corp.

Synchromesh Shift Controls

sion and rear of engine to be lowered.

5. Remove two bolts holding transmission mounting pad to transmission support. Leave mounting pad bolted to transmission.

6. With a padded jack under the engine, raise the unit until the transmission mounting pad just clears the transmission support.

7. Remove four bolts holding transmission support to body members. Remove support, then lower the jack to allow transmission to clear the underbody.

8. Remove upper left transmission to flywheel housing bolt and install a 7/16" x 14 x 4½" guide pin. Remove lower right bolt and install a 7/16" x 14 x 3½" guide pin.

9. Remove the other two transmission attaching bolts. Slide the transmission back until the drive gear shaft disengages the clutch disc and clears the flywheel housing. Lower the transmission.

10. Remove clutch throw-out bearing.

11. Disconnect release rod from the fork by removing clevis pin. Unhook fork boot from opening in housing.

12. Push inward on fork to free it from ball stud in the housing and remove the fork through the bottom.

13. Mark clutch cover and flywheel to assure proper indexing at the time of installation.

14. Remove clutch cover attaching bolts and remove the clutch assembly.

CLUTCH INSTALL

Install clutch by reversing removal procedure. Use a clutch aligning pilot or a spare main drive gear through the hub of driven plate and into the pilot bushing. Be sure to align the clutch cover-to-flywheel index marks.

CLUTCH LINKAGE ADJUST

Check pedal lash (free play) by pushing on the pedal with the hand. Lash should be 7/8" to 1" measured at the pedal pad.

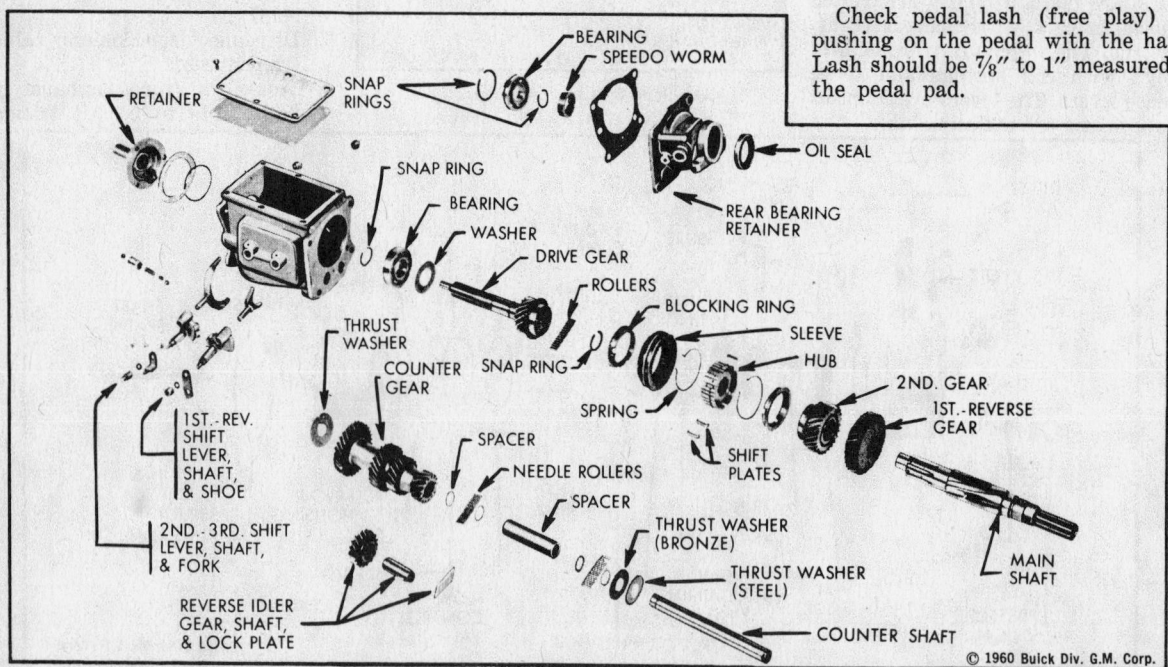

Synchromish Transmission

© 1960 Buick Div. G.M. Corp.

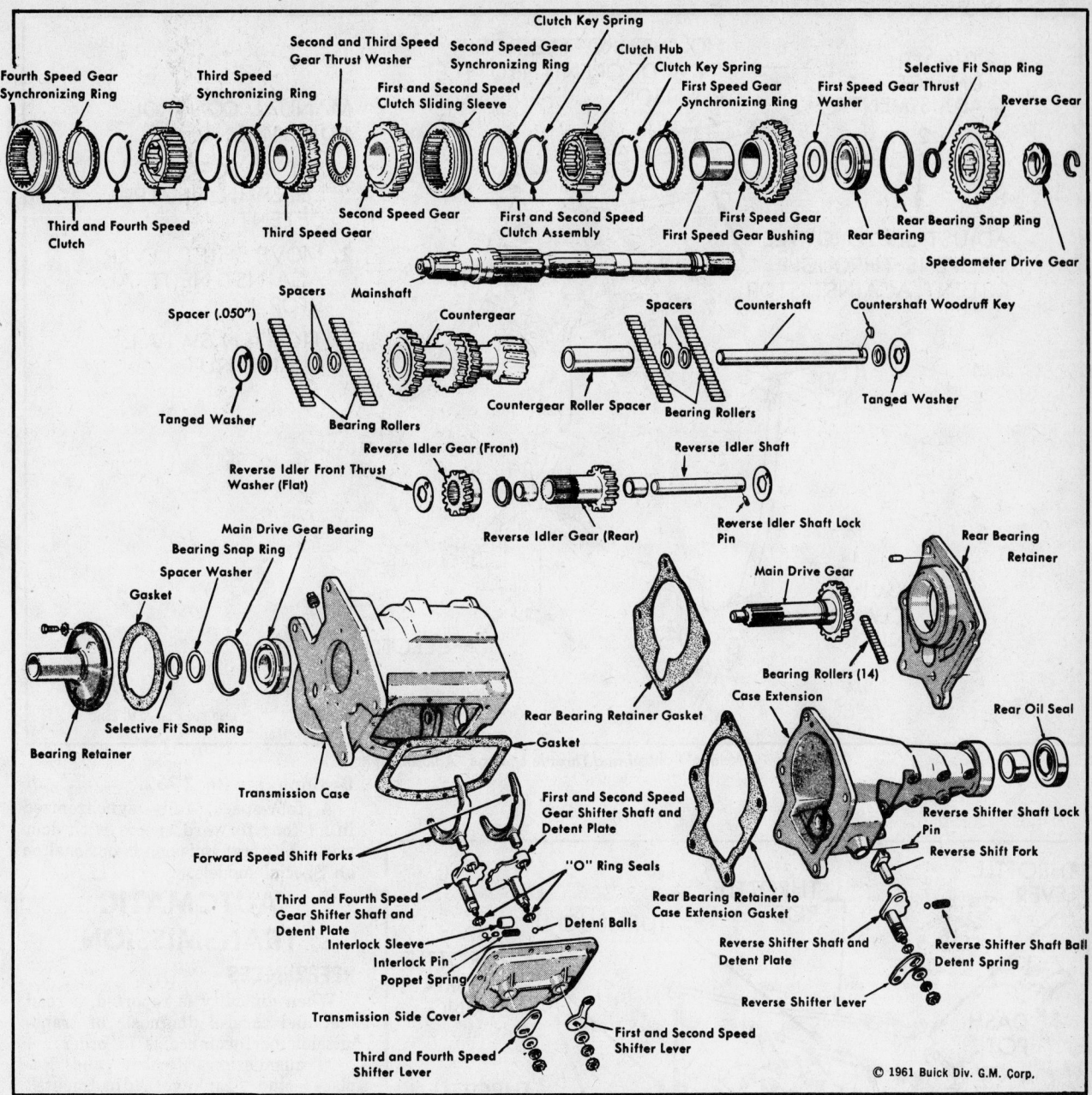

Fourth Speed Gear Synchronizing Ring

Third Speed Synchronizing Ring

Second and Third Speed Gear Thrust Washer

First and Second Speed Clutch Sliding Sleeve

Second Speed Gear Synchronizing Ring

Clutch Key Spring

Clutch Hub

Clutch Key Spring

First Speed Gear Synchronizing Ring

First Speed Gear Thrust Washer

Selective Fit Snap Ring

Reverse Gear

Third and Fourth Speed Clutch

Third Speed Gear

Second Speed Gear

First and Second Speed Clutch Assembly

First Speed Gear

First Speed Gear Bushing

Rear Bearing

Rear Bearing Snap Ring

Speedometer Drive Gear

Spacers

Spacer (.050")

Mainshaft

Countergear

Spacers

Countershaft

Countershaft Woodruff Key

Tanged Washer

Bearing Rollers

Countergear Roller Spacer

Bearing Rollers

Tanged Washer

Reverse Idler Gear (Front)

Reverse Idler Front Thrust Washer (Flat)

Reverse Idler Shaft

Reverse Idler Gear (Rear)

Reverse Idler Shaft Lock Pin

Main Drive Gear Bearing

Bearing Snap Ring

Spacer Washer

Gasket

Main Drive Gear

Rear Bearing Retainer

Bearing Rollers (14)

Case Extension

Rear Oil Seal

Selective Fit Snap Ring

Bearing Retainer

Rear Bearing Retainer Gasket

Gasket

Transmission Case

Rear Bearing Retainer to Case Extension Gasket

Reverse Shifter Shaft Lock Pin

Reverse Shift Fork

First and Second Speed Gear Shifter Shaft and Detent Plate

Forward Speed Shift Forks

"O" Ring Seals

Third and Fourth Speed Gear Shifter Shaft and Detent Plate

Interlock Sleeve

Interlock Pin

Poppet Spring

Detent Balls

Reverse Shifter Shaft and Detent Plate

Reverse Shifter Shaft Ball Detent Spring

Reverse Shifter Lever

Transmission Side Cover

First and Second Speed Shifter Lever

Third and Fourth Speed Shifter Lever

© 1961 Buick Div. G.M. Corp.

Four-speed synchromesh trans.

1. Make sure the pedal returns against the pedal bumper when the pedal is released.

2. With the car raised, pull outer end of the clutch fork rearward until throw-out bearing contacts clutch fingers. Free movement at outer end of fork should be 3/16". This should equal about 1 inch at the pedal.

3. If adjustment must be made, remove clevis pin from rear end of clutch release rod and rotate rod as needed to produce correct play.

4. Reinstall clevis and cotter pin.

STANDARD TRANSMISSION

The transmission is a conventional Synchromesh Transmission with 2nd & high synchronizing sleeve.

REMOVE AND INSTALL
See Clutch paragraph.

SHIFT CONTROLS

1. Place both shift levers in neutral detent position.
2. Loosen shift rod adjusting clamps and place both lower control shaft levers in horizontal positions. (Levers must be exactly parallel.)

3. Tighten 2nd-3rd shift rod adjusting clamp.

4. Lift manual control lever from 2nd-3rd range straight toward steering wheel into 1st-Reverse range. Do this several times to align 1st and Reverse lower control shaft lever. Then tighten 1st-Reverse shift rod adjusting clamp.

5. To recheck, depress clutch and shift transmission into each gear to check lower control shaft lever clearance in steering column jacket opening. Make sure that the manual lever movement from 2nd-3rd range into 1st-Reverse range is smooth and easy.

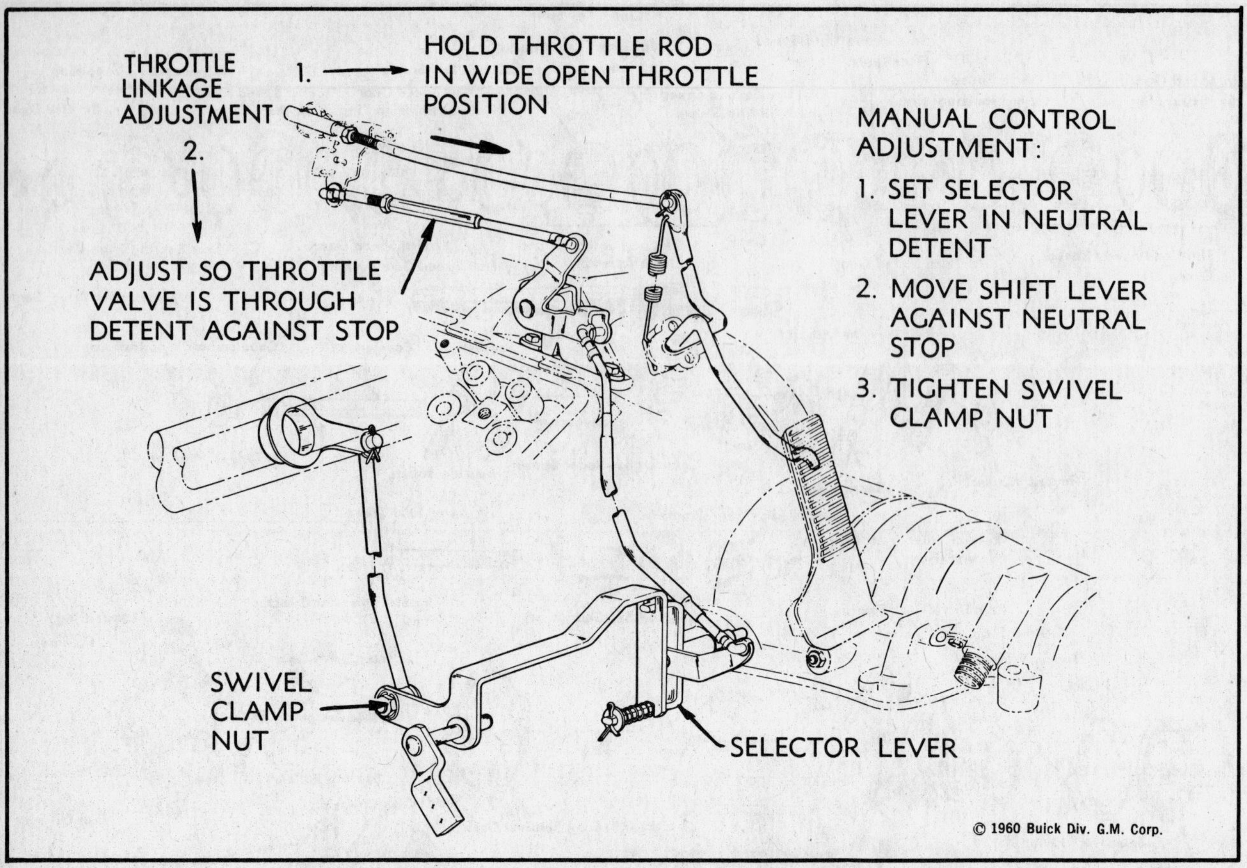

THROTTLE
LINKAGE
ADJUSTMENT

1. → HOLD THROTTLE ROD
IN WIDE OPEN THROTTLE
POSITION

2. ↓

ADJUST SO THROTTLE
VALVE IS THROUGH
DETENT AGAINST STOP

MANUAL CONTROL
ADJUSTMENT:

1. SET SELECTOR
LEVER IN NEUTRAL
DETENT

2. MOVE SHIFT LEVER
AGAINST NEUTRAL
STOP

3. TIGHTEN SWIVEL
CLAMP NUT

SWIVEL
CLAMP
NUT

SELECTOR LEVER

© 1960 Buick Div. G.M. Corp.

Manual Control and Throttle Linkage Adjustment

Beginning with 1962

A four-speed, fully synchronized in all four forward speeds with floor stick shift transmission is optional on all Special models.

AUTOMATIC TRANSMISSION

REFERENCES

When difficulty is reported, a road test and careful diagnosis of transmission performance is in order. "Transmission Remove and Replace" and "Linkage Adjustments" are covered in the following paragraphs. For "Test Procedures," "Transmission Recondition" and other detailed information see Unit Repair Section, Transmission Group of the manual.

THROTTLE LINKAGE ADJUSTMENT

1. Hold throttle rod in wide open throttle position, (against stop on carburetor).
2. Hold idler lever in full throttle valve position, (through detent to stop).
3. Adjust turn buckle so no lost motion exists in slide link. (Wide open throttle and throttle valve stop reached at the same time.)
4. Tighten nut on turnbuckle.

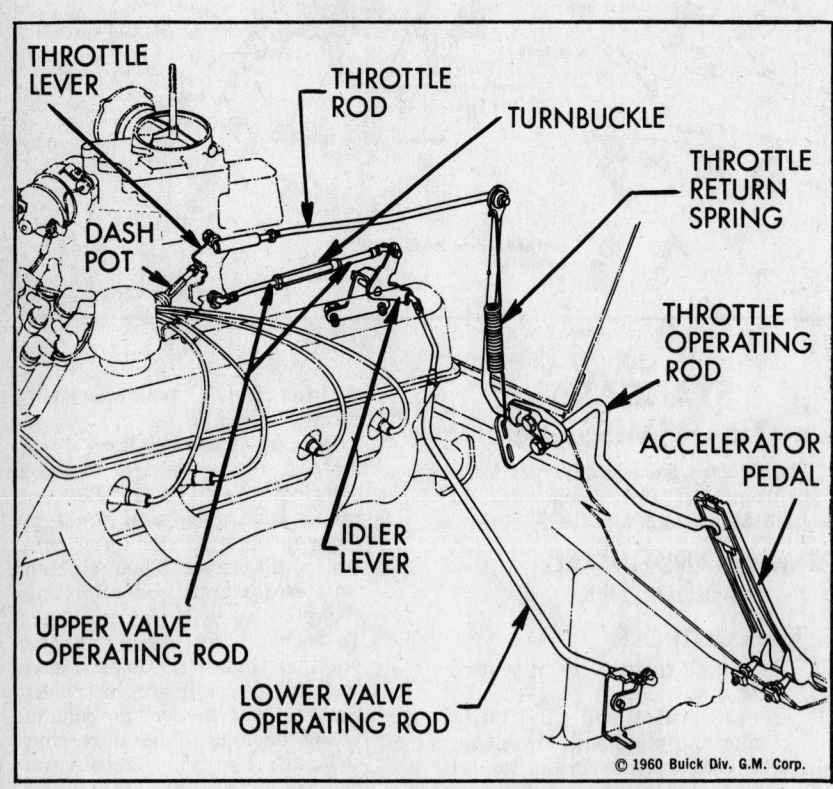

THROTTLE
LEVER

THROTTLE
ROD

TURNBUCKLE

THROTTLE
RETURN
SPRING

DASH
POT

THROTTLE
OPERATING
ROD

ACCELERATOR
PEDAL

IDLER
LEVER

UPPER VALVE
OPERATING ROD

LOWER VALVE
OPERATING ROD

© 1960 Buick Div. G.M. Corp.

Throttle and Transmission Linkage (Automatic Transmission)

TRANSMISSION, REMOVE

1. Raise the car and provide safe support front and rear.
2. Disconnect exhaust crossover pipe both ends and at transmission. Remove the pipe.
3. Remove universal joint "U" bolts and slide front propeller shaft rearward to separate universal joint at transmission.

Note: Support the propeller shaft so as to prevent the weight of the hanging shaft causing damage to the center universal joint.

4. Place a suitable jack under the transmission and fasten transmission to the jack.
5. Remove transmission mounting pad to crossmember bolts.
6. Remove transmission support crossmember-to-frame rail bolts at each end of crossmember. Remove crossmember.
7. Disconnect speedometer cable.
8. Loosen shift linkage adjusting swivel clamp nut. Remove cotter key spring and washer attaching equalizer to range selector outer lever. Remove equalizer.
9. Disconnect transmission filler pipe at the engine and at the transmission. Remove the filler pipe.
10. Support the engine with a padded jack under the oil pan.
11. Remove transmission cover pan-to-case tapping screws. Remove cover pan.
12. Mark flywheel and converter pump for reassembly in same relative position. Then remove three converter pump-to-flywheel bolts.
13. Remove transmission case-to-engine block bolts.
14. Move transmission rearward to provide clearance between converter pump and crankshaft.
15. Lower the transmission and remove it to a work bench or dismantling fixture. (Tool # J-7009 is handy.)

Note: Wire or otherwise secure the converter to the transmission case as soon as the assembly is clear of the flywheel. If converter is not secured, the converter can fall out if the transmission is tilted forward even slightly.

TRANSMISSION, INSTALL

1. Place the transmission, (with converter wired in place) assembly on a suitable transmission jack and raise into position.
2. Rotate flywheel or converter to permit attaching converter to flywheel with original relationship. Remove the temporary converter-to-transmission securing device.
3. Install transmission case-to-engine block bolts. Torque to 30-35 ft. lb.
4. Install flywheel-to-converter pump bolts. Torque to 18-25 ft. lb.
5. Install transmission support crossmember. Install mounting pad-to-crossmember bolts.
6. Remove transmission jack and engine support.
7. Install transmission cover pan with tapping screws.
8. Install transmission filler pipe and clamp using new "O" ring.
9. Connect speedometer cable.
10. Connect front propeller shaft to transmission companion flange and install "U" bolts.
11. Install exhaust crossover pipe.
12. Fill transmission, (see Capacities Chart).
    (A.) Add oil until the filler pipe is full.
    (B.) Start engine in "Park". Then continue pouring oil until 12 pints have been added.
13. With linkage properly adjusted and car warmed up, remove car for road test.

Note: For test procedures see Unit Repair Section, "Transmission Group."

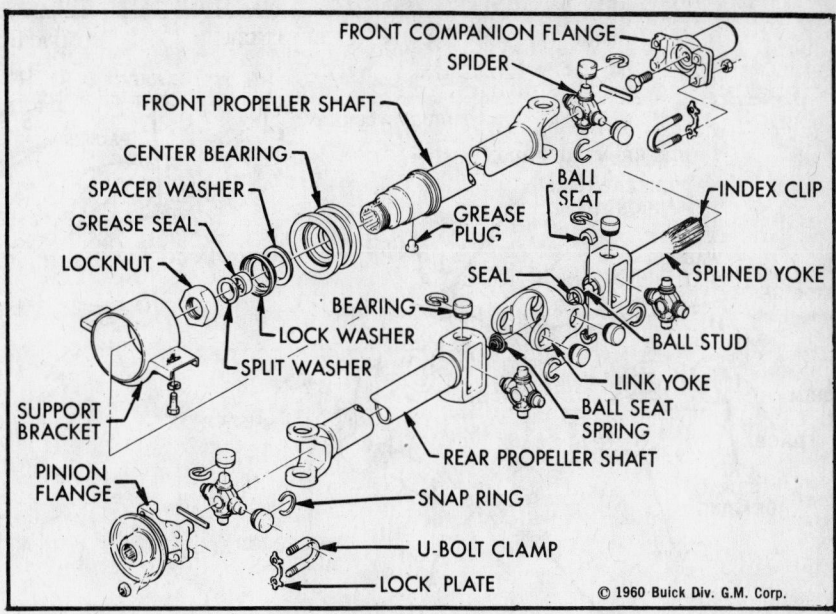

Universal Joint Plan

© 1960 Buick Div. G.M. Corp.

UNIVERSAL JOINTS AND DRIVE LINES

The drive line consists of a front propeller shaft, a rear propeller shaft, a standard universal joint at the extreme of each end and a double type, constant velocity universal joint in the center.

A center support bearing attaches the rear end of the front propeller shaft to the under side of the body. A splined front yoke on the front end of the rear propeller shaft extends into a splined coupling in the rear end of the front propeller shaft. This slip spline allows for the variety of lengths occurring in the propeller shaft due to road and torque conditions.

The propeller shaft assembly needs very little periodic service. The center bearing is lubricated for life and requires no additional lubrication. The universal joints are lubricated for life and cannot be lubricated while in the car. If a joint becomes noisy or worn a service kit must be installed which consists of a spider complete with bearing assemblies.

The center ball and socket cannot be lubricated in the car. Whenever the center joint is taken apart, the ball and socket must be lubricated with Multi-Purpose Grease E. P. # 1 Grade.

The slip spline must be lubricated with the same type grease every 10,000 miles. To lubricate the spline, remove the plug and install a temporary grease fitting. When grease appears at the slip joint nut, replace the grease fitting with the plug.

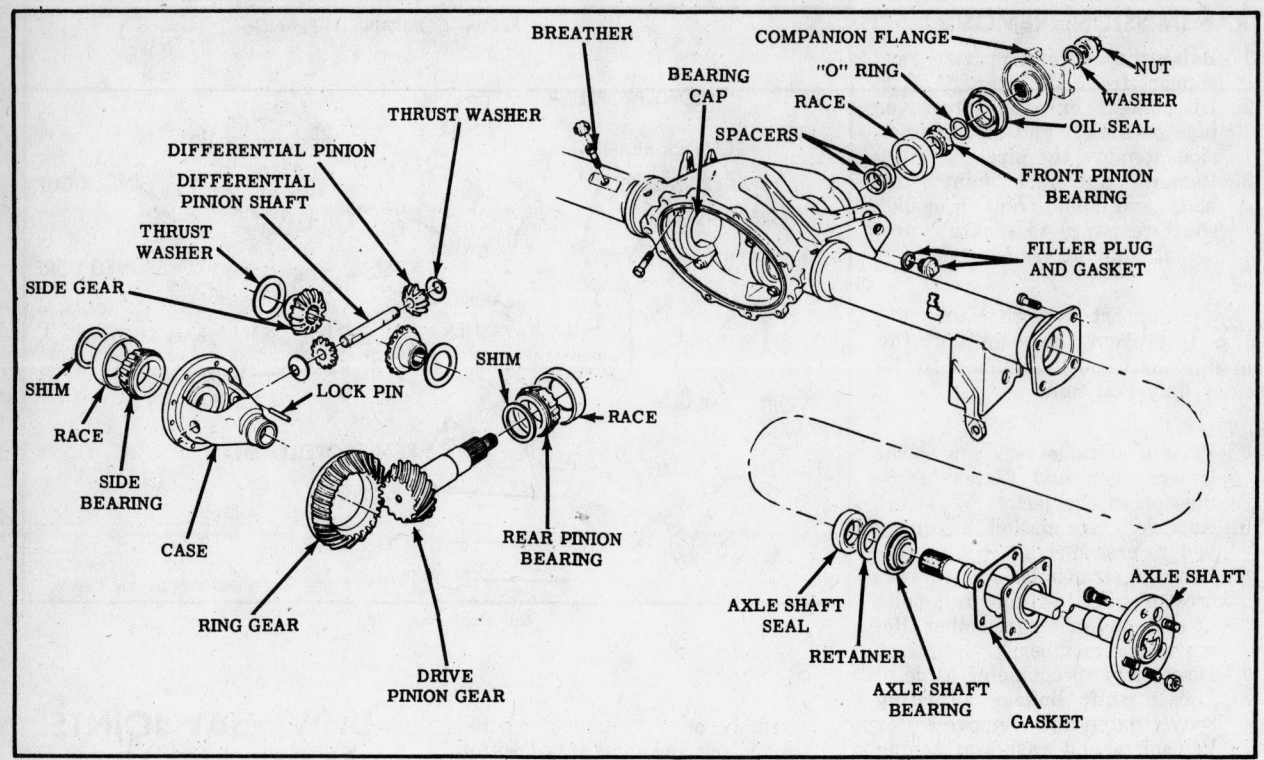

Rear axle assembly

REAR AXLE AND SUSPENSION

The rear axle assembly is of the semi-floating type in which the car weight is carried on the axle shafts through ball bearings in the rear axle tubes. Car drive is transmitted from the axle housing to body members through two lower and two upper control arms. Large rubber bushings at either end of these arms are designed to absorb vibration and noise. The arms also act as seats for the coil springs and are angle mounted to control sidewise movement of suspension.

REAR AXLE ASSEMBLY, REMOVE

It is not necessary to remove the rear axle assembly for normal repairs. However, if the housing is damaged, the rear axle assembly may be removed and installed using the following procedure.

1. Raise rear of car high enough to permit working under the car. Place a floor jack under center of axle housing so it just starts to raise rear axle assembly. Place car stands solidly under body members on both sides.

2. Mark rear universal joint and pinion flange for proper indexing at the time of installation. Then disconnect rear universal joint at pinion flange. Wire the propeller shaft back out of the way.

3. Disconnect parking brake cables at the sheave. Remove cable connector and two clips and slide cable back until free of body.

4. Disconnect rear brake hose at floor pan.

5. Disconnect shock absorbers at axle housing. Lower jack under housing until rear springs can be removed.

6. Disconnect upper control arms at axle.

7. Disconnect lower control arms at axle housing and roll rear axle assembly out from under the car.

INSTALL

Install in reverse order of removal.

RADIO

RADIO REMOVE & INSTALL

Note: Air conditioned cars require that the evaporator assembly be lowered, by removing both right and left bolts that hold the assembly up under the instrument panel. Then remove the brace that supports the radio, the screw which holds the two right sections of the air duct together and the glove box assembly. Radio and speaker may be removed through the glove box opening.

1. Disconnect antenna lead-in wire, speaker wire and battery wire from the receiver.

2. Remove knobs, escutcheons and retaining nuts from radio control shafts.

3. Remove the support bracket to receiver cap screw located at right side of receiver and lower receiver from under instrument panel.

4. Remove the two speaker to instrument panel nuts. These nuts are located at the front edge of the speaker mounting plate.

5. Remove speaker and mounting plate assembly.

6. Install by reversing removal procedure.

Page

AIR CONDITIONING

Service 1092

BRAKES, HYDRAULIC

Adjustments 938
References 80
Bleed brakes 941
Hand brake, adjust 938
Master cylinder, R & R 80
Master cylinder service 939
Parking brake 81

BRAKES, POWER

Power unit overhaul 954
Power unit, R & R 80
Trouble shooting 954

COOLING SYSTEM

Radiator core, R & R 83
Thermostat 84
Water pump, R & R 84

ELECTRICAL SYSTEM

Battery 78
Chassis 77
Distributor, R & R 77
Distributor specifications 73
Engine 77
Fuses and circuit breakers 76
Gauges 1024
Generator, R & R 78
Generator references 78
Generator service 1026
Generator specifications 73
Generator trouble shooting chart 1026
Ignition firing order & timing 71
Ignition timing procedure 77
Ignition timing specifications 72
Starter, R & R 78
Starter specifications 74
Starter systems 1046

ENGINE ASSEMBLY

Cylinder head, R & R 86
Engine assembly, R & R 84
Engine diagnosis 1012
Engine marking code 72
Engine references 84
Exhaust manifold, R & R 85
Inlet manifold, R & R 85
Oil filter element, R & R 86
Oil pan, R & R 86
Oil pressure specifications 76
Piston and rod, R & R 88
Piston and pin specifications 75
Rear main bearing oil seal 88
Rocker arm lubrication 76
Rocker arms & shaft 85
Specifications, general engine 76
Timing case cover & seal 90
Timing chain, R & R 89
Trouble shooting charts 1012

Page

ENGINE ASSEMBLY—continued

Tune-up specifications 72
Valve, R & R 86
Valve guide, R & R 86
Valve lifters. R & R 86
Valve specifications 76
Valve timing procedure 89

ENGINE LUBRICATION

Oil filter 86
Oil pan, R & R 86

EXHAUST SYSTEM

Exhaust pipe, R & R 83
Muffler, R & R 83
Tail pipe 83
Heat control valve 83

FUEL SYSTEM

Carburetors 972
Fuel gauge service 1024
Fuel pump pressure 72
Fuel pump, R & R 82
Fuel pump service 1020
Fuel system 82
Fuel tank, R & R 82

INSTRUMENTS

Instruments cluster, R & R 78
Windshield wiper motor, R & R ... 79

RADIO, R & R

References 100

REAR AXLE AND SUSPENSION

Axle assembly, R & R 100
Axle shaft 918
Axle shaft oil seal 918
Coil spring, R & R 99
Leaf spring, R & R 99
Pinion bearings 918
Ring gear & pinion 918
Trouble shooting 919

SPECIFICATIONS

Battery 74
Brake cylinder sizes 75
Capacities
    Axle, rear 74
    Cooling system 74
    Crankcase 74
    Fuel tank 74
    Transmission, automatic ... 74
    Transmission, manual 74
Chassis, general 75
Cylinder head tightening 75
Delcotron specifications 73
Distributor 73
Engine firing order & timing 71
Engine, general 76
Engine tune-up 72
Fuses and circuit breakers 76

Page

SPECIFICATIONS—continued

Generator regulators 73
Light bulbs 77
Main bearings 74
Model identification illustrations .. 70
Model year identification 72
Piston and pins 75
Quick reference specifications ... 71
Rod Bearings 74
Starters 74
Torque wrench 75
Tune-up 72
Valves 76
Wheel alignment 74

STEERING, MECHANICAL

Adjust gear housing 1052
Drag link check 94
Linkage 91
Horn ring. R & R 91
Steering wheel 91
Steering gear, R & R 94
Pitman shaft & seals 95

STEERING, POWER

Pump assembly 1058
Trouble shooting 1081
Unit overhaul 1058

SUSPENSION, FRONT

Alignment procedures 1082
Alignment specifications 74
King pins and bushings 1087
Knuckle supports 1087
References 90
Shock absorbers 1087
Support arms, pins and
    bushings 1037

TRANSMISSION, AUTOMATIC

References 95
General information 850
Hydramatic dual range service .. 850
Dual range linkage 95
Hydramatic dual coupling 860
Dual coupling linkage 96
Neutral switch 95
Transmission, R & R 96

TROUBLE CHECKS

Procedure 1

TUNE-UP

Procedures 1012
Specifications 72
Engine diagnosis 1012

UNIVERSAL JOINT AND DRIVE SHAFT

Disassemble U joint 97
U joint & drive shaft, R & R 97

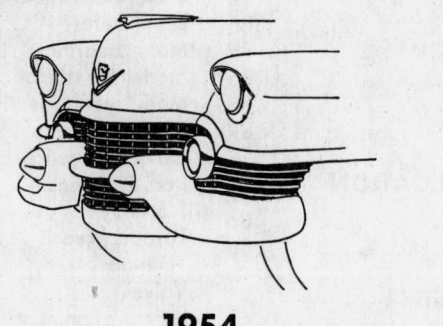

1954

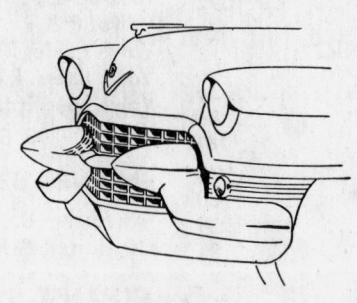

1955

1956

1957

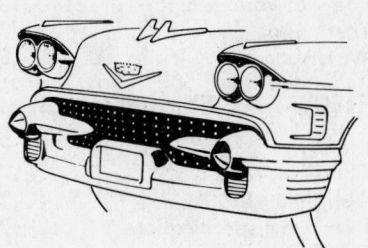

1958

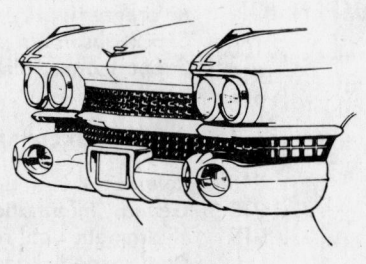

1959

1960

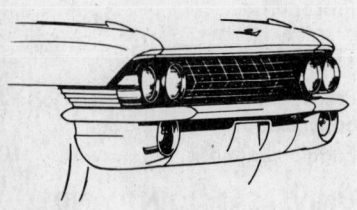

1961

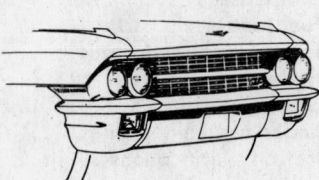

1962

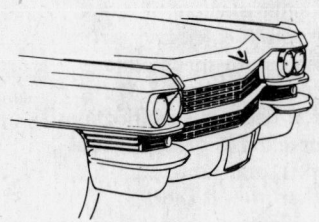

1963

QUICK WORKING SPECIFICATIONS

DISTRIBUTOR

Breaker Point Gap (In.)
1954-63 .... .015-.017

Cam Angle (Degrees)
1954-57 31
1958-63 30

SPARK PLUGS

Year	Type	Gap Inches
1954	46-5	.035
1955, ex. Eldorado	44-5	.035
1955, Eldorado	43-5	.035
1956-63	44	.035

IGNITION TIMING

(Spark occurs degrees before T.C.)

1954-55, ex. Eldorado ..2½ degrees
1955, Eldorado ....5 degrees
1956-57 ....5 degrees
1958-63, 1 carb ....5 degrees
1958-60, 3 carbs ....7½ degrees

GENERATOR & REGULATOR SPECIFICATIONS

YEAR AND SERIES	GENERATOR		REGULATOR		
	Field Current In Amperes 6 Volt	12 Volt	Cut-out Closing Voltage	Current Regulator Setting	Voltage Regulator Setting
1954-56	—	1.55	12.7	30	14.3±1.(A)
1959-63 W/O AC	—	1.72	12.6	35	14.3±1.(A)
W/AC	—	2.76	12.4	45	14.2±1.(A)

(A) Surrounding temperatures guide this voltage adjustment. Higher temperatures require lower settings and lower temperatures permit higher settings, within limits.

VALVES

Operating Tappet Clearance
All models, hydraulic lifters ....zero

COMPRESSION PRESSURE AT CRANKING SPEED

Variation between cylinders should not exceed 10 lbs. This is more important than actual reading or stated pressure.

1954 150
1955-56 175
1957-63 180

TORQUE WRENCH READINGS
(Ft. Lbs. & Thread Size)

Cylinder Head Bolts
1954-63 70-80

Main Bearing Bolts
1954-63 90-100

Rod Bearing Bolts
1954-63 40-45

Flywheel to Crankshaft Bolts
1954-63 75-80

Crankshaft Pulley Bolt
1954-63 65-70

WHEEL ALIGNMENT

Caster (Degrees)
1954-55 ....O to 1 N
1956-57 ....½ N to 1½ N
1958 ....1 N to O
1959-63 ....1½ N to ½ N

Camber (Degrees)
1954-63 ....⅜ N to ⅜ P

Toe-In (Inches)
1954-55 ....3/16 to ¼
1956-57 ....5/32 to 7/32
1958 ....3/16 to ¼
1958 air poise ....1/16 to ⅛
1959-63 all ....3/16 to ¾

King Pin Inclination (Degrees)
1954-56 ....6° @ 0° camber
1957-59 ....4° @ 0° camber
1960-63 ....6° @ 0° camber

Wheel Pivot Ratio
When outer wheel is turned to 20° then the inner wheel has turned to:
1954-63 ....22-2/3°

CAPACITIES

Engine Crankcase (Quarts)
Add 1 qt. for new Filter
1954-60 5
1961-63 4

Transmission, Synchro. (Pts.)
1954 ....3¾

Transmission, Hydramatic (Pts.)
1954-55 22
1956 23
1957-63 22

Rear Axle (Pints)
1954-63 5

Cooling System (Quarts)
1954 ....19¾
1955 18
1956 ....17½
1957-63 ....18½

For Heater
1954 Add ....One Quart
1955-56 Add ....Two Quarts
1957-63 Add ....One Quart

FIRING ORDER and TIMING

SPARK OCCURS:
1954-56, 2½° BTDC (Half Way Between "C" & "A")
1956-63, 5° BTDC—Standard Engine & Fuel

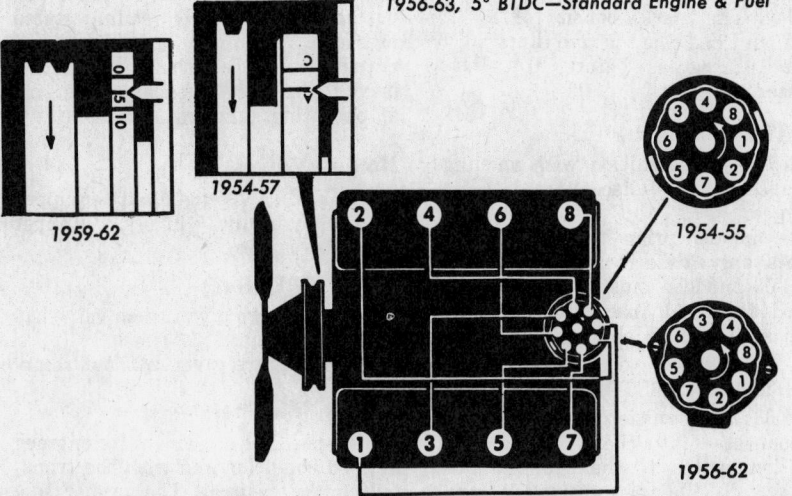

1959-62

1954-57

1954-55

1956-62

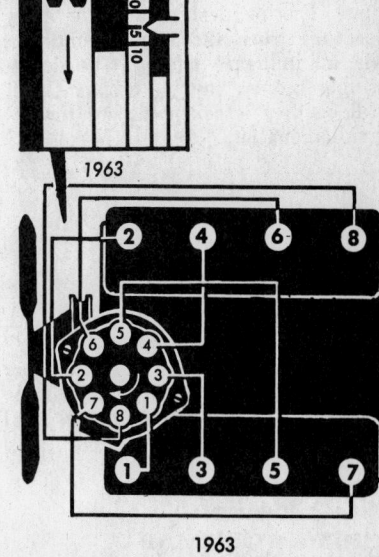

1963

NOTE:
THESE ARE APPROXIMATE SETTINGS. ENGINE DESIGN, ALTITUDE, TEMPERATURE, FUEL AND ENGINE CONDITION WILL ALL INFLUENCE TIMING. THE DETERMINING FACTOR, LIMITING ADVANCE, WILL STILL BE THE "KNOCK POINT" OF THE INDIVIDUAL ENGINE.

CADILLAC

CAR SERIAL NUMBER LOCATION AND ENGINE IDENTIFICATION

1954 THRU 1957

Each car has a serial number and an engine unit number. The car serial number is located on a plate attached to the left front door pillar post. ENGINE IDENTIFICATION IS STAMPED ON A MACHINED PAD AT THE FRONT, TOP EDGE OF THE RIGHTHAND BLOCK. The engine number has nine digits. The first two indicate the model year; the third and fourth, the series and the succeeding numbers, the individual car serial number. As an example: Engine unit number 546201140 would be a 1954, model 62, with a production numerical sequence of 01140.

1958

Identification is the same as above except, that a letter follows the first two digits of the engine unit number. This letter indicates the body style. All 1958 models were equipped with the same 4.000″ x 3.625″ (365 cu. in.) engine.

BEGINNING 1959

Identification same as above, however the engine size has been changed to 4.000″ x 3.875″ (390 cu. in.).

BEGINNING 1963

A new V8 engine of the same size, 390 cu. in. displacement, is used. This engine can be identified by the distributor mounting; it is at the front instead of the rear.

TUNE-UP SPECIFICATIONS

Year Model	Spark Plugs		Distributor (Note 1)			Ignition Timing (Note 2)	Compression Pressure Cranking (Note 3)	Valves (Note 4)				Engine Idle Speed Neutral (Note 5)
								Tappet Clearance Hot		Timing	Fuel Pump Pressure	
	Type	Gap	Cam Angle	Point Gap	Arm Spring Tension			Inlet	Exhaust	Inlet Opens		
1954 Series 60, 62, OHV, V8	46-5	.035	31	.016	19–23	2½B	150	Zero	Zero	22B	5	450
1955 Series 60, 62, OHV, V8	44-5	.035	31	.016	19–23	2½B	175	Zero	Zero	19B	5	450
Eldorado, OHV, V8..........	43-5	.035	31	.016	19–23	5B	175	Zero	Zero	19B	5	450
1956 Series 60, 62, OHV, V8..........	44	.035	31	.016	19–23	5B	175	Zero	Zero	39	6	450
1957 Series 60, 62, OHV, V8..........	44	.035	31	.016	19–23	5B	180	Zero	Zero	36	6	Note 6
1958-62 Series 60, 62, OHV, V8	44	.035	30	.016	19–23	Note 7	180	Zero	Zero	27B	5¾	Note 8
1963 Series All	44	.035	30	.016	19-23	Note 7	180	Zero	Zero	39B	5¾	Note 8

NOTES FOR TUNE-UP SPECIFICATIONS TABLE

NOTE: These are approximate settings. Engine design, altitude, temperature, fuel and engine condition will all influence timing. The determining factor, limiting advance, will still be the "knock point" of the individual engine.

Note 1: Distributor

POINT ADJUSTMENT

1956-63: Points can be adjusted with engine idling. Use a 1/8 inch "Allen" wrench thru window in distributor cap. Turn clockwise until engine misses, then counterclockwise until smooth.

Note 2: Ignition

TIMING MARKS AND THEIR LOCATION

1954-57: Marks are on the crankshaft pulley. The marks consist of "C" at Top Dead Center and an "A" at 5 deg. before T.D.C.
1958-63: Marks are on the crankshaft pulley. The marks consist of a "C" at Top Dead Center and lines at 5 and 10 degrees before Top Dead Center.

IGNITION TIMING

1954-63: Time ignition with vacuum advance line disconnected and plugged.
1956 models prior to Engine No. 033849 only: time at 2½ B.
1956-63 models must be accurately timed to avoid inaudible knock at high speed which can severely damage the engine.

IGNITION RESISTOR

1954-63: The ignition ballast resistor is connected into the wire from the ignition switch to the primary side of the coil. When the starter is operating the resistor is by-passed by means of a contact in the starter solenoid.

Note 3: Compression Pressure

All cylinders should read alike within 10 pounds. This is more important than actually reading stated pressure. Readings are taken at cranking speed with all plugs removed; throttle wide open and engine at operating temperature.

Note 4: Valves

All Cadillac V8 engines are equipped with Hydraulic lifters. Tappet clearance is zero.

INLET OPENS

1956-57: Figure given when valve has lifted .001 inch.
1958-63: Figure given without ramp.

Note 5: Idle Speed

Idle speeds as shown are for engines in good condition and with the transmission in neutral. The proper idle speed for an engine depends on its condition and also on whether or not it has an automatic transmission.

NOTES FOR TUNE UP SPECIFICATIONS—continued

Note 6: Idle Speed 1957

Adjust idle speed with transmission in either drive position. With 2 Carter 5 Brl. Carbs.—500 RPM:

With 1, Rochester or Carter, 4 Brl. Carb.—to 420.
If car has air conditioning it should be turned "ON" while adjusting idle speed.

Note 7: Ignition Timing 1958-63

Engines with Single Carburetors, 5B
Engines with Three 2-Brl. Carbs., 10B
Caution: The above settings are for use with 99 octane gas, or better. Gas below 98 octane should not be used in these engines.
For 98 octane gas set: single carb. engines at 2½B, Three carb. engines at 7½B.

For sections where gas of less than 98 octane must be used there are special pistons available. These lower the compression ratio.

Note 8: Idle Speed of 1958-63 Models

Set idle speed at 450 RPM with transmission in "Dr" range. If equipped with air conditioning the conditioner should be turned "OFF."

DELCO-REMY DISTRIBUTOR SPECIFICATIONS

YEAR	MODEL	DELCO-REMY NO.	ROTATION	CAM ANGLE DEGREES	BREAKER POINT GAP INCH	BREAKER ARM SPRING TENSION	GOVERNOR CONTROL @ DIST. R.P.M. ADV. STARTS	FULL ADV.	VAC. CONTROL DATA INCHES OF VACUUM TO START ADVANCE	INCHES OF VACUUM FOR FULL ADVANCE	MAX. ADV. OF DIST. IN DEGREES
1954	All	1110844	CC	29-33	.016	19-23	1 @ 400	12 @ 2000	7-9	16	14
1955	All	1110852	CC	29-33	.016	19-23	1 @ 450	12 @ 2000	6½-8½	16	14
1956	STD. ENG.	1110858	CC	29-33	.016	19-23	1 @ 475	10 @ 2000	6½-8½	17	18
1956	ELDORADO	1110859	CC	29-33	.016●	19-23	1 @ 475	10 @ 2000	6½-8½	17	18
1957	STD. ENG.	1110876	CC	29-33	.016●	19-23	1 @ 400	12 @ 2100	8	14½	13
1957	2 CARB. EARLY	1110877	CC	29-33	.016●	19-23	1 @ 400	12 @ 2100	8	14½	13
1957	2 CARB. LATE	1110898	CC	29-33	.016●	19-23	1 @ 400	11½ @ 2000	7½	13½	12½
1958	1 CARB. ENG.	1110909	CC	29-33	.016●	19-23	1 @ 400	15 @ 2000	9	14½	12
1958	3 CARB. ENG.	1110926	CC	29-33	.016●	19-23	1 @ 400	8 @ 2000	9	14½	12
1959-61	1 CARB. ENG.	1110932	CC	29-33	.016●	19-23	1 @ 600	8 @ 2000	8	14½	18
1959-60	3 CARB. EARLY	1110933	CC	29-33	.016●	19-23	1 @ 600	8 @ 2000	8½	15	12
1959-60	3 CARB. LATE	1110952	CC	29-33	.016●	19-23	1 @ 600	8 @ 2000	7½	15½	12¼
1962	1 CARB. ENG.	1110988	CC	29-33	.016●	19-23	1 @ 400	8 @ 2000	8-10	15¼	12¼
1963		1111001	C	29-33	.016●	19-23	1 @ 400	8 @ 2000	8-10	15¼	12¼

● Turn adjusting screw clockwise until engine misses. Then turn screw ½ turn in opposite direction.

GENERATOR AND REGULATOR SPECIFICATIONS

YEAR	GENERATORS Field Current in Amperes at 6 Volts	at 12 Volts	Brush Spring Tension	REGULATORS Cut-Out Relay Air Gap	Closing Voltage	Current & Voltage Regulator Air Gaps	Current Regulator Setting Amperes	Voltage Regulator Setting Volts
1954—56 All Series	......	1.55	26	.020	12.7	.075	30	14.3
1957—62 All Series WO/AC	.....	1.72	28	.020	12.6	.075	35	14.3
All Series W/AC		2.76	28	.020	12.4	Note 1	45	14.2

Note 1: Current and Voltage Regulator Air Gaps

A double contact voltage regulator is used on Air Conditioned Models. Air gap for the voltage regulator is .067. Air gap for the current regulator is .075. The lower voltage regulator points should be set at 14. volts.

Caution: Do not ground the generator field while the regulator is connected to it or the regulator points may be damaged.

DELCOTRON AND A.C. REGULATOR SPECIFICATIONS

Year 1963	Ground Polarity	Field Current Draw (Ampered)	CURRENT OUTPUT Engine R.P.M.	Amperes	Volts	RUNNING VOLTAGE Engine R.P.M.	Amperes	Volts @125°	REGULATOR Model Number	Point Gap	FIELD RELAY Armature Air Gap	Closing Voltage
Standard	Neg.	1.9 ot 2.2	1100	12.	14	6500	42	13.5-14.3	1119506	.015	.015	6.5-8.5
Heavy Duty	Neg.	4.1 to 4.5	1100	24.	14	6500	62	13.3-13.9	1119506	.015	.015	6-5-8.5

BATTERY AND STARTER SPECIFICATIONS

| YEAR | BATTERY | | | | STARTERS | | | | | | Brush Spring Tension |
| | Ampere Hour Capacity | Volts | Group Number | Terminal Grounded | Lock Test | | | No-Load Test | | | |
					Amps.	Volts	Torque	Amps.	Volts	R. P. M.	
1954—55 All Series	70	12	3EE	Neg.	460	5.2	11.5	75	10.3	6500	35
1956 All Series	70	12	3EE	Neg.	395	3.5	Locked	91	10.6	3900	35
1957 All Series	70	12	3KM	Neg.	395	3.5	Locked	91	10.6	3900	35
1958—63 All Series	70	12	3KM	Neg.	330	3.5	Locked	82	10.6	4400	35

FRONT WHEEL ALIGNMENT

| YEAR | CASTER | | CAMBER | | Toe-In | King-Pin | Wheel Pivot Ratio | |
	Range (Degrees)	Pref. Setting	Range (Degrees)	Pref. Setting	(Inches)	Inclination Degrees	Inner Wheel	Outer Wheel
1954—55 All Series V8	1N to 0		⅜N to ⅜P	A	3/16 to 1/4	6	22-2/3	20
1956 All Series V8	1½N to ½N	1.N	⅜N to ⅜P	A	5/32 to 7/32	6	22-2/3	20
1957 All Series V8	1½N to ½N	1.N	⅜N to ⅜P	A	5/32 to 7/32	4	22-2/3	20
1958 With Coil Springs With Air Springs	1N to 0 1N to 0	Equal Equal	⅜N to ⅜P ⅜N to ⅜P	A A	3/16 to 1/4 1/16 to 1/8	4 4	22-2/3 22-2/3	20 20
1959—63 All Series V8	1½N to ½N	1.N	⅜N to ⅜P	A	3/16 to 1/4	6	22-2/3	20

Note A: Preferred Camber Setting. 1954-63 — ¼ to ½ more positive camber on the left wheel than on the right will help cancel the right hand pull of a crowned road.

CRANKSHAFT BEARING JOURNAL SIZES

| YEAR | MAIN BEARING JOURNALS | | | | CONNECTING ROD BEARING JOURNALS | | |
	Journal Diameter	Oil Clearance	End Play of Shaft	End Play Held by	Journal Diameter	Oil Clearance	End Play
1954—55 All Series V8	2.500	.0016	.003	No. 5	2.25	.0013	.011
1956—62 All Series V8	2.625	.0016	.003	No. 5	2.25	.0013	.011
1963 All Series V8	3.000	.0018	.003	No. 5	2.249	.0013	.011

CAPACITIES

| YEAR | Engine Crankcase Add 1 Qt. for New Filter | Transmissions Pints to Refill After Draining | | Rear Axle Pints | Gasoline Tank Gallons | Cooling System Quarts |
		Manual	Automatic			
1954 All Series	5	3¾	22	5	20	19¾(A)
1955 All Series	5	N.U.	22	5	20	18(B)
1956 All Series	5	N.U.	23	5	20	17½(B)
1957-60 All Series	5	N.U.	22	5	20	18½(A)
1961—63 All Series	4	N.U.	22	5	21	18½(A)

Notes on Cooling:
(A)—Add 1 quart for heater.
(B)—Add 2 quarts for heater.

Note on Manual Transmissions:
NU—Manual Transmissions not used.

PISTON AND PIN SPECIFICATIONS

Year and Model	PISTON Skirt Clearance		PISTON PIN			
					FIT	
	TOP	BOTTOM	Diameter	Bushing	In Rod	In Piston
1954-55	.0020	.0030	1.000	None	Press	.0001
1956-58	.0005	.0020	1.000	None	Press	.0001
1959-63	.0005	.0020	.9994-.9997	None	Press	.0001

Piston and Rod Assembly

1954-61 Put word "REAR" on piston pin boss toward rear of engine while the number on the lower end of con. rod goes toward outer side of engine.

Piston Sizes

Pistons should be measured for size ⅛″ below the upper cross slot and ⅛″ to either side of the vertical slot, Fig. 9-25. Cylinders should be measured 1¼″ from the top, crosswise to the cylinder block.

The clearance should be .0008″ to .0012″ in this position at 70°F. Subtract .0001″ from measurement for every 6° above 70°F.

An identification letter is stamped on the valve lifter compartment cover rail next to the lower inside edge of the cylinder head. The letter may be to the right or left of each cylinder bore. This letter denotes the cylinder size as shown in the following table:

Letter	Cylinder Size	Piston Size
A	4.0000-4.0002	3.9990-3.9992
B	4.0002-4.0004	3.9992-3.9994
C	4.0004-4.0006	3.9994-3.9996
D	4.0006-4.0008	3.9996-3.9998
E	4.0008-4.0010	3.9998-4.0000
H	4.0010-4.0012	4.0000-4.0002
J	4.0012-4.0014	4.0002-4.0004
K	4.0014-4.0016	4.0004-4.0006
L	4.0016-4.0018	4.0006-4.0008
M	4.0018-4.0020	4.0008-4.0010

The table indicates ten piston sizes to match ten bore sizes, ranging in steps of .0002″ from 4.0000″ to 4.0020″. This makes it possible to maintain the .0008″ to .0012″ piston to cylinder block clearance.

GENERAL CHASSIS AND BRAKE SPECIFICATIONS

YEAR AND MODEL		CHASSIS		BRAKE CYLINDER BORE			
		Overall Length in Inches	Tire Size	Master Cyl. (Inch)		Wheel Cylinder Diameter (Inch)	
				Std.	Pow.	Front	Rear
1954 To 1955	V8, OHV - 60 Series	227½	8.00x15	1.0		1⅛	1.0
	V8, OHV - 62 Series	216½	8.00x15	1.0		1⅛	1.0
	V8, OHV - 62 Series	223½	8.00x15	1.0		1⅛	1.0
	V8, OHV - 75 Series	237⅛	8.20x15	1.0		1⅛	1.0
1956	V8, OHV - 60 Series	226.0	8.00x15		21/32	1⅛	1.0
	V8, OHV - 62 Series	222.0	8.00x15		21/32	1⅛	1.0
	V8, OHV - 75 Series	235¾	8.20x15		21/32	1⅛	1.0
1957	V8, OHV - 60 Sedan	224½	8.00x15		21/32	1⅛	1.0
	V8, OHV - 62 Convt.	220⅞	8.00x15		21/32	1⅛	1.0
	V8, OHV - 62 Eldorado	222¼	8.20x15		21/32	1⅛	1.0
	V8, OHV - 75-1 MP. Sedan	236¼	8.20x15		21/32	1⅛	1.0
1958	V8, OHV - 60 & 62 DeVille	225⅜	8.00x15		21/32	1⅛	1.0
	V8, OHV - 62 Sedan	216⅞	8.00x15		21/32	1⅛	1.0
	V8, OHV - 62 Coup & Convt.	223½	8.20x15		21/32	1⅛	1.0
	V8, OHV - 75 Sedan	237⅛	8.20x15		21/32	1⅛	1.0
1959	V8, OHV - 60 Fleetwood	225.0	8.00x15		21/32	1⅛	1.0
	V8, OHV - 62 Series, Ex.	225.0	8.00x15		21/32	1⅛	1.0
	V8, OHV - 62 Eldorado	225.0	8.20x15		21/32	1⅛	1.0
	V8, OHV - 75 Series	244⅞	8.20x15		21/32	1⅛	1.0
1960	V8, OHV - 60 Fleetwood	225.0	8.00x15		21/32	1⅛	1.1/16
	V8, OHV - 62 Ex. Eld.	225.0	8.00x15		21/32	1⅛	1.1/16
	V8, OHV - 62 Eldorado	225.0	8.20x15		21/32	1⅛	1.1/16
	V8, OHV - 75 Series	244⅞	8.20x15		21/32	1⅛	1.1/16
1961	Series 60, 62, 63	222.0	8.00x15*		1	1⅛	15/16
	67	222.0	8.00x15*		1	1⅛	15/16
	75	242.3	8.20x15		1	1⅛	1 1/16
1962–63	Series 60	222.0	8.00x15*		1	1 3/16	1.0
	62	222.0	8.00x15*		1	1 3/16	1.0
	75	242.3	8.20x15		1	1 3/16	1.0

* 8.20x15 Optional

ENGINE TORQUE SPECIFICATIONS

YEAR	Cylinder Head Bolts	Rod Bearing Bolts	Main Bearing Bolts	Crankshaft Pulley Bolt	Flywheel to Crankshaft Bolt	Manifolds	
						In.	Ex.
1954–63 All Series	70-80	40-45	90-100	65-70	75-80	25-30	25-30

Note for Torque Specification Table:
Some bolts and nuts are marked on the heads to indicate the grade of steel used. Do not use bolts of a lower grade than those originally installed. The marks consist of lines: SAE5—3 lines; SAE7—5 lines; SAE8—6 lines.

CYLINDER HEAD NUT TIGHTENING SEQUENCE

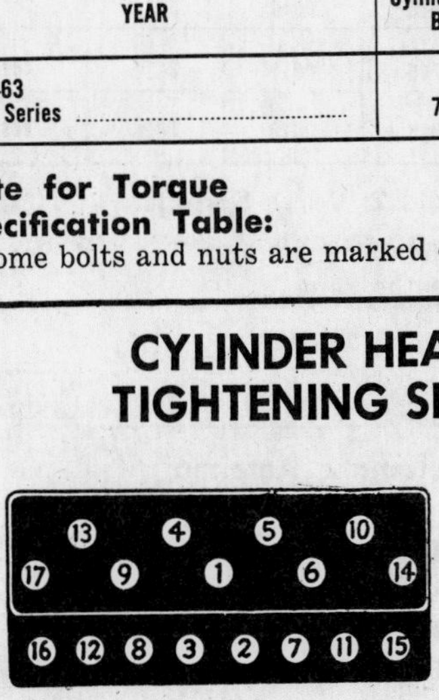

1954-63 All
Tighten to 70-80 ft. lbs.

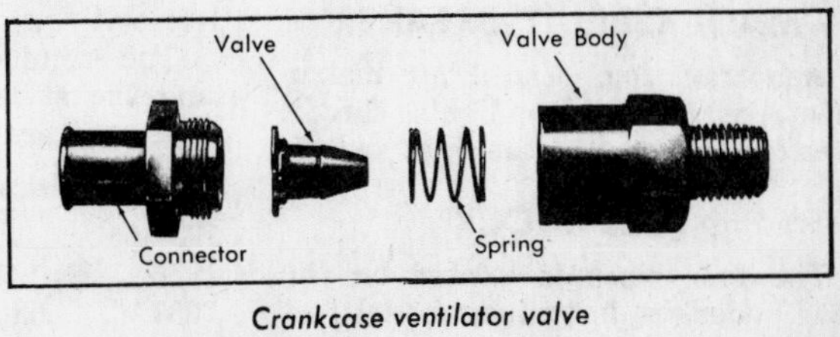

Crankcase ventilator valve

CADILLAC

GENERAL ENGINE SPECIFICATION

Year Model Engine Type	Bore and Stroke	Number of Main Bearings	Type of Valve Lifter Used	Cubic Inch Displacement	AMA Horsepower	Advertised Horsepower at Stated RPM	Advertised Torque at Stated RPM	Compression Ratio	Oil Pressure At 30 MPH (Note 1)	Cam Shaft Drive
1954										
All OHV, V8............	3¹³⁄₁₆x3⅝	5	Hydraulic	331	46.5	230@4400	330@2700	8.25–1	33	Chain
1955										
Series 60, 62, OHV, V8.........	3¹³⁄₁₆x3⅝	5	Hydraulic	331	46.5	250@4600	345@2800	9.0–1	33	Chain
Eldorado, OHV, V8............	3¹³⁄₁₆x3⅝	5	Hydraulic	331	46.5	270@4800	345@3200	9.0–1	33	Chain
1956										
Series 60, 62, OHV, V8.........	4x3⅝	5	Hydraulic	365	51.2	285@4600	400@2800	9.75–1	33	Chain
Eldorado, OHV, V8............	4x3⅝	5	Hydraulic	365	51.2	305@4700	400@3200	9.75–1	33	Chain
1957										
Series 60, 62, OHV, V8.........	4x3⅝	5	Hydraulic	365	51.2	300@4800	400@2800	10.0–1	33	Chain
Eldorado, OHV, V8............	4x3⅝	5	Hydraulic	365	51.2	325@4800	400@3300	10.0–1	33	Chain
1958										
Series 60, 62, OHV, V8......	4x3⅝	5	Hydraulic	365	51.2	Note 2	Note 3	10.25–1	33	Chain
1959-60										
All ex. Eldorado V8......	4x3⅞	5	Hydraulic	390	51.2	325@4800	435@3400	10.5–1	33	Chain
Eldorado "Q" V8	4x3⅞	5	Hydraulic	390	51.2	345@4800	430@3100	10.5–1	33	Chain
1961-63										
All	4x3⅞	5	Hydraulic	390	51.2	325@4800	430@3100	10.5–1	33	Chain

NOTES FOR GENERAL ENGINE SPECIFICATION TABLE

Note 1:

OIL FILTER TYPE

1954-59 ....Partial flow
1960-63 ....Full flow

ROCKER SHAFT OIL SUPPLY

1954-63:

Oil from the lengthwise header in the left block goes thru drilled passages in the front of the block and head to the left side hollow rocker shaft. Oil from the lengthwise header in the right bank goes thru drilled passages in the rear of the block and head to the right side hollow rocker shaft. Oil flows from the hollow shafts thru two holes at each rocker. One hole is perpendicular and lubricates the rocker bearing; the other is at an angle and meters oil flow to the push rod end of the rocker. Dribbles of oil flow across the rocker to provide lubrication at the valve end. The rocker shafts have indents at each end to indicate their proper position so that the oil holes for the rockers are properly positioned. These indents should point down and toward the center of the engine. The larger machined surface of each rocker arm bracket goes against the head.

Note 2: Horse Power of 1958 Models

Engines with Single Carburetors — 310 @ 4800 R.P.M.
Engines with Three 2-Barrel Carburetors — 335 @ 4800 R.P.M.

Note 3: Torque of 1958 Models

Engines with Single Carburetors — 405 @ 3100 R.P.M.
Engines with Three 2-Barrel Carburetors—405 @ 3400 R.P.M.

VALVE SPECIFICATIONS

Year	Seat Angle	Intake Valve Lift	Exhaust Valve Lift	Valve Spring Pressure Outer	Valve Spring Pressure Inner	Stem to Guide Clearance Inlet	Stem to Guide Clearance Exhaust	Stem Diameter	Are Valve Guides Removable
1954 All Series V8	44	.365	.365	61 @ 1.70	None	.0015	.0018	.342	Yes
1955 All Series V8	44	.411	.411	65 @ 1.70	None	.0015	.0018	.342	Yes
1956 All Series V8	44	.451	.451	63 @ 1.89	None	.0015	.0018	.342	Yes
1957-63 All Series V8	44	.451	.451	63 @ 1.94	None	.0018	.0018	.342	Yes

Note 1: Timing Sprocket Marks

Marks on camshaft and crankshaft sprocket should be aligned nearest each other and with the shaft centers.

Note 2: Valve Springs

1954-63: Inlet and Exhaust Springs are the same.

FUSES AND CIRCUIT BREAKERS

MAIN CIRCUIT BREAKER

Ash tray, fog, head, map, instrument, parking and stop lights: Circuit breaker is a part of the light switch.

FUSE BLOCK

The fuse block is located on the cowl under the instrument panel just left of the center.

The circuits protected by each fuse and the style and amperage of the fuse used are listed below.

Air Conditioner

1954-55 ....SFE20
1956 ....SFE25
1957 ....SFE20

1958-63 ....SFE25

Automatic Antenna

Thru 1956 ....SFE14
1957 ....SFE 9
1958-63 ....SFE14

Back-up Lights

1954-63 ....SFE 9

Instruments

1954-63 ....SFE 9

Heater

1954-63 ....SFE20

Radio

1954-63 ....AGA7½

Turn Signals and Stop Lights

1958-63 ....AGA9
1958-63 ....SFE9

Body Feed

Includes: Cigar Lighters, Clock, Dome, Glove Box, Map, Trunk.

1954-63 ....AGC25

Power Top

1954-63: 15 Amp. circuit breaker behind left kick pad.

Power Seats and Windows

1954-63: 40 Amp. circuit breaker behind left kick pad.

Power Trunk Lock

1956-63: 5 Amp. circuit breaker behind left kick pad.

Location of Horn Relay

1954-55—On engine side of dash.
1956—On radiator support at left.
1957-63—On right fender dust shield.

LIGHT BULBS

(C.P. MEANS CANDLE POWER)

Dash Lights for the Ash Tray, Ignition Switch and Cigar Lighters:

12 Volt, No. 53.
(One C.P. miniature bayonet fuse.)

Telltale Lights for Headlight Beam, Brake Warning, Generator, Oil Pressure, Trunk Lock and Hydramatic Quadrant together with the Clock, Glove Compartment and Instrument Cluster:

12 Volt, No. 57.
(2 C.P. single contact base.)

License Light and Rear Parking Light:

12 Volt, No. 67.
(4 C.P. single contact base.)

Radio Dial:

12 Volt, No. 1891.
(2 C.P. double contact base.)

Headlights—2 Only:

12 Volt, No. 5400.
(40 & 50 C.P. three contact base.)

Headlights—4 Only:

OUTER (Low and High Beam)
12 Volt, No. 4002.
(37.5-50 watts three contact base.)

INNER (High Beam Only)
12 Volt, No. 4001.
(37.5 watts double contact base.)

Dome Light, Corner Light, Rear Courtesy Light and Trunk Light:

12 Volt, No. 89.
(6 C.P. single contact base.)

Map Light on Dash:

12 Volt, No. 90.
(6 C.P. double contact base.)

Dome Light:

12 Volt, No. 1004.
(15 C.P. double contact base.)

Park and Direction Signal, Tail and Stop:

12 Volt, No. 1034.
(32-4 C.P. double contact base.)

TUNE-UP

Tune-Up, the returning of existing factors to factory specifications is dealt with in the "Unit Repair Section" of this manual under "Diagnosis, Professional Approach."

DISTRIBUTOR

Detailed information on: distributor drive, direction of distributor rotation; cylinder numbering; firing order; point gap; cam dwell; timing mark location; spark plugs, spark advance; ignition resistor location, and idle speed; will be found in the Tune-up Specifications table of this section.

INSTALL AND/OR ADJUST BREAKER POINTS

1956-63 Models

Points can be installed with the distributor on the car but a more satisfactory job can be done if the unit is removed.

In either case, using a screwdriver depress and turn the two cap retainers to release the cap from the body. Lift off the cap and wire assembly.

Remove the screw which holds the

two leads to the nylon insulating block on the point set. Remove the two screws which hold the point set to the breaker plate and lift off the points.

Install in reverse order, positioning the two leads carefully so as not to interfere with the centrifugal weights.

Set the breaker point gap to rough-

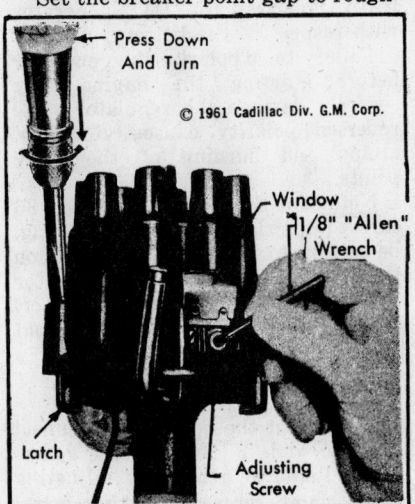

© 1961 Cadillac Div. G.M. Corp.

Press Down And Turn

Window ⅛" "Allen" Wrench

Latch

Adjusting Screw

Distributor starting with 1956 production. Showing how to release cap latches and how to adjust points with engine running

ly .016 inch (not the final setting). Start the engine and let warm up. Adjust idle speed to 425-475 R.P.M. With an Allen wrench, through the "window" in the side of the distributor cap turn the point adjusting screw inwards (clockwise) until the engine starts to slow down. Now turn the screw ½ turn (180°) in the opposite direction (counterclockwise) and this will be the correct contact gap and dwell angle. Close and secure the window.

REMOVAL OF DISTRIBUTOR

All Models

Remove distributor cap. Disconnect vacuum pipe. Disconnect primary lead at distributor.

Turn the engine to top dead center for No. 1 cylinder so that: the rotor points to the rear of the engine (which is where the wire from the No. 1 cylinder is inserted in the distributor cap); the pointer on the timing case cover points to the "C" mark on the crankshaft pulley.

Match mark the vacuum advance unit to the cylinder block so that the distributor body will be correctly replaced at reassembly.

CADILLAC

REPLACING DISTRIBUTOR
Starting with 1954 Production

Install rubber seal ring below distributor housing mounting flange.

Install the distributor so that the vacuum advance unit aligns with the match-mark made at removal. Turn the rotor slightly left of center so that as the gear engages the camshaft it will revolve into the proper position, pointing to No. 1 contact in the cap.

Note if the engine has been cranked, remove No. 1 spark plug Crank the engine until No. 1 piston is in firing position with the pointer and the "C" mark on the crankshaft pulley aligned. Then proceed as above.

Install the hold-down clamp. Connect the primary lead and install the cap.

Fill the distributor oiler tube with 10W oil.

Plug the distributor vacuum line to the carburetor.

Insert an adapter pin alongside No. 1 wire in the distributor cap and connect up a timing light.

Clean the crankshaft pulley markings and the pointer. Put a chalk mark midway between the "C" and "A" marks on the pulley for 1954 and 1955 models.

With engine warm and idling, turn distributor body until pointer and chalk mark appear to be aligned for 1954 and 1955 models. On 1956-57 models, adjust distributor so pointer and "A" mark are aligned. On 1958-63 models, the marks are at 5 and 10 degrees before top dead center. For a one-carburetor engine, time to 5 degree mark. For three-carburetor engines, time to the 7½ degree mark.

Insert an adapter pin alongside the wire from No. 6. Check relationship of pointer and chalk mark. If nearly the same as with the pin at No. 1 turn distributor body to divide the variance. If the variance is excessive the distributor needs overhauling.

Tighten clamp bolt to 15-18 ft lbs. Remove plug and reconnect the vacuum line to the advance unit.

GENERATOR AND REGULATOR

Detailed facts on the generator and the regulator can be found in the Generator and Regulator or Delcotron Specifications Table of this section.

General information on generator and regulator repair and trouble shooting can be found in the Unit Repair section under the heading Generators and Regulators, or under A.C. Generators.

Caution: Whenever the circuits of the D.C. generator, the regulator or the battery have been disconnected it is best to apply the following procedure:

Before the engine is started momentarily short from the "Bat" to the "Gen" terminals of the regulator with a screwdriver. This gives a momentary surge of current from the battery to the generator and so correctly polarizes the D.C. generator with respect to the battery.

Failure to so polarize the generator before starting the engine may severely damage the regulator since reversed polarity causes vibrating, arcing and burning of the relay points.

Note: On Series 75 and Series 86 cars equipped with air conditioning, be careful to insulate the brushes on the generator from the commutator before polarizing the D.C. generator. Note: Under no circumstances should the A.C. generator be polarized.

REMOVAL OF GENERATOR

Disconnect the battery. Disconnect the "A" and "F" leads at the generator. Remove generator adjusting strap clamp screw; mounting bolts; and drive belt. Remove generator from right exhaust manifold bracket thru 1956; from left exhaust manifold starting with 1957.

When reinstalling be sure to follow the polarizing procedure given under "Caution" above. Tighten mounting bolts to 15-18 ft lbs.

REGULATORS, AIR CONDITIONED CARS SERIES 75 & 86

These models use a double contact regulator and the following caution must be observed. Never ground the generator field with the regulator connected to the generator. To do so will instantaneously burn up the lower set of contact points in this type of regulator.

BATTERY AND STARTER

Detailed information on the battery and starter will be found in the Battery and Starter Specifications Table of this section.

A more general discussion of starters and their troubles can be found in the Unit Repair section under the heading Starters.

STARTER REMOVAL
All Models

Remove coil feed wire, battery cable, and starter button wire, at starter solenoid.

Remove the two starter mounting bolts at flywheel housing. Pull starter forward and remove from car.

INSTRUMENT PANEL CLUSTER AND SPEEDOMETER

REMOVAL OF PRINTED-CIRCUIT TYPE PANEL AND CLUSTER

1. Disconnect negative battery cable at the battery. Remove lower steering column cover and Hydra-Matic pointer. Remove the "U" clamp nuts and lower steering column.
2. Remove odometer: reset stem, knob and retaining nut.
3. Remove four instrument cluster to instrument panel mounting screws.
4. Remove two screws from the base of the heater control panel.
5. Cluster is now loose and may be tilted to replace bulbs. The bulb sockets should be twisted counterclockwise to remove.
6. Disconnect clock feed wire.
7. Carefully disconnect the two multiple connectors from in back of the cluster.

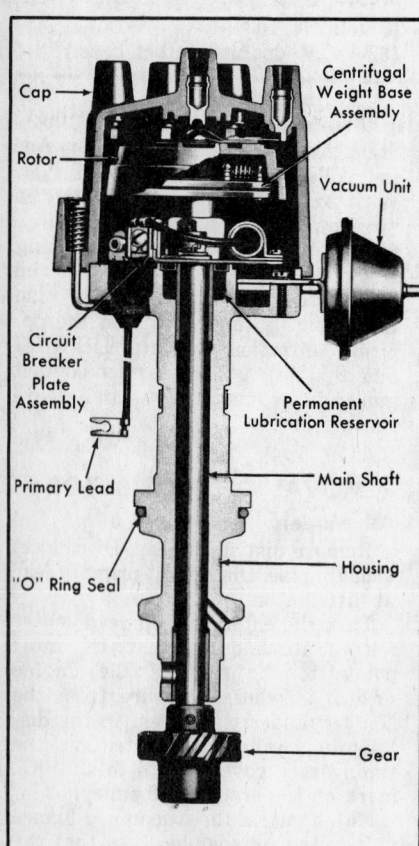

Cap
Rotor
Circuit Breaker Plate Assembly
Primary Lead
"O" Ring Seal
Centrifugal Weight Base Assembly
Vacuum Unit
Permanent Lubrication Reservoir
Main Shaft
Housing
Gear

distributor

8. Disconnect speedometer cable and remove the cluster to the bench.
9. Disconnect clock and Hydra-Matic indicator light wire connector.
10. Remove five printed circuit retaining screws to release the printed circuit.

Beginning 1962

1. Disconnect negative cable at battery.
2. Remove five screws holding upper panel cover to lower panel.
3. Raise upper panel high enough to disconnect 3-way connector for map light and 3-way connector for Guide-Matic phototube unit, if car is so equipped.
4. Pull cover rearward to disengage hooks at front of cover from retainers on cowl. Remove cover.
5. Loosen set screws holding radio manual selector and volume control knobs. Remove knobs, springs and speaker and tone control rings.
6. Using special radio control knob nut wrench, remove the retaining nut from manual, selector control shaft.
7. Disconnect one 6-way wire connector and one single connector from headlamp switch. On cars equipped with fog lamps, disconnect one 3-way connector also.
8. Disconnect light bulb socket and feed wire from clock.
9. Remove two bezel nuts from left side of bezel, near headlamp switch.
10. Remove bezel retaining screw from right side of bezel, near clock.
11. Remove bezel retaining nut from right side of bezel, near clock.
12. Remove screw holding bezel-to-cowl brace.
13. Disconnect gauge wires from back of fuel and temperature gauges.
14. Disconnect speedometer cable at the head.
15. Remove cluster bulb sockets.
16. Disconnect odometer reset cable from lower flange of instrument panel.

17. Remove four cluster retaining screws and remove cluster.
18. Install by reversing the above procedure.

Note:

The above procedure is required when service or replacement is needed on the speedometer head or any of the instruments.

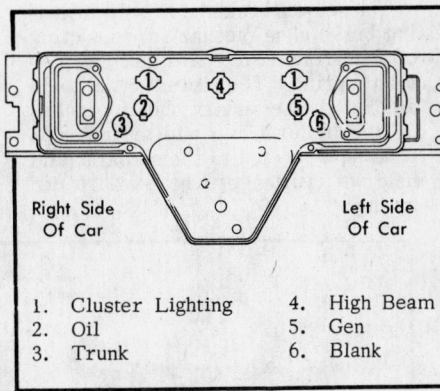

1. Cluster Lighting	4. High Beam
2. Oil	5. Gen
3. Trunk	6. Blank

Cluster Bulb Locations

WINDSHIELD WIPER MOTOR
1954-58

The windshield wiper motor is mounted on the firewall under the dash and near the steering column.

To remove the motor, first remove the wiper arms and blades. Then depress the wiper transmission pivot shafts to release the tension on the wiper cables. Now remove the heater defroster hoses for access to the wiper motor. Remove the cables from the motor, then take off the wiper motor mounting nuts and remove the motor from the firewall.

Reverse the removal procedure for installation. After the cables are attached to the motor, depress the wiper transmission pivot shafts to tighten the cables.

Beginning 1959

Remove wiper arm and blade assemblies using spanner wrench remove cam spanner nut and cam, then escutheon spanner nut and washer. LIFT escutcheon from grille, disconnect washer hose and remove escutcheon, raise hood, remove screws and LIFT grille from cowl.

Disconnect wiper-to-transmission control arm and three screws, then remove transmission with arm.

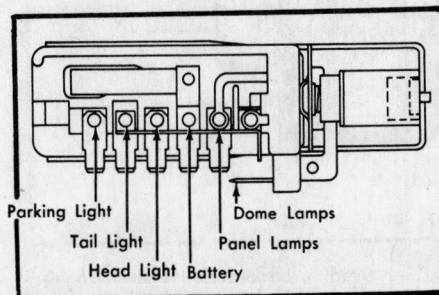

Headlamp Switch

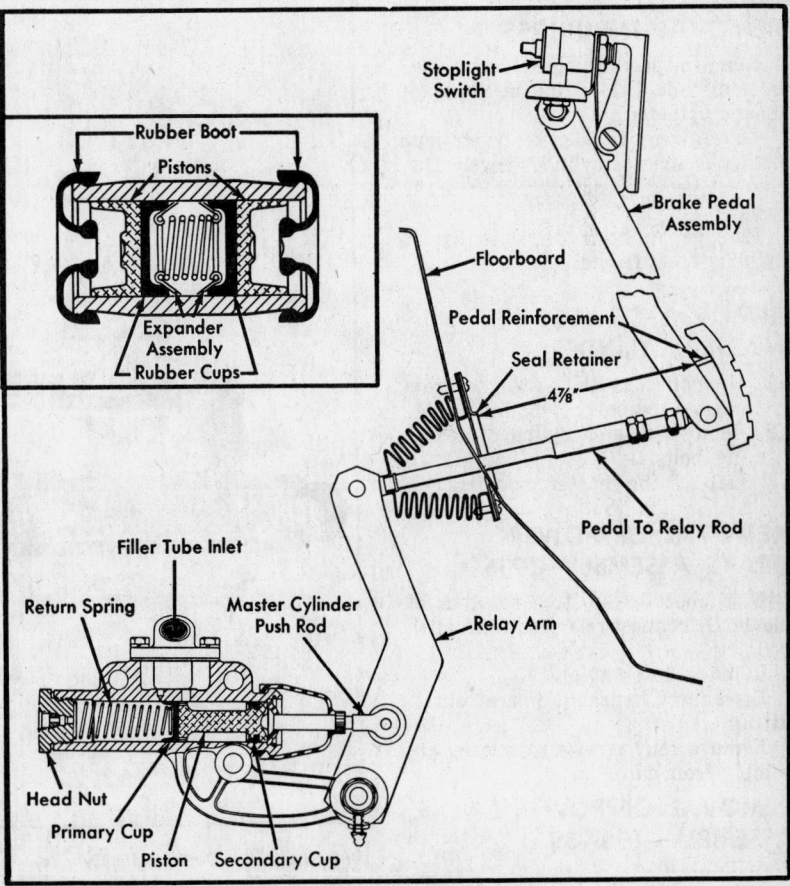

Power brake linkage—1957 models

Disconnect battery and separate multiple connector at wiper. Remove distributor cap, take out four mounting screws and lift out wiper motor. Reverse this procedure for installation.

BRAKE SYSTEM

Specific information on brake cylinder sizes can be found in the General Chassis and Brake Specifications Table at the beginning of this section.

Information on trouble shooting and overhauling power brakes can be found in the Unit Repair section under the heading: Brakes, Power. Starting with 1956 production all Cadillac cars are equipped with power brakes.

Information on the grease seals which may need replacement can be found in the Unit Repair section. The front wheel grease seals under the head: Suspension Front Repair. The rear wheel grease seals under the head: Axles, Rear.

Starting With 1957

To gain access to the front wheel star wheel adjustment, it will be necessary to remove the disc wheel (not the hub or drum).

MASTER CYLINDER REMOVAL THRU 1955

Remove splash shield from flywheel housing and brake line at front of master cylinder.

Loosen remote filler reservoir pipe fitting in master cylinder cover. Disconnect pedal operating rod at brake pedal.

Remove two bolts to release master cylinder from frame.

REMOVAL OF 1956-63 MASTER CYLINDER

1. Disconnect outlet fitting/s from master cylinder.
2. Remove master cylinder attaching bolts.
3. Lift off the master cylinder.

REMOVAL OF POWER BRAKE ASSEMBLY—1956

Disconnect relay to unit rod at clevis. Disconnect relay rod from push rod.

Remove hoses at unit.

Disconnect hydraulic line at outlet fitting.

Remove four screws to release assembly from car.

REMOVAL OF POWER BRAKE ASSEMBLY—1957-59

Disconnect remote filler tube from unit. Disconnect vacuum and brake lines from unit.

Remove four bolts to release assembly from cowl.

BEGINNING 1960 SELF ADJUSTING SERVICE BRAKE

The braking system on all models, starting with 1960 consists of a power-assisted, hydraulic service brake and a foot operated parking brake. The parking brake is applied at the rear wheels thru mechanical linkage.

The service brake has a self-adjusting brake shoe mechanism consisting of a link, actuator, pawl and pawl return spring. The actuator is held against the secondary shoe by means of a hold-down cup and spring. The pawl is connected to the actuator and held in position by the pawl return spring.

The automatic adjustment takes place only when the brakes are applied as the car is moving in a rearward direction.

Over-adjustment is prevented by the shoe-to-drum clearance limiting secondary shoe travel to a degree less than that required for the pawl to engage the next tooth of the starwheel.

Care must be used, that the correct starwheel assembly is installed at the proper wheel, to insure that the self-adjuster work correctly.

Starwheel adjusters with left hand threads have one groove on the long end of the starwheel adjuster and must be used on right side drums. Those with right-hand threads have two grooves and must be used on the left hand side of the car.

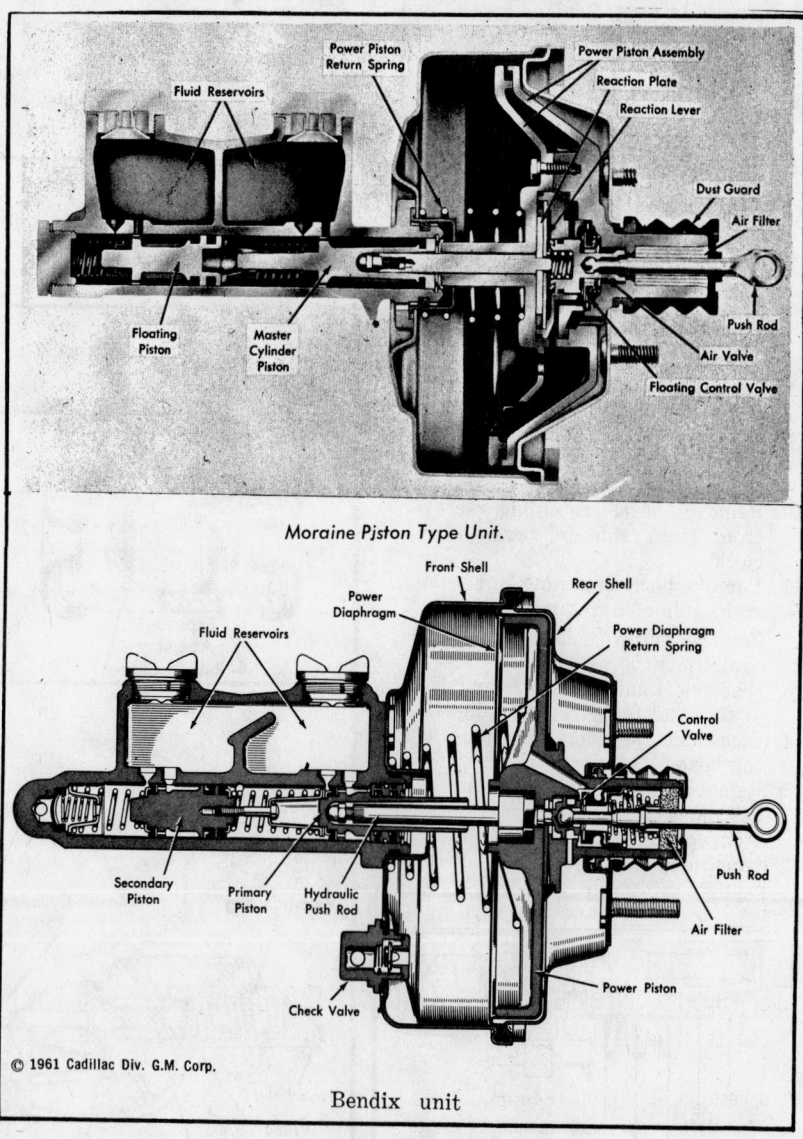

Moraine Piston Type Unit.

© 1961 Cadillac Div. G.M. Corp.

Bendix unit

1962-63 Cadillac Dual Master Cylinder. (It can be hooked up backwards; the proper hookup is as follows: the rear master cylinder should operate the front brakes; the front master cylinder should operate the rear brakes.)

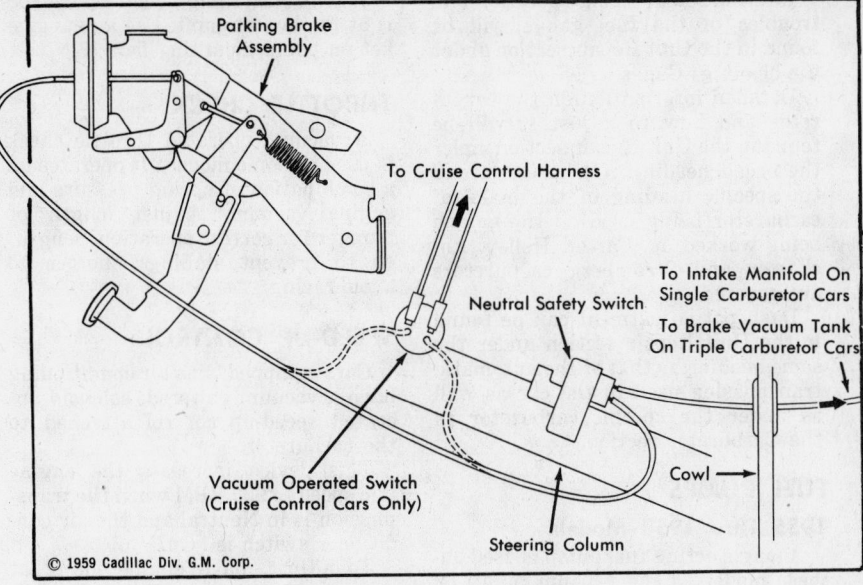

Schematic View – Vacuum Operated Parking Brake

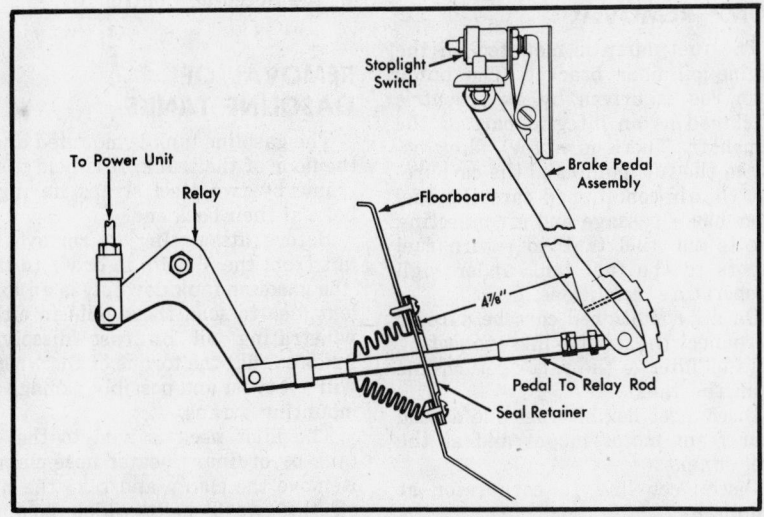

1958 Power Brake Pedal Linkage. With carpet removed distance from pedal reinforcement to seal retainer should be 4¾-5 inches. Adjust pedal to relay rod.

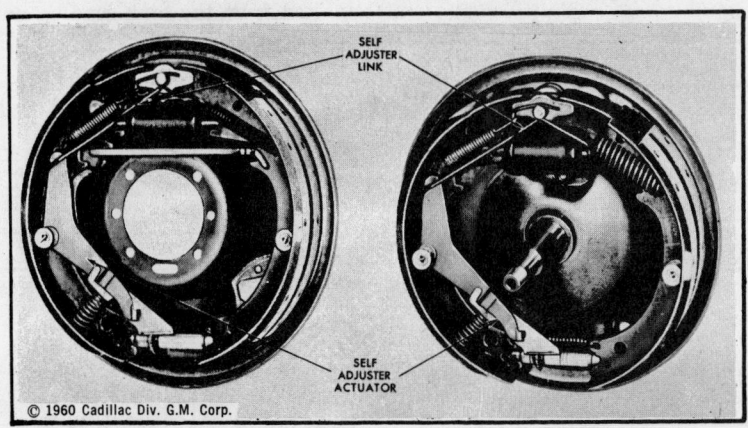

1961-63 Right Side Rear and Front Brakes with self adjusting mechanism.

CAUTION:

Fixed anchors are used starting with 1961 models.

Periodic wheel removal and lining inspection becomes more important to insure against drum and shoe damage due to neglect.

REMOVAL OF POWER BRAKE ASSEMBLY 1960-63

The master cylinder is part of the power unit on these models.

Disconnect output line from master cylinder of power unit.

Disconnect hoses from power units.

Remove clevis pin retaining power unit push rod to brake pedal relay lever.

Remove four screws to release power unit from car.

PARKING BRAKE

Removal of Hand Brake Handle Thru 1956

Remove bolt holding retaining plates over brake cable pin and brake lever at left side of cowl.

Disconnect clevis and cable from lever arm at the frame side bar.

Remove two bolts to release hand brake from instrument panel.

Lower assembly and disconnect brake-on light wire.

Remove unit from car by pulling cable and clevis thru rubber grommet in dash panel.

When reinstalling twist cable and clevis about 6 degrees counterclockwise so that sides of clevis fork are parallel to the ground. When properly adjusted a 55 lb. pull on the hand brake lever will move it 2¼ inches from the released position and should result in the car being held.

Removal of Foot Operated Parking Brake 1957-59

Disconnect clevis at bell crank relay on left frame side rail.

Disconnect vertical cable at pedal.

Remove four nuts holding parking pedal assembly to the cowl and remove from car.

When reinstalling check intermediate cable tension. There should

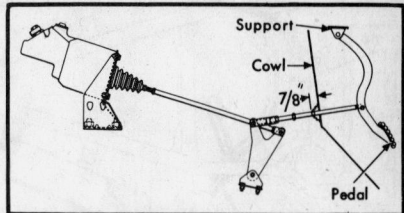

1956 Brake Pedal Linkage. Distance from front edge of groove to cowl must be 13/16 to 15/16. Screw pedal to relay rod into or out of trunnion to adjust.

be ⅛ inch between the rear edge of the lever and the end of the slot. Adjust cable link to suit.

When properly adjusted the pedal should travel 2½ to 2⅜ inches under 50 lbs. pressure. Measured at the relay lever, this travel would be ¾ inch.

1960-63 Vacuum Release Parking Brake

A vacuum release has been added to the foot operated parking brake. With the engine running, the brake automatically releases when the car is put into gear. This device eliminates the possibility of driving the car with the parking brake engaged, (see cut).

Beginning 1962

A dual master cylinder is used. The front reservoir supplying rear brakes and the rear one supplying the front brakes. This allows one pair of brakes to operate should there be a failure of the opposite pair. If lines have been disconnected be sure to reinstall in proper place, i.e. front to rear cylinder and rear to front.

With pressure bleeder the Bendix System can be bled from front reservoir by covering rear reservoir with solid cap. The Moraine type must be bled separately, front and rear.

Without pressure bleeder keep both reservoirs nearly full.

FUEL SYSTEM

A chart covering causes of excess fuel consumption will be found in the Unit Repair section under the heading: Fuel Consumption.

Data on capacity of the gas tank will be found in the Capacities table. Data on correct engine idle speed and and their trouble will be found in the Tune-Up Specifications table. Both the above tables can be found in this section.

General information on fuel pumps and their trouble will be found in the Unit Repair section under the heading: Fuel Pumps.

Information covering operation and troubles of the fuel gauge will be found in the Unit Repair section under the heading: Gages.

Detailed information on the carburetor and how to adjust it will be found in the Unit Repair section under the broad heading: Carburetors, and the specific heading of the make of carburetor being used on the engine being worked on. Carter, Holley, Rochester and Stromberg carburetors are covered.

Dash pot adjustment can be found in the Unit Repair section under the same heading as that of the automatic transmission used in the car as well as under the specific carburetor in the Carburetor section.

FUEL PUMPS

1955 Thru 1958 Models

A single acting fuel pump is used on these models. (The vacuum pump is an integral part of the oil pump and is in the crankcase.)

PUMP REMOVAL

The fuel pump is mounted on the engine oil filler bracket. The pump push rod is driven by an eccentric machined as an integral part of the camshaft. There is a fuel filter between the fuel pump and the carburetor. On air conditioned cars the fuel filter has a passage and a connecting line to the fuel tank to return fuel vapors to the fuel tank under high temperature conditions.

On air conditioned cars be sure to disconnect the flexible line connecting the fuel filter to the vapor return line from the tank.

Disconnect flexible fuel line at end near front motor mount and at the fuel pump.

Disconnect line to carburetor at the filter.

Remove two screws and flat washers holding the pump to the oil filler housing.

Remove pump and filter as an assembly.

When reinstalling be sure push rod is at the lowest point. Use a new gasket on pump mounting flange.

THROTTLE CHECK

A vacuum operated throttle check is used on some models. It operates on a combination of spring pressure and engine vacuum. Adjust length of plunger for correct operation: lengthen to prevent stalling; shorten to avoid racing.

SPEED-UP CONTROL

Cars equipped with air conditioning have a vacuum powered, solenoid operated speed-up control attached to the carburetor.

This device increases the engine idle speed to 900 RPM when the transmission is in Neutral and the air conditioner switch is "On."

To adjust, have engine idling at normal temperature. With transmission in Neutral turn on air conditioner. Adjust idle speed to 900 RPM at the Speed-up Control.

REMOVAL OF GASOLINE TANKS

The gasoline tank is mounted under the floor of the trunk. It is held to the frame by two steel straps having T bolts at their back end.

Before attempting to remove the nut from the T bolts in order to take the gasoline tank down, it is an excellent idea to soak these nuts in either penetrating oil or rust dissolving fluids so that the torque of the wrench will not twist and possibly damage the mounting straps.

The filler neck is held to the gas tank by ordinary heater hose clamps. Remove the clamp and take the nuts off the two T bolts which hold the strap to the back cross member and slowly lower the tank. After the tank has been lowered approximately a foot, the gage wire can be disconnected from the tank sending unit.

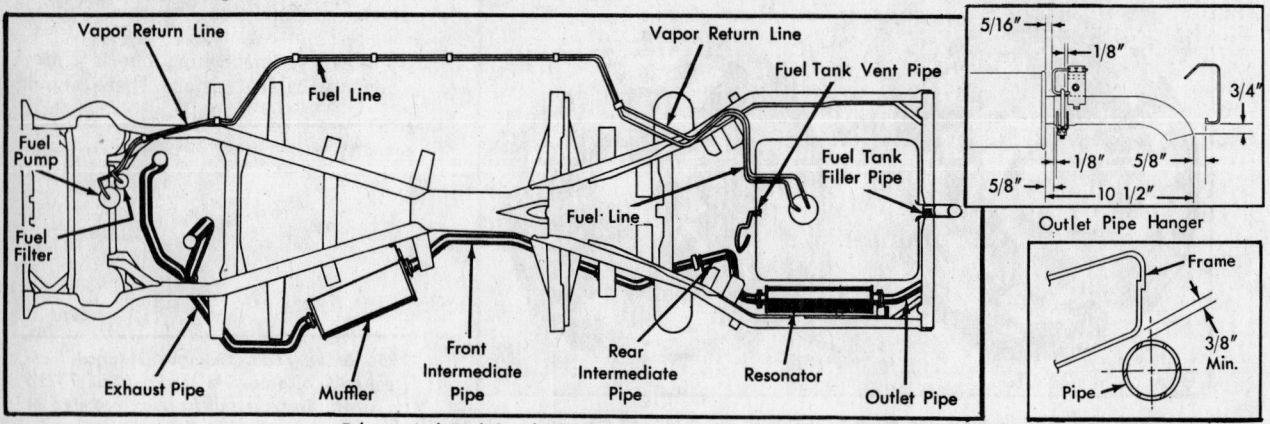

Exhaust And Fuel Supply Systems

Outlet Pipe Hanger

Rear Intermediate Pipe Hanger

EXHAUST SYSTEM

EXHAUST PIPE REMOVAL

Raise front of car and disconnect steering connecting rod at pitman arm.

Disconnect exhaust pipe from manifold. On left side remove heat control valve.

Loosen exhaust pipe to muffler coupling screws. On left side, remove slush deflector and loosen hanger clamp screw and slide clamp off hanger.

Remove exhaust pipe from muffler.

MUFFLER REMOVAL

Remove exhaust pipe as above.

Disconnect pad hanger at rear of muffler from the frame.

Loosen muffler to intermediate pipe coupling screws and remove muffler from the intermediate pipe.

RESONATOR REMOVAL

Remove resonator to intermediate pipe coupling screws. Remove the hanger at the rear of the resonator from the frame. Remove resonator from the intermediate pipe. Reinstall hanger to frame screws.

Loosen front screws of coupling at rear of resonator and slide resonator forward off the tail pipe.

REMOVAL OF INTER-MEDIATE PIPE THRU 1956

Remove resonator as described above.

Loosen muffler rear coupling screws and remove intermediate pipe.

REMOVAL OF FRONT INTERMEDIATE PIPE STARTING 1957

Raise car. Disconnect exhaust pipe at exhaust manifold and at hanger.

Remove clamp at rear muffler hanger.

Remove clamp connecting front and rear intermediate pipes.

Cut front intermediate pipe in two pieces.

Remove exhaust pipe-muffler assembly and front section of cut intermediate pipe. Remove the other section of the cut pipe from the rear intermediate pipe.

The replacement intermediate pipe comes in two sections.

REMOVAL OF REAR INTERMEDIATE PIPE STARTING WITH 1957

Raise rear of car and remove clamp at front end of rear intermediate pipe.

Drive rear intermediate pipe and resonator assembly rearward until tail pipe clears the front intermediate pipe. Now drive the rear intermediate pipe forward off the resonator and remove pipe from car.

REMOVAL OF TAIL PIPE

Remove resonator.

Remove hanger from frame cross bar. Slide tail pipe forward out of transition pipes to bumper and so out of car.

REMOVAL OF HEAT CONTROL VALVE

Remove left exhaust pipe support to bell housing screw.

Remove screws which hold left exhaust pipe to manifold.

Holding exhaust pipe down slightly from manifold, slide the heat control valve and its upper and lower gaskets down and out.

When reinstalling be sure to have part marked "Top" against left exhaust manifold. Tighten screws to 30-35 ft lbs.

COOLING SYSTEM

Detailed information on cooling system capacity can be found in the Capacities Table.

Information on the water temperature gauge can be found in the Unit Repair section under the heading: Gages.

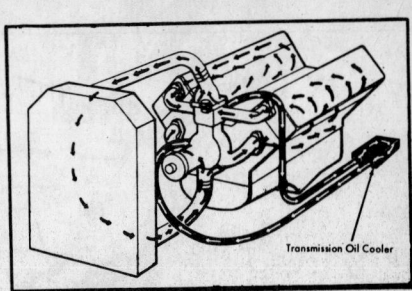

Coolant Flow 1957 Models Only.

COOLANT FLOW

1957 Models Only

When erratic overheating occurs on 1957 models one should check the transmission cooler lines. If either of these hoses were pinched water flow thru the thermostat by-pass would be slowed or stopped and overheating would occur until the thermostat opened fully. Pinching of the lines is most likely between the cowl and the rear of the engine.

In all other years, the water pump has a drilled by-pass hole to assure adequate flow into the heads while the thermostat is shut or only partially open. In the 1957 design the by-pass hole is omitted and the transmission oil cooler and lines act as the by-pass.

RADIATOR CORE REMOVAL

The space between the rear face of the radiator and the front edge of the fan blades should be from $\frac{1}{2}$ to 1 inch.

This is true of all models and is important for efficient fan operation.

1957-61 Models

To remove the radiator, drain the system and remove the upper and lower radiator hoses, disconnect the Hydramatic cooling lines, then remove the mounting bolts, or clamps, and lift the radiator up and out of the engine compartment.

All Models With Air Conditioning

Drain cooling system and disconnect radiator hoses.

Remove Freon hose retainer clip from right hand upper side of radiator cradle.

Remove four screws holding condenser and dehydrator-receiver to brackets on sides of radiator. Access to the lower right is obtained thru the grille.

Remove left tie bar between radiator cradle and hood lock plate.

Lift out condenser and attachments and taking advantage of the flexible lines which do not have to be disconnected, swing the assembly out of the way.

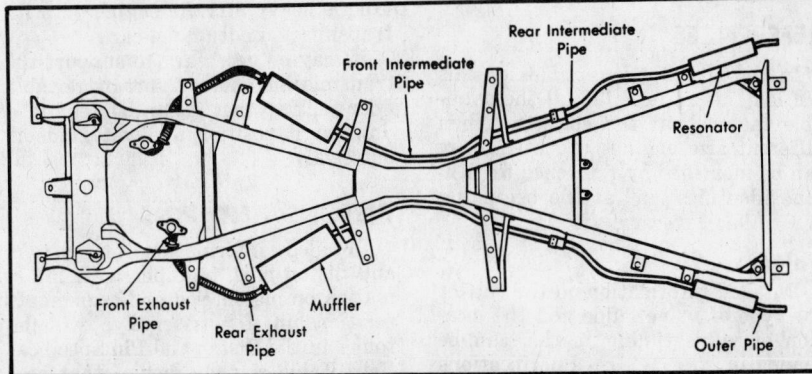

Typical Exhaust System 1957 Models

CADILLAC

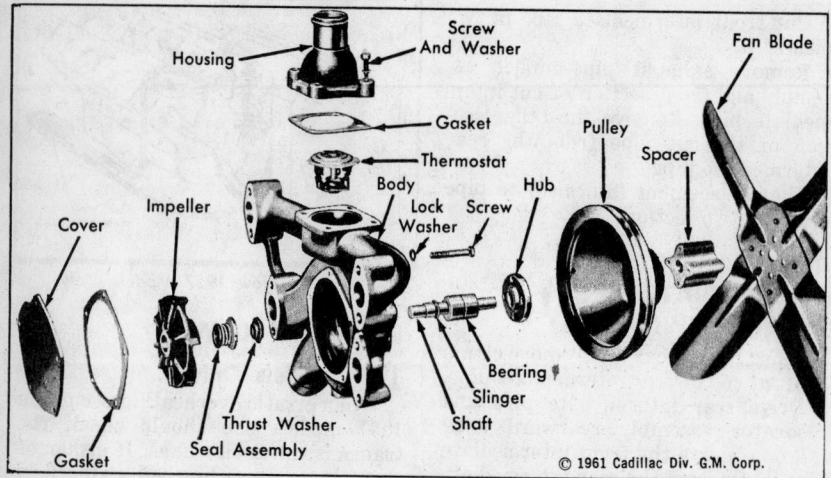

Typical Water Pump.

Remove six screws holding radiator assembly and condenser brackets to the radiator cradle. Remove the brackets.

Now pull radiator forward to clear the hoses and lift it up and out.

THERMOSTAT REMOVAL

The thermostat is located in the water manifold at the front of the block.

This thermostat is removed by disconnecting the upper radiator hose and taking off the four cap screws which hold the thermostat housing to the top of the water pump body.

INSTALLING THERMOSTAT

Install thermostat in opening at top of water pump with valve up. Be sure that the thermostatic spring strap is parallel to the centerline of the car (fore and aft). Install a new thermostat gasket with gasket cement.

Install thermostat housing and tighten cap screws to 13 ft lbs.

REMOVAL OF WATER PUMP

Models Without Air Conditioning

Drain the cooling system, then remove the fan and drive belts.

On power steering jobs, detach the power steering pump and bracket from the water pump.

Remove the radiator and heater hoses from the water pump, then take out the thermostat housing screws and remove the housing.

Now take out the water pump flange to cylinder block screws, then remove the water pump and gaskets.

Models With Air Conditioning and Air Suspension

Drain cooling system and remove upper half of fan shroud.

Remove drive belts from power-steering-air suspension unit, Freon compressor, and generator.

Disconnect radiator and heater hoses at the water pump.

Exhaust air from accumulator tank and disconnect air inlet and outlet lines at air suspension compressor.

Unfasten air-compressor-power-steering-pump assembly and brackets, no need to disconnect power steering hoses. Swing assembly aside.

Disconnect throttle return spring. Remove oil filter unit.

Remove the two water pump to block screws that hold the Freon compressor front mounting bracket.

Remove Freon compressor front mounting bracket to cylinder block screw and screw holding generator adjusting link to Freon compressor mounting bracket screw.

Loosen front Freon compressor adjusting link to mounting bracket screw and swing lower portion of front mounting bracket to right side of car.

Remove four fan retaining screws to release fan and pulley.

Remove four remaining water pump to cylinder block screws to release water pump from engine.

ENGINES

REFERENCES

In the specifications tables of this section there are listed all the available facts about the engines. When different size engines are used, they can be identified by reference to "Engine Identification" at the beginning of Cadillac coverage.

Valves

Detailed information on the valves, the type of valve guide and the location of valve timing marks, can be found in the Valve Specifications Table at the beginning of that section.

Bearings

Detailed information on engine bearings will be found in the Crankshaft Bearing Journal Sizes Table.

REMOVAL OF ENGINE ASSEMBLY

The engine is removed together with the transmission. Place the car on stand jacks and drain the cooling system, crankcase, and transmission. Disconnect the battery cables. Take a scribe and carefully mark the position of the hood hinges where they mount to the fender apron and remove the hood, complete with its hinge mechanism.

Disconnect the generator and remove the radiator core, fan and lower pulley. Disconnect the lines from the power steering pump at the pump. Disconnect the refrigerator lines on models with air conditioning, take out the heater hoses, the power brake vacuum line, the carburetor air cleaner, the carburetor and its linkage.

Remove the transmission gravel deflector and disconnect the levers and speedometer at the transmission, disconnect the fuel lines, take off the battery ground straps, the primary ignition wire, the oil pressure and cooling system temperature switch wires. Remove the ignition coil and take off the wires to the ignition resistor, disconnect the vacuum hoses to the manifold and windshield wipers.

Split the rear universal joint and slide the driveshaft off the back of the transmission. Remove the frame intermediate support, disconnect the starter and disconnect the exhaust pipe at the exhaust manifolds. Remove the bolts which hold the front motor supports at the frame and then take off the idler arm support screws and lower the idler arm and steering connecting link. Attach a lifting device and take up the slack until the lifting device has a little load on it. Then disconnect and remove the rear engine support bracket from the frame. Very carefully, since the engine is heavy, lift the engine with its transmission out of the car.

It may be necessary to support the transmission on some sort of movable floor jack so that it can be kept in a downward position and yet guide it out easily.

PISTONS AND PINS

Detailed information on pistons and piston pins, together with information on piston, rod and crankshaft relationship for assembly, will be found in the Piston and Pin Specifications Table at the start of that section.

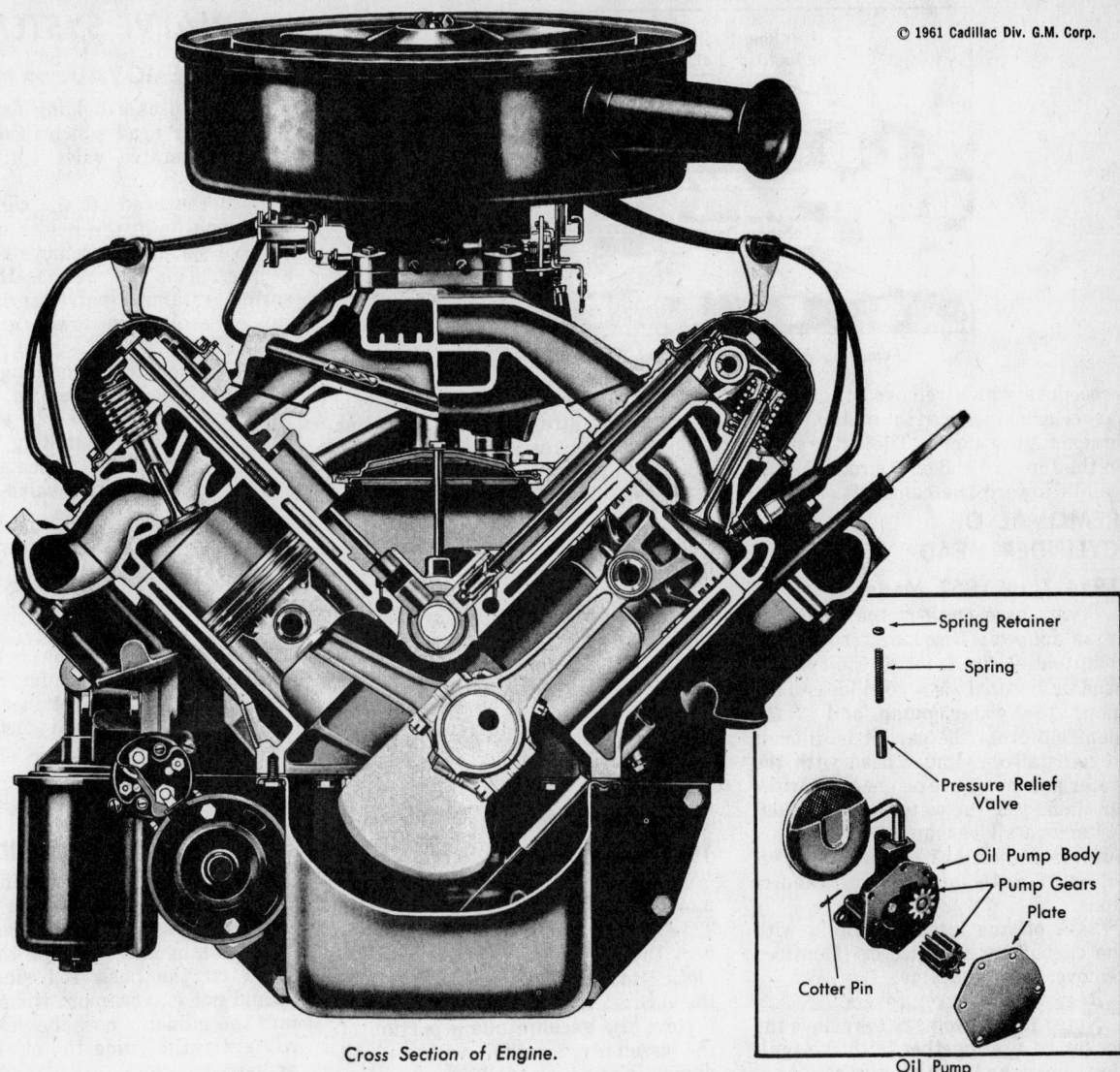

Cross Section of Engine.

Spring Retainer
Spring
Pressure Relief Valve
Oil Pump Body
Pump Gears
Plate
Cotter Pin
Oil Pump

ENGINE REASSEMBLY

Engine crankcase capacities are listed in the Capacities Table.

Approved torque wrench readings and head bolt tightening sequences are covered in the Torque Specifications Table of this section.

Information on the engine marking code will be found in the Model Year Identification Table at the start of this Cadillac section.

ENGINE MANIFOLDS

REMOVAL OF EXHAUST MANIFOLD

To remove either of the exhaust manifolds, detach the manifold at the exhaust pipe flange and, in the case of the right manifold, remove the generator and then remove the bolts which hold the manifold to the cylinder head.

On some models, particularly those with heater ducts, access to these bolts is said to be easier from underneath the car.

However, they can be reached if the air intake ducts of the heater system are detached at both ends.

REMOVAL OF INLET MANIFOLD

Remove throttle linkage, gas and vacuum lines and the carburetor.

Take off the ignition wires, unbolt and lift off the manifold.

CYLINDER HEAD

ROCKER SHAFT REMOVAL

The rocker shafts can be removed and serviced without disturbing the cylinder head or manifolds.

Simply get the spark plug wires out of the way and remove whatever heater or throttle linkage pass over the rocker cover and then unbolt and remove the rocker cover.

The rocker shafts are held on brackets, the bolts for which do not pass through the cylinder head. These bracket bolts hold the brackets to the head but do not hold the head on.

Unbolt and remove the rocker shafts, being careful to replace them on the head from which they were removed. If new rockers and/or shafts are to be installed, note the relative position the rocker occupies on the shaft so that if a new rocker is installed toward the center of the shaft the balance of the rockers will be put on in the proper order, having the correct springs between the rockers.

Clean the rocker springs and shafts up thoroughly before reinstalling.

The push rods can be pulled directly up through the cylinder heads for examination to make sure that they are straight and not badly worn at either end.

Reinstall the rockers, reversing the

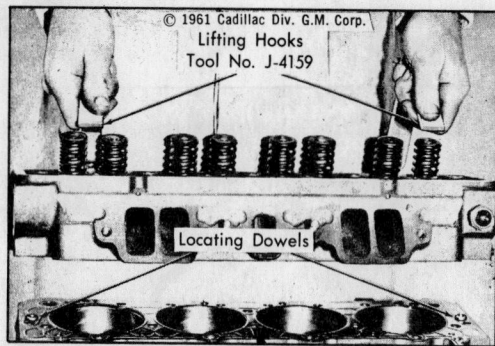

© 1961 Cadillac Div. G.M. Corp.
Lifting Hooks
Tool No. J-4159

Locating Dowels

Removing and installing cylinder head

procedure which removed them. The larger machined surface on the rocker bracket goes down. The little notch in the forward end of the rocker shaft points toward the camshaft.

REMOVAL OF CYLINDER HEAD

1954 Thru 1963 Models

With these engines the procedure is as follows: Disconnect the water manifold at the front of the cylinder head or heads. It is a good idea to remove the water pump and water manifold from the car. It is difficult to reinstall a cylinder head with the water pump in place on one head without damaging the water pump gasket.

Remove all vacuum lines and carburetor connections, disconnect all ignition, throttle and battery connections.

Take off the intake manifold with the carburetor in place or if desired remove the carburetor.

Remove the rocker covers.

Note: It is customary to remove the rocker covers together with the ignition wires and distributor cap as a unit unless service is to be done on the distributor.

Remove the generator if the right cylinder head is to be removed.

The exhaust manifolds may be disconnected either from the head or from the flange connection to the exhaust pipe. It is better to leave them connected to the head.

Remove the head bolts which hold the rocker assemblies to the cylinder head and lift off the rocker assemblies.

Take out the valve push rods.

Remove the balance of the cylinder attaching bolts and lift the head off. It is very important that the head be handled carefully so as not to damage or mark the head gasket surface.

ENGINE LUBRICATION

REMOVAL OF OIL PAN

On 1954 thru 1958 engines the exhaust pipe crossover must be removed to take down the oil pan. Otherwise proceed as follows.

Drain the oil, disconnect the battery ground strap, remove the wires from the starter and take off the starting motor.

On 1959 thru 1963 remove right exhaust pipe bracket.

Remove the steering idler support screws and lower the support from the frame side bar. Remove the water hose and clip from the frame crossmember. Remove the screws and nuts which hold the oil pan to the cylinder block and lower the pan to the floor.

When reinstalling tighten screws and nuts to 10-12 ft lb.

REMOVAL OF VACUUM PUMP

1955 Thru 1958 Models

Drain the engine and remove the oil pan as outlined under oil pan removal. Take out the oil pan baffle and disconnect the vacuum line at the engine block. Remove the screws that hold the vacuum pump at the oil pump and remove the vacuum pump portion of the assembly together with the oil pump idler gear and remove hex driveshaft and take off the vacuum line from the vacuum pump.

REPLACING OIL FILTER ELEMENT

The oil filter is at the upper front of the engine.

To replace the filter element:

Remove the filter cover screw complete with cover and gasket. Lift the old element out. Wipe all the sludge and old oil out of the reservoir. Wash and dry the reservoir and cover paying special attention to the gasket surfaces. Install a new element. Replace the gasket, cover and cover screw.

Run engine at fast idle and check unit for leaks. After five minutes operation stop engine and check oil level.

1960-63 Full Flow Oil Filter:

Starting with 1960 a Full Flow Filter is used. This is the disposable type and equipped with a by-pass safety valve.

VALVE SYSTEM

VALVE REMOVAL

Cadillac uses a holding fixture for the cylinder head which incorporates a pedal operated valve spring compressor.

With the head off the car and on the bench or in the holder compress a valve spring and remove the valve keepers. This will release the valve spring retainer, valve spring, and rubber seal from lower groove in valve stem.

Repeat for the remaining valves, being sure to keep them in order so they can be reinstalled in the same position. When reinstalling be sure that new rubber seal is seated in the groove closest to the valve head.

Check to see that seal is properly installed. Strike the ends of the valve stems to seat the keepers. Compress a suction cup over the spring retainer and valve stem to test for leakage past the seal.

If the rubber oil seal has been properly installed the vacuum cup will stick to the spring retainer due to suction. If there is no suction the seal is leaking and it will be necessary to remove the retainer and install another seal.

CHECKING VALVE GUIDES

Check valve stem to guide clearance using a 1/16 inch wide strip of .005 inch shim stock. Bend the end of the shim and hang in the valve guide on the push rod side. Shim should not extend more than 1/4 inch into the guide. If now the valve stem will enter the guide the clearance is excessive.

VALVE GUIDE REPLACEMENT

First make a pile of washers equal to the projection of the valve guide, and set aside. Drive out valve guides from the bottom side of the cylinder head.

Using an installer or suitable driver, with the pile of washers, lubricate outer surface of the guide and start it into the head. Enter the longest taper first, pointing toward the rocker arm side.

Press guide into head until the installer contacts the plate or the piston end of the guide is flush with the pile of washers.

REMOVAL OF VALVE LIFTERS

Lifters may be removed without taking off the cylinder head.

Remove throttle and gas lines from the carburetor, disconnect hoses, vacuum lines and wires which pass over the rocker covers. Remove the distributor cap and disconnect the wires at the spark plugs. Remove the

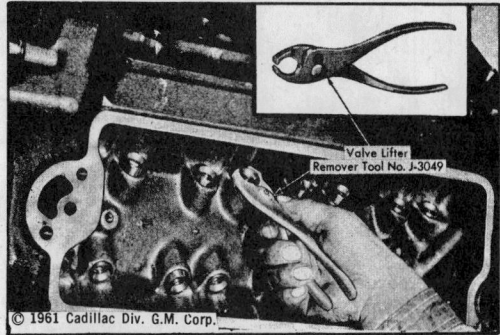

Removing valve lifters

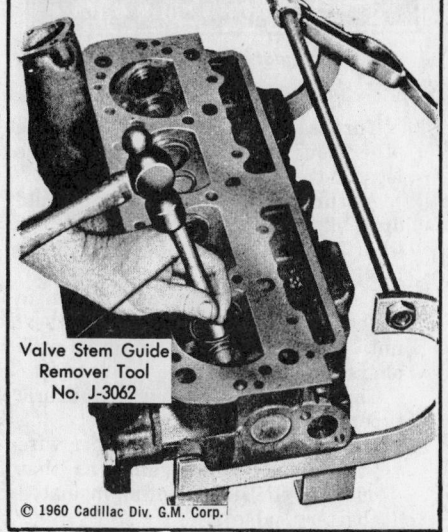

Valve Stem Guide
Remover Tool
No. J-3062

Removing valve guides

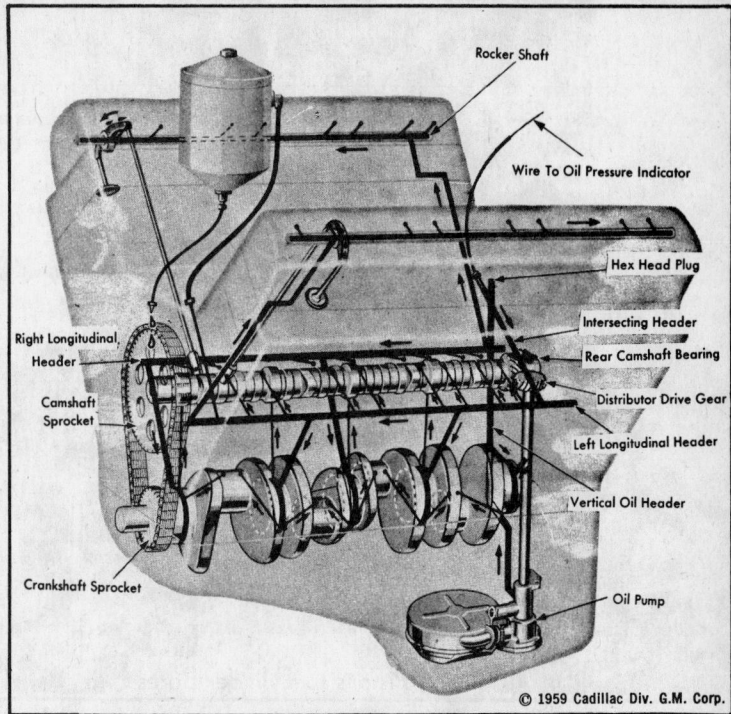

Engine Oiling System

bolts which hold the rocker covers to the cylinder head and lift off the rocker covers leaving the spark plug wires attached to them. Remove the

bolts which hold the intake manifold to the cylinder block and lift off the intake manifold. If desired, the carburetor can be detached from the manifold first, but this is not necessary. Remove the valve chamber cover plate. Remove the bolts which hold the rocker shafts to the cylinder head and lift off the rocker shafts. Pull up the push rods through the holes in the cylinder heads and the lifters can be pulled up out of their bores.

Sometimes gum residues form on the bottom of the lifter, making it very difficult to pull the lifter up out of its bore. If this condition is suspected before the job is started, put a good solvent in the engine oil and run the engine for the time specified by the manufacturer of the solvent in order to dissolve this gum before the job is started.

However, even when gum is present on the bottom of the lifter body it can be pulled up out of its bore using special pliers. These pliers are designed to grip the lifter body firmly without scoring or scratching it.

If a special tool isn't available, a good substitute can be made by grinding the teeth out of an ordinary pair of pliers and grinding a circle almost the size of the valve lifter body so that when the pliers are squeezed down on the lifter body it will contact a large surface of the lifter body, thus preventing scoring.

Arrangement of Valves and Valve Lifters

Measure piston ⅛" below cross slot

Measuring Piston Diameter

Pull Scale

Place feeler gauge at high spot of piston next to T-slot

Fitting Pistons to Cylinder Bores

Piston Measurements

Rear Main Bearing Oil Seal Installer Tool No. J-6349

Cutting rear main bearing oil seal

PISTONS, CONNECTING RODS AND MAIN BEARINGS

PISTON AND ROD REMOVAL

Rod and piston assemblies on all models are removed through the top of the block.

It is possible to replace any and all of the rod or main bearings from underneath the car without removing the crankshaft.

Clean out carbon from top of cylinder bore and ream off the ridge which will be found at the top of the bore. This will prevent breakage of the piston ring lands. Push the piston and rod assemblies up and out of the tops of the cylinders. Be careful not to nick the lower edge of the bores.

ASSEMBLING PISTONS TO CONNECTING RODS

Slippered-type pistons are used, but the piston has the word "rear" cast into the metal just beside the wrist pin hole. With the connecting rod mounted in the vise so that the number faces the operator, the word "rear" will go to his right hand on the odd numbered cylinders (left bank).

With the number on the connecting rod facing the operator, the word "rear" on the piston will go to his left hand on the even numbered pistons (right bank).

ASSEMBLING ROD AND PISTON ASSEMBLIES TO THE BLOCK

The numbers on the connecting rods face away from the camshaft; that is, the numbers on the left bank (odd numbers) face to the left; the numbers on the right bank (even numbers) face to the right. As a double check, the word "rear" stamped on the piston faces the rear of the engine on both banks.

WICK TYPE REAR MAIN BEARING OIL SEAL REPLACEMENT ALL MODELS TO 1958

The rear main bearing oil seal may be removed and replaced with the crankshaft installed.

Remove the oil pan and baffle. Disconnect the vacuum line from the combination oil and vacuum pump assembly and remove the pump from rear main bearing cap.

Remove the rear main bearing cap. Discard the seal.

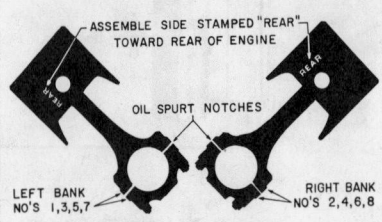

ASSEMBLE SIDE STAMPED "REAR" TOWARD REAR OF ENGINE

OIL SPURT NOTCHES

LEFT BANK NO'S 1,3,5,7

RIGHT BANK NO'S 2,4,6,8

Assembly of connecting rods to piston

Turn each of the bolts holding the other four bearing caps three turns loose.

At this point the crankshaft should drop slightly. If it does not, place a lever between the crankshaft and the block and force it to come down.

Use a bent rod or screwdriver to push on one end of the upper seal until the other end can be seized with pliers and pulled out.

To install the new woven fabric type seal:

1. Obtain a 12" piece of copper wire (about the same gauge as that used in the strands of an insulated battery cable).
2. Thread one strand of this wire thru the new seal, about ½" from the end, bend back and make secure.
3. Thoroughly saturate the new seal with engine oil.
4. Push the copper wire up thru the oil seal groove until it comes down on the opposite side of the bearing.
5. Pull (with pliers) on the protruding copper wire while the crankshaft is being turned and the new seal is slowly fed into place.
   <u>CAUTION</u>: This snaking operation slightly reduces the diameter of the new seal and care will have to be used to keep the seal from slipping too far thru the top half of the bearing.
6. When an equal amount of seal is extending from each side, cut off the copper wire close to the seal and tamp both ends of the seal up into the groove (this will tend to expand the seal again).
   <u>NOTE</u>: Don't worry about the copper wire left in the groove, it is too soft to cause damage.

Install the cap and tighten the bolts to 90-100 ft. lbs.

Be sure to tighten the other four bearing cap bolts to 90-100 ft. lbs.

Reinstall the combination oil and vacuum pump.

Replace baffle and oil pan.

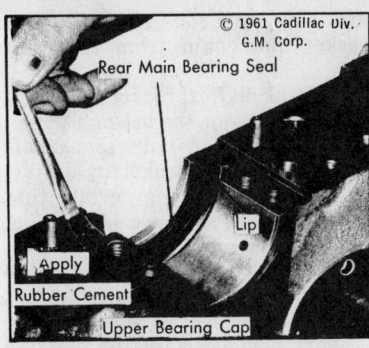

Applying Cement to Seal Surface

REAR MAIN BEARING OIL SEAL REPLACEMENT ALL MODELS FOLLOWING 1958

This oil seal has a lip and cannot be interchanged with the old type. The two seal halves are identical.

Remove the oil pan, baffle and combination oil and vacuum pump.

Remove the rear main bearing cap and loosen the bolts holding the other four bearings about three turns each. Remove the old rear main bearing seals.

Clean the groove in the cap and in the block.

Apply a slight coating of engine oil to the lips of the two seal halves.

Start the upper half into the groove in the block with the lip facing forward and rotate it into position using

Install the lower half of the seal care not to distort the seal. Press firmly on both ends to be sure it is protruding uniformly on each side. into the bearing cap with the lip facing forward and with one end of the seal over the ridge and flush with the split line. Hold one finger over this end to prevent it from slipping and push the seal into seated position by applying pressure to the other end. Be sure the seal is firmly seated and protrudes evenly on each side. Do not apply pressure to the lip as this may damage the effectiveness of the seal.

Apply rubber cement to the mating surfaces of the block and cap being careful not to get any of the cement on the bearing, the crankshaft or the seal. The cement coating should be about .010 thick, says Cadillac.

Install the bearing cap, tightening the bolts with the fingers only.

Move the crankshaft forward and rearward by pounding on the counterweight with a plastic hammer to assure alignment of the rear main bearing thrust surfaces.

Tighten the bearing bolts to 90-100 ft. lbs. Be sure to tighten the bolts of the other four bearings also.

Reinstall the combination oil and vacuum pump, the baffle and the oil pan.

TIMING CASE COVER—CHAINS AND SPROCKETS

REMOVAL OF TIMING CHAIN AND SPROCKETS

Remove the water pump and manifold assembly. Remove the engine oil pan. Remove the flywheel pulley. Remove the timing chain cover. Remove two screws and lockwashers to release the sprocket from the camshaft. Slide sprocket with chain off end of crankshaft.

When reinstalling align marks on the two sprockets nearest each other and in line with the shaft centers. The crankshaft sprocket is keyed to the crankshaft. The camshaft sprocket is located in the end of the camshaft by a dowel. Tighten camshaft sprocket screws to 15-18 ft lbs. Be careful when installing the timing case cover not to cut the felt oil seal on the key in the crankshaft. Tighten timing case cover screws to 10-12 ft. lbs. Tighten oil pan screws to 10-12 ft. lbs. and the nut to 15-18 ft. lbs. Tighten crankshaft pulley to 60-65 ft. lbs.

VALVE TIMING PROCEDURE

The chain and sprocket assembly used on all Cadillac models built since 1940 is such, that unless deliberately disturbed, the valve timing will remain as set by the factory, unless the chain and sprockets or both are badly worn or damaged.

Note: It is necessary to lower the oil pan in order to remove the crankshaft sprocket.

Remove the timing case cover.

If the timing chain and/or sprockets are being replaced because they are loose or noisy but the car is still

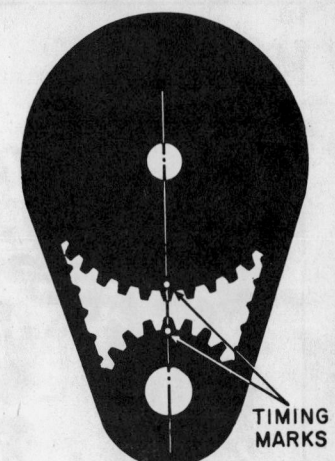

Timing gear location marks

in good operating condition, turn the crankshaft until the number 6 cylinder is in the firing position. With number 6 in the firing position the timing punch marks on the cam and crankshaft sprocket will be found to be in line with each other between the shafts centers. This is done to avoid the necessity of having to reset the ignition timing.

If it is found that the chain has "jumped" or is broken or damaged, first remove the old chain and sprocket and turn the camshaft so that the punch mark on the sprocket is pointing straight downwards with the ignition distributor rotor arm on number 6 cylinder segment. Then turn the crankshaft until number 6 piston is at top dead center. This will be when the timing punch mark on the crankshaft sprocket is pointing straight upwards.

Remove the two screws holding the camshaft sprocket to the cam-

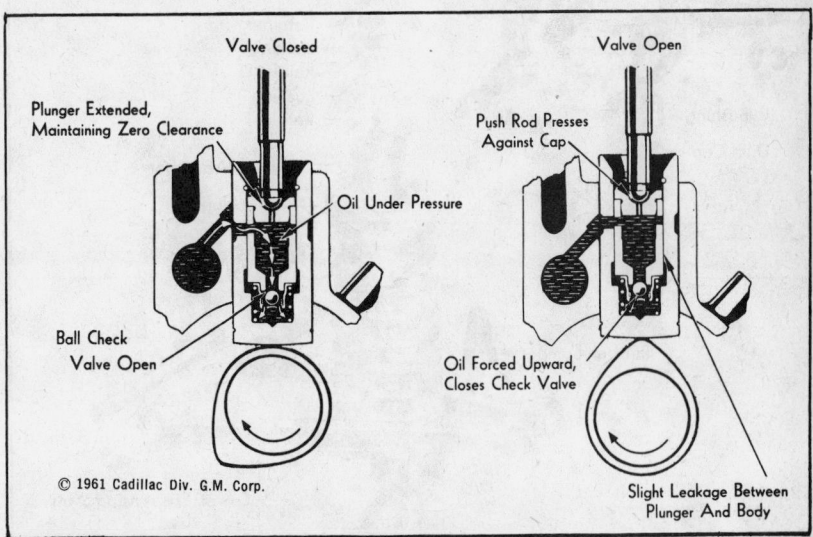

Operation of Hydraulic Valve Lifters

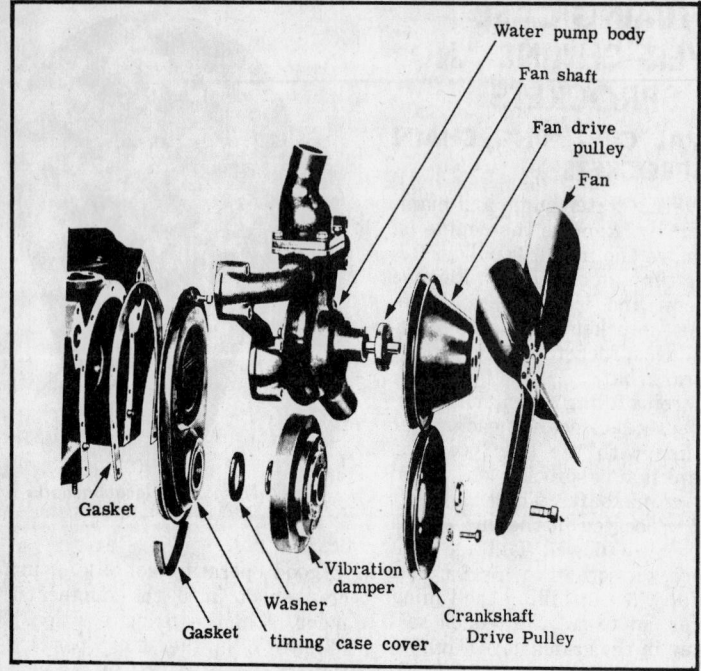

Timing Case Cover Assembly

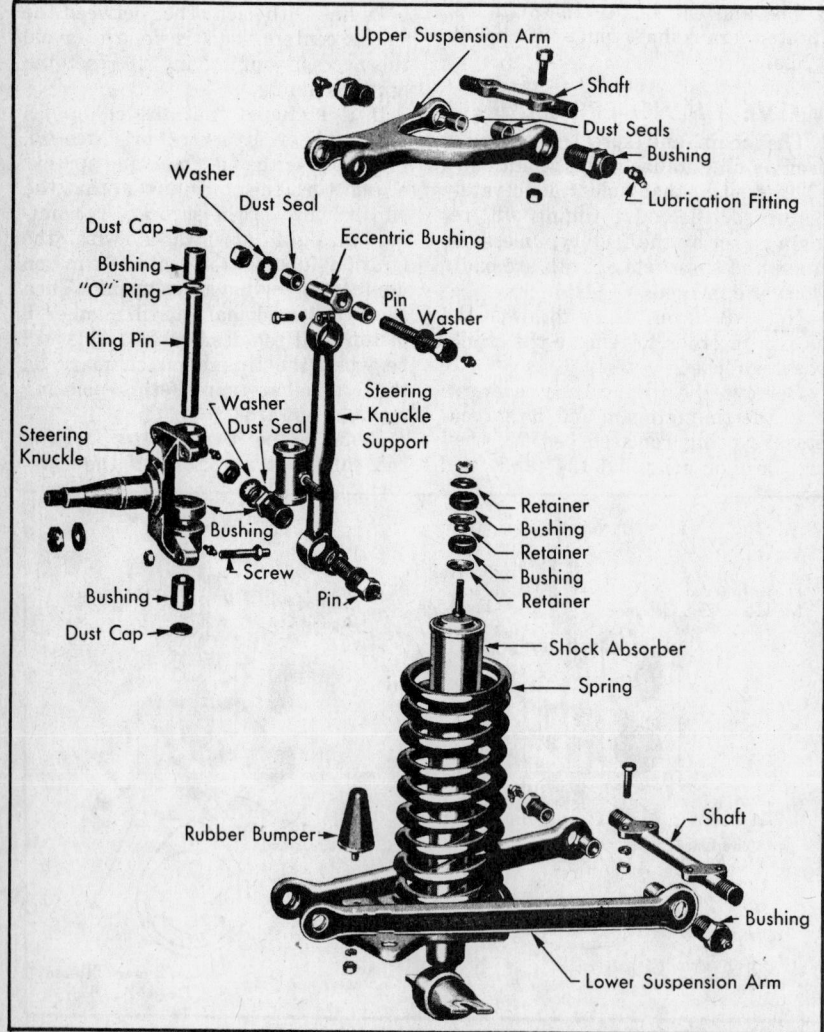

Front Suspension— 1954 thru 1956 models.

shaft and take off the camshaft sprocket and chain from the camshaft.

The crankshaft sprocket will come off readily without the use of a puller.

To replace, install crankshaft sprocket over the crankshaft until it engages the key, being certain that the timing punch mark is pointing straight upwards.

Mount the timing chain over the camshaft and the crankshaft sprocket and start the camshaft sprocket over the shaft being certain the aligning dowel is in a position where it will enter the hole in the camshaft freely and also that the timing marks on the sprockets are nearest each other and in line between shaft centers.

Camshaft sprockets sometimes go on a little stiffly; however, a comparatively easy way to install a tight fitting sprocket is to draw it on carefully with two bolts somewhat longer than the regular mounting bolts. By drawing alternately against each bolt and tapping gently with a plastic hammer even a very tight camshaft gear sprocket can be installed readily.

When the camshaft is secured, turn the engine two full revolutions until the timing marks again assume the original position and check to make certain that the punch marks, which are little round circles stamped into the front face of the sprockets, are in line between the shaft centers.

TIMING CASE COVER OIL SEAL

The engine front end oil seal is a felt ring retained in a slot in the cover and protected by a washer. Remove the cover as described above, pry out the old seal, press in the new and reinstall the cover.

FRONT SUSPENSION

REFERENCES

General instructions covering the front suspension and how to repair and adjust it, together with information on installation of front wheel bearings and grease seals, are given in the Unit Repair section under the heading: Suspension Front Repair.

Definitions of the points of steering geometry are covered in the Unit Repair section under the heading: Suspension Front Align. This article also covers trouble shooting front end alignment and irregular tire wear.

Figures covering the caster, camber, toe-in, king pin inclination, and turning radius can be found in the Front Wheel Alignment Table at the start of this section.

Over all length and tire size figures can be found in the General Chassis and Brake Specifications Table of this section.

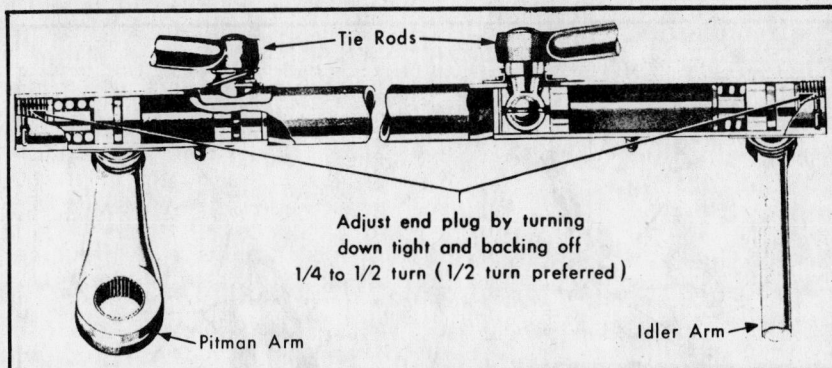

Adjust end plug by turning
down tight and backing off
1/4 to 1/2 turn (1/2 turn preferred)

Steering Drag Link.

STEERING

Power Steering Gear

Trouble shooting and repair instructions covering power steering gears are given in the Unit Repair section under the heading: Steering, Power.

Note: Power Steering Pump Belt Adjustment. Loosen pump to mounting bracket screws, move pump upward until belt is tight. Tighten mounting bracket screws with car in neutral and engine running faster than idle speed, turn steering wheel full right or left. If belt squeals it is too loose and should be tightened more.

REMOVAL OF HORN RING AND STEERING WHEEL

Disconnect horn wire at neutral safety switch on the steering column. Using an Allen wrench, loosen the screws on the underside of the steering wheel spokes near the center and remove the horn ring assembly.

Remove the nut holding the steering wheel to the steering shaft.

Use a puller to remove the steering wheel. Note the match-marking of the shaft and wheel.

When reinstalling, tighten nut to 45-50 ft. lbs.

REMOVAL AND DISASSEMBLY OF STEERING LINKAGE

Disconnect tie rod ends from steering arms at the wheels.

Remove idler arm support screws from frame side member.

Using a suitable puller, remove pitman arm from pitman shaft.

Remove steering connecting link (drag link) with tie rods, idler arm support and pitman arm attached.

Remove cotter pin, adjusting plug, stop plug, spring and ball seat from left end of drag link to release the pitman arm. Remove inside ball seat, spacer and tie rod outer ball seat to release left tie rod.

Remove cotter pin, plug and outer ball seat from right end of drag link to release idler arm. Remove inner ball seat, spring, stop plug, long spacer, cover, and ball seat to release right tie rod.

Loosen clamp screws and unscrew tie rod ends from tie rods.

Unscrew support to release idler arm from idler arm bushing. Remove bushing from idler arm cam.

When reassembling, tighten the end plugs in the drag link down tight and back off 1/4 to 1/2 turn. 1/2 turn is preferred. Tighten bushing in idler arm to 110-115 ft lbs. Turn idler-arm-support-with-seal into idler arm bushing until it bottoms and then back off 1/2 to 1 1/2 turns.

Tighten pitman arm to shaft bolt to 125-150 ft lbs.

Tighten idler arm support to frame bolts to 30 ft lbs. When connecting tie rod ends to steering arms tighten the nuts to 50-55 lbs. Check drag link height and that it is parallel to frame, then adjust toe-in. When adjusting toe-in be sure that clamp openings are aligned with slots.

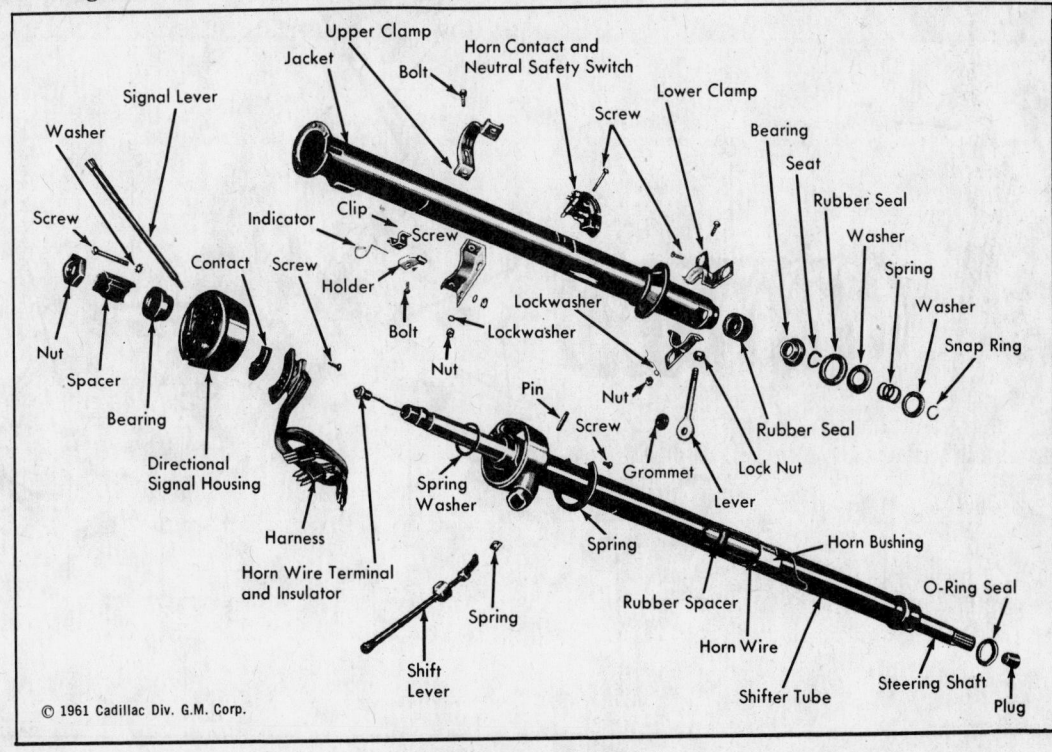

© 1961 Cadillac Div. G.M. Corp.

Steering Column Disassembled

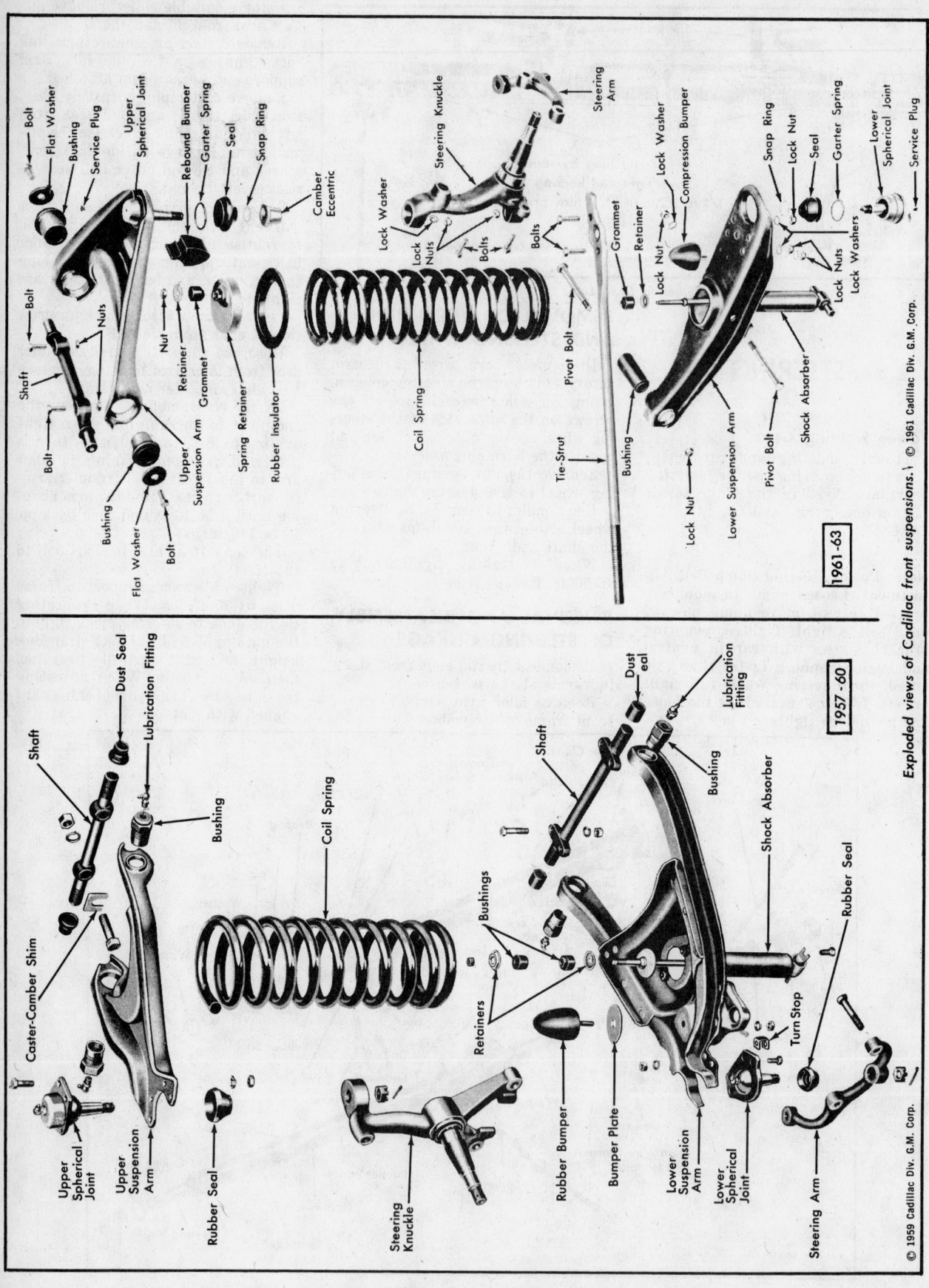

Exploded views of Cadillac front suspensions. © 1961 Cadillac Div. G.M. Corp.

1961-63

Bolt
Flat Washer
Bushing
Service Plug
Upper Spherical Joint
Rebound Bumper
Garter Spring
Seal
Snap Ring
Camber Eccentric
Steering Knuckle
Steering Arm
Lock Washer
Lock Nuts
Bolts
Bolts
Grommet
Retainer
Lock Nut
Compression Bumper
Lock Washer
Snap Ring
Lock Nut
Seal
Garter Spring
Lower Spherical Joint
Service Plug
Lock Nuts
Lock Washers
Bolt
Nuts
Nut
Retainer
Grommet
Spring Retainer
Rubber Insulator
Coil Spring
Pivot Bolt
Tie-Strut
Bushing
Shock Absorber
Pivot Bolt
Lower Suspension Arm
Lock Nut
Shaft
Bolt
Bushing
Flat Washer
Bolt
Upper Suspension Arm

1957-60

Dust Seal
Lubrication Fitting
Shaft
Dust Seal
Lubrication Fitting
Shaft
Bushing
Bushing
Shock Absorber
Coil Spring
Rubber Seal
Bushings
Turn Stop
Retainers
Bumper Plate
Lower Suspension Arm
Lower Spherical Joint
Steering Arm
Rubber Bumper
Steering Knuckle
Caster-Camber Shim
Upper Spherical Joint
Upper Suspension Arm
Rubber Seal

© 1959 Cadillac Div. G.M. Corp.

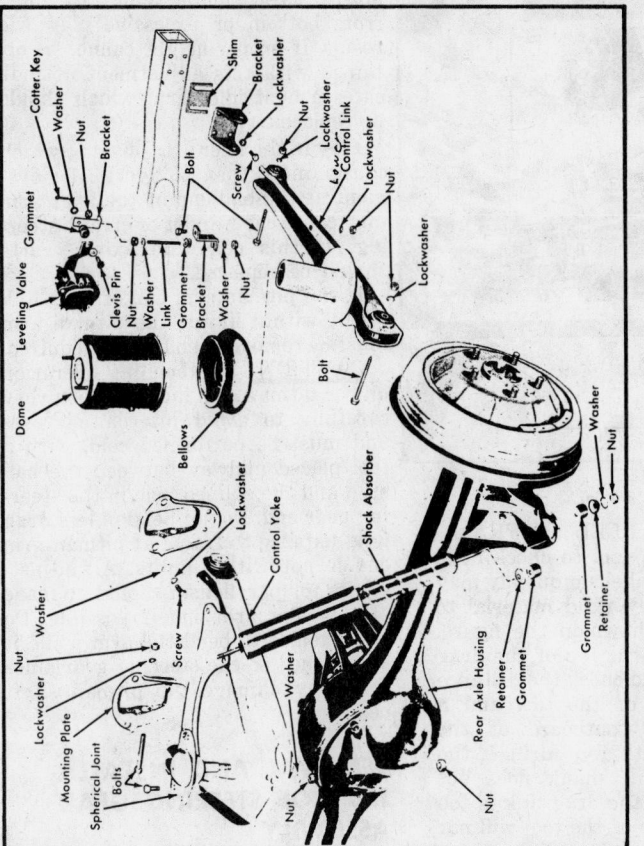

1958 Cadillac Rear Air Spring

1958 Cadillac Lift Valve Exploded

Tie Rod Clamp Position.

Tie Rod Assembly

Slots in Adjuster must line up with opening in clamps

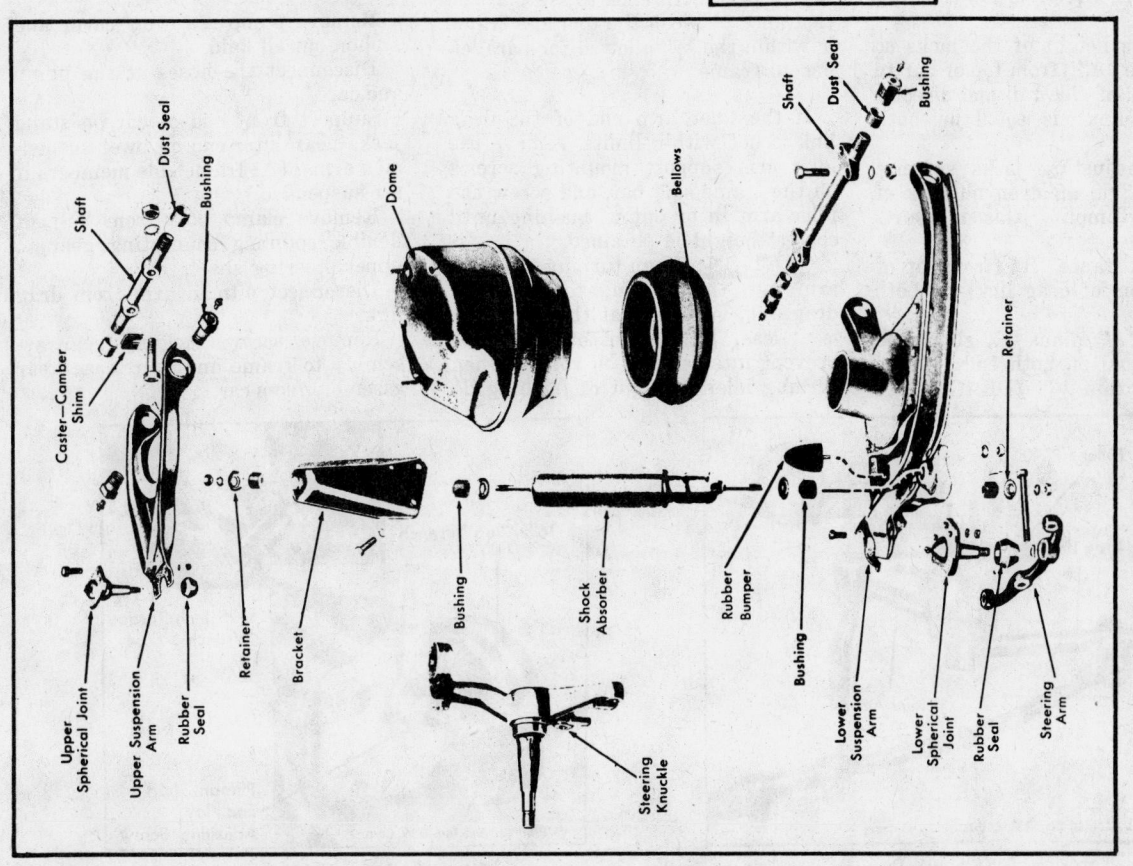

1958 Cadillac Front Air Spring

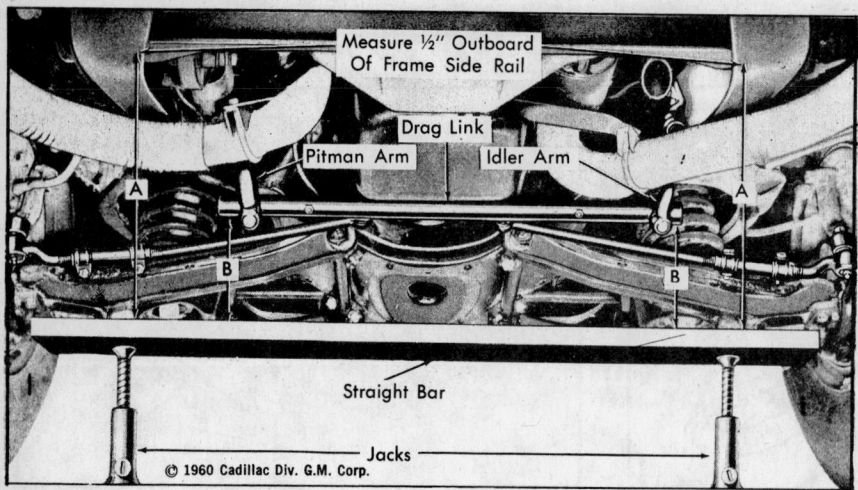

Checking that Drag Link is parallel to Frame within ⅛th inch.

CHECKING DRAG LINK HEIGHT AND THAT IT IS PARALLEL TO FRAME

The distance between the lower edge of the drag link and the flat spot on the frame side bar, directly above the drag link at each end, should be checked in cases of steering wander and instability after normal corrective adjustments have been made. The procedure outlined below may be used to measure these distances.

Place a straight bar across two adjustable jacks, directly below the drag link.

Adjust the height of the jacks so that distance "A" (from top of bar to ½" outboard of side rail and directly above drag link) is equal on both sides.

NOTE: Adjusting jacks so that distance "A" is an even number of inches will simplify this measurement.

Measure distance "B" (from top of bar to bottom of drag link) on both sides.

Distance "A" minus "B" should be 4½" and equal on both ends of the drag link within ⅛" (DRAG LINK MUST BE PARALLEL TO FRAME WITHIN ⅛"). A tool to check drag link to frame parallelism quickly may be made from any rigid material to the dimensions shown in the figure. Place the tool on the top of the drag link at the end, and check the distance between the tip of the tool and a point located ½" outboard of the frame side rail with a ¼" drill. If the tool plus the drill shank does not touch the frame, the drag link is too low, and if the tip of the tool will not fit in position, the drag link is too high. Check both ends to see that the clearance between the tool and frame is within the ⅛" allowed for parallelism to frame.

If the idler arm end of the drag link is not within limits, remove the idler arm support mounting screws on the frame side bar, and screw the idler arm in or out of bushing until correct height is obtained.

CAUTION: When turning the idler arm into the bushing to raise the drag link, be sure that the idler arm is at least ½ turn off of bottom to prevent interference on turns. When turning idler arm out of bushing do not unscrew more than 2½ turns from bottom or excessive play will result. If proper height cannot be obtained with this adjustment, it indicates a bent idler arm which should be replaced.

Play in the idler arm bushing which causes more than ⅛" vertical movement at the ball end of the idler arm may cause car wander or erratic steering. If this condition exists, parts should be replaced.

If the pitman arm end of drag link is not within limits, the pitman arm must be removed and bent as required.

CAUTION: The bending operation on the pitman arm must be done very carefully to avoid internal stresses and must be performed cold, with a tool placed midway between the ball stud and the splined hole in the steering gear end. Do not bend unless drag link distance to frame at pitman arm end is not within limits. All adjustments for parallelism should be made at the idler arm end if possible. Do not attempt to bend the arm while it is attached to the steering gear since this may damage the pitman shaft bearing.

REMOVAL AND INSTALLATION OF STEERING GEAR ASSEMBLY

Remove pump reservoir cover and siphon out all fluid.

Disconnect the hoses at the pump and cap.

Support front end of car on stand jacks near outer end of lower suspension arms. (At frame side members if air suspended.)

Remove clamp bolt from half of flexible coupling connecting gear to upper steering shaft.

Disconnect pitman arm from drag link.

Remove screws holding gear assembly to frame and so release gear assembly from car.

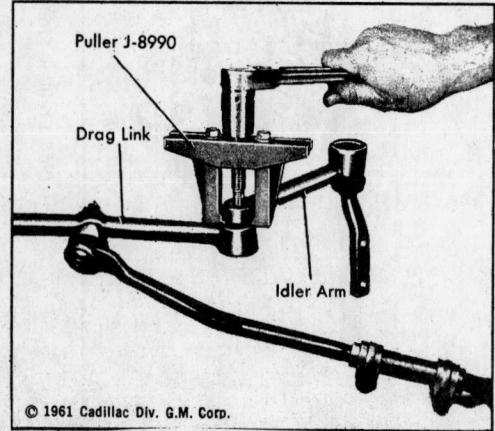

Removing Idler Arm From Drag Link

Pitman Shaft End Play Adjustment

When reinstalling tighten the clamp bolt in the upper half of the flexible coupling to 25-30 ft lbs. Reconnect the pitman arm to the drag link as described in Removal and Disassembly of Steering Linkage. Check that drag link is as described in Checking Drag Link Height and that it is Parallel to Frame.

Reconnect hoses. Be sure that flexible coupling is in a flat plane with no visible bend. If distorted in any way remove the lower steering column cover and lower clamp to jacket screw. Loosen the steering jacket clamp screws at the instrument panel and slide the steering column jacket up or down to relieve all distortion in the flexible coupling.

REPLACEMENT OF PITMAN SHAFT SEALS WITH STEERING GEAR IN PLACE IN CAR

Disconnect pitman arm from pitman shaft. Clean end of pitman shaft and housing. Tape the splines of the pitman shaft to keep them from cutting the seal. Use only one layer of tape. Too much tape will prevent passage of the seal. Using lock ring pliers remove the seal retaining ring.

Start the engine and turn the steering wheel to the right so that the oil pressure in the housing will force the seals out. Catch the seal and the oil in a container. Turn off the engine when the two seals are out.

This method of seal removal eliminates the possible scoring of the seal seats while attempting to pry them out.

Inspect the two old seals for damage to the rubber covering on the outside diameter. If it seems scored or scratched inspect the housing for burrs, etc. and remove them before installing the new seals.

Lubricate the two new seals with petroleum jelly. Put the one with a single lip in first, then put in a washer, drive seal in far enough to permit installation of double lip seal, washer and the seal retaining ring. The first seal is not supposed to bottom in its counterbore.

Fill reservoir to proper level, start engine, turn wheel to right and check for leaks.

Remove the tape and reinstall the pitman arm. Tighten nut to 100-125 ft lbs.

AUTOMATIC TRANSMISSION

QUICK SERVICE INFORMATION

The following units can be removed from the dual-coupling transmission

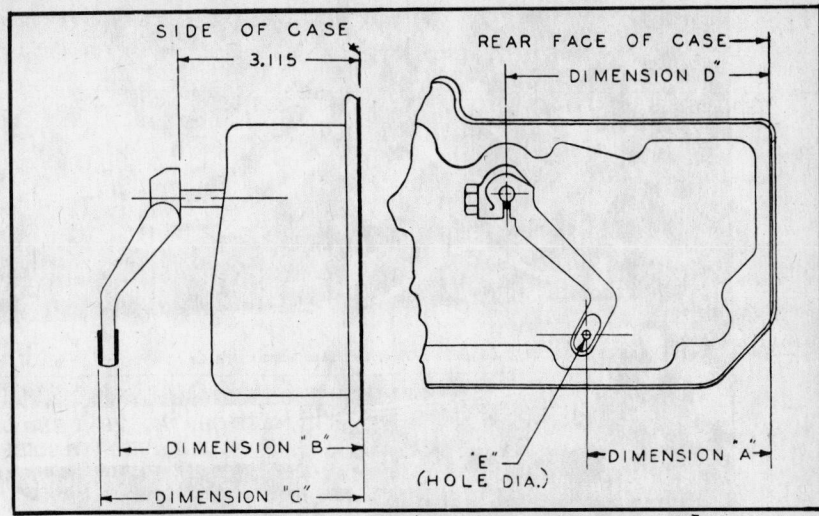

Fig. 2—Location of Throttle Lever on Dual-Range Hydramatic. The Dimension "A" is measured with the Lever against its stop

with the transmission remaining in the vehicle:

Control valve body
Accumulator and servo
Pressure regulator valve
Speedometer drive gear
Oil cooler
Governor
Parking brake bracket
Extension housing
Rear pump
Reverse stationary cone, piston, planet carrier, and internal gear

When automatic transmission trouble is reported, a road test and careful diagnosis is in order. "Transmission remove and replace" and "linkage adjustments" are covered here in the following paragraphs. For "test procedures," "transmission overhaul" and other detailed information, see "Unit Repair section," "transmission group" of this manual.

NEUTRAL SAFETY SWITCH, ALL MODELS

Check that the hand lever is correctly adjusted and that the neutral safety switch is properly positioned by this procedure.

Set the hand brake. Put the hand lever on the steering column in Drive position. Hold the ignition key (or starter button) on and slowly move the hand lever toward neutral until the starter cranks and the engine runs.

Without moving the lever further press the accelerator to determine whether or not the transmission is really in neutral.

If all is correct, the engine will have started when the hand lever got to the neutral position and the transmission will not be in gear.

Adjust the neutral safety switch by turning it and its mounting bracket until the above conditions have been met.

DUAL RANGE HYDRAMATIC 1954 THRU 1955

Table Showing Dimension "A" for Dual-Range Models

YEAR	DIMENSION "A" IN INCHES
CADILLAC	
1954	4½ in.
1955	4 in.

DUAL RANGE

Manual Linkage Adjustment

Disconnect the rod running from the thicker (the inner) of the two levers on the left side of the transmission to the lower shift lever on the steering column.

Set the hand lever in Neutral (N) position.

Move the thickest lever on the transmission as far forward as possible. (This will be Neutral position.)

Adjust the length of the rod which was disconnected from the lower shift lever, and reconnect it to the lever; so that the lever on the transmission and the hand lever have not and are not moved. Check that the hand lever can be moved freely from Neutral to Drive 4 and back and that the pointer indicates correctly.

Throttle Valve Linkage Adjustment

The theory of this adjustment is to arrange things so that the throttle valve in the carburetor is at the hot idle position when the lever on the transmission is all the way back against its stop. It sometimes happens that the lever gets bent while the transmission is being worked on.

Gauges are available which will permit rebending the lever to its proper position. Lacking the gauges, the dimension table may be used.

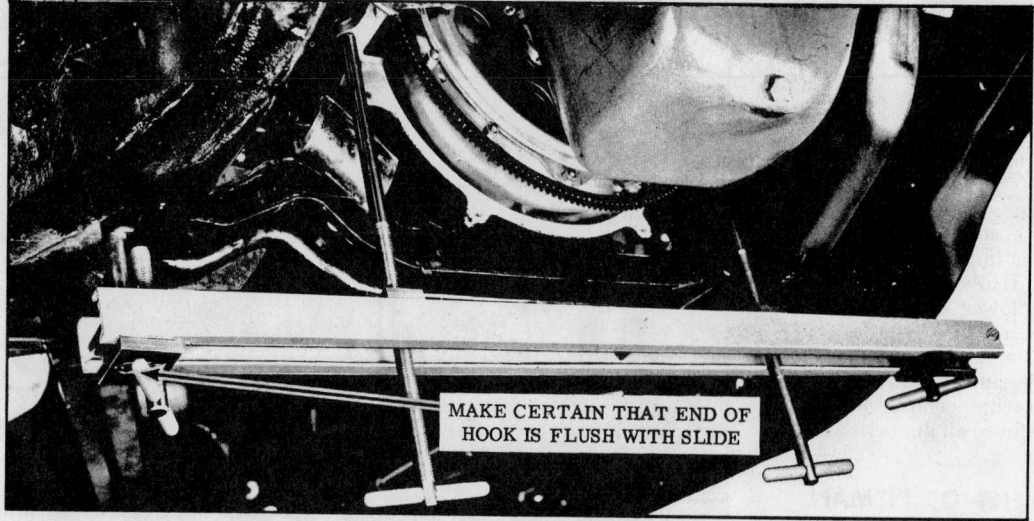

MAKE CERTAIN THAT END OF
HOOK IS FLUSH WITH SLIDE

Fig. 3—Install engine support–Dual-Coupling

Measurements are made with the connecting throttle rod removed and the lever held back against its rear stop. Fig. 2.

After the lever has been properly positioned according to the dimensions then adjust the rod running from the lever to the carburetor-accelerator linkage so that the throttle valve in the carburetor is at the hot idle position while the lever on the transmission is all the way back against its stop.

Notes for the Mechanic on Removal of Transmission

Removal of the unit from the car varies with the make and model. In general it involves the disconnection of the drive shaft and the removal of the frame cross members supporting the rear of the engine and the rear of the transmission. The flywheel housing is unbolted from the engine and the torus cover is unbolted from the flywheel.

The most important thing to remember to do is to remove the throttle and manual valve levers from the transmission before starting to remove the transmission from the car. It is very difficult to juggle the 250 pounds or more of transmission assembly around and not inadvertently bend these important levers.

For ease at reassembly the torus cover and flywheel should be match marked. The carburetor air cleaner should be removed before lowering the engine in order to remove the upper flywheel housing bolt.

DUAL-COUPLING
BEGINNING 1956

Manual Linkage Adjustment

Put the lever on the steering column in "Park" position.

Loosen adjusting nuts at the clevis on the rod running to the inner (manual) lever on the transmission.

Move the manual (inner) lever on the transmission fully forward to "Park" position.

Slide clevis of the manual lever along the rod toward the front of the car until all slack in the linkage is taken up.

Tighten lower adjusting nut against the clevis to further remove slack. Tighten upper nut.

Check that the hand lever moves freely from Park to Drive 4 and that the pointer is correctly set.

Throttle Valve Linkage Adjustment

Have engine and transmission at operating temperature. Adjust engine idle speed to 430-450 RPM.

At the transmission throttle valve lever (the outer one on the left side of the transmission). Loosen the two nuts which hold the trunnion on the rod. Hold the lever back against its stop and adjust the trunnion to suit. Tighten the lock nuts.

Upshifts will be at too high a speed if the throttle linkage is too short. Upshifts will be at too low a speed if the throttle linkage is too long.

Removal from the Car

Remove oil level stick. Drain transmission oil pan. Remove oil filler tube. The first fluid coupling can be drained now or later. Drain cooling system, disconnect battery, remove starter. Disconnect the controls at the transmission levers. Remove the levers so they won't be bent.

Remove two propeller shaft center-bearing-support-to-frame bolts, being careful to match mark the support at the frame to facilitate alignment at reassembly. Be careful also to identify the shim packs under each side of the support so they can be returned to their original position. The bent ends of the shims go down. Remove the "U" bolts and locks at the rear axle pinion. Slide the propeller shaft front yoke to the rear and so off the transmission output shaft. Tie the rear end of the double shaft up to the frame. The front portion can rest on the frame X member.

Install engine support and transmission jack. Fig. 3. Raise engine to take weight off rear engine mounts and remove mount-to-crossmember bolts. Unbolt and remove the crossmember. Lower engine enough to allow access to the upper bell housing bolts and remove them.

Remove the 4 flex plate-to-flywheel bolts. Match mark flywheel to flex plate.

Remove remaining flywheel housing bolts.

Move transmission ¾ inch to rear to clear the dowels and lower assembly down and away.

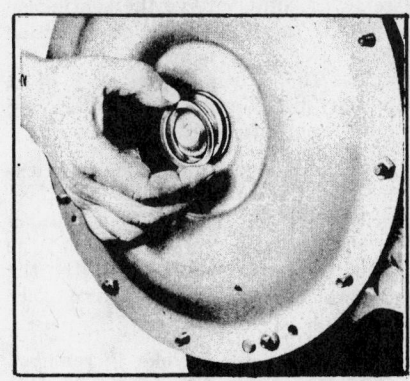

Fig. 4—Installing spacer on Flywheel Pilot in order to increase clearance between Flywheel and Flexplate to .013-.024

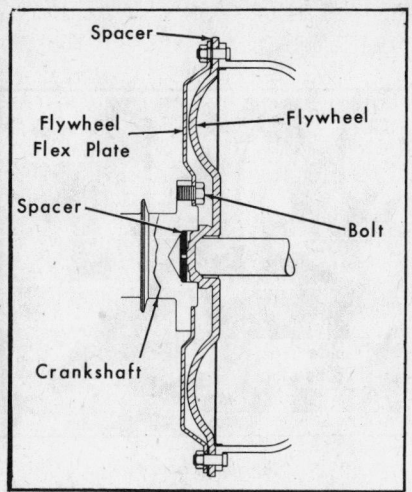

Installing Transmission to Crankshaft

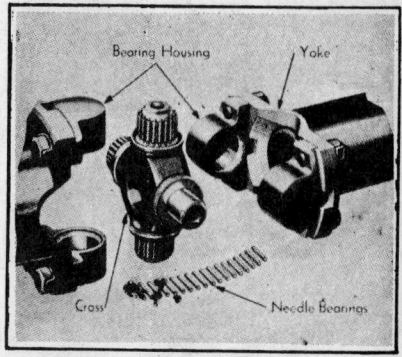

Universal Joint Showing Cross and Needle Bearings

Installation

Some models have a wick in the hole in the rear end of the crankshaft, which acts as a pilot for the first fluid coupling. Lubricate this hole or the wick with "Synthetic Oil Seal Lubricant."

Raise transmission to align with flex plate. Align match marks on flywheel and flex plate and move transmission assembly forward to engage dowels.

Install two of the lower flywheel housing bolts. Check that first fluid coupling assembly has some end play and that it is not binding in the pilot hole in the crankshaft. Push forward on the flywheel and measure clearance between a mounting pad on the flex plate and the front mounting face of the flywheel. This clearance should be between .013 and .024. If clearance is outside these limits install shims following one of the following procedures:

When Clearance Is Less Than .013

Install a spacer over flywheel pilot. Fig. 4. Then refasten the flywheel housing and again check that clearance between a mounting pad and the flywheel is between .013 and .024.

When Clearance Is More Than .024

Use vaseline coated shims on the flywheel mounting pads to reduce the clearance to between .013 and .024. Do not install the nuts but proceed to shim up the other mounting pad-to-flexplate surfaces to lie within the given limits. Try to keep the clearance equal.

Install the flywheel to flex plate

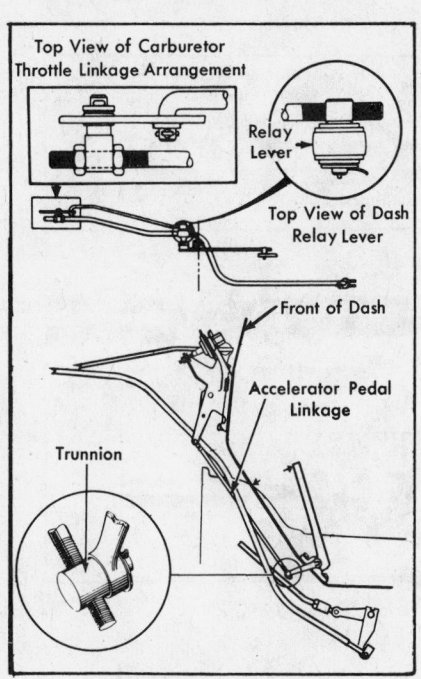

Manual Throttle Linkage

nuts and tighten evenly to 15-20 ft. lbs.

Reinstall engine support crossmember. Install the engine rear supports.

Remove engine support device and transmission jack.

Slide the drive shaft into place on the output shaft. Refasten the rear universal joint at the rear axle. Align the match marks at the drive shaft center support and install the two center bearing support-to-frame bolts.

Install the remaining flywheel housing-to-crankcase bolts and tighten evenly to 40-50 ft. lbs. Install the flywheel housing cover.

Reinstall the starter and the oil filler tube. Install the control linkages and levers, being careful to align the shaft and lever serrations before tightening.

Reconnect the cooling system, the speedometer cable, the battery; and refill the cooling system.

Pour 8 quarts of a good grade transmission fluid into the transmission. Run engine at fast idle (800 RPM) for a couple of minutes with hand lever in Neutral. Reduce speed to normal idle and add fluid to bring level to within $\frac{1}{4}$ inch of Full mark. Fluid level should be within $\frac{1}{4}$ inch of Full mark when cold; at Full mark when hot (150 degrees). From Low to Full on dipstick is one pint. It takes about 11 quarts to refill after overhaul.

UNIVERSAL JOINTS AND DRIVE LINES

REMOVE

Series 60 and 62 Thru 1956

To remove the drive shaft, disconnect, at the differential, the flange bearing from the pinion shaft yoke, lower the drive shaft and slide the front universal joint and its transmission yoke off the end of the transmission main shaft.

The universal joints may be disassembled by removing the lock rings which retain the bearings in the yoke. These lock rings are at the inner surface at the yoke and are formed like the letter C and can be driven out

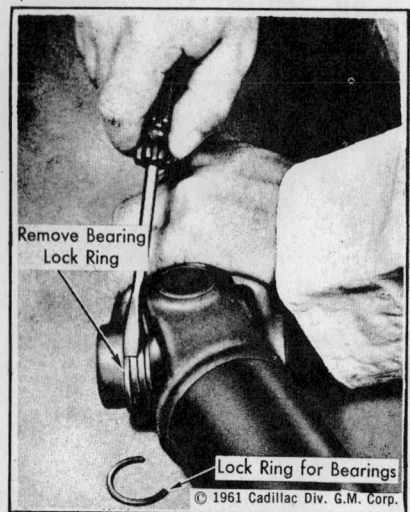

Removing bearings

Installing bearings

readily. When both sides have been removed, simply force the bearing on one side across to the other which will force that bearing out of the yoke. Then, using any kind of a dummy tool force the other bearing out the opposite side.

Usually very little difficulty is experienced in removing these bearings.

To replace the bearings simply mount the universal joint so that the bearings are pushed in with the fingers and squeeze them into place in a vise.

When the front yoke is removed from the transmission it is possible that the oil in the transmission will run out. If a dummy yoke or a piece of wood is available, the hole can be blocked up temporarily to prevent the oil from running on the floor.

All 75 Series Thru 1957 and All 1957-63 Models

Three universal joints are used on these models and there is a center bearing support.

To remove the propeller shaft assembly, first take out the center bearing support to frame bolts. Take out the U bolts and locks at the rear axle pinion universal joint. Split the rear universal joint and slide the propeller shaft and front yoke off the transmission main shaft and through the frame tunnel, removing it towards the rear. Note that on the series 75 thru 1956 the driveshaft slip joint is at the differential end of the propeller shaft.

<u>Caution</u>: Oil will probably drain out of the transmission. This can be avoided by plugging the hole where the universal joint yoke came out or

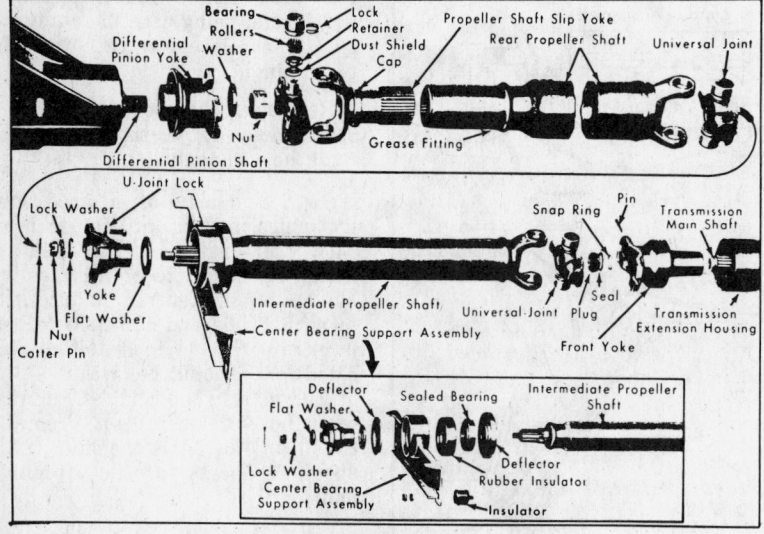

Propeller Shaft Series 75 thru 1956.

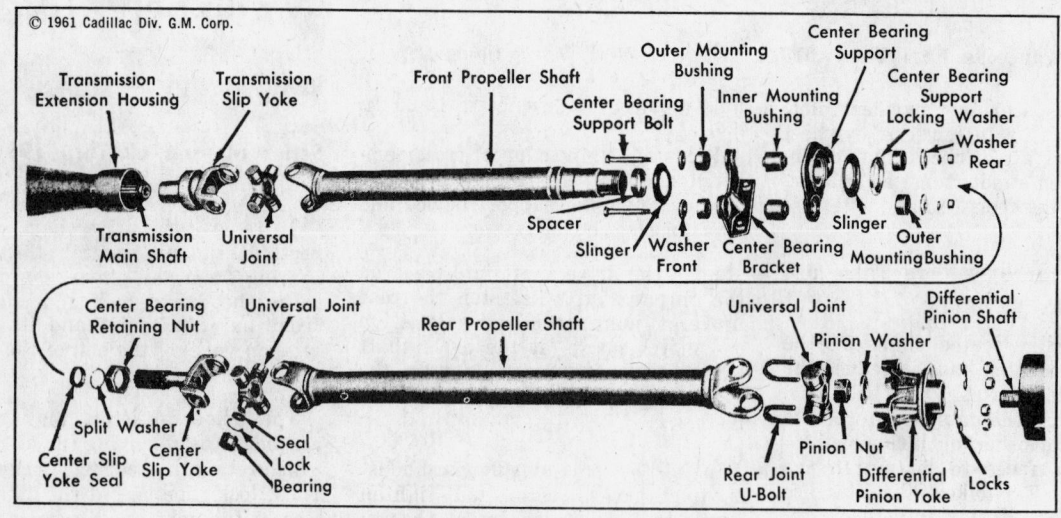

Propeller Shaft. All Models Starting with 1957.

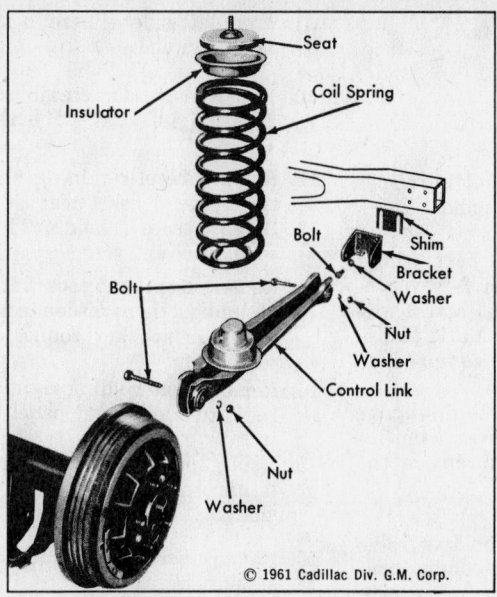

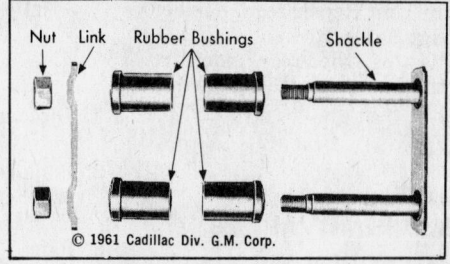

© 1961 Cadillac Div. G.M. Corp.

*Rear Spring Shackle and Rubber Bushings
Leaf Type.*

© 1961 Cadillac Div. G.M. Corp.

Rear Lower Control Link Starting in 1958.

catching the drip with a pan. Do not reuse the oil.

To replace any or all of the universal joints or the center bearing, first remove the propeller shaft from the vehicle as outlined above. For ease of handling, separate the front and rear propeller shafts by removing the center bearing nut from the intermediate joint which will permit the unit to split at that point. Universal joint cross bearings at the front and intermediate joint are held by C washers at the inner edge of each bearing. Simply drive out the C washers and driving from one side of the universal joint force the bearing out of the opposite side.

The rear universal joint bearings are held to the pinion shaft yoke by U bolts. However, they are retained in the propeller shaft in the same manner, that is, by C washers, in the driveshaft yoke.

REAR SUSPENSION

Leaf Spring Type
Thru 1957

On Cadillac models the rear spring is attached to the frame at the front and is mounted on rubber bushings and is shackled at the back to the rear end of the frame.

To remove the rear spring and/or shackle proceed as follows:

Jack up the car and bring the weight of the car on stand jacks on the frame in such a way that the

wheels are actually resting on the ground. In other words, do not jack the car high enough so that the wheels are hanging from their springs. This puts a strain on the spring shackles and makes them more difficult to take apart.

Another way to do this is to jack the car up so that the wheel does hang from its springs and then place a jack under the axle so that the spring can be located in the most advantageous position for removing the shackle.

Remove the nut from the front spring bolt and drive the bolt out through the hole in the frame.

Remove the two nuts which hold the back spring shackle one to the frame, the other to the spring.

Drive the spring shackle out of both the frame and the spring at the same time.

Disconnect the shock absorber from the lower mounting stud located on the spring U bolt plate.

Unbolt the spring U bolts and move the spring from under the car.

Note that rubber bushings are used at all mounting points on the spring. When a new spring or a new shackle is installed always use new rubber bushings.

Coil Spring Type
Starting 1958

Jack up the rear of the car and place stands under the rear housing near the differential and also under the frame. Now disconnect the shock absorber from the bracket which is welded to the rear housing. Disconnect the emergency brake cables at the clip on the rear support arm. Now place an hydraulic jack under the rear support arm at the spring. Remove the bolt that holds the rear support arm to the bracket that is welded on the rear housing. Then lower the support arm and remove the spring. To install a new spring, reverse the removal procedure.

REAR AXLE

Trouble Shooting and Adjustment

General instructions covering the troubles of the rear axle and how to repair and adjust it, together with information on installation of rear axle bearings and grease seals, are

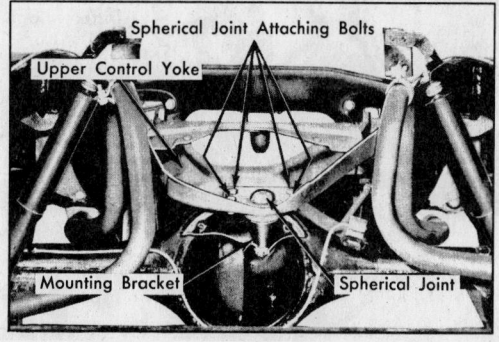

Rear Axle Upper Control Yoke Starting with 1958.

given in the Unit Repair section under the heading: Axles, Rear.

Capacities of the rear axle are given in the Capacities Tables of this section.

REAR AXLE ASSEMBLY REMOVAL

It is customary to remove the rear axle assembly from the Cadillac cars by disconnecting at the rear universal joint. It will be necessary to disconnect U bolts, stabilizer links, shock links, rear shackles, emergency brake cables and hydraulic lines. Starting with 1958 models, the rear support arms must be detached from the rear housing bracket.

Raise the back of the car high enough so that the rear will slide out with its wheels in place.

If this is impractical for the shop in which the job is being done the wheels can be taken off first, which will mean that the body has to be raised but very little in order to take out the rear axle assembly.

Cadillac does not supply internal parts for the differential carrier assembly.

They recommend that if the rear axle assembly has become damaged an entire new carrier be secured from the factory to be used as a replacement.

RADIO, R & R

1. Disconnect battery.

2. Remove five screws holding upper panel cover to lower panel.

3. Raise upper panel cover high enough to disconnect 3-way connector for map light and 3-way connector for Guide-Matic phototube unit, if car is so equipped.

4. Pull cover rearward to disengage hooks at front of cover from retainers on cowl and remove the cover.

5. Loosen set screws holding radio manual selector and volume control knobs. Remove knobs, springs, and speaker and tone control rings.

6. Using special wrench, remove retaining nut from manual selector control shaft.

7. Disconnect one 6-way wire connector and one single connector from headlamp switch. On cars equipped with fog lamps, disconnect one 3-way connector also.

8. Disconnect light bulb socket and feed wire connector from clock.

9. Remove two bezel retaining nuts from left side of bezel near headlamp switch.

10. Remove bezel retaining screw from right side of bezel near clock.

11. Remove bezel retaining nut from right side of bezel near clock.

12. Remove screw holding bezel-to-cowl brace and remove the brace.

13. Remove light bulb socket from top of radio, then disconnect front and rear speaker connectors.

14. Remove bolt holding right side of radio to instrument panel.

15. Using special wrench, remove retaining nut from volume control shaft.

16. Remove screw from radio-to-rear support bracket.

17. Move radio forward until volume control ferrule threads clear mounting bracket. Then lift radio from instrument panel sufficiently to gain access to electrical connectors.

18. Disconnect antenna lead-in cable and 4-way connector.

19. If so equipped, disconnect foot control unit from bottom of radio.

20. Remove the radio.

21. Install by reversing above procedure.

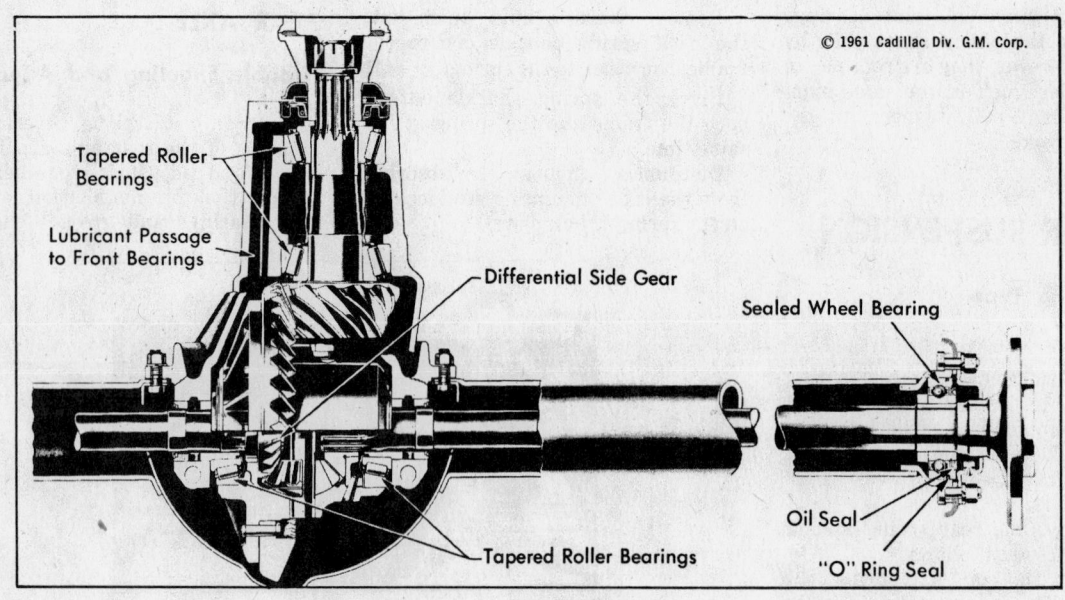

© 1961 Cadillac Div. G.M. Corp.

Tapered Roller Bearings

Lubricant Passage to Front Bearings

Differential Side Gear

Sealed Wheel Bearing

Tapered Roller Bearings

Oil Seal

"O" Ring Seal

Rear axle assembly—1958-63

Page

AIR CONDITIONING
Service 1092

BRAKES, HYDRAULIC
Adjustments 116
Bleed brakes 941
Master cylinder, R & R 116
Master cylinder service 939
Parking brake lever & cable ... 116
References 116

BRAKES, POWER
Power unit R & R 116
Power unit overhaul 954
Trouble shooting 954

CLUTCH
Clutch assembly, R & R 134
Clutch adjust 133
Pedal adjust 133

COOLING SYSTEM
Radiator core, R & R 119
Water pump, R & R 118

ELECTRICAL SYSTEM
Battery and starter, R & R 114
Engine electrical 112
Distributor reference 112
Delcotron reference 114
Delcotron specifications 105
Distributor, R & R 112
Distributor specifications 107
Fuses and circuit breakers 106
Gauges 1024
Generator, R & R 113
Generator and
    regulator specifications 105
Generator references 113
Generator service 1026
Generator trouble shooting chart 1026
Horn buttons 129
Ignition firing order & timing ... 103
Ignition timing procedure 113
Ignition timing specifications ... 104
Starter, R & R 114
Starter specifications 105
Starter systems 1046

ENGINE ASSEMBLY
Cylinder head, R & R 121
Engine assembly, R & R 119
Engine diagnosis 1012
Engine firing order & timing ... 103
Engine lubrication 127
Engine marking code 104
Engine references 119
Exhaust manifold, R & R 121
Inlet manifold, R & R 120
Main bearing, R & R 127
Main bearing oil seal, R & R ... 129
Oil filter, R & R 128
Oil pan, R & R 127
Oil pressure specifications 108
Oil pump 128

Page

ENGINE ASSEMBLY—continued
Piston and rod, R & R 126
Piston and pin specifications ... 110
Rocker arm lubrication 123
Rocker arms & shaft 123
Specifications, general engine ... 108
Specifications, tune-up engine ... 104
Timing case cover, R & R 125
Timing gear, R & R 125
Timing chain, R & R 126
Trouble shooting charts 1012
Tune-up specifications 104
Valve adjusting sequence 122
Valve specifications 110
Valves and guides 121

ENGINE LUBRICATION
Oil filter 128
Oil pan, R R 127
Oil pump, R & R 128

EXHAUST SYSTEM
Exhaust pipe, R & R 118
Muffler, R & R 118
Tail pipe, R & R 118

FUEL SYSTEM
Carburetors 972
Fuel gauge, R & R 1024
Fuel gauge service 1024
Fuel pump pressure 104
Fuel pump, R & R 117
Fuel pump service 1020
Fuel tank, R & R 117
References 117

INSTRUMENTS
Instrument cluster, R & R 114
Wiper motor, R & R 115

OVERDRIVES
Overdrive disassembly 914

REAR AXLE AND SUSPENSION
Axle assembly, R & R 142
Axle shaft 918
Axle shaft oil seal 918
Pinion bearings 918
Rear springs 142
Ring gear & pinion 918
Trouble shooting 919

SPECIFICATIONS
Battery 105
Brake cylinder sizes 106
Capacities
    Axle, rear 112
    Cooling system 112
    Crankcase 112
    Fuel tank 112
    Transmission, automatic ... 112
    Transmission, manual 112
Chassis, general 106
Cylinder head tightening 111
Delcotron specifications 105
Distributor 107
Engine, general 108
Engine, tune-up 104

Page

SPECIFICATIONS—continued
Fuses and circuit breakers 106
Generator regulators 105
Light bulbs 106
Main bearings 107
Model identification illustrations . 102
Model year identification 104
Piston and pin 110
Quick reference specifications .. 103
Regulator specifications 105
Rod bearings 107
Starters 105
Torque wrench 111
Tune-up 104
Valves 110
Wheel alignment 111
Adjust gear housing 1052

STEERING, MECHANICAL
Adjust gear housing 1052
Disassemble 131
Gear assembly, R & R 130
Horn button, R & R 129
Steering wheel, R & R 129

STEERING, POWER
Pump assembly 1058
Trouble shooting 1058
Unit overhaul 1058

SUSPENSION, FRONT
Alignment procedures 1082
Alignment 1082
Alignment specifications 111
Ball joints, R & R 1087
Coil springs 129
Intermediate steering arms ... 133
King pins and bushings 1087
Shock absorbers 1087
Support arms, pins and bushings 1087
Suspension references 129

TRANSMISSION, AUTOMATIC
Powerglide 748
Powerglide linkage adjustment .. 137
Powerglide, R & R 139
References 137
Turboglide 768
Turboglide linkage adjustment .. 139
Turboglide, R & R 140

TRANSMISSION, MANUAL SHIFT
Disassemble transmission 136
Linkage adjustments 134
Transmission, R & R 135

TROUBLE CHECKS
Procedures 1

TUNE-UP
Procedures 1012
Specifications 104
Engine diagnosis 1012

UNIVERSAL JOINT AND DRIVE SHAFT
Disassemble U joint 140
U joints & drive shaft, R & R ... 141

CHEVROLET

YEAR IDENTIFICATION

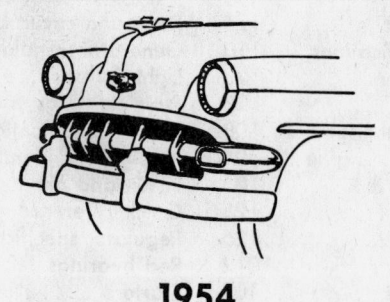

1954

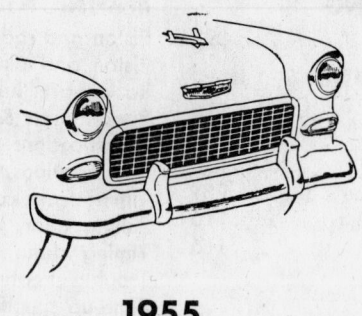

1955

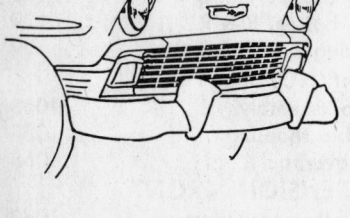

1956

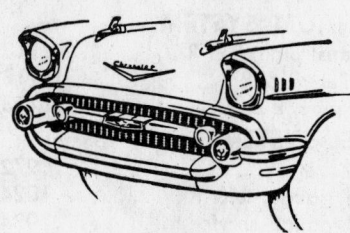

1957

1958

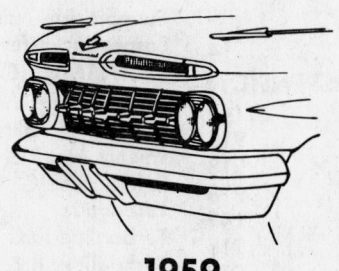

1959

1960

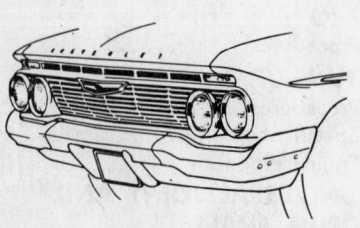

1961

1962

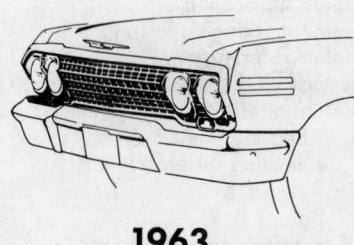

1963

QUICK WORKING SPECIFICATIONS

DISTRIBUTOR

Breaker Point Gap (In.)
1954, 6 cyl. ex. Corvette 6.... .015
1954-55, 6 cyl. Corvette ...... .016
1955, 6 cyl. ex. Corvette 6 ... .019
1956-63, all .... .019

Cam Angles (Degrees)
1954, all ex. Corvette 6 42
1954, 6 cyl. Corvette 44
1955-63, all 30

IGNITION TIMING
(Spark occurs degrees, at, before or after T.D.C.)

Dist. Vac. Line Disconnect for Initial Timing
1954, all 2A
1955-58, all 6 cyl. ....at T.D.C.
1959-63, all 6 cyl. 3-5B
1955-61, all V8 ex. those with spcl. camshaft 4B
1956-58, V8 with spcl. camshaft 12B
1959-63, V8 w/spcl. camshaft .14B
1962-63, 283 ....4B-8B
1962-63, 327 ex. Corvette ..4B-10B
1962-63, 327 Corvette 10B
1962-63, 409 V-8 ....12B

SPARK PLUGS

Year	Type	Gap
1954-55	44-5	.035 in.
1956-63	44-6	.035 in.

Note: Corvette 1954 used 43-5 and in 1955 used 43-5R, gap remained .035 in.

348 V8 W/Special Cam
1959-61 ....42—1 Comm.
1961-63, 409 V-8 ....43-N
1962-63, 327 W/Special Cam ..44-F

VALVES

Operating Tappet Clearance Mechanical Lifters (Hot)
1954 .... .010 .020
1955, 6 cyl. W/S .. .006 .013
1955, V8 W/S .... .008 .016
1955, Corvette 6 ... .006 .013
1955-56, Corvette V8 Std. .... .008 .018
1955-56, Corvette V8 Spcl. .... .012 .018
1956, V8 Spcl. ..... .008 .018
1957, "283," V8 Spcl. .012 .018
1958-62, all ..... .008 .018

Engines With Hydraulic Lifters Starting With 1958 (Hot)
All "6" adjust to remove free lash —then 1½ turn tighter.
All "V8" adjust to remove free lash—then ¾ turn tighter.

GENERATOR & REGULATOR

YEAR AND SERIES	GENERATOR		REGULATOR		
	Field Current In Amperes		Cut-out	Current Regulator Setting	Voltage Regulator Setting
	6 Volt	12 Volt	Closing Voltage		
1954 6 Cyl.	1.9	—	6.4	45	7.5
1955-57 All	—	1.5	12.8	25	14.3±1.(A)
1958-59 All	—	1.7	12.6	30	14.3±1.(A)
1960-63	—	1.7	12.6	30	14.2±1.(A)

(A) Surrounding temperatures guide this adjustment. Higher temperatures require lower settings and lower temperatures permit higher settings, within limits.

Note: Delcotron specifications, see succeeding spec. pages.

COMPRESSION PRESSURE

Variation between cylinders should not exceed 10 lbs. This is more important than actual reading.

CAPACITIES

Engine Crankcase (Quarts)
1954-63, 6 cyl. ....5 qt.
1955-63, V8 Ex. 327 ....4 qt.
1962-63, 327 ....5 qt.

Transmission, Synchro. (Pts.)
Add 1 Pint for Overdrive.
1954 ....1½
1955-63, 3 Speed 2
1958-63, 4 Speed 2½

Transmission, Automatic
Pints to refill after draining.
Note: Converter not drained starting 1953.
1954-63 Powerglide 10
1957-62 Turboglide 9

Rear Axle (Pints)
1954 ....3½
1955-63 4

Cooling System (Qts.)
1954-63, 6 cyl. 16
1955-58, V8 ex. 348 16
1959-61, all ex. 348 ....17½
1958, 348 cu. in. 22
1959-61, 348 cu. in. 21
1962-63, 6 cyl. 17
1962-63, V8 ex. 327 ....15½
1962-63, V8, 327 21
Add 1 qt. for heater

FIRING ORDER and TIMING

SPARK OCCURS:
1954-58, 6 Cyl.—Top Center (On the Ball)
1959-62, 6 Cyl.—5° BTC (First Line Clockwise from 0°)
1963— 6 Cylinder—4° BTDC (Second Line from 0°)
1955-63, V-8—4° BTC (Second Line from 0°)

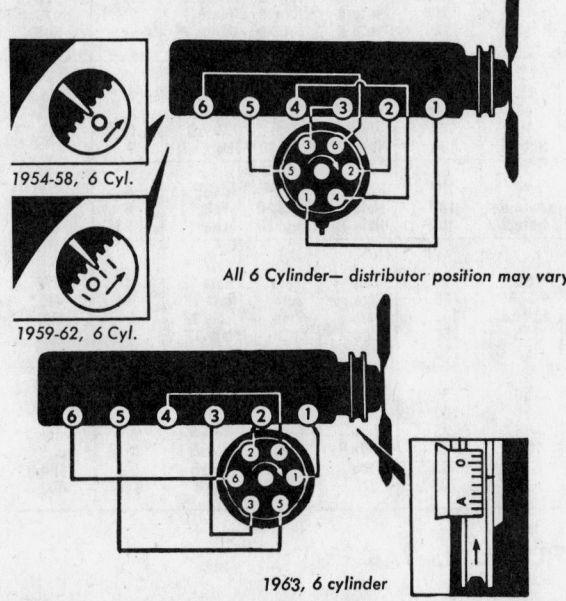

1954-58, 6 Cyl.

1959-62, 6 Cyl.

All 6 Cylinder— distributor position may vary

1963, 6 cylinder

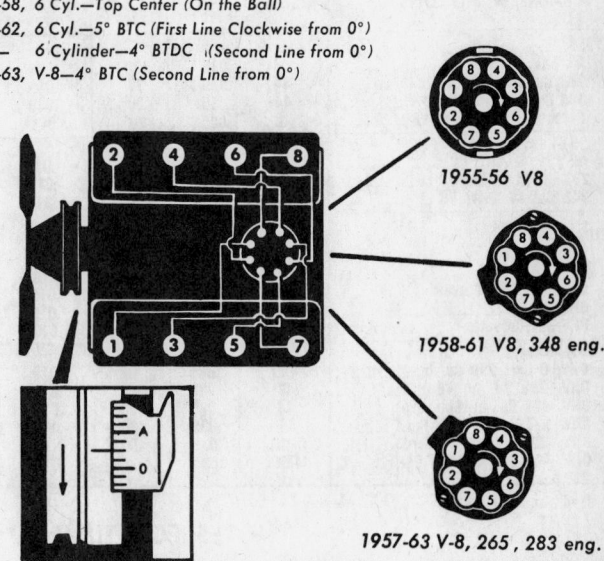

1955-56 V8

1958-61 V8, 348 eng.

1957-63 V-8, 265, 283 eng.
1962-63, 327

NOTE:
THESE ARE APPROXIMATE SETTINGS. ENGINE DESIGN, ALTITUDE, TEMPERATURE, FUEL AND ENGINE CONDITION WILL ALL INFLUENCE TIMING. THE DETERMINING FACTOR, LIMITING ADVANCE, WILL STILL BE THE "KNOCK POINT" OF THE INDIVIDUAL ENGINE.

CHEVROLET

CAR SERIAL NUMBER LOCATION AND ENGINE IDENTIFICATION

SERIAL NUMBER

SIX

Right side of engine at rear of distributor.

V-8:

Pad at the front, right cylinder block.

ENGINE IDENTIFICATION

NUMBER STAMPED IN FRONT, RIGHT HAND SIDE OF CYLINDER BLOCK CONTAINS A SUFFIX LETTER IDENTIFYING THE ENGINE USED.

IDENTIFICATION CHART		
	"Suffix"	cu. in. Displacement
SIX		
1954-56	"Z" or "Y"	235
1957-62	"A" or "B"	235
V-8		
1955-56	G or F	265
1957	C	265
1957	E, F, or G	283
1958-63	G, D, or E	283
1958-61	F, G, or H	348
1962-63	R or S	327
1961-63	Q	409

TUNE-UP SPECIFICATIONS

Year Model ENGINE TYPE	Spark Plugs Make and Number	Gap	Distributor Cam Angle	Point Gap	Arm Spring Tension	Note 1 Ignition Timing	Note 2 Compression Pressure Cranking	Valves Note 3 Tappet Clearance Hot Inlet	Exhaust	Timing Inlet Opens	Fuel Pump Pressure	Engine Idle Speed Neutral
1954												
W.O./P.G., OHV, 6 Cyl.	AC-44-5	.035	42	.015	19–23	2A	130	.010	.020	1A	4	475
W./P.G., OHV, 6 Cyl.	AC-44-5	.035	42	.015	19–23	2A	130	Zero	Zero	10½B	4	475
Corvette, OHV, 6 Cyl.	43-5 Com.	.035	44	.016	19–23	2A	130	.010	.020	19½B	4	500
1955												
W.O./P.G., OHV, 6 Cyl.	AC-44-5	.035	30	.019	19–23	TDC	130	.006	.013	1A	4	475
W./P.G., OHV, 6 Cyl.	AC-44-5	.035	30	.019	19–23	TDC	130	Zero	Zero	10½B	4	500
W.O./P.G., OHV, V8	AC-44-5	.035	30	.019	19–23	4B	150	.008	.016	12B	5	475
W./P.G., OHV, V8	AC-44-5	.035	30	.019	19–23	4B	150	Zero	Zero	18B	5	500
Corvette, OHV, 6 Cyl.	AC-43-5	.035	30	.016	19–23	TDC	130	.006	.013	19½B	4	500
Corvette, OHV, V8	AC-43-5R	.035	30	.019	19–23	4B	150	.008	.018	21½B	5	500
1956												
W.O./P.G., OHV, 6 Cyl.	AC-44	.035	32	.019	19–23	TDC	130	Zero	Zero	10½B	4	475
W./P.G., OHV, 6 Cyl.	AC-44	.035	32	.019	19–23	TDC	130	Zero	Zero	10½B	4	500
W.O./P.G., OHV, V8	AC-44	.035	32	.019	19–23	4B	150	Zero	Zero	18B	5	475
W./P.G., OHV, V8	AC-44	.035	32	.019	19–23	4B	150	Zero	Zero	26½B	5	500
W./2 F.B.C., OHV, V8	AC-44	.035	32	.019	19–23	12B	160	.008	.018	22B	5	500
Corvette, W.O./P.G., OHV, V8	AC-43Com.	.035	Note 6	.019	19–23	4B	150	Note 5	Note 6	Note 7	5	475
Corvette, W./P.G., OHV, V8	AC-43Com.	.035	Note 6	.019	19–23	4B	150	Note 5	Note 6	Note 7	5	500
1957												
All OHV, 6 Cyl.	AC-44	.035	32	.019	19–23	TDC	150	Zero	Zero	10½B	4	475
265 Cu. In., OHV, V8	AC-44	.035	30	.019	19–23	4B	150	Zero	Zero	18B	5	475
283 Cu. In., OHV, V8	AC-44	.035	30	.019	19–23	4B	155	Note 8	Note 8	Note 7	5	475
Corvette, W.O./P.G., OHV, V8	AC-44	.035	29	.018	19–23	Note 9	160	Note 8	Note 8	Note 7	5	475
Corvette, W./P.G., OHV, V8	AC-44	.035	29	.018	19–23	Note 9	160	Note 8	Note 8	Note 7	5	500
1958												
All OHV, 6 Cyl.	44	.035	30	.019	19–23	4B	130	Zero	Zero	10½B	4	475
283 Cu. In., OHV, V8	44	.035	30	.019	19–23	4B	160	Zero	Zero	12½B	6	475
348 Cu. In., OHV, V8	44	.035	30	.019	19–23	4B	160	Zero	Zero	18½B	6	475
Corvette 283 Cu. In., V8	46	.035	29	.018	19–23	Note 9	160	Note 10	Note 10	Note 7	6	475
1959-61												
All OHV, 6 Cyl.	44	.035	32	.019	19–23	4B	130	Zero	Zero	16B	4	475
283 Cu. In. OHV, V8	44	.035	30	.019	19–23	Note 9	160	Note 10	Note 10	Note 11	6	475
348 Cu. In. OHV, V8	44	.035	30	.019	19–23	Note 9	160	Note 10	Note 10	Note 11	6	475
1962												
OHV, 6 Cyl.	46	.035	32	.019	19–23	5B	130	Zero	Zero	Note 12	4	475
OHV, 283 V8	46	.035	30	.019	19–23	4B-8B	160	Zero	Zero	Note 12	6	475
OHV, 327 Exc. Corvette	44	.035	30	.019	19–23	4B-10B	160	Zero	Zero	Note 12	6	500
OHV, 409 V8	43N	.035	30	.019	19–23	12B	160	.008	.018	Note 12	9¾	700
OHV 327 Corvette	44	.035	30	.019	19–23	10B	150	Note 10	Note 10	Note 12	6	500
1963												
OHV, 6 Cyl., 230 Cu. In.	44N	.035	32	.019	19–23	3-5B	135	Zero	Zero	34B	4	475
OHV, 283 Cu. In. V8	46	.035	30	.019	19–23	4-8B	150	Zero	Zero	33B	6	475
OHV, 327 Cu. In. Standard*	44	.035	30	.019	19–23	3-6B	185	Zero	Zero	32½B	6	550
OHV, 327 Cu. In. High Per.*	44	.035	30	.019	19–23	10B	185	Zero	Zero	32½B	6	550
OHV, 409 Cu. In. Standard	C42N	.035	30	.019	19–23	12B	190	Zero	Zero	38½B	9¾	600
OHV, 409 Cu. In. High Per.	43N	.035	30	.019	19–23	12B	200	.018	.030	110B	6	600

* Used also in Corvette.

NOTES FOR TUNE-UP SPECIFICATIONS TABLE

Note 1:

All specifications are standard and should result in satisfactory performance. There are, however, factors that influence these settings, such as fuel octane value, air density, humidity, temperature, etc. Timing charts, like other specifications must be considered as averages, subject to modification.

Ignition Resistor

1955-63: A ballast resistor is used in

NOTES FOR TUNE-UP SPECIFICATIONS TABLE — continued

the primary ignition circuit of all cars equipped with 12 volt electrical system. A by-pass in the starter solenoid removes this resistor from the circuit only while the starter is operating. If the ignition switch is used to complete the circuit to the cranking motor while making underhood cranking tests, the distributor primary lead must be grounded to prevent the engine firing.

Note 2: Compression Pressure

All cylinders should read within 10 pounds. This is more important than the actual reading. Take the readings with all plugs removed, engine at normal operating temperature.

Note 3: Valves

"Zero" in the tappet clearance column indicates hydraulic lifters are standard equipment.

Note 4: 1956 Corvette Cam Angle

Dual breaker point distributor: 28-34 for each pair of breaker points.

Note 5: 1956 Corvette Tappet Clearance (Inlet)

.008 with standard camshaft
.012 with special camshaft

Note 6: 1956 Corvette Tappet Clearance (Exhaust)

.018 with any camshaft

Note 7: 1956-58 Corvette Valve Timing

12½ B with standard camshaft
35 B with special camshaft

Note 8: 1957 Tappet Clearance (Inlet)

Zero with standard camshaft
.012 with special camshaft

(Exhaust)

Zero with standard camshaft
.018 with special camshaft

Note 9: 1957-61 Ignition Timing

4 B with std. camshaft
12 B with spcl. camshaft plus either two 4 brl. carb. or fuel injection

Note 10: 1958-62 Tappet Clearance

Standard Models have Hydraulic Lifters, Zero Clearance.
Models with special Camshaft have solid lifters: Clearance: Inlet—.012; Exhaust—.018.

Note 11: 1959-61 V8 Valve Timing

WITH STANDARD CAMSHAFT
283 cu. in.: Inlet Opens 12½B
348 cu. in.: Inlet Opens 18½B

WITH SPECIAL CAMSHAFT
Both Engines: Inlet Opens 35B

Note 12:

6 Cyl.	62° BTC
283, V8	33° BTC
327, V8	32½° BTC*
327, V8 Spec. Cam	35° BTC*
409, V8	36° BTC

* Including Ramps.

BATTERY AND STARTER SPECIFICATIONS

| YEAR | BATTERY | | | | STARTERS | | | | | | Brush Spring Tension |
| | Ampere Hour Capacity | Volts | Group Number | Terminal Grounded | Lock Test | | | No-Load Test | | | |
					Amps	Volts	Torque	Amps	Volts	R.P.M.	
1954											
6 Cyl.	105	6	1	Neg.	550	3.2	11	80	5.6	5500	26
1955											
All ex. Corv.	50	12	2SM	Neg.	415	5.8	12	65	10.4	7900	37
Corvette 6 Cyl.	105	6	1	Neg.	600	3.0	14	70	5.0	5000	26
Corvette V8	50	12	2SM	Neg.	415	5.8	12.7	65	10.4	7900	37
1956											
6 Cyl.	53	12	2SM	Neg.	415	5.8	12.7	65	10.3	7900	37
V8	53	12	2SM	Neg.	415	5.8	12.7	65	10.4	8900	37
1957											
All Models	53	12	2SM	Neg.	290	4.2	Locked	75	10.3	6900	37
1958-61											
All ex. 348 Cu. In. V8	53	12	2SM	Neg.	290	4.2	Locked	75	10.6	7800	37
348 Cu. In. V8	63	12	2SM	Neg.	330	3.5	Locked	85	10.6	4300	37
1962-63											
6 Cyl.	53	12	2SMR	Neg.	330	3.5	Locked	65	10.6	6500	37
V8	61	12	2SMD	Neg.	330	3.5	Locked	65	10.6	7800	37
1963											
6 Cyl., 230 Cu. In.	44	12	2SMR	Neg.	330	3.5	Locked	63	10.6	7800	37
V8, 283 Cu. In.	44	12	2SMD	Neg.	330	3.5	Locked	63	10.6	7800	37
V8, 327 & 409 Cu. In.	61	12	2SMD	Neg.	330	3.5	Locked	83	10.6	4400	37

DELCOTRON AND A.C. REGULATOR SPECIFICATIONS

| Delcotron Model Number | Ground Polarity | Field Current Draw (Amperes) | CURRENT OUTPUT | | | RUNNING VOLTAGE | | | REGULAR | | FIELD RELAY | |
			Engine R.P.M.	Amperes	Volts	Engine R.P.M.	Amperes	Volts @ 125°	Model Number	Point Gap	Armature Air Gap	Closing Voltage (Cold)
1100600-13	Neg.	1.9 to 2.2	1100	12.	14	6500	42	13.5-14.3	1119502	.015"	.015	6.5-8.5
1100601	Neg.	1.9 to 2.2	1100	5.	14	6500	52	13.5-14.3	1119502	.015"	.015	6.5-8.5
*1117750-65	Neg.	4.1 to 4.5	1100	24.	14	6500	62	13.3-13.9	9000567	.027"	.014	5.0-9.5
1963												
1100628	Neg.	1.9 to 2.3	1100	12.	14	6500	37	13.5-14.4	1119512	.014"	.015	2.3-3.7

NOTE: Heavy Duty (6.2" diameter) models are identified in the above chart with an asterisk (*)

CHEVROLET

D.C. GENERATOR AND REGULATOR SPECIFICATIONS

YEAR	GENERATORS			REGULATORS				
	Field Current in Amperes		Brush Spring Tension	Cut Out Relay		Current and Voltage Regulator	Current Regulator Setting	Voltage Regulator Setting
	At 6 Volts	At 12 Volts		Air Gap	Closing Voltage			
1954 6 Cyl.	1.9	....	28	.020	6.4	.075	45	7.5
1955-57 All Models	....	1.5	28	.020	12.8	.075	25	14.3
1958-62 All Models	....	1.7	28	.020	12.6	.075(A)	30	14.3

(A): Voltage Regulator Air Gap

Double Contact Voltage Regulator: Lower Points—.067; Upper Points—.016

Caution: Never ground the generator field when the double contact voltage regulator is connected to the generator. To do so will burn up the upper set of voltage regulator contacts.

FUSE AND CIRCUIT BREAKERS

1954: All lights are protected by one 30 amp. circuit breaker on headlight switch.

1955-57: There are two 13 amp. circuit breakers in the light switch. The headlights and the parking lights are on one of these circuit breakers. All the other lights on the car are on the other. If any accessories are added there is available an optional fuse block for mounting on the upper inside of the dash panel to the left of the steering column.

1958-63: A 15-amp. circuit breaker in the lighting switch protects all driving and instrument lights. All other lights are protected thru fuses on the fuse block.

1956-58: Instrument Panel Lights: Fuse on switch AGA 3.

1957 Radio: SFE 7½.

1957 Heater, Back-up, Underhood, Spot, Brake on, Overdrive: SFE 9.

1957 Power Seats and Windows: HD Circuit Breaker.

1958-63:

Tail, Dome, Courtesy: ....10-amp. fuse
Manual Radio: .... 4-amp. fuse
Automatic Radio: ......7.5-amp. fuse
Heater: ....10-amp. fuse
Air Conditioning: ....20-amp. fuse
Back-up and Brake-on: ..10-amp. fuse
Power Antenna: ....15-amp. fuse

GENERAL CHASSIS and BRAKE SPECIFICATIONS

YEAR AND MODEL		CHASSIS		BRAKE CYLINDER BORE		
		Overall Length in Inches	Size Tire	Master Cyl. Inch	Wheel Cylinder Diameter Inch Front	Rear
Chevrolet						
1954	6 Cyl. All	196.4	6.70x15	⅞	1⅛	1.0
1955	6-8 Cyl. All	195.6	6.70x15	1.0	1⅛	1.0
1956	6-8 Cyl. All	197.5	6.70x15	1.0	1⅛	1.0
1957	6-8 Cyl. All	200.0	7.50x14	1.0	1⅛	1.0
1958	6-8 Cyl. Except Conv. & Sta. Wag.	209.1 209.1	7.50x14 8.00x14	1.0 1.0	1⅛ 1⅛	1.0 1.0
1959	6-8 Cyl. Except Conv. & Sta. Wag.	195.3 195.3	7.50x14 8.00x14	1.0 1.0	1⅛ 1⅛	1.0 1.0
1960	6-8 Cyl. Except Conv. & Sta. Wag.	210.8 210.8	7.50x14 8.00x14	1.0 1.0	1 3/16 1 3/16	1.0 1.0
1961	6-8 Cyl. Except Conv. & Sta. Wag.	210.8 210.8	7.50x14 8.00x14	1.0 1.0	1 3/16 1 3/16	1.0 1.0
1962	6-8 Cyl. Except Sta. Wag.	209.6 209.6	7.50x14 8.00x14	1.0 1.0	1 3/16 1 3/16	1.0 1.0
1963	6 Cyl. Sedans Convt. Sta. Wagon V8, 327 Cu. In. 409, Cu. In.	210.4 210.4 210.4 210.4 210.4	7.00x14 7.50x14 8.00x14 7.50x14 8.00x14	1.0 1.0 1.0 1.0 1.0	1 3/16 1 3/16 1 3/16 1 3/16 1 3/16	1.0 1.0 1.0 1.0 1.0
Corvette						
1955		167.0	6.70x15	1.0	1⅛	1.0
1956-57		168.0	6.70x15	1.0	1⅛	1.0
1958		177.2	6.70x15	1.0	1⅛	1.0
1959		177.2	6.70x15	1.0	1⅛	1.0
1960		177.2	6.70x15	1.0	1 3/16	1.0
1961		177.2	6.70x15	1.0	1⅛	⅞
1962		176.7	6.70x15	1.0	1 3/16	1.0
1963		175.3	6.70x15	1.0	1 3/16	1.0

LIGHT BULBS
(C.P. MEANS CANDLE POWER)

Telltale Lights for Headlamp Beam and the Direction Signals, also Ignition Switch Light:

6 Volt, No. 51; 12 Volt, No. 53. (One C.P. miniature bayonet base.)

Instrument Cluster Light, Glove Compartment Light, Radio Dial Light, Heater Control Light, Powerglide Quadrant and Telltale Lights for Generator and Oil Pressure:

6 Volt, No. 55; 12 Volt, No. 57. (2 C.P. miniature bayonet base.)

License, Clock and Dome Lights:

6 Volt, No. 63; 12 Volt, No. 67. (4 C.P. single contact base.)

Courtesy Light:

6 Volt, No. 81; 12 Volt, No. 89. (6 C.P. single contact.)

Rear Quarter Light:

6 Volt, No. 82; 12 Volt, No. 90. (6 C.P. double contact.)

Front Combination Park and Signal Light, also Combination Tail, Signal and Stop Light:

6 Volt, No. 1154; 12 Volt, No. 1034. (4 & 32 C.P. double contact.)

Headlight (Sealed Beam):

6 Volt, No. 5040; 12 Volt, No. 5400. (40 & 50 C.P. three contact.)

Headlight (Twin Sealed Beam):

High Beam (Inner): 12 Volt, No. 4001. (37.5 watts. Two contact base.)

Low and High Beam (Outer): 12 Volt, No. 4002. (37.5 & 50 watts. Three contact base.)

DELCO-REMY DISTRIBUTOR SPECS.

Year	Model	Delco-Remy No.	Rotation	Cam Angle Degrees	Breaker Point Gap Inch	Breaker Arm Spring Tension	Governor Control @Dist. R.P.M. Adv. Starts	Governor Control @Dist. R.P.M. Full Adv.	Vac. Control Data Inches of Vacuum To Start Advance	Vac. Control Data Inches of Vacuum for Full Advance	Vac. Control Data Max. Adv. of Dist. in Degrees
1954-55	Corvette	1112314	C	38-45	.016	19-23	1@375	13@1750	4-6	7½-10	7½
1954	Std. Trans.	1112388	C	38-45	.016	19-23	1@375	13@1750	7-8½	18½	10
	Powerglide	1112396	C	28-35	.019	19-23	1@375	13@1750	7-8½	18½	10
1955-56	Six	1112403	C	26-33	.019	19-23	1@375	13@1750	4-6	7½-10	7½
1955	V8	1110847	C	26-33	.019	19-23	1@400	16@1800	5-7	12-14½	11¾
1956	V8-Std. Tr.	1110847	C	26-33	.019	19-23	1@400	16@1800	5-7	12-14½	11¾
	V8 Powerglide	1110866	C	26-33	.019	19-23	1@325	8½@900	5-7	12-14½	11¾
	V8	1110866	C	26-33	.019	19-23	1@325	8½@900	5-7	12-14½	11¾
	Corvette	1110860	C	26-33	.019	19-23	1@350	14@1750	None	None	None
1957	Six	1112403	C	26-33	.019	19-23	1@375	13@1750	4-6	7½-10	7½
	V8-265 Eng.	1110874	C	28-32	.019	19-23	1@400	16@1800	5-7	16-18	12
	V8-283 Eng.	1110890	C	28-32	.019	19-23	1@400	14@1850	7-9	14-16	8½
	Corvette	1110891	C	28-32	.019	19-23	1@400	14@1850	None	None	None
1958	Six	1112403	C	26-33	.019	19-23	1@375	13@1750	4-6	7½-10	7½
	V8-283 Eng.	1110920	C	28-32	.019	19-23	1@300	14@1875	7-9	13½-16½	8½
	V8-348 Eng.	1110907	C	28-32	.019	19-23	1@300	13@2000	7-9	13½-16½	8½
	V8-283 Eng.	1110915	C	28-32	.019	19-23	1@325	15@1875	4-6	12½-14½	13
1959-61	Six	1112403	C	28.35	.019	19-23	1@375	13@1750	4-6	7½-10	6½-8½
	V8-283	1110947	C	28-32	.019	19-23	1@600	14@1875	7-8	14-15½	7½
●	Corvette	1110946	C	28-32	.019	19-23	1@600	14@1875	7-8	14-15½	7½
●●	Corvette	1110891	C	28-32	.019	19-23	1@400	14@1850	None	None	None
	348 Std. Eng.	1110948	C	28-32	.019	19-23	1@700	12@2300	7-8	14-15½	7½
●●●	283 Eng	1110914	C	28-32	.019	19-23	1@500	11@3000	None	None	None
●●●●	283 Eng	1110915	C	28-32	.019	19-23	1@325	14@1875	4-6	12½-14½	11-13
1962	Six	1112403	C	28.35	.019	19-23	1@600	13@1750	6	15½	11
	V8-283	1110947	C	26-33	.019	19-23	1@600	13@1875	8	15½	7½
	V8-327	1110987	C	26-33	.019	19-23	1@700	12@2300	8	15½	7½
	V8-409	1111006	C	26-33	.019	19-23	1@700	12@2300	8	15½	12
1963	Six	1110280	C	28-35	.019	19-23	1@600	13@1700	6	15½	11
	V8-283 Eng.	1111015	C	26-33	.019	19-23	1@600	13@1800	8	15½	7½
	V8-327 Std.*	1111016	C	26-33	.019	19-23	1@650	12@2300	8	15½	7½
	V8-327 High Per.*	1111016	C	26-33	.019	19-23	1@700	12@2300		None	None
	V8-409 Std.	1111023	C	26-33	.019	19-23	1@700	12@2350	8	15½	12
	V8-409 High Per.	1111023	C	26-33	.019	19-23	1@700	12@2350		None	None

Note: Starting with 1957, all V8 point adjustments are made by turning the adjustment in until the engine misses then back off ½ turn.
- ● Four barreled carburetor & dual exh.
- ●● Two four barreled carburetors.
- ●●● Fuel injection & special carburetors.
- ●●●● Fuel injection.
- * Used also in Corvette.

CRANKSHAFT BEARING JOURNAL SIZES

YEAR & ENGINE	MAIN BEARING JOURNALS Journal Diameter	MAIN BEARING JOURNALS Oil Clearance	MAIN BEARING JOURNALS End Play of Shaft	MAIN BEARING JOURNALS End Play Held by	CONNECTING ROD BEARING JOURNALS Journal Diameter	CONNECTING ROD BEARING JOURNALS Oil Clearance	CONNECTING ROD BEARING JOURNALS End Play
1954							
6 Cyl. All	Note 1	.0015	.006	No. 3	2.3115	.0017	.009
1955-57							
6 Cyl. All	Note 1	Note 2	.006	No. 3	2.3115	.0018	.007
V8 All	2.2983	.0021	.004	No. 5	1.9995	.0017	.011
1958-61							
6 Cyl.	Note 1	Note 2	.006	No. 3	2.3115	.0017	.007
283 Cu. In. V8	2.2983	.0021	.004	No. 5	1.9995	.0017	.011
348 Cu. In. V8	2.4985	.0019	.005	No. 5	2.1995	.0017	.011
1961-62							
409 Cu. In. V8	2.5001	.0019	.008	No. 5	2.1995	.0017	.018
1962							
6 Cyl.	Note 1A	Note 2	.0065	No. 3	2.3111	.0017	.0075
283-327 Cu. In. V8	2.3004	.0021	.004	No. 5	1.9995	.0017	.011
1963							
6 Cyl., 230 Cu. In.	2.3009●	.002	.004	No. 7	1.999-2.000	.0017	.011
V8, 283 Cu. In.	2.3004	.002	.004	No. 5	1.999-2.000	.0017	.011
V8, 327 Cu. In.	2.3009●●	.002	.004	No. 5	1.999-2.000	.0017	.011
V8, 409 Cu. In.	2.5001●●●	.002	.008	No. 5	2.1988-2.1998	.0017	.018

- ● Thrust Bearing (No. 7) 2.3004"
- ●● Thrust Bearing (No. 5) 2.3006"
- ●●● Thrust Bearing (No. 5) 2.5008"

CHEVROLET

NOTES FOR CRANKSHAFT BEARING JOURNAL TABLE

Note 1: Main Bearing Journal Diameter

1954-61 6 Cyl. Engines:
No. 1—2.6840; No. 2—2.7150
No. 3—2.7460; No. 4.—2.7770

Note lA: Main Bearing Journal Diameter

1962-63, 6 Cyl.:
No. 1 2.6856   No. 2 2.7166
No. 3 2.7478   No. 4 2.7788

Note 2: Main Bearing Journal Oil Clearance

1955-63, All 6 Cyl.:
No. 1 & No. 2—.0016
No. 3 & No. 4—.0018

GENERAL ENGINE SPECIFICATIONS

Year Model Engine Type	Bore and Stroke	Number of Main Bearings	Type of Valve Lifter Used	Cubic Inch Displacement	AMA Horsepower	Advertised Horsepower at Stated RPM	Advertised Torque at Stated RPM	Compression Ratio	Oil Pressure At 30 MPH (Note 1)	Cam Shaft Drive
1954										
W.O./P.G., OHV, 6 Cyl.........	3⁹⁄₁₆x3¹⁵⁄₁₆	4	Solid	235.5	30.4	115@3700	200@2000	7.5-1	45	Gear
W./P.G., OHV, 6 Cyl.........	3⁹⁄₁₆x3¹⁵⁄₁₆	4	Hydraulic	235.5	30.4	125@4000	200@2000	7.5-1	45	Gear
Corvette, OHV, 6 Cyl..........	3⁹⁄₁₆x3¹⁵⁄₁₆	4	Solid	235.5	30.4	150@4200	223@2400	8.0-1	45	Gear
1955										
W.O./P.G., OHV, 6 Cyl.........	3⁹⁄₁₆x3¹⁵⁄₁₆	4	Solid	235.5	30.4	123@3800	207@2000	7.5-1	30	Gear
W./P.G., OHV, 6 Cyl.........	3⁹⁄₁₆x3¹⁵⁄₁₆	4	Hydraulic	235.5	30.4	136@4200	209@2200	7.5-1	30	Gear
All OHV, V8..................	3¾x3	5	Note 2	265.0	45.0	Note 3	Note 4	8.0-1	30	Chain
Corvette, OHV, 6 Cyl.........	3⁹⁄₁₆x3¹⁵⁄₁₆	4	Solid	235.5	30.4	155@4200	225@2800	8.0-1	30	Gear
Corvette, OHV, V8............	3¾x3	5	Solid	265.0	45.0	195@5000	260@3000	8.0-1	30	Chain
1956										
All OHV, 6 Cyl...............	3⁹⁄₁₆x3¹⁵⁄₁₆	4	Hydraulic	235.5	30.4	140@4200	210@2400	8.0-1	30	Gear
All OHV, V8..................	3¾x3	5	Note 5	265	45.0	Note 6	Note 7	Note 8	30	Chain
Corvette, OHV, V8...........	3¾x3	5	Solid	265	45.0	Note 9	Note 10	9.25-1	30	Chain
1957										
All OHV, 6 Cyl...............	3⁹⁄₁₆x3¹⁵⁄₁₆	4	Hydraulic	235.5	30.4	140@4200	210@2400	8.0-1	30	Gear
OHV, V8 (Note 11)..........	3¾x3	5	Hydraulic	265	45.0	162@4400	257@2400	8.0-1	30	Chain
OHV, V8 (Note 12)..........	3⅞x3	5	Note 13	283	48.0	←————— Note 14 —————→			30	Chain
1958										
All OHV, 6 Cyl...............	3⁹⁄₁₆x3¹⁵⁄₁₆	4	Hydraulic	235.5	30.4	145@4200	215@2400	8.25-1	35	Gear
OHV, V8.....................	3⅞x3	5	Hydraulic	283.0	48.0	Note 15	Note 15	Note 15	35	Chain
Turbo-Thrust V8 Notes 19 & 20	4⅛x3¼	5	Hydraulic	348.0	54.5	Note 16	Note 16	Note 16	35	Chain
Corvette V8	3⅞x3	5	Note 17	283	48.0	Note 18	Note 18	Note 18	35	Chain
1959-61										
All OHV, 6 Cyl...............	3⁹⁄₁₆x3¹⁵⁄₁₆	4	Hydraulic	235.5	30.4	135@4000	217@2200	8.25-1	35	Gear
Std. OHV, V8................	3⅞x3	5	Note 17	283	48.0	185@4600	275@2400	Note 21	35	Chain
Turbo-Thrust V8, Notes 19 & 20 ...	4⅛x3¼	5	Note 17	348	54.5	250@4400	355@2800	Note 22	35	Chain
1962										
6 Cyl........................	3⁹⁄₁₆x3¹⁵⁄₁₆	4	Hydraulic	235.5	30.4	135@4000	217@2200	8.25-1	35	Gear
283 V8......................	3⅞x3	5	Hydraulic	283	48.0	170@4200	275@2200	8.05-1	35	Chain
327 V8......................	4x3¼	5	Note 17	327	51.2	300@5000	360@3200	Note 23	35	Chain
409 V8......................	4⁵⁄₁₆x3½	5	Solid	409	59.5	409@6000	420@4000	11.0-1	35	Chain
1963										
6 Cyl., 230 Cu. In...........	3⅞x3¼	7	Hydraulic	230	36	140@4400	220@1600	8.5-1	35	Gear
283 Cu. In..................	3⅞x3	5	Hydraulic	283	48	195@4800	285@2400	9.25-1	35	Chain
327 Cu. In. Standard*.......	4x3¼	5	Hydraulic	327	51.2	250@4400	350@2800	10.5-1	40	Chain
327 Cu. In. High Per.*......	4x3¼	5	Solid	327	51.2	300@5000	360@3200	11.25-1	40	Chain
409 Cu. In. Standard........	4⁵⁄₁₆x3½	5	Hydraulic	409	59.5	340@5000	420@3200	10.0-1	50	Chain
409 Cu. In. High Per........	4⁵⁄₁₆x3½	5	Solid	409	59.5	425@6000	425@4200	11.0-1	50	Chain

* Used also in Corvette

NOTES FOR GENERAL ENGINE SPECIFICATIONS TABLE

Note 1: Oil Flow

1954, 6 Cyl. W./P.G.
1955-57, All 6 Cyl.

The oil is supplied by a drilled passage in the rear camshaft bearing to a pipe under the push rod cover. From the pipe it enters a drilled passage at the top of the block, then thru a passage in the head to a pipe at the top center of the head to connect with the two hollow rocker arm shafts. From the rocker shafts it is distributed to the rocker arm bearings. A bleeder hole in each rocker arm supplies oil for lubrication of the valve stems and push rods. Oil for the hydraulic tappets comes from a tappet oil gallery.

1958-63, All 6 Cyl.

Oil is supplied through a drilled passage in the block from the tappet gallery to the hollow rocker shafts, eliminating the oil feed pipe used previously.

1955-63, V8 Without Hydraulic Lifters

A passage in each lifter allows oil from the lifter gallery to enter the hollow push rod. A metering hole at the top of the push rod sprays the oil over the stud mounted rocker and the valve mechanism.

1955-63, V8 With Hydraulic Lifters

An inertia type valve in each hydraulic lifter opens twice during each valve cycle allowing oil to pass into the push rod and so thru the metering hole in the top of the rod to lubricate the stud mounted rocker arm.

Note 2: 1955 V8, Valve Lifter Type

Hydraulic except when equipped with special camshaft. Solid when equipped with special camshaft.

Note 3: 1955 V8, Horsepower

Standard Engine ....162@4400
With 4 barrel carb. ....180@4600
With special camshaft ....195@5000

Note 4: 1955 V8, Torque

Standard Engine ....257@2200

NOTES FOR GENERAL ENGINE SPECIFICATIONS TABLE — continued

With 4 barrel carb. ....260@2800
With special camshaft ....260@3000

Note 5: 1956 V8, Valve Lifter Type
Standard Engine ....Hydraulic
With two 4 barrel carb. ....Solid

Note 6: 1956 V8, Horsepower
Standard Engine, with Synchromesh Transmission ..162@4400
With Powerglide Transmis-
sion ....170@4400
Engine with one 4 barrel
carb. and dual exhaust ....205@4600
Engine with two 4 barrel
carb. and dual exhaust ....225@5200

Note 7: 1956 V8, Torque
Standard Engine, with Synchromesh Transmission..257@2200
With Powerglide Transmis-
sion ....257@2400
Engine with one 4 barrel
carb. and dual exhaust ....268@3000
Engine with two 4 barrel
carb. and dual exhaust ....270@3600

Note 8: 1956 V8 Compression Ratio
Standard Engine ....8.0 to 1
With one or two 4 barrel
carb. ....9.25 to 1

Note 9: 1956 Corvette Horsepower
Standard Engine ....210@5200
With two 4 barrel carb. ......225@5200

Note 10: 1956 Corvette Torque
Standard Engine ....270@3200
With two 4 barrel carb. ......270@3600

Note 11: 1957, 265 Cubic Inch Engine Identification
The Engine Number of this V8 ends
in C, CD, or CE.

Note 12: 1957, 283 Cubic Inch Engine Identification.
The Engine Number of this V8 does
not end in C, CD, or CE.

Note 13: 1957 Valve Lifters on 285 Cu. In. V8
If the engine number ends in EK, EB,
EL, or EG the engine is equipped with
the special camshaft and has solid
lifters, otherwise it has hydraulic
lifters.

Note 14: 1957 V8, 283 Cu. In. Horsepower, Torque and Compression Ratio

WITH ONE 2 BARREL CARBURETOR
HP at stated RPM ....185@4600
Torque at stated RPM .....275@2400
Compression ratio ....8.5 to 1

WITH ONE 4 BARREL CARBURETOR
HP at stated RPM ....220@4800
Torque at stated RPM ....300@3000
Compression ratio ....9.5 to 1

WITH TWO 4 BARREL CARBURETORS
HP at stated RPM ....245@5000
Torque at stated RPM ....300@3800
Compression ratio ....9.5 to 1

WITH FUEL INJECTION
HP at stated RPM ....250@5000
Torque at stated RPM ....305@3800
Compression ratio ....9.5 to 1

WITH TWO 4 BARREL CARBURETORS AND SPECIAL CAMSHAFT
HP at stated RPM ....270@6000
Torque at stated RPM ....285@4200
Compression ratio ....9.5 to 1

WITH FUEL INJECTION AND SPECIAL CAMSHAFT
HP at stated RPM ....283@6200
Torque at stated RPM ....290@4400
Compression ratio ....10.5 to 1

Note 15: 1958 V8, 283 Cu. In. Engine Horsepower, Torque and Compression Ratio

WITH ONE 2 BARREL CARBURETOR
HP at stated RPM ....185@4600
Torque at stated RPM ....275@2400
Compression ratio ....8.5 to 1

WITH ONE 4 BARREL CARBURETOR
HP at stated RPM ....230@4800
Torque at stated RPM ....300@3000
Compression ratio ....9.5 to 1

WITH FUEL INJECTION
HP at stated RPM ....250@5000
Torque at stated RPM ....305@3800
Compression ratio ....9.5 to 1

Note 16: 1958 V8, 348 Cu. In. Engine Horsepower, Torque and Compression Ratio

WITH ONE 4 BARREL CARBURETOR
HP at stated RPM ....250@4400
Torque at stated RPM ....355@2800
Compression ratio ....9.5 to 1

WITH THREE 2 BARREL CARBURETORS
HP at stated RPM ....280@4800
Torque at stated RPM ....355@3200
Compression ratio ....9.5 to 1

Note 17: 1958-62 Corvette Valve Lifters and 1959 V8 Valve Lifters
Standard Engine ....Hydraulic
With Special Camshaft ....Solid

Note 18: 1958 Corvette Horsepower, Torque and Compression Ratio

WITH ONE 4 BARREL CARBURETOR:
HP at stated RPM ....230@4800
Torque at stated RPM   300@3000
Compression Ratio: ....9.5 to 1

WITH TWO 4 BARREL CARBURETORS:
HP at stated RPM ....245@5000
Torque at stated RPM ....300@3800
Compression Ratio: ....9.5 to 1

WITH FUEL INJECTION
HP at stated RPM ....250@5000
Torque at stated RPM ....305@3800
Compression Ratio: ....9.5 to 1

WITH TWO 4 BARREL CARBURETORS AND SPECIAL CAMSHAFT:
HP at stated RPM ....270@6000
Torque at stated RPM ....285@4200
Compression Ratio: ....9.5 to 1

WITH FUEL INJECTION AND SPECIAL CAMSHAFT:
HP at stated RPM ....290@6200
Torque at stated RPM ......290@4400
Compression Ratio: ....10.5 to 1

Note 19: Turbo-Thrust (348 Cu. In.) Engine Identification
The valve covers are curved due to
the staggered positions of the rockers.
This engine is called the "W" Engine.

Note 20: 348 Cu. In. Engine Head Angle
The top of the cylinder block is not
machined perpendicular to the cylinder bore. It is machined at an angle
of 16 deg. to the cylinder bore.

Note 21: 283 Cu. In. V8 Compression Ratio
Standard Engine .... 8.5 to 1
With Fuel Injection and
Special Camshaft .... 9.5 to 1

Note 22: 348 Cu. In. V8 Compression Ratio
Standard Engine .... 9.5 to 1
With Special Camshaft ....11.0 to 1

Note 23: 327 cu. in. V-8 Compression Ratio
Standard Engine ....10.5 to 1
With Special Camshaft ....11.0 to 1

VALVE SPECIFICATIONS

YEAR	Seat Angle		Intake Valve Lift	Exhaust Valve Lift	Valve Spring Pressure		Stem to Guide Clearance		Stem Diameter		Are Valve Guides Replaceable
	In	Ex			Outer	Inner	Inlet	Exhaust	Inlet	Exhaust	
1954											
6 Cyl. W/M ex. Corv.	31	46	.2941	.312	65@1.82	None	.0018	.0038	.3414	.3394	Yes
6 Cyl. W/A ex. Corv.	31	46	.4004	.400	65@1.91	None	.0018	.0038	.3414	.3394	Yes
Corvette	31	46	.4051	.414	55@1.88	25@1.81	.0018	.0038	.3414	.3394	Yes
1955											
6 Cyl. W/M ex. Corv.	31	46	.2941	.312	65@1.82	None	.0018	.0018	.3414	.3414	Yes
6 Cyl. W/A ex. Corv.	31	46	.4004	.400	78@1.86	None	.0018	.0018	.3414	.3414	Yes
6 Cyl. Corvette	31	46	.4051	.414	69@1.86	29@1.79	.0018	.0018	.3414	.3414	Yes
V8 W/M ex. Corv.	46	46	.3360	.334	75@1.70	None	.0018	.0023	.3419	.3414	No
V8 W/A ex. Corv.	46	46	.3240	.324	69@1.70	None	.0018	.0023	.3419	.3414	No
V8 Corvette	46	46	.4043	.414	75@1.70	None	.0018	.0023	.3419	.3414	No
1956											
6 Cyl. All	31	46	.4004	.400	78@1.86	None	.0018	.0018	.3414	.3414	Yes
V8 W/M ex. Corv.	46	46	.3336	.334	80@1.86	None	.0018	.0023	.3419	.3414	No
V8 W/A ex. Corv.	46	46	.3732	.396	80@1.70	Damper	.0018	.0023	.3419	.3414	No
V8 W/PP & Corvette	46	46	.4043	.414	74@1.70	Damper	.0018	.0023	.3419	.3414	No
1957											
6 Cyl. All	30	45	.4004	.400	78@1.86	None	.0018	.0018	.3414	.3414	Yes
265 Cu. In., V8	45	45	.3336	.334	80@1.70	None	.0018	.0023	.3419	.3414	No
283 Cu. In., V8	45	45	.3987	.399	74@1.70	Damper	.0018	.0023	.3419	.3414	No
283 Cu. In., V8 W/PP or F.I.	45	45	.3938	.399	74@1.70	Damper	.0018	.0023	.3419	.3414	No
1958											
6 Cyl. All	30	45	.4004	.400	78@1.86	None	.0018	.0018	.3414	.3414	Yes
283 Cu. In. V8, W.O./S.C.	45	45	.3987	.399	74@1.70	None	.0018	.0023	.3419	.3414	No
348 Cu. In. V8	45	45	.3987	.399	82@1.63	None	.0018	.0033	.3719	.3414	No
283 Cu. In. V8, W./S.C.	45	45	.3818	.399	75@1.70	Damper	.0018	.0023	.3419	.3414	No
1959-61											
All 6 Cyl.	31	46	.3275	.328	65@1.86	None	.0018	.0018	.3414	.3414	Yes
283 Cu. In., V8 W.O./S.C.	46	46	.3987	.399	74@1.70	None	.0018	.0023	.3419	.3414	No
283 Cu. In., V8 W/S.C.	46	46	.3937	.399	74@1.70	None	.0018	.0023	.3419	.3414	No
348 Cu. In., V8 W.O./S.C.	46	46	.3987	.411	82@1.63	None	.0018	.0033	.3719	.3714	No
348 Cu. In., V8 W/S.C.	46	46	.4058	.411	82@1.63	None	.0018	.0033	.3719	.3714	No
1962											
All 6 Cyl.	31	46	.3275	.328	65@1.86	None	.0018	.0018	.3414	.3414	Yes
283 Cu. In. V8	46	46	.3336	.334	80@1.70	None	.0018	.0023	.3414	.3414	No
327 Cu. In. V8	46	46	.3987	.399	74@1.70	None	.0018	.0023	.3414	.3414	No
409 Cu. In. V8	46	46	.4396	.473	134@1.68	22@1.49	.0018	.0033	.3719	.3714	No
1963											
6 Cyl., 230 Cu. In.	46	46	.3350	.335	88@1.66	None	.0021	.0023	.3410	.3410	No
283 Cu. In.	46	46	.3330	.333	78@1.70	None	.0018	.0023	.3414	.3414	No
327 Cu. In. Standard*	46	46	.3987	.399	82@1.66	None	.0018	.0021	.3410	.3414	No
327 Cu. In. High Per.*	46	46	.3987	.399	82@1.66	None	.0018	.0021	.3410	.3414	No
409 Cu. In. Standard	46	46	.4005	.4119	134@1.68	22@1.49	.0018	.0033	.3719	.3714	No
409 Cu. In. High Per.	46	46	.5069	.5185	134@1.68	22@1.49	.0018	.0033	.3719	.3714	No

* Used also in Corvette

PISTON AND PIN SPECIFICATIONS

Year and Model	Skirt Diameter		Pin Fit				
	TOP	BOTTOM	Diameter	Bushing	In Rod	In Piston	Lock
1954-62—6 cyl.	3.5625	3.5620-3.5614	.8660-8665	None	Slip	.00015-.00025	Rod Clamp
1963 6 cyl.	3.8746	3.8740	.9271	None	Press	.0007-.0027	Rod Clamp
1955-57—265 V8	3.750	3.7420	.9271	None	Press	.00015-.00025	Rod Press
1958-61—283 V8	3.8750	3.8742	.9271	None	Press	.00015-.00025	Rod Press
1958-61—348 V8	4.1250	4.1232	.9896	None	Press	.00015-.00025	Rod Press
1962-63—283 V8	3.8750	3.8742	.9271	None	Press	.00015-.00025	Rod Press
1962-63—327 V8	4.000	3.9982	.9271	None	Press	.00015-.00025	Rod Press
1962-63—409 V8	4.3125	4.3088	.9896	None	Press	.00015-.00025	Rod Press

Piston and Rod Assembly

1954-63, 6 Cyl. — Install pistons so that piston pin clamp and stamped number on connecting rod are on the camshaft side.

1954-63, V8—Cast depression in top of head and cast "F" marks on piston struts indicate front of piston and should be installed toward front of engine. The flange (heavy side) of the rod bearing should go toward the front of the engine on the left bank and toward the rear of the engine on the right bank.

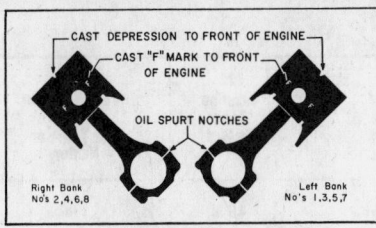

Correct Relation of Piston to Rod
265 to 283 Cu. In. Engine

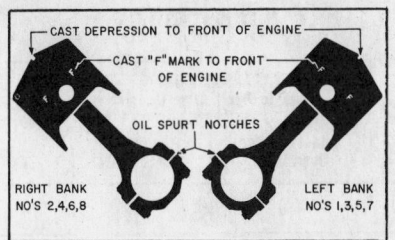

Correct Relation of Piston to Rod
327, 348, 409 Cu. In. Engine

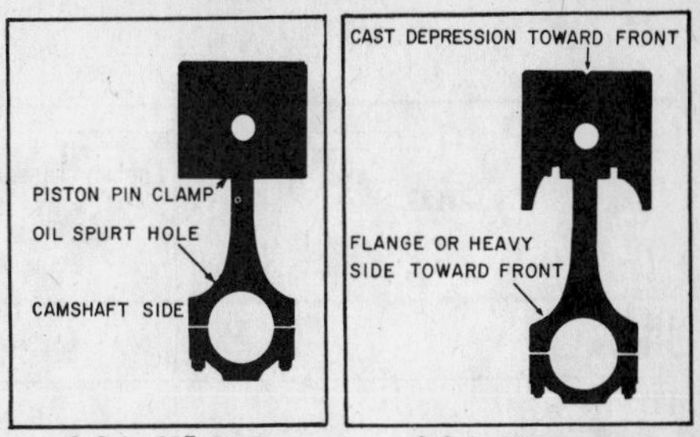

6 Cyl., 235 Cu. In.   6 Cyl., 230 Cu. In.
Correct Relation of Piston to Rod

TORQUE SPECIFICATIONS

YEAR	Cylinder Head Bolts	Rod Bearing Bolts	Main Bearing Bolts	Crankshaft Pulley Bolt	Flywheel to Crankshaft Bolts	Manifolds Intake	Manifolds Exhaust
1954-63							
All 6 Cyl.	90-95	35-45	100-110	45-55	55-65	25-35	Note 1
All V8	60-70	30-35	60-70	45-55	55-65	25-35	Note 1

Note 1. Exhaust Manifolds of All Engines
Tighten two middle to 25-30 ft. lbs.
Tighten four others to 15-20 ft. lbs.

Note for Torque Table
Some bolts and nuts are marked on the heads to indicate the grade of steel used. Do not use a lower grade than that used originally. The head marks consist of lines: SAE-5—3 lines; SAE-7—5 lines; SAE-8—6 lines.

CYLINDER HEAD NUT TIGHTENING SEQUENCE

1953-62 OHV 6 Cyl.:
Tighten to ...... 90-95 ft. lbs.

1963, OHV 6 Cyl.:
Tighten to ...... 90-95 ft. lbs.

1955-63, 265, 283 & 327 cu. in. V8's
Tighten to .... 60-70 ft. lbs.

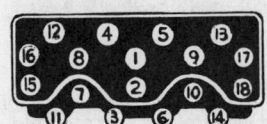

1958-63, Turbo-Thrust 348 and 409 cu. in.
V8 Tighten to .... 60-70 ft. lbs.

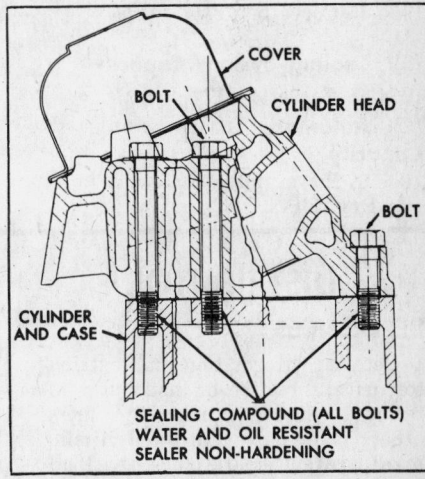

Cross Section of Cylinder Head and Case.
Typical of All V-8's Starting with 1957 Production.

FRONT WHEEL ALIGNMENT

YEAR	CASTER Range (Degrees)	CASTER Pref. Setting	CAMBER Range (Degrees)	CAMBER Pref. Setting	Toe-in (Inches)	King Pin Inclination (Degrees)	WHEEL PIVOT RATIO Inner Wheel	WHEEL PIVOT RATIO Outer Wheel
1954								
Conventional	0 to 1P	½P	0 to 1P	½P	⅛ to 3/16	3½ to 4½	24	20
Corvette	0 to 1P	½P	0 to 1P	½P	0 to ⅛	3½ to 4½	23	20
1955								
Conventional	½N to ½P	0	0 to 1P	½P	⅛ to 3/16	3½ to 4½	24	20
Corvette	0 to 1P	½P	0 to 1P	½P	0 to ⅛	3½ to 4½	23	20
1956–57								
Conventional	½P to 1½P	1P	0 to 1P	½P	⅛ to 3/16	3½ to 4½	24	20
Corvette	0 to 1P	½P	0 to 1P	½P	0 to ⅛	3½ to 4½	23	20
1958								
Conventional	½N to ½P	0	0 to 1P	½P	⅛ to ¼	6¾ to 7¾	20	18½
Corvette	2 1/16P to 2¼P	2⅛P	0 to 1P	½P	0 to ⅛	3½ to 4½	23	20
1959-63								
Conventional	½N to ½P	0	0 to 1P	½P	1/16 to ⅛	7¼	20	18
Corvette	1½P to 2½P	2P	½N to ½P	0	0 to ¼	3½ to 4½	23	20

CAPACITIES

YEAR	Engine Crankcase Add 1 Qt. for New Filter	TRANSMISSIONS Pints to Refill After Draining		Rear Axle Pints	Gasoline Tank Gallons	Cooling System Quarts Add 1 Qt for Heater
		Manual Add 1 Pt. for Over Drive	AUTOMATIC			
1954						
6 Cyl.	5	1½	10	3½	16(A)	16(B)
1955-57						
6 Cyl.	5	2	(C)	4	16(A)	16(B)
V8	4	2	(C)	4	16(A)	16(B)
1958						
6 Cyl.	5	2	9	4	20(D)	16
283 Cu. In. V8	4	2	(C)	4	20(D)	16
348 Cu. In. V8	4	2	(C)	4	20(D)	22
Corvette V8	5	(E)	9	4	16½	16
1959-61						
6 Cyl.	5	2	9	4	20(D)	17
283 Cu. In. V8	4	(E)	(C)	4	20(D)	17½
348 Cu. In. V8	4	(E)	(C)	4	20(D)	21
1962-63						
6 Cyl.	5	2	9	4	20(F)	17
283 Cu. In. V8	4	(E)	(C)	4	20(F)	17½
327 Cu. In. V8 Ex. Corvette	4	(E)	(C)	4	20(F)	17½
327 Cu. In. V8 Corvette	5	(E)	(C)	4	16½	16
409 Cu. In. V8	5	(E)	(C)	4	20(F)	17½

NOTES FOR CAPACITIES TABLE

(A): Gasoline Tank Capacity
1954-55 Corvette—17¼ gals.

(B): Cooling System Capacity
1954-55 Corvette—17¾ quarts

(C): Automatic Transmission Capacity
1955-57 Powerglide—Refill, 10 Pts. Dry 22 Pts.

1958-62 Powerglide "A"—Refill 9 Pts. Dry 21 Pts.

1962-63 Powerglide "B"—Refill 3 Pts. Dry 18 Pts.

1957 Turboglide—Refill 7 Pts. Dry 19 Pts.

1958-61 Turboglide—Refill 4 Pts. Dry 19 Pts.

(D): Gasoline Tank Capacity
Sta. Wagon—17 gals.

(E): Manual Transmission Capacity
Standard 3 speed—2 pints
Optional 4 speed—2½ pints

Note F: Station Wagon 1 gal. less

DISTRIBUTOR

REFERENCES

Detailed information on: distributor drive, direction of distributor rotation; cylinder numbering; firing order; point gap; cam dwell; timing mark location; spark plugs, spark advance; ignition resistor location, and idle speed; will be found in the Tune-up Specifications table of this section.

A further guide to trouble shooting can be found, beginning on page one of this manual. A professional approach to engine diagnosis is treated in the Unit Repair Section of the manual under "Engine Diagnosis".

REMOVAL OF DISTRIBUTOR FROM CAR

6 Cylinder Models

The distributor assembly is mounted on the right side of the block and is driven directly from the camshaft.

To remove the distributor first detach the vacuum lines to the vacuum advance unit and lift off the distributor cap.

The distributor body is held to the block by a single cap screw which holds the octane selector plate down against the block. Remove the retaining screw and lift the distributor out of the block.

V-8 Models

The distributor is located in between the two banks of cylinders at the back of the block.

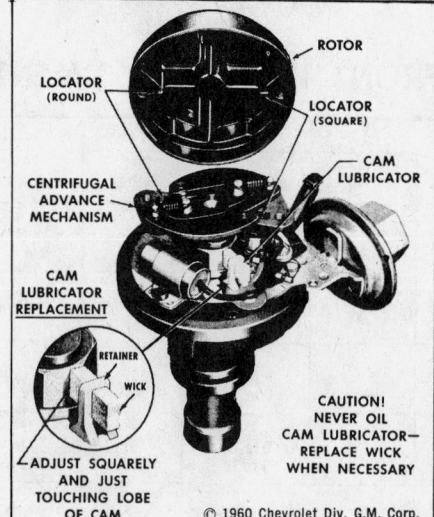

CAUTION! NEVER OIL CAM LUBRICATOR— REPLACE WICK WHEN NECESSARY

© 1960 Chevrolet Div. G.M. Corp.

V8 Distributor Showing Details of Cam Lubricator

The drive gear is attached to the distributor shaft so that if it becomes necessary to remove the distributor, mark carefully the position of the rotor so that, if the engine is not turned after the distributor is taken out it can be returned to the position from which it was removed without difficulty.

To remove the distributor take off the carburetor air cleaner, disconnect the coil primary wire and the vacuum line, remove the distributor cap, take out the single hold-down bolt located under the distributor body; with a pencil mark the position of the body relative to the block and then work the distributor up out of the block.

V8 DISTRIBUTOR CAM LUBRICATOR WICK

If the car has gone 20,000 miles or more the cam lubricator wick should be changed.

Take the distributor cap off. Using long nosed pliers, squeeze the wick assembly together at the base and lift it out. Wipe off the cam and install a new wick assembly so that the end of the wick just touches the cam lobes. Over lubrication at this point results when the wick presses too hard against the cam surface. Do not put oil on the wick.

INSTALLING 6 CYL. DISTRIBUTOR AFTER ENGINE HAS BEEN DISTURBED

Remove No. 1 spark plug and with finger on the plug hole crank the engine until compression is felt. Slowly continue cranking until the timing ball on the flywheel lines up with the pointer.

Position the distributor to its normal installed position. Turn the rotor clockwise not quite ⅛ of a turn and push the assembly down to engage the camshaft. It may be necessary to wiggle the rotor a bit to properly effect engagement. Holding the distributor down in place, use starter to turn motor to make sure oil pump shaft is engaged with the tongue of the distributor shaft. With holddown clamp at the octane selector drawn up tight, and the clamp screw loose, turn the distributor body until points are just slightly open and snug up the clamp screw.

Install the distributor cap, being sure that the rotor is pointing at the terminal for No. 1 spark plug. Use a timing light to check spark timing.

INSTALLING V8 DISTRIBUTOR AFTER ENGINE HAS BEEN DISTURBED

Remove No. 1 spark plug and with

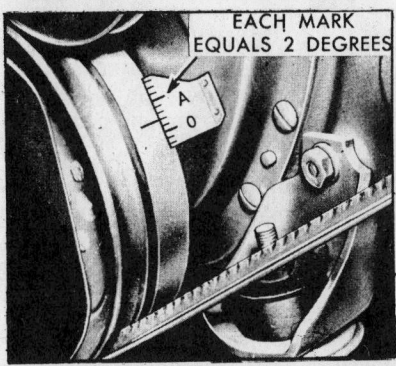

Ignition timing marks V8 engines

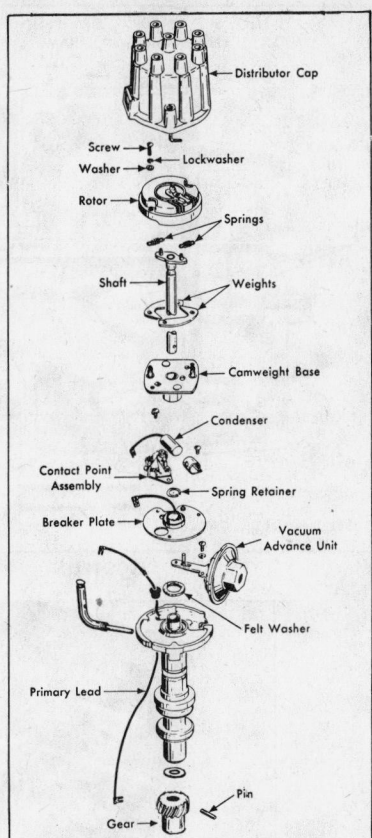

V-8 Distributor 1957-63

finger on plug hole crank the engine until compression is felt in No. 1 cylinder. Continue cranking until pointer lines up with the timing mark on the crankshaft pulley.

Position distributor to opening in the block in normal installed attitude, have rotor pointing to front of engine.

Turn the rotor counterclockwise about one-eighth of a turn (from straight front toward the left cylinder bank). Push the distributor down so as to engage the camshaft and while holding so, turn engine with the starter so that distributor shaft engages the oil pump shaft.

Return engine to compression stroke of No. 1 piston with timing mark on pulley aligned with the

pointer. Adjust the distributor so that the points are just opening. Install the cap being sure the rotor points to the contact for No. 1 spark plug. Connect up the timing light and check that spark occurs as timing mark and pointer are aligned.

CAUTION

V8, beginning 1955 the distributor body is involved in the engine lubricating system. The lubricating circuit can be interrupted to the right bank valve train by misalignment of the distributor body. This can cause serious trouble and may be hard to diagnose. See Firing Order and Timing illustrations for correct distributor positioning.

"D.C." GENERATOR AND REGULATOR

REFERENCES

Detailed facts on the generator and the regulator can be found in the Generator and Regulator Specifications Table of this section.

General information on generator and regulator repair and trouble shooting can be found in the Unit Repair section under the heading Generators and Regulators.

Generator Removal

Disconnect the battery. Disconnect the armature, field and ground wires at the generator. If the car has power steering the pump can be unbolted from the generator without disconnecting the power steering hoses.

Remove the generator brace bolt at the top of the generator. Push the assembly toward the engine and remove the belt.

Remove the two bolts holding the generator to the bracket and remove the generator.

Double Contact Regulator Caution

Never ground the generator or regulator field terminals when these units are connected together. To do so will burn up the upper set of contacts.

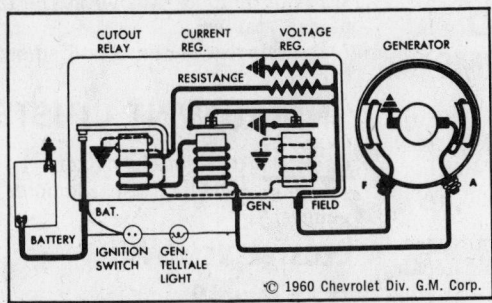

Generating Circuit, Single Contact Voltage Regulator

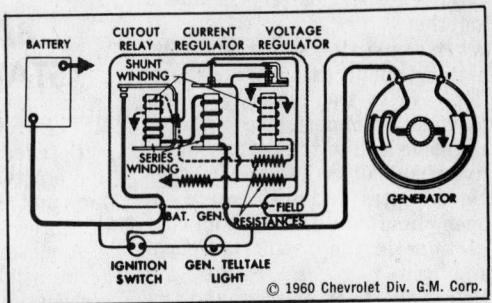

Generating Circuit, Double Contact Voltage Regulator

Polarity Caution

Whenever the circuits to the generator, the regulator or the battery have been disconnected it is best to use the following procedure:

Before the engine is started momentarily short from the "Bat" terminal to the "Gen" terminal on the regulator with a screwdriver. This gives a momentary surge of current from the battery to the generator and so correctly polarizes the generator with respect to the battery.

Failure to so polarize the generator before starting the engine may severely damage the regulator since reversed polarity causes vibration, arcing and burning of the relay points.

"AC" GENERATOR (DELCOTRON)

REFERENCES

Beginning 1962 "Delcotron," the AC generator by Delco-Remy is available on Chevrolet passenger cars and trucks. These units are furnished in two service types with companion voltage regulators. A three-unit regulator will be used with vehicles having a 42 or 52 ampere Delcotron. Vehicles such as police equipment, etc. will use a 62 ampere delcotron and be furnished with a two-unit transistorized regulator.

Repair and test details on the Delcotron and it's regulators are covered in the Unit Repair Section of this manual, under "Alternating Current Generators."

CAUTION:

Since the Delcotron and regulator are designed for use on only one polarity system, the following precautions must be observed:

1. The polarity of the battery, generator and regulator must be matched and considered before making any electrical connections in the system.
2. When connecting a booster battery, be sure to connect the negative battery terminals together and the positive battery terminals together.
3. When connecting a charger to the battery, connect the charger positive lead to the battery positive terminal. Connect the charger negative lead to the battery negative terminal.
4. Never operate the Delcotron on open circuit. Be sure that all connections in the circuit are clean and tight.
5. Do not short across or ground any of the terminals on the Delcotron regulator.

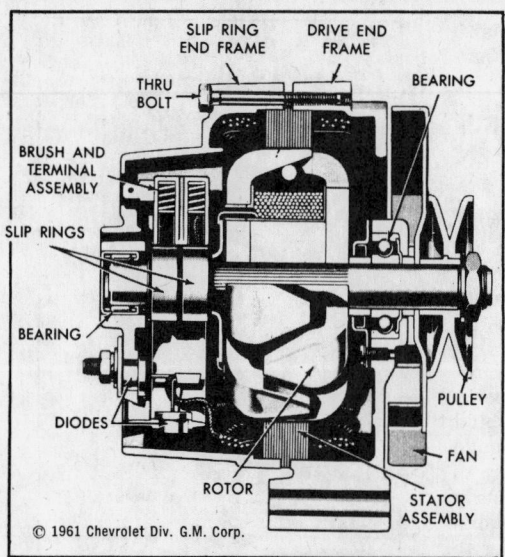

© 1961 Chevrolet Div. G.M. Corp.

5.5" DELCOTRON

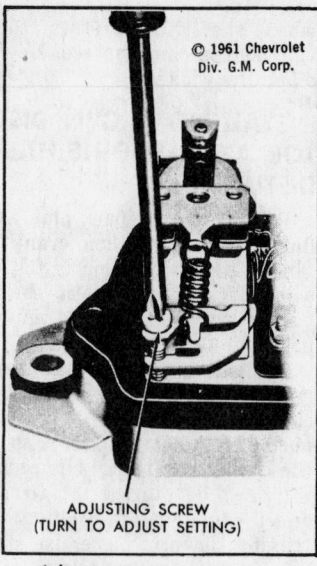

© 1961 Chevrolet Div. G.M. Corp.

ADJUSTING SCREW
(TURN TO ADJUST SETTING)

Adjusting Voltage Setting

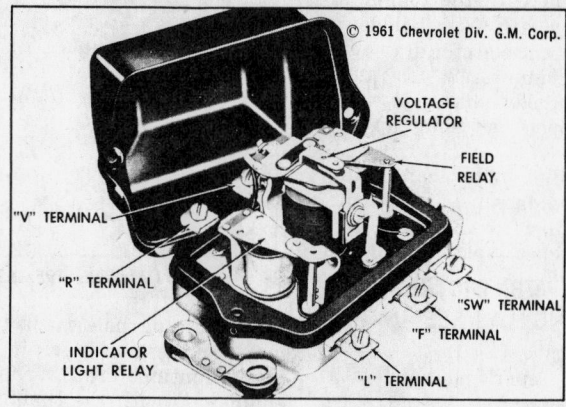

© 1961 Chevrolet Div. G.M. Corp.

Double Contact Regulator

6. Do not attempt to polarize the Delcotron.
7. Do not use test lamps of more than 12 volts for checking diode continuity.
8. Avoid long soldering times when replacing diodes or transistors. Prolonged heat is damaging to these units.
9. Disconnect the battery ground terminal when servicing any A.C. system. This will prevent the possibility of accidental reversing of polarity.

BATTERY AND STARTER SYSTEMS

REFERENCES

Detailed information on the battery and starter will be found in the Battery and Starter Specifications Table of this section.

A more general discussion of batteries will be found in the Unit Repair section under the heading "Engine Diagnosis."

A more general discussion of start-ers and their troubles can be found in the Unit Repair section under the heading: Starters.

Starter Removal

At the solenoid, disconnect the Violet wire from the "S" terminal; the Black wire from the "Bat" terminal; the Green wire from the "R" terminal; the Tan wire (for electric top, seat, windows) from the "Bat" terminal.

Remove the starter mounting bolt and lock washers. On V8's there is a stud nut and lock washer at the front of the starter.

Pull starter forward and so out of car.

INSTRUMENT CLUSTER

Caution; disconnect battery before starting work on speedometer or gauges.

CLUSTER REMOVAL

1954 Thru 1955

On these models the instruments are mounted on the dash in pairs

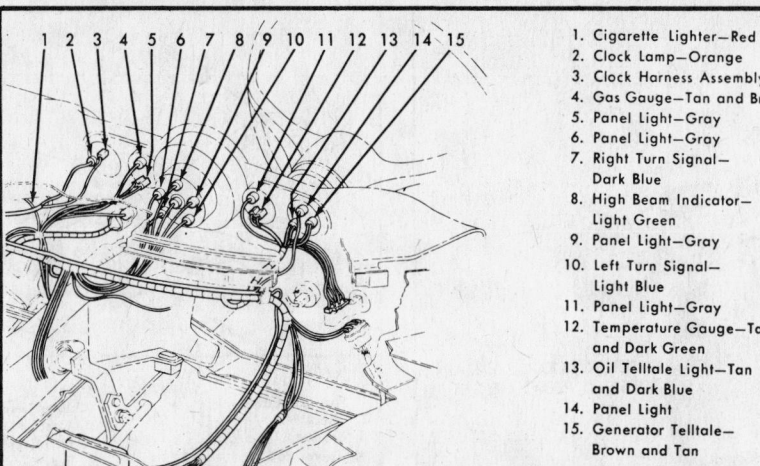

1. Cigarette Lighter—Red
2. Clock Lamp—Orange
3. Clock Harness Assembly
4. Gas Gauge—Tan and Brown
5. Panel Light—Gray
6. Panel Light—Gray
7. Right Turn Signal—Dark Blue
8. High Beam Indicator—Light Green
9. Panel Light—Gray
10. Left Turn Signal—Light Blue
11. Panel Light—Gray
12. Temperature Gauge—Tan and Dark Green
13. Oil Telltale Light—Tan and Dark Blue
14. Panel Light
15. Generator Telltale—Brown and Tan

Instrument Cluster Rear View—1959-60

called "bars." To remove any one instrument it is necessary to take out one bar which contains two instruments. Each bar is held in with four small screws. The speedometer may be removed as an individual item without removing any other obstacle since it is not mounted in a bar.

1956-1957

Each of the instruments is held to its cluster plate by its own screws and each can be removed separately. However, working under the dash is very tight quarters and the first thing to be done is disconnect the battery so that none of the instruments are accidentally short circuited.

There is, however, sufficient room under the dash to remove any or all of the instruments.

Starting With 1958

All component parts of the dash instruments are contained within the instrument cluster. The cluster may be removed as a whole or the instru-

ments can be removed separately. All the light bulb sockets are held by clips and can be easily snapped in or out of position. The fuel and temperature gages and the speedometer are held in place by screws.

Remove and tag the connectors and cables from the back of the cluster. Using a spanner wrench at the front of the dash, remove the light switch rod and the ferrule assembly.

From underneath the dash, remove the nut attaching the lighter assembly. Now take off the front trim plate. From under the dash, remove the four stud nuts attaching the bottom of the instrument cluster to the dash panel.

Now take out the six screws, two on each side and two at the top from the face of the instrument cluster.

Push the bottom of the cluster in to get off its studs, turn it slightly sideways and then pull the cluster assembly out towards the steering wheel.

When reinstalling work the cluster into the opening in the dash panel and engage the studs at the bottom of the cluster first, attach the stud nuts. Install the six screws, two at each side and two at the top of the cluster. Replace the trim plate, the light switch and the cigarette lighter. Make all electrical and speedometer connections in back of the cluster. These connections are all pin type.

When the instrument cluster is out of the vehicle the instruments can be tested and/or changed.

WIPER AND DRIVE REMOVAL
Thru 1955

The windshield wiper motor is mounted under the center of the dash and if the car is equipped with a radio the radio must be removed to gain access to the motor.

The windshield wiper transmission is of the bar type and can be removed without disturbing any of the connections or wires under the dash.

1956-1957

The windshield wiper motor, either vacuum or electric, is located on the engine side of the firewall just over the center of the engine. Access to the drive is through the glove compartment box to service the wiper drive.

If the operator is particularly adept at working in tight places it is possible to service the drive with the radio in place, but it is difficult and the quarters are rather close.

Starting With 1958

The windshield wiper motor is located under the dash on the rear side of the firewall in the middle.

The transmission is located under the ventilator grille just in front of the windshield.

Remove the glove compartment box and if the car is equipped with a radio, remove the radio.

This will give access to the motor.

Raise the hood and remove the screws which hold the air ventilator to the top of the cowl and lift off the air ventilator. This will give access

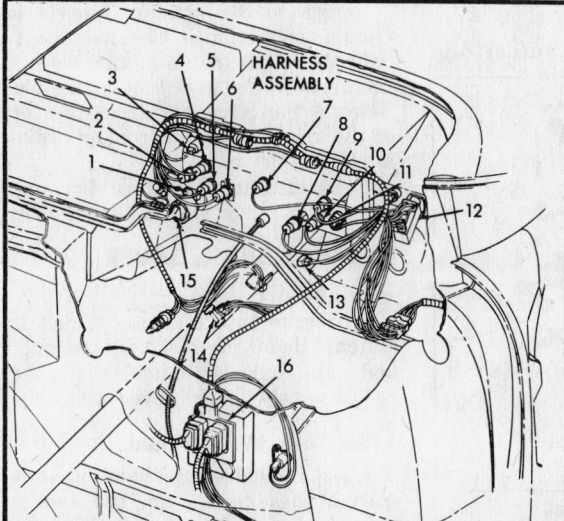

1. Ignition Switch Lamp—Gray
2. Right Turn Signal—Dark Blue
3. Cigarette Lighter—Red
4. Panel Light—Gray
5. Oil Pressure Indicator—Tan and Dark Blue
6. Parking Brake Lamp—Black
7. Panel Light—Gray
8. High Beam Indicator—Light Green
9. Panel Light—Gray
10. Generator Indicator—Tan and Brown
11. Left Turn Signal—Light Blue
12. Light Switch and Connector
13. To Horn Button Connector
14. Turn Signal Switch
15. Ignition Switch
16. Junction Block
17. Temperature Gauge, Connector—Tan and Dark Green
18. Temperature Gauge Light—Gray
19. Clock Connector—Red
20. Clock Light—Gray
21. Gas Gauge Connector—Tan and Brown
22. Gas Gauge Light—Gray

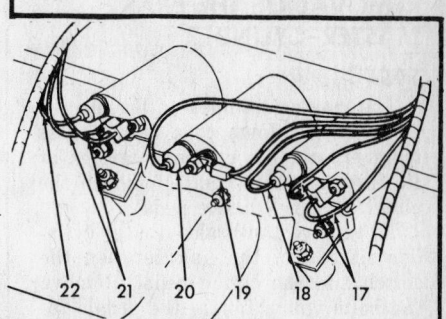

Instrument Cluster Rear View—1961-63

to the front of the driveshaft.

Disconnect the driveshaft from the transmission, working through the glove compartment opening remove the screws which hold the motor unit to the firewall, disconnect the control cables and vacuum line and remove the wiper motor.

No linkage rod adjustment is possible.

BRAKE SYSTEM

REFERENCES

Specific information on brake cylinder sizes can be found in the General Chassis and Brake Specifications Table.

Information on brake adjustments, band replacement, bleeding procedure, master and wheel cylinder overhaul can be found in the Unit Repair section under the heading: Brakes, Hydraulic.

Information on trouble shooting and overhauling power brakes can be found in the Unit Repair section under the heading: Brakes, Power.

Information on the grease seals which may need replacement can be found in the Unit Repair section. The front wheel grease seals under the head: Suspension, Front Repair. The rear wheel grease seals under the head: Axles, Rear.

POWER BRAKE UNIT REMOVAL

On V8's unfasten the vacuum line from the intake manifold on top of the engine.

On 6's unfasten the vacuum line from intake manifold on the left of the engine.

Now unfasten the other end of the vacuum line at the vacuum reservoir. Unfasten the brake line at the front of the unit.

In the driver's compartment, remove the brake lever to unit push rod retaining bolt, lock washer and nut.

Remove the four bolts and lock washers holding the power unit to the engine side of the dash and remove the power brake unit.

REMOVAL OF THE BRAKE MASTER CYLINDER

1954

The master cylinder on these models is bolted down to a frame cross member and the cylinder carries at its forward end a shaft for both the clutch and the brake pedal.

To remove the brake master cylinder disconnect the link between the clutch and the clutch pedal. Remove the bolts which fasten the pedals together. Disconnect the brake line at the back of the master cylinder. Un-

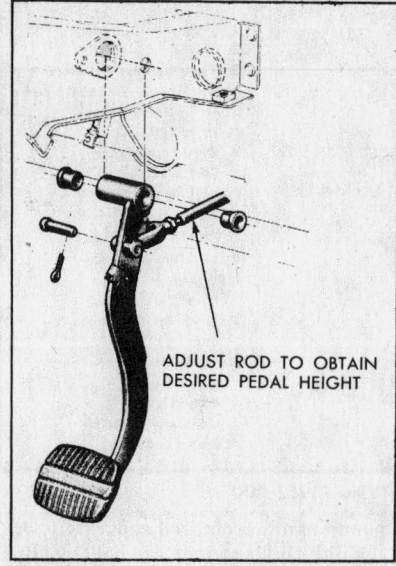

ADJUST ROD TO OBTAIN DESIRED PEDAL HEIGHT

Power Brake Push Rod to Brake Pedal Attachment

bolt the master cylinder from the frame and remove it from the car. Note that it is easier to overhaul this type while it is in place on the car. Remove the plug on the master cylinder from between the two shafts and, using a very thin punch or a piece of very stiff wire, pull the retaining pin out of the way so that both shafts can be slid out of the master cylinder.

New bushings are available for the clutch and brake cross shafts which can be inserted into the master cylinder as a job in addition to the servicing of the cylinder itself.

Starting with 1955

Starting with 1955 models the pedals were pivoted from underneath the dash panel. The master cylinder is located on the engine side of the fire wall.

To remove the master cylinder, dis-

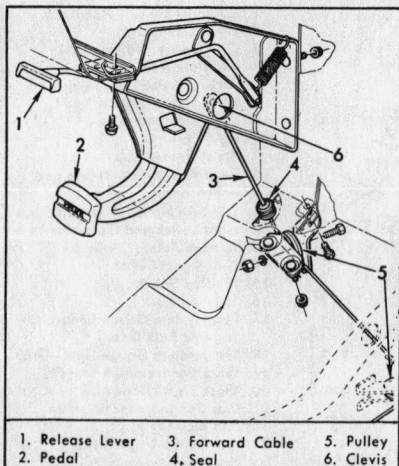

1. Release Lever   3. Forward Cable   5. Pulley
2. Pedal   4. Seal   6. Clevis

Parking Brake Pedal and Release Lever

connect the lines from under the hood, remove the clevis which holds the brake push rod to the brake pedal from under the dash.

Take out the four mounting bolts which hold the master cylinder to the fire wall and lift off the master cylinder.

REFILLING MASTER CYLINDER

1954

The master cylinder is filled through a port in the floor under the floor mat. When bleeding brakes, it is advisable not to let the fluid in the master cylinder get below the half way mark, as there is a possibility that air may be included in the bleeding process.

Starting With 1955 Production

Access to the master cylinder is from under the hood. The master cylinder is bolted to the engine side of the fire wall and is readily accessible. Remove the large nut from the top of the cylinder and fill from an ordinary filling device.

Be careful not to include dirt, grit or oil when filling the master cylinder.

PARKING BRAKE LEVER

1954 Models

The brake lever on these models is fastened under the dash with two nuts and bolts. A clevis pin holds the brake rod assembly to the lever assembly.

1955 Thru 1957 Models

A rod and cable type hand brake is used on these models and the lever is mounted on the left side of the dash.

Disconnect the cable at its lower end and pull the hand brake lever out

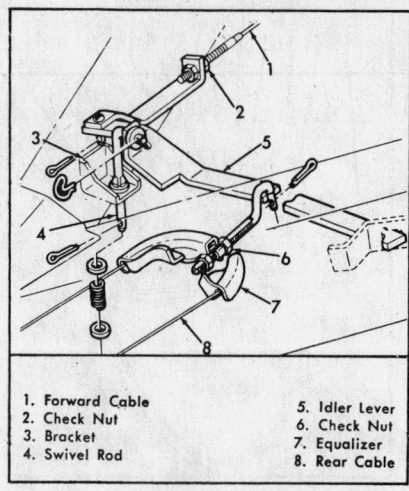

1. Forward Cable   5. Idler Lever
2. Check Nut   6. Check Nut
3. Bracket   7. Equalizer
4. Swivel Rod   8. Rear Cable

Parking Brake System
With brake off clearance between rear edge of arm (5) and end of guide slot should be ¼ inch

far enough and turn it so that the ball connection at the end of the cable can be disconnected from the hand brake rod.

Remove the bolts which hold the lower bracket to the toe board and the bolts which hold the upper bracket to the dash panel and lift off the hand brake lever.

Starting With 1958

The parking brake is applied by foot and released thru a hand operated lever. The control mechanism can be removed by taking out the three attaching bolts from the panel bracket and lowering the unit for easy access.

FUEL SYSTEM

REFERENCES

A chart covering causes of excess fuel consumption will be found in the Unit Repair section under the heading: Fuel Consumption Chart.

Data on capacity of the gas tank will be found in the Capacities Table. Data on correct engine idle speed and fuel pump pressure will be found in the Tune-up Specifications Table. Both the above tables can be found at the start of this section.

General information on fuel pumps and their troubles will be found in the Unit Repair section under the heading: Fuel Pumps.

Information covering operation and troubles of the fuel gauge will be found in the Unit Repair section under the heading: Gages.

Detailed information on the carburetor and how to adjust it will be found in the Unit Repair section under the broad heading: Carburetors, and the specific heading of the make

of carburetor being used on the engine being worked on. Carter, Holley, Rochester and Stromberg carburetors are covered.

Dash pot adjustment can be found in the Unit Repair section under the same heading as that of the automatic transmission used in the car as well as under the make of carburetor.

FUEL PUMP

The fuel pump is mounted on the right side of the engine towards the front.

It is secured to the side of the engine block with two screws.

To remove the fuel pump disconnect the input flex line and the output line to the carburetor. The fuel pump can then be detached from the side of the block and lifted off. On V8 models the pump is actuated by a push rod in the block.

CAUTION:

Fuel Pump Replacement V8

In a few instances a fuel pump has failed to function at the time of replacement. These cases have been the result of error in positioning or damage to the fuel pump push rod of the V8 engine. Design characteristics require that a push rod (or some other method of extension) be used to transmit camshaft lobe action to the pump activating arm. This rod can slip out of place during the process of pump replacement and result in no pump action from the newly replaced unit. Suggestion: Before tightening the fuel pump to the engine, have someone spin the engine with the starter while the machanic feels the fuel pump body for movement. If the pump and rod are in correct position, movement will be felt in the pump as the

push rod pressure is applied and released from the pump arm.

FUEL TANK AND SENDING UNIT

1954

The fuel tank is located under the trunk lid in the back of the car. It is held to the frame by two steel straps having T-bolts at their back end.

Soak the T-bolts in a rust dissolving fluid before attempting to take the nuts off.

Disconnect the hose clamps which tie the filler spout into the filler neck of the tank on models which use this flexible connection. Disconnect the gas line.

Look in the bottom of the trunk and see if there is a port over the fuel gage and if there is take the port off and disconnect the wire from the fuel gage.

Place a jack under the center of the gas tank and remove the two nuts from the T-bolts at the back cross member and slowly lower the tank down and out.

1955 Thru 1956 Models

From the front end of the gas tank disconnect the gas line. Remove the clamp which holds the metal filler neck to the frame.

Place a jack under the center of the tank to support its weight and loosen the bolts in the back which hold the tank supporting strap in place and lower both straps. Let the front end of the tank come down a sufficient amount to disconnect the gage.

Remove the filler neck cap and carefully thread the gas tank forward until the filler pipe comes out of the

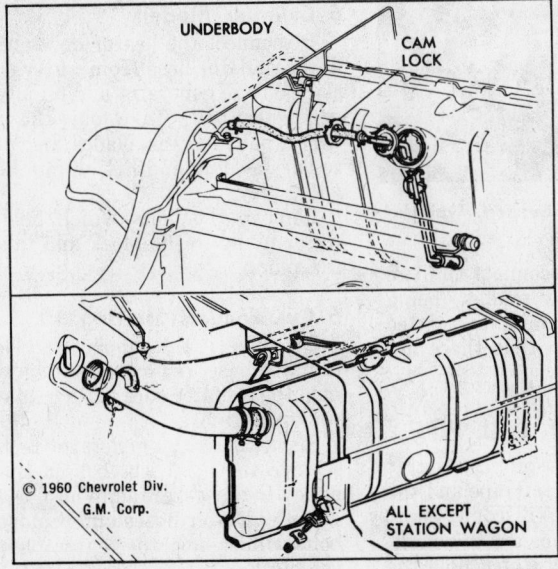
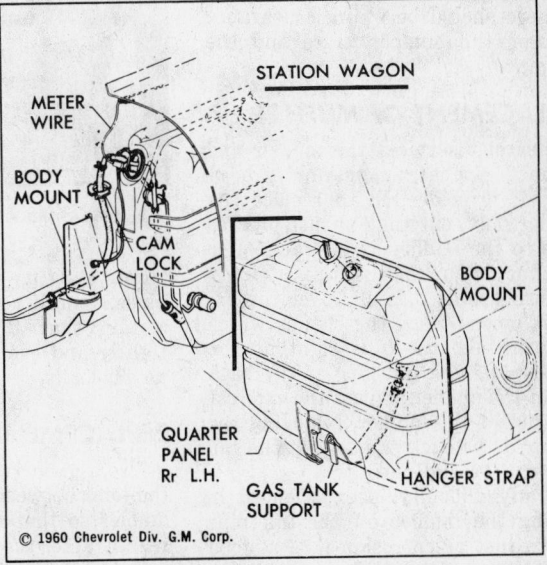

Passenger Car and Station Wagon Fuel Tank Installation

socket in the left rear fender. The tank is then lowered and twisted so that the filler neck will thread between the body and the frame.

Starting With 1957

Disconnect the gas line and the gauge line from the front of the tank. Disconnect the vent line at the back of the tank. Place a jack protected by a block of wood underneath the tank and then disconnect the two mounting strap bolts at the rear of the tank, slowly lower the front of the tank downwards and slide it forward to clear the filler neck.

Tank is installed in the reverse of this procedure.

EXHAUST SYSTEM

MUFFLER, EXHAUST PIPE AND TAIL PIPE

When installing an exhaust pipe, muffler or tail pipe assembly care should be taken to have these parts in proper relationship to each other and properly aligned.

Incorrect alignment of the exhaust system is frequently the cause of annoying rattles because of incorrect clearances. Many unusual noises very hard to locate are some times due to a change or obstruction to the normal flow of gases caused by improper mounting of any part of the exhaust system.

There are two points to consider when installing an exhaust or muffler assembly or a tail pipe. First, there should be ¾ inch clearance between the underside of the floor pan and the tail pipe at the pickup. Second, the tail pipe support must be in a vertical position. If it is at an angle the tail pipe might strike the bumper causing an annoying rattle.

There should be ¾ inch clearance between the bumper brace and the tail pipe.

REPLACEMENT OF MUFFLER

Chevrolet services the muffler and exhaust pipe as an assembly, however, if it is desired to replace the muffler only, cut the exhaust pipe as close to the muffler as is practical so that the new muffler will have plenty of purchase as it is slid over the exhaust pipe. Loosen the clamps which hold the exhaust pipe right at the muffler and the tail pipe at the back end of the muffler and cut the exhaust pipe out of the muffler, removing the clamp at the back end so that the tail pipe can be slid out.

If any difficulty is experienced in getting the muffler off the tail pipe due to rust or corrosion it is a good idea to let the joint soak in a good rust dissolving fluid for about ½ hour or so

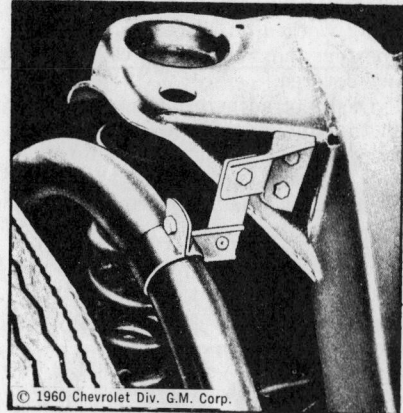

Tail Pipe Middle Mount. Typical 1958-63

Tail Pipe Rear Mount. Typical 1958-63

Tail Pipe and Muffler Support. Typical 1958-63

before starting to disconnect the two pipes. Install the new muffler, being certain that the clamps are fitted tightly and evenly so that there are no gas leaks.

REPLACEMENT OF TAIL PIPE

Use a good rust dissolving fluid at the joint between the tail pipe and the muffler so that they will come apart readily after the clamps are taken off.

Take off the clamps which hold the tail pipe to the body and frame and

spread them enough so that the tail pipe can be dropped out of them.

Drop out the tail pipe and, if sufficient rust dissolving fluid has been used the tail pipe will slide out of the muffler readily. It must be threaded between the housing and the rear axle assembly for easy removal.

On installing a new tail pipe make certain that all of the brackets hang straight down on the new pipe so that it does not rattle against either the body or the bumper assembly.

REPLACE EXHAUST PIPE

To replace the exhaust pipe it is customary to install an exhaust pipe and muffler assembly and the procedure is exactly the same as that for replacing a muffler except that the pipe is not cut. However, in many instances it will be found a lot easier to get the old unit down if the muffler is first cut away from the exhaust pipe and the exhaust pipe disconnected at the exhaust flange on the manifold.

COOLING SYSTEM

Detailed information on cooling system capacity can be found in the Capacities Table.

Information on the water temperature gauge can be found in the Unit Repair section under the heading: Gages.

Caution:

"Think"; when replacing a thermostat. It is possible to install it in the reverse position. The diaphram, or spring loaded end of the unit must be installed toward the engine.

WATER PUMP REMOVAL

6 Cylinder Models 1954

Disconnect the heater hose and the lower radiator hose from water pump, slack off the generator and remove the generator belt. Take out the bolts which hold the fan blades and pulley to the fan hub and lift off the blades and pulley.

Remove the bolts which hold the water pump to the block and take off the pump.

6 Cyl. Models Starting 1955

Disconnect the upper and lower radiator hose, remove the bolts which hold the radiator core to its cradle and remove the core.

Slack off on the generator belt and remove the bolts which hold the fan pulley to the water pump hub. Disconnect the heater hoses and remove the bolts which hold the water pump to the block.

Carefully scrape the gasket from

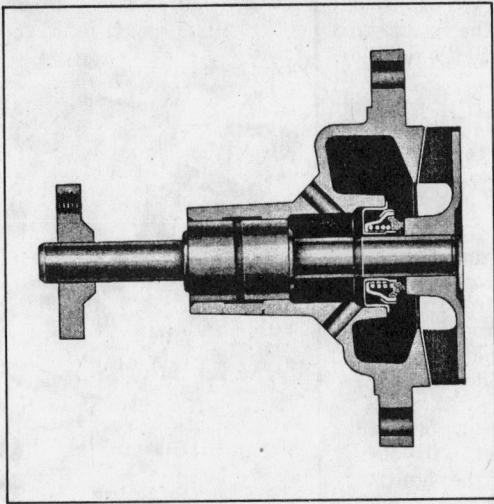

Water Pump, 6 Cylinder

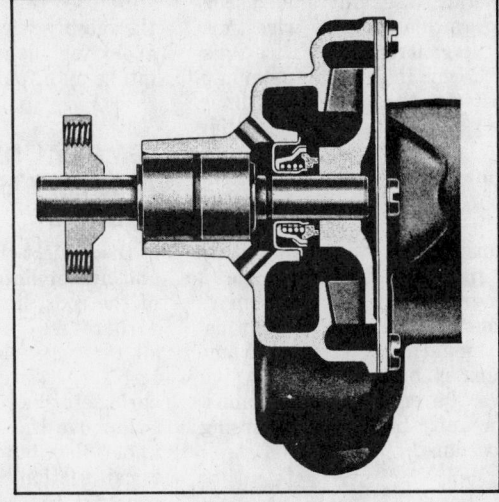

Water Pump, 283 cu. in., 8 Cylinder

the block. If a new pump is to be installed use a new gasket and it is good practice to put gasket compound on since this is a thin paper gasket.

V-8 Models

Slack off on the generator and remove the generator belt. Disconnect the heater hose and the lower radiator hose from the water pump manifold.

Remove the bolts which hold the fan blades and fan pulley to the hub and take off the blades and pulley.

Remove the bolts which hold the manifold to both cylinder heads and lift off the pump assembly.

Not necessary to remove the fan shroud on models so equipped but it is easier if the shroud and core are removed.

REMOVAL OF THE RADIATOR CORE

Thru 1955 Models

Drain the cooling system and remove the radiator drain cock and hose located at the bottom of the lower tank, disconnect and remove the upper and lower radiator hoses. Disconnect the transmission cooler lines.

Take off the air cleaner to allow room to tilt the radiator backwards.

Disconnect all wires which pass across the top of the radiator for the headlights and pull the harness out of the way.

Block the hood in the fully opened position and take out the bolts which attach the core to the support on each side.

Raise the core up and juggle the fan blades so that the bottom outlet of the radiator will clear the blades and, as the radiator comes to the well up position cock it backwards towards the engine so that the water outlet can be threaded past the radiator brace.

The radiator is installed in the re-

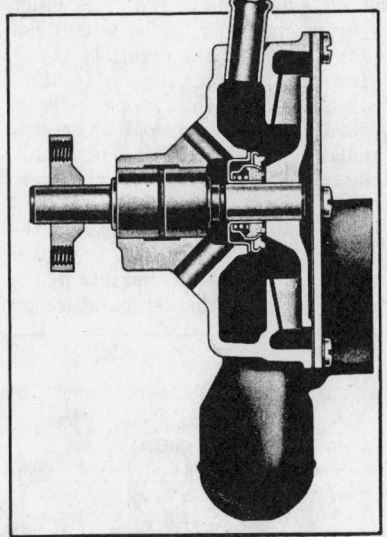

Water Pump, 348 cu. in., 8 Cylinder

verse of the above procedure.

6 Cylinder Models
Starting With 1956

Disconnect the upper and lower radiator hoses from the radiator and also disconnect the oil cooler lines at the bottom tank of the radiator on cars fitted with Power Glide.

From the front of the radiator baffle remove the bolts which hold the core to the baffle and pull the core straight forward and out.

1956 Thru 1957 V-8 Models

The procedure given above will also apply to the V-8 models except the mounting bolts are located on the engine side of the radiator cradle and the radiator core is lifted straight upwards.

V-8 Models Starting With 1958

Disconnect and remove the battery. Disconnect the upper and lower radiator hoses and the two oil cooler lines

at the bottom of the core.

Remove the bolts which hold the radiator core to its cradle and lift it straight up.

The new radiator core is reinstalled in reverse of the above procedure.

ENGINE

REFERENCES

In the specifications tables of this section are listed, most of the service references needed by the mechanic.

Where different sized engines are used, identification can be made by refering to "Car Serial Number Location And Engine Identification," near the beginning of this car section.

REMOVE & INSTALL

1954 to 1957

On these models it is necessary to remove the hood and radiator core and also the radiator cradle.

The engine is detached at the front universal joint after all connecting parts have been removed.

Starting With 1958

Remove hood assembly.

Remove the battery and the radiator core and its baffle. This will necessitate removing the battery wire from the regulator and feeding it thru the baffle and letting it hang on the right side of the car. The headlight wires on the right side can be pulled out of their pin socket, fed through the baffle and hung on the left side.

Horn wires can be disconnected at their pin connectors.

The baffle is bolted at the bottom to the frame, has one bolt in each fender skirt and two at the top.

Disconnect the hoses and remove the fan blades and fan hub.

Take off the air cleaner, disconnect

the temperature sending unit, disconnect the ignition primary wires, disconnect the generator lead wires, disconnect the gas line at the fuel pump, disconnect the throttle control lines, disconnect the oil pressure sending unit.

Disconnect the exhaust pipe at the flange and the crossover pipe on V8 models.

Disconnect the propeller shaft. Install lifting bolts in cylinder head. Raise engine slightly and remove front mounting bolts. Remove transmission mounting block to frame cross member bolts.

Remove the engine and transmission as a unit. Install by reversing above procedure.

MANIFOLDS

COMBINATION MANIFOLD USED ON 6 CYL. ENGINES

All Chevrolet 6 cylinder engines are equipped with a combination intake and exhaust manifold. The exhaust manifold is equipped with a heat riser valve which, when the engine is cold, deflects the hot exhaust gases against the intake manifold to assist in rapid warm up.

If the engine doesn't seem to warm up properly or when operated at a high speed it acts lean, it is a good idea to check this heat riser valve to be certain that it is functioning freely. Failure of the heat riser valve

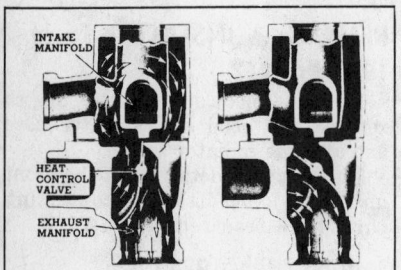

Manifold Heat Valve Used on 6 Cyl. Engines

to open will increase the time required to warm the engine. Failure of the heat riser valve to close after the manifold is hot will cause the engine to apparently run lean.

To remove the manifold assembly disconnect the exhaust pipe flange and remove all connections to the carburetor. Take off the vacuum lines at the manifold and also at the carburetor.

Remove the carburetor and the manifold may be unbolted from the side of the cylinder head using socket wrenches and box wrenches.

Before reinstalling the manifold thoroughly clean out the ports to avoid turbulence particularly on the intake manifold.

REMOVAL OF INLET MANIFOLD ASSEMBLY USED ON V8 ENGINES

Disconnect the upper radiator hose and heater hose and then remove all of the rods, lines and wires from the carburetor. While it is possible to take off the manifold with the carburetor in place, it is recommended that the carburetor be removed.

Remove the distributor as outlined under distributor removal in the electrical section. Remove the ignition coil and the heat indicating sender unit from the back of the manifold on the left side. Remove the bolts which hold the manifold to both cylinder heads and lift off the manifold.

The two passages at the front of the manifold and the two passages at the back of the manifold are water circulating passages. The four square holes on each side of the manifold are the inlet manifold passages.

The two holes in the center of the manifold are the exhaust crossover passages provided to maintain the manifold at operating temperature.

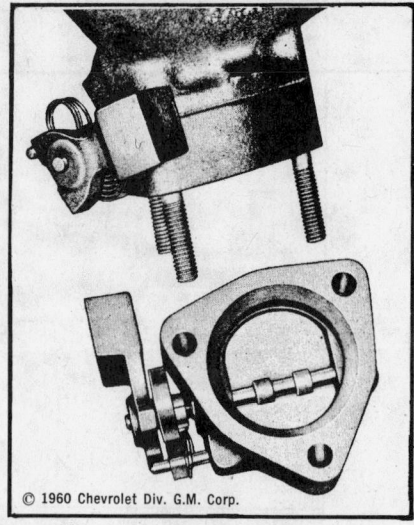

© 1960 Chevrolet Div. G.M. Corp.

Manifold Heat Valve Used on V8 Engines

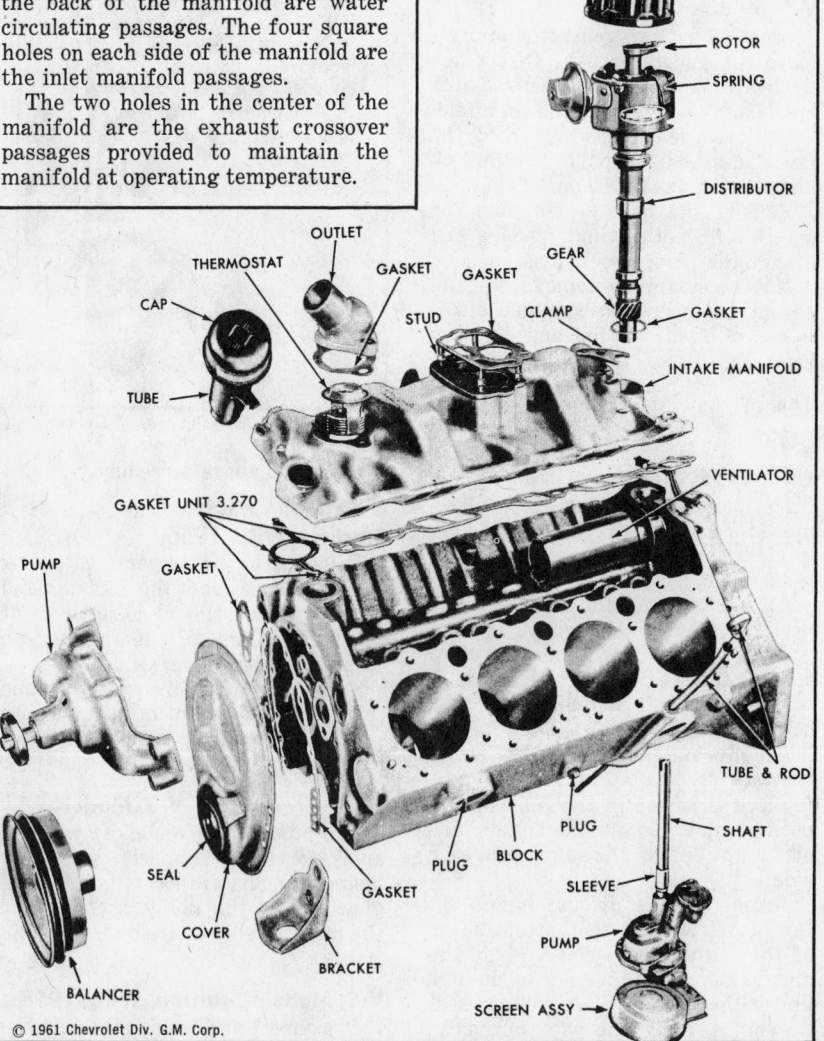

© 1961 Chevrolet Div. G.M. Corp.

Exploded View—V8 Engine External Parts

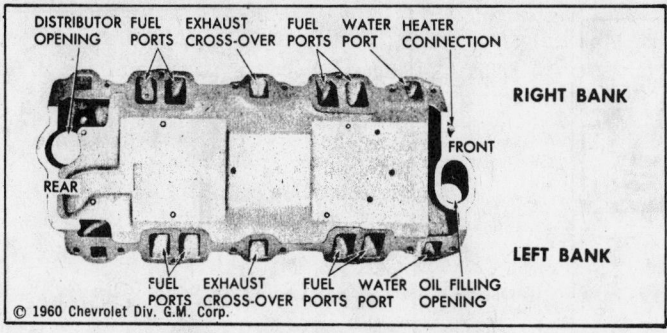

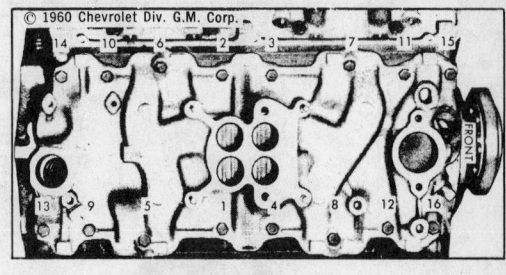

Intake Manifold Torque Sequence. 348 Cu. In. Engines Tighten to 25-35 ft. lbs.

348 Cu. In. V8 Intake Manifold Ports

REMOVAL OF EXHAUST MANIFOLD ASSEMBLY USED ON V8 ENGINES

Two exhaust manifolds are used and they are attached to the outside of each of the cylinder heads.

When removing either of the exhaust manifolds if any difficulty is experienced reaching the inside exhaust pipe flange bolt, it may be easier to disconnect the manifold first at the head and pull it away slightly from the cylinder block in order to get more easy access to the inner flange bolt.

CYLINDER HEAD

REMOVAL

6 Cylinder Models

To remove the cylinder head detach the air cleaner and all rods, lines and vacuum tubes at the carburetor and manifold.

Unbolt the manifold from the cylinder head but not from the exhaust pipe flange. The manifold is simply pulled away from the head.

Remove the engine side plate covers and the gas lines at the fuel pump. Unbolt and lift off the rocker cover, disconnect the oil line leads to the rockers.

Remove 4 bolts and 2 nuts on models prior to 1963 which retain the rocker arm assembly to the cylinder head and remove the rocker arm assembly. Beginning 1963 the rocker levers are supported separately and may be left intact until the head is removed.

Unbolt and lift off the cylinder head.

V-8 Models

Remove the carburetor, air cleaner and detach all lines and linkage at the carburetor rocker cover and distributor cap and wire assembly. Detach and remove distributor and upper water and heater hoses. Remove heat indicator sending unit.

Unbolt and lift off inlet manifold. Detach exhaust manifolds at both the head and the flange and lift off exhaust manifold.

Intake Manifild Torque Sequence. 265 and 283 Cu. In. Engine. Tighten to 25 to 35 ft. lbs.

Head can be unbolted without removing rockers by sliding the head up off the push rods.

Note: On 348 Cu. In. Engine the exhaust push rods are longer than the inlet push rods.

THE VALVE SYSTEM

Where some engines have hydraulic valve lifters and others do not, a means of determining which does and which does not is given in a note under the Tune-up Table.

Detailed information on the valves, the type of valve guide and valve timing information, can be found in the Valve Specifications Table of this section.

A general discussion of valve clearance and a chart showing how to read pressure and vacuum gauges when using them to diagnose engine troubles will be found in the Unit Repair section under the heading: Engine Diagnosis.

Valve tappet clearance for each engine is given in the Tune-up Specifications Table.

VALVE GUIDES

6 Cylinder Models, Prior to 1963

The clearance between the valve guide and the valve stem is very important.

Lack of power, noisy valves, poor idling, and generally noisy engine can sometimes be traced to worn valve guides.

A quick way to check the fit of the valve in its guide is to examine the valve stem carefully if there are signs of gum far enough down the valve stem that the gum entered the guide, then the guide is too loose and should be replaced.

Before driving out the old valve guide, carefully measure the distance from the top of the head to the guide or, better yet, secure a stack of flat washers which will fit over the guide and stack up just enough to make the washers come flush with the top of the valve guide and use this pile of washers as a stop for the valve guide driving tool.

The guides are knocked out from the top of the head into the combustion chamber portion. In other words, they are driven downwards.

The new guides are started also at the top of the head and driven downwards.

The best way to install a valve guide is in an arbor press, being very careful to note that the guide is at an angle to the machined surface of the cylinder head and the cylinder head must be supported at that angle in the arbor press so that the guide is pushed straight downwards.

When new guides have been installed, immediately try a new valve in the new valve guide and, if the slightest difficulty or the slightest binding is noticed, it will be necessary to pass a reamer through the guide since it has probably become distorted or riveted over because of the driver.

Whenever new valve guides are installed always lap in the valve so that it is concentric to the new guide.

Clearance between a worn valve and guide should not exceed .005. When new limits are .001-.003.

Beginning 1963, the valve guide is cast integral with the head.

V-8 Models Thru 1963

Separate valve guides are not used on the V-8 Chevrolet, instead the

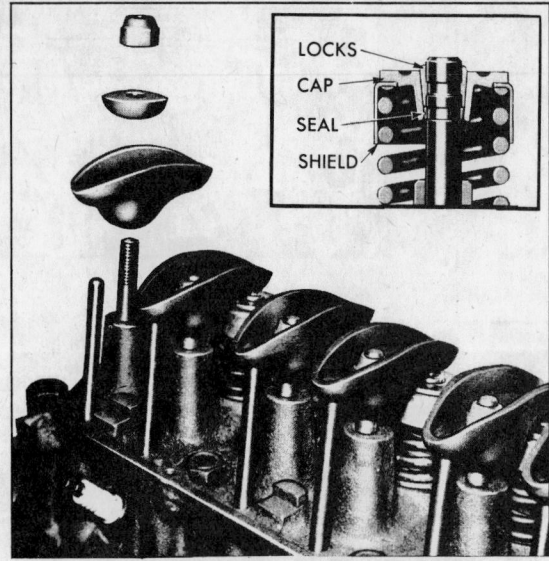

6 Cyl. Head & Rocker Arm Assembly
230 Cu. In.

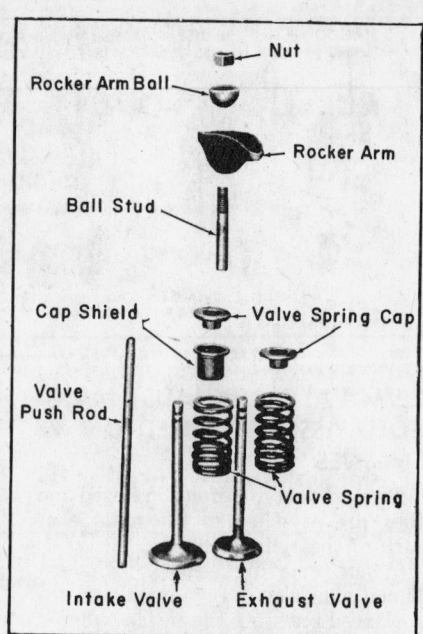

V-8 Engine Valve System

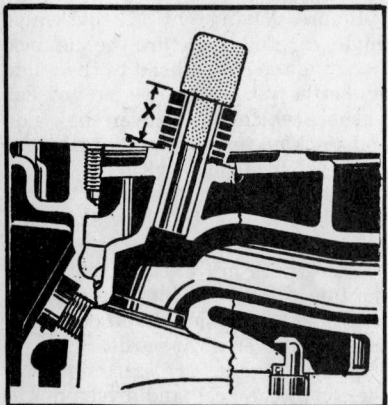

One method of controlling valve guide
depth—6 cyl. models

Correct Valve Installation
6 Cyl., 235 Cu. In.

valves are fitted directly into bores in the cylinder head.

Clearance of the valve stem to the bore should be .001 to .003 in. for inlet valves and .002 to .004 for exhaust valves. Clearance when worn should be within .002 of above limits.

This clearance should be checked by placing an indicator against the valve stem while gently pushing the valve from side to side so that the total clearance can be read in thousandths of an inch on the indicator.

If the clearance is found to be excessive as checked with the dial indicator, try a new valve in the bore to determine whether the bore is worn or the valve is worn. If it is found that the valve is worn, it will be necessary to install a new valve.

If it is found that the bore is worn, the bores can be reamed out since oversize valves are available having .003 in. oversize, .015 in. oversize, and .030 in. oversize.

Valve Replacement

With cylinder head on bench and the rockers removed, compress the valve spring and remove the valve lock, seal, spring cap and spring.

Line the valve springs up on a flat surface. They should all be the same height. Replace with new those that do not match.

When reinstalling the valves in the head there are available some asbestos washers with loading springs. These are placed over the intake valve stems onto the top of the valve guide before installation of the regular valve spring. It is said that these will aid when the guides are not too badly worn.

It is good practice to check that the contact between the seal at the end of the valve stem and the spring cap is air tight. The closed coil portion of the valve springs contact the head.

On six cylinder engines prior to 1963, the valve rockers have four different forms and it is well to check that they are in proper sequence before installing the rocker shaft as-

semblies to the head.

QUICK METHOD FOR VALVE TAPPET ADJUSTMENT ON ENGINES WITH HYDRAULIC LIFTERS

Adjust the rockers on both 6's and V8's until they just touch the valve stem.

Start the engine and back off a rocker adjustment until it clatters, tighten until no noise is heard and tighten further: 1 turn for 6's; ¾ of a turn for V8's. Repeat the procedure on all valves.

VALVE TAPPET ADJUSTMENT ENGINE STOPPED

6 Cylinder Engines

It is recommended that, since all Chevrolets have overhead valves, the

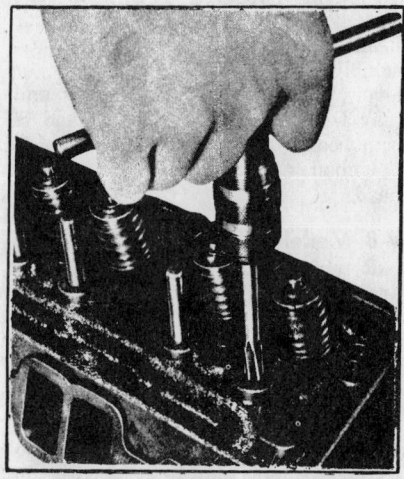

Reaming stud hole—V-8 Engines

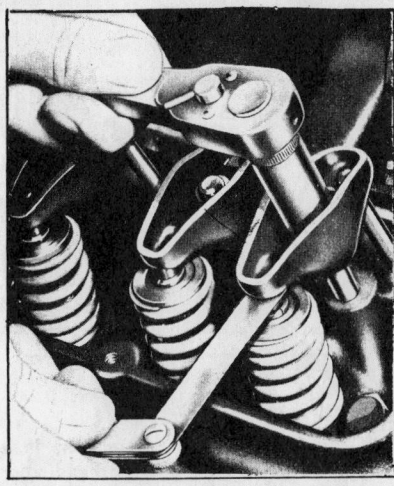

Adjusting valve clearance at the rocker arm on V-8 Engines

Adjusting Valve Clearance at Rocker Arms 6 Cyl., 230 Cu. In.

valves can be adjusted with the engine running at slow idle. This is generally conceded to be the easiest and best way to develop more accurate valve clearance.

However, if the operator desires to adjust the valves with the engine stationary, the following is the sequence for adjusting the valves which insures that the valve being adjusted will be on the base circle of the cam.

This sequence is also used for the initial adjustment of the 6 cylinder hydraulic valve lifters.

Turn the crank until No. 2 cylinder inlet valve is observed to start opening. Now turn the engine slowly and notice that No. 1 cylinder exhaust valve will also start to open. Continue cranking until No. 2 cylinder's intake valve is wide open, and then notice that No. 1 exhaust valve is also coming to the wide open position. No. 1 exhaust valve lags a little behind No. 2 inlet valve, but turn the crankshaft until both valves are wide open.

With these two valves wide open adjust:

No. 1 cylinder inlet
No. 2 cylinder exhaust
No. 3 cylinder both
No. 5 cylinder inlet
No. 6 cylinder exhaust

Now turn the crankshaft one full turn until No. 5 cylinder inlet is observed to start open. Lagging a little behind it will be No. 6 cylinder exhaust. Continue turning the crank until both of these valves are wide open and then adjust:

No. 1 cylinder exhaust
No. 2 cylinder inlet
No. 4 cylinder both
No. 5 cylinder exhaust
No. 6 cylinder inlet

V-8 Engines

For initial adjustment on the hydraulic valve lifters on the V-8 models or for the clearance adjustment of V-8 engines not equipped with hydraulic valve lifters the following sequence may be followed.

Keep in mind that the cylinders are numbered:

Left 1-3-5-7
Right 2-4-6-8

Turn the crank until No. 1 cylinder exhaust valve starts to open. As it approaches full open, notice that No. 7 cylinder inlet valve is also opening.

Turn the crank until both of these valves are in the wide open position and then adjust:

No. 1 cylinder inlet
No. 3 cylinder both
No. 4 cylinder inlet
No. 5 cylinder exhaust
No. 6 cylinder exhaust
No. 7 cylinder exhaust
No. 8 cylinder inlet

When these are adjusted satisfactorily, turn the crankshaft one full revolution to bring up No. 6 cylinder exhaust valve. Following No. 6 cylinder exhaust valve notice that No. 4 cylinder intake valve is also starting to open. When both of these valves are wide open, adjust:

No. 1 cylinder exhaust valve
No. 2 cylinder both
No. 4 cylinder exhaust valve
No. 5 cylinder inlet valve
No. 6 cylinder inlet valve
No. 7 cylinder inlet valve
No. 8 cylinder exhaust valve

Following the above sequence it is only necessary to turn the engine over once after the initial adjustment.

ROCKER ARM ASSEMBLIES

6 Cylinder Models, Prior to 1963

The formation of oil and gum deposits in the hollowed out rocker shaft will result in poor or inadequate lubrication to the rocker arms and may result in noisy and faulty operation of the valves. Therefore, any time it is necessary to remove the rocker assembly it is a good idea to disassemble the rocker arms from the shaft and thoroughly clean out the shaft and the oil holes which supply each rocker with oil.

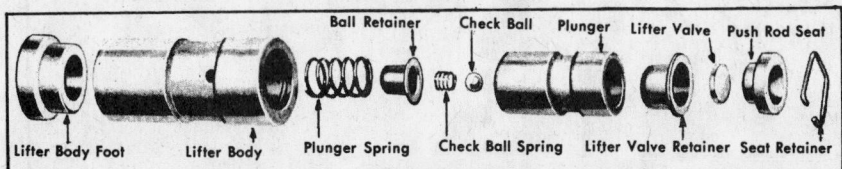

235 Cu. In. 6 Cylinder rocker arm shaft assembly

Typical Hydraulic Lifter Exploded

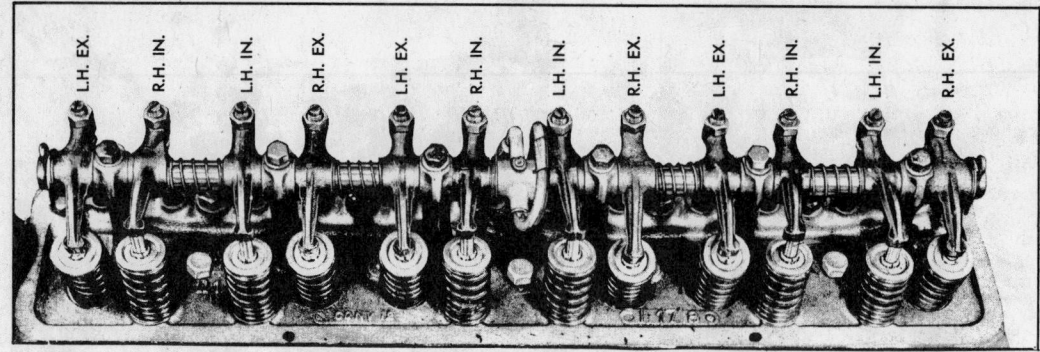

LH. EX. RH. IN. LH. IN. RH. EX. LH. EX. RH. IN. LH. IN. RH. EX. LH. EX. RH. IN. LH. IN. RH. EX.

235 Cu. In. 6 Cyl. Valve Rockers Correctly Installed

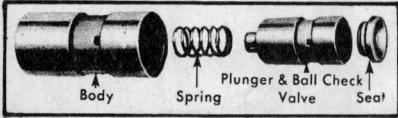

Body Spring Plunger & Ball Check Valve Seat

1963—Valve Lifter Components

Beginning 1963

The 6 cylinder, 230 cu. in. engine is equipped with a valve train and rocker lubrication design similar to the V8 engines. The rocker arms are supported upon individual pedestals with valve zero lash adjustment made at the rocker arm-to-pedestal ball seat and nut.

Rocker arm and cylinder head services are to be performed the same as on V8 engines.

To remove the rocker arms, simply take off the air cleaner, disconnect the rocker cover assembly and lift it off, (a new gasket must be used on reinstallation), disconnect the oil feed line at the center of the rocker arm, and remove the bolts which hold the rocker arm brackets to the top of the cylinder head.

When reassembling the rocker shafts to the engine be sure the open ends of the rocker shafts are connected to the oil fitting in the center.

The plugged ends face the front and the back.

The rocker arms should be marked which half is front and which half is back to avoid confusion on reassembly.

Since some of the early engines use three different types of rocker arms and 1954 engines use four different rocker arms, it will be necessary to mark them very carefully so that they will be installed properly in the engine.

On 1954 engines the rocker arms are stamped 1-2-5 or 6. The rocker arm stamped 1 is used for the exhaust on cylinders One, Three and Five.

The rocker stamped number 2 is used on the exhaust on cylinder Two, Four and Six.

The rocker stamped number 5 is used on the intake of cylinders Two, Four and Six.

The rocker stamped number 6 is used on the intake of cylinders of One, Three and Five.

However, if the rocker arms are tagged carefully from One to Twelve from the front of the engine, it will not be necessary to check on the stamp numbers on the rocker itself.

On reassembling the rocker shafts to the engine the open end of each shaft goes toward the center.

V-8 Models

The rocker arm on the V-8 models is formed of pressed steel with an oval hole in the center which fits over a stud having a spherical type nut at the top for adjustment.

Oil is fed through the hollowed out push rod and lies in the trough of the rocker arm providing adequate lubrication for the rocker arm spherical nut.

The rocker arm post is a pressed fit in the cylinder head and is available from Chevrolet stock in several oversizes for replacement purposes.

Chevrolet supplies special reamers with the oversize post. Reaming should be done with extreme care in order to get a press fit on the oversize stud.

TIMING CASE

CRANKSHAFT PULLEY REPLACEMENT

6 Cylinder Models

Remove the radiator core and the fan belt.

Use a screw type puller to remove the balancer-pulley assembly.

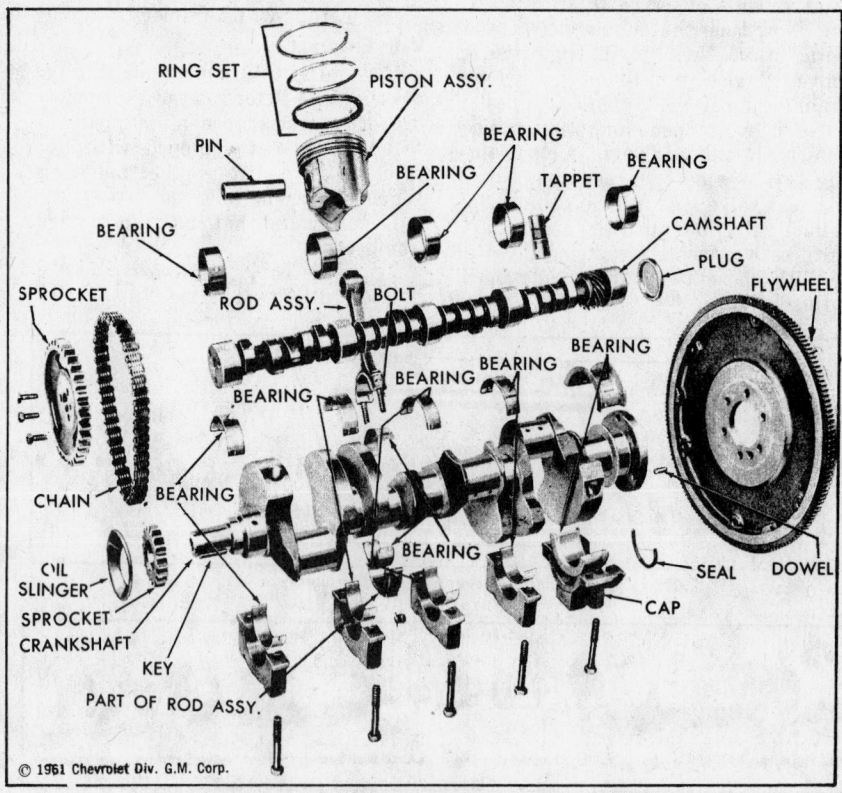

RING SET PISTON ASSY. PIN BEARING BEARING BEARING TAPPET BEARING CAMSHAFT PLUG FLYWHEEL SPROCKET ROD ASSY. BOLT BEARING BEARING BEARING BEARING CHAIN BEARING BEARING SEAL DOWEL OIL SLINGER CAP SPROCKET CRANKSHAFT KEY PART OF ROD ASSY.

Exploded View—V8 Engine Internal Parts

V-8 Models

Drain radiator and disconnect the hoses. Take off the fan belt, and the fan pulley assembly. Remove the battery.

Remove the fan shroud. Now remove the radiator core. Unbolt the pulley portion of the balancer-pulley assembly.

Install screw type puller and remove the balancer portion from the crankshaft.

TIMING CASE COVER AND FRONT END OIL SEAL REPLACEMENT

6 Cylinder Models

Remove the crankshaft pulley. Remove the oil pan.

Remove the timing case cover attaching screws and the two bolts that are installed from inside the engine through the front main bearing cap to hold the cover at the bottom.

Remove the cover and gasket. Pry the old seal out of the front side of the cover with a large screwdriver.

Install the new seal so that the open end of the seal is toward the inside of the cover. When reinstalling, be careful that cover is positioned to hold seal concentric to the shaft.

Tighten the screws and the two bolts inside the engine to 6-7½ ft. lbs.

V-8 Models

Remove the crankshaft pulley. Remove the oil pan. Remove the water pump. Remove the screws holding the timing case cover to the block and remove the cover and gaskets.

Use a large screwdriver to pry the old seal out of the front face of the cover.

Install the new seal so that open end is toward the inside of the cover.

Check that the timing chain oil slinger is in place against the crankshaft sprocket.

Install the cover carefully onto the locating dowels.

Tighten the attaching screws to 6-8 ft. lbs.

TIMING GEAR REPLACEMENT

6 Cylinder Engines

Chevrolet timing gears are arranged so that (unless deliberately disturbed) the valve timing will remain as set at the factory when the engine was assembled. Unless the gears are badly worn or seriously damaged the valve timing will remain constant within reasonable limits.

If it becomes necessary to replace the timing gears due to wear or damage, remove the radiator core, disconnect the front motor mounts and

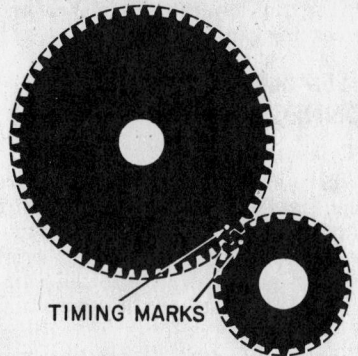

Timing Mark Alignment 6 Cyl.

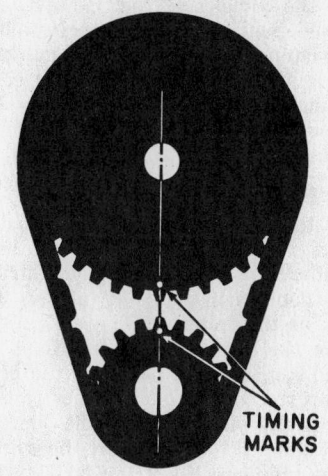

Timing Mark Alignment V-8

jack up the front of the engine. Remove the fan belt, fan pulley, oil pan and timing case cover.

NOTE: The Chevrolet Motor Car Company recommends that the camshaft be removed from the car in order to remove and replace the gear in an arbor press.

Many successful mechanics prefer removing the camshaft in order to avoid possible risk when attempting to press a gear onto the shaft in place on the car. Sometimes when the gear is being pressed on in place on the car, damage results to the thrust washer in back of the cam gear. Unfortunately this damage is not noticed until the engine is started.

To replace the gear by removing the camshaft, remove the rocker arm assemblies and the distributor, take out all of the push rods and take out all of the lifters. The camshaft may then be pulled out toward the front of the engine. It will be necessary to retime the ignition.

Runout of the timing gear should not exceed .004 inch. Backlash between the two gears should not be less than .004 inch nor more than .006 inch. End clearance of the thrust plate should be .001 to .005.

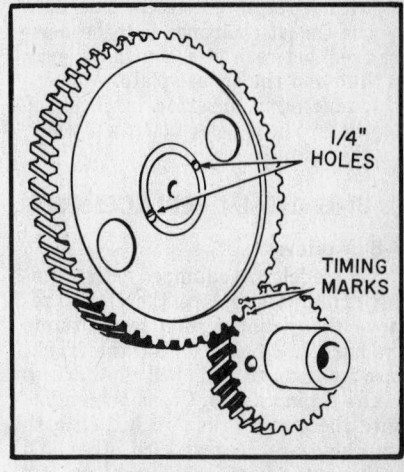

Time-saver for fast removal drill ¼" holes

⊙ CHILTON TIME-SAVER

A different approach to this situation and certainly a quicker one has proven successful in our practical experiments and is, as follows:

1. Very carefully center punch and drill two ¼" holes in opposite sides of the camshaft gear hub, as illustrated.
2. Break the fiber part of the camshaft gear away from the steel hub.
3. Split the steel hub with a cold chisel at the two newly drilled holes.
4. Remove broken camshaft gear and clean entire timing case area.
5. Place the new gear on the camshaft to line up with the keyway and the gear timing marks.
NOTE: Be sure to allow for the helical cut on the gear when aligning the marks for timing.
6. Have a RELIABLE helper, with the aid of a pinch bar, buck up against one of the camshaft lobes from underneath. (The success of the job depends upon this man's care in holding forward thrust on the camshaft. Failure on his part will allow the camshaft to be forced back and dislodge the oil sealing expansion plug in the back at the rear of the camshaft.)
7. With the aid of a 1¼" socket and a lead hammer, tap the new gear into place on the camshaft.
CAUTION: The use of a dial indicator will reduce the possibility of driving the gear too far onto the camshaft. This would alter the desired camshaft thrust clearance of .001" to .005". Use care when approaching the final position of the gear on the shaft as it is impossible to increase the thrust clearance without pulling the new gear. In the absence of a dial indicator, this end thrust can be measured

with a feeler gauge. In this case the thrust clearance is to be masured between the camshaft gear hub and the thrust plate. A feeler gauge strip, inserted in either of the two large gear holes, will reach this point.

TIMING CHAIN REPLACEMENT

V-8 Models

V-8 models are equipped with a timing chain. To replace the chain, remove the radiator core, water pump the harmonic balancer and the crankcase front cover. This will allow access to the timing chain. Crank the engine until the zero marks punched on both sprockets are nearest each other and in line between the shaft centers, and then take out the three bolts which hold the camshaft gear to the camshaft. This gear is a light press fit on the camshaft and will come off readily. It is located by a dowel.

The chain comes off with the camshaft gear.

A gear puller will be required to remove the crankshaft gear.

Without disturbing the position of the engine, mount the new crank gear on the shaft and then mount the chain over the camshaft gear. Arrange the camshaft gear in such a way that the timing marks will line up between the shaft centers and the camshaft locating dowel will enter the dowel hole in the cam sprocket.

Place the cam sprocket, with its chain mounted over it, in position on the front of the car and pull up with the three bolts which hold it to the camshaft.

After the gears are in place turn the engine two full revolutions to make certain that the timing marks are in correct alignment between the shaft centers.

End play of the V8 camshaft is zero.

PISTONS, CONNECTING RODS AND MAIN BEARINGS

PISTONS

Detailed information on pistons and piston pins, together with information on piston, rod and crankshaft relationship for assembly, will be found in the Piston and Pin Specifications Table of this section.

CONNECTING ROD BEARINGS

Chevrolet Motor Car Co. does not recommend adjusting the slip-in type rod bearing. However, this bearing may be adjusted for normal wear by installing a taper or feather type shim

between the lower bearing shell and the bearing cap.

ASSEMBLING PISTON TO CONNECTING ROD

6 Cylinder Engines

Where split skirt type pistons are being installed the split in the skirt of the piston should be placed opposite to the clamp screw of the wrist pin; this is also opposite to the number on the bottom of the connecting rod.

Where solid skirt slipper type pistons are being replaced it is immaterial which way the piston is mounted onto the connecting rod. However, if the old pistons are being reinstalled the piston should be carefully marked before it is detached from the connecting rod in order that it may be replaced on the same side from which it was removed.

V-8 Engines

Pistons are marked with a cast depression at the top of the piston and also the letter "F" on the piston strut. This depression and "F" always go towards the front.

For the left bank, pistons No. 1, 3, 5 and 7, the heavy flange at the bottom of the connecting rod goes on the side of the piston having the depression and "F" mark. For the right bank, cylinders No. 2, 4, 6 and 8, the heavy flange on the connecting rod goes to the side opposite the stamped letter "F" and the cast depression in the top of the piston.

ASSEMBLING PISTON AND ROD ASSEMBLY TO THE ENGINE

6 Cylinder Models, Prior to 1963

When assembling the piston and connecting rod assemblies to the en-

gine the number on the bottom of the connecting rod (also the clamp bolt on the wrist pin) should face the camshaft side of the engine.

Numbers are stamped on both the connecting rod and the connecting rod cap, both numbers facing the camshaft side.

V-8 Models

Place the piston and rod assemblies into the cylinder so that the depression cast into the top of the piston (and the letter "F" stamped on the boss of the piston) face front. Double check that the pistons are in the correct bank by noting that on the left bank, pistons No. 1, 3, 5 and 7, the heavy flange on the connecting rod will also face forward, but on the right bank, cylinders No. 2, 4, 6 and 8, the heavy flange on the connecting rod will face towards the rear.

CAUTION:

Some pistons, such as those used in the 348 engine with high lift camshaft, have a peculiar head shape. Where the standard piston is equipped with a gabled roof, or double slanted top, the high torque piston top has but one slanted side. This is a means of raising compression ratio from 9.5:1 to 11.0:1.

Use care in assembly as the piston head is clearance-bored to allow for the valve head.

6 Cyl. Models, Beginning 1963

When assembling the rods to the pistons and installing the pistons in their respective bores, be sure that the flange or heavy side of the rod at the bearing end is toward the front of the piston (cast depression in top of piston head). The oil hole in the connecting rod goes toward the camshaft side of the engine.

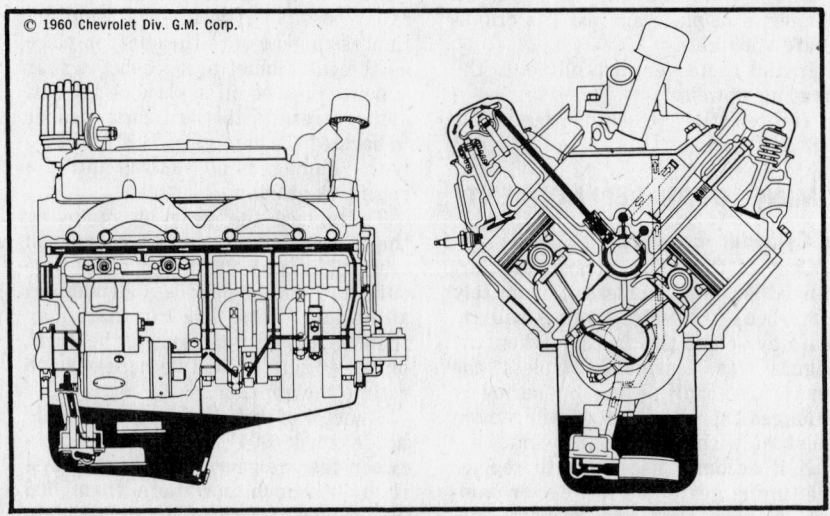

© 1960 Chevrolet Div. G.M. Corp.

265 and 283 Cu. In. V-8 Engine Lubrication

CRANKSHAFT MAIN BEARINGS

1954 Thru 1957
6 Cylinder Only

The main bearings on these models have a boss pressed into the outer rim of the oil hole in the center of the bearing. This boss fits up into a hole in the crankcase. In order to remove the upper half of the main bearing the crankshaft must be lowered somewhat to give this boss cast into the bearing a chance to clear the oil supply hole. Since the boss is a very small one, the bearing can be removed without too much difficulty.

Ordinary replacement bearings do not have this boss.

ENGINE LUBRICATION

OIL PAN REMOVAL

1954 6 Cylinder

To remove the oil pan, first remove the intermediate arm bracket and lower the arm and then unbolt and remove the oil pan. Make careful note of the shims used between the upper mounting bolt of the steering arm and the cross member so that the same number may be reinstalled.

1955 to 1957 6 Cylinder

Raise front of vehicle and place on stand jacks. Drain oil from engine.

Disconnect steering idler arm bracket from right hand frame side rail and drop for clearance.

Remove oil pan retaining bolts and screws and remove the oil pan. Crankshaft may have to be turned to allow clearance at front cross member.

When reinstalling tighten corner bolts to 12½ to 15 ft. lbs. and side rail screws to 6 to 7½ ft. lbs.

6 Cylinder Starting 1958

Chevrolet recommends the following procedure.

Scribe alignment marks on hood

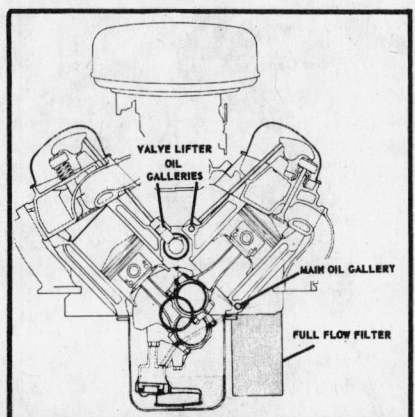

348 Cu. In. Turbo-Thurst V-8 Engine Lubrication

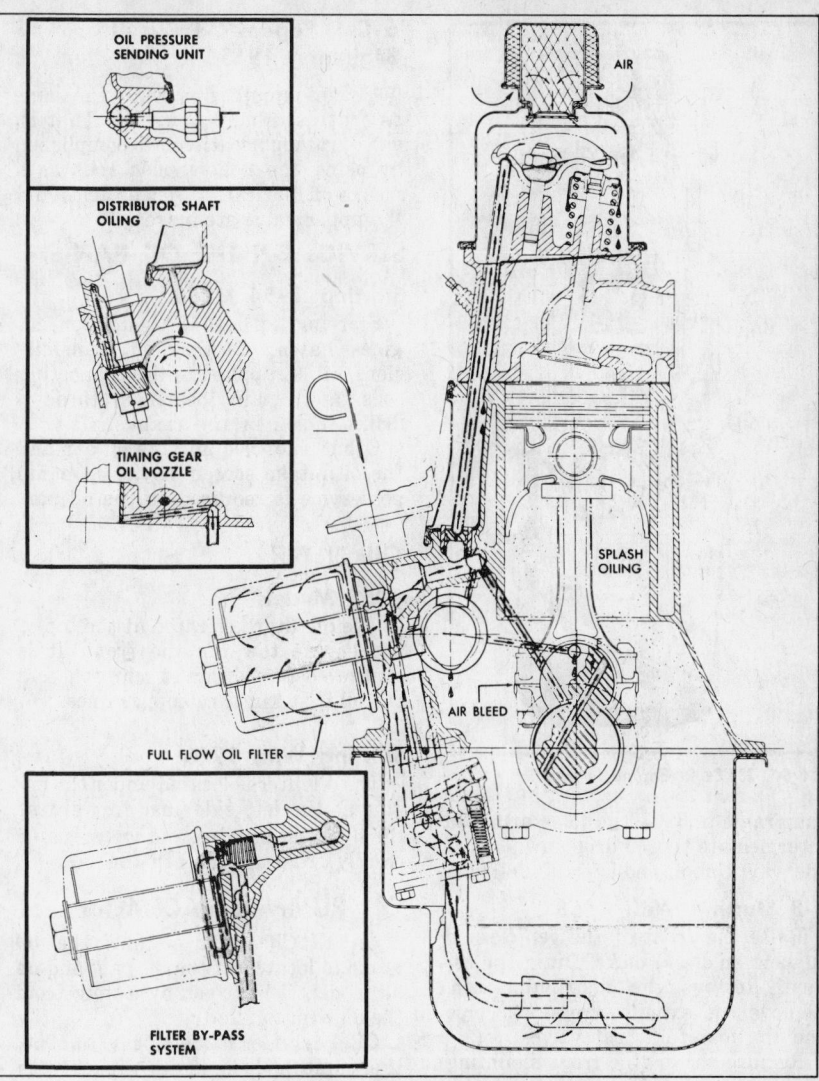

230 Cu. In. 6 Cylinder Engine Lubrication

around hood hinges and remove the hood.

Remove battery to engine ground cable. Disconnect gas line from tank at the fuel pump. Unfasten generator wires at the generator and loosen the fan belt. Drain radiator, disconnect hoses and lines and remove the radiator. Remove the radiator fan and pulley. Remove the valve cover and install a lift bolt. Hoist the engine up enough so front mount center bolts can be unfastened.

Unfasten exhaust pipe at manifold.

On Synchromesh models: Disconnect the clutch idler shaft bracket at the engine. Remove overdrive solenoid from transmission. Remove flywheel underpan extension. Disconnect shifter rods at the transmission.

On automatic models: Disconnect the oil cooler lines and the control linkage at the transmission.

Continuing for all models: Disconnect the propeller shaft at the differential, remove the center support

bolts and slide shaft to rear and so clear of transmission. Disconnect speedometer cable at the transmission. Drain the transmission and remove the transmission rear support and cross member.

Drain the oil from the engine, unbolt the oil pan and raise engine so that oil pan can clear the front cross member and be removed through the front of the engine compartment.

The crankshaft may have to be turned so that oil pan can clear the counterweights. In reinstalling, tighten corner bolts to 12½-15 ft. lbs. and side rail screws to 6-7½ ft. lbs.

⏻ CHILTON TIME-SAVER

Experience dictates the removal of the engine, to save time on this operation.

1955 to 1957 V-8

Jack up the car and drain the oil pan. Unbolt the steering idler arm at

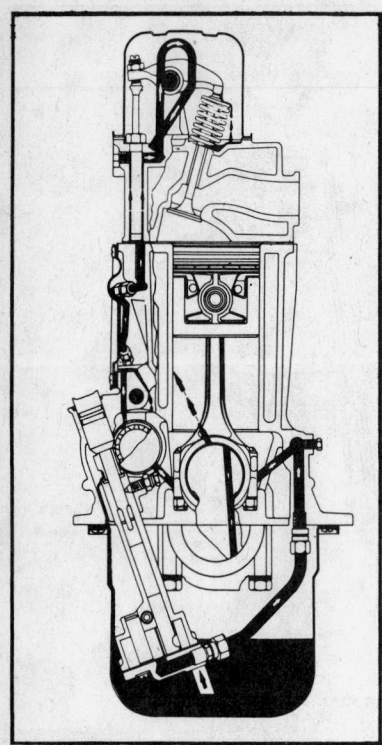

6 Cyl., 235 Cu. In. *Engine Lubrication*

the frame and let the idler arm and intermediate tie rod drop down out of the way. Unbolt and lower the oil pan.

V-8 Starting With 1958

Raise the front of the vehicle and support on stand jacks. Drain the engine. Remove the distributor cap. Remove the exhaust cross-over pipe and the manifold heat valve.

Remove the engine front mounting nuts, washers and bolts (one on each side holding mount to bracket).

Turn the crankshaft so that the crankshaft pulley keyway is at bottom of the engine. This will index crankshaft counterweights so baffle in oil pan can clear them.

Using a jack under the crankshaft pulley raise the engine at least three inches. Be careful that fan remains clear of shrouds.

Remove oil pan bolts using a universal socket and long speed handle. Tilt pan to remove from car.

When reinstalling, tighten bolts to 10-15 ft. lbs.

6 Cyl. Beginning 1963

1. Disconnect battery ground strap.
2. Drain crankcase oil.
3. Disconnect wires at solenoid, then remove starter.
4. Disconnect steering idler arm and lower linkage for pan clearance.
5. Remove the front crossmember.
6. Remove attaching bolts and drop oil pan. Install by reversing the removal procedure.

6 Cyl. Engine Oil Circuit Beginning 1963

The oil circuit is basically the same as that used on V8 engines. That is, valve train lubrication is accomplished by using the hollow push rods as a means of lubricating rocker arms and the upper valve stem area.

SERVICE ON THE OIL PAN

Starting 1954 Models

Starting with 1954 production engines having Powerglide transmissions, oil is supplied to the connecting rods and main bearings through drilled holes in the crankshaft.

Other than cleaning the oil pan and the oil intake screen of the oil pump no service is required on the oil pan.

OIL FILTER

1955 Models

The oil filter is located at the top of the engine towards the front. It is bracketed to the intake manifold and the oil is fed in thru copper lines.

Starting With 1956

The oil filter is located under the engine at the left side just forward of the flywheel housing and is accessible readily from underneath the car.

OIL PUMP REPLACEMENT

On all Chevrolet engines the oil pump is located in the oil pan, and on all models it is driven by a tang from the distributor shaft.

On 6 cylinder models prior to 1963, the pump is held in its socket with cap screw located just under the camshaft bearing.

Loosen this screw and the pump can be removed readily after the lines are disconnected.

Positive Ventilating System 1963 6 Cyl.

On 6 cyl. engines beginning 1963, the pump is flange-mounted to the under side of the crankcase with two cap screws.

On V-8 models the oil pump is bolted to the rear main bearing cap. Oil is fed from the pump up through the rear main bearing cap.

OIL PUMP DISASSEMBLY

Remove the oil pump from the engine to the bench.

Detach the oil pickup screen and clean it up thoroughly with a clean solvent. Remove the cover from the oil pump and slide off the idler gear.

With the main drive gear still left keyed to the shaft, thoroughly clean up the inside of the oil pump. Examine the inside of the pump body for deep scores or scratches, also the cover plate for scores or scratches. Replace the idler gear and check the clearance

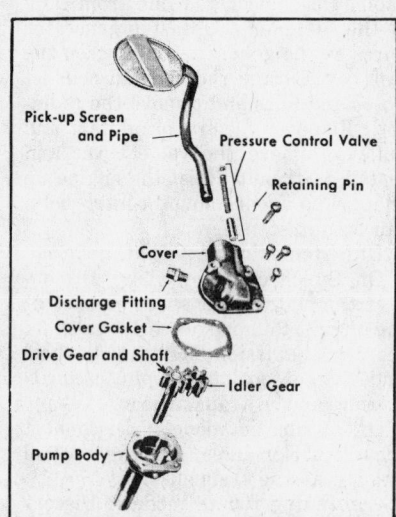

Layout of 6 Cyl. Oil Pump

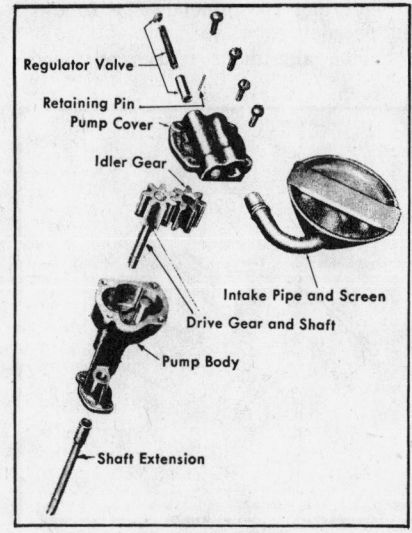

Layout of V8 Oil Pump

between the idler gear and the drive gear teeth at the point where they mesh. This clearance should not exceed two or three thousandths of an inch. The clearance around the outer rim of either of the gears should not exceed two or three thousandths of an inch.

If any of the parts are scored or badly worn and the engine has a reputation for developing low oil pressure, replace the gears and/or the housing, whichever shows wear.

REAR MAIN BEARING OIL SEAL REPLACEMENT

Wick Type Seal

Remove oil pan and oil pump. Remove rear main bearing cap, discarding lower seal.

Loosen the remaining bearing caps to allow the crankshaft to drop a slight amount. If the crankshaft does not drop place a lever between the shaft and block and so force the crankshaft down into the space provided.

Using a screwdriver or similar tool, push the seal out of upper bearing so end can be grabbed with pliers and pulled on out. Wiggle the crankshaft slightly to aid this operation.

Use the lower bearing cap to form the new upper seal into a semi-circle. Insert a wire (soft tag-type) through the seal about 1/4 inch in from the end. Wrap the wire around the end of the seal so it has a good grip.

Use a light coat of vaseline to lubricate the seal and insert the wire into the seal groove and up and over the crankshaft. Pull the seal gently into position. It may be needful to rotate the crankshaft to aid in getting the seal placed. With seal centered in the opening, cut off the ends so that they stick out 1/64 inch beyond the parting surface.

Install the lower seal in the groove and roll into place. Cut the small portions of the ends which protrude from the groove flush with the surface of the bearing cap. Install bearing cap over crankshaft onto the block.

Neoprene Seal

Remove rear main bearing cap and pry old seal from groove. Insert new seal with lubricant only on the lip. Do not get oil on the glue-treated parting

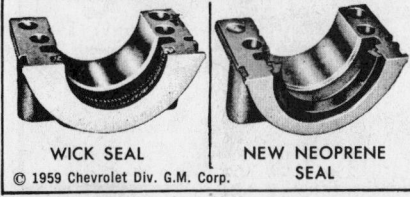

WICK SEAL NEW NEOPRENE SEAL
© 1959 Chevrolet Div. G.M. Corp.

Rear Main Bearing Seal

line surfaces. Lip faces front of engine.

Using a hammer and small punch persuade the upper half of the seal to revolve until it protrudes far enough to be removed with pliers.

Oil the seal except at the glue-treated ends, and using a hammer handle, roll the seal into place in the block.

These seals are made to size and require no trimming. Install the lower half over the crankshaft and in place onto the block.

Engine Front Mounts. Do not unbolt at "C".

FRONT SUSPENSION

REFERENCES

General instructions covering the front suspension and how to repair and adjust it, together with information on installation of front wheel bearings and grease seals, are given in the Unit Repair section under the heading: Suspension, Front Repair.

Definitions of the points of steering geometry are covered in the Unit Repair section under the heading: Suspension, Front Align. This article also covers trouble shooting front end geometry and irregular tire wear.

Figures covering the caster, camber, toe-in, king pin inclination, and turning radius can be found in the Front Wheel Alignment Table of this section.

Wheelbase, tread and tire size figures can be found in the General Chassis and Brake Specifications Table of this section.

FRONT SPRINGS

Remove & Install

1. With car supported high enough to permit the control arms to swing clear of the floor, remove wheel and tire assembly.
2. Remove front stabilizer bar and shock absorber.
3. Loosen lower ball joint-to-steering knuckle nut, and the two lower control arm cross shaft bushing bolts.
4. With a suitable spring compresser, compress the spring.
5. Disconnect lower ball joint from the steering knuckle, then lower the control arm with the compressed spring.

Caution:

This compressed spring is a potential danger, carefully release compression as soon as the spring is free of the car.

6. Install spring in the reverse order of removal.

Ball Joint Inspection and Services can be found in the Unit Repair section under "Suspension Front Repair."

HORN BUTTON

HORN BUTTON REMOVAL

1954 Models
With Standard Wheel

On these models the horn button is pried up.

1954 Models Deluxe Wheel

Pry off the medallion and remove the screws and large nut. Take off the steering wheel using a puller and the ring can then be separated from the steering wheel.

1955-56 Models

From under the center spoke remove the clutch head screw and then pry the horn blowing ring off the steering wheel.

1957 Models

Both the DeLuxe and standard horn button are simply pried out of the steering wheel.

Starting With 1958

The horn blowing ring is retained to the steering wheel by two screws from underneath the spokes of the wheel.

Remove the two screws and lift off the horn blowing ring.

HORN RELAY

1954 Models

The horn relay is mounted on the left side firewall under the hood.

1955 Thru 1957 Models

The horn relay is located on the left fender skirt below the generator regulator.

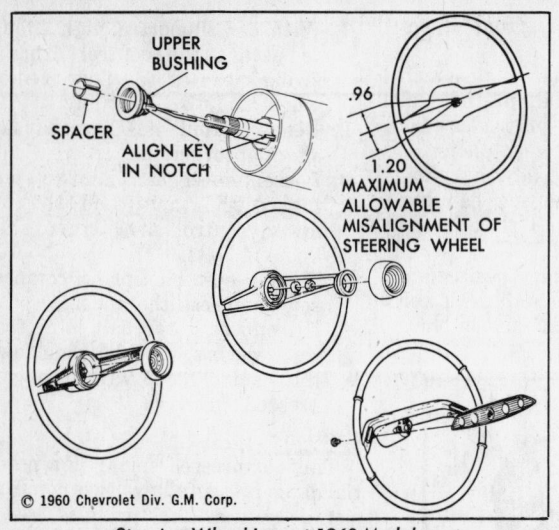

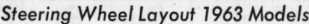

Steering Wheel Layout 1963 Models

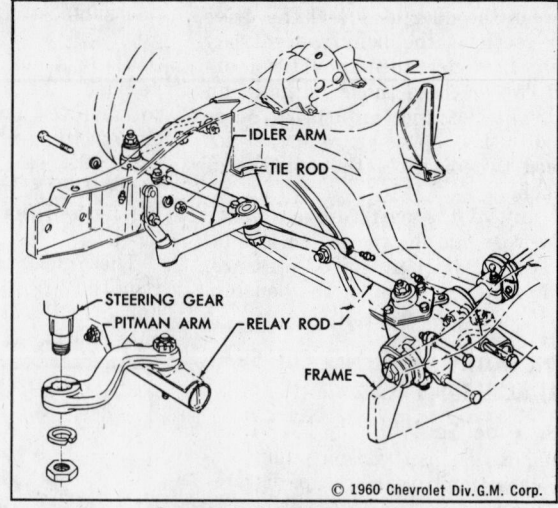

Steering Linkage 1963 Models

Starting With 1958 Models

The horn relay is located on the radiator core panel just above the generator regulator.

STEERING GEAR

MANUAL STEERING GEAR

Instructions covering the adjustment of the steering gear will be found in the Unit Repair section under the heading: Steering, Manual.

POWER STEERING GEARS

Trouble shooting and repair instructions covering power steering gears are given in the Unit Repair section under the heading: Steering, Power.

REMOVAL OF THE STEERING GEAR ASSEMBLY FROM THE CAR

1954 Models

Using a puller, remove the steering wheel.

Remove the clamp which fastens the column jacket to the instrument panel and remove the column jacket toe board grommet and seal from the toe board. Disconnect the gear shift control support from the column jacket and rotate the shifter housing with its control lever out of the way.

Unfasten the steering gear from the frame and, rotating it to clear the fender skirt, raise the gear bringing it upwards and forward to remove it from the engine compartment.

1955 Thru 1957 Models

Disconnect all electrical connections under the dash to the steering column, remove the back-up light switch on cars so equipped, pry out the horn button and remove the horn mechanism.

Using a puller, take off the steering wheel.

Remove the dash panel attaching bracket from the bottom of the mast jacket in the engine compartment. Do not remove the two bolts which hold the bracket to the engine side of the dash panel since this will necessitate realigning the gear. Just remove the bracket only.

Disconnect the transmission linkage from the shift lever at the bottom of the steering column.

Slide the rubber seal (driving compartment just in front of the instrument panel) away from the covers and then remove the lower cover retaining screws, below the instrument panel at the mast jacket; and then remove the upper cover located above the mast jacket just below the speedometer head.

Remove the mast jacket clamp which holds the upper end of the mast jacket to the underside of the instrument panel. Do not lose the shims. On Powerglide models, disconnect the indicator rod from the indicator lever and then remove the transmission control selector plate.

Pull the entire mast jacket assembly up off the steering tube.

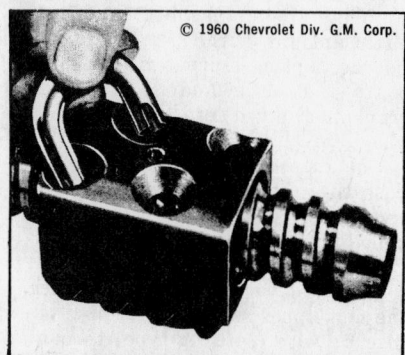

Removing Ball Guide

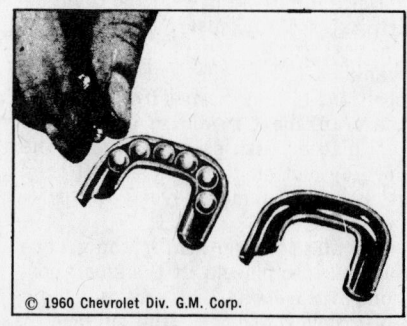

Filling Ball Guides

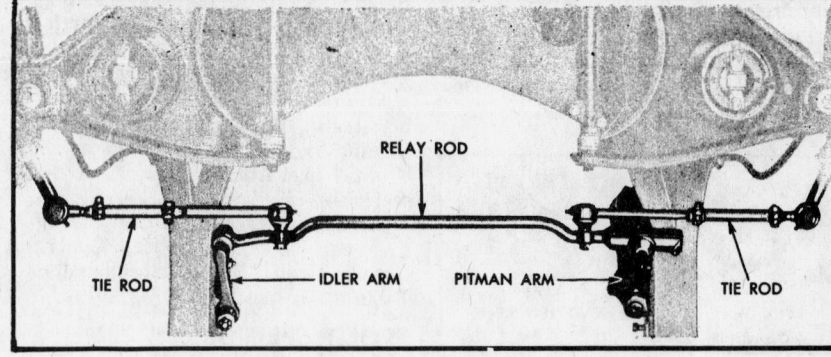

Steering Linkage starting with 1955

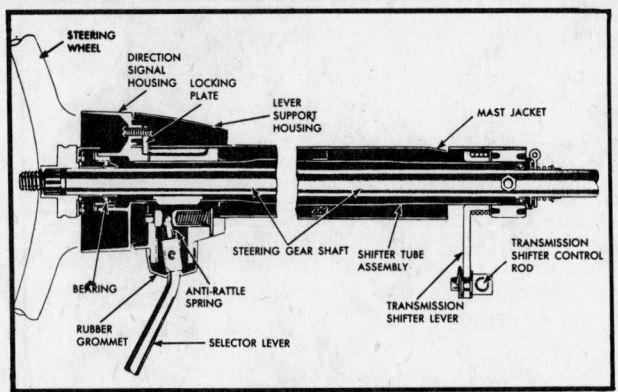

**Mast Jacket and Shifter Tube. Automatic Transmission Type.
1958 Shown.**

*Mast Jacket and Shifter Tube. Synchromesh Transmission Type.
1958 Shown.*

If desired the steering gear assembly can now be unbolted from the frame and removed.

Starting With 1958

From under the car, using a puller, remove the pitman arm from the steering cross shaft. Under the hood remove the clamp bolt which holds the lower steering shaft to the coupling.

Remove the bolts which retain the steering gear box to the frame, loosen the generator mounting bracket and tilt the generator up out of the way, slide the gear downwards a sufficient amount to separate it from the couple and pull the gear assembly and lower shaft up out of the engine compartment.

<u>Caution:</u> Any shims found between the casting and the mounting position on the frame should be retained since they are the aligning shims.

DISASSEMBLE, INSPECT, REPAIR

Remove the gear assembly from the vehicle as outlined in either of the above paragraphs.

Remove the gear housing to a bench. Remove the top cover, carrying with it the cross shaft. Once off the gear, slide the cross shaft off the cover adjusting screw.

Loosen the worm bearing adjuster lock nut and remove the worm bearing adjuster.

Take out the lower bearing and slide the steering shaft, together with its ball nut, out of the housing. The upper bearing may come out with the steering shaft or it may stay up in the housing. In either case, remove it.

Thoroughly clean up the housing assembly and the cross shaft in a good solvent.

Inspect the upper bearing race, which is still in the upper end of the housing, for pits and scratches, and if any are found the race will have to be driven out of the housing and a new one will have to be installed. Examine the upper and lower ball bearing for pits or flat spots on the balls. If any are found, replace the bearing.

Wash up the steering shaft and ball nut in clean solvent and then place on a clean piece of paper.

Now carefully turn the ball nut on the worm shaft, feeling for any roughness, binding or sticking. If the ball nut turns perfectly smooth on the worm and is neither loose nor binding, it will not be necessary to disassemble it.

The nut can be run to the top end of the worm and the lower end of the worm grooves examined. Then the nut

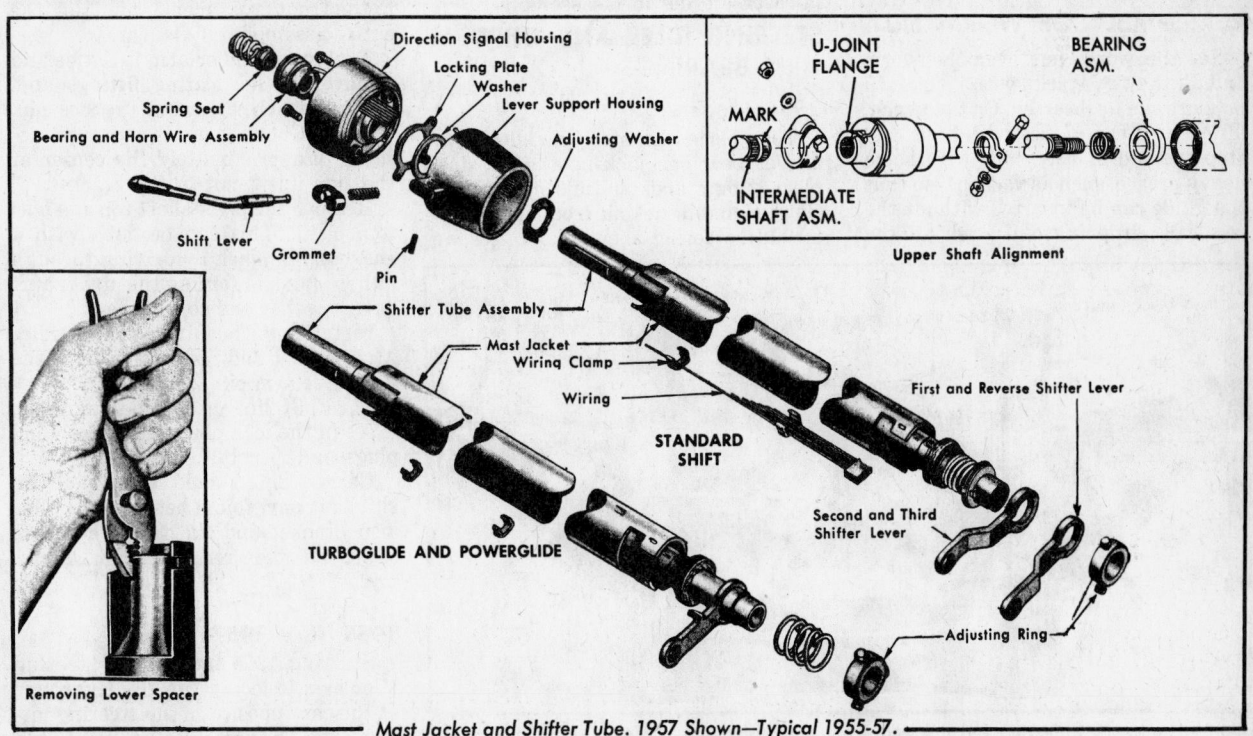

Mast Jacket and Shifter Tube. 1957 Shown—Typical 1955-57.

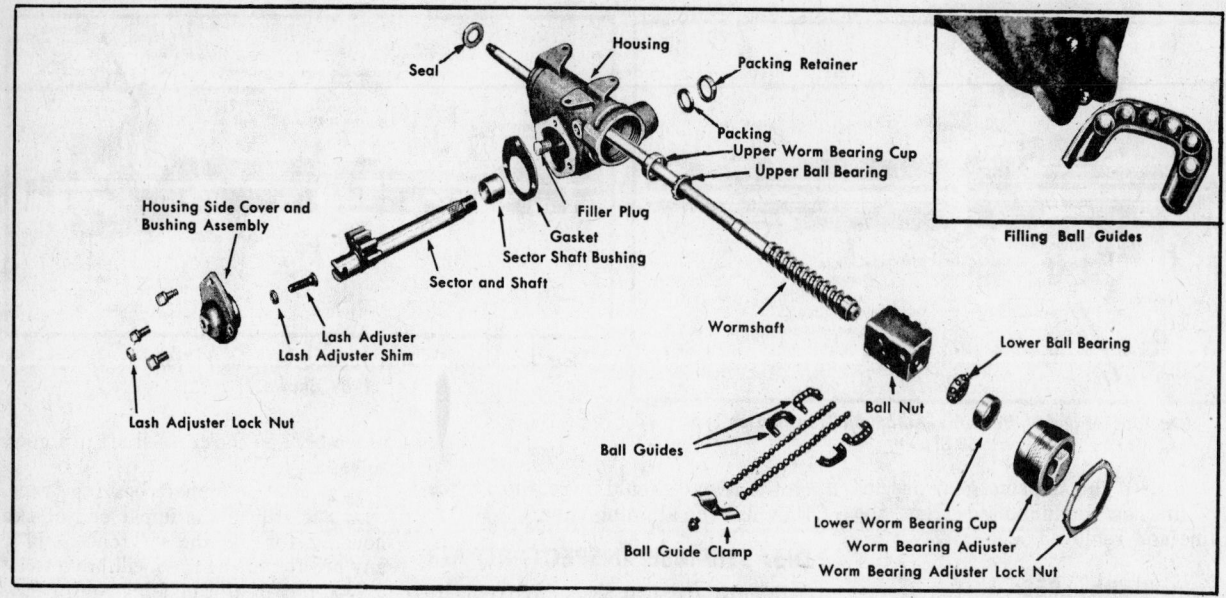

Ball and worm type—1955 thru 1963 models

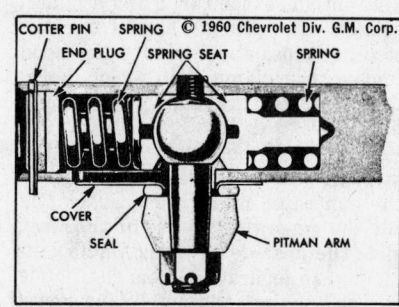

Pitman Arm attachment to Relay Rod

can be run to the lower end of the worm and the upper grooves examined. The grooves should be perfectly smooth, completely free of nicks and scratches.

If there is any roughness, or pits or scratches in the worm, new parts will have to be installed to replace the worn or damaged ones.

Disassemble the nut by removing the clamp which holds the ball guides to the nut, and by turning the worm shaft the balls can be worked up out of the holes.

Examine each of the balls for pits or flat spots.

REASSEMBLY OF WORM NUT

Set the worm nut over the worm and fill the two tracks with balls until no more can be inserted. On the bench, fill each of the guides with balls and stop the end of the guide with some heavy grease, such as vaseline, so that the guide can be inserted without the last balls dropping out. Push all the way in and reinstall the clamp. Again check that the worm turns smoothly.

Examine the cross shaft for wear and before installing the worm or worm shaft, put the cross shaft down on its bushings and check it for play: there should be no noticeable play. If there is, either the bushings or the cross shaft or both will have to be replaced.

A puller is required to remove either the upper or lower worm bearing race. The upper race is in the upper end of the housing; the lower race is in the upper end of the adjustment nut.

Reassemble the gear and reinstall in reverse order of disassembly.

STEERING IDLER AND THIRD ARM BEARINGS

1954 Models

To replace the steering idler arm and/or bearings jack up the car and place it on stands and disconnect the tie rods and drag link from the intermediate steering arm.

Remove the three bolts which retain the steering idler arm assembly to the front cross member and lift the entire assembly off the car.

Lock up the idler arm in a vise and remove the lubricating fittings and, using a punch, drive out the lock pin. <u>Note:</u> The lock pin is a tiny pin located in approximately the center of the arm itself, not in the bracket.

Remove the pivot shaft top and bottom plugs. This can be done with a sharp drift punch by driving through either plug and forcing the pivot shaft out the other end to remove it.

Install new bushings in the idler arm bracket and ream them to fit the new idler arm pin.

Carefully line up the lock pin hole, drive in the lock pin, replace both end plugs and reinstall on the car.

Careful note should be made of the shims, if any, found between the idler arm bracket and the frame as these shims must be reinstalled on assembly.

1955 Thru 1957 Models

Starting 1955 models the steering idler arm is located on the right side of the car opposite to the steering pitman arm. The arm is held to the frame

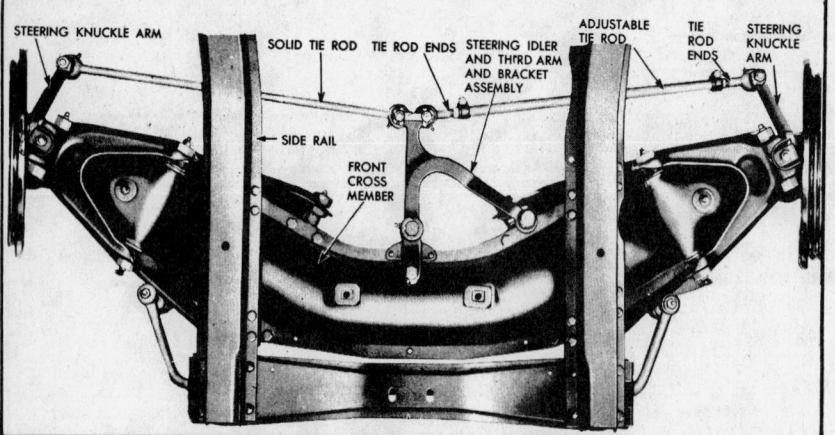

Steering Linkage and Front Suspension thru 1954

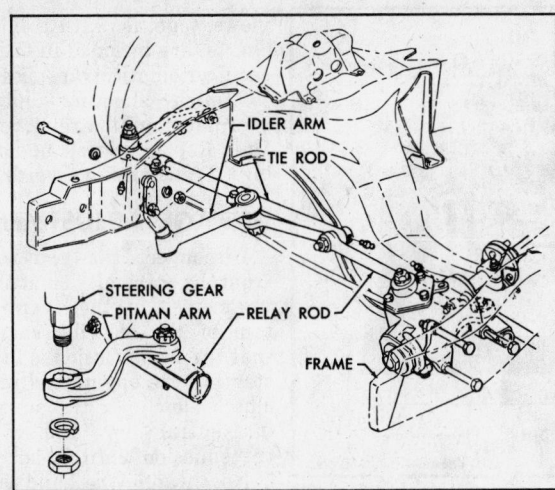

Steering Linkage 1963 Models

with a pivot bracket.

To remove the arm, take off the cotter pin and nut from each end of the idler arm and slide the idler arm off the frame bracket and out of the steering relay rod.

The pivot can then be unbolted from the frame.

Replace in reverse order.

Starting With 1958

The steering idler arm is bolted to the right front frame by two bolts.

It is connected to the center tie rod by a nonadjustable tie rod end which is an integral part of the intermediate steering arm.

The tie rod end portion is removed in the same manner as any tie rod end.

STEERING REACH ROD OR RELAY ROD REPLACE

1954 Models

On 1954 models, a steering reach rod was used which reached from the pitman arm to the intermediate steering arm located in the center of the frame.

Starting With 1955

On these models the relay rod reached from the steering pitman arm to the idler arm attached to the right frame side member.

On early models both ends of the relay rod were fitted with seats and springs, but on later models only the end connected to the pitman arm is adjustable.

Remove the cotter pin and the large adjusting screw from the end of the rod. The seats and spring assemblies can then be taken out of the tube.

Examine them for pits, scratches or wear, and if they cannot be adjusted so that they operate smoothly and easily they will have to be replaced.

It is unusual to find that these units require replacement and generally speaking they can be smoothed up to function well unless a distinct flat spot has been worn on the ball stud on the pitman arm.

CLUTCH ASSEMBLY

On most Chevrolet models with Synchromesh transmissions a diaphragm spring type clutch is used.

A ball bearing type throwout bearing is used and no provision is made for lubrication of this bearing as it was sealed full of lubricant at assembly.

The throwout fork pivots on a ball stud which is mounted in the rear face of the bell housing.

CLUTCH ADJUSTMENT

Free-travel is adjustable at one point on the clutch linkage. This free-travel adjustment will compensate for all normal clutch wear.

CLUTCH PEDAL FREE-TRAVEL

The pedal should travel 3/4 inch to 1 inch before the throwout bearing engages the diaphragm spring.

This should be checked at the pedal by hand. The check should be made by hand and not by foot as the feel is sensitive; 3/4 inch true free travel of the bearing will approximate one inch feel at the pedal.

The adjustment is made on the fork push rod running from the lever and shaft assembly to the clutch fork. On some models the adjustment is made at the fork end by changing the position of two jam nuts. On other models the adjustment is made at the front end of the rod by turning an adjustable swivel. On this type, one turn of the swivel equals approximately 3/16 inch at the pedal. Also on this type

the adjustment can be made by holding the fork push rod rearward to remove all lash and then adjusting the swivel to line up a conical point stamped on the swivel with a dimple which is stamped on the lever to which it attaches.

CLUTCH PEDAL HEIGHT

The top of the clutch pedal pad should be at least 7 inches above the deadener felt glued to the metal floor pan. Do not measure to the floor mat.

If less than seven inches, cut off the rubber pedal stop to obtain proper pedal height. On some models the rubber pedal stop is fastened to a metal piece held to the instrument panel brace by a bolt and nut. A slotted hole in the brace allows for adjustment of the bumper holding piece.

If there is more than seven inches of pedal travel it may be that the diaphragm spring is being overstressed. At any rate, to reduce pedal travel add a pad under the floor mat to reduce it.

CLUTCH PEDAL OVER-CENTER SPRING ADJUSTMENT

The pull back spring is attached to a hook at the front end. The rear connection is to an adjustable hook bolted to a bracket on the clutch pedal. The spring should be adjusted to 10 5/16 inches of installed length on cars beginning with 1958, and to a length which will provide movement of the pedal off its stop under 6 to 9 pounds pressure on earlier models.

CLUTCH RETRACTING SPRINGS

A rattle in the clutch assembly at idling speeds with the clutch released may be caused by insufficient tension on the pressure plate retracting

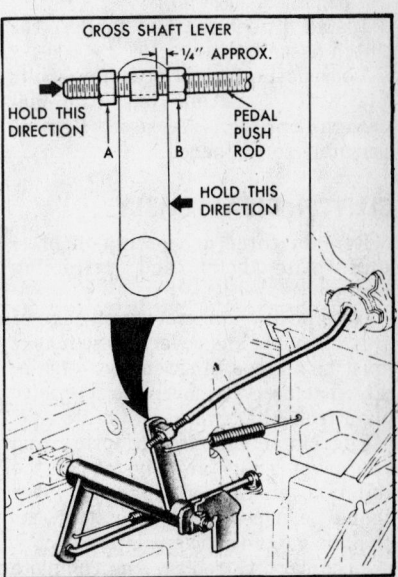

Typical Clutch Linkage

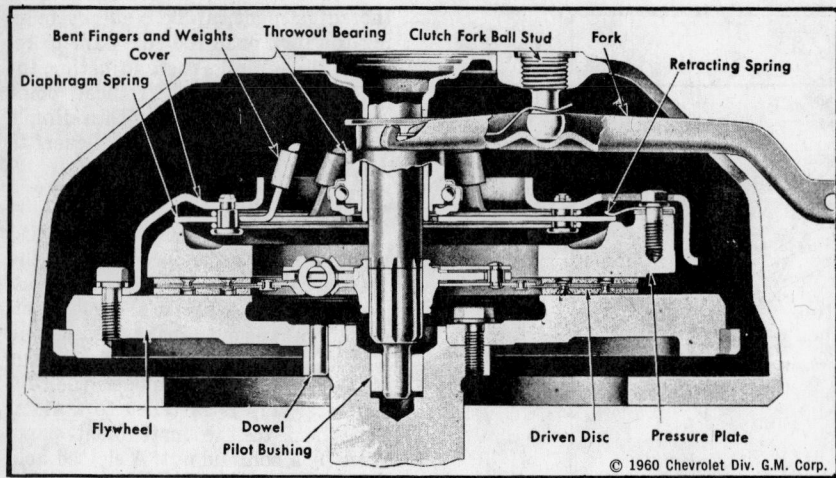

Typical V-8 Clutch Cross Section

Labels on diagram: Bent Fingers and Weights Cover, Throwout Bearing, Clutch Fork Ball Stud, Fork, Retracting Spring, Diaphragm Spring, Flywheel, Dowel, Pilot Bushing, Driven Disc, Pressure Plate. © 1960 Chevrolet Div. G.M. Corp.

springs.

The noise can be eliminated by replacing the springs.

Remove the clutch housing underpan. Crank the engine until one retracting spring attaching bolt is at the bottom. Remove the bolt and the pressure plate retracting spring and install a new spring.

Replace the other springs in the same way. Put back the underpan.

CLUTCH PILOT BEARING

The pilot bearing is an oil impregnated type pressed into the end of the crankshaft. It is replaceable.

CLUTCH ASSEMBLY REMOVAL

Remove the transmission. Remove the throwout bearing from the fork. Remove the tension spring and disconnect the push rod from the fork. Force the clutch fork toward the center of the car and so disconnet it from the ball stud.

Install a pilot shaft to support the clutch assembly.

Loosen the clutch attaching bolts one turn at a time until the diaphragm spring is released. Remove assembly to the bench.

CLUTCH DISASSEMBLY

Remove three drive-strap to pressure plate bolts and retracting springs.

Note position of grooves on edge of pressure plate and cover. These marks must be aligned in assembly to maintain balance. Remove the pressure plate from the cover.

The clutch diaphragm spring and two pivot rings are riveted to the clutch cover. Spring, rings and cover should be inspected for excessive wear or damage and if there is a defect it is necessary to replace the complete cover assembly.

CLUTCH ASSEMBLY

Install the pressure plate in the cover assembly, lining up the groove on the edge of the pressure plate with the groove on the edge of the cover.

Install pressure plate retracting springs and drive strap to pressure plate bolts. The drive straps should not be loose in the rivets or at the bolts. Tighten to 11 ft. lbs.

CLUTCH INSTALLATION

Turn crankshaft so the "X" mark on the flywheel is at the bottom.

With clutch fork in the housing but not on ball stud install the clutch disc, pressure plate and cover assembly and support on a pilot shaft.

Note that the longer portion of the hub of the driven disc goes toward the crankshaft.

Turn the clutch assembly until the "X" mark on the clutch cover flange lines up with the "X" mark on the flywheel. Align nearest bolt holes in clutch and flywheel and install bolts in every other hole (they are marked "L"). Tighten gradually and then install remaining 3 bolts. Remove the pilot shaft.

Pack the clutch fork ball seat with a small amount of high melting point grease.

Replace fork on ball stud. Lubricate the recess on the inside of the throwout bearing collar and coat the throwout fork groove with a small amount of graphite grease. Install throwout bearing assembly to the fork. Hook up linkage. Reinstall transmission.

STANDARD TRANSMISSION

Transmission refill capacities will be found in the Capacities Table of this section.

General information and exploded views, together with trouble shooting charts, are included in the articles on each automatic transmission.

Trouble shooting and repair of overdrive units are covered in the Unit Repair section under the heading: Transmission-Overdrive.

LINKAGE ADJUSTMENT

Disconnect the two rods coming from the transmission at their attaching swivels on the levers at the bottom of the steering column. Check that the transmission is in Neutral by starting the engine and releasing the clutch slowly. If transmission is not in Neutral move the levers at the transmission until it is.

Now wiggle the hand lever and be sure it is in Neutral position and works without binding. If it does bind, check the clamp on the steering column where it passes through the dash. The clamp is mounted on bolts through elongated holes and may be moved to relieve any binding of the column.

Next adjust the swivels so the rods can be easily reconnected to the steering column levers.

Reinstall swivels.

SPEEDOMETER DRIVEN GEAR OIL SEAL REPLACE

Disconnect speedometer cable, remove lock plate to housing bolt, lock washer and the plate. Insert screwdriver in lock plate slot in the gear assembly and pry it from the housing.

Pry the "O" ring oil seal from its groove on the gear assembly and install a new "O" ring.

Coat the assembly with transmission lubricant and insert in place in housing.

Hold the assembly so the slot in fitting is toward the lock plate boss in order that the lock plate can be inserted in the groove and attached to the housing.

TRANSMISSION REAR OIL SEAL REPLACEMENT

Remove the propeller shaft and disconnect the parking brake idler lever.

Using a punch against the exposed end of the seal drive seal out of extension.

Wash the counterbore with solvent and check for damage. Clean up any burrs with a stone.

Coat the new seal with a non-hardening oil-proof sealer, and being careful to keep the seal square with the counterbore, tap it into place. Reconnect the propeller shaft and parking brake.

TRANSMISSION SIDE COVER REPLACEMENT

Drain the transmission and disconnect the control rods at the levers. Unbolt and remove the side cover.

When replacing on case be sure that the transmission gears are in Neutral and that the shifter forks are in Neutral position. The pump on the rearward fork (1st and Reverse) must go to the rear of the car.

Coat the attaching screws with sealer and tighten to 15-18 ft. lbs.

4 SPEED TRANSMISSION

Starting with 1959 a four speed synchromesh transmission is available. It is designed to permit high speed operation with a minimum of heat and friction losses.

All four forward gears are provided with synchronizing clutches. They can be engaged while the car is in motion.

Gear ratios are 2.2:1 (first); 1.68:1 (second); 1.3:1 (third); 1.0:1 (fourth) and 2.25:1 (reverse). Reverse gear is not automatically syncronized and is of two-piece design.

TRANSMISSION REMOVAL

Drain the transmission. Disconnect the speedometer cable and the control levers. Disconnect the propeller shaft.

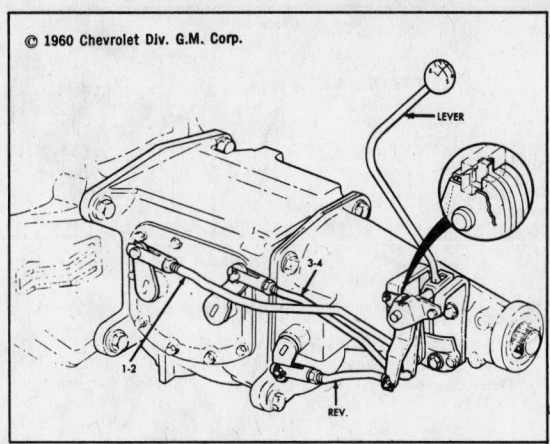

© 1960 Chevrolet Div. G.M. Corp.

Four Speed Transmission Gearshift Linkage

On models starting with 1958, remove two bolts attaching the center bearing to the frame. On all models starting with 1955 remove nuts and U bolts retaining the rear universal joint bearing to the differential pinion drive flange. Move the propeller shaft rearward to the left and under the rear axle housing to withdraw the front universal joint from the transmission output shaft. Support the rear of the engine on models through 1957. On models starting with 1958 remove the transmission rear mounting pad bolts and unbolt the support member from the frame.

On all models remove the two top transmission to clutch housing cap screws and insert guide pins to keep the weight of the transmission from falling on the clutch assembly.

Remove the lower transmission to clutch housing cap screws. Slide the transmission straight back on the

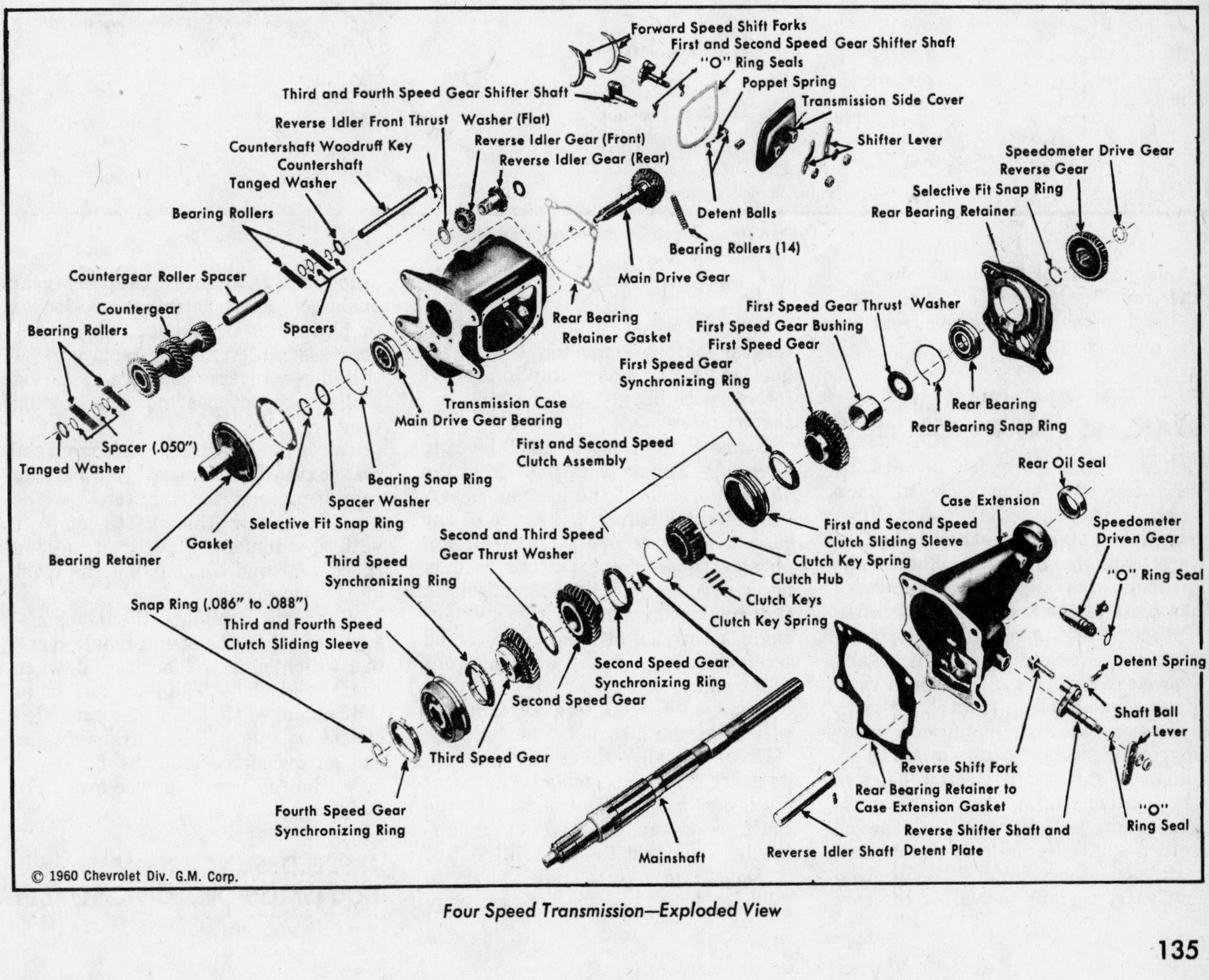

© 1960 Chevrolet Div. G.M. Corp.

Four Speed Transmission—Exploded View

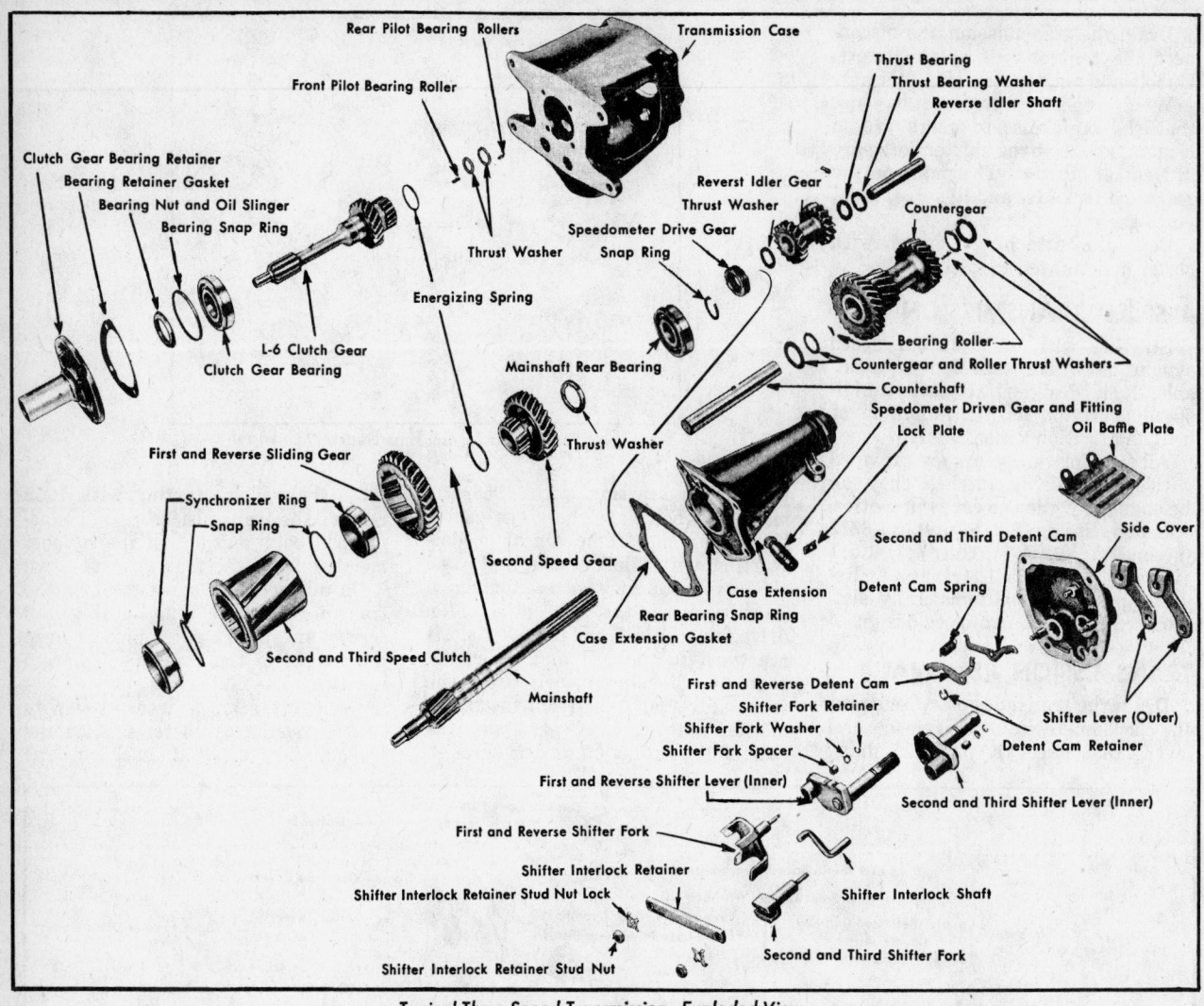

Typical Three Speed Transmission—Exploded View

guide pins until the input shaft of the transmission is free of the clutch.

Remove the transmission from under the car.

3 SPEED SYNCHROMESH TRANSMISSION DISASSEMBLY

Remove the side cover. Remove the rear extension along with the main shaft leaving the 2nd-and-3rd-clutch assembly along with the 1st-and-reverse-gear in the case. Rotate the mainshaft to align its splines with the teeth of the 2nd-and-3rd-clutch.

Slide 1st-and-reverse-gear from clutch sleeve and remove gear and sleeve separately through side of case Remove pilot rollers from clutch gear.

Remove the four clutch gear bearing retainer screws to release the retainer. Note that the screw holes in the retainer are unevenly spaced to assure proper alignment of the oil return slot with the hole in the case.

Remove the countershaft by driving it from front to rear of the case

and lower the countergear to the bottom.

It is necessary to lower the countergear before removing the clutch gear and bearing assembly to prevent interference between the bearing and the countergear.

Remove the clutch gear bearing snap ring. Tap on the front end of the shaft and remove the gear and bearing assembly through the rear of the case. The above operation while applicable to all transmissions is only necessary on 1958 V8 transmissions. On transmissions used with 6 cylinder engines the clutch gear and bearing assembly can be taken out the front of the case.

Remove the countergear complete with rollers and thrust washers.

Drive the idler shaft lock pin into its shaft. This is possible because the pin is not as long as the hole in the shaft. Now tap the idler shaft forward to drive out the plug in front of it. Do not permit the idler shaft to turn for if it does the lock pin may

drop through between the idler gear bushings. These bushings are locked in place and if damaged the whole gear assembly must be replaced.

Remove reverse idler gear, thrust washer, thrust bearing and bearing washer.

To remove the main shaft from the rear extension, expand the bearing snap ring and tap rear end of the shaft to bring the shaft, complete with speedometer drive gear, second speed gear and bearing, out the front of the extension.

When reassembling the transmission note that the countershaft has a flat which must be horizontal when shaft is in place. The flat must be at the bottom so that the rear extension can be installed, but if transmission has an overdrive unit the flat must be at the top to engage the overdrive adapter.

4 SPEED SYNCHROMESH TRANSMISSION, DISASSEMBLY

1. Remove 4 bolts and remove front bearing retainer.
2. Drive lock pin from reverse shifter lever boss, then pull shifter shaft out about ⅛". This disengages the reverse fork from reverse gear.
3. Remove 5 bolts holding the case extension to the rear bearing retainer. Tap the extension toward the rear and twist extension to left so that the reverse fork clears reverse gear. Remove extension and gasket.
4. The rear reverse idler and tanged thrust washer may now be removed.
5. Remove speedometer gear and reverse gear.
6. Remove the self locking bolt, attaching the rear bearing retainer to the transmission case. Remove the entire mainshaft assembly.
7. Unload bearing rollers from main drive gear and remove fourth speed synchronizer ring.
8. Lift front reverse idler and thrust washer from case.
9. Remove main drive gear snap ring and remove spacer washer.
10. Press main drive gear down from front bearing, then from inside the case, tap out front bearing and snap ring.

11. From front of case, press out the countershaft. Then remove the counter gear and both tanged washers.
12. Remove the 80 rollers, six .050" spacers and the roller spacer from the counter gear.
13. Remove mainshaft front snap ring and slide third and fourth speed clutch assembly, third speed gear and synchronizing ring, second and third speed gear thrust washer, second speed gear and second speed synchronizing ring from front of mainshaft.
14. Spread rear bearing snap ring and press mainshaft out of retainer.
15. Remove mainshaft rear snap ring. Support first and second speed clutch assembly and press on rear of mainshaft to remove shaft from rear bearing, first speed gear thrust washer, first speed gear, and synchronizing ring, first and second speed clutch sliding sleeve and first speed gear bushing.

To assemble the unit, reverse the disassembly procedure.

POWERGLIDE TRANSMISSION,

QUICK SERVICE INFORMATION

When automatic transmission trouble is reported, a road test and careful diagnosis is in order. "Transmission Remove and Replace" and "Linkage Adjustments" are covered here in the following paragraphs. For "Test Procedures", "Transmission Overhaul" and other detailed information, see "Unit Repair section", "transmission group" of this manual.

MANUAL LINKAGE ADJUSTMENT

1954

With hand lever in reverse loosen the nut holding the shift control rod to the swivel and lever at the bottom of the shifting shaft. Push the rod as far rearward as possible, to assure that the manual valve outside control lever at the rear of the transmission is truly in reverse. Then move the swivel and lever at the end of the shifting shaft until there is .090" clearance between the lever and the stop on its support. Still holding the rod rearward, tighten the nut which holds it to the swivel and lever.

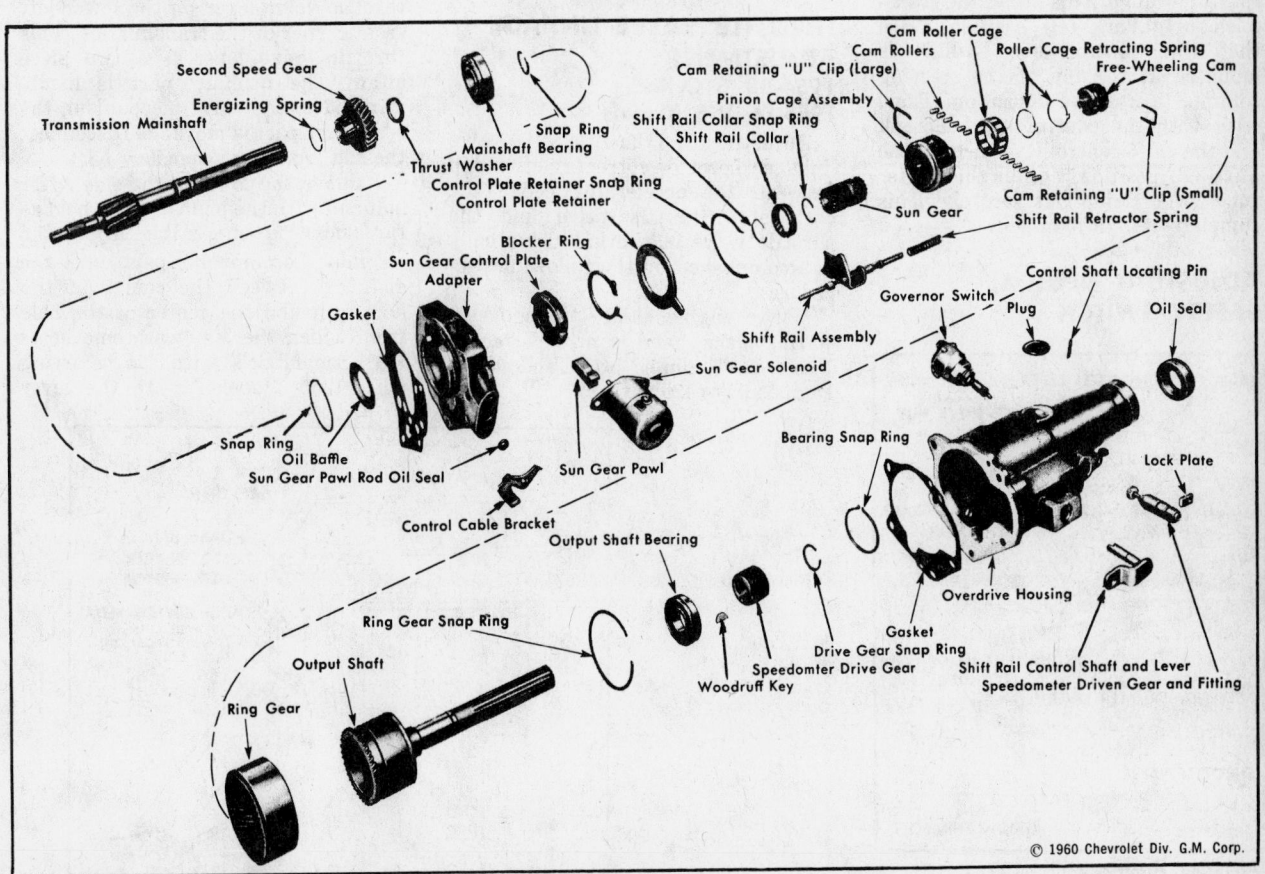

© 1960 Chevrolet Div. G.M. Corp.

Overdrive—Exploded View

137

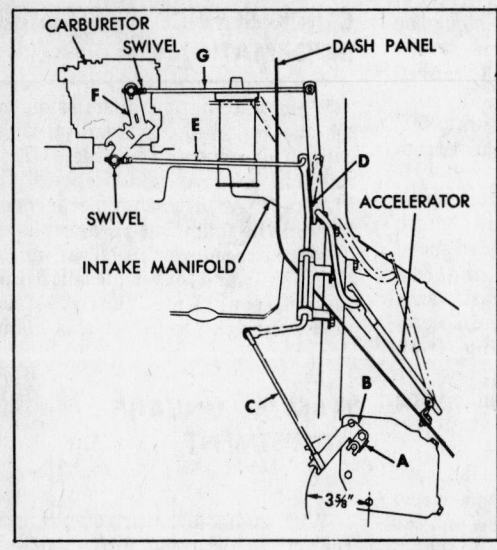

V8 Throttle Linkage Starting With 1957 Production. Hold Lever "A" Counterclockwise. Measure Distance From Outer End Of Lever "B" to Indicated Bolt Hole. It Should be 3 5/8".

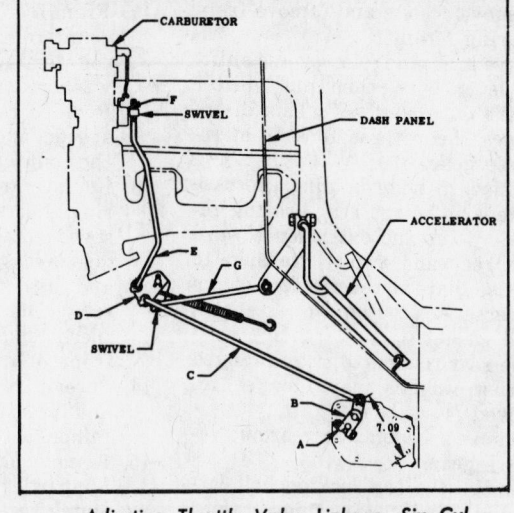

Adjusting Throttle Valve Linkage. Six Cyl. 1955-61 Hold Lever Counterclockwise

1955-62

Loosen the shifter tube lever clamp nut sufficiently to allow the upper control rod to move freely in the swivel. Push the control rod bellcrank, on the right side of the transmission case, toward the front of the car as far as it will go. This places the transmission in Park (P) position. Place the shift control lever, which is mounted at the top of the steering column, in Park (P) position. Then, with both the control rod bellcrank and the shift control lever held in the Park (P) position, tighten the shifter tube lever clamp nut securely. This completes the adjustment.

ADJUSTING NEUTRAL SAFETY SWITCH

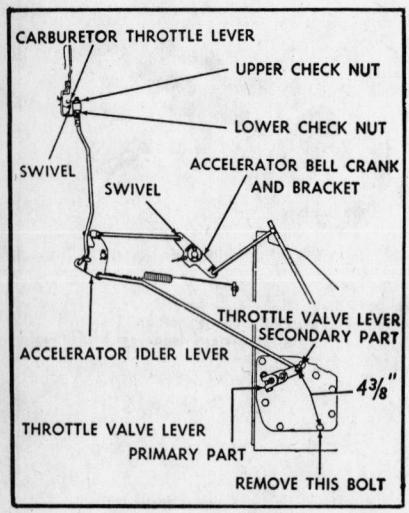

Adjusting Throttle Valve Linkage. 1953-54 Hold Lever Clockwise

Place hand lever in neutral and loosen the two switch mounting screws. Move the switch bracket so that a snug fitting pin can be inserted through the two locating holes. Tighten the screws to hold the switch securely and remove the pin. Note: Late models use two pins.

THROTTLE VALVE LINKAGE ADJUSTMENT
1954-58 6 Cylinder
1955-56 V-8 Models

Adjustment of the throttle valve linkage to provide correct relationship between the accelerator pedal, the carburetor throttle valve and the throttle valve in the low drive body is accomplished by the following procedure:

With engine and transmission warm, place hand control lever in Drive. Set the hand brake and adjust engine idle to 425 rpm.

Note: Automatic choke must be entirely off and throttle stop screw against low step on fast idle cam.

AT THE TRANSMISSION
1954-58 6 Cylinder
1955-56 V-8 Models

Disconnect the rod running from the accelerator idler lever to the throttle valve lever on the lower left front corner of the transmission. This throttle valve lever is a two piece affair. The primary part is firmly clamped to the valve mechanism, the secondary part is movable. Disconnect the rod from the secondary part.

Remove the lower right side cover bolt and with the primary part held as far clockwise as possible adjust the secondary or movable part until the distance between the center of the hole in it and the center of the hole from which the bolt was removed is 4⅜" for Models thru '54. Starting with 1955 Models rotate the lever

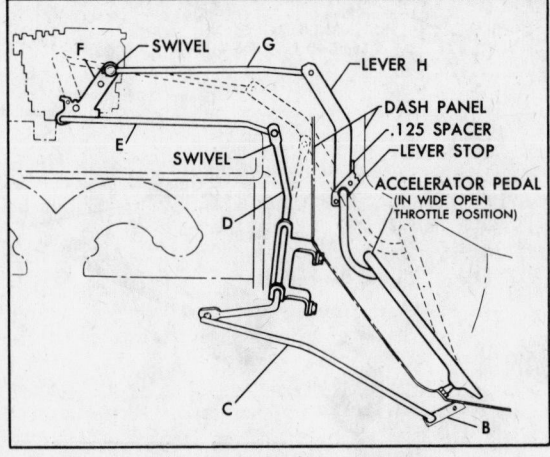

T.V. Linkage Adjustments 1962-63

counterclockwise. The distance measured otherwise in the same way should be 6⅜" for 1955 6 Cyl. and 7 3/32 for 1956-58 6 Cyl. It should be 2⅞" for V8 1955-56. Tighten the bolt which fastens the secondary part to the primary part. Reconnect the rod and replace the cover bolt. Tighten to 12-15 ft lbs.

1957-61 V8 Models

Remove rod "C." Loosen bolt holding Secondary Part of throttle valve lever "B" to Primary Part "A." Hold Primary Part "A" counterclockwise as far as it will go. Hold Secondary Part "B" so that the hole in the outer end is 3⅝ inches from the center of the lower left bolt in valve cover as shown in the cut. Tighten the bolt to fasten Secondary Part "B" to Primary Part "A" and install rod "C."

AT THE CARBURETOR

1954 Models Only

Now holding the throttle lever so the rod is as far toward the rear as can be adjust the rod which runs from the accelerator idler lever up to the carburetor for free entry of the swivel pin in the carburetor throttle lever. Shorten the rod three full turns of the upper check nut and tighten lower check nut to lock.

Next, insert a 3/16" diameter pin through the hole in the accelerator bell crank into the supporting bracket.

With the throttle valve lever still held rearward against its stop adjust the length of the rod running from the bell crank to the idler for free entry of its swivel into the bell crank.

Hold swivel from turning and lock check nut securely.

1955 61 Six Cylinder
1955-56 V-8 Models

With hand lever at "D" and brake set. Adjust idle speed with engine hot at 425 rpm. Shut off engine. Block carburetor throttle wide open. Hold rod from transmission throttle valve lever forward to stop. Adjust, one rod on sixes, two rods on eights, for free entry of pin in carburetor throttle lever.

After adjustment of the transmission throttle valve lever and the carburetor control rods as outlined above, adjust the accelerator linkage so the pedal is against the floor.

1957-61 V-8 Models

Disconnect rods "G" and "E" at their swivels. Move lever "F" so that throttle valve is wide open. Pull rod "E" forward as far as it will come. Adjust swivel on rod "E" for easy. attachment to lever "F" and attach.

Depress accelerator fully. The lowest point on accelerator rod should be ¾ inch above the toe pan. With throttle valve wide open adjust swivel on rod "G" for easy entry into lever "F" and attach.

Move lever "B" as far counterclockwise as it will go and then at carburetor check that throttle valve is wide open.

REMOVAL OF POWERGLIDE FROM CAR

Beginning 1954

1. Raise car on hoist. Remove oil and oil pan, then reattach pan with a few bolts.
2. Disconnect oil cooler lines, vacuum modulator line and the speedometer cable at the transmission.
3. Remove crankcase ventilator tube clamp bracket bolt, washer and nut from the transmission.
4. Disconnect manual and TV control lever rods from transmission.
5. Disconnect propeller shaft at transmission.
6. Install suitable transmission lift and support the transmission.
7. Disconnect engine rear mount on transmission extension, then remove transmission support crossmember.

<u>Caution:</u>

Note any shims which may be installed between the extension mounting boss and the crossmember. It is important that the exact same number of shims be reinstalled as these influence drive line angles.

8. Remove converter underpan, scribe flywheel-to-converter relationship for reassembly, then remove flywheel-to-converter attaching bolts.
9. Support engine at oil pan rail with a jack or other suitable brace for engine support safety.
10. Lower rear of transmission slightly so that the upper transmission housing-to-engine attaching bolts can be reached with a universal socket and long extension. Remove the upper bolts.

<u>Caution:</u>

On V-8 engines, use care not to lower the transmission too far as distributor-firewall interference may cause damage. Have a helper watch this area.

11. Remove the balance of the transmission attaching bolts.
12. Remove the transmission by lowering and moving the unit toward the rear. Be sure to use a converter holding strap, or some improvision, to keep converter from falling while removing the transmission unit.

Starter Must be Removed From V-8 Models For Access to the Flywheel-to-Converter Bolts

13. Install transmission unit by reversing the above procedure.

Powerglide—Type "A", Cast Iron Case
Powerglide—Type "B", Aluminum Case

1962

Powerglide (in type A) is used with 6 cylinder engines and the 283 cu. in. V-8 engines only. The 327 cu. in. engine is offered with the Powerglide (type B), aluminum case. Cars equipped with the 409 cu. in. engine are supplied with manual transmission only.

Beginning 1963

All models except those equipped with 409 cu. in. engines, are available with Powerglide "B" (aluminum case) transmissions. Powerglide "A" is no longer used in production.

TURBOGLIDE TRANSMISSION 1957-61 PRODUCTION
ADJUSTMENTS

MANUAL LINKAGE

Loosen the swivel connecting the rod from the transmission to the lever at the bottom of the steering column. Have lever on side of transmission at "N," which is the middle one of the five available positions. Put the hand control at "N." Now tighten the swivel to the lever.

Note that hand lever position is controlled by the transmission lever Neutral position and not by the gate on the mast jacket. When hand control is at Neutral and the inner one of the two transmission levers is at Neutral the gate on the mast jacket can be adjusted to suit.

Maladjustment of the linkage will result in partial pressure on the cones and clutches which will cause slippage and ultimate failure of the transmission.

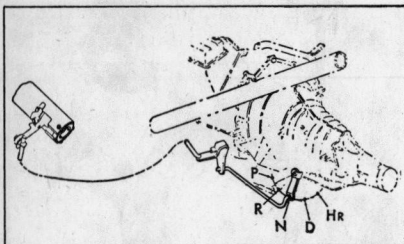

Manual Control Linkage Starting With 1957 Production

THROTTLE LINKAGE

This transmission does not have a throttle valve but the operation of the two-position stator in the converter is controlled by the correct relationship between the accelerator pedal, the carburetor throttle valve, and the stator control valve.

Disconnect rod "A" from the carburetor throttle lever "B" at the swivel. Block the throttle valve wide open. Check that accelerator does not hit floor before valve is open. If it does, adjust the upper swivel at lever "B" so that when the accelerator is against the floor the throttle valve is wide open. Now pull rod "A" forward, overcoming the stator control valve spring, so that lever "C" has moved as far back as possible. Adjust the swivel on rod "A" for easy attachment to lever "B" and attach. Let the carburetor throttle valve return to idle position. Push the accelerator to the floor and check that the throttle valve opened wide and the outer of the two levers on the transmission moved all the way counterclockwise.

NEUTRAL SAFETY SWITCH

The starter safety switch is at the bottom of the steering column. Place the hand lever at either "N" or "P." Check that the slot in the switch is on the center line of the shifter tube tang. Install cotter pins into the two holes in the switch on each side of the

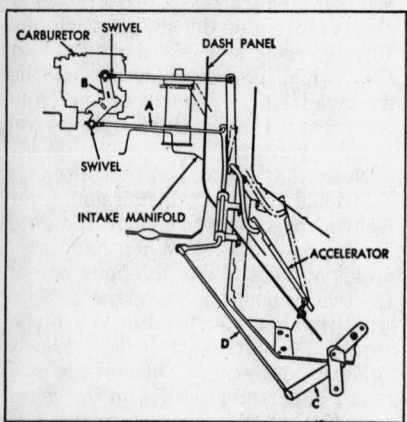

Throttle Linkage to Stator Control Valve Starting with 1957 Production

pointer. Center switch to pointer. Remove cotter pins. Check that starter will operate. If not, put hand lever at "N," loosen switch mounting screws and rotate switch until starter will operate, then retighten the mounting screws.

QUICK SERVICE INFORMATION

When automatic transmission trouble is reported, a road test and careful diagnosis is in order. "Transmission Remove and Replace" and "Linkage Adjustments" are covered here in the following paragraphs. For "Test Procedures", "Transmission Overhaul" and other detailed information, see "Unit Repair section", "transmission group" of this manual.

REMOVAL OF TURBOGLIDE TRANSMISSION FROM THE CAR

Starting With 1957 Production

Support the car on stand jacks. Remove toe pan plate from front compartment. Remove the spark plugs. Disconnect the battery and the wires from the solenoid on the starter. Remove the starter. Remove the transmission oil pan drain plug and drain the transmission case.

Unfasten the oil filler tube clamp and the nut holding the filler tube to the oil pan. Cover or plug the filler tube opening in the pan.

Disconnect the speedometer cable at the rear extension. Disconnect the oil cooler tubes at the thermal bypass valve. Disconnect the vacuum line at the vacuum diaphragm.

Disconnect the throttle control and the manual control at the levers on the transmission. Split the rear universal joint and slide the front joint and drive shaft rearward to release it from the transmission output shaft.

Disconnect the exhaust pipe at the crossover pipe. Disconnect the muffler at its support bracket. Tie assembly to left frame side member.

Remove converter underpan. Support the engine and unbolt the converter from the flywheel.

Raise and support the transmission in a cradle. Use of a cradle will prevent damage to the oil pan and valve body. Remove the supports at the rear extension. Unbolt the bell housing-transmission case from the block. (There are seven bolts in all.) Lift accelerator assembly toward the front and lay on the engine block. Tie or clamp converter to bell housing, so that it won't slip forward. Move transmission to the rear to release housing-case from the dowels on the

engine block. Lower transmission to the floor.

INSTALLATION OF TURBO-GLIDE TRANSMISSION IN THE CAR

Starting With 1957 Production

Put a film of lubriplate in the bore in the center of the flywheel.

Raise transmission, using a cradle to avoid distortion of pan and valve body, into approximate alignment with the locating dowels in the block. Remove the converter clamp. Align the "X" mark on the converter with the "X" mark on the flywheel and align the bolt holes.

Slide the bell housing transmission assembly onto the locating dowels and install one bolt on right of center near the top.

Replace accelerator assembly and fasten with two bolts. Install the remaining case to engine bolts and tighten to 25-30 ft. lbs. Install converter to flywheel bolts and nuts and tighten to 15-20 ft. lbs. Install converter underpan.

Install the rear supports and lower the engine into place. Remove the transmission jack and cradle. Reconnect the cooler tubes and the vacuum line. Install filler tube, starter and the controls.

Engage the internal splines of the front universal joint with the external splines of the transmission output shaft and slide the assembly into place so that the rear joint can be refastened. Reconnect the speedometer and install the exhaust pipe and muffler.

Reinstall the spark plugs, reconnect the battery and starter.

Pour three quarts of Type A transmission fluid. Start the engine and complete the filling with approximately 6½ quarts of Type A fluid. Check the oil level with the transmission at operating temperature, the hand lever in Drive and the engine idling. The level should be at the full mark on the dipstick. Adjust the controls as detailed in the section headed ADJUSTMENTS.

UNIVERSAL JOINT AND PROPELLER SHAFT

UNIVERSAL JOINT DISASSEMBLY

1954

Unhook the hand brake pull back spring, cable clevis and cable idler lever.

Remove the cap screws which retain the ball retaining collar to the

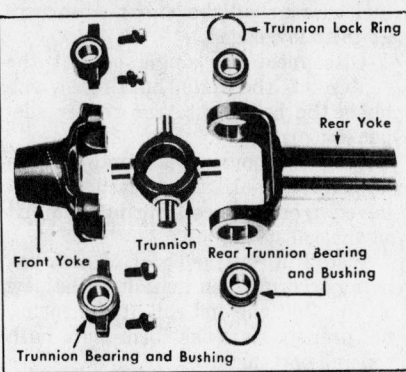

*Exploded view—Universal Joint—
Early Models*

transmission rear end and slide the collar and ball back on the propeller shaft housing. Remove the cap screws which fasten the front universal trunnion bearing to the front yoke on the transmission.

Support the propeller shaft and remove the two front yoke trunnion bearings and split the joint.

Take off the front yoke, remove the bolt and lock washer from the end of the transmission main shaft.

The two bearings on the universal joint, which attached to the propeller shaft yoke, are held with C washers on the inside surface of the bearing. These C washers can be driven out and the bearing knocked towards the outer side of the trunnion.

1955 Thru 1957

Starting with 1955 production, the Hotchkiss drive, or open driveshaft, type of drive line is used on all Chevrolet models.

Universal joint bearing jornals are held in place in the yokes by lock rings located on the outside of the joint.

Squeeze the lock rings together and remove them.

© 1960 Chevrolet Div. G.M. Corp.

*Disassembling Universal Joint—
Late Models*

The shaft is then pushed sideways which will force the bearing out of one side, and after that bearing is removed the shaft is forced in the opposite direction which will release the bearing on the opposite side.

When taking the universals down, in order to get at the transmission, it is generally customary to split the rear universal joint and slide the driveshaft right off the end of the transmission shaft.

Needle bearing type universal joint trunnions are used on all 1955 Chevrolets.

Starting With 1958

Three universal joints are used starting with the 1958 models. To remove the shaft and/or joint assemblies, first remove the bolts attaching the center bearing support to the frame crossmember.

At the rear universal joint split the joint by removing the trunnion bearing U clamps. Withdraw the propeller shaft and bearing assembly by moving it rearwards to the left under the axle housing assembly.

At the center universal joint remove the bearing lock rings and drive the universal joint cross from one side to the other to force out the bearing on the opposite side.

Repeat at all four of the bearings and then at the rear and front joint.

Reinstall by starting the driveshaft in up over the rear axle, down through the tunnel in the frame until the front universal joint spline slides up on the transmission output shaft.

Connect the rear universal joint by installing two U bolts. Be sure the trunnions are properly seated in the rear axle drive flange. Torque should be 14 to 18 ft. lbs.

On all units, except those with air suspension, with car at normal height the center bearing mounting should be allowed to fall freely into place over the slotted holes in the frame "X" member and then should be tightened at this position.

On air suspension models with springs full of air the center mounting should be forced forward ⅛ to ¼ inch from its free position before being bolted tight.

DRIVESHAFT ALIGNMENT STARTING WITH 1958

The relative angles formed by the two propeller shaft sections with the transmission output shaft and the pinion gear shaft are critical.

Consequently, in cases of propeller shaft vibration, collision, rear control arm replacement and such, the angles should be checked.

On cars with coil springs the angles should be, (in degrees).
Front Joint (A)
        2½ to 3½ with 2¾ pref.
Center Joint (B)
        0 to 1 N with ¾ N pref.
Rear Joint (C).....2 to 3 with 2¼ pref.
Axle Height (D) ....5⅞ to 6⅝ inches
On cars with air springs the angles should be, (in degrees).
Front Joint (A)
        2½ to 3½ with 2¾ pref.
Center Joint (B)
        1½ to 2½ with 2 pref.
Rear Joint (C) ....1 to 2 with 1½ pref.
Axle Height (D) ....3⅝ to 4⅜ inches
Do not use a frame contact hoist. Support car by tires or axle. Support front of car 6 inches higher than the rear.

Before checking the angles check the transmission support cross member. For correct assembly two conditions are important.

The taper in the top surface of the cross member must be toward the rear of the vehicle.

For Synchromesh and Turboglide transmissions the support must be attached to the frame by the upper holes in the frame brackets. For overdrive and Powerglide transmissions the support must be attached by the two lower holes in the frame brackets.

Use a bubble protractor to measure the degrees of angle.

Angle "A" is secured by subtracting the front propeller shaft angle from the engine angle.

Angle "B" is secured by subtracting the rear propeller shaft angle from the front propeller shaft angle.

Angle "C" is secured by subtracting the pinion shaft angle from the rear propeller shaft angle if the pinion shaft points up toward the engine. When the pinion shaft points forward toward the ground, the angle must be added to that of the rear propeller shaft to get angle "C."

If any of the joint angles are not within the limits given suitable shims should be added or removed at the transmission support and at the rear suspension upper control arm attaching point.

PROPELLER SHAFT VIBRATION

Excessive vibration of the propeller shaft may be due to: improper driveline angle; worn U joints; bent shaft; pinion flange runout; balance weights missing from shafts.

DRIVESHAFT CENTER BEARING REMOVAL

Starting With 1958

Remove the driveshaft from the vehicle as explained in the preceding

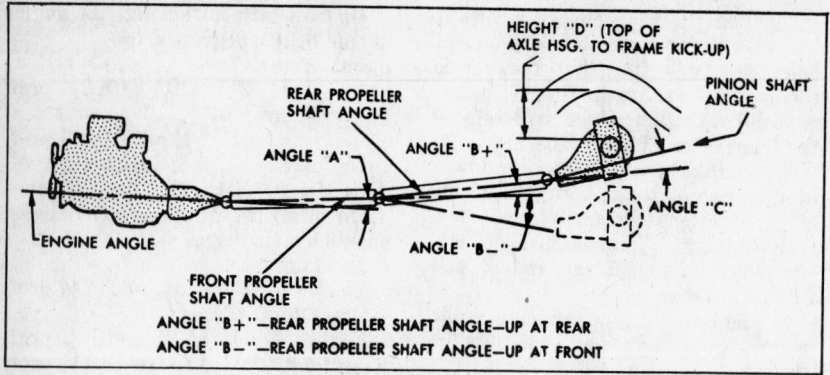

Driveline Angles

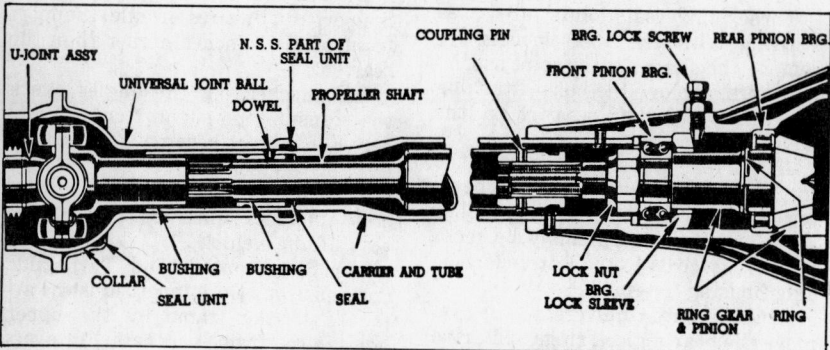

Cutaway of 1950-54 Propeller Shaft

and support assembly on the end of the shaft and press on the inner race, pressing it on until the bearing bottoms on the machined shoulder on the propeller shaft. Note: Depending on the transmission used, three front propeller shafts are used on the 1958 and later models. Turboglide and three-speed transmissions use a white color code; Powerglide engines use an orange color code; overdrive equipped cars use a blue color code.

TORQUE TUBE BEARING

1954

To replace the propeller shaft bushings it is necessary to remove the propeller shaft from the torque tube. To do this it is necessary to remove the differential carrier and propeller shaft as an assembly.

A dowel pin is used to retain the propeller shaft bearing to the torque tube. This pin will have to be driven out of place in order to remove the propeller shaft front bushings.

Corvette, Beginning 1963

Due to independent rear suspension, Corvette is equipped with a single, open, tubular propeller shaft and two universal joints, one joint at either end.

REAR AXLE AND SUSPENSION

LEAF TYPE REAR SPRING

Rear springs on all Chevrolets are mounted in a bracket at the front and a shackle at the back.

To remove the spring first jack the car up and place stand jacks under the frame in front of the rear spring.

Lower the jacking device sufficiently so that all strain is taken off the spring.

Remove the front bolt and drive it out of the bracket and then remove both nuts from the rear shackle, drive off the tie link and then drive the cross bar of the shackle out the opposite side.

Rubber bushings are used at all mounting parts on the Chevrolet springs. It will be necessary to press or drive the front bushing out of the springeye since it is a rubber bushing with metal core and OD.

Detach the shock absorber at the shackle plate and remove the U-bolt nuts which shackle the center of the spring to the rear axle housing.

Lift off the spring.

COIL TYPE REAR SPRING

Jack up the car to give sufficient room to work and place a second jack under the rear axle housing assembly. Disconnect the rear universal joint

and disconnect the shock absorbers at their lower end.

Disconnect the single bolt at the center of the axle housing which holds the housing to the center suspension arm.

Let the housing assembly come downwards until the pressure is relieved from the coil spring and lift off the coil spring.

Install in reverse order of renewal, being careful when installing the new spring that the end coil of the spring fits properly into the form plate both top and bottom.

Corvette, Beginning 1963

Corvette is equipped with an independent rear suspension. The differential is solidly attached to the car frame, the rear wheels being driven through tubular rear axles, each fitted with two universal joints. A transverse, multiple leaf rear spring affords rear suspension. Brake torque and driving forces are transmitted through radius arms to the frame. The spring supports vertical loads, while lateral forces, on turns etc., are taken by the axles and control rods to the fixed differential and to the frame.

For reconditioning procedures see Unit Repair Section, under Axles, Rear.

TROUBLE SHOOTING AND ADJUSTMENT

General instructions covering the troubles of the rear axle and how to repair and adjust it, together with information on installation of rear axle bearings and grease seals, are given in the general section under the heading: Axles, Rear.

Capacities of the rear axle are given in the Capacities Tables of this section.

REAR AXLE ASSEMBLY REMOVAL

Jack up the back of the car to allow sufficient room to work and then place another jack under the rear axle housing. Disconnect the drive shaft.

Remove the single bolt which holds the center support arm to the rear of the axle banjo housing on models starting with 1958. On earlier models remove spring "U" bolts and anchor plates.

Remove the wheel assemblies, disconnect the shocks at the lower end, and then slowly lower the rear axle housing down.

Remove the bolt on each side which holds the torque arm to the rear axle housing, disconnect the hand brake cable and the hydraulic line and the T fitting over the rear axle housing, then slide the housing assembly out from underneath the vehicle.

POSITRACTION DIFFERENTIAL

No special attention is required in this area except with the lubricant used.

Under no circumstances use anything but special G.M. #3758790 or 3758791 lubricant.

Failure to follow these instructions may result in permanent damage to the unit.

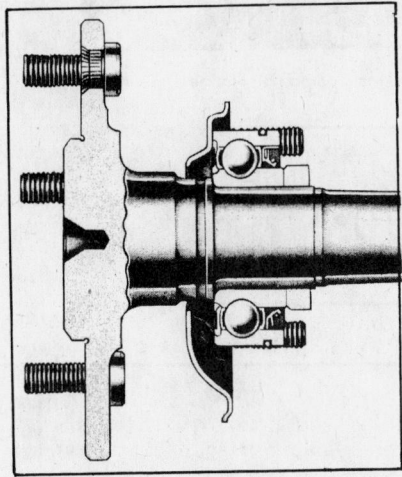

Rear Axle Shaft and **Bearing**

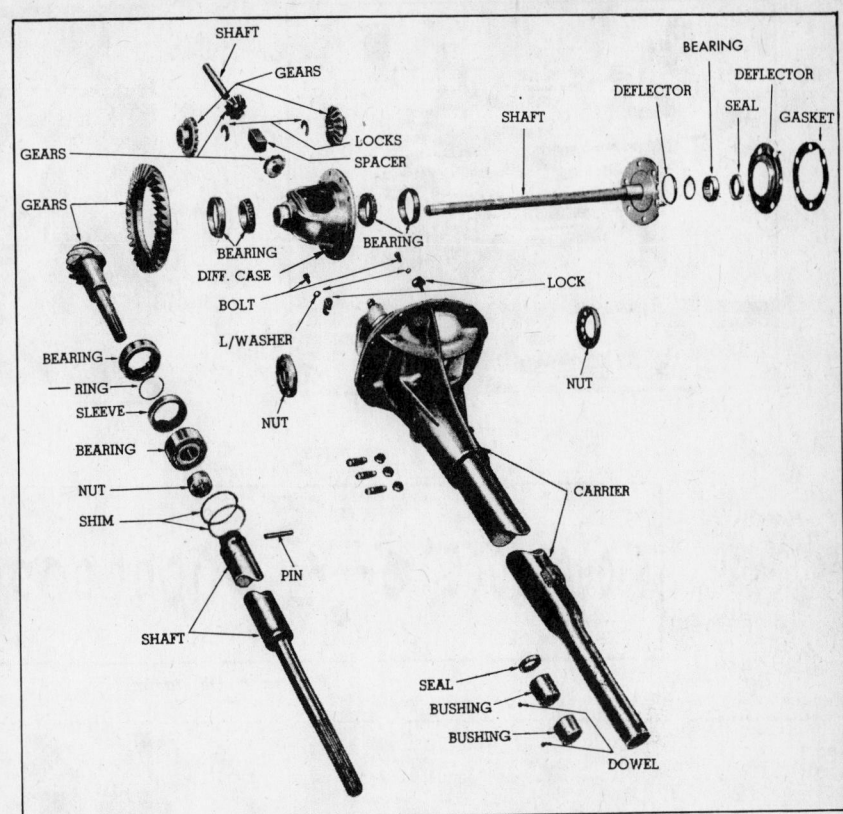

Exploded View—Rear Axle thru 1954

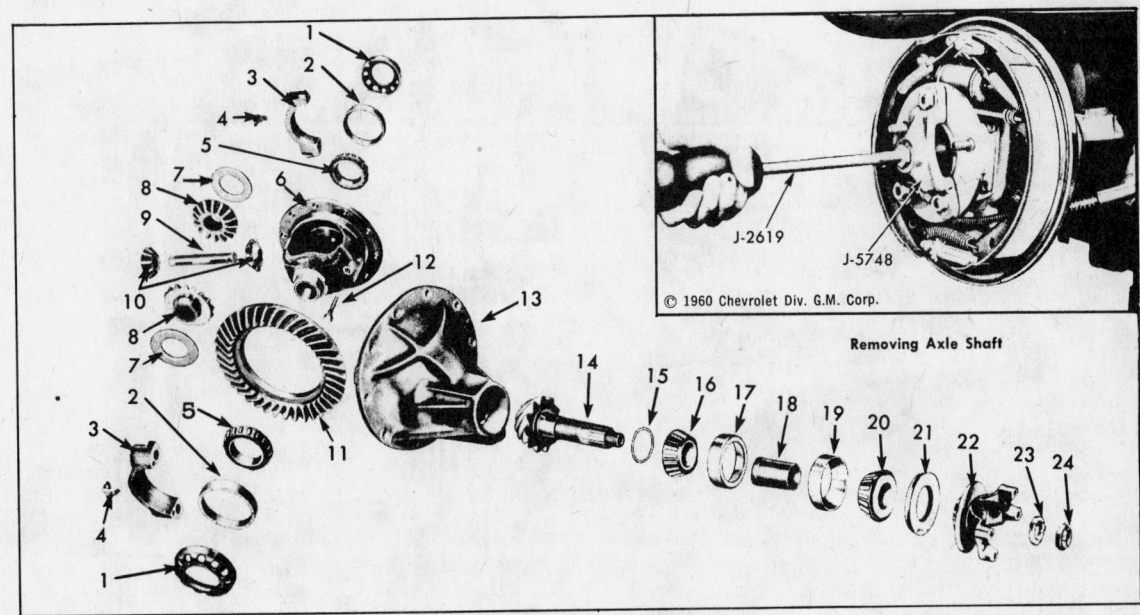

© 1960 Chevrolet Div. G.M. Corp.

Removing Axle Shaft

Rear Axle—Exploded View

1. Differential Bearing Adjusting Nut
2. Differential Bearing Outer Race
3. Differential Bearing Caps
4. Differential Bearing Adjusting Nut Lock
5. Differential Bearing Cone and Roller Assembly
6. Differential Case
7. Differential Side Gear Thrust Washer
8. Differential Side Gear
9. Differential Pinion Gear Shaft
10. Differential Pinion Gear
11. Ring Gear
12. Differential Pinion Gear Shaft Lock
13. Differential Carrier
14. Drive Pinion Gear
15. Pinion Depth Adjusting Shim
16. Rear Pinion Bearing Cone and Roller Assembly
17. Rear Pinion Bearing Outer Race
18. Pinion Bearing Spacer
19. Front Pinion Bearing Outer Race
20. Front Pinion Bearing Cone and Roller Assembly
21. Companion Flange Oil Seal
22. Companion Flange
23. Special Washer
24. Self Locking Nut

CHEVROLET

Installing Axle Shaft Bearing

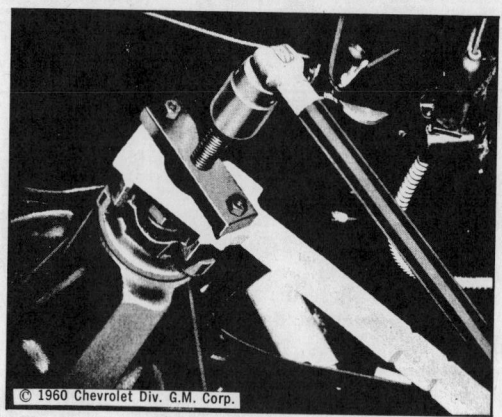

Removing Companion Flange

Positraction Differential

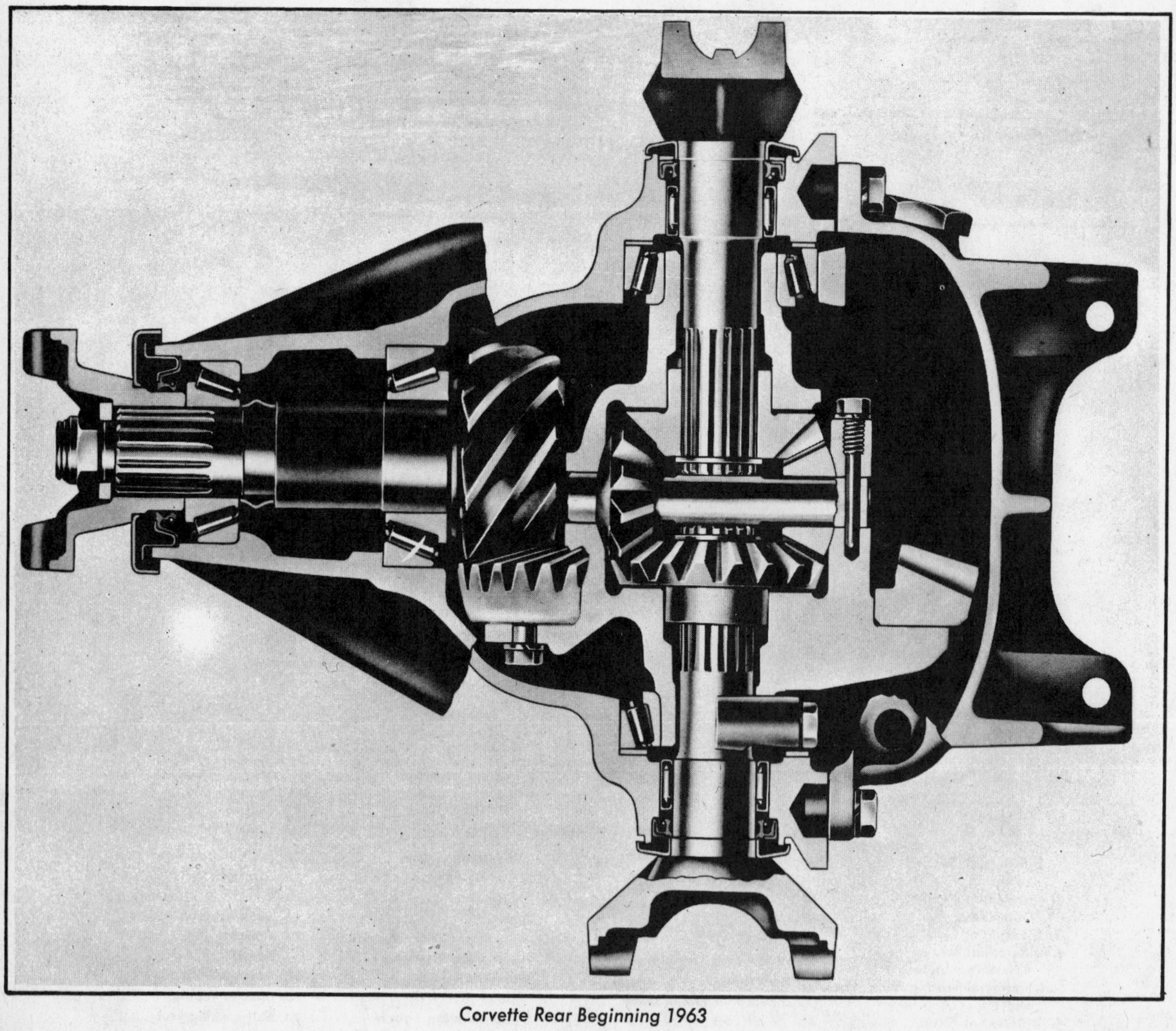

![Corvette Rear cutaway]

Corvette Rear Beginning 1963

CHEVY II INDEX

AIR CONDITIONING

Service .1092

BRAKES, HYDRAULIC

Adjustments 938
Bleed brakes 941
Brake references 152
Master cylinder service 939
Parking brake lever & cable . . .152

BRAKES, POWER

Power unit references 152
Power unit overhaul 954
Trouble shooting 954

CLUTCH

Clutch assembly, R & R 160

COOLING SYSTEM

Cooling system references 153
Radiator core, R & R 153
Thermostat 153
Water pump, R & R 153

ELECTRICAL SYSTEM

Battery .151
Delcotron references 150
Distributor references 149
Distributor, R & R 150
Distributor specifications 147
Fuses and circuit breakers 146
Gauges 1024
Generator, R & R 150
Generator and
    regulator specifications 147
Generator references 150
Generator service 1026
Generator trouble shooting chart 1026
Horn buttons 160
Ignition firing order & timing 146
Ignition timing procedure 149
Ignition timing specifications 147
Starter, R & R 151
Starter specifications 147
Starter systems 1046

ENGINE ASSEMBLY

Cylinder head, R & R 155
Engine assembly, R & R 153
Engine diagnosis 1012
Engine firing order & timing 146
Engine lubrication 157
Engine marking code 146
Engine references 153
Oil filter, R & R 157
Oil pan, R & R 158
Oil pressure specifications 148
Oil pump 157
Piston and rod, R & R 158
Piston and pin specifications 148

ENGINE ASSEMBLY—continued

Rocker arm lubrication 157
Rocker arms & shaft 155
Specifications, general engine . .148
Specifications, tune up engine . .147
Timing case cover, R & R 156
Timing gear, R & R 156
Timing chain, R R 156
Trouble shooting charts 1012
Tune-up specifications 147
Valve adjusting sequence 155
Valve specifications 148
Valves and guides 155

ENGINE LUBRICATION

Oil filter 157
Oil pan, R & R 158
Oil pump, R & R 157

EXHAUST SYSTEM

Exhaust pipe, R & R 153
Muffler, R & R 153
Tail pipe, R & R 153

FRONT END

Front end R & R 164

FUEL SYSTEM

Carburetors 972
Fuel gauge, R & R 1024
Fuel gauge service 1024
Fuel pump pressure 147
Fuel pump, references 152
Fuel pump service 1020
Fuel system references 152
Fuel Tank, R & R 152

INSTRUMENTS

Instrument references 151
Instrument cluster, R & R 151

REAR AXLE AND SUSPENSION

Axle assembly, R & R 163
Axle shaft 918
Axle shaft oil seal 918
Pinion bearings 918
Ring gear & pinion 918
Trouble shooting 919

SPECIFICATIONS

Battery .147
Brake cylinder sizes 148
Capacities
    Axle, rear 148
    Cooling system 148
    Crankcase 148
    Fuel tank 148
    Transmission, automatic 148
    Transmission, manual 148
Chassis, general 148
Cylinder head tightening 148

SPECIFICATIONS—continued

Delcotron specifications 147
Distributor 147
Engine, general 148
Engine, tune-up 147
Fuses and circuit breakers 146
Generator regulators 147
Light bulbs 146
Main bearings 148
Model identification illustrations .146
Model year identification 146
Piston and pin 148
Quick reference specifications . . .146
Rod bearings 148
Starters .147
Tune-up .147
Valves 148
Wheel alignment 147

STEERING, MECHANICAL

Adjust gear housing 1052
Gear assembly, R & R 160
Horn button, R & R 160
Steering wheel, R & R 160

STEERING, POWER

Pump assembly 1058
References 160
Trouble shooting 1081
Unit overhaul 1058

SUSPENSION, FRONT

Alignment procedures 1082
Alignment specifications 147
Ball joints, R & R 158
Coil springs, R & R 159
Riding height, adjust 158
Shock absorbers 1087
Support arms, pins and bushings 1087
Suspension references 158

TRANSMISSION, AUTOMATIC

Powerglide 758
Powerglide linkage adjustment . .161
Powerglide, R & R 161
References 161

TRANSMISSION, MANUAL SHIFT

Transmission, R & R 161

TROUBLE CHECKS

Procedures 1

TUNE-UP

Procedures 148
Specifications 147
Engine diagnosis 1012

UNIVERSAL JOINT AND DRIVE LINE

References 163

CHEVY II

YEAR IDENTIFICATION

Model identification of standard and deluxe series is illustrated in accompanying chart.

The vehicle number is located on the left front hinge pillar.

SERIAL NUMBER

A typical vehicle serial number tag yields vehicle type, model year, assembly plant and production unit sequence number.

ENGINE NUMBER

The engine number is located on a pad on the right hand side of the cylinder block at the rear of the distributor.

The engine number shows manufacturing plant, month and day of manufacture, and transmission type. A typical engine number would be F1210A, which would break down thus:

   F—Manufacturing Plant (F-Flint, T-Tonawanda)

   12—Month of manufacture (December)

   10—Day of manufacture (Tenth)

   A—Transmission Type.

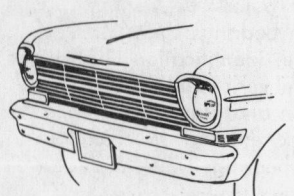

1962

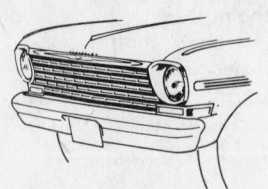

1963

Series Designation	Model No. 4 Cyl	Model No. 6 Cyl	Description
Chevy II 100	111	211	2-Dr. Sedan, 6-Passenger
	169	269	4-Dr. Sedan, 6-Passenger
	135	235	4-Dr. Station Wagon, 2-Seat
Chevy II 300	311	411	2-Dr. Sedan, 6-Passenger
	369	469	4-Dr. Sedan, 6-Passenger
	345	445	4-Dr. Station Wagon, 3-Seat
Nova 400	...	437	2-Dr. Sport Coupe, 5-Passenger
	...	467	2-Dr. Convertible, 5-Passenger
	...	435	4-Dr. Station Wagon, 2-Seat

Model Year[1]	Body Style[2]	Assembly Plant[3]	Unit Number[4]
2	0445	W	100025

[1] Last number of model year (1962).
[2] See Model Identification in this section.
[3] W—Willow Run.
[4] Unit numbering will start at 100,001 at all plants.

QUICK WORKING SPECIFICATIONS

IGNITION TIMING
4 Cyl. ....4° BTC
6 Cyl. ....8° BTC

DISTRIBUTOR
Point Gap ....019"
Cam Dwell ....30°±2°

SPARK PLUGS
Type 46N
Gap 035

VALVES
Face Angle ....45°
Seat Angle ....46°
Tappet Clearance ....Zero

CAPACITIES
Crankcase-4 cyl. ....3.5 Qt.
Crankcase-6 cyl. ....4 Qt.
Manual Trans. ....2 Pts.
Automatic Trans. ....15.2 Pts.
Rear Axle ....4 Pts.
Gasoline Tank ....16 Gals.
Cooling System
  4 Cyl. ....8½ Qts.
  6 Cyl. ....11½ Qts.

FUSES AND CIRCUIT BREAKERS
Headlamps & Parking Lamps
     15 Amp. Circuit Breaker
Tail, Stop and Dome Lamps
     15 Amp 3AG Fuse

Radio ....4 Amp. 3AG Fuse
Instr. Lamps ....3 Amp. 3AG Fuse
Windshield Wiper Motor
    20 Amp. Circuit Breaker

LIGHT BULBS
Headlamp 6012
Beam Indicator 53
Tail, Stop and Turn 1034
Parking and Turn 1034
License Plate 67
Instrument 1816
Gen., Oil., & Temp. 57
Courtesy 93

FIRING ORDER and TIMING

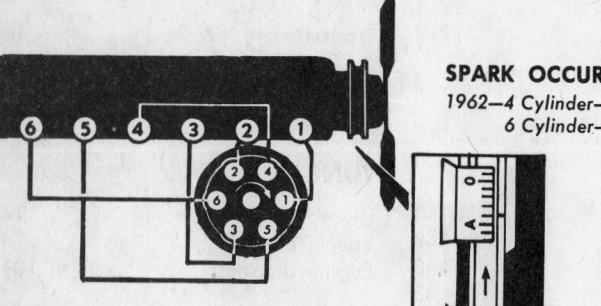

SPARK OCCURS:
1962—4 Cylinder—4° BTDC
      6 Cylinder—8° BTDC

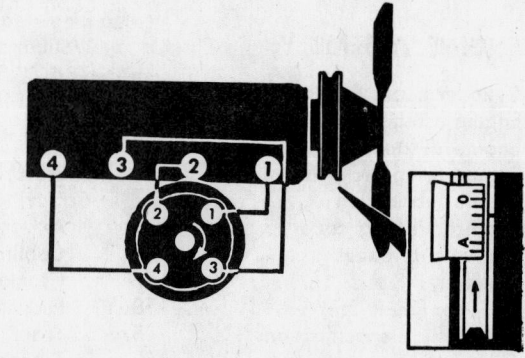

NOTE:
THESE ARE APPROXIMATE SETTINGS. ENGINE DESIGN, ALTITUDE, TEMPERATURE, FUEL AND ENGINE CONDITION WILL ALL INFLUENCE TIMING. THE DETERMINING FACTOR, LIMITING ADVANCE, WILL STILL BE THE "KNOCK POINT" OF THE ENGINE.

TUNE UP SPECIFICATIONS

| YEAR AND MODEL | SPARK PLUGS | | DISTRIBUTOR | | | Ignition Timing | Compression Pressure | VALVES | | | | Fuel Pump Pressure | Idle Speed |
| | Type | Gap | Cam Angle | Point Gap | Arm Spring Tension (Ounce) | | | Tappett Clearance | | Timing | | | |
								Intake	Exhaust	Note A			
1962-63—4 Cyl.	46N	.035	28°-32°	.019	19-23	4B	130	Zero	Zero	34B	3½-4½	500
6 Cyl.	46N	.035	28°-32°	.019	19-23	8B	130	Zero	Zero	34B	3½-4½	500

Note A: Including Cam Ramps.

Note:

All specifications are standard and should result in satisfactory performance. There are, however, factors that influence these settings, such as fuel octane value, air density, humidity, temperature, etc. Timing charts, like other specifications must be considered as averages, subject to modification.

DISTRIBUTOR SPECIFICATIONS

| YEAR AND MODEL | Delco-Remy Part Number | Rotation | Cam Angle Deg. | BREAKER | | GOVERNOR CONTROL At Dist. RPM | | VACUUM CONTROL DATA | | |
				Point Gap (Inch)	Arm Spring (Ounce)	Advance Starts	Full Advance	Inches Vacuum to Start	Inches Vacuum Full Adv.	Max. Dist. Advance Degrees
1962-63—4 Cyl.	1110268	C	28°-32°	.019	19-23	400	14 @ 1850	6	11-13½	11½
6 Cyl.	1110267	C	28°-32°	.019	19-23	400	13 @ 1125	6	11-13½	11½

GENERATOR AND REGULATOR SPECIFICATIONS

| YEAR AND MODEL | GENERATORS | | REGULATORS | | | | | | |
| | Field Current Amperes At 12 Volts | Brush Tension Spring | Cut-Out Relay | | Air Gap | | Current Regulator Setting | Voltage Regulator Setting |
			Air Gap	Closing Voltage	Reg. Current	Reg. Voltage		
1962—All	1.7	28	.020	12.6	.075	.075	30	14.3

DELCOTRON AND A.C. REGULATOR SPECIFICATIONS

| Delcotron Model Number | Ground Polarity | Field Current Draw (Amperes) | CURRENT OUTPUT | | | RUNNING VOLTAGE | | | REGULATOR | | FIELD RELAY | |
			Engine R.P.M.	Amperes	Volts	Engine R.P.M.	Amperes	Volts @ 125°	Model Number	Point Gap	Armature Air Gap	Closing Voltage
1100600	Neg.	1.9 to 2.2	1100	12.0	14	6500	42	13.5-14.3	1119502	.015	.015	6.5-8.5
1100601	Neg.	1.9 to 2.2	1100	5.0	14	6500	52	13.5-14.3	1119502	.015	.015	6.5-8.5
1117765*	Neg.	4.1 to 4.5	1100	24.0	14	6500	62	13.3-13.9	9000567	.027	.014	5.0-9.5
1100630	Neg.	1.9 to 2.3	1100	4.0	14	6500	32	14.0	1119512	.015	.014	2.3-3.7

Note: Standard Delcotron is 5.5" dia., heavy duty unit is 6.0" dia. (identified with *).

BATTERY AND STARTER SPECIFICATIONS

| YEAR AND MODEL | BATTERY | | | | STARTERS | | | | | | |
| | Amp. Hours Capacity | Volts | Delco Number | Terminal Grounded | LOCK TEST | | | NO LOAD TEST | | | Brush Spring Tension |
					Amp.	Volts	Torque	Amps.	Volts	RPM	
1962—All	42	12	1980454	N	Not Recommended			50-75	10.6	6452	35
1963—All	44	12	1980544	N	Not Recommended			49-76	10.6	7800	35

FRONT WHEEL ALIGNMENT

| YEAR AND MODEL | CASTER | | CAMBER | | Toe-In (Inches) | Kingpin Inclination (Degrees) | WHEEL PIVOT RATIO | |
	Range (Degrees)	Pref. Setting	Range (Degrees)	Pref. Setting			Inner Wheel	Outer Wheel
1962-63—All	0 to 1P	½P	½P to 1½P	1P	¼ to ⅜	8	20	18¾

CAPACITIES

YEAR AND MODEL	Crankcase Add 1 Qt. For New Filter	Transmission Pints to Refill After Draining		Rear Axle Shaft	Gasoline Tank Gallons	Cooling System Quarts Add ½ Qt. For Heater
		Manual	Automatic			
1962-63—4 Cyl.	3.5	2	15.2	4	16	8½
6 Cyl.	4	2	15.2	4	16	11½

GENERAL ENGINE SPECIFICATIONS

YEAR AND MODEL	Bore and Stroke	Number of Main Bearings	Type of Valve Lifter	Cubic Inch Displacement	AMA Horsepower	Adv. Horsepower	Adv. Torque	Compression Ratio	Oil Pressure at 30 MPH	Camshaft Drive
1962-63—4 Cyl.	3.88x3.25	5	Hydraulic	153	24	90 @ 4000	152 @ 2400	8.5-1	35	Gear
6 Cyl.	3.56x3.25	7	Hydraulic	194	30.5	120 @ 4400	177 @ 2400	8.5-1	35	Gear

CRANKSHAFT BEARING JOURNAL SIZES

YEAR AND MODEL	MAIN BEARING JOURNALS				CONNECTING ROD BEARING JOURNALS		
	Journal Diameter	Oil Clearance	End Play Of Shaft	End Play Held By	Journal Diameter	Oil Clearance	End Play
1962-63—4 Cyl.	2.3004	.016	.004	5	1.9999"	.0017"	.0011"
6 Cyl.	2.3004	.016	.004	7	1.9999"	.0017"	.0011"

PISTON AND PIN SPECIFICATIONS

YEAR AND MODEL	PISTON		PISTON PIN				
	Skirt Clearance		Diameter	Bushing	FIT		Lock
	Min.	Max.			In Rod	In Piston	
1962-63—All	.0006	.0010	.9272	None	Zero	.0002	In Rod

VALVE SPECIFICATIONS

YEAR AND MODEL	Seat Angle	Intake Valve Lift	Exhaust Valve Lift	VALVE SPRING PRESSUURE		STEM TO GUIDE CLEARANCE		Stem Diammeter	Are Guides Removable
				Outer	Inner	Intake	Exhause		
1962-63—All	46°	.335"	.335"	80 @ 1.696	None	.0015"	.0023"	.3411	No

GENERAL CHASSIS AND BRAKE SPECIFICATIONS

YEAR AND MODEL	CHASSIS		BRAKE CYLINDER BORE		
	Overall Length In Inches	Tire Size	Master Cylinder (Inch)	Wheel Cylinder (Inch)	
				Front	Rear
1962 & 1963 2 & 4 Door Sedans	183.	6.00x13	1	1	⅞
Spt. Coupe, Convt.	183.	6.50x13	1	1	⅞
Station Wagon	187.4	6.50x13	1	1	⅞

CYLINDER HEAD NUT TIGHTENING SEQUENCE

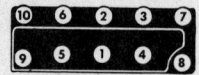

4 Cyl. *Tighten to* ......90-95 *ft. lbs.*

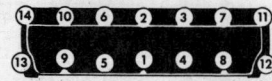

6 Cyl. *Tighten to* ......90-95 *ft. lbs.*

TUNE-UP

Tune-up and diagnosis operations are performed in the conventional manner regardless of engine being used. See charts on preceding pages for specifications.

Compression

1. Blow foreign matter from the plug wells. Then loosen all spark plugs one turn.
2. Start engine and accelerate a couple of times to blow out disturbed carbon.
3. Stop engine and remove plug wires and spark plugs.
4. Remove air cleaner and block choke and throttle in wide open position.
5. Hook up starter remote control cable and insert compression gauge in plug port.
6. Crank engine through about four compression strokes and record highest reading.
7. Do likewise with the remaining cylinders. The readings should

be about 130 lbs. and variation between cylinders should not exceed 20 lbs.

Note: A compression check is the first step in the tune-up procedure. Only if compression pressures are within limits, should tune-up be continued.

Spark Plugs

Use a good spark plug tester, if available. A visual check should disclose any worn electrodes, glazed, broken or blistered porcelains and heavy carbon deposits or oil damp. Clean or replace spark plugs as required (see tune-up chart for correct type), install new plug gaskets and torque to 20-25 ft. lbs.

Note: A good investment is the purchase of a spark plug thread tap. The size is 14 mm x 1.25 SAE. Use this tap (well greased) to clean cylinder head threads and prepare the plug hole for new or reconditioned spark plugs. This plug size is just about standard with American manufacturers of passenger cars and is a handy shop tool.

Ignition System

1. Replace brittle or otherwise damaged spark plug wires, (don't forget the coil-to-distributor cap wire).
2. Tighten all ignition system connections.
3. Remove distributor cap, clean cap and inspect for cracks, carbon tracks and burned or corroded terminals. Replace cap if necessary.
4. Clean rotor and inspect for damage.
5. Check distributor governor advance action by twisting the rotor in a clockwise direction as far as possible. Release the rotor to see if the spring tension is sufficient to return it to the retarded position. In the case of sluggish or partial return, the distributor must be disassembled for corrective measures.
6. Check vacuum spark control mechanism by pushing the breaker plate connecting lever against the diaphragm spring then release it to see if the spring returns it to full retard. Correct any interference or binding if present. The old suction and tongue method can be applied to the vacuum line to the distributor to check for cracks or porosity of the diaphragm.
7. Examine points, clean or replace as necessary.
8. Adjust distributor points, (see tune-up specifications chart).

Battery and Cables

1. Visually inspect battery case, cables and carrier for any condition which would interfere with good service. Make corrections.
2. Measure the specific gravity of the electrolite in each cell. If it is below 1.230 (at about 80° F) recharge the battery or further check for a drain or trouble in the charging circuit.
3. Connect a voltmeter across the battery terminals and measure the terminal voltage during cranking (coil secondary lead removed to prevent engine starting). If terminal voltage is less than 9.0 volts at room temperature, the battery should be further checked.

Fan Belt

1. Inspect condition of fan belt.
2. Check and adjust if necessary for correct tension, as follows.
   A. If a Tension gauge is available, check the belt tension between the water pump and the generator.
   B. Adjust generator bracket to obtain 90 lb. gauge reading for a new belt or 70 lb. for a belt that has been in service over 1,000 miles.

Generator

1. Lubricate both ends of the generator with a few drops of light engine oil.
2. Make sure generator wires have good electrical connections.

Note: Under no circumstances should the A.C. Generator, (Delcotron) be lubricated except at generator overhaul.

Manifold and Heat Riser

1. Tighten intake and exhaust manifold nuts. An intake leak at the manifold gaskets can ruin an otherwise good tune-up.
2. Be certain of the heat riser control valve. If the shaft is sticking, free it up with a suitable solvent and the help of a light persuader.

Fuel Supply

1. Inspect supply lines and connections for any leaks or defects and correct.

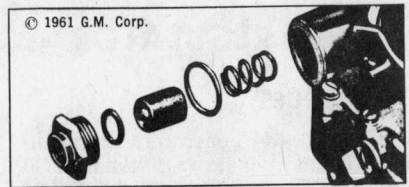

© 1961 G.M. Corp.

Carburetor Fuel Filter Components.

2. Clean or replace the fuel filter at the inlet connection of the carburetor.

Carburetor

For specifications and carburetor adjustments, see "Unit Repair Section," "Carburetors."

Linkage adjustments are contained in later paragraphs of this car section under "automatic transmission."

Valve Adjustment

Detailed instructions for adjusting for zero lash of these hydraulic valves will be found in a later paragraph of this car section under "the valve system."

Ignition Timing

1. Connect a timing light to #1 spark plug and battery, using extension at plug and tachometer at coil primary and ground.
2. Disconnect spark advance vacuum hose from distributor spark advance unit.
3. Use a short pencil as a plug or cover the hose end with a piece of tape to prevent vacuum leak.
4. Start engine and run at idling speed (500 R.P.M.).
5. Aim timing light at harmonic balancer. For timing specifications see "tune-up chart."

Idle Speed Adjustment

Note: This adjustment should be made with air cleaner installed.
1. Connect vacuum gauge to manifold.
2. On cars equipped with closed crankcase ventilation or power brakes, remove manifold connection and install gauge adapter.
3. Connect tachometer.
4. With engine operating at normal running temperature and choke wide open, adjust idle speed and mixture as follows:
5. **Set parking brakes.**
6. Adjust idle speed screw to produce 500 R.P.M. (automatic transmission in "drive" and manual transmission in "neutral").
7. Adjust idle mixture screw to produce highest steady vacuum reading at idle speed. This should be in the range of 17-21 inches.

DISTRIBUTOR

REFERENCES

Distributor design, (except for number of cam lobes and distributor cap) are quite similar for the unit used on the "L-4" and "L-6" engines. Mounting is on the right side of the engine, forward. Both units use centrifugal and vacuum control in their

Timing Mark, L-4 Engine.

design. Direction of rotation (as viewed from the top) is clockwise for both models. Other pertinent distributor specifications can be found in the "Tune-Up" and the "Distributor" charts at the beginning of this Chevy II section.

DISTRIBUTOR REMOVE

1. Remove distributor cap, primary wire and vacuum line at distributor.
2. Scribe a mark on the distributor body, locating the position of the rotor. Scribe another mark on the distributor body and engine block, showing the position of the body in the block.
3. Remove the distributor hold-down screw and lift the distributor up and out of the engine.

DISTRIBUTOR INSTALL

1. If the crankshaft has been rotated, turn the engine until the piston of #1 cylinder is to the top of its compression stroke.
2. Position the distributor to the block so that the vacuum control unit is in it's normal position.
3. Position the rotor to point toward the front of the engine (with distributor held out of the block, but in installed attitude). Turn rotor counterclockwise about ⅛ turn and push distributor down to engage camshaft drive. It may be necessary to move the rotor one way or the other to properly mesh the drive and driven gears.
4. While holding the distributor down in place, kick the starter a few times to make sure the oil pump shaft is engaged. Install hold-down clamb and bolt and snug up the bolt.
5. Once again, rotate the crankshaft until #1 cylinder is on the compression stroke and the harmonic balancer mark is on 0°.
6. Turn distributor body slightly until points just open. Tighten distributor clamp bolt.
7. Place distributor cap in position and see that the rotor lines up

with the terminal for #1 spark plug.
8. Install cap, distributor primary wire and double check plug wires in the cap towers.
9. Start engine and set timing according to the Tune-Up chart.
10. Reconnect vacuum hose to vacuum control assembly.

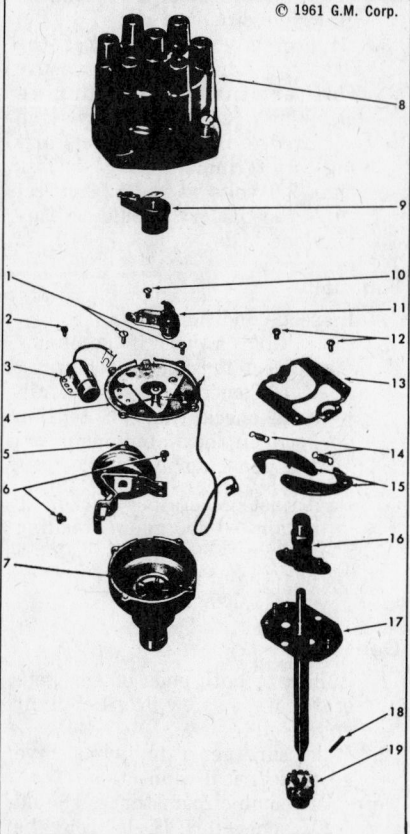

1. BREAKER PLATE ATTACHING SCREWS
2. CONDENSER ATTACHING SCREW
3. CONDENSER
4. BREAKER PLATE ASSEMBLY
5. VACUUM CONTROL ASSEMBLY
6. VACUUM CONTROL ATTACHING SCREWS
7. HOUSING
8. CAP
9. ROTOR
10. CONTACT POINT ATTACHING SCREW
11. CONTACT POINT ASSEMBLY
12. WEIGHT COVER ATTACHING SCREWS
13. WEIGHT COVER
14. WEIGHT SPRINGS
15. ADVANCE WEIGHTS
16. CAM ASSEMBLY
17. MAINSHAFT ASSEMBLY
18. ROLL PIN
19. DRIVE GEAR

Distributor Exploded View (Typical).

GENERATOR AND REGULATOR

REFERENCES

Two types of generators are available. In addition to the standard 30 amp. D.C. generator, 42, 52, or 62 amp. A.C. generators are options on all models. The D.C. generator is discontinued with the 1963 production.

Pertinent data on these generators and regulators are covered in the Unit Repair section under the heading, "Generators and Regulators" and "Alternating Current Generators."

GENERATOR REMOVE

1. Disconnect the armature, field terminal and ground wires from the generator.
2. Remove generator brace bolt, detach fan belt from pulley and lower the generator.
3. Remove the two generator-to-support bracket nuts and bolts and remove the generator.

GENERATOR INSTALL

1. Reverse above operation to install generator and brackets.
2. If no belt tension tool is available, force generator away from the engine until fan belt has 5/16" deflection when forced downward from normal position with a light pressure applied between the generator and the fan.
3. Tighten generator brace bolt with generator in this position, then tighten bracket bolts securely.

   Note: If belt tension tool is used, a strand tension of 75 lbs. is correct for new belts, (under 1,000 mile service) and 50 lbs. for used belts.
4. Connect brown positive generator lead to generator armature terminal. Connect dark blue field lead to generator field terminal and black ground wire to generator ground screw.

   Caution: On cars equipped with radio, connect radio by-pass condenser to generator armature terminal, **not** to the generator field terminal.

POLARIZING THE D.C. GENERATOR

After reconnecting leads, momentarily connect a jumper lead between the "GEN" and "BAT" terminals of the regulator. Failure to do this may result in damage to the equipment as reverse polarity causes vibration, arcing, and burning of the relay points.

A.C. GENERATOR

The following are a few precautions to observe in servicing the electrical system of cars equipped with the Delcotron (A.C.) generator and the regulator.

1. When installing a battery, be certain that the ground polarity of the battery and the ground polarity of the generator and regulator are the same.

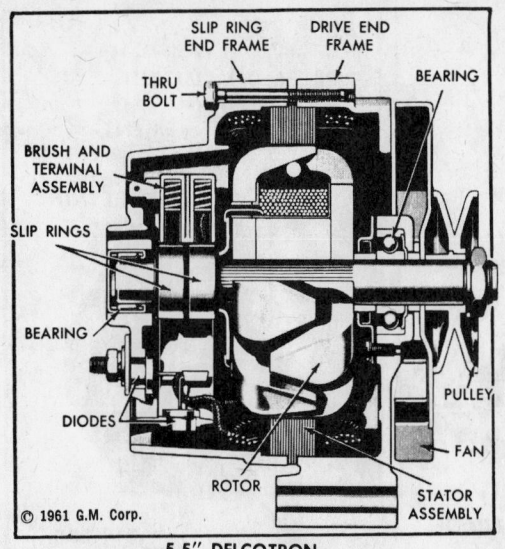

5.5" DELCOTRON

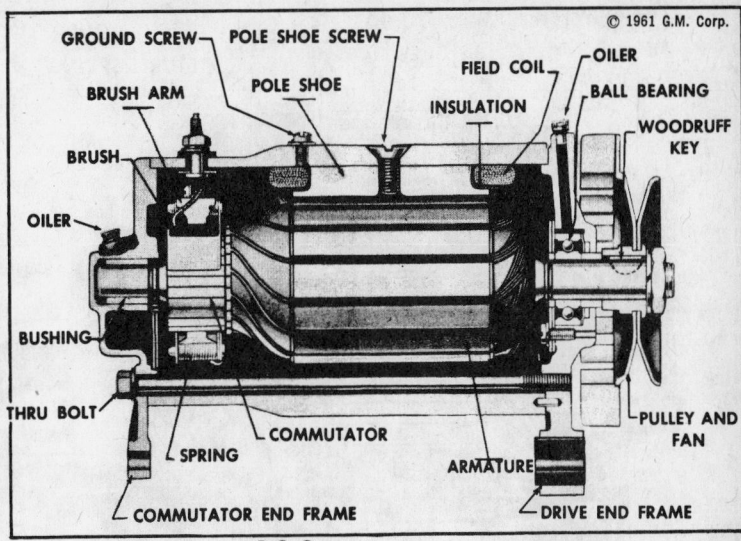

© 1961 G.M. Corp.

D.C. Generator.

2. When connecting a booster battery, be sure to connect the correct battery terminals together.
3. When hooking up a charger, connect the correct charged leads to the battery terminals.
4. Never operate the generator on open circuit. Be sure all connections in the charging circuit are tight.
5. Do not short across or ground any of the terminals on the generator or regulator.

INSTRUMENTS

REFERENCES

All instruments and gauges are contained in the instrument cluster. The entire cluster may be removed from the car for servicing any of the units. The temperature, oil pressure and generator indicator bulbs may be replaced without removing the cluster.

CLUSTER, REMOVE AND INSTALL

1. Loosen and lower the mast jacket from dash panel.

Note: Apply tape to upper mast jacket to prevent paint damage. Do not apply tape to instrument cluster.
2. Unscrew speedometer cable retaining collar.
3. Remove four screws holding cluster to dash panel. Cluster may now be pulled clear of dash.
4. Remove two harness clips from rear of cluster.

Note: Cluster may now be positioned face down for removal of fuel gauge.
5. Disconnect all indicator and illuminating bulb sockets carefully noting their location for proper reinstallation. Remove cluster.
6. To reinstall cluster, reverse above procedure.

BATTERY AND STARTER

BATTERY

The standard battery is a Delco 12 volt, 42 ampere hour (at 20 hr. rate) battery. It consists of 54 plates and is negative ground. Further battery information can be obtained from the Tune-Up paragraphs of this car section.

STARTER

The starter on all models is a pad mounted 12-volt extruded frame type. It has four pole shoes and four fields connected in series with the armature. The aluminum drive end housing is extended to enclose the entire shift lever and plunger mechanism. The flange mounted solenoid switch operates the overrunning clutch drive by means of linkage to the shift lever. This starter should require no lubrication or other maintenance between overhaul periods.

STARTER REMOVE AND INSTALL

Note: There is no problem here on either engine.
1. Disconnect lead wires from solenoid and battery terminals.

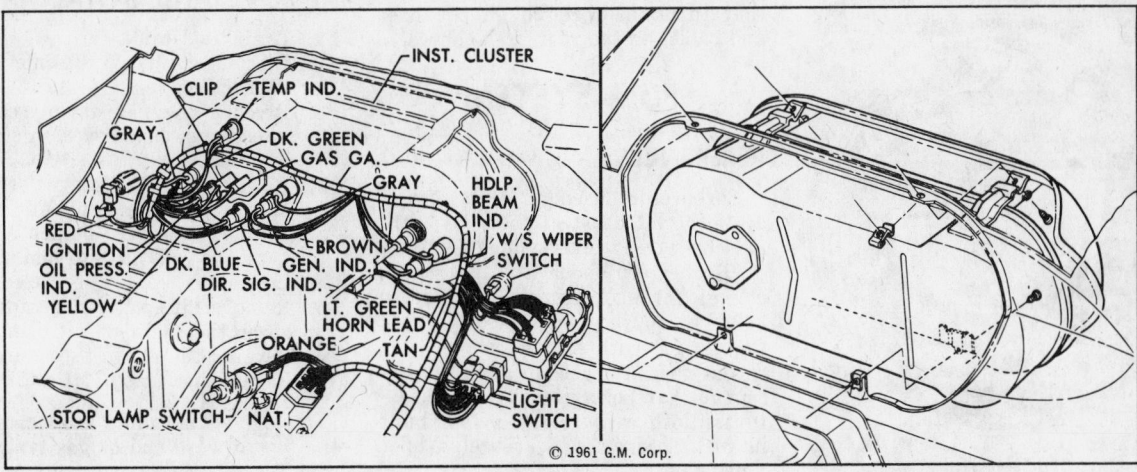

© 1961 G.M. Corp.

Cluster Removal.

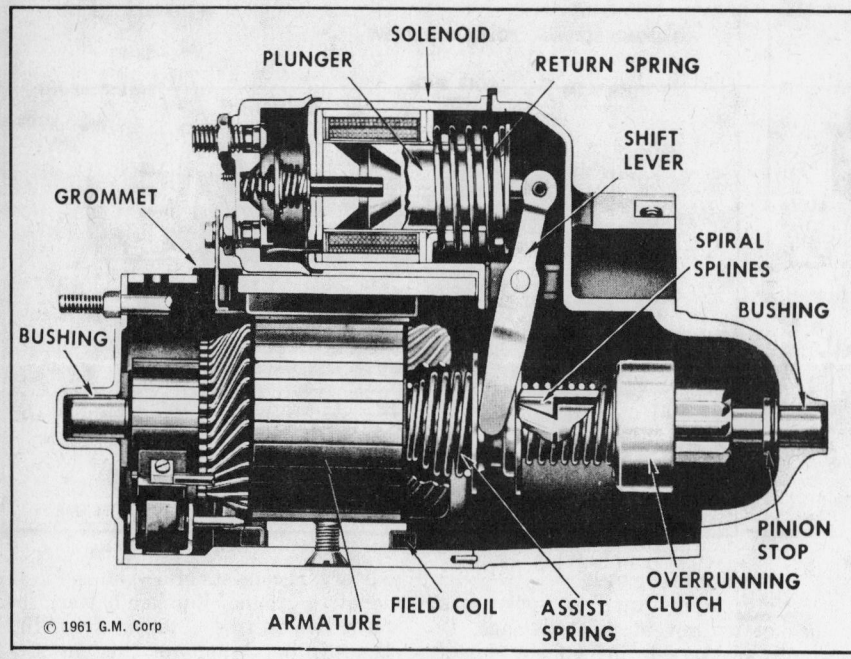

Starting Motor Cross Section

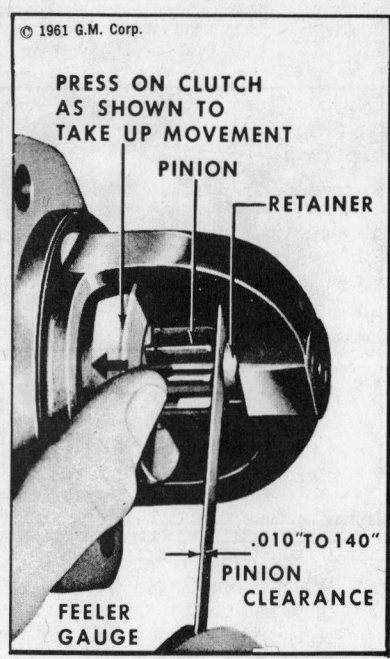

Checking Pinion Clearance

(note the color coding of lead wires to insure proper reinstallation).

2. Remove starter pad mounting bolts and washer. Remove stud nut and lockwasher at front of starting motor. Rotate bracket out of work area.

3. Pull starter assembly forward to clear housing and remove from engine compartment.

4. Install starter in reverse of the above order.

BRAKES

REFERENCES

As with other General Motors cars, Chevy II models are equipped with the Duo-Servo single anchor type

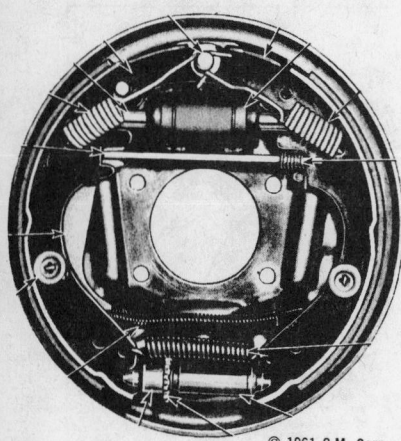

Duo-Servo Brake.

service brake. Brake shoe linings are bonded and the shoes are subject to the conventional type of periodic adjustment. Drums are of cast iron and have a contact area of 9″ in diameter by 2¼″ front and 1¾″ rear width.

Wheel cylinders are conventional double piston type.

The master cylinder consists of a single cylinder and reservoir mounted on the engine side of the firewall.

As an option, both Bendix or Moraine power brakes are available. Data on these two power brakes may be had from "Brakes, Power" in the "Unit Repair" section of this manual.

Parking Brake

The parking brake is hand operated by a lever attached to the dash panel, just to the right of the steering column.

It functions through an equalizer and cables to the rear brake shoes.

FUEL SYSTEM

REFERENCES

Carburetors used on 1962 models are either Rochester Model B (manual choke) for four cylinder engines or Rochester Model BC (automatic choke) for six cylinder engines. In 1963 the four cylinder model uses a Carter YF with manual choke. The carburetors are basically the same except for hand or automatic choke features. Both carburetors have a built in fuel filter at the carburetor inlet connection.

The fuel pump is the single action, AC diaphragm type and is mounted on the lower, right side of the engine, next to the distributor.

All models have a 16 gallon capacity fuel tank supported by two hinged metal straps. A fine mesh screen is located at the lower end of the fuel pick-up pipe. The tank can only be emptied by normal use, syphoning, or tank removal.

See "Carburetor Section" of Unit Repairs for all specifications and adjustments.

FUEL PUMP

See "Fuel Pumps" section of "Unit Repairs" for detailed information.

FUEL TANK
REMOVE AND INSTALL

1. Drain fuel tank.
2. Disconnect filler neck inlet hose connection.
3. Remove the gas gauge sending unit access hole cover on station wagons.
4. Disconnect gas gauge sending unit with tool #J-8950 or other suitable spanner, detach gauge wire and fuel pick-up line at gas tank.
5. Remove tank support straps and lower the tank.
6. Reverse the above procedure for installation.

Note: Sending units are located on the top forward end of gas tanks except for the three seat station wagons. These wagons have the units located at the rear of the tank.

EXHAUST SYSTEM

REFERENCES

A single exhaust system is used on all models and with either engine.

MUFFLER REMOVE AND INSTALL

1. Remove "U" bolt clamp at muffler mounting.
2. Remove muffler from exhaust pipe by cutting the pipe with a torch or hacksaw. Cut cleanly and close to the muffler inlet for ample surface for muffler replacement.
3. Remove the muffler from the tail pipe with a hammer.
4. Replace with a new muffler and/or tail pipe and exhaust pipe, as required.
5. Use existing hardware for replacement, plus a new "U" bolt and two nuts to secure the muffler to the tail pipe.
6. Attach a new clamp assembly to the muffler and exhaust pipe.
7. Neutralize, realign and check all clearances before finally tightening all fasteners.

COOLING SYSTEM

REFERENCES

A standard pressure cooling system is used on all models. The radiator cap is designed to maintain a cooling system pressure of about 13 pounds per square inch above atmospheric. Capacity of the system is 9 qts. (with heater) for the four cylinder engine and 12 qts. (with heater) for the six cylinder. The water pump requires no attention except to make certain the air vent at the top of the housing and the drain holes in the bottom do not become clogged.

RADIATOR REMOVE

1. Drain radiator.
2. Disconnect hoses.
3. Remove six radiator attaching bolts, (3 on each side) and lift radiator out of car.

RADIATOR INSTALL

1. Slide radiator into position.
2. Install attaching bolts.
3. Install hoses and close drain.
4. Fill cooling system, run engine until operating temperature has been reached. Again fill cooling system and check for leaks.

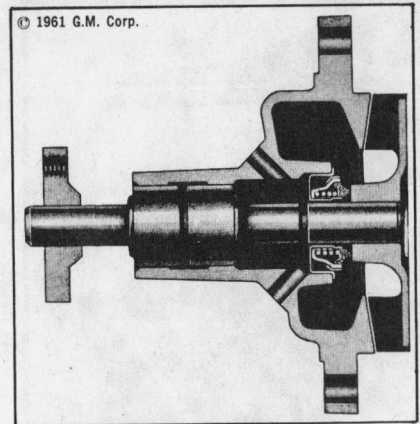

© 1961 G.M. Corp.

Water Pump, Cross-Section

WATER PUMP REMOVE AND INSTALL

1. Drain cooling system and remove inlet hose from pump. Loosen generator and remove fan belt.
2. On heater equipped cars, remove hose from pump housing.
3. Remove pump to cylinder block attaching bolts and remove pump from engine.
4. Install pump in the reverse of the above order.
5. Refill and bleed cooling system.

THERMOSTAT

When replacing thermostat, be sure to install unit with the business end (spring and body) toward the engine.

ENGINE

REFERENCES

Both the four and the six are entirely new in-line, overhead valve engines. The four cylinder, 153 cu. in. engine is used on the 100 and 300 models. The six cylinder, 194 cu. in. engine is used on the 200 and 400

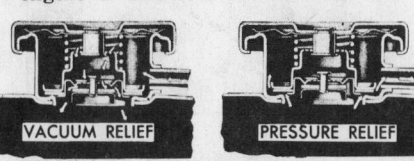

VACUUM RELIEF   PRESSURE RELIEF

© 1961 G.M. Corp.   *Pressure Cap*

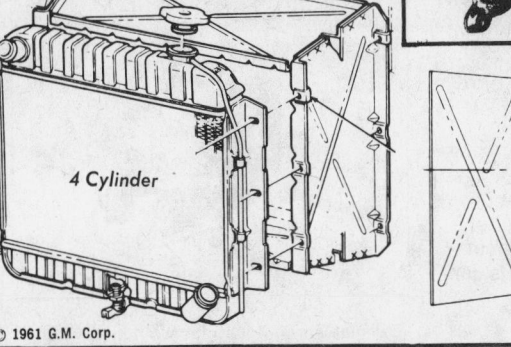

© 1961 G.M. Corp.

4 Cylinder

© 1961 G.M. Corp.   ←13/16"→

Radiator Shroud Assembly

Models. Cylinder numbering is from front to rear and the firing orders are 1-3-4-2 and 1-5-3-6-2-4 respectively.

The L-4 (4 cyl.) engine has five main bearings and the L-6 (6 cyl.) engine is equipped with seven mains. Both engines use hydraulic valve lifters and hollow push rods to operate the separately mounted rocker arms which pivot on ball seats.

A gear type oil pump is driven by the distributor shaft and supplies full pressure for each of these engines. The main oil gallery along hydraulic lifter areas passes oil through drilled passages to each cam and main bearing, through the hydraulic lifters and hollow push rods to the rocker arms.

Pertinent engine data can be found in the "specifications charts" or in the following paragraphs of this car coverage.

ENGINE R & R

Note: Unless otherwise stated the following operations cover both the 4 cyl. and 6 cyl. engines.

Engine Remove

1. Raise car and place on jackstand.
2. Drain cooling system and crankcase.
3. Scribe alignment marks on underside of hood, around hood hinges and remove hood from hinges.
4. Disconnect coolant and heater hoses at engine attachment.
5. Disconnect battery cables at battery.
6. Remove radiator and shroud assembly (on 4 cyl. engines) or radiator (on 6 cyl. engines).
7. Remove air cleaner.
8. Disconnect coil, starter and generator wires, engine-to-body ground strap, oil pressure and

© 1961 G.M. Corp.

Thermostat

Removing Fan Hub

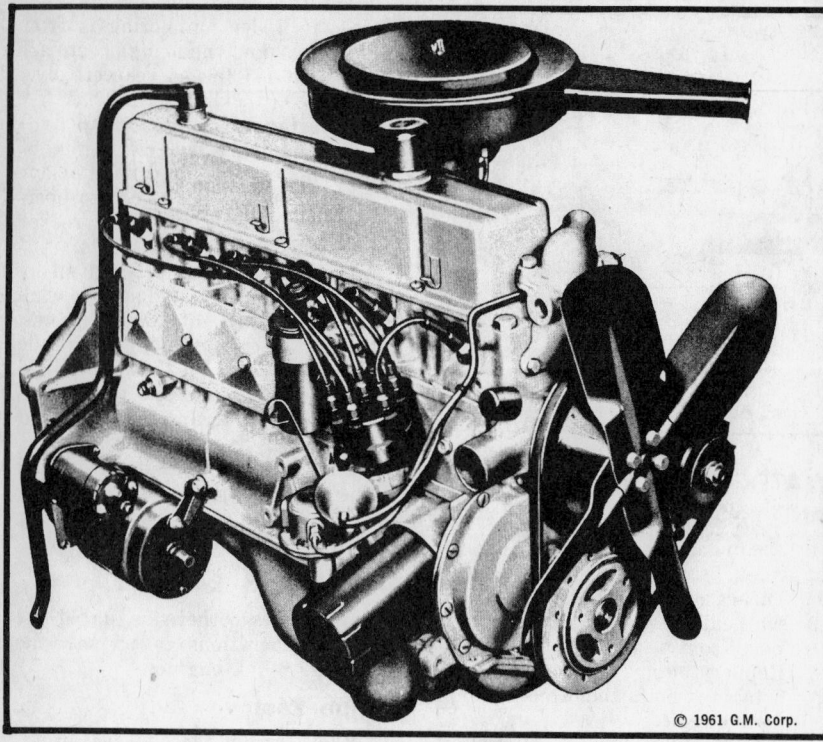

Chevy II 6 Cyl. Engine.

© 1961 G.M. Corp.

engine temperature sender wires.

9. Disconnect gas tank line at fuel pump.
10. Disconnect accelerator control linkage at firewall.
11. Disconnect hand choke linkage (4 cyl.).
12. Disconnect exhaust pipe from manifold.
13. Disconnect clutch shaft bracket at frame and disconnect clutch push rod, spring and pedal linkage. On automatic transmission models, remove transmission oil filler tube and plug the opening.
14. Remove rocker arm cover and road draft tube.
15. Attach engine lifting tool in two cylinder head bolt holes. Attach to hoist and secure the engine.
16. Remove drive shaft and plug the end of the transmission extension housing.
17. Disconnect steering linkage idler arm bracket from right side rail, then lower the linkage for clearance.
18. Remove engine rear mounting bolts.
19. Disconnect speedometer cable and transmission control rod linkage lower ends.
20. Loosen engine front mounting bolts.
21. Raise engine slightly and remove front engine mounting bolts.
22. Remove transmission crossmember and free the transmission rear mounting.
23. (On 4 cyl. only) remove front

crossmember.

24. Remove engine and transmission as a unit from the car.

SEPARATE TRANSMISSION AND CLUTCH FROM ENGINE

Manual Transmission

1. Remove clutch housing cover

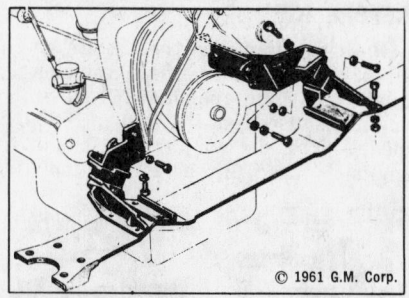

© 1961 G.M. Corp.

Engine Front Mounts Installation (4 Cyl.).

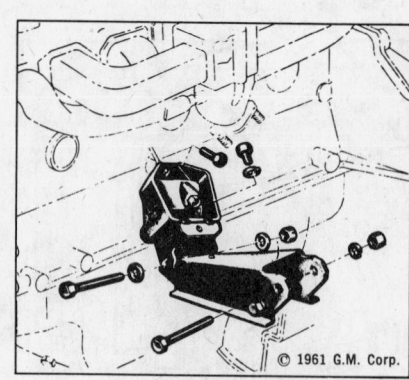

© 1961 G.M. Corp.

Engine Front Mounts Installation (6 Cyl.).

plate screws.

2. Remove bolts holding clutch housing to engine block. Remove clutch housing and transmission assembly.
3. Remove starter and clutch housing cover plate.
4. Loosen clutch-to-flywheel bolts, alternately, until spring pressure is released. Remove all bolts, clutch disc and pressure plate assembly.
5. Reattach transmission by reversing above process.

Automatic Transmission

1. Lower the engine and support it on suitable blocks.
2. Remove converter housing underpan bolts. Remove pan.
3. Remove flywheel-to-converter assembly attaching bolts.
4. Support transmission on blocks.
5. Remove transmission-to-engine mounting bolts.
6. With engine hoist attached, remove blocks from engine only and slowly guide the engine from the transmission.
7. Reattach automatic transmission by reversing above process.

ENGINE INSTALL

1. Position engine in car as follows:

4 Cylinder:

A. Install lifting tool J-4536-A (or substitute) to engine and lower the engine and transmission into the chassis as a unit to the approximate installed position.
B. Support transmission and install rear crossmember under transmission mounts.
C. Raise engine slightly and install front crossmember-to-frame rails. (on station wagons, bolt stabilizer bar in place).
D. Lower the engine, guiding front mounts into position over crossmember and install mount bolts.
E. Install rear mount bolts and remove lifting tool.

6 Cylinder:

A. Install engine lifting tool J-4536-A to engine and lower engine and transmission into chassis as a unit. Guide engine to align front engine mounts with mounts on frame.
B. Install one rear transmission crossmember side bolt, swing crossmember up under transmission mount and install bolt in opposite side rail.
C. Align and install rear mount bolts.
D. Install engine front mount bolts and remove lifting tool from engine.

2. Install drive shaft and "U" bolts at rear universal joint.
3. Make connections peculiar to the type of transmission used.

Manual Transmission Models:

A. Install clutch cross shaft on ball socket at block and bolt bracket to frame rail. Connect pedal and clutch fork push rods. Install return spring from clutch fork to left of engine mount.
B. Connect transmission control rods to shifter levers on transmission side cover. Adjust control rods.

Automatic Transmission Models:

A. Connect transmission control rod and throttle valve rod at transmission and adjust transmission linkage.
B. Install transmission filler tube and dipstick.
4. Connect carburetor choke linkage. (On 4 cyl. connect choke cable.)
5. Connect speedometer cable to driven gear at transmission.
6. Check transmission lubricant level. Fill if necessary.
7. Connect exhaust pipe to manifold and tighten.
8. Connect wire harness to heat sending unit, oil pressure sending unit and coil primary terminal.
9. Attach wires to generator.
10. Attach fuel line at fuel pump.
11. Attach wires and battery cable to starter solenoid.
12. Install radiator assembly (6 cyl.) and radiator and shroud assembly (4 cly.).
13. Refill radiator and crankcase.
14. Replace hood assembly, align previously scribed marks.
15. Adjust valve lash and perform necessary tune-up procedures and check for oil and coolant leaks.
16. Install rocker arm cover gasket, cover and road draft tube.

CYLINDER HEAD

Unless otherwise specified instructions are for both 4 cyl. and 6 cyl. engines.

Remove

1. Drain cooling system and remove air cleaner.
2. Disconnect choke cable (4 cyl.), accelerator pedal rod at bell crank on manifold, and fuel and vacuum lines at carburetor.
3. Disconnect exhaust pipe at manifold flange, then remove manifold bolts and clamps and remove manifolds and carburetor as an assembly.

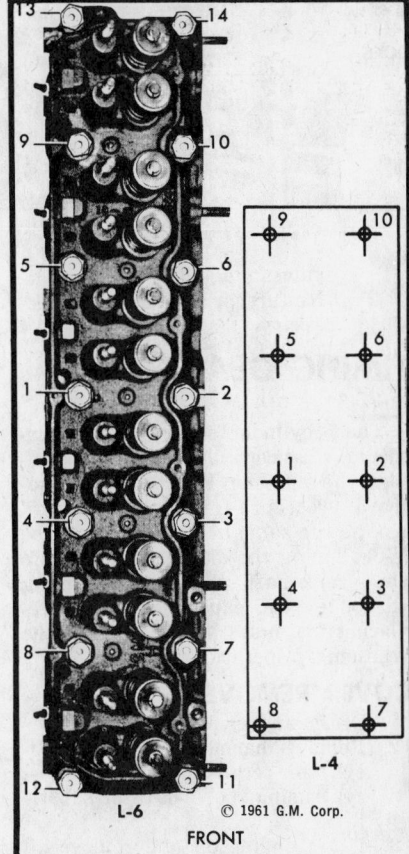

Cylinder Head Torque Sequence.

4. Remove fuel and vacuum line retaining clip from water outlet. Then disconnect wire harness from heat sending unit and coil, leaving harness clear of clips on rocker arm cover.
5. Disconnect radiator hose at water outlet housing and battery ground strap at cylinder head.
6. Disconnect wires and remove spark plugs. (On the 6 cyl. engine) disconnect coil to distributor primary wire lead at coil and remove the coil.
7. Remove rocker arm cover. Back off rocker arm nuts, pivot rocker arms to clear push rods and remove push rods.
8. Remove cylinder head bolts, cylinder head and gasket.

Install

1. Place a new cylinder head gasket over dowel pins in cylinder block.
2. Guide and lower cylinder head into place over dowls and gasket.
3. Oil cylinder head bolts, install and run them down just snug.
4. Tighten the cylinder head bolts a little at a time with a torgue wrench in the correct sequence. Final torque should be 90 to 95 ft. lbs.

5. Install valve push rods down through the cylinder head openings and seat them in their lifter sockets.
6. Install rocker arms, balls and nuts and tighten rocker arm nuts until all push rod play is taken up.
7. Install thermostat, thermostat housing and water outlet using new gaskets. Then connect radiator hose.
8. Install heat sending switch and torque to 15-20 ft. lbs.
9. Clean spark plugs or install new ones. Set gaps to .035".
10. Use new plug gaskets and torque to 20-25 ft. lbs.
11. Install coil (on 6 cyl. engine) then connect heat sending unit and coil primary wires, and connect battery ground cable at the cylinder head.
12. Clean surfaces and install new gasket over manifold studs. Install manifold. Install bolts and clamps and torque as illustrated.
13. Connect throttle linkage, and choke wire, (on 4 cyl. engine).
14. Connect fuel and vacuum lines to carburetor and secure lines in clip at water outlet.
15. Fill cooling system and check for leaks.
16. Adjust valve lash as outlined under "Valves."
17. Install rocker arm cover and position wiring harness in clips.
18. Clean and install air cleaner.

VALVES

REFERENCES

There is no mystery connected with this valve system as it has been tried, proven and used by G.M. for many years. It is a hydraulically operated tappet system with adjustable rocker nuts to obtain zero lash.

Valve specifications may be obtained from the "valve specifications" chart and the "tune-up" chart at the beginning of this Chevy II car section.

VALVE TAPPETS ADJUST

In the case of disassembly or any other cause for valve tappet adjustment, proceed as follows:

1. Adjust rocker arm nuts the amount necessary to eliminate lash.
2. This must be done when lifter is on base of circle of cam. Proceed as follows:
A. Remove distributor cap and crank engine until distributor rotor points to #1 cylinder terminal, with points open. This will insure both intake and exhaust lifters to be on

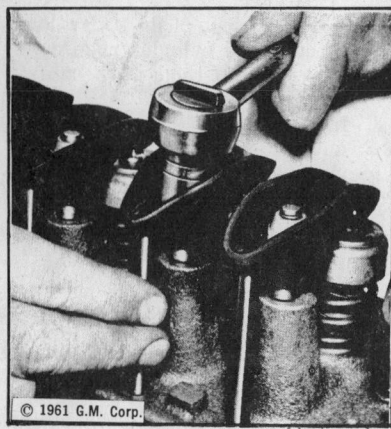

Adjusting valve clearance at the rocker

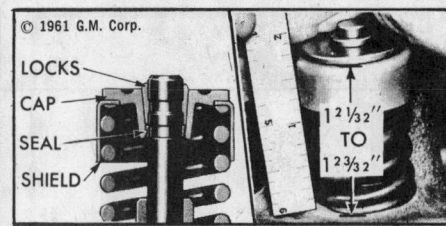

LOCKS
CAP
SEAL
SHIELD

1²¹/₃₂″ TO 1²³/₃₂″

Checking Valve Spring installed Height

the base circle of the camshaft cam lobe.

B. Now turn adjusting nut until all lash is removed from this particular valve train. This can be determined by checking push rod side play while turning the adjustment. When all play has **just** been removed, turn adjusting nut one more turn. This will place the lifter plunger in the center of its travel.

C. Follow steps A and B for each cylinder in order of firing and adjust remaining valves one cylinder at a time. No further adjustment is necessary.

TIMING GEAR COVER

Note:

The 6 cylinder engine uses a harmonic balancer that closely resembles the current V-8 type. The removal procedure for this "dampener" will be the same as that used for the V-8. Driving the dampener back onto the crankshaft without supporting the pulley can cause damage. A replacing tool must be used during the reassembly operation.

COVER REMOVE

1. Drain and remove radiator.
2. Remove harmonic balancer, (6 cyl.) or crankshaft pulley, (4 cyl.) using tool J-6978 or substitute.
3. Drain engine oil and remove oil pan.
4. Remove timing gear cover attaching screws and remove cover and gasket.

Oil Seal Replacement

1. After removing gear cover, pry oil seal out of front of cover with large screwdriver.
2. Install new lip seal with lip (open side of seal) inside of cover and drive or press seal into place with tool J-0995 or substitute.

Camshaft or Camshaft Gear Renew

1. In addition to removing the timing gear cover, remove the grille assembly.
2. Remove valve cover and gasket, loosen all the valve rocker arm nuts and pivot the arms clear of

TIMING MARKS

Oil Pan Removal.

the push rods.

3. Remove distributor.
4. Remove coil and side cover and gasket. Remove push rods and valve lifters.
5. Remove the two camshaft thrust plate retaining screws by working through holes in the camshaft gear.
6. Remove camshaft and gear assembly by pulling it out through the front of the block.

Note: If renewing either camshaft or camshaft gear, the gear must be pressed off of the camshaft. The replacement parts must be assembled in the same manner (under pressure). In placing the gear on the camshaft, press the gear onto the shaft until it bottoms against the gear spacer ring. The end clearance of the thrust plate should be .001" to .005".

7. Install camshaft assembly in the engine.
8. Turn crankshaft and camshaft so as to align and bring the timing marks together. Push the camshaft into this aligned position. Install camshaft thrust plate-to-block screws and torque them to 6-7½ ft. lbs.
9. Runout on either crankshaft or camshaft gear should not exceed .003".
10. Backlash between the two gears should be between .004" and .006".
11. Install timing gear cover and gasket.
12. Install oil pan and gaskets.
13. Install harmonic balancer.
14. Line up keyway in balancer with key on crankshaft and drive balancer onto shaft until it bottoms against crankshaft gear.
15. Install valve lifters and push rods. Install side cover with new gasket. Attach coil wires.
16. Install distributor and set timing as described under "Distributor" near the beginning of this car section.
17. Pivot rocker arms over push rods and lash the valves as described in a previous paragraph "Valve Tappets Adjust."
18. Add oil to the engine. Install and adjust fan belt.
19. Install radiator or shroud.
20. Install grille assembly.
21. Fill cooling system, start engine and check for leaks.
22. Check and adjust timing.

COVER INSTALL

1. Clean cover and block gasket surfaces.
2. Install centering tool J-0966 over end of crankshaft (or improvise with the harmonic balancer).
3. Coat gasket with light grease and position it to block.

4. Install cover and install cover screws. After being certain that the cover is centered, (with either the centering tool or harmonic balancer) torque attaching screws to 6-8 ft. lbs. remove centering tool.

Danger:

The 6 cyl. engine uses a harmonic balancer. Cases of breakage have come to our attention, where the balancer has been hammered back onto the crankshaft.

This balancer **must** be drawn back into place. Use tool J-8792 or a reasonable substitute.

5. Install harmonic balancer.
6. Install oil pan with new gaskets and seals.
7. Install radiator, connect hoses, fill cooling system, start engine and check for leaks.

ENGINE LUBRICATION

Lubrication is of the force feed design, with the gear type **oil pump** in the crankcase. This is a tried and proven system as used in other GM cars. Use of the accompanying charts should suffice in selecting the correct weight oil and to determine the periods for draining.

Under normal driving conditions the crankcase should be drained every 4,000 miles. However, adverse driving conditions, dusty operation, short trip winter driving, etc. make it advisable to change oil every month. Similar short trips in the summer make it advisable to change oil every two months.

OIL FILTER

A full flow oil filter is provided as optional equipment. The filter is the can and cartridge type and should be changed every 4,000 miles under normal conditions.

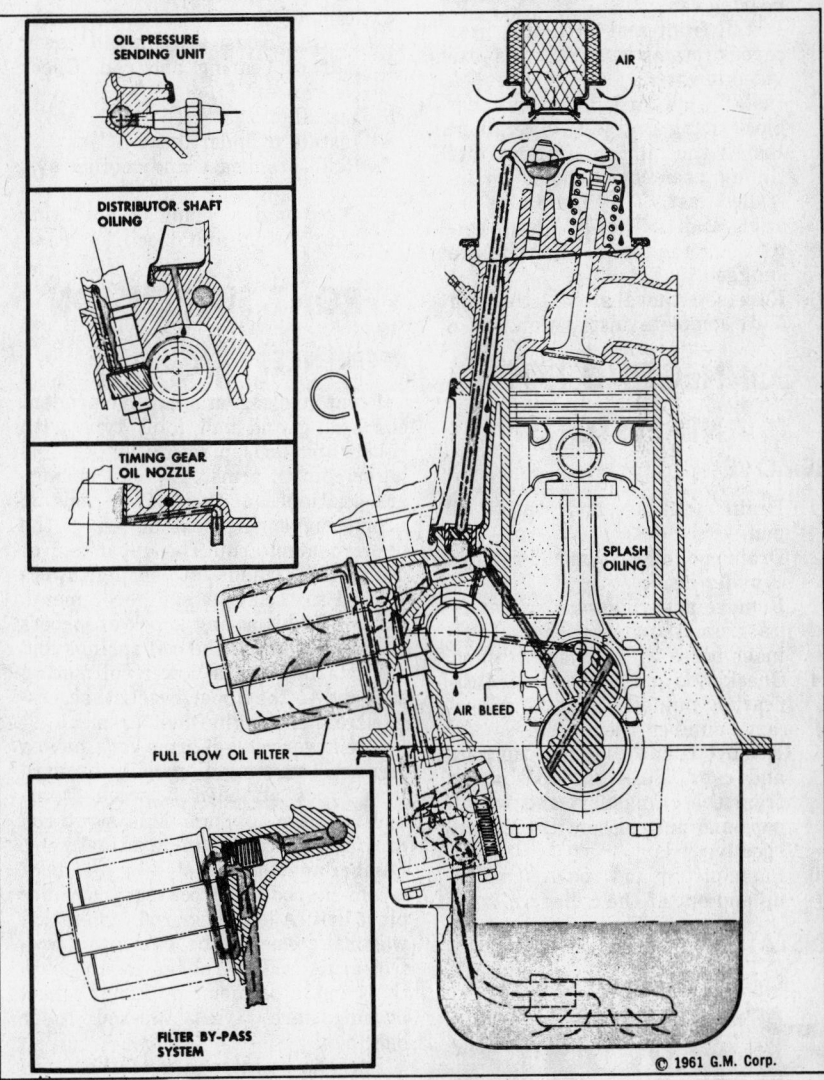

Oil Passage Diagram.

OIL PAN REMOVE AND INSTALL

Remove

1. Disconnect battery ground strap at battery.
2. Drain oil from engine.
3. Disconnect all wires from starter. Remove starter.
4. Disconnect steering idler arm bracket at right hand frame rail. Swing linkage down for pan clearance.
5. **(On 6 cyl. only)** remove front crossmember.

Note: On station wagon, let stabilizer bar hang while removing crossmember.

6. Remove oil pan bolts, drop the pan and clean off gaskets and end seals.

Install

1. Clean all gasket surfaces.
2. Install rear seal in rear main bearing cap.
3. Install front seal on timing gear cover pressing tips into holes provided in cover.
4. Install side gaskets on cylinder block using grease as a retainer.
5. Install the oil pan. (screws into timing gear cover should be installed last. They go in at an angle and the holes line up better after the rest of the bolts are snugged up.)
6. Reverse removal steps 1 through 5 to complete installation.

CONNECTING RODS AND PISTONS

REMOVE

1. Drain crankcase and remove oil pan.
2. Drain cooling system and remove cylinder head.
3. Remove any ridge and/or deposits from the upper end of cylinder bores with a ridge reamer.
4. Check rods and pistons for identification numbers and, if necessary, number them.
5. Remove connecting rod cap nuts and caps. Push the rods away from the crankshaft and install caps and nuts loosely to their respective rods.
6. Push piston and rod assemblies up and out of the cylinders.

INSTALL

1. Lightly coat pistons, rings and

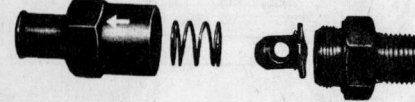

Positive Ventilation Valve

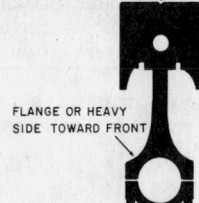

CAST DEPRESSION TOWARD FRONT

FLANGE OR HEAVY SIDE TOWARD FRONT

Correct Relation of Piston to Rod

cylinder walls with light engine oil.

2. With bearing caps removed, install Tool J-5239 or pieces of protective rubber hose on bearing cap bolts.
3. Install each piston in its respective bore using Tool J-5239 or other thread guards on each assembly. **The side of the piston with the cast depression in the head should be to the front. The oil hole in the connecting rod bearing is toward the camshaft.** Guide the rod bearing into place on the crankcase journal.
4. Remove thread guards from connecting rods and install lower half of bearing and cap. Check clearances.
5. Install oil pan.
6. Install cylinder head.
7. Refill crankcase and cooling system.
8. Start engine, bring to operating temperature and check for leaks.

FRONT SUSPENSION

REFERENCES

Front suspension is an independent coil spring and ball joint type with rubber bushed, pivoting upper and lower control arms. The coil springs are positioned at their lower ends on a pivoting spring seat bolted to the upper control arm. The upper end of the spring extends into spring towers formed in the front end sheet metal. Direct, double-acting shock absorbers are located inside the coil springs and are attached to the lower coil spring seat and to the upper bracket, accessible from the engine compartment.

The lower control arms each have a strut rod, running diagonally forward to a brace attached between frame and radiator support. This strut rod provides for **caster angle** adjustment. **Camber angle** is adjusted by means of a cam-shaped lower control arm inner pivot bolt. A stabilizer rod, on station wagons, connects the two lower control arms and is rubber mounted to the front crossmember. Front wheel bearings are Hyatt tapered roller bearings.

Periodic maintenance of the front suspension includes lubrication of the four ball joints, spring seat lower

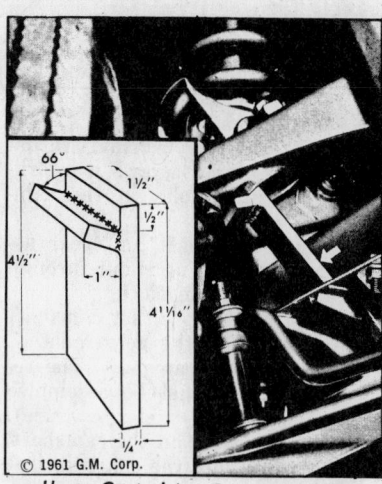

© 1961 G.M. Corp.

Upper Control Arm Support Installed.

pivot shafts and adjustment and lubrication of the front wheel bearings.

Further data on front end alignment can be obtained from the "Front Wheel Alignment" chart at the beginning of this car section and from "Suspension, Front Align" in the Unit Repair Section.

BALL-JOINT INSPECTION

The following on-the-car check is to determine ball joint wear.

Upper

Note: The upper ball joint is a loose fit when not connected to the steering knuckle. Wear may be checked without disassembling.

1. While car weight is still on the front wheels, insert upper control arm support as illustrated.
2. Raise car and allow wheel and tire to hang free.
3. Measure distance from tip of ball stud to top surface of control arm.
4. Place adjustable jackstand under tire and raise slightly to take up ball joint looseness.
5. Repeat step 3 and if the difference in measurements exceeds 3/32", the joint is excessively worn. It should be replaced.

Lower

1. With upper control arm support in position as in step 1 above, disconnect the lower ball stud from the steering knuckle.
2. Assemble nut to lower ball stud and check rotating torque with torque wrench. Specifications for new joints are 4-8 ft. lbs. If torque readings are very high or low, renew ball joint.

RIDING HEIGHT AND SPRING SAG

1. Position the car on a smooth level floor.

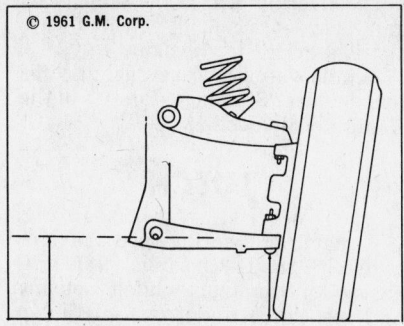

Height Adjusting Location

2. Bounce front of car to neutralize springs
3. Measure distance from floor to centerline of lower control arm pivot.
4. Measure the distance from the floor to the lower ball joint seat.
5. The difference of the distance between these two measurements should be 2½″ plus or minus ½″. This check should be made with gas tank full, spare tire in trunk but no passengers.
6. Measure the opposite side in the same way.
7. If riding height does not fall between these limits, replace front springs. Do not shim springs.

COIL SPRING OR SPRING SEAT REPLACE

Coil Spring Remove

1. Raise car and remove wheel.

2. Support lower control arm with adjustable jackstand and raise slightly from full rebound position.
3. Remove shock absorber.
4. Insert spring compressor J-6874-4-5 with adapters J-9512-1-2 into upper spring tower so that lower "U"-bolt fits into shock absorber mounting holes in spring seat. Secure the two lower studs to the spring seat with nuts.
5. Fit tool to upper pivot at top of spring and compress the spring by tightening the upper nut. Compress spring until the screw is bottomed out.
6. Remove lower spring seat retaining nuts, lift spring and seat assembly from control arm and guide it down and out through fender skirt.

Spring Seat

1. Release spring tension and disconnect spring compressor from spring seat.
2. Tap one bolt out of pivot shaft and remove rubber boots.
3. Unscrew pivot shaft, drawing the free end of the shaft through the threaded sleeve.
4. Inspect pivot shaft and sleeve for damage. Inspect rubber shaft boots for aging and replace if necessary.

Spring Seat Assembly

1. Screw pivot shaft into spring seat

sleeve until bolt hole centerlines are equal distance from spring seat.
2. Insert lip of rubber boot into groove in seat sleeve.
3. Insert bolt into pivot shaft and grease spring seat assembly through lube fitting.
4. Install spring seat to spring compressor.

Coil Spring Install

1. Install new spring into tool and compress spring until screw is bottomed out.

Note: Spring coil ends must be against spring stops in upper and lower seats.

Installing Spring Compressor.

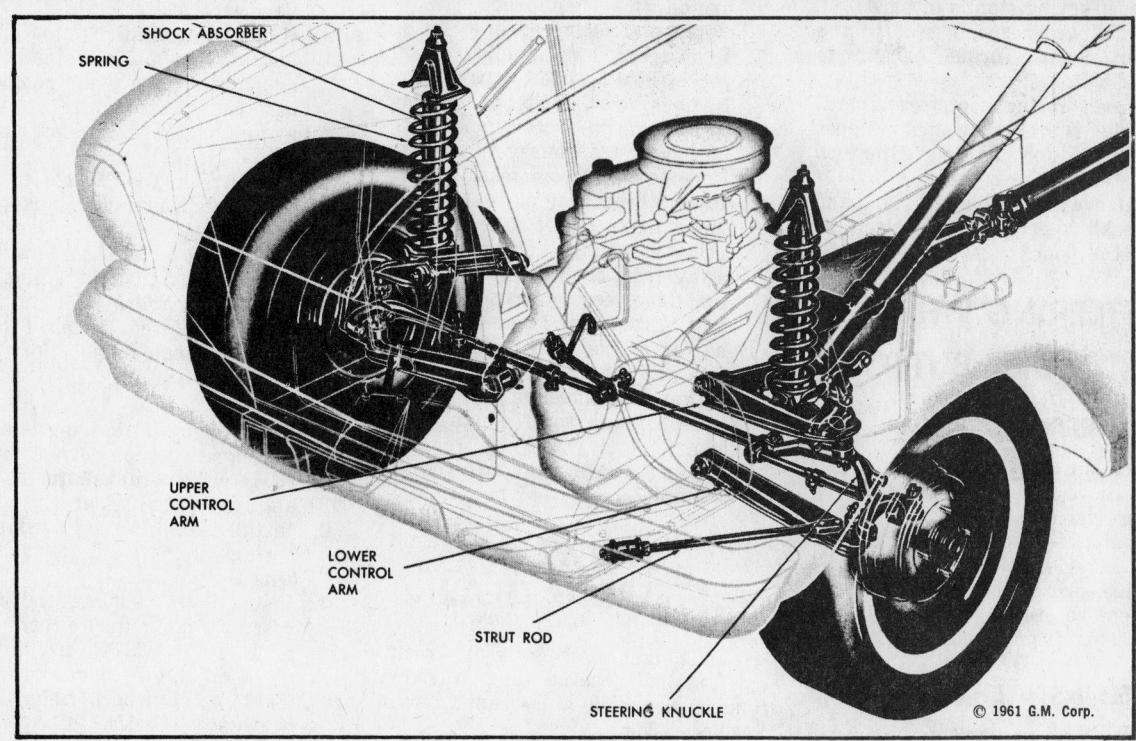

SHOCK ABSORBER

SPRING

UPPER CONTROL ARM

LOWER CONTROL ARM

STRUT ROD

STEERING KNUCKLE

Front Suspension

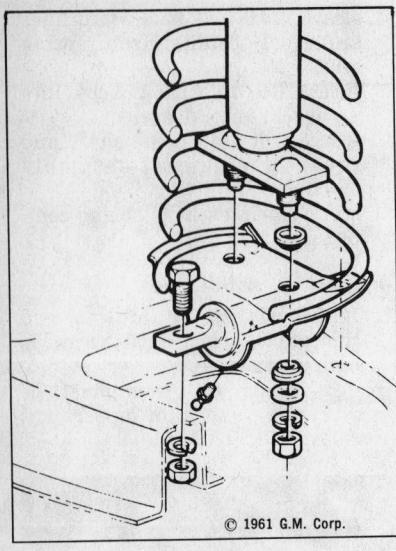

Spring and Seat Assembly.

© 1961 G.M. Corp.

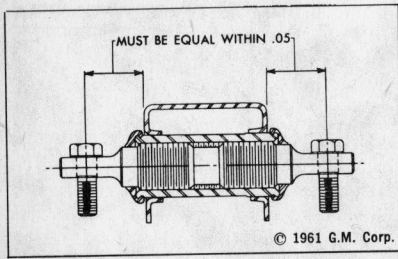

MUST BE EQUAL WITHIN .05

© 1961 G.M. Corp.

Pivot Shaft.

2. Lift spring and tool assembly into place and position so that the upper spring stop is inboard.
3. Install lower spring seat to the control arm. Torque the nuts to 25-35 ft. lbs.
4. Loosen spring compressor until spring is properly seated in upper spring tower and remove the tool.
5. Install shock absorber.
6. Remove adjustable jackstand and install wheel and tire. Lower car to the floor.

STEERING WHEEL AND HORN BUTTON

WHEEL REMOVE

1. Pry out horn button.
2. Remove three screws attaching receiver cup (or horn ring, if so equipped) and bushing spacer to steering wheel. Then remove bell-ville spring.
3. Remove steering wheel nut and washer from steering shaft.

WHEEL INSTALL

1. Install all components in reverse order of removal. There is an alignment mark on the steering

wheel shaft and on the wheel hub. Make certain these two marks are in register when installing the wheel. Torque the wheel retaining nut to 35-40 ft. lbs.

STEERING GEAR —MANUAL

There is no mystery in this area as the unit is of the tried and proven, recirculating ball type. This type gear has been used on G.M. cars for considerable time. Adjustment procedures may be found under "Steering—Manual" in the "Unit Repair Section."

STEERING GEAR R & R

Note: It will be necessary to remove power brake cylinder and/or clutch push rod if car is so equipped.

1. Remove pitman arm retaining nut. (mark an index mark on pitman arm and sector shaft so that the two parts can be reassembled in the same register.)
2. Remove pitman arm from sector shaft.
3. Disconnect transmission linkage from shift lever (S).
4. Remove the two lower steering gear-to-frame mounting bolts.
5. Disconnect external electrical wires from horn junction, directional switch and back-up lamp switch (if so equipped).
6. Remove steering wheel.
7. Remove screws holding mast jacket hole seal to toe panel.
8. Remove mast jacket-to-steering gear clamp on cars equipped with automatic transmission.
9. Remove nuts from mast jacket-to-dash brace clamp.
10. Move mast jacket and steering gear assembly downward and away from dash, pivoting on remaining steering gear mounting bolt. Move front seat to the rear as far as possible. Pull steering and mast jacket toward you, rotating it so that shift levers will pass through the toe pan opening.
11. Reverse above procedure for installing.

POWER STEERING GEAR

This equipment consists of a recirculating ball type steering gear and linkage to which a hydraulic assist has been added.

Hydraulic pressure is provided by a belt driven valve-type pump.

The steering gear is the same basic unit used on manually steered cars and is serviced in the same way.

Detailed service coverage may be found under "Steering—Power" in the "Unit Repair Section."

CLUTCH

A diaphragm spring-type clutch is used with the H-35 manual transmissions. An aluminum clutch housing encloses clutch and flywheel. Clutch maintenance and servicing are performed in the conventional way.

CLUTCH AND TRANSMISSION

Remove

1. Raise car and support on jackstands.
2. Support rear of engine with jackstand.
3. Remove propeller shaft.
4. Remove rear crossmember bolts from frame and transmission mounts and remove crossmember.
5. Disconnect transmission shift linkage, speedometer cable and clutch return spring. Clutch fork push rod will now hang free.
6. Remove clutch housing cover plate screws and let plate hang from starter gear housing.
7. Lower engine enough to gain access to clutch housing bolts at engine block, then remove all but uppermost bolt.
8. Hold transmission and clutch housing assembly against block over dowel pins while removing last bolt. Remove transmission and clutch housing as an assembly.
9. Install pilot Tool J-5824 to support clutch assembly during removal.
10. Loosen the 6 cover plate attaching screws, a little at a time, until clutch diaphragm spring tension is relieved. Remove bolts, clutch assembly and pilot tool.

Install

1. The clutch pilot bearing is an oil impregnated type bearing pressed into the crankshaft. Inspect and renew if necessary.
2. Install clutch disc so that damper springs are forward (toward flywheel).
3. Install pressure plate and cover assembly and support them with pilot Tool J-5824. Align "X" mark on clutch cover with "X" mark on flywheel, then align nearest bolt holes.
4. Install bolts in every other hole in cover and tighten alternately.

Then install remaining 3 bolts, tighten all 6.

5. Remove clutch pilot tool and check to see that it can be reinserted and moved freely.

6. Install clutch fork and dust boot into clutch housing. Lubricate throwout bearing with graphite grease.

7. Complete the reassembly of clutch housing and transmission by reversing removal method.

8. Adjust shifter and clutch release linkage.

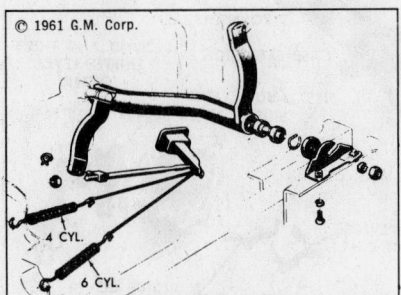

Cross Shaft Details.

STANDARD TRANSMISSION

A three-speed synchromesh transmission is used as standard equipment on all models. Gear shifting is manual through a steering column gearshift mechanism to the transmission side cover.

TRANSMISSION R & R

1. Drain transmission.

2. Disconnect speedometer cable at transmission. Disconnect shift control rods from shift levers at the transmission.

3. Remove propeller shaft assembly by disconnecting the rear "U" joint by removing trunnion bearing "U" bolts. (tape the bearing cups in place.)

4. Support rear of engine and remove transmission mounting block-to-support, (crossmember) bolts and washers. Remove sup-

port-to-frame bolts and remove support.

5. Remove two top transmission to clutch housing cap screws and install two long transmission guide pins, Tool J-1126, in these holes.

6. Remove the two lower transmission mounting cap screws.

7. Slide the transmission straight back on the guide pins until the clutch gear is free of splines in the clutch disc.

8. Remove transmission from under car.

9. Install transmission in reverse order of removal.

AUTOMATIC TRANSMISSION

REFERENCES

The Powerglide transmission, available as an option on all Chevy II models has an all aluminum case and extension. The driving characteristics of the transmission remain the same as those found in the established Powerglide, however some changes are in evidence.

LINKAGE ADJUSTMENTS

Shift Linkage

1. With engine stopped, lift up on the range selector lever and move the lever to the position where the **drive** detent is felt. Slowly release the lever to feel if the shaft lever tang freely enters the lock plate. Check **reverse** range in a similar manner. If the tang does not freely enter the lock plate in both **drive** and **reverse** ranges, it will be necessary to proceed as follows:

2. Position selector lever in driving compartment in "D" (Drive). Disconnect shift control rod at its swivel attachment to the shift control lever on the lower end of mast jacket by loosening the clamp nut.

3. Place transmission shift control outer lever in Drive position.

Note: Drive detent in the transmission is the first clockwise detent position from the fully counterclockwise detent or "L" position, (see illustration).

4. Hold the shift control lever, (at bottom of mast jacket) against the Drive stop of the range selector plate and with control rod through swivel, tighten the clamp nut.

5. Test transmission shifts in all ranges.

Throttle Linkage Adjustment

1. With the accelerator pedal depressed and dash lever "A", (see illustration) against a .06" spacer on the lever stop, rotate bell crank "B" to wide open position.

2. Adjust swivel on rod "C" to freely enter the hole in bell crank "B".

3. Rotate bell crank "B" and rod "C" to wide open position against spacer and lever stop.

4. Assemble rod "D" in transmission lever "E" and push on rod "D" to reach full detent at the transmission.

5. Adjust swivel on rod "D" to freely enter the hole in bell crank "B".

Safety Switch Adjustment

1. Place the selector lever in "N" position.

2. Loosen the screws holding the safety switch retainer, then while holding the ignition switch in "start," adjust the position of the switch until the engine cranks.

3. Hold safety switch in this position and tighten retainer screws.

4. Check adjustment by testing for engine cranking in both Neutral and Park.

TRANSMISSION R & R

1. Raise car on hoist and remove

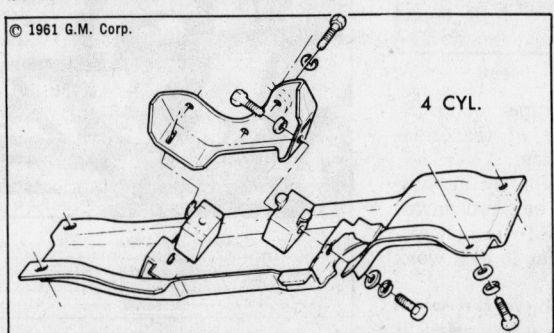

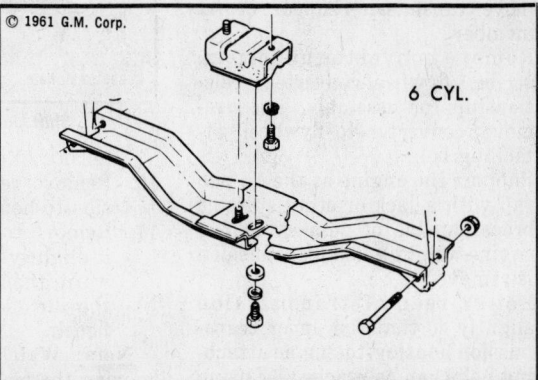

Removing Transmission Mounting Bolts

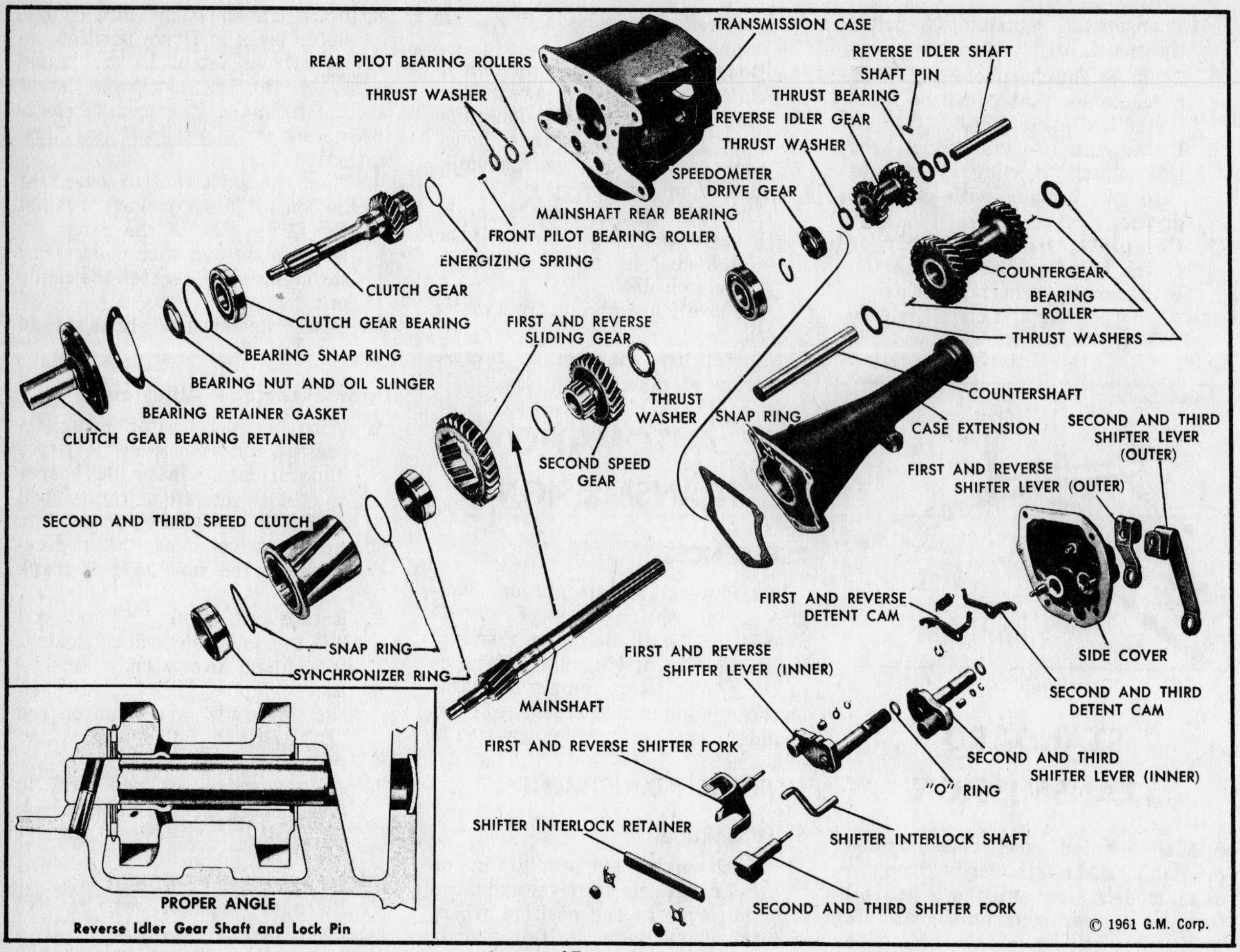

TRANSMISSION CASE

REAR PILOT BEARING ROLLERS

REVERSE IDLER SHAFT
SHAFT PIN

THRUST WASHER

THRUST BEARING

REVERSE IDLER GEAR

THRUST WASHER

SPEEDOMETER
DRIVE GEAR

MAINSHAFT REAR BEARING

FRONT PILOT BEARING ROLLER

ENERGIZING SPRING

CLUTCH GEAR

CLUTCH GEAR BEARING

BEARING SNAP RING

BEARING NUT AND OIL SLINGER

BEARING RETAINER GASKET

CLUTCH GEAR BEARING RETAINER

FIRST AND REVERSE
SLIDING GEAR

COUNTERGEAR
BEARING
ROLLER

THRUST WASHERS

THRUST
WASHER

SNAP RING

SECOND SPEED
GEAR

COUNTERSHAFT

CASE EXTENSION

SECOND AND THIRD
SHIFTER LEVER
(OUTER)

FIRST AND REVERSE
SHIFTER LEVER (OUTER)

SECOND AND THIRD SPEED CLUTCH

SNAP RING

SYNCHRONIZER RING

MAINSHAFT

FIRST AND REVERSE
SHIFTER LEVER (INNER)

FIRST AND REVERSE SHIFTER FORK

SHIFTER INTERLOCK RETAINER

FIRST AND REVERSE
DETENT CAM

SIDE COVER

SECOND AND THIRD
DETENT CAM

SECOND AND THIRD
SHIFTER LEVER (INNER)

"O" RING

SHIFTER INTERLOCK SHAFT

SECOND AND THIRD SHIFTER FORK

PROPER ANGLE
Reverse Idler Gear Shaft and Lock Pin

© 1961 G.M. Corp.

Layout of Transmission Parts.

transmission oil pan to drain oil, then replace pan with several bolts.

2. Disconnect vacuum modulator line and the speedometer drive cable at transmission. Tie lines out of way.

3. Disconnect manual and TV control lever rods from transmission.

4. Disconnect propeller shaft.

5. Install suitable transmission lift equipment.

6. Disconnect engine rear mount on transmission extension, then remove transmission support crossmember.

7. Remove converter underpan, scribe flywheel-converter relationship for assembly. Then remove converter-to-flywheel attaching bolts.

8. Support the engine at the oil pan rail with a jack or other suitable brace capable of supporting the engine weight when transmission is removed.

9. Lower rear of transmission slightly so that the upper transmission housing-to-engine attaching bolts can be reached by using a universal socket and a long ex-

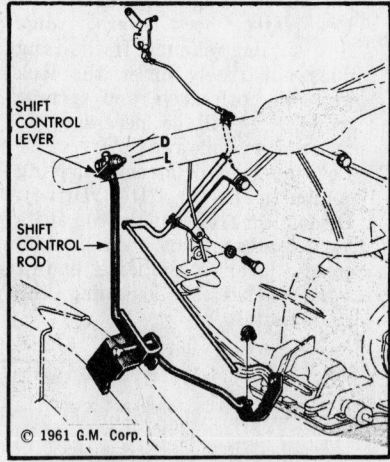

SHIFT
CONTROL
LEVER

SHIFT
CONTROL
ROD

© 1961 G.M. Corp.

Shift Linkage Adjustments.

tension. Remove upper bolts.

10. Remove remainder of transmission-to-housing bolts.

11. Remove transmission by moving it slightly to the rear and downward, then remove from beneath the car and transfer it to a work bench.

Note: Watch the converter when moving the transmission rearward. If it does not follow the transmission,

pry it free of the flywheel before proceeding.

Caution: Use some sort of holding strap to keep the converter from falling out of the transmission during transmission removal and handling.

12. Install transmission in the reverse order of removal.

© 1961 G.M. Corp.

CONVERTER HOLDING STRAP DIMENSIONS

⅛" O—¾" HOLE 18¹³⁄₁₆"

¾" 17³⅗₃₂" ±10

Converter Holding Tool.

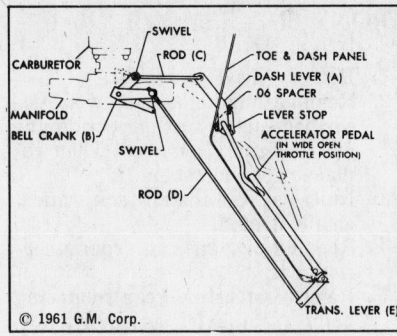

T-V Linkage Adjustments.

PROPELLER SHAFT AND "U" JOINTS

This is a Hotchkiss type drive with two universal joints and open propeller shaft. The joints are roller bearings and are lubricated at the factory. Maintenance calls for lubrication of the joints every 25,000 miles. This requires dismantling the joints.

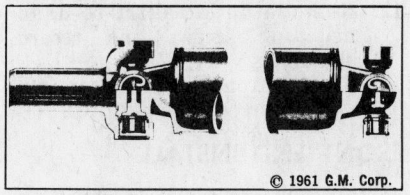

Propeller Shaft—Cross Section.

REAR AXLE AND SUSPENSION

The rear axle is a semi-floating, Hotchkiss Drive type with a stamped and welded steel banjo axle housing. The cast iron differential carrier is ribbed for strength and is as conventional as tradition warrants.

This differential is also optionally available in Positraction assembly. See "Unit Repair" section for reconditioning details.

REAR AXLE ASSEMBLY

Remove

1. Raise car and support with jackstands under frame side rails.
2. Remove rear wheels, brake drums and brake backing plates.
3. Remove two trunnion bearing "U"-bolts from the rear yoke and brake rear universal joint. Wire propeller shaft to exhaust pipe and tape trunnion bearing cups.
4. Disconnect hydraulic brake line at tee fitting on top of axle housing.
5. Support axle housing with hydraulic jack.
6. Remove shock absorber lower eye bolt and four nuts securing lower spring seat to axle housing.
7. Remove front spring eye bolts, lower rear spring and swing back. Remove spring seat pads.
8. Lower axle assembly and remove from under the car.

Install

1. Place axle assembly under car and raise into position.
2. Install spring seat pads and swing rear springs up into spring seats on axle housing, making sure upper seat pads are aligned in axle housing bracket.
3. Install front spring eye bolt and tighten, but do not torque at this point.
4. Install spring seat lower mounting bracket and torque four nuts to 45-55 ft. lbs. Insert shock absorber lower eye bolt, with threads to the rear, and torque to 45-55 ft. lbs.
5. Remove jack or hoist.
6. Install brake backing plates, brake drums, wheels and tires.
7. Reassemble rear universal joint to companion flange.
8. Fill carrier housing to plug level with recommended gear lubricant.
9. Connect brake line at tee on top of axle housing. Bleed brakes.
10. Lower car to floor and road test.

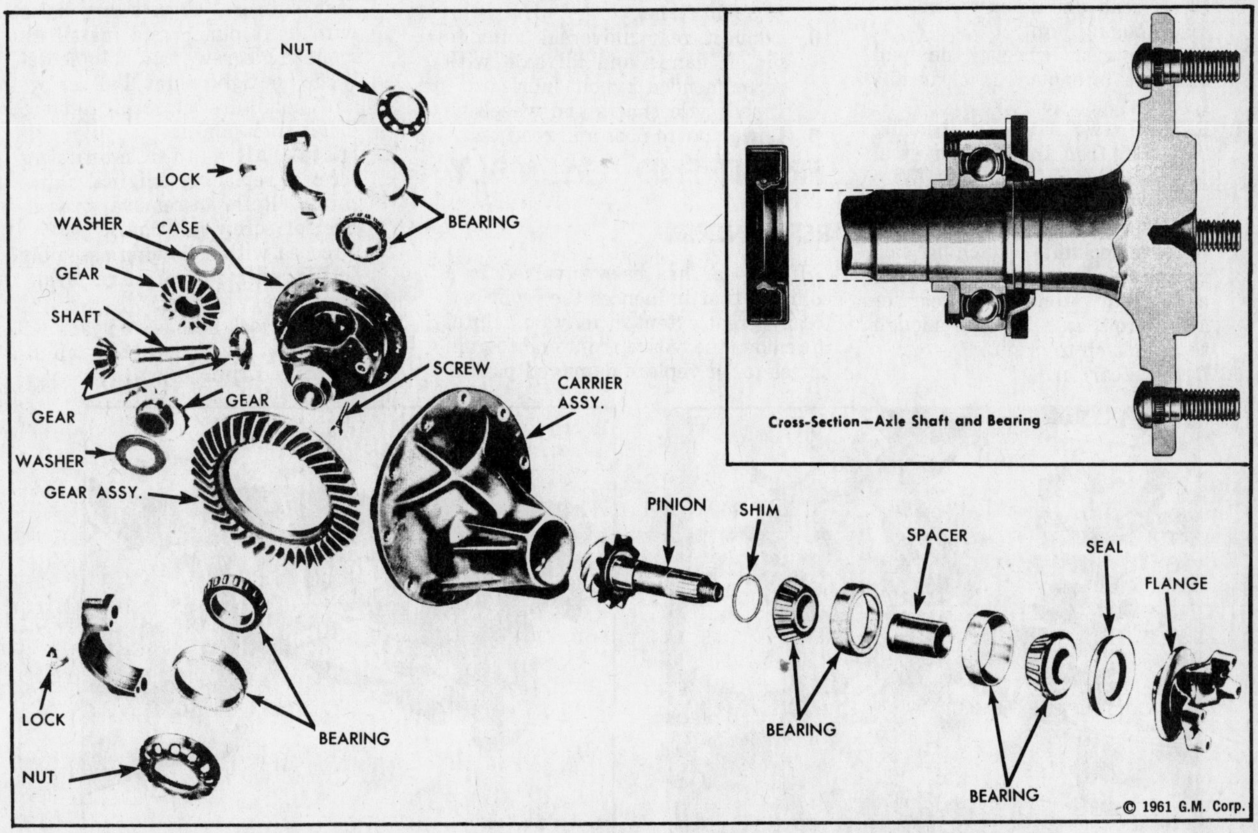

Cross-Section—Axle Shaft and Bearing

Rear Axle and Differential—Exploded.

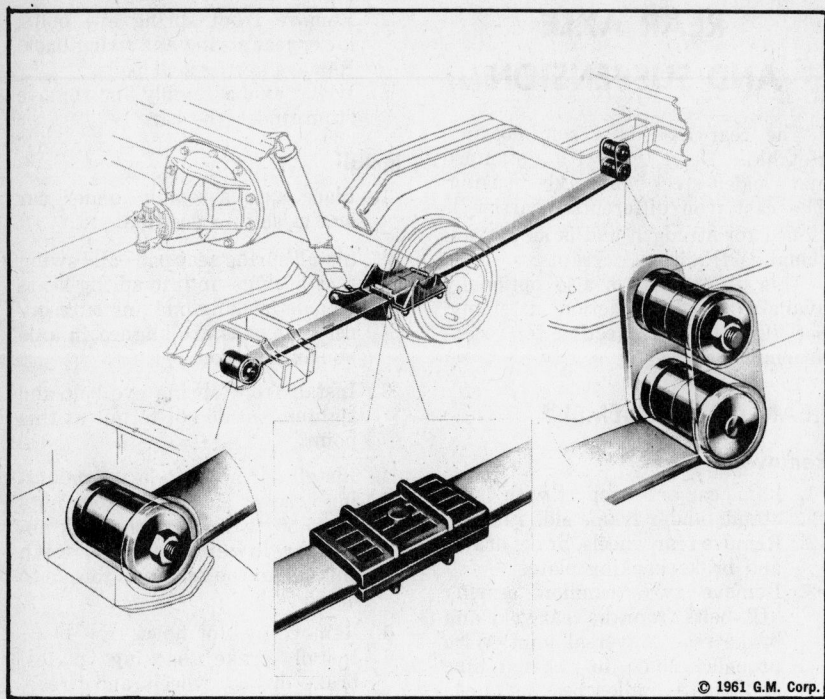

Rear Axle Assembly Installed.

FRONT END REMOVE

1. Remove hood assembly.
2. Remove engine assembly as described earlier in this section under "Engine, Remove." Then replace cross member.
3. Raise car and install jack stands, as illustrated.
4. Remove pitman arm from steering gear.
5. Remove steering gear mounting bolts from skirt assembly. Remove gear.
6. Remove 4 bolts holding each skirt assembly to lower dash brace.
7. Remove fender-to-rocker extension mounting screws and record shimming.
8. Remove brake hydraulic line and fuel line from right hand skirt.
9. Position floor jack or equivalent under front crossmember.
10. Remove hydraulic line from main cylinder.
11. Remove fender-to-cowl mounting screws and record shimming.
12. Remove upper skirt-to-dash mounting screws and record shimming.
13. Remove front end from car.

FRONT END INSTALL

1. Position front end assembly at upper dash mounts and lower dash support, align screw holes with drift punch and install all mounting screws and bolts loosely; do not tighten untill all screws and bolts are started. Replace original shimming.
2. Install all fender mounting screws, replacing original shimming. (Refer to removal procedure for screw location.)
3. Proceed with following assembly in the reverse order of removal.
4. Bleed brake system.
5. Remove jack stands and jack.
6. Perform hood and body alignment as required.

DIFFERENTIAL CARRIER

Remove

1. Raise car on hoist.
2. Clean road dirt from carrier-to-axle housing joint.
3. Remove rear wheels, and pull axle shafts enough to clear differential side gears.
4. Remove two trunnion bearing "U"-bolts from the rear universal joint and separate the joint. Wire propeller shaft to exhaust pipe and tape trunnion bearing cups.
5. Remove locknuts attaching carrier to axle housing. Discard nuts and clean studs. Pull carrier away from axle housing enough to permit oil to drain.
6. Remove carrier.

Install

1. Clean out axle housing and install new carrier gasket on axle housing.
2. Assemble carrier to housing, installing new locknuts and torque to 35-45 ft. lbs.
3. Connect rear universal joint to pinion flange and fill axle with recommended hypoid lubricant.
4. Install axle shafts and wheels.
5. Lower car to floor and road test.

FRONT END ASSEMBLY

REFERENCES

If the car has been involved in a collision that influences the front end to any great extent, it may be helpful to remove the entire front end to gain access to, or replace damaged parts.

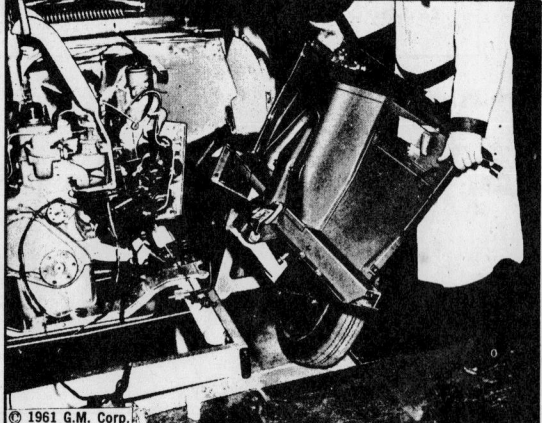

Removing Front End Assembly from Vehicle

CHRYSLER INDEX

Page

AIR CONDITIONING
Service 1092

BRAKES, HYDRAULIC
Adjustment 938
Bleed brakes 941
Hand brake, adjust 178
Master cylinder, R & R 177
Master cylinder service 939

BRAKES, POWER
Overhaul 954
Trouble shooting 954

CLUTCH
Clutch assembly, R & R 192
Clutch pedal, adjust 191

COOLING SYSTEM
Radiator core, R & R 180
Thermostat 180
Water manifolds 180
Water pump, R & R 180

ELECTRICAL SYSTEM
Alternator current generators,
   overhaul 1035
Alternator specifications 171
Distributor, R & R 176
Distributor specifications 172
Engine .176
Fuses and circuit breakers 175
Gauges 1024
Generator regulator specifications 171
Generator service 1026
Generator trouble shooting chart 1026
Generator References 176
Horn buttons 191
Ignition firing order & timing . . .167
Ignition timing procedure 170
Ignition timing specifications 169
Starter, R & R 176
Starter specifications 172
Starter systems 1046

ENGINE ASSEMBLY
Cylinder head, R & R 184
Engine assembly, R & R 182
Engine diagnosis 1012
Engine firing order & timing 167
Engine lubrication 186
Engine marking code 168
Engine references 182
Exhaust manifold, R & R 180
Inlet manifold, R & R 179
Oil filter, R & R 187
Oil pan, R & R 186
Oil pressure specifications 173
Piston and rod, assemble 188
Piston and rod, R & R 187
Piston and pins specifications . . .173
Rear main bearing oil seal 189
Rocker arm lubrication 173
Rocker arms & shaft 185

ENGINE ASSEMBLY—continued
Specifications, general engine . .173
Timing case cover, R & R 183
Timing chains, sprocket, R & R . . .183
Trouble shooting charts 1012
Tune-up specifications 169
Valve adjusting sequence 186
Valve lifters, hydraulic service . . .186
Valve specifications 168
Valves and guides 185
Valve timing procedures 183

ENGINE LUBRICATION
Oil filter, R & R 187
Oil pan, R & R 186

EXHAUST SYSTEM
Exhaust pipe 179
Manifolds 179
Muffler 179
Tail pipe 179

FUEL SYSTEM
Carburetors 972
Fuel gauge service 1024
Fuel pump pressure 169
Fuel pump service 1021
Fuel tank, R & R 179
Fuel consumption chart 1020

INSTRUMENTS
Speedometer, R & R 177

RADIO, R & R
References 200

REAR AXLE AND SUSPENSION
Axle shaft 918
Axle shaft oil seal 918
Pinion bearings 918
References 200
Ring gear & pinion 918
Shock absorbers, rear 200
Trouble shooting 919

SPECIFICATIONS
Alternators 171
Battery 172
Brake cylinder sizes 175
Capacities:
   Axle, rear 171
   Cooling system 171
   Crankcase 171
   Fuel tank 171
   Transmission, automatic 171
   Transmission, manual 171
Car serial & engine identification 168
Chassis, general 175
Cylinder head tightening 174
Distributor 172
Engine, general 173
Engine tune-up 169
Fuses and circuit breakers 175

SPECIFICATIONS—continued
Generator and regulators 171
Light bulbs 175
Main bearings 174
Model identification illustrations .166
Pistons and Pins 173
Quick reference specifications . . .167
Rod bearings 174
Starters 172
Torque wrench 174
Tune-up 169
Valves .168
Wheel alignment 170

STEERING, MANUAL
Adjust gear housing 1052
Gear assembly, R & R 191
Horn button, R & R 191
Steering wheel, R & R 191

STEERING, POWER
Pump assembly 1058
Trouble shooting 1081
Unit overhaul 1058

SUSPENSION, FRONT
Adjustments 190
Alignment procedures 1082
Alignment specifications 170
Ball joints, R & R 1087
Front Height 190
Intermediate steering arms 191
King pins and bushings 1087
References 189
Support arms, pins and bushings 1087
Torsion bar springs 189

TRANSMISSION, AUTOMATIC
Power Flite 778
Power Flite linkage 194
Power Flite transmission, R & R . .195
Torque Flite 788
Torque Flite linkage 197
Torque Flite transmission, R & R . .197
Push button controls, Power Flite .194
Push button controls, Torque Flite .197

TRANSMISSION, STANDARD
Disassemble transmission 192
Transmission, R & R 192

TROUBLE CHECKS
Procedures 1

TUNE-UP
Procedures 1012
Specifications 169
Engine diagnosis 1012

UNIVERSAL JOINT AND DRIVE SHAFT
Disassemble U joint 198
U joint & drive shaft, R & R 198

CHRYSLER

YEAR IDENTIFICATION

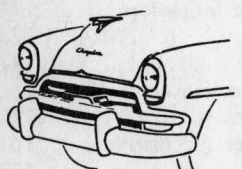
1954 Windsor
Model C-62 (6-Cyl.)

1954 New Yorker Deluxe
Model C-63-2 (V-8)

1954 New Yorker
Model C-63-1 (V-8)

1955 Windsor
Model C-67 (V-8)

1955 New Yorker
Model C-68 (V-8)

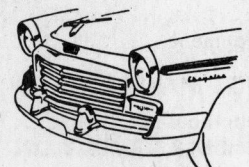
1956 Windsor
Model C-71 (V-8)

1956 New Yorker
Model C-72 (V-8)

1957 Windsor C-75-1
Saratoga C-75-2
New Yorker C-76

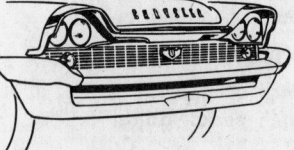
1958 Windsor
Model LCI-L (V-8)

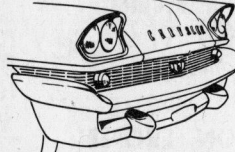
1958 Saratoga LC2-M
New Yorker LC3-H

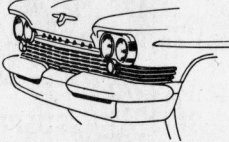
1959 Windsor MCI-L
Saratoga MC2-M
New Yorker MC3-H

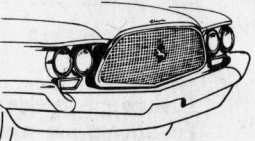
1960 Windsor
Model PC1-L

1960 New Yorker
Model PC3-H
PC2-M (Saratoga)

1961
Windsor—RC2-M
Newport—RC1-L

1961
New Yorker—RC3-H

1962 300 SC1-L
Newport SC2-M
New Yorker SC3-H

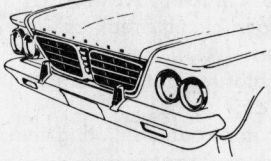
1963 300 TC1-L
Newport TC2-M
New Yorker TC3-H

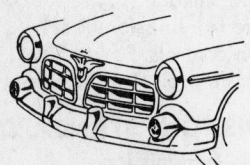
1955-56 Imperial
Model C-69 (1955), C-73 (1956)
C-70 (Crown Imperial)

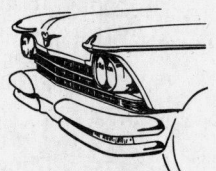
1957 Imperial
Model IM-1-2-4

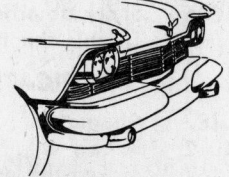
1958 Imperial LY1-L
Crown Imperial LY1-M
Imperial LeBaron LY1-H

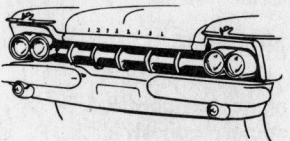
1959 Imperial MY1-L
Crown Imperial MY1-M
Imperial LeBaron MY1-H

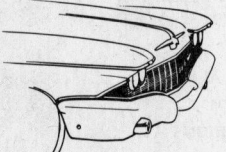
1960 Imperial PY1-L
Crown Imperial PY1-M
Imperial LeBaron PY1-H

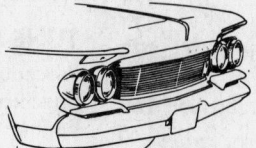
1961 Imperial RY1-L
Crown Imperial RY1-M
Imperial LeBaron RY1-H

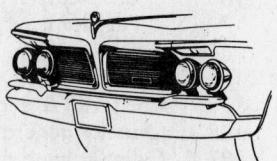
1962 Imperial SY1-L
Crown Imperial SY1-M
Imperial LeBaron SY1-H

1963 Imperial TY1-L
Crown Imperial TY1-M
Imperial Lebaron TY1-H

166

QUICK WORKING SPECIFICATIONS

DISTRIBUTOR

Breaker Point Gap (In.)

1954, 6 cyl. .... .018-.020
1954-59, V8 .... .015-.018
1960-63, all .... .017-.021

Cam Angle (Degrees)

1954-55, V8, set 27, Total both 34
1954, all 6 cyl. 39
1956-58, Windsor V8 Single 30½
1956-58, V8 Dual-each set 30½
Total both sets 37½
1959, all V8 Dual each set 37
Total both sets 39½
1960-63, all except PC4-300 27-32
1960-63, PC4-300
Dual points, one set ....27°-32°
Both sets ....34°-40°

IGNITION TIMING

1953-54, 6 cyl. ....................T.D.C.
1952-54, V8 ....4 deg. B
1955, all V8, ex. C-300 ....6 deg. B
1955, C-300, V8 ....10 deg. B
1956, C71, V8, Std. ....2 deg. B
1956, C71, V8, P.P. ....4 deg. B
1956, C70, 72, 73 ....4 deg. B
1956, C300, V8 ....8 deg. B
1957, all V8 exc. 300 ....6 deg. B
1957 300 ....4 deg. B
1958, Windsor V8 ....8 deg. B
1958, All others ....6 deg. B
1959-63, 361 cu. in. ....10 deg. B
1961-62 383 cu. in. ....7.5 deg.B
1963, 383 cu. in. ....10 deg. B
1963, 413 cu. in. ....10 deg. B

SPARK PLUGS

Year	Type	Gap
1954, V8	4GS-150	.035
1954, 6 cyl.	AR80	.035
1955, all exc. 300	AGR-51	.035
1955-57 300	AGR-41	.035
1956 Windsor	AR-52	.035
1956, N.Y & Imp.	AGR-41	.035
1957-58 Windsor	AR-42	.035
1957-58, All others exc. 300	AGR-42	.035
1958, 300	AGR-42	.035
1959, All exc. 300	A42	.035
1959 300 E	A-32	.035
1960-61, All	A42	.035
1962-63, 361, 383 cu. in.	J-12-Y	.035
413 cu. in.	J-9-Y	.035

GENERATOR AND REGULATOR

YEAR AND SERIES	GENERATOR Field Current In Amperes 6 Volt	12 Volt	REGULATOR Cut-out Closing Voltage	Current Regulator Setting	Voltage Regulator Setting
1954-55					
6 cyl.	1.7	—	6.6	51	7.3
Cr. Imp.	—	1.2	6.6	32	14.5(A)
All other	1.7	—	6.6	51	7.3
1956					
Cr. Imp.	—	1.2	13.4	45	14.5(A)
All other	—	1.2	13.4	35	14.5(A)
1957					
All models	—	1.2	13.4	35	14.5(A)
1958	—	1.2	13.4	30	14.5(A)
1959 All	—	1.5	13.1	35	14.6(A)
1960					
Imperial	—	1.5	13.0	30	14.6(A)
All other	—	1.5	13.0	35	14.6(A)

(A) Surrounding temperatures guide this adjustment, as much as 1 volt. Higher temperatures require lower settings and lower temperatures permit higher settings, within this limit.

VALVES

Tappet Clearance Hot (In.)

1954, all in-line engs. inlet .... .008
1954, all in-line engs. exhaust .. .010
1954-63, all V8, ex. 300 .... zero
1955-63, C300, V8, inlet .... .015
1955-63, C300, V8, exhaust .... .024

Mechanical Tappets are an option with the high performance 300 engine.

WHEEL ALIGNMENT

Caster (Degrees)

1954, all ....1 N to 3 N
1955-56, all ....0 to 2 N
1957, Manual ....1½ N to 1½ P
1958-63, Manual ....1N to 0
1957, Power ....0 to ½ P
1958, Power ....¾ N to ¾ P
1959-63, Power ....¼ P to 1¼ P

Camber (Degrees)

1954, all ....⅜ N to ⅜ P
1955-56, all ....⅛ N to ⅝ P
1957-63, Right wheel ..⅛ N to ⅛ P
1957-63, Left wheel ....⅛ P to ⅝ P

Toe-In (Inches)

1954-55, all ....0 to 1/16
1956-63, all ....3/32 to 5/32

CAPACITIES

Engine Crankcase (Quarts)

all 5

Note: Add 1 qt for new filter.

Transmission, Synchro. (Pints)

1950-57, all 2¾
1962-63, all 4½

Transmission, Automatic (Pints to refill after draining)

1954, M6 Hyd.ˣ 3
1954-57, Powerflite 22
1956-57, Torqueflite 20
1958-61 21
1962-63 18

ˣ Does not include converter.

Rear Axle (Pints)

1954, all 6 cyl. 3¼
1954-56, all Imperials 5
1954-63, all others 3½

Cooling System (Quarts)
Add one quart for heater

1954, 6 cyl. 15
1954-56, V8 ex. Windsor 25
1955-56, Windsor 24
1957-58, V8 ex. Windsor 24
1957-58, Windsor V8 21
1959-63 16

FIRING ORDER and TIMING

SPARK OCCURS:
A 1954-56— 4° BTDC
B 1957-58— 6° BTDC
C 1959-63—10° BTDC

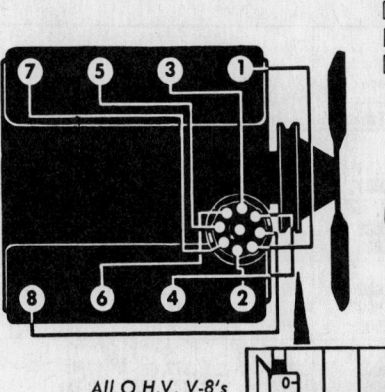

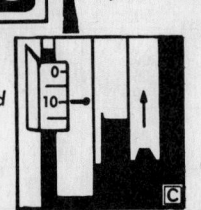

7 5 3 1
8 6 4 2
A
B
C
All O.H.V. V-8's w/front mounted distributor
2 4 6 8
1 3 5 7
All V-8's w/rear mounted distributor

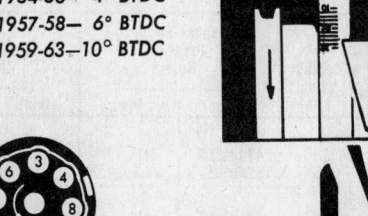

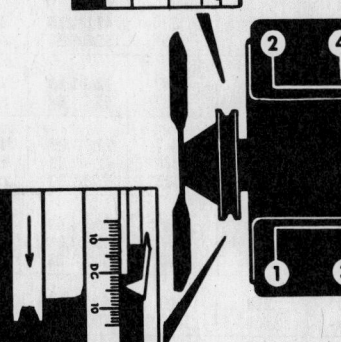

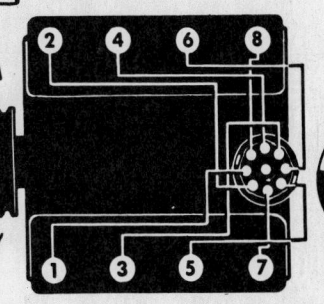

NOTE: THESE ARE APPROXIMATE SETTINGS. ALTITUDE, TEMPERATURE, FUEL AND ENGINE CONDITION WILL ALL INFLUENCE TIMING. THE DETERMINING FACTOR, LIMITING ADVANCE, WILL STILL BE THE "KNOCK POINT" OF THE ENGINE.

CHRYSLER

ENGINE IDENTIFICATION

ENGINE IDENTIFICATION IS CONTAINED IN THE ENGINE NUMBER.

STARTING ENGINE NUMBERS

1954, All 6 cyl. C54-1001
1954 New Yorker V8 . . .C541-8-1001
1954 New Yorker DeLV8 C542-8-1001
1954, All Imperials C542-8-1001

1955-57: Starting with 1955 production a revised engine numbering system has been used. This consists of a prefix and a number. The prefix consists of a letter for the model ("W" for Windsor, "L" for Saratoga, "N" for New Yorker, "C" for the two Imperials and "3N" for the "300"), "E" to indicate it is an engine number, two figures to show the year as "55" for 1955 and "56" for 1956. The actual number starts with 1001 for each model year, so CE561010 would be a 1956 Imperial, Engine No. 1010.

1958: Starting with 1958 production a second revision of the engine numbering system was devised. The prefix letters being the year, the next a digit, the model and the last numbers, 1001 being the actual engine number for the year. The lettering system indicates the following models: "W" Windsor, "S" Saratoga, "N" New Yorker, "N3" Chrysler 300D, "C" Imperial. Example: 58-W-1001, indicates a 1958 Windsor with a beginning engine number of 1001.

1959

Windsor: MC-1
Saratoga: MC-2
New Yorker: MC-3
Imperial Models: MY-1

1960

Windsor: PC-1
Saratoga: PC-2
New Yorker: PC-3
Imperial models: PY-1

1961-63

Beginning 1961 still another revision was made in identification. The engine numbers will provide the following information:

Newport R-36-8-4
Windsor R-38-8-4
New Yorker R-41-8-4
Chrysler 300 G R-41-8-4
Imperial R-41-8-4

R represents the 1961 model. The next two digits, represent the engine size, (36=361 cu. in.), (38=383 cu. in.) or ("41"=413 cu. in.). The next digit is the month built and the next digit is the day of the month.

CAR SERIAL NUMBER LOCATION
ALL MODELS

Plate attached to left front door hinge post.

ENGINE NUMBER
SIX CYLINDER—1954

The number is stamped on the left front side of the cylinder block.

ALL 8 CYLINDER—1954-63

The number is stamped on the top front end of the cylinder block.

ENGINE MARKING CODE

1954-63: A Maltese Cross on the engine number pad indicates that some main or rod bearings are .001 undersize. The position of these undersize bearings is stamped on the machined surface of No. 3 counterweight, with "M" indicating main bearing and "R" indicating rod bearing.

Also a diamond shaped mark on the engine numbering pad indicates that all tappet bodies are .008 oversize.

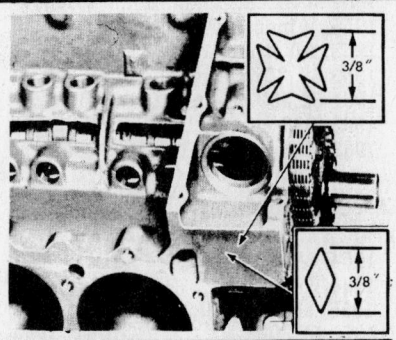

VALVE SPECIFICATIONS

YEAR Note 1	Seat Angle		Intake Valve Lift Note 2	Exhaust Valve Lift	Valve Spring Pressure Note 3		Stem to Guide Clearance		Stem Diameter		Are Valve Guides Replaceable
	In	Ex.			Outer	Inner	Inlet	Exhaust	Inlet	Exhaust	
1954											
6 Cyl.	45	45	.365	.365	43@1.75	None	.002	.003	.341	.340	Yes
Fire Power, V8	45	45	.378	.361	55@1.68	21.5@1.56	.002	.003	.372	.372	Yes
1955											
Spit Fire, V8	45	45	.381	.357	72@1.68	None	.002	.003	.372	.372	No
Fire Power, V8	45	45	.381	.357	55@1.68	22@1.56	.002	.003	.372	.372	Yes
1956											
Spit Fire, V8	45	45	.381	.357	72@1.69	None	.002	.003	.372	.372	No
Fire Power, V8	45	45	.381	.389	72@1.69	None	.002	.003	.372	.372	Yes
C-300, V8	45	45	.444	.435	72@1.69	28@1.53	.002	.003	.372	.372	Yes
1957-58											
Spit Fire, V8	45	45	.389	.389	83@1.69	None	.002	.003	.372	.372	No
Fire Power, V8	45	45	.389	.389	83@1.69	None	.002	.003	.372	.372	Yes
C-300, V8	45	45	.435	.442	60@1.66	28@1.53	.002	.003	.372	.372	Yes
1959-61											
All exc. 300 G	45	45	.389	.389	100@1.86	None	.002	.003	.372	.372	No
300 G	45	45	.430	.430	100@1.86	None	.002	.003	.372	.372	No
1962-63											
All exc. 300	45	45	.390	.390	100@1.86	None	.002	.003	.372	.372	No
300 exc. High Lift Cam	45	45	.390	.390	100@1.86	None	.002	.003	.372	.372	No
300 with High Lift Cam	45	45	.444	.456	90@1.86	Damper	.002	.003	.372	.372	No

NOTES FOR VALVE SPECIFICATIONS TABLE

Note 1: 1954-58 Engine Identification

"Fire Power Engine" has two rocker shafts per head.

"Spit Fire Engine" has one rocker shaft per head.

"C300 Engine" has standard camshaft with lift of .435.

Note 2: 1954-63 Position of Timing Sprocket Marks

Marks on camshaft and crankshaft sprockets should be aligned nearest each other and with the shaft centers.

Note 3: Valve Spring Pressures 1954-63

Intake and Exhaust Valve Springs are the same.

TUNE-UP SPECIFICATIONS

| Year Model | Spark Plugs | | Distributor (Note 1) | | | | Compression Pressure Cranking (Note 3) | Valves (Note 4) | | | Fuel Pump Pressure | Engine Idle Speed Neutral (Note 5) |
| | Number | Gap | Cam Angle | Point Gap | Arm Spring Tension | Ignition Timing (Note 2) | | Tappet Clearance Hot | | Timing | | |
								Inlet	Exhaust	Inlet Opens		
1954												
All L Head, 6 Cyl.	AR80	.035	39	.018–.020	17-20	TDC	125	.008	.010	12B	4¼	475
All OHV, V8	4GS150	.035	Note 1A	.015–.018	17-20	4B	150	Zero	Zero	15B	4¼	475
1955												
Windsor, OHV, V8, C67	AR51	.035	Note 1A	.016–.018	17-20	6B	155	Zero	Zero	15B	5¾	475
All V8 ex. C67, C300	AGR51	.035	Note 1A	.016–.018	17-20	6B	160	Zero	Zero	15B	5¾	475
C300, OHV, V8	AGR41	.035	Note 1A	.016–.018	17-20	10B	160	.015	.024	35B	5¾	500
1956												
Windsor, OHV, V8, C71	AR52	.035	30½	.015–.018	17-20	Note 2A	155	Zero	Zero	5B	5¾	475
All V8 ex. C71, C72-300	AGR42	.035	Note 1A	.015–.018	17-20	4B	160	Zero	Zero	15B	5¾	475
C72-300, OHV, V8	AGR41	.035	Note 1A	.015–.018	17-20	8B	160	.015	.024	35B	5¾	650
1957												
Windsor, OHV, V8, C75	AR42	.035	30½	.015–.018	17-20	6B	155	Zero	Zero	13B	6½	475
All V8 ex. C75, C76-300	AGR42	.035	Note 1A	.015–.018	17-20	6B	165	Zero	Zero	15B	6½	475
C76-300, OHV, V8	AGR41	.035	Note 1A	.015–.018	17-20	6B	165	.015	.024	35B	6½	635
1958												
Windsor, Saratoga V8	AR42	.035	30½	.015–.018	17-20	8B	165	Zero	Zero	13B	6½	475
300D V8	AGR42	.035	Note 1A	.015–.018	17-20	6B	165	.015	.024	32B	6½	625
New Yorker, Imperial V8	AGR42	.035	Note 1A	.015–.018	17-20	6B	165	Zero	Zero	15B	6½	475
1959												
Windsor, Saratoga V8	A42	.035	30	.015–.018	17-20	10B	165	Zero	Zero	15B	6½	475
New Yorker, Imperial V8	A42	.035	Note 1A	.015–.018	17-20	10B	165	Zero	Zero	15B	6½	475
300E V8	A32	.035	Note 1A	.015–.018	17-20	10B	165	Zero	Zero	20B	6½	475
1960-61												
Newport—ex. 300 H	A42	.035	30	.017–.021	17-20	10B	165	Zero	Zero	15B	4½	500
Others	A42	.035	30	.017–.021	17-20	10B	165	Zero	Zero	15B	4½	500
300 H	A32	.035	Note 1A	.017–.021	17-20	5B	165	Zero	Zero	20B	4½	550
1962												
Newport—300	J12Y	.035	30	.017–.021	17-20	10B	165	Zero	Zero	13B	4½	500
New Yorker, Imperial	J12Y	.035	30	.017–.021	17-20	10B	165	Zero	Zero	13B	4½	500
300 H	A32	.035	Note 1A	.017–.021	17-20	10B	165	.015	.024	22B	4½	500
1963												
Newport—361 cu. in.	J12Y	.035	30	.017–.021	17-20	10B	165	Zero	Zero	13B	4½	500
300, 383 cu. in.	J12Y	.035	30	.017–.021	17-20	10B	165	Zero	Zero	13B	4½	500
300 J, 413 cu. in.	J9Y	.035	Note 1A	.017–.021	17-20	10B	165	.015 Hot	.024 Hot	22B	4½	500
New Yorker, Imperial—413 cu. in.	J12Y	.035	30	.017–.021	17-20	10B	165	Zero	Zero	13B	4½	500

NOTES FOR TUNE-UP SPECIFICATIONS TABLE

Note:

All specifications are standard and should result in satisfactory performance. There are, however, factors that influence these settings, such as fuel octane value, air density, humidity, temperature, etc. Timing charts, like other specifications must be considerede as averages, subject to modification.

Note 1: Distributor

ROTATION VIEWED FROM THE TOP

1954, All ....Clockwise

1959-63, All ....Counter-Clockwise

DRIVE GEAR

1954, All 6 Cyl. & St. 8: Pinned to oil pump shaft.

1954-63, All V8: Pinned to an intermediate shaft which is slotted to receive distributor and oil pump shafts.

FIRING ORDER AND SPARK PLUG WIRE INSTALLATION

All Chrysler V8 engine cylinders are numbered from front to back: left bank, 1-3-5-7; right bank, 2-4-6-8. Using this numbering system the FIRING ORDER of the V8 engines is: 1-8-4-3-6-5-7-2.

The spark plug wires go into the distributor cap in the firing order.

On V8 engines with the distributor at the rear the direction of installation of the spark plug wires is clockwise.

On V8 engines with the distributor at the front of the engine the direction of installation of the spark plug wires is counter-clockwise.

All Chrysler 6 cylinder engine cylinders are numbered from front to back, starting with No. 1 cylinder at the front.

CHRYSLER

POINT GAP

When installing new points adjust to maximum gap to allow for wear-in of rubbing block.

Note 1A: Cam Angle

These OHV V8s have 2 sets of distributor points.

1954-55

Total Cam Angle	32-36
Each set Cam Angle	26-28

1956-58

Total Cam Angle	36-39
Each point set Cam Angle	29-32

1959-63

Total Cam Angle	34-40
Each point set Cam Angle	27-32

Note 2: Ignition

IGNITION TIMING MARK LOCATION

1954-61, All Engines

Marks are on crankshaft pulley. Pointer is on the chain cover. Marks consist of DC at Top Dead Center with 15 one-degree marks on each side.

IGNITION RESISTOR

1956-63—There is an ignition ballast resistor in the line between the ignition switch and the coil. The resistor is not by-passed during operation of the starter.

TIMING PROCEDURE

Adjust initial timing with engine operating at idle speed and distributor vacuum line connected except:

1955-59, 300 model. Disconnect distributor vacuum line. Idle engine at 500 RPM to make correct initial timing adjustment.

SPARK PLUGS

1955-58

The single rocker shaft Spitfire V8 uses a spark plug with a 3/8 inch reach.

The double rocker shaft Fire Power V8 uses a spark plug with a 3/4 inch reach. Do not use a spark plug gasket on this engine.

STARTING 1959 PRODUCTION

The use of Resistor Type Spark Plugs discontinued. The wires to the spark plugs have resistance built in. Although resistance varies with wire length it should not exceed 20,000 ohms for any one spark plug wire.

Do not use resistor type plugs on these engines.

For identification the cable has "RADIO" printed on it.

Note 2A: Ignition Timing

1956 Windsor C71, V8, Normal	2 B
1956 Windsor C-71, V8, with PowerPac	4 B

Note 3: Compression Pressure

All cylinders should read alike within 20 pounds. This is more important than the actual reading. Take the readings with all plugs removed, engine at normal operating temperature.

Note 4: Valves

1954-63, V8—TAPPET CLEARANCE

Zero in the tappet clearance column indicates Hydraulic Lifters.

Note 5: Idle Speed

Higher idle speeds are required for engines in poor condition and also for engines used with automatic transmissions.

NOTE: AIR CONDITIONED CARS CONDITIONED CARS

Set idle speed as shown, then with transmission in neutral, turn blower switch to first position and temperature control switch to second position. Engine should now be operating at 700-800 RPM. Turn round adjusting nut on fast idle diaphragm shaft to obtain correct setting.

Abbreviations Used:

6 Cyl.—Straight 6 Cylinder engine with valves in side of block.

V8—V shaped 8 Cylinder engine with valves in the heads.

FRONT WHEEL ALIGNMENT

YEAR	Caster Range (Degrees)	Caster Pref. Setting	Camber Range (Degrees)	Camber Pref. Setting	Toe-In (Inches) Note 3	King Pin Inclination (Degrees)	Wheel Pivot Ratio Inner Wheel	Wheel Pivot Ratio Outer Wheel
1954								
6 Cyl.	3N–1N	2N	3/8N–3/8P	Note 1	0–1/16	5 –6½	21½	20
V8 Exc. Imp.	3N–1N	2N	3/8N–3/8P	Note 1	0–1/16	5 –6½	21½	20
V8 Imp.	3N–1N	2N	3/8N–3/8P	Note 1	0–1/16	6½–8	21½	20
1955								
V8 Exc. Imp.	2N–0	Note 2	1/8N–5/8P	Note 1A	0–1/16	5 –6½	21½	20
V8 Imp.	2N–0	Note 2	1/8N–5/8P	Note 1A	0–1/16	6½–8	21½	20
1956								
V8 Exc. Imp.	2N–0	Note 2	1/8N–5/8P	Note 1A	3/32–5/32	5 –6½	21½	20
V8 Imp.	2N–0	Note 2	1/8N–5/8P	Note 1A	3/32–5/32	5 –6½	21½	20
V8 Crown Imp.	2N–0	Note 2	1/8N–5/8P	Note 1A	3/32–5/32	6½–8	21½	20
1957								
V8 Man. Strg.	1½N–1½P	Note 2A	Note 1B	Note 1B	3/32–5/32	5 –7	21½	20
V8 Pwr. Strg.	0–½P	Note 2A	Note 1B	Note 1B	3/32–5/32	5 –7	21½	20
1958								
V8 Man. Strg.	1½N–0	Note 2A	Note 1B	Note 1B	3/32–5/32	5 –7	20	18½
V8 Pwr. Strg.	3/4N–3/4P	Note 2A	Note 1B	Note 1B	3/32–5/32	5 –7	20	18¼
1959-63								
V8 Man. Strg.	1N–0	Note 2A	Note 1B	Note 1B	3/32–5/32	5 –7	21½	20
V8 Pwr. Strg.	¼P–1¼P	Note 2A	Note 1B	Note 1B	3/32–5/32	5 –7	21½	20

NOTES FOR FRONT WHEEL ALIGNMENT TABLE

Note 1: 1954, Preferred Camber

Set left side 3/8 higher than right.

Note 1A: 1955-56, Preferred Camber Settings

Set left side at ½P. Right side at 0.

Note 1B: 1957-63, Camber Range and Preferred Setting

Set right side at 1/8N—1/8P with 0 preferred.

Set left side at 1/8P to 5/8P with 3/8 preferred.

Note 2: 1955-56, Preferred Caster

Manual Steering 2N

Power Steering 0

Note 2A: 1957-63, Preferred Caster

Manual and Power Steering. Both side set equal.

Note 3: 1956-63, Preferred Toe-in

Manual and Automatic Steering 1/8.

GENERATOR and REGULATOR SPECIFICATIONS

| YEAR | Generators | | | Regulators | | | | |
| | Field Current In Amperes | | Brush Spring Tension | Cut Out Relay | | Current and Voltage Regulator Air Gap | Current Regulator Setting | Voltage Regulator Setting |
	At 6 Volts	At 12 Volts		Air Gap	Closing Voltage			
1954-55								
6 Cyl.	1.6–1.7	—	39	.033	6.6	.050	51	7.3
Crn. Imp. V8	—	1.1–1.3	39	.033	6.6	.050	32	14.5
All Other V8	1.6–1.7	—	39	.033	6.6	.050	51	7.3
1956								
Crn. Imp. V8	—	1.1–1.3	28	.033	13.4	.050	45	14.5
All Other V8	—	1.2–1.3	28	.033	13.4	.050	35	14.5
1957								
C75, V8	—	1.2–1.3	28	.033	13.4	.050	35	14.5
All Other V8	—	1.1–1.3	28	.033	13.4	.050	35	14.5
1958								
Imp. V8	—	1.1–1.3	28	.033	13.4	.050	30	14.5
All Other V8	—	1.2–1.3	28	.033	13.4	.050	30	14.5
1959								
All V8		1.4–1.7	28	.033	13.1	.050	35	14.6
1960								
All	—	1.4–1.7	38	.030	13.0	.050	35	14.6

ALTERNATOR (GENERATOR) AND ALTERNATOR REGULATOR AND SPECIFICATIONS

| Year and Model | Ground Polarity | ALTERNATOR | | CURRENT OUTPUT @ 15 Volts and 1250 Engine R.P.M. | VOLTAGE OUTPUT @ 15 Amp. Load and 1250 Engine R.P.M. | REGULATOR | |
		Ampere Rating	Field Current Draw, Amps.			Point Gap	Air Gap
1961-63							
Standard	Negative	35	Note ①	35 Ampere Min.	13.4-14.6 ②	.014-.016	.048-.052
Heavy Duty	Negative	40	Note ①	40 Ampere Min.	13.4-14.6 ②	.014-.016	.048-.052

NOTE ①
2.38-2.75 amps. minimum at 12 volts, while rotating the unit by hand or 2.97-3.43 amps. maximum at 15 volts at 70°F. with unit operating at 750 R.P.M.

NOTE ②
Run the engine at 1250 R.P.M. for about 15 minutes, with lights and accessories on to stabilize Regulator temperature. Turn of lights and accessories and read test voltmeter. With a fully charged battery and 15 amps. flowing in the circuit, the voltmeter reading should be within specs. shown in chart below. Temperature should be read within 2 inches of regulator.

Temp. in Degrees	0°	25°	48°	70°	95°	118°	140°
Volt Reading—Min.	14.0 to	13.9 to	13.8 to	13.7 to	13.6 te	13.5 te	13.4 to
Volt Reading—Max.	14.6	14.5	14.4	14.3	14.2	14.1	14.0

CAPACITIES

| YEAR | Engine Crankcase Add 1 Qt. For New Filter | Transmissions Pints to Refill After Draining | | Rear Axle Pints | Gasoline Tank Gallons | Cooling System Quarts Add 1 Qt. For Heater |
		Manual Note 1	Automatic			
1954						
6 Cyl.	5(C)	2¾	3	3¼	17	15
V8	5(C)	2¾	3(C)	3½(B)	20	25
1955						
Windsor	5	2¾	20	3½	20	24
Others	5	2¾	22	3½(B)	20	25
1956						
Windsor	5	2¾	20	3½	21	24
Others	5	Nu.	22	3½(B)	21	25
1957						
Windsor-Saratoga	5	2¾	18	3½	23(D)	21
Others	5	Nu.	21	3½	23(D)	24
1958						
Windsor-Saratoga	4	2¾	18	3½	23(D)	21
Others	5	Nu.	21	3½	23(D)	24
1959						
All	5	Nu.	21	3½	23(D)	16
1960						
All	5	Nu.	21	3½	23(D)	16
1961-63						
Windsor-Newport	5	4¼	21	3½	23(D)	16
New Yorker-Imperial—300	5	Nu.	21	3½	23(D)	16

NOTES FOR CAPACITIES TABLE

Note 1: Synchromesh Trans. Oil Type

1954-55 ....SAE 10
1956-58 ....Fluid Gear Lube SAE 80

(B) 1954-56 Imperial Rear Axle Capacity

Capacity is 5 pts.

(C) 1954 Automatic M6 Trans. with Self-fed Torque Converter

Figure is for M6 Case. Converter holds 21 pts.

(D) 1958-63 Town & Country Fuel Tank Capacity

Capacity is 22.

BATTERY and STARTER SPECIFICATIONS

YEAR	Battery Ampere Hour Capacity	Volts	(Note 1) Group Number	Terminal Grounded	Starters Lock Test Amps.	Volts	Torque	No-Load Test Amps.	Volts	R.P.M.	Brush Spring Tension
1954											
C62	120	6	2	POS	410	2.0	8.0	65	5.0	4300	48
C63, 64	135	6	2	POS	410	2.0	8.0	65	5.0	4300	48
C66	65	12	3HS	POS	140	4.0	4.0	21	10.0	4300	48
1955											
C67	120	6	2	POS	410	2.0	8.0	65	5.0	4300	48
C68, 69, 300	135	6	2	POS	410	2.0	8.0	65	5.0	4300	48
C70	65	12	3HS	POS	140	4.0	4.0	21	10.0	4300	48
1956											
C71	60	12	2SH	NEG	240	4	6.5	60	10.0	3200	48
Oll Other	70	12	2SH	NEG	240	4	6.5	60	10.0	3200	48
1957											
C75	60	12	2SH	NEG	225	4	6.0	85	4.0	3400	48
All Other	70	12	3SH	NEG	225	4	6.0	85	4.0	3400	48
1958											
Imp., 300D	70	12	3SH	NEG	225	4	6.0	85	11.0	3400	40
All Other	60	12	3SH	NEG	225	4	6.0	85	11.0	3400	40
1959											
All V8	70	12	3SH	NEG	350	4	8.5	80	11.0	3800	40
1960-61											
Imperial	70	12	3SH	NEG	350	4	8.5	80	11.0	3800	40
All Other	60	12	2SHB	NEG	350	4	8.5	80	11.0	3800	40
1962-63											
Newport	70	12	35H	NEG	350	4	8.5	80	11.0	3800	40
All Others	70	12	35H	NEG	475	4	24.0	85	11.0	1950	32-48

Note 1: Battery Group Numbers
Group numbers in table are SAE Numbers American Association Battery Manufacturers

DISTRIBUTOR SPECIFICATIONS

YEAR	MODEL	AUTO-LITE PART NO.	ROTATION	CAM ANGLE DEGREES	BREAKER POINT OPENING INCH	BREAKER ARM SPRING TENSION OUNCES	GOVERNOR CONTROL @ DIST. ADV. STARTS	R.P.M FULL ADVANCE	VACUUM CONTROL DATA INCHES OF VACUUM TO START ADVANCE	INCHES OF VACUUM FOR FULL ADVANCE	MAX. ADV. OF DIST. IN DEGREES
1954	6 cyl.	1AT-4102	C	36—40	.019	17—20	1 @ 350	10 @ 1425	6	15	8-10
	V-8	1AZ-4001-C	C	(A)	.017	17—20	1 @ 400	12 @ 2100	6	17	10½-12½
1955	V-8, C-67	1AZ-4001-E	C	(A)	.017	17—20	1 @ 350	12 @ 2100	6	17	10½-12½
	V-8, C-68	1AZ-4001-F	C	(A)	.017	17—20	1 @ 350	12 @ 1725	6	17	10½-12½
	V-8, C-300	1AZ-4001-G	C	(A)	.017	17—20	1 @ 350	8 @ 800	6	11	6-8
1956	V-8, C-71	1BJ-4303-A	C	29—32	.017	17—20	1 @ 350	14 @ 2020	6-7	15	10-12
	V-8, C-72	1BK-4301-A	C	(A)	.017	17—20	1 @ 350	9½ @ 2400	7-8	17	10½-12½
	V-8, C72-300	1BK-4301-C	C	(A)	.017	17—20	1 @ 400	8 @ 1200	7-8	13½	7-9
1957	V-8, C75	1BP-4002-A	C	29—32	.017	17—20	1 @ 350	13 @ 2050	16	16	9½-11½
	V-8, all other	1BK-4304	C	(A)	.017	17—20	1 @ 350	10 @ 2250	7½-8¾	18	10-12
1958	V-8, LC-1, LC-2	1BP-4002-F	C	29—32	.017	17—20	1 @ 400	10 @ 2200	8-9	16	10-12
	V-8, LC3-H, Imp.	1BS-4007-A	C	(A)	.017	17—20	1 @ 350	9½ @ 2400	7½-8½	16	10-12
	V-8, LC3-S(B)	1BS-4007	C	(A)	.017	17—20	1 @ 350	6½ @ 1050	7½-8½	12	6
	V-8, LC3-S (C)	1BS-4008	C	(A)	.017	17—20	1 @ 350	6½ @ 1050	7½-8½	12	6
1959	V-8, MC1, MC2	1BP-4006	CC	27—32	.017	17—21	1 @ 400	7½ @ 2350	7¼-9	16½	9½-12½
	V-8, MC3, 300E	1BS-4010	CC	(A)	.017	17—21	1 @ 350	6½ @ 1050	7½-9¼	18¼	11½-14½
	V-8, MY1-Imp.	1BS-4010-A	CC	(A)	.017	17—21	1 @ 350	9½ @ 2150	6¼-8	16½	11½-14½
1960	V-8, PC1, 2, 3	1BP-4006-C	CC	27—32	.017	17—21	1 @ 400	7½ @ 2350	7¼-9	15	8¼-11
	V-8, PY1-Imperial	1BP-4006-C	CC	27—32	.017	17—21	1 @ 400	7½ @ 2350	7¼-9	15	8¼-11
	V-8, PC4-C300	1BS-4011	CC	(A)	.017	17—21	1 @ 400	10½ @ 2400	7¼-9	14½	7½-10½
1961-62	RC1, 2 SC1, 2	1BP4005E	CC	27-32	.017	17-21	1 @ 350	11 @ 2050	6-8	16	10.5-13
	RC3, SC3	Note(D)	CC	27-32	.017	17-21	1 @ 350	9.5 @ 2300	7.5-9	15	8.5-11
	RY1, SY1	Note(D)	CC	27-32	.017	17-21	1 @ 350	9.5 @ 2300	7.5-9	15	8.5-11
1963	V-8, 361, 383 cu. in.	2095836	CC	28-33	.017	17-20	1 @ 350	11.5 @ 2150	5.5-8	16.5	11.5-14.5
	V-8, 383 cu. in. 4 bbl.	2095832	CC	(A)	.017	17-20	1 @ 350	12 @ 2050	7.5-9.2	16.0	9.5-12.5
	V-8, 361 cu. in. Power Pak.	2095836	CC	28-33	.017	17-20	1 @ 350	11.5 @ 2150	4.5-8	16.5	11.5-14.5
	V-8, 413 cu. in.	2098690	CC	28-33	.017	17-20	1 @ 400	9.5 @ 2300	6.0-9.0	13.0	6.0-8.5
	V-8, 413, Double Points	2098313	CC	(A)	.017	17-20	1 @ 400	10 @ 2400	7.2-8.9	14.5	7.5-10.5

(A) DUAL POINTS	EACH SET	TOTAL				(B) FOUR BARRELED CARB.
1954-55	26°—28°	32°—36°	1956-58	29°—32°	36°—39°	(C) FUEL INJECTORS
			1959-62	27°—32°	34°—40°	(D) CHRYSLER PART NUMBER 2095530

GENERAL ENGINE SPECIFICATIONS

Year Model Engine Type	Bore and Stroke	Number of Main Bearings	Type of Valve Lifter Used	Cubic Inch Displacement	AMA Horsepower	Advertised Horsepower at Stated RPM	Advertised Torque at Stated RPM	Compression Ratio	Oil Pressure At 30 MPH (Note 1)	Cam Shaft Drive
1954										
All 6 Cyl., L Head..............	3⁷/₁₆x4¾	4	Solid	264.5	28.4	119@3600	218@1600	7.0–1	50	Chain
Fire Power, V8, except C-63-1..	3¹³/₁₆x3⅝	5	Hydraulic	331.1	46.5	235@4400	330@2600	7.5–1	60	Chain
C-63-1, New Yorker, V8.........	3¹³/₁₆x3⅝	5	Hydraulic	331.1	46.5	195@4400	320@2000	7.5–1	60	Chain
1955										
Windsor, Spitfire, V8..........	3⅝x3⅝	5	Hydraulic	301	42.2	188@4400	275@2400	8.0–1	60	Chain
Fire Power, V8, except C-300....	3¹³/₁₆x3⅝	5	Hydraulic	331	46.5	250@4600	340@2800	8.5–1	60	Chain
C-300, Fire Power, V8..........	3¹³/₁₆x3⅝	5	Solid	331	46.5	300@5200	345@3200	8.5–1	60	Chain
1956										
Windsor, Spitfire, V8..........	3¹³/₁₆x3⅝	5	Hydraulic	331	46.5	225@4400	310@2400	8.5–1	60	Chain
Fire Power, V8, except C-300....	3¹⁵/₁₆x3⅝	5	Hydraulic	354	49.7	280@4600	380@2800	9.0–1	60	Chain
C-72-300, Fire Power, V8........	3¹⁵/₁₆x3⅝	5	Solid	354	49.7	340@5200	385@3400	9.0–1	60	Chain
1957										
Windsor, Spitfire, V8...........	3¹⁵/₁₆x3⅝	5	Hydraulic	354	49.7	285@4600	365@2400	9.25–1	60	Chain
Saratoga, Spitfire, V8..........	3¹⁵/₁₆x3⅝	5	Hydraulic	354	49.7	295@4600	390@2800	9.25–1	60	Chain
Fire Power, V8, except C-300....	4x3²⁹/₃₂	5	Hydraulic	392	51.2	325@4600	430@2800	9.25–1	60	Chain
C-76-300, Fire Power, V8.......	4x3²⁹/₃₂	5	Solid	392	51.2	375@5200	420@4000	10.0–1	60	Chain
1958										
Windsor V8	3¹⁵/₁₆x3⅝	5	Hydraulic	354	49.7	290@4600	385@2000	10.0–1	60	Chain
Saratoga V8	3¹⁵/₁₆x3⅝	5	Hydraulic	354	49.7	310@4600	405@2800	10.0–1	60	Chain
New Yorker V8	4.0x3²⁹/₃₂	5	Hydraulic	392	51.2	345@4600	450@2800	10.0–1	60	Chain
300D V8	4.0x3²⁹/₃₂	5	Hydraulic	392	51.2	Note 2	435@3600	10.0–1	60	Chain
Imperial V8	4.0x3²⁹/₃₂	5	Hydraulic	392	51.2	345@4600	435@3600	10.0–1	60	Chain
1959-60										
Windsor	4¹/₃₂x3¾	5	Hydraulic	383	52.2	305@4600	410@2400	10.0-1	60	Chain
Saratoga	4¹/₃₂x3¾	5	Hydraulic	383	52.2	325@4600	425@2800	10.0-1	60	Chain
New Yorker	4³/₁₆x3¾	5	Hydraulic	413	55.8	350@4600	470@2800	10.0-1	60	Chain
300	4³/₁₆x3¾	5	Hydraulic	413	55.8	380@5000	450@3600	10.0-1	60	Chain
Imperial	4³/₁₆x3¾	5	Hydraulic	413	55.8	350@4600	470@2800	10.0-1	60	Chain
1961										
Newport	4⅛x3⅜	5	Hydraulic	361	54.5	305@4800	395@3000	9.0-1	60	Chain
Windsor	4¼x3⅜	5	Hydraulic	383	57.8	325@4600	425@2800	10.0-1	60	Chain
New Yorker-Imperial, 300	4³/₁₆x3¾	5	Hydraulic	413	55.8	350@4600	470@2800	10.0-1	60	Chain
1962-63										
Newport	4⅛x3⅜	5	Hydraulic	361	54.5	305@4800	395@3000	9.0-1	60	Chain
300	4¼x3⅜	5	Hydraulic	383	57.8	325@4600	425@2800	10.0-1	60	Chain
New Yorker-Imperial,	4³/₁₆x3¾	5	Hydraulic	413	55.8	350@4600	470@2800	10.0-1	60	Chain

NOTES FOR GENERAL ENGINE SPECIFICATIONS TABLE

Note 1: Oil Flow

OIL PRESSURE

A pressure drop of 15-20 lbs. indicates a clogged filter.

FILTER TYPE

1954-63, All ....Full flow

ROCKER SHAFT OIL SUPPLY

1954-58, All OHV, V8

Oil from the pump flows thru the filter into the main oil gallery in the right hand bank. Oil from this gallery flows to the camshaft bearings.

Drilled passages from the number two and four camshaft bearings meter the oil into drilled passages in the block and head which carry the oil to the nearest rocker arm shaft bracket. From the brackets the oil flows into the hollow rocker shafts and thence into the drilled rockers. Oil is liberated from the rockers at the push rod ends.

1959-63, ALL OHV, V8

Oil flows from the pump thru the filter and then across the front of the block to the right oil gallery. From the right oil gallery oil flows to the main and camshaft bearings. From the No. 4 camshaft bearing oil flows thru drilled holes in the block and head of each bank to the hollow rocker shafts from which it is metered to the stamped rockers. A crossover passage at the rear of the block transfers oil to the left gallery. The oil pressure gage is connected into this crossover.

Note 2: 1958, 300D Horsepower With Two 4 Barrel Carburetors:

HP @ stated RPM: 380 @ 5200. **With Fuel Injection:** HP @ stated RPM: 390 @ 5200. **Identification Note:**

"Fire Power Engine"—Two rocker shafts per head.

"Spitfire Engine"—one rocker shaft per head.

PISTON AND PIN SPECIFICATIONS

Year and Model	PISTON			PISTON PIN			
	Skirt Clearance				FIT		
	Min.	Max.	Diameter	Bushing	In Rod	In Piston	Lock
1954 —6 Cyl.	.0002	.0012	.859	Yes	.0001-.0005	0-.0005	Ring
1954-58—V8	.0005	.0015	.9841-.9843	Yes	.0001-.0004	0-.0005	Ring
1959-63—V8	.0005	.0010	1.0935-1.0937	None	Press	.00045-.00075	Rod Press

NOTES FOR PISTON SPECIFICATIONS TABLE

Notes:

1954; All V8:

Install piston with letter F on side of piston toward front of engine. Install rods so largest chamfer on rod bearing is toward con rod journal fillet.

The "V" shaped oil spit hole in the connecting rods should always face to the top of engine, regardless of the bank they are installed in.

1955-63: All V8

Install piston on right bank with the indent on the piston head opposite the largest chamfer on the large end of the connecting rod. Assemble pistons on the left bank with the indent on the same side as the largest chamfer.

The indent on the piston should always face to the front when installed in the engine.

CRANKSHAFT BEARING JOURNAL SIZES

YEAR	MAIN BEARING JOURNALS				CONNECTING ROD BEARING JOURNALS		
	Journal Diameter	Oil Clearance	End Play Of Shaft	End Play Held By	Journal Diameter	Oil Clearance	End Play
1954							
6 Cyl.	2.500	.0010	.005	No. 4	2.1245	.0010	.009
V8	2.500	.0010	.005	No. 3	2.2495	.0010	.010
1955-56							
V8	2.500	.0010	.005	No. 3	2.2495	.0010	.010
1957-58							
S. Fire V8	2.500	.0010	.005	No. 3	2.2495	.0010	.010
F. Pwr. V8	2.69	.0010	.005	No. 3	2.3745	.0010	.010
1959-60							
V8	2.750	.0010	.005	No. 3	2.3745	.0010	.013
1961-63							
All V-8	2.6255	.0010	.005	No. 3	2.375	.0010	.013

TORQUE SPECIFICATIONS

YEAR	Cylinder Head Bolts	Rod Bearing Bolts	Main Bearing Bolts	Crankshaft Pulley Bolt	Flywheel To Crankshaft Bolt	Manifolds In.	Manifolds Ex.
1954							
6 Cyl.	65–70	45–50	80–85	55–60	108–112	20	20
V8	80–85	45–50	80–85	55–60	130–140	30	25
1955-58							
V8	80–85	45–50	80–85	55–60	130–140	30	25
1959-63							
V8	65–75	40–45	80–85	Note 1	130–140	40	30

Note 1   Vibration Damper Bolts 15 ft. lbs.   Bolt in end of Crankshaft 135 ft. lbs.

CYLINDER HEAD NUT TIGHTENING SEQUENCE

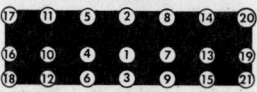

1954—All Windsor 6 cylinder
Tighten to 65-70 ft. lbs.

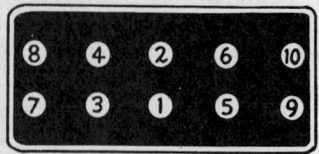

1954-58—All Firepower V-8
Tighten to 80-85 ft. lbs.

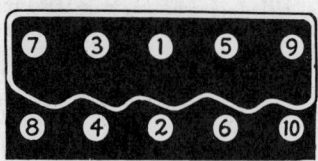

1955-58—All Spitfire V-8
Tighten to 80-85 ft. lbs.

1959-63—All V-8
Tighten to 70 ft. lbs.

LIGHT BULBS

(C.P. MEANS CANDLE POWER)

Ignition Key:

6 Volt, No. 51; 12 Volt, No. 53.
(One C.P. miniature bayonet base.)

Beam, Turn Signal, Indicators, Glove Box, Instruments:

6 Volt, No. 55; 12 Volt, No. 57.
(2 C.P. miniature bayonet base.)

License Plate:

6 Volt, No. 63; 12 Volt, No. 67.
(4 C.P. single contact base.)

Trunk Light:

12 Volt, No. 1003.
(15 C.P. single contact base.)

Map, Dome:

6 Volt, No. 210; 12 Volt No. 1004.
(15 C.P. double contact base.)

Front Combination Park and Signal; Combination Tail, Stop and Signal:

1954-55: ....6 Volt, No. 1154;
1956-63: ....12 Volt, No. 1034
(4 & 32 C.P. double contact base.)

Back-up:

Thru 1956: 6 Volt, No. 1129; 12 Volt, No. 1141.
(21 C.P. single contact base.)
For 1957-63, 12 Volt, No. 1073.
(32 C.P. single contact base.)

GENERAL CHASSIS AND BRAKE SPECIFICATIONS

YEAR AND MODEL		CHASSIS Overall Length in Inches	Tire Size	BRAKE CYLINDER BORE		
				Master Cyl. (Inch)	Wheel Cylinder Diameter (Inch)	
					Front	Rear
1954	6 Cyl. All	215⅝	7.60x15	1.0	2 Cyl. 1⅛	1⅛
	V-8, N. Yorker, N.Y. Delux	215⅝	8.00x15	1⅛	2 Cyl. 1⅛	1⅛
	V-8, Custom Imperial	223¾	8.20x15	1.0	2 Cyl. 1⅛	1⅛
	V-8, Crown Imperial	236⅜	8.90x15	1.0	2 Cyl. 1¼	2 Cyl. 1
1955	6 Cyl. All	218⅝	7.60x15	1.0	2 Cyl. 1⅛	1⅛
	V-8, N.Y. Delux, Chrysler 300	218⅞	8.00x15	1 1/16	2 Cyl. 1⅛	1⅛
	V-8, Imperial	224.0	8.20x15	1.0	2 Cyl. 1⅛	1⅛
	V-8, Crown Imperial	243⅝	8.90x15	1.0	2 Cyl. 1¼	2 Cyl. 1
1956	6 Cyl. All	219⅞	7.60x15	1⅛	2 Cyl. 1⅛	1⅛
	V-8, N. Yorker, Chrysler 300B	222¾	8.00x15	1⅛	2 Cyl. 1⅛	1⅛
	V-8, Imperial	229⅝	8.20x15	1⅛	2 Cyl. 1⅛	1⅛
	V-8, Crown Imperial	243⅝	8.20x15	1⅛	2 Cyl. 1⅛	1⅛
1957	V-8, Windsor, Saratoga	219¼	8.50x14	1⅛	2 Cyl. 1⅛	1⅛
	V-8, N. Yorker, 300	219¼	9.00x14	1⅛	2 Cyl. 1⅛	1⅛
	V-8, Imperial, Crown, LeBaron	224.0	9.50x14	1⅛	2 Cyl. 1⅛	1⅛
1958	V-8, Windsor	218⅛	8.00x14	1⅛	2 Cyl. 1⅛	1⅛
	V-8, Saratoga, 300D, N.Y.	220¼	9.00x14	1⅛	2 Cyl. 1⅛	1⅛
	V-8, Imperial, Crown, LeBaron	225¾	9.00x14	1⅛	2 Cyl. 1⅛	1⅛
1959	V-8, Windsor	216⅝	8.00x14	1⅛	2 Cyl. 1⅛	1⅛
	V-8, Saratoga	220⅝	8.50x14	1⅛	2 Cyl. 1⅛	1⅛
	V-8, New Yorker, 300	221.0	9.00x14	1⅛	2 Cyl. 1⅛	1⅛
	V-8, Imperial, Crown, LeBaron	226 5/16	9.50x14	1⅛	2 Cyl. 1⅛	1⅛
1960	V-8, Windsor	215.4	8.00x14	1⅛	2 Cyl. 1⅛	1⅛
	V-8, Saratoga	219.4	8.50x14	1⅛	2 Cyl. 1⅛	1⅛
	V-8, New Yorker, 300	219.6	9.00x14	1⅛	2 Cyl. 1⅛	1⅛
	V-8, Imperial, Crown, LeBaron	226.3	8.20x15	1⅛	2 Cyl. 1⅛	1⅛
1961	V-8, Newport	215.6	8.00x14	1⅛	2 Cyl. 1⅛	1⅛
	V-8, Windsor	215.6	8.50x14	1⅛	2 Cyl. 1⅛	1⅛
	V-8, New Yorker, 300G	219.6	9.00x14	1⅛	2 Cyl. 1⅛	1⅛
	V8, Imperial	227.3	8.20x15	1⅛	2 Cyl. 1⅛	1⅛
1962	V-8, Newport	214.9	8.00x14	1⅛	2 Cyl. 1⅛	1⅛
	V-8, 300	214.9	8.00x14	1⅛	2 Cyl. 1⅛	1⅛
	V-8, New Yorker	219.3	8.50x14	1⅛	2 Cyl. 1⅛	1⅛
	V-8, Imperial	227.1	8.20x15	1⅛	2 Cyl. 1⅛	1⅛
1963	Exc. Sta. Wagon & Imperial	215.3	8.00x14	1	1⅛	15/16
	Sta. Wagon	219.4	8.50x14	1	1⅛	15/16
	Imperial	227.8	8.20x15	1	1⅛	15/16

Radio Dial:

12 Volt, No. 1891.
(2 C.P. miniature bayonet base.)

Headlights: Two Light System

6 Volt, No. 5040; 12 Volt, No. 5400.
(40 & 50 C.P. three contact base.)

Headlights: Four Light System

Inner High Beam:
12 Volt, No. 4001. (37½ Watts.)

Outer High and Low Beam
12 Volt, No. 4002.
(50-37½ Watts.)

FUSES and CIRCUIT BREAKERS

All Lights Except Back-up:

Circuit Breakers on or near light switch.

Back-up Lights:

10 amp. Circuit Breaker on the windshield wiper switch.

Radio:

SFE 9 or 14 fuse in line back of instrument panel.

All Models Thru 1958

Automatic Top:

Circuit Breaker at switch.

Clock:

AGA 3 fuse at clock.

Window Lifts:

Circuit Breaker at left front kick pad.

Seat Motors:

Thru 1956 Circuit Breaker under seat. 1957-62—Circuit Breaker behind left front kick panel.

Air Conditioner Blower:

Circuit Breaker on switch.

All Models Starting 1959

All Lights:

22½ Amp. Circuit Breaker in Head Light Switch.

Fuse block behind dash to left of of radio. Carries:

Clock—1 Amp. Fuse.
Windshield Wiper—6 Amp. Circuit Breaker.
Radio—7½ Amp. Fuse.
Dome Light—6 Amp. Fuse.
Back-Up—6 Amp. Fuse.
Lighter—14 Amp. Fuse.
Rear Defroster—6 Amp. Fuse.
Heater—20 Amp. Circuit Breaker.

Air Conditioner;

Front—30 Amp. Circuit Breaker.
Rear—20 Amp. Circuit Breaker.
Dual—30 Amp. Circuit Breaker.

Terminal block behind left front kick pad. Carries:

Window Lifts—20-30 Amp. Circuit Breaker.
6-Way Seat — 40 Amp. Circuit Breaker.

CHRYSLER

DISTRIBUTOR

Detailed information on: distributor drive, direction of distributor rotation; cylinder numbering; firing order; point gap; cam dwell; timing mark location; spark plugs, spark advance; ignition resistor location, and idle speed; will be found in the Tune-up Specifications table of this section. Further information on trouble shooting, will be found in both the Trouble Checks section and the Tune-up and Diagnosis section of the manual.

SPARK PLUG CABLES STARTING WITH 1959 PRODUCTION

All 1959 and later Chrysler and Imperial engines incorporate conventional spark plugs (without resistors), along with resistance type spark plug cables to eliminate radio interference.

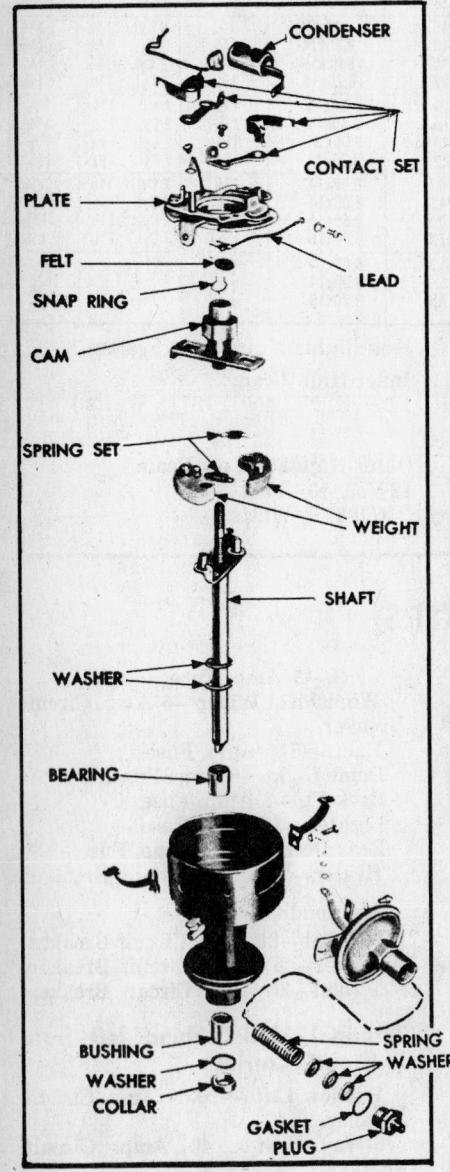

Distributor

For identification purposes, this new cable has "RADIO" printed on it.

The new cable uses a graphite or composition type conducting core replacing the copper wire found in the center of conventional spark plug cable. Full contact is made between the core and terminals by means of a short wire pin pushed into the ends of the cable.

Precautions must be observed in handling to prevent damage to the core. The cable should be removed from the spark plug by grasping the cable cover and pulling **straight off** with a steady, even pull. Pulling sideways could jam the terminal on the spark plug and cause the cable to separate from the terminal. The **cable** terminal should not be crimped to the point that excessive **force is re**quired to remove it from the **spark** plug.

The cables should never be removed by giving them a **quick jerk.** Doing so can stretch the core and cause a high resistance or open **cir**cuit. If a damaged core is **suspected,** a resistance check with an **ohmmeter** should be made. The resistance of the various plug cables will vary because of the different lengths.

Built-in Resistance of Cables

No. 1 Cable 8,300 to 16,600 Ohms
No. 2 Cable 5,500 to 11,000 Ohms
No. 3 Cable 8,100 to 16,200 Ohms
No. 4 Cable 6,000 to 12,000 Ohms
No. 5 Cable 8,800 to 17,600 Ohms
No. 6 Cable 6,300 to 12,600 Ohms
No. 7 Cable 9,400 to 18,800 Ohms
No. 8 Cable 7,200 to 14,400 Ohms

If any cable has appreciably more resistance than specified, check to be sure the terminals are in contact with the pin and the pin is in full contact with the core. If the terminals and pins are properly installed and the cable resistance is still more than specified, the cable should be replaced with a new resistance type cable.

A new terminal should never be attached to the resistance core cables unless the wire pin is in place; otherwise, contact will not be maintained with the core. This will result in arcing and burning of the core which will cause engine malfunctioning and radio interference.

Spark Plug Caution

Resistor type spark plugs are never to be used with the new resistance type cable. The added resistance of the spark plugs may cause malfunctioning of the ignition system. When replacing a spark plug, be sure to use the correct type specified for the particular engine.

Cable Troubles

If the radio develops excessive noise or if there is a pronounced engine miss, check for faulty or broken cables.

DISTRIBUTOR REMOVAL AND INSTALLATION

Removal Procedure

Disconnect vacuum advance pipe and primary wire. Lift off distributor cap and remove the holddown bolt, lock plate and distributor. (On cars with power brakes disconnect the brake vacuum line at the manifold.)

Installation Procedure

Make sure No. 1 piston is at top dead center and install the distributor so that the rotor is pointing to No. 1 firing position. Install the lock plate and screw, but not tightly. Rotate the crankshaft to align the specified degree mark on the crankshaft pulley with the pointer. Rotate distributor until contacts are just opening. Tighten the holddown bolt and reconnect the primary lead and the vacuum pipe. Check that timing is correct with a timing light.

GENERATOR AND REGULATOR

Detailed facts on the generator and the Alternator can be found in the Generator and Alternator Specifications Table of this section.

General information on generator and regulator repair and trouble shooting can be found in the Unit Repair section under the heading: Generators and Regulators.

D.C. GENERATOR POLARITY

Caution: Whenever the circuits to the D.C. generator or the regulator have been disconnected it is best to apply the following procedure:

Before the engine is started, momentarily short from the "Bat" to the "Gen" terminals of the regulator with a screwdriver. This gives a momentary surge of current from the battery to the generator and so correctly polarizes the generator with respect to the battery.

Failure to so polarize the D.C. generator before starting the engine may severely damage the regulator since reversed polarity causes vibration, arcing and burning of the relay points.

Caution:

Under no circumstances should the Alternator Circuit be Polarized.

STARTER, R & R

No problem here. Disconnect battery and starter wires. Remove attach bolts and lift out starter.

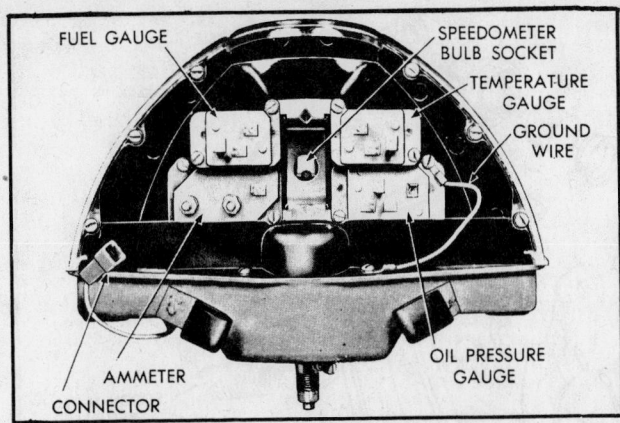

Intsrument Cluster Rear View —1960-62 Chrysler

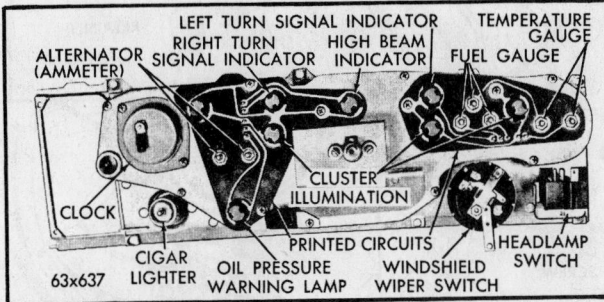

Instrument Cluster Rear View— 1963

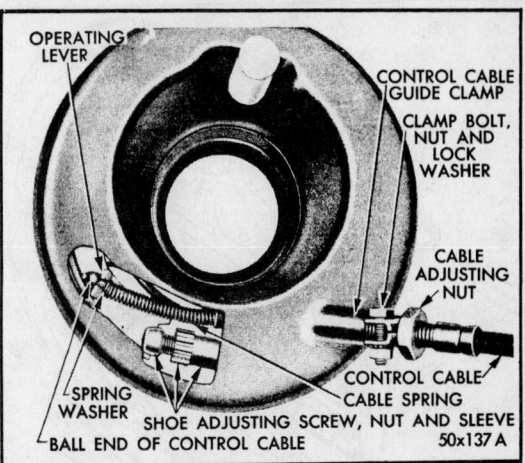

*Hand Brake Band Adjustment
Internal Type Hand Brake*

INSTRUMENTS

SPEEDOMETER REMOVAL

Imperial

Disconnect battery. Remove chrome retainer ring screw. Pull bottom of ring and raise retainer to release top tab. Remove screws holding cluster. Disconnect wires at connector and the Bowden wire at clock. Remove cluster to bench after disconnecting speedometer cable.

Other Models

Disconnect battery and speedometer cable. Remove transmission push button bezel then the button assembly.

Remove two studs from push button housing. Disconnect back-up light wires and push housing to one side. Disconnect panel lights. Remove steering column dash support to cowl panel brace. Disconnect horn and turn signal wires at connector under dash.

Remove four screws from speedometer to panel. Care must be used to prevent damage to speedometer face.

BRAKES

Specific information on brake cylinder sizes can be found in General Chassis and Brake Specifications Table of this section.

Information on trouble shooting and overhauling power brakes can be found in the Unit Repair section under the heading: Brakes, Power.

Information on the grease seals which may need replacement can be found in the Unit Repair section. The front wheel grease seals under the head: Suspension, Front Repair. The rear wheel grease seals under the head: Axles, Rear.

BRAKE TYPES

All Chrysler models use Lockheed internal expanding hydraulically operated brakes except the Imperial models of 1954 and 1955. On the 1954 and 1955 Imperial models a disc type, self adjusting brake was used.

Starting with 1963

A new Servo-contact, self-energizing brake is used. It uses a double-acting wheel cylinder at tops of shoes at each assembly.

It is also a self-adjusting brake. It operates thru a link, cable and return spring connected so that when brake is applied during reverse stops the link indexes the star wheel to maintain proper shoe clearance.

MASTER CYLINDER REMOVAL

1954

The master cylinder is bolted to the frame side rail and carries in its forward end the clutch and brake pedal shaft.

Disconnect the linkage to the clutch and brake pedal, including the clutch over-center spring, and drive off the "C" washer which holds the pedals to their shaft. Remove the lines from the master cylinder, remove the master cylinder mounting bolts in order to move the cylinder into a position convenient for driving out the clutch and brake pedal shaft. Drive out the clutch and brake pedal shaft and then lift off the master cylinder.

The master cylinder is filled through a hole in the floor boards.

Starting with 1955

Starting with 1955 models, the brake master cylinder is mounted on the front side of the fire wall under the hood. Remove the master cylinder and disconnect the lines and remove the clevis from the brake push rod from underneath the dash of the car.

The brake (and clutch) pedals are pivoted on a shaft which is mounted on the back and under the dash. To remove either or both shafts, disconnect the linkage including the clutch over-center spring, take out the shaft retaining washer, remove the shaft, and take off the pedals.

Starting with 1962

A new power brake unit is used. It features a direct pedal connection to a vacuum unit mounted on fire wall with master cylinder directly mounted to booster. Stoplight switch is mechanical and mounted at pedal. All units are readily accessible.

The booster chamber contains two diaphragms and is under constant engine vacuum. When brakes are applied the control valve is open to allow atmospheric pressure behind both diaphragms. This provides the power boost to the master cylinder rod.

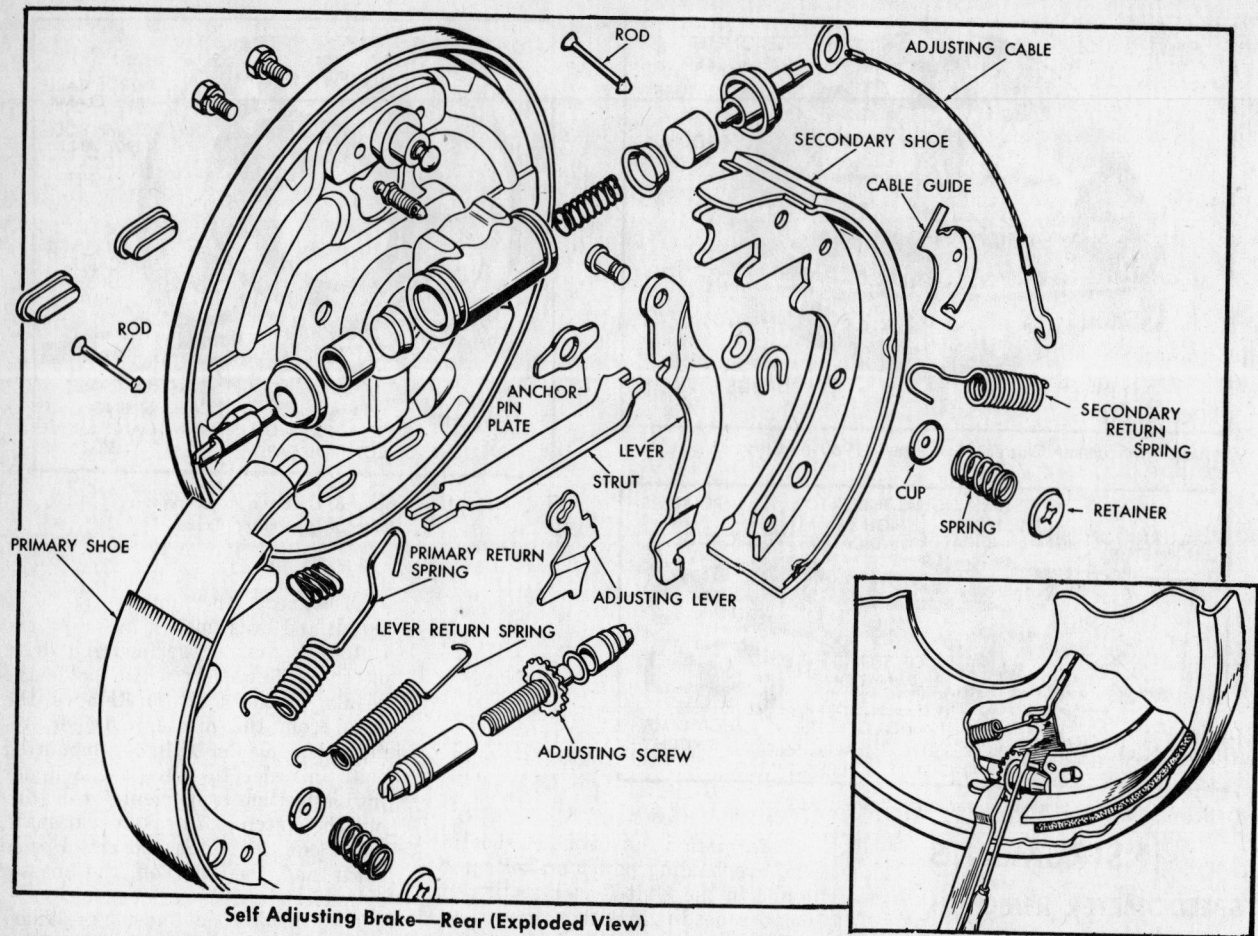

Self Adjusting Brake—Rear (Exploded View)

ROD

ADJUSTING CABLE

SECONDARY SHOE

CABLE GUIDE

SECONDARY RETURN SPRING

ROD

ANCHOR PIN PLATE

LEVER STRUT

CUP

RETAINER

SPRING

PRIMARY SHOE

PRIMARY RETURN SPRING

ADJUSTING LEVER

LEVER RETURN SPRING

ADJUSTING SCREW

Releasing Brake Adjustment

This vacuum-suspended system provides reserve against fade.

HAND BRAKE ADJUSTMENT

External Type Hand Brake

Fully release the hand brake lever and check the clearance at the brake between the anchor bracket and the drum. This clearance should not exceed .005 inch. Adjust the lining to drum clearance so there is between .015 and .020 in. clearance between the lining and the drum. After the lining is properly adjusted, pull all the slack out of the hand brake cable and reconnect.

Internal Type Hand Brake

Place the hand brake lever in the fully released position, and place the gear shift selector lever in the neutral position.

Detach the front half of the propeller shaft to permit the drum to be turned by hand and remove the adjusting plate cover from the brake dust plate.

Loose the cable guide clamping bolt and the adjusting nut.

Expand the shoes at the adjusting nut until a slight drag is felt and then back off approximately one notch. This will give approximately .010 in. clearance to the brake shoes.

The cable adjusting nut is positioned against the cable housing. See that there is from .005 to .010 inch clearance between the operating lever and the brake shoe cable.

Tighten the cable clamp and adjusting nut against the housing.

Starting with 1963

A new parking brake is used. It operates at the rear wheels thru a pedal, cable and shoe expanding link.

To adjust it, with cable not pulling, see that rear service brakes are properly adjusted. Tighten cable to produce slight drag. Then loosen cable just enough to be sure wheels are free.

FUEL SYSTEM

A chart covering causes of excess fuel consumption will be found in the Unit Repair section under the heading: Fuel Consumption Chart.

Data on capacity of the gas tank will be found in the Capacities table. Data on correct engine idle speed and fuel pump pressure will be found in the Tune-Up Specifications table. Both the above tables can be found in this section.

General information on fuel pumps and their troubles will be found in the Unit Repair section under the heading: Fuel Pumps.

Information covering operation and troubles of the fuel gauge will be found in the Unit Repair section under the heading: Gages.

Detailed information on the carburetor and how to adjust it will be found in the Unit Repair section under the broad heading: Carburetors, and the specific heading of the make of carburetor being used on the engine being worked on. Carter, Holley, Rochester and Stromberg carburetors are covered.

VAPOR SEPARATOR

Some air conditioned models are equipped with a vapor separator which is mounted on the carburetor.

Serviced only as a unit it consists of a steel can containing a filter screen. It has an inlet from the fuel pump and an outlet to the carburetor; it also has a metered vapor bleed hole which is piped back to the fuel tank.

When operating, the vapor separator is full of fuel. Any vapor which may form goes to the top of the can and, passing thru the metered orifice, returns to the fuel tank.

The unit cannot be serviced. If vapor lock is evident remove the return line at the top of the unit and insert a paper clip wire thru the orifice to clear it.

FUEL TANK

Thru 1956 Models

The fuel tank is located in the back of the car under the trunk floor. It is held by two steel straps having T-bolts at their back end.

Soak the T-bolts in rust dissolving fluid before attempting to remove them since this will greatly simplify the job and prevent possible damage to the steel straps.

Remove the hose clamps which connect the upper and lower filler neck (on models which have the flexible coupling) and disconnect the fuel line.

Look in the bottom of the trunk to determine if there is a cover over the fuel gage and if there is remove this cover and disconnect the fuel gage. Place a jack under the gas tank, detach fuel line and remove the nuts which hold the T-bolts to the back cross member and slowly lower the tank.

Starting with 1957

Disconnect the flex line and gage wire from the front of the tank and place a jack protected by a block of wood under the gas tank. Remove the two bolts which hold the tank straps at the back and let the straps go down. Remove the grommet from the top of the filler neck and thread the tank downwards and to the right.

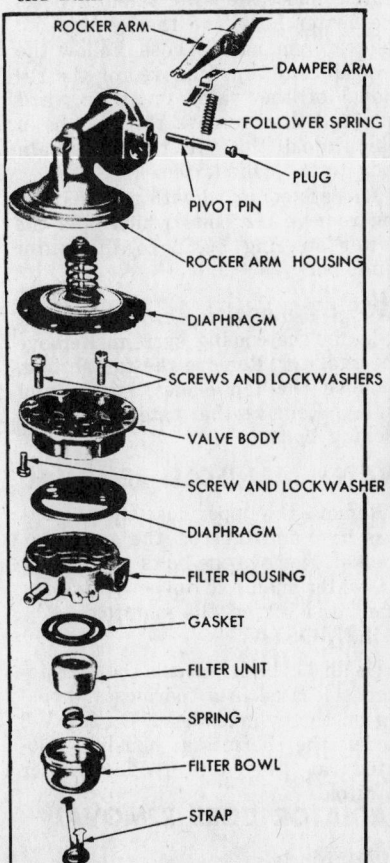

Exploded View of the 1958 Fuel Pump

INLET MANIFOLD

V-8 Models 1954

Remove the upper radiator hose and slack off on the fan belts and remove the generator.

Take off the air cleaner and remove all connections to the carburetor. Remove the ignition coil, the distributor

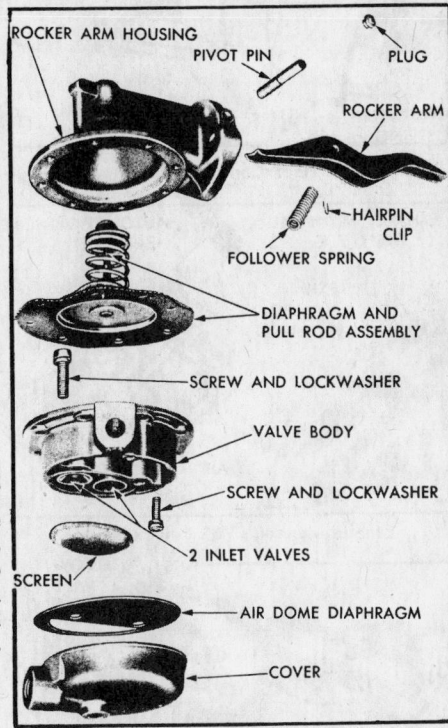

Exploded View of the 1957 Fuel Pump

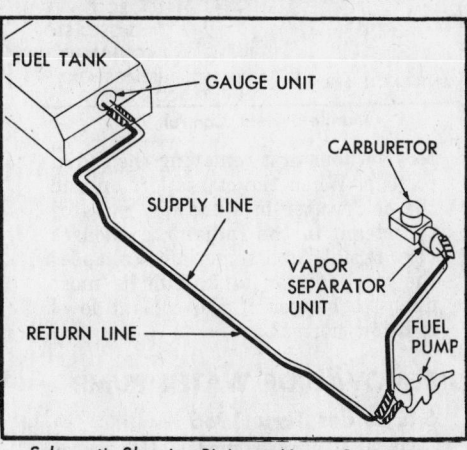

Schematic Showing Piping to Vapor Separator

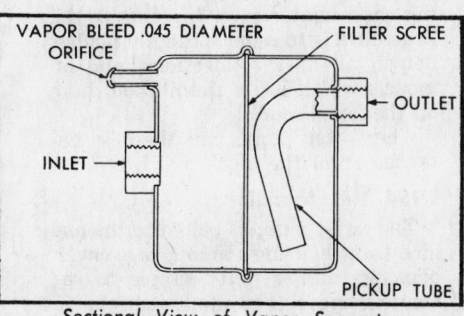

Sectional View of Vapor Separator.

vacuum lines, and the heat indicator. Disconnect automatic choke heat tube at the carburetor.

While the manifold can be removed with the carburetor in place, it is always better to take the carburetor off first.

Remove the bolts which hold the manifold to both cylinder heads and lift it off the cylinder heads. It is not necessary to take off the distributor.

V-8 Models Starting with 1955

Instructions given for the earlier V-8 models will also apply to the latest models except it is not necessary to disconnect the radiator hose.

EXHAUST SYSTEM

The exhaust pipe, muffler, and tail pipe are mounted by hangers which are installed to isolate vibration. A special clamp and adjustable hanger supports the tail pipe at the rear of the muffler. The rear of the tail pipe is supported by a clamp and hanger at the rear of the frame.

There should be one-half inch clearance between the exhaust system components and the frame, floor pan, bumper, shock absorber and fuel tank. Tighten bolts and brackets to 20 ft. lbs.

MANIFOLD HEAT VALVE

On 6 cyl. engines the intake and exhaust manifold are mounted on the right side of the engine and are jointed together just underneath the carburetor. A heat riser valve is used in the exhaust manifold to deflect the exhaust gases toward the intake manifold when the engine is cool. The heat riser valve is operated by a thermostatic spring which causes it to move to the off position when the engine reaches operating temperature.

On V8 models the manifold heat control valve is in the right exhaust manifold.

An inoperative valve may cause the engine to warm up slowly, resulting in excessive use of the choke, or it may cause the engine to apparently run lean when it is hot.

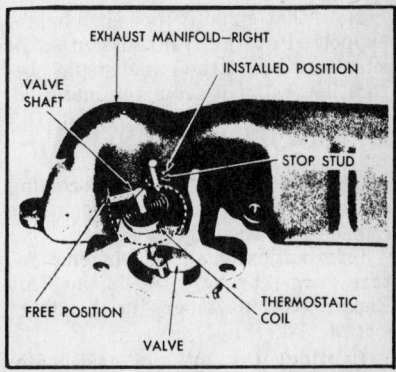

Positioning Thermostatic Coil Starting 1959

EXHAUST MANIFOLDS

V-8 Models 1954

Removing the exhaust manifolds on these models is a particularly difficult job because of the close clearance between the frame and the exhaust manifolds.

If the operator is particularly adept at working in close, tight places a box wrench can be altered and the manifold can be removed, but as stated before, the clearances are close and the job requires patience.

Many Chrysler mechanics agree that it is easier, and a much better job can be done, if the front motor mounts are loosened and the engine jacked up about 2 inches.

The exhaust flange can be reached readily from underneath the car and there is a sheet metal cover under the fender which can be detached and which gives some access to the manifold bolts.

V-8 Models 1955-56

Detach the exhaust pipe flange from underneath the car. The manifold bolts on firepower models are accessible from underneath the car. The spitfire bolts can be gotten from the top. Some slight difficulty may be experienced with the back bolts around the oil filter and also around the power steering gears, but these bolts can be removed without too much difficulty. However, the vacuum tank for the power brakes may have to be removed on 1956 Firepower models.

V-8 Models Starting with 1957

For the right exhaust manifold, remove the carburetor air cleaner and the oil filter can. Remove heat tube from exhaust manifold. Remove bolt and clamp holding ground cable and heat tube to cylinder head.

From under the car, remove the bolts which hold the exhaust pipes to the exhaust manifold. Remove the bolts which hold the manifolds to the cylinder head, loosen front engine mounts and jack up the engine to slide manifold off studs and away from cylinder head.

Note that exhaust pipe is no longer supported at the transmission so be sure to support the exhaust pipe before detaching it from the manifold.

COOLING SYSTEM

Detailed information on cooling system capacity can be found in the Capacities Table of this section.

Information on the water temperature gauge can be found in the Unit Repair section under the heading: Gages.

Caution: Do not run cold water over the outside of pressurized radia-

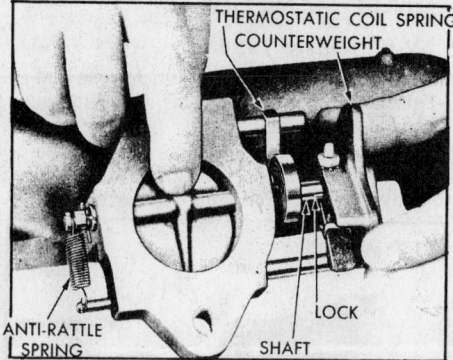

Installing the Heat Control Valve Counterweight

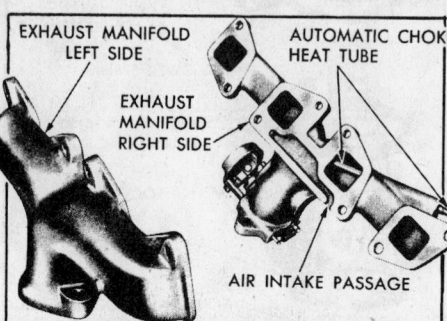

Exhaust Manifolds V8's thru 1958

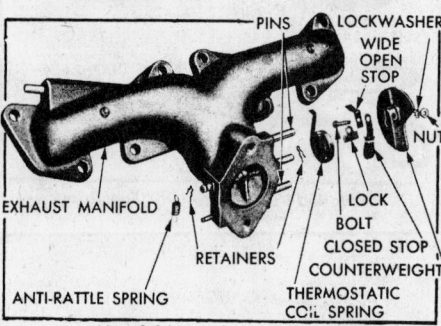

Manifold Heat Control Valve

tors without first removing the radiator cap. When the cap is left on and the cold water hits the hot radiator the steam in the radiator condenses very rapidly and sometimes collapses the top radiator tank. This is most likely to happen if the coolant level is below normal.

REMOVAL OF WATER PUMP

6 Cylinder Thru 1955

On all Chrysler models the water pump can be removed without removing the radiator core. In general, the procedure is to remove the fan blades, detach all hose connections, and on models which use a fan shroud, take off the fan shroud.

The water pump can then be detached from the block and lifted off.

1954 V-8 Models

The water pump is bolted to the engine front housing (timing case cover housing) and is quite simple to remove. Remove the radiator shroud if so equipped, slack off and remove the water pump belt, remove the bolts which hold the fan blades and pulley to the fan hub, take out the bolts which hold the pump body to the engine front cover and lift off the pump.

1955-56 V-8 Models

On 1955-56 V-8 models the water pump housing is an integral part of the water manifold.

To remove the water pump, first detach all of the hoses and heat indicator sending unit which connect to the water manifold, slack off and remove all the belts, remove the upper half of the fan shroud if the car is so equipped. Remove the bolts which hold the fan blades and pulley to the fan hub, take off the fan pulley and blades and then remove the bolts which hold the water manifold to the cylinder heads and block.

1957-58 Spitfire Engines

Slack off on the fan and power steering belts and remove the bolts which hold the fan spacer and pulley to the front of the water pump hub.

Remove the bolts which hold the front flange of the pump to the main body and lift off the front portion of the pump.

1957-58 Fire Power Engines

Disconnect the lower radiator hose, the heater hose, and the by-pass (to the water manifold) hose. Follow the procedure outlined above for the removal of the water pump forward half and then remove the four bolts which hold the water pump main body to the cylinder blocks.

On cars equipped with power steering remove the bolts which hold the power steering pump to the water pump body.

1959-63 Models

Drain the cooling system. Remove the radiator. Remove the fan shroud. Remove the fan blades, spacer and pulley. Remove the water pump attaching bolts.

WATER MANIFOLD REMOVAL

Remove the upper hose and the by-pass hose and take off the generator bracket. Remove the bolts which hold the water manifold to both cylinder heads and lift off the manifold.

THERMOSTAT

On all 6 cylinder models the thermostat is located in a thermostat housing on the cylinder head. On the V-8 models the thermostat housing is located at the top of the water manifold.

RADIATOR CORE REMOVAL

1954 Models

On these models the radiator core

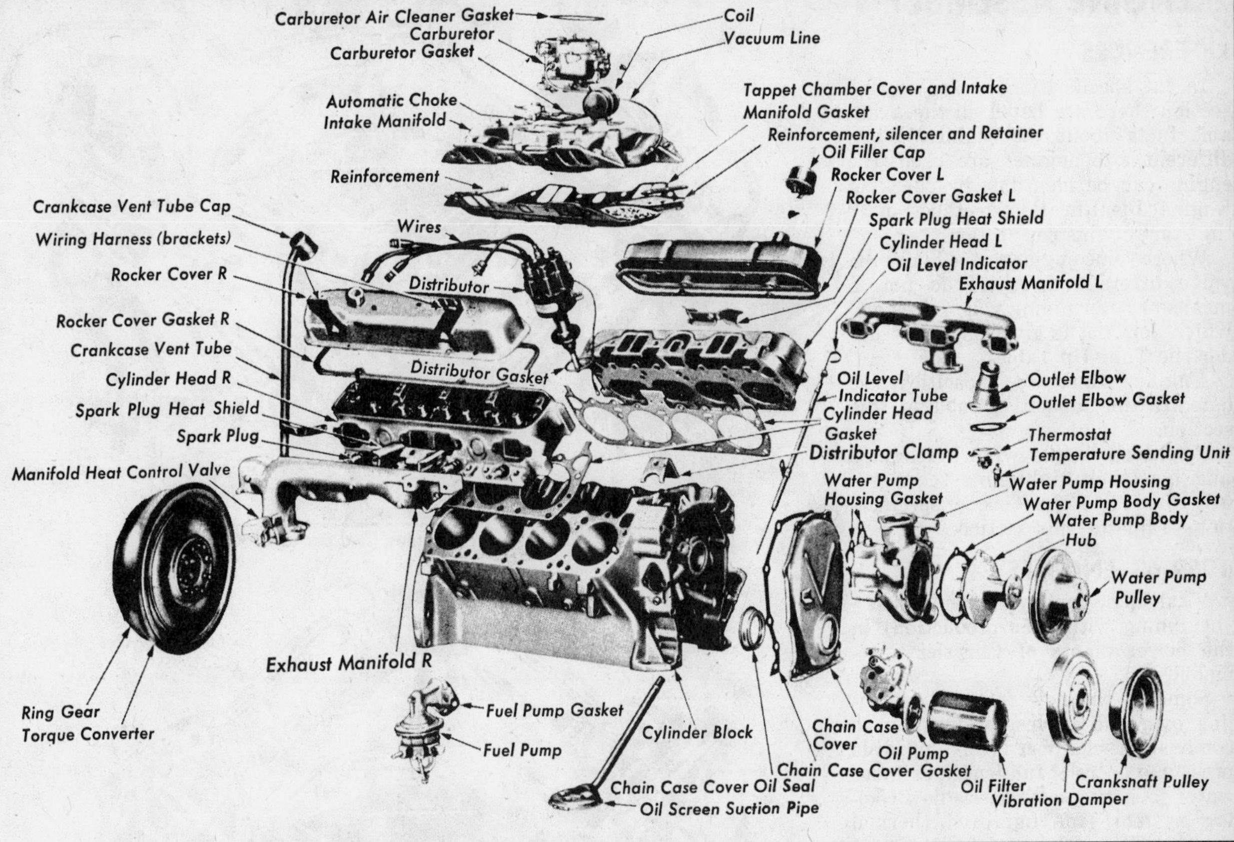

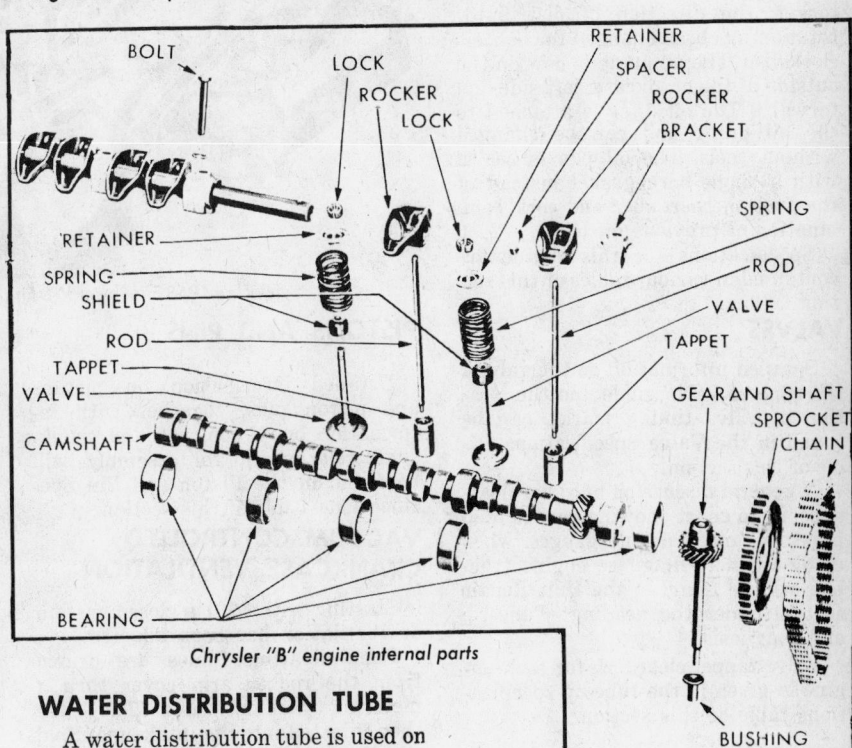

Carburetor Air Cleaner Gasket
Carburetor
Carburetor Gasket
Coil
Vacuum Line
Automatic Choke
Intake Manifold
Reinforcement
Tappet Chamber Cover and Intake Manifold Gasket
Reinforcement, silencer and Retainer
Oil Filler Cap
Rocker Cover L
Rocker Cover Gasket L
Spark Plug Heat Shield
Cylinder Head L
Oil Level Indicator
Exhaust Manifold L
Crankcase Vent Tube Cap
Wiring Harness (brackets)
Rocker Cover R
Wires
Distributor
Rocker Cover Gasket R
Crankcase Vent Tube
Cylinder Head R
Distributor Gasket
Spark Plug Heat Shield
Spark Plug
Manifold Heat Control Valve
Oil Level Indicator Tube
Cylinder Head Gasket
Distributor Clamp
Water Pump Housing Gasket
Outlet Elbow
Outlet Elbow Gasket
Thermostat
Temperature Sending Unit
Water Pump Housing
Water Pump Body Gasket
Water Pump Body
Hub
Water Pump Pulley
Exhaust Manifold R
Ring Gear
Torque Converter
Fuel Pump Gasket
Cylinder Block
Fuel Pump
Chain Case Cover
Oil Pump
Chain Case Cover Gasket
Chain Case Cover Oil Seal
Oil Screen Suction Pipe
Oil Filter
Crankshaft Pulley
Vibration Damper

1959-63 Chrysler "B" engine external parts. Note that distributor is at front of block

is mounted with two bolts on each side. These bolts pass through the radiator frame and into the side mounting of the sheet metal on the front end of the car. If the car is equipped with a heater the lower right hand mounting bolts will be difficult of access.

On some cars the bolt is driven from the front toward the back and may be reached by removing the shroud from between the radiator core and the grille. On other mountings the bolt is driven from the back toward the front and in order to get at this bolt it is necessary to remove the cover from underneath the fender (which gives access to the valves).

To take out the core remove these four bolts, disconnect the hoses and lift the core straight upward.

1955 Thru 1963 Models

Two bolts are used on each side to hold the radiator core to its cradle. The bolts on the right hand side can be reached easily, but it may be necessary to take out the lower left hand bolt from underneath the car.

Remove the fan shroud from cars which are equipped with a shroud in order to lift the radiator straight up. It is not necessary to take off the fan or fan blades.

BOLT
LOCK
ROCKER
LOCK
RETAINER
SPACER
ROCKER
BRACKET
RETAINER
SPRING
SHIELD
ROD
TAPPET
VALVE
CAMSHAFT
SPRING
ROD
VALVE
TAPPET
GEAR AND SHAFT
SPROCKET
CHAIN
BEARING
BUSHING

Chrysler "B" engine internal parts

WATER DISTRIBUTION TUBE

A water distribution tube is used on all 6 cylinder engines. On 6 cylinder engines the distributon tube is located immediately back of the water pump. It may be taken out by removing the radiator core and the water pump.

To remove tne tube, a rod is formed into a hook at one end and is slid into the distribution tube hooking one of the holes in the tube.

CHRYSLER

ENGINE ASSEMBLY

REFERENCES

In the specifications tables of this section there are listed all the available facts about the engines. When different size engines are used, the engine can be identified by checking Engine Identification methods near the start of this car section.

Where some engines have hydraulic valve lifters and others do not, a means of determining which does and which does not is given in a note under the Tune-Up Table.

Engine crankcase capacities are listed in the Capacities Table of this section.

Approved torque wrench readings and head bolt tightening sequences are covered in the Torque Specifications Table of this section.

1959-63 ENGINES

Vital changes have come to pass, (beginning with 1959 production) in the power plants of Chrysler automobiles.

Some of the new features are in-line overhead valves, wedge shaped combustion chamber (for improved pressure control), full length cylinder water jacketing with series flow cooling system (for improved thermal control). The distributor has been put up front where it belongs but don't forget, the direction of distributor rotation has been changed to counter-clockwise. The oil pump is now on the outside of the crankcase, left side and forward. The oil filter is attached to the oil pump and can be changed without tools. The oil pan is sealed with a single cork gasket instead of the four piece rubber and cork combination of previous models.

Specifications for this engine are contained in various tables of this section.

VALVES

Detailed information on the valves, the type of valve guide and the location of valve timing marks, can be found in the Valve Specifications Table of this section.

A general discussion of valve clearance and a chart showing how to read pressure and vacuum gauges when using them to diagnose engine troubles will be found in the Unit Repair section under the heading: Tune-Up and Diagnosis.

Valve tappet clearance for each engine is given in the tune-up specifications table of this section.

BEARINGS

Detailed information on engine bearings will be found in the Crankshaft Bearing Journal Sizes Table of this section.

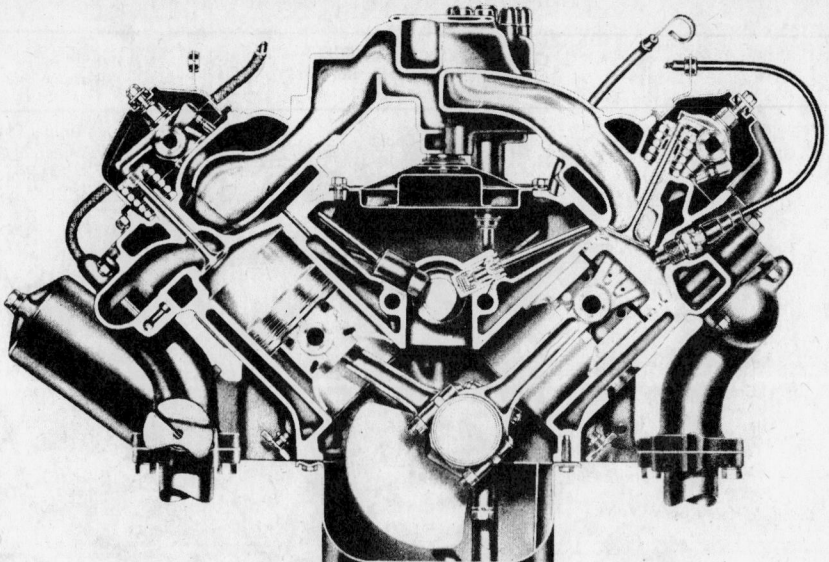

Thru 1958 SpitFire V-8 Engine (End Sectional View)

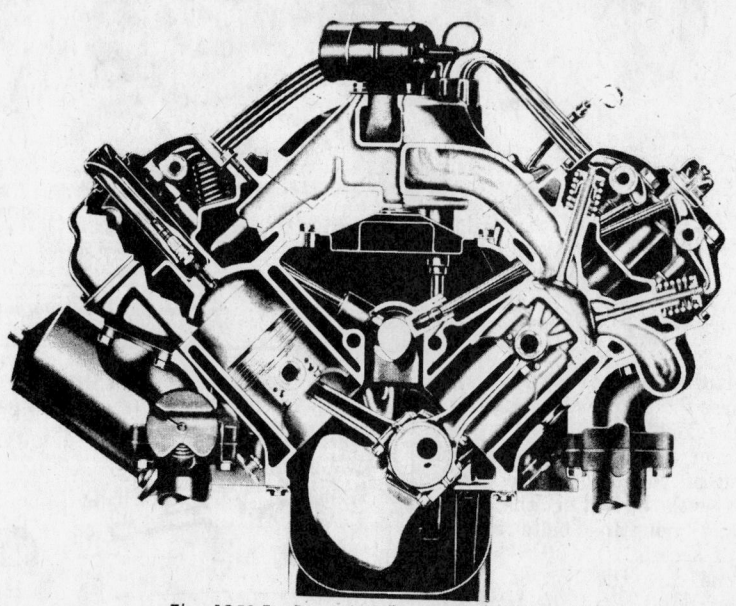

Thru 1958 FirePower V-8 Engine (End Sectional View)

PISTONS AND PINS

Detailed information on pistons and piston pins, together with information on piston, rod and crankshaft relationship for assembly, will be found in the Piston and Pin Specifications Table of this section.

VACUUM CONTROLLED CRANKCASE VENTILATION

Starting with 1961 a closed system of ventilation has been adopted.

Contaminating fumes are drawn from the rocker arm cover thru a metering vacuum valve. They are then injected into the intake manifold and thru combustion into the exhaust.

ENGINE REMOVAL

Remove the carburetor air cleaner and the carburetor. Remove the radiator and heater hoses and take out the radiator core. Remove the temperature gauge wires and the oil pressure gauge and disconnect the oil pressure line, disconnect power steering hoses and exhaust pipes at the flanges. Disconnect the battery connections, remove the generator assembly, disconnect ignition primary wires and fuel lines at the fuel pump. Scribe a line around the hood hinge plate for relocating purposes, remove the bolts and take off the hood.

From under the car, split the rear universal joint and remove the bolts which hold the front joint to the hand brake drum, drop the driveshaft, disconnect all clutch and transmission lines and speedometer cable. Disconnect the hand brake cable. Place a support under the transmission and take a light weight on the lifting device. Remove the rear crossmember to transmission support bolts and then remove the bolts which hold the cross member to the frame and take the member down. With a load taken on the lifting device and the back of the transmission supported by a roller jack, remove the front mounting brackets. Lift the engine and work it forward and upward out of the vehicle. It will come out complete with transmission.

TIMING CASE

COVER REMOVAL

V-8 Models 1954

On Chrysler V8 models the timing case cover is a fairly large housing in the front of the engine. In order to remove this housing it is necessary to take off the water pump, damper and damper pulley, damper dust seal, and the left engine bank exhaust pipe. Disconnect all fuel lines and remove the fuel pump. Take off the starter and the oil pan. Unbolt the timing case cover.

<u>Note:</u> One of the bolts which holds the timing case cover to the front of the cylinder block is located back of the water pump. It will be found in a little depression almost in the center of the water pump opening. Make certain this bolt is removed before attempting to pry the timing case cover off its dowel pins.

V-8 models thru 1954—chain case cover attaching cap screws

1955-56 V-8 Firepower and Spitfire Engines

Disconnect the radiator hoses and remove the fan shroud. Detach the bolts which hold the radiator core and lift off the radiator core. Note: Timing case cover can be removed with the radiator core in place, but it's so much simpler to take the radiator core out of there and it only takes a few minutes to remove the core.

Remove the bolts which hold the water manifold to the cylinder heads and block and lift off the water manifold. Detach the lines to the fuel pump and take off the fuel pump. Remove the vibration damper and the crankshaft pulley. Remove the bolts which hold the timing case cover to the block and lift the timing case cover

off the car. When replacing the cover, take care to seat it firmly against a new cork insert in the front of the oil pan. In fact, it might be a good idea to loosen the oil pan bolts and let the oil pan drop a little bit so that the timing case cover can be put on without interference and then the pan will go back into place again.

V8 Engines Starting with 1957

Remove the radiator core, the water pump and the water pump body. On cars fitted with power steering detach the power steering pump and move it out of the way. Remove the bolt from the center of the vibration damper and pull out the vibration damper.

The lower half of the timing case cover seals against the front of the oil pan. For this reason extreme care should be exercised in order to prevent damage to the small part of the oil pan gasket which contacts the flat surfaces of the timing case cover. A new half moon gasket should always be installed in the front end of the oil pan.

Remove the bolts which hold the timing case cover to the front of the engine block and lift off the timing case cover. Note: On reassembly, it may be necessary to align the timing case cover by using drift pins since the new half moon gasket in front of the oil pan will require a little compressing in order to effect a good seal.

Reassemble in reverse order.

VALVE TIMING PROCEDURE—REPLACEMENT OF CHAINS AND SPROCKETS

All V-8 Models

Remove the timing case cover, as outlined earlier in this text.

The procedure for installing a timing chain and/or sprockets on the V-8 model is essentially the same as it is for earlier models, with this exception: The camshaft gear is located to the shaft by means of a dowel pin which also passes through the gear and fuel pump eccentric, the eccentric is held in place with a single nut and lock washer.

It will be found, in some instances, that the fuel pump eccentric may be a little tight on the dowel pin and it will require tapping with a fibre hammer to remove.

In-Line Engines

To replace a timing chain and/or sprockets, or to retime the valves where the timing has jumped, proceed as follows: detach the camshaft sprocket, slide it off the shaft and remove the timing chain. Unless the crankshaft sprocket is to be replaced it will not be necessary to remove it from the shaft. Rotate the crankshaft

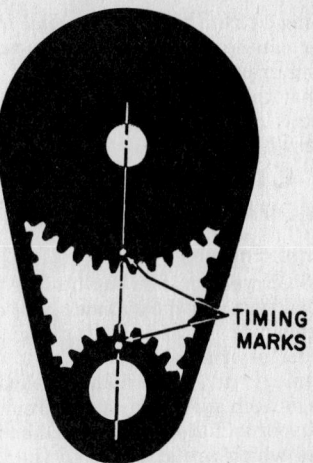

Timing Mark Alignment V-8

so that the mark on the crankshaft sprocket is toward the camshaft and in exact alignment between the shaft centers. Now install the timing chain over the cam sprocket so that the mark on the cam and the mark on the crank sprocket are nearest each other. Note that the cam sprocket bolt holes (in-line engines) are staggered in such a way that the sprocket will enter only one way and permit the bolt to enter through the threaded holes in the hub. Rotate the camshaft so that holes line up while the timing marks are still in line between the shaft centers.

Mount the sprocket on the hub and draw up the bolts. Turn the crankshaft two full revolutions and check to see that the marks are still in alignment between the shaft centers. When set in the manner described with the marks aligned between the two shaft centers it is immaterial which piston is at top dead center. It may be necessary, however, to retime the ignition at any time the chain setting is disturbed.

To Check Valve Timing

Remove the valve chamber cover and insert a feeler gauge, having considerably less thickness than the valve clearance, between the lifter and valve on No. 1 intake valve. Now crank the engine slowly until No. 1 cylinder is ready to commence its intake stroke. At this point the crankshaft should be turned very slowly at the exact point of rotation of the crankshaft noted when the lifter grips the feeler gauge. Then refer to the vibration damper which is marked in degrees (before and after top center) and note the degree mark which is under the pointer. If the reading noted is within 4 degrees of the specifications given in this Manual, the valve timing is within the prescribed limits.

When making this check on V-8 models, (with hydraulic lifters) operating at zero clearance, a dial indicator can be mounted over the valve spring or over the top of the push rod so that the lifting of the valve can be detected by motion at the indicator. Otherwise the procedure is the same.

CYLINDER HEAD
REMOVAL

In-Line Engines—6's

All Chrysler in-line engines are the L-head type and the cylinder head can be removed without disturbing the carburetor or manifold.

Remove all throttle and vacuum lines, detach spark plug wires, remove the upper radiator hose and all accessories which are attached to the cylinder head, take out the cylinder head bolts and lift off the head transferring it to a clean bench so that the gasket surface is not marked or scratched in any way.

Firepower V-8 Engines

Remove the inlet manifold, as explained in the paragraph earlier, remove the spark plug wire cover from both rocker covers and take off the spark plug wires and their long porcelain insulators. Caution: Be careful with the long insulators since they will crack readily if they are handled roughly.

Remove the bolts which hold the rocker cover to the cylinder head and take off the rocker cover.

Detach the exhaust manifolds at the exhaust pipe flange. These bolts are accessible from underneath the car.

Remove the bolts from the rocker brackets and take off the rocker assemblies. Pull out the push rods and lift off the cylinder head. Handle the head carefully so that the gasket surface is not marred or scratched in any way. This is very important.

Notice that the bolts which hold the rocker assemblies to the cylinder head also hold the head to the block.

While it is possible to switch the right cylinder head over to the left side, this practice is not recommended.

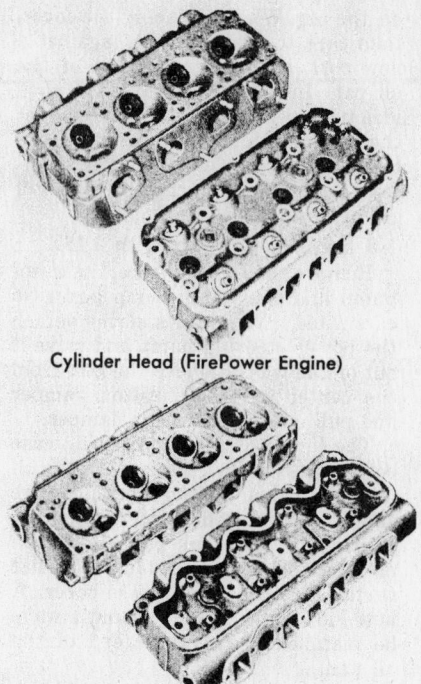

Cylinder Head (FirePower Engine)

Cylinder Head (SpitFire Engine)

The head should be marked and returned to the side from which it was removed.

Notice that on the top of the cylinder head one of the bolt holes has a small hole. This small hole is for the purpose of supplying lubricant to the rocker arms. Be certain in installing the rocker arms that the bracket with the mating hole is placed over this oil supply hole. If it is not so placed the rockers will be starved for oil and will fail quickly in service.

Spitfire V-8 Engines

Remove the inlet manifold, as explained earlier, detach the exhaust pipes from the manifold at the flange. These bolts are accessible from underneath the car. Remove the spark plug wires and the spark plug wire brackets.

Remove the rocker covers and take off the rocker shaft. Detach the bolts which hold the water manifold to the cylinder head being worked on. It is a good idea at this point to loosen the water manifold in the front because it may prove difficult to get the cylinder head back into place properly if it has to be pushed against that manifold when reinstalling it.

Remove the bolts which hold the cylinder head to the block and lift off the head.

All Engines Starting With 1959 Production

Drain the cooling system. Remove generator, carburetor air cleaner and fuel line. Disconnect the accelerator linkage. Remove the vacuum control tube at carburetor and distributor. Disconnect the distributor cap, coil wires and heater hose. Disconnect the heat indicator sending unit wire. Remove spark plugs located under the manifolds. Remove the intake manifold, ignition coil and carburetor as an assembly. Remove the tappet chamber cover. Remove cylinder head covers and gaskets.

NOTE: On air conditioned cars, number eight cylinder exhaust valve must be open to allow clearance between the right bank cylinder head cover and the heater housing.

Remove the generator. Remove exhaust manifolds. Remove the rocker arms and shaft assembly. Remove the push rods and place them in their respective slots in a holder. Remove the 17 head bolts from each cylinder head and remove cylinder heads.

When reinstalling, the small ends of the push rods go into the tappets. Be sure when tightening rocker shaft support bolts to allow time for tappets to bleed down. Tighten to 30 ft lbs.

The stamped arrow on the rocker shaft must be on top and the arrow must point toward the push rod socket of the rocker arm.

The two wide brackets must be installed with the oil feed grooves facing the push rod side of the rocker arm.

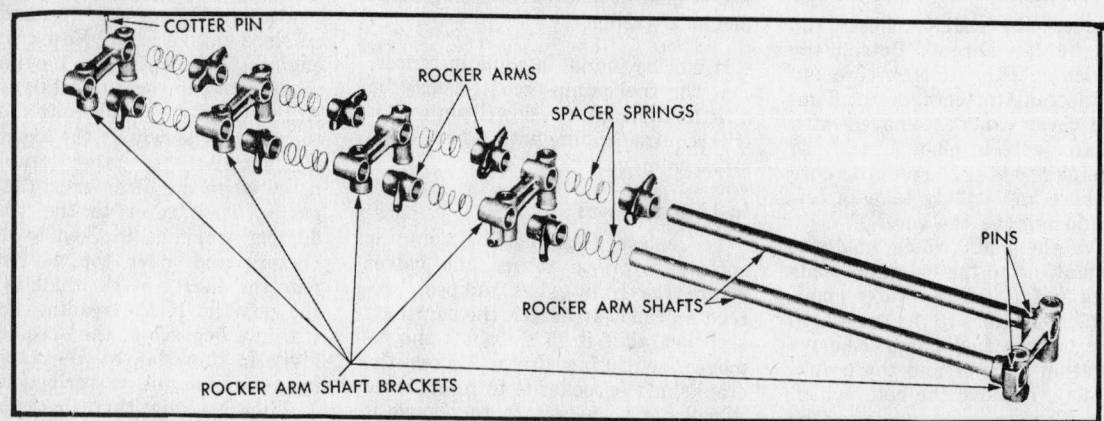

Rocker Shaft Assembly—1957-58 Firepower Engine

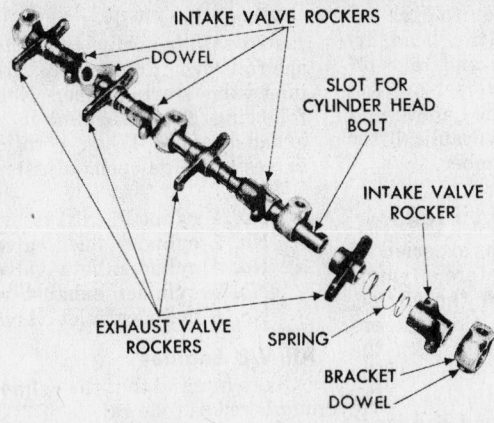

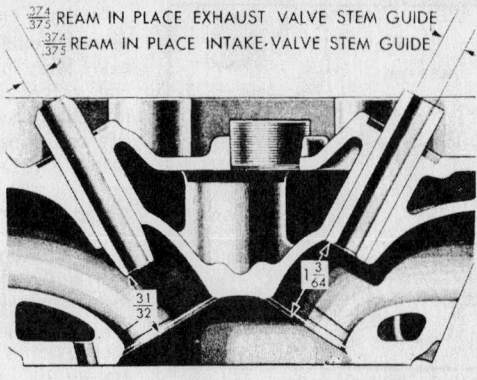

INTAKE VALVE ROCKERS
DOWEL
SLOT FOR CYLINDER HEAD BOLT
INTAKE VALVE ROCKER
EXHAUST VALVE ROCKERS
SPRING
BRACKET
DOWEL

Rocker Shaft Assembly 1957-58 Spitfire Engine

$\frac{.374}{.375}$ REAM IN PLACE EXHAUST VALVE STEM GUIDE
$\frac{.374}{.375}$ REAM IN PLACE INTAKE-VALVE STEM GUIDE

Valve stem guide assembly—1956-58 FirePower
Exhaust valve stem guide ($1\frac{7}{32}$) for 1954-55

REMOVAL OF ROCKER ARM AND SHAFTS

Firepower V-8 Engines

To remove the rocker arms and shafts, take off all of the carburetor controls and tubes which interfere with the removal of the rocker cover.

Pull out the spark plug insulating porcelains and remove the rocker cover.

Unbolt and lift off the rocker assembly.

Caution: The bolts which hold the rocker assembly to the head are also the bolts which hold the head to the cylinder block, therefore, it is advisable when removing the rockers to install a new cylinder head gasket.

This gasket is a very thin shim and requires extremely careful handling. Nicks or scratches on the cylinder head mating surfaces will almost certainly result in defective seating of this thin gasket.

To disassemble the rocker assemblies, carefully tag each of the rockers so that it can be reinstalled on the shaft and in the position from which it was removed.

Spitfire V-8 Engines

Remove the carburetor air cleaner and pull the wires off the spark plugs but not out of the spark plug bracket at the back of the cylinder heads. Remove the bolts which hold the rocker cover to the top of the rockers and lift off the rocker cover. Note: A new gasket must be used on reinstallation.

A little at a time, remove the bolts which hold the rocker brackets to the cylinder head and lift off the rocker assemblies as a unit.

The rocker shaft assemblies can then be unbolted from the cylinder head.

VALVE SYSTEM

All Chrysler in-line engines are L-head. The V-8 engine is equipped with overhead valves having hydraulic lifters. Valve tappet clearances are adjustable in the 300 engine, until 1958.

All 6 cylinder Chrysler models are fitted with mushroom type lifters which require that the camshaft be removed in order to take out any of the lifters.

On the V-8 model the valve lifters can be taken out after the rocker arms, push rods and manifolds have been removed.

REMOVAL OF VALVES

V-8 Models

To remove the valves on the V-8 models it is necessary to take off the cylinder head.

Follow the procedure given for cylinder head removal. The valves are taken out of the cylinder head on the bench.

REPLACEMENT OF VALVE GUIDES

All Engines Thru 1954, and 1955 Thru 1958 Firepower Engines

Whenever it is necessary to replace valve guides on Chrysler, or any other engine, it is always good practice to carefully measure the distance from the cylinder head to the edge of the valve guide before driving out the old guide. This measurement should be

carefully noted, both for the intake and the exhaust, so that when a new guide is installed, it can be inserted to exactly the same distance from the head as the old guide.

On all Chrysler engines the valve guide should be reamed after installation to provide the proper clearance for the valve stem.

On V-8 models equipped with removable guides, the valve guides are driven out into the combustion chamber. In other words, they are driven from the top of the head down to the bottom.

On all in-line engines the valve guides are pulled through the top of the block. New guides are installed by driving them from the top toward the bottom.

On V-8 engines new valve guides are driven from the combustion chamber up to the top of the head. The exhaust valve guide on the V-8 engine has a small oil hole at its upper end. This oil hole should face upwards.

1955 Thru 1958 Spitfire Engines and All V8 Starting with 1959

Separate guides are not used on these engines, instead the valve is fitted directly into a bore in the cylinder head.

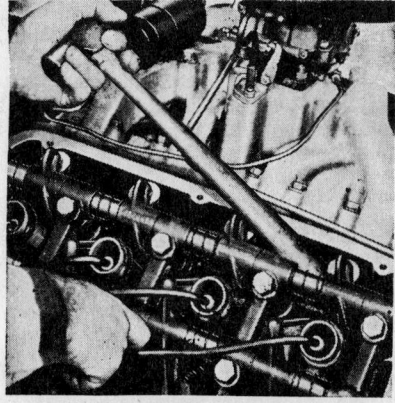

FirePower V8 models—applying side pressure against valve springs

FirePower V-8 models—check for valve tappet noise at rocker arm

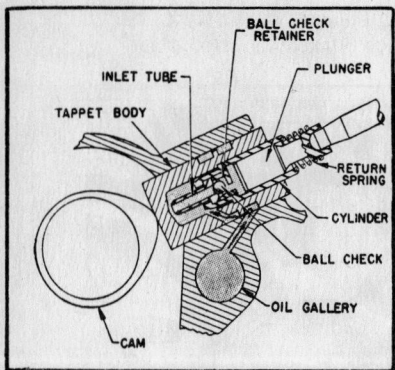

Hydraulic Tappet-valve open

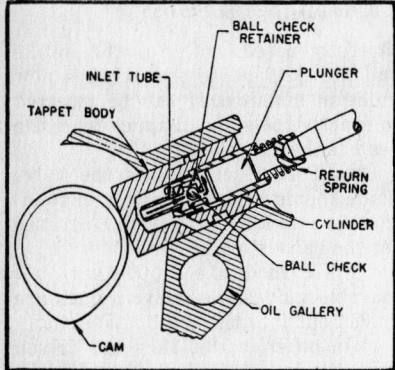

Hydraulic Tappet-valve closed
See "Valve Adjusting Sequence" V8 Models

VALVE SEAT INSERTS

All Chrysler engines are equipped with exhaust valve seat inserts made of a cast, heat resisting material, which cannot be cut successfully with a reamer. Exhaust valve seats must be ground and/or lapped to a perfect seal.

REMOVAL OF HYDRAULIC LIFTER PLUNGERS

All V-8 Models

Note: On some very early production V-8 engines it was necessary to remove the inlet manifold and the valve tappet cover in order to take out the hydraulic valve lifter unit. On later production and all present production engines, the push rod hole has been enlarged to permit passage of the hydraulic lifter unit.

Remove the rocker cover and, selecting the valves in the closed position, compress the valve springs sufficiently to move the rocker arm from the push rod and holding it in this position slide the rocker arm off to one side, which will permit withdrawal of the push rod and the lifter plunger assembly. This work can be done without removing the manifolds. This applies to the plunger portion of the lifter only. If the lifter body itself must be removed proceed as follows:

Remove the intake manifold, as explained earlier under the head Intake Manifold. Remove and take off the valve chamber cover. Now follow the procedure outlined above and lift the body of the hydraulic lifter into the valve cover chamber.

STUCK HYDRAULIC LIFTERS

If sticking has been experienced with hydraulic lifters, before attempting to take them out of the engine, first run a good solvent thru the engine by mixing the solvent with the engine oil in order to remove the gums, and tars, oil residues from the bottom of the lifter which will let it come up out of its bore easily. The residues of oil, such as gums and tars, sometimes make it very difficult to pull a lifter body up out of its bore

INITIAL ADJUSTMENT OF HYDRAULIC TAPPETS

To check to be certain the hydraulic lifter is operating some place near the middle of its stroke the Chrysler Motor Car Co. recommends that the length of the valve stem protruding from the cylinder head be checked with gauge No. C-3061. However, if this gauge is not available an emergency check can be made by turning the engine until the valve being checked is in the fully closed position and the lifter is on the bottom of the cam. Depress the push rod to force the lifter to leak down. Held in this position, there should be a minimum of .032 clearance between the rocker arm and the valve stem.

Maximum clearance should be approximately .070 inch. However, since all servicing on the hydraulic valves and valve train tend to decrease this clearance it is unlikely that the maximum will ever be encountered.

VALVE ADJUSTING SEQUENCE

6-Cylinder Engines

The following valve adjusting sequence is recommended as requiring the least turning of the engine and also the reasonable assurance that the valves being adjusted are at the bottom of their cams.

Turn the engine until No. 1 cylinder exhaust valve starts to open. Notice that right after it the No. 2 cylinder inlet valve will also start to open. When both of these valves are wide open, adjust:

No. 1 cylinder inlet valve
No. 2 cylinder exhaust valve
No. 3 cylinder both valves
No. 5 cylinder inlet valve
No. 6 cylinder exhaust valve

When these valves have been adjusted satisfactorily, turn the engine one full revolution until No. 5 cylinder inlet valve starts to open. Notice that following closely behind it is No. 6 exhaust valve. When both of these valves are wide open, adjust:

No. 1 cylinder exhaust valve
No. 2 cylinder inlet valve
No. 4 cylinder both valves
No. 5 cylinder exhaust valve
No. 6 cylinder inlet valve

All V-8 Engines

Keep in mind that the cylinders are numbered as follows:

Right front..........2-4-6-8
Left front............1-3-5-7

Using this numbering system, turn the engine until No. 1 cylinder exhaust valve starts to open. Notice that following a little behind it, No. 7 cylinder inlet valve will start to open. When both of these valves are wide open, adjust:

No. 1 cylinder inlet valve
No. 3 cylinder both valves
No. 4 cylinder inlet valve
No. 5 cylinder exhaust valve
No. 6 cylinder exhaust valve
No. 7 cylinder exhaust valve
No. 8 cylinder inlet valve

When these have been adjusted satisfactorily turn the engine one full revolution until No. 6 cylinder exhaust valve starts to open and notice that it will be followed by No. 4 cylinder inlet valve. When both of these valves are wide open, adjust:

No. 2 cylinder both valves
No. 4 cylinder exhaust valve
No. 5 cylinder inlet valve
No. 6 cylinder inlet valve
No. 7 cylinder inlet valve
No. 8 cylinder exhaust valve

The above sequence of the V-8 engine is given to be used for the initial setting of the hydraulic valve lifter.

ENGINE LUBRICATION

REMOVAL OF OIL PAN

V-8 Models 1954

Remove the oil level indicator and drain the oil. Remove the starting motor and the exhaust pipe crossover. Take out the cap screws and lower the pan.

When replacing the oil pan it is a good idea to tie the oil pan gasket with thin sewing cotton to each one of the mounting bolt holes so that it will not shift or move when it is being pushed up into place.

The sewing cotton will become embedded in the cork gasket and will be harmless.

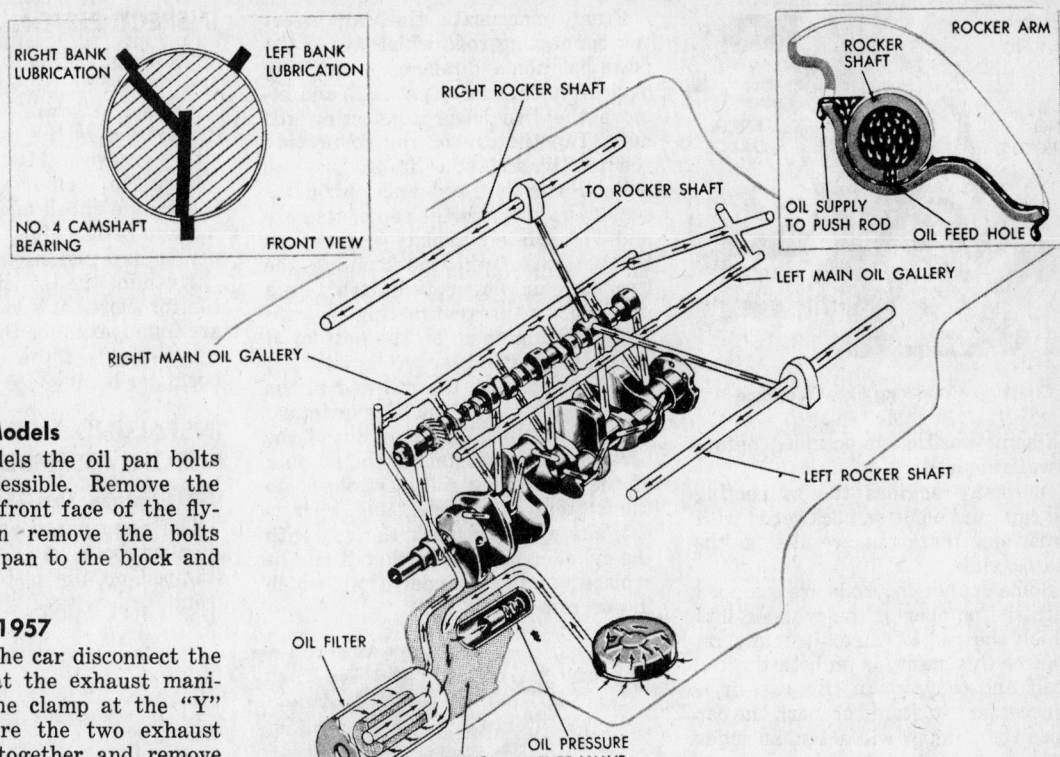

Engine Lubrication, V-8 with Front Mounted Distributor.

1955-56 V-8 Models

On these models the oil pan bolts are readily accessible. Remove the cover from the front face of the flywheel and then remove the bolts which hold the pan to the block and lower the pan.

Starting with 1957

From under the car disconnect the exhaust pipes at the exhaust manifolds. Loosen the clamp at the "Y" connection where the two exhaust pipes come in together and remove the "Y" exhaust pipes. Disconnect the steering idler arm and let the steering linkage drop down out of the way. Remove the starter and the transmission (or converter) dust shield at the front of the flywheel housing.

Place a jack under the engine and remove the engine front support bolts and then jack the engine up approximately one inch and block it in that position. Remove the bolts which hold the oil pan to the block, and by turning the crankshaft until the timing mark is 180° (one-half turn) removed from the indicator in order to get the counterweight out of the way, slide the oil pan backwards and down.

6 Cylinder Models

Crank engine until No. 1 piston is half way up the cylinder bore. Take down clutch underpan and the bolts around the oil pan. Lower the back of the pan and slide it back and out at the same time so that it will clear the oil pump screen.

Pan gasket end corks should protrude from ¼ in. to ½ in. above the oil pan. Do not cut off the protruding portions since the pan will compress it making a tight seal when it is bolted firmly in place.

OIL FILTER REPLACEMENT

V-8 Fire power Engines Thru 1954

The oil filter is located under the right bank of cylinders towards the rear. The element can be replaced by loosening the clamp around the top of the can and lifting off the can top.

If the can itself is to be replaced, it is held by four bolts to the crankcase. These bolts are accessible from underneath the car.

1955 Thru 1958 V-8 Firepower and Spitfire Engines

The oil filter is located below the right bank of cylinders towards the rear and is held by a single bolt which is accessible from the top of the can.

Starting with 1959

The oil filter is at the left lower front corner of the engine. Unscrew the filter from its base. Wipe the base clean. Screw new filter on base until gasket contacts base. Tighten ½ turn more by hand and check for leaks.

PISTONS, CONNECTING RODS AND MAIN BEARINGS

PISTON AND CONNECTING ROD ASSEMBLIES

If for any reason the connecting rod bearing cap is to be detached from the connecting rod it is essential that the cap and rod be marked so that the cap will be put back on the rod in

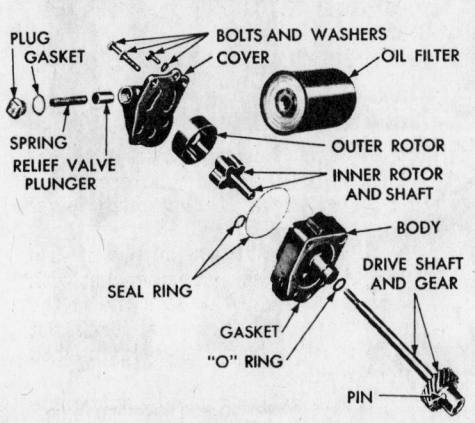

Exploded View of Oil Pump Starting with 1959 Production

Exploded View of the 1958 Oil Pump

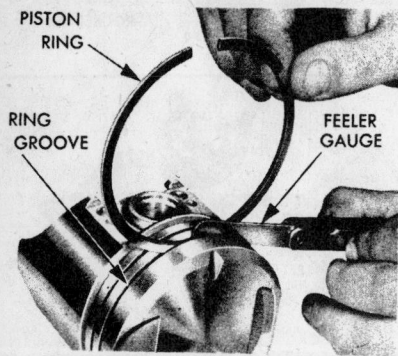

PISTON RING

RING GROOVE

FEELER GAUGE

Checking Piston Ring Side Clearance

the same position it occupied before it was removed.

On many engines the connecting rod cap can be put on backwards with sometimes disastrous results to the rod bearing.

Some connecting rods are stamped with the number of the cylinder into which the rod is fitted. In many instances this stamp is on both the rod itself and the cap. In this case it is unnecessary to stamp or mark the cap since the number will act as an index mark.

When working on piston and connecting rod assemblies which have been removed from the engine, it is always considered good practice to replace the cap on the bottom of the connecting rod as soon as it has been removed from the engine so that the cap will not become separated from its rod and the bearing shell will not be lost.

REMOVAL OF ROD AND PISTON ASSEMBLIES

All Models

Remove the cylinder head and oil pan. Select the two pistons in the down position and insert a good cylinder ridge reamer into those two cylinders and remove the ring ridge.

If a ridge reamer is not available, and the ridge is not too deep, say not more than .005 or .006 inch, it can be removed with a sharp bearing scraper.

Turn the crankshaft until two other pistons are in the same down position and repeat the ridge removing operation.

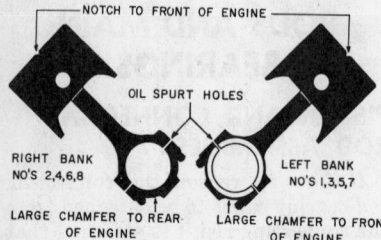

NOTCH TO FRONT OF ENGINE

OIL SPURT HOLES

RIGHT BANK NO'S 2,4,6,8

LEFT BANK NO'S 1,3,5,7

LARGE CHAMFER TO REAR OF ENGINE

LARGE CHAMFER TO FRONT OF ENGINE

Piston and connecting rod assembly.

From underneath the car, select two connecting rods which are in the down position and take off the locking device (cotter pin or pal nut) and remove the two lower connecting rod nuts. Tap the cap of the connecting rod gently and slide it off the two bolts. Push that rod and piston assembly up towards the top of its bore and immediately replace the cap on the bottom of the rod running the two nuts up finger tight. This is a precaution to prevent mixing the caps up or getting them on the bottom of the connecting rod the wrong way.

Before pushing the rod and piston assembly up out of the bore or immediately after pushing it up out of the bore check to ascertain if the number of the connecting rod is stamped on the bottom of the rod, and if it is not, either file or mark the rod with the cylinder number so that it can be replaced in the cylinder from which it was removed.

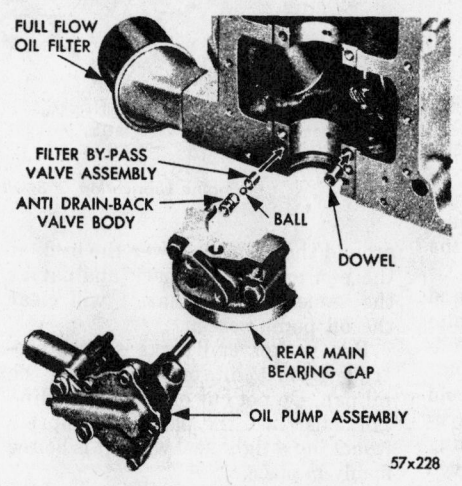

FULL FLOW OIL FILTER

FILTER BY-PASS VALVE ASSEMBLY

ANTI DRAIN-BACK VALVE BODY

BALL

DOWEL

REAR MAIN BEARING CAP

OIL PUMP ASSEMBLY

57x228

Oil Pump By Pass Valve, Rear Main Bearing—1957-58 Models

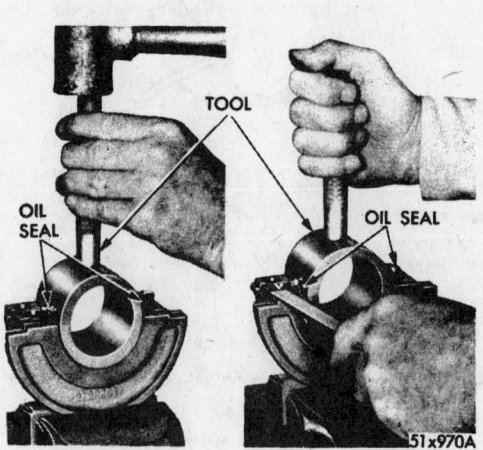

TOOL

OIL SEAL

OIL SEAL

51x970A

Installing Rear Main Bearing Oil Seal

INSPECT PISTONS

Thoroughly clean up the pistons and remove all traces of carbon from the ring grooves. Drill out the oil drain holes in the back of the lower ring grooves. Examine the ring grooves for bell mouth condition. If the groove is bell mouth it will either have to be machined to a square corner or new pistons installed.

Examine the thrust face of the piston for scores or scratches and if any are found, examine the cylinder to see whether or not the cylinder requires boring or honing.

INSTALLING ROD AND PISTON ASSEMBLIES

V-8 Engines Thru 1956

The pistons are assembled to the cylinder bore with the letter "F" stamped on the piston towards the front.

TOOL

BEARING

REMOVING

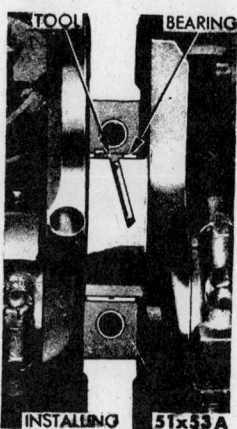

TOOL

BEARING

INSTALLING

51x53A

Removing and Installing Main Bearing Upper Shell

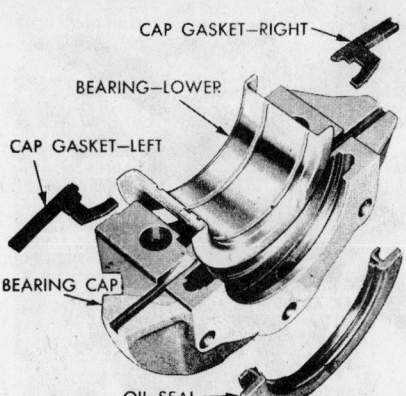

*Rear main bearing oil seal
6 cylinder type*

1957-63 Models

The pistons are assembled to the engine with the "V" notch in the head of the piston towards the front.

REAR MAIN BEARING OIL SEAL

All V-8 Engines

Braided asbestos is used to prevent oil escaping from the crank case on to the clutch and flywheel. To replace the lower half of this oil seal remove the rear main bearing cap and the old oil seal packing. Install the new packing in the connecting rod cap so that the packing protrudes lightly above the cap. Bolt the cap in place and torque it to approximately 60 ft. lbs. and then immediately take it down again. If the protruding part of the packing has "riveted over," cut off the riveted portion with a razor blade and again bolt the cap into place. Repeat this operation until the main bearing cap sets firmly in the block without riveting over the new portion of the oil seal.

To replace the upper half of the rear main bearing oil seal in the V-8 models it is necessary to remove the engine and the crankshaft.

● CHILTON TIME-SAVER

TOP HALF, REAR MAIN BEARING OIL SEAL REPLACEMENT —WICK TYPE

The following method has proven a distinct advantage in most cases and, if successful, saves many hours of labor.

1. Drain engine oil and remove oil pan.
2. Remove rear main bearing cap.
3. With a 6" length of 3/16" brazing rod, drive up on either exposed end of the top oil seal. When the opposite end of the seal starts to protrude, have a helper grasp it with pliers and pull gently while the driven end is being tapped. It is surprising how easily most of these seals can be removed by this method.

TO INSTALL THE NEW WOVEN FABRIC TYPE SEAL:

1. Obtain a 12" piece of copper wire (about the same gauge as that used in the strands of an insulated battery cable).
2. Thread one strand of this wire thru the new seal, about ½" from the end, bend back and make secure.
3. Thoroughly saturate the new seal with engine oil.
4. Push the copper wire up thru the oil seal groove until it comes down on the opposite side of the bearing.
5. Pull (with pliers) on the protruding copper wire while the crankshaft is being turned and the new seal is slowly fed into place.

<u>CAUTION</u>: This snaking operation slightly reduces the diameter of the new seal and care will have to be used to keep the seal from slipping too far thru the top half of the bearing.

6. When an equal amount of seal is extending from each side, cut off the copper wire close to the seal and tamp both ends of the seal up into the groove (this will tend to expand the seal again).

<u>Note</u>: Don't worry about the copper wire left in the groove, it is too soft to cause damage.

7. Replace the seal in the cap in the usual way and replace the oil pan.

All 6 Cylinder Models

The main bearing oil seal used in the 6 cylinder model is similar to that used in the V-8 model, and the seal is replaced in much the same manner. While it is sometimes possible to force the upper half of the oil seal out of its groove with the crankshaft in place, there is no certainty that such a procedure will be effective. In any case if an attempt has been made to drive the upper half of the seal out of its groove, and the attempt is not successful, it will then be necessary to remove the engine and crankshaft and install a new oil seal in the rear main bearing. Instructions given for the V-8 model also apply to the 6 cylinder models.

Beginning 1962

Beginning with 1962 production a new rear main bearing seal retainer and new self expanding type side seals are used. When exposed to engine oil, these laminated, composition side seals expand and should prevent any oil leakage at this point.

This type seal cannot be reused when once removed from an engine. New side seals must be installed.

FRONT SUSPENSION

REFERENCES

General instructions covering the front suspension and how to repair and adjust it, together with information on installation of front wheel bearings and grease seals, are given in the Unit Repair section under the heading: Suspension, Front Repair.

Definitions of the points of steering geometry are covered in the Unit Repair section under the heading: Suspension Front Align. This article also covers trouble shooting front end geometry and irregular tire wear.

Figures covering the caster, camber, toe-in, king pin inclination, and turning radius can be found in the Front Wheel Alignment Table of this section.

Overall car length and tire sizes can be found in the General Chassis and Brake Specifications Table of this section.

TORSION BAR SPRINGS

Contrary to appearance, the torsion bars are **not** interchangeable from "right" to "left." They are marked with an R or an L, according to their location.

Remove

1. Lift the car by the body only so that the front suspension is free of all load. If the car is to be raised with jacks, place jack under center of frame cross member and raise until suspension is free of all load.
2. Release load from torsion bar by backing off anchor adjusting nuts. Remove the adjusting nut and swivel bolt.
3. Remove the lower control arm strut.
4. Remove the lock spring from the rear of torsion bar rear anchor.
5. Install tool #C-3728, or other suitable clamp and remove torsion bar rearward by striking the clamping tool with a hammer.

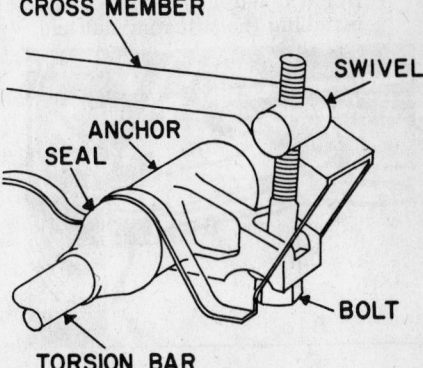

Torsion Bar Adjustment Bolt

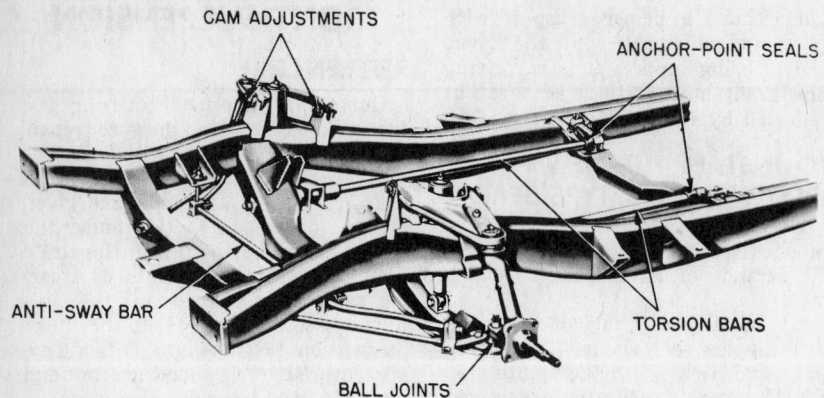

CAM ADJUSTMENTS

ANCHOR-POINT SEALS

ANTI-SWAY BAR

TORSION BARS

BALL JOINTS

Torsion bar front suspension.

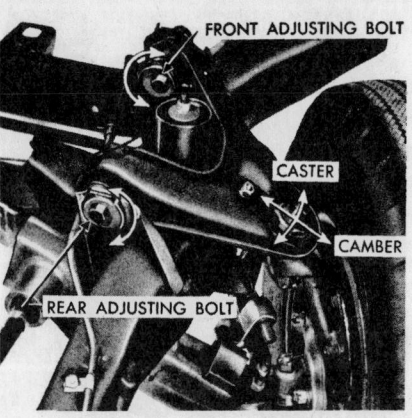

FRONT ADJUSTING BOLT

CASTER

CAMBER

REAR ADJUSTING BOLT

Caster and Camber Adjusting Points

Do not apply heat to the front or rear anchors. Do not scratch or otherwise mar the skin of the torsion bar during removal or installation.

6. Remove the clamping tool and slide the rear anchor balloon seal off the front end of the bar.

7. Remove torsion bar by sliding the bar rearward and out through the rear anchor.

Install

1. Clean the hex openings of both front and rear anchors, also clean the male ends of the torsion bar.

2. Feed the torsion bar through the rear anchor.

3. Slide the balloon type seal over the torsion bar, with the large cupped side of the seal facing the rear.

4. Coat both ends of the torsion bar with multi-purpose grease.

5. When starting the bar into the anchor in the lower control arm, position the adjusting arm about 60° below the horizontal plane. This will permit wind-up for future adjustment.

6. Install the lock ring in the rear anchor, then move torsion bar rearward until the bar contacts the lock ring.

7. Position swivel bolt on the control arm and hold in place while installing the adjusting nut and

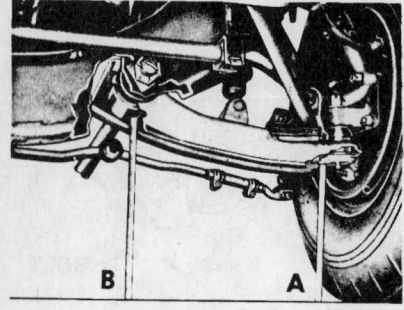

B   A

*Suspension Height, Checked at Ball Joint
and Lower Control Arm.*

seat. Tighten the adjustment about 10 turns before lowering car to the floor.

8. Pack the annular opening in the rear anchor with multi-purpose grease. Slide the rear anchor balloon type seal into position over the rear anchor until the lip of the seal fits in the groove.

9. Install lower control arm strut.

10. Lower car to the floor and adjust front suspension height.

FRONT HEIGHT

Adjustment, Without Gauge

1. Jounce the car and measure from the lower ball joint to the floor, (measurement "A").

2. Measure from the control arm torsion bar spring anchor housing to the floor, (measurement "B").

3. Subtract "A" from "B". The difference should be as follows:

4. Measure the other side in the same way.

1957-58	
All Others	2¼" ± ⅛"
Station Wagon	2¾" ± ⅛"
C-300	1¾" ± ⅛"
1959	
All Except Station Wagon	2⅛" ± ⅛"
1959-60	
Station Wagon	2½" ± ⅛"
1960-61	
All Except Sattion Wagon	2" ± ⅛"
1961	
Station Wagon	2⅜" ± ⅛"
1962-63	
All Except Station Wagon & 300 H	2" ± ⅛"
Station Wagon	2⅜" ± ⅛"
300 H (High Performance)	1¾" ± ⅛"

5. Adjust, if necessary, by turning the torsion bar anchor adjusting nut, clockwise to raise, and counter-clockwise to lower.

1959-63 FRONT SUSPENSION ALIGNMENT ADJUSTMENT

The upper control arms are fastened to brackets welded to the frame.

These brackets have lips against which the cam-like heads of the two arm attaching bolts make contact.

When the bolts are turned the cams push against the lips on the brackets and so the position of the upper control arm is altered. This provides the adjustment of caster and camber.

Full cam rotation is only one-half turn so it may be necessary to reverse the direction of bolt rotation to reach the correct setting.

Turning one bolt will alter the caster. Turning both an equal amount in the same direction will alter camber.

Before attempting adjustment be sure to soak the bolts with oil and solvent and brush off all dirt from the cams.

Turn one bolt and so bring caster to approximately the correct figure of: 1 N to O for Manual; ½ to 1¼ P for Power.

Now turn both bolts in the same direction (though not necessarily the same direction of rotation as was made for the caster setting) to set camber at the preferred figure of: O (range ⅛ N to ¾ P) for right wheel; ⅜ P (range ⅛ P to ⅝ P) for the left wheel.

Tighten the bolt lock nuts to 60-70 ft. lbs.

DRAINING

Depress the valve stem in the drain valve on the high pressure tank once a month.

RIDING HEIGHT

Riding height is measured between the axle housing and the rear of the rubber bumpers on the frame. Difference between sides should not exceed ½ inch. Height should be 4¾ inches on all except the Imperial, which should be 4⅜ inches. To adjust the leveling valve loosen the attaching nuts and rotate the cam on the lower stud. Tighten nuts to 8 ft. lbs.

COMPRESSOR

The compressor is connected into the engine oil lines. The oil pressure input line is at the rear of the compressor.

STEERING GEAR

Manual Steering Gear

Instructions covering the overhaul of the steering gear will be found in the Unit Repair section under the heading: Steering, Manual.

Power Steering Gears

Trouble shooting and repair instructions covering power steering gears are given in the Unit Repair section under the heading: Steering Power.

Starting with 1961 Models

The power steering pump belt is self-adjusting. The pump is mounted on a free-pivot bolt. When engine is off only weight of pump is on belt. As load is placed on pump the pull of belt tends to pull the pump down and away from engine. This tightens the belt in proportion to the load.

HORN BUTTON REMOVAL

1954 Models

On these models the horn blowing ring is held in place by four screws underneath the steering wheel.

1955-56 Models

To remove the horn button on these models, simply grasp the top of the button in the hand and turn it to the left.

If the car is equipped with a horn blowing ring, remove the medallion in the same manner as the horn button. The attaching screws for the horn ring are located under the medallion.

1957-63 Models

Disconnect the battery to prevent the horn from blowing and twist the horn blowing ring center medallion and lift it off.

Disconnect the wire and the three screws which hold the blowing ring to the steering wheel.

STEERING WHEEL REMOVAL

On all models of Chrysler the steering wheel can be removed by first taking off the horn button and horn wiring attaching pad. Remove the nut which holds the steering wheel to the steering tube, and use a puller to take off the steering wheel.

REMOVAL OF STEERING GEAR

Thru 1960

Although the steering column is divided and pinned at the steering gear assembly on power steering models it is easier to remove column jacket and gear as an assembly thru the driver's compartment.

Disconnect the battery. Disconnect the horn and turn signal wires at the instrument panel. Remove the steering wheel. Remove the steering jacket support clamp at the instrument panel. Remove the dust shield at the fire wall. Remove the floor opening panel. Disconnect the pitman arm from the shaft or the intermediate (drag) link. Remove the brake pedal pad. Disconnect the transmission controls. Remove the gear housing to frame bolts. Remove steering gear and mast jacket as an assembly thru the driver's compartment.

Starting 1961

Because of type of shaft coupling used the gear can be removed forward and down. Disconnect battery and steering arm. Remove bolt holding coupling to worm shaft.

Remove bolts holding steering gear to frame and lower gear toward front and remove.

In reinstalling be sure worm shaft is exactly on high spot, or one half way between two turning extremes. Align the master splines and insert in coupling.

INTERMEDIATE STEERING ARM BEARINGS

1954 Models

To replace the intermediate steering arm bearings, first detach the drag link from the intermediate steering arm and detach both tie rods from the intermediate steering arm.

Remove the bolts which hold the intermediate steering arm to the frame and work the arm out of the frame.

Mount the bracket in a vise and remove the nut and pin which hold the intermediate arm pin which goes down through the center of the intermediate steering arm bearings.

Pry the arm and bearings out of the bracket and remove the oil seals, bearings and, using a drift pin, drive out the bearing cups.

If either of the bearings are found to be defective it will be necessary to replace both bearings with new ones.

Install new bearing cups, bearings and oil seals and work the arm back into the bracket, installing a new pin and nut.

Take the entire assembly to the car

and work it back into the frame, replacing the bolts which hold the bracket to the frame.

Reconnect both of the tie rods and the drag link.

1955 Thru 1956 Models

On the 1955 and 1956 models the intermediate steering arm is mounted in a bracket which is bolted to the right side of the frame.

To replace the arm and/or its bushings, unbolt the bracket from the frame and the bracket and its bushing can be unscrewed from the top of the arm. The lower part of the arm can then be unscrewed from its bushing in the tie rod end and the bushings can later be unscrewed.

When installing a new arm and/or bushings, first insert the bushing in the steering reach rod and then screw the arm into the bushing in such a way that it is run up until it binds and then back off a full turn.

Do the same with the upper bushing and then bolt the upper bushing bracket to the frame.

1957-63 Models

Remove the nut from the intermediate steering arm bracket and take out the bolt. The arm can then be pried out of the bracket.

Remove the cotter pin and nut from the steering connector link and drive the link off the end of the intermediate steering arm. The arm can then be taken over to a bench, the bushing pressed out and a new one installed.

CLUTCH

The only practical service possible on the clutch assembly is to tighten up to prevent rattles and adjust the pedal toe board clearance. All other service requires the removal of the clutch assembly.

If the clutch assembly is being removed because of chatter or malfunction, it is advisable to check to see if there is any oil leaking from the rear main bearing or from the fluid coupling. Oil on the clutch facings will produce a noticeable chatter even taking into consideration the damping action of the hydraulic torque converter or the fluid couple.

Because of the damping action of the fluid couple service on the clutch is very rarely required.

CLUTCH PEDAL TOE BOARD CLEARANCE (THROWOUT BEARING CLEARANCE)

Thru 1956 Models

The clutch pedal toe board clearance is adjusted at the yoke, which is part of the rod between the throwout lever on the clutch itself and the clutch idler arm.

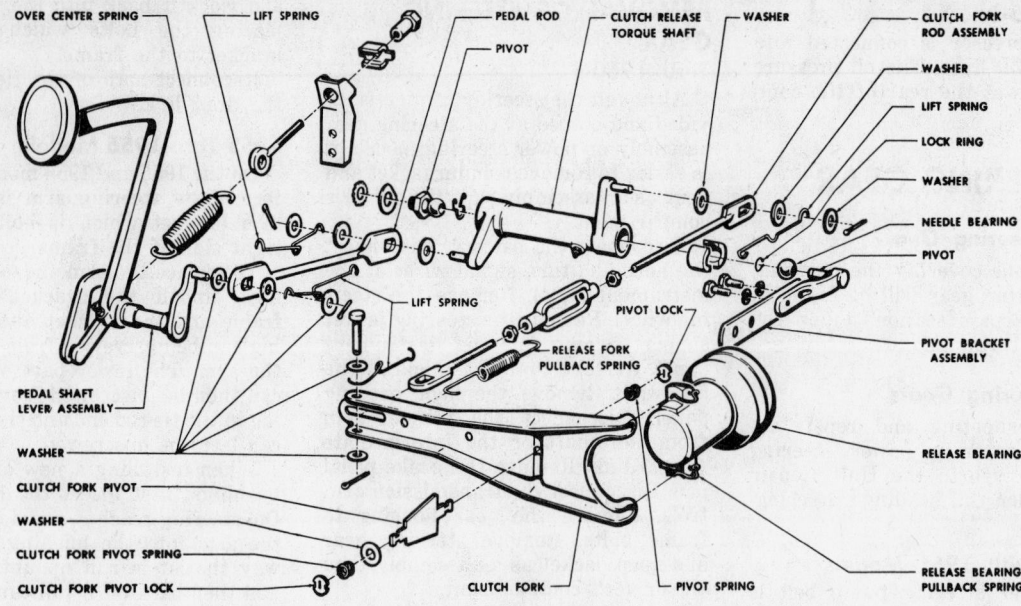

OVER CENTER SPRING — LIFT SPRING — PEDAL ROD — CLUTCH RELEASE TORQUE SHAFT — WASHER — CLUTCH FORK ROD ASSEMBLY — PIVOT — WASHER — LIFT SPRING — LOCK RING — WASHER — NEEDLE BEARING — PIVOT — LIFT SPRING — PIVOT LOCK — RELEASE FORK PULLBACK SPRING — PIVOT BRACKET ASSEMBLY — RELEASE BEARING — PEDAL SHAFT LEVER ASSEMBLY — WASHER — CLUTCH FORK PIVOT — WASHER — CLUTCH FORK PIVOT SPRING — CLUTCH FORK PIVOT LOCK — CLUTCH FORK — PIVOT SPRING — RELEASE BEARING PULLBACK SPRING

Clutch Linkage

Loosen the jam nut at both ends of the turnbuckle and turn the buckle until there is from ¾ to 1 inch free play of the clutch pedal, measured at the toe board, before the throwout bearing contacts the clutch fingers.

After the adjustment is secured, tighten the jam nuts at both sides of the adjusting link.

Starting with 1957

Starting with 1957 models this adjustment is done at the adjusting nut which connects the inner end of the idler lever to the clutch release fork. Remove the clevis pin in the release fork to permit turning the adjusting sleeve. Securely tighten the lock nut after the adjustment has been secured. There should be from one-half to three-quarter inch free travel of the pedal before the throwout bearing strikes the fingers of the clutch.

REMOVAL OF THE CLUTCH ASSEMBLY

Thru 1963

Split the rear universal joint and remove the four bolts which hold the front universal joint to the back of the brake drum. Remove the driveshaft. Disconnect the gear shift control rods and the speedometer cable and the back-up light switch. Take out the speedometer drive pinion. Disconnect the hand brake cable. Support the back of the transmission and remove the bolts which hold the transmission to the bell housing.

Some shops prefer to replace the two upper bolts with two long pilots so the transmission can be slid straight back on the pilots which eliminates the risk of bending the clutch disc.

On all models remove the transmission assembly, the clutch housing lower pan and the clutch throwout fork. The clutch cover assembly should be stamped, showing its relation to the flywheel so that it can be reassembled in the same position from which it was removed. The cover bolts should be removed a few turns at a time in order to avoid springing the clutch cover.

Disassembly service on the clutch requires special jigs and fixtures. Instructions in the use of the fixtures are supplied by the manufacturer of the tool.

STANDARD TRANSMISSION

Transmission refill capacities will be found in the Capacities Table of this section.

Thru 1956

Disconnect the propeller shaft at the front universal joint.

Disconnect all attaching parts such as speedometer cable, battery ground cable, gearshift control rods and gearshift selector cables. Support the rear of the engine on a padded jack and take off the transmission cross member.

Remove the nuts that hold the transmission to the clutch housing and lift the transmission assembly down and out.

1957-63 TRANSMISSION REMOVAL

Disconnect all attaching parts at the transmission.

Split the propeller shaft at the front universal joint and push back the universal joint yoke.

Support the rear of the engine on a padded jack and take off the transmission cross member.

Detach the transmission from the clutch housing and move down and out of the car.

Installation of Transmission

Important: Before installing transmission, check face of clutch housing and lower pan for alignment. If any misalignment is noted, loosen lower pan and align face of clutch housing and lower pan with a straight edge, then tighten the pan up securely. Unless the lower pan is in alignment with the face of the clutch housing properly the transmission will not fit tight against the clutch housing which may result in difficulty in shifting.

DISASSEMBLY OF 3 SPEED SYNCHROMESH TRANSMISSION

Thru 1956

Remove the two screws at the transmission cover which hold the shift rail detent springs and balls. Then take off the transmission side cover assembly.

Take off the universal joint companion flange and brake drum assembly.

Next take off the shifter fork guide rail. (This is a long thin rail which slides into the front face of the transmission and through the shifter fork. It is intended to guide the shifter fork. It is removed by unscrewing it to the left with a screw driver and sliding it out of the front face of the transmission.)

Set the transmission in neutral and loosen the shifter rails from the shifter forks. Then slide the shift rails out of the front of the transmission case (it will be necessary to remove the Welsh plug to get at the lower rail).

The shift rail interlock rod can be removed by taking out the single cap screw which is located at the top of the transmission toward the back, just to the right of the side cover. Take out the shifter forks. Unbolt the extension housing from the back of the transmission case and slide the case with the main shaft and gears connected to it out the rear of the transmission case.

The main shaft can now be disassembled by removing the synchronizer retaining snap ring and the synchronizer unit. The second speed gear and low speed gear can then be slid off the shaft.

The rear bearing is held in place with a snap ring. Take out the snap ring and the main shaft and bearing can be removed from the extension housing.

A new oil seal should be used at the rear end of the extension housing.

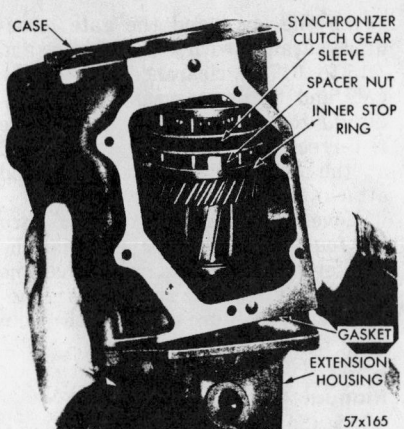

Removing Transmission Housing From Mainshaft Assembly—1957 Model

The countershaft is driven out toward the rear of the transmission case.

Note: A key is used in the rear end of the counter shaft to prevent it from turning. Be careful to pick up this key as soon as the shaft has been driven far enough to reach it.

Main drive pinion and bearing assembly can be pulled out of the front of the case after the counter shaft gear cluster has been dropped to the bottom of the case or removed.

Reverse idler gear shaft is driven toward rear of case.

Note: A locking key is also used on the idler shaft and it should be removed as soon as it is clear of the case.

Starting with 1957

Remove, the transmission side cover, together with the shift forks and shift levers. Caution: The interlock balls are spring loaded and may pop out.

From the front of the transmission, remove the sleeve over the main drive pinion. Leave the pinion in place at this time.

Temporarily reinstall the brake drum and set the transmission up on its own brake mount so it stands vertical. Loosen, but do not remove, the transmission case to extension case bolts.

With the transmission still in the vertical position, pull out the drive pinion shaft assembly from the front of the transmission.

Remove the extension housing bolts (which were loosened earlier) and place a nut between the synchronizer clutch gear sleeve and the inner stop ring which is to minimize any interference from the synchronizer clutch when the transmission case is removed from the extension housing assembly. The case is then lifted straight up off its own gears. This will require a little maneuvering to get the housing and cluster gears up past the synchronizing sleeve.

Remove the synchronizer clutch gear snap ring and drive mainshaft out of the extension housing by tapping the rear end of the shaft.

Drive countershaft towards the rear and up out of the transmission case. The key at the end of the shaft prevents the shaft from turning. Remove the key. Remove the adapter shaft from the transmission case, disassemble countershaft assembly by removing thrust washers, roller and spacer.

The transmission is assembled in reverse order of disassembly.

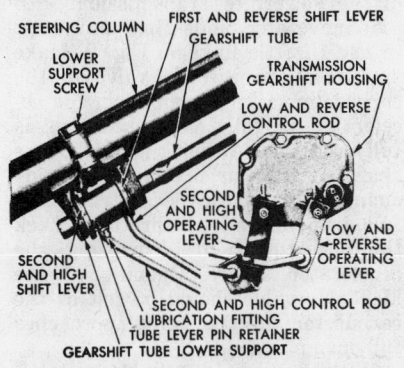

Shift mechanism synchromesh transmission: 1957-59

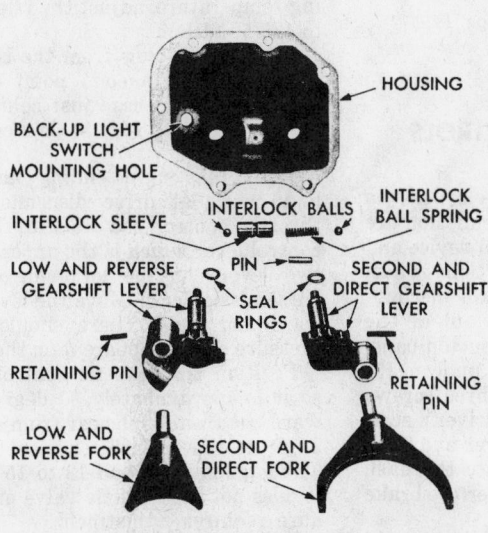

Gear Shift Housing Synchromesh Transmission

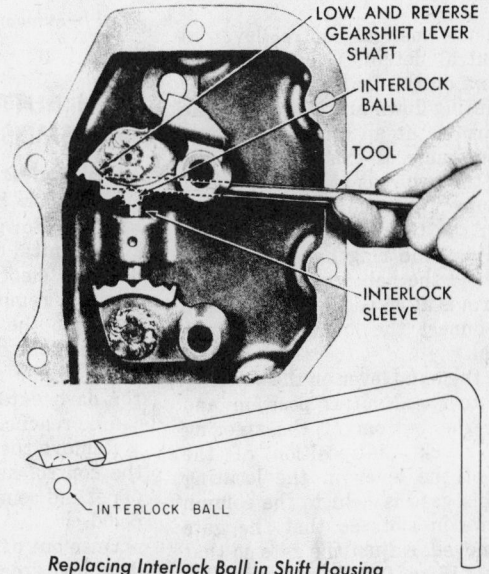

Replacing Interlock Ball in Shift Housing

AUTOMATIC TRANSMISSION, POWERFLITE

BEGINNING 1962

Transmission fluid is filtered through a, disposable type, external filter located in the cooler-to-transmission return line. The filter is equipped with an integral relief valve, which permits fluid to by-pass the filter if the element becomes clogged.

ADJUSTING THE ANTI-STALL

The anti-stall consists of a diaphragm and a plunger with a small orifice. The air trapped behind the diaphragm is bled out at a specific rate by the orifice. The device acts to keep the throttle from snapping shut during its last one-quarter inch of travel.

To check, open the throttle by hand and release. The closing of the throttle should be visibly slowed by the action of the anti-stall.

To adjust, have the engine at operating temperature and set adjusting screw so that the plunger has one-sixteenth of an inch travel after the throttle is fully closed.

ADJUSTING THE LINKAGE

Manual Control Adjustment 1954

The manual control lever is the bottom one of the two levers on the left side of the transmission case. When the lever is turned full back, counterclockwise, the transmission is in Reverse. The next detent forward, clockwise, is Neutral. The next detent is Drive and the last detent, when the lever is as far clockwise as it will go, is Low.

Place the manual control lever in the Neutral detent. Check that the bell crank on the frame has its lower arm pointing down and back while the upper arm is at an angle of 45 deg. with the frame. If this is not so, disconnect the two rods at the bell crank. Being sure that the manual control lever on the transmission is in Neutral, adjust the length of the lower rod to hold the bell crank so that its upper arm is at 45 deg. with the frame and reconnect the lower rod to the bell crank.

Move the hand lever on the steering column to the Neutral position and then at the bottom of the steering column check the position of the tongue of the lever in the locating gate. This gate is held to the column by screws in slots so that the gate can be moved. Adjust the gate so that there is .015 to .030 in. clearance be-

tween the lever and the gate measured parallel with the column and .015 to .017 in. clearance between the gate and the lever measured perpendicular to the column. When the gate is correctly set adjust the upper rod at the bell crank to fit easily and attach it.

Move the hand control lever thru the four positions and check that the pointer and the marks on the dial line up. If they do not: run thru the adjustment procedure again rather than bend the pointer.

Manual Control Adjustment 1955 (See Fig. 1)

On the forward end of the rod running forward from the dash control there is a swivel. Loosen this swivel.

At the transmission, move the manual control lever one notch forward from full rear position. This will be Neutral.

Put dash control in Neutral position and reconnect the swivel.

Check that lever moves freely.

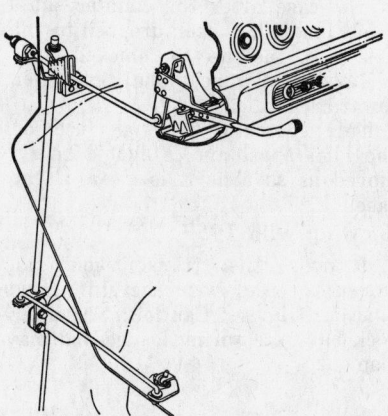

Fig. 1—Manual Control Linkage, 1955

PUSH BUTTON TRANSMISSION CONTROLS

1956 Models

The push button controls used on the 1956 PowerFlite transmission are a mechanical cam operated device and have no electrical connections whatever. To remove the control mechanism take the two screws out of the chrome base of the push button panel and the one screw from underneath the dash extension. All three screws can be reached from the driver's seat.

Remove the chrome cover and push the control mechanism into the dash panel and remove from over the brake pedal.

Once out of the dash panel it can be detached from the cable very easily.

1957-58 Models

To remove the push button assemblies from the 1957 model, first remove the Phillips head screw located on the cone strip just over the speedometer head. At the other end of this attaching strip there is another screw which goes into the push button housing. Remove this screw also. Remove the two screws which hold the bottom end of the push button housing to the front face of the dash panel and the one screw which holds the left side of the housing to the side of the car.

All of these screws are accessible from the driving compartment.

The push button housing assembly can then be pulled into the car and the cable disconnected readily.

Located directly in back of the push button mechanism is the starting switch.

Throttle Linkage and Throttle Valve Oil Pressure Adjustment

Accurate adjustment of the transmission throttle linkage and precise setting of the throttle valve oil pressure is required for proper operation of the Powerflite Transmission.

Remove any binds that may exist in the throttle linkage. Fig. 2. Make sure that the throttle valve in the carburetor is fully open when the accelerator is fully depressed and is fully released. Adjust the accelerator shaft to the carburetor to provide enough accelerator pedal travel for full open and closed throttle. Check the adjustment by depressing the accelerator slowly. Opening of the kickdown valve should be felt as the carburetor throttle valve approaches full open position.

With the hand lever at Neutral, the brakes set, and the engine at operating temperature, adjust the idle speed to 475-500 RPM.

Remove the plug from the throttle pressure test (takeoff) point on the right side of the case just behind the front servo. See Fig. 3. Connect in a pressure gage.

With the engine idling and the hand lever at drive disconnect the throttle control rod at the throttle control lever which is the upper of the two levers on the left side of the transmission case. Move the lever forward and back. There should be a pressure change apparent on the gage.

Position the throttle control lever so it is approximately 30 degrees toward the front of the car from a right angle to the transmission centerline. The gage should read 13 to 15 psi. If it does not the throttle valve oil pressure requires adjustment.

To adjust the throttle pressure, remove the throttle valve adjusting screw plug (Cover). It is the ⅜ in. pipe plug just below and forward of the back up light switch on the left side of the transmission case. Have a can handy as about a quart of transmission fluid will gush forth. Turn the adjusting screw, revealed by removal of the plug, clockwise to decrease the pressure and counterclockwise to increase it. Adjust the pressure to 14 psi.

Reinstall the plug and tighten to 20-25 ft. lbs. Reconnect the throttle control rod to the lever and depress the accelerator. The pressure should rise at once to 80 psi. If it does not and yet is 14 psi at idle the linkage requires adjustment.

Disconnect the swivel at the transmission end of the throttle valve control rod from the rod; leaving the swivel attached to the throttle control lever.

Now move the lever forward as far as it will come and then slowly move it back until a slight resistance is felt. From this point of slight resistance a slight forward movement of the lever should cause the pressure to rise to 80 psi. There at this point of slight resistance hold the lever and reconnect the control rod into the swivel. Push forward on the rod to remove any play in the linkage while making the connecting and tightening the swivel lock screw.

Again depress the accelerator and check that the pressure rises from 14 psi at an idle of 475-500 rpm to 80 psi at 1400-1500 rpm.

After removing the pressure gage tighten the ⅛″ pipe plug to 10-12 ft. lbs.

REMOVAL OF THE TRANSMISSION FROM THE CAR

Disconnect the battery. Drain the transmission and the converter. Unfasten the oil filler tube from the oil pan and remove the tube.

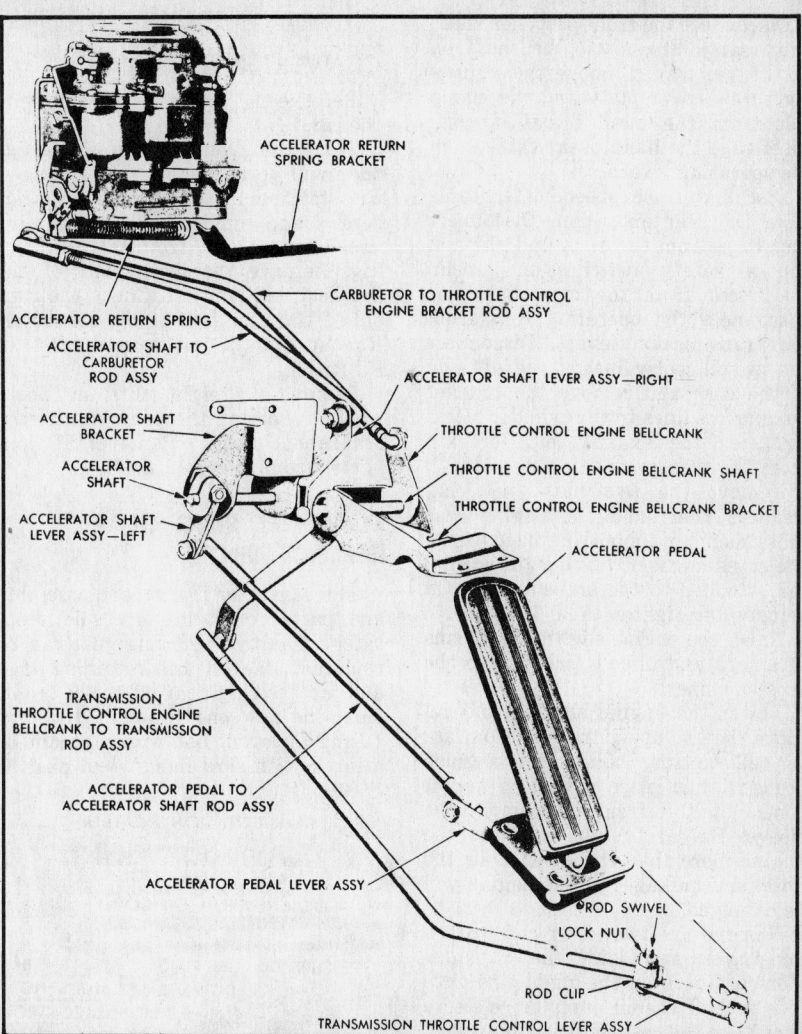

Fig. 2—Throttle Linkage typical of PowerFlite and TorgueFlite. The forward end of the accelerator return spring must be hooked to the flat of the control rod and not to the stud; failure to do so results in no-kickdown.

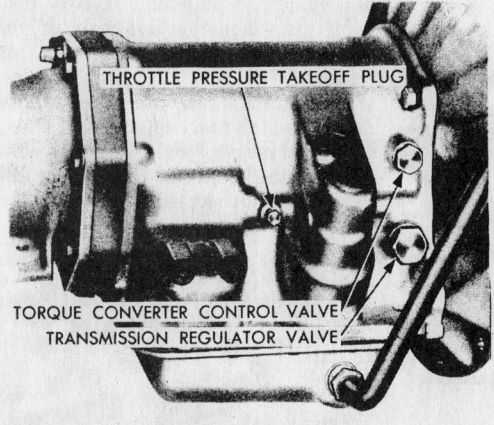

Fig. 3—View of right side of PowerFlite showing Throttle Pressure Takeoff Plug.

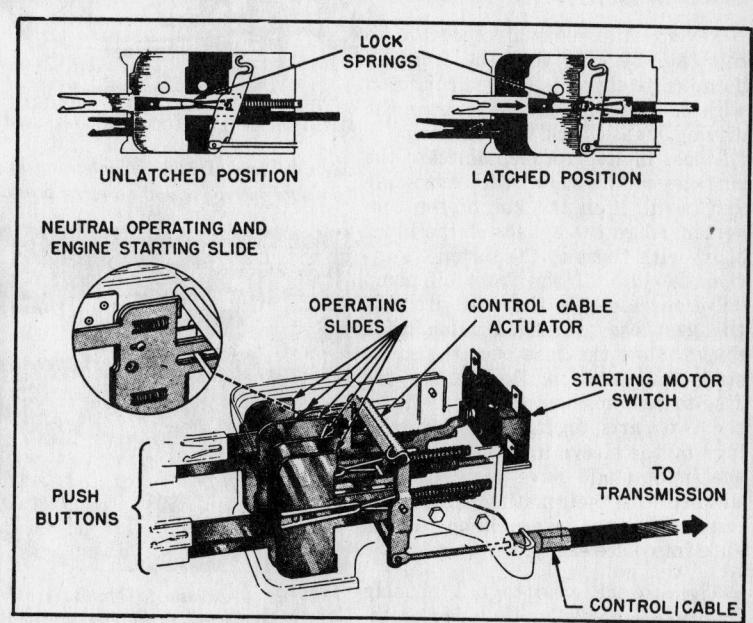

Typical Push Button Mechanism—1957-63 Models

195

CHRYSLER

Disconnect the front propeller shaft universal joint and tie the shaft up out of the way. Remove the adjusting screw cover plate and the clamp bolt from the hand brake support. Disengage the hand brake cable from the operating lever.

Disconnect the speedometer cable from the rear extension. Disconnect the wires from the back up light and neutral safety switches and unclip the wires from the cross member. Disconnect the operating rods from the transmission levers. Disconnect the two oil cooler lines at the left side of the case and remove the bracket holding the lines to the cylinder block. Unfasten the exhaust pipe bracket from the transmission case.

Remove the two nuts and lockwashers that hold the engine rear cross member supporting insulator to the cross-member, leaving the insulator attached to the transmission. On reinstalling tighten to 30-35 ft. lbs.

Raise the engine slightly by means of a jack and unbolt and remove the cross-member.

Lower the engine slightly and remove the two upper transmission case to bell housing bolts. Install guide studs in their place so that no weight comes on the front oil pump drive sleeve. Be careful not to lower the engine more than three inches or the hoses and linkages at the engine will be damaged.

Remove the two lower case to bell housing screws. Slide the transmission case back on the guide pins until it is free of the oil pump drive sleeve then take the case on down and away.

INSTALLATION OF THE TRANSMISSION

Reverse the removal procedure to reinstall. Be sure that the front oil pump drive sleeve is in good condition with no burrs or signs of wear on the driving lugs. Check the seal ring for freeness in its groove. Lubricate the surfaces of the sleeve with lubriplate and install it in the hub of the converter. Align the splines of the input shaft with those of the turbine. Position the lugs of the front oil pump drive gear so that they will properly engage those of the oil pump drive sleeve. Slide the case over the guide studs into position. Do not use the case-to-bell housing screws to bring the two parts together. If the drive lugs of the sleeve and the splines of the input shaft have been properly aligned with their mating parts in the converter the transmission should slide into place easily.

Tighten the case to bell housing screws of 45-50 ft. lbs., the cross-member to frame bolts to 50-55 ft.

lbs., the propeller shaft nuts to 33-37 ft. lbs.

CONVERTER REMOVAL

Remove the transmission case from the car.

Turn the front wheels as far as they will go to the right and remove the starting motor. Unfasten twelve screws and remove the transmission case adapter plate from the bell housing. Remove the lower half of the flywheel bell housing. Check the runout of the rear hub of the converter. Runout should not exceed .004 in F.I.R.

Remove the eight nuts and lockwashers holding the converter to the crankshaft flange. Remove the converter from the crankshaft.

FLYWHEEL RING GEAR REPLACEMENT

The converter is a welded assembly and parts for it are not sold separately. The flywheel ring gear can be replaced. File off the retaining lugs and tap the ring gear off to the front. Heat the new one to about 150 deg. (using an oven, hot water, steam or a torch with slow flame) and push it

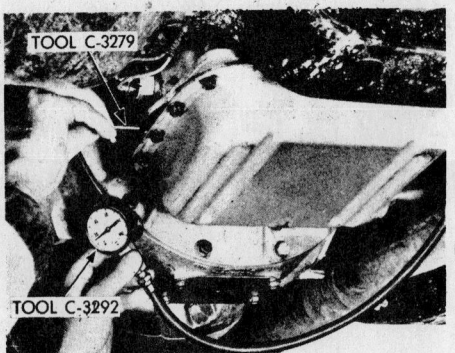

Left side view of PowerFlite showing location of line pressure test point and governor pressure test point

REAR EXTENSION BREATHER
OIL LINE TO OIL COOLER
OIL LINE FROM OIL COOLER
LINE PRESSURE TAKEOFF PLUG
KICKDOWN BAND ADJUSTING SCREW
THROTTLE CONTROL LEVER ASSY
MANUAL CONTROL LEVER ASSY
GOVERNOR PRESSURE TAKEOFF PLUG
BACK–UP LIGHT SWITCH
THROTTLE VALVE ADJUSTING SCREW PLUG
NEUTRAL STARTER SWITCH

TOOL C-3279
TOOL C-3292

Fig. 4—Adjusting Throttle, Pressure Gauge is connected to throttle pressure test point on right side of transmission.

onto the converter so that it contacts the flange all around. Weld the new ring gear in place using as much metal on the welds as was filed off and placing the welds in the same spots.

Do not use an acetylene or oxyhydrogen torch as these will harm the converter.

Do use a D.C. welder that is set at straight polarity or an A.C. welder. Use 200 Amps and a 5/32 in. rod equivalent to a Fleet Weld No. 47 or a G.E. No. W28.

The Arc should be directed at the intersection of the front face of the gear with the converter at an angle of 45 deg.

CONVERTER INSTALLATION

Check the runout of the crankshaft flange; it should not exceed .002 in. F.I.R. Reverse the procedure for removal to reinstall the converter. Check the runout of the rear hub of the converter after it has been bolted to the crankshaft flange. Runout should not exceed .004 in. F.I.R. See paragraph in Torque-Flite Section for corrective procedure.

TORQUEFLITE

ADJUSTMENTS

MANUAL CONTROL CABLE

Drain about two quarts of oil from the transmission and remove the starter safety switch. (Neutral starter switch Fig. 1) With the "R" button pushed in, remove the clip, flat washer, lock washer and screw which hold the cable sheath at the transmission. Block movement of the control lever inside the transmission by means of a screwdriver thru the starter safety switch hole. With the lever so held in reverse position move the cable sheath in as far as it will go and mark it where it enters the cable housing. Now pull cable sheath out as far as it will come and mark again. Now push cable into housing one half of distance between the two marks and fasten with the clip, washer, lock washer and screw. Reinstall starter safety switch and replace fluid. Check that starter will only operate when "N" button is in. In most cases distance will not exceed 3/32 inch.

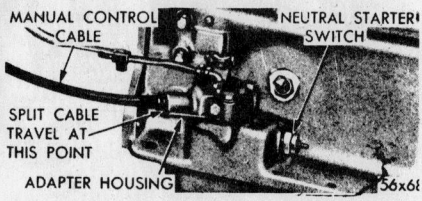

MANUAL CONTROL CABLE
NEUTRAL STARTER SWITCH
SPLIT CABLE TRAVEL AT THIS POINT
ADAPTER HOUSING

Fig. 1—Manual control cable adjustment at transmission

RENEW PUSH BUTTON UNIT LIGHT BULB

Remove the three bezel retaining screws (one screw is located on underside of unit) and the bezel. Pull the "D" button off its slider and so gain clearance to remove the bulb. Install new bulb. Compress ends of slider and push "D" button back in place thereon. Use a small screwdriver to assure that ends of slider are firmly seated in rear of plastic "D" button.

RENEW BACK-UP LIGHT SWITCH

The back-up light switch is fastened to the push button unit by four tabs. Remove the push button control unit from the dash. Straighten the tabs and remove the switch.

REMOVING PUSH BUTTON UNIT FROM DASH

Remove the three bezel retaining screws (one screw is located on underside) and remove bezel. Fig. 2. This will expose the two hex nuts and washers which hold the unit to the dash. Remove the unit to the back of the dash. Remove the two screws holding cable assembly bracket to the unit and then remove the clip which holds the cable to the unit. Unfasten the wires from the back-up light switch. Note that the wire to the light in the unit comes over the upper stud and down between the sliders. The bracket which holds the light fits over the upper stud. Reverse the procedure to reinstall.

THROTTLE LINKAGE ADJUSTMENT

With the engine idling in Neutral adjust idle speed to 475-500 rpm. Check that choke is fully open, after engine has run until it has reached normal operating temperature.

Stop engine and adjust throttle rod at carburetor so that throttle lever on transmission is back against its stop. Fig. 3. With rod preloaded to maintain transmission throttle lever at stop and carburetor throttle lever against idle-speed-adjusting-screw, tighten the throttle linkage adjusting screw to 7-9 ft. lbs. Do not disturb rod adjustment at transmission end.

Fig. 4—Push button unit behind dash

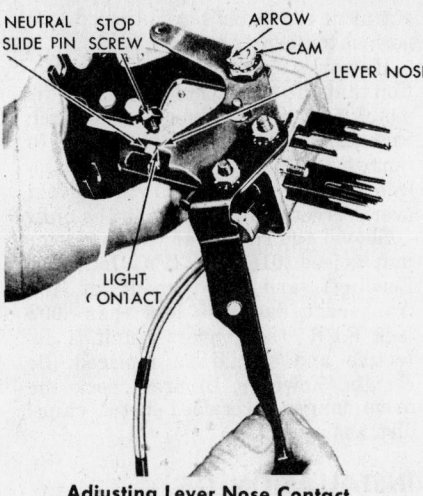

Adjusting Lever Nose Contact at Neutral Slide Pin

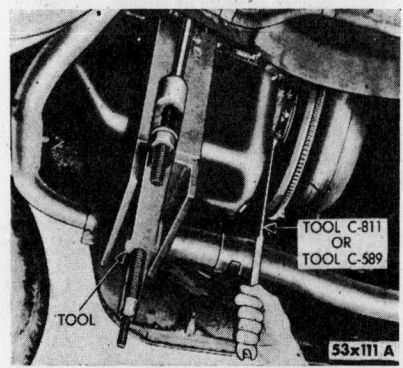

Fig. 3—Throttle lever and linkage

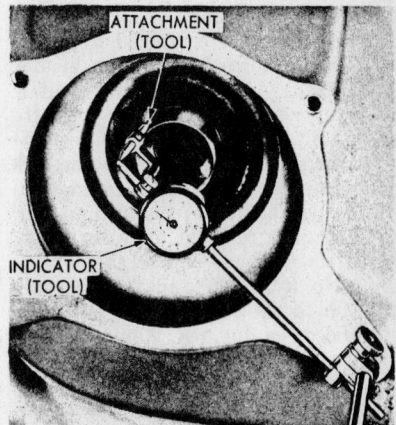

MANUAL CONTROL CABLE REMOVAL

Remove the push button control unit from the dash as in the preceding paragraph and remove the clip, screw and lock washer which holds the cable sheath to the housing on the left side of the transmission. Fig. 4.

Remove the plug in the side of the cable housing. Put a screwdriver thru the hole and release the spring lock, which fastens the cable to the lever,

Fig. 1—Removal of converter to flywheel stud nuts

at the same time pull the cable and sheath from the housing.

From inside the car pull the cable and sheath up thru the rubber grommet in the firewall.

Reverse procedure to reinstall and then apply paragraph on Manual Control Cable Adjustment.

PARTS THAT REQUIRE REMOVAL OF THE TRANSMISSION FROM THE CAR

REMOVAL OF TRANSMISSION AND CONVERTER

The transmission is removed as a unit first and then the torque converter.

Note: All Chrysler Corporation Torque Converters are welded units and require special equipment to rebuild.

Disconnect the battery. Push in the "1" button so the manual control cable can be removed. See paragraph on "Manual Control Cable Removal." Drain the transmission and converter. Disconnect the filler pipe. Disconnect the front universal joint and hang the propeller shaft up out of the way. Remove hand brake adjusting screw cover plate and disconnect hand brake cable and other parts as per paragraphs on "Rear Extension" and "Valve Bodies and Transfer Plate Assembly."

Remove the starter. Install engine support fixture. Raise engine slightly and remove crossmember. Replace two transmission case to torque converter housing bolts on right side with guide pins and then remove two case to housing bolts from left side. Slide transmission straight back to avoid damage to the front oil pump driving sleeve and lower transmission to the floor.

Unbolt and remove the converter housing bolts. Although most mechanics do not do so, it is recommend-

Fig. 2—Checking that runout of Torque Converter Hub does not exceed .004"

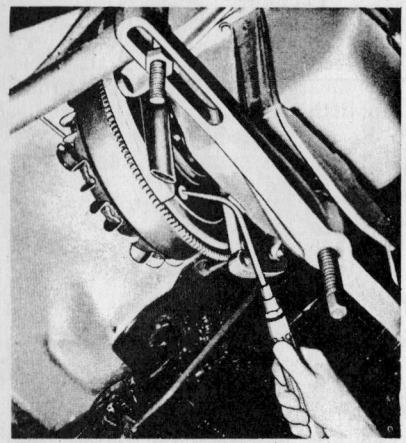

Fig. 3—Heat spot on front cover of converter opposite to mark on back face indicating low spot of converter hub

ed that the runout of the converter hub be checked before the converter is removed from the crankshaft. Using an indicator as shown in Fig. 2, check runout of converter hub (runout should not exceed .004 inch F.I.R.) and mark both converter and crankshaft flange so that the true source of any runout may be found. Be sure to match mark the converter to the shaft flange so that it may be assembled in the same position. Remove eight torque converter stud nuts and lock washers to release the converter from the crankshaft flange. See Fig. 1. Check runout of flange; it should not exceed .002 inch. If it does, use shims between converter and flange at reassembly to correct.

CORRECTING TORQUE CONVERTER RUNOUT

Note: Throughout this procedure the converter has no oil in it and the drain plugs are in place. This procedure is applicable to any Chrysler Corporation Torque Converter.

Runout of the converter hub should not exceed .004 inch. If it does, the condition may be corrected by using a torch as shown in Fig. 3 to heat a spot about ½ inch in diameter at a point on the front face of the converter opposite the low-spot of hub runout. The size of the spot to be heated depends on the amount of runout. It should be about ½ inch in diameter for .008 inch of total indicator reading. Using an acetylene torch containing a No. 3 tip set to maximum heat, apply it to the selected spot until the spot becomes dull red. Rapid heating and then cooling of an isolated area is the secret of the process. If all is well, the spot comes to color in a few seconds. The area is then quenched as rapidly as possible with a hose or wet rags. Do not attempt to recheck run-

out until converter has returned to a normal temperature.

If sparks are noted it is an indication that the torch is too close and the metal is starting to burn; move torch back slightly. Care should be taken to remove the torch the instant the selected spot becomes a dull red to avoid over-correction or damage to the unit.

Should the runout of the converter hub exceed .016 inch (Full Indicator Reading) and yet runout of the crankshaft flange is less than .002 inch F.I.R., the converter unit is defective and should be replaced. Be certain, however, to first check the drive flanges for raised metal, chips, dirt, and such.

INSTALLATION OF CONVERTER

When reinstalling, install the eight converter stud nuts and lock washers and tighten evenly (no specification for proper torque is given). Recheck that hub runout does not exceed .004 inch F.I.R. Place torque converter housing over the locating dowels and into position against the block-to-housing adapter plate. Install the housing to plate screws with lock washers and tighten evenly to 25-30 ft. lbs.

Note: The bore of the housing must be concentric to the hub of the converter within .010". Adjustment is made by turning the slot-ended housing-locating dowels or by installing different dowels available for the purpose. The rear face of the housing should be perpendicular to the converter hub within .008". Adjustment is made by shims between the housing and the adapter plate.

INSTALLATION OF TRANSMISSION

Install guide pins in the two transmission mounting holes in right side of torque converter housing. Lubricate and install front oil pump drive sleeve into transmission, making sure the driving lugs correctly engage the front oil pump pinion. Main position of drive sleeve will be flush with front of pump housing if sleeve is properly installed.

Position lugs on converter end of drive sleeve to engage drive lugs visible in hub of converter. Line up splines of reaction shaft and input shaft with those of stator and turbine in the converter.

Slide transmission along guide pins into place against converter housing. Check that the driving lugs and splines are properly engaged. Everything should go into place easily. If force seems necessary, it is likely that the input shaft or drive sleeve is not

properly aligned with splines or lugs in converter.

Install the two left hand transmission case to torque converter housing screws, but do not tighten. Remove the two guide pins and install the two right hand transmission case to torque converter housing screws and lock washers. Now tighten all four screws evenly and torque to 40-50 ft. lbs. Reinstall crossmember and tighten bolts to 50-55 ft. lbs. Lower engine and at the same time align mounting studs in insulator with holes in the crossmember. Install the two nuts and lock washers that hold the engine and transmission rear support insulator to the crossmember and torque from 30-35 ft. lbs. Remove the engine supporting device. Reinstall the other parts which were removed. Tighten oil pan to filler tube nut to 35-40 ft. lbs. Tighten propeller shaft flange nut to 200 ft. lbs. Tighten front universal joint nuts to 33-37 ft. lbs.

UNIVERSAL JOINTS AND DRIVE LINE

Thru 1956 Models

Universal joints on all Chrysler models built thru 1956 are the cross and yoke type and there is no adjustment provided for wear at any point.

If the universal joint requires service, new parts must be installed to correct for wear.

A quick check on the condition of the universal joint can be had by running the car very slowly on a very smooth road and depressing the clutch at about 15 miles per hour, letting the car slowly come down to about 8 miles an hour. A loose universal joint has a tendency to rattle at very low speed under no load.

If a little rattle goes out as soon as the clutch is engaged or if no rattle is heard if the clutch is left engaged, the universal joint will at least bear looking into.

Jack up the car sufficiently high so that the operator can work easily under the car. Examine either the front or the rear universal joint and notice that two of the bearing blocks on each universal joint are bolted to their yokes, the two front ones are bolted to the transmission yoke, the two back ones are bolted to the pinion shaft yoke.

Remove the bolts which hold these bearing blocks to their respective flanges, and the drive shaft can be lifted out from under the car.

Since each of these bearing blocks has a small tongue which is sometimes a tight fit, it may be necessary

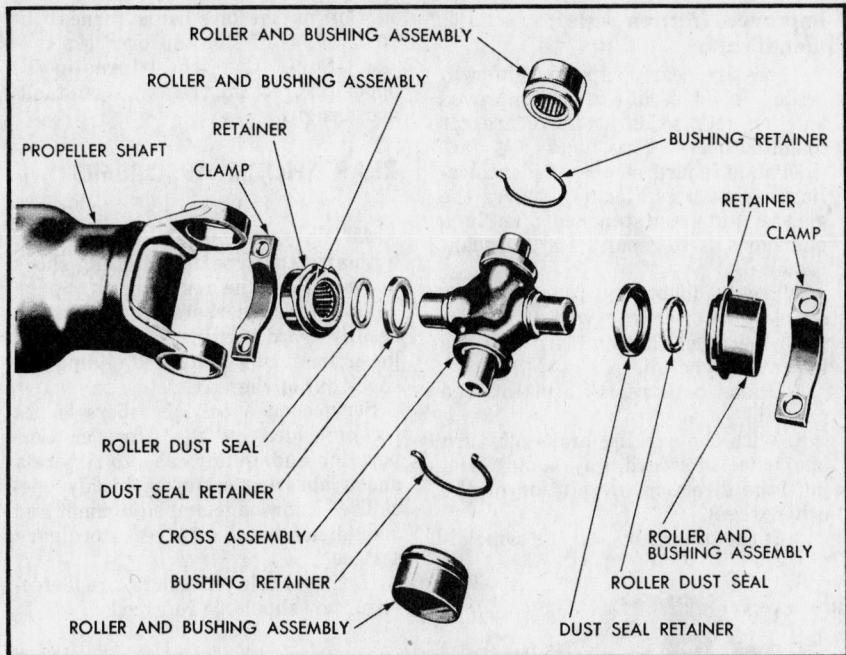

ROLLER AND BUSHING ASSEMBLY
ROLLER AND BUSHING ASSEMBLY
RETAINER
CLAMP
PROPELLER SHAFT
BUSHING RETAINER
RETAINER
CLAMP
ROLLER DUST SEAL
DUST SEAL RETAINER
CROSS ASSEMBLY
BUSHING RETAINER
ROLLER AND BUSHING ASSEMBLY
ROLLER AND BUSHING ASSEMBLY
ROLLER DUST SEAL
DUST SEAL RETAINER

Cross and Bearing Type Universal Point Similar to Cross and Yoke Type

to jolt the universal joint apart. However, it should not require a hammer, simply a jolt with the hand should be enough to free it. On the drive shaft yokes, the universal joint cross is held by lock rings on the inside of the bearing. These lock rings are fitted into grooves on the inside of the bearing cup. Drive out the lock rings and, using a flat punch, drive the universal joint from one side across to the other, which will knock the bearing out of the opposite side.

Once the bearing is taken out of the yoke, the cross can be driven toward the other side to knock out the opposite bearing.

To replace these two round bearings, it is customary to use an arbor press to insure that they start in a straight line.

They are sometimes difficult to replace, since the new oil seals found on new bearings have to be crushed somewhat against the universal joint cross.

This is the reason for using an arbor press to install the cross bearings.

The pillow block bearings are simply slipped on to the opposite side of the cross and unbolted in the reverse of the procedure which removed them.

Starting with 1957

A cross and bearing type universal joint is used at the back end of the driveshaft and a pin and trunnion type at the front end. The Imperial uses three cross type joints.

To remove the driveshaft and/or the universal joints, first remove the bolts which hold the rear universal joint cross bearing to the pinion shaft and split that universal joint.

Remove the four bolts which hold the housing at the front universal joint to the back of the hand brake drum and take the driveshaft down and to a bench.

On the bench remove the lock rings which hold the cross bearings to the rear end of the driveshaft and pressing the one side, press the bearing out the other side.

Once the first bearing is out, the opposite side bearing can be pressed out readily by pushing simply across to the other side.

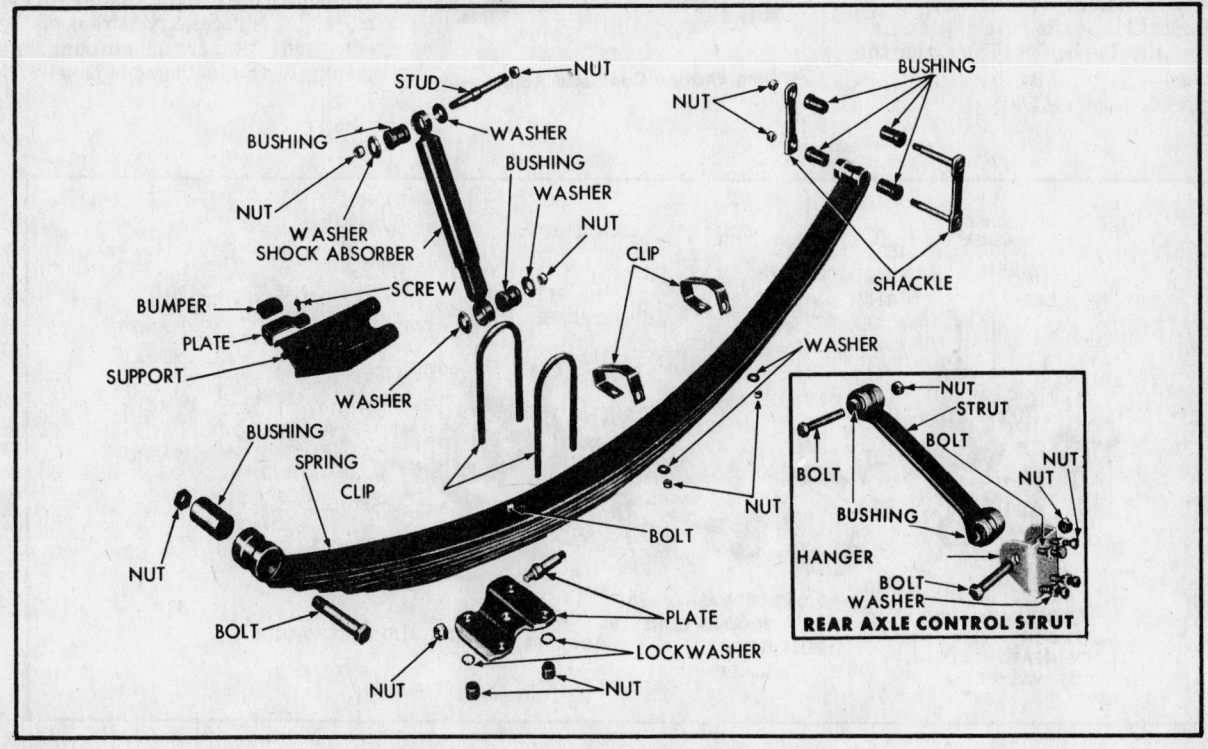

STUD
NUT
BUSHING
NUT
BUSHING
NUT
WASHER
BUSHING
WASHER
WASHER
NUT
SHOCK ABSORBER
CLIP
SHACKLE
BUMPER
SCREW
PLATE
WASHER
SUPPORT
WASHER
BUSHING
WASHER
SPRING
CLIP
NUT
BOLT
NUT
BOLT
PLATE
LOCKWASHER
NUT
NUT

REAR AXLE CONTROL STRUT
NUT
STRUT
BOLT
BOLT
NUT
NUT
BUSHING
HANGER
BOLT
WASHER

Rear Spring and Shackles (Disassembled View)

CHRYSLER

To disassemble the front universal joint slide the housing back off the trunnion balls, remove the two balls and then press the cross pin out of the front of the driveshaft ball.

The housing can then be slid off the front of the driveshaft.

UNIVERSAL JOINT CENTER BEARING

On most of the 8-passenger models and all of the Imperial models, a center bearing is used on the drive shaft. This center bearing is bolted to an insulator block to a frame cross member.

On these models it is necessary to unbolt the pillow block in order to lower the driveshaft.

However, the procedure for detaching the universal joints is the same except that it will be necessary to take down the pillow block in order to get the driveshaft out from under the car.

REAR AXLE AND SUSPENSION

TROUBLE SHOOTING AND ADJUSTMENT

General instructions covering the troubles of the rear axle and how to repair and adjust it, together with information on installation of rear axle bearings and grease seals, are given in the Unit Repair section under the heading: Axles, Rear.

Capacities of the rear axle are given in the Capacities Tables of this section.

Improved Traction Axle Identification

There are nearly as many different trade names used for the improved traction rear axles as there are car manufacturers. This, and the fact that no standard means of identification has been established, leaves the general auto maintenance man in a quandary as to repairs and lubricant required.

When in doubt, the following is a simple rule-of-thumb way to distinguish between the standard and the improved type units.

1. Raise both rear wheels off the ground.

2. With the parking brake off, turn one wheel forward (by hand) and note the direction of rotation of the other wheel.

3. If the other turns in the same direction as the one being turned, the rear axle is of the improved type.

4. If the other wheel turns in the opposite direction, the axle is of standard design.

REAR SHOCK ABSORBERS

All Chrysler models are equipped with airplane type direct acting shock absorbers on the rear axle.

The shock absorbers can be removed readily by detaching the upper and lower mounting bolts and sliding the shock out of the way.

Service on shock absorbers is not recommended by the Chrysler Corporation and, in any case, to service a shock absorber requires highly specialized knowledge and equipment and should not be attempted in ordinary service.

If the shock absorbers are defective, they should be replaced.

Scribing Bearing Caps and Adjusters

RADIO R & R

All Models

On Newport, Windsor, New Yorker, without Air Conditioning and all Imperials disconnect battery, remove support bracket, disconnect all lead wires, remove control knobs and shaft mountings and lower from under the panel.

On all with Air Conditioning except Imperial it is necessary to remove the radio and speaker up through the opening in the instrument panel.

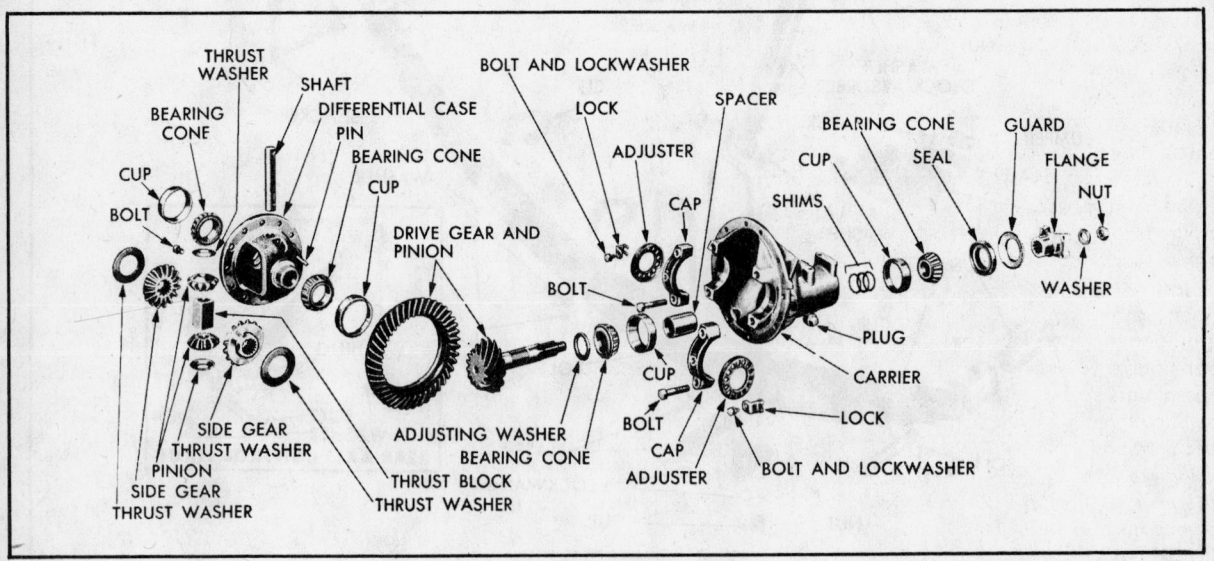

Rear Axle (Disassembled View)
(Pinion with Spacer)

BRAKES, HYDRAULIC

Adjustments	938
Bleed brakes	941
Foot brake	207
Parking brake lever & cable	207

COOLING SYSTEM

Blower, R & R	219
Oil cooler	209
Thermostat, R & R	209

CLUTCH

Clutch assembly, R & R	223
Clutch linkage, adjust	222

ELECTRICAL SYSTEM

Battery	207
Delcotron references	206
Distributor specifications	203
Fuses and circuit breakers	204
Gauges	1020
Generator regulator specifications	203
General regulators, R & R	205
Generator service	1026
Generator trouble shooting chart	1026
Ignition firing order & timing	202
Ignition timing procedure	205
Ignition timing specifications	203
Starter, R & R	207
Starter specifications	203
Starter system	207

ENGINE ASSEMBLY

Crankcase cover assembly	219*
Cylinder head, R & R	218
Cylinder head tightening sequence	217
Engine assembly	216
Engine disassemble	215
Engine firing order & timing	202
Engine references	214
Engine marking code	202
Oil pan, R & R	219
Oil pressure specifications	204
Piston and pin specifications	204
Rear housing, renew	217*
Rear main bearing oil seal	219
Specifications, general, engine	204
Specifications, tune-up, engine	203
Timing gears	216*
Tune-up specifications	203
Valve adjusting sequence	214
Valve lifters, hydraulic, service	214
Valve specifications	204
Valves	214

ENGINE LUBRICATION

Oil cooler	209
Oil pump	218

EXHAUST SYSTEM

Exhaust & tail pipe	209
Muffler, R & R	209

FUEL SYSTEM

Carburetors and linkage	207
Carburetor specifications	972
Fuel gauge service	1024
Fuel system	207
Fuel pump, R & R	209
Fuel pump service	1021
Fuely tank, R & R	209

INSTRUMENTS

Heat indicator	210
Ignition switch	206
Speedometer, R & R	206
Telltale light	210

POWER TRAIN

Assembling power train	213*
Power train, install	214*
Power train, remove	214*
Separating power train	212*

REAR AXLE AND SUSPENSION

Axle shaft and bearing	235
Differential carrier recondition	237*
Pinion shaft rear oil seal	237*
Rear wheel toe-in	219
Riding height	220
Ring gear and pinion adjustment	238*
Shock absorbers, rear	221
Side bearing adjusting sleeve	235
Spring, rear, R & R	221

SPECIFICATIONS

Battery	203
Brake cylinder sizes	203
Capacities:	
Axle, rear	204
Cooling system	204
Crankcase	204
Fuel tank	204
Transmission, automatic	204
Transmission, manual	204
Chassis, general	203
Delcotron specifications	203
Distributor	203
Engine, general	204
Engine tune-up	203
Fuses and circuit breakers	204
Generator regulators	203
Generators	203

SPECIFICATIONS—continued

Light bulbs	204
Main bearings	204
Model identification illustrations	202
Pistons and pins	204
Quick reference specifications	202
Rod bearings	204
Starters	203
Torque wrench	204
Tune-up	203
Valves	204
Wheel alignment	205

STEERING, MANUAL

Gear assembly, R & R	222
Steering gear, adjust	222
Steering wheel, R & R	222

SUSPENSION, FRONT

Alignment	1082
Alignment specifications	205
Ball joints, R & R	1087
Camber, adjust	1082
Caster, adjust	1082
Coil springs	220
Riding height	220
Support arms, pins and bushings	221
Toe-in, adjust	219

TRANSMISSION, AUTOMATIC

Assembly of transmission	232
Band adjustment	226
Control cable	227
Converter	232*
Disassembly of transmission	229*
General information	225
Governor & valve body	227
Safety switch adjustment	226
Shift linkage, adjust	225
Throttle linkage	226
Transmission, recondition	229*
Transmission, R & R	229*
Trouble shooting	234
Vacuum modulator	227

TRANSMISSION, STANDARD

Gearshift linkage, adjust	223
Transmission, R & R	224*

TUNE-UP

Carburetors	207
Engine diagnosis	1012
Procedures	205
Spark plugs	205
Specifications	203

UNIVERSAL JOINT AND AXLE

Universal joint and axle bearing 235
*Requires Power Train Removal

CORVAIR

YEAR IDENTIFICATION

SERIAL NUMBER

The serial number is located on the left front door lock pillar. This number identifies the vehicle type, model year, assembly plant and the production unit number.

ENGINE IDENTIFICATION

The engine number is stamped on top of the engine block, just forward of the generator—oil filter adapter. It consists of six units, the first unit is a letter and identifies the point of

manufacture. The next two digits show the month of manufacture and the next two digits show the day of manufacture. The last unit is a letter and identifies the type of transmission used.

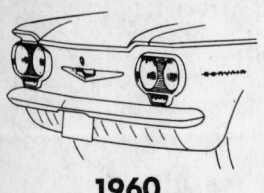
1960

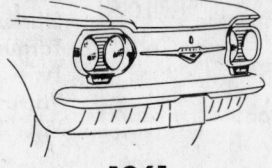
1961

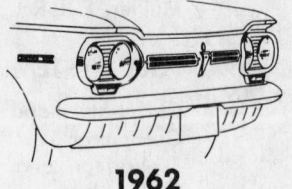
1962

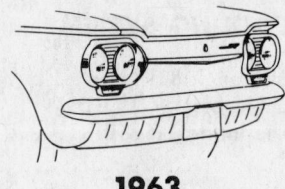
1963

QUICK WORKING SPECIFICATIONS

DISTRIBUTOR SPECIFICATIONS

Make	Delco-Remy
Type of advance	Centrifugal & Vacuum
Point gap 1960	.016″
1961-63	.019″
Point spring tension	19-23 oz.
Cam dwell	31°-35°

IGNITION TIMING

At idle Synchromesh 4° BTDC
Powerglide 13° BTDC
Superengine 13° BTDC

SPARK PLUGS

Year	Type	Gap
1960	44-FF	.035
1961-63	44-FF & 46-FF	.035

GENERATOR AND REGULATOR SPECIFICATIONS

D.C. GENERATOR

Delco-Remy	12 volt
Field current	1.50 to 1.60 amps. @ 80°F.
Brush tension	28 oz.

REGULATOR

Cut-out relay
Air gap	.020″
Closing voltage	11.8 to 13.5 volts
Current & voltage reg. air gap	.075″
Current regulator setting	27-33 amps.
Voltage regulator setting	13.8-14.8 volts @ 125°F

DELCOTRON SPECIFICATIONS
See Following Pages

COMPRESSION PRESSURE

1960	130 lbs.
1961-63	140 lbs.

CAPACITIES

Engine Crankcase (Qts.)
1960-63	4

Transmission, Synchro. (Pts.)
1960-63 3-speed	2
1961-63 4-speed	3⅓

Transmission, Automatic (Pts.)
1960-63 Refill	13

Rear Axle (in Pints)
1960-63	3.1

Gasoline Tank (Gallons)
1960	11
1961-63 exc. Sports Wagon	14
Sports Wagon	18½

FUSES AND CIRCUIT BREAKERS

A circuit breaker in the light control switch protects the headlamp circuit, thus eliminating one fuse. Other protection is comprised of fuses, located in a JUNCTION BLOCK, under the dash.

FUSES

Glove compartment lamp	
Heater blower	3 AG/AGC-10 amp.
Tail and stoplight, dome light	
Cigarette lighter	3 AG/AGC-10 amp.
Heater (total system)	
Back-up lamp	3 AG/AGC-15 amp.
Radio	3 AG/AGC-4 amp.
Instrument panel lamp	3 AG/AGC-3 amp.

VALVES

Operating Tappet Clearance
1960-63 all	Zero

WHEEL ALIGNMENT

Caster (Degrees)
1960-63	½P to 2P

Camber (Degrees)
1960-63	0 to 1P

Toe-In (inches) Front
1960	Total....⅛ to 3/16
1961-63	Total....¼ to ⅜

Toe-In (inches) Rear
1960	Total....0 to ¼
1961-63	Total....⅛ to ⅜

King Pin Inclination (Degrees)
1960-63	7°

FIRING ORDER and TIMING

SPARK OCCURS:

1960—First Type 1/3 Distance Between "O" and "A" Marks
1961-63—Second Type—4° BTDC
1962-63, Automatic Transmission 13° BTDC

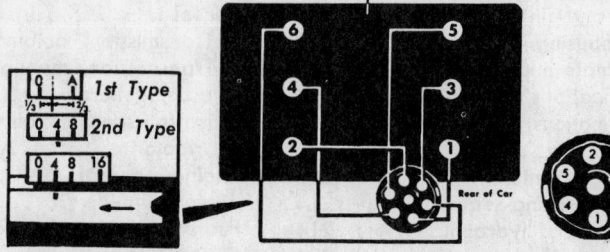

NOTE

THESE ARE APPROXIMATE SETTINGS. ENGINE DESIGN, ALTITUDE, TEMPERATURE, FUEL AND ENGINE CONDITION WILL ALL INFLUENCE TIMING. THE DETERMINING FACTOR, LIMITING ADVANCE, WILL STILL BE THE "KNOCK POINT" OF THE ENGINE.

TUNE-UP SPECIFICATIONS

Year		Spark Plug: Make and Number AC	Spark Plug: Gap	Distributor: Cam Angle	Distributor: Point Gap	Distributor: Arm Spring Tension	Ignition Timing	Compression Pressure Cranking	Valves Tappet Clearance Hot: Ex.	Valves Tappet Clearance Hot: In.	Timing Inlet Opens	Fuel Pump Pressure	Engine Speed Idle Neutral
1960		44FF	.035	33°	.016	21	4B	130	Hyd.	Hyd.	43B	.21	450-500
1961-1962	w/Synchromesh	46FF	.035	33°	.019	21	4B	140	Hyd.	Hyd.	43B	5¾	450-500
	w/Powerglide	46FF	.035	33°	.019	21	13B	140	Hyd.	Hyd.	43B	5¾	475-500
	High Cam Engine	46FF	.035	33°	.019	21	13B	140	Hyd.	Hyd.	54B	5¾	450-500
	Monza w/Powerglide	46FF	.035	33°	.019	21	13B	140	Hyd.	Hyd.	54B	5¾	450-500
1963	w/Synchromesh	46FF	.037	33°	.019	21	4B	130	Hyd.	Hyd.	43B*	5¾	500
	w/Pwr. Glide	46FF	.037	33°	.019	21	13B	130	Hyd.	Hyd.	43B*	5¾	500
	Monza w/Pwr. Glide	44FF	.037	33°	.019	21	13B	140	Hyd.	Hyd.	43B*	5¾	500
	Power Pack	44FF	.037	33°	.019	21	13B	140	Hyd.	Hyd.	54B*	5¾	600
	Turbo Charged	44FF	.037	33°	.019	21	24B	130	Hyd.	Hyd.	54B*	5¾	850

*Including Cam Ramps

DELCO-REMY DISTRIBUTOR SPECIFICATIONS

Year		Delco Remy No.	Rotation	Cam Angle Degrees	Point Gap (inches)	Breaker Arm Spring Tension	Governor Control: @ Dist. Adv. Starts	Governor Control: R.P.M. Full Adv.	Vacuum Control Data: Inches to Start Adv.	Vacuum Control Data: Inches for Full Adv.	Vacuum Control Data: Max. Adv. In Degrees
1960-61	w/Synchromesh	1110258	C	33	.016	21	1@200	16@1800	6	15¼	11½
	w/Powerglide	1110259	C	33	.016	21	1@850	10@1800	7	16¼	11½
	High Cam Engine	1110260	C	33	.016	21	1@350	12@2400	6	15¼	11½
1962	w/Synchromesh	1110269	C	33	.019	21	1@200	16@1800	6	15¼	11½
	w/Powerglide	1110271	C	33	.019	21	1@850	10@1800	7	16¼	11½
	High Cam Engine	1110272	C	33	.019	21	1@350	12@2400	6	15¼	11½
	Monza w/Powerglide	1110278	C	33	.019	21	1@925	10@2050	7	16¼	11½
1963	w/Synchromesh	1110294	C	33	.019	21	1@600	34@3600	6	16	24½
	w/Pwr. Glide	1110295	C	33	.019	21	1@1400	26@3700	7	17	24½
	Monza w/Pwr. Glide	1110297	C	33	.019	21	1@1600	22@4100	7	17	24½
	Power Pack	1110296	C	33	.019	21	1@700	26@4800	6	16	24½
	Turbo-charged	1110298	C	33	.019	21	1@3900	12@4500	—	—	

GENERATOR AND REGULATOR SPECIFICATIONS

Year	Generators: Field Current in Amperes at 6V	Generators: Field Current in Amperes at 12V	Generators: Brush Spring Tension	Regulators: Cut Out Relay Air Gap	Regulators: Cut Out Relay Closing Voltage	Regulators: Current and Voltage Regulator Air Gap	Regulators: Current Regulator Setting	Regulators: Voltage Regulator Setting
1960-63		1.5	28 oz.	.020	12.6	.075	30	14.3 ± .5

DELCOTRON AND A.C. REGULATOR SPECIFICATI ONS

Delcotron Model Number	Ground Polarity	Field Current Draw (Amperes)	Current Output: Engine R.P.M.	Current Output: Amperes	Current Output: Volts	Running Voltage: Engine R.P.M.	Running Voltage: Amperes	Running Voltage: Volts @ 125°	Regulator: Model Number	Regulator: Point Gap	Field Relay: Armature Air Gap	Field Relay: Closing Voltage
1100600	Neg.	1.9-2.2	1100	12.0	14	6500	42	13.5-14.3	1119502	.015	.015	6.5-8.5
1100601	Neg.	1.9-2.2	1100	5.0	14	6500	52	13.5-14.3	1119502	.015	.015	6.5-8.5
1117765*	Neg.	4.1-4.5	1100	24.0	14	6500	62	13.3-13.9	9000567	.027	.014	5.0-9.5

NOTE: Standard Delcotron is 5.5" dia., heavy duty unit is 6.0" dia. (heavy duty unit identified in chart by asterisk*).

BATTERY AND STARTER SPECIFICATIONS

Year	Battery: Ampere Hour Capacity	Battery: Volts	Battery: Group Number	Battery: Terminal Grounded	Starters: Lock Test Amps	Starters: Lock Test Volts	Starters: Lock Test Torque	Starters: No-load Test Amps	Starters: No-load Test Volts	Starters: No-load Test RPM	Starters: Brush Spring Tension
1960-63	35	12	NA	Neg.	NA	NA	NA	70	10.6	7100	35

CIRCUIT BREAKER

A circuit breaker in the light control switch protects the headlamp circuit. Where the current load is too heavy, the circuit breaker will rapidly open and close, protecting the circuit until the cause is found and corrected.

GENERAL CHASSIS AND BRAKE SPECIFICATIONS

Year and Model	Chassis: Overall Length in Inches	Chassis: Tire Size	Brake Cylinder Bore: Master Cylinder Inches	Brake Cylinder Bore: Wheel Cylinder—Inches Front	Brake Cylinder Bore: Wheel Cylinder—Inches Rear
1960-63	180	6.50x13*	1	⅞	15/16

* Sports Wagon, 7.00 x 14

FUSES and LIGHT BULBS

LIGHT BULBS

LAMP	NUMBER	VALUE
Headlamp Unit—		
Outer: High Beam	37½ watt	4002 Sealed Beam
Low Beam	50 watt	4001 Sealed Beam
Inner: High Beam	37½ watt	
Parking Lamp &		
Turn Signal	4-32 cp	1034
Tail, Stop &		
Turn Signal	4-32	1034
Back-up	32	1073
Instrument	3	GE-1816
Turn Signal Indicator	2	57
Temperature—Oil		
Pressure Signal	2	57
Generator—Fan Signal	2	57
Headlight Beam	1	53
Indicator		

Ignition Lock	1	53
Glove Compartment	2	57
Dome (Cartridge Type)	15	211
Courtesy	6	89
License Plate	4	67
Rapid Dial	2	GE-1891
Heater Control Panel	1	53

FUSES

The fuses located in the junction block beneath the dash are:

Equipment	Fuse Value
Radio Panel Lamp	(A)
Heater Control Panel Lamp	(A)
Instrument Panel Lamp	(A)

Radio	(B)
Heater	(C)
Glove Comp. Lamp	(C)
Tail and Stop Lamps	(C)
Dome Lamp	(C)
Cigarette Lighter	(C)
Heater, (Total System)	(D)
Back-up Lamps	(D)

Code to Fuse Values

(A) = 3AG/AGC— 3 AMP
(B) = 3AG/AGC— 4 AMP
(C) = 3AG/AGC—10 AMP
(D) = 3AG/AGC—15 AMP

CAPACITIES

Year	Crankcase Refill Add 1 Quart for Filter	Transmissions			Rear Axle Pints	Gasoline Tank Gallons	Cooling System Quarts Add 1 Quart for Heater
		Manual, Pints		Automatic, Pints			
		3 Speed	4 Speed				
1960	4	2	None	12½	3.1	11	Air Cooled
1961-63 Ex. Sports Wagon	4	2	3⅓	12½	3.1	14	Air Cooled
Sports Wagon	4	2	3⅓	12½	3.1	18½	Air Cooled

GENERAL ENGINE SPECIFICATIONS

Year	Bore and Stroke	No. of Main Bearings	Type of Valve Lifters	Cu. In. Displacement	AMA Horse Power	Advertised Torque at Stated R.P.M.	Advertised H.P. at Stated R.P.M.	Compression Ratio	Oil Pressure at 35 M.P.H.	Camshaft Drive
1960	3.375x2.6	4	Hyd.	140	27.3	80@4400	125@2400	8.0:1	35	Gear
1961-63	3.4375x2.6	4	Hyd.	145	28.4	80@4400	128@2300	8.0:1	35	Gear
1963 Std. Engine	3.4375x2.6	4		145	27.3	80@4400	128@2300	8.0:1	35	GEAR
Power Pak	3.4375x2.6	4		145	28.4	102@4400	134@2900	9.0:1	35	GEAR
Turbo-Charged	3.4375x2.6	4		145	28.4	150@4400	210@3100	8.0:1	35	GEAR

CRANKSHAFT BEARING JOURNAL SIZES

Year	Main Bearing Journals				Connecting Rod Bearing Journals		
	Diameter	Oil Clearance	End Play of Shaft	End Play Held By	Diameter	Oil Clearance	End Play
1960	Note 1	.0025"	.004"	#1	1.7995 ± .0005	.0025 ± .0005	.0075"
1961-63	Note 2	.0018"	.004"	#1	1.7995 ± .0005	.0015 ± .0008	.0075"

Note 1: All main bearing journals = 2.0983" ± .0005"
Note 2: #1 & 2 journals = 2.1008" ± .0005".—journals #3 & 4 = 2.1013" ± .0005"

TORQUE SPECIFICATIONS (Ft. Lbs.)

Year	Cylinder Head Bolts	Rod Bearing Bolts	Crankcase LH to RH (Main Bearing)	Crankshaft Pulley Bolt	Flywheel to Crankshaft Bolts	Manifold	
						Intake	Exhaust
1960-61	27-33	20-26	42.48	60-80	20-26	None	12-27

PISTON AND PIN SPECIFICATIONS

Year and Model	PISTON				PISTON PIN		
	Skirt Clearance		Diameter	Bushing	FIT		
	MIN.	MAX.			In Rod		In Piston
1960-63	.0011"	.0015"	.7999"-.8002"	None	Press		.00015"-.00025"

VALVE SPECIFICATIONS

Year	Seat Angle		Intake Valve Lift	Exhaust Valve Lift	Valve Spring Pressure		Stem to Guide Clearance		Stem Diameter		Are Valve Guides Replaceable
	In	Ex			Outer	Inner	In.	Ex.	In. Note 1	Ex. Note 1	
1960-63 Standard Cam	45	45	.314	.344	61@1.508	None	.0018	.0023	.3415-.3422	.3414-.3404	No
High Lift Cam	45	45	.380	.380	74@1.696	None	.0018	.0023	.3415-.3422	.3314-.3404	No

Note 1: Exhaust valve stems have .001" taper.

FRONT WHEEL ALIGNMENT

Year	Caster		Camber		To-in (Inches)	King Pin Inclination (Degrees)	Wheel Pivot Ratio	
	Range Degrees	Preferred	Range (Degrees)	Preferred			Inner Wheel	Outer Wheel
1960	1½P to 2P	Note 2	0 to 1P	Note 2	Note 1	7.	32¾°	29½°
1961-63	1½P to 2P	Note 2	0 to 1	Note 2	Note 1	7.	20°	18°

Note 1: Front toe-in, ⅛"-3/16" total. Rear toe-in, ⅛"-⅜" total.   Note 2: Within ¼° of opposite side.

TUNE-UP

Engine Tune-Up and Diagnosis Go Hand-in-Hand, Therefore, A Plan Of Approach Should Be Established To Best Serve Both Ends

1. Remove plug wires.
2. Blow foreign matter from around spark plugs with compressed air. Then loosen spark plugs one turn.
3. Replace plug wires, start engine and snap throttle open for one second. (This should clear the engine of dislodged carbon particles.)
4. Stop engine and remove plug wire, then remove spark plugs. (Use an "O" ring equipped, or a magnetized type plug socket to prevent dropping the plug into the engine shroud assembly.)
5. Remove air cleaner and both carburetors. (With the use of special compression gauge adapter, carburetor removal is not necessary.)
6. Hook up starter remote control cable and switch. Then crank the engine through about four compression strokes.
7. Check and record the maximum pressure of each cylinder. Minimum pressure should be 130 pounds and variation between cylinders should not exceed 20 pounds.

Note:

A compression check should be the the first step in the course of events to comprise a good engine tune-up. Only if compression is within limits, should the tune-up be continued.

SPARK PLUGS

Use a good spark plug tester, if available, and service or renew spark plugs. Detailed information on diagnosing spark plug troubles, and using spark plug condition as an aid in engine diagnosis, can be found in the Unit Repair section, under Tune-Up.

In spark plug installation, be sure of the following:
A. Use plugs of correct model, spaced properly.
B. Thoroughly clean cylinder head and spark plug threads.
C. Carefully torque the spark plugs to 20-25 ft. lb.

Note:

Be certain the spark plug covers are tightly in place. If any are loose, air pressure in the cooling system will be lost and serious engine overheating can result. A whistling sound may also develop that can be difficult to locate.

DISTRIBUTOR

The distributor is located on the right side of the engine, at the rear. It is driven through a helical gear by the crankshaft. The distributor shaft is extended into the crankcase area to drive the oil pump.

REMOVAL

1. Disconnect distributor primary wire.
2. Remove distributor cap.
3. Remove vacuum control line.
4. Mark position of rotor to simplify timing at the time of reinstallation.
5. Remove distributor clamp, then lift out distributor.
6. If removal of secondary wires from the cap is necessary, mark number "1" location on the cap tower. Consult the timing location and firing order diagram in this section for firing order and location data.

INSTALLATION, IF ENGINE HAS BEEN DISTURBED

1. With #1 piston coming up on compression stroke, continue cranking the engine until the pulley timing notch lines up with the "O" mark on the engine rear housing pad.
2. Position the distributor to the

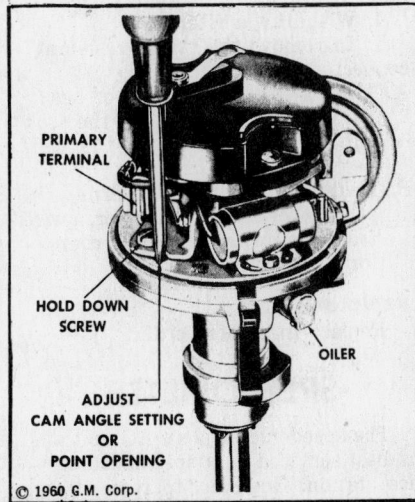

PRIMARY TERMINAL

HOLD DOWN SCREW

OILER

ADJUST CAM ANGLE SETTING OR POINT OPENING

© 1960 G.M. Corp.

Point Adjustment

opening in the block with the vacuum control unit at about 4 o'clock.
3. Point the rotor toward the rear of the engine (6 o'clock), then move the rotor counterclockwise slightly. This movement should permit distributor driven gear engagements with the crankshaft.
4. Press down on the distributor housing while kicking the starter a few times to insure distributor shaft engagement with the oil pump driven member.
5. Bring #1 piston back up on the compression stroke until the pulley notch lines up with the "O" mark on the engine rear housing pad. The rotor should point toward the distributor cap #1 tower, and the points should be just ready to break.
6 Install the hold down clamp and snug up the bolt.
7. Install distributor cap and check all secondary wire connections (spark plug and distributor cap ends.)
8. Connect vacuum line to distributor and primary coil wire to distributor.
9. Start the engine, allow time for normal warm-up and set timing according to tune-up chart.

"D.C." GENERATOR AND REGULATOR

Detailed facts on the generator and the regulator can be found in the Generator and Regulator Specification Table of this section.

General information on generator and regulator repair and trouble shooting can be found in the unit repair section under the heading: Generators and Regulators.

"D.C." GENERATOR CIRCUIT WIRING

Excessive resistance in the charging circuit will show up as voltage drop and will result in an undercharged battery.

GENERATOR REMOVE AND REPLACE

Remove
1. Disconnect ground cable from battery.
2. Disconnect armature and field terminal wires.
3. Loosen idler pulley on the belt

to allow slack for removal of belt from generator pulley.

4. Remove three generator mounting bolts. Lift off generator.

Replace

1. Lift generator into place and install attaching parts (Fig. 10). Leave the assembly loose.

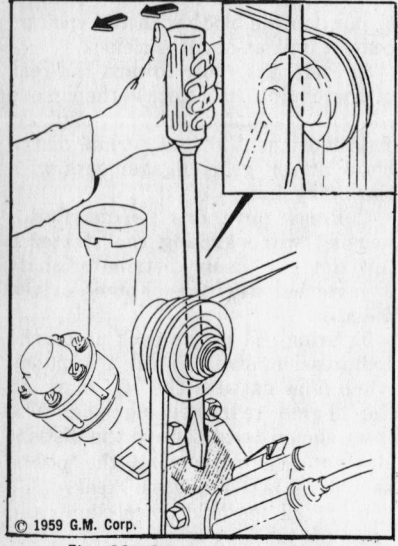

Fig. 10—Generator Installation Adjusting Blower Belt Torsion

2. Place blower belt over generator drive pulley, (don't tighten).

3. Secure the generator by torquing the bolts to 15-22 ft. lb. (Except the mounting bracket-to-generator. Bolt and nut, opposite the pulley end. This torque should be 8-11 ft. lb.)

4. Use a 16 inch screwdriver between the idler pulley and bracket. Locate the end of the screwdriver against the raised boss on the engine.

5. Exert a 25 pound pull on the screwdriver handle and tighten the idler pulley bolt and nut.

Note:

On cars with radio, connect the radio by-pass condenser to the armature (A) terminal, **not** to the field (F) terminal.

6. Polarize the generator by momentarily connecting a jumper between "Bat" and "Gen" terminals on the regulator.

"D.C." GENERATOR POLARITY

Whenever the circuits to the generator, the regulator or the battery have been disconnected it is best to apply the following procedure.

Before the engine is started momentarily short from the "Bat" to the "Gen" terminals of the regulator with a screwdriver. This gives a momentary surge of current from the battery to the generator and so correctly polarizes the generator with respect to the battery.

Failure to so polarize the generator before starting the engine may severely damage the regulator since reversed polarity causes vibration, arcing and burning of the relay points.

"A.C." GENERATOR (DELCOTRON)

REFERENCES

Beginning 1962 Delcotron, the AC generator by Delco-Remy is available on Corvair passenger cars and trucks. These units are furnished in two service types with companion voltage regulators. A three-unit regulator will be used with vehicles having a 42 or 52 ampere Delcotron. Vehicles such as Police equipment, etc., will use a 62 ampere Delcotron and be furnished with a two-unit transistorized regulator.

Repair and test details on the Delcotron and it's regulators are covered in the Unit Repair Section of this manual, under "Alternating Current Generators.

INSTRUMENT PANEL CLUSTER AND SPEEDOMETER

IGNITION SWITCH

The ignition switch is located in the right side of the instrument panel.

1. Disconnect battery cable at battery.

2. Remove the lock cylinder by turning the switch to the "lock" position. Then insert the end of a paper clip in the small hole of the cylinder face. Push in on the paper clip and turn the key counterclockwise until the lock cylinder can be removed.

3. Using spanner wrench (tool # J-7607), remove the front attaching nut.

4. Withdraw switch.

5. To remove the "theft resistant" connector:

A. Make a suitable tool out of heavy wire stock and press on the lock clip within the slot in the connector.

B. Holding the wire tool firmly in place, work the connector away from the switch until the connector is released.

Replace

Replace in reverse order.

SPEEDOMETER

The speedometer is an AC unit and is best serviced by a specialized service station. However, to remove and replace the head, proceed as follows:

1. Disconnect battery.

2. Remove the connectors from the back of instrument cluster. Unclip harness from retaining clips and disconnect speedometer cable at speedometer head.

3. Remove light switch. From beneath dash, remove attaching nut for lighter assembly and withdraw lighter.

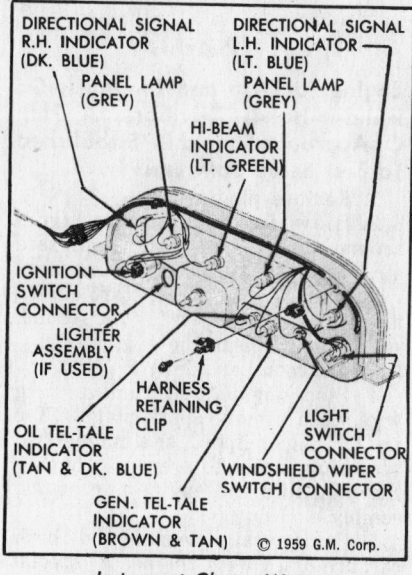

Instrument Cluster Wiring

4. Lower mast jacket and steering wheel assembly for clearance.

5. Remove the **eleven** cluster attaching screws.

6. Lift out instrument cluster, turn

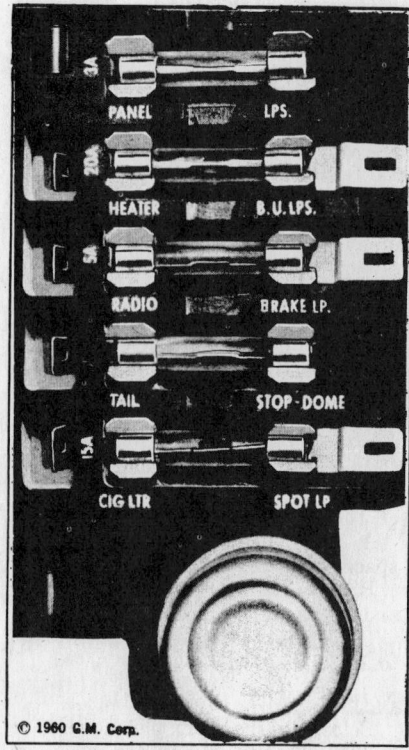

Junction Block

the unit slightly to clear the automatic transmission range selector, (if used).

7. Remove seven screws attaching the cluster back to the cluster.

8. Remove two screws and grommets holding the head of the cluster back.

9. Lift out the speedometer head.

Replace

Replace by reversing above procedure.

BATTERY AND STARTER

BATTERY

The standard battery is a 12 volt, 35 ampere hour battery with 7 plates per cell.

Detailed information on the battery and starter will be found in the Battery and Starter Specifications Table of this section.

A more detailed discussion of batteries will be found in the Unit Repair section under the heading: Tune-up and Diagnosis.

A more detailed discussion of starters and their troubles can be found in the Unit Repair section under the heading: Starters.

STARTER R. & R.

1. Disconnect battery ground at battery.

2. Jack-up and place studs under rear of car.

3. Disconnect rear throttle control rod from bell crank at transmission, and from the cross-shaft in the engine compartment.

4. Disconnect the three wires at the starter solenoid.

5. With a ⅜" drive—9/16" shallow socket on a 9" extension with ratchet, remove the two starter mounting bolts. Remove the upper bolt first. Then pull the starter forward and out of the engine.

6. Install starter in the reverse order of removal.

BRAKE SYSTEM

FOOT BRAKES

The service brakes, both front and rear of all models are the Duo-Servo single anchor type. This brake, except for size, is basically the same as that used on Chevrolet and should be serviced in the same way.

PARKING BRAKE

The parking brake apply lever is located on the dash, to the left of the steering column. A pull on the apply handle is transmitted through cables and an equalizer to the rear wheel brake shoes in the conventional manner.

Built into the parking brake mechanism is a self-adjusting feature. If the first full stroke of brake application is not enough to securely hold the car, a second and more solid stroke may be applied.

Release of the brake is by pulling a separate release handle which extends from under the dash to the left of the mast jacket. The release mechanism also provides a visual indication when the apply handle is pulled by causing the release handle to pop out about 2 inches during the first ½" of apply handle travel.

FUEL SYSTEM

Two identical Rochester Model "H" single-barrel downdraft carburetors are used, one located on each intake manifold. Neither carburetor is equipped with an automatic choke. The choke and fast idle is positioned in the centrally located air horn of the carburetor air cleaner. Two air tubes then direct the filtered air to the top of each carburetor.

The two carburetor throttle levers are connected by a cross shaft, actuated by the accelerator linkage. Care must be used to insure synchronized adjustment.

The automatic choke vacuum source is located at the mid point of the balance tube which extends between the two engine manifolds.

ACCELERATOR CONTROL LINKAGE ADJUSTMENT

(See Figs. 24 and 25)

1. Remove three screws and the mud guard over idler lever "A".

2. Disconnect swivel "D" from lever "A".

3. Disconnect swivel "B" from the left carburetor cross shaft "E".

4. Pull rod "C" to wide open throttle (through detent for Powerglide and against stop for standard transmission) and turn lever "E" in wide open throttle position (carburetor lever against the top). Adjust swivel "B" to align with the hole in lever "E". Now lengthen rod "C" by backing off swivel five full turns.

5. Position accelerator pedal by placing a block of wood between pedal end and floor mat. (**Power Glide** 1¼", **Standard** 1".)

6. Hold lever "A" in wide open position (through detent) turn swivel "D" to align with hole in lever "A". Install mud guard.

7. Remove the accelerator block.

SYNCHRONIZING CARBURETORS

1. Remove the air cleaner and air hoses as a unit.

2. Disconnect throttle rods from each carburetor as follows:

Right Carburetor—Remove the clip and disconnect the throttle rod from the throttle shaft lever.

Left Carburetor—Remove the clip and disconnect the throttle rod swivel from the left hand cross shaft lever.

3. Back off each carburetor idle screw until each throttle valve is fully closed.

4. With a .003" feeler between the idle screw and the throttle lever, turn the screw in until it just holds the gauge. Now turn the screw in one more turn. Do this on each carburetor.

5. On the right hand carburetor, connect and clip the throttle rod to the carburetor throttle lever.

6. With the left hand throttle lever held fully clockwise, adjust the swivel at the top of the rod so that it will

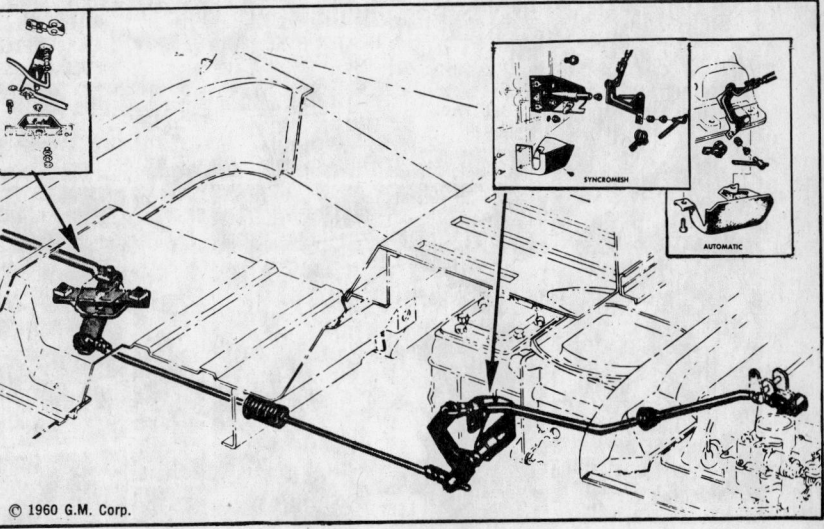

© 1960 G.M. Corp.

Fig. 24— Accelerator Linkage

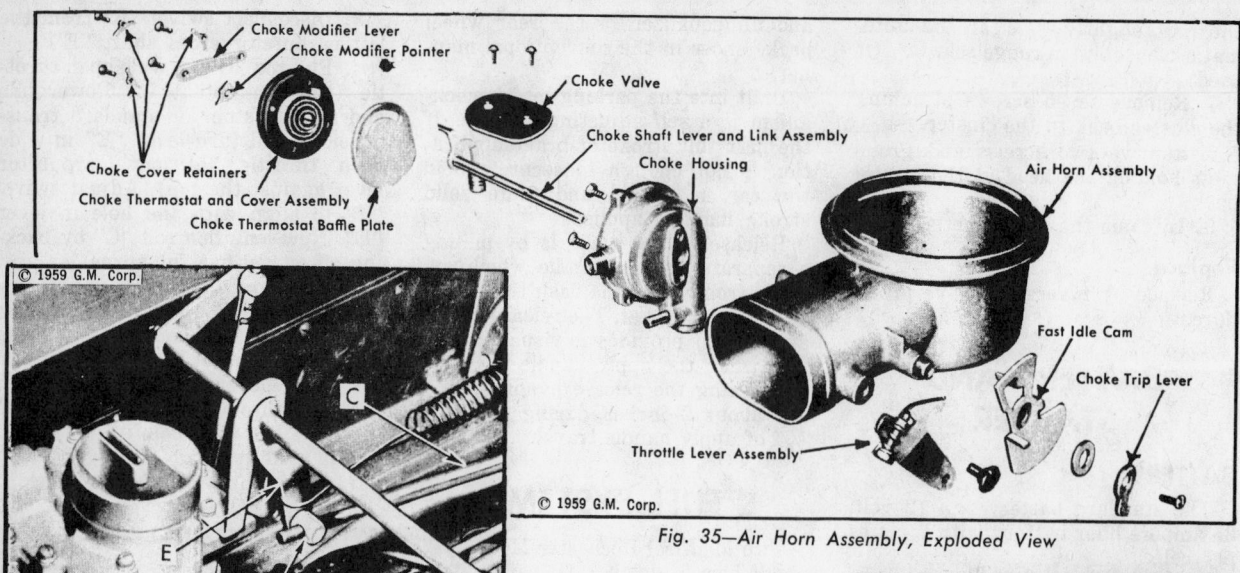

Fig. 35—Air Horn Assembly, Exploded View

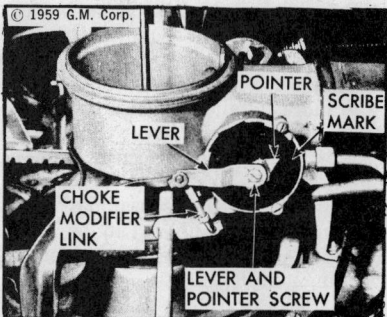

Fig. 33—Automatic Choke Adjustment

Fig. 25—Carburetor Linkage

freely enter the hole in the cross shaft lever. Clip it.

7. The carburetors are now synchronized and any change of idle adjustment must be in duplicate.

8. Replace the air cleaner and, hoses.

CHOKE MODIFIER AND FAST IDLE ADJUSTMENT

1. Synchronize carburetors and set idle speed.

2. Depress accelerator pedal and check carburetors for wide open

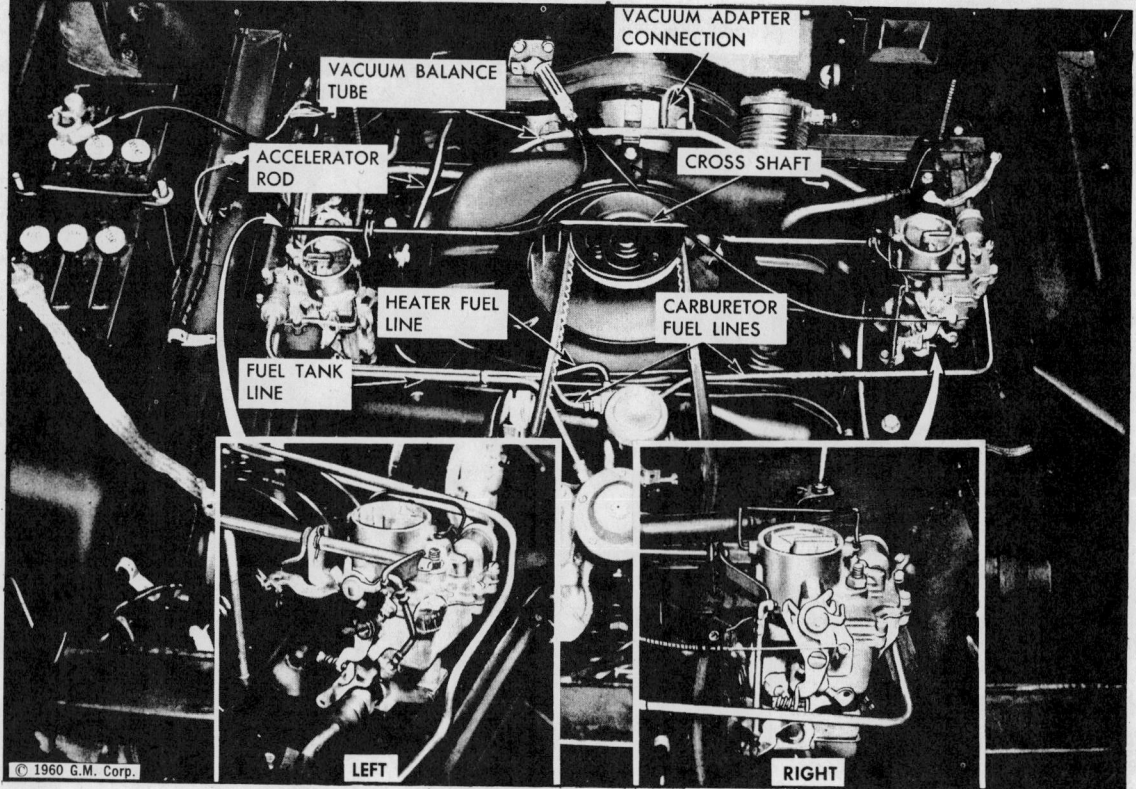

Fig. 28—Cross Shaft and Linkage to Carburetors, Fast Idle and Choke

throttle.

3. Place a ⅛" spacer between the throttle lever and adjusting screw at the RIGHT hand carburetor.

4. Remove the clip attaching the fast idle swivel to the fast idle lever, (Fig. 34).

5. Turn down fast idle screw until 5/16" of the screw threads projects beyond the lever.

6. Rotate the fast idle cam counterclockwise (viewed from left of vehicle), until the fast idle screw rests on the highest portion of the cam, (Fig. 34).

7. Holding the screw and lever in this position, adjust the swivel on the fast idle link so the pin will just enter the hole in the fast idle lever. Clip the swivel and link in this position.

8. Now remove the ⅛" spacer. Linkage clearances will have reduced this clearance, so readjust the fast idle screw until the ⅛" spacer can be reinstalled. This adjustment will provide the correct fast idle speed.

9. If unloading is still incorrect, bend the unloader tang.

10. As a final check, with the unloader actuated, clearance between the choke valve and the adjacent wall of the air horn should be ⅛".

IDLE SPEED AND MIXTURE ADJUSTMENT

1. Hook up a tachometer and vacuum gauge to the engine. Set the parking brake and put the transmission in Neutral.

2. Make sure the engine is warm, and that the choke and fast idle is off.

3. Start and allow the engine to idle. adjust engine idle to 450-500 RPM. (Idle Powerglide to 475-500 RPM in Drive).

4. Turn, but **do not force**, the idle mixture screw all the way in, then back it out two full turns. Using this position as a starting point, adjust the idle mixture screw on each carburetor independently for smoothest idle.

5. It may be necessary, at this time, to readjust for correct RPM and then set the idle mixture again.

6. Remove tachometer and vacuum gauge, then road test the car.

FUEL PUMP

The fuel pump is of the single acting diaphragm type. It is centrally located at the rear of the engine, directly over the crankshaft pulley. The drive is through a crankshaft eccentric and a spring loaded push rod.

Check fuel pump while on the car, in the conventional manner. The volume, **at starter cranking speed**, should be about one pint in 40 seconds. The pressure should be 4½ lb. minimum

and should remain constant **at running speeds** of 450 to 1,000 RPM.

The Pump is held in place by a lock screw and jam nut.

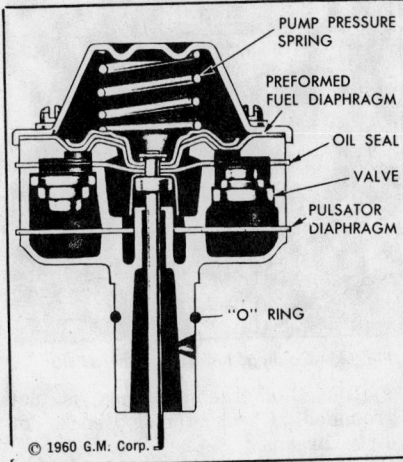

Fig. 37—Fuel Pump, Section View

FUEL TANK

The 11 gallon fuel tank is mounted just to the rear of the front cross-member and in front of the toe-pan. It is held in place by a single metal strap attached to the underbody at each end by an adjustable hook.

The fuel pick-up is part of the tank gauge sending unit located at the lower rght rear of the tank. A fine mesh screen is located at the end of the pick-up pipe. The tank has no drain plug, draining to be accomplished by removing the tank gauge.

Tank Remove

1. Drain fuel at gauge by loosening screws.

2. Disconnect feed line at the gauge Hose clamp connection, the gauge wire plug, the ground wire and, when equipped with a gas heater, dsconnect the pressure relief line at the "T" connector.

3. Remove the hex head screw holding the filler jelk bracket to the front sheet metal, just within the filler door on the left front fender.

4. Remove the nut on one end of the tank support strap that holds the support to the two tank support rods.

5. Lift the left side of the tank and work the tank down and out of its place, freeing the right side first.

Replace Tank in the reverse order of removal.

EXHAUST SYSTEM

The exhaust system is a single unit including exhaust pipes, muffler and tail pipe. The exhaust pipes are flange connected (and packed) to the exhaust manifolds. The packed flanges at the manifolds and the bracket at the engine comprise the entire exhaust mounting system.

Removal

1. Remove the four flange nuts
2. Remove muffler clamp bolt
3. Pull the muffler and exhaust pipe assembly from under the car.

Replace

In the reverse order of removal. Be sure the packing is in place at the two flanges. Torque nuts to 20-30 ft. lb. and bolt to 8-10 ft. lb.

COOLING SYSTEM

The engine is air cooled by a blower mounted on top of the crankcase cover. The engine is entirely shrouded with sheet metal pieces that attach directly to the engine and form a plenum chamber. Air leaving the blower, travels outward and downward over the cylinders and heads. The air then enters a duct under each bank from where it travels rearward to be exhausted at an opening at the rear of the engine.

Cooling is regulated by a bellows type thermostat in the lower part of the plenum. This thermostat operates a cooling air valve that moves in and out of the eye of the blower to control air flow. In the event of thermostat failure the air valve will remain open to prevent engine overheating.

The blower runs on a sealed, permanently lubricated ball bearing. It is belt-driven by a pulley mounted on the rear end of the crankshaft.

COOLING SYSTEM THERMOSTAT

In the event of thermostat failure, the cooling aid throttle valve, (Fig. 43) will remain open to prevent engine overheating.

When installing a new thermostat it is necessary to readjust the air throttle valve opening. This adjustment should be made with the engine warm so the thermostat rod can be easily pulled up against the pull of the thermostat bellows.

Adjustment

1. With the swivel inserted into the hinge lever, pull up on the thermostat rod until the bellows is stopped within its mounting bracket.

2. Adjust the swivel to produce a 1½" opening of the cooling air valve. This measurement is to be made directly opposite the hinge at the maximum opening.

OIL COOLER

An oil cooler, through which a portion of the cooling air passes before discharge, is mounted above the air exhaust duct near the left rear corner of the engine.

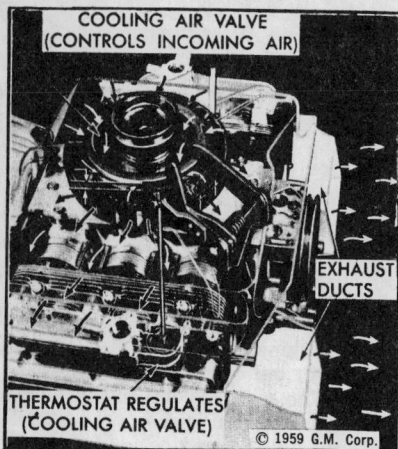

Fig. 43—Engine Cooling System

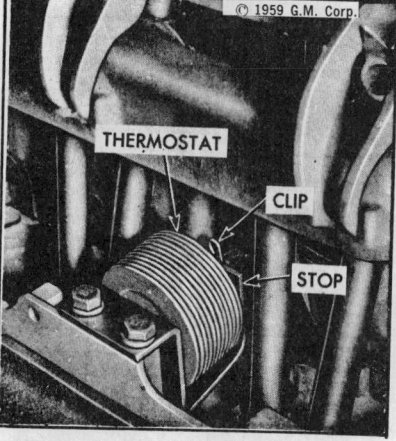

Fig. 45—Cooling Air Valve Thermostat

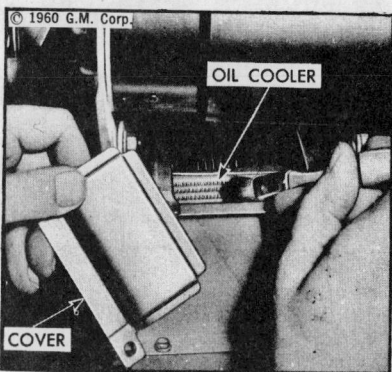

Removing Foreign Matter From Oil Cooler

It is important that the oil cooler be cleaned every 1,000 miles.

1. Remove oil cooler access hole cover and brush clean the cooler fins.

2. Insert and air hose under the cooler and blow up through the cooler fins.

3. Replace the cooler hole cover.

ENGINE TEMPERATURE INDICATOR

Excessive engine temperature or low oil pressure is indicated through the use of a telltale light in the instrument cluster. If engine (oil) temperature is high or oil pressure is low the telltale light will come on.

The indicator should light when the ignition switch is turned on and before the engine is started.

IGNITION ON, ENGINE STOPPED AND TELLTALE LIGHT OFF

1. Telltale light burned out, replace bulb.

2. Open circuit between light and ignition switch or between light and pressure switch.

3. Pressure switch stuck. Replace switch.

4. One of the switches is not grounded. Check for looseness or dirty threads.

TELLTALE LIGHT ON, ENGINE RUNNING

1. Oil pressure is low or oil temperature is high. First check oil level and apparent operating temperature of engine. If light is still on, remove the pressure sender and check oil pressure with a hydraulic gauge. If engine has cooled, and light remains on, temperature sending unit is bad.

2. Electric circuit is grounded between senders and telltale light.

3. Sender calibration is wrong. To check oil pressure sender, increase engine speed and see if light goes out. To check oil temperature sender, disconnect wire at Pressure sender and turn on ignition switch. With a jumper lead (7 ft. long) from temperature sender to the connector, remove the sender and immerse in container of hot oil. With a common kitchen cooking thermometer (400° scale) and the sending unit in the oil, heat the oil and note the temperature required to light the indicator. Temperature should be 280°-320°F.

POWER TRAIN

The power train comprises the engine, clutch, transmission and differential. Some of the components of this train are more easily serviced with the entire power train removed from the vehicle. However, many operations can be performed without disturbing the assembly to any great extent. The following are some of the COMPONENTS THAT REQUIRE THE REMOVAL OF THE POWER TRAIN for easier servicing:

Crankshaft
Camshaft
Connecting Rod
Flywheel
Flywheel Housing
Fuel Pump Eccentric
Rear Housing
Camshaft Drive Gear
Crankshaft Drive Gear
Distributor Drive Gear
Piston, Pins or Rings
Clutch Driving Plate
Clutch Driven Plate
Clutch Housing
Clutch Release Bearing
Manual Transmission
Automatic Transmission parts except those of the controls, the governor, the servo and valve body
Torque Converter
Differential

Power Train removal and installation points up the importance of using proper equipment and recommended procedures. The preferred way to remove and install the Power Train is with special Power Train cradle, tool number J-7894 mounted on a suitable

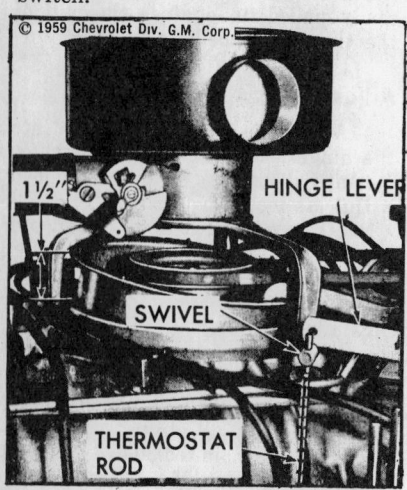

Cooling Air Throttle Valve Adjustment

Fig. 46—Oil Cooler Access Hole Cover

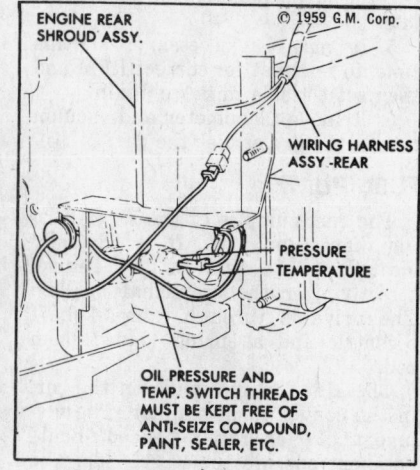

Oil Pressure and Temperature Senders

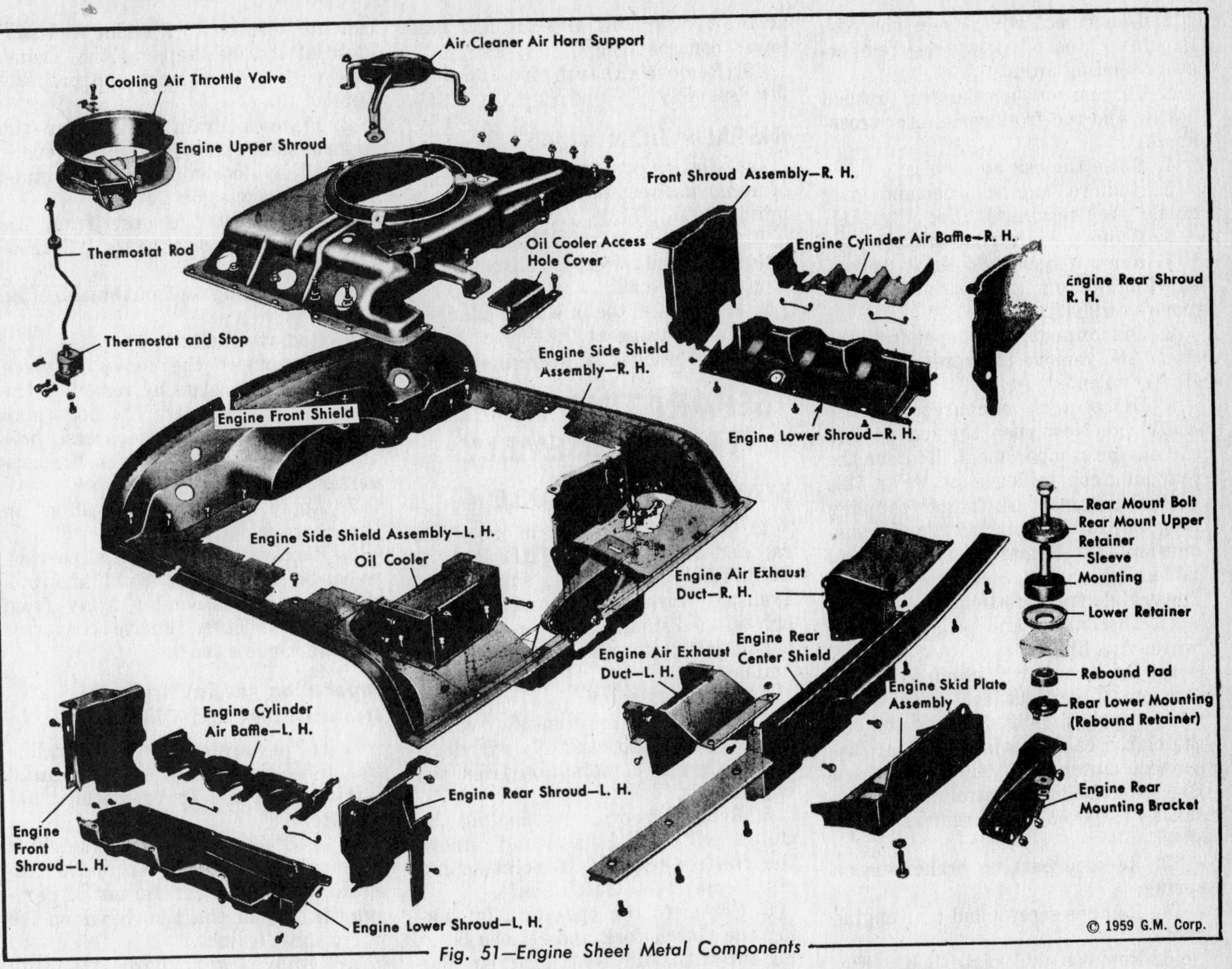

Air Cleaner Air Horn Support

Cooling Air Throttle Valve

Engine Upper Shroud

Front Shroud Assembly—R. H.

Engine Cylinder Air Baffle—R. H.

Engine Rear Shroud R. H.

Thermostat Rod

Oil Cooler Access Hole Cover

Thermostat and Stop

Engine Side Shield Assembly—R. H.

Engine Front Shield

Engine Lower Shroud—R. H.

Engine Side Shield Assembly—L. H.

Oil Cooler

Engine Air Exhaust Duct—R. H.

Rear Mount Bolt
Rear Mount Upper Retainer
Sleeve
Mounting
Lower Retainer

Engine Air Exhaust Duct—L. H.

Engine Rear Center Shield

Engine Skid Plate Assembly

Rebound Pad

Rear Lower Mounting (Rebound Retainer)

Engine Cylinder Air Baffle—L. H.

Engine Front Shroud—L. H.

Engine Rear Shroud—L. H.

Engine Rear Mounting Bracket

Engine Lower Shroud—L. H.

© 1959 G.M. Corp.

Fig. 51—Engine Sheet Metal Components

transmission jack, such as tool number J-8394 with the car on a hoist.

Equipment limitations may modify the approach to the operation but basic principles and precautions remain the same.

The following precautions must be observed:

1. Do not support the complete Power Train except at the engine pan rail. Support cradle J-7894 is designed to correctly support and lock the Power Train in a balanced position.

2. No jacking or lifting tool should

be used unless capable of supporting the weight of the power train assembly, about 460 lb.

3. No jacking device should be used unless sufficiently wide and stable to support the unit at its maximum height without tipping. The balance point of the complete Power Train is about 2/10″ behind the front face of the cylinder block.

4. No jack should be used that will not permit gradual and steady lowering and raising.

REMOVE
Note:

As a precaution, it is wise to insert a bolt through holes in the lid sup-

port to assure holding the lid open.

1. Disconnect ground cable from battery and ground straps to the engine.

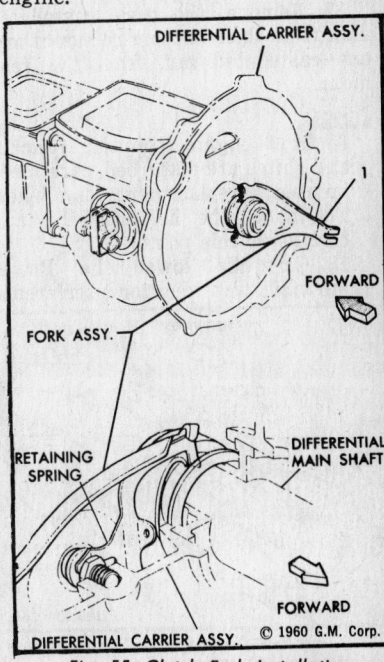

DIFFERENTIAL CARRIER ASSY.

FORWARD

FORK ASSY.

DIFFERENTIAL MAIN SHAFT

RETAINING SPRING

FORWARD

DIFFERENTIAL CARRIER ASSY.

© 1960 G.M. Corp.

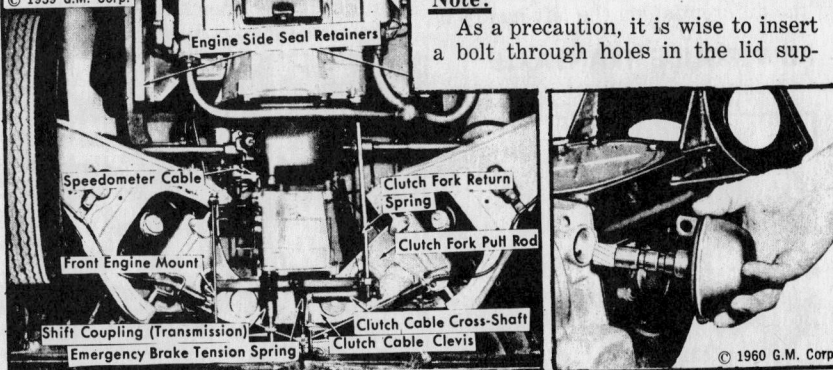

© 1959 G.M. Corp.

Engine Side Seal Retainers

Speedometer Cable

Clutch Fork Return Spring

Clutch Fork Pull Rod

Front Engine Mount

Shift Coupling (Transmission)

Emergency Brake Tension Spring

Clutch Cable Cross-Shaft

Clutch Cable Clevis

Fig. 53—Standard Transmission—Power Train Installation

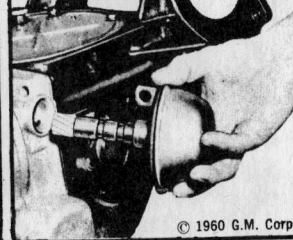

© 1960 G.M. Corp.

Fig. 58—Removing Governor

Fig. 55—Clutch Fork Installation

2. Disconnect wires from the coil, generator and oil pressure—Temperature sending units.

3. Disconnect accelerator return spring and rod from carburetor cross-shaft.

4. Raise the car on a hoist.

5. Remove engine side and rear shield seal retainers. (See Fig. 51).

6. Remove both rear wheels.

7. Remove rear axle shaft universal joints from differential and remove axle shafts.

8. Disconnect the speedometer shaft and remove the wires from the starter solenoid.

9. Disconnect carburetor cross shaft rod. Now push the rod up into the engine compartment. Remove the rear idler control lever rod. (Fig. 52).

10. Disconnect shift rod coupling (Fig. 53) on cars with standard transmission OR disconnect flex—control cable, T.V. and accelerator rod on Powerglide transmissions.

11. Disconnect and plug main and heater fuel lines.

12. On cars with standard transmission, disconnect the clutch fork return spring, (Fig. 53) and unhook the clutch cable clevis, (Fig.53). Disconnect clutch fork pull rod. Loosen Ball stud at clutch control cable cross-shaft, (Fig. 53) and remove cross-shaft.

13. Remove parking brake tension spring.

14. Remove screws and rear engine grille.

15. Remove skid plate bolt, (Fig. 52).

16. Position and secure transmission jack and cradle under the assembly. Raise slightly.

17. Remove the two castellated nuts from the front engine mount and one castellated nut from the rear mount.

Note:

If front engine mounting bracket and shims are disturbed, care must be used in replacement. Rear wheel Toe-in will be influenced by any change at this point.

18. Carefully lower the Power Train while watching for interference at the rear mount and the left rear lower control arm.

19. Remove exhaust pipe and muffler assembly.

INSTALLATION

Installation procedure is the reverse of removal, keeping the following in mind:

1. As with any other major installation, keep all wires, lines, levers and rods out of the way.

2. Rear wheel toe-in will be changed if the shim value at the engine front mounting bracket is altered.

SEPARATING POWER TRAIN ASSEMBLY

STANDARD TRANSAXLE

1. With the Power Train out of the car and secured to a STABLE AND SUBSTANTIAL fixture, support the Transaxle with a chain-hoist and properly applied sling.

2. Drain transmission and differential.

3. Remove starter.

4. Remove the differential to clutch housing bolts and carefully withdraw the Transaxle combination from the engine unit.

5. Remove two screws holding the clutch pull rod dust seal and remove the pull rod-to-clutch fork attaching pin. Remove the clutch shaft.

6. Complete the operation by taking the clutch fork and release bearing out of the differential carrier. The fork is attached to the carrier by a ball socket and spring retainer which is easily removed to permit the release bearing to be slipped off its shaft in the carrier.

Separation of Standard Transmission and Differential

To separate the STANDARD TRANSMISSION from the differential carrier simply requires the removal of the four attaching bolts shown in Fig. 56. Two of these attaching bolts are removed from the transmission, on the right-hand side. While two bolts are removed from the differential, on the left-hand side.

POWERGLIDE TRANSAXLE

1. With the Power Train out of the car and secured to a **stable and substantial** fixture, support the Transaxle with a chain-hoist and properly applied sling.

2. Place a drain pan under the transmission and remove transmission oil by loosening the filler tube at the transmission oil pan.

3. Disconnect the hose from the vacuum modulator tube to the carburetor balance tube.

4. Remove engine front shield, (Fig. 51).

5. Remove starter.

6. Disconnect the converter from the engine flex plate by removing the three attaching bolts. The bolts may be reached through the access hole at the 12 o'clock location in the converter housing.

7. Apply a slight lifting effort on the chain hoist and sling.

8. Remove the differential carrier-to-converter housing bolts and pull the Transaxle assembly away from the engine. Then remove converter and the turbine shaft.

Separation of Powerglide Transmission and Differential

1. To separate the Powerglide transmission from the differential carrier, place the Transaxle on a flat surface.

2. Carefully pull the turbine shaft through the transmission and differential carrier. Be careful not to damage the turbine shaft bushings on the pump shaft splines.

3. Remove governor attaching screw and lift out governor.

4. Remove the three remaining transmission-to-differential attaching screws. Carefully pull the transmission **Straight Away** from the carrier to prevent pump shaft and bushing damage.

5. Remove transmission-to-differential carrier gasket and remove governor drive gear and selective spacers from the pinion shaft of the differential carrier.

POWERGLIDE THRUST WASHER DETERMINATION

For proper operation of the Corvair Powerglide it is necessary that cor-

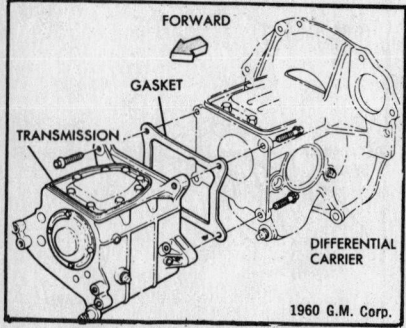

Fig. 56—Three Speed Transmission Differential Carrier Attachment

Fig. 57—Removing Turbine Shaft

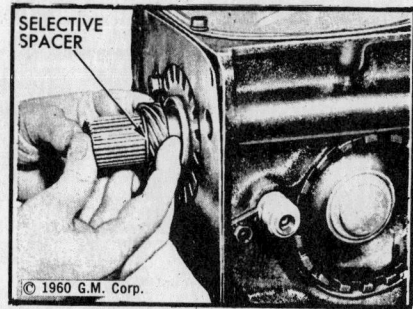

Fig. 59—Removing Governor Drive Gear and Spacers

rect end play be maintained within the unit. Selective thrust washers of various thickness are used at two locations to accomplish this.

A. At the front of the transmission between the front pump body and the clutch drum.

B. At the rear of the transmission between the rear face of the planet carrier hub and the front face of the governor gear.

From a service standpoint the use of selective washers at both front and rear is a great advantage. Final transmission end play can be controlled from either end of the transmission, whichever is most advantageous.

If the repair requires axle and transmission separation, make the washer selection at the rear.

Prior to reassembling the differential carrier to the Powerglide transmission after repairs requiring separation of these units, perform the following:

A. Properly adjust the low band to prevent disengagement or cocking apply linkage, then tip the transmission on end, (Fig. 61).

B. Install a dial indicator on support #J-8364 and install 3″ indicator extension.

C. Without gasket, place support on rear pump cavity surface so that dial indicator tip rests on planet carrier hub. Set indicator dial to zero.

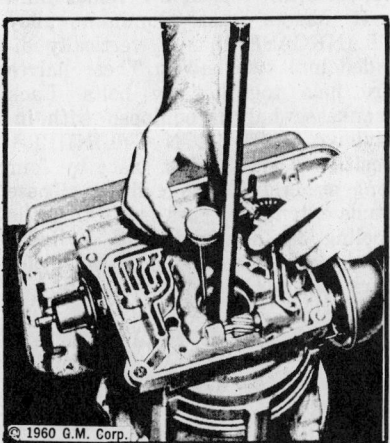

Fig. 61—Zeroing Dial Indicator on Output Shaft

Fig. 62—Measuring Mounting Difference With Indicator

D. Slowly raise support J-8364 and indicator off rear pump cavity and note its range of dial reading. The deflection should not exceed .050″.

E. Place J-8364 and dial indicator on governor gear of the differential pinion shaft, (Fig. 62) and lower the support slowly so that revolutions of the indicator needle can be counted. Measurement starts once the indicator needle again reaches zero. Fully depress support on governor gear, note reading and refer to chart for spacers to be installed on governor gear.

F. Install spacers on the governor gear as selected from chart, (Fig. 63).

ASSEMBLING THE POWER TRAIN ASSEMBLY

STANDARD TRANSMISSION TO DIFFERENTIAL

To assemble the standard transmission to the differential carrier:

1. Apply petroleum jelly to a new gasket and couple the transmission to the differential carrier. Use care in starting the transmission mainshaft in the internal splines of the differential pinion.

2. Secure the transmission to the differential carrier with the four bolts and torque to 24-32 ft. lb.

STANDARD TRANSAXLE TO ENGINE

1. Install the clutch bearing and the release fork on the differential carrier.

2. Bottom the clutch shaft in the Transaxle, then measure from the end of the clutch release bearing shaft to the end of the clutch shaft. This dimension should be 2-9/16″ ± 1/32″.

3. Support the Transaxle with a chain hoist and suitable sling. Align the Transaxle with the engine assembly and guide the clutch shaft splines into the clutch, then secure the differential carrier to the clutch housing with the attaching bolts.

4. Connect the clutch push rod to the clutch fork with pin, then attach the push rod dust seal assembly.

5. Install starter.

6. Fill transmission and differential carrier as prescribed.

POWERGLIDE TRANSMISSION TO DIFFERENTIAL

1. Apply a new gasket, with petroleum jelly, to the rear face of the transmission.

2. Align the transmission and carrier on a clean flat surface and guide the pump shaft through the differential carrier so as not to damage the bushing in the pinion. Then engage the splines of the pinion with the internal splines in the transmission.

3. Install the governor, then secure the transmission to the differential and torque the bolts to 24-32 ft. lb.

4. Install turbine shaft, using care to engage the forward splines, (clutch drum) and the rear splines, (planet gear set).

5. Install converter, Being sure to get full depth engagement of stator shaft, turbine shaft and front pump shaft.

Note:

After the converter is in place, improvise a device for securing the converter to the transaxle during further handling.

POWERGLIDE REAR THRUST SPACER USAGE CHART	
Indicator Reading	Spacers to Be Used
*.011—.038	NONE
.039—.053	.016
.054—.068	.031
.069—.083	.046
.084—.098	.046 + .016
.099—.113	.046 + .031
.114—.128	.046 + .046
.129—.145	.046 + .046 + .016
.146—.155	.046 + .046 + .031

*If initial indicator reading is below .011″, replace .088″ thrust washer at the clutch hub—front pump with an .076″ or .050″ thrust washer, then repeat entire rear thrust spacer selection procedure.

Spacer	Part No.
.016″	6256827
.031″	6256828
.046″	6255664

Fig. 63—Thrust Spacer Chart

POWERGLIDE TRANSAXLE TO ENGINE

1. Locate the transaxle next to the engine on a chain hoist and suitable sling.

2. Remove the converter-to-transaxle securing device and align the converter with the flex plate, (Fig. 67).

3. Guide the converter hub into the crankshaft, then align the mounting bolt holes of the differential housing and converter housing. Secure the two housing by installing the top left bolt, (11 o'clock) position.

4. Install the flex plate-to-converter bolt that is accessible at the 1 o'clock position, as a temporary measure.

5. Install and finish tightening the housing-to-carrier mounting bolts.

6. Install the starter motor.

7. Install the remaining two, and tighten all three converter-to-flex plate bolts via the acces hole in the converter housing.

8. Install the engine front shield.

9. If transmission filler tube was removed from the engine front shield, reinsert it thorugh the front shield at this time, then connect the vacuum

modulator to the carburetor balance tube with a short length of hose.

10. Connect filler tube to transmission oil pan and tighten.

11. Refill the transmission.

POWER TRAIN INSTALL

1. Position the Power Train jack and cradle with the Power Train attached under the engine compartment.

2. Raise Power Train until front and rear engine mounting brackets are in place on mounts, then install the nuts. Torque front mounts to 60-80 ft. lb. and the rear mount to 50-60 ft. lb. Install cotter pins at both mountings.

Standard Transmission

A. Install clutch control cable cross-shaft ball stud.

B. Attach clutch cable clevis to inboard lever.

C. Install transmission shift coupling and boot assembly.

D. Install clutch pull rod and adjust.

E. Hook up parking brake tension spring.

F. Connect and adjust throttle valve linkage.

Powerglide Transmission

A. Connect and adjust manual valve control cable.

B. Connect and adjust throttle valve linkage.

3. Disconnect cradle from Power Train, then lower and remove transmission jack.

4. Connect starter wires to solenoid and hook up speedometer cable.

5. Install axle shaft universal joints at differential.

6. Install rear wheel brake drums.

7. Install engine side and rear shield seal retainers. Place and tightened bolt in read skid plate. Install exhaust system.

8. Install rear engine grill and retaining screws.

9. Lower the car, then connect carburetor control rod and return spring.

10. Connect multiple harness connector and wires to the coil, generator and the oil pressure and temperature sending units.

11. Connect battery cable and radio ground cable.

12. Check engine oil, transmission oil and differential lubricant.

13. Start the engine, check for leaks and make necessary adjustments.

ENGINE

REFERENCES

The ENGINE is an horizontally-opposed, air cooled, 6 cylinder unit.

It has a cast aluminum alloy CRANKCASE that is vertically divided into two halves. These halves are held together by bolts. Each crankcase half is equipped with individual CAST IRON CYLINDERS, positioned and held in place by four long studs for each cylinder. These studs extend and pass freely thru the cooling fin structure and cylinder head, and serve to secure the cylinders and head to the crankcase.

VALVES, PUSH RODS AND TAPPETS

After removing the cylinder head, any service to valves, push rods or tappets can be handled in a conventional manner.

VALVE LASH

Note: Install distributor as outlined in this car section under "Distributor, Installation."

Rotate the crankshaft in its normal direction of rotation (counterclockwise), to bring #1 cylinder into firing position and the crankshaft pulley notch at "O" on the timing pad. Lash valves:

No. 1 Intake, No. 1 Exhaust
No. 3 Intake, No. 5 Exhaust
No. 4 Exhaust, No. 6 Intake

Lash adjustment is made by turn-

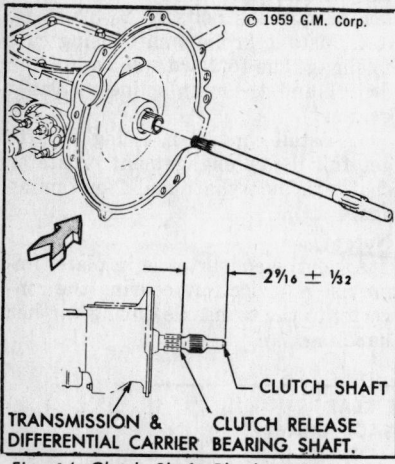

Fig. 64—Clutch Shaft Checking Dimensions

Fig. 65—Engaging Pinion Shaft-to-Transmission Planet Carrier Splines

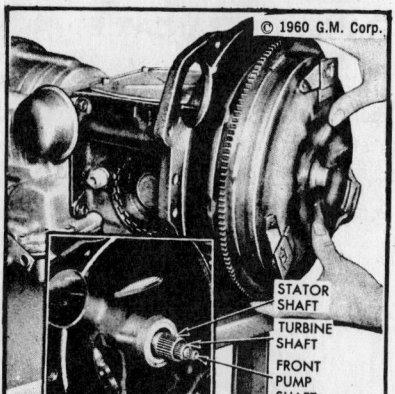

Fig. 66—Installing Converter on Transaxle

Fig. 67—Aligning Flex Plate and Converter

Fig. 88—Adjusting Valve Lash

ing down the rocker arm adjusting nut (with ⅝" deep socket), until there is no up-and-down movement felt in the push rod. Now turn adjusting nut ¾ turn more.

Rotate the crankshaft to the firing position for #2, with the pulley Notch at "O". Lash valves:

No. 3 Exhaust, No. 5 Intake
No. 2 Intake, No. 2 Exhaust
No. 4 Intake, No. 6 Exhaust

Install new gaskets in valve covers and attach covers to cylinder heads with torque of 40 to 60 in. lb.

ENGINE DISASSEMBLE

(Power Train Removed)

1. Separate Transmission from differential carrier.
2. Separate differential carrier from engine.
3. Separate clutch, (if equipped) from engine.
4. Remove carburetor induction hoses, choke hose, and air cleaner. Disconnect carburetor and choke linkage. Remove air horn and choke assembly and remove air horn support.
5. Disconnect throttle linkage and remove carburetor cross shaft.
6. Release belt tension and remove blower belt.
7. Disconnect fuel lines at carburetors and fuel pump. Loosen locknut at attaching screw and remove pump, push rod return spring from oil filter and generator adapter.
8. Remove generator.
9. Disconnect vacuum balance tube at engine front shield and carburetor mounting pad. Remove engine front shield. Remove vacuum balance tube.
10. Remove both carburetors.
11. Disconnect and remove cooling air throttle valve.
12. Remove fuel lines and oil level gauge.
13. Remove distributor cap and spark plug wiring harness.
14. Remove spark plugs.
15. Remove ignition coil and generator brace from cylinder head. Remove engine upper shroud, and left and right side shields.
16. Remove oil filter and generator

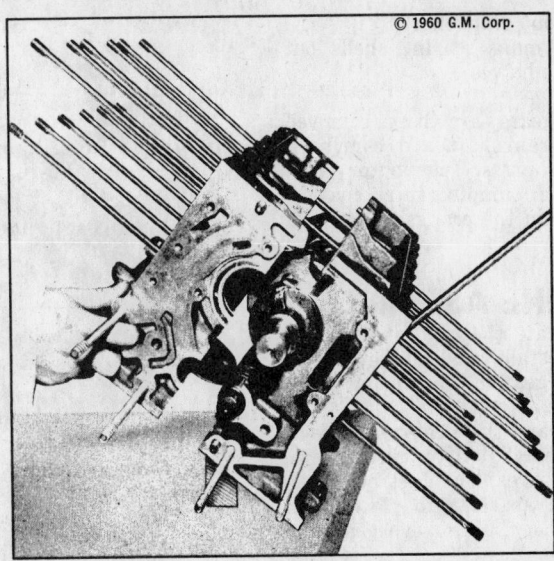

Fig. 77—Removal and Installation of Crankcase Sections

adapter retaining bolts and remove adapter, (throw the gasket away).

17. Remove blower and pulley from crankcase cover. Remove crankcase vent tube and gasket.
18. Remove crankcase cover and gasket, blower bearing, and the vent assembly.
19. Remove engine front and lower shrouds and exhaust ducts.
20. Turn engine upside down and remove oil pan and gasket.
21. Bend lock tabs back, remove nuts attaching nuts and clamps, and remove exhaust manifolds.
22. Remove manifold-to-cylinder head choke heat tube at right head.
23. Remove engine rear mounting bracket and engine skid plate at engine rear housing.
24. Remove valve rocker covers. Remove rocker arm nuts, balls and rocker arms.
25. Remove push rods and identify push rods for reinstallation, (oil holes up).
26. Remove push rod guide plates.
27. Remove valve rocker stubs, the chamfered washers, and discard the "O" rings.
28. Remove cylinder head nuts and flat washers.
29. Remove "O" rings from push rod drain tubes and remove drain tubes.
30. Remove cylinder head assemblies.

Note:

The cast iron cylinders will need a holding device when rotating the crankshaft for engine disassembly. Six pieces of ⅜" iron or galvanized pipe, 4¼" long can be used on the long cylinder stubs, (one to the cylinder). Six pieces of the same diameter pipe, 3½" long to be used on the short studs, (one to each cylinder).

31. Remove hydraulic lifters with a magnet or wire hook and identify them for reassembly.
32. With engine upside down, install two ⅜" x 16 bolts in crankshaft pulley, exactly ¼" deep.
33. Using a bar between the bolts, rotate the crankshaft to give access to the connecting rod bearing being worked on.
34. Mark the cylinder numbers on each rod and piston for identity for reassembly.
35. Remove cylinder holding device (long and short iron pipe), from one cylinder at a time.
36. Remove retainer springs on cylinder air baffle, and remove baffle.
37. Remove each cylinder with piston and rod assembly as a unit.
38. Remove the piston assembly from the cylinder bore with a hammer handle.
39. Remove cylinder ridge or deposits from the bore by mounting the cylinder barrel on an improvised jig, (a block of wood and four studs will do).
40. Remove pulley with puller, then remove engine rear housing bolts and remove rear housing.
41. Support engine on a couple of 2" x 4" wood strips, to protect the oil pump screen and pick-up tube.
42. Remove flywheel housing and gasket.
43. Remove front oil slinger snap ring and slinger.
44. Loosen crankshaft bolts (located on side of crankcase), 8 long and 3 short bolts. Support the crankcase at about a 15° angle (with a block of wood), so the crankshaft and camshaft will not fall out when the case halves are separated.
45. Remove left crankcase half.
46. Remove camshaft by turning while lifting.

47. Lift out crankshaft.

48. Slide main bearing shells out of crankcase halves.

<u>Note:</u>

Timing gears are best removed from the crankshaft and camshaft, in an arbor press. Distributor drive gear and fuel pump eccentric may be removed from the crankshaft with a puller.

ENGINE ASSEMBLE

1. Lubricate the crankshaft, **front end,** and install woodruff key. Press crankshaft gear in place using arbor press.

2. Lubricate the crankshaft, **rear end,** and install two woodruff keys. Locate and press the fuel pump eccentric and spacer into place, then press the distributor drive gear into place.

3. The crankshaft is serviced and the main bearings fitted in the conventional manner.

4. Place the bearing shells in their respective locations in the **left** half of the crankcase, lubricate with light engine oil.

5. Place the corresponding bearing shell halves in their locations in the **right** side of the crankcase, lubricate with light engine oil.

6. Carefully lay the crankshaft into place in the **left** crankcase half.

7. To install camshaft gear and thrust washer on camshaft, support the shaft at back of the front journal in an arbor press.

8. Lubricate gear hub of camshaft and install thrust washer and woodruff key.

9. Press gear onto shaft until it bottoms against the thrust washer.

TIMING GEAR MARKS

10. Install the camshaft assembly into the **left** crankcase half while indexing the two timing gears so that the timing marks line up. Lubricate camshaft and journals with light engine oil.

11. Install the other half of crankcase onto the crankshaft and camshaft, and torque to proper tightness in correct order. Torque eight, long 7/16" x 20 bolts 42-48 ft. lb. Torque three, small 5/16" x 18 bolts 7-13 ft. lb. Camshaft end play should be .003" to .007". End play is influenced by wear at the thrust washer or crankcase groove. Normal timing gear backlash is .002" to .004".

12. Install front crankshaft oil slinger and slinger snap ring.

13. Install main oil gallery plugs, with a good, non-hardening sealing compound.

14. Use a new gasket and install the flywheel to the crankcase with bolts and flat washers. Torque to 20 to 30 ft. lb.

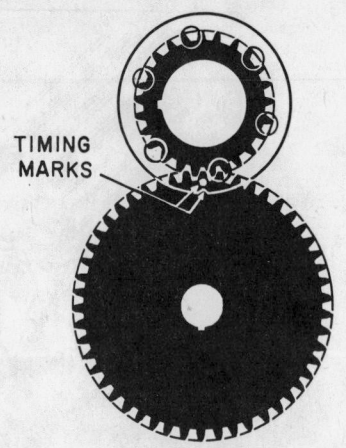

Fig. 78—Timing Marks

TIMING MARKS

15. Mount crankcase and flywheel housing assembly to suitable engine repair stand, if available.

16. Install one oil ring and two compression rings on each piston. (Notch on piston top must be installed toward the flywheel end, front,

NOTCH TOWARD FRONT OF ENGINE (FLYWHEEL END)

of each bank. Position the oil ring gap toward the top of the engine, and compression ring gaps 45° on either side of the oil ring gap.)

17. Lubricate rings, piston pin and skirt and install ring compressor.

18. Push piston assembly into the bore with a hammer handle until the piston head is slightly below the top of the cylinder bore.

19. With piston assemblies in the

Fig. 80—Torquing Connecting Rods— Showing Tubes Holding Opposite Cylinder

bores, put rod bearing inserts in place in the rods and caps.

20. Rotate the crankshaft to bring the crankpin in line with the piston and rod to be installed.

21. Protect the crankshaft journals by taping the rod bolt threads or sliding a piece of 5/16" I.D. plastic hose over the exposed rod bolts.

22. With a new copper cylinder gasket in place, start the cylinder and piston assembly on the long pilot bolts. With hammer handle pressure on the head of the piston, guide the cylinder into place on the crankcase. Tap the piston until firm rod-to-crankshaft journal contact is felt. Then install rod cap and torque to 20 to 26 ft. lb.

23. Install cylinder holding fixture tubes. Repeat this procedure on the remaining five cylinders. Side clearance at the connecting rod bearings should be .005" to .010".

24. Install cylinder air baffles with retainer springs.

25. Install new crankcase cover gasket. Install crankcase vent plate, then another crankcase cover gasket.

26. Install crankcase cover and blower bearing assembly and attach with sixteen bolts and flat washers. Torque to 7 to 13 ft. lb. Attach crankcase vent tube and gasket.

<u>Note:</u> If either a new or the original pump screen and tube assembly is to be installed in the original crankcase, the outside of the end of the tube must be tinned with solder before installation.

27. Drive oil pickup screen and tube assembly into the crankcase with tool #J-8369 (or substitute clamp) and a hammer. **Do not drive on the screen.** Align screen parallel to the oil pan rails. Install retaining clamp.

28. Coat threads on temperature and oil pressure sending units with non-hardening sealing compound and install sending units.

29. Remove cylinder holding fixture tubes from all cylinders of the bank to which the head is to be installed.

30. Install the three cylinder head gasket rings. Position cylinder head on studs and carefully lower head into place.

31. Install flat washers and nuts on the six long studs, next to the intake manifold). Lubricate and install six new "O" rings in the valve rocker stud counterbores. Coat rocker stud bore with anti-seize compound and install special flat washers and valve rocker studs.

32. Torque cylinder head nuts and valve rocker studs, in proper sequence, to 27-33 ft. lb.

33. With light oil, lubricate hydraulic lifters and install them in their proper bores.

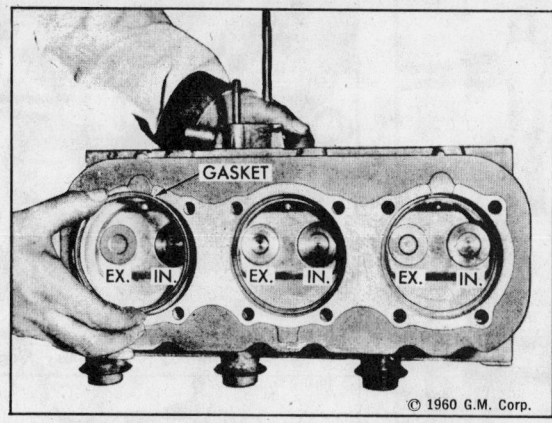

Fig. 82—Installation Cylinder Heat Gasket

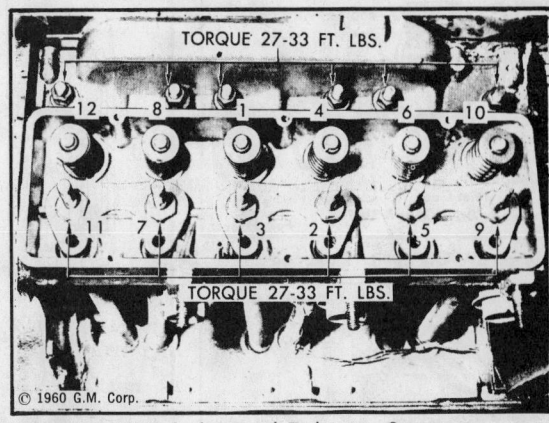

Fig. 84—Cylinder Head Tightening Sequence

34. Install push rod oil drain tubes through cylinder head. Place "O" rings, one on each end of the drain tube. Lubricate "O" rings and push tubes into place, at valve lifter bore and cylinder head. Install tube with long end toward cylinder head.

35. Install push rods with the side oil hole up, at the rocker arm socket. Install push rod guides in place over the rocker studs and push rods. Rod guide retaining bolts, torque to 60 to 80 in. lb.

36. Install rocker arms, balls and nuts loosely in place.

37. With a new gasket in place, position and attach the engine rear housing. Use flat washers and anti-seize compound on the attaching bolts. Torque to 7 to 13 ft. lb.

38. Block the crankshaft from turning with a wooden wedge. Lubricate and install pulley on the crankshaft with heavy washer and retaining bolt. **Draw** the pulley into place with retaining bolt. After bottoming the pulley, back screw off one turn, then torque to 50-60 ft. lb. Caution: Do not drive pulley onto shaft.

39. With new gasket in place, install oil cooler adapter with anti-seize compound on bolts and flat washers. Torque adapter bolts to 7 to 13 ft. lb. Install engine rear shroud. Install new seals in oil cooler adapter.

40. Install oil cooler, with anti-seize compound on the bolt and flat washer. Torque to 8 to 12 ft. lb.

41. With new gaskets in place, install exhaust manifolds. On the right bank, install heat tube in manifold. Install clamps, torque nuts to 10 to 20 ft. lbs.

42. With new gasket, install oil filter and generator adapter on the engine rear housing. With anti-seize compound on bolts and washers, secure and torque the adapter to 7 to 13 ft. lb. Install new oil filter cartridge and torque the attaching bolt, 9 to 15 ft. lb. Install engine right rear shroud.

Fig. 83—Installation of Cylinder Head

43. Install engine skid plate and rear mounting bracket, torque nuts, 20 to 30 ft. lb. Attach lifting adapter to rear engine mount.

44. Install blower and blower pulley to crankcase cover blower bearing hub assembly.

45. Install front shroud and exhaust ducts. Install left and right side shields.

46. Install upper shroud assembly. Turn blower and check clearance while tightening upper shroud retaining screws.

Fig. 86—Push Rod Installation

47. Install fuel lines and oil level gauge. Install thermostat and lower engine shrouds. Install cooling air throttle valve assembly.

48. Install idler bracket and pulley in place on the generator adapter. Be sure the adjusting slot is toward the front, (flywheel) end of the engine.

49. Install coil bracket, coil and generator brace on cylinder head. Install blower-generator belt and adjust according to procedure outlined in the "**Generator Remove and Replace**" department of this car section.

50. Install spark plugs, and torque to 20 to 25 ft. lb. Install plug and distributor wires. Install coil wires. Install carburetors.

51. Turn engine bottom up, and install oil pan with new gasket. Check crankcase-to-flywheel parting line to see if surface is conductive to good sealing. Torque oil pan bolts, 40 to 60 lb.

52. Lift the engine off the stand or bench and secure it to the cradle, tool #J-7894, in preparation for Power Train assembly and car installation.

53. Install fuel pump push rod and spring into the oil filter and generator adapter. Install fuel pump with new "O" ring seal. Secure pump with set screw and lock nut, both torqued 9 to 15 ft. lb.

54. Connect fuel lines, install engine front shield and support strap, connect vacuum balance tube to both carburetors. Connect choke heat tube, and fresh air tube.

55. Install carburetor cross-shaft and air horn support. Install air horn, air cleaner and air inlet hoses.

56. Refer to "Cooling System" in this car section for data on adjusting the cooling air throttle valve and thermostat.

Refer to Corvair Powerglide, Linkage Adjustments in this car section.

ENGINE REAR HOUSING—RENEW

The oil pump and pressure regulator are contained in the engine rear housing. The pump is driven by the extended distributor shaft. Any major service to the oil pump (including replacement of **early model** engine rear oil seals), requires engine removal.

Fig. 89—Oil Pump, Exploded

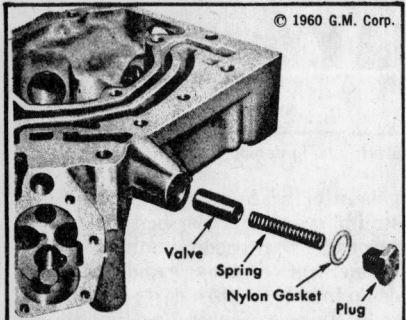
Fig. 90—Pressure Regulator, Exploded

CYLINDER HEAD R & R
(In The Car)

Valve conditioning, head gasket replacement or any other service directly connected to the cylinder head may be performed with the engine in the car.

LEFT BANK

1. Drain engine oil.
2. Disconnect battery and ground connection to the engine. Disconnect radio ground strap.
3. Remove air intake hose, connected to air cleaner and carburetor.
4. Remove carburetor accelerator return spring and disconnect accelerator rod from the carburetor.
5. Disconnect **left** side carburetor cross-shaft support from carburetor.
6. Disconnect fuel line and remove **left** carburetor. Remove the long, outboard stud from carburetor mounting.
7. Disconnect vacuum balance tube

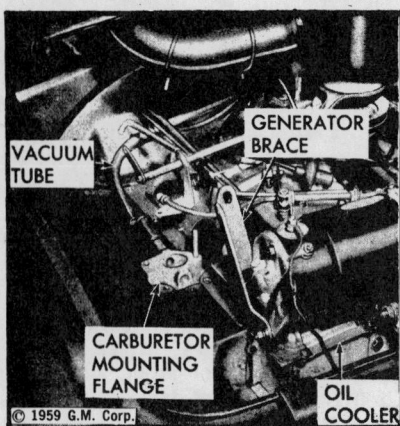
Fig. 95—Engine Compartment—Cylinder Head Removal and Installation

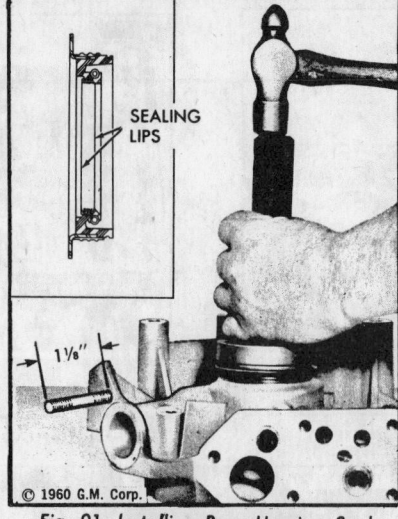
Fig. 91—Installing Rear Housing Seal, Using Tool J-270-6

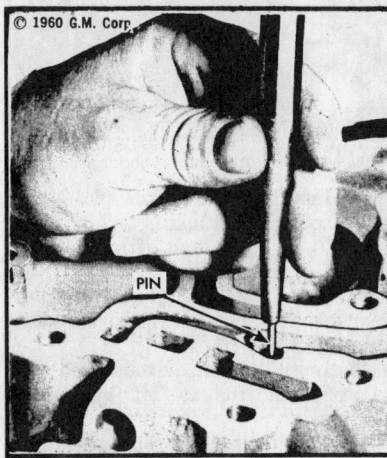
Fig. 92—Installing Oil Pressure Regulator Stop Groove Pin

at carburetor mounting flange. Remove generator mounting bolts and swivel bracket, up and away from the engine upper shroud.

8. Remove spark plugs and wires from cylinder head, throw away plug gaskets.
9. Loosen all engine side shield retaining screws and remove screw from engine side shield under carburetor in engine compartment, attached to cylinder head. Remove engine side shield.
10. Remove oil cooler access hole cover and remove oil cooler.
11. Raise car on a joist and attach lifting cradle and jack. Support the engine.
12. Remove both engine side seal retainers and engine rear seal retainers.
13. Remove engine rear center shield and seal assembly.
14. Remove lower engine shroud. Remove exhaust pipe to manifold nuts.
15. Remove clamps and exhaust manifold.

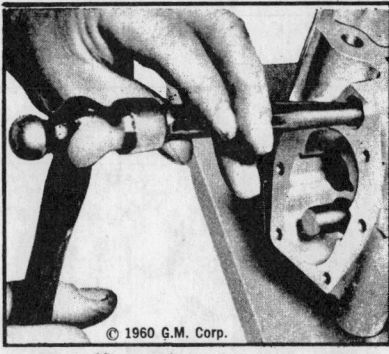
Fig. 93—Installing Oil Gallery Plug

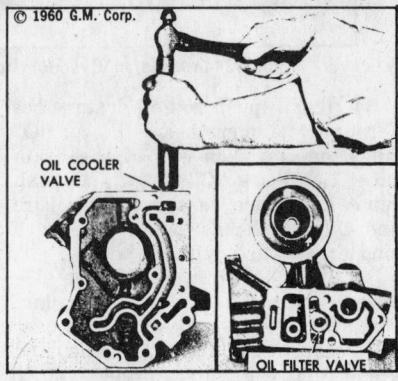
Fig. 94—Installing Oil Cooler By-Pass Valve

16. Remove engine-to-body rear mounting bracket.
17. Remove screws and lift off rocker arm cover, have oil drain pan in position to catch oil from head.
18. Remove rocker arm nuts, balls and rocker arms. Remove push rods and rod guides.
19. Remove rocker stubs, washers and "O" rings from cylinder head.
20. Remove "O" rings from bottom of push rod drain tubes with hooked tweezers, then remove tubes from cylinder head.
21. Remove nuts and washers from long cylinder head studs.
22. Carefully lower engine assembly about 3" to clear cylinder head carburetor flange.
23. Carefully remove cylinder head.

Immediately install cylinder holding

Fig. 96—Engine Assembly—Showing Access to Cylinder Head

fixture tubes and nuts to prevent possible cylinder barrel disturbance in the event of crankshaft rotation.

Reinstall

Install cylinder head in the reverse order of removal, using new gaskets, "O" rings and seals. For details and adjustments, see "ENGINE ASSEMBLY," cylinder head, in this car section.

RIGHT BANK

Removal and reinstallation of the right bank cylinder head is basically the same as the left. However the coil, oil pressure and temperature sending units, the choke heat pipe and the fresh air pipe from the exhaust pipe must be removed.

ENGINE REAR OIL SEAL

Unless the engine is of very early production, the rear oil seal can be changed without removing the engine. Early model engine rear housing seals were designed and installed with the seal flange located inside the housing, requiring engine removal. Later design provides for replacement from the outside by the following procedure:

1. Disconnect battery and drain engine oil.
2. Remove all side shield seal retainers.
3. Remove engine rear center shield. Remove engine skid bolt and attach cradle J-7894 to the underside of the engine, car raised on a hoist.
4. Remove engine rear body grille and engine rear mount.
5. On cars equipped with standard transmission, refer to "Clutch Linkage" description in this car section. Remove clutch return spring and disconnect control cable. Disconnect clutch pull rod.
6. Loosen the outboard stud nut and slide, part way, out of the engine front mounting bracket slot. Remove shift rod coupling.
7. Loosen front engine mounting nuts and lower engine until nuts are flush with the front engine mount studs.

<u>Note:</u> Do not remove front mounting nuts.

8. Lower engine just enough to remove engine rear mounting bracket.
9. Remove oil filter and belt from the pulley.
10. Remove crankshaft pulley with puller.
11. Remove engine rear oil seal by prying on the outer edge of the seal with a couple of screw drivers.
12. Clean rear housing seal seat with solvent and check for surface damage.
13. Lubricate the outside diameter

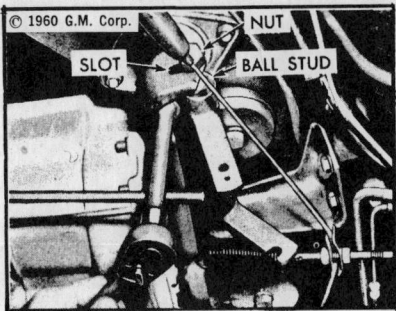

Fig. 99—Lowering Front Engine Mount

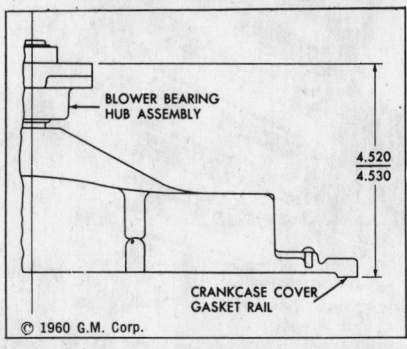

Fig. 101—Blower Bearing and Crankcase Cover

of the new seal and tap into place with a suitable tool.

14. Reassemble in the reverse order of removal.

BLOWER BEARING AND COVER

The blower bearing may be replaced without disturbing the Power Train by:

1. Disconnect battery.
2. Disconnect accelerator linkage and fuel lines.
3. Remove oil level gauge and fresh air choke at air cleaner. Remove choke pipe.
4. Remove air cleaner, air horn and support assembly.
5. Remove carburetor vacuum balance tube and retaining strap at engine upper shroud.
6. Remove blower belt and wire harness.
7. Disconnect cooling air throttle valve lever swivel.
8. Remove engine upper shroud and thermostat rod as an assembly.
9. Remove four bolts from blower pulley and lift off pulley and blower from blower bearing hub assembly.
10. Remove crankcase cover bolts and lift off the cover and bearing assembly.
11. Remove crankcase vent and gasket.

BLOWER BEARING REPLACEMENT

1. Carefully support the crankcase cover in an inverted position and

press out the old blower bearing shaft.

2. Install a new bearing hub assembly in the crankcase cover (cover in its normal operating position), using hypoid lubricant on the bearing shaft.
3. Press on the shaft (only), of the blower bearing until a height of 4.520"-4.530" from crankcase cover rail to the top of the blower bearing flange is reached.
4. Replace crankcase cover, crankcase vent and new gaskets by reversing the removal procedure. Torque blower pulley bolts to 20-25 ft. lb., crankcase cover bolts to 7-13 ft. lb.

OIL PAN REMOVE

Drain oil and remove in the conventional manner. Retorque attaching bolts to 40-60 in. lb.

FRONT SUSPENSION

Any major operations on the front suspension will be simplified by the use of a car hoist. The suspension should be permitted to swing free.

WHEEL ALIGNMENT

REFERENCES

With the exception of rear wheel toe-in, front wheel services and steering geometry are covered in the "Unit Repair Section" of this manual. Please refer to "Suspension, Front."

REAR WHEEL TOE-IN

Due to Corvair suspension design it is necessary to establish and maintain rear wheel toe-in.

This is controlled by adding or removing shims at the front edge of the transmission, and both rear wheels are affected by any shim change. Shims must be added or removed in pairs. A 1/16" shim added to each side will increase toe-in Removal of the 1/16" shim from each side will decrease toe-in.

Total rear wheel toe-in should be 0" to 1/4". However, manufacturing tolerances "stack-up" and it is possible to experience toe-out on one rear wheel and toe-in on the other rear wheel. In this case, adjust to bring the wheel with the toe-out as close to specifications as possible without letting the opposite wheel go out of limits. **Example:** One wheel toes-out by 1/4", then the opposite wheel must toe in enough to result in 0" to 1/4" overall toe-in.

<u>Caution:</u> If the case exceeds the above limits, look for bent or damaged parts or an uneven distribution of shims.

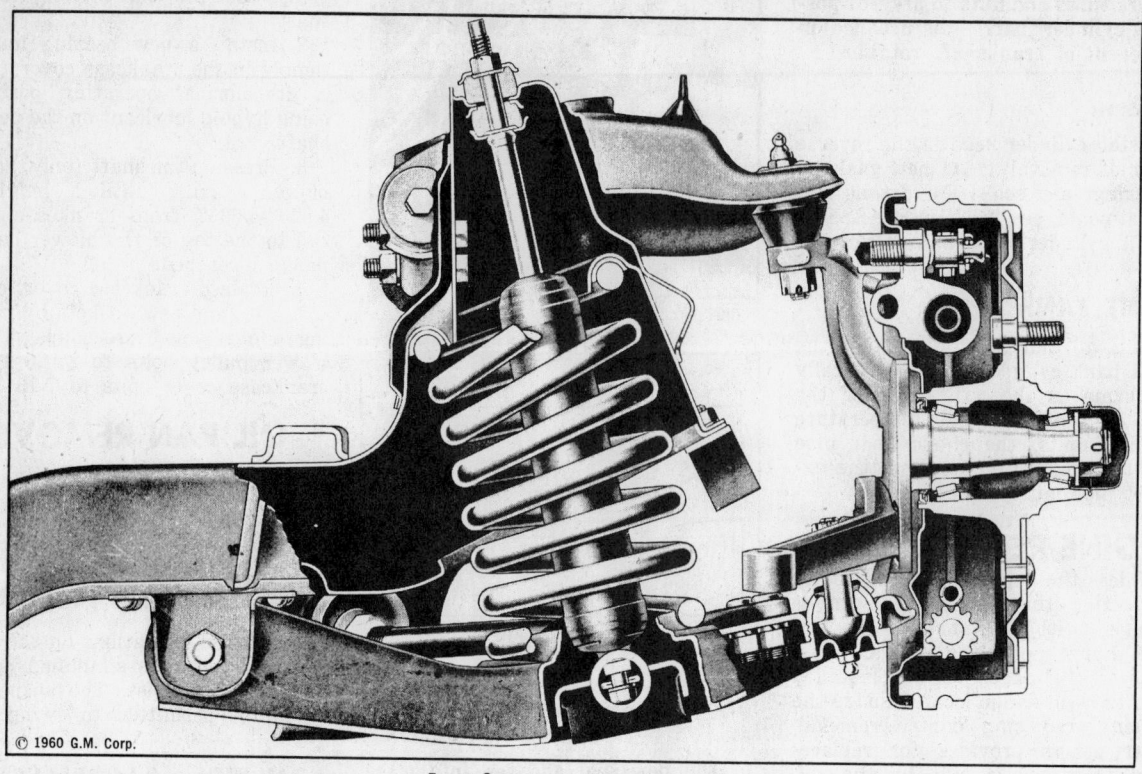

Front Suspension Cross Section

RIDING HEIGHT—SPRING SAG

1. Place the car on a smooth, level floor. (The car body should be empty except for spare tire.)

2. Bounce the car to normalize shock absorbers and springs.

3. Measure the height from the shop floor to the bottom of the rocker panel 27″ back of the centerline of the front wheel. This measurement indicates front spring condition and should be 9″ ± ½″.

4. Measure the height from the shop floor to the bottom of the rocker panel 29″ forward of the centerline of the rear wheel. This measurement indicates rear spring condition and should be 8¾″ ± ½″.

5. This check should be made on all four springs, and replacements made where necessary.

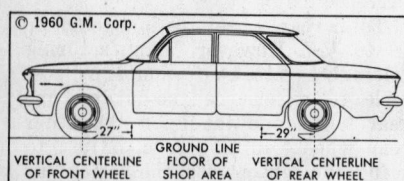

VERTICAL CENTERLINE OF FRONT WHEEL — GROUND LINE FLOOR OF SHOP AREA — VERTICAL CENTERLINE OF REAR WHEEL

Fig. 104—Check Riding Height

CONTROL ARMS AND SPRINGS —FRONT

COIL SPRING REMOVE

1. Place car on hoist so that the control arms can swing free.

2. Remove shock absorber.

3. Remove the two strut rod-to-control arm, nuts and lockwashers.

4. **Just loosen** the lower control arm inner pivot nut.

5. Place jack stand under lower control arm and take up slightly on spring pressure.

6. Remove control arm pivot nut and washer. Tap out pivot pin.

7. Carefully lower jackstand until spring is free. Lift out spring.

Note: A bar placed through the control arm and into the spring tower will keep the spring from slipping

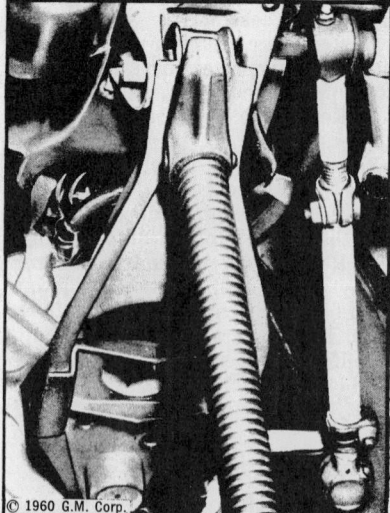

Fig. 105—Position of Jackstand For Spring Removal

until it is free.

FRONT SPRING INSTALL

1. Set control arm in place with the stud of the joint up through the steering knuckle. Install, tighten the nut and lock with cotter pin.

2. Position rubber spacer on top of coil spring and secure with friction tape. Contour of spacer and spring must match.

3. Place spring on control arm with spacer up. Rotate spring until upper end of spring and spacer finds its proper seat.

4. Using jack stand as in Fig. 107, raise control arm and install the lower control arm inner (pivot) bolt.

5. Attach strut rod to control arm with two attaching nuts and lock washers.

6. Install shock absorber.

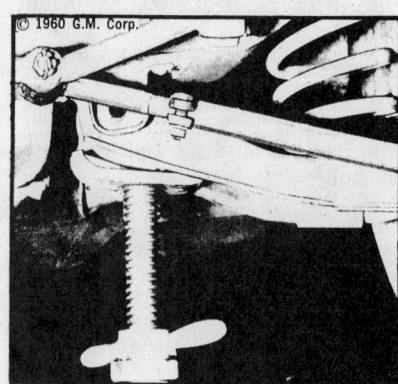

Fig. 107—Front Coil Spring Installation

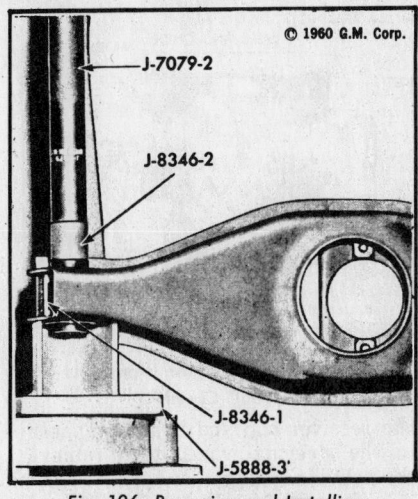

Fig. 106—Removing and Installing Lower Control and Bushings

7. Lower car to the floor. Neutralize by bouncing the car a few times. Then tighten the lower control arm inner pivot bolt and nut.

UPPER CONTROL ARM

1. Support the car weight at the outer end of the lower control arm.
2. Remove wheel assembly.
3. Remove cotter pin and nut from upper ball joint stud. Remove stud.
4. Remove two nuts holding the upper control arm cross shaft-to-front cross member. **Count number of shims at each bolt.**

UPPER CONTROL ARM BUSHINGS

The upper control shaft and/or bushings can be replaced by following the set-up as illustrated.

UPPER CONTROL ARM —INSTALL

1. Install upper control arm to the car.
2. Install two attaching nuts and lockwashers to the studs holding the upper control arm shaft to front cross member. **Install same number of shims as removed at each bolt.**
2. Install new rubber seal. Then install the bar stud through the knuckle, install the nut and cotter pin.
4. Install wheel assembly
5. Lower car to the floor and bounce the car to neutralize suspension.
6. Torque cross shaft bolts to 35-40 ft. lb.
7. Recheck caster and camber.

REAR SUSPENSION
SHOCK ABSORBERS

Rear shock absorber mounting and action is functionally the same as the front. **But, the rear shock absorber holds all of the rear spring compression.** When removing or installing rear shock absorbers, **the weight of the car must be resting on the tires.**

1. Place car on a "drive-on" (ramp type hoist, frame contact hoist or place jack stands under the body at each side rail, just foreward of the rear wheel openings.
2. Raise the body high enough to allow the rear wheels to hang free.
3. With a jack placed under the tire, raise the wheel to its normal position.
4. Now the shock absorber can be repaired without interference with the floor.

REAR SPRING—REPLACE

1. Raise car, by side rails, high enough for rolling floor jack to be placed under the brake drum.
2. Loosen control arm cross shaft bolts.
3. Remove the bolt that holds the brake hose bracket to the underbody.
4. Remove the wheel assembly.
5. Replace the wheel lug nuts to hold the drum in place.
6. Position the axle shaft as in Fig. 110. The side surface of the Universal joint yoke must be at 45° to the centerline of the axle case.
7. Place a rolling floor jack under the drum and backing plate.
8. Raise the floor jack slightly, detach and remove the shock absorber.
9. Carefully lower the floor jack until the spring is free. **Do not remove or lower the jack too far** as this will apply strain to the axle shaft and brake hose.

Install in the reverse order of removal.

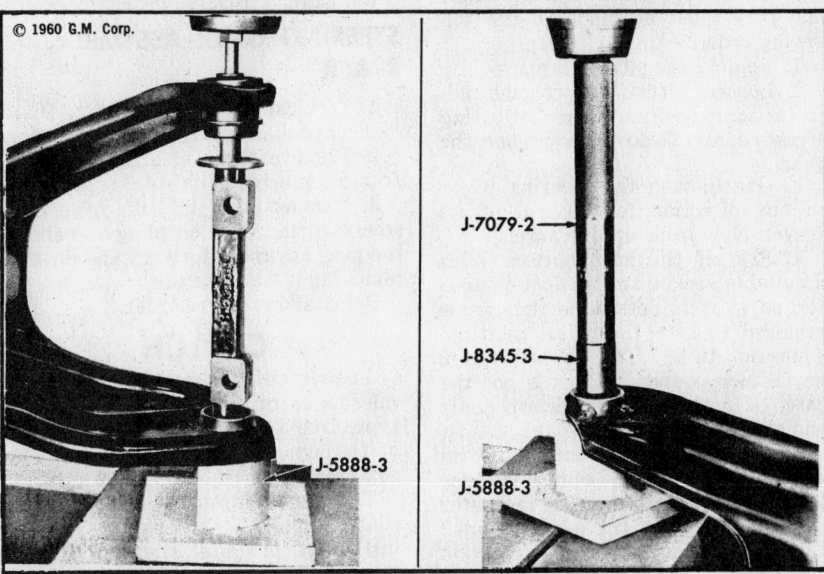

Fig. 108—Removing Upper Control Arm Bushings

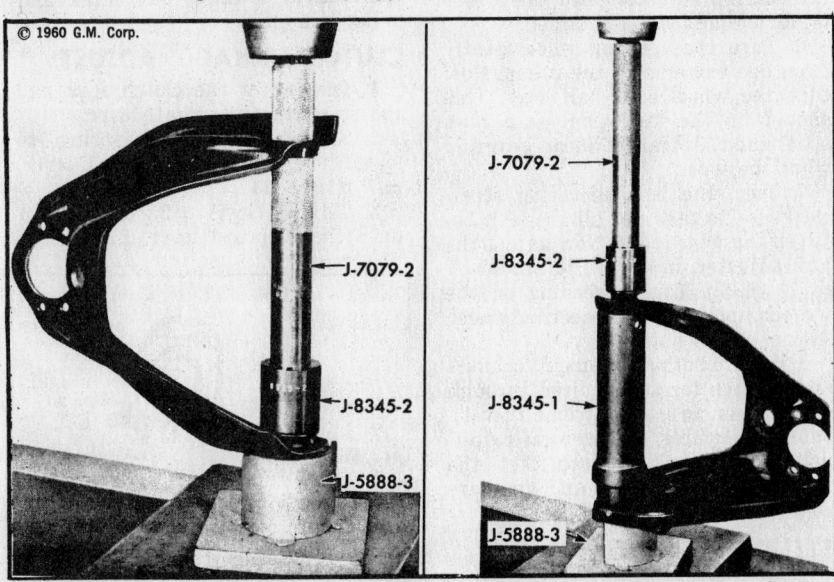

Fig. 109—Installing Upper Control Arm Bushings

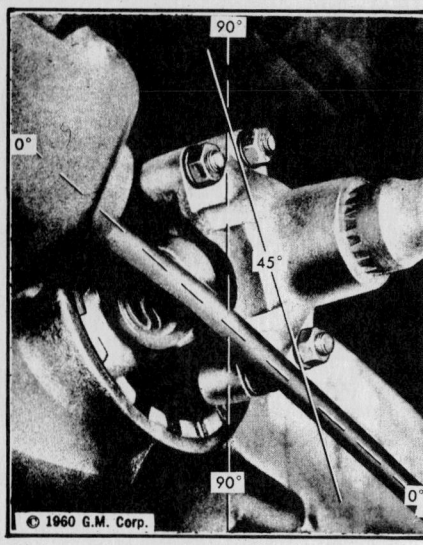

Rear Axle Positioning For Spring Removal

LOWER CONTROL ARM—R & R

1. Remove rear spring as outlined.
2. Support the control arm with a suitable stand high enough to prevent a strain on the brake hose.
3. Remove brake drum.
4. Pry the upper end of the brake shoe up and onto the brake anchor pin. This will permit the axle flange plate and shaft to be pulled out past the parking brake strut.
5. Remove the four backing plate attaching nuts and washers.
6. Pry between the axle flange plate and backing plate until the axle shaft and universal joint assembly can be pulled out of the axle case.
7. Disconnect the Universal joint at the "U" bolts.
8. Remove the universal joint flange retaining bolt and washers from the end of the axle and pull the joint flange.

Installing Shock Absorber and Coil Spring

9. Pull out the axle shaft.
10. Disconnect the backing plate and brake shoe assembly from the control arm and tie the assembly up, out of the way.
11. Remove the four bolts and nuts from the control Arm-to-crossmember. Remove the control arm.

Reinstall in the reverse order of removal.

STEERING GEAR AND LINKAGE

The steering gear is the recirculating ball type, basically the same as that used in Chevrolet. Linkage is of the relay type. The tie rod ends have self adjusting socket joints.

STEERING GEAR ADJUST

Only two adjustments are possible and they must be made in the following order:
1. Remove the pitman arm.
2. Loosen pitman shaft lash adjuster screw lock nut. Turn adjusting screw counterclockwise to unload the gear.
3. **Gently** turn the steering wheel in one direction to the end of its travel. Now back up one turn.
4. Pry off the horn button. With a suitable socket and an inch-pounds torque wrench, determine the torque required to keep the wheel rotating, (one full turn). This is between 2 and 6 inch pounds. If this is not the case, adjustment of the worm shaft end play is in order.
5. To adjust play out of worm shaft bearings and obtain proper load, loosen worm bearing adjuster lock nut and turn the adjuster until there is no play. Check shaft rotation pull with the torque wrench and turn the bearing adjuster until the 2 to 6 in. lb. torque load is obtained.
6. Turn the steering wheel **gently** from one extreme to the other. Now turn the wheel back half way. This should be the "steering gear high spot" and the straight ahead gear and wheel position.
7. Turn the lash adjusting screw clockwise to take out all the lash between the gear teeth. Now adjust the lash adjuster, in or out, to produce 7 to 12 in. lb. Torque reading on the wrench applied to the steering wheel, (worm shaft) nut.
8. Secure both adjustment locknuts and recheck torque required through entire steering gear extreme travel.
9. Reassemble pitman arm to pitman shaft, making sure that the wheels, steering wheel and gear are centered.

STEERING WHEEL, R & R

1. Pry off horn button.
2. Remove three screws holding

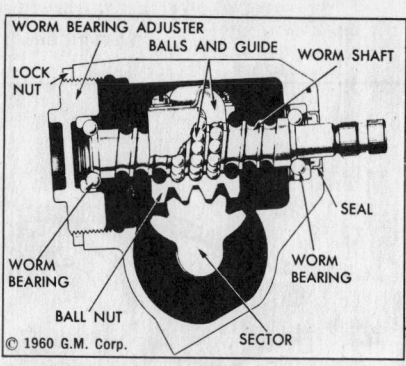

Fig. 113—Steering Gear Worm Nut and Ball Circuits

the receiver cup and bushing spacer to the steering wheel, then remove the bellville spring.
3. Remove steering wheel nut and washer from the wormshaft.
Reinstall in reverse order.

STEERING GEAR ASSEMBLY, R & R

1. Lift car on suitable hoist. Disconnect pitman arm from sector shaft.
2. Remove three steering gear-to-frame mounting bolts.
3. Remove nuts and bolts from the steering gear shaft coupling and slide the gear assembly forward and down, removing it from the car.
Reinstall in reverse order.

CLUTCH

The clutch for the standard transmission is of the diaphragm spring type. Due to the torsional flexibility of the input shaft, the driven disc is solid mounted.

The clutch is operated through a conventional clutch fork, by pulling instead of pushing. The clutch fork is pivoted on the axle housing and its operated by a cable, bell crank and pulley design.

CLUTCH LINKAGE, ADJUST

1. Disconnect the clutch fork pull rod from the cross shaft lever.
2. Attach the return spring to lower hole in the cross shaft lever, #3 of Fig. 117.
3. Adjust clevis #2, (Fig. 117.) until the outboard lever #3, on the

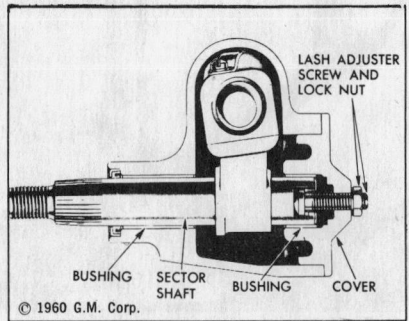

Fig. 114—Steering Gear Pitman Shaft

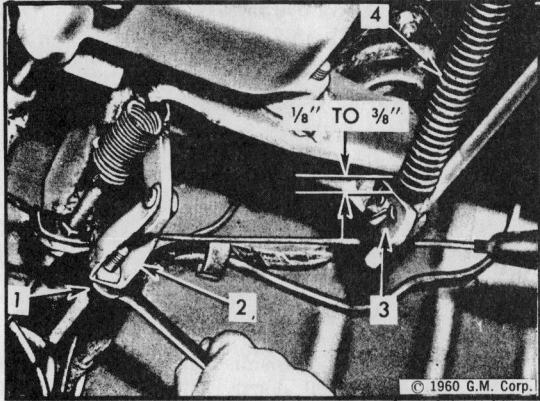

Fig. 117—Adjusting Clutch Cable

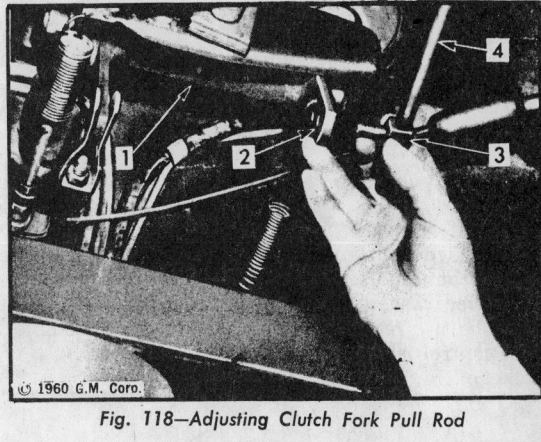

Fig. 118—Adjusting Clutch Fork Pull Rod

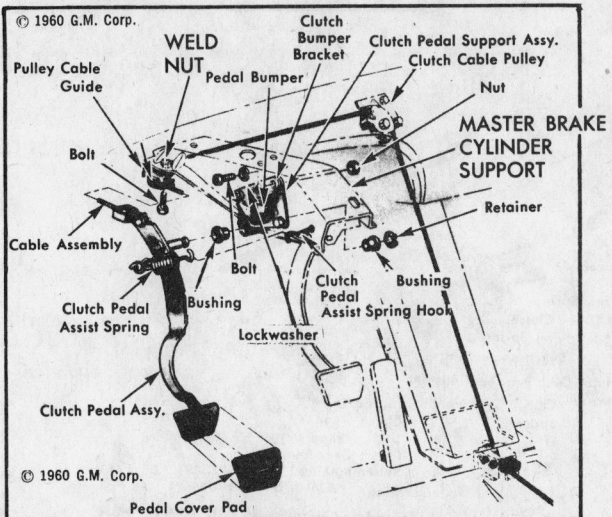

Fig. 120—Clutch Pedal and Cable, Exploded

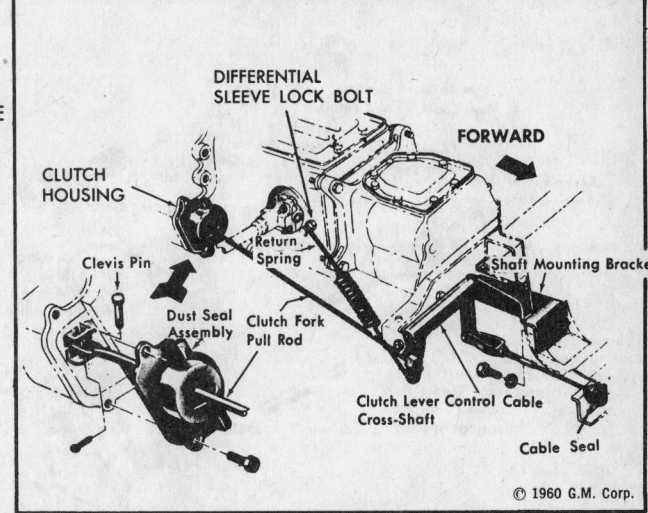

Fig. 121—Clutch Linkage, Exploded

clutch lever control cable cross shaft has a clearance of 1/8" to 3/8", as shown in Fig. 117.

4. Lock up the clevis jam nut.

5. Manually pull the fork pull rod #4, Fig. 118, until slack is out of the clutch fork. (The release bearing touching the diaphragm fingers.)

6. With the fork pull rod in this position, align the swivel #3, Fig. 118, with upper hole in outboard lever #2. Back off the swivel three full turns and assemble to lever #2, Fig. 118.

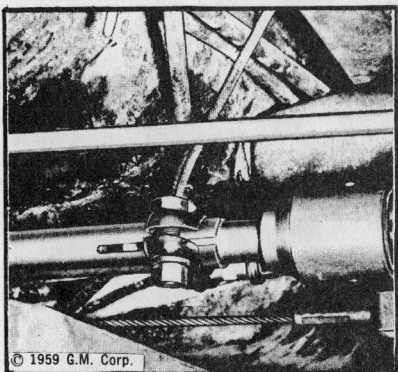

Fig. 123—Shift Rod Clamp

CLUTCH ASSEMBLY R & R

1. Remove Power Train.

2. Separate the transmission and axle units from the engine.

Note: The clutch fork, ball stud and clutch release bearing are removed with the axle housing.

3. Disconnect clutch fork from ball stud, and remove the release bearing from the clutch release shaft.

4. Loosen the six clutch attaching bolts, one turn at a time, until clutch spring pressure is zero.

5. Lift the clutch from the engine. **The pilot bearing is an oil impregnated type pressed into the crankshaft.**

Reinstall the clutch disc so that the cushion springs are toward the flywheel. Continue reinstallation of the clutch in reverse order of removal.

STANDARD TRANSMISSION

The standard transmission is basically the same as the Chevrolet Three Speed Unit except for the use of an input shaft that runs inside a hollow output shaft. Beginning with 1961, a 4-speed unit is available.

GEARSHIFT LINKAGE ADJUST

1. Loosen the "U"-joint clamp nut, (Fig. 123) then move the transmission shift shaft into reverse position.

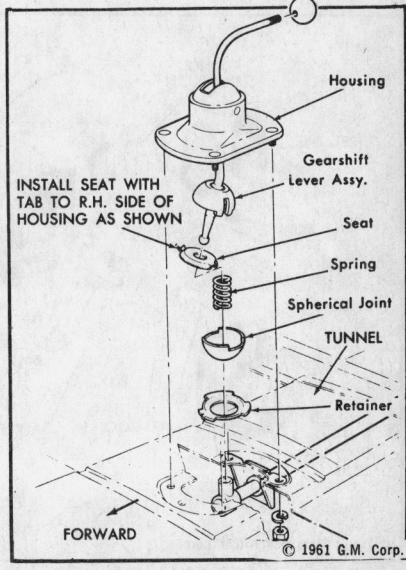

Fig. 124—Gearshift Lever Assembly

If doubtful about position, start the engine and slowly release the clutch.

2. With a helper holding the gearshift lever in reverse, tighten the "U"-joint clamp nut.

3. Test the shift in all ranges.

GEARSHIFT LEVER ASSEMBLY, REMOVE AND DISMANTLE

1. Remove the tunnel front plate.

2. Disconnect and remove the gearshift lever assembly from the floor pan. (The two rear nuts also hold the shift control shaft front mounting bracket.)

3. Lift the assembly up until its studs clear the floor, then remove the unit by lifting the floor mat at the center of the seat.

4. Unscrew the gearshift knob, then invert and gently clamp the gearshift housing in a vise.

5. Using a length of 1½" pipe, depress the retainer plate and rotate 1/3 turn.

6. Remove the lower ball joint, spring and seat, then lift the lever out of the housing.

Assemble and reinstall in reverse order.

TRANSMISSION REMOVE AND INSTALL

See, "Separating Power Train Assembly," in this section.

AUTOMATIC TRANSMISSION

The Corvair Powerglide is an air cooled unit. It has a three element torque converter which drives through an automatic shift, two speed planetary transmission.

The transmission is united to the differential carrier to form a Transaxle. The converter is therefore re-

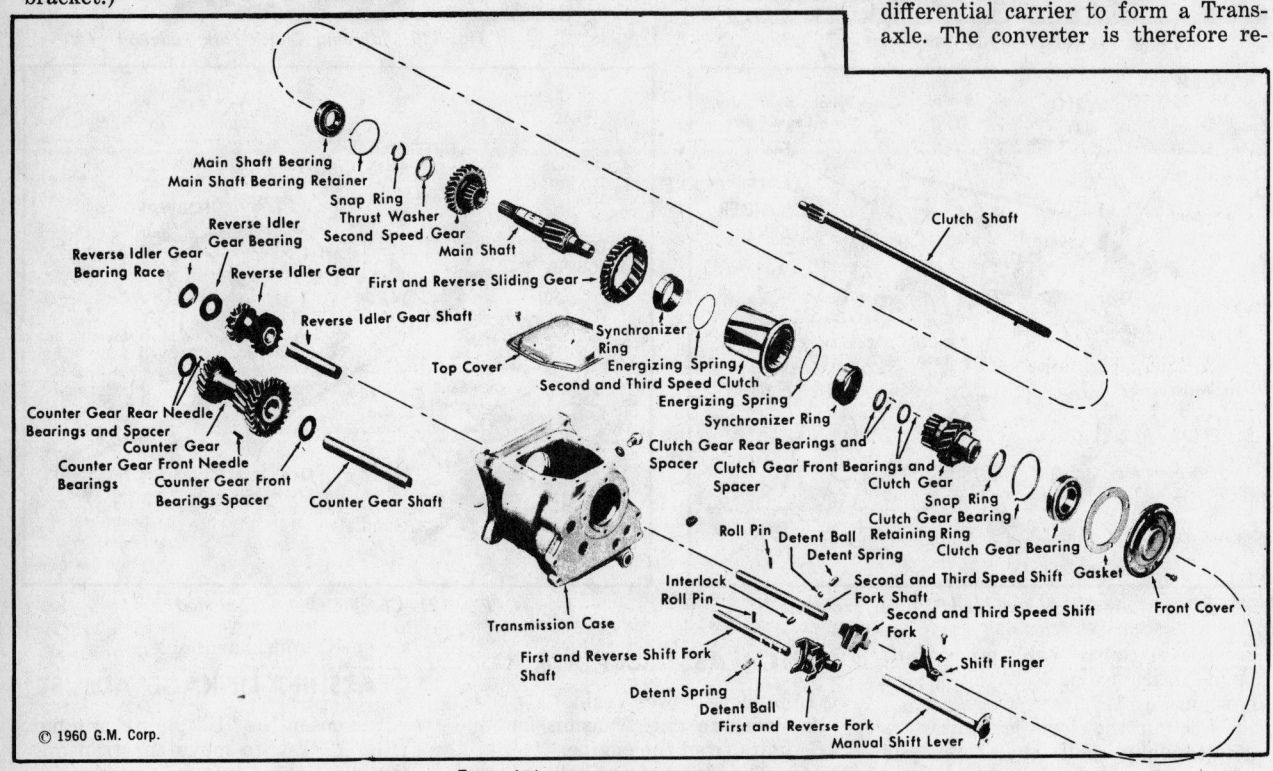

© 1960 G.M. Corp.

Typical Three Speed Transmission—Exploded View

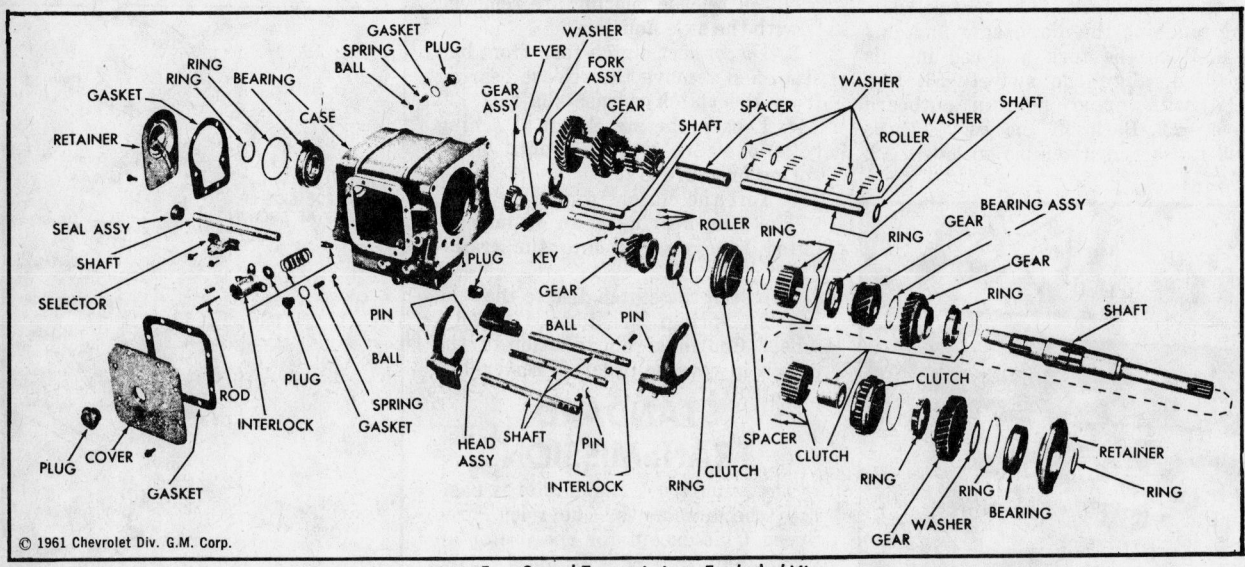

© 1961 Chevrolet Div. G.M. Corp.

Four Speed Transmission—Exploded View

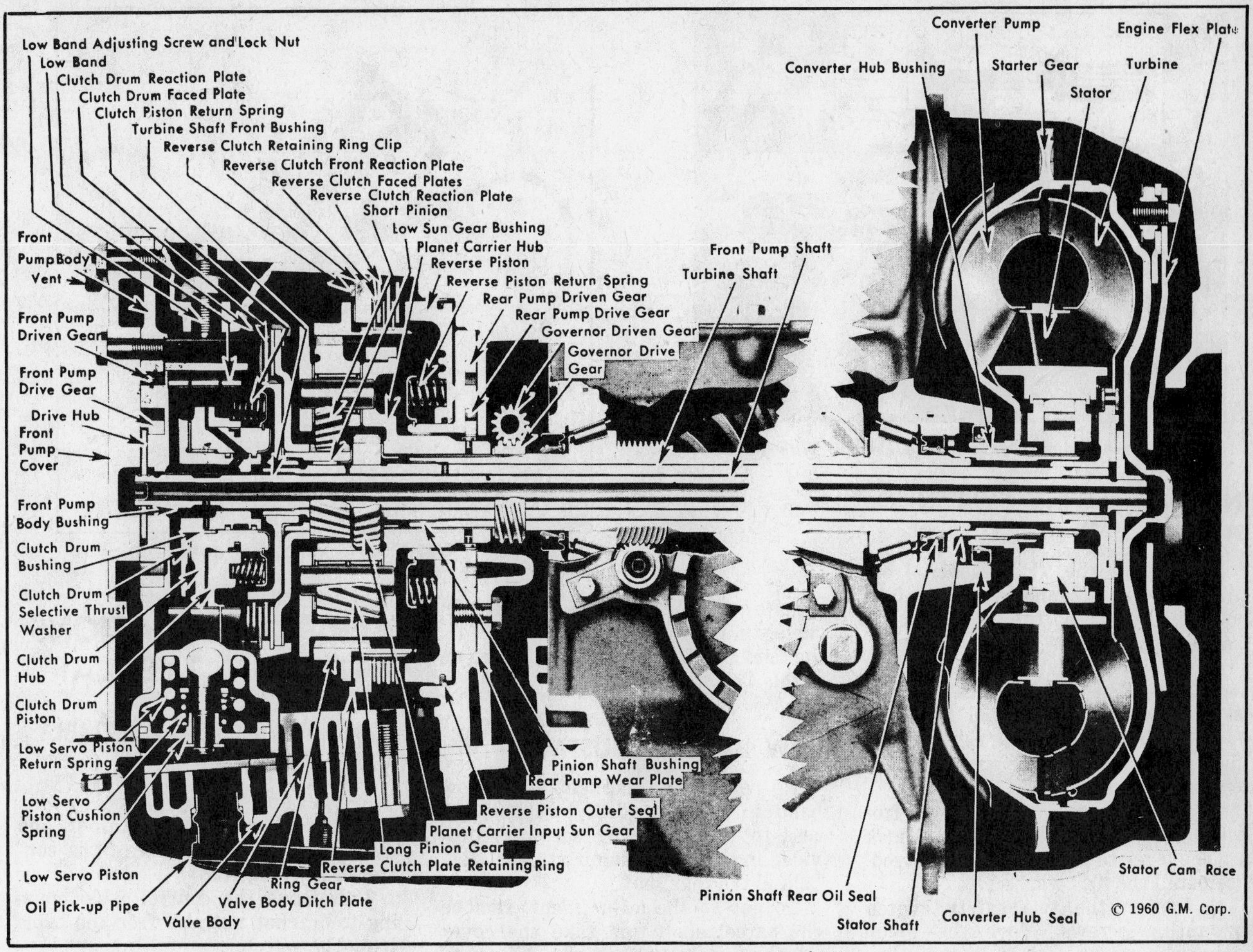

Low Band Adjusting Screw and Lock Nut
Low Band
Clutch Drum Reaction Plate
Clutch Drum Faced Plate
Clutch Piston Return Spring
Turbine Shaft Front Bushing
Reverse Clutch Retaining Ring Clip
Reverse Clutch Front Reaction Plate
Reverse Clutch Faced Plates
Reverse Clutch Reaction Plate
Short Pinion
Low Sun Gear Bushing
Planet Carrier Hub
Reverse Piston
Reverse Piston Return Spring
Rear Pump Driven Gear
Rear Pump Drive Gear
Governor Driven Gear
Governor Drive Gear

Front Pump Body
Vent

Front Pump Driven Gear

Front Pump Drive Gear

Drive Hub Front Pump Cover

Front Pump Body Bushing

Clutch Drum Bushing

Clutch Drum Selective Thrust Washer

Clutch Drum Hub

Clutch Drum Piston

Low Servo Piston Return Spring

Low Servo Piston Cushion Spring

Low Servo Piston

Oil Pick-up Pipe

Ring Gear

Valve Body Ditch Plate

Valve Body

Long Pinion Gear

Reverse Clutch Plate Retaining Ring

Planet Carrier Input Sun Gear

Reverse Piston Outer Seal

Pinion Shaft Bushing

Rear Pump Wear Plate

Front Pump Shaft

Turbine Shaft

Pinion Shaft Rear Oil Seal

Stator Shaft

Converter Hub Seal

Converter Hub Bushing

Converter Pump

Starter Gear

Stator

Engine Flex Plate

Turbine

Stator Cam Race

© 1960 G.M. Corp.

Fig. 125—"Corvair" Powerglide—Cross Sectional View

mote from the main transmission assembly, separated by the differential carrier. Two shafts run, one within the other, through the hollow pinion shaft. There is one from the converter cover hub to the front pump and the other from the turbine to the input sun gear. This shaft transmits converter torque to the transmission gear box.

Except for converter location, the Corvair Powerglide is, generally, a small version of comparable parts of the Conventional Powerglide. The use of a plate-type reverse clutch and a welded converter with integral starter ring gear are obvious differences.

Selector lever positions, from top to bottom are Reverse, Neutral Drive and Low. No park position is provided.

QUICK SERVICE INFORMATION

SHIFT LINKAGE CHECK

1. Start engine and run in neutral for about three minutes for warm-up.

2. With engine at normal idle and the parking brake set, slowly move the selector form "N" toward "R".

Note, by feel, the point at which the reverse clutch applies. If functioning properly, the reverse clutch should be felt to apply at the peak of the tooth separating "Neutral" and "Reverse" detents, (Fig. 126).

3. Repeat the check as in step "2" but move the selector from "N" to "D". If properly functioning, low band will be felt to apply as the selector lever follower is felt to be at the tooth peak between Neutral and Drive.

4. Unless shifts are obtained at the proper points the linkage should be adjusted. Use gauge #J-8365.

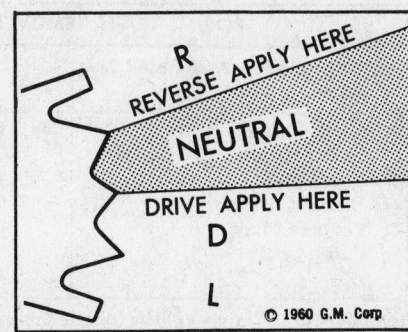

Fig. 126—Shift Linkage Check Diagram

SHIFT LINKAGE ADJUSTMENT

Adjustment of manual linkage may be necessary after any major transmission work is done or as a result of unit disturbances.

1. Drain the transmission at the filler tube nut. Remove transmission oil pan.

2. Indicate "D" at the selector indicator window.

3. Insert tool #J-8365 into the manual valve bore with the tab of the gauge upward and engaged in the forward port of the valve body, (Fig. 127).

4. With the adjusting tool in place, push forward on the manual valve. If properly adjusted, the tool will be held in place horizontally.

5. To adjust, loosen lock screw (Fig. 127), push the manual valve levers forward so that the tool is held in this horizontal position. Recheck the adjustment as outlined in step "4".

6. With adjustment complete, install oil pan and filler tube. Refill transmission to correct level.

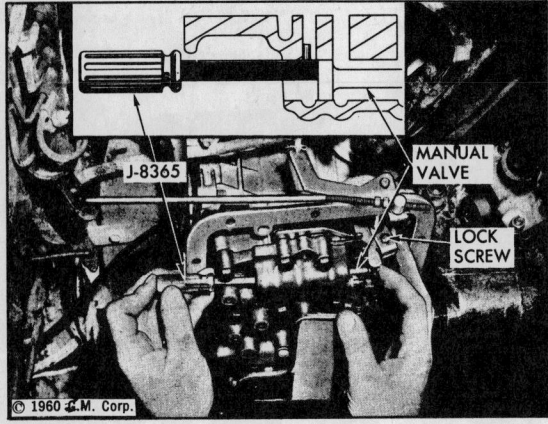

Fig. 127—Adjusting Manual Valve Linkage With J-8365

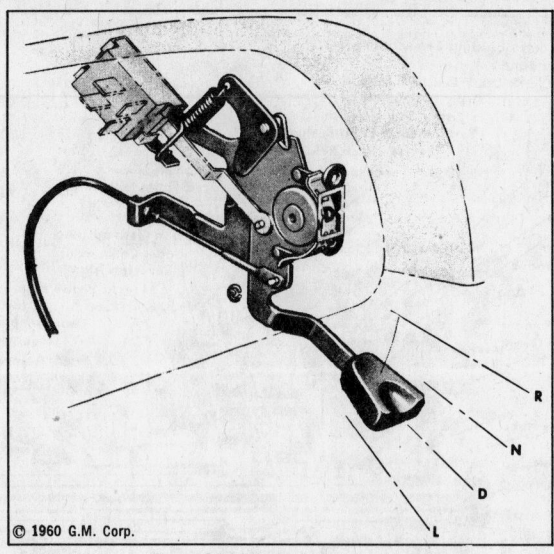

Fig. 128—Neutral Safety Switch

NEUTRAL SAFETY SWITCH ADJUSTMENT

1. Remove the "E" washer from the pin that connects the safety switch lever to the transmission range selector rod.

2. Put selector lever in Neutral.

3. Push the nylon block, in the safety switch, forward all the way.

4. Scribe a line on the right of the metal container in line with the rear end of the nylon block.

5. Pull the switch lever out (toward the rear of the car) and hook up the lever to the range selector rod. Reinstall the "E" washer.

6. Loosen the two safety switch mounting screws. Move the metal container so the scribed line will line up with the front end of the nylon block.

7. Tighten the two mounting screws and recheck the alignment of the scribed line with the nylon block.

8. Check operation of neutral safety switch. Starter should operate in neutral position only. If car is equipped with Back-Up lights, check their operation.

THROTTLE LINKAGE ADJUSTMENT

As special linkage is not used to actuate the transmission throttle valve, this subject will be covered in the Linkage text of the Fuel System of this Corvair section.

LOW BAND ADJUSTMENT

No periodic adjustment of the low band is recommended, however, access to the adjusting screw is provided in the parcel compartment area, behind the rear seat.

To get to the adjustment, remove the parcel shelf and take the cover off the access hole in the floor pan.

To adjust, loosen the lock nut and tighten the adjusting screw until it bottoms, finger tight. Then back off four turns, exactly. Hold the adjusting screw in this position and tighten the lock nut.

Note:

Adjustment is made easier by improvising a wrench for the lock nut, by welding two ¾″ tubular stamped steel spark plug wrenches end to end. The adjusting screw has a square head. It can be reached through the lock nut tubular socket, with a ⅜″ twelve point socket.

SERVICE OPERATIONS UNIT IN THE CAR

RANGE SELECTOR ASSEMBLY —REMOVE

1. Disconnect battery.

2. Remove the "E" retainer and disconnect the upper end of the control cable, (Fig. 128).

3. Remove the control cable housing-to-bracket nut and free the cable from the selector.

4. Remove the instrument cluster.

5. Disconnect the wires to the safety switch.

6. Remove two screws that hold the range selector to the instrument cluster, and remove the quadrant light from its clip on the selector.

Note:

The range selector is serviced only as an assembly.

REPLACE

Reverse above procedure for replacement.

SERVICE REFERENCE GUIDE

POWER TRAIN IN VEHICLE	POWER TRAIN REMOVED FROM VEHICLE	
	Transmission Assembled to Power Train	Transmission Separated from Power Train
Range Selector Assembly Control Cable Vacuum Modulator Governor Valve Body Low Servo Piston Throttle and Manual Valve Levers	Front Pump Clutch Drum Low Band Planet Carrier Turbine Shaft Pump Shaft	Rear Pump and Reverse Piston Assembly Rear Pump Wear Plate Governor Drive Gear Converter Assembly Transmission Case

NOTE: Above guide shows Transmission—Power Train—Vehicle relationship required to perform indicated service operations.

CONTROL CABLE ASSEMBLY

Removal

1. Disconnect the control cable and housing at the upper end.

2. Remove tunnel covers.

3. At the front of the car, remove cable housing from multiple clip (Fig. 131) at the toe-pan and remove upper toe-pan clip.

4. Remove cable housing from the three clips in the tunnel.

5. Remove grommet plate at the rear of the tunnel, free the cable sheath from the plate, and remove the clip in the underbody kick-up area.

6. Disconnect the throttle rods from the throttle valve lever on the transmission.

7. Complete cable removal by rotating the transmission T.V. lever counterclockwise to its full limit. Free the cable ball from the inner manual valve lever slot in the transmission and withdraw the cable.

Note:

The cable assembly with its two captive grommets is serviced only as an assembly.

Replace

1. With tunnel covers still removed, lay the cable out beneath the car in its proper form.

2. Insert the front end of the cable up and into the driver's compartment. The cable must then be snaked under the parking brake cable, then over the brake pipe to prevent chafing.

3. Connect the shift cable to the range selector.

4. Put selector in "D", attach the cable with the upper clip in the toe-pan, and secure the cable in the multiple clip at the base of the toe-pan.

5. Secure the cable with all three clips in the tunnel area. Guide the cable through the hole in the engine front support.

"Early Design"

A. With throttle rods disconnected from the T.V. lever on the transmission, rotate the lever fully counterclockwise and insert the cable ball into the slot of the transmission manual valve lever while guiding the cable sheath into the slot.

B. Insert and torque the cable sheath nut to 8-10 ft. lb.

"Late Design"

A. Install "O" ring seal (Fig. 133) on the cable. Lubricate the "O" ring with transmission fluid.

B. With throttle rods disconnected from the T.V. lever on the transmission, rotate the lever fully counterclockwise and insert the cable ball into the slot of the transmission manual valve lever.

C. Fully seat "O" ring and secure installation by installing cap screw and lock washer.

6. To check, exert a slight hand pressure in the counterclockwise and see that the hole in the notched arm of the T.V. lever is below the transmission oil pan rail, (Fig. 134). If hole is above the rail, installation is faulty.

7. Install cable rear grommet and plate in the rear of the tunnel.

8. Install clip on cable in rear kick-up area.

9. Check shift linkage for proper operation.

VACUUM MODULATOR

The vacuum modulator is mounted on the right side of the transmission and can be serviced from underneath the car.

Removal

1. Remove hose at vacuum modulator and unscrew the modulator with a thin, 1-inch end wrench.

2. Check modulator valve for nicks and other visual damage, however, a vacuum leak within the modulator can be troublesome and may cause loss of transmission fluid and smoky exhaust. The vacuum gauge of some distributor test equipment, may be used to check for modulator leak trouble, or a thorough look at the inside of the modulator hose should be oily if the modulator is leaking. If a leak is found, replace the modulator valve assembly.

Replace

Reverse above procedure for replacement.

GOVERNOR

The governor can be reached from under the car and is mounted on the left side.

Remove by taking out the lock screw from the governor retaining tab and lifting out the governor.

The only recommended service to the governor is the replacement of a driven gear, if necessary.

Fig. 136—Valve Body Installed

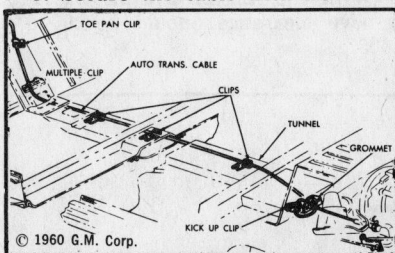

Fig. 131—Shift Control Cable Routing

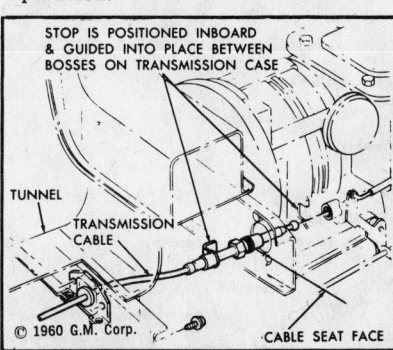

Fig. 132—Cable to Case Installation—Early Design

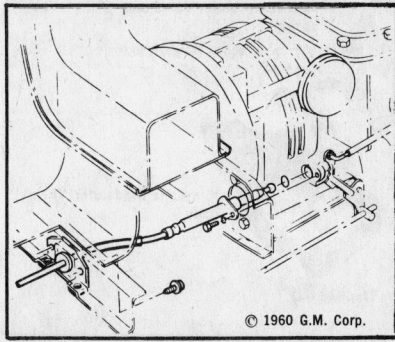

Fig. 133—Cable to Case Installation—Late Design

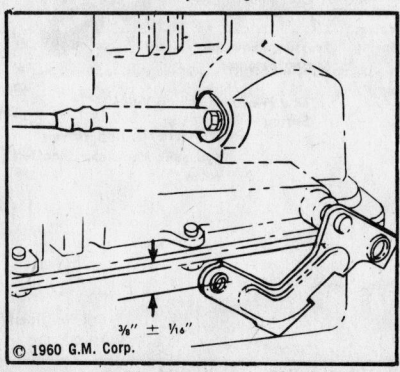

Fig. 134—Cable Installation Check Diagram

Fig. 135—Removing Vacuum Modulator and Valve

© 1960 G.M. Corp.

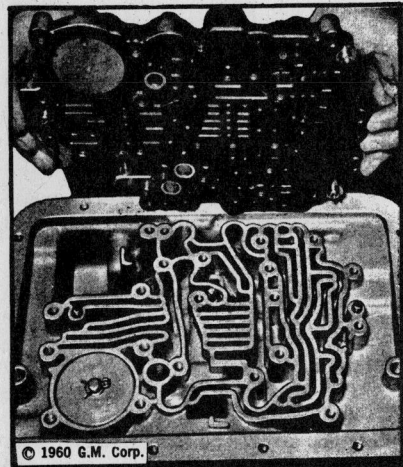

Fig. 137—Removing Valve Body

© 1960 G.M. Corp.

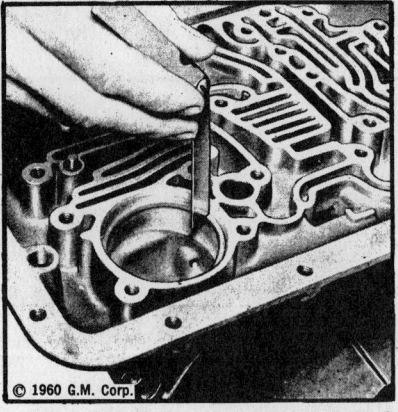

Fig. 138—Measuring Low Servo Piston Ring Gap

© 1960 G.M. Corp.

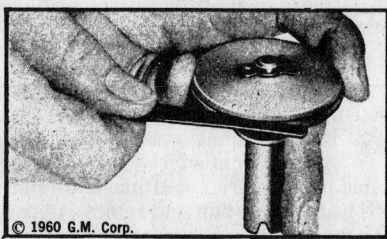

Fig. 139—Measuring Piston-to-Ring Clearance

© 1960 G.M. Corp.

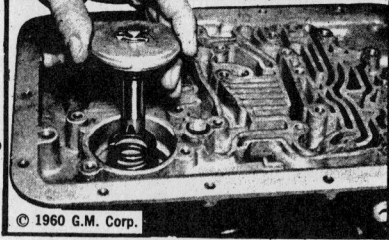

Fig. 140—Installing Low Servo Piston and Return Spring

VALVE BODY AND LOW SERVO

If service is required on the valve body or low servo piston while the transmission is still in the car, proceed as follows:

1. Remove the parcel compartment shelf, back of the rear seat.
2. Remove band adjusting hole cover and loosen the low band adjusting screw lock nut.
3. Drain transmission oil pan and remove filler pipe.
4. Disconnect control rods from T.V. lever on transmission.
5. Remove oil pan, gasket and pick-up pipes.
6. Remove valve body attaching bolts and jar the valve body assembly lightly with a soft hammer to loosen it from its locating dowels.

CAUTION

Carefully lower the valve body while tightening the low band adjusting screw. This must be done simultaneously with lowering the valve body, until the screw is fully tightened.

7. Remove the low servo piston by pulling downward on the hub of the piston shaft with a screwdriver.

Repairs—Valve Body

At present, only the manual valve of the valve body assembly is serviced separately, the other components being serviced as a complete unit.

Check the manual valve for freedom of movement and carefully remove any burrs with a slip stone.

Inspection and Repairs —Low Servo

Remove the hairpin retainer from the piston rod and disassemble the servo piston assembly. Transfer the piston ring from the piston to the servo bore and measure gap clearance. The gap should be .002"-.012".

With the ring on the piston, ring groove clearance should be .0005"-.005".

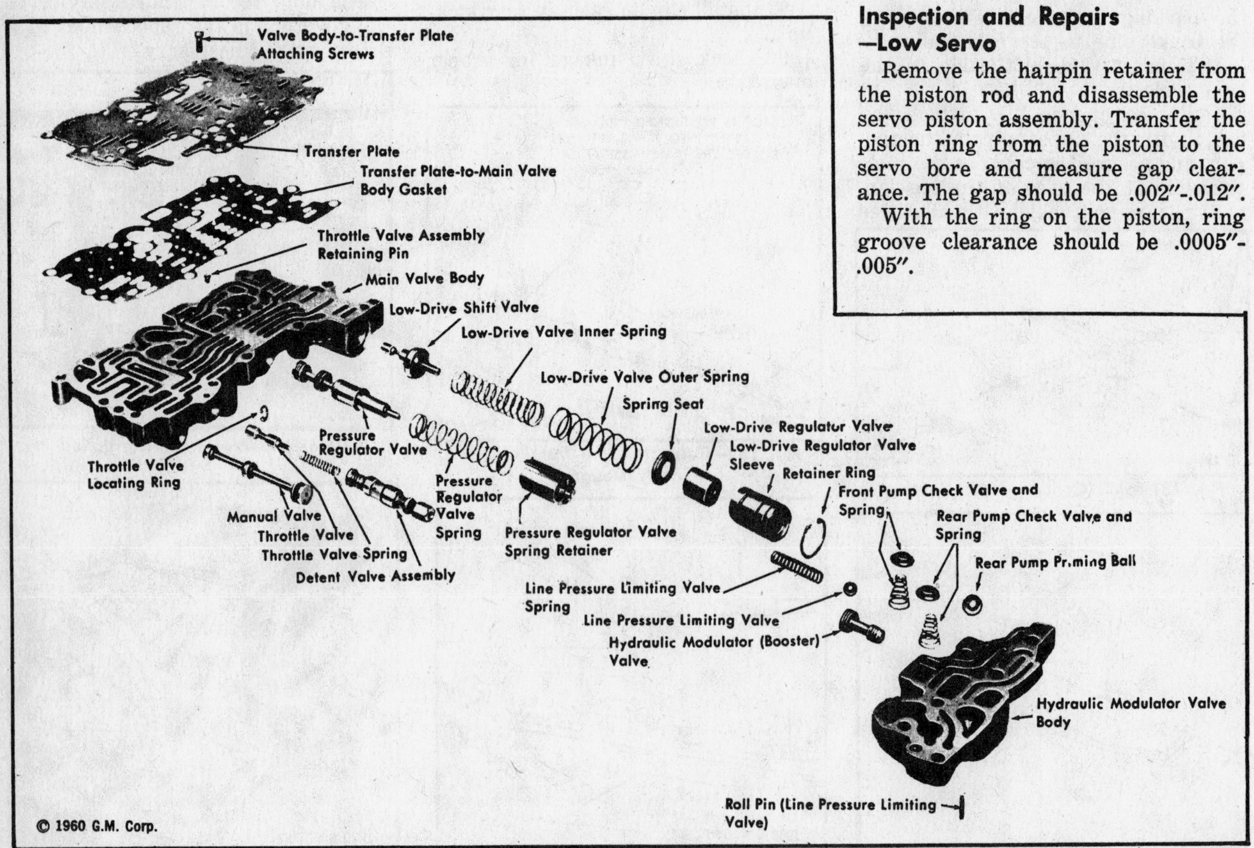

Valve Body-to-Transfer Plate Attaching Screws
Transfer Plate
Transfer Plate-to-Main Valve Body Gasket
Throttle Valve Assembly Retaining Pin
Main Valve Body
Low-Drive Shift Valve
Low-Drive Valve Inner Spring
Low-Drive Valve Outer Spring
Spring Seat
Low-Drive Regulator Valve
Low-Drive Regulator Valve Sleeve
Retainer Ring
Front Pump Check Valve and Spring
Rear Pump Check Valve and Spring
Rear Pump Priming Ball
Pressure Regulator Valve
Pressure Regulator Valve Spring
Pressure Regulator Valve Spring Retainer
Throttle Valve Locating Ring
Manual Valve
Throttle Valve
Throttle Valve Spring
Detent Valve Assembly
Line Pressure Limiting Valve Spring
Line Pressure Limiting Valve
Hydraulic Modulator (Booster) Valve
Hydraulic Modulator Valve Body
Roll Pin (Line Pressure Limiting Valve)
© 1960 G.M. Corp.

"Corvair" Powerglide Valve Body

VALVE BODY AND LOW SERVO—INSTALLATION

1. Assemble the piston and insert the piston assembly into its bore so the notch in the piston shaft engages the low band apply strut. Loosen the low band screw to permit the piston ring to seat in the case bore.

2. Install valve body in transmission; at the same time, loosening the low band screw until its is possible to align the valve body on the locating dowels. If manual valve is installed, index it with the manual valve lever in the case. Install the 20 attaching bolts and torque to 9-11 ft. lb.

3. Lubricate and install "O" ring seal in valve body and install oil pick-up pipe.

4. Install oil pan, torque to 3-4 ft. lb.

5. Tighten filler tube connection, refill transmission and adjust low range band.

TRANSMISSION REMOVE AND REPLACE

All of the following service operations are possible with the Power Train out of the car but not separated into individual assemblies, (Fig. 143). However to simplify illustration, these pictures show the transmission separate from the Power Train Assembly.

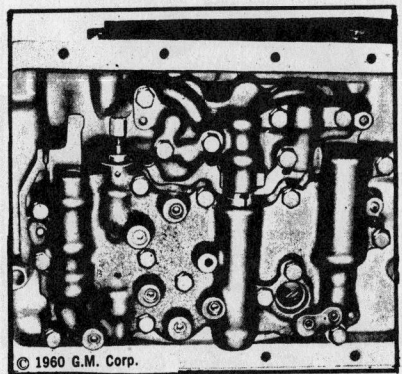

Fig. 141—Valve Body Attaching Bolts

Fig. 142—Installing Oil Pick-up in Valve Body

DISASSEMBLY OF TRANSMISSION

1. Drain oil by removing filler tube; then remove the 12 front pump-to-transmission case bolts.

2. If overhaul is being done with transmission attached to Power Train, loosen the low band adjustment jam nut and **fully tighten** the adjusting screw. (This will prevent the case components from being pulled out when the front pump is removed.)

3. With slide hammers (Fig. 147) remove the pump cover. Then remove the pump shaft.

4. Remove the front pump body from the transmission case. (**Don't drop the gears.**)

5. To remove the clutch drum, loosen the low band adjusting screw and remove the band and its components, (Fig. 149).

6. Remove the clutch drum, (Fig. 145).

Note:

If the work is being done without separating the transmission from the Power Train, care must be taken not to disengage the ring gear from the reverse clutch face plates unless renewal of either the ring gear or reverse plates is expected. Meshing the reverse plates and the ring gear is difficult while the unit is in the horizontal position.

7. Remove the planet carrier from the ring gear and remove the turbine shaft. On disassemblies made with the transmission separated from the axle, the turbine shaft is removed with the separation of the two components.

Note:

No further disassembly should take place with the transmission still attached to the Power Train. Though the reverse plates are accessible at this stage of tear-down, plate damage can usually be associated with trouble that requires the removal of the transmission from the Power Train.

The remainder of disassembly can only be done with the transmission removed from the Power Train.

8. Remove the ring gear from the reverse plates.

9. Remove the clip (Fig. 151), then the snap ring.

10. Remove all of the plates, (The thick reaction plate, three faced plates and the three, thin steel plates).

11. Remove the rear pump and reverse piston mounting bolts from the differential side of the transmission case (Fig. 153).

12. Remove the rear pump and reverse piston assembly by pulling with a twisting action.

13. Remove the rear pump wear plate.

INSPECTION AND REPAIRS

FRONT PUMP

1. Especially check the gear for wear at the inner bearing, where it mates with the pump journal.

2. Inspect the cover face and the pump body for nicks and scoring.

3. Install the pump gears and check the following:

A. Clearance, driven gear and body, .0025"-.005" (Fig. 156).

B. Clearance, driven gear and crescent, .003"-.009" (Fig. 157).

C. Check gear end clearance with a scale and feeler. Clearance should be, .0005"-.0015" (Fig. 158).

D. Check pump drive gear teeth for interference between end of gear teeth and the crescent.

4. Replace gasket and square-cut seal ring in O.D. of front pump cover. Also check condition of cast iron seal rings on pump body hub; replace if necessary.

5. Check condition of front pump body bushing. If worn, replace.

Fig. 143—Transmission in Holding Fixture

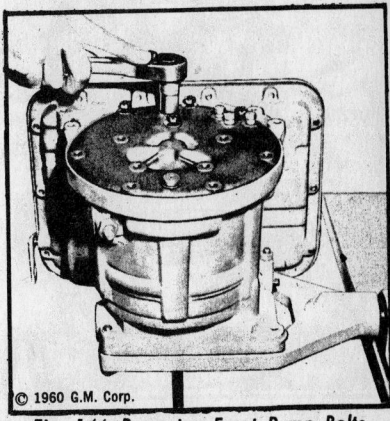

Fig. 144—Removing Front Pump Bolts

CLUTCH DRUM DISASSEMBLY, ASSEMBLY
Refer to Fig. 159

1. Remove clutch flange retaining ring.
2. Remove clutch flange and thrust washer.
3. Remove clutch hub, the nested plates and the hub front thrust washer.
4. Remove spring retainer (7) by placing the drum in a press and compressing the fifteen clutch piston return springs (#6). This is best accomplished with an adapter, as in Fig. 159, and removing snap ring (8) with lock ring pliers.
5. Release pressure on the press and remove retainer (7) and the fifteen springs.
6. Remove clutch piston (5) by pulling upward with a twisting motion. Then remove the piston seal (4).
7. Complete by removing piston inner seal (3) from hub of clutch drum (2).

Note:
Check all clutch components for damage and wear and replace as necessary.

Fig. 145—Removing Clutch Drum

INPUT SUN GEAR TO LOW SUN GEAR THRUST WASHER

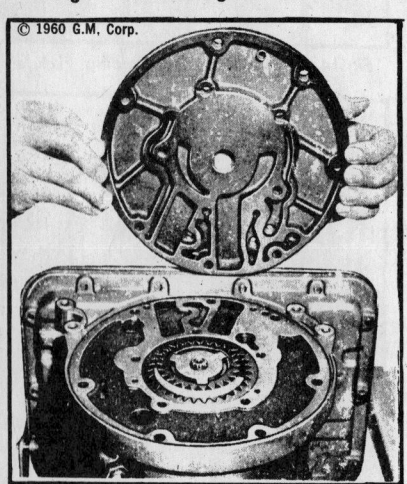

Fig. 146—Removing Front Pump Cover

Assembly
Assemble with care and in the reverse sequence of disassembly.

PLANET CARRIER
The planet carrier is serviced as a unit. If components fail, replace the assembly.

TURBINE SHAFT

In addition to normal inspection, make sure that the two lubrication holes are open. If necessary to replace the turbine shaft bushings, use care in locating them. The two bushings used are identical but are installed to different depths, as controlled by bushing installers and illustrated in Fig. 162.

The **front** bushing should be installed with tool #J-8360-6.

The **rear** bushing should be installed with tool #J-8360-7.

Fig. 147—Removing Front Pump with Slide Hammers

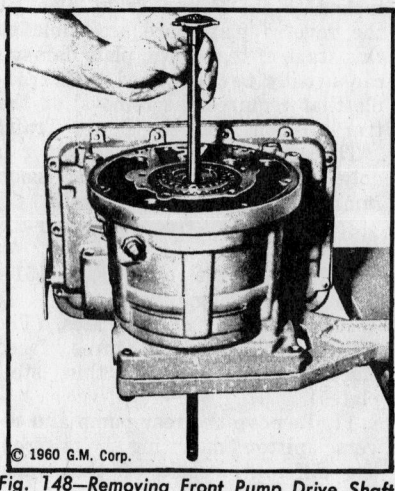

Fig. 148—Removing Front Pump Drive Shaft

PUMP SHAFT
Inspect in normal manner and replace parts as needed.

REAR PUMP AND REVERSE PISTON ASSEMBLY

Disassembly, Refer to Fig. 163

1. Remove drive gear, (9) and driven gear, (10) from pump body, (8).
2. Place the assembly in a press with the pump body on a wooden block, then compress the spring retainer, (2) as in Fig. 164.
3. Remove snap ring, (1). Now release pressure and remove retainer, (2) and springs, (4).
4. To remove reverse piston, (5) it is necessary to fill the snap ring groove in the hub of the rear pump body, (8) with string or, (temporarily) with an "O" ring. The rear pump body, (8) can then be pushed out of the reverse piston bore.
5. Remove the square cut piston inner seal, (3) and the outer seal, (6). The seals should be thrown away and new seals used in assembly.

Note:
If necessary to replace the rear pump body bushing, refer to Fig. 162. & Fig. 165.

Assembly
Assemble the rear pump and reverse piston assembly in the reverse order of disassembly.

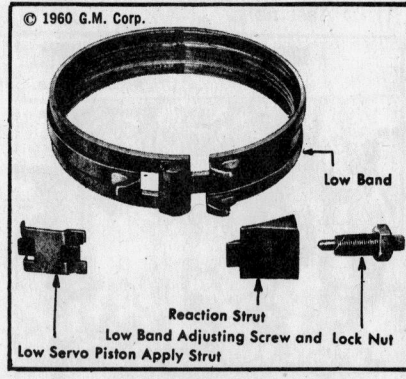

Low Band
Reaction Strut
Low Band Adjusting Screw and Lock Nut
Low Servo Piston Apply Strut

Fig. 149—Low Band Components

Fig 150—Removing Ring Gear

Fig.151—Reverse Clutch Pack
Retainer Ring and Clip

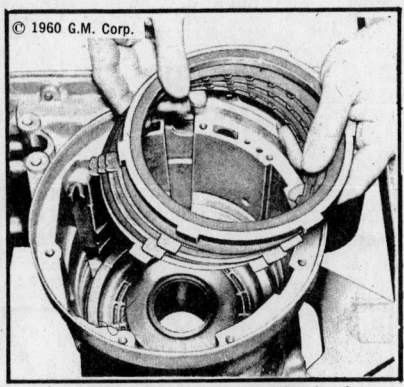

Fig. 152—Removing Reverse Clutch Plates

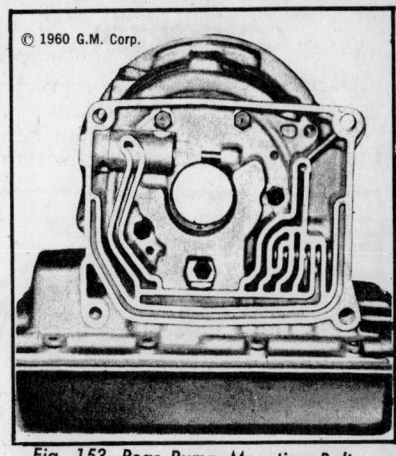

Fig. 153—Rear Pump Mounting Bolts

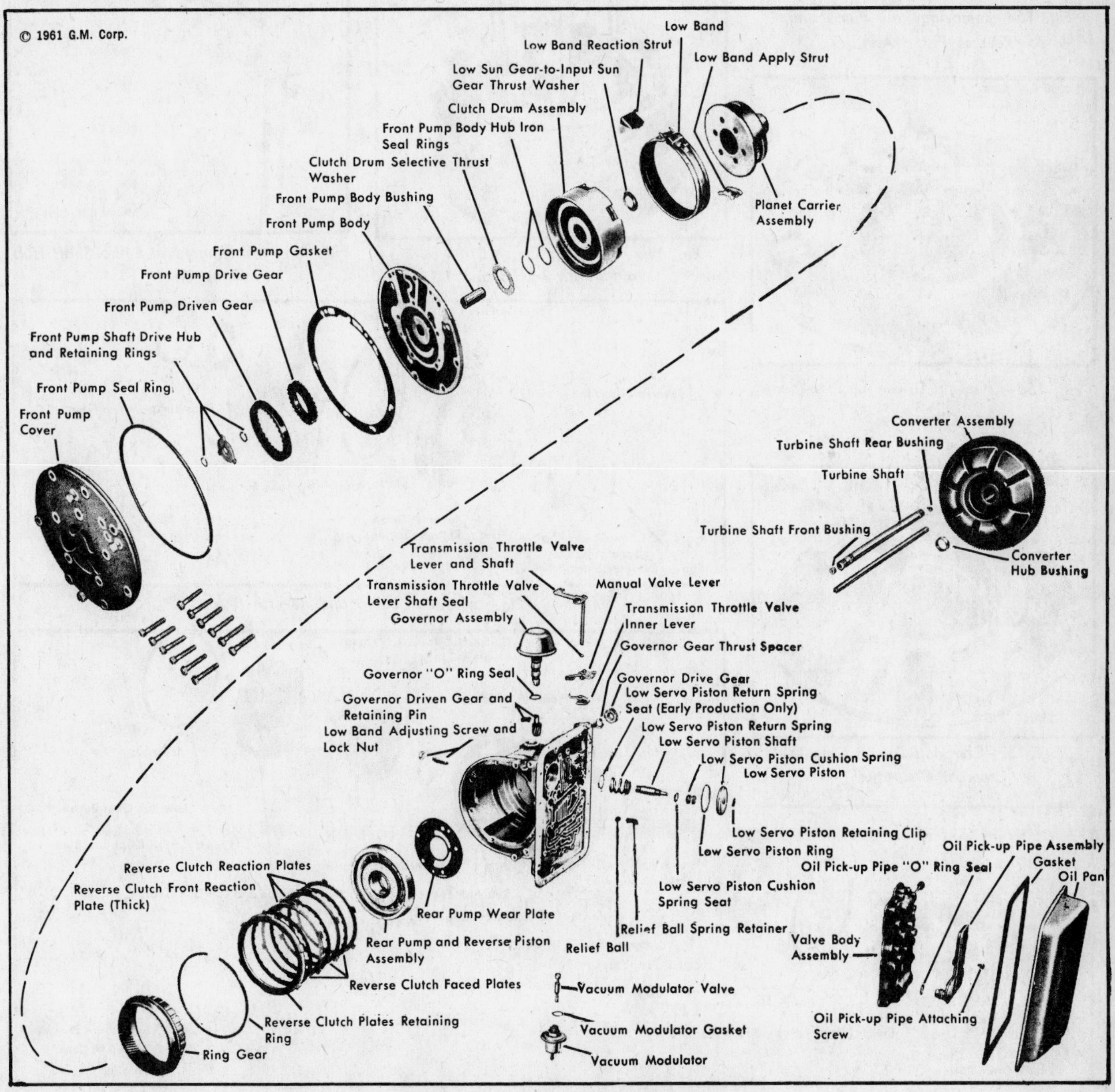

© 1961 G.M. Corp.

Low Band

Low Band Reaction Strut

Low Band Apply Strut

Low Sun Gear-to-Input Sun
Gear Thrust Washer

Clutch Drum Assembly

Front Pump Body Hub Iron
Seal Rings

Clutch Drum Selective Thrust
Washer

Front Pump Body Bushing

Planet Carrier
Assembly

Front Pump Body

Front Pump Gasket

Front Pump Drive Gear

Front Pump Driven Gear

Front Pump Shaft Drive Hub
and Retaining Rings

Front Pump Seal Ring

Front Pump
Cover

Converter Assembly

Turbine Shaft Rear Bushing

Turbine Shaft

Turbine Shaft Front Bushing

Converter
Hub Bushing

Transmission Throttle Valve
Lever and Shaft

Transmission Throttle Valve
Lever Shaft Seal

Manual Valve Lever

Governor Assembly

Transmission Throttle Valve
Inner Lever

Governor "O" Ring Seal

Governor Gear Thrust Spacer

Governor Drive Gear

Governor Driven Gear and
Retaining Pin

Low Servo Piston Return Spring
Seat (Early Production Only)

Low Band Adjusting Screw and
Lock Nut

Low Servo Piston Return Spring

Low Servo Piston Shaft

Low Servo Piston Cushion Spring

Low Servo Piston

Low Servo Piston Retaining Clip

Low Servo Piston Ring

Oil Pick-up Pipe Assembly

Oil Pick-up Pipe "O" Ring Seal

Gasket

Oil Pan

Reverse Clutch Reaction Plates

Reverse Clutch Front Reaction
Plate (Thick)

Rear Pump Wear Plate

Rear Pump and Reverse Piston
Assembly

Reverse Clutch Faced Plates

Relief Ball

Vacuum Modulator Valve

Vacuum Modulator Gasket

Vacuum Modulator

Low Servo Piston Cushion
Spring Seat

Relief Ball Spring Retainer

Valve Body
Assembly

Oil Pick-up Pipe Attaching
Screw

Reverse Clutch Plates Retaining
Ring

Ring Gear

Fig. 155—"Corvair" Powerglide, Exploded View

CONVERTER

During inspection of the converter it is well to remember that internal repairs are not practical and any malfunctioning of the unit, justifies re-

Fig. 154—Removing Rear Pump and Reverse Piston Assy.

Fig. 156—Checking Driven Gear-to-Pump Body Clearance

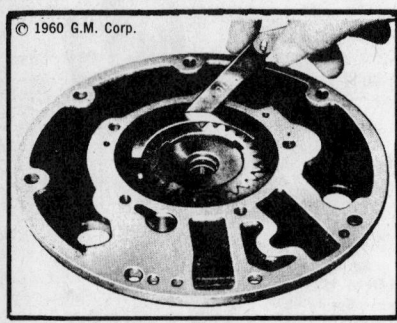

Fig. 157—Checking Driven Gear-to-Crescent Clearance

placing the assembly. The starter gear is an exception as is the converter hub bushing, see Fig. 162 & Fig. 166.

ASSEMBLY OF TRANSMISSION

Note:

The following procedure applies only when the transmission has been separated from the Power Train.

1. Attach the transmission case to a holding fixture, (Fig. 167).

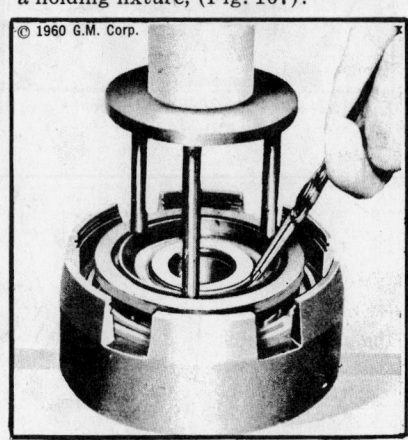

Fig. 160—Removing Clutch Drum Spring Retainer with J-5133 and J-7782

2. Install two 3-inch guide pins 5/16" x 18), in the rear pump bolt holes, then install the rear pump wear plate on the guide pins. Use a small quantity of petroleum jelly to hold the wear plate in place.

3. Insert the rear pump and reverse piston with guide pins into the case, then insert a length of 1/2" to 3/4" wide, .010"-.015" shim stock between the piston outer seal and the case. With the rear of the case downward and the piston entered into the case bore, use the shim stock (or long feeler gauge blade) in a sliding motion around the circumference of the

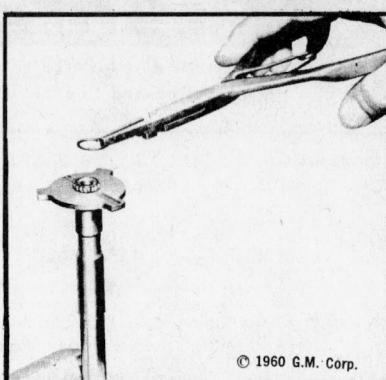

Fig. 161—Installing Front Pump Shaft Hub Snap Ring

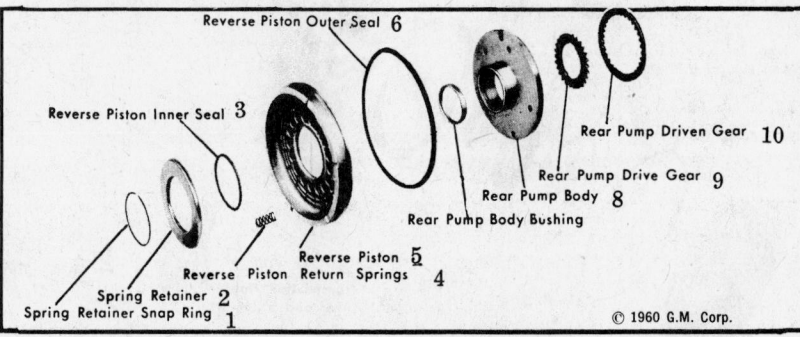

Fig. 163—Rear Pump and Reverse Piston

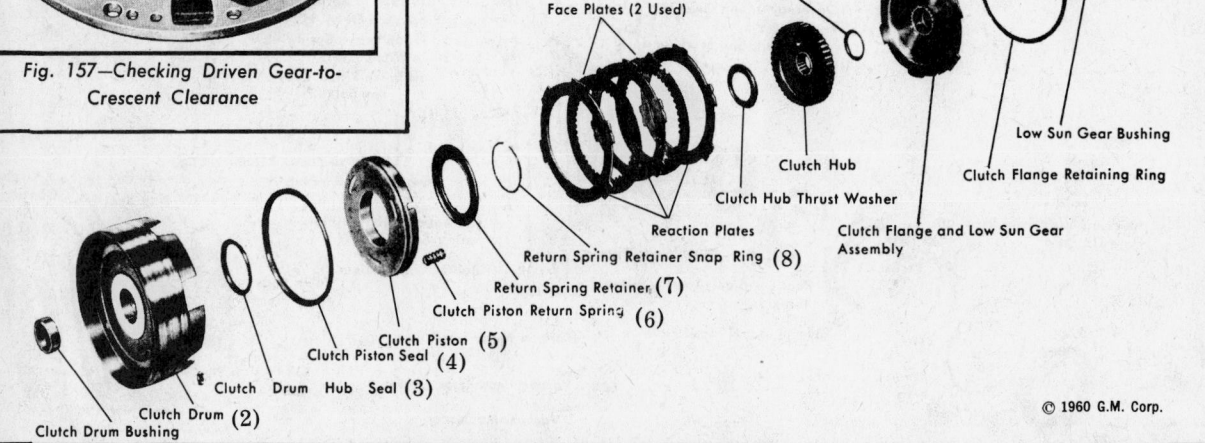

Fig. 159—Clutch Drum, Exploded View

Fig. 158—Installing Front Pump Bushing
with J-8360-5

J-5133

J-7782

Fig. 164—Removing Reverse Piston Return
Retainer with J-5133 and J-7782

Fig. 165—Installing Rear Pump Body Bushing
with J-8360-4 and Handle J-7079-2

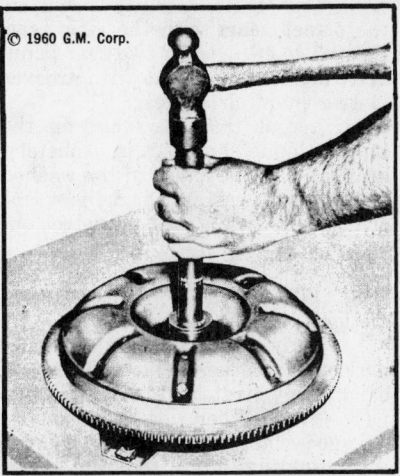

Fig. 166—Installing Converter Hub Bushing
with J-8360-1 and Handle J-7019-2

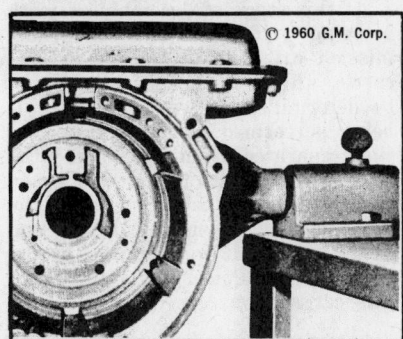

Fig. 167—Transmission Case Installed
in Holding Fixture J-7896

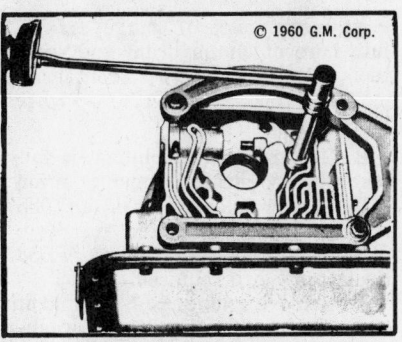

Fig. 168—Measuring Rear Pump and
Reverse Piston Bolt Torque

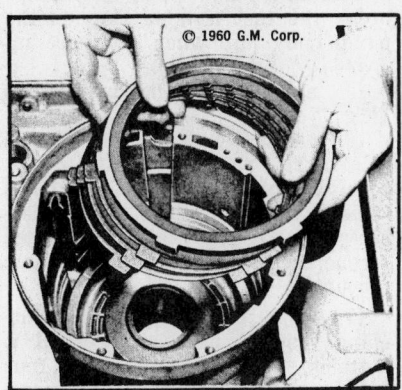

Fig. 169—Installing Reverse Clutch Plates

Fig. 170—Reverse Clutch Pack Retaining
Ring and Clip Installation

Fig. 171—Installing Ring Gear

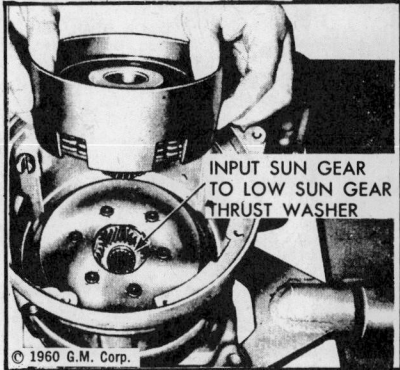

INPUT SUN GEAR
TO LOW SUN GEAR
THRUST WASHER

Fig. 172—Installing Clutch Drum

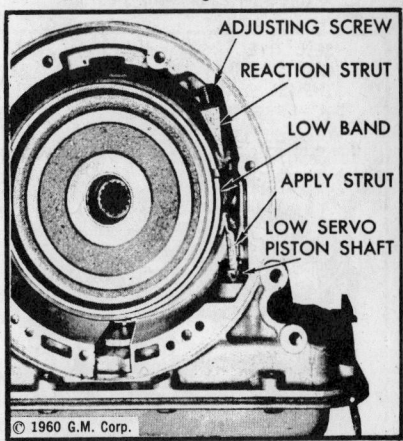

ADJUSTING SCREW

REACTION STRUT

LOW BAND

APPLY STRUT

LOW SERVO
PISTON SHAFT

Fig. 173—Low Band Components Installed

piston. This action, with a lubricated seal and a slight pressure on the piston, should depress the lip of the seal and allow the piston to enter the case bore.

4. Remove the guide pins and install five rear pump mounting bolts (Fig. 168), and torque to 9-11 ft. lb.

5. Install the clutch plate pack (Fig. 169), starting with a steel plate and alternating to finish with a faced plate. The notched lug of each steel (reaction) plate is installed so it is at the top of the groove and in the 4 o'clock position in the case, (with the transmission in normal running position). Then install the thick reaction plate with its square "dimple" on its lug engaging the 4 o'clock groove.

6. Install clutch plate retainer ring and the retainer ring clip, (Fig. 170).

7. Align the internal lands and grooves of the reverse face plates.

8. Start the ring gear in the reverse drive plates (Fig. 171), while jiggling the plates laterally.

9. If performing the assembly with the transmission installed on the Power Train, install the turbine shaft at this point.

10. Install the planetary unit with a slight twisting movement to engage the planet gears with the ring gear. Be sure to engage the two rear pump drive lugs on planet hub with grooves in rear pump drive gear.

11. Install thrust washer on the captive input sun gear in planetary gear set with the flange of the washer forward. If necessary, hold the washer in place with a daub of petroleum jelly.

12. Install clutch drum assembly (Fig. 172), with a slight twisting motion.

13. Turn the transmission to a horizontal position and install the low band, apply strut, and reaction strut, (Fig. 173). When low band apply linkage is completely installed, tighten the adjusting screw to keep struts from falling out of place.

Note:

At this stage of assembly, **if work is being performed with the transmission attached to the differential carrier,** thrust washer thickness must be determined. However, **if work is being performed with the transmission separated from the differential carrier,** install the thrust washer on the front pump hub and complete transmission assembly. Final end play adjustment to be made, as described in the Power Train portion of this car section.

TO DETERMINE THRUST WASHER THICKNESS

A. Insert pilot of gauge #J-8371 into bore of clutch drum and secure tool to case with two front pump mounting bolts, (Fig. 174). Tighten bolts fully.

B. Be sure that the plunger is fully seated then check plunger position:

If plunger is below flush, an .088" thrust washer is required.

If plunger is flush or above, A .058" thrust washer is required.

C. Remove gauge #J-8371 and install correct selective thrust washer on pump hub, (Fig. 175).

14. Use a new front pump gasket and install the front pump body. **Don't break the cast iron oil ring** on the pump body hub when they are indexed to the drum.

15. Install front pump drive shaft, (Fig. 176).

16. Install a new square-cut seal ring in the pump cover and install cover. Dip bolt heads in oil impervious sealer and torque them in a criss-cross pattern to 18 to 20 ft. lb. Then torque the five inner bolts the same amount.

17. Adjust the low band by tightening the adjusting screw until it bottoms, then back-off exactly four full turns and lock the adjustment.

TROUBLE SHOOTING

Pressure checks are not recommended on Corvair Powerglide at this time. Rather, the following diagnosis chart is provided to help identify the cause of troubles.

For trouble shooting, see "Powerglide "B", Diagnosis Guide, in the Automatic Transmission section of this manual.

ShiftPoint Plan

UPSHIFT	MPH
Minimum Throttle	10-12½
Full Throttle	41-47
Part Throttle (Detent Touch)	34-41

DOWNSHIFT	MPH
Closed Throttle	8-12
Full Throttle	38-44
Part Throttle (Detent Touch)	23-30
Manual Low, (Inhibited)	41-46

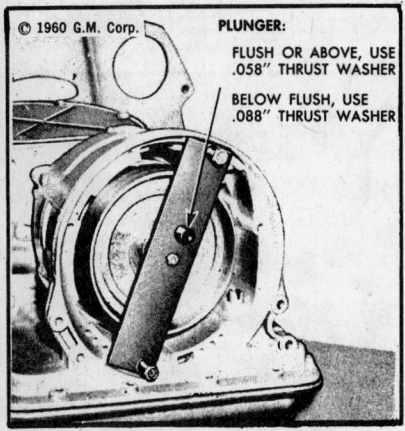

© 1960 G.M. Corp.

PLUNGER:
FLUSH OR ABOVE, USE .058" THRUST WASHER
BELOW FLUSH, USE .088" THRUST WASHER

Fig. 174—Gauging Clutch Drum Thrust Washer with J-8371

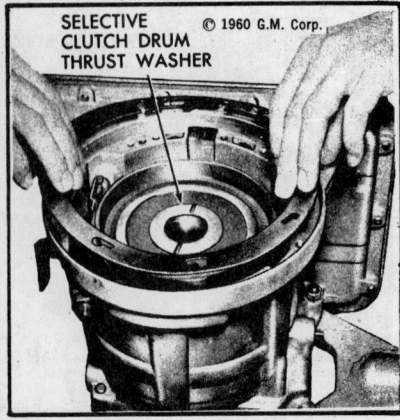

SELECTIVE CLUTCH DRUM THRUST WASHER   © 1960 G.M. Corp.

Fig. 175—Installing Front Pump Gasket

© 1960 G.M. Corp.

Fig. 176—Installing Front Pump Drive Shaft

© 1960 G.M. Corp.

Fig. 177—Installing Front Pump Cover

REAR AXLE ASSEMBLY

AXLE, AXLE BEARING AND UNIVERSAL JOINT

1. Jack up the car and remove the gear wheel.

2. Remove the four axle bearing retaining bolts, (through the access hole in the flange).

3. Pull the backing plate outward slightly then push it back onto the control arm studs to free it from the bearing retainer. Now pull the axle shaft out far enough to free the "U"-joint splines from the side gears in the rear axle.

4. Remove the four nuts from the "U"-bolts holding the "U"-joint.

5. Remove bolt and two washers attaching the yoke to the axle shaft and remove the yoke. Now, withdraw the axle shaft from the lower control arm.

AXLE SHAFT BEARING

1. Place the axle shaft and bearing in a press. Attach a split ring type puller between the axle flange and the bearing puller ring.

2. Pull oil deflector, bearing and puller ring.

3. To avoid damage in pressing the new bearing assembly into place, put a new puller ring and bearing on the axle. Now place the **old puller ring**, with it's flat face against the bearing inner race. Press the puller and bearing onto the axle.

4. Remove the old puller ring. Then press on the oil deflector.

SIDE BEARING ADJUSTER SEAL

The differential side bearing ad-

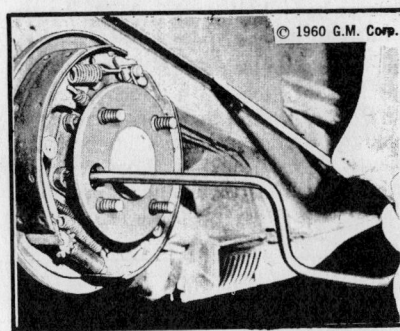

Fig. 179—Removing Axle Bearing Retainer Nuts

justing sleeve seal may be replaced while the axle shaft is out by:

1. Remove the universal joint from the side bearing adjusting sleeve.

2. Pry out the old seal, then install a new seal using a flat faced object as a driver, the seal mounts flush. The seal lips must face inward.

CARRIER DISASSEMBLE AND ASSEMBLE

For removal and installation procedures, see "Power Train" in this section.

1. Drain the differential carrier.

2. Remove speedometer driven gear assembly.

3. Remove six cover bolts and lift off the cover.

4. Remove the tab-locks and screw out the side bearing adjusting sleeves.

5. Unlock, then unscrew the pinion bearing adjusting sleeve.

6. Remove pinion with bearings by lifting the pinion shaft toward the transmission end of the carrier. Then remove the shaft and bearings through the carrier cover hole.

7. Remove the differential assembly from the carrier by angling the assembly through the carrier cover hole.

Planet Carrier Hub (Transmission Output)
Rear Selective End Play Spacers
Governor Driven Gear
Pinion Shaft Front Seal
Pinion Front Bearing and Race
Speedometer Drive Gear (Integral Part of Pinion Shaft)
Ring Gear

Converter Hub Seal
Pinion Shaft Rear Seal
Pinion Rear Bearing and Race
Selective Pinion Depth Shim
Pinion Gear
Vent

Drain Plug
Pinion Shaft
Speedometer Driven Gear Assembly
Governor Drive Gear
Transmission Front Pump Shaft
Transmission Turbine Shaft
Side Bearing Adjusting Sleeve
Side Bearing Adjusting Sleeve Seal
Stator Shaft
Stator Assembly
Differential Carrier Filler Plug
Side Bearing Adjusting Sleeve Lock Tab

© 1960 G.M. Corp.

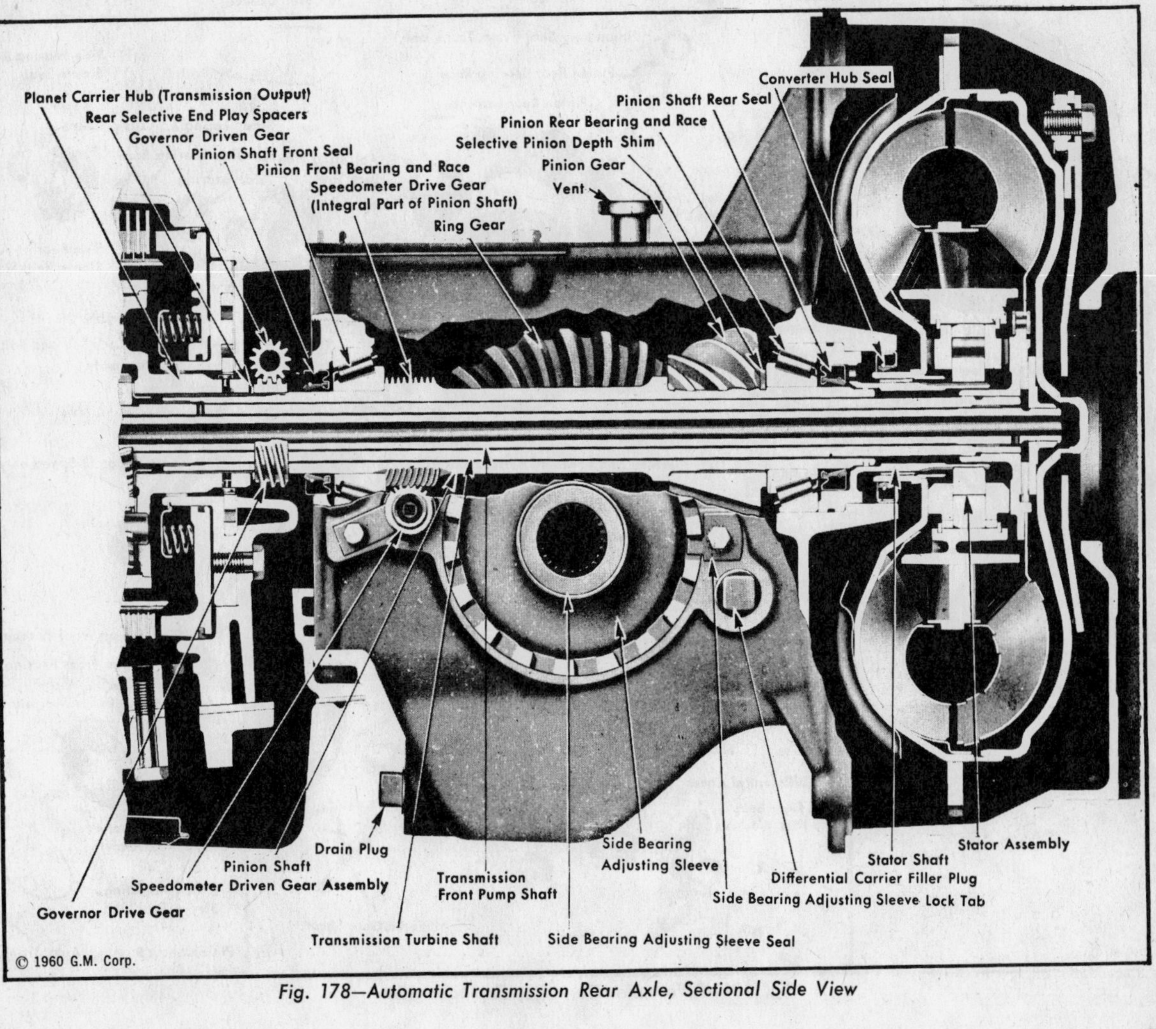

Fig. 178—Automatic Transmission Rear Axle, Sectional Side View

Further dismantling of components is done in the conventional manner and according to good mechanical logic.

NOTE:

There is a difference between some of the differential components used in cars equipped with standard transmissions and those used in automatic transmissions.

PINION OR BEARING REPLACE

In this area, special tools are required and should be used for best results.

1. To determine shim thickness to be used between the pinion bearing and pinion gear, proceed as follows:

A. Mount the differential carrier as in Fig. 183. Place pinion rear bearing to be used in assembly in carrier and rotate several times to seat it.

B. Insert adapter pilot J-6266-25 into bore of stator shaft or clutch bearing shaft. Place depth setting gauge plate J-6266-5 on rear bearing. Insert clamp bolt through the gauge plate and the pilot, then lightly tighten the nut. Work the plate and the bearing while tightening the nut to assure centering in the bore. Now tighten the clamp nut to 6 ft. lb.

C. Place gauge cylinder adapter, J-6266-18 in the unthreaded portion of the side bearing adjusting sleeve bore. Now insert gauge cylinder J-6266-01 in adapter with plunger and mounting post horizontal. Rotate the gauge body back and forth to insure that the adapter crescents and body are fully seated in the side bearing bores.

D. Place gauge J-6266-19 on the gauge plate so that it is centered beneath the gauge body. Loosen clamp screw in gauge and slide the plunger back and forth to obtain exact center between the low point of the gauge cylinder and the gauge plate. When this position is obtained, tighten the screw in the plunger and remove the plunger.

E. Using a 2" micrometer, measure the gauge plunger.

F. Check the pinion marking stamped on the front face of the pinion gear and the gauge plunger measurement obtained in procedure "E" with the following chart.

Example:

The gauge reading is 1.255" and the pinion marking is "15". Following the "Micrometer Reading" of 1.255", across the vertical "Pinion Marking" columns to the column headed "15", we find the indication 15. This indicates that for this particular pinion and gauge setting one .015" shim should be installed between the pinion rear bearing and the pinion gear.

Another Example:

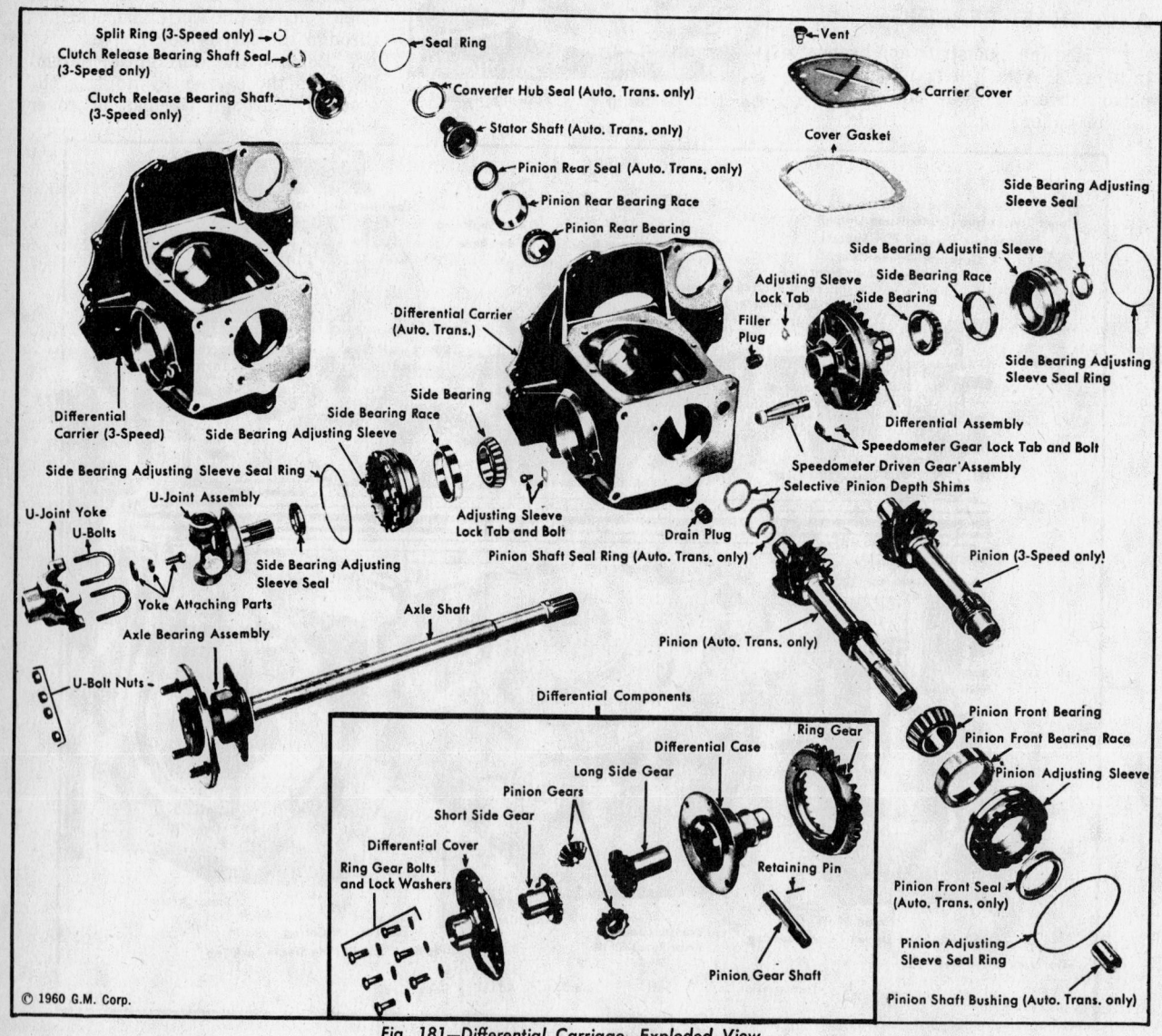

Fig. 181—Differential Carriage, Exploded View

© 1960 G.M. Corp.

If the "Gauge Reading" were the same but the "Pinion Marking" was "19", the chart would indicate "15 + 6" therefore one .015" shim and one .006" shim is required.

2. Assemble shim or shims on the rear face of the pinion gear, then install pinion rear bearing.

3. Install pinion front bearing.

PINION FRONT BEARING RACE

1. Remove the old bearing race from the pinion adjusting sleeve with a punch. On automatic transmission models it is necessary to remove the seal also.

2. Install new race in pinion adjusting sleeve using driver J-7137 and handle, if available.

3. On automatic transmission units, install new seal with tool #J-8340.

SIDE BEARING ADJUSTING SLEEVE SEAL

Pry out the old seal, then install new seal with the lips inward. Tap seal into place with a flat object.

SIDE BEARING ADJUSTING SLEEVE RACE

1. Punch mark the side bearing adjusting sleeve at two places, 180° apart and 9/16" outboard from the seal bore.

2. With a 1/8" to 3/16" drill, drill through the adjusting sleeve at the punch marks until the race is encountered.

3. Drive out the bearing race with a pin punch through the two drilled holes.

4. Deburr the race seat of the adjusting sleeve to insure positive race seating. Then drive a new bearing race into the sleeve until it is home and solidly seated.

5. Seal the drilled holes by using lead balls swaged into place with a punch. (These lead balls are available from your carburetor parts supplier.)

DIFFERENTIAL ASSEMBLY

RECONDITION

Differential reconditioning is conducted in the traditional way with the exception of the following procedures:

THREE SPEED TRANSMISSION AXLES

1. Remove the split ring and old seal from clutch release bearing shaft.

2. Drive a new seal, open side inward in shaft, (using an old 3/4" socket and soft hammer). Bottom the seal then install split ring in clutch release bearing shaft.

CLUTCH RELEASE BEARING SHAFT OR PINION BEARING RACE REPLACE

1. Press out both clutch release bearing shaft and pinion rear bearing race.

2. If a new clutch bearing release shaft is being installed, first install the inner seal. Install a new seal ring in groove on outer diameter of bearing shaft and lubricate with petroleum jelly.

3. Support the differential carrier (only on Boss) at clutch release bearing location with something cylindrical. Then place bearing rale on clutch release bearing shaft and press both into differential carrier. Press until cup is flush with adjacent surface inside the carrier.

AUTOMATIC TRANSMISSION REAR AXLES
Pinion Shaft or Converter Hub Oil Seal Replace

The pinion shaft front oil seal and converter hub oil seal are opposite each other (fore and aft), in the carrier.

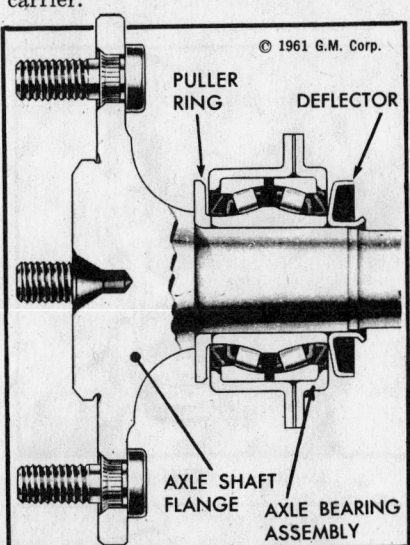

Fig. 180—Axle Bearing, Sectional View

© 1961 G.M. Corp.

PULLER RING   DEFLECTOR

AXLE SHAFT FLANGE   AXLE BEARING ASSEMBLY

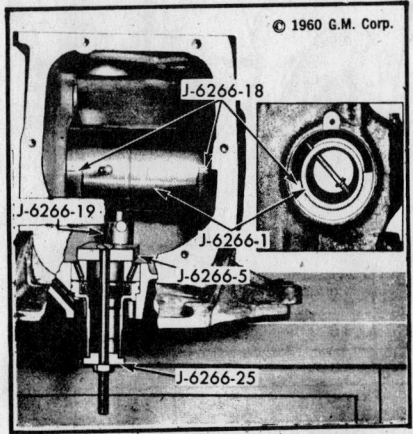

Fig. 182—Pinion Depth Shim Selection Gauges, Installed Views

© 1960 G.M. Corp.

J-6266-18
J-6266-19
J-6266-1
J-6266-5
J-6266-25

Their replacement involves the same basic operation with the same tool, J-8340. This tool is designed to install the pinion front seal, as this seal fits into the inner diameter of the tool for installation to a predetermined depth. When used to install the converter hub seal, the stop surface of J-8340 is used to drive the seal, as this seal is mounted flush.

1. Pry out the old seal.

2. Coat the outer diameter of the seal with non-hardening sealer, then install the new seal with tool J-8340.

PINION SHAFT REAR OIL SEAL REPLACE

1. Drive out the old seal with a punch inserted in the access hole in the stator shaft.

2. Install new seal by tapping until the seal bottoms.

PINION SHAFT BUSHING REPLACE

1. Remove the bushing with a chisel or other suitable tool.

2. Install new bushing to prescribed depth using tool #J-8333.

STATOR SHAFT AND PINION REAR BEARING RALE

1. Remove stator shaft and pinion bearing cup from carrier by using a press. Press downward on the end of the stator shaft.

2. Install seal ring in groove on outside diameter of stator shaft and lubricate with Petroleum Jelly. **This seal is not used on later models.**
Note:

When installing a new stator shaft it will be necessary to install a new pinion rear oil seal.

3. Align notch in stator shaft with drain passage in carrier. Place bearing rale on the shaft and press rale and stator shaft into housing carrier, using tool #J-7137.

ASSEMBLING THE CARRIER ASSEMBLY

1. Place differential assembly into carrier with side bearing cones in place on differential hubs.

2. Before any parts have been attached to the carrier, insert pinion through the cover hole.

3. Engage pinion with ring gear and carefully position the pinion rear bearing in the race. On automatic transmission models, care must be used to prevent damage to the seal at this location.

4. Install new "O" ring seals in side bearing adjusting sleeves, coat adjusting sleeves with non-hardening type sealer. Loosely install adjusting sleeves in the carrier with the side bearing in position.

5. On automatic transmission models, install a new "O" ring in the pinion adjusting sleeve, position pinion so its front bearing will pick up the bearing race in the adjusting sleeve. Then loosely install pinion adjusting sleeve in the carrier.

6. Tighten both side bearing adjusting sleeves and the pinion adjusting sleeve to the point of contact between bearings and races. At this point, there should be no preload on any of the bearings and the gear lash should be just enough to permit the differential to rotate freely and smoothly.

RING GEAR AND PINION BEARING ADJUSTMENT

1. Tighten **right** side bearing adjusting sleeve while rocking the differential assembly with one hand until there is zero backlash. Mark this point, then back off the adjustment **Three** notches to neutralize the "O" ring. Retighten the sleeve **two** notches and tab-lock.

2. Tighten the **left** side adjusting sleeve while chucking the differential side ways until all lash is gone. Mark the left side adjusting sleeve and carrier, then back off the sleeve adjustment three notches to neutralize the "O" ring. Retighten adjustment sleeve to the "No-lash" mark, then two to three additional notches and lock it up with the lock tab. This operation preloads the differential side bearings.

3. Tighten pinion bearing sleeve with spanner wrench until bearings are in good contact with their races. Then tighten pinion sleeve two additional notches. Measure pinion turning torque, using tool J-8362 adapter and inch-pound torque wrench. The finally adjusted pinion turning torque should be 5 to 15 inch-lb. for used bearings or 15 to 30 inch-lb. for new bearings.

4. When satisfied with preload, tab-lock the adjusting sleeve.

5. Engage the speedometer driven gear with the drive gear, then secure the driven gear assmbly in the carrier by tightening the lock tab.

RING GEAR-TO-PINION LASH

Ring gear-to-pinion lash should be .003" to .010", (.005"-.008" preferred). This critical measurement should be read with a dial indicator.

To reduce backlash, the ring gear and differential must be moved toward the pinion. To increase backlash, the ring gear and differential must be moved away from the pinion. One adjustment notch is equivalent to about .003" backlash change.

Example:

If the backlash were zero, turn the differential side bearing adjustment, (The side away from the pinion) counterclockwise two notches. Turn the side bearing adjustment, (the pinion side of the carrier) clockwise two notches.

By following this procedure the preload is maintained and the lash should now be .006".

RING GEAR AND PINION CONTACT PATTERN

Can be checked in the conventional manner as described under the heading "Rear Axles" section 25, in the "Unit Repair Section."

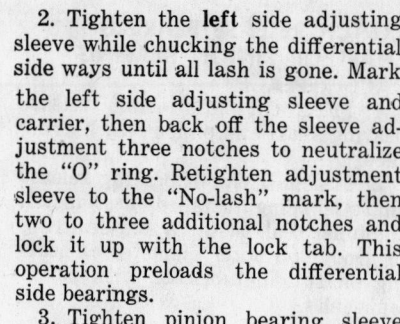

Fig. 184—Drilling Side Bearing Adjusting Sleeves for Race Removal

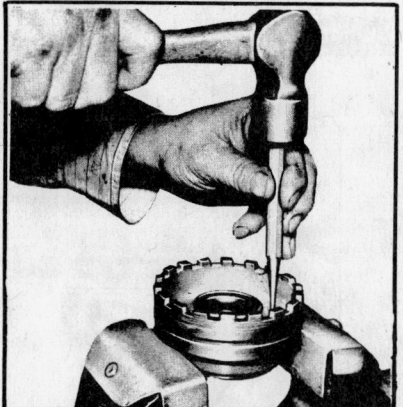

Fig. 185—Removing Side Bearing Race

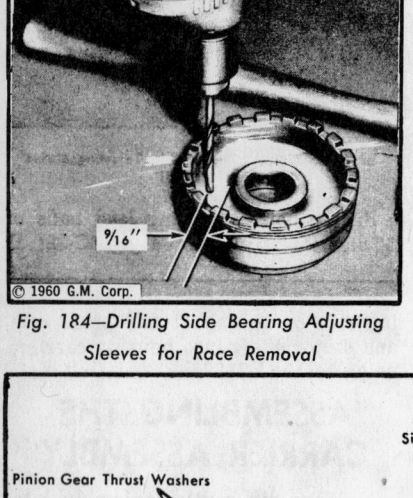

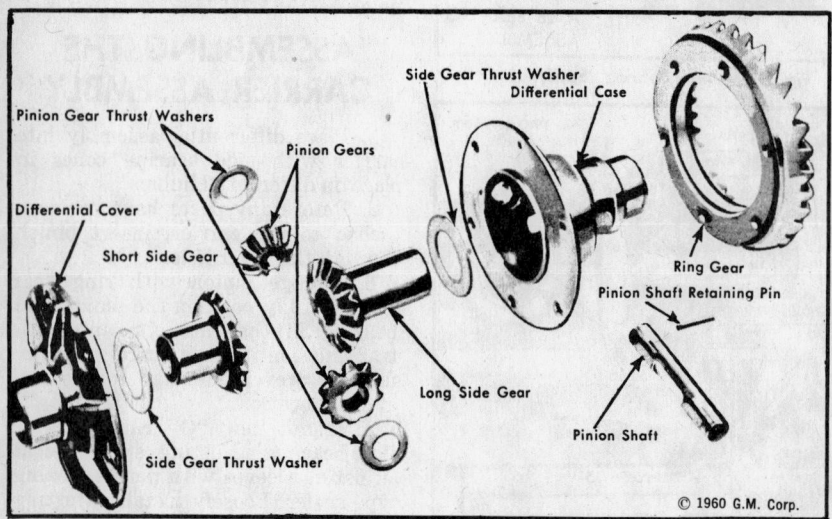

Fig. 186—Differential Assembly

Fig. 191—Measuring Pinion Turning Torque

Fig. 192—Measuring Ring Gear-to-Pinion Backlash

Page

AIR CONDITIONING
Service 1092

BRAKES, HYDRAULIC
Adjustments 938
Bleed brakes 941
Hand brake, adjust 260
Hand brake lever & cable 260
Master cylinder, R & R 259
Master cylinder service 939
Pedal clearance 259
References 259
Specifications 250

BRAKES, POWER
Power unit overhaul 954
References 260
Trouble shooting 954

CLUTCH
Clutch assembly, R & R 276
Clutch pedal, adjust 276

COOLING SYSTEM
References 263
Thermostat 263
Water pump, R & R 263

ELECTRICAL SYSTEM
Alternator overhaul 1035
Alternator specifications 245
Battery 259
Distributor, R & R 257
Engine 257
Fuses and circuit breakers 250
Gauges 1024
Generator regulator specifications 248
Generator references 258
Generator service 1026
Generator specifications 248
Generator trouble shooting chart 1026
Ignition firing order & timing 242
Ignition timing specifications 245
Ignition wires, replace 258
Starter, R & R 259
Starter specifications 249
Starter systems 1046

ENGINE ASSEMBLY
Cylinder head, R & R 264
Engine assembly, R & R 264
Engine diagnosis 1012
Engine firing order & timing 242
Engine marking code 244
Engine references 263
Exhaust manifold, R & R 262
Inlet manifold, R & R 262
Oil filter 271
Oil pan, R & R 270
Oil pressure specifications 251
Piston and rod, R & R 271
Piston and pins specifications 255
Rear main bearing oil seal 272
Rocker arms 265
Serial & engine numbers 244
Specifications, general, engine . . 251

ENGINE ASSEMBLY—continued
Timing case cover & seal 269
Timing chain, R & R 269
Trouble shooting charts 1012
Tune-up specifications 245
Valve adjusting sequence 267
Valve specifications 254
Valve springs 268
Valve and guides 268
Valve timing 269

ENGINE LUBRICATION
Oil filter 271
Oil pan, R & R 270
Oil pumps, R & R 271

EXHAUST SYSTEM
Exhaust pipe 262
Muffler 262
Tail pipe 262
Heat control valve 262

FUEL SYSTEM
Carburetors 972
Fuel gauge service 1024
Fuel pump pressure 245
Fuel pump, R & R 262
Fuel pump service 1020
References 261

INSTRUMENTS
Speedometer 259

OVERDRIVES
Overdrive disassembly 914
Trouble shooting 915

RADIO, R & R
References 286

REAR AXLE AND SUSPENSION
Axle assembly, R & R 286
Axle shaft 918
Axle shaft oil seal 918
Pinion bearings 918
Ring gear & pinion 918
Shock absorbers, rear 286
Trouble shooting 919
Rear spring, R & R 286

SPECIFICATIONS
Alternator specifications 245
Battery 249
Brake cylinder sizes 250
Capacities
 Axle, rear 255
 Cooling system 255
 Crankcase 255
 Fuel tank 255
 Transmission, automatic 255
 Transmission, manual 255
Chassis, general 250
Cylinder head tightening 250
Distributor specifications (DeSoto) 248
Distributor specifications (Dodge) 247
Engine firing order & timing 242
Engine, general 251
Engine tune-up 245

SPECIFICATIONS—continued
Fuses and circuit breakers 250
Generator regulators 248
Light bulbs 248
Main bearings 253
Model identification illustrations . 240
Piston and rings 255
Quick reference specifications . . 242
Rod bearings 253
Starters 249
Torque wrench 254
Valves 254
Wheel alignment 256

STEERING, MANUAL
Adjust gear housing 1052
Gear assembly, R & R 274
Steering wheel, R & R 274
Horn button, R & R 274

STEERING, POWER
References 274
Pump assembly 1058
Trouble shooting 1081
Unit overhaul 1058

SUSPENSION, FRONT
Adjustments 272
Alignment procedures 1082
Alignment specifications 256
Ball joints, R & R 1087
Height adjustments 272
Intermediate steering arms 275
King pins and bushings 1087
Shock absorbers 1087
Support arms, pins and bushings 1087
Torsion bars 273

TRANSMISSION, AUTOMATIC
Power Flite 778
 Linkage adjust 279
 R & R 281
Torque Flite "A" 788
 Linkage adjust 282
 R & R 282
Torque Flite "B" 802
 Linkage adjust 284
 R & R 284

TRANSMISSION, STANDARD
Disassemble transmission 277
Transmission, R & R 276
Manual shift adjustment 278

TROUBLE CHECKS
Procedures 1

TUNE-UP
Procedures 1012
Specifications 245
Engine diagnosis 1012

UNIVERSAL JOINT AND DRIVE LINE
Disassemble U joint 285
U joint & drive shaft, R & R 285

DE SOTO

1950

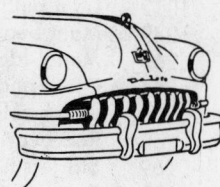

1951

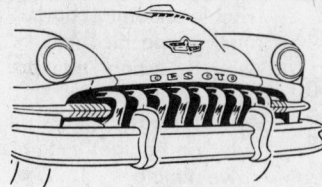

1952

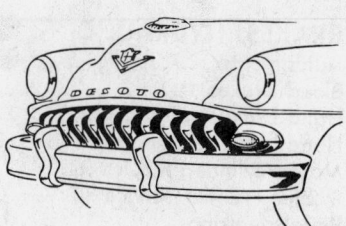

1953

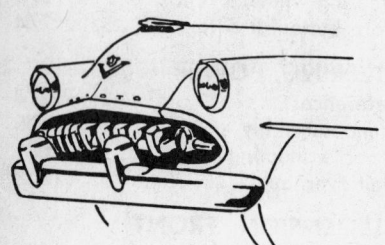

1954

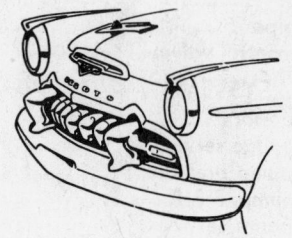

1955

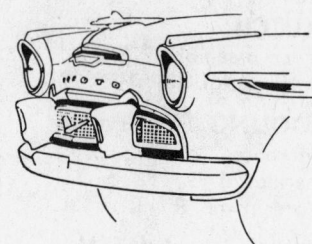

1956

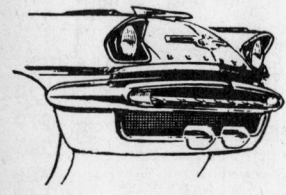

1957
Firedome—Model S25
Fireflite—Model S26

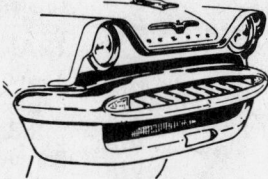

1957
Firesweep—Model S27

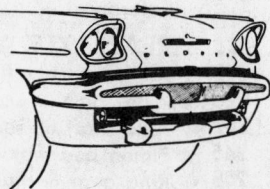

1958
Firedome—Model LS1-L
Fireflite—Model LS3-H
Adventurer—Model LS3-S

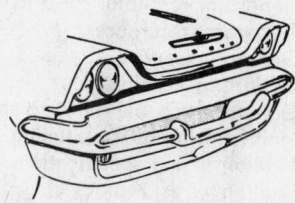

1958
Firesweep—Model LS1-L

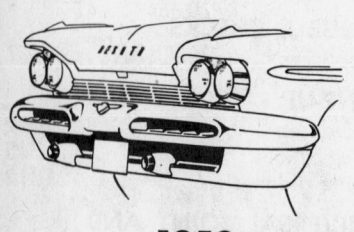

1959

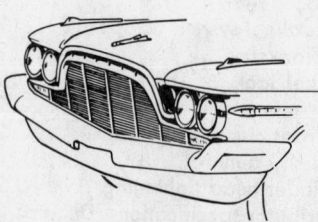

1960

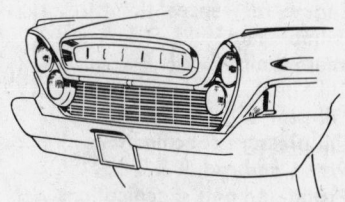

1961

YEAR IDENTIFICATION

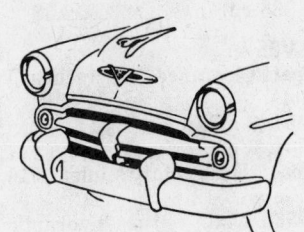

1954

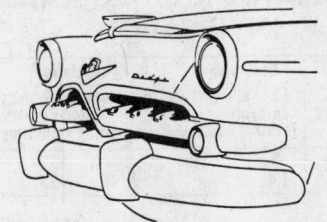

1955

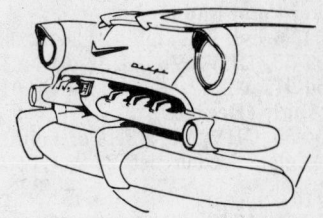

1956

1957

1958

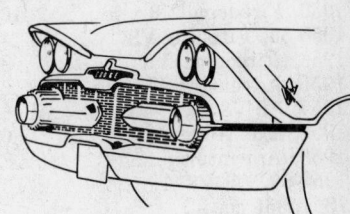

1959

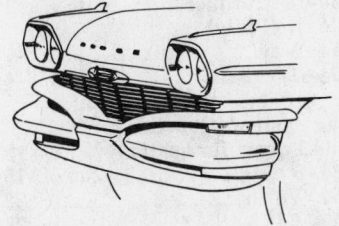

1960 — DODGE

1960 — DART

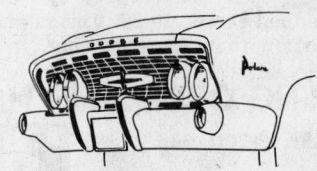

1961 — DODGE

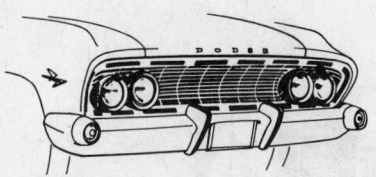

1961 - DART

1962

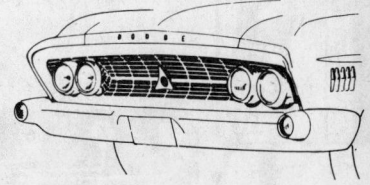

1962 — 880

1963

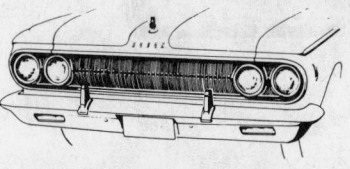

1963-880

DE SOTO

DE SOTO QUICK WORKING SPECIFICATIONS

DISTRIBUTOR
Breaker Point Gap (In.)
1954, 6 cyl. 018-.020
1954-59, OHV, V8 ....015-.018
1960-61, All 014-.019
Cam Angle (Degrees)
1954-55, OHV, V8, 2 sets of points:
Angle of each set 26-28, Total 32-36
1954, 6 cyl. 39
1956-61, OHV, V8 30
1960-61, All 014-.019

IGNITION TIMING
1952-54, OHV, V8 ....4B
1955, Firedome V8 ....10B
1955-56, Fireflite V8 ....4B
1956, Firedome V8 ....8B
1956, Adventurer V8 ....6B
1957, All V8 ....6B
1958, Exc. Adventurer 6B
1958, Adventurer 8B
1959-60, All V8 ....10B
1961, 361 cu. in. 10B
    383 cu. in. 7½B

COMPRESSION PRESSURE AT CRANKING SPEED IN POUNDS PER SQUARE INCH
<u>NOTE:</u> Variation between cylinders should not exceed 10 lbs. This is more important than actual reading.

GENERATOR AND REGULATOR SPECIFICATIONS

Year And Series	Generator		Regulator		
	Field Current In Amperes 6 Volt	12 Volt	Cut-out Closing Voltage	Current Regulator Setting	Voltage Regulator Setting
1954-55 ALL	1.45	—	6.5	40	7.2
1956-58 ALL	—	1.25	13.4	40	14.5±1.(A)
1959-60 ALL	—	1.55	13.5	35	14.6±1.(A)
1961 ALL		3.2	None	None	14

(A) Surrounding temperatures guide this adjustment. Higher temperatures require lower settings and lower temperatures permit higher settings, within limits.

SPARK PLUGS

Year	Type	Gap
1954, All	4S140	.035
1955, Firedome V8	4S140	.035
1955, Fireflite V8	4S165	.035
1956, Firedome V8	AR51	.035
1956, Fireflite; Adventurer	AR52	.035
1957, All V8	AR42	.035
1958, Exc. L53-S	AR42	.035
1958, L53-S Advr.	AR32	.035
1959 Ex. Advr.	A42	.035
1959 Advr.	A32	.035
1960, Fireflite, PS-1	A42	.035
1960, Adventurer, PS-3	A42	.035
1961, 361 cu. in.	A42	.035
383 cu. in.	A32	.035

VALVES
Tappet Clearance (in inches While Hot)
1954, 6 cyl. inlet 008
1954, 6 cyl. exhaust 010
Note: Heavy-duty: inlet .010, exhaust .012.
1954-61, all V8 use hydraulic lifters. Have zero clearance.

CAPACITIES
Engine Crankcase (Quarts)
(Add 1 qt. for new filter)
1954-57, all ex. 1956 V8 5
1956, V8 4
1958, V8 4
1959-61, V8 5

Transmission, Synchro. (Pts.)
(Add 1 pint for Overdrive)
1954-61 ....2¾

Transmission, Automatic (Pts.)
(Change every 20,000 miles or 2 years, whichever is first.)
1954-57, Powerflite 22
1956-57, TorqueFlite 18
1959-61, PowerFlite 20
1959-61, TorqueFlite 21
Rear Axle (Pints)
1954, 6 cyl. 3¼
1954-61, V8 ....3½

Cooling System (Quarts)
(Add 1 quart for heater)
1954, 6 cyl. 15
1954, V8 22
1955-56, V8 23
1957, V8 20
1959-61, V8 16

FIRING ORDER and TIMING

SPARK OCCURS:
V-8
[A] 1954-56— 4° BTDC
[B] 1957-58— 6° BTDC
[C] 1958 —6° BTDC
[D] 1959-61 10° BTDC

6 Cylinder
[E] 1954—2° BTDC

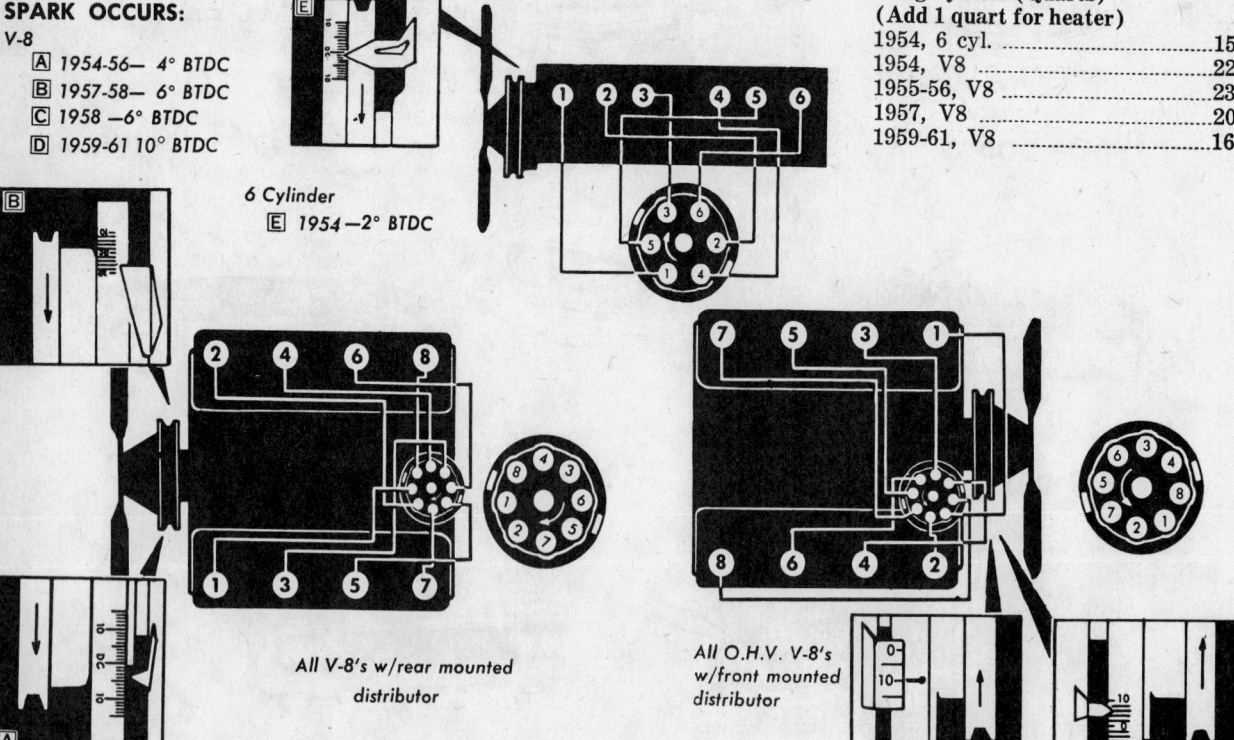

All V-8's w/rear mounted distributor

All O.H.V. V-8's w/front mounted distributor

NOTE:
THESE ARE APPROXIMATE SETTINGS. ENGINE DESIGN, ALTITUDE, TEMPERATURE, FUEL AND ENGINE CONDITION WILL ALL INFLUENCE TIMING. THE DETERMINING FACTOR, LIMITING ADVANCE, WILL STILL BE THE "KNOCK POINT" OF THE INDIVIDUAL ENGINE.

DODGE and DART QUICK WORKING SPECIFICATIONS
(1963 DART, SEE VALIANT)

DISTRIBUTOR
Breaker Point Gap (In.)
1954-63, 6 cyl. .... .018-.022
1954-59, V8 .... .015-.018
1960-63, V8 .... .015-.018

Cam Angle (Degrees)
1954-61, 6 cyl. 36-42
1962-63, 6 cyl. 40-45
1954-55, OHV, V8, has two sets of points: Angle for each set 26-28
          Total angle 32-36
1956-57, single rocker shaft V8's 31
1956, double rocker shaft V8 38
1957, double rocker shaft V8:
With one 4 barrel carb. 29-32
With two 4 barrel carbs., has two sets of points: Angle for each set
29-32 ....Total angle 32-36
1958-63, V8 27-32

IGNITION TIMING
1951-62, 6 cyl. 2B
1954-55, V8 ....4B
1956, D63-1, V8 ....4B
1956, D63-2-3, V8 ....6B
1956, D500, V8 ....2B
1957, all V8 ....6B
1958, V8 ....6B
1958, V8 & D500 PAC 8B
1959-63, all V8 ex. "318" 10B
1962-63, 318 cu. in. 5B

361 cu. in 10B
383 cu. in. 7½B

SPARK PLUGS
Year	Type	Gap
1954, all	4S140	.035
1955, 6 cyl.	4S140	.035
1955, all V8	4S165	.035
1956, cyl.	AR80	.035
1956, V8 ex. D500	AR52	.035
1956, D500	4S250	.035
1957-60, 6 cyl.	AR51	.035
1957, V8 ex. D500	AR42	.035
1957, D500, V8	AR32	.035
1957, D501, V8	AGR32	.035
1958, LD2	AGR42	.035
1958 LD3	AR42	.035
1958, V8 & D500 PAC	AR32	.035
1959, MD2	AR42	.035
1959-61, MD3-Matador- Polara	A42	.035
1959-61, 383 cu. in.	A32	.035
1960-61, Dart V8	A42	.035
1960-61, Slant 6	AG42*	.035
1962-63, Slant 6	N16Y	.035
1962-63, V-8 Exec, 413	J-12Y	.035
1962-63, 413 V-8	J9Y	.035

Note. * Use without gasket.

TAPPET CLEARANCE (HOT)
1954-59, 6 cyl.: In. & Ex. .... .010
1954-63, V8 (ex. 1956-D500) uses hydraulic lifters. Clearance is zero

1956, D500: In.—.012; Ex. 022
1960-63,
  Dart 6 ....In.—.010; Ex.—.020
1960-63,
  318 cu. in. ....In.—.010; Ex.—.018
  361, 383 cu. in. ....Hydraulic
1962-63, 413 V-8 ....Hydraulic

GENERATOR AND REGULATOR SEE DESOTO

ALTERNATOR SPECS., SEE SPECIFICATIONS CHARTS ON FOLLOWING PAGES

CAPACITIES
Engine Crankcase (Quarts)
(Add 1 qt. for new filter)
1954-57 5
1958, LD1, LD2 5
1958, LD3 4
1959-63, all V8 5
1960-63, Dart 6 4

Transmission, Synchro. (Pts.)
(Add 1 pint for Overdrive)
1954-61, all 2¾
1962-63 5

Rear Axle (Pints)
1954-63, all 3½

FIRING ORDER and TIMING

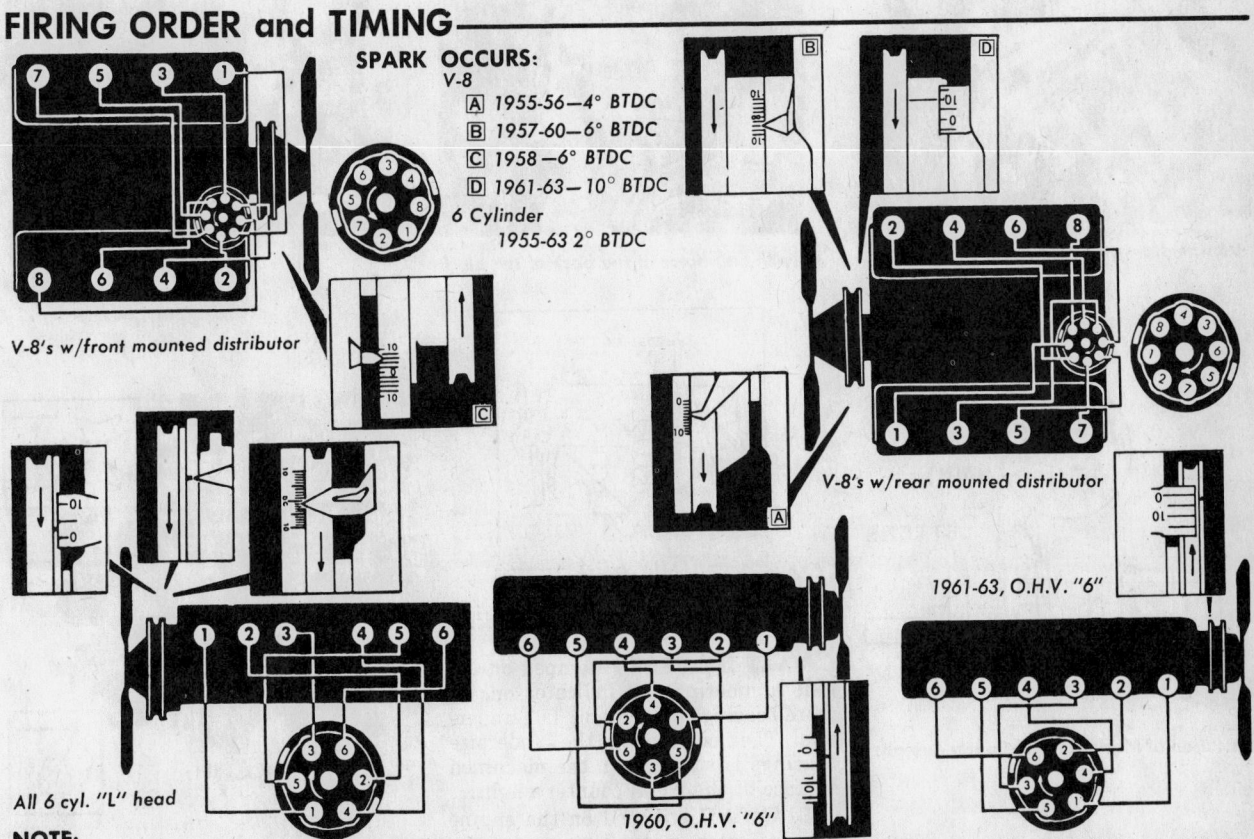

SPARK OCCURS:
V-8
[A] 1955-56—4° BTDC
[B] 1957-60—6° BTDC
[C] 1958—6° BTDC
[D] 1961-63—10° BTDC

6 Cylinder
1955-63 2° BTDC

V-8's w/front mounted distributor

V-8's w/rear mounted distributor

1961-63, O.H.V. "6"

All 6 cyl. "L" head

1960, O.H.V. "6"

NOTE:
THESE ARE APPROXIMATE SETTINGS. ENGINE DESIGN, ALTITUDE, TEMPERATURE, FUEL AND ENGINE CONDITION WILL ALL INFLUENCE TIMING. THE DETERMINING FACTOR, LIMITING ADVANCE, WILL STILL BE THE "KNOCK POINT" OF THE INDIVIDUAL ENGINE.

DE SOTO, DODGE & DART

CAR SERIAL NUMBER LOCATION AND ENGINE IDENTIFICATION

CAR SERIAL NUMBER LOCATION—1954-63 Plate on left front door hinge post.

THE ENGINE MAY BE IDENTIFIED THRU THE ENGINE NUMBER.

ENGINE NUMBERING SYSTEM

1954-57 ENGINE NUMBERING SYSTEM

All De Soto Engine Numbers consist of a prefix indicating the model and figures indicating the engine number. All engine numbers start at 1001. The model prefix is the same as that in the serial number table except in the case of the 1957 Firesweep, for which the prefix is KDS. For instance: Engine Number S19-1002 is the second engine of the 1954 Model S19, Firedome V8 run; while KDS-1001 is the first 1957 Firesweep V8 engine. (It could also be a 1957 Dodge Red Ram.)

1958 STARTING ENGINE NUMBERS

Beginning 1958 a more positive method of engine year and size identification has been adapted throughout the Chrysler corporation line.

The first segment of the engine number is a letter and identifies the year of production, such as:

Year	Symbol
1958	L
1959	M
1960	P
1961	R
1962	S
1963	T

The second segment of the engine number is a two or three digit number and identifies the size (cubic inch displacement) of the engine such as:

17	170 cu. in.
22	225 cu. in.
318	318 cu. in.
36	361 cu. in.
38	383 cu. in.
41	413 cu. in.

Therefore, an engine number prefix of S36 would be a 1962 car equipped with a 361 cu. in. engine. T318 would be a 1963 car equipped with a 3.8 cu. in. engine.

Engine numbers may be found in the following locations:

6 cyl. engines, right side of engine block at #1 cylinder.

V8 engines (except 3.8 engine) stamped on a boss on the right cylinder block, just back of the water pump.

V8, 318 engine, located on the front face of the left cylinder block.

ENGINE NUMBER LOCATION

V8 with distributor at the front of the block.

V8 with distributor at the back of the block

"L" Head 6 cyl.

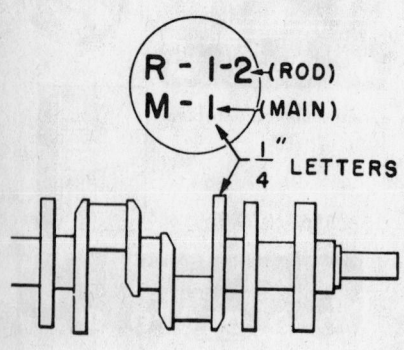

Location of Mark of No. 3 Counterweight

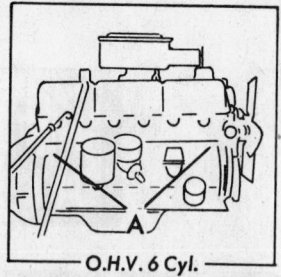

O.H.V. 6 Cyl.

ENGINE SIZE CODE

MALTESE CROSS stamped on engine numbering pad indicates one or more bearings are ground .001 undersize. The location of the undersize bearings is stamped on the machined surface of the No. 3 counterweight.

DIAMOND stamped on the engine pad indicates that all tappet bodies are .008 oversize.

Location of External Engine Numbering Pad

244

DE SOTO, DODGE & DART

(1963 DART, SEE VALIANT)

TUNE-UP SPECIFICATIONS

DE SOTO

Make Year Model	Spark Plugs Make and Number	Gap	Distributor (Note 1) Cam Angle	Point Gap	Arm Spring Tension	Ignition Timing	Compression Pressure Cranking	Valves (Note 4) Tappet Clearance Hot Inlet	Exhaust	Timing Inlet Opens	Fuel Pump Pressure	Engine Idle Speed Neutral
1954												
S18, S20, 6 Cyl., L Head	4S140	.035	39	.018–.020	17–20	2B	135	008	.010	12B	4¼	475
S16, S19, Firedome, V8	4S140	.035	Note 1A	.015–.018	17–20	4B	150	Zero	Zero	12B	4¼	475
1955												
S22, Firedome, V8	4S140	.035	Note 1A	.015–.018	17–20	10B	150	Zero	Zero	4A	5¾	475
S21, Fireflite, V8	4S165	.035	Note 1A	.015–.018	17–20	4B	150	Zero	Zero	12B	5¾	475
1956												
S23, Firedome, V8	AR51	.035	30	.015–.018	17–20	8B	155	Zero	Zero	4A	5¾	500
S24, Fireflite, V8	AR52	.035	30	.015–.018	17–20	4B	160	Zero	Zero	15B	5¾	500
S24, Adventurer, V8	AR52	.035	30	.015–.018	17–20	6B	165	Zero	Zero	35B	5¾	500
1957												
S25, Firedome, V8	AR42	.035	30	.015–.018	17–20	6B	160	Zero	Zero	15B	6½	500
S26, Fireflite, V8	AR42	.035	Note 1B	.015–.018	17–20	6B	160	Zero	Zero	Note 4A	6½	Note 5 A
S27, Firesweep, V8	AR42	.035	30	.015–.018	17–20	6B	140	Zero	Zero	10B	6½	500
1958												
All V8 ex. Adventurer	AR42	.035	30	.015–.018	17–20	6B	165	Zero	Zero	15B	6½	475
LS3-S, Adventurer	AR32	.035	Note 1C	.015–.018	17–20	8B	165	Zero	Zero	20B	6½	475
1959												
All V8 ex. Adventurer	A42	.035	30	.015–.018	17–20	10B	165	Zero	Zero	15B	6½	475
MS3-S Adventurer	A32	.035	30	.015–.018	17–20	10B	165	Zero	Zero	20B	6½	475
1960-61												
All V8	A42	.035	30	.014–.019	17–20	10B	165	Zero	Zero	15B	6½	450
Power Pak	A32	.035	Note 1D	.014–.019	17–70	7.5B	165	Zero	Zero	20B	6½	475

NOTES FOR TUNE-UP SPECIFICATIONS TABLE

Note:

All specifications are standard and should result in satisfactory performance. There are, however, factors that influence these settings, such as fuel octane value, air density, humidity, temperature, etc. Timing charts, like other specifications must be considered as averages, subject to modification.

Note 1A: Cam Angle (Dwell)
1954-55, OHV, V8, DE SOTO AND DODGE
Distributor with two sets of breaker points is used.
Cam angle for each set of
points 26-28
Total cam angle 32-36

Note 1B: Cam Angle (Dwell)
1957 DE SOTO FIREFLITE
Distributor with two sets of points is used.

Cam angle for single set 29-32
Total cam angle 36-40

Note 1D: Cam Angle (Dwell)
1960-61 DE SOTO w/RAM MANIFOLD

Note 1C: Cam Angle (Dwell)
1958 DE SOTO ADVENTURER

With single 4 barrel carburetor distributor had single set of points.
Cam angle 29-32
With dual 4 barrel carburetor, distributor had two sets of points.
Cam angle for each set
of points 29-32
Total cam angle 36-39
Distributor with two sets of points.
Cam angle for single set .... 27° to 32°
Total cam angle .... 34° to 40°

SPARK PLUGS

Beginning 1959, Engines do not use Resistor Type Plugs. The resistance is built into the spark plug wires. No one wire should exceed 20,000 Ohms.

Note 4: Valves

On engines with the distributor at the front the push rods have a diameter of 5/16 in. at the top end; ¼ in. at the bottom. If reversed the valves won't close.

Note 4A: 1957 Fireflite Valve Timing
Standard Camshaft 15B
Special Camshaft 35B

Note 5A: 1957 Idle Speed
Standard Camshaft 500
Special Camshaft 700

ALTERNATOR AND ALTERNATOR REGULATOR SPECIFICATIONS

Year and Model	Ground Polarity	ALTERNATOR Ampere Rating	Field Current Draw, Amps.	CURRENT OUTPUT @ 15 Volts and 1250 Engine R.P.M.	VOLTAGE OUTPUT @ 15 Amp. Load and 1250 Engine R.P.M.	REGULATOR Point Gap	Air Gap
1961-63							
Standard	Negative	35	Note A	35 ampere min.	13.4-14.6 B	.014-.016	.048-.052
Heavy Duty	Negative	40	Note A	40 ampere min.	13.4-14.6 B	.014-.016	.048-.052

245

DE SOTO, DODGE & DART

(1963 DART, SEE VALIANT)

NOTE A
2.38-2.75 amps. minimum at 12 volts, while rotating the unit by hand, or 2.97-3.43 amps. maximum at 15 volts at 70°F with unit operating at 750 R.P.M.

NOTE B
Run the engine at 1250 R.P.M. for about 15 minutes, with lights and accessories on to stabilize regulator temperature. Turn off lights and accessories and read test voltmeter. With a fully charged battery and 15 amps. flowing in the circuit, the voltmeter reading should be within specs. shown in chart below. Temperature should be read within 2 inches of regulator.

TEMPERATURE IN DEGREES	0°	25°	48°	70°	95°	118°	140°
Voltage—Minimum	14.0 to	13.9 to	13.8 to	13.7 to	13.6 to	13.5 to	13.4 to
Voltage—Maximum	14.6	14.5	14.4	14.3	14.2	14.1	14.0

TUNE-UP SPECIFICATIONS

DODGE and DART

Year Model	Spark Plugs Make and Number	Gap	Distributor Cam Angle	Point Gap	Arm Spring Tension	Ignition Timing	Compression Pressure Cranking	Valves (Note 4) Tappet Clearance Hot Inlet	Exhaust	Timing Inlet Opens	Fuel Pump Pressure	Engine Idle Speed Neutral
1954												
D51, D52, 6 Cyl., L Head	4S140	.035	39	.018–.022	17-20	2B	135	.010	.010	12B	4¾	475
D50, D53, Red Ram, V8	4S140	.035	Note 1A	.015–.018	17-20	4B	155	Zero	Zero	17B	4¾	475
1955												
D56, 6 Cyl., L Head	4S140	.035	39	.018–.022	17-20	2B	145	.010	.010	12B	5¼	475
D55-1, D55-2 Single Rocker Shaft, V8	4S165	.035	Note 1A	.015–.018	17-20	4B	155	Zero	Zero	14B	5¾	475
D-55-3 Double Rocker Shaft, V8	4S165	.035	Note 1A	.015–.018	17-20	4B	155	Zero	Zero	14B	5¾	475
1956												
D62, 6 Cyl., L Head	AR80	.035	39	.018–.022	17-20	2B	150	.010	.010	12B	4¾	475
D63-1 (270 cu. in.) Single Rocker Shaft, V8	AR52	.035	31	.015–.018	17-20	4B	155	Zero	Zero	14B	5¾	475
D63-2-3 (315 cu. in.) Single Rocker Shaft, V8	AR-52	.035	31	.015–.018	17-20	6B	155	Zero	Zero	11B	5¾	475
D500 (315 cu. in.) Double Rocker Shaft, V8	4S250	.035	38	.015–.018	17-20	2B	165	.012	.022	12B	5¾	475
1957												
D72, 6 Cyl., L Head	AR51	.035	39	.018–.022	17-20	2B	150	.010	.010	12B	5	475
D66-1-2, D67-1, D70, D71 Single Rocker Shaft, V8	AR42	.035	31	.015–.018	17-20	6B	155	Zero	Zero	10B	6½	475
D500 Double Rocker Shaft. V8	AR42	.035	Note 1B	.015–.018	17-20	6B	155	Zero	Zero	20B	6½	475
1958, Note 6												
LD1, 6 Cyl., L Head	AR51	.035	39	.018–.022	17-20	2B	150	.010	.010	12B	6½	475
LD2-L-M, (325 Cu. In.) Single Rocker Shaft, V8	AGR-42	.035	31	.015–.018	17-20	6B	155	Zero	Zero	10B	6½	475
LD3-H-L (350 Cu. In.) Single Rocker Shaft, V8	AR42	.035	31	.015–.018	17-20	6B	165	Zero	Zero	15B	6½	475
D500 Package (361 Cu. In.) Single Rocker Shaft, V8	AR32	.035	Note 1C	.015–.018	17-20	8B	165	Zero	Zero	15B	6½	475
1959												
MD1, 6 Cyl., L Head	AR51	.035	39	.018–.022	17-20	2B	150	.010	.010	12B	6½	475
MD2-L, V8, 326 Cu. In.	AR42	.035	30	.015–.018	17-20	10B	155	Zero	Zero	14B	6½	475
MD3, V8, 361 Cu. In.	A42	.035	30	.015–.018	17-20	10B	165	Zero	Zero	15B	6½	475
D500, V8, 383 Cu. In.	A32	.035	30	.015–.018	17-20	10B	165	Zero	Zero	20B	6½	475
1960-61												
Slant 6, OHV-225 cu. in.	AG42*	.035	36-42	.018–.020	17-20	2B	150	.010	.020	T.D.C.	6-7	475
Red Ram V-8 318 cu. in.	A42	.035	28-32	.014–.019	17-20	5B	155	.010	.018	17B	6-7	475
Super Red Ram V8 361 cu. in.	A42	.035	28-32	.014–.019	17-20	10B	155	Zero	Zero	15B	6-7	475
Ram Fire V8 383 cu. in.	A42	.035	28-32	.014–.019	17-20	10B	160	Zero	Zero	15B	6-7	500
Ram Induction D-500	A32	.035	28-32	.014–.019	17-20	7.5B	160	Zero	Zero	20B	6-7	530
1962												
Slant 6	N-16Y	.035	40-45	.017–.023	17-20	2.5B	150	.010	.020	T.D.C.	6-7	475
318 V-8	J-12Y	.035	27-32	.014–.019	17-20	5.0B	155	.010	.020	17B	6-7	475
361 V-8	J-12Y	.035	27-32	.014–.019	17-20	10.0B	160	Zero	Zero	15B	6-7	500
383 V-8	J-12Y	.035	27-32	.014–.019	17-20	10.0B	160	Zero	Zero	22B	6-7	500
413 V-8	J-9Y	.035	27-32	.014–.019	17-20	10.0B	165	Zero	Zero	22B	6-7	700
1963												
Slant 6, 225 cu. in.	N-12Y	.035	40-45	.017–.023	17-20	2.5B	150	.010	.020	8B	6-7	475
318, V8, std. trans.	J-12Y	.035	27-32	.014–.019	17-20	5.0B	160	.013	.021	17B	6-7	475
318, V8, auto. trans.	J-12Y	.035	27-32	.014–.019	17-20	10.0B	160	.013	.021	17B	6-7	475
361, V8, All	J-12Y	.035	27-32	.014–.019	17-20	10.0B	160	Zero	Zero	24B	6-7	500
383, V8, All	J-12Y	.035	27-32	.014–.019	17-20	10.0B	160	Zero	Zero	24B	6-7	500
413, V8, All	J-9Y	.035	27-32	.014–.019	17-20	15.0B	165	Zero•	Zero•	24B	6-7	700

* Use no gasket. Aluminum cup acts as gasket.
High performance options use mechanical tappets set as a cold clearance of .016″ (int.) & .028″ (exh.).

(1963 DART, SEE VALIANT)

NOTES FOR TUNE-UP SPECIFICATIONS TABLE

Note:

All specifications are standard and should result in satisfactory performance. There are, however, factors that influence these settings, such as fuel octane value, air density, humidity, temperature, etc. Timing charts, like other specifications must be considered as averages, subject to modification.

Note 1A: Cam Angle (Dwell)

1954-55, OHV, V8, DE SOTO AND DODGE

Distributor with two sets of breaker points is used.

Cam angle for each set of points 26-28

Total cam angle 32-36

Note 1B: Cam Angle (Dwell)

1957 DE SOTO FIREFLITE

1957, DODGE D500, OHV, V8

With single 4 barrel carburetor distributor had single set of points.

Cam angle 29-32

With dual 4 barrel carburetor, distributor had two sets of points.

Cam angle for each set of points 29-32

Total cam angle 36-39

Note 1C: Cam Angle (Dwell)

1958 DE SOTO ADVENTURER

1958 DODGE D500

Distributor with two sets of points is used.

Cam angle for single set 29-32

Total cam angle 36-40

Note 1D: Cam Angle (Dwell)

1960-61 DE SOTO w/RAM MANIFOLD

Distributor with two sets of points.

Cam angle for single set .... 27° to 32°

Total cam angle .... 34° to 40°

SPARK PLUGS

Beginning 1959, Engines do not use Resistor Type Plugs. The resistance is built into the spark plug wires. No one wire should exceed 20,000 Ohms.

Note 4: Valves

On engines with the distributor at the front the push rods have a diameter of 5/16 in. at the top end; 1/4 in. at the bottom. If reversed the valves won't close.

Note 4A: 1957 Fireflite Valve Timing

Standard Camshaft 15B

Special Camshaft 35B

Note 5A: 1957 Idle Speed

Standard Camshaft 500

Special Camshaft 700

Note 6: 1958 Tune Up

For 350 Cu. in. Engine with one 4 Brl. Carb. Set ignition timing at 6B (plus or minus 4 Deg.) at 450-500 R.P.M. For high speed or heavy duty use on AR 32 plug. For 361 Cu. In. Engine with two 4 Brl. Carbs. or fuel injection set ignition timing at 8B (plus or minus 4 Deg.) at 500-550 R.P.M. Use maximum setting only if Super Fuel is available. With Carb. use an AR32 plug; with Fuel Inj. an AR42 plug for high speed or heavy duty use AR32.

DODGE and DART DISTRIBUTOR SPECIFICATIONS, AUTO-LITE

Year	Model	Auto-Lite Part Number	ROTATION	Cam Angle in Degrees	Breaker Point Opening (Inch)	Breaker Arm Spring Tension (Ounces)	GOVERNOR CONTROL @ Dist. Advance Starts	GOVERNOR CONTROL R.P.M. Full Advance	VACUUM CONTROL DATA Inches of Vacuum To Start Advance	Inches of Vacuum For Full Advance	Max. Adv. of Dist. in Degrees
1954	6 Cyl., All	IAT-4011	C	38-40	.020	17-20	1 @ 350	10 @ 1425	4-6	14	7-9
	V8, All	IAZ-4003	C	(A)	.017	17-20	1 @ 350	15 @ 1750	5½-6½	17	10½-12½
1955	6 Cyl. Coronet	IAT-4101-B	C	36-41	.020	17-20	1 @ 425	8 @ 1350	5½-6½	14	7-9
	V8, Coronet, Royal	IAZ-4003-G	C	(A)	.017	17-20	1 @ 350	16 @ 1650	5½-6½	8½	3-5
	V8, Custom Royal	IAZ-4003-F	C	(A)	.017	17-20	1 @ 350	12 @ 1625	5½-6½	11	6-8
1956	6 Cyl., Coronet	IAT-4101-B	C	36-41	.020	17-20	1 @ 425	8 @ 1350	5½-6½	14	7-9
	V8, Coronet	IBJ-4303-B	C	29-32	.017	17-20	1 @ 350	15 @ 2350	5½-6½	12	7-9
	V8, Royal, Custom	IBJ-4303	C	29-32	.017	17-20	1 @ 350	16 @ 2350	6½-7½	15	10-12
	V8, Dodge "500"	IBK-4301-A	C	(B)	.017	17-20	1 @ 350	9½ @ 2400	7-8	17	10½-12½
1957	6 Cyl., Coronet	IBR-4001	C	36-41	.020	17-20	1 @ 350	8½ @ 1800	5¼-6¾	16	8½-10½
	V8, Coronet, Royal	IBP-4002	C	29-32	.017	17-20	1 @ 450	8½ @ 1700	5¼-6¾	18	12-14
	V8, Custom Royal	IBP-4002-B	C	29-32	.017	17-20	1 @ 350	8 @ 850	6½-7¾	18	12-14
	V8, Dodge "500"	IBP-4001-D	C	29-32	.017	17-20	1 @ 350	9 @ 2400	10-11	17¾	12-14
	V8, Dodge "500"	IBS-4005	C	(B)	.017	17-20	1 @ 400	8 @ 1200	8¼-9¾	18	9-11½
1958	6 Cyl., Coronet	IBR-4001	C	36-41	.020	17-20	1 @ 350	8½ @ 1800	5¼-6¾	16	8½-10½
	V8, Coronet, Royal	IBP-4002-E	C	29-32	.017	17-20	1 @ 350	9 @ 1650	6⅛-7¼	14	10-12
	V8, Sierra, C. Royal	IBP-4005	C	29-32	.017	17-20	1 @ 350	10 @ 2000	6¼-8	16½	11½-14½
	V8, Dodge "500"	IBS-4006-B	C	(B)	.017	17-20	1 @ 350	10 @ 2000	6¼-8	16½	11½-14½
1959	6 Cyl., Coronet	IBR-4001	C	36-42	.020	17-20	1 @ 350	8½ @ 1800	5¼-6¾	16	8½-10½
	V8, Coronet	JBP-4003-J	C	27-32	.017	17-20	1 @ 450	6½ @ 2300	5¾-7½	13¼	8½-11½
	V8, Royal, Custom	JBP-4005-B	CC	27-32	.017	17-20	1 @ 350	9½ @ 2150	7¼-9⅛	16½	9½-12½
	V8, S∠W, D500	IBS-4006-C	CC	(C)	.017	17-20	1 @ 450	9½ @ 2000	7½-9¼	18¼	11½-14½
1960	6 Cyl., 225 cu. in.	2095270*	C	36-42	.020	17-20	1 @ 400	11½ @ 2200	5-7	12	7¾-10¼
	V8, 318 cu. in.	IBP-4003-L	C	27-32	.017	17-20	1 @ 500	9 @ 2300	7½-8¾	17	12-14¾
	V8, 361 cu. in.	IBP-4005-C	CC	27-32	.017	17-20	1 @ 400	8 @ 2200	7½-9	15	0¼-11
	V8, 383 cu. in.	IBP-4005-D	CC	27-32	.017	17-20	1 @ 350	11 @ 2150	7½-9	15	8¼-11
	V8, 383 (D-500)	1BS-4006-E	CC	(C)	.017	17-20	1 @ 400	10 @ 2400	7¼-9	14½	7½-10½
1961	6 Cyl., 225 cu. in.	2095270	C	36-42	.020	17-20	1 @ 350	11½ @ 2200	5-7	12	7¾-10¼
	V8, 318 cu. in.	2095647	C	27-32	.017	17-20	1 @ 350	11½ @ 2300	6¾-9¼	17	12-15
	V8, 361 cu. in.	IBP-4005-E	CC	27-32	.017	17-20	1 @ 350	11 @ 2050	6-8	16	10½-13
	V8, 383 cu. in.	IBS-4006-E	CC	(C)	.017	17-20	1 @ 400	10 @ 2400	7¼-9	14½	7½-10½
1962	Slant 6, OHV	2095976	C	40-45	.020	17-21	1 @ 400	11½ @ 2300	5½	13	5-7½
	V8, 318 cu. in.	2095979	C	27-32	.017	17-21	1 @ 450	9 @ 2300	9	18	8½-11½
	V8, 361-383 cu. in.	2095983	CC	27-32	.017	17-21	1 @ 350	10 @ 2300	9	15	9½-12½
	Custom, 880	2095836	CC	27-32	.017	17-21	1 @ 350	11½ @ 2150	6	16½	11½-14½
	V8, 413 cu. in.	2098582	CC	(C)	.017	17-21	1 @ 500	12 @ 1000	None	None	None
1963	Slant 6, All	2098670	C	40-45	.020	17-21	1@400	11½@2500	6	13	5¼- 7½
	V8, 318, std. trans.	2098680	C	28-33	.017	17-21	1@400	9½@2000	9	15½	8½-11½
	V8, 318, auto. tran:	2098685	C	28-33	.017	17-21	1@400	8½@2600	9	15½	8½-11½
	V8, 361, 383, All	2095836	CC	28-33	.017	17-21	1@350	11½@2150	4½-8	16½	11½-14½
	V8, 413, All	2098620	CC	(C)	.017	17-21	1@600	5½@910	6-9	16½	7½-10½

(A) Dual Points: Each Set 26°—28°, Total Dwell 32°—36°. (B) Dual Points: Each Set 29°—32°, Total Dwell 36°—39°. (C) Dual Points: Each Set 27°—32°, Total Dwell 34°—40°.

DE SOTO, DODGE & DART

(1963 DART, SEE VALIANT)

DE SOTO DISTRIBUTOR SPECIFICATIONS, AUTO-LITE

Year	Model	Auto-Lite Number Part	ROTATION	Cam Angle in Degrees	Breaker Point Opening (Inch)	Breaker Arm Spring Tension (Ounces)	GOVERNOR CONTROL @ Dist. Advance Starts	R.P.M. Full Advance	Inches of Vacuum To Start Advance	Inches of Vacuum For Full Advance	Max. Adv. of Dist. in Degrees
1954	6Cyl., S-20	IAT-4102	C	36-42	.020	17-20	1 @ 350	10 @ 1425	5½-6½	15	8-10
	V8, Firedome, S-19	IAZ-4002-A	C	(A)	.017	17-20	1 @ 400	11 @ 1920	5½-6½	17	10½-12½
1955	V8, Firedome, S-22	IAZ-4001-D	C	(A)	.017	17-20	1 @ 375	17 @ 2300	5½-6½	17	10½-12½
	V8, Fireflight, S-21	IAZ-4002-C	C	(A)	.017	17-20	1 @ 375	8 @ 800	5½-6½	11	6-8
1956	V8, Firedome S-23	IBJ-4302-A	C	29-32	.017	17-20	1 @ 350	6 @ 800	5-6	15	10½-12½
	V8, Fireflight, S-24	IBJ-4302	C	29-32	.017	17-20	1 @ 350	8½ @ 2200	5-6	15	11½-13½
	V8, Adventure, S-24	IBK-4303	C	(B)	.018	17-20	1 @ 350	7-8	7-8	17½	10½-12½
1957	V8, Firesweep, S-27	IBP-4002	C	29-32	.017	17-20	1 @ 450	8½ @ 1700	6½-7½	18	12-14
	V8, Firedome, S-25	IBP-4001	C	29-32	.017	17-20	1 @ 350	10 @ 1700	10-11	18	14-16
	V8, Fireflight, S-26	IBP-4001-A	C	29-32	.017	17-20	1 @ 430	9 @ 2300	10-11	18	14-16
	V8, Adventurer, S-26	IBS-4004	C	(B)	.018	17-20	1 @ 350	8 @ 700	8¼-9	18	9-11½
1958	V8, Firesweep, LS1-L	IBP-4005	C	29-32	.017	17-20	1 @ 350	10 @ 2000	6¼-8	16½	11½-14½
	V8, Firedome, LS2-M	IBP-4005	C	29-32	.017	17-20	1 @ 350	10 @ 2000	6¼-8	16½	11½-14½
	V8, Fireflight, LS3-H	IBP-4005	C	29-32	.017	17-20	1 @ 350	10 @ 2000	6¼-8	16½	11½-14½
	V8, Adventurer, LS2-S	IBS-4006-B	C	(B)	.018	17-20	1 @ 350	10 @ 2000	6¼-8	16½	11½-14½
1959	Except Adventurer	IBP-4005-B	CC	27-32	.017	17-20	1 @ 350	9½ @ 2150	7¼-9	16½	9½-12½
	MS-3-H Adventurer	IBS-4005-H	CC	(C)	.018	17-20	1 @ 450	9½ @ 2000	7½-9¼	18¼	11½-14½
1960	V8, PS1-361 Eng.	IBP-4005-C	CC	27-32	.017	17-21	1 @ 400	8 @ 2200	7½-9	15	8¼-11
	V8, PS3-383 Eng.	IBP-4005-D	CC	27-32	.017	17-21	1 @ 350	11 @ 2150	7½-9	15	8¼-11
	V8, PS1 W/RAM	IBS-4006-E	CC	(C)	.017	17-21	1 @ 400	10 @ 2400	7¼-9	14½	7½-10½
1961	V8, 361 Cu. In.	IBP-4005-E	CC	27-32	.017	17-21	1@350	11@2050	6-8	16	10.5-13
	V8, 383 Cu. In.	IBS-4006-E	CC	27-32	.017	17-21	1@400	10@2400	7.5-10.5	14.5	7.5-10.5

(A) Dual Points: Each Set 26°—28°, Total Dwell 32°—36°.
(B) Dual Points: Each Set 29°—32°, Total Dwell 36°—39°.
(C) Dual Points: Each Set 27°—32°, Total Dwell 34°—40°.

GENERATOR and REGULATOR SPECIFICATIONS

DE SOTO, DODGE and DART

YEAR	GENERATORS			REGULATORS				
	Field Current in Amperes		Brush Spring Tension	Cut Out Relay		Current and Voltage Regulator Air Gap	Current Regulator Setting	Voltage Setting Regulator
	At 6 Volts	At 12 Volts		Air Gap	Closing Voltage			
1954-55 All Models	1.45	....	44	.032	6.5	.050	40	7.2
1956-58 All Models	....	1.25	27	.032	13.4	.050	40	14.5
1959 All Models	....	1.55	27	.032	13.5	.050	35	14.6
1960 All Models	....	1.55	27	.032	13.1 @ 1480	.050	35	14.3-14.9

LIGHT BULBS

DE SOTO, DODGE AND DART

(CP MEANS CANDLE POWER)

Ignition Key:
6 Volt, No. 51, 12 Volt, No. 53.
(One C.P. Miniature Bayonet Base)

Indicator Lights, Glove Box and Instrument Lights:
6 Volt, No. 55; 12 Volt, No. 57.
(C.P. Miniature Bayonet Base).

License Plate and Tail Light:
6 Volt, No. 63; 12 Volt, No. 67.
(4 C.P. Single Contact Base).

Map, Dome and Luggage Compartment:
6 Volt, No. 210; 12 Volt, No. 1004.
(15 C.P. Double Contact Base).

Front and Rear Signal and Park:
6 Volt, No. 1154; 12 Volt, No. 1034.
(4 & 32 C.P. 2 Contact Indexed Base).

Back-up Lights:
6 Volt, No. 1129, 12 Volt(No. 1141.
12 Volt, No. 1073.
(21 or 32 C.P. Single Contact Base).

Headlights, Sealed Beam:
6 Volt, No. 5040; 12 Volt, No. 5400.
(50 & 40 C.P. 3 Contact Base).

Headlights, Twin Sealed Beam:

OUTER (HIGH AND LOW BEAM)
12 Volt, No. 4002.
(37½—50 watts. 3 Contact Base).

INNER (HIGH BEAM)
12 Volt, No. 4001.
(37½ Watts. 2 Contact Base).

BATTERY and STARTER SPECIFICATIONS

| YEAR AND ENGINE TYPE | BATTERY | | | | STARTERS | | | | | | Spring Brush Tension |
| | Amp. Hour Cap. | Volts | Group No. | Term Grd. | Lock Test | | | No Load Test | | | |
					Amps.	Volts	Torque	Amps.	Volts	RPM	
DE SOTO											
1954											
6 Cyl.	120	6	2	Pos.	610	3.0	15.0	65	5.0	4900	48
V8	120	6	2	Pos.	335	2.0	6.5	65	5.0	4300	48
1955											
V8	120	6	2	Pos.	410	2.0	8.0	65	5.0	4300	48
1956											
V8	60	12	2SM	Neg.	240	4.0	6.5	60	10.0	3200	48
1957											
V8	60	12	2SM	Neg.	225	4.0	6.0	60	10.0	3200	48
1958											
Fire Sweep V8	60	12	2SM	Neg.	350	4.0	8.5	58	11.0	3800	40
All Other V8	60	12	2SM	Neg.	350	4.0	8.5	80'	11.0	3800	40
1959-61											
V8	60	12	2SHB	Neg.	350	4.0	8.5	80	11.0	3800	40
DODGE and DART											
1954–55											
6 Cyl. (A)	105	6	1	Pos.	500	3.0	11.0	57.5	6.0	4900	48
V8	105	6	1	Pos.	500	3.0	11.0	57.5	6.0	4900	48
1956											
Coronet 6 (B)	50	12	2SM	Neg.	210	4.0	5.0	50'	10.0	4400	48
Coronet V8 (B)	50	12	2SM	Neg.	240	4.0	6.5	60'	10.0	3200	48
Other V8	60	12	2SM	Neg.	240	4.0	6.5	60'	10.0	3200	48
1957											
6 Cyl. (C)	50	12	2SM	Neg.	210	4.0	5.0	50	11.0	3600	48
V8	53	12	2SM	Neg.	225	4.0	6.0	60	11.0	3400	48
1958											
Coronet 6	50	12	2SM	Neg.	210	4.0	5.0	50'	11.0	3600	48
Red Ram V8	50	12	2SM	Neg.	225	4.0	6.0	60	11.0	3400	48
Super Red Ram V8	60	12	25M	Neg.	350	4.0	8.5	58'	11.0	3800	48
1959											
6 Cyl. & Red Ram V8	50	12	2SHA	Neg.	355	4.0	9.0	50'	11.0	5500	48
Ram Fire & D500 V8's	60	12	2SHB	Neg.	350	4.0	8.5	58'	11.0	3800	48
1960											
Dart, Slant 6, 225 cu. in.	50	12	2SHA	Neg.	350	4.0	8.5	58	11.0	3800	48
Dart, V8, 318 cu. in.	50	12	2SHA	Neg.	355	4.0	9.0	50	11.0	5500	48
Dart, D500—Dodge, All	60	12	2SHB	Neg.	350	4.0	8.5	58	11.0	3800	48
1961											
225 cu. in. "6"	50	12	2SHA	Neg.	350	4.0	8.5	58	11.0	3800	48
318 cu. in. V8	50	12	2SHA	Neg.	350	4.0	8.5	78	11.0	3800	48
361, 383 cu. in V8	60	12	2SHA	Neg.	350	4.0	8.5	78	11.0	3800	48
1962											
Slant "6", 318 V8	48	12	HS48B	Neg.	475	4	8.5	85	11.0	1950	32-48
361 V-8, 413 V-8	59	12	HS59B	Neg.	475	4	8.5	85	11.0	1950	32-48
1963											
Slant 6, 225 cu. in.	48	12	MB24	Neg.	380	4	8:5	90	11.0	2950	32-48
V8, All Exc. 413 Engine	48	12	MB24	Neg.	475	4	8.5	90	11.0	2250	32-48
V8, 413 cu. in. Engine	59	12	MB24	Neg.	350	4	24.0	85	11.0	1950	32-48

NOTES FOR BATTERY AND STARTER SPECIFICATIONS TABLE

(A)—1954-55 Dodge 6:
When equipped with Powerflite transmission this model carries a Group 2 battery of 6 volts and 120 amp. hrs. capacity.

(B)—1956 Coronet 6 and V8:
When equipped with Powerflite or power steering or both these models have same battery and starter as other V8's.

(C)—1957 Coronet 6:
When equipped with Powerflite has same starter specs. as V8.

Ignition and Starter Switch

Like other members of the Chrysler family, De Soto and Dodge use a combination ignition and starter switch. The switch is key operated to complete the ignition primary circuit and to energize the solenoid and activate the starter. Peculiar to this system is a tie-in with the charging circuit that cuts out the starter when the generator speed increases on starting the engine. Voltage build-up opposes the current flow from the ignition and starter switch, preventing starter engagement while the engine is running.

This is accomplished by using a "starter relay" mounted on the left fender shield and connected into the primary starter solenoid circuit.

CAUTION: Don't overlook this area as a possible source of starter failure. It has not been a chronic point of trouble but the situation has presented itself in the past.

DE SOTO, DODGE & DART

(1963 DART, SEE VALIANT)

FUSES and CIRCUIT BREAKERS

DE SOTO, DODGE AND DART

All Lights Except Back-up:
Circuit Breakers on or near light switch.

Back-up Lights:
10 amp. Circuit Breaker on windshield wiper switch.

Radio:
SFE 9 or 14 fuse in line back of instrument panel.

Automatic Top:
Circuit Breaker at switch or at left front kick panel.

1962-63 production uses a printed instrument panel circuit.

1962-63

Headlights:
22.5 amp. circuit breaker.

Windshield Wiper Motor:
5 amp. circuit breaker.

All Other Circuits:
Fuses with ratings marked in easy access fuse box under dash.

Clock:
AGA 3 fuse at clock.

Window Lifts:
Circuit Breaker at left front kick pad.

Seat Motors:
Circuit Breaker under seat or at left front kick panel.

Air Conditioner Blower:
Circuit Breaker on switch.

DESOTO GENERAL CHASSIS AND BRAKE SPECIFICATIONS

YEAR & MODEL		CHASSIS		BRAKE CYLINDER BORE		
		Overall Length in Inches	Tire Size	Master Cyl. (Inch)	Wheel Cylinder Diameter (Inch) Front	Rear
1954	6 Cyl. and V-8, All	214½	7.60x15	1.0	2 Cyl. 1⅛	1⅛
1955	V-8, Firedome, Fireflight	216.0	7.60x15	1.0	2 Cyl. 1⅛	1⅛
1956	V-8, Firedome, FireFlight	218.0	7.60x15	1⅛	2 Cyl. 1⅛	1⅛
	V8, Adventurer	221.0	7.60x15	1⅛	2 Cyl. 1⅛	1⅛
1957	V-8, Firesweep	216½	8.00x14	1⅛	2 Cyl. 1⅛	1⅛
	V-8, All Others	218½	8.50x14	1⅛	2 Cyl. 1⅛	1⅛
1958	V-8, Firesweep	217¼	8.00x14	1⅛	2 Cyl. 1⅛	1⅛
	V-8, All Others	221¼	8.50x14	1⅛	2 Cyl. 1⅛	1⅛
1959	V-8, Firesweep	215½	8.00x14	1⅛	2 Cyl. 1⅛	1⅛
	V-8, FireFlite, Advent.	221⅛	8.50x14	1⅛	2 Cyl. 1⅛	1⅛
	V-8, Firedome	219½	8.50x14	1⅛	2 Cyl. 1⅛	1⅛
1960	V-8, FireFlite (A)	215 13/32	8.00x14	1⅛	2 Cyl. 1⅛	1⅛
	V-8, Adventure (A)	217.0	8.00x14	1⅛	2 Cyl. 1⅛	1⅛
1961	V-8, Adventure (A)	215 13/32	8.00x14	1⅛	2 Cyl. 1⅛	1⅛

Note A: 8.50x14 tires optional.

DODGE and DART GENERAL CHASSIS AND BRAKE SPECIFICATIONS

YEAR & MODEL		CHASSIS		BRAKE CYLINDER BORE		
		Overall Length in Inches	Tire Size	Master Cyl. (Inch)	Wheel Cylinder Diameter (Inch) Front	Rear
1954	6 Cyl. Meadowbrook	205½	6.70x15	1⅛	2 Cyl. 1⅛	1⅛
	6 Cyl. Coronet	205½	7.10x15	1⅛	2 Cyl. 1⅛	1⅛
	V-8, Meadowbrook, Coronet, Royal	205½	7.10x15	1⅛	2 Cyl. 1⅛	1⅛
	V-8, Coronet, Royal (Spts. Coupe)	196	7.10x15	1⅛	2 Cyl. 1⅛	1⅛
1955	6 Cyl. Coronet	212¼	6.70x15	1⅛	2 Cyl. 1⅛	1⅛
	V-8, Coronet, Royal, Custom Royal	212¼	7.10x15	1⅛	2 Cyl. 1⅛	1⅛
1956	6 Cyl. Coronet	212.0	6.70x15	1⅛	2 Cyl. 1⅛	1⅛
	V-8, All Except D500	212.0	7.10x15	1⅛	2 Cyl. 1⅛	1⅛
	V-8, Dodge "500"	212.0	7.60x15	1⅛	2 Cyl. 1⅛	1⅛
1957	6 Cyl. and V-8 Coronet	212¼	7.50x14	1⅛	2 Cyl. 1⅛	1⅛
	V-8, Others Except D500	214½	8.00x14	1⅛	2 Cyl. 1⅛	1⅛
	V-8, Dodge "500"	212¼	8.00x14	1⅛	2 Cyl. 1⅛	1⅛
1958	6 Cyl. and V-8 Coronet	213¾	7.50x14	1⅛	2 Cyl. 1⅛	1⅛
	V-8, All Others	213¾	8.00x14	1⅛	2 Cyl. 1⅛	1⅛
1959	6 Cyl. Except Convertible	217½	7.50x14	1⅛	2 Cyl. 1⅛	1⅛
	V-8, All Others	217½	8.00x14	1⅛	2 Cyl. 1⅛	1⅛
1960	Dart, All Except Station Wagon	208⅝	7.50x14	1⅛	2 Cyl. 1⅛	1⅛
	Dart, Station Wagon	214¾	8.00x14	1⅛	2 Cyl. 1⅛	1⅛
	Dodge, All Except Station Wagon	212⅝	8.00x14	1⅛	2 Cyl. 1⅛	1⅛
	Dodge, Station Wagon	214⅞	8.00x14	1⅛	2 Cyl. 1⅛	1⅛
1961	Dart, Exc. Sta. Wagon	209.4	750x14	1⅛	2 Cyl. 1⅛	1⅛
	Polara, Exc. Sta. Wagon	212.4	8.00x14	1⅛	2 Cyl. 1⅛	1⅛
	Station Wagon	214.8	8.00x14	1⅛	2 Cyl. 1⅛	1⅛
1962	6 cyl. Exc. Sta. Wagon	202.0	6.50x14	1	1	15/16
	V8, Exc. Sta. Wagon	202.0	7.00x14	1	1	15/16
	Station Wagon	209.9	7.00x14	1	1	15/16
	Custom 880	213.5	8.00x14	1⅛	2 Cyl. 1⅛	1⅛
	Custom 880 Sta. Wagon	215.0	8.50x14	1⅛	2 Cyl. 1⅛	1⅛
1963	All Exc. Sta. Wagon	208.2	7.00x14	1	1	15/16
	Sta. Wagon	210.7	7.00x14	1	1	15/16

CYLINDER HEAD NUT TIGHTENING SEQUENCE

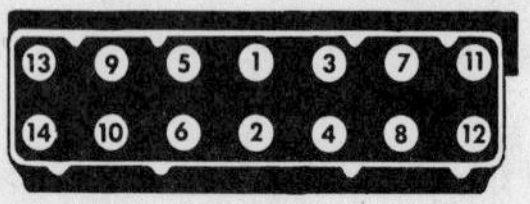

1960-63 Econo-Slant "6" O.H.V. Engine

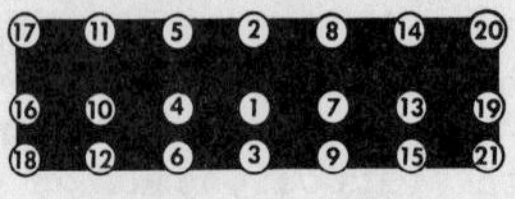

1950-59: All 6 cyl. "L" head
Tighten to 60-70 ft. lbs.

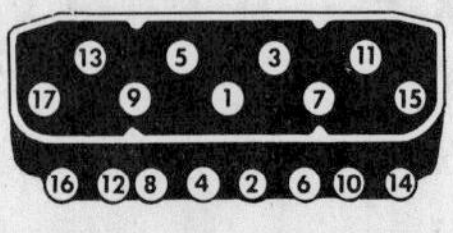

1958-63, V8 with one rocker shaft per head and distributor at front of engine.

DE SOTO, DODGE & DART
(1963 DART, SEE VALIANT)

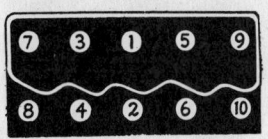

7 3 1 5 9
8 4 2 6 10

1955-63, V8 with one rocker shaft per head and distributor at rear of engine.

1954-57, V8 with two rocker shafts per head.

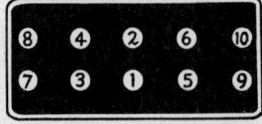

8 4 2 6 10
7 3 1 5 9

GENERAL ENGINE SPECIFICATIONS

DE SOTO

Year Model Engine Type	Bore and Stroke	Number of Main Bearings	Type of Valve Lifter Used	Cubic Inch Displacement	AMA Horsepower	Advertised Horsepower at Stated RPM	Advertised Torque at Stated RPM	Compression Ratio	Oil Pressure At 30 MPH (Note 2)	Cam Shaft Drive
1954—Note 3										
S20, 6 Cyl., L Head.............	3⁷⁄₁₆x4¹⁄₂	4	Solid	250.6	28.4	116@3600	208@1600	7-1	50	Chain
S19, Fire Dome, OHV, V8.......	3⁵⁄₈x3¹¹⁄₃₂	5	Hydraulic	276.1	28.4	170@4400	255@2400	7.5-1	50	Chain
1955—Note 3										
S22, Fire Dome, OHV, V8....	3²³⁄₃₂x3¹¹⁄₃₂	5	Hydraulic	291	44.3	185@4400	245@2800	7.5-1	50	Chain
S21, Fire Flite, OHV, V8........	3²³⁄₃₂x3¹¹⁄₃₂	5	Hydraulic	291	44.3	200@4400	274@2800	7.5-1	50	Chain
1956—Note 3										
S23, Fire Dome, OHV, V8.......	3²³⁄₃₂x3⁵¹⁄₆₄	5	Hydraulic	330	44.3	230@4400	305@2800	8.5-1	50	Chain
S24, Fire Flite, OHV, V8........	3²³⁄₃₂x3⁵¹⁄₆₄	5	Hydraulic	330	44.3	255@4400	350@3200	8.5-1	50	Chain
Adventure, OHV, V8............	3²⁵⁄₃₂x3⁵¹⁄₆₄	5	Hydraulic	341.4	45.7	320@5200	356@4000	9.25-1	50	Chain
1957—Note 3										
S25, Fire Dome, OHV, V8.......	3²⁵⁄₃₂x3⁵¹⁄₆₄	5	Hydraulic	341.4	45.7	270@4600	350@2400	9.25-1	50	Chain
S26, Fire Flite, OHV, V8........	3²⁵⁄₃₂x3⁵¹⁄₆₄	5	Hydraulic	341.4	45.7	295@4600	375@2800	9.25-1	50	Chain
S27, Fire Sweep, OHV, V8......	3¹¹⁄₁₆x3⁵¹⁄₆₄	5	Hydraulic	325	43.6	245@4400	320@2400	8.5-1	50	Chain
S26A, Adventurer, V8	3⁵¹⁄₆₄x3⁵¹⁄₆₄	5	Hydraulic	345	46.2	345@5200	355@3600	9.25-1	50	Chain
1958—Note 3										
LS1, Fire Sweep, OHV, V8	4¹¹⁄₁₆x3³⁄₈	5	Hydraulic	350	52.7	280@4600	380@2400	10.0-1	50	Chain
LS2, Fire Dome, OHV, V8	4¹⁄₈x3³⁄₈	5	Hydraulic	361	54.3	295@4600	390@2400	10.0-1	50	Chain
LS3, Fire Flite, OHV, V8	4¹⁄₈x3³⁄₈	5	Hydraulic	361	54.3	305@4600	400@2800	10.0-1	50	Chain
LS3-S, Adventurer, V8	4¹⁄₈x3³⁄₈	5	Hydraulic	361	54.3	345@5000	400@3600	10.0-1	50	Chain
1959—Note 3										
MS1, Fire Sweep, OHV, V8	4¹⁄₈x3³⁄₈	5	Hydraulic	361	54.4	290@4600	390@2400	10.0-1	50	Chain
MS2, Fire Dome, OHV, V8	4¹⁄₄x3³⁄₈	5	Hydraulic	383	57.8	305@4600	410@2400	10.1-1	50	Chain
MS3, Fire Flite, OHV, V8	4¹⁄₄x3³⁄₈	5	Hydraulic	383	57.8	325@4600	425@2400	10.1-1	50	Chain
MS3-S, Adventurer, V8	4¹⁄₄x3³⁄₈	5	Hydraulic	383	57.8	350@5000	425@3600	10.1-1	50	Chain
1960										
PS-1, Fire Flite, V-8	4.12x3.38	5	Hydraulic	361	54.3	295@4600	390@2400	10.0-1	55	Chain
PS-3, Adventurer, V-8	4.25x3.38	5	Hydraulic	383	57.8	305@4600	410@2400	10.0-1	55	Chain
1961										
RS1	4.12x3.38	5	Hydraulic	361	54.3	300@4800	390@3200	9.0-1	55	Chain
RS3	4.25x3.375	5	Hydraulic	383	57.8	325@4800	425@3200	10.0-1	55	Chain

NOTES FOR DE SOTO GENERAL ENGINE SPECIFICATIONS TABLE

Note 1: Valve Lifters

1954, Six-cylinder "L" head engines are equipped with adjustable valve tappets.

Starting with 1952, Eight cylinder overhead valve engines do not have adjustable valve tappets.

Note 2: Oil Flow

OIL FILTER TYPE

1954-57 ....Partial flow

1958-61, De Soto, All ....Full flow

ROCKER SHAFT OIL SUPPLY V8'S WITH DISTRIBUTOR AT REAR OF ENGINE

Oil is metered by the number two camshaft bearing to the left bank and the number four camshaft bearing to the right bank. Passages in the head and block carry the oil to drilled rocker cover studs on single rocker shaft engines, and drilled rocker shaft bracket bolts on two rocker shaft engines. The front one on the left bank; the rear one on the right bank. From the drilled studs (or bolts) it flows into the hollow rocker shafts and so into the drilled rockers. Holes at the rear of each head return the oil to the crankcase.

Rocker Shaft Oil Supply

V-8'S WITH DISTRIBUTOR AT FRONT OF ENGINE

Oil flows from the pump thru the filter and then across the front of the block to the right oil gallery. From the right oil gallery oil flows to the main and camshaft bearings. From the No. 4 camshaft bearing oil flows thru drilled holes in the block and head of each bank to the hollow rocker shafts from which it is metered to the stamped rockers. A crossover passage at the rear of the block transfers oil to the left gallery. The oil pressure gage is connected into this crossover.

Note 3: Engine Type—De Soto V8

1954-57, FIREDOME, OHV, V8:

This engine has 2 rocker shafts per head.

1955-57, FIREFLIGHT, OHV, V8:

This engine has 2 rocker shafts per head.

1957, FIRESWEEP, OHV, V8:

This engine has 1 rocker shaft per head.

1958-61, ALL DE SOTO V8

ENGINES

All these engines have 1 rocker shaft per head. The distributor is at the front of the engine.

DE SOTO, DODGE & DART

(1963 DART, SEE VALIANT)

GENERAL ENGINE SPECIFICATIONS

DODGE and DART

Year Model Engine Type	Bore and Stroke	Number of Main Bearings	Type of Valve Lifter Used (Note)	Cubic Inch Displacement	AMA Horsepower	Advertised Horsepower at Stated RPM	Advertised Torque at Stated RPM	Compression Ratio	Oil Pressure At 30 MPH	Cam Shaft Drive
1954										
All, 6 Cyl., L Head	3¼x4⅝	4	Solid	230.2	25.4	110@3600	190@1600	7.25–1	45	Chain
Red Ram, OHV, V8	3 7/16x3¼	5	Hydraulic	241.3	37.8	140@4400	220@2000		45	Chain
1955										
All, 6 Cyl., L Head	3¼x4⅝	4	Solid	230.2	25.2	123@3600	194@1600	7.4–1	45	Chain
Red Ram, OHV, V8	3⅝x3¼	5	Hydraulic	270	42.2	175@4400	246@2400	7.6–1	45	Chain
Super Red Ram, OHV, V8	3⅝x3¼	5	Hydraulic	270	42.2	183@4400	245@2400	7.6–1	45	Chain
1956										
All, 6 Cyl., L Head	3¼x4⅝	4	Solid	230.2	25.2	131@3800	203@2000	7.6–1	45	Chain
Red Ram, OHV, V8	3⅝x3¼	5	Hydraulic	270.2	42.2	189@4400	266@2400	8.0–1	45	Chain
Super Red Ram, OHV, V8	3⅝x3 51/64	5	Hydraulic	315	42.2	218@4400	309@2000	8.0–1	45	Chain
D500, OHV, V8	3⅝x3 51/64	5	Solid	315	42.2	260@4800	330@3000	9.25–1	45	Chain
1957										
All, 6 Cyl., L Head	3¼x4⅝	4	Solid	230.2	25.2	138@4000	208@1600	8.0–1	45	Chain
Red Ram, OHV, V8	3 11/16x3 51/64	5	Hydraulic	325	43.6	245@4400	320@2400	8.5–1	45	Chain
Super Red Ram, OHV, V8	3 11/16x3 51/64	5	Hydraulic	325	43.6	260@4400	335@2800	8.5–1	45	Chain
D500, OHV, V8	3 11/16x3 51/64	5	Hydraulic	325	43.6	285@4800	345@2800	8.5–1	45	Chain
D500, P.P., V8	3 11/16x3 51/64	5	Hydraulic	325	43.6	310@4800	350@3200	8.5–1	45	Chain
1958										
LD1, 6 Cyl., L Head	3¼x4⅝	4	Solid	230.2	25.2	138@4000	208@1600	8.01	45	Chain
LD2, Red Ram, OHV, V8	3 11/16x3 51/64	5	Hydraulic	325	43.6	252@4400	345@2400	8.5-1	45	Chain
LD3, Super Red Ram, V8	4 1/16x3⅜	5	Hydraulic	350	52.7	295@4600	385@2800	10.0-1	45	Chain
D500, Package	4⅛x3⅜	5	Hydraulic	361	54.3	305@4600	400@2800	10.0-1	45	Chain
1959										
MD1, 6 Cyl., L Head	3¼x4⅝	4	Solid	230.2	25.2	138@4000	208@1600	8.0-1	45	Chain
MD2, Red Ram, OHV, V8	3 61/64x3 5/16	5	Hydraulic	325	49.9	255@4400	350@2500	9.2-1	55	Chain
MD3, Ram Fire, OHV, V8	4⅛x3⅜	5	Hydraulic	361	54.3	305@4600	400@2800	10.0-1	55	Chain
D500, Package	4¼x3⅜	5	Hydraulic	383	57.8	320@4600	420@2800	10.0-1	55	Chain
1960										
P22, Slant 6, OHV	3.40x4.125	4	Solid	225	27.74	145@4000	215@2800	8.5-1	50	Chain
P318, Red Ram, V8	3.91x3.31	5	Solid	318	48.9	230@4400	340@2400	9.0-1	50	Chain
PL36, Super Red Ram, V8	4.12x3.38	5	Hydraulic	361	54.3	295@4600	390@2400	10.0-1	55	Chain
PL38, Ram Fire, V8	4.25x3.38	5	Hydraulic	383	57.8	330@4800	420@2800	10.0-1	55	Chain
1961										
Slant 6, RD 3	3.40x4.125	4	Solid	225	27.7	140@4000	215@2400	8.2-1	50	Chain
V8, 318 cu. in.	3.91x3.31	5	Solid	318	48.9	260@4400	345@2800	9.0-1	50	Chain
V8, 361 cu. in.	4.12x3.38	5	Hydraulic	361	54.3	300@4800	390@3200	9.0-1	55	Chain
V8, 383 cu. in.	4.25x3.375	5	Hydraulic	383	57.8	325@4800	425@3200	10.0-1	55	Chain
1962										
Slant 6	3.40x4.125	4	Solid	225	27.7	145@4000	215@2800	8.2-1	50	Chain
V8-318-2BBL.	3.91x3.31	5	Solid	318	48.9	230@4400	340@2400	9.0-1	50	Chain
V8-318-4BBL.	3.91x3.31	5	Solid	318	48.9	260@4400	345@2800	9.0-1	50	Chain
V8-361	4.25x3.375	5	Hydraulic	361	54.3	305@4800	395@3000	10.2-1	55	Chain
V8-413 cu. in.	4.19x3.75	5	Hydraulic	413	55.9	365@4600	460@2800	11.0-1	55	Chain
1963										
Slant 6	3.40x4.125	4	Solid	225	27.7	145@4000	215@2800	8.2-1	50	Chain
V8-318 cu. in.—2BBL.	3.91x3.31	5	Solid	318	48.9	230@4400	340@2400	9.0-1	50	Chain
V8-361 cu. in.	4.25x3.375	5	Hydraulic	361	54.3	305@4800	395@3000	9.0-1	55	Chain
V8-383 cu. in.	4.25x3.38	5	Hydraulic	383	57.8	325@4800	425@3200	10.0-1	55	Chain
V8-413 cu. in.	4.19x3.75	5	Hydraulic	413	55.9	365@4600	460@2800	11.0-1	55	Chain

NOTES FOR DODGE and DART GENERAL ENGINE SPECIFICATIONS TABLE

Note 1: Oil Flow Dodge and Dart Oil Filter Type. Starting with all 1954 Use Full Flow Filters

ROCKER SHAFT OIL SUPPLY ON DART-SLANT SIX ENGINES. From pump, thru filter, oil circulates thru block galleries to crankshaft mains. From #2 main to camshaft and front oil passages to rocker shaft and rocker lovors.

ROCKER SHAFT OIL SUPPLY ON DODGE AND DART V8 ENGINES. From pump, thru filter, oil circulates thru block galleries and camshaft to main bearings, from #4 camshaft bearing to shafts and rockers.

Note 2: Engine Type, Dodge V8

1954 RED RAM, OHV, V8:

This engine has 2 rocker shafts per head.

1955, RED RAM, OHV, V8:

This engine has 1 rocker shaft per head.

1955, SUPER RED RAM, OHV, V8:

This engine has 2 rocker shafts per head.

1956-57, RED RAM AND SUPER RED RAM:

These engines have 1 rocker shaft per head.

1956-57, D500, OHV, V8:

This engine has 2 rocker shafts per head.

1958-63, RED RAM, OHV, V8:

This engine has 1 rocker shaft per head. The distributor is at the rear of the engine.

(1963 DART, SEE VALIANT)

NOTES FOR DODGE and DART GENERAL ENGINE SPECIFICATIONS TABLE —continued

1960-63, ECONOMY SLANT 6 CYL. OHV:

This engine is mounted at a 30° angle to the right of vertical (viewed from the driving seat) and is 225 cu. in. in piston displacement. The basic engine design is used in the Dart, the Plymouth and the Valiant.

1960-63, RED RAM V8:

This engine has 318 cu. in. of displacement. It is equipped with mechanical tappets and is the popular V8 of the Dart series.

1960-63, SUPER RED RAM V8:

This engine has 361 cu. in. of displacement. It is equipped with hydraulic tappets and the distributor is front mounted.

1960, FIRE RAM V8:

This is the high output engine of the Dodge line. It is of 383 cu. in. capacity and has a front mounted distributor.

1958-63, SUPER RED RAM V8, RAM FIRE V8 AND D500 V8:

These engines have 1 rocker shaft per head. The distributor is at the front of the engine.

CRANKSHAFT BEARING JOURNAL SIZES

YEAR	MAIN BEARING JOURNALS				CONNECTING ROD BEARING JOURNALS		
	JOURNAL DIAMETER	OIL CLEARANCE	END PLAY	HELD BY	JOURNAL DIAMETER	OIL CLEARANCE	END PLAY
DE SOTO							
1954							
6 Cyl.	2.500	.0010	.005	No. 4	2.125	.0010	.0085
V8	2.375	.0010	.0045	No. 4	2.062	.0010	.010
1955							
V8	2.380	.0010	.0045	No. 3	2.062	.0010	.010
1956-57							
V8	2.500	.0010	.0045	No. 3	2.249	.0010	.010
1958-59							
All V8	2.625	.0010	.0045	No. 3	2.374	.0010	.013
1960-61							
All V8	2.650 ± .0005	.0010	.002-.007	No. 3	2.375	.0010	.013
DODGE							
1954							
6 Cyl. "L" Head	2.500	.0010	.005	No. 4	2.062	.0010	.0085
V8	2.375	.0010	.0045	No. 3	1.937	.0010	.010
1955							
6 Cyl. "L" Head	2.500	.0010	.005	No. 4	2.062	.0010	.0085
V8	2.380	.0010	.0045	No. 3	1.937	.0010	.010
1956							
6 Cyl. "L" Head	2.500	.0010	.005	No. 4	2.062	.0010	.0085
Red Ram. V8	2.375	.0010	.0045	No. 3	1.937	.0010	.010
Super Red Ram.	2.500	.0010	.0045	No. 3	2.250	.0010	.010
1957							
6 Cyl. "L" Head	2.500	.0010	.005	No. 4	2.062	.0010	.0085
V8	2.500	.0010	.0045	No. 3	2.250	.0010	.013
1958							
6 Cyl. "L" Head	2.500	.0010	.005	No. 4	2.062	.0010	.0085
Red Ram. V8	2.500	.0010	.0045	No. 3	2.250	.0010	.0010
All Other V8	2.625	.0010	.0045	No. 3	2.374	.0010	.013
1959							
6 Cyl. "L" Head	2.500	.0010	.0045	No. 4	2.062	.0010	.009
Red Ram. V8	2.500	.0010	.0045	No. 3	2.125	.0012	.0010
All Other V8	2.625	.0010	.0045	No. 3	2.375	.0010	.013
1960-62							
Slant 6 OHV	2.75	.0010	.003-.008	No. 3	2.1870	.0010	.010
361, 383 cu. in.	2.63	.0010	.002-.007	No. 3	2.375	.0010	.013
318 cu. in.	2.50	.0010	.002-.007	No. 3	2.126	.0010	.013
413 cu. in.	2.749	.0015	.002-.007	No. 3	2.376	.0015	.009
1963							
Slant 6	2.75	.0010	.002-.007	No. 3	2.187	.0010	.009
318 cu. in.	2.50	.0010	.002-.097	No. 3	2.125	.0010	.010
361 cu. in.	2.375	.0010	.002-.007	No. 3	2.375	.0010	.013
383 cu. in.	2.625	.0010	.002-.007	No. 3	2.125	.0010	.010
413 cu. in.	2.75	.0010	.002-.007	No. 3	2.375	.0015	.009

DE SOTO, DODGE & DART

(1963 DART, SEE VALIANT)

TORQUE SPECIFICATIONS

YEAR	Cylinder Head Bolts	Rod Bearing Bolts	Main Bearing Bolts	Crankshaft Pulley Bolt	Flywheel to Crankshaft Bolt	Manifolds	
						In	Ex
1954-63							
All 6 Cyl. exc. "Slant 6"	55–65	45–50	80–85	110–135	55–65	20	20
All V8 With Distributor at the back	80–85	45–50	80–85	110–135	55–65	30	25
All V8 With Distributor at the front	65-75	40–45	80–85	Note 1	55–65	40	30
"Slant 6"	65	45	85**	Press	65	10*	10

* Intake to exhaust, 17 ft. lbs.
**Aluminum Engine—50 ft. lb.

Note 1: Crankshaft Pulley Bolt
Vibration Damper Bolts __15 ft. lbs.
Bolt in end of crankshaft __135 ft. lbs.

VALVE SPECIFICATIONS

YEAR	Seat Angle		Intake Valve Lift Note 1	Exhaust Valve Lift	Valve Spring Pressure Note 2		Stem to Guide Clearance		Stem Diameter		Are Valve Guides Replaceable
	In	Ex			Inner	Outer	Inlet	Exhaust	Inlet	Exhaust	
DE SOTO											
1954											
6 Cyl.	45	45	.365	.361	43@1¾	None	.002	.004	.341	.340	Yes
V8	45	45	.365	.361	43@1 11/16	13@1 9/16	.002	.003	.372	.371	Yes
1955											
V8	45	45	.360	.360	28@1 11/16	22@1 9/16	.002	.003	.372	.372	Yes
1956											
V8 ex. Advtr.	45	45	.381	.357	72@1 11/16	None	.002	.003	.372	.372	Yes
Adventure V8	45	45	.431	.413	60½@1 21/32	28@1 17/32	.002	.003	.372	.372	Yes
1957											
V8 ex. F. Sweep	45	45	.398	.389	80½@1 11/16	Note 2A	.002	.003	.372	.372	Yes
V8 F. Sweep	45	45	.389	.435	72@1 11/16	None	.002	.003	.372	.372	Yes
1958											
V8 ex. Advtr.	45	45	.390	.389	80@1 55/64	None	.002	.003	.372	.372	No
Adventure V8	45	45	.390	.435	100@1 55/64	None	.002	.003	.372	.372	No
1959-61											
All V8	45	45	.390	.389	100@1 55/64	None	.002	.003	.372	.372	No
DODGE and DART											
1954											
6 Cyl. "L" Head	45	45	.365	.365	43@1¾	None	.002	.004	.340	.340	Yes
V8	45	45	.365	.365	41@1 11/16	22@1 9/16	.002	.003	.372	.371	Yes
1955											
6 Cyl. "L" Head	45	45	.365	.365	43@1¾	None	.002	.004	.340	.340	Yes
Red Ram, V8	45	45	.360	.360	53@1 11/16	None	.002	.003	.372	.371	No
Super Red Ram, V8	45	45	.360	.360	40@1 11/16	25@1 9/16	.002	.003	.372	.371	Yes
1956											
6 Cyl. "L" Head	45	45	.379	.365	43@1¾	None	.002	.004	.340	.340	Yes
V8 ex. D500	45	45	.360	.360	53@1 11/16	None	.002	.003	.372	.371	No
D500 V8	45	45	.400	.400	61½@1 21/32	28@1 17/32	.002	.003	.372	.371	Yes
1957											
6 Cyl. "L" Head	45	45	.379	.365	43@1¾	None	.002	.004	.340	.340	Yes
All V8	45	45	.389	.389	72@1 11/16	None	.002	.003	.372	.371	No
1958											
6 Cyl. "L" Head	45	45	.365	.365	42@1¾	None	.002	.004	.340	.340	Yes
V8 ex. D500	45	45	.389	.389	72@1 11/16	None	.002	.003	.372	.371	No
D500 V8	45	45	.390	.389	80@1 55/64	None	.002	.003	.372	.372	No
1959											
6 Cyl. "L" Head	45	45	.365	.365	42@1¾	None	.002	.004	.340	.340	Yes
Red Ram V8	45	45	.390	.386	72@1 11/16	None	.002	.003	.372	.372	No
Ram Fire V8	45	45	.390	.390	100@1 55/64	None	.002	.003	.372	.372	No
D500 V8	45	45	.390	.390	100@1 55/64	None	.002	.003	.372	.372	No
1960-62											
225 cu. in. Slant 6 OHV ..	45	45*	.375	.364	72@1 11/16	None	.002	.003	.372	.371	No
318 cu. in. V8	45	45	.389	.386	100@1 55/64	None	.002	.003	.372	.372	No
361 cu. in. V8	45	45	.389	.380	100@1 55/64	None	.002	.003	.372	.372	No
383 cu. in. V8—Note 3: ..	45	45	.389	.390	100@1 55/64	None	.002	.003	.372	.372	No
413 cu. in.	45	45	.444	.456	100@1 55/64	None	.002	.003	.37	.37	No
1963											
225 cu. in. Slant 6 OHV ..	45	45	.375	.364	53@1 11/16	None	.002	.003	.373	.372	No
318 cu. in.	45	45	.380	.386	83@1 11/16	None	.002	.003	.373	.372	No
361 cu. in.	45	45	.380	.386	100@1 11/16	None	.002	.003	.373	.372	No
413 cu. in.	45	45	.444	.456	100@1 55/64	None	.002	.003	.37	.37	No

Exhaust Valve Face—47° (2° Difference Between Exhaust Seat and Face).

(1963 DART, SEE VALIANT)

NOTES FOR VALVE SPECIFICATIONS TABLE

Note 1: Marks on camshaft and crankshaft gears should be aligned nearest each other and with the shaft centers.

Note 2: Intake and exhaust valve springs are the same. Except see below.

Note 2A: Adventure Model
Outer ....60 @ $1\frac{21}{32}$
Inner ....28 @ $1\frac{17}{32}$

Note 3: Not used in 1962.

PISTON AND PIN SPECIFICATIONS

DE SOTO

Year and Model	PISTON Skirt Clearance Min.	PISTON Skirt Clearance Max.	PISTON PIN Diameter	Bushing	FIT In Rod	FIT In Piston	Lock
1954—6 Cyl.	.0002	.0012	.8594	Yes	.0001-.0005	0-.0005	Ring
1954-57—V-8	.0005	.0015	.922	Yes	.0001-.0005	0-.0005	Ring
1958-61—V-8	.0005	.0010	1.0935-1.0937	None	Press	.00045-.00075	Rod Press

DODGE and DART

Year and Model	PISTON Skirt Clearance Min.	PISTON Skirt Clearance Max.	PISTON PIN Diameter	Bushing	FIT In Rod	FIT In Piston	Lock
1954-59—6 Cyl.	.0015	.002	.8494	Yes	Press	0-.0005	Ring
1954-56—V-8	.0005	.0015	.8592	Yes	.0001-.0004	0-.0005	Ring
1957-59—V-8	.0005	.0015	.922	Yes	.0001-.0004	0-.0005	Ring
1958—350—V-8	.0005	.0015	1.0936	None	Press	.00045-.00075	Rod Press
1959-63—361—V-8	.0005	.0010	1.0936	None	Press	.00015-.00065	Rod Press
1960-63—318—V-8	.0005	.0015	.9842	None	Press	0-.0005	Rod Press
1959-63—383—V-8	.0005	.0010	1.0936	None	Press	.00045-.00075	Rod Press
1960-62—225—Slant 6	.0005	.0015	.9008	None	Press	.00045-.00075	Rod Press
1962-63—413, V-8	.0035	.0045	1.0936	None	Press	.0006-.0009	Rod Press

CAPACITIES

DODGE and DART

YEAR	Engine Crankcase Add 1 Qt. for New Filter	TRANSMISSIONS Pints to Refill After Draining Manual	Automatic	Rear Axle Pints	Gasoline Tank Gallons	Cooling Systems Quarts Add 1 Qt. for Heater
1954						
All 6 Cyl.	5	2¾	20	3¼	17	14
All V8	5	2¾	20	3¼	17	19
1955						
All 6 Cyl.	5	2¾	20	3¼	17	13
All V8	5	2¾	20	3¼	17	19
1956						
All 6 Cyl.	5	2¾	20	3¼	17	13
Coronet D63-1, V8	5	2¾	20	3¼	17	19
All Other V8	5	2¾	20	3¼	17	20
1957						
All 6 Cyl.	5	2¾	20	3¼	20	13
All V8	5	2¾	18	3½	20	20
1958						
All 6 Cyl.	5	2¾	20	3¼	20 (C)	13
LD2, V8 (D)	5	2¾	(F)	3½	20 (C)	20
LD3, & D500 V8 (E)	4	2¾	21	3½	20 (C)	16
1959						
6 Cyl.	5	2¾	20	3¼	20 (C)	13
Red Ram V8	5	2¾	(F)	3½	20 (C)	20
Ram Fire V8	5	2¾	(F)	3½	20 (C)	16
1960-61						
Dart Slant 6 OHV	4	2¾	20	3¼	20(C)	14
Dodge & Dart with Red Ram	5	2¾	(F)	3½	20(C)	20
Dodge & Dart, All Other V-8	5	2¾	(F)	3½	20(C)	16
1962-63						
Slant 6	4	5	14	3½	20(C)	12
V8 Exc. Custom 880	4	5	19	3½	20(C)	20
Custom 880	5	5	19	4	23(C)	20

NOTES FOR DODGE AND DART CAPACITIES TABLE

(C)—Gasoline Tank Capacity
On all Station Wagons. Capacity is 22 gallons.

(F)—Automatic Transmissions
Power Flite ....20 Pints
Torque Flite: On-D2 ....18 Pints
Torque Flite: On-D3 ....21 Pints

DE SOTO, DODGE & DART
(1963 DART, SEE VALIANT)
CAPACITIES

DE SOTO

YEAR	ENGINE CRANKCASE ADD 1 QT. FOR NEW FILTER	TRANSMISSIONS PINTS TO REFILL AFTER DRAINING		REAR AXLE PINTS	GASOLINE TANK GALLONS	COOLING SYSTEM QUARTS ADD 1 QT. FOR HEATER
		MANUAL	AUTOMATIC			
1954						
6 Cyl.	5	2¾	24	3¼	17	15
V8	5	2¾	24	3½	17	22
1955						
All V8	5	2¾	20	3½	20	23
1956						
Fire Dome V8	4	2¾	20	3¼	21	23
Fire Flite V8	4	2¾	20	3½	21	23
1957						
Fire Sweep	5	2¾	(D)	3½	20	20
All Other V8	5	2¾	18	3½	23	20
1958						
Fire Sweep V8	4	2¾	(D)	3½	20	16
All Other V8	4	2¾	(E)	3½	23	16
1959-61						
Fire Sweep V8	5	2¾	(D)	3½	20	16
All Other V8	5	2¾	(E)	3½	23	16

NOTES FOR DE SOTO CAPACITIES TABLE

**(D)—Automatic Transmission
Used in Firesweep V8**
Either Power Flite or Torque Flite.
Power Flite holds 20 pints. Torque

Flite holds 18 pints.

(E)—Automatic Transmissions
Torque Flite _____ 21 pints
Power Flite _____ 20 pints

FRONT WHEEL ALIGNMENT

YEAR	FRONT END HEIGHT NOTE 6	CASTER		CAMBER		TOE-IN (INCHES)	KING PIN INCLINATION (DEGREES)	WHEEL PIVOT ANGLE	
		RANGE (DEGREES)	PREF. SETTING	RANGE (DEGREES)	PREF. SETTING			INNER WHEEL	OUTER WHEEL

DE SOTO

YEAR	FRONT END HEIGHT	CASTER RANGE	CASTER PREF	CAMBER RANGE	CAMBER PREF	TOE-IN	KING PIN INCL.	INNER WHEEL	OUTER WHEEL
1954									
All Models		3N to 1N	2N	⅜N to ⅜P	Note 1	0 to ¹⁄₁₆	5 to 6½	21½	20
1955									
Manual Strg.		2N to 0	2N	⅛N to ⅝P	Note 2	0 to ¹⁄₁₆	5 to 6½	21½	20
Power Strg.		2N to 0	0	⅛N to ⅝P	Note 2	0 to ¹⁄₁₆	5 to 6½	21½	20
1956									
Manual Strg.		2N to 0	2N	⅛N to ⅝P	Note 2	³⁄₃₂ to ⁵⁄₃₂	5 to 6½	21½	20
Power Strg.		2N to 0	0	⅛N to ⅝P	Note 2	³⁄₃₂ to ⁵⁄₃₂	5 to 6½	21½	20
1957									
Manual Strg.	2⅛" ± ⅛"	1½N to 0	Note 3	Note 4	Note 4	³⁄₃₂ to ⁵⁄₃₂	5½ to 7	21½	20
Power Strg.	2⅛" ± ⅛"	0 to 1½P	Note 3	Note 4	Note 4	³⁄₃₂ to ⁵⁄₃₂	5½ to 7	21½	20
1958-59									
Manual Strg.	2³⁄₁₆" ± ⅛"	1½N to 0	Note 3	Note 4	Note 4	³⁄₃₂ to ⁵⁄₃₂	5½ to 7	20	Note 5
Power Strg.	2³⁄₁₆" ± ⅛"	0 to 1½P	Note 3	Note 4	Note 4	³⁄₃₂ to ⁵⁄₃₂	5½ to 7	20	Note 5
1960-61									
Manual Strg.	2" ± ⅛"	1N to 0	Note 3	Note 4	Note 4	³⁄₃₂ to ⁵⁄₃₂	5½ to 7	20	Note 5
Power Strg.	2" ± ⅛"	¼P to 1¼P	Note 3	Note 4	Note 4	³⁄₃₂ to ⁵⁄₃₂	5½ to 7	20	Note 5

FRONT WHEEL ALIGNMENT

YEAR	FRONT END HEIGHT NOTE 6	CASTER		CAMBER		TOE-IN (INCHES)	KING PIN INCLINATION (DEGREES)	WHEEL PIVOT ANGLE	
		RANGE (DEGREES)	PREF. SETTING	RANGE (DEGREES)	PREF. SETTING			INNER WHEEL	OUTER WHEEL

DODGE and DART

YEAR	FRONT END HEIGHT NOTE 6	RANGE (DEGREES)	PREF. SETTING	RANGE (DEGREES)	PREF. SETTING	TOE-IN (INCHES)	KING PIN INCLINATION (DEGREES)	INNER WHEEL	OUTER WHEEL
1954 All Models		1N to 1P	0	⅜N to ⅜P	Note 1	0 to 1/16	5 to 6½	21½	20
1955 Manual Strg.		2N to 0	2N	⅛N to ⅝P	Note 2	0 to 1/16	5 to 6½	21½	20
Power Strg.		2N to 0	0	⅛N to ⅝P	Note 2	0 to 1/16	5 to 6½	21½	20
1956 Manual Strg.		2N to 0	2N	⅛N to ⅝P	Note 2	3/32 to 5/32	5 to 6½	21½	20
Power Strg.		2N to 0	0	⅛N to ⅝P	Note 2	3/32 to 5/32	5 to 6½	21½	20
1957 Manual Strg.	2¼" ± ⅛"	1½N to 0	Note 3	Note 4	Note 4	3/32 to 5/32	5½ to 7	21½	20
Power Strg.	2¼" ± ⅛"	0 to 1½P	Note 3	Note 4	Note 4	3/32 to 5/32	5½ to 7	21½	20
1958-59 Manual Strg.	2 3/16" ± ⅛"	1½N to 0	Note 3	Note 4	Note 4	3/32 to 5/32	5½ to 7	20	18¾
Power Strg.	2 3/16" ± ⅛"	0 to 1½P	Note 3	Note 4	Note 4	3/32 to 5/32	5½ to 7	20	18¾
1960-63 Manual Strg.	2½" ± ⅛"	1N to 0	Note 3	Note 4	Note 4	3/32 to 5/32	5½ to 7	20	18¾
Power Strg.	2½" ± ⅛"	¼P to 1¼P	Note 3	Note 4	Note 4	3/32 to 5/32	5½ to 7	20	18¾

NOTES FOR FRONT WHEEL ALIGNMENT TABLE

Note 1: 1954 De Soto and Dodge: Preferred Camber Setting:

Left Side ¼ more than Right Side.

Note 2: 1955 to 56 De Soto and Dodge: Preferred Camber Setting:

Left Side—½ P; Right Side 0.

Note 3: 1957-61 De Soto and Dodge: Preferred Caster Setting:

Both Sides—Equal.
1962 Driver Side ¾ less.

Note 4: 1957-61 De Soto and Dodge Camber Range and Preferred Setting:

Range of Left Side—⅛ P to ⅝ P.
Preferred Setting—⅜ P.
Range of Right Side—⅛ N to ⅜ P.
Preferred Setting—0.
1962 Preferred Left Side—½ P
1962 Preferred Right Side—¼ P

Note 5: 1958-61 De Soto Turning Radius Outer Wheel when Inner is 20:

Models with 122 inch wheelbase—18¾.
Models with 126 inch wheelbase—18½.

Note 6

To measure front end height see text.

DISTRIBUTOR

Detailed information on: distributor drive, direction of distributor rotation; cylinder numbering; firing order; point gap; cam dwell; timing mark location; spark plugs, spark advance; ignition resistor location and idle speed; will be found in the Tune-up Specifications table of this section. Further information on trouble shooting can be found in "Trouble Checks," at the beginning of the manual or in "Engine Diagnosis," in the Unit Repair Section.

DISTRIBUTOR ASSEMBLY REMOVAL

6 Cyl. "L" Head Engines

The distributor on these models is mounted on the left side of the engine block and is driven by the oil pump shaft which is slotted to receive the tongue of the distributor shaft.

To remove the distributor take off the cap and wire assembly and mark the position of the rotor with reference to the block with a piece of chalk so that the distributor can be returned to that position. After the distributor is removed from the car do not move the engine so that it can be returned exactly the way it was removed; this will save time in retiming the engine.

Disconnect the vacuum line at the

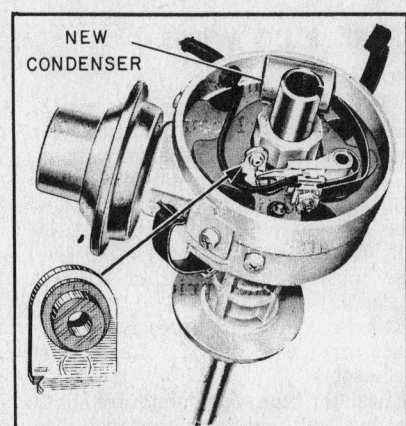

Beginning 1962—Dodge 8 Cylinder Distributor

vacuum advance mechanism and remove the one bolt which holds the distributor assembly down into the engine block.

Slant "6" Engine

The distributor is mounted on the right side of this 30° overhead valve engine. It is gear driven, directly from the camshaft and independent of the oil pump.

TO REMOVE THE DISTRIBUTOR

1. Take off the cap and wire assembly.
2. Disconnect the primary coil wire and vacuum control tube.
3. Mark the distributor and rotor relative positions.
4. Loosen the distributor mounting and lift out the distributor.

Note: To simplify reinstallation, do not disturb the engine while the distributor is out.

Reinstall by reversing the above procedure.

257

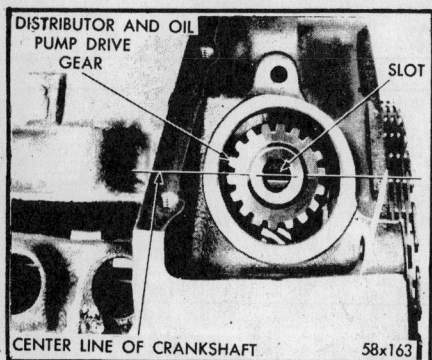

V-8 Engine with distributor at the front but typical of all V-8: Position of distributor drive gear with No. 1 piston at top of compression stroke.

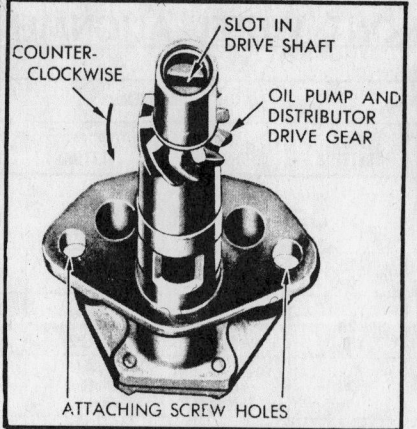

Positioning oil pump shaft for installation when No. 1 piston is at top dead center on the compression stroke. 6 Cyl. "L" Head

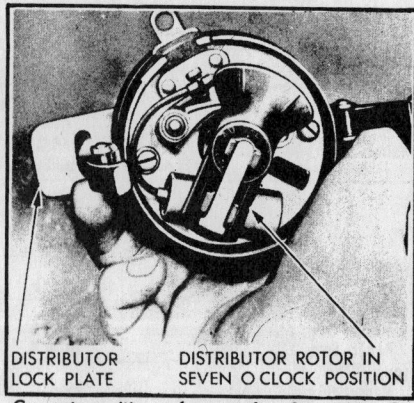

Correct position of rotor for firing No. 1 cylinder of 6 cylinder L-Head engine.

V8 Engines

To remove the distributor, take off the cap and wire assembly, disconnect the vacuum line, remove the ignition primary wire, take out the one mounting bolt which holds the distributor assembly down to the block and lift the assembly out of the block. Do not move the engine after the distributor has been removed so that it can be returned to the same position and thus save time in retiming the ignition.

DISTRIBUTOR REPLACEMENT WHEN ENGINE HAS BEEN DISTURBED

6 Cylinder "L" Head Engines

Remove No. 1 spark plug and with the thumb closing the hole rotate the engine until No. 1 piston is up on compression at top dead center as determined by the pressure on the thumb and the "DC" mark on the crankshaft pulley hub.

Turn the distributor rotor until it is in position to fire No. 1 cylinder.

Move the rotor back and forth slightly to allow the distributor shaft tongue to engage the slot in the oil pump shaft.

Slant "6" engine has a distributor driven gear of helical cut. The angle of this gear cut requires that a slight allowance of rotor position be made when meshing the distributor gear with the camshaft gear.

6 Cylinder "L" Head Engines

Set No. 1 piston at top dead center on the compression stroke as outlined above.

Turn the oil pump drive shaft so that the slot in the end of the shaft lines up with the bolt holes in the oil pump flange.

Now turn the drive gear one tooth counterclockwise. With distributor off engine, install the oil pump.

Turn distributor rotor to correct position for firing No. 1 cylinder. Wiggle the rotor slightly to engage the distributor shaft tongue with the slot in the oil pump shaft. Tighten distributor hold down bolt and check the timing with a timing light.

V8 Engine Distributor

Rotate the crankshaft until No. 1 cylinder is at top dead center. The pointer on the chain case cover should be over the "DC" mark on the crankshaft pulley. The slot in the intermediate shaft which carries the gear that drives the oil pump and the distributor should be parallel with the crankshaft.

Hold the distributor over the mounting pad on the cylinder block so that the distributor body flange coincides with the mounting pad and the rotor points to the No. 1 cylinder firing position.

Install the distributor while holding the rotor in position, only allowing it to move enough to engage the slot in the drive gear.

SPARK PLUG WIRES

Starting 1959

The spark plug wires have a non-metallic string type conductor for improved radio noise suppression. Care should be taken not to jerk the cables off the spark plugs or out of the distributor cap towers (especially if the engine is hot; otherwise, the cable may pull out of its terminal).

Check cables for excessive resistance or open circuit. Replace if necessary.

Resistor type spark plugs are not to be used with resistor type cables—otherwise poor engine performance will result.

If radio develops excessive noise or if there is a pronounced engine miss, check for defective cables—(broken).

Spark Plug Resistance

No. 1 Wire 8,300 to 16,600 Ohms
No. 2 Wire 5.500 to 11,000 Ohms
No. 3 Wire 8,100 to 16,200 Ohms
No. 4 Wire 6,000 to 12,000 Ohms
No. 5 Wire 8,800 to 17,600 Ohms
No. 6 Wire 6,300 to 12,600 Ohms
No. 7 Wire 9,400 to 18,800 Ohms
No. 8 Wire 7,200 to 14,400 Ohms

GENERATOR AND REGULATOR

Detailed facts on the generator and the alternator can be found in the Generator and Alternator Specifications Table of this section.

General information on D.C. and A.C. generator and regulator repair and trouble shooting can be found in Unit Repair section under the heading Generators and Regulators.

D.C. GENERATOR POLARITY
Caution:

Whenever the circuits to the generator, the regulator or the battery have been disconnected it is best to apply the following procedure.

Before the engine is started momentarily short from the "Bat" to the "Gen" terminals of the regulator with a screwdriver. This gives a momentary surge of current from the battery to the generator and so correctly polarizes the generator with respect to the battery.

Failure to so polarize the generator before starting the engine may severely damage the regulator since reversed polarity causes vibration, arcing and burning of the relay points.

Caution:

Under no circumstances, should the alternator be polarized.

(1963 DART, SEE VALIANT)

BATTERY AND STARTER

Detailed information on the battery and starter will be found in the Battery and Starter Specifications Table of this section.

A more general discussion of starters and their troubles can be found in the Unit Repair section under the heading Starters.

STARTER R & R

No problem here. Disconnect battery and starter wires. Remove attaching bolts and lift out starter.

SPEEDOMETER REMOVAL

All Models, 1960-63

Disconnect battery and speedometer cable. Remove transmission push button bezel then the button assembly.

Remove two studs from push button housing. Disconnect back-up light wires and push housing to one side.

Disconnect panel lights. Remove steering column dash support to cowl panel base. Disconnect horn and turn signal wires at connector under dash.

Remove four screws from speedometer to panel. Care must be used to prevent damage to speedometer face.

BRAKE SYSTEM

BRAKE INFORMATION

Specific information on brake cylinder sizes can be found in the General Chassis and Brake Specifications Table of this section.

Information on brake adjustments, band replacement, bleeding procedure, master and wheel cylinder overhaul can be found in the Unit Repair section under the heading: Brakes, Hydraulic.

Information on trouble shooting and overhauling power brakes can be found in the Unit Repair section under the heading: Brakes, Power.

Information on the grease seals which may need replacement can be found in the Unit Repair section. The front wheel grease seals under the head: Suspension, Front, Repair. The rear wheel grease seals under the head: Axles, Rear.

Starting with 1962 Except Custom 880

A new Servo-contact, self-energizing brake is used. It uses a double-acting wheel cylinder at tops of shoes at each assembly.

It is also a self-adjusting brake. It operates thru a link, cable and return spring connected so that when brake is applied during reverse stops the link indexes the star wheel to maintain proper shoe clearance.

BRAKE PEDAL CLEARANCE

1954 Thru April 1958

Adjust the master cylinder push rod so that there is 1/8 to 1/4 in. free play at the brake pedal.

This adjustment is made so that the pedal will travel 1/8 to 1/4 in. before the pedal rod starts actuating the master cylinder piston. Free play adjustment is to prevent any pressure build up of the brake pedal.

On all models thru 1954, this adjustment is made under the toeboard. Starting with 1955 the adjustment is made under the dash since the pedal is pendulum mounted.

Starting With March 1958

Cars built since March 9, 1958 with conventional brakes have a change incorporated in the brake master cylinder. With this change a pedal stop is built into the master cylinder. This eliminates the necessity of a free play adjustment on the master cylinder push rod.

The stop on the brake pedal, and the brake pedal return spring are also eliminated by this change. This results in a somewhat slower brake pedal return, when the brake is released, which is not detrimental. However, if a binding action is found at the brake pedal, the cause of binding should be eliminated.

Since the master cylinder piston determines the position of the brake pedal when the brakes are released, a free play at the pedal is no longer needed. However, if the pedal is pulled back by hand, same play may be noted, due to clearance allowed at the push rod eye for self-alignment of the push rod.

Pulling on the brake pedal, in a direction away from the master cylinder, with a force of 50 pounds or more, will result in deflection of the piston stop. Since this would result in excess pedal travel before any braking effort would be realized, this action should definitely be discouraged.

During disassembly, the master cylinder push rod cannot be removed from the piston, therefore, these parts along with the piston stop and boot retainer, are removed from the cylinder as an assembly and are also serviced as an assembly.

The new and old type master cylinders are not interchangeable, as the old type necessitates installing a pedal stop and a pedal return spring, as well as the adjustable push rod and nut.

REMOVAL OF MASTER CYLINDER

Thru 1954

On all DeSoto and Dodge cars thru 1954 the master cylinder is bolted to a bracket on the frame with three bolts and is held to the clutch and brake pedal at its front end.

To remove the master cylinder disconnect the brake lines and all linkage from the clutch and brake pedal including the clutch over-center spring. Remove the "C" washers which retain the shaft in the pedals. Remove the bolts which hold the master cylinder

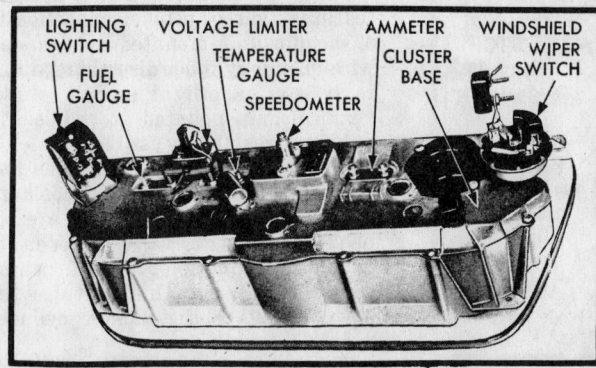

Instrument Cluster Removed (Rear View)

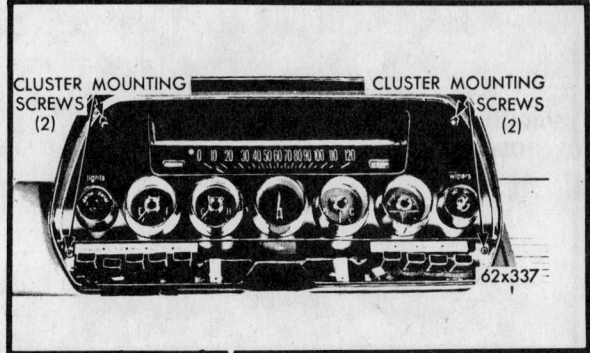

Instrument Cluster

DE SOTO, DODGE & DART

(1963 DART, SEE VALIANT)

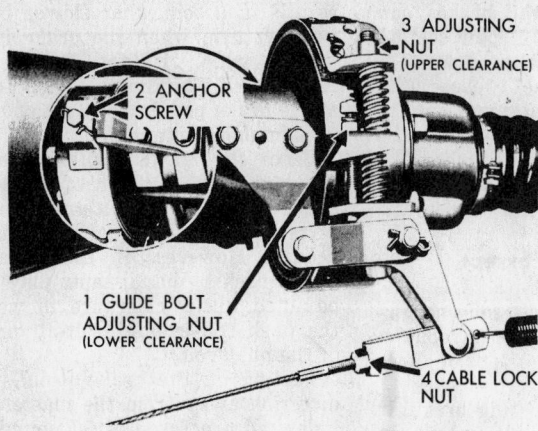

External type hand brake adjustment

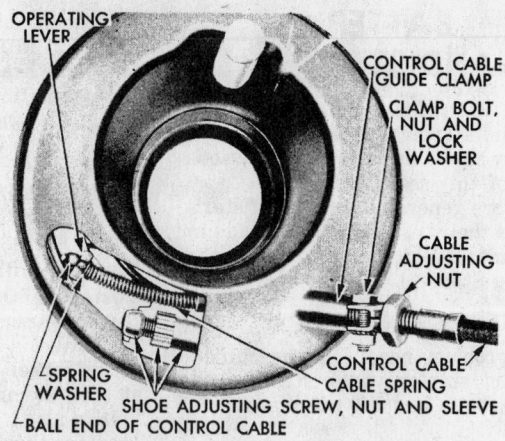

*Internal Type Hand Brake Adjusting Points.
Be sure the shoulders on adjusting nut are
seated in the grooves on the sleeve.*

to the frame and cock the master cylinder down to a convenient position for pushing out the pedal shaft from the front of the master cylinder. Leave the pedals hang up in the car and lift off the master cylinder.

Starting With 1955

The master cylinder is mounted on the front side of the firewall under the hood.

Disconnect the brake push rod and stop light wires from under the dash, remove the brake lines from under the hood, unbolt the master cylinder from the dash panel.

To remove the pedals, disconnect all linkage to the pedals, including the clutch over-center spring, remove the "C" washer which holds the shaft to the bracket under the dash, push the shaft out through the side and lower the pedals.

REFILLING MASTER CYLINDER

Thru 1954

The master cylinder is mounted to the frame directly under the floor panel on left side of the car, and is refilled by lifting the floor mat to one side and removing cut away cover in floor panel.

Starting With 1955

The master cylinder is located on the engine side of the firewall and can be filled by just raising the hood and removing the top from the master cylinder body.

INTERNAL HAND BRAKE ADJUSTMENT

<u>Note:</u> Incorrectly adjusted hand brake will effect automatic shifting.

Fully release hand brake and set shift lever in neutral. Detach front end of propeller shaft so brake drum may be turned by hand. Back off the cable adjusting nut and expand brake shoes until slight drag is felt. Now back off one notch with a special wrench C-3014 or a screwdriver to obtain .010 in. clearance. With cable adjusting nut against cable housing there should be .005 in. to .010 in. clearance between brake shoe cable and adjusting lever. Make certain the adjusting nut is securely tightened. Pull hand brake lever 4 to 6 notches and brake should be fully applied.

Starting with 1962 Exc. Custom 880

A new parking brake is used. It operates at the rear wheels through a peddle, cable and shoe expanding link.

To adjust it, with cable not pulling, see that rear service brakes are properly adjusted. Tighten cable to produce slight drag. Then loosen cable just enough to be sure wheels are free.

Starting with 1962

A new power brake unit is used. It features a direct peddle connection to a vacuum unit mounted on fire wall with master cylinder directly mounted to booster. Spotlight switch is mechanical and mounted at peddle. All units are readily accessible.

The booster chamber contains two diaphrams and is under constant engine vacuum. When brakes are applied the control valve is open to allow atmospheric pressure behind both diaphragms. This provides the power boost to the master cylinder rod.

This vacuum-suspended system provides preserve against fade. Peddle

Details of Brake Pedal and Power Cylinder Mounting

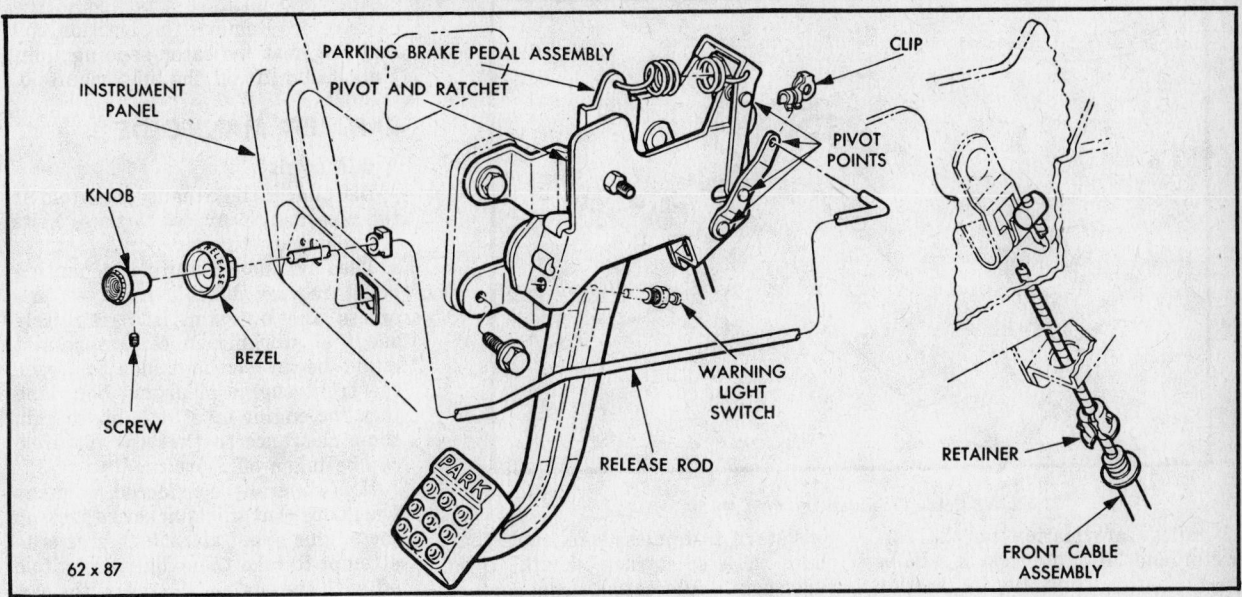

INSTRUMENT PANEL

PARKING BRAKE PEDAL ASSEMBLY

PIVOT AND RATCHET

CLIP

PIVOT POINTS

KNOB

BEZEL

SCREW

WARNING LIGHT SWITCH

RELEASE ROD

RETAINER

FRONT CABLE ASSEMBLY

62 x 87

linkages are eliminated. No additional vacuum storage tanks are needed.

FUEL SYSTEM

A chart covering causes of excess fuel consumption will be found in the Unit Repair section under the heading: Fuel Consumption Chart.

Data on capacity of the gas tank will be found in the Capacities table. Data on correct engine idle speed and fuel pump pressure will be found in the Tune-Up Specifications table. Both the above tables can be found in this section.

General information on fuel pumps and their troubles will be found in the Unit Repair section under the heading: Fuel Pumps.

Information covering operation and troubles of the fuel gauge will be found in the Unit Repair section under the heading: Gages.

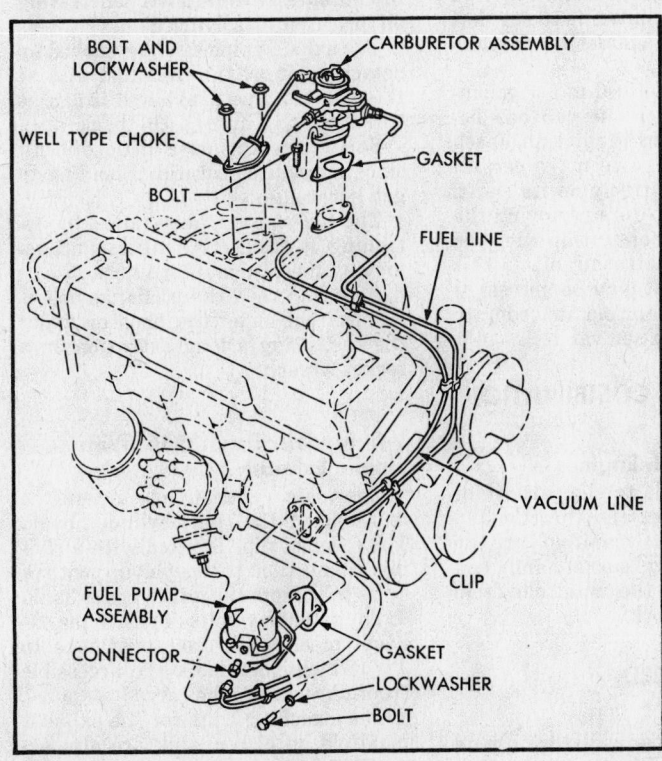

BOLT AND LOCKWASHER

CARBURETOR ASSEMBLY

WELL TYPE CHOKE

GASKET

BOLT

FUEL LINE

VACUUM LINE

CLIP

FUEL PUMP ASSEMBLY

CONNECTOR

GASKET

LOCKWASHER

BOLT

Slant "6" Fuel System

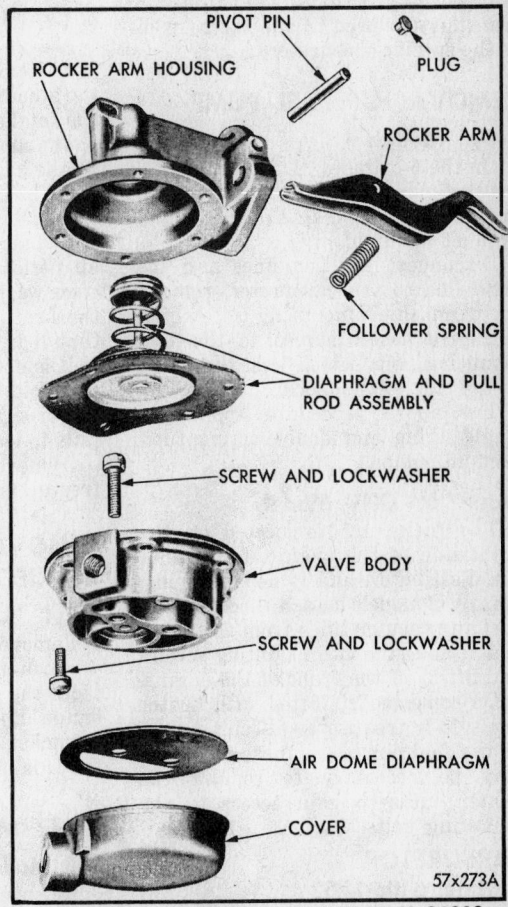

PIVOT PIN

PLUG

ROCKER ARM HOUSING

ROCKER ARM

FOLLOWER SPRING

DIAPHRAGM AND PULL ROD ASSEMBLY

SCREW AND LOCKWASHER

VALVE BODY

SCREW AND LOCKWASHER

AIR DOME DIAPHRAGM

COVER

57x273A

Fig. 2—Fuel Pump (Exploded View) M-2608S

DE SOTO, DODGE & DART

(1963 DART, SEE VALIANT)

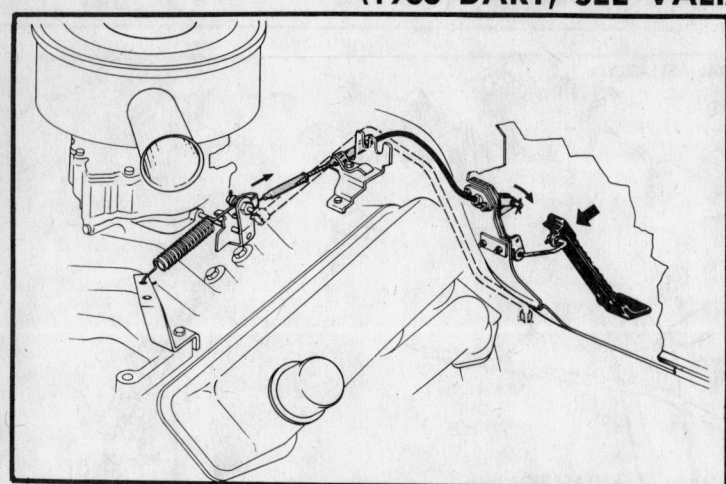

1962—V8-Cable Operated Throttle Control

Detailed information on the carburetor and how to adjust it will be found in the Unit Repair section under the broad heading: Carburetors, and the specific heading of the make of carburetor being used on the engine being worked on. Carter, Halley, Rochester and Stromberg carburetors are covered.

Dash pot adjustments can be found in the unit repair section under the same heading as that of the automatic transmission used in the car as well as the specific carburetor.

REMOVAL OF FUEL PUMP

6-Cyl. Models

On the 6-cylinder "L" head models, the fuel pump is fitted with a shield to protect the pump from the heat of the exhaust manifold.

Disconnect the flex lines and the rigid line to the carburetor, remove the pump shield mounting bolt, which will give easier access to the two mounting bolts which hold the pump to the side of the block.

The above procedure applies to single-acting and double-acting fuel-vacuum pumps.

Slant "6" OHV Models

The fuel pump is located on the right side of the engine, forward of the distributer, and is not shielded.

On V-8 models detach the flex lines, fuel and vacuum lines from the pump and remove the two mounting screws and lift it off the front of the engine.

On some models fitted with heater ducts it is frequently difficult to get at the fuel pump. On these models it may be necessary to remove the heater ducts to gain access to the mounting bolts.

CARBURETOR

Starting with 1962

The new throttle control is used. It consists of a stainless steel cable that slides in a steel rack sheath. It is permenently lubricated. Pedal contact is by roller. All lash or looseness common to most linkage is eliminated. Linkage conveyed noises are greatly reduced.

EXHAUST SYSTEM

MANIFOLD HEAT VALVE

6 Cylinder "L" Head

A heat riser control is incorporated in the exhaust manifold, to regulate the amount of heat bypassing around the intake manifold heat chamber.

The most common service required by the heat riser control is to see that it is free to turn against its thermostat spring.

If difficulty is noticed in the warm-up period, or after the car has become warm it seems to run lean, check the heat riser valve to make certain that it is turning freely on its shaft. If it is not, first, before removing the manifold, try to loosen it up with the use of a good penetrating oil. If this fails to loosen it, it may be necessary to remove the manifold in order to free up the heat riser valve.

REMOVAL OF COMBINATION MANIFOLD

6-Cyl. "L" Head Engines

Remove all leads to the carburetor—vacuum, gasoline and throttle. Detach the exhaust manifold at the flange and, using socket and box wrenches, unbolt the manifold from the side of the block.

INLET MANIFOLD

V-8 Models

Remove the upper radiator hose on models thru 1954. Disconnect the generator. Remove the carburetor air cleaner and all lines attached to the carburetor. Remove the ignition coil and the heat indicator sending unit. Unbolt and lift off the inlet manifold.

EXHAUST MANIFOLDS

V-8 Models

Disconnect the exhaust manifold at the pipe flange. Access to these bolts is underneath the car.

The exhaust manifold mounting bolts are very difficult of access, and unless the operator is particularly adept at working in close spaces it might be an excellent idea to loosen the front engine mounting bolts and jack the engine up a little bit to gain some clearance so that the manifold can be taken off more readily.

It is generally considered by many fine shops that it is quicker to jack up the engine about an inch than it is to attempt to take the exhaust manifold off with the engine in place on the car.

EXHAUST PIPE, MUFFLER AND TAIL PIPE

6-Cyl. Models

The oval muffler used on all models is of the straight through type. When installing a new muffler the word front stamped at one end is installed towards the front of the car.

If difficulty is experienced in separating the muffler from the exhaust and/or tail pipe, soak the joint for a few minutes with a good penetrating oil or a rust dissolving fluid.

The exhaust pipe can be removed by detaching it at the manifold and at the exhaust pipe flange and it can be threaded out through the back.

Sometimes this is a little difficult since it requires careful threading to get it through.

The tail pipe can be removed by detaching it from its hangers and removing the rear muffler clamp.

Access to the exhaust flange bolt is either from under the hood or under the car, using a long extension on a socket wrench.

V-8 Models Thru 1956 With Single Exhaust

The main exhaust pipe enters the manifold of the right cylinder bank. The exhaust pipe is fitted with a sliding connection to couple up with a cross tube from the left cylinder bank.

The attaching bolts of either the exhaust pipe or the cross-over tube to the left cylinder bank are accessible from underneath the car.

The attaching bolts for the exhaust manifold on either bank are also accessible from underneath the car.

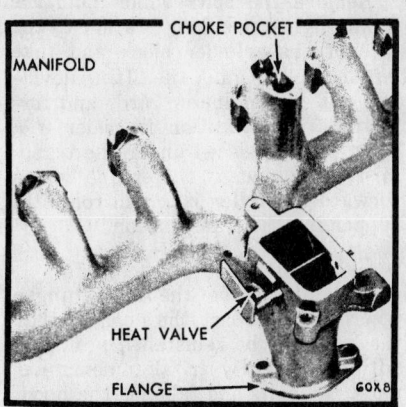

Slant "6" Manifold Heat Value

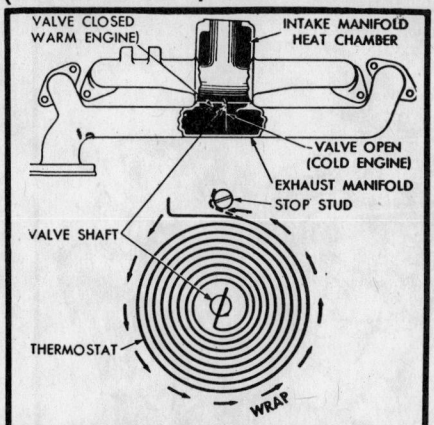

Diagram showing heat riser location & thermostat wrap 6 cyl. engines

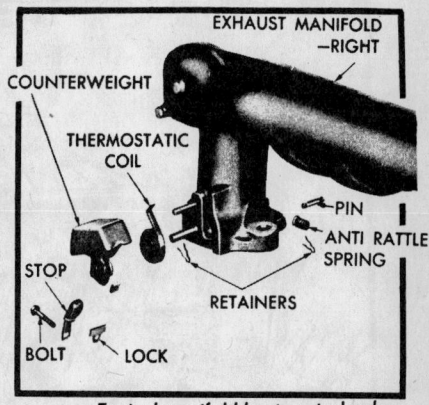

Typical manifold heat control valve

1957-63 V-8 Models With Single Exhaust

A "Y" type exhaust pipe is used to connect the two manifolds to a single exhaust line.

The "Y" connection can be taken down by removing the bolts which hold its flanges to the two exhaust flanges. A "U" type clamp is used to hold the "Y" connection to the exhaust pipe.

Dual Exhaust System

Starting with 1955 models, the dual exhaust system, together with the 4-barrel carburetor, is available on all V-8 models. The dual system is two separate systems, each going to its separate manifold, and there is no crossover pipe.

Otherwise, the service on the exhaust system is exactly the same as it is for the single muffler standard production car.

COOLING SYSTEM

Cooling System Information

Detailed information on cooling system capacity can be found in the Capacities Table of this section.

Information on the water temperature gauge can be found in the Unit Repair section under the heading: Gages.

WATER PUMP REMOVAL

6 Cylinder Models, All

The water pump may be removed on all models without removing the radiator core. This is accomplished by removing the fan blades, loosen generator and remove fan belt, disconnect the hoses, loosen nuts holding pump to block and by pass. Slide the pump off studs and lift out.

V-8 Models Thru 1954

Take off the radiator shroud, the fan and both belts and remove the fan belt pulley.

Disconnect the upper and lower radiator hoses.

Take out the bolts which attach the water pump to the chain case cover and lift off the pump.

It is not necessary to remove the radiator core in order to take off the pump.

V-8 Models Starting 1955

Slake off and remove the fan and generator belt. Remove the bolts which hold the fan blades and pulley to the fan hub. Detach water hose. Remove the bolts which hold the water pump body to the water manifold.

THERMOSTAT

On all models the thermostat is located in the water outlet elbow just under the upper radiator hose connection.

Caution:

Be sure to install thermostat with the bellows, or spring toward the engine.

ENGINE

REFERENCES

In the specifications table are listed the available facts about the engines. When different size engines are used a note under the General Engine Specifications Table will give an easy

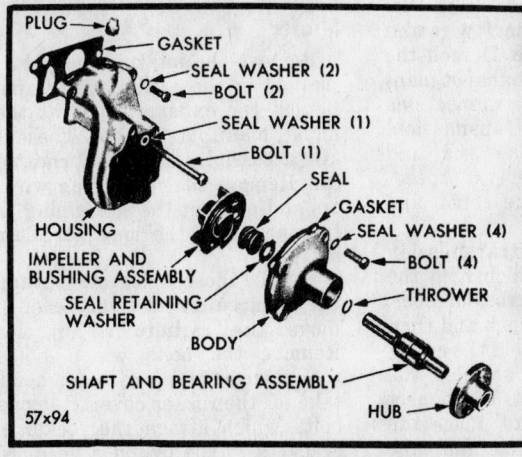

Six Cylinder Water Pump (Exploded View)

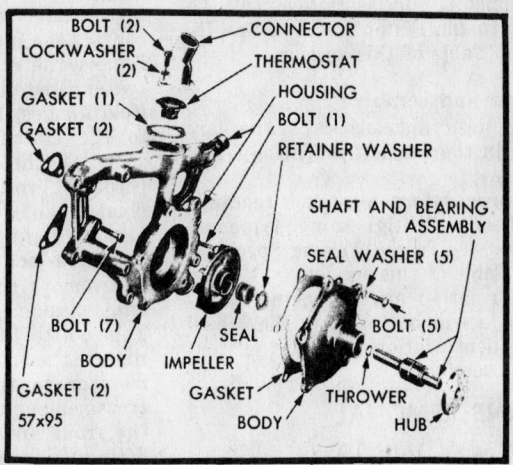

Eight Cylinder Water Pump

225 cu. in. Engine Assembly

means of determining which engine is which.

Where some engines have hydraulic valve lifters and others do not, a means of determining which does and which does not is given in a note under the Tune-Up Table.

Valves

Valve tappet clearance for each engine is given in the Tune-Up Specificatons Table of this section.

Bearings

Detailed information on engine bearings will be found in the Crankshaft Bearing Journal Sizes Table of this section.

Pistons and Pins

Detailed information on pistons and piston pins, together with information on piston, rod and crankshaft relationship for assembly, will be found in the Piston and Pin Specifications Table of this section.

Engine Reassembly

Engine crankcase capacities are listed in the Capacities Table of this section.

Approved torque wrench readings and head bolt tightening sequences are covered in the Torque Specifications Table of this section.

Information on the engine marking code will be found in the Model Year Identification Table at the start of this section.

ENGINE REMOVAL

V-8 Models Thru 1955

To remove the V-8 cylinder engine from the car detach all parts such as wires, transmission linkage, exhaust pipes, hood, battery, fuel lines, radiator hoses, all wires, etc.

Remove radiator shroud and core.

Split the front universal joint and take out the rear support mounting bolts and the cross member.

Raise the engine, and at the same time work it out of the chassis towards the left front fender. By moving towards the left front fender it will not be necessary to disturb the heater or duct work.

V-8 Models Starting With 1956

Scribe a line where the hood hinge connects to the hood so that reinstallation will be simplified and remove the bolts and take off the hood. Remove the carburetor air cleaner and all lines to the carburetor. Disconnect the battery and remove the heat indicater and engine ground lines. Disconnect the ignition primary wire and remove the radiator core. Detach the two exhaust pipes at the exhaust manifold flanges. Remove all connections to the clutch and/or transmission, such as the clutch idler rod and throwout rod, shift levers, speedometer cable, hand brake cable, and back-up light wires.

Place a jack under the transmission and remove the bolts which hold the transmission to the crossmember. Take a little load on the jack and then remove the bolts which hold the crossmember to the frame and let the crossmember come down. Disconnect the front universal joints. Place the lifting device on the engine and take a load on the lifter.

Remove the bolts which hold the front engine mounting bracket to the side of the cylinder block and take out the bolts. Crank the lifting device and pull the engine upwards and forwards. This operation is easier if a roller jack is placed under the transmission so that as the engine comes forward the roller jack will roll, still supporting the transmission.

6 Cyl. Engines

Carefully scribe the hood hinges where they contact the hood so that the hood can be reinstalled promptly without difficulty in alignment. Remove the bolts and take off the hood.

Remove the radiator core and take off the carburetor and generator.

Disconnect all fuel lines and heat indicator lines, battery ground straps, ignition primary wire and vacuum lines.

At the transmission, disconnect the clutch throwout rod and the transmission shift links. Remove the speedometer cable and hand brake cable. Disconnect the front universal joint. Disconnect the exhaust pipe at the flange. Place a roller jack under the transmission and take a slight load on the roller jack. Remove the bolts which hold the transmission to the crossmember and then take a slight load on the jack and remove the bolts which hold the crossmember to the frame and let the crossmember come down, leaving the weight of the transmission on the jack.

Attach the lifting device to the front part of the engine and take a slight load. Remove the bolts which hold the engine front motor mounts to the block and lift the engine upwards and forward.

The back of the engine will ride on the roller jack until it is clear.

CYLINDER HEAD
REMOVAL

Engines With Double Rocker Shafts

Remove the intake manifold as explained in the earlier paragraph and detach the exhaust pipes at the exhaust manifold flanges. These bolts are accessible from underneath the car. Remove the spark plug wire covers and pull out the spark plug wires, together with the long porcelain insulators.

Handle these insulators carefully as they can be cracked very easily. Remove the carburetor air cleaner. Remove the bolts which hold the rocker cover to the cylinder head and take off the rocker cover. Remove the bolts which attach the rocker shaft brackets to the cylinder head. <u>Note:</u> These bolts also hold the cylinder

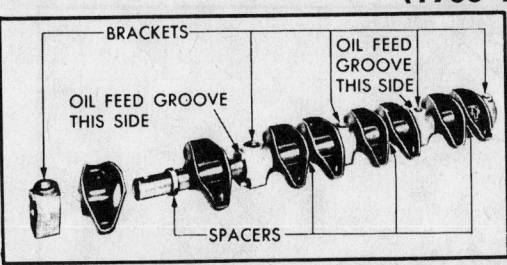

1960-63, V8, with front mounted distributor

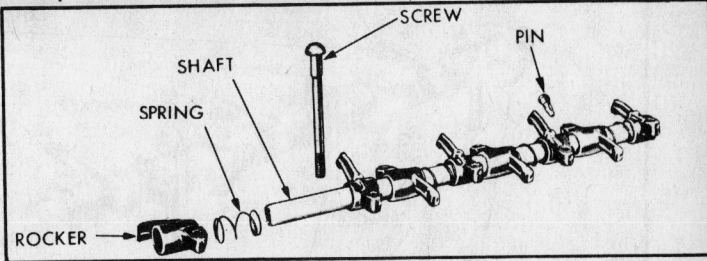

1960-63, V8, with rear mounted distributor

head to the block and any time the rockers are removed it would be necessary to remove the head entirely and install a new cylinder head gasket.

Pull out the push rods thru the top of the cylinder head and remove the balance of the bolts which hold the cylinder head to the block and lift off the head. Caution: The gasket used on this cylinder head is very thin and the head itself is critical of its machined surface; it should not be scarred or scratched in any way.

On reassembly notice that on each head one of the rocker bracket bosses has a small extension which contains a small hole. This hole supplies oil to the rocker shafts and MUST be indexed to the rocker bracket having a mating hole. If this is not done the rocker shafts will be starved for oil and will fail very shortly in service.

Absolute cleanliness is essential when reinstalling the cylinder heads since the gasket is a very thin shim.

Single Rocker Shaft Engines

Remove the carburetor air cleaner and disconnect the spark plug wires. Remove the bolts which hold the rocker cover to the cylinder head.

Note: A new gasket must be used on reinstallation.

Remove the bolts which hold the rockers to the cylinder head, each bolt a little at a time so as not to spring the shafts and lift off the rocker and shaft assemblies.

Note: The bolts which hold the rocker brackets do not hold the cylinder head to the block.

Remove the intake manifold as outlined earlier under "Inlet Manifold Removal" and detach the water manifold from the cylinder heads at the front of the heads and also loosen the bolts which hold the water manifold to the block so that the heads can be put back readily without springing against the water manifold.

Remove the heat indicator sending units. Remove the bolts which hold the cylinder heads to the block and lift off the heads.

ROCKER ARM ASSEMBLIES
De Soto V-8 Engines Thru 1957,
Dodge Red Ram V-8 Thru 1954,

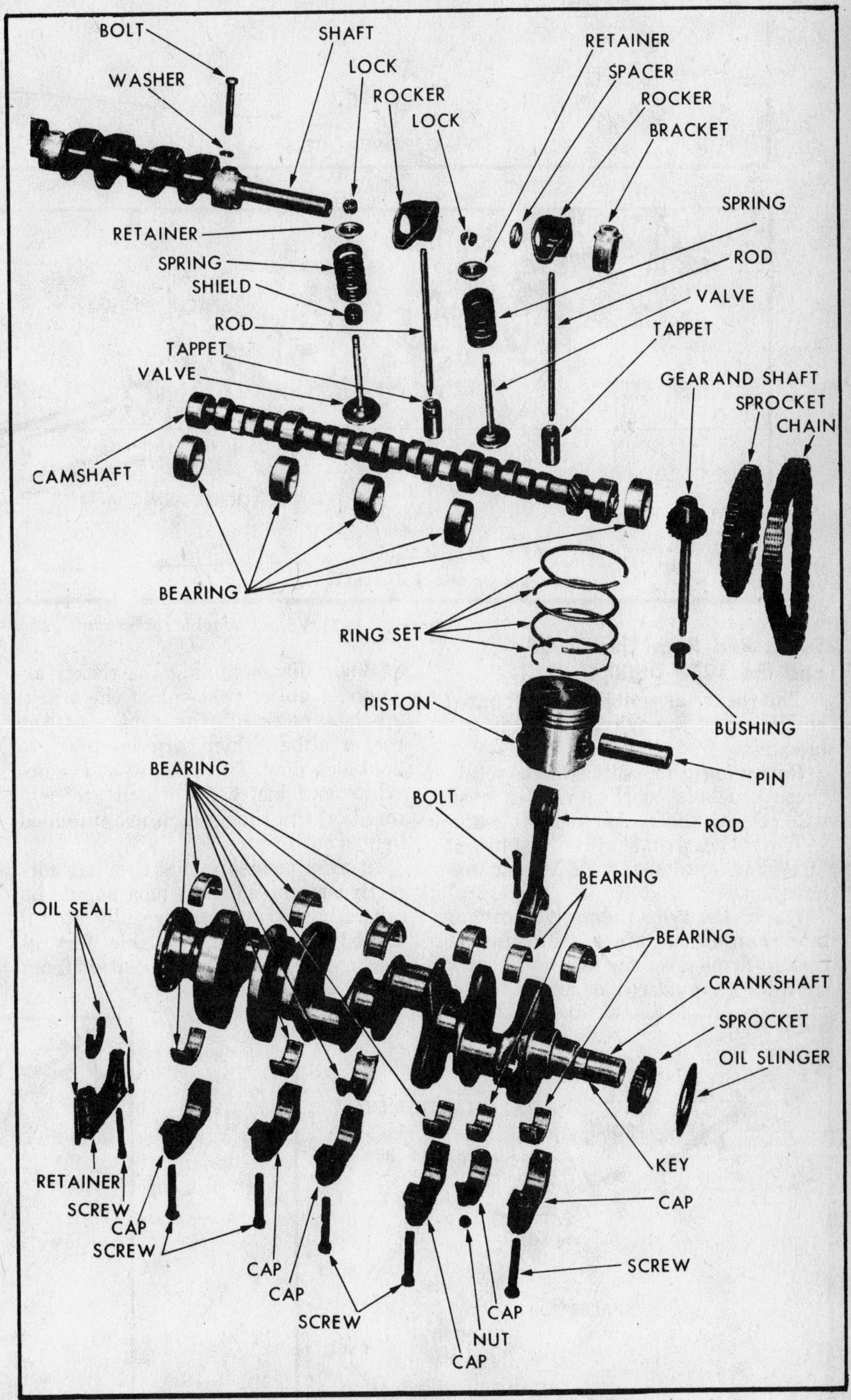

Exploded view—internal engine parts– 1958-63 V-8 (single rocker shaft)

V8 with distributor at the front of the block.

DE SOTO, DODGE & DART
(1963 DART, SEE VALIANT)

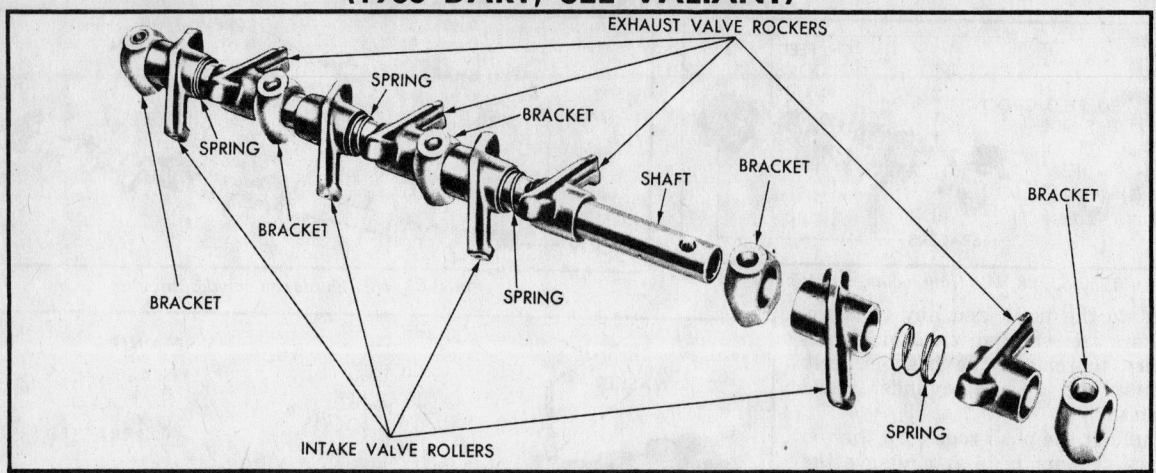

1954, V8

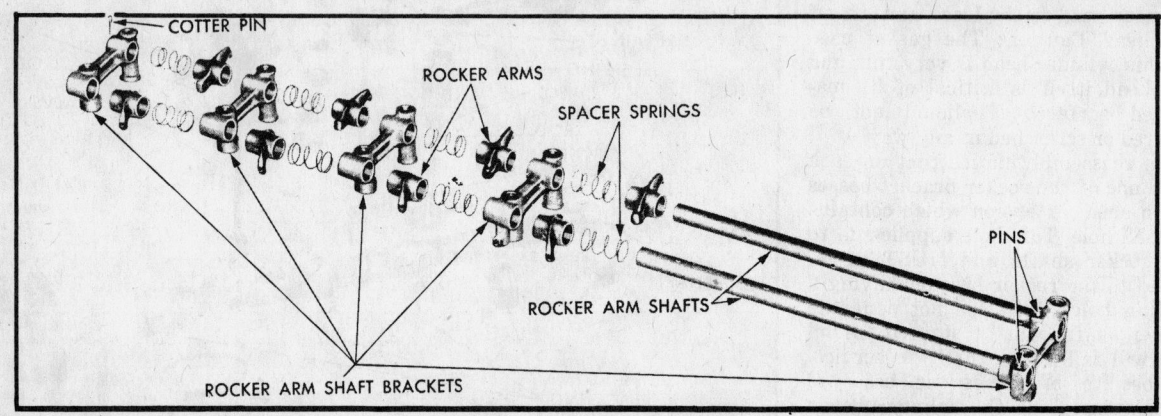

1955, V8, with double rocker shaft

Super Red Ram Thru 1955 and the 1957 D500

The rocker assemblies are mounted on the top of the cylinder head in five brackets.

Removing the bolts which retain these brackets to the cylinder head will release the rocker assemblies.

The rocker arm shafts are stamped "IN" for intake and "EX" for exhaust.

The rocker arms themselves are not interchangeable since the intake rocker arms are smaller or shorter than the exhaust rocker arms.

When disassembling the rocker assemblies notice that one of the brackets has holes off the center of the rocker tube, which are intended to hold lock pins. The bracket at the opposite end has holes which are centered on the tube which are intended to hold cotter pins.

In order to insure that they are correctly assembled, each part should be carefully marked or carefully stored so that it will be available for replacement in exactly the position from which it was removed.

1955 Thru 1957 Dodge Red Ram, 1956 Thru 1957 Super Red Ram and 1958-63 V-8 Engines

On these V-8 models a single rocker shaft is used which carries the rocker arms for both the intake and the exhaust valves. If the rockers are to be disassembled the rocker and springs should be marked or stored carefully so that they can be reassembled to the shaft in exactly the same position from which they were removed.

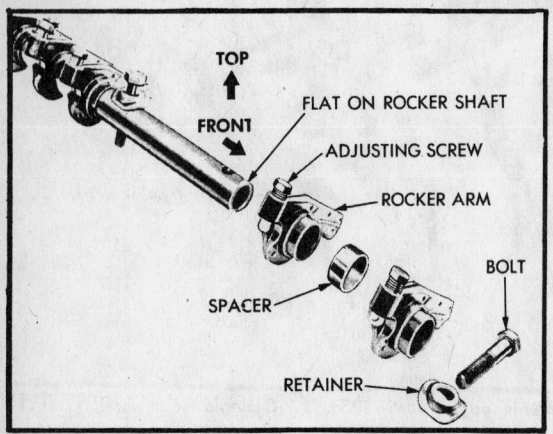

Slant "6" shaft and rockers

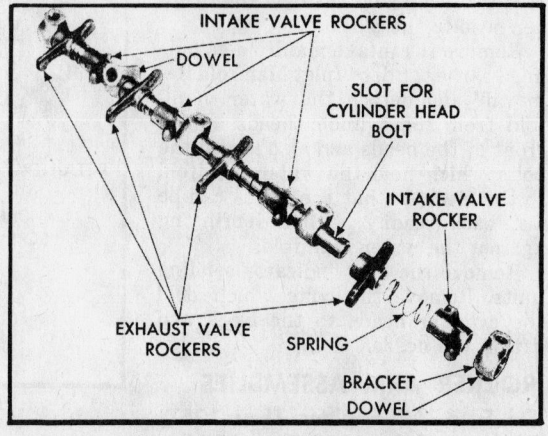

1955-60, V8, with single rocker shaft

266

(1963 DART, SEE VALIANT)

VALVE SYSTEM

6-Cyl. "L" Head Models

The valves, springs, and guides are accessible by removing the cylinder head and side valve covers.

When adjusting valve tappets the engine should be idling at normal operating temperature. Set the inlet valve tappets so that a .008 in. feeler will pass and a .009 in. feeler will stop; set exhaust valve tappets so that a .010 in. feeler will pass and a .011 in. feeler will stop. Where an engine is continually operated at high speed, it would be wise to allow the exhaust valves an additional .002 clearance to maintain satisfactory valve life.

VALVE ADJUSTING SEQUENCE

6-Cyl. Engines, All

In order to be reasonably certain that the valves being adjusted are at the bottom of the cam, the following sequence is recommended when adjusting valves with the engine stationary:

Turn the engine until No. 2 cylinder inlet valve starts to open. Notice that it will be followed closely by No. 1 cylinder exhaust valve. Turn engine until both of these valves are wide open and then adjust:

No. 1 cylinder inlet valve
No. 2 cylinder exhaust valve

No. 3 cylinder both valves
No. 5 cylinder inlet valve
No. 6 cylinder exhaust valve

When these valves have been adjusted satisfactorily, turn the engine one complete revolution until No. 5 cylinder inlet valve starts to open and notice that it will be followed by No. 6 cylinder exhaust valve. When both of these valves are wide open, adjust:

No. 1 cylinder exhaust valve
No. 2 cylinder inlet valve
No. 4 cylinder both valves

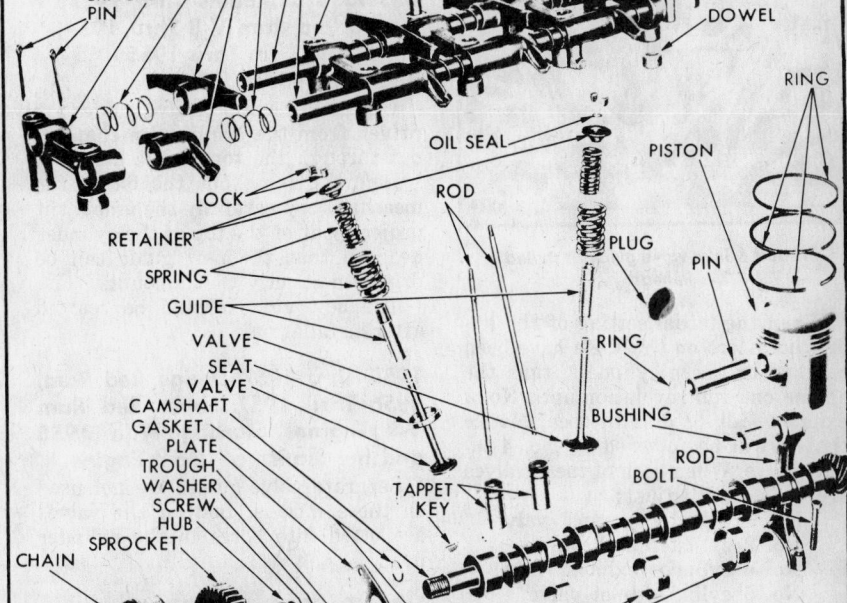

Exploded view—V8 with double rocker shafts

No. 5 cylinder exhaust valve
No. 6 cylinder inlet valve

V-8 Models

Keep in mind that the cylinders of the V-8's are numbered:

Front right 2-4-6-8
Front left 1-3-5-7

Using this numbering system, turn the engine until No. 1 cylinder exhaust valve starts to open and notice that it will be followed by No. 7 cylinder intake valve. When both of these valves are wide open, adjust:

No. 1 cylinder inlet valve
No. 3 cylinder both valves
No. 4 cylinder inlet valve
No. 5 cylinder exhaust valve
No. 6 cylinder exhaust valve
No. 7 cylinder exhaust valve
No. 8 cylinder inlet valve

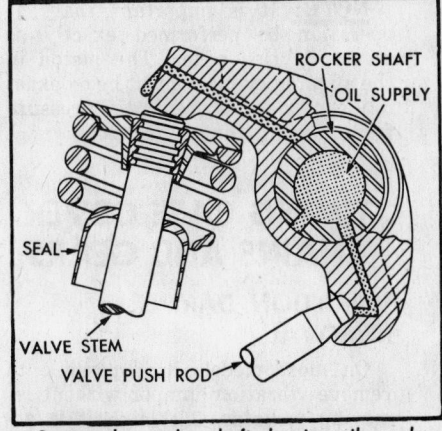

Section thru rocker shaft showing oil supply bores, V-8 models with distributor at the back

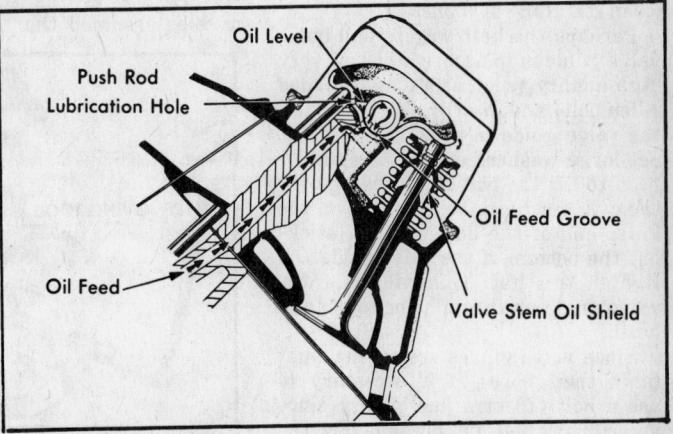

Rocker and shaft oil supply V8 engines with distributor in front

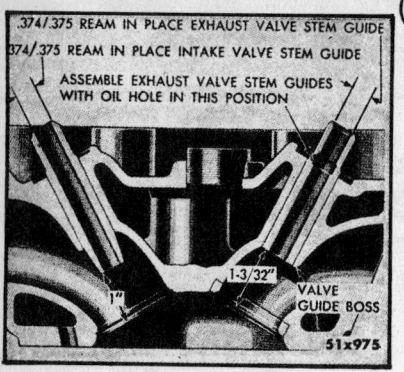

.374/.375 REAM IN PLACE EXHAUST VALVE STEM GUIDE

.374/.375 REAM IN PLACE INTAKE VALVE STEM GUIDE

ASSEMBLE EXHAUST VALVE STEM GUIDES WITH OIL HOLE IN THIS POSITION

1" 1-3/32" VALVE GUIDE BOSS 51x975

Exhaust & inlet valve guides installed in head

When the initial setting of the hydraulic lifters on the V-8's have been checked on these cylinders, turn the engine one full revolution until No. 3 exhaust valve starts to open. Notice that it will be followed by No. 4 intake valve. When both of these valves are wide open, adjust:

No. 1 cylinder exhaust valve
No. 2 cylinder both valves
No. 4 cylinder exhaust valve
No. 5 cylinder inlet valve
No. 6 cylinder inlet valve
No. 7 cylinder inlet valve
No. 8 cylinder exhaust valve

The above V-8 sequence is given for the purpose of checking the initial setting of the hydraulic valves.

REPLACEMENT OF VALVE GUIDES

6-Cyl. "L" Head Models

To replace the valve guides on the 6-cylinder models it is necessary to remove the cylinder head, the valve chamber covers, and take out the valve and spring assemblies.

Before installing new guides measure carefully the depth from the cylinder head to the top of the guide before taking the old guide out.

The guides are pulled upwards to the top of the block, and are driven downwards from the top of the block when installing new ones.

Perhaps the best way to pull out a valve guide is to secure a bolt of very high quality (such as a long threaded Allen bolt) and insert it down through the valve guide in place of the valve. Set large washers up on the cylinder head to lift the bolt head well up over the cylinder head. Screw a nut on the lower end of the bolt where it sticks out the bottom of the valve guide and tighten this nut. This will draw the valve guide up through the top of the head.

Since valve guides are a very tight fit in their bores, it is necessary to use a bolt of extra fine quality since an ordinary bolt will break before the valve guide will move.

There are, of course, special hydraulic tools made for the purpose of removing valve guides.

DeSoto V-8 Models Thru 1957, Dodge Red Ram V-8 Thru 1954, Super Red Ram Thru 1955 and the 1957 D500

On the V-8 engine, valve guides are driven from the combustion chamber out through the top of the block.

Before driving out the old guide, measure very carefully the amount it projects out of the top of the cylinder head so that the new guide can be driven in exactly that amount.

The new guide should be reamed after installation.

1955 Thru 1957 Dodge Red Ram, 1956 Thru 1957 Super Red Ram V-8 Engines Starting With 1958 and the Slant "6" OHV Engine

Separate valve guides are not used on these models. Instead the valves are fitted into bores in the cylinder head.

VALVE SEAT INSERTS

V-8 Models

Some of the earlier V-8 engines are equipped with exhaust valve seat inserts made of cast heat resisting material which cannot be cut successfully with a reamer.

Exhaust valve seats must be ground and/or lapped to a perfect seal.

1955 and 1956 Dodge Red Ram, 1956 Super Red Ram and 1958-63 V-8 engines do not have seat inserts.

VALVE SPRINGS

DeSoto and Dodge recommend that the valve springs be checked for free height and squareness rather than for pressure.

Perhaps the easiest way to do this is to lay the valve springs on a straight flat surface and compare one with the other. If all of the valve springs are of the same height it may be assumed that all are usable.

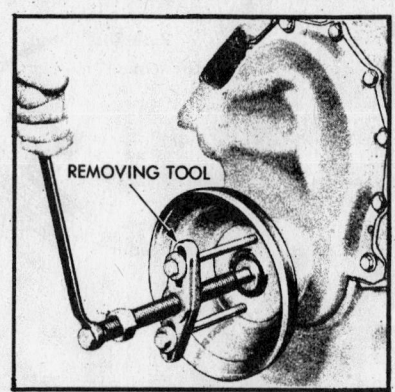

REMOVING TOOL

Puller used to take off crankshaft pulley, V-8 models

2

— Centering Tool C-522   2 — Cover and seal assembly

Use centering tool. L-head six

⏱ CHILTON TIME-SAVER

The following is a method for replacing valve springs, oil seals or spring retainers without removing the cylinder head.

1. Entirely dismantle a spark plug and save the threaded shell.

2. To this shell, braze or weld an air chuck.

3. Remove the valve rocker cover. Remove the rocker arm from the affected valve.

4. Remove the spark plug from the affected cylinder.

5. Turn the crankshaft to bring the piston of this cylinder down, away from possible contact with the valve head. Sharply tap the valve retainer to loosen the valve lock.

6. Then turn the crankshaft to bring the piston in this cylinder to the **Exact Top of its Compression Stroke.**

7. Screw in the chuck equipped spark plug shell.

8. Hook up an air hose to the chuck and turn on the pressure (about 200 lb).

9. With a strong and constant supply of air holding the valve closed, compress the valve spring and remove the lock and retainer.

10. Make the necessary replacements and reassemble.

NOTE: It is important that the operation be performed exactly as stated, in this order. The piston in the affected cylinder must be on exact top center to prevent air pressure from turning the crankshaft.

TIMING CASE COVER CHAINS AND GEARS

VIBRATION DAMPER REMOVAL

On most models it is possible to remove vibration damper without removing radiator. Although it is advisable to remove radiator core to

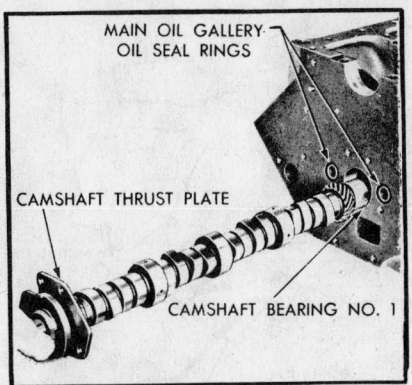

Removing camshaft
(V8 with distributor at the back of the block and single rocker shaft)

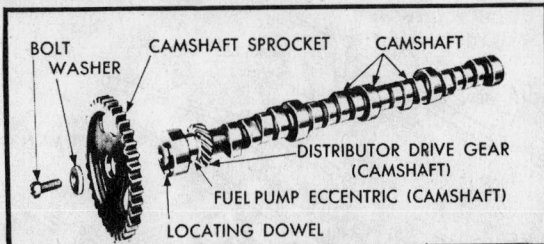

Camshaft and sprocket. V8 with distributor in the front

prevent accidental damage to the water tubes.

On the 1958 DeSoto and Super Red Ram the radiator must be removed and a puller used to take off the vibration damper.

TIMING CASE COVER REMOVAL

V-8 Engines With Double Rocker Shafts

The timing case cover on these models is also the water pump main body.

First remove the radiator core, take off the water pump for access to the bolt in back of the pump. Remove the vibration damper and lower fan pulley, take off the fuel pump.

Remove the bolts which hold the chain case cover to the front of the cylinder block. One of these bolts is located back of the water pump.

Note: The chain case cover is located to the front of the cylinder blocks with tight fitting dowel pins and it may be necessary to pry the case off the front of the block.

A special puller is available to remove the timing case.

V-8 Engines With Single Rocker Shafts

Slack off and remove the generator and water pump belts. Disconnect the upper and lower radiator hoses and unbolt and remove the water manifold. It is advisable to leave the water pump mounted in the manifold since the service is to be on the timing case cover.

Since the radiator core is held with four bolts only, it is a good idea to unbolt and remove the radiator core, although this is not absolutely necessary.

Remove the crankshaft drive pulley and unbolt and remove the timing case cover.

VALVE TIMING PROCEDURE

6 Cylinder Engines, All

To replace a timing chain, cam or crankshaft sprocket, or to retime valves where the timing has jumped, proceed as follows: Take off the radiator core, vibration damper and timing case cover. Remove the bolts from the camshaft gear, slide the camshaft sprocket off its hub and remove timing chain.

Note: Unless the crankshaft sprocket is to be replaced it will not

be necessary to remove it from the shaft.

Rotate the crankshaft so that the mark in the crankshaft sprocket is towards the camshaft and in exact alignment between the shafts center.

Now install the timing chain over the camshaft sprocket so that the mark in the cam and crankshaft sprocket are nearest each other.

The timing bolt holes are staggered in such a way that the camshaft sprocket will attach only one way and permit the bolt to enter through the threaded holes in the hub.

Rotate the camshaft so that the holes align up and the timing marks are still in line between the shaft center. Mount the gear on the hub and draw up the bolts.

Turn the crankshaft two full revolutions and check to see that the marks are still in alignment between the shaft centers.

When set in the manner described, with the marks aligned between the two shaft centers, it is immaterial which piston is at dead center. It is necessary, however, to retime the ignition at any time the camshaft setting is disturbed.

V-8 Engines

The valve timing procedure for V-8 models is essentially the same as that given for the 6-cylinder model with

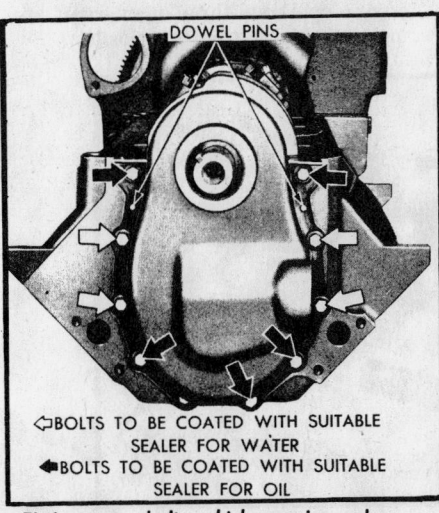

◁ BOLTS TO BE COATED WITH SUITABLE SEALER FOR WATER
◀ BOLTS TO BE COATED WITH SUITABLE SEALER FOR OIL

Timing case bolts which require sealer.

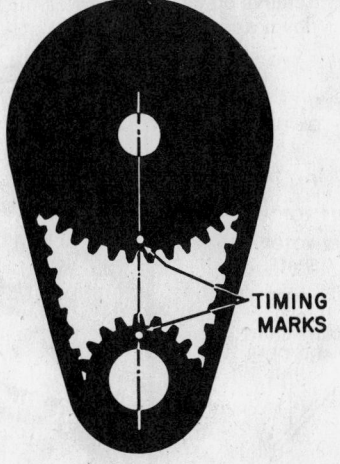

Aligning timing marks O.H.V. V8

Aligning timing marks 6 Cyl.

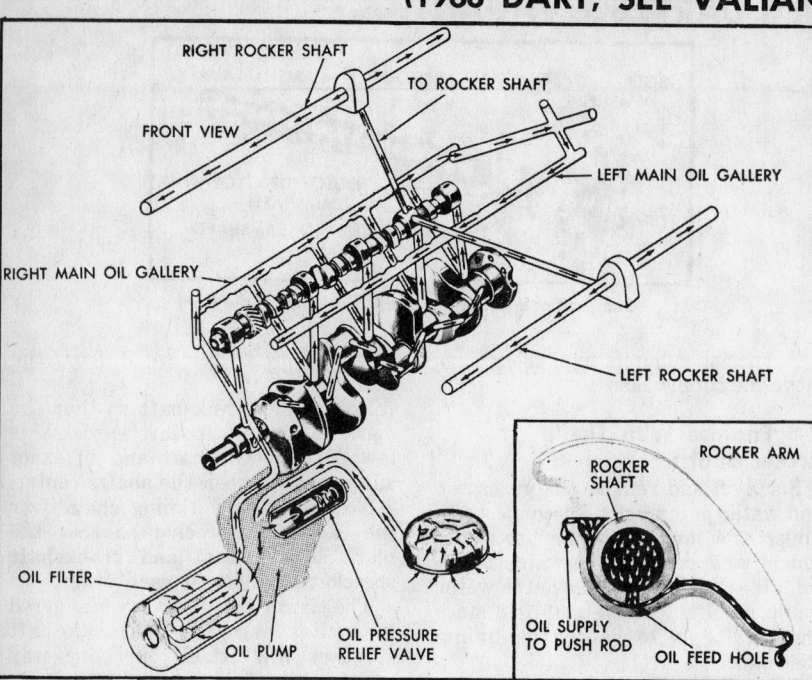

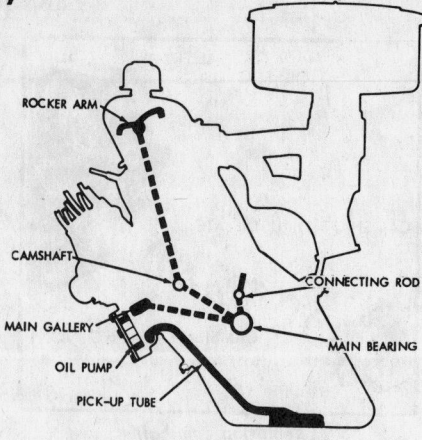

Slant "6" lubrication circuit

Engine lubrication. V8 with distributor at the front of the block.

this exception. After the camshaft gear has been placed on the shaft the fuel pump eccentric must be attached. This is the only important difference between the two jobs.

Bear in mind when removing the timing case cover from the V-8 models that it is necessary to first remove the water pump because the operation of removing the timing case cover is greatly simplified if the water pump is out of the way.

The camshaft gear is located on the camshaft by a very tight fitting dowel pin.

ENGINE LUBRICATION
OIL PAN REMOVAL
6-Cyl. "L" Head Engines

Rotate crankshaft until number one piston is half way up cylinder bore.

Remove clutch inspection pan.

Remove oil pan cap screws and slide pan back and down at the same time, holding oil pump screen up so oil pan will clear. When installing pan, the end corks should protrude $\frac{1}{8}$ to $\frac{1}{4}$ in. above oil pan. Tightening the pan will compress ends and make a tight seal.

Slant "6" OHV

To remove the oil pan on this engine the following procedure will prove helpful:

1. Remove the tie rod at the steering and idler arms.
2. Remove the two front engine mounting bolts.
3. Remove left side support, connecting converter housing and cylinder block.
4. Raise the engine about two inches.
5. Drain engine oil.
6. Remove oil pan bolts, lower the pan down and to the rear.

NOTE:

Do not turn the oil pick-up out of position.

V-8 Engines Thru 1954

In order to remove the oil pan on V-8 models it is necessary to remove the left side exhaust manifold and loosen the right side manifold.

Take the starter off the car and then unbolt and lower the oil pan.

1955 Thru 1956 V-8 Engines

Detach the tie rod end from the steering arm on either side and let the steering tie rod drop down a little. The pan can then be unbolted and removed readily. On some models it will be necessary to remove the cover plate from the front face of the flywheel.

1957 V-8 Engines

Turn the crankshaft until the timing indicator marks on the vibration damper are 180 degrees (one-half turn removed from the indicator mark).

Place a jack protected by a block of wood under the oil pan, loosen the front mounting bolts and jack the engine up about three-quarters of an inch and block it in this position.

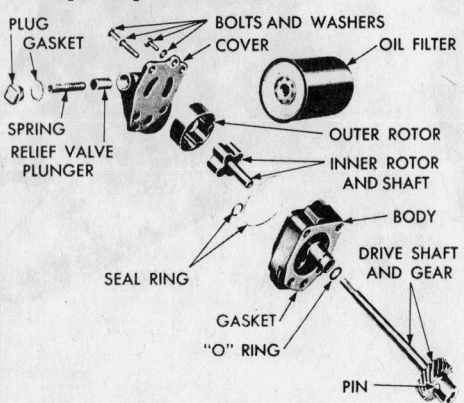

Oil pump for V8 with distributor at the front

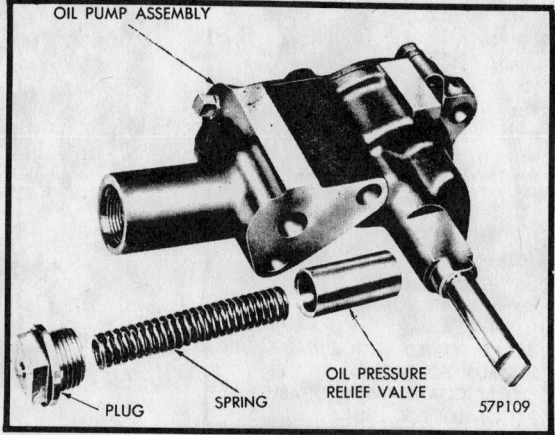

By-pass relief valve

Remove the jacks and then take out the bolts which hold the clutch cover plate to the front face of the flywheel. Remove the bolts which hold the oil pan to the cylinder block and drop the pan.

1958-63 V-8 Engines

Rotate the crankshaft until the timing marks are in the 5:00 o'clock position, as viewed from the front.

Disconnect the steering linkage at the idle arm bracket. On single exhaust systems, remove the crossover pipe. On Dodge, remove the starting motor. Also on Dodge, disconnect the front motor mount brackets and jack up the front of the engine about 1/2 inch.

Remove the oil pan bolts and work the pan to clear the crossmember.

OIL PUMP

6-Cyl. "L" Head Engines

On DeSoto and Dodge cars, the oil filter is located on the right side of the engine block.

The oil pressure relief-valve which is an integral part of the oiling system is positioned at the right side of the cylinder block.

To remove the oil pump, the two top cover bolts must be removed to clear frame.

To disassemble remove cover plate and rotate pump shaft to allow outer rotor to slip out. With a suitable pin punch, drive out the pin holding the oil pump and distributor drive gear to shaft.

Remove shaft and inner rotor from pump body.

If for any reason the position of the crankshaft has been changed after the oil pump is removed, it will be important to follow this procedure: Turn crankshaft until number one cylinder is at top dead center position. Rotate the pump drive shaft so that the slot in the oil pump shaft lines up with the pump body attaching bolt holes. Now move the drive gear counter-clockwise one tooth and loosen distributor lock bolt so distributor may be lifted to allow pump to be inserted. After all parts have been securely tightened adjust timing.

Slant "6' OHV

The oil pump is located low and externally, on the right side of the engine, with the oil filter. It is gear driven from the cam shaft and independent of the distributor. The oil pump has no effect on ignition or valve timing.

V-8 Engines With Distributor at the Back

In actual construction, the oil pump on the V-8 models is the same as that on the 6 cyl. " L" head, that is, it is a rotary gear type pump driven from the shaft of the distributor.

However, to service the pump on the V-8 models it is necessary to first remove the oil pan since the pump is located in the oil pan.

The pump relief valve is incorporated into the side of the pump casting.

The distributor drive gear does not come down with the pump. Therefore, when the pump is removed it has no effect whatever on ignition timing.

V-8 Engines With Distributor at the Front

The oil pump and filter assembly is mounted externally at the left front of the block. It is removed from underneath the engine by taking out the three short and one long attaching bolts.

When the pump is removed it has no effect on ignition timing.

OIL FILTER

V-8 Engines With Distributor at the Back

The oil filter is located under the right bank of cylinders towards the rear and, if only the element is to be replaced, the clamp which holds the lid on the filter pan can be loosened and removed and the top taken off the pan in order to replace the new element.

If it becomes necessary to replace the entire filter the filter unit may be detached from the block. It is held by four bolts which are accessible from underneath the car.

V-8 Engines With Distributor at the Front

The oil filter is located at the left front of the engine and is the "Throwaway" type. It is only necessary to unscrew the filter from the base by hand and discard.

Screw on the new filter until the gasket contacts the base, then tighten at least 1/2 turn more. Run the engine and check for leaks.

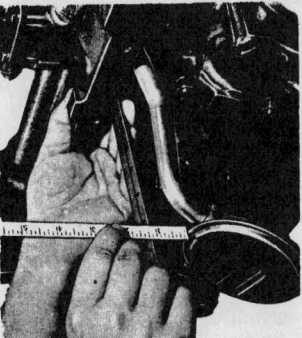

Positioning oil pick-up screen, 1 1/8"

PISTONS, CONNECTING RODS AND MAIN BEARINGS

REMOVAL OF ROD AND PISTON ASSEMBLIES

All Models

Remove the cylinder head and oil pan.

Insert a good cylinder ridge reamer into the top of the bores, that are accessible without turning the crankshaft, and remove the ridge. Detach the tool, turn the crankshaft, reattach the tool and remove the ridge on the next cylinder of your choice. Continue this process until all cylinder ridges have been removed.

CAUTION:

This is not a boring bar; merely remove the ridge.

From underneath the car, select the connecting rods in the down position and remove the locking device (pawl nut or cotter pin) and take off the two nuts which hold the cap to the lower end of the connecting rod. Tap the cap gently and slide it off the end of the bolts. Be careful not to lose the lower half of the rod bearing.

Start the connecting rod and piston assembly up towards the top of the bore, but before pushing it out replace the cap so that there isn't the slightest chance of it getting mixed up or put on in the wrong way.

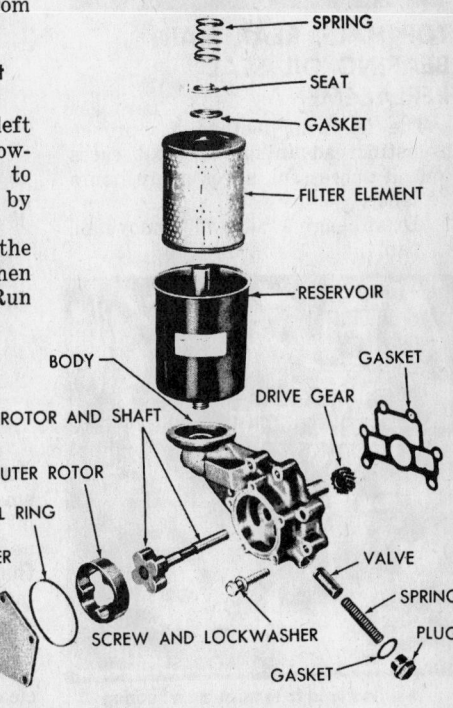

Oil pump. 6 cylinder 1960-63

DE SOTO, DODGE & DART
(1963 DART, SEE VALIANT)

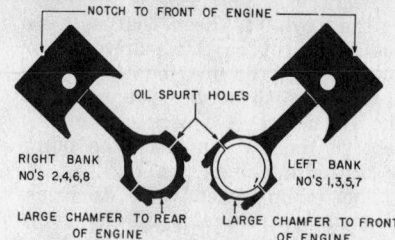

1954-63, V8

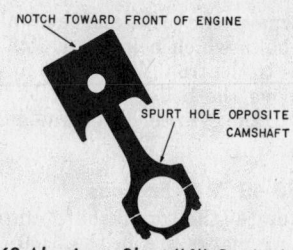

1960-62 Aluminum Slant "6". Beginning 1963, oil hole on cast-iron engine only is on opposite side.

1954-59: All 6 cyl. "L" head

At this point note whether or not the number of the cylinder is stamped on the connecting rod, and if it is not, some provision will have to be made to mark the rod, such as a file mark or a punch mark. Push the rod and piston assembly up until the rings snap out of the cylinder.

REAR MAIN BEARING OIL SEAL

6 Cylinder Models

The rear main bearing oil seal is attached to the bearing cap by three cap screws.

When replacing the oil seal the retaining cap screws are left loose and then tightened after the bearing cap has been torqued, this allows seal to seat properly around crankshaft.

V-8 Models

The rear main bearing oil seal is a braided asbestos wick.

The proper way to replace the upper half of the oil seal is to remove the crankshaft.

ⓘ CHILTON TIME-SAVER

TOP HALF, REAR MAIN BEARING OIL SEAL REPLACEMENT

The following method has proven a distinct advantage in most cases and, if successful, saves many hours of labor.

1. Drain engine oil and remove oil pan.

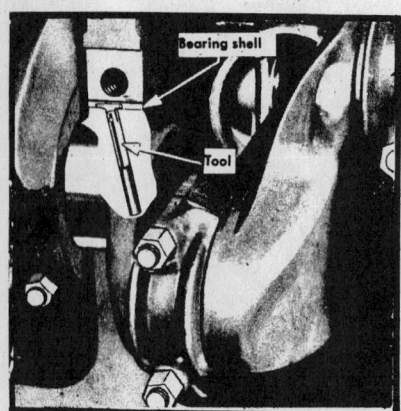

Method used to remove main bearing upper half

2. Remove rear main bearing cap.
3. With a 6" length of 3/16" brazing rod, drive up on either exposed end of the top half oil seal. When the opposite end of the seal starts to protrude, have a helper grasp it with pliers and pull gently while the driven end is being tapped. It is surprising how easily most of these seals can be removed by this method.

TO INSTALL THE NEW WOVEN FABRIC TYPE SEAL:

1. Obtain a 12" piece of copper wire about the same gauge as that used in the strands of an insulated battery cable.
2. Thread one strand of this wire thru the new seal, about ½" from the end, bend back and make secure.
3. Thoroughly saturate the new seal with engine oil.
4. Push the copper wire up thru the oil seal groove until it comes down on the opposite side of the bearing.
5. Pull (with pliers) on the protruding copper wire while the crankshaft is being turned and the new seal is slowly fed into place.
   CAUTION: This snaking operation slightly reduces the diameter of the new seal and care will have to be used to keep the seal from slipping too far thru the top half of the bearing.
6. When an equal amount of seal is extending from each side, cut off the copper wire close to the seal and tamp both ends of the seal up into the groove (this will tend to expand the seal again).
   NOTE: Don't worry about the copper wire left in the groove, it is too soft to cause damage.
7. Replace the seal in the cap in the usual way and replace the oil pan.

It is sometimes possible to seal up a small leak in the rear main bearing oil seal by installing a new lower half and letting it project slightly above the main bearing cap. The main bearing cap is then bolted tightly up into place and immediately taken down. The riveted over portion of the projecting lower half of the seal should be cleaned off and the cap again bolted up into place until the cap seats firmly

in the block without riveting over the oil seal.

The purpose of this is to squeeze the upper half of the oil seal more tightly into its groove and causing it to compress somewhat down on to the crankshaft.

This particular method is not always successful but has been used in many instances to prevent minor leaks.

FRONT SUSPENSION

ADJUSTMENT

General instructions covering the front suspension and how to repair and adjust it, together with information on installation of front wheel bearings and grease seals, are given in the Unit Repair section under the heading: Suspension, Front, Repair.

Definitions of the points of steering geometry are covered in the unit repair section under heading: Suspension, Front, Align. This article also covers trouble shooting front end geometry and irregular tire wear.

Figures covering the caster, camber, toe-in, king pin inclination, and turning radius can be found in the Front Wheel Alignment Table of this section.

Car length and tire size figures can be found in the General Chassis and Brake Specifications Table of this car section.

FRONT HEIGHT

Adjustment, Without Gauge

1. Jounce the car and measure

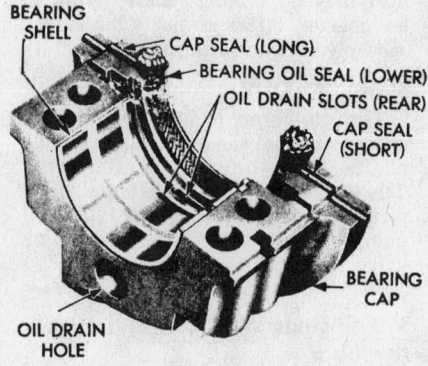

Rear main bearing oil seal

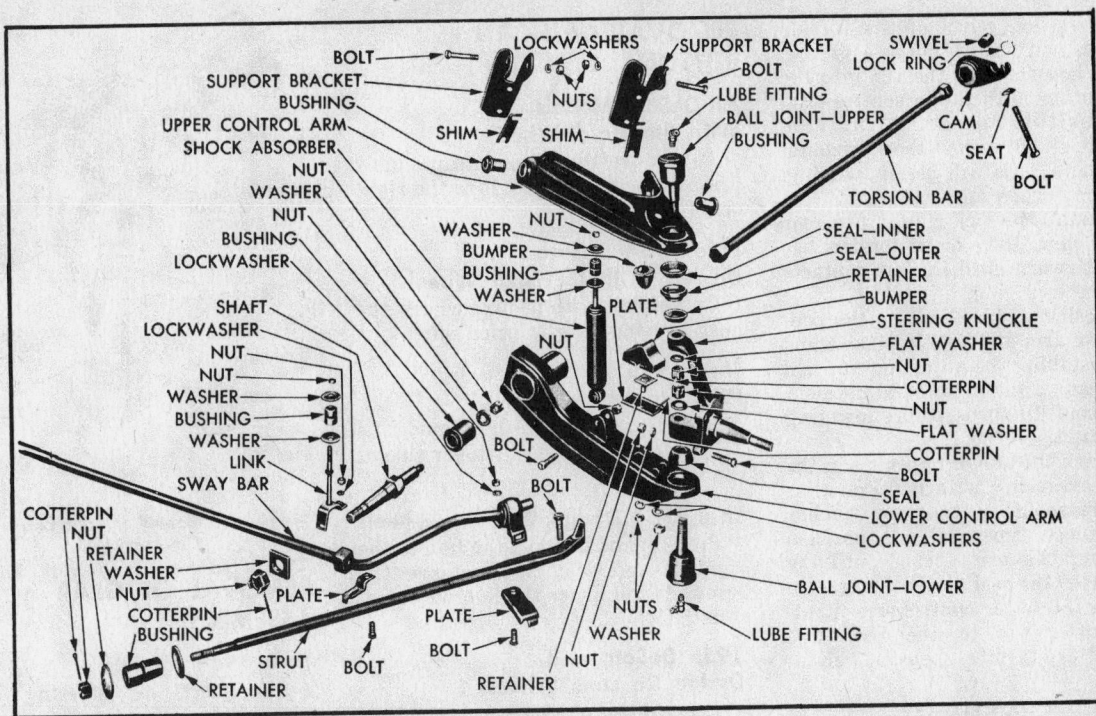

BOLT — LOCKWASHERS — SUPPORT BRACKET — SWIVEL
SUPPORT BRACKET — NUTS — BOLT — LOCK RING
BUSHING — SHIM — SHIM — LUBE FITTING — CAM
UPPER CONTROL ARM — BALL JOINT—UPPER — SEAT
SHOCK ABSORBER — BUSHING — BOLT
NUT
WASHER — TORSION BAR
NUT — WASHER — NUT — SEAL—INNER
BUSHING — BUMPER — SEAL—OUTER
LOCKWASHER — BUSHING — RETAINER
WASHER — BUMPER
SHAFT — PLATE — STEERING KNUCKLE
LOCKWASHER — NUT — FLAT WASHER
NUT — NUT
NUT — COTTERPIN
WASHER — NUT
BUSHING — FLAT WASHER
WASHER — COTTERPIN
LINK — BOLT — BOLT
SWAY BAR — SEAL
COTTERPIN — BOLT — LOWER CONTROL ARM
NUT — LOCKWASHERS
RETAINER
WASHER — BALL JOINT—LOWER
NUT — PLATE
COTTERPIN — NUTS
BUSHING — PLATE — WASHER — LUBE FITTING
STRUT — BOLT — BOLT — NUT
RETAINER — RETAINER

Exploded view of the front suspensions used on De Soto and Dodge cars, starting with 1957

from the lower ball joint to the floor, (measurement "A").

2. Measure from the control arm torsion bar spring anchor housing to the floor, (measurement "B").

3. Subtract "A" from "B". The difference should be as shown in specification table.

4. Measure the other side in the same way.

5. Adjust by turning the torsion bar anchor adjusting nut, clockwise to raise and counter-clockwise to lower.

TORSION BAR SPRINGS

Contrary to appearance, the torsion bars are **not** interchangeable from "right" to "left." They are marked with an R or an L, according to their location.

Remove

1. Lift the car by the body only so that the front suspension is free of all load. If the car is to be raised with jacks, place jack under center of frame cross member and raise until suspension is free of all load.

2. Release load from torsion bar by backing off anchor adjusting nuts. Remove the adjusting nut and swivel bolt.

3. Remove the lower control arm strut.

4. Remove the lock spring from the rear of torsion bar rear anchor.

5. Install tool #C-3728, or other suitable clamp and remove torsion bar rearward by striking the clamping tool with a hammer.

Do not apply heat to the front or rear anchors. Do not scratch

or otherwise mar the skin of the torsion bar during removal or installation.

6. Remove the clamping tool and slide the rear anchor balloon seal off the front end of the bar.

7. Remove torsion bar by sliding the bar rearward and out through the rear anchor.

Install

1. Clean the hex openings of both front and rear anchors, also clean the male ends of the torsion bar.

2. Feed the torsion bar through the rear anchor.

3. Slide the balloon type seal over the torsion bar, with the large

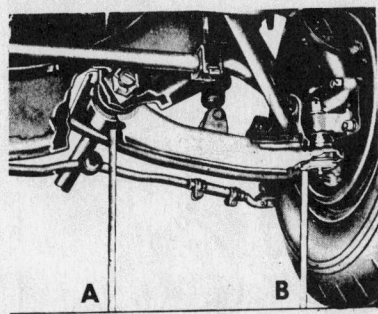

Checking Front Suspension Height at Ball Joint and Lower Central Arm

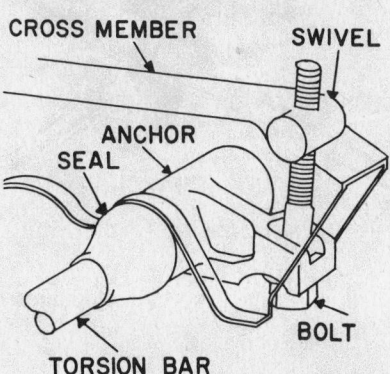

CROSS MEMBER — SWIVEL
ANCHOR
SEAL
TORSION BAR — BOLT

Torsion Bar Adjustment Bolt

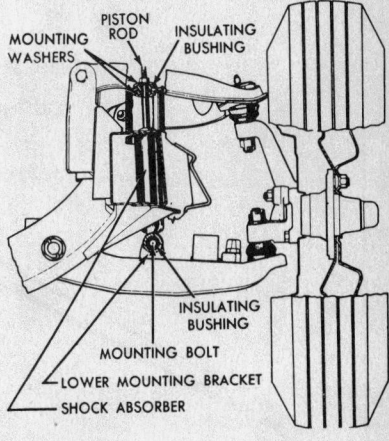

MOUNTING WASHERS — PISTON ROD — INSULATING BUSHING
INSULATING BUSHING
MOUNTING BOLT
LOWER MOUNTING BRACKET
SHOCK ABSORBER

Front shock absorber 1957-63

cupped side of the seal facing **(1963 DART, SEE VALIANT)**
the rear.

4. Coat both ends of the torsion bar with multi-purpose grease.
5. When starting the bar into the anchor in the lower control arm, position the adjusting arm about 60° below the horizontal plane. This will permit wind-up for future adjustment.
6. Install the lock ring in the rear anchor, then move torsion bar rearward until the bar contacts the lock ring.
7. Position swivel bolt on the control arm and hold in place while installing the adjusting nut and seat. Tighten the adjustment about 10 turns before lowering car to the floor.
8. Pack the annular opening in the rear anchor with multi-purpose grease. Slide the rear anchor balloon type seal into position over the rear anchor until the lip of the seal fits in the groove.
9. Install lower control arm strut
10. Lower car to the floor and adjust front suspension height.

STEERING

MANUAL STEERING GEAR

Instructions covering the overhaul of the steering gear will be found in the Unit Repair section under the heading: Steering, Manual.

POWER STEERING GEARS

Trouble shooting and repair instructions covering power steering gears are given in the Unit Repair section under the heading: Steering, Power.

REMOVAL OF HORN BUTTON

All DeSoto Models With Standard Wheels

To remove the horn button simply press it down and twist it to the right or left.

Thru 1954 DeSoto Models With De Luxe Wheels

On DeSotos with de luxe wheels the horn-blowing ring is pried off.

Thru 1955 Dodge Models With Standard Wheels

The horn button on these models is held by screws from the under side of the wheel hub.

Thru 1954 Dodge De Luxe Wheels

Press in and bayonet the hub to the right or left and then remove the screws found under the hub which retain the wheel.

1955 DeSoto and Dodge De Luxe Wheels

Press down on the horn trim ring and turn it counterclockwise. Lift off the medallion ring and spacer and underneath these will be found the screws which hold the De Luxe blowing ring in position on the steering wheel.

Starting With 1956

Remove the gear shift rod, shift the medallion to the center of the horn blowing device and lift off the medallion. Disconnect the horn wire and remove the screws which hold the blowing ring into the top of the steering wheel and lift off the ring.

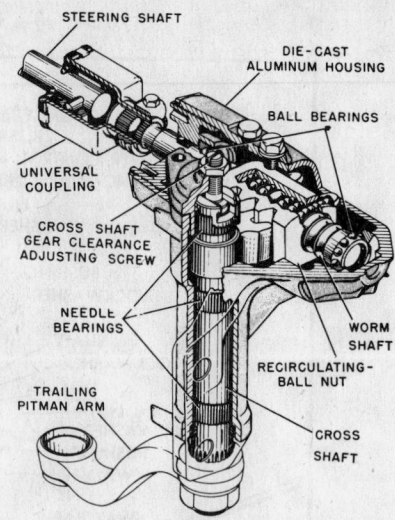

1962—63 Manual Steering Gear, Cut-Away View

REMOVAL OF GEAR ASSEMBLY

Thru 1954 Models

Disconnect all steering column wires, and remove the steering wheel.

Remove the jacket tube clamp to dash panel bracket and the gear shift bracket. Take off lower plate of directional signal housing and the screw from inside of housing.

Remove the signal contact unit by pulling the wire up through the jacket tube.

Remove the bear shift rod, shift lever, selector lever and brake cable clamp from jacket tube.

Take off pitman arm using special puller (C-143).

Remove steering gear to frame bolts.

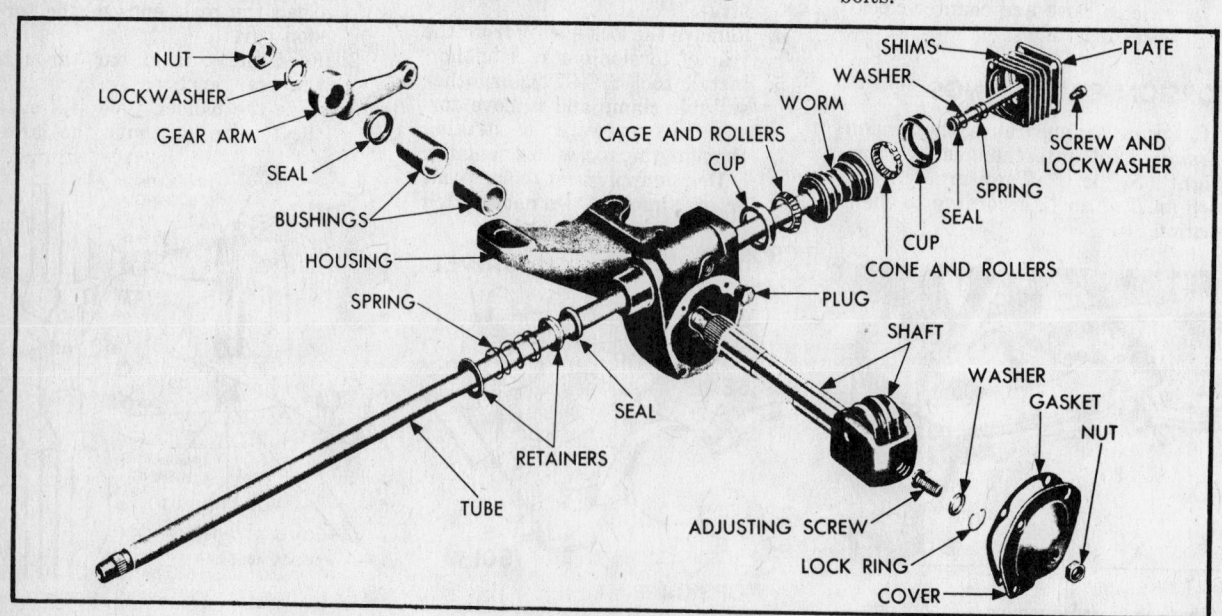

Disassembled view of steering gear

(1963 DART, SEE VALIANT)

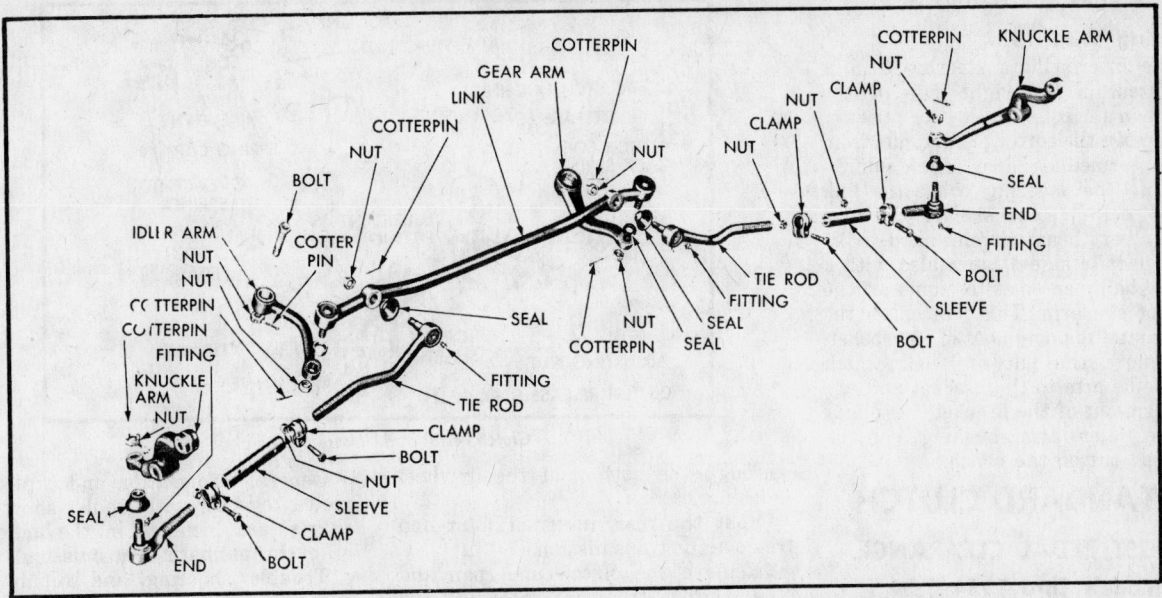

Exploded view—steering gear linkage 1957 thru 1961 models.

Remove the splash pan then lower gear assembly out of car.

1955-60

The steering assembly can be removed with the steering wheel intact by disconnecting the direction signals switch wires from under the dash, disconnecting the horn wire, disconnecting the gear shift links and levers from the engine compartment. Using a puller, detach the pitman arm from the bottom of the cross shaft, loosen the bracket which holds the steering mast jacket to the dash panel, remove the access plate in the toe board, remove the bolts which hold the gear

assembly to the frame and lift the entire gear assembly up through the inside of the car.

1961-63

The steering gear assembly can be removed without removing the column. Remove the steering gear arm. Disconnect coupling between worm shaft and column shaft. Loosen jacket clamp at instrument panel and slide column up to clear worm shaft.

Remove the gear to frame bolts and lift out through engine compartment on six cylinder models and from under car on V-8's.

REMOVAL AND DISASSEMBLY OF INTERMEDIATE STEERING ARM

1954 Thru 1956

The intermediate steering arm is a "U" shaped forging located on the right side of the frame. To replace the arms and/or bushings, disconnect the bracket from the frame and unscrew bracket and bushing from the upper end of the intermediate steering arm. The bushing can then be unscrewed from the bracket. Unscrew the arm from the lower bushing and the lower bushing can then be pulled out of the

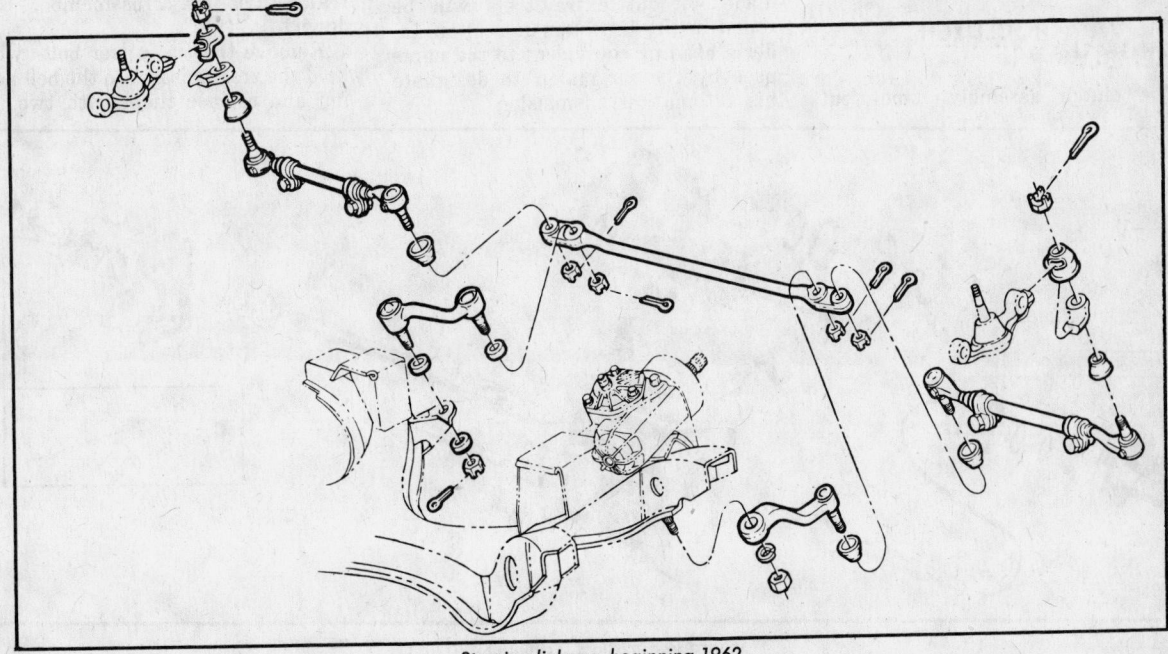

Steering linkage, beginning 1962

275

intermediate tie rod. Reassemble in reverse order and readjust toe-in.

(1963 DART, SEE VALIANT)

Starting With 1957

The intermediate steering arm is mounted on the right side of the frame in a bracket.

Remove the cotter pin and nut from the intermediate arm lower connection at the steering connector link and "back-up" the side of the arm with a very heavy hammer and strike the opposite side a blow, also with a heavy hammer, so as to "squeeze" the end of the arm. This will cause the taper stud to pop up out of the socket.

Remove the nut and bolt which holds the arm to the bracket and pry the arm out of the bracket.

The idler arm bushing can be pressed out on the bench.

STANDARD CLUTCH

ADJUST PEDAL CLEARANCE

All Models Thru 1954

Adjust the clutch throwout fork connecting link, under the toeboard, so that there is a three-quarter inch travel of the pedal measured at the toeboard before the throwout bearing contacts the clutch fingers.

Securely tighten the lock nut.

All Models Starting With 1955

From under the dash, remove the adjustable rod between the clutch idler shaft and the throwout fork by removing the clevis pin at the throwout fork. Adjust the link of this rod until there is approximately three-quarter inch pedal travel measured at the toeboard before the clutch throwout bearing strikes the fingers. Securely tighten the jam nut.

REMOVAL OF CLUTCH ASSEMBLY

The clutch assembly comes out

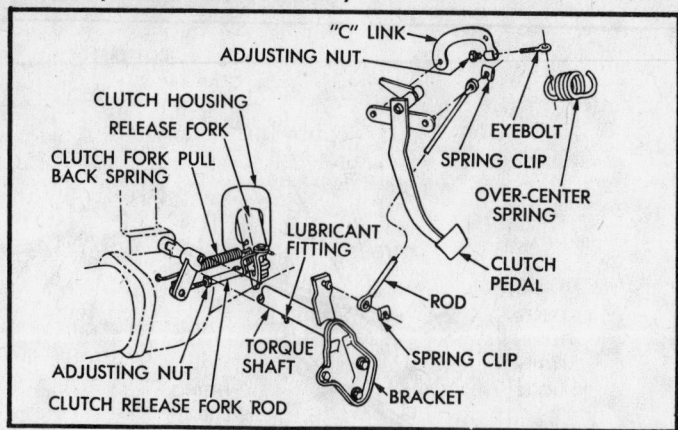

Clutch Pedal and Linkage Assembly

through the bottom of the flywheel housing.

Split the rear universal joint and remove the transmission.

Remove the clutch underpan and the clutch throwout bearing and sleeve. Reaching up from the bottom remove the bolts which hold the clutch cover to the flywheel, a little at a time so as not to spring the cover, until all pressure is removed and then remove the bolts and take the clutch out thru the bottom of the flywheel housing.

TRANSMISSIONS

Transmission refill capacities will be found in the Capacities Table of this section.

Automatic Transmission Linkage adjustment reduced to the simplest terms and with the basic theory explained so that adjustments can be made without extra tools will be found in the Unit Repair section under a heading equivalent to the name used by the car maker to designate his automatic transmission.

General information and exploded views, together with trouble shooting charts, are included in the articles on each automatic transmission.

Trouble shooting and repair of overdrive units are covered in the Unit Repair section under the heading: Transmission-Overdrive.

SYNCHROMESH TRANSMISION REMOVAL

Split the front universal joint and remove all attaching parts from the transmission such as speedometer cable, ground cables, shift levers and rods, hand brake cables, etc.

Place a jack under the back of the engine and take a slight load on the jack. Remove the bolts which hold the transmission to the frame crossmember and then take out the bolts which hold the crossmember to the frame. Let the crossmember come down.

Remove the two upper bolts which hold the transmission to the bell housing and replace them with two long

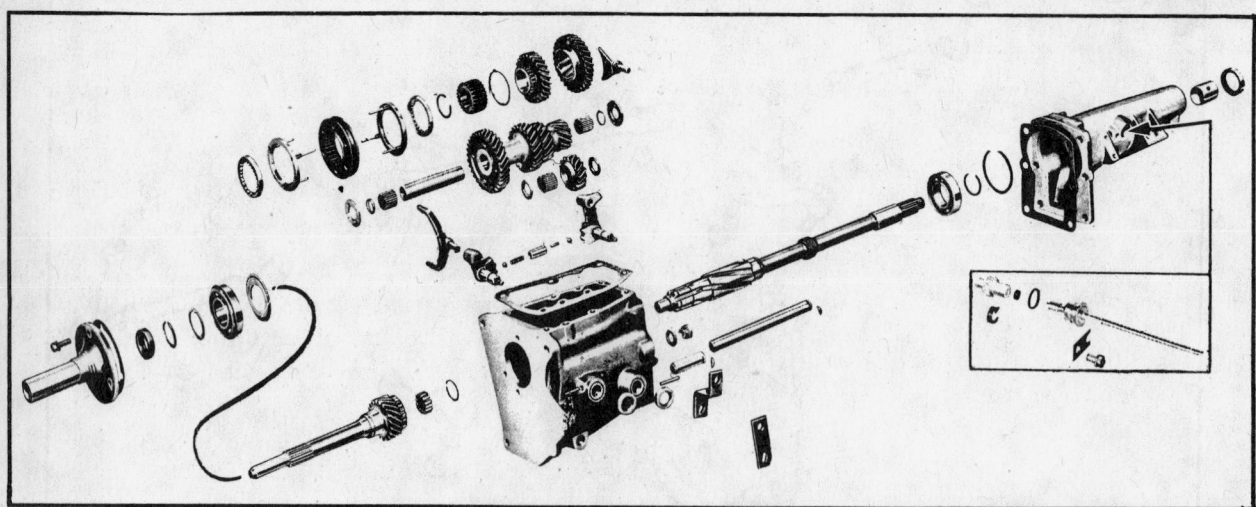

Standard transmission. 6 cylinder 1960-63

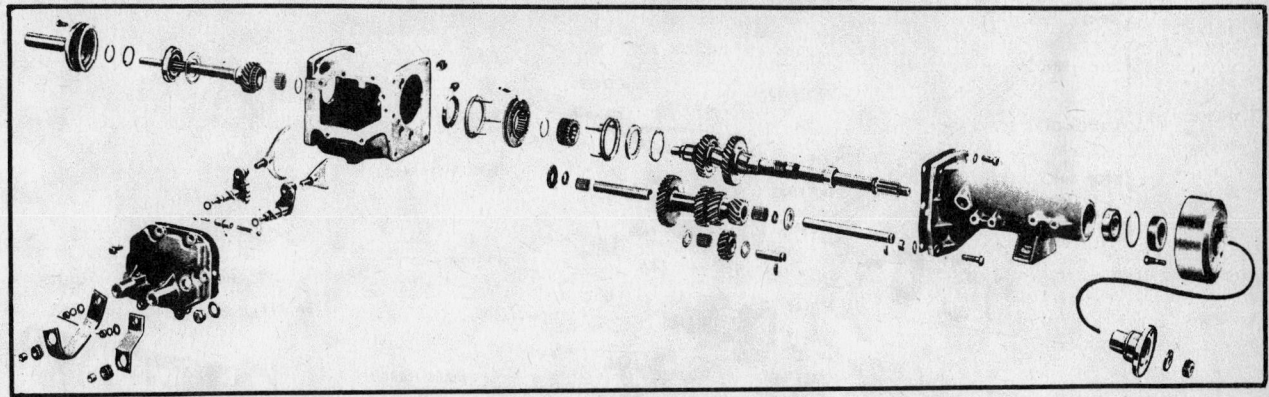

Standard Transmission 8 Cylinder 1957

pilot studs. Remove the two bottom bolts and slide the transmission assembly back along the two upper pilot studs until the clutch shaft clears the clutch hub. Slide off the end of the pilot shafts and lower to the floor.

SYNCHROMESH TRANSMISSION DISASSEMBLY

Remove transmission from the vehicle. Remove side cover assembly with its shift rails and forks. To disassemble the cover, drive out the pin which holds the outer levers to the shaft and pull the levers off the shafts. Push the shafts inwards which will release the detent balls.

Remove the forks from the shafts.

On the transmission case, remove the bolts which hold the front sleeve over the main drive gear and pull off the front sleeve.

Temporarily bolt the brake drum back to the back of the transmission and stand it on end.

Remove the main drive pinion. Remove the bolts which hold the rear ex-

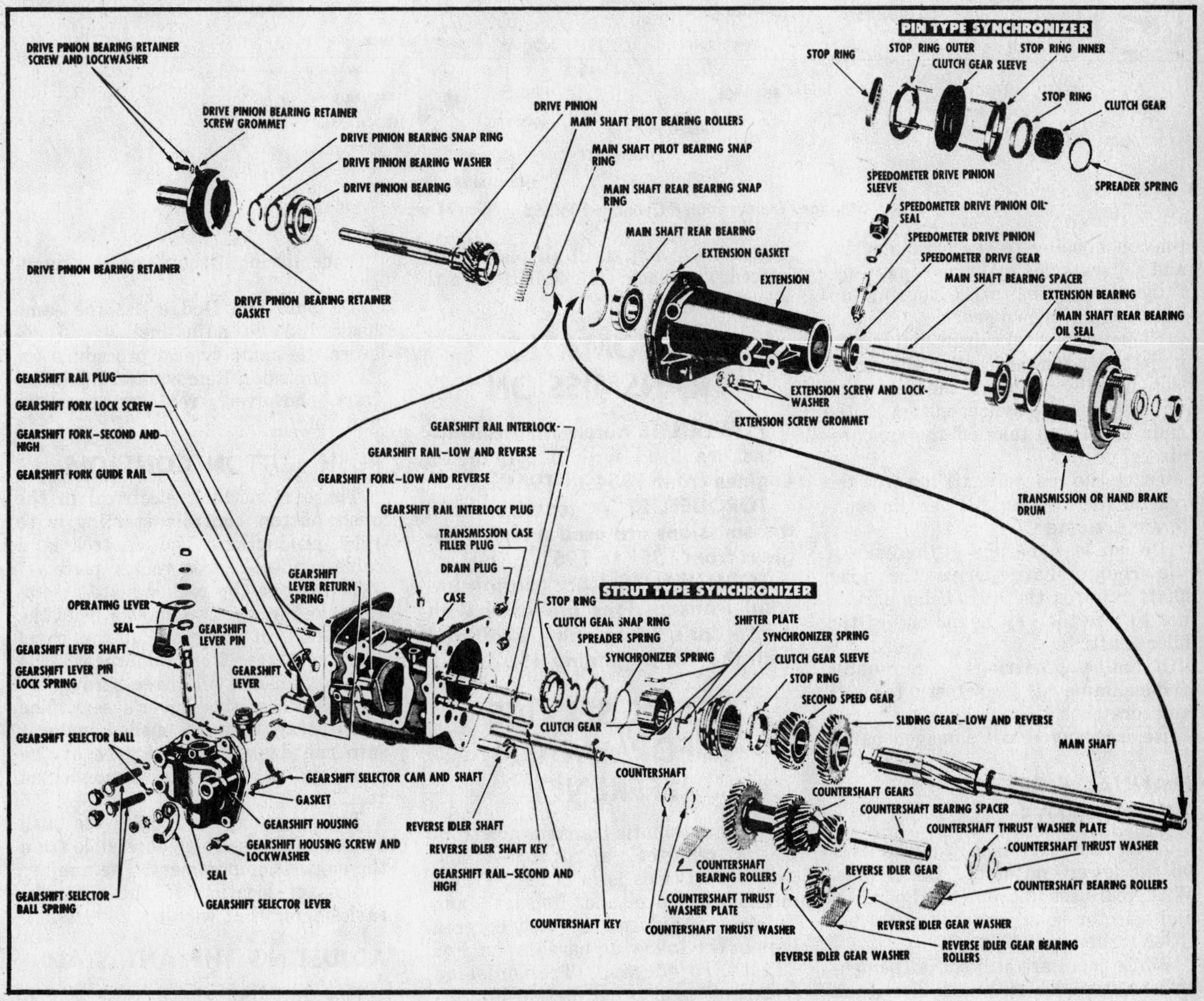

DRIVE PINION BEARING RETAINER SCREW AND LOCKWASHER
DRIVE PINION BEARING RETAINER SCREW GROMMET
DRIVE PINION BEARING RETAINER
DRIVE PINION BEARING SNAP RING
DRIVE PINION BEARING WASHER
DRIVE PINION BEARING
DRIVE PINION BEARING RETAINER
DRIVE PINION BEARING RETAINER GASKET
DRIVE PINION
MAIN SHAFT PILOT BEARING ROLLERS
MAIN SHAFT PILOT BEARING SNAP RING
MAIN SHAFT REAR BEARING SNAP RING
MAIN SHAFT REAR BEARING
EXTENSION GASKET
EXTENSION
EXTENSION SCREW AND LOCKWASHER
EXTENSION SCREW GROMMET

PIN TYPE SYNCHRONIZER
STOP RING
STOP RING OUTER
CLUTCH GEAR SLEEVE
STOP RING INNER
STOP RING
CLUTCH GEAR
SPREADER SPRING
SPEEDOMETER DRIVE PINION SLEEVE
SPEEDOMETER DRIVE PINION OIL SEAL
SPEEDOMETER DRIVE PINION
SPEEDOMETER DRIVE GEAR
MAIN SHAFT BEARING SPACER
EXTENSION BEARING
MAIN SHAFT REAR BEARING OIL SEAL
TRANSMISSION OR HAND BRAKE DRUM

GEARSHIFT RAIL PLUG
GEARSHIFT FORK LOCK SCREW
GEARSHIFT FORK—SECOND AND HIGH
GEARSHIFT FORK GUIDE RAIL
GEARSHIFT RAIL INTERLOCK
GEARSHIFT RAIL—LOW AND REVERSE
GEARSHIFT FORK—LOW AND REVERSE
GEARSHIFT RAIL INTERLOCK PLUG
TRANSMISSION CASE FILLER PLUG
DRAIN PLUG
CASE
GEARSHIFT LEVER RETURN SPRING
OPERATING LEVER
SEAL
GEARSHIFT LEVER PIN
GEARSHIFT LEVER SHAFT
GEARSHIFT LEVER PIN LOCK SPRING
GEARSHIFT LEVER
GEARSHIFT SELECTOR BALL
GEARSHIFT SELECTOR CAM AND SHAFT
GASKET
GEARSHIFT HOUSING
GEARSHIFT HOUSING SCREW AND LOCKWASHER
SEAL
GEARSHIFT SELECTOR BALL SPRING
GEARSHIFT SELECTOR LEVER
REVERSE IDLER SHAFT
REVERSE IDLER SHAFT KEY
GEARSHIFT RAIL—SECOND AND HIGH
COUNTERSHAFT KEY

STRUT TYPE SYNCHRONIZER
STOP RING
CLUTCH GEAR SNAP RING
SPREADER SPRING
SYNCHRONIZER SPRING
CLUTCH GEAR
SHIFTER PLATE
SYNCHRONIZER SPRING
CLUTCH GEAR SLEEVE
STOP RING
SECOND SPEED GEAR
SLIDING GEAR—LOW AND REVERSE
MAIN SHAFT
COUNTERSHAFT
COUNTERSHAFT GEARS
COUNTERSHAFT BEARING SPACER
COUNTERSHAFT THRUST WASHER PLATE
COUNTERSHAFT THRUST WASHER
COUNTERSHAFT BEARING ROLLERS
COUNTERSHAFT BEARING ROLLERS
REVERSE IDLER GEAR
COUNTERSHAFT THRUST WASHER PLATE
COUNTERSHAFT THRUST WASHER
REVERSE IDLER GEAR WASHER
REVERSE IDLER GEAR WASHER
REVERSE IDLER GEAR BEARING ROLLERS

Standard transmission. Through 1956

DE SOTO, DODGE & DART

(1963 DART, SEE VALIANT)

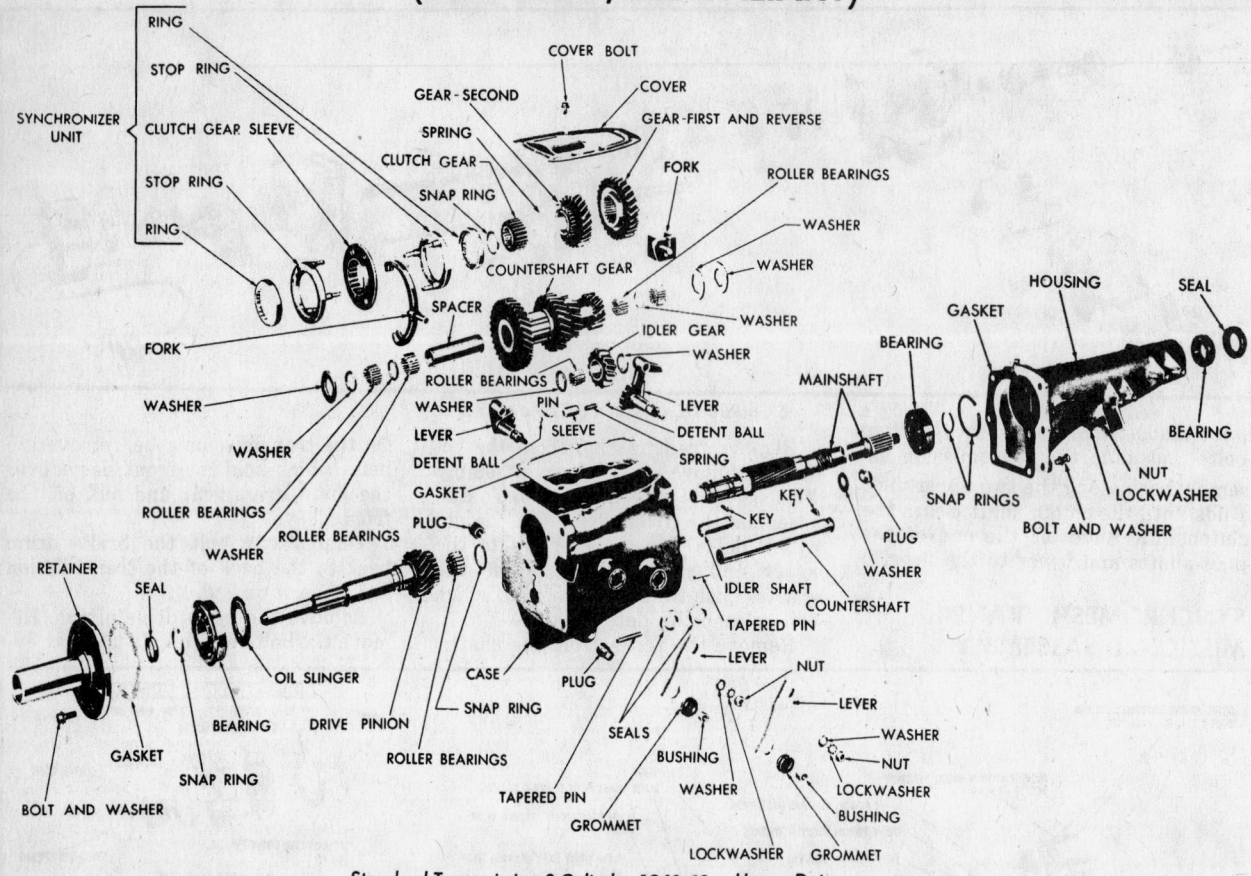

Standard Transmission 8 Cylinder 1960-63   Heavy Duty

tension housing to the main housing and separate the main housing. Carefully thread the main housing upwards off of its own gears.

Remove the brake drum and tap the main shaft forward out of the extension housing. Remove the snap ring which holds the synchronizers to the main shaft and take off the synchronizers.

Drive the countershaft towards the rear of the case and lift out the countershaft cluster.

Do not lose the key in the back of the countershaft. Drive the idler shaft towards the rear, being careful not to lose the key in the end of the idler shaft.

Examine all bearings for roughness and examine all gear teeth for pits and scratches.

Replace any or all damaged parts.

MANUAL SHIFT ADJUSTMENTS

Loosen the lock bolt at upper lever on the lower end of the jacket tube. With gears set in the neutral position and selector lever in a horizontal position tighten lock bolt.

While gears are still set in the neutral position loosen the lock nut on selector rod at transmission end.

Tighten the nut until all play is removed, and back off one-half turn to allow clearance.

AUTOMATIC TRANSMISSION

POWERFLITE automatic transmissions are used with 6 cyl. or V8 engines from 1954 to 1961.

TORQUEFLITE "A" (cast iron case) transmissions are used with V8 engines from 1957 to 1961.

TORQUEFLITE "B" (aluminum case) transmissions are used with the "Slant 6", beginning 1960 and with the V8, beginning 1962.

QUICK SERVICE INFORMATION REFERENCE

When automatic transmission trouble is reported, a road test and careful diagnosis is in order. "Transmission Remove and Replace" and "Linkage Adjustments" are covered here in the following paragraphs. For "Test Procedures," Transmission Overhaul" and other detailed information, see "Unit Repair Section,"

"Transmission Group" of this manual.

De Soto and Dodge use the same basic linkage adjustments and require the same typical procedure for "Transmission Remove and Replace". Dart, however, requires separate handling.

PUSH BUTTON CONTROLS

There is nothing electrical in the push button controls starting with 1956 production. The control is a cable connected to a rocker plate.

To remove the rocker plate assembly take out the two screws from the front face of the push button panel and one screw from underneath the dash extension, all three screws accessible from the driver's seat. The control can then be pushed inwards into the dash and once free of the dash the cable can be disconnected readily.

The mounting screws for the push button controls are all accessible from the engine compartment. The number and exact location of these screws varies somewhat with body styles.

ADJUSTING THE ANTI-STALL

The anti-stall consists of a diaphragm and a plunger with a small

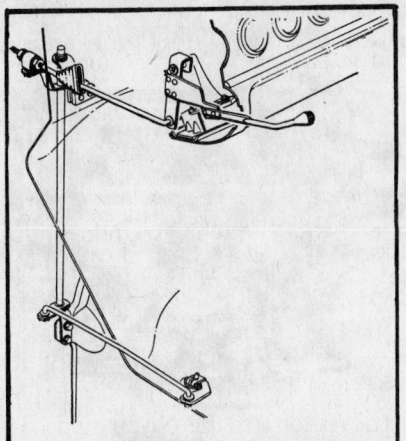

Fig. 1—Manual Control Linkage, 1955

orifice. The air trapped behind the diaphragm is bled out at a specific rate by the orifice. The device acts to keep the throttle from snapping shut during its last one-quarter inch of travel.

To check, open the throttle by hand and release. The closing of the throttle should be visibly slowed by the action of the anti-stall.

To adjust, have the engine at operating temperature and set adjusting screw so that the plunger has one-sixteenth of an inch travel after the throttle is fully closed.

ADJUSTING THE LINKAGE

Manual Control Adjustment Thru 1954

The manual control lever is the bottom one of the two levers on the left side of the transmission case. When the lever is turned full back, counterclockwise, the transmission is in Reverse. The next detent forward, clockwise, is Neutral. The next detent is Drive and the last detent, when the lever is as far clockwise as it will go, is Low.

Place the manual control lever in the Neutral detent. Check that the

bell crank on the frame has its lower arm pointing down and back while the upper arm is at an angle of 45 deg. with the frame. If this is not so, disconnect the two rods at the bell crank. Being sure that the manual control lever on the transmission is in Neutral, adjust the length of the lower rod to hold the bell crank so that its upper arm is at 45 deg. with the frame and reconnect the lower rod to the bell crank.

Move the hand lever on the steering column to the Neutral position and then at the bottom of the steering column check the position of the tongue of the lever in the locating gate. This gate is held to the column by screws in slots so that the gate can be moved. Adjust the gate so that there is .015 to .030 in. clearance between the lever and the gate measured parallel with the column and .015 to .017 in. clearance between the gate and the lever measured perpendicular to the column. When the gate is correctly set adjust the upper rod at the bell crank to fit easily and attach it.

Move the hand control lever thru the four positions and check that the pointer and the marks on the dial line up. If they do not: run thru the adjustment procedure again rather than bend the pointer.

Manual Control Adjustment 1955 (See Fig. 1)

On the forward end of the rod running forward from the dash control there is a swivel. Loosen this swivel.

At the transmission, move the manual control lever one notch forward from full rear position. This will be Neutral.

Put dash control in Neutral position and reconnect the swivel.

Check that lever moves freely.

Manual Control Adjustment Starting 1956

1. Raise car on hoist. Have a helper hold the "R" button firmly depressed.
2. Remove control cable adjustment wheel lock screw at the left side of transmission.
3. Back the adjustment wheel off on the cable guide until only two or three threads show behind the wheel on the guide.

   NOTE: Be sure the adjustment wheel turns freely on the guide. Lubricate the cable guide threads with transmission fluid.
4. Hold the control cable guide centered in the hole of the transmission case and apply only enough inward force (two to three pounds) to bottom the assembly at the reverse detent. While holding the cable bottomed, rotate the adjustment wheel clockwise until it just contacts the case.
5. Turn the wheel clockwise just enough to make the next adjustment hole in the wheel line up with the screw hole in the case.
6. Counting this hole as Number One, keep turning the wheel clockwise until the fifth hole lines up with the screw hole in the case.
7. Install lock screw and torque to 30 to 50 inch pounds.

Throttle Linkage and Throttle Valve Oil Pressure Adjustment

Accurate adjustment of the trans-

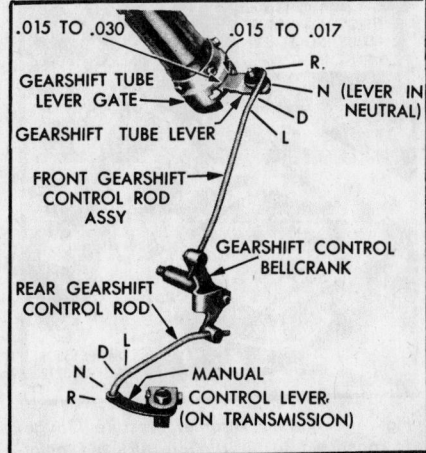

Manual control linkage thru 1954

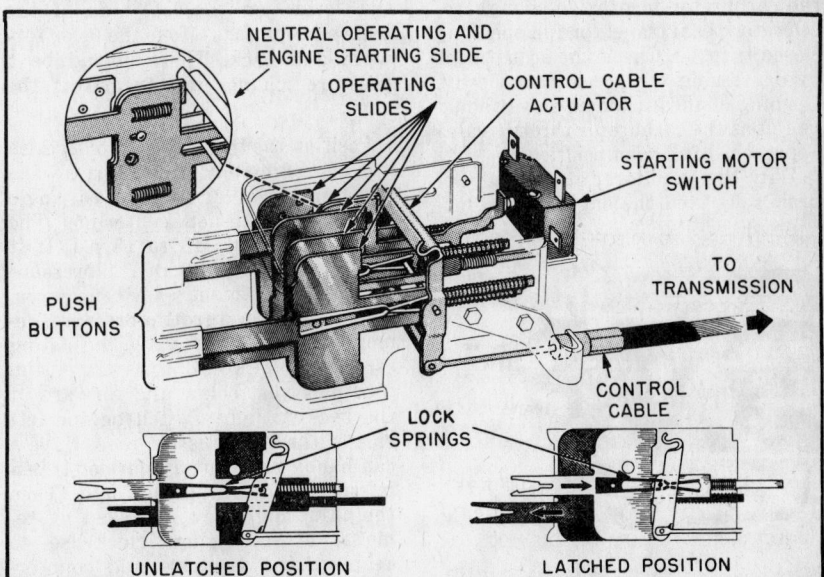

Operational sketch—push button gearshift control unit

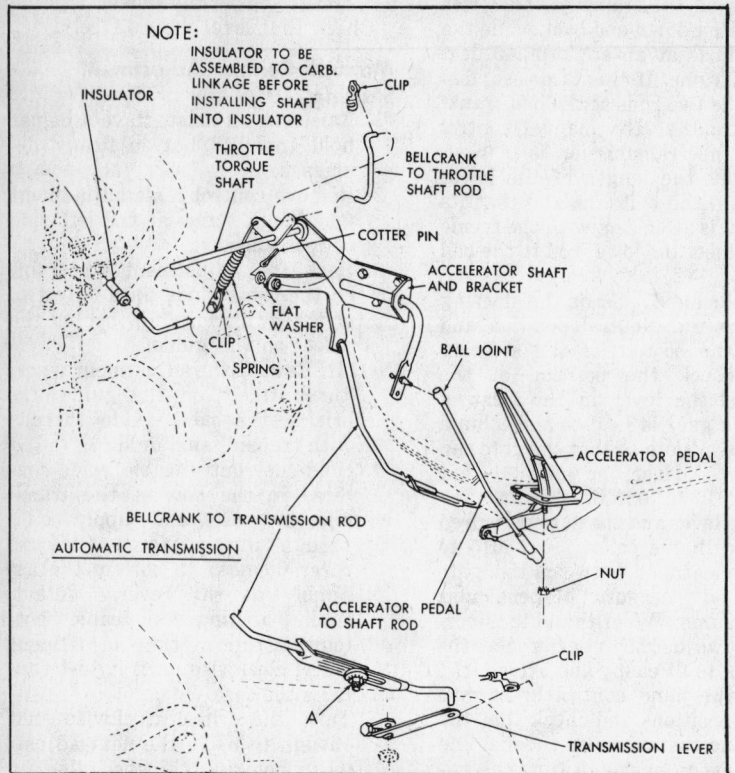

Fig. 2—Throttle Linkage typical of PowerFlite and TorqueFlite.

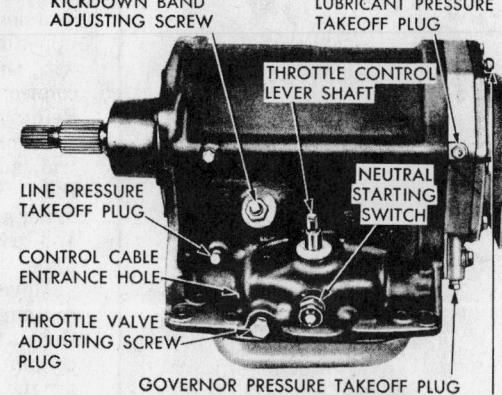

Left Side of Powerflite Transmission

Reinstall the plug and tighten to 20-25 ft. lbs. Reconnect the throttle control rod to the lever and depress the accelerator. The pressure should rise at once to 80 psi. If it does not and yet is 14 psi at idle the linkage requires adjustment.

Disconnect the swivel at the transmission end of the throttle valve control rod from the rod; leaving the swivel attached to the throttle control lever.

Now move the lever forward as far as it will come and then slowly move it back until a slight resistance is felt. From this point of slight resistance a slight forward movement of the lever should cause the pressure to rise to 80 psi. There at this point of slight resistance hold the lever and reconnect the control rod into the swivel. Push forward on the rod to remove any play in the linkage while making the connection and tightening the swivel lock screw.

Again depress the accelerator and check that the pressure rises from 14 psi at an idle of 475-500 rpm to 80 psi at 1400-1500 rpm.

After removing the pressure gage tighten the 1/8" pipe plug to 10-12 ft lbs.

mission throttle linkage and precise setting of the throttle valve oil pressure is required for proper operation of the Powerflite Transmission.

Remove any binds that may exist in the throttle linkage. Fig. 2. Make sure that the throttle valve in the carburetor is fully open when the accelerator is fully depressed and is fully closed when the accelerator is fully released. Adjust the accelerator shaft to the carburetor to provide enough accelerator pedal travel for full open and closed throttle. Check the adjustment by depressing the accelerator slowly. Opening of the kickdown valve should be felt as the carburetor throttle valve approaches full open position.

With the hand lever at Neutral, the brakes set, and the engine at operating temperature, adjust the idle speed to 475-500 RPM.

Remove the plug from the throttle pressure test (takeoff) point on the right side of the case just behind the front servo. See Fig. 3. Connect in a pressure gage.

With the engine idling and the hand lever at drive disconnect the throttle control rod at the throttle control lever which is the upper of the two levers on the left side of the transmission case. Move the lever forward and back. There should be a pressure change apparent on the gage.

Position the throttle control lever so it is approximately 30 degrees toward the front of the car from a right angle to the transmission centerline. The gage should read 13 to 15 psi. If it does not the throttle valve oil pressure requires adjustment.

To adjust the throttle pressure, remove the throttle valve adjusting screw plug (Cover). It is the 3/8 in. pipe plug just below and forward of the back-up light switch on the left side of the transmission case. Have a can handy as about a quart of transmission fluid will gush forth. Turn the adjusting screw, revealed by removal of the plug, clockwise to decrease the pressure and counterclockwise to increase it. Adjust the pressure to 14 psi. Fig. 4.

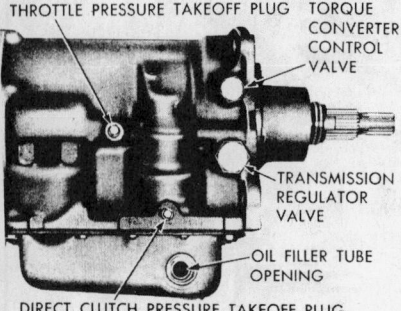

Fig. 3—View of right side of PowerFlite showing Throttle Pressure Takeoff Plug.

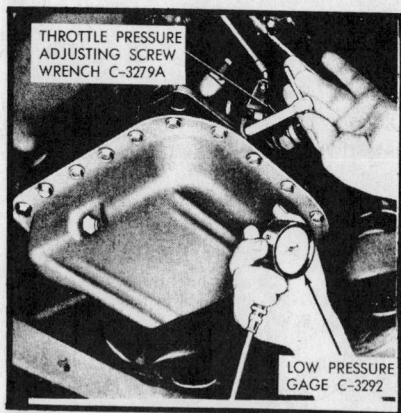

Fig. 4—Adjusting Throttle. Pressure Gauge is connected to throttle pressure test point on right side of transmission

REMOVAL OF THE TRANSMISSION FROM THE CAR

Disconnect the battery. Drain the transmission and the converter. Unfasten the oil filler tube from the oil pan and remove the tube.

Disconnect the front propeller shaft universal joint and tie the shaft up out of the way. Remove the adjusting screw cover plate and the clamp bolt from the hand brake support. Disengage the hand brake cable from the operating lever.

Disconnect the speedometer cable from the rear extension. Disconnect the wires from the back up light and neutral safety switches and unclip the wires from the cross member. Disconnect the operating rods from the transmission levers. Disconnect the two oil cooler lines at the left side of the case and remove the bracket holding the lines to the cylinder block. Unfasten the exhaust pipe bracket from the transmission case.

Remove the two nuts and lockwashers that hold the engine rear cross member support insulator to the cross-member, leaving the insulator attached to the transmission. On reinstalling tighten to 30-35 ft lbs.

Raise the engine slightly by means of a jack and unbolt and remove the cross-member.

Lower the engine slightly and remove the two upper transmission case to bell housing bolts. Install guide studs in their place so that no weight comes on the front oil pump drive sleeve. Be careful not to lower the engine more than three inches or the hoses and linkages at the engine will be damaged.

Remove the two lower case to bell housing screws. Slide the transmission case back on the guide pins until it is free of the oil pump drive sleeve then take the case on down and away.

INSTALLATION OF THE TRANSMISSION

Reverse the removal procedure to reinstall. Be sure that the front oil pump drive sleeve is in good condition with no burrs or signs of wear on the driving lugs. Check the seal ring for freeness in its groove. Lubricate the surfaces of the sleeve with lbriplate and install it in the hub of the converter. Align the splines of the input shaft with those of the turbine. Position the lugs of the front oil pump drive gear so that they wil properly engage those of the oil pump drive sleeve. Slide the case over the guide studs into position. Do not use the case-to-bell housing screws to bring the two parts together. If the drive lugs of the sleeve and the splines of

(1963 DART, SEE VALIANT)

the input shaft have been properly aligned with their mating parts in the converter the transmission should slide into place easily.

Tighten the case to bell housing screws of 45-50 ft lbs, the cross-member to frame bolts to 50-55 ft lbs, the propeller shaft nuts to 33-37 ft lbs.

CONVERTER REMOVAL

Remove the transmission case from the car.

Turn the front wheels as far as they will go. to the right and remove the starting motor. Unfasten twelve screws and remove the transmission case adapter plate from the bell housing. Remove the lower half of the flywheel bell housing. Check the runout of the rear hub of the converter. Runout should not exceed .004 in F.I.R.

Remove the eight nuts and lockwashers holding the converter to the crankshaft flange. Remove the converter from the crankshaft.

FLYWHEEL RING GEAR REPLACEMENT

The converter is a welded assembly and parts for it are not sold separately. The flywheel ring gear can be replaced. File off the retaining lugs and tap the ring gear off to the front. Heat the new one to about 150 deg. (using an oven, hot water, steam or a torch with slow flame) and push it onto the converter so that it contacts the flange all around. Weld the new ring gear in place using as much metal on the welds as was filed off and placing the welds in the same spots.

Do not use an acetylene or oxy-hydrogen torch as these will harm the converter.

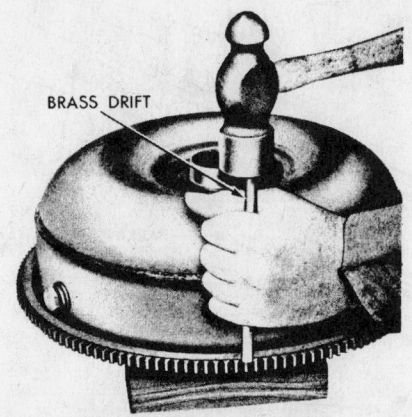

BRASS DRIFT

Tap the Flywheel Ring Gear Off to the Front of the Converter

Do use a D.C. welder that is set at straight polarity or an A.C. welder. Use 200 Amps and a 5/32 in. rod equivalent to a Fleet Weld No. 47 or a G.E. No. W28.

The Arc should be directed at the intersection of the front face of the gear with the converter at an angle of 45 deg.

CONVERTER INSTALLATION

Check the runout of the crankshaft flange; it should not exceed .002 in. F.I.R. Reverse the procedure for removal to reinstall the converter. Check the runout of the rear hub of the converter after it has been bolted to the crankshaft flange. Runout should not exceed .004 in. F.I.R. See paragragh in Torque-Flite Section for corrective procedure.

TORQUEFLITE TYPE A
ADJUSTMENTS

RENEW PUSH BUTTON UNIT LIGHT BULB

Remove the three bezel retaining screws (one screw is located on underside of unit) and the bezel. Fig. 2. Pull the "D" button off its slider and so gain clearance to remove the bulb. Install new bulb. Compress ends of slider and push "D" button back in place thereon. Use a small screwdriver to assure that ends of slider are firmly seated in rear of plastic "D" button.

RENEW BACK-UP LIGHT SWITCH

The back-up light switch is fastened to the push button unit by four tabs. Remove the push button control unit from the dash. Straighten the tabs and remove the switch.

REMOVING PUSH BUTTON UNIT FROM DASH

Remove the three bezel retaining screws (one screw is located on underside) and remove bezel. Fig. 2. This will expose the two hex nuts and washers which hold the unit to the dash. Remove the unit to the back of the dash. Remove the two screws holding cable assembly bracket to the unit and then remove the clip which holds the cable to the unit. Unfasten the wires from the back-up light switch. Note that the wire to the light in the unit comes over the upper stud and down between the sliders. The bracket which holds the light fits over the upper stud. Reverse the procedure to reinstall.

DE SOTO, DODGE & DART

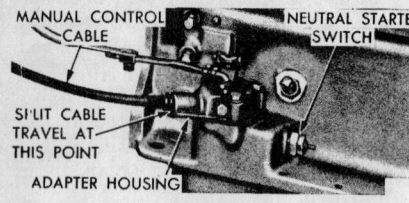

Fig. 1—Manual control cable adjustment at transmission

THROTTLE LINKAGE ADJUSTMENT

With the engine idling in Neutral adjust idle speed to 475-500 rpm Check that choke is fully open, after engine has run until it has reached normal operating temperature.

Stop engine and adjust throttle rod at carburetor so that throttle lever on transmission is back against its stop. Fig. 3. With rod preloaded to maintain transmission throttle lever at stop and carburetor throttle lever against idle speed-adjusting-screw, tighten the throttle linkage adjusting screw to 7-9 ft. lbs. Do not disturb rod adjustment at transmission end.

MANUAL CONTROL CABLE REMOVAL

Remove the push button control unit from the dash as in the preceding paragraph and remove the clip, screw and lock washer which holds the cable sheath to the housing on the left side of the transmission. Fig. 4.

Remove the plug in the side of the cable housing. Put a screwdriver thru

Fig. 2—Push button unit on dash

the hole and release the spring lock, which fastens the cable to the lever, at the same time pull the cable and sheath from the housing.

From inside the car pull the cable and sheath up thru the rubber grommet in the firewall.

Reverse procedure to reinstall and then apply paragraph on Manual Control Cable Adjustment.

PARTS THAT REQUIRE REMOVAL OF THE TRANSMISSION FROM THE CAR

REMOVAL OF TRANSMISSION AND CONVERTER

The transmission is removed as a unit first and then the torque converter.

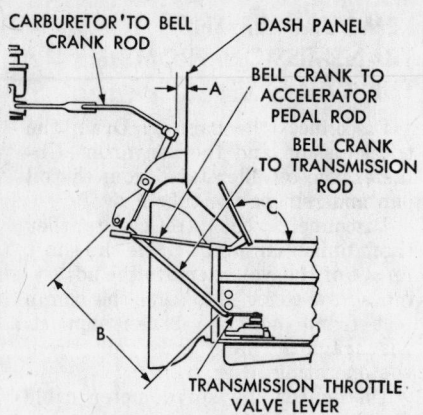

Fig. 3—Throttle lever and linkage

Note: All Chrysler Corporation Torque Converters are welded units and require special equipment to rebuild.

Disconnect the battery. Push in the "1" button so the manual control cable can be removed. See paragraph on "Manual Control Cable Removal." Drain the transmission and converter. Disconnect the filler pipe. Disconnect the front universal joint and hang the propeller shaft up out of the way. Remove hand brake adjusting screw cover plate and disconnect hand brake cable and other parts as per paragraphs on "Rear Extension" and "Valve Bodies and Transfer Plate Assembly."

Remove the starter. Install engine support fixture. Raise engine slightly and remove crossmember. Replace two transmission case to torque converter housing bolts on right side with

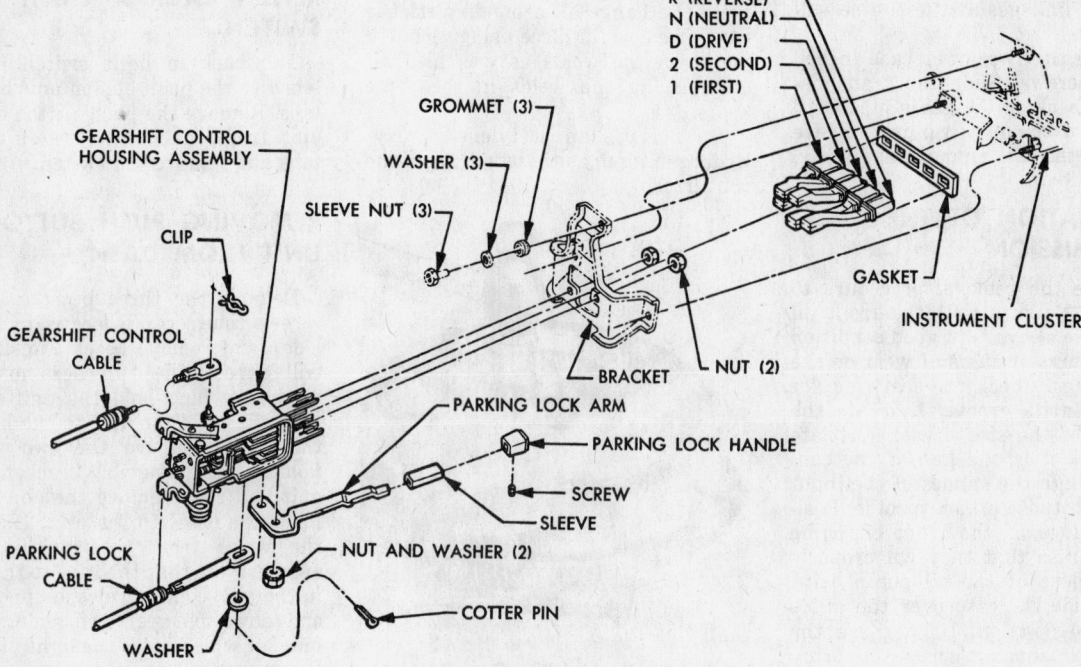

Push button selector unit

(1963 DART, SEE VALIANT)

guide pins and then remove two case to housing bolts from left side. Slide transmission straight back to avoid damage to the front oil pump driving sleeve and lower transmission to the floor.

Unbolt and remove the converter housing bolts. Although most mechanics do not do so, it is recommended that the runout of the converter hub be checked before the converter is removed from the crankshaft. Using an indicator as shown in Fig. 2, check runout of converter hub (runout should not exceed .004 inch F.I.R.) and mark both converter and crankshaft flange so that the true source of any runout may be found. Be sure to match mark the converter to the shaft flange so that it may be assembled in the same position. Remove eight torque converter stud nuts and lock washers to release the converter from the crankshaft flange. See Fig. 1. Check runout of flange; it should not exceed .002 inch. If it does, use shims between converter and flange at reassembly to correct.

CORRECTING TORQUE CONVERTER RUNOUT

Note: Throughout this procedure the converter has no oil in it and the drain plugs are in place. This procedure is applicable to any Chrysler Corporation Torque Converter.

Runout of the converter hub should not exceed .004 inch. If it does, the condition may be corrected by using a torch as shown in Fig. 3 to heat a spot about ½ inch in diameter at a point on the front face of the converter opposite the low-spot of hub runout. The size of the spot to be heated depends on the amount of runout. It should be about ½ inch in diameter for .008 inch of total indicator reading. Using an acetylene torch containing a No. 3 tip set to maximum heat,

apply it to the selected spot until the spot becomes dull red. Rapid heating and then cooling of an isolated area is the secret of the process. If all is well, the spot comes to color in a few seconds. The area is then quenched as rapidly as possible with a hose or wet rags. Do not attempt to recheck runout until converter has returned to a normal temperature.

If sparks are noted it is an indication that the torch is too close and the metal is starting to burn; move torch back slightly. Care should be taken to remove the torch the instant the selected spot becomes a dull red to avoid over-correction or damage to the unit.

Should the runout of the converter hub exceed .016 inch (Full Indicator Reading) and yet runout of the crankshaft flange is less than .002 inch F.I.R., the converter unit is defective and should be replaced. Be certain, however, to first check the drive flanges for raised metal, chips, dirt, and such.

INSTALLATION OF CONVERTER

When reinstalling, install the eight converter stud nuts and lock washers and tighten evenly (no specification for proper torque is given). Recheck that hub runout does not exceed .004 inch F.I.R. Place torque converter housing over the locating dowels and into position against the block-to-housing adapter plate. Install the housing to plate screws with lock washers and tighten evenly to 25-30 ft. lbs.

Note: The bore of the housing must be concentric to the hub of the converter within .010″. Adjustment is made by turning the slot-ended hous-

ing-locating dowels or by installing different dowels available for the purpose. The rear face of the housing should be perpendicular to the converter hub within .008″. Adjustment is made by shims between the housing and the adapter plate.

NSTALLATION OF TRANSMISSION

Install guide pins in the two transmission mounting holes in right side of torque converter housing. Lubricate and install front oil pump drive sleeve into transmission, making sure the driving lugs correctly engage the front oil pump pinion. Main position of drive sleeve will be flush with front of pump housing if sleeve is properly installed.

Position lugs on converter ends of drive sleeve to engage drive lugs visible in hub of converter. Line up splines of reaction shaft and input shaft with those of stator and turbine in the converter.

Slide transmission along guide pins into place against converter housing. Check that the driving lugs and splines are properly engaged. Everything should go into place easily. If force seems necessary, it is likely that the input shaft or drive sleeve is not properly aligned with splines or lugs in converter.

Install the two left hand transmission case to torque converter housing screws, but do not tighten. Remove the two guide pins and install the two right hand transmission case to torque converter housing screws and lock washers. Now tighten all four screws evenly and torque to 40-50 ft. lbs. Reinstall crossmember and tighten bolts to 50-55 ft. lbs. Lower engine and at the same time align mounting studs in insulator with holes in the crossmember. Install the two nuts and lock washers that hold

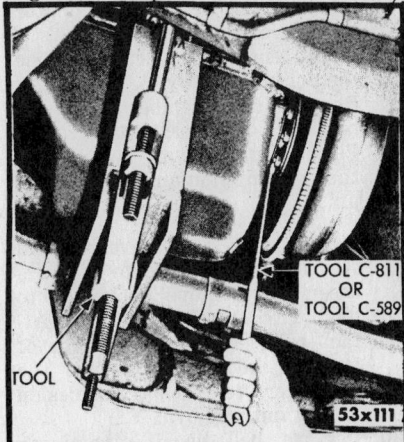

Fig. 1—Removal of converter to flywheel stud nuts

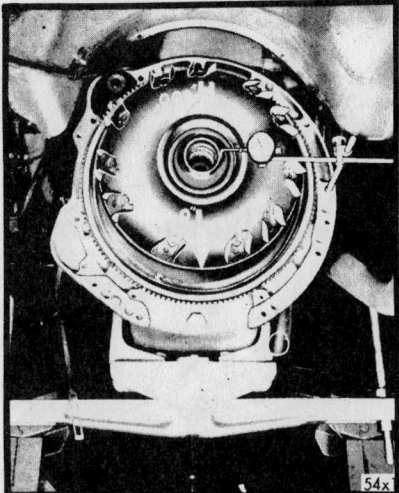

Fig. 2—Checking that runout of Torque Converter Hub does not exceed .004″

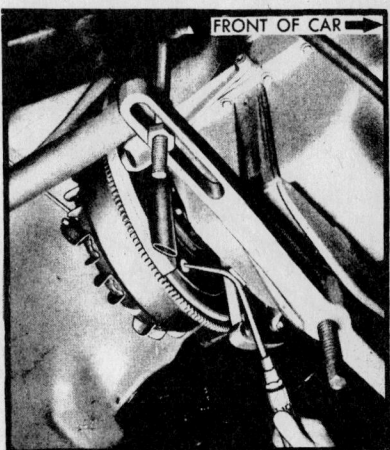

Fig. 3—Heat spot on front cover of converter opposite to mark on back face indicating low spot of converter hub

283

(1963 DART, SEE VALIANT)

the engine and transmission rear support insulator to the crossmember and torque from 30-35 ft. lbs. Remove the engine supporting device. Reinstall the other parts which were removed. Tighten oil pan to filler tube nut to 35-40 ft. lbs. Tighten propeller shaft flange nut to 200 ft. lbs. Tighten front universal joint nuts to 33-37 ft. lbs.

TORQUEFLITE TYPE B

In addition to POWERFLITE and TORQUEFLITE, the TORQUE-FLITE type "B" is used. This transmission was designed primarily, to accommodate the Slant "6" engine; and in 1962, to the V-8 engine. Detailed information on the TORQUE-FLITE type "B" may be found in the Unit Repair section, Transmission group of this manual.

THROTTLE LINKAGE ADJUSTMENT

1. With engine at operating temperature and carburetor off fast idle, adjust R.P.M. to 500.
2. Loosen lock nut "A" (Fig. 1) and move the transmission throttle control lever forward until it stops. Then retighten lock nut "A".
3. Adjust a spirit level protractor to 115 degrees, then place the protractor lengthwise and flat on the face of the accelerator pedal.
4. With the car on a LEVEL floor, disconnect the accelerator pedal rod and adjust the rod length to center the bubble in the spirit level. When the angle is correct reconnect the pedal rod.

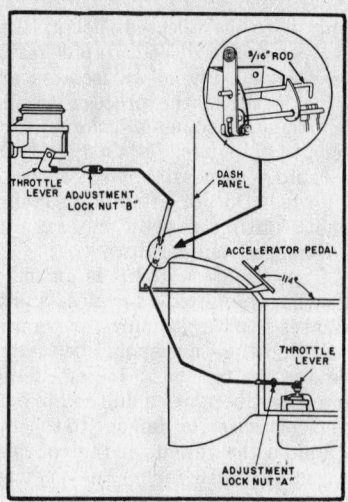

Fig. 1—Throttle linkage adjustments

Starting 1962

1. Disconnect ball socket (4).
2. Disconnect choke (1) or block it wide open, with throttle off fast idle cam.
3. With transmission lever forward against stop, adjust at ball joint (4) so that joint will enter directly and with no force on the rod, it must be held at same height for this measurement.
4. Check operation to be sure transmission lever is against stop when at curb idle and moves off stop immediately with throttle movement.
5. Follow steps 2, 3, 4 and 5 under manual transmission, above.

TORQUEFLITE "B", R & R

1. Disconnect a battery cable at the battery.
2. Depress "L" push button.
3. Remove starting motor.
4. Raise the car on a hoist.

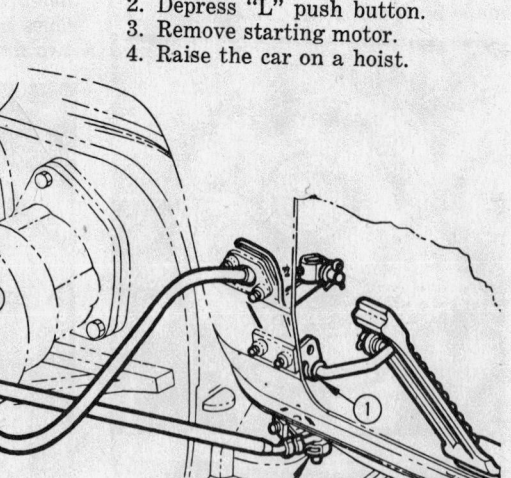

Fig. 2—Gearshift control cable and adjustment wheel

5. Remove cover plate from in front of converter.
6. Drain converter and transmission.
7. Disconnect wire and remove neutral starting switch.
8. Remove push button control cable to transmission adjusting plate screw.
9. Through the neutral starting switch opening, push a screw driver against the upper projecting portion of the cable lock spring. Pull outward on cable to remove cable from adapter and transmission case.
10. Loosen clamp screw and remove throttle link and lever assembly from the throttle shaft.
11. Disconnect oil cooler lines and remove oil filler tube.
12. Remove speedometer pinion and sleeve from transmission.
13. Disconnect front universal joint and tie propeller shaft out of the way.
14. Remove parking brake adjusting nut cover plate and loosen cable clamp bolt on brake support. Disengage the ball end of the cable from the operating lever and remove cable from the brake support.
15. Remove nut and washers holding transmission extension insulator at the crossmember.
16. Install engine support and raise the engine slightly.
17. Remove crossmember attaching bolts and the crossmember.
18. Place transmission jack under the transmission and support the unit.
19. Match mark the converter and the flex driving plate for reassembly. Remove converter to flex plate attaching screws. Attach a "C" clamp to the edge of the bell housing to secure the converter to the transmission during unit removal.
20. Remove bell housing retaining bolts. Carefully work the transmission and converter assembly rearward off the engine block

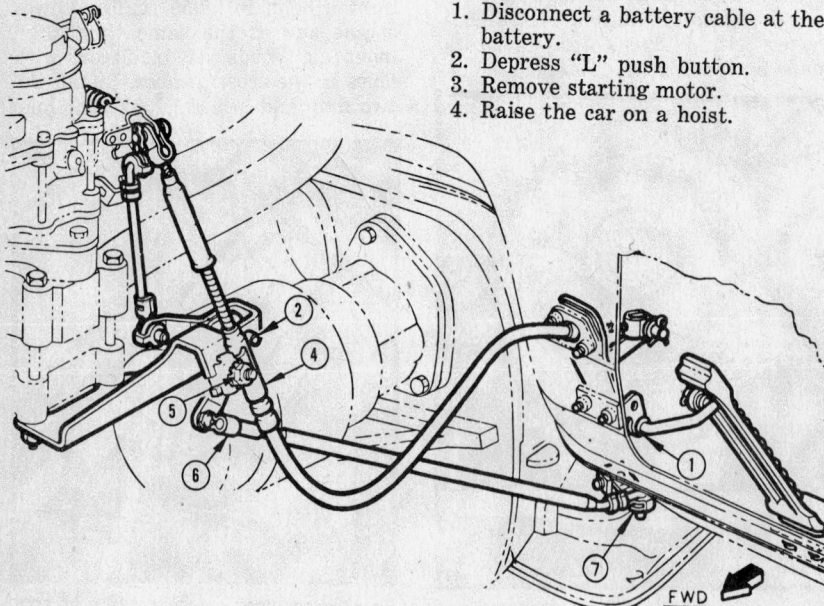

1962 cable throttle

(1963 DART, SEE VALIANT)

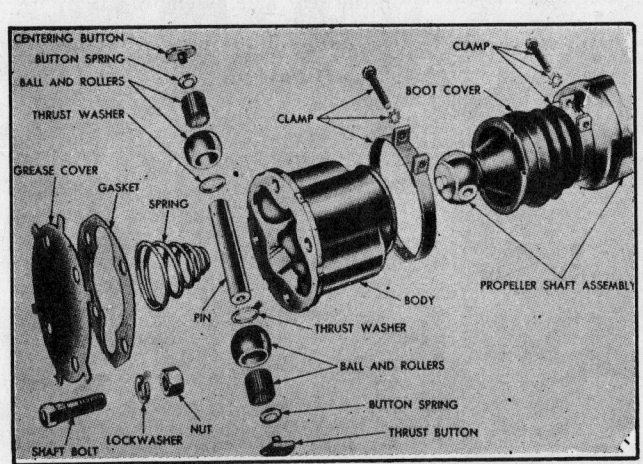

Exploded view—ball and trunnion type universal joint

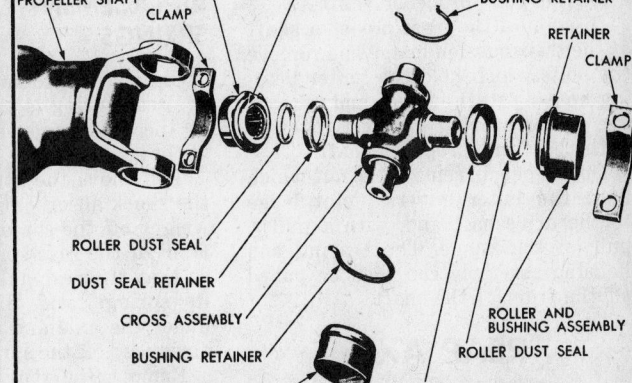

Exploded view—cross and bearing type universal joint

dowls and the converter hub out of the crankshaft.

21. Lower the transmission jack and remove the transmission and converter assembly.

Reinstall by Reversing above Procedure

UNIVERSAL JOINTS AND DRIVE LINE

DISASSEMBLY OF THE CROSS AND BEARING TYPE JOINT

The cross and bearing type joint can be identified readily since the joint is not covered.

To disassemble the joint, remove the four bolts which hold the two bearing assemblies to the companion flange and knock the bearings off the flange.

To remove the bearings from the yoke, first remove the bearing retainer lock washers or C washers, and then pressing on one of the bearings, press the bearing in towards the center of the joint which will force the cross to push the opposite bearing out of the universal joint yoke. After it has been pushed all the way out of the yoke, pull up the cross slightly and pack some washers under it and then press on the end of the cross from which the bearing was just removed to force the first bearing out of the yoke.

Perhaps the easiest way to reassemble is to start both bearing retainers into the yoke at the same time, hold the cross carefully in the fingers and squeeze both bearings in a vise or heavy C clamp. Driving the bearings into place usually cocks the little rollers greatly reducing the life of the bearings.

Reinstall the locking devices.

BALL AND TRUNNION TYPE JOINT

The housing of the ball and trunnion type joint is held to its companion flange by four bolts. Remove the four bolts and pry the cover assembly backwards away from the companion flange so that the shaft can be lowered. If two ball and trunnion type joints are used both must be disconnected from their companion flanges in order to get the driveshaft over to the bench.

Remove the grease cover which will release the centering spring.

Remove the centering button spring and the ball and roller assemblies from the cross pin. Supporting the propeller shaft ball, press out the cross pin.

The cover and boot assembly can then be slid off the end of the propeller shaft.

Some models of DeSoto and Dodge use a cross and bearing type joint at the rear joint and a ball and trunnion type at the front.

Ball and trunnion type universal joints do not require a slip yoke since the driveshaft can work back and forth in the universal joint housing.

PROPELLER SHAFT CENTER BEARING

Some models of the DeSoto and Dodge use a three universal joint drive line having two drive shafts

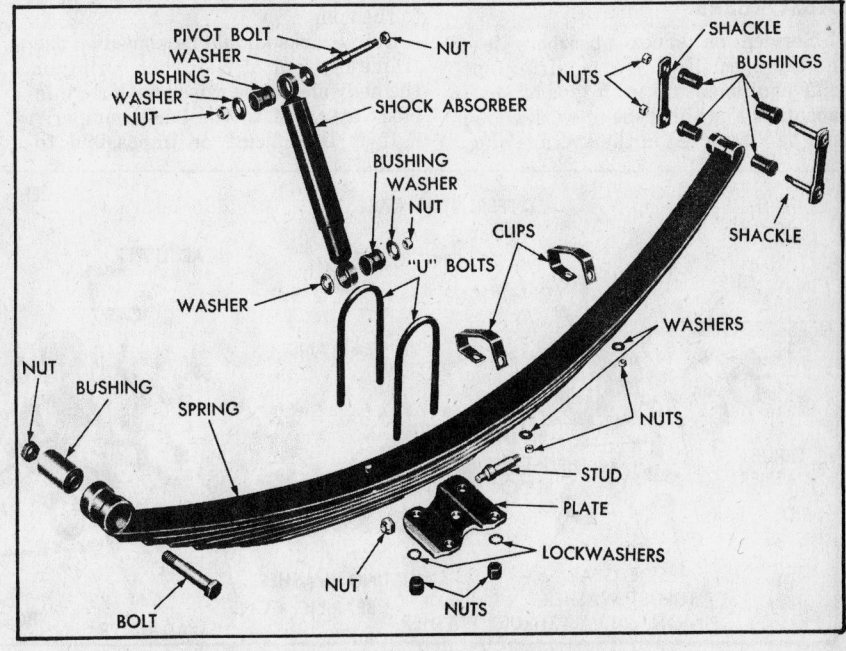

Rear Spring and Shackles (Disassembled View)

and a center support bearing. The center support bearing and housing assembly is removed with the front driveshaft.

Split the rear universal joint and remove the rear propeller shaft.

Disconnect the front propeller shaft at the transmission flange and remove the bolts which hold the center bearing housing to the frame and take off the center bearing housing, together with the front propeller shaft.

On the bench, remove the nut which holds the center universal joint flange to the driveshaft and, with a puller, pull off the flange. The bearing and housing assembly can then be pulled off the front of the shaft.

REAR AXLE

TROUBLE SHOOTING AND ADJUSTMENT

General instructions covering the troubles of the rear axle and how to repair and adjust it, together with information on installation of rear axle bearings and grease seals, are given in the general section under the heading: Axles, Rear.

Capacities of the rear axle are given in the Capacities Tables of this section.

REPLACEMENT OF REAR SHOCK ABSORBER

On all Desoto and Dodge models a direct acting shock absorber is used. To remove it simply detach at the top and bottom and lift off the car.

SERVICE ON SHOCK ABSORBERS

Service on shock absorbers is a highly specialized job requiring specific equipment for each type of shock absorber and this type of work should not be attempted in the average shop.

If the shock absorber is defective or inefficient, it should be replaced with a new or rebuilt one.

REPLACEMENT OF REAR SPRINGS

On all DeSoto and Dodge models the rear spring is hung on the frame at the front and through a shackle at the rear end.

To remove the spring, first remove the shock absorber and then take the weight off the car on a stand jack in front of the rear spring, high enough so that the rear axle will hang from its springs, and then place a jack under the axle and take some of the down-load off the spring.

Remove the four nuts which hold the U bolt to the axle housing and let the lockplate fall down.

Take out the two nuts which hold the rear shackle, the top one to the frame, the bottom one to the spring, and drive off the rear shackle.

Remove the single bolt which holds the spring at the front and lower the spring to the floor.

REMOVAL OF REAR AXLE ASSEMBLY

To remove the rear axle assembly on all Dodge and DeSoto models, detach the brake line at the T fitting, detach the rear universal joint, remove the rear shock absorbers, remove the nuts which hold the U bolts to the rear springs and rear axle housing and disconnect the spring at the back link and let the spring drop to the floor.

Stand jacks should be placed on the frame in front of the front spring or the body should be raised with a chain block attached to the back bumper.

If it is difficult or impossible to raise the car sufficiently high to let the rear wheels pass under the fenders, the rear wheels can be removed. Roll the rear axle assembly out from underneath the car.

On models which use a rear torsion bar it will be necessary to detach the torsion bar before removing the axle.

Replace the rear axle assembly by reversing the procedure which removed it.

RADIO R & R

Removing the Radio (Dodge)

To remove the radio, proceed as follows:

(1) Disconnect battery.

(2) Disconnect antenna lead, light lead and speaker leads.

(3) Remove control knobs.

(4) Remove shaft mounting nuts.

(5) Remove bracket-to-receiver attaching bolt.

(6) Remove speaker grille from top side of instrument panel by lifting up the left corner and sliding the grille out.

(7) Remove speaker mounting screws.

(8) Remove speaker assembly.

(9) Remove radio through the speaker opening of instrument panel.

Installing the Radio (Dodge)

To install the radio, proceed as follows:

(1) Enter radio receiver through instrument panel speaker opening.

(2) Install radio in instrument panel.

(3) Install shaft mounting nuts.

(4) Install bracket-to-receiver attaching bolt.

(5) Connect the antenna, light lead, lead and speaker leads.

(6) Install speaker assembly in instrument panel.

(7) Install speaker grille.

(8) Connect battery.

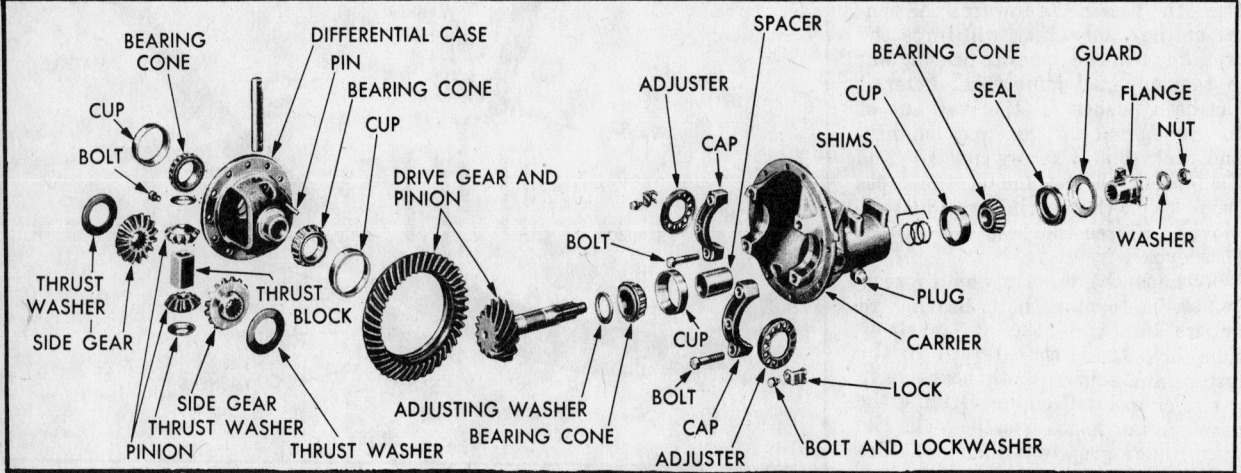

Rear Axle V-8—8¾ inch Ring Gear

Page

AIR CONDITIONING

Service 1092

BRAKES, HYDRAULIC

Adjustments 938
Bleed brakes 941
Parking brake lever & cable ... 295
Master cylinder, R & R 295
Master cylinder service 939
References 295

BRAKES, POWER

Power unit, R & R 296
Power unit overhaul 954
Trouble shooting 954

CLUTCH

Clutch assembly, R & R 308

COOLING SYSTEM

Radiator core, R & R 298
Thermostat 299
Water pump, R & R 299

ELECTRICAL SYSTEM

Battery 295
Distributor, R & R 293
Distributor specifications 289
Fuses and circuit breakers 289
Gauges 1024
Generator and regulator
    specifications 289
Generator, R & R 298
Generator service 1026
Generator truble shooting chart 1026
Horn buttons 307
Ignition firing order & timing .. 288
Ignition timing specifications ... 289
Instruments 295
Starter, R & R 295
Starter specifications 290
Starter systems 1046

ENGINE ASSEMBLY

Cylinder head, R & R 300
Cylinder head, tightening
    sequences 291
Engine assembly, R & R 299
Engine firing order & timing ... 288
Engine marking code 291
Engine diagnosis 1012
Engine references 299
Exhaust 297
Engine lubrication 305
Oil pan, R & R 305
Oil pressure specifications 290
Oil filter 305
Piston and rod, R & R 305
Piston specifications 290

Page

ENGINE ASSEMBLY—continued

Rocker arms & shaft 301
Specifications, general, engine .. 290
Timing chain & cover 303
Trouble shooting charts 1012
Tune-up specifications 289
Valve adjusting sequence 301
Valve specifications 290
Valve lifter hyd. 302
Valves and guides 301

ENGINE LUBRICATION

Oil filter 305
Oil pan, R & R 305

EXHAUST SYSTEM

Manifold, R & R 297
Tail & exhaust pipe 297

FUEL SYSTEM

Carburetors, adjustments 972
Carburetor references 297
Fuel gauge service 1024
Fuel pump pressure 289
Fuel pump, R & R 297
Fuel pump service 1020
Fuel tank, R & R 297

INSTRUMENTS

References 295
Instruments, R & R 295

REAR AXLE AND SUSPENSION

Axle shaft, R&R 312
Axle shaft oil seal 918
Pinion bearings 918
Ring gear & pinion 918
Rear spring 312
Trouble shooting 919

SPECIFICATIONS

Battery 290
Brake cylinder sizes 289
Capacities:
    Axle, rear 290
    Cooling system 290
    Crankcase 290
    Fuel tank 290
    Transmission, automatic ... 290
    Transmission, manual 290
Chassis, general 289
Distributor 289
Engine, general 290
Fuses and circuit breakers 289
General and regulators 289
Ignition timing 289
Main bearings 290
Model identification illustrations .288
Pistons 290
Quick reference specifications ... 288

Page

SPECIFICATIONS—continued

Rod bearings 290
Starters 290
Torque wrench 289
Tune-up 289
Valves 290
Wheel alignment 290

STEERING, MANUAL

Adjust gear housing 1052
Gear assembly, R & R 307
Horn button, R & R 307
Steering wheel, R & R 307

STEERING, POWER

Pump assembly 1058
Reference 308
Trouble shooting 1081
Unit overhaul 1058

SUSPENSION, FRONT

Alignment procedures 1082
Alignment specifications 290
Ball joints, R & R 1087
Camber, adjust 1087
Caster, adjust 1087
King pins and bushings 1087
Knuckle supports 1087
References 306
Support arms, pins and
    bushings 306
Toe-in, adjust 1082

TRANSMISSION, AUTOMATIC

Disassembly of Fordomatic
    transmission
    2 speed 838
Linkage, adjust Fordomatic 310
Transmission, R & R Fordomatic .. 311

TRANSMISSION, MANUAL SHIFT

Disassemble transmission 309
References 309
Transmission, R & R 308

TROUBLE CHECKS

Procedures 1

TUNE-UP

Carburetors 972
Procedures 291
Specifications 289
Engine diagnosis 1012

UNIVERSAL JOINT AND DRIVE LINE

Disassemble U joint 312
U joint & drive shaft, R & R 312

FAIRLANE AND METEOR

YEAR IDENTIFICATION

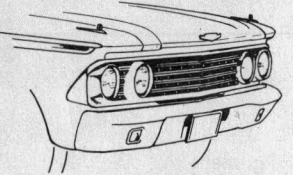

1962 FAIRLANE

1962 METEOR

1963 FAIRLANE

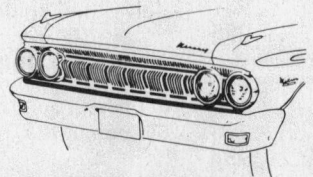

1963 METEOR

QUICK WORKING SPECIFICATIONS

Breaker Point Gap (In.)
1962-63 6-Cyl. .... .025
    221 cu. in. V8 .... .015
    260 cu. in. V8 .... .015

Cam Angle
1962-63 6-Cyl. .... 35°
    221 cu. in. V8 .... 26°
    260 cu. in. V8 .... 27°

Spark Plugs
	Type	Gap
1962-63 6-Cyl.	BF82	.035
221 cu. in. V8	BF92	.035
260 cu. in. V8	BF82	.035

GENERATOR AND REGULATOR SPECIFICATIONS

YEAR AND SERIES	GENERATOR Field Current In Amperes 6 Volt	12 Volt	Cut-out Closing Voltage	REGULATOR Current Regulator Setting	Voltage Regulator Setting
1962-63	—	1.5	12.8	25	15.0

(A) Surrounding temperatures guide this adjustment. Higher temperatures require lower settings. Lower temperatures permit higher settings, within limits.

Ignition Timing
Before Top Dead Center
  6-Cyl. Automatic ....12° BTC
  6-Cyl. Manual .... 6° BTC
  8-Cyl. All .... 6° BTC
Set idle at 500 RPM

Valves
Operating Tappet Clearance in Inches Hot

		Int.	Ex.
1962	6-Cyl.	.016	.016
	221 cu. in. V8	Zero	Zero
	260 cu. in. V8	Zero	Zero
1963	6-Cyl.	Zero	Zero
	221 cu. in.	Zero	Zero
	260 cu. in.	Zero	Zero

CAPACITIES

Engine Crankcase (Quarts)
  (Add 1 Qt. for new Filter)
1962-63 6-Cyl. 3½
    221 cu. in. V8 4
    260 cu. in. V8 4

Transmission, Manual (Pts.)
1962-63 6-Cyl. 2½
    221 cu. in. V8 3
    260 cu. in. V8 3

Transmission, Automatic (Pts.)
1962-63 All 13

Rear Axle (Pts.)
1962-63 All 4½

Gasoline Tank (Gallons)
1962-63 All 16

Cooling System (Quarts)
Add 1 Qt. for Heater
1962-63 6-Cyl. 8½
    221 cu. in. V8 .... 13½
    260 cu. in. V8 .... 13½

Torque Wrench Readings
(Foot Pounds)
Cylinder Head Bolts
1962-63 6-Cyl. 65-75
    221 cu. in. V8 65-70
    260 cu. in. V8 65-70

FIRING ORDER and TIMING

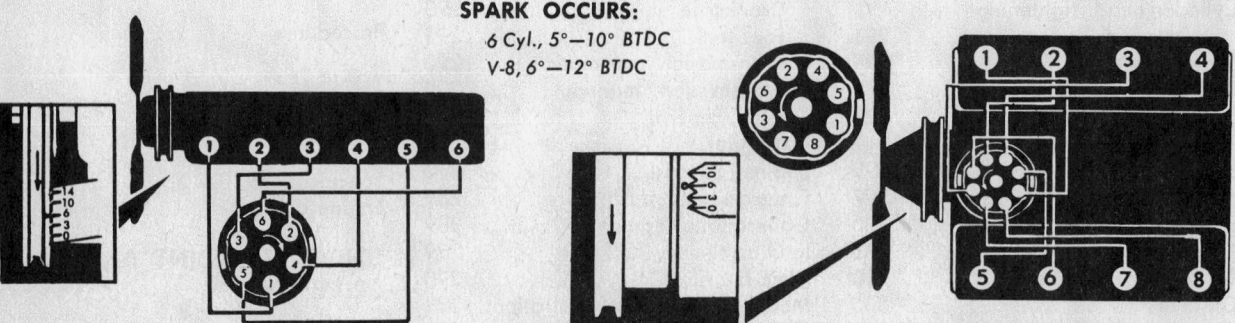

SPARK OCCURS:
6 Cyl., 5°—10° BTDC
V-8, 6°—12° BTDC

THESE ARE APPROXIMATE SETTINGS. ENGINE DESIGN, ALTITUDE, TEMPERATURE, FUEL AND ENGINE CONDITION WILL ALL INFLUENCE TIMING. THE DETERMINING FACTOR, LIMITING ADVANCE, WILL STILL BE THE "KNOCK POINT" OF THE INDIVIDUAL ENGINE.

TUNE UP SPECIFICATIONS

YEAR AND MODEL	SPARK PLUGS		DISTRIBUTOR			Ignition Timing	Compression Pressure Cranking	VALVES Tappet Clearance Hot		Inlet Opens	Fuel Pump Pressure	Engine Idle Speed
	Type	Gap	Cam Angle	Point Gap	Arm Spring Tension			Inlet	Exhaust			
1962-63, 6 Cyl.	BF82	.035	35	.025	17-20	Note 1	170	.016*	.016*	15°B	4.5	500
V-8, 221 cu. in.	BF92	.035	26	.015	17-20	Note 1	150	Zero	Zero	15°B	5	500
V-8, 260 cu. in.	BF82	.035	27	.015	17-20	Note 1	150	Zero	Zero	21°B	5	**500**

NOTE: See firing order and timing illustrations on previous page.

* Late production 1963, zero clearance hydraulic valve tappets are used.

DISTRIBUTOR SPECIFICATIONS

YEAR AND MODEL	Part Number	Rotation	Cam Angle	BREAKER		GOVERNOR CONTROL @ DIST. R.P.M.		VACUUM CONTROL		
				Point Gap (Inch)	Arm Spring (Ounces)	Advance Starts	Full Advance	Inches Vacuum To Start	Inches Vacuum For Full Advance	Max. Adv. of Dist. In Degrees
1962—6 Cyl. Std.	C1DF-12127B	C	36	.025	17-20	NONE	NONE	0.43	10.0	16½
6 Cyl. Auto.	C2DF-12127C	C	36	.025	17-20	NONE	NONE	0.35	10.0	11¾
V8 All	C20F-12127E	CC	26	.015	17-20	1 @ 525	12¾ @ 2000	5.00	20.0	10½
1963										
6 Cyl. Standard	CD3Z-12127-A	C	35	.025	17-20	None	None	0.43	10.0	16½
6 Cyl. Auto.	C30Z-12127-A	C	35	.025	17-20	None	None	0.35	10.0	11¾
V-8, 221 Cu. In.	C3AZ-12127U	CC	26	.015	17-20	1 @ 525	13 @ 2000	5.00	20.0	10½
V-8, Std. 260 Cu. In.	CD3Z-12127-B	CC	27	.015	17-20	1 @ 525	11 @ 2000	5.00	18.0	11
V-8, Auto. 260 Cu. In.	C20Z-12127-B	CC	27	.015	17-20	1 @ 525	13 @ 2000	5.00	18.0	11

GENERATOR AND REGULATOR SPECIFICATIONS

MODEL AND YEAR	GENERATORS				REGULATORS		
	Field Current in Amperes At 12 Volts	Brush Spring Tension	CUT OUT RELAY		Current And Voltage Regulators Air Gap	Current Regulator Setting	Voltage Regulator Setting
			Air Gap	Closing Voltage			
1962-63	1.5	32-40	A	12.8	A	25	14.6 @ 75°F

NOTE A: No Adjustment

ENGINE TORQUE SPECIFICATIONS

YEAR AND MODEL	Cylinder Head Bolts	Rod Bearing Bolts	Main Bearing Bolts	Crankshaft Pulley Bolt	Flywheel to Crankshaft Bolts	MANIFOLD	
						Intake	Exhaust
1962-63, 6 Cyl.	65-75	19-24	65-70	45-55	75-85	None	13-18
V-8, All	65-70	19-24	65-75	70-90	75-85	12-15	13-18

GENERAL CHASSIS and BRAKE SPECIFICATIONS

Year and Model	Chassis		Brake Cylinder Bore		
	Overall Length in Inches	Tire Size	Master Cyl. (Inch)	Wheel Cylinder Diameter—(Inch)	
				Front	Rear
1962-63 Fairlane 6 Cyl.	197	6.50 x 13	1	1⅛	29/32
Fairlane 8 Cyl.	197	7.00 x 13	1	1⅛	29/32
Meteor 6 Cyl.	203.8	6.50 x 14	1	1⅛	29/32
Meteor 8 Cyl.	203.8	7.00 x 14	1	1⅛	29/32

FUSES AND CIRCUIT BREAKERS

CIRCUIT	SIZE	LOCATION
Headlamp	12 Amp. Circuit Breaker	Switch
License Lamp	SFE 15	Fuse Panel
Rear, Tail, Stop	SFE 15	Fuse Panel
Dome Light	SFE 7.5	Fuse Panel
Turn Signals	SFE 14	Fuse Panel
Radio	SFE 7.5	Fuse Panel

FAIRLANE AND METEOR

BATTERY AND STARTER SPECIFICATIONS

YEAR AND MODEL	Battery				Starters						Brush Spring Tension
	Ampere Hour Capacity	Volts	Terminal Grounded		Lock Test			No-Load Test			
					Amps.	Volts	Torque	Amps.	Volts	R.P.M.	
1962-63	40	12	Neg.		67	Max. .6	15.5	70	12	9500	45

PISTON AND PIN SPECIFICATIONS

YEAR AND MODEL	SKIRT CLEARANCE		PISTON PINS			FIT		
	Top	Bottom	Diameter	Bushing	In Rod	In Piston	Lock
1962-63—All	.0025	.007-.0023	.912	None	Press	.0002	PRESS

VALVE SPECIFICATIONS

YEAR AND MODEL	Seat Angle		Intake Valve Lift	Exhaust Valve Lift	Valve Spring Pressure		Stem to Guide Clearance		Stem Diameter		Are Valve Guides Replaceable
	In	Ex			Outer	Inner	In.	Ex.	In.	Ex.	
1962-63											
6 cyl., 170 cu. in.	45°	45°	.344	.344	52 @ 1-19/32	None	.0016	.0026	.3104	.3094	No
V-8, 221 cu. in.	45°	45°	.380	.380	52 @ 1-19/32	None	.0016	.0026	.3104	.3094	No
V-8, 260 cu. in.	45°	45°	.380	.380	60 @ 1-49/64	None	.0016	.0026	.3104	.3094	No

FRONT WHEEL ALIGNMENT

YEAR	Caster		Camber		Toe-In (Inches)	King-Pin Inclination (Degrees)	Wheel Pivot Ratio	
	Range (Degrees)	Pref.	Range (Degrees)	Pref.			Outer Wheel	Inner Wheel
1962-63—All	½N to ½P	0	0 to ½P	½P	1/8	7¼	20°	21¾°

CAPACITIES

YEAR AND MODEL	Engine Crankcase Add 1 Qt. For New Filter	TRANSMISSION PINTS TO REFILL AFTER DRAINING			Rear Axle Pints	Gas Tank Gallons	Cooling System Quarts Add 1 Qt. For Heater
		Manual 3 Speed	Manual 4 Speed	Automatic			
1962-63							
6 cyl., 170 cu. in.	3½	2½	3	13	4½	16	8½
V-8, 221 cu. in.	4	3	3	13	4½	16	13½
V-8, 260 cu. in.	4	3	3	13	4½	16	13½

GENERAL ENGINE SPECIFICATIONS

YEAR AND MODEL	Bore And Stroke	No. Of Main Bearings	Type Valve Lifter	Cu. In Piston Displacement	AMA Horse Power	Advertised Horse Power At Stated RPM	Advertised Torque At Stated RPM	Compression Ratio	Oil Pressure At 30 MPH	Camshaft Drive
1962-63										
6 cyl., 170 cu. in.	3½ x 2-15/16	4	Mech. Adj.*	170	29.4	101 @ 4400	156 @ 2400	8.7-1	45	Chain
V-8, 221 cu. in.	3½ x 2⅞	5	Hydraulic	221	39.2	145 @ 4400	216 @ 2200	8.7-1	50	Chain
V-8, 260 cu. in.	3-51/64 x 2⅞	5	Hydraulic	260	46.2	164 @ 4400	258 @ 2200	8.7-1	55	Chain

* Late production 1963, zero clearance hydraulic valve tappets are used.

CRANKSHAFT BEARING JOURNAL SIZES

YEAR AND MODEL	MAIN BEARING JOURNALS				CONNECTING ROD BEARING JOURNALS		
	Journal Diameter	Oil Clearance	End Play of Shaft	End Play Held by	Journal Diameter	Oil Clearance	End Play
1962-63							
6 cyl., 170 cu. in.	2.2485	.0012	.006	3	2.1236	.0015	.007
V-8, 221 cu. in.	2.2485	.0012	.006	3	2.1236	.0015	.007
V-8, 260 cu. in.	2.2485	.0012	.006	3	2.1236	.0015	.007

CYLINDER HEAD NUT TIGHTENING SEQUENCE

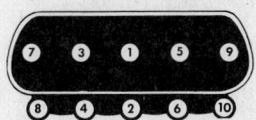

1962-63 V-8. Tighten in 3 steps.
Step 1. To 50 ft.-lb.
Step 2. To 60 ft.-lb.
Step 3. To 70 ft.-lb.

1962-63 Six Cyl. Tighten in 3 steps.
Step 1. To 55 ft.-lb.
Step 2. To 65 ft.-lb.
Step 3. To 75 ft.-lb.

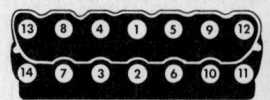

CAR SERIAL NUMBER LOCATION AND ENGINE IDENTIFICATION

ENGINE IS IDENTIFIED THRU CAR SERIAL NUMBER

Fairlane and Meteor **serial numbers** and other pertinent information are to be found on a plate riveted to the rear edge of the left front door.

The **engine number** is stamped on the top surface of the engine block near the crankcase breather pipe, (front left side).

The car serial number is composed of two sections, the first five units give the year, assembly plant, model, and the engine used. The second section of the number gives the consecutive order of production.

First, Digit "2" designates 1962, (3-1963 etc.).

Second, Letter—Assembly Plant:
"A"—Atlanta
"F"—Dearborn
"K"—Kansas City
"R"—San Jose
"S"—Pilot Plant

Third, Two Digits:
Fairlane
or
Meteor
31-2 Door
32-4 Door

Fairlane 500
or
Meteor Custom
41-2 Door
42-4 Door
Meteor
Sport
47-S-33

Fourth, Letter:
U—OHV-6, 170 cu. in. engine.
L—V8, 221 cu. in. engine.
F—V8, 260 cu. in. engine.
The remaining digits comprise the consecutive order of unit production.

TUNE-UP

TUNE-UP AND DIAGNOSIS OPERATIONS ARE PERFORMED IN THE CONVENTIONAL MANNER REGARDLESS OF ENGINE BEING USED. SEE SPECIFICATIONS CHARTS ON PRECEDING PAGES.

Compression

1. Blow foreign matter from plug wells. Then loosen all spark plugs one turn.
2. Start engine and accelerate a couple of times to blow out dislodged carbon particles.
3. Stop engine and remove plug wires and spark plugs.
4. Remove air cleaner and block choke and throttle in wide open position.
5. Hook up starter remote control cable and insert compression gauge in plug port.
6. Crank engine through about four compression strokes and record highest reading.
7. Do the same with the remaining cylinders. Compression pressures should be 170 ± 20 lbs. for the 6 cyl. engine and 150 ± 20 lbs. for the V-8 engines. Pressure variation between the high cylinder and low cylinder should not exceed 10 lbs.

Note:

A compression check should be the first step in tune-up procedure. Only if compression pressures are within limits, should tune-up be continued.

Spark Plugs

Use a good spark plug tester, if available. A visual check should disclose any worn electrodes, glazed, broken or blistered porcelains and heavy carbon deposits or oil damp. Clean or replace spark plugs as required. Install spark plugs and torque to 15-20 ft. lbs. (When new spark plugs are installed in a new replacement head, torque plugs to 20-30 ft. lbs.)

Ignition System

1. Examine and replace brittle or otherwise damaged spark plug wires, (don't forget the coil-to-distributor cap wire).
2. Tighten all ignition system connections.
3. Remove distributor cap, clean cap and inspect for cracks, carbon tracking and burnt or corroded terminals. Replace the cap if necessary.
4. Clean rotor and inspect for damage.
5. 6 Cyl. (Loadomatic Distributor) Check freedom of distributor vacuum advance action by pushing the breaker plate connecting lever hard against the diaphragm spring; then release it to see if spring tension will return the breaker plate to full retard. The old suction-and-tongue method can be applied at the vacuum line to the distributor to check for cracks or porosity of the vacuum control diaphragm.
5A. V-8 (Dual Advance Distributor) Check distributor governor ad-

vance action by twisting the rotor in a counterclockwise direction as far as possible. Release the rotor to see if spring tension is enough to return the cam to the fully retarded position. Check vacuum advance control mechanism in the same manner as in step 5, with the 6 cyl., Loadomatic Distributor.

6. Examine points, adjust or renew as necessary.

Note:

When setting used breaker points, use a dwell meter. It is nearly impossible to accurately adjust the gap of used points with a feeler gauge. This is due to irregularities of the point surfaces.

Battery and Cables

1. Visually inspect battery case, cables and carrier for any condition which would interfere with good service. Make corrections.
2. Measure the specific gravity of the electrolite in each cell. If it is below 1.230 (at about 80°F) recharge the battery and further check for a drain or trouble in the charging circuit.
3. Connect a voltmeter across the battery terminals and measure the terminal voltage during cranking (coil secondary lead removed to prevent engine starting). If terminal voltage is below 9.25 volts, make a test on the battery.

Fan Belt

1. Inspect condition of fan belt.
2. Check and adjust, if necessary, for correct tension as follows:
   A. If a tension gauge is available, locate the gauge on the belt between the fan pulley and generator pulley.
   B. Adjust generator position to obtain 90 lb. gauge reading for a new belt or 70 lb. reading for a belt that has been in service over 1,000 miles.
   C. If no gauge is available, adjust belt tension so as to obtain ½ inch belt deflection by applying 15 lb. thumb pressure to the belt midway between generator and fan pulleys.

Fuel Supply

1. Inspect supply lines and connections for leaks or defects and correct.
2. If a starving condition exists, check and compare pressures on the outlet side of the fuel pump against the outlet side of the fuel filter. The difference will indicate whether or not the filtering element is at fault and needs changing.

Carburetor

6 Cyl.
A single barreled, manual choke type carburetor is used.
V-8
A Ford two barreled, automatic choke equipped carburetor is used.

For specifications and carburetor adjustments, see "Unit Repair Section," "Carburetors." "Linkage Adjustments" are contained in later paragraphs of this car section under "Automatic Transmission."

Tappet Clearance

Detailed instructions for adjusting

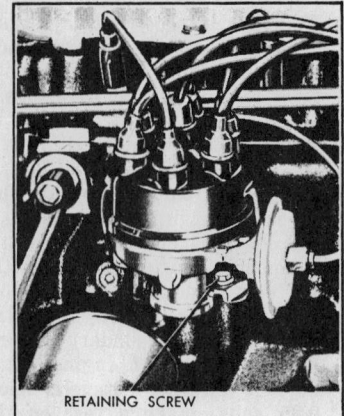

RETAINING SCREW

Distributor Installation, 6 Cyl.

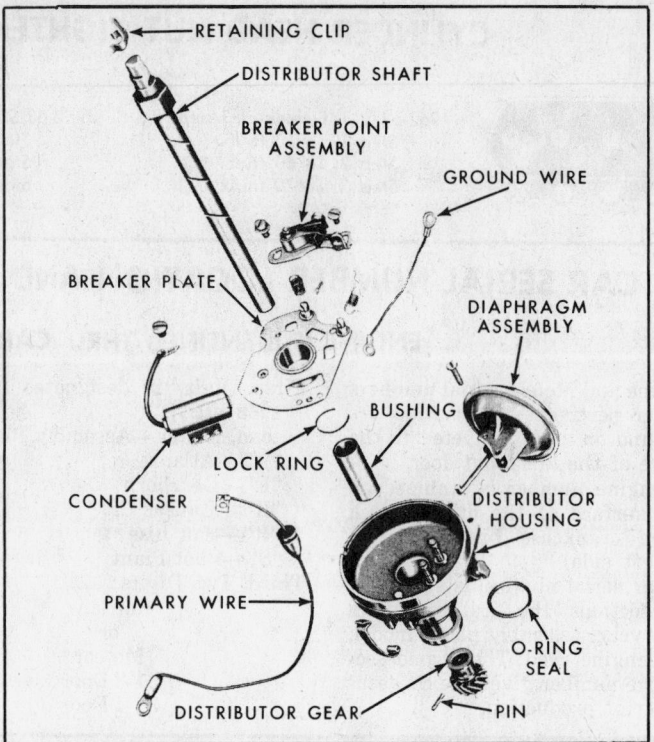

RETAINING CLIP

DISTRIBUTOR SHAFT

BREAKER POINT ASSEMBLY

GROUND WIRE

BREAKER PLATE

DIAPHRAGM ASSEMBLY

BUSHING

LOCK RING

CONDENSER

DISTRIBUTOR HOUSING

PRIMARY WIRE

O-RING SEAL

DISTRIBUTOR GEAR

PIN

Distributor Assembly, 6 Cyl.

the tappet operating clearance of both the 6 cyl. engine and V-8 engines, may be found later in this car section under the "Valve System."

Ignition Timing

Note:

Initial timing is based upon averages. It is merely a point at which to start making adjustments, influenced by existing conditions. The final setting will still be the "knock-point" of the individual engine.

1. Connect a timing light at #1 spark plug and battery.
2. Disconnect spark advance vacuum hose from distributor spark advance unit. Plug the vacuum line.
3. Operate the engine at idle. Be sure it is below 550 R.P.M. so that there will be no centrifugal advance on engines with Dual-Advance distributors (V-8 engine).
4. If the pointer does not align with the proper timing mark, rotate the distributor until the correct mark and the pointer are aligned.
   On the 6 cyl. engine, advance the timing by rotating the distributor body in a counterclockwise direction.
   On the V-8 engines, advance the timing by rotating the distributor body in a clockwise direction.

Note:

Initial timing may be advanced as much as 5° beyond recommended set-

ting. However, retarding the spark beyond 2° B.T.C. is not recommended.

5. Do not forget to hook up the vacuum line to the distributor before road testing the car for final timing adjustment.

Idle Speed and Mixture Adjustments

Note:

It is advisable to make idle fuel mixture adjustment with the air cleaner in place.

1. Run the engine for at least 20 minutes, or until normal operating temperature has been reached. On a car equipped with air conditioning, run the air conditioner for 15 minutes prior to adjusting the idle.
2. Securely set parking brake. Then place standard transmissions in "Neutral" position and automatic transmission in "Drive."
3. Check engine speed and adjust idle to specified R.P.M.
4. Make initial mixture adjustment by turning the mixture needle (2 needles on V-8) in until it is lightly seated. Then back out 1½ turns. **This is merely a starting point and finer adjustment will be likely to obtain ideal idling smoothness.**
5. Turn adjustment needle/s out until the engine begins to "roll" from the rich mixture. Then turn the needle/s in until the engine runs smoothly. In the case of the

two barrel carburetor, both needles should require similar setting within ½ turn of each other. Always favor a slightly rich mixture rather than a lean one.

6. Recheck idle speed and adjust to specifications.

DISTRIBUTOR

REFERENCES

There are two distinctly different types of distributor used, the "Loadomatic" as used with 6 cyl. engines and the Dual Advance distributor as used with either of the V8 engines.

6 CYL. LOADOMATIC

Ignition timing changes are entirely satisfied by the action of the breaker plate. The position of the plate is controlled by a vacuum-actuated diaphragm working against the tension of two accurately calibrated breaker plate springs. The diaphragm moves the breaker plate in a counterclockwise direction to advance the spark. The springs tend to counteract this movement to return timing to a retarded position. Cam and rotor rotation is in a clockwise direction as viewed from the top.

Distributor Remove

1. Remove distributor cap. Disconnect the primary wire at the coil and the vacuum control line at the distributor.
2. Scribe a mark on the distributor body, showing position of the rotor. Then scribe another mark

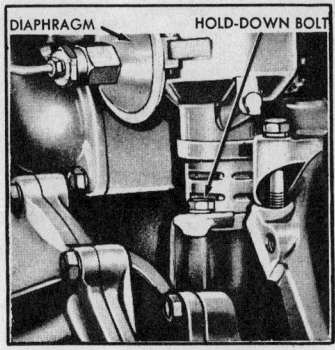

Distributor Installation, V-8.

on the distributor body and engine block, showing the position of the body in the block. These marks can be used to advantage when reassembling the distributor in an undisturbed engine.

3. Remove the screw, lockwasher and hold-down clamp and pull the distributor out of the block. **Do not rotate crankshaft while distributor is out of block** as it will then be necessary to retime ignition.

Distributor Install

1. If ignition timing is required, rotate the crankshaft to bring #1 piston to T.D.C. of its compression stroke.
2. Position the distributor in the block with the rotor at #1 firing position. **Be sure that the oil pump intermediate drive shaft is properly seated in the oil pump.**
3. Install, but do not tighten, the distributor retaining screw.
4. Rotate the distributor body counterclockwise until the breaker

points just start to open.
5. Tighten the retaining clamp screw.
6. Connect the distributor primary wire.
7. Install distributor cap.
8. Start the engine and check ignition timing with a timing light.
9. Connect the vacuum control line and check advance characteristics with the timing light when the engine is accelerated.

V-8 DUAL ADVANCE

The Dual Advance distributor has two independently operated spark timing control systems. A governor type and a vacuum type control is used on each distributor. Centrifugal weights cause the cam to advance or rotate ahead, relative to the distributor shaft.

The vacuum control mechanism operates through a spring loaded diaphragm and movable breaker plate, about the same as the Loadomatic distributor.

Distributor Remove

1. Disconnect primary wire at coil. Disconnect vacuum advance control line at distributor. Remove distributor cap.
2. Scribe a mark on the distributor body, showing position of the rotor. Then scribe another mark on the distributor body and engine block, to show the position of the body in the block. These marks can be used to an advantage when reassembling the distributor in an undisturbed engine.
3. Remove the distributor hold down cap screw and clamp. Then lift the distributor out of the block.

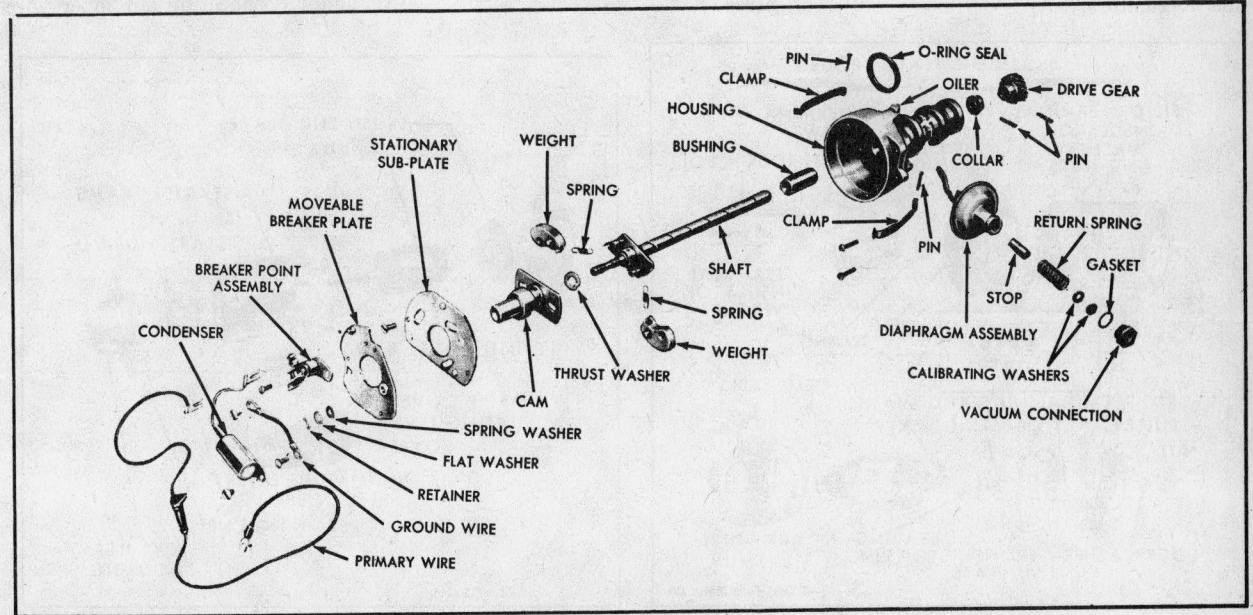

Distributor Assembly V-8.

Distributor Install

1. If ignition timing is required, rotate the crankshaft to bring #1 piston to T.D.C. of its compression stroke.
2. Position distributor in the block with the rotor at #1 firing position. **Be sure that the oil pump intermediate drive shaft is properly seated in the oil pump.**
3. Install, but do not tighten, the distributor retaining clamp and screw.
4. Rotate the distributor body, clockwise until the breaker points just start to open.
5. Tighten the retaining clamp screw.
6. Install distributor cap.
7. Connect distributor primary wire.
8. Start engine and run long enough to obtain engine operating temperature.
9. Idle engine to 500 R.P.M. Then, with a timing light, check the timing marks at the front pulley and make necessary corrections.
10. Connect the vacuum control line to the distributor and check advance characteristics with the timing light when the engine is accelerated.

GENERATOR AND REGULATOR

REFERENCES

The charging system may consist of a D.C. GENERATOR or the newer A.C. UNIT. More detailed information may be obtained on either of these systems from the "Unit Repair" section, under the heading, "Generators and Regulators."

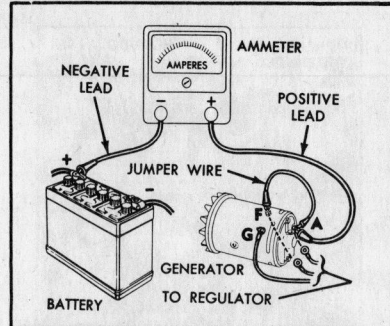

Generator Output Test.

The D.C. Generator uses a negative ground system. Output is controlled by a regulator which is connected between the generator armature and the field. The field is grounded internally.

The armature shaft is supported on both ends by permanently lubricated ball bearings which fit into the end plates.

"D.C." GENERATOR TEST, ON THE CAR

1. Disconnect regulator armature and field wires at the generator.
2. Connect a jumper wire from the generator armature terminal to the generator field terminal and the positive lead of a 0-50 ammeter to the generator armature terminal.
3. Start engine and while it is idling, connect the ammeter negative lead to the positive terminal of the battery.
4. Run engine at 1500 R.P.M. and read the current output on the ammeter. Generator output should reach or exceed 30 amperes.

Note:

Disconnect test leads as soon as test is completed to prevent overheating the generator. Then stop the engine.

GENERATOR REMOVE

1. Disconnect all wires from generator.
2. Remove generator attaching bolts, then remove the generator.

GENERATOR INSTALL

1. Clean mating surfaces of generator frame and mounting bracket.
2. Install generator in the mounting bracket with the two pivot bolts and lock washers.
3. Install the generator belt, and the adjustment arm to generator bolt. Adjust the belt tension and tighten all bolts securely.
4. Connect the armature, field, and ground leads to the generator terminals.
5. Start the engine and check generator operation.

POLARIZING THE "D.C." GENERATOR

To polarize a DC generator on the car, disconnect the field wire and the battery wire from the regulator. With the engine turned off, momentarily connect the two wires together.

Note:

Do not polarize a generator by any method that applies battery voltage to the field terminal of the regulator, such as shorting from the battery terminal to the field terminal of the regulator. Connecting a jumper wire

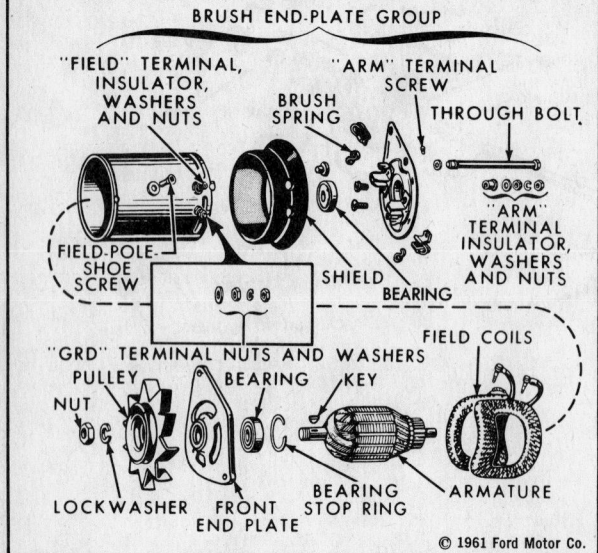

Exploded View of Generator.

© 1961 Ford Motor Co.

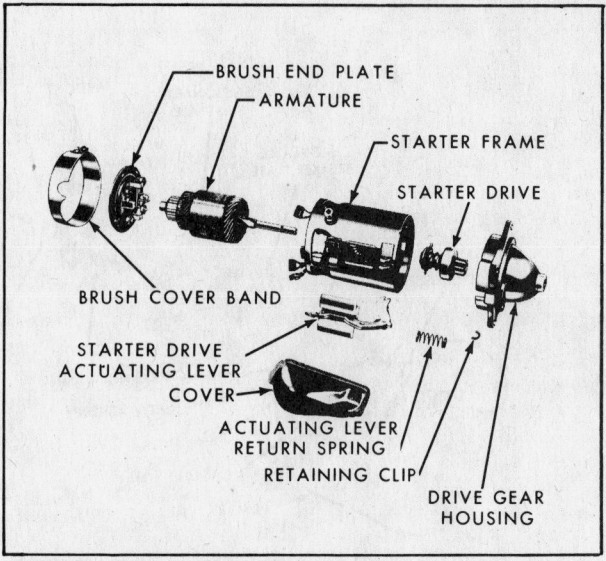

Starter Motor, Exploded View

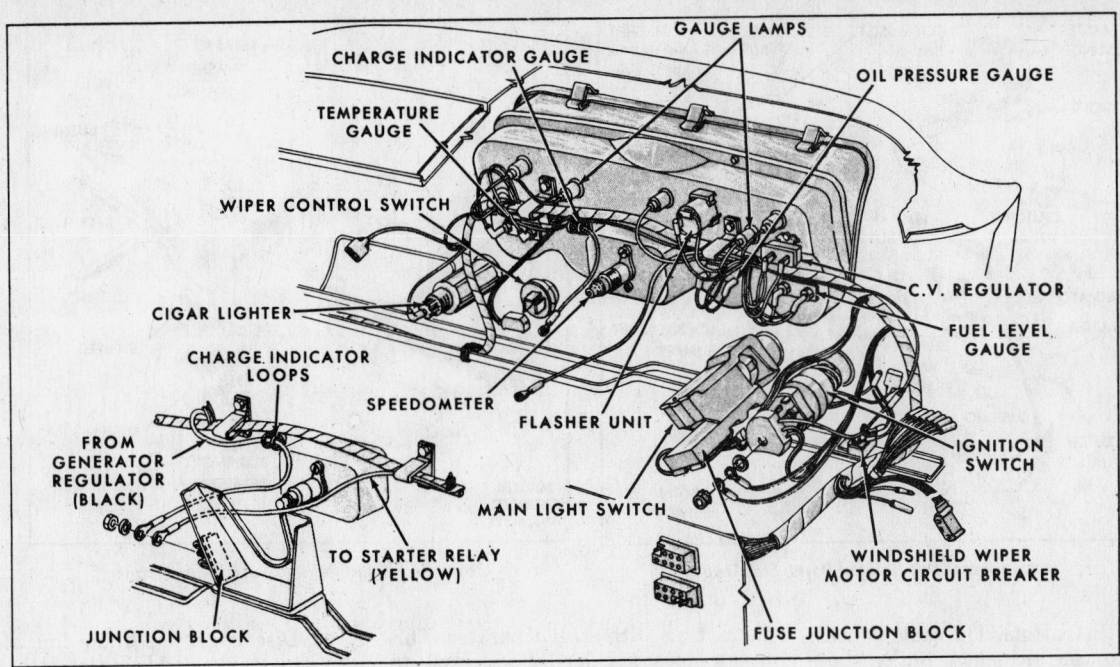

Instrument Panel, Rear View (Meteor).

directly from the battery to the generator field terminal is also taboo. The above practice will cause regulator damage.

Caution: Under no circumstances, should the AC generator be polarized.

INSTRUMENTS

REFERENCES

The instrument cluster includes a charge indicator light, fuel gauge, temperature gauge, oil pressure indicator light, high beam indicator and turn indicator lights and the speedometer. A gauge voltage regulator maintains a constant voltage supply to the fuel gauge and temperature gauge circuits. All of the instruments are electrically operated except the speedometer.

To replace the fuel gauges, temperature gauge, speedometer, and cluster dial, it is necessary to remove the cluster assembly.

Detailed information on the instruments may be found in the "Unit Repair" section under "Gauges."

INSTRUMENT CLUSTER REMOVE

1. Disconnect battery.
2. Disconnect speedometer cable at speedometer head.
3. Detach wiring harness from the two retaining clips at rear of cluster.
4. Protect steering column with shop cloth.
5. Remove cluster retaining screws from instrument panel. Pull out

the cluster and rest it on steering column.
6. Disconnect the wires to the fuel and temperature gauges, turn signal flasher, and constant voltage regulator.
7. Remove lights from instrument cluster.
8. Remove the cluster assembly.
9. Remove the instrument cluster-to-bezel attaching screws, and remove the bezel.
10. Instruments may now be removed.

INSTRUMENT CLUSTER INSTALL

1. Reverse the above procedure. Then check the operation of all gauges, lights and signals.

BATTERY AND STARTER

BATTERY

The battery is a 54 plate, 40 amp. hr., negative ground, 12 volt unit, mounted at the right front fender.

STARTER

Remove

1. Disconnect starter cable at starter.
2. Remove starter attaching screws and remove starter and rubber dust ring.

Install

1. Position rubber dust ring on the flywheel housing, so that the

flared part of the ring makes a good seal to the housing.
2. Position starter to flywheel housing and start the starter attaching screws. (On the 6 cyl. engine with automatic transmission, the transmission dip stick tube bracket is mounted under one of the starter attaching screws.)
3. Snug all attaching screws, then torque to 12-15 ft. lbs.
4. Connect starter cable.

BRAKES

REFERENCES

Single-anchor, internal-expanding, and self adjusting hydraulic brakes are used on all models.

An independent, hand operated parking brake works the rear wheel brake shoes through a mechanical cable linkage.

The self-adjusting brake mechanism consists of a cable, cable guide, adjusting lever, and adjuster spring. The cable is hooked over the anchor pin at the top and is connected to the

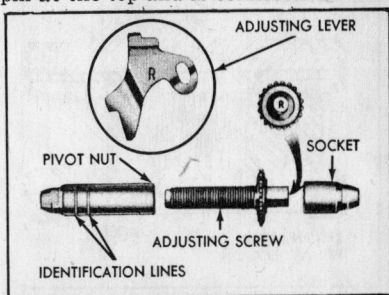

Adjusting Screw and Lever Identification.

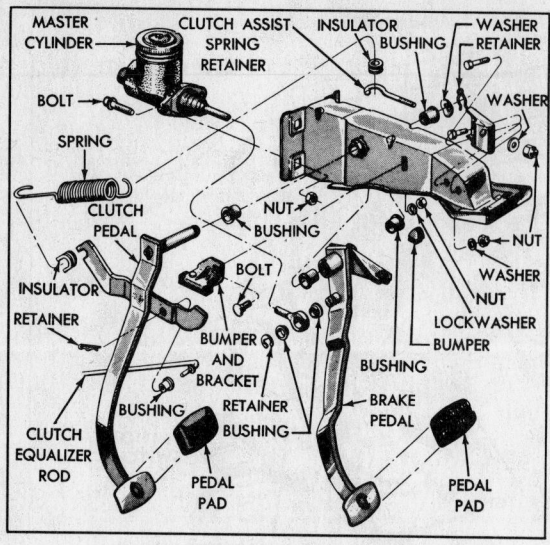

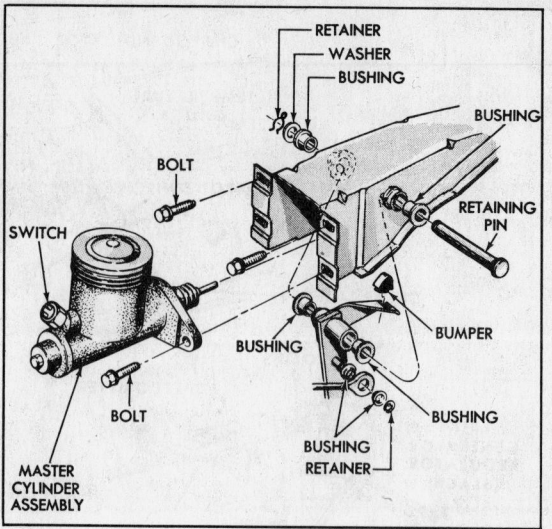

Brake Pedel and Related Parts, Std. Trans.

Brake Pedel and Related Parts, Auto. Trans.

lever at the bottom. The cable is connected to the secondary brake shoe by means of the cable guide. The adjuster spring is hooked to the primary brake shoe and to the lever.

The automatic adjuster operates only when the brakes are applied while the car is moving rearward.

With the car moving rearward and the brakes applied, the "wrapping" action of the shoes following the drum, forces the upper end of the primary shoe against the anchor pin. Action of the wheel cylinder moves the upper end of the secondary shoe away from the anchor pin. Movement of the secondary shoe causes the cable to pull the adjusting lever upward and against the end of a tooth on the adjusting screw star wheel. Upward travel of the lever increases as lining wear increases. When the lever can move far enough upward to pass over the end of the tooth, the adjuster spring pulls the lever downward causing the star-wheel to turn and expand the shoes. The star-wheel is turned one tooth at a time as the linings progressively wear.

Wheel cylinders are of the opposed

piston type with steel separator. This design does not lend itself well to honing.

The master cylinder consists of a single cylinder and reservoir, mounted on the engine side of the fire wall:

Information on brake adjustments, band replacement, bleeding procedure and cylinder reconditioning can be found in the "Unit Repair" section under the heading: "Brakes, Hydraulic."

Information on power brakes can be found in the "Unit Repair" section, under the heading: "Brakes, Power."

POWER BRAKES

A Midland Ross diaphragm type power brake is available on all models.

Power Unit Remove

1. Working inside the car below the instrument panel, disconnect booster valve operating rod from the brake pedal assembly.
2. Open the hood, and disconnect the wires from the stop light switch at the brake master cylinder.

3. Disconnect the brake line at the master cylinder outlet fitting.
4. Disconnect manifold vacuum hose from the booster unit.
5. Remove the four bracket-to-dash panel attaching bolts.
6. Remove the booster and bracket assembly from the dash panel, sliding the valve operating rod out from the engine side of the dash panel.

Power Unit Install

1. Mount the booster and bracket assembly to the dash panel by sliding the valve operating rod in through the hole in the dash panel and installing the attaching bolts.
2. Connect manifold vacuum hose to the booster.
3. Connect the brake line to the master cylinder outlet fitting.
4. Connect stop light switch wires.
5. Working inside the car below the instrument panel, install the rubber boot on the valve operating rod at the passenger side of the dash panel.

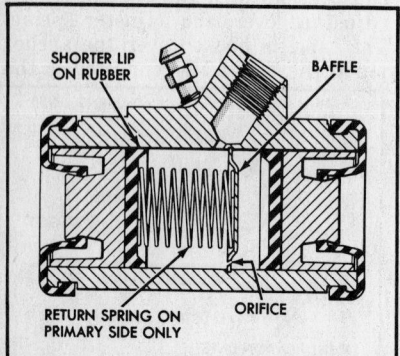

Cross Section of Front Brake Cylinder.

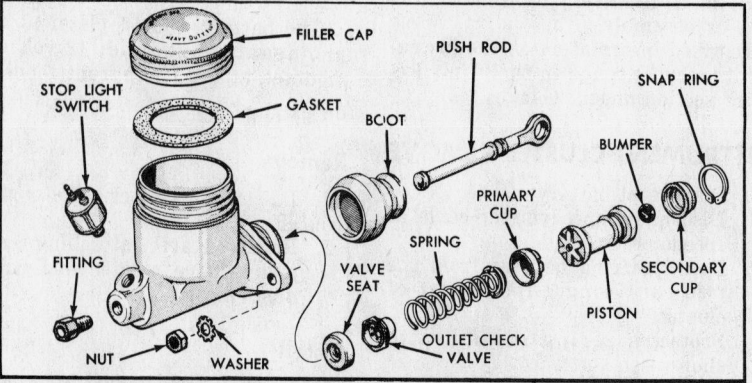

Layout of Master Cylinder

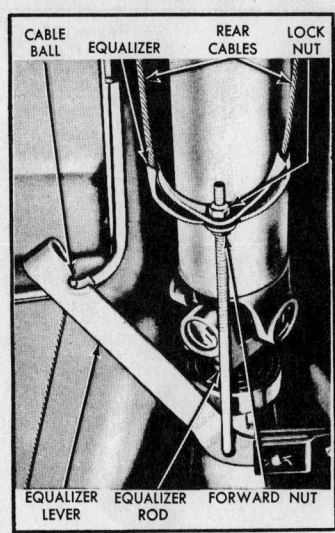

Parking Brake Linkage.

6. Connect the valve operating rod to the brake pedal with the bushings, eccentric shoulder bolt, and nut.
7. Adjust brake pedal height.

Power Pedal Adjust

1. Loosen lock nut on eccentric bolt, then rotate the bolt until the pedal height is about $1\frac{7}{8}$ inches above the accelerator pedal.
2. Hold the eccentric bolt securely and tighten the lock nut.
3. Recheck pedal height.

PARKING BRAKE ADJUST

In most cases, a rear brake shoe adjustment will provide satisfactory parking brake action. However, if parking brake cables are excessively loose after releasing the hand brake, proceed as follows:

1. Pull up the handle to the third notch.
2. Loosen lock nut on equalizer rod under the car. Then loosen the nut in front of the equalizer, several turns.
3. Turn the lock nut forward against the equalizer until the cables are just tight enough to stop forward rotation of the wheels.
4. When cables are properly adjusted, tighten both nuts against the equalizer.
5. Release the handle and feel for freeness of rear wheels.

FUEL SYSTEM

REFERENCES

The fuel supply system is identical on both Fairlane and Meteor. There is, however, a difference of fuel pump and filter mounting and a difference

of carburetor make between the 6 cyl. and V-8 engine applications.

Detailed information on fuel pumps may be found in the "Unit Repair" section under "Fuel Pumps."

Detailed repair and adjustment data may be found for both the "Holley Single-Barrel Carburetor and the Ford Dual Carburetor, in the "Unit Repair" section under "Carburetors."

FUEL TANK

Remove

1. Remove filler cap. Disconnect filler and vent tube.
2. Using necessary precautions, drain fuel into a clean container.
3. Disconnect fuel line at tank sending unit.
4. Loosen the two tank strap attaching bolts and lower the tank.

Install

1. If a new tank is to be installed, install the fuel gauge sending unit with a new gasket in the new tank. Install the tank drain plug.
2. Raise the tank into position against the body floor pan. Install fuel tank strap bolts.
3. Connect fuel gauge sending unit wire.
4. Connect fuel line to the fuel gauge sending unit.
5. Connect filler and vent tube. Then fill tank and check for leaks.

FUEL PUMP

No problem here. A single acting fuel pump is used for all models equipped with electric wipers, for either engine application. Mounting is on the left side of the engine.

For detailed information, see "Fuel Pumps," in the "Unit Repair" section.

CARBURETOR

Two carburetor models are used. The 6 cyl. engine, prior to 1963 uses a Holley single barreled, manual choke type carburetor. Beginning 1963, both 6 cyl. and V-8 engines use Ford automatic choke equipped carburetor

For specifications and carburetor adjustments, see "Unit Repair Section," "Carburetors." "Linkage Adjustments" are contained in later paragraphs of this car section under "Automatic Transmission."

EXHAUST SYSTEM

REFERENCES

The exhaust system consists of a muffler inlet pipe, an inlet extension pipe, and a muffler (with integral out-

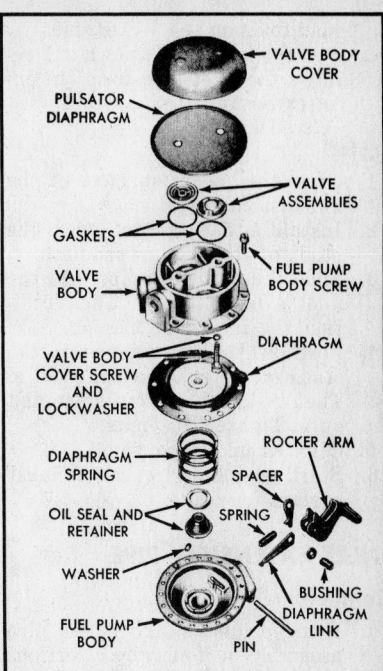

Fuel Pump Exploded View.

let pipe). The muffler inlet pipe used with V-8 engines is the Y-type in which the inlet pipe from the left exhaust manifold crosses over beneath the transmission. It is welded to the inlet pipe from the right exhaust manifold.

MUFFLER AND OUTLET PIPE

Remove

1. Remove inlet extension pipe clamp at muffler.
2. Remove bolts that attach the rear end of the muffler to the frame mounted bracket.
3. Separate the muffler from the inlet extension pipe and remove the muffler and outlet pipe assembly.

Install

1. Slide the new muffler and outlet pipe assembly on the inlet extension pipe. Position the inlet extension pipe clamp.
2. Position the muffler and outlet pipe assembly to the frame mounted bracket and install the retaining bolts. Tighten inlet extension pipe clamp.
3. Start engine and check exhaust system for leaks.

INLET PIPE

Remove

1. Remove inlet pipe clamp at inlet extension pipe.
2. Remove two nuts and lock washers holding the inlet pipe to the exhaust manifold (both exhaust

manifolds on the V-8 engines).

3. Pull the inlet pipe/s down and remove the inlet pipe from the inlet extension pipe.

Install

1. Clean the gasket surfaces of the exhaust manifold/s.
2. Install a new gasket over the studs of the exhaust manifold/s.
3. Slide the new inlet pipe into the inlet extension pipe. Then position the inlet pipe clamp.
4. Position the inlet pipe on the studs of the exhaust manifold/s. Then install the lock washers and nuts. Tighten the nuts.
5. Tighten inlet pipe clamp.
6. Start engine and check exhaust system for leaks.

INLET EXTENSION PIPE

Remove

1. Remove muffler and outlet pipe assembly by following directions given in previous paragraph, "Muffler and Outlet Pipe, Remove."
2. Remove the clamps at the inlet pipe and at the frame mounted bracket. Remove the inlet extension pipe.

Install

1. Slide the new inlet extension pipe on the inlet pipe.
2. Position the clamps at the inlet pipe and at the frame mounted bracket. Tighten the clamps.
3. Install the muffler and outlet pipe assembly by following steps 1 thru 3 of previous paragraph, "Muffler and Outlet Pipe, Install."

COOLING SYSTEM

The system uses a 12 to 15 lb. pres-

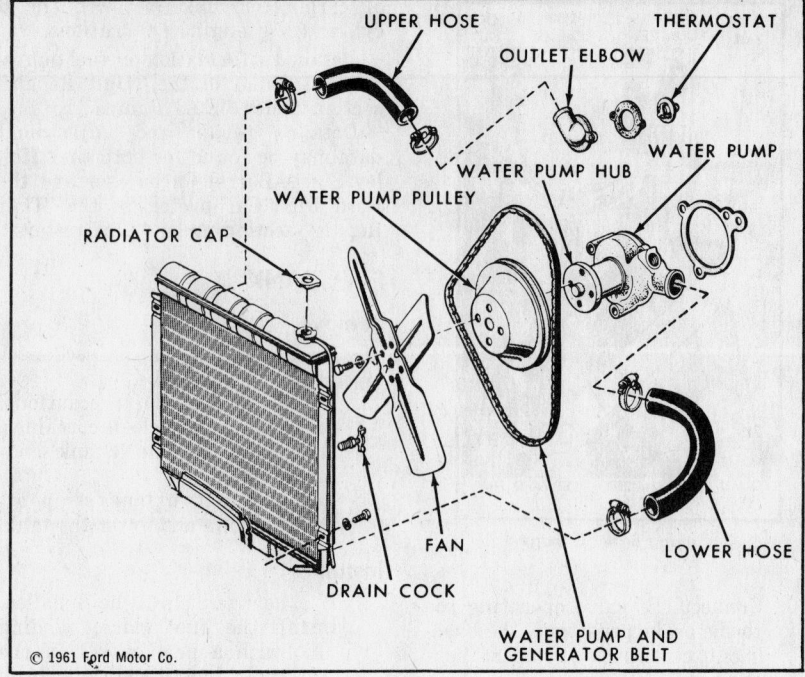

Water Circulation Components.

surized system. The cooling system capacity of heater equipped cars is 9½ qts. for the 6 cyl. engine and 14½ qts. for the V-8.

RADIATOR

Remove

1. Drain cooling system.
2. Disconnect upper and lower hoses at the radiator.
3. On automatic transmission equipped cars, disconnect oil cooler lines at radiator.
4. Remove radiator attaching bolts and lift out the radiator.

Install

1. If a new radiator is to be installed, transfer the petcock from the old radiator to the new one. On cars equipped with automatic transmissions, transfer the oil cooler from the old radiator to the new one.
2. Position the radiator and install, but do not tighten, the radiator support bolts. On cars equipped with automatic transmissions, connect the oil cooler lines. Then tighten the radiator support bolts.
3. Connect the radiator hoses. Close the radiator petcock. Then fill and bleed the cooling system.
4. Start the engine and bring to operating temperature. Check for leaks.

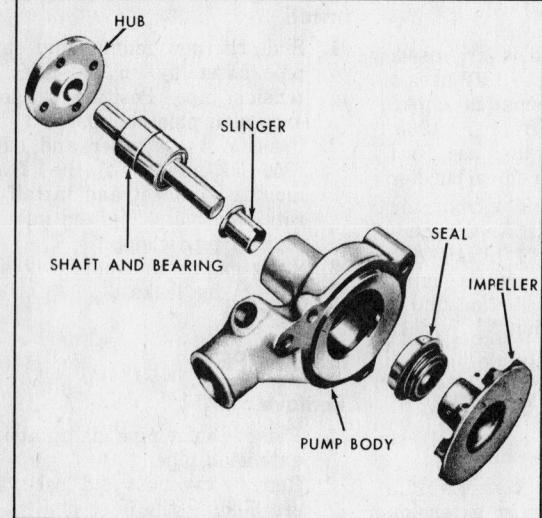

Water Pump—Six Cylinder.

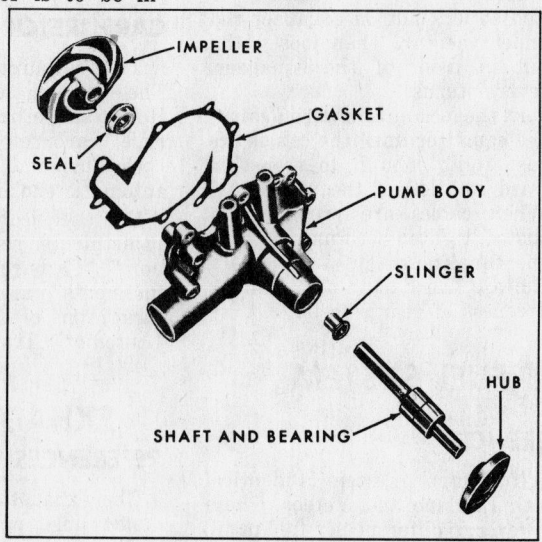

Water Pump—V-8.

5. On cars equipped with automatic transmissions, check the cooler lines for leaks and interference and check transmission fluid level.

THERMOSTAT

Both 6 cyl. and V-8 engines carry the thermostat inside the coolant outlet elbow.

The thermostat used in production is for use with water or permanent type anti-freeze. A lower reading thermostat is available for use with non-permanent type anti-freeze and water.

WATER PUMP

Water pumps for both the 6 cyl. and V-8 engines are similar and quite accessible, but not identical.

Remove

1. Drain the cooling system.
2. Disconnect lower hose and heater hose at the water pump.
3. Remove the drive belt, fan, fan spacer (if so equipped) and the pulley.
4. Remove the attaching bolts and lift off the pump, gasket, and the timing pointer, (from the V-8 engine).

Install

1. Clean mounting surfaces of both cylinder front cover and water pump.
2. Coat a new gasket on both sides, then position the gasket on the cylinder front cover and install the pump. (Position the timing pointer at the two lower mounting holes of V-8 engines.)
3. Install pump attaching bolts and torque to 12-15 ft. lbs.

ENGINE

REFERENCES

There are three engines available in both the Fairlane and Meteor mod-

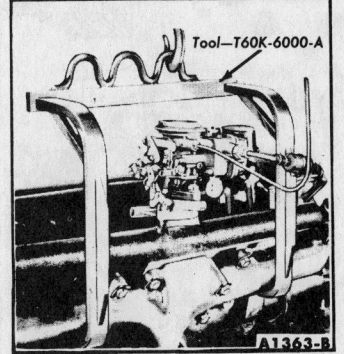

Engine Lifting Hook, 6 Cyl.

els. The 170 cubic inch, 6 cylinder engine, 221 cubic inch V-8, and 260 cubic inch V-8. Both V-8 engines are equipped with hydraulic valves.

ENGINE REMOVE

1. Scribe the hood hinge outline on the under-hood, disconnect the hood and remove.
2. Drain the entire cooling system and oil from the engine oil pan.
3. Remove the air cleaner, disconnect the battery at the cylinder head. On automatic transmission equipped cars, disconnect oil cooler lines at the radiator.
4. Remove upper and lower radiator hoses and remove radiator.
5. Remove fan, fan belt and upper pulley.
6. Disconnect the heater hoses at the water pump and the carburetor spacer.
7. Disconnect the generator wires at the generator, the starter cable at the starter, the accelerator rod at the carburetor and on the 6 cyl. engine, the choke control cable at the carburetor.
8. Disconnect fuel tank line at the fuel pump and plug the line.
9. Disconnect the coil primary wire at the coil. Disconnect wires at the oil pressure and water temperature sending units.
10. Remove the starter and dust seal.
11. On a car equipped with a manual-shift transmission, remove the clutch retracting spring. Disconnect the clutch equalizer shaft and arm bracket at the underbody rail and remove the arm bracket and equalizer shaft.
12. Raise the car. Remove the flywheel or converter housing upper retaining bolts thru the access holes in the floor pan.
13. Disconnect the exhaust pipe or pipes at the exhaust manifold. Disconnect the right and left motor mount at the underbody bracket. Remove the flywheel or converter housing cover.
14. On a car with manual shift, remove the flywheel housing lower retaining bolts.
15. On a car with Fordomatic, disconnect throttle valve vacuum line at the intake manifold, disconnect the converter from the flywheel. Remove the converter housing lower retaining bolts. On a car with power steering, disconnect power steering pump from cylinder head. Remove drive belt and wire steering pump out of the way.
16. Lower the car. Support the transmission and flywheel or converter housing with a jack.
17. Attach an engine lifting hook.

Lift the engine up and out of the compartment and onto an adequate work stand.

ENGINE INSTALL

1. Place a new gasket over the studs of the exhaust manifold/s.
2. Attach engine sling and lifting device. Then lift engine from work stand.
3. Lower the engine into the engine compartment. Be sure the exhaust manifold/s properly line up with the muffler inlet pipe/s and the dowels in the block engage the holes in the flywheel housing.
   On a car with automatic transmission, start the converter pilot into the crankshaft.
   On a car with manual-shift transmission, start the transmission main drive gear into the clutch disc. If the engine "hangs up" after the shaft enters, rotate the crankshaft slowly (with transmission in gear) until the shaft and clutch disc splines mesh.
4. Install the flywheel or converter housing upper bolts.
5. Install engine support insulator to bracket retaining nuts. Disconnet engine lifting sling and remove lifting brackets.
6. Raise front of car. Connect exhaust line/s and tighten attachments.
7. Position dust seal and install starter.
8. **On cars with manual-shift transmissions,** install remaining flywheel housing-to-engine bolts. Connect clutch release rod. Position the clutch equalizer bar and bracket and install retaining bolts. Install clutch pedal retracting spring.
8A. **On cars with automatic transmissions,** remove the retainer holding the converter in the housing. Attach the converter to the flywheel. Install the converter

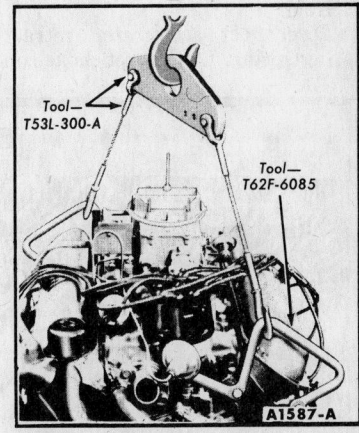

Engine Lifting Brackets and Sling, V-8.

housing inspection cover. Install the remaining converter housing retaining bolts.

9. Remove the support from the transmission and lower the car.

10. Connect engine ground strap and coil primary wire.

11. Connect water temperature gauge wire and the heater hose at coolant outlet housing. Connect accelerator rod at the bellcrank.

12. **On cars with automatic transmission,** connect the transmission filler tube bracket. Connect the throttle valve vacuum line.

12A. **On cars with power steering,** install the drive belt and power steering pump bracket. Install the bracket retaining bolts. Adjust drive belt to proper tension.

13. Remove plug from the fuel tank line. Connect the flexible fuel line and the oil pressure sending unit wire.

14. Install the pulley, belt, spacer, and fan. Adjust belt tension.

15. Tighten generator adjusting bolts. Connect generator wires and the battery ground cable.

16. Install radiator. Connect radiator hoses.

16A. **On cars with automatic transmissions,** connect oil cooler lines.

17. Install oil filter. Connect heater hose at water pump, after bleeding the system.

18. Bring crankcase to level with correct grade of oil. Run engine at fast idle and check for leaks. Install air cleaner and make final engine adjustments.

19. Install and adjust hood.

20. Road test car.

CYLINDER HEAD

6 CYL. HEAD, REMOVE

1. Drain coolant and remove air cleaner. Disconnect battery cable at cylinder head.

2. Disconnect exhaust pipe at manifold.

3. Disconnect accelerator retracting spring. Disconnect choke control cable and accelerator rod at carburetor.

4. Disconnect fuel line and distributor control vacuum line at the carburetor.

5. Disconnect coolant tubes from carburetor spacer. Disconnect coolant and heater hoses.

6. Disconnect distributor control vacuum line at distributor. Disconnect fuel inlet line at the filter. Remove lines as an assembly.

6A. **On an engine equipped with positive crankcase ventilation,** disconnect the emission exhaust tube at the regulator valve and crankcase outlet. Remove regulator valve and crankcase adapter.

7. Disconnect spark plug wires at the plugs and the small wire from the temperature sending unit.

8. Remove rocker arm cover.

9. Remove rocker arm shaft assembly. Remove valve push rods and keep them in sequence.

10. Remove one cylinder head bolt from each end and install two 7/16 x 14 guide studs.

11. Remove remaining cylinder head bolts, then remove cylinder head.

6 CYL. HEAD, INSTALL

1. Clean head and block surfaces.

2. Apply sealer to both sides of head gasket. Position gasket over guide studs.

3. Install new gasket on the exhaust pipe flange.

4. Lift the cylinder head over the guide studs and slide it carefully into place while guiding the exhaust manifold studs into the exhaust pipe flange.

5. Coat cylinder head attaching bolts with water resistant sealer and install (but do not tighten) the head bolts.

6. Replace the guide studs with the two remaining head bolts, then torque the head, in proper sequence and in three progressive steps, to 75 ft. lbs.

7. Lubricate both ends of the push rods and install them in their original bores and sockets.

8. Lubricate valve stem tips and rocker arm pads.

9. Install valve rocker arm shaft assembly and torque attaching pedestal bolts in progressive steps, to 30-35 ft. lbs.

10. Do a preliminary, cold, valve lash adjustment.

11. Install exhaust pipe-to-manifold nuts and lock washers. Torque to 17-22 ft. lbs.

12. Connect radiator and heater hoses. Connect coolant tubes at the carburetor spacer.

13. Connect distributor vacuum line and the carburetor fuel line. Connect battery cable to cylinder head.

13A. **On engines equipped with positive crankcase ventilation,** clean components thoroughly and install.

14. Connect accelerator rod pull-back spring. Connect choke control cable and the accelerator rod at the carburetor.

15. Connect distributor control vacuum line at distributor. Connect carburetor fuel line at fuel filter.

16. Connect temperature sending unit wire at sending unit. Connect spark plug wires.

17. Completely fill and bleed the cooling system.

18. Run engine for a minimum of 30 minutes at 1200 R.P.M. to stabilize engine temperature. Then check for coolant and oil leaks.

19. Adjust engine idle mixture and

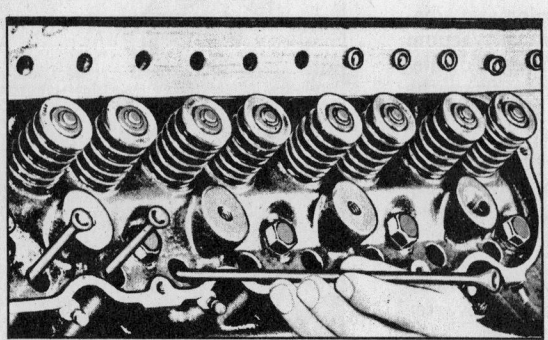

Push Rod Removal, 6 Cyl.

Push Rod Removal, V-8.

speed. Check valve lash and adjust, if necessary.

20. Install valve rocker arm cover, then the air cleaner.

V8 HEADS, REMOVE

Note:

Cylinder head removal and replacement procedures for the 221 cu. in. engine and the 260 cu. in. engine are to be considered identical unless otherwise stated. Right or left cylinder heads, on each specific engine, are interchangeable.

1. Remove intake manifold and carburetor as an assembly.
2. Disconnect battery cable at cylinder head.
3. Remove rocker arm cover/s.
3A. **On a car with power steering,** disconnect the steering pump bracket from the left clinder head and remove the drive belt. Wire the steering pump out of the way, (don't spill the oil).
4. Disconnect wires at generator. Remove generator and bracket as an assembly. Disconnect exhaust pipe/s at exhaust manifold/s.
5. Remove cylinder head attaching bolts from both ends of the head and install two 7/16 x 14 guide studs. Remove remaining cylinder head retaining bolts.
6. Raise cylinder head slightly, so that the rocker arms can be rotated to the side. Remove the push rods and store them in sequence. Remove the guide studs and lift the head off the block. Remove cylinder head gasket.

V8 HEADS, INSTALL

Reverse above procedure, (see valve lash adjustment under, "Valves," in the following paragraphs). Torque cylinder head bolts to 65 to 70 ft. lbs. (with lubricated threads).

VALVE SYSTEM

REFERENCES

The 6 cylinder, 170 cu. in. engine is equipped with tubular push rods, barrel type tappets and valve lash is controlled by self locking adjusting screws.

Early production 6 cylinder (170 cu. in.) engines are equipped with mechanical valve tappets, adjustable for lash and should be set to clearance specifications. The same as in previous models. However, later production engines incorporate a change to the hydraulic type of valve train. These valves are to operate at zero lash and can be adjusted as described in a following paragraph "Adjust 6 Cyl. Hydraulic Valves."

Both V8 engines use hydraulic tappets. The push rods in the V8s, also transfer oil under pressure to the friction areas of the rocker arms.

6 CYL., DISMANTLE

1. Remove cylinder head as described in previous paragraph.
2. Reach down thru the push rod area with a magnet, or other suitable extractor, and remove the tappets. Keep the tappets in order, that they can be installed in their original location.
3. Loosen all valve rocker arm adjusting screws two turns at a time, and in sequence.
4. Remove rocker arm shaft pedestal bolts and lift off rocker arm shaft assembly.
5. Dismantle shaft and rockers by removing pin and spring washer from each end of the shaft.
6. Slide rocker arms, springs and pedestals off the shaft. (Be sure to identify the parts for proper assembly sequence).

6 CYL., ASSEMBLE

1. Lubricate and assemble all rocker shaft components as per illustration.
2. If the end plugs were removed from the rocker shaft, install new plugs, cup side out, to each end of the shaft.
3. Do valve grinding job or any other service to the cylinder head, check valve spring condition, install new oil seals on valve stems, check springs and install valve assembly in place. Compress springs and install keepers.
4. Install valve tappets in their proper bores.
5. Apply cylinder head gasket sealer to both sides of a new gasket and locate gasket on cylinder block. Install cylinder head and torque, in three progressive steps, to 75 ft. lbs.
6. Apply lubriplate, or suitable substitute, to both ends of push rods, then install push rods into their respective places.
7. Install rocker arm and shaft. Tighten rocker shaft pedestal bolts in progressive steps to 30-35 ft. lbs.

Adjust Mechanical Valves—Primary Step

8. Make primary valve adjustment in the following manner. Then continue to install rocker covers and fill cooling system.

Note:

Tappets must be adjusted while on the low radius of the cam.

A. **If the distributor has not been disturbed** and ignition timing is reasonably correct, proceed as follows: Rotate crankshaft until the distributor rotor points to #1 plug wire tower of the distributor cap. Adjust valves in cylinder firing order according to rotor position.

B. **If the distributor is out of time or has been removed from the engine:** Turn the crankshaft until #1 piston is at the top of its compression stroke, (intake valve of #6 cylinder just beginning to open), and the crankshaft damper is on T.D.C. Make three chalk marks on the crankshaft damper, 120 degrees apart, starting with T.D.C. These marks will divide crankshaft travel into three parts, or six segments, of each engine cycle. Valve adjustment can then be made in

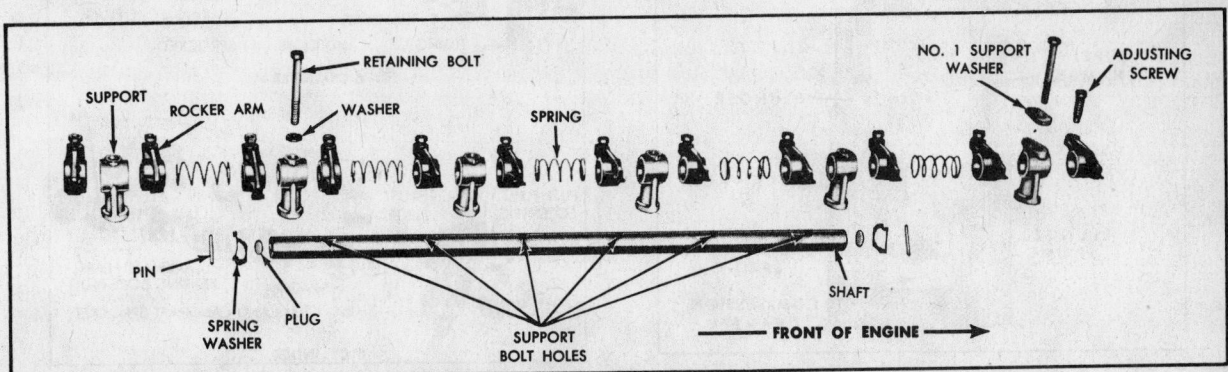

6 Cylinder Valve Rocker and Shaft arrangement

firing sequence, beginning with #1 on T.D.C. and progressing thru the regular order of firing by advancing one chalk mark, (120 crankshaft degrees) at a time.

Adjust Mechanical Valves—Final Step

Note:

Be sure engine is at regular operating temperature by running at least 30 minutes.

9. With engine idling, check valve clearance with a feeler gauge. Adjust clearance, if necessary, to 016" (hot) for both intake and exhaust.

Adjust 6 Cyl. Hydraulic Valves

The following procedure is performed with the engine running.

1. After the engine has been brought to operating temperature, remove the valve cover.
2. With engine at normal idle speed, back off the valve rocker arm adjusters, one at a time, until the rocker arm starts to clatter.
3. Turn the arm adjuster down until the clatter just stops.
4. Continue to turn down the adjuster exactly one turn, this will force the hydraulic lifter piston into the approximate center of its travel.
5. Install valve rocker cover.

V8—VALVE SYSTEM—DISMANTLE

1. Remove cylinder heads as described in previous paragraph.
2. Reach down thru the tappet bores with a magnet or other suitable extractor and remove the tappets. Keep tappets in order, that they can be reinstalled in their original location.

3. Support cylinder head on wooden blocks. With valves still installed to protect valve seats, wire brush the head clean, do not scratch gasket surfaces.
4. Remove rocker arm adjusting nuts, fulcrum seats, and rocker arms. Compress valve springs, remove spring retainer keys, retainers and springs. Remove and discard stem seals, and remove valves.
5. Remove the exhaust manifolds.
6. Inspect condition of manifolds and heads.
7. On the right exhaust manifold, be sure that the automatic choke air inlet and outlet holes are completely open. Clean the maze screen in the passage with cleaning solvent.
8. Perform necessary valve seating and guide services.
9. Check valve springs for squareness and free length. Springs should not be more than 5/64" out of square, or 1/8" shorter than a new spring. A more accurate spring value can be obtained with a spring tester (see valve specifications chart).
10. Check rocker arm studs in cylinder head for damage. Also check for evidence of coolant leak at stud base which may indicate a loose stud. Service replacements are available in standard size and .015" oversize. If any looseness is found, replace the stud.

HYDRAULIC TAPPET SERVICE—ALL MODELS

A. Remove lock ring from tappet body.
B. Remove push rod cup and metering valve disc.
C. Remove plunger from tappet body.

D. Invert the plunger and remove the check valve retainer by carefully prying up on it with a screwdriver.
E. Remove the check valve and the spring.
F. Remove the plunger spring from the tappet body.
G. Soak all tappet components in solvent (lacquer thinner works well on these tar and varnish substances).
H. After tappet parts have been thoroughly cleaned and blown dry, place the plunger upside down on a clean surface.
I. Place the check valve over the hole in the bottom of the plunger. Place check valve spring on top of the check valve.
J. Position check valve retainer over the spring and check valve, then push the retainer down into place on the plunger.
K. Place plunger spring and plunger into the tappet body.
L. Place metering valve disc and the push rod cup in the plunger. Depress plunger and install the lock ring.
M. Test all hydraulic tappets (both new and used) before installing them in an engine. The factory quotes a bleed-down time of from 10 to 80 seconds, using special test oil and their approved tester.

V8—VALVE SYSTEM—ASSEMBLE

1. Install hydraulic tappets into their respective bores.
2. Lubricate valve stems with engine oil and apply lubriplate to the tip of the valve stems.
3. Install each valve into its respective guide and install new oil seals on the stems.
4. Install valve springs, retainers and retainer keys.
5. Measure the assembled height of each valve spring, from the sur-

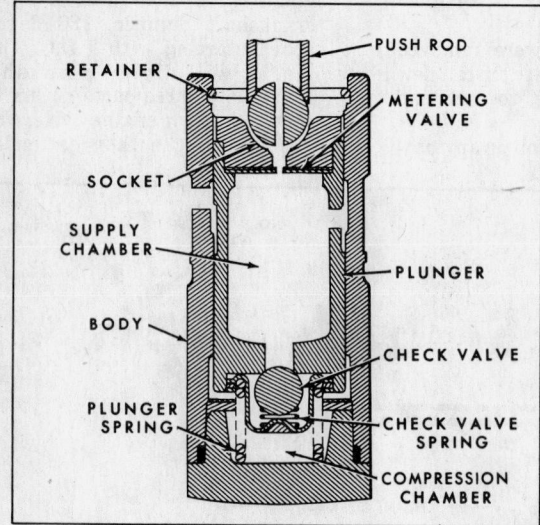

Hydraulic Tappet.

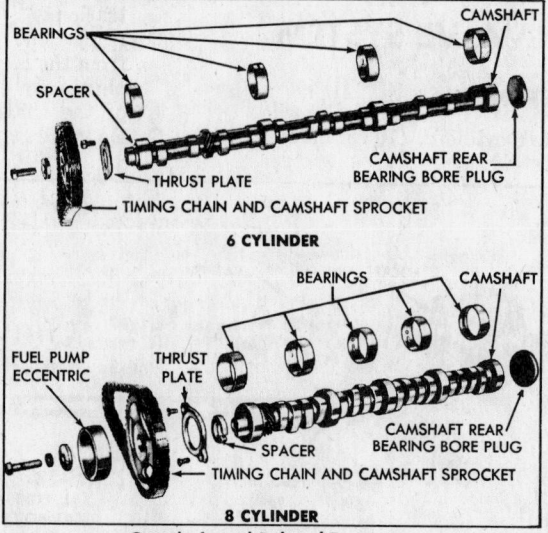

Camshaft and Related Parts.

face of the spring pad to the underside of the spring retainer. This measurement should be 1¾" to 1-25/32". If assembled height is not within limits, install necessary spacer/s between the spring pad and the spring to correct the measurement.

6. Install rocker arms and fulcrum seats. Install adjusting nuts, finger tight.

7. Install the exhaust manifold/s. Torque manifold bolts to 13-18 ft. lbs. and bend over the bolt locking tabs.

8. Position new sealer coated head gasket, install cylinder head, and progressively torque to 65-70 ft. lbs.

9. Lubricate both ends of push rods and install them into their respective tappets.

Adjust Valves

10A. Crank the engine to position #1 piston on T.D.C. of the compression stroke. With engine in this condition, the following valves may be adjusted:
No. 1—Intake
No. 1—Exhaust
No. 2—Exhaust
No. 3—Intake
No. 4—Exhaust
No. 5—Exhaust
No. 7—Intake
No. 8—Intake

B. Position a leverage tool on the rocker arm and slowly bleed down the tappet until the plunger is bottomed.

C. While holding the tappet in the collapsed position, turn rocker arm adjustment to obtain 0.082"-0.152" clearance between the valve stem and the rocker arm.

D. Crank the engine to position #6 piston on T.D.C. of the compression stroke. With engine in this condition, the following valves may be adjusted:
No. 2—Intake
No. 3—Exhaust
No. 4—Intake
No. 5—Intake
No. 6—Intake
No. 6—Exhaust
No. 7—Exhaust
No. 8—Exhaust

11. Coat intake manifold and cylinder block seal surfaces with oil resistant sealer. Position new seals on block and new gaskets on cylinder heads with the seal tabs interlocked with the slots in the gaskets.

12. To facilitate lining up the intake manifold properly, use two aligning studs. Lower the intake manifold onto the engine.

13. Install manifold attaching bolts. Torque bolts in a progressive manner to 14-16 ft. lbs.

14. Connect water pump by-pass hose to the pump and the water outlets housing, tighten the clamps.

15. Install generator and bracket assembly.

16. Install fuel pump and the fuel filter and adapter assembly.

17. Rotate crankshaft to bring #1 piston up to T.D.C. of the compression stroke.

18. Position distributor in the block with the rotor at #1 firing position and the points just opening. Install distributor hold-down clamp.

19. Install carburetor choke heat tube and the carburetor. Install distributor cap and plug wires as an assembly. Install ignition coil, and connect high tension lead at the coil.

20. Install and connect the fuel filter to carburetor line, the fuel pump to fuel filter line, and the distributor to carburetor vacuum line.

21 Check engine oil, fill and bleed cooling system, start engine, make final adjustments and road test car.

TIMING COVER AND CHAIN

6 CYL. COVER AND CHAIN—REMOVE

1 Drain cooling system, and disconnect radiator hoses.

2. Remove radiator.

3. Remove drive belt, fan and pulley.

4. Remove the crankshaft damper.

5. Remove timing chain cover and crankshaft front oil slinger.

6. Establish a reference point on the block. Now measure extreme slack in the loose side of the chain and record this measurement. Now, eliminate the slack by moving the camshaft sprocket within the chain slack limits and again take a measurement. The difference should not exceed ½ inch. More than ½ inch slack justifies renewal of chain and sprockets.

7. Crank the engine until timing marks are aligned, as shown in "Valve Timing Illustration."

8. Remove camshaft sprocket retaining bolt and washer. Then, slide both sprockets and chain forward and remove them as an assembly.

Cover Seal R & R (6 Cyl. & V8)

1. Drive out the old seal with a pin punch. Then, clean out the recess in the cover.

2. Coat a new seal with grease and drive it into place in the chain cover. Check that the spring is still properly positioned in the seal before installing cover.

6 CYL. COVER AND CHAIN—INSTALL

1. Position sprockets and chain on the camshaft and crankshaft with both timing marks on a centerline. Install camshaft sprocket retaining bolt and washer. Torque attaching bolt to 35-45 ft. lbs.

2. Install the oil slinger so that the pointer on the slinger is aligned with the camshaft sprocket timing mark.

3. Clean front cover and cylinder block of old gasket material. Apply sealer to a new cover gasket and position the gasket to the cover.

4. Install the front cover, using a crankshaft-to-cover alignment tool. Torque attaching bolts to 7-9 ft. lbs.

5. Install crankshaft damper and torque to 45-55 ft. lbs.

6. Install fan, fan pulley and drive belt. Adjust the belt.

7. Install radiator. Then, connect the hoses.

8. Fill and bleed cooling system.

9. Start engine and check for leaks and final adjustments.

V8 COVER AND CHAIN—REMOVE

1. Drain cooling system, remove air cleaner, and disconnect the battery.

2. Disconnect radiator hoses and remove the radiator.

3. Disconnect heater hose at water pump. Slide water pump by-pass hose clamp toward the pump.

4. Loosen generator mounting bolts at the generator. Remove the

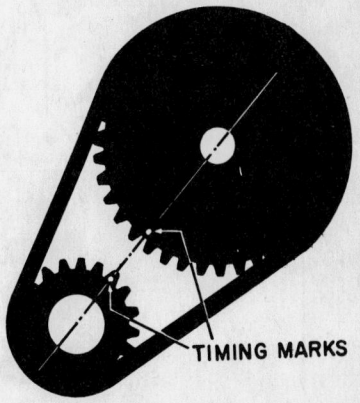

TIMING MARKS

Aligning Timing Marks—6 Cyl.

FAIRLANE and METEOR

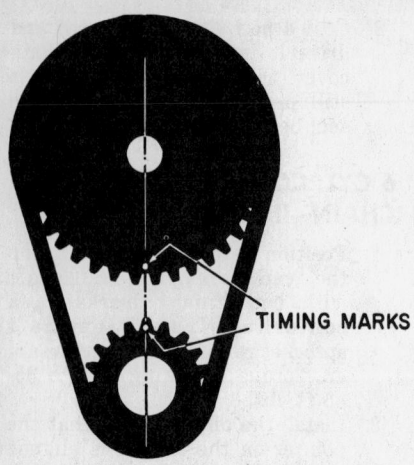

Aligning Timing Marks—V-8.

generator support bolt at the water pump.

5. Remove the fan, spacer, pulley, and drive belt. (On a car with **power steering,** remove the steering pump belt.) (On a car with **air conditioner,** remove the compressor belt.)

6. Remove pulley from crankshaft pulley adapter. Remove cap screw and washer from front end of crankshaft. Remove crankshaft pulley adapter with a puller.

7. Disconnect fuel pump outlet line at the pump. Remove fuel pump retaining bolts and lay the pump to the side.

8. Remove front cover attaching bolts and remove front cover and water pump as an assembly.

9. Remove crankshaft front oil slinger.

10. Rotate crankshaft in normal direction to remove slack from the chain, on the fuel pump side of the engine.

11. Establish a reference point on the block and measure from this point to the chain.

12. Back-up on crankshaft rotation to remove slack from the chain on the generator side of the engine. Force the fuel pump side of the chain out with the fingers and again take a measurement from chain to reference mark. Deflection is the difference between the two measurements. If deflection exceeds 1/2", a new chain and/or sprockets is warranted.

13. Crank engine until sprocket timing marks are aligned as shown in "Valve Timirg Illustration."

14. Remove camshaft sprocket cap screw, washers, and fuel pump eccentric. Slide both sprockets and chain forward and off of their shafts as an assembly.

V8 COVER AND CHAIN— INSTALL

1. Position sprockets and chain on the camshaft and crankshaft with both timing marks on a centerline. Install fuel pump eccentric, washers and sprocket attaching bolt. Torque the sprocket attaching bolt to 30-35 ft. lbs.

2. Install crankshaft front oil slinger.

3. Clean front cover and mating surfaces of old gasket material.

4. Coat a new cover gasket with sealer and position it on the block.

5. Install front cover, using a crankshaft-to-cover alignment tool. Torque attaching bolts to 12-15 ft. lbs.

6. Install fuel pump, torque attaching bolts to 23-28 ft. lbs., connect fuel pump outlet tube.

7. Install crankshaft pulley adapter and torque attaching bolt to 70-90 ft .bs. Install crankshaft pulley.

8. On a car with **power steering,** install pump drive belt. On a can with **air conditioning,** install and adjust drive belt.

9. Install water pump pulley, drive belt, spacer and fan.

10. Install generator support bolt at the water pump. Tighten generator mounting bolts. Adjust drive belt tension.

11. Install radiator and connect all coolant and heater hoses. Con nect battery cables.

12. Refill and bleed cooling system.

13. Start engine and operate at fast idle to operating temperature.

14. Check for leaks, install air cleaner. Adjust ignition timing and make all final adjustments.

Caution:

Due to the structure of the crankshaft, it is very important that the proper tools be used to draw the damper or pulley into place on the crankshaft. (**Do** not use a hammer, breakage of the cast crankshaft can result.)

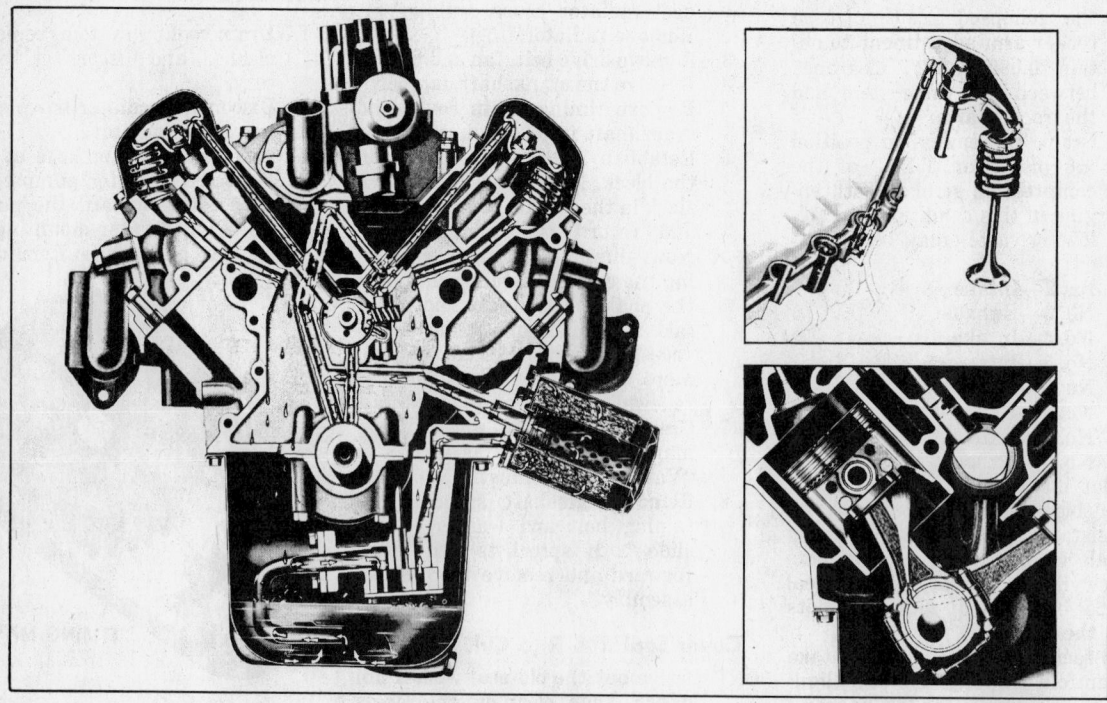

Engine Lubrication—V-8.

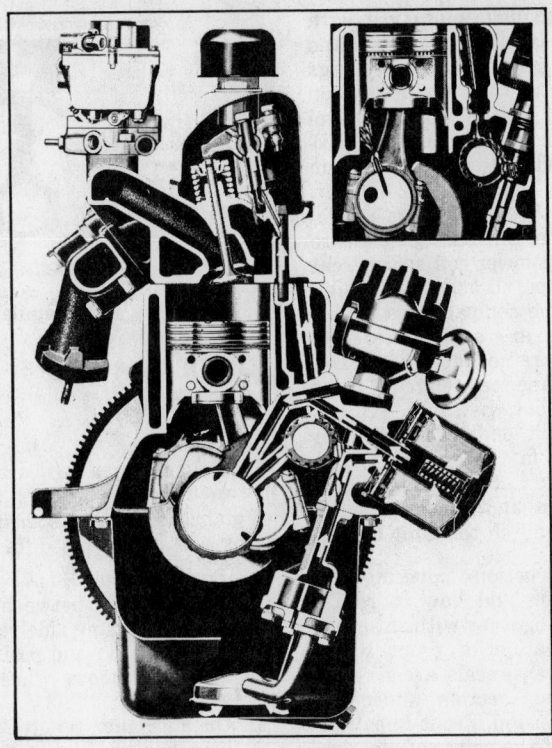

Engine Lubrication—6 Cyl.

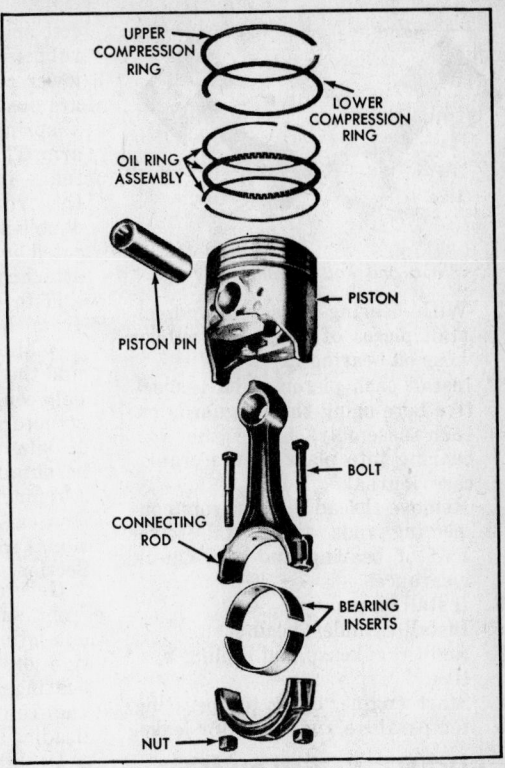

Piston and Rod Assembly.

ENGINE LUBRICATION

REFERENCES

All engines are equipped with full-flow type oil filters to condition the oil before it reaches the main bearings. The filter is equipped with an internal, relief, by-pass valve as a stoppage, safety precaution. The scheme of lubrication is best shown in the illustrations.

Under normal driving conditions, engine oil and oil filter should be changed at 6,000 mile intervals. However, adverse driving conditions, dusty operation, short trips, winter driving, etc., may justify the change at much shorter intervals.

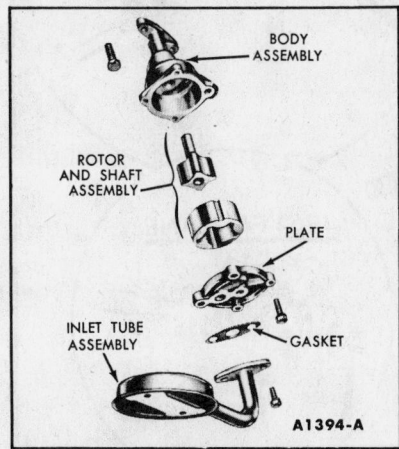

Oil Pump, Exploded View—6 Cyl.

OIL PAN R & R—6 CYL. & V8

1. Drain crankcase. Remove oil dipstick.
2. **Six cylinder with standard transmission,** remove clutch retracting spring.
3. Remove #2 crossmember retaining nuts and remove the crossmember.
4. **Six cylinder,** remove stabilizer bar-to-underbody retaining nuts and pull the bar downward.
5. **V-8 models,** remove starter motor.
6. Remove oil pan retaining bolts and crank the engine as required to obtain clearance, then remove the oil pan.
7. Install oil pan in the reverse order of removal. Torque the ¼" x 20 cap screws to 7-9 ft. lbs. and 5/16" x 18 cap screws to 9-11 ft. lbs.
8. Torque #2 crossmember attaching nuts to 27-39 ft. lbs.
9. Install oil dipstick. Fill crankcase to level, then run the engine and check for leaks.

CONNECTING RODS AND PISTONS

REMOVE

1. Drain crankcase and remove oil pan.
2. Drain cooling system and remove cylinder head or heads.
3. Remove any ridge and/or deposits from the upper end of cylinder bores with a ridge reamer.
4. Check rods and pistons for identification numbers and, if necessary, number them.
5. Remove connecting rod cap nuts and caps. Push the rods away from the crankshaft and install caps and nuts loosely to their respective rods.
6. Push piston and rod assemblies up and out of the cylinders.

INSTALL

1. Lightly coat pistons, rings and cylinder walls with light engine oil.

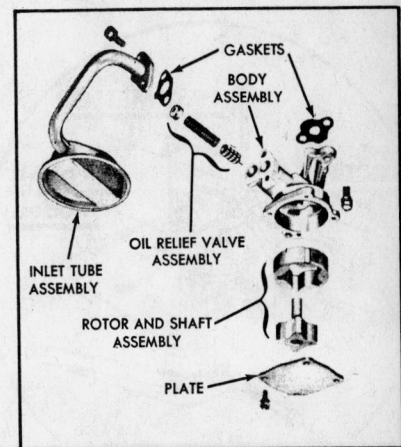

Oil Pump, Exploded View—V-8.

FAIRLANE AND METEOR

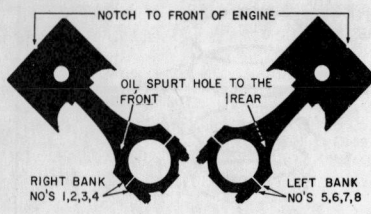

Piston and Rod Installation—V-8.

RIGHT BANK
NO'S 1,2,3,4

LEFT BANK
NO'S 5,6,7,8

NOTCH TO FRONT OF ENGINE

OIL SPURT HOLE TO THE
FRONT | REAR

2. With bearing caps removed, install pieces of protective rubber hose on bearing cap bolts.

3. Install each piston in its respective bore using thread guards on each assembly. Guide the rod bearing into place on the crankcase journal.

4. Remove thread guards from connecting rods and install lower half of bearing and cap. Check clearances.

5. Install oil pan.

6. Install cylinder head.

7. Refill crankcase and cooling system.

8. Start engine, bring to operating temperature and check for leaks.

FRONT SUSPENSION

REFERENCES

Front suspension is an independent coil spring and ball joint type with rubber bushed, pivoting upper and lower control arms. The coil springs are positioned at their lower ends on a spring seat in the upper control arm. The upper end of the spring extends into spring towers formed in the front end sheet metal. Direct, double-acting shock absorbers are located inside the loil springs and are attached at the lower coil spring seat and to the upper bracket, accessible from the engine compartment.

While there are some differences and the parts are not interchangeable between Fairlane and Meteor, basic structure is about the same.

Data on front end alignment can be obtained from the "Front Wheel Alignment" chart at the beginning of this car section and from "Suspension, Front Align" in the Unit Repair Section.

General instructions covering the front suspension and how to repair and adjust it, together with information on installation of front wheel bearings and grease seals, are given in the Unit Repair section under the heading: Suspension, Front Repair.

Definitions of the points of steering geometry are covered in the Unit Repair section under the heading: Suspension—Front Alignment. This article also covers trouble shooting front end geometry and irregular tire wear.

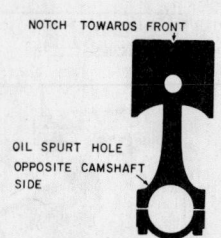

Piston and Rod Installation—6 Cyl.

NOTCH TOWARDS FRONT

OIL SPURT HOLE
OPPOSITE CAMSHAFT
SIDE

LOWER ARM AND BRACKET R & R

Note:

This is an area of design variation between the Fairlane and the Meteor. A glance at front suspension illustrations will show this difference.

1. Position tool #T57P-3006A (or a substitute) between the upper arm and frame side rail.

2. Raise the car and position safety stands. Remove wheel and tire assembly.

3. **On Fairlane,** remove the stabilizer bar and link retaining nut. Disconnect the bar from link and remove the link bolt.

4. **On Fairlane,** remove the strut to lower arm retaining nuts and

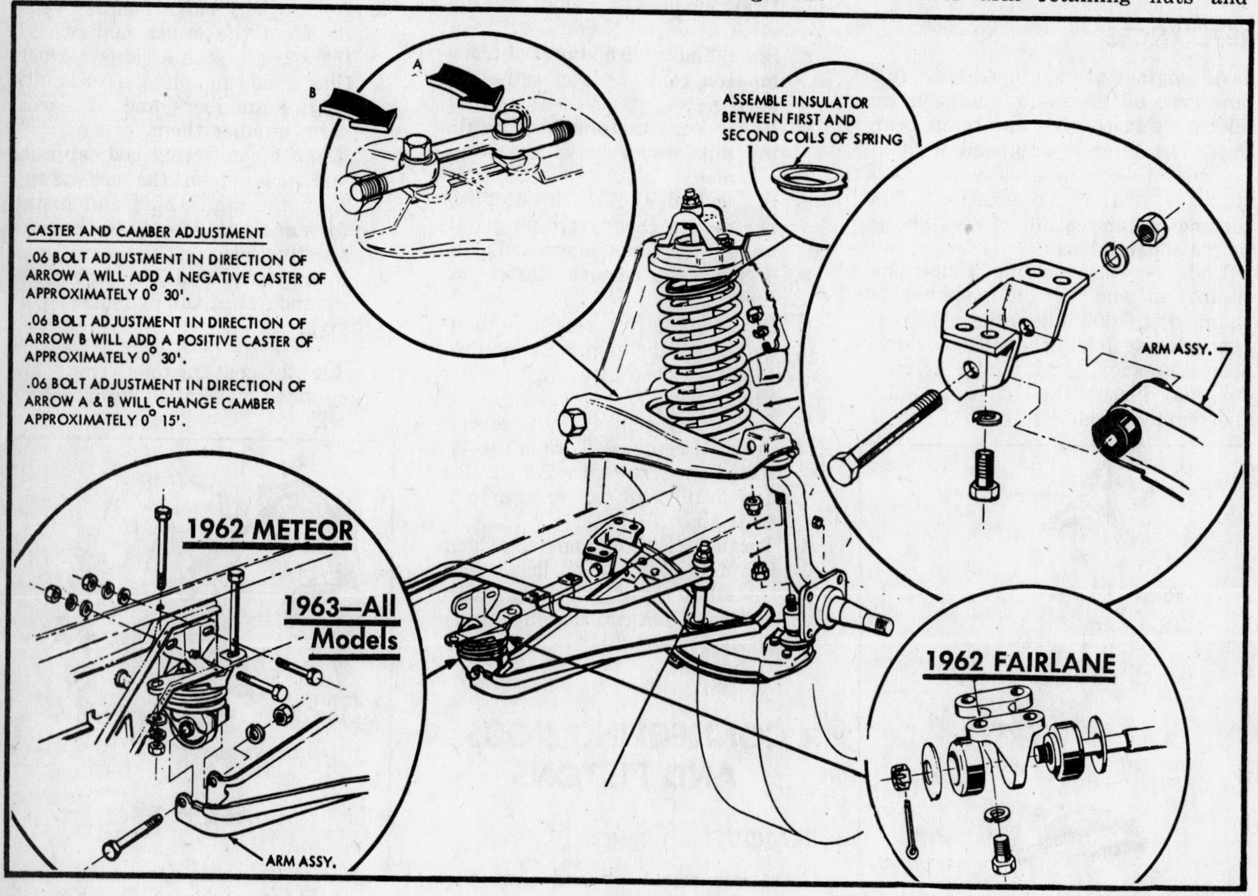

CASTER AND CAMBER ADJUSTMENT

.06 BOLT ADJUSTMENT IN DIRECTION OF ARROW A WILL ADD A NEGATIVE CASTER OF APPROXIMATELY 0° 30'.

.06 BOLT ADJUSTMENT IN DIRECTION OF ARROW B WILL ADD A POSITIVE CASTER OF APPROXIMATELY 0° 30'.

.06 BOLT ADJUSTMENT IN DIRECTION OF ARROW A & B WILL CHANGE CAMBER APPROXIMATELY 0° 15'.

ASSEMBLE INSULATOR BETWEEN FIRST AND SECOND COILS OF SPRING

ARM ASSY.

1962 METEOR

1963—All Models

ARM ASSY.

1962 FAIRLANE

Front Suspension

bolts. Disconnect the bar from the link and remove the link bolt.

5. **On Fairlane,** remove the strut to lower arm retaining nuts and bolts.

6. Remove cotter pin and loosen ball joint stud nut. Place ball joint removing tool in position, expand the tool to put tension on the ball stud. Then tap the spindle to free the tapered ball stud.

7. Remove nut from the lower ball joint stud.

8. **On Meteor,** remove the four rear pivot point bracket-to-body bolts.

9. Remove the complete lower arm assembly.

10. Install parts by reversing the removal procedure.

Front Pivot Point Bracket (Meteor Only)

A. Raise car and place support stands under the lower support arms.

B. Remove front pivot point to forward extension arm retaining bolt.

C. Remove the two vertical and horizontal front pivot point bracket-to-underbody retaining bolts.

D. Remove pivot point bracket assembly.

E. Install spacers (Tool 3069-M-7) between the side plates and main casting.

F. Put bracket assembly in a press. Support the unit with tool 6306-AC or other cylindrical substitute. By using a 15/16" socket and a six inch extension, the lower torsion bushing can be removed.

G. Place the bracket in a vise and compress one side of the coil spring. Compress the other side of the spring with a pair of vise grips.

H. Remove the side plate retaining nut, lockwasher, and bolt. Remove the side plates and main casting.

I. Relieve the coil spring by removing the vise grips and loosening the jaws of the vise.

The side plate of the bracket assembly that faces toward the front has the largest bushing hole.

STEERING WHEEL AND HORN RING

REMOVE AND INSTALL

1. Be sure that front wheels are straight ahead, and the battery disconnected.

Tool—3600-AA

Steering Wheel Removal

2. Remove horn ring by pressing it downward and turning it counter-clockwise.

3. Remove nut from the end of the steering shaft and remove steering wheel with a puller.

4. Install wheel, by lining up the index mark on the wheel hub with the mark on the steering shaft. Torque the attaching nut to 20-30 ft. lbs., then stake the nut.

5. Install horn ring by reversing the above procedure. Hook up the battery.

STEERING GEAR

REFERENCES

This is a tried and proven, recirculating ball type. It has been used on cars of Ford Motor Company manufacture for years. Adjustment procedures may be found under "Steering-Manual" in the "Unit Repair Section."

STEERING GEAR R & R

1. Raise front of car and install safety stands. **On a car with power steering, remove the power steering cylinder mounting bracket from the frame.**

2. Remove the sector shaft arm from the steering gear housing, if necessary, disconnect the muffler inlet pipe.

3. Remove flexible joint clamp bolts.

4. Remove steering gear housing attaching bolts, and remove the gear assembly.

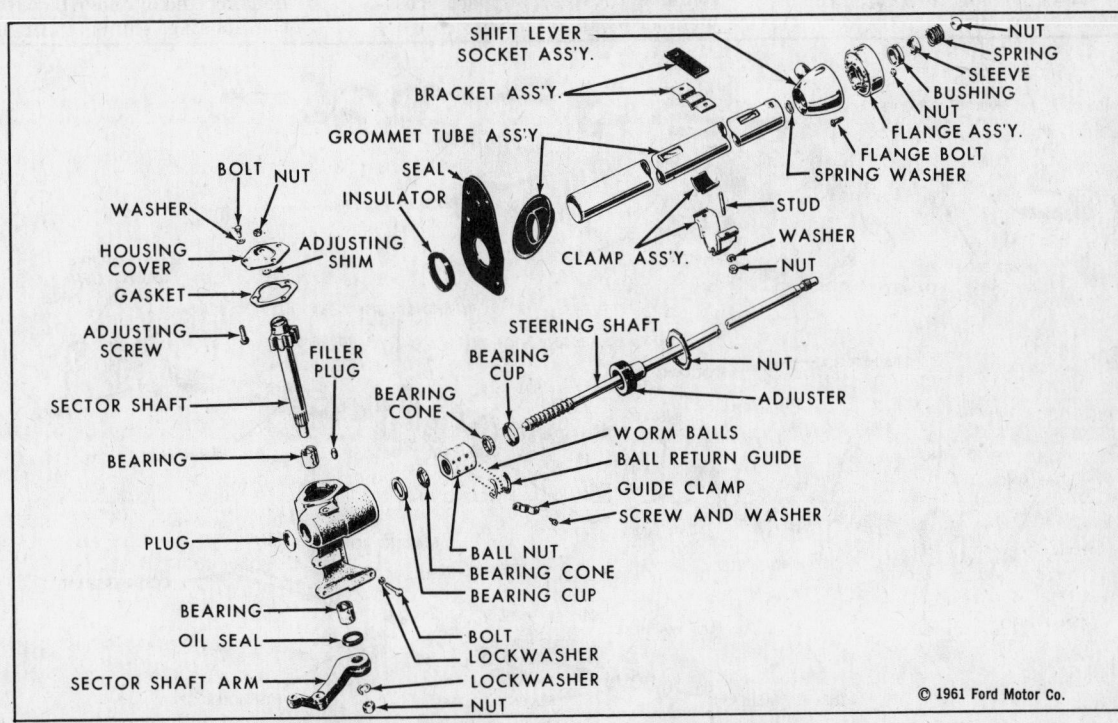

SHIFT LEVER SOCKET ASS'Y.
BRACKET ASS'Y.
GROMMET TUBE ASS'Y.
NUT
SPRING
SLEEVE
BUSHING
NUT
FLANGE ASS'Y.
FLANGE BOLT
SPRING WASHER
BOLT NUT
WASHER
SEAL
INSULATOR
STUD
WASHER
NUT
CLAMP ASS'Y.
HOUSING COVER
ADJUSTING SHIM
GASKET
ADJUSTING SCREW
FILLER PLUG
STEERING SHAFT
BEARING CUP
SECTOR SHAFT
BEARING CONE
NUT
ADJUSTER
BEARING
WORM BALLS
BALL RETURN GUIDE
GUIDE CLAMP
SCREW AND WASHER
PLUG
BALL NUT
BEARING CONE
BEARING CUP
BEARING
OIL SEAL
BOLT
LOCKWASHER
LOCKWASHER
SECTOR SHAFT ARM
NUT

© 1961 Ford Motor Co.

Manual Steering Gear and Steering Column Assembly, (Exploded View)

5. Reinstall by reversing above procedure.

POWER STEERING

REFERENCES

The power steering system includes a conventional steering gear, slightly modified linkage, a belt-driven pump, a reaction limiting type control valve, and a power cylinder.

Detailed information may be had by referring to "Steering-Power," in the "Unit Repair Section."

CLUTCH

REFERENCES

The clutch cover and pressure plate, and the clutch disc plan is dependent upon power and transmission application. The clutch disc used with the standard transmission and 6 cylinder engine has an O.D. of 8½ inches. The clutch disc used with the standard transmission and the V8 engines has an O.D. of 10 inches.

CLUTCH AND TRANSMISSION R & R

1. Raise the car.
2. Disconnect drive shaft at rear universal joint, remove the shaft.
3. Insert extension housing oil seal replacer, (tool #7657-G) into the tail shaft housing to retain the transmission oil.

Clutch Pedal Travel and Shift Linkage Adjustment Points.

4. Disconnect speedometer cable at the transmission.
5. Disconnect gearshift rods and interlock linkage at transmission.
6. Disconnect parking brake cable from crossmember and equalizer. Disconnect parking brake rear cable from the equalizer lever.
7. Remove rear support insulator bolts from the transmission extension housing.
8. Place a support stand under the engine and raise slightly. Support the transmission with a jack.
9. Remove transmission mounting bolts.
10. Remove the rear support crossmember as an assembly.

11. Remove the transmission by pulling rearward. Then lower the unit to the floor.
12. Remove clutch release lever retracting spring from the lever.
13. Slide release bearing and hub of the lever.
14. Disconnect battery, then disconnect starter cable at the starter.
15. Remove bolts, then remove starter and rubber dust shield.
15A. **On 6-cylinder equipped cars,** remove flywheel housing cover.
16. Remove flywheel housing-to-cylinder block attaching bolts. Remove flywheel housing (If shims are present between flywheel housing and cylinder block, mark the housing, shims, and cylinder

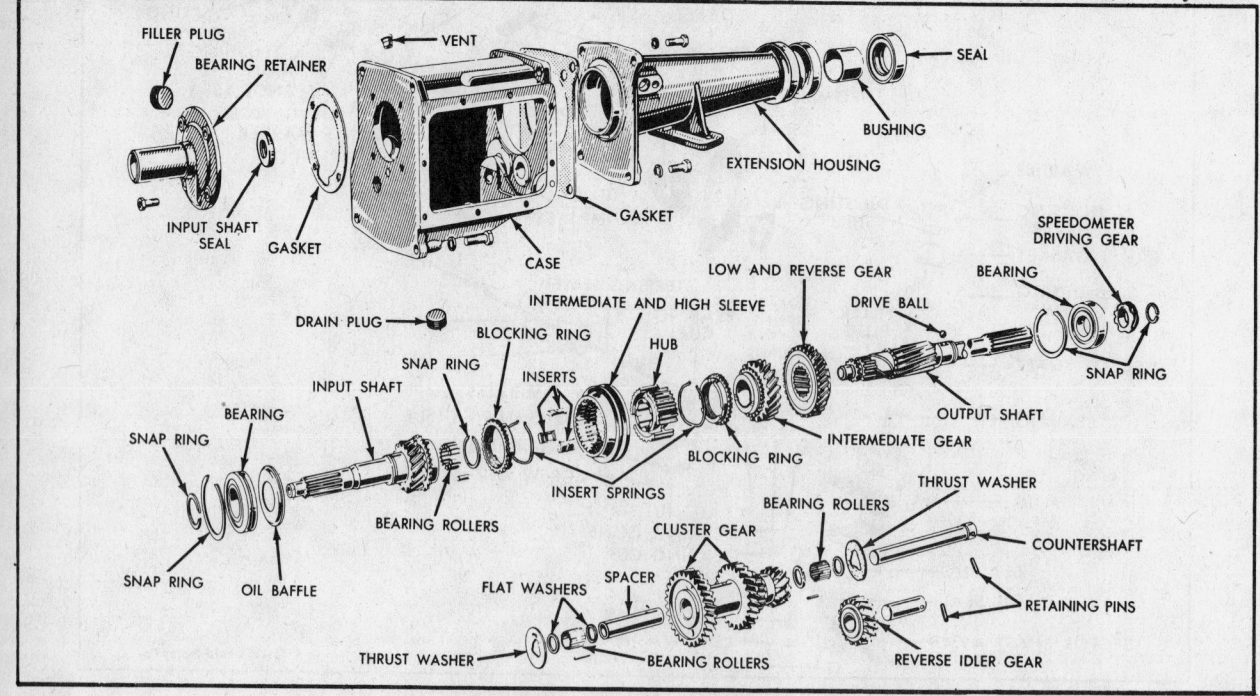

Standard Transmission, Exploded—V-8 Models.

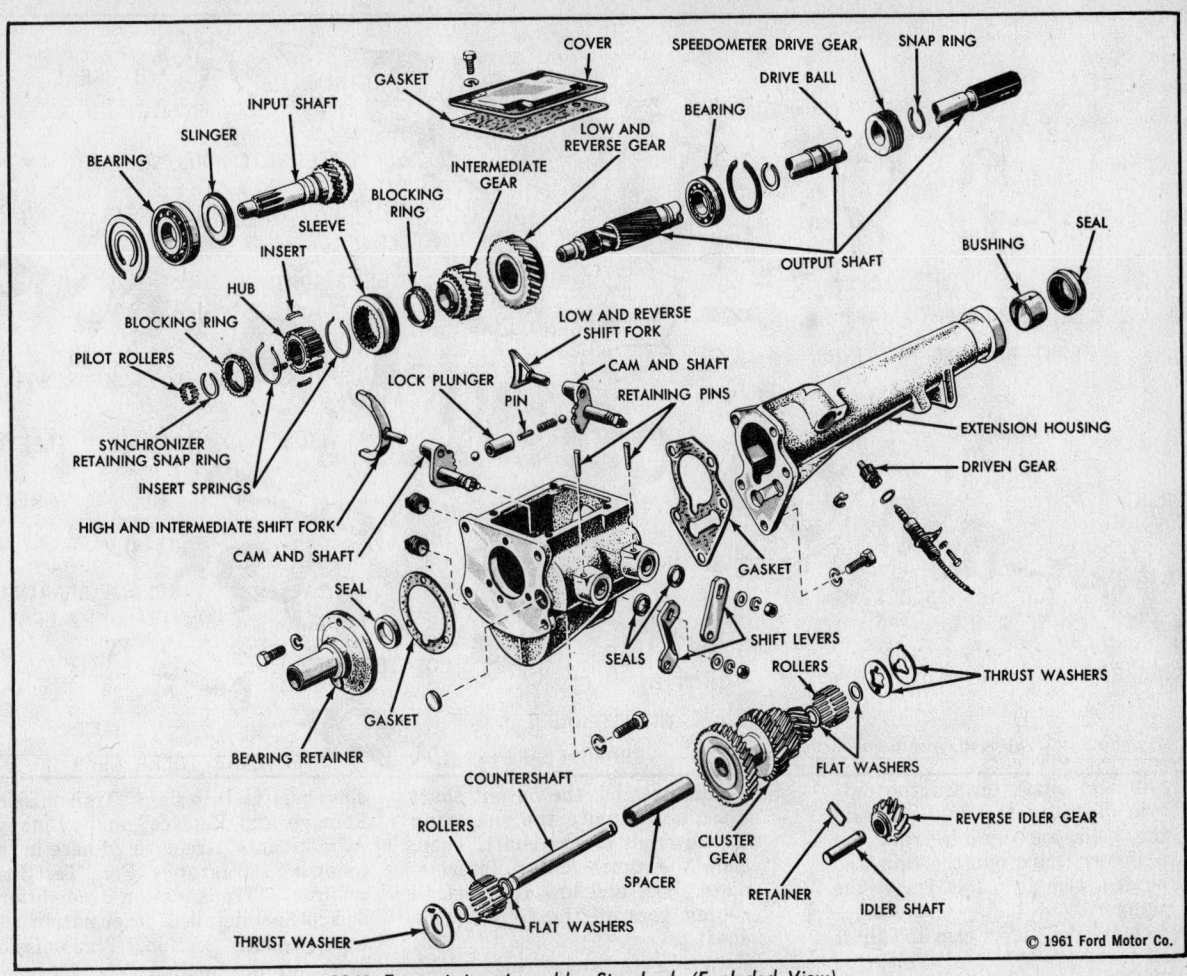

GASKET — COVER — SPEEDOMETER DRIVE GEAR — SNAP RING — DRIVE BALL — BEARING — INPUT SHAFT — LOW AND REVERSE GEAR — SLINGER — INTERMEDIATE GEAR — BEARING — SLEEVE — BLOCKING RING — BEARING — INSERT — OUTPUT SHAFT — BUSHING — SEAL — HUB — BLOCKING RING — LOW AND REVERSE SHIFT FORK — PILOT ROLLERS — LOCK PLUNGER — PIN — CAM AND SHAFT — RETAINING PINS — EXTENSION HOUSING — SYNCHRONIZER RETAINING SNAP RING — INSERT SPRINGS — DRIVEN GEAR — HIGH AND INTERMEDIATE SHIFT FORK — CAM AND SHAFT — GASKET — SEAL — GASKET — SHIFT LEVERS — SEALS — ROLLERS — THRUST WASHERS — BEARING RETAINER — GASKET — COUNTERSHAFT — FLAT WASHERS — ROLLERS — SPACER — CLUSTER GEAR — RETAINER — IDLER SHAFT — REVERSE IDLER GEAR — THRUST WASHER — FLAT WASHERS

© 1961 Ford Motor Co.

1962 Transmission Assembly—Standard, (Exploded View)

blocks for location identity in reassembly.)

17. Scribe marks on the flywheel and pressure plate cover to insure correct positioning at reassembly.

18. Loosen the six cover plate attaching bolts evenly. Remove the bolts and lower the clutch disc and the cover plate assembly from the car.

19. Reinstall components in the reverse order of removal.

20. Lower the car.

STANDARD TRANSMISSION

REFERENCES

There are two standard transmissions used. The one used with the 6 cylinder engine has a top cover. The one used with V-8 engines through 1962 has a side cover, and the fully synchronized one for the V-8 beginning 1963 has a top cover.

Overdrive, typical information is covered in the "Transmission Section" of the manual under "Overdrive Transmission."

BEGINNING 1963—3 SPEED FULLY SYNCHRONIZED SYNCHRO SMOOTH DRIVE

DISASSEMBLE & ASSEMBLE— TOP COVER TYPE

1. Drain the unit and remove transmission cover and gasket.

2. Remove outer shift levers and the interlock linkage.

3. Remove extension housing attaching bolts and remove the engine rear support bracket and the extension housing and gasket. (To prevent the output shaft from following the housing and dropping the needle bearings.) Tap the end of the output shaft with a soft hammer and withdraw extension housing.

4. Remove speedometer drive gear snap ring. Then remove the drive gear and drive ball from the output shaft.

5. Remove idler and countershaft retainer.

6. With a dummy shaft, drive the shaft out of the cluster gear and case. Leave the dummy shaft in the cluster, at rest, in the bottom of the case.

7. Remove input shaft bearing retainer and gasket.

8. Remove input shaft assembly and front synchronizer blocking ring from the case.

9. Remove synchronizer snap ring from the output shaft. Then, while holding the synchronizer assembly together, pull the output shaft out of the transmission case.

10. Lift the synchronizer assembly, intermediate, low and reverse sliding gears out of the case. Then remove the two shift forks.

11. Drive the reverse idler shaft out of the gear and rear of the case.

12. Lift reverse idler gear and the cluster gear out of the case.

13. From the underside of the case, drive out the tapered pins that hold the cam and shaft assemblies in the case.

14. Drive the intermediate and high

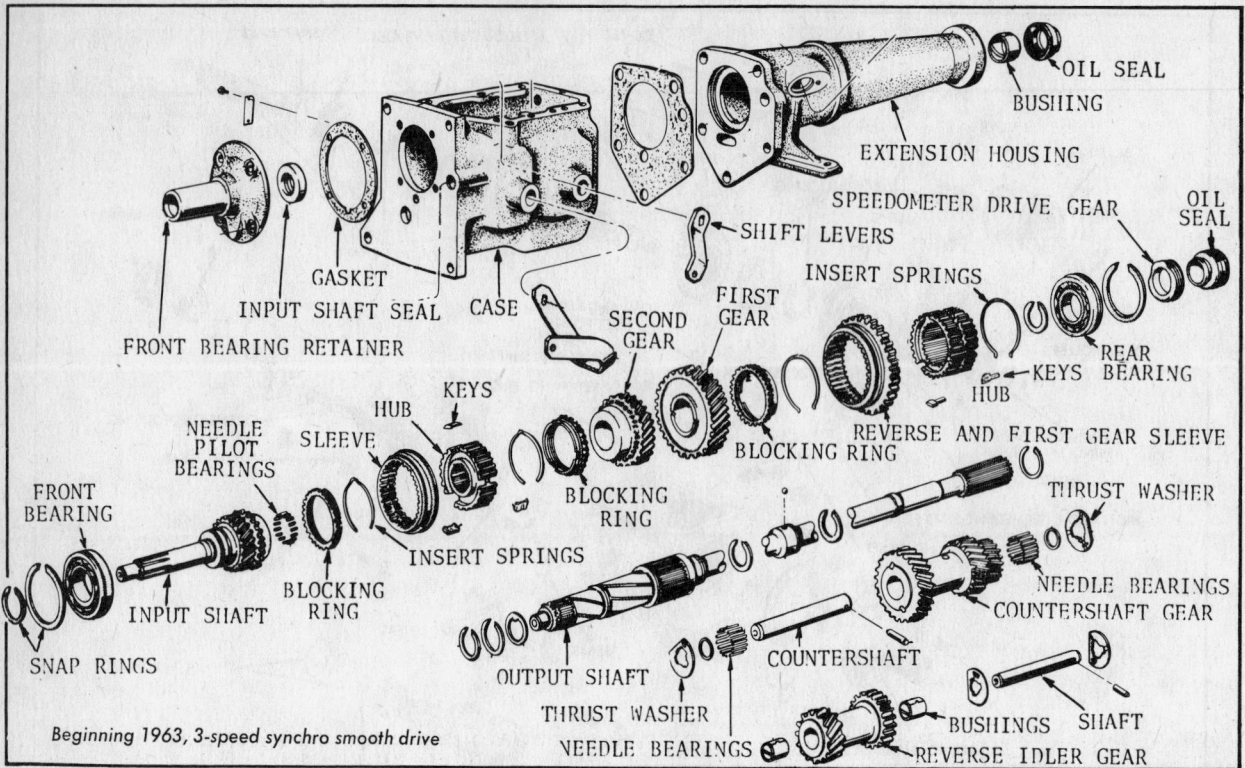

Beginning 1963, 3-speed synchro smooth drive

cam and shaft toward the outside of the case, then separate the balls and spring from the plunger. Drive out the cam and shaft assemblies, and remove the plunger.

15. Remove shift lever cam and shaft oil seals.

16. Remove snap ring and press the input shaft out of the bearing and oil slinger.

17. Remove snap ring, and remove the bearing from the output shaft.

18. Dismantle the components, such as: synchronizer, counter shaft cluster, etc. then clean and inspect parts.

19. To assemble, reverse the above procedure.

DISASSEMBLE & ASSEMBLE— SIDE COVER TYPE

1. Remove the cap screws that attach the gearshift housing to the transmission case. Remove the gearshift housing, housing gasket and two shifter forks.

2. Remove the four transmission case-to-extension housing bolts. Rotate the extension housing counterclockwise about 1/4 turn to expose end of countershaft.

3. With a dummy shaft, drive the shaft out of the cluster gear and case toward the rear. Leave dummy shaft in the cluster, at rest, in the bottom of the case.

4. Remove extension housing and output shaft from the case.

5. To disassemble the output shaft assembly, remove the snap ring at the front of the shaft. Then, slide the synchronizer, intermediate gear, and low and reverse sliding gear off the front of the shaft.

6. Remove the snap ring which holds the outer race in the extension housing, then tap the bearing and shaft out of the housing.

7. If output shaft bearing is to be replaced, remove speedometer gear snap ring, speedometer gear, and drive ball. Remove bearing retainer snap ring and press the old bearing off the shaft.

8. Remove main drive gear (input shaft) bearing retainer.

9. Tap drive gear and bearing out of the front of the transmission. Remove the pilot roller bearings.

10. Drive the reverse idler shaft toward the rear and out of the case. Lift out the reverse idler gear.

11. Dismantle the components to be serviced, such as: synchronizer, countershaft cluster, etc. Then clean and inspect all parts.

12. To assemble, reverse the above procedure.

AUTOMATIC TRANSMISSION

REFERENCES

When automatic transmission trouble is reported, a road test and careful diagnosis is in order. "Transmission Remove and Replace" and "Linkage Adjustments" are covered here in the following paragraphs. For "Test Procedures," "Transmission Recondition" and other detailed information see Unit Repair Section, Transmission Group of the manual.

LINKAGE ADJUSTMENT

"170-Six"

1. Apply parking brakes, and place the selector lever in "N" position.

2. Run the engine until it reaches normal operating temperature.

3. Hook up a tachometer and check engine idle speed. Idle speed should be less than 500 R.P.M.

4. With throttle in the hot-idle position, bottom the dashpot plunger and measure the clearance between the plunger and the throttle shaft lever. Dashpot clearance should be .060"~.150".

5. With engine stopped, adjust the carburetor throttle rod length to obtain an accelerator height of 4 5/16". This measurement is taken from the top of the accelerator pedal to the floor mat.

6. Disconnect throttle return spring and the downshift linkage return spring.

7. Loosen the adjusting lock on the downshift control rod.

8. Pull the control rod and throttle linkage "Z" bar up to the limit of their travel. Then, holding them in this position, slide the

adjustment lock down against the "Z" bar, and tighten the screw.

9. Install the return springs, and check the throttle and downshift linkage for full travel.

10. Test drive the car to check for proper up-shift and kickdown operations.

V-8 Engines

1. Apply parking brakes, and place the selector in "N."

2. Run engine at idle speed until normal operating temperature has been reached.

3. Hook up a tachometer and check idle speed. The R.P.M. should be under 500 with the fast idle cam in slow (hot) position.

4. With throttle in hot-idle position, bottom the dashpot plunger and measure the clearance between the plunger and the throttle shaft level. This clearance should be .060"-.090".

5. Engine stopped, disconnect the carburetor connecting link from the accelerator assembly.

6. Insert a ¼" drill rod through the gauging holes. Hold the carburetor conecting link forward, and adjust the sleeve until the link assembly fits freely in the accelerator assembly. Then rotate the sleeve counterclockwise one full turn. Remove the gauge pin.

MANUAL LINKAGE ADJUSTMENT

1. With engine stopped, loosen clamp at the shift lever so that the shift lever is free to slide in the clamp.

2. Put the selector in "D" position.

3. Shift the manual lever at the transmission into the "D" de-

CONVERTER SECURED TO TRANSMISSION CASE DURING REMOVAL AND INSTALLATION   D1278-A

Transmission Mounted in Jack.

tent, (second from the rear).

4. Tighten clamp on shift rod.

5. Recheck pointer alignment for all selector lever detent positions.

FORDOMATIC, R & R

Remove

1. Position the car on a suitable hoist but do NOT raise it at this time.

2. Pull back the front floor mat and remove the converter-housing-to-engine access hole covers. Remove the two upper bolts and lockwashers that hold the converter housing to the engine.

3. From under the hood, remove the two bolts that hold the throttle linkage bracket to the converter housing.

4. Remove the starter.

5. Now raise the car and remove the cover from the bottom of the converter housing.

6. Remove one of the converter drain plugs, turn the converter 180° and remove the other drain plug. (CAUTION) Do not attempt to

turn the converter with a wrench applied to the converter attaching nuts.

7. Remove the drain plug and drain the transmission.

8. Disconnect the driveshaft at the rear universal joint and remove the driveshaft. (By installing the extension housing oil seal replacing tool in the rear end of the extension housing, a sloppy mess can be avoided.)

9. Disconnect the manual throttle linkage at the transmission.

10. Disconnect the speedometer cable at the extension housing.

11. Disconnect the transmission oil filler tube and remove the bolt that attaches the extension housing to the rear support.

12. Disconnect the parking brake rod at the equalizer.

13. With a transmission jack attached to the transmission, lift enough to take the weight off the engine rear support member.

14. Remove the two bolts which hold the support member to the underbody. Remove the support member.

15. Lower the transmission and engine assembly again but support the rear of the engine.

16. Remove the four converter-to-flywheel attaching stud nuts. Back the converter off the flywheel as far as possible.

17. Remove the two lower converter housing to engine block bolts.

18. Work the converter housing off the engine block dowel pins and work the converter pilot out of the engine crankshaft.

19. Lash or otherwise secure the converter to the transmission and lower the transmission and converter assembly.

(CAUTION) Before proceeding

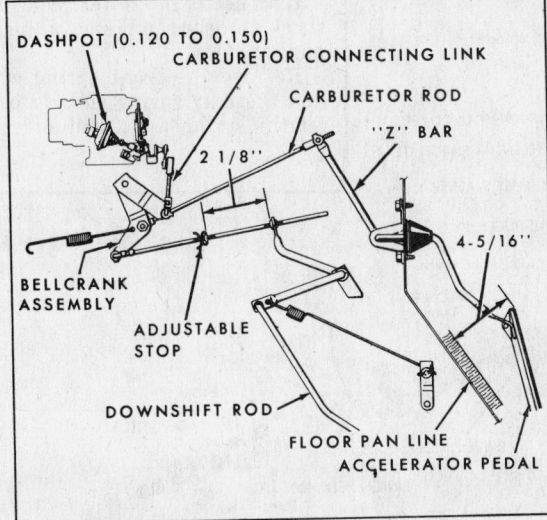

DASHPOT (0.120 TO 0.150)
CARBURETOR CONNECTING LINK
CARBURETOR ROD
"Z" BAR
2 1/8"
4-5/16"
BELLCRANK ASSEMBLY
ADJUSTABLE STOP
DOWNSHIFT ROD
FLOOR PAN LINE
ACCELERATOR PEDAL

Automatic Transmission Linkage—6 Cyl.

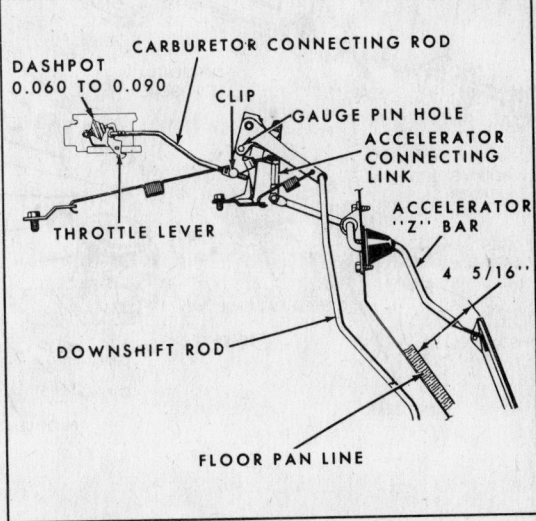

CARBURETOR CONNECTING ROD
DASHPOT 0.060 TO 0.090
CLIP
GAUGE PIN HOLE
ACCELERATOR CONNECTING LINK
ACCELERATOR "Z" BAR
THROTTLE LEVER
4 5/16"
DOWNSHIFT ROD
FLOOR PAN LINE

Automatic Transmission Linkage—V-8.

further with work on either the transmission or torque converter, thoroughly clean the outside of the units to prevent dirt from entering the mechanism and causing trouble. The Ford Motor Car Company is so particular about foreign matter entering the transmission or converter that they forbid the use of wiping rags for cleaning parts during transmission or converter assembly or repair.

TRANSMISSION OR CONVERTER, REPLACE

Replacement is a reverse procedure of removal.

Dismantling, overhaul, adjustments and test procedures are covered in the Unit Repair section under Two-Speed Fordomatic Transmission.

UNIVERSAL JOINTS AND PROPELLER SHAFT

REMOVAL OF THE REAR UNIVERSAL JOINT

The rear universal joint has two pillow blocks which are bolted to the pinion shaft flange.

Take out the four bolts which hold the bearing blocks to the pinion shaft and gently tap off the bearing blocks.

Lower the back end of the drive shaft and the front end can be slid out of the back of the transmission to-

gether with the transmission yoke portion of the front universal joint.

Carry the assembly—the front universal joint complete, the driveshaft and the rear universal joint, to the bench and remove the cross from the rear universal joint by taking out the lock rings from the inner side of the bearings. Using a large punch or an arbor press, drive one of the bearings in toward the center, which will force out the opposite bearing.

When it is pressed out far enough to grip it with a pair of pliers, grip it and pull it out of the driveshaft yoke.

Now drive the cross in the opposite direction until the opposite bearing has been driven far enough out for a purchase with a pair of pliers.

When both bearings have been taken out, the cross can be lifted from between the two yokes.

FRONT UNIVERSAL JOINT REMOVAL

Follow the procedure given above for the rear universal joint but leave the rear universal joint cross in place on the driveshaft if it is not to be removed.

Remove the lock rings from the inner side of two opposite bearings and press on the outer side of one of the bearings, forcing the cross over, which will force the bearings on the opposite side out of its yoke.

Remove the bearing which was forced out of the yoke and then press the cross in the opposite direction to press the other bearing out.

Repeat this procedure on the third and fourth bearing.

When installing the new bearings in the universal joint yoke, it is possible to put them in with a driver of some type, but it is recommended that this work be done in an arbor press since a heavy jolt on the needle bearings can very easly misalign them, which will greatly shorten their life.

REAR AXLE AND REAR SUSPENSION

TROUBLE SHOOTING AND ADJUSTMENT

General instructions covering the troubles of the rear axle and how to repair and adjust it, together with information on installation of rear axle bearings and grease seals, are given in the general section under the heading: Axles, Rear.

Capacities of the rear axle are given in the Capacities Tables at the start of this section.

REMOVAL OF REAR AXLE ASSEMBLY

Jack up the car sufficiently for clearance and support the vehicle with standjacks at the frame in front of the rear axle. Disconnect the lower end of the shock absorber and remove the spring U bolts and plate. Remove the rear spring front hanger stud and the rear shackle and remove the spring.

The rear axle assembly can be slid out on its own wheels.

REPLACE REAR SPRING

Jack up the side of the car being worked on and support the car at the frame in front of the rear axle.

Disconect the lower end of the shock absorber and remove the spring hanger plate.

Remove the front spring eye bolt and the rear spring shackle bolt and let the spring down and slide it out.

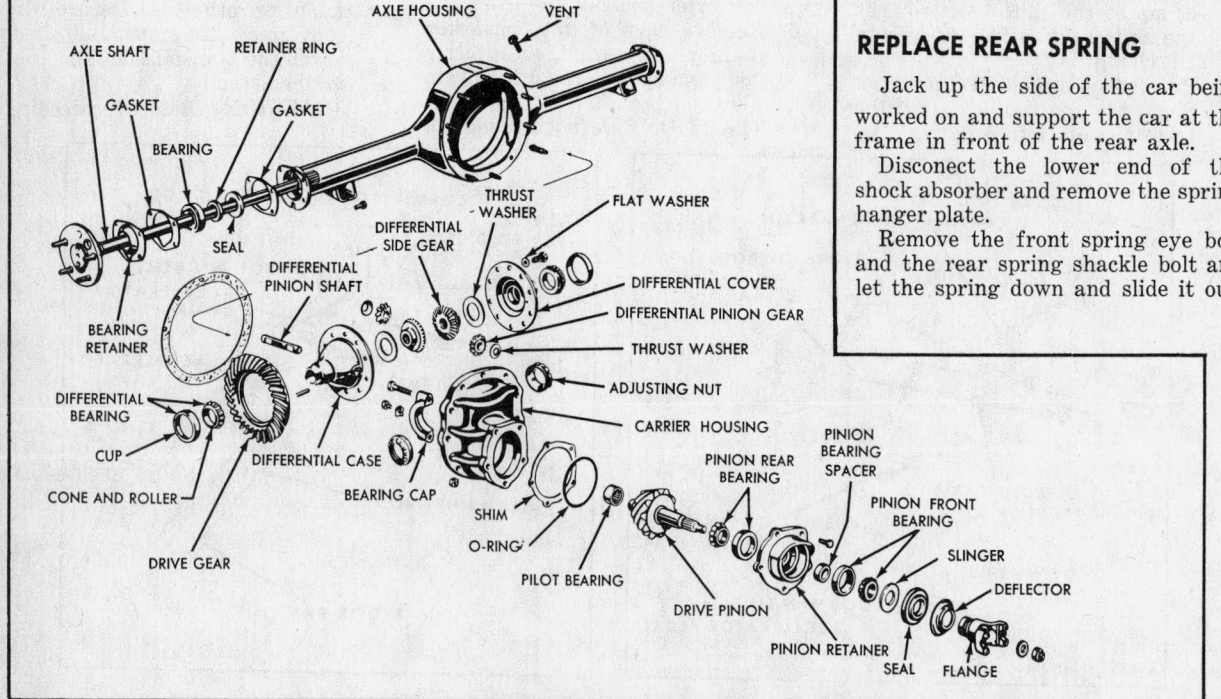

Rear axle assembly

Page

AIR CONDITIONING

Service 1092

BRAKES, HYDRAULIC

Adjustments 938
Bleed brakes 941
Master cylinder service 939
References 321

CLUTCH

Clutch assembly, R & R 333
Clutch pedal adjust 333

COOLING SYSTEM

Radiator, R & R 323
References 322
Thermostat 322
Water pump, R & R 323

ELECTRICAL SYSTEM

Distributor, R & R 318
Distributor specifications 315
Fuses and circuit breakers 316
Gauges 1024
Generator regulator
    specifications 315
Generator and regulators, R & R . 319
Generator service 1026
Generator specifications 315
Generator trouble chart 1026
Ignition firing order & timing ... 314
Ignition timing procedure 318
Ignition timing specifications ... 315
Starter, R & R 319
Starter specifications 316
Starter systems 1046

ENGINE ASSEMBLY

Cylinder head, R & R 324
Cylinder head tightening 317
Engine assembly, R & R 323
Engine diagnosis 1012
Engine firing order & Timing ... 314
Engine marking code 315
Engine references 323
Oil pan, R & R 329
Oil pressure specifications 316
Piston and rod, assembly 330
Piston specifications 317
Specifications, general, engine .. 316
Specifications, tune-up, engine .. 315
Timing case 328

Page

ENGINE ASSEMBLY—continued

Timing chain & cover 328
Trouble shooting charts 1012
Tune-up specifications 315
Valve references 325
Valve specifications 317
Valves 6 cyl., R & R 325
Valves V-8, R & R 327
Valves, hydraulic 327
Valve adjusting sequences 327

ENGINE LUBRICATION

Oil pan, R & R 329
References 329

EXHAUST SYSTEM

Muffler, R & R 322

FUEL SYSTEM

Carburetors 972
Fuel gauge service 1024
Fuel pump pressure 315
Fuel pump service 1020
Fuel tank, remove 321
References 321

INSTRUMENTS

Ignition switch 320
Oil pressure gauge 320
Speedometer, R & R 319
Temperature gauge 320

RADIO, R & R

References 338

REAR AXLE AND SUSPENSION

Axle assembly, R & R 338
Axle shaft 338
Axle shaft oil seal 918
Pinion bearings 918
Ring gear & pinion 918
Trouble shooting 919

SPECIFICATIONS

Battery 316
Brake cylinder sizes 316
Capacities:
    Axle, rear 316
    Cooling system 316
    Crankcase 316
    Fuel tank 316
    Transmission, automatic ... 316
    Transmission, manual 316
Chassis, general 316
Distributor 315
Engine, general 316
Engine tune-up 315
Fuses and circuit breakers 316

Page

SPECIFICATIONS—continued

General regulators 315
Generators 315
Light bulbs 316
Main bearings 316
Model identification illustrations .314
Pistons and pins 317
Quick reference specifications .. 314
Rod bearings 316
Starters 316
Torque wrench 317
Tune-up 315
Valves 317
Wheel alignment 317

STEERING, MANUAL

Adjust gear 1052
Gear assembly, R & R 333
Horn button, R & R 333
Steering wheel, R & R 333

SUSPENSION, FRONT

Alignment procedures 1082
Alignment specifications 317
Camber, adjust 1087
Caster, adjust 1087
Toe-in, adjust 1087
References 330

TRANSMISSION, AUTOMATIC

Disassembly of transmission ... 838
Linkage, adjust 336
Transmission, R & R 337
Trouble shooting 842

TRANSMISSION, STANDARD

Linkage, adjust 336
Transmission, R & R 333
Transmission, disassemble 335

TROUBLE CHECKS

Procedures 1

TUNE-UP

Procedures 317
Specifications 315
Engine diagnosis 1012

UNIVERSAL JOINT AND DRIVE LINE

Disassemble U joint 338
U joint & drive line, R & R 338

FALCON AND COMET

YEAR IDENTIFICATION

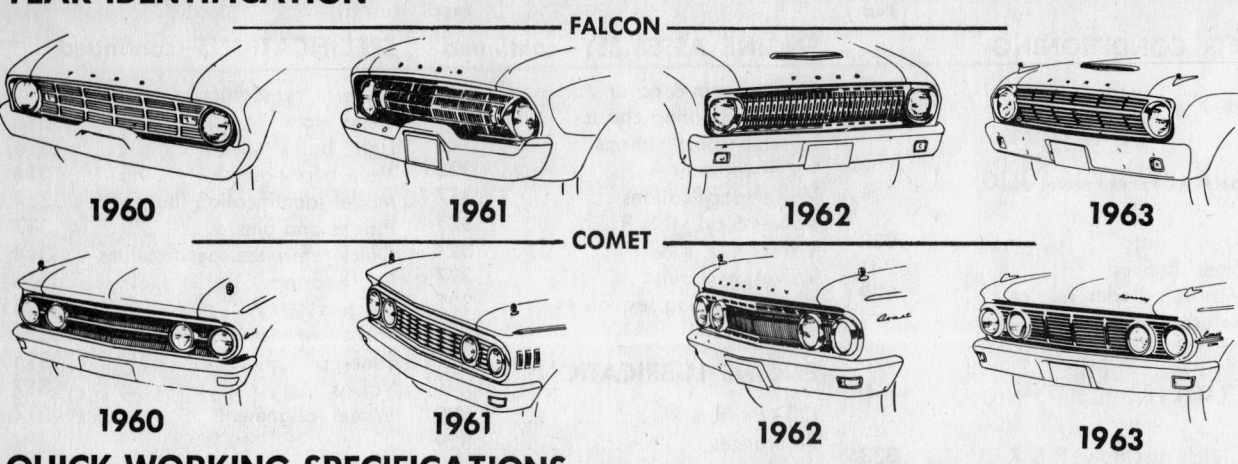

FALCON

1960   1961   1962   1963

COMET

1960   1961   1962   1963

QUICK WORKING SPECIFICATIONS

DISTRIBUTOR

Breaker Point Gap (In.)
1960-63, 6 cyl. 024-.026
1963, V-8 ....014-.016

Cam Angle (Degrees)
1960-63, 6 cyl. ....35°-38°
1963, V-8 ....26°-28½°

FIRING ORDER

Fires
1960-63, 6 cyl. 1-5-3-6-2-4
1963, V-8 1-5-4-2-6-3-7-8

IGNITION TIMING

(Spark occurs degrees at or before T.C.)
1960-63, 6 cyl. ....w/std. trans. 2 B
w/automatic 6 B
1963
260 V-8 ....2-11B
Idle speed for timing ....500 rpm

SPARK PLUGS

Year	Type	Gap
1960-63, 6 cyl.	BF-82	.034
1963, V8	BF-82	.034

VALVES

Operating Tappet Clearance in Inches Hot

	Int.	Ex.
1960-62	.016	.016
1963, 6 cyl. early	.016"	.016"
late	0"	0"
1963 All V8	zero	zero

GENERATOR AND REGULATOR

YEAR AND SERIES	GENERATOR Field Current In Amperes 6 Volt	12 Volt	REGULATOR Cut-out Closing Voltage	Current Regulator Setting	Voltage Regulator Setting
1960-63	—	1.5	12.8	25	15.0

(A) Surrounding temperatures guide this adjustment. Higher temperatures require lower settings. Lower temperatures permit higher settings, within limits.

CAPACITIES

Engine Crankcase (Quarts)
(Add 1 Qt. for new filter)
1960-63, 6 cyl. 3½
1963, V-8 4

Transmission, Synchro. (Pts.)
Add 1 pint for Overdrive.
1960-63, All 2½

Transmission, Automatic (Pts.)
1960-63, All 12½

Rear Axle (Pints)
1960-63, All 2

Gasoline Tank Gallons
1960-63, All 14

Cooling System (Quarts)
(Add 1 quart for heater)
1960-63, 6 cyl. 8¾
1963, V-8 ....13½

FIRING ORDER and TIMING

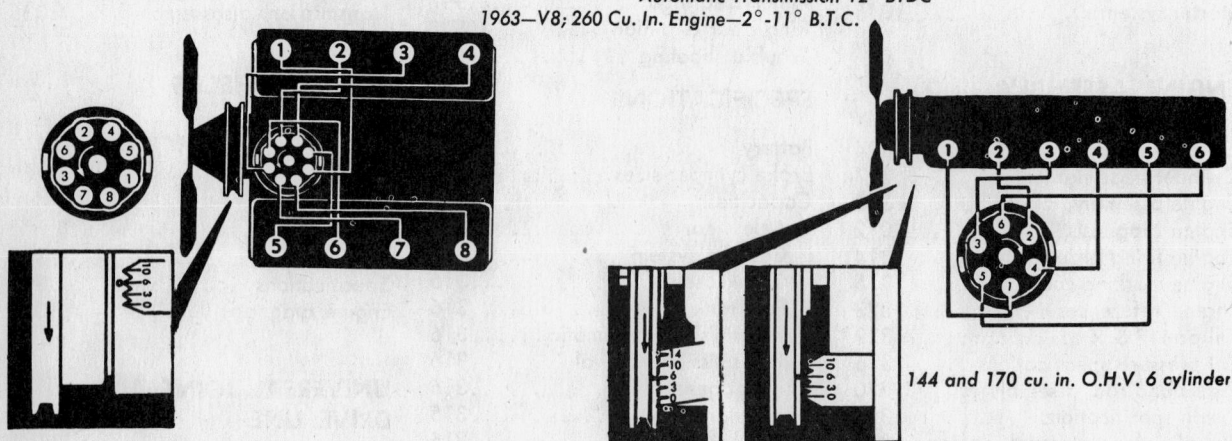

SPARK OCCURS: 1960-63 —6 Cyl., Standard Transmission 6° BTDC
Automatic Transmission 12° BTDC
1963—V8; 260 Cu. In. Engine—2°-11° B.T.C.

144 and 170 cu. in. O.H.V. 6 cylinder

NOTE:
THESE ARE APPROXIMATE SETTINGS. ENGINE DESIGN, ALTITUDE, TEMPERATURE, FUEL AND ENGINE CONDITION WILL ALL INFLUENCE TIMING. THE DETERMINING FACTOR, LIMITING ADVANCE, WILL STILL BE THE "KNOCK POINT" OF THE INDIVIDUAL ENGINE.

CAR SERIAL NUMBER LOCATION AND ENGINE IDENTIFICATION

ENGINE IS IDENTIFIED THRU CAR SERIAL NUMBER.

Falcon and Comet **serial numbers** and other pertinent information are to be found on a plate riveted to the rear edge of the left front door.

The **engine number** is stamped on the top surface of the engine block near the crankcase breather pipe, (front left side).

Beginning 1963 engine size can be determined by the color of the rocker arm cover and the air cleaner.

6 cyl. 144 cu. in. engine ....blue

170 cu. in engine ....red
260 cu. in. engine ....yellow
260 cu. in. Sprint ....chrome

The car serial number is composed of two sections, the first five units give the year, assembly plant, model, and the engine used. The second section of the number gives the consecutive order of production.

First, Digit "0" designates 1960, (1-1961 etc.).

Second, Letter—Assembly Plant:
"H"—Lorain
"K"—Kansas City
"R"—San Jose

S—Pilot Plant
T—Metuchen

Third, Two Digits:
11—Tow door sedan
12—Four door sedan
21—Two door wagon
22—Four door wagon
27—Ranchero

Fourth, Letter:
S—OHV-6, 144 cu. in. engine.
D—OHV-6, 144 cu. in. (Low compression).
U—OHV-6, 170 cu. in. engine.
The remaining digits comprise the consecutive order of unit production.

TUNE-UP SPECIFICATIONS

YEAR	SPARK PLUGS		DISTRIBUTOR			Ignition Timing	Compression Pressure Cranking	VALVES		Timing Inlet Opens	Fuel Pump Pressure	Engine Idle Speed
	Type	Gap	Cam Angle	Point Gap	Arm Spring Tension			TAPPET CLEARANCE HOT				
								Inlet	Exh.			
1960-62	BF-82	.034	35°	.025	17-20	Note 1	170	.016	.016	15°B	4.5	Note 2
1963 6 cyl.—All	BF-82	.034	35°	.025	17-20	Note 1	170	.016*	.016*	15°B	4.5	Note 2
V8—All	BF-82	.034	26-28½°	.015	17-20	Note 1	150	Zero	Zero	21°B	5.0	Note 2

NOTE 1. W/Std. Trans., 2°BTC. W/Automatic Trans., 6°BTC.
NOTE 2. W/Std. Trans., 500-525. W/Automatic Trans., In Drive, 475-500.
*Late production cars use zero Linkage Hydraulic Tappets.

DISTRIBUTOR SPECIFICATIONS

YEAR	Model	Part Number	Rotation	Cam Angle In Degrees	BREAKER		GOVERNOR CONTROL		VACUUM CONTROL, NOTE (A)		
					Point Opening (Inch)	Arm Spring In Ounces	@DIST.	R.P.M.	Inches of Vacuum To Start Advance	Inches of Vacuum For Full Advance	Max. Adv. of Dist. In Degrees
							Advance Starts	Full Advance			
1960	Std. Trans.	C0DF12127A	C	35	.025	17-20	None	None	0.33	5.35	15¾
	Auto. Trans.	C0DF12127B	C	35	.025	17-20	None	None	0.65	3.94	15¾
1961	144 cu. in. eng.	C1DF12127A	C	35	.025	17-20	None	None	0.33	5.35	16½
	170 cu. in. eng.	C1DF12127B	C	35	.025	17-20	None	None	0.65	3.94	15¾
1960-63	6 cyl. 144 cu. in.	C2DF12127A	C	35	.025	17-20	None	None	0.33	5.35	16½
	6 cyl. 170 cu. in.	C2DF12127C	C	37	.025	17-20	None	None	0.65	3.94	15¾
	V8, 260 Cu. IN.	C20F12127J	CC	27	.015	17-20	1 @ 525	11 @ 2000	5.00	18.0	11

NOTE (A)

Standard Transmission: Set test stand at 0° @ 300 R.P.M. and 0 in. (Hg.).
Automatic Transmission: Set test stand at 0° @ 600 R.P.M. and .48 in. (Hg.).

GENERATOR AND REGULATOR SPECIFICATIONS

YEAR	GENERATORS		REGULATORS						
	Field Current In Amperes at 12 Volts	Brush Spring Tension	Cut Out Relay		Air Gap		Current Reg. Setting	Voltage Reg. Setting
			Air Gap	Closing Voltage	Current Reg.	Voltage Reg.		
1960-63	1.5	32-40 oz.	(A)	12.8	(A)	(A)	25	14.6 @ 75°F

(A) NO ADJUSTMENT
NOTE: Surrounding temperatures and driving habits influence the above adjustments and must be considered by the mechanic. Higher temperatures or turnpike conditions permit lower adjustments; lower temperatures or city type driving conditions require higher settings, within limits.

Note:

All specifications are standard and should result in satisfactory performance. There are, however, factors that influence these settings, such as fuel octane value, air density, humidity, temperature, etc. Timing charts, like other specifications must be considered as averages, subject to modification.

315

FALCON AND COMET

BATTERY AND STARTER SPECIFICATIONS

YEAR		BATTERY			STARTER							
		Amp. Hour Capacity	Volts	Terminal Grounded	LOCK TEST			NO-LOAD TEST				Brush Spring Tension
					Amps.	Volts	Torque	Amps.	Volts	R.P.M.		
1960-62		40	12	Neg.	37½	3	8.4	70	12	6000		52 oz.
1963	6 cyl.	40	12	Neg.	54	4.2	14	50	12	9500		50 oz.
	V8	40	12	Neg.	67	5.6	15.5	70	12	9500		50 oz.

CAPACITIES

YEAR		Engine Crankcase Add 1 qt. For New Filter	Transmission Pints To Refill After Draining		Rear Axle Pints	Gasoline Tank Gallons	Cooling System Quarts
			Manual	Automatic			
1960-62		3½	2½	12½	2	14	8¾
1963	6 cyl.—All	3½	2½	12½	2	14	..8¾
	V8—All	4	2½	12½	2	14	13½

LIGHT BULBS

BULB CHART

ILLUMINATION

	Power	Part #
Headlamps	50/40w	6012
Fr. turn sig. & prk.	32/4 c.p.	1034
Rr. turn, stop & tail	32/4 c.p.	1034
Tail only (inboard)	4 c.p.	67
License plate	4 c.p.	67
Cluster	2 c.p.	57
Radio dial	1.5 c.p.	1445
Dome lamp	1.5 c.p.	1003

INDICATOR

High Beam	1.5 c.p.	1445
Oil pressure	1.5 c.p.	1445
Generator	1.5 c.p.	1445
Turn signal	1.5 c.p.	1445

GENERAL CHASSIS AND BRAKE SPECIFICATIONS

YEAR AND MODEL		CHASSIS		BRAKE CYLINDER BORE		
		Overall Length In Inches	Tire Size	Cyl. Master (Inch)	Wheel Cylinder Diameter (Inch)	
					Front	Rear
1960-63	Falcon—Sedan	181.2	6.00x13	1.0	1¹⁄₁₆	13⁄16
	Falcon—Ranch Wagon	189.0	6.50x13	1.0	1¹⁄₁₆	⅞
	Comet—Sedan	194.9	6.00x13	1.0	1¹⁄₁₆	13⁄16
	Comet—Ranch Wagon	191.8	6.50x13	1.0	1¹⁄₁₆	⅞

FUSE AND CIRCUIT BREAKER CHART

Circuit		
Headlamps	SFE-7.5 Fuse	
Dome & Rear Parking	SFE-14 Fuse	
Turn Signals	Circuit Breaker	
Radio		
Heater Blower		
Electric w/s Wiper	**Location**	
Fuse or Breaker	Headlight Switch	
Circuit Breaker	Fuse Panel on Light Switch	
3 AG-15 Fuse	Fuse Panel on Light Switch	
SFE-14 Fuse	Fuse Panel on Light Switch	
	Fuse Panel on Light Switch	
	Instrument Panel	

GENERAL ENGINE SPECIFICATIONS

YEAR AND MODEL		Bore and Stroke	No. of Main Bearings	Type of Valve Lifter Used	Cu. In. Piston Displacement	AMA Horsepower	Advertised Horsepower At Stated RPM	Advertised Torque At Stated RPM	Compression Ratio	Oil Pressure At 30 MPH	Camshaft Drive
1960-62	144 cu. in.	3½ x 2½	4	Mech. Adj.	144.3	29.4	90 @ 4200	138 @ 2000	8.7:1	45	Chain
1961-62	170 cu. in.	3½ x 2¹⁵⁄₁₆	4	Mech. Adj.	170.0	29.4	N.A.	N.A.	8.7:1	45	Chain
1963											
	6 cyl., 144 cu. in.	3½ x 2½	4	Mech.*	144.3	29.4	90 @ 4200	138 @ 2000	8.7:1	45	Chain
	6 cyl., 170 cu. in.	3½ x 2¹⁵⁄₁₆	4	Mech.*	170.0	29.4	101 @ 4400	156 @ 2400	8.7:1	45	Chain
	V8, 260 cu. in.	3-51/64 x 2⅞	5	Hydraulic	260	46.2	164 @ 4400	258 @ 2200	8.7-1	55	Chain

*Late production models use zero clearance Hyd. Tappets.

CRANKSHAFT BEARING JOURNAL SIZES

YEAR	MAIN BEARING JOURNALS					CONNECTING ROD BEARING JOURNALS		
	Journal Diameter	Oil Clearance	of Shaft	End Play End Play Held By		Journal Diameter	Oil Clearance	End Play
1960-62	2.2485	0.0010	0.006	3		2.1236	0.0015	0.007
1963								
6 cyl.—All	2.2485	0.0010	0.006	3		2.1236	0.0015	0.007
V8, 260 cu. in.	2.2485	.0012	.006	3		2.1236	.0015	.007

PISTON AND PIN SPECIFICATIONS

Year and Model	PISTON		Diameter	Bushing	PISTON PIN			
	Skirt Clearance				FIT			
	Min.	Max.			In Rod	In Piston	Lock	
1960-63—All	.0021	.0027	.9120	None	Press	.0001-.0003	Rod Press	

Skirt clearance measured at bottom of skirt 0.0024
To test clearance by ribbon method use ½" wide shim, .002" thick. The pull required is approximately 6 to 8 pounds.

VALVE SPECIFICATIONS

YEAR	Seat Angle		Intake Valve Lift	Exhaust Valve Lift	Valve Spring Pressure		Stem to Guide Clearance		Stem Diameter		Valve Guides Replaceable
	In.	Ex.			Outer	Inner	Inlet	In.	Ex.	Exhaust	
1960-62	45°	45°	0.2405	0.344	52 @ 1¹⁹⁄₃₂	None	.0016	.0026	.3104	.3094	No
1963											
6 cyl., 144 cu. in.	45°	45°	0.344	0.344	52 @ 1¹⁹⁄₃₂	None	.0016	.0026	.310	.309	No
6 cyl., 170 cu. in.	45°	45°	0.344	0.344	52 @ 1¹⁹⁄₃₂	None	.0016	.0026	.310	.309	No
V8, 260 cu. in.	45°	45°	.380	.380	60 @ 1-49/64	None	.0016	.0026	.3104	.3094	No

TORQUE SPECIFICATIONS

YEAR	Cylinder Head Bolts	Rod Bearing Bolts	Main Bearing Bolts	Crankshaft Pulley Bolt	Flywheel To Crankshaft Bolt	MANIFOLD	
						In.	Ex.
1960-62	65-75	19-24	65-75	45-55	75-85	None	13-18
1963							
6 cyl.—All	65-75	19-24	60-70	45-55	75-85	None	13-18
V8	65-70	19-24	60-70	70-90	75-85	12-15	13-18

FRONT WHEEL ALIGNMENT SPECIFICATIONS

YEAR	CASTER		CAMBER		Toe-In (Inches)	King Pin Inclination (Degrees)	WHEEL PIVOT RATIO	
	Range (Degrees)	Preferred	Range (Degrees)	Preferred			Outer Wheel	Inner Wheel
1960-63	1½P to ½P	1P	0 to ½P	¼P	³⁄₁₆	7	20°	21¾°

CYLINDER HEAD NUT TIGHTENING SEQUENCE

6 Cyl.—65-75 Ft. lbs.

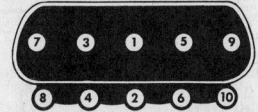

V8—65-70 ft. lbs.

TORQUE SPECIFICATIONS
(Foot Pounds)

Oil pan to crankcase 7-9
Timing case cover 7-9
Valve rocker arm cover 3-5
Rocker shaft support to cyl. head.......................................30-35
Valve adjusting screw (minimum torque required) 3

Engine Front Support:
Insulator assy. to engine bolts 23-28
Insulator assy. to attaching bracket locknut 11-15
Engine Rear Support:

Support retainer to insulator locknuts 11-15
Support assembly to body locknuts 10-15
Bracket & Number 2 crossmember to body locknut ..24-32

TUNE-UP

Engine tune-up and diagnosis are closely enough related to justify coverage under one head and to establish an approach that will best serve both ends.

1. Blow foreign matter from around the plugs. Remove plug wires and then remove spark plugs.

2. Hook up starter remote control cable and switch. Then crank the engine through about four compression strokes while reading the compression gauge.

3. Record and compare the individual cylinder pressures. A variation of 15 pounds or more should not be tolerated.

NOTE:

A compression check should be the first step in the course of tune-up events. Only if compression pressures are within limits should the tune-up be continued.

Spark Plugs

Use a good spark plug tester,, if available, and service or renew the plugs. Detailed information on diagnosing spark plug troubles, and using spark plug condition as an aid in engine diagnosis can be found in the Unit Repair section under Diagnosis.

IN SPARK PLUG INSTALLATION:

A. Use plugs of correct model, spaced properly.

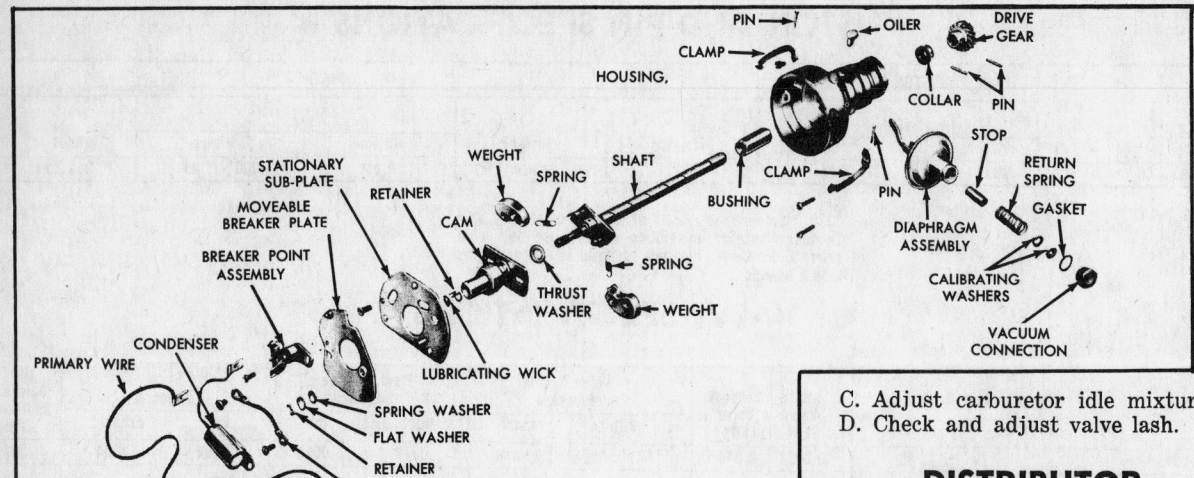

Distributor Assembly—V8

B. Thoroughly clean the cylinder head and spark plug threads and seats, (no gaskets used).
C. Torque the spark plugs to 15-20 ft. lb.

Generator Drive Belt

Check the condition of the belt and adjust tension to ½" deflection when 15 pounds pressure is applied midway between the water pump and the generator pulley.

Battery

A. Check the condition of the battery.
B. Clean, lubricate and tighten cable connections, both ends.

Electrical

A. Check Generator output.
B. Check regulator.
C. Check starter motor current draw.
D. Check ignition coil output.
E. Check ignition wiring.
F. Test primary circuit resistance.
G. Test spark intensity at each plug wire.

Cooling System

A. Examine for radiator and engine coolant leaks.
B. Check radiator and heater hoses.
C. Look for coolant contamination (Rust, oil, etc.) in the radiator.
D. Recharge cooling system with anti-freeze or rust inhibitor.

Distributor

A. Replace and/or reset breaker points.
B. Lubricate distributor cam.
C. Lubricate distributor shaft bushing at the oil cup.
D. Check and adjust vacuum control.
E. Inspect and clean distributor rotor and cap.

Fuel System

A. Clean pump sediment bowl.
B. Check Pump pressure and capacity, (fuel filter may be partially obstructed).
C. Clean carburetor bowl and adjust float.

FINAL ADJUSTMENTS

A. Set ignition timing with a light. Then modify the prescribed setting (within limits) to accomodate the variables of engine and operating conditions, and fuel anti-knock valve. This last adjustment is made in the shop but as a result of road test.
B. Check and adjust engine idle speed.

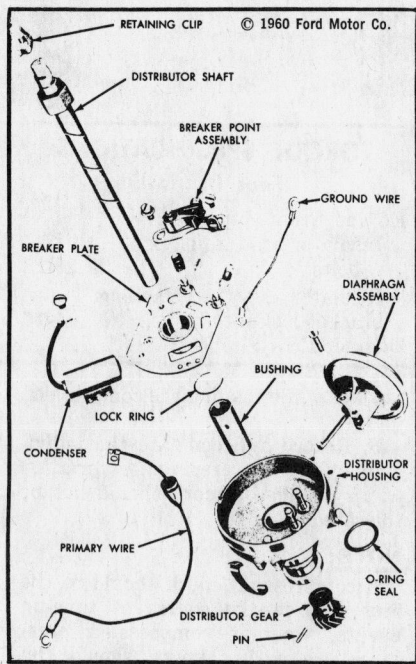

Distributor Assembly—6 Cyl.

C. Adjust carburetor idle mixture.
D. Check and adjust valve lash.

DISTRIBUTOR

Detailed information on: distributor drive, direction of distributor rotation; cylinder numbering; firing order; point gap; cam dwell; timing mark location; spark plugs, spark advance; ignition resistor location, and idle speed; will be found in the Tune-Up Specifications table at the start of this section.

SET IGNITION TIMING

The timing marks are on the crankshaft pulley, each mark represents two degrees.

These marks will coincide with the ignition from No. 1 cylinder.

Connect the neon timing light to No. 1 cylinder and adjust the body of the distributor so that the spark occurs as follows:

6 cyl. Std. Trans.   —2° Before
6 cyl. Auto. Trans.   —6° Before
8 cyl., all   —2° -11° Before

DISTRIBUTOR REMOVAL

For convenience, remove the air cleaner.

Take off the distributor cap, disconnect the vacuum line from the side of the distributor and the ignition primary wire. Crank the engine until the distributor rotor points to a definite point on the engine so that it can be installed properly without having to retime the ignition. Mark the position of the rotor and the distributor body. Remove the holddown bolt and lift the distributor out of the engine.

RETIME IGNITION

If the timing relationship has been completely fouled up proceed to retime the ignition as follows: Bring No. 1 cylinder up into the firing position. This can be checked by removing the spark plug, place your thumb in the spark plug hole and then crank the engine until the compression attempts to blow by your thumb, now slowly bring the crankshaft around until the TDC mark on the crankshaft pulley lines up with the pointer. This is firing position for No. 1 cylinder.

Remove the distributor cap and mark on the outside of the distributor the position of the rotor. The wire from No. 1 spark plug should be placed in the socket just above the rotor. Now, working in the direction of the distributor rotation, place the spark plug wires into the cap according to the firing order of the engine.

"Looking from above"

6 cyl. turns clockwise

8 cyl. turns counterclockwise.

GENERATOR AND REGULATOR

REFERENCES

Detailed facts on the generator and regulator can be found in the specification table in this section.

General repair and trouble shooting can be found in the Unit Repair section under the heading; Generators and Regulators.

GENERATOR REMOVE

1. Disconnect the negative (ground) cable from the battery.

2. Disconnect armature, field, and ground wires at the generator terminals.

3. Remove adjustment arm to generator bolt. Remove the two pivot bolts from the mounting bracket, (from underneath the car). Remove generator and belt.

GENERATOR INSTALL

1. Reverse the above procedure.

2. **Polarize the generator** by disconnecting the wire from the **field** terminal of the regulator and momentarily touch it to the **bat** terminal of the regulator. The quick surge of current will correctly polarize the generator. <u>CAUTION</u>: Do not use a "jumper" wire to polarize the generator. The regulator points may be burned if you do.

3. Adjust fan belt tension so as to obtain ¼" belt deflection when applying 10 lb. thumb pressure to the belt, midway between the generator and fan pulleys.

STARTER

The starter is a four-brush, series-parallel wound unit. The circuit is completed by means of a relay controlled switch which is part of the ignition switch.

STARTER AND STARTER DRIVE REMOVE

1. Disconnect the starter cable at the starter.

2. Remove the starter-to-flywheel housing attaching screws and remove the starter.

3. Loosen and remove the brush cover band and the starter drive actuating lever cover.

4. Loosen the through bolts enough to permit the removal of the gear housing and the starter drive actuating lever return spring.

5. Remove the pivot pin holding the starter drive actuating lever and remove the lever.

6. Remove the drive gear retaining spring clip from the end of the armature shaft and remove the drive gear assembly.

Install

1. Install the drive gear assembly on the armature shaft and install the retaining clip.

2. Position the starter gear actuating lever on the starter frame and install the retaining pivot pin.

3. Position the starter drive actuating return spring and drive gear housing to the starter frame, then tighten the through bolts.

4. Attach the starter drive lever cover and the brush cover band.

5. Place the rubber dust ring on the flywheel housing.

6. Position the starter to the flywheel housing and start the attaching screws. On a car with automatic

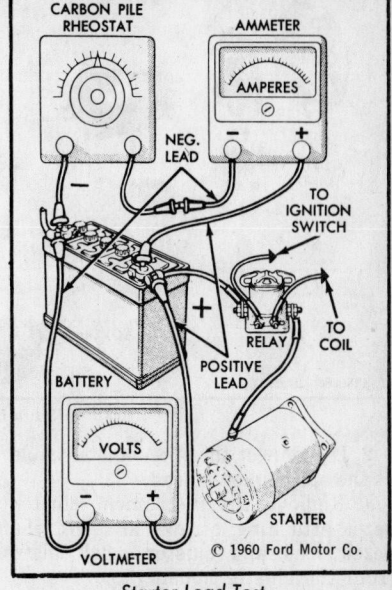

Starter Load Test.

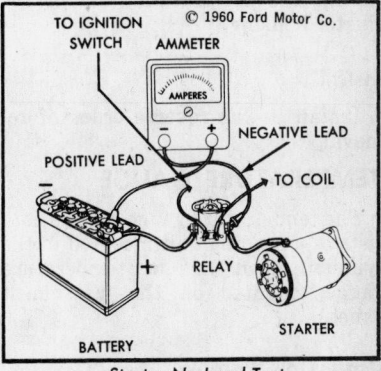

Starter No-Load Test.

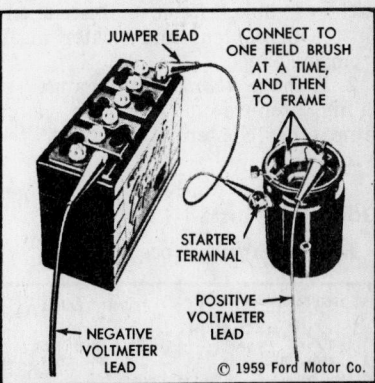

Field Open Circuit Test.

transmission, the transmission dipstick tube bracket is mounted under the starter side mounting bolt. Snug attaching bolts, then tighten, starting with the middle bolt.

INSTRUMENTS

SPEEDOMETER

Remove

1. Disconnect the battery.

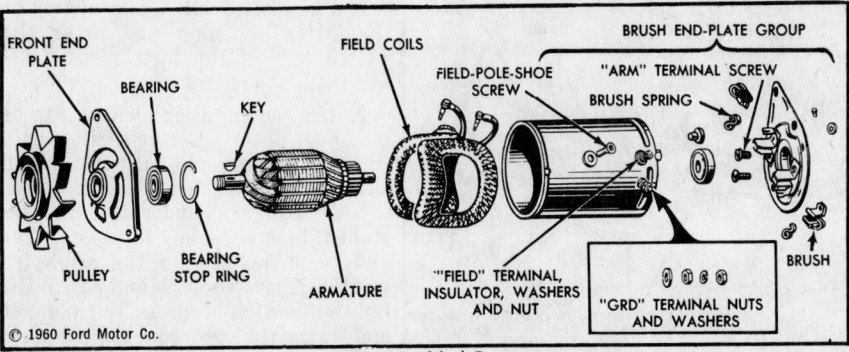

Disassembled Generator.

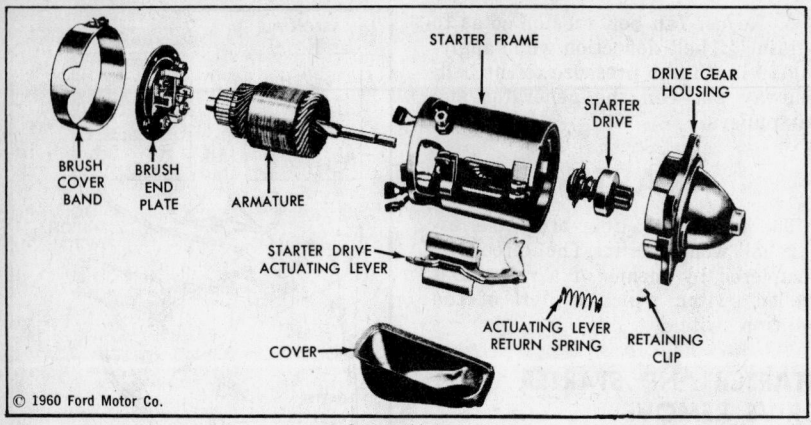

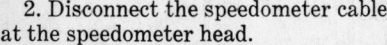

Starter Motor.

2. Disconnect the speedometer cable at the speedometer head.

3. Remove the instrument cluster bezel attaching screws and lift the bezel, lens and cluster mask plate from the cluster housing.

4. Remove speedometer retaining screws and lift the head out of the cluster housing.

Install

Install in the reverse order of removal.

TEMPERATURE GAUGE

The temperature gauge system consists of a sending unit mounted in the cylinder head and a temperature gauge mounted on the instrument panel.

Dash Unit Remove

1. Disconnect negative (ground) battery cable. Remove instrument cluster bezel, lens and cluster mask from the panel.

2. Remove temperature gauge retaining screws and pull the gauge from the cluster. Disconnect the wires.

Dash Unit Install

Reverse above procedure.

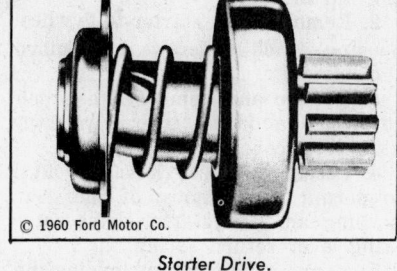

Starter Drive.

OIL PRESSURE GAUGE

All models are equipped with a red indicator light on the dash.

To test the oil pressure switch (sending unit) on the engine, turn the ignition on, engine not running, the light should come on. If the indicator does not come on, short the terminal of the oil pressure switch to ground. If the light now comes on, the oil pressure switch is probably defective. If the light still does not come on, the bulb is burned out or the wires from the bulb to the ignition switch and oil pressure switch are bad.

IGNITION SWITCH AND LOCK

Remove

1. Disconnect negative battery cable.

2. Turn ignition key to accessory

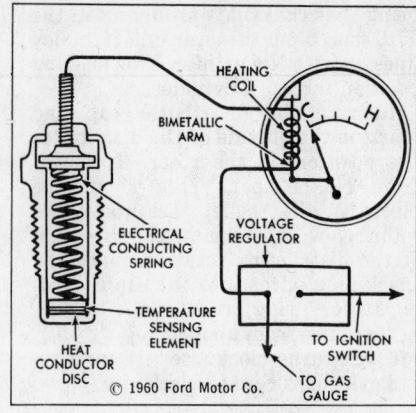

Temperature Gauge Circuit.

position.

3. With a paper clip end inserted in the cylinder release pin hole, depress the pin and turn the key and cylinder counterclockwise while withdrawing the cylinder.

If only the cylinder is to be replaced, proceed to installation, step 4.

4 From under the panel, take the nut from the back of the ignition switch.

5. Remove the wire from the accessory terminal of the switch. Pull off the insulated plug from the rear of the switch.

6. Press in on the rear of the switch and turn the switch ¼ turn counterclockwise. Remove the switch.

Ignition Switch Removal.

Install

1. Position the retainer on the switch with the open face away from the switch.

2. Place the switch and spacer to the switch opening and press the switch toward the instrument panel and install the bezel.

3. If a new ignition switch is to be installed, insert a screwdriver into the lock opening and turn the slot all the way counterclockwise.

4. If a new cylinder is to be installed, insert the key in the cylinder and turn the key to the accessory position. Place the lock and key in the ignition switch, depress the plunger and turn the key counterclockwise. Push the cylinder into the switch.

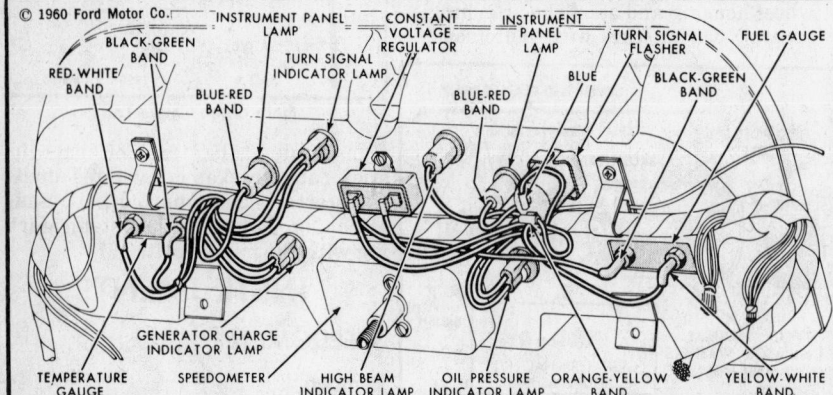

Instrument Cluster Rear View.

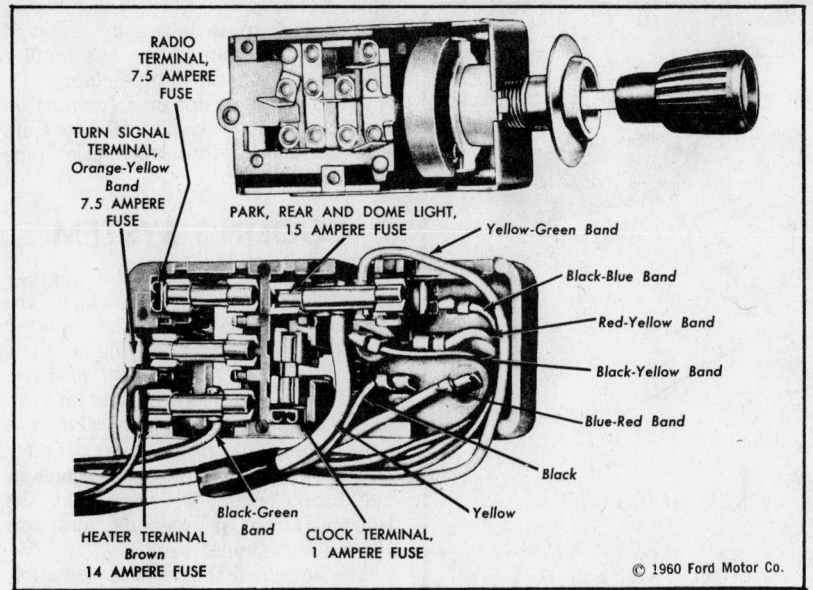

Headlight Switch.

Turn the key to check lock cylinder operation.

5. Connect the insulated plug with wires attached to the back of the switch.

6. Position the accessory and gauge wires into the switch stud and install retaining nut.

7. Connect the battery cable and check ignition switch and accessories operation.

BRAKES

Single-anchor, internal-expanding hydraulic brakes are used on all models. Self-energizing primary and secondary brake shoes with duo-servo action expand to contact against the inside surfaces of cast iron brake drums.

Beginning in March 1962, a new design front wheel brake cylinder and piston is used. These pistons have an O-Ring installed in an anular groove on the outer diameter. The O-Ring type piston has proven quite effective

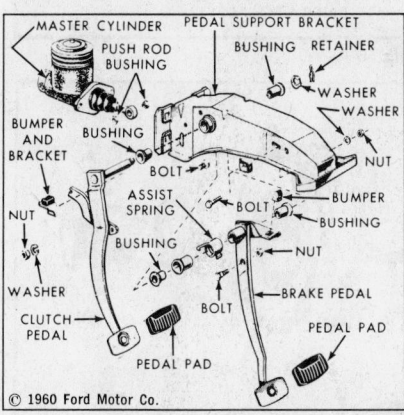

Brake Pedal and Related Parts Standard Transmission.

in reducing brake squeal and can be used in earlier production automobiles.

Note:

Any time these wheel cylinders are serviced, the O-Rings on the pistons must be replaced.

This design does not lend itself well to honing.

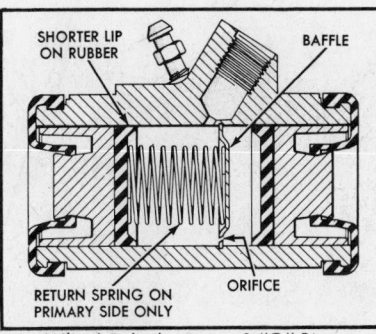

Wheel Cylinder Piston & "O" Ring

Beginning 1963

Self adjusting brake shoes are used. More detailed brake information may be obtained by refering to "Brakes, Hydraulic" in the "Unit Repair Section."

An independent hand operated parking brake operates the rear wheel brake shoes through a mechanical cable linkage.

The foot brakes are adjusted in the conventional manner through a star wheel and adjusting screw.

FUEL SYSTEM

Fuel System Information

A chart covering causes of excess fuel consumption will be found in the Unit Repair section under the head-ing: Fuel Consumption Chart.

Data on capacity on the gas tank will be found in the Capacities Table. Data on correct engine speed and fuel pump pressure will be found in the Tune-up Specifications table. Both the above tables can be found in this car section.

General information on fuel pumps and their troubles will be found in the Unit Repair section under the heading: Fuel Pumps.

Information covering operation and troubles of the fuel gauge will be found in the Unit Repair section under the heading: Gauges.

Detailed information on the carburetor and how to adjust it will be found in the Unit Repair section under the heading: Carburetors, and the specific heading of the make of carburetor being used on the engine being worked on.

FUEL PUMP

A combination fuel and vacuum booster pump is standard equipment on cars with vacuum operated windshield wipers. However, a single action pump is optional on cars equipped with electric wipers.

A disposable-type in-line filter is attached to the outlet side of the pump to clean the fuel before entering the carburetor.

FUEL TANKS

Removal

1. Raise rear of car.

2. Remove drain plug and empty the tank.

3. Disconnect fuel gauge sending unit wire.

4. Loosen hose clamp, slide clamp forward and disconnect the fuel line

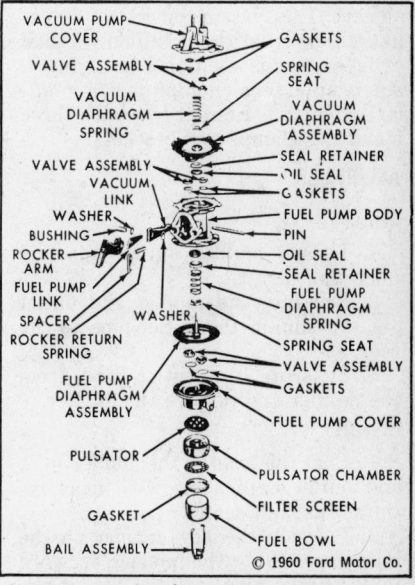

Fuel and Vacuum Booster Pump Disassembled.

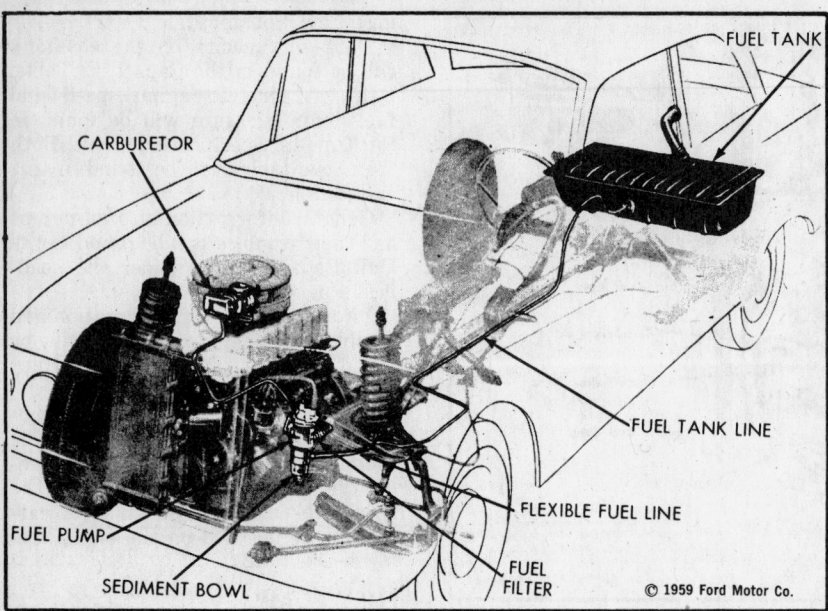

Fuel System Installation.

must not exceed 1¾". Check for possible interference between "kick-up" and the floor pan. Align the muffler and tighten the inlet pipe clamp.

3. Slide the outlet pipe forward on the muffler extension until the slots are blocked. Tighten the outlet pipe clamp.

COOLING SYSTEM

Both the 6 cyl. and V-8 engines employ cooling systems which are basically similar.

In the 6 cylinder engine, coolant flows from the cylinder head, past the thermostat (if it is open), and into the radiator upper tank. In the V-8 engine, coolant from each cylinder head flows through water passages in the intake manifold, then past the thermostat (if it is open), and into the radiator upper tank.

The standard thermostat operating temperature is 177°-182°F, however, a low reading thermostat of 157°-

at the gauge sending unit.

5. If the gauge is to be removed, turn the unit retaining ring counterclockwise and withdraw the unit.

6. Remove the spare tire from the luggage area. Remove the trunk floor mat.

7. Remove the fuel tank filler neck retaining screws.

8. Loosen filler neck to tank hose clamps. Remove filler neck, mounting gasket, and filler neck to tank hose.

9. Remove fuel tank to luggage area floor pan retaining screws.

10. Move the fuel tank up and out through the luggage compartment area.

EXHAUST SYSTEM

A single exhaust system is used on all cars. The system consists of an exhaust pipe from the manifold, (a dual exhaust pipe is used on V-8 engines). An inlet extension pipe and a muffler and a muffler outlet pipe with three mounting clamps and brackets.

MUFFLER

Remove

1. Loosen muffler outlet pipe and inlet pipe clamps.

2. Separate the muffler and outlet pipe by sliding the outlet pipe to the rear.

3. Separate the outlet pipe from the muffler and remove the muffler.

Install

1. Coat the ends of the muffler inlet and outlet extensions with heat resistant asphalt sealer.

2. Position the new muffler on the inlet pipe. Slide the muffler forward into the inlet pipe until the slots in the muffler extension are blocked. Overlap

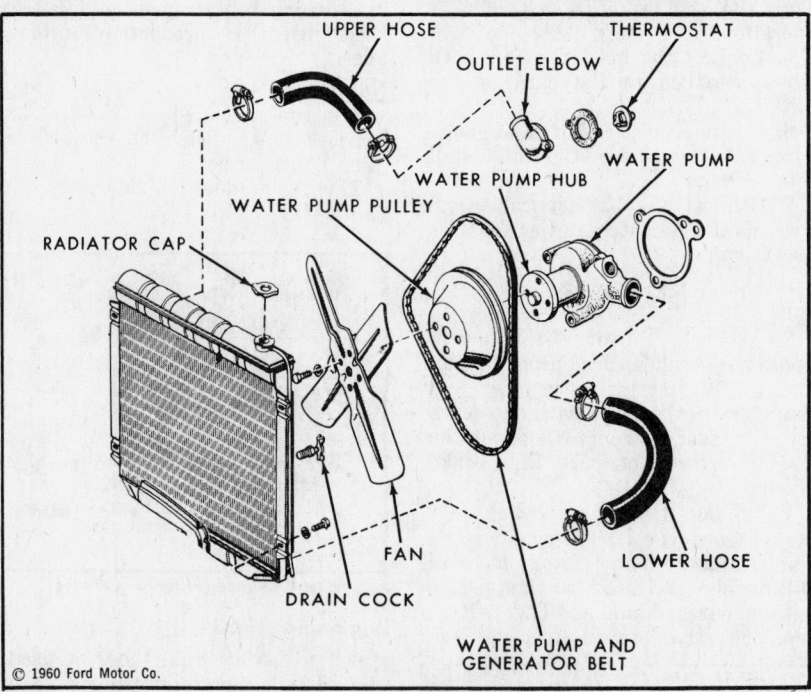

Radiator and Related Parts.

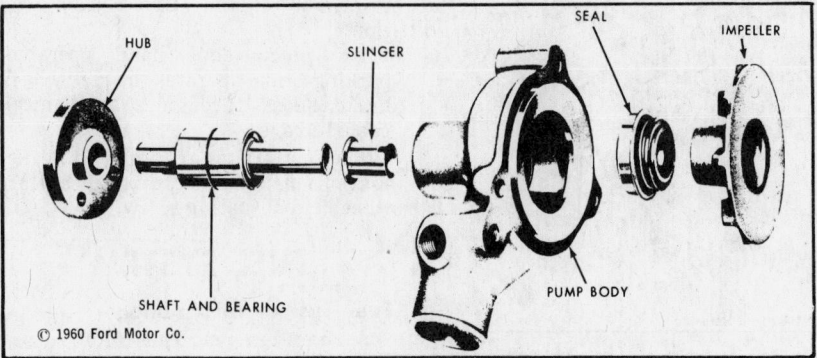

Water Pump Assembly. 6 Cyl.

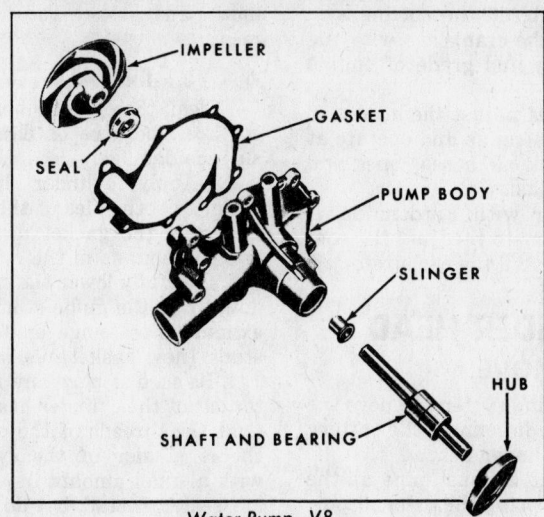

IMPELLER

GASKET

SEAL

PUMP BODY

SLINGER

HUB

SHAFT AND BEARING

Water Pump—V8

162°F is available for use with non-permanent-type anti freeze solutions.

A single water pump assembly is used. The pump has a sealed bearing integral with the water pump shaft. The bearing requires no lubrication. There is a bleed hole in the water pump housing. **This is not a lubrication hole.**

WATER PUMP
Remove

1. Drain cooling system.
2. Disconnect radiator lower hose at the water pump. Remove drive belt, fan, and water pump pulley.
3. Disconnect the heater hose at the water pump.
4. Remove the pump.

Install

1. Install in reverse order of removal.
2. Adjust fan belt so that 15 lb. pressure applied to the belt midway between the generator and water pump pulley will cause ½" deflection.

RADIATOR
Remove

1. Drain cooling system. Disconnect upper and lower hoses at the radiator.
2. Remove radiator to support bolts and remove the radiator.

Install

1. Position the radiator and install the bolts.
2. Connect upper and lower hoses.
3. Close drain cock. Fill and bleed the cooling system.
4. Operate engine and check for leaks.

ENGINE
References

Beginning 1963, both Falcon and Comet are available with the following power:

6 Cylinder, 144 cu. in. over head valve engine, 6 Cylinder, 170 cu. in. over head valve engine, V-8, 221 cu. in. valve-in-head engine, and V-8, 260 cu. in. valve-in-head engine.

General description which follows applies to all engines unless otherwise noted.

On the 6 cyl. engines, a rocker arm and shaft arrangement is used. On the V-8's, each rocker arm pivots on its individual folcrum seat, supported by a stud pressed into the cylinder head. The valve guides are an integral part of the head and are, therefore, not replaceable.

The 6 cylinder engines use mechanical tappets which, until 1963, were adjustable for running clearance. Early production, 1963 models still use mechanical, adjustable tappets, however, later production models employ a hydraulic tappet that operates at zero clearance.

The V-8 engines use hydraulic tappets and tubular push rods. Valves operate at zero clearance.

The 170 cubic inch engine is available with either the Manual or Fordomatic transmissions. It is supposed to operate satisfactorily on standard grade fuels, has a compression ratio of 8.7:1, has a single throat downdraft carburetor and a single exhaust.

It can be identified by a **red** air cleaner and rocker covers and by a quarter panel name script with "170" superimposed on "Special."

The 170 cubic inch engine can be had in either Falcon or Comet and differs from the 144 cubic inch version in the following features:

1. Different crankshaft to accommodate the stroke increase.
2. Different connecting rods to accommodate the stroke increase.
3. Different slipper type pistons.

4. Different cylinder head, revised to maintain the 8.7:1 compression ratio, has larger intake ports and valve heads with larger fuel passages (runners) for proper distribution of fuel mixture.
5. Larger intake valves.
6. Different distributor and calibration.
7. Different main bearings, water pump pulley and impeller and a 15" fan.

ENGINE, R & R

1. Scribe the hood hinge outline on the under-hood, disconnect the hood and remove.
2. Drain the entire cooling system and oil from the engine oil pan.
3. Remove the air cleaner, disconnect the battery at the cylinder head.
4. Remove upper and lower radiator hoses and remove radiator.
5. Remove fan, fan belt and upper pulley.
6. Disconnect the heater hoses at the water pump and the carburetor spacer.
7. Disconnect the generator wires at the generator, the starter cable at the starter, the accelerator rod at the carburetor and the choke control cable at the carburetor.
8. Disconnect the windshield wiper hose at the vacuum pump. Remove the fuel sediment bowl. Disconnect the fuel line at the tank.
9. Disconnect the coil primary wire at the coil. Disconnect wires at the oil pressure and water temperature sending units.
10. Remove the starter and dust seal.
11. On a car equipped with a manual-shift transmission, remove the clutch retracting spring. Disconnect the clutch equalizer shaft and arm bracket at the underbody rail and remove the arm bracket and equalizer shaft.
12. Raise the car. Remove the flywheel or converter housing upper retaining bolts thru the access holes in the floor pan.
13. Disconnect the exhaust pipe at the exhaust manifold. Disconnect the right and left motor mount at the underbody bracket. Remove the flywheel or converter housing cover.
14. On a car with manual shift, remove the flywheel housing lower retaining bolts.
15. On a car with Fordomatic, disconnect the converter from the flywheel. Remove the converter housing lower retaining bolts.
16. Lower the car. Support the transmission and flywheel or converter housing with a jack.
17. Attach an engine lifting hook. Lift the engine up and out of the com-

partment and onto an adequate work stand.

INSTALLATION

1. Install guide pins in the flywheel or converter housing bolt holes in the rear of the engine. Place a new gasket over the studs of the exhaust manifold.

2. Carefully lower the engine into the engine compartment.

3. Be sure the studs on the exhaust manifold are aligned with the holes in the exhaust pipe and the guide pins in the block engage the holes in the flywheel housing.

4. On cars with Fordomatic, start the converter pilot into the crankshaft.

5. On cars equipped with manual-shift transmissions, start the transmission main drive gear into the splines of the clutch disc. It may be necessary to adjust the alignment of the transmission with the engine if the input shaft is opposed to easily entering the clutch disc or the pilot bearing in the crankshaft.

6. After the engine is in place in the chassis, remove the engine lifting hooks and install the flywheel or converter housing upper retaining bolts.

7. Remove jack from the transmission and raise the car.

8. Remove guide pins and install flywheel or converter housing lower retaining bolts.

9. On cars with Fordomatic, attach the converter to the flywheel and properly torque the retaining nuts.

10. Install flywheel or converter housing dust cover.

11. Install the engine left and right mount to the body bracket. Replace the sediment bowl on the fuel pump.

12. Reconnect the fuel line at the tank. Install the manifold to muffler exhaust pipe retaining lockwashers and nuts.

13. Lower the car. Connect the oil pressure and temperature sending unit wires. Connect the coil primary wire. Connect the windshield wiper vacuum hose to the vacuum pump. Connect the accelerator rod and the choke control cable to the carburetor.

14. Install the starter motor and dust seal and connect the starter cable. Connect the generator wires and connect the heater hose at the water pump and carburetor spacer. Reconnect the battery ground cable to the cylinder head.

15. Install hte fan, fan pulley and drive belt. Adjust the drive belt to a tension requiring about 5 lb. downward thumb pressure, between the generator and the fan pulley to produce ½" deflection. Install the radiator and install upper and lower radiator hoses.

16. Fill and bleed the cooling system and refill the crankcase with the proper quantity and grade of engine oil.

17. Install and adjust the hood.

18. Start the engine and operate at fast idle. Check all hoses, lines and gaskets for leaks.

19. On a car with Fordomatic, it will be necessary to readjust the control linkage. Install the carburetor air cleaner.

CYLINDER HEAD

6 CYL., REMOVE

1. Drain cooling system, remove the air cleaner and disconnect the battery cable at the cylinder head.

2. Disconnect exhaust pipe at the manifold end, spring the exhaust pipe down and remove the flange gasket.

3. Disconnect the fuel and vacuum lines from the carburetor. Disconnect the intake manifold line at the intake manifold.

4. Disconnect the accelerator and retracting spring at the carburetor. Disconnect the manually operated choke cable.

5. Disconnect the carburetor spacer outlet line at the spacer. Disconnect the radiator upper hose and the heater hose at the water outlet elbow. Disconnect the radiator lower hose and the heater hose at the water pump.

6. Disconnect the distributor vacuum control line at the distributor. Disconnect the gas filter line on the inlet side of the filter and the vacuum line at the fuel pump. Remove these three lines as an assembly, then remove the windshield wiper line at the vacuum pump.

7. Disconnect the spark plug wires and remove the plugs.

8. Remove the rocker arm cover.

9. Back off all of the tappet adjusting screws to relieve tension on the rocker shaft. Loosen the rocker arm shaft attaching bolts and remove the rocker arm and shaft assembly. Remove the valve push rods, in order, and keep them that way.

10. Remove one cylinder head bolt from each end of the head, at opposite corners, and install cylinder head guide studs. Remove the remaining cylinder head bolts and lift off the cylinder head.

(NOTICE) The day of hammer and chisel tactics is passing in favor of easier and better methods of operation. This includes the correct removal procedure for cylinder heads. Two 6 inch, 7/16 x 14 bolts with the heads cut off and the head end slightly tapered and slotted for installation and removal with a screwdriver will reduce the possibility of damage during head replacement. These guide studs make a handy tool during head re-

moval and gasket and head replacement.

6 CYL., INSTALL

1. Clean the cylinder head and block surfaces, be sure of flatness and no surface damage.

2. Apply cylinder head gasket sealer to both sides of the new gasket and slide the gasket down over the two guide studs in the cylinder block.

3. Carefully lower the cylinder head down over the guide studs. Enter the exhaust pipe flange on the manifold studs (new gasket, please).

4. Be sure to blow any foreign matter out of the cylinder head bolt holes. Coat the threads of the end bolts for the right side of the cylinder head with a small amount of water resistant sealer. Install, but do not tighten, two head bolts at opposite ends to hold the head gasket in place. Remove the guide studs and install the remaining bolts.

5. Cylinder head torquing should proceed in three steps and in prescribed order. Tighten to 55 ft. lb., then give them a second tightening to 65 ft. lb. The final step is to 75 ft. lb. at which they should remain undisturbed.

6. Lubricate both ends of the push rods and install them in their original locations.

7. Apply a petroleum jelly type lubricant to the rocker arm pads and the valve stem tips and position the rocker arm shaft assembly on the head. <u>BE SURE THE OIL HOLES IN THE SHAFT ARE IN A DOWN POSITION.</u>

8. Tighten all the rocker shaft retaining bolts to 30-35 ft. lb. and do a preliminary valve adjustment (make sure there are no tight valve adjustments).

9. Hook up the exhaust pipe.

10. Reconnect the heater and radiator hoses.

11. Reposition the distributor vacuum line, the carburetor gas lone and the intake manifold vacuum line on the engine. Hook them up to their respective connections and reconnect the battery cable to the cylinder head.

12. Connect the accelerator rod and retracting spring. Connect the choke control cable and adjust the choke.

13. Reconnect the vacuum line at the distributor. Connect the fuel inlet line at the fuel filter and the intake manifold vacuum line at the vacuum pump. Connect the windshield wiper vacuum line to the other side of the vacuum pump.

14. Lightly lubricate the spark plug threads, install them and torque to 25 ft. lb. Connect spark plug wires and be sure the wires are all the way down in their sockets.

15. Fill the cooling system and bleed. Run the engine for about ½ hr. at a good fast idle to stabilize ALL engine parts temperatures.

16. Adjust engine idle speed and idle fuel-air adjustment.

17. Reset valve tappet adjustment to .016" for a hot adjustment of both intake and exhaust valves.

18. Coat one side of a new rocker cover gasket with oil resistant sealer. Lay the treated side of the gasket on the cover and install the cover. Be sure the gasket seals evenly all around the cylinder head.

V8 HEADS, REMOVE

Note:

Right and left cylinder heads are interchangeable.

1. Remove intake manifold and carburetor as an assembly.
2. Disconnect battery cable at cylinder head.
3. Remove rocker arm cover/s.
3A. **On a car with power steering,** disconnect the steering pump bracket from the left cylinder head and remove the drive belt. Wire the steering pump out of the way, (don't spill the oil).
4. Disconnect wires at generator. Remove generator and bracket as an assembly. Disconnect exhaust pipe/s at exhaust manifold/s.
5. Remove cylinder head attaching bolts from both ends of the head and install two 7/16 x 14

guide studs. Remove remaining cylinder head retaining bolts.
6. Raise cylinder head slightly, so that the rocker arms can be rotated to the side. Remove the push rods and store them in sequence. Remove the guide studs and lift the head off the block. Remove cylinder head gasket.

V8 HEADS, INSTALL

Reverse above procedure, (see valve lash adjustment under, "Valves," in the following paragraphs). Torque cylinder head bolts to 65 to 70 ft. lbs. (with lubricated threads).

VALVE SYSTEM

REFERENCES

The 6 cylinder engines are equipped with tubular push rods, barrel type tappets and valve lash is controlled by self locking adjusting screws.

Early production 1963, 6 cylinder engines use mechanical adjusters, however, later production engines incorporate hydraulic tappets with zero lash running clearance.

V-8 engines use hydraulic tappets. The push rods in the V-8s also transfer oil under pressure to the friction areas of the rocker arms.

6 CYL., DISMANTLE

1. Remove cylinder head as described in previous paragraph.
2. Reach down thru the push rod

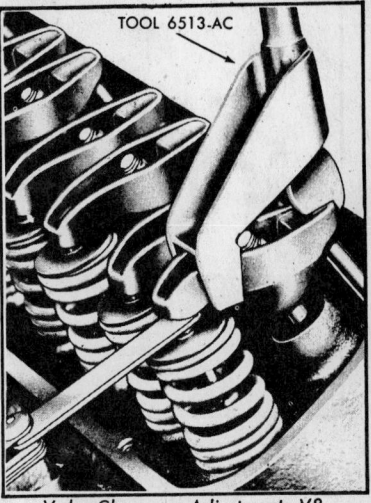

Valve Clearance Adjustment—V8

area with a magnet, or other suitable extractor, and remove the tappets. Keep the tappets in order, that they can be installed in their original location.

3. Loosen all valve rocker arm adjusting screws two turns at a time, and in sequence.
4. Remove rocker arm shaft pedestal bolts and lift off rocker arm shaft assembly.
5. Dismantle shaft and rockers by removing pin and spring washer from each end of the shaft.
6. Slide rocker arms, springs and pedestals off the shaft. (Be sure to identify the parts for proper assembly sequence).

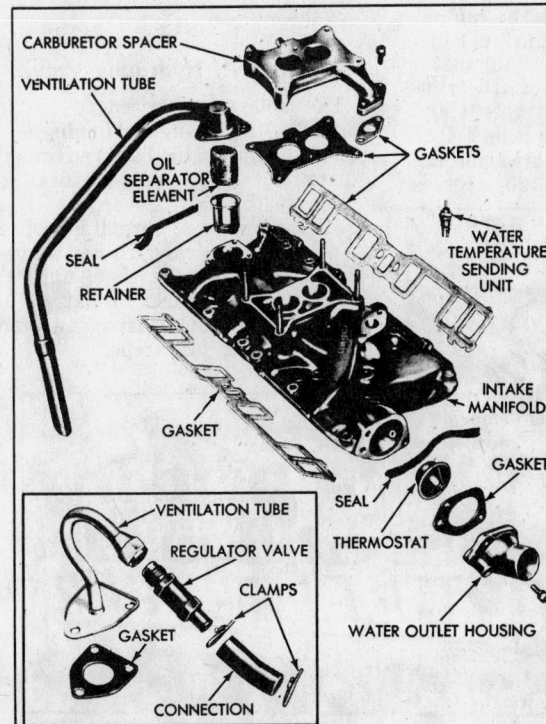

Intake Manifold—V8

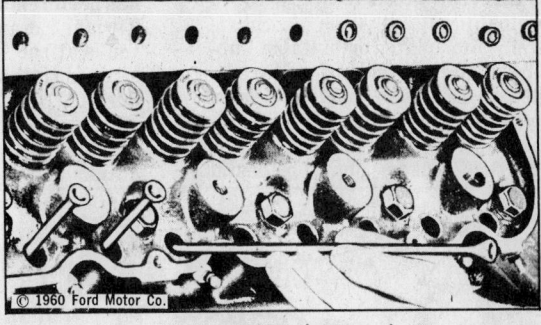

Valve Push Rod, removal—V8

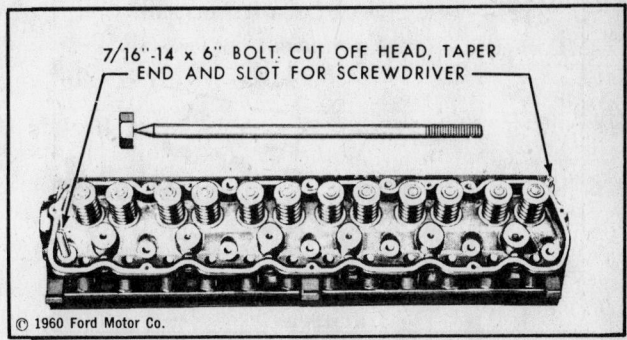

Cylinder Head Guide-Studs-6 Cyl.

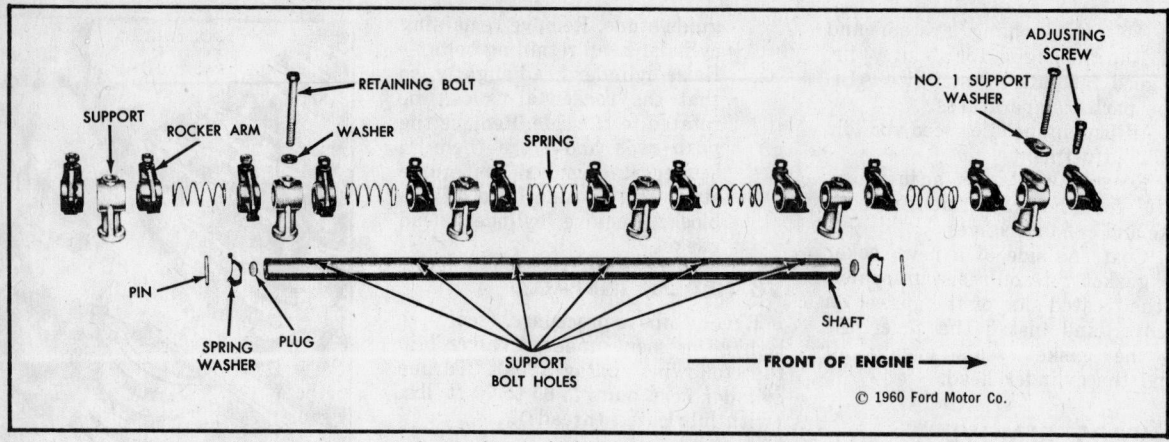

Valve Rocker and Shaft Arrangement 6 Cyl.

6 CYL., ASSEMBLE

1. Lubricate and assemble all rocker shaft components as per illustration.
2. If the end plugs were removed from the rocker shaft, install new plugs, cup side out, to each end of the shaft.
3. Do valve grinding job or any other service to the cylinder head, check valve spring condition, install new oil seals on valve stems, check springs and install valve assembly in place. Compress springs and keepers.
4. Install valve tappets in their proper bores.
5. Apply cylinder head gasket sealer to both sides of a new gasket and locate gasket on cylinder block. Install cylinder head and torque, in three progressive steps, to 75 ft. lbs.
6. Apply lubriplate, or suitable substitute, to both ends of push rods, then install push rods into their respective places.
7. Install rocker arm and shaft. Tighten rocker shaft pedestal bolts in progressive steps to 30-35 ft. lbs.

Adjust Mechanical Valves— Primary Step

8. Make primary valve adjustment in the following manner. Then continue to install rocker covers and fill cooling system.

Note:

Tappets must be adjusted while on the low radius of the cam.

A. **If the distributor has not been disturbed** and ignition timing is reasonably correct, proceed as follows: Rotate crankshaft until the distributor rotor points to #1 plug wire tower of the distributor cap. Adjust valves in cylinder firing order according to rotor position.

B. **If the distributor is out of time or has been removed from the engine:** Turn the crankshaft until #1 piston is at the top of its compression stroke, (intake valve of #6 cylinder just beginning to open), and the crankshaft damper is on T.D.C. Make three chalk marks on the crankshaft damper, 120 degrees apart, starting with T.D.C. These marks will divide crankshaft travel into three parts, or six segments, of each engine cycle. Valve adjustment can then be made in firing sequence, beginning with #1 on T.D.C. and progressing thru the regular order of firing by advancing one chalk mark, (120 crankshaft degrees) at a time.

Adjust Mechanical Valves— Final Step

Note:

Be sure engine is at regular operating temperature by running at least 30 minutes.

9. With engine idling, check valve clearance with a feeler gauge. Adjust clearance, if necessary, to .016" (hot) for both intake and exhaust.

Adjust 6 Cyl. Hydraulic Valves

The following procedure is performed with the engine running.

1. After the engine has been brought to operating temperature, remove the valve cover.
2. With engine at normal idle speed, back off the valve rocker arm adjusters, one at a time, until the rocker arm starts to clatter.
3. Turn the arm adjuster down until the clatter just stops.

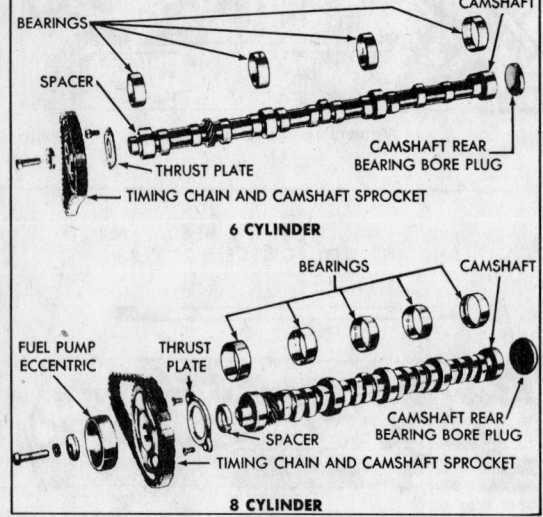

Camshaft and Related Parts

Removing rocker arm assembly 6 Cyl.

4. Continue to turn down the adjuster exactly one turn this will force the hydraulic lifter piston into the approximate center of its travel.
5. Install valve rocker cover.

V8—VALVE SYSTEM—DISMANTLE

1. Remove cylinder heads as described in previous paragraph.
2. Reach down thru the tappet bores with a magnet or other suitable extractor and remove the tappets. Keep tappets in order, that they can be reinstalled in their original location.
3. Support cylinder head on wooden blocks. With valves still installed to protect valve seats, wire brush the head clean, do not scratch gasket surface.
4. Remove rocker arm adjusting nuts, fulcrum seats, and rocker arms. Compress valve springs, remove spring retainer keys, retainers and springs. Remove and discard stem seals, and remove valves.
5. Remove the exhaust manifolds.
6. Inspect condition of manifolds and heads.
7. On the right exhaust manifold, be sure that the automatic choke air inlet and outlet holes are completely open. Clean the maze screen in the passage with cleaning solvent.
8. Perform necessary valve seating and guide services.
9. Check valve springs for squareness and free length. Springs should not be more than 5/64" out of square, or 1/8" shorter than a new spring. A more accurate spring valve can be obtained with a spring tester (see valve specifications chart).
10. Check rocker arm studs in cylinder head for damage. Also check for evidence of coolant leak at stud base which may indicate a loose stud. Service replacements are available in standard size and .015" oversize. If any looseness is found, replace the stud.

HYDRAULIC TAPPETS—SERVICE ALL MODELS

A. Remove lock ring from tappet body.
B. Remove push rod cup and metering valve disc.
C. Remove plunger from tappet body.
D. Invert the plunger and remove the check valve retainer by carefully prying up on it with a screwdriver.
E. Remove the check valve and the spring.

F. Remove the plunger spring from the tappet body.
G. Soak all tappet components in solvent (lacquer thinner works well on these tar and varnish substances).
H. After tappet parts have been thoroughly cleaned and blown dry, place the plunger upside down on a clean surface.
I. Place the check valve over the hole in the bottom of the plunger. Place check valve spring on top of the check valve.
J. Position check valve retainer over the spring and check valve, then push the retainer down into place on the plunger.
K. Place plunger spring and plunger into the tappet body.
L. Place metering valve disc and the push rod cup in the plunger. Depress plunger and install the lock ring.
M. Test all hydraulic tappets (both new and used) before installing them in an engine. The factory quotes a bleed-down time of from 10 to 80 seconds, using special test oil and their approved tester.

V8—VALVE SYSTEM—ASSEMBLE

1. Install hydraulic tappets into their respective bores.
2. Lubricate valve stems with engine oil and apply lubriplate to the tip of the valve stems.
3. Install each valve into its respective guide and install new oil seals on the stems.
4. Install valve springs, retainers and retainer keys.
5. Measure the assembled height of each valve spring, from the surface of the spring pad to the underside of the spring retainer. This measurement should be 1¾" to 1-25/32". If assembled height is not within limits, install necessary spacer/s between the spring pad and the spring to correct the measurement.
6. Install rocker arms and fulcrum seats. Install adjusting nuts, finger tight.
7. Install the exhaust manifold/s. Torque manifold bolts to 13-18 ft. lbs. and bend over the bolt locking tabs.
8. Position new sealer coated head gasket, install cylinder head, and progressively torque to 65-70 ft. lbs.
9. Lubricate both ends of push rods and install them into their respective tappets.

Adjust Valves

10A. Crank the engine to position #1 piston on T.D.C. of the compression stroke. With engine in this condition, the following valves may be adjusted:

No. 1—Intake
No. 1—Exhaust
No. 2—Exhaust
No. 3—Intake
No. 4—Exhaust
No. 5—Exhaust
No. 7—Intake
No. 8—Intake

B. Position a leverage tool on the rocker arm and slowly bleed down the tappet until the plunger is bottomed.
C. While holding the tappet in the collapsed position, turn rocker arm adjustment to obtain 0.082"-0.152" clearance between the valve stem and the rocker arm.
D. Crank the engine to position #6 piston on T.D.C. of the compression stroke. With engine in this condition, the following valves may be adjusted:

No. 2—Intake
No. 3—Exhaust
No. 4—Intake
No. 5—Intake
No. 6—Intake
No. 6—Exhaust
No. 7—Exhaust
No. 8—Exhaust

11. Coat intake manifold and cylinder block seal surfaces with oil resistant sealer. Position new seals on block and new gaskets on cylinder heads with the seal tabs interlocked with the slots in the gasket.
12. To facilitate lining up the intake manifold properly, use two aligning studs. Lower the intake manifold onto the engine.
13. Install manifold attaching bolts. Torque bolts in a progressive manner to 14-16 ft. lbs.
14. Connect water pump by-pass hose to the pump and the water outlets housing, tighten the clamps.
15. Install generator and bracket assembly.
16. Install fuel pump and the fuel filter and adapter assembly.
17. Rotate crankshaft to bring #1 piston up to T.D.C. of the compression stroke.
18. Position distributor in the block with the rotor at #1 firing position and the points just opening. Install distributor hold-down clamp.
19. Install carburetor choke heat tube and the carburetor. Install distributor cap and plug wires as an assembly. Install ignition coil, and connect high tension lead at the coil.
20. Install and connect the fuel filter to carburetor line, the fuel pump to fuel filter line, and the distributor to carburetor vacuum line.
21. Check engine oil, fill and bleed cooling system, start engine, make final adjustments and road test car.

FALCON AND COMET

TIMING COVER AND CHAIN

6 CYL. COVER AND CHAIN—REMOVE

1. Drain cooling system, and disconnect radiator hoses.
2. Remove radiator.
3. Remove drive belt, fan and pulley.
4. Remove the crankshaft damper.
5. Remove timing chain cover and crankshaft front oil slinger.
6. Establish a reference point on the block. Now measure extreme slack in the loose side of the chain and record this measurement. Now, eliminate the slack by moving the camshaft sprocket within the chain slack limits and again take a measurement. The difference should not exceed ½ inch. More than ½ inch slack justifies renewal of chain and sprockets.
7. Crank the engine until timing marks are aligned, as shown in "Valve Timing Illustration."
8. Remove camshaft sprocket retaining bolt and washer Then, slide both sprockets and chain forward and remove them as an assembly.

Cover Seal R & R (6 Cyl. & V8)

1. Drive out the old seal with a pin punch. Then, clean out the recess in the cover.
2. Coat a new seal with grease and drive it into place in the chain cover. Check that the spring is still properly positioned in the seal before installing cover.

6 CYL. COVER AND CHAIN—INSTALL

1. Position sprockets and chain on the camshaft and crankshaft with both timing marks on a centerline. Install camshaft sprocket retaining bolt and washer. Torque attaching bolt to 35-45 ft. lbs.
2. Install the oil slinger so that the pointer on the slinger is aligned with the camshaft sprocket timing mark.
3. Clean front cover and cylinder block of old gasket material. Apply sealer to a new cover gasket and position the gasket to the cover.
4. Install the front cover, using a crankshaft-to-cover alignment tool. Torque attaching bolts to 7-9 ft. lbs.
5. Install crankshaft damper and torque to 45-55 ft. lbs.
6. Install fan, fan pulley and drive belt. Adjust the belt.
7. Install radiator. Then, connect the hoses.
8. Fill and bleed cooling system.

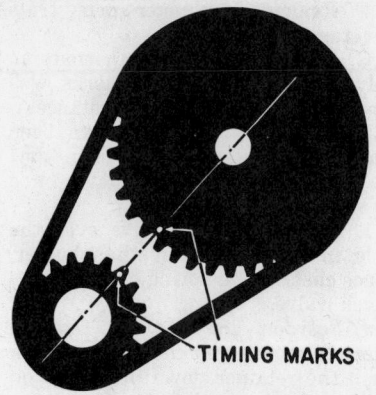

TIMING MARKS

Timing Mark Alignment—6 Cyl.

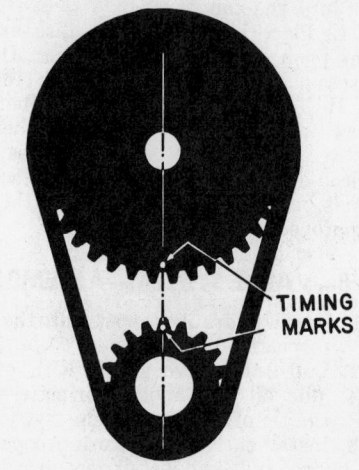

TIMING MARKS

Timing Mark Alignment—V8

9. Start engine and check for leaks and final adjustments.

V8 COVER AND CHAIN—REMOVE

1. Drain cooling system, remove air cleaner, and disconnect the battery.
2. Disconnect radiator hoses and remove the radiator.
3. Disconnect heater hose at water pump. Slide water pump by-pass

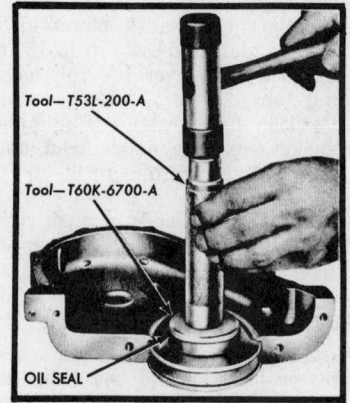

Tool—T53L-200-A

Tool—T60K-6700-A

OIL SEAL

Crankshaft Front Oil Seal Replacement—Typical 6 Cyl.

hose clamp toward the pump.
4. Loosen generator mounting bolts at the generator. Remove the generator support bolt at the water pump.
5. Remove the fan, spacer, pulley, and drive belt.
6. Remove pulley from crankshaft pulley adapter. Remove cap screw and washer from front end of crankshaft. Remove crankshaft pulley adapter with a puller.
7. Disconnect fuel pump outlet line at the pump. Remove fuel pump retaining bolts and lay the pump to the side.
8. Remove front cover attaching bolts and remove front cover and water pump as an assembly.
9. Remove crankshaft front oil slinger.
10. Rotate crankshaft in normal direction to remove slack from the chain, on the fuel pump side of the engine.
11. Establish a reference point on the block and measure from this point to the chain.
12. Back-up on crankshaft rotation to remove slack from the chain on the generator side of the engine. Force the fuel pump side of the chain out with the fingers and again take a measurement from chain to reference mark. Deflection is the difference between the two measurements. If deflection exceeds ½", a new chain and/or sprockets is warranted.
13. Crank engine until sprocket timing marks are aligned as shown in "Valve Timing Illustration."
14. Remove camshaft sprocket cap screw, washers, and fuel pump eccentric. Slide both sprockets and chain forward and off of their shafts as an assembly.

V8 COVER AND CHAIN—INSTALL

1. Position sprockets and chain on the camshaft and crankshaft with both timing marks on a centerline. Install fuel pump eccentric, washers and sprocket attaching bolt. Torque the sprocket attaching bolt to 30-35 ft. lbs.
2. Install crankshaft front oil slinger.
3. Clean front cover and mating surfaces of old gasket material.
4. Coat a new cover gasket with sealer and position it on the block.
5. Install front cover, using a crankshaft-to-cover alignment tool. Torque attaching bolts to 12-15 ft. lbs.
6. Install fuel pump, torque attaching bolts to 23-28 ft. lbs., con-

nect fuel pump outlet tube.

7. Install crankshaft pulley adapter and torque attaching bolt to 70-90 ft. lbs. Install crankshaft pulley.
8. Install water pump pulley, drive belt, spacer and fan.
9. Install generator support bolt at the water pump. Tighten generator mounting bolts. Adjust drive belt tension.
10. Install radiator and connect all coolant and heater hoses. Connect battery cables.
11. Refill and bleed cooling system.
12. Start engine and operate at fast idle to operating temperature.
13. Check for leaks, install air cleaner. Adjust ignition timing and make all final adjustments.

ENGINE LUBRICATION

REFERENCES

All engines are equipped with full-flow type oil filters to condition the oil before it reaches the main bearings. The filter is equipped with an internal, relief, by-pass valve as a stoppage, safety precaution. The scheme of lubrication is best shown in the illustrations.

Under normal driving conditions, engine oil and oil filter should be changed at 6,000 mile intervals. However, adverse driving conditions, dusty operation, short trips, winter driving, etc., may justify the change at much shorter intervals.

OIL PAN R & R—6 CYL. & V8

1. Drain crankcase. Remove oil dipstick.
2. **Six cylinder with standard transmission**, remove clutch retracting spring.
3. Remove #2 crossmember retaining nuts and remove the crossmember.
4. **Six cylinder**, remove stabilizer bar-to-underbody retaining nuts and pull the bar downward.
5. **V-8 models**, remove starter motor.
6. Remove oil pan retaining bolts and crank the engine as required to obtain clearance, then remove the oil **pan.**
7. Install oil pan in the reverse order of removal. Torque the ¼" x 20 cap screws to 7-9 ft. lbs. and 5/16" x 18 cap screws to 9-11 ft. lbs.
8. Torque #2 crossmember attaching nuts to 27-39 ft. lbs.
9. Install on dipstick. Fill crankcase to level, then run the engine and check for leaks.

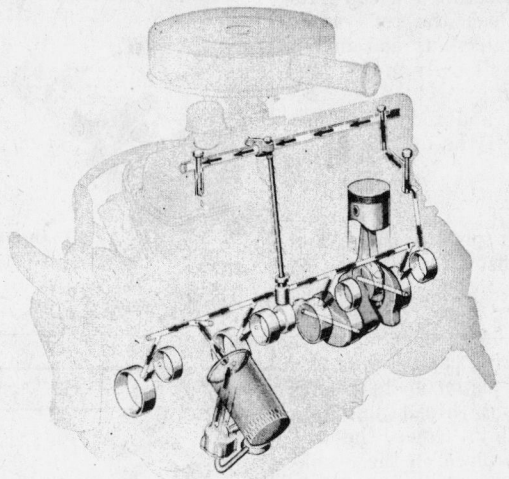

Engine Oiling—6 Cyl.

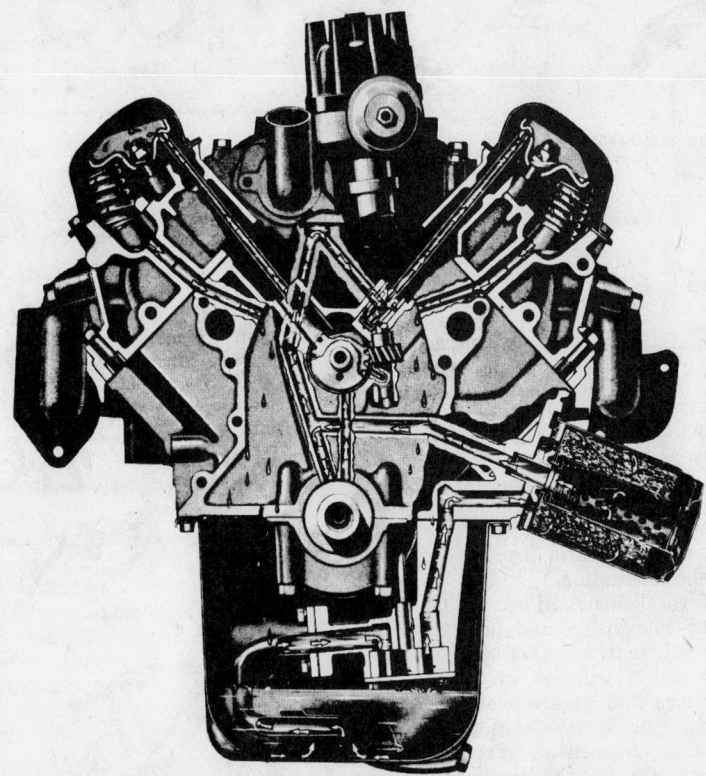

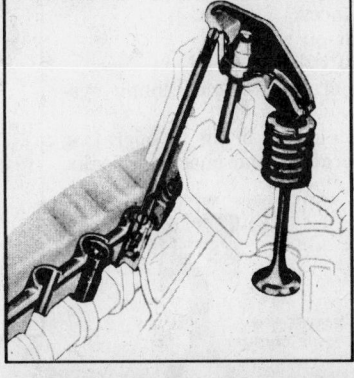

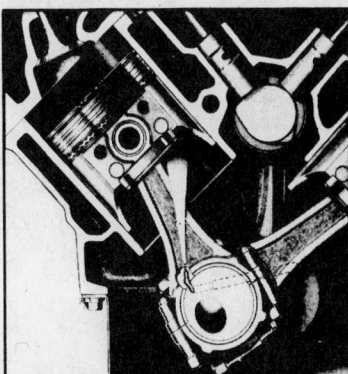

Engine Oiling—V8

CONNECTING RODS AND PISTONS

REMOVE

1. Drain crankcase and remove oil pan.
2. Drain cooling system and remove cylinder head or heads.
3. Remove any ridge and/or deposits from the upper end of cylinder bores with a ridge reamer.
4. Check rods and pistons for identification numbers and, if necessary, number them.
5. Remove connecting rod cap nuts and caps. Push the rods away from the crankshaft and install caps and nuts loosely to their respective rods.
6. Push piston and rod assemblies up and out of the cylinders.

INSTALL

1. Lightly coat pistons, rings and cylinder walls with light engine oil.
2. With bearing caps removed, install pieces of protective rubber hose on bearing cap bolts.
3. Install each piston in its respective bore using thread guards on each assembly. Guide the rod bearing into place on the crankcase journal.
4. Remove thread guards from connecting rods and install lower half of bearing and cap. Check clearances.
5. Install oil pan.
6. Install cylinder head.
7. Refill crankcase and cooling system.
8. Start engine, bring to operating temperature and check for leaks.

NOTCH TOWARDS FRONT

OIL SPURT HOLE
OPPOSITE CAMSHAFT
SIDE

Relation of Piston & Rod—6 Cyl.

FRONT SUSPENSION REFERENCES

Comet and Falcon springs are mounted on TOP of the upper control arm to a tower in the sheet metal of the body. This type of mounting provides good stability. The lower arm and stabilizing strut substitute for the conventional "A" frame and serves to guide the lower part of the spindle thru its cycle of up and down move-

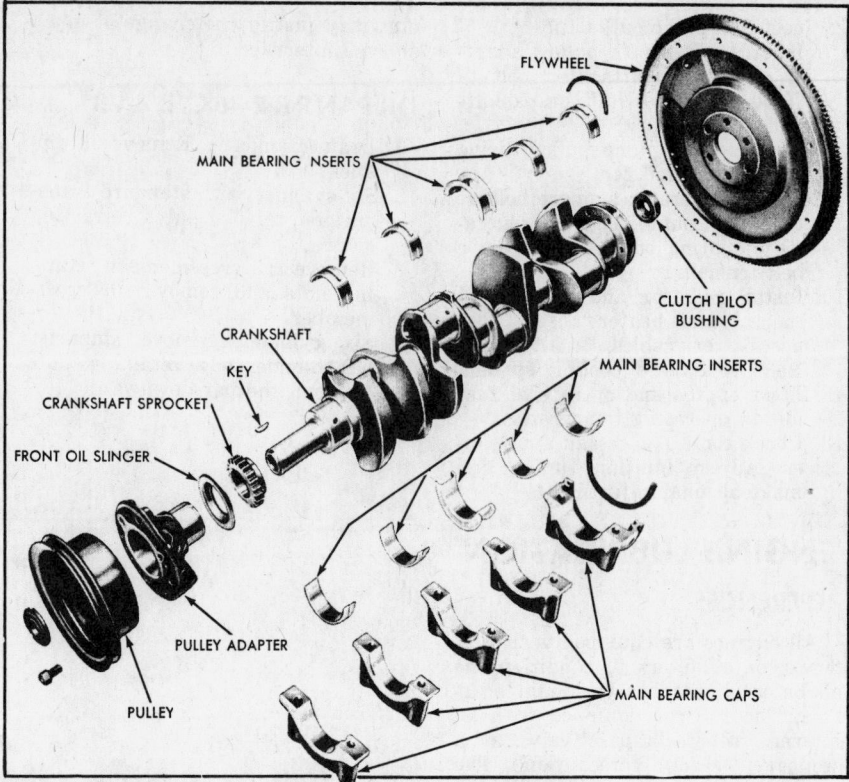

FLYWHEEL

MAIN BEARING INSERTS

CLUTCH PILOT BUSHING

CRANKSHAFT

KEY

MAIN BEARING INSERTS

CRANKSHAFT SPROCKET

FRONT OIL SLINGER

PULLEY ADAPTER

PULLEY

MAIN BEARING CAPS

Crankshaft & Related Parts—V8 Engine

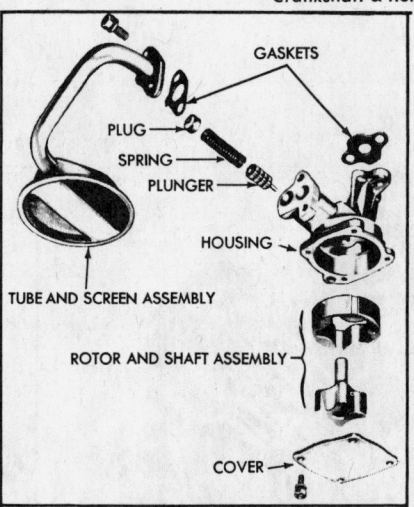

GASKETS

PLUG

SPRING

PLUNGER

HOUSING

TUBE AND SCREEN ASSEMBLY

ROTOR AND SHAFT ASSEMBLY

COVER

Oil Pump Assembly—V8 Engine

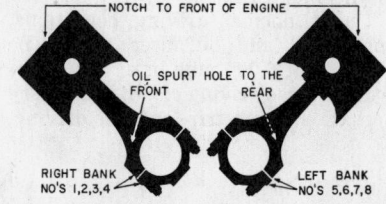

NOTCH TO FRONT OF ENGINE

OIL SPURT HOLE TO THE FRONT   REAR

RIGHT BANK NO'S 1,2,3,4   LEFT BANK NO'S 5,6,7,8

Relation of Piston & Rod—V8

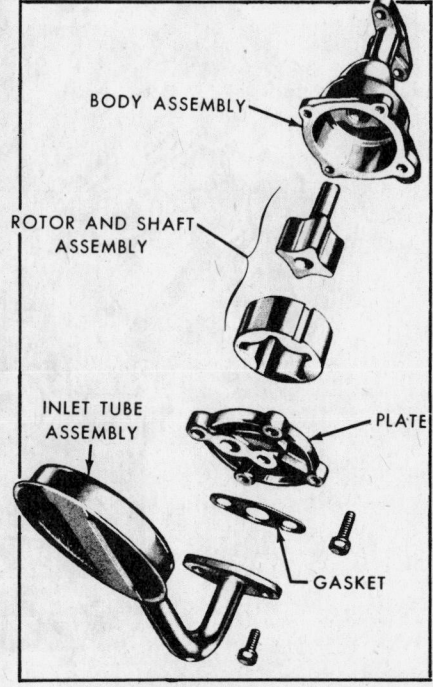

BODY ASSEMBLY

ROTOR AND SHAFT ASSEMBLY

INLET TUBE ASSEMBLY

PLATE

GASKET

Oil Pump Assembly—6 Cyl. Engine

ment. The rod type stabilizing strut is mounted between two rubber buffer pads, at the front end to cushion fore and aft thrust of suspension. The effective length of this rod is variable and must be considered in maintenance. Ball joints are of the usual steel construction.

General instructions covering the front suspension and how to repair and adjust it, together with information on installation of front wheel bearings and grease seals, are given in the Unit Repair section under the heading: Suspension, Front Repair.

Definitions of the points of steering geometry are covered in the Unit Re-

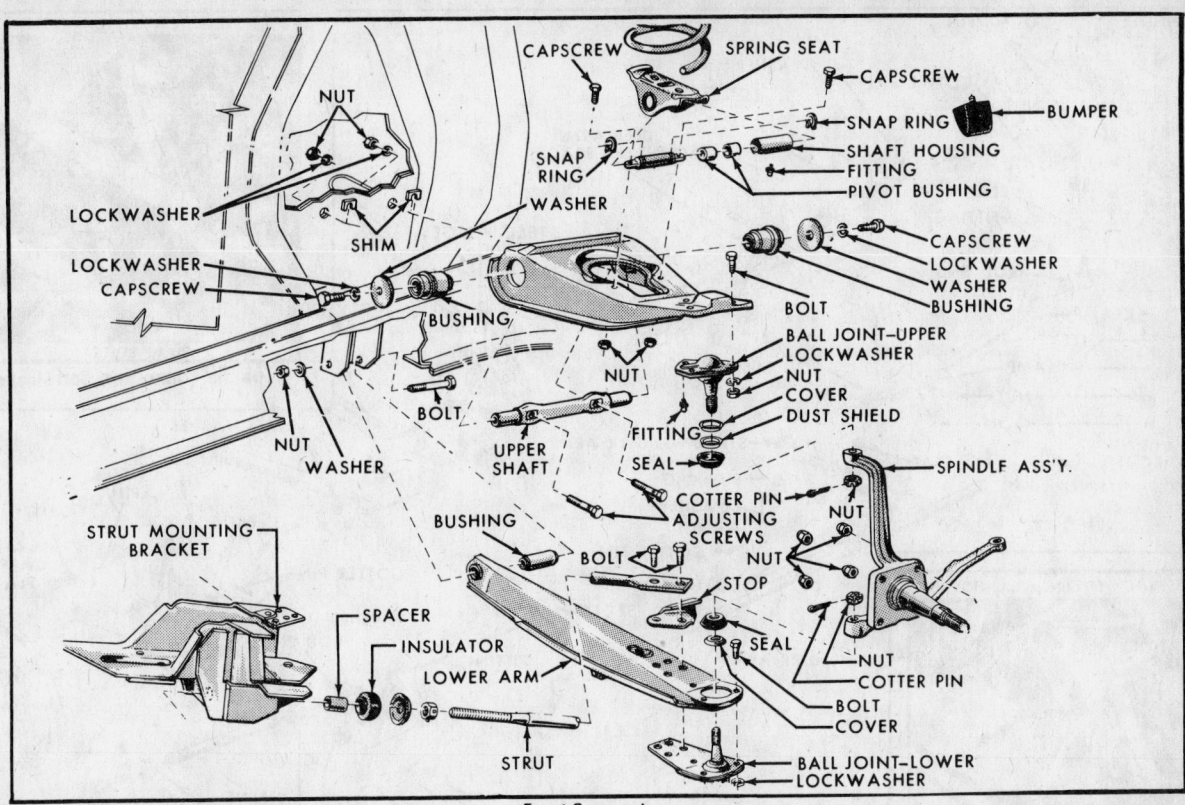

Front Suspension.

pair section under the headings: Suspension, Front Align. This article also covers trouble shooting front end geometry and irregular tire wear.

Figures covering the caster, camber, toe-in, king pin inclination, and turning radius can be found in the Front Wheel Alignment Table of this section.

Tire size figures can be found in the General Chassis and Brake Specifications Table of this section.

WHEEL ALIGNMENT

Caster and Camber values are both maintained by changing the location, or by the addition or subtraction, of shims between the inner shaft of the front suspension upper arm and the underbody. Shims are available in 1/32" and 1/8" thicknesses.

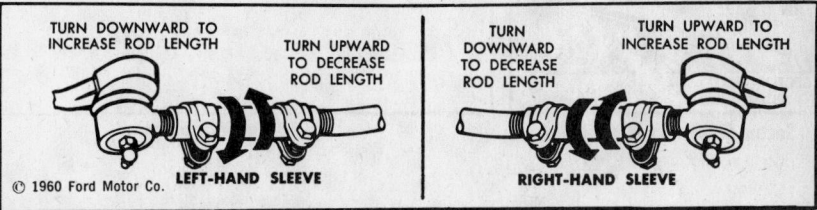

© 1960 Ford Motor Co.

Spindle Connecting Rod Adjustments.

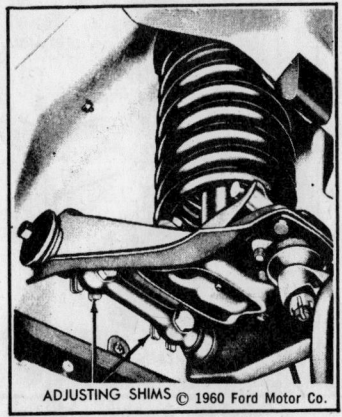

Upper Arm Assembly.

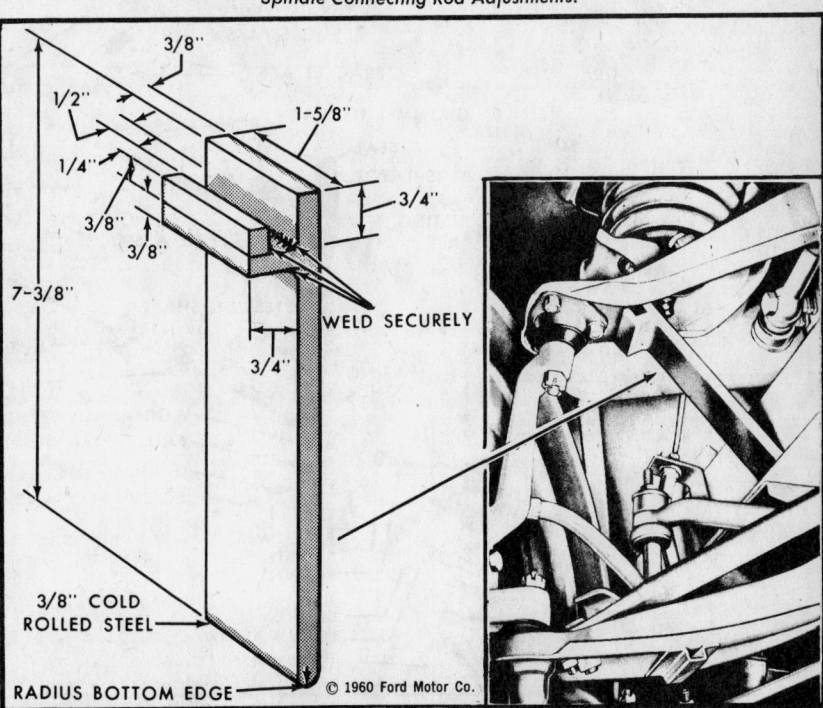

Upper Control Arm Support

331

FALCON and COMET

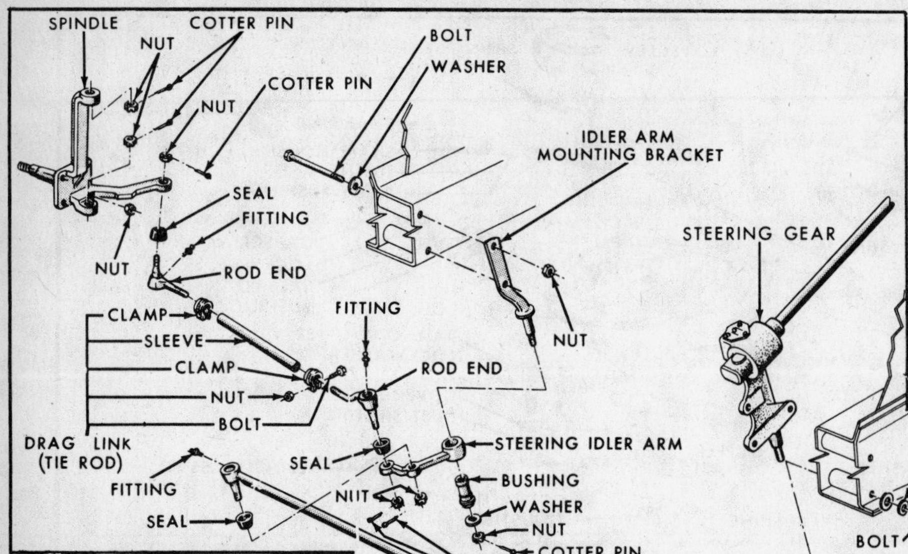

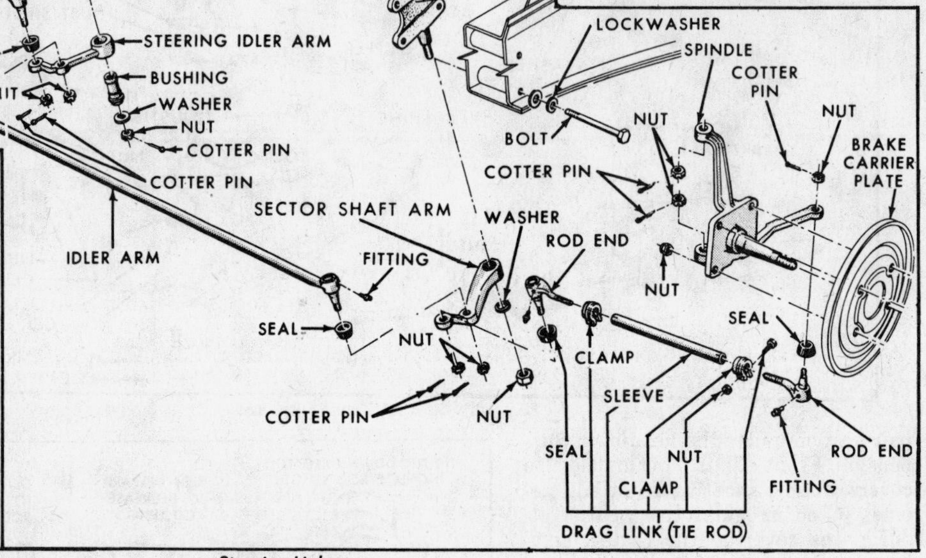

SPINDLE **COTTER PIN** **BOLT** **NUT** **NUT** **COTTER PIN** **WASHER**

IDLER ARM MOUNTING BRACKET

SEAL **FITTING** **ROD END**

NUT

CLAMP **SLEEVE** **CLAMP** **NUT** **BOLT**

FITTING **ROD END**

DRAG LINK (TIE ROD) **FITTING** **SEAL**

NUT

SEAL

STEERING IDLER ARM **BUSHING** **WASHER** **NUT** **COTTER PIN** **COTTER PIN**

IDLER ARM

STEERING GEAR

SLEEVE

CLAMP BOLTS

Spindle Connecting Rod Sleeve

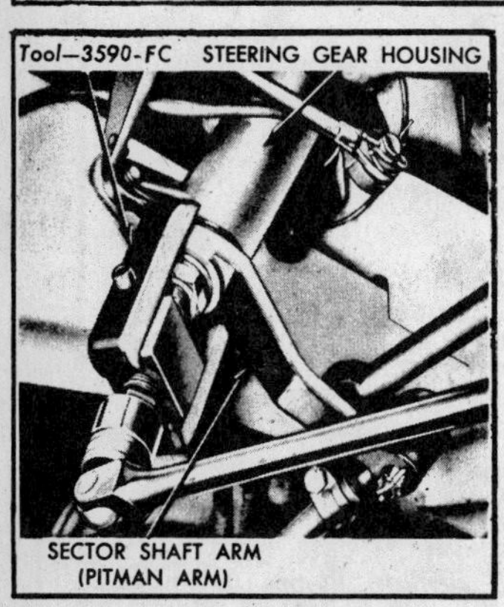

LOCKWASHER **SPINDLE** **COTTER PIN** **NUT**

BOLT **NUT** **BRAKE CARRIER PLATE**

COTTER PIN **COTTER PIN**

SECTOR SHAFT ARM **WASHER** **ROD END** **NUT**

FITTING **SEAL**

SEAL **NUT** **CLAMP** **SLEEVE** **SEAL** **ROD END**

COTTER PIN **NUT** **NUT** **CLAMP** **FITTING**

DRAG LINK (TIE ROD)

Tool—3590-FC **STEERING GEAR HOUSING**

SECTOR SHAFT ARM (PITMAN ARM)

Sector Shaft Arm Removal

Steering Linkage.

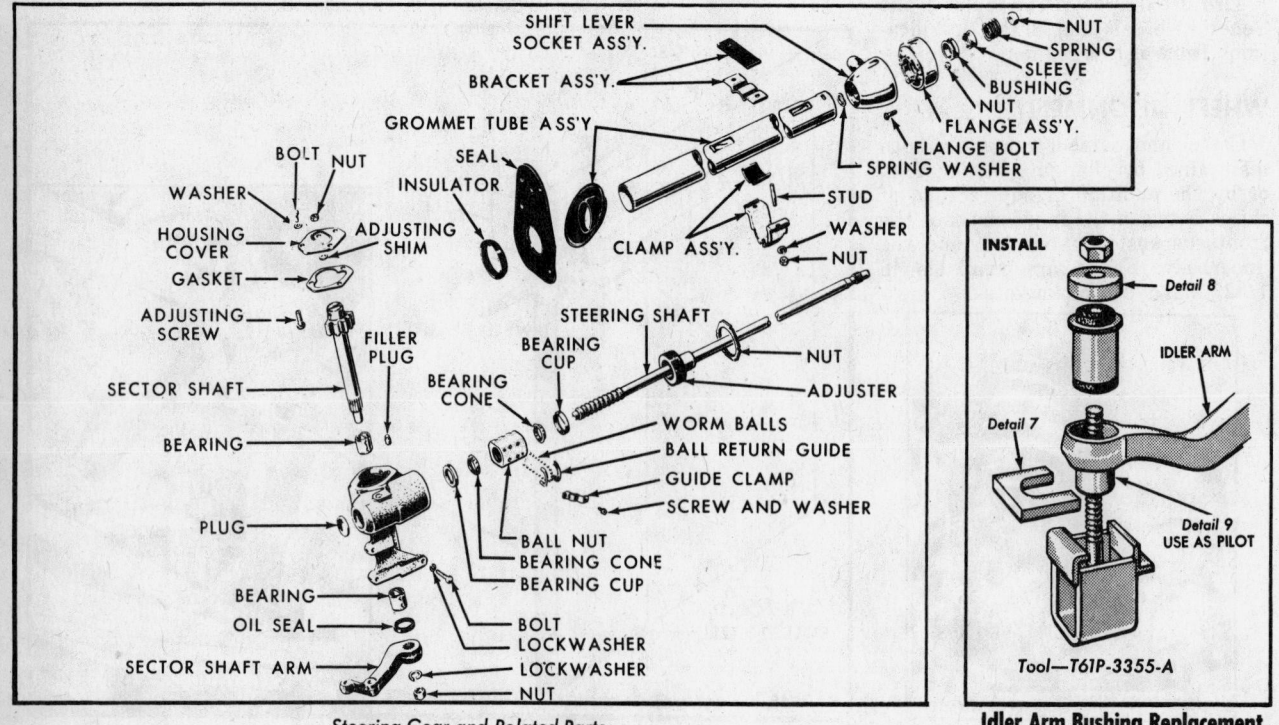

SHIFT LEVER SOCKET ASS'Y. **NUT** **SPRING** **SLEEVE** **BUSHING** **NUT** **FLANGE ASS'Y.**

BRACKET ASS'Y.

GROMMET TUBE ASS'Y. **SEAL** **INSULATOR**

FLANGE BOLT **SPRING WASHER**

BOLT **NUT** **WASHER** **HOUSING COVER** **GASKET** **ADJUSTING SHIM**

STUD **WASHER** **NUT**

CLAMP ASS'Y.

ADJUSTING SCREW **FILLER PLUG** **SECTOR SHAFT** **BEARING**

STEERING SHAFT **BEARING CUP** **BEARING CONE** **NUT** **ADJUSTER**

PLUG **BEARING CONE**

WORM BALLS **BALL RETURN GUIDE** **GUIDE CLAMP** **SCREW AND WASHER**

BEARING **OIL SEAL** **SECTOR SHAFT ARM**

BALL NUT **BEARING CONE** **BEARING CUP** **BOLT** **LOCKWASHER** **LOCKWASHER** **NUT**

Steering Gear and Related Parts.

INSTALL

Detail 8

IDLER ARM

Detail 7

Detail 9 **USE AS PILOT**

Tool—T61P-3355-A

Idler Arm Bushing Replacement

Toe-In and Steering Wheel Alignment

Check steering wheel spoke position with the front wheels straight ahead. If the spoke position is not normal, the steering wheel can be properly adjusted while toe-in is being adjusted. See Unit Repair section for complete toe-in to steering wheel relation adjustment.

STEERING GEAR

A recirculating ball type steering gear is used. Instructions for adjusting this assembly can be found in the Unit Repair section under the heading: Steering, Manual.

GEAR ASSEMBLY
Remove

1. Raise front of and place on safety stands.
2. Remove sector shaft.
3. Remove steering gear bolts from the underbody.
4. Disconnect shift rods from the shift levers.
5. Pull up the rubber seal on the column, fold back the floor mat and move the dash insulation out of the way. Then take out weather seal retaining screws and the column cover plates and gasket.
6. Disconnect the horn and turn-signal wires under the instrument panel. Remove the steering wheel.
7. Remove the upper bearing sleeve and spring and turn indicator lever.
8. Remove the clamp to instrument column bolts, then the clamp and insulator, and slide the tube from the steering gear shaft.
9. Remove the assembly through the engine compartment.

Install

Install by reversing the above procedure.

STEERING WHEEL AND HORN BUTTON

HORN BUTTON REMOVAL

The horn button or ring can be removed by pressing down evenly and twisting to the left.

STEERING WHEEL REMOVAL

To remove the steering wheel, first remove the horn button or ring and the steering wheel nut and use proper puller. Be sure turn signal switch is neutral.

CLUTCH

PEDAL ADJUSTMENT

1. To check pedal assist spring ten-

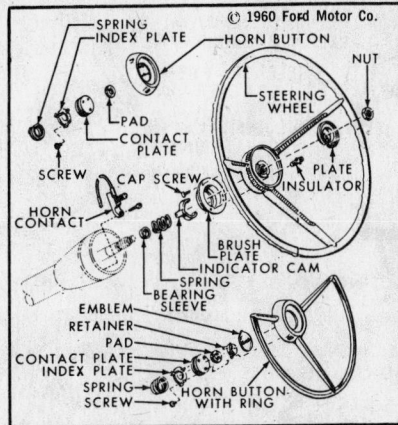

Steering Wheel, Horn, and Related Parts.

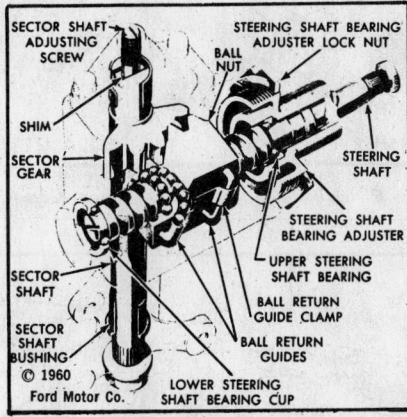

Recirculating Ball Type Steering Gear.

sion, measure the distance between the inside radius of the spring hook and the front face of the link. This distance should be 1-3/16″. Turn the nut on the retainer to get proper pedal assist.

2. Measure the total pedal travel. If the total travel is not within 6-6½ inches, move the pedal bumper and bracket up or down as necessary. <u>NOTE:</u> Always check and adjust total travel before checking free travel.

3. To check pedal free travel, start to depress the pedal slowly until the release fingers contact the release bearing. Measure this distance with a rule. The difference between this reading and the reading when the pedal is released is free travel. To obtain the required ⅞-1⅛ inch free travel, loosen the pedal-to-equalizer rod nuts and rotate the equalizer bar as needed. Then secure both equalizer bar nuts.

CLUTCH AND/OR TRANSMISSION REMOVE

1. Disconnect and remove starter and dust ring, if the clutch is to be removed.
2. Raise the car.
3. Disconnect the drive shaft at the

rear universal joint and remove the drive shaft.

4. Disconnect the speedometer cable at the transmission extension.
5. Disconnect the gear shift rods from the transmission shift levers.
6. Remove the bolt holding the extension housing to the rear support, and remove the muffler inlet pipe bracket to housing bolt.
7. Remove the two rear support bracket insulator nuts from the underside of the cross member.
8. Place a jack, (equipped with a protective piece of wood) under the rear of the engine oil pan. Raise the engine slightly.
9. Remove transmission-to-flywheel housing bolts. Thread two guide studs into the bottom attaching bolt holes.
10. Slide the transmission back and out of the car.
11. Remove release lever retracting spring and disconnect pedal at the equalizer bar.
12. Remove the release bearing and hub.
13. Remove the flywheel housing.
14. Remove the pressure plate and clutch disc from the flywheel.

CLUTCH AND/OR TRANSMISSION INSTALL

1. Wash flywheel surface with alcohol.
2. Attach the clutch disc and pressure plate assembly to the flywheel with the bolts finger tight.
3. Align the clutch disc with the pilot bushing. Then torque the cover bolts to 23-28 ft. lb.
4. Lightly lubricate the release lever fulcrum ends. Install the release lever in the flywheel housing and install the dust shield.
5. Apply very little lubricant on the release bearing retainer journal. Attach the release bearing and hub on the release lever.
6. Install the flywheel housing and torque the attaching bolts to 40-50 ft. lb. Install the dust cover and torque the bolts to 17-20 ft. lb.
7. Connect the release rod and the retracting spring. Connect the pedal-to-equalizer rod at the equalizer bar.
8. Install starter and dust ring.
9. Start the transmission extension housing up and over the rear support. After moving the transmission back just far enough for the pilot shaft to clear the clutch housing, move it upward and into position on the transmission guide studs.
10. Move the transmission forward and into place against the flywheel housing.
11. Remove guide studs and attach the transmission with a torque of 32-36 ft. lb.

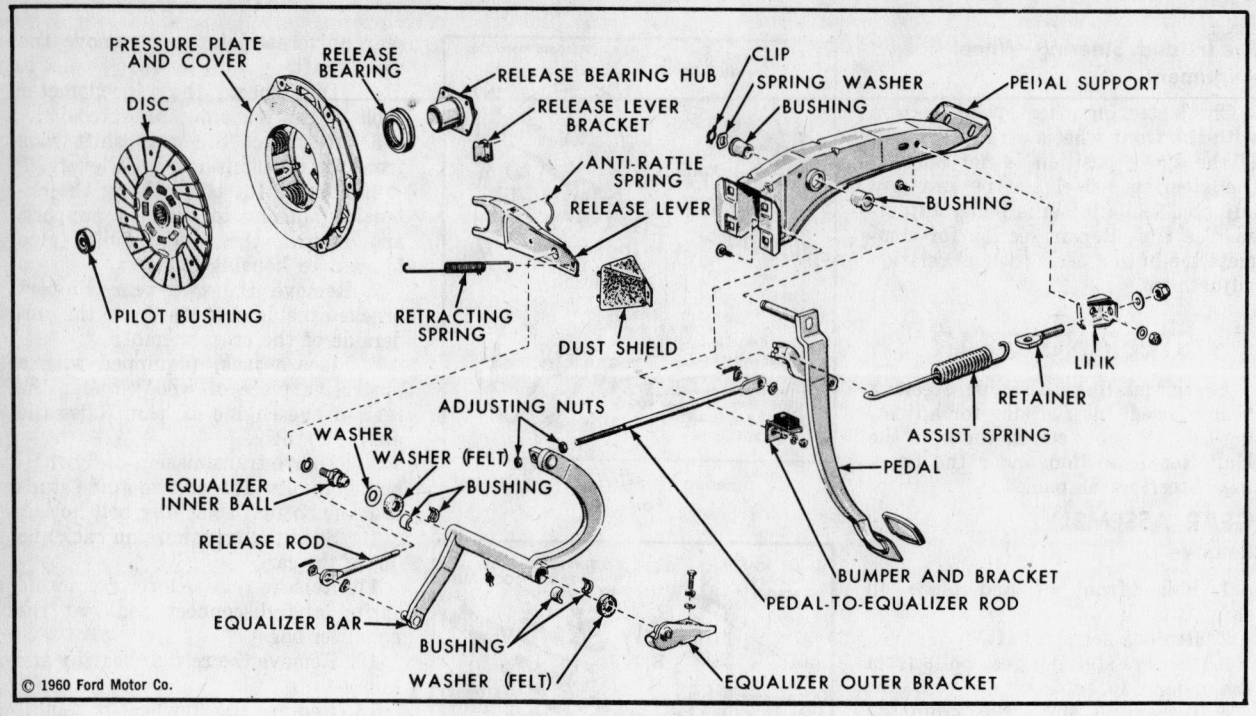

PRESSURE PLATE AND COVER

DISC

RELEASE BEARING

RELEASE BEARING HUB

RELEASE LEVER BRACKET

CLIP

SPRING WASHER

BUSHING

PEDAL SUPPORT

ANTI-RATTLE SPRING

RELEASE LEVER

BUSHING

PILOT BUSHING

RETRACTING SPRING

DUST SHIELD

ADJUSTING NUTS

LINK

RETAINER

ASSIST SPRING

WASHER

WASHER (FELT)

BUSHING

EQUALIZER INNER BALL

PEDAL

RELEASE ROD

BUMPER AND BRACKET

PEDAL-TO-EQUALIZER ROD

EQUALIZER BAR

BUSHING

WASHER (FELT)

EQUALIZER OUTER BRACKET

© 1960 Ford Motor Co.

Clutch Pedal Mounting and Linkage—Comet.

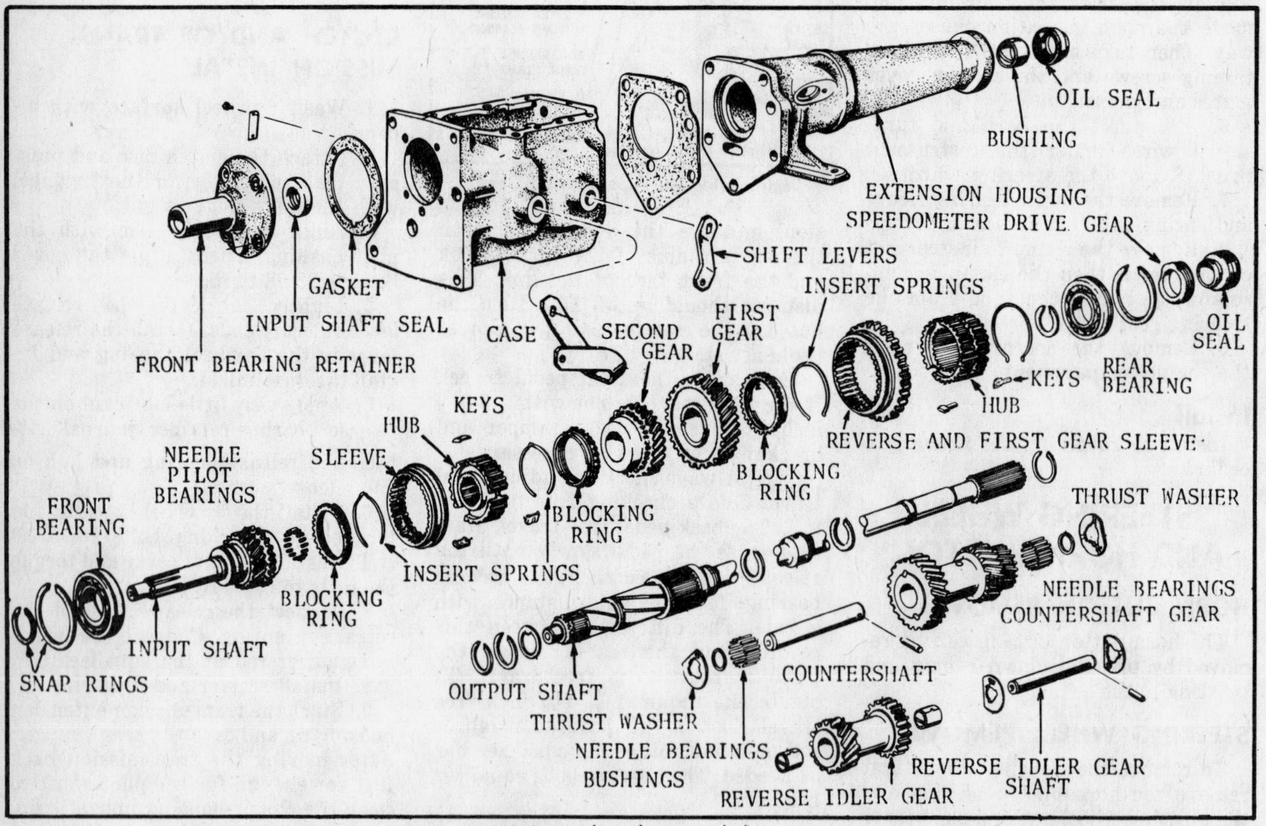

OIL SEAL

BUSHING

EXTENSION HOUSING

SPEEDOMETER DRIVE GEAR

SHIFT LEVERS

INSERT SPRINGS

OIL SEAL

GASKET

INPUT SHAFT SEAL

CASE

SECOND GEAR

FIRST GEAR

REAR BEARING

KEYS

HUB

FRONT BEARING RETAINER

KEYS

HUB

REVERSE AND FIRST GEAR SLEEVE

NEEDLE PILOT BEARINGS

SLEEVE

BLOCKING RING

BLOCKING RING

THRUST WASHER

FRONT BEARING

INSERT SPRINGS

NEEDLE BEARINGS

COUNTERSHAFT GEAR

BLOCKING RING

INPUT SHAFT

SNAP RINGS

OUTPUT SHAFT

THRUST WASHER

NEEDLE BEARINGS

BUSHINGS

COUNTERSHAFT

REVERSE IDLER GEAR

REVERSE IDLER GEAR

REVERSE IDLER GEAR SHAFT

Beginning 1963, 3-speed synchro smooth drive

12. Slowly lower the engine onto the cross member.

13. Install and torque the insulator-to-cross member nuts to 23-29 ft. lb.

14. Connect gear shift rods and the speedometer cable.

15. Hook up the drive shaft.

16. Refill transmission to proper level.

STANDARD TRANSMISSION

REFERENCES

There are three types of standard

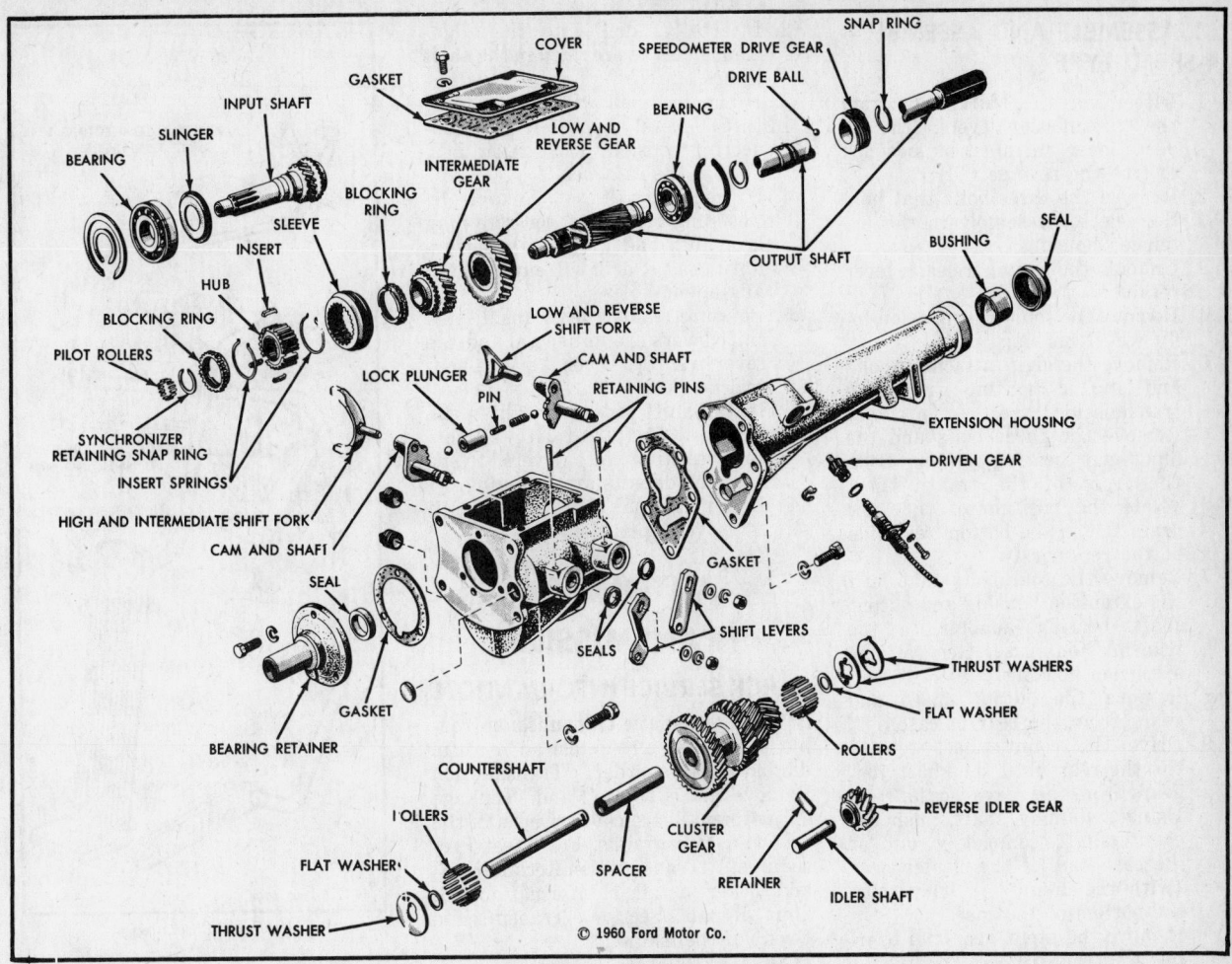

GASKET • COVER • SPEEDOMETER DRIVE GEAR • SNAP RING • DRIVE BALL • BEARING • INPUT SHAFT • SLINGER • BEARING • LOW AND REVERSE GEAR • INTERMEDIATE GEAR • BLOCKING RING • SLEEVE • INSERT • HUB • BLOCKING RING • PILOT ROLLERS • SYNCHRONIZER RETAINING SNAP RING • INSERT SPRINGS • HIGH AND INTERMEDIATE SHIFT FORK • CAM AND SHAFT • SEAL • BEARING RETAINER • GASKET • LOCK PLUNGER • PIN • LOW AND REVERSE SHIFT FORK • CAM AND SHAFT • RETAINING PINS • EXTENSION HOUSING • DRIVEN GEAR • BUSHING • SEAL • OUTPUT SHAFT • GASKET • SEALS • SHIFT LEVERS • THRUST WASHERS • FLAT WASHER • ROLLERS • REVERSE IDLER GEAR • COUNTERSHAFT • CLUSTER GEAR • RETAINER • IDLER SHAFT • ROLLERS • SPACER • FLAT WASHER • THRUST WASHER • © 1960 Ford Motor Co.

Conventional Drive Transmission Details.

transmission used, the original 3-speed (synchronized in 2nd & 3rd speeds) with top cover, the 4-speed (fully synchronized) with side cover, and beginning 1963, the 3-speed (fully synchronized transmission) with top cover.

DISASSEMBLE AND ASSEMBLE— 3-SPEED TYPE

Note:

The following procedure is for the original, 3-speed (2nd & 3rd speed synchronized) top cover transmission. However, service procedure on the 3 speed, fully synchronized, standard transmission is almost identical with former 3-speed types. Separate disassembly and assembly instructions should not be necessary.

1. Drain the unit and remove transmission cover and gasket.

2. Remove outer shift levers and the interlock linkage.

3. Remove extension housing attaching bolts and remove the engine rear support bracket and the extension housing and gasket.

(To prevent the output shaft from following the housing and dropping the needle bearings.) Tap the end of the output shaft with a soft hammer and withdraw extension housing.

4. Remove speedometer drive gear snap ring. Then remove the drive gear and drive ball from the output shaft.

5. Remove idler and countershaft retainer.

6. With a dummy shaft, drive the shaft out of the cluster gear and case. Leave the dummy shaft in the cluster, at rest, in the bottom of the case.

7. Remove input shaft bearing retainer and gasket.

8. Remove input shaft assembly and front synchronizer blocking ring from the case.

9. Remove synchronizer snap ring from the output shaft. Then, while holding the synchronizer assembly together, pull the output shaft out of the transmission case.

10. Lift the synchronizer assembly, intermediate, low and reverse sliding gears out of the case.

Then remove the two shift forks.

11. Drive the reverse idler shaft out of the gear and rear of the case.

12. Lift reverse idler gear and the cluster gear out of the case.

13. From the underside of the case, drive out the tapered pins that hold the cam and shaft assemblies in the case.

14. Drive the intermediate and high cam and shaft toward the outside of the case, then separate the balls and spring from the plunger. Drive out the cam and shaft assemblies, and remove the plunger.

15. Remove shift lever cam and shaft oil seals.

16. Remove snap ring and press the input shaft out of the bearing and oil slinger.

17. Remove snap ring, and remove the bearing from the output shaft.

18. Dismantle the components, such as: synchronizer, counter shaft cluster, etc., then clean and inspect parts.

19. To assemble, reverse the above procedure.

FALCON and COMET

DISASSEMBLE AND ASSEMBLE—4-SPEED TYPE

1. Disconnect the shift rods from the transmission levers, (the reverse lever nut must be loosened to free the reverse rod).
2. Remove the three bolts that hold the selector assembly to the extension housing.
3. Unhook the clutch release lever retainer.
4. Remove the four transmission-to-fly wheel housing bolts.
5. Remove the eight attaching bolts and shifter housing from the transmission case.
6. Remove the three bolts and the input gear bearing retainer from the front of the transmission. (Note the position of the lube drain slot in the bottom rear side of the retainer.)
7. Remove the four bolts that hold the extension housing and output shaft bearing adapter to the transmission. case. Remove the extension housing.
8. Remove the output shaft and gears from the rear of case.
9. Drive the countershaft toward the the the rear until the shaft just gears from the rear of case. Using a dummy shaft, push the countershaft completely out of the case and let the cluster gear (with the dummy in it) rest in the bottom of the case.
10. Remove the input gear and bearing from the front of the case.
11. Lift the countershaft gear assembly out through the cover opening of the case.
12. Remove the idler gear shaft with a puller, then remove the idler gear.
13. If the input gear bearing needs replacing, remove it.
14. Straighten the output shaft nut lock tab and remove the nut and lock.
15. Remove the speedometer gear and drive ball. Remove speedometer gear spacer.
16. Place the output shaft assembly in a press and press off the bearing, adapter, first gear, first and second synchronizer assembly and second gear.
17. Remove the snap ring on the output shaft in front of the 3-4 synchronizer. Press the 3-4 synchronizer off the shaft. Remove the front and rear insert springs from both synchronizer assemblies. Slide sleeves off the hubs. Remove the hub inserts.
18. Reassemble in the reverse order of disassembly.

GEAR SHIFT LINKAGE, ADJUST

1. Put selector lever in neutral, then raise car on hoist.

2. Insert ¼" drill into the alignment holes as provided in the shift levers.
3. If the ¼" drill will not enter all three levers, check for bent connecting rods, or loose lever lock nuts at the rod ends.
4. If necessary, reset linkage by loosening the three rod-retaining lock nuts and moving the levers until the ¼" drill will enter all the alignment holes.
5. Be sure that the transmission shift levers are in neutral and the reverse shifter lever is in the neutral detent.
6. Install shift rods and tighten the lock nuts to 15-20 ft. lb. torque.
7. Operate the shift levers to be sure the detents are engaging.
8. Lower car and check for smooth crossover operation.

AUTOMATIC TRANSMISSION

QUICK SERVICE INFORMATION

When automatic transmission trouble is reported, a road test and careful diagnosis is in order. "Transmission Remove and Replace" and "Linkage Adjustments" are covered here in the following paragraphs. For "Test Procedures," "Transmission Recondition" and other detailed information see Unit Repair Section, Transmission Group of the manual.

THROTTLE LINKAGE ADJUSTMENT

Preliminary Adjustment, (see Unit Repair Group for pressure method of adjustment).

1. Apply parking brake, place selector in "N," (Neutral) position, and start engine.
2. Hook up a tachometer.
3. Adjust engine idle to 475—500

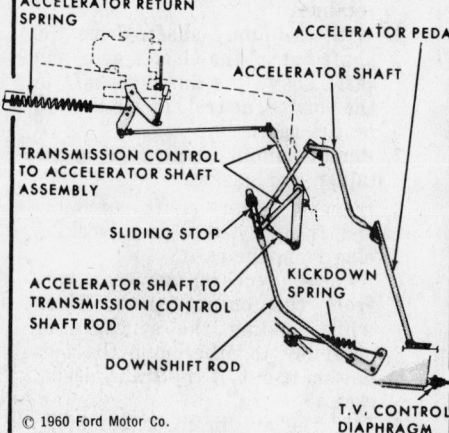

1961-62, Throttle Linkage.

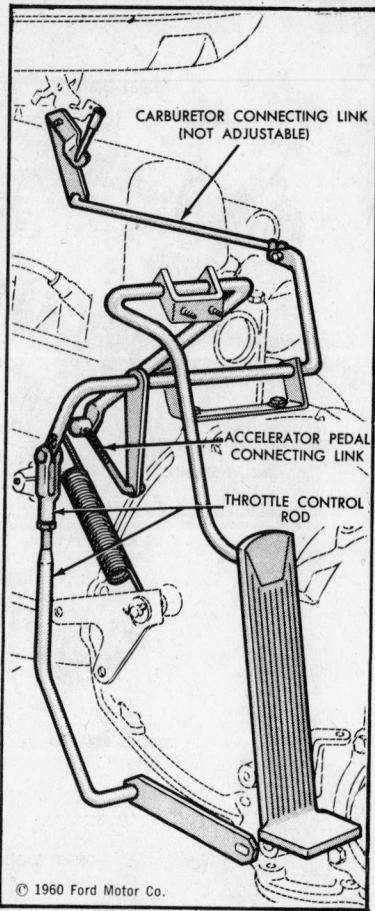

© 1960 Ford Motor Co.

1960 Throttle Linkage.

R.P.M. with operating temperature at normal and selector in "D" position.

4. Bottom the dashpot plunger and check its clearance between the plunger and the throttle lever. Clearance should be .060"—.090" with hot engine.

5. Stop the engine, disconnect the throttle control rod at the clevis end, then loosen the clevis locknut.

6. Push down on the throttle control rod to hold the throttle lever against the stop inside the transmission.

7. Holding down on the rod, adjust its length so the clevis pin has a free fit. From this length, shorten the throttle rod at the clevis, 3½ turns and install the clevis pin.

8. Adjust accelerator pedal height to 4½ inches. Adjustment is made at the trunion end of the accelerator connecting link.

BEGINNING 1961 VACUUM CONTROLS

During 1961, two-speed transmission design has gone to vacuum controls instead of the manually controlled throttle valve previously used. The following adjustments are required.

LINKAGE ADJUSTMENT

"144-Six" and "170-Six"

1. Apply parking brakes, and place the selector lever in "N" position.
2. Run the engine until it reaches normal operating temperature.
3. Hook up a tachometer and check engine idle speed. Idle speed should be less than 500 R.P.M.
4. With throttle in the hot-idle position, bottom the dashpot plunger and measure the clearance between the plunger and the throttle shaft lever. Dashpot clearance should be .060"-.090" on Falcon, (.130"-.150" on Comet).
5. With engine stopped, adjust the carburetor throttle rod length to obtain an accelerator height of 4 5/16". This measurement is taken from the top of the accelerator pedal to the floor mat.
6. Disconnect throttle return spring and the downshift linkage return spring.
7. Loosen the adjusting lock on the downshift control rod.
8. Pull the control rod and throttle linkage "Z" bar up to the limit of their travel. Then, holding them in this position, slide the adjustment lock down against the "Z" bar, and tighten the screw.
9. Install the return springs, and check the throttle and downshift linkage for full travel.
10. Test drive the car to check for proper up-shift and kickdown operations.

V-8 Engines

1. Apply parking brakes, and place the selector in "N."
2. Run engine at idle speed until normal operating temperature has been reached.
3. Hook up a tachometer and check idle speed. The R.P.M. should be under 500 with the fast idle cam in slow (hot) position.
4. With throttle in hot-idle position, bottom the dashpot plunger and measure the clearance between

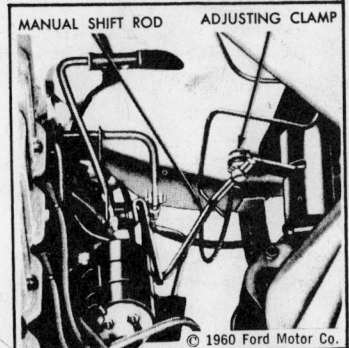

MANUAL SHIFT ROD   ADJUSTING CLAMP

© 1960 Ford Motor Co.

Fig. 3 —Manual Linkage.

the plunger and the throttle shaft lever. This clearance should be .060"-.090".
5. Engine stopped, disconnect the carburetor connecting link from the accelerator assembly.
6. Insert a ¼" drill rod through the gauging holes. Hold the carburetor connecting link forward, and adjust the sleeve until the link assembly fits freely in the accelerator assembly. Then rotate the sleeve counterclockwise one full turn. Remove the gauge pin.

MANUAL LINKAGE ADJUSTMENT

1. With engine stopped, loosen clamp at the shift lever so that the shift lever is free to slide in the clamp, (Fig. 3).
2. Put the selector in "D" position.
3. Shift the manual lever at the transmission into the "D" detent, (second from the rear).
4. Tighten clamp on shift rod.
5. Recheck pointer alignment for all selector lever detent positions.

STARTER NEUTRAL SWITCH

1. Check starter circuit in all selector lever positions. The circuit must be open in all positions except "N" and "P."
2. To adjust, loosen the neutral switch to steering column attaching screws, (Fig. 4). Locate the switch so that the starter circuit is closed when the selector is at "N" and "P" only.

AUTOMATIC TRANSMISSION (FORDOMATIC)

The automatic transmission used as optional equipment on the FALCON

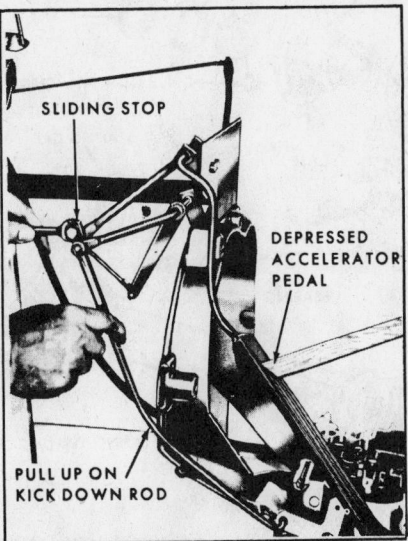

SLIDING STOP

DEPRESSED ACCELERATOR PEDAL

PULL UP ON KICK DOWN ROD

Adjusting the Kickdown Rod

—COMET is an air cooled and reduced version of the two-speed Ford automatic transmission.

FORDOMATIC, R & R

Remove

1. Position the car on a suitable hoist but do NOT raise it at this time.
2. Pull back the front floor mat and remove the converter-housing-to-engine access hole covers. Remove the two upper bolts and lockwashers that hold the converter housing to the engine.
3. From under the hood, remove the two bolts that hold the throttle linkage bracket to the converter housing.
4. Remove the starter.
5. Now raise the car and remove the cover from the bottom of the converter housing.
6. Remove one of the converter drain plugs, turn the converter 180° and remove the other drain plug.

(CAUTION) Do not attempt to turn the converter with a wrench applied to the converter attaching nuts.

7. Remove the drain plug and drain the transmission.
8. Disconnect the driveshaft at the rear universal joint and remove the driveshaft. (By installing the extension housing oil seal replacing tool in the rear end of the extension housing, a sloppy mess can be avoided.)
9. Disconnect the manual throttle linkage at the transmission.
10. Disconnect the speedometer cable at the extension housing.
11. Disconnect the transmission oil filler tube and remove the bolt that attaches the extension housing to the rear support.
12. Disconnect the parking brake rod at the equalizer.
13. With a transmission jack attached to the transmission, lift enough to take the weight off the engine rear support member.
14. Remove the two bolts which hold the support member to the underbody. Remove the support member.
15. Lower the transmission and engine assembly again but support the rear of the engine.
16. Remove the four converter-to-flywheel attaching stud nuts. Back the converter off the flywheel as far as possible.
17. Remove the two lower converter housing to engine block bolts.
18. Work the converter housing off the engine block dowel pins and work the converter pilot out of the engine crankshaft.
19. Lash or otherwise secure the converter to the transmission and lower the transmission and converter assembly.

(CAUTION) Before proceeding further with work on either the transmission or torque converter, thoroughly clean the outside of the units to prevent dirt from entering the mechanism and causing trouble. The Ford Motor Car Company is so particular about foreign matter entering the transmission or converter that they forbid the use of wiping rags for cleaning parts during transmission or converter assembly or repairs.

TRANSMISSION OR CONVERTER, REPLACE

Replacement is a reverse procedure of removal.

Dismantling, overhaul, adjustments and test procedures are covered in the Unit Repair section under Two-Speed Fordomatic Transmission.

UNIVERSAL JOINT AND DRIVE LINE

This drive line with universals are, in general, similar to Ford models.

To inspect or replace U-joints follow this method.

1. Disconnect the rear U-joint from the pinion flange. Pull the drive shaft toward rear until the front joint comes out of the transmission extension housing. (Installing the seal driver will prevent loss of transmission lubricant).

2. Remove snap rings that retain the bearings in the yokes.

3. Place the joint in vise or press.

4. Use two sockets. One of slightly smaller outside diameter than the joint bearing and one of an inside diameter larger than the bearing outside diameter.

5. With the sockets opposite each other, alternately press both bearings out of the yoke.

6. Rotate the shaft ¼ turn and use the same method for the remaining bearings.

7. For installation, reverse the above procedure. The splines should be lubricated and care taken not to damage the rear transmission extension seal.

REAR AXLE AND SUSPENSION

TROUBLE SHOOTING AND ADJUSTMENTS

General instructions covering troubles of the rear axle with repair methods and adjustments are given in the Unit Repair section under: Axles, Rear.

All service operations on the differential case and pinion assembly can be done with the axle in the car.

AXLE SHAFT, DRIVE SHAFT AND COVER REMOVAL

1. Raise car and support it on the pads in front of rear springs, so the rear axle drops as low as allowed by the rear shock absorbers and springs.

2. Remove the cover from the rear. Drain lubricant.

3. Remove both rear wheels.

4. Loosen rear brake shoe adjustments and take off the drums.

5. Working thru the holes in the axle flanges remove the nuts holding the wheel bearing retainers.

6. Pull the axle shafts.

7. Disconnect the drive shaft at the pinion flange. Differential and pinion assemblies can now be removed.

RADIO, R & R

1. Pull the radio and control knobs off and remove the nuts and washers retaining the radio to the instrument panel.

2. Disconnect the antenna lead at the right side of the radio.

3. Disconnect the speaker lead.

4. Disconnect the radio lead wire at the fuse panel, and disconnect the pilot light wire. Remove the lead wire from the retaining clips.

5. Remove the radio right support bracket to radio retaining bolt. Remove the radio left support bracket to radio retaining nut. One bracket only on the Bendix radio.

6. Remove the radio assembly from the instrument panel.

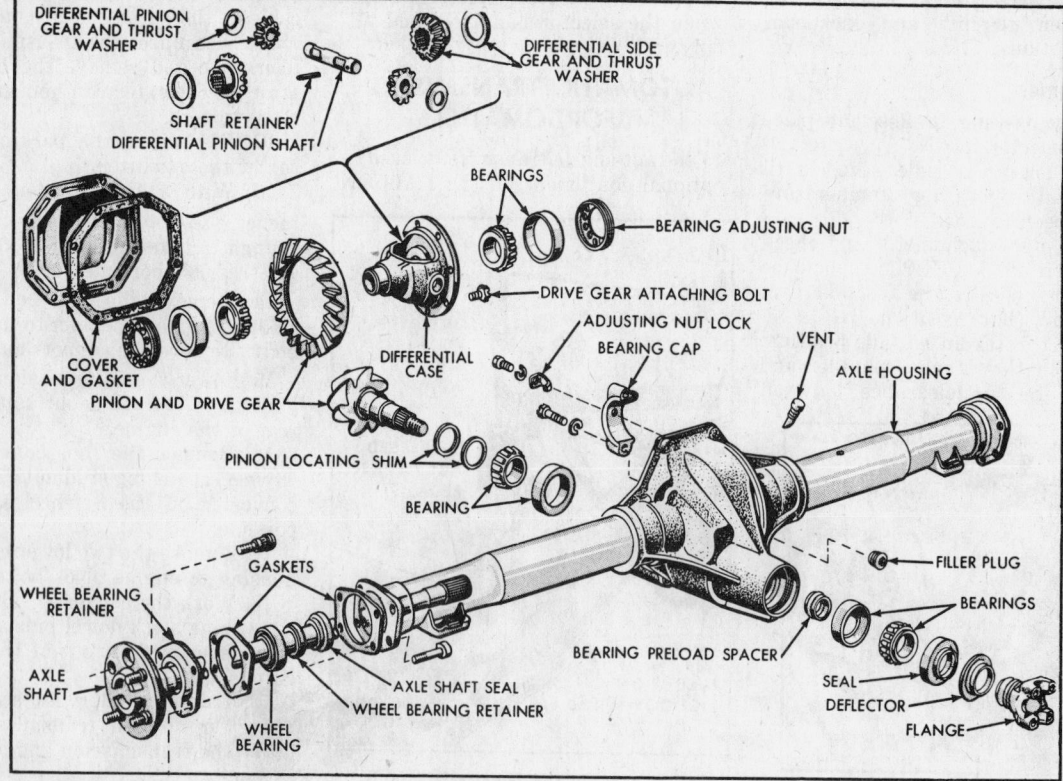

Dissambled Rear Axle.

AIR CONDITIONING
Service 1092

BRAKES, HYDRAULIC
Adjustments 938
Bleed brakes 941
Parking brake level & cable 353
Pedal adjust 351
Master cylinder, R & R 351
Master cylinder service 939
References 351

BRAKES, POWER
Power unit overhaul 954
Trouble shooting 954

CLUTCH
Clutch assembly, R & R 368
Clutch pedal, adjust 368

COOLING SYSTEM
Radiator core, R & R 355
Thermostat 354
Water pump, R & R 354

ELECTRICAL SYSTEM
Battery 350
Distributor, R & R 349
Distributor specifications 344
Fuses and circuit breakers 347
Gauges 1024
Generator and regulator
    specifications 345
Generator and regulators 349
Generator service 1028
Generator trouble shooting chart 1026
Horn buttons 367
Ignition firing order & timing 341
Ignition timing specifications 343
Instruments 350
Starter, R & R 350
Starter specifications 343
Starter systems 1046
Transistor, ignition 1018

ENGINE ASSEMBLY
Crankcase ventilation 355
Cylinder head, R & R 358
Cylinder head, tightening
    sequences 348
Engine assembly, R & R 356
Engine firing order & timing 341
Engine marking code 342
Engine diagnosis 1012
Engine references 355
Exhaust 354
Exhaust manifold, R & R 354
Inlet manifold, R & R 354
Engine lubrication 362
Mechanics data 1136
Oil pan, R & R 363
Oil pressure specifications 348
Oil filter 364
Piston and rod, R & R 365
Piston specifications 345
Pistons, inspect 365

ENGINE ASSEMBLY—continued
Rear main bearing oil seal 365
Rocker arms & shaft 357
Specifications, general, engine . .348
Timing chain, R & R 362
Timing cover, R & R 361
Transistor, Ignition 1018
Trouble shooting charts 1012
Tune-up specifications 343
Valve references 359
Valve adjusting sequence 361
Valve specifications 347
Valve springs 361

ENGINE LUBRICATION
References 362
Oil filter 364
Oil pan, R & R 363

EXHAUST SYSTEM
Manifolds, R & R 354

FUEL SYSTEM
References 353
Carburetors, adjustment 972
Fuel gauge service 1020
Fuel pump pressure 343
Fuel pump, R & R 354
Fuel pump service 1020
Fuel tank, R & R 354

INSTRUMENTS
Speedometer, R & R 350
Instruments, R & R 350

RADIO, R & R
References 380

REAR AXLE
Axle shaft 918
Axle shaft oil seal 918
Pinion bearings 918
Ring gear & pinion 918
Shock absorbers, rear 379
Spring, R & R 379
Trouble shooting 919

SPECIFICATIONS
Battery 343
Brake cylinder sizes 349
Capacities:
    Axle, rear 342
    Cooling system 342
    Crankcase 342
    Fuel tank 342
    Transmission, automatic 342
    Transmission, manual 342
Chassis, general 349
Distributor 344
Engine, general 348
Fuses and circuit breakers 347
Generator and regulators 345
Light bulbs 346
Main bearings 344
Model identification illustrations . .340
Pistons 345

SPECIFICATIONS—continued
Quick reference specifications . . .341
Rod bearings 344
Starters 343
Torque wrench 345
Tune-up 343
Valves 347
Wheel alignment 346

STEERING, MANUAL
Adjust gear housing 1052
Gear assembly, R & R 367
Horn button, R & R 367
Steering wheel, R & R 367

STEERING, POWER
Pump assembly 1058
Trouble shooting 1081
Unit overhaul 1058

SUSPENSION, FRONT
Adjustments 366
Alignment procedures 1082
Alignment specifications 346
Ball joints, R & R 1087
Camber, adjust 1089
Caster, adjust 1089
King pins and bushings 1087
Knuckle supports 1087
Shock absorbers 1087
Support arms, pins and bushings
    bushing 1089
Toe-in, adjust 1089

TRANSMISSION, AUTOMATIC
Fordomatic 3 speed 820
    Linkage adjust 371
    Transmission, R & R 373
    Transmission and converter,
        R & R 374
Cruis-o-matic 820
    Linkage adjust 374
    Transmission, R & R 375
Fordomatic 2 speed 838
    Linkage adjust 377

TRANSMISSION, MANUAL SHIFT
Disassemble transmission 369
Shift linkage 369
Transmission, R & R 368

TROUBLE CHECKS
Procedures 1

TUNE-UP
Carburetors 972
Procedures 1012
Specifications 343
Engine diagnosis 1012

UNIVERSAL JOINT AND DRIVE SHAFT
Disassemble U joint 378
U joint & drive shaft, R & R 378

FORD and THUNDERBIRD

YEAR IDENTIFICATION

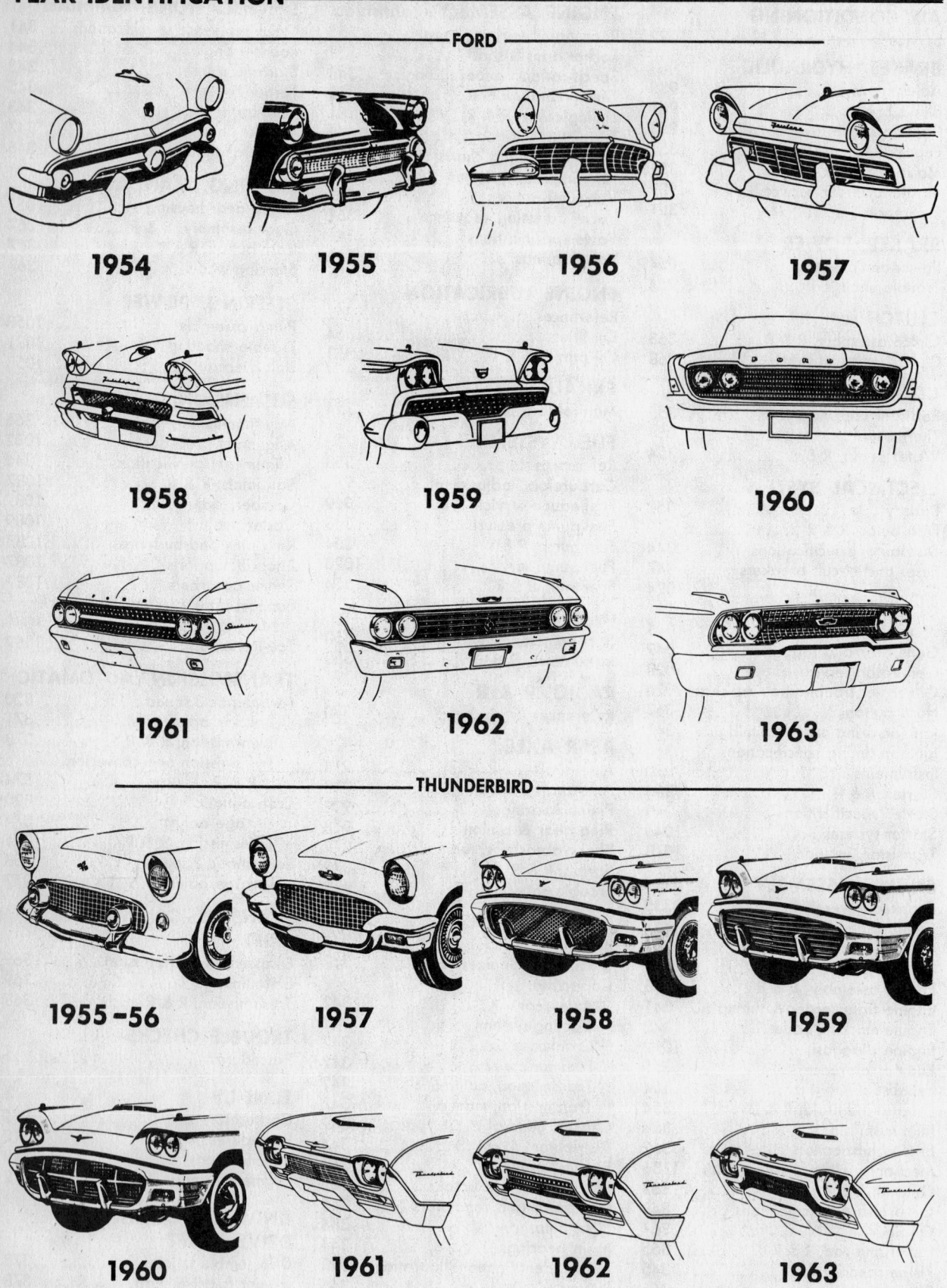

FORD

1954

1955

1956

1957

1958

1959

1960

1961

1962

1963

THUNDERBIRD

1955–56

1957

1958

1959

1960

1961

1962

1963

QUICK WORKING SPECIFICATIONS

DISTRIBUTOR

Breaker Point Gap

1954-63, 6 cyl. .... .024-.026
1954-63, V-8 .... .014-.016

Cam Angle

1954-63, 6 cyl. 37
1954-63, 6 cyl. 37

IGNITION TIMING

1954-55

6 Cyl. .... 4°
V-8, Std. Trans. .... 4°
V-8, Auto. Trans. .... 6°

1956-60

6 Cyl. & V-8, Std. Trans. .... 4°
6 Cyl. & V-8, Auto. Trans. .... 6°

1961-62

6 Cyl. & V-8, Std. Trans. .... 4°
6 Cyl. & V-8, Auto. Trans. .... 10°
V-8, 390—High Perf. Option .... 13°
V-8, 406—High Perf. Option .... 10°

1960

6 Cyl., Std. Trans. .... 4°
6 Cyl., Auto. Trans. .... 10°
V-8, 260 cu. in. Engine—All .... 6½°
V-8, Exc. 260, Std. Trans. .... 4°
V-8, Exc. 260, Auto. Trans. .... 10°
V-8, 390, High Perf. Option .... 13°
V-8, 406, High Perf. Option .... 10°

SPARK PLUGS

Year	Type	Gap
1954, 6 cyl. OHV	H10	.035
1954-57, OHV, V8	870	.035
1955-61, 6 cyl.	870	.035
1958-61, 292 cu. in.	FI4Y	.035
1958-61, V8 ex. 292	F11Y	.035
1962, 6 cyl. and 292	BF82	.035
1962-63, 352 & 390	BF42	.035
1963, 6 cyl., 260 & 289	BF82	.035
1963, 406-V8	BF32	.035

GENERATOR AND REGULATOR

YEAR AND SERIES	GENERATOR Field Current In Amperes 6 Volt	12 Volt	REGULATOR Cut-out Closing Voltage	Current Regulator Setting	Voltage Regulator Setting
1954-55 Ex.T.Bird	2.0	—	6.3	35	7.6
T. Bird	2.0	—	6.3	40	7.6
1956-63 All		1.5	12.4	30	15.0±1(A)

(A) Surrounding temperatures guide this adjustment. Higher temperatures require lower settings and lower temperatures permit higher settings, within limits.

For A.C. Generator Specs., see following pages

TORQUE WRENCH READINGS

Cylinder Head Bolts

1954-63, 6 cyl. 65-75

1954-57, V8 65-75
1958-62, 292 V8 65-75
1958-63, 332, 352, 260, 289, 390 80-90
1959-63, 430, 406 cu. in. 95-105

CAPACITIES

Engine Crankcase (Quarts)
(Add 1 qt. for new filter)

1954-63, 6 cyl. 4
1954-63, V8, OHV. 5

Synchromesh Trans. (Pints)
(Add 1½ pts. for overdrive)

1954-56, All 3
1957, All 3¼
1958, All 3½
1959-63, All 3

Automatic Trans. (Pints)

1954, All 19
1955-56, 6 cyl. 18½
1955-56, V8 .... 19½
1957, All 21½
1958, 6 cyl. 18
1958, V8 All 20
1959-63
2 speed Fordomatic 20
3 speed cruise o matic 22

Cooling System (Quarts)
(Add 1 qt. for heater)

1954-63, 6 cyl. 15
1954, V8 20
1955-59, V8 ex. T Bird 19
1955-59, T Bird V8 20
1960-63, V8 All 19

FIRING ORDER and TIMING

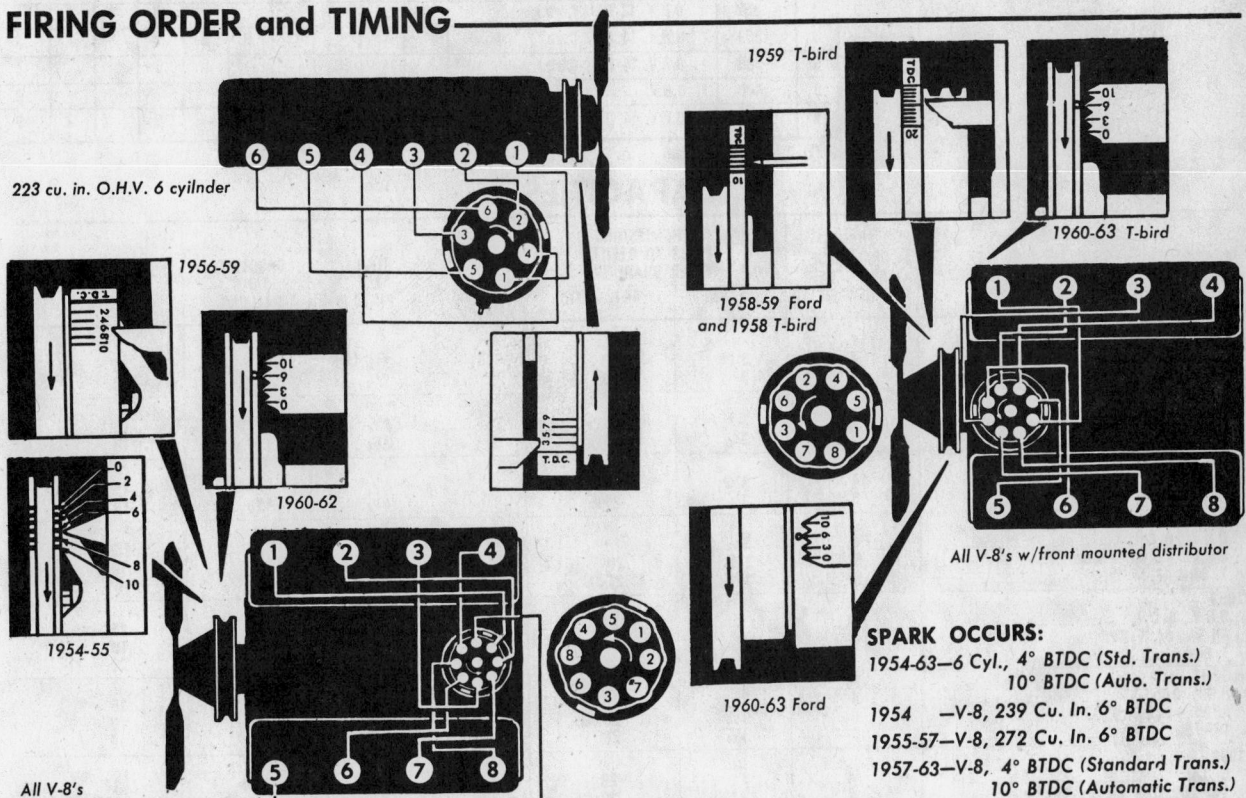

223 cu. in. O.H.V. 6 cyilnder

1959 T-bird

1960-63 T-bird

1956-59

1958-59 Ford and 1958 T-bird

1960-62

All V-8's w/front mounted distributor

1954-55

1960-63 Ford

All V-8's w/rear mounted distributor

SPARK OCCURS:

1954-63—6 Cyl., 4° BTDC (Std. Trans.)
10° BTDC (Auto. Trans.)
1954 —V-8, 239 Cu. In. 6° BTDC
1955-57—V-8, 272 Cu. In. 6° BTDC
1957-63—V-8, 4° BTDC (Standard Trans.)
10° BTDC (Automatic Trans.)

NOTE

THESE ARE APPROXIMATE SETTINGS. ENGINE DESIGN, ALTITUDE, TEMPERATURE, FUEL AND ENGINE CONDITION WILL ALL INFLUENCE TIMING. THE DETERMINING FACTOR, LIMITING ADVANCE, WILL STILL BE THE "KNOCK POINT" OF THE INDIVIDUAL ENGINE.

FORD and THUNDERBIRD

CAR SERIAL NUMBER LOCATION AND ENGINE IDENTIFICATION

ON ALL FORDS THE SERIAL NUMBERS AND THE ENGINE NUMBERS ARE ONE AND THE SAME.

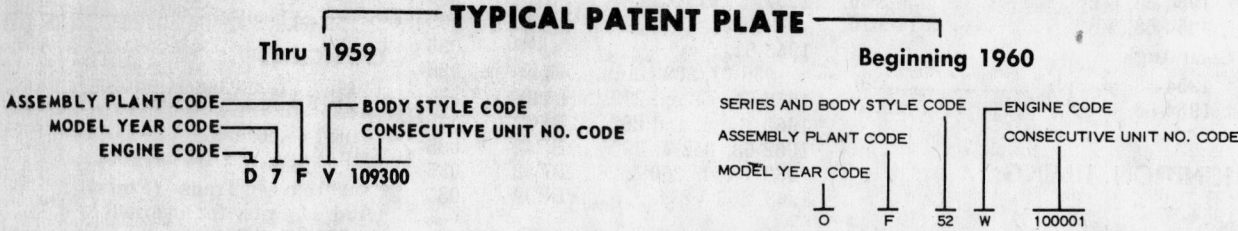

— **TYPICAL PATENT PLATE** —

Thru 1959

ASSEMBLY PLANT CODE
MODEL YEAR CODE
ENGINE CODE
BODY STYLE CODE
CONSECUTIVE UNIT NO. CODE

D 7 F V 109300

Beginning 1960

SERIES AND BODY STYLE CODE
ASSEMBLY PLANT CODE
MODEL YEAR CODE
ENGINE CODE
CONSECUTIVE UNIT NO. CODE

O F 52 W 100001

ENGINE IS IDENTIFIED THRU CAR SERIAL NUMBER. (See Chart) →

SERIAL NUMBER LOCATION

1954-63—On left front door pillar.
1955-63—Thunderbird on firewall under hood.

1963 — Air Cleaner & Valve Rocker Cover

223 cu. in. Engine	Red
260 cu. in Engine	Yellow
289 cu. in Engine	Ivory
352 cu. in. Engine	Blue
390 cu. in. Engine	Gold
427 cu. in. Engine	Chrome
406 cu. in. Engine	Silver

ENGINE IDENTIFICATION CODE

No. Cyls.	Cu In. Displ.	Type	1954	1955	1956	1957	1958	1959	1960	1961	1962	1963
6	223	O.H.V.	A	A	A	A	A	A	V	V	V	V
8	239	O.H.V.	U									
8	260	O.H.V.										F
8	272	O.H.V. (4 Bbl. Carb.)		M*								
8	272	O.H.V. (2 Bbl. Carb.)		U	U	B						
8	289	O.H.V. (2 Bbl. Carb.)										
8	289	O.H.V. (4 Bbl. Carb.)										
8	292	O.H.V. (2 Bbl. Carb.)					C	C	C	W	W	W
8	292	O.H.V. (4 Bbl. Carb.)		P	M							
8	312	O.H.V. (4 Bbl. Carb.)			P	D						
8	312	O.H.V. (Two, 4 Bbl. Carbs.)				E						
8	312	O.H.V. (Blower, 4 Bbl. Carb.)				F						
8	332	O.H.V. (2 Bbl. Carb.)					B	B				
8	332	O.H.V. (4 Bbl. Carb.)					G					
8	352	O.H.V. (2 Bbl. Carb.)							X	X	X	
8	352	O.H.V. (4 Bbl. Carb.)					H	H	Y			X
8	390	O.H.V. (4 Bbl. Carb.)						J	J			Z
8	406	O.H.V.										B
8	430	O.H.V. (4 Bbl. Carb.)								Z	Z	F

NOTE: * 182 HP—Special

CAPACITIES

YEAR	ENGINE CRANKCASE ADD 1 QT. FOR NEW FILTER	TRANSMISSIONS PINTS TO REFILL AFTER DRAINING		REAR AXLE PINTS	GASOLINE TANK GALLONS	COOLING SYSTEM QUARTS
		MANUAL	AUTOMATIC			
1954						
O.H.V. 6 Cyl.	4	3	19	3½	17	15
OHV, V8	5	3	19	3½	17½	20
1955-56						
O.H.V. 6 Cyl.	4	3	18½	3½	17½	15
O.H.V. V8	5	3	19½	3½	17½	19
1957						
O.H.V. 6 Cyl.	4	3¼	21½	4½	20	15
O.H.V., V8	5	3¼	21½	4½	20	19
1958						
O.H.V., 6 Cyl.	4	3½	18	5½	20	15
O.H.V., V8, ex. T Bird	5	3½	20	5½	20	19
T Bird	5	3¾	21	5½	20	19½
1959						
O.H.V., 6 Cyl.	4	3	20	4½	20	15
All V8, ex. T Bird	5	3	20A	4½	20	19
T Bird	5	3	20	5½	20	20
1960-62						
O.H.V., 6 Cyl.	4	3	20	4½	20	15
All V8, ex. T Bird	5	3¼	20 (A)	4½	20	19
T. Bird	5	3¼	20	5½	20	19
1963						
6 Cyl.	4	3	20	4½	20	15
V8, 260, 289 Cu. In. Engine	4	3	20	4½	20	13½
V8, All Others	5	3¼(B)	20	4½	20	19

(A) 1959-61 automatic transmission capacities are relative to the transmission used—Fordomatic, 20 pts.—Cruise-o-matic, 22 pts.
(B) 4-Speed Manual Transmission,—3½ Pints

TUNE-UP SPECIFICATIONS

YEAR	Spark Plugs Make and Number	Gap	Distributor Cam Angle	Point Gap	Arm Spring Tension	Ignition Timing (Note 1)	Compression Pressure Cranking	Valves Tappet Clearance Hot ex.-"C" for Cold Inlet	Exhaust	Timing Inlet Opens	Fuel Pump Pressure	Engine Idle Speed Neutral
1954												
6 Cyl., OHV	CH-H10	.035	36	.025	17–20	3B	120	.015	.019	13B	4.5	485
V8, OHV	CH-870	.035	27	.015	17–20	6B	130	.019	.019	8B	5	485
1955												
6 Cyl., OHV	CH-870	.035	36	.025	17–20	3B	125	.015	.019	13B	4.5	485
V8, OHV	CH-870	.035	27	.015	17–20	6B	130	.019	.019	12B	5	485
T Bird, V8, OHV	CH-870	.035	27	.015	17–20	6B	135	.018	.018	12B	5	485
1956												
6 Cyl., OHV	CH-870	.035	36	.025	17–20	Note 1	135	.019	.019	24B	4.5	485
V8, OHV	CH-870	.035	27	.015	17–20	Note 1	135	.019	.019	12B	5	485
1957												
6 Cyl., OHV	CH-870	.035	36	.025	17–20	Note 1	150	.019	.019	17B	4.0	485
V8, OHV	CH-870	.035	27	.015	17–20	Note 1	160	.019	.019	18B	5	485
1958												
6 Cyl., OHV	870	.035	37	.025	17–20	Note 1	150	.019	.019	17B	4.5	485
Y-V8, OHV	F14Y	.035	27	.015	17–20	Note 1	160	.019	.019	18B	4.5	485
Interceptor V8's	F11Y	.035	27	.015	17–20	Note 1	180	.026	.026	22B	5.5	600
1959												
6 Cyl., 223 Cu. In.	870	.035	37	.025	17-20	Note 1	150	.019	.019	17B	4.5	485
V8, 292 Cu. In.	F14Y	.035	27	.015	17-20	Note 1	160	.018	.018	12B	5.0	600
V8, 332 Cu. In.	F11Y	.035	27	.015	17-20	Note 1	170	Zero	Zero	22B	5.0	600
V8, 352 Cu. In.	F11Y	.035	27	.015	17-20	Note 1	180	Zero	Zero	22B	5.0	600
V8, T. Bird, 430 Cu. In.	F11Y	.035	27	.015	17-20	Note 1	180	Zero	Zero	22B	5.5	450
1960												
6 Cyl., 223 Cu. In.	870	.035	37	.025	17-20	Note 1	150	.019	.019	17B	4.5	485
V8, 292 Cu. In.	F14Y	.035	27	.015	17-20	Note 1	160	.019	.019	12B	5.0	600
V8, 352 Cu. In.	F11Y	.035	27	.015	17-20	Note 1	180	Zero	Zero	22B	5.0	600
V8, T. Bird, 430 Cu. In.	F11Y	.035	27	.015	17-20	Note 1	180	Zero	Zero	22B	5.5	450
1961												
6 Cyl., 223 cu. in.	870	.035	37	.025	17-20	Note 1	150	.019	.019	17B	4.5	485
V-8, 292 cu. in.	F14Y	.035	27	.015	17-20	Note 1	160	.019	.019	12B	5.0	600
V-8, 352, 390 cu. in.	F11Y	.035	27	.015	17-20	Note 1	180	Zero	Zero	26B	5.0	600
1962												
6 Cyl., 223 Cu. In.	BF-82	.035	37	.025	17-20	Note 1	150	.019	.019	17B	4.5	485
V8, 292 Cu. In.	BF-82	.035	27	.015	17-20	Note 1	160	.019	.019	12B	5.0	600
V8, 352, 390 Cu. In.	BF-42	.035	27	.015	17-20	Note 1	180	Zero	Zero	26B	5.0	600
1963												
6 Cyl., 223 Cu. In.	BF-82	.035	37	.025	17-20	Note 1	150	Zero	Zero	23B	4.5	485
V8, 260 Cu. In.	BF-82	.035	27	.015	17-20	Note 1	150	Zero	Zero	21B	5.0	550
V8, 289	BF-82	.035	27	.015	17-20	Note 1	160	Zero	Zero	20B	5.0	550
V8, 352, 390 Cu. In.	BF-42	.035	27	.015	17-20	Note 1	180	Zero	Zero	26B	5.0	600
V8, 406, Cu. In.*	BF-32	.035	27	.015	17-20	Note 1	180	Zero	Zero	24B	5.0	600

* High performance option uses BTF-1 spark plugs at .025" gap and is equipped with adjustable mechanical valve lifters, set at .025" hot.

NOTES FOR TUNE-UP SPECIFICATIONS TABLE

Note:

All specifications are standard and should result in satisfactory performanance. There are, however, factors that influence these settings, such as fuel octane value, air density, humidity, temperature, etc. Timing charts, like other specifications must be considered as averages, subject to modification.

Note 1: Ignition Timing

See Pictorial "Firing Order and Timing" specifications on previous page.

BATTERY and STARTER SPECIFICATIONS

YEAR	BATTERY Ampere Hour Capacity	Volts	Group Number	Terminal Grounded	Starters Lock Test Amps.	Volts	Torque	No-Load Test Amps.	Volts	R.P.M.	Brush Spring Tension
1954-55											
All ex. T. Bird	100	6	2N	Pos.	700	3.5	16.0	70	6	4000	52
T Bird	100	6	2N	Pos.	700	3.5	14.2	70	6	5000	52
1956											
All Models	55	12	4N	Neg.	550	5.0	15.5	120	12	4800	52
1957											
All Models	55	12	4N	Neg.	550	5.0	15.5	85	12	4500	52
1958-63 Note A											
All Models	55	12	4N	Neg.	550	5.0	15.5	80	12	4500	52

Note A: Optional Equipment 65 and 70 Ampere-Hour Capacity

FORD and THUNDERBIRD

DISTRIBUTOR SPECIFICATONS

Year	Model	Part Number	Rotation	Cam Angle Degrees	Breaker Point Opening Inch	Breaker Arm Spring Tension Ounces	Governor Control @ Dist. R.P.M.		Vacuum Control Data		
							Adv. Starts	Full Adv.	Inches of Vacuum To Start Advance	Inches of Vacuum For Full Advance	Max. Adv. of Dist. in Degrees
1954	6 Cyl.	FAA-12127C	C	35-38	.025	17-20	None	None	4 @ .50	6.00	11¾
1954	V-8	FAE-12127A	CC	26-28	.016	17-20	None	None	4½ @ .72	4.40	14½
1955	6 Cyl.	FDH-12127A	C	35-38	.025	17-20	None	None	4 @ .50	6.00	11¾
	V-8	FDJ-12127C	CC	26-28	.016	17-20	None	None	2 @ .40	4.60	15¾
	T. Bird	FEA-12127E	CC	26-28	.016	17-20	None	None	1 @ .19	2.00	14¾
1956	6 Cyl.	FDR-12127A	C	35-38	.025	17-20	None	None	2¼ @ .50	6.00	13¾
	V-8 272	FDS-12127A	CC	26-28	.016	17-20	None	None	¾ @ .28	4.60	16½
	V-8 292	FDT-12127B	CC	26-28	.016	17-20	None	None	½ @ .29	2.20	13½
1957	6 Cyl.	FEG-12127B	C	35-38	.025	17-20	None	None	½ @ .22	3.40	13¼
	V-8 272	FEH-12127B	CC	26-28	.016	17-20	1 @ 300	17 @ 1500	1 @ 10.00	21.00	12
	V-8 292	FEH-12127A	CC	26-28	.016	17-20	1 @ 375	18 @ 2000	1 @ 5.00	20.00	12
	V-8 312	FEH-12127C	CC	26-28	.016	17-20	1 @ 300	15 @ 2000	1 @ 5.00	20.00	9
1958	6 Cyl.	FEG-12127D	C	35-38	.025	17-20	None	None	3 @ .55	3.40	12¼
	V-8 292	FEU-12127A	CC	26-28	.016	17-20	1 @ 350	17 @ 2000	2 @ 6.00	20.00	11½
	V-8 332	FEU-12127B	CC	26-28	.016	17-20	1 @ 450	15 @ 2000	1 @ 6.00	15.00	11
	V-8 352	FEU-12127H	CC	26-28	.016	17-20	1 @ 400	11 @ 2000	2 @ 6.00	20.00	11½
	T. Bird 352	FEU-12127N	CC	26-28	.016	17-20	1 @ 500	15 @ 2000	2 @ 8.00	14.00	10
1959	6 Cyl.	FET-12127D	C	35-38	.025	17-20	None	None	3 @ .79	5.99	11
	V-8 292	B9FA-12127A	CC	26-28	.016	17-20	1 @ 450	15 @ 2000	@ 6.50	15.00	11
	V-8 332	FEU-12127J	CC	26-28	.016	17-20	1 @ 500	15 @ 2000	2 @ 6.00	16.00	11½
	V-8 352	FEU-12127J	CC	26-28	.016	17-20	1 @ 500	15 @ 2000	2 @ 8.00	14.00	10
	T. Bird 430	FEW-12127H	CC	26-28	.016	17-20	1 @ 400	15 @ 2000	2 @ 6.50	16.00	12½
1960	6 Cyl.	FET-12127C	C	35-38	.025	17-20	None	None	1 @ .32	6.00	13¾
	V-8 292	9FA-12127A	CC	26-28	.015	17-20	1 @ 350	15 @ 2000	1 @ 2.0	9.00	11
	V-8 352	FEU-12127J	CC	26-28	.015	17-20	1 @ 500	15 @ 2000	1 @ 2.0	7.5	11
	T. Bird 430	FEU-12127H	CC	26-28	.016	17-20	1 @ 400	15 @ 2000	2 @ 6.50	16.00	12½
1961-62	6 Cyl. 223	CIAF-12127D	CC	35-38	.025	17-20	None	None	1 @ .5	6.5	13
	V-8 292	COAF-12127A	C	26-28	.015	17-20	1 @ 500	11 @ 2000	1 @ 7.0	20.0	11
	V-8 352	COAF-12127D	CC	26-28	.015	17-20	1 @ 500	12.2 @ 2000	1 @ 5.0	17.0	11
	V-8 390	CISF-12127A	CC	26-28	.015	17-20	1 @ 500	11.5 @ 2000	1 @ 9.0	17.0	9
1963	6 Cyl. 223	C3AF-12127-H	C	35-38	.025	17-20	None	None	1 @ .5	6.5	13
	V-8 260	C3AZ-12127-U	CC	26-28	.015	17-20	1 @ 1050	12.5 @ 2000	1 @ 5.0	18.0	11
	289	C3BY-12127-R	CC	26-28	.015	17-20	1 @ 500	12.5 @ 2000	1 @ 5.0	18.0	11
	V-8 352	COAF-12127-D	CC	26-28	.015	17-20	1 @ 500	12.2 @ 2000	1 @ 5.0	17.0	11
	V-8 390	CZAF-12127-A	CC	26-28	.015	17-20	1 @ 500	11.5 @ 2000	1 @ 9.0	17.0	9
	V-8 406	COAF-12127K	CC	26-28*	.020	17-20	1 @ 750	12.2 @ 2175	None	None	None

NOTE:
* Dual point distributor is used.

CRANKSHAFT BEARING JOURNAL SIZES

YEAR	MAIN BEARING JOURNALS				CONNECTING ROD BEARING JOURNALS		
	JOURNAL DIAMETER	OIL CLEARANCE	END PLAY OF SHAFT	END PLAY HELD BY	JOURNAL DIAMETER	OIL CLEARANCE	END PLAY
1954							
OHV, 6 Cyl.	2.4984	.0013	.006	No. 3	2.298	.0013	.005
OHV, V8	2.4980	.0013	.004	No. 3	2.188	.0018	.004
1955-57							
OHV, 6 Cyl.	2.4984	.0013	.006	No. 3	2.298	.0013	.005
OHV, V8 ex. 312 Cu In. V8	2.4984	.0017	.004	No. 3	2.188	.0013	.004
312 Cu. In. T. Bird V8	2.6239	.0017	.004	No. 3	2.188	.0013	.004
1958							
OHV, 6 Cyl.	2.4984	.0015	.006	No. 3	2.298	.0014	.006
Y-V8, OHV	2.4984	.0017	.004	No. 3	2.1884	.0018	.011
Interceptor V8's	2.7488	.0018	.004	No. 3	2.4384	.0019	.011
1959-62							
OHV, 6 Cyl.	2.4984	Note 1	.006	No. 3	2.2984	.0014	.006
292, Cu. In. V8	2.4984	.0017	.004	No. 3	2.1884	.0018	.011
332, 352, Cu. In. V8	2.7488	.0018	.004	No. 3	2.4384	.0019	.011
430, Cu. In. V8	2.8998	.0019	.006	No. 3	2.5996	.0016	.010
1963							
OHV, 6 Cyl.	2.4984	Note 1	.006	No. 3	2.2984	.0014	.006
260, 289 Cu. In. V8	2.2484	.0016	.006	No. 3	2.1236	.0017	.011
352, 390, 406, V8	2.7488	.0020	.006	No. 3	2.4384	.0019	.011

Note 1: 6 Cyl. Crankshaft Oil Clearance   Journals 1, 2, 3. Clearance—.0005-.0025.

D.C. GENERATOR & REGULATOR SPECIFICATIONS

	GENERATORS					REGULATORS		
	FIELD CURRENT IN AMPERES		BRUSH SPRING TENSION	CUT OUT RELAY		CURRENT AND VOLTAGE REGULATOR AIR GAP	CURRENT REGULATOR SETTING	VOLTAGE REGULATOR SETTING
YEAR	AT 6 VOLTS	AT 12 VOLTS		AIR GAP	CLOSING VOLTAGE			
1954-55 All ex. T. Bird	2.0	—	30	.025	6.3	(A)	35	7.6
T Bird	2.0	—	30	.025	6.3	(A)	40	7.6
1956-57 All Models	—	1.5	30	.025	12.4	(A)	30	15.0
1958-59 All Models	—	1.5	30	.025	12.4	(A)	30	15.0
1960-63 All Models	—	1.5	30	.025	12.4	(A)	30	15.0

A.C. GENERATOR & REGULATOR SPECIFICATIONS

Year and Model	Ground Polarity	ALTERNATOR		CURRENT OUTPUT @ 15 Volts and 2950 Engine R.P.M.	VOLTAGE OUTPUT @ 15 Amp. Load and 2950 Engine R.P.M.	REGULATOR	
		Ampere Rating	Field Current Draw, Amps.			Point Gap	Air Gap
1963 All Models	Neg.	40	2.9-3.1	40 Amp.	15	.015-.022	.022-.030

(A) Current and Voltage Regulator Air Gap

CURRENT REGULATOR AIR GAP—.025
VOLTAGE REGULATOR AIR GAP—.035

TORQUE SPECIFICATIONS

YEAR	CYLINDER HEAD BOLTS	ROD BEARING BOLTS	MAIN BEARING BOLTS	CRANKSHAFT PULLEY BOLT	FLYWHEEL TO CRANKSHAFT BOLT	Manifolds, FT. LB. In.	Ex.
1954-57							
Allex. 312 Cu. In. V8	65-75	40-50	92-105	85- 90	75-80	NA	NA
312 Cu. In. T. Bird	65-75	40-50	92-105	130-145	75-80	NA	NA
1958							
6 Cyl. & Y-V8	65-75	45-50	95-105	85-90	75-85	26	26
Interceptor V8's	80-90	45-50	95-105	130-145	75-85	26	26
1959-60							
6 Cyl. & 292 Cu. In. V8	65-75	45-50	95-105	85-95	75-85	26	26
332, 352 Cu. In. V8's	80-90	45-50	95-105	130-145	75-85	26	26
430 Cu. In. V8	95-105	45-50	95-105	75-90	75-85	26	26
1961-62							
6 Cyl. & 292 V8	65-75	45-50	95-105	85-95	75-85	26	26
352 & 390 V8	80-90	45-50	95-105	130-145	75-85	26	26
1963							
6 Cyl. O.H.V.	65-75	40-45	95-105	70-90	75-85	26	26
260, 289 Cu. In.	65-70	40-45	65-75	70-90	75-85	15*	15
352, 390, 406 Cu. In.	80-90	40-45	95-105	70-90	75-85	15*	26

NOTE: 35 ft. lbs Torque when cast iron manifold is used.

PISTON AND PIN SPECIFICATIONS

Year and Model	PISTON Skirt Clearance Min.	Max.	PISTON PIN Diameter	Bushing	FIT In Rod	In Piston	Lock
1954-63 223 6 Cyl.	.0008	.0026	.9120	Yes	.0001-.0005	.0001-.0003	Ring
1954-57 V8	.0008	.0026	.9120	Yes	.0001-.0005	.0001-.0003	Ring
1958 V8	.0008	.0026	.9750	Yes	.0001-.0005	.0001-.0003	Ring
1959-62 V8, Ex. 430 Cu. In.	.0008	.0026	.9750	Yes	.0001-.0005	.0001-.0003	Ring
1959-62 V8, 430 Cu. In.	.0008	.0026	.9749	No	Press	.0001-.0003	None
1963 V8, Ex. 260, 289 & 406	.0008	.0026	.9750	Yes	.0001-.0005	.0001-.0003	Ring
1963 V8, 260, 289 Cu. In.	.0008	.0026	.9120	No	Press*	.0001-.0003	None*
1963 V8, 406 Cu. In.	.0008	.0026	.9750	No	Press*	.0001-.0003	None*

NOTE:
* A special piston pin installing tool, #T60K-6135-A or it's equivalent, should be used when assembling the piston to the connecting rod.

FORD and THUNDERBIRD

LIGHT BULBS
(C.P. MEANS CANDLE POWER)

1954-57: ALL MODELS

Telltales for Headlight Beam, Direction Signal, Oil Pressure, Generator, Light for Instruments, Ignition Lock, Radio Dial, Glove Compartment, Fuel Gage, Heater Control, Cigar Lighter, Clock:

6 Volt, No. 55; 12 Volt, No. 57.
(2 C.P. miniature bayonet base.)

Trunk Compartment:

6 Volt, No. 81; 12 Volt, No. 89.
(6 C.P. single contact base.)

License Plate Light, Map Light, Ford-omatic Quadrant:

6 Volt, No. 63; 12 Volt, No. 67.
(4 C.P. single contact base.)

Dome Light:

6 Volt, No. 209; 12 Volt, No. 1003.
(15 C.P. single contact base.)

Front Combination Parking and Signal Light, Rear Combination Tail, Signal and Stop Light:

6 Volt, No. 1154; 12 Volt, No. 1034.
(4 & 32 C.P. double contact indexed base.)

Back-up Lights:

6 Volt, No. 1133; 12 Volt, No. 1073.
(32 C.P. single contact base.)

Headlights:

6 Volt, No. 5040; 12 Volt, No. 5400.
(40 & 50 C.P. three contact base.)

1958-63: ALL MODELS

Radio Dial, Turn Indicator, Cluster, Lighter, Heater Button, Clock, Key, Lights:

12 Volt, No. 57.
(2 C.P. miniature bayonet base.)

Inboard Tail, License Plate, Map Lights:

12 Volt, No. 67.
(4 C.P. single contact base.)

Back-up on Courier and Ranchero, Dome Lights:

12 Volt, No. 1003.
(15 C.P. single contact base.)

Combination Turn Signal and Park (Front) Tail and Stop (Rear) Lights:

12 Volt, No. 1034.
(4 & 32 C.P. 2 contact indexed base.)

Headlights, Oil Pressure, Generator, Top Cycle, Indicator Lights:

12 Volt, No. 1445.
(One C.P.)

Back-up Light on All Ex Courier and Ranchero:

12 Volt, No. 1141.
(21 C.P. single contact base.)

Four Headlight System

LOW BEAM (OUTER)
12 Volt, No. 4002.
(50 & 37½ watts, 3 contact base.)

HIGH BEAM (INNER)
12 Volt, No. 4001.

(37½ watts 2 contact base.)

1958 Retractable Hardtop

There is circuit breaker in the control circuit feed between the ignition switch and the indicator light. There is a circuit breaker in the common motor feed behind the dash at the left. There is a circuit breaker at the ground feed of each of the seven motors. All of the power relays are housed in a metal box behind the rear seat back.

Other Fuses Have Been Used As Listed Below:

CLOCK:
At or near clock 1954-55, AGA 3; 1956-63, AGA 1.

Direction Signal:

Back of dash between ignition switch and flasher. 1954-55, SFE 14; 1956-63, SFE 7½.

Heater:

In a fuse holder back of dash. 1954-55, SFE 20; 1956-63, SFE 14.

Overdrive:

In clips on engine side of dash. 1954-55, AGC 30; 1956-57, AGC 15; 1958-63, AG 15.

Park and Tail Light:

Fuse behind instrument panel to right of charge indicator. 1956, AGC 15.

Windshield Wiper

At the wiper motor 1952 only, SFE 20.

FRONT WHEEL ALIGNMENT

YEAR	CASTER		CAMBER		Toe-In (Inches	KING PIN INCLINATION (DEGREES)	TURNING RADIUS	
	RANGE (DEGREES)	PREF. SETTING	RANGE (DEGREES)	PREF. SETTING			OUTER WHEEL	INNER WHEEL
1954 All Models	0 to 1P		0 to 1P		1/16 to 1/8	7 1/10	20	24½
1955 All Models	½P to 1½P		¼P to 1¼P		1/16 to 1/8	7 1/10	20	24½(A)
1956 All Models	½P to 1½P	Note 1	¼P to 1¼P	Note 2	1/16 to 1/8	7 1/10	20	24¼(A)
1957 All Models	½P to 1½P	Note 1	½P to 1½P	Note 2	1/16 to 1/8	7 1/10	20	24½(A)
1958 All Models	½P to 1½P	Note 1	½P to 1½P	Note 2	1/16 to 1/8	7 1/10	20	24¼(B)
1959 All ex. T Bird	0 to 1P	Note 1	½P to 1½P	Note 2	1/32 to 1/8	6¾	20	24½
T Bird	½P to 1½P	Note 1	½P to 1½P	Note 2	1/16 to 1/8	7½	17¼	20
1960 All ex. T. Bird	½N to ½P	Note 1	½P to 1½P	Note 2	1/8 to 5/32	6¾	20	24½
T Bird	½P to 1½P	Note 1	½P to 1½P	Note 2	1/16 to 1/8	7½	17⅛	20
1961-63 All Ex. T-Bird	½N to ½P	Note 1	¼P to 1P	Note 2	1/8 to 5/32	6¾	20	24½
T-Bird	½P to ½P	Note 1	¼P to 1P	Note 2	1/16 to 1/8	7½	17⅛	20

NOTES FOR FRONT WHEEL ALIGNMENT TABLE

Note 1: Preferred Caster Setting

Equal wheel to wheel within ½ degree.

Note 2: Preferred Camber Setting

Equal wheel to wheel within ¼ degree.

(A)—1955-57 Thunderbird Turning Radius

When outer wheel has turned 20 degrees inner wheel should have turned 25 degrees.

(B)—1958 Thunderbird Turning Radius

When inner wheel has turned to 20 degrees the outer wheel will have turned 17⅛ degrees.

FUSES and CIRCUIT BREAKERS

1954-63 Lights:

Headlight circuit breakers are part of headlight switch. A fuse block with one or two fuses is fastened to it. Of the two fuses, one is SFE 14 amp. to protect parking, tail, and instrument lights, the other is SFE 14 amp. to protect the dome and stoplights. If only one fuse is used (an SFE 14 amp. for 6 volt system, an AGC 7½ amp. for 12 volt systems) it is to protect the map and dome lights.

1954-57 Power Top:

40 amp. circuit breaker on right front fender apron.

1958-63 Power Top:

Circuit breaker on instrument panel near switch.

1954-63 Power Windows:

30 amp. circuit breaker on engine side of firewall. Also 15 amp. circuit breaker in control line near ignition switch.

Also a 15 amp. circuit breaker is at each motor.

1957 Power Seat:

15 amp. circuit breaker under dash and a 30 amp. circuit breaker on seat motor.

1958-63 Power Seat:

15 amp. and 30 amp. circuit breakers under the dash and a ground circuit breaker at the motor.

VALVE SPECIFICATIONS

YEAR	Seat Angle		Intake Valve Lift	Exhaust Valve Lift	Valve Spring Pressure		Stem to Guide Clearance		Stem Diameter		Are Valve Guides Repraceable
	In	Ex			Outer	Inner	Inlet	Exhaust	Inlet	Exhaust	
1954											
6 Cyl. OHV	45	45	.329	.325	58@1¹³⁄₁₆		.0015	.0025	.3420	.3410	No.
OHV, V8	45	45	.331	.331	58@1¹³⁄₁₆		.0015	.0025	.3420	.3410	No.
1955											
6 Cyl. OHV	45	45	.331	.325	58@1¹³⁄₁₆		.0015	.0025	.3420	.3410	No.
OHV, V8	45	45	360	.331	58@1¹³⁄₁₆		.0015	.0025	.3420	.3410	No.
1956											
6 Cyl. OHV	45	45	.370	.370	75@1²⁵⁄₃₂		.0015	.0025	.3420	.3410	No.
OHV, V8	45	45	.386	.384	75@1²⁵⁄₃₂		.0015	.0025	.3420	.3410	No.
1957											
6 Cyl. OHV	45	45	.370	.370	75@1²⁵⁄₃₂		.0015	.0025	.3419	.3407	No
OHV, V8	45	45	.401	.421	75@1²⁵⁄₃₂		.0015	.0025	.3419	.3407	No
1958											
6 Cyl. OHV	45	45	.369	.370	75@1²⁵⁄₃₂		.0017	.0030	.3419	.3407	No
V8, 292 Cu. In.	45	45	.400	.421	75@1²⁵⁄₃₂		.0017	.0030	.3419	.3407	No
V8, 332, 352 Cu. In.	30	45	.399	.408	99@1⁵³⁄₆₄	Damper	.0017	.0035	.3715	.3697	No.
1959											
6 Cyl. OHV	45	45	.369	.370	75@1²⁵⁄₃₂		.0017	.0035	.3419	.3403	No
V8, 292 Cu. In.	45	45	.359	.357	75@1²⁵⁄₃₂		.0017	.0030	.3419	.3403	No
V8, 332,352 Cu. In.	30	45	.408	.408	99@1⁵³⁄₆₄		.0017	.0035	.3715	.3697	No
V8, 430 Cu. In.	45	45	.408	.408	Note 1		.0017	.0035	.3715	.3697	No
1960											
6 Cyl. OHV	45	45	.369	.370	75@1²⁵⁄₃₂		.0017	.0035	.3419	.3403	No
V8, 292 Cu. In.	45	45	.359	.357	75@1²⁵⁄₃₂		.0017	.0030	.3419	.3403	No
V8, 352 Cu. In.	30	45	.408	.408	99@1⁵³⁄₆₄		.0017	.0035	.3715	.3697	No
V8, 430 Cu. In.	45	45	.408	.408	Note 1		.0017	.0035	.3715	.3697	No
1961-62											
OHV6, 223 cu. in.	45	45	.369	.370	75@1²⁵⁄₃₂	None	.0017	.0035	.3419	.3403	No
V8, 292 cu. in.	45	45	.359	.357	75@1²⁵⁄₃₂	None	.0017	.0030	.3419	.3403	No
V8, 352, 390 cu. in.	45	45	.408	.408	99@1⁵³⁄₆₄	None	.0017	.0035	.3715	.3697	No
1963											
OHV 6, 223 cu. in.	45	45	.369	.369	100@1²⁵⁄₃₂	None	.0017	.0035	.3420	.3402	No
V8, 260, 289 cu. in.	45	45	.380	.380	60@1⁴⁹⁄₆₄	None	.0017	.0026	.3104	.3094	No
V8, 352, 390 cu. in.	45	45	.408	.408	80@1¹³⁄₁₆	None	.0017	.0035	.3715	.3697	No
V8, 406 cu. in.	30	45	.500	.500	85@1⁵³⁄₆₄	None*	.0017	.0027	.3715	.3705	No

* Inner springs are optional 30@1²³⁄₃₂.

NOTES FOR VALVE SPECIFICATIONS TABLE

Note 1: Valve Springs

Intake ....72@1⁵³⁄₆₄
Exhaust ....70@1⁵³⁄₆₄

FORD and THUNDERBIRD

GENERAL ENGINE SPECIFICATIONS

Year Note 1	Bore and Stroke	Number of Main Bearings	Type of Valve Lifter Used	Cubic Inch Displacement	AMA Horsepower	Advertised Horsepower at Stated RPM	Advertised Torque at Stated RPM	Compression Ratio	Oil Pressure At 30 MPH	Cam Shaft Drive
1954										
6 Cyl., OHV, Symbol A	$3\frac{5}{8}x3\frac{19}{32}$	4	Mech. Adj.	223	31.5	115@3900	193@1600	7.2–1	45–55	Chain
OHV, V8, Symbol U	$3\frac{1}{2}x3\frac{7}{64}$	5	Mech. Adj.	239	39.2	130@4200	214@2000	7.2–1	45–55	Chain
1955										
6 Cyl., OHV, Symbol A	$3\frac{5}{8}x3\frac{19}{32}$	4	Mech. Adj.	223	31.5	120@4000	195@1800	7.5–1	45–50	Chain
OHV, V8, Symbol U	$3\frac{5}{8}x3\frac{19}{64}$	5	Mech. Adj.	272	42.0	162@4400	258@2200	7.6–1	45–50	Chain
T Bird, OHV, V8, Symbol M ..	$3\frac{3}{4}x3\frac{19}{64}$	5	Mech. Adj.	292	45.0	193@4400	280@2600	8.1–1	45–50	Chain
1956										
6 Cyl., OHV, Symbol A	$3\frac{5}{8}x3\frac{19}{32}$	4	Mech. Adj.	223	31.5	137@4200	202@2200	8–1	45–50	Chain
OHV, V8, Symbol M, Fairlane .	$3\frac{3}{4}x3\frac{19}{64}$	5	Mech. Adj.	292	45.0	200@4600	285@2600	8.4–1	45–50	Chain
OHV, V8, Symbol U	$3\frac{5}{8}x3\frac{19}{64}$	5	Mech. Adj.	272	42.0	173@4400	260@2400	8.4–1	45–50	Chain
OHV, V8, Symbol P, T Bird ...	$3\frac{51}{64}x3\frac{7}{16}$	5	Mech. Adj.	312	46.2	215@4600	317@1700	8.4–1	45–50	Chain
OHV, V8, Symbol M, T Bird ..	$3\frac{3}{4}x3\frac{19}{64}$	5	Mech. Adj.	292	45.0	202@4600	289@2600	8.4–1	45–50	Chain
1957										
6 Cyl., OHV, Symbol A	$3\frac{5}{8}x3\frac{19}{32}$	4	Mech. Adj.	223	31.5	144@4200	212@2400	8.6–1	45–50	Chain
OHV, V8, Symbol D, Optional .	$3\frac{51}{64}x3\frac{7}{16}$	5	Mech. Adj.	312	46.2	245@4500	332@3200	9.7–1	45–50	Chain
OHV, V8, Symbol C, Fairlane ..	$3\frac{3}{4}x3\frac{19}{64}$	5	Mech. Adj.	292	45.0	215@4500	297@2700	9.1–1	45–50	Chain
OHV, V8, Symbol B, Custom ..	$3\frac{5}{8}x3\frac{19}{64}$	5	Mech. Adj.	272	42.0	190@4600	270@2400	8.6–1	45–50	Chain
1958 Note 7										
6 Cyl., OHV, Symbol A	$3\frac{5}{8}x3\frac{19}{32}$	4	Mech. Adj.	223	31.5	145@4200	212@2100	8.6-1	45–50	Chain
Y-V8, Symbol C	$3\frac{3}{4}x3\frac{19}{64}$	5	Mech. Adj.	292	45	205@4500	295@2400	9.5-1	45–50	Chain
Interceptor V8, Symbol G	$4x3\frac{19}{64}$	5	Mech. Adj.	332	51.2	240@4600	340@2400	9.5-1	45–50	Chain
T. Bird Special V8, Symbol H	$4x3\frac{1}{2}$	5	Hydraulic	352	51.2	300@4600	395@2800	10.2-1	45–50	Chain
1959 Note 7										
6 Cyl., OHV 223 Cu. In.	$3\frac{5}{8}x3\frac{19}{32}$	4	Mech. Adj.	223	31.5	145@4200	206@2200	8.4-1	45-50	Chain
V8, OHV, 292 Cu. In.	$3\frac{3}{4}x3\frac{19}{64}$	5	Mech. Adj.	292	45.0	200@4400	285@2200	8.8-1	45-55	Chain
V8, OHV, 332 Cu. In.	$4x3\frac{19}{64}$	5	Hydraulic	332	51.2	225@4400	325@2200	8.9-1	43-54	Chain
V8, OHV, 352 Cu. In.	$4x3\frac{1}{2}$	5	Hydraulic	352	51.2	300@4600	380@2800	9.6-1	43-54	Chain
V8, T. Bird, Special 430 Cu. In.	$4\frac{19}{64}x3\frac{45}{64}$	5	Hydraulic	430	59.1	350@4800	490@3100	10.0-1	43-54	Chain
1960 Note 7										
6 Cyl., OHV, 223 Cu. In.	$3\frac{5}{8}x3\frac{19}{32}$	4	Mech. Adj.	223	31.5	145@4000	206@2200	8.4-1	45-50	Chain
V8, OHV, 292 Cu. In.	$3\frac{3}{4}x3\frac{19}{64}$	5	Mech. Adj.	292	45.0	185@4200	292@2200	8.8-1	45-55	Chain
V8, OHV, 352 Cu. In. 2V	$4x3\frac{1}{2}$	5	Hydraulic	352	51.2	235@4400	350@2800	9.6-1	43-54	Chain
V8, OHV, 352 Cu. In. 4V	$4x3\frac{1}{2}$	5	Hydraulic	352	51.2	300@4600	381@2800	8.9-1	43-54	Chain
V8, T. Bird, 430 Cu. In.	$4\frac{19}{64}x3\frac{45}{64}$	5	Hydraulic	430	59.1	350@4600	490@2800	10.0-1	43-54	Chain
1961-62										
6 Cyl., 223 cu. in	3.62x3.60	4	Note 1	223	31.5	135@4000	200@2000	8.4-1	45	Chain
V-8, 292 cu. in.	3.75x3.30	5	Mech. Adj.	292	45.0	175@4200	279@2200	8.8-1	45	Chain
V-8, 352 cu. in.	4.00x3.50	5	Hydraulic	352	51.2	220@4400	376@2400	8.9-1	45	Chain
V-8, 390 cu. in.	4.05x3.784	5	Hydraulic	390	52.5	300@4600	427@2800	9.6-1	45	Chain
1963										
6 Cyl., 223 Cu. In.	3.62x3.60	4	Note 1	223	31.5	138@4200	203@2200	8.4-1	45	Chain
V8, 260 Cu. In.	3.80x2.87	5	Hydraulic	260	46.2	164@4400	258@2200	8.7-1	45	Chain
V8, 289 Cu. In.	4.00x2.87	5	Hydraulic	289	51.2	195@4800	282@2400	8.7-1	45	Chain
V8, 352 Cu. In.	4.00x3.50	5	Hydraulic	352	51.2	220@4300	336@2600	8.9-1	45	Chain
V8, 390 Cu. In.	4.05x3.78	5	Hydraulic	390	52.5	300@4600	427@2800	9.6-1	45	Chain
V8, 406 Cu. In.	4.13x3.78	5	Hydraulic*	406	54.6	405@5800	448@3500	10.9-1	45	Chain

* Except high performance options, where solid tappets are used with .025" lash.

NOTES FOR GENERAL ENGINE SPECIFICATIONS TABLE

Note 1:

Beginning 1962, 6 cyl. engines are equipped with mechanical, zero lash, self adjusting valve tappets.

CYLINDER HEAD NUT TIGHTENING SEQUENCE

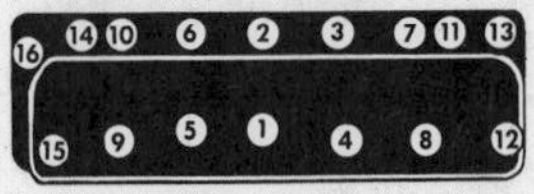

1954-63, OHV 6 cyl.

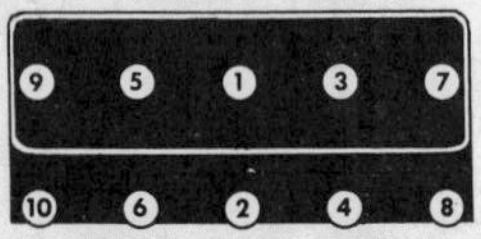

1954-63, V-8, Exc. 260

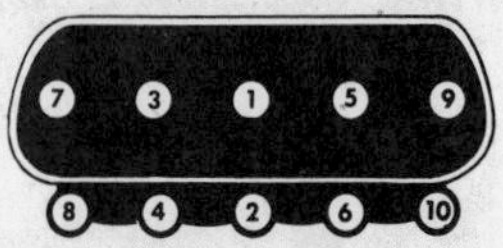

1963, V-8, 260 cu. in. and 289 cu. in. Engines

DISTRIBUTOR

Detailed information on: distributor drive, direction of distributor rotation; cylinder numbering; firing order; point gap; cam dwell; timing mark location; spark plugs, spark advance; ignition resistor location, and idle speed; will be found in the Tune-up Specifications table of this section.

All 6-Cylinder Starting 1954

On these models the distributor is located on the right side of the cylinder block.

First mark the position of the rotor and body and, to remove it, lift off the cap and wire assembly, disconnect the ignition primary wire, disconnect the vacuum line to the carburetor, remove the distributor hold down bolt and pull the distributor out of the side of the block.

All V8 with Distributor at the Rear Of the Block Starting with 1954

On these engines the distributor is located in back of the right bank of cylinders. It rotates counterclockwise. The procedure for removal is exactly the same, however, take off the distributor cap and wire assembly, detach the vacuum line and the ignition primary wire, take out the distributor hold down bolt and lift the distributor off the back of the engine.

The job of removing the distributor is greatly simplified if the air cleaner and the ignition coil are removed.

All distributor service is given in the distributors and ignition system section, see index.

All V8 with Distributor at the Front Of the Block Starting with 1958

On these models the distributor is located in the front of the engine and is easily accessible.

First mark the position of the rotor and also the position of the body with

GENERAL CHASSIS AND BRAKE SPECIFICATIONS

YEAR AND MODEL		CHASSIS		BRAKE CYLINDER BORE			
		Overall Length in Inches	Tire Size	Master Cyl. (Inch)		Wheel Cylinder Diameter (Inch)	
				Std.	Pow.	Front	Rear
1954		198⁵⁄₁₆	6.70x15	1.0		1⅛	⅞
1955	Pass	198½	6.70x15	1.0		1⅛	⅞
	Sta. Wagons	198½	6.70x15	1.0		1⅛	15⁄16
	Thunderbird	175⁵⁄₁₆	6.70x15	1.0		1⅛	⅞
1956	Pass	175⅞	6.70x15	1.0		1⅛	⅞
	Sta. Wagons	198⁹⁄₁₆	6.70x15	1.0		1⅛	15⁄16
	Thunderbird	185⅛	6.70x15	1.0		1⅛	15⁄16
1957	Custom	201¾	7.50x14	1.0	1⅛	1⅛	⅞
	Fairlane	207¾	7.50x14	1.0	1⅛	1⅛	⅞
	Sta. Wagons	207.0	8.00x14	1.0	1⅛	1⅛	15⁄16
	Thunderbird	181⁷⁄₁₆	7.50x14	1.0	1⅛	1⅛	15⁄16
1958	Custom	202.0	7.50x14	1.0	1⅛	1⅛	⅞
	Fairlane	207.0	7.50x14	1.0	1⅛	1⅛	⅞
	Sta. Wagons	207.0	8.10x14	1.0	1⅛	1⅛	15⁄16
	Thunderbird	205⅜	8.00x14	1.0	1⅛	1⅛	⅞
1959	6-8 Cyl. Pass.	208.0	7.50x14	1.0	1⅛	1⅛	⅞
	Sta. Wagons	208.0	8.10x14	1.0	1⅛	1⅛	
	Thunderbird	205⅜	8.00x14	1.0	1⅛	1³⁄₃₂	2⁹⁄₃₂
1960	Pass	213¾	7.50x14	1.0		1³⁄₃₂	15⁄16
	Sta. Wagons	213¾	8.00x14	1.0		1³⁄₃₂	15⁄16
	Thunderbird	205⅜	8.00x14	1.0		1³⁄₃₂	2⁹⁄₃₂
1961-63	Pass	209²⁹⁄₃₂	7.50x14	1.0	1.0	1³⁄₃₂	15⁄16
	Sta. Wagons	209²⁹⁄₃₂	8.00x14	1.0	1.0	1³⁄₃₂	15⁄16
	Thunderbird	205⅜	8.00x14	1.0	1.0	1³⁄₃₂	15⁄16

relation to the block. Disconnect the ignition primary wire, the vacuum lead, the distributor cap, and then take out the hold down bolt which holds the distributor down in the block and lift it up out of the block.

Do not disturb the engine after the distributor has been removed so as not to disturb the ignition timing.

IGNITION PRIMARY RESISTOR

Starting with 1956 12-volt models, a resistance is used in the primary circuit of the ignition. The resistor is mounted immediately adjacent to the coil on both 6's and 8's. Any time difficulty is experienced with the ignition system it is a good idea to check the resistor.

GENERATOR AND REGULATOR

Detailed facts on the generator and the regulator can be found in the Gen-

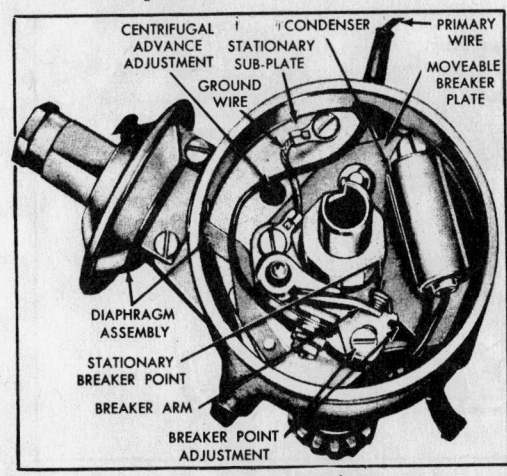

Dual Advance Distributor

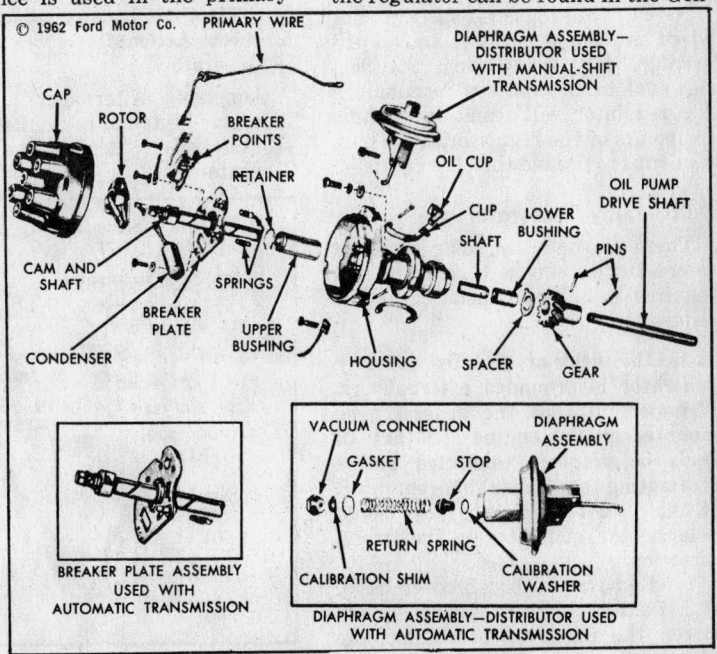

Loadomatic Distributor Assembly

349

FORD and THUNDERBIRD

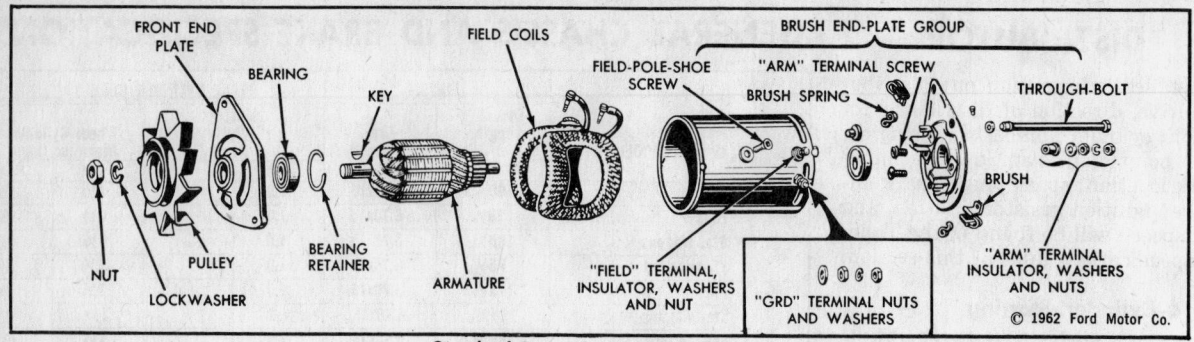

Standard Generator-Disassembled view

erator and Regulator Specifications Table of this section.

General information on generator and regulator repair and trouble shooting can be found in the Unit Repair section under the heading Generators and Regulators.

"D.C." Generator Polarity, Ford & Bosch

Caution. Whenever the circuits to: the generator; the regulator; or the battery have been disconnected it is best to apply the following procedure:

Before the engine is started disconnect the field wire and the battery wire from the regulator and momentarily connect the two wires together, engine not running. This gives a momentary surge of current from the battery to the generator and so correctly polarizes the generator with respect to the battery.

Failure to so polarize a "D.C." generator before starting the engine may severely damage the regulator since reversed polarity causes vibration, arcing and burning of the relay points.

Note: Ford generators are not wired as other generators and so polarizing by shorting from the field terminal to the battery terminal on the regulator will result in burning the points of the regulator as the current runs to ground thru the points.

Delco-Remy Generator

There are, however, some instances where Delco-Remy is used. This unit requires a different polarizing procedure.

As the field of the Delco Remy generator is grounded externally, it is important that the generator be mounted on the engine and that all leads be properly connected before attempting to polarize this generator. If this it not done, it is possible to polarize the generator in the wrong direction.

1. Remove the brush cover band.
2. Place a piece of insulation between the insulated brush and the commutator.

3. Momentarily connect a jumper lead between the BAT and GEN terminals of the regulator.

This method of polarizing a generator is to be used only with the Delco Remy D.C. generator.

Beginning 1963

Some cars are equipped with Alternating Current Generators. This charging system is different from the "D.C." circuit and requires certain precautions.

1. **Reversing Battery Connections** will cause damage to the one-way electrical valves, the rectifiers.
2. **Booster Battery Connections** must be made as follows: the negative terminal of the booster battery must be connected to the negative terminal of the car battery. The positive terminal of the booster battery must be connected to the positive battery of the car battery.
3. **Fast Chargers** should never be used as boosters. To start AC circuit equipped cars.
4. **When Servicing the Battery** with with a fast charger, always disconnect car battery cables.
5. **Never Attempt to Polarize an AC Generator.**

Complete Alternating servicing data may be found in the Unit Repair section under "Alternating Current Generators."

BATTERY AND STARTER

Detailed information on the battery and starter will be found in the Battery and Starter Specifications Table at the start of this section.

A more general discussion of starters and their troubles can be found in the Unit Repair Section under the heading starters.

STARTER, R & R

1954

Disconnect cable at starter. On V8's with manual transmission remove oil pan-to-starter attaching bracket screw. On six cylinder cars remove starter to flywheel housing screw. On 1954 V8's dropping the steering idler arm will help.

On all models loosen through bolts and lift starter out.

Flywheel clearance can be gained by tilting starter.

1955-63

Remove cable from starter. Remove mounting screws and lift starter out. Tilt starter for better flywheel clearance.

SPEEDOMETER HEAD, R & R

1957-53 Except Thunderbird

1. Disconnect battery.

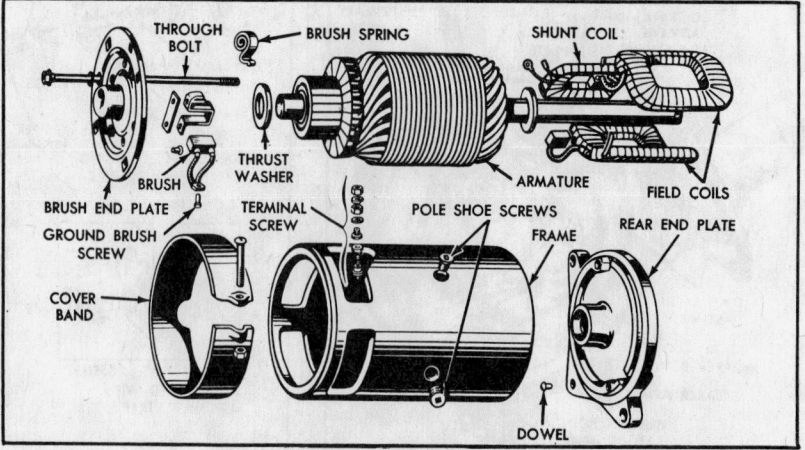

Disassembled Startor Motor

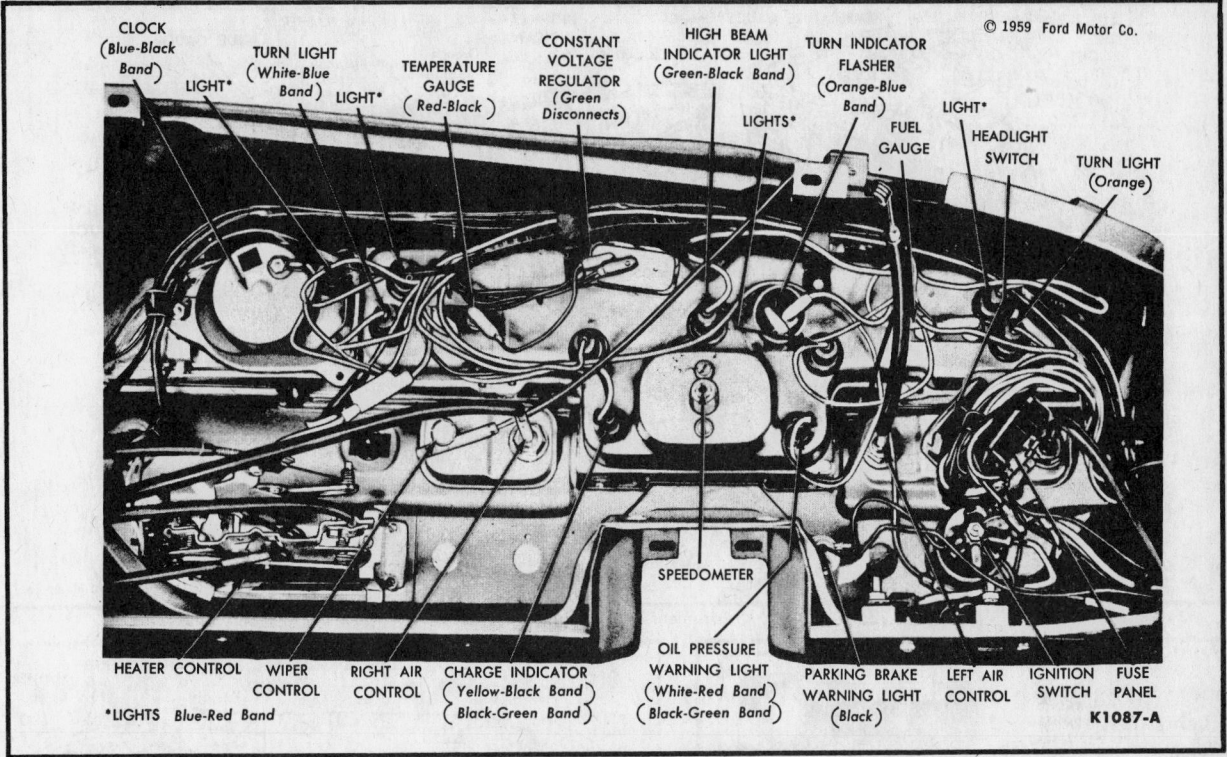

© 1959 Ford Motor Co.

CLOCK (Blue-Black Band)
LIGHT*
TURN LIGHT (White-Blue Band)
LIGHT*
TEMPERATURE GAUGE (Red-Black)
CONSTANT VOLTAGE REGULATOR (Green Disconnects)
HIGH BEAM INDICATOR LIGHT (Green-Black Band)
TURN INDICATOR FLASHER (Orange-Blue Band)
LIGHTS*
FUEL GAUGE
LIGHT*
HEADLIGHT SWITCH
TURN LIGHT (Orange)

SPEEDOMETER

HEATER CONTROL
WIPER CONTROL
RIGHT AIR CONTROL
CHARGE INDICATOR (Yellow-Black Band) (Black-Green Band)
OIL PRESSURE WARNING LIGHT (White-Red Band)
PARKING BRAKE WARNING LIGHT (Black-Green Band)
LEFT AIR CONTROL
IGNITION SWITCH
FUSE PANEL

*LIGHTS Blue-Red Band

K1087-A

Instrument Panel Wiring 1960

2. Disconnect speedometer cable, at speedometer.

3. Remove instrument cluster assembly from the front of the instrument panel, unhooking the wiring harness from the harness clips.

4. Lay the cluster assembly on the steering column and remove the lights, turn-indicator flasher and constant voltage regulator wires from the speedometer head mounting plate.

5. Remove the cluster back plate from the cluster body.

6. The speedometer head may now be removed from the back plate.

7. To replace, reverse above procedure.

1958-63 Thunderbird

Pull bezel from instrument panel. Remove four mounting screws and pull speedometer out enough to disconnect cable and pilot lights. Instrument is now free for removal.

BRAKE SYSTEM

BRAKE INFORMATION

Specific information on brake cylinder sizes can be found in the General Chassis and Brake Specifications Table of this section.

Information on brake adjustments, band replacement, bleeding procedure, master and wheel cylinder overhaul can be found in the Unit Repair section under the heading: Brakes,

Hydraulic.

Information on trouble shooting and overhauling power brakes can be found in the Unit Repair section under the heading: Brakes, Power.

Information on the grease seals which may need replacement can be found in the Unit Repair section. The front wheel grease seals under the head: Suspension, Front Repair. The rear wheel grease seals under the head: Axles, Rear.

REMOVAL OF MASTER CYLINDER
Starting with 1954

To remove the master cylinder, remove the pin which holds the master

cylinder push rod to the brake pedal. This is accessible from under the dash.

Working in the engine compartment, remove the brake lines from the back end of the master cylinder and take out the master cylinder mounting bolts.

BRAKE PEDAL ADJUSTMENT

Establish approximately $\frac{1}{2}$ inch free pedal travel, measured at the toe board by turning the eccentric bolt, which attaches the brake pedal assembly to the master cylinder push rod assembly. Rotate this eccentric bolt until the play is between $\frac{1}{4}$ and $\frac{1}{2}$ inch.

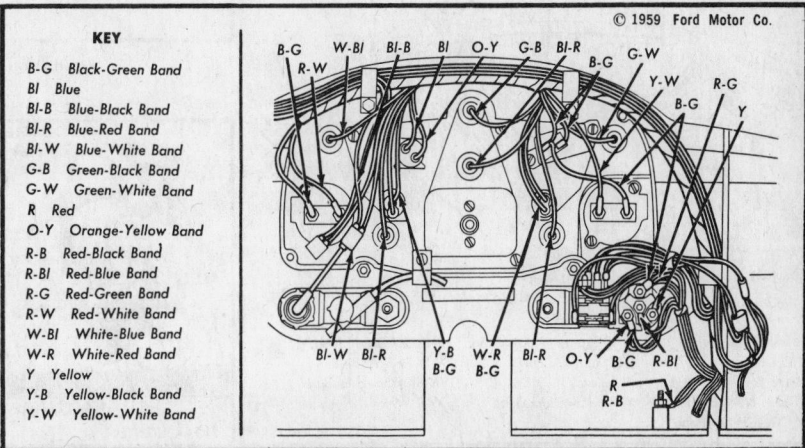

© 1959 Ford Motor Co.

KEY

B-G   Black-Green Band
Bl   Blue
Bl-B Blue-Black Band
Bl-R Blue-Red Band
Bl-W Blue-White Band
G-B   Green-Black Band
G-W   Green-White Band
R   Red
O-Y   Orange-Yellow Band
R-B   Red-Black Band
R-Bl Red-Blue Band
R-G   Red-Green Band
R-W   Red-White Band
W-Bl White-Blue Band
W-R   White-Red Band
Y   Yellow
Y-B   Yellow-Black Band
Y-W   Yellow-White Band

Instrument Panel Wiring 1959

FORD and THUNDERBIRD

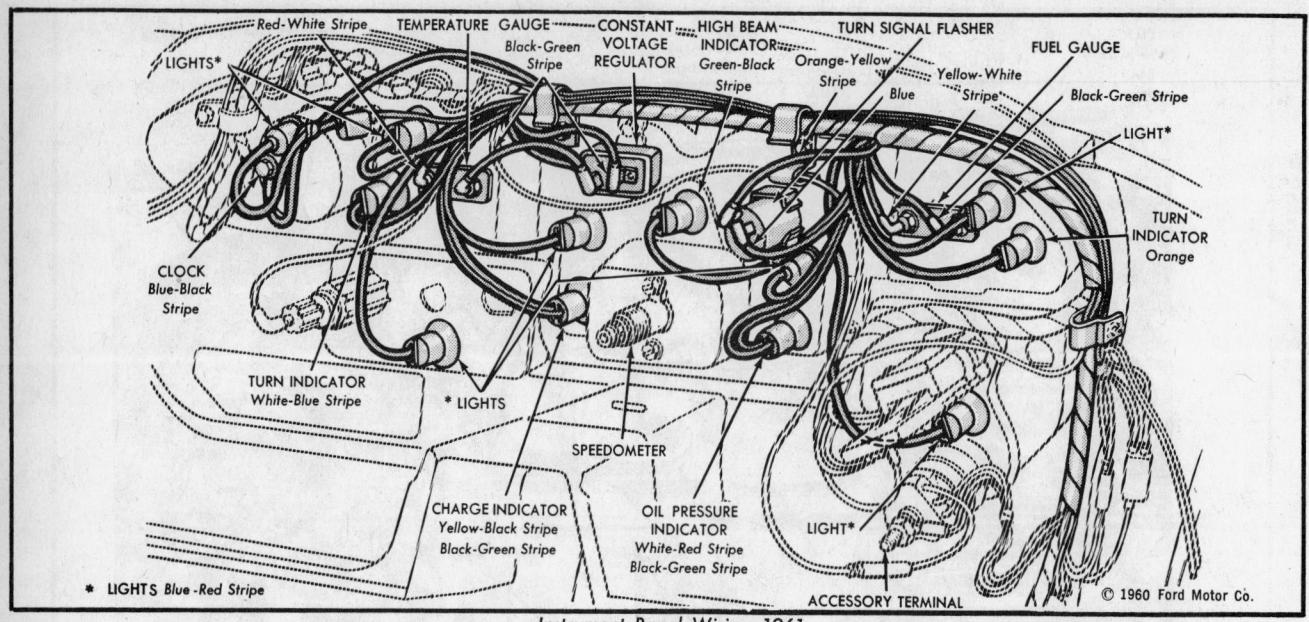

TEMPERATURE GAUGE
Black-Green Stripe

Red-White Stripe

CONSTANT VOLTAGE REGULATOR

HIGH BEAM INDICATOR
Green-Black Stripe

TURN SIGNAL FLASHER

FUEL GAUGE

LIGHTS*

Orange-Yellow Stripe

Yellow-White Stripe

Blue

Black-Green Stripe

LIGHT*

TURN INDICATOR
Orange

CLOCK
Blue-Black Stripe

TURN INDICATOR
White-Blue Stripe

* LIGHTS

SPEEDOMETER

CHARGE INDICATOR
Yellow-Black Stripe
Black-Green Stripe

OIL PRESSURE INDICATOR
White-Red Stripe
Black-Green Stripe

LIGHT*

ACCESSORY TERMINAL

* LIGHTS Blue-Red Stripe

© 1960 Ford Motor Co.

Instrument Panel Wiring 1961

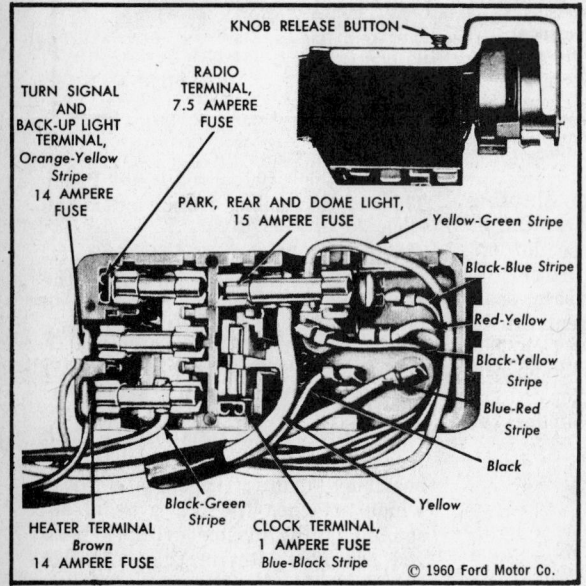

KNOB RELEASE BUTTON

RADIO TERMINAL, 7.5 AMPERE FUSE

TURN SIGNAL AND BACK-UP LIGHT TERMINAL, Orange-Yellow Stripe 14 AMPERE FUSE

PARK, REAR AND DOME LIGHT, 15 AMPERE FUSE

Yellow-Green Stripe

Black-Blue Stripe

Red-Yellow

Black-Yellow Stripe

Blue-Red Stripe

Black

HEATER TERMINAL Brown 14 AMPERE FUSE

Black-Green Stripe

CLOCK TERMINAL, 1 AMPERE FUSE Blue-Black Stripe

Yellow

© 1960 Ford Motor Co.

Headlight and Dome Light Switch 1961

TURN INDICATOR
W-Bl

G-W

FUEL GAUGE
Y   B-G

FLASHER
Bl

HI-BEAM   G-B

O-Y
B-R

CLOCK
Bl-B

RADIO SUPPRESSION CHOKE
B - G

WASHER SWITCH LEADS
B, W

HEADLIGHT SWITCH

OIL PRESSURE INDICATOR
W-R, B-G

SPARK COIL PRIMARY RESISTOR
P

TEMPERATURE GAUGE
R-W, B-G

KEY

Bl-B	Blue-Black Stripe
W-Bl	White-Blue Stripe
G-W	Green-White Stripe
G-B	Green-Black Stripe
B-G	Black-Green Stripe
Bl	Blue
Y-B	Yellow-Black Stripe
O-Y	Orange-Yellow Stripe
B-R	Black-Red Stripe
B	Black
W	White
R-W	Red-White Stripe
W-R	White-Red Stripe
P	Pink

NOTE: BULB SOCKETS NOT IDENTIFIED ARE FOR INSTRUMENT ILLUMINATION

IGNITION SWITCH

CHARGE INDICATOR
Y-B, B-G

WINDSHIELD WASHER PUMP

PARKING BRAKE WARNING LIGHT SWITCH LEADS
B

HEATER
TURN SIGNAL
RADIO
CLOCK

FUSE PANEL ON L.H AIR DUCT

DOME, REAR AND PARKING LIGHTS

CIGAR LIGHTER

© 1960 Ford Motor Co.

Instrument Panel Wiring 1961 T-bird

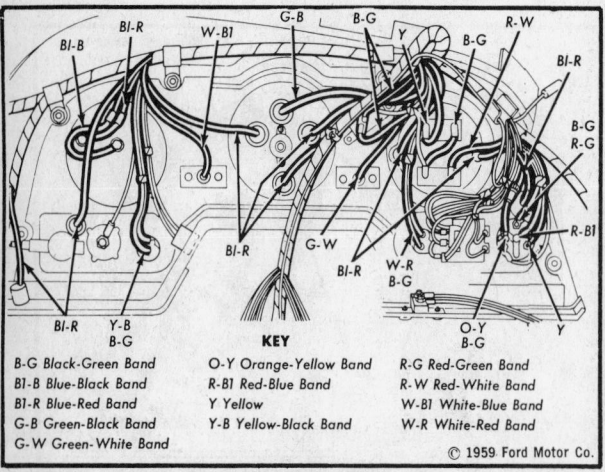

Bl-R   Bl-R   W-Bl   G-B   B-G   Y   B-G   R-W

Bl-B

Bl-R

B-G
R-G

R-B1

Bl-R   G-W   Bl-R

W-R
B-G

Bl-R   Y-B
B-G

O-Y
B-G

Y

KEY

B-G Black-Green Band	O-Y Orange-Yellow Band	R-G Red-Green Band
Bl-B Blue-Black Band	R-Bl Red-Blue Band	R-W Red-White Band
Bl-R Blue-Red Band	Y Yellow	W-Bl White-Blue Band
G-B Green-Black Band	Y-B Yellow-Black Band	W-R White-Red Band
G-W Green-White Band		

© 1959 Ford Motor Co.

Instrument Panel Wiring 1960 T-bird

CLOCK

SPEEDOMETER

CONSTANT VOLTAGE REGULATOR

FUEL GAUGE

TEMPERATURE GAUGE

LIGHT SWITCH

IGNITION SWITCH

CIGAR LIGHTER

© 1959 Ford Motor Co.

Rear View of Instrument Custer 1960 T-bird

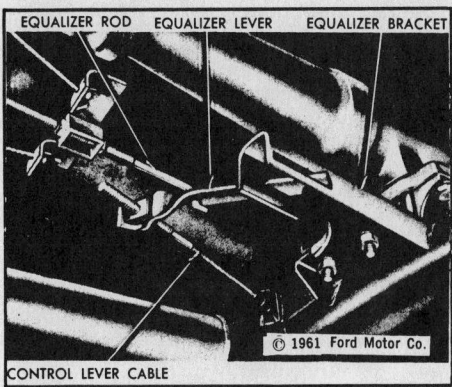

EQUALIZER ROD EQUALIZER LEVER EQUALIZER BRACKET

© 1961 Ford Motor Co.

CONTROL LEVER CABLE

Parking Brake Linkage

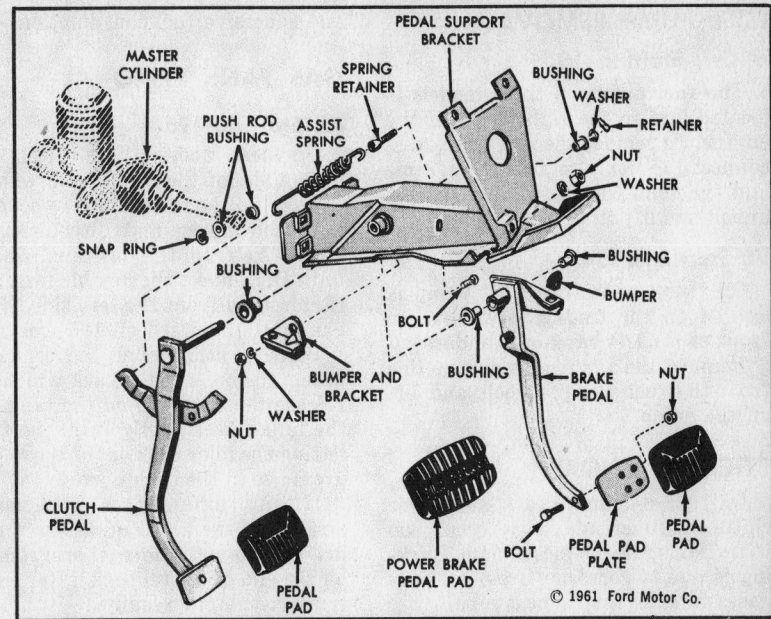

Brake Pedal and Related Parts

Note:

1960 Foot Brake Adjustment

The star wheel adjustment rotation is reversed on the left rear wheel only. To tighten the brakes on the left rear wheel, reverse the normal star wheel rotation.

PARKING BRAKE LEVER REMOVAL

Hand Operated Lever

Remove the brackets which hold the lever assembly up under the dash, slide the end of the cable ball joint out of its conection in the end of the lever and lift the lever off the vehicle.

Foot Operated Lever

The foot operated lever is mounted under the left side of the instrument panel. Slack off on the brake cable and remove the clevis which holds the cable to the top part of the lever. Remove the brackets which hold the lever assembly to the side of the body and lift off the lever.

⏻ CHILTON TIME-SAVER

REMOVING STUBBORN REAR BRAKE DRUMS

Occasional cases of rear wheel drums, frozen to the rear axle flange, require much time and effort to remove, without damage.

If a rear drum resists normal efforts to remove by tapping, try the following method:

1. Drive 2 or 3 of the serrated hub bolts out of the drum and into the brake shoe area.

2. With an old screw driver or other suitable wedge forced between the drum and axle flange thru these bolt holes, tap and wedge the drum from the axle flange.

3. After the drum is removed the bolts can be recovered and returned to their respective places in the axle flange.

Any damage to the drum can usually be corrected by a few taps with a hammer.

FUEL SYSTEM

FUEL SYSTEM INFORMATION

A chart covering causes of excess fuel consumption will be found in the Unit Repair Section under the heading: Fuel Consumption Chart.

Data on capacity of the gas tank will be found in the Capacities Table. Data on correct engine idle speed and fuel pump pressure will be found in the Tune-up Specifications table. Both the above tables can be found in this car section.

General information on fuel pumps and their troubles will be found in the Unit Repair section under the heading: Fuel Pumps.

Information covering operation and troubles of the fuel gauge will be

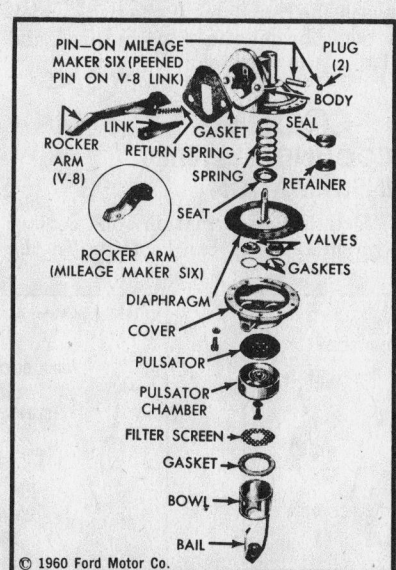

© 1960 Ford Motor Co.

Single Action Fuel Pump

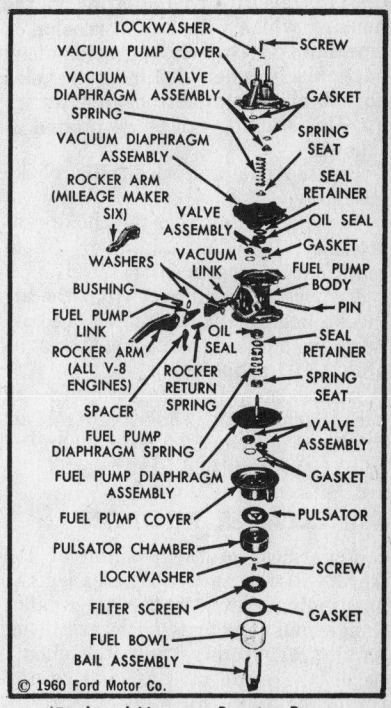

© 1960 Ford Motor Co.

Fuel and Vacuum Booster Pump

found in the Unit Repair section under the heading: Gages.

Detailed information on the carburetor and how to adjust it will be found in the Unit Repair section under the heading: Carburetors, and the specific heading of the make of carburetor being used on the engine being worked on. Carter, Holley, Rochester and Stromberg carburetors are covered.

Dash pot adjustment can be found in the Unit Repair section under the same heading as that of the automatic transmission used in the car.

FORD and THUNDERBIRD

FUEL PUMP REMOVAL

6 Cyl. Starting 1954

The fuel pump on these models is located low on the right front of the engine. To remove the fuel pump, disconnect the flex line from the frame and the solid line to the carburetor, unbolt and lift off the fuel pump.

V8 Starting 1954

On these models the fuel pump is located on the timing case cover in front of the left bank of cylinders.

Remove the input and output line from the fuel pump, unbolt and lift off the pump.

STICKING CHOKE

On 1956 8-cylinder cars, automatic choke malfunctioning may occur due to a sticking choke mechanism. Sticking is due to corrosion from exhaust gases entering a split heat tube.

This sticking can also be due to excessive moisture condensation in the housing which will cause corrosion or freezing of the choke mechanism, particularly when distances traveled do not allow complete engine warm-up. This sticking can be eliminated as follows:

Disassemble and clean the choke assembly.

Remove and discard the choke control air intake tube and elbow (from manifold into carburetor).

Remove the grommet from the air intake hole in the bottom of the carburetor and plug the hole with a suitable 9/16" rubber plug.

Install the deflector assembly and the thermostatic choke control air intake (Ford No. B7A-9492-A) in the end of the manifold heat tube.

AIR CLEANER POSITION

Regardless of the position of the word FRONT on the air cleaner the positioning notch in the air cleaner flange must engage the locating lug on the carburetor. The notch should be on the same side as, and on the centerline of, the air intake.

Improperly assembled air cleaners may be a contributing factor in accelerator binding, carburetor icing,

and excessive fuel consumption.

GAS TANK REMOVAL

All Starting 1954

On these models the fill neck is in the middle of the back of the vehicle.

Take up the trunk mat, remove the port hole cover and disconnect the gage wire from the gas tank sending unit. Disconnect the flexible tank ventilator pipe from the left side of the gas tank (not used on 1954 models).

Place a jack under the tank and loosen the bolts at the back which will release the straps from the tank. Let the tank lower gently from the front letting the filler neck out of the rubber grommet in the deck apron.

If any difficulty is experienced straighten the neck out, take a screwdriver and pry the rubber grommet off the end of the fill neck, after which it will come out readily.

EXHAUST SYSTEM

REMOVAL OF ENGINE MANIFOLDS

All 6 Cylinder Engines

Disconnect all lines to the carburetor, including gas, vacuum, throttle, and governor lines. Remove the air cleaner and unbolt and lift off the carburetor.

Detach the exhaust pipe at the flange, remove the bolts which secure the manifold to the header block and lift off the manifold.

EXHAUST MANIFOLD

Unbolt and remove both exhaust pipe flanges. These bolts are accessible with a long extension from underneath the car. Remove the bolts which attach the manifold to the head and lift off the manifold.

COOLING SYSTEM

COOLING SYSTEM INFORMATION

Detailed information on cooling system capacity can be found in the

Capacities Table.

Information on the water temperature gauge can be found in the Unit Repair section under the heading: Gages.

Caution: Do not run cold water over the outside of pressurized radiators without first removing the radiator cap. When the cap is left on and the cold water hits the hot radiator the steam in the radiator condenses very rapidly and sometimes collapses the top radiator tank. This is most likely to happen if the coolant level is below normal.

THERMOSTAT REPLACEMENT

V8 Engines Starting 1954

The thermostat is located in the forward part of the inlet manifold between the two cylinder heads. The thermostat housing is held to the manifold by two bolts. To replace, loosen the lower end of the upper radiator hose and the little by-pass hose at the thermostat housing, remove the thermostat housing and lift out the thermostat. A lock wire is sometimes used to hold the thermostat in the housing.

6 Cyl. Engines Starting 1954

Disconnect the upper radiator hose and heater hose and disconnect the two bolts which hold the thermostat housing to the cylinder head and lift off the housing.

The thermostat is installed with the operating mechanism toward the engine.

REMOVAL OF WATER PUMP

V8 Starting 1954

To remove the pump, take off the fan belt, fan blades and fan pulley, disconnect the water hose, unbolt and lift off the pump.

6 Cylinder Starting 1954

To remove the water pump, take off the fan belt, fan and pulley. Disconnect the hoses and remove the cap screws which hold the water pump assembly to the block and lift the pump.

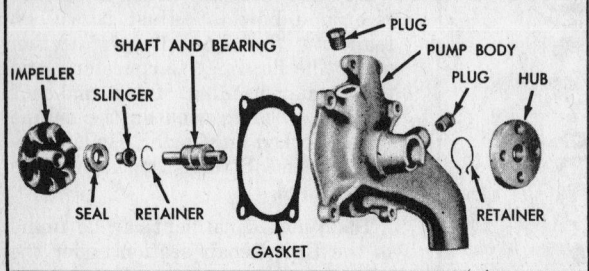

Water pump assembly—8 cylinder engine—1957

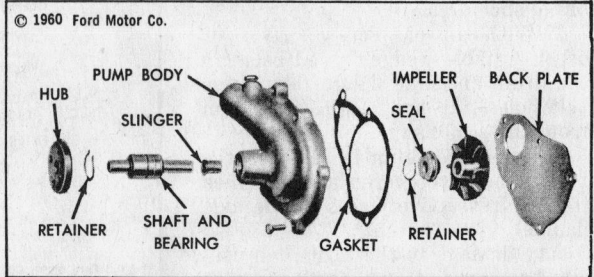

Water pump assembly—6 cylinder engine

use a separate regulator valve in its circuit. The V-8 engines all use a control valve in the circuit to meter the emission flow. It prevents the fuel mixture from being too lean at idle (high manifold vacuum). It allows enough flow at open throttle to draw contaminations from the crankcase. This contaminous fog is passed back into the combustion chamber where it is burned and discharged thru the exhaust.

REFERENCES

In the specifications tables of this section there are listed all the available facts about the engines. When different size engines are used a note under the General Engine Specifications Table will give an easy means of determining which engine is which.

Valves

Detailed information on the valves, can be found in the Valve Specifications Table at the beginning of this car section.

A general discussion of valve clearance and a chart showing how to read pressure and vacuum gauges when using them to diagnose engine troubles will be found in the Unit Repair section under the heading: Tune-Up and Diagnosis. Under the same head will be found a chart on engine trouble shooting.

Valve tappet clearance for each engine is given in the Tune-up Specifications Table at the beginning of the car section.

Bearings

Detailed information on engine bearings will be found in the Crank-

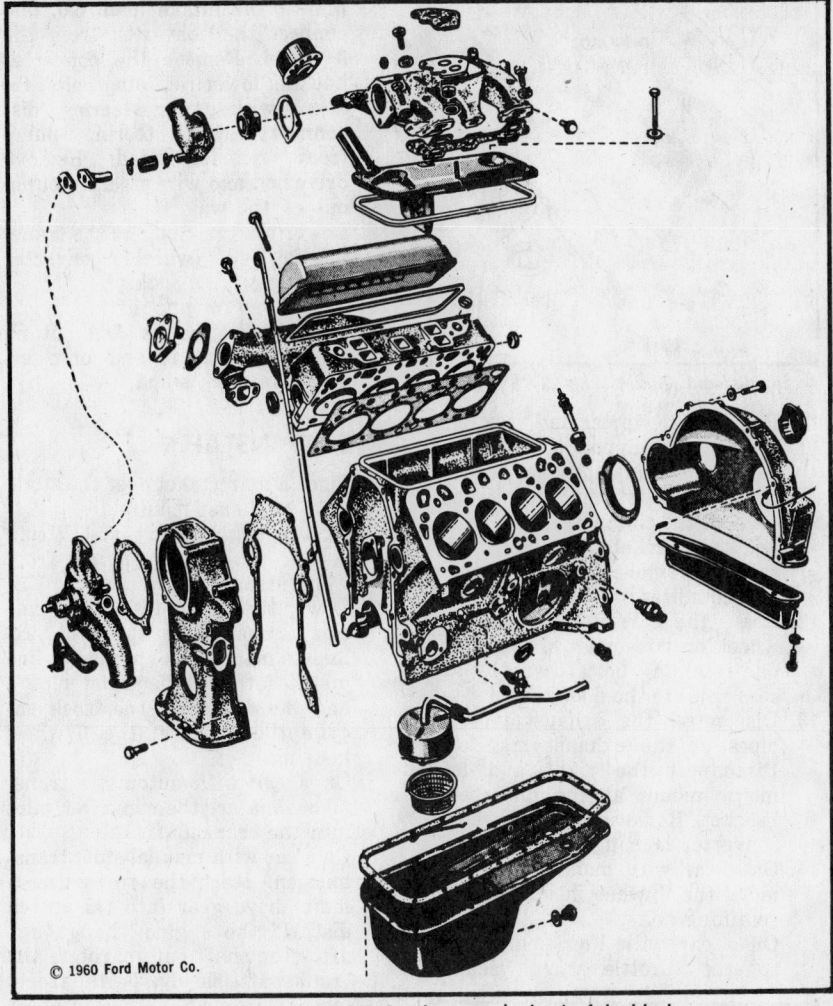

© 1960 Ford Motor Co.

External parts. V8 with distributor at the back of the block.

RADIATOR CORE REMOVAL

Disconnect the upper and lower radiator hoses and take out the center air deflector side screws on models with air deflector and then taking out the cap screws that secure each side of the radiator to the front fender apron support. The core can then be lifted straight up and off the vehicle.

ENGINE

VACUUM CONTROLLED CRANKCASE VENTILATION

Starting with 1963 a vacuum controlled crankcase breather is standard on Ford and Thunderbird engines.

Unburned fuels and exhaust gases passing the rings contribute to sludge formation in the crankcase and oil passages. By applying manifold vacuum to the crankcase this condition is reduced.

The 6 cylinder engine uses an emission system which includes the carburetor air cleaner. This type of positive crankcase ventilation does not

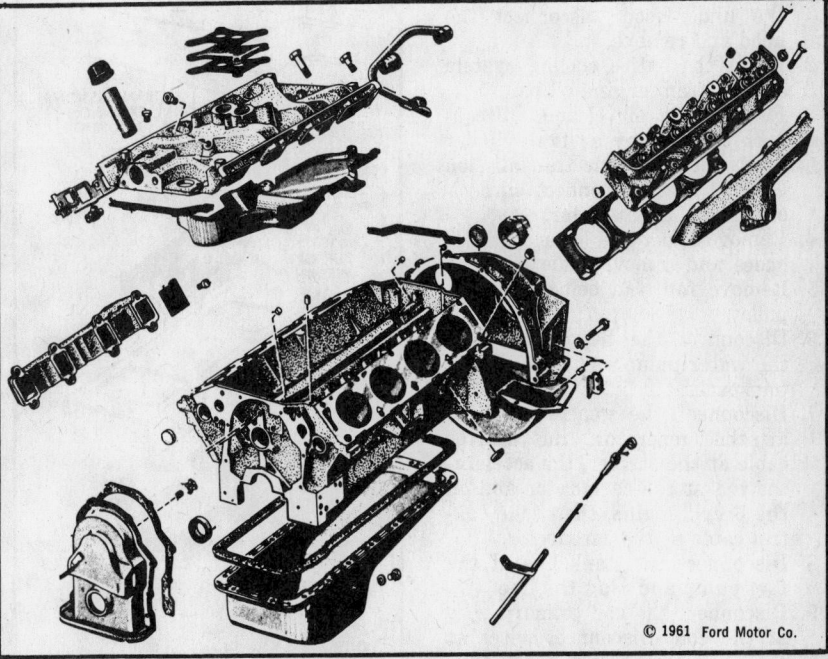

© 1961 Ford Motor Co.

External parts. V8 with distributor at the front of the block.

shaft Bearing Journal Sizes Table at the start of the car section.

Pistons and Pins

Detailed information on pistons and piston pins, together with information on piston, rod and crankshaft relationship for assembly, will be found in the Piston and Pin Specifications Table at the start of this section.

Engine crankcase capacities are listed in the Capacities Table in this car section.

Approved torque wrench readings and head bolt tightening sequences are covered in the Torque Specifications Table of this car section.

ENGINE REMOVE

All Engines Thru 1957

Either the 6 cylinder or the 8 cylinder engine can be taken from the chassis after removing the hood, radiator core and battery.

Disconnect all attaching parts such as generator wire, oil pressure sender wire, ignition switch wire, temperature sender wire, and also fuel and carburetor connections including the choke wire, throttle linkage and accelerator rods.

Support the transmission on a jack and disconnect the engine at the transmission. The engine assembly and clutch can then be slid forward in the frame off of the clutch pilot shaft and rocked slightly and lifted up out of the car.

All Engines 1958-63

1. Scribe the hood hinge outline on the under-hood, disconnect the hood and remove.
2. Drain the entire cooling system and oil from engine oil pan.
3. Remove the air cleaner, disconnect the battery at the cylinder head. On automatic transmission equiped cars, disconnect oil cooler lines at the radiator.
4. Remove upper and lower radiator hoses and remove radiator.
5. Remove fan, fan belt and upper pulley.
6. Disconnect the heater hoses at the water pump and the carburetor spacer.
7. Disconnect the generator wires at the generator, the starter cable at the starter, the accelerator rod at the carburetor and on the 6 cyl. engine, the choke control cable at the carburetor.
8. Disconnect fuel tank line at the fuel pump and plug the line.
9. Disconnect the coil primary wire at the coil. Disconnect wires at the oil pressure and water temperature sending units.

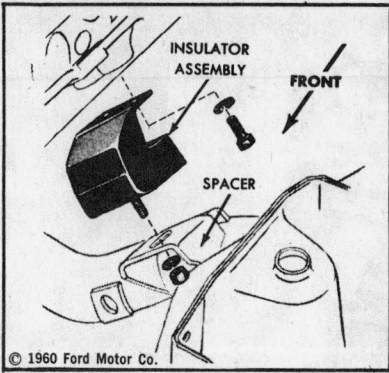

Engine front support 1958-62 V8 models

10. Remove the starter and dust seal.
11. On a car equipped with a manual-shift transmission, remove the clutch retracting spring. Disconnect the clutch equalizer shaft and arm bracket at the underbody rail and remove the arm bracket and equalizer.
12. Raise the car. Remove the flywheel or converter housing upper retaining bolts thru the access holes in the floor pan.
13. Disconnect the exhaust pipe or pipes at the exhaust manifold. Disconnect the right and left motor mount at the underbody bracket. Remove the flywheel or converter housing cover.
14. On a car with manual shift, remove the flywheel housing lower retaining bolts.
15. On a car with Fordomatic, disconnect throttle valve vacuum

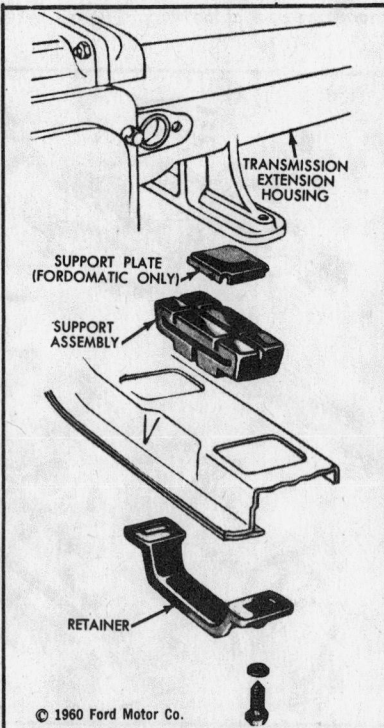

Rear Engine Support 1957-62

line at the intake manifold, disconnect the converter from the flywheel. Remove the converter housing lower retaining bolts. **On a car with power steering,** disconnect power steering pump from cylinder head. Remove drive belt and wire steering pump out of the way.

16. Lower the car. Support the transmission and flywheel or converter housing with a jack.
17. Attach an engine lifting hook. Lift the engine up and out of the compartment and onto an adequate work stand.

ENGINE INSTALL

1. Place a new gasket over the studs of the exhaust manifold/s.
2. Attach engine sling and lifting device. Then lift engine from work stand.
3. Lower the engine into the engine compartment. Be sure the exhaust manifold/s properly line up with the muffler inlet pipe/s and the dowels in the block engage the holes in the flywheel housing.

   On a car with automatic transmission, start the converter pilot into the crankshaft.

   On a car with manual-shift transmission, start the transmission main drive gear into the clutch disc. If the engine "hangs up" after the shaft enters, rotate the crankshaft slowly (with transmission in gear) until the shaft and clutch disc splines mesh.
4. Install the flywheel or converter housing upper bolts.
5. Install engine support insulator to bracket retaining nuts. Disconnect engine lifting sling and remove lifting brackets.
6. Raise front of car. Connect exhaust line/s and tighten attachments.
7. Position dust seal and install starter.
8. **On cars with manual-shift transmissions,** install remaining flywheel housing-to-engine bolts. Connect clutch release rod. Position the clutch equalizer bar and bracket and install retaining bolts. Install clutch pedal retracting spring.
8A. **On cars with automatic transmissions,** remove the retainer holding the converter in the housing. Attach the converter to the flywheel. Install the converter housing inspection cover. Install the remaining converter housing retaining bolts.
9. Remove the support from the transmission and lower the car.

10. Connect engine ground strap and coil primary wire.
11. Connect water temperature gauge wire and the heater hose at coolant outlet housing. Connect accelerator rod at the bellcrank.
12. **On cars with automatic transmission,** connect the transmission filler tube bracket. Connect the throttle valve vacuum line.
12A. **On cars with power steering,** install the drive belt and power steering pump bracket. Install the bracket retaining bolts. Adjust drive belt to proper tension.
13. Remove plug from the fuel tank line. Connect the flexible fuel line and the oil pressure sending unit wire.
14. Install the pulley, belt, spacer, and fan. Adjust belt tension.
15. Tighten generator adjusting bolts. Connect generator wires and the battery ground cable.
16. Install radiator. Connect radiator hoses.
16.A. **On cars with automatic transmissions,** connect oil cooler lines.
17. Install oil filter. Connect heater hose at water pump, after bleeding the system.
18. Bring crankcase to level with correct grade of oil. Run engine at fast idle and check for leaks. Install air cleaner and make final engine adjustments.
19. Install and adjust hood.
20. Road test car.

Beginning 1960 Engine Rear Mount

A new engine rear mount (integral with the frame) has been introduced into production to better arrest engine-to-frame vibration.

REPLACEMENT ENGINES

Both new and factory approved rebuilt engines are available for all of these models.

Ordinarily, a factory approved rebuilt engine does not include the manifolds, oil pan or flywheel. Short blocks are also available which include the block assembly less the timing case cover and flywheel.

CYLINDER BLOCK CORE HOLE PLUGS

O.H.V. 6 Cyl.

There are two large cylinder block core hole plugs located in the back of the clutch bell housing. In order to service either or both of these plugs it is necessary to remove the clutch bell housing. This job is best accomplished by removing the engine.

REMOVAL OF ROCKER ARMS

O.H.V. 6 Cyl.

Remove the rocker chamber cover and then remove the screws which hold the oil feed lines to the rocker shaft and remove the feed lines by prying up with a pair of pliers out of the cylinder head.

Back off on the rocker arm adjusting screws until the pressure is taken off the valve springs and then unbolt the rocker shaft assembly.

V8 Engines with Distributor at the Back 1954-62

Remove the rocker cover assemblies and carefully scrape off the gasket.

A little bit at a time, release the bolts which hold the rocker support brackets to the cylinder head so as to let the tension off evenly. Continue loosening the bolts until the push rods are entirely free of tension. Take the bolts out, lift off the complete rocker shaft assembly, together with

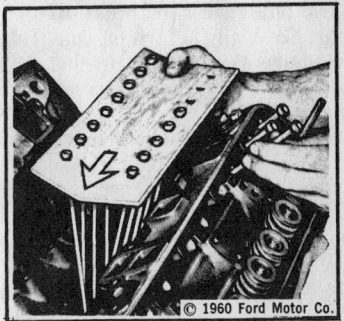
Removing push rods.

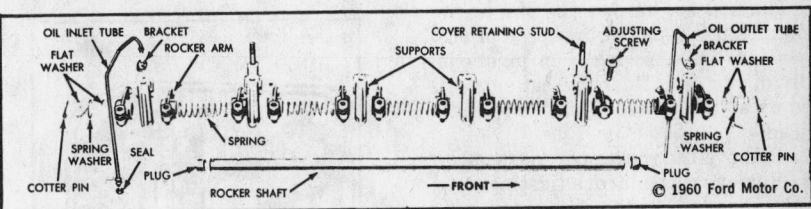
6 Cylinder rocker arm shaft assembly

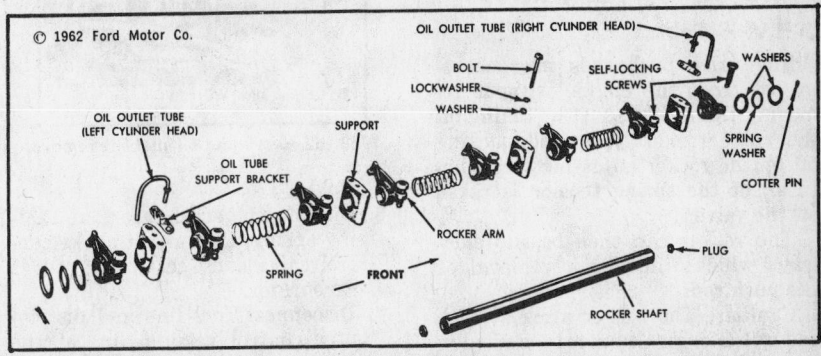
Adjustable rocker arms & parts. V8 with distributor at the front of the block. 1958-62

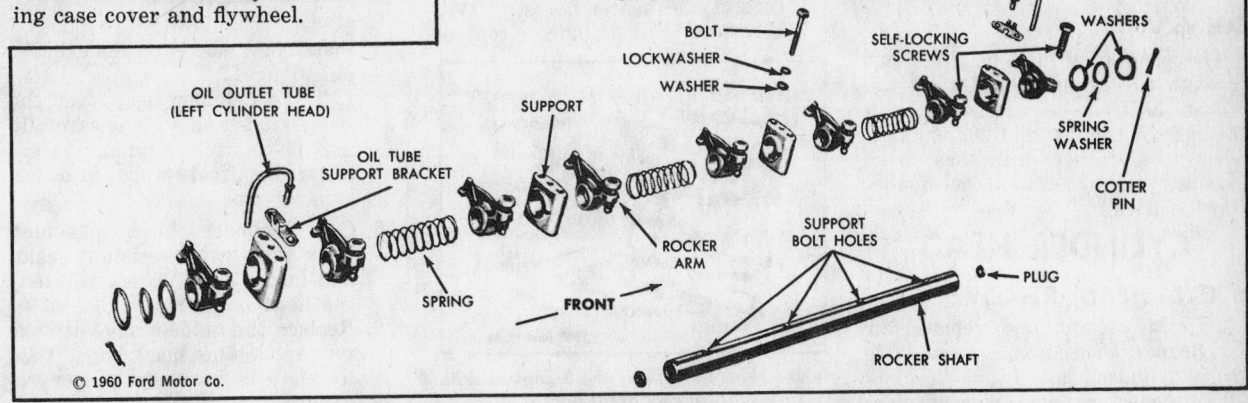
Adjustable rocker arms & parts. V8 with distributor at the back of the block

its oil outlet tubes.

If for any reason the rocker shaft is to be disassembled, carefully mark each piece so that it can be reassembled, carefully mark the position from which it was removed.

V8 Engines with Distributor at the Front Starting with 1958

Remove the rocker cover assembly. It may be necessary to disconnect the spark plug wires in order to get it clear. Carefully scrape off the gasket.

Remove the rocker bracket bolts, a little at a time, so as to remove the tension slowly.

Once the tension is removed, take out the bolts and lift the rocker assembly off onto the bench.

If the rockers are to be disassembled, carefully mark the position of each unit as it is taken off so that it can be reinstalled in the position from which is was removed. Reinstall in reverse order.

Beginning 1963

The 260 cu. in. and the 289 cu. in. engines use separate rocker arm suspension. Each rocker arm pivots individually on a fulcrum seat supported by a stud pressed into the cylinder head.
1. Remove the rocker cover assembly.
2. Remove rocker arm adjusting nuts, fulcrum seats and rocker arms.

REMOVAL OF PUSH RODS

O.H.V. 6 Cyl.

The valve push rods may be removed from the engine without removing the rocker shaft by taking off the valve rocker cover and backing off on the rocker adjusting screw until all of the spring tension is taken off the valve.

The rocker can then be slid sideways which will permit removal of the push rod.

Caution: The rocker arms at each end of the engine cannot be shifted in this manner and the two end push rods cannot be removed until after the cylinder head has been taken off.

O.H.V. V8

The push rods may be lifted out through the cylinder head after the rocker shaft has been removed, or in the case of the 260 and 289 engines, when the rocker arm has been loosened and turned to an out-of-the-way position.

CYLINDER HEAD

6 CYL. HEAD, REMOVE

1. Drain coolant and remove air cleaner. Disconnect battery cable at cylinder head.
2. Disconect exhaust pipe at man-

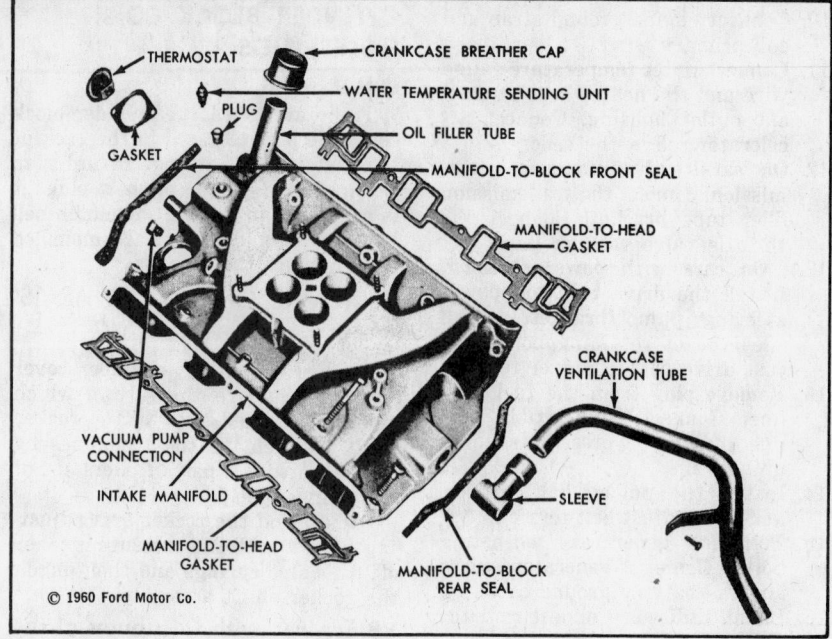

Intake Manifold Typical of V8 Engines With Distributor at the Front of the block.

1958 -62 -6 cylinder oil inlet line removal

ifold.
3. Disconnect accelerator retracting spring. Disconnect choke control cable and accelerator rod at carburetor.
4. Disconnect fuel line and distributor control vacuum line at the carburetor.
5. Disconnect coolant tubes from carburetor spacer. Disconnect coolant and heater hoses.
6. Disconnect distributor control

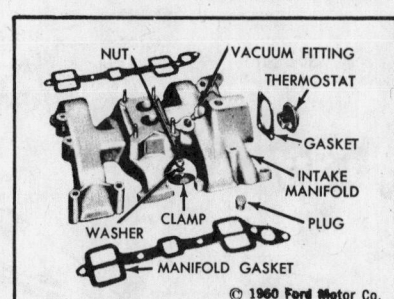

Intake Manifold Typical of V8 Engines With Distributor at the Back.

vacuum line at distributor. Disconnect fuel inlet line at the filter. Remove lines as an assembly.
6A. **On an engine equipped with positive crankcase ventilation,** disconnect the emission exhaust tube.
7. Disconnect spark plug wires at the plugs and the small wire from the tempermature sending unit.
8. Remove rocker arm cover.
9. Remove rocker arm shaft assembly. Remove valve push rods and keep them in sequence.
10. Remove one cylinder head bolt from each end and install two 7/16 x 14 guide studs.
11. Remove remaining cylinder head bolts, then remove cylinder head.

6 CYL. HEAD, INSTALL

1. Clean head and block surfaces.
2. Apply sealer to both sides of head gasket. Position gasket over guide studs.
3. Install new gasket on the exhaust pipe flange.
4. Lift the cylinder head over the guide studs and slide it carefully into place while guiding the exhaust manifold studs into the exhaust pipe flange.
5. Coat cylinder head attaching bolts with water resistant sealer and install (but do not tighten) the head bolts.
6. Replace the guide studs with the two remaining head bolts, then torque the head, in proper sequence and in three progressive

steps, to 75 ft. lbs.

7. Lubricate both ends of the push rods and install them in their original bores and sockets.

8. Lubricate valve stem tips and rocker arm pads.

9. Install valve rocker arm shaft assembly and torque attaching pedestal bolts in progressive steps, to 30-35 ft. lbs.

10. Do a preliminary, cold, valve lash adjustment.

11. Install exhaust pipe-to-manifold nuts and lock washers. Torque to 17-22 ft. lbs.

12. Connect radiator and heater hoses. Connect coolant tubes at the carburetor spacer.

13. Connect distributor vacuum line and the carburetor fuel line. Connect battery cable to cylinder head.

13A. **On engines equipped with positive crankcase ventilation,** clean components thoroughly and install.

14. Connect accelerator rod pull-back spring. Connect choke control cable and the accelerator rod at the carburetor.

15. Connect distributor control vacuum line at distributor. Connect carburetor fuel line at fuel filter.

16. Connect temperature sending unit wire at sending unit. Connect spark plug wires.

17. Completely fill and bleed the cooling system.

18. Run engine for a minimum of 30 minutes at 1200 R.P.M. to stabilize engine temperature. Then check for coolant and oil leaks.

19. Adjust engine idle mixture and speed. Check valve lash and adjust, if necessary.

20. Install valve rocker arm cover, then the air cleaner.

V8 HEADS, REMOVE

1. Remove intake manifold and carburetor as an assembly.

2. Disconnect battery cable at cylinder head.

3. Remove rocker arm cover/s.

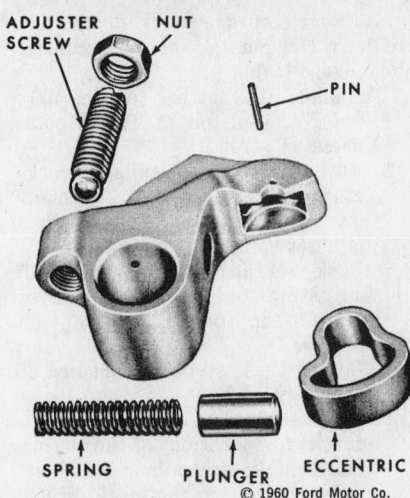

Mechanical adjuster—disassembled

3A. **On a car with power steering,** disconnect the steering pump bracket from the left cylinder head and remove the drive belt. Wire the steering pump out of the way, (don't spill the oil).

4. Disconnect wires at generator. Remove generator and bracket as an assembly. Disconnect exhaust pipe/s at exhaust manifold/s.

5. Remove cylinder head attaching bolts from both ends of the head and install two 7/16 x 14 guide studs. Remove remaining cylinder head retaining bolts.

6. Raise cylinder head slightly, so that the rocker arms can be moved to the side. Remove the push rods and store them in sequence. Remove the guide studs and lift the head off the block. Remove cylinder head gasket.

V8 HEADS, INSTALL

Reverse above procedure, (see valve lash adjustment under, "Valves," in the following paragraphs).

VALVE SYSTEM

REFERENCES

Beginning 1963 all Ford built engines will operate at zero clearance with the exception of some power options. These special high out-put engines are equipped with provision for adjustment and should operate efficiently with about .025" lash. All other engines use hydraulic valve lifts except the 6 cyl., 223 cu. in. engine. This model uses a zero lash mechanical adjuster built into the rocker arm.

6 CYL., DISMANTLE

1. Remove cylinder head as described in previous paragraph.

2. Reach down thru the push rod area with a magnet, or other suitable extractor, and remove the tappets. Keep the tappets in order, that they can be installed in their original location.

3. Loosen all valve rocker arm adjusting screws two turns at a time, and in sequence.

4. Remove rocker arm shaft pedestal bolts and lift off rocker arm shaft assembly.

5. Dismantle shaft and rockers by removing pin and spring washer from each end of the shaft.

6. Slide rocker arms, springs and pedestals off the shaft. (Be sure to identify the parts for proper assembly sequence).

6 CYL., ASSEMBLE

1. Lubricate and assemble all rocker shaft components as per illustration.

2. If the end plugs were removed from the rocker shaft, install new plugs, cup side out, to each end of the shaft.

3. Do valve grinding job or any other service to the cylinder head, check valve spring condition, install new oil seals on valve stems, check springs and install valve assembly in place. Compress springs and install keepers.

4. Install valve tappets in their proper bores.

5. Apply cylinder head gasket sealer to both sides of a new gasket

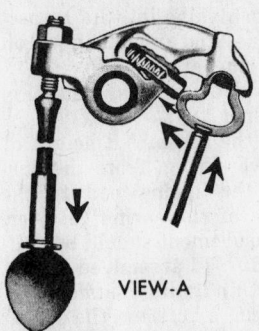
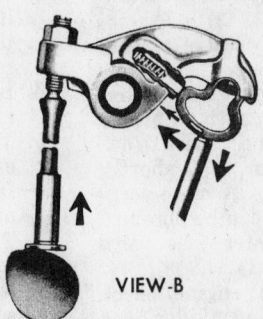
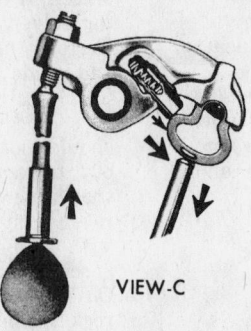
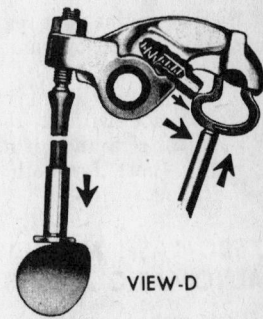

—Sectional View of Valve Rocker Arm Assembly

and locate gasket on cylinder block. Install cylinder head and torque, in three progressive steps, to 75 ft. lbs.

6. Apply lubriplate, or suitable substitute, to both ends of push rods, then install push rods into their respective places.

7. Install rocker arm and shaft. Tighten rocker shaft pedestal bolts in progressive steps to 30-35 ft. lbs.

Adjust Mechanical Adjustable Valves—Primary Step

8. Make primary valve adjustment in the following manner. Then continue to install rocker covers and fill cooling system.

Note:

Tappets must be adjusted while on the low radius of the cam.

A. **If the distributor has not been disturbed** and ignition timing is reasonably correct, proceed as follows: Rotate crankshaft until the distributor rotor points to #1 plug wire tower of the distributor cap. Adjust valves in cylinder firing order according to rotor position.

B. **If the distributor is out of time or has been removed from the engine:** Turn the crankshaft until #1 piston is at the top of its compression stroke, (intake valve of #6 cylinder just beginning to open), and the crankshaft damper is on T.D.C. Make three chalk marks on the crankshaft damper, 120 degrees apart, starting with T.D.C. These marks will divide crankshaft travel into three parts, or six segments, of each engine cycle. Valve adjustment can then be made in firing sequence, beginning with #1 on T.D.C. and progressing thru the regular order of firing by advancing one chalk mark, (120 crankshaft degrees) at a time.

Adjust Mechanical Adjustable Valves—Final Step

Note:

Be sure engine is at regular operating temperature by running at least 30 minutes.

9. With engine idling, check valve clearance with a feeler gauge. Adjust clearance, if necessary, to .016" (hot) for both intake and exhaust.

ZERO LASH MACHANICAL AUTOMATIC ADJUSTERS

This rocker arm has an eccentric at the valve stem end. It is held against the stem by a spring loaded plunger.

As wear occurs or parts expand due to heat the plunger-loaded eccentric holds zero lash.

To make initial setting (engine off):

1. Set No. 1 piston at T.D.C. compression stroke.
2. Adjust intake and exhaust rockers for No. 1 cylinder by tightening screw until eccentric pushes plunger completely into bore.
3. Back out adjusting screw until adjusting mark is directly over valve stem. Torque locknut to 35 ft. lbs.
4. Repeat these steps for balance of cylinders.
5. Start engine and idle. Make recheck for location of adjusting mark. Make any minor readjustment to position the mark directly over valve stem.

V8—VALVE SYSTEM— DISMANTLE

1. Remove cylinder heads as described in previous paragraph.
2. Reach down thru the tappet bores with a magnet or other suitable extractor and remove the tappets. Keep tappets in order, that they can be reinstalled in their original location.
3. Support cylinder head on wooden blocks or the bolts described in Chilton Time Savers. With valves still installed to protect valve seats, wire brush the head clean, do not scratch gasket surfaces.
4. Remove rocker arm adjusting nuts, fulcrum seats, and rocker arms. From the 260 cu. in. engine, remove rocker shaft assemblies from the others. Compress valve springs, remove spring retainer keys, retainers and springs. Remove and discard stem seals, and remove valves.
5. Remove the exhaust manifolds.
6. Inspect condition of manifolds and heads.
7. On the right exhaust manifold, be sure that the automatic choke air inlet and outlet holes are completely open. Clean the maze screen in the passage with cleaning solvent.
8. Perform necessary valve seating and guide services.
9. Check valve springs for squareness and free length. Springs should not be more than 5/64" out of square, or 1/8" shorter than a new spring. A more accurate spring value can be obtained with a spring tester (see valve specifications chart).
10. On the 260 cu. in. engine, check rocker arm studs in cylinder head for damage. Also check for evidence of collant leak at stud base

which may indicate a loose stud. Service replacements are available in standard size and .015" oversize. If any looseness is found, replace the stud.

Hydraulic Tappets—Service

A. Remove lock ring from tappet body.

B. Remove push rod cup and metering valve disc.

C. Remove plunger from tappet body.

D. Invert the plunger and remove the check valve retainer by carefully prying up on it with a screwdriver.

E. Remove the check valve and the spring.

F. Remove the plunger spring from the tappet body.

G. Soak all tappet components in solvent (lacquer thinner works well on these tar and varnish substances).

H. After tappet parts have been thoroughly cleaned and blown dry, place the plunger upside down on a clean surface.

I. Place the check valve over the hole in the bottom of the plunger. Place check valve spring on top of the check valve.

J. Position check valve retainer over the spring and check valve, then push the retainer down into place on the plunger.

K. Place plunger spring and plunger into the tappet body.

L. Place metering valve disc and the push rod cup in the plunger. Depress plunger and install the lock ring.

M. Test all hydraulic tapets (both new and used) before installing them in an engine. The factory quotes a bleed-down time of from 10 to 80 seconds, using special test oil and their approved tester.

V8—VALVE SYSTEM— ASSEMBLE

1. Install hydraulic tappets into their respective bores.
2. Lubricate valve stems with engine oil and apply lubriplate to the tip of the valve stems.
3. Install each valve into its respective guide and install new oil seals on the stems.
4. Install valve springs, retainers and retainer keys.
5. Measure the assembled height of each valve spring, from the surface of the spring pad to the underside of the spring retainer. This measurement should be 1¾" to 1-25/32". If assembled height is not within limits, install necessary spacer/s between the spring pad and the spring to correct the measurement.

6. On the 260 cu. in. engine install rocker arms and fulcrum seats. Install adjusting nuts, finger tight.

7. Position new sealer coated head gasket, install cylinder head, and progressively torque to 65-70 ft. lbs.

8. Lubricate both ends of push rods and install them into their respective tappets.

9. Install the exhaust manifold/s. Torque manifold bolts to 13-18 ft. lbs. and bend over the bolt locking tabs.

10. On all other V-8's, install rocker shafts and torque to 40-45 ft. lbs.

Adjust Valves, 260 and 289 cu. in. Engines

10A. Crank the engine to position #1 piston on T.D.C. of the compression stroke. With engine in this condition, the following valves may be adjusted:
No. 1—Intake
No. 1—Exhaust
No. 2—Exhaust
No. 3—Intake
No. 4—Exhaust
No. 5—Exhaust
No. 7—Intake
No. 8—Intake

B. Position a leverage tool on the rocker arm and slowly bleed down the tappet until the plunger is bottomed.

C. While holding the tappet in the collapsed position, turn rocker arm adjustment to obtain 0.082"-0.152" clearance between the valve stem and the rocker arm.

D. Crank the engine to position #6 piston on the T.D.C. of the compression stroke. With engine in this condition, the following valves may be adjusted:
No. 2—Intake
No. 3—Exhaust
No. 4—Intake
No. 5—Intake
No. 6—Intake
No. 6—Exhaust
No. 7—Exhaust
No. 8—Exhaust

All V8's

11. Coat intake manifold and cylinder block seal surfaces with oil resistant sealer. Position new seals on block and new gaskets on cylinder heads with the seal tabs interlocked with the slots in the gaskets.

12. To faciliate lining up the intake manifold properly, use two aligning studs. Lower the intake manifold onto the engine.

13. Install manifold attaching bolts. Torque bolts in a progressive manner to 14-16 ft. lbs.

14. Connect water pump by-pass hose to the pump and the water outlets housing, tighten the clamps.

15. Install fuel pump and the fuel filter and adapter assembly.

17. Rotate crankshaft to bring #1 piston up to T.D.C. of the compression stroke.

18. Position distributor in the block with the rotor at #1 firing position and the points just opening. Install distributor hold-down clamp.

19. Install carburetor choke heat tube and the carburetor. Install distributor cap and plug wires as an assembly. Install ignition coil, and connect high tension lead at the coil.

20. Install and conect the fuel filter to carburetor line, the fuel pump to fuel filter line, and the distributor to carburetor vacuum line.

21. Check engine oil, fill and bleed cooling system, start engine, make final adjustments and road test car.

VALVE ADJUSTMENT— ROCKER SHAFT TYPE HYDRAULIC

Valve stem to rocker arm (operating) clearance is zero, however, conditions may change the original setting and adjustment become necessary.

Clearance must be determined by measuring the clearance between the closed valve stem and the rocker arm, (with the tappets empty). The clearance should be from .078" to .226."

The most accurate way to check these clearances is to take the feeler gauge reading of the valves, cylinder by cylinder, with each piston at top dead center of its compression stroke. This is best accomplished by following the regular firing order.

If changes must be made, grind the valve stem end to increase this clearance or replace the push rod with the next shorter push rod. These short rods are available from your local dealer.

VALVE SPRINGS

Valve springs should be checked for pressure at any time they are removed.

There is, however, a quick easy way to check valve springs if they have all been removed from the car, and that is to lay all the valve springs along side of each other on a level flat surface, and if they are all the same height, only one of the springs need to be checked, if the one spring comes up to specifications it can be safely assumed that the rest of them will also if they are the same height as the one which tested O.K.

TIMING CASE

TIMING GEAR COVER REMOVAL

O.H.V. 6 Cyl.

The timing case cover is located to the front of the cylinder block by two dowel pins. It is held in place with ten hex head screws. There are also two screws fed up from the oil pan into the timing case cover. The cover is also used as the engine front support.

To remove the timing case cover it is recommended that the oil pan be removed because the oil pan gasket contacts the bottom of the timing case cover and it is an extremely difficult job to remove the timing case cover without destroying or damaging the gasket so that it is no longer fit for service.

Take out the engine front support bolts and support the engine on a jack Take off the radiator core and the fan assembly, remove the vibration damper and unbolt the timing case cover.

O.H.V. V8

To remove the timing case cover from the front of these engines it is recommended that the oil pan also be removed since there is a gasket between the lower part of the timing case cover and the oil pan and it will be very difficult to prevent oil leaks if the oil pan is left in place and an attempt is made to seal between the bottom of the timing case cover and the oil pan.

Remove the radiator core, the fan, fan pulley, the water pump and the water by-pass pipe back of the water pump. Take off the crankshaft pulley and the fuel pump.

(On 1957 Models. Take the weight of the engine on a jack and remove the engine front mounting bolts which pass into the engine steady rest plate in front of the timing case cover.)

Take off the bolts which hold the timing case cover to the front of the block and slide the cover off the

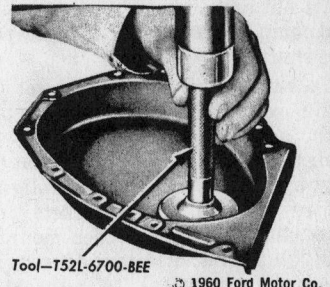

Tool—T52L-6700-BEE   Ⓒ 1960 Ford Motor Co.

Oil Seal Installation— O.H.V. 6 Cyl.

361

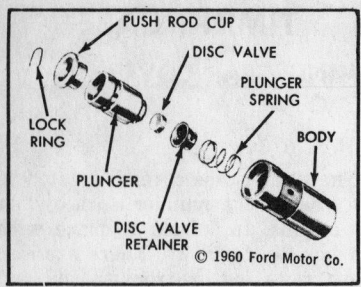

Hydraulic valve lifters. 332, 352, 390 and 430 cu. in. V8 engine

crankshaft.

It is always good practice to install a new oil seal when replacing the timing case cover.

Caution: Due to the structure of the crankshaft, it is very important that the proper tools be used to draw the damper or pulley into place on the crankshaft. (Do not use a hammer, breakage of the cast crankshaft can result.)

TIMING CASE OIL SEAL REPLACEMENT

All Models

To replace the oil seal it is necessary to take off the timing case cover and drive the seal out with a pin punch. Clean out the recess in the cover and install a new seal using a special driving tool.

Coat the new seal with grease to reduce friction when installing and starting the car.

TIMING SPROCKET AND/OR CHAIN

O.H.V. 6 Cyl.

To replace the timing chain for wear or looseness, first align the timing marks so that there are 12 pins of the chain between the mark on the cam and the mark on the crankshaft sprocket. These should be measured on the driving, upper, side of the chain. Now remove the camshaft sprocket retaining nut and the crankshaft nut and slide the two sprockets and chain as one unit off their respective shafts.

To reinstall the chain first set the chain over both sprockets and start both sprockets simultaneously on their two shafts being certain that the keyways are very carefully aligned before starting the sprockets into place. After they have been mounted fully on their shafts turn the engine two full revolutions to recheck to make certain that there are seven links of the timing chain between the

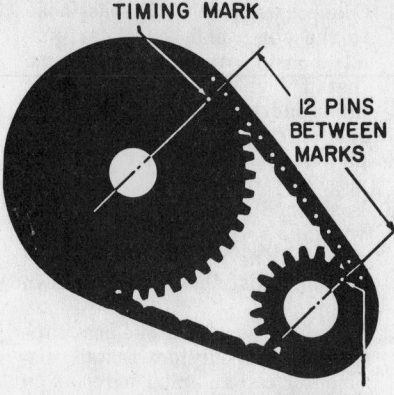

Timing Gear Marks, O.H.V., 6 Cyl.

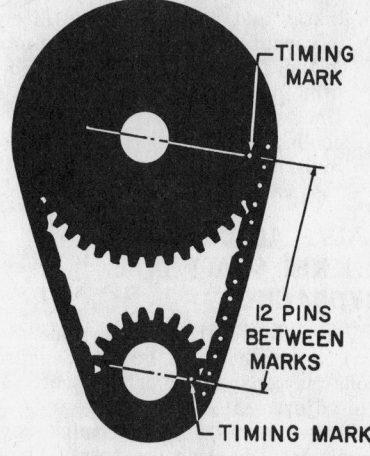

Timing Gear Marks, V-8 with Rear Mounted Distributor

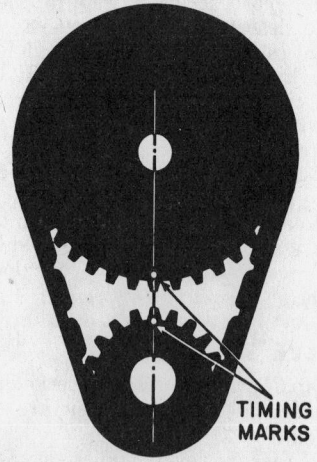

Timing Gear Marks, V-8 with Front Mounted Distributor

mark on the cam and the mark on the crankshaft sprocket, counting the link at each mark.

Check the chain for wear or looseness.

O.H.V. V8 with Distributor At the Back of the Block

Remove the timing case cover as outlined under the paragraph devoted to this subject and remove the cam and crankshaft sprockets.

Before taking the sprockets off, however, arrange them so that the marks (little round punch marks) on the sprockets are pointing approximately horizontally towards the left side of the engine in such a way that the marks will straddle 12 pins of the timing chain. That is, there will be 12 pins of the timing chain between the mark on the cam and the mark of the crank sprocket.

Thru 1954 the chain is marked either with a brass disc on two of the links or with two link plates of a different color. These marked links go on the sprockets at the index punch mark on the face of the sprocket.

Remove the cam and crankshaft sprocket.

Arrange the new chain and/or sprockets on the bench to occupy the same relative position just explained.

Now carefully start the sprockets upon the shafts with the chain in place and after being certain that they are started straight push them all the way onto the shafts and secure.

Turn the engine two full revolutions to make sure that the timing marks are in the correct position.

ENGINE LUBRICATION

6 Cyl.—No Oil Pressure

A few instances of no oil pressure have come to our recent attention on the six cylinder engine.

Design characteristics and wear bring about the failure responsible for this condition.

The gear-type oil pump is entirely within the crankcase, in line with and driven by the distributor gear, through a hex shaft.

This shaft is pinned in the lower end of the distributor drive shaft by a roll pin. The bottom end of the hex shaft seats in the female end of the oil pump drive. It is possible for the roll pin to shear or work out of place. This will allow the hex drive shaft to slip down and out of the distributor drive and cause oil pump failure.

⏻ CHILTON TIME-SAVER

In the event of no-oil-pressure, remove the distributor and check the condition of this hex drive. If the above situation exists, it may be possible to recover the hex shaft with the aid of a magnet or a mechanical finger tool. If recovery is possible, the shaft can be reattached to the distributor with a new roll pin. The alternative is to drop the oil pan and remove the oil pump to retrieve the hex.

FORD and THUNDERBIRD

OIL PAN REMOVAL

O.H.V. 6 Cyl., 1954 Thru 1955

To remove the oil pan first disconnect the steering drag link and remove the engine front mounting bolts. Jack the engine up about an inch and block it in that position.

The oil pan may now be unbolted and lowered to the floor.

1956 Thru 1962 6 Cylinder

Drain the crankcase and pull out the dipstick. Take off the left and right front splash aprons and the flywheel housing inspection cover.

Remove the oil pan, screws, and drop the pan.

1954 Thru 1955 V8 Engines

On these models the oil pan can be removed by detaching the steering idler arm bracket from the frame and letting the idler arm and the tie rods drop down.

Disconnect the large oil line at its back end and remove the sheet metal splasher which is fastened to the frame under the radiator in front of the oil pan. Remove the bolts which hold the oil pan to cylinder block and, by carefully turning the crankshaft, the oil pan can be worked forward and out towards the front.

1956 Thru 1962 V8 Models

Drain the crankcase and take out the dipstick. Take off both engine front splash pans. On Fordomatic models remove the converter housing

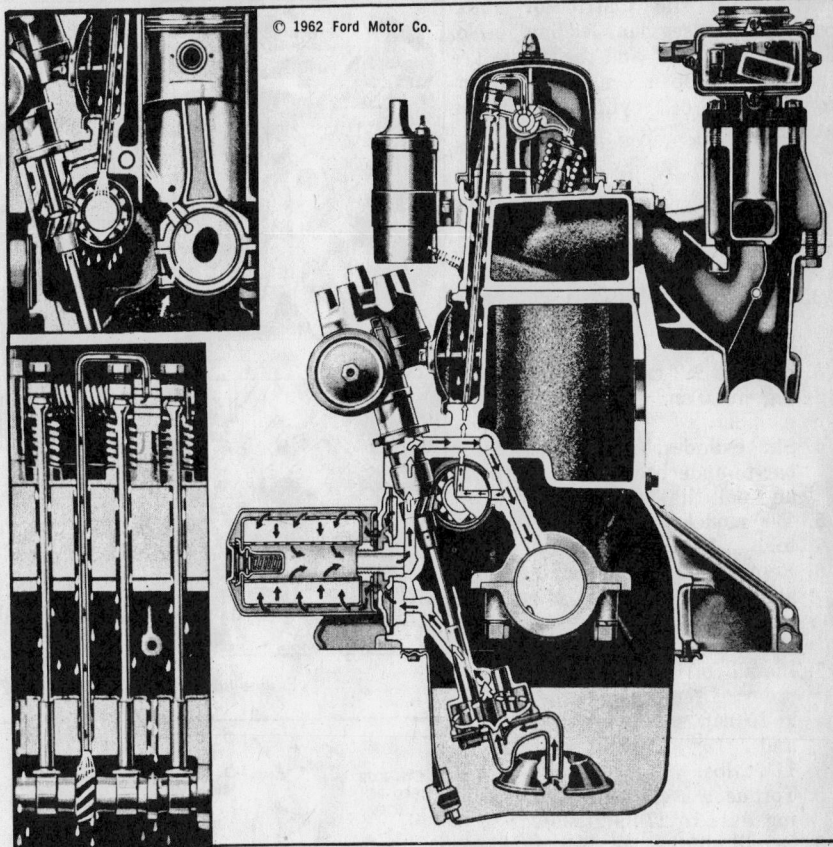

© 1962 Ford Motor Co.

Engine lubrication. Typical all O.H.V. 6 cyl.

cover assembly.

Disconnect the oil pump inlet tube at the oil pump. Remove the oil ring from the pump end of the tube. Take out the oil pan retaining screws and

nuts and drop the pan. Note: on 1957 models No. 5 cylinder must be at approximately top dead center so that the pan will clear the crankshaft throws. To accomplish this, turn the

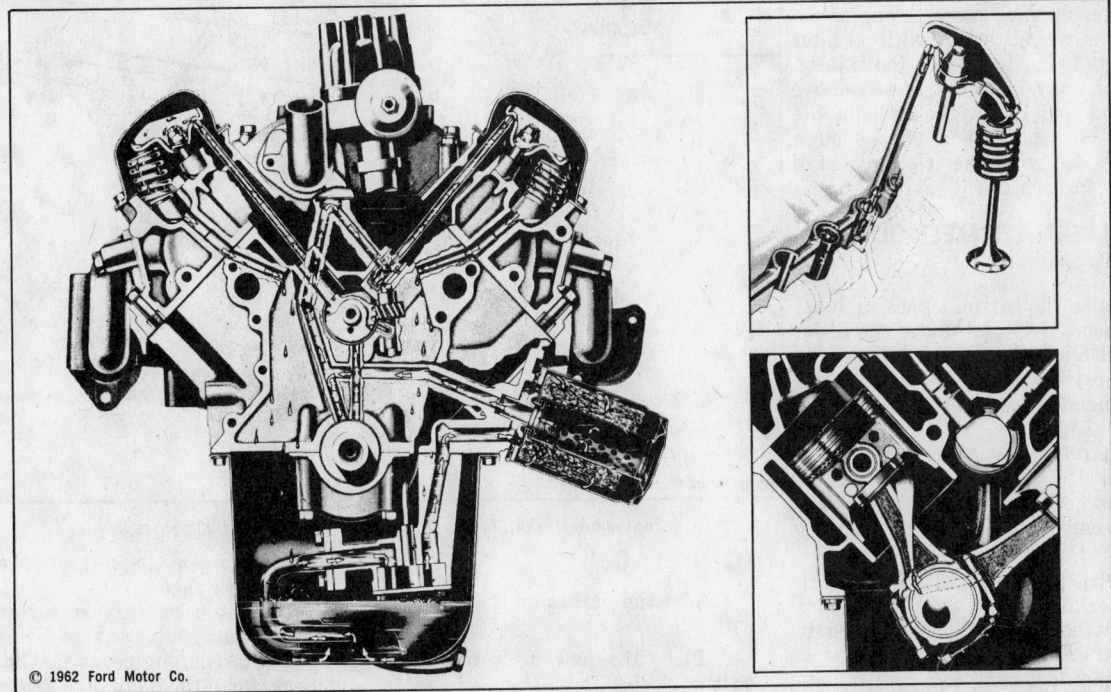

© 1962 Ford Motor Co.

Engine Lubrication—260 cu. in. and 289 cu. in. Engines

363

crank until the distributor rotor points to the segment leading to No. 5 spark plug wire and the points are just about to open. On 1958 Interceptor engines No. 1 cylinder should be at top center.

1963
Oil Pan R & R—6 Cyl. & V8

1. Drain crankcase. Remove oil dipstick.
2. **Six cylinder with standard transmission**, remove clutch retracting spring.
3. Remove #2 crossmember retaining nuts and remove the crossmember.
4. **Six cylinder**, remove stabilizer bar-to-underbody retaining nuts and pull the bar downward.
5. **V-8 models**, remove starter motor.
6. Remove oil pan retaining bolts and crank the engine as required to obtain clearance, then remove the oil pan.
7. Install oil pan in the reverse order of removal. Torque the ¼" x 20 cap screws to 7-9 ft. lbs. and 5/16" x 18 cap screws to 9-11 ft. lbs.
8. Torque #2 crossmember attaching nuts to 27-39 ft. lbs.
9. Install oil dipstick. Fill crankcase to level, then run the engine and check for leaks.

OIL FILTER

⏱ CHILTON TIME-SAVER

A few cases of difficulty in oil filter replacement have come to our attention. The trouble starts with oil filter elements being turned on too tightly. The unit may be too tight to remove by hand and it may collapse in the grip of a tool that applies enough squeeze to grip the element hard enough to turn it.

AN ALTERNATE METHOD OF REMOVAL:

1. Raise the car on a jack or hoist and place a drip pan under the filter.
2. With a 12 inch to 14 inch slender punch drive a hole in the element from one side to the other.

NOTE: Before punching the hole, consider the angle required for the punch to act as a lever, with the least interference.

3. With the drift all the way thru the filter and acting as a lever, turn the unit counterclockwise enough to break it loose.
4. Final loosening and removal can now be accomplished by hand.

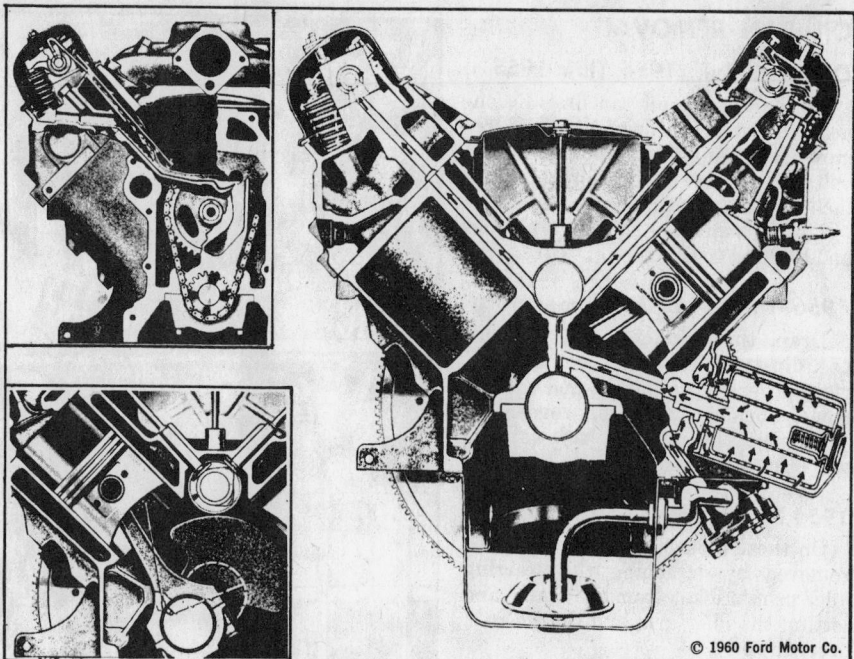

Engine lubrication. Typical of V8-239, 272, 292 and 312 cu. in. engine

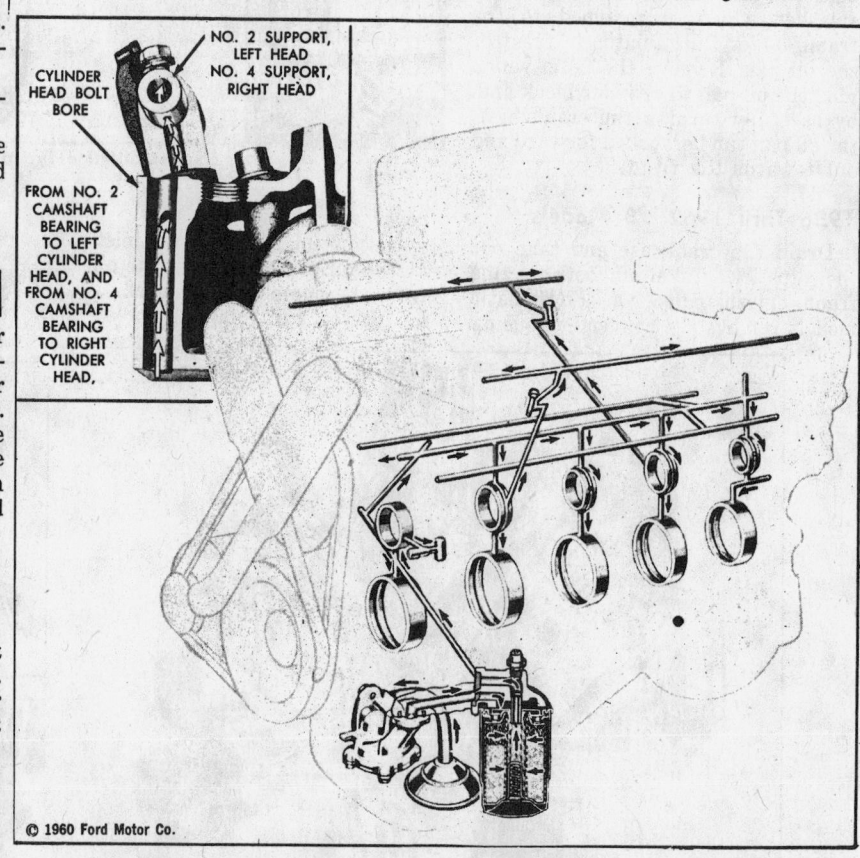

Engine lubrication. Typical of V8-332, 352, 390 and 430 cu. in. engine

TO REPLACE

1. Coat the gasket on the new filter with oil.
2. Place the new filter in position on the block.
3. Hand tighten until contact is made between the filter gasket and the adapter face.
4. Tighten by further turning the filter ½ turn.
5. Run the engine at fast idle and check for oil leaks.
6. Check the oil and bring crank-

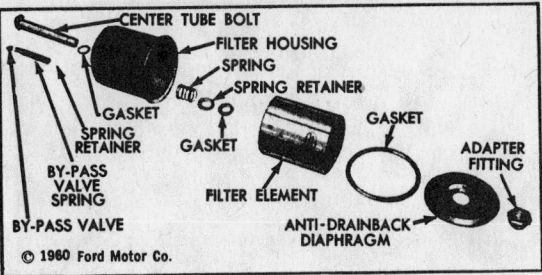

Oil filter. All engines 1954-56

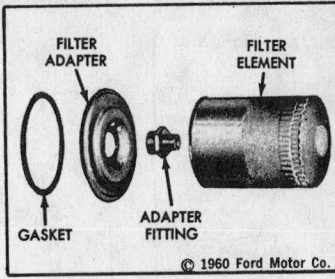

*Oil filter. V8 292 and six cyl.
1957-62*

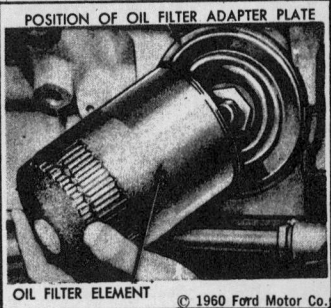

*Check filter adaptor plate for
proper position*

case to level if necessary.

CONNECTING RODS
AND PISTONS
REMOVAL ALL MODELS

Take off the cylinder heads and oil pan. Select the pistons in the down position and using a good cylinder ridge reamer remove the ridge from the top of the cylinder. Turn the crankshaft one-half revolution to gain access to the cylinders whose pistons were at first at the top.

From underneath the car, remove the two bolts from the connecting rod cap on the rods which are in the down position. Push the connecting rod and piston assembly part way up the bore and immediately replace the cap on the bottom of the connecting rod. This is to eliminate the possibility of either losing the bearing or getting the caps mixed up.

INSPECTION OF PISTONS
ALL MODELS

Carefully inspect the pistons, particularly the thrust face, for scratches or scores. Do not confuse an ordinary wear pattern with scoring. Scoring on the piston is generally accompanied

by a comparable scoring on the cylinder walls, whereas the wear pattern usually leaves a perfectly smooth and, in fact, somewhat glassy cylinder wall.

Cylinders showing the slightest scoring will have to be rebored and pistons with scores will have to be resized or replaced.

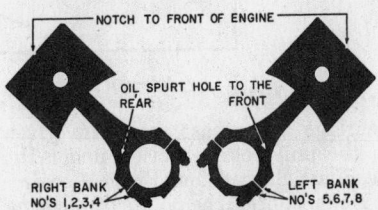

Piston & Rod Installation V8

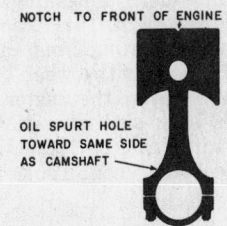

Piston & Rod Installation 6 Cyl.
FITTING RINGS

Complete instructions are supplied by each ring manufacturer with each package set of rings. These instructions should be followed very carefully since the ring manufacturer knows, better than anyone else, how

to get the best possible service from his product.

REAR MAIN BEARING
OIL SEAL

On both 6 and 8 cylinder models a packing type seal is used in back of the rear main bearing. To replace the upper half of the seal it is necessary to remove the crankshaft. The lower half of the seal may be replaced by taking down the rear main bearing cap and inserting new packing, letting the packing protrude approximately 1/16 inch above the cap at either side. Bolt the cap into place and immediately take it down to determine if the seal has riveted over. If it has riveted over, trim off with a razor blade just the riveted portion and bolt the cap back up again and again remove it to determine if the main bearing cap is seating properly in the block. The reason for permitting the oil seal packing to protrude is so that it will tend to compress the upper half of the packing more tightly into the retainer in the cylinder block. In this way it is sometimes possible to prevent leaks at the rear main bearing without replacing the upper half of the oil seal.

CAMSHAFT BEARING
REPLACEMENT

V8 Engines with Distributor at the Back

It is necessary to remove the engine from the chassis to replace the camshaft bearings. The need for camshaft bearing replacement on these engines will show up as a lack of rocker arm lubrication. When the rocker arm shafts start to run dry the No. 3 camshaft bearing has turned and closed off the oil feed hole to the rocker shafts.

After removing the engine, remove the crankshaft and the camshaft.

Drill a ½ inch hole in the rear camshaft bearing plug and remove the plug.

Remove the camshaft bearings.

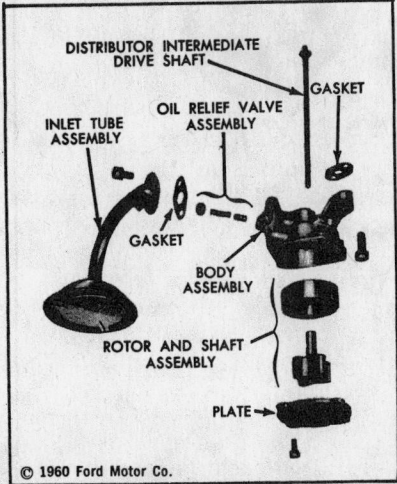

*Oil pump for V8 with distributor at
the front*

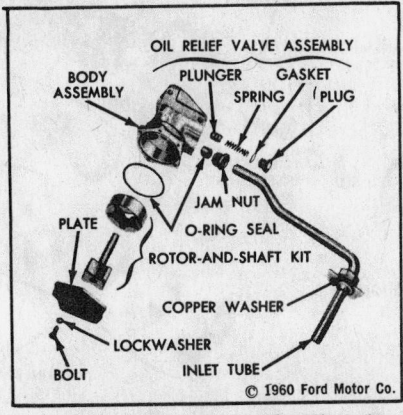

*Externally mounted oil pump for V8 engines
with distributor at the back.*

FORD and THUNDERBIRD

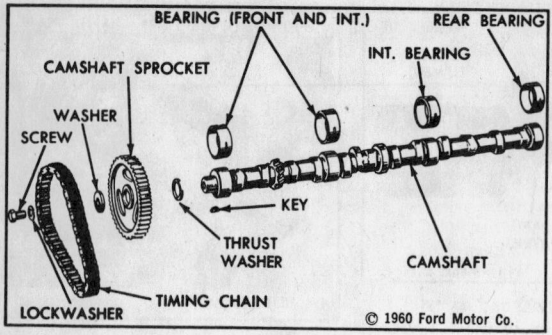

Camshaft and related parts. O.H.V. six

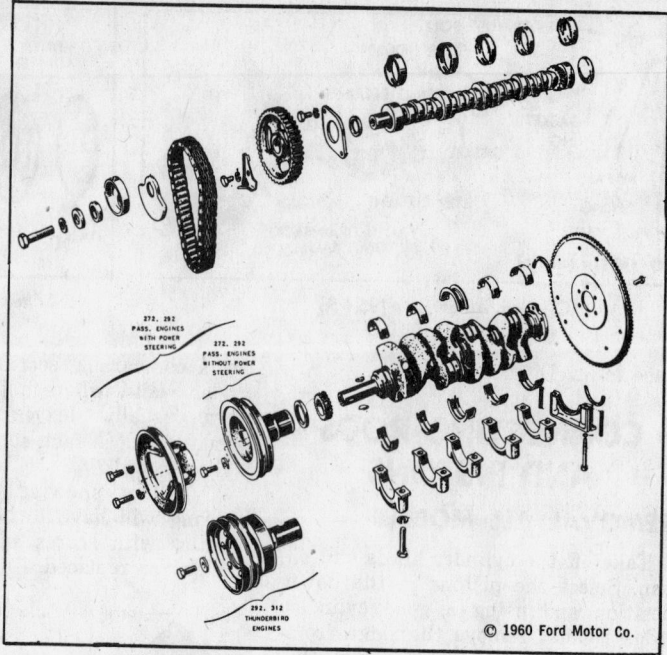

Internal engine parts. 1954-57 V8's and 1958-62 292 V8

Press the new camshaft bearings into place, being careful to align the oil holes in the bearings with those in the block.

The No. 1 bearing is not interchangeable with the others. When installed the No. 1 bearing must be .005 to .020 inch below the front face of the cylinder block to allow room for the camshaft gear thrust washer.

Oil is fed to the rocker shafts of both banks from the No. 3 camshaft bearing. Be sure the holes are properly aligned and that the passages are open before reinstalling the camshaft and crankshaft.

1955 and 1956 camshafts are not interchangeable. 1956 camshafts have grooved journals. 1955 camshafts have oil holes in the journals. Use sealer when installing the plug at the rear end of the camshaft.

V8 Engines with Distributor at the Front

The procedure is the same as that for the other type V8's only none of the bearings are interchangeable.

FRONT SUSPENSION

ADJUSTMENT

General instructions covering the front suspension and how to repair and adjust it, together with information on installation of front wheel

bearings and grease seals, are given in the unit repair section under the heading: Suspension, Front Repair.

Definitions of the points of steering geometry are covered in the unit repair section under the headings: Suspension, Front Align. This article also covers trouble shooting front end geometry and irregular tire wear.

Figures covering the caster, camber, toe-in, king pin inclination, and turning radius can be found in the Front Wheel Alignment Table of this section.

Tire size figures can be found in the General Chassis and Brake Specifications Table of this section.

Extended Lubrication

Starting with 1961 the following front suspension and steering parts will require lubrication only after long mileage periods; Two upper ball joints, two lower ball joints, one idler arm joint, two cross link joints, four tie rod ball joints, one power steering valve joint.

These places are factory packed

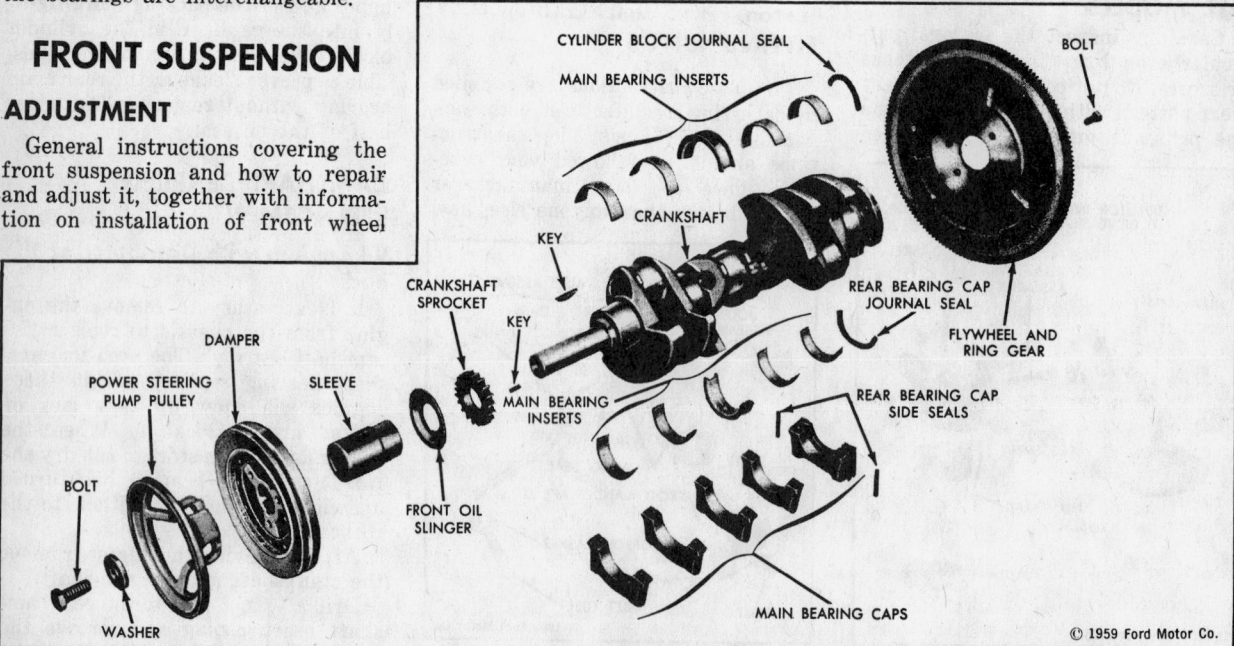

Crankshaft and related parts 1958-62, 332, 352, 390 and 430

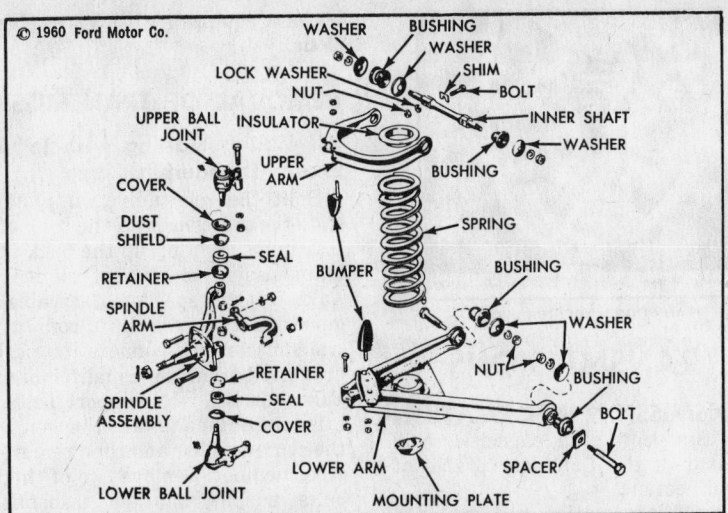

Typical ball joint front suspension starting with 1954

with a special compound and when replaced ONLY the original type lubricant should be used.

STEERING

Steering Gear Adjustment

Instructions covering the adjustment of the steering gear will be found in the Unit Repair section under the heading: Steering, Manual.

Power Steering Gears

Trouble shooting and repair instructions covering power steering gears are given in the Unit Repair section under the heading: Steering, Power.

REMOVAL OF MANUAL STEERING GEAR ASSEMBLY FROM THE CAR

Thru 1955 Models

Disconnect the pitman arm and remove the steering wheel. Then disconnect the steering column from the instrument panel. Disconnect the lower shift levers from the rod adjusting nuts. Remove the cap screws from the bracket that secures the gear shift tube to the steering column tube and remove the bracket which will permit removal of the gear shift tube pin and the gear shift levers.

Take out the steering column clamp and pull the jacket tube off the gear shaft. Take out the bolts holding the gear housing to the frame.

Then the steering gear may be taken out through the bottom, from underneath the car.

Starting with 1956

Disconnect and tag the wire from the column underneath the dash. Remove the horn ring and take off the steering wheel.

Remove the turn indicator lever and the gear shift lever from the top of the steering column. If equipped with automatic transmission, remove the selector dial and cover. Throw back the floor mat and take off the floor cover plate. Disconnect the speedometer cable from the instrument panel and remove the right hand cover plate from the cable. Disconnect the gear shift rods at the bottom of the steering column. Disconnect the neutral safety switch wire at the bottom of the clutch return spring bracket.

On cars with single exhaust systems, disconnect the exhaust pipe for access to the pitman arm and remove the pitman arm. Remove the bolts which hold the steering mast jacket to the under side of the dash panel and then remove the bolts which hold the gear box itself to the frame. Lift the steering gear assembly out thru the engine compartment on standard transmission jobs, up into the body on automatic transmission cars.

Thunderbird Models

Disconnect the wires from the bottom of the gear housing, loosen the lower steering column clamp and remove the screws from the upper steering column bracket. Remove the horn ring from the steering wheel and take off the upper steering column, upper steering shaft and steering wheel, as an assembly from the car. Remove the pitman arm and take out the bolts which hold the steering gear housing to the frame side member in order to remove the lower steering gear assembly from the car.

HORN BUTTON REMOVAL

Starting with 1954

The horn ring can be removed by pressing down evenly on the button and turning it counterclockwise until it lifts out.

Horn Ring Models

The horn ring is removed by first removing the two screws at the back of the steering wheel. The horn ring can then be lifted off.

STEERING WHEEL REMOVAL

The steering wheel is removed, using a puller designed for the purpose, after the horn button and the steering

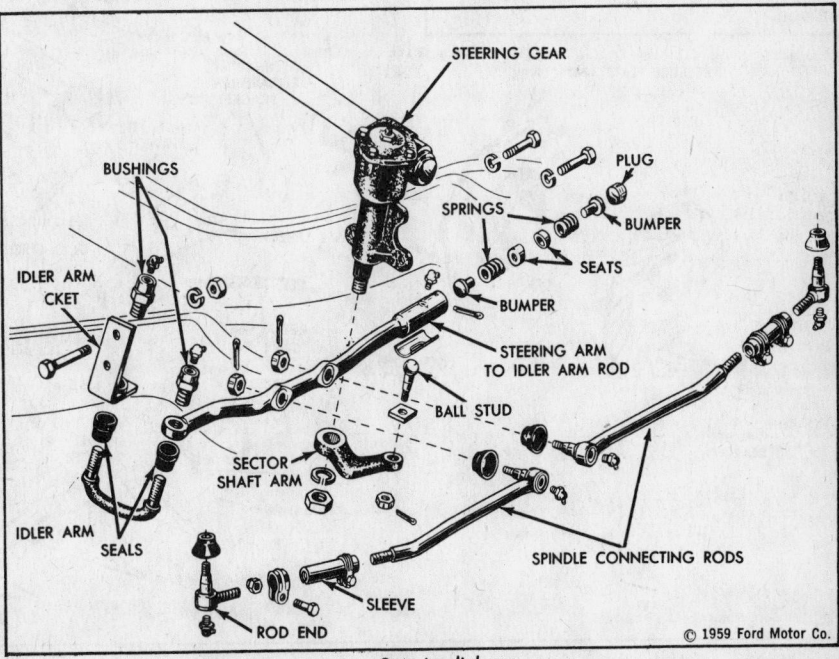

Steering linkage

wheel nut have been taken off.

If the car is equipped with direction signals it will be necessary to set the direction signals in the Neutral position.

CLUTCH

CLUTCH PEDAL ADJUSTMENT

The clutch release fork rod should be adjusted so that there is from 1 to 1½ inch free play of the clutch pedal, measured at the toe board. This is the only practical adjustment which can be made with the clutch mounted in the car.

All other adjustments require that the clutch be removed.

CLUTCH REMOVAL

Except Thunderbird

Take off the transmission, disconnect the clutch pedal release rod and take off the flywheel housing.

It will be necessary to support the back of the engine on a jack. The clutch can then be unbolted from the flywheel.

Ford Motor Co. recommends that wedges be set behind each of the clutch fingers in order to prevent bending the clutch cover when taking out the mounting bolts.

If inspection of the clutch reveals that there is oil on the facings it is a good idea to replace the rear main bearing oil seal. When replacing the clutch the cap screws should be tightened to 17-20 ft. lb. torque. If the original clutch is to be replaced it should be marked showing its relationship to the flywheel so that it can be replaced in the position from which it was removed.

Steering Wheel Puller © 1959 Ford Motor Co.

Steering wheel removal

TRANSMISSIONS

TRANSMISSION INFORMATION

Transmission refill capacities will be found in the Capacities Table of this car section.

General information and exploded views, together with trouble shooting charts, are included in the Unit Repair Section on each automatic transmission.

Beginning with 1959, a 2 speed ("Fordomatic") transmission has been added to the line. See the Unit Repair section for coverage.

Trouble shooting and repair of overdrive units are covered in the Unit Repair section under the heading: Transmission—Overdrive.

Beginning 1963 a fully synchronized 3 speed manual transmission is available. A 4-speed, fully synchronized transmission is also available on

all cars equipped with V8 engine options.

REMOVAL OF TRANSMISSION

All Models Starting with 1954 Except Thunderbirds

Split the rear universal joint and slide the driveshaft off the back of the transmission. Plug up the back of the transmission to prevent oil leakage. Take off the speedometer cable and gear and the gear shift rods at the transmission. Disconnect the parking brake rod from the equalizer bracket. Take out the rear support bolts and raise the engine to take the weight off the crossmember and then remove the crossmember. Remove two of the four bolts which hold the transmission case to the flywheel housing and replace these two bolts with long pilot studs. Lower the engine and the back of the transmission for clearance and remove the two upper bolts which hold the transmission to the bell housing and then slide the transmission assembly off the two guide pins. Using the guide pins will prevent the heavy transmission from springing downwards with possible damage to the clutch disc.

Thunderbird Models

Perhaps the easiest way to remove the transmission on Thunderbird

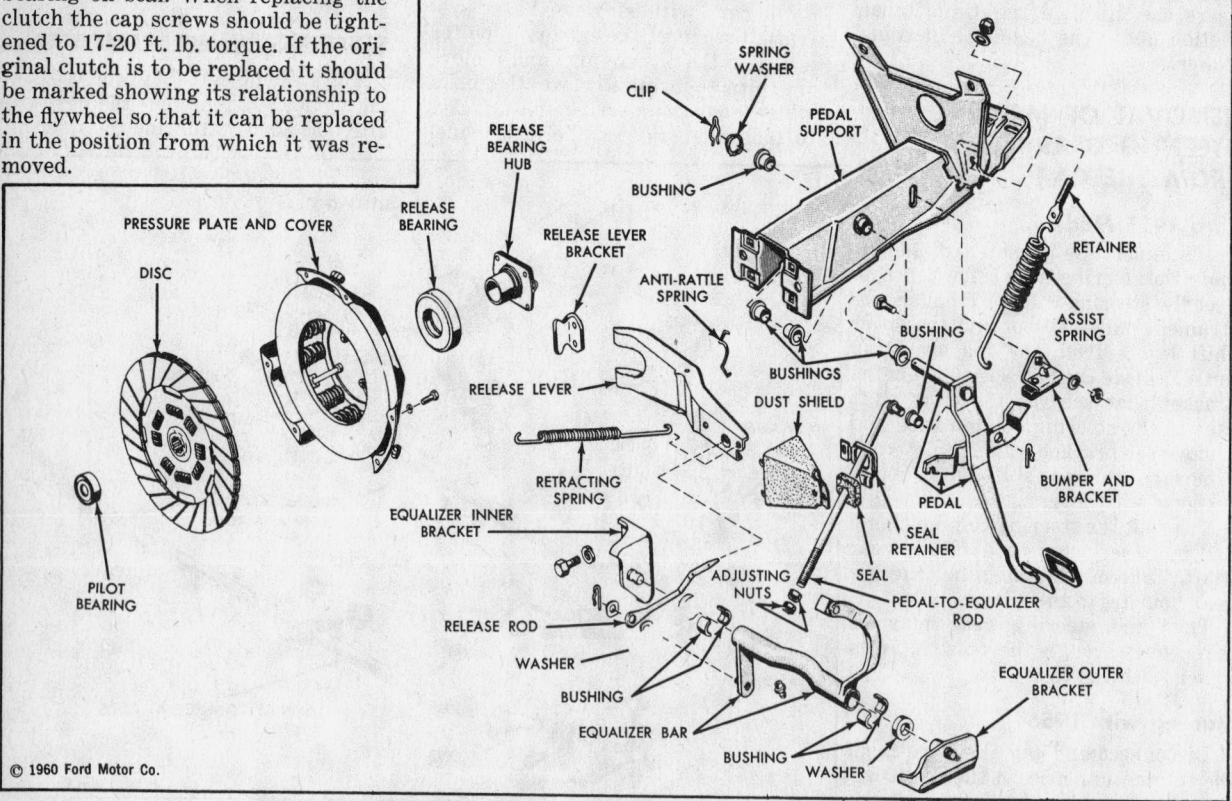

PRESSURE PLATE AND COVER — DISC — PILOT BEARING — RELEASE BEARING — RELEASE BEARING HUB — RELEASE LEVER BRACKET — RELEASE LEVER — RETRACTING SPRING — EQUALIZER INNER BRACKET — RELEASE ROD — WASHER — BUSHING — EQUALIZER BAR — BUSHING — WASHER — ADJUSTING NUTS — CLIP — SPRING WASHER — PEDAL SUPPORT — BUSHING — ANTI-RATTLE SPRING — BUSHINGS — DUST SHIELD — SEAL RETAINER — PEDAL — SEAL — PEDAL-TO-EQUALIZER ROD — RETAINER — ASSIST SPRING — BUMPER AND BRACKET — EQUALIZER OUTER BRACKET

© 1960 Ford Motor Co.

Exploded view of the complete clutch and pedal assembly.

models is to take the engine and transmission assembly out as a unit.

However, the transmission can be removed with the engine in the car as follows. Disconnect all linkage from the transmission and clutch including the shift levers, the clutch pedal rods, speedometer cable and, when equipped with overdrive, disconnect the wires and rods to the overdrive.

Split the universal joints and remove the driveshaft. Support the weight of the engine on a jack and remove the bolts from the transmission rear mounting and then take off that mounting crossmember.

Remove the bolts which hold the transmission to the bell housing and slide the transmission back as far as it will go. Now with the transmission supported back as far as it will go, reach up through the bottom of the clutch housing and remove the clutch assembly from the flywheel. With the clutch out, remove the bolts which hold the clutch housing to the engine bell housing and move the clutch housing backwards, tilted forward, and bring it out from the bottom of the car in front of the transmission main driveshaft.

The transmission can now be slid forward and down out of the car.

DISASSEMBLY OF SYNCHROMESH THRU 1962

Remove the transmission cover assembly and unbolt the extension housing. Drive the pin out of the transmission case which holds the counter shaft and the reverse idler gear shaft. This pin is located at the back by the bottom of the case. Turn the extension housing one-quarter turn clockwise, which will permit the removal of the counter shaft. The counter shaft is driven out through the rear of the case permitting the counter set cluster gear to drop to the bottom of the case.

Now the extension housing and the main shaft assembly can be pulled out from the rear of the transmission case.

The reverse idler shaft can now be driven out through the rear of the case. The main drive gear is removed by taking off the bearing cover and pulling the shaft and bearing out the front of the case. Remove the snap ring which holds the main shaft assembly in the extension case. (This snap ring is located at the front of the extension case. It is the snap ring which holds the bearing into the extension case.)

Tap the mainshaft out of the extension case. Next take off the speedometer gear and the mainshaft rear bearing.

To dis-assemble the synchronizer push the synchronizer hub out of the sleeve which will release the three synchronizer blocks. The main drive gear bearing can be pressed off the main drive gear after the snap ring is removed.

Inspect all parts for nicks and roughness and check all bearings for smooth operation.

When the transmission is disassembled always place a new oil seal at the back of the housing.

3-SPEED SYNCHROMESH TRANSMISSION SHIFT LINKAGE ADJUSTMENT

To adjust the shift rods, disconnect the rods from the steering column levers and loosen the lock nuts. Turn the clevices either clockwise or counterclockwise whichever is required, so that with the gears in neutral and the two levers on the steering column in line with each other, the clevices will just enter the hole in the shift lever.

BEGINNING 1961—4 SPEED FULLY SYNCHRONIZED

Disassemble

1. Remove shift linkage rods at transmission levers and remove the linkage and levers from the extension housing as a unit.
2. Remove gear shift housing cover with the shift forks.
3. Drive out the reverse lever shaft lock pin and pull the shaft out of the extension housing about ⅛". This will free the reverse shift fork from the reverse sliding gear.
4. Remove the extension-to-case retaining bolts. Slide the extension housing rearward and rotate counter-clockwise to remove the extension.
5. Remove the reverse rear idler gear from the back of the case.
6. Remove the bolt holding the adapter plate to the transmission, then remove the output shaft assembly along with the adapter plate.
7. Remove the fourth speed synchronizer blocking ring.
8. Remove the reverse gear front idler and thrust washer from the case.

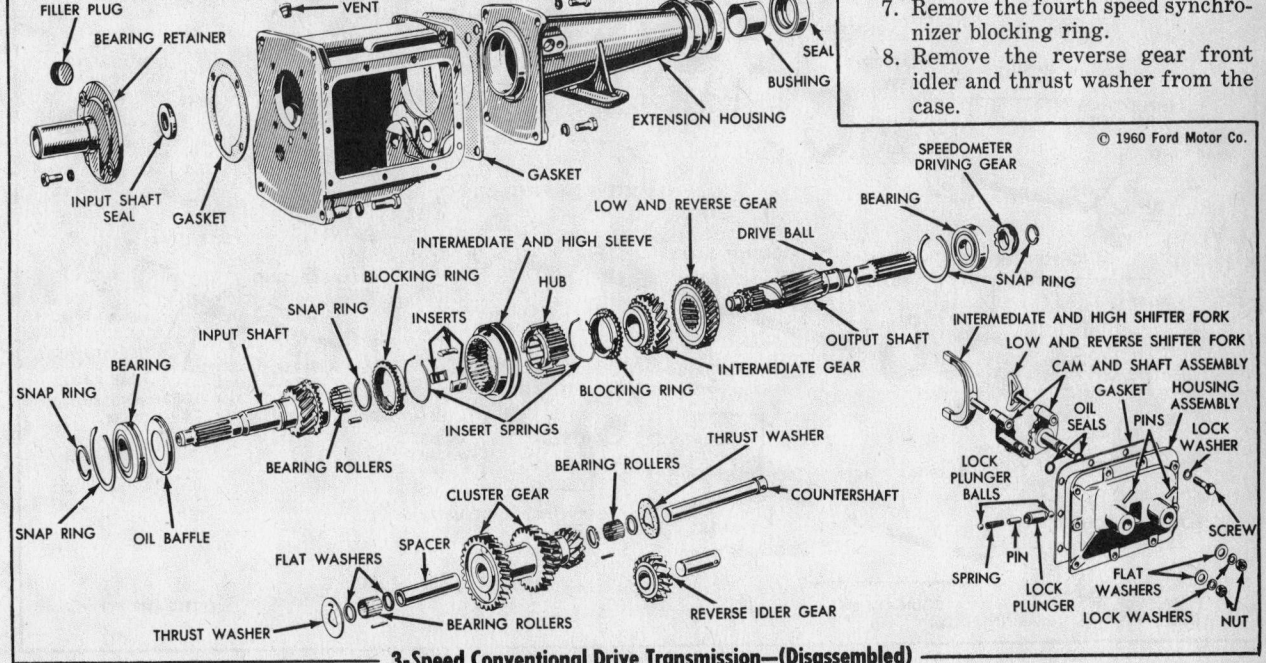

© 1960 Ford Motor Co.

3-Speed Conventional Drive Transmission—(Disassembled)

9. Drive the countershaft rearward to free the front of the case, then with a dummy shaft, push out the countershaft. Leave the dummy shaft remain in the countershaft.

10. Remove the input shaft retainer. Remove the input shaft bearing retaining snap ring, and push the input shaft and bearing inward, out of the bearing bore. Remove the input shaft assembly from the case.

11. Remove cluster assembly from the case.

12. Disassemble the cluster gear.

13. Remove input shaft bearing retainer oil seal.

14. To dismantle the input shaft, remove bearing snap ring and spacer washer. Press off the bearing.

15. To dismantle the output shaft, remove the snap ring from front of shaft. Slide off the third and fourth speed gear synchronizer assembly, third speed gear synchronizer blocking ring, third speed gear, second speed gear, second and third speed thrust bearing, second speed gear, and second speed synchronizer blocker ring.

16. Remove output shaft rear oil rubber seal from the shaft. Press off the speedometer drive gear. Slide reverse gear off the shaft.

17. Spread the retaining snap ring and press the adapter plate off the output shaft rear bearing.

18. Remove the snap ring holding the output shaft rear bearing to the output shaft.

19. Remove the snap ring holding the output shaft rear bearing to the output shaft and press the bearing off the shaft.

20. Complete disassembly of the output shaft by sliding off the balance of components.

21. Place an index mark on the hub and clutch sleeve for reassembly reference.

22. Disassemble first and second speed and third and fourth speed synchronizers by sliding the clutch sleeves off the hubs and removing the three inserts and two insert springs in each assembly.

Note:

Unless transmission lock-up or jumping out of gear is included in the complaint, the shifter housing is generally left intact.

23. To disassemble the shifter housing, remove the shift levers from the cam and shaft assemblies. Pull forks and shafts out of the gear shift housing. With shafts removed, the interlock balls, retainer, and spring will fall out of the gearshift housing. Pull the shifter forks out of the cams, and remove the seal rings from the

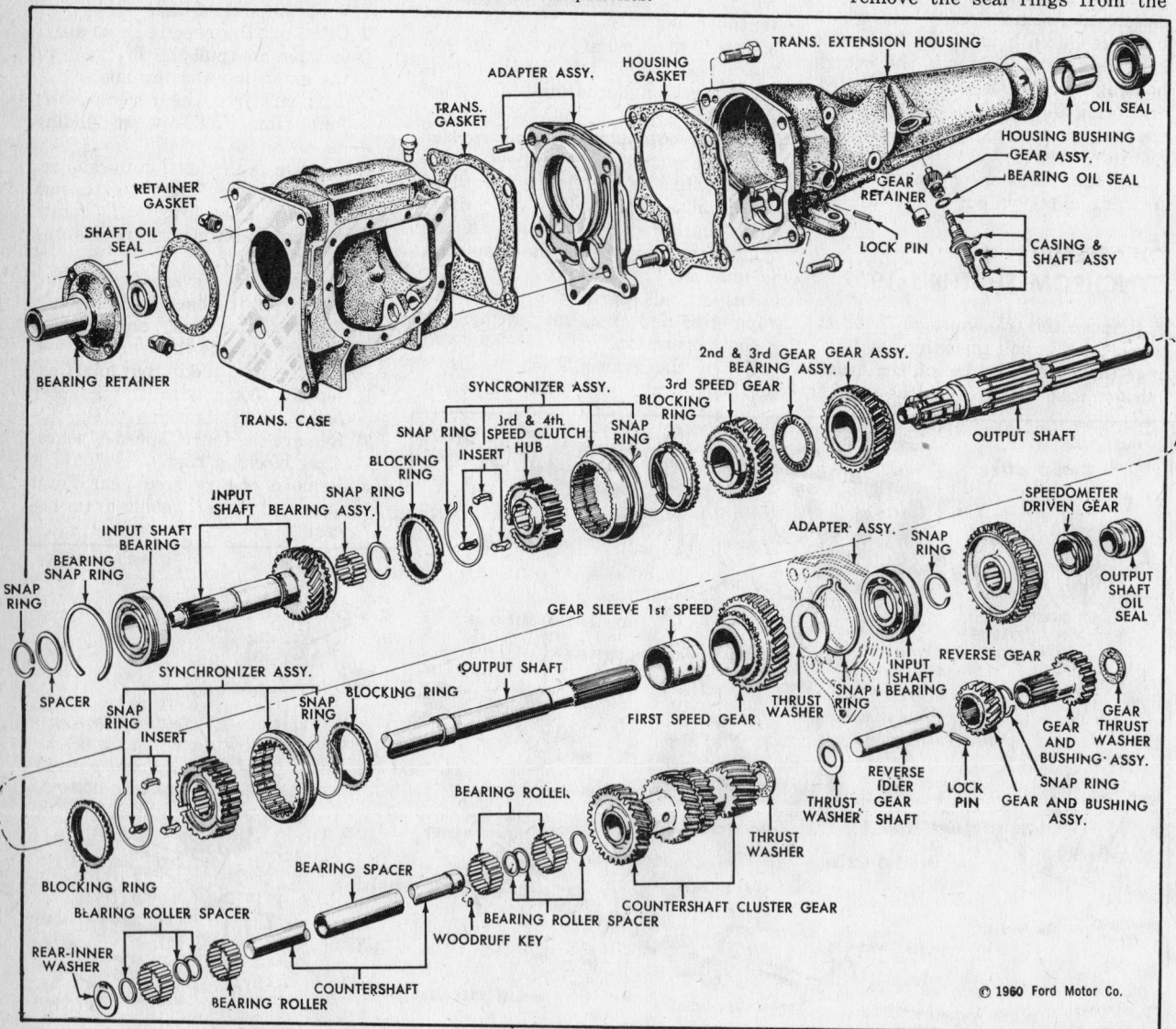

© 1960 Ford Motor Co.

Manual 4-Speed Transmission

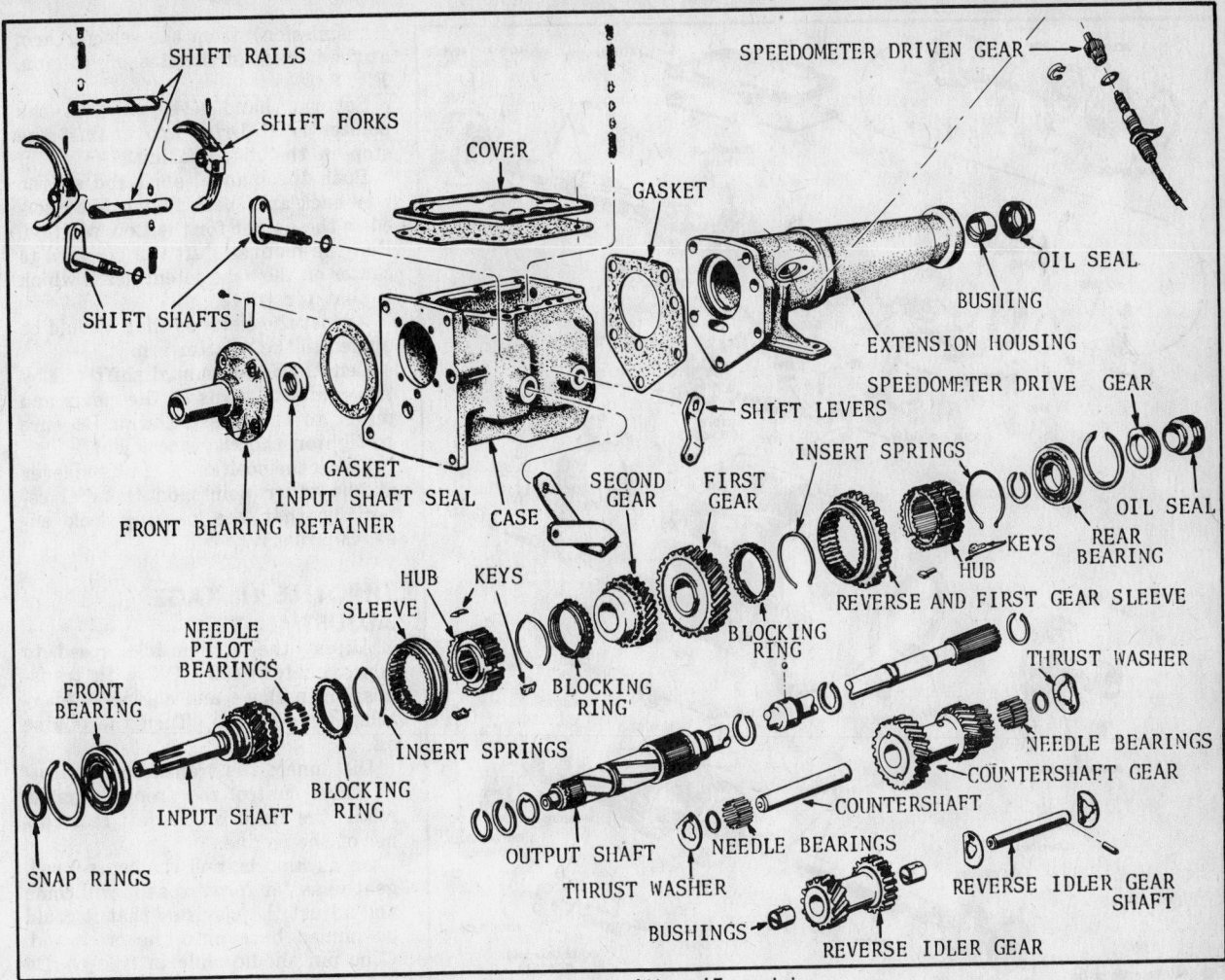

3-Speed, Fully Synchronized Manual Transmission

cam shafts. Inspect balls and springs for defects. Check detent notches for wear.

24. To disassemble extension housing, first remove the oil seal and bushing.

25. Pull the reverse fork from the reverse shift lever shaft and cam. remove the reverse shift lever and tap the shaft and cam into the housing, allowing the ball and spring to drop out of the detent bore.

26. Remove "O" ring seal from the reverse shift lever shaft.

27. Remove the reverse idler shaft by driving the retaining pin inward until it bottoms. Then, pull the shaft from the extension housing by tapping it with a soft hammer.

28. Reassemble by reversing above procedure.

4 SPEED LINKAGE, ADJUST

1. Place selector lever in neutral, then raise car on a hoist.

2. Try to insert a 1/4" drill, or rod, into the lever alignment holes in the shifter levers.

3. If the rod will not enter all of the way, check for poor adjustment or bent rods.

4. Repair or replace any damaged parts.

5. Reset linkage by loosening the three rod-retaining lock nuts and position the three transmission shift levers in neutral.

6. Move the linkage levers until the 1/4" gauge rod, or drill, will enter the alignment holes. (All of the levers must be in neutral.)

7. Retighten the rod-retaining lock nuts and remove the gauge pin from the lever alignment holes.

8. Lower the car and check for correct shifting operation of the transmission.

BEGINNING 1963—3 SPEED FULLY SYNCHRONIZED

Service procedure on the 3 Speed, fully synchronized, standard Transmission is almost identical with former 3-speed types. Separate disassembly and assembly instructions should not be necessary.

AUTOMATIC TRANSMISSION

QUICK SERVICE INFORMATION

When automatic transmission trouble is reported, a road test and careful diagnosis is in order. "Transmission Remove and Replace" and "Linkage Adjustments" are covered here in the following paragraphs. For "Test Procedures", "Transmission Overhaul" and other detailed information, see "Unit Repair Section," "Transmission Group" of this manual.

NEUTRAL SAFETY SWITCH ADJUSTMENT

Loosen the switch to steering column attaching screws and position the switch so that the starter circuit is closed when the hand lever is at Neutral. Retighten screws.

MANUAL LINKAGE ADJUSTMENT

Unpin the clevis of the manual shift rod (which runs back to the

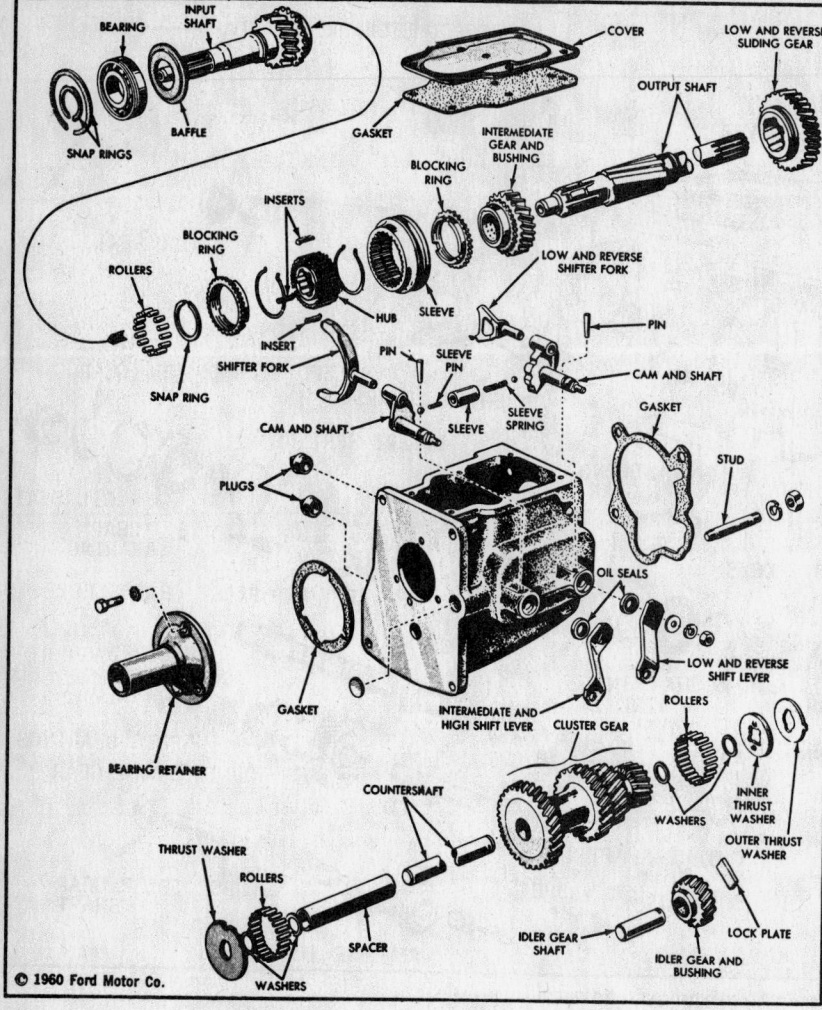

© 1960 Ford Motor Co.

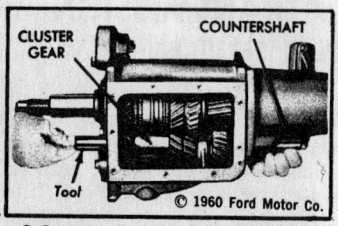

3-Speed Countershaft Removal

Overdrive Housing Removal

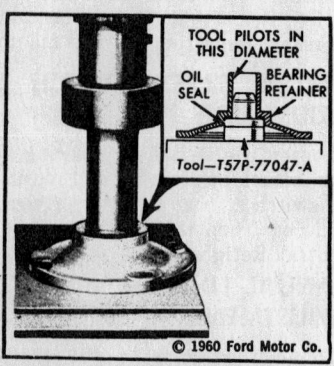

Input Shaft Seal Installation

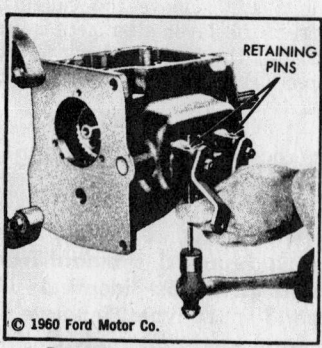

Retaining Pin Removal

transmission) from the selector arm at the bottom of the steering column. Fig. 3.

Set the hand lever so that the pointer is at Drive and against the stop in the dial housing.

Push the manual shift rod all the way back and check that it is centered in the detent for the Low position. Pull the manual shift rod forward to center on the next detent notch which is that for Drive.

Adjust the clevis so that it could be pinned to the selector arm.

Lengthen the manual shift rod by two complete turns of the clevis and pin it to the selector arm. Be sure to tighten the clevis lock nut.

Check the position of the hand lever at the other points on the dial especially that the parking lock engages properly.

THROTTLE LINKAGE ADJUSTMENT

Adjust the engine idle speed to approximately 450 RPM with transmission in Drive and engine at operating temperature. Turn the engine off.

Disconnect the transmission throttle valve control rod from the cross rod at the clevis on the left rear corner of the engine.

On all models, pull the control rod, gently, as far forward as it will come and adjust the clevis so that it could be pinned back onto the cross rod. (The pin should slide in freely.) Do not repin at this point.

Now lengthen the rod by turning the clevis counterclockwise between 2½ and 3 complete turns and repin the rod.

On all models if there is slippage after the above adjustment, lengthen the throttle control rod to a total of not over 4 turns.

Should the transmission still show signs of slippage the trouble could be due to a bent rod or inaccurately adjusted accelerator to carburetor linkage or malfunctioning of the valve unit in the transmission.

If the transmission fails to kick down adjust the accelerator pedal height according to the table below.

The measurement of height is made from the top side of the tip of the pedal to the metal floor pan.

Accelerator Pedal Height

	Thru '55	1956	'57-'58
6 cyl. Pass. Car	4 9/16	4 9/16	3⅛
V8 Pass. Car	3 11/16	3⅝	3⅛
Thunderbird	4¼	4¼	4⅞
Trucks ex. Parcel Del.	2⅝		2¾

Parcel Delivery

Pedals should just touch detent

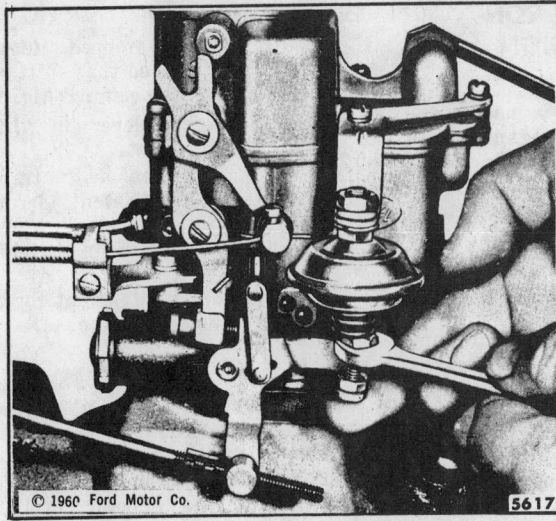

Fig. 1—Turn dash pot adjusting screw to bottom of its travel

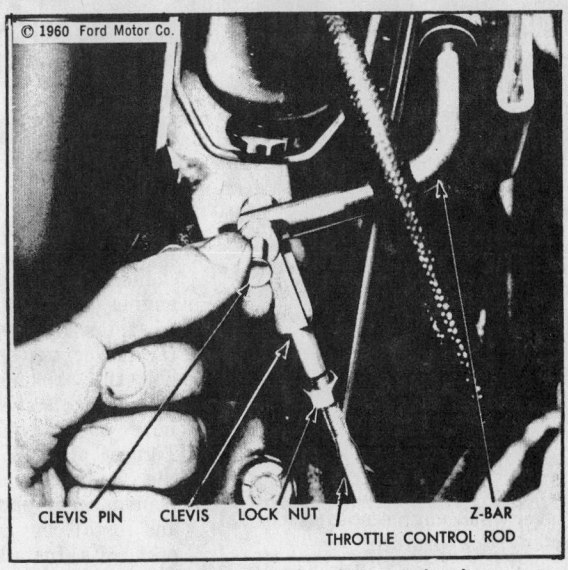

CLEVIS PIN CLEVIS LOCK NUT Z-BAR
THROTTLE CONTROL ROD

Fig. 3—Adjusting throttle valve control rod

stem when valve in carburetor hits wide open stop.

Make the adjustment at the accelerator assembly to carburetor control connecting link.

If a road test demonstrates that shifts are rough, the transmission throttle valve control rod should be shortened by one-half turn of the clevis.

In other words, tighten to come in quicker; loosen to delay shift. Total travel 4 turns either way.

It is well to note in making these adjustments that the thread on the carburetor throttle rod is finer than that on the transmission throttle rod so that small adjustments can be made more easily at the carburetor than they can at the transmission. The adjustments are rather sensitive so that a few turns of the carburetor throttle rod swivel are all that should be needed.

REMOVAL OF TRANSMISSION FROM THE CAR

On most models the transmission can be removed without removing the converter. However, on Thunderbird models the transmission and the converter cannot be removed with the engine in the car. On Thunderbird models the engine must be removed first or the engine, converter and transmission can be removed as an assembly.

On Sunliner Models, due to the frame, the transmission will not clear the converter and the two must be removed as a unit.

Thunderbird Only: Removal

If the converter and transmission have been removed with the engine,

they can be detached from the engine by removing the converter-to-flywheel bolts and then removing the four converter housing-to-engine bolts.

If the engine was removed separately, remove the two bolts at the rear extension. Disconnect the speedometer cable at the transmission. Disconnect the manual shift linkage at the transmission. Move the assembly forward and remove the drive shaft. Then remove the converter and the transmission from the car.

Thunderbird Only—Installation

The converter and transmission assembly must be installed in the car before the engine or the assembly can be installed on the engine first. To attach the converter and transmission to the engine before assembly into car; align the converter pilot to the hole in the crankshaft, and the con-

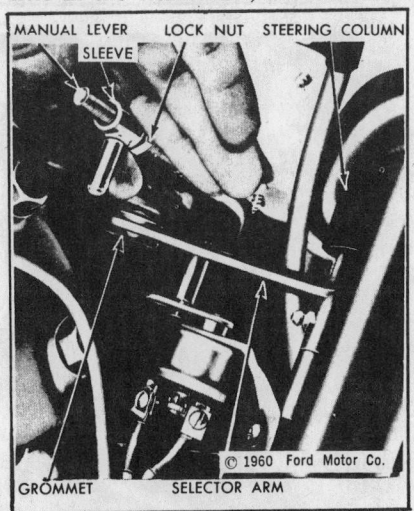

MANUAL LEVER LOCK NUT STEERING COLUMN
SLEEVE

© 1960 Ford Motor Co.

GROMMET SELECTOR ARM

Fig. 2—Adjusting manual control valve linkage

verter housing to the dowel pins. Be sure that the hole in the crankshaft is clean and apply a light coating of Lubricate to the converter pilot. Too much grease in the pilot bore will force the converter rearward and score the transmission front oil pump. Install the four converter housing-to-engine bolts and tighten to 40-45 ft. lbs. Align the marks on the flywheel and the converter cover and tighten the converter-to-flywheel bolts to 25-28 ft. lbs.

All Models Except Thunderbird

The engine cannot be removed with the transmission attached to it.

The transmission can be removed with the converter or separately on all cars except Sunliners. On Sunliners, the transmission input shaft will not clear the converter. To remove the transmission alone, drain the transmission oil pan. Disconnect the drive shaft at the differential and remove the drive shaft. Disconnect the oil cooler lines at the transmission. Arrange a support under the engine. Disconnect the speedometer cable and the control linkage at the transmission. Remove the two bolts holding the rear extension to the rear support. Position a cradle under the transmission and raise it slightly. Unbolt and remove the rear crossmember. Remove four transmission case-to-converter housing bolts. Move the transmission straight back to disengage it from the converter and then lower it to the floor. Be careful to support the transmission so that its weight does not fall on the oil pan. Damage to the oil pan may bend it into contact with the valve block which can distort the lower valve body cover and cause the 1-2 shift valve to stick.

Installation of Transmission, Except Thunderbird

Use guide pins in the two top holes in the converter housing. Align the splines of the shaft and turbine and the lugs of the converter with the slots in the front oil pump drive gear. Slide the transmission into place against the converter housing and install the attaching bolts. Tighten the bolts to 40-45 ft. lbs. Reinstall the rear crossmembers and refasten the rear extension to the support. Slide the front universal joint yoke onto the output shaft and refasten the drive shaft to the differential. Refasten the oil cooler lines, the control linkages and speedometer cable. Fill the transmission with fluid and check the level when engine reaches normal operating temperature.

CONVERTER AND TRANSMISSION ASSEMBLY REMOVAL

This procedure for converter-transmission assembly removal is applicable to all models except Thunderbirds.

Remove the two upper converter housing-to-engine bolts. Drain the transmission oil pan. Remove the plate at the lower front of the converter housing and remove the two converter drain plugs. Drain the converter. Disconnect the drive shaft at the rear axle and remove the shaft. Remove the flywheel to converter bolts. Wedge the converter in place in the housing. Disconnect the battery ground strap. Disconnect the starter cable at the starter and the transmission-to-body ground cable at the transmission. Remove the starter. Disconnect the oil cooler lines at the transmission. Disconnect the control linkages and the speedometer cable at the transmission.

Arrange a support for the engine. Remove the bolts holding the rear extension to the rear support. Support the transmission on the transmission cradle-jack. Unbolt and remove the rear crossmember. On V8 models, loosen and drop the exhaust system to allow the converter to clear the muffler inlet pipe. Tilt the rear of the converter-transmission assembly upward and remove the six bolts holding the flywheel to the crankshaft and remove the flywheel. This is done on some models to provide clearance.

Lower the converter-transmission assembly to the floor. Remove the wedge holding the converter in the housing and pull the converter out of the housing. Do not rock it, as to do so is hard on the seals.

INSTALLATION OF CONVERTER-TRANSMISSION ASSEMBLY

Wedge the converter in place in the housing. Using the transmission cradle-jack raise the transmission assembly into place. Install the flywheel onto the crankshaft. Tighten the bolts to 75-85 ft. lbs.

Install the converter housing-to-engine lower bolts and tighten to 40-45 ft. lbs. Remove the retainer securing the converter in the housing and bolt the converter to the flywheel. Be sure to have washers under the nuts to prevent converter float. Tighten all to 25-28 ft. lbs. Reinstall the rear crossmember. Lower the transmission onto the rear support and install the two extension-to-support bolts. Install the converter drain plugs and access plates. Reconnect the cooler lines. Install the drive shaft onto the transmission output shaft and refasten the shaft at the rear axle. Reconnect the control linkages and speedometer cable. Install the starter and connect: the transmission-to-frame ground; the starter cable; and the battery ground. Install the two upper converter housing to engine bolts and tighten to 40-45 ft. lbs.

Connect and adjust the manual and throttle controls.

Put 5 quarts of Type A fluid into the transmission and allow to idle for 2 minutes. Now add 5 more quarts and let idle until it reaches its normal operating temperature. Do not race the engine.

CRUIS-O-MATIC

BEGINNING 1959

MANUAL LINKAGE ADJUSTMENT

Except Thunderbird

1. With engine stopped, loosen clamp at shift lever so that shift rod is free to slide in the clamp, (Fig. 1).
2. Place selector lever in "D1" position.
3. Shift manual lever at the transmission into the "D1" detent, (second from rear).
4. Tighten the clamp on the shift rod.
5. Check pointer alignment for all selector lever detent positions.

Thunderbird

1. With engine stopped, disconnect the upper end of the manual shift rod and clevis from the shift selector lever.
2. Position the selector lever so that the pointer is down against the steering column stop in the "D1" position.
3. Shift the manual lever on the transmission to the "D1" detent position, (second from the bottom).
4. Rotate the clevis on the manual shift rod until it can be easily installed on the selector lever pin. Then, lengthen the rod at the clevis, three turns.
5. Lock the clevis, and connect the rod and clevis to the selector lever.
6. Check the pointer alignment for all positions of the selector lever.

THROTTLE LINKAGE ADJUSTMENT

All Models

1. With selector in "N" position and parking brake set securely, start the engine.
2. Hook up a tachometer and run the engine at fast idle until normal operating temperature has been reached. Slow down to normal idle.
3. Adjust idle speed to 450-475

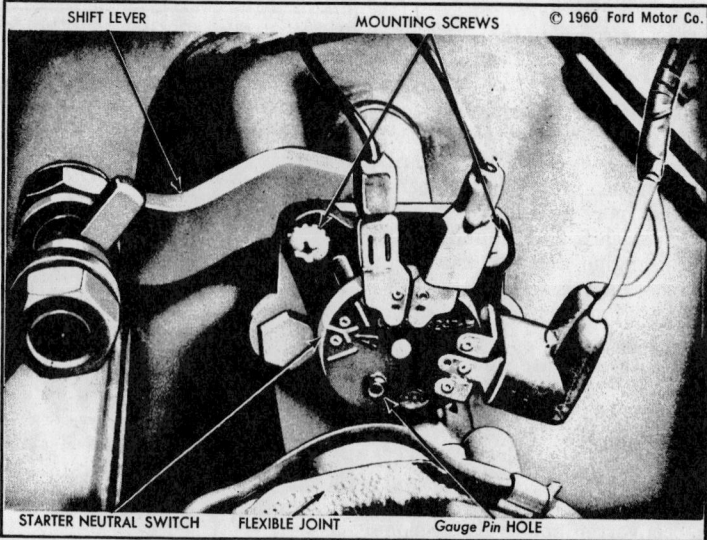

Fig. 1—Manual Linkage and Starter Neutral Switch

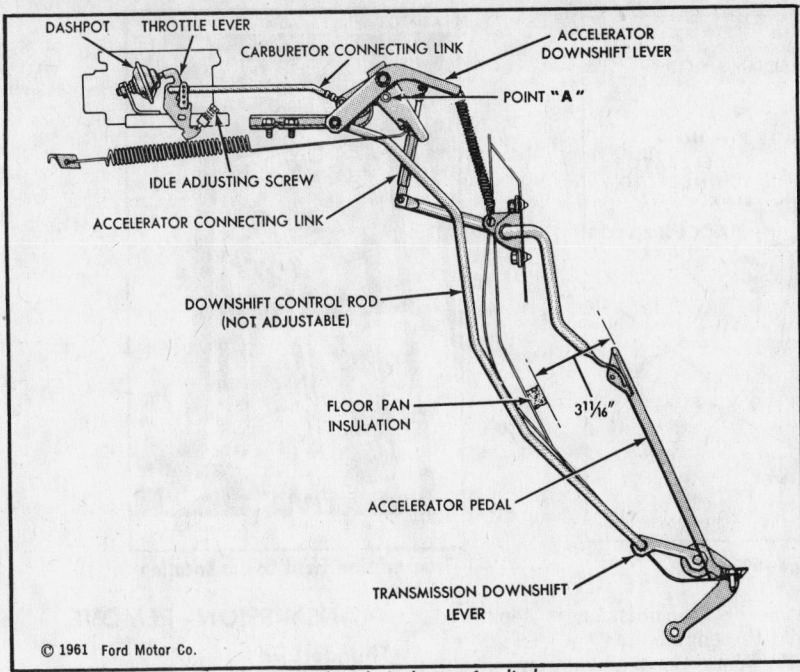

Fig. 2—Throttle Linkage—6 cylinder

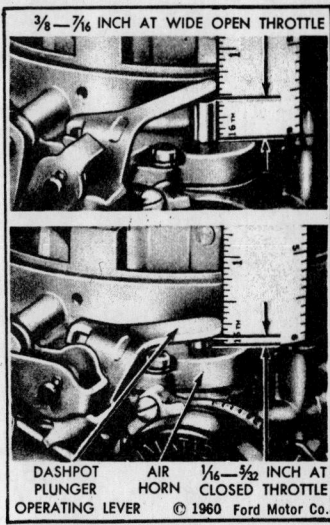

Fig. 4—Dashpot Adjustment on Carter Carburetor

R.P.M. With the transmission selector in "D1" or "D2". Make sure the throttle lever is against the adjusting screw and not hung up by the fast idle or the dashpot plunger.

4. After idle speed has been properly set, stop the engine and adjust dashpot clearance. On cars with external type dashpot (Fig. 2 & 3) bottom the dashpot plunger against it's spring and then adjust the clearance between the bottomed plunger and the throttle lever to .060-.090 inch.

On cars with internal type dashpot (Carter carburetor), the adjustment is checked at closed-throttle and wide-open throttle positions (Fig. 4). With the primary throttle plates closed, (hot idle position), there should be 1/16" to 5/32" clearance between the dashpot plunger operating lever and the top surface of the air horn, (Fig. 4).

With the primary throttle plates wide open, there should be a clearance of 3/8" to 7/16" between the dashpot plunger operating lever and the top surface of the air horn.

5. Disconnect the throttle control rod clevis from the accelerator assembly.

6. Disconnect the carburetor connecting link from the accelerator assembly.

7. Insert a gauge pin, (1/4" drill) through the gauging holes, (Fig. 3).

8. With forward pressure on the carburetor connecting link, adjust it's length so that the trunion can be freely fitted into the accelerator assembly lever. Now rotate the trunion one full turn counterclockwise, remove the gauge pin and connect the link to the accelerator assembly lever.

9. Recheck the alignment of the gauge pin holes after snapping the throttle open and having it return to idle position by its own spring tension. If necessary, readjust the carburetor connecting link.

10. Remove the gauge pin and adjust the throttle control rod. Pull upward on the rod to hold the transmission lever against its internal stop.

11. Adjust the clevis until the clevis pin freely fits the accelerator assembly lever. Further lengthen the throttle rod three turns and connect the throttle control rod to the accelerator assembly lever.

12. Adjust the accelerator connecting link to obtain a pedal height of 3½", (4½" on T. Bird). Measure from the top corner of the pedal to the floor.

TRANSMISSION—REMOVE

All, Except Thunderbird

1. Raise the car and remove the cover from the bottom of the converter housing.

2. Drain the converter through both (180° apart), drain plugs.

3. Drain transmission oil pan.

4. Disconnect propeller shaft at rear universal joint. Slide propeller shaft and front "U" joint to the rear and out of the transmission extension housing. Install extension housing seal replaced in extension housing seal.

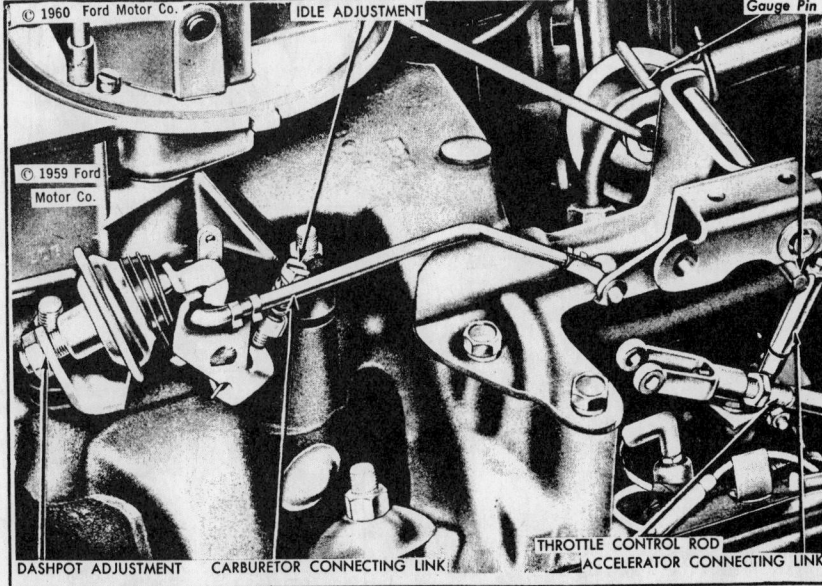

Fig. 3—Throttle Linkage—8 cylinder

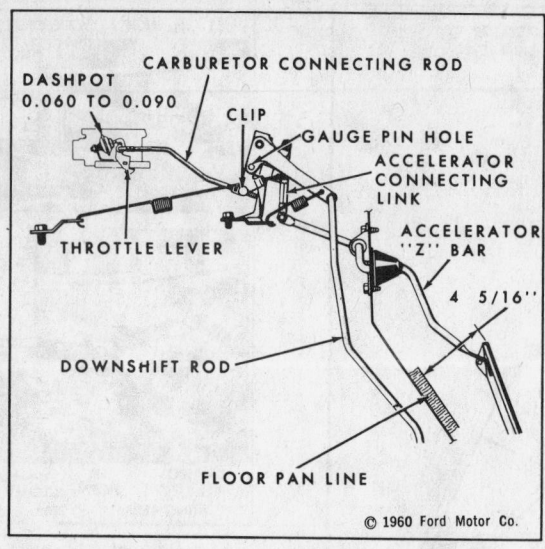

Automatic Transmission Linkage—8 Cylinder

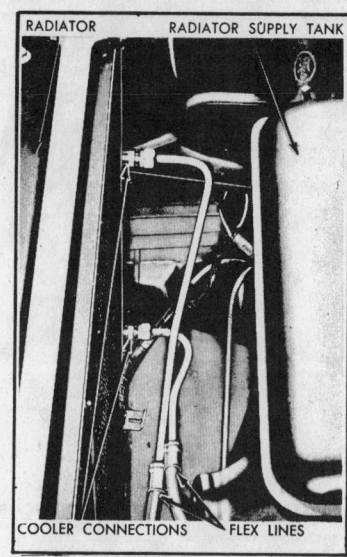

Transmission Fluid Cooler Location

5. Disconnect the manual and throttle linkage at transmission.

6. Disconnect speedometer cable at extension housing.

7. Disconnect oil cooler lines at the transmission. Loosen line clamp at engine block, and remove the lines.

8. Disconnect oil filler tube at transmission.

9. Disconnect cable and remove the starter.

10. Disconnect parking brake cable at equalizer.

11. Remove two engine rear support bolts from extension housing, then remove the support clamp.

12. Place a transmission jack under the transmission and raise the unit just enough to relieve the weight from the crossmember. Support the rear of the engine in this position with an engine support bar or stand.

13. Remove the crossmember.

14. Remove the three converter-to-flywheel bolts.

15. Remove converter housing to engine block bolts.

16. Secure the converter to the transmission so it will not fall out

when the transmission is separated from the engine.

17. Work the transmission off the engine block dowels and toward the rear until the converter pilot clears the crankshaft.

18. Lower the transmission and converter assembly and remove it from the car.

TO INSTALL, REVERSE ABOVE PROCEDURE.

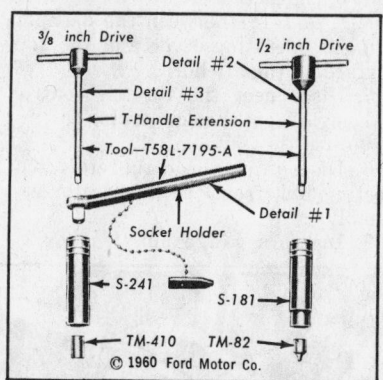

Front and Rear Band Adjusting Tool

TRANSMISSION—REMOVE

Thunderbird

This is the cruise-o-matic transmission but due to car design and exhaust circuit interference, replacement differs somewhat from other car models.

1. Remove the upper four converter housing to engine block bolts.

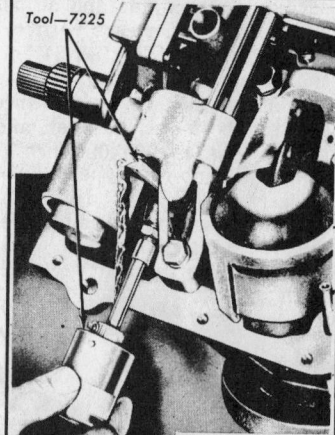

Front Band Adjustment

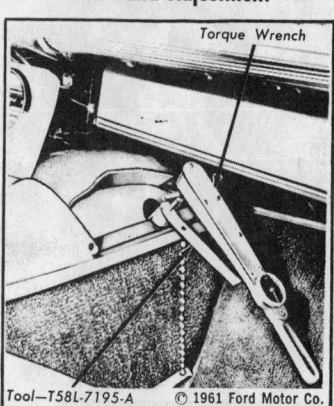

Rear Band Adjustment

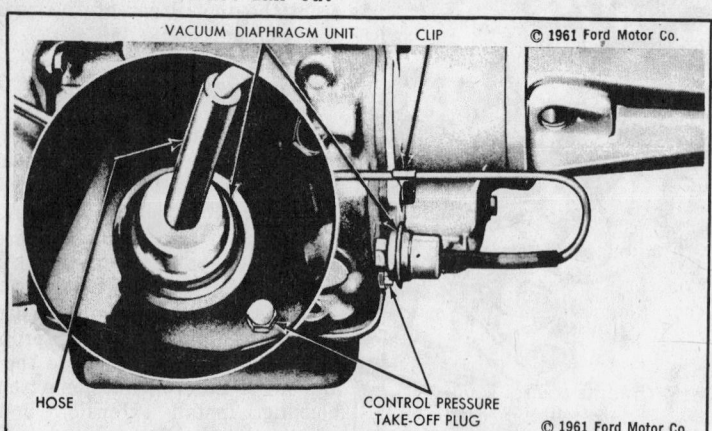

Vacuum Diaphragm and Control Pressure Connecting Point

Remove the upper (2) starter mounting bolts.

2. Raise the car and drain the transmission pan.

3. Disconnect the muffler front inlet pipes at both engine exhaust manifolds. Separate the muffler front inlet pipe assembly from the rear inlet pipes.

4. Remove the starter.

5. Remove the converter housing lower cover. Drain the converter.

6. Remove the converter to flywheel stud nuts, (4).

7. Disconnect drive shaft and the speedometer cable.

8. Disconnect throttle and manual linkage at the transmission.

9. Disconnect oil cooler lines.

10. Remove parking brake equalizer lever from it's bracket. Remove parking brake cable housing from its retainer.

11. Remove two bracket-to-engine rear support member bolts.

12. On each bracket, remove the upper (2) bracket-to-underbody bolt nuts. These bolts are pressed into a plate, (Fig. 5). Push the bolts out of the brackets.

13. Raise the transmission with a jack, so that the engine rear support member is clear of the brackets.

14. On each bracket, remove the lower (2) bracket-to-underbody bolt nuts. Remove the brackets. With the brackets removed from the underbody, the transmission can be removed with the support member still attached to the extension housing.

15. Lower the transmission and engine, until the engine rests on the tubular crossmember.

16. Remove the two remaining converter housing-to-engine block bolts.

17. Move the converter housing back and away from the engine block and see that the converter follows the transmission away from the flywheel. Secure the converter to the converter housing to prevent dropping it during handling.

18. Lower the transmission and remove it from under the car.

19. Remove the converter.

20. Remove the converter housing from the transmission case.

21. Remove the vent tube.

22. Remove engine rear support from the transmission extension housing.

TO INSTALL, REVERSE ABOVE PROCEDURE.

2 SPEED FORDOMATIC

1959-63

MANUAL LINKAGE ADJUSTMENT

"223 Six and V8 Engines"

1. With engine stopped, loosen clamp at shift lever so that shift rod is free to slide in the clamp, (Fig. 1).

2. Place selector so the pointer lines up in the "D" position.

3. Shift manual lever at the transmission into the "D" detent position, (second from the rear).

4. Tighten the clamp on the shift rod.

5. Check pointer alignment for all selector lever detent positions.

THROTTLE LINKAGE ADJUSTMENT

"223 Six Cylinder Engine"

1. With engine stopped and carburetor at hot idle position, remove the lock from the clevis pin on the upper end of the throttle control rod. Loosen clevis olck nut, (Fig. 2).

2. Remove clevis and pull upward, to hold the throttle lever against the stop inside the transmission.

3. Turn the throttle rod clevis until the clevis pin enters the hole in the lever. Now lengthen the throttle rod 3½ turns.

4. Connect the throttle control rod to the accelerator shaft and secure it.

5. Adjust accelerator height by turning the threaded trunion on the accelerator connecting link until the top of the pedal is 3½ inches from the floor mat.

V8 Engines

1. With engine stopped, disconnect the throttle control rod from the accelerator, at the top, (Fig. 3).

2. Insert a ¼ inch drill, or rod, through the gauge holes, (Fig. 3).

3. Disconnect the carburetor connecting link from the accelerator assembly.

4. Lift the carburetor connecting link to its normal position and hold forward pressure on it so the throttle lever is held against the idle adjusting screw.

5. Adjust it's length to permit the trunion to fit freely into the accelerator assembly lever. Now lengthen the link one full turn. Remove the gauge pin, (¼ inch drill or rod) and connect the link to the accelerator assembly lever.

6. Recheck alignment of the gauge pin holes. Snap the throttle open and allow the retracting spring to return the linkage to normal. Now, the pin must enter freely. If necessary, readjust the carburetor connecting link for a free pin fit.

7. Remove the pin and adjust the throttle control rod. Pull upward on the rod to hold the transmission lever against its stop in the transmission.

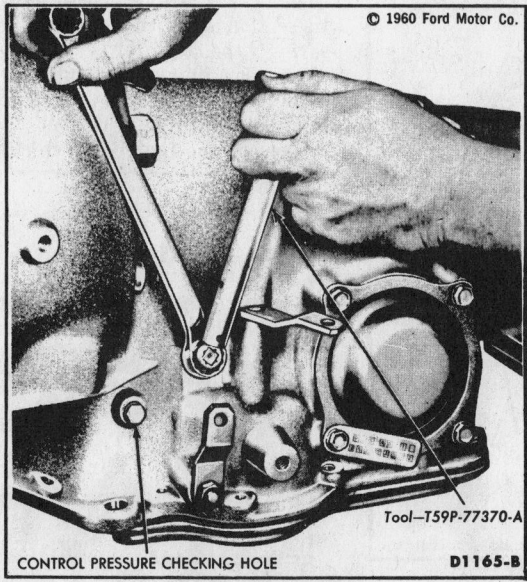

Low Band Adjustment

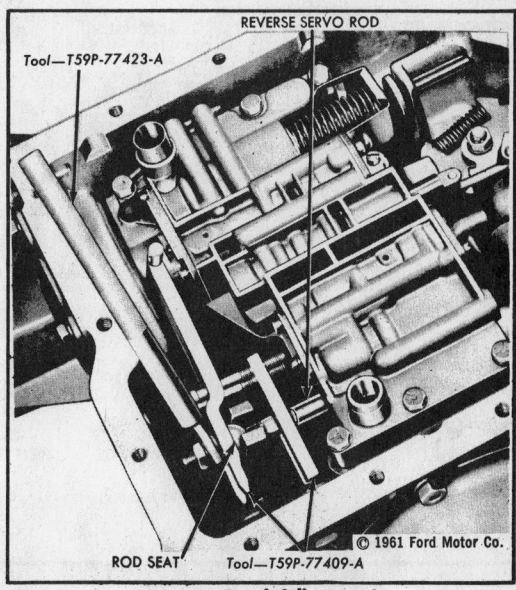

Reverse Band Adjustment

8. Turn the clevis until the clevis pin freely fits the accelerator assembly lever. Now lengthen the throttle control rod by turning the clevis 3 turns.

9. Connect the throttle control rod to the accelerator assembly lever.

10. Adjust the accelerator connecting link to obtain a pedal height of 3½ inches from the top of the pedal to the floor mat.

BEGINNING 1961 VACUUM CONTROLS

During 1961, two-speed transmission design has gone to vacuum controls instead of the manually controlled throttle valve previously used. The following adjustments are required.

LINKAGE ADJUSTMENT

"223" Six Cylinder Engine

1. With engine stopped, check accelerator pedal height (measuring from top edge of pedal to floor mat). If height is not 3¾", turn the threaded trunion on the accelerator connecting link until the correct height is reached.

2. Disconnect the downshift control rod from the bellcrank.

3. Block the accelerator pedal to the floor.

4. Push the downshift control rod down to the limit of its travel. Then adjust the sleeve on the rod until the end of the rod enters the bellcrank freely. Connect the linkage after adjustment is complete, then tighten the locknut.

V-8 Engines

1. Apply parking brakes, and place the selector in "N."

2. Run engine at idle speed until normal operating temperature has been reached.

3. Hook up a tachometer and check idle speed. The R.P.M. should be under 500 with the fast idle cam in slow (hot) position.

4. With Throttle in hot-idle position, bottom the dashpot plunger and measure the clearance between the plunger and the throttle shaft lever. This clearance should be .060"-.090".

5. Engine stopped, disconnect the carburetor connecting link from the accelerator assembly.

6. Insert a ¼" drill rod through the gauging holes. Hold the carburetor connecting link forward, and adjust the sleeve until the link assembly fits freely in the accelerator assembly. Then rotate the sleeve counterclockwise one full turn. Remove the gauge pin.

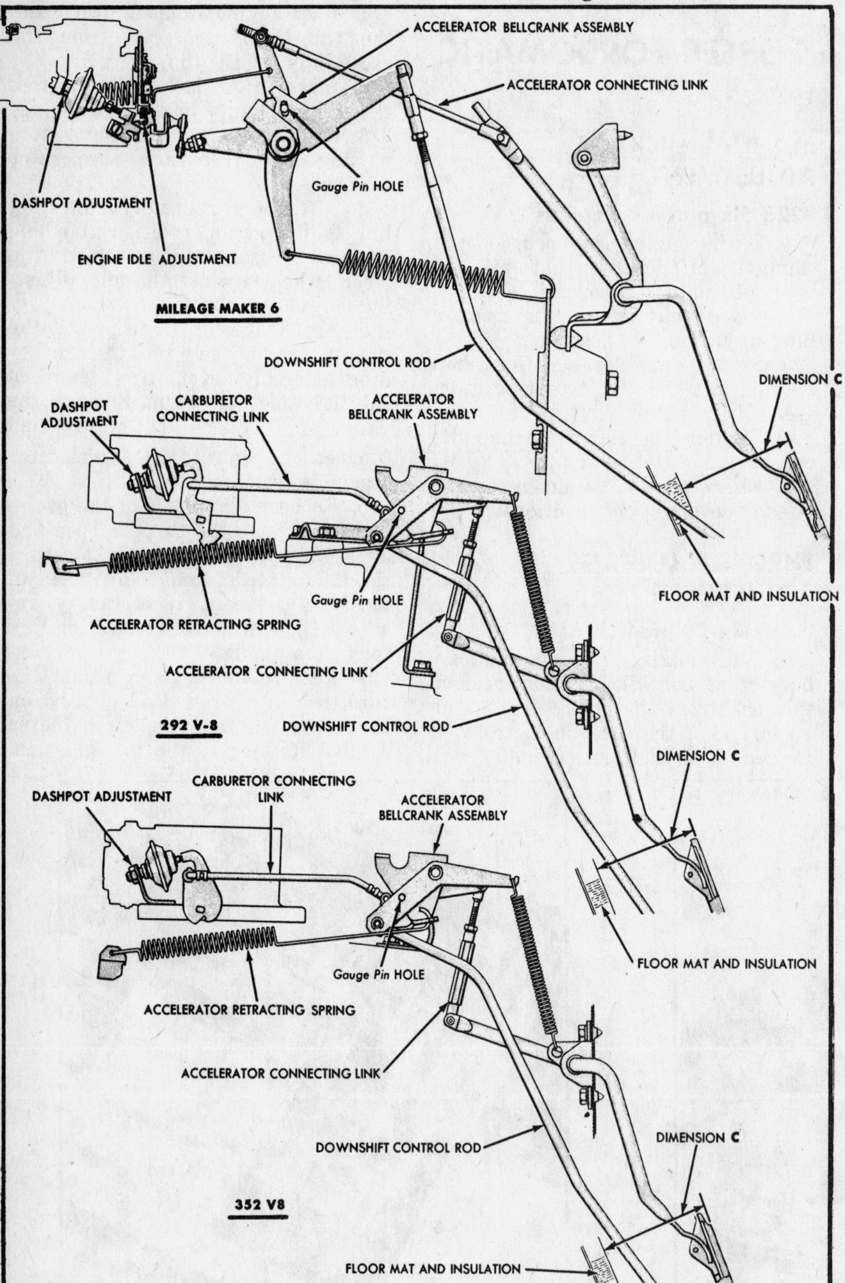

UNIVERSAL JOINTS AND PROPELLER SHAFT

REAR JOINT REMOVAL

The universal joints on all Fords in this section are of the cross and needle bearing type.

The rear universal joint has two pillow blocks which are bolted to the pinion shaft flange.

Take out the four bolts which hold

Figure (Throttle Linkage Diagram)

ACCELERATOR BELLCRANK ASSEMBLY

ACCELERATOR CONNECTING LINK

DASHPOT ADJUSTMENT

Gauge Pin HOLE

ENGINE IDLE ADJUSTMENT

MILEAGE MAKER 6

DOWNSHIFT CONTROL ROD

DIMENSION C

DASHPOT ADJUSTMENT

CARBURETOR CONNECTING LINK

ACCELERATOR BELLCRANK ASSEMBLY

Gauge Pin HOLE

ACCELERATOR RETRACTING SPRING

FLOOR MAT AND INSULATION

ACCELERATOR CONNECTING LINK

292 V-8

DOWNSHIFT CONTROL ROD

DIMENSION C

DASHPOT ADJUSTMENT

CARBURETOR CONNECTING LINK

ACCELERATOR BELLCRANK ASSEMBLY

Gauge Pin HOLE

FLOOR MAT AND INSULATION

ACCELERATOR RETRACTING SPRING

ACCELERATOR CONNECTING LINK

DOWNSHIFT CONTROL ROD

DIMENSION C

352 V8

FLOOR MAT AND INSULATION

© 1961 Ford Motor Co.

Ford Car Fordomatic Throttle Linkage

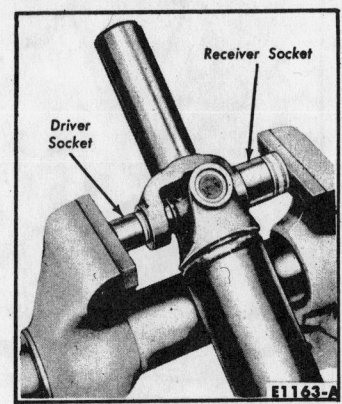

Receiver Socket

Driver Socket

E1163-A

U-Joint Removal

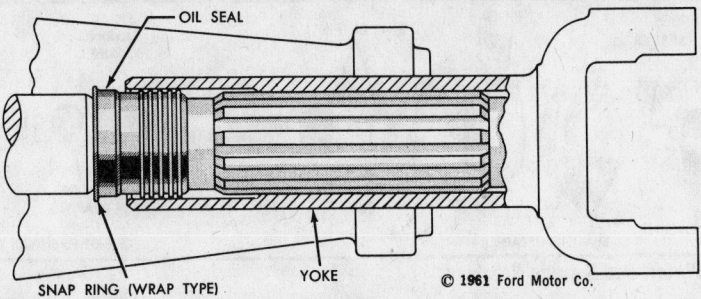

OIL SEAL

SNAP RING (WRAP TYPE)   YOKE   © 1961 Ford Motor Co.

Output Shaft Spline Seal

the bearing blocks to the pinion shaft and gently tap off the bearing blocks.

Lower the back end of the drive shaft and the front end can be slid out of the back of the transmission together with the transmission yoke portion of the front universal joint.

Carry the assembly—the front universal joint complete, the driveshaft and the rear universal joint, cross over to the bench and remove the cross from the rear universal joint by taking out the lock rings from the inner side of the bearings. Using a large punch or an arbor press, drive one of the bearings in toward the center, which will force the opposite bearings.

When it is pressed out far enough to grip it with a pair of pliers, grip it and pull it out of the driveshaft yoke.

Now drive the cross in the opposite direction until the opposite bearing has been driven far enough out for a purchase with a pair of pliers.

When both bearings have been taken out, the cross can be lifted from between the two yokes.

FRONT UNIVERSAL JOINT REMOVAL

Follow the procedure given above for the rear universal joint but leave the rear universal joint cross in place on the driveshaft if it is not to be removed.

Remove the lock rings from the inner side of two opposite bearings and press on the outer side of one of the bearings, forcing the cross over, which will force the bearing on the opposite side out of its yoke.

Remove the bearing which was forced out of the yoke and then press the cross in the opposite direction to press the other bearing out.

Repeat this procedure on the third and fourth bearing.

When installing the new bearings in the universal joint yoke, it is possible to put them in with a driver of some type, but it is recommended that this work be done in an arbor press since a heavy jolt on the needle bearings can very easily misalign them, which will greatly shorten their life.

REAR AXLE

TROUBLE SHOOTING AND ADJUSTMENT

General instructions covering the troubles of the rear axle and how to repair and adjust it, together with information on installation of rear axle bearings and grease seals and data on the equa-lock differential are given in the Unit Repair section under the heading: Axles, Rear.

Capacities of the rear axle are given in the Capacities Tables of this section.

REAR SPRING REMOVAL

To remove rear springs disconnect the shock absorber at the spring clip plate and remove the U bolt nuts.

Take out the stud at the front hanger and the two bolts at the rear shackle.

The spring can then be lifted out from under the car.

Note: When installing a new spring the short end of the spring goes toward the front of the car.

The short end of the spring is the one having the shortest distance from the spring eye to the center bolt.

Spring clips should be tightened to 45-50 ft. lbs. torque.

REPLACEMENT OF REAR SHOCK ABSORBERS

Rear shock absorbers on all Fords are straddle mounted and are held to rubber bushings at both the top and bottom connections. Simply remove the nuts from the top and bottom of the shock absorber and lift the shock absorber off the car.

Service on shock absorbers after they have been removed from the car is a highly specialized job requiring specialized equipment. There is no practical way for the average shop to

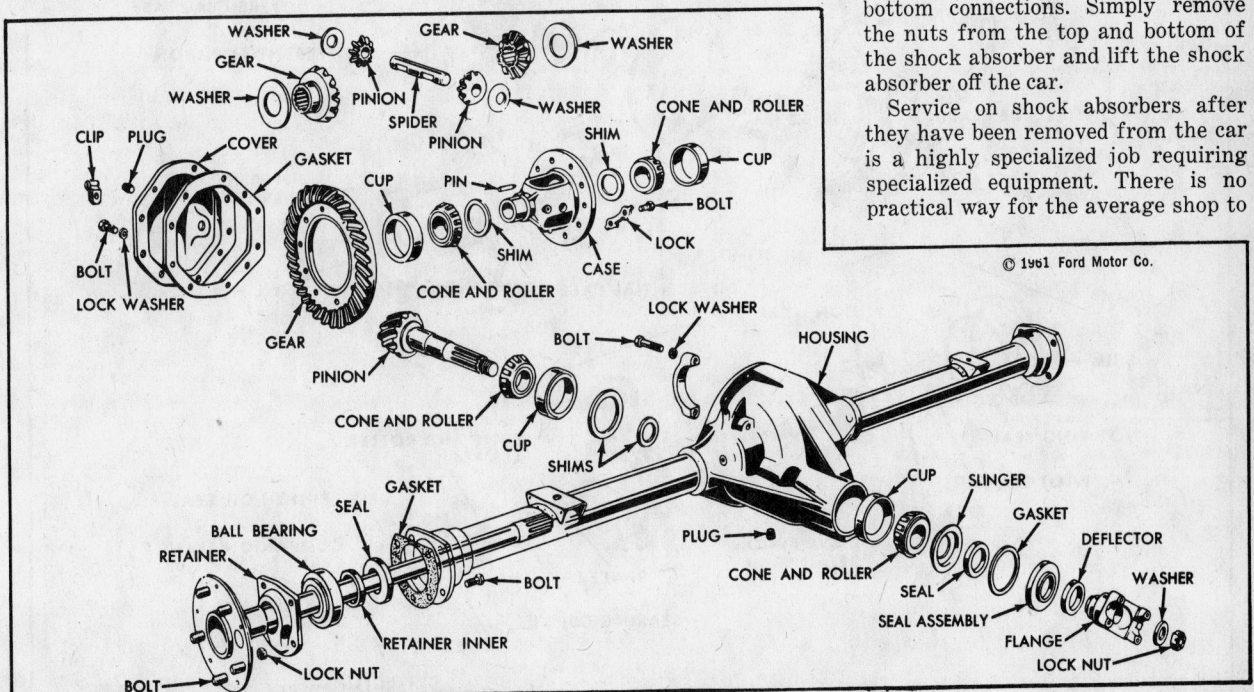

Integral housing rear axle. 1951-56 station wagon and 1955-56 T-bird

FORD and THUNDERBIRD

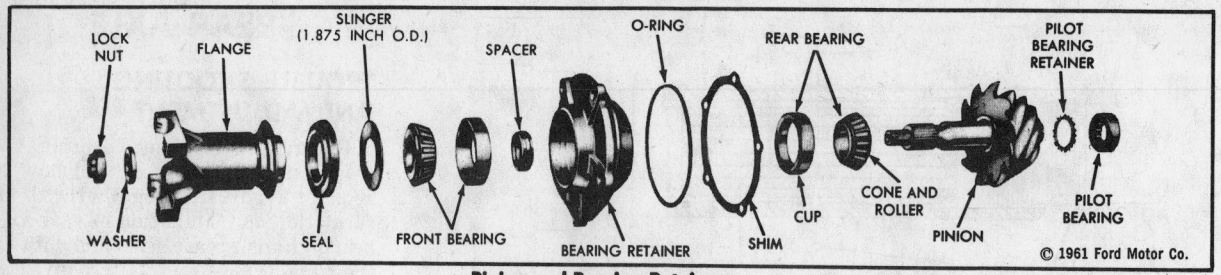

LOCK NUT — FLANGE — SLINGER (1.875 INCH O.D.) — SPACER — O-RING — REAR BEARING — PILOT BEARING RETAINER

WASHER — SEAL — FRONT BEARING — BEARING RETAINER — SHIM — CUP — CONE AND ROLLER — PINION — PILOT BEARING

© 1961 Ford Motor Co.

Pinion and Bearing Retainer

rebuild or service a shock absorber.

If tests show that the shock is weak or inefficient, it should be replaced with a new or rebuilt one.

RADIO R & R

REMOVE

To remove the receiver from a car equipped with a Select-Air Conditioner, remove the glove box liner, radio speaker, radio right mounting support, and remove the radio through the speaker opening.

Remove the receiver as follows:
1. Pull off radio control knobs and remove the nuts and washers holding the radio to the instru-

ment panel.
2. Disconnect antenna lead at the right side of the radio.
3. Disconnect the speaker lead and disconnect the pilot light wire at the harness.
4. Disconnect radio lead wire at the fuse panel and remove the wire from the retaining clips.

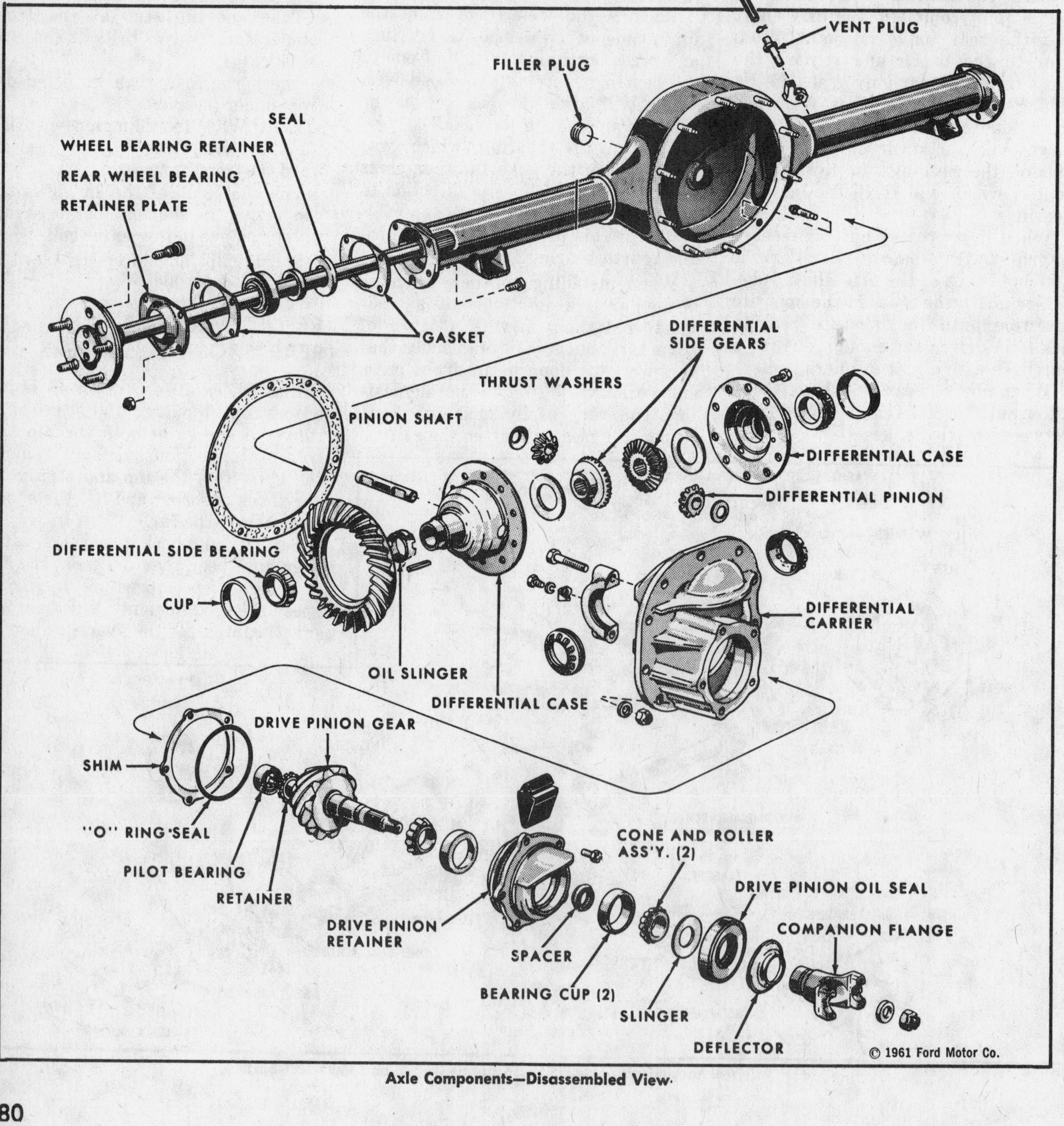

VENT PLUG

FILLER PLUG

SEAL

WHEEL BEARING RETAINER

REAR WHEEL BEARING

RETAINER PLATE

GASKET

DIFFERENTIAL SIDE GEARS

THRUST WASHERS

PINION SHAFT

DIFFERENTIAL CASE

DIFFERENTIAL PINION

DIFFERENTIAL SIDE BEARING

CUP

OIL SLINGER

DIFFERENTIAL CASE

DIFFERENTIAL CARRIER

SHIM

DRIVE PINION GEAR

"O" RING SEAL

PILOT BEARING

RETAINER

DRIVE PINION RETAINER

CONE AND ROLLER ASS'Y. (2)

DRIVE PINION OIL SEAL

COMPANION FLANGE

SPACER

BEARING CUP (2)

SLINGER

DEFLECTOR

© 1961 Ford Motor Co.

Axle Components—Disassembled View

380

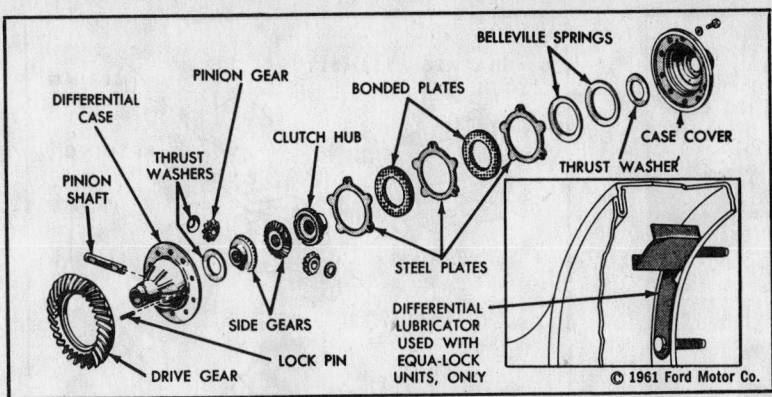

Equa-Lock Differential Assembly

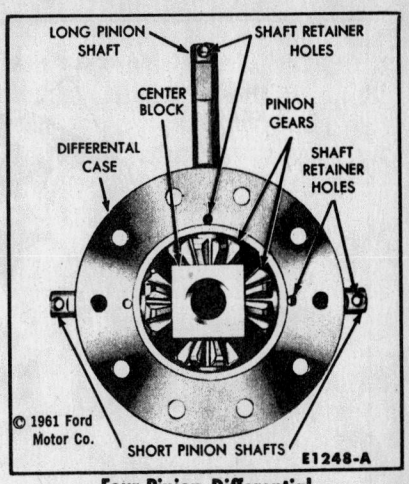

Four-Pinion Differential

5. Remove the radio back support bracket-to-radio retaining nut. Remove radio unit from the instrument panel.

INSTALL

1. Position the radio to the instrument panel, then install the washers and retaining nuts at the knob shafts.
2. Install the radio support bracket retaining nut. Torque all nuts to 25-30 in. lbs.
3. Conect the antenna lead.
4. Connect the speaker lead, then connect the pilot light wire at the harness.
5. Connect the lead wire at the fuse panel mounted on the headlight switch.
6. Install radio control knobs, then check radio performance.

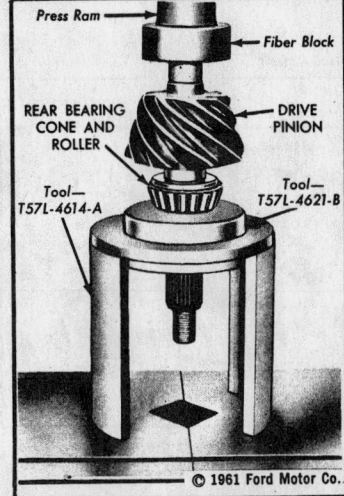

Pinion Bearing Cone Installation

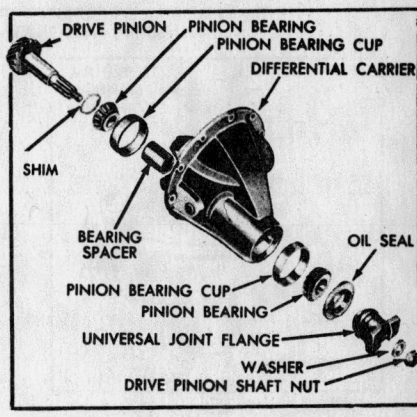

Pinion and carrier assembly 1953-56 passenger car

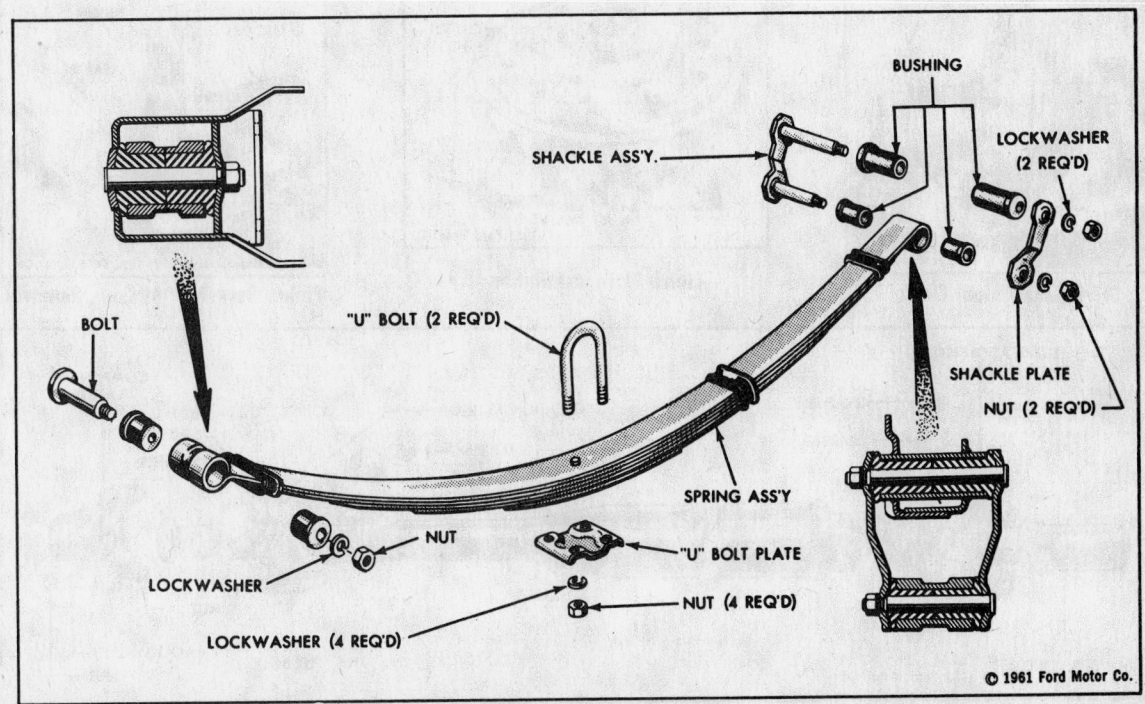

Rear Spring Assembly

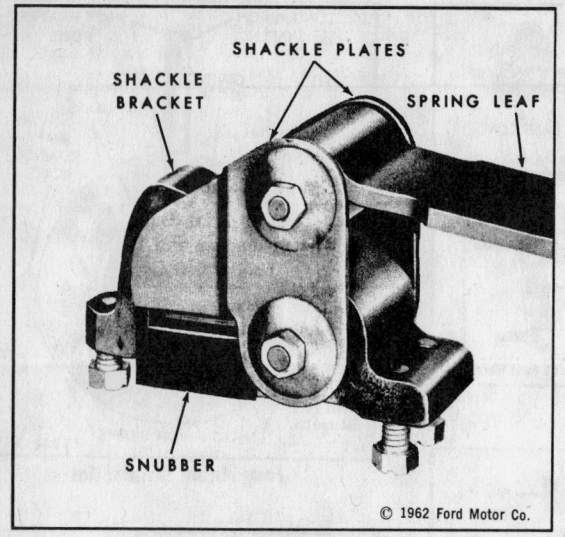

Rear Spring Front Shackle

Rear Spring Front Shackle Details

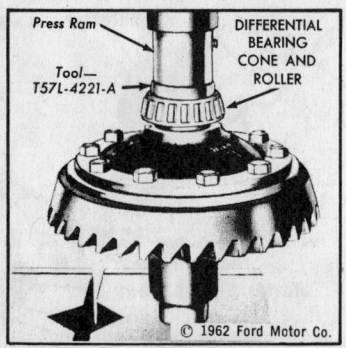

Differential Bearing Installation

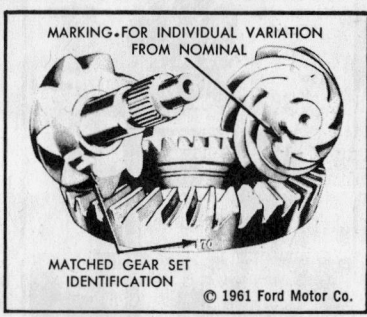

Pinion and Drive Gear Markings

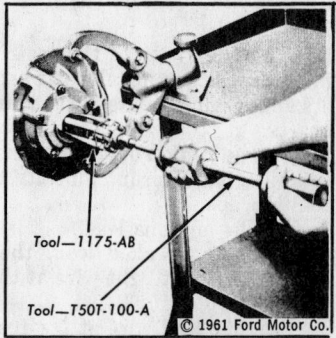

Pinion Seal Removal

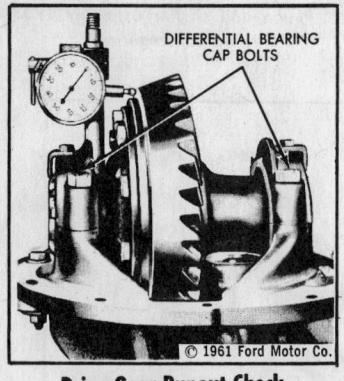

Drive Gear Runout Check

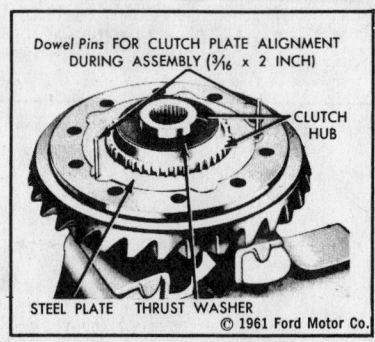

Clutch Plate Installation

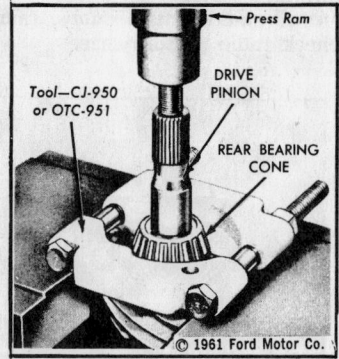

Pinion Rear Bearing Cone Removal

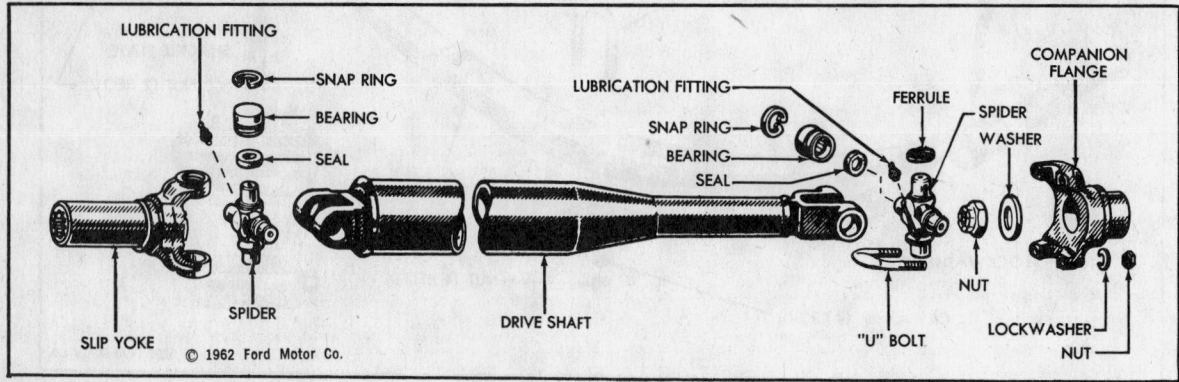

Drive Shaft and Universal Joint Assembly

AIR CONDITIONING

Service 1092

BRAKES, HYDRAULIC

Adjustments 393
Bleed brakes 941
Brake specifications 390
Parking brake, adjust 393
Parking brake cable 393
Master cylinder service 393
Master cylinder, R & R 393

BRAKES, POWER

Power unit overhaul 954
Trouble shooting 954

COOLING SYSTEM

Radiator core, R & R 394
Water pump, R & R 394

ELECTRICAL SYSTEM

Distributor, R & R 391
Distributor specifications 387
Fuses and circuit breakers 390
Gauges 1024
Generator and regulator
  specifications 387
Generator and regulators 391
Generator service 1026
Generator trouble
  shooting chart 1026
Horn button, R & R 401
Ignition firing order & timing .. 385
Ignition timing procedure 391
Ignition timing specifications .. 386
Ignition wires, replace 391
Starter, R & R 391
Starter specifications 387
Starter systems 1046
Windshield wipers 410

ENGINE ASSEMBLY

Cylinder head, R & R 397
Cylinder head tightening 390
Engine assembly, R & R 396
Engine firing order & timing .. 385
Engine marking code 385
Engine references 395
Exhaust manifold, R & R 394
Inlet manifold, R & R 394
Oil filter, R & R 399
Oil pan, R & R 398
Oil pressure specifications 388
Piston and rod, R & R 399
Piston specifications 389
Rear main bearing oil seal 400
Rocker arm lubrication 397

ENGINE ASSEMBLY—continued

Rocker arm, R & R 397
Specifications, general, engine 388
Timing chain and case 398
Trouble shooting charts 1012
Tune-up specifications 386
Valve adjusting sequence 397
Valve specifications 389
Valve springs 397
Valve system 397

ENGINE LUBRICATION

Multi-luber 392
Oil filter, R & R 399
Oil pan, R & R 398

EXHAUST SYSTEM

Manifolds, R & R 394

FUEL SYSTEM

Carburetors 972
Fuel gauge service 1024
Fuel pump pressure 386
Fuel pump, R & R 394
Fuel pump service 1020
Fuel system 394
Fuel tank, R & R 394

INSTRUMENTS

Instrument, R & R 392
Speedometer, R & R 392

RADIO, R & R

References 410

REAR AXLE AND SUSPENSION

Axle assembly, R & R 409
Axle shaft 918
Axle shaft oil seal 918
Pinion bearings 918
Ring gear & pinion 918
Springs, rear, R & R 409
Trailing arm, R & R 409
Trouble shooting 919

SPECIFICATIONS

Battery 387
Brake cylinder sizes 390
Capacities:
  Axle, rear 388
  Cooling system 388
  Crankcase 388
  Fuel tank 388
  Transmission, automatic .. 388
  Transmission, manual 388
Chassis, general 390

SPECIFICATIONS—continued

Distributor 387
Engine, general 388
Fuses and circuit breakers 390
Generator and regulators 387
Light bulbs 390
Main bearings 387
Model identification
  illustrations 384
Pistons 389
Quick reference specifications . 385
Rod bearings 387
Starters 387
Torque wrench 386
Tune-up 386
Valves 389
Wheel alignment 389

STEERING, MANUAL

Adjust gear housing 1052
Gear assembly, R & R 401
Horn button, R & R 401
Steering wheel, R & R 401

STEERING, POWER

Pump assembly 1058
Trouble shooting 1081
Unit overhaul 1058

SUSPENSION, FRONT

Alignment procedures 1082
Alignment specifications 389
Ball joints, R & R 1087
Camber, adjust 1082
Caster, adjust 1082
Intermediate steering arms ... 402
King pins and bushings 1087
Knuckle supports 1087
References 401
Shock absorbers 1087
Support arms, pins & bushings 1087

TRANSMISSION, AUTOMATIC

Quick information 402
Turbo drive linkage, adjust ... 403
Turbo drive, R & R 405

TUNE-UP

Specifications 386
Engine diagnosis 1012

UNIVERSAL JOINT AND DRIVE SHAFT

Disassemble U joint 406
U joint & drive line, R & R 406

LINCOLN and CONTINENTAL

YEAR IDENTIFICATION

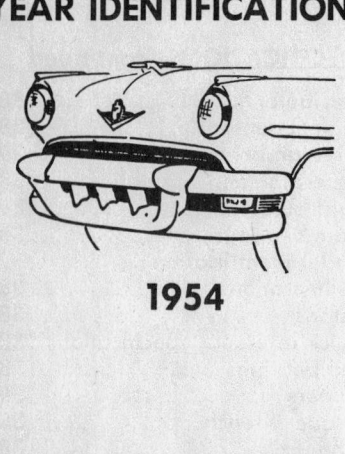

1954

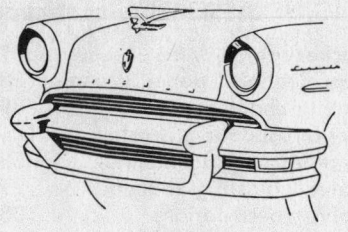

1955

1956 Lincoln

1957 Lincoln

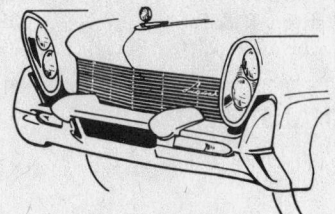

1958 Lincoln

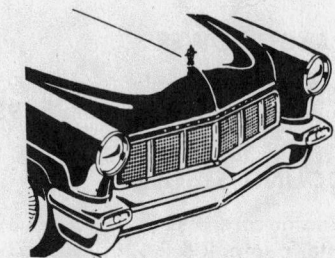

1956-57 Continental

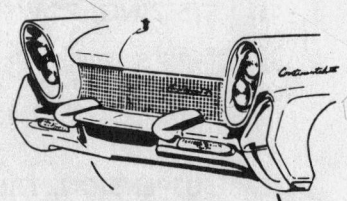

1958 Continental

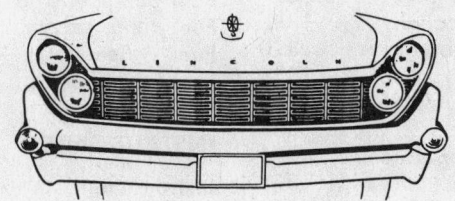

1959 Lincoln

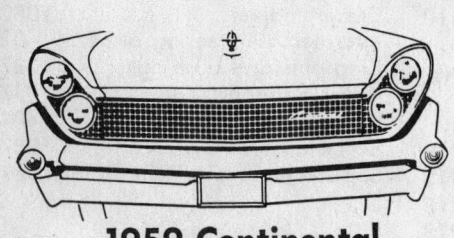

1959 Continental

1960 Lincoln

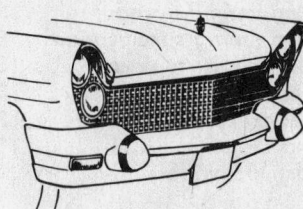

1960 Continental

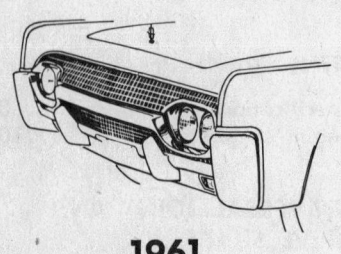

1961

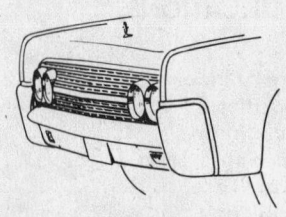

1962

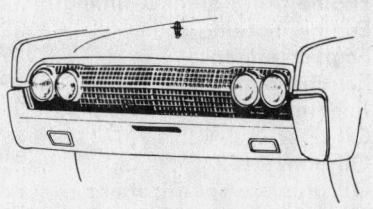

1963

CAR SERIAL NUMBER LOCATION AND ENGINE IDENTIFICATION

SERIAL NUMBERS AND MOTOR NUMBERS ARE ONE AND THE SAME.

SERIAL NUMBER LOCATION
1954: Right front door hinge post.
1955-63: Left front door hinge post.

ENGINE IDENTIFICATION
ENGINE IDENTIFICATION IS THRU CAR SERIAL NUMBER.

No complications, Lincoln-Continental offers one engine per model year.

1954-57 Lincoln,
first two digits—Year
1956-57 Continental,
first two digits—Year
1958-63 Lincoln & Continental,
first digit—Year

QUICK WORKING SPECIFICATIONS

DISTRIBUTOR
Breaker Point Gap (In.)
1954-63 .... .014-.016
Cam Angle (Degrees)
1954-63 27

SPARK PLUGS

Year	Type	Gap
1954, OHV, V8	H10	.035
1955, OHV, V8	870	.035
1956-57, OHV, V8 ..	860	.035
1958-61	F-11-Y	.035
1962-63	BF42	.035

IGNITION TIMING
(Sparks occurs degrees before T.C.)
1954, ... 3B
1955-57 .... 5B
1958-62 .... 6B
1963 .... 4B

COMPRESSION PRESSURE AT CRANKING SPEED
Variations between cylinders should not exceed 10 lbs. This is more important than actually reading stated pressure.
1954-55 135
1956-57 150
1958-63 180

GENERATOR AND REGULATOR SPECIFICATIONS

Year and Series	Generator Field Current In Amperes 6 Volt	Generator Field Current In Amperes 12 Volt	Regulator Cut-Out Closing Voltage	Regulator Current Regulator Setting	Regulator Voltage Regulator Setting
1954-55 All	2.4	—	6.3	40	7.6
1956-57 Ex. Continental	—	1.55	12.4	30	15.0
Continental	—	1.55	12.4	40	15.0
1958-62 All	—	1.55	12.4	40	15.0

NOTE: Surrounding temperatures and driving habits influence the above adjustments and must be considered by the mechanic. Higher temperatures or turnpike conditions permit lower adjustments; lower temperatures or city type driving conditions require higher settings, within limits.

For A.C. Generator Specifications See Following Pages

WHEEL ALIGNMENT
Caster
1954-56, all V8 .... 1½ N to O
1957, OHV, V8 .... ½ N to O
1958-63 .... 1½ N to O

Camber
1954-63 .... O to ¾P

Toe-In
1954-57, all except Capri & Premiere .... 3/32 to 5/32
1956-57, Capri, Premiere .... 1/32 to 3/32
1958-63 .... 1/16 to 3/16

CAPACITIES
Engine Crankcase (Quarts)
(Add 1 qt. for new filter)
1954-63 5

Transmission Synchro. (Pts.)
1954-63, all .... Not used

Automatic Trans. (Pints)
1954, Hydramatic 22
1955-56, Turbo-Drive 20
1957, Turbo-Drive 22½
1958-60, Turbo-Drive 21
1961-63, Turbo-Drive 23

Rear Axle (Pints)
1954-60 4
1961-63 .... 4¾

Cooling System (Quarts)
Add for heater
1954 .... 22½
1955-60 23
1961-63 22

FIRING ORDER and TIMING

SPARK OCCURS:
1954 —Rear Mounted Distributor 3° BTDC
1955-57—Rear Mounted Distributor 5° BTDC
1958-62—Rear Mounted Distributor 6°-10° BTDC
1963—4° B

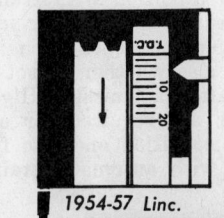

1954-57 Linc.

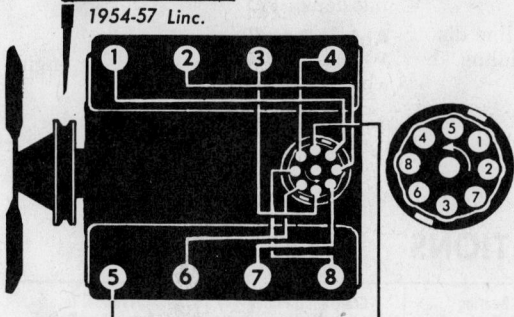

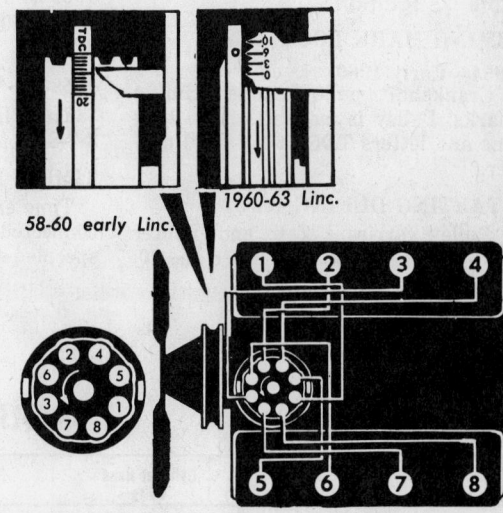

58-60 early Linc.

1960-63 Linc.

NOTE:
THESE ARE APPROXIMATE SETTINGS. ENGINE DESIGN, ALTITUDE, TEMPERATURE, FUEL AND ENGINE CONDITION WILL ALL INFLUENCE TIMING. THE DETERMINING FACTOR, LIMITING ADVANCE, WILL STILL BE THE "KNOCK POINT" OF THE ENGINE.

TUNE-UP SPECIFICATIONS

Year Engine Type	Spark Plugs		Distributor (Note 1)				Ignition Timing (Note 2)	Compression Pressure Cranking (Note 3)	Valves (Note 4)			Fuel Pump Pressure	Engine Idle Speed Neutral (Note 5)
	Make and Number	Gap	Cam Angle	Point Gap	Arm Spring Tension				Tappet Clearance Hot		Timing		
									Inlet	Exhaust	Inlet Opens		
1954 All V8, OHV..................	CH-H10	.035	27	.015	17–20		3B	135	Zero	Zero	18B	4	450
1955 All V8, OHV.................	CH-870	.035	27	.015	17–20		5B	135	Zero	Zero	8B	4	450
1956–57 All V8, OHV.................	CH-860	.035	27	.015	17–20		5B	150	Zero	Zero	18B	5	450
1958-61 All V8, OHV	F-11-Y	.035	26-28.5	.015	17-20		Note 2A	180	Zero	Zero	22B	5-6	450
1962-63 All	BF42	.035	26-28.5	.015	17-20		Note 2A	180	Zero	Zero	22B	5-6	450

NOTES FOR TUNE-UP SPECIFICATIONS TABLE

Note:

All specifications are standard and should result in satisfactory performance. There are, however, factors that influence these settings, such as fuel octane value, air density, humidity, temperature, etc. Timing charts, like other specifications must be considered as averages, subject to modification.

Note 1: Distributor

ROTATION (VIEWED FROM THE TOP)

1954-63, All OHV ....Counterclockwise

DRIVE GEAR
1954-63

Gear pinned to distributor shaft has slot which engages centered tongue of oil pump extension shaft. Oil pump has tongue which engages slot in this extension shaft (sometimes called Distributor Intermediate Shaft).

Note 2: Ignition

TIMING MARK LOCATION

1954—Early 1960

Crankshaft pulley carries timing marks. Pulley is marked with a long line and letters TDC at top dead center.

STARTING DURING 1960

Pulley carries a Zero and pointer on case has graduations; 0, 3, 6 and 10.

IGNITION RESISTOR

1956-62—Engines with 12 volt electrical systems.

There is a resistor in the primary ignition circuit between the coil and the ignition switch. When the starter switch is operated this resistor is bypassed. Be careful to ground the primary ignition circuit when using the starter to turn the engine for adjustment.

Firing Order and Spark Plug Wire Installation

1954-63, V8, OHV

All Lincoln V8, OHV engine cylinders are numbered from front to back: left bank, 5-6-7-8; right bank, 1-2-3-4. Using this numbering system, spark plug wires go into the distributor cap in the FIRING ORDER and in a counter clockwise direction.

1954-57

The FIRING ORDER is: 1-5-4-8-6-3-7-2.

1958-63, V8

The FIRING ORDER is: 1-5-4-2-6-3-7-8.

TIMING PROCEDURE

Time engine with Vacuum line disconnected and plugged while idling at specified speed.

Note 2A: 1958-63 Ignition Timing

Normal setting is 6B. If available fuel is below 98 octane setting can be retarded to 3B but no lower. A distributor modification package for use with low octane fuel is available.

With high octane fuel setting can be advanced but no earlier than 10B. 4° B for 1963.

Note 3: Compression Pressure

All cylinders should read alike within 10 pounds. This is more important than the actual reading. Take the readings with all plugs removed, engine at normal operating temperature.

Note 4: Valves

Zero in the tappet clearance column indicates hydraulic lifters are standard equipment.

Note 5: Idle Speeds

Idle speeds as shown are for engines in good condition with transmission in Neutral. The proper idle speed for an engine depends on its condition and also whether or not it has an automatic transmission. Higher idle speeds are required for engines in poor condition and also for engines used with automatic transmissions.

Abbreviations Used

V8, OHV—V shaped 8 cylinder engine with valves in the heads.

TORQUE SPECIFICATIONS

	Cylinder Head Bolts	Rod Bearing Bolts	Main Bearing Bolts	Crankshaft Pulley Bolt	Flywheel to Crankshaft Bolt
1954-57 All Models	80–90	45–50	120–130	130–145	75–85
1958-63 All Models	85-105	45–50	95–105	75-90	75–85

LINCOLN—DISTRIBUTOR SPECIFICATIONS—CONTINENTAL

Year	Model	Part Number	Rotation	Cam Angle in Degrees	BREAKER Point Opening (Inch)	BREAKER Arm Spring in Ounces	GOVERNOR CONTROL @ Dist. Advance Starts	GOVERNOR CONTROL R.P.M. Full Advance	VACUUM CONTROL DATA Inches of Vacuumn To Start Advance	VACUUM CONTROL DATA Inches of Vacuum For Full Advance	VACUUM CONTROL DATA Max. Adv. of Dist. in Degrees
1954	V-8, All	FAF-12127B	CC	26-28	.015	17-20	None	None	.51	2.65 @ 2000	12¼-13½
1955	V-8, All	FDL-12127B	CC	26-28	.015	17-20	None	None	.62	2.35 @ 2000	12¼-13½
1956	V-8, Lincoln	FDU-12127B	CC	26-28	.015	17-20	None	None	.46	1.88 @ 2000	12¾-14
	V-8, Continental	FER-12127A	CC	26-28	.015	17-20	None	None	.46	1.88 @ 2000	12¾-14
1957	V-8, Lincoln	FEL-12127A	CC	26-28	.015	17-20	1 @ 300	13½ @ 2000	5.0	20.0	7-9
	V-8, Continental	FEK-12127C	CC	26-28	.015	17-20	1 @ 300	11 @ 2000	5.0	20.0	7-9
1958	V-8, Lincoln	FEW-12127A	CC	26-28	.015	17-20	1 @ 300	13½ @ 2000	6.0	18-20	10-12
	V-8, Continental	FEW-12127E	CC	26-28	.015	17-20	1 @ 300	13½ @ 2000	6.0	18-20	10½-12½
1959-60	V-8, All	FEW-12127H	CC	26-28	.015	17-20	1 @ 350	15 @ 2000	6.0	15-17	9½-12½
1961-63	All	CIVF-12127A	CC	26-28½	.015	17-20	1 @ 550	15 @ 2000	7	18	9½-12½

NOTE: HOLLEY DIST. USED 1954-57
FORD DIST. USED 1958-63

D.C. GENERATOR and REGULATOR SPECIFICATIONS

YEAR	GENERATORS Field Current in Amperes At 6 Volts	GENERATORS Field Current in Amperes At 12 Volts	GENERATORS Brush Tension Spring	REGULATORS Cut Out Relay Air Gap	REGULATORS Cut Out Relay Closing Voltage	REGULATORS Current And Voltage Regulator Air Gap	REGULATORS Current Regulator Setting	REGULATORS Voltage Regulator Setting
1954—55 All OHV, V8	2.4		30	.018	6.3	.035	40	7.6
1956—57 All ex. Continental		1.55	30	.018	12.4	.035	30	15.0
Continental		1.55	30	.018	12.4	.035	40	15.0
1958-62 All OHV, V8		1.55	34	.018	12.4	.035	40	15.0*

* Starting 1961—15.6 volts.

A.C. GENERATOR & REGULATOR SPECIFICATIONS

Year and Model	Ground Polarity	ALTERNATOR Ampere Rating	ALTERNATOR Field Current Draw, Amps.	CURRENT OUTPUT @ 15 Volts and 2950 Engine R.P.M.	VOLTAGE OUTPUT @ 15 Amp. Load and 2950 Engine R.P.M.	REGULATOR Point Gap	REGULATOR Air Gap
1963 All Models	Neg.	40	2.9-3.1	40 Amp.	15	.015-.022	.022-.030

BATTERY and STARTER SPECIFICATIONS

YEAR	BATTERY Ampere Hour Capacity	BATTERY Volts	BATTERY Group Number	BATTERY Terminal Grounded	STARTERS Lock Test AMPS	STARTERS Lock Test Volts	STARTERS Lock Test Torque	STARTERS No Load Test Amps	STARTERS No Load Test Volts	STARTERS No Load Test R.P.M.	Brush Spring Tension
1954 All OHV, V8	110	6	3N	Pos.	700	3.5	14.5	70	6.0	4750	52
1955 All OHV, V8	110	6	3N	Pos.	700	3.5	14.0	70	6.0	4750	52
1956 All OHV, V8	65	12	5N	Neg.	550	5.0	15.5	120	12.0	4800	52
1957 All OHV, V8	65	12	5N	Neg.	550	5.0	15.5	85	12.0	4500	52
1958-60 All OHV, V8	72	12	5N	Neg.	550	5.0	15.5	85	12.0	4500	52
1961-63, All	80	12		Neg.	525	4.0	14.0	70	12.0	9500	52

CRANKSHAFT BEARING JOURNAL SIZES

YEAR	MAIN BEARING JOURNALS Journal Diameter	MAIN BEARING JOURNALS Oil Clearance	MAIN BEARING JOURNALS End Play of Shaft	MAIN BEARING JOURNALS End Play Held By	CONNECTING ROD BEARING JOURNALS Journal Diameter	CONNECTING ROD BEARING JOURNALS Oil Clearance	CONNECTING ROD BEARING JOURNALS End Play
1954-57 OHV, V8	2.6235-2.6243	.0017	.006	#3	2.2482-2.2490	.0014	.010
1958-63 OHV, V8	2.8994-2.9002	.0019	.006	#3	2.5992-2.600	.0016	.010

LINCOLN and CONTINENTAL

GENERAL ENGINE SPECIFICATIONS

Year Model Engine Type	Bore and Stroke	Number of Main Bearings	Type of Valve Lifter Used	Cubic Inch Displacement	AMA Horsepower	Advertised Horsepower at Stated RPM	Advertised Torque at Stated RPM	Compression Ratio	Oil Pressure At 30 MPH (Note 1)	Cam Shaft Drive
1954 All V8, OHV..........	$3\frac{13}{16}$x$3\frac{1}{2}$	5	Hyd. Adj.	317.5	46.2	205@4200	305@2300	8.0-1	40	Chain
1955 All V8, OHV..........	$3\frac{15}{16}$x$3\frac{1}{2}$	5	Hyd. Adj.	341	49.6	225@4400	342@2500	8.5-1	45	Chain
1956 All V8, OHV..........	4x$3\frac{21}{32}$	5	Hyd. Adj.	368	51.2	285@4600	402@3000	9.0-1	35	Chain
1957 All V8, OHV..........	4x$3\frac{21}{32}$	5	Hyd. Adj.	368	51.2	300@4800	415@3000	10.0-1	45	Chain
1958-Note 2 All V8, OHV........	$4\frac{19}{64}$x$3\frac{45}{64}$	5	Hyd.	430	59.7	375@4800	490@3100	10.5-1	50	Chain
1959 Note 2 All V8, OHV	$4\frac{19}{64}$x$3\frac{45}{64}$	5	Hyd.	430	59.7	350@4400	490@2800	10.0-1	50	Chain
1960 All	$4\frac{19}{64}$x$3\frac{45}{64}$	5	Hyd.	430	59.7	315@4100	465@2200	10.0-1	50	Chain
1961-62 All	$4\frac{19}{64}$x$3\frac{45}{64}$	5	Hyd.	430	59.7	300@4100	465@2000	10.0-1	50	Chain
1963 All	$4\frac{19}{64}$x$3\frac{45}{64}$	5	Hyd.	430	59.7			10.0-1	50	Chain

NOTES FOR GENERAL ENGINE SPECIFICATIONS TABLE

Note 1: Oil Pressure
FILTER TYPE
1954-63, All ....Full flow

ROCKER SHAFT OIL SUPPLY

Oil from the pump flows thru the filter to the main oil passage in the left side of the block. Oil from this passage flows to the camshaft bearings.

The RIGHT rocker arm assembly receives oil thru a drilled passage from No. 4 camshaft bearing which lines up with a hole in the cylinder head that directs oil thru No. 2 rocker shaft support. The LEFT rocker arm assembly is supplied similarly from No. 2 camshaft bearing and No. 3 rocker shaft supports. From the rocker shaft supports the oil flows thru the rocker shafts where it is directed thru drilled holes to lubricate each rocker arm. Overflow pipes located at the front of the right bank and at the rear of the left bank rocker arm assemblies allow excess oil to drain into the push rod chamber thru holes provided in the corners of the cylinder heads.

Note 2: Engine Design

Starting with 1958 production the top of each cylinder bank is cast at an angle of 10 degrees to the piston.

If the date code on the right rear oil pan rail is 4-82R or higher the block is .020 inch higher and requires only one gasket.

CAPACITIES

	Engine Crankcase Add 1 Qt. for New Filter	Transmissions Pints to Refill After Draining		Rear Axle Pints Note 2	Gasoline Tank Gallons	Cooling System Quarts Note 1
		Manual	Automatic			
1954 All Models	5	NA	22	4	20	22½(B)
1955-56 All ex. Continental	5	NA	20	4	20	23 (B)
Continental	5	NA	20	4	25	23 (B)
1957 All ex. Continental	5	NA	22½	4	20	23 (C)
Continental	5	NA	22½	4	25	23 (C)
1958-60 All Models	5	NA	21	4	25	23 (C)
1961-63 All Models	5	NA	23	4.8(A)	21	22(C)

NOTES FOR CAPACITIES TABLE

Note 1: 1954-63 Cooling System Capacity

(B)—Add 2 qts. for heater.
(C)—Add 3 qts. for heater.

Note 2: Rear Axle Lubricant

Draining the rear axle is not recommended.

When differential has been overhauled be sure to refill with a lead-sulpher base grease equivalent to Lincoln Part No. LA-19581.

(A)—No drain plug.

Abbreviations Used

N.A.—Not available on these models.

PISTON AND PIN SPECIFICATIONS

| Year and Model | PISTON | | | | PISTON PIN | | |
| | Skirt Clearance | | Diameter | Bushing | FIT | | Lock |
	Min.	Max.			In Rod	In Piston	
1954	.0002	.002	.9120	Yes	.0002-.0005	.0001-0003	Ring
1955-57	.0004	.0007	.9120	Yes	.0008	.0008	Ring
1958-63	.0011	.0017	.9750	None	Press	.0008-.0016	Rod Press

1954-57, ALL OHV, V8

Tighten to 80-90. ft. lbs.

1958-63

Tighten to 105 ft. lbs. in 3 steps cold. Follow the sequence shown for each step. Step 1: to 85 ft. lbs. Step 2: to 95 ft. lbs. Step 3: to 105 ft. lbs.

Piston Fitting Ribbon Thickness and Spring Scale Pull

1954-57: ½ inch wide; 10 inches long; .0015 inch thick; pull of 6-12 pounds.
1958-63: ½ inch wide; 10 inches long; .002 inch thick; pull of 5 to 10 pounds.

Piston and Rod Assembly

All engines: The indentations in the head of the piston must be toward the front of the engine. The bearing lock slots must be toward the outside of the engine. If the rods are numbered the numbers go to the outside of the engine.

VALVE SPECIFICATIONS

| YEAR | Seat Angle | | Intake Valve Lift Note 1 | Exhaust Valve Lift | Valve Spring Pressure Note 2 | | Stem to Guide Clearance | | Stem Diameter | | · Are Valve Guides Replaceable |
	In	Ex.			Outer	Inner	Inlet	Exhaust	Inlet	Exhaust	
1954 V8, OHV	45	45	.354	.354	67@1.80	None	.0015	.0025	.3420	.3410	No
1955 V8, OHV	45	45	.384	.384	71@1.80	None	.0015	.0025	.3420	.3420	No
1956 V8, OHV	45	45	.417	.417	71@1.80	None	.0015	.0025	.3420	.3410	No
1957 V8, OHV	45	45	.417	.417	71@1.80	None	.0017	.0030	.3420	.3410	No
1958 V8, OHV	30	45	.441	.441	70@1.83	Damper	.0017	.0035	.3715	.3695	No
1959-63 OHV-V8	45	45	.408	.408	70@1.83	Damper	.0017	.0035	.3715	.3697	No

NOTES FOR VALVE SPECIFICATIONS TABLE

Note 1: Timing Sprocket or Gear Marks

ALL OHV, V8

Marks on camshaft and crankshaft sprockets should be aligned nearest each other and with the shaft centers.

Note 2: Valve Springs

ALL OHV, V8

Inlet and exhaust springs are the same.

FRONT WHEEL ALIGNMENT

| YEAR | CASTER | | CAMBER | | Toe-In (Inches) | King Pin Inclination (Degrees) | WHEEL PIVOT RATIO | |
	Range (Degrees)	Pref. Setting	Range (Degrees)	Pref. Setting			Inner Wheel	Outer Wheel
1954—55 All Models	1½N to 0		0 to ¾P	Note 1	3/32 to 5/32	7⅛	23½	20
1956 Capri, Premiere	1½N to 0	Note 2	0 to ¾P	Note 1	1/32 to 5/32	7 1/16	24½	20
Continental	¾P to 1¼P	Note 2	0 to ¾P	Note 1	3/32 to 5/32	7⅛	25¾	20
1957 Capri, Premiere	½N to 0	Note 2	0 to ¾P	Note 1	1/32 to 5/32	7 1/16	24⅓	20
Continental	¾P to 1¼P	Note 2	0to ¾P	Note 1	3/32 to 5/32	7⅛	25¾	20
1958-60 All Models	1½N to 0	Note 2	0 to ¾P	Note 1	1/16 to 3/16	7½	23	20
1961-63 All Models	1½N to 0	Note 2	0 to ¾P	Note 1	1/16 to 3/16	7	23	20

NOTES FOR FRONT WHEEL ALIGNMENT TABLE

Note 1: 1954-63 Preferred Camber Setting

Not to vary more than ½ degree from one side to the other.

Note 2: 1956-63 Preferred Caster Setting

Not to vary more than ¼ degree from one side to the other.

LINCOLN and CONTINENTAL

LIGHT BULBS

(C.P. MEANS CANDLE POWER)
1954-57
Pilot Light of Automatic Headlight Dimmer, Heater Control Light, and Transmission Quadrant Light:

6 Volt, No. 51; 12 Volt, No. 53.
Telltale Lights for High Beam, Oil Pressure, Generator, Turn Signals,
(1 C.P. miniature bayonet base.)
Brake-on, Instrument Panel Lights, Heater Controls, Radio Dial, Ignition Switch Light, Glove Compartment Light, Air Conditioner Control Panel Light:

6 Volt, No. 55; 12 Volt, No. 57.
(2 C.P. miniature bayonet base.)
License Plate, Trunk, Front Parking, Utility Lights:

6 Volt, No. 63; 12 Volt, No. 67.
(4 C.P. single contact base.)
Courtesy Light, Map Light:

6 Volt, No. 81; 12 Volt, No. 89.
(6 C.P. single contact base.)
Dome Light, Engine Comparment Light:

6 Volt, No. 209; 12 Volt, No. 1003.
(15 C.P. single contact base.)
Rear Turn Signal, Tail, Stop Lights:

6 Volt, No. 1154; 12 Volt, No. 1034.
(4 and 32 C.P. double contact indexed base.)
Front Turn Signal:

6 Volt, No. 1133; 12 Volt, No. 1034.
Back-up Lights:

6 Volt, No. 1129; 12 Volt, No. 1141.
(21 C.P. single contact base.)
Headlights:

6 Volt, No. 5040; 12 Volt, No. 5400.
(40 and 50 C.P. three contact base.)
1958-63
12 Volt	Low	No. 4002
12 Volt	High	No. 4001

GENERAL CHASSIS and BRAKE SPECIFICATIONS

| YEAR AND MODEL | CHASSIS | | BRAKE CYLINDER BORE | | |
| | Overall Length in inches | Tire Size | Master Cyl. (inch) | Wheel Cylinder Diameter (inch) | |
				Front	Rear
1954-55 Cosmopolitan & Capri	214¾	8.00x15	1.0	1⅛	1⁵⁄₁₆
1956 Continental	218½	8.00x15	2½₂	1³⁄₃₂	1⁵⁄₁₆
Capri & Premiere	222¾	8.00x15	1.0	1⅛	1⁵⁄₁₆
1957 Continental	218½	8.00x15	2½₂	1³⁄₃₂	1⁵⁄₁₆
Capri & Premiere	224¾	8.00x15	2½₂	1³⁄₃₂	1⁵⁄₁₆
1958 All Except Convt.	229.0	9.00x14	2½₂	1³⁄₃₂	1⁵⁄₁₆
Continental Convt.	229.0	9.50x14	2½₂	1³⁄₃₂	1⁵⁄₁₆
1959-60 All	227¼	9.50x14	2½₂	1³⁄₃₂	1⁵⁄₁₆
1961-62 Sedans	212¹³⁄₃₂	9.00x14	2½₂	1³⁄₃₂	1⁵⁄₁₆
Convt. & Sedans with A.C.	212¹³⁄₃₂	9.50x14	2½₂	1³⁄₃₂	1⁵⁄₁₆
1963 Sedans	213	9.00x14	2½₂	1³⁄₃₂	1⁵⁄₁₆
Convt. & Sedans with A.C.	213	9.50x14	2½₂	1³⁄₃₂	1⁵⁄₁₆

CYLINDER HEAD NUT TIGHTENING SEQUENCE

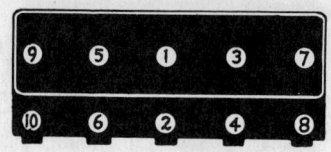

1954-57
Tighten to 80-90. ft. lbs
1958-63
Tighten to 105 ft. lbs. in 3 steps cold. Follow the sequence shown for each step.
Step 1: to 85 ft. lbs.
Step 2: to 95 ft. lbs.
Step 3: to 105 ft. lbs.

1958-63

Instrument, Ignition, Glove Box, Ash Tray, Push Buttons

12 Volt, No. 57.
(2 C.P. miniature bayonet base.)
License

12 Volt, No. 67.
(4 C.P. single contact base.)
Dome
12 Volt, No. 1003.
(15 C.P. single contact base.)
Courtesy, Trunk

12 Volt, No. 89.
(6 C.P. single contact base.)
Parking Signal, Tail Combination
12 Volt, No. 1034.
(4 & 32 C.P. 2 contact indexed base.)

Headlight, Oil Pressure, Generator, Turn, Brake-on, Radio, Shiftplate, Fuel, Lighter, Doorlock, Decklock, Indicator Lights

12 Volt, No. 1445.
1½ C.P.
Back-up

12 Volt, No. 1141.
21 C.P.
Headlights (Four Light System)
LOW BEAM
12 Volt, No. 4002.
(50 & 37½ Watts, 3 contact base.)

HIGH BEAM
12 Volt, No. 4001.
(37½ Watts. 2 contact base.)

FUSES and CIRCUIT BREAKERS

CIRCUIT BREAKERS
(ALL ARE UNDER DASH)
Headlights and Beam Telltale:
1954-55—30 Amp.
1956-57—12 Amp.
1958-63—18 & 12 Amp.
Parking, Tail, Stop, License Plate, Instruments, Ignition, Clock and Trunk Lights:
1954-55—15 Amp.
1956-63—12 Amp.
Electric Windows and Seat:
One 30 amp. line protector; one 15 amp. each window motor; one 15 amp. common to both seat motors. One 5 amp. at each ventpane.
Air Conditioner:
1954-55—20 Amp.
1952-63—20 Amp.

Power Top:
With manual header locks—30 amp. With electric header locks—one 40 amp. motor line protector, one 20 amp. motor protector, one 10 amp. switch protector.
FUSES
Almost all the fuses are under the dash. On models thru 1954 the fuses were adjacent to the lines involved. Starting with 1955 production the fuses are mounted in a panel together with the turn signal flasher. This panel will be found under the dash near the steering column. A rectangular shaped Flasher is specified for 1958.
Cigar Lighter:
1954-55, Thermal fuse plus AGC 30 fuse.
1956, Thermal fuse plus AGC 15 fuse.

1957, 1 Sulphur Disc on Lincoln, SFE 20 fuse on Mark 2.
1958-63, AGC—15
Clock:
1954, AGA 3 fuse.
1957, SFE 7.5 fuse.
Underhood Lamp:
1957-63, SFE 7.5 fuse.
Turn Signal
1954-55, SFE 9; 1956-59, SFE 7½.
1960-63, SFE 14.

Glove Box, Map, Dome and Courtesy Light:
1954-55, SFE 9.
1956-62, SFE 14.
Automatic Headlight Dimmer:
Thru 1956, AGC 5 fuse.
1957, AGC 3 fuse.

FUSES

Automatic Radio Antenna:
Single 3 AG 10.
Double SFE 20.

Radio:
SFE 7½.

Windshield Washer
1955, AGA 3; 1956-60, SFE 7½.

Heater Motors:
2 SFE 14.
Starting 1960—20 AM C.B.

Back-up Light:
SFE 7.5.

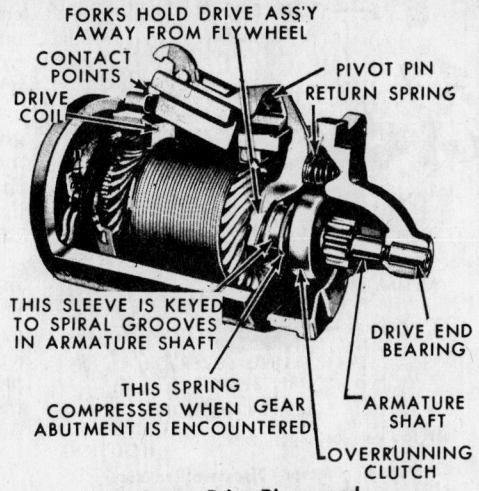

FORKS HOLD DRIVE ASS'Y AWAY FROM FLYWHEEL
CONTACT POINTS
DRIVE COIL
PIVOT PIN
RETURN SPRING
THIS SLEEVE IS KEYED TO SPIRAL GROOVES IN ARMATURE SHAFT
THIS SPRING COMPRESSES WHEN GEAR ABUTMENT IS ENCOUNTERED
DRIVE END BEARING
ARMATURE SHAFT
OVERRUNNING CLUTCH

Starter Drive Disengaged

DISTRIBUTOR

Detailed information on: distributor drive, direction of distributor rotation; cylinder numbering; firing order; point gap; cam dwell; timing mark location; spark plugs, spark advance; ignition resistor location, and idle speed; will be found in the Tune-up Specifications Table of this section. Further information on trouble shooting, general tune-up procedures, how to replace ignition wires, how to install points and condensers, how to choose the proper spark plug, adjust timing, will be found in the Unit Repair section under the heading: Ignition-Distributor-Tune-up.

IGNITION PRIMARY RESISTOR

On all Lincoln and Continental models 12-volt systems a resistor is used in the primary circuit in the ignition coil. It is mounted immediately adjacent to the coil. If any difficulty is experienced with the ignition, first check to make certain that the resistor itself is functioning properly.

DISTRIBUTOR REMOVAL

1954 Thru 1957

On these models the distributor is located at the back of the engine block, just back of the left cylinder head. An 8 load cam is used having a single set of breaker points.

To remove the distributor, take off the air cleaner and distributor cap and wire assembly and disconnect the ignition primary wire. Disconnect the vacuum line to the vacuum advance mechanism and take out the bolt which retains the distributor housing to the block and lift off the distributor.

Starting With 1958

The distributor is located in the front of the engine between the cylinder banks.

Remove the carburetor air cleaner, take off the ignition primary lead, and the vacuum advance lead, care-

fully mark the position of the rotor in relation to the body of the distributor and mark the position of the body of the distributor relative to the chamber cover, remove the bolt which holds the distributor down into the engine and lift it out. The marks are made so that the distributor can be reinstalled without having to retime the ignition.

IGNITION TIMING

ALL OHV, V8

On these models the ignition timing is marked on the vibration damper and it is recommended that neon type timing light be used to determine the exact point of ignition.

REPLACING IGNITION WIRES

1954 Thru 1957

The best way to replace ignition wires is to put them in one at a time and use the old wire as a "come along" for the new wire. However, if all the wires are removed and it is necessary to replace them, proceed as follows: remove the spark plug from No. 1 cylinder and crank the engine with the thumb in the cylinder hole until compression is felt to blow by the thumb. Continue turning the engine very slowly until the ignition timing mark comes up on the vibration damper. This places No. 1 cylinder in firing position.

Remove the distributor cap and note the position of the rotor by marking its position on the cap. Place the first wire in the socket directly over the tip of the rotor and put that wire on No. 1 plug. Now, moving in a counterclockwise direction, place the wires in the cap and to the spark plugs according to the firing order of the engine, which is: 1-5-4-8-6-3-7-2. Keep in mind that the cylinders are numbered:

Right front 1-2-3-4
Left front 5-6-7-8

1958-63 Lincoln and Continental Models

The precedure given above for the models through 1957 will apply to the 1958-63 models except that the firing order is 1-5-4-2-6-3-7-8. Except for the difference in firing order, the procedure is exactly the same.

REPLACE SPARK PLUGS

1955 Thru 1957 Models

On these models the spark plugs are located below the exhaust manifolds on both banks and on cars fitted with power steering the No. 8 spark plug on the left bank is particularly difficult of access. Most shops specializing in this type of work agree that it is slightly less difficult if the plug is removed from underneath the car.

Starting With 1958

On these models the plugs are above the exhaust manifolds and can be reached with relative ease.

GENERATOR AND REGULATOR

Detailed facts on the generator and the regulator can be found in the Generator and Regulator Specifications Table of this section.

General information on generator and regulator repair and trouble shooting can be found in the Unit Repair section under the heading Generators and Regulators.

GENERATOR POLARITY

Caution: Whenever the circuits to: the generator; the regulator; or the battery have been disconnected it is best to apply the following procedure:

Before the engine is started momentarily short from the "Bat" to the "Gen" terminals of the regulator with a screwdriver. This gives a momentary surge of current from the battery to the generator and so correctly polarizes the generator with respect to the battery.

Failure to so polarize the generator before starting the engine may severely damage the regulator since reversed polarity causes vibration, arcing and burning of the relay points.

The charging system may consist of a D.C. GENERATOR or the newer AC UNIT. More detailed information may be obtained on either of these systems from the "Unit Repair" section, under the heading, "Generators and Regulators."

BATTERY AND STARTER

A more general discussion of batteries will be found in the Unit Repair section under the heading: Ignition-Distributors-Tune-Up.

LINCOLN and CONTINENTAL

A more general discussion of starters and their troubles can be found in the Unit Repair section under the heading: Starters.

STARTER, R & R

1954-55

Disconnect battery and starter cables. Drop steering idler arm. Remove end plate cap screws and pull starter out and down.

1956-57

Disconnect starter cable. Remove mounting bolts. Remove starter, turning front wheels to extreme right for clearance.

1958

Disconnect Battery. Remove two upper end plate screws. Raise car. Remove rear engine support stud nut and jack up rear of engine about one inch. Remove cable from starter. Remove lower end plate screw. Work starter down and forward through suspension arms. Where power lubricator is used remove bracket nuts and move to one side for clearance.

1959-60

Remove battery and support. Disconnect transmission control rod at accelerator bracket. Drain coolant from block. Remove front engine mounting bolt nuts and raise front of engine as high as possible.

Remove right exhaust manifold. Remove mounting bolts and lift out starter.

1961-63

Follow 1957 instructions. Then tilt up rear of starter and lower between cooler line and No. 2 cross member.

BATTERY LOCATION

1954 Thru 1957
Lincoln Models

The battery is located under the right toe board and is accessible by lifting the floor mat and pulling up the cover in the right toe board.

The battery itself is held into its case in the usual manner with wing nuts.

Continental Mark II

The battery is located between the two cylinder banks in back of the engine under the hood.

1958-63, Lincoln and Continental

Battery is located under the hood on the right front fender skirt.

MULTI-LUBER

Description and Operation

The production installed Multi-

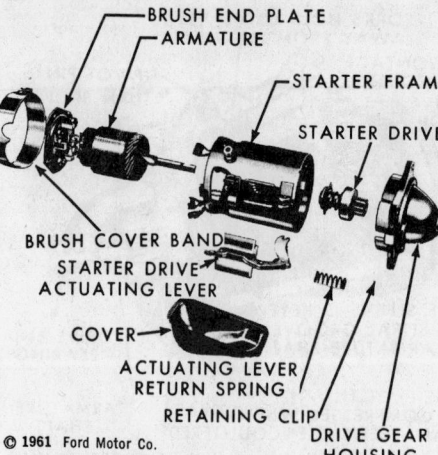

© 1961 Ford Motor Co.

Starting Motor—Disassembled View

Luber used on the 1958 Lincoln and Continental Mark III has been modified to operate automatically with each engine start. Formerly the lubrication cycle was initiated by a push button mounted on the instrument panel. This change was incorporated in production the second week of May, 1958. The automatic cycling system eliminates the push button mounted on the dash.

The Multi-Luber is a vacuum powered pump which provides pressure lubrication for all front suspension and steering points. Designed to cycle each time the engine is started. On each engine start, manifold vacuum actuates a pump diaphragm which forces a pump plunger through its pumping cycle. The plunger, which is hollow, has a cross-drilled hole and passage groove around its circumference which acts as a metering valve. The plunger is held at the end of its pumping cycle by manifold vacuum until the engine is stopped. At this time the plunger is returned to its original position by two coil springs, this action also introduces a fresh change of lubricant for the next cycle.

In addition to the automatic cycling feature, the Multi-Luber has a low level indicator which lights the instrument panel lube light bulb when the lubricant container becomes

empty. The light will remain "ON" until the empty container is replaced by a full container. The indicator lamp will also light each time the ignition switch is turned on; however, it will go out when the engine starts and the manifold vacuum is sufficient to start the lubrication cycle. The indicator light circuit is protected by an SFE 7.5 amp fuse located in the fuse panel.

Nylon lubricant feed lines, extending from the outlet ports of the pump body are connected directly to the grease fittings by means of leak-proof snap-on couplers. Lubricant is supplied from a replaceable 7-oz. container located at the right front fender apron support.

INSTRUMENTS

SPEEDOMETER AND INSTRUMENT REMOVAL

Lincoln Models and Continental Mark II

Since any work under the instrument panel is of necessity done in very close quarters, it is a particularly difficult job to take out the instrument panel from these models.

First, disconnect the battery and if the car has a radio disconnect the radio speaker and remove it and the radio.

Reach up under the dash and disconnect the speedometer cable, now remove the five bolts which hold the entire cluster under the dash panel and lift the instrument panel up into the car as far as the wires will permit it to go. This will be approximately 3 or 4 inches and will permit comparatively easy access to the rest of the instruments.

Once up into the car, any one of the instruments can be removed without too much difficulty.

Starting With 1960

To remove lamps, speedometer or printed circuit it is necessary to remove the instrument cluster Hood. Remove the three retaining screws. (with Air Conditioning it is necessary to remove conditioner grille).

Caution: Do not reconnect the battery until the instrument is back in place so as to avoid possible short circuits.

SPEEDOMETER R & R

Removal or replacement of the speedometer head requires the following procedure:

1. Disconnect battery ground cable.
2. Remove instrument panel top cover plate (7 screws).
3. Disconnect wiring and bulb sockets in the speedometer area (for clearance).

Note: Make note of color codes of these wires for accuracy in reassembly.

L.H. TURN INDICATOR LAMP HIGH BEAM INDICATOR LAMP R.H. TURN INDICATOR LAMP

CHARGE INDICATOR LAMP INSTRUMENT LAMPS OIL PRESSURE WARNING LAMP

© 1960 Ford Motor Co

Speedometer Housing Lamp Locations

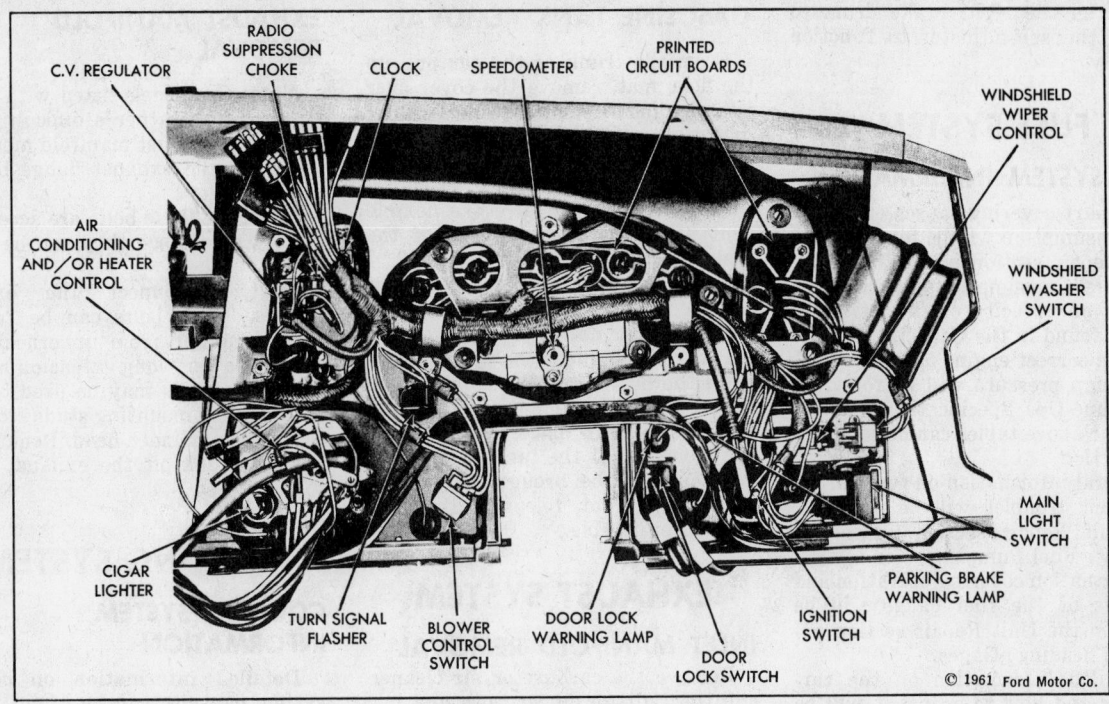

C.V. REGULATOR — RADIO SUPPRESSION CHOKE — CLOCK — SPEEDOMETER — PRINTED CIRCUIT BOARDS — WINDSHIELD WIPER CONTROL — AIR CONDITIONING AND/OR HEATER CONTROL — WINDSHIELD WASHER SWITCH — CIGAR LIGHTER — TURN SIGNAL FLASHER — BLOWER CONTROL SWITCH — DOOR LOCK WARNING LAMP — DOOR LOCK SWITCH — IGNITION SWITCH — PARKING BRAKE WARNING LAMP — MAIN LIGHT SWITCH

© 1961 Ford Motor Co.

1961-62 Instrument Panel—Rear View

4. Disconnect speedometer drive cable.

5. Remove instrument panel left, lower cover plate.

6. Disconnect trip reset from bottom of instrument panel.

7. Take out 6 screws that mount speedometer head.

Note: 2 of these screws are used to hold the constant voltage regulator and 2 are used to hold the S.I.P. relay.

8. Lift out speedometer head.

9. Reinstall by reversal of above sequence.

A magnetic or patented type screwdriver will simplify the replacement of the 6 mounting screws as they are rather difficult to start.

BRAKE SYSTEM

Information on brake adjustments, band replacement, bleeding procedure, master and wheel cylinder overhaul can be found in the General Section under the heading: Brakes, Hydraulic.

Information on trouble shooting and overhauling power brakes can be found in the Unit Repair section under the heading: Brakes, Power.

Information on the grease seals which may need replacement can be found in the Unit Repair section under the heading. The front wheel grease seals under the head: Suspension, Front Repair. The rear wheel grease seals under the head: Axles, Rear.

BRAKE PEDAL CLEARANCE

The pedal clearance on these cars is adjusted at the brake push rod and should allow approx. ¾" to 1" free motion of the pedal before the master cylinder piston starts to move.

ADJUSTMENT OF PARKING BRAKE CABLES

To adjust the parking brake cables expand the rear brake shoes at the star wheel until they are tight against the drum and then, with the parking brake lever in the fully released position adjust the length of the brake cables until they will just enter their clevises. This should be done with all slack pulled out of the cable.

REMOVAL OF THE BRAKE MASTER CYLINDER

Starting With 1954

On these models the master cylinder is located on the engine side of the firewall under the hood.

Disconnect the lines from the back of the master cylinder, and, under the dash, remove the clevis pin which holds the push rod to the brake lever, remove the mounting bolts and lift off the cylinder.

Starting with 1959 Models

A self-adjuster has been added to the service brake mechanism.

General Description

The automatic adjusters operate only when the brakes are applied as the car is moving rearward. The wrap-around action of the shoes following the drum while moving rearward forces the upper end of the primary shoe against the anchor pin and the secondary shoe away from the anchor pin.

The link holds the top of the actuator stationary, forcing the actuator to pivot on the secondary shoe. The pivoting action forces the pawl downward against the end of a tooth on the starwheel adjusting screw, which turns the star wheel and expands the shoes.

The greater the clearance between the brake drum and the lining, the greater the travel of the secondary shoe away from the anchor. The further the secondary shoe moves, the greater the adjustment. When the brakes are adjusted correctly, there will not be sufficient travel of the secondary shoe to permit the actuator to pivot and force the pawl to engage against the end of a tooth of the starwheel adjusting screw, and turn the wheel to expand the shoe.

When the brakes are applied as the car is moving forward, the self-adjuster does not operate because the wrap-around action of the shoes forces the secondary shoe against the anchor pin.

The rear brake assembly is basically the same as the front brake, except that the conventional parking brake operating lever, spring, and parking brake strut rod are used in the rear brake. The anchor pin on all brakes can be adjusted when necessary.

Whenever removing or replacing a starwheel assembly, special care must be exercised to be certain that the correct starwheel assembly is in-

LINCOLN and CONTINENTAL

stalled on the right brake drum to enable the self-adjuster to function properly.

FUEL SYSTEM

FUEL SYSTEM INFORMATION

A chart covering causes of excess fuel consumption will be found in the Unit Repair section under the heading: Fuel Consumption Chart.

Data on capacity of the gas tank will be found in the Capacities Table. Data on correct engine idle speed and fuel pump pressure will be found in the Tune-Up Specifications Table. Both the above tables can be found in this section.

General information on fuel pumps and their troubles will be found in the Unit Repair section under the heading: Fuel Pumps.

Information covering operation and troubles of the fuel gauge will be found in the Unit Repair section under the heading: Gages.

Detailed information on the carburetor and how to adjust it will be found in the Unit Repair section under the broad heading: Carburetors, and the specific heading of the make of carburetor being used on the engine being worked on. Carter, Holley, Rochester and Stromberg carburetors are covered.

Dash pot adjustment can be found in the Unit Repair section under the same heading as that of the automatic transmission used in the car.

REMOVAL OF THE FUEL PUMP

1954 Thru 1957

The fuel pump is located in front of the left bank of cylinders down low and is driven by an eccentric on the front of the cam gear.

To remove the pump, disconnect the fuel and vacuum lines and the pump can then be unbolted and lifted off.

On power steering models the bolts are accessible from under the car.

1958-63

The fuel pump is mounted on the top portion of the engine front cover.

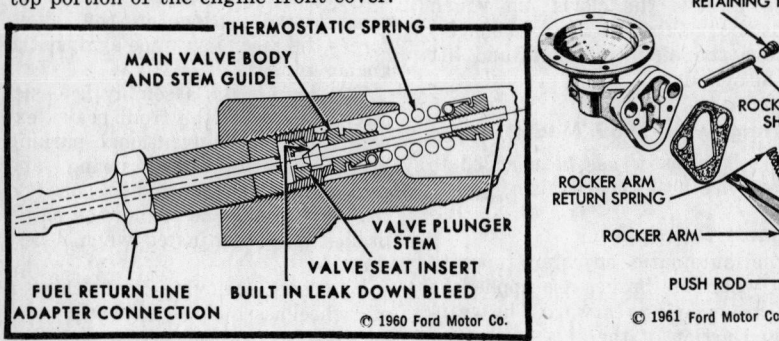

Thermostatic valve assembly

GASOLINE TANK REMOVAL

From the trunk of the car pull up the floor mat, remove the cover over the gage and disconnect the gage wire.

From underneath the car in the front end of the gas tank remove the main feed line. From the left side underneath the car remove the flexible vent line from the left side of the tank.

From the back of the car on the outside remove the rubber grommet from the filler neck.

Place a jack under the tank and remove the bolts from the front end of the tank which hold the straps and hold the tank in place. Slowly lower the front end of the tank so that the gas tank can be brought down and toward the front, releasing the filler neck from its hole.

EXHAUST SYSTEM

INLET MANIFOLD REMOVAL

Remove the carburetor air cleaner and the radiator upper hose and by-pass hose. Remove all lines to the carburetor, including the throttle rods, and take off the carburetor. Remove the ignition coil and the carburetor throttle rod bracket from the manifold. Disconnect the heat sending unit wire and the power brake vacuum lines. Disconnect all attaching lines to the intake manifold, unbolt and lift off the manifold.

On 1958 and later models it is more convenient to remove the distributor.

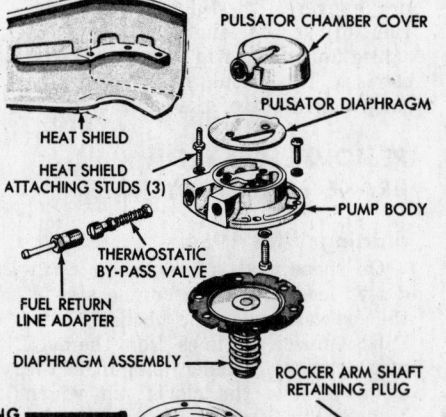

Fuel pump, exploded

EXHAUST MANIFOLD REMOVAL

Note: On models fitted with power steering it is rather a difficult job to get to the exhaust manifold mounting bolts and the exhaust flange bolt on the left side.

However, these bolts are accessible, and with patience they can be taken out.

First, disconnect the exhaust flanges. These bolts can be reached perhaps easier from underneath the car with a very long extension handle.

Short sockets may be used to take the manifold mounting studs from the side of the cylinder head. Remove the studs and lift off the exhaust manifolds.

COOLING SYSTEM

COOLING SYSTEM INFORMATION

Detailed information on cooling system capacity can be found in the Capacities Table of this section.

Information on the water temperature gauge can be found in the Unit Repair section under the heading: Gages.

Caution: Do not run cold water over the outside of pressurized radiators without first removing the radiator cap. When the cap is left on and the cold water hits the hot radiator the steam in the radiator condenses very rapidly and sometimes collapses the top radiator tank. This is most likely to happen if the coolant level is below normal.

Starting with 1961

The Radiator is cellular-tubular cross flow. The coolant tanks provide a means of cooling the power steering fluid and the transmission fluid. A supply tank provides a means of controlling surge and permits lowering of hood line. The ignition coil is mounted under this tank.

A power booster fan is used on air-conditioned cars.

RADIATOR CORE REMOVAL

On all models the radiator is removed in practically the same way. Disconnect the radiator hoses, disconnect the wires from the radiator frame and take out the bolts which hold the radiator core to its mounting and lift it straight up.

WATER PUMP REMOVAL

All Models

Disconnect the water pump lower hose and remove the fan belt. Take off the fan blades in order to prevent

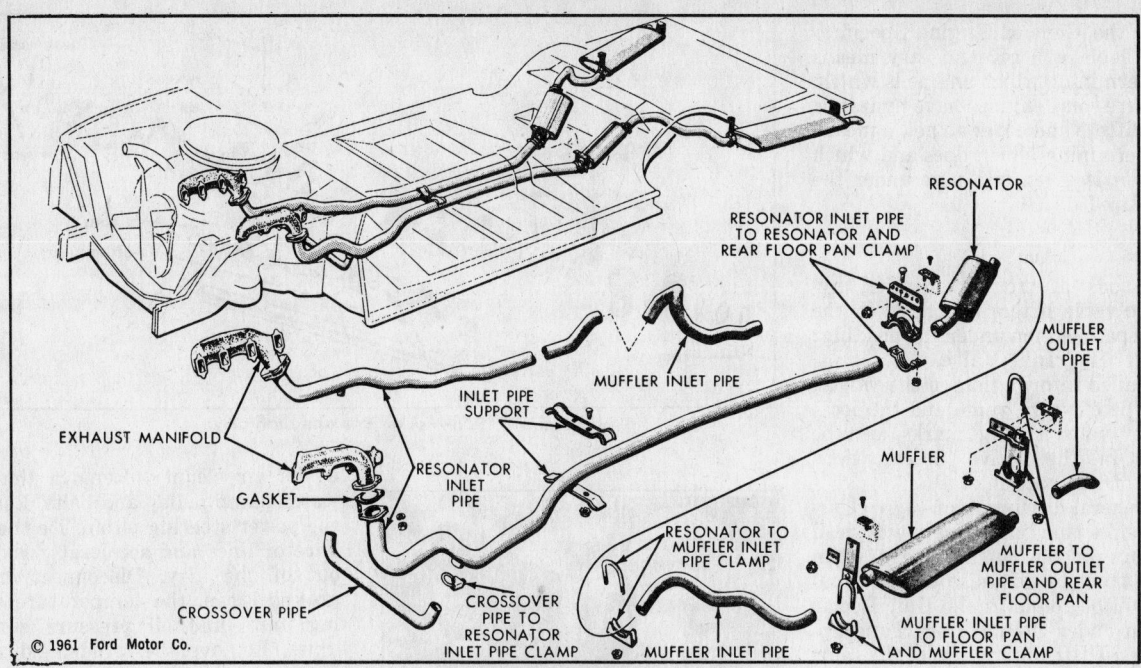

© 1961 Ford Motor Co.

1958-61 Exhaust System

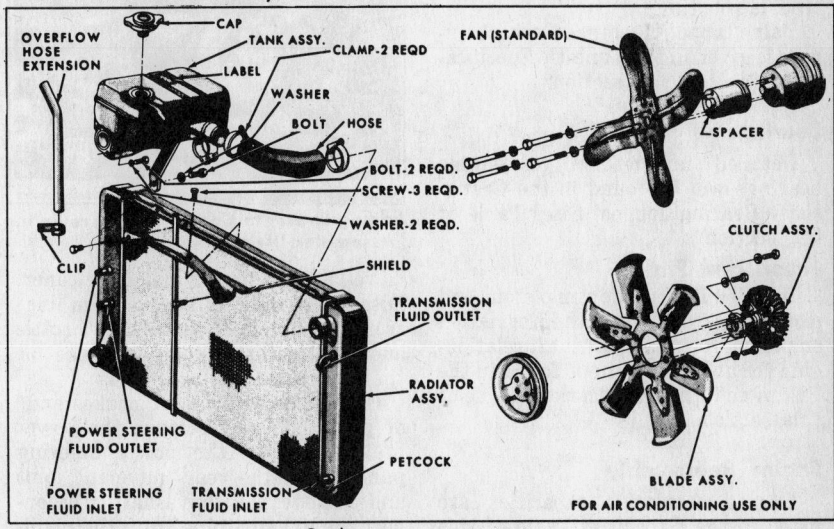

Cooling system components

damaging the radiator core and un-bolt the water pump body and re-move it from the timing case front plate.

Slack off on the generator and power steering belts. Remove the bolts which hold the fan blades and hub extension to the water pump hub and take off the fan blades, extension and water pump pulley. Slide the belts off the vehicle, disconnect the water by-pass hose, and heater hose if car is so equipped.

Remove the bolts which hold the power steering pump to the engine front cover and pull the power steer-ing pump out of the way. Remove the rest of the bolts which hold the water pump to the engine front cover and lift off the pump.

It is not necessary to disconnect the power steering pump lines.

With Power Booster Clutch and Fan

In addition to the above, remove the fan shield. Loosen compressor bracket bolts and adjusting bracket and move compressor inward toward engine. Remove the clutch, fan and pulley as a unit.

Remove coolant supply tank. Loosen and push generator inward. Discon-nect hose. Remove pump retaining bolts and lift out by clearing power steering pump and dipstick bracket.

ENGINE

REFERENCES

In the specifications tables of this section there are listed all the avail-able facts about the engines. When different size engines are used a note

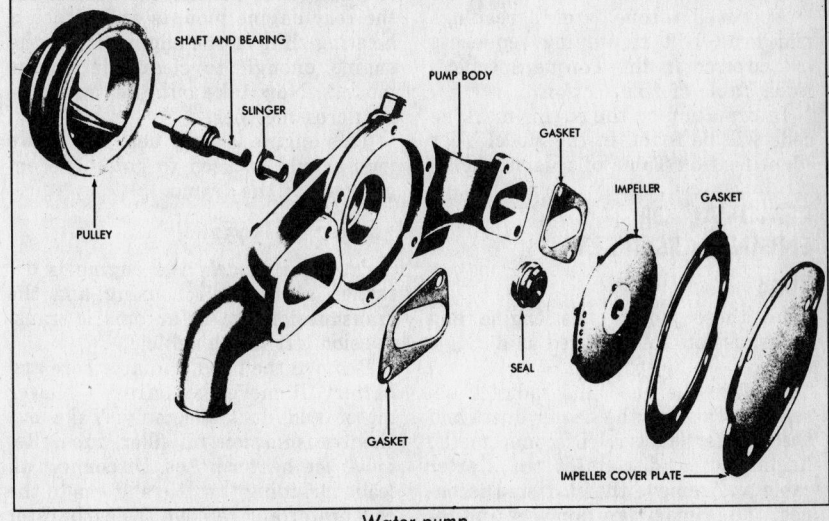

Water pump

LINCOLN and CONTINENTAL

under the General Engine Specifications Table will give an easy means of determining which engine is which.

Where some engines have hydraulic valve lifters and other do not, a means of determining which does and which does not is given in a note under the Tune-Up Table.

Valves

Methods of trouble shooting hydraulic valve lifters are given in the unit repair section under the heading: Lifters, Hydraulic Valve.

Detailed information on the valves, the type of valve guide and the location of valve timing marks, can be found in the Valve Specifications Table of this section.

A general discussion of valve clearance and a chart showing how to read pressure and vacuum gauges when using them to diagnose engine troubles will be found in the Unit Repair section under the heading: Tune-Up-Ignition-Distributors. Under the same head will be found a chart on engine trouble shooting.

Valve tappet clearance for each engine is given in the Tune-Up Specifications Table of this section.

Bearings

Detailed information on engine bearings will be found in the Crankshaft Bearing Journal Sizes Table of this section.

Piston and Pins

Detailed information on pistons and piston pins, together with information on piston, rod and crankshaft relationship for assembly, will be found in the Piston and Pin Specifications Table of this section.

Engine Reassembly

Engine crankcase capacities are listed in the Capacities Table of this section.

Approved torque wrench readings and head bolt tightening sequences are covered in the Torque Specifications Table of this section.

Information on the engine marking code will be found in the Model Year Identification Table of this section.

REMOVAL OF ENGINE ASSEMBLY

1954

On these models the engine and transmission are removed as a single unit.

Remove the hood and radiator assembly. Take off the heater ducts and the heater motor. Disconnect the heater hoses, disconnect the starter cable and remove the starter. Disconnect the primary ignition wire and re-

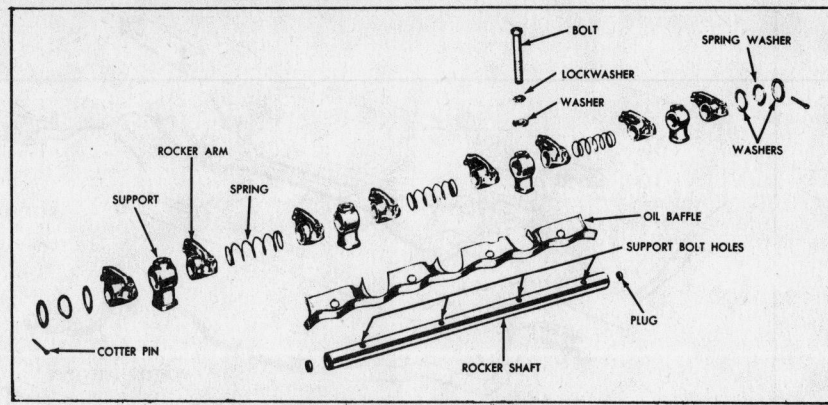
Beginning 1958—Rocker arm and shaft assy.

Adding Spacer to Correct the Valve Spring Assembled Height—Typical

move the carburetor and air cleaner. Disconnect the fuel and vacuum lines from the pump. Remove the throttle and accelerator linkage and take off the carburetor.

On models with power brakes and/or power steering remove the power brake unit and the power steering pump. Split the rear universal joint and remove the driveshaft. Disconnect the exhaust pipe from the manifold and remove the oil filter. Take out the rear engine mounts and attach a hoisting sling to the engine. Raise the engine enough to clear the engine mounts. Now take out the transmission crossmember.

This engine is very heavy and two men should be used to guide the engine out of the frame.

1955 Thru 1957

On these models the engine is detached at the bell housing and the transmission and/or automatic transmission left in the vehicle.

Remove the hood, radiator core and battery. Remove the defroster blower motor and duct assembly. Take out the transmission oil filler tube. Remove the heater hoses. Disconnect all leads including throttle and gas to the carburetor and remove the carburetor

at its air cleaner. Remove the fan, water pump pulley and belts. Remove the power steering pump. Tie the carburetor lines and accelerator rods up out of the way. Disconnect engine ground strap, the temperature sending units and oil pressure sending units. Remove the windshield wiper hose at the vacuum pipe, remove the starter, take off the radiator splash shield, remove the oil filter, take the lower cover off the bottom of the converter and remove the bolts securing the converter to the flex plate. Take out the radio speaker. Fold back the front center floor carpet and remove the two rubber plugs from the access hole in the dash panel. Place a jack under the transmission. Remove the two converter housing to cylinder block cap screws through these two holes. Disconnect the engine front mounting brackets and attach an engine hoist and position the sling to balance the engine after the transmission is off it. Lift the engine slightly and push it forward to clear the dash panel. A helper will probably be required to guide the engine out of the vehicle.

Starting With 1958

On these models the engine and transmission assembly are removed as a unit, they are split at the front universal joint.

Except for those instructions which apply to the detaching of the bell housing and the transmission, the above instructions for 1957 models will apply to 1958 and later models.

Replacement Engines

Replacement engines are available for all Lincoln models and they are also available in factory approved rebuilt types. Short blocks are also stocked which consist of simply a block assembly having pistons, pins, rings, valves and timing sprockets.

Engine assemblies are sold without oil pan, flywheel or inlet manifold.

CYLINDER HEAD

REMOVAL OF ROCKER ASSEMBLIES

Raise the hood and remove the carburetor air cleaner. Disconnect the ignition wires where they cross over the rocker cover. Remove the bolts which hold the rocker cover to the cylinder head, lift off the rocker cover and carefully scrape off its gasket.

Now working a little at a time loosen the bolts which hold the rocker brackets to the cylinder head so that the tension of the valve springs will be left off a little at a time. Once the tension is removed, remove the screws and lift the rocker assemblies up off the cylinder head.

If the rockers are to be disassembled they should be laid out carefully on a bench, disassembled and carefully marked so that they can be reassembled in the same manner in which they were removed. Rocker assemblies are reinstalled in reverse order of removal.

REMOVAL OF ROCKER ARMS

Take off the air cleaner.

Remove the two acorn nuts which hold the rocker cover to the top of the cylinder head and lift off the rocker cover.

Disconnect the oil lines to the rocker shaft and, turning a little at a time, turn out the bolts which hold the rocker shaft brackets to the cylinder head and lift off the rocker shafts.

ROCKER OILING

Oil is fed to the rocker shaft through the passage in the block which lines up with the hole in the cylinder head that indexes through the No. 1 rocker shaft support on the right bank and the No. 2 support on the left bank, from there it goes up into the hollowed out rocker shafts.

CYLINDER HEAD REMOVAL

All OHV Engines

Follow the procedure given for the rocker shafts and the procedure given for the inlet manifolds. Disconnect the exhaust pipes at their flanges, remove the bolts which retain the cylinder heads to the cylinder blocks and lift off the heads.

VALVE SYSTEM

All Models

To replace the valve lifter it is only necessary to take the rocker cover off of the side affected and take off the intake manifold and the valve chamber cover.

With the push rod pulled up out of the way the lifter may be lifted up out of its bore.

<u>Caution:</u> The hydraulic valve lifters are not to be interchanged from one bore to the other. They should be carefully marked so that they will be returned to the bore from which they were removed.

None of the internal parts of the lifters are interchangeable with any other lifter.

VALVE ADJUSTING SEQUENCE

1954 Thru 1957

The initial adjustment of the hydraulic lifter, should be done with the lifter on the base circle of its cam. Now turn adjusting screw clockwise and while rotating push rod remove all slack. Do not force down into hydraulic lifter. With slack removed turn adjusting screw an additional $2\frac{1}{2}$ turns and tighten lock nut.

To insure as near as practical that the lifter will be on the base circle of its cam and with a minimum turning of the engine, proceed as follows: turn the engine until No. 1 cylinder exhaust valve starts to open. Notice that it will be followed closely by No. 7 cylinder inlet valve. When both of these valves are wide open, adjust:

No. 1 cylinder inlet valve
No. 3 cylinder exhaust valve
No. 4 cylinder inlet valve
No. 5 cylinder inlet valve
No. 6 cylinder exhaust valve
No. 7 cylinder exhaust valve
No. 8 cylinder both valves

Now turn the engine one full revolution until No. 6 cylinder exhaust valve starts to open. Notice that it will be followed closely by No. 4 cylinder inlet valve. When both of these valves are wide open, adjust:

No. 1 cylinder exhaust valve
No. 2 cylinder both valves
No. 3 cylinder inlet valve
No. 4 cylinder exhaust valve
No. 5 cylinder exhaust valve
No. 6 cylinder inlet valve
No. 7 cylinder inlet valve

Keep in mind that these cylinders are numbered:

Right front 1-2-3-4
Left front 5-6-7-8

VALVE SPRINGS

All Models

A quick easy way to check the condition of the valve springs is to lay the springs alongside each other on a flat surface. Check with the straight edge to see whether all springs are the same height, and if they are it can be

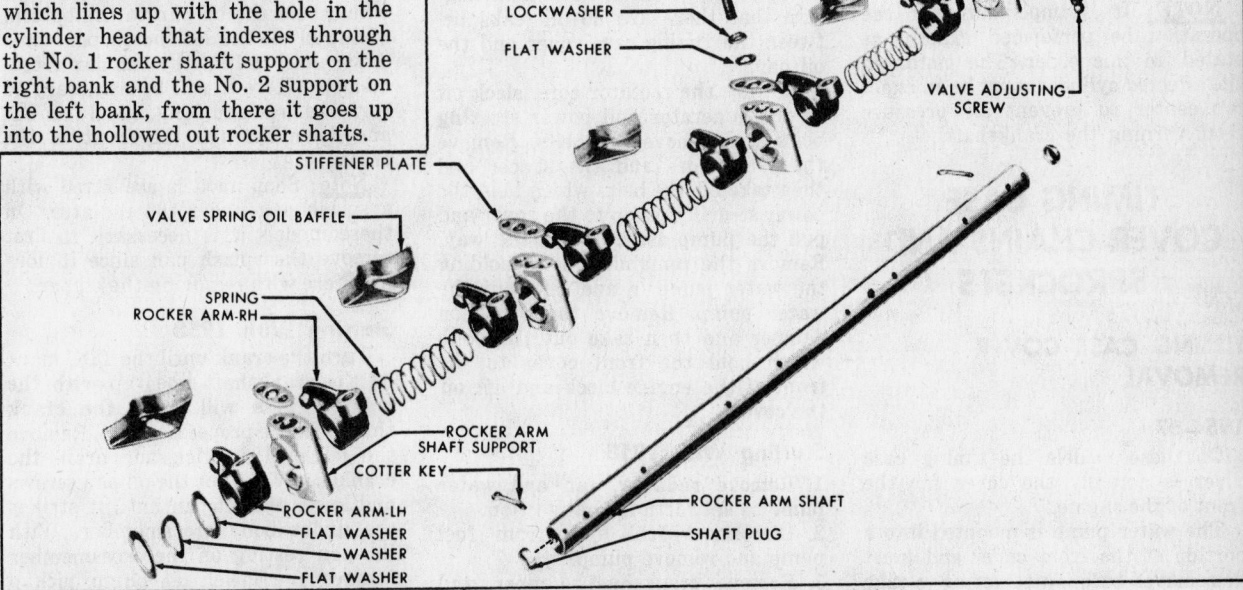

NUT
BOLT
LOCKWASHER
FLAT WASHER
VALVE ADJUSTING SCREW
STIFFENER PLATE
VALVE SPRING OIL BAFFLE
SPRING
ROCKER ARM-RH
ROCKER ARM SHAFT SUPPORT
COTTER KEY
ROCKER ARM-LH
FLAT WASHER
WASHER
FLAT WASHER
ROCKER ARM SHAFT
SHAFT PLUG

Exploded view of the rocker assembly, Typical 1954-57 Models

assumed with a high degree of accuracy that the springs are in good condition since it is extremely unlikely that all of the springs will collapse the same amount.

If, however, any of the springs are shorter than the rest, the free length will have to be checked against a new spring. Only those springs whose free length is equal to the free length of a new spring should be reused; others should be replaced.

⏱ CHILTON TIME-SAVER

The following is a method for replacing valve springs, oil seals or spring retainers without removing the cylinder head.

1. Entirely dismantle a spark plug and save the threaded shell.
2. To this shell, braze or weld an air chuck.
3. Remove the valve rocker cover. Remove the rocker arm from the affected valve.
4. Remove the spark plug from the affected cylinder.
5. Turn the crankshaft to bring the piston of this cylinder down, away from possible contact with the valve head. Sharply tap the valve retainer to loosen the valve lock.
6. Then turn the crankshaft to bring the piston in this cylinder to the **Exact Top of its Compression Stroke.**
7. Screw in the chuck equipped spark plug shell.
8. Hook up an air hose to the chuck and turn on the pressure (about 200 lb).
9. With a strong and constant supply of air holding the valve closed, compress the valve spring and remove the lock and retainer.
10. Make the necessary replacements and reassemble.

NOTE: It is important that the operation be performed exactly as stated, in this order. The piston in the affected cylinder must be on exact top center to prevent air pressure from turning the crankshaft.

TIMING CASE COVER CHAINS AND SPROCKETS

TIMING CASE COVER REMOVAL

1954-57

On these models the timing case cover is actually the cover for the front of the engine.

The water pump is mounted into a portion of the front cover and must be removed before attempting to take the cover off.

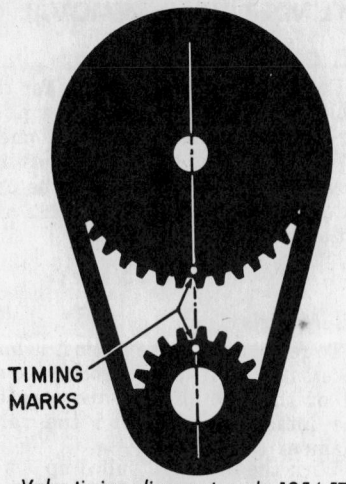

Valve timing alignment marks 1954-57

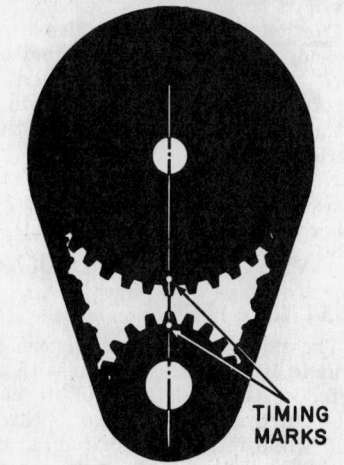

Valve timing alignment marks 1958-63

The lower part of the cover is connected to the oil pan gasket and, if the cover is removed and the gasket disturbed it will be necessary to remove the oil pan in order to make certain that there are no oil leaks between the timing case cover and the oil pan. Remove the radiator core, slack off on the generator and power steering belts and remove the belts. Remove the fan blades and the spacer and then take off the belts which hold the power steering pump to the cover and pull the pump aside out of the way. Remove the remaining bolts holding the water pump in and take out the water pump. Remove the vibration damper and then take out the bolts which hold the front cover to the front of the engine block and lift off the cover.

Starting With 1958

1. Remove radiator, fan and water pump as set forth in that section.
2. Disconnect fuel lines from fuel pump and remove pump.
3. Remove crankshaft damper and key.

4. Remove cup type plug from top of front cover and remove fuel pump push rod.
5. Remove front cover. **Note:** Care must be used not to damage gasket between cover and oil pan. Should this be broken it will be necessary to remove the oil pan and replace the gasket.
To Replace: Reverse the above.

VALVE TIMING PROCEDURE AND/OR TIMING SPROCKET REPLACEMENT

Remove the radiator core, vibration damper and timing case cover, as explained in paragraphs devoted to these subjects.

Turn the crankshaft so the mark on the crankshaft and the mark on the cam sprocket are nearest each other and in line between shaft centers and then remove the camshaft sprocket and chain. Arrange the chain on the old (or new) sprockets so that the marks will be nearest each other and in line between the shaft centers and then replace the camshaft sprocket with the chain fitted over it onto the camshaft and bolt in place. Turn the engine two full revolutions, then make certain that the marks on the sprockets are in line between the shaft centers.

ENGINE LUBRICATION

OIL PAN REMOVAL

1954 Thru 1957

Disconnect the large oil line from the oil pump outside of the oil pan, remove the flywheel cover plate from the front face of the flywheel (on models so equipped), remove the bolts which hold the oil pan to the bottom of the block and let the oil pan come down until it hits the tubular crossmember. Here it will be necessary to turn the crank to feed the oil pan out and down through the front of the engine.

Note: Some models are fitted with a splash pan under the radiator. On these models it is necessary to first remove the splash pan since it does interfere with removing the oil pan.

Starting With 1958

Turn the crank until the TDC mark on the crankshaft lines up with the pointer. This will place the crank throws in the proper position. Remove the oil level dipstick and drain the crankcase. Take out the oil pan screws and lower the oil pan until it strikes the under body crossmember. With the pan resting on the crossmember remove the lower oil pump pickup tube and loosen the upper tube and

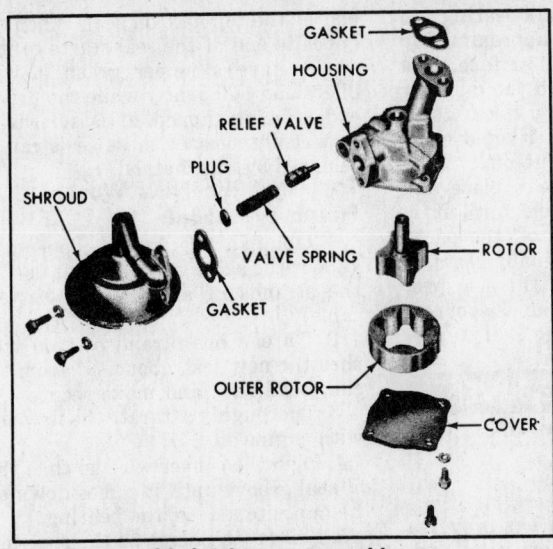

Disassembled Oil Pump Assembly

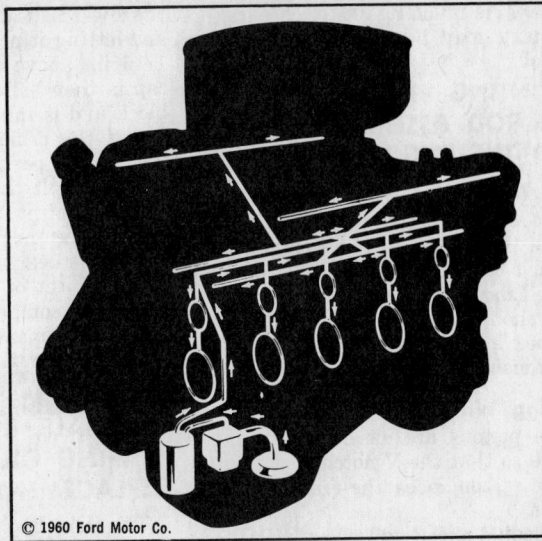

Lubrication system.

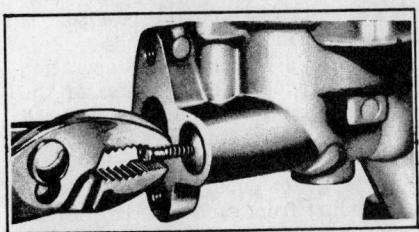

Removing Relief Valve Plug

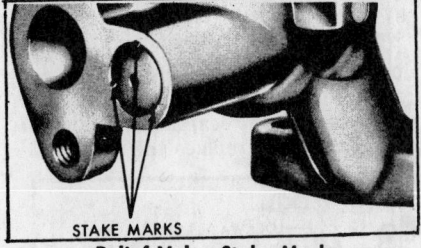

Relief Valve Stake Marks

screen assembly bolts. This allows the screen assembly to swing forward to clear the oil pan baffles. Remove the oil pan in a lowering forward motion. Carefully scrape the gasket from the block and the oil pan. Replace the pan, using a new gasket, in the reverse order that removed it.

OIL FILTER REPLACEMENT

1954 Thru 1956

The oil filter is located on the left side of the crankcase below and in back of the steering gear. It is held by a single bolt.

Jack up the car and cramp the wheels hard to the right and loosen the one bolt which holds the oil filter can to the crankcase and let the oil filter can drain. Remove the bolt. Now carefully thread the oil filter down between the flywheel housing and the tie rods. Sometimes this is rather a tedious job, but it can be done without dropping the tie rods.

1957 Lincoln and 1957 Continental Mark II

A disposable element type filter is used on these models. No tools are required to place the element; it is on a bayonet joint and it is simply untwisted from the engine and the element removed and a new one installed.

Starting 1958 Models

The oil filter is located on the left side of the engine towards the front and is simply unscrewed from its fitting. Access to the filter is from under the vehicle.

CONNECTING RODS AND PISTONS

REMOVAL OF ROD AND PISTON ASSEMBLY

On all Lincoln and Continental models the rod and piston assemblies are removed through the top of the block.

Remove the oil pan and cylinder heads.

Start with any pistons that are down and remove the ring ridge from the top of the cylinder wall with a ring ridge reamer or a good bearing scraper.

From underneath the car take off the lower half of the connecting rod on those rods where the ridge has been taken from the top of the cylinder. Carefully mark the cap so that it can be replaced in the same position on the same rod or better yet, or install the cap on the rod immediately.

Push the upper half of the rod and piston assembly up out of the top of the block.

Repeat on the rest of the cylinders and piston assemblies.

PISTON INSPECTION

Examine the piston, particularly the thrust surface for scores and

scratches, and if any are found immediately examine the cylinder wall to see if there are matching scratches on the cylinder wall. If there are, the cylinder will have to be rebored or honed.

If there are scores or scratches on the piston but none on the cylinder wall, the piston can usually be dressed down, providing of course it isn't enough to spoil the fit.

WRIST PINS

Thru 1957 Models

The wrist pins used in the above models are of the full floating type. They are retained in the piston by lock wires at each end of the pin.

Wrist pins require ream or hone fit and must be fitted with extreme care.

Hone or diamond boring is recommended for fitting wrist pins.

Starting With 1958

The wrist pin is a press fit in the connecting rod, the bearing is in the piston.

If the pin can be moved in the connecting rod with less than 20 ft. lbs. torque the press fit between the piston and the rod is insufficient and either the pin or the connecting rod or both must be replaced.

The pin should be pressed in so that the connecting rod is nicely centered between the bosses of the piston without the pin protruding at either side.

CONNECTING RODS

Connecting rods used in all Lincoln engines are fitted with an individual type connecting rod bearing.

The Lincoln Division does not recommend adjusting these rod bearings. However, it is possible to secure a good working adjustment by placing a feather or taper type shim between the lower part of the rod bearing and the cap. As much as .004 inch excessive play may be taken up by this method.

MOUNTING PISTON AND ROD ASSEMBLIES INTO THE ENGINE

Thru 1957

The letter F or the dimple stamped at the top of the piston should face forward on both banks.

All Lincoln piston and connecting rods should be assembled with the rod bearing spit hole UP, or facing the camshaft.

Starting With 1958

The pistons are assembled to the engine so that the V notch at the top of the piston faces the front of the engine.

A double check will show that the numbers at the bottom of the connecting rods face away from the camshaft on both banks.

REAR MAIN BEARING OIL SEAL

All Models

The rear main bearing oil seal on all models of Lincoln is a packing type seal which requires the removal of the crankshaft to replace the upper half. The lower half may be replaced, however, by removing the crankshaft rear main bearing cap and inserting a new packing into the packing retainer. It is sometimes possible to correct an oil leak at the rear main bearing by installing new packing in

the lower half of the main bearing cap and letting it protrude approximately 1/16 in. above the cap surface. The cap is then bolted up to the cylinder block and is immediately taken down and if the packing has riveted over, the riveted portion is cut off.

Again bolt the cap into place and keep repeating this cycle until it is either necessary to cut off the packing or the bearing cap finally seats.

The object of letting the seal protrude is to compress the upper portion of the rear main bearing seal to prevent a leak at that point.

⏱ CHILTON TIME-SAVER

TOP HALF, REAR MAIN BEARING OIL SEAL REPLACEMENT

The following method has proven a distinct advantage in most cases and, if successful, saves many hours of labor.

1. Drain engine oil and remove oil pan.
2. Remove rear main bearing cap.
3. With a 6″ length of 3/16″ brazing rod, drive up on either exposed

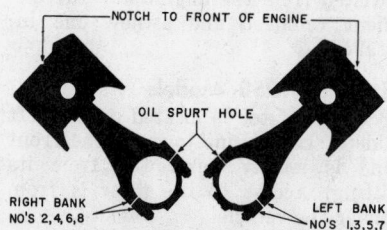

1958-63—Position of Oil Squirt Hole

end of the top half oil seal. When the opposite end of the seal starts to protrude, have a helper grasp it with pliers and pull gently while the driven end is being tapped. It is surprising how easily most of these seals can be removed by this method.

To Install the New Woven Fabric Type Seal:

1. Obtain a 12″ piece of copper wire (about the same guage as that used in the strands of an insulated battery cable).
2. Thread one strand of this wire thru the new seal, about ½″ from the end, bend back and make secure.
3. Thoroughly saturate the new seal with engine oil.
4. Push the copper wire up thru the oil seal groove until it comes down on the opposite side of the bearing.
5. Pull (with pliers) on the protruding copper wire while the crankshaft is being turned and the new seal is slowly fed into place.

CAUTION: This snaking operation slightly reduces the diameter of the new seal and care will have to be used to keep the seal from slipping too far thru the top half of the bearing.

6. When an equal amount of seal is extending from each side, cut off the copper wire close to the seal and tamp both ends of the seal up into the groove (this will tend to expand the seal again) Don't worry about the copper wire left in the groove, it is too soft to cause damage.

7. Replace the seal in the cap in the usual way and replace the oil pan.

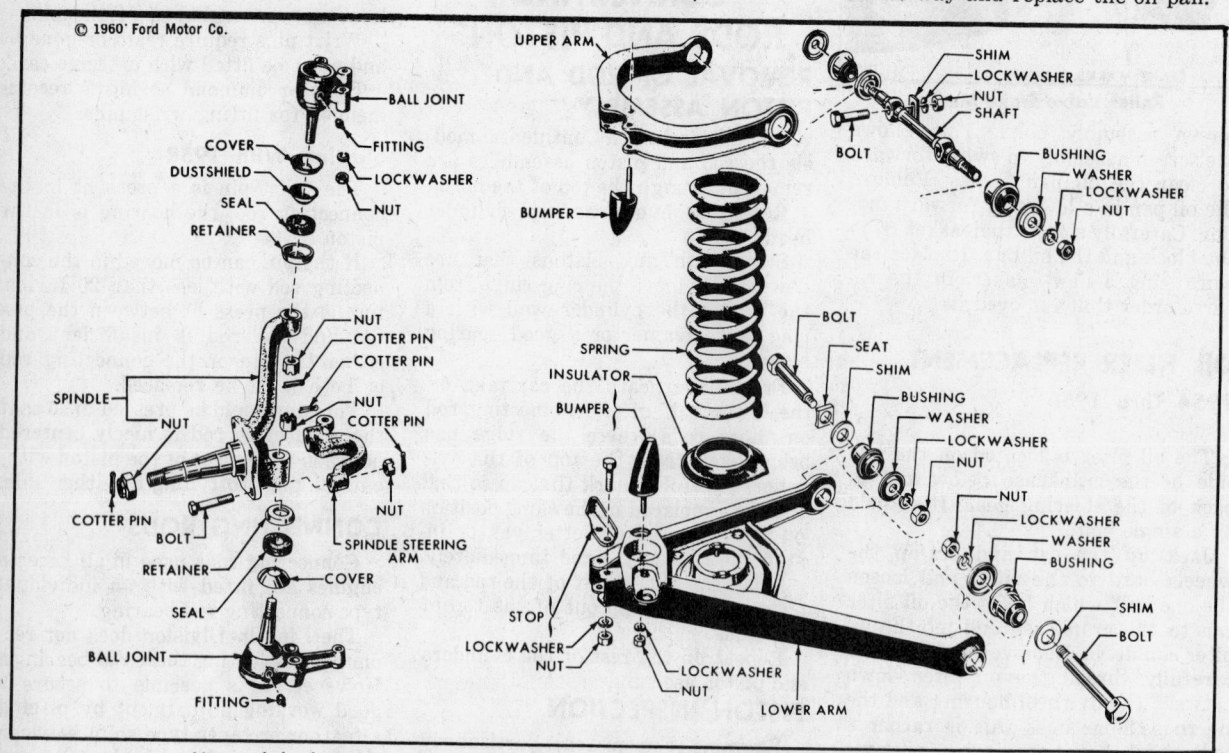

Views of the front suspension used on 1956-57 models. Typical of all Lincoln ball joint suspensions.

FRONT SUSPENSION

REFERENCES

General instructions covering the front suspension and how to repair and adjust it, together with information on installation of front wheel bearings and grease seals, are given in the Unit Repair section under the heading: Suspension, Front Repair.

Definitions of the points of steering geometry are covered in the Unit Repair section under the heading: Suspension, Front Align. This article also covers trouble shooting front end geometry and irregular tire wear.

Figures covering the caster, camber, toe-in, king pin inclination and turning radius can be found in the Front Wheel Alignment Table of this section.

Wheelbase, tread and tire size figures can be found in the General Chassis and Brake Specifications Table of this section.

STEERING WHEEL AND HORN BUTTON

REMOVAL OF STEERING WHEEL

All Models

Remove cap and emblem assembly by simply prying it up off the steering wheel. Remove the steering wheel nut and, using a puller, pull the steering wheel off the sector shaft.

REMOVAL OF HORN BUTTON HORN BLOWING RINGS

First look to see if the horn ring is mounted on top of or underneath the steering wheel. If it is mounted underneath the steering wheel, pry up the medallion, remove the steering wheel and the horn blowing ring can then be detached from the top of the steering column.

If the horn blowing ring is mounted on top of the steering wheel; simply pry off the medallion in the center, which will give access to the wheel nut which holds the blowing ring in place.

STEERING GEAR ASSEMBLY

Manual Steering Gear

Instructions covering the overhaul of the steering gear will be found in the Unit Repair section under the heading: Steering, Manual.

Power Steering Gears

Trouble shooting and repair instructions covering power steering gears are given in the Unit Repair section under the heading: Steering, Power.

ADJUSTMENT OF STEERING MECHANISM

All Models

Complete instructions on the ad-

© 1962 Ford Motor Co.

justment of this and all other manual steering gears is given in the Manual Steering Gear section of the manual, see index.

REMOVAL OF STEERING GEAR ASSEMBLY FROM VEHICLE

Continental Mark II Models

Remove the steering wheel and the pitman arm. Disconnect the battery and take out the cover plate and insulator from the bottom end of the steering column in the engine compartment. Disconnect the shift rods at the bottom of the steering column. Remove the dash panel trim pad and the trim panel from the steering column where it connects to the instrument panel. Disconnect the wires from

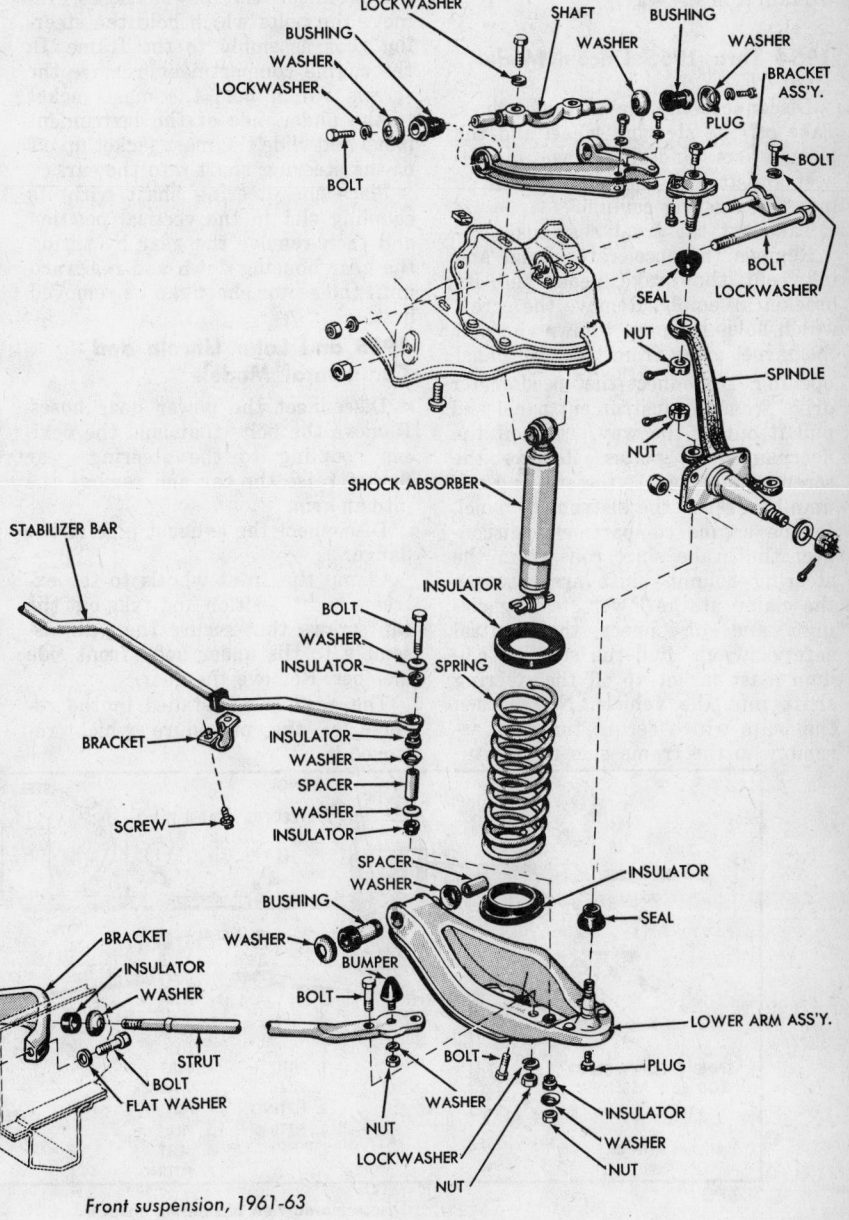

Front suspension, 1961-63

under the dash which go into the steering column. Disconnect the neutral safety and back-up light switch. Remove the screws which secure the mast jacket tube to the lower side of the instrument panel. In the engine compartment, take off the air cleaner and the air duct as an assembly and remove the exhaust manifold on that side of the car. Disconnect the power hoses and remove the screws which hold the gear housing to the frame.

Inside the car, slide the steering column tube up off the steering shaft and into the car.

In the engine compartment, turn the gear around so that the cross shaft faces up. Now lift the gear assembly upwards between the fender apron and the engine and remove it over the top of the radiator.

Cover the seat assembly so as not to stain it in any way.

1954 Thru 1955 Lincoln Models

Disconnect the power brake lines. Take off the steering wheel and the pitman arm. Under the dash, disconnect and tag all the wires which go into the steering column.

Take out the front seat cushion.

Remove the accelerator pedal and take out the brake pedal and its bracket assembly. Remove the screw which holds the carpet down and pull the carpet away from the dash panel opening. Disconnect the speedometer drive from the instrument panel and pull it out of the way. Take off the floorpan cover plates. Remove the screws which secure the steering column bracket to the instrument panel. In the engine compartment, disconnect the brake shift rods from the steering column shift arm. Loosen the clamp at the lower steering column and disconnect the neutral safety switch. Pull the steering column mast jacket up off the steering shaft into the vehicle. Now loosen the bolts which secure the gear assembly to the frame side rail.

Pull the unit up into the driving compartment.

1956 Thru 1957 Lincoln Models

Remove the steering wheel and the pitman arm. Under the dash, disconnect and tag the wires which go into the steering column. Under the dash, remove the radio speaker, disconnect the speedometer cable at the speedometer head, the accelerator rod at the clevis connection, and remove the brake pedal pad. Pull back the floor carpet and remove the clamps from the bottom of the steering column. Take off the floor access hole cover. At the bottom of the steering column disconnect the shift rods from the shaft. Disconnect the exhaust pipe and the exhaust manifold. Take out the spark plugs on the left bank of cylinders.

Disconnect the power hoses, remove the bolts which hold the steering gear assembly to the frame. In the engine compartment, remove the screws which hold the mast jacket to the under side of the instrument panel and slide the mast jacket up off of the steering shaft into the car.

Place the steering shaft with its coupling slot in the vertical position and then remove the gear by tilting the gear housing down and rearward until the sector shaft can be removed first.

1958 and Later Lincoln and Continental Models

Disconnect the power gear hoses. Remove the bolts that hold the flexible coupling to the steering gear flange, raise the car and remove the pitman arm.

Disconnect the exhaust pipe at the flange.

Clamp the front wheels to the extreme right position and take out the cap screws that secure the gear assembly to the under body front side member. Remove the gear.

The gear is reinstalled in the reverse of the procedure which removed it.

REPLACEMENT OF INTERMEDIATE STEERING ARM

The intermediate steering arm is held to the frame by a bolted on bracket. This bracket is roughly "S" shaped on some of the earlier models "U" shaped on the 1954 thru 1956 models and "L" shaped on the 1957 to 1963 models.

To remove it, detach the bracket from the frame and then unscrew the bracket from the upper end of the intermediate arm. The arm itself can then be unscrewed from the tie rod bushing. After which the bushings can be unscrewed from the bracket and the tie rod arm.

TURBO-DRIVE TRANSMISSION

A "Turbo-Drive" automatic transmission is used on all models.

GENERAL INFORMATION APPLICABLE TO TURBO-DRIVE

LINKAGE ADJUSTMENTS
Starting 1955

Linkage adjustments should be made according to the following sequence. (Fig. 2.)
1. Adjust engine idle speed.
2. Adjust carburetor to control shaft rod.
3. Adjust accelerator shaft to transmission control shaft rod.
4. Adjust transmission control shaft to transmission rod.
5. Manual linkage.

IDLE SPEED

1. Apply parking brake. Start engine and place selector lever in ("DR" for turbo-drive or "DR 2" for twin range turbo-drive) position.
2. Hook up tachometer.

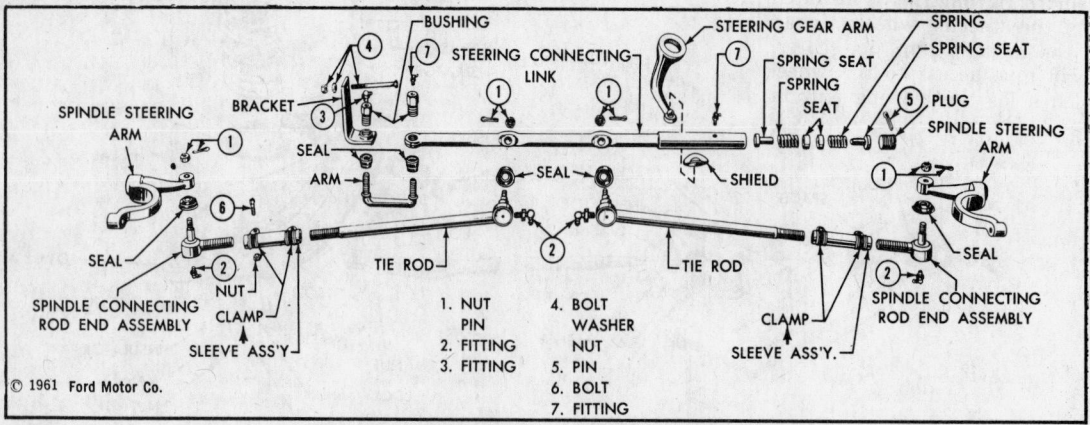

Disassembled view of steering linkage

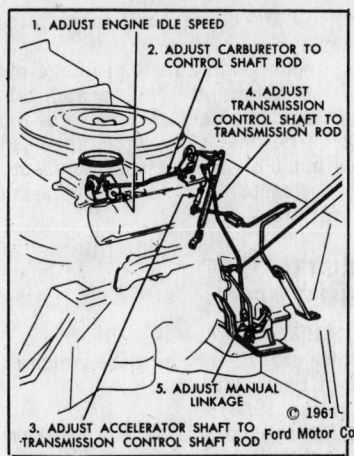

Fig. 2—Sequence of Linkage Adjustments

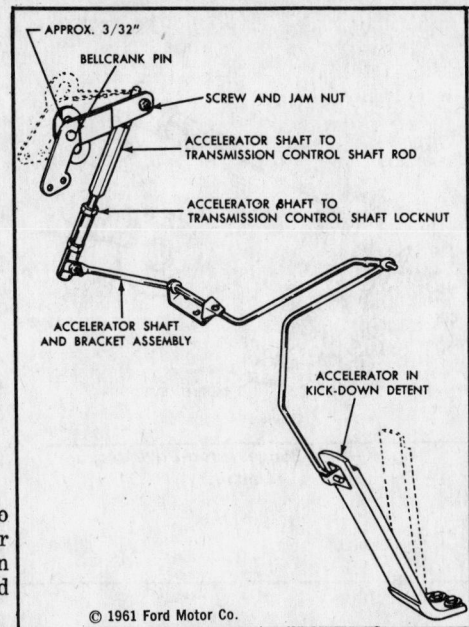

Fig. 4—Accelerator Shaft to Transmission Control Shaft Rod Adjustment

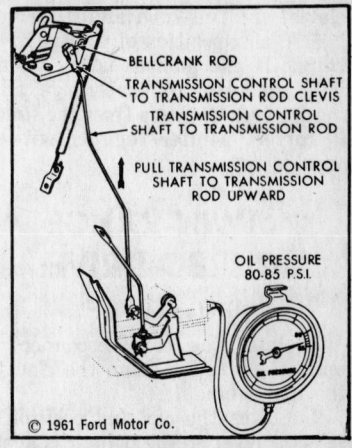

Fig. 5—Transmission Control Shaft to Transmission Rod Adjustment

3. Disconnect the carburetor to control shaft rod from the carburetor lever and disconnect the transmission control shaft to transmission rod from the bellcrank rod. (Fig. 3).

4. With engine at normal operating temperature and the carburetor lever against the hot idle screw, adjust the hot idle screw to 450-475 R.P.M. (in "DR" for turbo-drive or "DR 2" for twin-range turbo-drive) position.

CARBURETOR TO TRANSMISSION CONTROL SHAFT ROD ADJUSTMENT

1. Adjust anti-stall dashpot, (Fig. 3). Clearance between dashpot button and carburetor lever should be .067".

2. Insert a ¼" diameter gauge pin through the bellcrank bracket and tab, (as in Fig. 2-4).

3. Holding the carburetor lever against the hot-idle screw, adjust the carburetor rod to a length that will permit the rod pin to enter the carburetor lever freely. Lengthen the carburetor rod one complete turn and reassemble to the carburetor lever.

4. Remove the ¼" gauge pin.

ACCELERATOR SHAFT-TO-TRANSMISSION CONTROL SHAFT ROD ADJUSTMENT

1. With ignition key "off" push the accelerator to full kickdown position. Check the position of the bellcrank slot and pin. Check alignment of the accelerator shaft to transmission control shaft rod, (Fig. 4). The control shaft pin must be within 3/32" from the top of the bellcrank slot.

2. It is quite important that no binding exists at either end of the vertical, accelerator shaft to transmission control shaft rod. Adjust the screw and jam-nut, so that this rod is vertical, relative to the sides of the car. If it is not, binding will result.

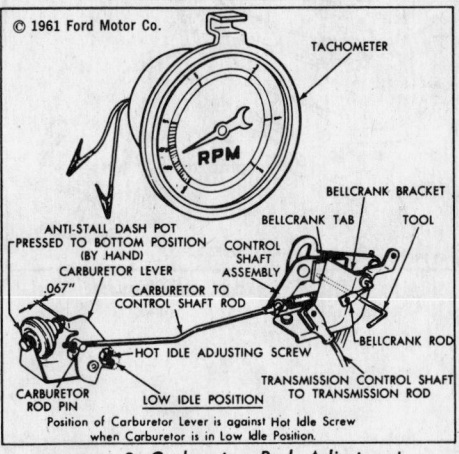

Fig. 3—Carburetor Rod Adjustment

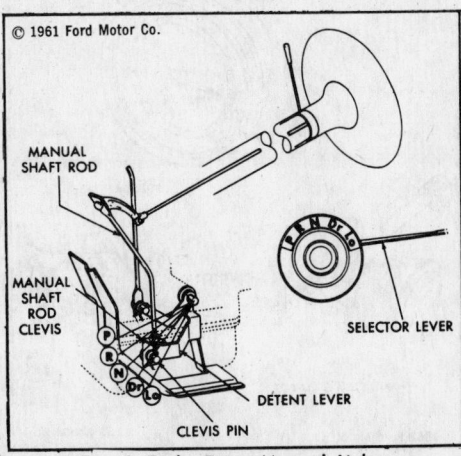

Fig. 6—Turbo-Drive Manual Linkage

TRANSMISSION CONTROL SHAFT TO TRANSMISSION ROD ADJUSTMENT

1. Raise the car and hook-up a pressure gauge at the rear of the transmission.

2. Lower the car. Pull up on the transmission control shaft to transmission rod, firmly but gently, (Fig. 5). Adjust the clevis at the bellcrank rod so the clevis pin enters freely. Lengthen the clevis, three full turns, and reassemble.

3. Start the engine, and with the **foot brake** (service brake) applied firmly, place the selector lever in "DR" for turbo-drive or "DR-2" for twin-range turbo-drive.

4. Accelerate the engine to 1,000 R.P.M. Pressure gauge must read 80-85 P.S.I., (Fig. 5). To change the pressure, adjust the length of the transmission control shaft to transmission rod. Lengthen the rod to increase pressure, shorten the rod to reduce pressure.

CAUTION:

Make these pressure surges quickly and return the selector to neutral to avoid serious transmission damage.

5. Raise the car and remove the gauge.

MANUAL LINKAGE ADJUSTMENT TURBO-DRIVE— REFER TO FIG. 6

1. Raise the car. Disconnect the manual shaft rod from the clevis pin.

2. Lower the car and position the selector lever so the pointer is against the stop in drive range. (This position must be held all during manual linkage adjustment.)

3. Place the detent lever, in the second position from the bottom, (drive position).

4. Adjust the manual shaft rod clevis so the clevis pin enters clevis and detent lever freely. Lengthen the

clevis, one full turn and reassemble.

5. Check position of pointer in each range. If the pointer is not lined up with the letters in each range, adjust the letters. **Do not adjust the linkage to correct pointer register with letters.**

TWIN-RANGE TURBO-DRIVE:

Refer to Fig. 7

1. Raise the car. Disconnect the manual shaft rod from the clevis, at the clevis pin.

2. Lower the car and position the selector lever so the pointer is against the stop in "RD 2" range. (This position must be maintained throughout the manual adjustment.)

3. Position the detent lever in the third position ("DR 2" detent) from the bottom. (The second detent is "DR 1" and the bottom detent is "low".)

4. Adjust the manual shaft rod clevis so the clevis pin enters the clevis detent and lever freely. Lengthen the clevis one full turn and reassemble.

5. Check the position of the pointer in each range. If the pointer does not line up with the letters in each range, adjust the letters. **Do not adjust the linkage to correct pointer register with letters.**

Beginning 1959 Engine R.P.M.

1. Apply parking brake, start engine and place selector lever in "DR 2" position.

2. Hook-up tachometer.

3. Check dashpot for bottom clearance, (Fig. 8). Hold carburetor lever against hot idle screw and depress dashpot plunger by hand. Clearance should be .060" to .090", (refer to "dashpot adjustment").

4. With engine at normal operating temperature and the primary throttle shaft lever against the hot idle screw, adjust the screw to 450-475 R.P.M. engine speed, with selector lever in "DR 2" position.

CARBURETOR ROD ADJUSTMENT

1. Disconnect the transmission throttle rod at "C" and carburetor rod at "A."

2. Insert ¼" gauge pin through alignment holes in bellcrank bracket and tab at "D", (Fig. 9).

3. Hold carburetor lever against hot idle screw, adjust length of carburetor rod between "A" and "B" for free fit into carburetor lever. Lengthen the rod one turn.

4. Remove ¼" gauge pin from

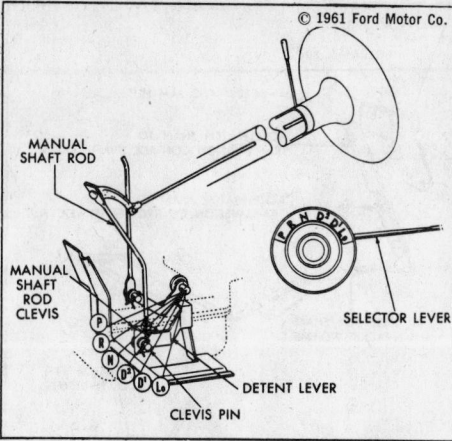

Fig. 7—Twin-Range Turbo-Drive Manual Linkage

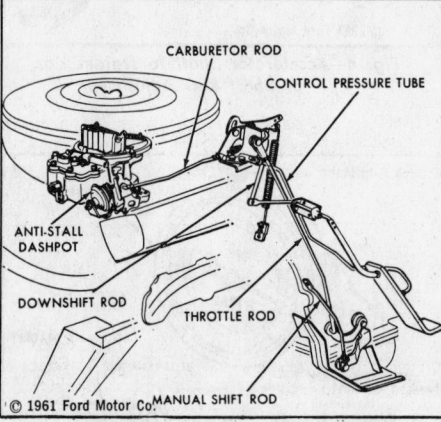

Fig. 8—Linkage Adjustments

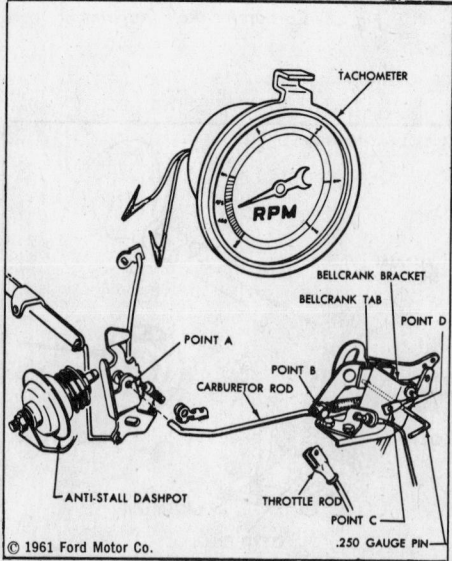

Fig. 9—Carburetor Rod Adjustment

bellcrank and connect rod to carburetor lever.

5. Recheck alignment of gauge pin holes in bellcrank bracket and tab. Further adjustment of carburetor rod may be needed. (The ¼" gauge pin holes must be in alignment to assure correct carburetor - to - transmission calibration.

THROTTLE ROD ADJUSTMENT

1. (1959 Cars):
Raise car. Install pressure gauge at rear of transmission.
(Begining 1960):
Raise the hood. Connect pressure gauge to bellcrank fitting, (Fig. 10).

2. Pull up on throttle rod, (Fig. 10). Adjust clevis at "C" so the clevis pin enters freely. Lengthen clevis 3½ turns and reassemble throttle rod. (**This is a preliminary setting only. Final setting must be made with pressure gauge reading of 80-85 P.S.I. at 1,000 R.P.M.**).

3. Start engine, set foot brake firmly and place selector lever at "D2".

4. Accelerate engine to 1,000 R.P.M. Pressure gauge reading must be 80-85 P.S.I. Lengthen the clevis to increase pressure, shorten the clevis to reduce pressure.

<u>CAUTION:</u>
These checks must be made quickly. The selector must be returned to neutral and the throttle closed after each check to avoid overheating and damage to the transmission.

5. Remove pressure gauge and seal up the fitting.

DOWNSHIFT ROD ADJUSTMENT

1. With ignition key "off", push accelerator to full kick-down position. Check position of bellcrank slot and pin. The pin must be within 3/32" from the top of the bellcrank slot. (Release accelerator pedal when making adjustment.)

2. It is important that no binding exists at either end of downshift rod, (Fig. 11). If downshift rod is not vertical and free, binding will result and travel will be restricted. After adjustment tighten jam nuts.

3. With the accelerator again depressed the top of the bellcrank pin must be within 3/32" from the top of the bellcrank slot. To adjust, disconnect the downshift rod at "F", (Fig. 11). Lengthen or shorten the rod, as needed, to obtain correct linkage travel.

DASHPOT ADJUSTMENT, FIG. 9

With the carburetor lever held firmly against the hot idle screw, de-

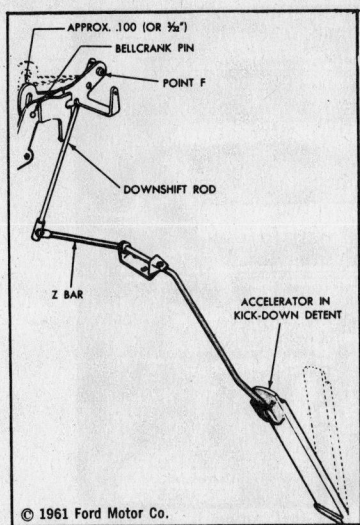

Fig. 11—Downshift Rod Adjustment

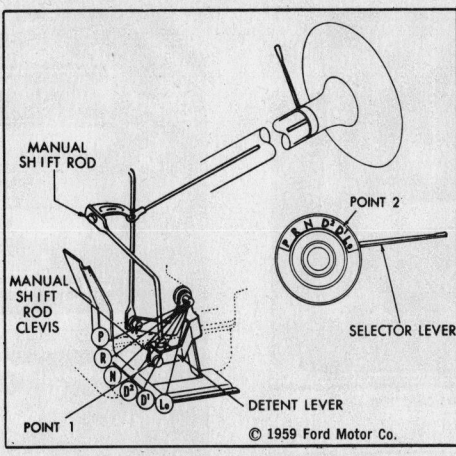

Fig. 12—Manual Linkage Adjustment

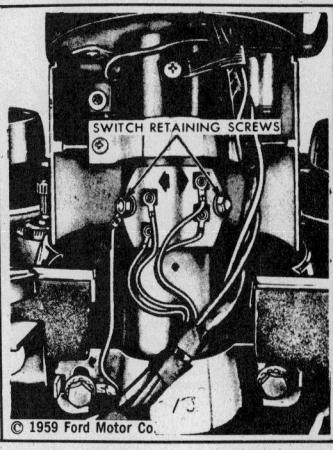

Fig. 13—Starter Neutral Switch

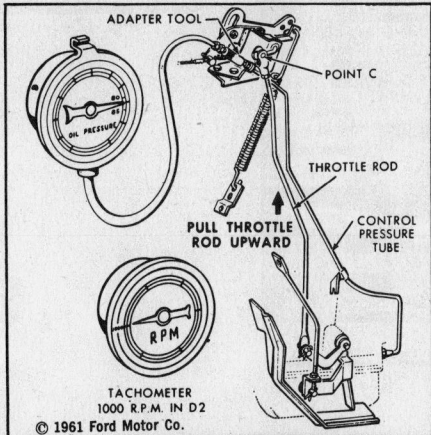

Fig. 10—Throttle Rod Adjustment

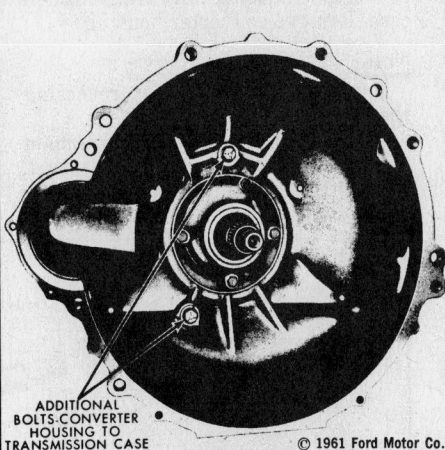

Fig. 14—Additional Bolts Attaching Converter Housing to Transmission Case

press dashpot plunger by hand and check clearance between lever and plunger. Clearance should be .060"-.090".

2. Adjust clearance by loosening the lock nut and turning the dashpot in its mounting bracket.

3. When clearance is correct, tighten the locknut.

MANUAL LINKAGE ADJUSTMENT (FIG. 12)

1. Raise the car. Disconnect the manual rod clevis at point "1".

2. Lower the car and position the selector lever at point "2", so the pointer is against the stop in "D1" range. (Hold this position throughout manual adjustment.)

3. Position the detent lever in the second position, ("D1") from the bottom.

4. Adjust the manual rod clevis so the clevis pin enters the detent lever freely. Lengthen the clevis one full turn and reassemble.

5. Check position of pointer through the full shifting range. If pointer does not line up with quadrant indicator letters, adjust the letters.

STARTER-NEUTRAL SWITCH ADJUSTMENT, (FIG. 13)

The starter-neutral switch is located on the under side of the steering column, inside of the passenger compartment.

1. Remove two lower steering column shroud attaching screws and remove the shroud.

2. Loosen starter-neutral switch to steering column retaining screws.

3. Position switch so that the starter circuit is closed when the selector is in the "N" and "P" positions. Circuit must be open in all positions except "neutral" and "park".

4. Tighten switch retaining screws. Double check selector position relative to open and closed starter—neutral switch circuits.

5. Install steering column lever shroud.

REMOVE & REPLACE TRANSMISSION

TURBO-DRIVE

Note:

1956-57 Continental Mark II requires that the engine be removed to accomplish the removal of the transmission.

REMOVE AND REPLACE

To remove the transmission from any Lincoln or Lincoln Continental it is necessary to remove the gear box and converter housing assembly as a unit. Two additional converter housing-to-transmission case bolts are located behind the converter assembly and are not accessible until after the converter has been removed, (Fig. 14).

Refer to (Fig. 15) for identity of underbody components.

1. Raise the hood and disconnect accelerator linkage (downshift rod) from bellcrank.

2. Remove 2 upper bolts and one bolt from right side of converter housing to engine block.

3. Remove one inner upper bolt attaching the starter motor to the converter housing.

4. Install remote control starter switch to the starter solenoid and put the transmission in neutral. Raise the car.

5. Disconnect the engine stabilizer bar bracket from the converter housing, (Fig. 16). Remove converter housing lower plate.

6. Drain the converter.

7. Disconnect the fluid filler tube at the transmission and drain transmission.

8. Remove exhaust cross-over pipe.

9. Disconnect oil cooler lines at transmission.

10. Index mark the rear universal joint and pinion flange to help upon reassembly. Disconnect propeller shaft at rear universal joint and remove the shaft.

11. Disconnect parking brake cables and the spring from equalizer bar. Remove the bar.

12. Remove two remaining bolts

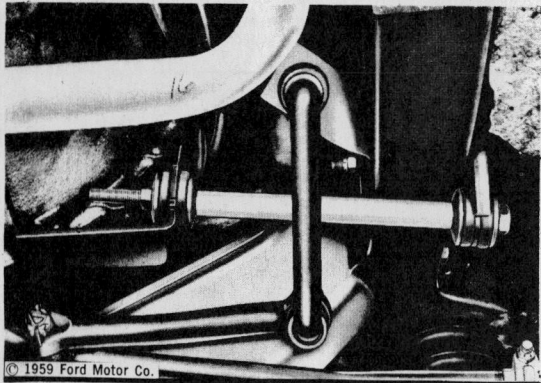

Fig. 16—Engine Stabilizer Bar Installation

Fig. 17—Transmission Jack in Position

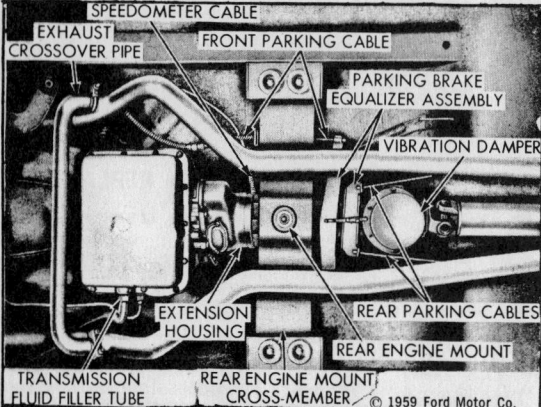

Fig. 15—Transmission and Under Body Components

UNIVERSAL JOINTS AND DRIVE LINE

REMOVAL OF THE UNIVERSAL JOINTS AND DRIVE SHAFTS

All Except Mark II Thru 1960

Remove the four bolts which hold the bearing pillow block to the rear axle pinion, lower the drive shaft and slide it out off the end of the transmission. It will come off complete with the front universal joint.

The entire assembly can be carried to the bench. The cross is held into the drive shaft yoke by lock rings at the outside of the bearings.

Remove the lock ring and drive the right side bearing across so that the left side bearing comes out.

Now drive the cross across to the right side bearing, driving it out.

Both of the universal joints are split in this manner.

from starter motor to converter housing. Disconnect starter cable from electrical power box. Slide starter motor forward over the crossmember and secure out of the way.

13. Remove control linkage splash shield. Disconnect manual and throttle control linkage from the transmission.

14. Disconnect speedometer at transmission.

15. Remove nut and washer from engine rear mount lower stud.

16. Secure transmission jack under, and raise the transmission off the rear mount crossmember, (Fig. 17).

17. Remove two attaching bolts from the rear mount to the transmission extension housing.

18. Remove four attaching bolts and nuts from the crossmember to underbody brackets, (Fig. 15).

19. Remove the rear mount from the crossmember. Then remove the crossmember by sliding it over the left exhaust pipe to the rear of the left mounting bracket.

20. Lower the transmission jack slightly and remove the remaining three converter housing to engine block bolts.

21. Move transmission toward the rear, lower, and remove from under the car.

22. Remove converter from converter housing.

23. Remove six bolts holding the converter housing to transmission case. Remove converter housing.

Note:

Replace transmission by reversing the above procedure.

For further detail and overhaul data on "turbo-drive" transmissions, see **Unit Repair Section—Transmission Group.**

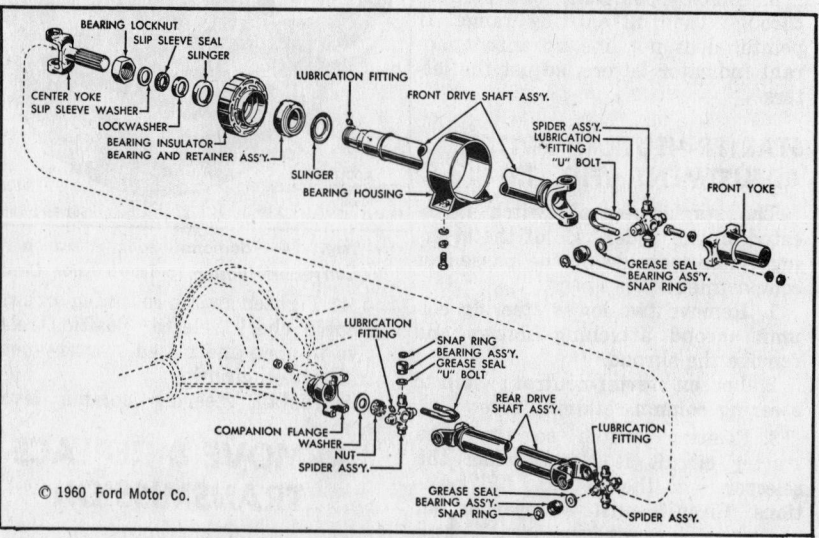

Drive shaft and universal joints, Continental Mark II

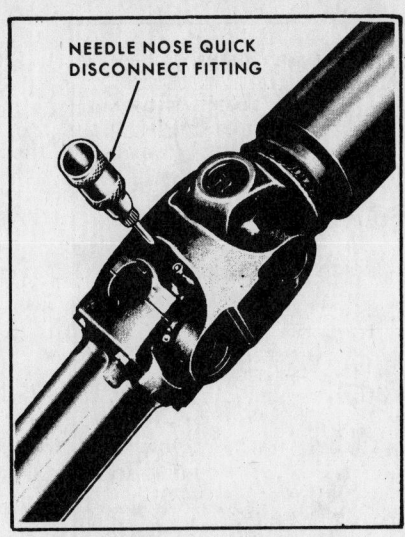

Adapter for Lubricating Centering Socket Yoke

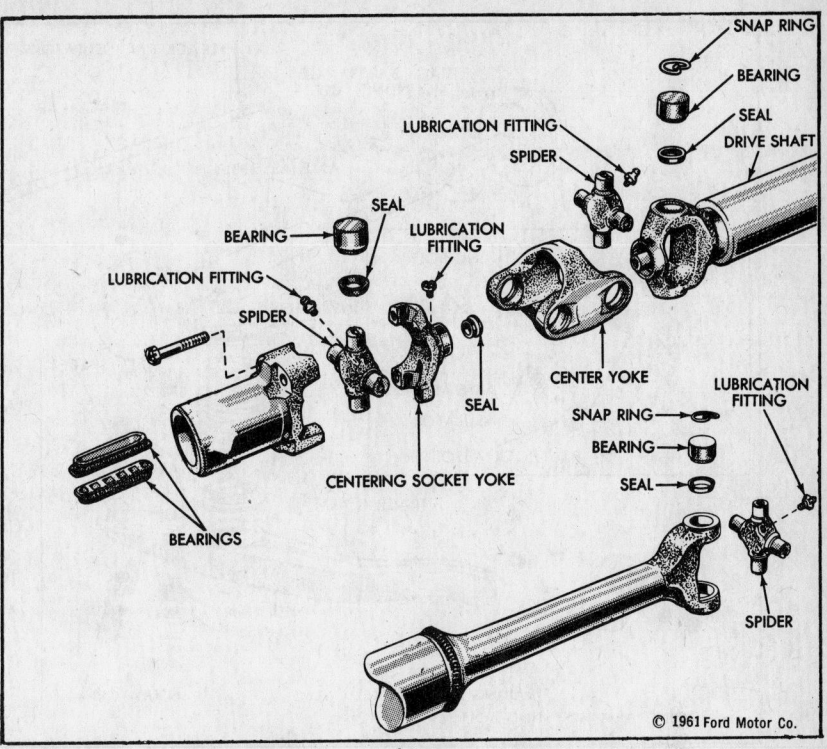

© 1961 Ford Motor Co.

Drive Shaft and Universal Joints

Continental Mark II

Remove the U bolts which attach the front universal joint to the transmission yoke. Remove the U bolts which attach the rear universal joint to the companion flange.

Take out the two cap screws that secure the driveshaft center bearing to the frame. Lower the rear end of the driveshaft and remove the entire assembly out from under the car.

Starting 1961

A Hotchkiss type drive line is used with three universal joints. A single cross and needle type at rear and a double one at front. To remove the assembly:

1. Mark the slip yoke, companion flange and drive shaft so reassembly will be in original position to maintain drive line balance.

The spring can then be slid from under the car.

Replace in reverse of the procedure which removed it.

1958 and 1959

Coil springs are used at the rear on these models.

To replace the coil spring raise the vehicle and place stand jacks under the jack pads under the body.

2. Disconnect rear bearing U-Bolts.
3. Remove cap screws holding front joint to slip yoke and slide slip yoke forward onto transmission output shaft.
4. Lower front end first.

DISASSEMBLY OF DRIVESHAFT

Continental Mark II Models

From just in back of the center bearing bend up the tabs and remove the nut. This will permit sliding the slip yoke of the rear driveshaft out of the front driveshaft. Now the front driveshaft can be slid out of the center bearing.

Set the universal joint up in a vise so that the cross bearing is in a horizontal position. Remove the lock rings from the bearings.

Now using a blunt punch drive the right hand bearing over towards the left which will drive out the left bearing. Now driving again with a blunt punch against the cross on the left drive out the right bearing.

An arbor press, vise or good heavy "C" clamp can be used to reinstall the bearings.

Do not drive the bearings into position since this frequently cocks the little rollers and leads to early destruction of the universal joint cross.

Commencing With 1961

The rear joint is serviced in the conventional way.

The two front joints and centering yoke are similarly serviced. A special adapter is required for lubricating the centering yoke. (See illustration).

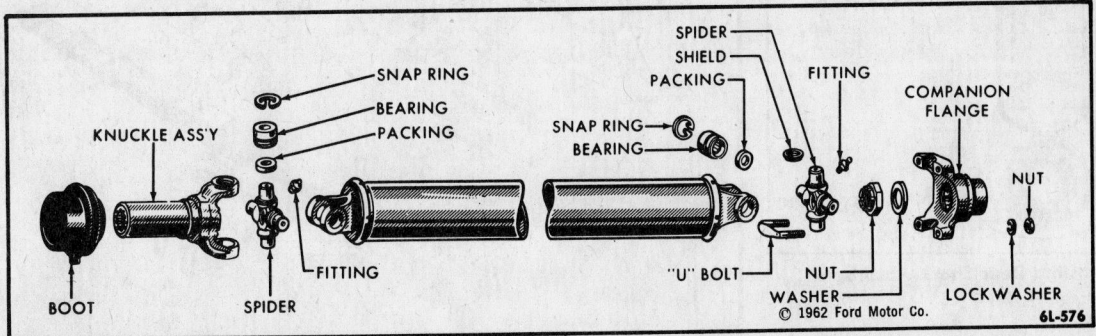

© 1962 Ford Motor Co.   6L-576

Drive Shaft and Universal Joins All Models Except Mark II

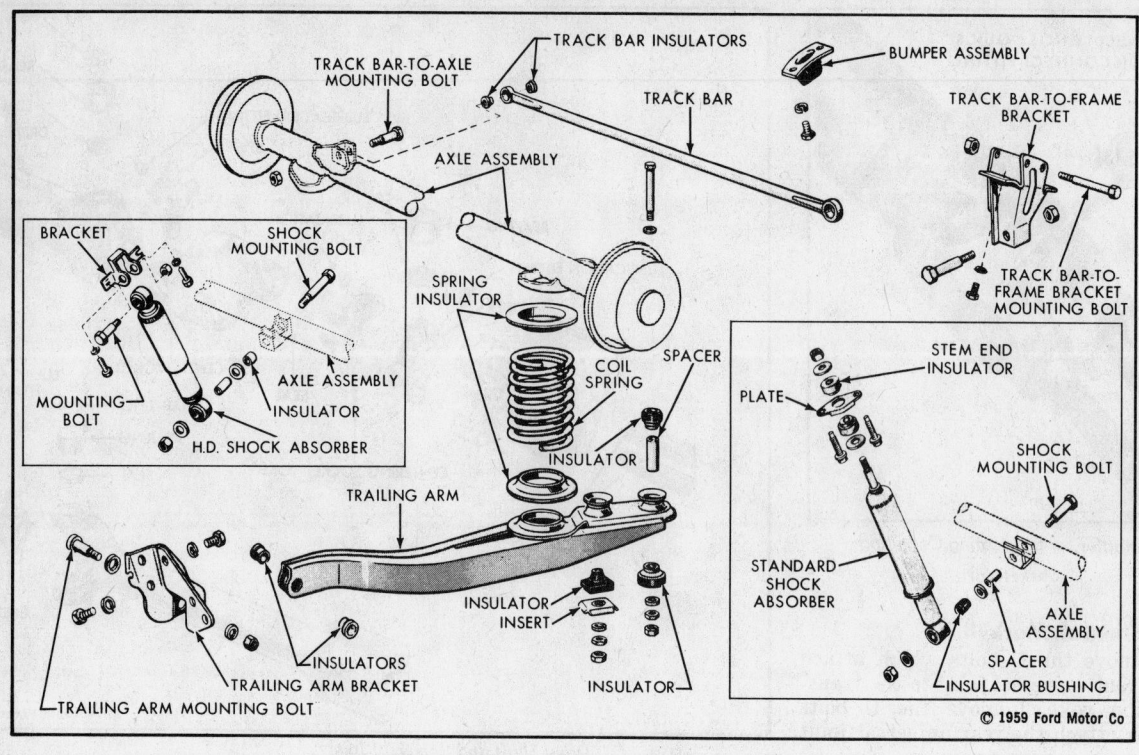

1958-59 Exploded View of Rear Suspension

© 1959 Ford Motor Co

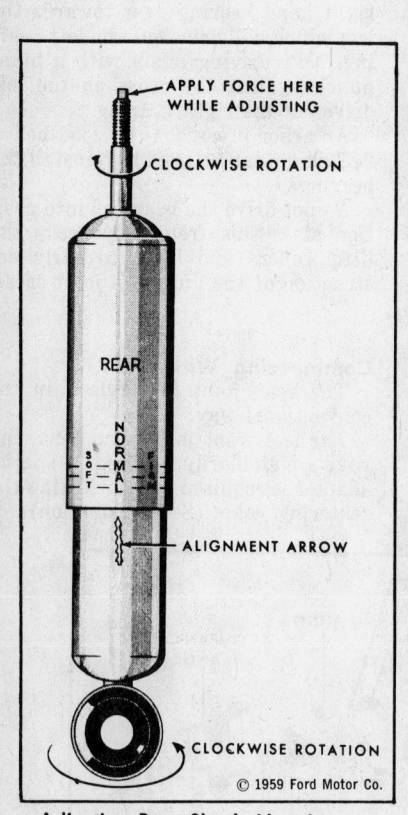

Adjusting Rear Shock Absorbers

© 1959 Ford Motor Co.

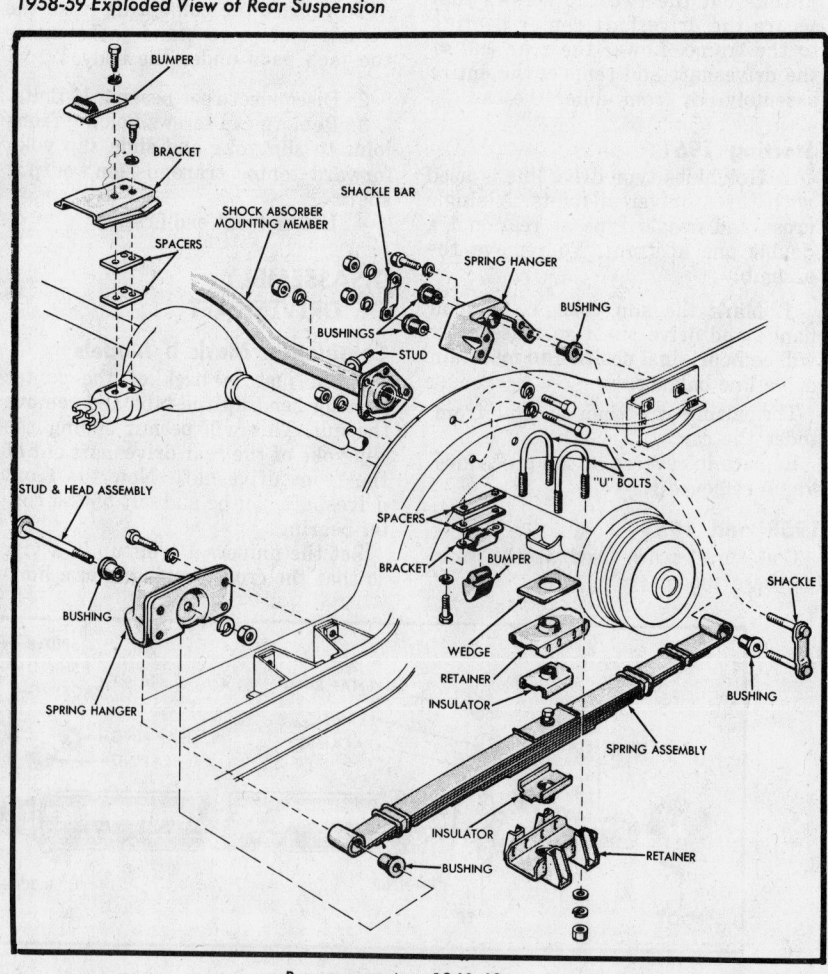

Rear suspension, 1960-63

REAR AXLE AND SUSPENSION

REPLACEMENT OF REAR SPRING

1954 Thru 1957 and 1960-63

Longitudinal leaf springs are used on these models.

They are held with a single bolt at the front and a shackle at the back.

Take the weight of the car on a frame in front of the rear spring. Unbolt and remove the rear shackle. Disconnect the rear shock absorber and remove the 4 U-bolts from each side of the spring saddle where the spring is held to the rear axle housing, lower the spring to the ground, remove the nut which holds the front pin into the frame bracket and drive the front spring pin out.

Use a floor jack, raise the differential housing and disconnect the lower end of the shock absorber. Place a jack under the trailing arm and then remove the nut and washer which retains it to the differential housing. Now lower the trailing arm just sufficiently to take the pressure off the coil spring and remove the spring.

A new spring is replaced in reverse order, being certain that the end coil of the spring fits into the notch in both the trailing arm and the under body.

Disconnect the brake lines and brake cables from the trailing arm to be disconnected. Disconnect the lower end of the shock absorber.

Place a jack under the trailing arm and remove the nut and washer which retain it to the rear axle housing and slowly lower the trailing arm until the pressure is off the coil spring.

Now disconnect the bolts which hold the trailing arm to the front bracket and remove the arm.

The arm is replaced in reverse order of removal.

REPLACE REAR AXLE TRAILING ARM

Lincoln and Continental Models

Jack up the vehicle and place floor jacks exactly under the jacking pads indicated under the under body.

REMOVAL OF THE REAR AXLE ASSEMBLY

1954 Thru 1957 and 1960-63

To remove the rear axle on these models, take the weight of the car on the frame in front of the rear spring

and split the rear universal joint. Disconnect the brake hoses and brake lines, disconnect the shock absorbers, unbolt and remove the rear spring back shackles.

Remove the four U-bolts which hold the spring to the axle housing and disconnect the shock absorber.

Lower both springs to the floor and the rear axle assembly can be slid out from under the car.

All service procedure on this rear axle is given in the rear axle section, see index.

1958 and 1959

Jack up the rear axle high enough that the rear can be slid out from under the vehicle and place stand jacks exactly under the pack pads marked on the under body.

Disconnect the lower end of the shock absorbers and the stalilizer bar. Disconnect the brake lines and the parking brake cables.

Place a jack under one of the trailing arms and disconnect the trailing arm from the rear axle housing and slowly let it come down until the tension is off the spring. Do the same with the other trailing arm. Now spilt the rear universal joint and slide the rear axle assembly out from under the vehicle.

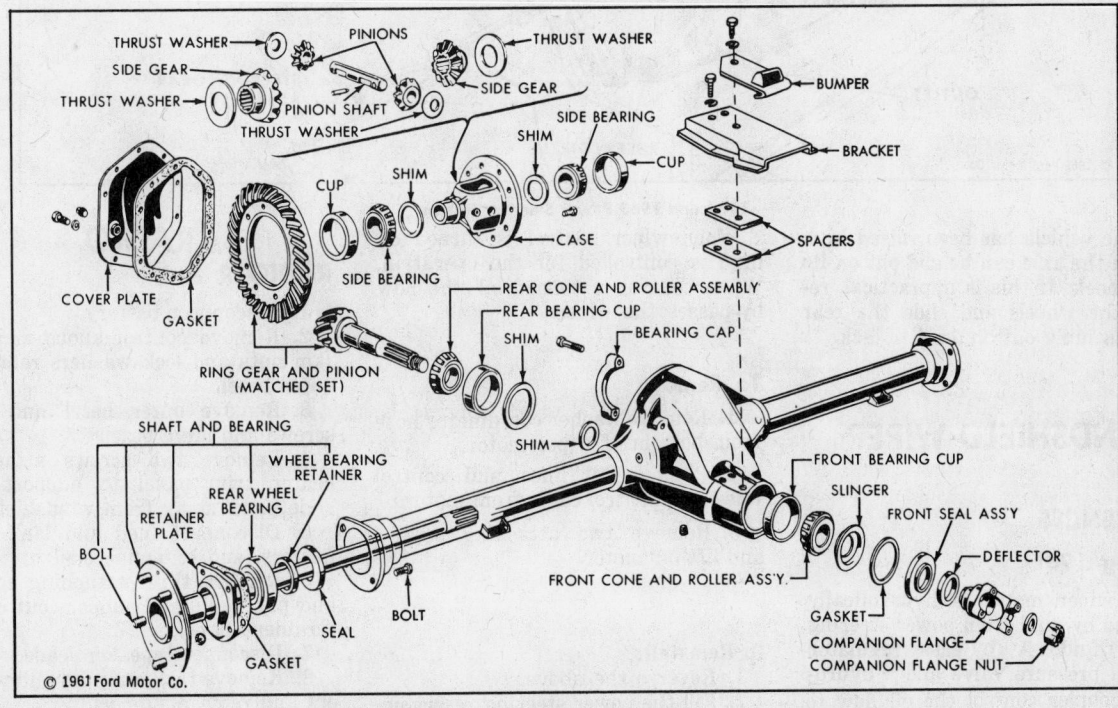

Rear Axle Assembly Used in 1956 thru 1963 Lincoln & Continental Models

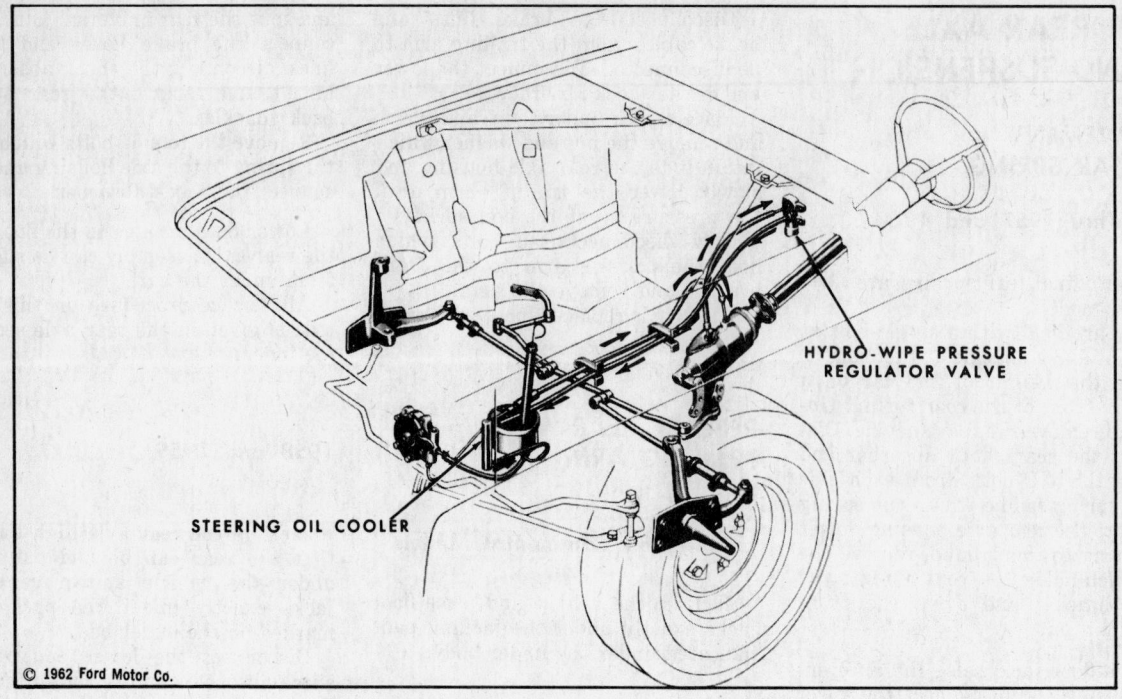

HYDRO-WIPE PRESSURE
REGULATOR VALVE

STEERING OIL COOLER

© 1962 Ford Motor Co.

1961 Power Steering System

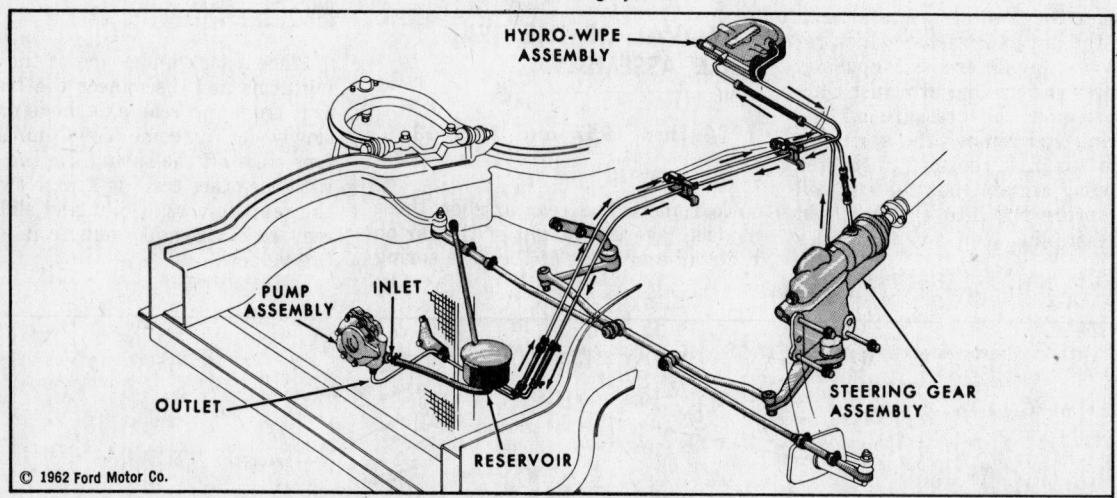

HYDRO-WIPE
ASSEMBLY

PUMP
ASSEMBLY

INLET

OUTLET

RESERVOIR

STEERING GEAR
ASSEMBLY

© 1962 Ford Motor Co.

1962 and 1963 Power Steering System

If the vehicle has been raised high enough the axle can be slid out on its own wheels. If this is impractical, remove the wheels and slide the rear axle assembly out on a roller jack.

WINDSHIELD WIPER

REFERENCES

Starting 1961

The wiper motor is hydraulically operated by fluid from power steering return fluid. A by-pass regulator valve, a pressure valve and a hydro-static coupler control the oil flow to the wiper motor.

When wiper control is turned on fluid is controlled for the operation. When control is turned off the flow by-passes the wiper.

To Remove

1. Remove washer coordinator hose from bottom of wiper motor.

2. Remove oil lines and control lines, and control cable from motor.

3. Remove two attaching screws and lift off motor.

To Reinstall:

1. Reverse the above.

2. Fill the power steering reservoir and bleed the lines.

RADIO
RADIO R & R

1. Disconnect battery.

2. Remove control knobs and two jam nuts and lock washers retaining outer bezel.

3. Remove outer bezel and four screws and large bezel.

4. Remove two screws attaching center trim panel to support and slide panel away from windshield.

5. Disconnect feed and lamp connectors, and antennae lead in.

6. Remove three attaching screws and pull radio and support out of instrument panel.

7. Disconnect speaker leads.

8. Remove two jam nuts and washers and remove support.

To Reinstall: Reverse the above.

MERCURY INDEX

AIR CONDITIONING

Service .1092

BRAKES, HYDRAULIC

Adjustments 423
References 423
Bleed brakes 941
Parking brake, adjust 424
Parking brake level & cable 424
Master cylinder, R & R 424
Master cylinder service 939

BRAKES, POWER

Power unit overhaul 954
Trouble shooting 954

CLUTCH

Clutch assembly, R & R 435
Clutch pedal, adjust 435

COOLING SYSTEM

Automatic fan 426
Radiator core, R & R 426
Thermostat 425
Water pump, R & R 425

ELECTRICAL SYSTEM

Distributor, R & R 421
Distributor specifications 416
Fuses and circuit breakers 416
Gauges 1024
Generator and regulator
    specifications 416
Generator and regulators 1026
Generator, R & R 421
Generator trouble shooting chart 1026
Horn buttons 434
Ignition firing order & timing 413
Ignition timing specifications 414
Starter, R & R 421
Starter specifications 415
Starter systems 1046

ENGINE ASSEMBLY

Cylinder head, R & R 427
Cylinder head tightening 420
Engine assembly, R & R 426
Engine diagnosis 1012
Engine firing order & timing 413
Exhaust manifold, R & R 425
References 426
Inlet manifold, R & R 425
Model year identification 414
Oil filter, R & R 431
Oil pan, R & R 430
Oil pressure specifications 420
Oil pump 431
Piston and rod, R & R 432
Piston specifications 418
Rear main bearing oil seal 433
Rocker arm lubrication 428
Rocker arms & shaft 427

ENGINE ASSEMBLY—continued

Specifications, general, engine . .420
Timing chain & cover, R & R 429
Trouble shooting chart 1012
Tune-up specifications 414
Valve adjusting sequence 429
Valve specifications 419
Valve springs 428
Valve and guides 428

ENGINE LUBRICATION

Oil filter, R & R 431
Oil pan, R & R 430
Oil pump 431

EXHAUST SYSTEM

Manifolds, R & R 425
Muffler, R & R 424
Pipes, R & R 424

FUEL SYSTEM

Carburetors 972
Fuel gauge, R & R 1024
Fuel gauge service 1024
Fuel pump pressure 414
Fuel pump, R & R 424
Fuel pump service 1020
Fuel tank, R & R 424

INSTRUMENTS

Instruments, R & R 422
Speedometer, R & R 422

RADIO, R & R

References 446

REAR AXLE AND SUSPENSION

Axle assembly, R & R 445
Axle shaft 918
Axle shaft oil seal 918
Pinion bearings 918
Ring gear & pinion 918
Shock absorbers, rear 446
Spring, rear, R & R 444
Trouble shooting chart 919

SPECIFICATIONS

Battery 415
Branke cylinder sizes 417
Capacities:
    Axle, rear 419
    Cooling system 419
    Crankcase 419
    Fuel tank 419
    Transmission, automatic 419
    Transmission, manual 419
Chassis, general 417
Distributors 416
Engine, general 420
Fuses and circuit breakers 416
Generator and regulator 416
Light bulbs 417

SPECIFICATIONS—continued

Main bearings 418
Model identification illustrations .412
Pistons 418
Quick reference specifications . . .413
Rod bearings 418
Starters 415
Torque Wrench 418
Tune-up 414
Valves 419
Wheel alignment 417

STEERING, MANUAL

Adjust gear housing 1052
Gear assembly, R & R 434
Horn button, R & R 434
Steering wheel, R & R 434

STEERING, POWER

Pump assembly 1058
Pump, R & R 435
Trouble shooting 1081
Unit overhaul 1058

SUSPENSION, FRONT

Alignment procedures 1082
Alignment specifications 417
Ball joints, R & R 1087
Camber, adjust 1082
Caster, adjust 1082
King pins and bushings 1087
Knuckle supports 1087
References 433
Support arms, pins and bushings 1087

TRANSMISSION, AUTOMATIC

Merc-o-matic 3 speed 820
    Linkage adjust 439
    R & R 440
Multi-drive 820
    Linkage adjust 440
    R & R 442
Merc-o-matic 2 speed 838
    Linkage adjust 443
    R & R 443

TRANSMISSION, STANDARD

Linkage adjustment 437
Disassemble transmission 436
Transmission, R & R 436

TROUBLE CHECKS

Procedure 1

TUNE-UP

Carburetors 972
Specifications 414
Engine diagnosis 1012

UNIVERSAL JOINT AND DRIVE SHAFT

Disassemble U joint 444
U joint & drive shaft, R & R 444

MERCURY

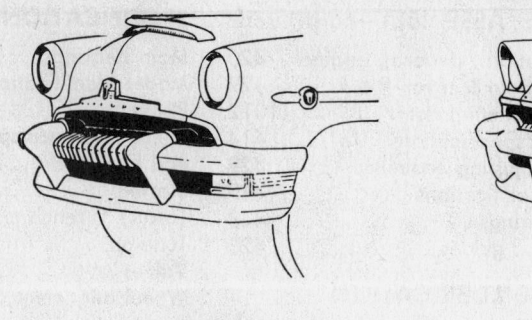

1954

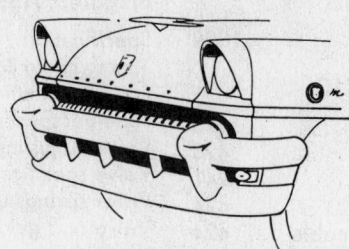

1955

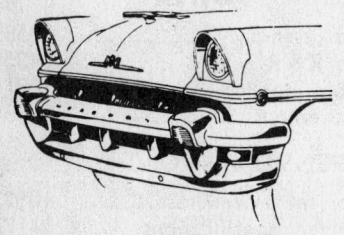

1956

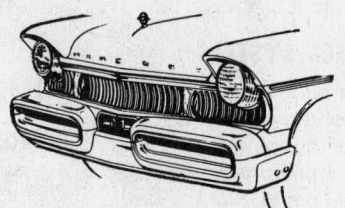

1957

1958

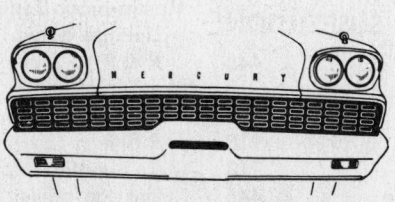

1959

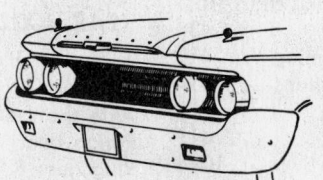

1960

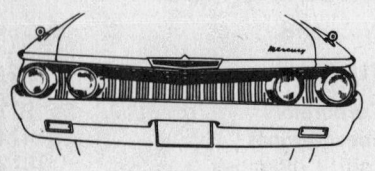

1961

1962

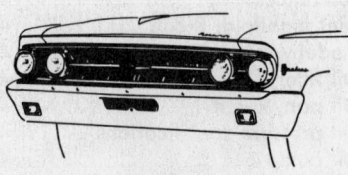

1963

QUICK WORKING SPECIFICATIONS

DISTRIBUTOR

Breaker Point Gap (In.)
1954-63, V8 ....014-.016
1961-62, 6 cyl. 024-.026

Cam Angle (Degrees)
1954-63, V8 27
1961-62, 6 cyl. 37

SPARK PLUGS

Year	Type	Gap
1954	H10	.030
1955-57	870	.034
1958-60, All ex. 312	F11Y	.035
1958-60, 312 cu. in.	F14Y	.035
1961, 6 Cyl.	870	.035
1961, 292 cu. in.	F14Y	.035
1961, 352, 390 cu. in.	F11Y	.035
1962, 6 Cyl.	BTF6	.034
1962, 292 cu. in.	BF82	.034
1962, 352, 390 cu. in.	BF42	.034
cu. in.	BF42	.034
1963, 390, 406 cu. in.	PF32	.034

IGNITION TIMING

1956-60
V-8, Std. Trans. ....4°
V-8, Auto. Trans. ....6°

1961-62
6 Cyl. & V-8, Std. Trans. ....4°
6 Cyl. & V-8, Auto. Trans. ....10°
V-8, 390—High Perf. Option ....13°
V-8, 406—High Perf. Option ....10°

1963
V-8, 390, High Perf. Option ......13°
V-8, 406, High Perf. Option ......10°

VALVES

Operating Tappet Clearance (Hot)

Year	Inlet	Exhaust
1954-57	.019	.019

1957 Optional: Hydraulic, clearance is zero.
1958-60, All V8 ex. 312: Hydraulic, clearance is zero.
312 ....019 inlet and exhaust
1961-62, 6 Cyl. Self Adj.
292 V8 In, Ex. 019
Others ....Zero
1963, All ....Zero

GENERATOR & REGULATOR SPECIFICATIONS

Year and Series	GENERATOR		REGULATOR		
	Field Current In Amperes		Cut-out Closing Voltage	Current Regulator Setting	Voltage Regulator Setting
	6 Volt	12 Volt			
1954-55 All	2.3	—	6.3	40	7.6
1956-62 All	—	1.5	12.4	35	15.0

NOTE: Surrounding temperatures and driving habits influence the above adjustments and must be considered by the mechanic. Higher temperatures or turnpike conditions permit lower adjustments; lower temperatures or city type driving conditions require higher settings, within limits.

WHEEL ALIGNMENT

Caster (Degrees)
1954-60 ....1½ N to 0
1961-63 ....½ N to ½ P

Camber (Degrees)
1954-60 ....0 to ¾ P
1961-63 ....¼ P to 1 P

Toe-In (Inches)
1954-56 ....3/32 to 5/32
1957-60 ....1/16 to 3/16
1961-63 ....⅛ to ¼

King Pin Inclination (Degrees)
1954-63 7

CAPACITIES

Engine Crankcase (Quarts)
(Add 1 qt. for new filter)
1954-63, V8 5
1961-62, 6 Cyl. 4

Transmission, Synchro. (Pts.)
Add 1¼ Pts. for Overdrive.
1954-58 ....3½
1959-63 ....3¼

Transmission, Automatic (Pts.)
1954 19
1955 20
1956-57 21
1958, ex. Park Lane 20
1963, 4 Speed 3

FIRING ORDER and TIMING

SPARK OCCURS:
1961-62—6 Cyl., 223 Cu. In. 3° BTDC (Std. Trans.)
10° BTDC (Auto. Trans.)

1954-63—V-8—All, 4° BTDC (Std. Trans.)
10° BTDC (Auto. Trans.)

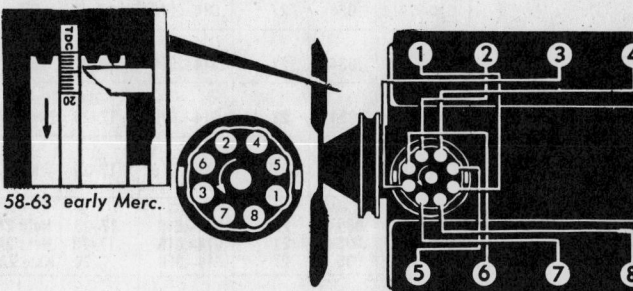

58-63 early Merc.

All O.H.V. V-8's., Front Mounted Distributor

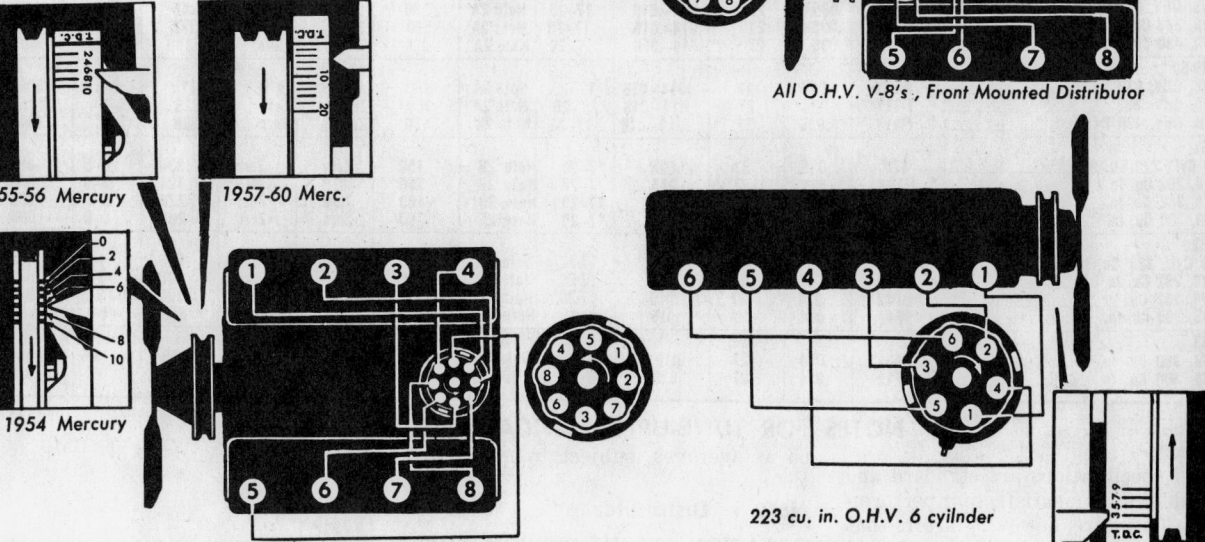

55-56 Mercury

1957-60 Merc.

1954 Mercury

All V-8's w/rear mounted distributor

223 cu. in. O.H.V. 6 cyilnder

NOTE:
THESE ARE APPROXIMATE SETTINGS. ENGINE DESIGN, ALTITUDE, TEMPERATURE, FUEL AND ENGINE CONDITION WILL ALL INFLUENCE TIMING. THE DETERMINING FACTOR, LIMITING ADVANCE, WILL STILL BE THE "KNOCK POINT" OF THE INDIVIDUAL ENGINE.

MERCURY

CAR SERIAL NUMBER LOCATION AND ENGINE IDENTIFICATION

MERCURY SERIAL NUMBERS AND ENGINE NUMBERS ARE ONE AND THE SAME.

SERIAL NUMBER LOCATION

1954-63

On plate on left front door pillar.

ENGINE IDENTIFICATION

ENGINE IS IDENTIFIED THRU CAR SERIAL NUMBER.

The engine is identified by a prefix to the serial number. 1954-57, two digits represent the year. Beginning 1958, a letter and a digit, (or two letters) represent the engine used. (See accompanying chart).

Year	Prefix	Engine Used
1954	54	V-256
1955	55	V-292
1956	56	V-312

Year	Prefix	Engine Used	
1957	57	V-312	
"	57	V-368	A
1958	L8	V-312	
"	M8	V-383	B
"	K8	V-430	B
"	J8	V-430	C
1959	P9	V-312	
"	N9	V-383	D
"	M9	V-383	B
"	L9	V-430	
1960	O9	V-312	
"	ON	V-383	
"	OM	V-430	
1961	1V	6-223	
"	1W	V-292	
"	1X	V-352	

Year	Prefix	Engine Used	
"	1L	V-390	
1962	2V	6-223	
"	2W	V-292	
"	2X	V-352	
"	2Z	V-390	
1963		V-390	D
"		V-390	B
"		V-406	B
"		V-406	C

NOTES:

A—Turnpike Cruiser.
B—4 Bbl. Carb.
C—Three 2-Bbl. Carbs.
D—2 Bbl. Carb.

TUNE-UP SPECIFICATIONS

Year	Spark Plugs		Distributor (Note 1)				Ignition Timing (Note 2)	Compression Pressure Cranking (Note 3)	Valves (Note 4)			Fuel Pump Pressure	Engine Idle Speed Neutral
									Tappet Clearance Hot		Timing		
	Type	Gap	Cam Angle	Point Gap	Arm Spring Tension				Inlet	Exhaust	Inlet Opens		
1954 V8, OHV	CH-H10	.030	27	.014–.016	17–20		3B	115	.019	.019	15B	4–5	485
1955 V8, OHV	CH-870	.034	27	.014–.016	17–20		3B	135	.019	.019	12B	4–5	485
1956 V8, OHV	CH-870	.034	27	.014–.016	17–20		5B	155	.019	.019	12B	4–5	485
1957 V8, OHV, 312 Cu. In. Std.	CH-870	.034	27	.014–.016	17–20		Note 2A	165	.019	.019	18B	4–5	485
1957—Note 6 V8, OHV, 368 Cu. In. Opt.	CH-870	.034	27	.014–.016	17–20		5B	160	Zero	Zero	18B	4–5	485
1958 V8, OHV, 312 Cu. In.	F-11Y	.035	27	.014–.016	17–20		Note 2A	190	.019	.019	34B	5–6	485
V8, 383 Cu. In.	F-11Y	.035	27	.014–.016	17–20		Note 2A	190	Zero	Zero	27B	5–6	485
V8, 430 Cu. In.	F-14Y	.035	27	.014–.016	17–20		Note 2A	190	Zero	Zero	18B	4–5	485
1959-60 V8, OHV, 312 Cu. In.	F-14Y	.035	27	.014–.016	17–20		Note 2A	160	.019	.019	12B	4–5	500
V8, OHV, 383	F-11Y	.035	27	.014–.016	17–20		Note 2A	160	Zero	Zero	22B	5–6	485
V8, OHV, 430 Cu. In.	F-11Y	.035	27	.014–.016	17–20		Note 2A	180	Zero	Zero	22B	5–6	485
1961 6 Cyl., 223 Cu. In.	870	.035	37	.025	17–20		Note 2B	150	Zero	Zero	23B	4–5	485
V8, 292 Cu. In.	F-14Y	.035	27	.015	17–20		Note 2B	160	.019	.019	12B	5–0	600
V8, 352 Cu. In.	F-11Y	.035	27	.015	17–20		Note 2B	180	Zero	Zero	22B	5–0	600
V8, 390 Cu. In.	F-11Y	.035	27	.015	17–20		Note 2B	180	Zero	Zero	26B	5–0	600
1962 6 Cyl., 223 Cu. In.	BTF6	.034	37	.026	17-20		Note 2B	150	Zero	Zero	23B	4-5	485
V8, 292 Cu. In.	BF82	.034	27	.015	17-20		Note 2B	160	Zero	Zero	12B	5-0	600
V8, 352 Cu. In	BF42	.034	27	.015	17-20		Note 2B	180	Zero	Zero	22B	5-0	600
V8, 390 Cu. In.	BF42	.034	27	.015	17-20		Note 2B	180	Zero	Zero	26B	5-0	600
1963 V8, 390 Cu. In.	BF42	.034	27	.015	17-20		Note 2B	180	Zero	Zero	26B	5	600
V8, 406 Cu. In.	BF32	.034	27	.020	27-32		10B	180	.025	.025	24B	6	600

NOTES FOR TUNE-UP SPECIFICATIONS TABLE

Note:

All specifications are standard and should result in satisfactory performance. There are, however, factors that influence these settings, such as fuel octane value, air density, humidity, temperature, etc. Timing charts, like other specifications must be consider-ed as averages, subject to modification.

Note 1: Distributor

ROTATION (VIEWED FROM THE TOP)

6 Cyl. .... Clockwise
V8 .... Counterclockwise

DRIVE GEAR

1954-55:

Gear is pinned to distributor shaft. An extension of the distributor shaft engages a tongue on the oil pump shaft.

NOTES FOR TUNE UP SPECIFICATIONS—continued

1956-63:

Gear is pinned to distributor shaft. Oil pump is driven by hexagonal-shaped intermediate shaft which contacts hex-shaped sockets in the distributor and oil pump shafts.

Note 2: Ignition
TIMING MARKS AND THEIR LOCATION

TIMING PROCEDURE

Disconnect the vacuum line. Operate engine at 475 R.P.M. and adjust timing to specified advance. If 98 Octane Fuel is not available retard to 3B but no further.

IGNITION RESISTOR
1956-63, All Models

An ignition ballast resistor is mounted on the ignition coil in the line between the coil and the ignition switch. A contact in the starter solenoid by-passes this resistor when the starter is operating. Therefore, be careful to ground the primary circuit before attempting work on the engine that requires using the starter to turn the engine; otherwise, the engine can fire and cause injury even though the ignition is OFF.

Note 2A: Ignition Timing

All V8

With Manual Trans. ....3B to 7B
With Auto. Trans. ....6B to 10B

Note 2B
1961-62, 6 Cyl.
With Synchromesh Trans. ......3°BTC
With Auto. Trans. ....10°BTC
V8
With Synchromesh Trans. ....4°BTC
With Auto. Trans ....10°BTC

Note 3: Compression Pressure

All cylinders should read alike within 10 pounds. This is more important than the actual reading. Take readings with all plugs removed and engine at normal operating temperature.

Note 4: Valves

1954-57

All OHV engines ex 1957 optional engine have mechanical lifters. Valve clearance and adjustment is obtained with the adjusting screw found on the rocker arm.

1957

Optional 368 cubic inch engine, has valve cover painted red. Shows zero tappet clearance indicating hydraulic lifters are standard.

1958

383 Cu. In. V8 engines built after date Code 4-7BE have inlet valve opening at 22B.

430 Cu. In. V8 engines opening at 22B.

1958-60

All engines are equipped with hydraulic lifters and have zero clearance, exc. 312 Eng. which has .019 clearance.

1961-62, 6 cyl. engines have self-adjusting mechanical rockers; 292, V8 has adjustable rocker set to .019" and others are hydraulic with zero clearance.

Note 6: Engine Size

The 368 cubic inch OHV engine used in 1957 has the valve covers painted red. It is similar to the 1956 Lincoln engine.

BATTERY and STARTER SPECIFICATIONS

YEAR	BATTERY				STARTERS						
					Lock Test			No-Load Test			
	Ampere Hour Capacity	Volts	Group Number	Terminal Grounded	Amps	Volts	Torque	Amps	Volts	R.P.M.	Brush Spring Tension
1954 OHV, V8	100	6	2N	Pos.	700	3.5	16	70	6	4500	52
1955 OHV, V8	100	6	2N	Pos.	700	3.5	14	70	6	5500	52
1956–57 All ex. Crusier	55	12	4N	Neg.	550	5	15.5	120	12	4800	52
Cruiser, V8	65	12	5N	Neg.	550	5	15.5	85	12	4500	52
1958 All Exc. Park Lane	55	12	5N	Neg.	550	5	15.5	85	12	4500	52
Park Lane	65	12	5N	Neg.	550	5	15.5	85	12	4500	52
1959-60 All Exc. Monterey	65	12	4NB	NEG.	550	5	15.5	80	12	4500	52
Monterey	55	12	4NA	NEG.	550	5	15.5	85	12	4500	52
1961-62 223,292 Cu. In.	55	12	4NF	NEG.	580	5	14.8	110	12	5200	52
352,390 Cu. In.	65	12	4NF	NEG.	580	5	14.8	110	12	5200	52
1963 390 Cu. In. M/T	55	12		Neg.	580	5	14.8	110	12	5200	52
390 Cu. In. A/T	65	12		Neg.	580	5	14.8	110	12	5200	52
406 Cu. In.	70	12		Neg.	580	5	14.8	110	12	5200	52

A.C. GENERATOR & REGULATOR SPECIFICATIONS

Year and Model	Ground Polarity	ALTERNATOR		CURRENT OUTPUT @ 15 Volts and 2950 Engine R.P.M.	VOLTAGE OUTPUT @ 15 Amp. Load and 2950 Engine R.P.M.	REGULATOR	
		Ampere Rating	Field Current Draw, Amps.			Point Gap	Air Gap
1963 All Models	Neg.	40	2.9-3.1	40 Amp.	15	.015-.022	.022-.030

D.C. GENERATOR and REGULATOR SPECIFICATIONS

YEAR	GENERATORS					REGULATORS		
	Field Current in Amperes		Brush Spring Tension	Cut Out Relay		Current and Voltage Regulator Air Gap	Current Regulator Setting	Voltage Regulator Setting
	At 6 Volts	At 12 Volts		Air Gap	Closing Voltage			
1954–55 All Models	2.3		30	.025	6.3	.035	40	7.6
1956-58 All Models		1.5	30	.025	12.4	.035	30	15.0
1959-60 312 Cu. In.		1.5	36	.025	12.4	.035	30	1.50
383,430 Cu. In		1.5	36	.025	12.4	.035	37	1.50
1961-62 All Models		1.5	36	.025	12.4	.035	28-32	15.0

*Note: Setting varies depending on equipment. Standard transmissions,30 amp. thru Air-conditioned models, 45 amps.

DISTRIBUTOR SPECIFICATIONS

Year	Model	Part Number	ROTATION	Cam Angle in Degrees	BREAKER		GOVERNOR CONTROL		VACUUM CONTROL DATA		
					Point Opening (Inch)	Arm Spring in Ounces	Advance Starts	Full Advance	INCHES OF VACUUM		Max Adv. of Dist. in Degrees
									To Start Advance	For Full Advance	
1954	All	FDC-12127A	CC	26–28	.015	17–20	None	None	.24 @ 500	1.50 @ 2000	15–15½
1955	All	FEC-12127B	CC	26–28	.015	17–20	None	None	.75 @ 700	2.19 @ 2000	14–15¼
1956	All	FDT-12127B	CC	26–28	.015	17–20	None	None	.29 @ 400	2.19 @ 2000	14–15¼
1957	312 cu. in. eng.	FEK-12127A	CC	26–28	.015	17–20	1 @ 450	12½ @ 2000	5.0	19–21	11–13
	368 cu. in. eng.	FEL-12127A	CC	26–28	.015	17–20	1 @ 400	13½ @ 2000	5.0	19–21	7–9
1958	312 cu. in. eng.	FEW-12127F	CC	26–28	.015	17–20	1 @ 450	13 @ 2000	5.0	19–21	11–13
	383 cu. in. eng.	FEW-12127D	CC	26–28	.015	17–20	1 @ 350	13 @ 2000	6.0	18–20	10½–12½
	430 cu. in. eng.	FEW-12127E	CC	26–28	.015	17–20	1 @ 350	13 @ 2000	6.0	18–20	10½–12½
1959	312 cu. in. eng.	B9FA-12127A	CC	26–28	.015	17–20	1 @ 450	13 @ 2000	6.0	18–19	10–12
	383 & 430 cu. in.	FEW-12127H	CC	26–28	.015	17–20	1 @ 400	15 @ 2000	6.0	15–17	9½–12½
1960	312 cu. in. eng.	B9FA-12127A	CC	26–28	.015	17–20	1 @ 450	11 @ 2000	6.0	18–19	10–12
	383 cu. in. eng.	COMF-12127C	CC	26–28	.015	17–20	1 @ 400	15 @ 2000	6.0	15–17	9½–12½
	430 cu. in. eng.	B9MF-12127B	CC	26–28½	.015	17–20	1 @ 400	15 @ 2000	6.0	14–16	9½–12½
1961-62	223 cu. in. A/T	CIAF-12127D	C	35-38	.025	17–20	None	None	1.08	6.50	13
	223 cu. in. S/T	COAF-12127G	C	35-38	.025	17–20	None	None	.38	5.99	10¼–11¼
	292 cu. in.	COAF-12127A	CC	26-28½	.015	17–20	1 @ 750	11 @ 2000	7	20	9½–12½
	352 cu. in. A/T	COAF-12127D	CC	26-28½	.015	17–20	1 @ 500	12¼ @ 2000	5	17	9½–12½
	352 cu. in. S/T	COAF-12127E	CC	26-28½	.015	17–20	1 @ 775	12¼ @ 2000	5	17	9½–12½
	390 cu. in.	CISF-12127A	CC	26-28½	.015	17–20	1 @ 400	11½ @ 2000	9	17	6–9
1963	390 cu. in.	C2AF-12127A	CC	27	.015	17-20	1 @ 500	11.5 @ 2000	1 @ 9.0	17.0	9
	406 cu. in.	COAF-12127K	CC	27	.020	17-20	1 @ 750	12.2 @ 2175	None	None	None

FUSES and CIRCUIT BREAKERS

CIRCUIT BREAKERS

Headlights and Telltale:

Behind instruments near steering column.
30 amp. C.B. for 6 volt systems;
12 amp. C.B. for 12 volt systems.
18 amp. C.B. for dual lamps.

Parking, Tail, Stop, License, Instrument, Clock and Trunk Lights:

Behind instruments near steering column.
15 amp. C.B. for 6 volt systems;
12 amp. C.B. for 12 volt systems.

Convertible Top:

In engine compartment.
40 amp. C.B. for 6 volt systems;
30 amp. C.B. for 12 volt systems.

Power Seats and Windows:

30 amp. C.B. in the feed line plus a 15 amp. C.B. at each motor.

Air Conditioning Unit:

In the blower motor circuit.
20 amp. C.B.

FUSES

Fuses are used for the following devices. In 1954 these fuses were in the lines under the dash near the items protected. Starting in 1955 they are mounted in a fuse block (along with the turn signal flasher) under the dash near the steering column. The items protected and the fuse values are as follows:

Clock:

1954-55, 1AG3;
1956-63, 1AG2.

Radio:

1957, SFE 7½.
1958-63, 1AG5.

Turn Signals:

1954-55, SFE 9;
1956-63, SFE 7½ or AGW 7½.

Dome, Courtesy, Glove Box:

1954-55, SFE 9;
1956-63, SFE 7½ or AGW 7½.

Windshield Washer:

1955, AGA 3;
1956-63, SFE 7½.

Back-up Lights:

1955, SFE 9;
1956-63, SFE 7½.

Automatic Headlight Dimmer:

1955, AGC 5;
1956-63, AGC 3.

Heater:

1954-55, SFE 20:
1956-63, SFE 14.

LIGHT BULBS

Automatic Headlight Dimmer Pilot Light, and Merc-o-matic Quadrant:

6 Volt, No. 51; 12 Volt, No. 53.
(One C.P. miniature bayonet base.)

Telltale Lights for Headlamp Beam, Brake-on, Multiluber, Turn Signals, together with all instrument lights and lights for the Ignition Lock, Clock, Radio Dial, Glove Compartment, Heater, Air Conditioning Controls:

6 Volt, No. 55; 12 Volt, No. 57.
(2 C.P. miniature bayonet base.)

License Plate Light:

6 Volt, No. 63; 12 Volt, No. 67.
(4 C.P. single contact base.)

Map and Courtesy Light:

6 Volt, No. 81; 12 Volt, No. 89.
(6 C.P. single contact base.)

Instrument, Clock, Radio Dial, Glove Compartment, Push Buttons

12 Volt, No. 57.
(2 C.P. miniature bayonet base.)

Engine Compartment and Dome Light:

6 Volt, No. 209; 12 Volt, No. 1003.
(15 C.P. single contact base.)

Front Combination Park and Signal Light, Rear Combination Tail, Stop and Signal Light:

6 Volt, No. 1154; 12 Volt, No. 1034.
(4 & 32 C.P. double contact indexed base.)

Hand Spot and Trouble Light:

6 Volt, No. 4516; 12 Volt, No. 4416.
(30 watt screw type base.)

Headlights (Two Light System):

6 Volt, No. 5040; 12 Volt, No. 5400.
(40 & 50 C.P. three contact base.)

(Four light system)

Low beam #2. 50/37.5 W. #4002—3 contact base.
High beam # 1. 37.5 W, #4001—2 contact base.

Headlight Beam, Turn, Oil Pressure, Generator, Indicator Lights:

12 Volt, No. 1445. (1.5 C.P. single contact base.)

Under Hood Light:

12 Volt, No. 93. (15 C.P. single contact base.)

Dome Light:

12 Volt, No. 1003.
(15 C.P. single contact base.)

Parking, Tail, Stop, Turn, Combination Lights:

12 Volt, No. 1034.
(4 & 32 C.P. 2 contact indexed base.)

Back-up Light:

12 Volt, No. 1141. (21 C.P. No. 1073 single contact base.)

FRONT WHEEL ALIGNMENT

YEAR	CASTER		CAMBER		Toe-In (Inches)	King Pin Inclination (Degrees)	WHEEL PIVOT RATIO	
	Range (Degrees)	Pref. Setting Note A	Range (Degrees)	Pref. Setting			Inner Wheel	Outer Wheel
1954–56 All Models	1½N to 0	Note A	0 to ¾P	Note B	3/32 to 5/32	7	25	20
1957 All Models	1½N to 0	Note A	0 to ¾P	Note B	1/16 to 3/16	7	24¾	20
1958-60 All Models	1½N to 0	Note A	0 to ¾P	Note B	1/16 to 3/16	7	20	17⅓
1961-63 All	½N to ½P	Note A	¼P to 1P	Note B	⅛ to ¼	7	24¼	20

Note A: Preferred Caster Within ½° one side to other. **Note B: Preferred Camber** Within ¼°

GENERAL CHASSIS AND BRAKE SPECIFICATIONS

YEAR AND MODEL		CHASSIS		BRAKE CYLINDER BORE		
		Overall Length in Inches	Tire Size	Master Cyl. (Inch)	Wheel Cylinder Diameter (Inch)	
					Front	Rear
1954-55	All	203¾	7.10x15	1.0	1⅛	15/16
1956	All	206½	7.10x15	1.0	1⅛	⅞
1957	All	209⅛	8.00x14	1.0	1⅛	15/16
1958	Medalist	213¼	7.50x14	(A)	1⅛	29/32
	Monterey-Montclair	213¼	8.00x14	(A)	1⅛	31/32
	Park Lane	220¼	8.50x14	21/32	1⅛	31/32
1959	Monterey	217¾	8.00x14	1.0	1⅛	31/32
	Montclair	217¾	8.50x14	1.0	1⅛	31/32
	Park Lane	222¾	8.50x14	1.0	1⅛	31/32
1960	Monterey	219¼	8.00x14	1.0	1⅛	31/32
	Montclair	219¼	8.50x14	1.0	1⅛	31/32
	Park Lane	222¾	8.50x14	1.0	1⅛	31/32
1961	All	214.6	7.50x14	1.0	1 3/32	15/16
1962	All	215.5	7.50x14*	1.0	1 3/32	15/16
1963	Sedan	215.0	7.50x14	1.0	1 3/32	15/16
	Sta. Wagon	209.9	8.00x14	1.0	1 3/32	15/16

* Convertible & Station Wagon 8.00x14.

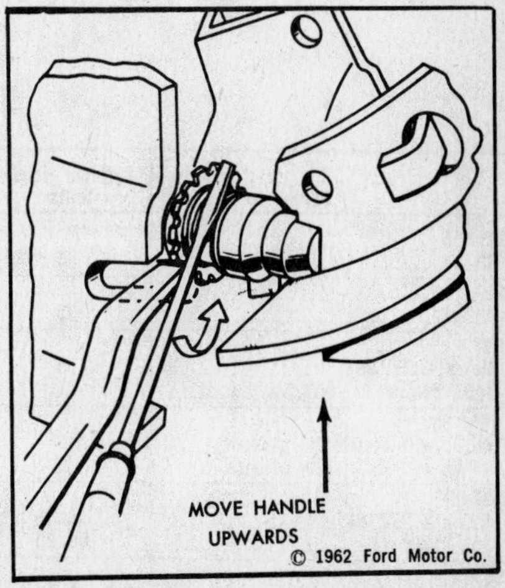
MOVE HANDLE
UPWARDS
© 1962 Ford Motor Co.

Backing Off Brake Adjustment

CRANKSHAFT BEARING JOURNAL SIZES

YEAR	MAIN BEARING JOURNALS				CONNECTING ROD BEARING JOURNALS		
	Journal Diameter	Oil Clearance	End Play of Shaft	End Play Held by	Journal Diameter	Oil Clearance	End Play
1954 All OHV, V8	2.498	.0013	.004	No. 3	2.188	.0012	.011
1955 All OHV, V8	2.499	.0013	.004	No. 3	2.188	.0013	.011
1956 All OHV, V8	2.623	.0017	.004	No. 3	2.188	.0018	.011
1957 Standard OHV, V8	2.623	.0017	.006	No. 3	2.188	.0013	.011
Optl. 368 cu. in., OHV, V8	2.623	.0017	.006	No. 3	2.248	.0016	.010
1958 OHV, V8, 383, 430 Cu. In.	2.8998	.0019	.006	No. 3	2.5996	.0016	.010
OHV, V8, 312 Cu. In.	2.6239	.0017	.006	No. 3	2.1884	.0016	.010
1959 OHV, V8, 312 Cu. In.	2.6239	.0017	.006	No. 3	2.1884	.0016	.010
OHV, V8, 383, 430, Cu. In.	2.8998	.0019	.006	No. 3	2.5996	.0016	.010
1961-62 223 Cu. In. OHV 6	2.4984	.0015	.006	No. 3	2.2984	.014	.006
292 Cu. In. V8	2.4984	.0017	.004	No. 3	2.1884	.018	.011
352, 390 Cu. In. V8	2.7488	.0018	.004	No. 3	2.4384	.019	.011
1963 390, 406 Cu. In.	2.7488	.0020	.006	No. 3	2.4384	.019	.019

PISTON AND PIN SPECIFICATIONS

Year and Model	PISTON		PISTON PIN				
	Skirt Clearance				FIT		
	MIN.	MAX.	Diameter	Bushing	In Rod	In Piston	Lock
1954-55	.0009	.0017	.9120	Yes	.0002-.0004	.0001-.0003	Ring
1956-60—"312"	.0004	.0007	.9120	Yes	.0001-.0003	.0008	Ring
1957—368	.0008	.0026	.9120	Yes	.0001-.0003	.0008	Ring
1958-60—383	.0011	.0029	.9750	None	Press	.0001-.0003	Rod Press
1959-60—430	.0011	.0029	.9750	None	Press	.0001-.0003	Rod Press
1961-62—6 Cy.	.0008	.0026	.9120	Yes	.0001-.0005	.0001-.0003	Ring
1961-62—V8	.0008	.0026	.9750	Yes	.0001-.0005	.0001-.0003	Ring
1963—390 cu. in.	.0008	.0020	.9750	Yes	.0001-.0005	.0001-.0003	Ring
406 cu. in.	.0043	.0049	.9750	Yes	.0003-.0005	.0001-.0003	Ring

Piston Fitting Ribbon Thickness and Spring Scale Pull

1954-63 ENGINES WITH DISTRIBUTOR AT BACK: ex. 1957, 368 Cu. In. V8

½ inch wide; .0015 inch thick; 10 inches long; 5-10 pounds pull.

1957, 368 CU. IN. V8

½ inch wide; .0015 inch thick; 10 inches long; 6-12 pounds pull.

1958-63, ENGINES WITH DISTRIBUTOR AT FRONT

½ inch wide, .002 inch thick. Pull of 5 to 10 pounds.

Piston Assembly

ALL:

The indentation on top of the piston goes to the front of the engine. The squirt hole in the rod faces the camshaft. The bearing lock slots go towards the outside of the engine.

TORQUE SPECIFICATIONS

YEAR	Cylinder Head Bolts	Rod Bearing Bolts	Main Bearing Bolts	Crankshaft Pulley Bolt	Flywheel to Crankshaft Bolt	Manifolds	
						Ex.	In.
1954-55 All V8	65	45–50	80–90	85–95	75–85	26	26
1956 All V8	75	45–50	95–105	85–95	75–85	26	26
1957 All ex. Optl., 368	75	45–50	95–105	130–145	75–85	26	26
Optl., 368 cu. in., OHV, V8	90	45–50	120–130	130–145	75–85	26	26
1958-60 All V8 with distributor at front	105	45–50	95–105	130–145	75–85	26	26
All V8 with distributor at back	75	45–50	95–105	130–145	75–85	26	26
1961-62 6 Cyl. & 292 V8	65–75	45–50	95–105	85–95	75–85	26	26
352 & 390 V8	80–90	45–50	95–105	130–145	75–85	26	26
1963 390, 406 V8	80–90	45–50	95–105	130–145	75–85	26	26

VALVE SPECIFICATIONS

Year and Model	Seat Angle In	Ex	Valve Lift Note 1 In	Ex	Valve Spring Pressure Note 2 Outer	Inner	Stem to Guide Clearance In	Ex	Stem Diameter In	Ex	Replaceable Valve Guides
1954	45	45	.333	.326	$58@1\frac{57}{64}$	None	.0015	.0025	.342	.341	No
1955	45	45	.377	.375	$58@1\frac{57}{64}$	None	.0015	.0025	.342	.341	No
1956	45	45	.386	.384	$75@1\frac{25}{32}$	None	.0015	.0025	.342	.341	No
1957											
312 cu. in.	45	45	.401	.421	$64@1\frac{25}{32}$	None	.0017	.0030	.342	.341	No
368 cu. in	45	45	.417	.417	$60@1\frac{51}{64}$	None	.0017	.0030	.342	.341	No
1958											
312 cu. in.	45	45	.401	.421	$71@1\frac{53}{64}$	None	.0010	.0028	.3711	.3718	No
383 cu. in.	30	45	.403	.403	$71@1\frac{53}{64}$	None	.0024	.0042	.3693	.3700	No
430 cu. in.	30	45	.441	.441	$71@1\frac{53}{64}$	None	.0017	.0031	.342	.3407	No
1959											
312 cu. in.	45	45	.406	.404	$75@1\frac{25}{32}$	None	.0017	.0031	.342	.3407	No
383 cu. in.	45	45	.408	.408	$72@1\frac{53}{64}$	None	.0017	.0035	.3715	.3697	No
430 cu. in.	45	45	.408	.408	$72@1\frac{53}{64}$	None	.0017	.0035	.3715	.3697	No
1960											
312 cu. in.	45	45	.358	.356	$75@1\frac{25}{32}$	None	.0017	.0031	.342	.3407	No
383 cu. in.	45	45	.408	.408	$72@1\frac{53}{64}$	None	.0017	.0035	.3715	.3697	No
430 cu. in.	45	45	.408	.408	$72@1\frac{53}{64}$	None	.0017	.0035	.3715	.3697	No
1961-62											
223 cu. in.	45	45	.370	.370	$75@1\frac{25}{32}$	None	.0017	.0035	.3419	.3403	No
292 cu. in.	45	45	.377	.375	$75@1\frac{25}{32}$	None	.0017	.0030	.3419	.3403	No
352, 390 cu. in.	45	45	.408	.408	$99@1\frac{53}{64}$	None	.0017	.0035	.3715	.3697	No
1963											
390 cu. in.	45	45	.408	.408	$85@1\frac{53}{64}$	Opt.	.0017	.0027	.3715	.3705	No
406 cu. in.	30	45	.500	.500	$95@1\frac{53}{64}$	Opt.	.0017	.0027	.3715	.3705	No

NOTES FOR VALVE SPECIFICATIONS TABLE

Note 1: Camshaft Sprocket Index Marks

1954-63, ALL OHV, V8 WITH DISTRIBUTOR AT THE BACK ex. 368 cu. in. optional 1957 Engine. With the marks on the camshaft and crankshaft sprockets set to the left of the engine; there should be 7 links of the chain from one mark to the other including the marks.

1957, 368 CU. IN. OPTIONAL ENGINE AND 1958-59, ALL OHV, V8 WITH DISTRIBUTOR AT THE FRONT

Align the marks on the camshaft and crankshaft sprockets nearest each other and with the shaft centers.

1958-63, ALL OHV, V8 exc. 312 Cu. In.

Align the marks on the camshaft and crankshaft sprockets nearest each other and with the shaft centers.

Note 2: Valve Springs

Intake and exhaust valve springs are the same.

CAPACITIES

YEAR	Engine Crankcase Add 1 Qt. for New Filter	Transmissions Pints to Refill After Draining Manual	Automatic	Rear Axle Pints	Gasoline Tank Gallons	Cooling System Quarts Add 1 Qt. for Heater
1954 All OHV, V8	5	3½	19	3.5	19	19
1955 All OHV, V8	5	3½	20	3.5	18	19
1956-57						
All ex. Optional, V8	5	3½	21	5	20	20
Optional, 368 cu. in., V8	5	3½	21	5	20	23
1958						
All ex. Park Lane	5	3½	20	5	20	20½
Park Lane	5	NU	23	5	20	20½
1959-60						
OHV, V8, 312 cu. in.	5	3¼	20	4.5	20	20
OHV, V8, 383 cu. in.	5	NU	22	4.5	20	20½
OHV, V8, 430 cu. in.	5	NU	21	4.5	20	20½
1961-62						
6 Cyl., 223 cu. in.	4	3¼	20	4.5	20	15
V8, 292, 352, 390 cu. in.	5	3¼	20A	4.5	20	19
1963						
390 cu. in.	5	3¼B	20	4.5	20	
406 cu. in.	5	3	NU	4.5	20	

N.U.—Not Used.
(A) Automatic transmission capacities vary with type used.
(B) With 4-Speed Manual—3 Pts.

MERCURY

CYLINDER HEAD NUT TIGHTENING SEQUENCE

1961-63 OHV 6
Tighten to 65-75 ft. lbs.

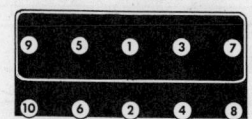

All OHV, V8 with Distributor at the back except the 1957 368 Cu. In. V8 Tighten to 75 ft. lbs. The 1957 368 Cu. In. V8 Tighten to 90. ft. lbs

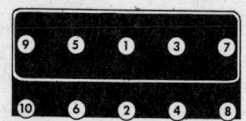

All OHV, V8 with Distributor at the front Tighten to 105 ft. lbs. in 3 steps cold. Follow the sequence shown for each step. Step 1: to 85 ft. lbs. Step 2: to 95 ft. lbs. Step 3: to 105 ft. lbs.

GENERAL ENGINE SPECIFICATIONS

Year	Bore and Stroke	Number of Main Bearings	Type of Valve Lifter Used	Cubic Inch Displacement	AMA Horsepower	Advertised Horsepower at Stated RPM	Advertised Torque at Stated RPM	Compression Ratio	Oil Pressure At 30 MPH (Note 2)	Cam Shaft Drive
1954										
V8, OHV	$3\frac{5}{8}$x$3\frac{3}{32}$	5	Mech. Adj.	256	42.05	161@4400	238@2500	7.5–1	40–50	Chain
1955										
V8, OHV, Montclair	$3\frac{3}{4}$x$3\frac{19}{64}$	5	Mech. Adj.	292	45.0	198@4400	286@2500	8.5–1	40–50	Chain
1955										
V8, OHV, Cust. Montclair	$3\frac{3}{4}$x$3\frac{19}{64}$	5	Mech. Adj.	292	45.0	188@4400	274@2500	7.6–1	40–50	Chain
1956										
V8, OHV	$3\frac{51}{64}$x$3\frac{7}{16}$	5	Mech. Adj.	312	46.2	Note 3	Note 4	Note 5	40–50	Chain
1957										
V8, OHV, 312 Cu. In.	$3\frac{51}{64}$x$3\frac{7}{16}$	5	Mech. Adj.	312	46.2	255@2600	340@2600	9.7–1	40–50	Chain
V8, OHV, 368 Cu. In.	4:00x$3\frac{21}{32}$	5	Hydraulic	368	51.2	290@4600	405@2600	10–1	40–50	Chain
1958										
V8, OHV, 312 Cu. In.	$3\frac{51}{64}$x$3\frac{7}{16}$	5	Mech. Adj.	312	46.21	255@2600	340@2600	9.7–1	45–50	Chain
V8, OHV, 383 Cu. In.	$4\frac{19}{64}$x$3\frac{19}{64}$	5	Hydromatic	383	59.2	Note 6	Note 7	10.5–1	45–50	Chain
V8, OHV, 430 Cu. In.	$4\frac{19}{64}$x$3\frac{45}{64}$	5	Hydromatic	430	59.2	360@4600	480@3000	10.5–1	45–50	Chain
1959										
V8, OHV, 312 Cu. In.	$3\frac{51}{64}$x$3\frac{7}{16}$	5	Mech. Adj.	312	46.21	210@4400	325@2200	9.0–1	45–50	Chain
V8, OHV, 383 Cu. In.	$4\frac{19}{64}$x$3\frac{19}{64}$	5	Hydraulic	383	59.17	322@4600	420@2800	10–1	45–50	Chain
V8, OHV, 430 Cu. In.	$4\frac{19}{64}$x$3\frac{45}{64}$	5	Hydraulic	430	59.17	345@4400	480@2800	10–1	45–50	Chain
1960										
V8, OHV, 312 Cu. In.	$3\frac{51}{64}$x$3\frac{7}{16}$	5	Mech. Adj.	312	46.21	205@4000	328@2100	8.9–1	45–50	Chain
V8, OHV, 383 Cu In.	$4\frac{19}{64}$x$3\frac{19}{64}$	5	Hydraulic	383	59.17	280@4200	405@2200	8.5–1	45–50	Chain
V8, OHV, 430 Cu. In.	$4\frac{19}{64}$x$3\frac{45}{64}$	5	Hydraulic	430	59.17	310@4100	460@2200	10.0–1	45–50	Chain
1961										
6 Cyl., 223 Cu. In.	3.625x3.6	4	Note 8	223	31.54	135@4000	200@2000	8.4–1	45	Chain
V8, 292 Cu. In.	3.75x3.3	5	Mech. Adj.	292	45.0	175@4200	279@2200	8.8–1	45	Chain
V8, 352 Cu. In.	4.00x3.5	5	Hydraulic	352	51.2	220@4400	376@2400	8.9–1	45	Chain
V8, 390 Cu. In.	4.05x3.784	5	Hydraulic	390	52.5	300@4600	427@2800	9.6–1	45	Chain
1962										
6 Cyl., 223 Cu. In.	3.625x3.6	4	Note 8	223	31.54	138@4200	203@2200	8.4–1	45	Chain
V8, 292 Cu. In.	3.75x3.3	5	Mech. Adj.	292	45.0	170@4200	279@2200	8.8–1	45	Chain
V8, 352 Cu. In.	4.00x3.5	5	Hydraulic	352	51.2	220@4300	336@2600	8.9–1	45	Chain
V8, 390 Cu. In.	4.05x3.784	5	Hydraulic	390	52.5	300@4600	427@2800	9.6–1	45	Chain
1963										
V8, 390 Cu. In.	4.05x3.78	5	Hydraulic	390	52.5	300@4600	427@2800	9.6–1	45	Chain
V8, 406 Cu. In.	4.13x3.78	5	Mech. Adj.	406	54.58	385@5800	444@2800	10.9–1	45	Chain

NOTES FOR GENERAL ENGINE SPECIFICATIONS

Note 1: Valve Lifters

1954-57: All except 1957 optional 368 cubic inch engine have mechanical lifters.

1957: Optional 368 cubic inch engine has hydraulic lifters standard. Valve cover is painted Red.

1958-63: All Engines have hydraulic lifters as standard equipment. Exc. 312 and 406 Cu. In. Engines. See note 8, for 6 Cyl.

Note 2: Oil Flow

OIL FILTER TYPE

1954-63, All ....Full flow

ROCKER SHAFT OIL SUPPLY
All OHV Engines With Distributor at the back

The right bank rocker shaft assembly receives oil through a drilled passage that starts at No. 3 cam bearing and directs oil through No. 2 rocker arm shaft support. The left bank rocker arm assembly receives its oil from No. 3 cam bearing and No. 3 rocker arm shaft support. The oil then, through a system of holes and passages, lubricates rocker arm bushings, valve and ball joint ends, tappets, push rods and push rod seats.

Excess oil finds its way into the rocker arm to the push rod and valve push rod chamber through holes in the heads and two overflow pipes, one at the front of the right bank and one at the rear of the left bank.

Oil from the left bank overflow pipe, rockers, tappets, and push rod chamber, drains through a large hole at the rear of the block that directs the oil to the distributor drive gears and down in the pan.

Oil from the right bank overflow pipe and push rod chamber is directed through a system of holes and channels to lubricate the timing chain and sprockets.

All OHV Engines With Distributor at the front

Oil flows from the main oil gallery through a passage to parallel galleries, on each side, for the hydraulic tappets.

From each gallery, oil flows upward through a passage to two rocker arm shaft supports and into the rocker arm shafts.

Oil flows through the rocker arm shafts and is forced through metered holes in the shafts to the rocker arms. Metered holes in the rocker arms intermittently align with the holes in the rocker arm shaft. Allowing oil under pressure to flow through the

assembly. The discharged oil flows down the valves and is deflected by the seal into a trough in the cylinder heads where it is directed through a hole in the cylinder head to the valve tappet chamber. Oil also runs down the push rods to the tappet chamber reservoir.

Note 3: 1956 Horse Power

All with standard trans ....210 @ 4600
All with Mercomatic trans. 220 @ 4600

Note 4: 1956 Torque

All with standard trans. ....312 @ 2600
All with Mercomatic trans 320 @ 2600

Note 5: 1956 Compression Ratio

All with standard trans. 8-1
All with Mercomatic trans. 8.4-1

Note 6: 1958 Horse Power

Monterey ....312 @ 4600
Montclair ....330 @ 4800

Note 7: 1958 Torque

Monterey ....405 @ 2900
Montclair ....425 @ 3000

Note 8:

The 223 cu. in. 6 cyl. engine has mechanical self adjusting valve rocker arms.

DISTRIBUTOR

1954 Thru 1957 Models

The distributor is located at the back of the block between the two cylinder banks.

To remove it, remove the air cleaner, the distributor cap and wire assembly, disconnect the vacuum line from the carburetor and the linkage lines, remove the ignition primary wire and take out the bolt which holds the distributor down to the engine block.

Lift off the distributor.

Service on distributors is given in the distributor and ignition system section in this manual, see index.

1958-60 Models

On these models the distributor is located at the front of the engine.

To remove it, first remove the cap and mark the position of the rotor in relation to the distributor body and then mark the position of the distributor body in relation to the block so that the unit can be reinstalled without having to retime the ignition.

Disconnect the vacuum advance line and the ignition wire and then remove the holddown bolt and pull the distributor up out of the block.

1961-63 Models

Removal procedure is same as noted for the 1960 models. However the distributor for the 223 cu. in. 6 is on the right side. It is at the rear of the 292 cu. in. V8 and at the front of the 352 and 390 cu. in. engines.

Firing Order

See "TUNE-UP" Specifications.

Timing Mark Location

See "TUNE-UP" Specifications.

IGNITION PRIMARY RESISTOR

Starting with 1956 12-volt models, a resistance is used in the primary circuit of the ignition coil. This resistor is mounted immediately adjacent to the coil.

If any difficulty is experienced with ignition, make absolutely certain that the primary resistor is functioning properly.

Spark Plug Wire Replacement

See "TUNE-UP" section of manual.

GENERATOR AND REGULATOR

Generator Service

See "Generator and Regulator" Specifications.

1954 Thru 1962 Models

The generator is located on the right bank of cylinders at the front under the side of the cylinder head, on V8's. On the 6 cylinder model it is mounted on the left side.

To remove it, loosen the bolt which holds the tension bar on the generator to release the belt tension and slip the belt off the pulley. Remove the wires, and the generator may be detached either at the bracket or the two swivel bolts may be removed. On these models it is easier to take out the bracket than it is to separate the generator from its swivel.

The charging system may consist of a D.C. GENERATOR or the newer A.C. UNIT. More detailed information may be obtained on either of these systems from the "Unit Repair" section, under the heading, "Generators and Regulators."

BATTERY AND STARTER

STARTER SYSTEM SERVICE

See "Starter Systems" Section.

STARTER, R & R

1954-56

Disconnect battery. Raise car. Then disconnect starter cable. Drop idler arm and bracket. Remove end plate to housing screws and work starter down and out. In some cases turning front wheels to extreme right will help.

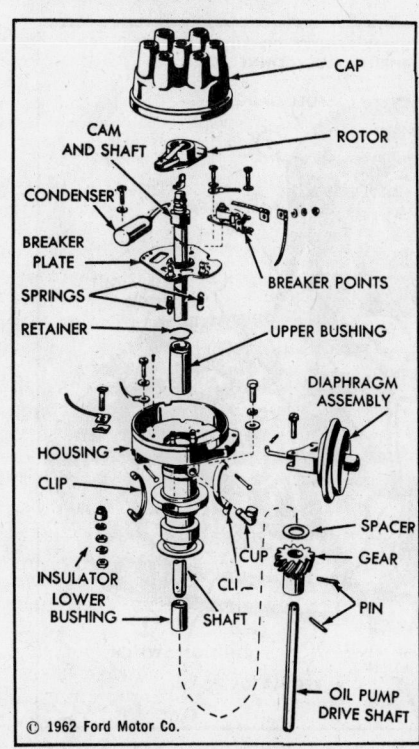

CAP
ROTOR
CAM AND SHAFT
CONDENSER
BREAKER PLATE
SPRINGS
RETAINER
BREAKER POINTS
UPPER BUSHING
DIAPHRAGM ASSEMBLY
HOUSING
CLIP
SPACER
GEAR
CUP
CLI..
PIN
INSULATOR LOWER BUSHING
SHAFT
OIL PUMP DRIVE SHAFT
© 1962 Ford Motor Co.

Distributor assembly

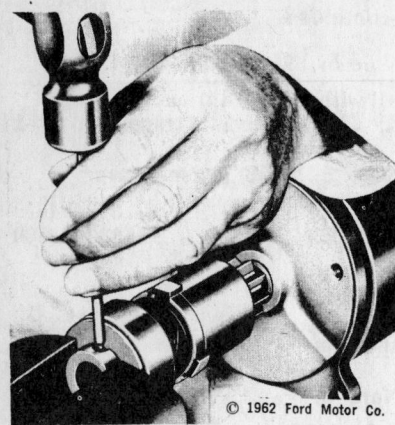

Removing the Starter Drive

1957

Disconnect battery, starter cable and cable bracket below No. 4 spark plug. Turn front wheels full right. Remove attaching screws. Pull starter out and up and while in vertical position rotate unit to permit end plate lug clearance. Lower between idler and tie rod.

1958

Disconnect battery. Raise car and with wheels turned full right disconnect starter cable. Remove both exhaust pipes (Right only, if dual exhaust) from manifold and muffler. Unbolt starter and pull forward and upward between engine and Apron. By holding in vertical position and slightly twisting, starter can be low-ered between idler arm and tie rod. When installing be sure rubber seal is in place. Always tighten outer cap screw first to assure proper starter alignment.

1959-63

Disconnect battery and throttle linkage at bell crank. Raise car. Disconnect starter cable. Remove front splash shield and front engine insulator nuts. Raise front of engine about one inch. Use wood block on jack to prevent engine damage. Unbolt starter and lower between idler and tie rod with drive end down.

When reinstalling be sure rubber seal is in proper position.

INSTRUMENTS

DASH INSTRUMENTS

Since all work on an instrument cluster is of necessity done in very tight quarters, it is imperative that the battery be disconnected before any attempt is made to work under the dash to avoid short-circuiting any of the wires with possible injury to the operator.

Perhaps the easiest way to work on any or all of the instruments is to take the entire instrument cluster out and pull it into the driver's compartment.

Remove the screws from the upper front flange (in the driver's compartment) of the instrument panel and, from underneath the dash, re-move the two nuts from each side of the cluster and then the entire cluster can be pulled into the car a sufficient amount to permit working on the instruments under perhaps less difficult conditions than working under the dash itself.

The wires are sufficiently long to permit pulling the cluster into the car approximately three inches after the speedometer cable has been disconnected.

On the most recent models remove wires from under clips. Protect the finish with cloth or masking tape. Remove upper cluster screws, pull the upper cluster outward and support on covered column. Disconnect gauge wires and lamp assemblies. Complete removal of cluster.

SPEEDOMETER R & R

Always disconnect the battery, on the ground side, before starting any work that involves the instrument panel.

1. Remove the two screws holding the hood and speedometer head to the instrument cluster.

2. Raise the hood and speedometer head up off the dowel pins and disconnect speedometer cable.

3. Disconnect the speedometer light wiring at the four-way connector and remove the speedometer and hood assembly.

On later cars, after upper cluster has been removed, the speedometer may be removed from the case.

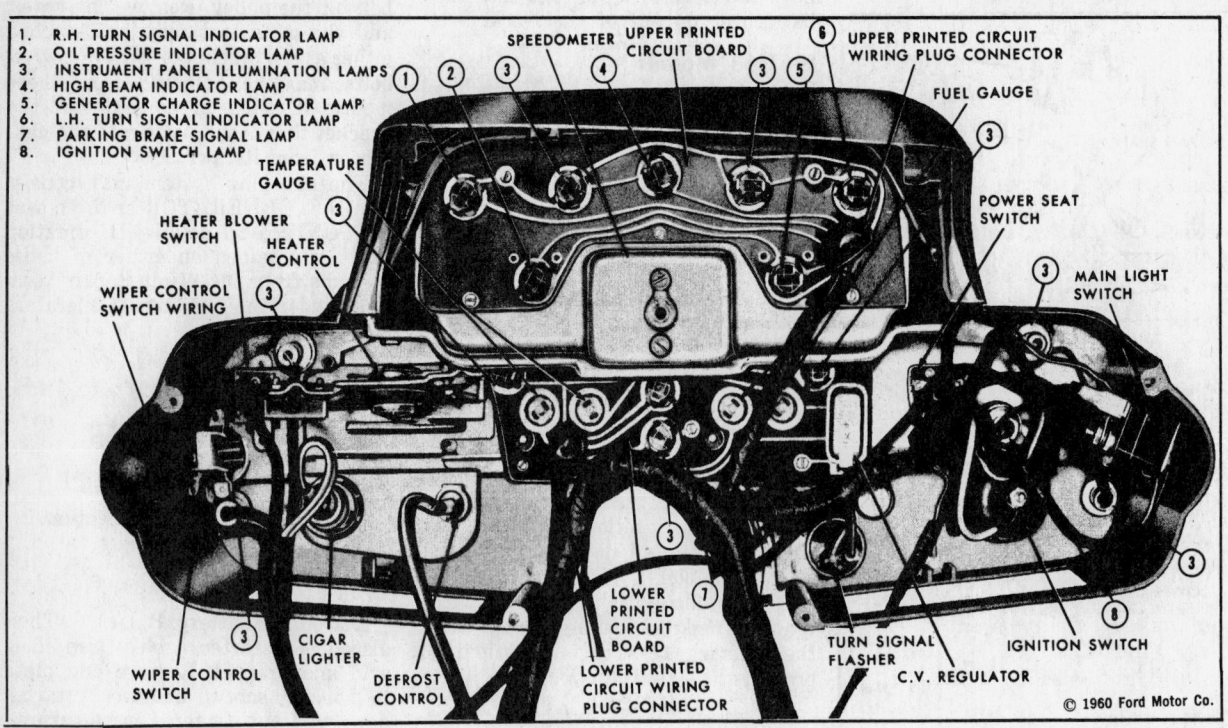

1. R.H. TURN SIGNAL INDICATOR LAMP
2. OIL PRESSURE INDICATOR LAMP
3. INSTRUMENT PANEL ILLUMINATION LAMPS
4. HIGH BEAM INDICATOR LAMP
5. GENERATOR CHARGE INDICATOR LAMP
6. L.H. TURN SIGNAL INDICATOR LAMP
7. PARKING BRAKE SIGNAL LAMP
8. IGNITION SWITCH LAMP

Instrument Cluster Rear View—1960

© 1960 Ford Motor Co.

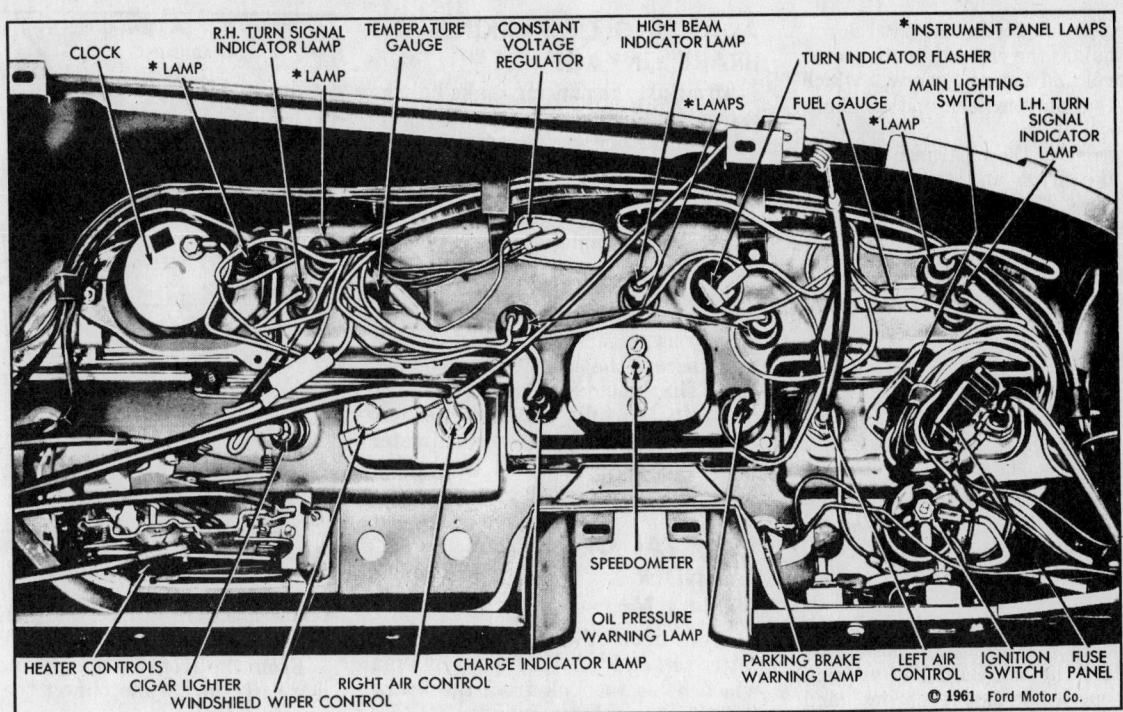

CLOCK · R.H. TURN SIGNAL INDICATOR LAMP · *LAMP · *LAMP · TEMPERATURE GAUGE · CONSTANT VOLTAGE REGULATOR · HIGH BEAM INDICATOR LAMP · *LAMPS · *INSTRUMENT PANEL LAMPS · TURN INDICATOR FLASHER · FUEL GAUGE · MAIN LIGHTING SWITCH · *LAMP · L.H. TURN SIGNAL INDICATOR LAMP · SPEEDOMETER · OIL PRESSURE WARNING LAMP · HEATER CONTROLS · CIGAR LIGHTER · WINDSHIELD WIPER CONTROL · RIGHT AIR CONTROL · CHARGE INDICATOR LAMP · PARKING BRAKE WARNING LAMP · LEFT AIR CONTROL · IGNITION SWITCH · FUSE PANEL · © 1961 Ford Motor Co.

Intsrument Cluster Rear View—1961

DISASSEMBLY & ASSEMBLY

Record the lamp wiring color codes to reduce the possibility of error in reassembly.

1. Remove socket assemblies from back of speedometer. **Note:** on safety speed monitor speedometers, loosen the driven gear set screw and slide the gear and chain off of the shaft.

2. Remove four screws holding speedometer head to the hood and remove hood.

3. Remove one screw from either end of trim plate and remove trim plate, glass and dial.

4. Remove the three screws from the bottom of the speedometer housing and remove the speedometer from the housing.

5. To assemble, merely reverse disassembly procedure.

BRAKES

All Mercury models, through early 1955, are equipped with Bendix type two-shoe hydraulically actuated brakes having an adjustable anchor. Late 1955 thru 1957 models have the same type brakes but the anchor pins are not adjustable. The hand brake on all models actuates the shoes at the rear wheels.

Starting With 1958 Models

Starting with 1958 models a Bendix brake having a fixed anchor but self-adjusting feature is used on Mercury models.

BRAKE PEDAL ADJUSTMENT

Adjust the brake pedal so that there is approximately ½ inch free play of the pedal before the push rod contacts the piston in the master cylinder. This adjustment is made at the eccentric bolt which holds the brake push rod to the brake pedal under the dash.

BRAKE ADJUSTMENT

All adjustment and service on these brakes is given in Unit Repair section.

STARTING WITH 1958 SELF ADJUSTERS

The service brake has a self-adjusting brake shoe mechanism consisting of a link, actuator, pawl, and pawl re-

turn spring. The looped end of the link is attached to the achor pin, and the hooked end to the actuator. The actuator is held against the secondary shoe by means of the holddown cup and spring. The pawl is connected to the actuator and held in position by the pawl return spring.

The automatic adjusters operate only when the brakes are applied as the car is moving rearward. The wrap-around action of the shoes following the drum while moving rearward forces the upper end of the primary shoe against the anchor pin and the secondary shoe away from the anchor pin.

The link holds the top of the actuator stationary, forcing the actuator to pivot on the secondary shoe. The

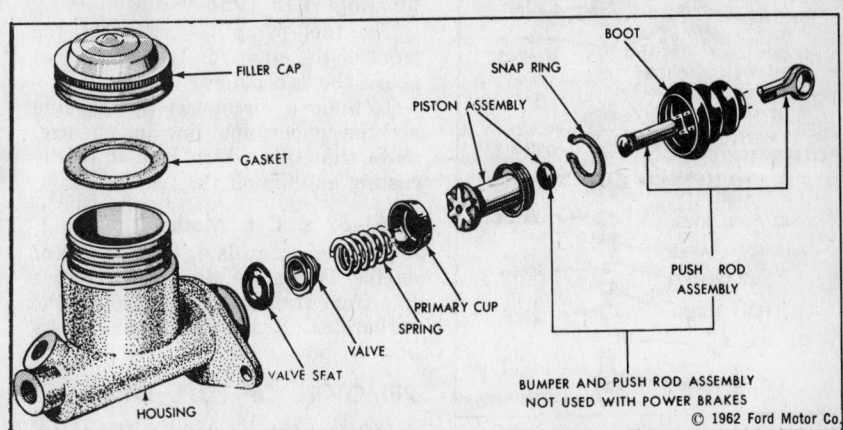

FILLER CAP · GASKET · SNAP RING · PISTON ASSEMBLY · BOOT · PUSH ROD ASSEMBLY · PRIMARY CUP · SPRING · VALVE · VALVE SEAT · HOUSING · BUMPER AND PUSH ROD ASSEMBLY NOT USED WITH POWER BRAKES · © 1962 Ford Motor Co.

Exploded view of brake master cylinder—typical

pivoting action forces the pawl downward against the end of a tooth on the starwheel adjusting screw, which turns the star wheel and expands the shoes.

The greater the clearance between the brake drum and the lining, the greater the travel of the secondary shoe away from the anchor. The further the secondary shoe moves, the greater the adjustment. When the brakes are adjusted correctly, there will not be sufficient travel of the secondary shoe to permit the actuator to pivot and force the pawl to engage against the end of a tooth of the starwheel adjusting screw, and turn the wheel to expand the shoe.

When the brakes are applied as the car is moving forward, the self-adjuster does not operate because the wrap-around action of the shoe forces the secondary shoe against the anchor pin.

The rear brake assembly is basically the same as the front brake, except that the conventional parking brake operating lever, spring, and parking brake strut rod are used in the rear brake. The anchor pin on all brakes can be adjusted when necessary.

Whenever removing or replacing a star wheel assembly, special care must be exercised to be certain that the correct star wheel assembly is installed on the right brake drum to enable the self-adjuster to function properly.

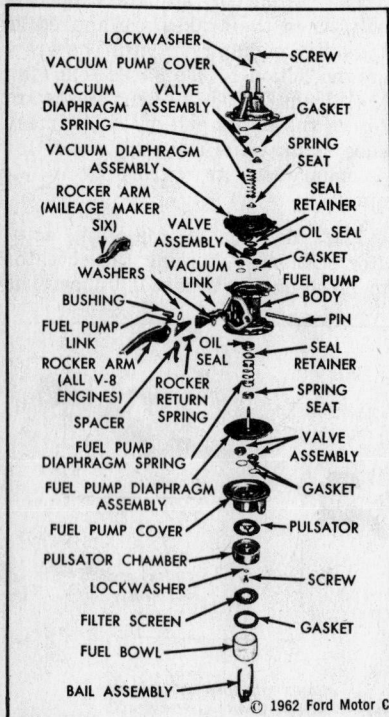

Typical Combination Vacuum Booster and Fuel Pump

ADJUSTING OF PARKING BRAKE LINKAGE

To adjust the parking brake linkage expand the rear shoes at the star wheel until they are very tight at the drum. This should be done with the brake cable disconnected at the equalizer nut. By hand, pull up all the slack in the cables and adjust the forward nut on the brake pull shaft until it just touches the equalizer bracket when it is being pulled back as tightly as possible. Run the rear nut up to secure the equalizer in the position. This should be done with the brake in the fully released position. Back off on the star wheel adjuster on each rear wheel until the brakes are just free.

REMOVAL OF MASTER CYLINDER
1954-63 Models

From under the dash, remove the cotter pin and take out the clevis pin which holds the link from the brake pedal to the master cylinder.

Under the hood of the car in the engine compartment, remove the hydraulic lines from the master cylinder and take out the three bolts which hold the master cylinder up to the dash.

Lift off the master cylinder.

FUEL SYSTEM

FUEL PUMP

1954 Thru 1957 Models

On these models, the fuel pump is located on the left side of the engine front case. Disconnect the fuel and vacuum lines from the fuel pump, remove the two mounting bolts and lift the pump off of the engine.

Service on fuel pumps is given in the fuel pump section of this manual, see index.

Starting With 1958 V-8 Models

The fuel pump is located at the front of the engine in the center just above the fan pulley.

To remove, disconnect the flex line and the copper input line and then remove the bolts which hold it to the casting and lift off the fuel pump.

1961-62 6 Cyl. Models

The fuel pump is on right front of engine. To remove, disconnect flexible line from frame and solid line to the carburetor. Remove mounting bolts and lift off.

REMOVAL OF FUEL TANK

Lift the floor mat from the trunk and force the cover plate down in the

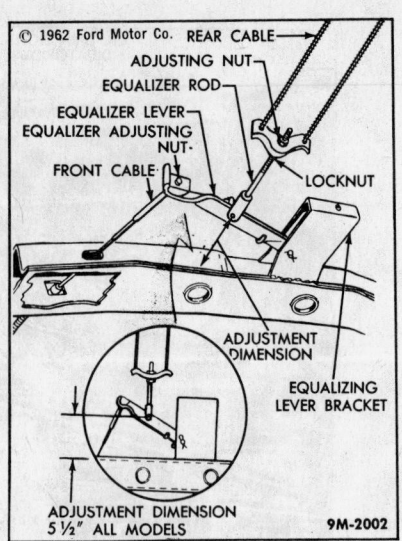

Parking Brake Linkage

trunk floor from over the gage connection and disconnect the gage.

From the front of the gas tank underneath the car disconnect the gasoline feed line.

From the left side of the gas tank, also underneath the car, disconnect the flexible vent line.

Place a jack under the tank and remove the bolts which hold the tank straps at the back of the tank and then slowly lower the front of the tank so that the neck will thread out through the rubber grommet. If difficulty is experienced, take the grommet off.

EXHAUST SYSTEM
EXHAUST PIPE REPLACEMENT

Starting With 1955 Models

The exhaust manifold flange bolts are accessible from underneath the car with a long extension. On some production 1955 and 1956 models a flexible tube is wrapped around the outside of the rigid exhaust line.

Work plenty of derusting oil around the joint between the exhaust pipe and the muffler, then disconnect the flange bolts, remove the clamp which holds the exhaust pipe to the muffler and separate the pipe with the muffler under the car. The pipe can then be threaded out from under the car. On cars with dual exhaust systems each pipe can be removed separately. On models with single exhaust systems the crossover is accomplished in back of the transmission just ahead of the muffler.

REMOVAL OF MUFFLER

Disconnect the exhaust pipe at the flange and squirt plenty of penetrat-

REMOVAL OF INLET MANIFOLDS

Starting With 1954 Models

Remove the air cleaner in the upper radiator hose, disconnect all lines to the carburetor, including gas, vacuum and throttle lines and take off the carburetor. Remove the ignition coil and throttle rod bracket. Disconnect the temperature sending units. Disconnect the thermostat by-pass hose, unbolt and lift off the inlet manifold.

ing oil or derusting oil around the joint between the exhaust pipe and the muffler and between the muffler and the tail pipe. Then remove the clamps which hold these two together. Pull the exhaust pipe forward until it comes out of the muffler and then tilt the muffler downward and pull it off the tail pipe.

REPLACEMENT OF TAIL PIPE

Starting With 1954 Models

Some models are fitted with a resonator which is an integral part of the tail pipe; it is not sold separately.

Remove the brackets which hold the tail pipe up to the under side of the car, squirt plenty of derusting oil on the joint between the muffler and the tail pipe, remove the clamp and separate the tail pipe from the muffler, threading the entire unit toward the front of the car.

REMOVAL OF EXHAUST MANIFOLDS

Starting With 1954 Models

Disconnect the exhaust pipe flanges, the bolts are accessible from underneath the car. Remove the bolts which hold the exhaust manifolds to the head and lift off the manifolds.

On cars equipped with power steering thru 1957, the back bolts on the left manifold are somewhat difficult of access but they can be reached.

On models equipped with a heater, many shops prefer to disconnect the heater when working on the right side

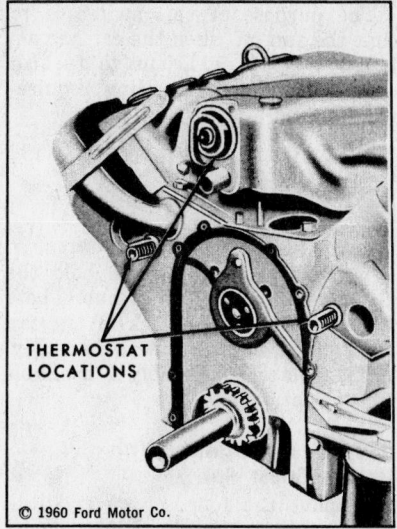

THERMOSTAT LOCATIONS

© 1960 Ford Motor Co.

Cylinder Block Thermostats

exhaust manifold. While the manifold can be taken off with the heater in place, many shops feel it is easier to take the heater off first.

COOLING SYSTEM

A pressure type cooling system is used on all Mercury models.

REMOVAL OF THERMOSTAT

1954-57 and 1961-63 Models

The thermostat is located in the thermostat housing in the front of the intake manifold. Disconnect the upper radiator hose at its lower end and the by-pass hose. Unbolt and lift off the thermostat housing and then take out the thermostat.

1958 Thru 1960 Models

1958 thru 1960, three thermostats are used on the Mercury engines from 1958 to 1960.

One: The "normal" thermostat is located back of the water outlet elbow in front of the manifold.

The other two thermostats are located back of the two legs of the

water pump where they butt against the cylinder block.

The two small thermostats in back of the water pump legs are rated at 140 degrees Fahrenheit. The thermostat at the water outlet elbow is rated at 180 degrees Fahrenheit. This is the one to change to accommodate the use of non-permanent type antifreeze.

FUNCTION OF THE THREE THERMOSTATS

When the engine starts up cold all three thermostats are closed and the two thermostats located in back of the pump legs cause the water to circulate through the intake manifold only.

As the engine warms up to 140 degrees, these two thermostats open permitting water to circulate through the block and the manifold.

As the engine water temperature reaches 180 degrees the main thermostat opens permitting water to circulate out of the engine into the radiator.

The upper thermostat is replaced in the usual manner, disconnect the lower end of the upper radiator hose, remove the bolts which hold the goose neck to the intake manifold, lift off the goose neck and take out the thermostat. The other two thermostats can be lifted out of the block after the water pump is removed, see "Water Pump Removal."

REMOVAL OF WATER PUMPS

1954 Thru 1957 Models

A single water pump is used on these models, mounted in the front of the engine front case.

To remove the water pump, slack off and remove the fan belt, remove the bolts which hold the fan plate to the fan hub, disconnect the radiator and heater hoses, remove the bolts which hold the by-pass line at the top of the pump, take out the bolts which hold the water pump to the front case and lift off the pump.

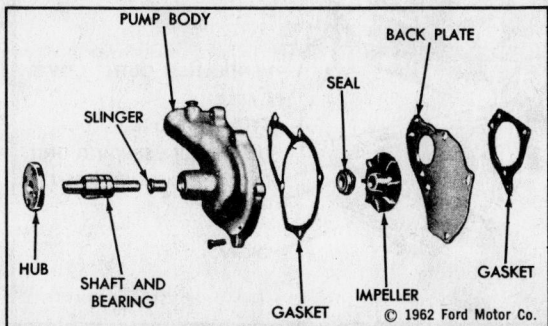

PUMP BODY
BACK PLATE
SEAL
SLINGER
HUB
SHAFT AND BEARING
GASKET
IMPELLER
GASKET
© 1962 Ford Motor Co.

Water Pump Assembly—6 Cylinder Engine.

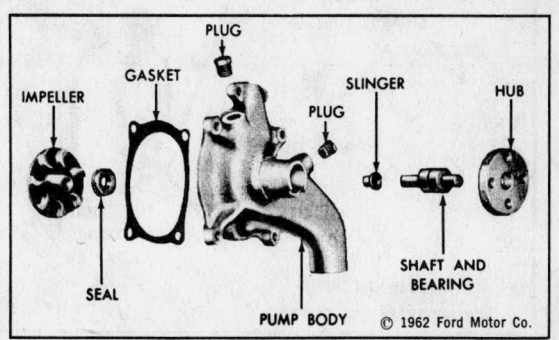

PLUG
GASKET
IMPELLER
SLINGER
HUB
PLUG
SEAL
SHAFT AND BEARING
PUMP BODY
© 1962 Ford Motor Co.

Water Pump Assembly—8 Cylinder Engine.

Starting With 1958 Models

Drain the radiator and remove the upper, lower and bypass hose. Loosen the generator belt and take off the generator support bracket at the water pump housing. Remove the fan blade assembly and its spacer. Remove the cap screws which attach the water pump to the engine and lift off the pump. Scrape off the gasket carefully from both the engine and the water pump, check the condition of the two thermostats located in back of the legs of the water pump.

POWER SURGE AUTOMATIC COOLING FAN

1957 Models

A fully automatic fan controlled by a thermostat is used on some 1957 Turnpike Cruisers. A thermostat located in the center of the pump impeller prevents the fan from turning by declutching it when the engine is cool.

1958 Thru 1960 With 430 Cu. In. Engine

On these models a power boost fan is used which has a power boost air switch. The air switch is located to the right front face of the left cylinder head.

At 27 miles per hour air speed, sufficient air will pass into the air switch to cause it to go to the "fan off position." "Fan off" position is indicated on the instrument panel.

The purpose of this switch is to shut the fan off when the car has attained a speed sufficient to furnish enough air for the cooling requirements.

REMOVAL OF AUTOMATIC FAN

Some 1957 Turnpike Cruisers

Remove the bolts which hold the fan assembly to the fan hub. These bolts are located in back of the fan mechanism, but in front of the pulley.

The complete assembly is available for replacement.

1958-1960 Engines With Power Boost Fan

Remove the four screws and lock washers attaching the power boost fan assembly to the water pump hub and remove the boost assembly.

Remove the four nuts and lock washers which attach the fan proper to the power boost fluid unit and take off the fan blade assembly. Reassemble in reverse order.

REMOVAL OF RADIATOR CORE

1954 Thru 1963 Models

Detach the top and bottom radiator hoses at the radiator, remove the bolts at the side which hold the radiator to the radiator support and lift the radiator assembly straight up.

ENGINE

REFERENCES

1954 Thru 1960 Models

An overhead valve V type 8-cylinder engine is used on all of the above models.

1961-62

In addition to the overhead valve V8 an overhead valve 6-cylinder engine is used.

REMOVAL OF ENGINE ASSEMBLY

Starting With 1954 Models

Remove the hood, carburetor air cleaner, and carburetor assembly. Place protecting covers over the painted parts of the car so they are not damaged.

Remove the water hoses and as a precaution take off the radiator core and fan blades. Disconnect and remove the battery, the starter cables and starter, and the Automatic Transmission filler tube bracket disconnect the wires at the coil, the water temperature gauge, the oil pressure gauge, disconnect the flexible fuel lines and the windshield vacuum lines.

Disconnect the clutch pedal equalizer bars from the engine and let the equalizer bar and clutch rods hang from the frame.

If the vehicle has power brakes, remove the power brake unit.

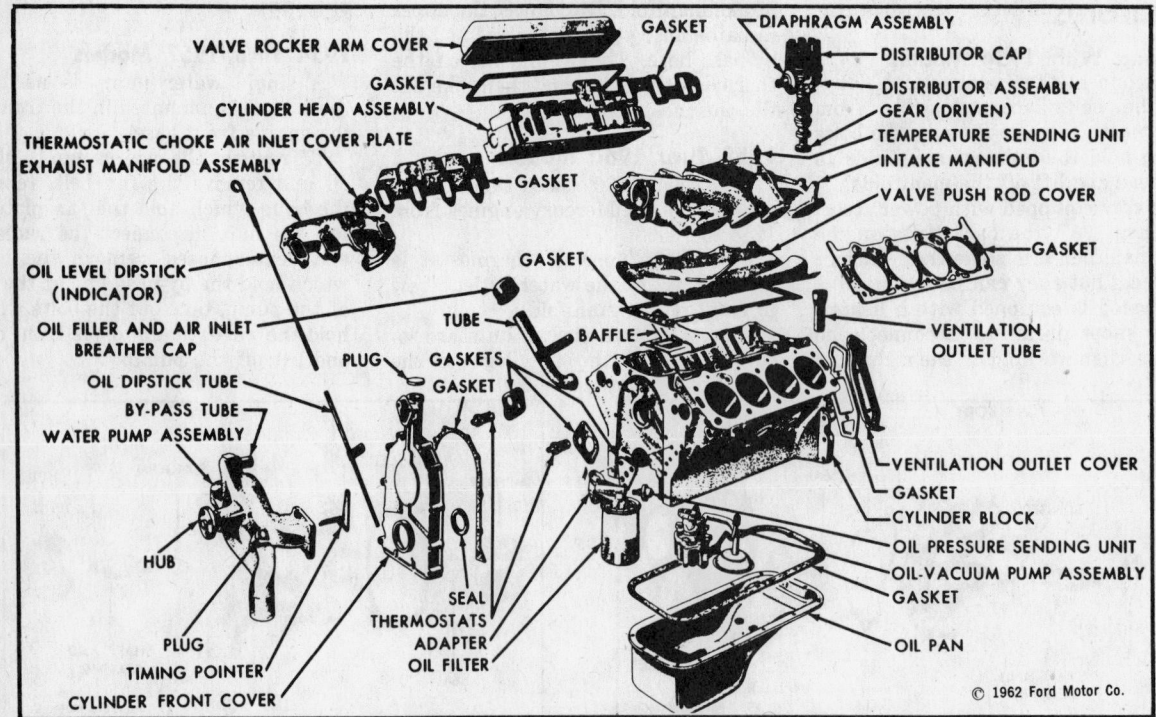

Cylinder block and related parts—typical 1954-60

© 1962 Ford Motor Co.

If equipped with Automatic Transmission, disconnect the linkage from the engine to the Transmission.

Disconnect the wires at the generator and disconnect the exhaust pipe at the flanges.

Place a jack under the transmission to hold it in place after the engine is removed and take out the two screws on each side which hold the engine to the cross member.

From the inside of the vehicle on early models, take up the floor carpet and remove the two rubber grommets covering the openings which gives access to the two upper cap screws which hold the engine assembly to the flywheel housing and take out those cap screws. Remove the nut of the flywheel housing screws.

Raise the engine slightly and slide it forward off the front of the transmission.

VACUUM CONTROLLED CRANKCASE VENTILATION

Starting with 1961 the 390 cu. in. engine will have a vacuum controlled crankcase breather. It will be an optional feature on the other engines.

Starting with 1963 this system is standard equipment on all models.

This system draws the fumes from the crankcase vent tube by means of manifold vacuum and injects them into the intake manifold. It is then combined with fuel mixture and ejected thru the exhaust.

A valve is mounted in the line to manifold to control flow. It prevents too lean intake mixture at idle (maximum vacuum), and allows enough flow at open throttle to draw off the contamination.

CYLINDER HEAD

REMOVAL OF CYLINDER HEADS

Starting With 1954 V-8 Models

Remove the inlet and exhaust manifolds as explained elsewhere in this text. Disconnect the wires from the spark plugs and take off the distributor cap wire assembly.

Remove the rocker cover pans. Disconnect the oil feed line at the rocker arms and remove the bolts which hold the rocker shaft to the cylinder head and lift off the rocker shafts.

These bolts should be turned out a little at a time until the valve spring pressure is released from the rocker shaft. The rockers must be returned to the head from which they were removed.

Remove the bolts which hold the cylinder head to the block and lift off the head.

1961-63 6-Cyl. Models

Follow procedure to remove rocker arms. Next remove temperature sending unit, coil, carburetor, vacuum and fuel lines. Disconnect water outlet hose. Remove cylinder head bolts and lift off head.

REMOVAL OF THE ROCKER ARMS AND SHAFTS

1954 Thru 1957 Models

Take off the carburetor air cleaner and remove the rocker chamber cover from the cylinder head. Disconnect the oil line which feeds the rocker shafts, unbolt the rocker shaft brackets a little at a time so as to release the spring pressure gradually and lift off the rocker shaft.

Starting with 1958 V-8 Models

Remove the carburetor air cleaner and disconnect the ignition wires where they go over the rocker cover. Remove the rocker cover assembly and, a little bit at a time, loosen the screws which hold the rocker brackets down to the cylinder head.

When spring pressure has been released, remove the screws and lift off

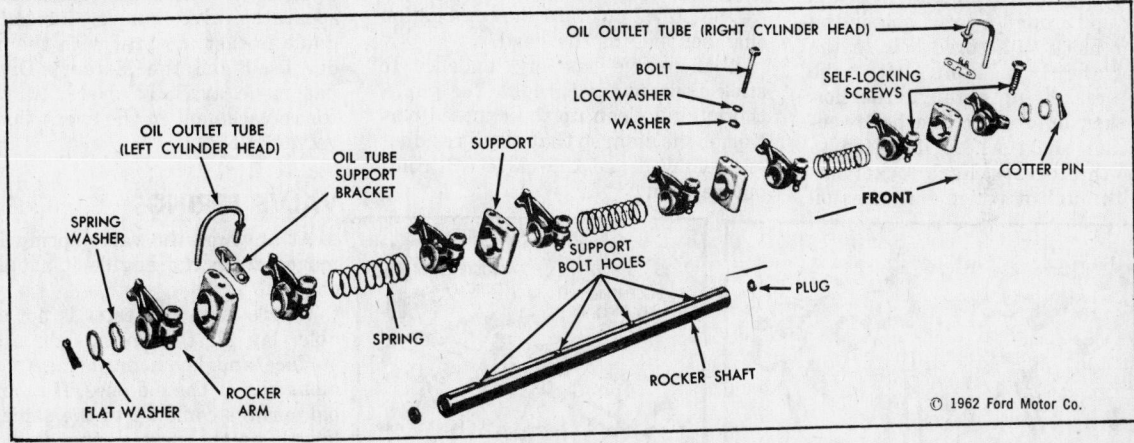

Rocker Arm Shaft, V-8 with Rear Mounted Distributor.

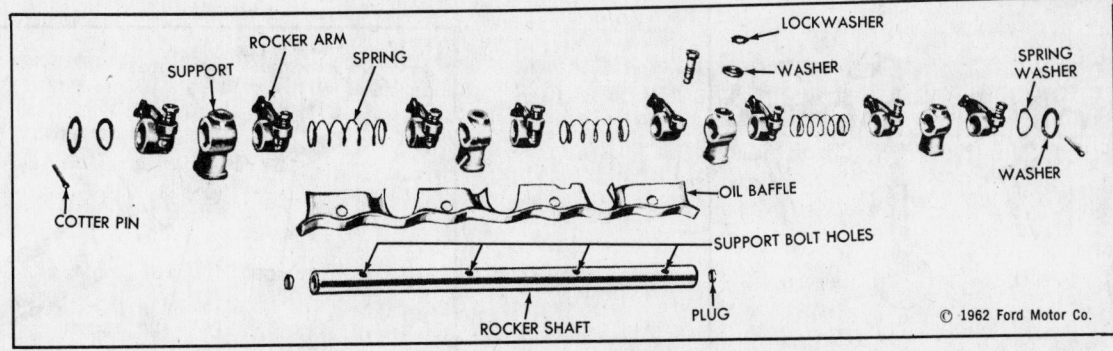

Rocker Arm Shaft Assembly, V-8 with Front Mounted Distributor.

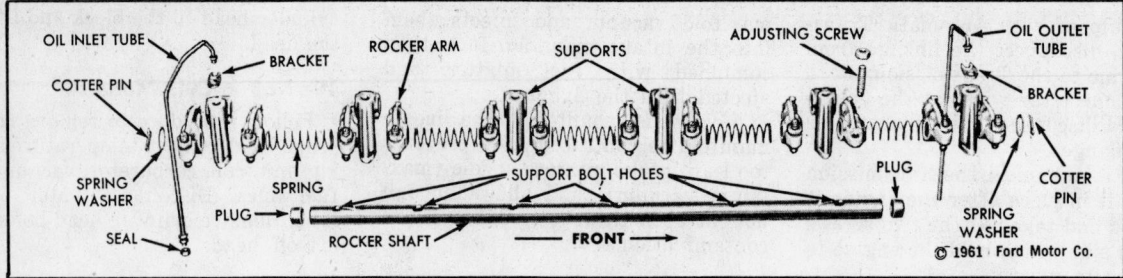

6 Cylinder Rocker Arm Shaft Assembly.

the rocker shaft assembly.

If the rockers are to be disassembled they should be marked carefully where each piece goes so that it can be returned in the position from which it was removed.

1961-62 6-Cyl. Models

Remove chamber cover. Remove screws that hold oil feed lines to rocker shaft and pry lines with pliers to remove from cylinder head. Loosen rocker bracket bolts gradually and in rotation till pressure is off then remove bolts and lift assembly from engine.

ROCKER LUBRICATION

All Models

The rockers are lubricated by oil coming up through a cored hole in the cylinder block to a cored hole in the cylinder head indexing with the rocker bracket, up through the hollow rocker bracket to the hollowed-out rocker shaft where it is fed to each of the rockers. Each rocker has a hole through it which furnishes oil

to the end of the push rod where it runs down the push rod and helps lubricate the outside of the lifter assembly.

THE VALVE SYSTEM

Starting With 1954 Models

Starting with 1954 production, overhead valves are used on all Mercury engines. Adjusting screws are provided in the push rod end of the valve rocker on the 8 cylinder 292, 312 and 406 cu. in. and the 6 cylinder models. The other V8's are hydraulic.

The valves are removed by taking off the cylinder head, transferring it to a bench, and using a C type or lever type valve spring compressor, compress the spring and remove the key, release the spring and the valve can be pulled out into the combustion chamber side of the head.

If the valve has any tendency to stick as it comes through the guide, thoroughly clean up the exposed portion of the stem so that all oil residues are removed and the valve will come out readily.

Starting 1963

A valve rotator is used on exhaust valves.

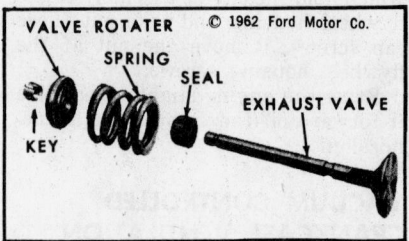

Valve Components Showing Rotator

REPLACEMENT OF VALVE GUIDES

Starting With 1954 Models

The cylinder head does not have separate valve guides, instead the guide is cast integral with the cylinder head and the Mercury Division has made available oversized valves for replacement in the event that the valve fits badly.

VALVE SPRINGS

At anytime the valve spring is removed from the engine it should be checked.

Where a spring tester is not available, lay all the springs on a level surface and lay a brand new spring alongside of the old ones. If all of the old springs come up to the same free length as the new spring, it can be assumed with a very great degree of

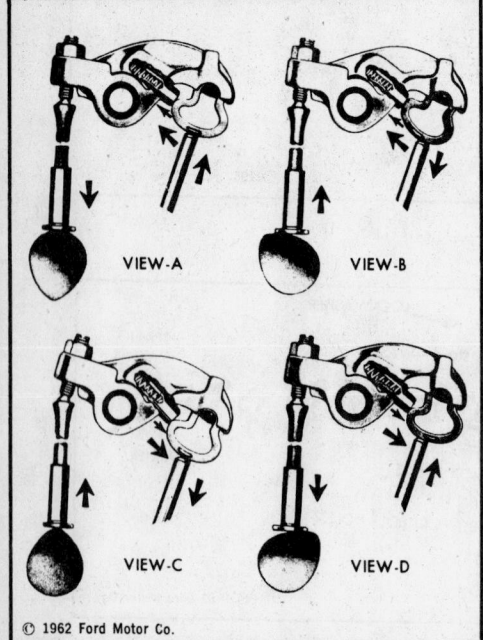

Fig. 1—Sectional of Zero Lash Rocker Arms

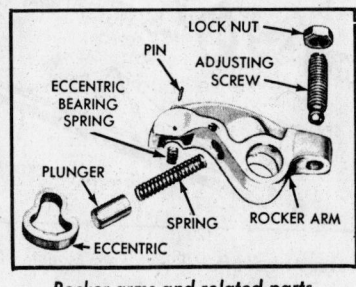

Rocker arms and related parts

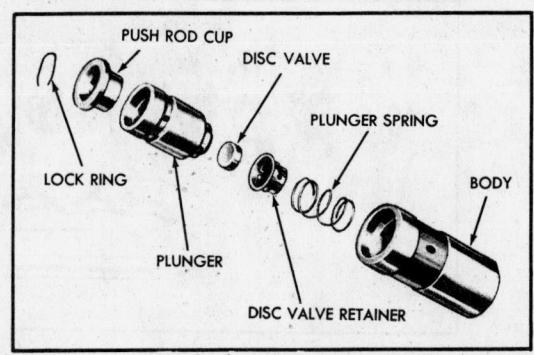

Typical Hydraulic Valve Lifter

safety that all of the springs are O.K. If one or more of the springs are shorter than the new one, they should all be tested with a spring tester and the defective ones replaced.

HYDRAULIC VALVE LIFTERS

Overhead Valve V-8 Models

The lifters can be pulled up out of their bores after the push rods and the inlet manifold have been removed.

If there is any tendency of the lifter to stick in its bore a little penetrating oil should be tried before they are forced out of their bores with a pair of pliers or some such tool. Any hard steel tool may tend to nick or scratch the outside of the lifter and since it is a tight fit in the bore this may cause the lifter to stick.

VALVE ADJUSTMENT

1954 Thru 1963 Models

On those engines using adjustable valves, loosen the clamp screw and turn the rocker adjusting screw until there is the clearance specified in the tables at the beginning of this section between the other end of the rocker shaft and the top of the valve stem.

This adjustment should be made with the engine running at slow idle.

However, if it is desired to develop the valve clearance with the engine stationary, the following sequence will give reasonable assurance that the valve being adjusted is on the down portion of its cam.

VALVE ADJUSTING SEQUENCE, 292, 312 AND 406 CU. IN. ENGINES

On the overhead valve models it is recommended that the valves be adjusted with the engine running at slow idle. However, if it is desired to adjust them with the engine stationary the following sequence will give

reasonable assurance that the valves being adjusted are at the base of the camshaft. The following applies to all Mercurys: All Mercury cylinders are numbered:

    Front right 1-2-3-4
    Front left 5-6-7-8

Using this numbering system, turn the crank until No. 1 exhaust valve starts to open and notice that following it No. 7 intake valve will also start to open. When both of these valves are wide open, adjust:

    No. 1 inlet valve
    No. 3 exhaust valve
    No. 4 inlet valve
    No. 5 inlet valve
    No. 6 exhaust valve
    No. 7 exhaust valve
    No. 8 both valves

Now turn the crank one full revolution until No. 6 cylinder exhaust valve starts to open and notice that it will be followed closely by No. 4 cylinder inlet valves. When both of these valves are wide open, adjust:

    No. 1 cylinder exhaust valve
    No. 2 cylinder both valves
    No. 3 cylinder inlet valve
    No. 4 cylinder exhaust valve
    No. 5 cylinder exhaust valve
    No. 6 cylinder inlet valve
    No. 7 cylinder inlet valve

ZERO LASH MECHANICAL ADJUSTERS

Starting with the 1961 OHV 6 cylinder engine, some zero lash mechanical rocker arms are used.
This rocker arm has an eccentric in the valve stem end held against the stem by a spring loaded plunger. As wear occurs or parts expand thru heat, the plunger loaded eccentric holds zero lash.

To make initial setting (engine off);

1. Set No. 1 piston at T.D.C. compression stroke.
2. Adjust intake and exhaust rockers for No. 1 cylinder by tightening screw until eccentric pushes plunger completely into bore.
3. Back out adjusting screw until adjusting mark is directly over valve stem. Torque locknut to 35 ft. lbs.
4. Repeat these steps for balance of cylinders.
5. Start engine and at idle make recheck for location of adjusting mark. Make any minor readjustment to position it directly over valve stem.

TIMING CASE

VIBRATION DAMPER REMOVAL

In order to take off the vibration damper, first remove the radiator core and then unbolt and remove the vibration damper. If the engine has settled down on its mounts it may be necessary to jack it up slightly in order to clear the front cross member.

VALVE TIMING AND/OR REPLACEMENT OF TIMING GEARS

1954 Thru 1957—312 Cu. In. Models

On these models a timing chain is used.

Remove the radiator core, water pump, and timing case cover as outlined under Timing Case Cover Remove. Turn the crankshaft until the timing marks on the cam and crankshaft sprockets are roughly in a horizontal position. (If the timing chain is broken, arrange the sprockets by hand so that the marks are approximately in a horizontal position,

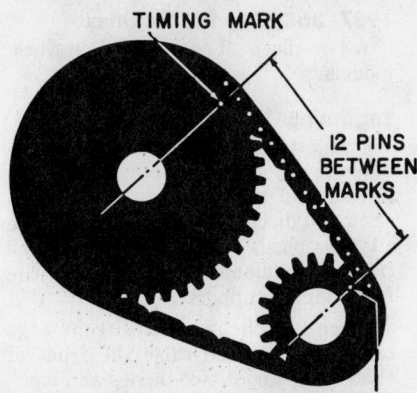

Timing Gear Marks, O.H.V., 6 Cyl.

Timing Gear Marks, V-8 with Front Mounted Distributor

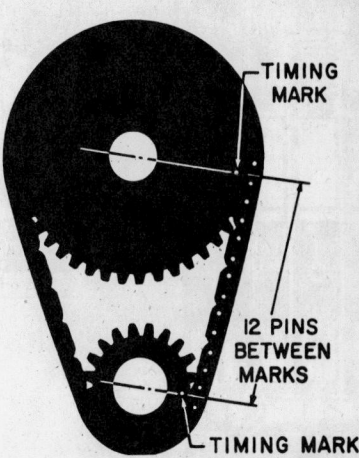

Timing Gear Marks, V-8 with Rear Mounted Distributor

pointing toward the drivers side of the engine.)

Remove the camshaft sprocket and arrange the new chain over the sprocket so that there will be 12 pins of the timing chain straddling the marks on the cam and crankshaft sprockets.

Install the camshaft sprocket and secure in place.

Turn the engine two full revolutions and recheck to make sure of the position of the timing chain pins.

Note: Most Mercury timing chains are marked with either a brass washer or a lighter colored link side plate to identify the marked link on the timing chain.

1957 368 Cu. In. Engines And All 1958-1963, V8 Models

The instructions given above for the 1957 models will also apply except that the marks on the crank and camshaft sprocket should be nearest each other and in line between the shaft centers. Except for this arrangement of the sprockets, the procedure given above will apply.

TIMING GEAR COVER REMOVAL

1954 Thru 1957 Models

The timing gear cover is an engine

front cover pan and it contains at its upper end the water pump assembly.

The lower end of the cover seats on the oil pan.

Remove the upper and lower radiator hoses and take out the radiator core.

Remove the fan blades, fan hub and take off the fan assembly.

Remove the oil pan as outlined under the Oil Pan Removal.

Take off the vibration damper. Unbolt and remove the timing case cover.

The reason the oil pan is removed is that it is almost impossible to secure a good seal between the timing case cover and the oil pan unless the oil pan too is removed and a new gasket installed.

Starting With 1958 Models

Remove the fan and generator belt and, for convenience, pull the radiator core. Take off the water pump assembly and remove the crankshaft pulley.

On models with power steering, remove the power steering pump from the front of the timing case cover.

Remove the bolts which hold the timing case cover to the front of the engine block and also to the oil pan and slide the cover off the front of the crankshaft.

To reinstall, keep in mind that the

oil pan seals against the bottom of the timing case cover and unless extreme care is used it is quite possible that the oil pan will leak after the timing case cover is installed.

Good leak insurance is to remove the oil pan first, install a new gasket and reattach the oil pan after the timing case cover is in place.

ENGINE LUBRICATION
REMOVAL OF OIL PAN

1954 Thru 1956 Models

To remove the oil pan, first take off the sheet metal underpan found under the radiator immediately in front of the oil pan and then remove the bolts which hold the oil pan to the block, tilt the oil pan downward at the front and slide it forward off the top of the crossmember.

It will be necessary to turn the crank throws to clear the back edge of the pan.

If the engine has settled so that it is difficult to clear the front end sheet metal with the oil pan, try removing the rear motor mounts and jacking the back of the engine up just a little bit which will allow the oil pan to tilt at steeper angle.

1957 312 Cu. In. Engines

Remove the front stabilizer bar. Take off the sheet metal underpan (on some models) found under the radiator immediately in front of the oil pan. Now take out the bolts which hold the oil pan to the block and take the oil pan downward at the front and slide it forward off the crossmember.

It will be necessary to turn the crank throws in order to clear the back edge of the pan.

If too much difficulty is experienced getting the pan down, try removing the rear motor mounts and jacking the back of the engine up just a little bit which will allow the engine pan to tilt at a steeper angle.

1957 368 Cu. In. Engines

A two-piece oil pan is used on these models.

Beginning With 1958 Models

Crank the engine until No. 1 cylinder is in the firing position. Drain the oil and remove the oil level dipstick and disconnect the battery. Take off the splash shield from the frame front crossmember. Disconnect the front engine supports.

Place a jack under the front edge of the oil pan and raise the front of the engine about two inches and block it in that position.

Disconnect the right hand stabilizer mounting brackets from the

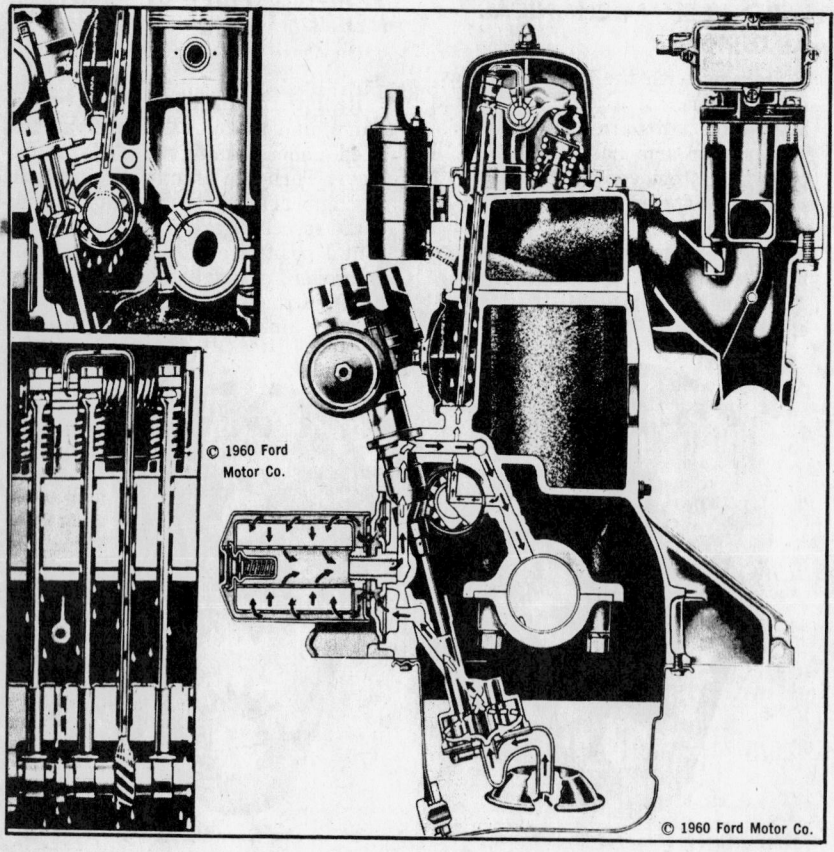

© 1960 Ford Motor Co.

© 1960 Ford Motor Co.

Engine Lubrication, O.H.V. 6 Cyl.

frame. Pull the stabilizer down out of the way.

Remove the oil pan retaining screws and lower the pan until it touches the crossmember. Reaching in over the pan remove the lower and loosen the upper oil pump inlet tube and screen assembly screws. This will allow the tube and screen assembly to swing freely, permitting the oil pan baffle to clear. Or, remove both bolts and let the screen drop into the pan. Lower oil pan to floor.

The pan is reinstalled in reverse order which removed it. It should have a new gasket and the block should be carefully cleaned of the old gasket.

Set the oil pan up on the crossmember and then tighten the oil pump upper and lower screws.

OIL PUMP ASSEMBLY

1957 Models

The oil pump on the 1957 models is designed so that the screen is an integral part of the cover assembly and cannot be separately renewed. If the screen is damaged or unusable a new cover will have to be installed.

Starting With 1958 Models

The oil pump is accessible after the oil pan has been removed. It is located in the oil pan at the extreme front of the block.

The oil pump flange is bolted up to the underside of the block.

OIL FILTER ASSEMBLY

1954-56 Models

The oil filter is located on the lower left side of the crankcase just in back of the steering gear box. Cramp the

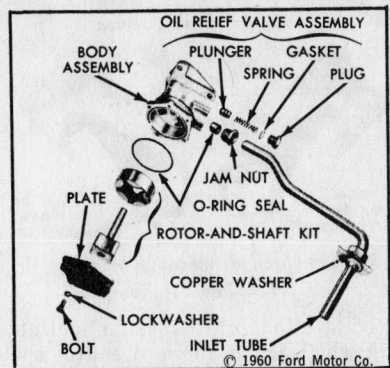

Oil Pump Assembly, V-8 with Rear Mounted Distributor.

wheels hard to the right and by reaching up through the tie rods remove the one bolt which holds the oil pan to the crankcase. Slide the filter can back a little bit and let it drain and then carefully thread it down between the tie rods and the flywheel housing.

Some of the oil filters are marked "top" and so is the block. When installing a new filter make sure to index the two tops together.

Starting With 1957 Models

Full flow, disposable type filters are used, no tools are required to change this filter.

ⓘ CHILTON TIME-SAVER

A few cases of difficulty in oil filter replacement have come to our attention. The trouble starts with oil filter elements being turned on too tightly. The unit may be too tight to remove by hand and it may collapse in the grip of a tool that applies enough squeeze to grip the element hard enough to turn it.

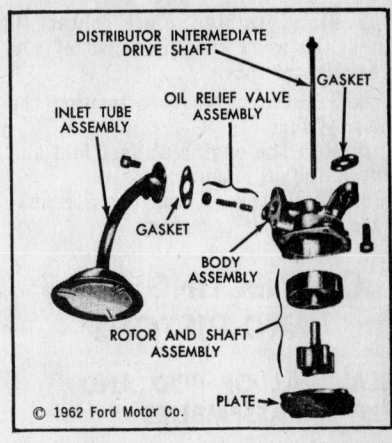

Oil Pump, V-8 with Front Mounted Distributor.

AN ALTERNATIVE METHOD OF REMOVAL:

1. Raise the car on a jack or hoist and place a drip pan under the filter.
2. With a 12 inch to 14 inch slender punch drive a hole in the element from one side to the other.

NOTE: Before punching the hole, consider the angle required for the punch to act as a lever, with the least interference.

3. With the drift all the way thru the filter and acting as a lever, turn the unit counterclockwise enough to break it loose.
4. Final loosening and removal can now be accomplished by hand.

TO REPLACE

1. Coat the gasket on the new filter with oil.
2. Place the new filter in position on the block.

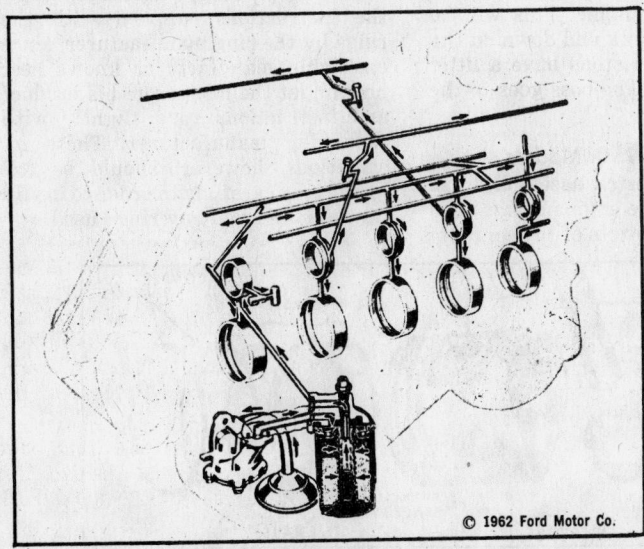

Engine Lubrication, V-8 with Front Mounted Distributor.

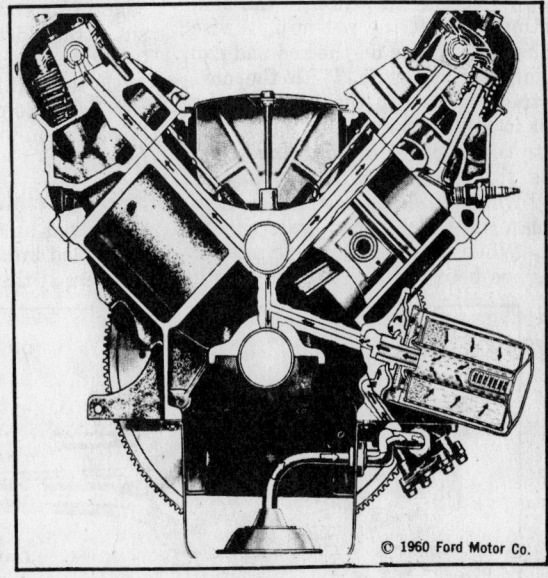

Engine Lubrication, V-8 with Rear Mounted Distributor.

3. Hand tighten until contact is made between the filter gasket and the adapter face.

4. Tighten by further turning the filter ½ turn.

5. Run the engine at fast idle and check for oil leaks.

6. Check the oil and bring crankcase to level if necessary.

CONNECTING RODS AND PISTONS

REMOVAL OF ROD AND PISTON ASSEMBLIES

All Models

Remove the cylinder heads and oil pan. With a ring ridge cutter, cut the ring ridge from the top of the cylinders whose pistons are in the down position. Working from underneath the car, disconnect the rod caps from the cylinders which have had the ring ridge removed and push the rod and piston assembly up out of the top of the cylinder.

Mark the rod cap so that it can be returned to the same rod and in the same position as it was removed.

Repeat on all the rod and piston assemblies.

Most shops bolt the bearing cap back on the rod before or just after the piston assembly is out of the bore so that neither the cap nor the bearing shells get lost or damaged.

ASSEMBLING THE PISTONS TO CONNECTING ROD

Thru 1957 Models

To assemble the piston to the connecting rod, set the rod up in a vise with the numbers on the rod end cap facing the mechanic. With the connecting rod held in that position the split in the skirt in the piston should be to the mechanic's right hand. If a solid skirt or slipper type piston is used which does not have a slot, it is immaterial which way it goes on the rod. When the old pistons and/or rods are being used, however, it is a

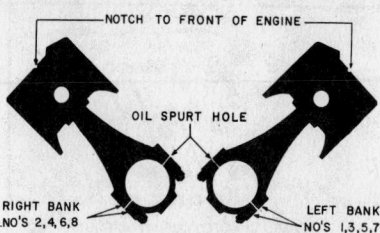

Rod and Piston Identification Markings with Front Mounted Distributor

good idea to mark the piston, indicating which is the forward end of the piston and if it is marked in this manner the mark on the piston will be on the same side as the number on the connecting rod.

Starting With 1958 Models

Set the connecting rod up in a vise so that the numbers on the bottom of the rod face the mechanic. With the rod held in this position the notch at the top of the piston will go to the mechanic's left hand on the left bank of cylinders, and to his right hand on the right bank of cylinders. This will place the oil squirt hole of the rod on the side facing the camshaft when the pistons are mounted in the engine.

ASSEMBLING ROD & PISTON ASSEMBLIES TO THE ENGINE

Thru 1957 Models

On all Mercury engines the cylinders are numbered 1, 2, 3 and 4 on the right bank, starting at the radiator. The left bank is numbered 5, 6, 7 and 8, starting at the radiator. The piston and rod assemblies should be placed in the engine so that the numbers on the connecting rods face forward and the slit in the skirt of the piston faces the left side of the engine. This will be up on the right bank and down on the left bank. Some pistons have a little boss cast on top. The boss goes to the front.

Starting With 1958 Models

The rod and piston assemblies are assembled into the engine so that the numbers at the bottom of the connect-

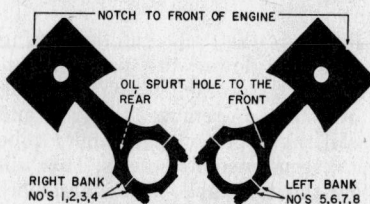

Rod and Piston Identification Markings, with Rear Mounted Distributor

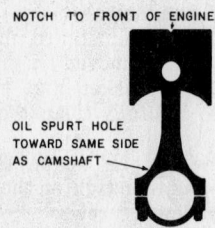

Rod and Piston Identification Markings, O.H.V., 6 Cyl.

ing rod will face away from the camshaft on both banks. As a double check, this will place the notch at the top of the piston forward on both banks.

WRIST PINS

Starting With 1958 Models

Not less than 20 ft. lbs. torque should be required to push the pin out of its press fit in the rod. If less than 20 ft. lbs. are required it is too loose a fit and either the rod should be rebushed or an oversized wrist pin used.

PISTON RINGS

When replacing piston rings, follow the instructions supplied with the rings by the ring manufacturer, since each ring manufacturer knows best how to get the most from his product and instructions vary slightly with each ring manufacturer. These instructions, however, should be followed very carefully in order to insure best results from any rings used.

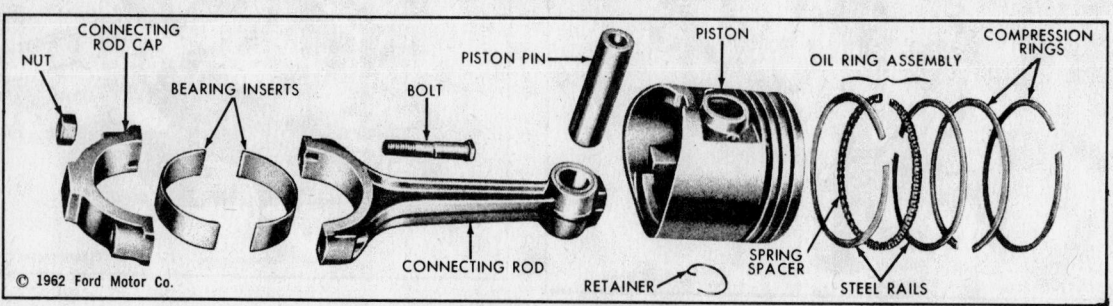

Piston and Connecting Rod Assembly

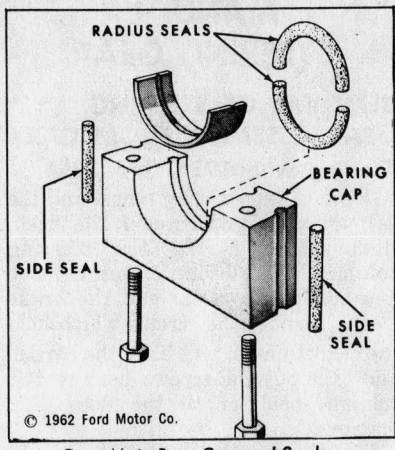

Rear Main Bear Cap and Seals

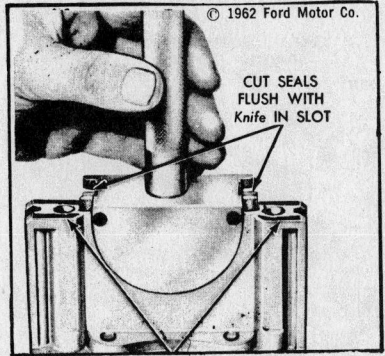

Installing Crankshaft Rear Oil Seal.

REAR MAIN BEARING OIL SEAL

A packing type oil seal is used in back of the rear main bearing. The lower half of this oil seal is held in place by the flywheel front plate. The upper half is mounted in a container which is fitted to a tongued out portion of the cylinder block itself. To replace the rear main bearing oil seal it is necessary to remove the engine from the car and disassemble the flywheel and flywheel front plate.

CHILTON TIME-SAVER

TOP HALF, REAR MAIN BEARING OIL SEAL REPLACEMENT—WICK TYPE

The following method has proven a distinct advantage in most cases and, if successful, saves many hours of labor.

1. Drain engine oil and remove oil pan.
2. Remove rear main bearing cap.
3. With a 6" length of 3/16" brazing rod, drive up on either exposed end of the top half oil seal. When the opposite end of the seal starts to protrude, have a helper grasp it with pliers and pull gently while the driven end is being tapped. It is surprising how easily most of these seals can be removed by this method.

TO INSTALL THE NEW WOVEN FABRIC TYPE SEAL:

1. Obtain a 12" piece of copper wire (about the same gauge as that used in the strands of an insulated battery cable).
2. Thread one strand of this wire thru the new seal, about ½" from the end, bend back and make secure.
3. Thoroughly saturate the new seal with engine oil.

4. Push the copper wire up thru the oil seal groove until it comes down on the opposite side of the bearing.
5. Pull (with pliers) on the protruding copper wire while the crankshaft is being turned and the new seal is slowly fed into place.
CAUTION: This snaking operation slightly reduces the diameter of the new seal and care will have to be used to keep the seal from slipping too far thru the top half of the bearing.
6. When an equal amount of seal is extending from each side, cut off the copper wire close to the seal and tamp both ends of the seal up into the groove (this will tend to expand the seal again).
Note: Don't worry about the copper wire left in the groove, it is too soft to cause damage.

7. Replace the seal in the cap in the usual way and replace the oil pan.

FRONT SUSPENSION

See "Suspension, Unit Repair" Section.

Cushion-Link Suspension

Starting with 1961 all Mercurys except the "600" series have "Cushion-Link" suspension at all four wheels.

This suspension allows the wheels to move rearward as well as upward as a better means to insulate shock.

In the front, the Cushion-Link is at the front pivot of the lower arm. It is an arrangement of two pivot pins in shackle form. The upper pin is in a large elliptical rubber bushing and controls horizontal movement. The shackle is positioned in neutral unless disturbed by road bumps.

When road shock is encountered, fore and aft, as well as vertical movement is permitted.

At the rear a rubber insulated tension shackle is mounted at the front of each rear spring. Again rearward movement is allowed to cushion the shock when a road bump is encountered.

Extended Lubrication

Starting with 1961 the following front suspension and steering parts will require lubrication only after

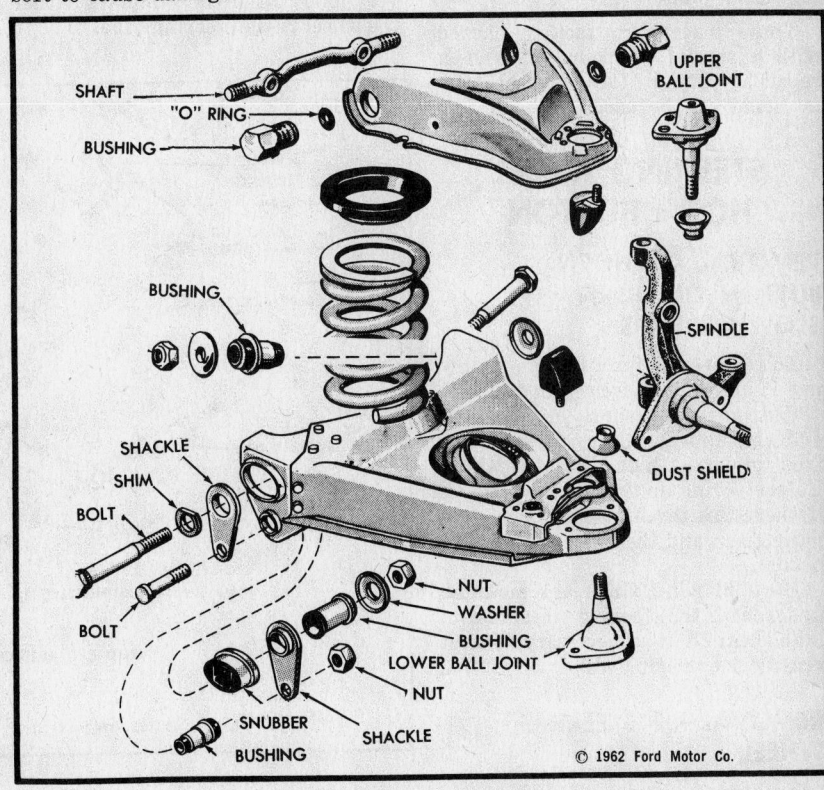

Exploded View of Cushion-Link Suspension.

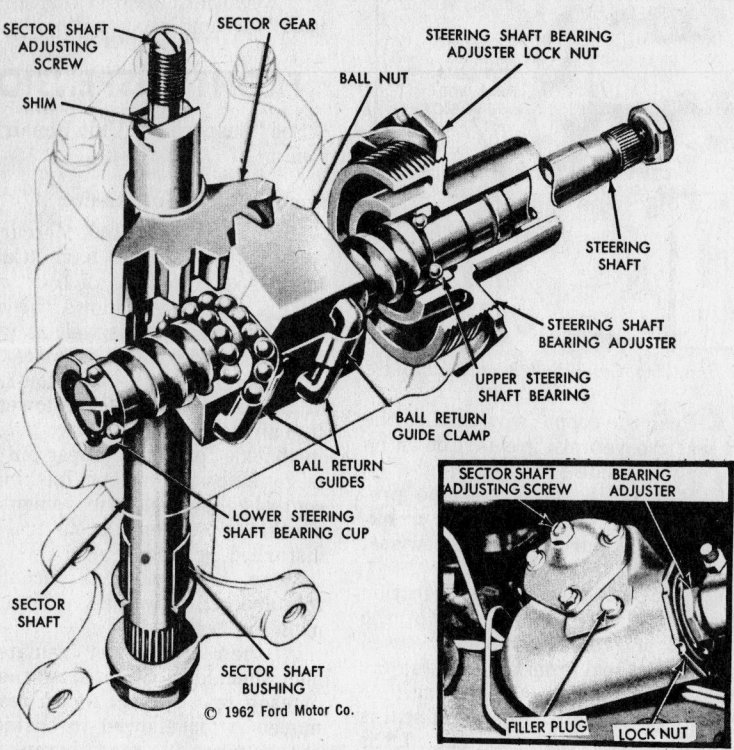

Cutaway view—steering gear 1957-61

© 1962 Ford Motor Co.

MANUAL STEERING GEAR

REMOVAL OF STEERING GEAR ASSEMBLY FROM CAR

Starting with 1954 Thru 1958

Remove the steering wheel and the pitman arm. From under the dash, disconnect and tag the steering column electrical connections. Remove the accelerator pedal and the brake pedal. Remove the screws which hold the carpet down, pull back the carpet and take out the screws holding the column insulator to the floor pan opening.

Disconnect the speedometer cable from the instrument panel and pull it out of the way. On jobs with automatic transmissions, remove the cotter pins and release the shift rod from the steering column shift arm. Also loosen the clamp on the lower steering column and raise the column sufficiently to disconnect the wires at the neutral switch. Remove the bolts which clamp the steering mast jacket to the dash and pull the mast jacket up into the inside of the vehicle. Now loosen the bolts that secure the gear assembly to the frame side rail. Caution: If any shims are found they should be returned to the position from which they were taken. Now the unit can be lifted up thru the passenger compartment.

It is customary to mask the dash

long mileage periods; Two upper ball joints, two lower ball joints, one idler arm joint, two cross link joints, four tie rod ball joints, one power steering valve joint.

These places are factory packed with a special compound and when repacked ONLY the original type lubricant can be used.

STEERING WHEEL HORN BUTTON

REMOVAL OF HORN BUTTON OR HORN BLOWING RING

To remove the horn button, simply pry it up on all Mercury models.

Caution: On some models the emblem cap was held by three screws from underneath the steering wheel. Before prying up the cap check to see if there are three screws; if so, remove them and then lift off the horn button.

Horn blowing rings are mounted underneath the steering wheel and to take them off it is necessary to first remove the steering wheel.

REMOVAL OF STEERING WHEEL

To remove the steering wheel pry up the emblem cap and take off the

nut which mounts the steering wheel to the steering tube. A puller should always be used when taking off the steering wheel since driving it off will very likely result in damaging either the wheel or the steering tube.

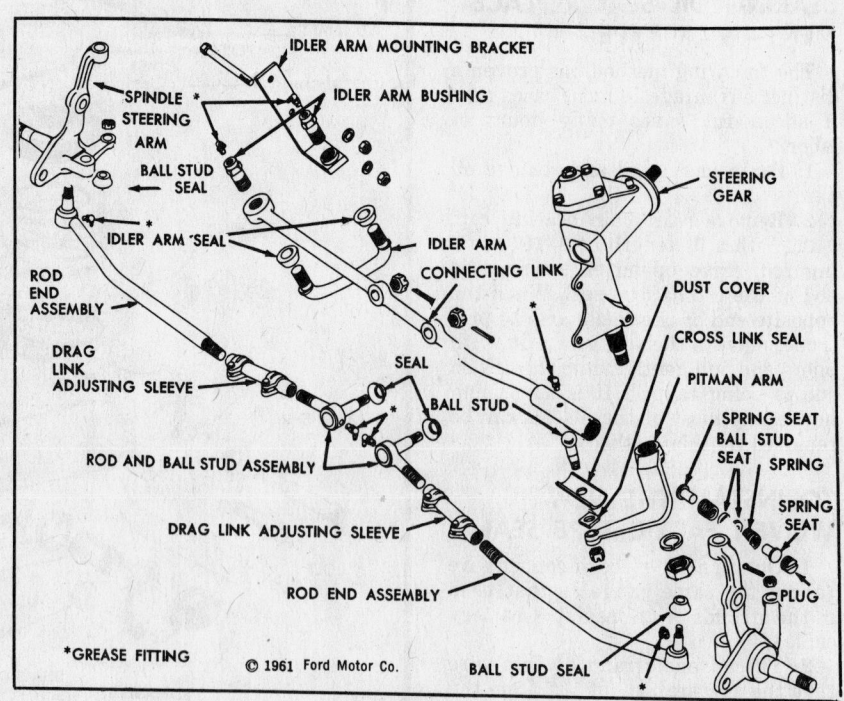

© 1961 Ford Motor Co.

*GREASE FITTING

Typical Steering Linkage.

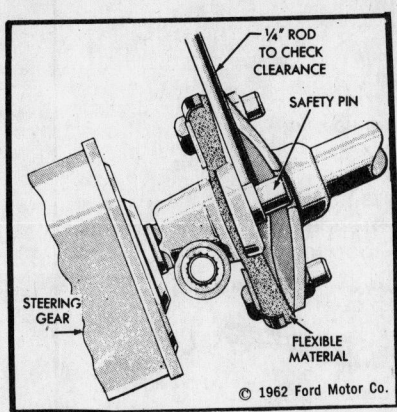

Checking Clearance Between Steering
Gear and Steering Shaft

panel and take some precautions to
protect the seat.

Starting 1959

A flexible shaft coupling is used.
On these models the coupling can be
separated, the pitman arm removed
and mounting bolts to frame removed.
Then gear may be lifted out without
disturbing upper column and controls.

All Models

Complete instructions for adjusting
this and all other steering gears is
given in the Unit Repair Section under
Steering, Manual.

POWER STEERING

All service on the power steering
gear is given in the Unit Repair Section under Steering, Power.

REMOVAL OF POWER STEERING PUMP

Starting With 1958 Models

On these models the power steering
pump is driven directly off the front
of the crankshaft and is mounted on
the front of the timing case cover.

For convenience, remove the radiator core. Slack off and remove the
generator belt.

Disconnect the power steering
pump intake line under the reservoir
by loosening the clamp and disconnecting the rubber line. Disconnect
the output shaft at the pump.

Remove the vibration damper and
then take out the bolts which hold the
power steering pump to the front of
the engine.

Now using a draw type puller, with
its two bolts fed into the two threaded
holes, one top and one bottom, on the
power pump body, pull the steering
pump off the front of the crankshaft.

STANDARD CLUTCH

The standard clutch in all Mercury
models is of the single plate, dry disc
type having a coil spring pressure
plate.

REMOVAL OF CLUTCH ASSEMBLY

Remove the transmission assembly
and disconnect the clutch linkage. Remove the pan from under the clutch
housing for access to the clutch
mounting bolts which hold the clutch
cover to the flywheel. Match mark the
clutch and flywheel.

Remove the mounting bolts a little
at a time to release the pressure plate
spring pressure, take the bolts out
and lower the clutch pressure plate
and disc through the bottom of the
housing.

REPLACEMENT OF CLUTCH ASSEMBLY

A clutch pilot shaft will simplify
clutch reassembly.

Raise the pressure plate and disc
assembly up through the bottom of
the flywheel housing and enter the
pilot shaft through the back of the
flywheel housing so as to engage the
center of the clutch disc.

Align the splines on the pilot shaft
and clutch disc so that the pilot shaft
may be moved forward, through the
clutch disc and into the pilot bearing
in the rear end of the crankshaft.
Some wiggling motion may be necessary to obtain this result.

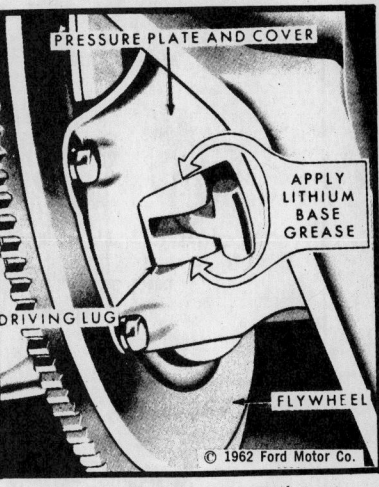

Clutch Pressure Plate Finger Lubrication

Attach the cover at its match
marks and start the flywheel bolts,
tightening them up a little at a time
so as not to distort the clutch cover.

Securely tighten the cover to the
flywheel and remove the pilot shaft.
The transmission may now be lifted
into place and secured.

ADJUSTMENT OF CLUTCH PEDAL

The clutch pedal link should be adjusted so that there is approximately
1 inch free play of the clutch pedal
(measured at the toe board) before
the throw out bearing engages the
fingers.

Adjust at the adjusting rod at the
clutch fork.

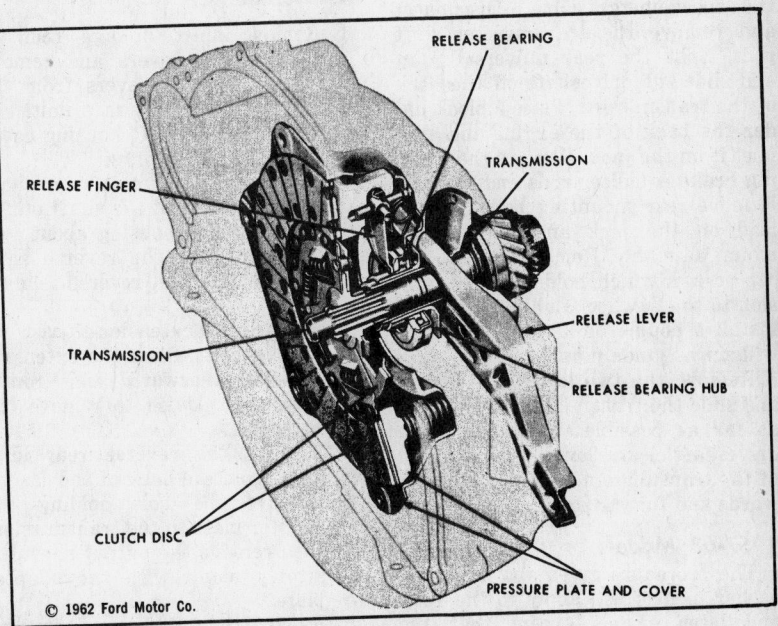

Clutch assembly—cut away view

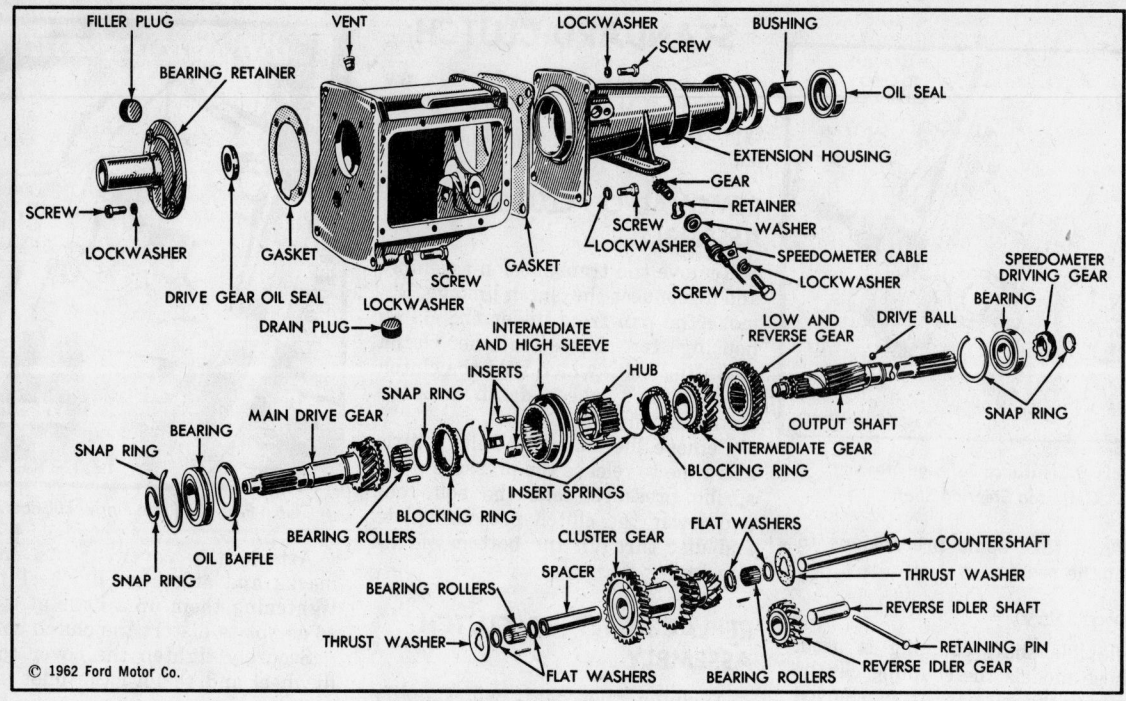

FILLER PLUG — VENT — LOCKWASHER — BUSHING
BEARING RETAINER — SCREW — OIL SEAL
EXTENSION HOUSING
GEAR
SCREW — RETAINER — WASHER
LOCKWASHER — SPEEDOMETER CABLE
SCREW — LOCKWASHER
SCREW — LOCKWASHER
SCREW — GASKET
DRIVE GEAR OIL SEAL — LOCKWASHER
DRAIN PLUG
SPEEDOMETER DRIVING GEAR
BEARING
LOW AND REVERSE GEAR — DRIVE BALL
INTERMEDIATE AND HIGH SLEEVE — HUB
INSERTS
SNAP RING — OUTPUT SHAFT
MAIN DRIVE GEAR — INTERMEDIATE GEAR
SNAP RING
BEARING — BLOCKING RING
SNAP RING — INSERT SPRINGS
BEARING ROLLERS — BLOCKING RING
OIL BAFFLE — CLUSTER GEAR — FLAT WASHERS — COUNTER SHAFT
SNAP RING — SPACER — THRUST WASHER
BEARING ROLLERS — REVERSE IDLER SHAFT
THRUST WASHER — RETAINING PIN
FLAT WASHERS — BEARING ROLLERS — REVERSE IDLER GEAR

© 1962 Ford Motor Co.

Disassembled standard 3-speed transmission

STANDARD TRANSMISSION

REMOVAL OF THE STANDARD TRANSMISSION

1954 Thru 1956 Models

Drain transmission and remove the overdrive and kickdown switch retainer. Now push the switch up thru the floor pan. On overdrives remove the governor, solenoid, control cable and electrical connections. Take out the speedometer cable. Disconnect and remove the transmission shift rods. Split the rear universal joint and slide the driveshaft off the back of the transmission. Place a block under the back of the engine and support it on the jack. Remove the parking brake equalizer rods and springs. Remove rear mounting bolts, take a load on the jack and remove the mount assembly. Remove the two top cap screws which hold the transmission to the flywheel and in their place install a couple of long studs which will act as guide pins.

Remove the two lower cap screws and slide the transmission to the rear as far as possible. When the main driveshaft clears, lower the front end of the transmission and slide it downwards and forwards.

1957-63 Models

The procedure given above for the earlier models will apply to the 1957 and later models except that the frame crossmember supporting the rear of the transmission can be re-

moved. Simply take a load on the jack supporting the back of the engine. Remove the bolts which hold the transmission to the crossmember and raise the transmission slightly to take the weight off the crossmember. Then unbolt the crossmember from the frame and remove it. The transmission can then be slid down and out.

BEGINNING 1961—4 SPEED FULLY SYNCHRONIZED

Disassemble

1. Remove shift linkage rods at transmission levers and remove the linkage and levers from the extension housing as a unit.
2. Remove gear shift housing cover with the shift forks.
3. Drive out the reverse lever shaft lock pin and pull the shaft out of the extension housing about 1/8". This will free the reverse shift fork from the reverse sliding gear.
4. Remove the extension-to-case retaining bolts. Slide the extension housing rearward and rotate counter-clockwise to remove the extension.
5. Remove the reverse rear idler gear from the back of the case.
6. Remove the bolt holding the adapter plate to the transmission, then remove the output shaft assembly along with the adapter plate.
7. Remove the fourth speed synchronizer blocking ring.
8. Remove the reverse gear front

idler and thrust washer from the case.
9. Drive the countershaft rearward to free the front of the case, then with a dummy shaft, push out the countershaft. Leave the dummy shaft remain in the countershaft.
10. Remove the input shaft retainer. Remove the input shaft bearing retaining snap ring, and push the input shaft and bearing inward, out of the bearing bore. Remove the input shaft assembly from the case.
11. Remove cluster assembly from the case.
12. Disassemble the cluster gear.
13. Remove input shaft bearing retainer oil seal.
14. To dismantle the input shaft, remove bearing snap ring and spacer washer. Press off the bearing.
15. To dismantle the output shaft, remove the snap ring from front of shaft. Slide off the third and fourth speed gear synchronizer assembly, third speed gear synchronizer blocking ring, third speed gear, second speed gear, second and third speed thrust bearing, second speed gear, and second speed synchronizer blocker ring.
16. Remove output shaft rear oil rubber seal from the shaft. Press off the speedometer drive gear. Slide reverse gear off the output shaft.
17. Spread the retaining snap ring

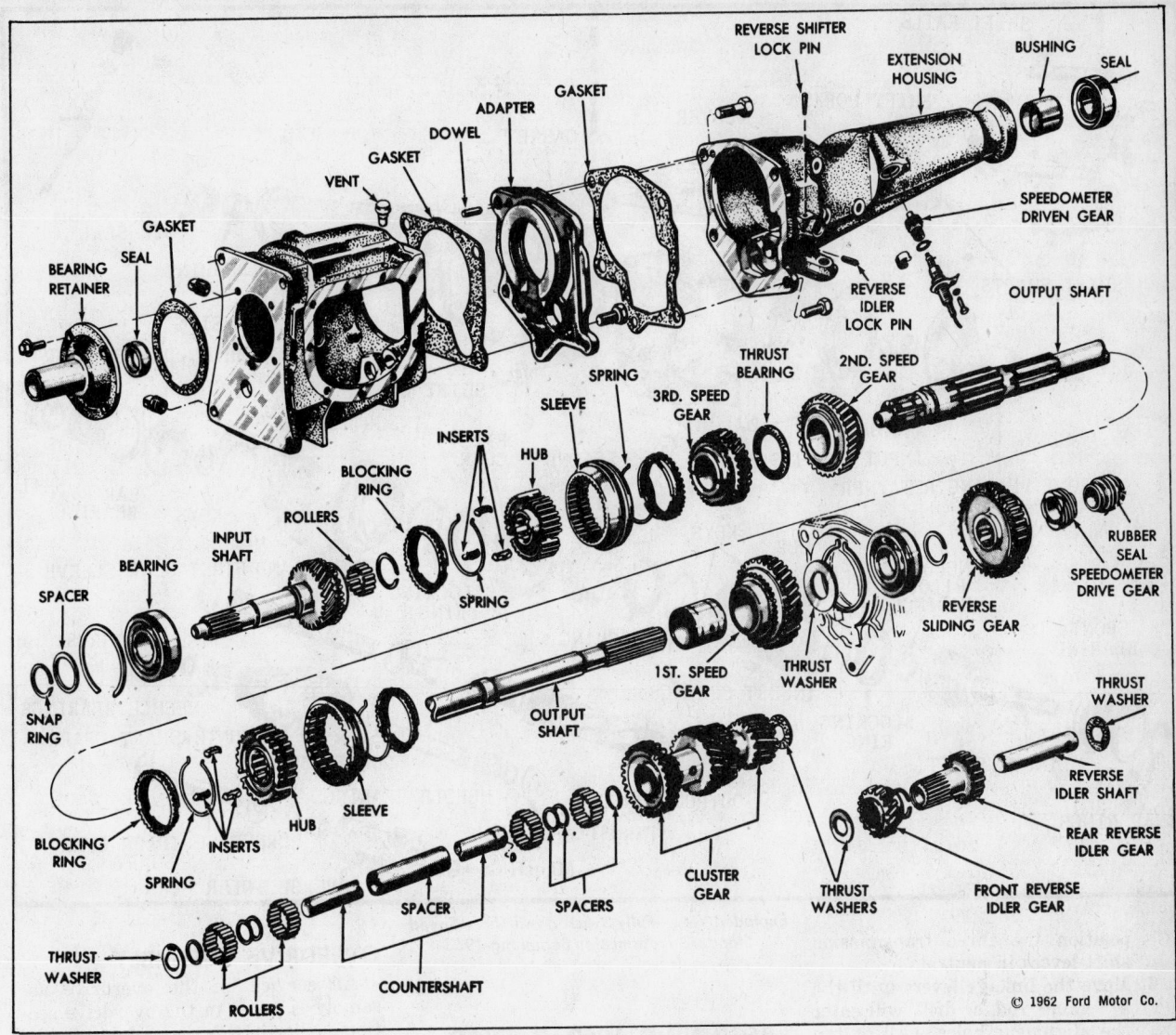

Exploded View—Four Speed Transmission

REVERSE SHIFTER LOCK PIN · EXTENSION HOUSING · BUSHING · SEAL · ADAPTER · GASKET · DOWEL · GASKET · VENT · GASKET · SPEEDOMETER DRIVEN GEAR · GASKET · SEAL · BEARING RETAINER · REVERSE IDLER LOCK PIN · OUTPUT SHAFT · SPRING · THRUST BEARING · 2ND. SPEED GEAR · SLEEVE · 3RD. SPEED GEAR · INSERTS · HUB · BLOCKING RING · ROLLERS · INPUT SHAFT · RUBBER SEAL SPEEDOMETER DRIVE GEAR · BEARING · SPRING · REVERSE SLIDING GEAR · SPACER · 1ST. SPEED GEAR · THRUST WASHER · THRUST WASHER · SNAP RING · OUTPUT SHAFT · REVERSE IDLER SHAFT · BLOCKING RING · HUB · SLEEVE · INSERTS · REAR REVERSE IDLER GEAR · SPRING · SPACER · SPACERS · CLUSTER GEAR · THRUST WASHERS · FRONT REVERSE IDLER GEAR · THRUST WASHER · COUNTERSHAFT · ROLLERS

© 1962 Ford Motor Co.

and press the adapter plate off the output shaft rear bearing.

18. Remove the snap ring holding the output shaft rear bearing to the output shaft.

19. Remove the snap ring holding the output shaft rear bearing to the output shaft and press the bearing off the shaft.

20. Complete disassembly of the output shaft by sliding off the balance of components.

21. Place an index mark on the hub and clutch sleeve for reassembly reference.

22. Disassemble first and second speed and third and fourth speed synchronizers by sliding the clutch sleeves off the hubs and removing the three inserts and two insert springs in each assembly.

Note:

Unless transmission lock-up or jumping out of gear is included in

the complaint, the shifter housing is generally left intact.

23. To disassemble the shifter housing, remove the shift levers from the cam and shaft assemblies. Pull forks and shafts out of the gear shift housing. With shafts removed, the interlock balls, retainer, and spring will fall out of the gearshift housing. Pull the shifter forks out of the cams, and remove the seal rings from the cam shafts. Inspect balls and springs for defects. Check detent notches for wear.

24. To disassemble extension housing, first remove the oil seal and bushing.

25. Pull the reverse fork from the reverse shift lever shaft and cam. remove the reverse shift lever and tap the shaft and cam into the housing, allowing the ball and spring to drop out of the detent bore.

26. Remove "O" ring seal from the reverse shift lever shaft.

27. Remove the reverse idler shaft by driving the retaining pin inward until it bottoms. Then, pull the shaft from the extension housing by tapping it with a soft hammer.

28. Reassemble by reversing above procedure.

4 SPEED LINKAGE, ADJUST

1. Place selector lever in neutral, then raise car on a hoist.

2. Try to insert a ¼" drill, or rod, into the lever alignment holes in the shifter levers.

3. If the rod will not enter all of the way, check for poor adjustment or bent rods.

4. Repair or replace any damaged parts.

5. Reset linkage by loosening the three rod-retaining lock nuts and

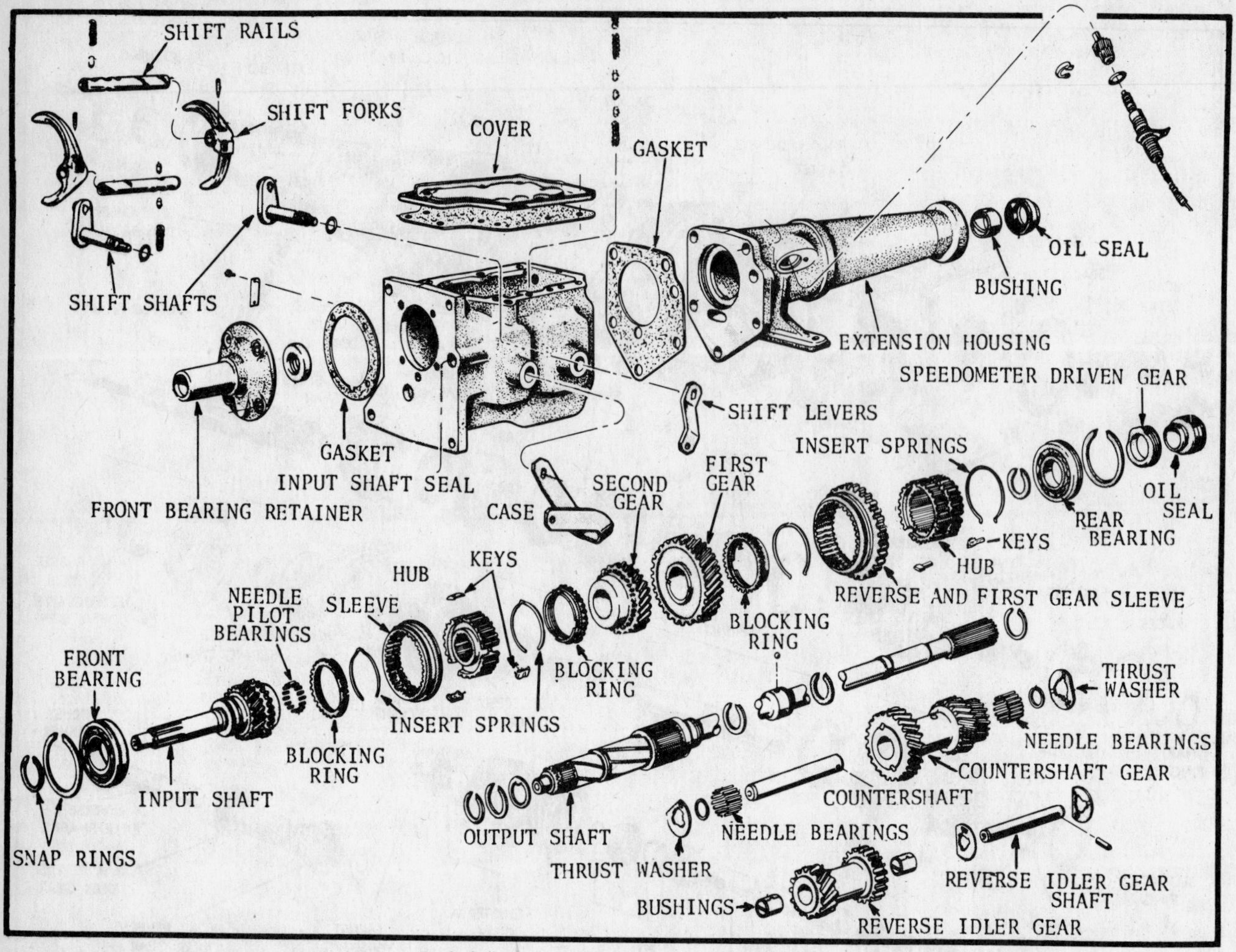

SHIFT RAILS

SHIFT FORKS

COVER

GASKET

SHIFT SHAFTS

OIL SEAL

BUSHING

EXTENSION HOUSING

SPEEDOMETER DRIVEN GEAR

GASKET

INPUT SHAFT SEAL

FRONT BEARING RETAINER

CASE

SHIFT LEVERS

INSERT SPRINGS

SECOND GEAR

FIRST GEAR

OIL SEAL

REAR BEARING

KEYS

HUB

REVERSE AND FIRST GEAR SLEEVE

NEEDLE PILOT BEARINGS

HUB

KEYS

SLEEVE

BLOCKING RING

BLOCKING RING

FRONT BEARING

INSERT SPRINGS

THRUST WASHER

BLOCKING RING

NEEDLE BEARINGS

COUNTERSHAFT GEAR

INPUT SHAFT

COUNTERSHAFT

SNAP RINGS

OUTPUT SHAFT

THRUST WASHER

NEEDLE BEARINGS

REVERSE IDLER GEAR SHAFT

BUSHINGS

REVERSE IDLER GEAR

Exploded View—Fully Syncronized Three Speed Standard Transmission Beginning-1963

position the three transmission shift levers in neutral.

6. Move the linkage levers until the ¼″ gauge rod, or drill, will enter the alignment holes. (All of the levers must be in neutral.)

7. Retighten the rod-retaining lock nuts and remove the gauge pin from the lever alignment holes.

8. Lower the car and check for correct shifting operation of the transmission.

BEGINNING 1963—3 SPEED FULLY SYNCHRONIZED

Service procedure on the 3 Speed, fully synchronized, standard Transmission is almost identical with former 3-speed types. **SEE FORD**

OVERDRIVE ASSEMBLY

All service on the overdrive assembly is given in the overdrive section earlier in this manual, see index.

3 SPEED MERC-O-MATIC TRANSMISSION

Complete instructions on the Merc-O-Matic transmission are given in the automatic transmission portion of this manual, see index.

2-speed Fordomatic transmission is thoroughly covered in the Unit Repair section of this manual, see index.

QUICK SERVICE INFORMATION

When automatic transmission trouble is reported, a road test and careful diagnosis is in order. "Transmission Remove and Replace" and "Linkage Adjustments" are covered here in the following paragraphs. For "Test Procedures," "Transmission Overhaul" and other detailed information, see "Unit Repair Section," "Transmission Group" of this manual.

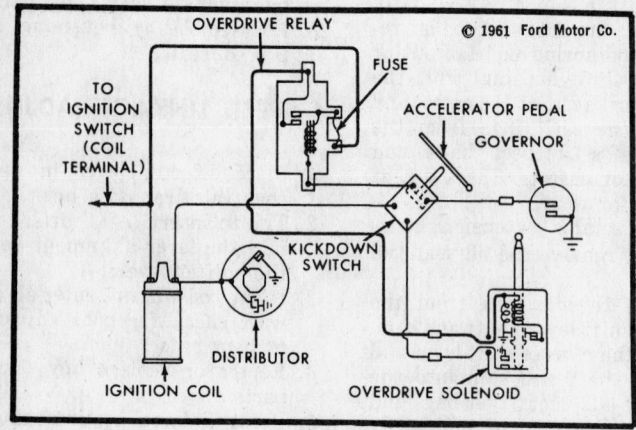

OVERDRIVE RELAY

© 1961 Ford Motor Co.

FUSE

TO IGNITION SWITCH (COIL TERMINAL)

ACCELERATOR PEDAL

GOVERNOR

KICKDOWN SWITCH

DISTRIBUTOR

IGNITION COIL

OVERDRIVE SOLENOID

Overdrive Electrical Control System

ANTI-STALL DASH POT ADJUSTMENT

Hold the throttle in closed position, and turn the dash pot adjusting screw counterclockwise (out) until the dash pot rod has reached the end of its travel.

Turn the adjusting screw clockwise (in) 1½ to 2 turns.

Clearance should now be .045-.064 inches.

Do not forget to tighten the lock nut.

Note on Carter Type Dash Pot

Hold the primary throttle wide open.

Measure the distance from the top of the air horn to the top of plunger. The distance should be 7/16″. Bend the lug to adjust.

NEUTRAL SAFETY SWITCH ADJUSTMENT

Loosen the switch to steering column attaching screws and position the switch so that the starter circuit is closed when the hand lever is at Neutral. Retighten screws.

MANUAL LINKAGE ADJUSTMENT

Unpin the clevis of the manual shift rod (which runs back to the transmission) from the selector arm at the bottom of the steering column.

Set the hand lever so that the pointer is at Drive and against the stop in the dial housing.

Push the manual shift rod all the way back and check that it is centered in the detent for the Low position. Pull the manual shift rod forward to center on the next detent notch which is that for Drive.

Adjust the clevis so that it could be pinned to the selector arm.

Lengthen the manual shift rod by two complete turns of the clevis and pin it to the selector arm. Be sure to tighten the clevis lock nut.

Check the position of the hand lever at the other points on the dial especially that the parking lock engages properly.

THROTTLE LINKAGE ADJUSTMENT

Theory of Throttle Linkage Adjustment

The intent of throttle control rod adjustment is to coordinate the movement of three things:
1. The throttle valve in the carburetor.

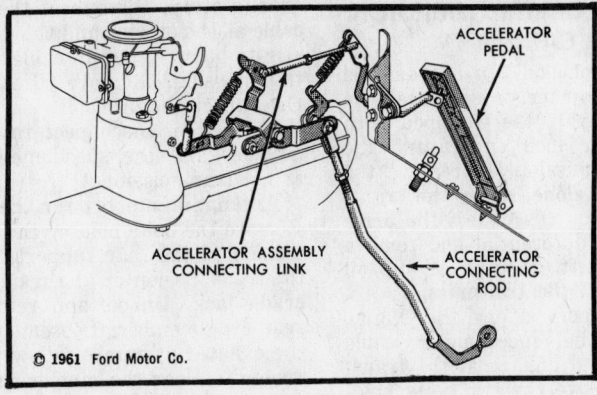

Engine Throttle Lever

2. The throttle valve in the transmission.
3. The accelerator pedal.

The two valves should be wide open when the accelerator is against the floor.

The two valves should be closed when the accelerator pedal is released. In the released position the accelerator pedal should be a certain distance from the steel floor. There are two methods of throttle control adjustment. One is by trial and error; the other is based on the transmission throttle pressure. The trial and error adjustment is easier.

Trial and Error Adjustment of The Throttle Control

Adjust the engine idle speed to approximately 450 RPM with transmission in Drive and engine at operating temperature. Turn the engine off.

Disconnect the transmission throttle valve control rod from the cross rod at the clevis on the left rear corner of the engine.

On all models, pull the control rod, gently, as far forward as it will come and adjust the clevis so that it could be pinned back onto the cross rod. (The pin should slide in freely.) Do not repin at this point.

Now lengthen the rod by turning the clevis counterclockwise between 2½ and 3 complete turns and repin the rod.

On all models if there is slippage after the above adjustment, lengthen the throttle control rod to a total of not over 4 turns.

Should the transmission still show signs of slippage the trouble could be due to a bent rod or inaccurately adjusted accelerator to carburetor linkage or malfunctioning of the valve unit in the transmission.

If the transmission fails to kick down adjust the accelerator pedal height according to the table below.

The measurement of height is made from the top side of the tip of the pedal to the metal floor pan.

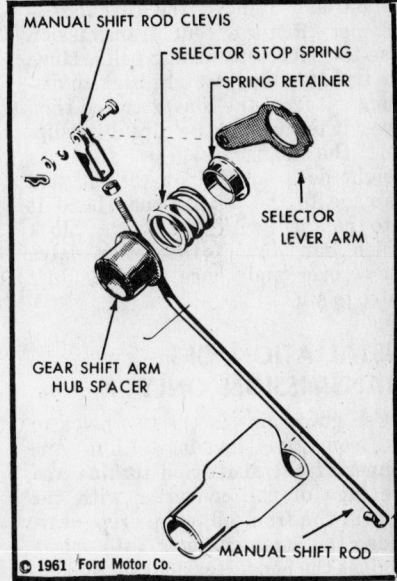

Selector Lever

Accelerator Pedal Height

1955-60	4
1961-63	3½

Make the adjustment at the accelerator assembly to carburetor control connecting link.

If a road test demonstrates that shifts are rough, the transmission throttle valve control rod should be shortened by one-half turn of the clevis.

In other words, tighten to come in quicker; loosen to delay shift. Total travel 4 turns either way.

It is well to note in making these adjustments that the thread on the carburetor throttle rod is finer than that on the transmission throttle rod so that small adjustments can be made more easily at the carburetor than they can at the transmission. The adjustments are rather sensitive so that a few turns of the carburetor throttle rod swivel are all that should be needed.

REMOVAL OF TRANSMISSION FROM THE CAR

The transmission can be removed with the converter or separately on all cars except those equipped with the 430 cubic inch engine and the "PBB" transmission. To remove the transmission alone, drain the transmission oil pan. Disconnect the drive shaft at the differential and remove the drive shaft. Disconnect the oil cooler lines at the transmission. Arrange a support under the engne. Disconnect the speedometer cable and the control linkage at the transmission. Remove the two bolts holding the rear extension to the rear support. Position a cradle under the transmission and raise it slightly. Unbolt and remove the rear crossmember. Remove four transmission case-to-converter housing bolts. Move the transmission straight back to disengage it from the converter and then lower it to the floor. Be careful to support the transmission so that its weight does not fall on the oil pan. Damage to the oil pan may bend it into contact with the valve block which can distort the lower valve body cover and cause the 1-2 shift valve to stick.

INSTALLATION OF TRANSMISSION ONLY

Use guide pins in the two holes in the converter housing. Align the splines of the shaft and turbine and the lugs of the converter with the slots in the front oil pump drive gear. Slide the transmission into place against the converter housing and install the attaching bolts. Tighten the bolts to 40-45 ft. lbs. Reinstall the rear crossmembers and refasten the rear extension to the support. Slide the front universal joint yoke onto the output shaft and refasten the drive shaft to the differential. Refasten the oil cooler lines, the control linkages and speedometer cable. Fill the transmission with fluid and check the level when engine reaches normal operating temperature.

CONVERTER AND TRANS-MISSION ASSEMBLY REMOVAL

This procedure for converter-transmission assembly removal is applicable to all models.

Remove the two upper converter housing-to-engine bolts. Drain the transmission oil pan. Remove the plate at the lower front of the converter. Disconnect the drive shaft at the rear axle and remove the shaft. Remove the flywheel to converter bolts. Wedge the converter in place in the housing. Disconnect the battery ground strap. Disconnect the starter cable at the starter and the transmission-to-body ground cable at the transmission. Remove the starter. Disconnect the oil cooler lines at the transmission. Disconnect the control linkages and the speedometer cable at the transmission.

Arrange a support for the engine. Remove the bolts holding the rear extension to the rear support. Support the transmission on the transmission cradle-jack. Unbolt and remove the rear crossmember. Loosen and drop the exhaust system to allow the converter to clear the muffler inlet ppe. Tilt the rear of the converter-transmission assembly upward and remove the six bolts holding the flywheel to the crankshaft and remove the flywheel. This is done on some models to provide clearance. Lower the converter-transmission assembly to the floor. Remove the wedge holding the converter in the housing and pull the converter out of the housing. Do not rock it, as to do so is hard on the seals.

INSTALLATION OF CONVERTER-TRANSMISSION ASSEMBLY

Wedge the converter in place in the housing. Using the transmission cradle-jack raise the transmission assembly into place. Install the flywheel onto the crankshaft. Tighten the bolts to 75-85 ft. lbs.

Install the converter housing-to-engine lower bolts and tighten to 40-45 ft. lbs. Remove the retainer securing the converter in the housing and bolt the converter to the flywheel. Be sure to have washers under the nuts to prevent converter float. Tighten all to 25-28 ft. lbs. Reinstall the rear crossmember. Lower the transmission onto the rear support and install the two extension-to-support bolts. Install the converter drain plugs and access plates. Reconnect the cooler lines. Install the drive shaft and refasten the shaft at the rear axle. Reconnect the control linkages and speedometer cable. Install the starter and connect: the transmission-to-frame ground; the starter cable; and the battery ground. Install the two upper converter housing to engine bolts and tighten to 40-45 ft. lbs.

Connect and adjust the manual and throttle controls.

Put 5 quarts of Type A fluid into the transmission and allow to idle for 2 minutes. Now add the remaining fluid and let idle until it reaches its normal operating temperature. Do not race the engine.

BEGINNING 1959

Two transmissions are available, the Merc-o-Matic and the Multi-Drive. The two transmissions are similar, however, Multi-Drive differs from Merc-o-Matic in clutch and control system design and operation. Multi-Drive has one additional manually selected driving range, (Figs. 4 and 5.)

LINKAGE ADJUSTMENTS

Throttle Linkage must be adjusted in the following steps:
1. Engine idle.
2. Carburetor rod.
3. Anti-stall dashpot.
4. Throttle rod.
5. Accelerator pedal height.

ENGINE IDLE

1. Set parking brake. Start engine and place transmission selector in "D" position for Merc-o-Matic or "D2" for Multi-Drive.

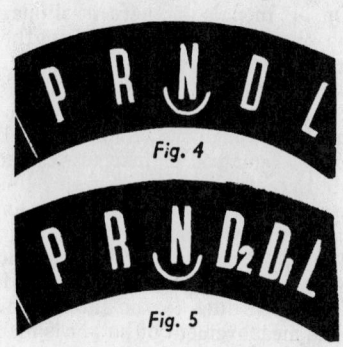

Fig. 4

Fig. 5

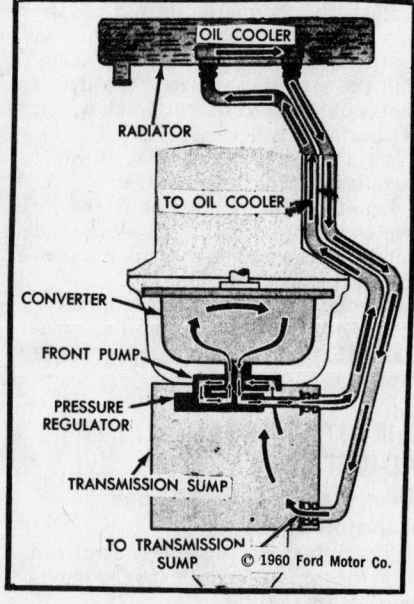

Transmission Cooling System

2. Hook up tachometer.

3. Check dashpot clearance.

4. With engine at operating temperature and the primary throttle shaft lever against the hot idle screw, set R.P.M. to 450-475.

CARBURETOR ROD ADJUSTMENT, (SEE FIG 6)

1. Disconnect transmission throttle rod at "C".

2. Disconnect carburetor rod assembly at "A".

3. Insert ¼ inch drill or rod through alignment holes in bellcrank bracket and tab at "D".

4. With carburetor lever held against hot idle adjusting screw, adjust length of carburetor rod between "A" and "B" for free fit into carburetor lever. Then lengthen the rod one turn.

5. Remove ¼ inch gauge, (or drill)

from bellcrank and connect the carburetor rod to the carburetor lever.

6. Recheck alignment of gauge pin holes in bellcrank. Further adjustment of the carburetor rod length may be required to obtain perfect gauge pin hole alignment.

THROTTLE ROD ADJUSTMENT

1. Raise hood. Connect pressure gauge to transmission tube fitting at bellcrank, (Fig. 7).

2. Pull up on throttle rod and adjust clevis at "C" so the clevis pin enters freely.

3. Lengthen clevis 3½ turns and reassemble throttle rod.

4. Start engine and set the foot brake firmly. Place selector lever in "D" for Merc-o-Matic or "D2" for Multi-Drive.

5. Accelerate engine to 1,000 R.P.M. Pressure gauge must read 80-85 P.S.I. To change the pressure, lengthen the rod clevis to increase pressure or shorten the rod clevis to decrease pressure.

CAUTION: These checks must be made quickly, the engine R.P.M. returned to idle and the selector returned to neutral to prevent transmission damage.

6. Remove pressure gauge and replace valve cap on tube fitting.

ACCELERATOR PEDAL HEIGHT ADJUSTMENT

1. Pedal height adjustment must be done at the accelerator rod **only**. (Fig. 6).

2. Measure the distance from the pedal to the bare floor pan. Measurement should be 4-3/16 inch. Shorten the rod to raise the pedal or lengthen the rod to lower the pedal.

3. After pedal is adjusted, check the "Kickdown." To do this, have someone depress the accelerator all the way. Watch for additional movement of the transmission control shaft after the throttle is fully opened. The added movement of the shaft will cause the pin to over-ride the full throttle position in the slot in the transmission control-to-accelerator shaft assembly. (Refer to point "E" of Fig. 6). If kickdown is not obtained, shorten the accelerator rod slightly to increase pedal travel.

ANTI-STALL DASHPOT ADJUSTMENT

1. Adjust dashpot at "F", (Fig. 6). With carburetor lever held against hot idle screw, push dashpot plunger in by hand and check clearance between lever and plunger. Clearance should be .060—.090 inch.

2. To adjust, turn dashpot into or out of the mounting bracket.

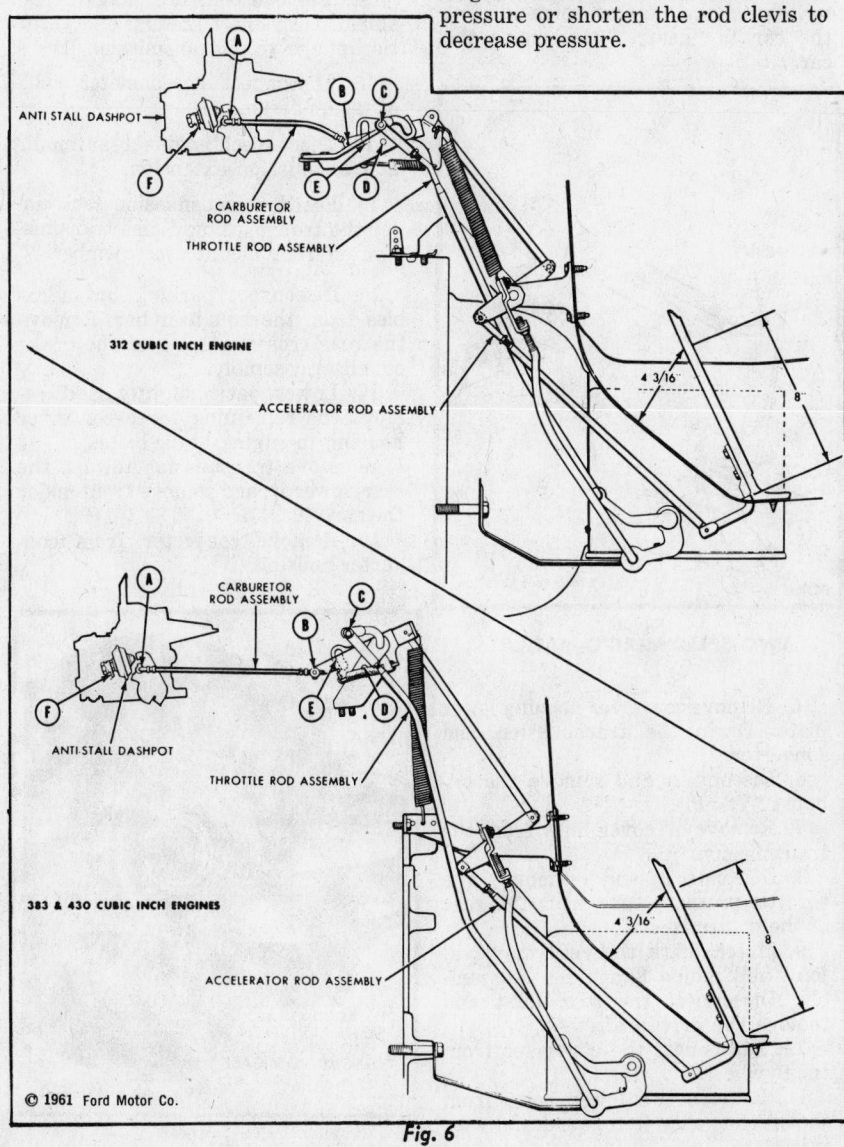

ANTI STALL DASHPOT

CARBURETOR ROD ASSEMBLY

THROTTLE ROD ASSEMBLY

312 CUBIC INCH ENGINE

ACCELERATOR ROD ASSEMBLY

4 3/16

CARBURETOR ROD ASSEMBLY

ANTI-STALL DASHPOT

THROTTLE ROD ASSEMBLY

383 & 430 CUBIC INCH ENGINES

ACCELERATOR ROD ASSEMBLY

4 3/16

© 1961 Ford Motor Co.

Fig. 6

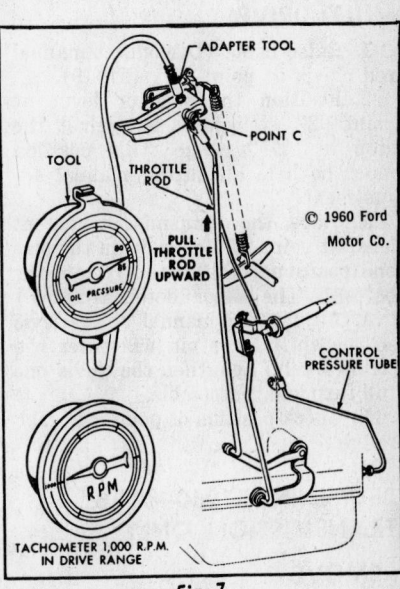

ADAPTER TOOL

POINT C

TOOL

THROTTLE ROD

© 1960 Ford Motor Co.

PULL THROTTLE ROD UPWARD

OIL PRESSURE

CONTROL PRESSURE TUBE

RPM

TACHOMETER 1,000 R.P.M. IN DRIVE RANGE

Fig. 7

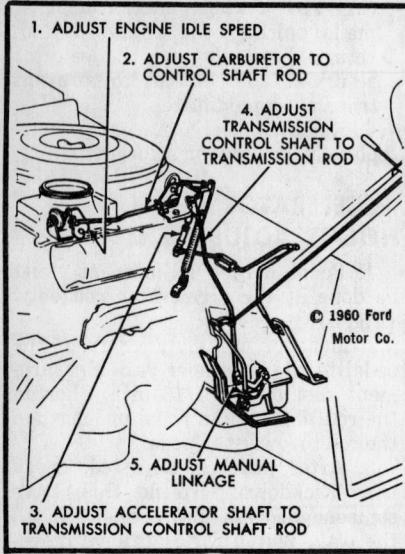

1. ADJUST ENGINE IDLE SPEED

2. ADJUST CARBURETOR TO CONTROL SHAFT ROD

4. ADJUST TRANSMISSION CONTROL SHAFT TO TRANSMISSION ROD

© 1960 Ford Motor Co.

5. ADJUST MANUAL LINKAGE

3. ADJUST ACCELERATOR SHAFT TO TRANSMISSION CONTROL SHAFT ROD

Sequence of Linkage Adjustments

MANUAL LINKAGE— MERC-O-MATIC

1. Raise Hood. Disconnect manual rod clevis at point "1", (Fig. 8).

2. Place selector lever at point "2", so pointer is against the stop in "Drive" range. This position must be held all during manual adjustment.

3. Place the transmission detent lever at point "3", in the second position (Drive Detent) from the bottom. Bottom detent is "low."

4. Adjust the manual shift clevis so the shift lever pin will enter the clevis freely. Lengthen the clevis one full turn and reassemble.

5. Check position of pointer in each range.

MANUAL LINKAGE— MULTI-DRIVE

1. Raise hood. (Disconnect manual rod clevis at point "1", (Fig. 9).

2. Position the selector lever at point "2", so pointer is against the stop in "D1" range. This position must be held all during manual adjustment.

3. Place the transmission detent lever at point "3", (Fig. 9) in the second position ("D1" detent) from the bottom. (The bottom detent is "Low.)

4. Adjust the manual shift clevis so the shift lever pin will enter the clevis freely. Lengthen the clevis one full turn and reassemble.

5. Check position of pointer in each range.

BEGINNING 1960—"PBB" TRANSMISSION ONLY

REMOVE

When removing the transmission

from cars equipped with the 430 cubic inch engine it is necessary to pull the transmission and converter housing as one unit. The gear box and transmission housing cannot be separated while in the vehicle. Two additional case bolts, located behind the converter, make accessibility impossible until the converter is removed. (See Fig. 10).

1. Open the hood. Disconnect accelerator linkage at bellcrank on engine. Disconnect transmission pressure tube from bellcrank bracket.

2. Remove two upper bolts and one bolt from right side of converter housing-to-engine block.

Note:

On air conditioned cars this area is limited but the bolts can be removed from under the car if necessary.

3. Remove one upper bolt holding the starter to the converter housing.

4. Connect remote control starter switch to the starter solenoid. Put the car in "neutral" and raise the car.

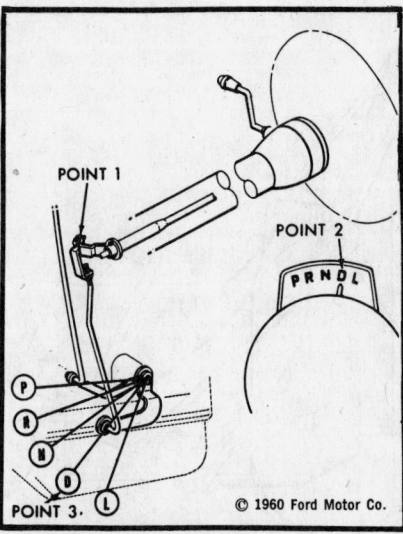

POINT 1

POINT 2

PRNDL

P
R
N
D
L

POINT 3

© 1960 Ford Motor Co.

Fig. 8

TWO-SPEED MERC-O-MATIC

5. Remove converter housing lower plate. Drain the transmission and converter.

6. Disconnect and remove the exhaust "Y" pipe.

7. Remove oil cover lines from the transmission.

8. Disconnect and remove the throttle pressure tube from the rear of the transmission.

9. Match mark the rear universal joint and pinion flange for reassembly. Disconnect the rear joint and remove the driveshaft.

10. Disconnect the converter from the flywheel.

11. Remove two lower bolts from the starter, slide it forward and wire it in place.

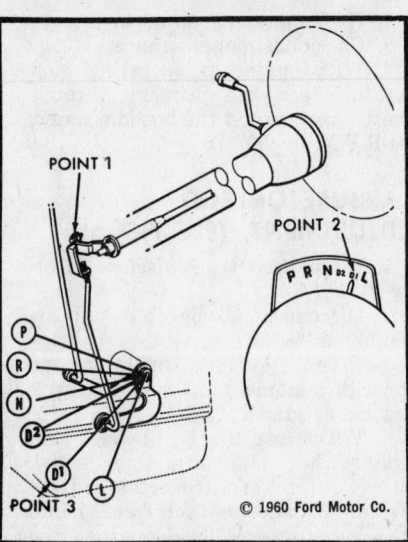

POINT 1

POINT 2

P R N D² L

P
R
N
D²
D1
L

POINT 3

© 1960 Ford Motor Co.

Fig. 9

MULTI-DRIVE

12. Remove control linkage splash shield. Disconnect manual and throttle linkage from transmission levers.

13. Disconnect speedometer cable at transmission.

14. Disconnect engine rear mount at transmission extension.

15. Position transmission jack under the transmission. Raise transmission off rear mount crossmember.

16. Disconnect parking brake cables from the equalizer bar. Remove the rear crossmember and the brake equalizer assembly.

17. Lower jack slightly and remove the remaining three converter housing-to-engine block bolts.

18. Move transmission toward the rear, lower it, and remove from under the car.

19. Remove converter from converter housing.

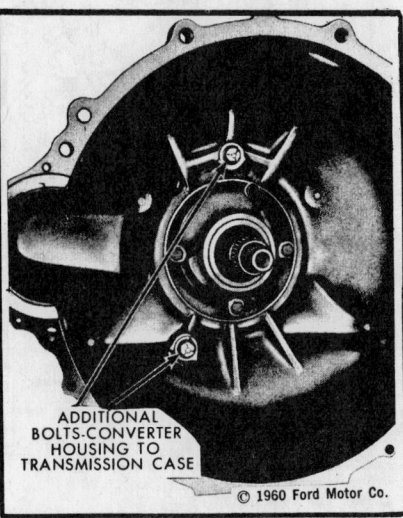

ADDITIONAL BOLTS-CONVERTER HOUSING TO TRANSMISSION CASE

© 1960 Ford Motor Co.

Fig. 10

20. Remove six converter housing-to-transmission attaching bolts, and remove converter housing.

Note:

For reconditioning information see Unit Repair Section, Transmission Group.

REPLACE

Reverse above procedure for replacement.

2 SPEED MERC-O-MATIC TRANSMISSION

TRANSMISSION—REMOVE

1. Raise the car and remove the cover from the bottom of the converter housing.

2. Drain the converter through both (180° apart), drain plugs.

3. Drain transmission oil pan.

4. Disconnect propeller shaft at rear universal joint. Slide propeller shaft and front "U" joint to the rear and out of the transmission extension housing. Install extension housing seal replaced in extension housing seal.

5. Disconnect the manual and throttle linkage at transmission.

6. Disconnect speedometer cable at extension housing.

7. Disconnect oil cooler lines at the transmission. Loosen line clamp at engine block, and remove the lines.

8. Disconnect oil filler tube at transmission.

9. Disconnect cable and remove the starter.

10. Disconnect parking brake cable at equalizer.

11. Remove two engine rear support bolts from extension housing, then remove the support clamp.

12. Place a transmission jack under the transmission and raise the unit just enough to relieve the weight from the crossmember. Support the rear of the engine in this position with an engine support bar or stand.

13. Remove the crossmember.

14. Remove the three converter-to-flywheel bolts.

15. Remove converter housing to engine block bolts.

16. Secure the converter to the transmission so it will not fall out when the transmission is separated from the engine.

17. Work the transmission off the engine block dowels and toward the rear until the converter pilot clears the crankshaft.

18. Lower the transmission and converter assembly and remove it from the car.

TO INSTALL, REVERSE ABOVE PROCEDURE.

BEGINNING 1961 VACUUM CONTROLS

During 1961, two-speed transmission design has gone to vacuum controls instead of the manually controlled throttle valve previously used. The following adjustments are required.

LINKAGE ADJUSTMENT

"223" Six Cylinder Engine

1. Apply parking brake and place the selector lever in "N" position.
2. Disconnect the kickdown rod from the bellcrank and start the engine.
3. Idle the engine until normal operating temperature has been reached.

4. Hook up a tachometer and place the selector in "D" position.

5. With the throttle shaft lever against the hot idle screw, adjust engine idle to just under 500 R.P.M. **Be sure carburetor is off fast idle.**

6. With engine off and the throttle shaft lever held tight against the hot idle adjusting screw, fully depress the dashpot plunger. Then check clearance between the plunger and the lever. Clearance should be .060"-.090".

7. Obtain proper clearance by loosening the locknut and turning the dashpot in its mounting bracket. Retighten the dashpot mounting lock nut.

8. Set accelerator pedal height to about 3¾". To do this, adjust the rod between the bellcrank and "Z" bar.

9. Insert a ¼" gauge pin. (a drill will do) through the bellcrank and kickdown rod lever alignment holes. Adjust the length of the kickdown rod until a free fit is obtained in the bellcrank lever. Normally, the kickdown valve spring will hold the lever against its stop and the lever will be in the "up" position. However, pull up on the kickdown rod gently to make sure that there is no bind.

V-8 Engines

The Eight cylinder linkage adjustment procedures are the same as those used on the Multi-Drive Merc-O-Matic (dual range, three speed).

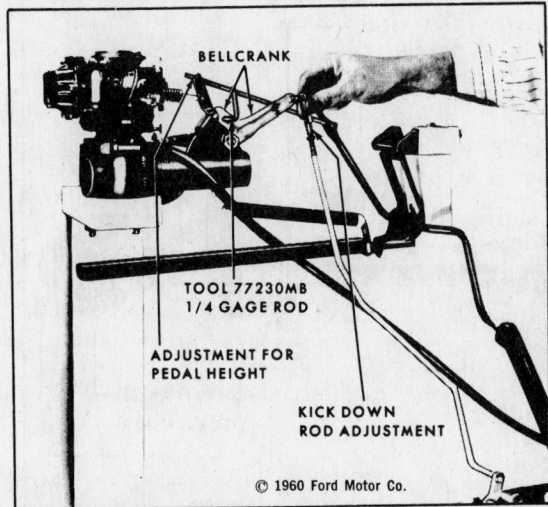

Throttle Linkage—223 Cu. Inch Engine with Vacuum Type T.V. Two-Speed Transmission

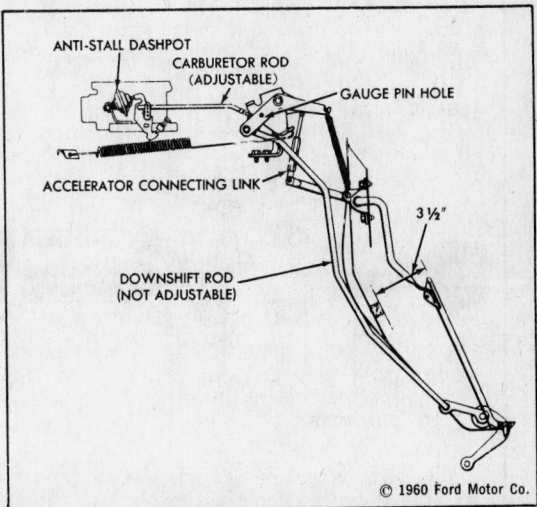

Throttle Linkage—Eight Cylinder Engine with Vacuum Type T.V. Two-Speed Transmission

MERCURY

UNIVERSAL JOINTS AND DRIVE LINES

REMOVAL OF UNIVERSAL JOINTS AND/OR DRIVE SHAFT

All Models

Remove the bolts which attach the rear universal joint to the pinion shaft companion flange, which will release the bearing block from the rear universal joint cross. Part the universal joint at the companion flange and lower the rear end of the drive shaft to the floor. Pull the drive shaft complete with its front universal joint off the end of the transmission (or overdrive) main shaft.

DISASSEMBLY OF THE UNIVERSAL JOINTS

All Models

With the drive shaft and joint assemblies on the bench, remove the lock rings which hold the bearings at the outer end of the yokes.

Lock the universal joint up in a vise and, driving with a large punch from the right, drive the left side bearing out of the yoke. Now, drive on the cross on the left side to drive the right side bearing out of the yoke. Repeat this at all four of the bearings.

No adjustment is possible on the universal joint. If any of the parts are worn they must be replaced with new parts.

It is customary to use an arbor press to install the bearings in the yokes. Driving the bearings with a bushing driver or broad-faced tool is somewhat risky since the needle bearings may be cocked in their cage, which will greatly shorten their life. A very strong heavy duty C clamp can be used to install the needle bearing cages if an arbor press is not available.

REAR AXLE AND SUSPENSION

Note description of Cushion-Link described under 'Front Suspension."

REPLACEMENT OF REAR SPRING

Thru 1956 Models

Support the weight of the car on jacks on the frame. Detach the shock absorber at the bottom and remove

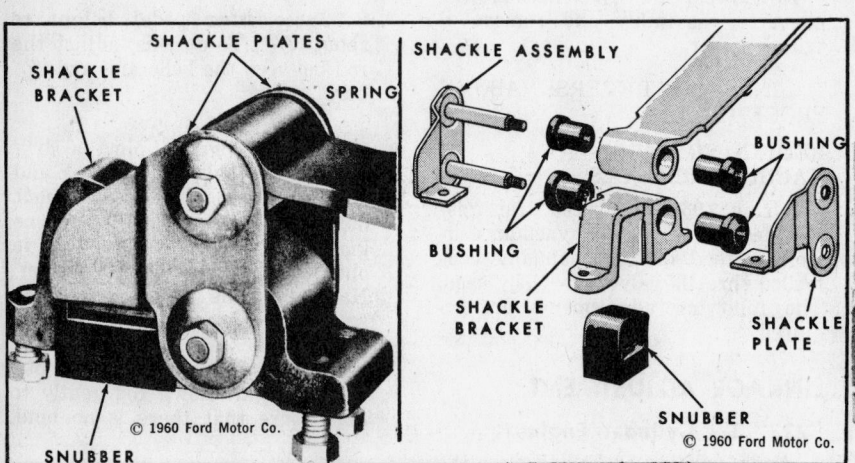

1961 Rear Spring Front Shackle

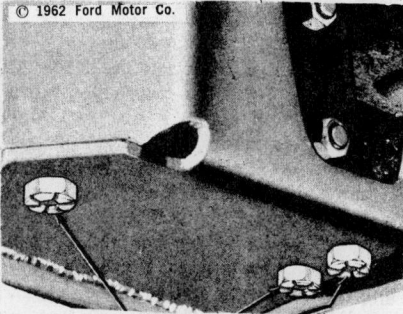

SHACKLE BRACKET RETAINING BOLTS

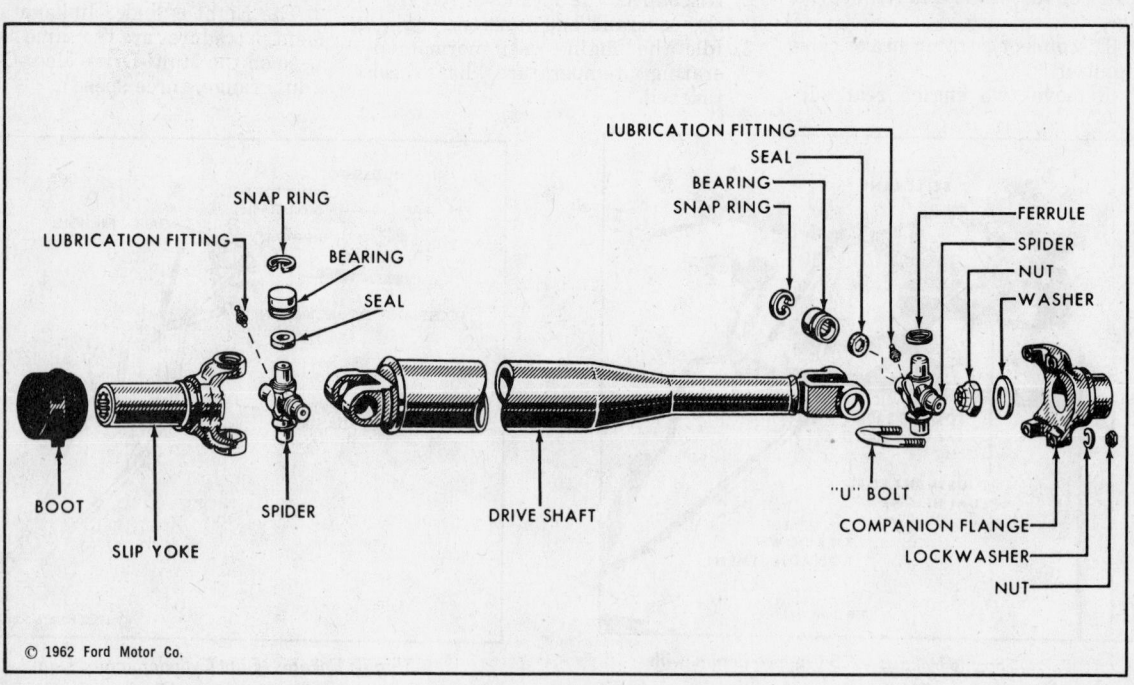

Drive Shaft and Universal Joint Assembly

444

the U clips which hold the rear spring to the rear axle housing and remove the bolts which retain the spring to the shackle at the back and then take out the bolt which holds it to the frame bracket at the front and remove the spring.

Rubber bushings are used in all Mercury rear end spring shackles.

1957 Thru 1963 Models

Support the weight of the car on a frame rail and disconnect the rear shackle. Remove the four nuts which

fold the rear spring front hanger to the frame.

Remove the four U bolts which hold the spring to the axle housing and remove the spring.

The rear spring rubber hanger is held together at the center by a pinch bolt.

REAR AXLE ASSEMBLY REMOVAL FROM VEHICLE

All Models

Disconnect all brake tubes and

brake cables at the rear axle. Disconnect the lower end of the shock absorbers and push them up out of the way.

Split the rear universal joint and let the drive shaft lower to the floor.

Support the weight of the car on the frame in front of the rear springs and remove the rear spring rear shackles.

Remove the U-bolt nuts which hold the spring to the axle tubes and let the two springs lower down to the floor.

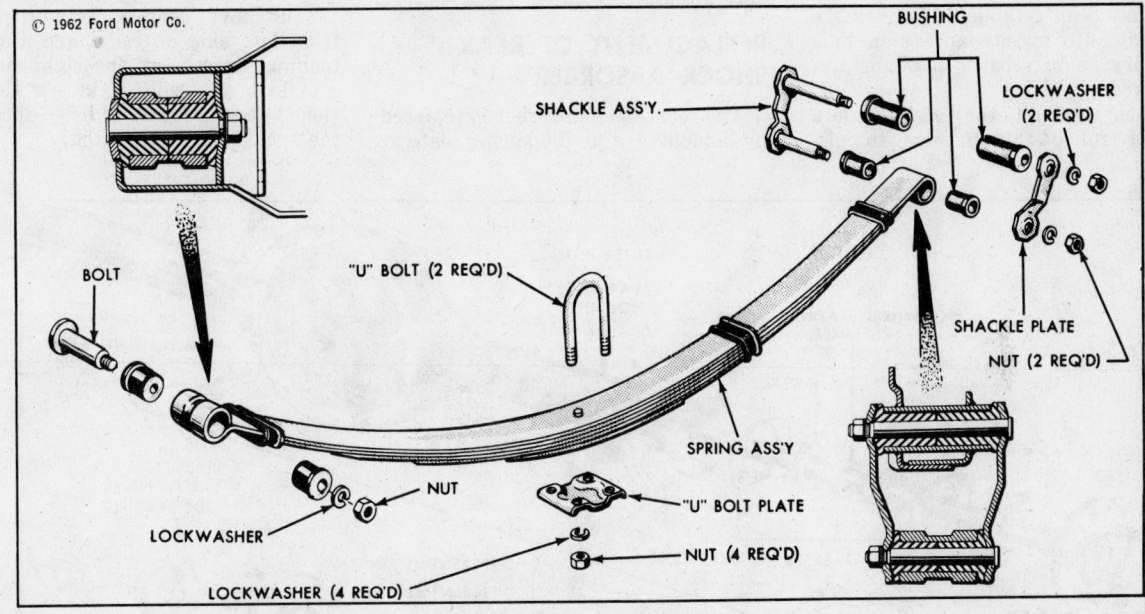

Rear Spring Assembly

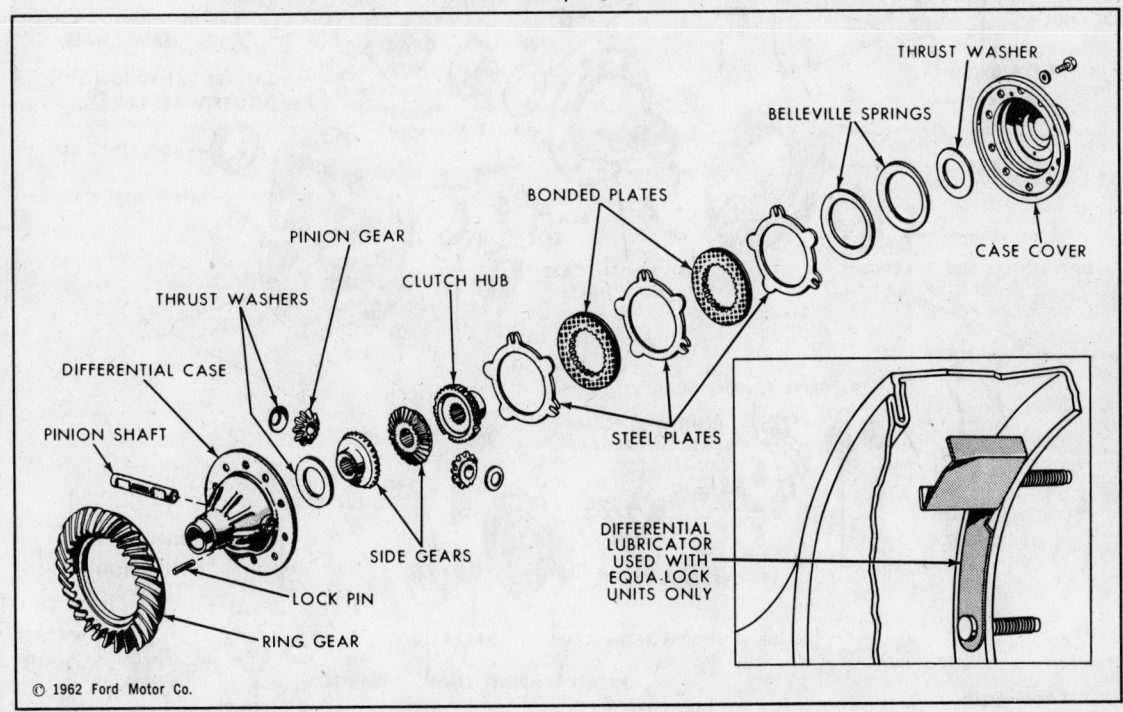

Power Transfer Differential Details

MERCURY

The axle assembly can now be slid out from under the car.

If the vehicle can be raised high enough, the wheels can be left on and the assembly can be rolled on its own wheels out from under the car.

IMPROVED TRACTION AXLE IDENTIFICATION

There are nearly as many different trade names used for the improved traction rear axles as there are car manufacturers. This, and the fact that no standard means of identification has been established, leaves the general auto maintenance man in a quandry as to repairs and lubricant required.

When in doubt, the following is a simple rule-of-thumb way to distinguish between the standard and the improved type units.

1. Raise both rear wheels off the ground.

2. With the parking brake off, turn one wheel forward (by hand) and note the direction of rotation of the other wheel.

3. If the other wheel turns in the same direction as the one being turned, the rear axle is of the improved type.

4. If the other wheel turns in the opposite direction, the axle is of standard design.

REPLACEMENT OF REAR SHOCK ABSORBER

The rear shock absorber is replaced by detaching it at the spring plate at the bottom and from the frame at the top. Rubber grommets are used top and bottom on the shock absorber.

RADIO REMOVE AND INSTALL

1. Disconnect the battery.

2. With Air Conditioning remove glove box liner.

3. Disconnect antennae lead, speaker plug, dial lamp lead at bullet connector and power lead at main junction block.

4. Remove control knobs, with two nuts and washers from front of radio.

5. Remove bracket retaining nut from left side of radio and the attaching screw from the right side.

6. Lift out radio. (On Air Conditioned Cars the radio is lifted through the speaker grille opening).

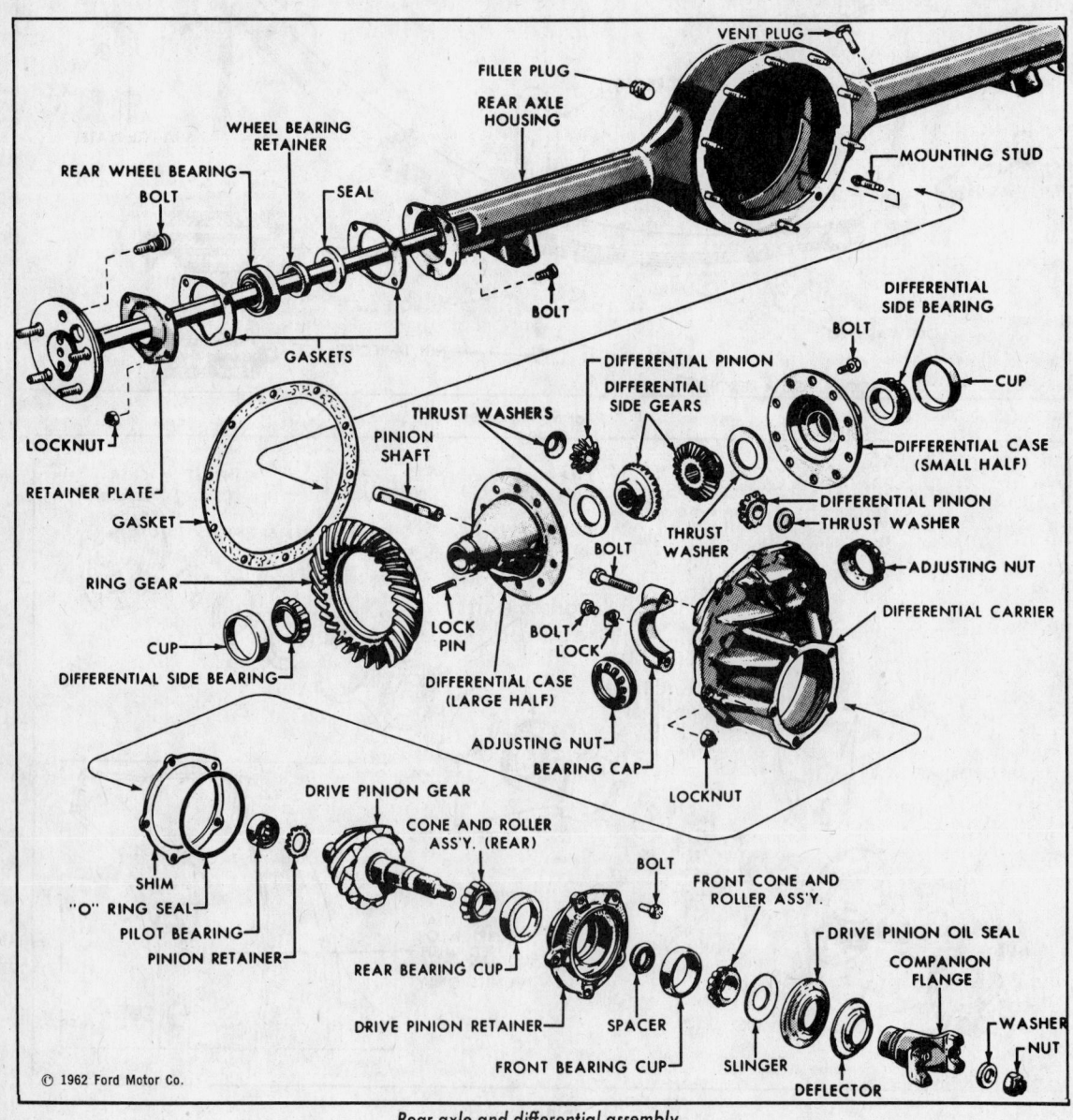

© 1962 Ford Motor Co.

Rear axle and differential assembly

Page

AIR CONDITIONING
Service 1092

BRAKES, HYDRAULIC
Adjustments 938
References 458
Bleed brakes 941
Brake pedal clearance 458
Hand brake, adjust 458
Hand brake lever and cable .. 458
Master cylinder service 939
Parking brake 458

BRAKES, POWER
Power brake, R & R 458
Power unit overhaul 954
Trouble shooting 954

CLUTCH
Clutch assembly, R & R 467
Clutch pedal, adjust 467

COOLING SYSTEM
Radiator core, R & R 459
Thermostat 459
Water pump, R & R 459

ELECTRICAL SYSTEM
Delcotron references 456
Delcotron specifications 450
Distributor, R & R 455
Distributor, specifications 451
Fuses and circuit breakers 452
Gauges 1024
Generator, R & R 456
Generator service 1026
Generator specifications 450
Generator trouble shooting
    chart 1026
Horn buttons 465
Ignition firing order & timing .. 449
Ignition timing procedure 455
Ignition timing specifications .. 450
Starter, R & R 456
Starter specifications 451
Starter systems 1046

ENGINE ASSEMBLY
Cylinder head, R & R 461
Cylinder head tightening 454
Engine assembly, R & R 460
Engine diagnosis 1012
Engine firing order & timing ... 449
Engine marking code 449
Engine references 460
Exhaust manifold, R & R 461
Inlet manifold, R & R 460
Oil filter, R & R 463
Oil pan, R & R 463
Oil pressure specifications 453
Piston and rod, R & R 464
Piston and pin specifications .. 452
Rear main bearing oil seal 463
Rocker shaft lubrication 461
Rocker shaft, R & R 461
Specifications, general engine . 453
Timing case cover, R & R 462

Page

ENGINE ASSEMBLY—continued
Timing chain, R & R 462
Trouble shooting charts 1012
Tune-up specifications 450
Valve lifters, hydraulic,
    R & R service 462
Valve specifications 454
Valve springs 462
Valve and guides 462
Valve timing procedure 462

ENGINE LUBRICATION
Oil filter, R & R 463
Oil pan, R & R 463

EXHAUST SYSTEM
Exhaust manifold, R & R 461
Inlet manifold, R & R 460

FUEL SYSTEM
Carburetors 972
Fuel gauge, R & R 456
Fuel gauge service 1024
Fuel pump pressure 450
Fuel pump service 1020
Fuel pump, R & R 459
Fuel system 458
Fuel tank, R & R 459

INSTRUMENTS
Ammeter 456
Speedometer 457

RADIO, R & R
References 474

REAR AXLE AND SUSPENSION
Axle assembly, R & R 474
Axle shaft 918
Axle shaft oil seal 918
Pinion bearings 918
Ring gear & pinion 918
Shock absorbers, rear 473
Trouble shooting 919
Coil spring, R & R 473
Leaf spring, R & R 473

SPECIFICATIONS
Battery 451
Brake cylinder sizes 452
Capacities:
    Axle, rear 453
    Cooling system 453
    Crankcase 453
    Fuel tank 453
    Transmission, automatic .. 453
    Transmission, manual 453
Chassis, general 452
Cylinder head tightening 454
Delcotron specifications 450
Distributor 451
Engine firing order & timing .. 449
Engine, general 453
Engine tune-up 450
Fuses and circuit breakers 452
Generator regulators 450
Light bulbs 451

Page

SPECIFICATIONS—continued
Main bearings 454
Model identification 449
Model identification
    illustrations 448
Piston and pins 452
Rod bearings 454
Quick reference specifications . 449
Starters 451
Torque wrench 454
Tune-up 450
Valves 454
Wheel alignment 455

STEERING, MANUAL
Adjust gear housing 1052
Gear assembly, R & R 465
Horn button, R & R 465
Steering wheel, R & R 465

STEERING, POWER
Gear assembly, R & R 466
Pump assembly, R & R 466
Trouble shooting 1081
Unit overhaul 1058

SUSPENSION, FRONT
Alignment procedures 1082
Alignment specifications 455
Ball joints, R & R 1087
Camber, adjust 1082
Caster, adjust 1082
Coil springs 465
King pins and bushings 1087
Knuckle supports 1087
Pitman shaft & seals 466
Suspension references 464
Support arms, pins and
    bushings 1087
Toe-in, adjust 1082

**TRANSMISSION,
HYDRA-MATIC**
Dual range 850
    Linkage adjust 468
    R & R 470
Hydramatic, 4 speed 860
    Linkage adjust 469
    R & R 470
Hydramatic, 3 speed 886
    R & R 471

TRANSMISSION, STANDARD
Disassemble transmission 468
Transmission, R & R 467

TROUBLE CHECKS
Procedures 1

TUNE-UP
Procedures 1014
Specifications 450
Engine diagnosis 1012

**UNIVERSAL JOINT AND
DRIVE LINES**
Disassemble U joint 472
U joint & drive line, R & R ... 472

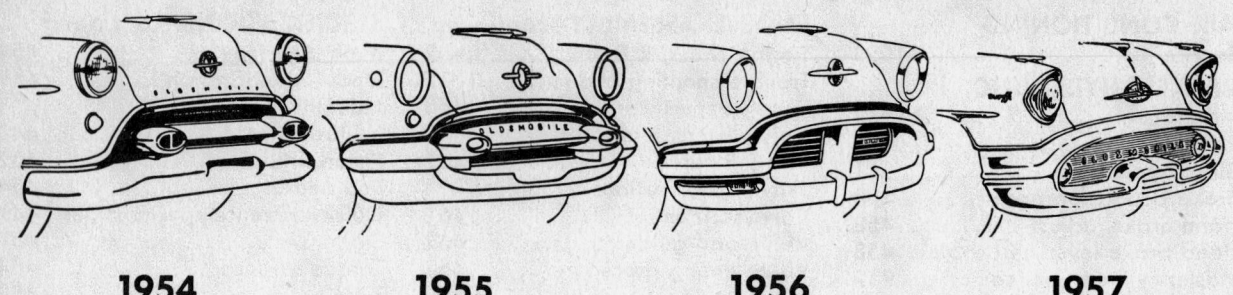

1954   **1955**   **1956**   **1957**

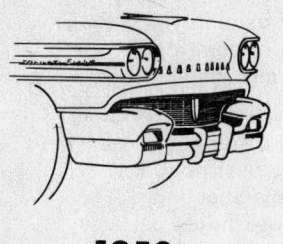   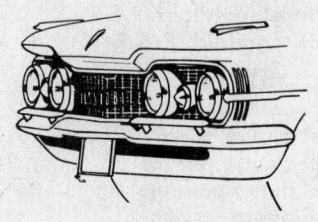   

1958   **1959**   **1960**

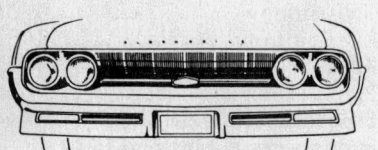
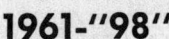
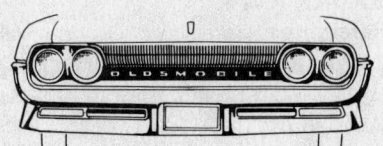

1961-"98"   **1961-"88"**   **1962**

   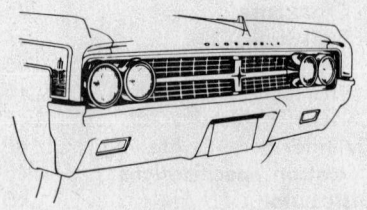   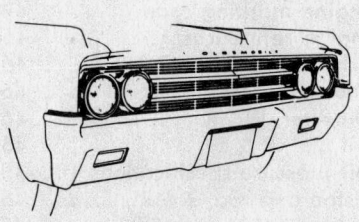

1963
DYNAMIC "88"

1963
SUPER "88"

1963
"98"

OLDSMOBILE

QUICK WORKING SPECIFICATIONS

DISTRIBUTOR

Breaker Point Gap (In.)
1954-63, V-8 .... .015-.017

Cam Angle (Degrees)
1954-63, V8 30

SPARK PLUGS

Year	Type	Gap
1954, V8	46-5	.030 in.
1955-63, V8	44-45	.030 in.

TIMING INDICATOR MARK AND LOCATION

1954-63, V8 notch in crankshaft pulley

IGNITION TIMING

(Spark occurs)
1954-60 V8 ....5 B
1961-63 ...... 88 ....5 B
1961-63, Super 88, 98 .... 5 B

COMPRESSION PRESSURE

Variation between cylinders should not exceed 10 lbs. This is more important than actually reading stated pressure.
1954, V8 136
1955, V8 140
1956-60, V8 150
1961-63 V8 185

GENERATOR AND REGULATOR SPECIFICATIONS

YEAR AND SERIES	GENERATOR Field Current in Amperes		REGULATOR Cut-Out Closing Voltage	Current Regulator Setting	Voltage Regulator Setting
	6 Volt	12 Volt			
1954-57 All		1.55	12.8	30	14.5
1958 All		1.55	12.8	35	14.5
1959-63 88, S88, 98		1.72	12.8	35	14.5

NOTE: Surrounding temperatures and driving habits influence the above adjustments and must be considered by the mechanic. Higher temperatures or turnpike conditions permit lower adjustments; lower temperatures or city type driving conditions require higher settings, within limits.

FRONT WHEEL ALIGNMENT

Caster (Degrees)
1954-56, all ....0 to ¾ N
1957, all ....¾ P to 0
1958-63, all ....1 N to 0

Camber (Degrees)
1954-63, all ....¼ N to ¾ P

Toe-In (Inches)
1954-57, all ....1/16 to ⅛
1958-63 ....0 to ⅛

King Pin Inclination (Degrees)
1954-56, all 5⅞
1957-58, all 7
1959-63, all 10

CAPACITIES

Engine Crankcase (Quarts)
(Add 1 qt. for new filter)
1954-57, V8 5
1958-63 4

Transmission Synchro (Pints)
1954-63 ....2½

Transmission, Automatic (Pints)
1954-55 20
1956-60 22
1961-63 18

Rear Axle (Pints)
1954-58 ....5¼
1959-63 ....5½

Gasoline Tank (Gallons)
1954-63 20

Cooling System (Quarts)
Add 1 quart for heater.
1954-55, V8 ....20½
1956-60, V8 20
1961-63, V8 ....19¼

CAR SERIAL NUMBER LOCATION AND ENGINE IDENTIFICATION

ENGINE NUMBER LOCATION

1954-58—All V-8 engines. on left cylinder block between No. 1 & 7 exhaust ports.
1959-63—All V-8 engines, on left side center of left cylinder head. This number indicates detail information such as: Transmission combination, compression ratio, etc.

SERIAL NUMBER LOCATION

1954-63—On left front door hinge post. Prefixes to this number are used to identify: First, the model year. The next is a letter indicating the series on engine used.

YEAR—ENGINE IDENTIFICATION CHART

Year	Prefix	Engine cu. in.
1954-56	7, 8 or 9	V-8 324.3
1957-58	7, 8, or 9	V-8 371.
1959-60	7	V-8 371.
	8 or 9	V-8 394
1961-63	2, 5 or 8	V-8 394

Note:
1954-60—Prefix Symbol,
6—"76" series, 6 cyl.
7—"88" series
8—"Super 88"
9—"98" series
1961-63—Prefix Symbol,
2—"88" series
5—"Super 88"
8—"98" series

FIRING ORDER and TIMING

SPARK OCCURS:
1954-61—V-8, All 5°-10° BTDC
1963   —V-8, All 2½° BTDC (Std. Trans.)
5° BTDC (Auto. Trans.)

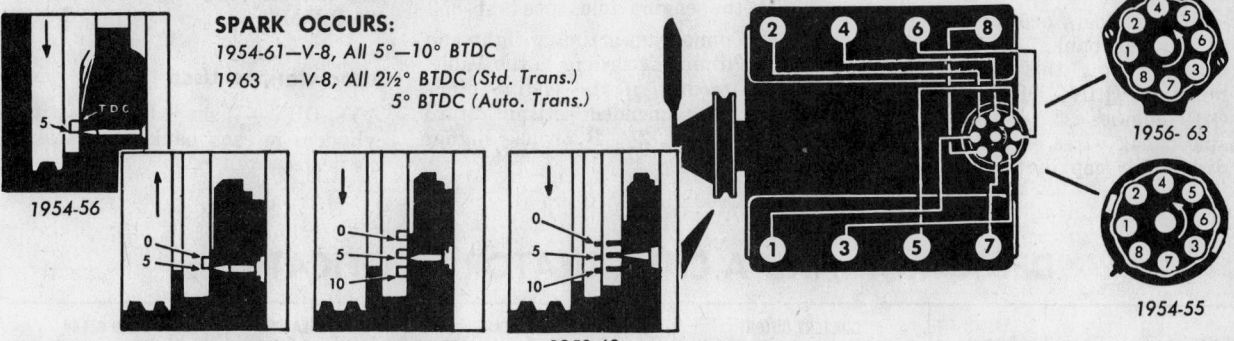

1954-56   1957 Early Models   Late 1957-58   1959-63   1956-63   1954-55

NOTE:
THESE ARE APPROXIMATE SETTINGS. ENGINE DESIGN, ALTITUDE, TEMPERATURE, FUEL AND ENGINE CONDITION WILL ALL INFLUENCE TIMING. THE DETERMINING FACTOR, LIMITING ADVANCE, WILL STILL BE THE "KNOCK POINT" OF THE ENGINE.

TUNE-UP SPECIFICATIONS

Year	Spark Plugs		Distributor (Note 1)				Compression Pressure Cranking (Note 3)	Valves (Note 4)				
								Tappet Clearance Hot		Timing	Fuel Pump Pressure	Engine Idle Speed Neutral (Note 5)
	Type	Gap	Cam Angle	Point Gap	Arm Spring Tension	Ignition Timing (Note 2)		Inlet	Exhaust	Inlet Opens		
1954 All V8, OHV	46.5	.030	30	.016	19-23	5B	136	Zero	Zero	13½B	4½	425
1955 All V8, OHV	44	.030	30	.016	19-23	5B	140	Zero	Zero	13½B	4½	425
1956 All V8, OHV	44	.030	30	.016	19-23	5B	150	Zero	Zero	11½B	4½	425
1957 All V8, OHV	44	.030	30	.016	19-23	5B	150	Zero	Zero	13½B	5½	450
1958-60 All V8, OHV	44	.030	30	.016	19-23	5B	150	Zero	Zero	16B	5½	460
1961-63 88	45	.030	30	.016	19-23	5B	185	Zero	Zero	14B	5½	460
Super 88, 98	44	.030	30	.016	19-23	5B	185	Zero	Zero	11B	5½	460

NOTES FOR TUNE-UP SPECIFICATIONS TABLE

Note:

All specifications are standard and should result in satisfactory performance. There are, however, factors that influence these settings, such as fuel octane value, air density, humidity, temperature, etc. Timing charts, like other specifications must be considered as averages, subject to modification.

Note 1: Distributor

ROTATION (VIEWED FROM THE TOP)

All ....Counterclockwise

DRIVE GEAR

1954-63 All OHV, V8's

Gear is pinned to distributor shaft. Oil pump extension shaft sockets in gear.

FIRING ORDER AND SPARK PLUG WIRE INSTALLATION

1954-63, All, V8, OHV Engines

The cylinders are numbered front to back: left bank, 1-3-5-7; right bank, 2-4-6-8. Using this numbering system the FIRING ORDER for all V8, OHV engines is: 1-8-7-3-6-5-4-2. The spark plug wires enter the OHV, V8 distributor cap in the FIRING OR-DER and in a counterclockwise direction.

Note 2: Ignition

IGNITION TIMING MARKS AND THEIR LOCATION

1954-56, All V8, OHV:

Notch in crankshaft pulley. The leading edge of the notch is 5° before TDC. The trailing edge is at TDC.

1957, All V8, OHV:

Three notches in the crank shaft pulley. One at Top Dead Center. One at 5 degrees Before. One at 10 degrees Before.

1958-63, All V8 AHV:

Two notches in the crankshaft pulley. One at Top Dead Center. One at 5 degrees Before.

V8 ENGINE TIMING PROCEDURE

Disconnect the vacuum line at the vacuum unit on the distributor and close it with a small plug.

Set the engine idle speed at 850 RPM. Connect up a timing light and set the timing according to the Table. On all models, if the engine pings at the recommended setting retard the timing to 2½ B or use higher octane fuel.

At high altitudes the timing can be advanced to, but not over 7½ B.

Note 3: Compression Pressure

All cylinders should read alike within 10 pounds. This is more important than the actual reading. Take the readings with plugs removed, engine at normal operating temperature.

Note 4: Valves

"Zero" in the tappet clearance column indicates hydraulic lifters to be standard equipment.

Note 5: Idle Speed

Idle speeds as shown are for engines in good condition with the transmission in Neutral. The proper idle speed for an engine depends on its condition and also whether or not it has an automatic transmission. Higher idle speeds are required for engines in poor condition and also engines used with automatic transmissions. If engine has air conditioning set idle at 520 R.P.M.

Abbreviations Used

V8, OHV—V shaped engine with 4 cylinders in each bank and valves in the heads.

DELCOTRON AND A.C. REGULATOR SPECIFICATIONS

Delcotron Model Number	Ground Polarity	Field Current Draw (Amperes)	CURRENT OUTPUT			RUNNING VOLTAGE			REGULATOR		FIELD RELAY	
			Engine R.P.M.	Amperes	Volts	Engine R.P.M.	Amperes	Volts @ 125°	Model Number	Point Gap	Armature Air Gap	Closing Voltage
1100622	Neg.	1.9 to 2.2	1100	12.	14	6500	42	13.5-14.3	1119506	.015	.015	6.5-8.5
1100633	Neg.	4.1 to 4.5	1100	24.	14	6500	62	13.3-13.9	1119506	.015	.015	6.5-8.5

GENERATOR and REGULATOR SPECIFICATIONS

	GENERATORS			REGULATORS					
	Field Current in Amperes		Brush Spring Tension	Cut Out Relay		and Voltage Current Regulator Air Gap	Current Regulator Setting	Voltage Regulator Setting	
YEAR	At 6 Volts	At 12 Volts		Air Gap	Closing Voltage				
1954–57 All Models		1.55	28	.020	12.8	.075	30	14.5	
1958 All Models		1.55	28	.020	12.8	.075	35	14.5	
1959-62 Series 88, S88 & 98, OHV, V8		1.72	28	.020	12.8	.075	35	14.5	

NOTE: Surrounding temperatures and driving habits influence the above adjustments and must be considered by the mechanic. Higher temperatures or turnpike conditions permit lower adjustments; lower temperatures or city type driving conditions require higher settings, within limits.

DISTRIBUTOR SPECIFICATIONS, DELCO—REMY

YEAR	MODEL	Delco-Remy Part Number	ROTATION	Cam Angle in Degrees	BREAKER		GOVERNOR CONTROL @ Dist. R.P.M.		VACUUM CONTROL DATA		
					Point Opening (Inch)	Arm Spring In	Advance Starts	Full Advance	Inches of Vacuum To Start Advance	Inches of Vacuum For Full Advance	Max. Adv. of Dist. in Degrees
1954	V8-OHV, All	1110843	CC	26–33	.016	19–23	1 @ 400	14 @ 1725	4½–6½	15–16	9–11
1955	V8-OHV, All	1110850	CC	26–33	.016	19–23	1 @ 400	14 @ 1725	4½–6½	15–17	9¼–10¾
1956	V8-OHV, All	1110857	CC	26–33	.016	19–23	1 @ 400	11 @ 2000	4½–6½	16–18	9–11
1957	V8-OHV, All	1110883	CC	30	.016	19–23	1 @ 400	12 @ 2200	4½–6½	15–17	9–11
1958	V8-OHV, All	1110929	CC	30	.016	19–23	1 @ 400	12 @ 2200	8–10	15–17	11–13
1959	V8-OHV, All	1110931	CC	30	.016	19–23	1 @ 400	12 @ 2200	8–10	19–21	10–12
1960-62	V8-OHV, All	1110968	CC	30	.016	19–23	1 @ 400	12 @ 2200	8–10	19–21	10–12
1963	V8-OHV, All	1110976	CC	30	.016	19–23	1 @ 400	12 @ 2200	8–10	18–20	10–12

BATTERY and STARTER SPECIFICATIONS

YEAR	BATTERY				STARTERS						Brush Spring Tension
	Ampere Hour Capacity	Volts	Group Number	Terminal Grounded	Lock Test			No-Load Test			
					Amps	Volts	Torque	Amps	Volts	R.P.M.	
1954–56 All OHV, V8	70	12	3KM	Neg	460	5.2	11	95	10.1	3500	26
1957–58 All OHV, V8	70	12	3KM	Neg.	Note A	Note A	Note A	100	10.6	3600	35
1959 Series 88, OHV, V8	70	12	3KM	Neg.	Note A	Note A	Note A	83	10.6	3600	35
S88 & 98, OHV, V8	70	12	3KM	Neg.	Note A	Note A	Note A	100	10.6	3900	35
1960-63 Dynamic 88, Model 32*	62	12	3KMA	Neg.	Note A	Note A	Note A	83	10.6	3600	35
Super 88, Model 35	70	12	3KMB	Neg.	Note A	Note A	Note A	100	10.6	3900	35
98, Model 38	70	12	3KMB	Neg.	Note A	Note A	Note A	100	10.6	3900	35

* 1960 only—1961-63 use 70 Amp—3KMB in all Models.   Note. A   Not Recommended

LIGHT BULBS
(C.P. MEANS CANDLE POWER)

Ash Tray Light, Beam Telltale:

12 Volt, No. 53.
(1 C.P. miniature bayonet base.)

Brake-on, Clock, Turn Signal Telltale, Radio Dial, Ignition Key, Glove Compartment, Instrument Lights:

12 Volt, No. 57.
(2 C.P. miniature bayonet base.)

License Light:

12 Volt, No. 67.
(3 C.P. single contact base.)

Trunk and Engine Compartment Lights:

12 Volt, No. 89.
(6 C.P. single contact base.)

Courtesy and Dome Lights:

12 Volt, No. 90.
(6 C.P. double contact base.)

Combination Front Park and Turn Signal, Combination Rear Stop, Tail and Turn Signal:

12 Volt, No. 1034.
(32 & 4 C.P. double contact indexed base.)

Back-up Light:

12 Volt, No. 1073.
(32 C.P. single contact base.)

Headlights: (Single Sealed Beam)

12 Volt, No. 5400.
(50 & 40 C.P. three contact base.)

Headlight: (Twin Sealed Beam)
High Beam: 12 Volt, No. 4001.
(3.75 Watts Two contact base.)

Low and High Beam: 12 Volt, No. 4002.
(37.5-50 Watts. Three contact base.)

451

OLDSMOBILE

FUSES and CIRCUIT BREAKERS

Head and Parking Lights:

1954-63—20 amp. circuit breaker on switch.

Instrument Lights:

1954-55—SFE 2; 1956-58—AGA 2. 1959-63—AGA 3

Dome and Stop Light:

1954-58—AGC 25.
1959-63—AGA or SFE 20 series 88 and super 88.
AGC 25—Series 98.
In main fuse block.

Radio:

1954-57—AGW 7½.
On main fuse block.
1958-63—AGW 4.
Deluxe and Trans-portable.
AGW 7½ Super Deluxe.

Heater:

1954-57—SFE 20; 1958-63—AGC 20. or SFE 20. In main fuse block.

1958-63—SFE 9.
In main fuse block.

Engine Compartment Light:

1954-63—SFE 9. In main fuse block.

Turn Signal:

1954-63—SFE 9. In main fuse block. Flasher is on fuse block.

Cigar Lighter:

1954-63—SFE 20. On back of the lighter.

Clock:

1954-57—AGA 2. 1958-63—AGA 3. In fuse block.

GENERAL CHASSIS and BRAKE SPECIFICATIONS

YEAR AND MODEL		CHASSIS		BRAKE CYLINDER BORE		
		Overall Length (Inches)	Tire Size	Master Cyl. Inch	Wheel Cylinder Diameter (Inch) Front	Rear
1954	V-8 Super 88 & 88	205¼	7.60x15	1.0	1 3/32	31/32
	V-8 98	214¼	7.60x15	1.0	1 3/32	31/32
1955	V-8 88	203½	7.10x15	1.0	1 3/32	31/32
	V8 Super 88	203½	7.60x15	1.0	1 3/32	31/32
	V-8 98	213½	7.60x15	1.0	1 3/32	31/32
1956	V-8 88	203¼	7.10x15	1.0	1 3/32	31/32
	V-8 Super 88	203¼	7.60x15	1.0	1 3/32	31/32
	V-8 98	212¼	7.60x15	1.0	1 3/32	31/32
1957	V-8 88	207¾	8.50x14	1.0	1 3/32	31/32
	V-8 Super 88	207¾	8.50x14	1.0	1 3/32	31/32
	V-8 98	216¼	8.50x14	1.0	1 3/32	31/32
1958	V-8, Dynamic & Super 88	208¼	8.50x14	1.0	1 3/32	31/32
	V-8 98	216¾	8.50x14	1.0	1 3/32	31/32
1959	V-8 Dynamic 88	218½	8.50x14	1(A)	1⅛	1.0
	V-8 Super 88	218½	9.00x14	1(A)	1⅛	1.0
	V-8 98	223—	9.00x14	1(A)	1⅛	1.0
1960	V-8 Dynamic 88	217½	8.50x14	1.0	1⅛	1.0
	V-8 Super 88	217½	8.50x14	1.0	1⅛	1.0
	V-8 98	220¾	9.00x14	1.0	1⅛	1.0
1961	V-8 Dynamic & Super 88	212	8.00x14	1.0	1⅛	1.0
	98	218	8.50x14	1.0	1⅛	1.0
1962-63	V-8 Dynamic & Super 88	213.9	8.00x14	1.0	1⅛	1.0
	98	220	8.50x14	1.0	1⅛	1.0
1963	V-8 Dynamic & Super 88	214.4	8.00x14	1.0	1⅛	1.0
	98	221.5	8.50x14	1.0	1⅛	1.0
	Convertible	214.4	8.50x14	1.0	1⅛	1.0

(A) Power Brake 21/32

Glove Box Light:

1954-63—SFE 9. In main fuse block.

Back-up Light:

1954-57—SFE 9; 1958—SFE 19;

Autronic Eye:

1954-63—SFE 9. Under amplifier cover.

Air Conditioner:

1954—SFE 2. In line to solenoid valve near the valve.
1955-58—AGC 25; 1959-63—AGC 20 or—SFE 20. In fuse block.

Window Switches and Antenna:

1954-63—SFE 20. In fuse block.

Window, Seat and Top Motors:

1962-63—SFE 20.

Special Note On Fuse Block

The arrangement of fuses and the circuits they protect are shown on fuse block. **Thru** 1961 fuse block is on dash under instrument panel. **Starting** 1962 on engine side of fire wall.

PISTON AND PIN SPECIFICATIONS

Year and Model	PISTON Skirt Clearance Min	Max.	PISTON PIN Diameter	Bushing	FIT In Rod	In Piston	Lock
1954-56	.0005	.0010	.9805	Yes	.0003-.0005	0-.0002	Ring
1957-59—371″	.00075	.00125	.9805	Yes	.0003-.0005	0-.0002	Ring
1959-63—394″	.00075	.00125	.9805	Yes	.0003-.0005	.0003-.0005	Ring

Piston Fitting Ribbon Thickness and Spring Scale Pull

1954-56, ALL OHV, V8 ENGINES:
12 inches long; ½ inch wide; .0015 inch thick; pull of 5 to 12 pounds.

1957-63, ALL OHV, V8 ENGINES:
12 inches long, ½ inch wide; .0015 inch thick; pull of 2 to 6 pounds for the 4 in. piston and 3 to 12 pounds for the 4⅛ in. piston.

1954-63, ALL OHV, V8:
Assemble so that F Marks near pin hole are to the front. Rods have a boss on one side. Put boss to rear on left bank; front on right bank.
Oil spit holes should face towards the camshaft on both banks.

CAPACITIES

YEAR	Engine Crankcase Add 1 Qt. for New Filters	Transmissions Pints to Refill After Draining		Rear Axle Pints	Gasoline Tank Gallons	Cooling System Quarts Add 1 Qt. for Heater
		Manual	Automatic			
1954-55 All OHV, V8	5	2½	20	5¼	20	20½
1956-57 All OHV, V8	5	2½	22	5¼	20	20
1958 All OHV, V8	4	2½	22	5¼	20	20
1959-60 All OHV, V8	4	2½	22	5½	20	20
1961-63 All OHV, V8	4	2½	18	5½	20A	19¼

*1963-21 Gal.

GENERAL ENGINE SPECIFICATIONS

Year	Bore and Stroke	Number of Main Bearings	Type of Valve Lifter Used	Cubic Inch Displacement	AMA Horsepower	Advertised Horsepower at Stated RPM	Advertised Torque at Stated RPM	Compression Ratio	Oil Pressure At 30 MPH (Note 1)	Cam Shaft Drive
1954										
V8, OHV, Series 88	3⅞x3 7/16	5	Hyd. No Adj.	324.3	48	170@4000	295@2000	8.25–1	35	Chain
V8, OHV Series, Super 88, 98	3⅞x3 7/16	5	Hyd. No Adj.	324.3	48	185@4000	300@2000	8.25–1	35	Chain
1955										
V8, OHV, Series 88	3⅞x3 7/16	5	Hyd. No Adj.	324.3	48	185@4000	320@2000	8.5–1	35	Chain
V8, OHV, Super 88, 98	3⅞x3 7/16	5	Hyd. No Adj.	324.3	48	202@4000	332@2400	8.5–1	35	Chain
1956										
V8, OHV, Series 88	3⅞x3 7/16	5	Hyd. No Adj.	324.3	48	230@4400	340@2400	9.25–1	35	Chain
V8, OHV Series, Super 88, 98	3⅞x3 7/16	5	Hyd. No Adj.	324.3	48	240@4400	350@2800	9.25–1	35	Chain
1957										
V8, OHV, All Series	4x3 11/16	5	Hyd. No Adj.	371	51	277@4400	400@2800	9.25–1	35	Chain
1958										
V8, OHV, All Series	4x3 11/16	5	Hyd. No. Adj.	371	51	←Note: 2→		10.0–1	35	Chain
1959 Note 3										
V8, OHV, Series 88	4x3 11/16	5	Hyd. No. Adj.	371	51	270@4600	390@2400	9.75–1	35	Chain
V8, OHV, Series, Super 88, 98	4⅛x3 11/16	5	Hyd. No. Adj.	394	54	315@4600	435@2800	9.75–1	35	Chain
1960										
V8, OHV, Series 88	4x3 11/16	5	Hyd. No Adj.	371	51	240@4600	375@2400	8.75–1	35	Chain
V8, OHV, Series, Super 88, 98	4⅛x3 11/16	5	Hyd. No Adj.	394	54	315@4600	435@2800	9.75–1	35	Chain
1961										
Dynamic 88	4⅛x3 11/16	5	Hyd.	394	54	250@4200	405@2400	8.75-1	35	Chain
Super 88, 98	4⅛x3 11/16	5	Hyd.	394	54	325@4600	435@2800	10.0–1	35	Chain
1962-63										
Dynamic 88	4⅛x3 11/16	5	Hyd.	394	54	280@4400	430@2400	10.25–1(4)	35	Chain
Super 88, 98	4⅛x3 11/16	5	Hyd.	394	54	330@4600	440@2800	10.25–1	35	Chain

NOTES FOR GENERAL ENGINE SPECIFICATIONS TABLE

Note 1: Oil Flow

OIL FILTER TYPE

1954-63

All OHV engines ....Full flow

ROCKER SHAFT OIL SUPPLY

The oil supply to the rocker arms is furnished from No. 2 and No. 4 cam bearings, through a core hole in the cylinder heads into No. 2 rocker shaft bracket on the left bank and No. 3 bracket on the right bank. A hole in each bracket lines up with a hole in each rocker arm shaft which allows oil to flow through the shafts and into the rockers.

Note 2: 1958 Horsepower and Torque

WITH ONE TWO BARREL CARBURETOR.

H.P.—265 @ 4400.
Torque—390 @ 2400.

WITH ONE FOUR BARREL CARBURETOR

H.P.—305 @ 4600.

Torque—410 @ 2800.

WITH 3 TWO BARREL CARBURETORS

H.P.—312 @ 4600.

Torque—415 @ 2800.

Note 3: 1959-63 Eng. Identification

The 371 cubic inch engine has gold painted valve covers. The 394 cubic inch engine has green painted valve covers.

Note 4: An 8.75-1 Compression Ratio is Optional on Dynamic 88; An 8.5-1 on 1963 Starfire

OLDSMOBILE

TORQUE SPECIFICATIONS

YEAR	Cylinder Head Bolts	Rod Bearing Bolts	Main Bearing Bolts	Crankshaft Pulley Bolt	Flywheel to Crankshaft Bolt	Manifolds In.	Ex.
1954-58 All Models	60–70	45–50	100–140	45–50	85–95(A)	28	22
1959-63 All Models	60–80	38–48	90–120(B)	100	85–95(A)	23	22

(A)—1957-63, Fly wheel to Flex-plate: 60 lb.

(B)—1959-63 Main Bearings Bolts
Nos. 1 thru 4: 90-120
No. 5: 130-160

CYLINDER HEAD NUT TIGHTENING SEQUENCE

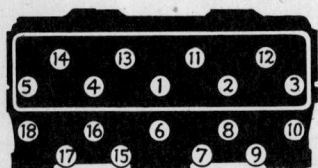

1959-63 OHV, V8
1. *Tighten numbered bolts to 50 to 60 ft. lbs.*
2. *Tighten lettered bolts 14 to 22 ft. lbs.*
3. *Retighten numbered bolts to 60 to 80 ft. lbs.*
4. *Retighten lettered bolts 14 to 22 ft. lbs.*

1954-58 All OHV, V8 *Tighten to 60-70 ft. lbs.*

CRANKSHAFT BEARING JOURNAL SIZES

YEAR	MAIN BEARING JOURNALS				CONNECTING ROD BEARING JOURNALS		
	Journal Diameter	Oil Clearance	End Play of Shaft	End Play Held By	Journal Diameter	Oil Clearance	End Play
1954-56 All OHV, V8	Note: 1	.0027(A)	.006	No. 5	2.250"	.0019	.007
1957-58 All OHV, V8	2.750"	Note: 2	.006	No. 5	2.250"	.0020	.007
1959-63 All OHV, V8	3.000"	Note: 2	.006	No. 5	2.500"	.0015	.007

NOTES FOR CRANKSHAFT BEARING JOURNAL SIZE TABLE

Note 1: 1954-56, V8 Main Bearing Journal Diameter No's. 1, 2, 3, & 4—2 1/12
No. 5—2 5/8

(A): 1954-56, OHV, V8 Main Bearing Oil Clearance Figure is given for rear bearing only. All others are .0017

Note 2: Main Bearing Oil Clearance 1957-58 No. 1—.0013; Nos. 2, 3, 4—.0018; No. 5—.0022
1959-63 Nos. 1, 2, 3, 4—.0016; No. 5 —.0023

VALVE SPECIFICATIONS

Year and Model	Seat Angle In.	Ex.	Valve Lift Note: 1 In.	Ex.	Valve Spring Pressure Note: 2 Outer	Inner	Stem to Guide Clearance In.	Ex.	Stem Diameter In.	Ex.	Are Guides Replaceable
1954 All	45	45	.366	.366	90 @ 1⁵³⁄₆₄	None	.0032	.0036	.342	.393	Yes
1955 All	45	45	.403	.403	90 @ 1⁵³⁄₆₄	None	.0032	.0036	.342	.393	Yes
1956 All	45	45	.418	.418	100 @ 1⅞	None	.0026	.0034	.342	.393	Yes
1957 All	45	45	.419	.435	100 @ 1⅞	None	.0026	.0034	.342	.393	Yes
1958 All	45	45	.419	.435	110 @ 1⁵³⁄₆₄	None	.0018	.0023	.343	.394	Yes
1959 All	45	45	.419	.435	90 @ 1⁵³⁄₆₄	None	.0018	.0023	.343	.394	Yes
1960-61 88	45	45	.427	.435	90 @ 1⁵³⁄₆₄	None	.0018	.0023	.343	.394	Yes
Super 88 & 98	45	45	.437	.435	90 @ 1⁵³⁄₆₄	None	.0018	.0023	.343	.394	Yes
1962-63 88	45	45	.428	.435	90 @ 1⁵³⁄₆₄	None	.0018	.0023	.343	.394	Yes
Super 88 & 98	45	45	.435	.437	90 @ 1⁵³⁄₆₄	None	.0018	.0023	.343	.394	Yes

NOTES FOR VALVE SPECIFICATIONS

Note 1: Valve Timing Marks
Align marks on camshaft and crankshaft sprockets closest each other and in line with a center line thru both shafts.

Note 2: Valve Springs
Intake and exhaust valve springs are identical.

FRONT WHEEL ALIGNMENT

YEAR	Caster		Camber		Toe-In (Inches)	King Pin Inclination (Degrees)	Wheel Pivot Ratio	
	Range (Degrees)	Pref. Setting	Range (Degrees)	Pref. Setting			Inner Wheel	Outer Wheel
1954-56 All, OHV, V8	¾N to 0	⅜N	¼N to ¾P	¼P	1/16 to ⅛	5⅝	23	20
1957 All, OHV, V8	0 to ¾P	⅜P	¼N to ¾P	¼P		7	'23	20
1958 All, OHV, V8	1N to 0	½N	¼N to ¾P	¼P	0 to ⅛	7	23	20
1959-63 All	1N to 0	½N	¼N to ¾P	⅛P	0 to ⅛	10	23	20

Caster and Camber Setting   Maximum variation side to side should not exceed ½°.

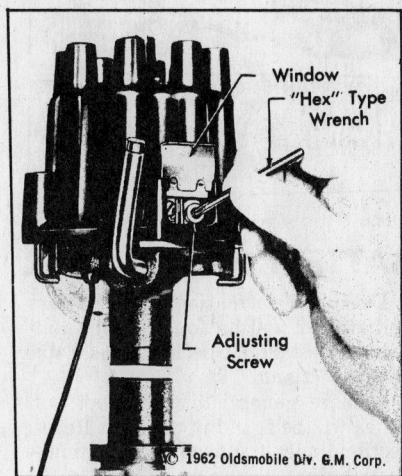

Adjusting Distributor Points.

DISTRIBUTOR

Detailed information on: distributor drive, direction of distributor rotation; cylinder numbering; firing order; point gap; cam dwell; timing mark location; spark plugs, spark advance; ignition resistor location, and idle speed; will be found in the Tune-up Specifications table of this section. Further information on trouble shooting, general tune-up procedures, how to replace ignition wires, how to install points and condensers, how to choose the proper spark plug, adjust timing, will be found in the Unit Repair Section under the heading: Tune-up.

DISTRIBUTOR REMOVAL

V8 Engines Thru 1955

On V8 engines the distributor is located in back of the intake manifold.

To remove it, take off the air cleaner, remove the distributor cap and wire assembly and take off the vacuum line to the distributor. Remove the ignition primary wire and take out the one bolt which holds the distributor down to the block. Lift off the distributor.

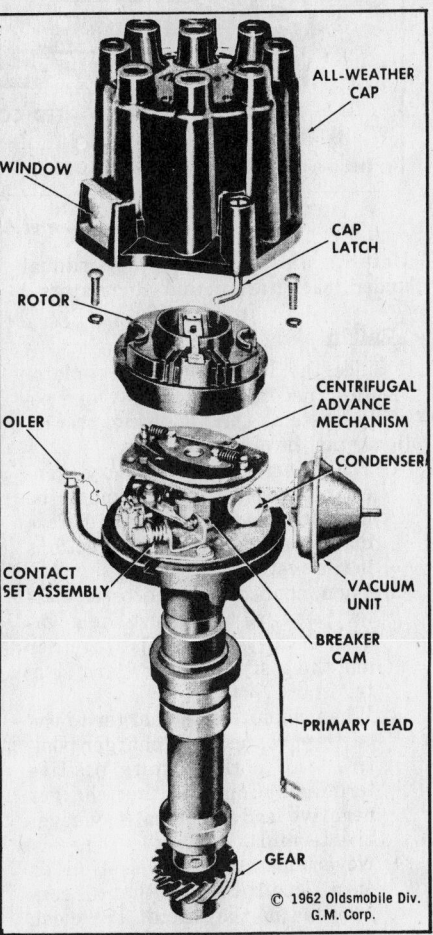

Distributor details, Externally Adjusted Type

A movable breaker plate type distributor is used on all V8 rocket engines.

V8 Engines Starting with 1956

Take off the air cleaner and the distributor cap and wire assembly. Mark the position of the rotor in relation to the body and the body in relation to the block so retiming is simplified. Do not move the engine after the distributor is removed. Disconnect the vacuum line at the distributor and remove the primary wire. Take out the bolt which holds the distributor to the block and lift off the distributor.

These models are fitted with an externally adjusted type distributor having a "window" in the distributor cap. Final adjustment of the breaker points is done with the engine running.

The breaker points are set roughly to the correct gap and the distributor installed on the vehicle and the engine started and run at fast idle.

An electric type dwell meter can be attached to the distributor.

Raise the "window" in the cap and, reaching thru the "window" with the engine running, turn the adjusting screw until a dwell angle of 30 degrees is obtained.

If a dwell meter is not available, turn the screw inwards until the engine slows down and outwards until the engine slows down, counting the number of turns between the two positions. Set the points midway between these two positions.

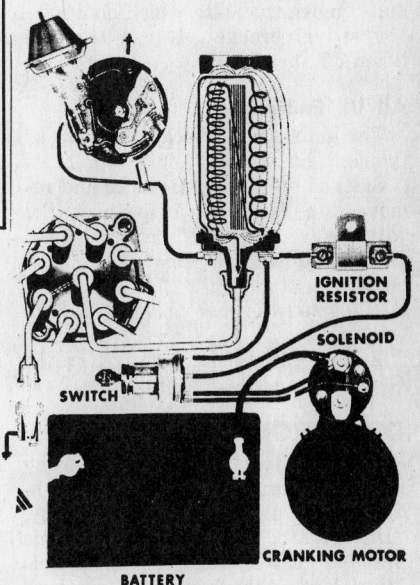

Ignition System

OLDSMOBILE

GENERATOR AND REGULATOR

Detailed facts on the generator and the regulator can be found in the Generator and Regulator Specifications Table of this section.

General information on generator and regulator repair and trouble shooting can be found in the Unit Repair section under the heading: Generators and Regulators.

GENERATOR POLARITY

Caution: whenever the circuits to the generator, the regulator, or the battery have been disconnected it is best to apply the following procedure:

Before the engine is started momentarily short from the "Bat" to the "Gen" terminals of the regulator with a screwdriver. This gives a momentary surge of current from the battery to the generator and so correctly polarizes the generator with respect to the battery.

Failure to so polarize the generator before starting the engine may severely damage the regulator since reversed polarity causes vibration, arcing and burning of the relay points.

GENERATOR REMOVAL

All In-Line Engines

On all in-line engines the generator is located on the left side of the engine and is driven by the fan belt.

Loosen the tension bolt on the generator and rock the generator up so that the fan belt can be released from the generator pulley.

Disconnect the wires to the generator, let the generator drop downwards and remove the bolts which hold it to the swivel bracket. It can then be lifted off the car.

All V8 Engines

The generator is located on top of the right bank of cylinders.

Slacken off on the tensioner and remove the fan belt, disconnect the wires to the generator, let the generator rock down and remove the swivel bolts.

The generator may now be lifted off the car.

All generator service is given in the Generator and Regulator section.

DELCOTRON (A.C. Generator)

Beginning with 1962, an alternating current generator is being made available. This unit is the Delco-Remy, "DELCOTRON." The purpose of this unit is to satisfy the increase in electrical loads that have been imposed upon the car battery by modern conditions of traffic and driving patterns.

The DELCOTRON is covered in the

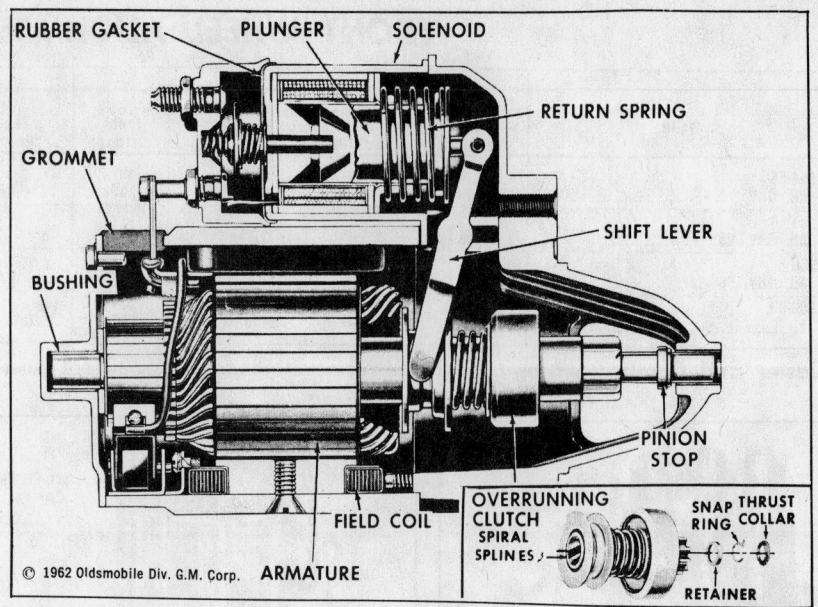

© 1962 Oldsmobile Div. G.M. Corp.

Starter Assembly.

Unit Repair section of this manual under "Generators and Regulators."

Caution

Since the Delcotron and regulator are designed for use on only one polarity system, the following precautions must be observed:

1. The polarity of the battery, generator and regulator must be matched and considered before making any electrical connections in the system.
2. When connecting a booster battery, be sure to connect the negative battery terminals together and the positive battery terminals together.
3. When connecting a charger to the battery, connect the charger positive lead to the battery positive terminal. Connect the charger negative lead to the battery negative terminal.
4. Never operate the Delcotron on open circuit. Be sure that all connections in the circuit are clean and tight.
5. Do not short across or ground any of the terminals on the Delcotron regulator.
6. Do not attempt to polarize the Delcotron.
7. Do not use test lamps of more than 12 volts for checking diode continuity.
8. Avoid long soldering times when replacing diodes or transistors. Prolonged heat is damaging to these units.
9. Disconnect the battery ground terminal when servicing any A.C. system. This will prevent the possibility of accidental reversing of polarity.

BATTERY AND STARTER

Detailed information on the battery and starter will be found in the Battery and Starter Specifications Table of this section.

A more general discussion of batteries will be found in the Unit Repair section under the heading: Ignition—Distributors—Tune-up.

A more general discussion of starters and their troubles can be found in the Unit Repair section under the heading: Starters.

STARTER, R & R

Disconnect battery at junction block and solenoid wire from harness. Raise car. Where engine filler plate is used remove it too. With dual exhaust remove pipe from manifold. Remove mounting bolts and lift out starter. Cable will slide thru sleeve.

DASH INSTRUMENT REMOVAL

1955 Models

Since all work under the dash is done in necessarily close quarters, the first thing to do is disconnect the battery to avoid an accidental short circuit. Remove the speedometer drive cable from the back of the speedometer.

The ammeter and temperature gage are located on the left and are contained in a single plate. Three bolts hold this plate to the instrument cluster and both instruments are pulled down at the same time. The same is true of the right side which holds the fuel and oil pressure gage.

The speedometer can also be removed from under the dash.

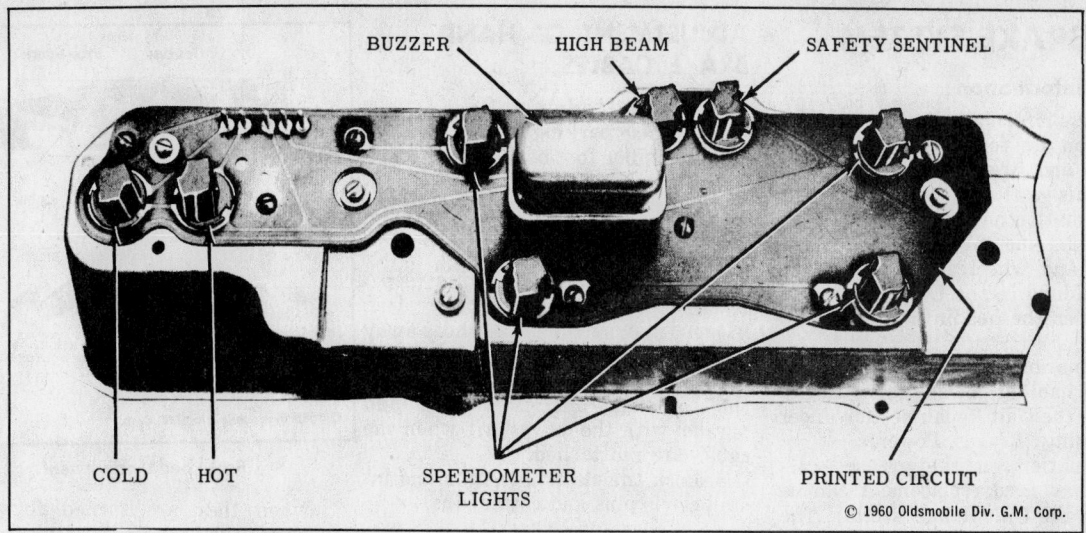

BUZZER   HIGH BEAM   SAFETY SENTINEL

COLD   HOT   SPEEDOMETER LIGHTS   PRINTED CIRCUIT

© 1960 Oldsmobile Div. G.M. Corp.

Speedometer Head Printed Circuit

There are four bolts holding the entire cluster up to the dash and the entire cluster assembly can be taken down as a unit. This is a rather difficult job due to the many wires and cables under the dash.

1956 Models

Actually there is only one "instrument" used in the 1956 model, and that is the fuel tank gage. The other instruments make use of colored lights operated from relays and are not in the strict sense of the word instruments at all.

These colored bulbs can be removed readily from under the dash.

The gas gage can be removed without disturbing anything, but if it becomes necessary to take out the speedometer it is first necessary to remove the Hydramatic shift indicator needle before attempting to remove the speedometer.

The speedometer is removed by taking the entire cluster assembly down from under the dash and removing the speedometer out through the front of the cluster.

1957 Thru 1963 Models

1957 instrument cluster is a printed circuit. All electrical instruments and lights are connected to the wire harness by a plug located at the rear of the cluster.

The generator, temperature and oil pressure indicators are simply colored lights. The light sockets can be removed readily by turning the socket an eighth of an inch clockwise.

SPEEDOMETER REMOVAL

1. Disconnect printed circuit connector.
2. Disconnect cable from head.
3. Remove three cluster attaching screws.
4. Remove cluster through front of panel.

To Reinstall: Reverse the above.

Starting 1963

The speedometer is driven by cable running from left front wheel through engine compartment and to speedometer. Spindle is hollow, allowing cable to pass through and engage with dust cap.

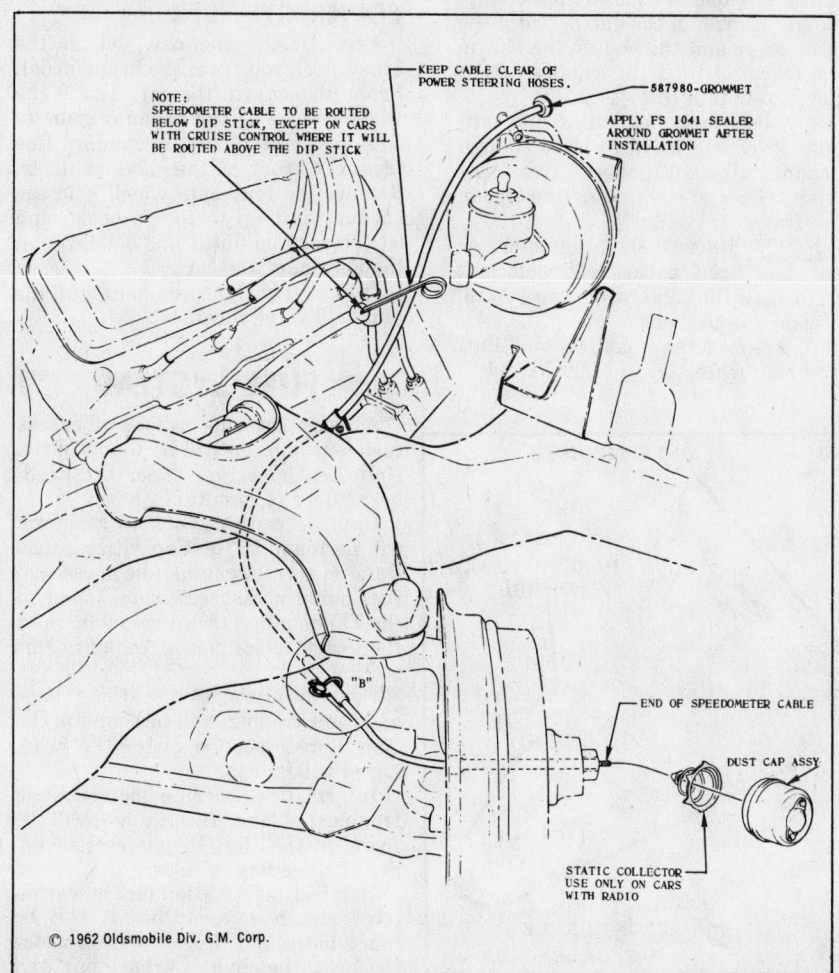

NOTE:
SPEEDOMETER CABLE TO BE ROUTED BELOW DIP STICK, EXCEPT ON CARS WITH CRUISE CONTROL WHERE IT WILL BE ROUTED ABOVE THE DIP STICK.

KEEP CABLE CLEAR OF POWER STEERING HOSES.

587980—GROMMET

APPLY FS 1041 SEALER AROUND GROMMET AFTER INSTALLATION

"B"

END OF SPEEDOMETER CABLE

DUST CAP ASSY

STATIC COLLECTOR USE ONLY ON CARS WITH RADIO

© 1962 Oldsmobile Div. G.M. Corp.

Speedometer Drive 1963

OLDSMOBILE

BRAKE SYSTEM

Brake Information

Specific information on brake lining sizes can be found in the General Chassis and Brake Specifications Table of this section.

Information on brake adjustments, band replacement, bleeding procedure, master and wheel cylinder overhaul can be found in the Unit Repair section under the heading: Brakes, Hydraulic.

Information on trouble shooting and overhauling power brakes can be found in the Unit Repair section under the heading: Brakes, Power.

Information on the grease seals which may need replacement can be found in the Unit Repair section. The head: Suspension, Front Repair. The rear wheel grease seals under the head: Axles, Rear.

BRAKE PEDAL CLEARANCE

Before adjusting the brakes, make certain there is 1/2" to 3/4" free pedal travel (measured at the toe-board). This adjustment is secured at the master cylinder push rod.

Starting with 1962

All Oldsmobiles with power brakes are of the self-adjusting type. Adjustment is accomplished thru a link, actuator and pawl that operate when brake is applied while reversing car.

STARTING WITH 1963

Self adjusting brakes are standard on all models.

ADJUSTMENT OF HAND BRAKE CABLES

Thru 1958 Models

1. Release parking brake.
2. Do minor foot brake adjustment.
3. Adjust front cable so that the intermediate lever is held from seating on its released seat, in the left hand "X" member, by 1/16".
4. Adjust rear brake cables (separately) to remove all of their slack without moving the brake shoes away from the off position. Divide the adjustment of these rear cables so that the equalizer link is neutral and parallel with the driveshaft when the cables are reattached.
5. Lock the clevis lock-nuts and install clevis pins and cotter pins.

1959-63

The parking brake is controlled by a separate foot pedal design. Adjust as follows:

1. Release parking brake.
2. Do minor service brake adjustment.
3. Check for proper length of intermediate cable by inserting a 1/4" gauge, or drill, in the gap between the relay lever and the end of the slot in the frame. Adjust this cable at front clevis to obtain this 1/4" fit.
4. Loosen brake equalizer nut until relay lever will move forward enough to admit a 1-3/16" gauge between the relay lever and the rear of the slot in the frame.
   NOTE: Be sure that the equalizer nut has been backed off sufficient to slack the cable when the 1-3/16" gauge is in place.
5. Tighten the equalizer nut until the rear wheels are nearly locked up

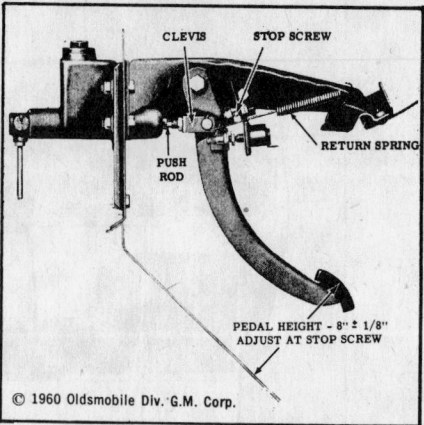

Brake pedal adjustment

when they are turned forward by hand.
6. Remove 1-3/16" gauge from slot.
   NOTE: If instructions have been followed and the linkage and cables are free, the parking brake pedal should travel about 2 1/4" to solidly set the brakes.

REMOVAL OF POWER CYLINDER

From inside the car, detach the brake push rod from the brake pedal. From underneath the car, detach the vacuum hose at the vacuum cylinder and disconnect the hydraulic line from the front of the slave cylinder. Remove the four nuts which hold the vacuum unit up to the toeboard and let the vacuum unit come out through the bottom of the car.

It is pretty tight quarters, but the unit will come down.

FUEL SYSTEM

A chart covering causes of excess fuel consumption will be found in the Unit Repair section under the heading: Fuel Consumption Chart.

Data on capacity of the gas tank will be found in the Capacities Table. Data on correct engine idle speed and fuel pump pressure will be found in the Tune-up Specifications table. Both the above tables can be found in this section.

General information on fuel pumps and their troubles will be found in the Unit Repair section under the heading: Fuel Pumps.

Information covering operation and troubles of the fuel gauge will be found in the Unit Repair section under the heading: Gages.

Detailed information on the carburetor and how to adjust it will be found in the Unit Repair section under the broad heading: Carburetors, and the specific heading of the make of carburetor being used on the engine

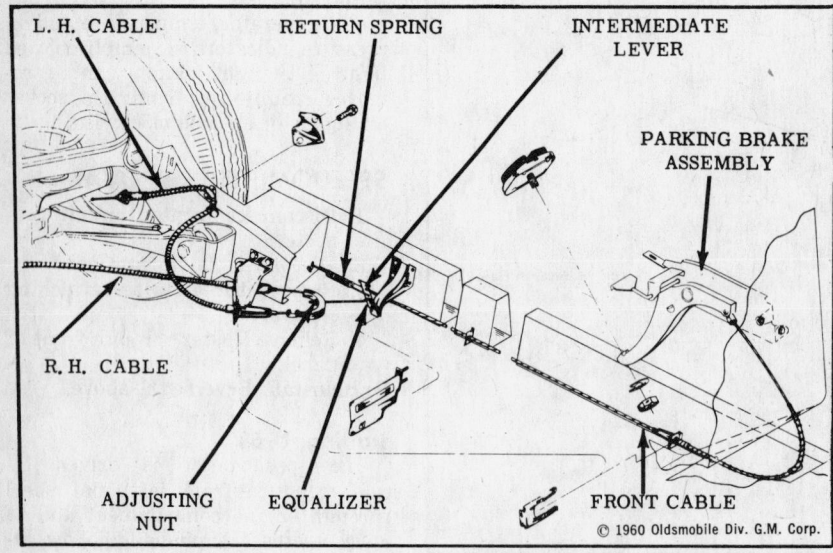

Parking Brake Linkage

458

TIP FUEL PUMP AND
POSITION ARM UNDER
FUEL PUMP ECCENTRIC

© 1962 Oldsmobile Div. G.M. Corp.

Fuel Pump Installation

being worked on. Carter, Holley, Rochester and Stromberg carburetors are covered.

Dash pot adjustment can be found in the general section under the same heading as that of the automatic transmission used in the car, and carburetor section.

REMOVAL OF FUEL PUMPS
All V8 Models

On V8 models the fuel pump is located in front of the right bank of cylinders.

To remove it, disconnect the fuel and vacuum lines, take out the two mounting bolts which hold it to the timing case cover and lift off the pump.

The back bolt can be reached with a universal socket and short extension.

FUEL TANK REMOVAL
1954 Models

Remove the fuel line from the fuel tank and drain the fuel, on models which have a flexible filler pipe disconnect the hose clamp from the flexible pipe. Place a jack under the tank using a block of wood between the jack and the tank so as not to dent the tank in any way.

Remove the strap mounting bolts and let the tank come down slowly until the gage wire is accessible and remove the gage wire. Continue lowering the tank to the floor.

1955 Thru 1958 Models

Disconnect the main feed line from the gas tank on the left front corner at the top. Place a jack under the tank and remove the strap bolts from the back of the tank and slowly lower the tank a sufficient amount to permit removing the gage wire. Let the tank come down on the right side so that the fill neck can be threaded out of the tinware on the left side.

Starting with 1959 Models

Follow above method except disconnect Fuel Line and gauge wire thru trunk compartment.

COOLING SYSTEM
COOLING SYSTEM INFORMATION

Detailed information on cooling system capacity can be found in the Capacities Table of this section.

Information on the water temperature gauge can be found in the unit repair section under the heading: Gages.

Caution: Do not run cold water over the outside of pressurized radiators without first removing the radiator cap. When the cap is left on and the cold water hits the hot radiator the steam in the radiator condenses very rapidly and sometimes collapses the top radiator tank. This is most likely to happen if the coolant level is below normal.

REMOVAL OF RADIATOR CORE

Note: On models with an oil cooler the oil cooler lines will have to be disconnected and capped.

On models with the horns attached to the core brackets, remove the horns.

The radiator core can be removed from all Oldsmobile models without taking off the water pump. Remove the radiator upper baffle plate and radiator hoses, headlight wires, hood cables, etc., and unbolt the core assembly from its support and raise it up out of the car. It may be necessary to rotate the fan blades in order to keep them out of the way.

REMOVAL OF WATER PUMP

Drain the cooling system and slack off the generator and power steering belts, remove the fan and fan pulley, remove bolts which hold the water pump to front of engine and lift off pump.

Only one side of the gasket should be coated with gasket compound when reinstalling.

It is a good idea to dip the bolts in sealer before inserting them into the pump.

THERMOSTATS

On V8 engines the thermostat is located under the water outlet elbow in the water manifold at the front of the block.

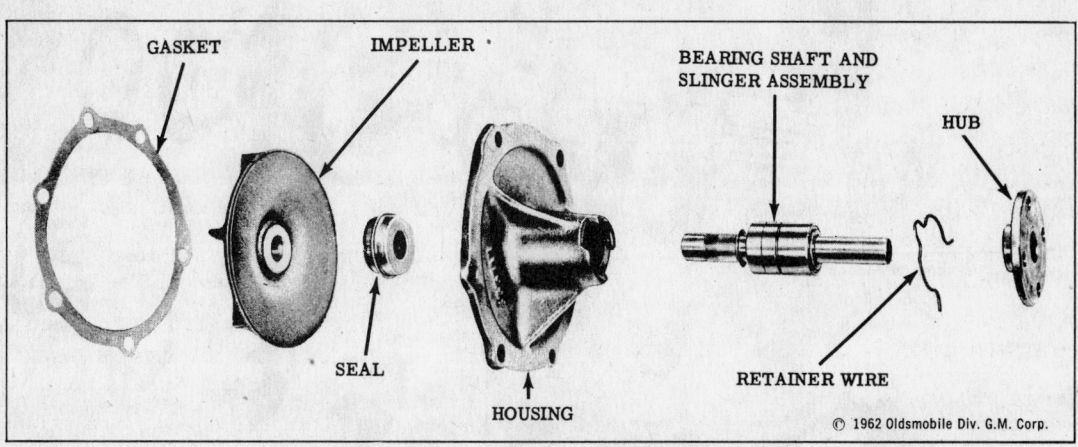

GASKET IMPELLER BEARING SHAFT AND SLINGER ASSEMBLY HUB

SEAL HOUSING RETAINER WIRE

© 1962 Oldsmobile Div. G.M. Corp.

Water Pump Assembly

OLDSMOBILE

ENGINE

REFERENCES

In the specifications tables of this section there are listed all the available facts about the engines. When different size engines are used a note under the General Engine Specifications Table will give an easy means of determining which engine is which.

Where some engines have hydraulic valve lifters and others do not, a means of determining which does and which does not is given in a note under the Tune-up Table.

Valve Information

Methods of trouble shooting hydraulic valve lifters are given in the Unit Repair section under the heading Lifters, Hydraulic Valve.

Detailed information on the valves, the type of valve guide and the location of valve timing marks, can be found in the Valve Specifications Table of this section.

A general discussion of valve clearance and a chart showing how to read pressure and vacuum gauges when using them to diagnose engine troubles will be found in the Unit Repair section under the heading: Tune-up—Ignition — Distributors. Under the same head will be found a chart on engine trouble shooting.

Valve tappet clearance for each engine is given in the Tune-up Specifications Table of this section.

Bearing Information

Detailed information on engine bearings will be found in the Crankshaft Bearing Journal Sizes Table of this section.

Pistons and Pin Information

Detailed information on pistons and piston pins, together with information on piston, rod and crankshaft relationship for assembly, will be found in the Piston and Pin Specifications Table of this section.

Engine Reassembly Information

Engine crankcase capacities are listed in the Capacities Table of this section.

Approved torque wrench readings and head bolt tightening sequences are covered in the Torque Specifications Table of this section.

Information on the engine marking code will be found in the Model Year Identification Table of this section.

Camshaft end play on these engines is controlled by a block and spring loaded plunger.

ENGINE REMOVAL

1. Remove hood, radiator and battery.
2. Disconnect all electrical connections.
3. Disconnect fuel lines and gauge connections.
4. Disconnect exhaust lines at manifolds.
5. Remove carburetor and connect lifting device.
6. Remove the starter and lower flywheel housing and disconnect the flex-plate to flywheel attaching nuts. (Note position of Dowels for reassembly.) On standard transmission remove the transmission to clutch housing bolts.
7. Remove engine mount nuts and lift out engine.

To Reinstall: Reverse the above.

ENGINE MANIFOLDS

INLET MANIFOLD REMOVAL

Remove the carburetor air cleaner and disconnect the upper radiator hose. Take the wires from the spark plugs and disconnect the spark plug wire supports. Take distributor cap and high tension wires off the distributor. Disconnect the throttle, vacuum and gas lines from the carburetor and take off the carburetor. If equipped with power steering, remove pump and bracket. Remove the bolts which hold the intake manifold to the two cylinder heads. The coil can be left on the intake manifold.

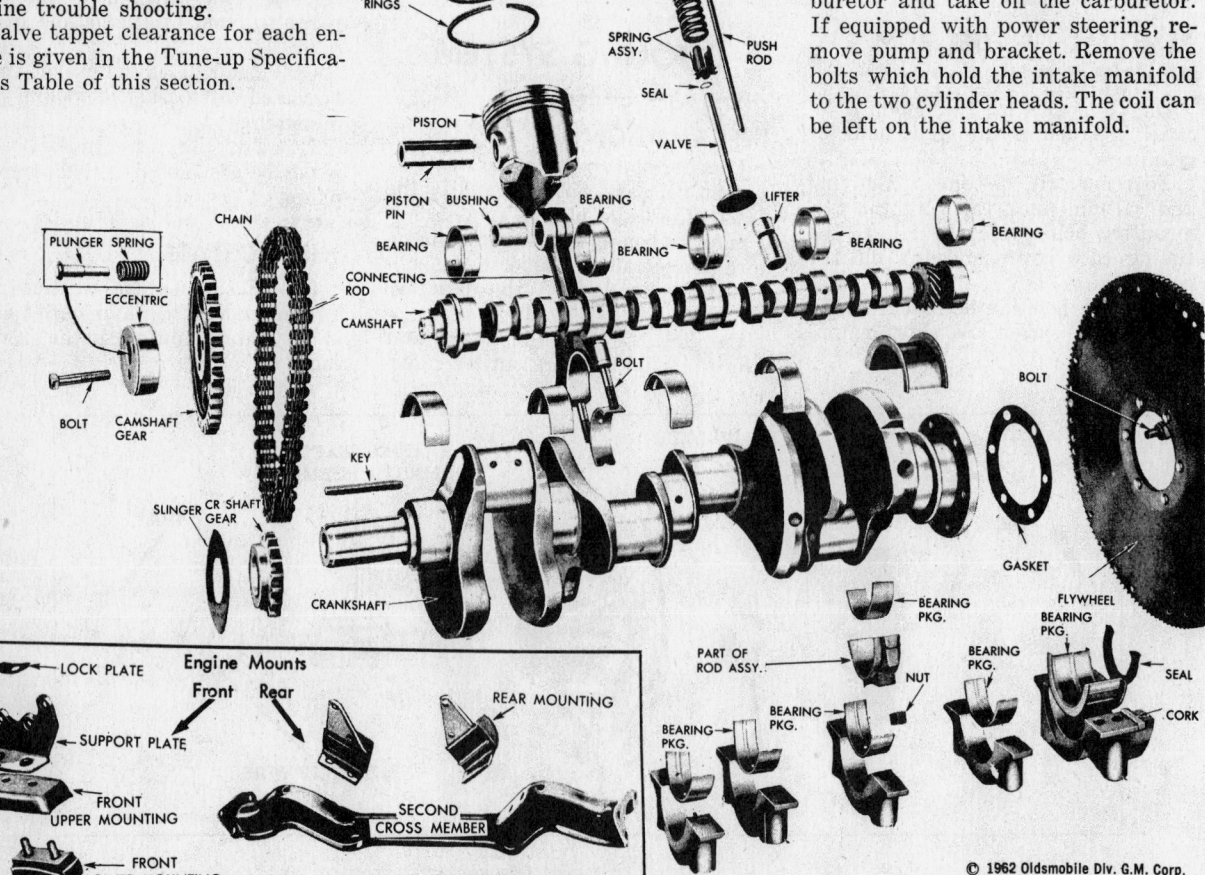

© 1962 Oldsmobile Div. G.M. Corp.

Internal Layout of Rocket V-8 Engine

460

EXHAUST MANIFOLD REMOVAL

All V8 Models

Remove the bolts from the exhaust manifold flanges on both sides and take off the cross over pipe. On the Right Side, remove generator and bracket. Remove the bolts which hold the exhaust manifold to the cylinder head and lift off the exhaust manifolds.

CYLINDER HEAD

ROCKER SHAFT REMOVAL

All V8 Models

Remove the bolts which hold the rocker cover assembly to the cylinder head and lift off the rocker cover.

A little at a time, loosen the bolts which hold the rocker brackets to the cylinder head and lift off the rocker assemblies.

If the push rods are to be pulled up through the cylinder head, be careful to break the seal created by the oil down at the lifter plunger in order to prevent pulling the lifter plunger up with the push rod.

On some models it may be necessary to loosen the heater motor and core assembly in order to pull out the push rods in No. 8 cylinder. Do not bend the push rod in any way in order to force it past the heater motor.

This condition varies with body styles.

ROCKER SHAFT LUBRICATION

Lubrication is supplied to the rocker shafts through a core hole in the cylinder head to the rocker shaft bracket, through the rocker shaft bracket to a hole in the rocker shaft which indexes with the hole in the bracket and thus to each of the rockers.

The bracket through which the oil now passes is doweled to the rocker shaft. It will be found to be the second bracket on the left bank, and the third bracket on the right bank.

CYLINDER HEAD REMOVAL

All Models

1. Drain radiator and cylinder block.
2. Remove air cleaner, carburetor and intake manifold.
3. Remove generator.
4. Disconnect exhaust pipes and remove crankcase vent tube.
5. Remove rocker arm covers.

Note: With air conditioner, remove compressor bracket bolts and tip compressor toward rear. With power

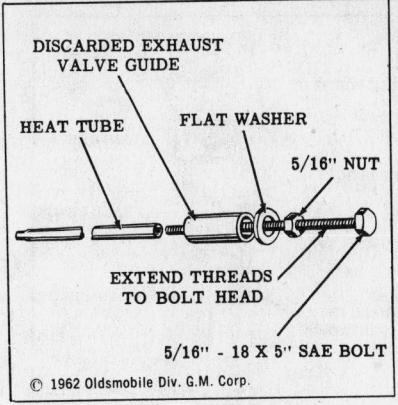

Heat Tube Removing Tool

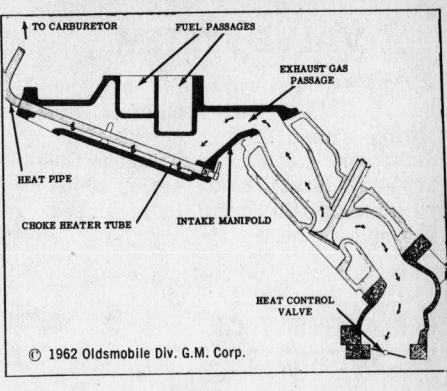

Exhaust Flow (Heat Control Closed)

steering, remove bracket bolts and hold assembly to one side.

6. Remove rocker arm shaft assemblies. Disconnect cylinder head ground strap.

7. Remove push rods. Keep them in proper rotation for installation in original location.

8. Remove head bolts and lift off heads with exhaust manifolds attached.

To Reinstall: Reverse the above. Oldsmobile recommends use of a sealer on both sides of head gaskets and on head bolts. Two guide studs will allow easier location of heads.

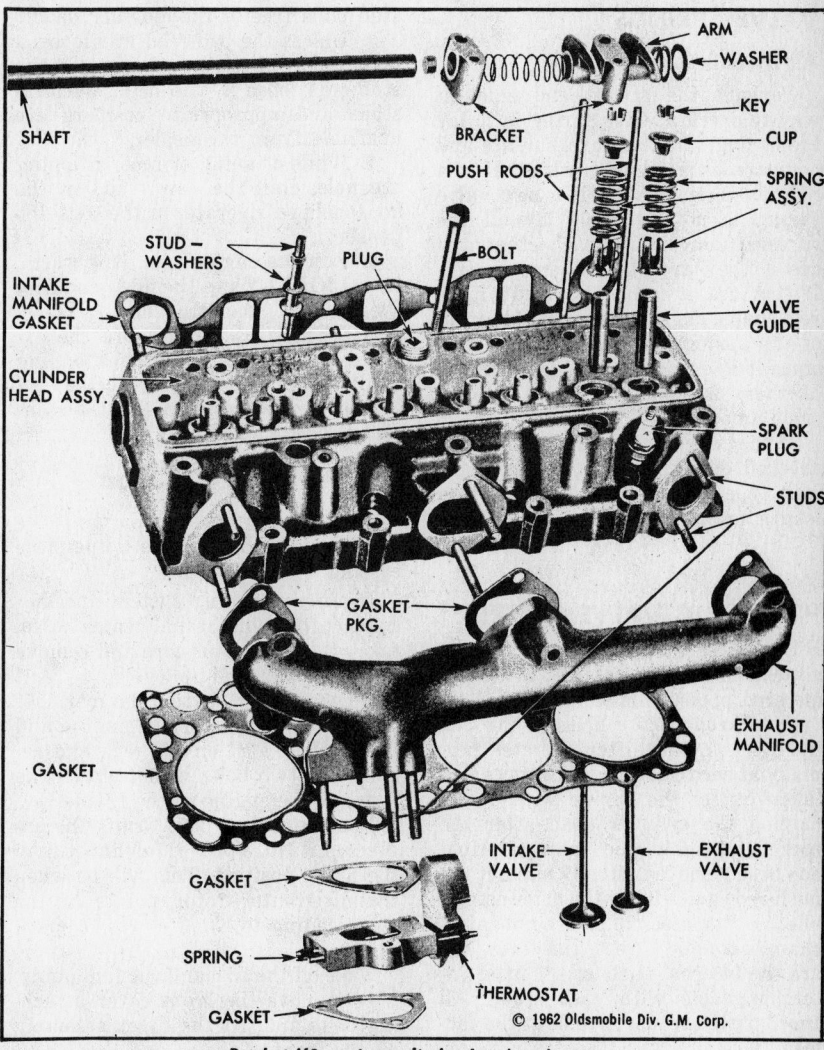

Rocket V8 engine cylinder head and parts

OLDSMOBILE

VALVE SYSTEM

On V8 models work on the cylinder head on the bench, compress the spring with a C type or lever type valve spring compressor, remove the key and release the valve spring which will permit the valve to be pulled through the head.

REPLACEMENT OF VALVE GUIDES

V8 Models

On V-8 models the old valve guide is driven out through the top of the cylinder head and the new one is installed by driving from the top of the cylinder head down toward the firing chamber.

After the new guides have been driven into place immediately try a valve down in the guide to make sure it was not warped or twisted in the driving process. If it is it will be necessary to ream it to the correct size.

VALVE SPRINGS

All Models

Perhaps the easiest and quickest way to check a valve spring is to lay the spring on a flat, level surface and compare its free length with that of a new valve spring. Or if a new valve spring is not available lay all the springs alongside of each other and see if they are all the same length. If they are, it can be assumed with a reasonable degree of accuracy that all of the springs are in good condition since it is extremely unlikely that all of them would collapse exactly the same amount.

If they vary in length they must be checked either on a spring compression type checker or tested for free length against a new valve spring.

HYDRAULIC VALVE LIFTERS

Hydraulic valve lifters are used on all Oldsmobile V-8 engines. Oil under metered pressure is supplied to these valves through core holes in the cylinder block. The lifter operates normally at zero clearance. Lifters can be taken out of the engine without removing the cylinder head after the rocker assembly and inlet manifold has been removed. Simply pull out the push rods and lift out the lifter assemblies. Lifter assemblies are not interchangeable one bore to the other, nor are the internal parts of the lifter interchangeable with each other. All these parts are selective fit at the factory.

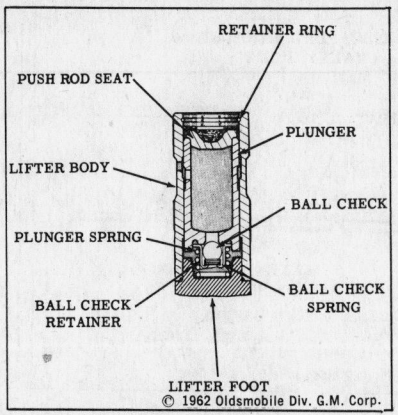

RETAINER RING
PUSH ROD SEAT
LIFTER BODY
PLUNGER
PLUNGER SPRING
BALL CHECK
BALL CHECK SPRING
BALL CHECK RETAINER
LIFTER FOOT
© 1962 Oldsmobile Div. G.M. Corp.

Hydraulic Valve Lifter

⏻ CHILTON TIME-SAVER

Field experience indicates the need for quick replacement data on worn, loose or thread damaged valve rocker arm studs.

1. Place a thin walled socket and a flat washer over the bad stud.
2. Turn the stud nut on until the stud pulls free of the cylinder head.
3. Unless the bad stud was loose, a standard stud can be replaced. If the stud was loose in the head, oversize studs and appropriate reamers are available from the dealer.
4. While cleaning or reconditioning the hole, chill the new stud (in the household refrigerator or the soda dispenser).
5. Run the engine until it is warm, then LIGHTLY tap the new stud into the cylinder head stud hole.

NOTE: Carefully measure the exposed length of the corresponding studs. If the new stud is inserted to a greater depth than necessary, a ruined head may result.

TIMING CASE

The timing case cover and the water pump housing are a one-piece casting.

Drain the cooling system and disconnect the radiator and heater hoses, take off the radiator core and remove the fan blades and pulley.

Remove the vibration damper.

Place a jack under the engine and take a light load on the jack and remove the two bolts which attach the front of the engine to the frame.

Remove the oil pan. Crank the engine until No. 3 or No. 7 cylinder is in the firing position. This will be when the distributor rotor points to the wire leading to No. 3 or No. 7 spark plug.

Take off the fuel and vacuum pump. Now remove the front cover attaching bolts and lift the cover assembly off the front of the engine.

VALVE TIMING PROCEDURE

On all Oldsmobile models a chain is used to drive the camshaft. The construction is such that the chain can be worn even badly without seriously affecting the valve timing. If the chain is worn badly enough that the timing jumps or it becomes necessary to replace either the chain or the sprockets or both, proceed as follows:

Remove the timing case cover and take off the camshaft gear.

<u>Note:</u> The fuel pump operating cam is bolted to the front of the camshaft sprocket and the sprocket is located to the camshaft by means of a dowel.

Remove the timing chain and the camshaft sprocket and if the crankshaft sprocket is to be replaced remove it also at this time.

Reinstall the crank sprocket being careful to start it with the keyway in perfect alignment since it is rather difficult to correct for misalignment after the gear has been started on the shaft. Turn the timing mark on the crankshaft gear until it points directly toward the center of the camshaft. Mount the timing chain over the camshaft gear and start the camshaft gear up on to its shaft with the timing marks nearest each other and in line between the shaft centers. Rotate the camshaft sufficient to align the shaft with the new gear.

A dowel pin is used for alignment. Secure the camshaft gear and check to see that the mark on the crank sprocket and the mark on the cam sprocket are nearest each other in line between shaft centers. Valves timed in this manner are correct regardless of which piston is at top center. It may be necessary, however, to retime the ignition since there is a possibility it will be 180 degrees out of position.

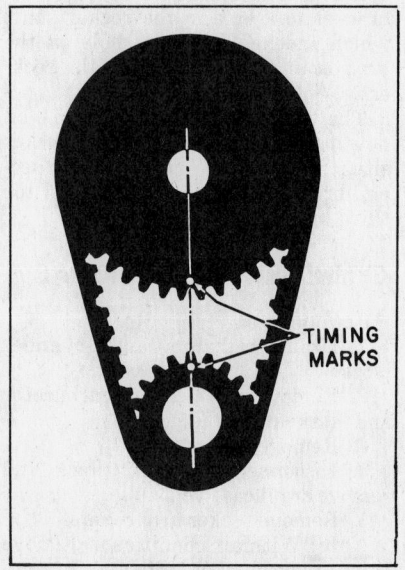

TIMING MARKS

Timing chain and sprockets—V-8 models

ENGINE LUBRICATION

ENGINE OIL PAN REMOVAL

All V8

Remove the engine side splash pans on models so equipped, remove starting motor and the exhaust cross-over pipe, detach and lower the idler arm from the frame for easy clearance. The oil pan may then be unbolted.

Models with dual exhaust do not have a cross-over pipe.

On later models it is necessary to remove two front engine mount nuts and raise front of engine. Do not allow engine to contact cowl. Wood blocks may be inserted between exhaust manifolds and front crossmember for support.

OIL FILTER REMOVAL

1955 Thru 1957

The oil filter is located under the right bank of cylinders toward the back and is accessible from underneath the car.

Remove the one bolt which holds the oil filter can in place, let the oil drain out and then take the bolt all the way out and lift off the oil filter can and element.

Starting with 1958

A full flow disposable filter is used, no tools are required for change.

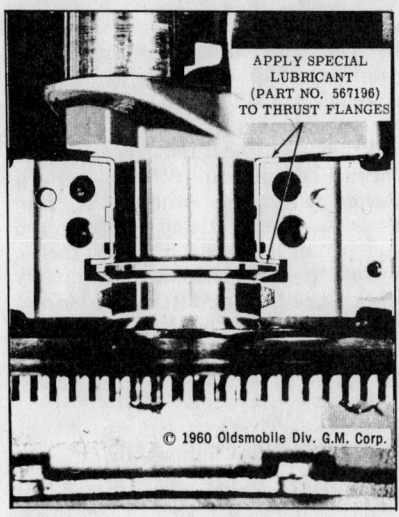

APPLY SPECIAL LUBRICANT (PART NO. 567196) TO THRUST FLANGES

© 1960 Oldsmobile Div. G.M. Corp.

Rear Main Bearing

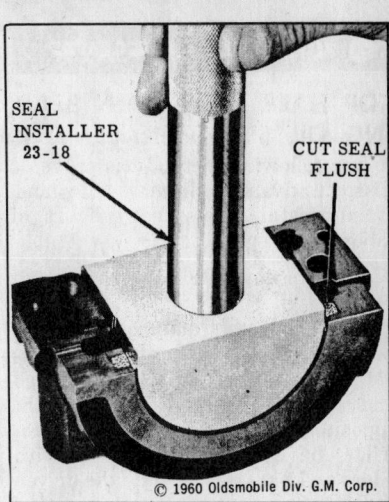

SEAL INSTALLER 23-18

CUT SEAL FLUSH

© 1960 Oldsmobile Div. G.M. Corp.

Installing Oil Seal

REAR MAIN BEARING OIL SEAL

A packing type rear main bearing oil seal is used in all models of Oldsmobile. *To replace the upper half of this seal, the factory recommends the removal of the engine and crankshaft.* The lower half of the seal may be replaced, however, by removing the rear main bearing cap, take out the old packing and install new packing, permitting it to protrude slightly from the bearing cap. Bolt the bearing cap up into place and immediately remove it to determine if the extended packing has riveted over, preventing the cap from seating properly. If it has, trim off the riveted over portion only and rebolt the cap. Repeat this operation until the cap seats firmly without riveting over the protruding portion of the oil seal. The reason this is done is so that the lower oil seal will have a tendency to compress the upper oil seal, forcing it to a tighter fit around the upper half of the crankshaft. In this way it is frequently possible to prevent an oil leak in the upper half of the rear main bearing packing without actually replacing the packing.

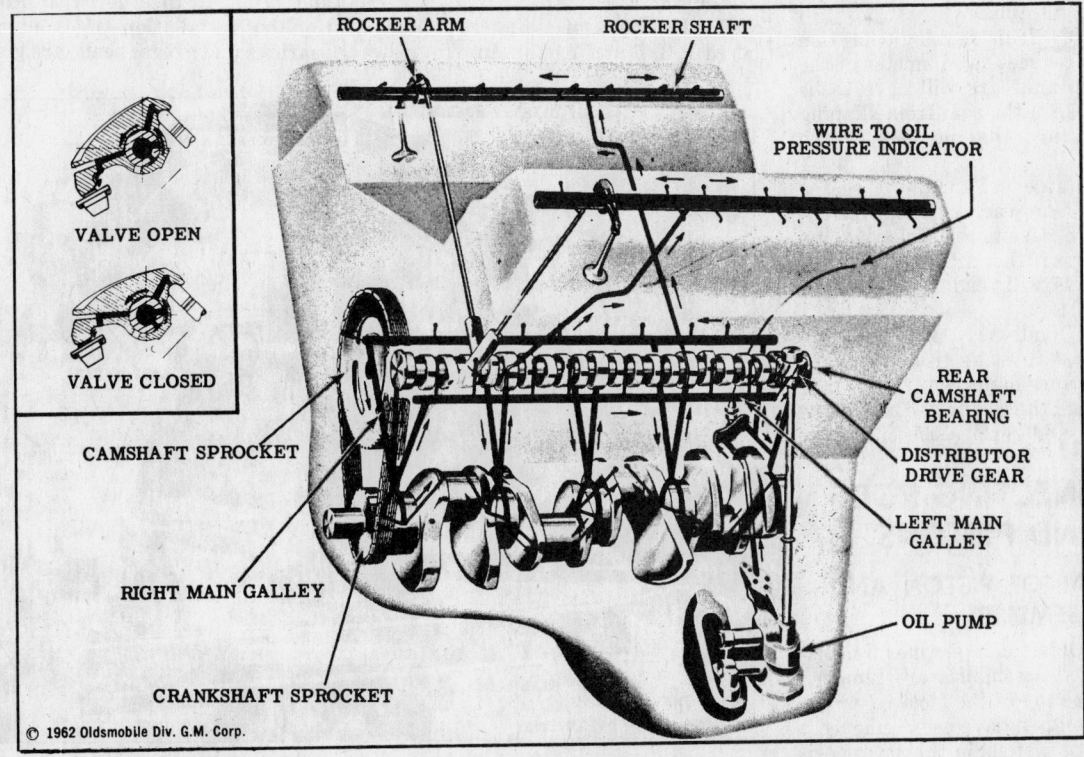

ROCKER ARM   ROCKER SHAFT

WIRE TO OIL PRESSURE INDICATOR

VALVE OPEN

VALVE CLOSED

REAR CAMSHAFT BEARING

DISTRIBUTOR DRIVE GEAR

LEFT MAIN GALLEY

CAMSHAFT SPROCKET

RIGHT MAIN GALLEY

CRANKSHAFT SPROCKET

OIL PUMP

© 1962 Oldsmobile Div. G.M. Corp.

Engine lubrication.

OLDSMOBILE

⏻ **CHILTON TIME-SAVER**

TOP HALF, REAR MAIN BEARING OIL SEAL REPLACEMENT

The following method has proven a distinct advantage in most cases and, if successful, saves many hours of labor.

1. Drain engine oil and remove oil pan.
2. Remove rear main bearing cap.
3. With a 6" length of 3/16" brazing rod, drive up on either exposed end of the top half oil seal. When the opposite end of the seal starts to protrude, have a helper grasp it with pliers and pull gently while the driven end is being tapped. It is surprising how easily most of these seals can be removed by this method.

TO INSTALL THE NEW WOVEN FABRIC TYPE SEAL:

1. Obtain a 12" piece of copper wire (about the same gauge as that used in the strands of an insulated battery cable).
2. Thread one strand of this wire thru the new seal, about ½" from the end, bend back and make secure.
3. Thoroughly saturate the new seal with engine oil.
4. Push the copper wire up thru the oil seal groove until it comes down on the opposite side of the bearing.
5. Pull (with pliers) on the protruding copper wire while the crankshaft is being turned and the new seal is slowly fed into place.
   CAUTION: This snaking operation slightly reduces the diameter of the new seal and care will have to be used to keep the seal from slipping too far thru the top half of the bearing.
6. When an equal amount of seal is extending from each side, cut off the copper wire close to the seal and tamp both ends of the seal up into the groove (this will tend to expand the seal again).
   NOTE: Don't worry about the copper wire left in the groove, it is too soft to cause damage.
7. Replace the seal in the cap in the usual way and replace the oil pan.

CONNECTING RODS AND PISTONS

REMOVAL OF PISTON AND ROD ASSEMBLIES

On all Oldsmobile engines the piston and rod assemblies are removed through the top of the block after the head and oil pan have been removed. Select the pistons in the down position and, using a ridge reamer cut out the ring ridge from the top of the cylinder. If a ridge reamer is not available a good bearing scraper will cut the ridge.

From underneath the car remove the rod bearing cap from the rod and piston assemblies where the ring ridge has been cut and push the rod and piston assembly up through the top of the block and out. Immediately replace the bearing cap on the bottom of the rod so that neither the bearing nor the bearing nuts become lost or damaged. Repeat on the rest of the cylinders.

INSPECT PISTONS AND CYLINDER BORES

Inspect the thrust surface of the piston for scratches and scores. Do not confuse the normal wear pattern with scratches.

If scoring or scratching is observed on the piston, immediately inspect the cylinder wall to see whether or not there are corresponding marks on the wall.

If there are, the cylinder will have to be rebored or refinished.

Scratches on the piston which are not transferred to the cylinder wall can be removed by lightly sanding the piston smooth.

ASSEMBLING PISTON TO CONNECTING ROD

V-8 Engines

The left bank of cylinders is numbered 1, 3, 5 and 7, starting from the

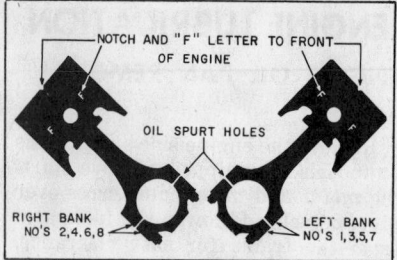

Relation of piston to connecting rod V8 Engines

front. The right bank of cylinders is numbered 2, 4, 6 and 8. Pistons are stamped with the letter "F" just alongside the wrist pin hole and the piston is assembled to the connecting rod as follows: on the right bank of pistons (2, 4, 6, 8) the letter "F" on the piston is assembled to the same side as the machined boss on the connecting rod (at the lower bearing).

On the left bank of cylinders (1, 3, 5, 7) the letter "F" on the piston is mounted to the connecting rod on the side opposite to the boss at the big end of the rod. The oil spit holes in the connecting rods should face the camshaft on both banks of the engine while the letter "F" on the piston should face to the front.

FRONT SUSPENSION

REFERENCES

General instructions covering the front suspension and how to repair and adjust it, together with information on installation of front wheel bearings and grease seals, are given in

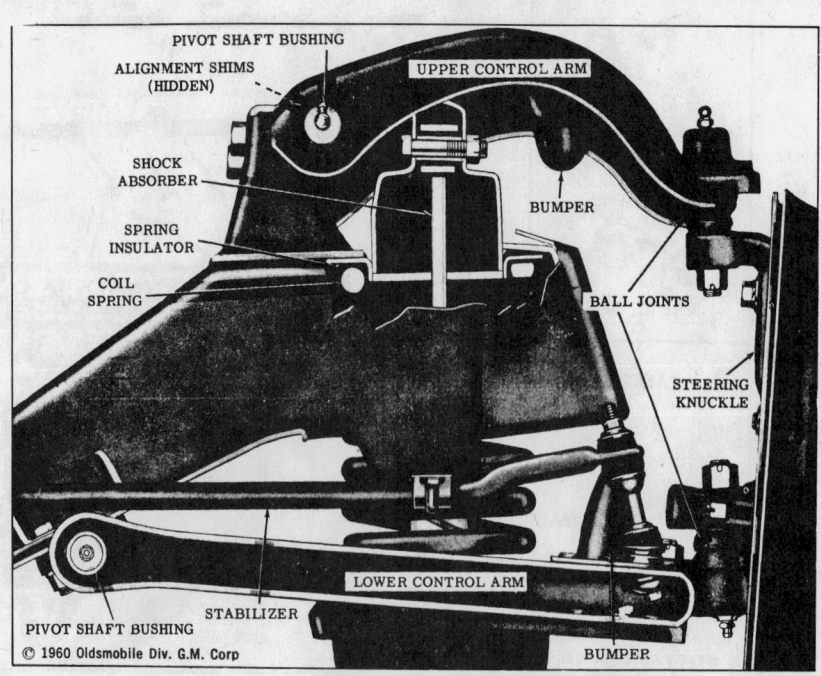

Ball Joint Front Suspension

the Unit Repair section under the heading: Suspension, Front Repair.

Definitions of the points of steering geometry are covered in the Unit Repair section under the heading: Suspension, Front Align. This article also covers trouble shooting front end geometry and irregular tire wear.

Figures covering the caster, camber, toe-in, king pin inclination and turning radius can be found in the Front Wheel Alignment Table of this section.

Overall length, brake cylinder and tire size figures can be found in the General Chassis and Brake Specifications Table at the start of this section.

FRONT SPRING REMOVAL

1. Raise front of car and place floor stands under frame.
2. Remove wheel.
3. Disconnect stabilizer link from control arm.
4. Remove shock absorber.
5. With jack under control arm between spring seat and ball joint, raise to support lower control arm.
6. Disconnect lower arm ball joint from knuckle. Tool J-8806 will simplify this job.
7. Slowly lower jack until spring is fully extended, then remove spring. **Do not** interchange right and left springs.

To Reinstall:

1. Tape insulator to top of spring in at least six places. Top of spring has flat coil.
2. While holding spring and insulator against pilot in frame crossmember, tilt spring so it will pilot in lower arm. Rotate spring so bottom coil will index edge of hole in control arm seat. Do not cover any portion of hole.
3. While placing jack between ball joint and spring seat install chain, upper control arm to jack base.
4. Raise jack and control arm until the ball joint is in steering knuckle. Install nut and tighten to 40 ft. lbs. minimum. Tighten further if needed to install cotter pin.
5. Install shock absorber, connect stabilizer link and install wheel. Lower car to floor.

STEERING WHEEL AND HORN BUTTON

1954 De Luxe Models

The horn button is held in by a bayonet type connection. To remove, place the hand squarely on the horn button, press firmly and turn slightly in a counterclockwise direction which will release the horn button.

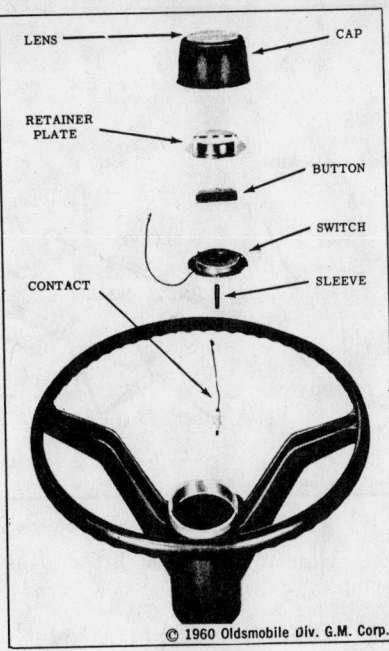

Starting 1961 Standard Steering Wheel

1955 De Luxe Wheels

There are two spring clips on the ends of the horn button which engage the horn ring hub. They are accessible from the under side of the wheel. Relieve the spring pressure on the clips and lift up the horn button from its seat.

1955 Standard Models

On standard models the horn button is simply pried up.

Starting with 1956

Pry up the center medallion and remove the nut which holds the steering wheel in place. This also holds the horn blowing ring contacts.

DeLuxe horn ring caps are retained to the horn ring hub by a screw which is accessible from underneath the cap.

STEERING WHEEL REMOVAL

On all Oldsmobile models it is necessary to use a puller to take off the steering wheel.

MANUAL STEERING GEAR

REFERENCES

Instructions covering the overhaul of the steering gear will be found in the Unit Repair section under the heading: Steering, Manual.

REMOVAL

1954 Thru 1956 Models

Remove the steering wheel and

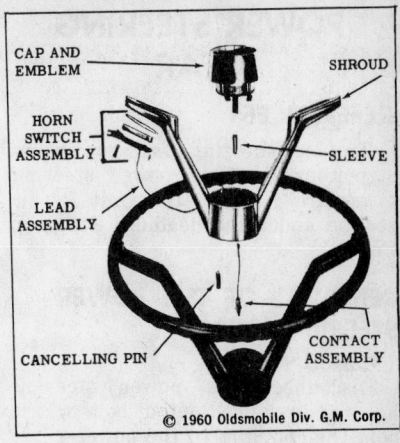

Starting 1961 Deluxe Steering Wheel

turn back the floor mat, take off the mast jacket cover plate attaching screws. Loosen the upper and lower mast jacket clamps. Remove the pitman arm from the bottom of the gear (on some cars it will be necessary to take off the engine splash pan to do this).

Take off the bolts which mount the steering gear housing to the frame.

The gear is removed downwards out of the mast jacket.

1957 Thru 1963 Models

Remove the steering wheel assembly, turn back the floor mat and remove the mast jacket cover plate attaching screws. Take out the upper mast jacket clamps and disconnect the shift linkage from the lower end of the mast jacket.

Pull the pitman arm off the bottom of the steering gear and take out the bolts which hold the steering gear to the frame. Remove the gear assembly and mast jacket by pulling it up thru the floor.

To get the mast jacket off the gear, loosen the lower clamp and simply slide it off.

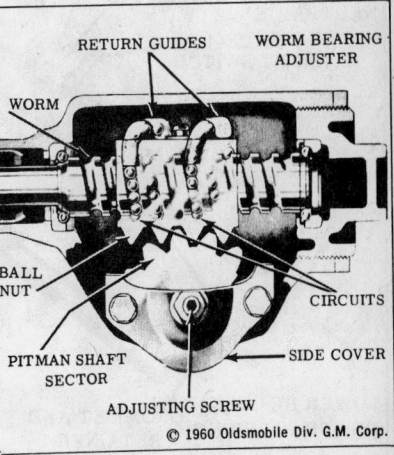

Manual Steering Gear

POWER STEERING GEAR

REFERENCES

Trouble shooting and repair instructions covering power steering gears are given in the Unit Repair section under the heading: Steering, Power.

REMOVAL OF THE POWER STEERING GEAR

1958-63 Models

Disconnect the power steering hoses and remove the four bolts which hold the coupling to the power gear. Remove the nut from the cross shaft and pull off the pitman arm.

From underneath the vehicle, remove the bolts which hold the power gear assembly to the frame and let the power gear come down through the bottom.

REMOVAL OF POWER STEERING PUMP

Remove and cap the two hoses which run through the pump, loosen the clamp bolts so that the pump can be slid along its adjusting slot and take the belt off. Remove the three bolts which hold the pump bracket to

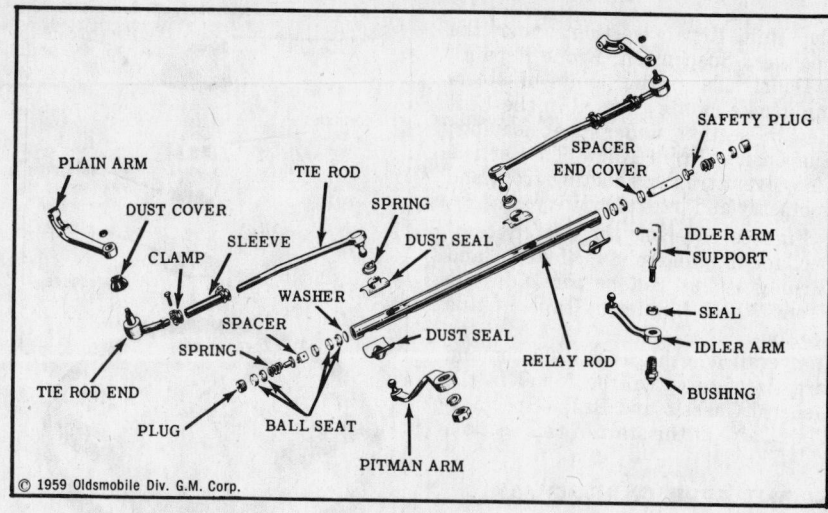

Steering Linkage

the cylinder heads and lift off the pump.

REPLACEMENT OF PITMAN SHAFT SEALS WITH POWER STEERING GEAR IN PLACE IN CAR

Disconnect pitman arm from pitman shaft. Clean end of pitman shaft and housing. Tape the splines of the pitman shaft to keep them from cut-

ting the seal. Use only one layer of tape. Too much tape will prevent passage of the seal. Using lock ring pliers remove the seal retaining ring.

Start the engine and turn the steering wheel to the right so that the oil pressure in the housing will force the seals out. Catch the seal and the oil in a container. Turn on the engine when the two seals are out.

This method of seal removal eliminates the possible scoring of the seal seats while attempting to pry them out.

Inspect the two old seals for damage to the rubber covering on the outside diameter. If it seems scored or scratched inspect the housing for burrs, etc. and remove them before installing the new seals.

Lubricate the two new seals with petroleum jelly. Put the one with a single lip in first, then put in a washer, drive seal in far enough to permit installation of double lip seal, washer and the seal retaining ring. The first seal is not supposed to bottom in its counterbore.

Fill reservoir to proper level, start engine, turn wheel to right and check for leaks.

Remove the tape and reinstall the pitman arm. Tighten nut to 90-110 ft. lbs.

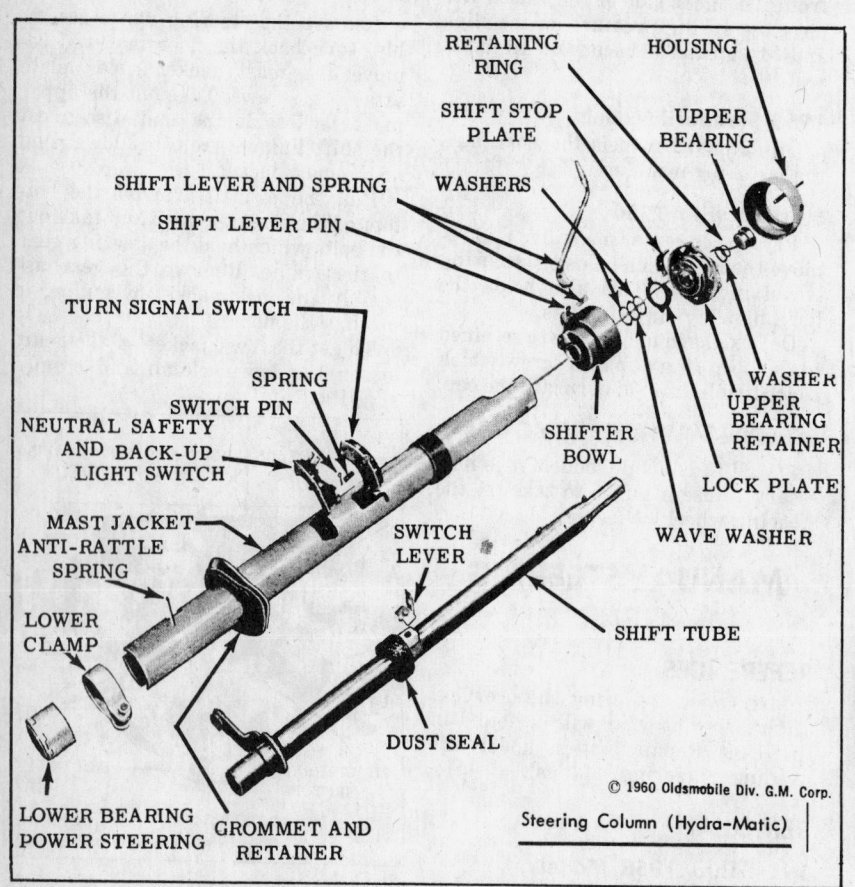

1959-63 Steering column shown—typical 1957-58

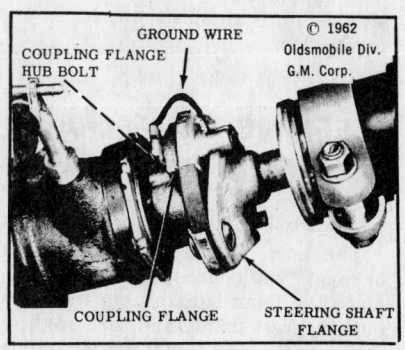

Alignment marks—typical 1956 thru 63

When installing a new belt the tension should be set so that the pulley will slip in the belt when 40-45 ft. lbs. torque is applied to pulley nut. With a used belt the torque should be 30-35 ft. lbs.

CLUTCH ASSEMBLY

CLUTCH PEDAL ADJUSTMENT

The clutch pedal should be adjusted so that there is from one-half to three-quarter inch free play at the clutch pedal before the throwout bearing engages the clutch fingers. This adjustment is made under the car at the clutch adjustable rod just in front of the throwout fork. Loosen the jam nut and turn the adjusting screw until the desired clearance is obtained and then tighten the jam nut.

REMOVAL OF CLUTCH FROM CAR

Remove the transmission assembly and take out the throwout bearing sleeve from the back of the clutch housing. Remove the clutch return spring and disconnect the clutch linkage at the yoke. Take out the left engine filler plate, the breather pipe and the lower flywheel housing bolts. Support the back of the engine and remove the rear engine mounting bolts at the clutch housing. Take a load on

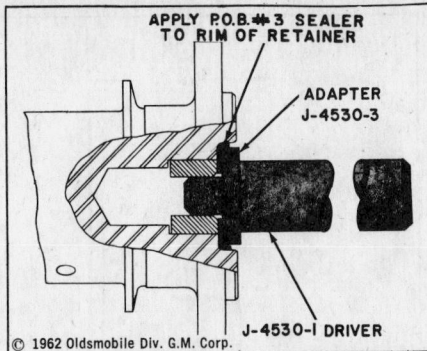

APPLY P.O.B. #3 SEALER TO RIM OF RETAINER

ADAPTER J-4530-3

J-4530-I DRIVER

© 1962 Oldsmobile Div. G.M. Corp.

Pilot Bearing Retainer Installation

the jack and remove the frame crossmember which supports that housing.

Remove the bolts which secure the clutch housing to the flywheel housing and take down the clutch housing.

Now take out a little at a time the bolts which hold the clutch cover to the flywheel. **Note:** Always mark the clutch cover and the flywheel so that the clutch can be reassembled to the position from which it was removed.

Install in reverse order.

STANDARD TRANSMISSION

REFERENCES

Transmission refill capacities will be found in the Capacities Table of this section.

Trouble shooting and repair of overdrive units are covered in the General Section under the heading: Transmission—Overdrive.

REMOVAL OF TRANSMISSION

All Models Thru 1956 and 1961-63

Drain the transmission and disconnect the shift levers and speedometer cable. Split the rear universal joint and slide the front universal joint off the back of the transmission. Remove the two upper bolts which hold the transmission to the clutch housing and replace with two long pilot studs.

Remove the two lower bolts and then slide the transmission assembly back off the two long pilot studs. The studs are used to prevent damaging the main drive gear or clutch plate.

1957 Thru 1960

Drain the transmission and disconnect the control rods and the speedometer cable at the transmission. At the center bearing of the driveshaft mark the position of the center bearing in relation to the frame so that it can be replaced in that position. Disconnect the front and rear companion flanges at the center bearing, support the frame attaching bolts and slide the propeller shaft assembly out of the frame.

Remove the two upper transmission to clutch housing bolts and replace them with two long pilot studs.

CLUTCH RING RING
WASHER WASHER GEAR, 1st & reverse RING SPACER
BEARING GEAR RING
RING RING
WASHER RING GEAR (clutch gear)
RETAINER
WASHER SHAFT, (main) RING
SHAFT WASHER WASHER
BEARING WASHER BEARING GEAR, drive
RETAINER BEARING SPACER COUNTERSHAFT BEARING
WASHER, countershaft gear thrust WASHER WASHER
WASHER WASHER
BEARING
WASHER CAP, breather SEAL
BUSHING GEAR SHAFT SCREW BUSHING
GEAR WASHER BUSHING
BEARING RETAINER, rear bearing
GASKET BOLT
PIN INTERLOCK GEAR ASSY., speedometer
CASE, transmission SCREW SHAFT SCREW, shifter yoke
SCREW LEVER BALL
PLUG, expansion SPRING YOKE, 1st & reverse shifter
PLUG, drain SCREW
SCREW, shifter yoke SPRING, shift lever
RETAINER YOKE EXTENSION, return spring
SHAFT, 1st & reverse shifter LEVER
SHAFT, selector shift SEAL WASHER, shift lever
STEEL BALL LEVER BOLT, shift lever
SPRING, shifter shaft poppet ball PIN SHAFT & LEVER
© 1962 Oldsmobile Div. G.M. Corp. LEVER, gear shift selector outer →

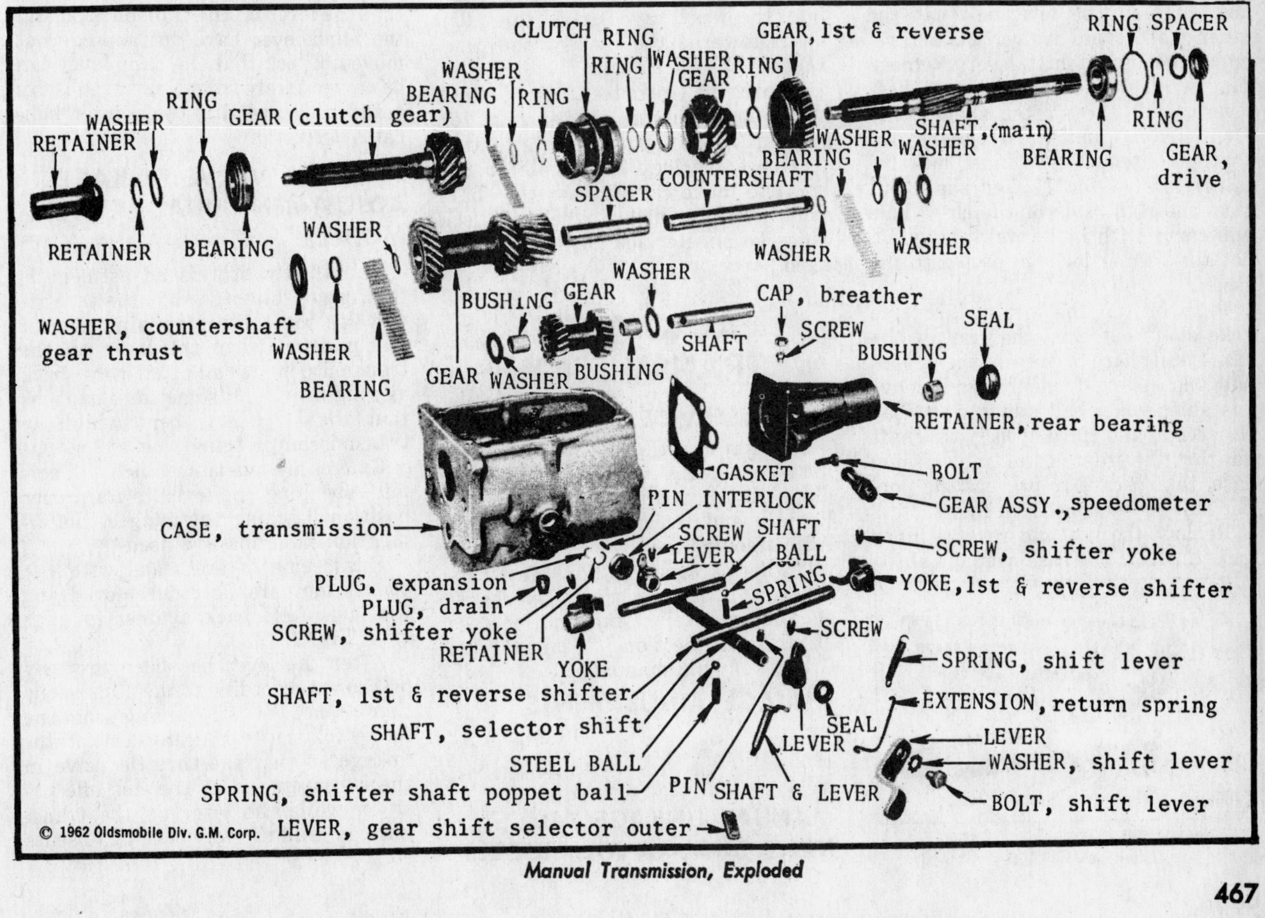

Manual Transmission, Exploded

Remove the two lower bolts and then slide the transmission assembly back along the two pilot studs so as not to spring the main driveshaft or the clutch plate.

Reassemble in reverse order.

DISASSEMBLY OF SYNCHRO-MESH TRANSMISSION

On the bench, remove the cover from the top of the transmission. A puller will be needed to remove the universal joint companion flange from the back of the transmission shaft.

Remove the speedometer driven gear, remove the rear bearing retainer and gasket. Remove the set screws from the two shifter yokes and move the mainshaft rearward until the rear bearing clears the case.

Remove the synchronizer clutch from the mainshaft and take out the snap ring holding the second speed gear onto the mainshaft. Rotate the wire ring in the snap ring groove until the ring gap lines up with the key on the second speed thrust washer.

Remove the thrust washer, the second speed gear, and the rear thrust washer from the mainshaft. Take off the low and reverse gear retaining snap ring and slide these gears off the mainshaft. Now pull the mainshaft out of the rear of the case.

Loosen the outer shift lever bolt and position the lever so that the inner shaft levers are vertical and remove the outer shift lever. Remove the set screws from the inner shaft levers. Pull the shifter shaft away from second and third speed yoke shaft and remove the inner lock retainer. Drive the shifter shaft out thru the right side of the case. This will carry with it the welch plug. Do not allow inner locks to drop into the case.

Push or tap the low and reverse yoke shaft out thru the rear of the case taking care to prevent the poppet ball and spring from flying. Remove the shift yoke, ball and spring. Tap the second and third speed yoke shaft out thru the front of the transmission case, taking care to prevent the poppet ball and spring from flying.

Remove the low and reverse inner lock pin from the case near the shift-

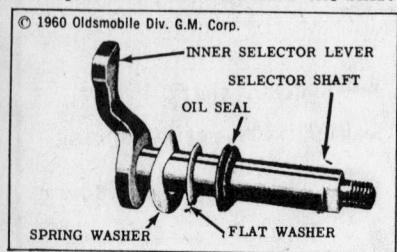

© 1960 Oldsmobile Div. G.M. Corp.

INNER SELECTOR LEVER
SELECTOR SHAFT
OIL SEAL
SPRING WASHER
FLAT WASHER

Inner Selector Lever and Shaft

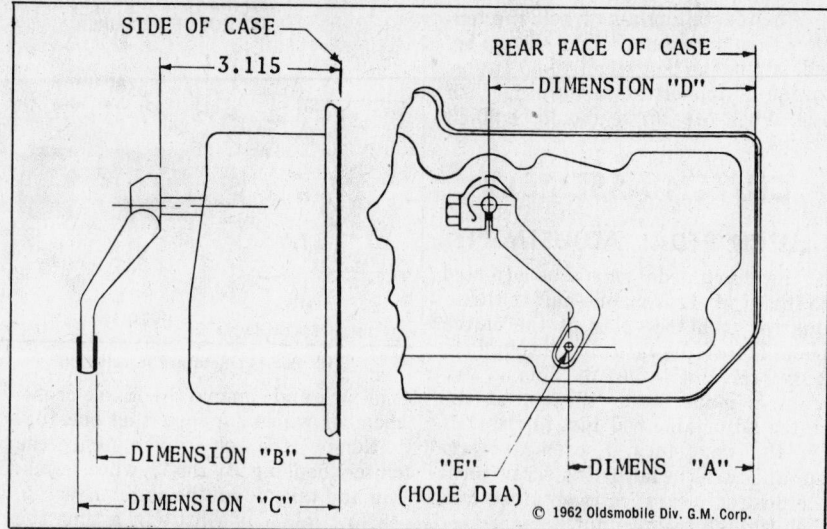

SIDE OF CASE — 3.115

REAR FACE OF CASE — DIMENSION "D"

DIMENSION "B"
DIMENSION "C"
"E" (HOLE DIA)
DIMENS "A"

© 1962 Oldsmobile Div. G.M. Corp.

Fig. 1—Location of Throttle Lever on Dual- Range Hydramatic. The Dimension "A" is measured with the Lever against its stop

er shaft seal. Drive the counterset gear shaft lock pin into the shaft. Drive the countershaft out thru the rear end of the case. Remove the snap ring from the main drive gear bearing outer race and tap the drive gear and bearing assembly towards the rear of the case. Lift it out. Now remove the cluster gear assembly from the case. Remove the transmission outer-selector lever and then remove the inner selector shaft and lever assembly. Drive the idler shaft lock pin into the shaft and drive the idler shaft towards the rear of the case. Lift out the idler gears.

Examine all gear teeth for pits and scores and examine all bearings for roughness. Pay particular attention to where the lock rings go into the shaft to make certain that the shaft isn't broken or nicked where the lock rings go on. Replace any or all damaged parts.

AUTOMATIC TRANSMISSION

QUICK SERVICE INFORMATION

When automatic transmission trouble is reported, a road test and careful diagnosis is in order. "Transmission Remove and Replace" and "Linkage Adjustments" are covered here in the following paragraphs. For "Test Procedures," "Transmission Overhaul" and other detailed information, see "Unit Repair Section," "Transmission Group" of this manual.

LINKAGE ADJUSTMENTS

1954	6½ in.
1955	6¾ in.

MANUAL LINKAGE ADJUSTMENT DUAL-RANGE MODELS

Disconnect the rod running from the thicker (the inner) of the two levers on the left side of the transmission to the lower shift lever on the steering column.

Set the hand lever in Neutral (N) position.

Move the thickest lever on the transmission as far forward as possible. (This will be Neutral position.)

Adjust the length of the rod which was disconnected from the lower shift lever, and reconnect it to the lever; so that the lever on the transmission and the hand lever have not and are not moved. Check that the hand lever can be moved freely from Neutral to Drive 4 and back and that the pointer indicates correctly.

THROTTLE VALVE LINKAGE ADJUSTMENT DUAL-RANGE MODELS

The theory of this adjustment is to arrange things so that the throttle valve in the carburetor is at the hot idle position when the lever on the transmission is all the way back against its stop. It sometimes happens that the lever gets bent while the transmission is being worked on.

Gauges are available which will permit rebending the lever to its proper position. Lacking the gauges, the dimension table may be used.

Measurements are made with the connecting throttle rod removed and the lever held back against its rear stop. Fig. 1.

After the lever has been properly positioned according to the dimensions then adjust the rod running from the lever to the carburetor-accelerator linkage so that the throttle valve in the carburetor is at the hot idle position while the lever on the transmission is all the way back against its stop.

LINKAGE, STARTING WITH 1956 PRODUCTION

Constant change dictates the use of typical adjustments and illustrations to be used in the linkage area.

Linkage adjustments must be made in the following order, with the carburetor throttle valves closed and the choke lever blocked open.

THROTTLE LINKAGE ADJUSTMENTS

1. Adjust T.V. Lever Position at Transmission (Fig. 2)

A. Raise car and disconnect the lower T.V. Rod "C" from T.V. lever ("A") at transmission.

B. Place T.V. lever gauge J-8497 against machined surface of rear of transmission case. While holding lever at rear of its travel, align the gauge rod with the hole in the T.V. lever, (Fig. 3.).

C. If gauge rod does not align with the T.V. lever hole, bend the lever with tool number, J-6373 or J-6373-01, recheck and hook-up T.V. rod to lever.

D. Car may now be lowered.

2. Adjust Carburetor Rod, Throttle Lever to Auxiliary Bellcrank (B, Fig. 2)

Measure clearance as shown in (Fig. 4). (Four Barrel) or Fig. 4a

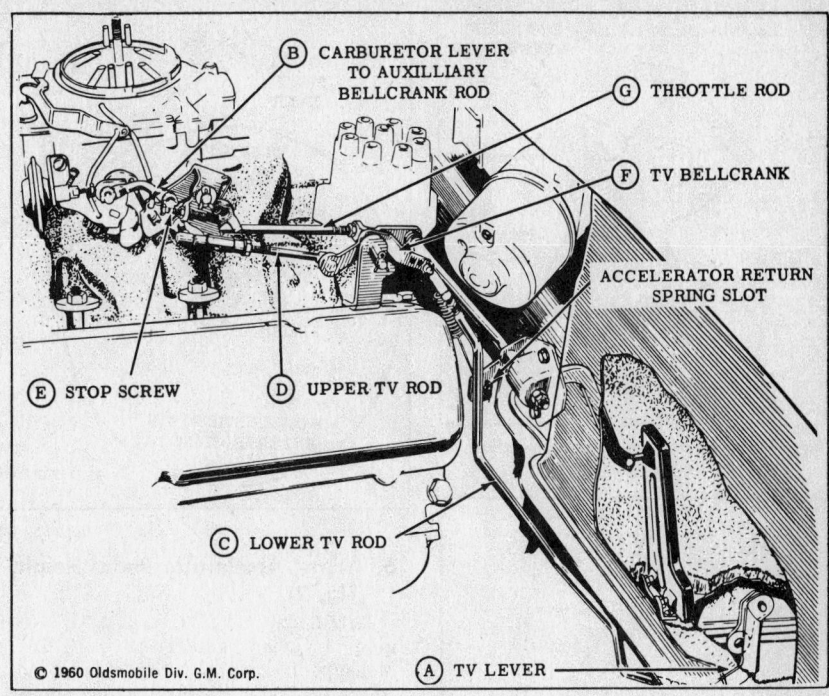

Fig. 2—T.V. Adjustment.

(Two Barrel) with feeler gauge. To obtain proper clearance of .020" to .040" remove the rod and bend. Reinstall rod and recheck clearance.

3. Adjust Lower T.V. Rod (C, Fig. 2)

A. Loosen jam nut on lower T.V. rod and remove both rods from bellcrank "F."

B. With both bellcrank and transmission lower T.V. rod held against their rearward stops, adjust lower T.V. rod clevis so that the clevis pin will enter freely into the holes of the clevis and bellcrank (Fig. 5).

C. Install cotter pin and lock jam nut on lower T.V. rod.

4. Adjust Upper T.V. Rod (D, Fig. 2)

A. Lubricate sockets and install upper throttle rod on ball studs. Adjust rod by rotating ball socket assembly until bellcrank is .002" to

.005" off it's stop with the throttle valves closed. (Fig. 5) Do not apply pressure on linkage while making this adjustment.

B. Lock the jam nut.

C. Remove blocking device holding the choke open, start engine and allow it to develop normal operating temperature. With throttle return check holding fixture J-6342-01 in place, set slow idle speed with automatic transmission in "DR" position, at 460 R.P.M. (add 60 R.P.M. if car is equipped with air conditioning).

5. Adjust Throttle Downshift Stop Screw (E, Fig. 2)

A. Loosen jam nut and back out stop screw. Push rearward on accelerator pedal level until throttle valves are wide open. Hold in this position with hand on carburetor throttle lever. Rotate T.V. bellcrank counterclockwise with the other hand to the point of maximum transmission lever travel. This point is a matter of feel

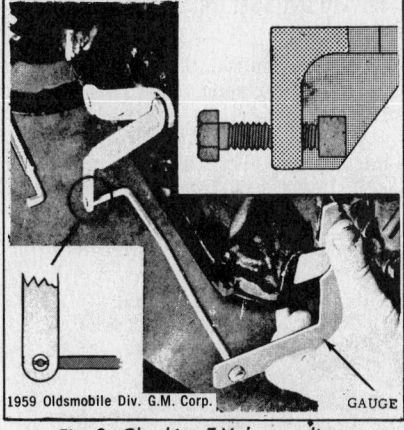

Fig. 3—Checking T.V. lever adjustment

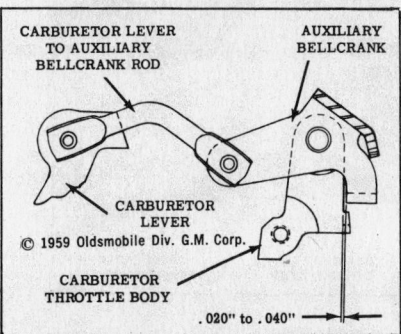

Fig. 4—Checking carburetor rod (4B6L)

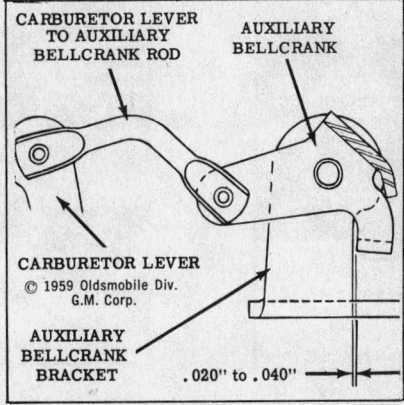

Fig. 4a—Checking carburetor rod (2B6L)

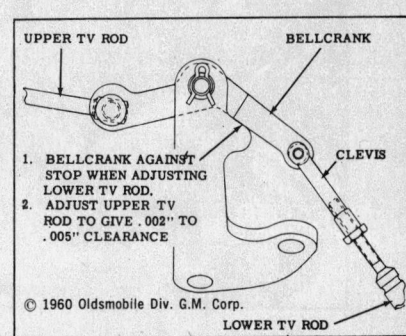

Fig. 5 Adjusting lower and upper T.V. rods

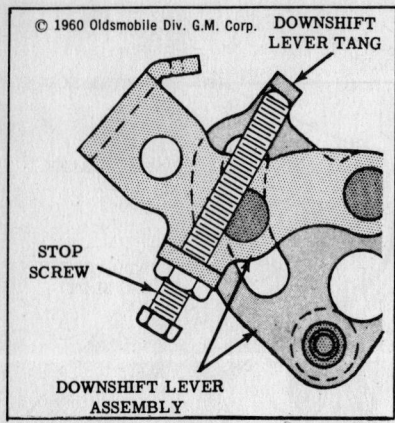

Fig. 6—Throttle downshift stop crew adjustment

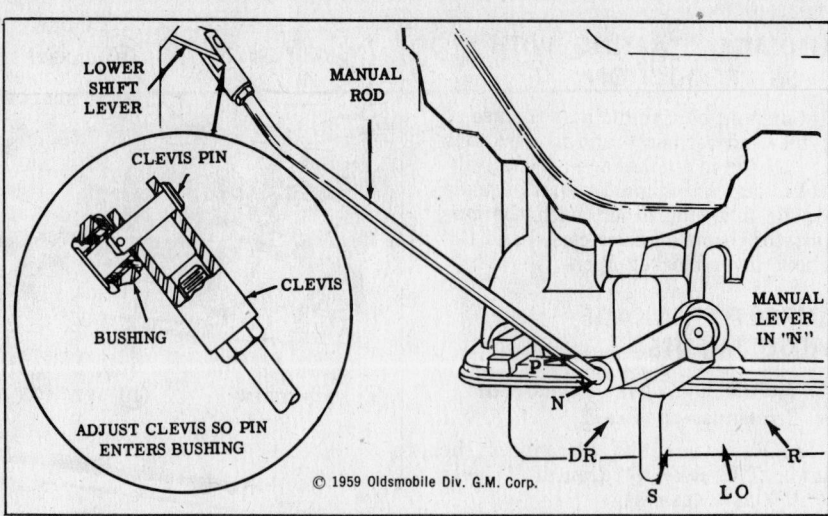

Fig. 8—Manual lever adjustments

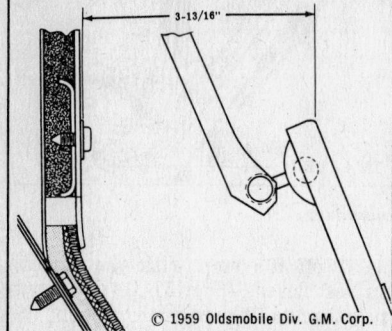

Fig. 7—Accelerator pedal height

and good judgment. Do not force linkage at this point.

B. With linkage held in this position, adjust stop screw "E" to just touch the tang on the downshift lever.

C. Permit the throttle valves to return to a closed position, then turn screw "E" in 1½ to 2 turns and tighten jam nut, (Fig. 6).

6. Adjust Accelerator Pedal Height (Fig. 2)

A. Adjust throttle rod ("G") to give a measurement of 3-13/16". Measure from upper top side of accelerator pedal to flat washer under metal screw in dash insulator just ahead of pedal (Fig. 7). One turn of throttle rod adjuster moves accelerator pedal 1/16".

B. Lubricate linkage pivot points with light engine oil.

C. Remove throttle return check holding tool J-6342-01, unblock choke and install air cleaner.

MANUAL LEVER ADJUSTMENT

The following adjustment provides proper clearance between the neutral detent in the transmission and the manual shifter lever stop in the upper steering column.

1. Place transmission manual lever in neutral detent position.

2. Disconnect manual rod from lower shift lever.

3. Hold lower shift lever upward so selector level is positioned against stop in upper steering column.

4. Adjust manual rod end so pin will enter about ⅛" into lower shift lever bushing with selective lever against stop. (Fig. 8)

5. Lengthen clevis 2½ turns.

6. Connect manual rod to lower shift lever and lock up clevis jam nut.

REMOVING HYDRA-MATIC TRANSMISSION
4 Speed

The transmission, torus cover and flywheel are removed from the car as an assembly.

1. Disconnect battery and transmission oil filler tube at engine.

2. Raise car (on jacks or hoist)

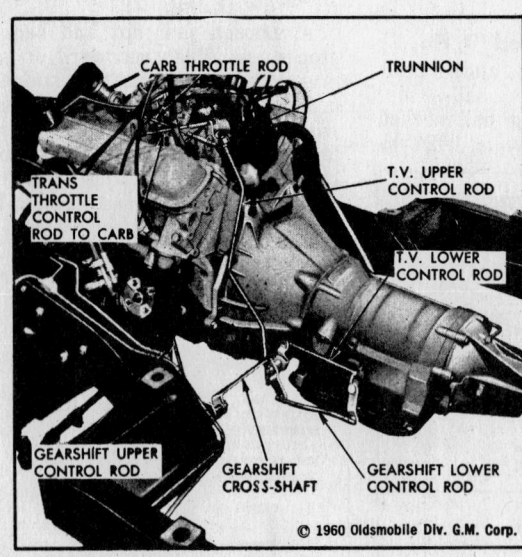

Throttle Control Linkage 4-Speed
Hydra-Matic

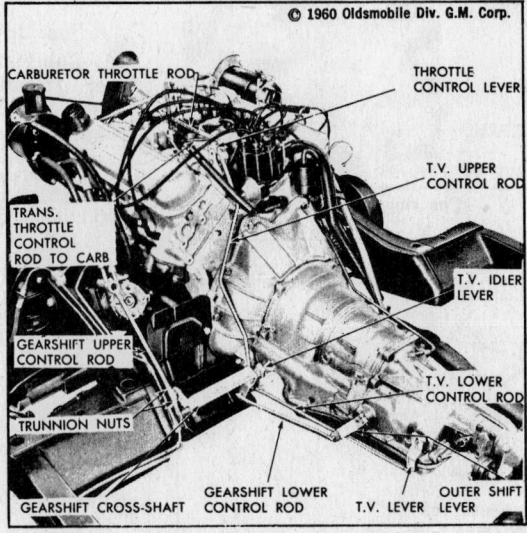

Throttle Control Linkage 3-Speed
Hydra-Matic

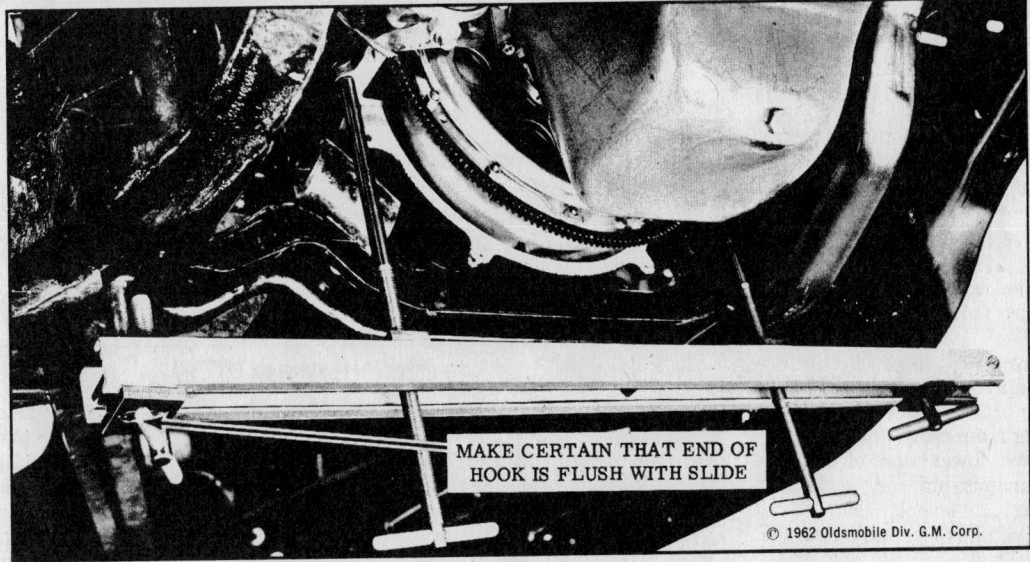

MAKE CERTAIN THAT END OF
HOOK IS FLUSH WITH SLIDE

© 1962 Oldsmobile Div. G.M. Corp.

Fig. 9—Engine support bar

remove filler pipe and drain transmission.

3. Disconnect speedometer cable, manual and throttle linkage from transmission.

4. Remove crankcase breather outlet tube.

5. Scribe a line from the propeller shaft center bearing support to frame member (for later center bearing support alignment).

6. Remove propeller shaft center bearing support bolts and shims. Identify the shims for proper relocation.

7. Raise the center bearing assembly so it will clear the frame member and slide the front propeller shaft and bearing assembly about 2 inches to the rear on the slip joint. (The bearing mounting plate will rest on the frame and keep the propeller shaft from dropping down.)

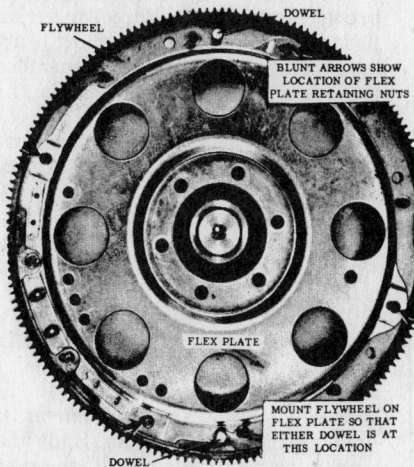

FLYWHEEL   DOWEL

BLUNT ARROWS SHOW
LOCATION OF FLEX
PLATE RETAINING NUTS

FLEX PLATE

MOUNT FLYWHEEL ON
FLEX PLATE SO THAT
EITHER DOWEL IS AT
THIS LOCATION

DOWEL

© 1959 Oldsmobile Div. G.M. Corp.

Fig. 10—Flex plate to cover location

8. Remove starter and lower flywheel housing.

9. Remove the four flex plate-to-flywheel attaching nuts and note position of flywheel dowels relative to flex plate.

10. Install engine support bar with support screw pilots seated into lower flywheel housing screw holes. (Fig. 9).

11. Support the transmission with a transmission lift and an adapter that will securely hold this unit during removal.

12. Raise the engine enough to relieve weight from the rear engine mounts. Remove engine mount to cross member attaching bolts.

13. Remove cross member to frame attaching bolts, then remove cross member.

14. Remove torus oil plug and drain torus. Reinstall Plug and Torque to 6 to 7 ft. lb.

15. Lower the transmission—Lift until it is free of transmission oil pan.

16. Lower engine (using support bar adjusting screws), not to exceed 1½ inches, to permit removal of the two upper bell housing-to-block bolts.

17. Disconnect oil cooler hoses from lines. Cap the lines immediately.

18. Raise transmission-lift until it supports the unit.

19. Remove remaining flywheel housing-to-block bolts.

20. Move transmission rearward about ¾" to clear the dowels.

21. Lower the transmission from the car.

Note: Standard, threaded holes adjacent to the dowels are provided for installing bolts to push the housing off the dowels.

INSTALLING HYDRA-MATIC TRANSMISSION
4 Speed

To install, reverse removal procedure and include the following:

Lubricate the crankshaft pilot bore and wick in the pilot bore with synthetic oil seal lubricant.

To assemble flex plate to flywheel, align one dowel in flywheel with the small recess adjacent to the small ear in the flex plate. (Fig. 10) Cross tighten and torque flex plate-to-flywheel attaching nuts, 17 to 22 ft. lb.

After transmission is installed, pour in 10 qts. of hydra-matic fluid. Set parking brake and with selector in "N", run the engine until oil has reached operating temperature. Add enough fluid to bring level to the "Full" mark on the dipstick.

Note: Transmission capacity, about 10 qts. (for oil change with oil pan removed). The transmission will take about 11½ qts. (after a complete overhaul).

REMOVING HYDRA-MATIC TRANSMISSION

3 Speed

Before raising the car on the lift, remove one cable (either one) from the battery, since the starter must be removed, and release the emergency brake.

1. Remove the filler tube and drain the transmission. Push the filler tube up toward its upper bracket out of the way.

2. Disconnect propeller shaft from transmission:

    a. Remove "U" bolt nuts, lock plates, and "U" bolts from rear

OLDSMOBILE

axle drive pinion flange.

b. Use a suitable rubber band or tape to hold bearings on "U" joint journals if tie wire is broken.

c. Slide propeller shaft rearwards off transmission output shaft.

3. Disconnect speedometer cable from speedometer driven gear.

4. Remove gearshift control lower rod.

5. Remove lower end of gearshift control upper rod by removing "E" ring.

6. Remove the 2 cross-shaft bracket to frame attaching bolts and then remove the bracket, cross-shaft lever, and bushing from car.

7. Remove lower end of throttle control transmission rod (engine to transmission idle lever).

8. Remove idler lever to outer T.V. lever control rod.

9. Remove throttle control idler lever.

10 Remove parking brake return spring and brake cable guide hook from frame crossmember.

11. Remove oil cooler lines.

12. Loosen exhaust pipe to manifold bolts about 1/4 inch.

13. Remove both starter cables.

14. Remove the starter and the splash shield by removing the 2 attaching bolts.

15. Remove bottom cover from bottom of case cover (3 attaching bolts).

16. Remove the 4 bolts hiding the flywheel front cover plate to the transmission case cover.

17. Place special automatic transmission jack under transmission and raise it enough to support the transmission.

18. Remove 2 rear mount support to frame crossmember nuts and raise transmission so studs clear the crossmember.

19. Remove the two bolts at each end of the frame crossmember and re-

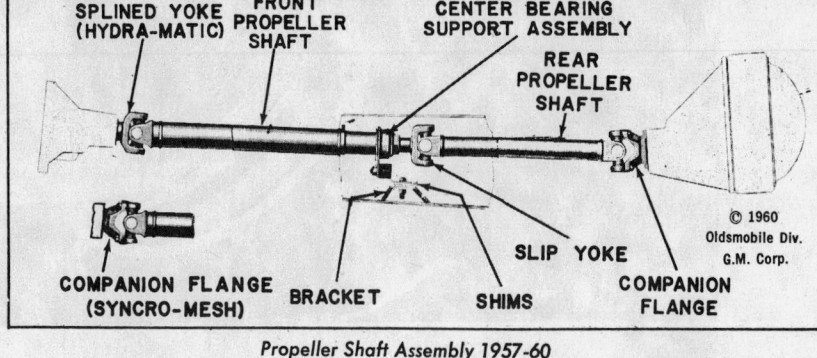

Propeller Shaft Assembly 1957-60

move crossmember.

20. Lower the transmission until the jack is barely still supporting it.

21. Remove breather pipe clip bolt and remove pipe from transmission.

22. Using a long wrench extension with a "U" joint, remove the remaining 6 transmission case over to engine attaching bolts.

23. Raise transmission to its normal position, slide forward from the engine and flywheel, and lower it away from the car.

24. Remove rear mount support from rear mount by removing a nut from each insulator.

25. Remove 4 rear mount to rear bearing retainer attaching screws.

INSTALL

3 Speed

Install by reversing above procedure.

UNIVERSAL JOINTS AND DRIVE LINE

Cross and bearing type universals are used on all Oldsmobile models.

REMOVAL OF UNIVERSAL JOINT

All Models Thru 1956 and 1961-63

Remove the four bolts which hold

the rear universal filler blocks to the pinion shaft flange and pry the universal joint off the pinion flange, lowering the back end of the shaft to the floor.

It is customary to tape the bearing blocks to the universal joints so that they don't get lost or get a lot of dirt in them.

The front end of the shaft can then be slid off the back of the transmission shaft and carried to the bench.

The bearings are held into the yokes by two lock plates one on each side.

Take out the nut which holds the lock plate in position and lift off the lock plate. The bearing can then be driven from one side across to the other which will drive the opposite side bearing out. Once the opposite side bearing has been removed, drive on the cross itself to drive out the first bearing.

It is recommended when reinstalling bearings that an arbor press or a very heavy "C" clamp he used to replace these bearings since driving on them has a tendency to distort the outer race of the needle bearings.

1957 Thru 1960

These models are fitted with two propeller shafts and three universal joints. There is a center support bearing mounted at a frame crossmember just back of the X member on the frame.

Both Saginaw and Spicer type universal joints are used, mixed in production.

The Saginaw joints have their snap ring on the inside of the bearing, whereas the Spicer joints have a snap ring on the outside of the bearing.

To remove the rear propeller shaft, pry up the retainer on the nut just in front of the middle universal joint and unscrew the nut. Remove the U bolts which connect the rear universal joint to the pinion flange. Split the rear universal joint and slide the rear propeller shaft out of the center bearing.

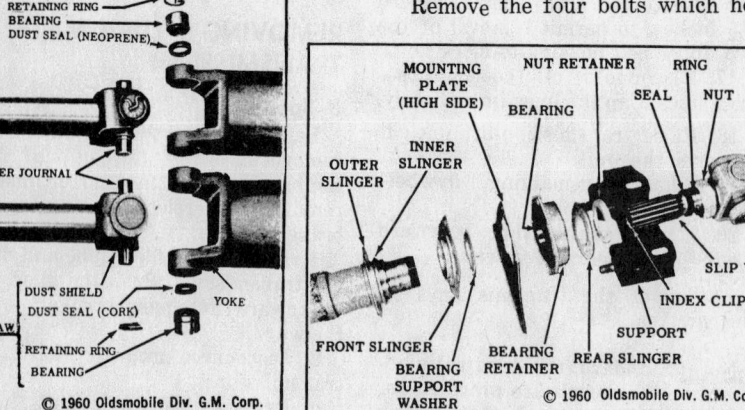

Layout of universal joints

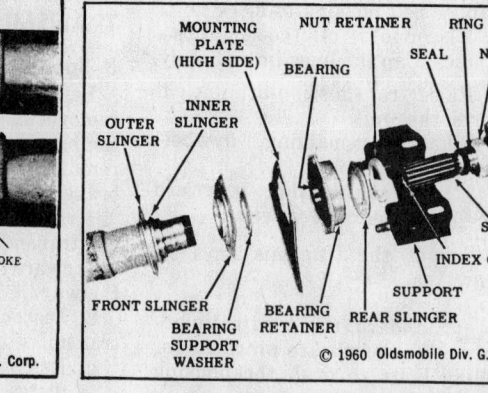

1957-60 center bearing assembly

To remove the entire propeller assembly. First, scribe a vertical line on the center support and one on the frame member so that alignment can be had while reassembling. Remove the center bearing support bolts and the shims from the frame member. Be careful not to lose the shims.

Remove the U bolts from the companion flanges at both the transmission and the differential. Split these universal joints. The complete assembly can now be slid rearward and out from under the car.

To disassemble the universal joints, remove the retaining washers from the bearings and set the joint up in a vise. Drive the cross downwards, driving out one side bearing.

When that bearing is removed, drive in the opposite direction until the other bearing comes out. The cross can then be readily slipped out.

REAR AXLE AND SUSPENSION

SERVICE ON SHOCK ABSORBERS

To service a shock absorber requires highly specialized equipment and knowledge.

Unless such equipment is available service on the shock absorber should not be attempted. If the shock is defective or inefficient it should be replaced with a new or rebuilt one.

Oldsmobile recommends that shock absorbers be replaced in pairs.

REPLACEMENT OF REAR SHOCK ABSORBERS

The rear shock absorbers on all Oldsmobiles are direct acting airplane type shocks. They are held at the bottom to the spring saddle with a single bolt and are held at the top in rubber bushings to a single bolt.

Remove both of these bolts and the shock absorbers can be lifted off the car.

REPLACEMENT OF THE REAR COIL SPRING

Disconnect the shock absorber link and raise the car sufficiently high to take the pressure off the coil spring and, reaching down through the coil spring, remove the bolt which holds the bottom of the spring to the insulating pad on the rear axle.

Working through the coil spring upwards, take out the upper bolt which holds the spring to the frame at the top.

If the car has been raised sufficient-

Removing Rear Spring Shackle Bolt

Rear Spring Front Bolt

ly high the spring can then be lifted out.

LEAF SPRINGS

On models having leaf springs, disconnect the spring from the rear shackle supporting the weight of the car at the frame in front of the spring front shackle. Disconnect the shock absorber. Disconnect the front shackle and remove the spring clip bolts which retain the spring to the axle housing. Lift off the spring.

REAR AXLE

TROUBLE SHOOTING AND ADJUSTMENT

General instructions covering the troubles of the rear axle and how to repair and adjust it, together with information on installation of rear axle bearings and grease seals, are

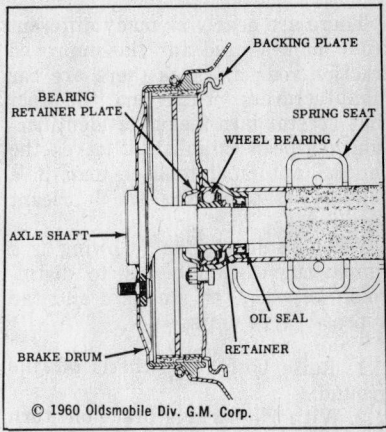

Axle Shaft and Related Parts

given in the Unit Repair section under the heading: Axles, Rear.

Capacities of the rear axle are given in the Capacities Tables of this section.

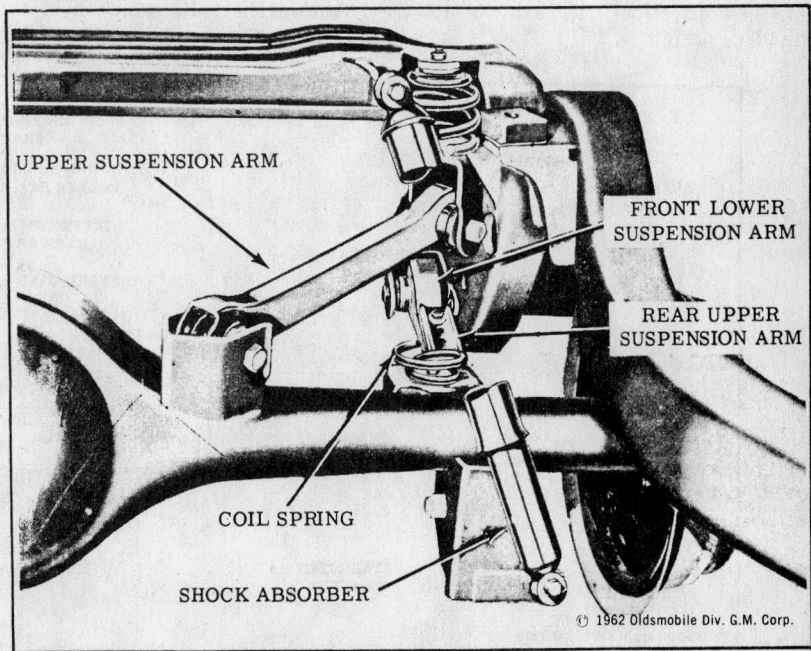

Rear Suspension

OLDSMOBILE

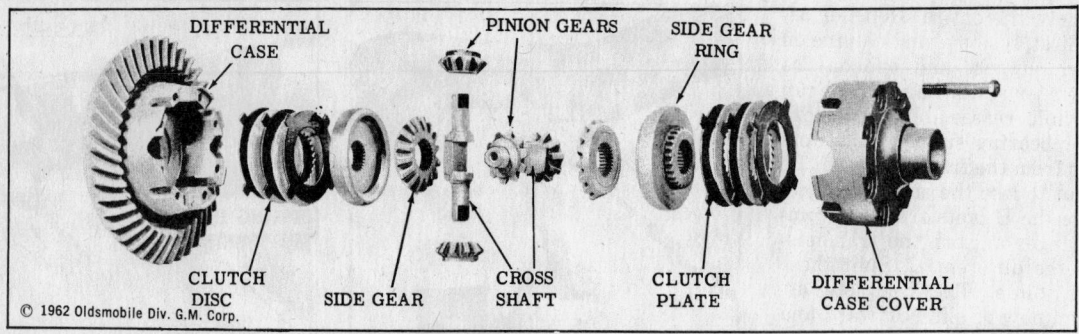

DIFFERENTIAL CASE — PINION GEARS — SIDE GEAR RING

CLUTCH DISC — SIDE GEAR — CROSS SHAFT — CLUTCH PLATE — DIFFERENTIAL CASE COVER

© 1962 Oldsmobile Div. G.M. Corp.

Anti-Spin Differential Assembly

IMPROVED TRACTION AXLE IDENTIFICATION

There are nearly as many different trade names used for the improved traction rear axles as there are car manufacturers. This, and the fact that no standard means of identification has been established, leaves the general auto maintenance man in a quandry as to repairs and lubricant required.

When in doubt, the following is a simple rule-of-thumb way to distinguish between the standard and the improved type units.

1. Raise both rear wheels off the ground.

2. With the parking brake off, turn one wheel forward (by hand) and note the direction of rotation of the other wheel.

3. If the other wheel turns in the same direction as the one being turned, the rear axle is of the improved type.

4. If the other wheel turns in the opposite direction, the axle is of standard design.

REMOVAL OF THE REAR AXLE ASSEMBLY

Models with Rear Leaf Springs

To remove the rear axle assembly, take the weight of the car on the frame in front of the rear spring and remove the bolt which holds the lower end of the shock absorber to the spring saddle.

Disconnect the brake cables and brake lines at the rear axle. Split the rear universal joint as explained in the paragraph under universal joints and remove the two bolts from the rear spring shackle and take out the shackle. Take off the four bolts on each side which hold the U-bolts through the spring seat to the rear axle housing and lower the springs and roll the rear axle assembly out from under the car.

Models with Rear Coil Springs

Disconnect the rear shock absorbers and raise the car sufficiently to take all the pressure off the rear springs.

Remove the bolts which hold the torsion bars to the rear axle housing and then take out the one bolt which holds the coil spring to the coil spring saddle.

This is a left hand thread on one side and a right hand thread on the other. Disconnect the brake lines and cables at the rear axle, split the rear universal joint, disconnect the sway bar and roll the rear axle assembly from under the car.

RADIO

REMOVE AND INSTALL

1. Disconnect "A" (Green) lead from harness.

2. When equipped with rear speaker, disconnect speaker lead.

3. Disconnect antennae thru opening in top of glove box.

4. When equipped with foot selector switch, disconnect plug-in connector from right side of receiver.

5. Remove control knobs and nuts from front of panel.

6. Disconnect bracket from side of receiver and remove receiver.

To Reinstall: Reverse the above.

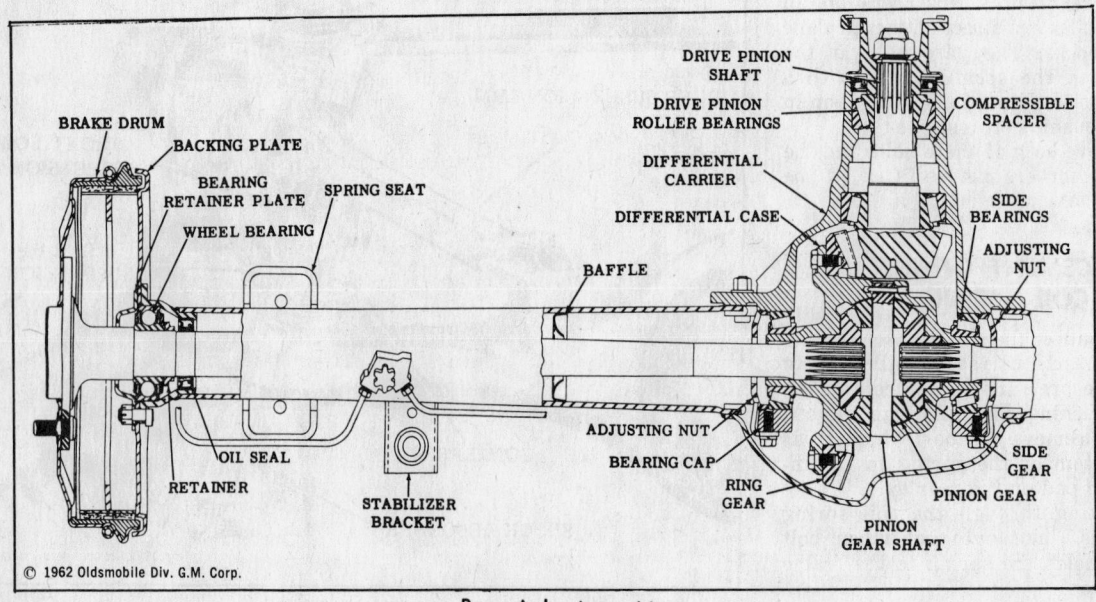

BRAKE DRUM — BACKING PLATE — BEARING RETAINER PLATE — SPRING SEAT — WHEEL BEARING — OIL SEAL — RETAINER — STABILIZER BRACKET — BAFFLE — ADJUSTING NUT — BEARING CAP — RING GEAR — PINION GEAR SHAFT — PINION GEAR — SIDE GEAR — DRIVE PINION SHAFT — DRIVE PINION ROLLER BEARINGS — DIFFERENTIAL CARRIER — DIFFERENTIAL CASE — COMPRESSIBLE SPACER — SIDE BEARINGS — ADJUSTING NUT

© 1962 Oldsmobile Div. G.M. Corp.

Rear Axle Assembly

Page | Page | Pag

AIR CONDITIONING

Service 1092

BRAKES, HYDRAULIC

Adjustments 938
Bleed brakes 941
Brake references 482
Hand brake lever & cable 482
Master cylinder service 939

BRAKES, POWER

Power unit overhaul 954
Trouble shooting 954

CLUTCH

Clutch assembly, R & R 491
Clutch linkage 492
Clutch pedal, adjust 492

COOLING SYSTEM

Water pump, R & R 484

ELECTRICAL SYSTEM

Battery 481
Delcotron specifications 477
Distributor, R & R 480
Distributor specifications 477
Engine 479
Engine firing order & timing 476
Engine tune-up specifications 477
Fuses and circuit breakers 476
Gauges 1024
Generator and regulator
   specifications 477
Generator and regulators 480
Generator service 1026
Generator trouble shooting chart 1026
Horn button 490
Ignition timing procedure 479
Instruments 481
Starter, R & R 482
Starter specifications 477
Starter systems 1046

ENGINE ASSEMBLY

Cylinder head, R & R 485
Engine assembly, R & R 484
Engine firing order & timing 476
Engine marking code 477
Exhaust manifold, R & R 483
Inlet manifold, R & R 484
Lubrication 487
Oil filter 487
Oil pan, R & R 487
Oil pressure specifications 478
Oil pump 487
Piston & pin specifications 478
Piston and rod, assemble 487
References 484
Rocker arms & shaft 485

ENGINE ASSEMBLY—continued

Specifications, general, engine .. 478
Specifications, tune-up, engine .. 477
Timing case 485
Timing chain 486
Trouble shooting charts 1012
Tune-up 479
Valve lifters 485
Valve specifications 478

ENGINE LUBRICATION

Oil filter 487
Oil pan, R & R 487
Oil pump 487

EXHAUST SYSTEM

Exhaust manifold 483
Intake manifold 484

FUEL SYSTEM

Carburetor adjustments 482
Carburetor specifications 972
Fuel gauge service 1024
Fuel pump pressure 477
Fuel pump 483
Fuel tank, R & R 483
References 482

INSTRUMENTS

Fuel gauge, R & R 481
Instrument cluster, R & R 481
Speedometer 481
Starter switch, R & R 481
Sending unit references 484

RADIO, R & R

References 496

REAR AXLE AND SUSPENSION

Axle assembly, R & R 496
Axle shaft 918
Axle shaft oil seal 918
Pinion bearings 918
Ring gear & pinion 918
Spring, rear R & R 496
Trouble shooting 919

SPECIFICATIONS

Battery 477
Brake cylinder sizes 478
Capacities:
   Axle, rear 478
   Cooling system 478
   Crankcase 478
   Fuel tank 478
   Transmission, automatic 478
   Transmission, manual 478
Chassis, general 478
Delcotron specifications 477
Distributor 477

SPECIFICATIONS—continued

Engine, general 478
Engine, tune-up 477
Fuses and circuit breakers 476
Generator and regulators 477
Ignition timing specifications ... 477
Light bulbs 476
Main bearings 478
Model identification illustration .. 476
Piston and pin 478
Quick reference specifications ... 476
Rod bearings 478
Starters 477
Torque wrench 479
Valves 478
Wheel alignment 478

STEERING, MANUAL

Adjust gear housing 1052
Gear assembly, R & R 490
Horn button, R & R 490
Steering wheel, R & R 490

STEERING, POWER

Pump assembly 1058
References 491
Trouble shooting 1081
Unit overhaul 1058

SUSPENSION, FRONT

Alignment procedures 1082
Alignment specifications 478
Ball joints, R & R 489
Coil springs 489
References 488

TRANSMISSION, AUTOMATIC

Disassembly of transmission 893
General information 886
Manual control adjust 494
References 493
Throttle linkage, adjust 494
Transmission, R & R 494
Trouble shooting 892

TRANSMISSION, MANUAL SHIFT

Disassemble transmission 493
Shift controls 493
Transmission, R & R 493

TUNE-UP

Carburetor 972
Engine diagnosis 1012
Specifications 477

UNIVERSAL JOINT AND DRIVE LINE

U joint & drive line, R & R 495

OLDSMOBILE F-85

YEAR IDENTIFICATION

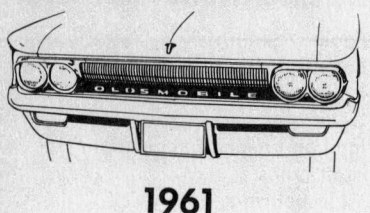
1961

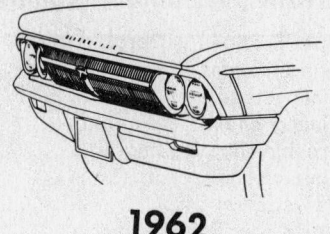
1962

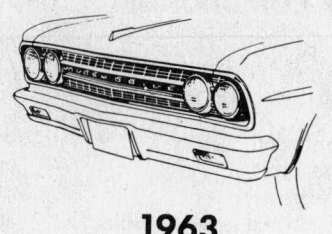
1963

QUICK WORKING SPECIFICATIONS

DISTRIBUTOR SPECIFICATIONS

Make ....Delco-Remy
Type of Advance
..........Centrifugal & Vacuum
Point Gap 016
Point Spring Tension ......19-23 oz.
Cam Dwell .... 28°-32°

IGNITION TIMING ....5°BTDC

SPARK PLUGS

Year	Type	Gap
1961-63	46FF	.035″

GENERATOR AND REGULATOR SPECIFICATIONS

Year and Series	Generator		Regulator		
	Field Current in Amperes @ 12 Volts	Cut-Out Closing Voltage	Current Regulator Setting	Voltage Regulator Setting
1961-63	1.74	12.8	35	14.4

(A) Surrounding temperatures guide this adjustment. Higher temperatures require lower settings and lower temperatures permit higher settings, within limits.

Regulator

Cut-out Relay
Air Gap ....020″

Closing Voltage ...12.8 @ 1450 RPM
Current and Voltage Regulator
Air Gap ....075″
Current Regulator
Setting ....31-36 @ 125°F.

COMPRESSION PRESSURE

Cranking ....140 P.S.I.

CAPACITIES

Engine Crankcase (Qts.)
1961-63 4

Transmission, Manual (Pts.)
1961-63 ....2.1

Transmission, Automatic (Pts.)
1961-63 12

Rear Axle (Pts.)
1961-63 ....2½

Gas Tank (Gals.)
1961-63 16

Cooling System (Qts.)
Less Heater 11
With Heater 12.5

VALVES

Seat Angle
1961-63 ....45°

Operating Tappet Clearance
1961-63—All Hydraulic ....Zero

Valve Timing (Inlet Opens)
1961-63 ....22°BTC

BULB SPECIFICATIONS

Head Lamps

	Candle Power	Number
Outer:		
High Beam ...37½ W		4002
Low Beam .....50 W		
Inner:		
High Beam ..37½ W		4001

Other Lamps

Headamp Indicator	2	158
Parking & Front Turn	4/32	1034
Tail, Stop & Rear Turn	4/32	1034
Turn Indicator	2	158
License Plate	3	67
Instrument	2	1816
Dome Light	15	211

CIRCUIT BREAKER

A 15-amp circuit brake protects head and front parking lamps. It is mounted on light switch.

FUSES

(Located on block under left side of instrument panel)

Stoplights, Directional Lights
& Indicator ....20 Amp—1¼″
Panel Lights
& Rheostat .... 3 Amp—1¼″
Wiper & Washer
Motor ....25 Amp—1¼″
Tail, License & Dome
Lights .... 9 Amp— ⅞″
Back Up Lights
(if used) .... 9 Amp— ⅞″
Heater Blower
(if used) ....20 Amp—1¼″

FIRING ORDER and TIMING

SPARK OCCURS:

1961-63—V-8, All 5° With Vacuum Line
Disconnected, 850 Engine R.P.M.

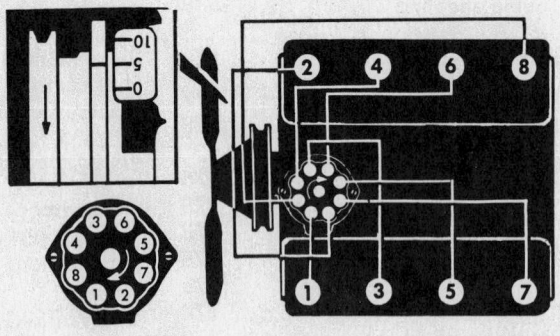

NOTE:
THESE ARE APPROXIMATE SETTINGS. ENGINE DESIGN, ALTITUDE, TEMPERATURE, FUEL AND ENGINE CONDITION WILL ALL INFLUENCE TIMING. THE DETERMINING FACTOR, LIMITING ADVANCE, WILL STILL BE THE "KNOCK POINT" OF THE INDIVIDUAL ENGINE.

CAR SERIAL NUMBER LOCATION AND ENGINE IDENTIFICATION

ENGINE NUMBER

ENGINE IDENTIFICATION IS THRU CAR SERIAL NUMBER.

The engine number is stamped on the front of the right cylinder head. The starting unit number is S-001001.

Suffix "E" is used for an export, low compression engine option.

SERIAL NUMBER LOCATION

A vehicle identification plate is located on the left front door pillar. Each identification number is prefixed by three digits. The first two indicate the year, the third designates the series ("O," standard F-85—1, deluxe F-85). The next is a letter and indicates the assembly plant ("M" for Lansing and "C" for South Gate). The vehicle number is next and each plant's starting number is 01001.

TUNE UP SPECIFICATIONS

| YEAR AND MODEL | SPARK PLUGS | | DISTRIBUTOR | | | Ignition Timing | Compression Pressure Cranking | VALVES | | | | Fuel Pump Pressure | Engine Idle Speed (R.P.M.) |
| | TYPE | Gap | Cam Angle | Point Gap | Arm Spring Tension | | | Tappet Clearance | | Timing Inlet Opens | | |
								In.	Ex.			
1961-63	46FF*	.035	30°	.016	19-23	5B	140	Zero	Zero	22B	4-5¼	525

*=45FF with 4 BBL Carb.

Note:

All specifications are standard and should result in satisfactory performance. There are, however, factors that influence these settings, such as fuel octane value, air density, humidity, temperature, etc. Timing charts, like other specifications must be considered as averages, subject to modification.

DISTRIBUTOR SPECIFICATIONS

| YEAR AND MODEL | Delco-Remy Part Number | Rotation | Cam Angle Degrees | BREAKER | | GOVERNOR CONTROL @ DIST. R.P.M. | | VACUUM CONTROL DATA | | |
				Point Opening (Inch)	Arm Spring (Ounce)	Advance Starts	Advance Full	Inches Vacuum To Start Advance	Inches Of Vacuum For Full Advance	Max. Advance Of Dist. In Degrees
1961-63	1110975	C	28-32	.016	19-23	1°@400	15°@2200	5-7	16	12

GENERATOR AND REGULATOR SPECIFICATIONS

| YEAR AND MODEL | GENERATORS | | REGULATORS | | | | |
| | Field Current Amperes At 12 Volts | Brush Spring Tension | Cut-Out Relay | | Current and Voltage Regulator Air Gaps | Current Regulator Setting | Voltage Regulator Setting |
			Air Gap	Closing Voltage			
1961-62	1.74	28	.020"	12.8	.075"	35	14.4

DELCOTRON AND A.C. REGULATOR SPECIFICATIONS

| Delcotron Model Number | Ground Polarity | Field Current Draw (Amperes) | CURRENT OUTPUT | | | RUNNING VOLTAGE | | | REGULATOR | | FIELD RELAY | |
			Engine R.P.M.	Amperes	Volts	Engine R.P.M.	Amperes	Volts @ 125°	Model Number	Point Gap	Armature Air Gap	Closing Voltage
1962—63 1100622	Neg.	1.9 to 2.2	1100	12.	14	6500	42	13.5-14.3	1119506	.015	.015	6.5-8.5
1100633	Neg.	4.1 to 4.5	1100	24.	14	6500	62	13.3-13.9	1119506	.015	.015	6.5-8.5

BATTERY AND STARTER SPECIFICATIONS

| YEAR AND MODEL | BATTERY | | | | STARTERS | | | | | | Brush Spring Tension |
| | Amp. Hour Capacity | Volts | Group Number | Terminal Grounded | LOCK TEST (Note 1) | | | NO-LOAD TEST | | | |
					Amps.	Volts	Torque	Amps.	Volts	R.P.M.	
1961-63	40*	12	N.A.	Neg.	300	4	N.A.	70	10.6	7675	35

NOTE 1: Not recommended by Oldsmobile.
*1963—44 Amp.

OLDSMOBILE F-85

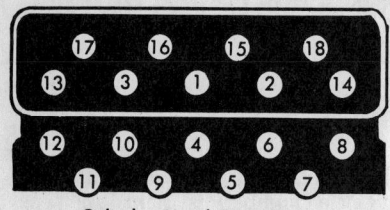

Cylinder Head Torquing

GENERAL CHASSIS AND BRAKE SPECIFICATIONS

YEAR AND MODEL	CHASSIS			BRAKE CYLINDER BORE		
	Overall Length In Inches	Tire Size	Master Cylinder (Inch)	Wheel Cylinder (Inch)		
					Front	Rear
1961-63	188.2*	6.50x13	1.00		1.00	⅞

*1963—192.2"

TORQUE SPECIFICATIONS

YEAR	Cylinder Head Bolts	Rod Bearing Bolts	Main Bearing Bolts	Crankshaft Pulley Bolt	Flywheel to Crankshaft Bolts	MANIFOLDS	
						In.	Ex.
1961-63	50-55	30-35	50-60(A)	150	85-95	25-30	18-24

(A) No. 5 Main—65-70 Ft. Lbs.

GENERAL ENGINE SPECIFICATIONS

YEAR AND MODEL	Bore And Stroke	No. Of Main Bearings	Type Of Valve Lifter	Cubic Inch Displacement	AMA Horse Power	Advertised Horse Power At Stated R.P.M.	Advertised Torque At Stated R.P.M.	Compression Ratio	Oil Pressure At 35 MPH	Cam Shaft Drive
1961-63	3.5x2.8	5	Hydraulic	215	39.2	155@4800(A)	210@3200(B)	8.75-1(C)	35	Chain

(A) w/4Bbl—185@4800 (B) w/4Bbl—230@3200 (C) 1962—w/4BBL—10.25-1, 1963—w/4BBL—10.75-1.

CRANKSHAFT BEARING JOURNAL SIZES

YEAR AND MODEL	MAIN BEARING JOURNALS				CONNECTING ROD BEARING JOURNALS		
	Journal Diameter	Oil Clearance	End Play Of Shaft	End Play Held By	Journal Diameter	Oil Clearance	End Play
1961-63	2.2983	.0005"-.0020"	.006	3	2.000"	.0005"-.0020"	.006"-.0140"

PISTON AND PIN SPECIFICATIONS

YEAR AND MODEL	PISTON		PISTON PIN				
	Skirt Clearance				FIT		
	Min.	Max.	Diameter	Bushing	In Rod	In Piston	Lock
1961-63	.0005	.0011	.8750	No	.0007-.0013	.0003-.0005	Rod Press

VALVE SPECIFICATIONS

YEAR AND MODEL	Seat Angle	Intake Valve Lift	Exhaust Valve Lift	VALVE SPRING PRESSURE		STEM TO GUIDE CLEARANCE		Stem Diameter	Are Guides Removable
				Outer	Inner	Inlet	Exhaust		
1961-63	45°	.384	.384	75#@1¾	None	.001"-.025"	.015"-.003"	Note 1	Yes

NOTE 1: EXHAUST .3427" TOP; .3417" BOTTOM.
           INTAKE .3432" TOP; .3427" BOTTOM.

FRONT WHEEL ALIGNMENT

YEAR AND MODEL	CASTER		CAMBER		Toe-In (Inches)	King Pin Inclination (Degrees)	WHEEL PIVOT RATIO	
	Range (Degrees)	Pref. Setting	Range (Degrees)	Pref. Setting			Inner Wheel	Outer Wheel
1961-63	¾°N-1¾°N	1½N	⅜°N-⅜°P	0°	⅛	7½	23°	20°

CAPACITIES

YEAR AND MODEL	Engine Crankcase Add 1 Qt. For New Filter	Transmission Pints To Refill After Draining		Rear Axle Pints	Gasoline Tank Gallons	Cooling System Quarts
		Manual	Automatic			
1961-63	4	2.1	12	2.5	16	11.0(A)

(A) Add 1½ qts. for heater.

TUNE-UP

ENGINE TUNE-UP AND DIAGNOSIS ARE SO CLOSELY RELATED THAT ONE PROCEDURE SHOULD SERVE BOTH PURPOSES

Compression Check

1. Remove the plug wires.
2. Blow foreign matter from around the spark plugs with compressed air. Then loosen the plugs one turn.
3. Replace plug wires, start engine and snap throttle open for one or two seconds. (This should clear the engine of dislodged carbon particles.)
4. Stop engine and remove the plug wires and spark plugs.
5. Remove the air cleaner. Then block the carburetor throttle wide open.
6. Hook up a starter remote-control cable and switch. Then crank the engine through about four strokes for each cylinder while reading the compression pressure on a reliable cylinder compression gauge.
7. Record the maximum pressures of each cylinder. Variation between cylinders should not exceed 15 lbs.

Note: A compression check should be the first step in the course of tune-up events. Only if compression is within limits, should tune-up be continued.

Spark Plugs

Use a good plug tester, if available and service or renew the spark plugs. Detailed information on diagnosing spark plug troubles can be found in the Unit Repair section, under Tune-Up.

In spark plug installation, be sure of the following:
1. Use plugs of correct model, gapped properly, and threads lightly oiled.
2. Thoroughly clean the cylinder head and spark plug threads.
3. Carefully torque the spark plugs to 12-17 ft. lb.

Generator Drive Belt

Check the condition of the belt and adjust tension to ½" deflection when 15 pounds pressure is applied midway between the water pump and the generator pulley.

Battery

1. Check condition of battery.
2. Clean, lubricate and tighten cable connections both ends.
3. Clean carburetor bowl and adjust float.

Final Adjustments

1. Set ignition timing with a light.
2. Then road test the car and, if necessary, modify the prescribed setting within limits to accommodate the variables of engine and operating conditions and fuel anti-knock valve.
   Note: This final timing adjustment is made in the shop but as a result of road test.
3. Check and adjust engine idle speed.
4. Adjust carburetor idle mixture.

Other Electrical

1. Check Generator output.
2. Check Regulator.
3. Check Starter Motor current draw.
4. Check Ignition Coil output.
5. Check Ignition Wiring.
6. Test Primary Circuit resistance.
7. Test spark intensity at each plug wire.

Cooling System

1. Examine for coolant leaks, (engine, radiator, pump, heater and all hoses).
2. Look for coolant contamination, (rust, oil, etc.) in the radiator.
3. Recharge cooling system with anti-freeze or rust inhibitor.

Distributor

1. Replace and/or reset breaker points.
2. Lubricate distributor cam.
3. Lubricate distributor shaft bushing at the oil cup.
4. Check and adjust vacuum control.
5. Inspect and clean distributor rotor and cap.

Fuel System

1. Clean pump sediment bowl.
2. Check pump pressure and capacity, (fuel filter may be partially obstructed).

CAP

WINDOW

ROTOR

CAP LATCH

CENTRIFUGAL ADVANCE MECHANISM

VACUUM UNIT

CONDENSER

BREAKER CAM

ADJUSTING SCREW

© 196u Oldsmobile Div. G.M. Corp.

PRIMARY LEAD

GEAR

Distributor Exploded

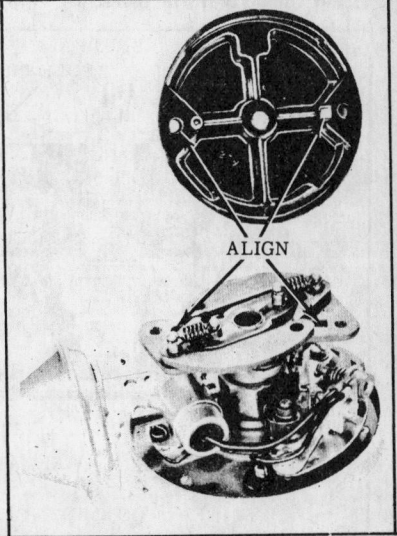

ALIGN

Rotor Installation

DISTRIBUTOR

REFERENCES

Detailed information on: distributor drive, direction of distributor rotation; cylinder numbering; firing order; point gap; cam dwell; timing mark location; spark plugs, spark advance; ignition resistor location, and idle speed; will be found in the Tune-up Specifications table of this section. Further information on trouble shooting, general tune-up procedures, how to replace ignition wires, how to install points and condensers, how to choose the proper spark plug, adjust timing, will be found in the Unit Repair Section under the heading: Ignition-Distributors-Tune-up.

The distributor is located between the two cylinder banks, up front. The rotor turns in a clockwise direction, as viewed from the top.

Engine timing requirements are satisfied by the action of the breaker plate which is controlled by the effort of a vacuum diaphragm working against spring tension. The diaphragm moves the breaker plate in a counter-clockwise direction to advance the timing, and the springs move the plate in a clockwise direction to retard the timing. The degree of timing, within automatic control limits, is determined by the amount of vacuum applied to the spring loaded diaphragm and breaker plate.

DISTRIBUTOR REMOVE

1. Remove distributor cap, primary wire and vacuum line at the distributor.
2. Scribe a mark on the distributor body, locating the position of the rotor and scribe another mark on the distributor body and engine block, showing the position of the body in the block.

3. Remove the hold-down screw and lift the distributor out of the block.

DISTRIBUTOR INSTALL

1. If engine has been disturbed rotate the crankshaft to bring the piston of number one cylinder to the top of its compression stroke.
2. Position the distributor in the block with the rotor at #1 firing position. Make sure the oil pump intermediate drive shaft is properly seated in the oil pump.
3. Install the distributor lock but do not tighten.
4. Rotate the distributor body clockwise until the breaker points are just starting to open. Tighten the retaining screw.
5. Connect the primary wire and the vacuum line to the distributor, then install distributor cap.
6. Start the engine and check the timing with a timing light.

GENERATOR AND REGULATOR

Detailed facts on the generator and regulator can be found in the specification table in this section.

General repair and trouble shooting can be found in the Unit Repair section under the heading; Generators and Regulators.

DELCOTRON (A.C. Generator)

Beginning with 1962, an alternating current generator is being made available. This unit is the Delco-Remy, "DELCOTRON." The purpose of this unit is to satisfy the increase in electrical loads that have been imposed upon the car battery by modern conditions of traffic and driving patterns.

The DELCOTRON is covered in the Unit Repair section of this manual under "Generators and Regulators."

Caution:

Since the Delcotron and regulator are designed for use on only one polarity system, the following precautions must be ovserved:

1. The polarity of the battery, generator and regulator must be matched and considered before making any electrical connections in the system.
2. When connecting a booster battery, be sure to connect the negative battery terminals together and the positive battery terminals together.
3. When connecting a charger to the battery, connect the charger positive lead to the battery positive terminal. Connect the charger negative lead to the battery negative terminal.
4. Never operate the Delcotron on open circuit. Be sure that all connections in the circuit are clean and tight.
5. Do not short across or ground any of the terminals on the Delcotron regulator.
6. Do not attempt to polarize the Delcotron.
7. Do not use test lamps of more than 12 volts for checking diode continuity.
8. Avoid long soldering times when replacing diodes or transistors. Prolonged heat is damaging to these units.
9. Disconnect the battery ground terminal when servicing any A.C. system. This will prevent the possibility of accidental reversing of polarity.

GENERATOR REMOVE

1. Disconnect the positive cable from the battery.
2. Disconnect armature, field, and ground wires at the generator terminals.
3. Remove adjustment arm to generator bolt. Remove the two pivot bolts from the mounting bracket. Remove generator and belt.
   Reinstall: Install by reversing above procedure.

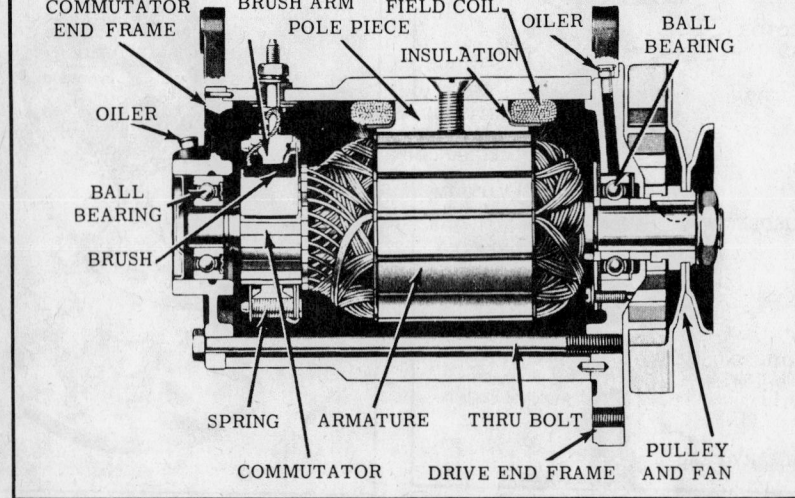

COMMUTATOR END FRAME — BRUSH ARM — FIELD COIL — OILER — BALL BEARING — POLE PIECE — INSULATION — OILER — BALL BEARING — BRUSH — SPRING — ARMATURE — THRU BOLT — COMMUTATOR — DRIVE END FRAME — PULLEY AND FAN

Generator

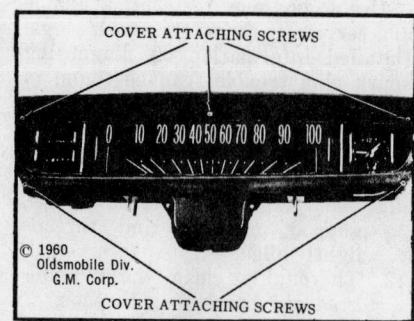

COVER ATTACHING SCREWS

© 1960 Oldsmobile Div. G.M. Corp.

COVER ATTACHING SCREWS

Instrument Cluster

INSTRUMENTS

The instrument cluster includes the speedometer head, the generator charge indicator, the oil pressure indicator and the temperature indicator. The fuel gauge, light switch, wiper and washer switch, starter and ignition switch and the cigarette lighter.

CLUSTER REMOVE AND INSTALL

1. Disconnect positive battery cable at the battery.
2. Remove cluster cover attaching screws. Disconnect the wiring harness, clock, and speedometer cable at the cluster.
3. Remove four cluster attaching nuts and lock washers from under the panel. Then remove cluster from the top of instrument panel.

Install by reversing above procedure.

Note: Exercise care to prevent damage to the printed circuit.

SPEEDOMETER

Remove

1. With the cluster removed from the car, remove the 6 instrument cluster bezel-to-case attaching screws and remove bezel and face from the cluster.
2. Remove 2 speedometer head holding screws from the case assembly and remove speedometer head from front of case.

PRINTED CIRCUIT

Remove

1. Remove all cluster lamp sockets, and 5 circuit attaching screws.
2. Remove 2 hex nuts from fuel gauge mounting studs.
3. Lift printed circuit from cluster.

Install

When installing, reverse removal procedure. Do not overtighten attaching screws or nuts. This could cause cracking and opening the circuit.

FUEL GAUGE

Remove

The fuel gauge can be removed without removing the instrument cluster as follows:

1. Disconnect positive battery cable.
2. Remove cluster cover.
3. Disconnect fuel gauge wiring connector and the light socket from the printed circuit.
4. Remove the two attaching nuts and withdraw fuel gauge from front of the cluster.

Install

To install the gauge, use extreme care to prevent damage.

HEADLIGHT SWITCH

Remove

1. Disconnect positive battery cable at battery.
2. Disconnect wiring from light switch.
3. Remove knob and rod by pulling knob out to "Headlight" position, then depress button on top of switch assembly and pull rod out.
4. Remove escutcheon with tool #J-6592-01.
5. Remove headlight switch from rear of instrument panel.

Install

Install by reversing removal procedure.

IGNITION—STARTER SWITCH

Remove

1. Remove escutcheon from instrument panel with tool #J-6592-01 or substitute tool made from 16 gauge metal 4" long, 13/16" wide and 1/16" thick. Then remove switch assembly from rear of panel.
2. Disconnect connector from back of ignition switch.

Note: The switch wiring connector is locked to the back of the ignition

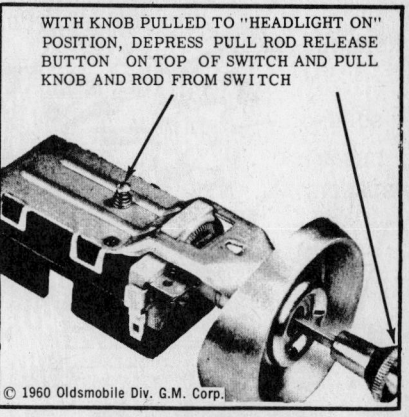

WITH KNOB PULLED TO "HEADLIGHT ON" POSITION, DEPRESS PULL ROD RELEASE BUTTON ON TOP OF SWITCH AND PULL KNOB AND ROD FROM SWITCH

© 1960 Oldsmobile Div. G.M. Corp.

Headlight Switch

switch with a special terminal tang which fits in a hole in the terminal for the accessory wire. The connector plastic insulation has a slot in it to permit access to the tang. To remove the connector, insert a small punch through the slot and depress the tang. Then disengage it from the terminal and pull the connector from the ignition switch. The tang automatically engages the terminal when the connector is reinstalled.

Note: To remove the lock cylinder, insert key and turn to the left. Push a paper clip in hole in face of lock cylinder. Turn cylinder to left as far as it will go and withdraw cylinder.

BATTERY AND STARTER

BATTERY

A Delco 12 volt battery is used in all models. The battery has 6 cells with 9 plates each and a capacity of 40 ampere-hours.

STARTER

The starter circuit consists of the battery, battery cables, starting motor, starter motor solenoid switch, ignition-starter switch and the neu-

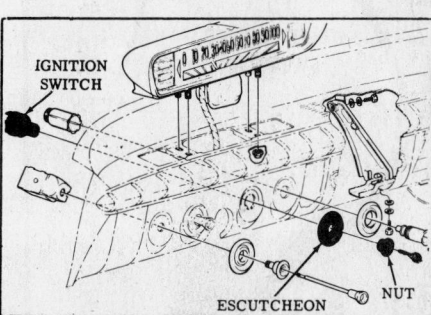

IGNITION SWITCH

ESCUTCHEON   NUT

Ignition Starter Switch

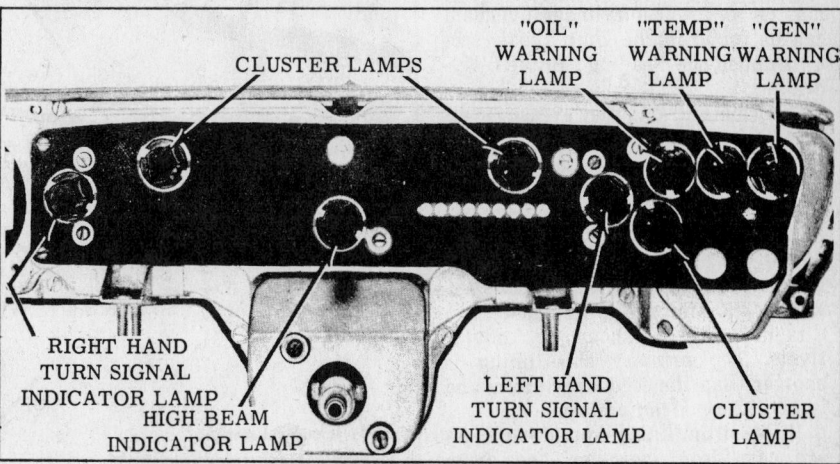

CLUSTER LAMPS

"OIL" WARNING LAMP   "TEMP" WARNING LAMP   "GEN" WARNING LAMP

RIGHT HAND TURN SIGNAL INDICATOR LAMP

HIGH BEAM INDICATOR LAMP

LEFT HAND TURN SIGNAL INDICATOR LAMP

CLUSTER LAMP

Back of Cluster

OLDSMOBILE F-85

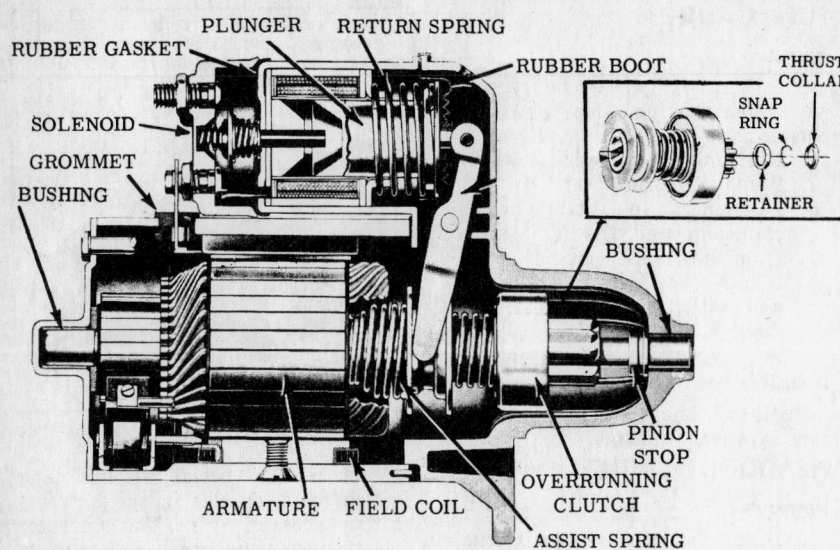

RUBBER GASKET — PLUNGER — RETURN SPRING — RUBBER BOOT — THRUST COLLAR — SNAP RING — RETAINER — SOLENOID — GROMMET BUSHING — BUSHING — PINION STOP — OVERRUNNING CLUTCH — ASSIST SPRING — ARMATURE — FIELD COIL

© 1960 Oldsmobile Div. G.M. Corp.

Starter Motor and Solenoid

tral safety switch, (used on cars with automatic transmission).

The starting motor and solenoid assembly is mounted on the flywheel upper housing, left side.

The solenoid switch closes the circuit between the battery and the starting motor. It also operates the shift lever that moves the drive pinion into mesh with the flywheel ring gear.

STARTER, R & R

No problem here. Disconnect battery. Remove starter cable from junction block and solenoid wire from harness. Unbolt starter and lift out. Cable loom will slide through support tube.

BRAKES

Specific information on brake lining sizes can be found in the General Chassis and Brake Specifications Table of this section.

Information on brake adjustments, band replacement, bleeding procedure, master and wheel cylinder overhaul can be found in the Unit Repair section under the heading: Brakes, Hydraulic.

Information on the grease seals which may need replacement can be found in the Unit Repair section. The head: Suspension, Front Repair. The rear wheel grease seals under the head: Axles, Rear.

The service brakes are of the conventional type, hydraulically operated. The lining is molded and attached to the shoes by tubular rivets. The primary shoe lining is shorter than the secondary lining and is of different composition.

Brake drum lining-contact-surfaces are cast iron, however, the drum

proper is pressed steel.

The parking brake uses a hand operated control lever, enclosed cables, rear wheel brake shoe levers and struts to the rear wheel shoes. The parking brake is released by turning the apply handle to the right. Starting 1963 they are self-adjusting.

FUEL SYSTEM

A chart covering causes of excess fuel consumption will be found in the Unit Repair section under the heading: Fuel Consumption Chart.

Data on capacity of the gas tank will be found in the Capacities Table. Data on correct engine idle speed and fuel pump pressure will be found in the Tune-up Specifications table. Both the above tables can be found in this section.

General information on fuel pumps and their troubles will be found in the Unit Repair section under the heading: Fuel Pumps.

Information covering operation and troubles of the fuel gauge will be found in the Unit Repair section under the heading: Gages.

Detailed information on the carburetor and how to adjust it will be found in the Unit Repair section under the broad heading: Carburetors, and the specific heading of the make of carburetor being used on the engine being worked on. Carter, Holley, Rochester and Stromberg carburetors are covered.

Dash pot adjustment can be found in the general section under the same heading as that of the automatic transmission used in the car.

CARBURETOR

The carburetor is a Rochester two barrel down draft compart unit mounted centerally between the two cylinder heads.

Idle and Choke Adjustments

Carburetor adjustments should not be attempted until it is known that all other items affecting engine performance are correct.

1. Adjust needle (idle mixture)

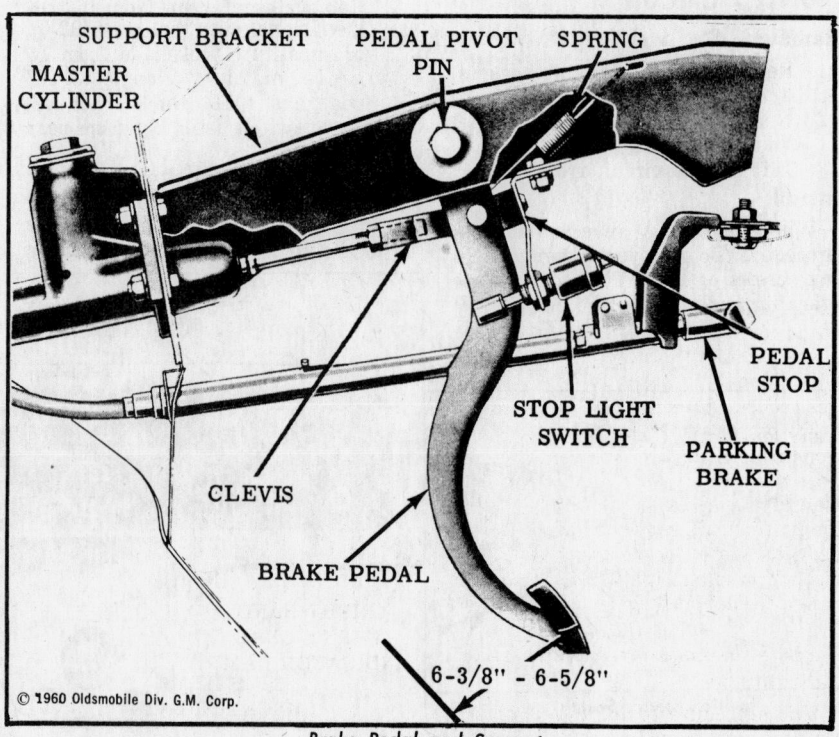

SUPPORT BRACKET — PEDAL PIVOT PIN — SPRING — MASTER CYLINDER — PEDAL STOP — STOP LIGHT SWITCH — PARKING BRAKE — CLEVIS — BRAKE PEDAL — 6-3/8" - 6-5/8"

© 1960 Oldsmobile Div. G.M. Corp.

Brake Pedal and Support

482

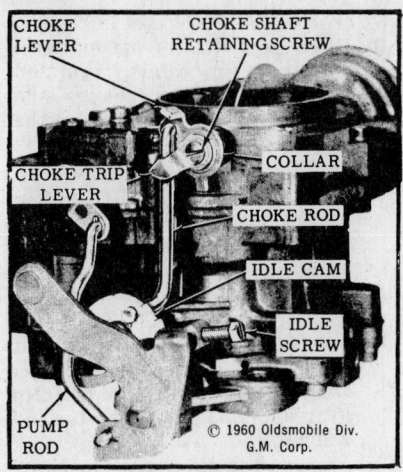

CHOKE LEVER

CHOKE SHAFT RETAINING SCREW

CHOKE TRIP LEVER

COLLAR

CHOKE ROD

IDLE CAM

IDLE SCREW

PUMP ROD

© 1960 Oldsmobile Div. G.M. Corp.

Rochester Carburetor

valves all the way in, until they are just seated. Then back off one complete turn. This is a temporary setting.

2. Back off the throttle stop screw and hold fast idle cam in **Hot** (wide open) position so that throttle valves are fully closed.

3. Turn throttle stop screw in, (clockwise) until it just contacts, then turn the screw in one complete turn. This should provide an approximate idling speed so the engine can be warmed up for final adjustment.

4. Now, with the engine at normal operating temperature and idling at 525 RPM, turn the needle valve "in" until the engine just begins to lag.

5. Then turn the needle out until the engine just begins to roll or gallop.

6. Then, slowly turn the needle in again and hunt for the position that produces the smoothest engine idle. Repeat this procedure on the idle mixture of the other barrel.

7. Readjust the throttle stop screw to obtain a hot idle of 525 RPM.

The choke thermostat is calibrated to work in conjunction with regular fuel when it is adjusted to original factory index. When it is necessary to adjust the thermostat, loosen the cover attaching screws and move the cover one point at a time until the desired results are obtained.

Do not try to accommodate for old and heat fatigued thermostats by adjustment. Original physical properties of the thermostat change after long use. Unit replacement is necessary to again obtain correct calibration throughout the choke operating range. Renew old choke thermostats.

Throttle Linkage and Dash Pot Adjustments

The procedure for adjusting throttle linkage is identical on "Standard"

or "Automatic" transmission cars. On automatic transmission cars, however, the linkage actuates other linkage connected to a valve in the transmission. Also, automatic transmission cars have a dash pot to prevent engine stalling from too-quick release of the accelerator pedal.

1. To adjust throttle linkage, make sure the accelerator pedal is free and in good linkage condition.

2. On automatic transmission equipped cars, see "Throttle Linkage Adjustment" of "Automatic Transmission," on the next few pages of this car section.

3. Disconnect rear end of throttle rod from throttle operating lever.

4. While a helper presses the accelerator firmly against the floor, hold throttle in wide open position. Hold rear end of throttle rod at hole in throttle operating lever. The rod end must be 1/16" short of entering the hole in the lever. Adjust throttle rod length to obtain this condition.

5. Connect throttle rod to operating lever and attach cotter pin.

6. Now, press accelerator to the floor and recheck throttle for wide open position.

7. Hold choke valve closed and move throttle lever to wide open position to check adjustment of choke unloader.

8. Finally check that there is a full opening of the throttle valve as the accelerator pedal just strikes the floor.

9. Now adjust the dash pot by turning the plunger until it just touches the throttle lever.

10. With the gear selector in "Drive" and the brakes firmly set, jab the accelerator and release it quickly. Note engine operation as the throttle closes.

11. If engine stalls due to too quick deceleration, move the dash pot plunger toward the throttle lever until the stalling is corrected. If too much time is required for throttle to close, move the plunger away from the throttle lever.

12. If correct control cannot be obtained, renew the dash pot.

FUEL PUMP

An AC Type HQ fuel pump is used. It is mounted on the left side of the timing chain cover in an inverted position. The pump lever works from the underside of a camshaft eccentric. It is of the single action diaphragm type and is equipped with a pulsation dampening chamber for stabilizing fuel flow.

FUEL FILTER

The tank gauge unit has a Saran

fuel filter on the end of the suction pipe. This filter prevents the entry of dirt or water into the fuel lines. The filter is a push pit and should be pressed on about 1-11/16" so that the pipe bottoms on the shoulder inside the filter.

Note: It is necessary to drop the gas tank to replace this filter or service the gas gauge, tank unit.

FUEL TANK

The fuel tank is attached by two strap type supports to the body under the trunk compartment.

The gas tank filler is soldered into an opening at the center of the left side of the tank. It is accessible through a door in the left rear quarter.

The stand pipe and fuel gauge sending unit are integral and require tank removal for replacement.

Tank Remove

1. Remove the gasoline by syphoning into a clean container.

2. Remove vent pipe.

3. Remove hoses and clips.

4. Disconnect the vent pipe from the breather pipe.

5. Disconnect gauge sending unit wire at the connector.

6. Disconnect support straps at their rear ends and lower the tank.

Tank Install

Install in reverse order of removal.

EXHAUST SYSTEM

EXHAUST MANIFOLD

Remove

1. Disconnect exhaust pipe.

2. For the **right manifold,** remove the rear generator mounting bolt, road draft tube, and disconnect the heat tube.

3. For the **left manifold,** disconnect the dipstick tube, remove power steering hoses (if so equipped) and raise the steering column.

4. Remove manifold-to-head attaching nuts and washers and remove the manifold.

Install

1. Apply a thin coating of graphite grease to the cylinder head and manifold surfaces.

2. Install manifold to head and torque nuts to 18-24 ft. lbs.

3. Reconnect other disconnected parts.

OLDSMOBILE F-85

PIPES AND MUFFLER

The single exhaust system is standard on all models. The front exhaust pipe is a one piece assembly which is attached to both exhaust manifolds. Before tightening any part of the exhaust system align for sufficient body clearance. See illustration for exhaust circuit plan.

COOLING SYSTEM

The cooling system is pressurized to 15 lb. Coolant temperature is controlled by a 170° thermostat housed in the forward (outlet) end of the intake manifold. This pellet type thermostat controls circulation and temperature in the intake manifold as well as the engine proper. A 180° thermostat is available for use with non-volatile type, permanent anti-freeze solutions.

WATER PUMP

The water pump cover is die cast aluminum into which the water pump bearing outer race is shrunk fit. Therefore, the cover, shaft bearing and hub are not replaceable. The shaft seal and the impeller are the only replaceable parts.

Remove

1. Drain cooling system.
2. Loosen belt or belts, then remove fan blades and pulley or pulleys from hub on water pump shaft. Remove belt or belts.
3. Disconnect hose from water pump inlet and heater hose from nipple. Remove bolts, then remove pump and gasket from the timing case cover.
4. Check pump shaft bearings for end play or roughness. If bearings are not serviceable, the assembly must be replaced.

Install

1. Install pump assembly with new gasket. Bolts and lock washers must be torqued evenly.
2. Connect radiator hose to pump inlet and heater hose to nipple. Fill cooling system and check all points of possible coolant leaks.
3. Install fan pulley or pulleys and fan blade. Install belt or belts and adjust for correct tension.

ENGINE TEMPERATURE AND OIL PRESSURE SENDING UNITS

A temperature switch located in right front of the intake manifold controls the operation of the "Temp" indicator light located in the instrument cluster.

If the engine cooling system is not working properly and the coolant temperature reaches 248°, the "Temp" indicator light will burn in the instrument cluster.

The oil pressure sending unit is located in the oil pump cover and operates an indicator light in the instrument cluster.

If engine oil pressure drops below a safe level during operation, the circuit is completed through the sending unit to ground. This will cause the "Oil" indicator light in the cluster to burn.

ENGINE

REFERENCES

This V-8 aluminum engine has a displacement of 215 cubic inches. The bore and stroke is 3.5" x 2.8" which produces 155 brake horsepower at 4800 RPM. Developed torque is 210 foot pounds at 3200 RPM with a compression ratio of 8.75:1. This should permit the use of regular type fuel, under normal operating conditions. The engine weighs about 318 pounds.

The pistons are aluminum alloy, anodized for long lasting surface finish. They operate within cast iron cylinder bores that are cast in the aluminum cylinder block. These sleeves are locked in place by grooves turned into their O.D.

Beginning Mid-1962

An optional engine is available, using the same basic 215 cu.in. engine and adding a turbo-charger and fluid injection system with 10:25-1 compression ratio, 215 H.P. @ 4600 R.P.M. is delivered. Presently available premium gasolines are utilized.

Caution: To help prevent thread damage, all bolts used in aluminum must be free of grit and well lubricated before installation. This caution applies particularly to cylinder head and main bearing cap bolts.

"Special Thread Lubricant" is available for this purpose. Sealing compound is also available and should be used as a non-hardening sealer and lubricant to prevent coolant seepage at the cylinder head bolts.

ENGINE REMOVE

When necessary to remove the engine from the car, the following items should be disconnected and the body raised off the engine and suspension.

1. Disconnect front exhaust pipe from the rear exhaust pipe.
2. Disconnect speedometer cable, front of propeller shaft, and shift linkage from transmission.
3. Disconnect clutch and equalizer on Synchro-Mesh equipped cars.
4. Disconnect battery cable from starter and the engine ground strap.
5. Disconnect accelerator linkage.
6. Disconnect wires from oil pressure sending unit, ignition switch, temperature gauge and disconnect the fuel line at the pump.
7. Drain cooling system and disconnect all water hoses. If air conditioned, remove the pressure hoses from the compressor and fan shroud.
8. Disconnect stabilizer brackets from the frame rail.
9. Disconnect and plug the front brake hoses.
10. Disconnect steering shaft from gear and raise up into steering column.
11. Remove the air cleaner and carburetor cover.
12. Place a block of wood between the front cross bar and the front of the engine oil pan. Remove the rear transmission mount cross support. Then support the rear of the transmission with a stand.
13. With the front wheels on the floor, remove the 3 isolation mount bolts and carefully raise the body off the engine and suspension.

ENGINE INSTALL

Installation is just the reverse of removal.

CYLINDER HEADS

INTAKE MANIFOLD REMOVE

1. Drain cooling system.
2. Remove carburetor air cleaner. Disconnect all tubes and hoses from the carburetor. Disconnect and remove the coil.
3. Disconnect temperature indicator wire from sending unit.
4. Disconnect accelerator and transmission linkage at carburetor. Disconnect throttle return spring.

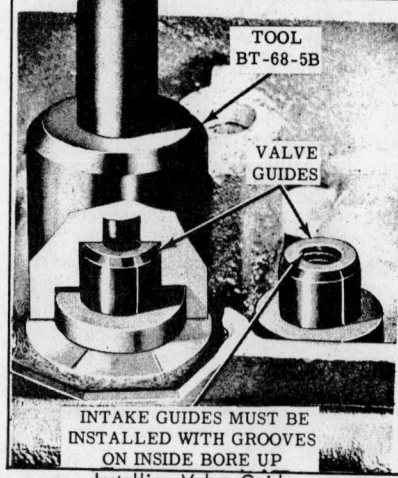

INTAKE GUIDES MUST BE INSTALLED WITH GROOVES ON INSIDE BORE UP
Installing Valve Guides

5. Slide front thermostat by-pass hose clamp back on the hose. Disconnect upper radiator hose at outlet.

6. Disconnect heater hose at the temperature control valve inlet. Force the end of the hose down to permit coolant to drain from intake manifold.

7. Remove 12 manifold-to-head attaching bolts.

8. Remove intake manifold and carburetor as an assembly by sliding rearward to disengage the thermostat by-pass hose from the water pump. Remove intake manifold gasket sound absorber.

9. Be sure there is no coolant present. Then remove intake manifold gasket clamps and remove the gasket. Remove rubber gasket seal.

INTAKE MANIFOLD INSTALL

Install by reversing above plan. Torque to 25-30 ft. lb.

EXHAUST MANIFOLD REMOVE

(Cylinder Heads Off)

1. Remove exhaust manifold-to-exhaust pipe attaching bolts.

2. **On the right side,** remove generator rear attaching bolt.

3. Unlock and remove exhaust manifold-to-cylinder head bolts. Remove the manifold.

EXHAUST MANIFOLD INSTALL

Install by reversing above plan. Torque to 18-24 ft. lb.

ROCKER ARMS AND SHAFT REMOVE

1. Pull spark plug wire retainers from brackets on rocker arm cover. Disconnect plug wires at the spark plugs and tie back out of the way.

2. Remove four screws holding the rocker arm cover to the cylinder head. **On the right side,** remove vent pipe. Remove rocker arm cover and gasket.

3. Remove four rocker arm shaft bracket-to-cylinder head attaching bolts. Remove rocker arm and shaft assembly. (Vent pipe oil baffle is mounted under rear bolts on right rocker arm and shaft assembly.)

4. Remove the push rods.

5. If lifters are to be serviced, remove them. If not, protect them with clean cloth.

ARMS AND SHAFT INSTALL

Install in reverse order of removal. Torque rocker shaft bracket bolts to 45-55 ft. lbs. Valve cover bolts to 3-5 ft. lbs.

Intake Manifold Torque Sequence

CYLINDER HEAD REMOVE

1. Drain cooling system.
2. Remove intake manifold.
3. Disconnect exhaust pipe.
4. Disconnect plug wires and remove the valve cover.

5. Right Cylinder Head Removal

a. Remove generator rear mounting bolt.

b. Remove ground straps at front and rear of cylinder head.

c. When equipped with a heater, remove all head bolts except rear

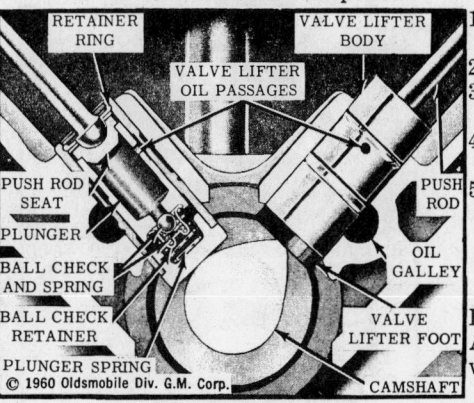

Hydraulic Valve Lifter

rocker arm shaft bracket bolt. (Blower motor prevents this.)

d. Loosen rear rocker shaft bracket bolt and raise the shaft from the head. Then remove all push rods but #16.

e. Lift #16 rod to within 1" of the blower and tape to rocker shaft.

f. Lift head, rocker shaft assembly and exhaust manifold off dowel pins and move forward to clear blower case.

6. Left Cylinder Head Remove

a. Remove power steering belt if so equipped.

b. Remove 2 power steering pump bracket-to-cylinder head bolts.

c. Remove rocker arm shaft assembly and remove push rods.

d. Remove cylinder head bolts and remove cylinder head with exhaust manifold attached.

CYLINDER HEAD INSTALL

Reverse the removal procedure. All head bolt threads must be coated with P.O.B. No. 4 Sealer or equivalent. Torque head bolts to 45-55 ft. lbs. and torque exhaust manifold to head bolts to 18-24 ft. lbs. Follow illustrated torque sequence.

Note: The cylinder head is equipped with removable valve guides and valve seat inserts.

Proceed with valve grinding and general cylinder head reconditioning in the conventional manner.

VALVE LIFTERS

Removal

1. Remove rocker cover, arms and shafts as above.

2. Lift out push rods, keep in proper sequence for reinstallation.

3. Remove lifters, if stuck with varnish apply good solvent and soak for several minutes. Tool BT-39 is an aid for hard removal.

Reinstall: Reverse the above.

Cleaning Lifters

1. Remove retaining spring with screw driver or Tool BT-31.

2. Remove push rod seat.

3. Remove plunger and spring. Use solvent if necessary.

4. Remove check ball retainer, then ball and spring.

5. Clean **thoroughly** in clean solvent. Be sure no foreign matter remains. If any parts are defective replace entire lifter assembly.

To reassemble: Reverse the above. Fill with oil and check for leak down. Always replace in same location from where removed.

ENGINE FRONT COVER

The front cover contains the timing chain and sprockets. It consists of part of the water pump, oil pump and filter mounting, distributor mounting and the mounting for the fuel pump.

FRONT COVER REMOVE

1. Drain cooling system.

2. Disconnect heater hose, by-pass hose and both radiator hoses. Disconnect oil pressure switch wire.

3. Remove crankshaft pulley, fan and fan pulley, and all belts.

4. Remove distributor cap, vacuum hose, generator and mounting bracket.

5. Remove fuel pump hoses, fuel pump and 2 front oil pan bolts.

6. Remove 9 cover-to-block attaching bolts and remove cover.

Note: Whenever the front cover is removed it is necessary to remove the oil pump cover and completely pack the pump gear housing with petrolatum. This is to prime the oil pump and insure immediate oil pressure to engine parts.

FRONT COVER INSTALL

1. Install new cover gasket with a good sealing compound.
2. Install the cover.
3. Oil attaching bolts and install. Torque evenly to 20-25 ft. lbs.
4. Apply special seal lubricant on pulley seal surface.
5. Install pulley, pulley bolt and pull the pulley into place. Torque to 140-160 ft. lbs.
6. Connect oil pressure switch.
7. Install generator mounting bracket and adjust the link.
8. Install fuel pump, using a new gasket and sealer.
9. Oil fuel pump bolts and torque to 20-25 ft. lbs.
10. Connect fuel lines.
11. Install distributor (see "Distributor" paragraph in this car section.)
12. Connect vacuum advance hose and primary wire.
13. Install distributor cap and wires.
14. Connect all of the hoses.
15. Install fan pulley, fan and 4 bolts.
16. Install and adjust belts.
17. Refill and bleed cooling system.

FRONT COVER SEAL

Remove

A wick type front cover seal is used.
1. Remove the seal retainer with a drift (timing case cover on the bench).

Install

1. Assemble the wick seal in the retainer.
2. Support front cover on block of wood. Apply P.O.B. No. 4 sealer to outside of seal retainer.
3. Place seal and retainer in cover with seal joint toward top of cover and stake until seated. Stake the retainer securely.
4. **Important:** Place tool #J-8753-2 in seal and push tool a little at a time from both sides until the tool goes through and sizes the seal.

TIMING CHAIN

Remove

1. With front cover removed, install harmonic balancer bolt and washer to the end of crankshaft. Rotate crankshaft so sprockets are positioned as for timing, (shafts and sprocket "O" marks on a centerline). Now remove harmonic balancer bolt with a sharp rap on the wrench handle to prevent changing the position of the sprockets.

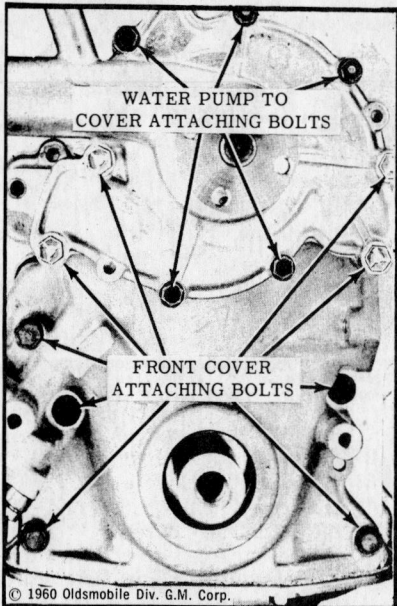

Engine Front Cover Bolts

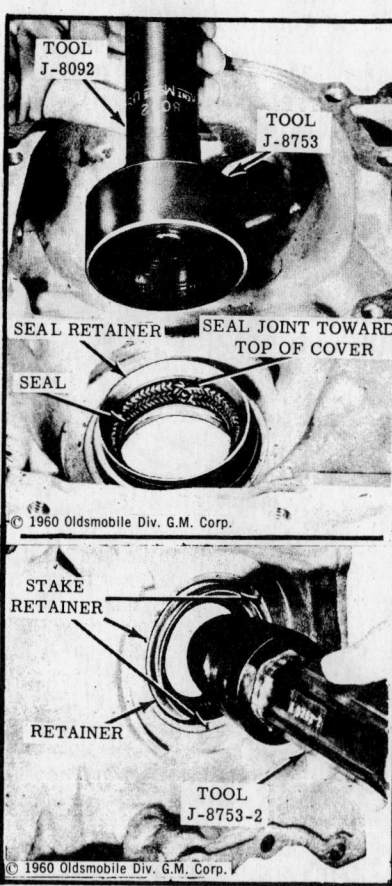

Front Oil Seal Install

2. Remove front crankshaft oil slinger.
3. Remove bolt and special washer holding the camshaft distributor drive gear and fuel pump eccentric to the camshaft. Slide gear and eccentric off the shaft.

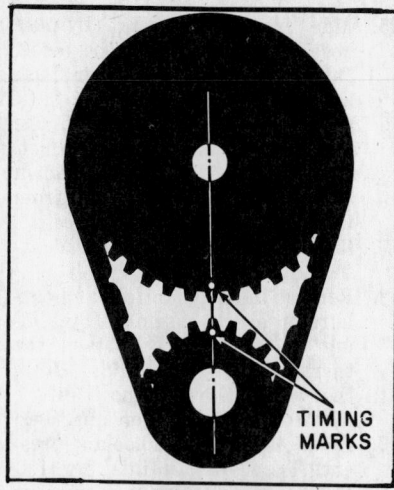

Valve Timing Plan

Fuel Pump and Distributor Drive

4. Use two large screwdrivers to alternately pry the camshaft sprocket then the crankshaft sprocket forward and off their respective shafts.
5. Thoroughly clean the sprockets, distributor drive gear, fuel pump eccentric and crankshaft oil slinger.

Install

1. Make sure, with sprockets temporarily installed, that #1 piston is at top dead center and the camshaft sprocket "O" mark straight down and on a centerline of both shafts.
2. Remove the camshaft sprocket and assemble the timing chain on both sprockets. Then slide the sprockets-and-chain assembly on the shafts with the "O" marks in their closest together position and on a centerline with the sprocket hubs.
3. Assemble slinger on crankshaft with I.D. against the sprocket, (concave side toward front of engine).

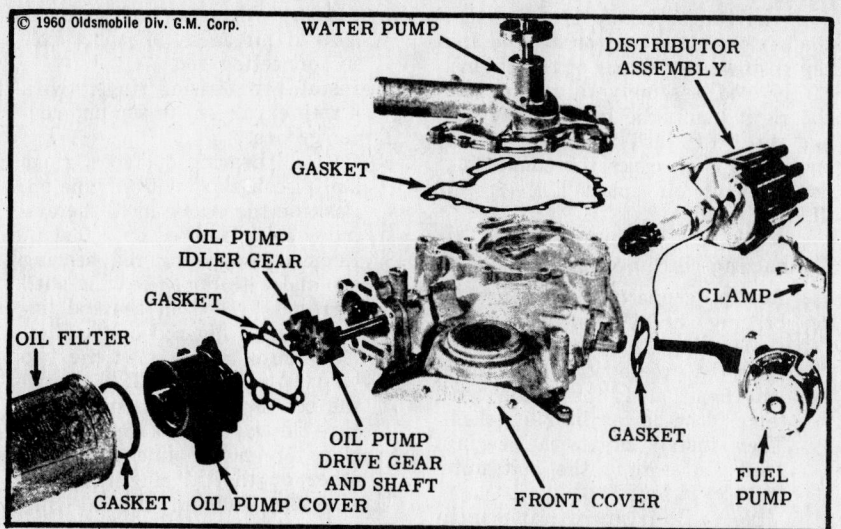

Engine Front Cover

4. Slide fuel pump eccentric on camshaft and Woodruff key with oil groove forward.
5. Install distributor drive gear.
6. Install drive gear and eccentric bolt and retaining washer. Torque to 40-45 ft. lb. See previous paragraph on "Front Cover Install."

ENGINE LUBRICATION

The engine lubrication system is the force feed type where oil is supplied under pressure to the crankshaft, connecting rods, camshaft bearings and valve lifters. Oil is supplied under controlled volume to the rocket arm bearings and push rods. All other moving engine parts are lubricated by gravity flow or splash.

OIL PUMP

The oil pump is located in the engine front cover where it is connected by a drilled passage in the cylinder crankcase to an oil screen housing and stand pipe assembly.

Oil is drawn into the pump through the screen and pipe. Oil is discharged from the pump to the oil pump cover assembly. The cover assembly con-

sists of an oil pressure relief valve, an oil filter by-pass valve and a nipple for installation of an oil filter. The oil pressure relief valve limits oil pressure to a maximum of 33 pounds per square inch. The oil filter by-pass valve opens if the filter becomes clogged to the extent that 4½ to 5 pounds pressure difference exists between the filter inlet and exhaust. This is a safeguard for oil passage to the main engine oil galleries in case of filter stoppage. See engine front cover.

OIL FILTER

A full flow oil filter is mounted on the oil pump at the right front corner of the engine. The filtering element should be changed every 6,000 miles unless conditions warrant earlier attention.

OIL PAN REMOVE AND INSTALL

1. Raise car and support on stands.

2. Drain engine oil.
3. Disconnect exhaust pipe at cross-over.
4. If standard transmission equipped, loosen clutch equalizer-to-frame attaching bolts.
5. Remove steering idler arm bracket-to-suspension crossmember attaching bolts.
6. Support engine with a padded jack under the oil pan.
7. Remove bolts and nuts attaching engine mounts to mount brackets.
8. Raise engine and insert bolts through bracket bolt holes, then lower engine so mounts rest on bolts or use support tool as illustrated.
9. Remove flywheel housing bolts. Then remove housing.
10. Remove oil pan bolts and lower the oil pan enough to remove oil pump pipe and screen-to-cylinder block attaching bolts.
11. Rotate crankshaft to provide maximum clearance at the front end of oil pan. Move the front of the pan to the right and lower the pan through opening between crossmember and steering linkage intermediate shaft.
12. Install by reversing removal procedure. Torque to 6-15 ft. lbs.

CONNECTING RODS AND PISTONS

REMOVE PISTON ASSEMBLIES

1. Remove cylinder heads.
2. Remove oil pan.
3. Examine cylinder bores for top ridge. If ridge exists, remove it before taking pistons out.
4. Number all the pistons, connecting rods and caps. Starting at

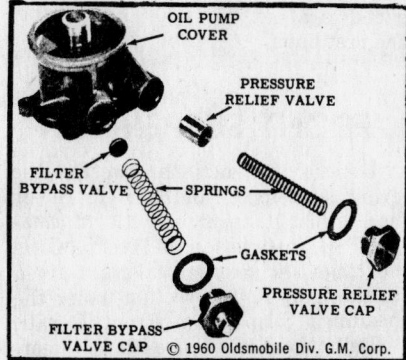

Oil Pump Assembly

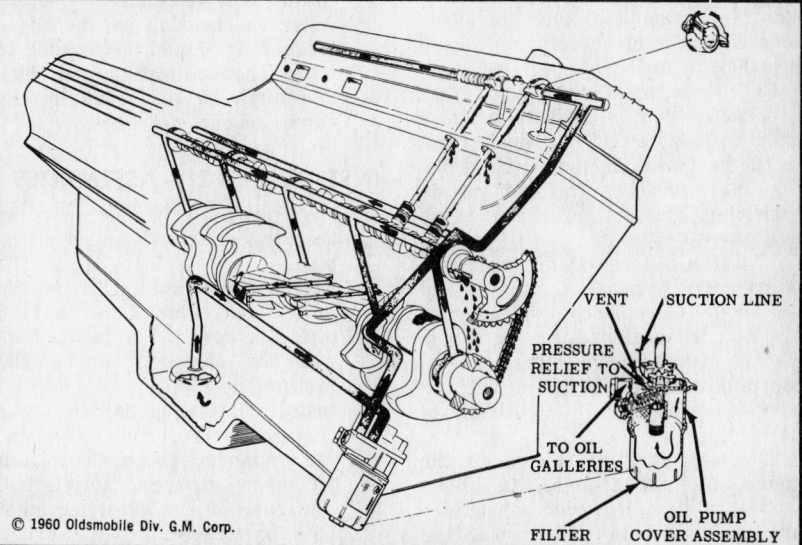

Engine Oil Flow

the front, the **right bank** is numbered 2-4-6-8. The **left bank** is numbered, 1-3-5-7.

5. With number 4 crankpin straight down, remove cap and bearing shell from #1 connecting rod. Install connecting rod bolt guides to hold upper half of the bearing shell in place.

6. Push piston and rod assembly up out of the cylinder. Then remove bolt guides and reinstall cap and bearing shell on the rod.

7. Remove the remaining rod and piston assemblies in the same manner.

8. Carefully remove old rings with

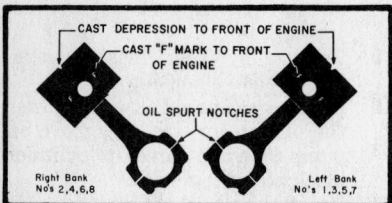

Piston and Rod Arrangement

piston ring expander.

9. Carefully press out the old pin.

Note: Check the cylinder bores for out-of-round, taper or other damage. Any cylinders requiring attention may be bored or honed the same as any conventional cast iron cylinder block. Maximum allowable taper is .010″.

Fitting Rings and Pins

When new rings are installed without reboring the cylinders, cylinder wall glaze should be broken. This can be done by using the finest grade stones in a cylinder hone.

New piston rings must be checked for clearance in piston grooves and for cap in cylinder bores.

When fitting new rings to new pistons the side clearance for compression rings should be .003″ to .005″. Side clearance of the oil ring should be .0005″ to .0055″.

Check end gap of compression rings by placing them in the bore in which they will operate. Then push them to the bottom of the bore with a piston. Now measure the end gap in each ring. The end gap should be no less than .015″.

If piston pin bosses are worn out of round or oversize, the piston and pin should be replaced. Oversize pins are not practical because the pin is a press fit in the connecting rod. Piston pins must fit the piston with an easy finger push at 70° F, (.0007″ to .0013″).

In assembling the piston to the connecting rod a press, (as illustrated) is ideal. However, substitutes are available that will answer the purpose.

If the rod assembly is to go into the **left bank**, the **boss on the rod** and cap go toward the **rear** of the engine. If the rod assembly is to go into the **right bank**, the **boss on the rod** and cap go toward the **front** of the engine. In both cases the connecting rod bearing oil spurt holes point "UP."

Connecting Rod Bearings

1. Remove connecting rod cap with bearing shell. Wipe all oil from the bearing area.

2. Place a piece of Plastigage lengthwise along the bottom center of the lower bearing shell. Then install cap with bearing shell and torque the bolt nuts to 30-35 ft. lb.

   Note: Do not turn crankshaft.

3. Remove the cap and shell. The gauge material will be found flattened and adhering to either the bearing shell or the crankpin. **Do not remove it.**

4. Using the scale that comes with the gauge, measure the flattened gauge material at its widest point. The number within the graduation which comes closest to the width of the gauging material indicates the bearing to crankpin clearance in thousandths of an inch.

5. Desired clearance for a new bearing is .0002″ to .0022″. If the bearing has been in service, it is wise to install a new bearing if clearance exceeds .0035″.

6. If a new bearing is required, try a "standard," then each undersize bearing in turn until one is found that is within specifications.

7. With the proper bearing selected, clean off the gauging material, reinstall the bearing cap and torque to 40-45 ft. lb.

8. After the bearing cap has been torqued, it should be possible to move the connecting rod back and forth on the crankpin, the extent of end clearance.

INSTALL PISTON ASSEMBLIES

1. Carefully assemble the piston to the connecting rod (press in the pin).

2. Remove piston and rod from the press. Rock the piston on the pin to be sure pin or piston boss was not damaged during the pressing operation.

3. Install ring expander in lower ring groove. Position the ends of the expander above the piston pin where groove is not slotted. The ends of the expander must butt together.

4. Install oil ring rails over expander with gaps "up" on same side of piston as oil spurt hole in connecting rod.

5. Install compression rings, (with a ring expander) in top and center groove.

6. Coat all bearing surfaces, rings and piston skirt with engine oil.

7. Position the crankpin of the cylinder being worked on, "Down."

8. Remove connecting rod bearing cap and with upper bearing shell correctly seated in the rod, install connecting rod bolt guides.

9. Make sure the gaps in the two oil ring rails are "UP" toward the center of the engine. Make sure the gaps of the compression rings are **not** in line with each other or the oil ring rails. Be sure the ends of the oil ring spacer-expander are butted and not overlapped.

10. With a good ring compressor, install the piston and rod assembly into the cylinder bore and carefully TAP down until the rod bearing is solidly seated on the crankpin.

11. Remove the connecting rod bolt guides and install cap and lower bearing shell. Torque to 30-35 ft. lb.

12. Install other piston and rod assemblies in the same manner. When the assemblies are all installed, the oil spurt holes will be "UP". The rib on the edge of the rod cap will be on the same side as the conical boss on the connecting rod web. These marks will be toward the other connecting rod on the same crankpin.

13. Accumulated end clearance between rod bearings on any crankpin should be .006″ to .014″.

14. Install oil screen and oil pan.

15. Install cylinder heads.

Note: Before starting a new or reconditioned engine it is advisable to pack the oil pump with petroleum jelly to insure pump priming for immediate lubrication. See "Engine Front Cover Install" in this section.

After starting the engine, avoid high speed but do not run on slow idle for a while. A better break-in speed is about 800-1,000 R.P.M. for the first hour.

FRONT SUSPENSION

General instructions covering the front suspension and how to repair and adjust it, together with information on installation of front wheel bearings and grease seals, are given in the Unit Repair section under the heading: Suspension, Front Repair.

Definitions of the points of steering geometry are covered in the Unit

Repair section under the heading: Suspension, Front Align. This article also covers trouble shooting front end geometry and irregular tire wear.

Figures covering the caster, camber, toe-in, king pin inclination and turning radius can be found in the Front Wheel Alignment Table of this section.

Overall length, brake cylinder and tire size figures can be found in the General Chassis and Brake Specifications Table at the start of this section.

The Oldsmobile F-85 front suspension is of the ball joint, independent type. It differs from the conventional Oldsmobile system in that it is attached to the body by 3 isolation mounts, (see illustration). The engine is supported by two mounts attached to the cross bar of the front suspension system. The entire system can be removed from the car as a unit. However, most parts can be serviced with the unit undisturbed.

BALL JOINT

The upper ball joint is spring loaded in its socket. If the upper stud has any noticeable shake, or if it can be twisted in its socket with the fingers, the ball joint should be replaced.

Remove

1. Raise front of car. Remove wheel with hub and drum assembly.
2. Remove cotter pin from the nut on ball joint tapered stud. Loosen nut but do not remove.
3. Force of chassis spring will be in favor of disengaging tapered stud from steering knuckle. Rap knuckle sharply with a hammer in the area of the tapered stud to disengage stud from knuckle.
4. Support lower control arm with jack and remove nut from ball joint stud. Raise upper control arm and remove tapered stud from knuckle.
5. Using a wire, hold the brake backing plate and steering knuckle assembly out of the way and to prevent damage to the brake hose.
6. With a 1-9/16" socket, remove the ball joint from tne control arm.

Install

1. Install new ball joint into control arm and tighten until hex section of ball joint seats firmly into arms.
2. Turn stud to align the cotter pin hole fore and aft and assemble rubber dust shield over stud.
3. Remove tie-back wire from steering knuckle and backing plate assembly and assemble tapered

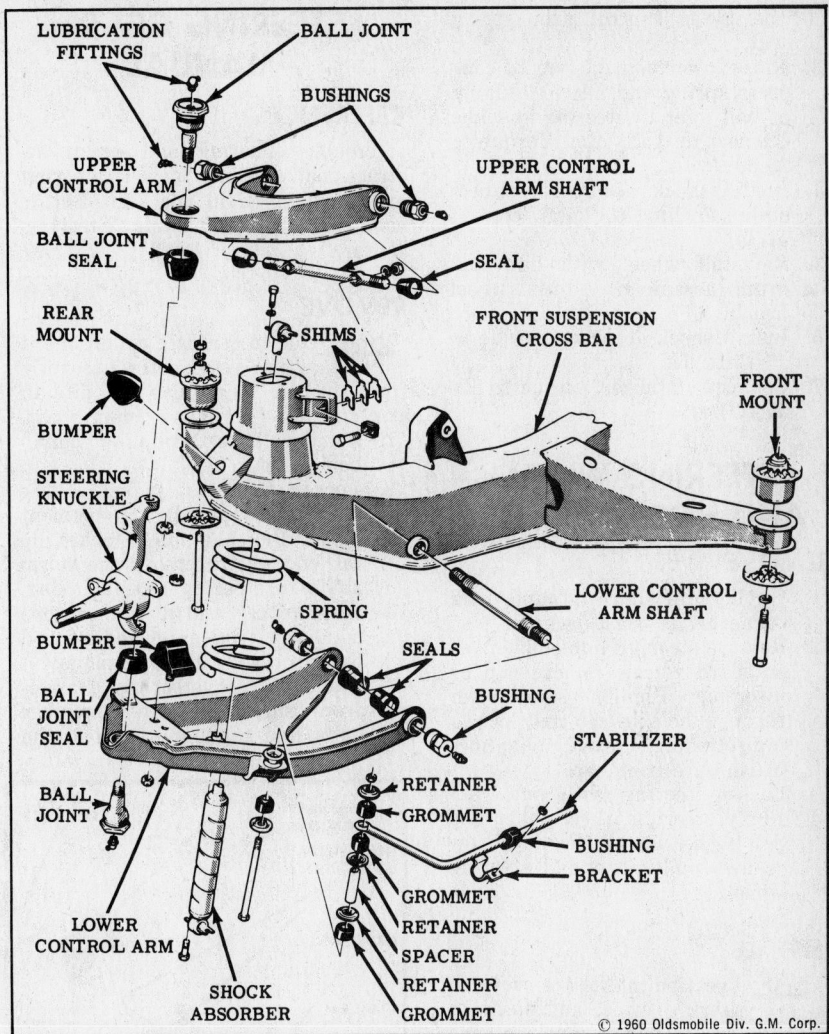

Front Suspension

© 1960 Oldsmobile Div. G.M. Corp.

stud to knuckle. Install castellated nut, torque to 35-60 ft. lb. and install cotter pin.
4. Reinstall wheel with hub and drum.

Note: Upper and lower joints look alike but are not interchangeable. Upper joints are spring loaded. Lower joints depend on the force of the chassis spring to keep the ball loaded.

FRONT SPRINGS

Because of weight variations due to undercoating, optional equipment, etc. the spring dimension given is for the standard car only. Curb weight, (height) includes fuel, oil, coolant and a spare tire but no passengers.

Spring Remove

1. Raise front of car. Remove wheel with hub and drum.
2. Disconnect stabilizer bar and remove front shock absorber.
3. Disconnect lower control arm ball joint from steering knuckle.
4. Lower jack until spring is fully extended and remove coil spring.

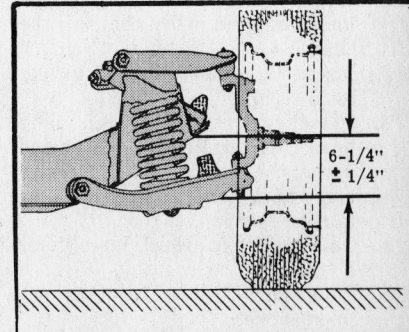

CARRYING HEIGHT AT CURB HEIGHT TO BE MEASURED FROM LOWER SIDE OF GAGE HOLE IN LOWER CONTROL ARM TO METAL SURFACE OF UPPER SPRING HOUSING.
© 1960 Oldsmobile Div. G.M. Corp.

Trim Height Front

Spring Install

1. Tape the insulator to top of spring. (Top of spring coil is flat.)
2. Position spring and insulator up in front suspension cross member. Rotate the spring to index the end of the bottom coil with

the lower control arm spring seat.

3. Raise lower control arm to compress spring and allow assembly of ball joint to steering knuckle. Connect up ball joint. Torque to 35-60 ft. lbs.
4. Install shock absorber. Connect stabilizer link to lower control arms.
5. Reinstall wheel with hub and drum assembly. Adjust wheel bearings.
6. Install shock absorber, torque to 15-25 ft. lbs.
7. Connect stabilizer, torque to 13-17 ft. lbs.

STEERING WHEEL AND HORN BUTTON

REMOVE

1. Unplug the horn ground wire connector at mast jacket.
2. Remove steering hub emblem, on standard wheels remove cap by inserting Phillips screwdriver through hole in cap and loosening retaining screw. Unplug horn brush wire from cap.
3. Loosen steering wheel nut.
4. Apply steering wheel puller and pull wheel up to the nut. Now remove puller, nut and steering wheel.

INSTALL

Note: Location marks are provided on the steering wheel and shaft to simplify proper indexing at the time of installation.

1. Install wheel with the location mark aligned with that of the shaft.
2. Install the wheel nut and torque to 25 ft. lb.
3. On the standard wheel, plug horn wire terminals together and install the cap assembly on steering wheel hub. Tighten the retaining screw.
4. On the deluxe wheel, install emblem.
5. Plug horn wires together on mast jacket.

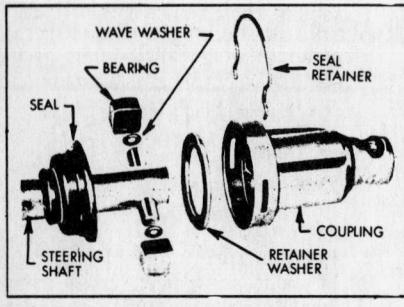

Coupling Assembly

STEERING GEAR —MANUAL

REFERENCES

Trouble shooting and repair instructions covering power steering gears are given in the Unit Repair section under the heading: Steering, Power.

REMOVE

Note: Due to compact conditions it is necessary to remove the assembly from the car to remove the pitman arm and nut from the pitman shaft.

1. Remove lower coupling clamp bolt and nut.
2. Loosen the mast jacket at the toe pan and the instrument panel. Pull the mast jacket up far enough to remove the worm shaft to steering gear coupling.
3. Jack up car and disconnect pitman arm from intermediate rod by unscrewing the end plugs.
4. Remove four steering gear-to-front suspension cross member bolts and nuts and remove the gear assembly.

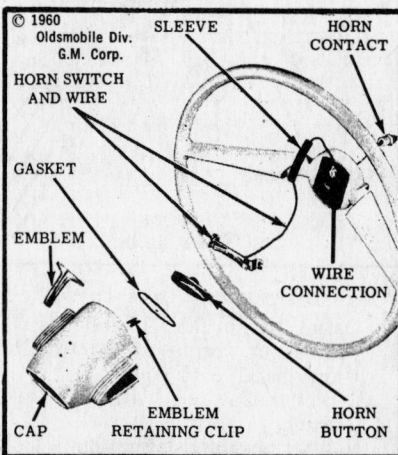

Standard Wheel

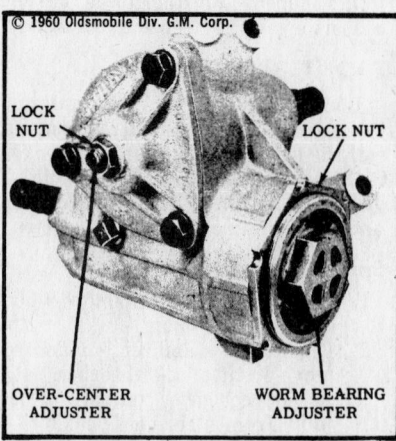

Manual Steering Gear Adjusting Points

Note: Do not remove pitman arm from gear unless shaft or seal are to be removed.

5. Grasp pitman arm in vise and remove pitman arm nut.
6. Remove pitman arm from shaft with a puller.

INSTALL

Install in reverse order of removal. Torque coupling clamp bolt to 35-40 ft. lbs.

ADJUST IN CAR

There are two adjustments on the steering gear: Worm bearing preload and pitman shaft overcenter preload.

The wheel should turn smoothly through its entire range. Roughness indicates internal trouble requiring disassembly. Binding (especially in straight ahead position) indicates too tight an adjustment. Steer alignment or linkage adjustment should be corrected before bear adjustment.

1. Be sure the steering gear-to-cross member bolts are torqued to 55 ft. lb.
2. Disconnect intermediate rod from pitman arm by unscrewing end plug until bearings will release ball socket.
3. Turn steering wheel slowly from one extreme to the other. **Never turn the wheel hard against the stopping point.**
4. Remove emblem or cap from steering wheel.

Worm Bearing Preload

5. Check worm bearing preload by turning the steering wheel gently in one direction until it stops. This positions the gear away from the "High Point" load.
6. Attach a 15/16" socket and "inch-pounds" torque wrench to the steering wheel nut. Turn the worm shaft with the wrench, through a one revolution range from either extreme. Torque required to keep the wheel moving through either one—revolution extreme should be 2-7 inch pounds.
7. Be sure the gear case side cover bolts are torqued to 30 ft. lb.

Straight Ahead Preload

8. Turn steering wheel from one extreme to the other while counting total turns. Then turn the wheel back exactly midway. This positions the steering gear on the "High Spot" or straight ahead position. A slight "drag" should exist at this point.
9. Check torque used to rotate the wheel through the "High Point" range. Torque should be 4 to 8

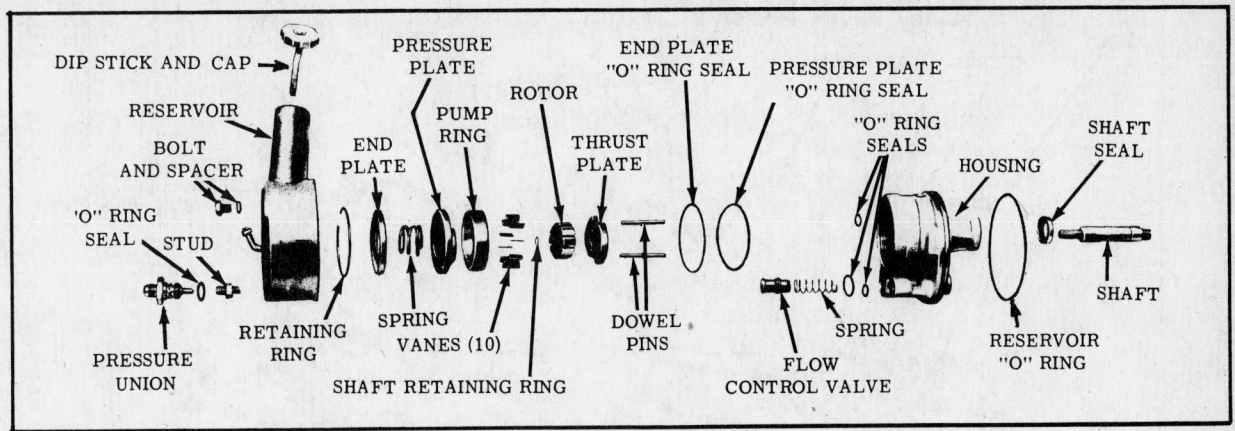

Power Steering Pump Assembly

DIP STICK AND CAP
RESERVOIR
BOLT AND SPACER
"O" RING SEAL
STUD
PRESSURE UNION
RETAINING RING
END PLATE
PRESSURE PLATE
PUMP RING
ROTOR
THRUST PLATE
SPRING VANES (10)
SHAFT RETAINING RING
DOWEL PINS
END PLATE "O" RING SEAL
PRESSURE PLATE "O" RING SEAL
"O" RING SEALS
FLOW CONTROL VALVE
SPRING
HOUSING
RESERVOIR "O" RING
SHAFT SEAL
SHAFT

inch pounds **higher than worm bearing preload.** The total "over-center" pull should not exceed 13 inch pounds.

10. Adjust pitman shaft overcenter preload by loosening lock nut and turning pitman shaft lash adjuster screw to obtain 4 to 8 inch pounds higher than worm bearing preload.

11. Tighten lock nut. Rotate steering wheel through its entire range. Then recheck for the maximum 13 inch pounds torque while passing through the straight ahead position.

STEERING GEAR —POWER

<u>Note:</u> Steering linkage for power steering is the same as that used with manual steering except for the pitman arm. The arm used with power steering has a larger splined hole to fit the power steering gear shaft.

The rotary valve power steering is optional on all models.

For more detailed information, see the Unit Repair Section, Steering—Power, Section 11.

PUMP

The Rotary Valve Power Steering Pump is mounted on the engine and belt driven from crankshaft pulley. The reservoir is integral with the pump housing.

The pump housing encloses the flow control valve and the rotor assembly. The flow control valve and spring are retained in the pump housing by the pressure union. This permits servicing the flow control valve without removing the pump.

The rotor assembly consists of a drive shaft, a thrust plate, a rotor with ten vanes, a pump ring and a pressure plate. The shaft is held to the rotor by a retaining ring. Oil enters the rotor section on the housing through a reservoir hole in the housing.

CLUTCH

A single plate, 9½" dry disc clutch is used in cars with manual transmissions. The unit is conventional in design with coil springs and three release levers. The levers are counterbalanced and are not adjustable.

CLUTCH REMOVE

1. Mark universal joint and transmission shaft companion flange for proper indexing at time of installation. Remove two "U" bolts and disconnect driveshaft at the front joint. Slide the driveshaft rearward as far as possible and tie to one side.

2. Disconnect shift linkage from transmission by first removing equalizer spring. Slide shift equalizer to full left position to disengage it from 2nd-3rd shift lever. Then slide equalizer to right to remove from support pin. Remove transmission 1st-reverse shift lever from shift shaft.

3. Disconnect speedometer cable at transmission.

Power Steering Gear

RETAINING RING
LOCK NUT
OIL SEAL
ADJUSTER PLUG
"O" RING
SIDE COVER
THRUST BEARING
THRUST WASHER
LOCK NUT
BOLTS AND LOCKWASHERS
"O" RING
ADJUSTER RETAINER
SHIM
SCREWS AND LOCKWASHERS
ADJUSTER SCREW
BALL RETURN GUIDE
PLUG
"O" RING
DUST SEAL
BEARING
TEFLON OIL RINGS
SPOOL VALVE SPRING
VALVE BODY
PITMAN SHAFT
SPRING
CLAMP
BALLS
"O" RING
SPOOL VALVE
"O" RINGS
LOWER SHAFT
"O" RING
WORM SHAFT
THRUST WASHERS
BEARING HOUSING
NEEDLE BEARING
WASHERS
RACK PISTON
OIL SEALS
TEFLON OIL SEAL
RETAINING RING
HOUSING END COVER
"O" RING
RETAINER RING

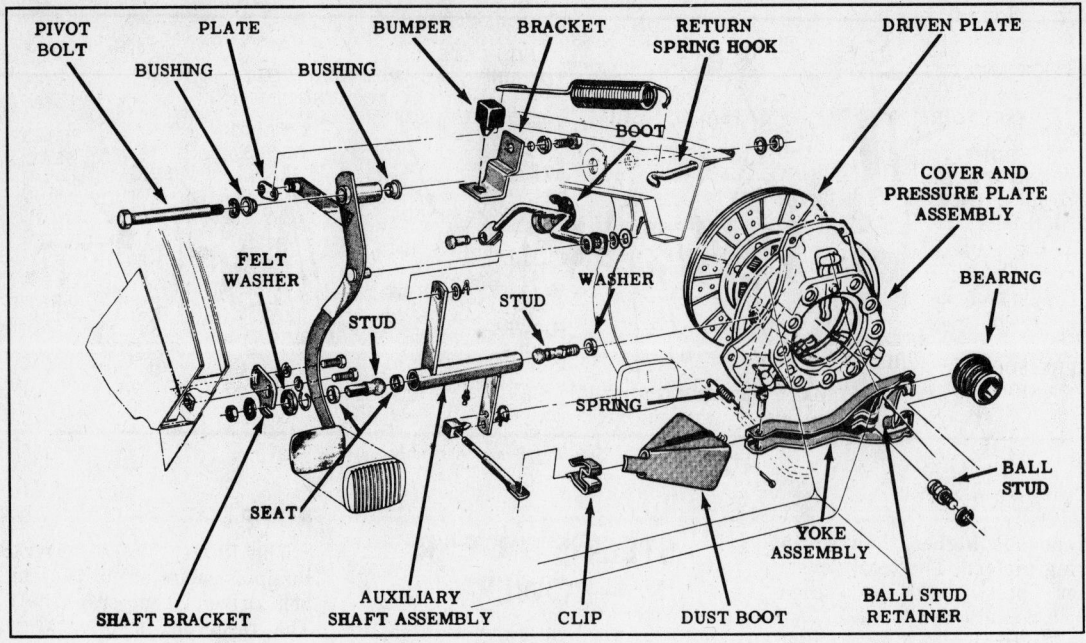

Clutch Linkage

PIVOT BOLT — PLATE — BUMPER — BRACKET — RETURN SPRING HOOK — DRIVEN PLATE — BUSHING — BUSHING — BOOT — COVER AND PRESSURE PLATE ASSEMBLY — BEARING — FELT WASHER — WASHER — STUD — STUD — SPRING — BALL STUD — SEAT — YOKE ASSEMBLY — BALL STUD RETAINER — SHAFT BRACKET — AUXILIARY SHAFT ASSEMBLY — CLIP — DUST BOOT

4. Loosen all three exhaust pipe ball joints to permit transmission and rear of engine to be lowered.
5. Remove two bolts holding transmission mounting pad to transmission support. Leave mounting pad bolted to transmission.
6. With a padded jack under the engine, raise the unit until the transmission mounting pad just clears the transmission support.
7. Remove four bolts holding transmission support to body members. Remove support, then lower the jack to allow transmission to clear the underbody.
8. Remove upper left transmission to flywheel housing bolt and install a 7/16" x 14 x 4½" guide pin. Remove lower right bolt and install a 7/16" x 14 x 3½" guide pin.
9. Remove the other two transmission attaching bolts. Slide the transmission back until the drive gear shaft disengages the clutch disc and clears the flywheel housing. Lower the transmission.
10. Remove clutch throw-out bearing.
11. Disconnect release rod from the fork by removing clevis pin. Unhook fork boot from opening in housing.
12. Push inward on fork to free it from ball stud in the housing and remove the fork through the bottom.
13. Mark clutch cover and flywheel to assure proper indexing at the time of installation.
14. Remove clutch cover attaching bolts and remove the clutch assembly.

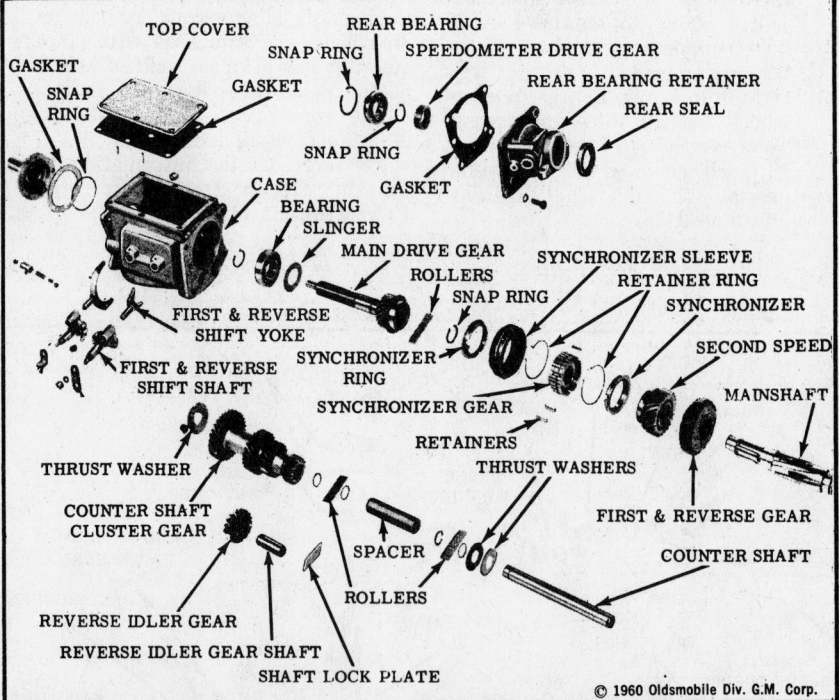

Synchromesh Transmission - 3 Speed

TOP COVER — REAR BEARING — SNAP RING — SPEEDOMETER DRIVE GEAR — GASKET — GASKET — REAR BEARING RETAINER — SNAP RING — REAR SEAL — SNAP RING — GASKET — CASE — BEARING SLINGER — MAIN DRIVE GEAR — SYNCHRONIZER SLEEVE — ROLLERS — RETAINER RING — SNAP RING — SYNCHRONIZER — FIRST & REVERSE SHIFT YOKE — SECOND SPEED — SYNCHRONIZER RING — MAINSHAFT — FIRST & REVERSE SHIFT SHAFT — SYNCHRONIZER GEAR — RETAINERS — THRUST WASHER — THRUST WASHERS — COUNTER SHAFT CLUSTER GEAR — FIRST & REVERSE GEAR — SPACER — COUNTER SHAFT — ROLLERS — REVERSE IDLER GEAR — REVERSE IDLER GEAR SHAFT — SHAFT LOCK PLATE — © 1960 Oldsmobile Div. G.M. Corp.

CLUTCH INSTALL

Install clutch by reversing removal procedure. Use a clutch aligning pilot or a spare main drive gear through the hub of driven plate and into the pilot bushing. Be sure to align the clutch cover-to-flywheel index marks.

TORQUES:

Clutch-to-flywheel 15 ft. lb. Rear transmission mount 35 ft. lb. Rear mount to cross bar 30 ft. lb. Cross bar to body 30 ft. lb. "U" bolt nuts 16 ft. lbs.

CLUTCH LINKAGE INSTALL

Check pedal lash (free play) by pushing on the pedal with the hand. Lash should be ⅞" to 1" measured at the pedal pad.

1. Make sure the pedal returns against the pedal bumper when the pedal is released.
2. With the car raised, pull outer end of the clutch fork rearward until throw-out bearing contacts clutch fingers. Free movement at outer end of fork should be

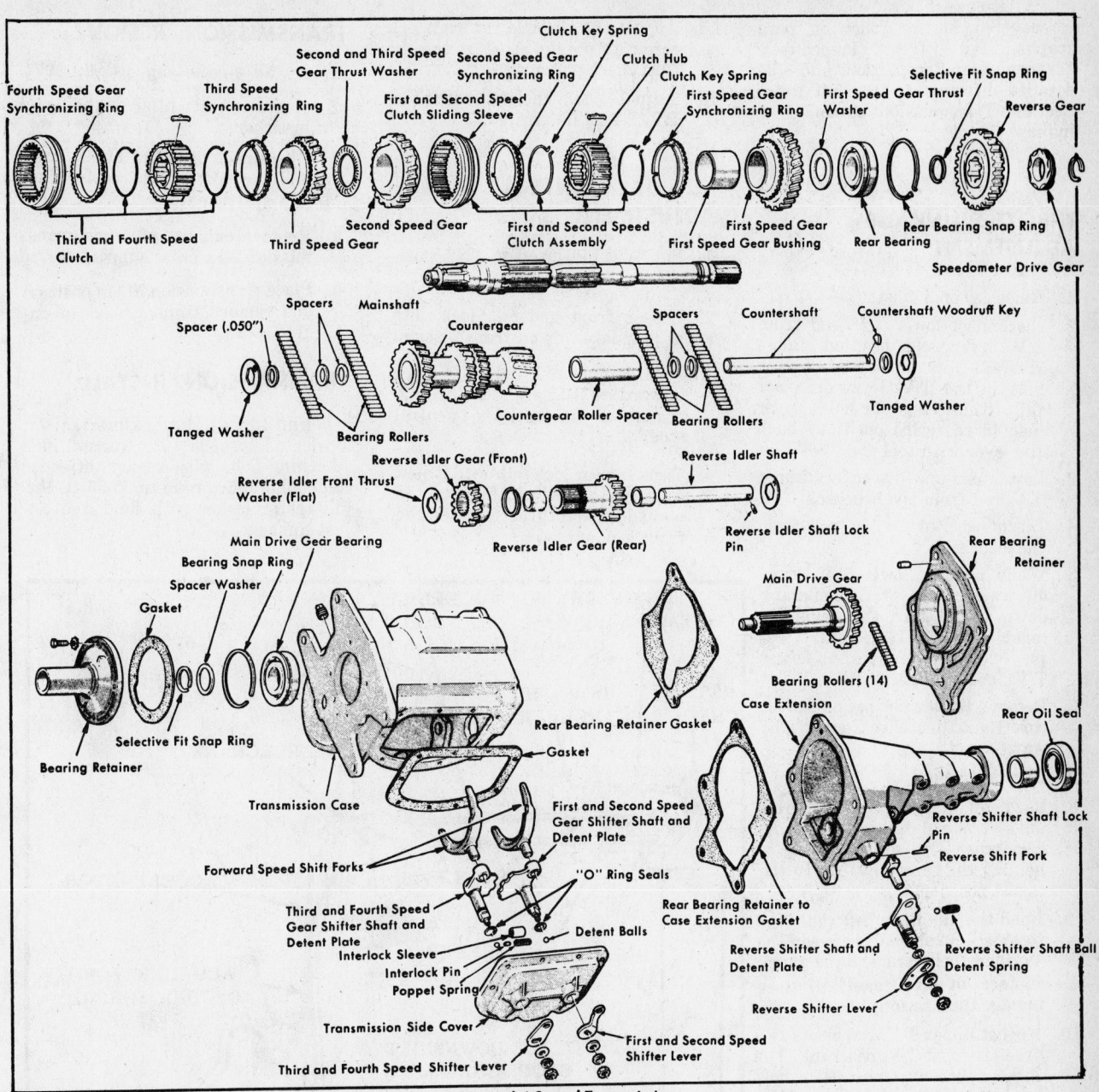

Manual 4-Speed Transmission

3/16". This should equal about 1 inch at the pedal.

3. If adjustment must be made, remove clevis pin from rear end of clutch release rod and rotate rod as needed to produce correct play.

4. Reinstall clevis and cotter pin.

STANDARD TRANSMISSION

The transmission is a conventional Synchromesh Transmission with 2nd & high synchronizing sleeve.

REMOVE AND INSTALL

See Clutch paragraph.

SHIFT CONTROLS

1. Place both shift levers in neutral detent position.
2. Loosen shift rod adjusting clamps and place both lower control shaft levers in horizontal positions. (Levers must be exactly parallel.)
3. Tighten 2nd-3rd shift rod adjusting clamp.
4. Lift manual control lever from 2nd-3rd range straight toward steering wheel into 1st-Reverse range. Do this several times to align 1st and Reverse lower control shaft lever. Then tighten 1st-Reverse shift rod adjusting clamp.
5. To recheck, depress clutch and

shift transmission into each gear to check lower control shaft lever clearance in steering column jacket opening. Make sure that the manual lever movement from 2nd-3rd range into 1st-Reverse range is smooth and easy.

AUTOMATIC TRANSMISSION

REFERENCES

When difficulty is reported, a road test and careful diagnosis of transmission performance is in order.

"Transmission Remove and Replace" and "Linkage Adjustments"

are covered in the following paragraphs. For "Test Procedures," "Transmission Recondition" and other detailed information see Unit Repair Section, Transmission Group of the manual.

THROTTLE LINKAGE ADJUSTMENT

1. Raise car on a hoist.
2. Disconnect lower T.V. rod from T.V. lever and position gauge #BT-33-2 as illustrated. If the hole in the T.V. lever does not fall within the gauge hole, (lever held in rearward position) bend the lever with tool #BT-33-7.
3. Lower car and disconnect upper T.V. rod from the bellcrank.
4. Disconnect lower T.V. rod from the bellcrank.
5. While holding lower T.V. lever downward and T.V. bellcrank down at the rear, the clevis pin must fit freely. If necessary, adjust clevis, then hook up lower T.V. lever to bellcrank.
6. Remove the air cleaner and pivot throttle return check out of the way.
7. Block choke open.
8. Back off idle adjusting screw until it is not touching the idle cam when the return spring is holding the throttle valves in the closed position.
9. Bend the auxiliary bellcrank link to obtain .020"-.040" between the auxiliary bellcrank and the gauge surface of the manifold, (see linkage illustration).
10. Adjust upper T.V. rod clevis to a free pin fit at T.V. bellcrank. The T.V. bellcrank must be held against its stop at the rear. Then adjust the clevis ½ turn longer.
11. Loosen the throttle down shift stop screw lock nut and back-off stop screw about 6 turns. With accelerator lever, move the throttle to wide open. This will overtravel the linkage to point of maximum transmission T.V. lever travel.
12. Holding accelerator lever in wide open position, set the stop screw to just touch the down-shift lever tang. Then screw the stop screw in an additional 1½ turns.
13. With the idle cam hold the choke in the "Off" position and adjust the idle speed.
14. Reposition throttle return check.

15. Adjust the throttle return check screw to obtain .020" at the return check plunger.
16. Adjust pedal height with tool BT-33-2 as illustrated.

MANUAL CONTROL ADJUSTMENT

1. Put selector lever in "N" position.
2. Loosen front and rear lock nuts at manual lever on transmission.
3. Hold manual rod and shift lever upward so the selector lever is positioned against the neutral stop.
4. Tighten rear lock nut until it just contacts the swivel, then tighten two additional turns. Tighten the front lock nut.

TRANSMISSION, REMOVE

1. Install engine support #J-8974.
2. Remove oil filler tube and breather.
3. Disconnect propeller shaft, shift and throttle linkage, cooler lines and speedometer cable.
4. Remove exhaust pipe and transmission rear cross support bar.
5. Place transmission lift in position and remove transmission to engine bolts.

TRANSMISSION, INSTALL

When installing transmission, lubricate threads of transmission attaching bolts with a good anti-seize compound and torque to 30-35 ft. lbs. Fill transmission with fluid and adjust linkage.

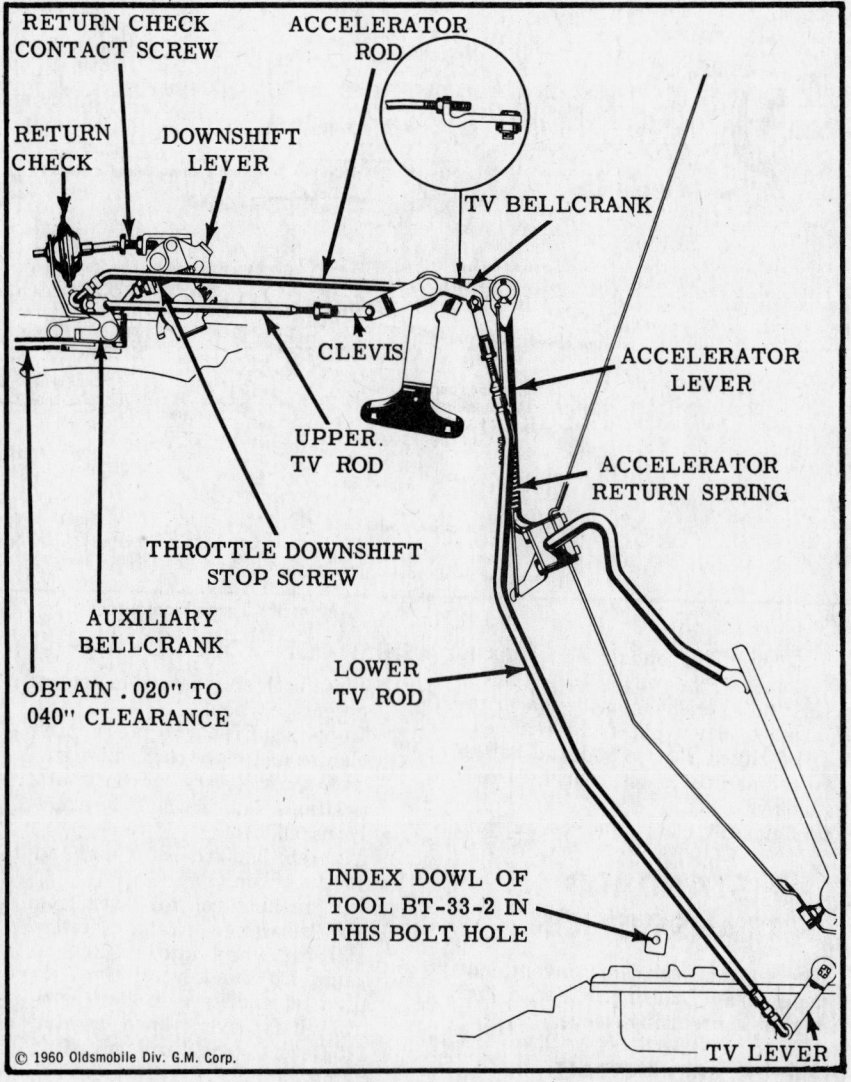

RETURN CHECK CONTACT SCREW
ACCELERATOR ROD
RETURN CHECK
DOWNSHIFT LEVER
TV BELLCRANK
CLEVIS
ACCELERATOR LEVER
UPPER TV ROD
ACCELERATOR RETURN SPRING
THROTTLE DOWNSHIFT STOP SCREW
AUXILIARY BELLCRANK
LOWER TV ROD
OBTAIN .020" TO 040" CLEARANCE
INDEX DOWL OF TOOL BT-33-2 IN THIS BOLT HOLE
© 1960 Oldsmobile Div. G.M. Corp.
TV LEVER

Throttle Linkage

UNIVERSAL AND DRIVE LINE

The drive line consists of a front propeller shaft, a rear propeller shaft, a standard universal joint at the extreme of each end and a double type, constant velocity universal joint in the center.

A center support bearing attaches the rear end of the front propeller shaft to the under side of the body. A splined front yoke on the front end of the rear propeller shaft extends into a splined coupling in the rear end of the front propeller shaft. This slip spline allows for the variety of lengths occurring in the propeller shaft due to road and torque conditions.

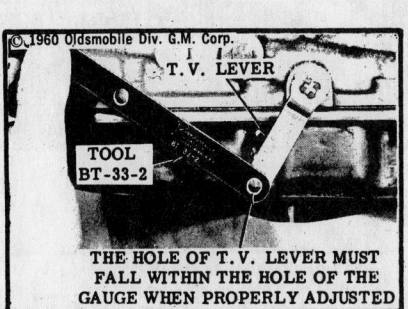

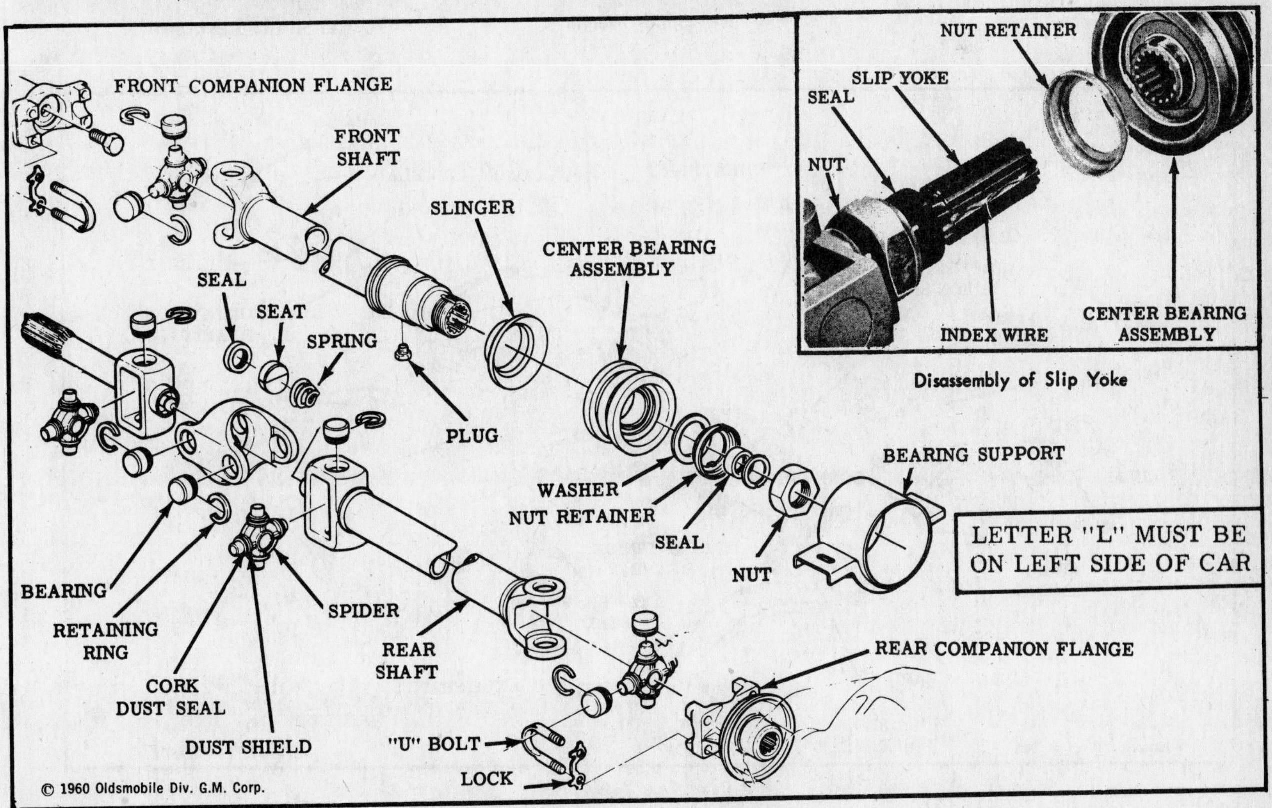

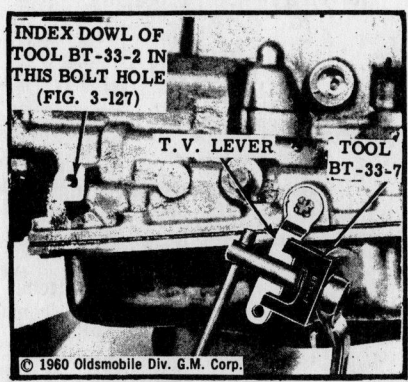

INDEX DOWL OF TOOL BT-33-2 IN THIS BOLT HOLE (FIG. 3-127)
T.V. LEVER
TOOL BT-33-7
© 1960 Oldsmobile Div. G.M. Corp.
Bending T.V. Lever

The propeller shaft assembly needs very little periodic service. The center bearing is lubricated for life and requires no additional lubrication. The universal joints are lubricated for life and cannot be lubricated while in the car. If a joint becomes noisy or worn a service kit must be installed which consists of a spider complete with bearing assemblies.

The center ball and socket cannot be lubricated in the car. Whenever the center joint is taken apart, the ball and socket must be lubricated with Multi-Purpose Grease E.P. # 1 Grade.

© 1960 Oldsmobile Div. G.M. Corp.
T.V. LEVER
TOOL BT-33-2
THE HOLE OF T.V. LEVER MUST FALL WITHIN THE HOLE OF THE GAUGE WHEN PROPERLY ADJUSTED
Checking T.V. Lever

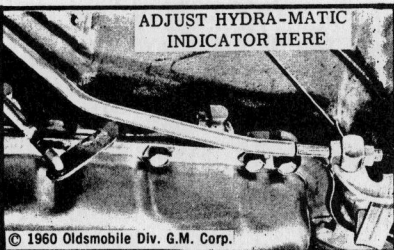

ADJUST HYDRA-MATIC INDICATOR HERE
© 1960 Oldsmobile Div. G.M. Corp.
Indicator Adjustment

The slip spline must be lubricated with the same type grease every 10,000 miles. To lubricate the spline, remove the plug and install a temporary grease fitting. When grease appears at the slip joint nut, replace the grease fitting with the plug.

Propeller Shaft Torques

"U" bolts 16 ft. lbs. Center bearing to body 14 ft. lbs. Slip yoke nut 50-75 ft. lbs.

REAR AXLE AND SUSPENSION

The rear axle assembly is of the semi-floating type in which the car weight is carried on the axle shafts through ball bearings in the rear axle tubes. Car drive is transmitted from the axle housing to body members through two lower and two upper control arms. Large rubber bushings at either end of these arms are designed to absorb vibration and noise. The arms also act as seats for the coil springs and are angle mounted to control sidewise movement of suspension.

NUT RETAINER
SLIP YOKE
SEAL
NUT
INDEX WIRE
CENTER BEARING ASSEMBLY
Disassembly of Slip Yoke
FRONT COMPANION FLANGE
FRONT SHAFT
SLINGER
CENTER BEARING ASSEMBLY
SEAL
SEAT
SPRING
PLUG
WASHER
NUT RETAINER
SEAL
NUT
BEARING SUPPORT
LETTER "L" MUST BE ON LEFT SIDE OF CAR
BEARING
RETAINING RING
CORK DUST SEAL
DUST SHIELD
SPIDER
REAR SHAFT
"U" BOLT
LOCK
REAR COMPANION FLANGE
© 1960 Oldsmobile Div. G.M. Corp.
Universal Joint Plan

OLDSMOBILE F-85

REAR AXLE ASSEMBLY, REMOVE

It is not necessary to remove the rear axle assembly for normal repairs. However, if the housing is damaged, the rear axle assembly may be removed and installed using the following procedure.

1. Raise rear of car high enough to permit working under the car. Place a floor jack under center of axle housing so it just starts to raise rear axle assembly. Place car stands solidly under body members on both sides.

2. Mark rear universal joint and pinion flange for proper indexing at the time of installation. Then disconnect rear universal joint at pinion flange. Wire the propeller shaft back out of the way.

3. Disconnect parking brake cables at the sheave. Remove cable connector and two clips and slide cable back until free of body.

4. Disconnect rear brake hose at floor pan.

5. Disconnect shock absorbers at axle housing. Lower jack under housing until rear springs can be removed.

6. Disconnect upper control arms at axle.

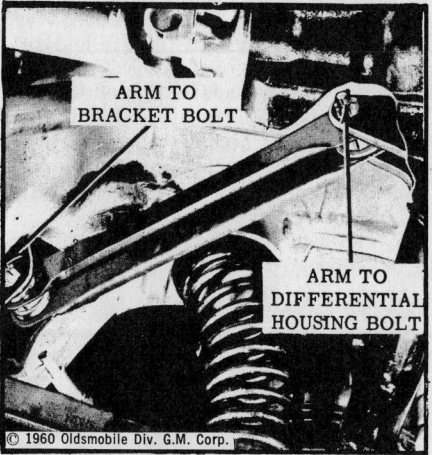

© 1960 Oldsmobile Div. G.M. Corp.

Upper Suspension Arm

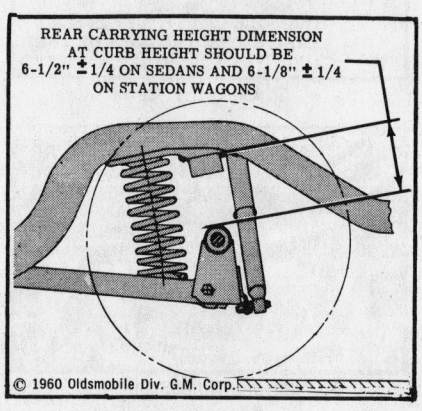

REAR CARRYING HEIGHT DIMENSION AT CURB HEIGHT SHOULD BE 6-1/2" ±1/4 ON SEDANS AND 6-1/8" ±1/4 ON STATION WAGONS

© 1960 Oldsmobile Div. G.M. Corp.

Rear Spring Height

7. Disconnect lower control arms at axle housing and roll rear axle assembly out from under the car.

REAR AXLE ASSEMBLY, INSTALL

Install in reverse order of removal. **Note:** For detailed information on rear axle see Unit Repair Section, xles Rear.

REAR SPRING REMOVE

1. Disconnect shock absorber at lower bracket.
2. Slack off parking brake at brake equalizer.
3. Raise the rear of the car until the coil spring can be removed.

REAR SPRING INSTALL

Reverse removal procedure.

RADIO

RADIO REMOVE AND INSTALL

1. Disconnect lead from wiring harness.
2. Disconnect antennae and speaker leads.
3. Remove control knobs, escutcheons and supportnuts from front panel.
4. Support unit and remove rear bracket, then lower and remove assembly.

To Reinstall: Reverse the above.

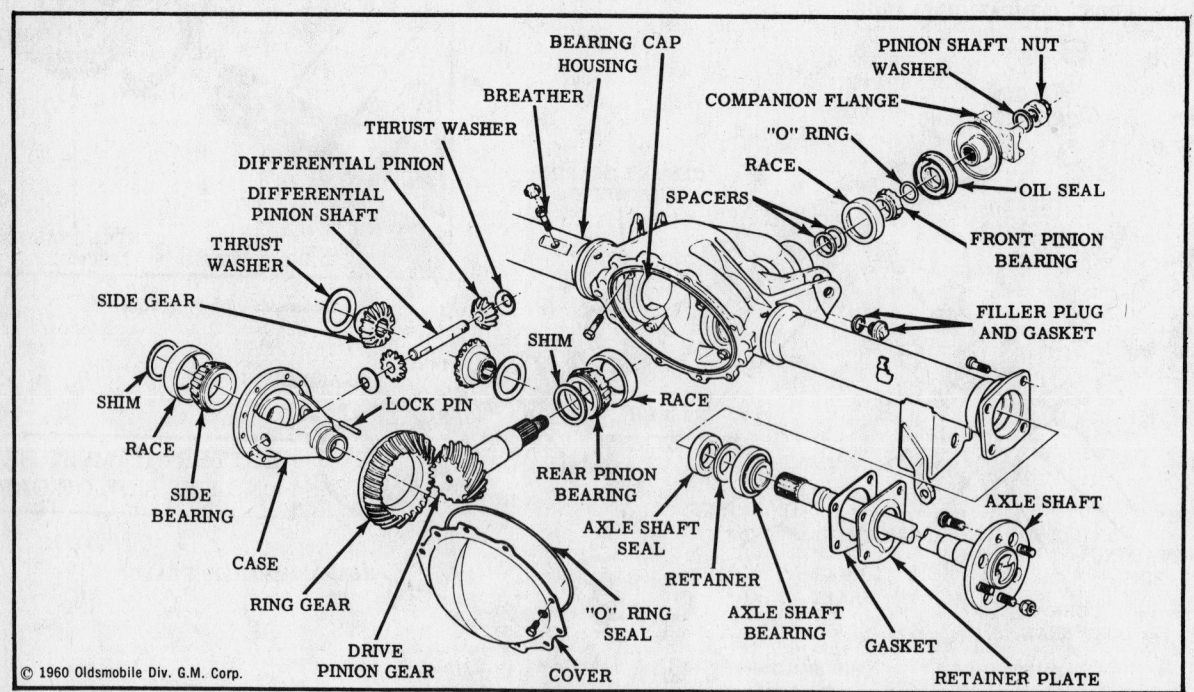

© 1960 Oldsmobile Div. G.M. Corp.

Rear Axle Assembly

Page

AIR CONDITIONING
Service 1092
BRAKES, HYDRAULIC
Adjustments 938
References 509
Bleed brakes 941
Hand brake, adjust 511
Hand brake lever & cable 510
Master cylinder, R & R 510
Master cylinder service 939
Hand brake 510
BRAKES, POWER
Power unit overhaul 954
Trouble shooting 954
CLUTCH
Clutch assembly, R & R 524
Clutch pedal, adjust 525
COOLING SYSTEM
Cooling system 514
Radiator core, R & R 514
Water manifolds 514
Water pump, R & R 514
Water distribution tube 514
ELECTRICAL SYSTEM
Alternator overhaul 1035
Alternator, R & R 509
Alternator specifications 500
Distributor, R & R 508
Distributor specifications 502
Engine 508
Fuses and circuit breakers 504
Light Bulbs 503
Gauges 1024
Generator regulators
  specifications 500
Generator service 1026
Generator specifications 500
Generator trouble shooting
  chart 1026
Horn buttons 524
Ignition firing order & timing ..499
Ignition timing specifications ..501
Starter, R & R 509
Starter specifications 503
Starter systems 1046
ENGINE ASSEMBLY
Cylinder head, R & R 517
Cylinder head tightening 507
Engine assembly, R & R 516
Engine diagnosis 1012
Engine firing order & timing ..499
Engine marking code 500
Engine references 515
Exhaust manifold, R & R 513
Inlet manifold, R & R 513
Oil pan, R & R 520
Oil pressure specifications 505
Piston and rod, R & R 521
Piston and pin specifications ..506
Rocker arms & shaft, R & R ...516
Rocker cover, R & R 516
Rear main bearing oil seal 521
Specifications, general engine .505

Page

ENGINE ASSEMBLY—continued
Timing case cover & seal, R & R 519
Timing chain, R & R 519
Trouble shooting charts 1012
Tune-up specifications 501
Valve specifications 507
Valve springs 519
Valves and guides 519
Valves, R & R 518
Valve system 517
ENGINE LUBRICATION
Oil pan 520
EXHAUST SYSTEM
Exhaust pipe 513
Muffler 513
Tail pipe 513
Heat control valve 513
Manifolds, R & R 513
FUEL SYSTEM
Carburetors 972
Fuel filters 513
Fuel gauge service 1024
Fuel pump pressure 501
Fuel pump service 1020
Fuel pump, R & R 512
Fuel tank, R & R 512
Fuel system 511
References 511

INSTRUMENTS
Fuel gauge 509
Speedometer 509
Temperature gauge 509
Windshield wiper motor 509
OVERDRIVE
Overdrive disassembly 914
Trouble shooting 915
RADIO, R & R
References 534

REAR AXLE AND SUSPENSION
Axle assembly, R & R 534
Axle shaft 918
Axle shaft oil seal 918
Pinion bearings 918
Ring gear & pinion 918
Shock absorbers 534
Trouble shooting 919

SPECIFICATIONS
Alternators 500
Battery 503
Brake cylinder sizes 503
Capacities:
  Axle, rear 504
  Cooling system 504
  Crankcase 504
  Fuel tank 504
  Transmission, automatic ..504
  Transmission, manual 504
Chassis, general 503
Cylinder head tightening 507
Distributor 502
Engine firing order & timing ..499

Page

SPECIFICATIONS—continued
Engine, general 505
Engine tune-up 501
Fuses and circuit breakers 504
Generator regulators 500
Light bulbs 503
Main bearings 506
Model identification
  illustrations 498
Model year identification 498
Piston and pins 506
Quick reference specifications .499
Rod bearing 506
Starters 503
Torque wrench 507
Tune-up 501
Valves 507
Wheel alignment 508
STEERING, MANUAL
Adjust gear housing 1052
Gear assembly, R & R 523
Horn button, R & R 524
STEERING, POWER
Pump assembly 1058
Trouble shooting 1081
Unit overhaul 1058
SUSPENSION, FRONT
Alignment procedures 1082
Adjustments 522
Alignment specifications 508
Ball joints, R & R 1087
Front height 523
King pins and bushings 1087
Knuckle supports 1087
Support arms, pins and
  bushings 1087
Torsion bars 522
TRANSMISSION, AUTOMATIC
Powerflite 778
  Linkage, adjust 527
  Transmission, R & R 528
  Converter, R & R 529
Torqueflite "A" 788
  Linkage, adjust 530
  Push button, R & R 530
  Transmission, R & R 530
  Converter, R & R 531
Torqueflite "B" 802
  Linkage, adjust 532
  Transmission, R & R 533
TRANSMISSION, STANDARD
Disassemble transmission 525
Transmission, R & R 525
TROUBLE CHECKS
Procedures 1
TUNE-UP
Procedures 1012
Specifications 501
Engine diagnosis 1012
UNIVERSAL JOINT AND
DRIVE LINES
Disassemble U joint 534
U joint & drive lines, R & R ...534

PLYMOUTH

YEAR IDENTIFICATION

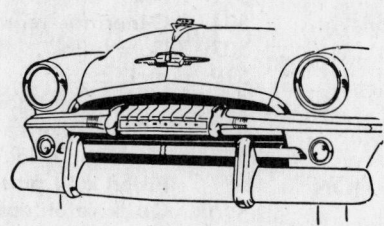

1954

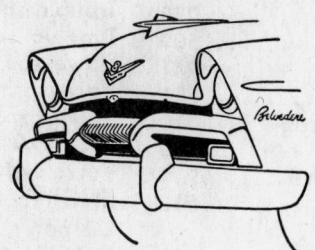

1955

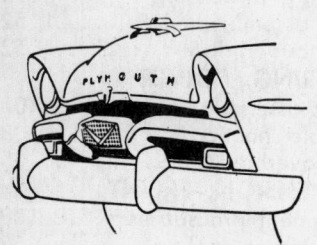

1956

1957

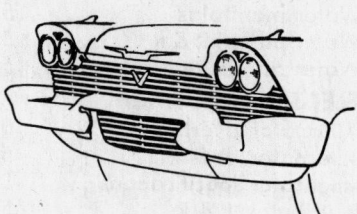

1958

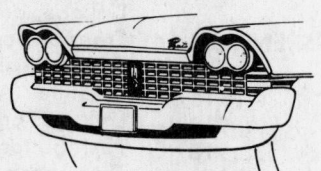

1959

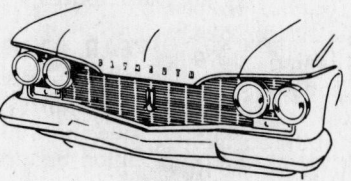

1960

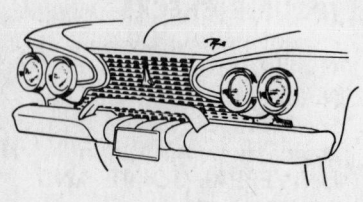

1961

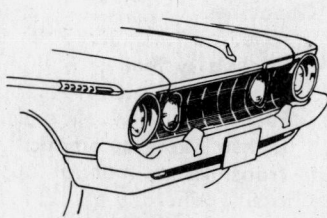

1962

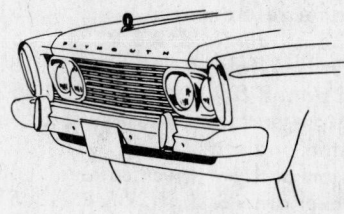

1963

QUICK WORKING SPECIFICATIONS

DISTRIBUTOR

Breaker Point Gap (In.)
1954-59, 6 Cyl. .... .018-.022
1955-59, V8 .... .016-.018
1960-63, 6 Cyl. .... .017-.023
1960-63, V8 .... .014-.019

Cam Angle (Degrees)
1954-56, 6 Cyl. 36
1957-63, 6 Cyl. 40
1955, V8, 2 sets: ea. set 26-28
   Total Dwell 32-36
1956-57, V8, Exc. Fury 31
1956-57, Fury V8 .... 37½
1958-63, V8 30
1958-63, Fury & Commando 38
   For 2 sets, one set 30

IGNITION TIMING

1953-56, 6 cyl. 2B
1955-56, V8 .... 4B
1957, 6 cyl. .... TDC
1957, 277 Cu. In. V8 .... 4B
1957, 301, 318 Cu. In. V8 .... 8B
1958, 6 cyl. 2B
1958-59, V8 ex. Commando 10B
1958, Commando 8B
1959, 6 cyl. 2B
1959, Commando 7½B
1960 V-8 Dist. in Front-MT 5B
1960 V-8 Dist. in Front-AT 10B
1960 V-8 Dist. in Rear 5B
1960, Slant 6 .... 5B
1961-63 Slant "6" 2½B
1961-63,
  V-8 Dist. in Front-2BBL 10B
1961-63,
  V-8 Dist. in Front-4BBL 5B
1961-63 V-8 Dist. in Rear 10B

SPARK PLUGS

Year	Type	Gap
1954-56, 6 cyl.	AR80	.035
1957-59, 6 cyl.	AR51	.035
1955, V8	AR51	.035
1956, V8, ex. Fury	AR52	.035
1956, Fury, V8	4S-250	.035
1957, V8, ex. Fury	AR52	.035
1957, Fury, V8	AR32	.035
1958, all V8 ex. Com.	AR42	.035
1958-59, Com. V8	AR32	.035
1959, all V8 ex. Com.	AR51	.035
1960-61, Slant "6"	AG 42	.035
1954-62 "318"	A42	.035
1960-61 "361"	A32	.035
1962-63, V8	J12Y	.035
1962-63, Slant "6"	N12Y	.035

VALVES

Mechanical Lifters (Hot)
1954-59, 6 cyl. ....in. .010 ; ex. .010
1956, "277" V8, w/Power
  Pack ....in. .012 ; ex. .020
1956, Fury ....in. .010 ; ex. .018
1958, V8 ....in. .012 ; ex. .018
1959-63, V8 ....in. .010 ; ex. .018
1960-63, 6 cyl. ....in. .010 ; ex. .020

ALTERNATOR

1961-63—An alternator instead of the conventional generator is supplied as standard equipment.

GENERATOR AND REGULATOR

YEAR AND SERIES	GENERATOR Field Current In Amperes 6 Volt	12 Volt	REGULATOR Cut-out Closing Voltage	Current Regulator Setting	Voltage Regulator Setting
1954-55 All	1.45	—	6.6	40	7.3
1956-59 All	—	1.25	13.4	35	14.6±1.(A)
1960 All	—	1.25	13.2	34	14.5±1.(A)
1961 All		3.2	None	None	14.0

(A) Surrounding temperatures guide this adjustment. Higher temperatures require lower settings. Lower temperatures permit higher settings, within limits.

CAPACITIES

Engine Crankcase (Quarts)
(Add 1 Qt. for new filter)
1954-61, all ex. '58 Commando 5
1958, Commando 4
1960-63, Slant "6" 4
1962-63, V8 4

Transmission, Synchro. (Pts.)
(Add 1 pint for Overdrive)
1954-59 .... 2¾
1960-63 5

Cooling System (Quarts)
(Add 1 quart for heater)
1954-61, all 6 cyl. 13
1962-63, Slant "6" 12
1955, V8 19
1956-63, V8's exc. below 20
1956, 270, V8 19
1958-61, Commando V8 16

FIRING ORDER and TIMING

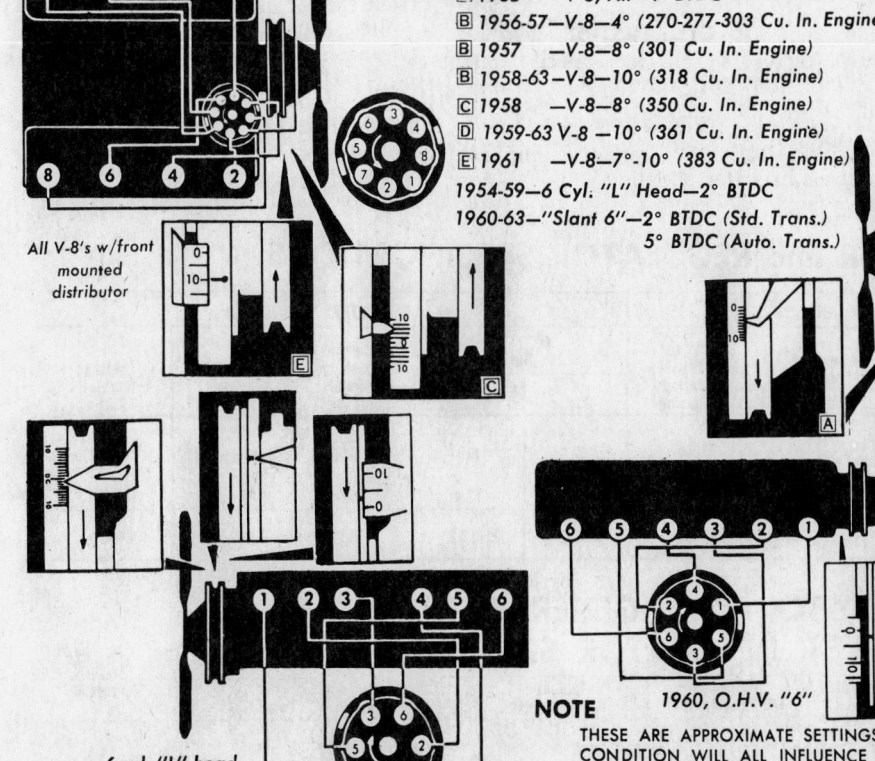

SPARK OCCURS:
A 1955 —V-8, All—4° BTDC
B 1956-57—V-8—4° (270-277-303 Cu. In. Engine)
B 1957 —V-8—8° (301 Cu. In. Engine)
B 1958-63—V-8—10° (318 Cu. In. Engine)
C 1958 —V-8—8° (350 Cu. In. Engine)
D 1959-63 V-8 —10° (361 Cu. In. Engine)
E 1961 —V-8—7°-10° (383 Cu. In. Engine)
1954-59—6 Cyl. "L" Head—2° BTDC
1960-63—"Slant 6"—2° BTDC (Std. Trans.)
     5° BTDC (Auto. Trans.)

All V-8's w/front mounted distributor

All V-8's w/rear mounted distributor

1961-63, O.H.V. "6"

1960, O.H.V. "6"

6 cyl. "L" head

NOTE
THESE ARE APPROXIMATE SETTINGS. ALTITUDE, TEMPERATURE, FUEL AND ENGINE CONDITION WILL ALL INFLUENCE TIMING. THE DETERMINING FACTOR, LIMITING ADVANCE, WILL STILL BE THE "KNOCK POINT" OF THE INDIVIDUAL ENGINE.

PLYMOUTH

MODEL YEAR IDENTIFICATION

1954
Ser.: P-25-1, P-25-2, P-25-3,

6 Cyl. L Head
13,506,001; 20,658,001
25,163,001; 25,590,001

1955
Ser.: P-26-1, P-26-2, P-26-3,
6 Cyl. L Head
13,835,001; 20,745,001; 25,180,001
Ser.: P-27-1, P-27-2, P-27-3, OHV, V8
15,663,001; 22,182,001; 26,524,001

1956
Ser.: P-28-1, P-28-2, P-28-3,
6 Cyl. L Head
14,720,001; 20,820,001; 25,202,001
Ser.: P-29-1, P-29-2, P-29-3, OHV, V8
15,873,001; 22,247,001; 26,552,001

1957
Ser.: P-30-1, P-30-2, P-30-3,
6 Cyl. L Head
14,280,001; 20,860,001; 25,215,001
Ser.: P-31-1, P-31-2, P-31-3, OHV, V8
16,083,001; 22,330,001; 26,595,001

1958
Ser: LP1-H, LP1-L, LP1-M
6 Cyl. L Head
Ser: LP2-H, LP2-L, LP2-M
OHV, V8

1959
Ser: M1-3, M1-5, M1-7, M1-8
6 Cyl. L Head
Ser.: M2-3, M2-5, M2-6, M2-7, M2-8, M2-9
OHV, V8

1960
Ser: PP1-L, PP1-M, PP1-H
Slant "6" OHV
Ser: PP2-L, PP2-M, PP2-H
OHV, V8

1961
Ser: RP1-L, RP1-M, RP1-H
Slant "6" OHV
Ser: RP2-L, RP2-M, RP2-H
V-8

1962
Ser: SP1-L, SP1-M, SP1-H
Slant "6" OHV
Ser: SP2-L, SP2-M, SP2-H, SP2-P
V-8

1963
Ser: TP1-L, TP1-M, TP1-H
Slant "6" OHV
Ser: TP2-L, TP2-M, TP-2-H, TP2-P
V-8

CAR SERIAL NUMBER LOCATION AND ENGINE IDENTIFICATION

SERIAL NUMBER

Attached to left front door hinge post. The car serial number tells the make of car (first digit), car model (second digit), year (third digit), assembly plant (fourth digit), and the consecutive number of production (last six digits).

NOTE: 1954-57 ENGINE IDENTIFICATION WAS THRU CAR SERIAL NUMBER. BEGINNING 1958, CU. IN. DISPLACEMENT IS PART OF ENGINE NUMBER.

ENGINE NUMBER LOCATION

WITH
CUBIC INCH DISPLACEMENT

6 CYL. 1954-60
Upper left side of block, near front. ("L" head) 230 cu. in.

6 CYL. 1961-63
Right side of block, near front. ("Slant 6" OHV) 225 cu. in.

V-8—1955
P27: 241, 260—Front of engine just back of water pump.

V-8—1956
P29: 270—Top of Engine near filler pipe.
277—Left front face of block.

V-8—1957-58
P31 and LP2: 277, 301, 318—Left front face of block.
LP2: 350—Right side of block between coil and distributor.

V-8—1959-63
M2, PP2, RP2, SP2: 318—Left front face of block.
361, 383—Right side of block between coil and distributor.

GENERATOR and REGULATOR SPECIFICATIONS

| YEAR | GENERATORS | | | REGULATORS | | | | |
| | Field Current In Amperes | | Brush Spring Tension | Cut Out Relay | | Current and Voltage Regulator Air Gap | Current Regulator Setting | Voltage Regulator Setting |
	At 6 Volts	At 12 Volts		Air Gap	Closing Voltage			
1954-55 All Models	1.45		44	.032	6.6	.050	40	7.3
1956-59 All Models	—	1.25	27	.032	13.4	.050	35	14.6
1960 All Models	—	1.25	27	.032	13.2	.050	34	14.5

ALTERNATOR (A.C. GENERATOR) AND ALTERNATOR REGULATOR SPECIFICATIONS

YEAR AND MODEL	ALTERNATOR Rated Amps	Field Current At 12V	Output At 1250 Engine RPM	Output At 2200 Engine RPM	REGULATOR Air Gap	Point Gap	Voltage At 70°F
1961-63 All	35	3.2	35	N A	.050"	.015"	14
W/air Conditioner	40	3.2	40	N A	.050"	.015"	14

TUNE-UP SPECIFICATIONS

Year	Spark Plugs: Type	Spark Plugs: Gap	Distributor (Note 1): * Cam Angle	Distributor (Note 1): Point Gap	Distributor (Note 1): Arm Spring Tension	Ignition Timing (Note 2)	Compression Pressure Cranking (Note 3)	Valves: Tappet Clearance Hot: Inlet	Valves: Tappet Clearance Hot: Exhaust	Valves: Timing: Inlet Opens	Fuel Pump Pressure	Engine Idle Speed Neutral (Note 5)
1954-55												
P24, P25, P26, 6 Cyl., L Head	AR80	.035	36	.018–.022	17–20	2B	125	.010	.010	12B	4¾	450
P27, 240 cu. in., OHV, V8	AR51	.035	27	.017–.019	17–20	4B	130	Zero	Zero	14B	5¾	475
P27, 260 cu. in., OHV, V8	AR51	.035	27	.017–.019	17–20	4B	135	Zero	Zero	14B	5¾	475
1956												
P28, 6 Cyl., L Head	AR80	.035	36	.018–.022	17–20	2B	125	.010	.010	12B	4¾	475
P29, 270 cu. in., OHV, V8	AR52	.035	30½	.016–.018	17–20	4B	130	Zero	Zero	14B	6½	475
P29, 277 cu. in., OHV, V8	AR52	.035	30½	.016–.018	17–20	4B	135	Zero	Zero	14B	6½	475
Fury, 303 cu. in., OHV, V8	4S-250	.035	37½	.016–.018	17–20	4B	145	.010	.018	9B	6½	475
1957												
P30, 6 Cyl., L Head	AR51	.035	39	.018–.022	17–20	TDC	130	.010	.010	12B	5	475
P31, 277 cu. in., OHV, V8	AR52	.035	31½	.016–.018	17–20	4B	135	.008	.018	8B	6½	475
P31, 301 cu. in., OHV, V8	AR52	.035	31½	.016–.018	17–20	8B	140	.008	.018	8B	6½	475
Fury, 318 cu. in., OHV, V8	AR32	.035	31	.016–.018	17–20	8B	145	.008	.018	17B	6½	475
1958												
LP1, 6 Cyl, "L" Hd.	AR-51	.035	39	.018–.022	17–20	2B	130	.010	.010	12	6½	475
LP2, V8 only	AR-42	.035	30	.015–.018	17–20	10B	135	.012	.018	8	6½	475
LP2, Fury	AR-42	.035	31	.015–.018	17–20	10B	140	.017	.018	17	6½	475
Commando, V8, Pkg.	AR-32	.035	31	.015–.018	17–20	8B	165	Zero	Zero	15	6½	475
1959												
MP1, 6 Cyl., "L" Hd.	AR-51	.035	39	.018–.022	17–20	2B	130	.010	.010	12	6½	475
MP2, V8	AR-51	.035	30	.015–.018	17–20	10B	135	.010	.018	17	6½	475
MP2, Sports Fury	AR-51	.035	30	.015–.018	17–20	10B	140	.010	.018	13	6½	475
Commando, V8, Pkg.	AR-32	.035	29½	.015–.018	17–20	7-10B	165	Zero	Zero	20	6½	475
1960												
6 Cyl., 225 cu. in., Std. Trans.	AG-52	.035	39	.017-.023	17-21	2½B	145	.010	.020	8°B	4½	550
6 Cyl., 225 cu. in., Auto. Trans.	AG-52	.035	39	.017-.023	17-21	5B	145	.010	.020	8°B	4½	500
V8, 318 cu. in., Std. Trans.	A-42	.035	30	.014-.019	17-21	5B	145	.010	.018	17°B	6	500
V8, 318 cu. in., Auto. Trans.	A-42	.035	30	.014-.019	17-21	10B	145	.010	.018	13°B	6	500
V8, 361 cu. in., Gold Com.	A-32	.035	30*	.014-.019	17-21	10B	165	Zero	Zero	20°B	4½	500
V8, 361 cu. in., Sonar Com.	A-32	.035	30*	.014-.019	17-21	5B	165	Zero	Zero	20°B	4½	750
1961												
6 Cyl., Slant "6"	AG-52	.035	39	.017-.023	17-21½	2½B	145	.010	.020	8°B	4½	550
V8, 318 cu. in., Std. Trans.	A-42	.035	30	.014-.019	17-21½	5B	145	.010	.018	17°B	6	500
V8, 318 cu. in., Auto. Trans.	A-42	.035	30	.014-.019	17-21½	10B	145	.010	.018	13°B	6	500
V8, 361 cu. in.	A-32	.035	30*	.014-.019	17-21½	10B	150	Zero	Zero	20°B	5½	500
V8, 383 cu. in.	A-32	.035	30*	.014-.019	17-21½	7½B	165	Zero	Zero	20°B	5½	750
1962												
6 Cyl., Slant "6"	AG-52	.035	42	.017-.023	17-21½	2½B	145	.010	.020	8°B	4½	550
V8, 318 cu. in., Std. Trans.	A-42	.035	31	.014-.019	17-21½	5B	145	.013	.020	19°B	6	500
V8, 318 cu. in., Auto. Trans.	A-42	.035	31	.014-.019	17-21½	10B	145	.013	.021	19°B	6	500
V8, 361 cu. in.	A-32	.035	30*	.014-.019	17-21½	10B	150	Zero	Zero	22°B	4½	500
V8, 413 cu. in., Std. Trans.	J-9Y	.035	37	.014-.019	17-21½	10B**	145	Zero	Zero	22°B	4½	750
V8, 413 cu. in., Opt.	J-9Y	.035	37	.014-.019	17-21½	10B***	145	.020	.032	25°B	9	750
1963												
6 Cyl., Slant "6"	N-14Y	.035	42	.017-.023	17-20	2½B	145	.010	.020	8°B	4½	550
V8, 318 cu. in., Std. Trans.	J-12Y	.035	31	.014-.019	17-20	5B	145	.013	.021	19°B	6	500
V8, 318 cu. in., Auto. Trans.	J-12Y	.035	31	.014-.019	17-20	10B	145	.013	.021	19°B	6	500
V8, 361 cu. in.	J-12Y	.035	31	.014-.019	17-20	10B	150	Zero	Zero	13°B	4½	500
V8, 383 cu .in., 2-Bbl.	J-12Y	.035	30*	.014-.019	17-21½	10B	150	Zero	Zero	13°B	4½	500
V8, 383 cu. in., 4-Bbl.	J-12Y	.035	30*	.014-.019	17-21½	7½B	165	Zero	Zero	24°B	4½	500

* On models with dual points set 1955 @ 32°-36°; 1957-58 @ 36°-39°; 1959-63 @ 34°-40°

** At 500 R.P.M.

*** At 800 R.P.M.

NOTES FOR TUNE-UP SPECIFICATIONS TABLE

Note:

All specifications are standard and should result in satisfactory performance. There are, however, factors that influence these settings, such as fuel octane value, air density, humidity, temperature, etc. Timing charts, like other specifications must be considered as averages, subject to modification.

Note 1: Distributor

FIRING ORDER AND SPARK PLUG WIRE INSTALLATION

The cylinders of all Plymouth 6 cylinder engines are numbered from front to back starting with No. 1 cylinder at the front. Using this numbering system, the FIRING ORDER of the 6 cylinder engine is: 1-5-3-6-2-4. The spark plug wires go into the distributor cap in the firing order and in a clockwise direction.

The cylinders of all Plymouth V8 engines are numbered from front to back: left bank, 1-3-5-7; right bank, 2-4-6-8. Using this numbering system, the FIRING ORDER of the V8 engines is: 1-8-4-3-6-5-7-2. The spark plug wires go into the V8 distributor cap in the firing order and in a clockwise direction on all engines except the 1958-60 Commando V8. On the 1958-61 Golden Commando V8 the wires go into the cap in the same FIRING ORDER but in a counterclockwise direction.

Note 1A: Cam Dwell

1955, OHV, V8

These engines have 2 sets of distributor points.

Total Cam Dwell	32-36
Cam Dwell of each set	26-28

Note 2: Ignition

IGNITION TIMING MARKS AND THEIR LOCATION

1954-63, All engines: Crankshaft pulley is marked D.C. at T.D.C. with 5 marks at 2 degree intervals before and after. (Some early models had 15 marks at 2 degree intervals on each side.)

Note 2A: Cam Dwell

1957 Fury OHV, V8

Double Breaker. Total dwell.... 36-39

Note 3: Compression Pressure

All cylinders should read alike within 15 pounds. This is more important than the actual reading. Take the readings with all plugs removed, engine at normal operating temperature.

Note 4: Ignition Timing

w/mt	2B
w/at	5B

Note 5: Idle Speed

Idle speeds as shown are for engines in good condition with the transmission in Neutral. The proper idle speed for an engine depends on its condition and also on whether or not it has an automatic transmission. Higher idle speeds are required for engines in poor condition and also for engines used with automatic transmissions.

Note 7: V8 Engine Identification 1956, OHV, V8's

270 CUBIC INCH V8

Has open type intake manifold. Oil filler pipe is in center of block.

277 CUBIC INCH V8

Intake manifold and valve tappet cover combined in one piece. Oil filler pipe is in front end of left rocker cover. When equipped with power pack (4 barrel carburetor) this engine has solid adjustable tappets instead of hydraulic tappets.

Note 6: V8 Engine Identification 1955, OHV, V8

241 cubic inch V8
Valve cover painted red
260 cubic inch V8
Valve cover painted silver

303 CUBIC INCH ENGINE

Called the Fury, this engine has an "F" as the first letter of the engine number.

Note 8: Tappet Clearance 1956 277 Cubic Inch OHV, V8

This engine normally has hydraulic lifters and zero tappet clearance. When equipped with power pack (4 barrel carburetor) it has solid adjustable tappets:

Intake .012; exhaust .020.

Note 9: V8 Engine Identification 1957, OHV, V8

277 CUBIC INCH V8
Engine number has prefix LP-31.
301 CUBIC INCH V8
Engine number has prefix P-31.

Note 10: 1958 Fury and Commando Cam Angle

These OHV V8's have 2 sets of distributor points.
Total Cam Angle 36-40
Each Set Cam Angle 29-32

Note 11: V8 Engine Identification

318 CUBIC INCH V8
Engine number has prefix LPZ for 1958, MP8 for 1959.
Fury version prefix LPZ-H for 1958. For 1959 the SERIAL Prefix is M26 for Fury and M29 for Sports Fury.

350 CUBIC INCH COMMANDO V8
Engine number has prefix LPZ-O.

361 CUBIC INCH COMMANDO V8
Engine number has prefix ML361.

Note 12: 1959-61 Commando Cam Angle

This OHV, V8 has 2 sets of distributor points.
Total Cam Angle 34-40
Each Set Cam Angle 27-32

IGNITION RESISTOR

1956-63, OHV, V8 Engines Only

On these engines there is an ignition ballast resistor in the line between the ignition switch and the coil. The resistor is not by-passed during operation of the starter.

SPARK PLUGS

1959, 361 Cubic Inch Commando does not use Resistor Type Plugs. The resistance is built into the spark plug wires. No one plug wire should test over 20,000 ohms resistance.

PLYMOUTH DISTRIBUTOR SPECIFICATIONS

Year	Model	Part Number	Rotation	Cam Angle in Degrees	Breaker Point Opening (Inch)	Breaker Arm Spring in Ounces	Governor Control @ Dist. R.P.M.		Vacuum Control Data		
							Advance Starts	Full Advance	Inches of Vacuum To Start Advance	Inches of Vacuum For Full Advance	Max. Adv. of Dist. in Degrees
1954	P-24 & P-25	IAT-4101	C	36-42	.020	17-20	1 @ 350	10 @ 1425	5½-6½	13-15	7-9
1955	P-26, 6, L. Head	IAT-4101B	C	36-42	.020	17-20	1 @ 400	8 @ 1350	6-8	13-15	7-9
	P-27, V8	IAZ-4003E	C	(A)	.018	17-20	1 @ 350	18 @ 1900	4½-6½	10-12	6-8
1956	P-28, 6, L. Head	1AT-4101B	C	36-42	.020	17-20	1 @ 400	8 @ 1350	6-8	13-15	7-9
	P-29, V8	IBJ-4301A	C	26-28	.018	17-20	1 @ 350	15 @ 2150	4½-6½	12-16	11½-13½
1957	P-30, 6, L. Head	IBR-4001	C	36-42	.020	17-20	1 @ 400	8 @ 1800	6-8	15-17	8½-10½
	P-31-1, V8	1BP-4003C	C	29-32	.018	17-20	1 @ 400	15 @ 2150	6-8	15-17	11½-13½
	P-31-2, P-31-3	IBP-4003	C	29-32	.018	17-20	1 @ 400	9½ @ 2200	6-8	17-19	12-14
	P-31, Fury	IBS-4003	C	(B)	.017	17-20	1 @ 400	8 @ 1000	7-8	17-19	9-11
1958	LP1, 6, L. Head	IBR-4001	C	36-42	.020	17-20	1 @ 400	8 @ 1800	6-8	15-17	8½-10½
	LP2, V8	IBP-4003F	C	29-32	.018	17-20	1 @ 450	9 @ 2300	6½-7	15-17	12-14
	LP2, Power P.	IBP-4003D	C	29-32	.018	17-20	1 @ 350	11 @ 2400	6-7	15-17	12-14
	LP2, Fury	IBS-4003	C	(B)	.017	17-20	1 @ 400	8 @ 1000	7-8	17-19	9-11
1959	MP1, 6, L. Head	IBR-4001	C	36-42	.020	17-20	1 @ 400	8 @ 1800	7-8	15-17	8½-10½
	MP2, V8	IBP-4003F	C	29-32	.018	17-20	1 @ 450	9 @ 2300	6½-7	15-17	12-14
	MP2, Power P.	IBP-4003H	C	27-32	.018	17-20	1 @ 350	8½ @ 2200	4½-6½	12-14	8½-11½
	MP2, G. Commando	IBS-4006C	CC	(C)	.017	17-20	1 @ 450	9½ @ 2000	7½-9¼	18¼	11½-14½
1960	PP1, Slant "6" OHV	2095270*	C	36-42	.020	17-21	1 @ 350	11½ @ 2200	5-7	12	7¾-10¼
	PP2, 318 Cu. In. V8	BPI-4003L	C	27-32	.017	17-21	1 @ 550	9 @ 2300	7½-8¾	17	9½-12½
	PP2, 361 Cu. In. V8	IBS-4006D	CC	(C)	.017	17-21	1 @ 450	9½ @ 2400	7½-9¼	16	12-14¾
1961	225 Cu. In. Slant 6	2095270*	C	36-42	.020	17-21	1 @ 350	11½ @ 2200	5-7	12	7¾-10¼
	318 Cu. In. V8, Manual Trans.	2095647*	C	27-32	.017	17-21	1 @ 350	11½ @ 2300	6¾-9¼	17	12-15
	318 Cu. In. V8, Auto. Trans.	1838505*	C	27-32	.017	17-21	1 @ 450	9 @ 2300	6¾-9¼	17	12-15
	361 Cu. In. V8	IBP-4005E	CC	27-32	.017	17-21	1 @ 350	11 @ 2050	6-8	16	10½-13
1962											
	225 Cu. In. Slant 6	2095976	C	40-45	.020	17-21	1 @ 400	11½ @ 2300	5½	13	5-7½
	318 Cu. In. V8	2095979	C	27-32	.017	17-21	1 @ 450	9 @ 2300	9	18	8½-11½
	361 Cu. In. V8	2095983	CC	27-32	.017	17-21	1 @ 350	10 @ 2300	9	15	9½-12½
1963											
	Slant 6, 225 Cu. In.	2098670*	C	40-45	.020	17-21	1@400	11½@2500	6	13	5¼-7½
	V-8, 318—Std. Trans.	2098680*	C	28-33	.017	17-21	1@375	9½@2000	9	15½	8½-11½
	V-8, 318—Auto. Trans	2098685*	C	28-33	.017	17-21	1@400	8½@2600	9	15½	8½-11½
	V-8, 361—All	2095836*	CC	28-33	.017	17-21	1@350	11½@2100	6½	16½	11½-14½
	V-8, 383—All	2095832*	CC	28-33	.017	17-21	1@350	12 @2050	8½	16	9½-12½

(A) Dual Points Each Set, 26°-28° Total, 32°-36° (B) Dual Points Each Set, 29°-32° Total, 36°-39° (C) Dual Points Each Set, 27°-32° Total, 34°-40°

* Mopar number.

BATTERY and STARTER SPECIFICATIONS

YEAR	BATTERY Ampere Hour Capacity	Volts	Groupe Number	Terminal Grounded	STARTERS Lock Test Amps.	Volts	Torque	No-Load Test Amps.	Volts	R.P.M.	Brush Spring Tension
1954 All 6 Cyl.	105	6	1	Pos.	335	2	6	57	6	4900	48
1955											
6 Cyl. W./M.	105	6	1	Pos.	500	3	11	57	5½	4900	48
6 Cyl. W./A.	120	6	2	Pos.	500	3	11	57	5½	4900	48
O.H.V., V8	105	6	1	Pos.	500	3	11	57	5½	4900	48
1956 All Models	53	12	2SM	Neg.	210	4	5	50	10	4400	48
1957 All Models	53	12	2SM	Neg.	210	4	5	50	11	3600	48
1958											
6 Cyl. W./M.	50	12	NA	Neg.	210	4	5	50	11	3600	48
6 Cyl. W./A.	50	12	NA	Neg.	225	4	6	60	11	3400	48
V8 ex. Comm.	50	12	NA	Neg.	210	4	5	50	11	3600	48
Commando V8	50	12	NA	Neg.	350	4	8.5	58	11	3800	48
1959											
All, exc. Comm.	50	12	2SHA	Neg.	355	4	9	50	11	5500	48
Commando, V8	60	12	2SHB	Neg.	350	4	8.5	58	11	3800	48
1960											
Slant "6", OHV	50	12	2SHA	Neg.	350	4	8.5	58	11	3800	48
V8, 318 Cu. In.	50	12	2SHA	Neg.	355	4	9	50	11	5500	48
V8, 361 Cu. In.	60	12	2SHB	Neg.	350	4	8.5	58	11	3800	48
1961											
225 Cu. In. Slant 6	50	12	2SHA	Neg.	350	4.0	8.5	58	11.0	3800	48
318 Cu. In. V8	50	12	2SHA	Neg.	350	4.0	8.5	78	11.0	3800	48
361 Cu. In. V8	60	12	2SHB	Neg.	350	4.0	8.5	78	11.0	3800	48
1962-63											
Slant "6". 318 V8	48	12	HS48B	Neg.	475	4	24.0	85	11.0	1950	32-48
361, 383 cu. in. V8	59	12	HS59B	Neg.	475	4	24.0	85	11.0	1950	32-48

LIGHT BULBS

(C.P. MEANS CANDLE POWER)

Beam and Turn Signal Telltales, Clock, Glove Box, Ignition Key, Instruments, Generator, Oil Pressure, Power Flite Quadrant Lights:

6 Volt, No. 55; 12 Volt, No. 57
(2 C.P. miniature bayonet base.)

Parking Light (without Turn signals) and License Plate Light:

6 Volt, No. 63; 12 Volt, No. 67.
(4 C.P. single contact base.)

Brake-on Warning Light:

6 Volt, No. 82; 12 Volt, No. 90.
(6 C.P. double contact base.)

Under Hood and Trunk Lights:

6 Volt, No. 209; 12 Volt, No. 1003.
(15 C.P. single contact base.)

Dome and Courtesy Lights:

6 Volt, No. 210; 12 Volt, No. 1004.
(15 C.P. double contact base.)

Parking Light (with Turn Signals), Combination Tail, Stop, and Turn Signal:

6 Volt, No. 1154; 12 Volt, No. 1034.
(32 and 4 C.P. 2 contact indexed base.)

GENERAL CHASSIS and BRAKE SPECIFICATIONS

YEAR AND MODEL	CHASSIS Overall Length In Inches	Tire Size	BRAKE CYL. BORE Master Cyl. Inch	Wheel Cylinder Diameter (Inch) Front	Rear
1954 6 Cyl., All, P25-1-2-3	193½	6.70x15	1⅛	1⅛—1⅛	1⅛
1955 6 & V8, All P26-1-2-3, P27-1-2-3	203¾	6.70x15	1⅛	1⅛—1⅛	1⅛
1956 6 Cyl., All P28-1-2-3	204¾	6.70x15	1⅛	1⅛—1⅛	1⅛
V-8, Except Fury, P29-1-2-3	204¾	6.70x15	1⅛	1⅛—1⅛	1⅛
V-8, Fury, P29-3	204¾	7.10x15	1⅛	1⅛—1⅛	1⅛
1957 6 Cyl. All P30-1-2-3	204¾	7.50x14	1⅛	1⅛—1⅛	1⅛
V-8, Except Fury, P31-1-2-3	204¾	7.50x14	1⅛	1⅛—1⅛	1⅛
V-8, Fury, P31-Fury	206⅛	8.00x14	1⅛	1⅛—1⅛	1⅛
1958 6 Cyl., All, LP1-L-M-H	206.0	7.50x14	1⅛	1⅛—1⅛	1⅛
V-8, Except Sub., LP2-L-M-H	206.0	7.50x14	1⅛	1⅛—1⅛	1⅛
All Suburbans & Fury	213½	8.00x14	1⅛	1⅛—1⅛	1⅛
1959 6 Cyl. "L" Head, MP1-L-M	210.0	7.50x14	1⅛	1⅛—1⅛	1⅛
V-8, Except Suburbans	210.0	7.50x14	1⅛	1⅛—1⅛	1⅛
All Suburbans	214.0	7.50x14	1⅛	1⅛—1⅛	1⅛
1960-61 Slant "6" & V-8, Sedans	209½	7.50x14	1⅛	1⅛—1⅛	1⅛
Slant "6" & V-8, Station Wagons	215.0	8.00x14	1⅛	1⅛—1⅛	1⅛
1962 All, exc. Sta. Wagon	202.0	6.50x14	1	1	15/16
Stations Wagons	210.0	7.00x14	1	1	15/16
1963 All, exc. Sta. Wagon	205.0	7.00x14	1	1	15/16
Station Wagon	210.1	7.00x14	1	1	15/16

Plymouth is equipped with independent wheel cylinders for each front brake shoe thru 1961.

Back-up Light:

6 Volt, No. 1129; 12 Volt, No. 1141.
(21 C.P. single contact base.)

Radio Dial:

6 Volt, No. 44; 12 Volt, No. 1891.
(2 C.P. miniature bayonet base.)

Headlights: 2 Only

6 Volt, No. 5040; 12 Volt, No. 5400.

(50 and 40 C.P. three contact base.)

Headlights: 4 Only

LOW AND HIGH BEAM

12 Volt, No. 4002
(37.5-50 watts three contact base.)

HIGH BEAM ONLY

12 Volt, No. 4001
(37.5 Watts double contact base.)

FUSES and CIRCUIT BREAKERS

1954: LIGHTS

30 amp. circuit breaker on instrument panel near headlight switch.

Tail, License, Instrument, Clock Lights:

10 amp. circuit breaker on light switch.

1955: LIGHTS

Head, Beam Indicator, Parking, Ignition Key Lights:

25 amp. circuit breaker on light switch.

Stop, Dome, Glove Box, Courtesy

10 amp. circuit breaker on light switch.

Back-up Light:

10 amp. circuit breaker in windshield wiper switch.

1956-58—ALL LIGHTS:

15 amp. circuit breaker on headlight switch.

1959-1963: LIGHTS

Head, Beam Indicator, Parking Lights:
22.5 amp. circuit breaker.
Tail, Stop, License, Instrument, Dome Lights:
15 amp. circuit breaker.
Both on headlight switch.

OTHER CIRCUITS

Clock:

1954-55—AGA 3 fuse in wire at clock.
1956-58—Internally protected or AGA 2 fuse in wire at clock.
1959-63—AGA—2 fuse.

Overdrive:

1954-55—SFE fuse in wire to relay under hood on dash.
1956-58—SFE 14 in wire to relay under hood on dash.

Radio:

1954-55—SFE 14 in wire at set.
1956-58—SFE 9 in wire at set.
1959-63—SFE 7.5.

Windshield Wiper Motor and Back-up Light:

1954-55—10 amp. circuit breaker built into wiper switch.

1956-63—5 amp. circuit breaker built into wiper switch.

Power Seat, Top and Windows:

Circuit breakers, one for each electric motor, are all located behind the left cowl panel.

1962-63

Headlights:
22.5 amp. circuit breaker.

Windshield Wiper Motor:
5 amp. circuit breaker.

All Other Circuits:

Fuses with ratings marked in easy access fuse box under dash.
1962 production uses a printed instrument panel circuit.

CAPACITIES

YEAR	Engine Crankcase Add 1 Qt. for New Filter	TRANSMISSIONS Pints to Refill After Draining		Rear Axle Pints	Gasoline Tank Gallons	Cooling System Quarts Add 1 Qt. for Heater
		Manual Add 1 Pt. for Over Drive	AUTOMATIC			
1954						
All 6 Cyl.	5(A)	2¾	(A)	3¼	17	13
1955						
All 6 Cyl.	5	2¾	20	3¼	17	13
All V8	5	2¾	20	3¼	17	19
1956						
All 6 Cyl.	5	2¾	20	3¼	17	13
270 Cu. In. V8	5	2¾	20	3¼	17	19
All Other V8	5	2¾	20	3¼	17	20
1957						
All 6 Cyl.	5	2¾	20	3¼	20	13
All V8	5	2¾	(B)	3¼	20	20
1958-59						
All 6 Cyl.	5	2¾	20	3¼	(D)	13
All V8 ex. Comm.	5	2¾	(C)	3½	(D)	20
Commando V8	(E)	2¾	21	3½	(D)	16
1960-61						
Slant "6"	4	5	18	3¼	(D)	13
All V8 ex. Comm.	5	5	18	3½	(D)	20
V8 Commando	5	5	21	3½	(D)	16
1962-63						
Slant "6"	4	5	14	3½	20(D1)	12
V8	4	5	19	3½	20(D1)	20

NOTES FOR CAPACITIES TABLE

(A) 1954 Crankcase and Automatic Transmission Capacity Hy-Drive Transmission

Converter uses oil from the engine crankcase so Engine requires 10 qts. of oil to fill it after draining crankcase and converter.

(B) 1957 V8 Automatic Transmission Capacity

PowerFlite—20 pints.
TorqueFlite—22 pints.

(C) 1958 V8 Automatic Transmission Capacity

PowerFlite—20 pints.
TorqueFlite—18 pints.

(D) 1958-63 Gasoline Tank Capacity

Suburban—22 gallons.
Exc. Sub.—20 gallons.

(E) 1958-60 Crankcase Capacity

1958 Commando—4 quarts.
1959 Commando—5 quarts.

GENERAL ENGINE SPECIFICATIONS

Year	Bore and Stroke	Number of Main Bearings	Type of Valve Lifter Used	Cubic Inch Displace-ment	AMA Horse-power	Advertised Horsepower at Stated RPM	Advertised Torque at Stated RPM	Com-pression Ratio	Oil Pressure At 30 MPH (Note 1)	Cam Shaft Drive
1954										
P24, P25, 6 Cyl., L Head	3¼x4⅜	4	Mech. Adj.	217.8	25.4	100@3600	177@1200	7.1-1	30	Chain
1955										
P26, 6 Cyl., L Head	3¼x4⅝	4	Mech. Adj.	230	25.4	Note 2		7.4-1	30	Chain
P27, 240 cu. in., OHV, V8	3⁷⁄₁₆x3¼	5	Hyd. Non Adj.	240	37.9	157@4400	217@2400	7.6-1	30	Chain
P27, 260 cu. in., OHV, V8	3⁹⁄₁₆x3¼	5	Hyd. Non Adj.	260	40.6	167@4400	231@2400	7.6-1	30	Chain
1956										
P28, 6 Cyl., L Head	3¼x4⅝	4	Mech. Adj.	230	25.4	Note 3		7.4-1	40	Chain
P29, 270 cu. in., OHV, V8	3⅝x3¼	5	Hyd. Non Adj.	270	42.2	180@4400	260@2400	8.0-1	45	Chain
P29, 277 cu. in., OHV, V8	3¾x3⅛	5	Note 4	277	45	Note 5		8.0-1	45	Chain
Fury, 303 cu. in., OHV, V8	3¹³⁄₁₆x3⁵⁄₁₆	5	Mech. Adj.	303	46.5	240@4800	310@2800	9.25-1	45	Chain
1957										
P30, 6 Cyl., L Head	3¼x4⅝	4	Mech. Adj.	230	25.4	132@3600	205@1600	8.0-1	40	Chain
P31, 277 cu. in., OHV, V8	3¾x3⅛	5	Mech. Adj.	277	45	197@4400	270@2400	8.0-1	45	Chain
P31, 301 cu. in., OHV, V8	3²⁹⁄₃₂x3⅛	5	Mech. Adj.	301	48.9	Note 6		8.5-1	45	Chain
Fury, 318 cu. in., OHV, V8	3²⁹⁄₃₂x3⁵⁄₁₆	5	Mech. Adj.	318	48.9	290@5400	325@4000	9.25-1	45	Chain
1958										
LP1, 6 Cyl. "L" Hd.	3¼x4⅝	4	Mech. Adj.	230	25.3	132@3600	205@1200	8.0	40	Chain
LP2, V8, OHV	3²⁹⁄₃₂x3⁵⁄₁₆	5	Mech. Adj.	318	48.9	Note 7		9.0	50	Chain
LP2, Fury, V8	3²⁹⁄₃₂x3⁵⁄₁₆	5	Mech. Adj.	318	48.9	290@5200	330@3600	9.25	50	Chain
Commando, V8, Pkg.	4¹⁄₁₆x3⅜	5	Hyd. Non Adj.	350	52.7	Note 8		10.0	50	Chain
1959										
MP1, 6 cyl. "L" Hd.	3¼x4⅝	4	Mech. Adj.	230	25.3	132@3600	205@1200	8.0-1	40	Chain
MP2, V8, OHV	3²⁹⁄₃₂x3⁵⁄₁₆	5	Mech. Adj.	318	48.9	Note 9		9.0-1	55	Chain
MP2, Sports Furry	3²⁹⁄₃₂x3⁵⁄₁₆	5	Mech. Adj.	318	48.9	260@4400	345@2800	9.0-1	55	Chain
Commando, V8, Pkg.	4⅛x3⅜	5	Hyd. Non Adj.	361	54.3	305@4600	395@3000	10.0-1	55	Chain
1960										
PP1, Slant "6", OHV	3¹³⁄₃₂x4⅛	4	Mech. Adj.	225	27.7	145@4000	215@2800	8.5-1	40	Chain
PP2, V8, OHV	3²⁹⁄₃₂x3⁵⁄₁₆	5	Mech. Adj.	318	48.9	Note 9		9.0-1	55	Chain
PP2, V8, OHV Commando	4⅛x3⅜	5	Hyd. Non Adj.	361	54.3	305 @ 4600	395 @ 3000	10.0-1	55	Chain
1961										
RP1 Slant "6"	3¹³⁄₃₂x4⅛	4	Solid	225	27.7	140 @ 4000	215 @ 2400	8.2-1	50	Chain
RP2 V8—318	3²⁹⁄₃₂x3⁵⁄₁₆	5	Solid	318	48.9	260 @ 4400	345 @ 2800	9.0-1	50	Chain
RP2 V8—361	4⅛x3⅜	5	Hydraulic	361	54.3	300 @ 4800	390 @ 3200	9.0-1	50	Chain
RP2 V8—383	4¼x3⅜	5	Hydraulic	383	57.8	325@4800	425 @ 3200	10.0-1	55	Chain
1962-63										
Slant "6"	3 13/32x4⅛	4	Solid	225	27.7	145@4000	215 @ 2800	8.2-1	50	Chain
V8 318-2BBL	3 29/32x3 5/16	5	Solid	318	48.9	230@4400	340 @ 2400	9.0-1	50	Chain
V8—361	4⅛x3⅜	5	Hydraulic	361	54.3	305@4800	395 @ 3000	10.2-1	55	Chain
V8 383	4¼x3⅜	5	Hydraulic	383	57.8	305@4600	410@2400	10.04	55	Chain

NOTES FOR GENERAL ENGINE SPECIFICATIONS TABLE

Note 1: Oil Flow

OIL FILTER TYPE

1954-59, All ex. Commando . . . . Partial flow

1959 Golden Commando . . . . Full flow

1960-63, Slant "6" OHV. & Commando 361 cu. in. engine has full flow oil filter. The small V8-318 cu. in. engine has shunt type.

ROCKER SHAFT OIL SUPPLY ALL V8, OHV EXC. COMMANDO

Left Bank:

Oil flows thru the No. 2 main bearing to the adjacent camshaft bearing and thence thru holes in the block and head to the second-from-front rocker shaft support bolt on the left bank. The bolt is smaller than the hole in the bracket. The oil flows around the bolt into the hollow rocker shaft and so to the drilled rockers. Be sure to check that hole in rocker and hole in rocker bushing are aligned.

Right Bank:

Oil flows thru the No. 4 main bearing to the adjacent camshaft bearing and thence to the second-from-rear rocker shaft support bolt on the right bank. The bolt is smaller than the hole in the bracket. The oil flows around the bolt into the hollow rocker shaft and thence to the drilled rockers. Check each rocker to be sure that passage and hole in bushing are aligned.

ROCKER SHAFT OIL SUPPLY 1958-63, V8, OHV COMMANDO

Oil flows from the pump thru the filter and then across the front of the block to the right oil gallery. From the right oil gallery oil flows to the main and camshaft bearings. From the No. 4 camshaft bearing oil flows thru drilled holes in the block and head of each bank to the hollow rocker shafts from which it is metered to the stamped rockers. A crossover passage at the rear of the block transfers oil to the left gallery. The oil pressure gage is connected into this crossover.

Hydraulic Valve Lifter Oil Supply

1955-56, OHV, V8 and 1958-61, Golden Commando V8

Oil is fed to the lifters from oil galleries running the length of each side of the block.

Note 2: Horse Power and Torque 1956, 6 Cyl. "L" Hd

STANDARD ENGINE

H.P.—117@3600.
T.—194@1600

WITH POWER PACK:

H.P.—177@4400.
T.—231@2800.

Note 3: Horse Power and Torque 1956, 6 Cyl. "L" Hd

STANDARD ENGINE

H.P.—125@3600.
T.—200@1600.

WITH POWER PACK:

H.P.—131@3600.
T.—203@2000

Note 4: Type of Valve Lifter Used

1956, 277 cubic inch OHV, V8
(Oil filler pipe in front end of left rocker cover)

STANDARD ENGINE:

Hydraulic Lifters and Non-Adjustable Tappets.

WITH POWER PACK:

Solid Lifters and Adjustable Tappets.

PLYMOUTH

NOTES FOR GENERAL ENGINE SPECIFICATIONS—continued

Note 5: Horse Power and Torque 1956, 277 Cubic Inch, OHV, V8

STANDARD ENGINE:
H.P.—187@4400.
T.—265@2400

WITH POWER PACK:
H.P.—200@4400.
T.—272@2400

Note 6: Horse Power and Torque 1957, 301 Cubic Inch, OHV, V8

STANDARD ENGINE:
H.P.—215@4400.
T.—285@2800

WITH POWER PACK:
H.P.—235@4400.
T.—305@2800

Note 7: Horse Power and Torque 1958, 318 Cubic Inch, OHV, V8
WITH ONE TWO BARREL CARBURETOR
H.P.—225@4400
Torque—330@2800

WITH ONE FOUR BARREL CARBURETOR

H.P.—250@4400
Torque—340@2800

Note 8: Horse Power and Torque 1958 Golden Commando 350 Cubic Inch, V8
WITH TWO FOUR BARREL CARBURETORS
H.P.—305@5000
Torque—370@3600

WITH FUEL INJECTION

H.P.—315@5000
Torque—370@3600

Note 9: Horse Power and Torque 1959-63, 318 Cubic Inch, OHV, V8

WITH ONE TWO BARREL CARBURETOR
H.P.—230@4400
Torque—340@2400

WITH ONE FOUR BARREL CARBURETOR
H.P.—260@4400
Torque—345@2800

WITH TWO FOUR BARREL CARBURETORS (THE FURY)
H.P.—290@5200
Torque—330@3600

CRANKSHAFT BEARING JOURNAL SIZES

YEAR	MAIN BEARING JOURNALS				CONNECTING ROD BEARING JOURNALS		
	Journal Diameter	Oil Clearance	End Play of Shaft	End Play Held by	Journal Diameter	Oil Clearance	End Play
1954 All 6 Cyl. "L" Hd.	2.500	.0010	.005	No. 4	2.0625	.0010	.009
1955 All 6 Cyl. "L" Hd.	2.500	.0010	.005	No. 4	2.0625	.0010	.009
All OHV, V8	2.375	.0010	.005	No. 3	1.9375	.0010	.010
1956 All 6 Cyl. "L" Hd.	2.500	.0015	.005	No. 4	2.0625	.0010	.009
All V8 ex., 270 Cu. In.	2.500	.0015	.005	No. 3	2.1250	.0015	.010
270 Cu. In., V8	2.375	.0010	.005	No. 3	1.9375	.0010	.010
1957 All 6 Cyl. "L" Hd.	2.500	.0010	.005	No. 4	2.0625	.0010	.009
All OHV, V8	2.500	.0010	.005	No. 3	2.1250	.0010	.010
1958–59 All 6 Cyl. "L" Hd.	2.500	.0010	.005	No. 4	2.0625	.0010	.009
All V8 ex. Com.	2.500	.0010	.005	No. 3	2.1250	.0012	.010
Commando, V8	2.6250	.0010	.005	No. 3	2.3745	.0010	.013
1960-63 Slant "6", OHV, 225 Cu. In.	2.750	.0010	.005	No. 3	2.187	.0010	.009
V8, 318 Cu. In.	2.500	.0010	.005	No. 3	2.125	.0010	.010
V8, 361 & 383 cu. in.	2.6250	.0010	.005	No. 3	2.375	.0010	.013

PISTON AND PIN SPECIFICATIONS

Year and Model	PISTON				PISTON PIN			
	Skirt Clearance		Diameter	Bushing	FIT			Lock
	MIN.	MAX.			In Rod	In Piston		
1954—6 Cyl.	.0002	.0012	.8592	Yes	Slip	0—.0005		Ring
1955-59—6 Cyl.	.0005	.0015	.8592	Yes	.0001—.0004	0—.0005		Ring
1955—V8	.0005	.0015	.8592	Yes	.0001—.0004	0—.0005		Ring
1956—270"	.0005	.0015	.8592	Yes	.0001—.0004	0—.0005		Ring
1956-57—277"	.0005	.0015	.922	Yes	.0001—.0005	0—.0005		Ring
1957—301"	.0005	.0015	.9841	Yes	.0001—.0005	0—.0005		Ring
1957-63—318"	.00075	.00125	.9841	None	Press	0—.0005		Rod—Press
1958-63—350" & 361"	.0005	.0015	1.0936	None	Press	.00045—.00075		Rod—Press
1960-63 Slant 6	.0005	.0015	.9008	None	Press	.00045—.00075		Rod—Press
1961—383"	.0005	.0010	1.0936	None	Press	.00045—.00075		Rod—Press

PISTON SPECIFICATIONS

Piston Fitting Ribbon Thickness and Spring Scale Pull

1954-59, ALL 6 CYL. "L" HD.:
10 inches long; ½ inch wide; .002

inch thick; pull of 5 to 10 pounds.

1955-56, OHV, V8:
10 inches long; ½ inch wide; .0015 inch thick; pull of 5 to 10 pounds.

Assembling Piston and Rod

1954-59, ALL 6 CYL. "L" HD.:

Assemble so that slot in piston is away from valve side and spurt hole in rod is toward valve side.

1960-63, SLANT "6"

Assemble the piston to the rod so as to result in the notch on top of the piston pointing forward and the squirt hole in the connecting rod facing the manifold side of the engine. This is the side away from the camshaft.

1955-63, ALL OHV, V8:

Indent on head of piston goes toward front of engine in both banks. The connecting rods have a larger chamfer on one side of the bearing than on the other. The chamfer should go toward the journal fillet. That is, toward the rear on the right bank; toward the front on the left bank.

VALVE SPECIFICATIONS

YEAR	Seat Angle In	Seat Angle Ex	Intake Valve Lift	Exhaust Valve Lift	Valve Spring Pressure Outer	Valve Spring Pressure Inner	Stem to Guide Clearance Inlet	Stem to Guide Clearance Exhaust	Stem Diameter Inlet	Stem Diameter Exhaust	Are Valve Guides Replaceable
1954											
6 Cyl. "L" Hd.	45	45	.365	.365	42½@1¾	None	.002	.004	.3405	.3405	Yes
1955											
6 Cyl. "L" Hd.	45	45	.365	.365	42@1¾	None	.002	.003	.3405	.3405	Yes
OHV, V8	45	45	.360	.360	35@1¹¹⁄₁₆	None	.002	.003	.3725	.3715	No
1956											
6 Cyl. "L" Hd.	45	45	.365	.365	42@1¾	None	.002	.004	.3405	.3405	Yes
270 Cu. In., V8	45	45	.360	.360	53@1¹¹⁄₁₆	None	.002	.003	.3725	.3715	No
277 Cu. In., V8	45	45	.374	.380	72@1¹¹⁄₁₆	None	.002	.003	.3725	.3715	No
303 Cu. In., V8	45	45	.379	.376	72@1¹¹⁄₁₆	None	.002	.003	.3725	.3715	No
1957											
6 Cyl. "L" Hd.	45	45	.365	.365	42@1¾	None	.002	.004	.3405	.3405	Yes
All V8 ex. Fury	45	45	.405	.405	72@1¹¹⁄₁₆	None	.002	.003	.3725	.3715	No
Fury, V8	45	45	.387	.387	90@1²¹⁄₃₂	None	.002	.003	.3725	.3715	No
1958											
6 Cyl. "L" Hd.	45	45	.365	.365	42@1¾	None	.002	.004	.3405	.3405	Yes
All V8, ex. Com.	45	45	.405	.405	72@1¹¹⁄₁₆	None	.002	.002	.3725	.3715	No
Commando	45	45	.390	.390	80@1⁵⁵⁄₆₄	None	.002	.003	.3725	.3715	No
1959											
6 cyl. "L" Hd.	45	45	.365	.365	42@1¾	None	.002	.004	.34	.34	Yes
All V8, ex. Com.	45	45	.390	.386	72@1¹¹⁄₁₆	None	.002	.003	.37	.37	No
Commando	45	45	.390	.390	100@1⁵⁵⁄₆₄	None	.002	.002	.37	.37	No
1960-61											
Slant "6", OHV, 225 Cu. In.	45	45	.375	.368	72@1¹¹⁄₁₆	None	.002	.003	.3725	.3715	No
V8, 318 Cu. In.	45	45	.370	.368	83@1¹¹⁄₁₆	None	.002	.003	.3725	.3715	No
V8, 361 Cu. In.	45	45	.430	.430	100@1⁵⁵⁄₆₄	None	.002	.003	.3725	.3715	No
1962-63											
Slant "6" 225 cu. in.	45	45	.371	.364	83@1¹¹⁄₁₆	None	.002	.003	.3725	.3715	No
V8 318 cu. in.	45	45	.380	.386	83@1¹¹⁄₁₆	None	.002	.003	.3725	.3715	No
V8 361 cu. in.	45	45	.444	.456	100@1⁵⁵⁄₆₄	None	.002	.003	.3725	.3715	No
V8 383 cu. in.	45	45	.389	.389	100@1⁵⁵⁄₆₄	None	.002	.003	.3725	.3715	No

ENGINE TORQUE SPECIFICATIONS

YEAR	Cylinder Head Bolts	Rod Bearing Bolts	Main Bearing Bolts	Crankshaft Pulley Bolt	Flywheel to Crankshaft Bolt	Manifolds In.	Manifolds Ex.
1954-63							
All 6 Cyl. "L" Head exc. slant 6	65–70	45–50	80–85	100–135	55–60	30	25
All V8 ex. Comm.	80–85	45–50	80–85	100–135	55–60	30	25
Commando V8	65–70	40–45	80–85	100–135	55–60	40	30
Slant "6" Aluminum Eng.	65–70	45–50	55–58	100–135	55–60	17	10

CYLINDER HEAD NUT TIGHTENING SEQUENCE

1954-59 6 Cyl. "L" Head

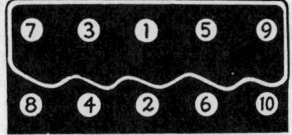

1955-63 OHV, V8

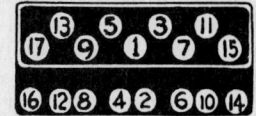

1958-63 Golden Commando V8

1960-63 Slant Six Tighten to 65

V-8—Front Mounted Distributor Tighten to 80-85

PLYMOUTH

FRONT WHEEL ALIGNMENT

YEAR	Front End Height Note 7	Caster		Camber		Toe-In (Inches)	King Pin Inclination (Degrees)	Wheel Pivot Ratio	
		Range (Degrees)	Pref. Setting	Range (Degrees)	Pref. Setting			Inner Wheel	Outer Wheel
1954 6 Cyl. "L" Hd.		1N to 1P	0	⅜N to ⅜P	Note 1	0 to 1⁄16	5½	20	18¾
1955 All Models		2N to 0	Note 2	⅛N to ⅝P	Note 3	0 to 1⁄16	5½	20	18¼
1956 All Models W./M. All Models W./P.		2N to 0 2N to 0	2N 0	⅛N to ⅝P ⅛N to ⅝P	Note 3 Note 3	3⁄32 to 5⁄32 3⁄32 to 5⁄32	5½ 5½	20 20	18¼ 18¼
1957 All Models W./M. All Models W./P.	2 3⁄16″ ± ⅛″ 2 3⁄16″ ± ⅛″	1½N to 0 0 to 1½P	Note 4 Equal	Note 5 Note 5	Note 6 Note 6	3⁄32 to 5⁄32 3⁄32 to 5⁄32	6½ 6½	20 20	18¼ 18¼
1958-59 All W./Manual All W./Power	2 3⁄16″ ± ⅛″ 2 3⁄16″ ± ⅛″	1½N to 0 ¾N to ¾P	Equal Equal	Note 5 Note 5	Note 6 Note 6	3⁄32 to 5⁄32 3⁄32 to 5⁄32	6½ 6½	20 20	18¾ 18¾
1960-63 Manual Power	2″ ± ⅛″ 2″ ± ⅛″	1N to 0 ¼P to 1¼P	Equal Equal	⅛P to ⅝P ⅛N to ⅜P	⅜P ⅛P	1⁄16 to 3⁄32 1⁄16 to 3⁄32	6½-7½ 6½-7½	21½ 21½	20 20

NOTES FOR FRONT WHEEL ALIGNMENT TABLE

Note 1: 1954 Preferred Camber Setting
Left ⅜ higher than the Right.

Note 2: 1955 Preferred Caster Setting
Left Wheel—⅜N.
Right Wheel—O.

Note 3: 1955-56 Preferred Camber Setting
Left Wheel—½P.

Right Wheel—O.

Note 4: 1957 Preferred Caster Setting With Power Steering
Left ⅜ more negative than the Right.

Note 5: 1957-59 Camber Range
Left Wheel—O to ½P.
Right Wheel—¼N to ¼P.

Note 6: 1957-61 Preferred Camber

Setting
Left Wheel—⅜P.
Right Wheel—O.

1962-63 Preferred Camber Setting
Left Wheel—½°
Right Wheel—¼°

Note 7: To Measure Front End Height See Text.

DISTRIBUTOR

Detailed information on: distributor drive, direction of distributor rotation; cylinder numbering; firing order; point gap, cam dwell; timing mark location; spark plugs, spark advance; ignition resistor location, and idle speed; will be found in the Tune-up Specifications table of this section. Further information on trouble shooting, general tune-up procedures, how to replace ignition wires, how to install points and condensers, how to choose the proper spark plug, adjust timing, will be found in the Unit Repair section under the heading: Ignition—Distributors—Tune-up.

DISTRIBUTOR REMOVAL

All Models

To remove the distributor, take off the cap and wire assembly and remove the ignition primary wire.

Disconnect the vacuum line from the carburetor and remove the bolt which holds the distributor into the engine block.

Lift off the distributor.

1959-63, V8 Engines

The spark plug wires have a non-metallic string type conductor for im-proved radio noise suppression. Care should be taken not to jerk the cables off the spark plugs or out of the distributor cap towers (especially if the engine is hot; otherwise, the cable may pull out of its terminal).

Check cables for excessive resistance or open circuit. Replace if necessary.

Resistor type spark plugs are not to be used with resistor type cables—otherwise poor engine performance will result.

If radio develops excessive noise or if there is a pronounced engine miss, check for defective cables—(broken).

SPARK PLUG WIRE RESISTANCE

No. 1 Wire 8,300 to 16,600 Ohms
No. 2 Wire 5,500 to 11,000 Ohms
No. 3 Wire 8,100 to 16,200 Ohms
No. 4 Wire 6,000 to 12,000 Ohms
No. 5 Wire 8,800 to 17,600 Ohms
No. 6 Wire 6,300 to 12,600 Ohms
No. 7 Wire 9,400 to 18,800 Ohms
No. 8 Wire 7,200 to 14,400 Ohms

IGNITION PRIMARY RESISTOR

1956 Thru 1957 All Models

The ignition primary resistor is located on top of the ignition coil.

No by-pass connector is used to shunt the resistor during starter operation.

Ballast (primary) resistor used on V8

All Models Starting 1958

The ignition primary resistor is mounted on the lower right master cylinder stud.

No by-pass connection is used to shunt the resistor during starter operation.

GENERATOR AND REGULATOR

Detailed facts on the generator and the regulator can be found in the Generator and Regulator Specifications Table of this section.

General information on generator and regulator repair and trouble shooting can be found in the Unit Repair section under the heading: Generators and Regulators.

GENERATOR ASSEMBLY

6 Cylinder Models Thru 1960

The generator assembly on all 6 cyl. Plymouths is located on the left side of the cylinder block and is driven by the fan belt. To remove it, disconnect the wires and remove the generator belt tensioner.

Lift the belt off the generator pulley, let the generator swivel down and remove the two pivot bolts, one on the front and one on the back of the generator and lift the generator off the car.

All service on generators is given in the generator and regulator section of this manual, see index.

1955 Thru 1960 V8 Models

The generator is located on top of the right bank of cylinder head towards the front. Slack off on the tension bar and remove the fan belt. Disconnect the wires to the generator and remove the generator either from the bracket or remove the bracket from the cylinder head. Either set of bolts are readily accessible.

ALTERNATOR AND GENERATOR

REFERENCES

Details on Alternator and Regulator can be found in Specification Table of this section.

General information on Alternator and Regulator repair and trouble shooting can be found in the Unit Repair section.

Removal

To remove alternator:
1. Disconnect battery.
2. Disconnect "BAT" and "FLD" leads from alternator.
3. Remove alternator by removing two mounting bolts and belt tensioner bracket bolt.
To reinstall: Reverse the above.
Never attempt to polarize an alternator, nor short the regulator.

D.C. GENERATOR POLARITY

Caution: Whenever the circuits to: the generator; the regulator; or the battery have been disconnected it is best to apply the following procedure:

Before the engine is started momentarily short from the "Bat" to the "Gen" terminals of the regulator with a screwdriver. This gives a momentary surge of current from the battery to the generator and so correctly polarizes the generator with respect to the battery.

Failure to so polarize the generator before starting the engine may severely damage the regulator since reversed polarity causes vibration, arcing and burning of the relay points.

BATTERY AND STARTER

Detailed information on the battery and starter will be found in the Battery and Starter Specifications Table of this section.

STARTER R & R

No problem here. Disconnect battery and starter wires. Remove attaching bolts and lift out starter.

DASH INSTRUMENTS

1956 Thru 1960 Models

Strictly speaking there are only two instruments used on the 1956 thru 1960 models: they are the fuel gage and the temperature gage.

Since all work under the dash is necessarily done in tight places, it is advisable, in fact, necessary to first disconnect the battery in order to avoid the possibility of short circuits with consequent injury to the operator.

Each instrument is held separately under the dash with two screws.

Remove the screws and the instrument can be pulled out under the dash.

The charge indicator and the oil pressure indicator are actually bulbs operated by relays and it is quite a simple matter to replace them since they are simply snap-in sockets which can be removed readily and the bulb replaced.

The oil pressure tell-tale lamp grounds through the oil pressure sending unit located just below the distributor on the back of the block.

The battery charge indicating light grounds through the relay or voltage control unit located high up on the firewall on the left side.

Electrical connections to the fuel and temperature gauge are push pin type.

Starting with 1961
Removal:

1. Disconnect battery.

2.
From below remove retaining nuts and washers holding cluster to panel.
3. Disconnect wires and connectors.
4. Protect steering column with cloth to prevent scratching.
5. Carefully pull cluster from front of panel.
Note: An ammeter is used in connection with models using alternators.
Reinstall: Reverse the above.

WINDSHIELD WIPER MOTOR

1958-63 Models

The windshield wiper motor is located under the dash and to the right of the glove box.

To remove the motor, detach the wires from the wiper switch, remove the clips from the wiper arms at the motor, then take out the four mounting bolts that hold the motor and mounting plate to the mounting bracket. Lower the motor and plate from under the dash.

Thru 1961

Starting with 1962 it is necessary to remove the radio, speaker and speaker grille.

SPEEDOMETER

Thru 1961

The speedometer can be replaced in Plymouth by disconnecting the drive cable and housing from the speedometer head and the mounting screws that hold the head to the back of the instrument panel. The unit can now be removed from the rear of the panel.

Starting with 1962
Removal:

After removing cluster as described under Instruments, the Speedometer can be removed by taking out two mounting screws.

BRAKE SYSTEM

BRAKES

Information on brake adjustments, band replacement, bleeding procedure, master and wheel cylinder overhaul

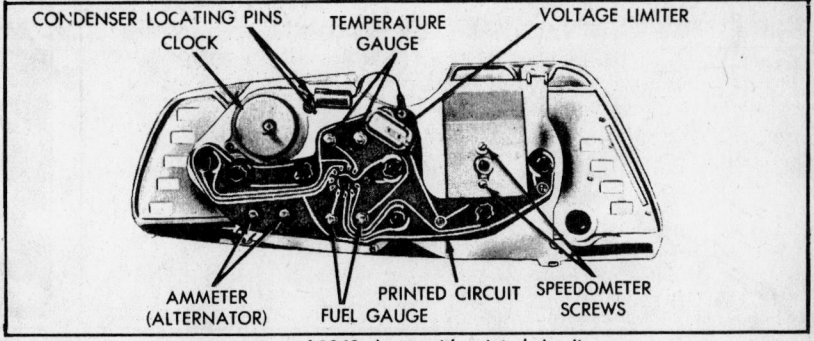

Rear view of 1962 cluster with printed circuits

PLYMOUTH

can be found in the Unit Repair Section under the heading: Brakes, Hydraulic.

Information on trouble shooting and overhauling power brakes can be found in the Unit Repair Section under the heading: Brakes, Power.

Information on the grease seals which may need replacement can be found in the Unit Repair Section. The front wheel grease seals under the head: Suspension, Front Repair. The rear wheel grease seals under the head: Axles, Rear.

Starting with 1962

A new Servo-contact, self-energizing brake is used. It uses a double-acting wheel cylinder at tops of shoes at each assembly.

It is also a self-adjusting brake. It operates thru a link, cable and return spring connected so that when brake is applied during reverse stops the link indexes the star wheel to maintain proper shoe clearance.

REMOVAL OF THE MASTER CYLINDER

1954

To remove the master cylinder, disconnect the push rod at the clevis pin on the brake pedal and disconnect the lines from the back of the master cylinder and tape them up to prevent dirt and foreign matter from falling into the tube.

Remove the clutch and brake pedal shaft and disconnect the master cylinder mounting bolts and remove it from the car.

On installation, it will be necessary to readjust the clutch pedal linkage and the brake pedal free play.

Starting 1955

The master cylinder is located on the front side of the firewall. To remove it, disconnect the brake push rod at the clevis from under the dash, disconnect the stop light wires and the line running to the master cylinder from under the hood and remove the bolts which mount the master cylinder to the firewall.

MASTER CYLINDER CHANGE

Beginning 1958

Cars built since March 9, 1958 with conventional brakes have a change incorporated in the brake master cylinder. With this change a pedal stop is built into the master cylinder. This eliminates the necessity of a free play adjustment on the master cylinder push rod.

The stop on the brake pedal, and the brake pedal return spring are also eliminated by this change. This results in a somewhat slower brake pedal return, when the brake is released, which is not detrimental. However, if a binding action is found at the brake pedal, the cause of binding should be eliminated.

Since the master cylinder piston determines the position of the brake pedal when the brakes are released, a free play at the pedal is no longer needed. However, if the pedal is pulled back by hand, some play may be noted, due to clearance allowed at the push rod eye for self-alignment of the push rod.

Pulling on the brake pedal, in a direction away from the master cylinder, with a force of 50 pounds or more, will result in deflection of the piston stop. Since this would result in excess pedal travel before any braking ef-

fort would be realized, this action should definitely be discouraged.

During disassembly, the master cylinder push rod cannot be removed from the piston, therefore, these parts along with the piston stop and boot retainer, are removed from the cylinder as an assembly and are also serviced as an assembly.

The new and old type master cylinders are not interchangeable, as the old type necessitates installing a pedal stop and a pedal return spring, as well as the adjustable push rod and nut.

PARKING BRAKE

Thru 1956

A ratchet type hand brake is used on these models.

Two bolts are used to mount the cable under the dash. The cable fastens to the lever assembly with a clevis pin.

The cable and conduit is held by a bracket which is screwed to the fire wall under the dash.

The brake end of the cable is held to the transmission by a mounting bracket.

A yoke is screwed to the lower end of the cable and forms the lever cable adjustment. This in turn is held with a clevis pin to the brake operating mechanism.

A new cable and conduit assembly does not include the yoke.

1957 Thru 1959

The cable lever is held with a clevis pin to a bracket under the dash. The hand brake rod itself is pivoted to a bracket immediately under the instrument panel. The pin of this bracket is held with a simple push clamp.

To replace the cable, remove the clevis from the lever under the dash and loosen the clamp screw, also under the dash, which holds the hand brake

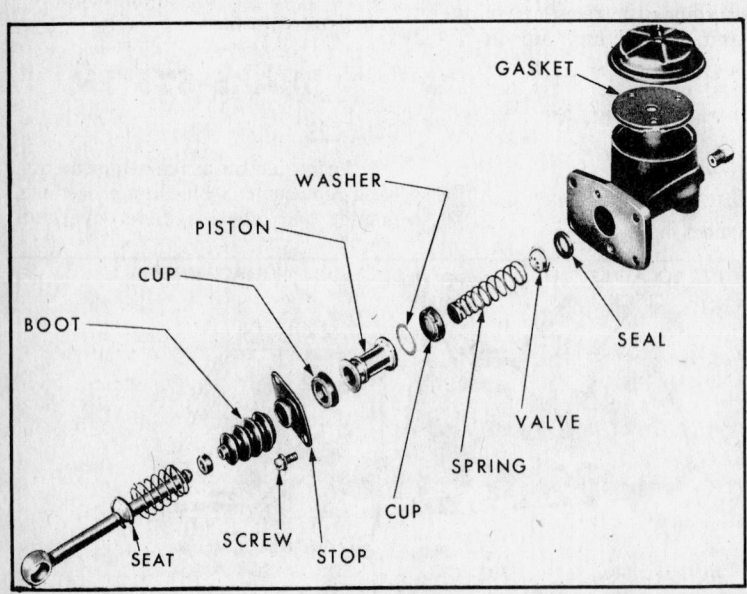

Master Cylinder

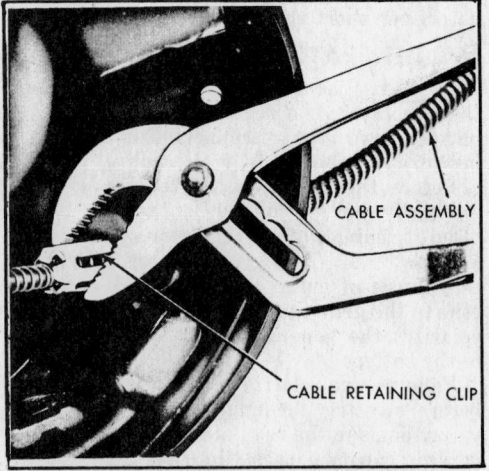

Removing Brake Cable from Support Plate

conduit. Pull the upper end of the cable forward into the engine compartment and then remove the clamp which holds the conduit to the side of the transmission.

Disconnect the lower end of the cable at the transmission hand brake. The adjustable end of the cable is at the transmission. Install a new cable in reverse order.

Starting 1960

A Step-on parking brake lever is used. Adjustment are the same as with the hand lever types. Replacement is also similar and reference to the adjoining cut is self-explanatory.

HAND BRAKE ADJUSTMENT

External Type Hand Brake

Fully release the hand brake lever and check the clearance at the brake between the anchor bracket and the drum. This clearance should not exceed .005 inch. Adjust the lining to drum clearance so there is between .015 and .020 in. clearance between the lining and the drum. After the lining is properly adjusted, pull all the slack out of the hand brake cable and reconnect.

Internal Type Hand Brake

NOTE: Incorrectly adjusted hand brake will effect automatic shifting.

Fully release hand brake and set shift lever in neutral. Detach front end of propeller shaft so brake drum may be turned by hand. Back off the cable adjusting nut and expand brake shoes until slight drag is felt. Now back off one notch with a special wrench C-3014 or a screwdriver to obtain .010 in. clearance. With cable adjusting nut against cable housing there should be .005 in. to .020 in. clearance between brake shoe cable

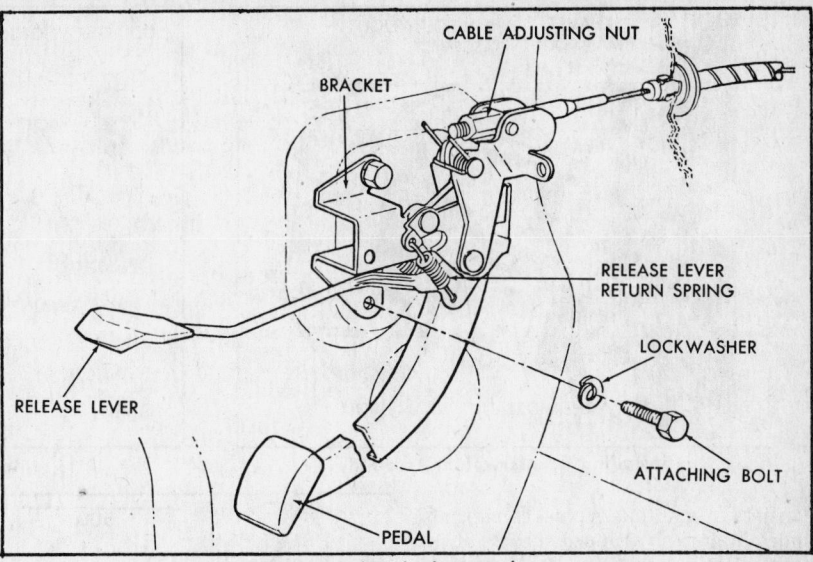

Step on parking brake control

and adjusting lever. Make certain the adjusting nut is securely tightened. Pull hand brake lever 4 to 6 notches and brake should be fully applied.

Starting with 1962

A new parking brake is used. It operates at the rear wheels thru a pedal, cable and shoe expanding link.

To adjust it, with cable not pulling, see that rear service brakes are properly adjusted. Tighten cable to produce slight drag. Then loosen cable just enough to be sure wheels are free.

FUEL SYSTEM

FUEL SYSTEM INFORMATION

A chart covering causes of excess fuel consumption will be found in the Unit Repair section under the heading: Fuel Consumption Chart.

Data on capacity of the gas tank will be found in the Capacities Table. Data on correct engine idle speed and fuel pump pressure will be found in the Tune-up Specifications table.

General information on fuel pumps and their troubles will be found in the Unit Repair section under the heading: Fuel Pumps.

Information covering operation and troubles of the fuel gauge will be found in the Unit Repair section under the heading: Gages.

Detailed information on the carburetor and how to adjust it will be found in the Unit Repair section under the heading: Carburetors.

Dash pot adjustment can be found in the Unit Repair section under the same heading as that of the automatic transmission used in the car.

CARBURETOR
Starting with 1962

A new throttle control is used. It

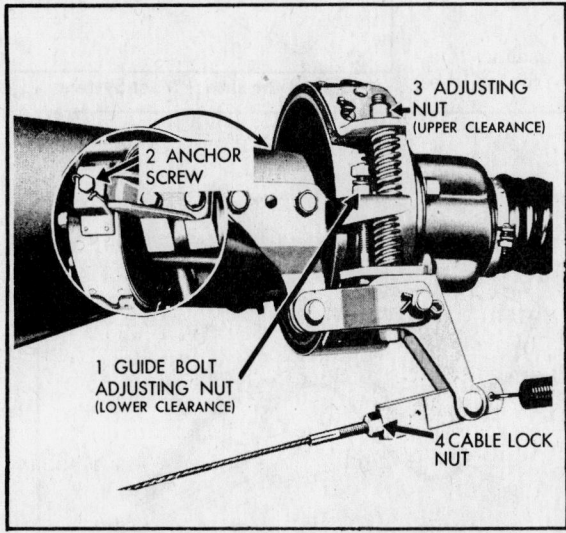

External type hand brake adjusting point

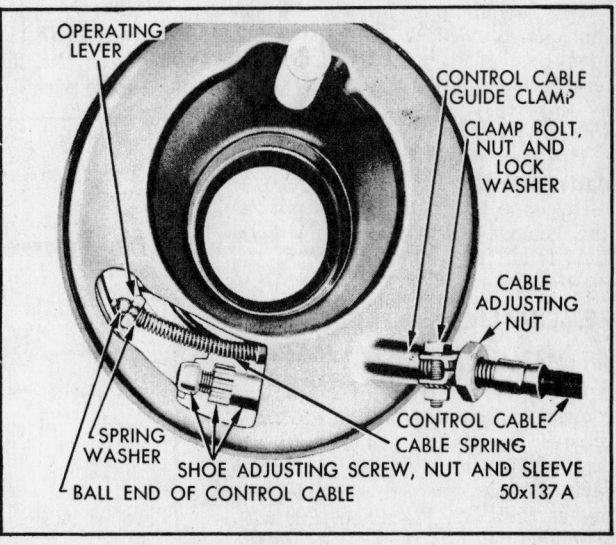

Internal type hand brake adjusting point

PLYMOUTH

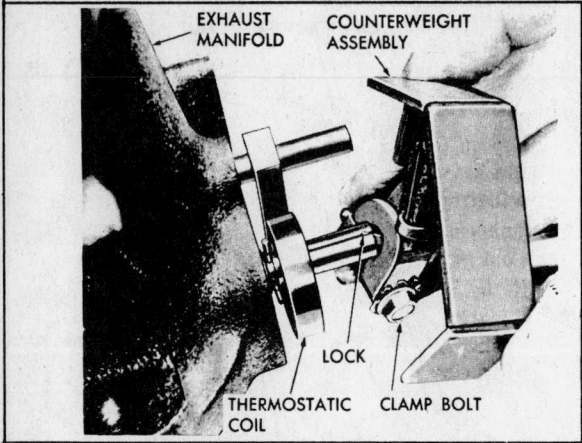

Installing Counterweight Assembly

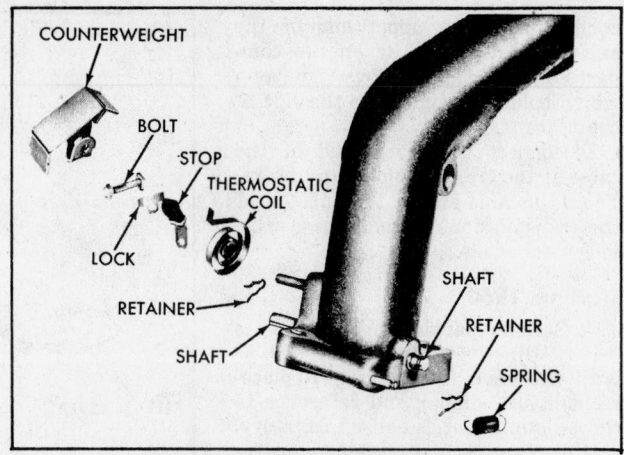

Manifold Heat Control Valve

consists of a stainless steel cable that slides in a steel wrapped sheath. It is permanently lubricated. Pedal contact is by roller. All lash or looseness common to most linkage is eliminated. Linkage conveyed noises are greatly reduced.

FUEL PUMP

6 Cyl. "L" Head Models Thru 1959

On all Plymouths the fuel pump is located on the right side of the engine towards the front under the exhaust manifold.

A steel baffle plate is used between the manifold and the fuel pump to reduce the possibility of vapor lock in the fuel pump.

Remove the lines to the fuel pump and take out the two mounting bolts which hold the fuel pump to the block.

On some models there is a small vertical stud between the fuel pump and the steel baffle. On these models disconnect the vertical stud and lift off the fuel pump.

Slant "6" OHV

This fuel pump is placed in the conventional 6 cyl. location and has the advantage of no exhaust pipe interference.

1955 Thru 1963 V8 Models

The fuel pump is located on the right front of the engine.

Disconnect the input and output gas line, remove the two mounting bolts and lift off the fuel pump.

REMOVAL OF FUEL TANK

All Models Thru 1956

To remove the fuel tank, first disconnect the gas line at the tank and remove the clamps which hold the flexible filler neck to the tank filler neck and disconnect the flexible vent line at the tank. Place the jack with a wooden block on top of it under the fuel tank and then disconnect the

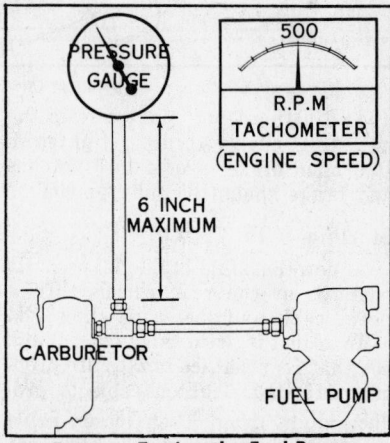

Pressure Testing the Fuel Pump

straps which hold the tank up into position. Slowly lower the tank until the gauge wire is accessible and remove the gauge wire. Continue lowering the tank.

It may be necessary to thread the tank a little to get it past the springs and frame cross members.

Gage wire is also accessible from the port hole in the floor of the trunk.

Starting 1957

Remove the flexible gasoline line and gauge wire from the front of the

tank and place a jack protected by a block of wood under the tank.

Remove the two hook bolts from the rear end and let the T straps come down. Remove the rubber grommet from the top of the filler neck and then thread the tank downwards somewhat. Continue threading the tank downwards and to the right to get the filler neck out of the tube which passes thru the trunk. The access hole has been eliminated, making it necessary to lower tank to remove gauge unit.

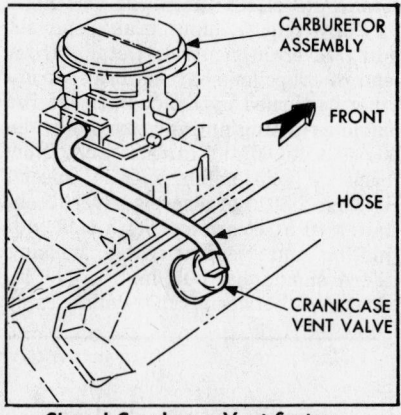

Closed Crankcase Vent System

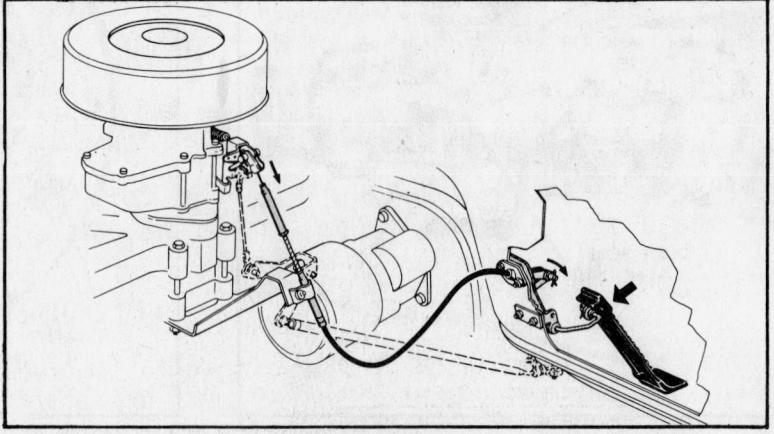

1962 Throttle Linkage.

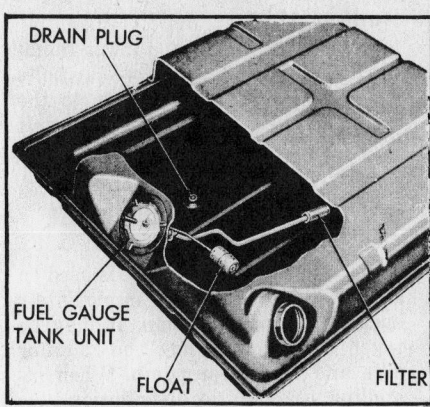

Fuel tank and filter starting with 1957

FUEL FILTERS

For many years attention has been drawn to the fact that certain automobile fuels, exposed to adverse conditions, are prone to develop gum. These deposits can be very troublesome, especially to ceramic fuel filters. In extreme cases the ceramic has been discarded in favor of no filter at all. In most cases this gum film is invisible but thoroughly stops the passage of fuel through the pores of the filter.

⏻ CHILTON TIME-SAVER

Soak the offending ceramic in undiluted alcohol for about ½ hour and blow out with an air hose. (Yes, antifreeze alcohol will do.)

EXHAUST SYSTEM

All 6 cylinder Plymouth models use a single muffler.

Some V-8 models are fitted with a dual exhaust.

REMOVAL OF MUFFLER

6 Cylinder Models, All

Before attempting to remove a muffler, look to see whether or not the joints in the muffler between the exhaust pipe and tail pipe are badly corroded, and if they are, squirt plenty of penetrating oil or rust dissolving fluid on these joints before loosening the clamps.

Loosen the clamps and drive the muffler and its tail pipe backwards until the muffler is released from the exhaust pipe.

Now drop the mufiler downwards and then drive it forward off the tail pipe.

If the tail pipe is to be replaced with the muffler, remove the hangers which hold the tail pipe up under the body and thread the tail pipe and muffler assembly out from underneath the car in a single unit.

The car will have to be jacked up

considerably to do this since it is sometimes a difficult job.

V8 Models

On these models the muffiler is fitted with a short extension pipe which is welded into the front of the muffler.

Replacements are supplied having a muffler and separate extension pipe.

Be sure of the type of replacement being used before taking the old muffler off the car.

It may be necessary to cut the exhaust pipe at a convenient point in order to install a new muffler.

REPLACEMENT OF EXHAUST PIPE

6 Cyl. Models Thru 1963

From underneath the car detach the exhaust pipe from the muffler as explained in the paragraph on muffler removal and then jack the car up considerably and disconnect the exhaust pipe at the flange on the manifold. Now thread the exhaust pipe downwards and to one side and out from under the car.

1955 Thru 1963 V8 Models

The exhaust pipe on these models comes from each bank of cylinders to a common outlet at the center where it is connected to the muffler extension pipe. A slip joint is provided at this point and the exhaust pipe can be replaced by detaching it from both manifold flanges and then, after using plenty of penetrating oil, separating the "Y" shaped exhaust pipe from the muffler extension pipe.

MANIFOLDS

6 Cylinder "L" Head Models

On all Plymouth engines the intake and exhaust manifold are mounted on the right side of the engine and are

joined together just underneath the carburetor. A heat riser valve is used in the exhaust manifold to deflect the exhaust gases toward the intake manifold when the engine is cool. The heat riser valve is operated by a thermostatic spring which causes it to move to the off position when the engine reaches operating temperature. The only service required by the heat riser is to see that the valve is free and operates freely.

An inoperative valve may cause the engine to warm up slowly, resulting in excessive use of the choke, or it may cause the engine to apparently run lean when it is hot.

To remove the manifolds, take off the carburetor and all its attaching parts, remove all lines from the manifolds, disconnect the exhaust manifold at the exhaust pipe flange, unbolt the manifold from the side of the block and lift it off.

INLET MANIFOLD REMOVAL

V8 Models

Remove the carburetor air cleaner and take off the throttle, gas and vacuum lines from the carburetor and unbolt the carburetor.

Remove the heater hose and the vacuum lines from the intake manifold. Disconnect and remove the ignition coil. Remove the bolts which attach the intake manifold to both cylinder heads and lift off the manifold.

EXHAUST MANIFOLDS REMOVAL

V8 Models

From underneath the car, using a long extension, remove the bolts which hold both exhaust pipe flanges to the exhaust manifold. Remove the choke heater tube and the generator from the right manifold and then take

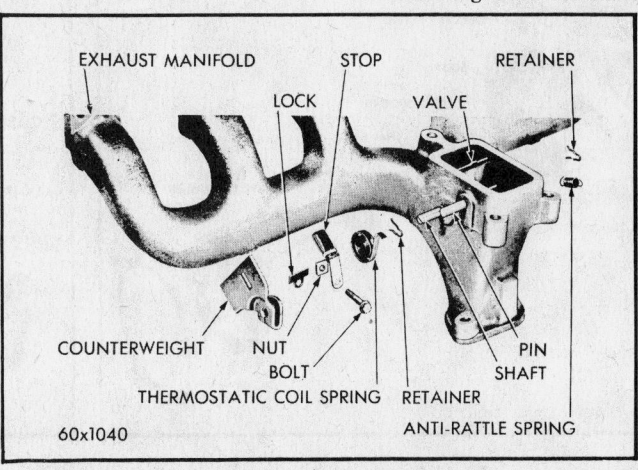

Thermostatic Coil Spring—6 Cyl. Engine

PLYMOUTH

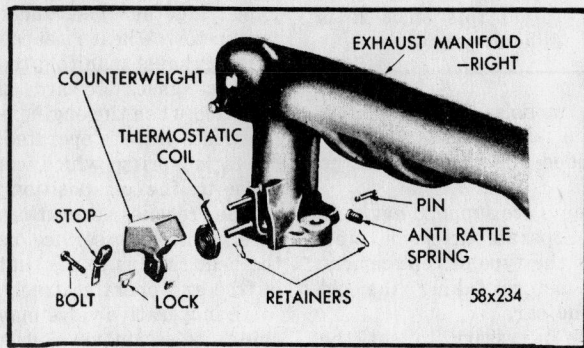

Thermostatic Coil Spring—V-8 Engine

out the bolts which hold the manifolds to the cylinder head and lift off.

COOLING SYSTEMS

Detailed information on cooling system capacity can be found in the Capacities Table of this section.

Information on the water temperature gauge can be found in the Unit Repair section under the heading: Gages.

Caution: Do not run cold water over the outside of pressurized radiators without first removing the radiator cap. When the cap is left on and the cold water hits the hot radiator the steam in the radiator condenses very rapidly and sometimes collapses the top radiator tank. This is most likely to happen if the coolant level is below normal.

REMOVAL OF WATER PUMP

6 Cyl. Models

On all Plymouth models the water pump can be removed without removing the radiator core. In general the procedure is to remove the fan blades, detach all hose connections, and on models which use a fan shroud, take off the fan shroud.

The water pump can then be detached from the block and lifted off.

V8 Models

Slack off on the generator belt and remove the bolts which hold the fan, blades, spacer and pulley to the fan hub.

Remove the lower radiator hose, the by-pass hose and the heater hose.

Remove the bolts which hold the pump assembly to the engine front cover and lift off the pump.

RADIATOR CORE REMOVAL

1954 Models

The radiator core is removed after taking off the water hoses, headlight wires, fan shroud (if any) and the water pump assembly.

Note: It will be necessary to remove the upper and lower radiator shield on the 1954 models. The radiator can then be unbolted from its side mountings and lifted up and over the engine.

Starting 1955

Remove the upper and lower radiator hoses and take out the four bolts which hold the radiator core to the cradle and lift the core straight up. It it not necessary to remove the fan shroud.

WATER DISTRIBUTION TUBE

6 Cyl. "L" Head Models

A water distribution tube is used on all models and is located immediately back of the water pump. It may be taken out by removing the radiator core and the water pump. When installing a new water distribution tube it is essential that the new tube be flared on the end in a manner similar to the old tube.

To remove the tube, a rod is formed into a hook at one end and is slid into the distribution tube hooking one of the holes in the tube. If the distribution tube seems to be stuck or corroded in place it is a good idea to thoroughly flush out the block rather than attempting to force the tube out of the block.

WATER MANIFOLD REMOVAL

1955 V8 Models

Slack off on the generator and remove the fan belt. Take off the fan blades and fan hub and remove the water pump. Remove the upper and lower radiator hoses and the by-pass hose.

Support the weight of the front of the engine on a jack and remove the motor mounting bolts which are just under the water manifold.

Remove the bolts which hold the water manifold to the block and heads and lift off the manifold.

1956 V8 Models

Slack off on the generator and re-

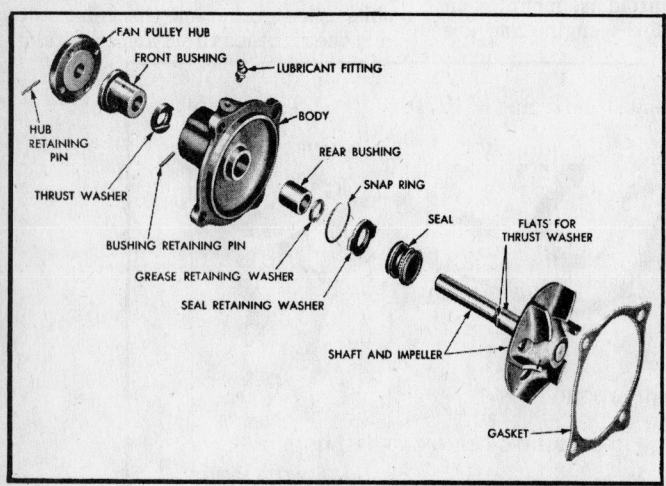

Hy Fire V-8 Water Pump—Disassembled Bushing Type
(241 and 260 Cu. In. Engine)

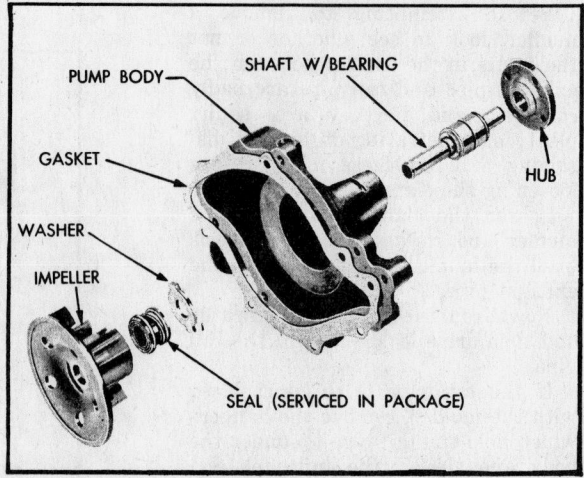

Water Pump Disassembled
(Typical 277, 301 and 318 Cu. In. Engine)

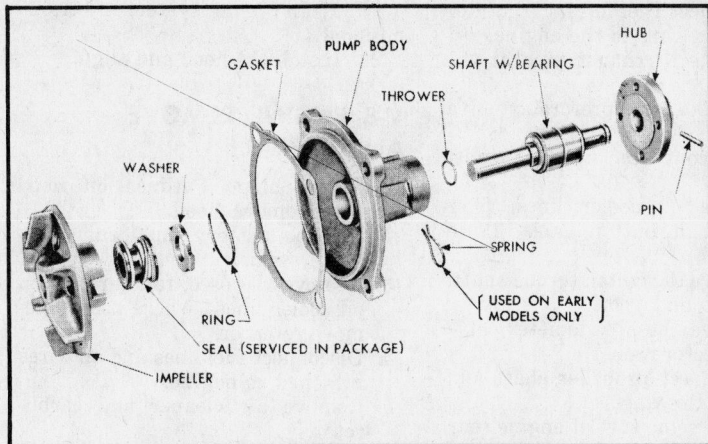

Hy Fire V-8 Water Pump—Disassembled Ball Bearing Type (260 and 270 Cu. In. Engine)

Water Pump—Disassembled (Typical of 350 Cu. In. V-8 Engine)

move the fan belt. Take off the fan blades and fan hub and remove the water pump. Remove the upper and lower radiator hoses and the by-pass hose and then disconnect the water manifold from the heads and block and lift off.

V8 Models Starting 1957

Remove the water pump and the fuel pump.

Take off the crankshaft pulley. Note: This job is a good deal easier if the core is removed first.

Remove the bolts which hold the front cover to the block and the two bolts which hold the front cover to the oil pan and lift off the cover. Note: It is very difficult to secure a good seal at the front of the oil pan if the cover is removed without first removing the oil pan.

It is recommended that the oil pan be removed first in order to insure an oil tight seal at the front of the oil pan.

ENGINES

REFERENCES

Starting 1960 power is supplied by

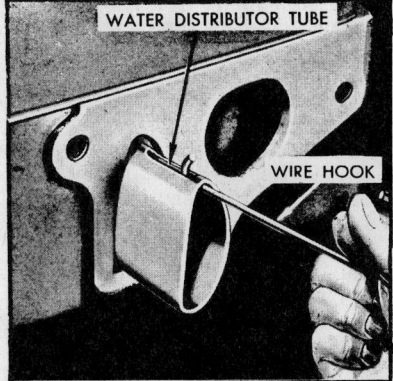

Removing water distributor tube from 6 cyl. engine block

three basic engines, with variations.

The most spectacular of the line is the overhead valve, 6 cylinder engine. It is mounted in the frame at a 30° angle toward the right, from vertical. This engine is in the 225 cubic inch class and referred to as the 30-D economy "6" or the Slant "6" engine.

The next size in power plant is the 318 cubic inch V8 engine. This is the standard Fury engine, however, variations of this engine are available in the V-800 with super pak (4-barrel carburetor etc).

The 361 cubic inch Golden Commando engine is optional on all Plymouth models. It is available with single 4-barrel carburetor, dual exhaust, special radiator and clutch and heavy duty battery. A heavy-duty manual transmission is standard. A

modified version of Torque-Flite and a higher shifting governor is also optional with this engine.

The "Sonoramic Commando V8" is a high performance version of the 361 basic engine. It develops about 10 percent greater torque, (in the 1800 to 3600 R.P.M. range) than the Golden Commando and accomplishes this added power through RAM induction.

Engine Information

In the Specifications Tables of this section there are listed all the available facts about the engines. When different size engines are used a note under the General Engine Specifications Table will give an easy means of

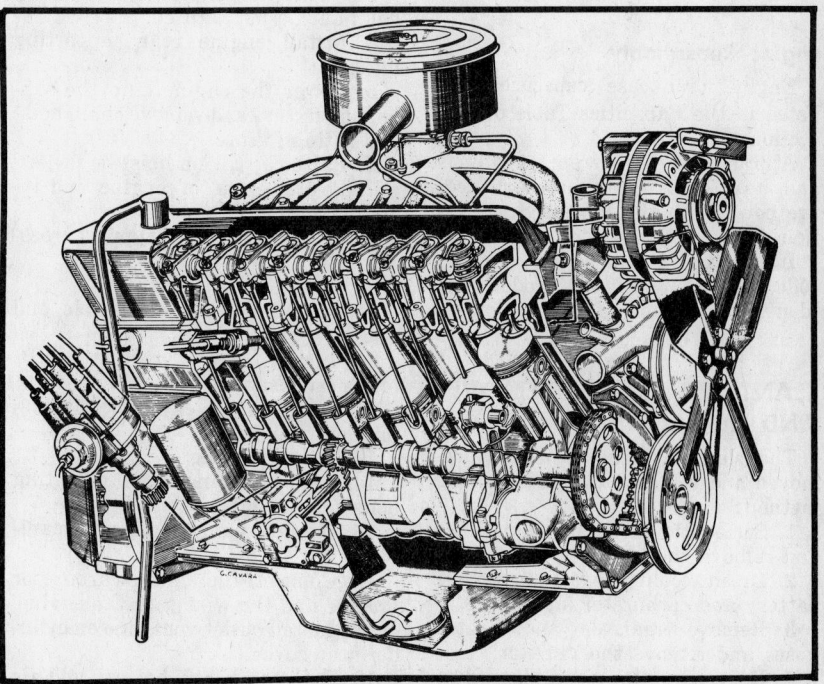

225 cu. in. Engine Assembly

determining which engine is which.

Where some engines have hydraulic valve lifters and others do not, a means of determining which does and which does not is given in a note under the Tune-Up Table.

Valves

Detailed information on the valves, the type of valve guide and the location of valve timing marks, can be found in the Valve Specifications Table of this section.

A general discussion of valve clearance and a chart showing how to read pressure and vacuum gauges when using them to diagnose engine troubles will be found in the Unit Repair section under the heading: Tune-Up —Ignition—Distributors. Under the same head will be found a chart on engine trouble shooting. Valve tappet clearance for each engine is given in the Tune-Up Specifications Table of this section.

Bearings

Detailed information on engine bearings will be found in the Crankshaft Bearing Journal Sizes Table of this section.

Pistons and Pins

Detailed information on pistons and piston pins, together with information on piston, rod and crankshaft relationship for assembly, will be found in the Piston and Pin Specifications Table of this section.

Engine Reassembly

Engine crankcase capacities are listed in the Capacities Table of this section.

Approved torque wrench readings and head bolt tightening sequences are covered in the Torque Specifications Table of this section.

Information on the engine marking code will be found in the Model Year Identification Table of this section.

SLANT "6" ENGINE REMOVE AND REPLACE

The slant "6" engine is best removed and replaced by the following method:

1. Scribe the hood hinge outlines and remove the hood.
2. Drain cooling system, remove battery and carburetor air cleaner.
3. Remove radiator and heater hoses and remove the radiator.
4. Remove outlet vent pipe from cylinder head cover.

5. Disconnect fuel lines, carburetor linkage and wiring to the engine.
6. Disconnect exhaust pipe at the manifold.
7. Raise the car, preferably on a hoist.
8. Drain converter and transmission.
9. Remove oil cooler lines, filler tube and push button cable, if so equipped.
10. Remove the clutch torque shaft, brake cables and rods.
11. Remove the speedometer cable and gear selector rods.
12. Disconnect propeller shaft and tie it out of the way.
13. Install some sort of engine rear support that will permit safe removal of rear engine mount.
14. Remove engine rear support crossmember.
15. Remove transmission bolts from clutch housing.
16. Remove the transmission.
17. Lower the car.
18. Attach engine lifting fixture and hook up chain hoist to fixture eyebolt.
19. Remove engine rear support fixture.
20. Remove engine front mounting bolts.
21. Lift engine from chassis and place on adequate repair stand.

TO REPLACE:

1. Attach engine lifting fixture and hook up chain hoist to fixture eyebolt.
2. Lower the engine into the chassis until the front of the engine is in position on the front engine mounts.
3. Install engine front mounting bolts but do not tighten.
4. Install engine rear supporting fixture.
5. Lower the engine onto the supporting fixture and remove chain hoist and lifting fixture.
6. Raise the car on hoist or jacks.
7. Position rear of engine and install the transmission.
8. Install engine rear support crossmember.
9. Connect propeller shaft.
10. Install speedometer cable and selector rods.
11. Install clutch torque shaft, brake cables and rods.
12. Install oil cooler lines and transmission filler tube.
13. Lower the car.
14. Torque engine front mounting bolts (85 ft. lb.).
15. Connect exhaust pipe to manifold.
16. Connect fuel lines, carburetor linkage and the wiring to the engine.
17. Install outlet vent pipe on cylinder head cover.
18. Reinstall hoses, battery and air cleaner.

19. Refill cooling system and transmission.
20. Install the hood and align.

V-8 ENGINE REMOVE AND REPLACE

1. Scribe hinge outlines on hood then remove hood.
2. Remove battery and drain cooling system.
3. Remove all hoses, fan shroud and oil cooler lines (where used). Remove radiator.
4. Disconnect fuel lines and all wires attached to engine.
5. Remove air cleaner and carburetor.
6. Attach lifting fixture, tool C-3466, or equivalent to carburetor flange studs.
7. Attach rear engine support, tool C-3487, and remove rear engine support.
8. Disconnect exhaust pipes at manifolds.
9. Disconnect propeller shaft, wires, cables linkage and cooler lines and remove transmission.
10. Remove engine front mount nuts. Attach crane or other suitable lifting tool to manifold fixture and lift out engine.

To Replace: Reverse above procedure.

CYLINDER HEAD
ROCKER COVER REMOVAL

Slack off on the generator and lift off the fan belt, then rock the generator back towards the fender. Remove the spark plug wires from the plugs, tag them carefully or leave them in the wire bracket. Take out the bolts which hold the rocker covers to the cylinder head and lift off the cover.

ROCKER SHAFT REMOVAL, SLANT "6" ENGINE

Stamped steel rocker arms are arranged on a single rocker arm shaft. Hardened steel spacers are used between the pairs of arms. The rocker shaft is secured by bolts and stamped steel retainers attached to seven integral brackets on the cylinder head.

The removal of the rocker arms or shaft requires no peculiar attention, however, assembly and reinstallation does.

1. The rocker arms and shaft assembly must be installed correctly. The flat on the end of the rocker shaft must be on top and point toward the front of the engine. This is necessary to provide proper lubrication to the rocker assemblies.
2. Install the shaft retainers with

the wide retainer in the center.

3. Install the rocker shaft retaining bolts with the long bolt at the rear of the engine.

4. Torque rocker shaft bolts to 30 ft. lb.

5. Warm up the engine and adjust the tappets to .010", intake and .020, exhaust.

V8 Models

A single rocker shaft is used on each cylinder head. Remove the rocker cover as outlined above, and then a little at a time turn out the bolts which hold the rocker brackets to the cylinder head and lift off the rocker shafts.

They should be returned to the head from which they were removed and at the position from which they were removed.

CYLINDER HEAD REMOVAL

6 Cylinder "L"-head Models

Disconnect the water outlet hose and water by-pass, remove the carburetor air cleaner, disconnect all spark plug wires and heater hoses, remove all linkage to the carburetor and dis-

tributor which pass over the cylinder head, take out the cylinder head bolts and lift the head off.

Slant "6" Models

1. Drain cooling system.
2. Remove rocker cover, rocker arms and shaft as above.
3. Disconnect accelerator linkage, vacuum control, heater and by pass hose and heat gauge sending unit.
4. Disconnect exhaust pipe at flange and remove intake manifold and carburetor as an assembly.
5. Remove push rods.
6. Remove 14 head bolts and lift off head.
   Reinstall: Reverse above procedure.

Starting with 1955 V8 Model

To remove the cylinder head, follow the instructions given above for the intake manifold and the rocker cover, and, in addition, disconnect the exhaust pipes at their flanges. On 1955 models support the weight of the front of the engine on a jack and remove the bolts which hold the water manifold to both the cylinder head and the block. (On 1956 models it is

not necessary to support the engine) if the water manifold is not loosened at the block, it will be extremely difficult to get the head back in the proper alignment when it is being reinstalled.

Remove the bolts which hold the cylinder head to the block and lift off the head.

VALVE SYSTEM

6 Cylinder "L" Head Models

All 6 cylinder engines up to and including 1959, are of the inline L-head variety and are fitted with mushroom type lifters which require that the camshaft be removed in order to take out any of the lifters.

Slant "6" Models

The Slant "6" is an overhead valve engine and does **not** use the mushroom type lifters. The straight sided tappets are replaceable with the same ease as a hydraulic tappet.

V8 Models

Overhead valves are used on all V8 models.

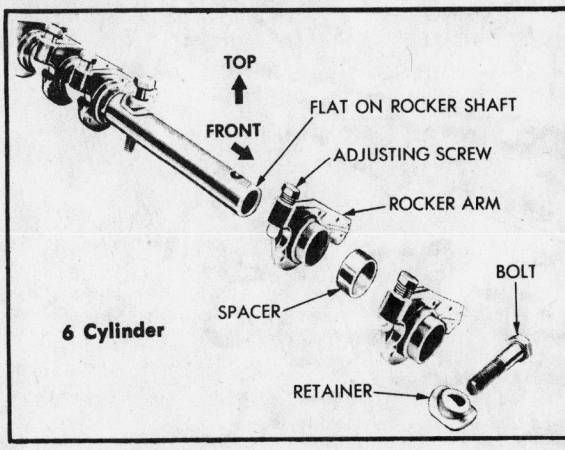

Rocker Arm and Shaft Assembly

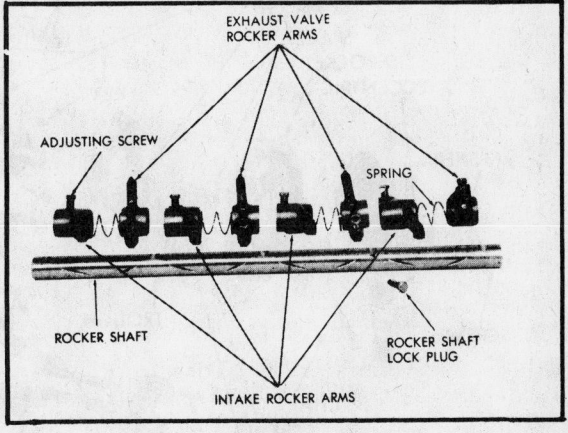

Rocker shaft assembly 277, 301, 318 cubic inch capacity V8's

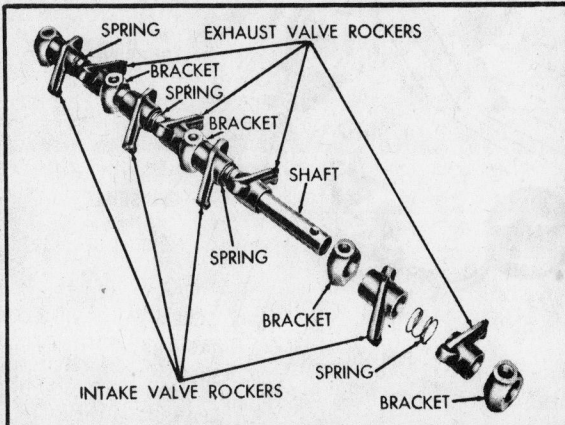

*Rocker shaft assembly
241, 260, 270 cubic inch capacity V8's*

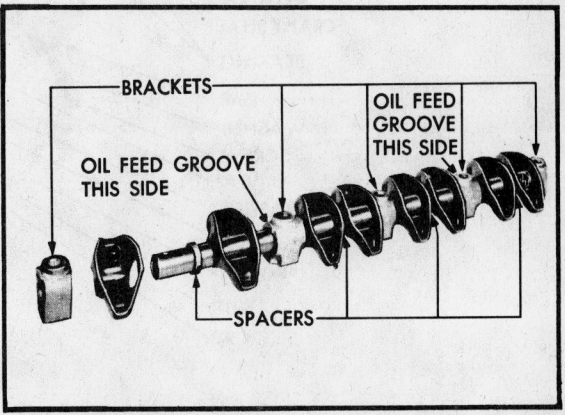

Rocker Shaft Assembly Commando V8's

PLYMOUTH

REMOVAL OF VALVES

6 Cylinder "L" Head Models

Take off the cylinder head and the valve chamber side cover.

Some models of Plymouth are fitted with a removable shield under the right wheel. Jack up the car, remove the wheel and take off this shield for easy access to the valve chamber.

Using a valve spring lifter, select valves in the closed position and raise the valve spring and remove the keeper from the bottom of the valve stem.

Release the valve spring and the valve can be pulled up and out of the cylinder block.

Slant "6" and V8 Models

On these models the valves are in the cylinder head. Remove the cylinder head as outlined in an earlier paragraph and take it to a bench. The valves may then be released by depressing the valve springs and taking out the keeper.

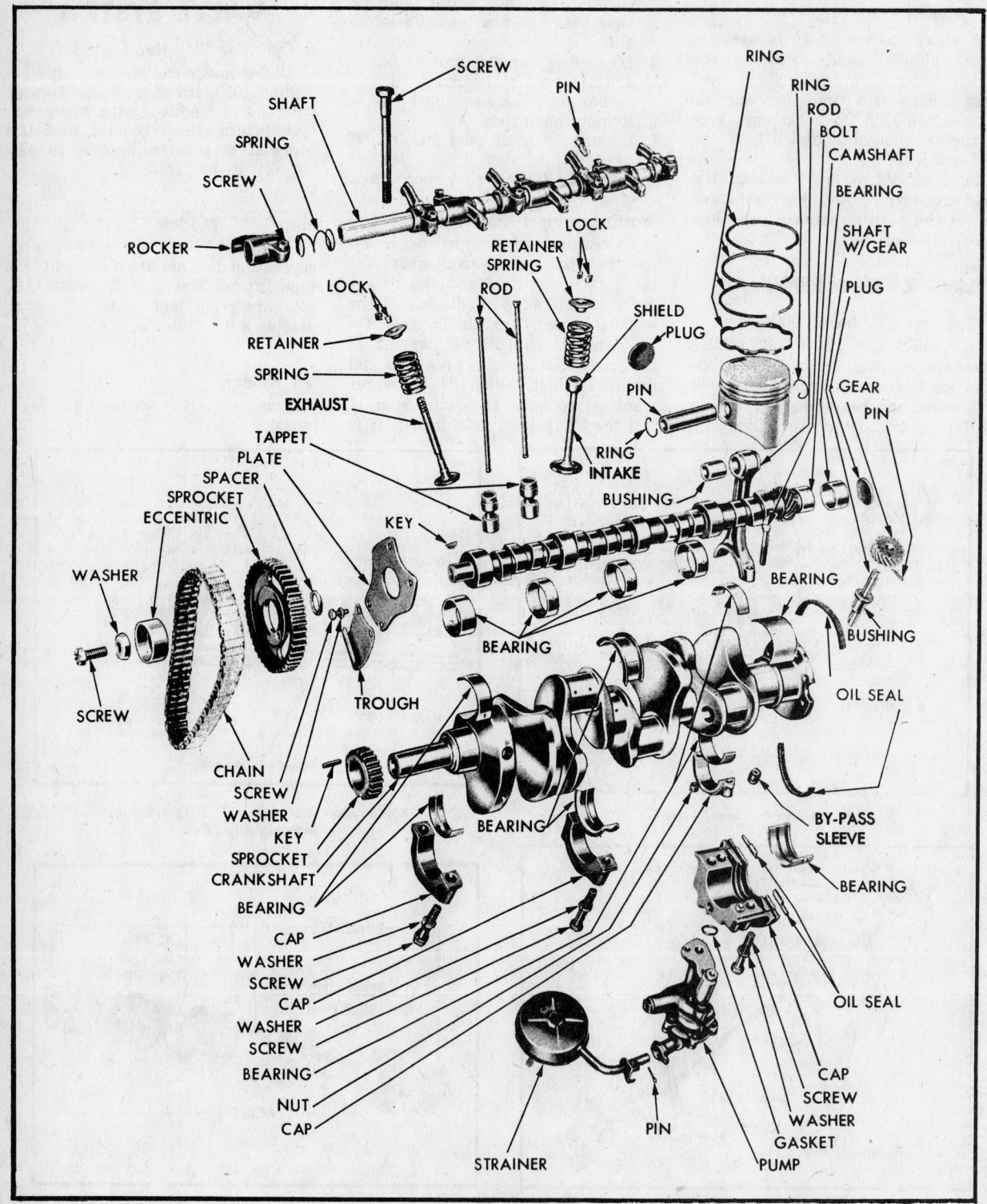

Crankshaft and Related Parts—V-8 Engine—277, 301 and 318 cu. in. Engine

REPLACEMENT OF VALVE GUIDES

6 Cylinder "L" Head Models

Whenever it is necessary to replace valve guides on Plymouth, or any other engine, it is always good practice to carefully measure the distance from the cylinder head to the edge of the valve guide before driving out the old guide. This measurement should be carefully noted, both for the intake and the exhaust, so that when a new guide is installed, it can be inserted to exactly the same distance from the head as the old guide.

On all Plymouth engines the valve guide should be reamed after installation to provide the proper clearance for the valve stem.

The data tables of this Plymouth section give the diameter of valve stems for all models and the guide should be reamed to provide a clearance of approximately .0015 inch.

On all 6 cyl. "L" head engines the valve guides are pulled through the top of the block. New guides are installed by driving them from the top toward the bottom.

Slant "6" & V8 Models

These models do not use a separate valve guide. Instead, the guides are cast integral with the cylinder head. If the valve stem is a poor fit in the guide, first determine whether or not the valve or guide is worn by inserting a new valve down into the guide. If it fits well it means the valves will have to be replaced.

If the new valve fits poorly it will be necessary to secure oversize valves and ream the cylinder head to a running fit of approximately .0015 inch.

VALVE SPRINGS

A quick way to check the condition of the valve springs when they have been removed is to lay them all in a row on a level surface and determine that all of them are the same height by placing a straight edge across the top of all the springs.

If it is found that the springs vary in height it will be necessary to secure one new spring and then check all the others against the new one. They should be exactly the same length as the new one. If they are not, they require replacement.

Checking the valve springs against the new spring is generally considered to be a fairly accurate way of checking the general condition of the spring itself, when regular spring pressure testers are not available.

ADJUSTING VALVES

6 Cylinder "L" Head Models

Remove the road wheel and the access hole cover under the fender to service the valves in the most convenient manner. Take off the valve chamber cover.

Starting in 1958 the access hole cover was discontinued. Because of this change it is necessary to remove the right front fender shield when servicing valve tappets.

A self-locking tappet screw is used on all adjustable Plymouth models.

TIMING CASE

TIMING CASE COVER REMOVAL

6 Cylinder "L" Head Models

On these models, to remove the timing case cover it is necessary to take off the radiator core, water pump, fan and vibration damper.

Slant "6" Engines

These models do not require water pump removal.

1955 V8 Models

Support the weight of the front of the engine on a jack and remove the radiator core and the water manifold. The water pump can be left intact in the manifold. Remove the bolts which hold the front motor mount to the frame and lift off the motor mount together with the water manifold.

Take off the crankshaft pulley and then unbolt and lift off the timing case cover.

It is not necessary to separate the motor mount from the water manifold.

1956-58 V8 Models

1. Remove radiator core.
2. Remove generator, fan blades and hub, fuel pump and water pump.
3. Loosen oil pan bolts and lower to clear cover.
4. Remove damper and pulley.
5. Remove cover.

To Reinstall: Reverse the above. Be sure of positive gasket seal between cover and oil pan.

1959-63 V8 Models

1. Remove radiator core, fan and belt.
2. Remove water pump and housing as an assembly.
3. Remove crank shaft pulley.
4. Remove fuel pump and line.
5. Remove cover, using care not to damage oil pan gasket.

To Reinstall: Reverse the above.

VALVE TIMING PROCEDURE— REPLACEMENT OF CHAINS AND SPROCKETS

To replace a timing chain and/or sprockets, or to retime the valves where the timing has jumped, proceed as follows: Remove the timing case cover and oil pan and detach the camshaft sprocket, slide it off the shaft and remove the timing chain. Unless the crankshaft sprocket is to be replaced it will not be necessary to remove it from the shaft. Rotate the crankshaft so that the mark on the crankshaft sprocket is toward the camshaft and in exact alignment between the shaft centers. Now install

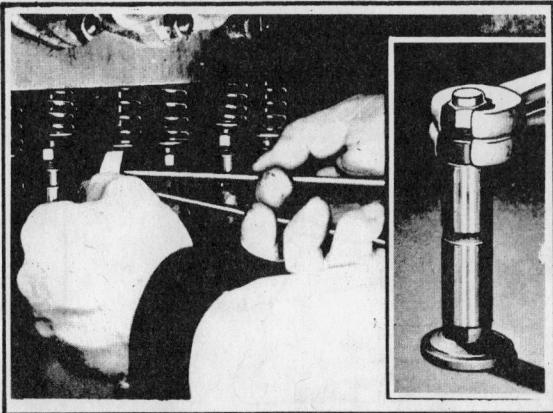

Tappet adjustment, 6 cyl. "L" head engines

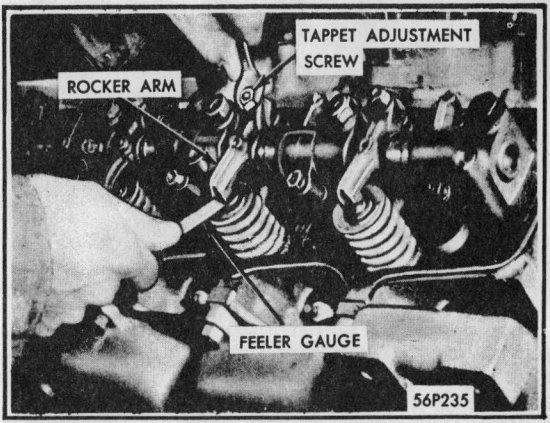

Typical tappet adjustment, V8 and Slant "6" engines

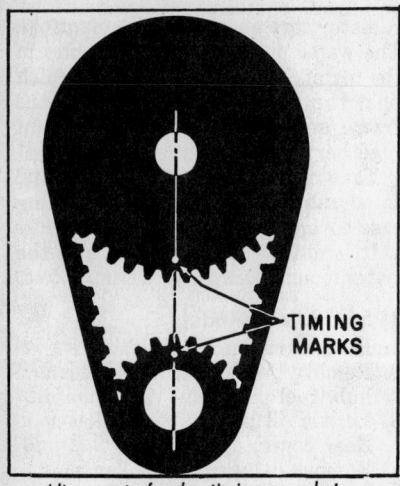

Alignment of valve timing sprockets— All V8' engines

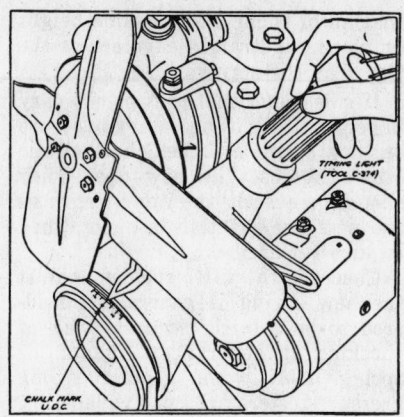

Timing light in use—note degree marks on damper rim

the timing chain over the cam sprocket so that the mark on the cam and the mark on the crank sprocket are nearest each other. Note that the cam sprocket bolt holes ("L" head engines) are staggered in such a way that the sprocket will enter only one way and permit the bolt to enter through the threaded holes in the hub. Rotate the camshaft so that the holes line up while the timing marks are still in line between the shaft centers.

Mount the sprocket on the hub and draw up to bolts. Turn the crankshaft two full revolutions and check to see that the marks are still in alignment between the shaft centers. When set in the manner described with the marks aligned between the two shaft centers it is immaterial which piston is at top dead center. It may be necessary, however, to retime the ignition at any time the chain setting is disturbed.

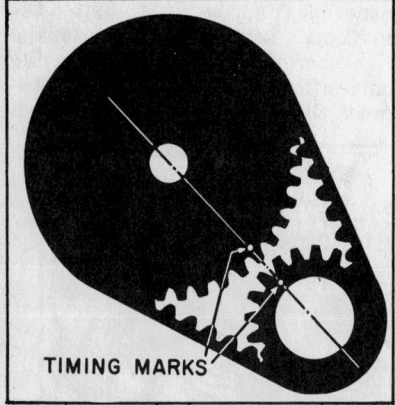

TIMING MARKS

Alignment of valve timing sprockets— All 6 cyl. engines

Slant "6" Engines

Proceed the same as with the "L" head engine except that the camshaft sprocket is secured with one 7/16 inch lock bolt. Torque this bolt to 35 ft. lb.

ENGINE LUBRICATION

REMOVAL OF OIL PAN

6 Cylinder Models Thru 1955

Crank engine until No. 1 piston is half way up the cylinder bore. Take down clutch underpan and the bolts around the oil pan. Lower the back of the pan and slide it back and out at the same time so that it will clear the oil pump screen.

New pan gasket end corks should protrude from ¼ in. to ½ in. above the oil pan. Do not cut off the protruding portions since the pan will compress it making a tight seal when it is bolted firmly in place.

6 Cyl. "L" Head Models Starting 1956

Remove the little plate in the front of the clutch housing and take down the intermediate steering arm. Disconnect the tie rods at the pivot arm and let the tie rods drop down a little.

If the front motor mats have sagged any it may be necessary to take out the front mounting bolts, jack the engine up an inch or two and block it in that position so that the front of the pan can be made to clear the throws. Remove the bolts which hold the oil pan to the crankcase and lower the pan.

Slant "6" Engine
Removal:

1. Disconnect the tie rod at both ends.
2. Remove the engine front mounting bolts, (2).
3. Remove left side support, connecting the converter housing and cylinder block.
4. Raise engine about two inches.
5. Drain engine oil.
6. Remove oil pan bolts, lower the pan down and to the rear. (Caution) Do not bump or turn oil pick-up out of position.

INSTALLATION:

1. Install the oil pan.
2. Lower the engine to position.
3. Install left side support.
4. Install engine front mounting bolts and torque to 85 ft. lb.
5. Reinstall the tie rod.
6. Refill crankcase to proper capacity.

1955 Thru 1956 V8 Models

Remove the steering idler arm bracket from the frame and let the bracket idler arm and tie rods drop downwards. Disconnect the left exhaust pipe at the flange and slip the crossover pipe out of the right side exhaust line. Remove the pan from the front of the flywheel housing, unbolt and lower the oil pan.

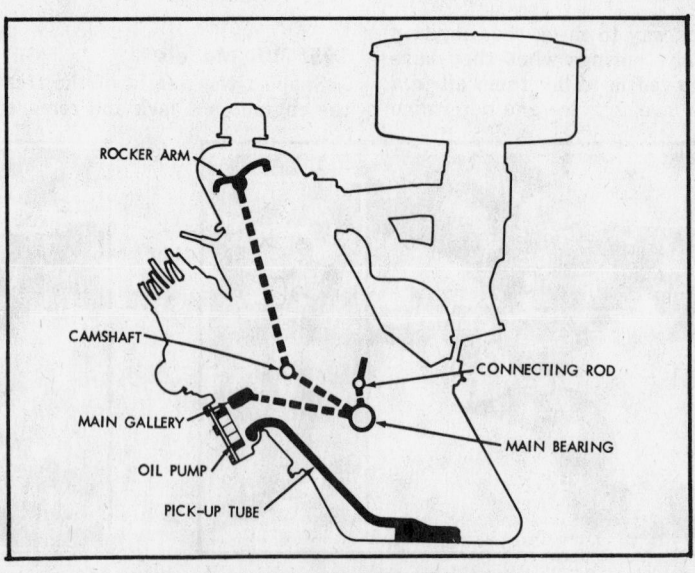

ROCKER ARM

CAMSHAFT

CONNECTING ROD

MAIN GALLERY

MAIN BEARING

OIL PUMP

PICK-UP TUBE

Slant "6" Engine Oil Passage Diagram

V8 Models 1957-61

Remove the little pan from the front of the clutch housing, disconnect the tie rods at the pitman arm and the intermediate steering arm and let the tie rods drop down out of the way. Remove the engine front mounting bolts and jack the front of the engine about ¾ inch. Remove the bolts which hold the oil pan to the cylinder block and drop the pan. Turn the crankshaft if necessary to clear the counterweights.

V8 Models 1962-63

1. Remove dip stick and disconnect battery.
2. Raise car and drain oil.
3. Remove brace, engine to converter housing.
4. Remove cross-over pipe on single exhaust models.
5. Remove idler and steering ball joint from center link.
5. Remove pan bolts and lower pan.

PISTONS, CONNECTING RODS AND MAIN BEARINGS

REMOVAL OF THE ROD AND PISTON ASSEMBLY

Remove the cylinder head and oil pan and, selecting pistons in the down position, cut the ring ridge from the top of the cylinder using a good ring ridge reamer.

If a ring ridge tool is not available, the ridge can be cut off with a good sharp bearing scraper.

From underneath the car, mark the connecting rod and the cap, take the cap off the rod and push the rod and piston assembly up out of the top of the block. Immediately reattach the rod bearing cap to the rod so that the bolts do not get lost or the threads damaged.

REAR MAIN BEARING OIL SEAL

Braided asbestos is used to prevent oil escaping from the crank case on to

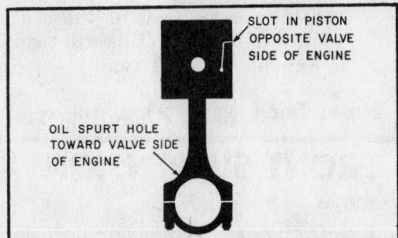

Piston and Rod Assembly Six Cyl. "L" Head

Piston and Rod Assembly Slant Six O.H.V. Beginning 1963 all iron 6 cyl. engines, oil hole on right.

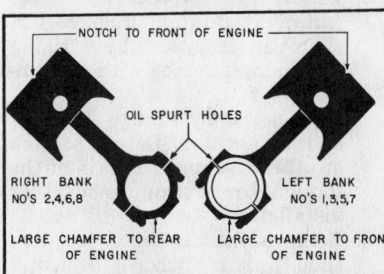

Piston and Rod Assembly V-8 Engines

the clutch and flywheel. To replace the lower half of this oil seal remove the rear main bearing cap and the old oil seal packing. Install the new packing in the main bearing cap so that the packing protrudes slightly above the cap. Bolt the cap in place and torque it to approximately 60 ft. lbs. and then immediately take it down again. If the protruding part of the packing has "riveted over," cut off the riveted portion with a razor blade and again bolt the cap into place. Repeat this operation until the main bearing cap sets firmly in the block without riveting over the new portion of the oil seal.

TOP HALF, REAR MAIN BEARING OIL SEAL REPLACEMENT —WICK TYPE

The following method has proven a distinct advantage in most cases and, if successful, saves many hours of labor.

1. Drain engine oil and remove oil pan.
2. Remove rear mail bearing cap.
3. With a 6" length of 3/16" brazing rod, drive up on either exposed end of the top half oil seal. When the opposite end of the seal starts to protrude, have a helper grasp it with pliers and pull gently while the driven end is being tapped. It is surprising how easily most of these seals can be removed by this method.

TO INSTALL THE NEW WOVEN FABRIC TYPE SEAL:

1. Obtain a 12" piece of copper wire (about the same gauge as that used in the strands of an insulated battery cable).
2. Thread one strand of this wire thru the new seal, about ½" from the end, bend back and make secure.
3. Thoroughly saturate the new seal with engine oil.
4. Push the copper wire up thru the oil seal groove until it comes down on the opposite side of the bearing.
5. Pull (with pliers) on the protruding copper wire while the crankshaft is being turned and the new seal is slowly fed into place.

CAUTION: This snaking operation slightly reduces the diameter of the new seal and care will have to be used

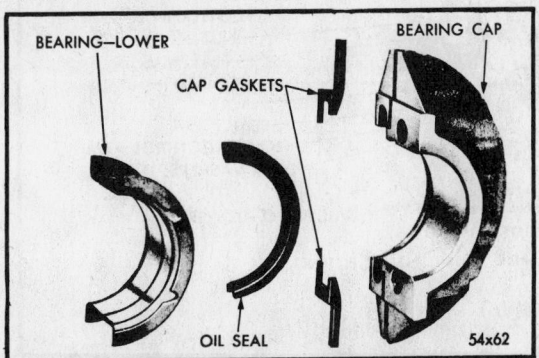

Rear main bearing oil seals—6 Cylinder Engine

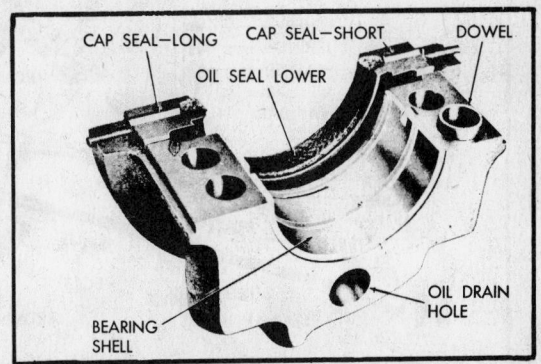

Rear main bearing oil seal—V8 engines

PLYMOUTH

to keep the seal from slipping too far thru the top half of the bearing.

6. When an equal amount of seal is extending from each side, cut off the copper wire close to the seal

and tamp both ends of the seal up into the groove (this will tend to expand the seal again).

Note: Don't worry about the cop-

per wire left in the groove, it is too soft to cause damage.

7. Replace the seal in the cap in the usual way and replace the oil pan.

ADJUSTMENT

General instructions covering the front suspension and how to repair and adjust it, together with information on installation of front wheel bearings and grease seals, are given in the Unit Repair section under the heading: Suspension, Front Repair.

Definitions of the points of steering geometry are covered in the Unit Repair section under the heading: Suspension, Front Align. This article also covers trouble shooting front end geometry and irregular tire wear.

Figures covering the caster, camber, toe-in, king pin inclination, and turning radius can be found in the Front Wheel Alignment Table of this section.

Overall car length and tire size figures can be found in the General Chassis and Brake Specifications Table of this section.

TORSION BAR SPRINGS

Contrary to appearance, the torsion bars are **not** interchangeable from "right" to "left." They are marked with an R or an L, according to their location.

FRONT SUSPENSION

Remove

1. Lift the car by the body only so that the front suspension is free of all load. If the car is to be raised with jacks, place jack under center of frame cross member and raise until suspension is free of all load.
2. Release load from torsion bar by backing off anchor adjusting nuts. Remove the adjusting nut and swivel bolt.
3. Remove the lower control arm strut.
4. Remove the lock spring from the rear of torsion bar rear anchor.
5. Install tool #C-3728, or other suitable clamp and remove torsion bar rearward by striking the clamping tool with a hammer.

   Do not apply heat to the front or rear anchors. Do not scratch or otherwise mar the skin of the torsion bar during removal or installation.
6. Remove the clamping tool and slide the rear anchor balloon seal off the front end of the bar.
7. Remove torsion bar by sliding the bar rearward and out through the rear anchor.

Install

1. Clean the hex openings of both front and rear anchors, also clean the male ends of the torsion bar.
2. Feed the torsion bar through the rear anchor.
3. Slide the balloon type seal over the torsion bar, with the large cupped side of the seal facing the rear.
4. Coat both ends of the torsion bar with multi-purpose grease.
5. When starting the bar into the anchor in the lower control arm, position the adjusting arm about 60° below the horizontal plane. This will permit wind-up for future adjustment.
6. Install the lock ring in the rear anchor, then move torsion bar rearward until the bar contacts the lock ring.
7. Position swivel bolt on the control arm and hold in place while installing the adjusting nut and seat. Tighten the adjustment about 10 turns before lowering car to the floor.
8. Pack the annular opening in the rear anchor with multi-purpose grease. Slide the rear anchor

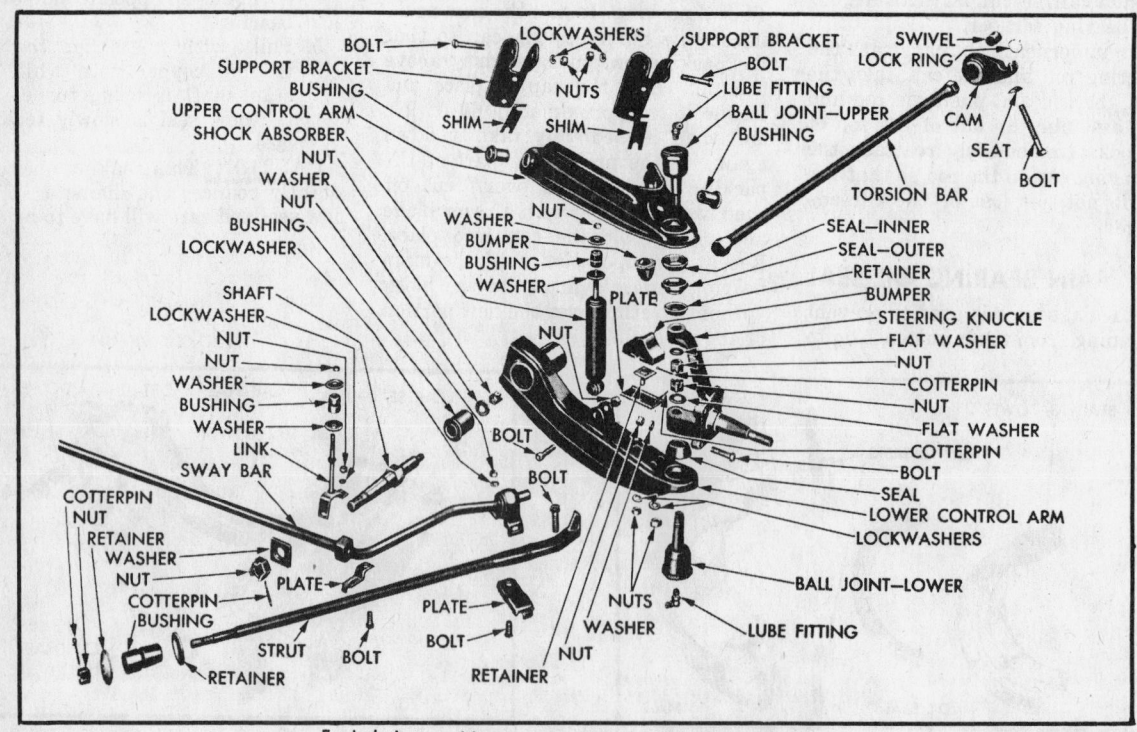

Exploded view of front suspension starting 1957 production

balloon type seal into position over the rear anchor until the lip of the seal fits in the groove.

9. Install lower control arm strut.
10. Lower car to the floor and adjust front suspension height.

FRONT HEIGHT

Adjustment, Without Gauge

1. Jounce the car and measure from the lower ball joint to the floor, (measurement "A").
2. Measure from the control arm torsion bar spring anchor housing to the floor, (measurement "B").
3. Subtract "A" from "B". The difference should be $1\frac{1}{2}'' \pm \frac{1}{8}''$.
4. Measure the other side in the same way.
5. Adjust, if necessary, by turning the torsion bar adjusting bolt, in to raise and out to lower height.

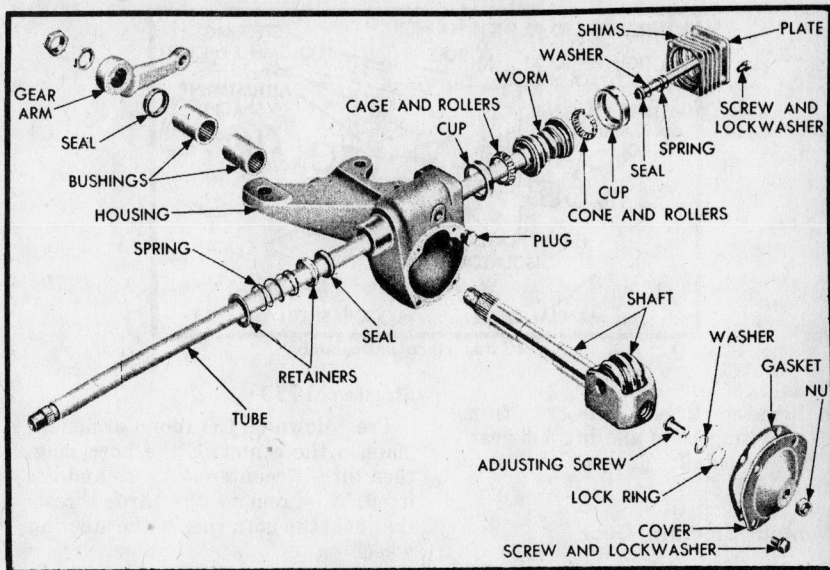

1959-60   Manual Steering Gear Assembly, (Exploded View)

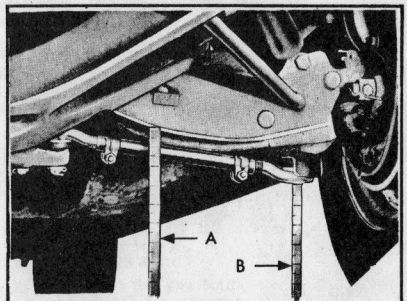

Measuring front suspension height

STEERING GEAR ASSEMBLY

STEERING GEAR ASSEMBLY REMOVAL

1954 Thru 1956

On these models the steering gear mechanism is lifted up into the car after all attaching parts have been removed, such as the shift mechanism, directional signal wires, pitman arm, steering wheel, horn button wires, toe board cover plate, etc.

Turn signal wires go to push pin connectors under the dash. They should be tagged carefully so as to simplify replacement.

1957-61

Remove the horn blowing ring and steering wheel.

From under the dash remove the two bolts which hold the steering column to the under side of the instrument panel. These two bolts can be reached from under the dash.

The wires coming out of the top of the steering column under the dash are disconnected at the junction block.

Caution: Tag each wire carefully so that it can be returned properly to the socket from which it was removed.

Pull up the floor mat and take off the grommets and plates under the floor mat.

Remove the bolt which holds the pitman arm to the bottom of the steering gear and pull off the pitman arm.

Disconnect the shifting rods from the shift levers at the bottom of the steering column. Remove the bolts which hold the steering gear box to the frame and pull the entire steering gear up into the car.

Caution: Cover the seat in the driving compartment to prevent the grease from the lower end of the steering gear from staining the upholstery.

Starting 1962

1. Remove steering gear arm.
2. Remove bolt from coupling clamp.
3. Loosen column jacket to panel clamp bolts, enough to disengage tab on clamp from column jacket slot and slide column up just enough to clear coupling. Note: use care not to scratch column. It is not necessary to disconnect the shift

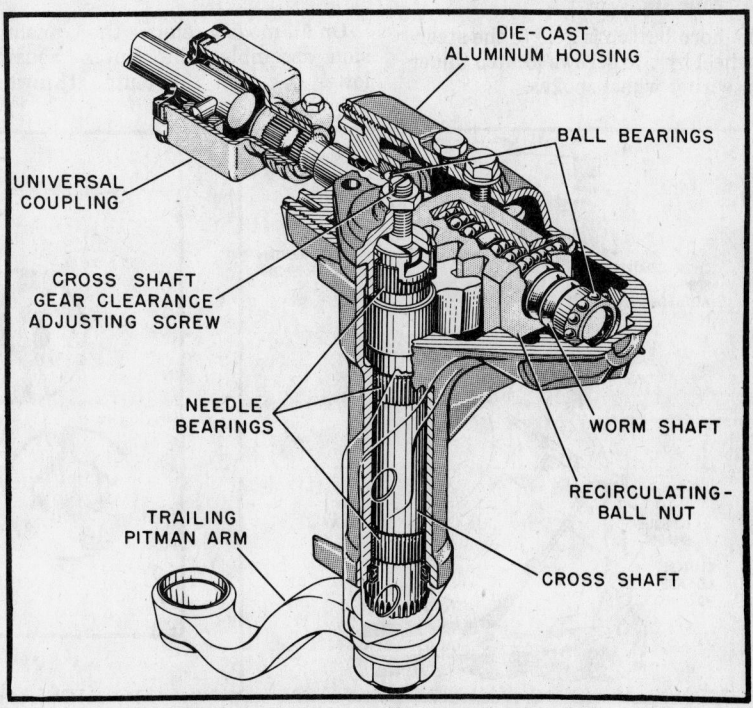

1962—Manual Steering Gear,   Cut-Away View

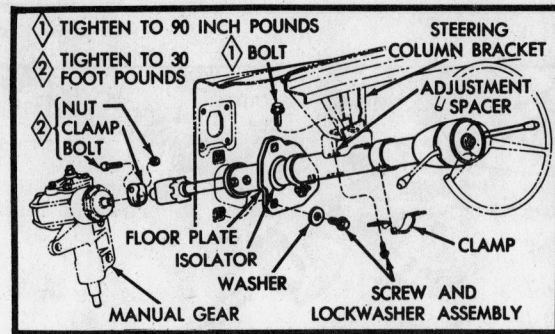

1962 steering column assembly

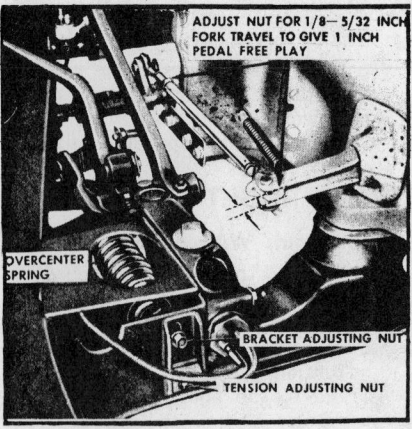

Clutch Linkage—Hy Drive Equipped Cars Only

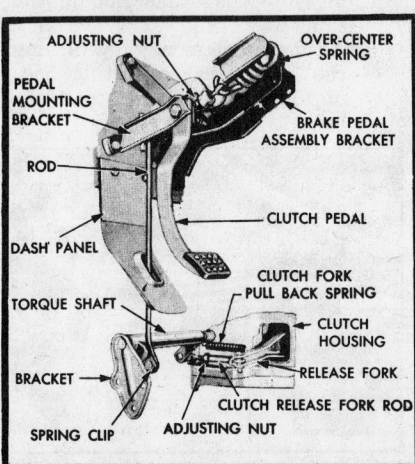

Use adjusting nut on clutch release fork rod to adjust clutch free play. 3/16 inch free movement of outer end of release fork will give correct pedal free play

1957-61 (Typical).

linkage.

4. Remove three gear to frame mounting bolts and lift out gear.
To Reinstall: Reverse the above procedure.

Manual Steering Gear

Instructions covering the overhaul of the steering gear will be found in the Unit Repair section under the heading: Steering, Manual.

Power Steering Gears

Trouble shooting and repair instructions covering power steering gears are given in the Unit Repair section under the heading: Steering, Power.

REMOVAL OF HORN BUTTON

1955 Thru 1956 Models

Pry up the medallion in the center of the steering wheel which will uncover the screws which hold the horn blowing ring in place on the wheel.

1957 Models

The horn button is held to the steering wheel by two screws located under the steering wheel spokes.

Starting 1958

Press down on the round ornament plate in the center of the horn ring, then turn it counterclockwise and lift it off. Now remove the three screws that hold the horn ring to the steering wheel.

CLUTCH ASSEMBLY

The only practical service possible on the clutch assembly is to tighten up to prevent rattles and adjust the pedal toe board clearance. All other service requires the removal of the clutch assembly.

If the clutch assembly is being removed because of chatter or malfunction, it is advisable to check to see if there is any oil leaking from the rear main bearing. Oil on the clutch facings will produce a noticeable chatter.

REMOVAL OF THE CLUTCH ASSEMBLY

On all models remove the transmission assembly, the clutch housing lower pan and the clutch throwout

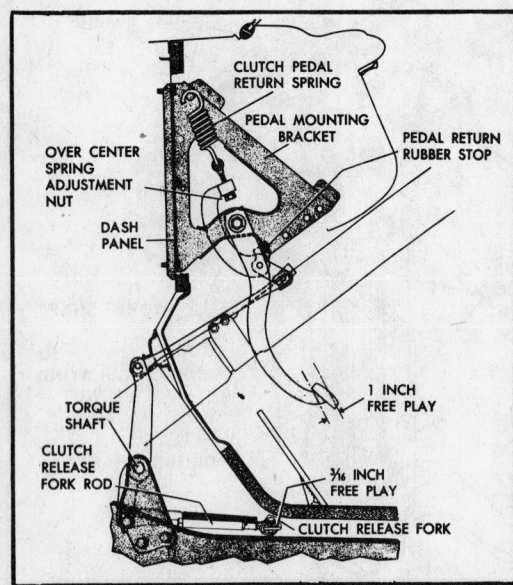

Clutch pedal free play adjustment for 1955-56

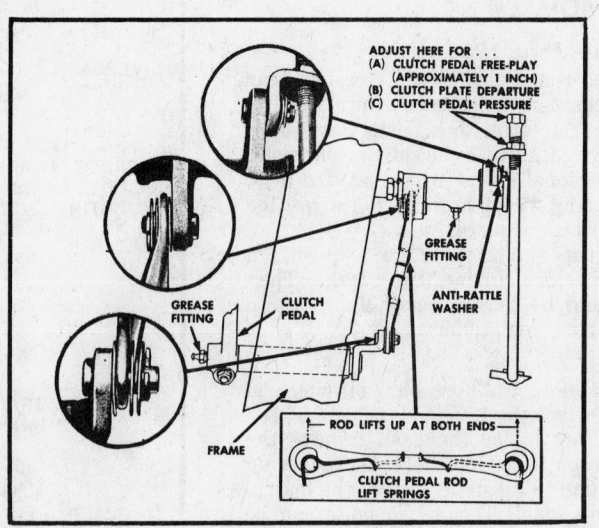

Typical Clutch Pedal Linkage Without Overcenter Spring

bearing. The clutch cover assembly should be marked, showing its relation to the flywheel so that it can be reassembled in the same position from which it was removed. The cover bolts should be removed a few turns at a time in order to avoid springing the clutch cover.

Disassembly service on the clutch requires special jigs and fixtures. Instructions in the use of the fixtures are supplied by the manufacturer of the tool.

CLUTCH PEDAL ADJUSTMENT

Pedal toe-board adjustment for clutch throwout bearing clearance is provided at the adjusting rod which connects the clutch idler lever to the clutch throwout fork. This adjustment is readily accessible from underneath the car. Remove the clevis pin, turn the adjusting yoke to the correct position, replace the clevis pin and tighten the jam nut. There should be approximately three-quarter inch free pedal motion before the throwout bearing strikes the clutch fingers.

TRANSMISSIONS

General information and exploded views, together with trouble shooting charts, are included in the articles on each automatic transmission.

Trouble shooting and repair of overdrive units are covered in the Unit Repair section under the heading: Transmission—Overdrive.

STANDARD TRANSMISSION REMOVAL

Disconnect the propeller shaft at the front universal joint.

Disconnect all attaching parts such as speedometer cable, battery ground cable, gear shift control rods and gear shift selector cables.

Remove the nuts which hold the transmission to the clutch housing and lift the transmission assembly down and out.

DISASSEMBLY OF THE SYNCROMESH TRANSMISSION

Remove the two screws at the transmission cover which hold the

shift rail detent springs and balls. Then take off the transmission side cover assembly.

Take off the universal joint companion flange and brake drum assembly.

Next take off the shifter fork guide rail. (This is a long thin rail which slides into the front face of the transmission and through the shifter fork. It is intended to guide the shifter fork. It is removed by turning it counterclockwise with a screw driver and sliding it out of the front face of the transmission.)

Set the transmission in neutral and loosen the shifter rails from the shifter forks. Then slide the shift rails out of the front of the transmission case (it will be necessary to remove the Welsh plug to get at the lower rail).

The shift rail interlock rod can be removed by taking out the single cap screw which is located at the top of the transmission toward the back, just to the right of the side cover. Take out the shifter forks. Unbolt the

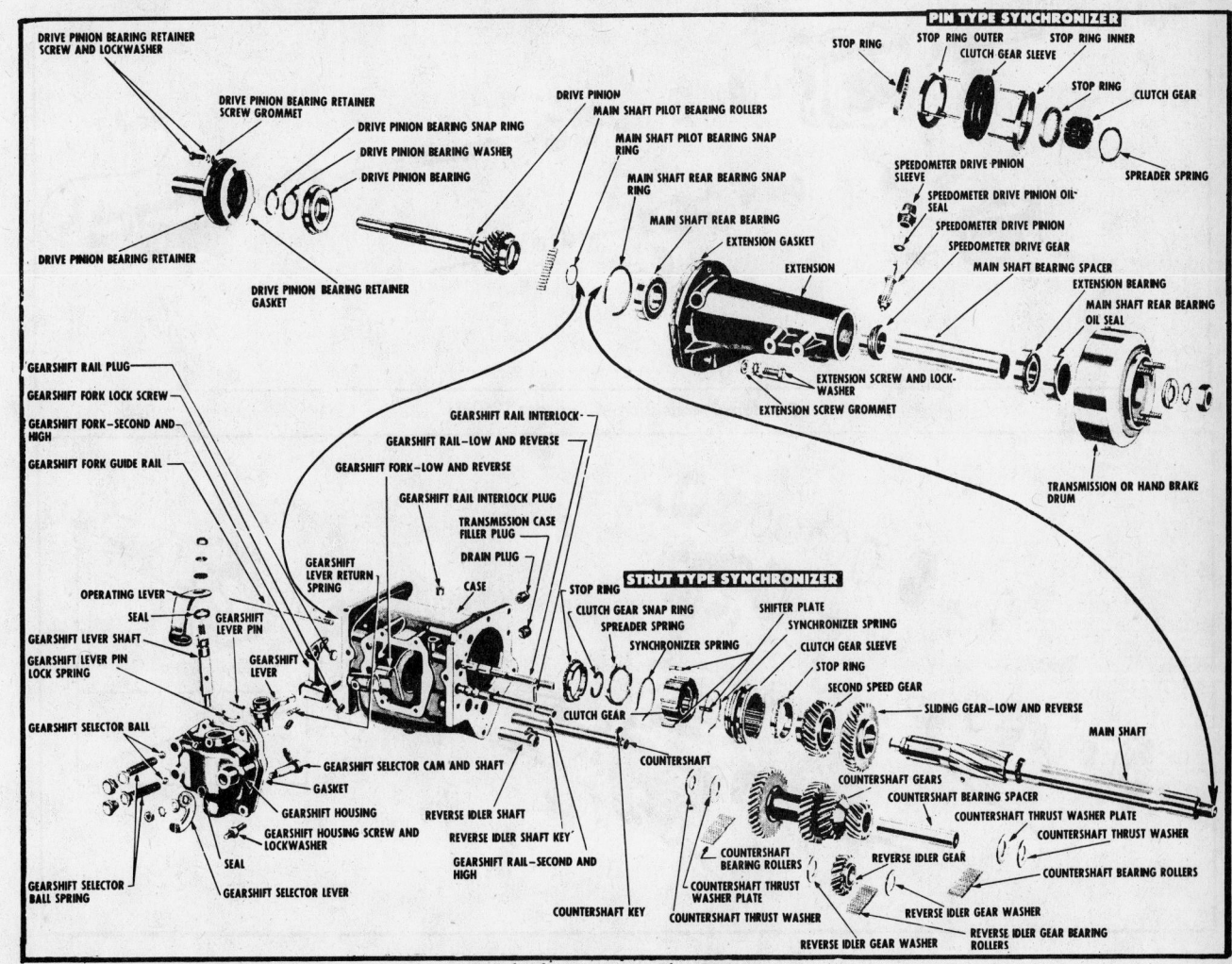

Standard transmission. Thru 1956

extension housing from the back of the transmission case and slide the case with the main shaft and gears connected to it out the rear of the transmission case.

The main shaft now can be disassembled by removing the synchronizer retaining snap ring and the synchronizer unit. The second speed gear and low speed gear can then be slid off the shaft.

The rear bearing is held in place with a snap ring. Take out the snap ring and the main shaft and bearing can be removed from the extension housing.

The countershaft freewheel unit is held together by a snap ring also.

The countershaft is now removed from the countershaft gear cluster by tapping the shaft with a bronze drift toward the rear. At this point a pilot shaft (the same diameter as the countershaft and the same length as the cluster gear plus the 2 thrust washers), should be used. If care is exercised in following the counter-

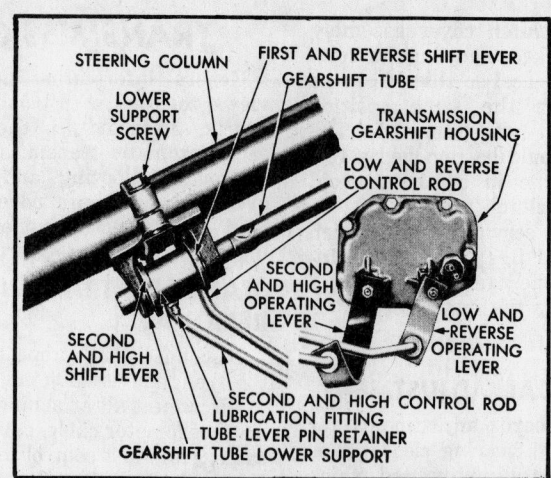

Shift mechanism synchromesh transmission: 1957-59

shaft with this arbor (or dummy) the cluster may be lowered to the bottom of the case with the needle bearings and washers in place. **Note:** a key is used to position both the reverse idler shaft and the countershaft.

Be careful to pick up and save these keys as soon as the shafts are driven clear of the case.

The main drive pinion and bearing assembly can now be removed from the front of the case after lowering

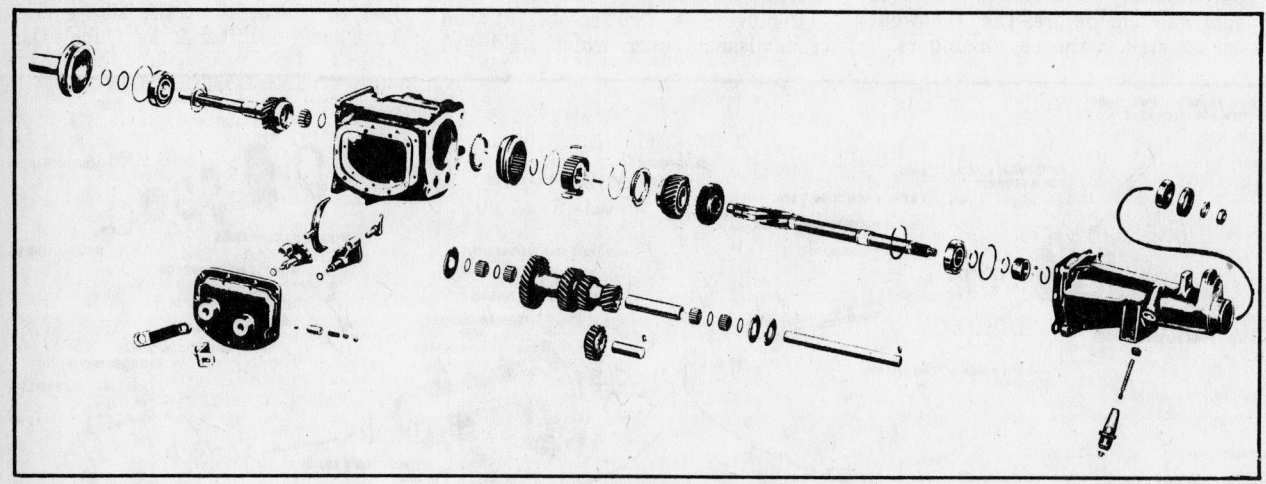

Standard Transmission—8 Cylinder 1960-63

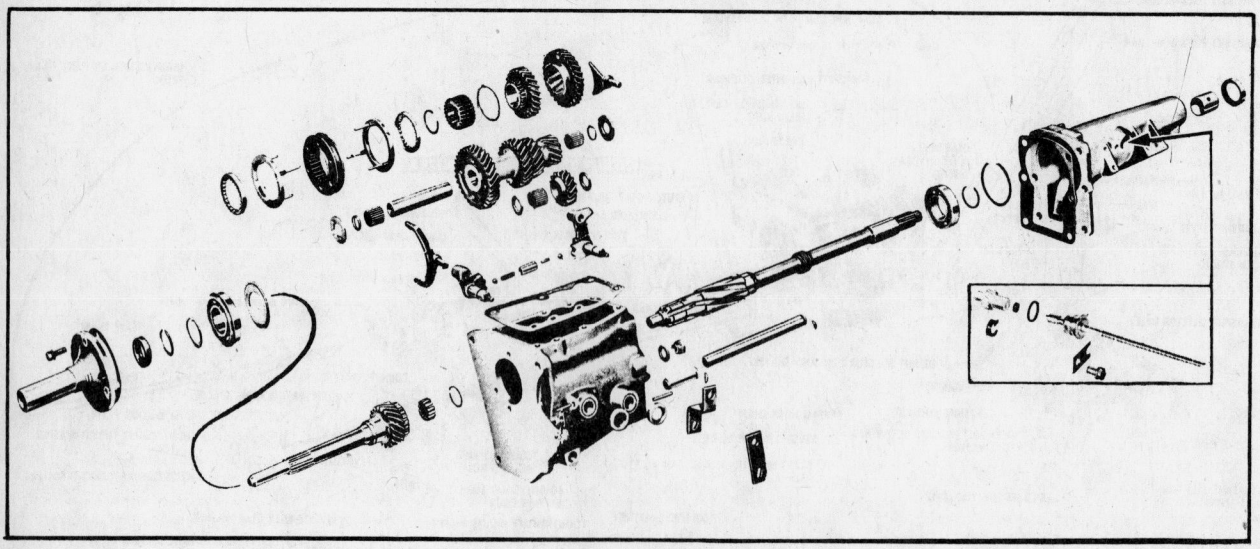

Standard Transmission—6 Cylinder 1960-63

the countershaft gear cluster to clear the pinion.

There is a single cap screw at the top of the case, just to the right of the cover assembly which covers the hole containing the shift interlock pin. Remove the cap screw and turn the case over, permitting the interlock pin to drop out. On assembly do not fail to place the interlock pin back into the transmission as this pin prevents the transmission from going into two gears at one time.

On assembly, all parts should be thoroughly cleaned with a good solvent and blown off with compressed air.

In general the transmission is reassembled in the reverse of the disassembly procedure.

AUTOMATIC TRANSMISSION

Starting during 1962 production an Automatic Transmission Oil Filter has been added for better control of impurities in these transmissions.

QUICK SERVICE INFORMATION

When automatic transmission trouble is reported, a road test and careful diagnosis is in order. "Transmission Remove and Replace" and "Linkage Adjustments" are covered here in the following paragraphs. For "Test Procedures", "Transmission Overhaul" and other detailed information, see "Unit Repair Section", "Transmission Group" of this manual.

POWERFLITE TRANSMISSION

ADJUSTMENTS

Adjusting the Anti-Stall

The anti-stall consists of a diaphragm and a plunger with a small orifice. The air trapped behind the diaphragm is bled out at a specific rate by the orifice. The device acts to keep the throttle from snapping shut during its last one-quarter inch of travel.

To check, open the throttle by hand and release. The closing of the throttle should be visibly slowed by the action of the anti-stall.

To adjust, have the engine at operating temperature and set adjusting screw so that the plunger has one-sixteenth of an inch travel after the throttle is fully closed.

MANUAL CONTROL ADJUSTMENT

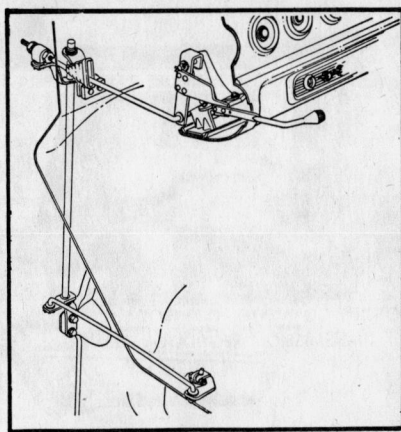

Fig. 1—Manual Control Linkage, 1955

1954

The manual control lever is the bottom one of the two levers on the left side of the transmission case. When the lever is turned full back, counter-clockwise, the transmission is in Reverse. The next detent forward, clockwise, is Neutral. The next detent is Drive and the late detent, when the lever is as far clockwise as it will go, is Low.

Place the manual control lever in the Neutral detent. Check that the bell crank on the frame has its lower arm pointing down and back while the upper arm is at an angle of 45 deg. with the frame. If this is not so, disconnect the two rods at the bell crank. Being sure that the manual control lever on the transmission is in Neutral, adjust the length of the lower rod to hold the bell crank so that its upper arm is at 45 deg. with the frame and reconnect the lower rod to the bell crank.

Move the hand lever on the steering column to the Neutral position and then at the bottom of the steering column check the position of the tongue of the lever in the locating gate. This gate is held to the column by screws in slots so that the gate can be moved. Adjust the gate so that there is .015 to .030 in. clearance between the lever and the gate measured parallel with the column and .015 to .017 in. clearance between the gate and the lever measured perpendicular to the column. When the gate is correctly set adjust the upper rod at the bell crank to fit easily and attach it.

Move the hand control lever thru the four positions and check that the pointer and the marks on the dial line up. If they do not: run thru the adjustment procedure again rather than bend the pointer.

1955 (See Fig. 1)

On the forward end of the rod running forward from the dash control there is a swivel. Loosen this swivel.

At the transmission, move the manual control lever one notch forward from full rear position. This will be Neutral.

Put dash control in Neutral position and reconnect the swivel.

Check that lever moves freely.

Starting 1956

1. Raise car on hoist. Have a helper hold the "R" button firmly depressed.
2. Remove control cable adjustment wheel lock screw at the left side of transmission.
3. Back the adjustment wheel off on the cable guide until only two or three threads show behind the wheel on the guide.
NOTE: Be sure the adjustment wheel turns freely on the guide. Lubricate the cable guide threads with transmission fluid.
4. Hold the control cable guide centered in the hole of the transmission case and apply only enough inward force (two to three pounds) to bottom the assembly at the reverse detent. While holding the cable bottomed, rotate the adjustment wheel clockwise until it just contacts the case.
5. Turn the wheel clockwise just enough to make the next adjustment hole in the wheel line up with the screw hole in the case.
6. Counting this hole as Number One, keep turning the wheel clockwise until the fifth hole lines up with the screw hole in the case.
7. Install lock screw and torque to 30 to 50 inch pounds.

THROTTLE LINKAGE AND THROTTLE VALVE OIL PRESSURE ADJUSTMENT

Accurate adjustment of the transmission throttle linkage and precise setting of the throttle valve oil pressure is required for proper operation of the Powerflite Transmission.

Remove any binds that may exist in the throttle linkage. Fig. 2. Make sure that the throttle valve in the carburetor is fully open when the accelerator is fully depressed and is fully closed when the accelerator is fully released. Adjust the accelerator shaft to the carburetor to provide enough accelerator pedal travel for full open and closed throttle. Check the adjustment by depressing the accelerator slowly. Opening of the kickdown valve should be felt as the carburetor throttle valve approaches full open position.

With the hand lever at Neutral, the brakes set, and the engine at operating temperature, adjust the idle speed to 475-500 RPM.

Remove the plug from the throttle pressure test (takeoff) point on the right side of the case just behind the front servo. See Fig. 3. Connect in a pressure gage.

With the engine idling and the hand lever at drive disconnect the throttle control rod at the throttle control lever which is the upper of the two levers on the left side of the transmission case. Move the lever forward and back. There should be a pressure change apparent on the gage.

Position the throttle control lever so it is approximately 30 degrees toward the front of the car from a right angle to the transmission centerline. The gage should read 13 to 15 psi. If it does not the throttle valve oil pressure requires adjustment.

To adjust the throttle pressure, remove the throttle valve adjusting screw plug. (Cover) It is the 3/8 in. pipe plug just below and forward of the back up light switch on the left

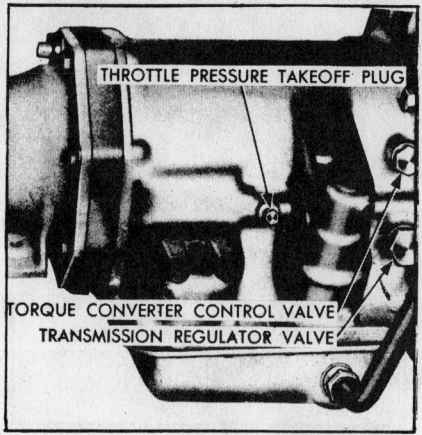

Fig. 3—View of right side of PowerFlite showing Throttle Pressure Takeoff Plug.

side of the transmission case. Have a can handy as about a quart of transmission fluid will gush forth. Turn the adjusting screw, revealed by removal of the plug, clockwise to decrease the pressure and counterclockwise to increase it. Adjust the pressure to 14 psi. Fig. 4.

Reinstall the plug and tighten to 20-25 ft lbs. Reconnect the throttle control rod to the lever and depress the accelerator. The pressure should rise at once to 80 psi. If it does not and yet is 14 psi at idle the linkage requires adjustment.

Disconnect the swivel at the transmission end of the throttle valve control rod from the rod; leaving the swivel attached to the throttle control lever.

Now move the lever forward as far as it will come and then slowly move it back until a slight resistance is felt. From this point of slight resistance a slight forward movement of the lever should cause the pressure to rise to 80 psi. There at this point of slight resistance hold the lever and reconnect the control rod into the swivel. Push forward on the rod and remove any play in the linkage while making the connection and tightening the swivel lock screw.

Again depress the accelerator and check that the pressure rises from 14 psi at an idle of 475-500 rpm to 80 psi at 1400-1500 rpm.

After removing the pressure gage tighten the 1/8" pipe plug to 10-12 ft. lbs.

REMOVAL OF THE TRANSMISSION FROM THE CAR

Disconnect the battery. Drain the transmission and the converter. Unfasten the oil filler tube from the oil pan and remove the tube.

Disconnect the front propeller shaft universal joint and tie the shaft up out of the way. Remove the adjusting screw cover plate and the clamp bolt from the hand brake support. Disengage the hand brake cable from the operating lever.

Disconnect the speedometer cable from the rear extension. Disconnect the wires from the back up light and neutral safety switches and unclip the wires from the cross member. Disconnect the operating rods from the transmission levers. Disconnect the two oil cooler lines at the left side of the case and remove the bracket holding the lines to the cylinder block. Unfasten the exhaust pipe bracket from the transmission case.

Remove the two nuts and lockwashers that hold the engine rear cross member support insulator to the cross-member, leaving the insulator attached to the transmission. On reinstalling tighten to 30-35 ft lbs.

Raise the engine slightly by means of a jack and unbolt and remove the cross-member.

Lower the engine slightly and remove the two upper transmission case to bell housing bolts. Install guide

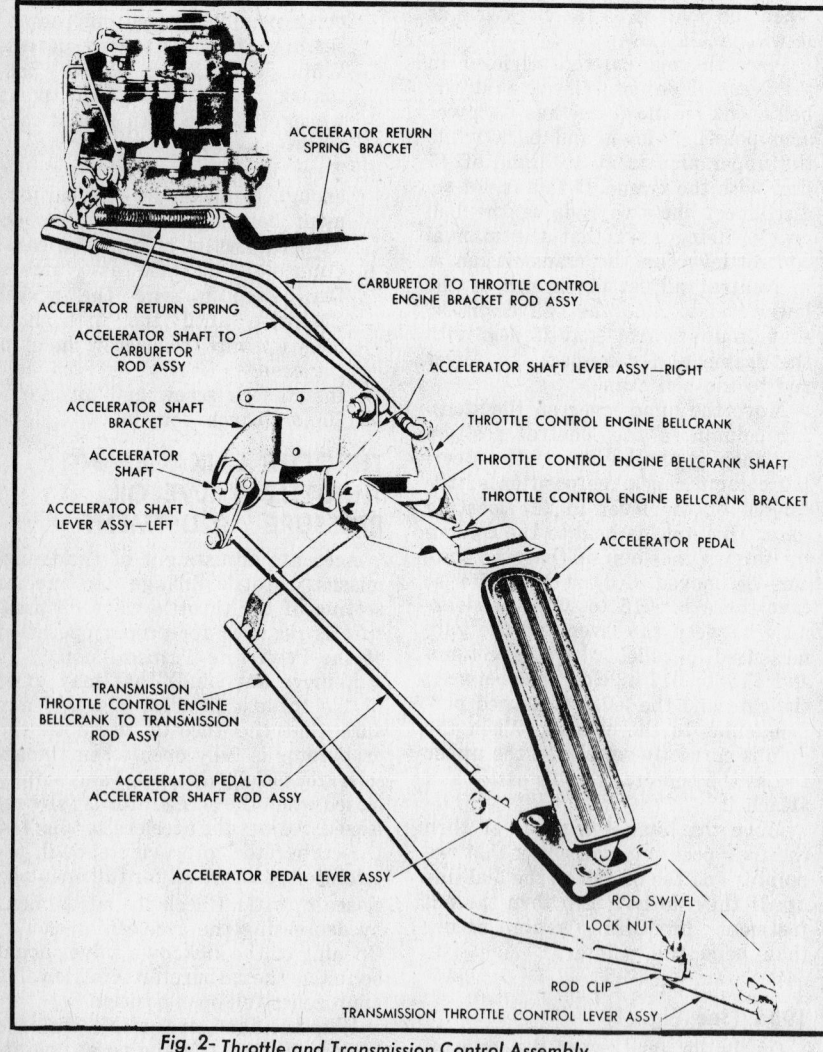

ACCELERATOR RETURN SPRING BRACKET

ACCELRATOR RETURN SPRING

ACCELERATOR SHAFT TO CARBURETOR ROD ASSY

ACCELERATOR SHAFT BRACKET

ACCELERATOR SHAFT

ACCELERATOR SHAFT LEVER ASSY—LEFT

CARBURETOR TO THROTTLE CONTROL ENGINE BRACKET ROD ASSY

ACCELERATOR SHAFT LEVER ASSY—RIGHT

THROTTLE CONTROL ENGINE BELLCRANK

THROTTLE CONTROL ENGINE BELLCRANK SHAFT

THROTTLE CONTROL ENGINE BELLCRANK BRACKET

ACCELERATOR PEDAL

TRANSMISSION THROTTLE CONTROL ENGINE BELLCRANK TO TRANSMISSION ROD ASSY

ACCELERATOR PEDAL TO ACCELERATOR SHAFT ROD ASSY

ACCELERATOR PEDAL LEVER ASSY

ROD SWIVEL

LOCK NUT

ROD CLIP

TRANSMISSION THROTTLE CONTROL LEVER ASSY

Fig. 2- Throttle and Transmission Control Assembly

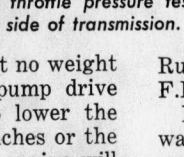

Fig. 4—Adjusting Throttle. Pressure Gauge is connected to throttle pressure test point on right side of transmission.

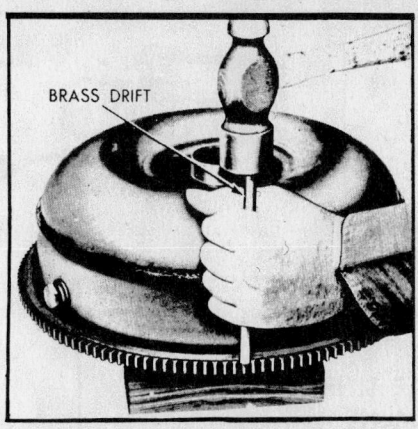

Fig. 6—Tap the Flywheel Ring Gear Off to the Front of the Converter

studs in their place so that no weight comes on the front oil pump drive sleeve. Be careful not to lower the engine more than three inches or the hoses and linkages at the engine will be damaged.

Remove the two lower case to bell housing screws. Slide the transmission case back on the guide pins until it is free of the oil pump drive sleeve then take the case on down and away.

INSTALLATION OF THE TRANSMISSION

Reverse the removal procedure to reinstall. Be sure that the front oil pump drive sleeve is in good condition with no burrs or signs of wear on the driving lugs. Check the seal ring for freeness in its groove. Lubricate the surfaces of the sleeve with lubriplate and install it in the hub of the input shaft with those of the turbine. Position the lugs of the front oil pump drive gear so that they will properly engage those of the oil pump drive sleeve. Slide the case over the guide studs into position. Do not use the case-to-bell housing screws to bring the two parts together. If the drive lugs of the sleeve and the splines of the input shaft have been properly aligned with their mating parts in the converter, the transmission slide into place easily.

Tighten the case to bell housing screws of 45-50 ft lbs, the crossmember to frame bolts to 50-55 ft lbs, the propeller shaft nuts to 33-37 ft lbs.

CONVERTER REMOVAL

Remove the transmission case from the car.

Turn the front wheels as far as they will go to the right and remove the starting motor. Unfasten twelve screws and remove the transmission case adapter plate from the bell housing. Remove the lower half of the flywheel bell housing. Check the runout of the rear hub of the converter.

Runout should not exceed .004 in F.I.R.

Remove the eight nuts and lockwashers holding the converter to the crankshaft flange. Remove the converter from the crankshaft.

FLYWHEEL RING GEAR REPLACEMENT

The converter is a welded assembly and parts for it are not sold separately. The flywheel ring gear can be replaced. File off the retaining lugs and tap the ring gear off to the front. See Fig. 6. Heat the new one to about 150 deg. (using an oven, hot water, steam or a torch with slow flame) and push it onto the converter so that it contacts the flange all around. Weld the new ring gear in place using as much metal on the welds as was filed off and placing the welds in the same spots.

Do not use an acetylene or oxy-hydrogen torch as these will harm the converter.

Do use a D.C. welder that is set at straight polarity or an A.C. welder. Use 200 Amps and a 5/32 in. rod equivalent to a Fleet Weld No. 47 or a G.E. No. W28.

The Arc should be directed at the intersection of the front face of the gear with the converter at an angle of 45 deg.

CONVERTER INSTALLATION

Check the runout of the crankshaft flange; it should not exceed .002 in. F.I.R. Reverse the procedure for removal to reinstall the converter. Check the runout of the rear hub of the converter after it has been bolted to the crankshaft flange. Runout should not exceed .004 in. F.I.R. See paragraph in Torque-Flite Section for corrective procedure.

TORQUEFLITE TRANSMISSION STARTING WITH 1956

ADJUSTMENTS

Manual Control Cable

Drain about two quarts of oil from the transmission and remove the starter safety switch. (Neutral starter switch Fig. 1) With the "R" button pushed in, remove the clip, flat washer, lock washer and screw which hold the cable sheath at the transmission. Block movement of the control lever inside the transmission by means of a screwdriver thru the starter safety switch hole. With the lever so held in reverse position move the cable sheath in as far as it will go and mark it where it enters the cable housing. Now pull cable sheath out as far as it will come and mark again. Now push cable into housing one half of distance between the two marks and fasten with the clip, washer, lock washer and screw. Re-install starter safety switch and replace fluid. Check that starter will only operate when "N" button is in. In most cases distance will not exceed 3/32 inch.

RENEW PUSH BUTTON UNIT LIGHT BULB

Remove the three bezel retaining screws (one screw is located on underside of unit) and the bezel. Fig. 2 Pull the "D" button off its slider and so gain clearance to remove the bulb. Install new bulb. Compress ends of slider and push "D" button back in place thereon. Use a small screwdriver to assure that ends of slider are firmly seated in rear of plastic "D" button.

RENEW BACK-UP LIGHT SWITCH

The back-up light switch is fastened to the push button unit by four tabs. Remove the push button control

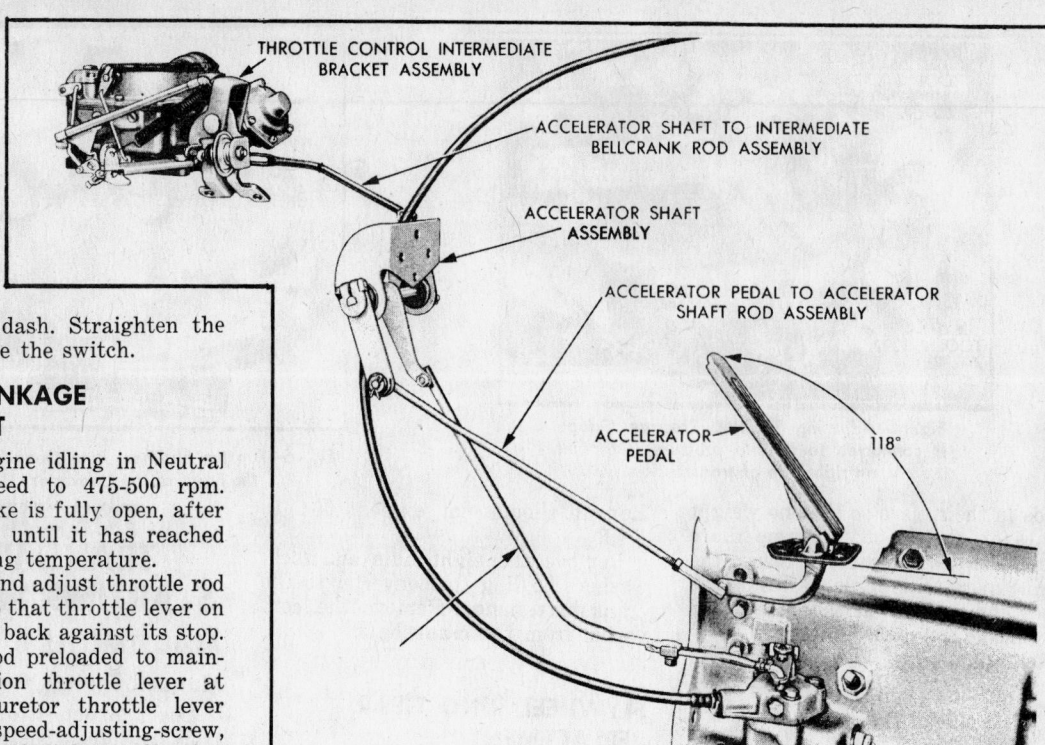

THROTTLE CONTROL INTERMEDIATE
BRACKET ASSEMBLY

ACCELERATOR SHAFT TO INTERMEDIATE
BELLCRANK ROD ASSEMBLY

ACCELERATOR SHAFT
ASSEMBLY

ACCELERATOR PEDAL TO ACCELERATOR
SHAFT ROD ASSEMBLY

ACCELERATOR
PEDAL

118°

Fig. 3—Throttle lever and linkage

unit from the dash. Straighten the tabs and remove the switch.

THROTTLE LINKAGE ADJUSTMENT

With the engine idling in Neutral adjust idle speed to 475-500 rpm. Check that choke is fully open, after engine has run until it has reached normal operating temperature.

Stop engine and adjust throttle rod at carburetor so that throttle lever on transmission is back against its stop. Fig. 3. With rod preloaded to maintain transmission throttle lever at stop and carburetor throttle lever against idle-speed-adjusting-screw, tighten the throttle linkage adjusting screw to 7-9 ft. lbs. Do not disturb rod adjustment at transmission end.

REMOVING PUSH BUTTON UNIT FROM DASH

Remove the three bezel retaining screws (one screw is located on underside) and remove bezel. Fig. 2. This will expose the two hex nuts and washers which hold the unit to the

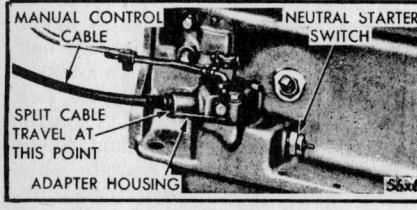

MANUAL CONTROL CABLE

NEUTRAL STARTER SWITCH

SPLIT CABLE TRAVEL AT THIS POINT

ADAPTER HOUSING

Fig. 1—Manual control cable adjustment at transmission

Fig. 2—Push button unit on dash

dash. Remove the unit to the back of the dash. Remove the two screws holding cable assembly bracket to the unit and then remove the clip which holds the cable to the unit. Unfasten the wires from the back-up light switch. Note that the wire to the light in the unit comes over the upper stud and down between the sliders. The bracket which holds the light fits-over the upper stud. Reverse the procedure to reinstall.

MANUAL CONTROL CABLE REMOVAL

Remove the push button control unit from the dash as in the preceding paragraph and remove the clip, screw and lock washer which holds the cable sheath to the housing on the left side of the transmission. Fig. 4.

Remove the plug in the side of the cable housing. Put a screwdriver thru the hole and release the spring lock, which fastens the cable to the lever,

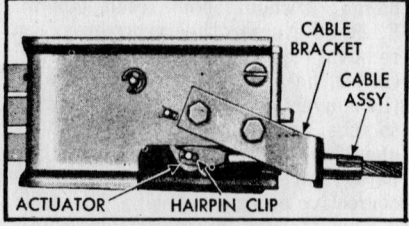

CABLE BRACKET

CABLE ASSY.

ACTUATOR   HAIRPIN CLIP

Fig. 4—Push button unit behind dash

at the same time pull the cable and sheath from the housing.

From inside the car pull the cable and sheath up thru the rubber grommet in the firewall.

Reverse procedure to reinstall and then apply paragraph on Manual Control Cable Adjustment.

REMOVAL OF THE TRANSMISSION FROM THE CAR

The transmission is removed as a unit first and then the torque converter.

Note: All Chrysler Corporation Torque Converters are welded units and require special equipment to rebuild.

Disconnect the battery. Push in the "1" button so the manual control cable can be removed. See paragraph on "Manual Control Cable Removal." Drain the transmission and converter. Disconnect the filler pipe. Disconnect the front universal joint and hang the propeller shaft up out of the way. Remove hand brake adjusting screw cover plate and disconnect hand brake cable and other parts as per paragraphs on "Rear Extension" and "Valve Bodies and Transfer Plate Assembly."

Remove the starter. Install engine support fixture. Raise engine slightly and remove crossmember. Replace two transmission case to torque con-

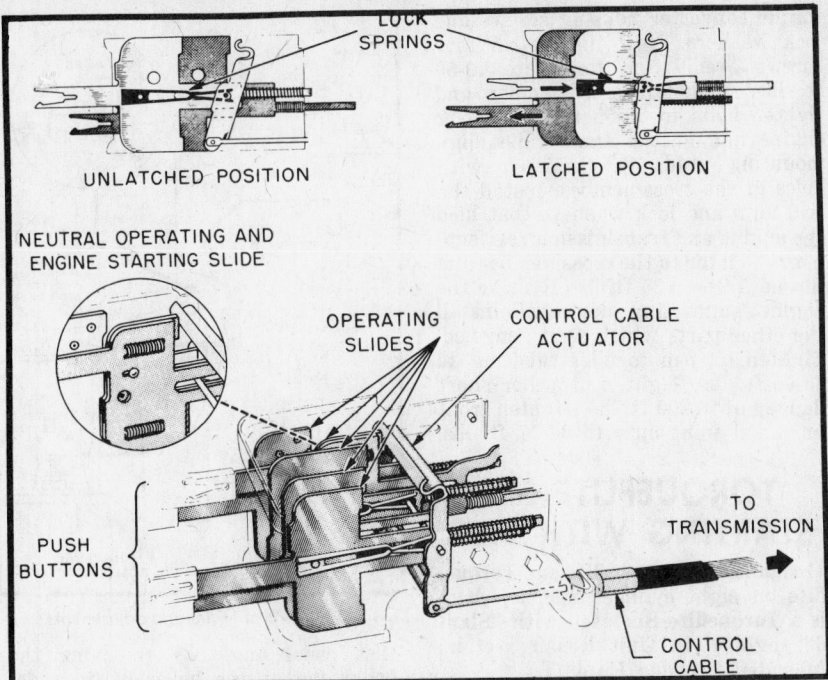

LOCK SPRINGS

UNLATCHED POSITION   LATCHED POSITION

NEUTRAL OPERATING AND ENGINE STARTING SLIDE

OPERATING SLIDES   CONTROL CABLE ACTUATOR

PUSH BUTTONS

TO TRANSMISSION

CONTROL CABLE

Typical Gearshift Control Unit

point on the front face of the converter opposite the low-spot of hub runout. The size of the spot to be heated depends on the amount of runout. It should be about ½ inch in diameter for .008 inch of total indicator reading. Using an acetylene torch containing a No. 3 tip set to maximum heat, apply it to the selected spot until the spot becomes dull red. Rapid heating and then cooling of an isolated area is the secret of the process. If all is well, the spot comes to color in a few seconds. The area is then quenched as rapidly as possible with a hose or wet rags. Do not attempt to recheck runout until converter has returned to a normal temperature.

If sparks are noted it is an indication that the torch is too close and the metal is starting to burn; move torch back slightly. Care should be taken to remove the torch the instant the selected spot becomes a dull red to avoid over-correction or damage to the unit.

Should the runout of the converter hub exceed .016 inch (Full Indicator Reading) and yet runout of the crankshaft flange is less than .002 inch F.I.R., the converter unit is defective and should be replaced. Be certain, however, to first check the drive flanges for raised metal, chips, dirt, and such.

INSTALLATION OF CONVERTER

When reinstalling, install the eight converter stud nuts and lock washers and tighten evenly (no specification for proper torque is given). Recheck that hub runout does not exceed .004 inch F.I.R. Place torque converter housing over the locating dowels and into position against the block-to-housing adapter plate. Install the housing to plate screws with lock washers and tighten evenly to 25-30

verter housing bolts on right side with guide pins and then remove two case to housing bolts from left side. Slide transmission straight back to avoid damage to the front oil pump driving sleeve and lower transmission to the floor.

Unbolt and remove the converter housing bolts. Although most mechanics do not do so, it is recommended that the runout of the converter hub be checked before the converter is removed from the crankshaft. Using an indicator as shown in Fig. 6, check runout of converter hub (runout should not exceed .004 inch F.I.R.) and mark both converter and crankshaft flange so that the true source of any runout may be found. Be sure to match mark the converter to the shaft flange so that it may be assembled in the same position. Remove eight torque converter stud nuts and

Fig. 6—Checking that runout of Torque Converter Hub does not exceed .004"

lock washers to release the converter from the crankshaft flange. See Fig. 5. Check runout of flange; it should not exceed .002 inch. If it does, use shims between converter and flange at reassembly to correct.

CORRECTING TORQUE CONVERTER RUNOUT

Note: Throughout this procedure the converter has no oil in it and the drain plugs are in place. This procedure is applicable to any Chrysler Corporation Torque Converter.

Runout of the converter hub should not exceed .004 inch. If it does, the condition may be corrected by using a torch as shown in Fig. 7 to heat a spot about ½ inch in diameter at a

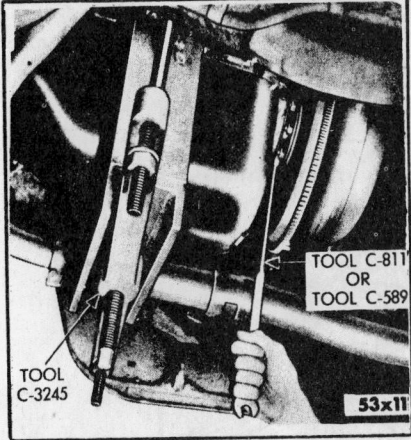

TOOL C-811 OR TOOL C-589

TOOL C-3245

53x11

Fig. 5—Removal of converter to flywheel stud nuts

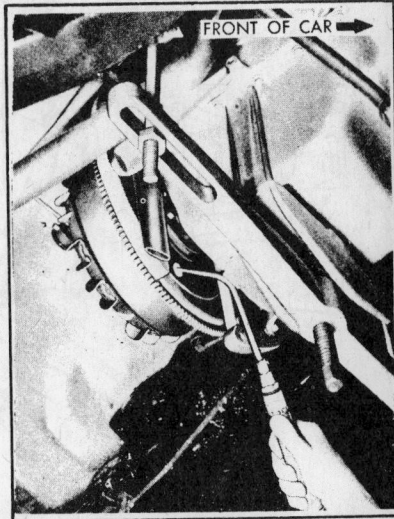

FRONT OF CAR

Fig. 7—Heat spot on front cover of converter opposite to mark on back face indicating low spot of converter hub

ft. lbs.

Note: The bore of the housing must be concentric to the hub of the converter within .010″. Adjustment is made by turning the slot-ended housing-locating dowels or by installing different dowels available for the purpose. The rear face of the housing should be perpendicular to the converter hub within .008″. Adjustment is made by shims between the housing and the adapter plate.

INSTALLATION OF TRANSMISSION

Install guide pins in the two trans-of torque converter housing Lubricate and install front oil pump drive mission mounting holes in right side sleeve into transmission, making sure the driving lugs correctly engage the front oil pump pinion. Main position of drive sleeve will be flush with front of pump housing if sleeve is properly installed.

Position lugs on converter end of drive sleeve to engage drive lugs visible in hub of converter. Line up splines of reaction shaft and input shaft with those of stator and turbine in the converter.

Slide transmission along guide pins into place against converter housing. Check that the driving lugs and splines are properly engaged. Everything should go into place easily. If force seems necessary, it is likely that the input shaft or drive sleeve is not properly aligned with splines or lugs in converter.

Install the two left hand transmission case to torque converter housing screws, but do not tighten. Remove the two guide pins and install the two right hand transmission case to

torque converter housing screws and lock washers. Now tighten all four screws evenly and torque to 40-50 ft. lbs. Reinstall crossmember and tighten bolts to 50-55 ft. lbs. Lower engine and at the same time align mounting studs in insulator with holes in the crossmember. Install the two nuts and lock washers that hold the engine and transmission rear support insulator to the crossmember and torque from 30-35 ft. lbs. Remove the engine supporting device. Reinstall the other parts which were removed. Tighten oil pan to filler tube nut to 35-40 ft. lbs. Tighten propeller shaft flange nut to 200 ft. lbs. Tighten front universal joint nuts to 33-37 ft. lbs.

TORQUEFLITE SIX STARTING WITH 1960

(In addition to **Powerflite** and **Torqueflite** on eight cylinder models, there is a **Torqueflite Six** used with "Slant 6" engine). In Unit Repair section, indicated "Torque Flite (B)".

1. With the engine at operating temperature and carburetor off fast idle, adjust r.p.m. to 500.

2. Loosen both "A" and "B" lock nuts, (Fig. 1), on the carburetor rod and the transmission throttle rod.

3. Insert a 3/16″ rod or drill bit in the hole and open slot of the accelerator shaft bracket and into the elongated hole of the throttle lever.

4. With rod in position, hold the transmission throttle valve lever all the way foreward, (closed position) and tighten transmission to accelerator lever assembly rod adjusting locknut "A".

5. Remove 3/16″ rod from accelerator lever, shaft and bracket assembly.

6. With the carburetor off "fast idle", move the rear half of the carburetor rod rearward until the stop in the transmission is felt. Tighten locknut "B" (Fig. 1).

7. The accelerator pedal should be at an angle of 115° to the horizontal, (113°—114° on powerflite transmissions). If correction is necessary, ad-

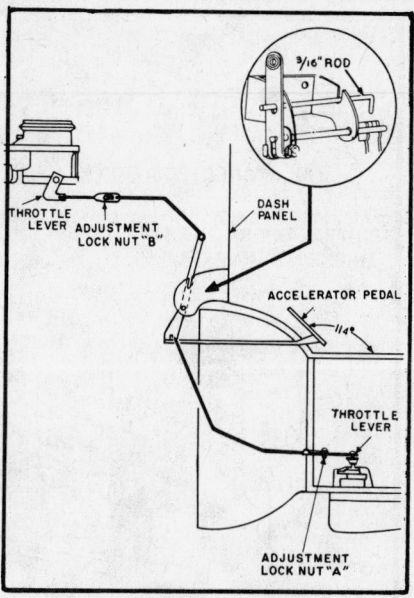

Fig. 1—Throttle linkage adjustments

just pedal angle by removing the pedal end of the bellcrank to pedal rod, and adjusting the length of the rod at the swivel. Reinstall the rod and tighten the locknut.

Starting 1962

The slant "6" Plymouth uses a cable operated throttle control (See diagram). Linkage adjustments are as follows:

1. Disconnect ball socket (4).
2. Disconnect choke (1) or block it wide open, with throttle off fast idle cam.
3. With transmission lever forward against stop, adjust at ball joint (4) so that joint will enter directly and with no force on the rod, it must be held at same height for this measurement.
4. Check operation to be sure transmission lever is against stop when at curb idle and moves off stop immediately with throttle movement.
5. Follow steps 2, 3, 4 and 5 under manual transmission, above.

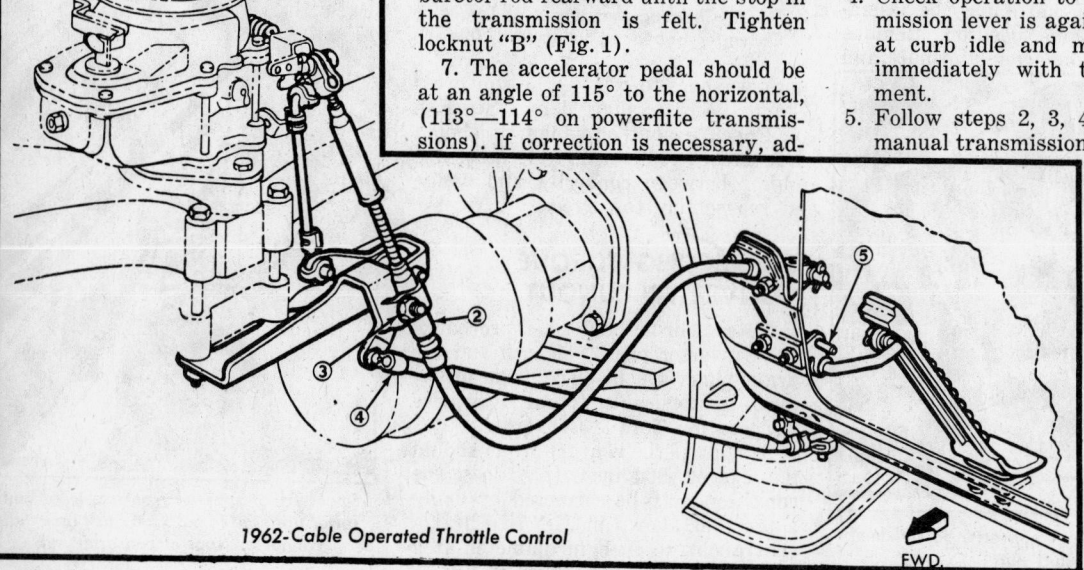

1962-Cable Operated Throttle Control

SHIFT CONTROL ADJUSTMENT

Beginning 1959

1. Raise car on hoist. Have an assistant hold the "R" button fully depressed.

2. Drain about three quarts of fluid from the transmission.

3. Remove control cable adjustment wheel lock screw.

4. Remove neutral starting switch, washer and seal.

5. Back the adjustment wheel off on cable housing, (counterclockwise) until only two or three threads are showing behind the wheel on the housing, (Fig. 2).

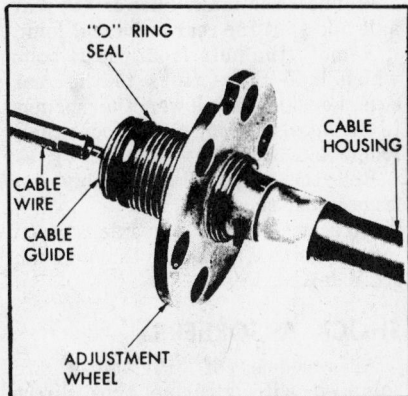

Fig. 2—Gearshift control cable and adjustment wheel

6. Hold the cable guide centered in the hole of the transmission with just enough force to overcome "O" ring friction and to bottom the assembly. Holding the cable in this position, rotate the adjusting wheel to just contact the case squarely.

7. Release inward pressure on the cable, rotate the wheel, (clockwise) to the next hole that lines up with the case hole, then turn an additional 4 holes clockwise. Install and tighten lockscrew.

8. Install neutral starting switch. Then refill the transmission with type "A" suffix "A" fluid to proper level.

NEUTRAL STARTING SWITCH

1. With the neutral button depress-

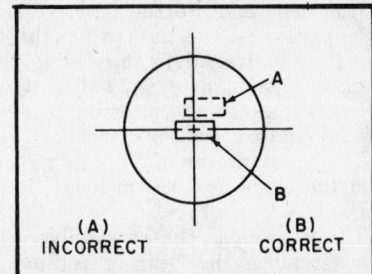

Fig. 3—Lever alignment

ed and the switch lever properly aligned in the center of the neutral switch hole, (Fig. 3) Hook up a test light to the switch. With a test light connected between the battery and the switch terminal, screw in the switch until the light goes on. Then tighten the switch an additional 1/8 to 1/2 turn. This should produce satisfactory operation of the switch. If not modifications must be made to the switch lever inside the transmission, (Fig 3) or to the switch itself, (Fig. 4).

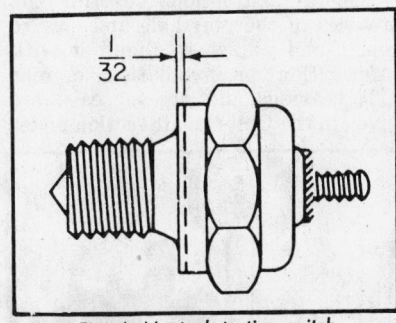

Fig. 4—Neutral starting switch

Modifying the switch lever consists of bending the lever with a screw driver or small pry bar, to it's correct location. Modifying the switch, consists of seating the switch deeper by cutting off 1/32" from the seating surface of the switch or adding a thin flat washer before the cupped washer and seal.

TRANSMISSION R. & R.

TORQUEFLITE

1. Disconnect the battery.

2. Depress "R" push button (Torqueflite). Depress "L" push button (Torqueflite six).

3. Remove starting motor.

4. Raise car on a hoist.

5. Remove converter coverplate and drain converter and transmission.

6. Disconnect wire and remove starter neutral switch.

7. Remove push button control cable to transmission adjusting plate screw.

8. With a screw driver in the neutral switch hole, (Fig. 5) push a screw driver against the upper projecting portion of the cable lockspring. Pull outward on the cable to remove the cable from the adapter and transmission case.

9. Loosen and remove the throttle link and lever from the throttle shaft.

10. Disconnect oil cooler lines at the transmission and remove oil filler tube.

11. Remove speedometer pinion and sleeve from the transmission.

12. Disconnect propeller shaft at the front joint and tie it out of the way.

13. Remove parking brake adjusting nut cover plate and loosen cable clamp bolt on brake support, (Fig. 6). Disengage the ball end of the cable from the operating lever and remove the cable from the brake support.

14. Disconnect the extension housing insulator at the crossmember.

15. Install rear engine support fixture and raise the engine slightly.

16. Disconnect and remove the crossmember.

17. Place transmission jack under the unit to support the assembly.

18. Match mark the converter and flex drive plate for reassembly. Remove converter to flex plate attaching screws. Attach a small "C" clamp to edge of bell housing to hold converter in place during removal of transmission.

19. Remove bell housing retaining bolts. Work the transmission rearward off the engine block dowels and to disengage the converter hub from out of the crankshaft.

20. Lower transmission and con-

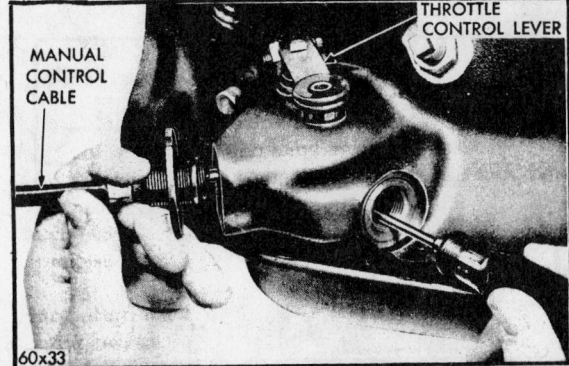

Fig. 5—Removing gearshift control cable

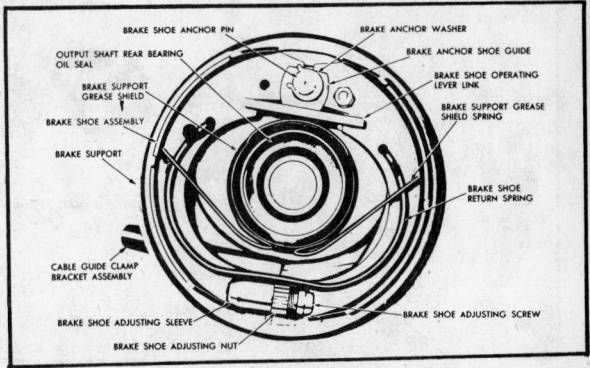

Fig. 6—Internal expanding parking brake (drum removed)

PLYMOUTH

verter assembly down and free of the car.

Reverse above procedure for installation and refill with fluid type "A" suffix "A".

TRANSMISSION R. & R. POWERFLITE—BEGINNING 1960

Procedure remains basically the the same as with former models.

UNIVERSAL JOINTS AND DRIVE LINES

REMOVAL OF THE DRIVE SHAFT AND UNIVERSAL JOINTS

Thru 1956 Models

From under the car, remove the bolts which hold the rear universal joint housing to the rear axle pinion flange and lower the rear end of the drive shaft to the floor.

Repeat the operation at the front universal joint and slide the drive shaft assembly complete with both universal joint body assemblies out from under the car and remove to a bench.

On the bench, remove the grease boot and slide the housing assembly back, which will permit easy removal of the ball and needle bearing assemblies.

If the cross pin is to be removed, an arbor press should be used since this pin is a pressed fit in the drive shaft ball.

To reinstall, reverse the order of removal, using a new grease boot at both universal joints.

Starting 1957

From under the car, remove the bolts which hold the rear cross and bearing type universal to the axle pinion flange, then lower the rear end

of the driveshaft to the floor.

Now remove the nuts which hold the front universal joint housing to transmission flange and slide the driveshaft assembly out from under the car and place it on a bench.

The front universal joint is serviced the same as 1956 models. (See above.)

To disassemble the rear universal joint, remove the bearing retainer, then push one bearing assembly towards the cross spider forcing out the opposite bearing assembly. Now push on the cross spider to remove the other bearing assembly. (It may be necessary to remove the dust seal from the cross spider to remove the spider from the yoke.)

REAR AXLE AND SUSPENSION

TROUBLE SHOOTING AND ADJUSTMENT

General instructions covering the troubles of the rear axle and how to repair and adjust it, together with information on installation of rear axle bearings and grease seals, are given in the Unit Repair section under

Installing Universal Joint Pin

the heading: Axles, Rear.

Capacities of the rear axle are given in the Capacities Tables of this section.

REMOVAL OF THE REAR AXLE ASSEMBLY FROM THE CAR

All Models

Jack up the car and take the weight of the car on jacks on the frame in front of the rear spring.

Disconnect and remove the rear spring shackle and sway bars and take off the rear shock absorbers. Disconnect the brake lines at the rear axle and split the rear universal joint.

Remove the nuts from the U bolts which hold the springs to the rear axle housing and lower the springs to the floor, pivoting them about their front bolts.

Roll the rear axle assembly out from under the car.

All service on the rear axle is given in the rear axle section in this manual, see index.

SHOCK ABSORBERS

All models of Plymouth are equipped with airplane type direct acting shock absorbers.

Since disassembly service on shock absorbers is a highly specialized job, it is recommended that if difficulty is experienced with the shock absorber they be removed from the car and replaced with either a new or rebuilt unit.

RADIO REMOVE AND INSTALL

1. Disconnect "A" lead, antennae, light lead, and speaker lead.
2. Remove control knobs and shaft mounting nuts.
3. Remove bracket attaching bolt.
4. Remove speaker grille, heater push button assembly and speaker opening.
5. Remove radio through speaker opening.

To reinstall: Reverse the above.

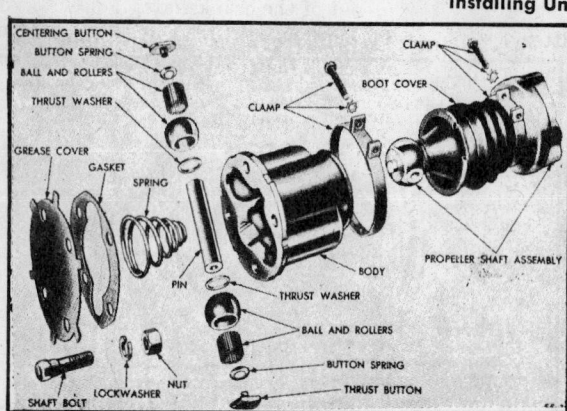

Exploded view—ball and trunnion type universal joint

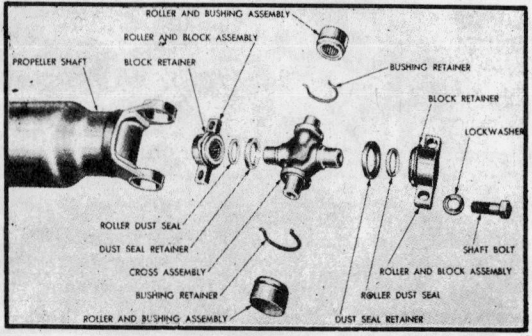

Exploded view—cross and bearing type universal joint

PONTIAC INDEX

AIR CONDITIONING

Service 1092

BRAKES, HYDRAULIC

Adjustments 938
Brake information 547
Bleed brakes 941
Parking brake, adjust 548
Parking brake lever & cable ... 548
Master cylinder, R & R 548
Master cylinder service ... 939

BRAKES, POWER

Power unit overhaul 954
Trouble shooting 954

CLUTCH

Clutch assembly, R & R 557
Clutch pedal, adjust 557

COOLING SYSTEM

Capacities 541

ELECTRICAL SYSTEM

Delcotron generator 546
Distributor, R & R 545
Distributor specifications ... 539
Fuses and circuit breakers ... 540
Gauges 1024
Generator and regulator
  specifications 539
Generator and regulators .. 546
Generator service 1026
Generator trouble shooting chart 1026
Horn buttons 555
Ignition firing order & timing ... 537
Ignition timing procedure ... 538
Ignition timing specifications ... 538
Starter, R & R 546
Starter specifications 540
Starter systems 1046
Transistor ignition 1018

ENGINE ASSEMBLY

References 549
Cylinder head, R & R 550
Cylinder head tightening ... 545
Engine assembly, R & R ... 549
Engine firing order & timing ... 537
Engine marking code 538
Engine diagnosis 1012
Exhaust manifold, R & R ... 548
Inlet manifold, R & R 549
Oil filter, R & R 554
Oil pan, R & R 553
Oil pressure specifications ... 542
Piston and rod, R & R 555
Piston specifications 544
Rear main bearing oil seal ... 554
Rocker arms & shaft 550
Specifications, general, engine ... 542
Timing chain & case 552

ENGINE ASSEMBLY—continued

Trouble shooting charts ... 1012
Tune-up specifications 538
Valve lifters, hydraulic, removal .552
Valve specifications 544
Valve springs 551
Valves and guides 551

ENGINE LUBRICATION

Oil pan removal 553
Oil filter 554

EXHAUST SYSTEM

Exhaust manifold, R & R ... 548
Intake manifold, R & R ... 549

FUEL SYSTEM

Carburetor 972
Fuel gauge service 1024
Fuel pump pressure 538
Fuel pump, R & R 548
Fuel pump service 1020
Fuel tank, R & R 548

INSTRUMENTS

Instruments, R & R 546
Speedometer, R & R 547
Wiper motor 547

RADIO, R & R

References 564

REAR AXLE AND SUSPENSION

Axle assembly, R & R 563
Axle shaft 918
Axle shaft oil seal 918
Pinion bearings 918
Rear spring 564
Ring gear & pinion 918
Trouble shooting 919

SPECIFICATIONS

Battery 540
Brake cylinder sizes 541
Capacities:
  Axle, rear 541
  Cooling system 541
  Crankcase 541
  Fuel tank 541
  Transmission, automatic ... 541
  Transmission, manual ... 541
Chassis, general 541
Distributor 539
Engine, general 542
Fuses and circuit breakers ... 540
Generator and regulators .. 539
Light bulbs 541
Main bearings 543
Model identification illustrations .536
Pistons 544
Quick reference specifications ... 537
Rod bearings 543

SPECIFICATIONS—continued

Starters 540
Torque wrench 545
Tune-up 538
Valves 544
Wheel alignment 545

STEERING, MANUAL

Adjust gear housing 1052
Gear assembly, R & R 555
Horn button, R & R 555
Steering wheel, R & R 555

STEERING, POWER

Power gear, R & R 556
Pump assembly 1058
Pump removal 556
Trouble shooting 1081
Unit overhaul 1058

SUSPENSION, FRONT

Alignment procedures 1082
Alignment specifications .. 545
Ball joints, R & R 1087
King pins and bushings ... 1087
Knuckle supports 1087
References 555
Shock absorbers 1087
Support arms, pins and bushings .1087
Toe-in, adjust 1082

TRANSMISSION, HYDRA-MATIC

Quick service information .. 559
Dual range 850
  Linkage adjust 559
  Transmission, R & R 560
Hydramatic 4 speed 860
  Linkage adjust 560
  Transmission, R & R 561
Hydramatic 3 speed 886
  Transmission, R & R 562

TRANSMISSION, MANUAL SHIFT

Disassemble transmission .. 558
References 557
Transmission, R & R 558

TROUBLE CHECKS

Procedures 1

TUNE-UP

Procedures 1012
Specifications 538
Engine diagnosis 1012

UNIVERSAL JOINT AND DRIVE LINE

U joint & drive shaft, R & R ... 562

535

PONTIAC

1954

1955

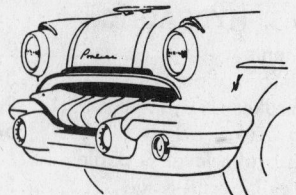

1956

1957

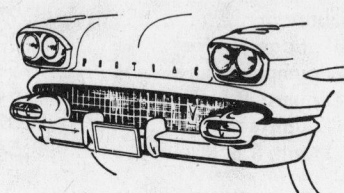

1958

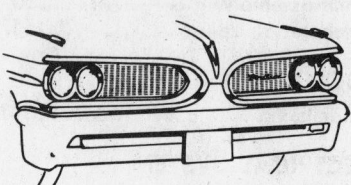

1959

1960

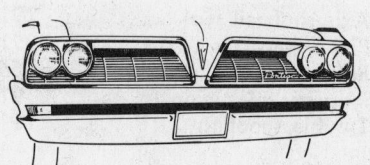

1961

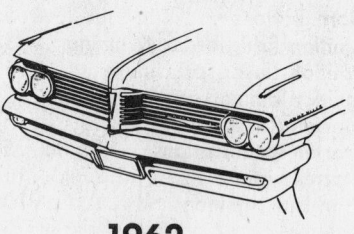

1962

1962 GRAND PRIX

1963

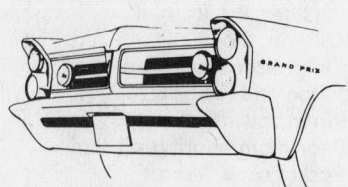

1963 GRAND PRIX

QUICK WORKING SPECIFICATIONS

DISTRIBUTOR

Breaker Point Gap (In.)
1954-63, All 016

Cam Angles (Degrees)
1954, all 25½
1955-63, V8 30

SPARK PLUGS

Year	Type	Gap
1954, all	44-5	.025 in.
1955, all	44-5	.035 in.
1956, all	44	.035 in.
1957, Norm.	44-5	.035 in.
1957, Xtra H.P.	44	.035 in.
1958-59	45	.035 in.
1960-63	45S	.035 in.

IGNITION TIMING

(Spark occurs degrees before TC)
1954, 6 cyl. 3B
1953-54, St. 8 with Std. Hd. 6B
1953-54, St. 8 with Opt. Hd. 3B
1955-56, V8 ....5B
1957-63, V8 ....6B

VALVES

Operating Tappet Clearance (Hot)
1954, all 012
1955-63, V8, Clearance is zero.

GENERATOR & REGULATOR

Year and Series	Generator Field Current in Amperes 6 Volt	Generator Field Current in Amperes 12 Volt	Regulator Cut-out Closing Voltage	Regulator Current Regulator Setting	Regulator Voltage Regulator Setting
1954 All	1.9	—	6.4	45	7.4
1955-57 All	—	1.55	12.7	26	14.3±1.(A)
1958 All	—	1.55	12.7	30	14.0±1.(A)
1959-61 All	—	1.69	13.2	30	14.2±1.(A)
1962-63	—	1.69	13.2	35	14.2±1.(A)

(A) Surrounding temperatures guide this adjustment. Higher temperatures require lower settings and lower temperatures permit higher settings, within limits.

For A.C. Generator Specifications See Following Pages

WHEEL ALIGNMENT

Caster (Degrees)
1954, all ....½N to ½ P
1955-57, all ....½ N to ½ N
1958, all ....1 N to 0
1959-63, all ....2 N to 1 N

Camber (Degrees)
1954-58, all ....0 to 1 P
1959-63, all ....¼ N to ¾ P

Toe-In (In.)

1954-63, all ....0 to 1/16

CAPACITIES

Engine Crankcase (Qts.)
Add 1 qt. for new filter.
1954-60 5
1961-63 4

Transmission, Synchro. (Pts.)
1954-55 ....1¾
1956-57 ....1½
1958-63-3 speed 2
1961-63-4 speed 2½

Transmission, Automatic (Pts.)
1954 22
1955-56 19
1957-63 ....18½

Rear Axle
1954-56 ....3¼
1957 5
1958-63 ....5½

Cooling System (Qts.)
(Add 1 qt. for heater)
1954, 6 cyl. 18
1954, all 18½
1955 24
1956-57, V8 ....21¾
1958-60, V8 ....21½
1961-63 ....18½

FIRING ORDER and TIMING

SPARK OCCURS:
1954 — 6 Cyl. "L" Head—3° BTDC
1954 — Straight 8—6° BTDC
1955-56—V-8, All—5°BTDC
1957-63—V-8, All—6°BTDC

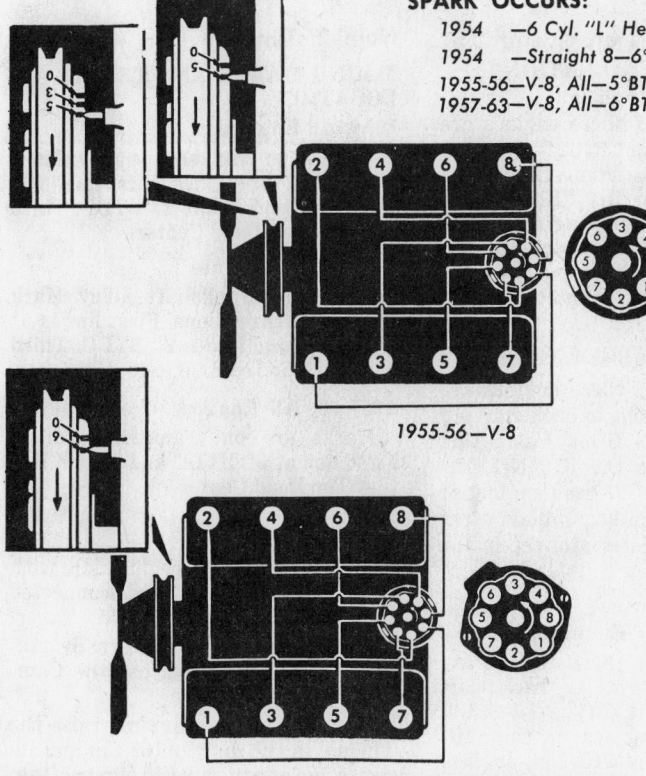
1955-56 —V-8

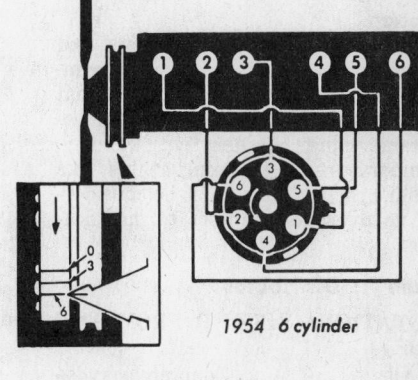
1954 6 cylinder

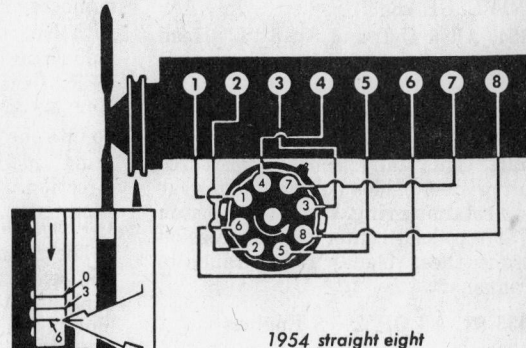
1954 straight eight

1957-63 —V-8

NOTE:
THESE ARE APPROXIMATE SETTINGS. ENGINE DESIGN, ALTITUDE, TEMPERATURE, FUEL AND ENGINE CONDITION WILL ALL INFLUENCE TIMING. THE DETERMINING FACTOR, LIMITING ADVANCE, WILL STILL BE THE "KNOCK POINT" OF THE INDIVIDUAL ENGINE.

PONTIAC

CAR SERIAL NUMBER LOCATION AND ENGINE IDENTIFICATION

SERIAL NUMBER LOCATION

Left front door post. This number is identical with the engine number and furnishes information such as model year and chassis, (Power) used.

ENGINE NUMBER LOCATION
1954:

All in-line engines—Left front face of cylinder block.
1955-63:

All V-8 engines—Front of right bank.

ENGINE IDENTIFICATION

There is no problem here. Model year identity and engine type used, (6, straight 8 or V-8) will establish the engine size used in any specific model.

TUNE-UP SPECIFICATIONS

Year	Spark Plugs		Distributor (Note 1)			Ignition Timing (Note 2)	Compression Pressure Cranking (Note 3)	Valves (Note 4)				Fuel Pump Pressure	Engine Idle Speed Neutral (Note 5)
								Tappet Clearance Hot		Timing			
	Type	Gap	Cam Angle	Point Gap	Arm Spring Tension			Inlet	Exhaust	Inlet Opens			
1954													
6 Cyl., L Head	44-5	.025	25½	.016	19–23	3B	132	.012	.012	12½B	4-5	475	
St.8, L Head	44-5	.025	25½	.016	19–23	Note 6	132	.012	.012	5B	4-5	475	
1955													
OHV, V8	44-5	.035	30	.016	19–23	5B	140	Zero	Zero	22B	4-5	475	
1956													
OHV, V8	44	.035	30	.016	19–23	5B	150	Zero	Zero	Note 7	4-5	475	
1957													
OHV, V8, Normal	44-5	.035	30	.016	19–23	6B	160	Zero	Zero	22	4-5	Note 8	
OHV, V8, Extra H.P.	44	.035	30	.016	19–23	6B	160	Zero	Zero	29	4-5	Note 8	
1958-59													
OHV, V8	45	.035	30	.016	19–23	Note 6	180	Zero	Zero	Note 7	5-6½	Note 8	
1960-1963													
OHV, V8	45S	.035	30	.016	19–23	Note 6	180	Zero	Zero	Note 7	5-6½	Note 8	

Note Dist. Vac. Line Disconnect for Initial Timing

NOTES FOR TUNE-UP SPECIFICATIONS TABLE

Note:

All specifications are standard and should result in satisfactory performance. There are, however, factors that influence these settings, such as fuel octane value, air density, humidity, temperature, etc. Timing charts, like other specifications must be considered as averages, subject to modification.

Note 1: Distributor

ROTATION (VIEWED FROM THE TOP)

All ....Counterclockwise

DRIVE GEAR

1954, All 6 Cyl. and St. 8 "L" Head Engines

The gear is a press fit on the oil pump shaft. Distributor shaft is slotted to receive drive tang of oil pump shaft. This tang consists of three spring steel blades held in top of gear by a retaining ring. When No. 1 piston is at top dead center on compression stroke these blades run parallel to crankshaft.

1955-63, All OHV, V8 Engines

The gear is pinned to distributor shaft. There is an intermediate shaft with a slot on each end which takes the drive from the distributor shaft to the pump shaft.

FIRING ORDER AND SPARK PLUG WIRE INSTALLATION

6 Cyl. "L" Head Engines

The cylinders of these engines are numbered from front to back, starting with No. 1 at the front. Using this numbering system the FIRING ORDER of the 6 cylinder engine is: 1-5-3-6-2-4. The spark plug wires go into the 6 cylinder distributor cap in the firing order and in a counterclockwise direction.

St. 8 "L" Head Engines

The cylinders of these engines are numbered from front to back starting with No. 1 at the front. Using this numbering system the FIRING ORDER of the St. 8 "L" head engine is: 1-6-2-5-8-3-7-4. The spark plug wires go into the St. 8 distributor cap in the firing order and in a counterclockwise direction.

1955-63, OHV, V8 Engines

The cylinders of these engines are numbered from front to back: left bank, 1-3-5-7; right bank, 2-4-6-8. Using this numbering system the FIRING ORDER of the OHV, V8 engines is: 1-8-4-3-6-5-7-2. The spark plug wires go into the OHV, V8 distributors in the firing order and in a counterclockwise direction.

Note 2: Timing

TIMING MARKS AND THEIR LOCATION

1954, All Engines

Mark is on crankshaft pulley. Mark consists of three lines. First line is 6° BTDC. Second line is 2° BTDC. Third line is at Top Dead Center.

1955-56, All Engines

Mark is on crankshaft pulley. Mark consists of three lines. First line is 5° BTDC. Second line is 3° BTDC. Third line is at Top Dead Center.

1957-63, All Engines

Marks are on crankshaft pulley. First line at 6° BTDC and second line is at Top Dead Center.

Timing Procedure

Adjust timing at specified idle with distributor vacuum line disconnected and plugged.

If the car has an Externally Adjustable Point Gap adjust the Cam dwell as follows:

With the engine running, raise the window in the distributor cap and insert a hexagonal shaped wrench into the adjusting screw. Turn the adjusting screw clockwise until the engine begins to misfire. Now turn the screw

NOTES FOR TUNE UP SPECIFICATIONS—continued

one-half turn counterclockwise. This will give the proper dwell angle.

In all cases loosen distributor clamp screw and rotate distributor until timing light shows that pointer is at proper mark on crankshaft pulley. Tighten clamp screw to 12-15 ft lbs.

When retarding the spark to compensate for low octane fuel do not retard beyond T.D.C. as overheating and excessive power loss would result.

IGNITION RESISTOR

1955-63: A resistor is provided in the primary ignition circuit to limit the flow of current to the ignition coil and so protect the distributor points at high speeds. A contact in the ignition switch by-passes the resistor allowing more current to the coil to facilitate easier starting. Be sure to disconnect and ground the distributor lead when using the starter to turn the engine.

Note 3: Compression Pressure

All cylinders should read alike within 10 pounds. This is more important than the actual reading. Take the readings with all plugs removed, engine at normal operating temperature.

Pontiac suggests that engine needs attention if variation between the highest and lowest readings is more than 20 per cent of the highest.

10.25:1 and 10.75:1 205
8.6:1 165

Note 4: Valves

Zero in the tappet clearance column indicates hydraulic lifters are standard equipment.

Note 5: Idle Speed

Idle speeds as shown are for engines in good condition with the synchromesh transmission in Neutral. Add 25 RPM to figure given for engines with Hydramatic. The proper idle speed for an engine depends on its condition and also on whether or not it has an automatic transmission. Higher idle speeds are required for an engine in poor condition and also for engines used with automatic transmissions.

Note 6: Ignition Timing

Refer to "Firing Order and Timing" Illustrations.

When car has air conditioning R.P.M. should be adjusted with AC system turned off. Idle speed of cars with air conditioning should be 40 R.P.M. higher than figure in table.

1958, OHV, V8
All 6B

1959-63, OHV, V8
All ex. 420E 6B
420E, Opt. Eng. 4B

Note 7: Valve Timing

1956, OHV, V8
With Synchromesh Trans. .... 22 B

Dist. Vac. Line Disconnect for Initial Timing

With Hydramatic Trans. .... 27 B

1958, OHV, V8
With Manual Trans. .... 22 B
With Hydramatic Trans. .... 30 B
1959-63, OHV, V8
Std. Eng. W/S 22B
Std. Eng. W/A 30B
420 A, Opt. Eng. 29B
420 E, Opt. Eng. 41B

Note 8: Idle Speed

1957, OHV, V8
In Neutral with Synchromesh 460
In Neutral with Hydramatic 500
1958, OHV, V8
In Neutral with Synchromesh 460
In Drive with Hydramatic 490
1959, 63
In Neutral with Synchromesh 490
In Drive with Hydramatic 500

Abbreviations Used

6 Cyl. L Hd.—Straight six cylinder engine with valves in side of block.
St. 8 L Hd.—Straight eight cylinder engine with valves in side of block.
OHV, V8—V-shaped eight cylinder engine with valves in the heads.
BTDC—Before top dead center.
W/S—With Synchromesh Transmission.
W/A—With Automatic Transmission.
Opt. Eng.—Optional Engine.
Std. Eng.—Standard Engine.

PONTIAC—DISTRIBUTOR SPECIFICATIONS, DELCO-REMY

Year	Model	Delco-Remy Part Number	Rotation	Cam Angle in Degrees	Point Opening (inch)	Arm Spring in Ounces	Governor Control @ Dist. Advance Starts	R.P.M. Full Advance	Inches of Vacuum To Start Advance	Inches of Vacuum For Full Advance	Max. Adv. of Dist. in Degrees
1954	6 Cyl.	1110234	CC	38-45	.016	19-23	1 @ 400	11 @ 1950	4-6	19½-20½	11-13
	St. 8	1110831	CC	22-30	.016	19-23	1 @ 400	11 @ 1950	7-9	19½-21½	9-11
1955	OHV, V8 All	1110828	CC	26-33	.016	19-23	1 @ 250	15 @ 1700	4-6	12½-13½	7-9
1956	OHV, V8 All	1110862	CC	26-33	.016	19-23	1 @ 300	10 @ 1800	4-6	12½-13½	7-9
1957	OHV, V8 All	1110871	CC	30	.016	19-23	1 @ 300	13 @ 2125	6-8	14-15¾	10-12
1958	V8, Std. Eng.	1110924	CC	30	.016	19-23	1 @ 350	14 @ 2300	6-8	14-15¾	10-12
	V8, H. Com. Eng.	1110913	CC	30	.016	19-23	1 @ 450	11 @ 2300	6-8	13-15	9-11
1959	OHV, V8	1110941	CC	30	.016	19-23	1 @ 300	9 @ 1450	7-9	13-15	9-11
1960-61	V8, 389 cu. in. std.	1110971	CC	30	.016	19-23	1 @ 350	11 @ 1800	6-8	13-15	9-11
	V8, 389 cu. in. h/com.	1110970	CC	30	.016	19-23	1 @ 325	10 @ 1450	8-10	15-17	9-11
1962-63	V8, 389 cu. in. std.	1110997	CC	30	.016	19-23	1 @ 350	11 @ 1800	6-8	13-15	9-11
	V8, 389 cu. in. h/com.	1110996	CC	30	.016	19-23	1 @ 325	10 @ 1450	8-10	15-17	9-11

A.C. GENERATOR and REGULATOR SPECIFICATIONS

Year and Model		GENERATOR D-R Number	Field Current	Cut-In	Hot-Out-Put	REGULATOR D-R Number	Voltage @ 125°
1963	Standard	1100634	1.9-2.3 Amp	At Idle	42 Amp	1119511	14.4
	Heavy Duty	1100627	1.9-2.3 Amp	At Idle	52 Amp	1119511	14.4

D.C. GENERATOR and REGULATOR SPECIFICATIONS

| YEAR | GENERATORS | | | REGULATORS | | | | |
| | Field Current in Amperes | | Brush Spring Tension | Cut Out Relay | | Current and Voltage Regulator Air Gap | Current Regulator Setting | Voltage Regulator Setting |
	At 6 Volts	At 12 Volts		Air Gap	Closing Voltage			
1954 All Series	1.9		28	.020	6.4	.075	45	7.3
1955 All Series		1.55	28	.020	12.7	.075	25	14.3±1.0(A)
1956–57 All Series		1.55	28	.020	12.7	.075	26	14.3±1.0(A)
1958 All Series		1.55	28	.020	12.7	.075	30	14.0±1.0(A)
1959-61 All Series	—	1.69	28	.020	13.2	.075	30	14.2±1.(A)
1962	—	1.69	28	.020	13.2	.075	35	14.2±(A)

(A) Surrounding temperatures guide this adjustment. Higher temperatures require lower settings and lower temperatures permit higher settings, within limits.

BATTERY and STARTER SPECIFICATIONS

| YEAR | BATTERY | | | | STARTERS | | | | | | Brush Spring Tension |
| | Ampere Hour Capacity | Volts | Group Number | Terminal Grounded | LOCK TEST | | | NO-LOAD TEST | | | |
					Amps	Volts	Torque	Amps	Volts	R.P.M.	
1954 All 6 Cyl.	120	6	2E	Neg.	550	3.25	11.0	80	5.6	5500	26
All St. 8	120	6	2E	Neg.	600	3.0	15.0	60	5.0	6000	26
1955 All Engines	60	12	2SM	Neg.	440	5.4	12.5	85	10.2	4200	38
1956 All Engines	60	12	2SM	Neg.	440	5.4	12.5	85	10.2	3500	38
1957 All Engines	60	12	2SM	Neg.	←——— Note 1 ———→			83	10.6	4400	38
1958-61 with Synchromesh	53	12	2SM	Neg.	←——— Note 1 ———→			100	10.6	3600	35
with Hydramatic	60	12	2SM	Neg.	←——— Note 1 ———→			120	10.6	3900	35
1962-63 with Synchromesh	53	12	2SM	Neg.			Note 1	100	10.6	3600	35
with Hydramatic	61	12	2SM	Neg.			Note 1	120	10.6	4700	35

Note 1: 1957-63 Starter Lock Test   Pontiac does not recommend use of Lock Test on these Starters.

FUSES and CIRCUIT BREAKERS

1954 MAIN BLOCK

The main block is on the engine side of the dash on the left side near the generator regulator. It has three sets of clips. The top set holds a spare SFE 14 fuse. Circuits protected on main fuse block are as follows:

Tail, License, Instrument and Hydramatic Quadrant Lights:

SFE 14 fuse held in middle (gold colored) set of clips.

Stop, Dome, Trunk Lights:

SFE 14 fuse held in bottom (grey collored) set of clips.

1954 AUXILIARY BLOCK

The auxiliary (accessory) fuse block is on the passenger side of the firewall just above the accelerator. The inside of the cover of this block carries information as to which fuse protects

what. The block carries a spare SFE 20 fuse. Circuits protected on auxiliary block are as follows:

Radio:

SFE 14

Electric Antenna:

SFE 30

Hood Ornament and Ash Tray:

SFE 20

Fog Lamps:

SFE 20

Courtesy, Underhood Clock Mechanism, Glove Box:

SFE 20

Heater Motor and Brake-on Light:

SFE 20

Back-up and Turn Signal:

SFE 20

Heater Dial and Radio Dial:

SFE 20

Clock Dial:

SFE 20

1954 ADDITIONAL CIRCUITS

Head, Park, Tail Lights:

30 amp. fuse on the headlight switch.

Autronic Eye:

SFE 14 fuse under amplifier cover. Amplifier is on right side of engine side of firewall.

Turn Signal Flasher:

Behind instrument panel.

Cigar Lighter:

Special thermal fuse in base.

1955-63 ONE FUSE BLOCK

FUSES AND CIRCUIT BREAKERS—Continued

Fuses for all circuits are located in one fuse block on firewall on passenger side above and to left of steering column. The circuits supplied by each fuse are shown on the block. Stop, Dome, Trunk and Courtesy Lights are fed by the same fuse. Tail and License Lights have the same fuse. All the fuses are SFE 14 except the SFE 4 fuse for the instrument lights rheostat. A spare SFE 14 is at the bottom of the block. Note HD means Hydramatic Quadrant, and "orn" means ornaments.

1955-63 ADDITIONAL CIRCUITS

Head, Beam, Telltale, Parking Lights:

22 amp. circuit breaker on headlight switch.

Electric Antenna:

SFE 14 fuse in line holder above the fuse block.

Air Conditioner:

SFE 30 fuse in a line holder on the defroster core housing.

Cigar Lighter:

1955 special thermal fuse in base;

1956-63 some models circuit breaker in base.

Turn Signal Flasher:

Clamped to steering column.

Electric Windshield Wiper:

18 amp. circuit breaker built into the upper motor together with an SFE 25 fuse in a line holder next to the fuse block.

Clock:

AGA 14 fuse on clock.

CAPACITIES

YEAR	Engine Crankcase Add 1 Qt. For New Filter	Transmissions Pints to Refill After Draining		Rear Axle Pints	Gasoline Tank Gallons	Cooling System Quarts Add 1 Qt. for Heater
		Manual	Automatic			
1954						
All 6 Cyl.	5	1¾	22	3¼	17½	18
All St. 8	5	1¾	22	3¼	20	18½
1955						
All OHV, V8	5	1¾	19	3¼	20	24
1956						
All OHV, V8	5	1½	19	3¼	20	22½
1957						
All OHV, V8	5	1½	18½	5	20	21¾
1958						
All OHV, V8	5	2	18½	5½	20	21¼
1959						
All OHV, V8	5	2	18½	5½	21½	21¼
1960						
All exc. Safari	5	2	18½	5½	23	21½
Safari	5	2	18½	5½	20	21½
1961-63						
All Exc. Safari	4	(A)	18½	5½	25	18½
Safari	4	2	18½	5½	19	18½

(A): Manual Trans. Capacity—3 Speed, 2 Pts.—4 Speed, 2½ Pts.

GENERAL CHASSIS and BRAKE SPECIFICATIONS

Year and Model	Chassis		Brake Cylinder Bore		
	Overall Length in Inches	Tire Size	Master Cyl. (Inch)	Wheel Cylinder Diameter (Inch)	
				Front	Rear
1954 6 & Str. 8	202⅝	7.10x15	1.	1¹⁄₁₆	⅞
Str. 8 Star Chief	213⅝	7.10x15	1.	1¹⁄₁₆	⅞
1955 V8, Chieftain	203¼	7.10x15	1.	1¹⁄₁₆	¹⁵⁄₁₆
V8, Star Chief	210¼	7.10x15	1.	1¹⁄₁₆	¹⁵⁄₁₆
1956 V8, All Ex. Star Chief	205⅝	7.10x15	1.	1¹⁄₁₆	¹⁵⁄₁₆
V8, Star Chief	212⅝	7.10x15	1.	1¹⁄₁₆	¹⁵⁄₁₆
1957 V8, All Ex. Star Chief	206⅞	7.50x14	1.	1¹⁄₁₆	¹⁵⁄₁₆
V8, Star Chief	213⅞	8.00x14	1.	1¹⁄₁₆	¹⁵⁄₁₆
1958 V8, Chieftain	210½	8.00x14	1.	1⅛	1.
V8, Bonneville	211¾	8.00x14	1.	1⅛	1.
V8, Super & Star Chief	215½	8.00x14	1.	1⅛	1.
1959 V8, Catalina	213¾	8.00x14	1.	1³⁄₁₆	1.
V8, Bonneville & Star Chief	220¾	8.00x14	1.	1³⁄₁₆	1.
1960 V8, Catalina, Ventura	213¾	8.00x14	1.	1³⁄₁₆	1.
V8, Bonneville & Star Chief	220¾	8.00x14	1.	1³⁄₁₆	1.
1961 V8, Catalina, Ventura	210	8.00x14	1.	1³⁄₁₆	1.
V8, Bonneville, Star Chief	217	8.00x14	1.	1³⁄₁₆	1.
1962 V8, Catalina, Grand Prix	211.6	8:00x14	1.	1³⁄₁₆	1.
V8, Bonneville, Star Chief	218.6	8:00x14	1.	1³⁄₁₆	1.
1963 V8, Catalina, Grand Prix	212.1	8.00x14	1.	1³⁄₁₆	1.
V8, Bonneville, Star Chief	219.1	8.00x14	1.	1³⁄₁₆	1.
V8, Station Wagon	212.7	8.00x14	1.	1³⁄₁₆	1.

LIGHT BULBS

Beam Telltale, Hood Ornament, Ash Tray, Ignition Key Lights:

6 Volt, No. 51; 12 Volt, No. 53.
(1 C.P. miniature base.)

Hydramatic Quadrant, Brake-on, Air Conditioning Panel, Heater Panel, Glove Box, Radio Dial, Clock, Instruments, Turn Signal Telltale Lights:

6 Volt, No. 55; 12 Volt, No. 57.
(2 C.P. miniature base.)

License Plate Light:

6 Volt, No. 63; 12 Volt, No. 67.
(4 C.P. single contact base.)

Courtesy Lights:

6 Volt, No. 81; 12 Volt, No. 89.
(6 C.P. single contact base.)

LIGHT BULBS —Continued

Underhood Lights:

6 Volt, No. 82; 12 Volt, No. 90.
(6 C.P. double contact base.)

Trunk Lights:

6 Volt, No. 209; 12 Volt, No. 1003.
(15 C.P. single contact base.)

Dome Light:

6 Volt, No. 210; 12 Volt, No. 1004.
(15 C.P. double contact base.)

Front Park and Turn; Rear Stop, Tail and Turn:

6 Volt, No. 1154; 12 Volt, No. 1034.
(32 & 4 C.P. double contact indexed base.)

Back-up Light:

6 Volt, No. 1133; 12 Volt, No. 1073.
(32 C.P. single contact base.)

Headlights, Two Light System

6 Volt, No. 5040; 12 Volt, No. 5400.
(50 & 40 C.P. triple contact base.)

Headlights, Four light System

LOW AND HIGH BEAM

12 Volt, No. 4002.
(37.5-50 watts three contact base.)

HIGH BEAM ONLY

12 Volt, No. 4001.
(37.5 watts double contact base.)

GENERAL ENGINE SPECIFICATIONS

Year	Bore and Stroke	Number of Main Bearings	Type of Valve Lifter Used	Cubic Inch Displacement	AMA Horsepower	Standard Advertised Horsepower at Stated RPM	Advertised Torque at Stated RPM	Compression Ratio	Oil Pressure At 30 MPH (Note 1)	Cam Shaft Drive
1954										
6 Cyl., L Head W/S	3⁹⁄₁₆x4	4	Mech. Adj.	239.2	30.4	115@3800	193@2200	7-1	30	Chain
6 Cyl., L Head W/H	3⁹⁄₁₆x4	4	Mech. Adj.	239.2	30.4	118@3800	197@2000	7.7-1	30	Chain
St.8, L Head W/S	3³⁄₈x3³⁄₄	5	Mech. Adj.	268.4	36.4	122@3800	226@2200	7.7-1	30	Chain
St.8, L Head W/H	3³⁄₈x3³⁄₄	5	Mech. Adj.	268.4	36.4	127@3800	234@2200	7.7-1	30	Chain
1955—Note 2										
OHV, V8, Std.	3³⁄₄x3¹⁄₄	5	Hydraulic	287.2	45.0	180@4600	264@2400	8-1	30	Chain
OHV, V8, Optl.	3³⁄₄x3¹⁄₄	5	Hydraulic	287.2	45.0	173@4400	256@2400	7.4-1	30	Chain
1956—Note 2										
OHV, V8, Std.	3¹⁵⁄₁₆x3¹⁄₄	5	Hydraulic	316.6	49.6	227@4800	312@3000	8.9-1	30	Chain
OHV, V8, Optl.	3¹⁵⁄₁₆x3¹⁄₄	5	Hydraulic	316.6	49.6	205@4600	294@4600	7.9-1	30	Chain
1957—Note 3										
1.—OHV, V8 W/S	3¹⁵⁄₁₆x3⁹⁄₁₆	5	Hydraulic	347	49.6	244@4800	338@2700	8.5-1	30	Chain
2.—OHV, V8 W/H	3¹⁵⁄₁₆x3⁹⁄₁₆	5	Hydraulic	347	49.6	270@4800	359@2800	10-1	30	Chain
3.—OHV, V8 W/S	3¹⁵⁄₁₆x3⁹⁄₁₆	5	Hydraulic	347	49.6	227@4600	333@2300	8.5-1	30	Chain
4.—OHV, V8 W/H	3¹⁵⁄₁₆x3⁹⁄₁₆	5	Hydraulic	347	49.6	252@4600	354@2400	10-1	30	Chain
1958										
All OHV, V8	4¹⁄₁₆x3⁹⁄₁₆	5	Hydraulic	370	52.8	← Note 4 →			40	Chain
1959										
All OHV, V8	4¹⁄₁₆x3³⁄₄	5	Hydraulic	389	52.8	Note 5			35	Chain
1960 (Note 5)										
All V8 Exc. Bonneville	4¹⁄₁₆x3³⁄₄	5	Hydraulic	389	52.8	215@3600	390@2000	8.6-1	35	Chain
V8 Bonneville	4¹⁄₁₆x3³⁄₄	5	Hydraulic	389	52.8	281@4400	407@2800	8.6-1	35	Chain
1961-63 (Note 5)										
All Exc. Bonneville	4¹⁄₁₆x3³⁄₄	5	Hydraulic	389	52.8	215@3600	390@2000	8.6-1	35	Chain
Bonneville	4¹⁄₁₆x3³⁄₄	5	Hydraulic	389	52.8	235@3600	402@2000	8.6-1	35	Chain

NOTES FOR GENERAL ENGINE SPECIFICATIONS TABLE

Note 1: Oil Flow

OIL FILTER TYPE

1954, All "L" Head Engines

Pontiac Settling Type installed in the crankcase.

1955-63, OHV, V8 .... Full flow

Note 2: Engine Identification

1955-56, OHV, V8 Only

Low compression optional engine is designated by the letter "L" with a circle inscribed around it, stamped alongside the Engine Number. High compression standard engine has no such mark.

Note 3: Engine Identification

1957, OHV, V8

Super Chief and Star Chief with synchromesh transmission and 4 bar-
rel carburetor. There will be the letter "L" with a circle around it alongside the Engine Number.

Note 4: 1958 Horsepower, Torque and Compression Ratio

WITH ONE TWO BARREL CARBURETOR AND STANDARD HEAD.

H.P.—204 @ 4500.
Torque—354 @ 2600.
C.R.—8.6 to 1.

WITH ONE FOUR BARREL CARBURETOR AND STANDARD HEAD.

H.P.—255 @ 4500.
Torque—360 @ 2600.
C.R.—8.6 to 1.

WITH ONE TWO BARREL CARBURETOR AND HIGH COMPRESSION HEAD

H.P.—270 @ 4600.
Torque—388 @ 2800.
C.R.—10. to 1.

WITH ONE FOUR BARREL CARBURETOR AND HIGH COMPRESSION HEAD

H.P.—285 @ 4600.
Torque—395 @ 2800.
C.R.—10. to 1.

WITH THREE TWO BARREL CARBURETORS

H.P.—300 @ 4600.
Torque—400 @ 3000.
C.R.—10.5 to 1.

WITH FUEL INJECTION

H.P.—310 @ 4800.
Torque—400 @ 3400.
C.R.—10.5 to 1.

Note 5: 1959-63 Horsepower,

NOTES FOR GENERAL ENGINE SPECIFICATIONS—continued

Torque and Compression Ratio

WITH ONE TWO BARREL CAR-
BURETOR, STANDARD HEAD
AND CAMSHAFT
H.P.—245 @ 4200.
Torque—392 @ 2000.
C.R.—8.6 to 1.

WITH ONE FOUR BARREL CAR-
BURETOR, STANDARD HEAD
CAMSHAFT
H.P.—260 @ 4200.
Torque—400 @ 2800.
C.R.—8.6 to 1.

WITH ONE TWO BARREL CAR-
BURETOR, OPTIONAL HEAD AND
HYDRAMATIC CAMSHAFT
H.P.—280 @ 4400.
Torque—408 @ 2800.
C.R.—10.0 to 1.

WITH ONE FOUR BARREL CAR-
BURETOR, OPTIONAL HEAD AND
HYDRAMATIC CAMSHAFT
H.P.—300 @ 4600.
Torque—420 @ 2800.
C.R.—10.0 to 1.

WITH THREE TWO BARREL CAR-
BURETORS, OPTIONAL HEAD
AND HYDRAMATIC CAMSHAFT
H.P.—315 @ 4600.
Torque—425 @ 3200.
C.R.—10.5 to 1.

WITH ONE FOUR BARREL CAR-
BURETOR, OPTIONAL HEAD AND
SPECIAL CAMSHAFT (TEMPEST
420A ENGINE)
H.P.—330 @ 4800.
Torque—420 @ 2800.

C.R.—10.5 to 1.

WITH ONE TWO BARREL CAR-
BURETOR, STANDARD HEAD
AND SPECIAL CAMSHAFT (TEM-
PEST 420E ENGINE)
H.P.—215 @ 3600.
Torque—390 @ 2000.
C.R.—8.6 to 1.

1961-63
WITH TWO BARREL CARBURE-
TOR, OPTIONAL HEAD AND
HM 61-10 TRANSMISSION*
H.P.—267@4200.
Torque—405@2400.
C.R.—10.25 to 1.

WITH TWO BARREL CARBURE-
TOR, OPTIONAL HEAD AND HM
315 TRANSMISSION*
H.P.—283@4400.
Torque—413@2800.
C.R.—10.25 to 1.

WITH FOUR BARREL CARBURE-
TOR, OPTIONAL HEAD AND HM
315 TRANSMISSION*
H.P.—303@4600.
Torque—425@2800.
C.R.—10.25 to 1.

WITH FOUR BARREL CARBURE-
TOR, OPTIONAL HEAD AND HM
61-10 TRANSMISSION*
H.P.—287@4400.
Torque—417@2400.
C.R.—10.25 to 1.

WITH THREE TWO BARREL CAR-
BURETORS, OPTIONAL HEAD
AND ALL TRANSMISSIONS
H.P.—318@4600.
Torque—430@3200.
C.R.—10.75 to 1.

WITH TWO BARREL CARBURE-
TOR, STANDARD HEAD AND HM
61-10 OR HM 315 TRANSMISSION*,
(425E ENGINE)
H.P.—230@4000.
Torque—380@4800.
C.R.—8.6 to 1.

WITH FOUR BARREL CARBURE-
TOR, OPTIONAL HEAD AND ALL
TRANSMISSIONS (425A ENGINE)
H.P.—333@4800.
Torque—425@2800.
C.R.—10.75 to 1.

WITH THREE TWO BARREL CAR-
BURETORS, OPTIONAL HEAD
AND ALL TRANSMISSIONS (425A
ENGINE)
H.P.—348@4800.
Torque—380@2000.
C.R.—10.75 to 1.
*HM 61-10—Hydramatic Trans. for
Catalina and Ventura Series
HM 315—Hydramatic Trans. for
Bonneville and Star Chief Series.

Abbreviations Used

6 cyl. "L" Hd.—Straight 6 cylinder
engine with valves in the block.
St. 8 "L" Hd.—Straight 8 cylinder
engine with valves in the block.
OHV, V8—V-shaped 8 cylinder engine
with valves in the head.
W/S—With Synchromesh Transmission.
W/H—With Hydramatic Transmission.
Mech. Adj.—Solid valve lifters with
adjustable tappets.
Hyd. Adj.—Hydraulic valve lifters
with adjustable rockers.

CRANKSHAFT BEARING JOURNAL SIZES

| YEAR | Main Bearing Journals | | | | Connecting Rod Bearing Journals | | |
	Journal Diameter	Oil Clearance	End Play of Shaft	End Play Held By	Journal Diameter	Oil Clearance	End Play
1954 6 Cyl., "L" Head St. 8, "L" Head	Note 1. Note 2.	.0013 .0013	.006 .006	No. 3 No. 4	2.125 2.000	.0011 .0011	.010 .010
1955 V8, OHV	2.2498	Note 3.	.007	No. 4	2.250	.0019	.009
1956 V8, OHV	2.2498	Note 4.	.007	No. 4	2.250	.0019	.009
1957-58 V8, OHV	2.6235	Note 5.	.007	No. 4	2.250	.0019	.009
1959-63 V8, OHV	3.00	Note 5.	.006	No. 4	2.250	.0015	.009

NOTES FOR CRANKSHAFT BEARING JOURNAL

Note 1: 1954 6 Cyl. Main Bearing
Journal Diameters

Bearing No. 1—2.4989
Bearing No. 2—2.5299
Bearing No. 3—2.5294
Bearing No. 4—2.6237

Note 2: 1954 St. 8 Main Bearing
Journal Diameters
Bearing No. 1—2.3737
Bearing No. 2—2.4049
Bearing No. 3—2.4362
Bearing No. 4—2.4674
Bearing No. 5—2.6237

Note 3: 1955, OHV, V8 Main Bearing Oil Clearance

No. 1, No. 2, No. 3, No. 4— .0018
No. 5—.0021

Note 4: 1956, OHV, V8 Main Bearing Oil Clearance

PONTIAC

NOTES FOR CRANKSHAFT BEARING JOURNAL —Continued

Bearing No. 1—.0015
Bearings No. 2, No. 3, No. 4—.0018
Bearing No. 5—.0021

Note 5: 1957-63, OHV, V8 Main Bearing Oil Clearance

Bearing No. 1—.0015
Bearings No. 2, No. 3, No. 4, No. 5—.0018

VALVE SPECIFICATIONS

YEAR	Note 3 Seat Angle		Intake Valve Lift Note 1	Exhaust Valve Lift	Valve Spring Pressure Note: 2		Stem to Guide Clearance		Stem Diameter		Are Valve Guides Replaceable
	In	Ex.			Outer	Inner	Inlet	Exhaust	Inlet	Exhaust	
1954											
6 Cyl., "L" Head	30	45	.319	.319	59½@1 29/32	None	.006	.006	.311	.311	Yes
St. 8, "L" Head	30	45	.300	.300	62½@1 23/32	None	.006	.006	.311	.311	Yes
1955											
All Engines	30	45	.327	.327	58 @1 17/32	26@1 31/64	.005	.005	.340	.340	Yes
1956											
V8 OHV, W/A	30	45	.403	.403	58 @1 17/32	26@1 31/64	.005	.005	.340	.340	No
V8 OHV W/M	30	45	.373	.373	58 @1 17/32	26@1 31/64	.005	.005	.340	.340	No
1957											
V8 OHV W/M	30	45	.373	.373	58 @1 17/32	26@1 31/64	.0019	.0024	.340	.340	No
V8 OHV W/A	30	45	.373	.409	59 @1 33/64	33@1 31/64	.0019	.0024	.340	.340	No
1958											
V8 OHV W/M	30	45	.373	.373	60 @1 5/32	26@1 5/32	.0025	.0030	.340	.340	No
V8 OHV W/A	30	45	.407	.411	60 @1 5/32	26@1 5/32	.0025	.0030	.340	.340	No
1959-63 Note 3											
V8 OHV W/M	30	45	.370	.370	60@1 33/64	26@1 31/64	.0025	.0030	.340	.340	No
V8 OHV W/A	30	45	.400	.400	60@1 33/64	26@1 31/64	.0025	.0030	.340	.340	No
420A	30	45	.400	.400	62@1 33/64	32@1 31/64	.0025	.0030	.340	.340	No
420B, 425E, Note 4	30	45	.330	.330	60@1 33/64	26@1 31/64	.0025	.0030	.340	.340	No

Note 1: Camshaft Sprocket Marks

Marks on camshaft and crankshaft sprockets should be aligned nearest each other and with shaft centers.

Note 2: Valve Springs

Intake and exhaust valve springs are the same.

Note that near the center bolt hole of each head is a casting number. Stamped above this number:

Note 3: 1959-60 Identification

The Tempest engines have special camshafts. Shown by a decalcomania on the left valve cover towards the center of the V.

Note 4: 1960-63 The 425E Engine Uses No Inner Valve Springs

x—indicates 3 carburetors.
xx—indicates fuel injection.

Stamped to right of the number an "O" indicates extra heavy valve springs.

W/M—With Manual Transmission.

W/A—With Automatic Transmission.

PISTON AND PIN SPECIFICATIONS

YEAR	PISTON				PISTON PIN		
	SKIRT CLEARANCE		Diameter	Bushing	FIT		Lock
	Min.	Max.			In Rod	In Piston	
1954 6 Cyl.	.0007	.0012	.9372	Yes	.0004-.0006	0-.0002	Ring
1954 Str. 8	.0005	.0010	.9372	Yes	.0004-.0006	0-.0002	Ring
1955 V8	.0007	.0012	.9805	Yes	.0003-.0005	0-.0002	Ring
1956-57 All	.0007	.0017	.9805	Yes	.0001-.0006	0-.0004	Ring
1958-63 All	.0007	.0013	.9802	None	Press	.0003-.0005	Rod Press

PISTON FITTING RIBBON THICKNESS AND SPRING SCALE PULL

Ribbon should be 10 inches long; ½ inch wide; .0015 inch thick; pull of 8 to 15 pounds. Cylinder and piston clean and dry.

PISTON AND ROD ASSEMBLY

1954, All St. 8

Rods are not offset, can be installed either way. Rods and caps should be returned to their original positions.

1954, 6 Cyl. Only

Piston pin is offset in piston. Install piston to connecting rod with "F" on front of piston and notch on top of piston toward front of engine. Oil squirt hole in connecting rod points toward camshaft.

1955-63, All OHV, V8:

Notch in piston head and F mark on side of piston go toward front of engine. (Note that when engine number has an L with a circle around it, the pistons are dished-out.) The large machined boss on lower end of connecting rod goes: to the FRONT on LEFT BANK; to the REAR on RIGHT BANK.

This means that the large machined bosses face each other on the same crank pin. When correctly installed, the oil groove between the rod and cap will be on the left on even numbered rods and on the right on odd numbered rods.

TORQUE SPECIFICATIONS

YEAR	Cylinder Head Bolts	Rod Bearing Bolts	Main Bearing Bolts	Crankshaft Pulley Bolt	Flywheel to Crankshaft Bolt	Manifolds In.	Manifolds Ex.
1954 All Series	50–60	35–45	85–95(A)	95	90–105	30	25
1955-63 All Series	80–95	35–45	85–95(A)	160	90–95	40	30

(A)—Tighten Rear Main to 120

CYLINDER HEAD NUT TIGHTENING SEQUENCE

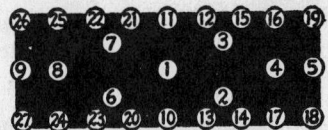

1954, 6 Cyl. Engine "L" Head Tighten to 60 ft. lbs.

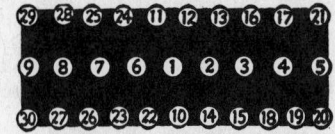

1954, Straight 8 "L" Head Tighten to 60 ft. lbs.

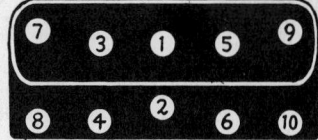

1955-63, OHV V-8 Engine Tighten to 95 ft. lbs.

FRONT WHEEL ALIGNMENT

YEAR	Caster Range (Degrees)	Caster Pref. Setting	Camber Range (Degrees)	Camber Pref. Setting	Toe-In (Inches)	King Pin Inclination (Degrees)	Wheel Piot Ratio Inner Wheel	Wheel Piot Ratio Outer Wheel
1954 All Series	½N–½P	0	0–1P	½P	0–1/16	4½	22	20
1955 All Series	1½N–½N	1N	0–1P	½P	0–1/16	4½	22½	20
1956-57 All Series	1½N–½N	1N	0–1P	½P	0–1/16	4½	22½	20
1958 All Series	1N–0	½N	0–1P	½P	0–1/16	4½	21½	20
1959-63 All Series	2N–1N	1½N	¼N–¾P	¼P	0–1/16	4½	20	18

DISTRIBUTOR

Detailed information on: distributor drive, direction of distributor rotation; cylinder numbering; firing order; point gap; cam dwell; timing mark location; spark plugs, spark advance; ignition resistor location, and idle speed; will be found in this section. Further information on trouble shooting, general tune-up procedures, how to replace ignition wires, how to install points and condensers, how to choose the proper spark plug and how to adjust timing will be found in the Unit Repair Section under the heading: Tune-Up.

REMOVAL OF DISTRIBUTOR

St. 8 and 6 Cyl.

The distributor is on the left side of the block to the rear of the engine.

To remove the distributor, take off the cap and wire assembly, disconnect the ignition primary wire and the vacuum line to the carburetor, remove the one bolt which holds the distributor to the engine and lift the distributor off.

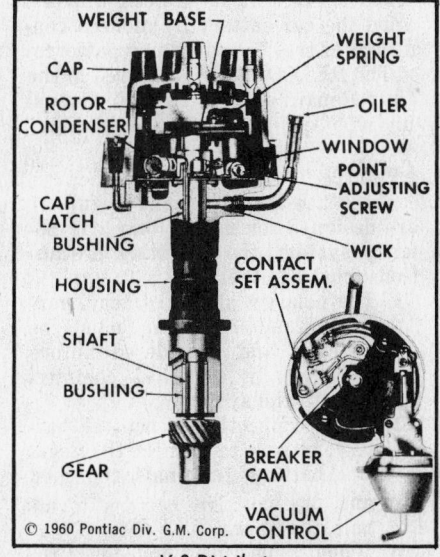

© 1960 Pontiac Div. G.M. Corp.

V-8 Distributor

The distributor shaft is slotted to allow the tongue in the oil pump shaft to drive the distributor. The gear is on the oil pump.

All V8

The distributor is located in the back of the block. To take it off remove the air cleaner and the distributor cap and wire assembly, mark the position of the rotor relative to the distributor body and the body relative to the block for easy replacement. Do not move the engine after taking off the distributor. Detach the vacuum lines and the ignition primary wire from the distributor and remove the bolt which holds the distributor down into the block. The unit can then be lifted up. On the V-8 models the drive gear is located on the bottom of the distributor. When replacing it, it will be necessary to index the groove in the bottom of the distributor shaft with the oil pump drive shaft.

PONTIAC

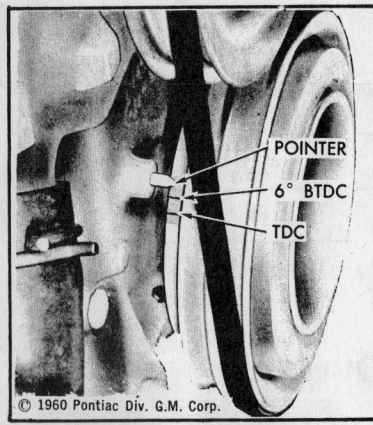

© 1960 Pontiac Div. G.M. Corp.

Ignition timing marks V8 engines

DISTRIBUTOR OPERATION

An external adjustment type distributor is used. The cap has a window for adjusting dwell time (cam angle) with the cap in place.

Adjustment of dwell is made on the car while the engine is operating or while the distributor is being checked on a distributor tester. The centrifugal advance parts have been relocated above the breaker plate and cam. This plan permits the cam and breaker lever to be located closer to the upper bearing for greater stability.

The breaker plate is of one piece construction and rotates on the outer diameter of the upper bearing. The plate is held in position by a retainer clip in the upper shaft bushing. The molded rotor serves as a cover for the centrifugal advance mechanism. The vacuum control unit is mounted under the movable breaker plate to the distributor housing.

The point set has the breaker lever spring tension and point alignment pre-set and is serviced as an assembly. Only the dwell angle requires adjustment after replacement.

Under part throttle operation, manifold vacuum is enough to actuate the vacuum control diaphragm. This causes the movable plate to advance the spark and aid fuel economy. During acceleration or on a heavy pull, the vacuum is insufficient to move the plate. The plate is spring-loaded, thru the vacuum control diaphragm, and remains in the retarded position.

The centrifugal advance is conventional and operates thru two spring-loaded weights.

GENERATOR AND REGULATOR

Detailed facts on the generator and the regulator can be found in the Generator and Regulator Specification Table of this section.

General information on generator and regulator repair and trouble shooting can be found in the Unit Repair section under the heading: Generators and Regulators.

GENERATOR REMOVAL

1954 Models

Detach the wires, then release the belt tension by removing the bolt which holds the tension bar to the generator. Remove the belt from the generator pulley and then let the generator swivel down so that the pivot bolts can be removed. Lift off the generator.

Starting with 1955

The generator is located above the right cylinder head.

Slack off on the belt tension, remove the belt, disconnect the wires from the distributor and remove the two bolts which hold it to its swivel bracket.

GENERATOR POLARITY

Whenever the circuits to the generator, the regulator or the battery have been disconnected it is best to apply the following procedure.

Before the engine is started momentarily short from the "Bat" to the "Gen" terminals of the regulator with a screwdriver. This gives a momentary surge of current from the battery to the generator and so correctly polarizes the generator with respect to the battery.

Failure to so polarize the generator before starting the engine may severely damage the regulator since reversed polarity causes vibration, arcing and burning of the relay points.

DELCOTRON (A.C. Generator)

Beginning with 1962, an alternating current generator is being made available. This unit is the Delco-Remy, "DELCOTRON." The purpose of this unit is to satisfy the increase in electrical loads that have been imposed upon the car battery by modern conditions of traffic and driving patterns.

The DELCOTRON is covered in the Unit Repair section of this manual under "Generators and Regulators."

Caution:

Since the Delcotron and regulator are designed for use on only one polarity system, the following precautions must be observed:

1. The polarity of the battery, generator and regulator must be matched and considered before making any electrical commections in the system.
2. When connecting a booster battery, be sure to connect the negative battery terminals together and the positive battery terminals together.
3. When connecting a charger to the battery, connect the charger positive lead to the battery positive terminal. Connect the charger negative lead to the battery negative terminal.
4. Never operate the Delcotron on open circuit. Be sure that all connections in the circuit are clean and tight.
5. Do not short across or ground any of the terminals on the Delcotron regulator.
6. Do not attempt to polarize the Delcotron.
7. Do not use test lamps of more than 12 volts for checking diode continuity.
8. Avoid long soldering times when replacing diodes or transistors. Prolonged heat is damaging to these units.
9. Disconnect the battery ground terminal when servicing any A.C. system. This will prevent the possibility of accidental reversing of polarity.

BATTERY AND STARTER

Detailed information on the battery and starter will be found in the Battery and Starter Specifications Table of this section.

A more general discussion of batteries will be found in the Unit Repair section under the heading: Tune-up.

A more general discussion of starters and their troubles can be found in the Unit Repair section under the heading: Starters.

STARTER REMOVAL

From underneath the vehicle, disconnect the battery cable, the main feed cable, and the starter control cable.

Remove the bolts which hold the starter to the bell housing and remove the starter with its solenoid assembly attached.

INSTRUMENTS

INSTRUMENT PANEL

1954

Any one instrument is mounted on a plate with one other instrument and it is necessary to take two out in order to remove any one.

They are mounted from the front end toward the back on the plate and the plate in its turn is mounted to the inside of the dash panel.

Starting with 1955

For safety first disconnect the battery. On these models removing the instruments is comparatively easy. Each pair of instruments is held with either two or three screws which are readily accessible from underneath the dash.

In the case of the left side instruments containing the heat indicator unit, it will be necessary to disconnect the sending unit in the engine side and thread it thru the dash towards the inside of the car after the instrument has been disconnected from the dash panel.

The speedometer also can be disconnected readily after the cable and the mounting bolts have been removed.

To remove either the charge indicator or the heat indicator it is merely necessary to disconnect the leads and remove the three attaching nuts from the back of the instrument panel.

REMOVAL OF SPEEDOMETER HEAD

1957 Models

Remove the radio knobs and the radio to trim plate attaching nuts. Take out the heater blower switch from the rear of the instrument panel. Remove the attaching screws and take out the instrument panel trim plate. Take out the nuts which each of the gauge clusters to the bracket underneath the instrument panel. Disconnect the speedometer cable. From the face of the instrument panel, remove two screws, one on each side. which retain the speedometer head to the instrument panel.

Pull the instrument cluster assembly out of the instrument panel. Detach gauge clusters and light sockets from the speedometer head and remove the speedometer head.

1958 Thru 1960

Remove instrument cluster (from below).

1. Disconnect battery.
2. Remove four 7/16" mounting nuts and washers.
3. Disconnect speedometer cable.
4. Push cluster thru instrument panel opening to gain access to wiring.

NOTE: Protect dash panel with cloth or other means to prevent scratching.

5. Begin at the top of cluster and remove bulbs and wiring, (make note of colors).
6. Remove cluster.
7. Remove two 7/16" speedometer retaining nuts.
8. Remove speedometer head.

Replace by reversing the above procedure.

Starting 1961

1. Disconnect Safeguard cable, on cars so equipped, then pull

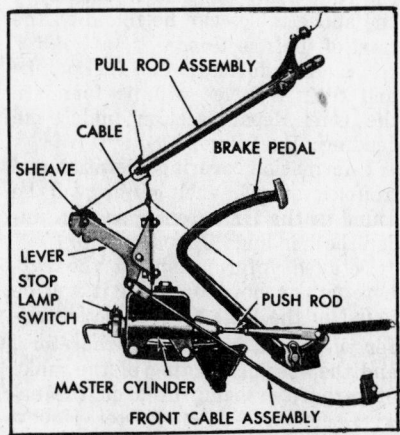

Hand brake mechanism 1955-1956

straight out.

2. Remove speedometer cluster assembly.
3. Remove face plate and lense by unsnapping.
4. Remove three screws at back of cluster.

WINDSHIELD WIPER MOTOR

Starting with 1954

The windshield wiper motor is located on the firewall under the hood.

It can be removed readily from underneath the hood.

The wiper transmission is accessible from underneath the dash panel with no more than the usual difficulties found working under any dash panel.

BRAKE SYSTEM

Specific information on brake cylinder sizes can be found in the General Chassis and Brake Specifications Table of this section.

Information on brake adjustments, band replacement, bleeding procedure, master and wheel cylinder overhaul can be found in the Unit Repair section under the heading: Brakes, Hydraulic.

Information on trouble shooting and overhauling power brakes can be found in the Unit Repair section under the heading: Brakes, Power.

Information on the grease seals which may need replacement can be found in the Unit Repair section. The front wheel grease seals under the head: Suspension, Front Repair. The rear wheel grease seals under the head: Axles, Rear.

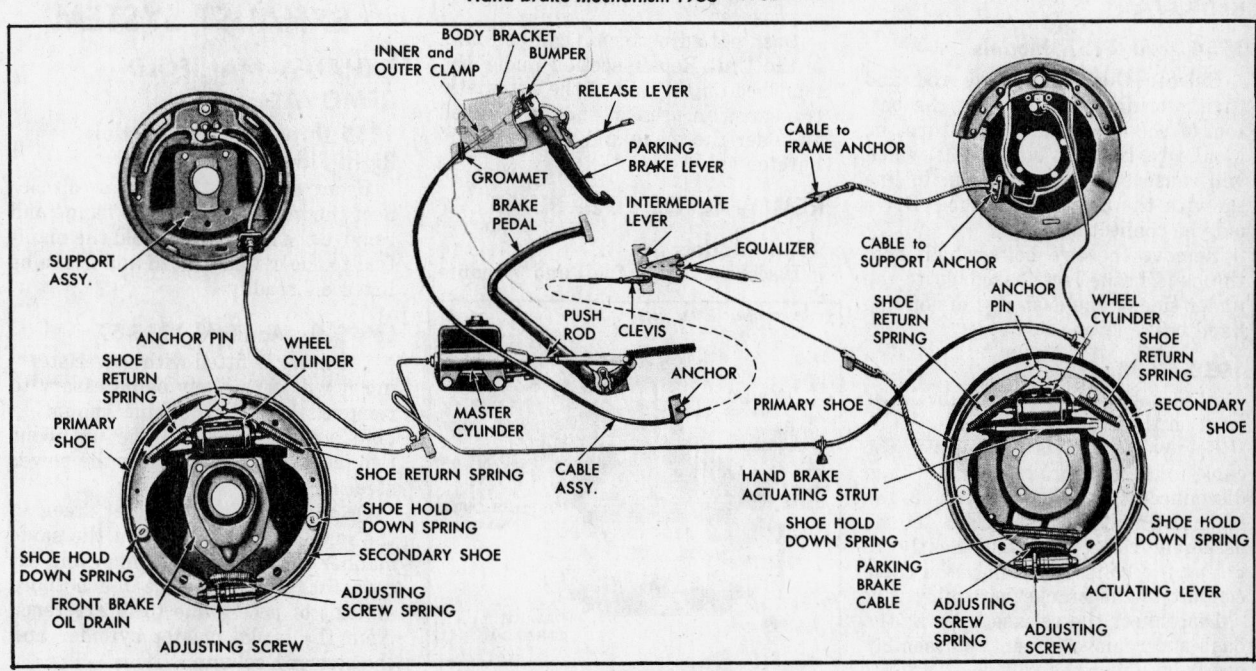

Diagram of complete brake system—1957

PONTIAC

MASTER CYLINDER REMOVAL

1954 thru 1957 Models

The master cylinder is refilled from the engine compartment and is located below and behind the steering column.

From under the car, remove the clevis from the brake pedal to push rod and disconnect the brake lines. Take off the stop light switch wires and remove the bolts which hold the master cylinder to the frame and lift off the master cylinder.

1958-63 Models

The master cylinder is located in the engine compartment just above the steering column.

From under the dash, disconnect the brake pedal from the master cylinder. From under the hood, disconnect the hydraulic line and the stoplight wire.

Remove the bolts which hold the master cylinder to the cowl panel and lift off the master cylinder.

The unit is installed in reverse order of removal.

HAND BRAKE ADJUSTMENT

Expand the shoes on the rear wheel until the wheels can just barely be turned by hand with the hand brake cable disconnected. Now pull all of the slack out of the hand brake clevis so that the clevis pin will just enter. Secure the clevis pin and back off on the star wheel adjuster on each back wheel until the wheels are just free.

PARKING BRAKE LEVER REMOVAL

1954 thru 1957 Models

Release the hand brake rod and then, working way down at the bottom of the hand brake tube, turn the handle to the left somewhat, which will cause the connecting pin to line up with the holes in the tube. Drive out the connecting pin.

Remove the two bolts which hold the hand brake lever assembly to the under side of the dash and lift off the hand brake lever.

1958-63 Models

A foot operated parking brake is used on these models.

Remove the clevis which holds the cable to the foot brake lever and then disconnect the bolts which hold the lever assembly to the bracket. Let the assembly come down sufficiently to get at the bolts which hold the cable conduit to the bracket assembly.

Disconnect the release lever at the dash and remove the entire assembly out from under the vehicle.

HAND BRAKE CABLE

1954 thru 1963 Models

Follow the instructions given for hand or foot lever to disconnect the cable from the end of the brake lever and then carefully thread the cable out over its pulleys and disconnect it at the hand brake end.

It is always an excellent idea to tie a string or cord or something to the cable so that the "route" of the old cable can be followed when replacing it with a new one.

FUEL SYSTEM

A chart covering causes of excess fuel consumption will be found in the Unit Repair section under the heading: Fuel Consumption Chart.

Data on capacity of the gas tank will be found in the Capacities Table. Data on correct engine idle speed and fuel pump pressure will be found in the Tune-up Specifications table. Both the above tables can be found at the start of their sections.

General information on fuel pumps and their troubles will be found in the Unit Repair section under the heading: Fuel Pumps.

Information covering operation and troubles of the fuel gauge will be found in the Unit Repair section under the heading: Gages.

Detailed information on the carburetor and how to adjust it will be found in the Unit Repair section under the broad heading: Carburetors, and the specific heading of the make of carburetor being used on the engine being worked on. Carter, Holley, Rochester and Stromberg carburetors are covered.

Dash pot adjustments can be found in the Unit Repair section under the same heading as that of the automatic transmission used in the car as well as under the make and model of carburetor.

REMOVAL OF FUEL PUMP

1954 Models

Disconnect the fuel and vacuum

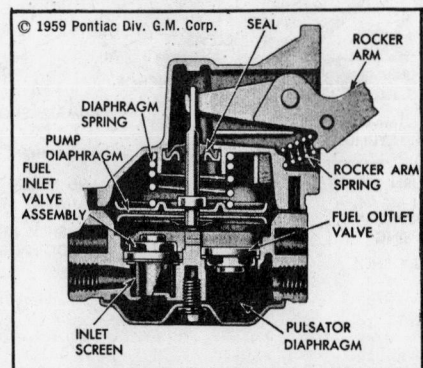

© 1959 Pontiac Div. G.M. Corp.

SEAL

ROCKER ARM

DIAPHRAGM SPRING

PUMP DIAPHRAGM

FUEL INLET VALVE ASSEMBLY

ROCKER ARM SPRING

FUEL OUTLET VALVE

INLET SCREEN

PULSATOR DIAPHRAGM

Fuel Pump Starting 1959

lines from the fuel pump, remove the two mounting bolts and lift the fuel pump off the car.

1955 thru 1957 Models

For convenience, disconnect the battery cables and remove the battery. Disconnect the fuel lines and fittings from the pump and take out the pump body attaching screws. Lower the pump and then remove the vacuum lines from the pipes on the pump.

Starting with 1958

From the left front side of the engine, disconnect the input and output line from the fuel pump and disconnect the vacuum line. Starting 1959 a single type pump is used.

Remove the bolts which hold the fuel pump to the timing case cover and lift off the pump.

On models equipped with power steering it is possible, but somewhat difficult, to reach the mounting bolts with the steering pump in place. It may pay to slack off on the power steering pump, remove its mounting bolts and with it still connected to its lines lift it up out of the way.

REMOVAL OF FUEL TANK

Remove the fuel line from the tank, disconnect the clamp which holds the flexible filler neck to the tank neck on models with flexible connection, place a wooden block on the top of a jack and support the tank and then remove the mounting strap bolts. Lower the tank sufficiently for access to the gauge wire, remove the gauge wire and continue lowering the tank.

EXHAUST SYSTEM

EXHAUST MANIFOLD REMOVAL

1955 thru 1957 V-8 Models
Right Side Manifold

From underneath the car disconnect the manifold from the flange and remove the bolts which hold the manifold to the cylinder head and it can be lifted off readily.

Left Side Manifold 1955-57

If the car is fitted with power steering it will very likely be necessary to remove the front engine mounting bolts and jack the engine up about two inches in order to clear the power steering gear.

On models without power steering the manifold is removed in the same manner as the right side manifold except that the bolts are much more difficult of access due to interference from the brake master cylinder and the steering column.

V8 Starting with 1958—Left Side Manifold

If the car is equipped with power steering, disconnect the power steering pump but leave it attached to its hoses and simply pull it up out of the way.

From underneath the vehicle, disconnect the exhaust crossover pipe flange.

If the car is equipped with power brakes, the rear bolts of the manifold are a little tough to reach but they can be reached with a box wrench.

Remove the bolts which hold the manifold to the left cylinder head and take off the manifold.

V8 Starting with 1958—Right Side Manifold

From underneath the vehicle, disconnect the upper flange from the right manifold. This is the upper flange where the cross manifold and exhaust pipe and right manifold join.

From underneath the vehicle, remove the bolts which hold the manifold to the head on the back two flanges. The front flange can be removed from the top of the car with a box wrench.

INTAKE MANIFOLD REMOVAL

V-8 Models

Remove the air cleaner, the generator, the upper radiator hose, the ignition coil, the heater connection, the temperature indicating sending unit, and on models fitted with power steering disconnect the pump from its mounting on the cylinder head in order to get it out of the way and then remove the lines and rods to the carburetor and take off the carburetor.

Remove the bolts which hold the intake manifold to both cylinder heads and lift off the manifold.

EXHAUST CROSSOVER PIPE

V-8 Models

The flange bolts which holds the exhaust crossover pipe to the manifolds are accessible from underneath the car.

On some 1955 models engine side pars were used, and these sometimes make it difficult to get at the flange bolts from the bottom.

ENGINE

REFERENCES

In the specifications tables of this section there are listed all the available facts about the engines. When different size engines are used a note under the General Engine Specifications Table will give an easy means of determining which engine is which.

Valves

Detailed information on the valves, the type of valve guide and the location of valve timing marks, can be found in the Valve Specifications Table of this section.

A general discussion of valve clearance and a chart showing how to read pressure and vacuum gauges when using them to diagnose engine troubles will be found in the Unit Repair section under the heading: Tune-up-Ignition-Distributors. Under the same head will be found a chart on engine trouble shooting.

Valve tappet clearance for each engine is given in the Tune-up Specifications Table of this section.

Pistons and Pins

Detailed information on pistons and piston pins, together with information on piston, rod and crankshaft relationship for assembly, will be found in the Piston and Pin Specifications Table of this section.

Engine Reassembly

Engine crankcase capacities are listed in the Capacities Table of this section.

Approved torque wrench readings and head bolt tightening sequences are covered in the Torque Specifications Table of this section.

Information on the engine marking code will be found in the Model Year Identification Table of this section.

REMOVAL OF ENGINE ASSEMBLY

The engines on all Pontiac models are removed in practically the same manner. The engine and transmission assembly are removed as a unit. Drain the water, the engine oil and the transmission oil. Remove the hood, battery, air cleaner, radiator core, power steering pump and carburetor. As a safety measure remove the generator and starter. Disconnect oil pressure, heat indicator and vacuum lines. Remove the engine side aprons and crankcase ventilator outlet pipe.

On cars with power steering remove pump drive belt and pump with bracket. Do not disconnect hoses. Locate pump with hoses out of area to prevent damage as engine is lifted.

Disconnect the exhaust pipes from the flanges.

Remove all gear shift linkage from the transmission and disconnect the clutch linkage at the clutch fork.

On models with clutch control countershaft, remove the bracket from the flywheel housing. Split the rear universal joint and slide the driveshaft off the back of the transmission. Place the lifting device on the engine and

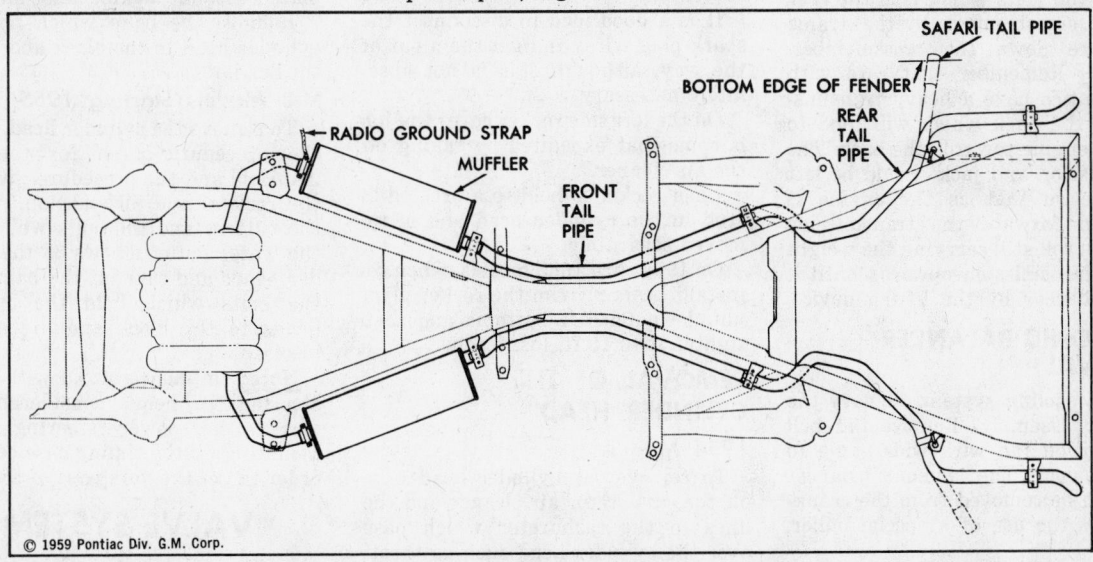

Typical Exhaust System

© 1959 Pontiac Div. G.M. Corp.

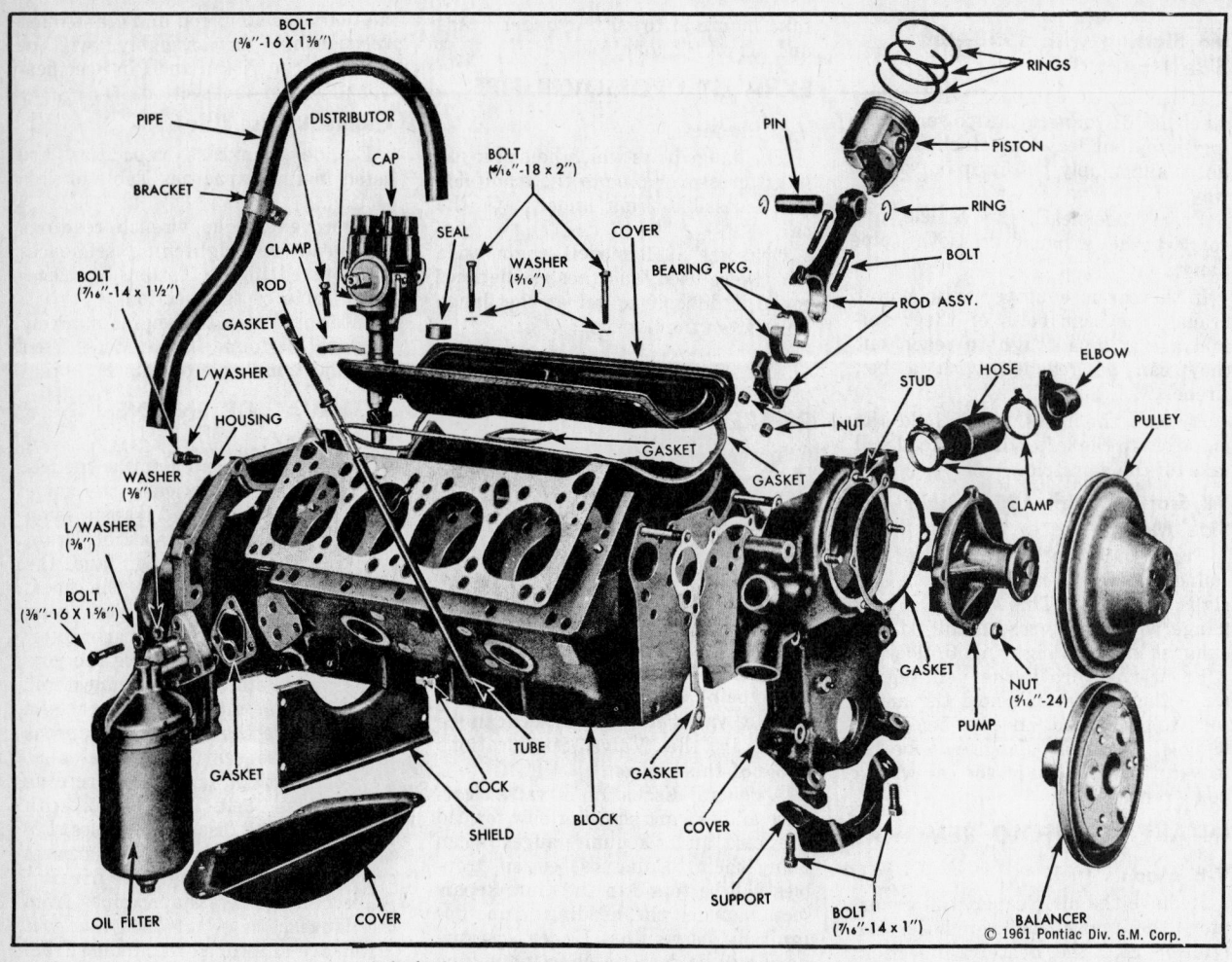

Cylinder block and related parts—typical of all V8 engines,

take a slight load on the lifting device. Remove the screws holding the front and rear insulators to their cross-members. On models with hydramatics, place a jack under the hydramatic, take a load on the jack and remove the bolts which hold the rear support crossmember to the frame and take down the crossmember. **Caution:** Remember that cars with hydramatics have a heavy transmission at the back which will tend to tilt the engine towards the back. The transmission and jack should be left in place so that as the engine is threaded forward the transmission jack will roll still carrying the weight of the transmission upwards until it is lifted clear by the lifting device.

HARMONIC BALANCER REMOVAL

Drain cooling system. Remove the radiator assembly. Remove fan belt and position fan with wide angle to clear balancer. The harmonic balancer can then be removed from the crankshaft by the use of a special puller.

CYLINDER HEAD

REMOVAL OF ROCKER COVERS AND ROCKERS

Remove the four bolts which hold the rocker cover assembly to the cylinder head and lift off the rocker cover.

It is a good idea to disconnect the spark plug wires and get them out of the way, although this is not absolutely necessary.

On the left side rocker cover the job is somewhat expedited by taking off the air cleaner.

Each rocker is held to a pressed-in stud in the cylinder head and is removed separately.

On 1956 thru 1963 models, when reinstalling simply run the rocker pivot nut down until it bottoms and then tighten it to 15 ft. lbs. torque.

REMOVAL OF THE CYLINDER HEAD

1954 Models

To remove the cylinder head take off the carburetor air cleaner and the lines to the carburetor which pass over the cylinder head such as throttle, vacuum and gasoline lines. Dis-

connect the water hose and remove all heater hoses which connect to the cylinder head.

Carefully mark on the head the brackets and braces which are mounted to it so that they can be replaced without making false starts.

Remove the bolts which hold the cylinder head to the block and lift off the head.

V-8 Models Starting 1955

To remove the cylinder head, follow the procedure given for the inlet manifold and the procedure given for the rockers and, in addition, remove the battery and the bolts which hold the water outlet elbows to the cylinder heads and take off the balance of the bolts which hold the cylinder heads to the block and lift off the heads.

Note: On models fitted with power steering it helps considerably to loosen the power steering pump mounting on the timing case cover in order to get the pump out of the way.

VALVE SYSTEM

REMOVAL OF VALVES

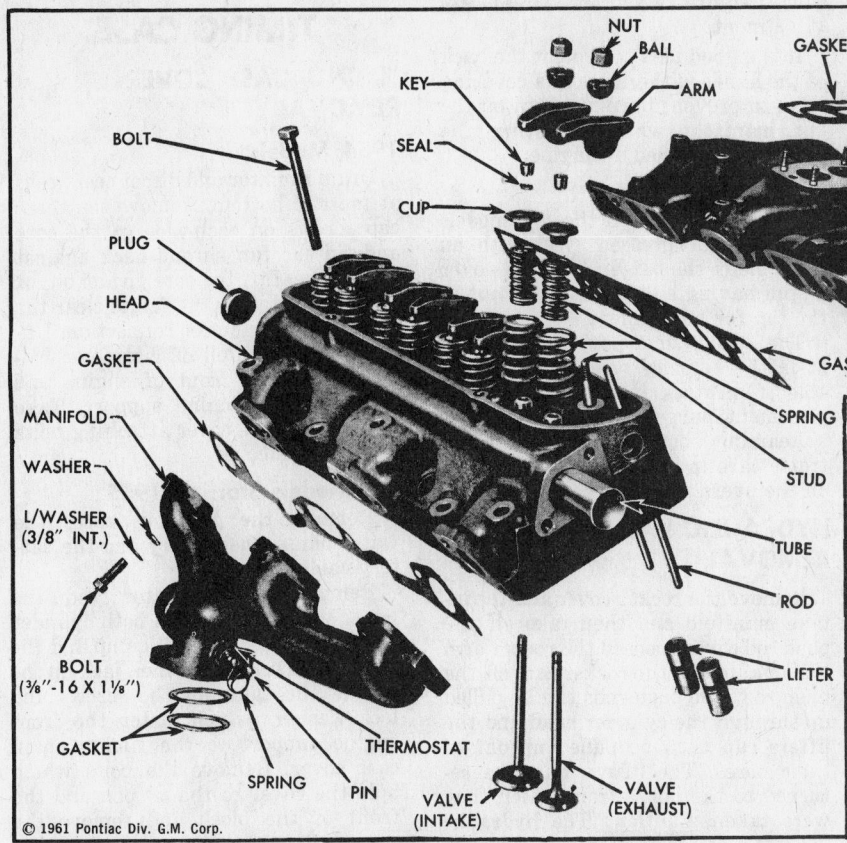

Cylinder head, manifolds and related parts, V8 engines.

1954 Models

Remove the cylinder head and the valve chamber side cover.

With a valve ring compressor, compress the springs on any of the valves which are in the down position and remove the keeper from the bottom of the valve stem.

Release the pressure from the valve spring and pull the valve up through the top of the block.

If the valve tends to bind coming out of the guide, push it back in again and dissolve the gums and tars formed on the bottom of the valve stem and then it will come up readily. Do not attempt to force the valve out of the guide.

V-8 Models Starting 1955

Remove the head from the engine and take it over to a bench. The valve springs can be compressed using a lever type compressor in order to remove the valve keepers. Release the springs and pull out the valves.

VALVE GUIDE REMOVAL

1954 Models

Removable tapered valve guides are used in all engines. The upper end of the guide is slightly larger than the lower end which will permit a closer fit at the bottom of the valve guide, where less clearance is desirable and at the same time provides sufficient clearance at the upper end of the guide to allow for the necessary expansion of the parts, resulting from the heat developed during operation. Pull the guides up to remove them from the engine. The new guides are pressed into place from the top of the engine. The valve guides taper .001 inch and the valves should be installed to give from a free fit to .0006 inch.

Pontiac replacement valve guides have undersize holes and necessitate reaming to secure proper fit of valve stem.

Whenever it is determined to replace valve guides, carefully measure the distance from the top of the cylinder block to the edge of the valve guide before removing the old guide. The measurement should be carefully noted for both intake and exhaust valve guides so a new guide can be inserted exactly the same distance from the top of the block as the old guide.

1955 V-8 Models

Remove the cylinder head to the bench and take out the valves and valve springs. Now carefully measure the distance that the guide protrudes from the head so that the new ones can be driven in to just that distance. The guides should be driven out toward the combustion chamber and the new one driven in from the combustion chamber side of the cylinder head.

The guides are made with a tapered hole with the large end toward the bottom. This allows for expansion of the guide.

V-8 Engines Starting 1956

The guides on these models are cast integral with the head and are not replaceable.

Pontiac supplies valves in .001, .003 and .005 inch oversize, together with special reamers for fitting these valve stems.

VALVE SPRINGS

All Models

In order to check on the condition of the valve springs, lay all of the springs on a flat surface and carefully measure across the top of the intake springs with a straight edge to see that all are the same height. If all are the same height it may safely be assumed that they are all in good condition since it is very unlikely that they will all collapse an equal amount.

If one or more is found to be a different height from the rest of the springs, it is a good idea to get one new spring and carefully measure all of the old springs against the one new one. Those which come up to the same height as the new spring may be considered to be in good condition. Those

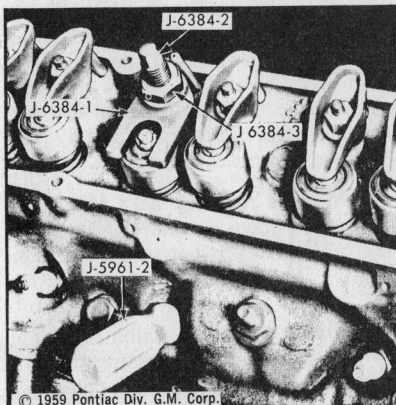

Valve Spring Compressed

which do not should be replaced.

Where regular spring testing equipment is not available, this is generally considered to be a good, safe way to check the condition of the valve springs.

⏱ CHILTON TIME-SAVER

REPLACEMENT OF INTAKE OR EXHAUST VALVE STEM OIL SEAL OR SPRING, WITHOUT REMOVING CYLINDER HEAD

1. Remove rocker arm cover and any other item of interference.
2. Remove the spark plug from the affected cylinder.
3. Remove distributor cap and crank the engine to the firing position of the affected cylinder.
4. Remove the rocker arm, lubricate the rocker arm stud and attach spring compressor to the stud and compress the valve spring.
5. Some type of valve holder must be used thru the spark plug hole.

NOTE: It will require the use of special tools, peculiar to the make of car being serviced. In the case of Pontiac:

Compressor stud ....#J-6384-2
Compressor stud nut ..#J-6348-3
Compressor ....#J-6384-1
Valve Holder ....#J-5961-2

With some study of our transverse engine cross section illustration and a view of the cylinder head and rocker levers with the above tools attached, the resourceful mechanic can improvise in the event of lack of tools.

VALVE ADJUSTMENT

1954 Models

The valves can be reached, with some difficulty, from under the hood. Remove the valve chamber covers and the valves may be adjusted without removing any other unit.

Tappets are of the self-locking type

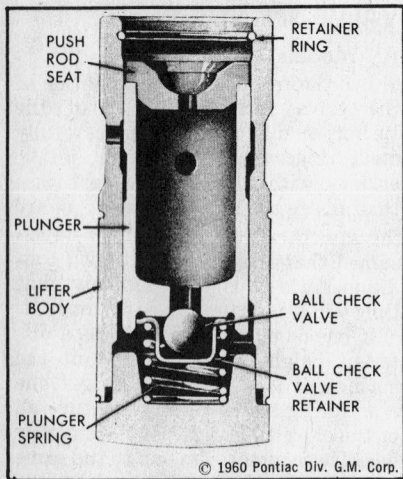

Sectional view of valve lifter

PUSH ROD SEAT
RETAINER RING
PLUNGER
LIFTER BODY
BALL CHECK VALVE
BALL CHECK VALVE RETAINER
PLUNGER SPRING
© 1960 Pontiac Div. G.M. Corp.

which require two wrenches only for adjustment.

It is a good idea to protect the back of the hands with gloves or a covering so as to prevent burning them on the hot manifold when adjusting the valves in a warmed up engine.

V-8 Models

The rocker arm on the V-8 models is formed of pressed steel with an oval hole in the center which fits over a stud having a spherical type nut at the top for adjustment.

The rocker arm post is a pressed fit in the cylinder head and is available from stock in oversizes for replacement purposes.

Reaming should be done with extreme care in order to get a press fit on the oversize stud.

HYDRAULIC VALVE LIFTER REMOVAL

Remove the rocker cover and the intake manifold and then take off the push rod cover. Loosen the rocker arm ball nut and lift the rocker arm off the push rod. The push rods can be pulled up through the cylinder head and the lifters can then be pulled up out of their bores. The lifters must be returned to the bores from which they were taken. **Caution:** The hydraulic lifter is a complete assembly which is match-mated at the factory and the bore of one lifter positively cannot be used in the body of another. These parts should not be mixed. **Note:** The rear-most push rod on the left bank cannot be lifted out on cars equipped with a defroster unit. However, the push rod can be lifted up far enough to permit removal of the hydraulic lifter.

INITIAL ADJUSTMENT OF THE HYDRAULIC LIFTER

1955 V-8 Models

First make certain that the lifter assembly is on the base circle of the cam and that the lifter contains oil and is not completely depressed.

Tighten down on the rocker adjusting nut until there is zero clearance between the rocker and the valve and then turn the adjusting nut one complete turn. This will place the hydraulic lifter in approximately the center of its operating range.

V-8 Models Starting with 1956

Tighten down on the rocker adjusting nut until it bottoms and then tighten it to 15-25 ft. lbs. torque.

There is a shoulder on the mounting stud which is precision machined to give the correct operating position when this operation is performed.

TIMING CASE

TIMING CASE COVER REMOVAL

1954 Models

Drain radiator and disconnect hoses at top and bottom. Remove the three cap screws on each side of the core and tip the fan shroud back against the engine. Lift the core up and out of the shell, rotating the fan to clear the radiator water outlet connection. Unbolt mud pan. Pull off harmonic balancer. Support front of engine and remove front engine support. Take out timing case cover attaching bolts and remove cover.

V-8 Models Starting 1955

Remove the radiator core, the water pump, the battery and the battery cables.

Remove the generator and the water inlet elbows from both cylinder heads. Take off the fuel pump and the vibration damper and then jack up the engine and take out the screws and lock washers which fasten the front engine support to the timing chain case cover. Remove the bolts which hold the cover to the oil pan and the front of the block and remove the cover. **Caution:** When taking the weight of the engine on its own oil pan use extreme care to pad the jack carefully so as not to damage the oil pan.

TIMING CHAIN AND SPROCKET REMOVAL

Remove the radiator core, water pump and the vibration damper. Support the front of the engine with a jack protected by a wooden block and remove the front engine support retaining bolts. Take off the engine support. Take out the oil pan front screws

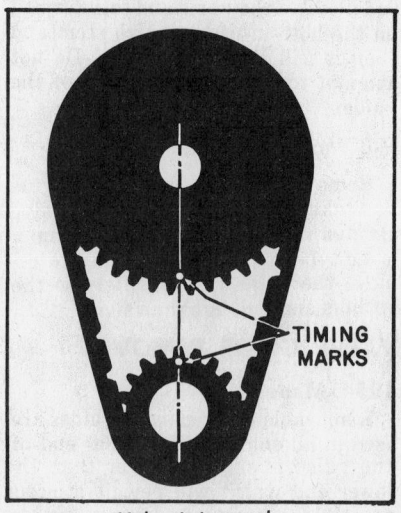

TIMING MARKS

Valve timing marks

and remove the timing cover bar. Now unbolt and remove the timing case cover.

Turn the crank and camshaft (if the chain is broken) until the two timing marks are in line between the shaft centers. Now remove the nut from the front of the camshaft sprocket.

Using a puller, pull the sprocket off the front of the camshaft.

Arrange the new chain on the sprocket and set the sprocket up over the camshaft by looping the chain over the crank sprocket so that when the cam sprocket engages its key the timing marks are nearest each other and in line between the shaft centers. Secure the camshaft sprocket in this position.

When reassembling the timing case cover extra care should be taken to insure that the oil seal between the bottom of the timing case cover and the front of the oil pan is still a good one. Plenty of gasket cement should be used at this point to prevent oil leaks.

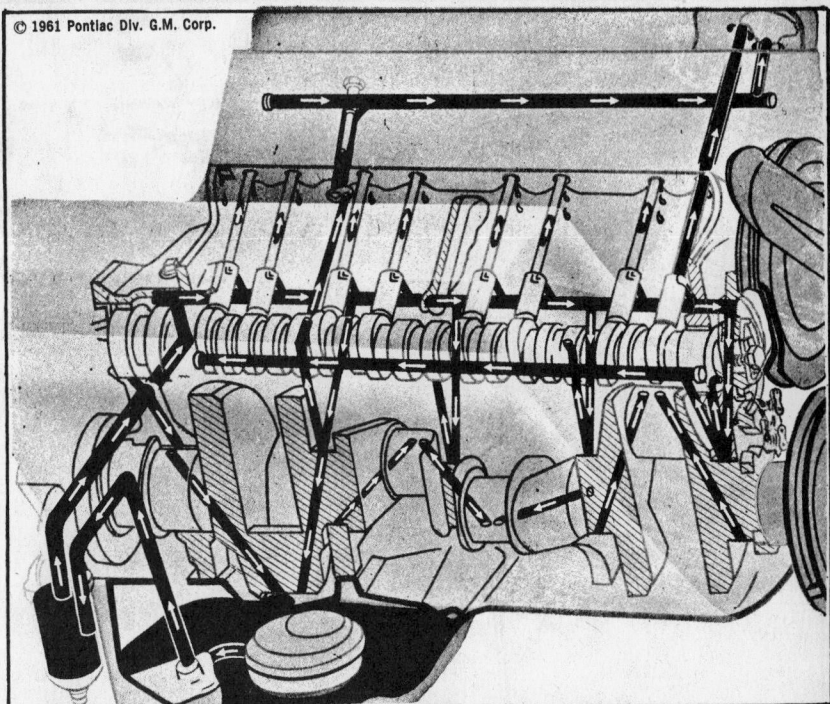

© 1961 Pontiac Div. G.M. Corp.

Engine Lubrication

ENGINE LUBRICATION
OIL PAN REMOVAL
1954 Models

Drain the oil. On the eight cylinder engine it is necessary to remove the front cross member to the radiator support aprons, which will give access to mounting screws at the front end of the pan. The right and left sheet metal aprons may be lifted out in a circular movement, right to right, and left to left, from inside engine compartment, after attaching screws are all removed.

V-8 Models Starting 1955

Remove both engine side aprons and take off the steering idler lever bracket and lower the steering linkage. Disconnect the exhaust crossover pipe from both manifolds. This may require some jockeying to get it down after it is unbolted. Remove the flywheel housing front shield and the lower cover screws and remove cover. Loosen ventilator brace. Remove the oil pan screws and remove pan.

1960 Models
Remove:

1. Remove the engine fan.
2. Drain cooling system and remove radiator hoses.
3. Raise front of car and place on stands.
4. Drain engine oil.
5. Disconnect exhaust crossover pipe at the left exhaust manifold and at the right exhaust manifold connections.
6. Remove crossover pipe.
7. Disconnect exhaust pipe from the right hand exhaust manifold.
8. If equipped with dual exhausts, disconnect both exhaust pipes from exhaust manifolds.
9. Remove the flywheel housing front shield by removing two screws into the flywheel housing and two screws into the rear of the oil pan.
10. Remove the flywheel housing lower cover screws and remove the cover.
11. On synchro-mesh transmissions, disconnect the clutch linkage.
12. Disconnect steering idler arm from frame.
13. Remove front engine mount-to-frame bolts and loosen rear engine mount-to-frame nuts.
14. Disconnect oil cooler lines at the timing case cover.
15. Loosen transmission filler tube bracket on Hydra-Matic models to allow clearance between oil tube and the floor pan.

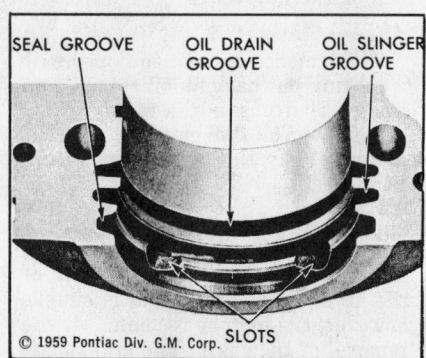

SEAL GROOVE   OIL DRAIN GROOVE   OIL SLINGER GROOVE

© 1959 Pontiac Div. G.M. Corp.   SLOTS

Rear Main Bearing Cap

16. With a well padded jack, under the crankshaft pulley, raise the front of the engine sufficiently to allow the engine oil pan to clear the rear upper edge of the engine support cross member. At this height the jack may be removed by supporting the front of the engine with two stands placed at the right and left hand front corners of the crankcase.
17. Remove the oil pan screws and the oil pan.
18. Clean the pan and remove all traces of gasket from every mating surface.
19. Apply oil resistant gasket cement to rear main bearing cap groove and secure a new gasket.
20. Apply gasket cement to the oil pan and position new gasket, (make sure the front gasket overlaps the side gaskets.

Replace:

Reverse above procedure and refill crankcase to prescribed capacity.

Beginning 1961

1. Remove hood and air cleaner.
2. Drain oil pan and radiator.
3. Disconnect battery.
4. Disconnect radiator hose.
5. Remove fan guard and upper radiator support.
6. Remove coil mounting bolts to suspend coil out of way.
7. Remove exhaust pipe and crossover pipe bolts from manifolds.
8. Remove idler arm mounting bolts and lower arm and tie rods.
9. Remove front engine mount bolts.
10. Remove starter mounting bolts

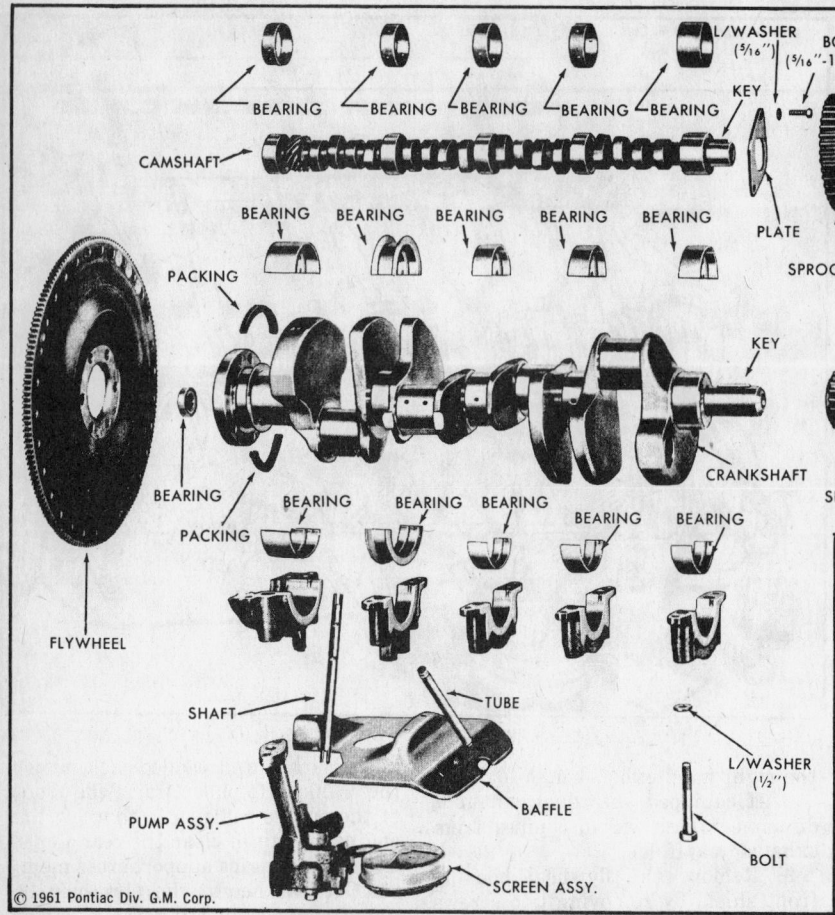

© 1961 Pontiac Div. G.M. Corp.

Camshaft, crankshaft and related parts, V8 engine.

and lower starter.

11. Remove lower clutch housing cover.
12. Remove oil pan bolts.
13. Support front of engine by chain hoist, hooking under front of intake manifold and raise as far as possible.
14. Lower oil pan as far as possible.
15. Remove front main bearing cap.
16. Turn crank shaft until No. 1 throw is up.
17. Hold crossover pipe and tie rod down and clear oil pan.

Replace: After cleaning and installing new gaskets, reverse the above.

OIL FILTER

Beginning with 1960 Models

All engines have full-flow disposable type filters. No tools are required to change it.

REAR MAIN BEARING OIL SEAL

1954—6 Cylinders

Two annular grooves are machined in the block and cap just behind the rear main bearing on the six cylinder engines. A formed asbestos oil seal packing is assembled in the rear groove. Oil escaping from the rear

bearing is first thrown off the crankshaft oil throw ridge into the first groove which is constructed to drain the oil back into the crankcase. The formed asbestos packing is compressed in the rear groove of the block and bearing cap. Any stray drops of oil which pass the first groove are stopped by the asbestos oil seal.

Note: On 1954 models one end of the groove in the bearing cap is recessed to prevent the packing turning with the crankshaft. When installing new packing be sure one end of seal is packed into the recess at the end of the groove.

1954—Straight 8

These models are not equipped with a packing but have an oil return pipe. The oil that passes the main bearing contacts the oil slinger and is returned to the oil pan through the oil return line.

All V-8 Models

A wick packing is used to seal the rear main bearing. Replacement of the lower half of this seal is simple, however, the factory recommends the removal of the engine and crankshaft to replace the upper half. An alterna-

tive factory method is to remove the oil pan and transmission, loosen all of the main bearing caps and lower the crankshaft about 3/8″. This will allow the removal of the old upper half rear bearing seal and the installation of a new one.

ⓤ CHILTON TIME-SAVER

TOP HALF, REAR MAIN BEARING OIL SEAL REPLACEMENT

The following method has proven a distinct advantage in most cases and, if successful, saves many hours of labor.

1. Drain engine oil and remove oil pan.
2. Remove rear main bearing cap.
3. With a 6″ length of 3/16″ brazing rod, drive up on either exposed end of the top half oil seal. When the opposite end of the seal starts to protrude, have a helper grasp it with pliers and pull gently while the driven end is being tapped. It is surprising how easily most of these seals can be removed by this method.

TO INSTALL THE NEW WOVEN FABRIC TYPE SEAL:

1. Obtain a 12″ piece of copper wire (about the same gauge as that used in the strands of an insulated battery cable).
2. Thread one strand of this wire thru the new seal, about 1/2″ from the end, bend back and make secure.
3. Thoroughly saturate the new seal with engine oil.
4. Push the copper wire up thru the oil seal groove until it comes down on the opposite side of the bearing.
5. Pull (with pliers) on the protruding copper wire while the crankshaft is being turned and the new seal is slowly fed into place.

CAUTION: This snaking operation slightly reduces the diameter of the new seal and care will have to be used to keep the seal from slipping too far thru the top half of the bearing.

6. When an equal amount of seal is extending from each side, cut off the copper wire close to the seal and tamp both ends of the seal up into the groove (this will tend to expand the seal again).

NOTE: Don't worry about the copper wire left in the groove, it is too soft to cause damage.

7. Replace the seal in the cap in the usual way and replace the oil pan.

PISTON AND ROD ASSEMBLIES

1954 Straight Eights

All models employ tin-plated pistons of chrome nickel alloy iron, having two tin-plated compression rings above the wrist pin and an oil control ring in the skirt. Wrist pins, are locked in piston boss at one end; the opposite end is slotted to permit it to move in its piston boss allowing for expansion and contraction.

Connecting rods are of the I-beam type, rifle drilled for pressure oiling to the wrist pins.

1954 6 Cylinder

Cam ground aluminum pistons having two steel struts are used on these models. The pistons are tin plated and all three of the rings are located above the wrist pin.

All V-8 Models

Slipper skirt tin plated aluminum pistons having steel struts are used.

All three rings are located above the wrist pin. The letter "F" and the depression in the edge of the piston goes to the front of the engine in all cases.

REMOVAL OF ROD AND PISTON ASSEMBLIES

Remove the head and oil pan and, selecting pistons which are in the down position, cut the cylinder ring ridge from the top of the cylinder using a good ring ridge reamer.

If no reamer is available, the ridge can be taken off with a good sharp bearing scraper.

From underneath the car, mark the connecting rod cap and the rod itself on the camshaft side so that they can be replaced in the same cylinder and in the same position that they occupied before they were removed. Remove the bolts and push the piston assemblies up out of the top of the block. Immediately replace the rod bearing cap back on the rod so that

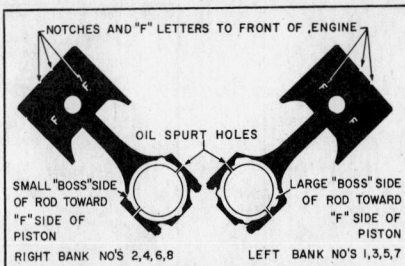

NOTCHES AND "F" LETTERS TO FRONT OF ENGINE

OIL SPURT HOLES

SMALL "BOSS" SIDE OF ROD TOWARD "F" SIDE OF PISTON

LARGE "BOSS" SIDE OF ROD TOWARD "F" SIDE OF PISTON

RIGHT BANK NO'S 2,4,6,8   LEFT BANK NO'S 1,3,5,7

Correct assembly of rod to piston

the bearing shells do not get lost or the threads in the rod get damaged.

FRONT SUSPENSION

REFERENCES

General instructions covering the front suspension and how to repair and adjust it, together with information on installation of front wheel bearings and grease seals, are given in the Unit Repair section under the heading: Suspension, Front Repair.

Definitions of the points of steering geometry are covered in the Unit Repair section under the heading: Suspension, Front Align. This article also covers trouble shooting front end geometry and irregular tire wear.

Figures covering the caster, camber, toe-in, king pin inclination, and turning radius can be found in the Front Wheel Alignment Table of this section.

Overall length and tire size figures can be found in the General Chassis and Brake Specifications Table of this section.

STEERING WHEEL AND HORN BUTTON
HORN BUTTON RENEW

Standard Horn Buttons or Ornament

Press down on one side of the horn

J-3044

© 1959 Pontiac Div. G.M. Corp.

Remove steering wheel

button and pry up on the other side. It will pry right out of the steering wheel.

Horn Blowing Rings

Turn the ring counterclockwise and it will lift off the steering wheel. Some are held by a plate which is visible when ornament has been removed. Two nuts hold the plate.

REMOVAL OF STEERING WHEEL

Remove the horn button as outlined above and take off the nut and lock washer, horn ring and horn insulator from under the horn button.

Use a puller to remove the steering wheel so as not to damage the hub.

MANUAL STEERING GEAR

REFERENCES

Instructions covering the overhaul of the steering gear will be found in the Unit Repair section under the heading: Steering, Manual.

REMOVAL OF MANUAL STEERING GEAR ASSEMBLY FROM VEHICLE

1954-57 Models

On cars equipped with power brakes, remove the power brake unit.

Remove the steering wheel, the left engine side pan and the pitman arm. Disconnect all wires under the dash which run into the steering column.

Roll back the floor mat and remove the cover plates where the gear passes thru the flooring. Disconnect the horn and neutral safety switch wire. Remove the gear shift lever.

Disconnect the gear shift and selector rods at the bottom of the steering column. Remove the bolts which hold the steering column to the bracket on the instrument panel and then remove the bolts which hold the steering gear housing to the frame. The gear is then brought down thru the floor board, over the steerage linkage towards the right front wheel.

1958-60 Models

1. Remove steering wheel.
2. Disconnect directional signal harness at connector under panel and remove lever.
3. Remove lower column finish plate, roll back floor mat and remove felt.
4. Remove horn wire and neutralizer switch wire.
5. Remove shift lever and disconnect rods from column.
6. Remove splash apron, floor pan cover and turn signal wires.
7. Remove pitman arm.

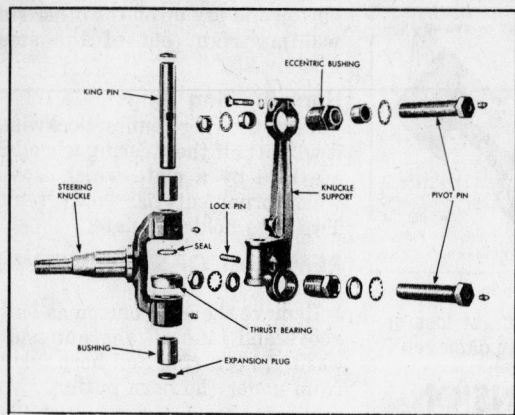

1954-1957

Steering Knuckle and Related Parts

Starting 1958

8. Remove upper steering column bracket.
9. Remove three gear mounting bolts. Be sure to note shims and reinstall in the same position as removed.

Replace: Reverse the above procedure.

1961-63 Models

1. Disconnect pitman arm.
2. Scribe position of steering shaft on worm shaft flange and disconnect lower flange from shaft.
3. Remove three gear to frame bolts and lift out gear.

Replace:

1. Align scribe marks at shaft and flange.
2. Position gear assembly. Install three gear to frame bolts and tighten to 80-90 ft. lb.
3. Install pitman arm. Tighten nut to 100-125 ft. lbs.
4. Install two flange nuts and lock washers and tighten to 10-20 lbs.

Note: In connecting and aligning shaft and jacket avoid metal to metal contacts to avoid noise transmission to driver.

REPLACEMENT OF PITMAN

SHAFT SEALS WITH STEERING GEAR IN PLACE IN CAR

Disconnect pitman arm from pitman shaft. Clean end of pitman shaft and housing. Tape the splines of the pitman shaft to keep them from cutting the seal. Use only one layer of tape. Too much tape will prevent passage of the seal. Using lock ring pliers remove the seal retaining ring.

Start the engine and turn the steering wheel to the right so that the oil pressure in the housing will force the seals out. Catch the seal and the oil in a container. Turn off the engine when the two seals are out.

This method of seal removal eliminates the possible scoring of the seal seats while attempting to pry them out.

Inspect the two old seals for damage to the rubber covering on the outside diameter. If it seems scored or scratched inspect the housing for burrs, etc. and remove them before installing the new seals.

Lubricate the two new seals with petroleum jelly. Put the one with a single lip in first, then put in a washer, drive seal in far enough to permit installation of double lip seal, washer and the seal retaining ring.

The first seal is not supposed to bottom in its counterbore.

Fill reservoir to proper level, start engine, turn wheel to right and check for leaks.

Remove the tape and reinstall the pitman arm. Tighten nut to 90-110 ft. lbs.

POWER STEERING GEAR

REFERENCES

Trouble shooting and repair instructions covering power steering gears are given in the Unit Repair section under the heading: Steering, Power.

POWER STEERING PUMP REMOVAL

Disconnect and cover the two hoses at the back of the pump. Remove the bolt from the tensioner bracket and take off the drive belt.

Tilt the pump in towards the engine and remove the bolts which hold its bracket to the cylinder head.

REMOVAL OF POWER GEAR ASSEMBLY
Thru 1956 Models

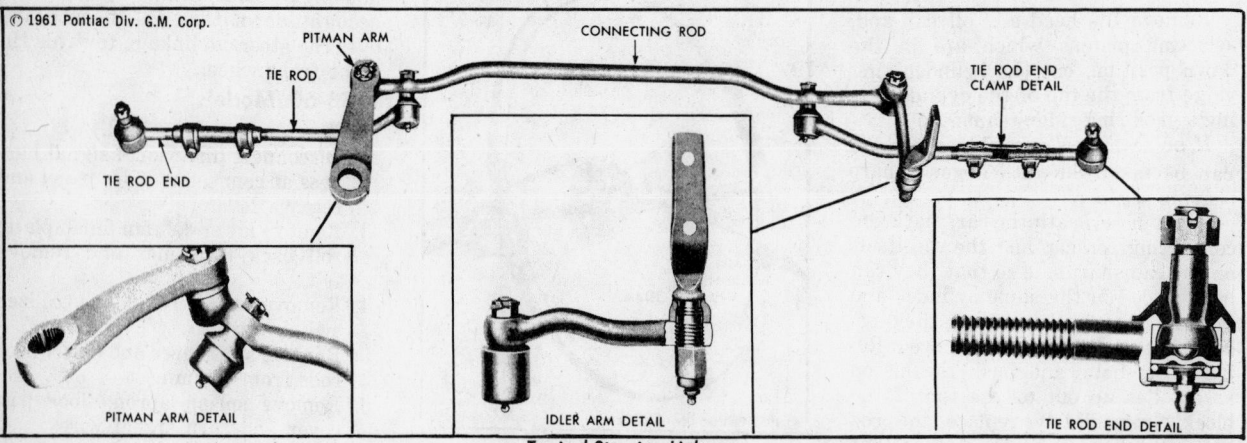

Typical Steering Linkage.

Note: If equipped with power brakes remove power brake unit.

1. Using load positioning tool J-5571, hold front end in five passenger load position.
2. Remove steering wheel.
3. Remove gear shift and turn signal livers.
4. Remove column bracket.
5. Slide rubber grommet up column, roll back carpet and remove pedal plates.
6. Remove back up and neutralizer switches.
7. Disconnect shift and selector rods, and directional signal wires.
8. Disconnect power steering oil lines at gear and tie ends high to prevent draining pump. Cover holes in gear to keep out dirt.
9. Raise car on hoist.
10. Remove starter.
11. Remove pitman arm.
12. Remove left tie rod end and lower linkage.
13. Remove left engine side pan.
14. Remove brake pedal hairpin spring retainer, slide pedal to right.
15. Remove steering gear attaching bolts (the front upper one last), and lower assembly. Be sure to note shims for proper reinstalling.

Replace: Reverse the above procedure.

1957 Thru 1963

1. Scribe alignment mark on shaft and worm shaft flange and remove two nuts and washers.
2. Disconnect oil lines from valve body.
3. Remove pitman arm.
4. Remove gear to frame bolts and lift out gear.

Replace: Reverse above procedure. When installing mounting bolts, tighten finger tight only until proper alignment is obtained.

CLUTCH ASSEMBLY

CLUTCH PEDAL FREE PLAY ADJUSTMENT

On all models the clutch pedal free play adjustment should be between $7/8$ inch to $1\frac{1}{4}$ inch measured at pedal pad.

CLUTCH REMOVAL

Remove transmission being sure that its weight is not allowed to rest on the hub of the clutch disc.

On all models, unhook the clutch pedal, pull back spring, and take out

the clutch fork ball support, the clutch fork and the clutch throwout bearing. Be sure and mark the flywheel and clutch cover so that the assembly can be made in the same relative position in order to preserve the clutch balance. A little at a time, loosen bolts holding clutch to flywheel and remove clutch.

STANDARD TRANSMISSIONS

TRANSMISSION INFORMATION

Transmission refill capacities will be found in the Capacities Table of this section.

Trouble shooting and repair of overdrive units are covered in the Unit Repair section under the heading: Transmission-Overdrive.

4 SPEED TRANSMISSION

Starting with 1962 a four speed synchromesh is optional. It has syncronizing clutches for all forward gears. Gear engagement is thus possible in any forward range while in

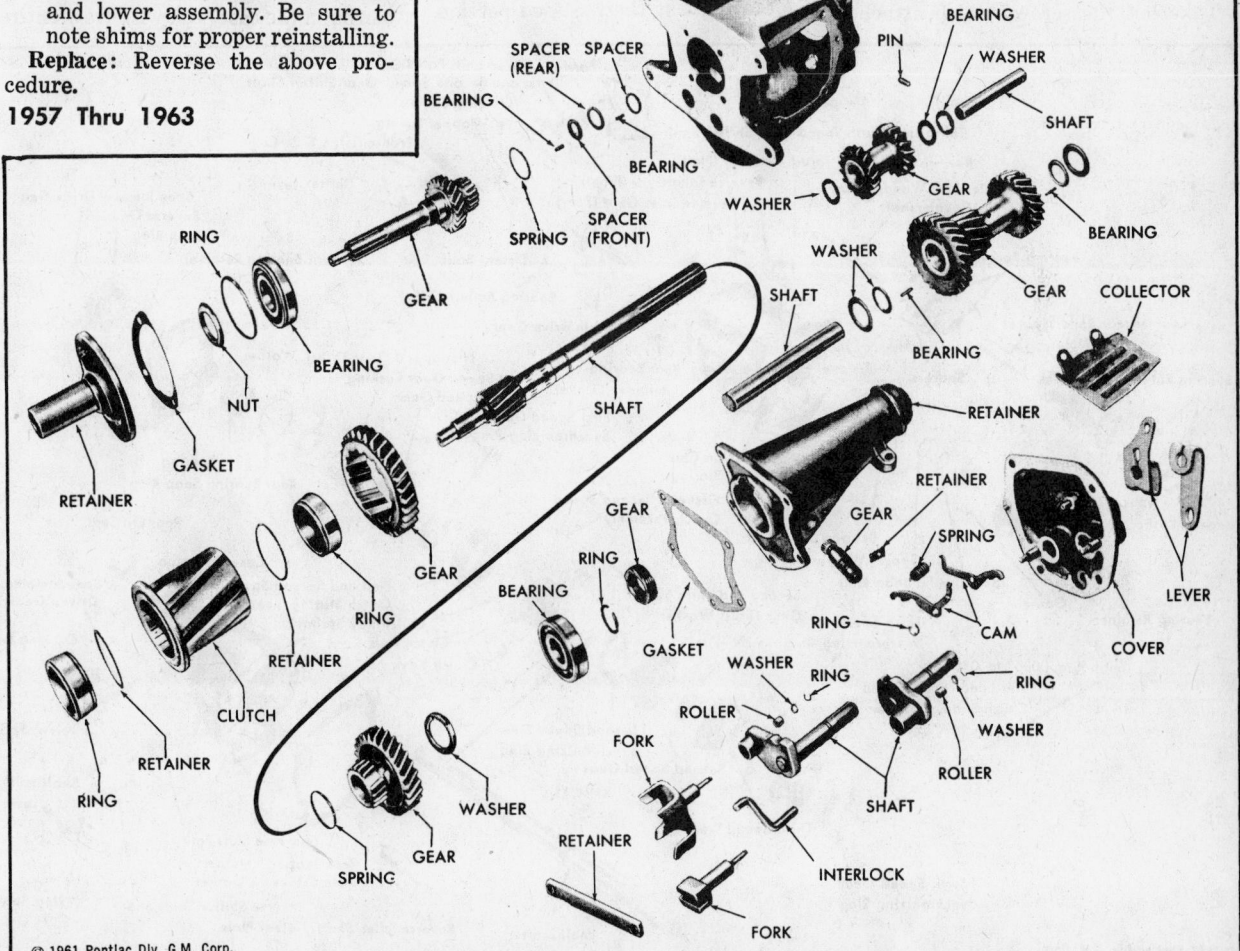

Exploded view of 3-speed synchromesh transmission.

© 1961 Pontiac Div. G.M. Corp.

motion.

Removal and repairs are similar to that of the three speed syncromesh.

TRANSMISSION ASSEMBLY REMOVAL FROM THE VEHICLE

Disconnect the speedometer cable, the gear shift selector rod and the control rod. Split the rear universal joint and (on 1958-61 models with three universal joints split the rear joint, remove the center bearing support bolts and slide the shaft and joints off the end of the transmission) slide the front universal joint off the back of the transmission shaft. To gain access to the upper cap screws remove the transmission shift lever spring yoke and its extension.

To give clearance to the lower cap screws remove the transmission outer selector lever. Now take out the upper cap screws and in their place install two long transmission guide pins. Remove the lower cap screws and move the transmission towards the rear, bringing the rear bearing retainer into the intersection of the frame X member (on models with X members) until the main drive gear is free, then lower the front of it to the floor.

Take out the screws which attach shifter shaft lever to the selector shaft, and remove lever, the spring tension, the spring yoke and its springs. Lift case cover and speedometer drive gear, the sleeve and shaft assembly.

Shift transmission into high gear position to prevent the sliding sleeve and the first and reverse gear from dropping into the case. Remove rear bearing retainer screws and withdraw rear bearing retainer, main shaft and second speed gear as a unit out through the rear of the case.

Take out the shifter fork lock screws. Shift the selector shaft to neutral and remove the shifter lever lock screws. Then slide the shaft out through the rear of the case, being careful not to lose the poppet bolts and springs. Lift out the sliding sleeve and the low and reverse sliding gear.

SYNCHROMESH TRANSMISSION
Disassembly

Loosen the clamping screw which fasten the selector shaft lever and remove lever. This is necessary to allow the transmission selector inner lever to disengage the recess in the selector shaft as the shaft is removed from the case. To prevent the recessed portion of the selector shaft from damaging the oil seal which is pressed into the left side of the case, the shaft must be removed from the right side of the case and installed from the left side.

To remove the selector shaft, drive it from the left side of case, which will knock out the welsh plug from right side of case. When reinstalling, use a new welsh plug. Also, when re-installing the inner selector shaft, check the order of assembling the oil seal and washers. The leather oil seal is pressed into left side of case with the lip of the seal toward the inside of the case.

Drive countershaft to rear until it just clears the hole in front of the case. Then, with a dummy shaft which is exactly the same length as the cluster gear and thrust washers, drive out the regular countershaft, leaving dummy shaft in place so as to prevent losing the needle rollers at each end of the cluster. The cluster gear is allowed to lie in the bottom of the case until after the main drive gear has been removed.

To remove the main drive gear assembly, take out the snap ring which retains the front bearing and tap the main drive gear, with the bearing, through the case, and withdraw entire

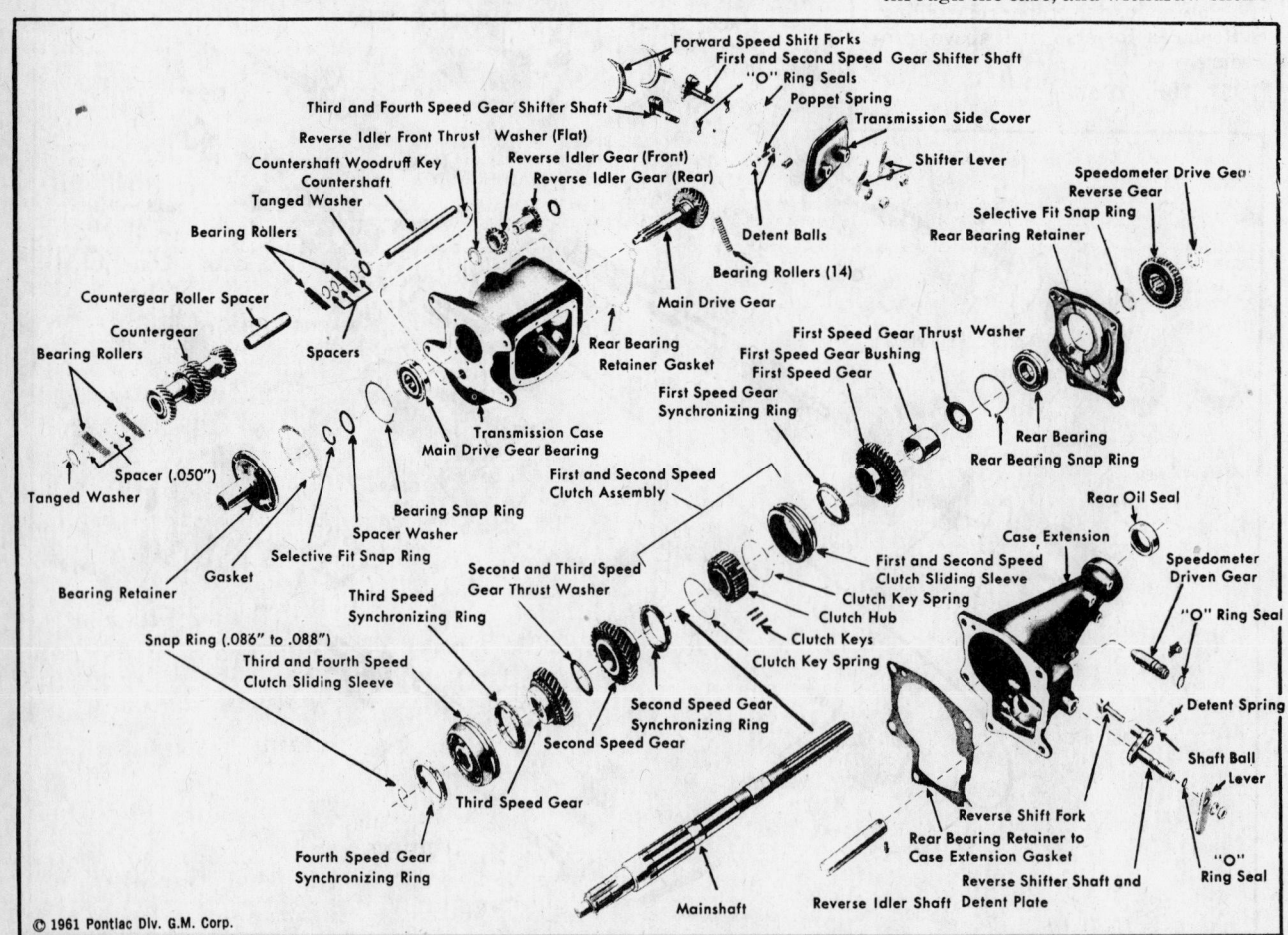

Four Speed Transmission—Exploded View

assembly.

To take out the reverse idler gear, drive the retaining pin through the shaft into the inside of the transmission and remove the shaft and gear. Then to disassemble the second speed gear, expand the wire retainer and slide the drum off the end of the shaft, leaving the retainer in the drum. Take off the mainshaft snap ring and thrust washer from in front of gear and slide off front end of shaft.

To disassemble the main drive gear, expand the wire retainer and remove the synchronizing drum. Remove the front bearing retainer snap ring and spring washer. Take out the bearing by bumping the shaft on a block of wood.

Reassembly

To reassemble the main drive gear bearing, make sure that the shielded side is placed "toward" the gear.

Press the bearing firmly in place, using a tube placed over the gear shaft and pressing on the "inner" race of the bearing. Make sure that the high and second speed clutch slides freely on mainshaft. The synchronizing drum must be smooth and free from scores. They must also show the heaviest contact on the large diameters for best results when synchronizing. Make sure that the oil grooves are cleaned and free of dirt. To reassemble the countergear, insert the dummy shaft in place of regular countershaft and insert "25" (twenty-five) needle rollers at each end of the gear, after using a liberal supply of vaseline

or lubriplate to hold them in position. Coat the bearing retainers and thrust washers with lubricant and position them at each end of cluster. Then lay the countershaft assembly in the bottom of case until the main drive gear is installed.

When this has been done, position the cluster gear assembly and install the countershaft from the rear of case, pushing the dummy shaft out through the front. Align the slots in the case and the shaft and insert the lock ball before driving the countershaft to its final position.

Note: When installing the idler shaft pin, its outer end should be ¾ inch from the outside of case.

ADJUSTMENT OF GEAR SHIFT

Between the shoulder of control shaft upper bearing and top of the support a clearance of ⅛ inch should be had so there will be no interference at this point when selecting gears.

To adjust clearance remove pivot pin and shift lever from upper bearing, now screwing the bearing out ½ turn will increase clearance 1/32 inch.

The distance between the shaft lever and steering wheel should be 2¾ inch plus or minus ⅛ inch. To adjust, back off the adjusting bolt that fastens selector contact and levers together. Holding selector rod in its rearmost position (second and high), and set shift lever to desired position. Secure bolt and recheck lever position.

PONTIAC

AUTOMATIC TRANSMISSION
QUICK SERVICE INFORMATION

When automatic transmission trouble is reported, a road test and careful diagnosis is in order. "Transmission Remove and Replace" and "Linkage Adjustments" are covered here in the following paragraphs. For "Test Procedures", "Transmission Overhaul" and other detailed information, see "Unit Repair Section", "Transmission Group" of this manual.

Note that starting with 1959 production, cars equipped with Hydra-Matic cannot be started by pushing as the use of a Rear Pump has been discontinued.

GENERAL INFORMATION APPLICABLE TO DUAL-RANGE MODELS ONLY

MANUAL LINKAGE ADJUSTMENT

Disconnect the rod running from the thicker (the inner) of the two levers on the left side of the transmission to the lower shift lever on the steering column.

Set the hand lever in Neutral (N) position.

Move the thickest lever on the transmission as far forward as possible. (This will be Neutral position.)

Adjust the length of the rod which was disconnected from the lower shift lever, and reconnect it to the lever; so that the lever on the transmission and the hand lever have not and are not moved. Check that the hand lever can be moved freely from Neutral to Drive 4 and back and that the pointer indicates correctly.

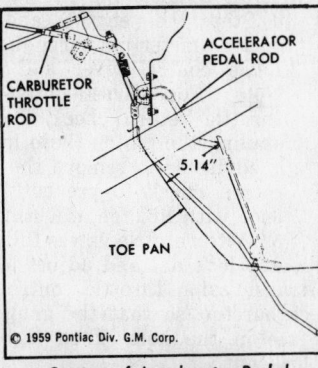
Setting of Accelerator Pedal

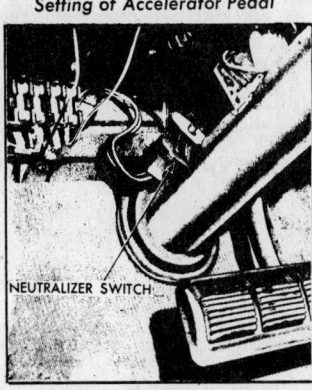
Neutral Starter Switch

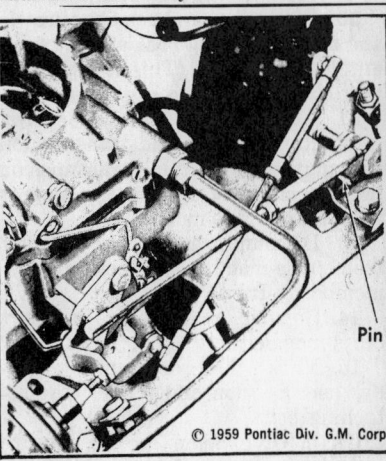
Linkage Pin Installed

Throttle Control Linkage

559

THROTTLE VALVE LINKAGE ADJUSTMENT DUAL-RANGE MODELS

The theory of this adjustment is to arrange things so that the throttle valve in the carburetor is at the hot idle position when the lever on the transmission is all the way back against its stop. It sometimes happens that the lever gets bent while the transmission is being worked on.

Gauges are available which will permit rebending the lever to its proper position.

Measurements are made with the connecting throttle rod removed and the lever held back against its rear stop.

After the lever has been properly positioned according to the dimensions then adjust the rod running from the lever to the carburetor-accelerator linkage so that the throttle valve in the carburetor is at the hot idle position while the lever on the transmission is all the way back against its stop.

TRANSMISSION REMOVE

Removal of the unit from the car varies slightly with model changes but follows a logical and rather typical course.

1. Disconnect one of the battery cables at the battery.
2. Raise the car on a hoist.
3. Disconnect side pan at rear and remove starter.
4. Remove exhaust pipe bracket and ventilator tube bracket from bell housing.
5. Remove oil pan plug and drain transmission.
6. Remove flywheel lower half and drain the torus member.
7. Remove transmission filler tube on models where the tube interferes.
8. Disconnect lower end of speedometer cable.
9. Remove propeller shaft.
10. Disconnect and remove throttle and manual control rods at the transmission bellcrank. (This is a precaution against damage.)
11. Attach engine real support tool.
12. Raise engine and transmission assembly on a suitable transmission jack, enough to relieve the weight from rear engine mounts.
13. Disconnect rear engine mount from cross-member and remove cross-member-to-frame bolts.
14. Remove rear engine support cross-member.
15. Mark the torus member-to-flywheel location and remove the attaching bolts.
CAUTION: Some models require draining the radiator and removing the top radiator hose to prevent damage when tilting the engine.
16. Lower the engine and transmission assembly enough to permit access to the bell housing upper bolts.
16A. Remove nuts from six torus cover and flywheel to flex plate attaching bolts.
17. Remove the remainder of the bolts holding the flywheel housing halves together.
18. Double check that the engine support tool is in place and the transmission jack is sustaining all of the transmission weight.
19. Back the transmission away from the engine until the locating dowels are free and clear.
20. Lower transmission to complete removal operation.

LINKAGE ADJUSTMENTS
Beginning 1956

CAUTION: Satisfactory linkage operation can not prevail if binding or excessive wear exists.

THROTTLE LINKAGE

1. Remove carburetor air cleaner.
2. Loosen lock nuts at top of transmission throttle control rod trunnion.
3. With engine at normal operating temperature and selector in "drive," adjust idle to 480-500 RPM, (540-560 with air conditioning).
4. Stop the engine and install proper diameter pin through holes in throttle control lever and bracket.
Note: Four-barrel units have a throttle return check, Before installing the pin on these models, it is advisable to remove the throttle return check to prevent interference with linkage adjustment.
5. With throttle valves fully closed, loosen lock nut and adjust length of transmission throttle control rod to carburetor, so that the gauge pin is free in the hole. Then tighten the lock nut.
6. Push throttle control rod to transmission, (T.V. rod) downward until the outer throttle lever is felt to touch the end of it's travel.
CAUTION: Make sure that, when the lever is in this position, the upper lock nut is not interfering with the trunnion.
7. While holding the throttle rod to transmission in this position, tighten upper and lower trunnion lock nuts finger tight. Shorten throttle control rod to transmission by backing off the lower trunnion nut 2½ turns and tighten upper nut securely. Remove gauge pin.

8. Loosen lock nut on carburetor throttle rod. Adjust carburetor throttle rod to obtain 5 9/64", (5.140") from roller end of pedal rod to body toe board.
9. Tighten lock nut on carburetor throttle rod.
10. Reinstall the air cleaner.
11. To complete throttle linkage adjustment, road test the car. Modify the adjustment as required by shortening or lengthening the throttle control rod to transmission, (T.V. rod) ½ turn at a time to obtain the best shift pattern.

SELECTOR LEVER LINKAGE

1. With upper shift control lever and transmission lever in park, ("P") position, and with the transmission outer shift lever trunnion nuts backed clear of the trunnion, pull the shift rod down toward the transmission all the way. While holding the rod in this position, run the trunnion upper nut down to just contact the trunnion.
2. Holding the shift rod, shift transmission into reverse, ("R") using upper shift lever, and observe the position of upper trunnion nut.
3. If the upper nut is short of trunnion, then the transmission will be short of full travel to reverse detent by that same amount. Screw the upper nut down to just contact the trunnion and then screw it down two additional turns to assure necessary reserve. Tighten the lower nut.
If the upper nut is contacting the trunnion, count the number of turns the nut can be backed off and still contact the trunnion. If less than two turns, turn nut down two turns against the trunnion from the "just contact" position and lock the lower nut. If more than two turns, turn upper nut down against the trunnion from the "just contast" position to the original or starting position and lock the lower nut.
4. After completing above adjustment, check transmission parking lock with car on ramp or grade to insure positive lock.
5. The selector indicator must not be off index register more than 1/16" after adjustment is complete.

STARTER SAFETY SWITCH

1. Place selector in neutral position.
2. Loosen switch mounting screw.
3. Adjust safety switch to index with selector lever. Starter must not operate when ignition key is turned to start position with selector indicator in any "drive" or "reverse" position.
4. Test to see that the engine will start with the selector in "P" or "N" position.

5. When adjustment is complete, tighten the switch mounting screw.

REMOVE TRANSMISSION
Beginning 1956

This is a typical operation and may vary slightly with model changes, however, the basic procedure is the same.

1. Remove transmission oil level indicator.

2. Drain transmission by disconnecting filler pipe from right side of oil pan. The torus assembly can be drained at the same time or it can be drained after transmission removal.

3. Disconnect oil cooler adapter, with lines attached, and move away from transmission. Plug holes in adapter and transmission to stop oil flow.

NOTE: A copper washer is used under the head of the bolt at the through hole and a steel lock washer is used on the bolt at the blind hole.

4. Remove exhaust cross-over pipe if necessary (single exhaust only).

5. Disconnect propeller shaft from transmission output shaft by:

(a) Unscrew center bearing bracket support bolts several turns.

(b) Disconnect propeller shaft at rear axle pinion flange, (universal joint).

(c) Use a suitable rubber band, or substitute, to hold needle bearings onto journals if the wire has been removed from rear universal joint.

(d) Remove complete drive line assembly by sliding the shaft rearward out of the frame tunnel to disengage splines of transmission output shaft.

6. Disconnect speedometer shaft at transmission.

7. Remove flywheel housing bottom cover and crankcase ventilator outlet filter.

8. Pull clevis pin, freeing gearshift control rod trunnion from transmission outer shift lever and unsnap throttle control rod from transmission outer throttle lever ball stud.

9. Support rear end of engine.

10. Remove nuts from six torus cover and flywheel-to-flex plate attaching bolts.

11. Position and attach transmission jack under transmission.

12. Remove bolts attaching transmission to cross member and insulator assembly.

13. Remove transmission cross member to frame bolts and remove cross member and insulator assembly from frame.

14. Raise transmission jack slightly to take load off rear flywheel housing attaching screws.

15. Remove attaching bolts with a 7/16" socket and an 18" to 22" socket extension to reach the bolts.

16. Work the transmission rearward to disengage dowels from front flywheel housing, then lower the transmission from the car.

17. Straighten clip at extension housing to free breather pipe. Remove breather pipe.

REINSTALL TRANSMISSION

1. Raise transmission until engine flex plate and transmission flywheel and torus cover are at the same level.

2. Rotate torus cover to align dowels in the cover and flywheel with holes in flex plate. (Torus cover and flex plate can be fastened in either of two positions.)

3. Move transmission into position engaging rear flywheel housing dowels into front flywheel housing.

4. Install and tighten two rear flywheel housing attaching screws.

Note: If the pilot on the flywheel has entered the end of the crankshaft properly, flywheel and torus cover should move back and forth slightly.

5. Rotate flywheel to bring one flex plate mounting pad down to lowest position. Push flywheel forward lightly to seat it against crankshaft. Measure clearance between pad on flex plate and flywheel with feeler gauge. Clearance should be .015" minimum.

If clearance is less than .015", move transmission away from engine and install special spacer (part #522975) over flywheel pilot. Then move transmission back into place, install and tighten flywheel housing attaching bolts.

6. Attach transmission cross member and insulator assembly to frame.

7. Lower transmission and install two bolts through insulator and into extension housing.

8. Remove transmission jack.

9. Install flex plate-to-flywheel and torus cover, torque to 15 ft. lb.

10. Install crankcase ventilator filter and flywheel housing bottom cover.

11. Connect filler pipe to transmission oil pan and install oil level indicator.

12. Remove temporary plugs from oil cooler adapter and transmission and attach adapter to transmission. **Copper washer must be used under head of bolt at through hole in transmission case.**

13. Install exhaust cross-over pipe, on single exhaust systems.

14. Connect up speedometer cable.

15. Connect throttle control rod onto transmission outer throttle lever ball stud and connect gearshift control rod trunnion to outer shift lever with clevis pin.

16. Install propeller shaft.

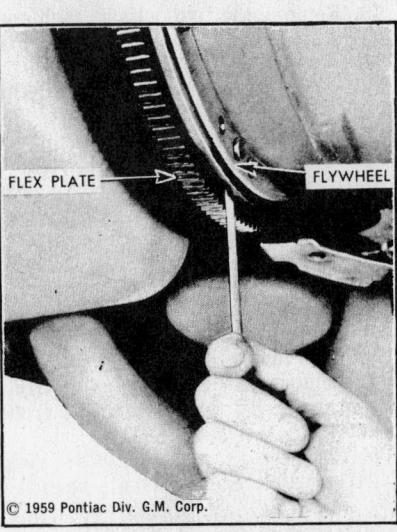

Clearance Between Flywheel and Flex Plate

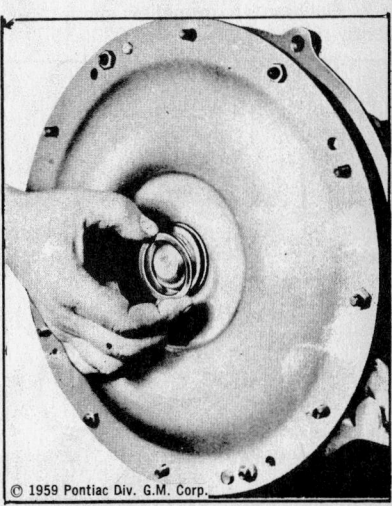

Spacer on Flywheel Pilot

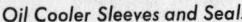

Oil Cooler Sleeves and Seals

PONTIAC

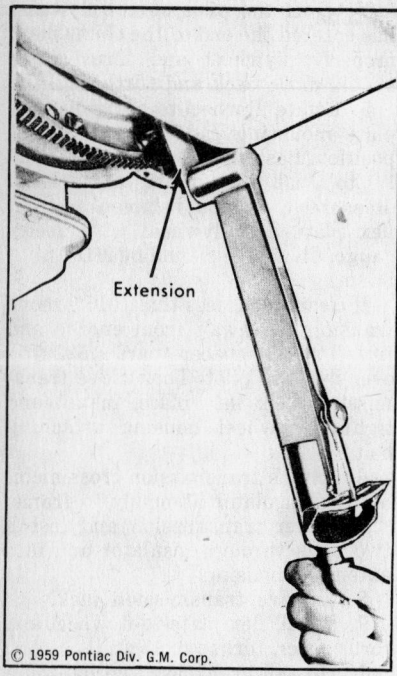

Using Torque Wrench Extension

17. Refill transmission, using proper procedure, (see Unit Repair section).
18. Adjust throttle and shift linkage.
19. Test transmission oil pressure, (as outlined in Unit Repair section) and road test the car.

REMOVAL OF TRANSMISSION
3 SPEED HYDRA-MATIC

Before raising the car on the lift, remove one cable (either one) from the battery, since the starter must be removed, and release the emergency brake.

1. Remove the filler tube and drain the transmission. Push the filler tube up toward its upper bracket out of the way.
2. Disconnect propeller shaft from transmission:

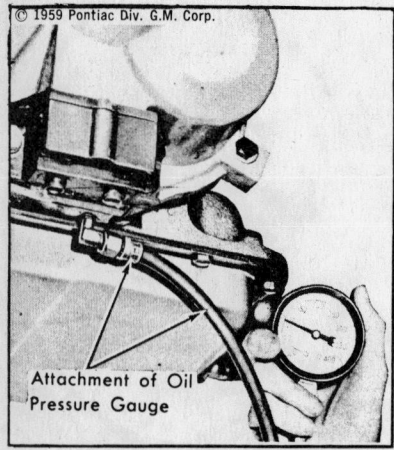

Attachment of Oil Pressure Gauge

a. Remove "U" bolt nuts, lock plates, and "U" bolts from rear axle drive pinion flange.
b. Use a suitable rubber band or tape to hold bearings on "U" joint journals if tie wire is broken.
c. Slide propeller shaft rearwards off transmission output shaft.
3. Disconnect speedometer cable from speedometer driven gear.
4. Remove gearshift control lower rod.
5. Remove lower end of gearshift control upper rod by removing "E" ring.
6. Remove the 2 cross-shaft bracket to frame attaching bolts and the remove the bracket, cross-shaft lever, and bushing from car.
7. Remove lowre end of throttle control transmission rod (engine to transmission idler lever).
8. Remove idler lever to outer T.V. lever control rod.
9. Remove throttle control idler lever.
10. Remove parking brake return spring and brake cable guide hook from frame crossmember.
11. Remove oil cooler lines.
12. Loosen exhaust pipe to manifold bolts about ¼ inch.
13. Remove both starter cables.
14. Remove the starter and the splash shield by removing the 2 attaching bolts.
15. Remove bottom cover from bottom of case cover (3 attaching bolts).
16. Remove the 4 bolts holding the flywheel front cover plate to the transmission case cover.
17. Place special automatic transmission jack under transmission and raise it enough to support the transmission.
18. Remove 2 rear mount support to frame crossmember nuts and raise transmission so studs clear the crossmember.
19. Remove the two bolts at each end of the frame crossmember and remove crossmember.
20. Lower the transmission until the jack is barely still supporting it.
21. Remove breather pipe clip bolt and remove pipe from transmission.
22. Using a long wrench extension with a "U" joint, remove the remaining 6 transmission case cover to engine attaching bolts.
23. Raise transmission to its normal position, slide rearward from the engine and flywheel, and lower it away from the car.
24. Remove rear mount support from rear mount by removing a nut from each insulator.
25. Remove 4 rear mount to rear bearing retainer attaching screws.

INSTALL

Install by reversing above procedure.

UNIVERSAL JOINTS AND DRIVE LINES
1954 thru 1957 and 1961-63

Cross and bearing type universals are used on all Pontiacs.

There are two types used, however, one type held with a C shaped lock ring; the other held with a lock plate.

From under the car, remove the four bolts which hold the two rear universal joint pillow blocks to the rear axle pinion shaft flange. Tap the pillow blocks until they come off the flange. Lower the rear end of the driveshaft and slide the front end off the splines of the transmission, together with the front universal joint.

Take the entire assembly to the bench. If lock type bearings are used, remove the screws which hold the lock plates over the bearing. If lock ring types are used, remove the lock rings. Set the back end of the driveshaft up in a vise so that the two bearings which remain in the end of the driveshaft are in a horizontal position. With the two bearings in a horizontal position take a blunt punch and drive the bearing on the right inwards which will force the bearing on the left out of the yoke. When the left bearing has been taken out pack a couple of washers under the cross and driving from the left side drive the cross against the right side bearing which will drive it out.

On reassembling the bearings to the universal joint cross a press or a very heavy C clamp should be used to press the bearings into position. They should not be driven into position since this tends to cock the little rollers in the pillow blocks, resulting in early failure of the universal joint.

1958 Thru 1960

Three universal joints are used on these models. At the rear universal joint remove the U bolts which hold the bearing to the pinion shaft and tap the bearings off the pinion shaft.

Let the driveshaft come down. At the frame bracket, remove the bolts which hold the universal center bearing support to the frame and slide the complete assembly out from underneath the vehicle. **Caution:** Be careful of the shims which may be found under the bearing support between the bearing support and the frame.

On the bench, remove the lock rings which retain the universal joint bearing to the yoke and, driving on one yoke, drive the bearing inwards forcing the cross to drive the opposite bearing out of the yoke.

With the first bearing out, turn the unit over and drive the opposite way to drive out the bearing which was just driven in.

Repeat at all the universal joints.

Some models are fitted with a splash shield in the frame tunnel. On these models remove the splash shield.

Starting with 1962

Two basic designs are used, one is a typical solid shaft with two joints. The other incorporates five rubber torsional dampeners. The accompaning diagram shows the rubber dampeners inserted between the solid and tubular sections.

REAR AXLE AND SUSPENSION

TROUBLE SHOOTING AND ADJUSTMENT

Starting with 1961 a Four Link Pivoted Control Arm suspension system is used.

General instructions covering the troubles of the rear axle and how to repair and adjust it, together with information on installation of rear axle bearings and grease seals, are given in the Unit Repair section under the heading: Axles, Rear.

Capacities of the rear axle are given in the Capacities Tables of this section.

REMOVAL OF REAR AXLE ASSEMBLY FROM THE CAR

Thru 1957

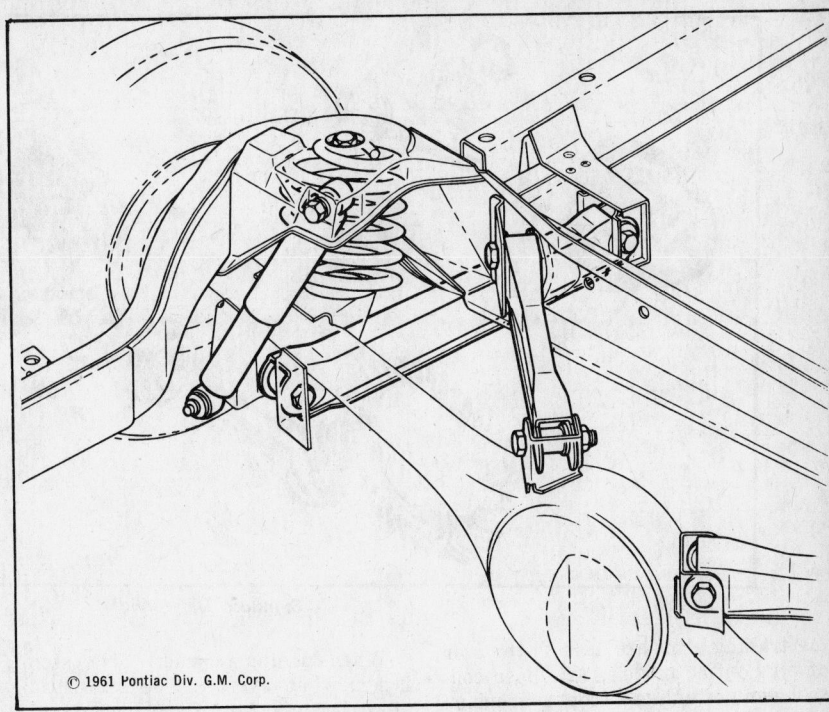

© 1961 Pontiac Div. G.M. Corp.

1962 Pontiac rear suspension.

Take the weight off the car on jacks on the frame in front of the rear spring. Disconnect the brake lines and brake cables at the rear axle and split the rear universal joint.

Take the nuts off the rear shackle and drive the rear shackle off the back of both the rear springs.

Disconnect the shock absorber at its lower end and push it up out of the way.

Remove the U bolts nuts which hold the rear spring to the rear axle housing and lower the spring down, pivoting about the front bolt.

Disconnect torsion and sway bars and then the rear axle assembly can be rolled out from under the car.

Starting with 1958

Starting in 1958, coil springs hav-

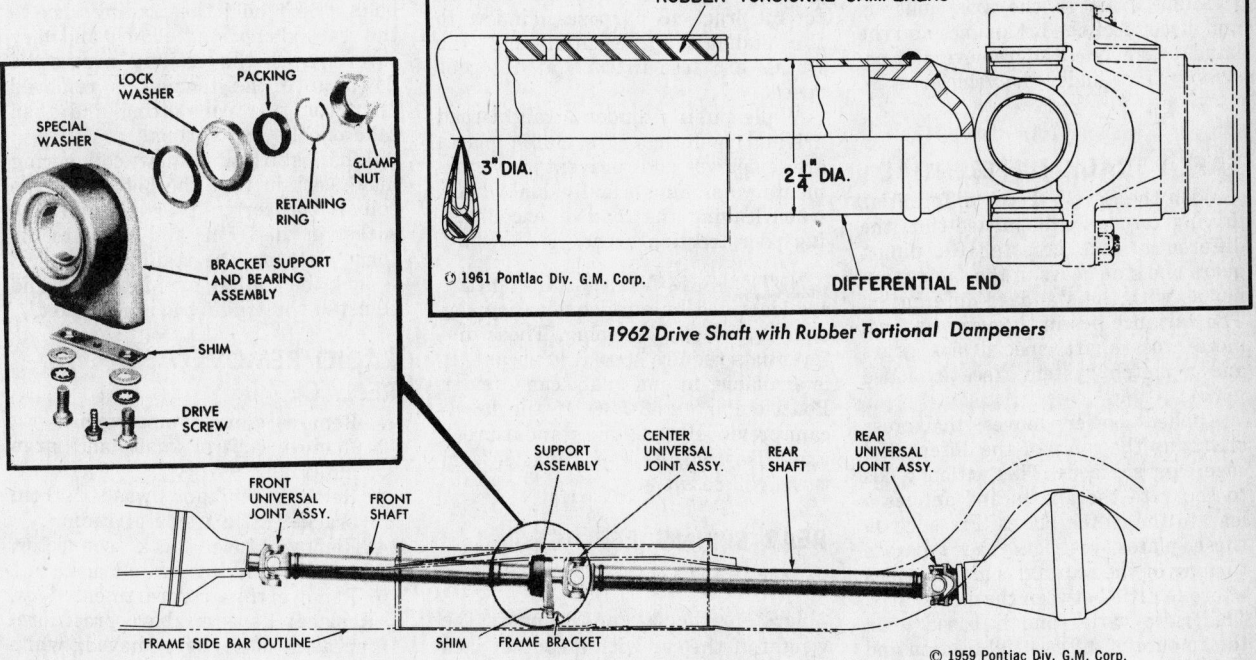

RUBBER TORSIONAL DAMPENERS

3" DIA.

$2\frac{1}{4}$" DIA.

© 1961 Pontiac Div. G.M. Corp.

DIFFERENTIAL END

1962 Drive Shaft with Rubber Tortional Dampeners

LOCK WASHER

PACKING

SPECIAL WASHER

CLAMP NUT

RETAINING RING

BRACKET SUPPORT AND BEARING ASSEMBLY

SHIM

DRIVE SCREW

FRONT UNIVERSAL JOINT ASSY.

FRONT SHAFT

SUPPORT ASSEMBLY

CENTER UNIVERSAL JOINT ASSY.

REAR SHAFT

REAR UNIVERSAL JOINT ASSY.

FRAME SIDE BAR OUTLINE

SHIM

FRAME BRACKET

© 1959 Pontiac Div. G.M. Corp.

Drive Shaft with Three Universal Joints 1958-60

Standard Differential

© 1961 Pontiac Div. G.M. Corp.

ing trailing arms are used on the rear of all Pontiac models. An upper control arm not unlike a front suspension upper control arm is used at the center of the rear axle housing.

To remove the rear axle assembly, jack up the car and take the weight of the car on jacks in front of the frame kickup. Split the rear universal joint.

Disconnect the lower end of the shock absorbers and remove the bolt which holds the upper control arm to the rear axle banjo housing.

Now let the assembly come downwards until the tension is released from the coil spring. Now remove the bolts which hold the lower control arm (trailing arm) to the axle housing, and disconnect the brake lines and the hand brake line and remove the assembly from under the vehicle.

SAFE-T-TRACK DIFFERENTIAL

With the Safe-T-Track differential, driving force is transmitted thru the differential case, cross shafts, pinion gears and side gears in the same manner as with the standard differential. The variance lies in the use of a two-piece cross shaft, special side gears and a clutch system, (see exploded view).

Applied power moves the cross shafts up the ramp of the differential case cam surfaces. This action tends to separate the shafts and applies a load to the clutch plates. Pressure on these plates restricts the separate turning of the rear axles and provides a torque ratio between the axle shafts. This ratio varies and is based upon the amount of differential friction and the degree of load that is being applied to the differential.

When turning a corner, this system is somewhat reversed. The differential gears become part of a planetary set. The gear on the inside of the curve becomes the fixed gear of the planetary train. The outer gear of this set overruns, as does the outside wheel on the curve, having a further distance to travel. With the outer gear overrunning and the inner gear fixed, the cross shafts attempt to rotate but are restricted by the fixed gear and they must move the pinion cross shafts back down the ramp. This action relieves the thrust load on the clutch plates. So when turning a corner, the Safe-T-Track differential is, for all practical purposes, similar to the standard differential and the wheels are free to turn at different speeds.

While pulling, under straight-road driving conditions, the clutch plates are engaged and prevent any momentary spinning of individual wheels when leaving the road or encountering poor traction areas.

NOTE: Safe-T-Track differentials are identified by an identification tag next to the oil filter plug. These differentials require special lubricant. It is available, in one quart cans, under Pontiac Part #531536. If the lubricant previously used for standard rear axles is used, severe "chatter" on turns will result.

REAR SPRING REPLACE

Leaf Springs

Jack up the car and support the weight of the car with a contact jack against the frame in front of the kickup.

Disconnect the lower end of the shock absorber, and on models with a torsion bar disconnect the torsion bar.

Remove the bolt from the rear shackle and let the back end of the spring come down.

Remove the front shackle bolt and then take out the four U bolts which hold the leaf spring to the rear axle housing and let the spring down.

Coil Springs

Jack up the back of the car and support both sides of the car on stand jacks on the frame in front of the rear axle. Place a jack under the lower trailing arm and remove the bolts which hold the trailing arm to the rear axle housing. Slowly and very carefully let the trailing arm come down until the tension is removed from the rear coil spring and then take off the coil spring.

When starting a new coil spring make certain that the bottom of the coil is properly inserted into the socket in the frame and also into the form plate on the trailing arm.

Jack the trailing arm into place and reinstall the trailing arm rear bolt.

RADIO REMOVE AND REPLACE

1. Remove glove compartment.
2. Remove control knobs and large nuts.
3. Remove nut and washer from bracket at left side of radio.
4. Remove fuse block connector, speaker and antennae leads.
5. Remove thru compartment door.

Replace: Reverse above procedure. If speaker is to be removed, while radio is out, remove four nuts holding to panel and lift out.

AIR CONDITIONING
Service 1092
BRAKES, HYDRAULIC
Adjustments 938
References 576
Bleed brakes 941
Parking brake lever, R & R 577
Parking brake cable, R & R 577
Master cylinder, R & R 577
Master cylinder service 939
BRAKES, POWER
Power unit overhaul 954
Trouble shooting 954
CLUTCH
Clutch assembly, R & R 587
Clutch pedal, adjust 587
"E-stick" clutch, R & R 587
COOLING SYSTEM
Radiator core, R & R 579
Thermostat, R & R 579
Water pump, R & R 579
ELECTRICAL SYSTEM
Distributor references 574
Distributor, R & R 575
Distributor specifications 569
Fuses and circuit breakers ...571
Gauges 1024
Generator regulator
 specifications 570
Generator regulators 1026
Generator, R & R 575
Generator service 1026
Generator specifications 570
Generator trouble shooting
 chart 1026
Horn button, R & R 585
Ignition firing order & timing .567
Ignition timing procedure 568
Ignition timing specifications ..568
Starter specifications 570
Starter systems 1046
Starter assembly, R & R 575
ENGINE ASSEMBLY
Cylinder head tightening 574
Cylinder head, R & R 582
Engine diagnosis 1012
Engine references 579
Engine marking code 568
Engine firing order & timing ..567
Engine assembly, R & R 580
Inlet manifold, R & R 580
Exhaust manifold, R & R 580
Oil pan, R & R 582
Oil pressure specifications 572
Piston and rod, assembly 584
Piston and rod, R & R 584
Piston and pin specifications ..573
Rocker assembly, R & R 580
Rear main bearing oil seal ...582
Specifications, general, engine .572
Timing case cover & seal, R & R 583
Timing chain, R & R 584
Vibration damper, R & R 583
Trouble shooting charts 1012

ENGINE ASSEMBLY—continued
Tune-up specifications 568
Valve specifications 573
Valve, R & R 583
Valve springs 583
Valves and guides 583
ENGINE LUBRICATION
Oil pan, R & R 582
EXHAUST SYSTEM
Exhaust pipe 578
Muffler 578
Tail pipe 578
Heat control valve 606
Manifolds 580
FUEL SYSTEM
References 577
Carburetors 972
Fuel gauge service 1024
Fuel pump pressure 568
Fuel pump service 1020
Fuel pump, R & R 577
INSTRUMENTS
Speedometer, R & R 576
OVERDRIVES
Overdrive disassembly 914
Overdrive, R & R 914
Overdrive wiring 914
Trouble shooting 915
RADIO, R & R
References 594
REAR AXLE AND SUSPENSION
Axle assembly, R & R 594
Axle shaft 918
Axle shaft oil seal 918
Pinion bearings 918
Ring gear & pinion 918
Rear spring, R & R 592
Shock absorber, R & R 594
Trouble shooting 919
SPECIFICATIONS
Battery 570
Brake cylinder sizes 572
Capacities:
 Axle, rear 570
 Cooling system 570
 Crankcase 570
 Fuel tank 570
 Transmission, automatic ...570
 Transmission, manual 570
Chassis, general 572
Cylinder tightening 574
Distributor 569
Engine firing order & timing ..567
Engine, general 572
Engine tune-up 568
Fuses and circuit breakers ...571
Generator regulators 570
Light bulbs 571
Main bearings 574
Model identification
 illustrations 566
Model year identification 568
Piston and pins 573

SPECIFICATIONS—continued
Quick reference specifications .567
Rod bearings 574
Starters 570
Torque wrench 571
Tune-up 568
Valves 573
Wheel alignment 574
STEERING, MANUAL
Adjust gear housing 1052
Gear assembly, R & R 585
Horn button, R & R 585
Steering wheel, R & R 585
STEERING, POWER
Pump assembly, R & R 587
Pump assembly 1058
Trouble shooting 1081
Unit overhaul 1058
SUSPENSION, FRONT
Alignment 1082
Alignment specifications 574
Ball joints, R & R 1087
Camber, adjust 1082
Caster, adjust 1082
King pins and bushings 1087
Knuckle supports 1087
References 585
Shock absorbers 1087
Support arms, pins and
 bushings 1087
Toe-in, adjust 1082
Trunnions, upper & lower ...1087
TRANSMISSION, AUTOMATIC
Quick service information 589
Dual-range hydra-matic 850
 Disassembly 850
 Linkage, adjust 589
 Transmission, R & R 591
 Trouble shooting 853
Flashaway hydra-matic 860
 Disassembly 864
 Linkage, adjust 589
 Transmission, R & R 591
 Trouble shooting 884
Flash-o-matic (Borg-Warner) .820
 Disassembly 826
 Linkage, adjust 589
 Transmission, R & R 591
 Trouble shooting 824
TRANSMISSION, STANDARD
Transmission, R & R 588
Shaft linkage adjustment 589
TROUBLE CHECKS
Procedures 1
TUNE-UP
Procedures 1012
Specifications 568
Engine diagnosis 1012
**UNIVERSAL JOINT AND
DRIVE LINE**
Disassemble U joint 591
U joint & drive line, R & R ...591

YEAR IDENTIFICATION

1953-54
Series 10
Rambler

1955
Series 10
Rambler

1956
Series 10
Rambler

1957
Series 10
Rambler

1958 Series 10 Rambler
Series 20 Rambler Rebel

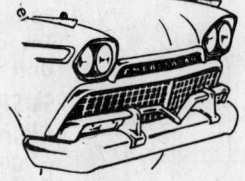

1958 Series 80
Rambler Ambassador

1959 Series 10 Rambler
Series 20 Rambler Rebel

1959 Series 80
Rambler Ambassador

1960 Series 80
Rambler Ambassador

1960 Series 10 Rambler
Series 20 Rambler Rebel

1958-60
Series 01 American

1961
Series 01 American

1961
Rambler Classic

1961 Series 80
Rambler Ambassador

1962 Rambler Ser. 10 & 80
Classic & Ambassador

1962
Series 01 American

1963
Series 01 American

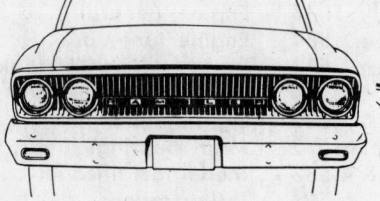

1963
Rambler Ser. 10

1963 Series 80
Rambler Ambassador

QUICK WORKING SPECIFICATIONS

DISTRIBUTOR

Breaker Point Gap

1954-55, All .... .021-.023
1956-63, All .... .017-.020

Cam Angle

1954-55, All 34
1956, All 32
1957, All 30
1958-63, Series-10 32-38
1958-63, Series-20-80 30-34

IGNITION TIMING

1954-55—6 cyl. "L" Head .... 4° A.T.D.C.
1958-63—6 cyl. "L" Head .... 3° B.T.D.C.
1956-57—6 cyl. O.H.V. All ..0° T.D.C.
1958-59—6 cyl. O.H.V. All .... 5° B.T.D.C.
1960-63—6 cyl. O.H.V. Std. Tr. .... 5° B.T.D.C.
1960-63—6 cyl. O.H.V. Auto Tr. .... 8° B.T.D.C.
1960 —V8-Rebel, All .... 0° T.D.C.
1960 —V8-Ambassador All .... 5° B.T.D.C.
1961-63—V8- Std. Tran. .... 0° T.D.C.
1961-63—V8-Auto. Tran. .... 5° B.T.D.C.

VALVES

Seat Angle

1954-63, All 6 cyl. ...In.-45; Ex.-45
1957-63, All V8 ....In.-30; Ex.-45

Operating Tappet Clearance (Hot)

1954-55, All .... .015
1956-63, 6 cyl. OHV
In.-.012; Ex.-.016
1957, V8 .... In.-.012; Ex.-.014
1958-63 Series-20, V8
In.-.012; Ex.-.016
1958-63 Series-80, V8 Hydraulic
Zero
1958-63, 6 cyl. L Hd.
In.-.016C; Ex.-.018C

CAMSHAFT SPROCKET MARKS

1954-63, All Engines: Align the marks on the camshaft and crankshaft sprockets nearest each other and with the shaft centers.

GENERATOR & REGULATOR

Year and Series	Generator Field Current in Amperes 6 Volt	Generator Field Current in Amperes 12 Volt	Regulator Cut-out Closing Voltage	Regulator Current Regulator Setting	Regulator Voltage Regulator Setting
1954-55 All	1.9	—	6.6	48	7.2
1956 All	—	1.5	13.2	29	14.3±1.(A)
1957-58 All	—	1.5	12.6	30	14.3±1.(A)
1959-63 Ser. 10 & 20	—	1.5	12.7	25	14.3±1.(A)
Ser. 80	—	1.65	12.7	30	14.3±1.(A)

(A) Surrounding temperatures guide this adjustment. Higher temperatures require lower settings and lower settings permit higher settings, within limits.

CAPACITIES

Engine Crankcase (Quarts)

(Add 1 qt. for new filter)
1954-57, All 6 cyl. 4
1957, All V8 5
1959-63, All Engines 4

Synchromesh Trans. (Pints)

(Add 1¼ pts. for overdrive)
1954-55, All 1½
1956-57, All 2¼
1958-63, Series-10-11 .... 1½
1958-63, Series-20 .... 2¼
1958-63, Series-80 4

Hydramatic Trans. (Pints)

1954-57, All 6 cyl. 17
1957, All V8 23

Flash-O-Matic Trans. (Pints)

1957, All V8 19
1958-63, Series-10-20 & 01 20
1958-63, Series-80 22

Rear Axle (Pints)

1954-63, All 6 cyl. 3
1957-63, All V8 4
1958-63, Series-20-80 4

Cooling System (Quarts)

(Add 1 qt. for heater)
1954-55, All 11
1956-63, All 6 cyl. 10
1957-61, All Series-20 20
1958-63, Series 80, Ambassador V8 19

FIRING ORDER and TIMING

SPARK OCCURS:

1954-55—6 Cyl. "L" Head—0°—4° ATDC
1956-57—6 Cyl. "O" Head—0° (TDC)
1958-63—6 Cyl. "L" Head—3° BTDC
1958-63—6 Cyl. "O" Head—5° BTDC
1957-63—V-8, All—5° BTDC

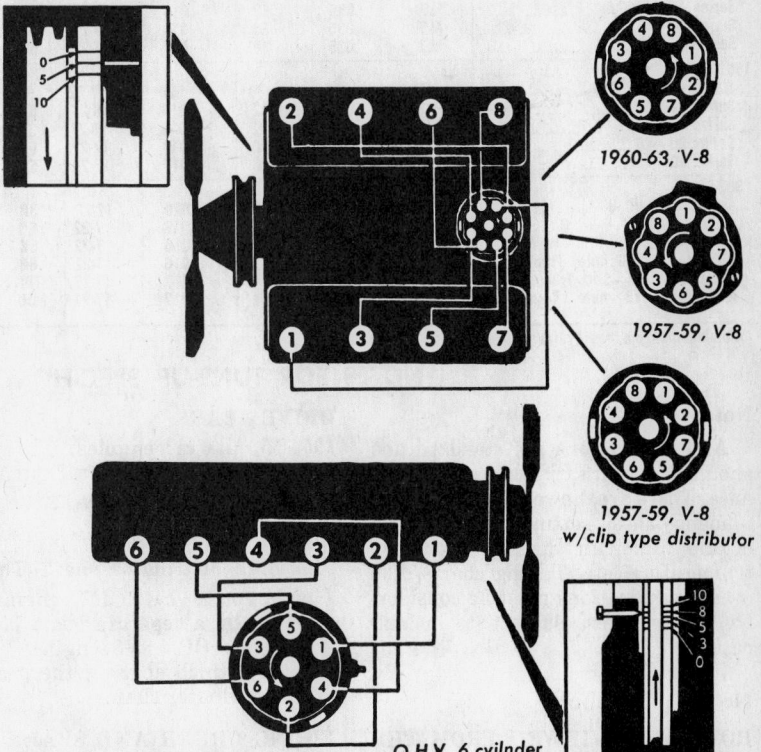

1960-63, V-8

1957-59, V-8

1957-59, V-8 w/clip type distributor

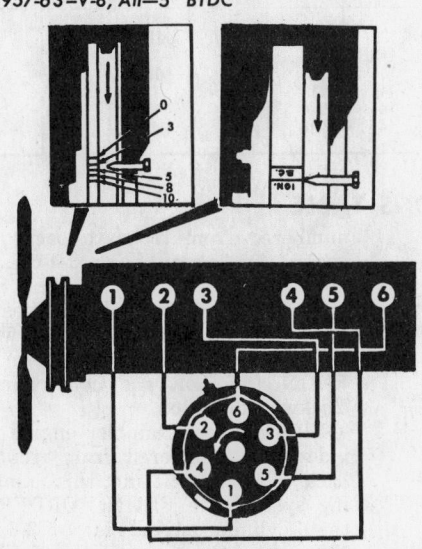

All 6 cyl. "L" head

O.H.V. 6 cyilnder

NOTE:
THESE ARE APPROXIMATE SETTINGS. ENGINE DESIGN, ALTITUDE, TEMPERATURE, FUEL AND ENGINE CONDITION WILL ALL INFLUENCE TIMING. THE DETERMINING FACTOR, LIMITING ADVANCE, WILL STILL BE THE "KNOCK POINT" OF THE INDIVIDUAL ENGINE.

RAMBLER

CAR SERIAL NUMBER LOCATION AND ENGINE IDENTIFICATION

ENGINE IDENTIFICATION
6 CYL. "L" HEAD
	cu. in. Disp.
1954	184.0
1955-63—All 6 cyl.	195.6

V-8 OHV
1957-63—"Rebel"	250.0
1958-63—Ambassador	327.0

SERIAL NUMBER LOCATION
1954-63:
On firewall under hood.

ENGINE NUMBER LOCATION
6 CYL.
Upper left front corner of block.
V-8
1957-58—Lower front corner of block .

1959-63—Tag attached to generator support bracket.

TUNE-UP SPECIFICATIONS

Year	Spark Plugs Type	Gap	Distributor (Note 1) Cam Angle	Point Gap	Arm Spring Tension	Ignition Timing (Note 2)	Compression Pressure Cranking (Note 3)	Tappet Clearance Hot Inlet	Exhaust	Timing Inlet Opens	Fuel Pump Pressure	Engine Idle Speed Neutral (Note 4)
1954												
Series 10, 6 Cyl., L Head	AL-A7	.030	34	.022	17–21	4A	120	.015	.015	10B	4	500
1955												
Series 10, 6 Cyl., L Head	AL-A7	.030	34	.022	17–21	4A	120	.015	.015	10B	4	550
1956												
Series 10, 6 Cyl., OHV	AL-A7	.030	32	.016	19–23	TDC	120	.012	.016	12½B	4½	550
1957												
Series 10, 6 Cyl., OHV	AL-A7	.035	30	.016	19–23	TDC	120	.012	.016	12½B	4½	550
Series 20, V8, OHV	AL-A7	.035	30	.016	19–23	5B	140	.012	.014	12½B	4½	550
1958-59												
Series 01—L. Hd. 6	AL7	.035	32	.016	19–23	3B	120	.012	.018	10B	4½	550
Series 10—OHV 6	AL7	.035	32	.016	19-23	5B	120	.012	.016	12½B	4½	550
Series 20—V8	AL7	.035	30	.016	17–22	5B	140	.012	.016	12½B	4½	550
Series 80—V8	AL7	.035	30	.016	17–22	5B	140	Zero	Zero	12½B	4½	550
1960												
Series 01—L. Hd. 6	AL7	.035	39	.020	17–22	3B	120	.012	.016	10B	4½	550
Series 01—OHV 6	H18Y	.035	32	.016	19-23	5B	120	.012	.016	12½B	4½	550
Series 10—OHV 6	AL7	.035	32	.016	19-23	5B	120	.012	.016	12½B	4½	550
Series 20—V8	AL7	.035	30	.017	17–22	5B	140	.012	.016	12½B	4½	550
Series 80—V8	AL7	.035	30	.017	17–22	5B	140	Zero	Zero	12½B	4½	550
1961												
Series 01—L. Hd. 6	AL7	.035	39	.020	17–22	3B	120	.012	.016	10B	4½	550
Series 01—OHV 6	H18Y	.035	32	.016	19-23	5B	120	.012	.016	12½B	4½	550
Series 10—OHV 6	AL7	.035	32	.016	19-23	3B	120	.012	.016	10B	4½	550
Series 20—V8	AL7	.035	30	.017	17–22	5B	140	.012	.016	12½B	4½	550
Series 80—V8	AL7	.035	30	.017	17–22	5B	140	Zero	Zero	12½B	4½	550
1962-63												
American—L.HD.-6	H10	.035	39	.020	17–22	3B	130	.016	.018	10B	4½	550
American—O.H.V.-6	H18Y	.035	32	.016	17–22	8B	145	.012	.016	12½B	4½	550
Classic—O.H.V.-6 Std. Trans.	H10	.035	32	.016	17–22	5B	145	.012	.016	12½B	4½	550
Classic—O.H.V.-6 Auto. Trans.	H-10	.035	32	.016	17–22	8B	145	.012*	.016	12½B	4½	500
Ambassador V8—Std. Trans.	H18Y	.035	34	.017	17–22	TDC	145	Zero	Zero	12½B	4½	550
Ambassador V8—Auto. Trans.	H18Y	.035	34	.017	17–22	5B	145	Zero	Zero	12½B	4½	500

*Aluminum engine has hydraulic tappets, at zero clearance

NOTES FOR TUNE-UP SPECIFICATIONS TABLE

Note:

All specifications are standard and should result in satisfactory performance. There are, however, factors that influence these settings, such as fuel octane value, air density, humidity, temperature, etc. Timing charts, like other specifications must be considered as averages, subject to modification.

Note 1: Distributor

ROTATION (VIEWED FROM THE TOP)
All ....Counterclockwise

DRIVE GEAR

1954-55, All 6 cyl. engines:
Pinned to oil pump shaft. Distributor shaft has offset tongue.

1956-63, All engines:
Pinned to distributor shaft. The oil pump on 6 cyl. OHV engines is driven by a separate gear. The oil pump on OHV, V8 engines has a tongue which engages the gear on the distributor shaft.

FIRING ORDER AND SPARK PLUG WIRE INSTALLATION

All Rambler V8 engine cylinders are numbered from front to back: left bank, 1-3-5-7; right bank, 2-4-6-8. Using this numbering system the FIRING ORDER of the V8 engines is: 1-8-4-3-6-5-7-2. The spark plug wires go into the V8 distributor cap in the FIRING ORDER and in a counter-clockwise direction.

All 6 cylinder Rambler engine cylinders are numbered from front to back; 1-2-3-4-5-6. Using this numbering system the FIRING ORDER of the 6 cylinder engines is: 1-5-3-6-2-4. The spark plug wires go into the 6 cylinder distributor cap in the FIRING ORDER and in a counterclockwise direction.

NOTES FOR TUNE UP SPECIFICATIONS—continued

Note 2: Ignition
IGNITION TIMING MARKS AND
THEIR LOCATION
1954-63, All 6 Cyl.:
On the crankshaft pulley. Mark is a line indicating Top Dead Center.

1958-63, OHV, V8
On the crankshaft pulley. Mark is a line five degrees before Top Dead Center.

IGNITION RESISTOR
1956-63: A ballast resistor is used in the primary ignition circuit of all cars equipped with 12-volt electrical systems. A by-pass in the starter solenoid removes this resistor from the circuit only while the starter is operating. If the ignition switch is used to complete the circuit to the cranking motor while making underhood cranking tests, the distributor primary lead must be grounded to prevent the engine firing.

Note 3: Compression Pressure

All cylinders should read alike within 10 pounds. This is more important than the actual reading. Take the reading with all plugs removed, engine at normal operating temperature.

Note 4: Idle Speed
Idle speeds as shown are for engines in good condition with the transmission in Neutral. If equipped with Air If equipped with Air Conditioning unit should be "ON" when setting idle.

DISTRIBUTOR SPECIFICATIONS, DELCO-REMY

Year	Model	Delco-Remy Part Number	Rotation	Cam Angle in Degrees	Breaker		Governor Control		Vacuum Control Data		
					Point Opening (Inch)	Arm Spring in Ounces	@ Dist. Advance Starts	R.P.M. Full Advance	Inches of Vacuum To Start Advance	Inches of Vacuum For Full Advance	Max. Adv. of Dist. in Degrees
1954-55	6 cyl. L head	1112382	cc	31-37	.022	17-21	1 @ 300	11 @ 1400	4-6	10-12	4½-6½
1956-57	6 cyl. O.H.V.	1110242	cc	28-35	.016	19-23	1 @ 375	16 @ 1600	5-7	11-12½	4-6
1957	V8, Ser. 5720	1110884	cc	28-32	.016	19-23	1 @ 350	19 @ 1700	5½-7½	13½-15½	11-13
	V8, Ser. 5730	1110887	cc	28-32	.016	19-23	1 @ 325	18 @ 1900	5-7	14¼-15¾	9-11
1958-59	6 cyl. L head	1112426	cc	28-35	.016	17-21	1 @ 500	7 @ 2100	4-6	10-12	4½-6½
	6 cyl. O.H.V.	1110246	cc	28-35	.016	17-21	1 @ 500	10½ @ 2100	6-8	16-17	6½-8½
	V8, O.H.V. Ser. 20	1110923	cc	28-32	.016	19-23	1 @ 350	18 @ 2000	5½-7½	13¼-15½	11-13
	V8, O.H.V. Ser. 80	1110887	cc	28-32	.016	19-23	1 @ 325	18 @ 1900	5-7	14¼-15¾	9-11
1960	6 Cyl., O.H.V. American Custom	1112434	CC	28-35	.016	19-23	1 @ 500	11 @ 2100	6	16-17	11
	6 Cyl., O.H.V. Rambler	1110246	CC	28-32	.016	19-23	1 @ 500	11 @ 2100	6	16-17	11
1961	6 Cyl., O.H.V. American Cust.	1112434	CC	28-35	.016	19-23	1 @ 500	11 @ 2100	6	16-17	11
	6 Cyl., O.H.V. Rambler Classic	1112434	CC	28-35	.016	19-23	1 @ 500	11 @ 2100	6	16-17	11
1962-63	6 Cyl., O.H.V. American "400"	1112435	CC	28-35	.016	19-23	1 @ 500	11 @ 2100	6	16-17	11
	6 Cyl., O.H.V. Rambler Classic	1112435	CC	28-35	.016	19-23	1 @ 500	11 @ 2100	6	16-17	11

DISTRIBUTOR SPECIFICATIONS, AUTO-LITE

Year	Model	Auto-Lite Part Number	Rotation	Cam Angle in Degrees	Breaker		Governor Control		Vacuum Control Data		
					Point Opening (Inch)	Arm Spring in Ounces	@ Dist. Advance Starts	R.P.M. Full Advance	Inches of Vacuum To Start Advance	Inches of Vacuum For Full Advance	Max. Adv. of Dist. in Degrees
1960	6 Cyl., L. Head American	IAT-4402	CC	37-41	.020	17-22	1 @ 425	7 @ 2000	5	11	5½
	V8, Rambler Rebel	IPB-4104-A	CC	28-32	.017	17-22	1 @ 315	18 @ 2000	6-7	14	12
	V8, Ambasdr.	IPB-4104	CC	28-32	.017	17-22	1 @ 300	18 @ 1900	6	15	10
1962-63	6 Cyl., L. Head American	IAT-4402-1	CC	37-41	.020	17-22	1 @ 425	7 @ 2000	5	11	5½
	V8, Rambler, Classic	IPB-4107	CC	28-32	.017	17-22	1 @ 300	18 @ 1900	6	10	15
	V8, Rambler Ambassdr.	IPB-4107	CC	28-32	.017	17-22	1 @ 300	18 @ 1900	6	10	15
1961	6 Cyl., L. Head American	IAT-4407	CC	37-41	.020	17-22	1 @ 425	7 @ 2000	5	11	5½
	V8, Rambler Ambasdr.	IPB-4109	CC	33-35	.017	17-22	1 @ 300	18 @ 1900	6	10	15

RAMBLER

GENERATOR and REGULATOR SPECIFICATIONS

YEAR	GENERATORS					REGULATORS		
	Field Current in Amperes		Brush Spring Tension	Cut Out Relay		Current and Voltage Regulator Air Gap	Current Regulator Setting	Voltage Regulator Setting
	At 6 Volts	At 12 Volts		Air Gap	Closing Voltage			
1954–55 All Series	1.9		30	.020	6.6	.075	48	7.2
1956 All Series		1.5	30	.020	13.2	.075	29	14.3
1957–58 All Series		1.5	30	.020	12.6	.075	30	14.3
1959–63 All 6 Cyl.		1.5	28	.020	12.7	.060	25	14.3
Series 20, V8, OHV		1.65	28	.020	12.7	.060	30	14.3
Series 80, V8, OHV		1.65	28	.020	12.7	.075	30	14.3

BATTERY and STARTER SPECIFICATIONS

YEAR	BATTERY				STARTERS						Brush Spring Tension
	Ampere Hour Capacity	Volts	Group Number	Terminal Grounded	Lock Test			No-Load Test			
					Amps	Volts	Torque	Amps	Volts	R.P.M.	
1950–55 All Series, 10	105	6	1	Pos.	550	3	12	65	6	5500	26
1956–58 All Series	53	12	2SM	Neg.	435	6	11	75	10	6900	57
1959											
Series 01, 6 Cyl. L Hd.	40	12	2MS	Neg.	290	4.25	10.5	63	10.6	7800	35
Series 10, 6 Cyl. OHV	45	12	2HS	Neg.	290	4.25	10.5	63	10.6	7800	35
Series 20, V8, OHV	50	12	2HS	Neg.	290	4.25	10.5	63	10.6	7800	35
Series 80, V8, OHV	50	12	2HS	Neg.	330	3.5	10.5	83	10.6	4400	35
1960-62											
Series 01, 6 cyl. L Hd.	40	12	2MS	Neg.	285	4.0	6.5	48	10.0	5300	35
Series 01, 6 Cyl. OHV	40	12	2MS	Neg.	385	3.5	10.5	112	10.6	3240	35
Series 10	45	12	2HS	Neg.	385	3.5	10.5	112	10.6	3240	35
Series 20	50	12	2HS	Neg.	285	4.0	6.5	48	10.0	5300	48
Series 80	50	12	2HS	Neg.	405	4.0	9.0	60	10.0	4200	48
1963											
6 Cyl., L. Head American	40	12	2-SM	Neg.	285	4.0	6.5	48	10.0	5300	35
6 Cyl., O.H.V. American	45	12	2-SM	Neg.	385	3.5	10.5	112	10.6	3240	35
6 Cyl., O.H.V. Rambler Classic	45	12	2-SM	Neg.	385	3.5	10.5	112	10.6	3240	48
V8, Rambler Ambassador	60	12	2-SMH	Neg.	405	4.0	9.0	60	10.0	4200	48

CAPACITIES

YEAR	Engine Crankcase Add 1 Qt. for New Filter	TRANSMISSIONS Pints to Refill After Draining		Rear Axle Pints	(See Note 2) Gasoline Tank Gallons	Cooling System Quarts Add 1 Qt. for Heater
		Manual Add 1 Pt. for Over Drive	AUTOMATIC			
1954–55 Series 10, 6 Cyl. L Hd.	4	1½	17	3	20	11
1956–57						
Series 10, 6 Cyl., OHV	4	2¼	17	3	20	10
Series 20, V8, OHV	5	2¼	Note 1	4	20	20
1958						
Series 01, 6 Cyl. L Hd.	4	1½	20	3	20	11
Series 10, 6 Cyl., OHV	4	1½	20	3	20	10
Series 20, V8, OHV	4	2¼	20	4	20	20
Series 80, V8, OHV	4	4	22	4	20	19
1959-63						
Series 01, 6 Cyl. L Hd.	4	1½	20	3	20	11
Series 10, 6 Cyl. OHV	4	1½	20	3	20	10
Series 20, V8, OHV	4	2¼	20	4	20	20
Series 80, V8, OHV	4	4	22	4	20	19

NOTES FOR CAPACITIES TABLE

Note 1—1957 Series 20 Automatic Tranmission Capacity

With Hydra-Matic ....23 pints

With Flashomatic ....19 pints

Note 2—1960

All ....22 gallons

FUSES and CIRCUIT BREAKERS

1957-63 MODELS

Head and Tail Lights:
Two circuit breakers in the light switch.

Interior Lighting Circuit:
7.5 amp. fuse on light switch.

Stop Light and Turn Signals:
30 amp. circuit breaker on the ceiling of the cowl beneath the dash panel.

Radio:
AGA-5 fuse in line to set.

Overdrive:
AGC-15 fuse on relay.

Power Windows:
30 amp. circuit breaker under the instrument panel on each side of the car.

1954-56 MODELS

All Lights Except the Stop Light and the Turn Signals:
On light switch; AGC 30 fuse.

Turn Signals and Stop Light:
Under hood on left fender skirt; SFE 30 fuse.

Radio:
At the set. AGC 18 fuse.

Overdrive
On relay. AGC 30 fuse.

LIGHT BULBS

1954-57 MODELS

Hydramatic Quadrant:

6 Volt, No. 44; 12 Volt, No. 1891.
(2 C.P. miniature bayonet base.)

Beam Indicator, Generator, Oil Pressure, Turn Indicator, Clock:

6 Volt, No. 51; 12 Volt, No. 57.
(1 C.P. or 2 C.P. miniature bayonet base.)

Instrument Lights:

6 Volt, No. 55; 12 Volt, No. 57.
(2 C.P. miniature bayonet base.)

Front Park, License Plate and Courtesy Lights:

6 Volt, No. 63; 12 Volt, No. 67.
(4 C.P. single contact base.)

Dome Light:

6 Volt, No. 81; 12 Volt, No. 89.
(6 C.P. single contact base.)

Back-up Light:

6 Volt, No. 1133; 12 Volt, No. 1073.
(32 C.P. single contact base.)

Combination Front Turn and Park or Rear Turn, Tail and Stop Lights:

6 Volt, No. 1154; 12 Volt, No. 1034.
(32 and 4 C.P. 2. contact indexed base.)

Headlamps—Two Only:

6 Volt, No. 5040; 12 Volt, No. 5400.
(50 and 40 C.P. three contact base.)

1958-63 MODELS

Instrument, Headlamp Beam Indicator, Clock, Glove Box, Turn Signal Indicator, Generator Charge, Oil Pressure Lights:

12 Volt, No. 57.
(2 C.P. miniature bayonet base.)

License Light:

12 Volt, No. 67.
(4 C.P. single contact base.)

Dome and Courtesy Lights:

1958

12 Volt, No. 89.
(6 C.P. single contact base.)
1959-63
12 Volt, No. 1003
(15 C.P. single contact base.

Tail, Stop, Turn Signal and Parking:

12 Volt, No. 1034.
(32 and 4 C.P. 2 contact bayonet indexed base.)

Back-up Lights:

12 Volt, No. 1073.
(32 C.P. single contact base.)

Headlights—4 Only:

OUTER (Low and High Beam)
12 Volt, No. 4002.
(37.5-50 watts three contact base.)

INNER (High Beam Only)
12 Volt, No. 4001.
(37.5 watts double contact base.)

Headlights—2 Only:

12 Volt, No. 5400.
(40 and 50 C.P. three contact base.)

TORQUE SPECIFICATIONS

YEAR	Cylinder Head Bolts	Rod Bearing Bolts	Main Bearing Bolts	Crankshaft Pulley Bolt	Flywheel to Crankshaft Bolt	Manifolds In	Ex
1954-60							
All 6 Cyl.	60	30	70	80	105	20	25
All OHV, V8	65	50	85(A)	80	105	25	25
1961-63							
6 Cyl. Iron	60	30	70	80	105	20	25
6 Cyl. Alumium	50	30	58	80	105	(B)	(C)
V8, All	60	50	85(A)	80	105	20	25

NOTE FOR TORQUE SPECIFICATIONS TABLE

(C) Manifold
End Nuts=10 Ft. Lb.
Center Flange=25 Ft. Lb.

(A) 1957-63 V8 Bearing Bolt Torque
Figure given is for bearing No.'s 1, 2, 3 & 4. Tighten No. 5 (Rear Main) to 55 ft. lbs.

(B) Manifold
Cover Screw, 5/16"=15 Ft. Lb.
1/4"=11 Ft. Lb.

GENERAL CHASSIS and BRAKE SPECIFICATIONS

Year and Model		Chassis		Brake Cyl. Bore		
		Overall Length in Inches	Tire Size	Master Cyl. (Inch)	Wheel Cylinder Diameter (Inch) Front	Wheel Cylinder Diameter (Inch) Rear
1954	6 Cyl. Series 10 (2 door)	185⅜	6.40x15	1.0	1.0	13/16
	6 Cyl. Series 10 (4 door)	193⅜	6.40x15	1.0	1.0	13/16
1955	6 Cyl. Series 10 (2 door)	178¼	6.40x15	1.0	1.0	13/16
	6 Cyl. Series 10 (4 door)	186¼	6.40x15	1.0	1.0	13/16
1956	6 Cyl. Series 10 All	191⅛	6.40x15	1.0	1 1/16	⅞
1957	6 Cyl. Series 10	191⅛	6.40x15	1.0	1.0	13/16
	V8, Series 20, 30	191⅛	6.70x15	1.0	1.0	13/16
1958-59	6 Cyl. Series 01 (L Head)	178 11/32	5.90x15	1.0	1.0	13/16
	6 Cyl. Series 10 (OHV)	191 5/32	6.40x15	1.0	1.0	13/16
	V8, Series 20	191 5/32	7.50x14	1.0	1⅛	⅞
	V8, Series 80	200 5/32	8.00x14	1.0	1⅛	⅞
1960						
	Series 01	178 11/32	5.90x15	1.0	1.0	13/16
	Series 10	189½	6.40x15	1.0	1.0	13/16
	Series 20	189½	7.50x14	1.0	1⅛	⅞
	Series 80	198½	8.00x14	1.0	1⅛	⅞
1961						
	American, All	173.1	6.00 x 15	1.0	1.0	13/16
	Rambler, Classic-6	189.8	6.50 x 15	1.0	1.0	13/16
	Rambler, Classic-V8	189.8	7.50 x 14	1.0	1⅛	⅞
	Rambler, Ambassador-V8	199.0	8.00 x 14	1.0	1⅛	⅞
1962-63						
	American, All	173.1	6.00 x 15	1.0	1.0	13/16
	Rambler, Classic-6	190.0	6.50 x 15	1.0	1⅛	13/16
	Rambler, Ambassador-V8	190.0	7.50 x 14	1.0	1⅛	⅞

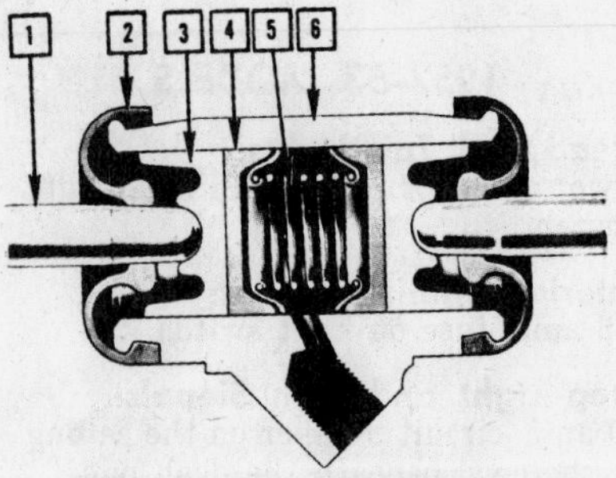

1. Boot
2. Piston
3. Cup
4. Cylinder
5. Spring
6. Bleeder Screw

Front Wheel Cylinder

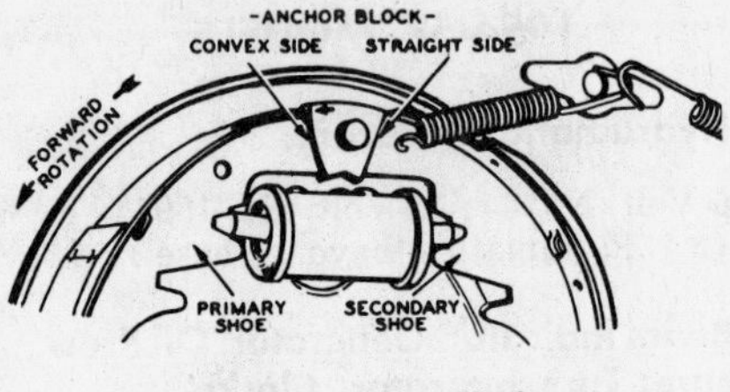

Anchor Block Installation

GENERAL ENGINE SPECIFICATIONS

Year	Bore and Stroke	Number of Main Bearings	Type of Valve Lifter Used	Cubic Inch Displacement	AMA Horsepower	Advertised Horsepower at Stated RPM	Advertised Torque at Stated RPM	Compression Ratio	Oil Pressure At 30 MPH (Note 1)	Cam Shaft Drive
1953–54										
Series 10, 6 Cyl. L Head	3⅛x4	4	Mech. Adj.	184	23.4	85@3800	150@1600	7.3–1	50	Chain
1955										
Series 10, 6 Cyl. L Head	3⅛x4¼	4	Mech. Adj.	195	23.4	90@3800	150@1600	7.3–1	50	Chain
1956										
Series 10, 6 Cyl. OHV	3⅛x4¼	4	Mech. Adj.	195	23.4	120@4200	170@1600	7.5–1	50	Chain
1957										
Series 10, 6 Cyl. OHV	3⅛x4¼	4	Mech. Adj.	195	23.4	← Note 2 →			50	Chain
Series 20, V8 OHV	3½x3¼	4	Mech. Adj.	250	39.2	190@4900	240@2500	8.0–1	50	Chain
1958										
Series 01, 6 Cyl. L Head	3⅛x4¼	4	Mech. Adj.	195.6	23.4	90@3800	150@1600	8.0–1	50	Chain
Series 10, 6 Cyl. OHV	3⅛x4¼	4	Mech. Adj.	195.6	23.4	← Note 3 →			50	Chain
Series 20, V8 OHV	3½x3¼	5	Mech. Adj.	250	39.2	215@4900	260@2500	8.7–1	55	Chain
Series 80, V8 OHV	4 x3¼	5	Hyd. Non-Adj.	327	51.2	270@4700	360@2600	9.7–1	55	Chain
1959-60										
Series 01, 6 Cyl., L Head	3⅛x4¼	4	Mech. Adj.	195.6	23.4	90@3800	150@1600	8.0–1	50	Chain
Series 10, 6 Cyl. OHV	3⅛x4¼	4	Mech. Adj.	195.6	23.4	← Note 3 →		8.7–1	50	Chain
Series 20, V8 OHV	3½x3¼	5	Mech. Adj.	250	39.2	215@4900	260@2500	8.7–1	55	Chain
Series 80, V8 OHV	4 x3¼	5	Hyd. Non-Adj.	327	51.2	270@4700	360@2600	8.7–1	55	Chain
1961										
Series 01, L Head	3⅛x4¼	4	Mech. Adj.	195.6	23.4	125@4200	180@1600	8.0-1	50	Chain
Series 10, Single Carb	3⅛x4¼	4	Mech. Adj.	195.6	23.4	127@4200	180@1600	8.7-1	50	Chain
Series 10, 2 Brl. Carb	3⅛x4¼	4	Mech. Adj.	195.6	23.4	138@4500	185@1800	8.7-1	50	Chain
Series 20, 2 Brl. Carb	3½x3¼	5	Mech. Adj.	250.0	39.2	200@4900	245@2500	8.7-1	50	Chain
Series 20, 4 Brl. Carb	3½x3¼	5	Mech. Adj.	250.0	39.2	215@4900	260@2500	8.7-1	50	Chain
Series 80, 2 Brl. Carb	4 x3¼	5	Hyd. Non-Adj.	327.0	51.2	250@4700	340@2600	8.7-1	50	Chain
Series 80, 4 Brl. Carb	4 x3¼	5	Hyd. Non-Adj.	327.0	51.2	270@4700	360@2600	9.7-1	50	Chain
1962-63										
6 Cyl., L Head	3⅛x4¼	4	Mech. Adj.	195.6	23.4	90@3800	160@1600	8-0-1	50	Chain
6 Cyl., OHV	3⅛x4¼	4	Mech. Adj.	195.6	23.4	127 @ 4200	180@1600	8-7-1	50	Chain
V8, OHV	4 x3¼	5	Hyd. Non-Adj.	327.0	51.2	250@4700	340@2600	8-7-1	50	Chain
V8, OHV	4 x3¼	5	Hyd. Non-Adj.	327.0	51.2	270@4700	360@2600	9-7-1	50	Chain

NOTES FOR GENERAL ENGINE SPECIFICATIONS TABLE

Note 1: Oil Flow

OIL FILTER TYPE

1954-57, All	Partial flow
1958, 6 cyl. OHV	Partial flow
1958, V8, OHV	Full flow
1959, 6 cyl. L Head	Partial flow
1960-63, 6 cyl., OHV	Partial flow
1959-63, V8 OHV	Full flow

ROCKER SHAFT OIL SUPPLY

1956-63, 6 cyl. OHV

The oil under pressure from the main oil gallery is directed through drilled passages in the block and head, then through the front rocker shaft support and into the hollow rocker shaft to lubricate each rocker arm.

1957-63, OHV, V8

Passages at the front of the engine and in the camshaft thrust plate connect the main central oil gallery with the left and right bank tappet oil galleries. At the rear of each tappet oil gallery a passage connects upward to the rear rocker arm shaft support retaining bolt. These bolts are drilled to permit oil flow to the rocker arm shafts, rocker arms, push rods, valve stems and guides. Two drain holes in the lower corners of the heads return the oil to the sump.

Note 2: 1957 Series 10 Horsepower and Torque

WITH SINGLE BORE CARB.:

H.P.—125@4200.

Torque—175@1600.

WITH TWO BORE CARB.:

H.P.—135@4500.

Torque—180@1800.

Note 3: 1958-63 Series 10 Horsepower and Torque

WITH SINGLE BORE CARB.:

H.P.—127@4200.

Torque—180@1600.

WITH TWO BORE CARB.:

H.P.—138@4500.

Torque—185@1800.

Abbreviations Used

MECH. ADJ.—Solid Lifter with adjustable tappets.

H.P.—Horse Power.

C.R.—Compression Ratio.

PISTON AND PIN SPECIFICATIONS

Year and Model		PISTON				PISTON PIN			
		Skirt Clearance		Diameter	Bushing	FIT			Lock
		TOP	BOTTOM			In Rod	In Piston		
1954	Six	.0015	.0018	.8595	None	0	.0002		Clamp
1955-56	All	.0009	.0009	.8595	None	0	.0002		Clamp
1957	All	.0009	.0009	.8595	None	Press	Palm Press		Rod Press
1957	V8	.0017	.0012	.9306	None	Press	Palm Press		Rod Press
1958-60	Six	.0012	.0009	.8595	None	Press	Palm Press		Rod Press
1958-60	V8	.0017	.0012	.9306	None	Press	Palm Press		Rod Press
1961-63	Six	.0017	.0012	.8595	None	Press	Palm Press		Rod Press
1961-63	V8	.0025	.0015	.9306	None	Press	Palm Press		Rod Press

VALVE SPECIFICATIONS

YEAR	Seat Angle		Intake Valve Lift Note 1	Exhaust Valve Lift	Valve Spring Pressure Note: 2.		Stem To Guide Clearance		Stem Diameter		Are Valve Guides Replaceable
	In.	Ex.			Outer	Inner	Inlet	Exhaust	Inlet	Exhaust	
1954											
Series 10, 6 Cyl., "L" Hd.	45	45	.325	.325	39@1¾	None	.0031	.0031	.341	.341	Yes
1955											
Series 10, 6 Cyl., "L" Hd.	45	45	.340	.340	39@1¾	None	.0023	.0023	.341	.341	Yes
1956											
Series 10, 6 Cyl. OHV	45	45	.366	.361	68@1¹³⁄₁₆	None	.0025	.0030	.341	.341	Yes
1957											
Series 10, 6 Cyl., OHV	45	45	.366	.361	68@1¹³⁄₁₆	None	.0028	.0033	.341	.341	Yes
Series 20, V8, OHV	30	45	.375	.375	88@1	None	.0021	.0026	.341	.341	Yes
1958											
Series 10, 6 Cyl., OHV	45	45	.366	.361	68@1¹³⁄₁₆	None	.0028	.0033	.341	.341	Yes
Series 20, V8, OHV	30	45	.375	.375	88@1¹³⁄₁₆	None	.0021	.0026	.341	.341	Yes
Series 80, V8, OHV	30	45	.375	.375	88@1¹³⁄₁₆	None	.0021	.0026	.341	.341	Yes
Series 01, 6 Cyl., "L" Hd.	45	45	.324	.322	39@1¾	None	.0023	.0023	.341	.341	Yes
1959-60											
Series 01, 6 Cyl., "L" Hd.	45	45	.324	.322	39@1¾	None	.0018	.0018	.341	.341	Yes
Series 10, 6 Cyl., OHV	45	45	.366	.361	68@1¹³⁄₁₆	None	.0018	.0033	.341	.341	Yes
Series 20 & 80, V8, OHV	30	45	.375	.375	88@1¹³⁄₁₃	None	.002	.002	.372	.372	Yes
1961-63											
American, 6 Cyl., "L" Head	45	45	.340	.340	39@1¾	None	.0025	.0025	.341	.341	Yes
Amer. & Classic, 6 Cyl.—Iron	45	45	.371	.369	68@1¹³⁄₁₆	None	.0025	.0030	.3415	.341	Yes
Classic, Cyl. O.H.V.—Aluminum	45	45	.388	.388	68@1¹³⁄₁₆	None	.0025	.0030	.3415	.341	Yes
Ambassador V-8, OH..V.	30	45	.375	.375	88@1¹³⁄₁₆	None	.0025	.0020	.372	.372	Yes

NOTES FOR VALVE SPECIFICATIONS TABLE

Note 1: Camshaft Sprocket Index Marks

1954-63, All Engines—Align the marks on the camshaft and crankshaft sprockets nearest each other and with the shaft centers.

Note 2: Valve Springs

1954-63, All—Intake and Exhaust Springs are the same.

CRANKSHAFT BEARING JOURNAL SIZES

YEAR	MAIN BEARING JOURNALS				CONNECTING ROD BEARING JOURNALS		
	Journal Diameter	Oil Clearance	End Play of Shaft	End Play Held By	Journal Diameter	Oil Clearance	End Play
1954-55							
Series 10, 6 Cyl., "L" Hd.	2.4794	.0018	.005	No. 1	2.0952	.0015	.010
1956							
Series 10, 6 Cyl., OHV	2.4794	.0012	.005	No. 1	2.0952	.0015	.010
1957							
Series 10, 6 Cyl., OHV	2.4794	.0012	.005	No. 1	2.0952	.0015	.008
Series 20, V8, OHV	2.4987	.0014	.005	No. 1	2.2486	.0015	.008
1958							
Series 01, 6 Cyl. L Head	2,4794	.0012	.005	No. 1	2.0952	.0015	.008
Series 10, 6 Cyl., OHV	2.4794	.0012	.005	No. 1	2.0952	.0015	.008
Series 20, V8, OHV	2.4987	.0014	.005	No. 1	2.2486	.0015	.008
Series 80, V8, OHV	2.4987	.0014	.005	No. 1	2.2486	.0015	.008
1959-63							
All 6 Cyl.	2.4794	.0012	.005	No. 1	2.0952	.0012	.010
All V8	2.4988	.0015	.005	No. 1	2.2486	.0017	.010

CYLINDER HEAD NUT TIGHTENING SEQUENCE

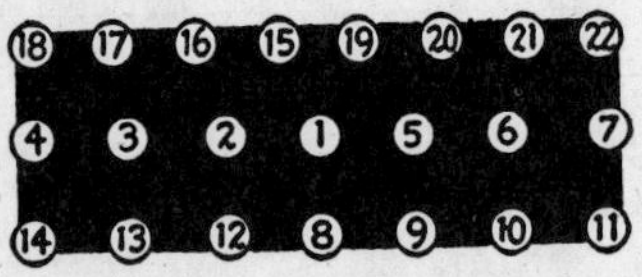

All 6 Cyl. L Head

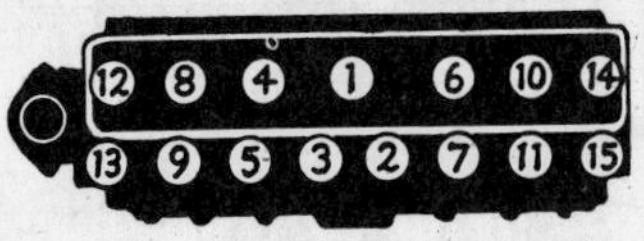

All 6 Cyl. OHV

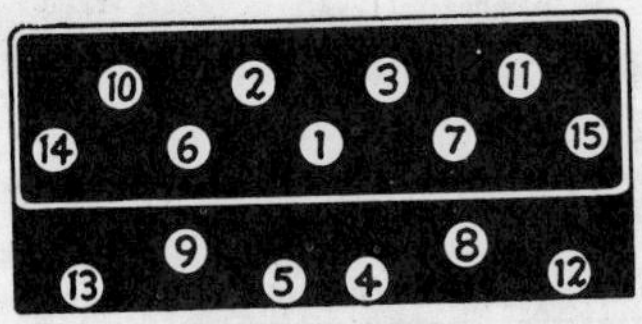

All OHV, V8

FRONT WHEEL ALIGNMENT

YEAR	CASTER		CAMBER		Toe-In (Inches)	King Pin Inclination (Degrees)	Wheel Pivot Ratio	
	Range (Degrees)	Pref. Setting	Range (Degrees)	Pref. Setting			Inner Wheel	Outer Wheel
1954								
Series 10, 6 Cyl., "L" Hd.	¾P–1¼P	1P	¼P–¾P	½P	⅛–¼	8	21½	20
1955								
Series 10, 6 Cyl., "L" Hd.	¾P–1¼P	1P	¼P–¾P	½P	1/16–⅛	8	21	20
1956-58								
All Models, W/Manual	0 – ½P	½P	¼P–¼N	0	1/16–3/16	6⅙	22½	20
All Models W/Power	½ –1 P	1P	¼P–¼N	0	1/16–3/16	6⅙	22½	20
Series 01, 6 Cyl., "L" Hd.	0 – ½P	½	¼N–¼P	0	1/16–3/16	8	20	17½
1959-61								
Series 01, 6 Cyl., "L" Hd. WO/PS	0 – ½P	½P	¼N–¼P	0	1/16–3/16	8	20	17½
Series 01, 6 Cyl., "L" Hd. W/PS	½P–1P	1P	¼N–¼P	0	1/16–3/16	8	20	17½
Series 10, 6 Cyl., OHV WO/PS	0 – ½P	½P	¼N–¼P	0	1/16–3/16	6½	20	17¼
Series 10, 6 Cyl., OHV W/PS	½P–1P	1P	¼N–¼P	0	1/16–3/16	6½	20	17¼
All OHV V8 WO/PS	0..– ½P	½P	¼N–¼P	0	1/16–3/16	6½	20	17¼
All OHV V8 W/PS	½P–1P	1P	¼N–¼P	0	1/16–3/16	6½	20	17¼
1962-63								
Series 01, W/P.S.	1½-2 P	2P	¼N–¼P	0	⅛	8	25	22
Series 01, WO/P.S.	¼N– ¼P	0	¼N–¼P	0	⅛	8	25	22
Series 10, 80, W/P.S.	½ –1 P	1P	¼N–¼P	0	⅛	6½	25	22
Series 10, 80, WO/P.S.	¼N– ¼P	0	¼N–¼P	0	⅛	6½	25	22

DISTRIBUTOR

Detailed information on: distributor drive, direction of distributor rotation; cylinder numbering; firing order; point gap; cam dwell; timing mark location; spark plugs, spark advance; ignition resistor location, and idle speed; will be found in the Tune-up Specifications table at the start of this section. Further information on trouble shooting, general tune-up procedures, how to choose the proper spark plug, adjust timing, will be found in the Unit Repair section under the heading: "Tune-Up and Diagnosis."

Begining with 1960, Rambler uses both Auto-Lite and Delco-Remy Distributors.

DISTRIBUTOR REMOVAL

6 Cyl. Models

The distributor is mounted on the side of the engine. Remove the distributor cap and mark the position of the rotor relative to the distributor body and then mark the distributor body relative to the block. Remove the distributor holddown screw, disconnect the ignition primary wire and the vacuum advance tube and lift the distributor out of the block.

V8 Models

On these models the distributor is located at the back of the block in between the two banks of cylinders. Remove the distributor cap, mark the position of the rotor relative to the distributor body and mark the body relative to the block. Remove the carburetor air cleaner and the distributor primary wire and the distributor vacuum tube.

Remove the holddown bolt and take the distributor up out of the block.

The rotor and body are marked so that they can be returned to the position from which they were removed. Do not turn the engine after the distributor has been taken off.

IGNITION RESISTOR

All 12 Volt Models

The resistor is a white porcelain unit located on the dash panel above and behind the engine.

GENERATOR AND REGULATOR

Detailed facts on the generator and the regulator can be found in the Generator and Regulator Specifications Table of this section.

General information on generator and regulator repair and trouble

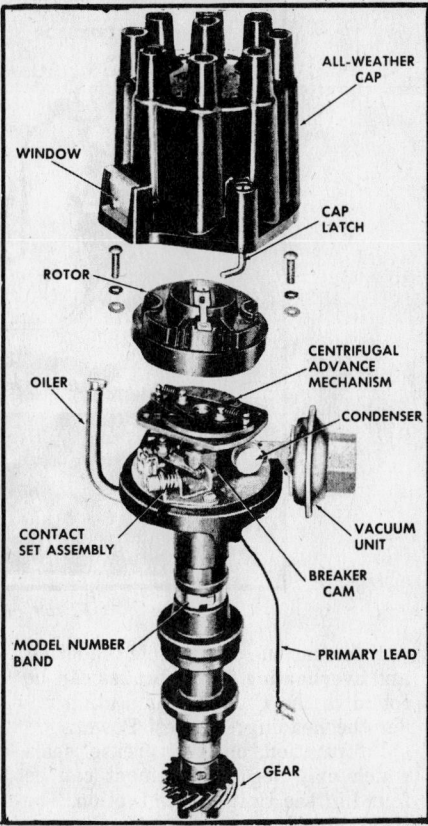

1958 V8 distributor assembly

shooting can be found in the Unit Repair section under the heading: Generators and Regulators.

GENERATOR POLARITY

Caution: Whenever the circuits to: the D.C. generator; the regulator; or the battery have been disconnected it is best to apply the following procedure:

Before the engine is started momentarily short from the "Bat" to

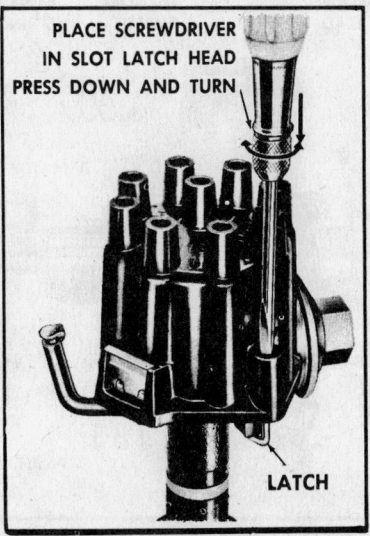

Removing distributor cap

the "Gen" terminals of the regulator with a screwdriver. This gives a momentary surge of current from the battery to the generator and so correctly polarizes the generator with respect to the battery.

Failure to so polarize the D.C. generator before starting the engine may severely damage the regulator since reversed polartiy causes vibration, acting and buring of the relay points.

GENERATOR REMOVAL

Models With Front Mounted Water Pump

Disconnect the wires from the generator and disconnect the water pump coupling. Loosen the fan clamp and remove the tension on the fan belt.

Remove the bolt from the clamp which holds the generator to the side of the engine and lift off the generator. It can be slid out of the water pump coupling.

Models With Side Mounted Water Pumps

Disconnect and insulate the wires from the generator, loosen the tension strap nut and take the tension off the fan belt, remove the fan belt from the generator pulley, let the generator rock down and remove the bolts which hold it to the swivel and lift off the generator.

REGULATOR REMOVAL

Disconnect and carefully tag the wires which run to the regulator, remove the two metal screws which hold the regulator to the sheet metal and lift off the regulator.

BATTERY AND STARTER

Detailed information on the battery and starter will be found in the Battery and Starter Specifications Table of this section.

A more general discussion of batteries will be found in the Unit Repair section under the heading: Tune-Pp and Diagnosis.

A more general discussion of starters and their troubles can be found in the Unit Repair section under the heading: Starters.

STARTER ASSEMBLY REMOVAL

Models With Side Mounted Water Pumps

Disconnect the water pump coupling at the pump and remove the bolts which hold the pump to the block.

Remove the oil filler pipe.

Disconnect the starter and tape the wire up out of the way.

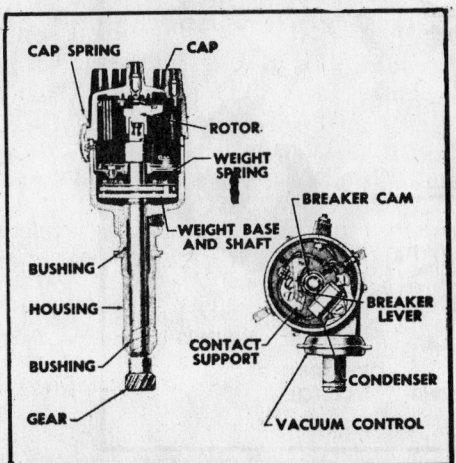

Distributor used on 6 cylinder engines

Disconnect the battery cable from the starter. From under the hood, remove the top bolt, and from under the vehicle, remove the bottom bolt, slide the starter back and out of its housing.

6 Cyl. Models With Front Mounted Pump

Remove the oil filler pipe, disconnect the battery lead from the starter and the solenoid lead from the starter and from underneath the vehicle, remove the bolts which hold the starter to the bell housing and lift off the starter.

V8 Models

Disconnect the battery wire and the solenoid wire at the starter. From underneath the vehicle, remove the bolts which hold the starter to the flywheel housing and lift off the starter.

INSTRUMENTS

SPEEDOMETER REMOVAL

Disconnect battery and speedometer cable. Disconnect instrument wiring and pilot lights. Remove cluster mounting screws and remove cluster to bench.

BRAKE SYSTEM

Specific information on brake cylinder sizes can be found in the General Chassis and Brake Specifications Table of this section.

Information on brake adjustments, band replacement, bleeding procedure, master and wheel cylinder overhaul can be found in the Unit Repair section under the heading: Brakes, Hydraulic.

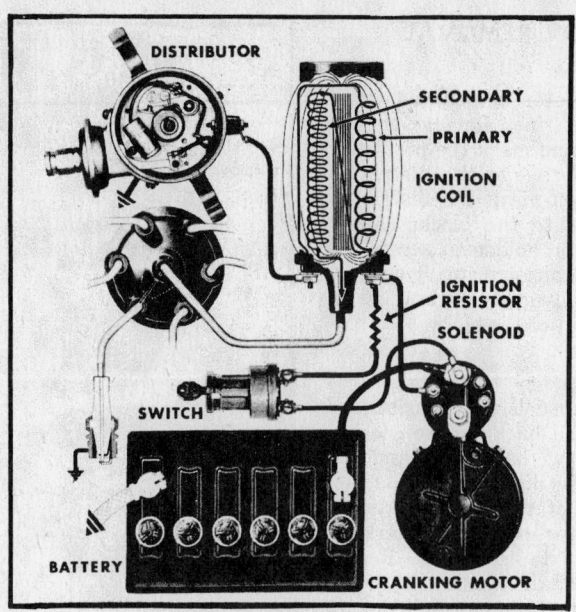

12 volt ignition circuit

Information on trouble shooting and overhauling power brakes can be found in the Unit Repair section under the heading: Brakes, Power.

Information on the grease seals which may need replacement can be found in the Unit Repair section. The front wheel grease seals under the head: Suspension, Front Repair. The rear wheel grease seals under the head: Axles, Rear.

Starting Late 1957

The rear axle splines cut serrations into the inner diameter of the rear wheel hub. If the hub is to be removed match mark the hub to the axle so that the job of aligning the serrations and splines will be easier. If this is not done the axle will cut new splines which may be so near the old that

the hub will move on the axle with resultant damage to the hub, axle and differential gears.

REAR WHEEL HUB INSTALLATION

Slide the hub onto the axle shaft aligning the serrations of the hub with those of the shaft. Now install the nut and tighten the hub onto the shaft until the face of the hub is 3/16" from the outer taper of the shaft.

The 3/16" measurement also applies to a new replacement hub which is not serrated. The serrations will be cut in the hub as it is installed on the shaft.

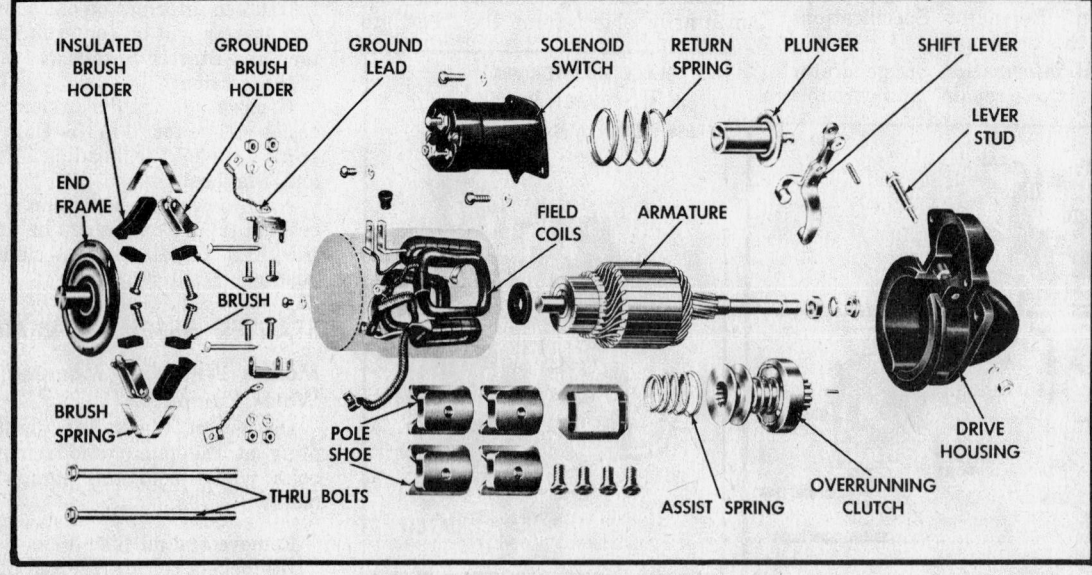

12 volt starting motor

MASTER CYLINDER POWER UNIT REMOVAL

1956 Thru 1963 Models

Remove the clevis pin from the power unit operating rod, disconnect the vacuum line and the hydraulic lines from the power unit, remove the stoplight wires, remove the mounting bolts and lift off the power cylinder.

PARKING BRAKE LEVER REMOVAL

Hand Operated Lever

Remove the brackets which hold the lever assembly up under the dash, slide the end of the cable ball joint out of its connection in the end of the lever and lift the lever off the vehicle.

Foot Operated Lever

The foot operated lever is mounted under the left side of the instrument panel. Slack off on the brake cable and remove the clevis which holds the cable to the top part of the lever. Remove the brackets which hold the lever assembly to the side of the body and lift off the lever.

PARKING BRAKE CABLE REPLACE

All Models

Disconnect the lower end of the cable at the cross shaft or equalizer, disconnect it at the hand brake end as outlined under Hand Brake Removal, remove the brackets which retain it to the body and firewall and thread it out of the vehicle.

When a new cable is to be installed it is always a good idea to tie the new one to the end of the old one so that it will thread through in the same route as the old one. This sometimes will require the service of a helper to guide it.

STARTING 1959 AUTOMATIC ADJUSTERS

Series 20 and 80 cars are presented with an option of automatically adjusted service brakes. This is the Bendix Duo-Servo brake. It automatically adjusts for lining wear, as the case requires. This continuous adjustment maintains a constant pedal height and is a decided safety and economic factor thru the entire lining life.

The adjuster is operated by the movement of the secondary shoe during reverse brake application. The automatic mechanism is attached to and works thru the standard type star wheel adjuster, therefore, care must be used during a reline or major brake job to assure freedom of adjuster parts movement. Care must also be

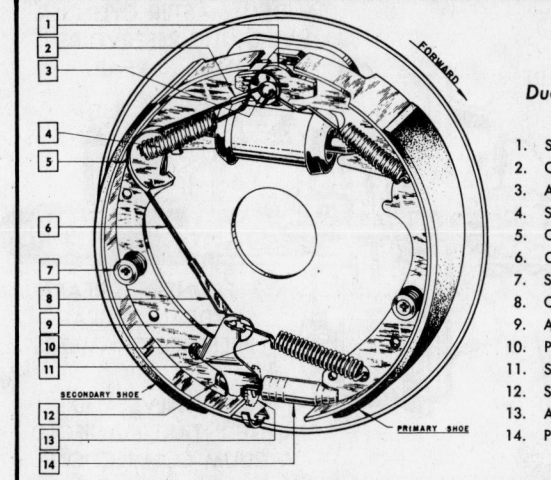

Duo-Servo Brake Assembly with Automatic Adjuster

1. Shoe guide plate
2. Cable anchor fitting
3. Anchor pin
4. Spring-anchor to shoe
5. Cable guide
6. Cable
7. Shoe hold down spring assy.
8. Cable hook
9. Adjusting lever
10. Pivot hook
11. Spring-automatic adjuster
12. Socket
13. Adjusting screw
14. Pivot nut

used to eliminate the mixing of right with left hand parts.

BEGINNING 1961

The 10 series (6 cyl. Rambler) includes an automatic adjuster. This adjuster is designed to operate on the Primary Shoe instead of the conventional secondary type. Incorporating the automatic adjuster into the primary shoe causes the brake adjustment to be made upon forward brake application instead of reverse, which is the case with most other designs of brake automatic adjusters.

Starting 1962

A dual master cylinder is used. The front reservoir supplying rear brakes and the rear one supplying the front brakes. This allows one pair of brakes to operate should there be a failure of the opposite pair. If lines have been disconnected be sure to reinstall in proper place. i.e. front to rear cylinder and rear to front.

With pressure bleeder the Bendix System can be bled from front reservoir by covering rear reservoir with solid cap. The Moraine type must be bled separately, front and rear.

Without pressure bleeder keep both reservoirs nearly full.

FUEL SYSTEM

INFORMATION

A chart covering causes of excess fuel consumption will be found in the Unit Repair section under the heading: Fuel Consumption Chart.

Data on capacity of the gas tank will be found in the Capacities table. Data on correct engine idle speed and fuel pump pressure will be found in the Tune-Up Specifications table. Both the above tables can be found in this section.

General information on fuel pumps and their troubles will be found in the

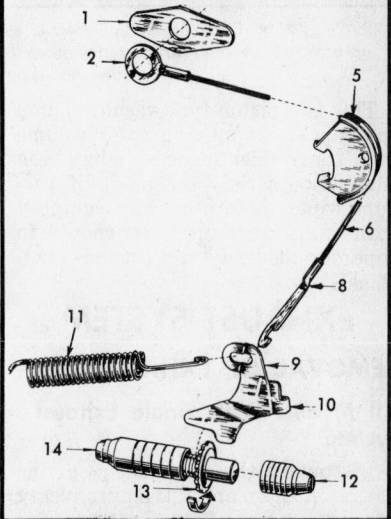

Automatic Adjuster Brake Parts

Unit Repair section under the heading: Fuel Pumps.

Information covering operation and troubles of the fuel gauge will be found in the Unit Repair section under the heading: Gages.

Detailed information on the carburetor and how to adjust it will be found in the Unit Repair section under the board heading: Carburetors.

FUEL PUMP REMOVAL

Disconnect both gas lines from the fuel pump, disconnect the vacuum line if it is a vacuum pump, remove the two bolts which hold it to the block and lift off the pump.

STARTING 1961 FUEL PUMP—CARTER

A newly designed fuel-vacuum pump is used on Classic and Ambassador models.

The outward appearance of this pump is traditional and looks not unlike Carter's earlier double purpose pumps, however, the vacuum pumping mechanism is quite different.

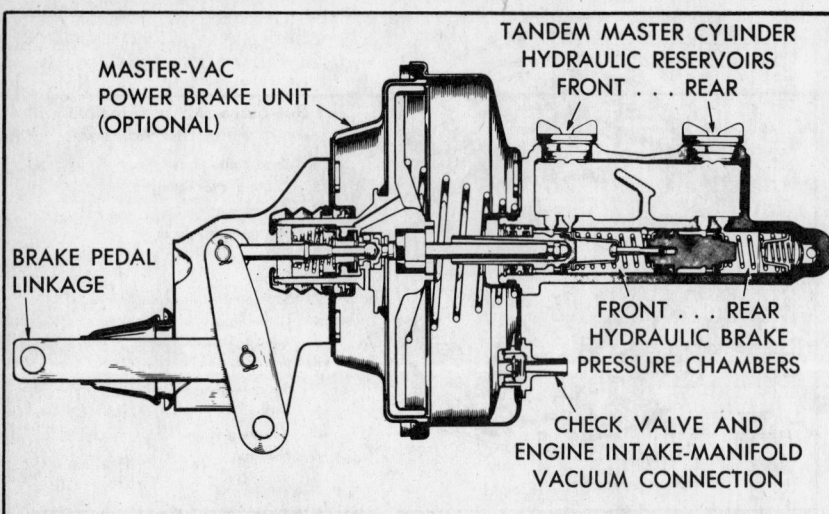

MASTER-VAC
POWER BRAKE UNIT
(OPTIONAL)

TANDEM MASTER CYLINDER
HYDRAULIC RESERVOIRS
FRONT . . . REAR

BRAKE PEDAL
LINKAGE

FRONT . . . REAR
HYDRAULIC BRAKE
PRESSURE CHAMBERS

CHECK VALVE AND
ENGINE INTAKE-MANIFOLD
VACUUM CONNECTION

1962 Power Dual Master Cylinder. (It can be hooked up backwards; the proper hook-up is as follows: the rear master cylinder should operate the front brakes; the front master cylinder should operate the rear brakes.)

This is a piston type vacuum pump and capable of much greater volume than some older models. It has been adapted to satisfy the needs of vacuum wiper motors on cars equipped with blades large and heavy enough to wipe our modern wrap around windshields.

EXHAUST SYSTEM

REMOVAL OF EXHAUST PIPE

All Models With Single Exhaust System

Disconnect the exhaust pipe at the flange on the manifold. Squirt plenty of penetrating oil between the muffler and the exhaust pipe, or if it is frozen too solidly turn a little heat on it.

Remove the clamps which hold the

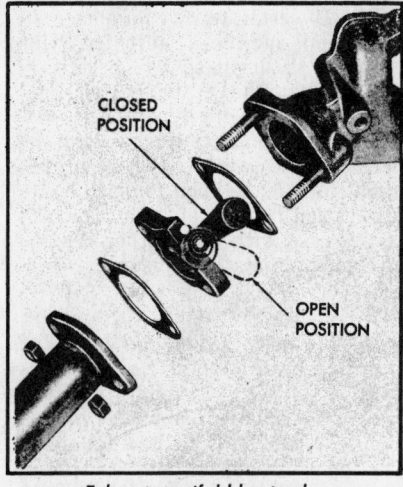

CLOSED
POSITION

OPEN
POSITION

Exhaust manifold heat valve

exhaust pipe to the muffler and slide the exhaust pipe out the front of the muffler. It can be threaded out from underneath the car.

Reinstall the new exhaust pipe so that the pipe extends past the slots in the muffler connections.

INSTALL MUFFLER

Squirt a good penetrating or de-rusting oil at the joint between the exhaust pipe and the muffler and the joint between the muffler and the tail pipe.

Let this oil work in. Remove the clamps which hold the muffler to the exhaust pipe and the muffler to the tail pipe. Loosen the tail pipe hanger bracket so that tail pipe can be slid backwards slightly so that it can be cleared from the muffler.

Let the tail pipe clear, bend the muffler downwards and slide it off the back of the exhaust pipe.

Reinstall in reverse order and tighten all of the clamps which were loosened to permit removal of the muffler.

INSTALL TAIL PIPE

Squirt plenty of penetrating oil where the tail pipe joins the muffler and remove the clamp.

Remove the hangers which hold the tail pipe up to the under-body and slide the front of the tail pipe out of the back of the muffler.

When the new tail pipe is installed slide it far into the muffler to cover the slots in the muffler joint.

Arrange the muffler so that it hangs on each of its hangers approximately equally, that is, don't leave one hanger carrying all the weight so that it can rattle on the other one.

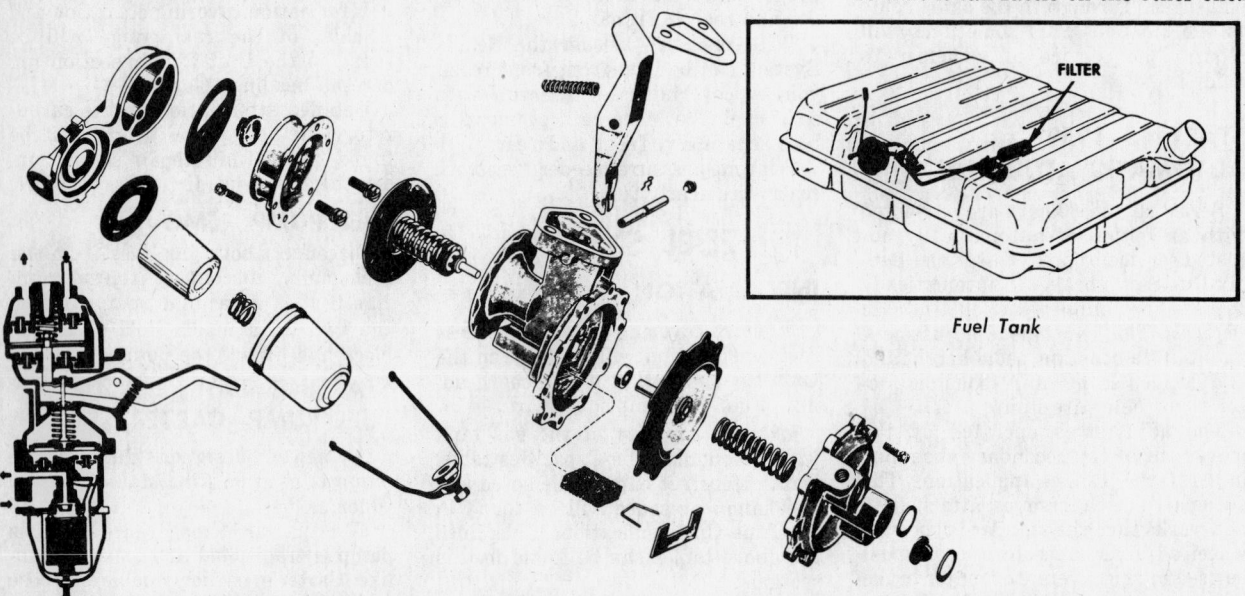

FILTER

Fuel Tank

Starting 1960 fuel-vacuum pump

Exploded view combination fuel and vacuum pump and ceramic filter assembly used on Series 10

This can be accomplished easily by twisting the muffler slightly so that pressures are reasonably equal on all hangers. This will prevent rattles.

COOLING SYSTEM

Detailed information on cooling system capacity can be found in the Capacities Table of this section.

Information on the water temperature gauge can be found in the Unit Repair section under the heading: Gages.

RADIATOR CORE REMOVAL

Raise the hood, drain the radiator, remove the upper and lower radiator hose, take out the bolts which hold the radiator to its cradle and, if the car is fitted with an oil cooler on the transmission, disconnect the oil cooler lines and lift the core up and out.

WATER PUMP REMOVAL

Side Mounted Pumps

Disconnect the coupling between the pump and the generator, remove the hose from the pump, take out the cap screws which mount the pump to the block and lift the pump off.

Front Mounted Pumps

Slack off and remove the fan belt, take out the bolts which hold the fan pulley to the hub and remove the fan blades and hub assembly. The water pump can then be unbolted from the manifold and lifted off.

THERMOSTAT REMOVAL

The thermostat is located in the water outlet housing at the top of the cylinder head or on V8 models in front of the manifold.

Disconnect the upper radiator hose and remove the bolts which hold the water outlet neck to the engine and remove the thermostat.

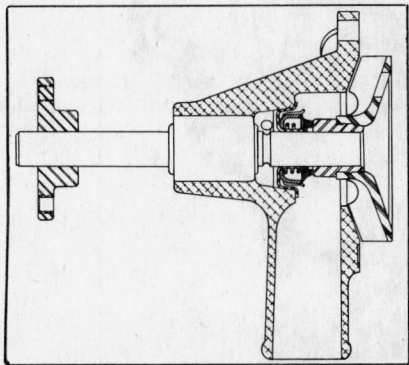

Water pump -Series 10

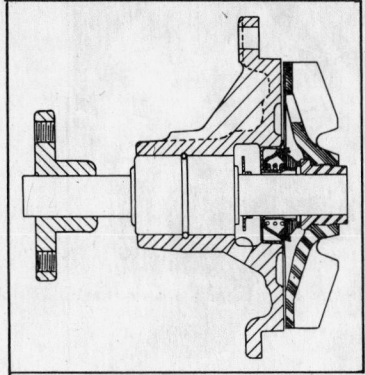

Water Pump 80 Series

ENGINE

REFERENCES

In the specifications tables of this section there are listed all the available facts about the engines. The General Engine Specifications Table will give an easy means of engine identity.

Where some engines have hydraulic valve lifters and others do not, a means of determining which does and which does not is given in the Tune-Up Table.

Engine crankcase capacities are listed in the Capacities Table of this section.

Approved torque wrench readings and head bolt tightening sequences are covered in the Torque Specifications Table of this section.

Information on the engine marking code will be found in the Model Year Identification Table of this section.

Valves

Detailed information on the valves, the type of valve guide and the location of valve timing marks, can be found in the Valve Specifications Table of this section.

A general discussion of valve clearance and a chart showing how to read pressure and vacuum gauges when using them to diagnose engine troubles will be found in the Unit Repair section under the heading: Tune-Up and Diagnosis. Under the same head will be found a chart on engine trouble shooting.

Valve tappet clearance for each engine is given in the Tune-up Specifications Table of this section.

Bearings

Detailed information on engine bearings will be found in the Crankshaft Bearing Journal Sizes Table of this section.

Pistons and Pins

Detailed information on pistons and piston pins, together with information on piston, rod and crankshaft relationship for assembly, will be found in the Piston and Pin Specifications Table

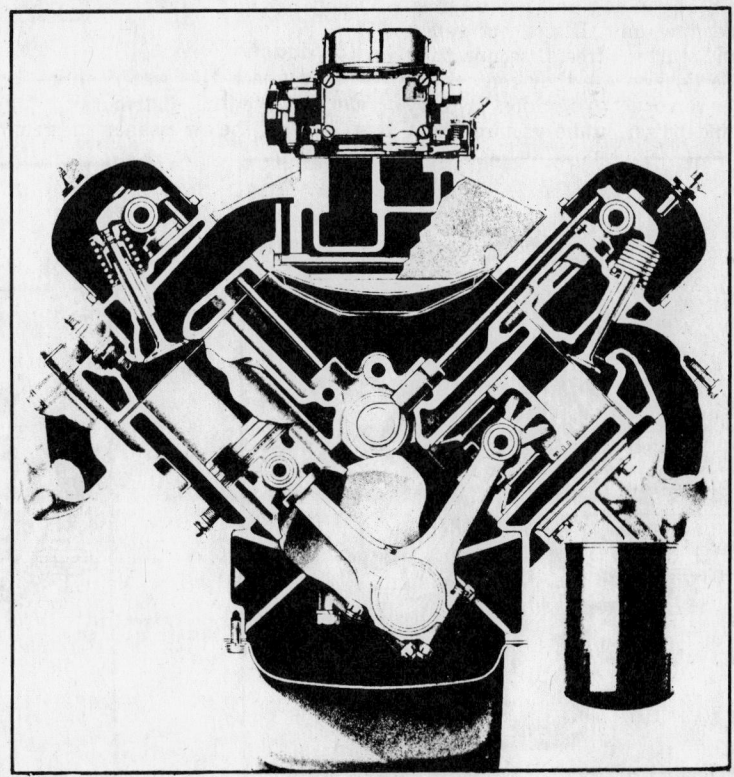

Cross-sectional view of Rambler overhead valve V-8 Engine which started in 1957

On Rambler models thru 1955 the engine is removed by unbolting the cross members from the side rails and lowering the engine down and so out of the car as shown

of this section.

REMOVAL OF ENGINE

All Models Starting 1956

Remove the transmission assembly and the radiator core and hood. Take off the air cleaner and carburetor. Disconnect the gas line at the fuel pump and disconnect the exhaust pipe flange. Disconnect and remove the battery, disconnect the wires leading to the heat sending unit and oil pressure sending unit. Disconnect generator and starter wires. Disconnect the throttle lines where they contact the engine, remove the ignition primary wire and power brake vacuum lines.

Disconnect windshield vacuum lines. Place a lifting device on the engine, remove the mounting bolts and lift the engine forward, up and out.

ENGINE MANIFOLDS

INTAKE MANIFOLD

All "L" Head Engines

On these models the intake manifold is cast integral with the cylinder head.

V8 Models

Disconnect the water outlet tube and remove the distributor.

Take off the air cleaner and remove the carburetor.

Disconnect all throttle lines across the cylinder head.

Disconnect the vacuum lines, the coil and ignition primary leads.

Remove the bolts which hold the intake manifold to both cylinder heads and lift off the manifold.

EXHAUST MANIFOLD REMOVAL

In-line Engines

The exhaust manifold on these models is actually the exhaust pipe held at the side of the cylinder head. Remove the caps which hold the pipe to the cylinder head, split the pipe at the flange and remove it from the vehicle.

V8 Models

Two exhaust manifolds are used, one on each bank. Disconnect the exhaust pipe at the flange, remove the bolts which hold the manifold to the cylinder head and lift the manifold off.

CYLINDER HEAD

ROCKER ASSEMBLY REMOVAL

"L" Head Engines

Remove the carburetor air cleaner and take off the wing nuts which hold the rocker cover to the cylinder head and carefully remove the gasket from both the hood and the cover.

Now working a few turns at a time, remove the bolts which hold the rocker assembly brackets to the cylinder head until the valve spring tension has been removed.

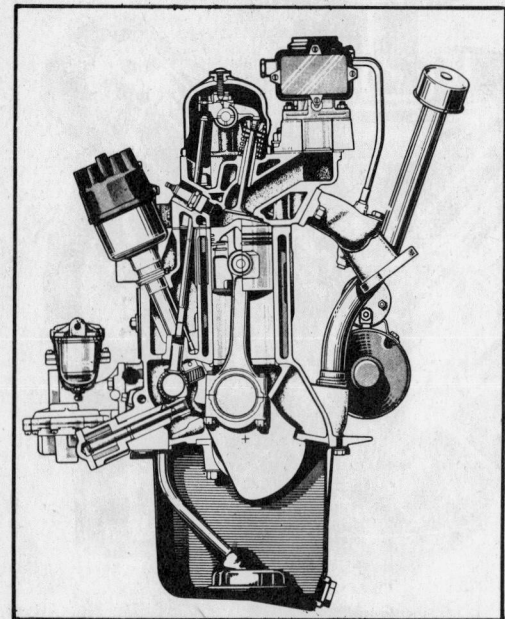

Rambler 6 Cyl. overhead

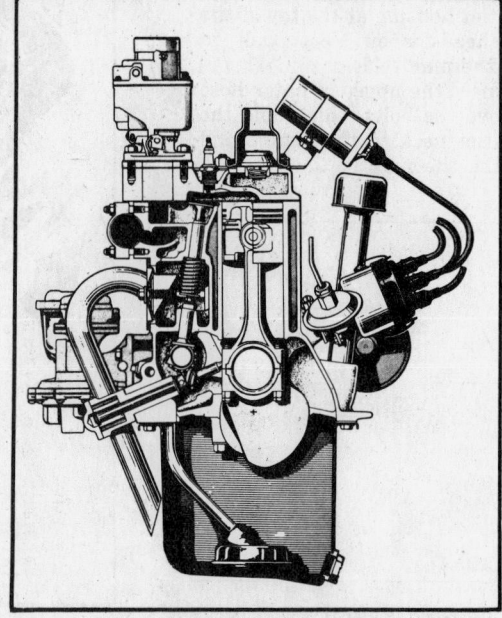

Economy Champ 6 Cyl. "L" head Rambler American

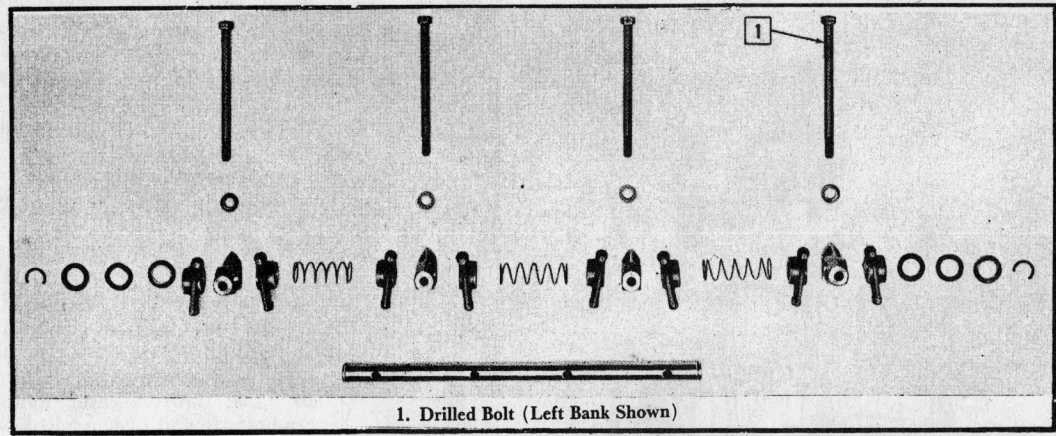

1. Drilled Bolt (Left Bank Shown)

Valve Rocker Arm Assembly 80 Series

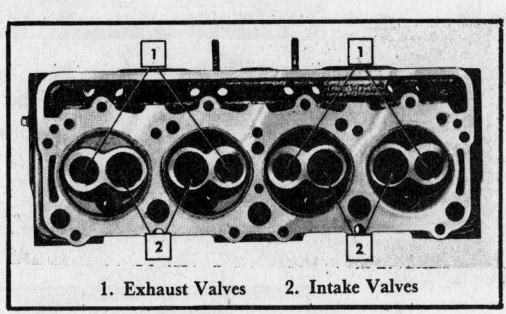

1. Exhaust Valves   2. Intake Valves

Valve   sequence V8

Checking Valve Guide to Stem Clearance

```
FRONT OF ENGINE    VALVES
    I E E I I E E I I E E I

    I- INTAKE VALVE
    E- EXHAUST VALVE
```

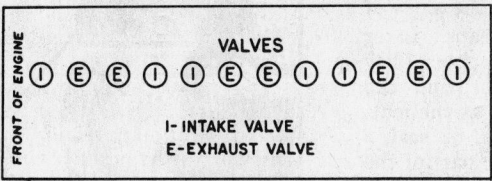

Valve Sequance 6cyl. "L" Head

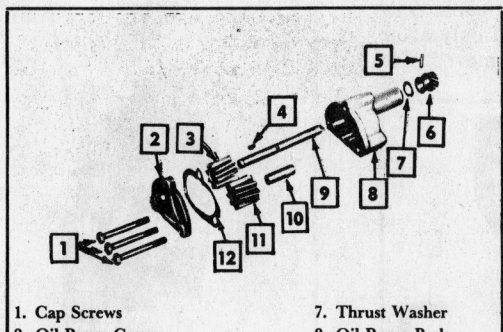

1. Cap Screws	7. Thrust Washer
2. Oil Pump Cover	8. Oil Pump Body
3. Drive Gear (in Pump)	9. Oil Pump Drive Shaft
4. Key	10. Oil Pump Idle Shaft
5. Oil Pump Drive Gear Pin	11. Idle Gear
6. Oil Pump Drive Gear	12. Gasket

6 cylinder oil pump

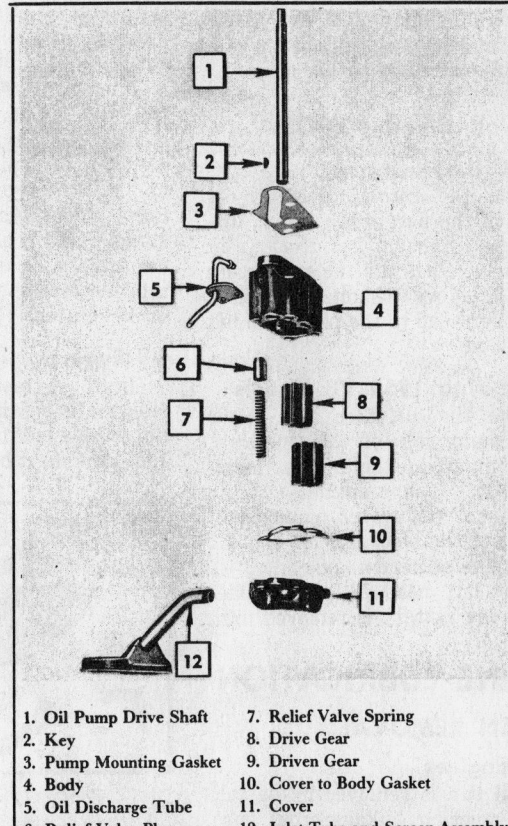

1. Oil Pump Drive Shaft	7. Relief Valve Spring
2. Key	8. Drive Gear
3. Pump Mounting Gasket	9. Driven Gear
4. Body	10. Cover to Body Gasket
5. Oil Discharge Tube	11. Cover
6. Relief Valve Plunger	12. Inlet Tube and Screen Assembly

V-8 oil pump

581

RAMBLER

Die-cast Aluminum block 6 cyl. 1962

Continue to remove the bolts until the rocker assembly is clear.

V8 MODELS

The procedure given above for the in-line engine will apply to the V8 except that in most cases it is not necessary to take the air cleaner off.

CYLINDER HEAD REMOVAL

In-line O.H.V. Engines

Remove the rocker assembly as outlined in the paragraph above, disconnect the exhaust manifold from the cylinder head, pull the spark plug wires and remove the bolts which hold the cylinder head to the block and lift off the head.

Starting With 1955 V8 Models

Remove the oil filler and power steering pump, take off the generator, the inlet manifold, the exhaust manifold and the rocker shafts.

Disconnect the water manifold at the front of the block, unbolt and lift off the cylinder heads.

On the left head it is sometimes easier if the battery is removed first.

ENGINE LUBRICATION

OIL PAN REMOVAL

In-line Engines

The oil pan is removed by detaching the steering linkage cross tube, take out the oil pump attaching bolts and remove the oil pan.

582

REAR MAIN BEARING OIL SEAL

In-line Engines

Several different kinds of rear main bearing oil seals are used, such as wood, rubber, felt and packing. Wooden plugs are used to seal the sides of the rear main bearing caps. Later models use synthetic rubber key strips overlapping the bearing cap and seal the sides as well as the mating surfaces. As an actual oil seal, a slinger, that is an integral part of the crankshaft, is used to throw the oil into the trough so that it cannot get on the clutch.

V8 Engines

On these models a packing type rear main bearing seal is used. The upper half can be replaced only after the crankshaft has been removed. The

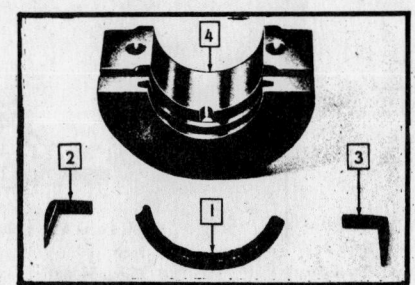

Rear main bearing oil seal, 6 cyl.
1. Hemp packing
2. & 3. Cap side seals
4. Main bearing cap

lower half can be replaced any time the rear main bearing cap is taken down. To replace the lower half, take down the oil pan and remove the rear main bearing cap. Remove the oil packing and set the new packing into the cap so that it protrudes a little at both ends and temporarily bolt it up into place. This will probably cause the upper portion of the oil seal to compress and rivet over just a little bit. Trim off the riveted portion and again insert the cap into position. The reason this is done is that sometimes the compression from the brand new oil seal will cause the upper seal to come down tighter against the crankshaft and prevent leaks even in the upper half which has not been replaced.

⏱ CHILTON TIME-SAVER

Top Half, Rear Main Bearing Oil Seal Replacement—Wick Type

The following method has proven a distinct advantage in most cases and, if successful, saves many hours of labor.
1. Drain engine oil and remove oil pan.

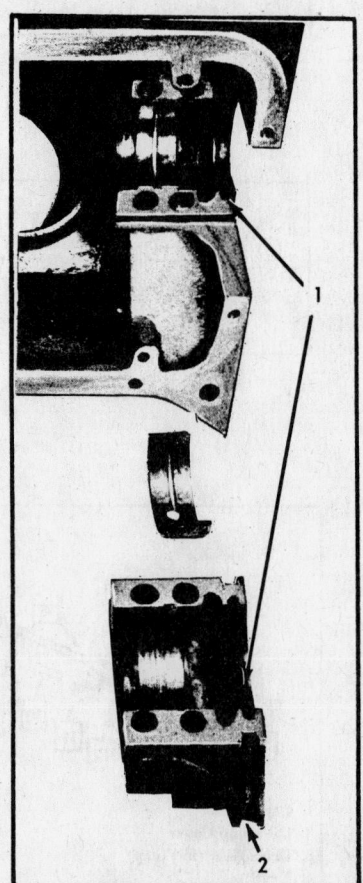

Rear main bearing oil seal, V8
1. Grooves for hemp packing
2. Side seal grooves

2. Remove rear main bearing cap.
3. With a 6" length of 3/16" brazing rod, drive up on either exposed end of the top half oil seal. When the opposite end of the seal starts to protrude, have a helper grasp it with pliers and pull gently while the driven end is being tapped. It is surprising how easily most of these seals can be removed by this method.

To Install the New Wick Type Seal:

1. Obtain a 12" piece of copper wire (about the same gauge as that used in the strands of an insulated battery cable).
2. Thread one strand of this wire thru the new seal, about ½" from the end, bend back and make secure.
3. Thoroughly saturate the new seal with engine oil.
4. Push the copper wire up thru the oil seal groove until it comes down on the opposite side of the bearing.
5. Pull (with pliers) on the protruding copper wire while the crankshaft is being turned and the new seal is slowly fed into place. CAUTION: This snaking operation slightly reduces the diameter of the new seal and care will have to be used to keep the seal from slipping too far thru the top half of the bearing.
6. When an equal amount of seal is extending from each side, cut off the copper wire close to the seal and tamp both ends of the seal up into the groove (this will tend to expand the seal again). NOTE: Don't worry about the copper wire left in the groove, it is too soft to cause damage.
7. Replace the seal in the cap in the usual way and replace the oil pan.

VALVE SYSTEM

VALVE REMOVAL

L-Head Engines

Remove the cylinder head and the valve chamber cover. Using a valve spring compressor, compress the valve spring and remove the keeper. This is done, of course, with the valves in the closed position.

Let the valve spring come down and pull the valve up out of the top of the cylinder.

Thoroughly clean up the valve and examine the seat for pits and scratches and if any are found the valve face should be ground on a facing machine. When refaced, examine carefully to make sure that too much metal was not removed from the valves since a sharp corner on the

head of the valve will not last long in an engine.

There should be plenty of metal above the seat.

Examine the valve stem for wear and if necessary mike the valve stem in two or three places to check the amount of wear.

Overhead Valve Engines

Remove the cylinder head and carry it to a bench. Compress the valve spring and remove the keeper. Release the pressure from the spring and push the valve out.

VALVE SPRING CHECK

Valve spring pressure specifications are given in the General Engine Specification Table.

However, a quick check can be made by laying all of the inlet springs alongside of each other on a straight edge,

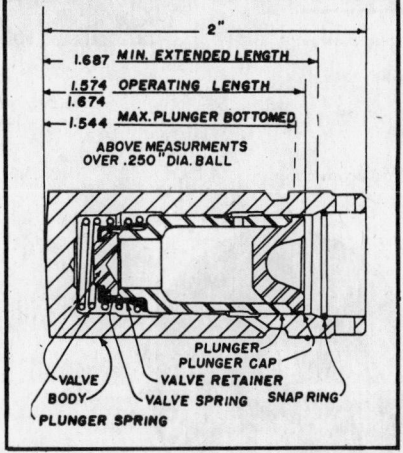

Sectional view of hydraulic tappet assembly.

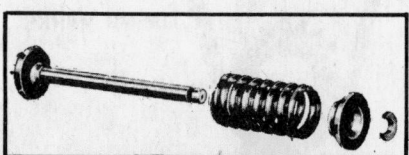

Valve Assembly Sequence

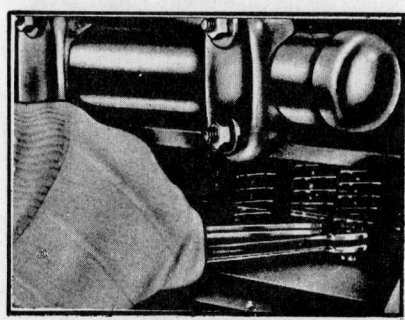

Valve Adjustment
(cold setting .016" intake, .018" Exhaust)

and if they all come up to the same height it can be presumed with a fair degree of accuracy that all the valve springs are in good condition since it is unlikely that all of them would collapse the same amount.

VALVE GUIDE REMOVAL

L-Head Engines

Remove the valves and, using a draw-type puller, pull the valve guide up through the top of the bore. Before the guide is pulled the distance from the top of the cylinder head to the top of the guide should be measured and noted so that a new guide can be driven in just that amount. Sometimes driving a new guide into the bore disturbs the top of the guide somewhat making it necessary to ream the guide so that the valve will fit properly. Any time a new valve guide is installed the valve should be reseated to make certain that the seat is concentric with the new guide.

Overhead Valve Engines

With cylinder head off remove the valves and carefully measure the distance from the top of the cylinder head to the top of the valve guide and then drive the guide out into the combustion chamber.

A new guide is driven in from the top towards the combustion chamber the distance noted before the old guide was removed.

Sometimes driving the guide disturbs it somewhat making it necessary to ream for a good fit on the valve.

TIMING CASE

VIBRATION DAMPER REMOVAL

All Models

Remove the radiator core and the water pump. Remove the nut from the center of the pulley and, using a puller, pull the pulley off the front of the crankshaft.

TIMING CASE COVER REMOVAL

V8 Models

Remove the radiator core and the vibration damper. Take off the water pump and the water manifold. Remove the bolts which holds the timing case cover to the front of the block and lift off the cover.

TIMING COVER OIL SEAL REPLACE

The oil seal can be replaced readily once the timing case cover has been

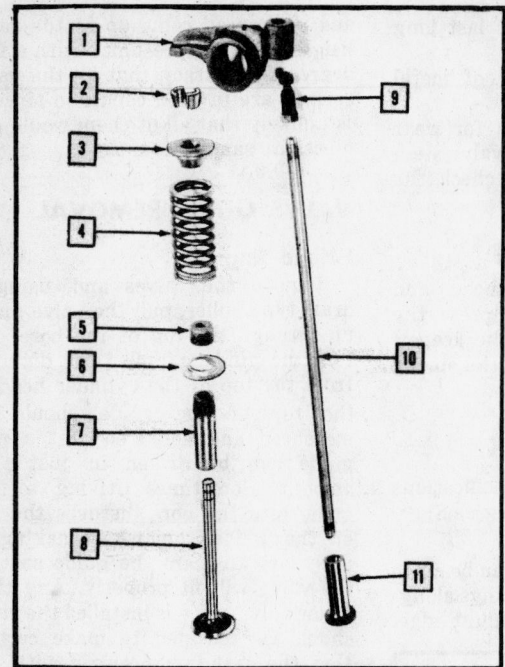

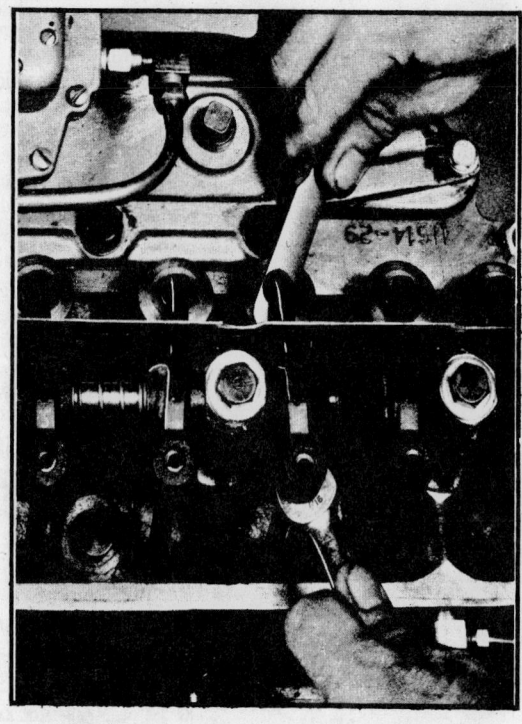

1. Rocker Arm
2. Valve Locks
3. Valve Spring Upper Retainer
4. Valve Spring
5. Oil Deflector
6. Valve Spring Lower Retainer
7. Valve Guide
8. Valve
9. Adjusting Screw
10. Push Rod
11. Tappet

6 cyl. valve assembly sequence. Starting with 1956 production

Valve Adjustment with Engine "Hot" and Running Intake .012"—Exhaust .016"

removed.

RETIME CAMSHAFT AND/OR INSTALL TIMING CHAIN

All Models

Remove the timing case cover and turn the engine until the mark on the crankshaft sprocket points upwards and the mark on the camshaft sprocket points downwards. They should be near each other and in-line between the shaft centers.

Now remove the bolts which hold the camshaft sprocket to the camshaft and start a puller over the crank gear.

Pull the crank gear off the front of the crankshaft.

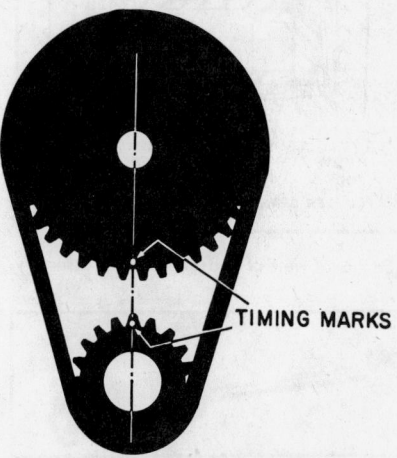

V8 camshaft and crankshaft sprockets. Marks should be adjacent and in line with shaft centers

Now, on the bench, arrange the new chain over the sprockets so that the marks are nearest each other and in line between their own centers and then carry this to the engine. Start the crank gear up on its key and arrange the camshaft so that when the three bolts line up the marks are between shaft centers.

Secure the cam gear to the camshaft and force the crankshaft gear all the way on the shaft.

Reassemble the front of the engine.

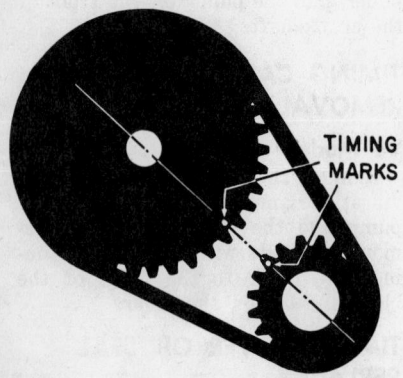

6 cylinder sprockets. Marks should be adjacent and in line with shaft centers

PISTONS, CONNECTING RODS AND MAIN BEARINGS

ROD AND PISTON ASSEMBLY REMOVAL

Remove the cylinder head and oil pan and crank the engine so that one pair of pistons is in the down position. Use a cylinder ring ridge remover and cut the ridge off the top of the cylinders where the piston is down.

Now working from underneath the car, remove the two bolts which hold the rod bearing cap, remove the cap and push the rod and piston assembly up out of the block. Immediately replace the cap and run the nuts up finger-tight so that the cap will not get turned in or the bearing lost.

ASSEMBLE PISTON TO CONNECTING ROD

On engines using split skirt pistons the slit in the skirt must be installed opposite to the oil squirt hole in the connecting rod. Solid skirt pistons are assembled so that the boss or dimple (and in some instances the letter F) at the top of the piston is on the same side of the connecting rod as the boss which will be found on the connecting rod channel about halfway up the rod.

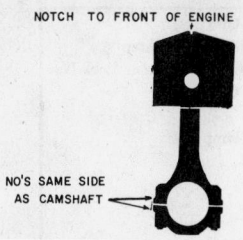

NOTCH TO FRONT OF ENGINE

NO'S SAME SIDE AS CAMSHAFT

Piston and rod assembly. 6 cylinder engine

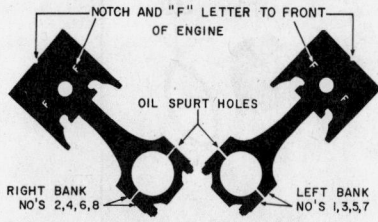

NOTCH AND "F" LETTER TO FRONT OF ENGINE

OIL SPURT HOLES

RIGHT BANK NO'S 2,4,6,8

LEFT BANK NO'S 1,3,5,7

Piston and rod assembly, V8 Engines

INSTALLING PISTONS AND ROD ASSEMBLIES

The piston and rod assemblies are assembled to the engine from the top and the dimple or dot on the top of the piston goes toward the front. On those engines having split skirt pistons, the slit in the skirt of the piston goes to the left side of the engine.

FRONT SUSPENSION

REFERENCES

General instructions covering the front suspension and how to repair and adjust it, together with information on installation of front wheel bearings and grease seals, are given in the Unit Repair section under the heading: Suspension, Front Repair.

Definitions of the points of steering geometry are covered in the Unit Repair section under the heading: Suspension, Front Align. This article also covers trouble shooting front end geometry and irregular tire wear.

Figures covering the caster, camber, toe-in, king pin inclination, and turning radius can be found in the Front Wheel Alignment Table of this section.

Overall car length and tire size figures can be found in the General Chassis and Brake Specifications Table of this section.

STEERING WHEEL AND HORN BUTTON

HORN BUTTON REMOVAL

All Models

On all models the horn button is simply twisted or pried out of the steering wheel.

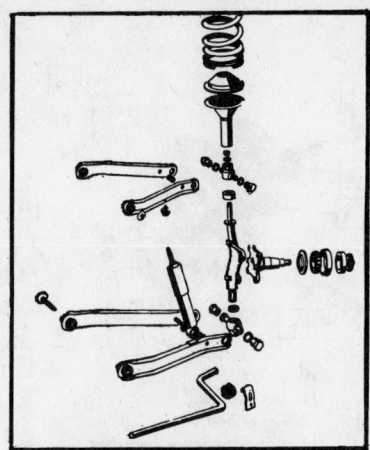

Details of front suspension Starting with 1956 production.

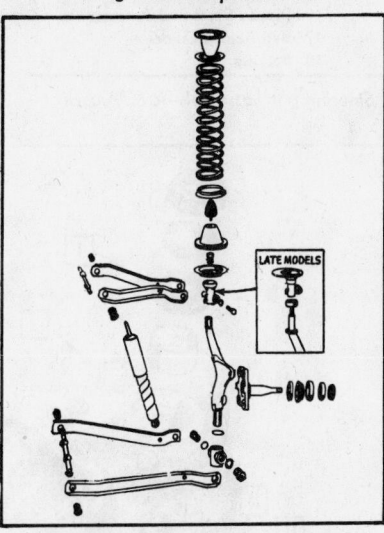

LATE MODELS

Front suspension 1954-55 and Ser. 01

STEERING WHEEL REMOVAL

Remove the horn button or horn blowing ring, take off the nut which holds the steering wheel to the top of the steering tube. Pull the wheel.

STEERING

Manual Steering Gear

Instructions covering the overhaul of the steering gear will be found in the Unit Repair section under the heading: Steering Manual.

Power Steering Gears

Trouble shooting and repair instructions covering power steering gears are given in the Unit Repair section under the heading: Steering, Power.

STEERING GEAR REMOVAL

Thru 1955 Models

Drain the radiator and remove the lower radiator hose.

Remove the steering wheel.

Jack up the car to gain clearance and remove the bolts and clamps which hold the gear assembly to the frame and slide the gear assembly out of the bottom of the vehicle, leaving the mast jacket in the car.

1956 Thru 1963 Models Except 1958-63 Series 80

Disconnect the battery and remove the steering wheel and take off the toeboard plate.

Remove the screws which hold the upper steering jacket to the lower steering jacket.

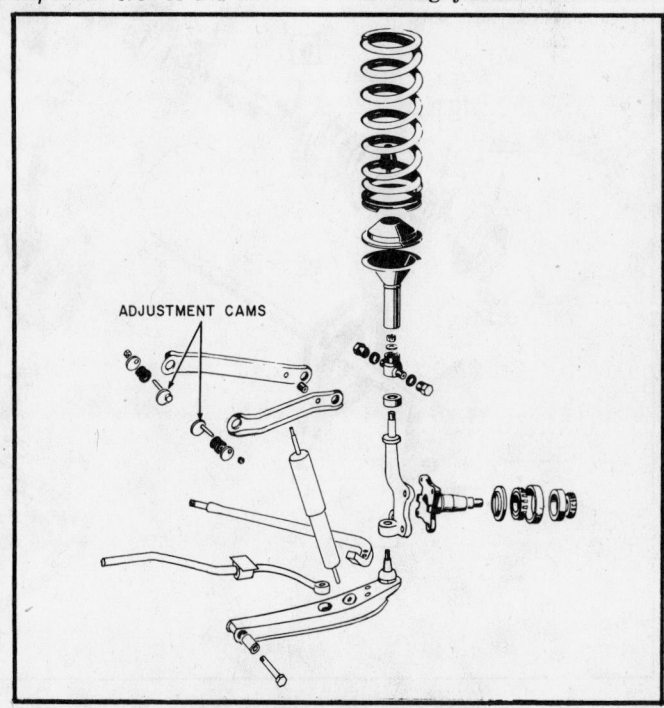

ADJUSTMENT CAMS

Details of front suspension 1962

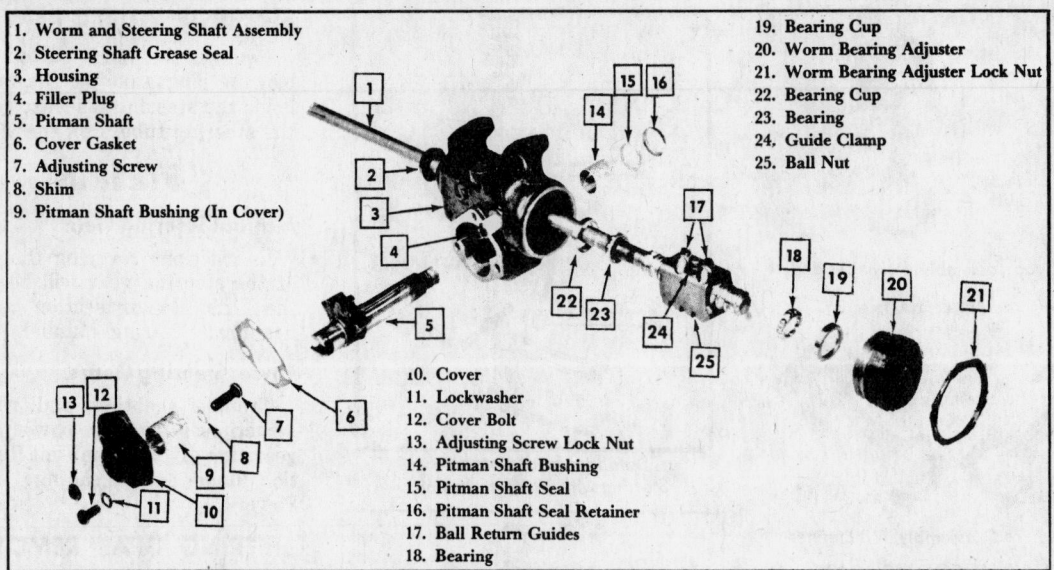

1. Worm and Steering Shaft Assembly
2. Steering Shaft Grease Seal
3. Housing
4. Filler Plug
5. Pitman Shaft
6. Cover Gasket
7. Adjusting Screw
8. Shim
9. Pitman Shaft Bushing (In Cover)

19. Bearing Cup
20. Worm Bearing Adjuster
21. Worm Bearing Adjuster Lock Nut
22. Bearing Cup
23. Bearing
24. Guide Clamp
25. Ball Nut

10. Cover
11. Lockwasher
12. Cover Bolt
13. Adjusting Screw Lock Nut
14. Pitman Shaft Bushing
15. Pitman Shaft Seal
16. Pitman Shaft Seal Retainer
17. Ball Return Guides
18. Bearing

Steering gear assembly—exc. American

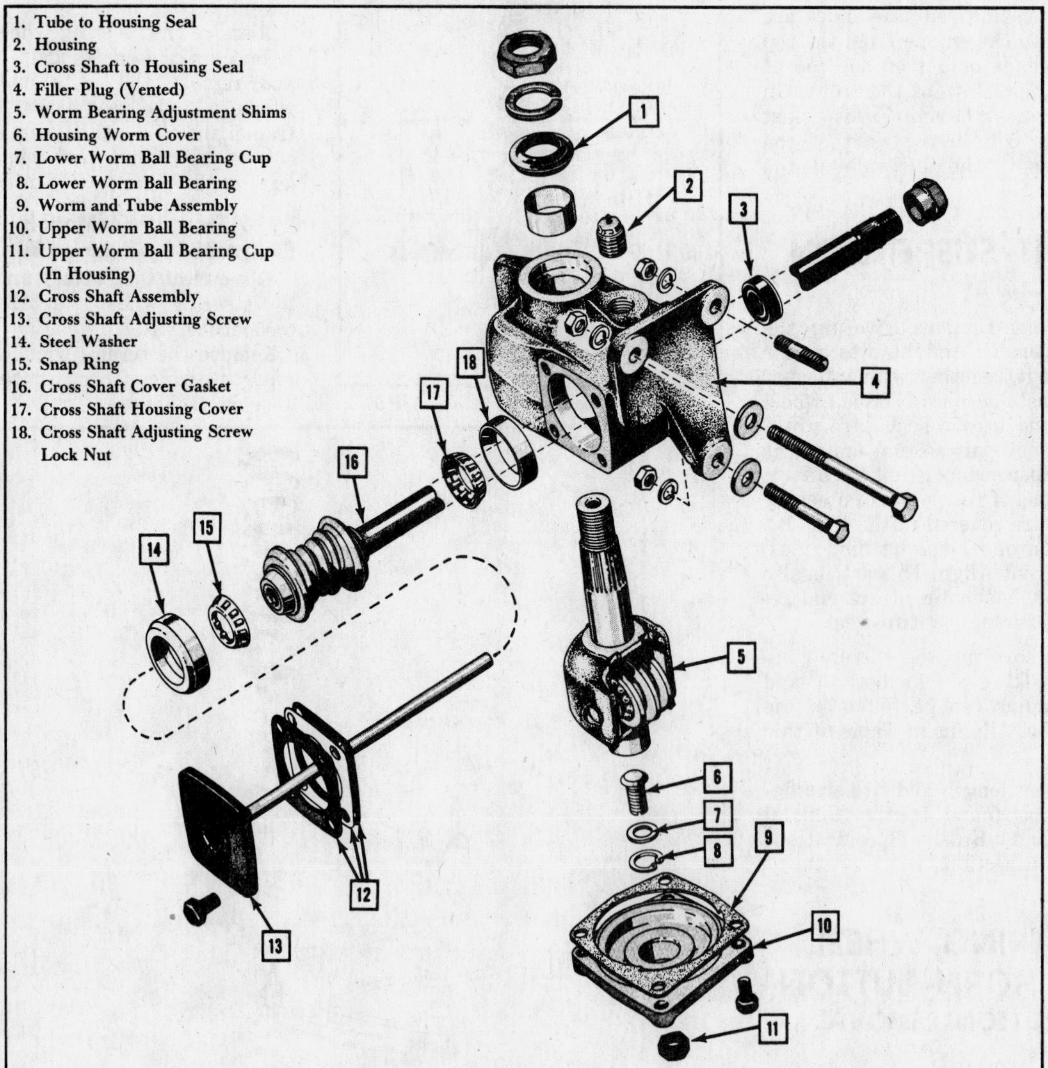

1. Tube to Housing Seal
2. Housing
3. Cross Shaft to Housing Seal
4. Filler Plug (Vented)
5. Worm Bearing Adjustment Shims
6. Housing Worm Cover
7. Lower Worm Ball Bearing Cup
8. Lower Worm Ball Bearing
9. Worm and Tube Assembly
10. Upper Worm Ball Bearing
11. Upper Worm Ball Bearing Cup (In Housing)
12. Cross Shaft Assembly
13. Cross Shaft Adjusting Screw
14. Steel Washer
15. Snap Ring
16. Cross Shaft Cover Gasket
17. Cross Shaft Housing Cover
18. Cross Shaft Adjusting Screw Lock Nut

Steering gear assembly—American

Remove the pitman arm. Place a jack under the front of the engine and take out the engine front support crossmember.

Mark the turning radius stop plate and then take the plate off. Remove the screws which hold the gear housing to the frame and pull the steering gear assembly down and out through the bottom.

1958 Thru 1963 Ambassador Series 80

Remove the steering wheel.

Jack up the car and remove the left front wheel. Mark the location of the turning radius stop plate and then remove the stop plate. Loosen the gear in the housing and then remove the pitman arm. Take off the left exhaust manifold. Support the front of the engine and remove the left engine support mounting bracket. Take down the front crossmember, leaving the stabilizer bar attached. Remove the gear housing screws which hold the gear to the frame and pull the gear down and out the bottom.

POWER GEAR PUMP REMOVAL

Disconnect the pressure hoses from the pump, slack off on the adjusting bracket and remove the bracket bolts which hold the pump to the side of the engine and lift off the pump.

On Eton pumps, to separate the oil reservoir from the pump body, remove the cover, the element, the hollow stud, the two attaching screws, the element baffle and the reinforcement plate. On Vicars pumps take the cover off the reservoir and remove the two cap screws which hold the reservoir to the pump.

CLUTCH

ADJUST PEDAL CLEARANCE

Adjust the free play of the clutch pedal to ½-¾ inch. This is done by changing the length of the link between the throwout lever and the clutch lever.

CLUTCH ASSEMBLY REMOVAL

Remove the transmission and disconnect the clutch linkage, unbolt the clutch inspection pan. Release the pedal rod and return spring which will permit removing the throwout shaft so that the release bearing can be removed through the transmission opening. On all models release the clutch mounting bolts evenly and remove the assembly from the flywheel. Reverse procedure to replace using a pilot shaft to align the clutch disc with the pilot bushing.

"E-STICK" CLUTCH

Beginning with 1962 an optional clutch, engaged by engine oil pressure is used. This pressure is controlled through a valve body so arranged that engine vacuum raises or lowers the pressure as driving conditions demand. In turn, the position of the gear shift lever controls a solenoid which changes applied manifold vacuum; this, through the valve body, regulates the required oil pressure.

With engine off and gear shift lever in neutral a retracting spring releases pressure on clutch fingers, throwout bearing and driven plate.

With engine idling and gear shift lever in neutral the solenoid prevents vacuum from applying any pressure.

With engine idling and gear shift lever in any driving position the solenoid allows a controlled pressure (approximately 7 P.S.I.) through the valve body to servo piston. This piston in turn, applies slight pressure to the throwout lever, throwout bearing, clutch cover fingers, cover plate and driven plate. The slight pressure takes up drive line slack. It is also enough pressure to hold clutch engagement for engine braking.

As engine is accelerated, controlled vacuum and controlled oil pressure increase clutch pressures so that

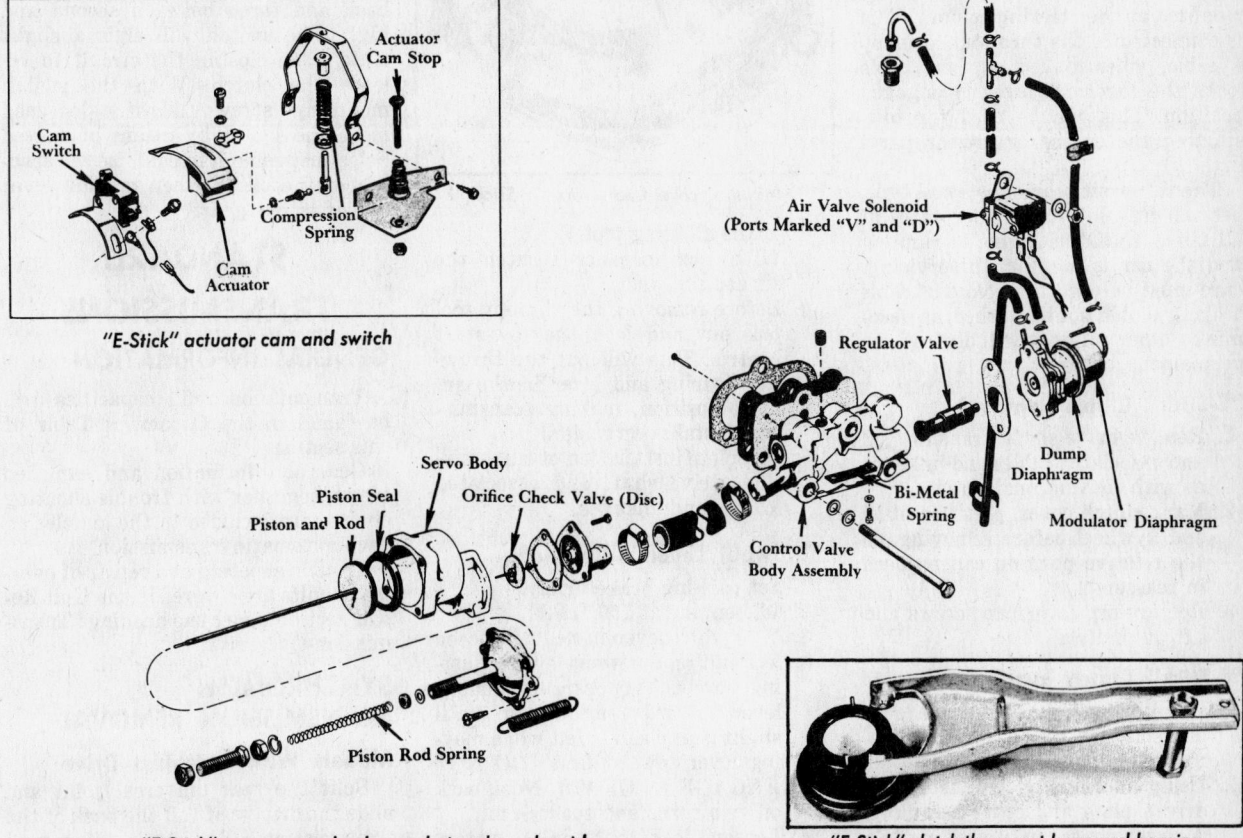

"E-Stick" actuator cam and switch

"E-Stick" servo, control valve and air valve solenoid

"E-Stick" clutch throw-out lever and bearing

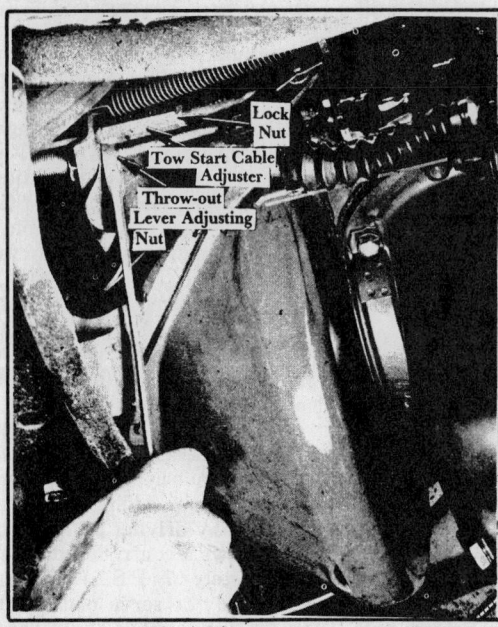

Adjusting throw-out lever—"E-Stick"

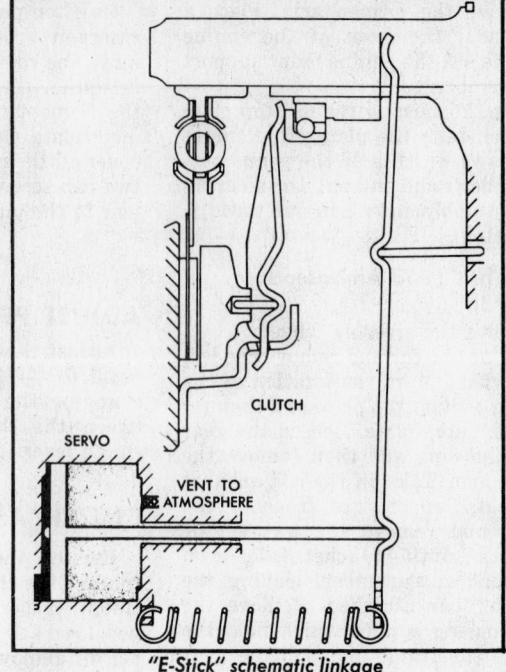

"E-Stick" schematic linkage

there is positive clutch engagement.

Releasing of accelerator increases vacuum. This now reduces oil pressure to the point of clutch release for gear shifting. When gear shift is returned to neutral a cam switch actuates the solenoid and controls the oil pressure thru the valve body.

A Tow Start Control Handle is mounted at the steering column. This is connected to the throwout lever by a cable, when pulled out the cable locks the throwout lever in engaged position. This can be used for tow-starting the engine or in-gear parking.

The throwout bearing is a ball type, permanently lubricated. It rotates at all times that the engine is running and the car is in gear. In servicing, care must be used to avoid dirt. This bearing should not be washed, as gasoline or other solvents will destroy the permanent lubricant.

"E-Stick" Clutch Removal

1. Remove drive shaft, transmission and associated cables and linkages as with conventional clutch.
2. Mark clutch cover, pressure plate and flywheel before removing, so the relative position can be used in reassembly.
3. Remove six cover cap screws and lift out clutch.

"E-Stick" Clutch Installation

1. Check freeness of driven plate on transmission clutch shaft and remove any burrs with a stone.
2. Using an aligning tool install the driven plate and cover assembly. A clutch shaft can be used in place

Installing cover and levers—"E-Stick"

of the aligning tool.

3. With tool in place tighten the six cap screws.
4. Before removing the aligning tool pull out and lock the tow-start control. This will put the throw-out bearing and lever in the applied position, making transmission installation easier.
5. Complete installation of transmission, drive shaft and associated cables and linkages.

Throwout Lever Adjustment

1. Set parking brake firmly.
2. Idle engine at 550 R.P.M.
3. With shift lever in neutral loosen lock nut on throwout lever adjusting screw. Turn screw to move lever toward rear of car until slight gear clash is felt when moving lever toward first (DO NOT ENGAGE IN GEAR). Now, back off two turns and set lock nut.
4. Loosen lock nut on tow-start

cable. Adjust hexagon adjuster until pivot clears throwout lever by 1/8". Tighten lock nut.

Actuator Cam Adjustment

This switch is mounted on column below instrument panel and must be set properly to release clutch when shifting gears. Move gear shift lever back and forth between second and high. The switch will emit a slight click when closing the circuit to release the clutch. With the switch mounting screws slightly loosened move the switch by means of slotted holes just enough to equalize the spacing of the clicks when moving lever out of either gear.

STANDARD TRANSMISSIONS

GENERAL INFORMATION

Transmission refill capacities will be found in the Capacities Table of this section.

General information and exploded views, together with trouble shooting charts, are included in the articles on each automatic transmission.

Trouble shooting and repair of overdrive units are covered in the Unit Repair section under the heading: Transmission-Overdrive.

SYNCHROMESH TRANSMISSION REMOVAL

Models With Hotchkiss Drive

Split the rear universal joint and slide the driveshaft off the back of the transmission (See text "Universal

Joints and Drive Lines")

Remove shift mechanism linkage to the transmission and disconnect the clutch linkage.

Disconnect the overdrive mechanism (if so equipped) and remove the rear mounts. Take out the transmission support crossmember, remove the two studs which hold the transmission to the bell housing and replace these two studs with two long pilot studs. Take out the two bottom studs and slide the transmission assembly along the pilot studs and out of the car.

Models With Torque Tubes

While it is possible to remove the transmission with the torque tube in the car by prying the torque tube back as far as it will go, it is probably easier to do so with the rear axle removed (See text "Universal Joints and Drive Lines").

Disconnect the brake lines and brake cables. Jack the car sufficiently high so that the operator can work under it.

Remove the bolts which hold the front flange at the torque tube to the back of the transmission, detach the rear end of the springs and the shock absorbers, remove the U bolts which hold the rear axle assembly to the leaf spring and roll the rear axle assembly back a couple of inches to clear the transmission.

Disconnect the shift levers at the transmission speedometer cable, and if equipped with overdrive, the overdrive wiring.

Support the back of the engine and remove the bolts which hold the back of the transmission to the crossmember and take out the crossmember.

Remove the bolts which hold the transmission to the bell housing and replace two of the bolts with long guide studs. Slide the transmission out along the guide studs and down and out of the car.

SHIFT LINKAGE ADJUSTMENT

Position the levers at the transmission in Neutral and position the shift lever at the top of the steering column in Neutral. Now adjust the link of the adjustable rods so that the clevises will just enter without shifting the rods out of position.

AUTOMATIC TRANSMISSION

QUICK SERVICE INFORMATION

When automatic transmission trouble is reported, a road test and careful diagnosis is in order. "Transmission Remove and Replace" and "Linkage

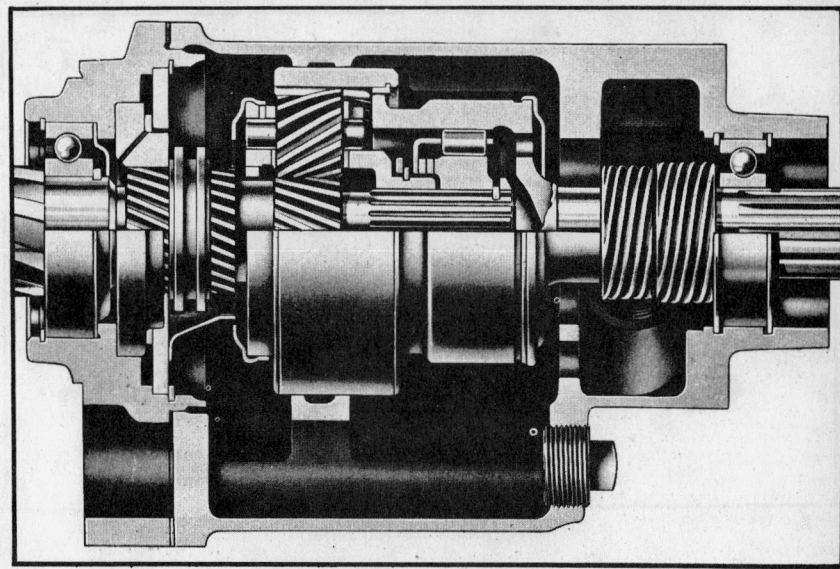

Overdrive Assembly (10 and 20 Series)

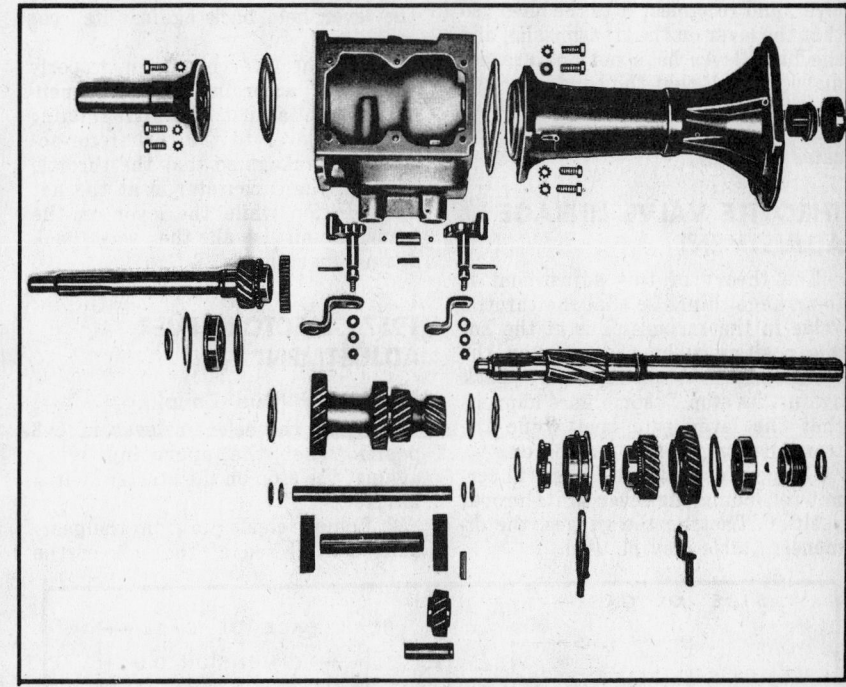

20 Series Transmission

Adjustments" are covered here in the following paragraphs. For "Test Procedures," "Transmission Overhaul" and other detailed information, see "Unit Repair section," "Transmission Group" of this manual.

LINKAGE ADJUSTMENTS

TABLE SHOWING DIMENSION "A" FOR DUAL-RANGE MODELS

Year	Dimension "A" In Inches
RAMBLER	
1954-56	7¼ in.

GENERAL INFORMATION APPLICABLE TO HYDRAMATIC MODELS ONLY

MANUAL LINKAGE ADJUSTMENT

Disconnect the rod running from the thicker (the inner) of the two levers on the left side of the transmission to the lower shift lever on the steering column.

Set the hand lever in Neutral (N) position.

Move the thickest lever on the transmission as far forward as possible. (This will be Neutral position.)

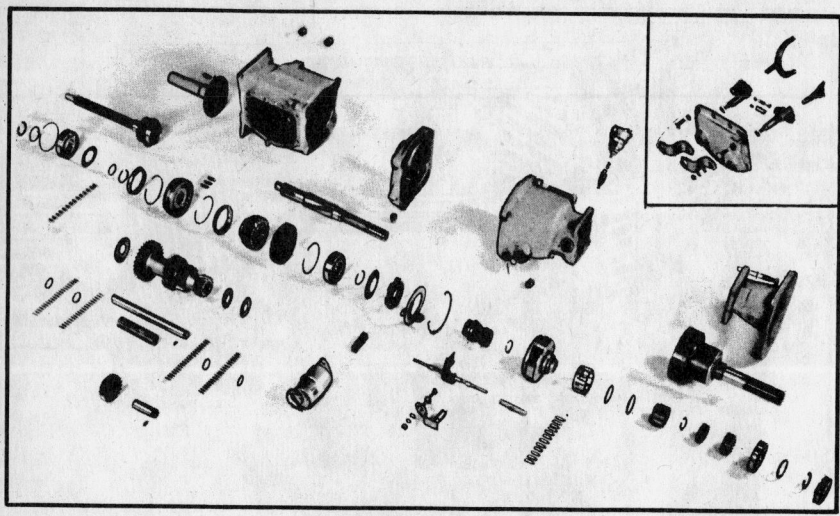

Overdrive Transmission (80 Series)

Adjust the length of the rod which was disconnected from the lower shift lever, and reconnect it to the lever; so that the lever on the transmission and the hand lever have not and are not moved. Check that the hand lever can be moved freely from Neutral to Drive 4 and back and the the pointer indicates correctly.

THROTTLE VALVE LINKAGE ADJUSTMENT

The theory of this adjustment is to arrange things so that the throttle valve in the carburetor is at the hot idle position when the lever on the transmission is all the way back against its stop. It sometimes happens that the lever gets bent while the transmission is being worked on.

Gauges are available which will permit rebending the lever to its proper position. Lacking the gauges, the dimension table may be used.

Measurements are made with the connecting throttle rod removed and the lever held back against its rear stop. Fig 1.

After the lever has been properly positioned according to the dimensions then adjust the rod running from the lever to the carburetor-accelerator linkage so that the throttle valve in the carburetor is at the hot idle position while the lever on the transmission is all the way back against its stop.

1957 SELECTOR LEVER ADJUSTMENT

Flashaway (Dual-Coupling)

1. With the selector lever in D-3 position set the operating lever against the stop on the starter switch bracket.

2. Remove clevis pin from the gearshift control rod at the side of the

transmission and remove the shift lever.

3. Place the transmission outer shift lever in the D-3 position.

4. Adjust clevis so that clevis pin passes freely through hole in lever with operating lever against the stop on the starter switch bracket. Then remove clevis and lengthen the control rod two full turns, replace clevis and pin.

Hydramatic (Dual Range)

1. With the selector lever in "R," disconnect clevis at transmission lever, and set transmission and lever in reverse position.

2. Adjust clevis-to-transmission lever so that the pin passes freely through the hole in the lever.

3. Check selector lever pointer in all positions going through "P," "N," "D-2," "D-1," "L," and "R" to be sure pointer is set correctly. If pointer does not line up, remove bottom half of jacket tube and adjust pointer to line up with center of letter "N."

FLASH-O-MATIC BEGINNING WITH 1957 ALL MODELS

Vacuum and Solenoid Control

The vacuum and solenoid control unit is threaded into the left rear corner of the transmission case. It's purpose is to regulate pressures, shift pattern and down shift. The control unit is activated by vacuum, through a tube, from the intake manifold.

To provide the preliminary vacuum control adjustment, locate the unit to a 3/8" measurement on the "10" and "20" series; 23/64" on the "80" series. This measurement is between the back face of the transmission case and the front edge of the control unit.

1. Connect a **vacuum** gauge to a fitting with a "T" connection between the control unit and the vacuum line tube.

2. Remove the 1/8" pipe plug located at the left front lower side of the transmission case. Install a pressure gauge line connector at this location connected to a **pressure** test gauge. Start the engine and put the selector in D-1 range.

Apply the parking and service brakes and accelerate the engine until 10.5" of vacuum is obtained on the vacuum gauge for the "10" series car, 12.1" of vacuum for the "20" series car and 13.8" of vacuum for the "80" series car.

At this time, check the reading on the **pressure gauge**. The correct pressure should be 100 lb. ± 3 lb. for the "10" series and 85 lb. ± 3 lb. for the "20" and "80" series.

If the correct reading is not ob-

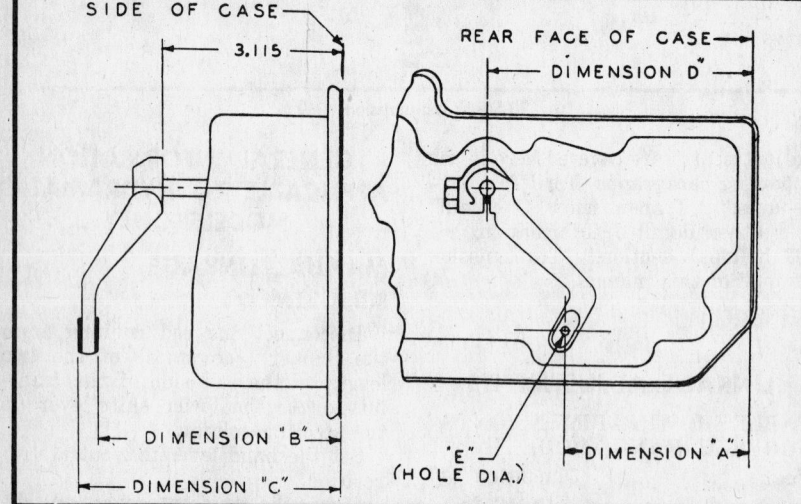

Fig. 1—Location of Throttle Lever on Dual-Range Hydramatic. The Dimension "A" is measured with the Lever against its stop

tained, it will be necessary to adjust the vacuum control unit. **Rotating the vacuum unit clockwise increases the pressure and counterclockwise decreases the pressure.**

NOTE: Do not operate the engine over ten seconds at any one time when performing the above test.

With a properly tuned engine, the engine r.p.m. and vacuum reading at sea level should be:

Series	R.P.M. In Neutral	Approx. Vacuum
10	475	18½
20 & 80	475	18½

REMOVE AND REPLACE

TRANSMISSION, BELL HOUSING AND CONVERTER

Removal of the unit from the car varies with the make and model. In general it involves the disconnection of the drive shaft and the removal of the frame cross members supporting the rear of the engine and the rear of the transmission. The flywheel housing is unbolted from the engine and the torus cover is unbolted from the flywheel.

The most important thing to remember to do is to remove the throttle and manual valve levers from the transmission before starting to remove the transmission from the car. It is very difficult to juggle the 250 pounds or more of transmission assembly around and not inadvertently bend these important levers.

For ease at reassembly, the torus cover and flywheel should be match marked. The carburetor air cleaner should be removed before lowering the engine in order to remove the upper flywheel housing bolt.

REMOVE

Flash-O-Matic Beginning 1957

Involvement may require that the transmission, bell housing, and converter assembly be removed as a unit. The following procedure is in order:

1. Disconnect a battery cable, at the assembly.
2. Remove starter motor.
3. Raise car on a hoist, place stands under the rear of the car at body sills.
4. Disconnect oil filler tube at the oil pan and drain the transmission.
5. Remove one converter drain plug, rotate the converter ½ turn and remove the other plug, ("20" & "80" series). The "10" series has only one drain plug.
6. Disconnect the oil cooler lines on the "20" & "80" series.
7. Disconnect the vacuum line and terminal wire at the vacuum unit of the transmission.
8. Disconnect speedometer cable at the transmission.
9. Disconnect the rear brake hose bracket from the floor panel.
10. Disconnect the manual cable shift linkage at both levers on the transmission.
11. Remove shift cable bracket from transmission.
12. Disconnect rear shock absorbers at the rear axle.
13. Disconnect the torque tube, propeller shaft, and parking brake cable.
14. Lower rear axle and move rearward to separate torque tube and propeller shaft from transmission.
15. Attach a transmission jack to the underside of the transmission and apply a slight lifting effort.
16. Remove the crossmember to side sill bolts.
17. Lower the engine and bellhousing assembly. Block the engine on both sides from top ledges of the oil pan to the side sill crossmember. These blocks should be 2″ x 2″ x 5″.
18. Remove the bell housing-to-engine bolts and bell housing lower mud pan.
19. Remove six cap screws that hold the converter to the drive plate.
20. With the transmission jack holding the transmission in alignment, pull the unit to the rear to disengage the housing and converter from the engine.
21. Lower the complete assembly and remove from the car.

NOTE: The converter cannot be taken apart and is only serviced as a unit.

REPLACE

Flash-O-Matic Beginning 1957

1. With the bell housing, converter and rear crossmember attached to the transmission, locate and secure the transmission to the transmission jack.
2. Raise the transmission to an approximate installation height.
3. Align the bell housing with the engine. Install the two lower engine-to-bell housing bolts in the engine block. This is to guide the bell housing dowels into place.
4. Move the entire assembly forward, guiding the converter pilot into the crankshaft.
5. Install the plain washers, long washers, and nuts on the two lower bolts and install the three upper bell housing-to-engine bolts and tighten securely.
6. Raise the transmission and install the transmission-to-side sill bolts. Then remove the two 2″ x 2″ x 5″ blocks from engine and side sill crossmember.
7. Remove transmission jack.
8. Connect the exhaust pipe ("20"

& "80" series with single exhaust system), torque tube, propeller shaft, and shock absorbers.
9. Connect the manual cable bracket and shift linkage, rear brake hose bracket, and speedometer cable.
10. Connect the vacuum line and terminal wire to the vacuum unit.
11. Connect the drive plate to the torque converter and tighten the six attaching screws to 23-28 ft. lb.
12. Install the bell housing lower mud pan.
13. Connect the filler tube to the oil pan.
14. Connect the oil cover lines, ("20" & "80" series).
15. Lower the car from the hoist, replace the starter, and connect the battery.
16. Refill transmission to prescribed level.
17. Road test car for shift pattern, manual cable linkage adjustment, and leaks.

UNIVERSAL JOINTS AND DRIVE LINES

OPEN TYPE DRIVE LINE

To Remove

An open tubular shaft is used with a slip joint at front. The rear joint uses a coupling to the rear axle pinion shaft. Both joints are the cross and trunnion type.

1. To remove assembly, raise and place stands under rear of body.
2. Disconnect parking brake cable.
3. Disconnect rear shock absorbers.
4. Disconnect rear brake line at body bracket.
5. Disconnect rear spring U-bolts.
6. Remove coupling nut (Fig. 1).
7. Shift rear axle assembly to rear to allow front joint to slide from transmission shaft and separate at rear coupling.

To Reinstall

1. Place the shaft and coupling on the rear axle pinion shaft until the center of the joint yoke bearing is 4-3/16″ from the front face of the pinion shaft housing (see Fig. 2).
2. Tighten coupling nut to 300 foot-pounds.
3. Slide the front slip joint onto the transmission output shaft.
4. Reposition rear axle assembly.
5. Reinstall U-bolts.
6. Reconnect brake line, parking brake cable and shock absorbers.
7. Bleed brakes.
8. Lower car to floor.

TORQUE TUBE TYPE DRIVE LINE

Fig. 1-American Series 01 Rear Joint

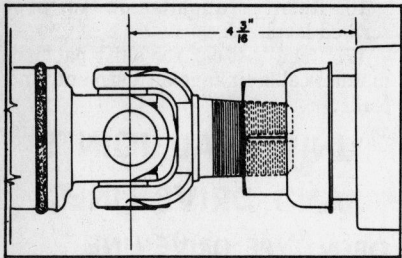

Fig. 2-American Series 01 Coupling Location

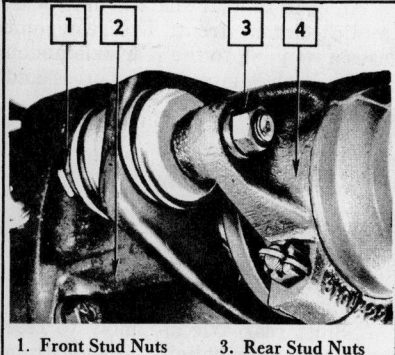

1. Front Stud Nuts   3. Rear Stud Nuts
2. Adapter   4. Trunnion Bracket

Fig. 3-Series 10 Front Joint on Standard
or Overdrive Transmission

To Remove

Two types of drive line are used on series 10, 20 and 80. Both are torque tube drives, one with a solid shaft and one with a tubular shaft (Figs. 5 & 6).

1. To remove assembly raise and place stands under rear of body.
2. Disconnect parking brake cable.
3. Disconnect rear stabilizer bar.
4. Disconnect lower ends of shock absorbers.
5. Disconnect truss rods at center bracket.
6A **On solid shaft types**, remove trunion bracket rear nuts (Fig. 3).
6B **On tubular shaft types**, disconnect torque tube from front adapter.
7. Move the rear axle and drive line assembly to the rear and disconnect the torque tube from the rear axle housing.
8. Move the tube forward to release rear slip joint. On cars using torque tube drive no rear spring U-bolts are used. The spring is held in place by car weight and shock absorber travel limits.

Note:

The solid shaft type uses a slip joint as in Fig. 5. It also has a center bearing as in Fig. 4, held in place by a snap ring. The tubular shaft uses a slip joint as in Fig. 6.

To Reinstall

On both torque tube types reverse the removal procedures above. Use care when inserting at slip joints not to damage oil seals.

UNIVERSAL JOINT REPAIRS

Remove the lock rings from the inner side of two opposite bearings and press on the outer side of one of the bearings, forcing the cross over, which will force the bearing on the

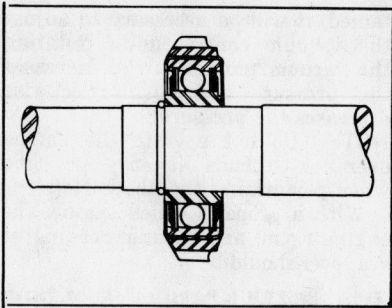

Fig. 4-Center Bearing used on Solid
Shaft type with Torque Tube

opposite side out of its yoke.

Remove the bearing which was forced out of the yoke and then press the cross in the opposite direction to press the other bearing out.

Repeat this procedure on the third and fourth bearing.

When installing the new bearings in the universal joint yoke, it is possible to put them in with a driver of some type, but it is recommended that this work be done in an arbor press since a heavy jolt on the needle bearings can very easily misalign them, which will greatly shorten their life.

REAR AXLE AND SUSPENSION

REAR SUSPENSION

Rear Spring Removal

Jack up the car and place stand jacks at the frame in front of the rear axle. Disconnect the lower end of the shock absorber and the torsion bar.

Disconnect the spring at its front hanger and rear shackle and remove the U bolts which hold the spring to the axle housing and remove the spring. On cars using torque tube drive no rear spring U-bolts are used.

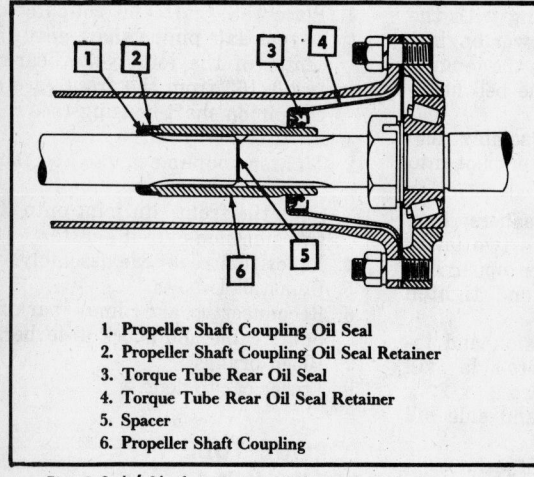

1. Propeller Shaft Coupling Oil Seal
2. Propeller Shaft Coupling Oil Seal Retainer
3. Torque Tube Rear Oil Seal
4. Torque Tube Rear Oil Seal Retainer
5. Spacer
6. Propeller Shaft Coupling

Fig. 5-Solid Shaft in Torque Tube, series 10, 20 and 80

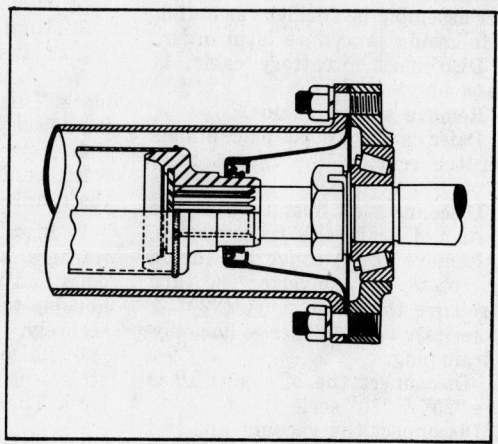

Fig. 6-Tubular Shaft in Torque Tube,
series 10, 20 and 80

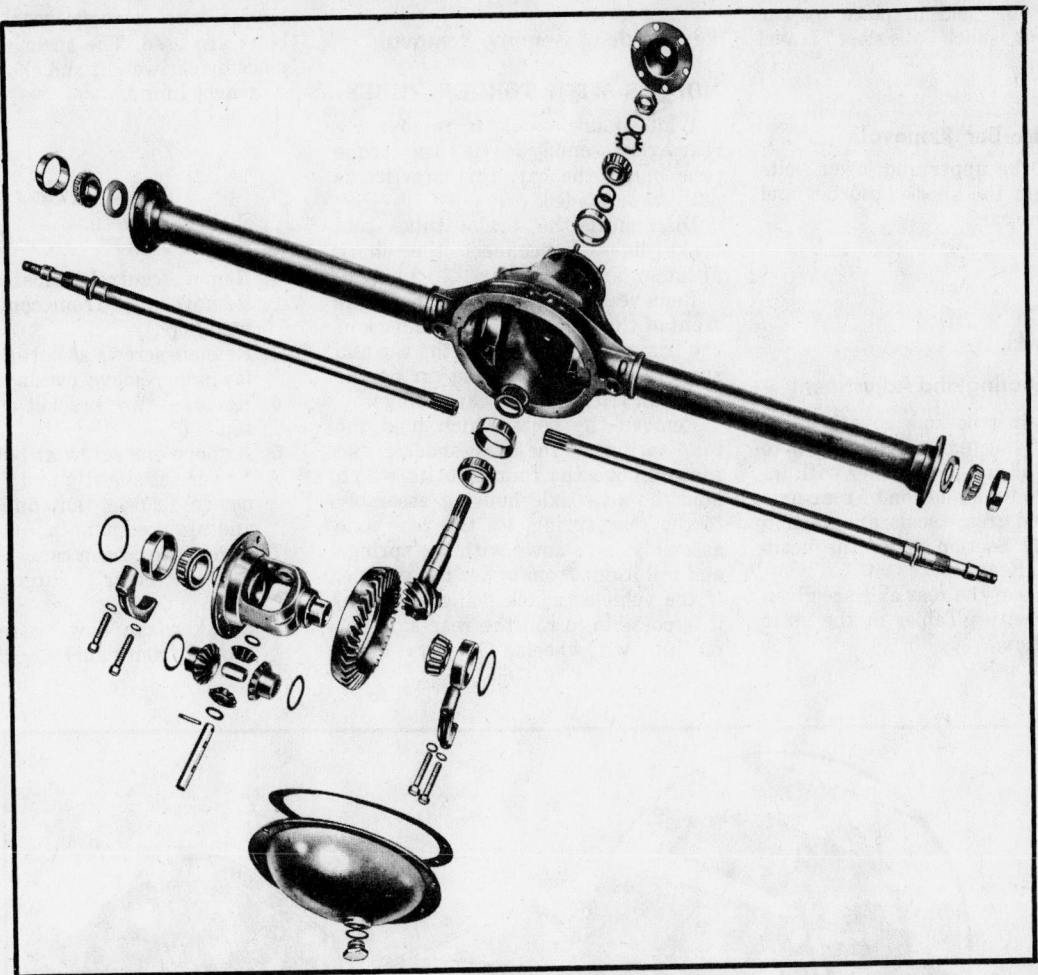

Rear Axle Assembly

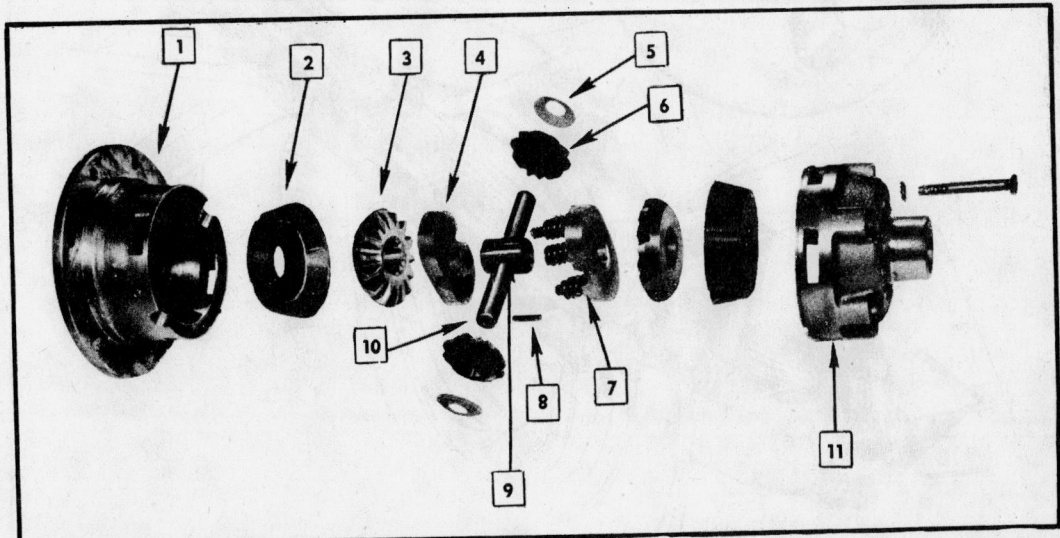

1. Case, Ring Gear Flange Half
2. Cone
3. Side Gear
4. Spring Thrust Block
5. Pinion Gear Thrust Washer
6. Pinion Gear
7. Thrust Block Springs (6 Large, 2 Small)
8. Pinion Shaft Retaining Dowel
9. Axle Shaft Thrust Block
10. Pinion Gear Shaft
11. Case, Cap Half

"Twin-Grip" Differential Assembly —10 Series

RAMBLER

The spring is held in place by car weight and shock absorber travel limits.

Shock Absorber Removal

Remove the upper and lower bolts which retain the shock absorber and lift it off the car.

REAR AXLE

Trouble shooting and Adjustment

General instructions covering the troubles of the rear axle and how to repair and adjust it, together with information on installation of rear axle bearings and grease seals, are given in the General Section under the heading: Axles, Rear.

Capacities of the rear axle are given in the Capacities Tables at the start of this section.

Rear Axle Assembly Removal

MODELS WITH TORQUE TUBES

While it is possible to remove the rear axle assembly leaving the torque tube under the car, this practice is not recommended.

Disconnect the brake tubes and brake lines. Disconnect the shock absorber and sway bar.

Remove the bolts which hold the front of the torque tube to the back of the transmission. Jack up the car and support the weight of the car on the frame in front of the rear springs.

Remove the bolts which hold the rear spring to the rear shackle and then remove the four U bolts which hold the rear axle housing assembly to the rear spring, let the rear axle assembly come down with the springs and roll it out from under the vehicle. If the vehicle is jacked high enough, it is possible to roll the rear axle out on its own wheels. On cars using torque tube drive no rear spring u-bolts are used. The spring is held in place by car weight and shock absorber travel limits.

RADIO

REMOVE

1. Remove control knobs.
2. Remove nuts from control shaft bushings.
3. Remove screws at bottom of overlay and remove overlay.
4. Remove two bracket screws at top.
5. Remove one screw at bottom rail.
6. Lower set slightly and disconnect power lead-in, antennae lead-in and speaker plug-in.
7. Remove set from car.
8. Remove cigar lighter and ash tray.
9. Speaker can now be readily removed from panel.

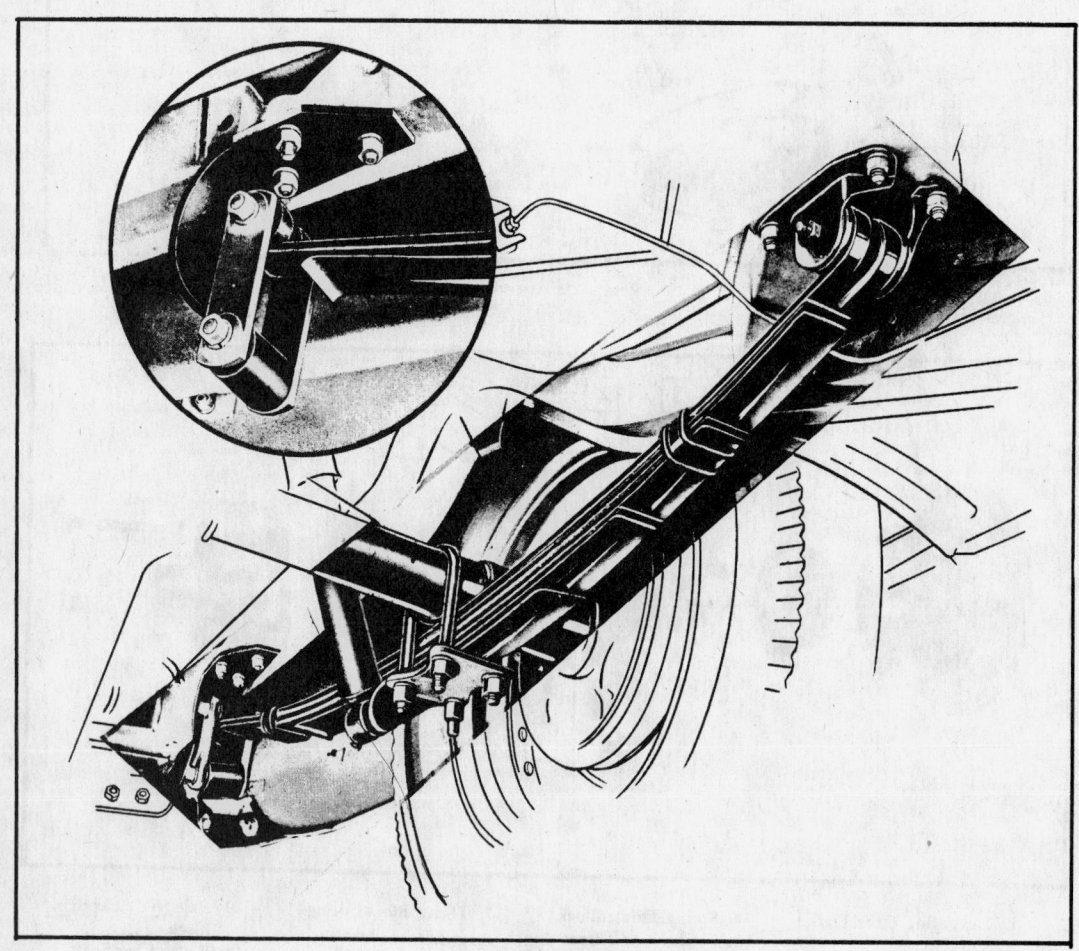

Spring Mounting

Page

BRAKES, HYDRAULIC

Pedal adjustment 606
References 606
Bleed brakes 941
Master cylinder service 939

BRAKES, POWER

Power unit overhaul 954
Trouble shooting 954

CLUTCH

Clutch assembly, R & R 615
Clutch pedal, adjust 615

COOLING SYSTEM

Radiator core, R & R 607
Thermostat 608
Water manifolds 608
Water pump, R & R 608

ELECTRICAL SYSTEM

Distributor, R & R 604
Distributor specifications 599
Fuses and circuit breakers 599
Gauges 1024
Generator and regulator
    specifications 600
Generator service 1026
Generator trouble shooting chart 1026
Horn buttons 614
Ignition firing order 605
Ignition timing procedure 1012
Ignition timing specifications 598
Starter, R & R 605
Starter specifications 600
Starter systems 1046

ENGINE ASSEMBLY

Cylinder head, R & R 610
Cylinder head tightening 602
Engine assembly, R & R 608
Engine firing order & timing 597
Model identification 598
Exhaust manifold, R & R 607
Inlet manifold, R & R 607
Oil filter, R & R 611
Oil pan, R & R 610
Oil pressure specifications 601
Oil pump 611
Piston and rod, R & R 612
Rear main bearing oil seal 613
References 608
Rocker arm lubrication 609
Rocker arms & shaft 609
Specifications, general, engine . .601
Timing case & sprockets 612
Trouble shooting charts 1012
Tune-up specifications 598
Valve specifications 603

Page

ENGINE ASSEMBLY—continued

Valve springs 612
Valves and guides 611

ENGINE LUBRICATION

Oil filter 611
Oil pan, R & R 610
Oil pump, R & R 611

EXHAUST SYSTEM

Manifolds, R & R 607

FUEL SYSTEM

Carburetors 972
Fuel gauge service 1024
Fuel pump pressure 598
Fuel pump, R & R 606
Fuel pump service 1020
Fuel tank, R & R 607

INSTRUMENTS

Instruments, R & R 605
Speedometer, R & R 606
Windshield wiper motor, R & R . .606

OVERDRIVES

Overdrive disassembly 914
Trouble shooting 915

REAR AXLE AND SUSPENSION

Axle assembly, R & R 622
Axle shaft 918
Axle shaft oil seal 918
Pinion bearings 918
Ring gear & pinion 918
Trouble shooting 919

SPECIFICATIONS

Battery .600
Brake cylinder sizes 603
Capacities:
    Axle, rear 604
    Cooling system 604
    Crankcase 604
    Fuel tank 604
    Transmission, automatic 604
    Transmission, manual 604
Chassis, general 603
Engine, general 601
Distributor 599
Fuses and circuit breakers 599
Generator and regulators 600
Light bulbs 600
Main bearings 602
Model identification illustrations. .596
Piston and pin 602
Quick reference specifications . . .597
Rod bearings 602

Page

SPECIFICATIONS—continued

Starters .600
Torque wrench 602
Tune-up 598
Valves .603
Wheel alignment 604

STEERING, MANUAL

Adjust gear housing 1052
Gear assembly, R & R 614
Horn button, R & R 614
Steering wheel, R & R 614

STEERING, POWER

References 615
Pump assembly 1058
Trouble shooting 1081
Unit overhaul 1058

SUSPENSION, FRONT

Alignment procedures 1082
Alignment specifications 604
Camber, adjust 1082
Caster, adjust 1082
Intermediate steering arms 615
King pins and bushings 1087
Knuckle supports 1087
References 613
Support arms, pins and bushings 1087
Toe-in, adjust 1082

TRANSMISSION, AUTOMATIC

Studebaker automatic 906
    Anti-creep adjust 617
    Linkage adjust 619
    Transmission, R & R 619
Flightomatic 820
    Linkage adjust 620
    Transmission, R & R 621

TRANSMISSION, MANUAL SHIFT

Disassemble transmission 616
Transmission, R & R 615

TROUBLE CHECKS

Procedures 1

TUNE-UP

Procedures 1012
Specifications 598
Engine diagnosis 1012

UNIVERSAL JOINT AND DRIVE SHAFT

Disassemble U Joint 621
U joint & drive shaft, R & R 621

STUDEBAKER

YEAR IDENTIFICATION

1954
Commander "V8" Model 5H
Champion "6" Model 15G

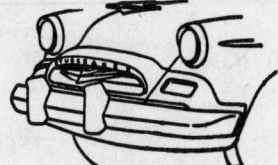

1955
President "V8" Model 6H
Commander "V8" Model 16G8
Champion "6" Model 16G6

1956
President "V8" Model 56H
Commander "V8" Model 56B
Champion "8" Model 56G

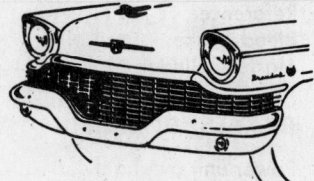

1957
President "V8" Model 57H
Commander "V8" Model 57B
Champion "6" Model 57G

1958
President "V8" Model 58H
Commander "V8" Model 58B
Champion "6" Model 58G

1959
Lark VI—Model 59S
Lark VIII—Model 59V

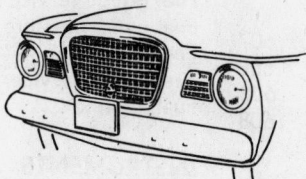

1960
Lark VI—Model 60S
Lark VIII—Model 60V

1961
Lark VI—Model 61S
Lark VIII—Model 61V

1962

1963

——— HAWK SERIES ———

1956-57

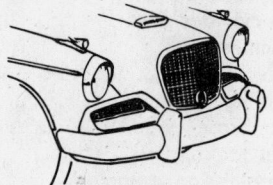

1958

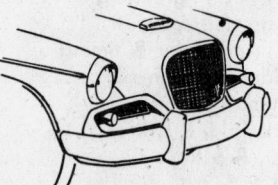

1959-61

1962

1963

1963
AVANTI

QUICK WORKING SPECIFICATIONS

DISTRIBUTOR

Breaker Point Gap (In.)

1954-63, Champion & Lark,
6 cyl., All .... .020
1954, All V8 .... .015
1955, All V8 .... .013
1956-63, All V8 .... .015

Cam Angle (Degrees)

1954-63, Champion & Lark,
6 cyl., All .... .39
1954-63, All V8 .... .31

SPARK PLUGS

Year	Type	Gap
1954, All 6 cyl.	J7	.025
1954-63, All V8 ex. G. H.	H18Y	.035
1955-60, All 6 cyl.	J7	.030
1956, Golden Hawk	N18	.035
1957-58, Golden Hawk	H10	.035
1959-60, Golden Hawk	H11	.035
1961-63, All	H14Y	.035

IGNITION TIMING

1954-60, 6 cyl. "L" Hd. 2B
1961-63, 6 cyl. OHV 4B
1954, V-8 .... 4B
1955, Commander V-8 .... 8B
1955, President V-8 .... 4B
1956, All V-8 exc. G.H. 4B
1956, Golden Hawk V-8 .... 5B
1957-63, All V-8 .... 4B

TIMING INDICATOR MARK AND LOCATION

1954-63 .... Crankshaft Pulley

GENERATOR & REGULATOR SPECIFICATIONS

YEAR AND SERIES	GENERATOR Field Current In Amperes		REGULATOR Cut-out Closing Voltage	Current Regulator Setting	Voltage Regulator Setting
	6 Volt	12 Volt			
1954-55 Champ.	1.7	—	6.6	45	7.3
All V8	1.95	—	6.5	45	7.5
1956 Champ.	—	1.25	13.4	30	14.6±1.0(A)
V8, Ex. G.H.	—	1.55	13.0	30	15.1±1.0(A)
V8, G. Hwk.	—	1.25	13.4	30	14.6±1.0(A)
1957-63 All 6 Cyl.	—	1.25	13.4	30	14.6±1.0(A)
All V8	—	1.55	13.0	30	15.1±1.0(A)

(A) Surrounding temperatures guide this adjustment. Higher temperatures require lower settings and lower temperatures permit higher settings, within limits.

VALVES

Operating Tappet Clearance (Cold)

Intake and Exhaust are the same.
1954-63, All 6 cyl. .... .016
1954-63, All V8 ex. G. H. .... .026
1956, Golden Hawk Hydr : ...... Zero
1959-60, 6 cyl. L Hd. .... .018
1961-63, 6 cyl. OHV .... .024

COMPRESSION PRESSURE

1954, All 130
1955, Champion 6 140
1955, All V8 130
1956-63, All 140-150

WHEEL ALIGNMENT

Caster

1954-60 .... 2½N to 1N
1961-63 .... ¾P to ¾N

Camber

1954-63 .... 0 to 1P

Toe-In

1954-63 .... 1/16 to ⅛

King Pin Inclination

1954-63 .... 6°

CAPACITIES

Engine Crankcase (Quarts)

Add 1 qt. for new filter.
1954-63, Champion & Lark,
6 cyl. 5
1954-55, all V8 6
1956-63, all V8 5

Transmission, Synchro. (Pts.)

1954-56, All 6 cyl. 1.5
1954-56, All V-8 .... 2.5
1957-63, All 6 cyl. 2.3
1957-63, All V-8, 3-speed 3.8
1961-63, All 4-speed 2.5

Transmission, Automatic (Pts.)

1954-55, All 19
1956, ex. Gld. Hawk 18
1956, Golden Hawk 22
1957-63, All 18

Rear Axle (Pints)

1954-59, Champion 6 .... 2½
1954, Commander 3
1955, President V8 3
1955, All V8 ex. President 2½
1956-63, All 3

Gasoline Tank (Gallons)

1954-63, All 18

Cooling System (Quarts)

Add 1 quart for heater.
1954-55, Champion 10
1954-56, all V8 ex. 1956 G. H. .. 17¼
1956, Golden Hawk V8 25
1956-63, 6 cyl. 11
1957-63, All V8 17

FIRING ORDER and TIMING

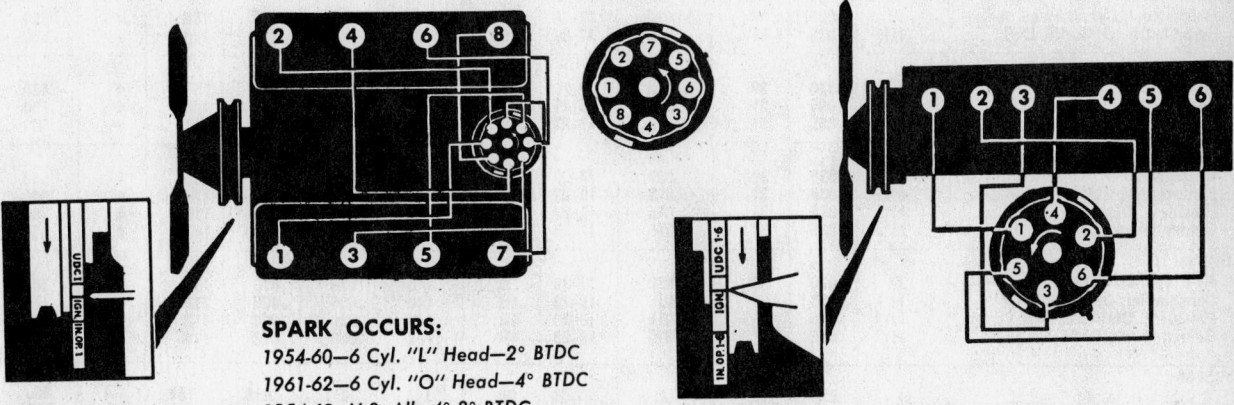

SPARK OCCURS:
1954-60—6 Cyl. "L" Head—2° BTDC
1961-62—6 Cyl. "O" Head—4° BTDC
1954-62—V-8, All—4°-8° BTDC

NOTE:
THESE ARE APPROXIMATE SETTINGS. ALTITUDE, TEMPERATURE, FUEL AND ENGINE CONDITION WILL ALL INFLUENCE TIMING. THE DETERMINING FACTOR, LIMITING ADVANCE, WILL STILL BE THE "KNOCK POINT" OF THE INDIVIDUAL ENGINE.

CAR SERIAL NUMBER LOCATION AND ENGINE IDENTIFICATION

SERIAL NUMBER LOCATION
1954-63:
  All, Plate on left front door post.

ENGINE NUMBER LOCATION
6 CYL., ALL:
  Upper left side of cylinder block.

V-8, ALL:
  Top side front of cylinder block.

YEAR	MODEL AND SIZE	Starting Engine Number	Starting Serial Number
1954	15G—Champion, 170"	1090001	G-1274001
	5H—Commander, 232"	V-282501	8354901
1955	16G6—Champion, 185"	1138001	G-1316501
	16G8—Commander, 224"	V-312701	8380601
	6H—President, 259"	P-101	7150001
1956	56G—Champion and Flight Hawk, 185"	1180251	G-1357501
	56B—Commander and Power Hawk, 259"	V-363751	8429601
	56H—President and Sky Hawk, 289"	P-22001	7171001
	56J—Golden Hawk, 352"	F-1001	6030001
1957	57G—Champion and Silver Hawk, 185"	1202101	G-1379201
	57B—Commander, 259"	V-390001	8454101
	57H—President, 289"	P-39601	7188901
	57HK—Golden Hawk, 289"	PS-1001	G-100001
1958	58G—Champion and Silver Hawk, 185"	1228401	G-1405401
	58B—Commander, 259"	V-407501	8471601
	58H—President, 289"	P-60701	7210001
	58HK—Golden Hawk, 289"	PS-5501	6104501
1959	59S—Lark and Hawk, 170"	59S-10001	59S-1001
	59V—Lark and Hawk, 259"	59V-14701	59V-1001
1960	60S—Lark, 170"	S-106001	60S-1001
	60V—Lark, 259"	V-454701	60V-1001
	60V—Lark and Hawk, 289"	P-70501	60V-1001
1961	61S—Lark, 170"	S-172601	61S-1001
	61V—Lark, 259"	V-510401	61V-1001
	61V—Hawk, 289"	P-74701	61V-1001
1962	62S—Lark, 170"	S-210901	62S-1001
	62V—Lark, 259"	V-534901	62V-1001
	62V—Hawk, 289"	P-79801	62V-1001
1963	63S—Lark, 170"	V-1001	63S-1001
	63V—Lark, 259"	V-1001	63V-1001
	63V—Hawk, 289"	P-1001	63V-1001

TUNE-UP SPECIFICATIONS

Year	Spark Plugs TYPE	Gap	Distributor (Note 1) Cam Angle	Point Gap	Arm Spring Tension	Ignition Timing (Note 2)	Compression Pressure Cranking (Note 3)	Valves (Note 4) Tappet Clearance Hot Inlet	Exhaust	Timing Inlet Opens	Fuel Pump Pressure	Engine Idle Speed Neutral (Note 5)
1954												
Champion, 6 Cyl., L Head, A-L	J7	.025	39	.020	17–20	2B	130	.016	.016	15B	4½	550
Commander, OHV, V8, D-R	H11	.035	31	.015	17–21	4B	130	.026	.026	11B	4½	550
1955												
Champion, 6 Cyl., L Head, A-L	J7	.030	39	.020	17–20	2B	140	.016	.016	15B	4¾	550
Commander, OHV, V8, D-R	H11	.035	31	.013	17–21	8B	130	.026	.026	19B	4¾	550
President, OHV, V8, D-R	H11	.035	31	.013	17–21	4B	130	.026	.026	11B	4¾	550
1956												
Champion, 6 Cyl., L Head, A-L	J7	.030	39	.020	17–20	2B	140	.016	.016	15B	4	550
Commander, OHV, V8, D-R	H11	.035	31	.015	19–23	4B	140	.026	.026	11B	4	550
President, OHV, V8, D-R	H11	.035	31	.015	19–23	4B	140	.026	.026	11B	4	550
Golden Hawk, OHV, V8, D-R	N18	.035	31	.015	17–20	5B	140	Zero	Zero	14B	4	450
1957-58												
All 6 Cyl., L Head, A-L	J7	.030	39	.020	17–20	2B	140	.016	.016	15B	4	550
Commander, OHV, V8, D-R	H11	.035	31	.015	19–23	4B	140	.026	.026	11B	4	550
President, OHV, V8, D-R	H11	.035	31	.015	19–23	4B	140	.026	.026	11B	4	550
Golden Hawk, OHV, V8, D-R	H10	.035	31	.015	19–23	4B	140	.026	.026	11B	6½	550
1959-60												
6 Cyl., L Head, A-L	J7	.030	39	.020	17–20	2B	140	.018	.018	15B	4	550
OHV, V8, D-R	H18-Y	.035	31	.015	19–23	4B	140	.026	.026	11B	4	550
1961-63												
6 Cyl., OHV, A-L	H14Y	.035	39	.020	17-20	4B	150	.024	.024	15B	4	550
OHV, V8, D-R	H14Y	.035	31	.015	19-23	4B	140	.026	.026	11B	4	550

NOTES FOR TUNE-UP SPECIFICATIONS TABLE

Note:

All specifications are standard and should result in satisfactory performance. There are, however, factors that influence these settings, such as fuel octane value, air density, humidity, temperature, etc. Timing charts, like other specifications must be considered as averages, subject to modification.

Note 1: Distributor

ROTATION VIEWED FROM THE TOP

1954-63, All ....Counterclockwise

DRIVE GEAR

1954-63, All "L" Hd. Engines and OHV-6: Gear is pinned to oil pump shaft. Distributor shaft has matching tongue.

1954-63, All OHV-V8 Engines: Gear is pinned to distributor shaft. An intermediate shaft carries drive to oil pump shaft.

Note 2: Ignition

1956-63, V8: A ballast resistor is used in the primary ignition circuit of all V8 cars equipped with a 12 volt electrical system. A by-pass in the starter solenoid removes this resistor from the circuit only while the starter is operating. If the ignition switch is

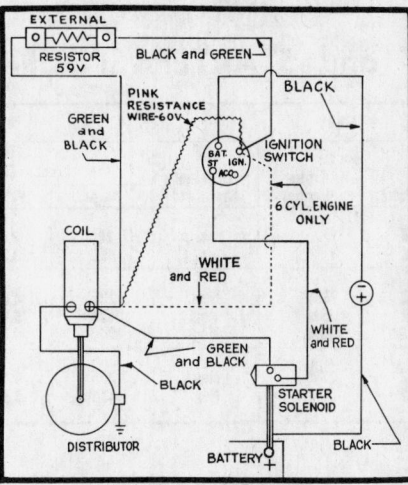

IGNITION CIRCUIT

used to complete the circuit to the cranking motor while making underhood cranking tests, the distributor primary lead must be grounded to prevent the engine firing.

Note 3: Compression Pressure

All cylinders should read alike within 10 pounds. This is more important than the actual reading. Take the readings with all plugs removed, engine at normal operating temperature.

Note 4: Valves

"Zero" in the tappet clearance column indicates hydraulic lifters are standard equipment.

Note 5: Idle Speed

Idle speeds as shown are for engines in good condition with the transmission in Neutral. The proper idle speed for an engine depends on its condition and also on whether or not it has an automatic transmission. Higher idle speeds are required for engines in poor condition and also for engines used with automatic transmissions.

DISTRIBUTOR SPECIFICATIONS, DELCO-REMY

YEAR	MODEL	Delco-Remy Part Number	Rotation	Cam Angle in Degrees	Breaker Point Opening (Inch)	Breaker Arm Spring in Ounces	Governor Control & Dist. R.P.M. Advance Starts	Governor Control & Dist. R.P.M. Full Advance	Vacuum Control Data Inches of Vacuum To Start Advance	Vacuum Control Data Inches of Vacuum For Full Advance	Vacuum Control Data Max. Adv. of Dist. in Degrees
1954-55	V8, All	1110839	CC	28-34	.015	19-23	1 @ 300	16 @ 1450	4-6	10-11½	7-9
1956-59	V8, Ex. G. Hawk	1110864	CC	28-34	.015	19-23	1 @ 500	12 @ 1125	4-6	10-11½	7-9
1960-63	V8, All	1110969	CC	28-32	.016	19-23	1 @ 500	12 @ 1200	4-6	12	16

DISTRIBUTOR SPECIFICATIONS, AUTO-LITE

YEAR	MODEL	Auto-Lite Part Number	Rotation	Cam Angle in Degrees	Breaker Point Opening (Inch)	Breaker Arm Spring in Ounces	Governor Control & Dist. R.P.M. Advance Starts	Governor Control & Dist. R.P.M. Full Advance	Vacuum Control Data Inches of Vacuum To Start Advance	Vacuum Control Data Inches of Vacuum For Full Advance	Vacuum Control Data Max. Adv. of Dist. in Degrees
1954	6 Cyl. All	IAT-4010	CC	38-40	.020	17-20	1 @ 400	7 @ 1400	3-5	11-13	8-10
1955-58	6 Cyl. All	IAT-4201	CC	38-40	.020	17-20	1 @ 400	7 @ 1400	3-5	12	8-10
1959-60	6 Cyl. All	IAT-4403	CC	38-40	.020	17-20	1 @ 400	7 @ 1400	3-5	12	8-10
1961-63	6 Cyl. OHV	IAT-4403B	CC	37-41	.020	17-20	1 @ 325	13 @ 1800	7-9	13	7-9
1962-63	V-8	1BP-0108	CC	27-31	.014-.019	17-22	1 @ 500	12 @ 1200	4-6	12	16

FUSES and CIRCUIT BREAKERS

Head, Beam Telltale, Parking, Tail, License, Instruments, Clock and Trunk Lights:

20 amp. circuit breaker on headlight switch.

Clock:

AGA 3 fuse back of clock.

Radio:

1954-55, SFE 14; 1956-60, AGW 7½; 1961-63, AGW 4, fuse in wire near set.

Overdrive:

SFE 20 fuse on overdrive relay on left engine side of firewall near steering column. Starting with 1957, SFE 14.

STUDEBAKER

FUSES AND CIRCUIT BREAKERS—continued

Stop, Dome, Glove Lights:

15 amp. circuit breaker on headlight switch.

Power Seats and Top:

Circuit breaker on left passenger side of firewall near steering column.

Turn Signals:

SFE 15 fuse on flasher mounting behind instrument panel near instruments.

Heater:

SFE 14 fuse on heater switch.

Windshield Wiper:

5 amp. circuit breaker built into wiper motor.

Anti-creep:

SFE 14 fuse on left engine side of firewall at lower corner.

BATTERY and STARTER SPECIFICATIONS

YEAR	BATTERY				STARTERS						Brush Spring Tension
	Ampere Hour Capacity	Volts	Group Number	Terminal Grounded	Lock Test			No-Load Test			
					Amps.	Volts	Torque	Amps.	Volts	R.P.M.	
1954-55											
Champion, 6 Cyl.	105	6	1	Pos.	280	2.0	4.4	70	5.5	4300	48
All V8	105	6	1	Pos.	550	3.3	11.0	65	5.7	5000	26
1956											
Champion, 6 Cyl.	53	12	2SM	Neg.	235	4.0	5.2	50	10.0	5200	48
All V8 ex. Gld. Hk.	60	12	2SM	Neg.	435	5.8	14.0	75	10.0	5000	37
Golden Hawk	60	12	2SM	Neg.	240	4.0	6.5	60	10.0	3200	48
1957-63											
All 6 Cyl.	50	12	2SM	Neg.	235	4.0	5.2	50	10.0	5200	37
All V8 Models	50	12	2SM	Neg.	435	5.8	14.0	75	10.0	5000	35

GENERATOR and REGULATOR SPECIFICATIONS

YEAR	GENERATORS			REGULATORS					
	Field Current in Amperes		Brush Spring Tension	Cut Out Relay		Current and Voltage Regulator Air Gap	Current Regulator Setting	Voltage Regulator Setting
	At 6 Volts	At 12 Volts		Air Gap	Closing Voltage			
1954-55								
Champion, 6 Cyl.	1.7		28	.032	6.6	.050	45	7.3
All V8	1.95		28	.020	6.5	.075	45	7.5
1956								
Champion, 6 Cyl.		1.25	28	.032	13.4	.050	30	14.6
All V8 ex. Gld. Hk.		1.55	28	.020	13.0	.075	30	15.1
Golden Hawk, V8		1.25	28	.032	13.4	.050	30	14.6
1957-62								
All 6 Cyl.		1.25	28	.032	13.4	.050	30	14.6
All V8		1.55	28	.020	13.0	.075	30	15.1

LIGHT BULBS

(C.P. MEANS CANDLE POWER)

Beam and Turn Telltales, Automatic Transmission Quadrant, Cigar Lighter:

6 Volt, No. 51; 12 Volt, No. 53.
(1 C.P. miniature bayonet base.)
Starting with 1957, No. 1445.

Clock, Instrument, Glove Box, Brake-on:

6 Volt, No. 55; 12 Volt, No. 57.
(2 C.P. miniature bayonet base.)

License Plate Light:

6 Volt, No. 63; 12 Volt, No. 67.
(4 C.P. single contact base.)

Trunk Light:

6 Volt, No. 209; 12 Volt, No. 1003.
(15 C.P. single contact base.)
Starting 1957, No. 67, 12 C.P.

Combination Front Park and Signal; Combination Rear Signal, Stop and Tail:

6 Volt, No. 1154; 12 Volt, No. 1034.
(32 & 4 C.P. double contact indexed base.)

Back-up Lights:

6 Volt, No. 1133; 12 Volt, No. 1073.
(32 C.P. single contact base.)
Starting 1959, No. 1141.

Radio Dial:

6 Volt, No. 44; 12 Volt, No. 1891.
(2 C.P. miniature bayonet base.)

Headlights—Two Only:

6 Volt, No. 5040; 12 Volt, No. 5400.
(50 & 40 C.P. triple contact base.)

Headlights—Four Only:

LOW AND HIGH BEAM (OUTER)
12 Volt, No. 4002
(37.5-50 watts three contact base.)

HIGH BEAM ONLY (INNER)
12 Volt, No. 4001
(37.5 Watts double contact base.)

GENERAL ENGINE SPECIFICATIONS

Year	Bore and Stroke	Number of Main Bearings	Type of Valve Lifter Used	Cubic Inch Displacement	AMA Horsepower	Advertised Horsepower at Stated RPM	Advertised Torque at Stated RPM	Compression Ratio	Oil Pressure At 30 MPH (Note 1)	Cam Shaft Drive
1954										
Champion, 6 Cyl., L Head	3x4	4	Mech. Adj.	169	21.6	85@4000	138@2400	7.5–1	40	Gear
Commander, OHV, V8	3⅜x3¼	5	Mech. Adj.	232	36.4	120@4000	190@2000	7.5–1	40	Gear
1955										
Champion, 6 Cyl., L Head	3x4⅜	4	Mech. Adj.	185	21.6	101@400	152@1800	7.5–1	40	Gear
Commander, OHV, V8 (Note 6)	3⁹⁄₁₆x2¹³⁄₁₆	5	Mech. Adj.	259	40.6	140@4500	202@2800	7.5–1	40	Gear
President, OHV, V8	3⁹⁄₁₆x3¼	5	Mech. Adj.	259	40.6	185@4500	258@3000	7.5–1	40	Gear
1956										
Champion, 6 Cyl., L Head	3x4⅜	4	Mech. Adj.	185	21.6	101@4000	152@1800	7.8–1	40	Gear
Commander, OHV, V8	3⁹⁄₁₆x3¼	5	Mech. Adj.	259	40.6	←—— Note 2 ——→		7.8–1	40	Gear
President, V8, OHV	3⁹⁄₁₆x3⅝	5	Mech. Adj.	289	40.6	←—— Note 3 ——→		7.8–1	40	Gear
Golden Hawk, V8, OHV	4x3½	5	Hyd. Non Adj.	352	51.2	275@4600	380@2800	9.5–1	40	Chain
1957–58										
All 6 Cyl., L Head	3x4⅜	4	Mech. Adj.	185	21.6	101@4000	152@1800	7.8–1	40	Gear
Commander, V8, OHV	3⁹⁄₁₆x3¼	5	Mech. Adj.	259	40.6	←—— Note 4 ——→		8.0–1	40	Gear
President, OHV, V8	3⁹⁄₁₆x3⅝	5	Mech. Adj.	289	40.6	←—— Note 5 ——→		8.3–1	40	Gear
Golden Hawk, OHV, V8	3⁹⁄₁₆x3⅝	5	Mech. Adj.	289	40.6	275@4800	333@3200	7.5–1	40	Gear
1959-60										
All 6 Cyl., L Head	3x4	4	Mech. Adj.	170	21.6	90@4000	145@2000	8.3–1	40	Gear
All OHV, V8 Exc. Hawk	3⁹⁄₁₆x3¼	5	Mech. Adj.	259	40.6	Note 4		8.8–1	40	Gear
Hawk	3⁹⁄₁₆x3⅝	5	Mech. Adj.	289	40.6	225@4500	300@2800	8.8-1	40	Gear
1961										
All 6 Cyl., OHV	3x4	4	Mech. Adj.	169.6	21.6	112@4500	225@4500	8.5-1	40	Gear
All OHV, V8 Exc. Hawk	3⁹⁄₁₆x3¼	5	Mech. Adj.	259.0	40.6	Note 4		8.8-1	40	Gear
Hawk	3⁹⁄₁₆x3⅝	5	Mech. Adj.	289.0	40.6	154@2000	300@2800	8.8-1	40	Gear
1962-63 6 Cyl.	3x4	4	Mech. Adj.	169.6	21.6	112@4500	225@4500	8.25-1	40	Gear
V8, exc. Hawk	3⁹⁄₁₆x3¼	5	Mech. Adj.	259.0	40.6	Note 4		8.5-1	40	Gear
Hawk	3⁹⁄₁₆x3⅝	5	Mech. Adj.	289.0	40.6	154@2000	300@2800	8.5-1	40	Gear

NOTES FOR GENERAL ENGINE SPECIFICATIONS TABLE

Note 1: Oil Flow

OIL FILTER TYPE

1954-63 ....Partial flow

ROCKER SHAFT OIL SUPPLY

1954-63, All OHV, V8 except 1956 Golden Hawk

Oil from the right main oil gallery flows through drilled passages in the block and head to the rear rocker shaft undercut mounting bolt. Around the undercut bolt and through the bracket to the hollow shaft. The oil pressure supply for the left bank rocker arm assembly is from the front main bearing through drilled passages in the block and head to the front rocker shaft undercut mounting bolt. Around the undercut bolt and through the bracket to the hollow shaft.

1956, GOLDEN HAWK V8, OHV

The oil supply for the left bank rocker arm assembly is taken from the left main oil gallery at the front camshaft bearing. The oil flows through connecting passages in the block and head and passes around the undercut stem of the front rocker arm shaft mounting bolt and into the hollow rocker arm shaft.

The right bank rocker arm assembly lubrication is taken from the vertical oil gallery passage at the rear camshaft bearing. Oil passes through the block and head to the rear rocker arm shaft undercut mounting bolt. Around the undercut bolt and through the bracket to the hollow shaft.

Note 2: Horsepower and Torque

1956, Commander, OHV, V8

WITH 2 BARREL CARBURETOR:
H.P.—170@4500;
Torque—260@2800

WITH 4 BARREL CARBURETOR:
H.P.—185@4500;
Torque—265@2800

Note 3: Horsepower and Torque

1956, President, OHV, V8

WITH 2 BARREL CARBURETOR:
H.P.—195@4500;
Torque—286@2800

WITH 4 BARREL CARBURETOR:
H.P.—210@4500;
Torque—292@2800

Note 4: Horsepower and Torque

1957-58, Commander, OHV, V8
1959-63, OHV, V8

WITH 2 BARREL CARBURETOR:
H.P.—180@4500;
Torque—260@2800

WITH 4 BARREL CARBURETOR:
H.P.—195@4500;
Torque—265@3000

Note 5: Horsepower and Torque

1957-58, President, OHV, V8

WITH 2 BARREL CARBURETOR:
H.P.—210@4500;
Torque—300@2800

WITH 4 BARREL CARBURETOR:
H.P.—225@4500;
Torque—305@3000

Note 6: Commander Series 16G8

The 1955 Commander engine started with size as shown. After engine numbers: 8,397,201; 8,843,001; 8,958,101; the engine was changed to the same engine as the 1955 President except that: H.P. is only 162@4500, T. is only 250@2800.

Abbreviations Used

GLD. HK. OHV, V8—Golden Hawk V-shaped 8 cylinder engine with valves in head.

In 1956 this engine was a Packard design. In 1957-58 it is of Studebaker design.

CRANKSHAFT BEARING JOURNAL SIZES

YEAR	Main Bearing Journals				Connecting Rod Bearing Journals		
	Journal Diameter	Oil Clearance	End Play of Shaft	End Play Held By	Journal Diameter	Oil Clearance	End Play
1954							
Champion, 6 Cyl.	2.437	.0015	.005	No. 1	1.812	.0012	.007
All V8	2.500	.0015	.005	No. 1	2.000	.0012	.010
1955							
Champion 6 Cyl.	3.062	.0015	.005	No. 1	1.812	.0012	.007
All V8	2.500	.0015	.005	No. 1	2.000	.0012	.010
1956							
Champion, 6 Cyl.	3.062	.0015	.005	No. 1	1.812	.0012	.007
All V8 ex. Gld. Hk.	2.500	.0015	.005	No. 1	2.000	.0012	.010
Golden Hawk, V8	2.500	.0015	.006	No. 5	2.250	.0015	.007
1957-58							
All 6 Cyl.	3.062	.0015	.005	No. 1	1.812	.0012	.007
All V8	2.500	.0015	.005	No. 1	2.000	.0015	.010
1959-63							
All 6 Cyl.	3.062	.0015	.005	No. 1	1.812	.0012	.007
All V8	2.500	.0015	.005	No. 1	2.000	.0015	.010

TORQUE SPECIFICATIONS

YEAR	Cylinder Head Bolts	Rod Bearing Bolts	Main Bearing Bolts	Crankshaft Pulley Bolt	Flywheel to Crankshaft Bolt
1954-55					
All 6 Cyl.	46–50	28–32	88–93	130–140	33–55
All V8	46–50	52–54	88–93	130–140	33–55
1956					
All 6 Cyl.	46–50	28–32	88–93	130–140	33–55
All V8 ex. Gld. Hk.	46–50	52–54	88–93	130–140	33–55
Golden Hawk, V8	55–60	40–45	90–95	130–150	55–60
1957-60					
All 6 Cyl.	46–50	28–32	85–95	130–140	33–55
All V8	55–65	52–54	85–95	130–140	33–55
1961-63					
All 6 Cyl., OHV	46–50	28–32	85–95	130–140	33–55
All V8	55–65	52–54	85–95	130–140	33–55

CYLINDER HEAD NUT TIGHTENING SEQUENCE

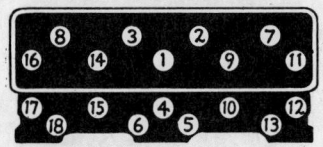

1954-63 V8 ex. 1956 Golden Hawk V8
Tighten to 55-65 ft. lbs.

1956 Golden Hawk V8 Only
Tighten to 55-60 ft. lbs.

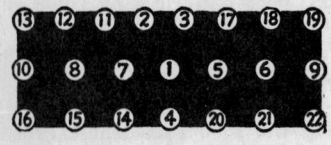

1954-60 All 6 Cyl.
Tighten to 46-50 ft. lbs.

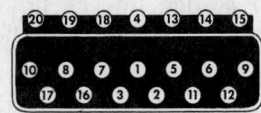

1961-63 OHV 6 Cyl.
Tighten to 46-50 ft. lbs.

PISTON AND PIN SPECIFICATIONS

Year and Model	PISTON			PISTON PIN			
	Skirt Clearance TOP BOTTOM	Diameter	Bushing	FIT In Rod	FIT In Piston	Lock
1954-63 6 Cyl.	Note A	.7493	None	0	.0001-.0003	Clamp
1954-63 V8	Note A	.8743	None	0	.0001-.0003	Clamp

NOTE "A": Use 1" x .002" Feeler—7 to 12 lbs. pull.

VALVE SPECIFICATIONS

YEAR	Seat Angle In.	Seat Angle Ex.	Intake Valve Lift	Exhaust Valve Lift	Valve Spring Pressure Inner	Valve Spring Pressure Outer	Stem to Guide Clearance Inlet	Stem to Guide Clearance Exhaust	Stem Diameter Inlet	Stem Diameter Exhaust	Are Valve Guides Replace-able
1954											
Champion, 6 Cyl.	45	45	.344	.344	52@1 21/32	None	.0025	.0025	.3125	.3125	Yes
Commander, V8	45	45	.359	.359	50@2 1/32	None	.0025	.0025	.3438	.3438	Yes
1955											
Champion, 6 Cyl.	45	45	.344	.344	52@1 21/32	None	.0025	.0025	.3125	.3125	Yes
All V8 Models	45	45	.359	.359	50@2 1/32	None	.0025	.0025	.3438	.3438	Yes
1956											
Champion, 6 Cyl.	45	45	.344	.344	52@1 21/32	None	.0025	.0025	.3125	.3125	Yes
All V8 ex. Golden Hawk	45	45	.359	.359	50@2 1/32	None	.0025	.0025	.3438	.3438	Yes
Golden Hawk, V8	30	45	.398	.398	92@1 3/4	None	.0015	.0025	.3725	.3715	No
1957-58											
Champion, 6 Cyl.	45	45	.344	.344	52@1 21/32	None	.0025	.0025	.3125	.3125	Yes
All V8 Models	45	45	.359	.359	50@2 1/32	None	.0025	.0025	.3438	.3438	Yes
1959-60											
All 6 Cyl.	45	45	.344	.344	52@1 21/32	None	.0025	.0025	.3125	.3125	Yes
All V8	45	45	.359	.359	50@2 1/32	None	.0025	.0025	.3438	.3438	Yes
1961-63											
All OHV, 6 & 8 Cyl	45	45	.375	.375	50@2 1/32	None	.0025	.0025	.3438	.3438	Yes

GENERAL CHASSIS and BRAKE SPECIFICATIONS

Year	Model	Chassis: Overall Length in Inches	Chassis: Tire Size	Brake Cylinder Bore: Master Cyl. (Inch)	Wheel Cylinder Diameter (Inch) Front	Wheel Cylinder Diameter (Inch) Rear
1954	6 Cyl. Champion	198 5/8	6.40x15	1.0	1.0	7/8
	V8, Commander	198 5/8	6.40x15	1.0	1 1/16	7/8
	V-8, Land Cruiser	202 5/8	7.10x15	1.0	1 1/16	7/8
1955	6 Cyl. Champion	204 7/16	6.40x15	1.0	1.0	7/8
	V8, Commander	204 7/16	6.70x15	1.0	1.0	7/8
	V8, President	206 1/4	7.10x15	1.0	1.0	7/8
1956	6 Cyl. Champion	200 3/4	6.40x15	1.0	1.0	13/16
	6 Cyl. Flight Hawk	203 15/16	6.40x15	1.0	1.0	13/16
	6 Cyl. Pelham	196 3/4	6.70x15	1.0	1.0	13/16
	V8, Commander	200 3/4	6.70x15	1.0	1 1/16	7/8
	V8, Power Hawk	203 15/16	6.70x15	1.0	1 1/16	7/8
	V8, Parkview	196 3/4	6.70x15	1.0	1 1/16	7/8
	V8, President	200 3/4	6.70x15	1.0	1 1/16	7/8
	V8, Classic	204 3/4	7.10x15	1.0	1 1/16	7/8
	V8, Sky Hawk	203 15/16	6.70x15	1.0	1 1/16	7/8
	V8, Pinehurst	196 3/4	6.70x15	1.0	1 1/16	7/8
	V8, Golden Hawk	203 15/16	7.10x15	1.0	1 1/16	7/8
1957	6 Cyl. Champion	202 3/8	6.40x15	1.0	1.0	13/16
	6 Cyl. Silver Hawk	203 15/16	6.40x15	1.0	1.0	13/16
	6 Cyl. Pelham	202 3/8	6.70x15	1.0	1.0	13/16
	V8, Commander-Provincial	202 3/8	6.70x15	1.0	1 1/16	7/8
	V8, Parkview-Broadmoor	202 3/8	6.70x15	1.0	1 1/16	7/8
	V8, President	200 3/4	6.70x15	1.0	1 1/16	7/8
	V8, Classic	206 3/8	7.10x15	1.0	1 1/16	7/8
	V8, Silver Hawk	203 15/16	6.70x15	1.0	1 1/16	7/8
	V8, Golden Hawk	203 15/16	7.10x15	1.0	1 1/16	7/8
1958	6 Cyl. Scotsman	202 3/8	6.40x15	1.0	1.0	13/16
	6 Cyl. Champion S. Hawk	203 15/16	6.40x15	1.0	1.0	13/16
	V8, President (4 door)	206 3/8	8.00x14	1.0	1 1/16	7/8
	V8, President (2 door)	202 3/8	7.50x14	1.0	1 1/16	7/8
	V8, President (coupe, S. Hawk)	203 15/16	7.50x14	1.0	1 1/16	7/8
	V8, Stude. Golden Hawk	203 15/16	8.00x14	1.0	1 1/16	7/8
	V8, Packard Hawk	205 1/16	8.00x14	1.0	1 1/16	7/8
1959-61	6 Cyl. Lark, Sedans and H. Top	175.0	5.90x15*	1.0	1.0	13/16
	V8, Lark, Sedans and H. Top	175.0	6.40x15*	1.0	1 1/16	7/8
	6 Cyl. Hawk	204.0	6.40x15	1.0	1.0	13/16
	V8, Hawk	204.0	6.70x15	1.0	1 1/16	7/8
	6 Cyl. Station Wagons	184 1/2	6.40x15	1.0	1.0	13/16
	V8, Convertibles	175.0	6.70x15	1.0	1 1/16	7/8
1962–63	All 2-door Sedans and H. Top Conv.	184.0	6.00x15*	1.0	Note A	
	All 4-door Sedans	188.0	6.00x15	1.0	Note A	
	All Station Wagons	187.0	6.00x15	1.0	Note A	
	All Hawk Models	204.0	6.70x15	1.0	Note A	

* Convertibles 6.50 x 15 NOTE "A": All 6 Cyl. 1" Front, 13/16" Rear; All 8 Cyl. 1 1/16" Front, 7/8" Rear.

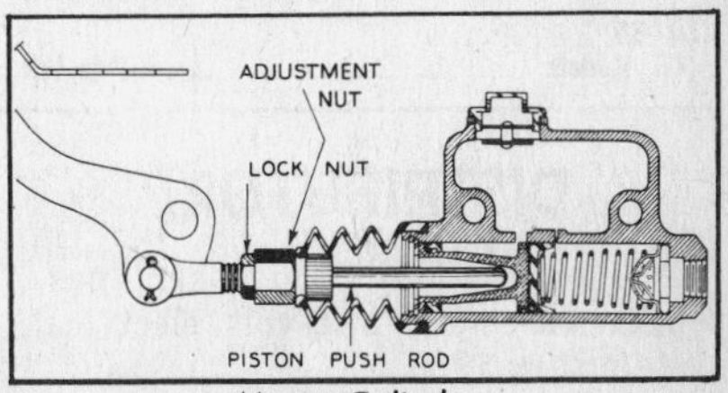

Master Cylinder

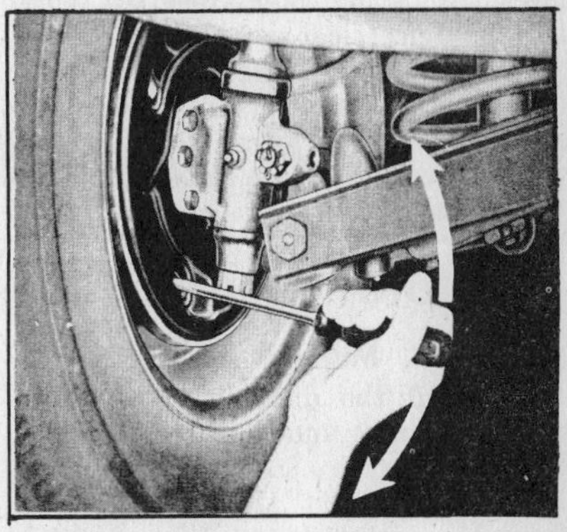
Brake Adjustment

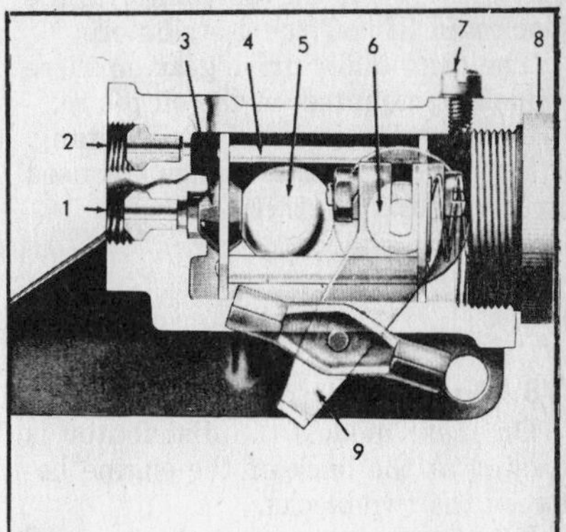

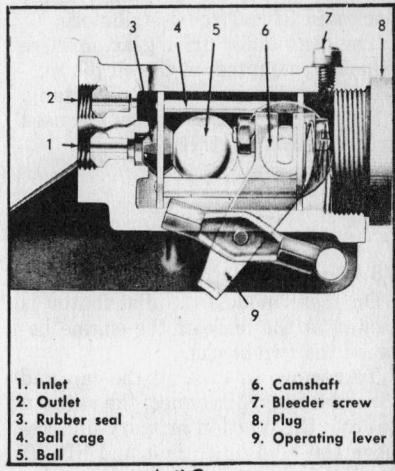

1. Inlet
2. Outlet
3. Rubber seal
4. Ball cage
5. Ball
6. Camshaft
7. Bleeder screw
8. Plug
9. Operating lever

Anti-Creep

CAPACITIES

YEAR	Engine Crankcase Add 1 Qt. For New Filter	Transmissions Pints to Refill After Draining		Rear Axle Pints	Gasoline Tank Gallons	Cooling System Quarts Add 1 Qt. For Heater
		Manual Note 1	Automatic			
1954-55						
All 6 Cyl.	5	1½	19	2½	18	10
All V8	6	2½	19	3	18	17¼
1956						
All 6 Cyl.	5	1½	18	2½	18	11
All V8 ex. Golden Hawk	5	2½	18	2½	18	17¼
Golden Hawk, V8	5	2½	22	2½	18	11
1957-63						
All 6 Cyl.	5	2.3	18	3	18	11
All V8	5	3.8	18	2½	18	17

NOTE 1: 1961-63, 4-speed—2.5.

FRONT WHEEL ALIGNMENT

YEAR	Caster		Camber		Toe-In (Inches)	King Pin Inclination (Degrees)	Wheel Pivot Ratio	
	Range (Degrees)	Pref. Setting	Range (Degrees)	Pref. Setting			Inner Wheel	Outer Wheel
1954-60 All Models	2½N to 1N	1¾N	0 to 1P	½P	1/16 to ⅛	6	20	17½
1961-63 All Models	¾P to ¾N	Zero	0 to 1P	½P	1/16 to ⅛	6	23	20

DISTRIBUTOR

All production Studebaker passenger cars use a 6-volt electrical system thru 1955.

Starting with 1956 production, all models of Studebaker are fitted with a 12-volt electrical system.

This in no way affects the service on the electrical system except that no part except the spark plugs on 1956 models are interchangeable with any of the earlier models.

DISTRIBUTOR REMOVAL

All 6 Cyl. Models

Take off the distributor cap and wire assembly and remove the ignition primary wire from the side of the block. Disconnect the vacuum line from the carburetor and remove the bolt which holds the distributor to the block and lift off the distributor.

The distributor drive gear on these models is mounted on the oil pump.

The distributor is driven by a tang.

Stationary breaker plates are used on all in-line engines.

V8 Models

On these models the distributor is located at the back of the engine between the two blocks.

To remove it, take off the cap and wire assembly, disconnect the vacuum line and the ignition primary line, remove the hold down bolt and lift off the distributor.

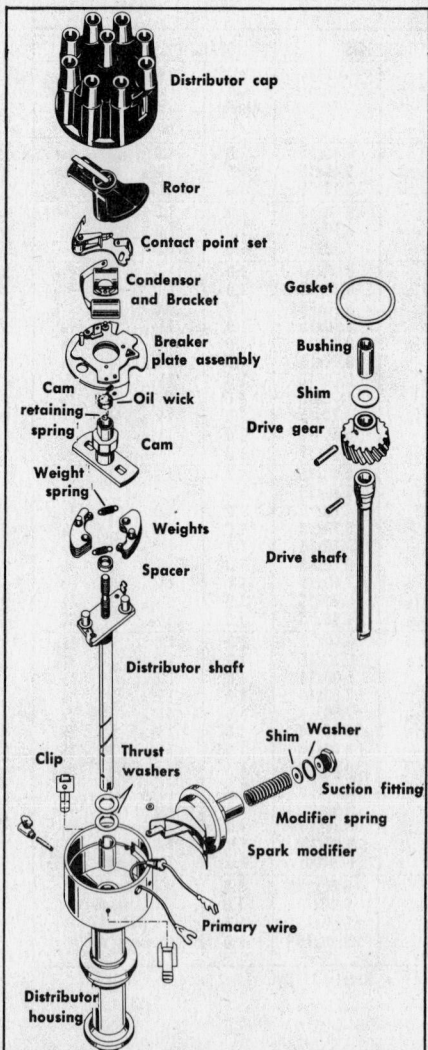

Distributor cap

Rotor

Contact point set

Condensor and Bracket

Gasket

Breaker plate assembly

Bushing

Cam retaining spring

Oil wick

Shim

Cam

Drive gear

Weight spring

Weights

Spacer

Drive shaft

Distributor shaft

Shim Washer

Clip

Thrust washers

Suction fitting

Modifier spring

Spark modifier

Primary wire

Distributor housing

Disassembled view of distributor V-8 models

DISTRIBUTER INSTALLATION

6 Cyl. Models

Insert shaft into block opening and enter shaft slot on oil pump shaft tongue. Position the distributor clamp at block and install screw loosely. Position the clamp so that the center of adjusting slot is in line with the screw hole in block. Connect wires and spark modifier vacuum line. Install distributor cap and reset timing.

V8 Models

Set No. 1 cylinder on firing position with pointer directly at IGN mark. With rotor toward front of engine and modifier connection to the right side, start to lower into position. Now turn rotor approximately 30° clockwise and complete lowering assembly. As distributor gear teeth start to engage camshaft gear the rotor will turn counterclockwise and the tongue on the oil pump drive shaft will engage the slot in the oil pump. This should aline the rotor directly with No. 1 terminal of the car. If trouble is experienced meshing pump shaft, turning engine slightly will help.

Keep slight pressure on distributor during this alignment until mesh is secured.

Install cap, wires and clamp. Reset timing. Finally reinstall the modifier vacuum line.

IGNITION PRIMARY RESISTOR

1956 Thru 1959 Models

Starting with 1956 production, a primary ignition resistor is used on

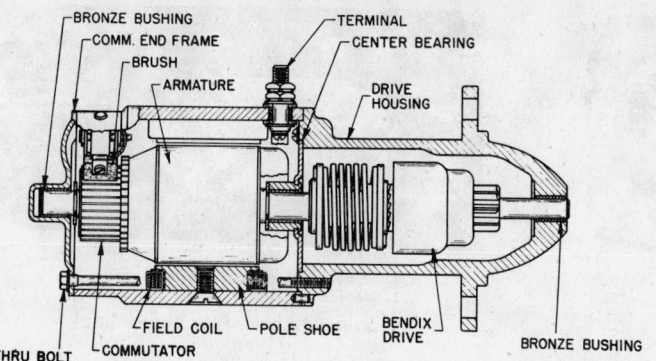

Starter Motor

all 12-volt models. The resistor is located almost in the center of the dash just above the distributor.

Starting with 1960—V8 a resistance type wire to the coil is used with 1.40 to 1.65 ohms value.

IGNITION FIRING ORDER

All 6-Cylinder Engines

All 6-cylinder Studebakers fire 1-5-3-6-2-4. The distributor turns in a counterclockwise direction on all 6-cylinder models.

All V8 Models

On V8 models the cylinders are numbered:

Front right 2-4-6-8
Front left 1-3-5-7

Using this numbering system, the engine fires 1-8-4-3-6-5-7-2 and turns counterclockwise.

REPLACE IGNITION WIRES

The easiest way to replace ignition wires is to do the job one wire at a time and in this way the old wire can be used as a pilot to locate it properly in the distributor cap.

However, if this method cannot be used and it is necessary to replace all the wires at once, proceed as follows:

Remove the spark plug from number 1 cylinder and bring that cylinder up on compression by placing the thumb in the spark plug hole and turning the engine over until compression is felt to blow by the thumb.

As the compression is blowing by the thumb bring the engine around very slowly and notice when the ignition timing mark lines up with the pointer. This is the firing position of number 1 cylinder. Now remove the cap from the distributor and notice the position of the rotor.

Place the first spark plug wire in the distributor cap socket just above the rotor. Now go around the distributor cap in the direction of distributor rotation and follow the firing order.

Thus on 6-cylinder cars the wires would be placed 1-5-3-6-2-4 around the cap, and on V8 models the wires would be placed 1-8-4-3-6-5-7-2 around the cap.

GENERATOR AND REGULATOR

All service on generators is given in the Generator and Regulator section, see index.

BATTERY & STARTER

All service on the starters is given in the Starter and Starter Switch section, see index.

Starter Remove

Disconnect battery, (on 6-cylinder models remove oil level gauge and tube). Disconnect the cable and wires. Remove cap screws and lift out starter.

DASH INSTRUMENTS

1956 Thru 1963 Models
Except Hawks

There are four instruments mounted on the dash, the ammeter and oil pressure gauge are telltale lights and are not in the strict sense of the word instruments.

Each of the other two instruments is separately mounted on the dash and held in place with two nuts.

Since all work under the dash is done in necessarily close quarters, the battery should first be disconnected before attempting any work of any nature under the dash.

Remove the nuts which hold the instruments to the under side of the dash panel and pull the instruments back out of the dash panel and down towards the floor.

Push pin type electrical connections are used on all instruments.

1956 Thru 1963 Hawk Models
Instruments

On Hawk models each instrument comes out separately. Remove the nuts from the wire connection and the

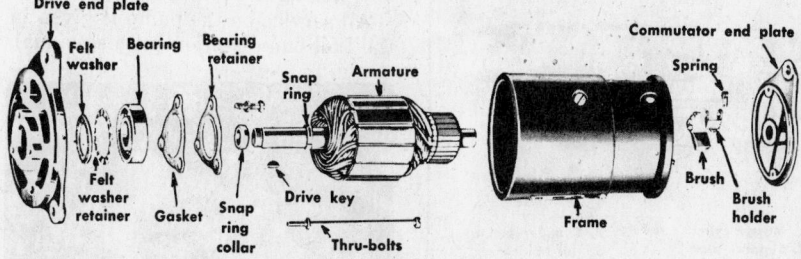

Generator, Exploded View

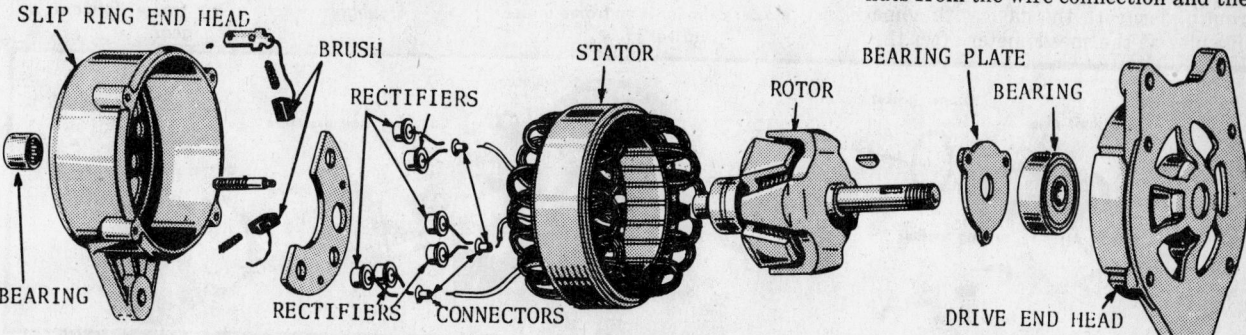

Alternator, Exploded View

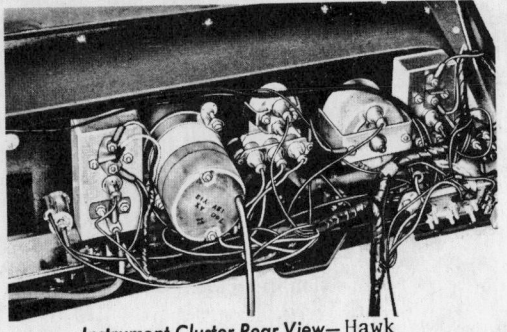

Instrument Cluster Rear View— Hawk

1. Cluster stud nuts and brackets
2. Speedometer case stud nuts and brackets

Instrument Cluster Rear View— Lark

lock nut underneath the wire connection and the instrument can then be pulled forward into the car. This is true of each of the instruments.

WINDSHIELD WIPER MOTOR

1958 Models

The windshield wiper motor is mounted on the firewall just above the distributor. To remove the motor, disconnect the wiper arms which are attached to the motor with clips and can be easily taken out from under the dash. Remove the wires from the motor and take out the two motor mounting screws and remove the motor from the firewall.

1959-63 Models

The wiper motor may be electric or vacuum operated. In either case, the presence of a radio will require the radio to be taken out of the dash to permit removal of the wiper motor and linkage.

SPEEDOMETER

SPEEDOMETER REMOVAL

1956 Thru 1963 Models
Except Hawks

Since all work under the dash is done in necessarily close quarters, the first thing to do is to disconnect the battery so that there is not an accidental short circuit.

The speedometer is held to the upper surface of the dash panel by two screws. The screws can be removed from underneath the dash with some difficulty at the speedometer after the

cable is disconnected and lifted up into the car.

1956 Thru 1963 Hawk Models
Speedometer Removal

From underneath the dash, remove the cable from the back of the speedometer and then take out the two bolts which hold the speedometer box up to the instrument panel and pull the speedometer into the car.

BRAKES

The service brakes are of the conventional type, hydraulically operated. The lining is molded and attached to the shoes by tubular rivets. The primary shoe lining is shorter than the secondary lining and is of different composition.

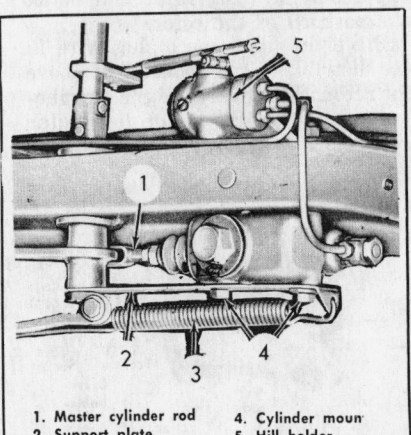

1. Master cylinder rod
2. Support plate
3. Clutch pedal spring
4. Cylinder moun
5. Hill holder

Master cylinder is on frame under driver's feet

The parking brake uses a hand operated control lever, enclosed cables, rear wheel brake shoe levers and struts to the rear wheel shoes. The parking brake is released by turning the apply handle to the right.

Starting with 1961, a suspended pedal type, with master cylinder on fire wall is used on all Lark models.

Repair methods can be found in Unit Repair section.

BRAKE PEDAL ADJUSTMENT

There should be from $\frac{1}{2}$ inch to $\frac{3}{4}$ inch free motion of the brake pedal before the master cylinder rod contacts the piston. This adjustment is made at the master cylinder piston rod.

FUEL SYSTEM

FUEL PUMP REMOVAL

All 6 Cylinder Models

The fuel pump is located on the right side of the block towards the front. Disconnect the intake and output gas lines, remove the two bolts which hold the pump to the block and lift off the pump.

All service on the pump is given in the fuel pump section in this manual.

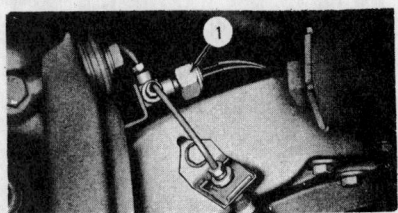

Stoplight switch is on frame forward of steering gear

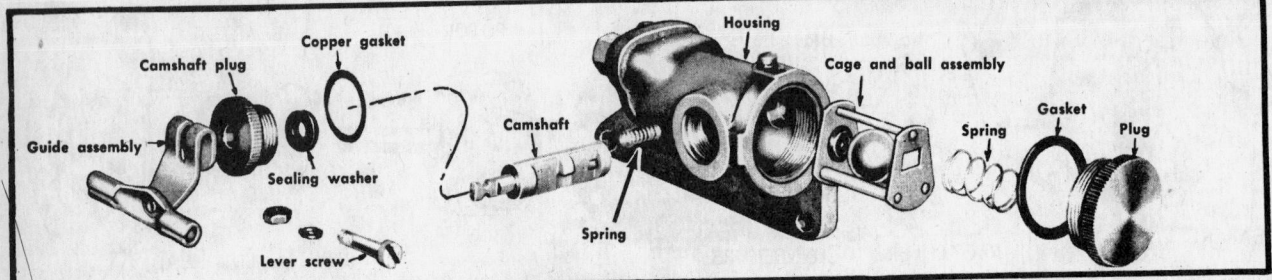

Exploded View of Hill Holder

Guide assembly — Camshaft plug — Copper gasket — Sealing washer — Lever screw — Camshaft — Spring — Housing — Cage and ball assembly — Spring — Gasket — Plug

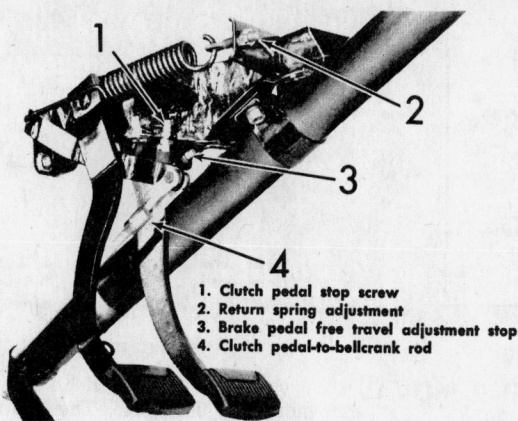

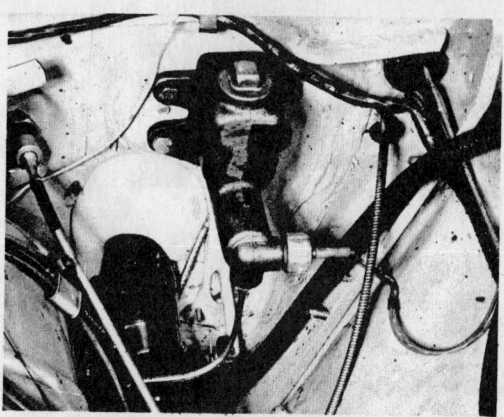

1. Clutch pedal stop screw
2. Return spring adjustment
3. Brake pedal free travel adjustment stop
4. Clutch pedal-to-bellcrank rod

Suspended pedal and master cylinder plan Starting 1961—Except Hawk

All V-8 Models

The pump is located on the left side of the engine towards the front. Disconnect the gas lines and remove the bolts which hold the pump to the timing case cover and then lift off the pump.

REMOVAL OF GAS TANK

Disconnect the filler neck at the flexible fitting on the left side of the gas tank.

From in the trunk of the car pull off the cover over the port hole in the trunk floor and remove the gauge wire from the gas tank.

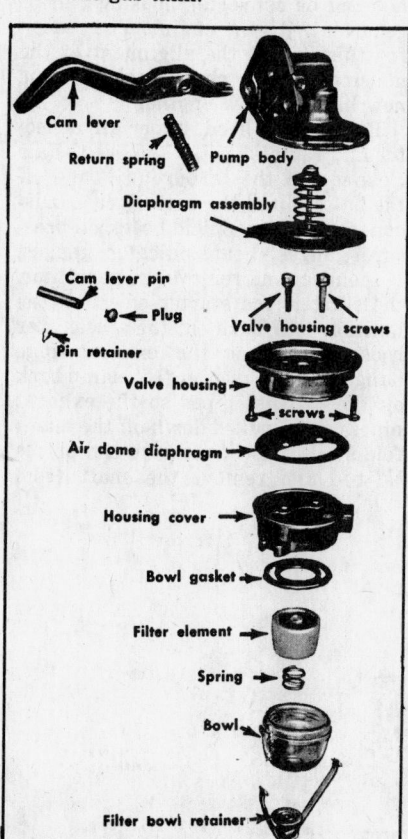

Disassembled view of fuel pump

Cam lever
Return spring
Pump body
Diaphragm assembly
Cam lever pin
Plug
Valve housing screws
Pin retainer
Valve housing
screws
Air dome diaphragm
Housing cover
Bowl gasket
Filter element
Spring
Bowl
Filter bowl retainer

Disconnect the main gas feed line from the gas tank and then remove the bolts from both sides of the gas tank after having placed a jack under the tank to prevent it from falling down when the last bolt is removed.

Lower the tank straight down and out from under the car.

EXHAUST SYSTEM

All Models

The exhaust system is removed in the conventional manner. When removing the tailpipe, it is best to let the rear housing assembly hang free. This can be accomplished by placing stands under the frame.

EXHAUST MANIFOLD REMOVAL

All V-8 Models

From underneath the car detach the exhaust pipe flanges on both sides. Disconnect and remove the generator.

Remove bolts which hold power steering pump to the front of the block and pull the pump up out of the way. On models fitted with power brakes access to the bolts is rendered somewhat difficult because of the location on the power brake cylinder.

However, on these models the bolts can be reached from underneath the car.

Remove the bolts which hold the manifold to the cylinder head and take off the exhaust manifolds.

Inlet Manifold Removal
ALL V-8 MODELS

Remove the carburetor air cleaner and take off all the lines to the carburetor, including gas, vacuum and throttle. Remove the vacuum lines at the manifold. Remove the bolts which hold the manifold hold-down brackets and lift off the intake manifold.

COOLING SYSTEM
RADIATOR CORE REMOVAL

1954 Models

The radiator core on these models is removed after the hose clamps are disconnected, and the water outlets in the block removed. The core is held with six sheet metal screws and can be lifted up after these screws are taken out.

1955 Thru 1963 Models

On models which have a fan shroud, unclip the wires from the radiator fan shroud and remove the junction block from the fan shroud without disconnecting the wires from the block. Disconnect the upper and lower radiator hose and the oil cooler lines on super charged models and take out the bolts which hold the radiator shroud and core to the cradle. Slide the shroud over the fan and lift the radiator straight up.

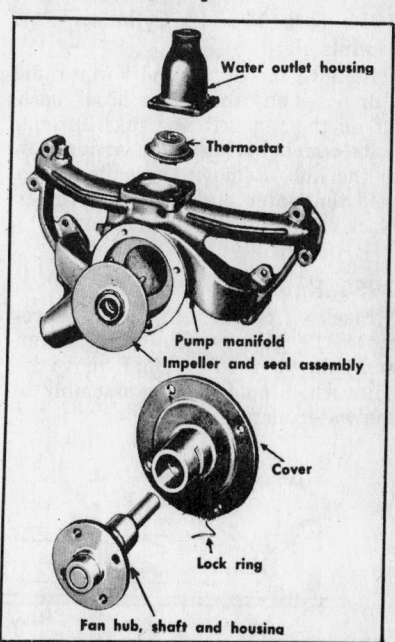

Water outlet housing
Thermostat
Pump manifold
Impeller and seal assembly
Cover
Lock ring
Fan hub, shaft and housing

Water pump assembly V8 Engines

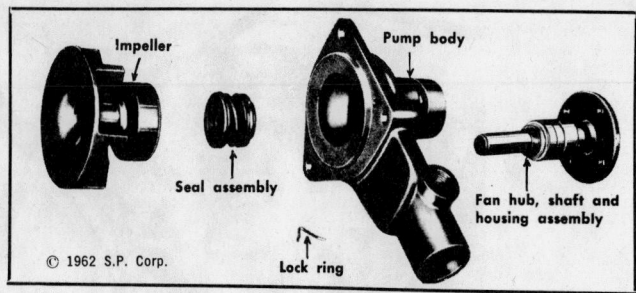

Exploded view of water pump—6 cyl. Engine

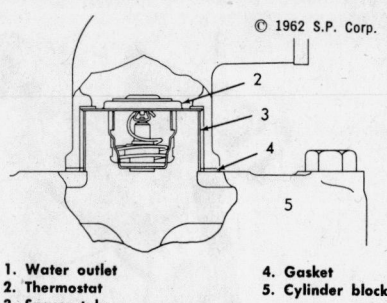

1. Water outlet
2. Thermostat
3. Spacer tube
4. Gasket
5. Cylinder block

Thermostat

THERMOSTATS

On all Studebaker models the thermostats are contained in water outlet housings at the top of the cylinder block or water manifold.

To replace the thermostat remove the water outlet elbow and take out the thermostat.

WATER PUMP REMOVAL

1954 Models
Except V-8's

On the earlier models remove the hood side panel and take off the fan blades, fan belt and pulley and disconnect the pump and either hoses. Remove the bolts which hold the pump to the engine block and lift off the water pump.

All V-8 Models

Remove the fan belt and fan pulley, disconnect the inlet and outlet water hoses, take out the screws which hold the water pump to the block and lift off the pump.

1955 Thru 1963 6 Cylinder Models

Remove the upper and lower radiator hoses and the heater hose. Slack off on the fan belt and take out the bolts which hold the fan and pulley to the hub. Remove the bolts which hold the water pump to the cylinder block and pull off the water pump.

1955 Thru 1963 V-8 Models

Slack off on the generator and remove the bolts which hold the fan and pulley to the fan hub. Remove the bolts which hold the fan assembly to the water manifold.

WATER MANIFOLD REMOVAL

1955 Thru 1963 V-8 Models

Remove the upper and lower radiator hoses and the heater hose. Slack off on the generator belt and remove the bolts which hold the fan and pulley to the hub and take off the water pump.

ENGINE

Starting with the 1961 model, the Lark Six will have an overhead valve engine.

The basic sizes follow the former Lark L-Head six but increased power and economy are delivered.

Features contributing are larger valves, staggered to increase air intake. A ram-type intake manifold and a kidney-shaped combustion chamber aid to better breathing and reduced detonation. Efficent operation can be had with regular gas.

A redesigned cam shaft is also part of this improved operation.

ENGINE REMOVAL

1954 V-8 Engines

In order to remove the engine on these models it is recommended that the transmission first be removed from the car. Remove the hood and radiator core and all engine attaching parts such as exhaust flange, flange crossover pipes, electrical connections to the starter and engine, fuel lines,

accelerator linkage, and engine mounting bolts, etc. The engine then can be lifted upwards and out of the car.

6 Cylinder Engines

If the engine is being removed to work on the engine and replace the same engine, it is best to disconnect it at the bell housing, leaving the clutch attached to the engine.

On models with automatic drive the torque converter should be disconnected from the engine drive plate so that the torque converter will remain on the transmission when the engine is removed.

If, however, the engine is being removed so that a new block or a new engine can be installed, the clutch housing or converter housing can be removed with the engine. The reason for this is that the alignment of the housings can be checked against the new block or new engine.

Remove the hood, upper air deflector and radiator core. Remove the air cleaner and the carburetor. Take off the battery and the battery case. Disconnect the windshield hoses, oil pressure gauges, heat indicator gauges. Disconnect and remove the generator, the starter, the starter solenoid, the ignition coil. Take out the accelerator rods, disconnect the exhaust pipe flange and remove the "U" clamp back on the exhaust pipes so the exhaust pipes can be pulled down off the manifold studs. Disconnect one end of the tie rod and remove the shaft from

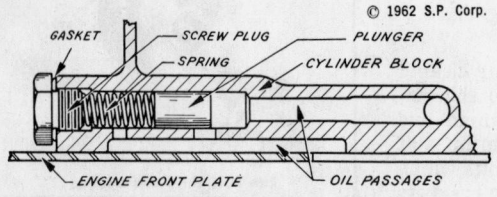

6 cyl. engine oil pump Valve

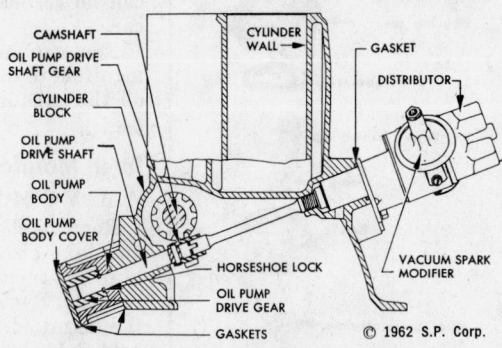

Oil pump assembly 6 cylinder models

the steering bellcrank. Move the bell-crank out of the way to provide clearance for the oil pan. Disconnect the gas lines and attach a lifting device to the engine. Now raise the engine just enough to take the weight off the front supports. Disconnect the wires from the anticreeps on the transmission and disconnect the throttle control to the transmission. Remove the converter housing lower plate if the job has automatic transmission and disconnect the torque converter driven plate. If it has a clutch, remove the clutch housing to engine bolts and drive out the clutch housing dowel pins. Raise the engine slightly and move it forward sharply to break it loose from the clutch housing. Contine to push the engine forward until the transmission spline is clear of the clutch assembly and then lift the engine out of the car.

1955 Thru 1963 V8 Models

If the engine is being removed so that work can be done on the engine and it will be returned to the chassis, it is best to disconnect it at the bell housing, leaving the clutch attached to the flywheel if the job has a clutch. If the job has an automatic transmission it is easier to disconnect the bell housing and disconnect the torque converter from the flywheel.

If, however, a new engine is to be installed or a new block is to be installed, it is better to take the transmission assembly or the automatic transmission bell housing along with the engine so that it can be aligned properly.

Remove the hood, radiator core, radiator air deflector, battery, battery box, starter, carburetor and air cleaner, water pump and water manifold.

Disconnect all lines to the engine such as vacuum lines, heat indicator lines, oil pressure gauge and oil pressure gauge line, wires to the generator. Remove the distributor cap and take off the ignition wires, remove the fuel pump.

Disconnect the exhaust pipes at their flanges and let the pipes come down, remove the "U" clamp where the two pipes run together, and separate the exhaust pipe and take it off the vehicle.

Disconnect the wires to the distributor and ignition coil, pull the accelerator linkage off the car. On overdrive cars, disconnect the wire at the kickdown switch. On automatic drive cars disconnect the throttle control rod which runs to the transmission.

Attach a lifting device to the engine and take a little load on the lifting device. Now remove the converter drive plate if the job has automatic

transmission and take out the plate to converter bolts. On models with standard transmission remove the bolts which hold the back of the engine to the bell housing. Now take out the nuts from the engine support insulators and take a further lift on the engine. Disconnect the steering linkage and let it drop down out of the way. Take another hitch on the lifting device and push the engine forward off of the splines at the transmission and lift it up out of the vehicle.

CYLINDER HEAD

REMOVAL OF ROCKER COVERS

V-8 Models

Remove the carburetor air cleaner and, for convenience, take off the distributor cap and wire assembly. Remove the bolts which hold the rocker covers to the cylinder heads and take off the rocker covers.

On models fitted with power steering it helps somewhat to loosen the power steering pump mounting bolts and pull the pump slightly out of the way.

It also helps to take out the battery.

DISASSEMBLY

Before disassembling, mark the rocker arms, brackets and shafts so that they can be reassembled in their original position.

To separate, compress the outer flat washer at one end of the assembly so that the cotter pin can be taken out. Remove the cotter pin and take off the first of the rockers.

Again compressing the rocker, remove the cylinder head cap screw which passes through the bracket and slide the bracket off. Repeat this process until all the rockers have been separated from the shaft.

Before reassembly make absolutely certain that the oil holes in the rocker shaft are free so that plenty of lubrication reaches them.

ROCKER ASSEMBLIES

All V-8 and OHV 6 Cyl. Engines

To remove the rocker assemblies take off the carburetor air cleaner, disconnect the spark plug wires from the plugs and drain the cooling system.

Take off the crown nuts which hold the rocker arm cover and lift the cover off the rocker arm bracket screws.

Remove the four rocker arm bracket screws and lock washers from the rocker arm assembly. Then unscrew the four cylinder head cap screws which also pass down through the rocker assemblies. Lift the rocker arm assembly off with the cylinder head cap screws remaining through the shaft.

When properly assembled to the engine, the flat on one end of the rocker shaft will be at the rear on the right bank and at the front on the left bank.

ROCKER ARM OILING SYSTEM

At the back of the right block there is a passage drilled down into the oil gallery in the block. This passage indexes with the hole in the cylinder head around the shank of a relief bolt

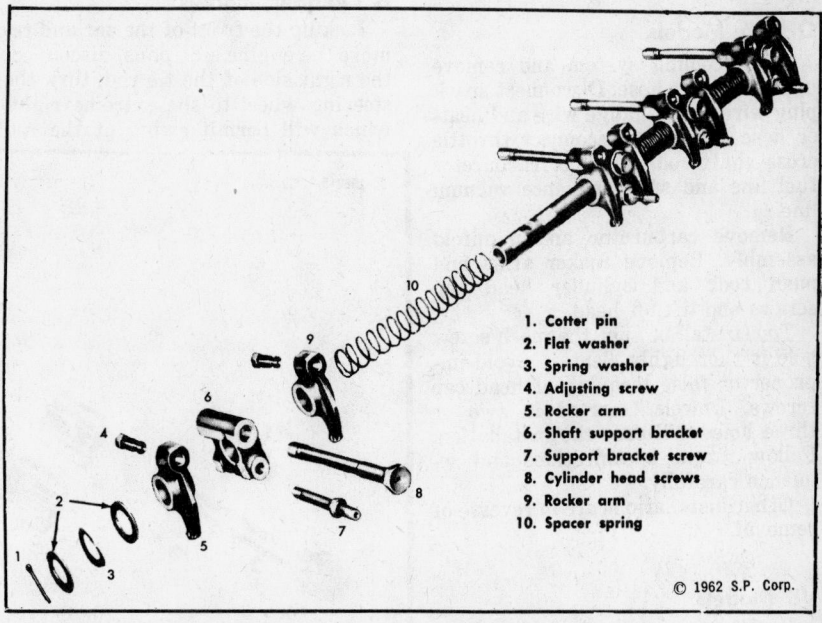

1. Cotter pin
2. Flat washer
3. Spring washer
4. Adjusting screw
5. Rocker arm
6. Shaft support bracket
7. Support bracket screw
8. Cylinder head screws
9. Rocker arm
10. Spacer spring

© 1962 S.P. Corp.

Rocker Arm and Shaft Assembly, V-8 Models

STUDEBAKER

© 1962 S.P. Corp.

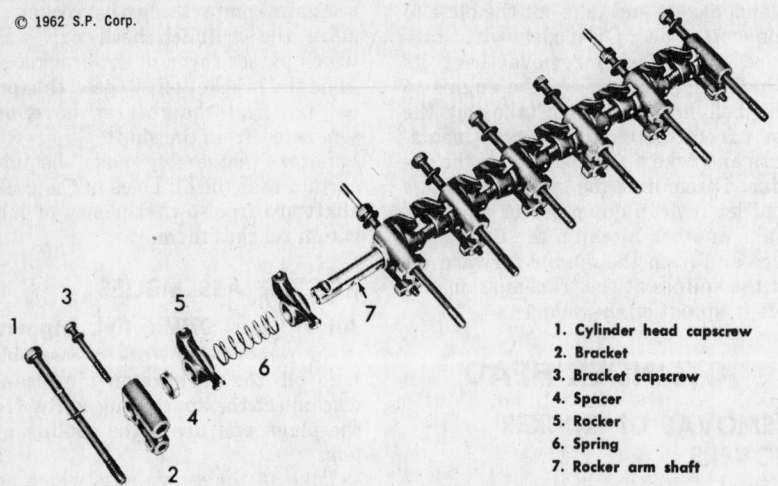

1. Cylinder head capscrew
2. Bracket
3. Bracket capscrew
4. Spacer
5. Rocker
6. Spring
7. Rocker arm shaft

Rocker Arm and Shaft Assembly, OHV 6

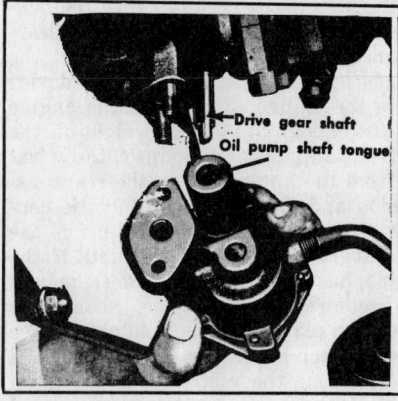

V8 oil pump removal

to the rocker arm shaft rear bracket. The bracket in turn is drilled to connect the cap screw hole with the rocker arm shaft hole. The oil then flows through the hollowed out rocker shaft and flows to the rocker arms through small holes drilled in the rocker arm shaft. Oil then flows through these holes to the rocker arms themselves, which in turn are drilled, supplying oil to the lifters.

The same system is used on the left bank except the oil is supplied from the front of the left bank.

Be sure when installing the lifter brackets to use a relief bolt in the back bracket of the right head and the front bracket of the left head.

REMOVAL OF CYLINDER HEAD

OHV-6 Models

Drain cooling system and remove upper radiator hose. Disconnect spark plug wires, heat gauge wire and heater hose at head. Disconnect throttle cross shaft rod, pump to carburetor fuel line and spark advance vacuum line.

Remove carburetor and manifold assembly. Remove rocker arms and push rods and cylinder head cap screws and lift off head.

To reinstall be sure that each screw hole is thoroughly clean to avoid improper or false torquing of head cap screws. Dowels inserted in two or three holes will ease the installation. Follow torque specifications and sequence carefully.

Other installations are in reverse of removal.

V8 Models

Remove the inlet manifold and the rocker assemblies as explained in pre-

vious paragraphs. Disconnect the exhaust pipes at their flanges. Remove the four bolts which hold the water manifold to the two cylinder heads and loosen the bolts which hold the same water manifold to the cylinder block so that the water manifold can be moved forward just slightly in order to facilitate removing the head.

Remove the bolts which hold the heads to the cylinder block and lift off the heads.

The push rods can be pulled up through the head without disturbing it or, with a little maneuvering, the head can be pulled off the push rods.

ENGINE LUBRICATION

OIL PAN REMOVAL

6 Cylinder Models

Jack up the front of the car and remove the engine side pans, disconnect the right side of the tie rod, turn the steering wheel to the extreme right, which will permit swing of the rod

rearward to an out of the way position.

Unbolt and slide out the oil pan.

Note: On short wheel base models remove the intermediate steering arm.

1954 V-8 Models

Disconnect the right end of the right tie rod and the front end of the drag link and swing the steering linkage to an out of the way position. Disconnect the engine exhaust system and lower to the floor. Remove the oil pan bolts and the oil pan.

Note: On station wagon and sedan models remove the intermediate steering arm.

1955 Thru 1963 V-8 Models

Remove the oil level gauge and its adapter tube. Disconnect the battery and remove the starter on coupe (short wheel base) models, swing the wheels to the right to move the steering bellcrank out of the way.

On station wagons and sedan models (long wheel base) remove the steering bellcrank assembly from the vehicle. Take out the exhaust cross-

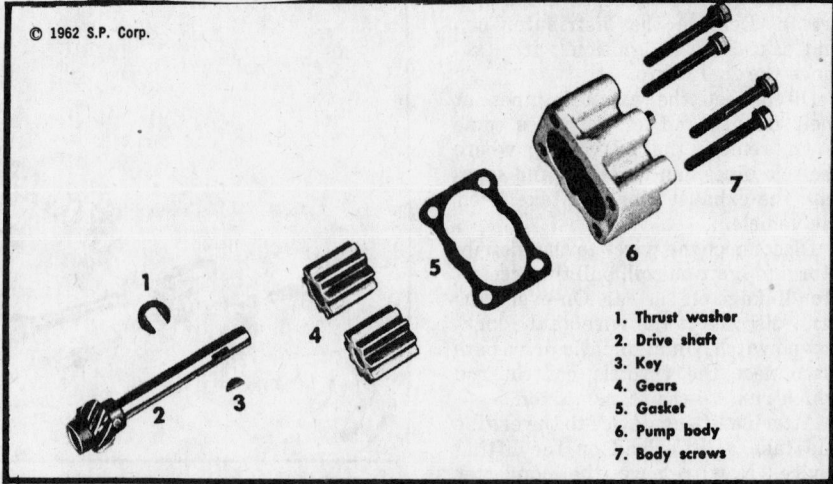

© 1962 S.P. Corp.

1. Thrust washer
2. Drive shaft
3. Key
4. Gears
5. Gasket
6. Pump body
7. Body screws

Oil Pump, Exploded View OHV 6

© 1962 S.P. Corp.

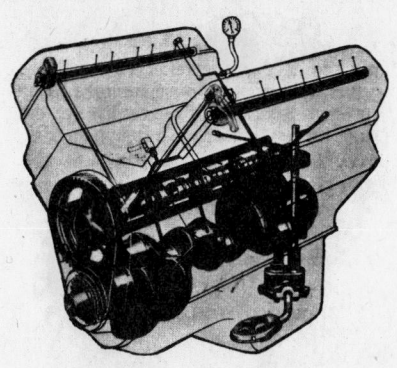

Oiling system, V8 engines

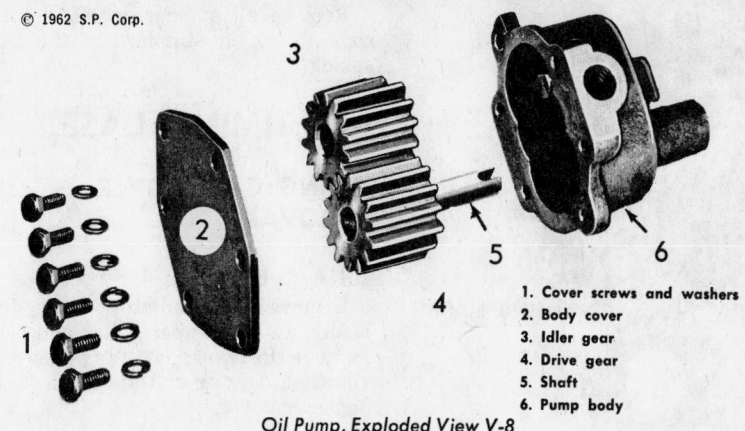

1. Cover screws and washers
2. Body cover
3. Idler gear
4. Drive gear
5. Shaft
6. Pump body

Oil Pump, Exploded View V-8

over pipe, remove the oil pan cap screws and drop the pan.

OIL PUMP REMOVAL

6 Cylinder Models

Remove the right engine side pan. Take off the pump cover and the idler gear. Remove the driven gear and the Woodruff key from the shaft and then the pump body can be unbolted and removed from the block.

If necessary to remove the oil pump shaft, the oil pan will have to be taken down.

All V8 Models

On these models the oil pump is attached to the main bearing caps, to remove it take off the oil pan and unbolt and remove the pump.

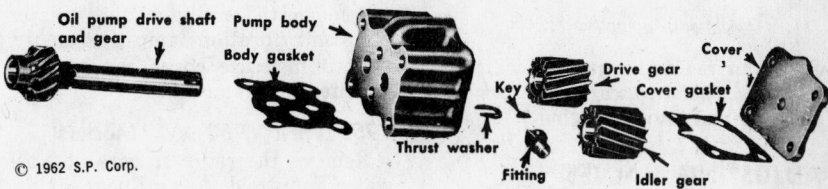

© 1962 S.P. Corp.

Oil pump assembly 6 cylinder models

OIL FILTER REMOVAL

Thru 1960-63 Models

On models which are equipped at the factory, the oil filter is mounted on the oil filler tube on top of the engine between the cylinder blocks. It is removed readily by disconnecting the mounting bolts and lines.

Either the entire filament or the element only can be replaced.

VALVE SYSTEM

On all 1954 in-line engines the valves are of the L head type and are equipped with mechanical mushroom type lifters. Starting with 1951 production an 8 cylinder V type overhead valve engine is used on Commander production. Mechanical valve lifters are used on all Studebaker V8 engines.

All 6 cyl. L-head engines use mushroom type lifters. All OHV engines use barrel type lifters. The 1956 Golden Hawk uses hydraulic lifters.

REPLACEMENT OF VALVE GUIDES

L-Head Engines

Before removing the old valve guides measure carefully the distance from the top of the guide to the top of the cylinder block and drive the new guide down to exactly that distance.

On the in-line engines valve guides are pulled up out of the top of the block and are driven in from the top of the block toward the valve chamber.

OHV Models

Valve guides are driven from the combustion chamber towards the top of the block. Always measure carefully the distance the guide protrudes from the cylinder head before removing it so that the new guide can be inserted just this distance. The new guide is driven in from the top of the head towards the combustion chamber. The chamfered edge of the guide should be started first. It may be nec-

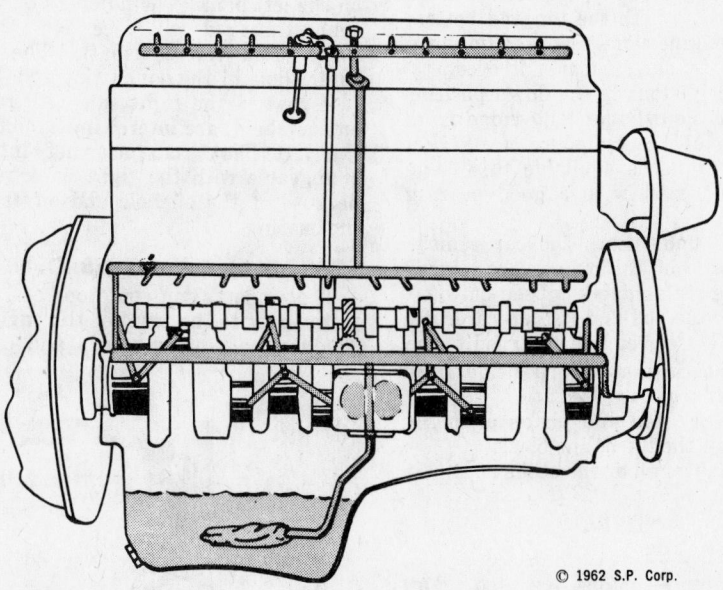

© 1962 S.P. Corp.

Engine Lubrication OHV 6

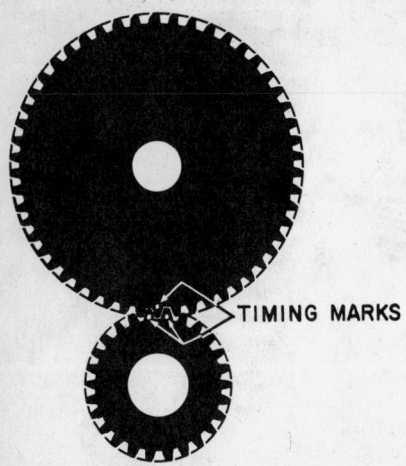

Aligning Timing Marks, V-8

essary to ream the guide since they sometimes tend to warp a little when being driven into an engine.

ADJUSTING VALVES

V-8 Models

A self locking screw is used on the rocker arms of the V8 models. The head of the screw is located underneath the rocker. The engine should be thoroughly warmed before any attempt is made to adjust the valve clearance.

VALVE SPRINGS

The best way to check the condition of a valve spring is to take a compression test. The specifications for the pressure on the valve spring are given in the Valve Specifications Table of Studebaker.

However, if a spring tester is not available, take all of the intake valves and lay them alongside of each other on a flat surface and measure the height of each spring with a straight edge. If all springs are the same height it may safely be assumed that the springs are in good condition since it is unlikely that they will all collapse exactly the same amount. Repeat the same test on the exhaust springs.

If one or more of the springs are different height, it will be necessary to compare them with a new spring to determine which of the springs has collapsed.

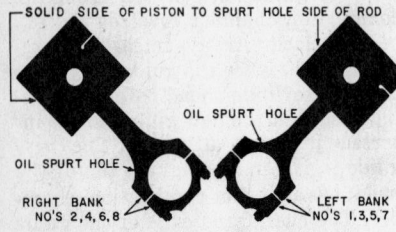

Piston and Rod Installation V-8

Replace all springs which do not come up to the standard of the new spring.

TIMING CASE

TIMING CASE COVER REMOVAL

All 6 Cyl. Models

Remove the radiator core, fan blades, and the upper pulley and belt. Remove the crankshaft fan pulley and vibration damper and unbolt the timing gear cover.

1954 V8 Models

Remove the radiator core, water pump and vibration damper assembly. The timing case cover can then be unbolted and removed.

1955 Thru 1963 V-8 Models

Remove the radiator core and the water manifold as outlined earlier. Remove the vibration damper and take out the bolts which hold the timing case cover to the front of the engine and lift off the cover.

CONNECTING ROD AND PISTONS

REMOVAL OF ROD AND PISTON ASSEMBLIES

First remove the cylinder head and oil pan.

Note: on models where the engine must be removed in order to take off the oil pan it is generally considered an easier job to lay the engine on its side so that both the top and bottom of the engine can be worked on without continuously turning it over.

Select pistons in the down position and cut the cylinder ring ridge from the top of the cylinder. If no ring ridge reamer is available this ridge can be cut off with a good bearing scraper.

From underneath the car remove the caps from the rods on the pistons that the ring ridge has been cut off.

Mark the rod and its cap carefully so that the cap can be returned to the same rod in the same position from which it was removed.

Push the rod and piston assembly up out of the top of the block.

Repeat on all of the other rods.

PISTON AND ROD ASSEMBLIES

Aluminum pistons are used in all Studebaker models. Wrist pins are locked in the rod on all Studebaker models.

Aligning Timing Marks, 6 Cyl.

Connecting rod bearings are of the slip in type and are available in .001, .005, .010 and .020 undersizes.

PISTON ASSEMBLY

6 Cylinder Engines:

On 6 cyl. engines the rod and piston assemblies are assembled so that the oil squirt hole and the number stamped on the rod are facing the camshaft side of the engine and the split in the skirt of the piston faces away from the camshaft.

V-8 Engines, All Ex. 1956 Golden Hawk

On V8 models the left bank is numbered 1, 3, 5 and 7, the right bank is numbered 2, 4, 6 and 8. When assembling the rod and pistons to the engine the T slot in the piston is always on the left side of the engine. This will be up on the right bank and down on the left bank. The numbers on the connecting rod will face downward away from the camshaft. The oil squirt hole in the connecting rod will face toward the right side. All rods on each bank are interchangeable but the left bank rods are not interchangeable with the right bank rods because of the oil hole and offset of the bearing.

1956, Golden Hawk V8 Only:

The indentation on top of the piston goes to the front of the engine. The numbers on the rods and caps

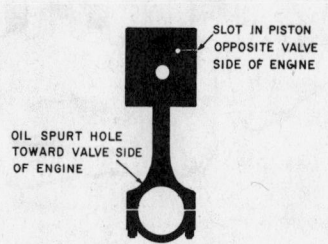

Piston and Rod Installation 6 Cyl.

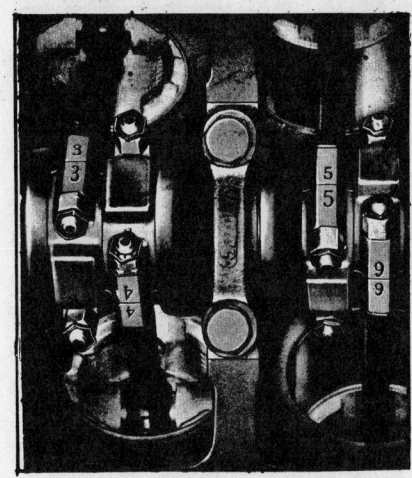

Connecting rod numbering sequence

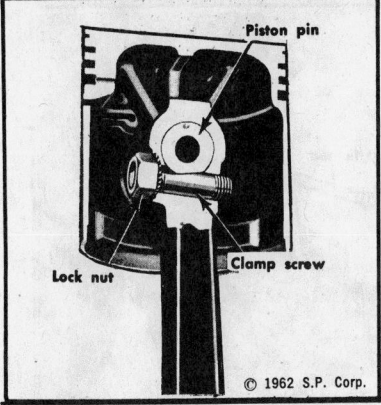

Cross section of typical piston

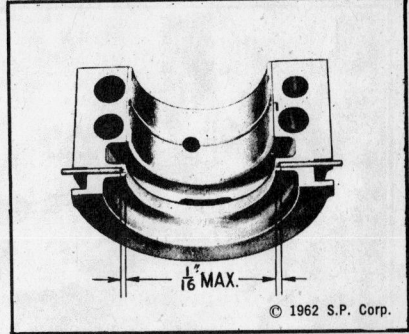

Installing upper rear main bearing oil seal

face down and toward the outside of the banks in which they are located. The oil squirt holes face toward the camshaft.

ASSEMBLY OF PISTON TO THE CONNECTING ROD

6 Cylinder Models

Assemble with T-slot away from camshaft. The oil squirt hole and number on rod should be on solid side of piston.

V8 Models

On the right bank, cylinders Nos. 2, 4, 6 and 8, the T slot in the piston is placed on the side opposite the numbers on the cap. On the left bank, cylinders Nos. 1, 3, 5 and 7, the T slot in the piston is placed on the same side as the numbers on the cap.

ASSEMBLING ROD AND PISTON ASSEMBLIES TO ENGINE

6 Cylinder Models

On all In-Line engines the rod and piston assemblies are assembled so that the number stamped on the rod and cap is facing the camshaft side of the engine and the split in the skirt of the piston faces away from the camshaft side of the engine.

V8 Models

On V8 models the left bank is numbered 1, 3, 5 and 7, the right bank is numbered 2, 4, 6, and 8. When assembling the rod and pistons to the engine the T slot in the piston is always on the left side of the engine. This will be up on the right bank and down on the left bank. The numbers on the connecting rod will face downward away from the camshaft. The oil squirt hole in the connecting rod will face toward the right on both banks.

WRIST PINS

A taper pin is used in the connecting rod to retain the wrist pin. This taper pin is threaded at both ends and to remove it the procedure is to take the nut off the taper bolt and mount it on the opposite side of the taper bolt using the nut as a puller to pull the taper bolt out of the connecting rod. If the bolt is apparently stuck in the connecting rod and it is found to be difficult to break it loose, first insert wrist pin clamp through the center of the wrist pin and tighten securely.

Mount the clamp in a vise and rotate the connecting rod so that the taper pin will come into true index with the flat on the wrist pin. It will then be comparatively simple to remove the wrist pin clamp screw.

The reason the taper pin tends to stick is that, in service the wrist pin may rock somewhat, causing the edge of the flat on the wrist pin to dig into the taper clamp screw. Holding the wrist pin with a clamp in a vise and rocking the rod will release the dug-in portion and permit the wedged pin to come out more readily.

On early models which did not have

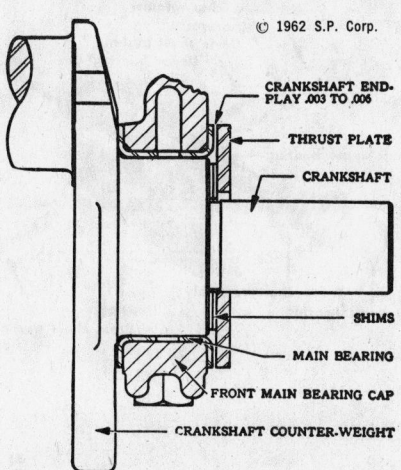

Crankshaft end play is controlled by shims

© 1962 S.P. Corp.

CRANKSHAFT END-PLAY .003 TO .006

THRUST PLATE

CRANKSHAFT

SHIMS

MAIN BEARING

FRONT MAIN BEARING CAP

CRANKSHAFT COUNTER-WEIGHT

a hole in the side of the piston there was no easy way of driving out the pin. On these models it is customary to drill a 3/8 in. hole in the skirt of the piston, just opposite to the wrist pin clamp screw in order to drive out the screw with a drift.

REAR MAIN BEARING OIL SEAL

A Brummer type one or two piece rubber oil seal is used at the rear main bearing. This oil seal can be replaced readily by removing the rear main bearing cap and letting the crankshaft come down just the slightest amount.

The old oil seal can then be pulled down and a new one inserted. The purpose of the rubber oil seal is to prevent oil which might escape from the slinger from getting onto the clutch.

FRONT SUSPENSION

REFERENCES

General instructions covering the front suspension and how to repair and adjust it, together with information on installation of front wheel bearings and grease seals, are given in the Unit Repair section under the heading: Suspension, Front Repair.

Definitions of the points of steering geometry are covered in the Unit Repair section under the heading: Suspension—Front Alignment. This article also covers trouble shooting front

Typical front suspension

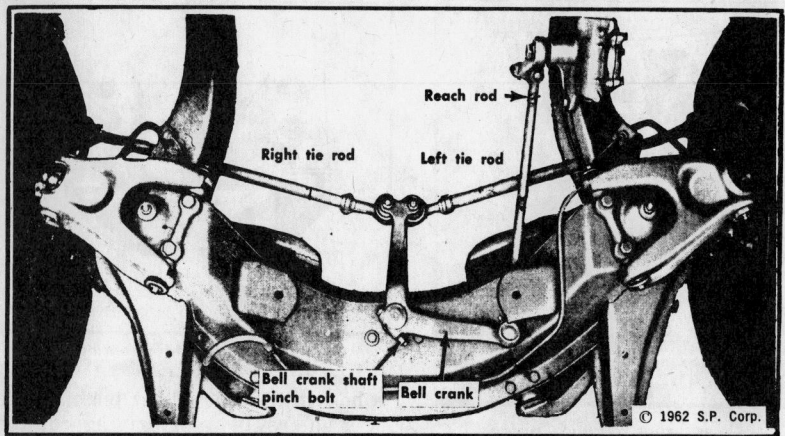

Top view of front suspension

Removing spindle from upper arm

end geometry and irregular tire wear.

Figures covering the caster, camber, toe-in, king pin inclination, and turning radius can be found in the Front Wheel Alignment Table of this section.

Tire size figures can be found in the General Chassis and Brake Specifications Table.

STEERING WHEEL AND HORN BUTTON

REMOVAL OF HORN BUTTON ASSEMBLY

All Models

Push down on the horn button and at the same time turn the button one-third of a turn. This will release it from its bayonet connectors.

STEERING WHEEL REMOVAL

All Models

Remove the horn button as outlined above and take off the horn wire terminals. Remove the nut which holds the steering wheel to the shaft and, using a puller, pull the steering wheel off of the steering shaft.

MANUAL STEERING GEAR

REMOVAL OF STEERING GEAR ASSEMBLY

1955 Models

Disconnect the battery, and on Commander and President models remove the battery and its battery box. From underneath the car take off the pitman arm.

Under the dash disconnect all wires running into the steering gear. Remove the steering wheel. Disconnect the bolts which hold the steering column under the dash and on President and Commander models remove the left front engine support cushion and raise the left front corner of the engine approximately two inches. Do this cautiously since the exhaust lines are still connected. Pull back the floor mat and remove the cover from the toeboard. Now disconnect the bolts

which hold the steering mechanism to the frame and pull the steering mechanism up into the vehicle.

Starting with 1956 Models

Disconnect the battery and on Commander and President models disconnect the starter cable at the starter.

On Golden Hawk, Power Hawk and Sky Hawk models, take out the battery and the battery case. Disconnect all shift linkage at the bottom of the steering column and remove all wires from under the dash which go into the steering column. Pull back the toeboard rug and remove the hole cover from the bottom of the steering column. Disconnect all shift linkage at the bottom of the steering column.

Remove the clamp bolt from under the dash and on Golden Hawk, Power Hawk, and Sky Hawk models remove the left front engine support cushion and raise the left front corner of the engine approximately two inches. Do this cautiously since the exhaust lines are still connected.

Take off the pitman arm and remove the bolts which hold the steering gear housing to the frame and the

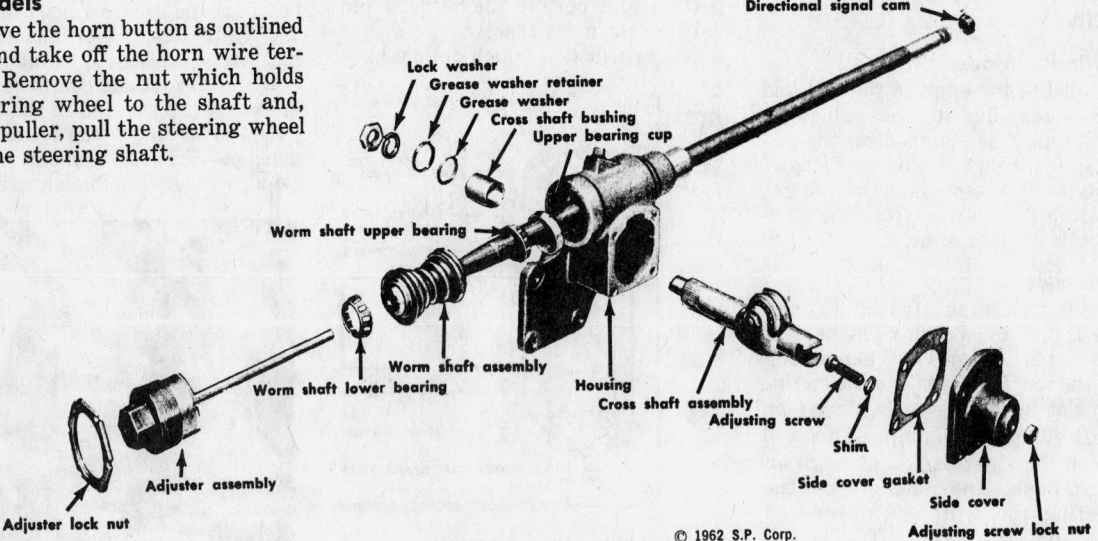

Typical steering gear—Exploded view 1960

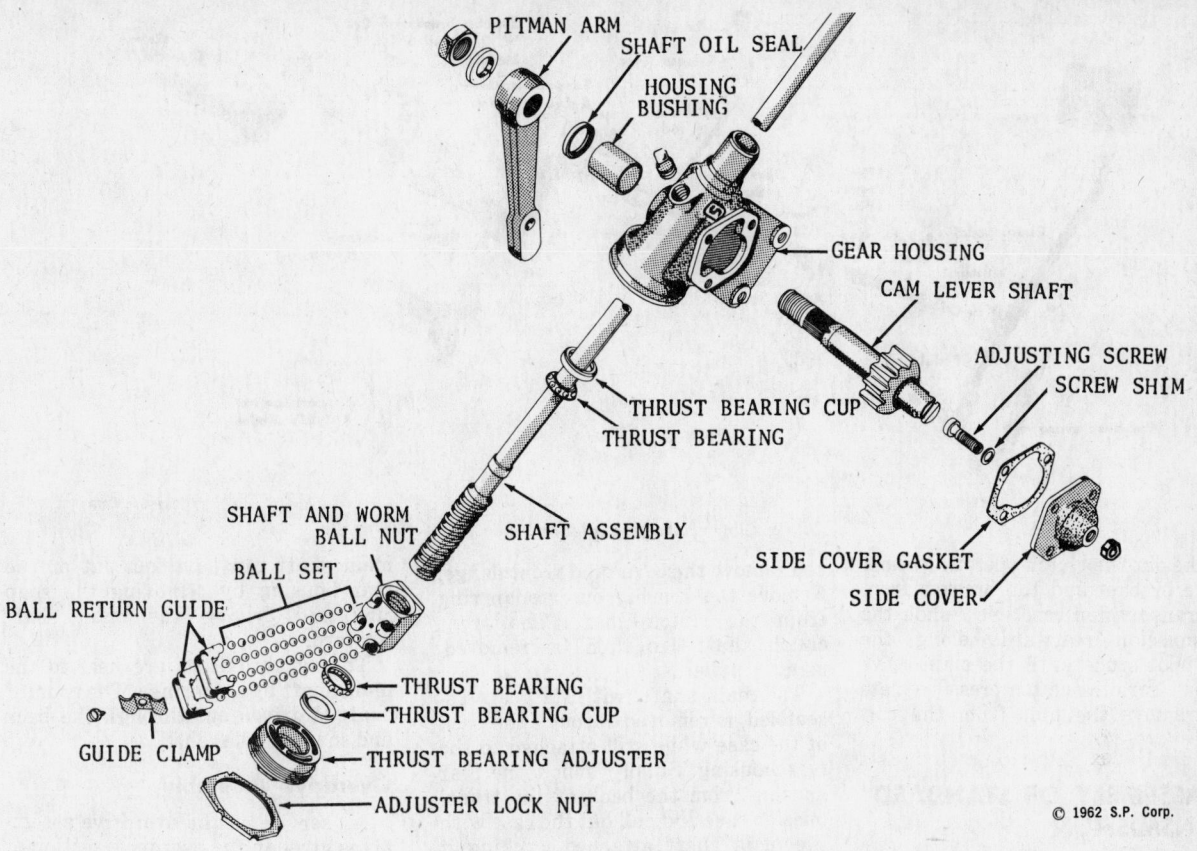

PITMAN ARM
SHAFT OIL SEAL
HOUSING BUSHING
GEAR HOUSING
CAM LEVER SHAFT
ADJUSTING SCREW
SCREW SHIM
THRUST BEARING CUP
THRUST BEARING
SHAFT AND WORM
BALL NUT
SHAFT ASSEMBLY
BALL SET
SIDE COVER GASKET
SIDE COVER
BALL RETURN GUIDE
THRUST BEARING
THRUST BEARING CUP
GUIDE CLAMP
THRUST BEARING ADJUSTER
ADJUSTER LOCK NUT

© 1962 S.P. Corp.

Typical steering gear—Exploded view -1961

gear can be brought up into the vehicle.

INTERMEDIATE STEERING ARM REMOVAL

All Models

Disconnect both tie rods and the steering drag link. From under the car, remove the pinch bolt which holds the bell crank to the shaft. This is located on top of the frame member.

Remove the bolts which hold the bracket to the frame and slip the shaft down out of the bell crank. The bell crank will then lay on top of the frame and it can be lifted off. Remove the assembly to the bench to complete disassembly of the shaft from the bracket.

POWER STEERING GEAR

Two types of power steering are used; Saginaw and Bendix. Detail information is covered in the Unit Repair section under the heading: Steering, Power.

CLUTCH

A single plate dry disc clutch is used on all Studebaker models, except those equipped with automatic transmissions.

CLUTCH PEDAL ADJUSTMENT

On all standard clutches adjust the clutch pedal so that there is a minimum of ¾ in. to 1 in. free motion of the clutch pedal before the throw-out bearing engages the fingers.

REMOVAL OF CLUTCH

All Models

Disconnect battery. On 6 cyl. models, remove oil level gauge and tube. Remove starter. Remove operating shaft and transmission. Place small hydraulic jack at rear of oil pan (use wooden pa). Remove two bolts from engine rear support to crossmember. Raise engine slightly to take weight from crossmember and remove it.

On the V-8 remove housing cover plate. Remove housing bolts or screws and then housing. On the 6 cyl. car remove the dowel bolts first.

The clutch cover can now be removed in conventional way.

To reassemble be sure to draw the 6 cyl. dowel bolts into place. Do not drive them. Complete installation by reversing removal operations.

STANDARD TRANSMISSION

Three-speed transmissions and three-speed transmissions with overdrive are available as optional equipment on all Studebaker models. A four speed transmission is available starting in 1961.

REMOVAL

Drain the transmission. On two-piece drive shafts, disconnect the front joint and center bearing studs and move end of shaft to one side. On one-piece shaft models disconnect the rear joint and slide out of transmission.

Disconnect the shaft rods, shift levers, speedometer cable, and in the case of overdrive the solenoids and wires. Remove the bolts which hold the transmission case to the clutch housing, substituting for the two top bolts two long studs.

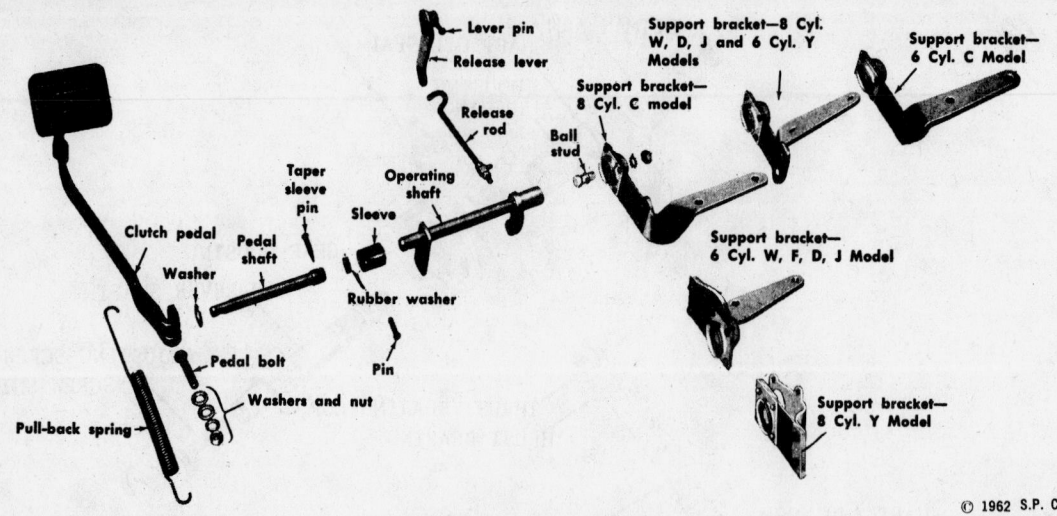

Lever pin
Release lever
Release rod
Ball stud
Taper sleeve pin
Sleeve
Operating shaft
Support bracket—8 Cyl. C model
Support bracket—8 Cyl. W, D, J and 6 Cyl. Y Models
Support bracket—6 Cyl. C Model
Clutch pedal
Washer
Pedal shaft
Rubber washer
Support bracket—6 Cyl. W, F, D, J Model
Pedal bolt
Pin
Washers and nut
Pull-back spring
Support bracket—8 Cyl. Y Model

© 1962 S.P. Corp.

Clutch Linkage, Exploded View

Take out the clutch operating shaft at the bracket and the bracket from the transmission case. Now slide the transmission rearwards along the long pilot studs until the main drive pinion clears the clutch pressure plate and remove the unit from the car.

DISASSEMBLY OF STANDARD TRANSMISSION

Mount the transmission in a vise and remove the cover and front flange. Remove the bearing outer snap ring from the clutch shaft. The front clutch shaft can then be removed, using a puller.

The main shaft, with its gears assembled, is removed through the back of the case while still attached to the rear housing. Simply unbolt the rear housing from the back of the transmission case and pull out the case with the main shaft attached, cocking it slightly to clear the shift yokes. The main shaft can be taken out of the rear housing by removing the snap ring and driving the main shaft forward.

The synchronizers are held to the main shaft by snap rings. The counter shaft is driven out through the back and so is the idler shaft.

Overdrive Assembly

All service on the overdrive assembly is given in the overdrive section of this manual, see index.

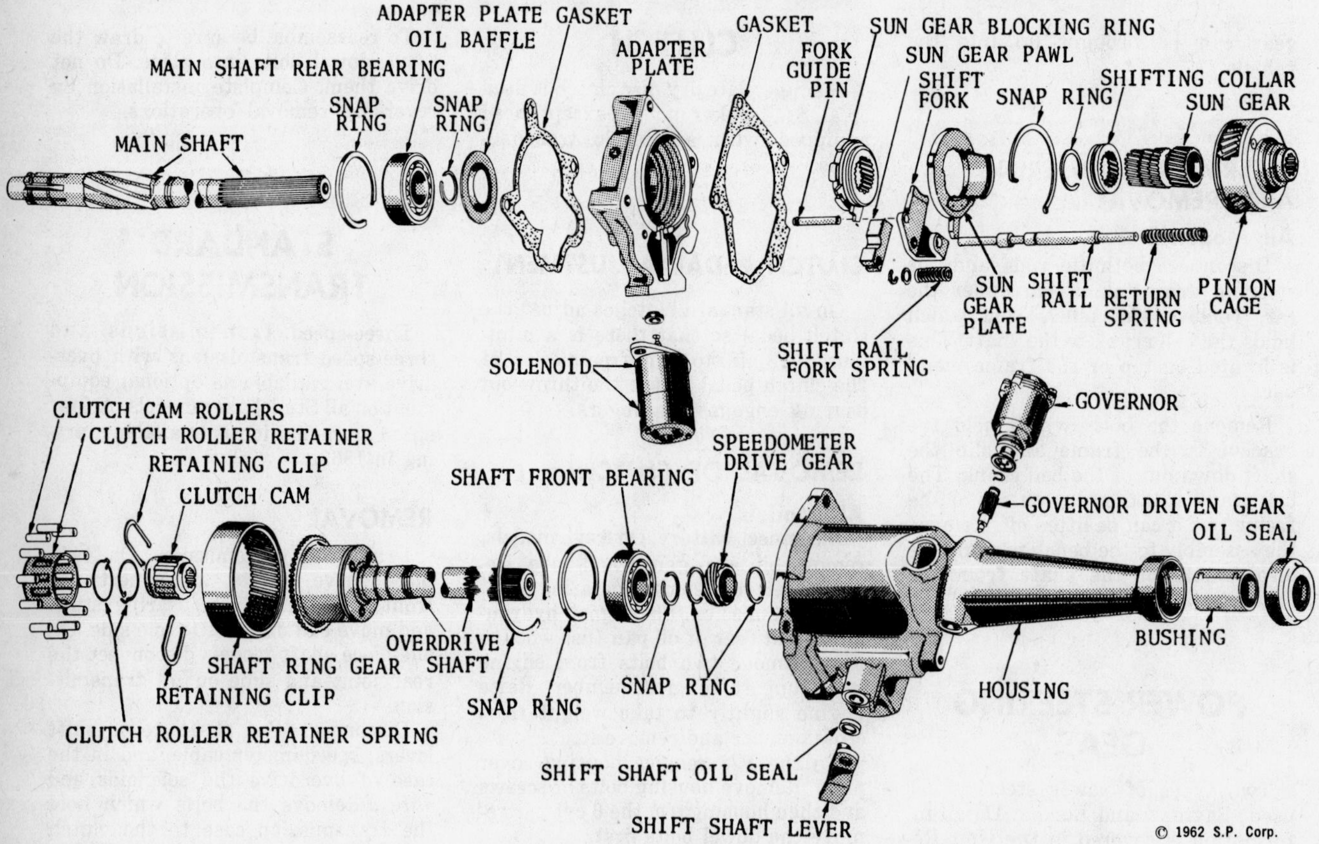

ADAPTER PLATE GASKET
OIL BAFFLE
MAIN SHAFT REAR BEARING
SNAP RING
SNAP RING
ADAPTER PLATE
GASKET
FORK GUIDE PIN
SUN GEAR BLOCKING RING
SUN GEAR PAWL
SHIFT FORK
SNAP RING
SHIFTING COLLAR
SUN GEAR
MAIN SHAFT
SUN GEAR PLATE
SHIFT RAIL
RETURN SPRING
PINION CAGE
SHIFT RAIL FORK SPRING
SOLENOID
GOVERNOR
SHAFT FRONT BEARING
SPEEDOMETER DRIVE GEAR
GOVERNOR DRIVEN GEAR
OIL SEAL
CLUTCH CAM ROLLERS
CLUTCH ROLLER RETAINER
RETAINING CLIP
CLUTCH CAM
SHAFT RING GEAR
OVERDRIVE SHAFT
RETAINING CLIP
SNAP RING
SNAP RING
HOUSING
BUSHING
CLUTCH ROLLER RETAINER SPRING
SHIFT SHAFT OIL SEAL
SHIFT SHAFT LEVER

© 1962 S.P. Corp.

Overdrive assembly

AUTOMATIC TRANSMISSION

1954-55

Complete details on the servicing of Studebaker automatic transmissions is given in the Unit Repair section.

GENERAL INFORMATION

HILL HOLDER

The hill holder is built into the transmission in the No. 2 and No. 3 drums and functions by means of two sprag type free wheeling clutches to prevent rearward movement of the car whenever the hand lever is set at the Drive position.

ANTI-CREEP

The anti-creep functions only after the brakes have been applied with the motor idling and the car standing still. Under such conditions the fluid pressure put on the brake lines by the application of the pedal is trapped and retained in the lines to the rear brakes. This keeps the car from moving while permitting the operator to release the pedal. The retention of the fluid pressure in the lines to the rear brakes is done by means of a solenoid valve located just behind the brake master cylinder.

ANTI-CREEP ADJUSTMENT

The No. 1 anti-creep switch is a part of the idling adjustment screw on some models. On other models it contacts a plate on the accelerator to carburetor cross shaft. Fig. 1. The basic theory of the adjustment is that it should contact when the engine is idling and the accelerator pedal is

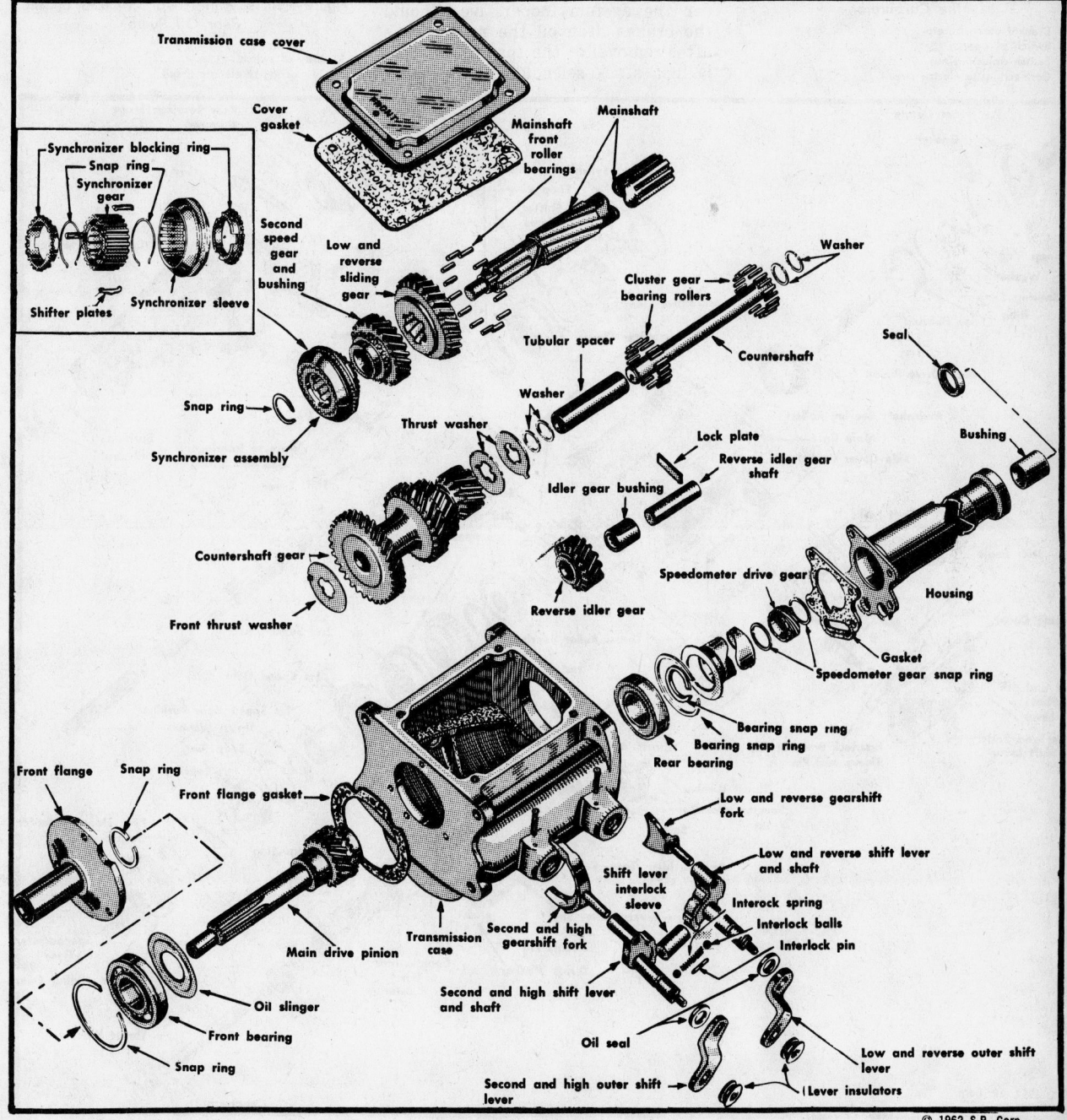

Standard Transmission, 3 Spd.

© 1962 S.P. Corp.

STUDEBAKER

Fig. 1—No. 1 Anti-Creep Switch may be at the Carburetor

1. Bracket on carburetor.
2. Switch plunger.
3. Switch adjusting nut.
4. Connections to electric circuit.

released and should not contact the moment the accelerator pedal is depressed. With the accelerator releasd, loosen the No. 1 switch lock nut. Turn on the ignition and screw the switch in or out until a click is heard in the solenoid. Then tighten the lock nut. The switch cuts the anti-creep electrical circuit thus releasing the solenoid valve in the rear brake line. Cases of dragging brakes can be caused by a grounded, stuck, or improperly adjusted No. 1 anti-creep switch. A fuse to protect the circuit is located in the line on the engine side of the fire wall just above the steering column. Removal of the fuse will render the system inoperative. Should the brakes drag on the rear wheels after removal of the fuse the trouble is in a stuck solenoid valve or poor

Fig. 2—No. 2 Anti-Creep Switch is on the Rear Oil Pump

1. Body of switch.
2. Connection to electric circuit.

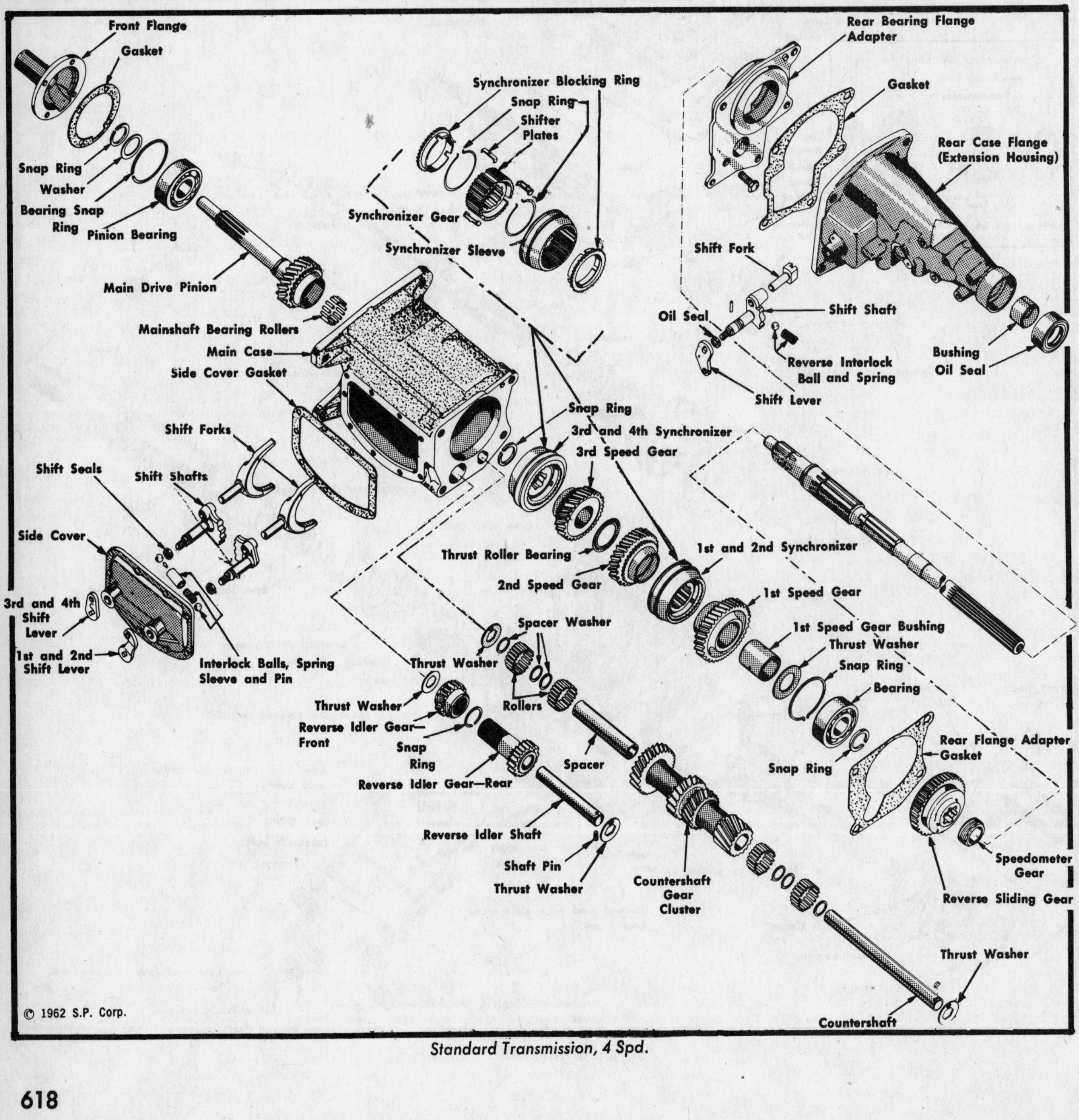

© 1962 S.P. Corp.

Standard Transmission, 4 Spd.

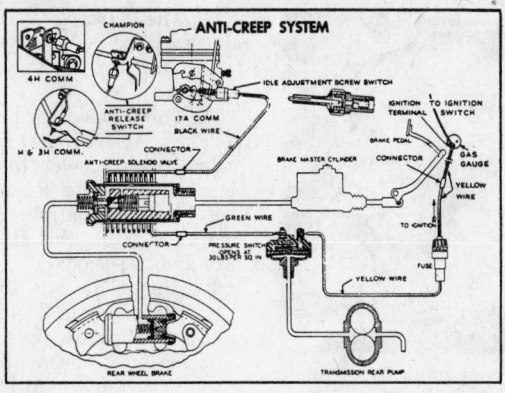

Fig. 3—Schematic Diagram of Anti-Creep System

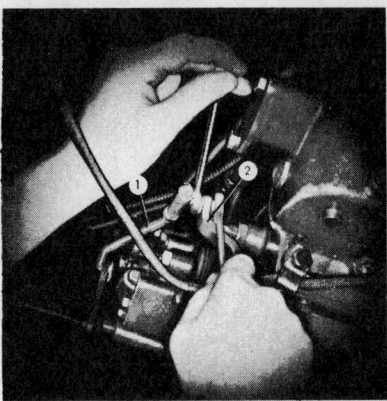

Fig. 6—Disconnect Ball Joint at Manual
Valve Control Lever

1. Rod from bell crank
2. Manual Valve Control Lever.

brake adjustment. Switch No. 2 is a pressure operated switch that breaks the Anti-creep circuit when the car moves forward. Fig. 2.

GOVERNOR VALVE (THROTTLE VALVE) LINKAGE ADJUSTMENT

The governor valve lever is the rearward of the two levers on the left rear of the transmission case. It is connected into the linkage from the accelerator to the carburetor so that the governor valve's action is modified in accord with the position of the throttle. The principal function of the lever is to shift the transmission down to intermediate gear for passing and fast acceleration.

Position the accelerator so that the throttle is wide open but the over-travel spring is not compressed at all. Check this at the swivel end of the overtravel spring; it is important that the spring does not move. Adjust the carburetor to accelerator linkage as necessary to achieve this result.

With the accelerator so held, go under the car to the governor valve control lever. The rod coming back to the lever will be in the outer of the two holes (after 1951 Commander Serial No. 8133626). Disconnect the rod and turn the lever clockwise until the resistance of the detent is felt. Fig. 5. Lengthen or shorten the rod, by turning the ball joint, until it can be refastened without moving the lever out of the detent.

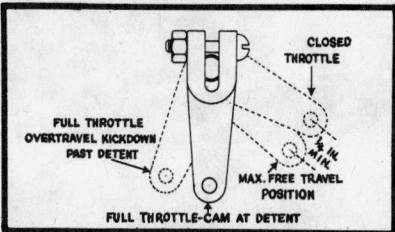

Fig. 5—Governor Valve Control Lever Should
Be at Detent When Carburetor Throttle
Valve Is Open

To check the adjustment push the accelerator to the floor. The lever should move clockwise to the kick-down point as shown. Release the accelerator and the lever should move to the closed throttle position.

GOVERNOR ADJUSTMENT

If on road testing the car it is found that upshift at wide open throttle occurs at too high a speed, the governor requires adjustment.

Remove the acord nut from the rear face of the rear extension. This will expose the governor adjusting screw and lock nut. Loosen the lock nut and turn the adjusting screw in (clockwise) until the condition has been corrected. Turning the screw clockwise lowers the upshift point. Turning it counterclockwise raises the upshift point. Turning the screw one-quarter turn changes the shift speed approximately two miles per hour.

NEUTRAL SAFETY SWITCH ADJUSTMENT

Loosen the switch to steering column attaching screws and position the switch so that the starter circuit is closed when the hand lever is at Neutral.

MANUAL LINKAGE ADJUSTMENT

The manual valve control lever is the forward lever of the two levers at the left rear of the transmission.

Disconnect the ball joint at the lever. Move the hand lever on the steering column to the Reverse position. Move the manual valve control lever on the transmission all the way clockwise. The ball joint stud should fit back in the hole in the lever. If it does not, adjust the clevis at the bell crank just forward of the No. 1 servo until it does.

To check the adjustment disconnect the ball joint again. Move the manual

valve control lever counterclockwise all the way. Check that the parking ratchet is engaged. Now move the hand lever to Park position. Check that the ball joint can be reconnected to the lever. If it cannot, attempt a compromise adjustment at the clevis. If more than ½ a turn of the clevis is required, check the entire linkage for wear, looseness, binding, or distortion.

PARKING LOCK ADJUSTMENT

Move the manual valve lever on the side of the transmission full forward to Park (counterclockwise). Now move the lever back (clockwise) one detent to neutral. Now turn the "U" joint while moving the lever forward again. If the parking lock pawl is correctly adjusted, a slight ratcheting will be felt as the lever moves forward out of neutral and the pawl hits the gear.

If an adjustment is needed, remove the transmission oil pan. Loosen the lock nut on the parking rod and turn the rod counterclockwise to move the pawl away from the gear. Turn it clockwise to move it nearer the gear. Tighten the lock nut to 3-4 ft. lbs. torque.

TRANSMISSION REMOVAL

The bell housing, converter, and transmission case are to be removed as an assembly. Remove the floor mat and the transmission inspection hole cover. Remove the spark plugs. Drain the transmission case and the converter. Disconnect the starter and remove it. Disconnect the manual and the throttle rods at the transmission and tie them up out of the way.

Disconnect the wires from the No. 2 Anti-Creep switch on the rear pump. Disconnect the speedometer cable at the rear extension. Unfasten the muffler and tail pipe assembly and move them out of the way. Unfasten the front "U" joint yoke and move the drive shaft to one side.

Take the weight of the engine on a suitable pad and jack. Remove the nuts holding the rear engine support blocks to the frame cross member. Raise the engine, unbolt, and remove the frame cross member.

Lower the engine by means of the jack and unbolt the bell housing from the block. Support the transmission assembly on a jack. It weighs 200 lbs.

Remove the nuts holding the converter to the flywheel plate. Move the transmission back and then down away from the engine. Do not let the converter slide off the main shaft. Be careful of the two bell-housing-to-block locating dowels. One stays in the block and one in the housing. Be sure to protect the hands from the sharp edges of the converter.

TRANSMISSION INSTALLATION

Reverse the removal procedure to reinstall. Be careful not to let the converter slide forward on the transmission main shaft while it is being raised into position.

Fasten the bell housing to the block first. It should be fitted up snug and flat against the block before the bolts are installed. There are no aligning marks between the converter and the crankshaft drive plate.

FLIGHTOMATIC

REFERENCES

Details of Flightomatic repairs will be found in the Unit Repair section.

ANTI-STALL DASH POT ADJUSTMENT

Starting 1956

Hold the throttle in closed position, and turn the dash pot adjusting screw counterclockwise (out) until the dash pot rod has reached the end of its travel. Fig. 1.

Turn the adjusting screw clockwise (in) 1½ to 2 turns.

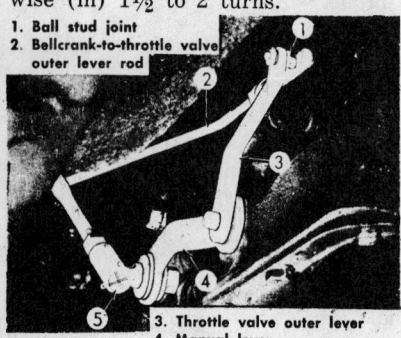

1. Ball stud joint
2. Bellcrank-to-throttle valve outer lever rod
3. Throttle valve outer lever
4. Manual lever
5. Shift lever-to-manual lever rod

Fig. 2—Adjusting manual control valve linkage

1. Lock nut
2. Plunger
3. Throttle lever

Fig. 1—Turn dash pot adjusting screw to bottom of its travel

Clearance should now be .045-.064 inches.

Do not forget to tighten the lock nut.

Note on Carter Type Dash Pot

Hold the primary throttle wide open.

Measure the distance from the top of the air horn to the top of plunger. The distance should be 7/16". Bend the lug to adjust.

NEUTRAL SAFETY SWITCH ADJUSTMENT

Loosen the switch to steering column attaching screws and position the switch so that the starter circuit is closed when the hand lever is at Neutral. Retighten screws.

MANUAL LINKAGE ADJUSTMENT

Unpin the clevis of the manual shift rod (which runs back to the transmission) from the selector arm at the bottom of the steering column. Fig. 2.

Set the hand lever so that the pointer is at Drive and against the stop in the dial housing.

Push the manual shift rod all the way back and check that it is centered in the detent for the Low position. Pull the manual shift rod forward to center on the next detent notch which is that for Drive.

Adjust the clevis so that it could be pinned to the selector arm.

Lengthen the manual shift rod by two complete turns of the clevis and pin it to the selector arm. Be sure to tighten the clevis lock nut.

Check the position of the hand lever at the other points on the dial especially that the parking lock engages properly.

THEORY OF THROTTLE LINKAGE ADJUSTMENT

The intent of throttle control rod adjustment is to coordinate the movement of three things:

1. The throttle valve in the carburetor.
2. The throttle valve in the transmission.
3. The accelerator pedal.

The two valves should be closed when the accelerator pedal is released. In the released position the accelerator pedal should be a certain distance from the steel floor. There are two methods of throttle control adjustment. One is by trial and error; the other is based on the transmission throttle pressure. The trial and error adjustment is easier. The pressure adjustment is more accurate.

TRIAL AND ERROR ADJUSTMENT OF THE THROTTLE CONTROL

Adjust the engine idle speed to approximately 450 RPM with transmission in Drive and engine at operating temperature. Turn the engine off.

Disconnect the transmission throttle valve control rod from the cross rod at the clevis on the left rear corner of the engine. Fig. 3.

On Studebakers hold the lever at the transmission back against its stop and shorten the rod 4 complete turns. Repin. The adjustment is made at the transmission and not in the engine compartment as on the other cars.

On all models if there is slippage after the above adjustment, lengthen the throttle control rod to a total of not over 4 turns.

Should the transmission still show signs of slippage the trouble could be due to a bent rod or inaccurately adjusted accelerator to carburetor linkage or malfunctioning of the valve unit in the transmission.

If the transmission fails to kick down adjust the accelerator pedal. The measurement of height is made from the top side of the tip of the pedal to the metal floor pan.

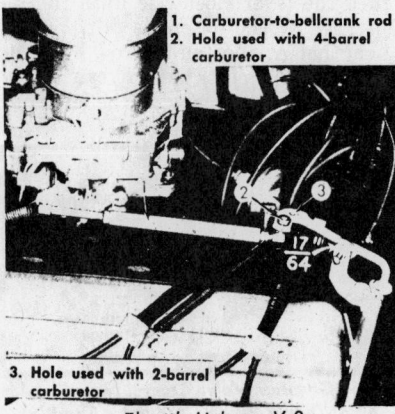

1. Carburetor-to-bellcrank rod
2. Hole used with 4-barrel carburetor

17/64

3. Hole used with 2-barrel carburetor

Throttle Linkage, V-8

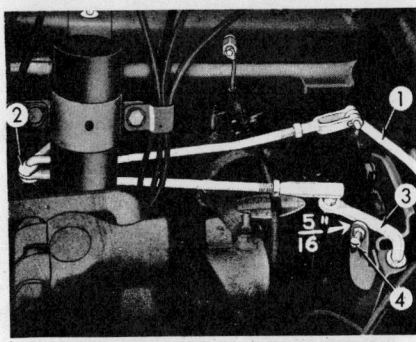

Throttle Linkage, 6 Cyl.

1. Accelerator bracket
2. Auxiliary bellcrank
3. Main bellcrank
4. Adjusting screw

PRESSURE METHOD OF THROTTLE LINKAGE ADJUSTMENT

The results in a custom adjustment of the linkage which compensates for all variables in the linkage system.

Have engine and transmission at operating temperature. Set the hand brake. Raise the car and connect a 0 to 250 pound capacity pressure gauge to the throttle pressure take off which is just forward of the transmission levers.

With all four wheels back on the ground, the gauge held so that it can be read from the drivers seat, together with an engine tachometer, set the hand brake and start the engine.

Put the hand lever at Drive and run engine up to 1000 RPM. The pressure gauge should read between 80 and 85. If it is under 80 lengthen the throttle control a turn at a time. If it is over 85 shorten the rod a turn at a time. In either case adjust the rod length so that the pressure on a 1000 engine RPM is between 80 and 85 psi.

Now let the engine return to idle. which should be 425 to 450 RPM with the hand lever in Drive.

When idle pressure is too high and the linkage cannot be shortened the throttle lever internal stop should be bent away from the valve body.

If the idle pressure is low lengthen the rod, but if the pressure is erratic the transmission requires overhaul.

CONVERTER AND TRANSMISSION ASSEMBLY

REMOVAL

This procedure for converter-transmission assembly removal is applicable to all models.

Remove the two upper converter housing-to-engine bolts. Drain the transmission oil pan. Remove the plate at the lower front of the converter housing and remove the two converter drain plugs. Drain the converter. Disconnect the drive shaft at the rear axle and remove the shaft. Remove the flywheel to converter bolts. Wedge the converter in place in the housing. Disconnect the battery ground strap. Disconnect the starter cable at the starter and the transmission-to-body ground cable at the transmission. Remove the starter. Disconnect the oil cooler lines at the transmission. Disconnect the control linkages and the speedometer cable at the transmission.

Arrange a support for the engine. Remove the bolts holding the rear extension to the rear support. Support the transmission on the transmission cradle-jack. Unbolt and remove the rear crossmember. On V8 models, loosen and drop the exhaust system to allow the converter to clear the muffler inlet pipe. Tilt the rear of the converter-transmission assembly upward and remove the six bolts holding the flywheel to the crankshaft and remove the flywheel. This is done on some models to provide clearance. Lower the converter-transmission assembly to the floor. Remove the wedge holding the converter in the housing and pull the converter out of the housing. Do not rock it, as to do so is hard on the seals.

INSTALLATION

Wedge the converter in place in the housing. Using the transmission cradle-jack raise the transmission assembly into place. Install the flywheel onto the crankshaft. Tighten the bolts to 75-85 ft. lbs.

Install the converter housing-to-engine lower bolts and tighten to 40-45 ft. lbs. Remove the retainer securing the converter in the housing and bolt the converter to the flywheel. Be sure to have washers under the nuts to prevent converter float.

Tighten all to 25-28 ft. lbs. Reinstall the rear crossmember. Lower the transmission onto the rear support and install the two extension-to-support bolts. Install the converter drain plugs and access plates. Reconnect the cooler lines. Install the drive shaft onto the transmission output shaft and refasten the shaft at the rear axle. Reconnect the control linkages and speedometer cable. Install the starter and connect: the transmission-to-frame ground; the starter cable; and the battery ground. Install the two upper converter housing to engine bolts and tighten to 40-45 ft. lbs.

Connect and adjust the manual and throttle controls.

Put 5 quarts of Type A fluid into the transmission and allow to idle for 2 minutes. Now add 5 more quarts and let idle until it reaches its normal operating temperature. Do not race the engine.

UNIVERSAL JOINTS AND DRIVE LINE

Thru 1957 Models

Cross and bearing type universal joints are used on all Studebaker models listed above. All are fitted with two driveshafts having three universal joints. The slip yoke is at the center universal joint. The center bearing is mounted on the face of a frame crossmember.

Starting with 1958 Models

A one-piece drive shaft with two universal joints is used.

REMOVAL OF THE UNIVERSAL JOINT AND DRIVESHAFT ASSEMBLY

To remove the two-piece assembly, mark the yokes to locate in original position. Disconnect the rear joint from rear axle pinion flange. Remove the center support nuts and washers. Disconnect the front joint from the transmission flange. The assembly can now be moved rearward through the center crossmember.

The one-piece assembly can be removed by removing the "U" bolts at

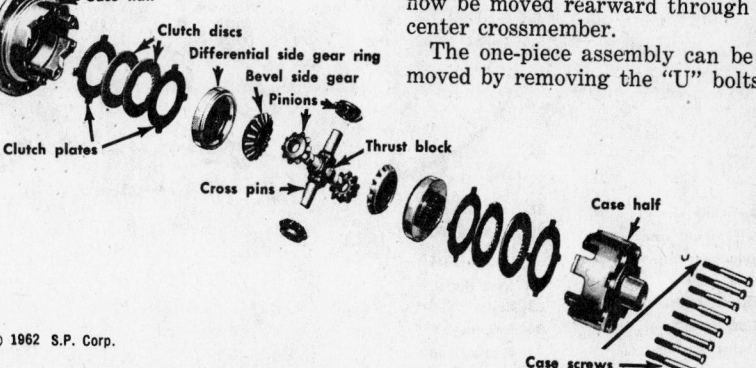

© 1962 S.P. Corp.

Exploded view—twin traction differential

the rear flange and sliding toward rear, out of transmission. Again be sure to mark locations.

DISASSEMBLY OF THE DRIVESHAFT

All Models Thru 1958

On the bench, remove the large nut from the back end of the front driveshaft which will let the slip yoke of the center universal joint come out of the front driveshaft.

Take the center universal joint, together with the rear driveshaft, over to the bench and remove the lock rings which hold the bearing blocks in the yokes. Set the yokes up in a vise so that two of the bearings are in a horizontal plane and, driving the right bearing inwards, force the left bearing out.

Now pack some washers under the right bearing and drive against the cross on the left side driving the right bearing out.

Turn the driveshaft 180 degrees to set the other pair of bearings in the vise and repeat.

The universal joint yokes of both

© 1962 S.P. Corp.

front and rear driveshafts are separated in exactly the same manner.

REAR AXLE AND SUSPENSION

Shims are used for all adjustments including preloading of the pinion and differential side bearings.

SERVICE ON THE REAR AXLE

All service on the rear axle including the replacement of axle shafts, all oil seals, replacement of bearings and pinion and ring gear is given in the Unit Repair section of this manual, see index.

REMOVAL OF THE REAR AXLE ASSEMBLY

Support the weight of the car on jacks to the frame directly in front of both rear springs. Disconnect the brake lines and brake cables and split the rear universal joint at the rear axle pinion flange. Disconnect the shock absorbers from the spring plate and the stabilizer bar on models which use one. Disconnect the rear springs

at the rear shackle and remove the nuts from the U-bolts which hold the spring to the rear axle housing and slide the rear axle housing out from under the car.

Tap the bearings off the rear axle companion flange and let the back end of the driveshaft come down. At the front universal joint disconnect the bearing pillow block from the transmission flange and tap those bearings off the end of the shaft. Now carefully scribe the position of the center bearing hanger on the frame so it can be replaced in the same place, and remove the bolts which hold the center bearing to the frame and pull the complete driveshaft out from underneath the vehicle.

TWIN-TRACTION DIFFERENTIAL

The name twin-traction is applied to Studebaker-Packard improved traction differentials. This is confusing because it covers two different types of clutching application. See "Non-Slip Differentials" in the Rear Axles segment of the Unit Repair section for further details.

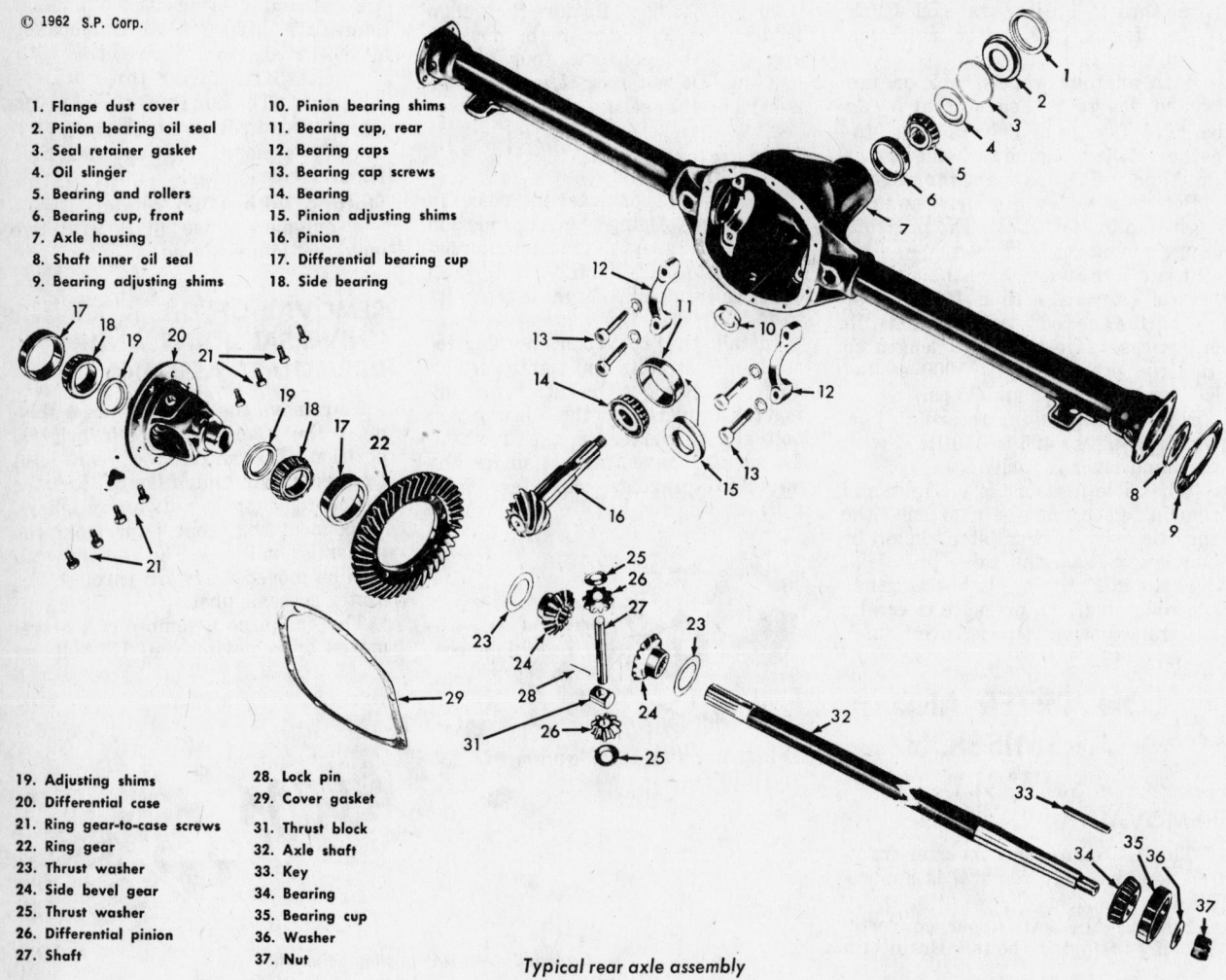

1. Flange dust cover	10. Pinion bearing shims
2. Pinion bearing oil seal	11. Bearing cup, rear
3. Seal retainer gasket	12. Bearing caps
4. Oil slinger	13. Bearing cap screws
5. Bearing and rollers	14. Bearing
6. Bearing cup, front	15. Pinion adjusting shims
7. Axle housing	16. Pinion
8. Shaft inner oil seal	17. Differential bearing cup
9. Bearing adjusting shims	18. Side bearing

19. Adjusting shims	28. Lock pin
20. Differential case	29. Cover gasket
21. Ring gear-to-case screws	31. Thrust block
22. Ring gear	32. Axle shaft
23. Thrust washer	33. Key
24. Side bevel gear	34. Bearing
25. Thrust washer	35. Bearing cup
26. Differential pinion	36. Washer
27. Shaft	37. Nut

Typical rear axle assembly

Page

AIR CONDITIONING
Service 1092

BRAKES, HYDRAULIC
Adjustments 938
Bleed brakes 941
Brake references 629
Parking brake lever & cable 629
Master cylinder service 939

BRAKES, POWER
Power unit overhaul 954
Trouble shooting 954

CLUTCH
Clutch assembly, R & R 639
Clutch pedal, adjust 639

COOLING SYSTEM
Radiator, R & R 632
Thermostat 632
Water pump, R & R 632

ELECTRICAL SYSTEM
Battery 627
Delcotron specifications 625
Distributor, R & R 628
Distributor specifications 625
Engine 627
Engine firing order & timing . . . 624
Fuses and circuit breakers 624
Gauges 1024
Generator and regulator
   specifications 625
Generator and regulators 628
Generator service 1026
Generator, R & R 628
Generator trouble shooting chart 1026
Horn button 638
Ignition firing order 624
Ignition timing procedure 627
Instruments 629
Starter, R & R 629
Starter specifications 626
Starter systems 1046

ENGINE ASSEMBLY
Cylinder head, R & R 633
Engine assembly, R & R 632
Engine diagnosis 1012
Engine firing order & timing . . . 624
Engine marking code 625
Lubrication 635
Oil pan, R & R 635
Oil pressure specifications 626
Oil pump 636
Piston and rod, assemble 636
References 632
Rocker arms & shaft 633
Specifications, general, engine . 626
Specifications, tune-up, engine . 625
Timing case 634
Timing chain 634
Trouble shooting charts 1012
Tune-up 627

Page

ENGINE ASSEMBLY—continued
Valve guides 634
Valve specifications 626

ENGINE LUBRICATION
Oil pan, R & R 635
Oil pump 636

EXHAUST SYSTEM
Crossover pipe, R & R 631
Exhaust pipe, R & R 632
Muffler, R & R 632

FUEL SYSTEM
Carburetor adjustments 630
Carburetor specifications 972
Fuel filter 631
Fuel gauge service 1024
Fuel pump pressure 625
Fuel pump 631
Fuel tank, R & R 631

INSTRUMENTS
Fuel gauge 629
Ignition and starter switch 629
Instrument cluster, R & R 629
Speedometer 629

RADIO, R & R
References 656

REAR AXLE AND SUSPENSION
Axle assembly references 654
Axle shaft, R & R 656
Axle "U" joint service 656
Differential side bearing oil seal . 654
Spring, rear, R & R 656

SPECIFICATIONS
Battery 626
Brake cylinder sizes 627
Capacities:
   Axle, rear 626
   Cooling system 626
   Crankcase 626
   Fuel tank 626
   Transmission, automatic 626
   Transmission, manual 626
Chassis, general 627
Delcotron specifications 625
Distributor 625
Engine, general 626
Engine, tune-up 625
Fuses and circuit breakers 624
Generator and regulators 625
Ignition timing specifications . . . 625
Light bulbs 626
Main bearings 626
Model identification illustrations . 624
Piston and pin specification 627
Quick reference specifications . . 624
Rod bearings 626
Starters 626
Torque wrench 627
Tune-up 625

Page

SPECIFICATIONS—continued
Valves 626
Wheel alignment 627

STEERING, MANUAL
Adjust gear housing 1052
Gear assembly, R & R 638
Horn button, R & R 638
Steering wheel, R & R 638

STEERING, POWER
Pump assembly 1058
References 639
Trouble shooting 1081
Unit overhaul 1058

SUSPENSION, FRONT
Alignment procedures 1082
Alignment specifications 627
Ball joints, R & R 637
Coil springs 637
Cross member, R & R 637
References 637
Shock absorbers 637
Upper control arm, R & R 637

TRANSMISSION, AUTOMATIC
Adjustments, "on car" 646
Disassembly 648
General information 646
Overhaul 651
References 646
Throttle linkage, adjust 646
Transmission, R & R 643
Trouble shooting 654

TRANSMISSION, MANUAL SHIFT
Disassemble transmission 645
Shift controls 643
Transmission, R & R 643

TRANSMISSION, EXTENSION ASSEMBLY
Remove 643
References 643

TRANSMISSION, DIFFERENTIAL ASSEMBLY
Assembly, R & R 643

TROUBLE CHECKS
Procedures 1

TUNE-UP
Carburetor 972
Procedures 627
Specifications 625
Engine diagnosis 1012

PROPELLER SHAFT AND TORQUE TUBE
Standard transmission, R & R . . . 640
Automatic transmission, R & R . . 642
Bearing insulators, R & R 640

TEMPEST
YEAR IDENTIFICATION

1961

1962

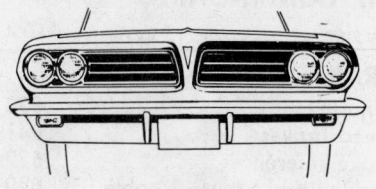

1963

QUICK WORKING SPECIFICATIONS

DISTRIBUTOR SPECIFICATIONS

Make ....Delco-Remy
Type of
  Advance .Centrifugal and Vacuum
Point Gap ....016"
Point Spring Tension ......19-23 oz.
Cam Dwell
  1961-62 4 cyl. ....73°-77°
  1963 4 cyl. ....31°-34°
  V-8 ....28°-32°

SPARK PLUGS

1961-63—4 cyl. .....45 S.....035
1961-62—V8 ....45 FFS....032
1963—V8 ....45 S......032

IGNITION TIMING

4 cyl. ....6°BTDC
V-8 ....5°BTDC

Operating Tappet Clearance

All, Hydraulic ....Zero

VALVE TIMING (INLET OPENS)

1961-63
4 cyl. Standard Trans. . .14°B.T.D.C.
  Automatic Trans. ....30°B.T.D.C.
1961-62
V-8, All Trans. ....29°B.T.D.C.
1963
V-8, All ....22°B.T.D.C.

GENERATOR AND REGULATOR SPECIFICATIONS
Generator

Delco-Remy ....12 Volt
Field Current
    ....1.50 to 1.60 amps @ 80°F
Brush Tension ....28 oz.

Regulator

Cut-Out Relay
  Air Gap ....020"
  Closing Voltage 11.8 to 13.6 @ 1250
Current & Voltage
  Reg. Air Gap ....075"
Current Regulator
  Setting ....27-33 Amps
Voltage Regulator Setting
  .....13.8-14.8 Volts @ 125°F
See specification chart for 1963 A.C. Delcotron generator and regulator details.

FUSES AND CIRCUIT BREAKERS

A circuit breaker in the light control switch protects the headlamp and parking light circuit. Other protection is by fuses located in a junction block under the dash.

FUSES

Tail Light, License Plate . 9 amp.
Stop Light, Dome Light .. 9 amp.

Turn Indicator, Back-Up . 20 amp.
Instrument Light,
  Radio Dial, Heater Panel,
  Shift Indicator .... 4 amp.
Heater Blower, Air
  Cond. Blower ....20 amp.
Radio Power ....7½ amp.
W/S Wiper, W/S Washer,
  Parking Brake Signal . 25 amp.
Cigar Lighter .... 20 amp.
Air Cond. Control ......7½ amp.
Spot Light .... 14 amp.

CIRCUIT BREAKERS

Head Lamps ....22 amp.
Parking Lamp ....22 amp.
Beam Indicator ....22 amp.

CAPACITIES

Engine Crankcase (qts.) 4
Transmission-Synchro. (pts.) ...3
4 speed 3¾
Transmission-Auto. (pts.) 12
Rear Axle (pts.) 3
Gasoline Tank (gallons) 16
  1963 20
Cooling System (qts.) 11.6

FIRING ORDER and TIMING

SPARK OCCURS:
1961-63—4 Cyl. 6° BTDC
1961-63—V-8—5° BTDC

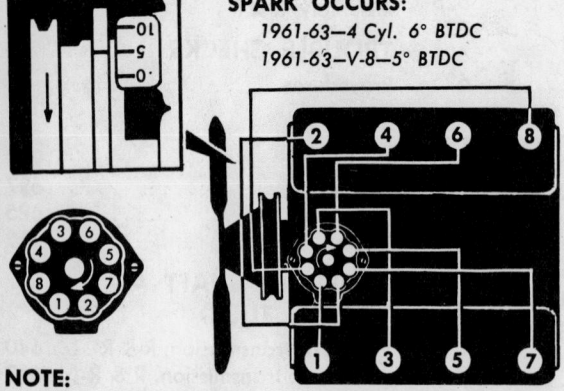

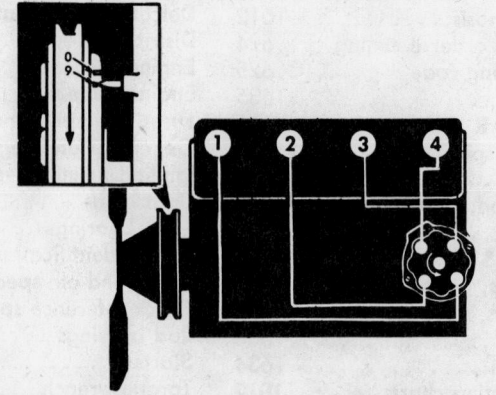

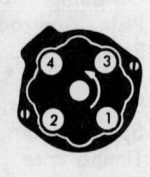

NOTE:
THESE ARE APPROXIMATE SETTINGS. ENGINE DESIGN, ALTITUDE, TEMPERATURE, FUEL AND ENGINE CONDITION WILL ALL INFLUENCE TIMING. THE DETERMINING FACTOR, LIMITING ADVANCE, WILL STILL BE THE "KNOCK POINT" OF THE ENGINE.

CAR SERIAL NUMBER LOCATION AND ENGINE IDENTIFICATION

SERIAL NUMBER LOCATION

1961-63:

Plate attached to left front hinge pillar. This number gives the series, model year, assembly plant, and sequence of assembly.

ENGINE NUMBER LOCATION

1961-63:

The number is stamped on the front, right hand side of the cylinder block.

THERE IS NO ENGINE IDENTIFICATION PROBLEM here as power is supplied by either the Standard 4 cylinder, 194.5 cu. in engine or the optional V-8, 215 cu. in. engine, in 1961-62 and a 326 cu. in. V-8 in 1963.

TUNE UP SPECIFICATIONS

YEAR AND MODEL	SPARK PLUGS		DISTRIBUTOR			Ignition Timing	Compression Pressure @ Cranking Speed	VALVES			Fuel Pump Pressure	Engine Idle Speed
	Type	Gap	Cam Angle	Point Gap	Arm Spring Tension (Oz.)			Tappett Clearance		Inlet Opens		
								In.	Ex.			
1961-63 4-Cyl.	45S	.035	75°	.016	19-23	6°B	145	Hyd.	Hyd.	14B*	4-5¼	Note "A"
V8	45FFS△	.032	30°	.016	19-23	5°B	150▢	Hyd.	Hyd.	29B**	4-5¼	

NOTE A: 4-cyl. engine std. trans. 680-700 R.P.M.—neutral.
       4-cyl. engine auto. trans. 580-600 R.P.M.—in drive.
       V-8 engine std. trans. 580-600—neutral

V-8 engine auto. trans. 580-600—in drive.
▢1962-63—160 P.S.I.
△1963—45S.

**1963—22°B.
*With 4 cyl. engine and automatic trans. 30°B.

Note:

All specifications are standard and should result in satisfactory performance. There are, however, factors that influence these settings, such as fuel octane value, air density, humidity, temperature, etc. Timing charts, like other specifications must be considered as averages, subject to modification.

DISTRIBUTOR SPECIFICATIONS

YEAR AND MODEL		Delco-Remy Part Number	Rotation	Cam Angle In Degrees	BREAKER		GOVERNOR CONTROL @ DIST. R.P.M.		VACUUM CONTROL DATA		
					Point Gap (Inch)	Arm Spring (Ounce)	Advance Starts	Full Advance	Inches Vacuum To Start Advance	Inches Vacuum Full Advance	Max. Advance In Distributor Degrees
1961	4-Cyl. 1 BBL. Carb.	1110254	CC	73-77	.016	19-23	1 @ 410	10 @ 2200	6-8	14	10
	4-Cyl. 4 BBL. Carb.	1110261	CC	73-77	.016	19-23	1 @ 410	10 @ 2200	6-8	14	10
	V-8 2 BBL. Carb.	1110977	C	28-32	.016	19-23	1 @ 350	13 @ 1850	6-8	14	10
1962	4-Cyl.—Std.	1110282	CC	74-76	.016	19-23	1 @ 400	13 @ 2125	6-8	14	10
	4-Cyl.—HI-Comp	1110283	CC	74-76	.016	19-23	1 @ 400	10 @ 2200	6-8	14	10
	V-8	1110983	C	28-32	.016	19-23	1 @ 500	13 @ 1850	6-8	15	8
1963	4-Cyl.—Std.	1110284	CC	31-34	.016	19-23	1 @ 650	13 @ 2125	6-8	20	14
	4-Cyl.—HI-Comp	1110300	CC	31-34	.016	19-23	1 @ 650	11 @ 2300	6-8	20	14
	V-8	1111020	C	28-32	.016	19-23	1 @ 650	12 @ 2200	6-8	20	14

GENERATOR & REGULATOR SPECIFICATIONS

YEAR AND MODEL	GENERATORS		REGULATORS				
	Cut In Engine R.P.M. (Hot)	Brush Spring Tension (Ounce)	Cutout Relay		Current And Voltage Regulator Air Gaps	Current Regulator Setting	Voltage Regulator Setting
			Air Gap	Closing Voltage			
1961-62 4-Cyl.	580	28	.020	12.7	.075	30	14.3
V-8	525	28	.020	12.7	.075	30	14.3

DELCOTRON & A.C. REGULATOR SPECIFICATIONS

Year and Model		GENERATOR				REGULATOR	
		D-R Number	Field Current	Cut-In	Hot Output	D-R Number	Voltage
1963	4-Cyl.	1100632 (A)	1.9 to 2.3 Amp	At Idle	37 Amp	1119511	14.3
	V-8	1106637 (B)	1.9 to 2.3 Amp	At Idle	37 Amp	1119511	14.3

(A) 4-Cyl. with Air Conditioning—42 Amp Output.
(B) 8-Cyl. with Air Conditioning—42 Amp Output.

BATTERY AND STARTER SPECIFICATIONS

YEAR AND MODEL	BATTERY				STARTERS						
	Amp. Hour Capacity	Volts	Group Number	Terminal Grounded	Lock Test			No-Load Test			Brush Spring Tension
					Amps.	Volts	Torque	Amps.	Volts	R.P.M.	
1961-62 4-Cyl.	42	12	17M2	Neg.	Lock Test Not Recommended			49-76	10.6	6200-9400	35
V-8	42	12	17M2	Neg.				80	10.6	6750	35
1963 4-Cyl.	44	12	17M1	Neg.	Lock Test Not Recommended			49-76	10.6	6200-9400	35
V-8	53	12	25MB	Neg.				65-100	10.6	3600-5100	35

CAPACITIES

YEAR AND MODEL	Engine Crank-case Add 1 Qt. For New Filter	TRANSMISSION Pints to Fill After Draining		Rear Axle Pints	Gasoline Tank Gallons	Cooling System Quarts Add 1 Qt. For Heater
		Manual	Automatic			
1961-63 All	4	3*	12△	3	16□	11.6

* 4 Speed—3¾ Pints
□ 1963—20 Gal.
△ 12 Pts., Dry Fill—6 Pts., Drain—Refill.

GENERAL ENGINE SPECIFICATIONS

YEAR AND MODEL	Bore And Stroke	No. Of Main Bearings	Type Of Valve Lifter	Cubic Inch Dis-place-ment	AMA Horse Power	Advertised Horsepower At Stated R.P.M.	Advertised Torque At Stated R.P.M.	Com-pres-sion Ratio	Oil pres-sure At 35 MPH	Cam-Shaft Drive
1961-62 4-Cyl.	4.06x3.75	5	Hyd.	194.5	26.4	110 @ 3800	190 @ 2000	8.6-1	35	Chain
1961 V-8	3.5x2.8	5	Hyd.	215	39.2	155 @ 4600	220 @ 2400	8.8-1	35	Chain
1962 V-8	3.5x2.8	5	Hyd.	215	39.2	185 @ 4800	230 @ 2800	10.25-1	35	Chain
1963 4-Cyl.	4.06x3.75	5	Hyd.	194.5	26.4	115 @ 4000	195 @ 2000	8.6-1	35	Chain
V-8	3.72x3.75	5	Hyd.	326	44.3	264 @ 4800	352 @ 2800	10.25-1	35	Chain

CRANKSHAFT BEARING JOURNAL SIZES

YEAR AND MODEL	MAIN BEARING JOURNALS				CONNECTING ROD BEARING JOURNALS		
	Journal Diameter	Oil Clearance	End Play Of Shaft	End Play Held By	Journal Diameter	Oil Clearance	End Play
1961-63 4-Cyl.	3.00	.0005-.0025	.0060	4	2.250	.0005-.0025	.0065
1961-62 V-8	2.30	.0005-.0021	.0060	3	2.000	.0002-.0022	.0010
1963 V-8	3.00	.0005-.0020	.0060	4	2.250	.0005-.0025	.0085

VALVE SPECIFICATIONS

YEAR AND MODEL	VALVE SEAT ANGLE		Int. Valve Lift	Ext. Valve Lift	VALVE SPRING PRESSURE		STEM TO GUIDE CLEARANCE		Stem Dia.	Remov-able Guides
	Inlet	Exhaust			Inner	Outer	Inlet	Exhaust		
1961-62 4-Cyl.—M/Trans.	30°	45°	.33	.33	None	80 @ 1.53	.0021-.0038	.0026-.0043	.34	No
4-Cyl.—A/Trans.	30°	45°	.40	.40	26 @ 1.48	60 @ 1.52	.0021-.0038	.0026-.0043	.34	No
V-8—All	45°	45°	.38	.38	None	64 @ 1.64	.0005-.0030	.0015-.0045	.34	Yes
1963 4-Cyl.— 1 BBL. Carb.	30°	45°	.33	.33	None	83 @ 1.52	.0021-.0038	.0026-.0043	.34	No
4-Cyl.— 4 BBL. Carb.	30°	45°	.40	.40	27 @ 1.47	60 @ 1.52	.0021-.0038	.0026-.0043	.34	No
V-8	30°	45°	.37	.37	27 @ 1.47	60 @ 1.52	.0021-.0038	.0026-.0043	.34	Yes

LIGHT BULBS

Headlamp Unit—Outer:

	Candlepower	No.
High Beam	37½W	4002
Low Beam	50W	

Inner:

High Beam	37½W	4001
Parking and Turn Signal	32-4	1034

Tail and Stop Light	32-4	1034
Back-Up	32	1073
Instrument	2	57
Turn Indicator	2	57
Oil Pressure	2	57
Eng. Temperature	2	57
Gen. Tell-Tale	2	57
High Beam Indicator	1	53
Glove Compartment	2	57
Dome Light	15	1004
License Plate	4	67
Radio Dial	1	1881
Heater Panel	2	57
Parking Brake Signal	2	57

FRONT WHEEL ALIGNMENT

YEAR AND MODEL	CASTER		CAMBER		Toe-in (Inches)	Inclination (Degrees)	WHEEL PIVOT RATIO	
	Range (Degrees)	Pre-ferred	Range (Degrees)	Pre-ferred			Inner Wheel	Outer Wheel
1961-63 All	1⅔±½	1¼N	0±½	Note A	0 To ⅛	6½	20°	19°

Note A: Preferred L. ¼° more than R.

PISTON AND PIN SPECIFICATIONS

YEAR AND MODEL	PISTON			PISTON PIN				
	Skirt Clearance				Fit			
	Top	Bottom	Diameter	Bushing	In Rod	In Piston	Lock	
1961-62 4-Cyl.	.0014	.0009	.9802	None	Press	.0003-.0005	In Rod	
V-8	.0008	.0010	.8748	None	Press	.0001-.0005	In Rod	
1963 All	.0013	.0012	.9802	None	Press	.0003-.0005	In Rod	

TORQUE SPECIFICATIONS

YEAR AND MODEL	Spark Plugs	Cylinder Head	Rod Bearing	Main Bearing	Crank-shaft Pulley	Flywheel To Crankshaft	Manifolds	
							In.	Ex.
1961-63 4-Cyl.	25	80-95	35-45	85-95(A)	160	90 95	40	30
V-8	15-20	50-55	30-35	50-55	140-160	50-60	25-30	10-15

(A) REAR MAIN 120.

TUNE-UP

Engine tune-up and diagnosis go hand-in-hand therefore, a plan of approach should be established to best serve both ends.

SPARK PLUGS

1. Remove plug wires and blow foreign particles from the plug wells with compressed air.
2. Use a good plug tester, (before or after plug removal, depending on equipment). Visually check plugs. Renew and/or gap them to specifications.
3. Connect a jumper wire between distributor terminal of coil and ground to prevent high tension sparking.

COMPRESSION TEST

4. Attach a good compression gauge in the spark plug port.
5. With the throttle held wide open, crank engine three or four revolutions to determine highest compression reading. Record this reading.
6. Repeat this test on all cylinders. Engine design and atmospheric variables prevent establishing a positive cranking speed cylinder pressure. **Pressure variation** between cylinders is the most important factor and should not exceed 15 pounds.

    Note: A compression check should be the first step in the course of tune-up events. Only if compression is within limits

GENERAL CHASSIS AND BRAKE SPECIFICATIONS

YEAR AND MODEL	CHASSIS		BRAKE CYLINDER BORE		
	Overall Length In Inches	Tire Size	Master Cylinder (Inch)	Wheel Cylinder (Inch)	
				Front	Rear
1961-62 All	189.3	6.00x15	1.	1¹¹⁄₁₆	¹⁵⁄₁₆
1963 All	194.3	6.00x15	1.	1¹⁄₁₆	¹⁵⁄₁₆

should tune-up be continued.
7. Lightly lubricate the spark plug threads, install them and torque to specifications.
    4 cyl. spark plug torque 25 ft. lb.
    V-8 spark plug torque 20 ft. lb.
8. Carefully install the resistance type plug wires.

BATTERY AND CABLES

9. Check physical and electrical condition of battery and cables. Recharge or replace as necessary.
10. Test cranking ability of starter and starter circuit.
11. Check neutral safety switch.

DISTRIBUTOR

The **4 cylinder** engine distributor is high on a centerline of the engine and to the rear of the air cleaner.

The **V-8 engine** distributor is mounted in the top of the timing chain case, between cylinder banks but favoring the left side.
12. Disconnect distributor primary wire and vacuum advance tube at the distributor.
13. Remove distributor cap and mark position of rotor on distributor body for reference in reassembly.

14. Remove distributor clamp. Then lift out distributor.
15. Examine contact points for pits and burned appearance. Excessively pitted points should be replaced as they cannot be cleaned and aligned satisfactorily.
16. Check for breaker plate, distributor shaft and bushing wear and advise reconditioning as necessary.
17. Reinstall distributor.

    Note: If the engine has been disturbed;
    A. With #1 piston coming up on compression stroke, continue cranking the engine until the pulley timing mark indexes with the stationary mark.
    B. Position the distributor to the opening in the block with reference to the firing order sequence shown in the firing order illustrations of this Tempest Section.
    C. Point the rotor toward distributor cap #1 tower location. Then slightly retard the distributor rotor position.
    D. Press down on distributor housing until seated and

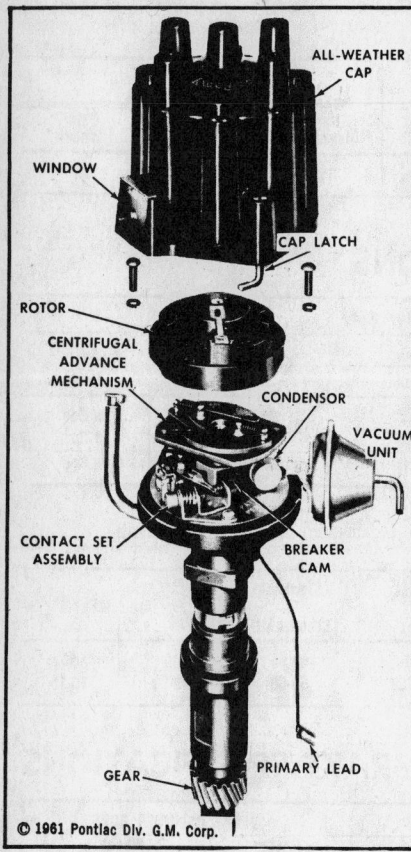

ALL-WEATHER CAP

WINDOW

CAP LATCH

ROTOR

CENTRIFUGAL ADVANCE MECHANISM

CONDENSOR

VACUUM UNIT

CONTACT SET ASSEMBLY

BREAKER CAM

GEAR

PRIMARY LEAD

© 1961 Pontiac Div. G.M. Corp.

4 cyl. engine distributor

clamp unit in place.

18. Check initial timing, centerfugal and vacuum advance characteristics and engine vacuum.
19. Test fuel pump.
20. Check and/or replace fuel filter.
21. Adjust carburetor.
22. Road test and make final adjustments.

DISTRIBUTOR

REMOVE

1. Disconnect distributor primary wire.
2. Remove distributor cap. (Unlatch the cap by using a screwdriver to disengage the latches.)
3. Crank engine so the rotor is in #1 position and the crankshaft pulley timing mark in line with the pointer.
4. Disconnect vacuum line at distributor.
5. Remove distributor clamping screw and hold-down clamp.
6. Lift out distributor and distributor-to-block gasket. Notice the slight rotation of the rotor as the distributor is removed from the block. (The four cylinder engine rotor will tend to rotate clockwise as the unit is withdrawn from the block. The V-8 rotor will tend to rotate counter-

clockwise as the unit is withdrawn from the block.)

INSTALL

Install in reverse order of removal. See previous paragraph, "Tune-Up," "Distributor."

GENERATOR AND REGULATOR

The generator, regulator and charging circuit is basically the same whether used with the four or the eight cylinder engine. It is a 30 amp. two brush unit.

Detailed facts on the generator and regulator can be found in the specification table in this section.

General repair and trouble shooting can be found in the Unit Repair section under the heading; Generators and Regulators.

GENERATOR REMOVE

1. Disconnect the negative (ground) cable from the battery.
2. Disconnect armature, field, and ground wires at the generator terminals.
3. Remove adjustment arm to generator bolt. Remove the two pivot bolts from the mounting bracket. Remove generator and belt.

GENERATOR INSTALL

1. Reverse the above procedure.
2. **Polarize the generator:** Attach **bat, gen, field** and ground leads to regulator and polarize generator by momentarily touching a jumper wire to **bat** and **gen** terminals on the regulator before starting the engine.
3. Adjust fan belt tension so as to obtain ½" belt deflection when applying 15 lb. thumb pressure to the belt, midway between the generator and fan pulleys.

REGULATOR AMBIENT TEMPERATURE	VOLTAGE		
	LOW		HIGH
165° F	13.1	—	13.9
145° F	13.5	—	14.3
125° F	13.8		14.7
105° F	14.0	—	14.9
85° F	14.2	—	15.2
65° F	14.4	—	15.4
45° F	14.5	—	15.6
	NORMAL SPECIFICATION RANGE ■ INDICATES PUBLISHED SPECIFICATIONS		

© 1961 Pontiac Div. G.M. Corp.

Voltage regulator correction chart

DELCOTRON (A.C. Generator)

Beginning with 1962, an alternating current generator is being made available. This unit is the Delco-Remy, "DELCOTRON." The purpose of this unit is to satisfy the increase in electrical loads that have been imposed upon the car battery by modern conditions of traffic and driving patterns.

The DELCOTRON is covered in the Unit Repair section of this manual under "Generators and Regulators."

Caution:

Since the Delcotron and regulator are designed for use on only one polarity system, the following precautions must be observed:

1. The polarity of the battery, generator and regulator must be considered before making any electrical connections in the system.
2. When connecting a booster battery, be sure to connect the negative battery terminals together and the positive battery terminals together.
3. When connecting a charger to the battery, connect the charger positive lead to the battery positive terminal. Connect the charger negative lead to the battery negative terminal.
4. Never operate the Delcotron on open circuit. Be sure that all connections in the circuit are clean and tight.
5. Do not short across or ground any of the terminals on the Delcotron regulator.
6. Do not attempt to polarize the Delcotron.
7. Do not use test lamps of more than 12 volts for checking diode continuity.
8. Avoid long soldering times when replacing diodes or transistors. Prolonged heat is damaging to these units.
9. Disconnect the battery ground terminal when servicing any A.C. system. This will prevent the possibility of accidental reversing of polarity.

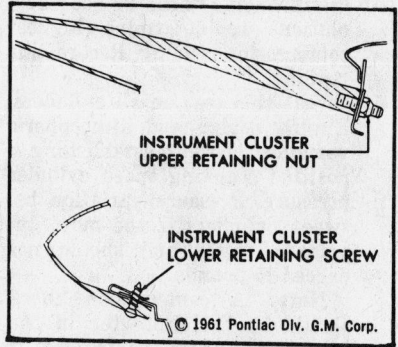

INSTRUMENT CLUSTER UPPER RETAINING NUT

INSTRUMENT CLUSTER LOWER RETAINING SCREW

© 1961 Pontiac Div. G.M. Corp.

Instrument cluster fasteners

INSTRUMENTS

The instrument cluster includes the speedometer head, the generator charge indicator, the oil pressure indicator and the temperature indicator. The fuel gauge, light switch, wiper and washer switch, starter and ignition switch and the cigarette lighter.

CLUSTER REMOVE AND INSTALL

1. Disconnect battery.
2. Remove 2 upper retaining nuts.
3. Remove 4 screws at lower edge of cluster.
4. Remove 2 screws from lower steering column bezel.
5. Disconnect speedometer cable.
6. Pull cluster and housing out from instrument panel to gain access to wiring.
7. Starting at the top, remove bulbs and wiring.
8. Remove 4 screws holding cluster to housing and remove the cluster.
9. To install reverse above procedure.

SPEEDOMETER

(Cluster Removed From Car)

1. Remove 8 screws.
2. Remove screws retaining speedometer head.
3. Replace by reversing above steps.

FUEL GAUGE

1. Remove wire connector and bulb.
2. Remove 2 screws and lift out gauge.
3. Replace by reversing above steps.

IGNITION AND STARTING SWITCH

1. Remove switch from the dash by unscrewing the switch ferrule with a special spanner wrench, tool #J-5893.
2. Remove switch from back of instrument panel and disconnect wires.
3. Replace switch by reversing above method.

BATTERY AND STARTER

BATTERY

A Delco 12 volt battery is used in all models.

STARTER

The starter circuit consists of the battery, battery cables, starting motor, starter motor solenoid switch. ignition-starter switch and the neutral safety switch, (used on cars with automatic transmission).

The starting motor and solenoid assembly is mounted on the flywheel upper housing, left side.

The solenoid switch closes the circuit between the battery and the starting motor. It also operates the shift lever that moves the drive pinion into mesh with the flywheel ring gear. Two models of starting motors are used, one for the 4 cyl. engine and a different one for the V-8, see illustrations. However the systems are basically the same.

STARTER, R & R

No problem here. Disconnect battery and starter wires. Remove attaching bolts and lift out starter.

BRAKES

The service brakes are of the conventional type, hydraulically operated. The lining is molded and attached to the shoes by tubular rivets. The primary shoe lining is shorter than the secondary lining and is of different composition.

Brake drum lining-contact-surfaces are cast iron, however, the drum proper is pressed steel. Brake drum diameter is 9 inches.

The parking brake uses a foot operated control lever, enclosed cables, rear wheel brake shoe levers and struts to the rear wheel shoes. The parking brake is released by turning the apply handle to the right.

Information on brake adjustments, band replacement, bleeding proce-

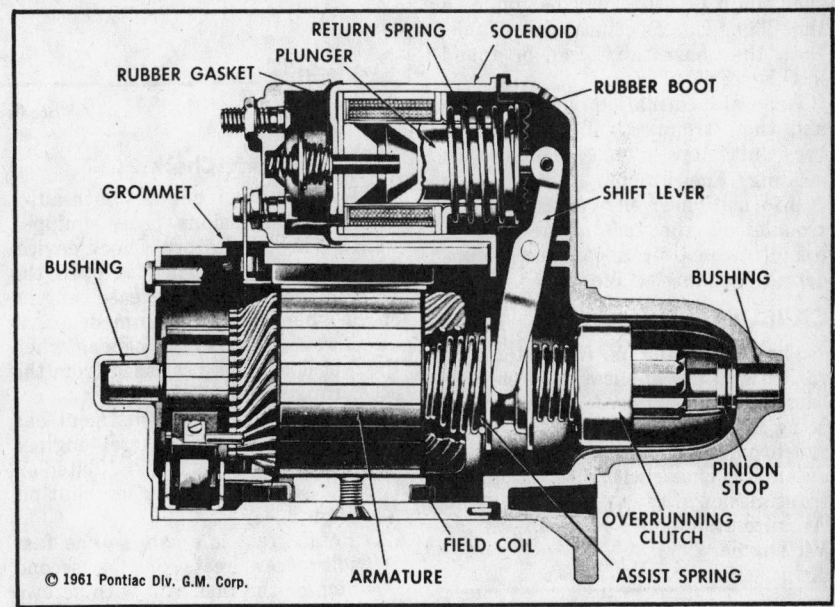

V-8 engine starting motor and solenoid

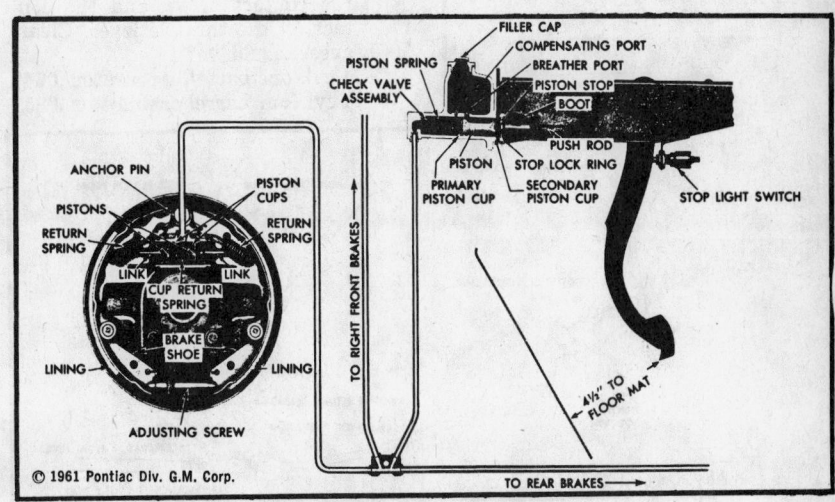

Schematic diagram of service brake system

dure, master and wheel cylinder overhaul can be found in the General Section under the heading: Brakes, Hydraulic.

Information on the grease seals which may need replacement can be found in the Unit Repair section. The front wheel grease seals under the head: Suspension, Front Repair. The rear wheel grease seals under the head: Axles, Rear.

FUEL SYSTEM

FUEL SYSTEM INFORMATION

A chart covering causes of excess fuel consumption will be found in the Unit Repair section under the heading: Fuel Consumption Chart.

Data on capacity of the gas tank will be found in the Capacities Table. Data on correct engine idle speed and fuel pump pressure will be found in the Tune-Up Specifications Table. Both the above tables can be found in this section.

General information on fuel pumps and their troubles will be found in the Unit Repair section under the heading: Fuel Pumps.

Information covering operation and troubles of the fuel gauge will be found in the Unit Repair section under the heading: Gages.

CARBURETOR

The carburetor is Rochester but varies with the application, from one barrel to four barrels. A manual choke being furnished as standard with the synchromesh transmission, and an automatic choke with the automatic transmission of the 4 cylinder version. An automtaic choke is used with the V-8 engine.

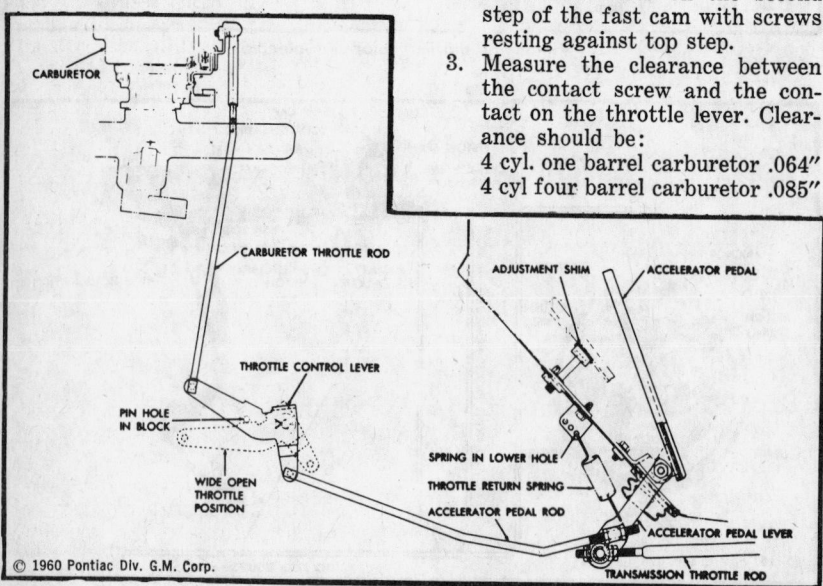

4 cyl. accelerator linkage

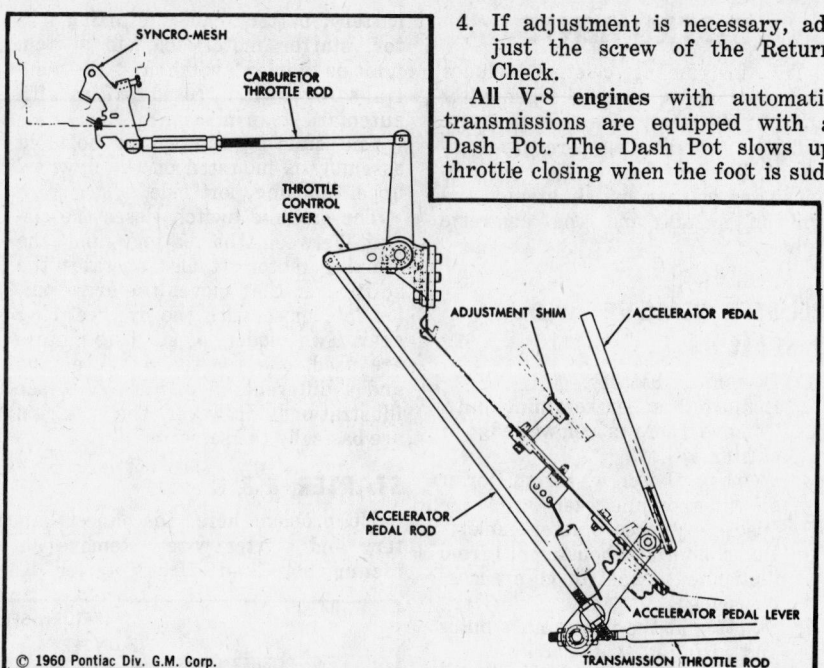

V-8 accelerator linkage

Throttle Return Check

All of the 4 cyl. engines with automatic transmissions are equipped with a Throttle Return Check device. This device is designed to open the throttle valves to increase engine speed when engine vacuum drops. It also slows down throttle closing when the foot is suddenly released from the accelerator pedal.

1. Be sure fast idle adjustment has been made on 4 barrel engines and hot idle has been adjusted on one barrel engines, then shut off engine.
2. Rotate fast idle cam so the fast idle screw rests on the second step of the fast cam with screws resting against top step.
3. Measure the clearance between the contact screw and the contact on the throttle lever. Clearance should be:
   4 cyl. one barrel carburetor .064″
   4 cyl four barrel carburetor .085″
4. If adjustment is necessary, adjust the screw of the Return Check.

All V-8 engines with automatic transmissions are equipped with a Dash Pot. The Dash Pot slows up throttle closing when the foot is suddenly taken from the accelerator pedal.

1. The Dash Pot should not be adjusted until the carburetor and transmission linkage are properly adjusted. The carburetor idle speed should be adjusted and the engine at operating temperature.
2. Place idle screw on high step of fast idle cam.
3. Adjust Dash Pot until there is a clearance of .000″ to .010″ between Dash Pot and throttle lever. Be sure Dash Pot is aligned with throttle lever.
4. Place selector lever in Drive and, with brakes firmly set, jab accelerator pedal and release rapidly. Note engine operation as throttle closes.

Throttle Valve Linkage
Adjustments

The following procedure is to be used to obtain correct relationship between the carburetor, accelerator pedal and the transmission throttle valve shaft.

When making this adjustment on standard transmission equipped cars, omit part "D" in steps 5 and 6.

1. Check accelerator pedal stop. It should be 1 11/16″. If incorrect, adjust by loosening lock nut and resetting to correct height.
2. Attach a .060″ shim on the top of the pedal stop, then:
3. Disconnect carburetor throttle rod at the carburetor.
4. Disconnect accelerator rod and

throttle valve rod at accelerator pedal lever beneath the car.

5. **On 4 cyl cars:**

A. Rotate throttle control lever to wide open position. Hold this position by inserting pin #J-7687 in hole in block so that flat on throttle lever rests against pin.

B. Manually open carburetor to wide open throttle and adjust length of throttle rod so that it freely engages with carburetor throttle lever.

C. From beneath the car, pull accelerator pedal to wide open throttle position against shim. Adjust trunnion so it will slip into upper hole of pedal lever. Tighten securely.

D. With the pedal still against the stop, push rearward on throttle valve rod until T.V. lever in transmission bottoms solidly. Adjust trunnion to slip into lower hole of accelerator pedal lever. Tighten securely.

6. **On V-8 cars:**

A. Rotate throttle control lever to wide open position. Hold this position by installing tool #J-9257 over the lever.

B. Manually open carburetor to wide open throttle and adjust length of carburetor throttle rod so that it freely engages with carburetor throttle lever.

C. From beneath the car, pull accelerator pedal to wide open position against shim. Ad-

just trunnion so it will slip into upper hole of accelerator pedal lever. Tighten securely.

D. With the pedal still against the stop, push rearward on throttle valve rod until T.V. lever in transmission bottoms. Adjust trunnion to slip into lower hole of accelerator pedal lever. Tighten securely.

7. Remove shim from accelerator pedal stop and the linkage pin from throttle control lever.

8. As a final check, push pedal to stop and check that carburetor is wide open and T.V. lever is against stop.

FUEL PUMP

An AC Type HQ fuel pump is used. It is mounted on the left side of the timing chain cover in an inverted position. The pump lever works from the underside of a camshaft eccentric. It is of the single action diaphragm type and is equipped with a pulsation dampening chamber for stabilizing fuel flow.

FUEL FILTER

The filter is contained in the fuel tank and is integral with the stand pipe and gas gauge—tank unit.

The fuel tank must be dropped to gain access to the fuel filter, gas gauge—tank unit or the stand pipe.

FUEL TANK

The fuel tank is attached by two

strap type supports to the body under the trunk compartment.

The gas tank filler is soldered into an opening at the center of the left side of the tank. It is accessible through a door in the left rear quarter.

The stand pipe and fuel gauge sending unit are integral and require tank removal for replacement.

Tank Remove

1. Remove the gasoline by syphoning to a clean container.
2. Remove vent pipe.
3. Remove hoses and cups.
4. Disconnect the vent pipe from the breather pipe.
5. Disconnect gauge sending unit wire at the connector.
6. Disconnect support straps at their rear ends and lower the tank.

Tank Install

Install in reverse order of removal.

EXHAUST SYSTEM

CROSSOVER PIPE—R & R

4 Cyl. Engine

1. Disconnect crossover pipe from manifold.
2. Remove two nuts from "U" bolt and remove "U" bolt.
3. Disconnect and remove exhaust crossover pipe from connection.
4. Replace crossover pipe by using new gaskets and reversing above steps. Torque bolts at each end of pipe to 15-25 ft. lbs.

V-8 Engine

1. Remove four bolts holding exhaust crossover pipe to exhaust manifold.
2. Remove clamp connecting exhaust crossover pipe to exhaust pipe.
3. Remove exhaust crossover pipe from car.
4. Replace exhaust crossover pipe by reversing above steps. Torque bolts connecting the crossover pipe to the manifold to 15-25 ft. lbs. Torque nuts on clamp to 10-15 ft. lbs.

CONNECTOR—R & R

4 Cyl. Engine

1. Remove two bolts holding the crossover pipe to the connector.
2. Remove two bolts holding the exhaust pipe to the connector.
3. Remove two bolts holding connector to exhaust manifold.
4. Replace connector, using new gaskets, by reversing above steps. Torque bolts to 15-25 ft. lbs.

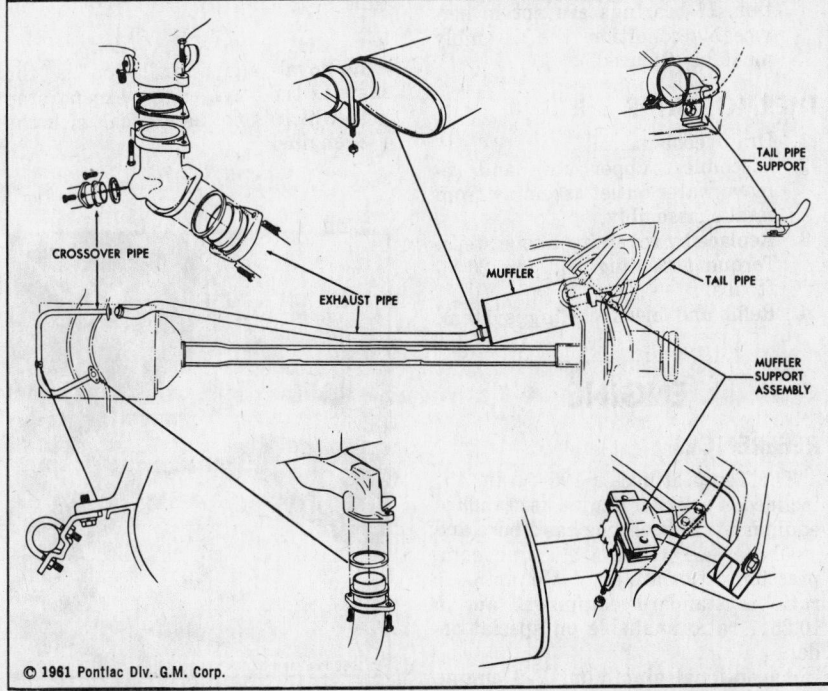

© 1961 Pontiac Div. G.M. Corp.

4 cyl. exhaust system

EXHAUST PIPE—R & R

4 Cyl. Engine

1. Remove two bolts from exhaust pipe to connector.
2. Remove clamp holding exhaust pipe to muffler.
3. Remove exhaust pipe.
4. Replace pipe by reversing above steps. Torque exhaust pipe-to-connector bolts to 15-25 ft. lbs. Torque, clamp "U"-bolt nuts to 10-15 ft. lbs.

V-8 Engine

1. Remove clamps at both ends of exhaust pipe.
2. Remove exhaust pipe from car.
3. Replace by reversing above steps. Torque nuts to 10-15 ft. lbs.

MUFFLER—R & R

All Models

1. Remove clamp from support assembly and from front of muffler.
2. Remove muffler.
3. Replace by reversing above steps. Torque clamp nuts to 10-15 ft. lbs.

COOLING SYSTEM

RADIATOR

There are four different radiators used, depending upon application, (4 or 8 cyl., standard or air conditioned). A drain cock is located at the inside lower left hand corner of the radiator. The core is of the down-flow tube and center type and is constructed of copper.

Note:

Use caution in selecting anti-freeze and cleaning solutions for use with aluminum. Most well-known brand commercially available anti-freezes are acceptable but beware of the off-brands.

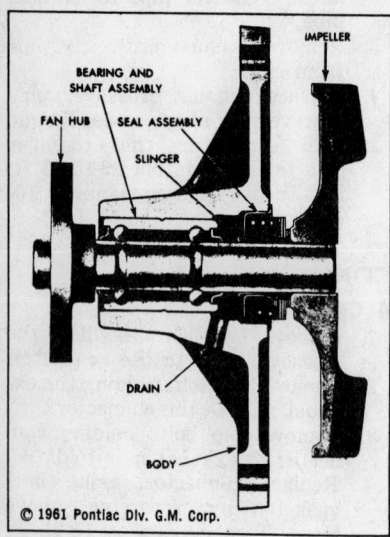

4 cyl. water pump

© 1961 Pontiac Div. G.M. Corp.

Radiator R & R

1. Drain cooling system.
2. Disconnect overflow, upper and lower radiator hoses.
3. Remove radiator fan shield.
4. Remove radiator.
5. To replace, reverse removal steps.

WATER PUMP R & R

4 Cyl. Engine

Note:

The pump is serviced only as an assembly.

1. Drain cooling system.
2. Loosen generator at adjusting strap and remove fan belt.
3. Remove fan and pulley.
4. Remove pump.
5. Install pump by reversing above steps. When pump is installed, drain hole will be at bottom. Torque pump attaching nuts to 15 ft. lbs. Adjust fan belt.

V-8 Engine

The pump cover is die cast aluminum into which the water pump bearing outer race is shrunk fit. Therefore, the cover, shaft bearing and hub are not replaceable. The shaft seal and impeller are the only replaceable parts of the water pump.

1. Drain cooling system.
2. Remove fan blade and pulley or pulleys from the pump hub.
3. Disconnect hose from the pump inlet and heater hose from nipple. Remove pump assembly and gasket from timing chain cover.
4. Check pump shaft bearings for end play or roughness of operation. If bearings are not in serviceable condition, the assembly must be replaced.

THERMOSTAT R & R

1. Drain coolant.
2. Disconnect upper hose and remove water outlet assembly from intake assembly.
3. Replace by reversing above steps. Torque attaching bolts to 20-35 ft. lbs.
4. Refill and bleed cooling system.

ENGINE

REFERENCES

The Tempest uses a 195 cu. in. 45° inclined, 4 cylinder engine as standard equipment. This engine has a bore and stroke of 4-1/16" x 3¾". Two compression ratios are available, an 8.6:1 ratio is standard equipment and a 10.25:1 ratio available on special order.

An optional aluminum V-8 engine is also available on special order.

ENGINE R & R

4 Cylinder

1. Remove hood.
2. Drain cooling system and remove radiator.
3. Disconnect heater hoses at the engine.
4. Disconnect wiring harness at generator, ignition coil starter solenoid, heater blower, thermogauge and oil pressure switch.
5. Disconnect ground strap at both sides of the engine.
6. Disconnect fuel line at fuel pump.
7. Disconnect vacuum modulator line at automatic transmission, at hose connection and at clip on flywheel housing.
8. Remove front fender cross brace.
9. Remove fan and fan pulley.
10. Disconnect accelerator rod at engine lever.
11. Raise front of car.
12. Disconnect exhaust pipe at manifold.
13. Disconnect clutch linkage on Synchromesh.
14. Position wooden block at rear of engine to prevent distributor damage if engine rocks to the rear.

Disconnect propeller shaft and torque tube from rear of engine.

15. Disconnect engine support at crossmember.
16. Raise engine with chainfall. Move forward to clear the firewall and heater.
17. Lift and remove engine.

Replace by reversing the removal procedure. Give special care to installing the propeller shaft and torque tube

V-8

Removal and installation is the same as the 4 cyl. engine except, step #14 which is not as critical with the V-8 engine.

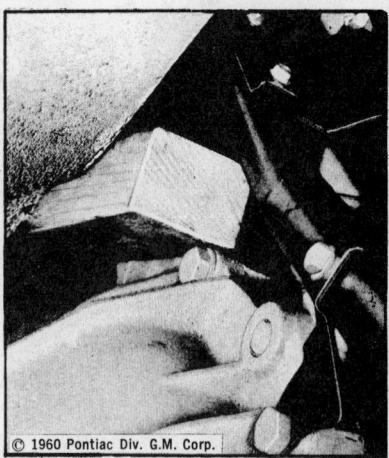

Wooden block at rear of engine

© 1960 Pontiac Div. G.M. Corp.

CYLINDER HEAD

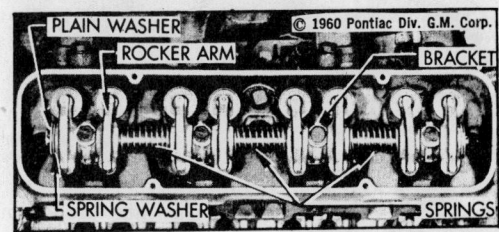

Rocker Arm Shaft Assembly

4 CYL. REMOVE

1. Remove intake manifold assembly.
2. Disconnect breather pipe and remove push rod cover.
3. Remove exhaust manifold-to-cylinder head attaching bolts.
4. Remove rocker arm cover assembly.
5. Loosen rocker arm nuts and rotate rocker arms so the push rods can be removed.
6. Remove push rods and store them so they can be installed in their original locations.
7. Disconnect spark plug wires.
8. Remove cylinder head bolts.
9. Lifter off the head.
10. Remove cylinder head gasket.

4 CYL. INSTALL

1. Position new cylinder head gasket on block, on locating dowels.
2. Place cylinder head in position.

Note:
Three different length bolts are used. When they are properly located, they will project an equal amount from their bosses. Do not use sealer on these bolt threads.

3. Install cylinder head attaching bolts. Torque to 95 ft. lbs.
4. Install push rods in original location and position.
5. Position rocker arms and torque rocker arm nuts to 15-25 ft. lbs.
6. Install rocker arm cover.
7. Install exhaust manifold-to-cylinder head bolts and torque to 30 ft. lbs.
8. Install push rod cover and crankcase breather outlet pipe.
9. Install intake manifold.
10. Connect spark plug wires.

V-8 REMOVE

1. Remove intake manifold.
2. Remove spark plug wire retainers from rocker arm covers. Gently disconnect plug wires at plugs. Then swing wires and loom out of the way.
3. Remove rocker arm covers and gaskets. On right side of engine, remove the vent pipe.
4. Remove rocker arm shaft bracket to cylinder head attaching bolts (4 to each cylinder head). Remove rocker arm and shaft assemblies.
5. Remove push rods. Store them so that they may be installed in their original location.
6. Protect lifters and camshaft area from dirt.
7. Disconnect exhaust manifold at exhaust pipe.
8. Disconnect battery ground strap at front right outer cylinder head bolt stud.
9. Remove 14 cylinder head bolts and rear generator attaching bolt.
10. Remove cylinder head, head gasket and exhaust manifold as an assembly.

V-8 INSTALL

1. Wipe all gasket surfaces and blow out bolt holes with an air hose.
2. Install new head gasket on block dowels. **Do not** use sealer.
3. Place cylinder head on the block dowels.
4. Clean and coat head bolts with special non-hardening sealing compound.
   Caution: Failure to use sealing compound at this point can result in coolant seepage into the cylinders.
5. Install short, medium, and long cylinder head bolts (as illustrated).
6. Just snug down head bolts. Then, in the proper sequence, torque to 50-55 ft. lbs.
7. Install push rods in original location and position.
8. Wipe bases of rocker arm shaft brackets and bracket basses on cylinder head clean.
9. Check notch on one end of rocker arm shaft to be certain it is "up." Set rocker arm and shaft assembly in place and start one or two attaching bolts.
10. Tilt rocker arms towards push rods and locate top of push rod in it's rocker arm seat.
11. Draw down rocker arm and shaft assembly a little at a time. Torque to 25-35 ft. lbs.
12. Install rocker arm cover and gaskets. On right side, install vent pipe.
13. Connect spark plug wires.
14. Connect battery ground strap at the right front of the engine.

ROCKER ARM STUD
REPLACE—4 CYL.

This operation does not apply to the V-8 engine as a rocker arm shaft is used instead of rocker arm studs. Studs are replaceable providing a press of two tons capacity or more is available.

1. Remove engine cylinder head.
2. With rocker arm removed, fill two slots 3/32" to 1/8" deep on opposite sides of the rocker arm stud. Top of slots should be 1/4"

Bolt length location

Head bolt tightening sequence

Locating rocker shaft notch

to ⅜" below thread travel.

3. Place washer #J-8934-3 at bottom of rocker arm stud.
4. Position Rocker Arm Stud Remover #J-8934-1 on rocker arm stud and tighten screws securely with Allen wrench.
5. Place spacer #J-8934-2 over Stud Remover #J-8934-1.
6. Thread a ⅞" standard nut on Stud Remover and turn nut until stud is out of head.
7. Remove cylinder head oil gallery plugs and thoroughly flush and blow out the gallery.
8. Position rocker arm on new rocker arm stud and place Rocker Arm Stud Installer #J-8927 on stud in place of rocker arm ball.
9. Coat the new rocker arm stud with white lead and oil and with the head mounted in press so studs are vertical, position the stud with rocker arm and Rocker Arm Stud Installer over hole in cylinder head.
10. Carefully press stud into head until it is in about half way (7/16").
11. Position Valve Train Gauge #J-8928 in push rod hole so that it seats properly in the rocker arm.
12. With valve seated, slowly press

the rocker arm stud into the cylinder head until the gauge projects about midway between the end of the gauge and the step with respect to the gasket surface of the cylinder head.

13. Remove stud installer, rocker arm and ball.
14. Blow air through oil hole in new stud to insure that the passage is not restricted.
15. Blow air through oil gallery to remove any foreign matter.
16. Replace plugs in ends of oil gallery.
17. Clean and inspect cylinder head and valves.
18. Install rocker arm and ball and install nut loosely.
19. Replace cylinder head.

VALVE GUIDES

4 Cyl. Engine

The cylinder head is cast iron and the guides are cast as part of the head. There are oil seals used on both intake and exhaust valve stems. Both inner and outer valve springs are used. No valve seat inserts are used with this engine. The valves are refaced and the head reseated in the conventional manner. The intake valve seat angle is 30°. The exhaust valve seat angle is 45°. The intake valve face angle is 29°. The exhaust valve face angle is 44°.

V-8 Engine

The cylinder heads are aluminum and carry removable valve guides and have valve seat inserts. The valves are refaced and the head reseated in the conventional manner. The valve seat angle, both intake and exhaust is 45°.

VALVE TAPPETS

The valve lifters are virtually the same on the 4 cyl. and V-8 engines.

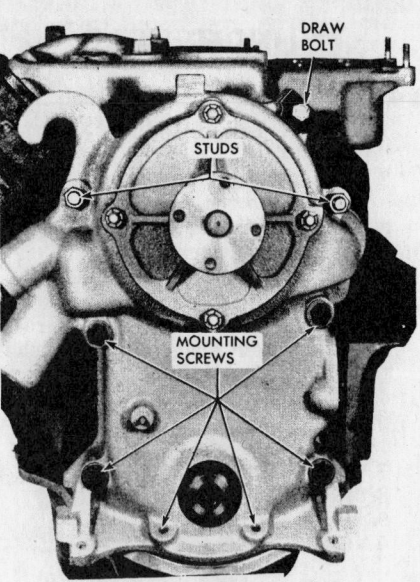

4 cyl. Timing case cover

TIMING CASE

CHAIN OR SPROCKETS R & R

4 Cyl. Engine

1. Drain cooling system.
2. Remove generator and mounts.
3. Remove crankshaft balancer.
4. Remove fuel pump.
5. Disconnect lower radiator and heater hose at the case cover.
6. Remove timing cover attaching bolts.
7. Loosen timing cover-to-intake manifold draw bolt and remove cover.
8. Remove fuel pump eccentric bushing and crankshaft oil seal.
9. Remove fuel pump eccentric.
10. Remove chain tensioner spring and bumper.

Note:

To avoid damage to the spring, re-

File slots in rocker arm stud

Removing rocker arm stud

V-8 engine front cover assembly

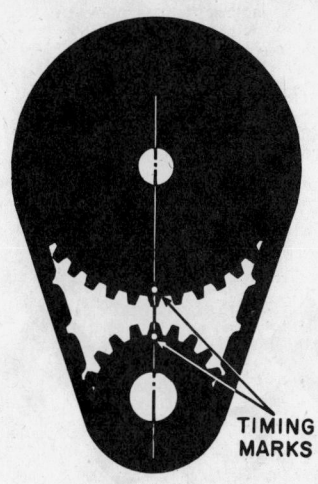

V-8 align timing marks

move right hand bumper before attempting to remove spring.

11. Align timing marks on sprockets to simplify correct chain replacement.
12. Slide timing chain and sprockets off ends of crankshaft and camshaft.
13. Install new chain and/or sprockets. Be sure timing marks are aligned exactly on a straight center line through the two shafts. Camshaft must extend through the sprocket so that the hole in fuel pump eccentric will locate on the shaft.
14. Inspect tensioner bumpers; if worn replace. Install chain tensioner assembly.
15. Install crankshaft oil seal, fuel pump eccentric bushing and timing cover.
16. Install oil pan-to-cover screws and tighten to 15 ft. lbs. torque.
17. Connect coolant and heater hoses.
18. Install harmonic balancer.
19. Install generator, brackets and fan belt.
20. Fill and bleed cooling system.

V-8 Engine

1. Drain cooling system.
2. Disconnect lower radiator hose and heater hose at water pump.
3. Remove fan, fan pulley and belt, or belts.
4. Remove harmonic balancer.
5. If car has power steering, remove pump brackets, bolts to chain cover and loosen or remove other bolts to permit pump to be moved out of the way.
6. Disconnect fuel lines and remove fuel pump.
7. Remove generator and brackets.
8. Remove distributor cap and pull spark plug wire retainers off fasteners on rocker arm covers. Swing cap and wires out of the way. Disconnect primary distributor lead.
9. Loosen and slide front clamp on thermostat by-pass hose rearward.
10. Remove chain cover attaching bolts. Remove two oil pan to cover bolts.
11. Lift off the timing case cover.
12. Remove oil slinger from crankshaft.
13. Temporarily install the harmonic balancer bolt in the crankshaft. Turn crankshaft to align timing marks on sprockets for easy assembly. Then remove the harmonic balancer bolt by sharply rapping an attached wrench to loosen the bolt without disturbing the sprocket timing marks.
14. Remove bolt and special washer from camshaft and slide off distributor drive gear and fuel pump eccentric.
15. Slide sprockets and chain forward and off the two shafts. Clean all parts thoroughly and install by reversing the removal procedure.

V-8 OIL SEAL

V-8 Engine

With chain cover off

1. Remove old oil seal and shedder from chain cover with vise grip pliers.
2. Coil new packing around opening so ends of packing are at top. Drive in new shedder.
3. Stake shedder in three places.

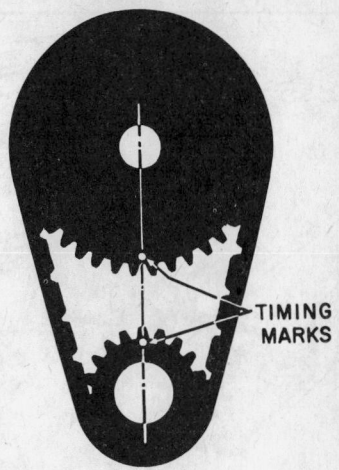

4 cyl. Align timing marks

ENGINE LUBRICATION

OIL PAN, R & R

4 Cyl. Engine

1. Drain the crankcase.
2. Remove exhaust crossover pipe.
3. With the front of car raised, install blocks or jack stands under front crossmember is such a way that crossmember will be supported when free of car.
4. Install suitable engine support.
5. Remove front wheels.
6. Disconnect steering linkage at tie rod ends.
7. Disconnect engine mounts at crossmember.
8. Remove ground straps from crossmember on both sides.
9. Disconnect brake lines at junc-

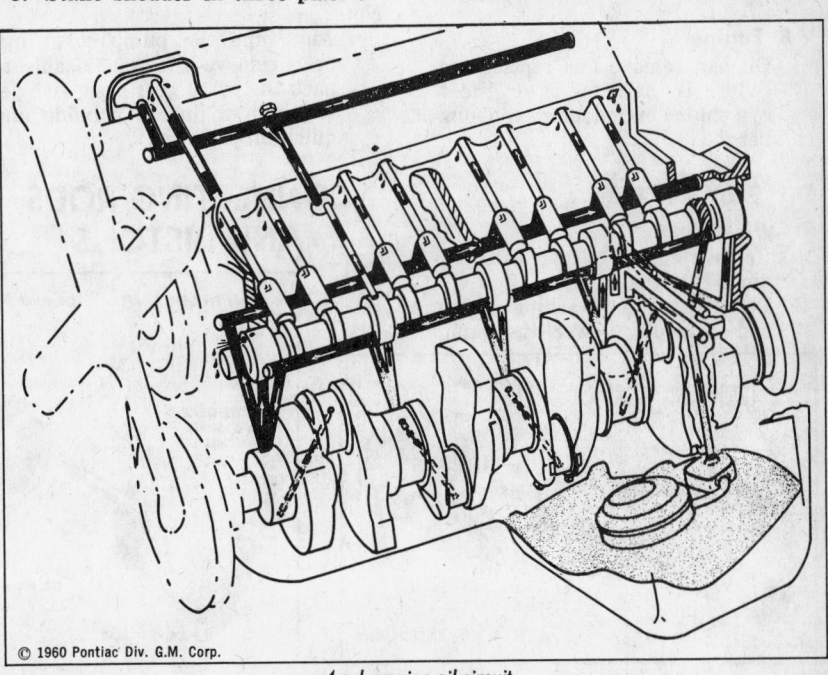

© 1960 Pontiac Div. G.M. Corp.

4 cyl. engine oil circuit

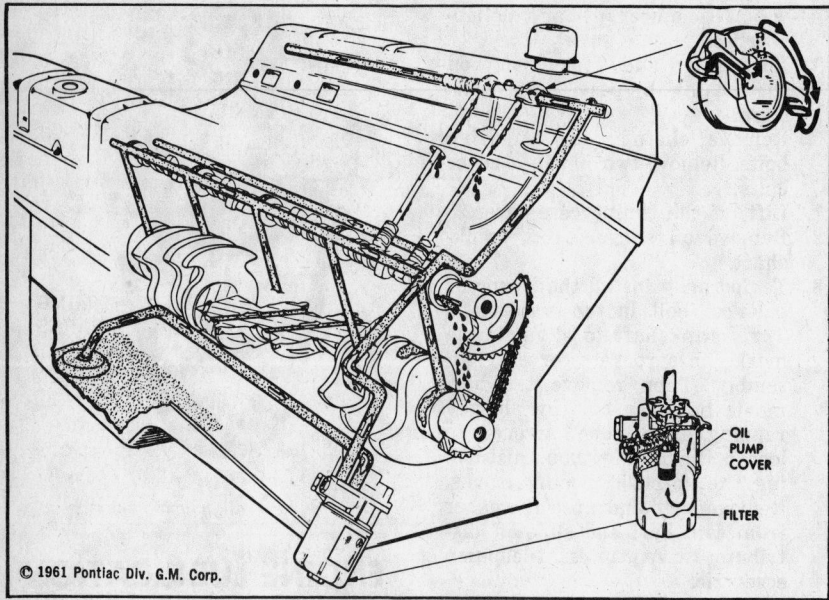

© 1961 Pontiac Div. G.M. Corp.

V-8 engine oil circuit

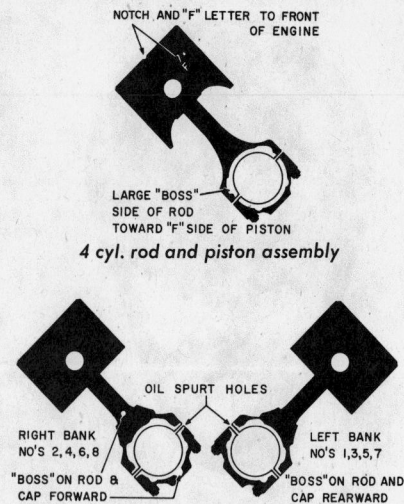

NOTCH AND "F" LETTER TO FRONT OF ENGINE

LARGE "BOSS" SIDE OF ROD TOWARD "F" SIDE OF PISTON

4 cyl. rod and piston assembly

OIL SPURT HOLES

RIGHT BANK NO'S 2, 4, 6, 8   LEFT BANK NO'S 1, 3, 5, 7

"BOSS" ON ROD & CAP FORWARD   "BOSS" ON ROD AND CAP REARWARD

V-8 rod and piston assembly

tion block on crossmember.

10. Disconnect fuel line from crossmember clip.

11. Remove three crossmember retaining bolts on each side of crossmember

12. Raise car to permit removal of crossmember assembly.

13. Remove flywheel housing front shield and lower cover.

14. Remove oil pan bolts and remove the oil pan.

To replace reverse the removal outline plus bleeding brakes. Torque three crossmember retaining bolts to 70-85 ft. lbs. The engine mount bolts to 30-45 ft. lbs. and the tie rod end nuts to 55-70 ft. lbs.

V-8 Engine

Oil pan remove and replace procedure is the same as on the 4-cyl. engine except, omit step number 2.

OIL PUMP R & R

4 Cyl. Engine

1. Remove engine oil pan (see previous paragraph).

2. Remove pump attaching screws and carefully lower the pump

while removing the pump drive shaft.

3. Reinstall in reverse order.

V-8 Engine

The oil oil pump is easily accessible on this model. It is mounted on the lower part of the timing case cover, right side.

1. Remove oil filter.

2. Disconnect wire from oil pressure indicator switch in filter bypass valve cap.

3. Remove screws attaching oil pump cover assembly to timing chain cover. Remove cover assembly and slide out oil pump gears.

Note:

Any time the pump cover has been removed, it is advisable to pack the pump gear area with petrolatum to insure priming and quick oil pressure.

CONNECTING RODS AND PISTONS

REMOVE AND REPLACE

All Models

1. Remove engine oil pan as outlined in previous paragraph.

2. Remove intake manifold.

3. Remove cylinder head.

4. To get at #3 and #4 connecting rod caps (4 cyl. engine) it is necessary to remove the pump screen and oil baffle.

5. Rotate crankshaft to bring bearing case of interest straight up.

6. Remove bearing cap and install rod bolt guide.

7. Carefully remove connecting rod and piston assembly by pushing the assembly toward the cylinder head end of the bore.

8. Service pistons, rings, pins and bearings in the conventional manner.

Note:

See specifications charts for various fits and clearances.

4-cyl. engines:

The pistons have an "F" cast on the front side. There is also a notch cast in the top of the high compression piston head and two notches cast in top of low compression piston head

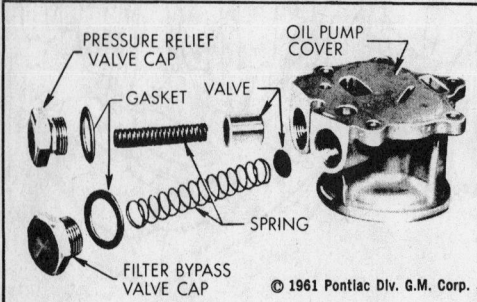

PRESSURE RELIEF VALVE CAP   OIL PUMP COVER

GASKET   VALVE

SPRING

FILTER BYPASS VALVE CAP   © 1961 Pontiac Div. G.M. Corp.

V-8 oil pump cover assembly

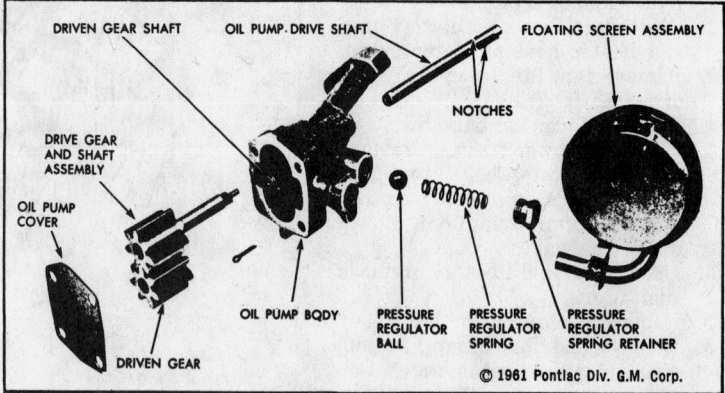

DRIVEN GEAR SHAFT   OIL PUMP DRIVE SHAFT   FLOATING SCREEN ASSEMBLY

NOTCHES

DRIVE GEAR AND SHAFT ASSEMBLY

OIL PUMP COVER

OIL PUMP BODY   PRESSURE REGULATOR BALL   PRESSURE REGULATOR SPRING   PRESSURE REGULATOR SPRING RETAINER

DRIVEN GEAR   © 1961 Pontiac Div. G.M. Corp.

4 cyl. oil pump and screen

at the front to help in proper installation. The piston assemblies should be installed with the notch or notches "front."

One side of the connecting rod will have large machines bosses. This side of the rod goes toward the front of the engine.

V-8 engines:

Assemble piston to connecting rod so that the assembly will be installed with the connecting rod bearing spurt hole "up." The rib on the edge of the rod cap will be on the same side as the conical boss on the connecting rod web. These ribs and bosses will be toward the other connecting rod on the same crankpin.

9. Replace by reversing above procedure.

FRONT SUSPENSION

The crossmember may be removed as an assembly, including wheels and brakes or after all components have been removed from the assembly.

CROSSMEMBER R & R

1. Raise front of car and install blocks or jack stands under the crossmember assembly in such a way that crossmember will be supported when free of the car.
2. Install suitable engine support.
3. Remove the wheels.
4. Disconnect steering linkage at tie rod ends.
5. Disconnect engine mounts at crossmember.
6. Remove ground straps from crossmember on both sides.
7. Disconnect brake lines at junc-

tion block on crossmember.
8. Disconnect fuel line from clip on the member.
9. Remove three crossmember retaining bolts on each side of crossmember.
10. Raise car to permit removal of crossmember assembly.
11. Reinstall by reversing removal steps plus bleeding brakes. Torque the three crossmember retaining bolts to 70-85 ft. lbs. Engine mount bolts to 30-45 ft. lbs. and the tie rod end nuts to 55-70 ft. lbs.

COIL SPRING REMOVE

1. Place car on suitable hoist which supports car at side rails. The front control arms must be allowed to swing free and positioned so that the control arms may be raised or lowered with the hoist.
2. Remove shock absorber.
3. Remove two strut rods to control arm nuts. The studs are pressed into the end of the strut rod.
4. Place stand under control arm and take up slightly on spring compression.
5. Remove lower ball stud from steering knuckle.
6. Carefully raise hoist until spring is free. Remove the spring.
7. Remove lower control arm inner pivot nut and bolt and remove the arm. To move steering linkage out of the way, turn wheel to the right.

COIL SPRING INSTALL

1. Set rubber insulator in place in crossmember spring tower.

2. Place spring on control arm.
3. Using jack stand under outer end of arm, raise control arm by lowering the hoist.
4. Install ball study into steering knuckle. Tighten nut to 55-70 ft. lbs. Torque.
5. Attach strut rod to control arm with two nuts and washers. Torque to 40-55 ft. lbs. The studs are pressed into the end of the strut rod.

   Note: Do not touch the large nuts at the grommet end of the strut rod as these control caster adjustment.
6. Install shock absorber.
7. Lower the vehicle to the floor. Bounce front end to neutralize the suspension, then tighten lower control arm. Pivot bolt and nut to 75-90 ft. lb. at curb height position.

UPPER CONTROL ARM REMOVE

1. Support car weight at outer end of lower control arm.
2. Remove wheel and tire.
3. Remove cotter pin and nut from upper control arm ball stud.
4. Remove the stud from the knuckle with tool J-6627 or suitable substitute.
5. Remove two nuts holding the upper control arm cross shaft to front crossmember. Count number of shims at each bolt.
6. Remove sheet metal access hole plugs opposite control arm retaining bolts. Remove bolts through access holes.

UPPER CONTROL ARM INSTALL

1. Install bolts through access holes and install upper control arm to crossmember.
2. Install two nuts and washers to the bolts holding the upper control arm shaft to front cross-

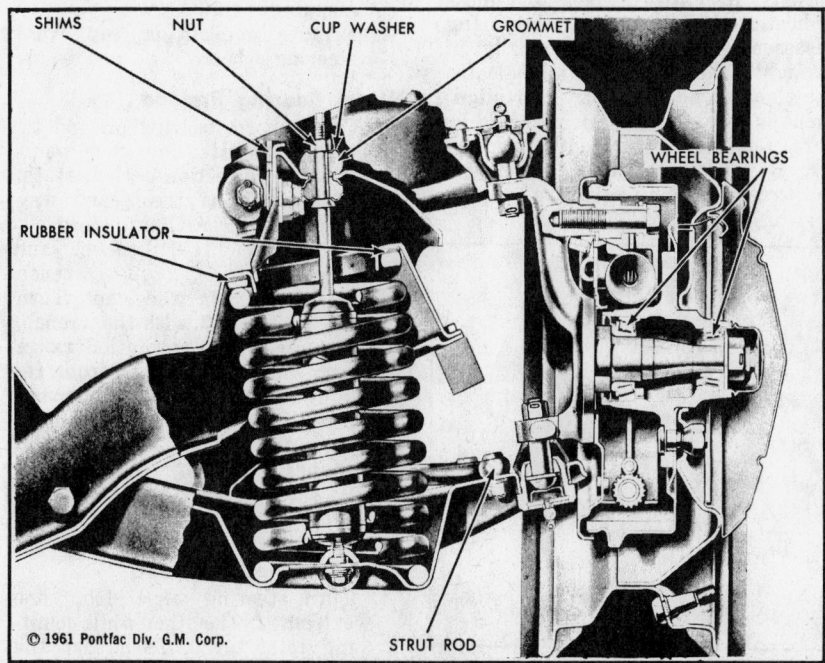

Front wheel and suspension

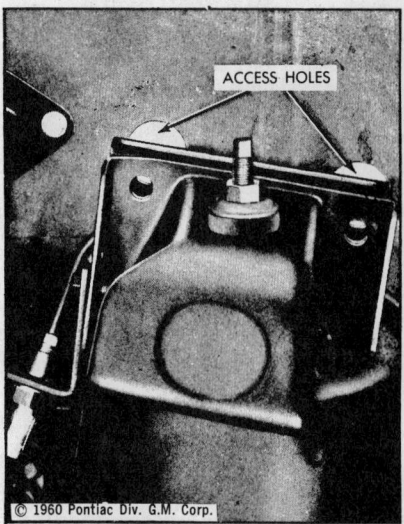

Control arm access holes

member. Install same number of shims as removed at each bolt. Torque bolts to 55-70 ft. lbs. Replace access hole plugs.

3. Install new rubber seal on ball joint stud and lubricate ball with chassis lube.
4. Install ball joint stud through knuckle, install nut and torque to 55-70 ft. lbs.
5. Install wheel and tire assembly.
6. Lower car to floor.
7. Bounce car to neutralize front end suspension and torque cross shaft nuts to 35-40 ft. lbs. Install cotter pins.
8. Be sure: Recheck Caster and Camber.

STEERING WHEEL AND HORN BUTTON

REMOVE

1. Disconnect the battery.
2. Lift ornament to remove.
3. Remove two nuts from steering shaft.
4. Remove spacer bushing.
5. Remove horn ring (deluxe wheel) or receiver cup (standard wheel).
6. Remove pivot ring (deluxe wheel) and bellville spring.
7. Remove contact assembly.
8. Remove steering wheel with puller.

INSTALL

1. Reverse removal procedure. Torque wheel attaching nut to 25-30 ft. lbs.
2. Reconnect battery.

STEERING GEAR— MANUAL

REMOVE

1. Remove steering wheel as previously outlined.
2. Remove steering gear housing-to-side rail attaching bolts.
3. Remove gear and shaft from car.

4. Remove plastic collar and felt seal from steering column.

INSTALL

1. Install shaft, with felt seal and plastic collar into steering column and secure gear to side rail with three bolts and spacers. Torque bolts to 70-90 ft. lbs. Use shims as necessary to align shaft with steering column jacket.
   Note: On power steering cars be sure to secure booster cylinder shaft bracket with two lower steering gear housing-to-side rail bolts.
2. Install felt seal and plastic collar into steering gear column jacket.
   Note: Install upper column bearing prior to installing seal and collar.

ADJUST IN CAR

There are two adjustments on the steering gear: Worm bearing preload and pitman shaft overcenter preload.

The wheel should turn smoothly through its entire range. Roughness indicates internal trouble requiring disassembly. Binding (especially in straight ahead position) indicates too tight an adjustment. Steer alignment or linkage adjustment should be corrected before bear adjustment.

1. Be sure the steering gear-to-cross members bolts are torqued to 70-90 ft. lbs.

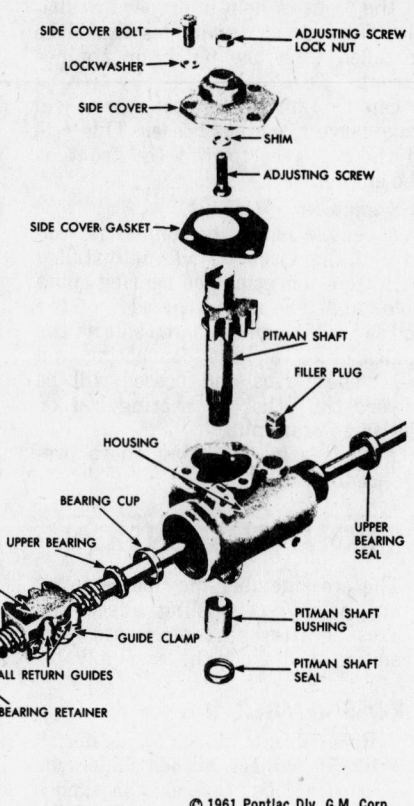

© 1961 Pontiac Div. G.M. Corp.

Steering gear—Manual

2. Disconnect intermediate rod from pitman arm by unscrewing end plug until bearings will release ball socket.
3. Turn steering wheel slowly from one extreme to the other. **Never turn the wheel hard against the stopping point.**
4. Remove emblem or cap from steering wheel.

Worm Bearing Preload

5. Check worm bearing preload by turning the steering wheel gently in one direction until it stops. This positions the gear away from the "High Point" load.
6. Attach a 15/16" socket and "inch-pounds" torque wrench to the steering wheel nut. Turn the worm shaft with the wrench, through a one revolution range from either extreme. Torque required to keep the wheel moving through either one—revolution extreme should be 2-7 inch pounds.
7. Be sure the gear case side cover bolts are torqued to 30 ft. lb.

Straight Ahead Preload

8. Turn steering wheel from one extreme to the other while counting total turns. Then turn the wheel back exactly midway. This

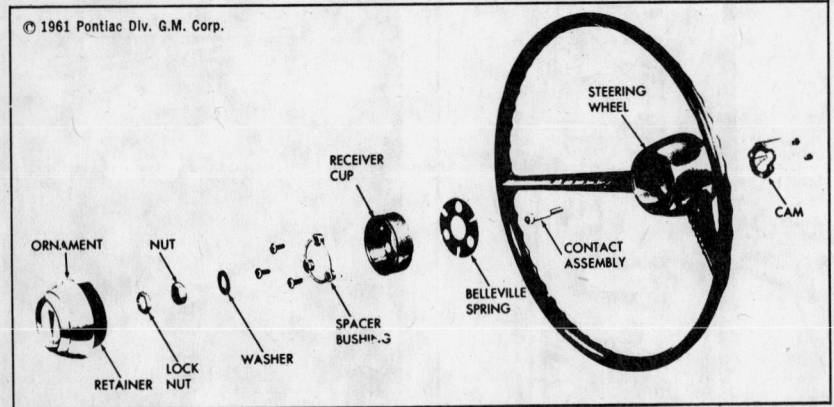

© 1961 Pontiac Div. G.M. Corp.

Standard steering wheel and horn contact

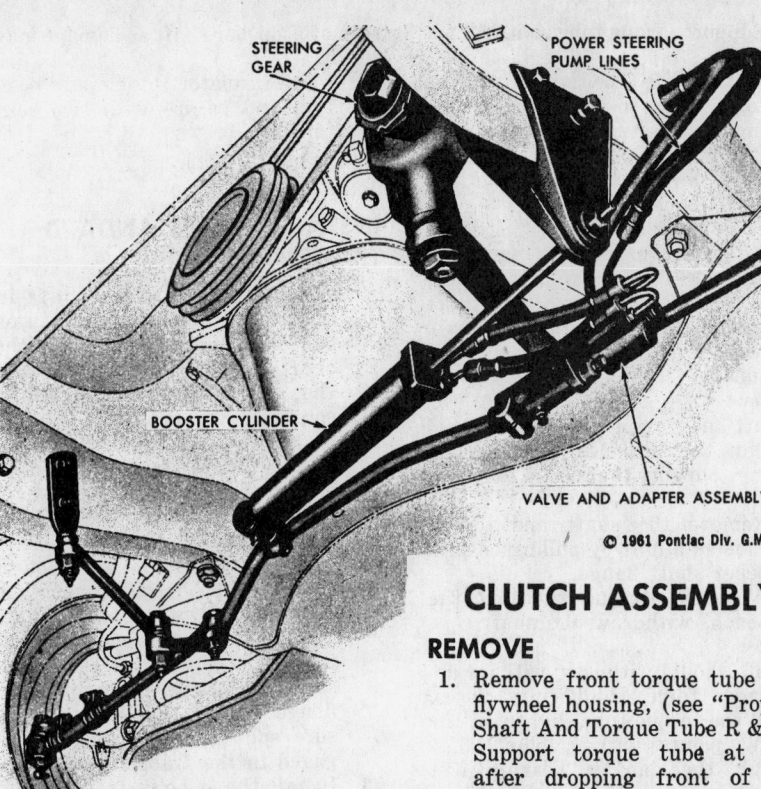

Power steering plan

positions the steering gear on the "High Spot" or straight ahead position. A slight "drag" should exist at this point.

9. Check torque used to rotate the wheel through the "High Point" range. Torque should be 4 to 8 inch pounds **higher than worm bearing preload**. The total "overcenter" pull should not exceed 13 inch pounds.

10. Adjust pitman shaft overcenter preload by loosening lock nut and turning pitman shaft wash adjuster screw to obtain 4 to 8 inch pounds higher than worm bearing preload.

11. Tighten lock nut. Rotate steering wheel through it's entire range. Then recheck for the maximum 13 inch pounds torque while passing through the straight ahead position.

STEERING GEAR— POWER

The hydraulic power steering system consist of a pulley driven vane type pump, an oil reservoir which is part of the pump assembly, a double-acting hydraulic power booster cylinder and a control valve.

The pump and linkage mounting plan is illustrated.

For detailed information on the power steering and pump, see Unit Repair Section—"Power Steering."

CLUTCH ASSEMBLY

REMOVE

1. Remove front torque tube from flywheel housing, (see "Propeller Shaft And Torque Tube R & R"). Support torque tube at front after dropping front of tube enough to permit access to the clutch assembly.
2. Disconnect accelerator linkage.
3. Remove cotter pin from clutch rod at fork end.
4. Remove washer and spring from clutch rod.
5. Remove "C" shaped retainer and washer, clutch rod-to-lever assembly.
6. Disconnect clutch anti-rattle spring from clutch rod.
7. Remove clutch rod from lever assembly and clutch fork.
8. Remove clutch housing cover.
9. Remove fork spring.
10. Remove fork cover plates.
11. Remove fork ball support bolt.
12. Remove retaining plate bolts.
13. Remove clutch drive shaft and plate.
14. Remove clutch release bearing support.
15. Remove release bearing.
16. Remove ball nut from release fork.
17. Remove clutch pressure plate and cover and the clutch driven plate.

   Caution: Index the pressure plate and cover to the flywheel for reference in installation location.

18. Remove clutch fork.

INSTALL

Install by reversing above procedure.

Reminders:

A. Install driven plate with longer flange toward engine.

B. Use clutch drive shaft as an alignment pilot while mounting and torquing the cover plate.

C. Torque cover plate to previously indexed flywheel to 20-35 ft. lbs.

D. Coat ball nut with wheel bearing grease and install the fork.

E. Install release bearing and support. Be sure to coat the support surface with a light coating of wheel bearing grease.

F. Lightly coat splines of clutch drive shaft with wheel bearing grease and install shaft and retaining plate. Torque bolts to 10-25 ft. lbs.

G. Install lubricated dust shields on release fork.

H. Install ball nut bolt and torque to 30-45 ft. lbs.

I. Install fork spring.

J. Install clutch housing cover. Torque bolts to 10-20 ft. lbs.

K. Lubricate and install clutch rod in lever and fork assemblies. Secure rod to lever with "C" shaped retainer.

L. Hook anti-rattle spring to clutch rod.

M. Install spring, washer and cotter pin at the fork end.

N. Connect accelerator linkage.

O. Adjust clutch pedal linkage.

LINKAGE ADJUST

1. Back off silencer bumper so it does not touch the pedal.
2. Adjust position of stop bracket

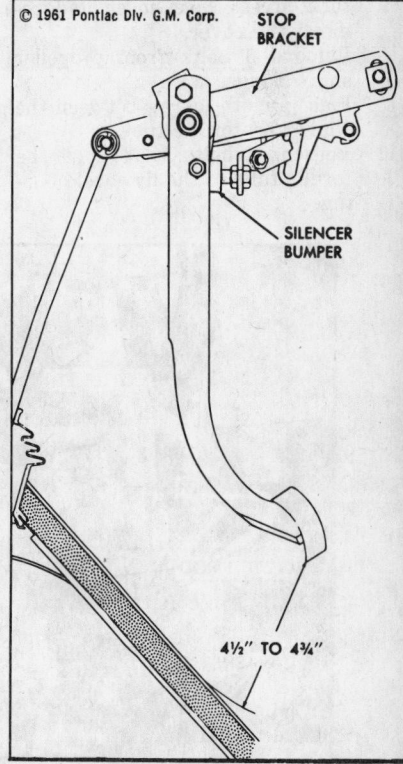

Clutch pedal clearance

TEMPEST

4 Cyl. Engine

4½ turns for installation of new plate.
3½ turns for adjustment with worn plate.

V-8 Engine

4½ turns for installation of new plate.
3 turns for adjustment with worn plate.

4. Tighten jam nuts to 6-10 ft. lbs. Torque.
5. Adjust silencer bumper so the overcenter lever is just lifted off stop pin. Tighten jam nuts to 6-10 ft. lbs. Torque.

PROPELLER SHAFT AND TORQUE TUBE

REMOVE WITH STANDARD TRANSMISSION

1. Remove bolts holding the shaft damper bearings.
2. Remove parking brake cable from torque tube.
3. Remove exhaust crossover pipe (V-8 engine).
4. Disconnect transmission control rod from transmission.
5. Remove three bolts from gearshift lever housing and remove housing and control rod.
6. Remove flywheel housing bottom cover.
7. Support rear of engine with stand or other suitable device.
8. Remove the screws from torque tube access hole cover and remove the cover.
9. Remove 6 bolts from propeller shaft flange.
10. Place a cloth or rag between the shaft and torque tube.
11. Loosen 6 bolts that hold the torque tube to the flywheel housing.

12. Support torque tube so it will not fall.
13. Remove the 6 bolts that hold the torque tube to the flywheel housing.
14. Pry torque tube and propeller shaft away and down from flywheel housing.
15. Place block of wood (3″ square) between transmission extension and car floor to position transmission for reassembly. Support torque tube with stand.
16. Remove 6 bolts connecting torque tube to transmission.

Caution:
Shaft and torque tube are now held only by the bearings in extension housing. Support the torque tube and shaft.

17. Remove the shaft and torque tube as a unit by pulling on propeller shaft flange.
18. With the torque tube on the bench, withdraw the shaft.

Note:
Shaft should withdraw without using undue force. If difficulty arises, spread the torque tube slightly at the bearing points with a blunt drift through the damper bearing bolt holes.

Note:
Propeller shaft damper bearings and shaft are serviced as an assembly. No attempt should be made to remove the bearings from the shaft.

Bearing Insulators R & R

1. Remove two screws from the bearing insulator retainer.
2. Remove rubber insulator from each bearing.
3. Install rubber insulator on each bearing, starting with bearing toward flange first.

Caution:
Do not scratch or nick coating or

skin of propeller shaft as damage may result.

4. Place insulator retainers in position and secure with two self-tapping screws.

INSTALL WITH STANDARD TRANSMISSION

1. Assemble propeller shaft in torque tube and place a cloth or rag between the front of the shaft and torque tube to protect the skin of the shaft against scratches or nicks.
2. Install the shaft into the transmission. Care must be used to engage the spline of the shaft into transmission and the journal diameter into transmission extension bearings so as not to damage the journal surface. A visual check of propeller shaft alignment into transmission extension is required and if necessary, the rearward on the front flange with a soft hammer. **Be sure splines are completely engaged in the transmission.**
3. Install the 6 bolts from torque tube to transmission extension. Torque to 30-45 ft. lbs.
4. Remove block of wood, between the transmission and the floor.
5. Insert propeller shaft in place on clutch drive shaft and secure with 6 bolts, just finger tight.
6. Remove rag from inside torque tube.
7. Secure torque tube to flywheel housing with 6 bolts, just finger tight.
8. Tighten bolts securing propeller shaft flange to clutch drive shaft and torque tube to flywheel housing to 30-45 ft. lbs.
9. Install eight screws in torque

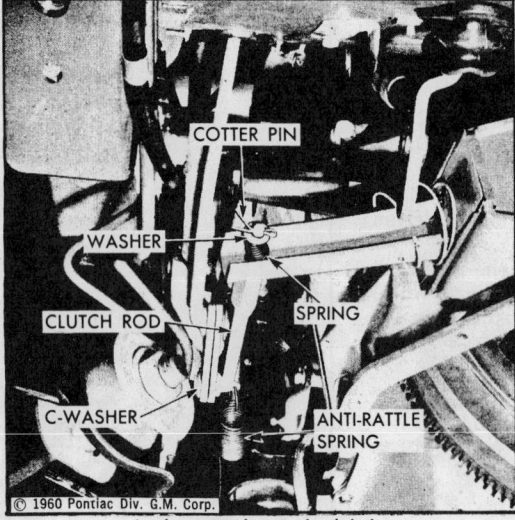
4 cyl. engine lower clutch linkage

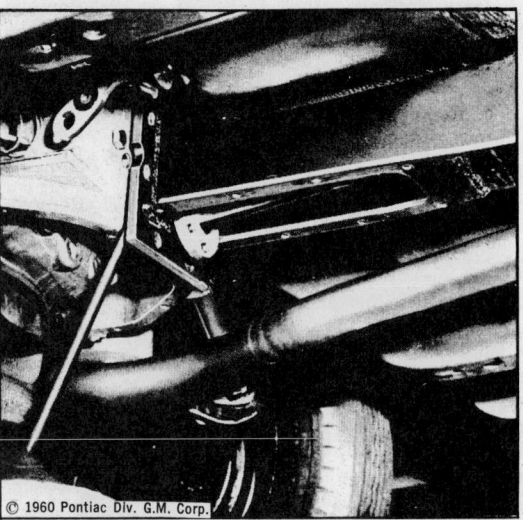
Pry torque tube and propeller shaft from clutch housing

tube access cover. Torque to 40-80 in. lbs.

10. Install and adjust gearshift housing and control rod, as described under "Gearshift Control."

11. Idle the engine about one minute to neutralize drive line bearings

12. Install and tighten damper bearing retainer bolts to 8-12 ft. lbs. torque.

REMOVE WITH AUTOMATIC TRANSMISSION
1961-62 All
1963—4 Cylinder

Remove the propeller shaft and torque tube from cars equipped with automatic transmission by following the same basic procedure as on standard transmission equipped cars.

1. Remove bolts holding propeller shaft damper bearings.

2. Remove parking brake cable and vacuum line from torque tube. T.V. linkage from transmission. Remove stabilizer bar.

3. Remove exhaust crossover pipe, V-8 engine only.

4. Remove flywheel bottom cover from engine.

5. Support rear of engine with stand or other suitable device.

6. Remove 6 bolts holding the propeller shaft to the flywheel.

7. Back out, about halfway, bolts that connect torque tube to flywheel housing.

8. Place cloth or rag between the shaft and torque tube to prevent damage to coating or skin on the propeller shaft.

9. Pry the propeller shaft flange to the rear far enough for pilot to clear recess in flywheel.

10. Remove 6 bolts holding torque

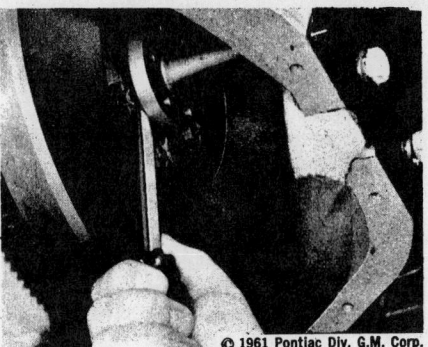

Removing Propeller Shaft From Flywheel

tube to flywheel housing.

11. Pull torque tube and propeller shaft down and away from flywheel housing.

12. Place 3" block of wood between the transmission extension and the car floor to position the extension for reassembly.

13. While supporting the torque tube, remove 6 bolts that hold the torque tube to the transmission.

14. Remove propeller shaft and torque tube as a unit by pulling on the shaft flange.

15. Place the assembly on a bench and pull propeller shaft out of torque tube.

INSTALL WITH AUTOMATIC TRANSMISSION
1961-62 All
1963—4 Cylinder

1. Install propeller shaft in torque tube and place a cloth or rag between front of propeller shaft and torque tube so that shaft coating will not be damaged.

2. Install propeller shaft into transmission. Care must be used to engage the spline into transmission and the journal diameter into the transmission extension bearings so as not to damage the journal surface. A visual check of shaft alignment into transmission is required and, if necessary, use a soft rubber hammer on the front shaft flange to move the shaft into place. Be sure splines are completely engaged in the transmission.

3. Install 6 bolts from torque tube to transmission. Torque to 30-45 ft. lbs.

4. Remove the block of wood from top of transmission extension.

5. Install propeller shaft in place on flywheel and secure with 6 bolts just finger tight.

6. Remove rag from inside torque tube.

7. Secure torque tube to flywheel housing with 6 bolts, just finger tight.

8. Torque bolts from shaft flange to flywheel and from torque tube to flywheel housing to 30-45 ft. lbs.

9. Install flywheel cover.

10. Install T.V. linkage to transmission and adjust.

11. Remove support from rear of engine.

12. Install exhaust crossover pipe (V-8 engine only).

13. Idle engine for about one minute to neutralize bearings.

14. Install and torque shaft bearing bolts and torque to 8-12 ft. lbs.

15. Install parking brake cable and vacuum line. Adjust parking brake cable.

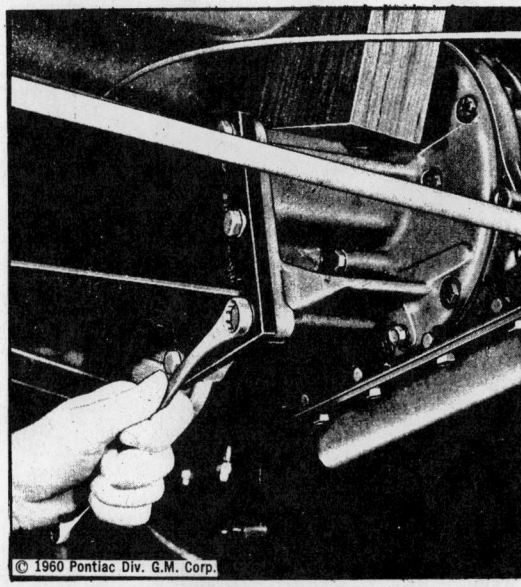

Stabilizing block, transmission to body

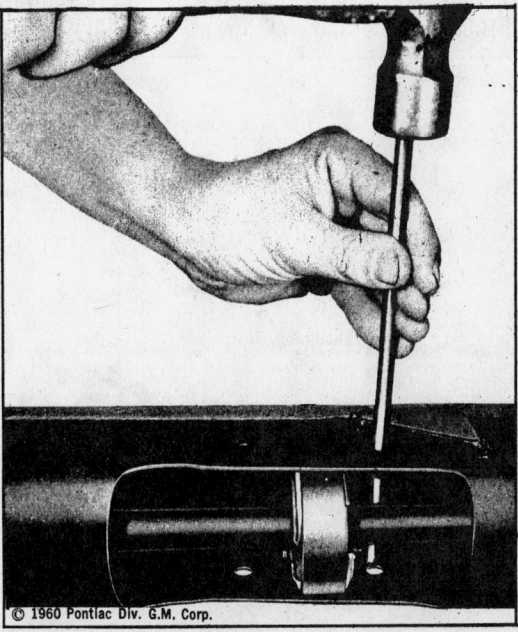

Spreading the torque tube

REMOVE—WITH AUTOMATIC TRANSMISSION

1963—V8 Engine

1. Raise car so that rear wheels hang free.
2. Drain transmission and remove filler tube.
3. Remove rear wheels and brake drums.
4. Remove four nuts securing axle shaft bearing retainer to brake backing plate.
5. Pull axle shafts outward far enough to remove universal joints from differential and carrier.
6. Disconnect speedometer cable, transmission control cable, downshift electrical connector, retaining clip, vacuum modulator line and parking lock control cable.
7. Remove parking brake cable from torque tube and disconnect exhaust system from rear tail pipe hanger.
8. Remove flywheel bottom cover.
9. Remove six bolts securing propeller shaft flange to flywheel.
10. Place a short piece of rubber hose or rag between propeller shaft and torque tube to prevent damage to coating on drive line.
11. Support torque tube and trans-axle separately.
12. Remove six bolts connecting torque tube to flywheel housing.
13. Remove six axle support crossmember to insulator bolts.
14. Disconnect rear lower control arms from differential housing by removing control arm to attachment bracket bolts.
15. Remove axle support crossmember from trans-axle assembly by lowering trans-axle slightly, permitting access to four attachment bolts.
16. Lower trans-axle until top of torque converter clears gasoline tank and pull rearward until propeller shaft emerges from flywheel housing.
17. Remove six bolts connecting torque tube to transmission extension.

<u>CAUTION</u>: **Propeller shaft and torque tube are now held in place only by the bearings in the transmission extension and must be supported to prevent bearing or propeller shaft damage.**

18. Remove propeller shaft and torque tube as a unit by pulling on propeller shaft flange.

<u>CAUTION</u>: **Pull propeller shaft straight out of transmission so that shaft will not bind in transmission or transmission extension.**

19. Place propeller shaft and torque tube on bench and pull propeller shaft out of torque tube.

INSTALL—WITH AUTOMATIC TRANSMISSION

1963—V8 Engine

1. Install propeller shaft in torque tube and place a short piece of rubber hose or rag between front of propeller shaft and torque tube so that coating on propeller shaft will not be damaged.
2. Support torque tube separately and secure torque tube to flywheel housing with six attachment bolts.
3. Remove rag or short piece of rubber hose from inside of torque tube.
4. Install propeller shaft in place on flywheel and secure front flange of propeller shaft to flywheel with six attachment bolts.
5. Replace trans-axle support crossmember on trans-axle assembly.
6. Coat spline generously with transmission fluid and take care introducing shaft into extension seal. Never allow weight of shaft to rest on seal. Install propeller shaft into transmission.
7. Replace six bolts connecting torque tube to transmission extension and tighten.
8. Replace four bolts attaching trans-axle support crossmember to rear crossmember by raising trans-axle until mounting holes in ends of trans-axle support line up with insulator bolt holes.
9. Connect control arms to differential housing. Tighten attachment bolts.
10. Replace transmission control cable, downshift electrical connector, retaining clip, speedometer cable, vacuum modulator line and parking lock control cable.
11. Install axle shaft universal joint splines in differential and carrier assembly using extreme care so as not to damage side cover oil seals.
   Coat lips of seal and splines with hypoid oil to prevent damage to seal.
12. Connect parking brake cable to torque tube and exhaust system at rear tail pipe hanger.
13. Replace transmission lubricant filler tube.
14. Install four nuts securing axle bearing retainer to brake backing plate via access hole in axle shaft flange.
15. Install wheels and brake drums and secure with five nuts.

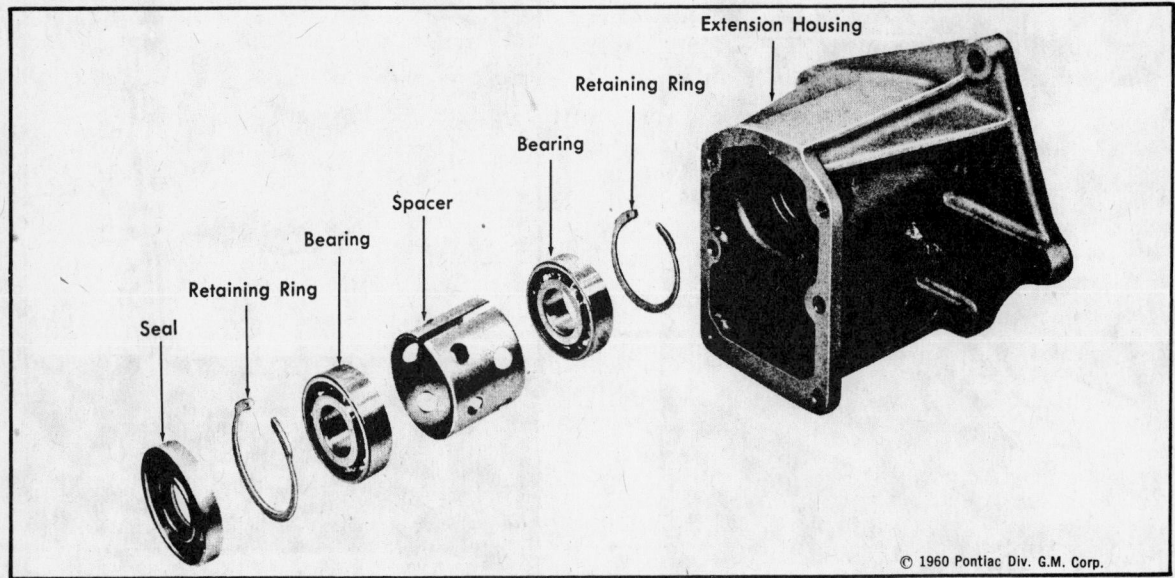

© 1960 Pontiac Div. G.M. Corp.

Transmission extension

16. Replace flywheel housing access plate.
17. Refill transmission with proper amount of recommended lubricant.
18. Remove all stands and supports and lower car.

TRANSMISSION EXTENSION ASSEMBLY

Contary to conventional form, this unit is attached to the forward end of the transmission but may be serviced **on the car.**

1. Remove propeller shaft and torque tube.
2. Remove transmission extension bearing seal.
3. Remove bearing retaining ring.
4. Remove bearings (2) and spacer.
5. Install by reversing above steps.

TRANSMISSION— DIFFERENTIAL ASSEMBLY

REMOVE ASSEMBLY

1. Raise car so that rear wheels hang free.
2. Drain both differential and carrier assembly and transmission.
3. Remove transmission filler tube (Automatic Transmission).
4. Remove rear wheels and brake drums.
5. Remove four nuts securing axle shaft bearing retainer to brake backing plate. Nuts are accessible through hole in axle shaft flange.
6. Pull axle shafts outward far enough to remove universal joints from differential and carrier assembly.
7. Disconnect speedometer cable.
8. Disconnect transmission control cable, downshift electrical connector, retaining clip, vacuum modulator line and parking lock control cable, (Automatic Transmission).
9. Support torque tube and transaxle separately.
10. Remove six bolts connecting torque tube to transmission extension.

CAUTION: Propeller shaft and torque tube are now held in place only by the bearings in the transmission extension and must be supported to prevent bearing or propeller shaft damage.

11. Remove six axle support crossmember to insulator bolts.
12. Disconnect rear lower control arms from attachment bracket on differential housing by removing control arm pivot bolts.

13. Disconnect shift tube from transmission (Synchro-Mesh Transmission).
14. Disconnect exhaust system from rear tail pipe hanger.
15. Remove axle support crossmember from trans-axle assembly by lowering trans-axle slightly, permitting access to four attachment bolts.
16. Separate trans-axle assembly from torque tube and propeller shaft.

CAUTION: Pull trans-axle assembly straight off propeller shaft so that propeller shaft will not bind in transmission.

17. Carefully lower trans-axle assembly from car.

INSTALL ASSEMBLY

1. Coat spline generously with transmission oil and take care introducing shaft into extension seal. Never allow weight of shaft to rest on seal. Install propeller shaft into transmission. Care must be used to engage spline of propeller shaft into transmission and journal diameter into transmission extension bearings so as not to damage journal surface. Visual check of propeller shaft alignment into transmission extension is required and if absolutely necessary, tap front flange lightly with a soft rubber hammer. Be sure splines are completely engaged in transmission.
2. Replace six bolts connecting torque tube to transmission extension and tighten.
3. Replace trans-axle support crossmember on trans-axle assembly. Tighten four attaching bolts.
4. Replace four bolts attaching trans-axle support crossmember to rear crossmember by raising trans-axle until mounting holes in ends of trans-axle support line up with insulator bolt holes.
5. Connect control arms to differential housing.
6. Connect exhaust system at rear tailpipe hanger.
7. Connect shift tube to transmission (Synchro-Mesh Transmission).
8. Connect speedometer cable.
9. Replace transmission control cable, downshift electrical connector, retaining clip, vacuum modulator line and parking lock control cable (Automatic Transmission).
10. Install axle shaft universal joint splines in differential and carrier assembly using extreme care so as not to damage side cover oil seal.

NOTE: Coat lip of seal and splines with hypoid oil to prevent damage to seal.

11. Install four nuts securing axle bearing retainer to brake backing plate via access hole in axle shaft flange.
12. Replace transmission lubricant filler tube (Automatic Transmission).
13. Install wheels and brake drums and secure with five nuts.

STANDARD TRANSMISSION

GEARSHIFT CONTROL REMOVE

1. Loosen clamp nut holding control rod to control rod coupling.
2. Remove bolts holding the gearshift lever and housing to the torque tube.
3. Move the gearshift lever and housing toward the front of car.
4. Remove cotter pin and clevis pin that holds the control rod coupling to manual shift shaft.
5. Remove coupling from shaft.
6. Remove boot.

GEARSHIFT CONTROL INSTALL

1. Position manual shift shaft in first gear position. Locate first

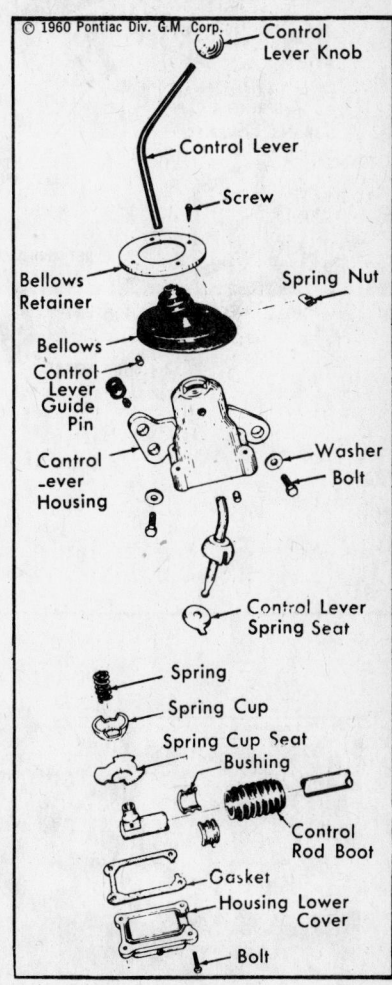

© 1960 Pontiac Div. G.M. Corp.

Control Lever Knob
Control Lever
Screw
Bellows Retainer
Spring Nut
Bellows
Control Lever Guide Pin
Control Lever Housing
Washer
Bolt
Control Lever Spring Seat
Spring
Spring Cup
Spring Cup Seat
Bushing
Control Rod Boot
Gasket
Housing Lower Cover
Bolt

Lever and housing

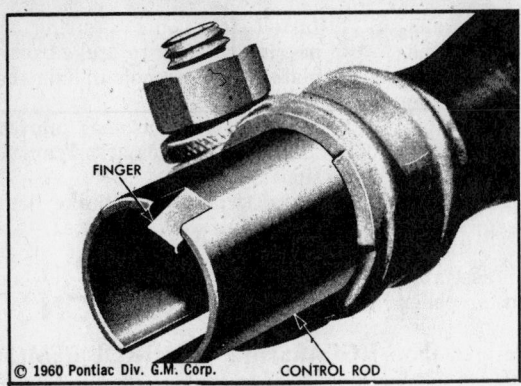

FINGER

© 1960 Pontiac Div. G.M. Corp.

CONTROL ROD

Coupling finger

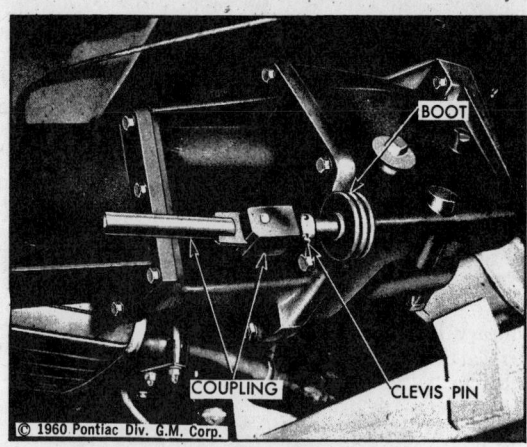

BOOT

COUPLING   CLEVIS PIN

© 1960 Pontiac Div. G.M. Corp.

Control rod coupling

1-2 DETENT BALL, SPRING AND CAP
TRANSMISSION CASE
CLUTCH GEAR BEARING RETAINING RING
SEAL
SNAP RING
SELECTOR SHAFT
SHIFTER SELECTOR
3-4 DETENT BALL, SPRING & CAP
TRANS. COVER GASKET
TRANS. CASE COVER

THRUST WASHER   COUNTERSHAFT GEAR
REVERSE IDLER GEAR
SHIFTER LEVER
REVERSE FORK
SHIFTER SHAFT
REVERSE IDLER GEAR SHAFT
SLEEVE   NEEDLE BEARINGS
SHAFT
BEARING WASHERS
THRUST WASHER

RING   WASHER   3-4 CLUTCH HUB & KEYS
CLUTCH GEAR BLOCKER RING
3-4 SLIDING SLEEVE   SNAP RING
PLUNGER, SPRING & PLUG
DETENT BALL, BALL SEAT, SPRING & PLUG
THIRD SPEED GEAR   SECOND SPEED GEAR
BLOCKER RING   RING
RADIAL NEEDLE BEARINGS   BLOCKER RING
MAIN SHAFT

REVERSE SHIFTER HEAD
DETENT SPRING & BALL
ROLL PIN
RETAINING PIN
RETAINING PIN
3-4 SHIFT FORK
3-4 SHIFT FORK SHAFT
INTERLOCK
INTERLOCK PIN
1-2 SHIFT FORK SHAFT
INTERLOCK
REVERSE SHIFTER HEAD SHAFT
1-2 CLUTCH HUG & KEYS
1-2 SHIFT FORK
SLEEVE
1-2 SLIDING SLEEVE   RING
FIRST SPEED GEAR
BLOCKER RING
THRUST WASHER
BEARING
RETAINER RING
SNAP RING
BEARING RETAINER

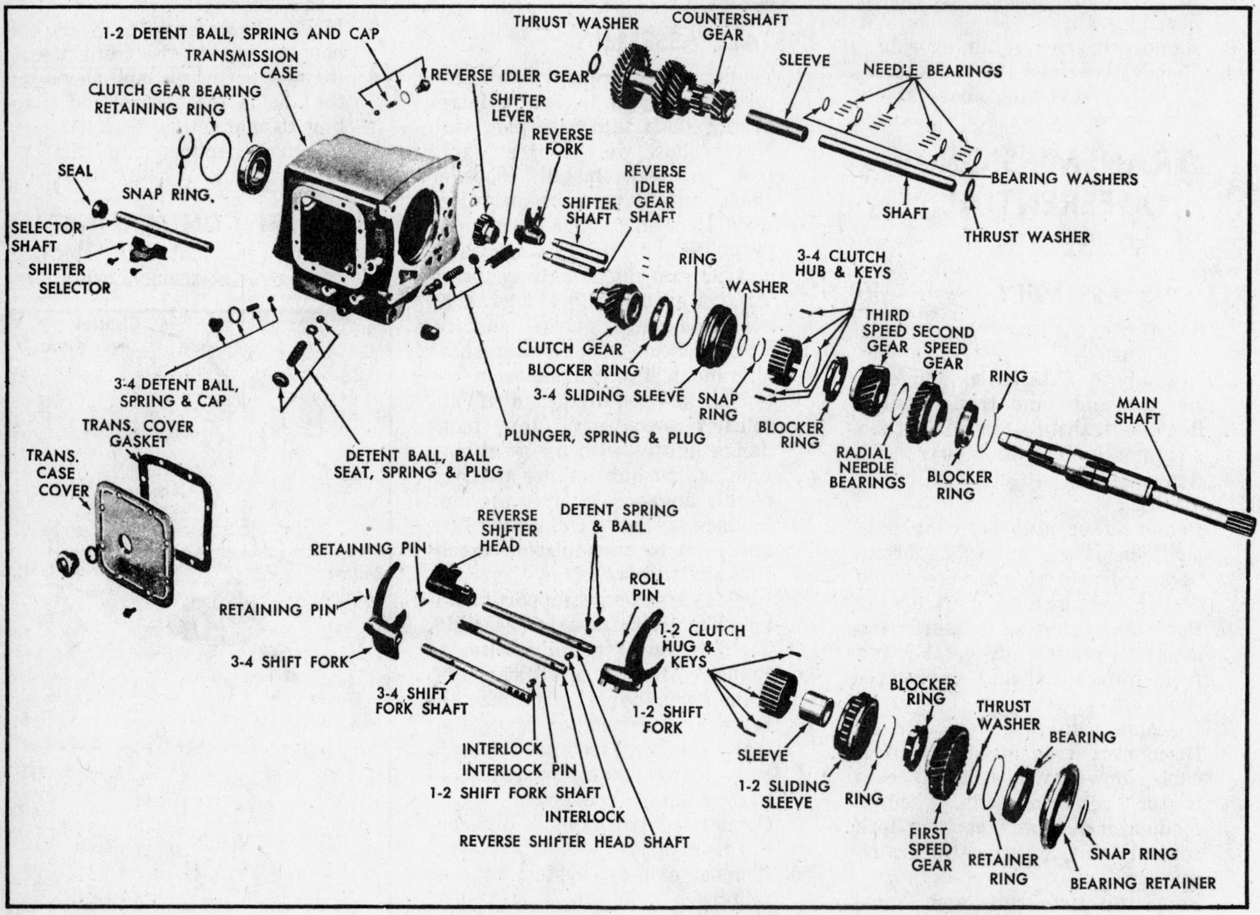

Exploded View—Four Speed Transmission

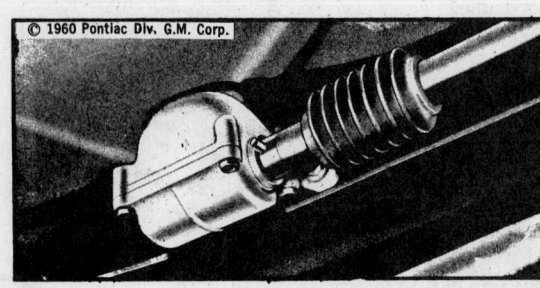

© 1960 Pontiac Div. G.M. Corp.

Gearshift lever and housing location

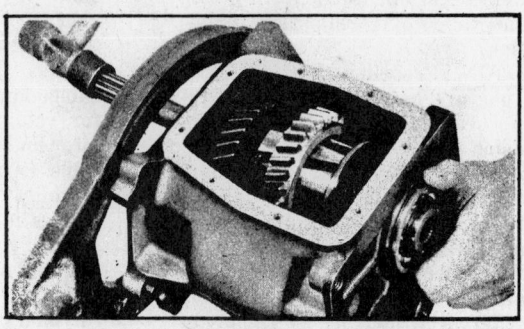

Drive out clutch gear and bearing

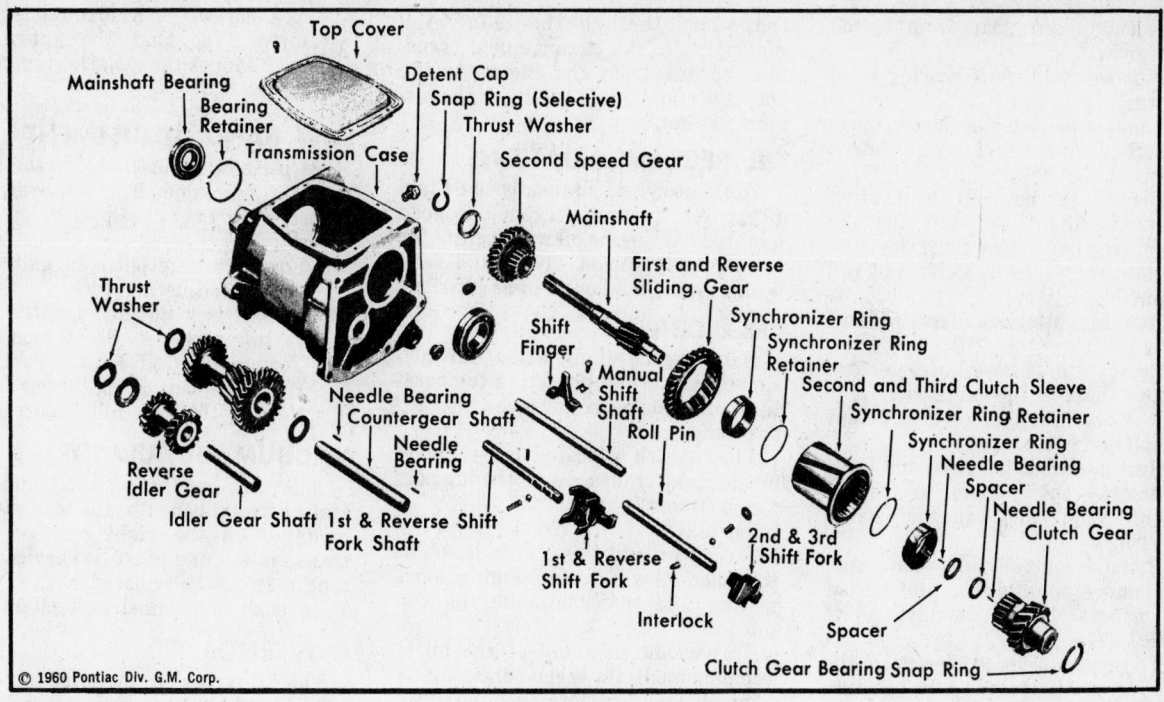

Synchro-mesh transmission

gear position in transmission by placing shift in "Neutral," turn counterclockwise, and pull shaft to full forward position.

2. Install shift shaft and control rod coupling boot.
3. Install control rod coupling on manual shift shaft and secure with clevis pin and cotter pin.

Note: Slot in control rod coupling should be in "UP" position.

4. Slide control rod on rod coupling with control rod finger in coupling slot.
5. Secure gear shift lever and housing to torque tube. Torque bolts to 10-15 ft. lbs.

6. Install pin in control rod alignment hole and push control rod forward into gearshift lever and housing, until pin hits flange of housing.
7. Secure control rod to coupling by torquing clamp nut to 10-20 ft. lbs.
8. Remove pin from control rod alignment hole and position the rod boot over housing shoulder.

TRANSMISSION DISASSEMBLE

1. Mount transmission on a holding fixture.
2. Remove filler plug.

3. Remove top cover and gasket.
4. Remove snap ring from main shaf groove at rear of case.
5. Drive out clutch gear bearing and clutch gear by driving on main shaft. Remove clutch gear and bearing.
6. Continue to drive main shaft out of transmission and remove thrust washer.

Caution: Be sure synchronizer ring tangs are aligned with the main shaft splines, otherwise damage to ring and shaft will occur.

7. Remove second speed gear, first and reverse, and second and third speed clutch sleeve from the case through top cover hole. Remove

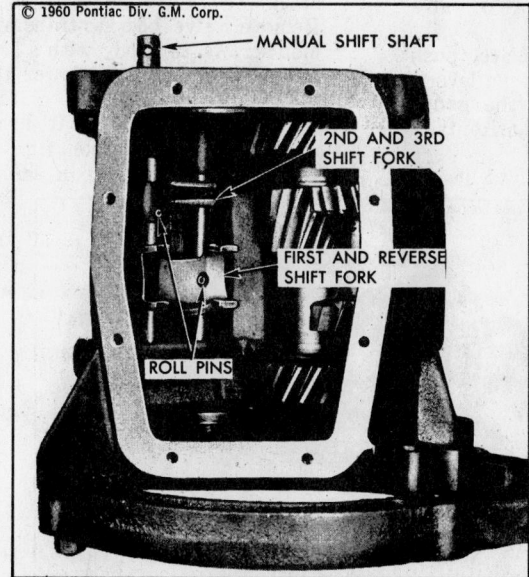

Shift forks

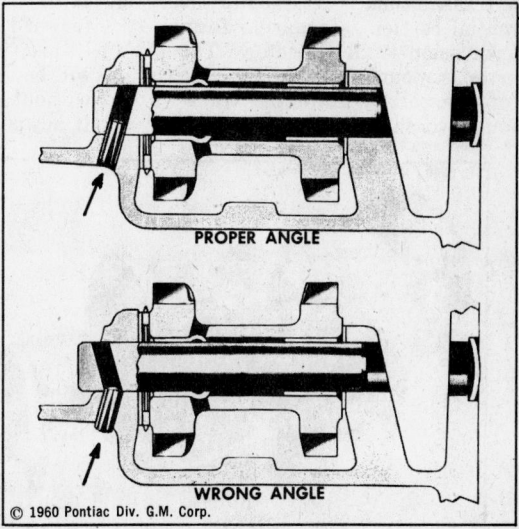

Reverse idler and locking plan

645

second speed gear from clutch sleeve.

8. Remove main shaft bearing from case.
9. Remove detent plug and remove second and third gear detent spring and ball.
10. Drive out the roll pin holding second and third shift fork to shaft. Then drive shaft forward and remove fork, shaft and roll pin.
11. Remove interlock from detent cavity.
12. Remove first and reverse fork and shaft in the same way.
13. Remove first and reverse detent ball and spring.
14. Remove two cap screws and locks holding shift finger to manual shift shaft and pull shaft from case.
15. Remove manual shift shaft seal.
16. Remove countergear and thrust washers with dummy shaft #J-5777.
17. To remove reverse idler, drive the reverse idler shaft lock pin into the shaft far enough to clear the case. Then drive the gear shaft out of the case with a drift from the through hole at rear of case.
18. Remove caged needle bearing and thrust washer used at the rear of the reverse idler gear.
19. Remove main shaft bearing retaining ring from the case.

TRANSMISSION ASSEMBLE

Reverse disassemble procedure.

AUTOMATIC TRANSMISSION

The automatic transmission consists of an air cooled, three element torque converter and a two speed planetary transmission.

The transmission is attached to the differential carrier assembly to form a transmission—axle assembly. The converter is mounted on the opposite side of the carrier from the transmission. Two shafts run, one within the other, through the differential pinion shaft. This arrangement transmits torque from the engine to the converter and back to the transmission assembly.

OIL RECOMMENDATIONS

Use Automatic Transmission Fluid (Type A). In an emergency, a good quality 20W engine oil will operate for a temporary period. Drain and refill with regular fluid as soon as possible.

Check Oil Level

Have engine idling with transmission oil at normal operating temperature and the selector lever in "N" position.

The dipstick is located under a plate in the right front area of the luggage compartment.

Important:

Do not overfill this transmission as too much oil will cause foaming, overheating and malfunctioning of the unit.

No periodic draining of the oil is recommended. However, draining is accomplished by loosening the filler tube attaching nut in the oil pan.

THROTTLE VALVE LINKAGE ADJUSTMENT

Due to design peculiar to this transmission and controls the throttle valve linkage adjustments are covered in the "Fuel System" department of this text, under "Carburetor—throttle valve linkage adjustment.

SHIFT LINKAGE ADJUSTMENT

1. Drain transmission oil and remove pan.
2. Place range selector indicator in "D" position.
3. Insert tool into manual valve bore with tab of gauge "UP" so it engages forward port of valve body.
4. With the gauge in place, push forward on manual valve levers. If properly adjusted the gauge will be held in place horizontally without support.
5. If adjustment is required, loosen lock screw, push manual levers forward so that the gauge is held in position. Retighten lock screw.

LOW BAND ADJUSTMENT

No periodic adjustment of the low band is recommended, however, if necesary it may be performed as follows:

1. Lower transmission to gain access to adjusting screw.
2. Loosen lock nut and tighten adjusting screws to 35-45 inch lbs. Torque, back off 4 turns exactly. Hold the adjusting screw and tighten the lock nut securely.

VACUUM MODULATOR

This unit can be removed and installed from beneath the car. It is mounted on the right side of the transmission and must be serviced as a unit. It can be replaced with a thin 1" wrench or channel lock pliers.

GOVERNOR

The governor is mounted on the left side of the transmission and can be removed from underneath the car. It is attached to the transmission with a tab and lock screw.

VALVE BODY AND LOW SERVO—REMOVE

1. Drain transmission and remove filler pipe.
2. Disconnect throttle valve rods from T.V. lever on transmission.
3. Remove oil pan by removing 14 screws.
4. Remove retainer screw, oil screw and "O" ring.
5. Loosly install a servo piston retainer. (This is improvised with any short stiff piece of strip steel.)
6. Remove valve body-to-transmission screws, tap body with a soft hammer are carefully lower the valve body about 1/16". Rotate retainer into place so it holds servo piston hub. Then tighten the retainer with a pan screw.

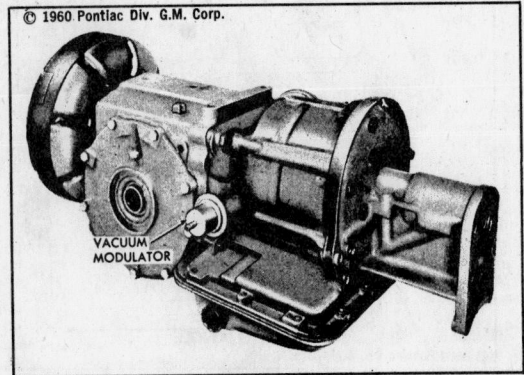

Vacuum modulator

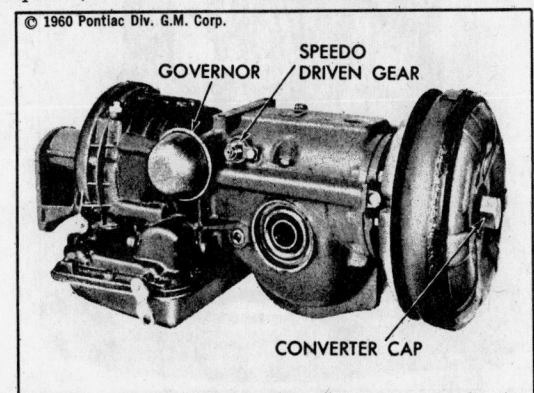

Speedometer gear and governor

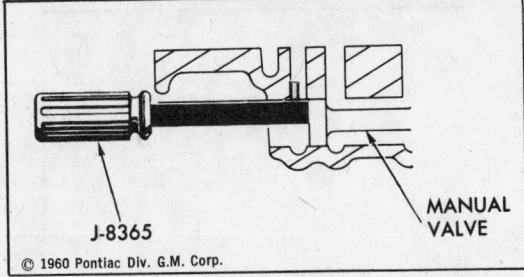

Manual valve gauge

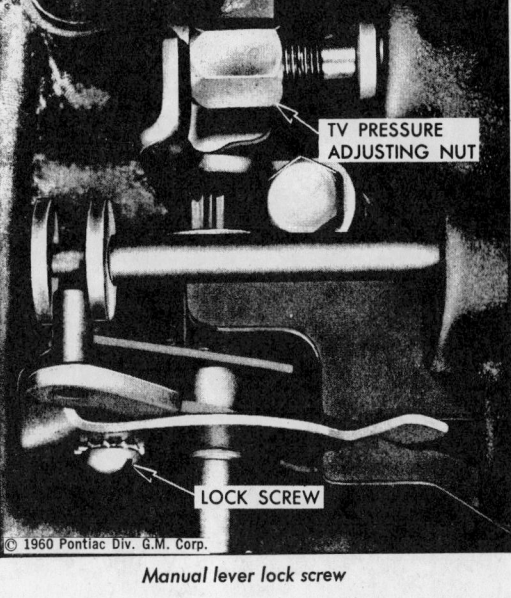

Manual lever lock screw

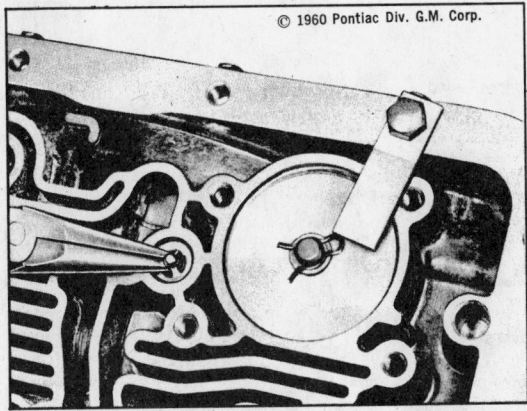

Servo piston retainer

This prevents the servo piston from slipping down out of it's bore and losing contact with low band apply components.

7. Remove valve body and gasket.
8. If necessary, remove downshift timing valve and install new valve.
9. If necessary to remove low servo, tighten low band adjusting screw fully. Remove retainer and pull downward on piston shaft with screwdriver.
10. If necessary to replace, the float air bleed ball can be removed by removing retainer with needle nose pliers.

VALVE BODY DISASSEMBLE

1. Remove manual valve.
2. Remove two clutch head screws holding hydraulic modulator valve body and separate modulator body from main valve body.
3. Remove pressure regulator valve spring retainer, spring and pressure regulator valve.
4. From hydraulic modulator body, remove rear pump priming ball and front and rear pump, check valves and springs. Remove hydraulic modulator valve.
5. Drive roll pin from modulator valve body and remove line pressure limiting valve spring and valve from their bore in modulator valve body.
6. Remove two remaining clutch head screws separate transfer plate and gasket from main valve body.

7. To remove low drive shift valve components, remove retainer ring, then release pressure and remove low drive sleeve, spring seat, and inner and outer springs. Lightly tap main valve body with rubber hammer to remove low drive shift valve from it's bore.
8. To remove T.V. valve parts, pry the retaining pin out of the main valve body. Remove detent valve assembly and throttle valve spring. Complete disassembly of valve body by removing "E" ring from throttle valve and removing throttle valve from main valve body.

Valve Body Assemble

1. Drop line pressure limiting valve into bore of modulator, then install spring. Compress spring slightly and install roll pin.
2. Install modulator valve in it's bore in the modulator valve body.
3. Place rear pump priming ball into modulator valve body, then place front and rear pump check valves and springs into modulator body.
4. Lower transfer plate onto assembled components in modulator valve body so as not to knock front and rear pump check valves from their springs. Secure transfer plate to modulator valve body with two clutch head screws. Tighten screws to 38-50 inch pounds.
5. Install low drive shift valve parts in main valve body. Place low

drive shift valve into it's main valve body bore. Then assemble inner and outer low drive springs and place them in the bore. Put spring seat over open end of sleeve, and insert this assembly into bore in main valve body, compressing inner and outer springs and secure by installing retainer ring.
6. Install throttle valve into it's bore in main valve body, then install locating ring in groove in throttle valve. Be sure throttle valve is fully seated in it's bore.
7. Place throttle valve spring and detent assembly in throttle valve bore. Depress detent valve assembly and secure to valve body by tapping retaining pin into main valve body.
8. Using a new transfer plate-to-main valve body gasket, apply a light coating of petroleum jelly to main body and install gasket onto the valve body.
9. Install pressure regulator valve in main valve body with spring and spring retainer. Fully compress pressure regulator valve spring so that spring retainer enters bore of main valve body. Position main valve body onto assembled transfer plate—hydraulic modulator body, align mounting screw holes in transfer plate and main valve body. Secure with two remaining clutch head screws. Torque screws to 38-50 inch pounds.
10. Install manual valve in main valve body.

VALVE BODY AND LOW SERVO—INSTALL

1. Install low servo piston and re-

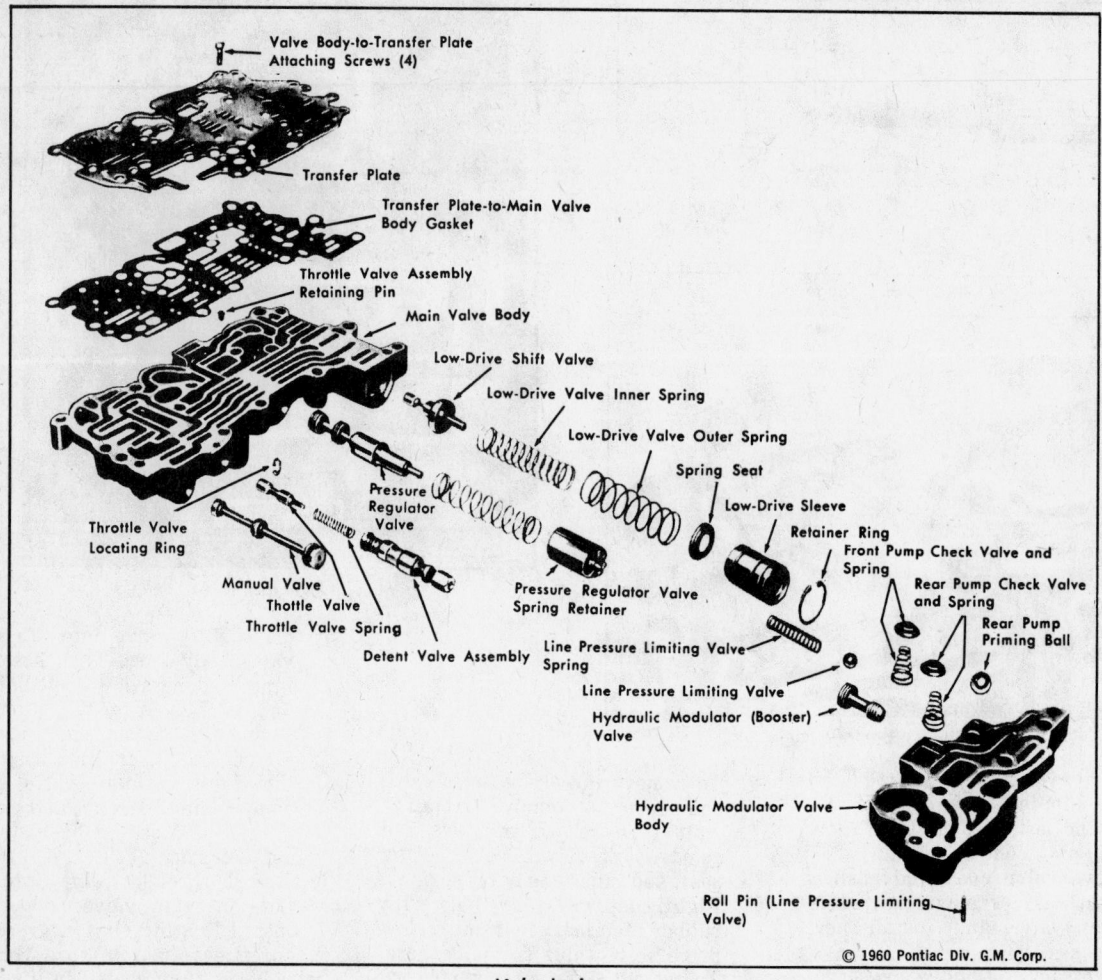

Valve Body-to-Transfer Plate Attaching Screws (4)

Transfer Plate

Transfer Plate-to-Main Valve Body Gasket

Throttle Valve Assembly Retaining Pin

Main Valve Body

Low-Drive Shift Valve

Low-Drive Valve Inner Spring

Low-Drive Valve Outer Spring

Spring Seat

Low-Drive Sleeve

Retainer Ring

Front Pump Check Valve and Spring

Rear Pump Check Valve and Spring

Rear Pump Priming Ball

Throttle Valve Locating Ring

Pressure Regulator Valve

Manual Valve

Thottle Valve

Throttle Valve Spring

Detent Valve Assembly

Pressure Regulator Valve Spring Retainer

Line Pressure Limiting Valve Spring

Line Pressure Limiting Valve

Hydraulic Modulator (Booster) Valve

Hydraulic Modulator Valve Body

Roll Pin (Line Pressure Limiting Valve)

© 1960 Pontiac Div. G.M. Corp.

Valve body

turn spring in bore in transmission and engage notch in piston shaft with low band apply strut, loosening low band screw slightly to permit piston ring to seat in case bore and permit installation of valve body.

2. Install retainer to hold servo piston in bore.
3. Position new gasket on valve body.
4. Position valve body in transmission indexing on dowels, then remove retainer. Be sure manual valve indexes with pin on inner shaft lever.
5. Secure valve body with 20 screws. Torque to 9-11 ft. lbs.
6. Install oil pick-up screen and "O" ring in valve body and secure with screw.
7. Position manual valve lever in full reverse so it is held securely by wedging devile in transfer plate. Engage shift control cable and secure.
8. Using new gasket, install the oil pan and torque attaching bolts to 3-4 ft. lbs.
9. Tighten filler tube attaching nut, then refill transmission as pre-

scribed.
10. Readjust low band as previously outlined.

AUTOMATIC TRANSMISSION— REMOVED

DISASSEMBLY

1. Remove converter cover cap assembly. Remove converter retaining ring and converter.

<u>Note:</u>

Reinstall cap on converter after removal and place converter cap side down to retain oil.

2. Remove speedometer drive gear.
3. Remove governor assembly and "O" ring.
4. Remove turbine drive shaft.
5. Remove remaining screws that hold the transmission to the differential carrier assembly.
6. Separate transmission and differential carrier.
7. Remove vacuum modulator and modulator valve.
8. Mount transmission in a holding fixture.

9. Loosen low band adjusting screw jam nut and fully tighten low band adjusting screw.
10. Remove 12 housing attaching screws.
11. Using a soft hammer, tap off extension housing.
12. Remove thrust washer and coupling.
13. Remove converter pump drive shaft. It is not necessary to remove drive key unless it is to be replaced.
14. Remove thrust washer from pump body.
15. Remove pump gears. Stack them so they may be reassembled with same face up.
16. Remove pump body and gasket.
17. Remove pump body-to-clutch drum thrust washer.
18. Loosen low band adjusting screw and remove low band, apply strut and reaction strut.
19. Remove clutch drum assembly.
20. Remove clutch drum-to-sun gear thrust washer.
21. Remove panet carrier assembly from ring gear.
22. Remove ring gear from engagement with reverse clutch plates.

23. Remove clip mounted on thick reverse reaction plate between the ends of reverse clutch snap ring and remove snap ring.
24. Remove thick reverse reaction plate, three drive plates (faced) and three reaction plates (steel).
25. Rotate transmission to a horizontal position and remove rear pump and reverse piston mounting bolts at rear of case.
26. Remove rear pump and reverse piston assembly.
27. Remove rear pump wear plate.

ASSEMBLY

1. Install transmission case in holding fixture.
2. Install two #J-3387-2 guide pins in rear pump bolt holes, then install rear pump wear plate on guide pins.
3. Insert rear pump and reverse piston with guide pins into the case. Insert a length of .010" shim stock between piston outer seal and case. Run shim stock around entire outer edge of seal to seat the seal.
4. Remove guide pins and install five rear pump mounting bolts. Torque to 9-11 ft. lbs.

Note:

Check rear pump for freedom to turn before proceeding with assembly.

5. Install reverse clutch drive and reaction plates alternately, starting with a steel plate and finishing with a faced plate. Notched lug in each steel plate is installed so it is at top of groove at 4 o'clock position in the case. Install the thick reaction plate. It has a rectangular "Dimple" on it's lug which engages the 4 o'clock case groove.
6. Install reverse clutch plate retainer ring in such a way that the open ends of the ring are at 12 o'clock position, then insert the retainer ring clip on thick reaction plate between the ends of snap ring.
7. With rear of transmission case downward, align internal lands and grooves of reverse face plates.
8. Engage ring gear to reverse drive plates. Engagement must be made by feel while moving the drive plates laterally.
9. Install planetary unit with a twisting motion to engage planet gears with ring gear. Be sure to engage two rear pump drive lugs on planet hub with grooves in rear pump drive gear.
10. Install thrust washer on captive input sun gear in planetary gear

set with flange of thrust washer toward front of transmission.
11. Install clutch drum assembly, using a slight twist to engage low sun gear to the planet gears in the planetary gear set.
12. Turn transmission to a horizontal position, then install the low band, apply strut, and reaction strut. When low band linkage is all installed, tighten low band adjusting screw to prevent band struts from falling out of place. Then shake clutch drum slightlly to center band and linkage.
13. Replace original thrust washer or new washer of same thickness if original one is damaged. Final end play adjustment will be performed at governor drive gear prior to assembly of transmission to carrier.
14. Install new front pump gasket, then locate and install front pump body.
15. Install inner and outer pump gears with drive notches on inner gear facing up, and outer gear with same face up as removed.
16. Install thrust washer in pump body.
17. Install converter pump drive shaft.
18. Position coupling on end of pump drive shaft.
19. Position coupling thrust washer in extension housing. Washer is retained by light press fit.
20. Install new square-cut seal ring in extension housing. Then position extension housing, dip bolt heads in oil impervious sealer and install mounting bolts loosely. Tighten outer bolts alternately, then torque them to 15-20 ft. lbs. Then tighten the five inner bolts and torque the same amount. Check pump for freedom of operation before proceeding.
21. Adjust low band by tightening

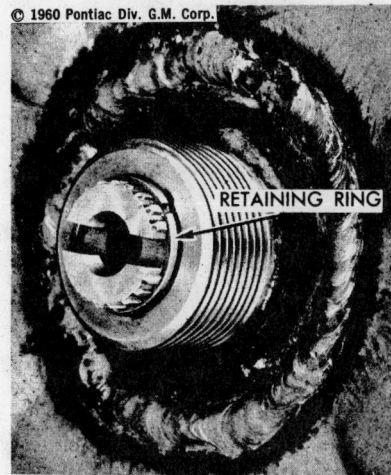

Converter Retaining Ring

Unit Mounted in Holding Fixture

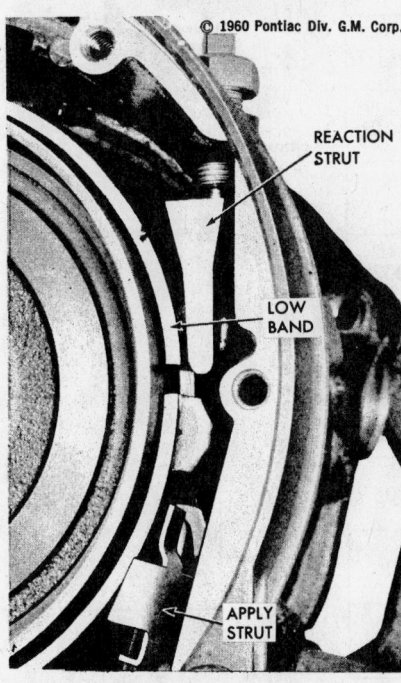

Low Band and Struts

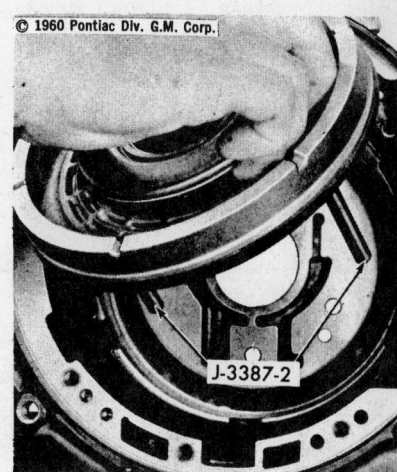

Installing Rear Pump and Reverse Piston

© 1960 Pontiac Div. G.M. Corp.

4 O'CLOCK GROOVE

NOTCH

Installing Reverse Clutch Reaction Plates

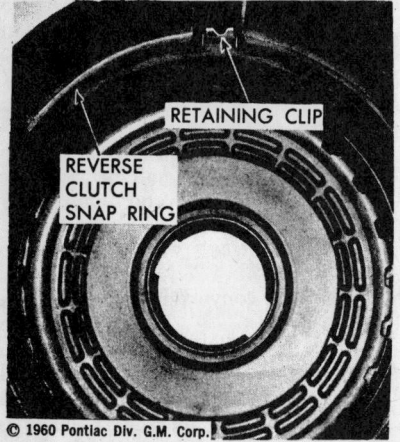

RETAINING CLIP

REVERSE CLUTCH SNAP RING

© 1960 Pontiac Div. G.M. Corp.

Snap Ring Retaining Clip

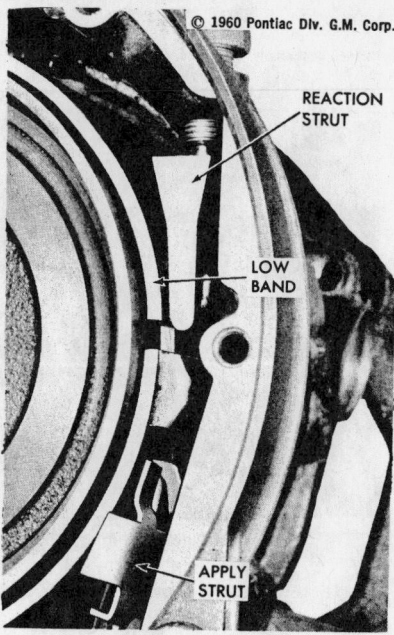

© 1960 Pontiac Div. G.M. Corp.

REACTION STRUT

LOW BAND

APPLY STRUT

Location of Apply and Reaction Struts

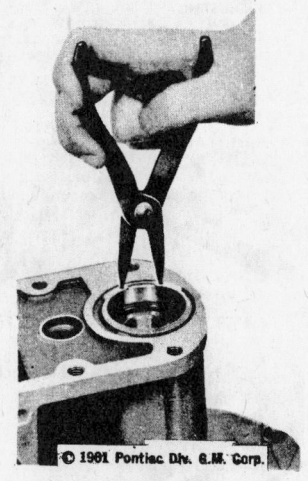

© 1961 Pontiac Div. G.M. Corp.

Removing Bearing Retainer Ring

© 1960 Pontiac Div. G.M. Corp.

J-8364

Zeroing the Indicator on Planet Carrier Hub

J-8364

© 1960 Pontiac Div. G.M. Corp.

Measuring for Shim Thickness Requirements

the adjusting screw to 40 ± 5 inch-lbs. Then back off the adjusting screw 4 full turns. Hold screw and lock up the jam nut.

Note:

Prior to reassembly of the carrier to the transmission it is necessary to determine required thickness of shim pack to be installed at front face of governor drive gear.

22. Follow this procedure:

A. Install dial indicator on support #J-8364 and install 3" indicator extension.

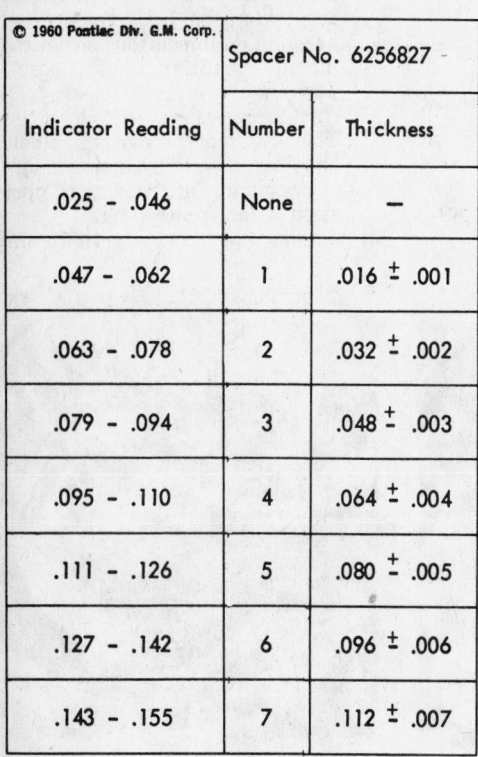

© 1960 Pontiac Div. G.M. Corp.

Indicator Reading	Spacer No. 6256827	
	Number	Thickness
.025 – .046	None	–
.047 – .062	1	.016 ± .001
.063 – .078	2	.032 ± .002
.079 – .094	3	.048 ± .003
.095 – .110	4	.064 ± .004
.111 – .126	5	.080 ± .005
.127 – .142	6	.096 ± .006
.143 – .155	7	.112 ± .007

Spacer Thickness Chart

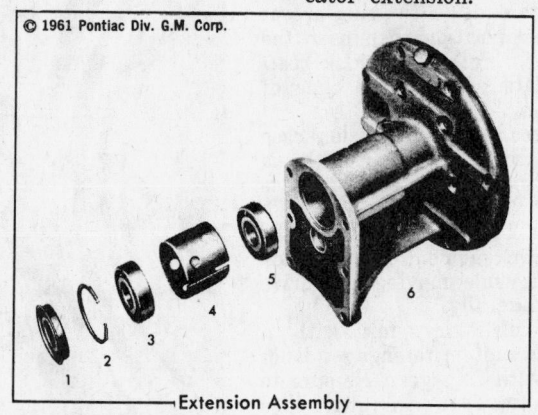

© 1961 Pontiac Div. G.M. Corp.

─ Extension Assembly ─

1. Seal
2. Retainer Ring
3. Bearing Assembly
4. Bearing Spacer
5. Bearing Assembly
6. Extension Housing

Assembling Transmission to the Carrier

Installing Spacers

Installing Converter and Turbine Shaft

B. Without gasket, place support on rear pump cavity surface of transmission case with transmission on front end so that dial indicator tip rests on planet carrier hub. Adjust indicator on support #J-8364 so as to permit maximum indicator travel and set indicator dial to zero.

Note:

Front of transmission must face downward when indicator is zeroed.

C. Slowly lift support and indicator off transmission and note its range of needle movement from zero. Properly positioned on support, indicator should not deflect more than .050″ (one half turn) when removed; otherwise, raise or lower dial indicator on support post as required and again zero gauge as described in step B.

D. Now place support #J-8364 and dial indicator on governor gear without spacers on the differential carrier pinion shaft and lower support slowly so that revolutions of indicator needle can be counted. Measurement starts when the indicator needle again reaches zero. Fully depress support on governor gear, note in-

dicator reading and refer to chart for spacers to be installed on governor gear.

E. Install spacers selected on the governor gear, then check that proper total thickness has been installed by again measuring with the indicator combination as described in step D. If shim stack is correct, indicator reading will now be between .025″—.038″; otherwise add or remove spacers until reading is within this range.

23. Apply a new gasket to either carrier or rear face of transmission with petroleum jelly.

24. Remove transmission from holding fixture and align carrier and transmission on a flat surface, then guide pump shaft through differential carrier so as not to damage bushing in pinion. Engage splines of the pinion shaft with planet carrier internal splines in transmission.

25. Install governor and "O" ring seal and secure transmission to carrier with four screws. Drive two screws from the carrier side first to reduce change of cocking

mating surfaces of the transmission and carrier. Torque screws to 30-35 ft. lbs.

26. Install turbine shaft into converter and then install converter and turbine shaft. It is necessary to use caution in engaging splines in converter and at end of turbine shaft.

27. Install converter retaining ring on the protruding end of the turbine shaft.

28. Install converter cap and seal. Torque to 60-70 ft. lbs. Use a strap wrench to hold the converter while tightening.

29. Install modulator valve and vacuum modulator assembly.

30. Install transmission and axle assembly as previously outlined.

OVERHAUL TRANSMISSION COMPONENTS

Rear Pump and Reverse Piston—Disassemble

1. Remove drive and driven gear from the rear pump body. Stack so they may be reassembled with same faces up.

2. Compress spring retainer with tool #J-6129, J-4670-C and J-8765 or

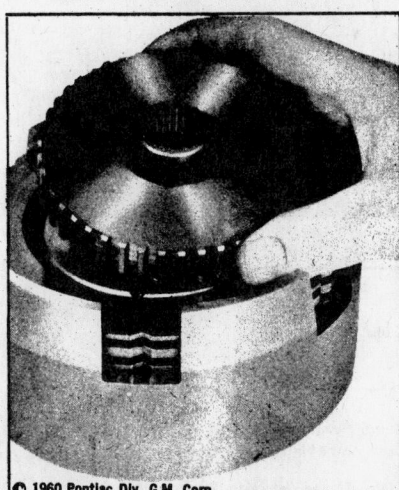

Removing Clutch Hub

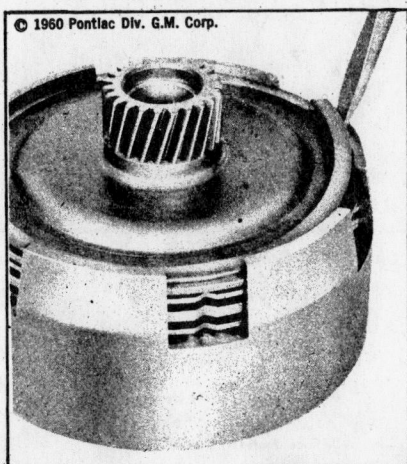

Clutch Drum Retainer Ring

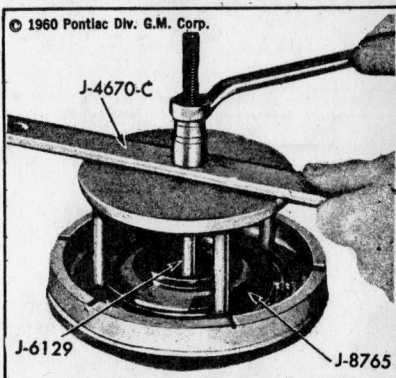

Compressing Reverse Piston Springs

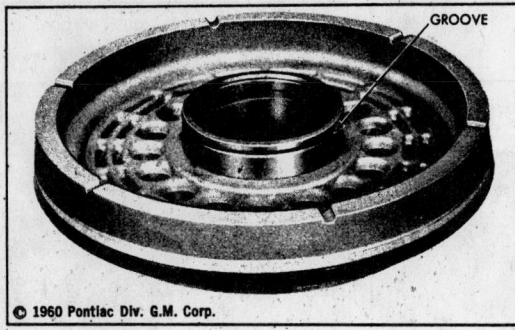

GROOVE

© 1960 Pontiac Div. G.M. Corp.

Reverse Piston Ring Groove

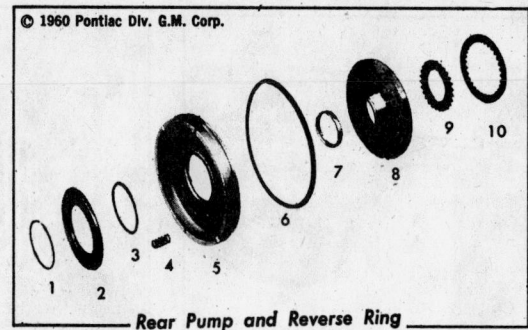

© 1960 Pontiac Div. G.M. Corp.

Rear Pump and Reverse Ring

1. Spring Retainer Snap Ring
2. Spring Retainer
3. Reverse Piston Inner Seal
4. Reverse Piston Return Springs (17 Used)
5. Reverse Piston
6. Reverse Piston Outer Seal (Lip Type)
7. Rear Pump Body Bushing
8. Rear Pump Body
9. Rear Pump Drive Gear
10. Rear Pump Driven Gear

other "stool" type compressor.

3. With retainer compressed until springs bottom, remove the snap ring. Carefully release pressure. Remove spring retainer and 17 return springs.

4. To permit removal of reverse piston, it is necessary to fill snap ring groove in hub of rear pump body with string or some other bulk material. When the groove is filled flush, rear pump body can be pushed out of reverse piston bore.

5. Remove square cut piston inner seal and piston outer seal. Seals should be discarded and new seals installed at reassembly.

Rear Pump and Reverse Piston—Assemble

1. Install inner seal in reverse piston.
2. Install outer seal in piston with lip

of seal toward pump body (opposite from spring seats in piston).

3. Install reverse piston on rear pump body. It is not necessary to fill snap ring groove on pump body hub for installation of piston. Pitch of groove for snap ring is favorable for installation.

4. Position 17 return springs in their seats on reverse piston, then place retainer on springs.

5. Hook up "stool" type compressor and compress springs.

6. With springs fully compressed, install snap ring in its groove in the pump body.

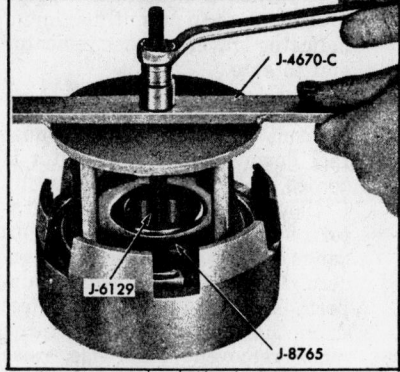

J-4670-C
J-6129
J-8765

Compressing Clutch Springs

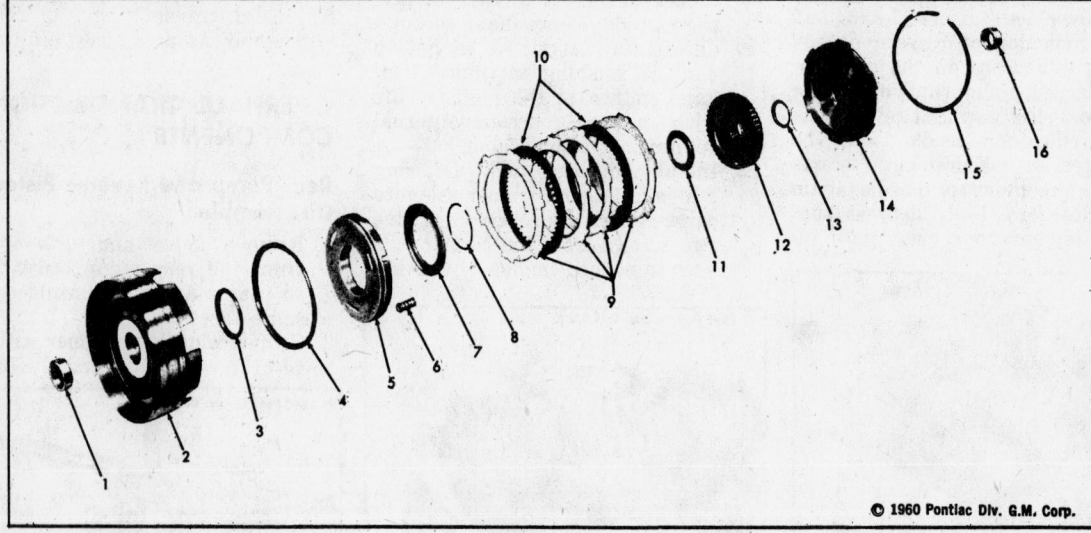

© 1960 Pontiac Div. G.M. Corp.

Clutch and Drum Assembly—Exploded

1. Clutch Drum Bushing
2. Clutch Drum
3. Clutch Drum Hub Seal (Lip Type)
4. Clutch Piston Seal (Lip Type)
5. Clutch Piston
6. Clutch Piston Return Spring (15 Used)
7. Return Spring Retainer
8. Return Spring Retainer Snap Ring
9. Reaction Plates (4 Used)
10. Face Plates (2 Used)
11. Clutch Hub Thrust Washer
12. Clutch Hub
13. Clutch Hub-to-Clutch Flange Thrust Washer
14. Clutch Flange and Low Sun Gear Assembly
15. Clutch Flange Retaining Ring
16. Low Sun Gear Bushing

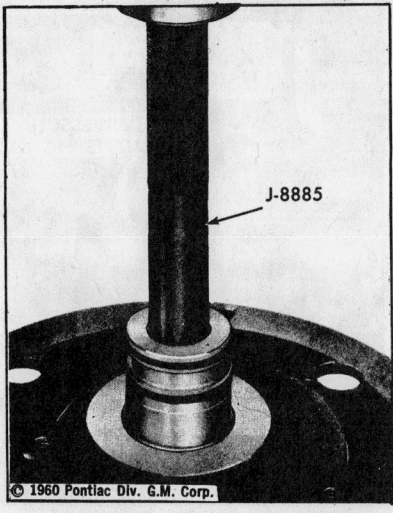

Removing Front Pump Body Bushing

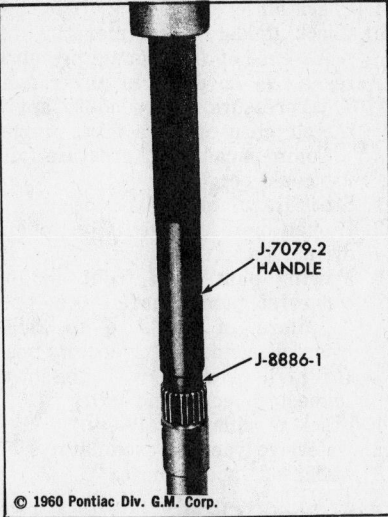

Installing Front Turbine Shaft Bushing

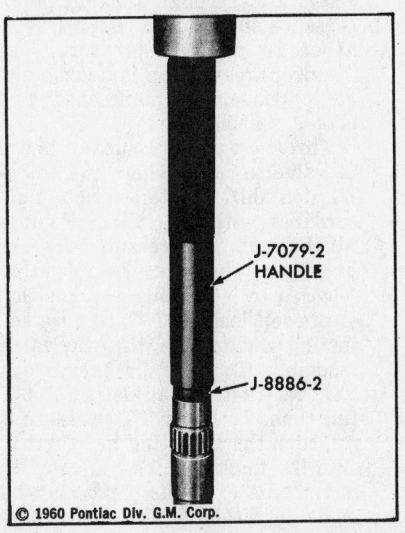

Installing Rear Turbine Shaft Bushing

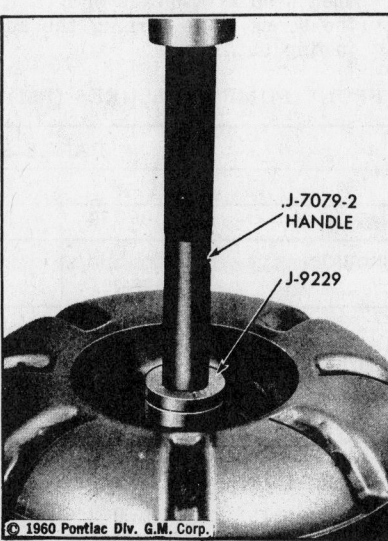

Installing Converter Bushing

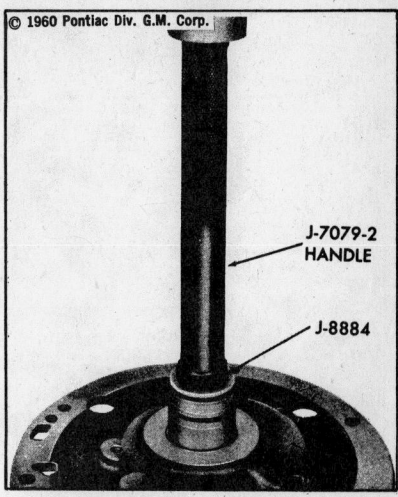

Installing Front Pump Body Bushing

7. Complete assembly by installing drive gear and driven gear in their respective bores in the pump body.

Clutch Drum—Disassemble

1. Remove retainer ring holding low sun gear and clutch flange assembly to clutch drum.
2. Remove low sun gear clutch flange and hub to flange thrust washer.
3. Lift out clutch hub, then remove nested drive and reaction plates and hub thrust washer.
4. To remove spring retainer, compress the springs using "stool" type compressor, J-6129, J-4670-C and adapter ring J-8765. Remove the snap ring.
5. Carefully release pressure, then remove spring retainer and return springs.
6. To remove clutch piston, pull upward with a twisting motion on the center. Remove piston seal.
7. Complete disassembly by removing piston inner seal from hub of clutch drum.

Note: The low clutch drum bushing and the low sun gear bushing are both replaceable.

Clutch Drum—Assemble

1. Install piston inner seal in hub of the clutch drum. Be sure seal lips are downward (or toward front of transmission).
2. Install a new piston seal in clutch piston. Be sure seal lips are toward front of transmission (clutch drum) when installed. Lubricate both piston inner seal and piston seal, then install clutch piston in clutch drum with a twisting motion.
3. Pace 15 return springs in position on clutch piston. Place retainer on springs.
4. Compress springs with stool type compressor and install snap ring

in groove on clutch drum hub.
5. Install hub front thrust washer with its lip toward clutch drum. Install clutch hub.
6. Install steel reaction plate, faced drive plate, **two steel plates,** faced plate then steel plate.
7. Install hub rear thrust washer with its flange toward low sun gear, then install low sun gear and clutch flange assembly and secure with retainer ring. Opening of retainer ring should be adjacent to one of the clutch drum lands.
8. Check assembly by turning clutch hub to insure its freedom to rotate.

Front Pump and Extension Housing—Disassemble

Note:

Front pump and extension housing were separated during disassembly of components from case, step 11 of "Disassembly Procedure."

1. Pry out the oil seal.
2. Remove bearing retaining ring.
3. Invert extension housing. Using a suitable socket as a driver, tap out the front bearing, spacer sleeve and the rear bearing.

Note:

The front pump body bushing is replaceable in the customary bushing service fashion.

Front Pump and Extension Housing—Assemble

1. Press or tap the rear drive line bearing in the pump cover.
2. Install spacer sleeve.
3. Install front drive line bearing using suitable socket as installer.
4. Install retaining ring.
5. Using soft hammer, tap in new drive line oil seal.
6. Install new square cut oil ring on OD of pump cover.

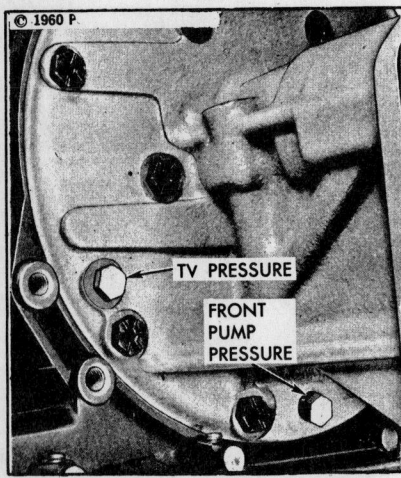

Pressure Tap Locations

Planet Carrier

If trouble is experienced in the planet carrier, replace the carrier as an assembly.

Turbine Shaft

Inspect splined areas for wear or other damage. Check to see that lube holes are open. If bushings are bad, replace in the customary fashion.

Converter

It is unnecessary to drain the converter as it is a welded unit and no internal repairs can be made. However, the converter hub bushing can be replaced in the customary fashion, and light welding repairs can be made to the converter body.

TROUBLE DIAGNOSIS

All tests can be made without driving the car on the road by pursuing the following steps:
1. Raise the car to clear the floor.
2. Hook up pressure gauges at pressure tap locations.
3. Warm up transmission.

4. Check oil level.
5. Check linkage adjustment.

Absence of front pump pressure results in no drive in any range. This pressure is needed to apply the clutch used for a given range.

Common causes of pressure failure could be:
1. Stuck regulator valve.
2. Broken or disengaged front pump drive lugs.
3. Missing plug from front end of converter pump shaft.

Failure of pressure to raise when disconnecting vacuum hose (or high pressure with the hose connected) could indicate:
1. Stuck modulator valve.
2. Defective vacuum modulator.
3. Collapsed vacuum hose.

Rear Pump Check

With the rear wheels clear of the floor, place selector in "D" and accelerate the engine. Front pump pressure should drop to 0-5 PSI at about 20 mph. If pressure does not drop, rear pump is disengaged or clogged, or rear pump check ball is not seating.

Throttle valve pressure tests are of value in cases where the transmission shift points are not in accordance with the "Shift Point—MPH Chart." If pressures are not as shown, they may be raised or lowered by adjusting the position of the self locking TV pressure adjusting nut on the throttle valve assembly. To **raise** TV pressure 3 PSI, back off the adjusting nut 1 full turn. To **lower** TV pressure 3 psi, turn the adjusting nut further onto its shaft 1 full turn. Smaller increments of adjustment may be made in either direction by partial turns of the nut. The end of the TV adjusting screw has an allen head as a means of holding the screw while turning the adjusting nut.

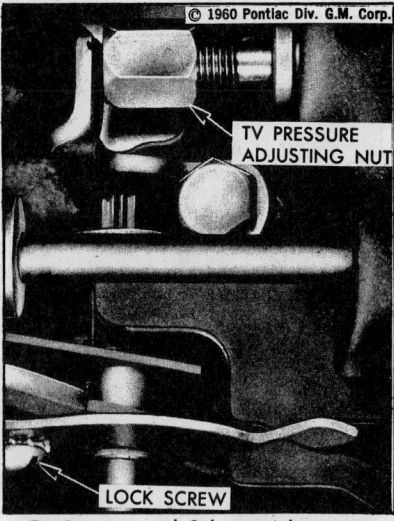

TV Pressure and Selector Adjustments

SHIFT POINT—MPH CHART

Upshifts	MPH
Minimum Throttle	12-15
Full Throttle	43-50
Part Throttle (detent touch)	35-45
Downshifts	**MPH**
Closed Throttle	9-15
Full Throttle	39-46
Part Throttle (detent touch)	21-33

The above shift points are based on 3.55:1 axle ratio.

REAR AXLE AND SUSPENSION

The differential and carrier assembly used with both the standard transmission and automatic transmission are identical except for the drive pinion shaft, front pinion bearing adjusting nut, rear pinion bearing retainer and oil seals.

MINOR REPAIRS—REAR AXLE
Differential Side Bearing Oil Seal R & R
1. Drain oil from differential.

FRONT PUMP PRESSURES (PSI)

CONDITION	RANGE SELECTOR POSITION			
	R	N	D	L
At idle (16" Hg)	106-130	55-67	55-67	124-137
At idle, with vacuum hose disconnected at vacuum modulator	198-222	101-114	101-114	124-137

THROTTLE VALVE (TV) PRESSURE (PSI)

CONDITION	R	N	D	L
Disconnect TV rod at carburetor and vacuum hose at vacuum modulator. Depress accelerator to W.O.T.*	0	0	50-52	119-132

*By disconnecting TV rod at carburetor, engine remains at idle speed throughout test.

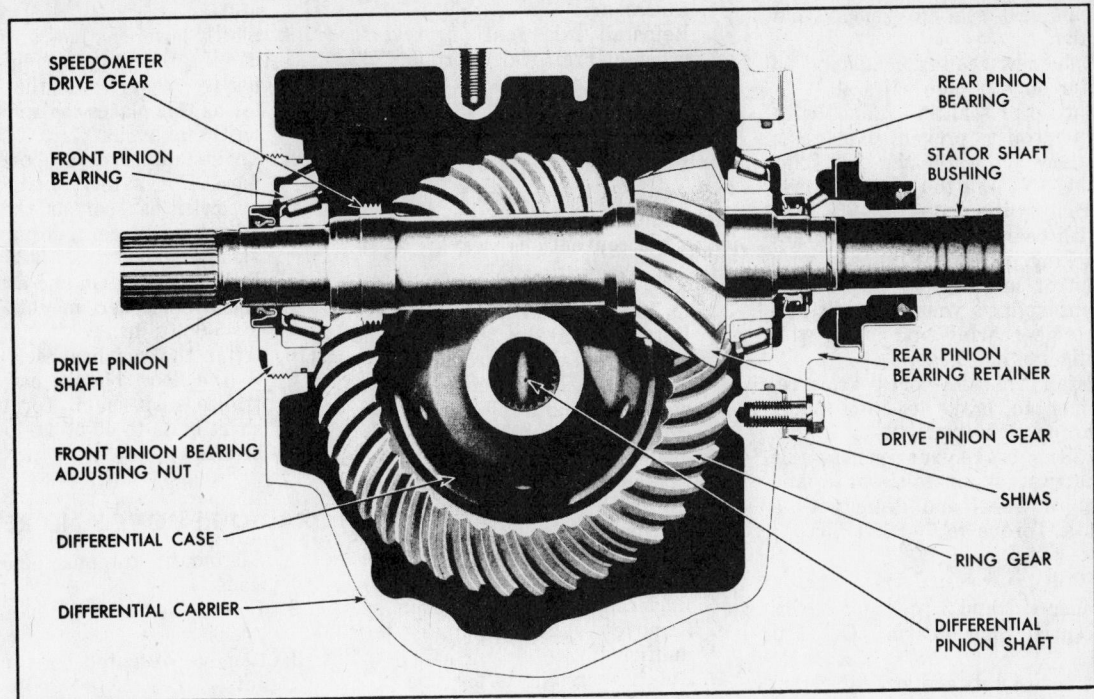

Differential Assembly

2. Remove wheel and brake drum.
3. Remove four nuts holding the axle bearing retainer to the brake backing plate. Nuts are accessible through hole in axle shaft flange.
4. Pull axle shaft and universal joint outward far enough to remove universal joint from differential and carrier assembly.
5. Remove side bearing oil seals by prying out with a small chisel or screwdriver.

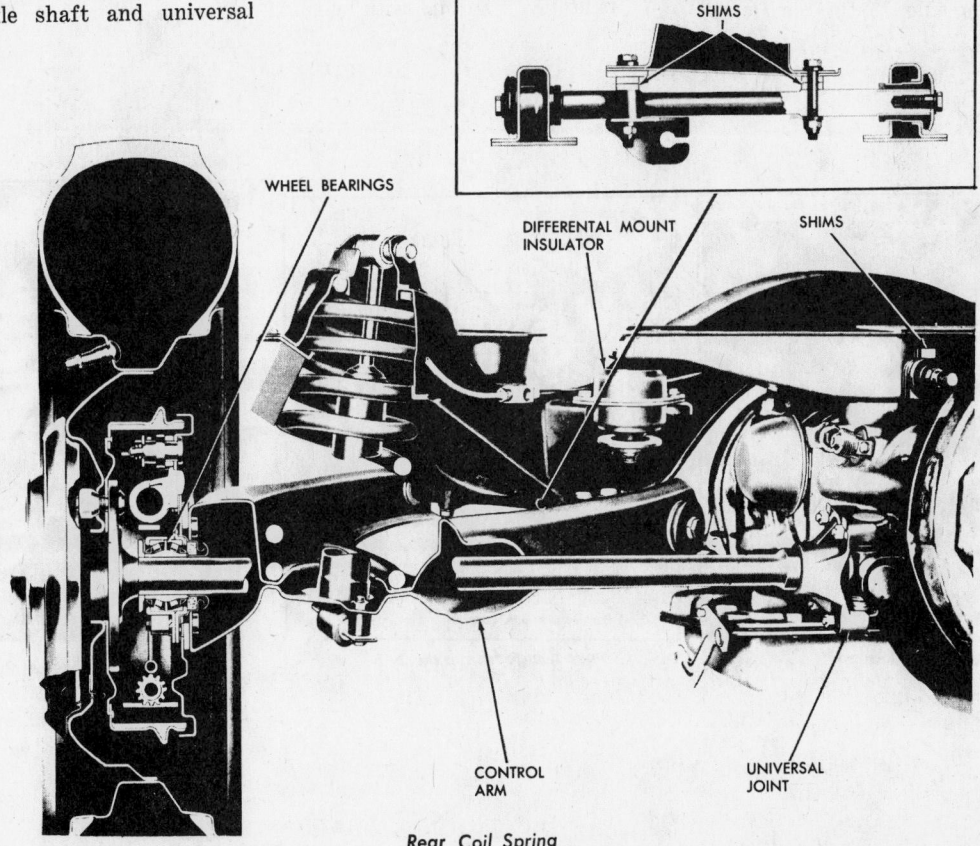

Rear Coil Spring

6. Clean seal seat to remove old sealer.
7. Apply new sealing compound to outer edge of new oil seal.
8. Coat lip of seal and splines with hypoid oil to prevent damage to seal by splines of the "U" joint yoke. Drive in the new seal, preferably with driver #J-8889.
9. With bearing retainer and brake backing plate holes aligned with control arm studs, insert "U" joint splined yoke through seal at side bearing and index with splines of side gear.
10. Install 4 nuts to hold bearing retainer to brake backing plate. Torque all nuts to 30-45 ft. lbs.
11. Position brake drum on rear axle shaft studs, install wheel, and secure wheel and drum with 5 nuts. Torque to 70-85 ft. lbs.

Axle Shaft R & R

Number 1, 2 and 3 the same as for "Differential Side Bearing Oil Seal R & R."

4. Remove 4 nuts and lock tabs from "U" bolts, attaching "U" joint assembly to rear axle flange.
5. Pull axle flange out enough to separate flange from "U" bolts.
6. Remove capscrew, lock washer, and flat washer, holding flange to axle shaft.
7. Remove flange from shaft with a puller.
8. Remove axle shaft from lower control arm.
9. Reinstall axle shaft in reverse order of removal. Torque "U" joint flange to axle, 20-35 ft. lbs. 'U' joint nuts 14-20 ft. lbs.

Repack Axle "U"-Joints

Proceed with foregoing paragraphs then handle the universal joint service in the conventional way.

REAR COIL SPRING R & R

1. Raise the car by the body side rails so that the control arms may swing free. The car must be high enough so that a rolling floor jack can be placed under the wheel drum.
2. Loosen the control arm cross shaft bolts (in ends of shaft). Disconnect brake hose from brake line at junction point. Remove wheel and tire assembly, Replace nuts to hold the drum on.
3. Remove exhaust pipes and muffler.
4. Rotate rear axle to position "U" joint in suitable position. This will permit sufficient down swing of the control arm to reduce pressure on spring.
5. Place a rolling floor jack under the drum and brake flange.
6. Raise the jack slightly to place a light load on the coil spring. Remove shock absorber.
7. Index coil spring with spring seat.
8. Slowly lower the jack until spring is free, then pry spring out. Do not remove or lower the jack too far as this places too much strain on the axle shaft and "U" joint.
9. **To install,** reverse above procedure. For safety, install shock absorber as soon as the spring is put in place. Torque bottom attaching bolts to 15-25 ft. lbs. Raise control arm and attach top shock absorber mount. Torque to 45-60 ft. lbs.
10. After the car has been lowered to the floor, bounce car to neutralize suspension. Torque cross shaft bolts to 45-55 ft. lbs. Bleed brakes.

RADIO REMOVE AND REPLACE

1. Disconnect antennae and power leads.
2. Loosen hex screws and remove knobs.
3. Remove escutcheon retaining nuts.
4. Remove screw holding receiver to panel bracket. **Note:** With air conditioner, left evaporator and glove box must be removed.
5. Remove speaker by disconnecting output connector and mounting bracket screws.
6. Reverse above procedure to reinstall.

U-Bolts Installed

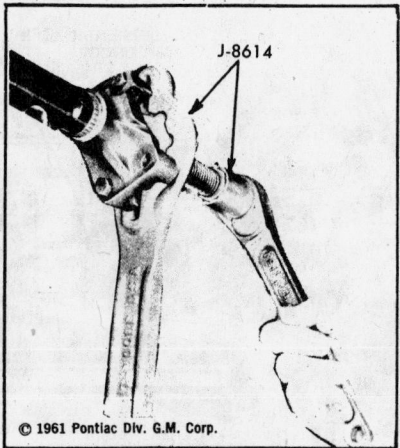

Remove flange from axle shaft

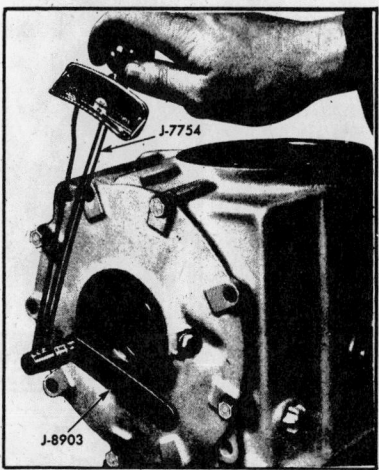

Checking Side Bearing Preload

Page   Page   Page

AIR CONDITIONING
Service 1092

BRAKES, HYDRAULIC
Adjustments 938
Bleed brakes 941
Parking brake, adjust 663
Master cylinder service 939
References 663

BRAKES, POWER
Power unit overhaul 954
Trouble shooting 954

CLUTCH
Clutch assembly, R & R 673
Clutch pedal, adjust 674

COOLING SYSTEM
Thermostat 666
Water pump, R & R 666

ELECTRICAL SYSTEM
Alternator current generator . 1035
Alternator regulator
   specification 659
Alternator and regulators ... 1035
Alternator, R & R 662
Distributor, R & R 662
Distributor specifications 659
Gauges 1024
Horn buttons 673
Ignition firing order & timing . 658
Ignition timing specifications .. 659
Starter references 662
Starter, R & R 662
Starter specifications 660
Starter systems 1046
Voltage regulator adjustments 1035

ENGINE ASSEMBLY
Cylinder head, R & R 666
Cylinder head tightening 666
Engine assembly, R & R 666
Engine diagnosis 1012
Engine firing order & timing . 658
Engine tune-up 661
Engine references 666
Exhaust manifold, R & R 665
Inlet manifold, R & R 665
Oil pan, R & R 668
Oil pressure specifications 660
Oil filter 669
Piston and rod, assembly 669
Piston and pins, specifications . 660
Rocker arms & shaft 667
Specifications, general, engine . 660
Specifications, tune-up, engine . 659
Timing case 668
Timing chain 668
Trouble shooting charts 1012
Tune-up specifications 659

ENGINE ASSEMBLY—continued
Valve specifications 660
Valves and guides 667

ENGINE LUBRICATION
Oil pan, R & R 668
Oil pump 669
Oil filter 669

EXHAUST SYSTEM
Manifolds 665
Muffler & tail pipe 665

FUEL SYSTEM
Carburetors 972
Fuel gauge service 1024
Fuel pump pressure 659
Fuel pump service 1020
Fuel tank, R & R 664
Pump pressure test 663

INSTRUMENTS
References 662
Fuel and temperature gauges . 662
Speedometer 663

RADIO, R & R
References 680

REAR AXLE AND SUSPENSION
Axle assembly, R & R 680
Axle shaft 918
Axle shaft oil seal 918
Pinion bearings 918
Ring gear & pinion 918
Trouble shooting 919

SPECIFICATIONS
Alternator generators 659
Alternator regulators 659
Battery 660
Brake cylinder sizes 661
Capacities:
   Axle, rear 661
   Cooling system 661
   Crankcase 661
   Fuel tank 661
   Transmission, automatic .. 661
   Transmission, manual 661
Chassis, general 661
Distributor 659
Engine, general 660
Engine tune-up 659
Fuses & circuit breakers 660
Light bulbs 660
Main bearings 660
Model identification
   illustrations 658
Model year identifications ... 659
Piston & pins 660
Quick reference specifications . 658

SPECIFICATIONS—continued
Rod bearings 660
Starters 660
Torque wrench 661
Tune-up 659
Valves 660
Wheel alignment 661

STEERING, MANUAL
Adjust gear 671
Horn button, R & R 673
References 671
Steering wheel, R & R 673

STEERING, POWER
Pump assembly 1058
Trouble shooting 1081
Unit overhaul 1058

SUSPENSION, FRONT
Alignment procedures 1082
Alignment specifications 661
Ball joints, R & R 1087
Camber, adjust 1087
Caster, adjust 1087
Height adjustment 670
King pins and bushings 1087
Knuckle supports 1087
References 670
Shock absorbers 1087
Support arms, pins & bushings 1087
Toe-in, adjust 1087
Torsion bars 670

TRANSMISSION, AUTOMATIC
Disassembly of transmission .. 802
Linkage, adjust 678
General information 802
Push button adjustment 677
References 676
Transmission, R & R 678
Trouble shooting 817

TRANSMISSION, STANDARD
Disassemble transmission ... 674
Shift linkage 674
Transmission, R & R 674

TROUBLE CHECKS
Procedures 1

TUNE-UP
Procedures 661
Specifications 659
Engine diagnosis 1012

UNIVERSAL JOINT AND DRIVE LINE
Disassemble U joint 680
U joint & drive line, R & R ... 680

VALIANT–LANCER–DART

YEAR IDENTIFICATION

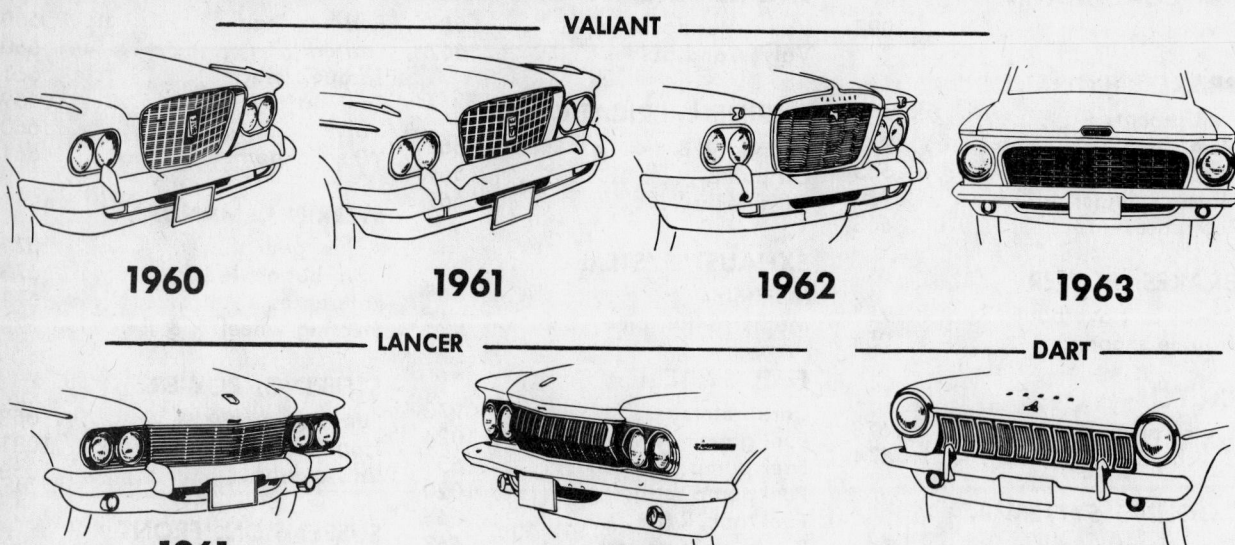

VALIANT

1960   1961   1962   1963

LANCER

1961   1962

DART

1963

QUICK WORKING SPECIFICATIONS

DISTRIBUTOR

Breaker Point Gap
1960-63 020

Cam Angle (Degrees)
1960-61 63-42
1962-63 40-45

IGNITION TIMING

1960-63 ....2½°B.T.D.C.

SPARK PLUGS

Year	Type	Gap
1960-62	AG52 or N12Y	.035
1963	N14Y	.035

ALTERNATOR

1960-63
An alternator instead of the conventional generator is supplied as standard equipment.

VALVES

1960-63 ....intake, hot .010"
1960-63 ......exhaust, hot .020"

COMPRESSION PRESSURE

(Cylinders should read alike within 10 pounds. This is more important than the actual reading.)
1960-63 145

CAPACITIES

Engine Crankcase (Quarts)
(Add 1 qt. if new filter installed)
1960-63 4

Synchromesh Trans. (Pints)
1960-63 5

3 Speed Automatic Trans. (Pints)
1960-61 14
1962-63 15

Rear Axle (Pints)
1960-63 2

Cooling System (Quarts)
1960 13
1961-63 170 cu. in. 11
225 cu. in. 12

FIRING ORDER and TIMING

SPARK OCCURS:
① 1960-63—"Slant 6"—2½° BTDC (170 Cu. In.)
"Slant 6"—2½° BTDC (225 Cu. In.)

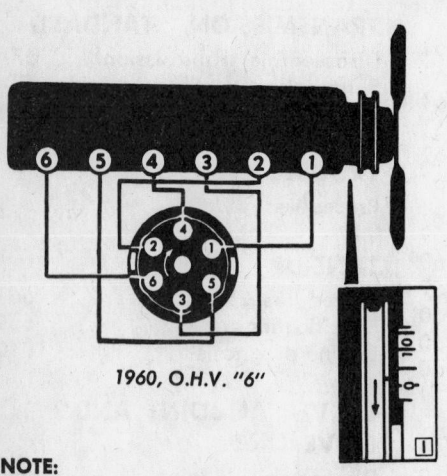

1960, O.H.V. "6"

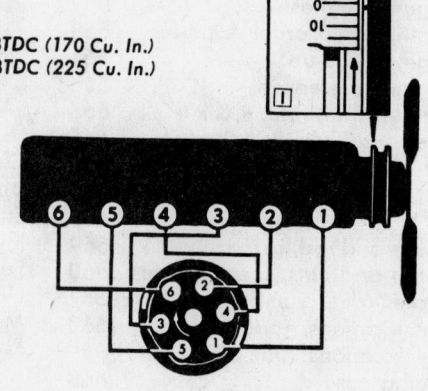

1961-63 O.H.V. "6"

NOTE:
THESE ARE APPROXIMATE SETTINGS. ENGINE DESIGN, ALTITUDE, TEMPERATURE, FUEL AND ENGINE CONDITION WILL ALL INFLUENCE TIMING. THE DETERMINING FACTOR, LIMITING ADVANCE, WILL STILL BE THE "KNOCK POINT" OF THE INDIVIDUAL ENGINE.

CAR SERIAL NUMBER LOCATION AND ENGINE IDENTIFICATION

ENGINE NUMBER LOCATION

Stamped forward on right side of block just below cylinder head.

SERIAL NUMBER LOCATION

Tag attached to left front hinge pillar.

ENGINES MAY BE INDENTI-FIED BY ENGINE NUMBER PRE-

FIXES:
1. Engine model, (P-1960, R-1961).
2. Cubic inch displacement, (17-170, 22-225).
3. Manufacturing date.

TUNE-UP SPECIFICATIONS

YEAR AND MODEL	SPARK PLUGS (NOTE 1)		DISTRIBUTOR			Ignition Timing	Compression Pressure Cranking	VALVES					Engine Idle Speed In Neutral
								Tappet Clearance Hot		Timing Inlet Opens	Fuel Pump Pressure		
	Type	Gap	Cam Angle	Point Gap	Arm Spring Tension			In.	Ex.				
1960-61, All	N12Y	.035	36-42	.020	20 oz.	2½° B	145	.010	.020	8 B	3½-5	Note 2	
1962-63	N12Y	.035	40-45	.020	17-21	2½° B	145	.010	.020	8 B	3½-5	Note 2	

NOTE 1: AG52 WAS ALSO USED IN EARLY PRODUCTION 1963 N14Y   NOTE 2: MANUAL TRANSMISSION....550 R.P.M.   AUTOMATIC TRANSMISSION.....500 R.P.M. IN "D"

Note:

All specifications are standard and should result in satisfactory performance. There are, however, factors that influence these settings, such as fuel octane value, air density, humidity, temperature, etc. Timing charts, like other specifications must be considered as averages, subject to modification.

DISTRIBUTOR SPECIFICATIONS

YEAR AND MODEL	Part Number	Rotation	Cam Angle (Degrees)	Point Gap (Inches)	Arm Spring Tension (Ounces)	GOVERNOR @ DIST. R.P.M.		VACUUM CONTROL		
						Advance Starts	Full Advance	Inches Vacuum To Start	Inches Vacuum For Full Advance	Maximum Dist. Advance Degrees
1960-61										
170 cu. in.	1889750	C	36-42	.020	20	1 @ 400	12.5 @ 1925	4.7-7.1	9.5-12.5	14.5
225 cu. in.	2095270	C	36-42	.020	17-21	1 @ 350	11.5 @ 2200	5-7	12	7¾-10¼
1962										
170 cu. in.	2095974	C	40-45	.020	17-21	1 @ 400	13.5 @ 2200	5-7	12.5	11
225 cu. in.	2095976	C	40-45	.020	17-21	1 @ 400	11.5 @ 2300	5-7	13	5¼-7½
1963										
170 cu. in. Std. Trans.	2095974	C	40-45	.020	17-21	1 @ 400	13.5 @ 2200	5-7	12.5	11
170 cu. in. Auto Trans.	2098524	C	40-45	.020	17-21	1 @ 400	13.5 @ 2200	5-7	12.5	9½-12½
225 cu. in.	2095976	C	40-45	.020	17-21	1 @ 400	11.5 @ 2300	5-7	12.5	5¼-7½
1963										
170 cu. in Std. Trans.	2098665	C	40-45	.020	17-21	1 @ 450	13.5 @ 2200	5-7	10	6-8½
170 cu. in. Auto. Trans.	2098675	C	40-45	.020	17-21	1 @ 400	13.5 @ 2200	5-7	10	6-8½
225 cu. in.-All	2098670	C	40-45	.020	17-21	1 @ 475	11.5 @ 2500	5-7	13	5¼-7½

ALTERNATOR (GENERATOR) AND ALTERNATOR REGULATOR SPECIFICATIONS

YEAR AND MODEL	ALTERNATOR				REGULATOR		
	Rated Amperage	Field Current At 12V	Output at 1250 Engine RPM	Output at 2200 Engine RPM	Air Gap	Point Gap	Voltage At 70°F.
1960-63							
170 cu. in.	35	2.56	28A @ 14.6V	33A @ 15.0V	.050"	.015"	14.0
225 cu. in.	35	3.2	35A @ 14.6V	N A	.050"	.015"	14.0

NOTE: Surrounding temperatures and driving habits influence the above adjustments and must be considered by the mechanic. Higher temperatures or turnpike conditions permit lower adjustments; lower temperatures or city driving require higher setting, within limits.

VALIANT—LANCER—DART

LIGHT BULBS

Headlights	Sealed Beam	Stop	1034	Turn Signal	
Outer Lamp	4002	Tail	1034	Indicator	57
Inner Lamp	4001	Turn Signal		Parking	1034
Headlamp Beam Indicator	57	Front	1034	Instruments	57
Rear License Plate	67	Rear	1034	Dome	1004

BATTERY AND STARTER SPECIFICATIONS

YEAR AND MODEL	BATTERY			STARTERS						Brush Spring Tension
	Ampere-Hour Capacity	Volts	Terminal Grounded	LOCK TEST			NO-LOAD TEST			
				Amps.	Volts	Torque	Amps.	Volts	R.P.M.	
1960-61, All	50	12	Neg.	350	4	8.5	58	11.0	3800	32-48 oz.
1962-63	48	12	Neg.	475	4	24.0	85	11.0	1950	32-48 oz.
1963	38	12	Neg.	425	4	20.0	90	11.0	2950	32-48 oz.

FUSES AND CIRCUIT BREAKERS

Circuit Breakers
(at H.L. Switch)   Amps.
Head Lamps, Parking Lights ... 22
Fuses (in junction block under dash)
Tail Light, License Plate Lamp .. 9

Stop Light, Dome Light 9
Turn Indicator, Back Up Light .. 20
Instrument Light, Radio Dial,
    Heater Panel, Shift Indicator . 4
Heater Blower, Air
    Conditioner Blower 14

Power Radio 7½
w/s Wiper, w/s Washer,
    Parking Brake Signal 25
Cigar Lighter 20
Air Conditioner Control 7½
Spot Light 14

GENERAL ENGINE SPECIFICATIONS

YEAR AND MODEL	Bore And Stroke	No. Of Main Bearings	Type Valve Lifter	Cu. In. Displacement	AMA Horsepower	Horsepower At R.P.M.	Advertised Torque At R.P.M.	Compression Ratio	Oil Pressure At 40 M.P.H.	Camshaft Drive
1960-63										
170 cu. in.	3¹³⁄₃₂ x 3⅛	4	Mech. Adj.	170	27.74	101@4400	155@2400	8.2-1*	45	Chain
225 cu. in.	3¹³⁄₃₂ x 4⅛	4	Mech. Adj.	225	27.74	145@4000	215@2400	8.2-1	45	Chain

* 1960—170 cu. in. 8.6-1

CRANKSHAFT BEARING JOURNAL SIZES

YEAR AND MODEL	MAIN BEARING JOURNALS					CONNECTING ROD BEARING JOURNALS		
	Journal Diameter	No. Of Main Bearings	Oil Clearance	End Play Of Shaft	End Play Held By	Journal Diameter	Oil Clearance	End Play
1960-63, All	2.750	4	.001	.0045	No. 3	2.1870	.0010	.009

PISTON AND PIN SPECIFICATIONS

Year and Model	PISTON			PISTON PIN				
	Skirt Clearance					FIT		
	Min	Max	Diameter	Bushing	In Rod	In Piston	Lock	
1960-63 All	.0005	.0015	.9008	None	Press	.00045-.00075	Rod Press	

VALVE SPECIFICATIONS

YEAR AND MODEL	Seat Angle		Intake Valve Lift	Exhaust Valve Lift	Valve Spring Pressure		Stem To Guide Clearance		Stem Diameter		Are Valve Guides Replaceable
	In.	Ex.			Outer	Inner	In.	Ex.	In.	Ex.	
1960-63, All	45	47	.371	.364	83@1¹¹⁄₁₆"	None	.002	.003	.372	.372	No

CAPACITIES

YEAR AND MODEL	Engine Crankcase Add 1 Qt. For Filter	TRANSMISSION PINTS TO REFILL		Rear Axle Pints	Gasoline Tank Gallons	Cooling System Quarts Add 1 Qt. For Heater
		Manual	Automatic			
1960 170 cu. in.	4	5	14	2	13	13
1961-63 170 cu. in.	4	5	15	2	13	12
1961-63 225 cu. in.	4	5	14	2	13	11

TORQUE SPECIFICATIONS

YEAR AND MODEL	Cylinder Head Bolts	Rod Bearing Bolts	Main Bearing Bolts	Crankshaft Pulley	Flywheel To Crankshaft Bolts	Manifolds (Note A)	
						In.	Ex.
1960-63, All	65	45	85	Press Fit	55	10	10

NOTE A: Torque intake to exhaust bolts to 15 ft. lb.

CYLINDER HEAD NUT TIGHTENING SEQUENCE

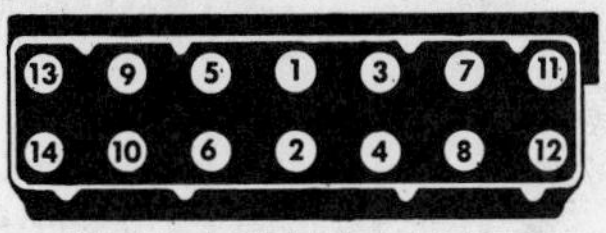

Tighten in Sequence to 65 ft. lbs.

GENERAL CHASSIS AND BRAKE SPECIFICATIONS

YEAR AND MODEL	CHASSIS		BRAKE CYLINDER SIZES		
	Overall Length In Inches	Tire Size	Master Cylinder Inches	Wheel Cylinder—Inches	
				Front	Rear
1960-62					
VALIANT	184.0	6.50 x 13	1	1	13/16
LANCER	188.8	6.50 x 13	1	1	13/16
1963					
VALIANT	184.0	6.50 x 13	1	1	13/16
DART	195.9	6.50 x 13	1	1	13/16

FRONT WHEEL ALIGNMENT

YEAR AND MODEL		Front End Height Note 2	CASTER		CAMBER		Toe-In Inches	Steering Axis Inclination	WHEEL PIVOT RATIO	
			Range Degrees	Pref. Setting	Range (Degrees)	Pref. Setting			Inner Wheel	Outer Wheel
1960-63	Manual	1¾″±⅛″	1 N to 0	½° N	Note 1		⅛	7½°	20°	17⅔°
	Power	1¾″±⅛″	¼ P to 1¼ P	½° P	Note 1		⅛	7½°	20°	17⅔°

NOTE 1: Right Side, ⅛° N to ⅜° P; Left Side, ⅛° P to ⅝° P. **NOTE 2: To measure front end height see text.**

ENGINE TUNE-UP

Engine tune-up and diagnosis are closely enough related to justify coverage under one head, and to establish an approach that will best serve both ends.

The following steps are suggested as a guide toward systematic engine tune-up. Circumstances, however, may alter this list.

1. Remove the spark plugs and tubes. Keep the plug positions relative to the cylinders from which they were removed for future reference.
2. Hook up starter remote control cable and switch. Then crank the engine through about four **compression** strokes while reading the compression gauge.
3. Record and compare the individual cylinder pressures. A variation of 15 pounds or more should not be tolerated and further progress along tune-up lines discontinued.
4. During compression test, make both vacuum and pressure test on **fuel pump**. Also check fuel lines and connections.
5. Test **battery** and connections with a voltmeter. Also with the voltmeter in series and all electrical units off, check for battery drain.
6. With voltmeter in series, test **starter** current draw.
7. Clean and reoil **carburetor air cleaner.**
8. Inspect **distributor** points and replace if burned or pitted. Test

condenser and replace if necessary. Check for distributor shaft and breaker plate play. Align and gap the points, check governor and vacuum advance and reset point gap with dwell meter.

9. Test continuity and **coil** output. Test voltage to the ignition coil, (a drop of over 1/10 volt indicates a loose connection or resistance in the wiring).

10. Clean, rinse and air dry **carburetor** parts, reset to specifications.

11. Inspect **automatic choke** for free operation and proper calibration.

12. Inspect **manifold heat control valve**, free up and adjust if necessary.

13. Inspect the removed **spark plugs**. If plugs are in satisfactory condition, sand blast them. Whether the old plugs are used or new ones installed, gap them to specifications. Install the plug and sleeve and torque to 30 ft. lb.

14. Measure the ohm resistance of each **spark plug wire** and replace if outside of specifications.

15. **Start engine** and during warm-up period check the following items:

   A. Fast idle adjustment
   B. Radiator hose
   C. Heater hose
   D. Leaking or worn water pump
   E. Worn or loose fan belt
   F. Leaky head or manifold gaskets
   G. Check alternator out-put

16. With engine at operating temperature, remove the valve cover and **adjust the tappets**.

17. Clean and reoil **crankcase breather**.

18. With engine at operating temperature, **adjust fuel-air mixture** and readjust **idle speed**.

19. Now adjust **ignition timing** with vacuum line disconnected and plugged.

20. Hook up distributor vacuum line. **Road test** the car.

DISTRIBUTOR

REMOVAL

1. Remove distributor cap.
2. Disconnect primary wire.
3. Disconnect vacuum line.
4. Remove hold-down bolt and remove distributor.

INSTALLATION

1. Rotate crankshaft until mark on inner edge of crankshaft pulley is in line with the "O" (TDC) mark on timing chain case cover.
2. With distributor gasket in position, hold distributor over the mounting pad.

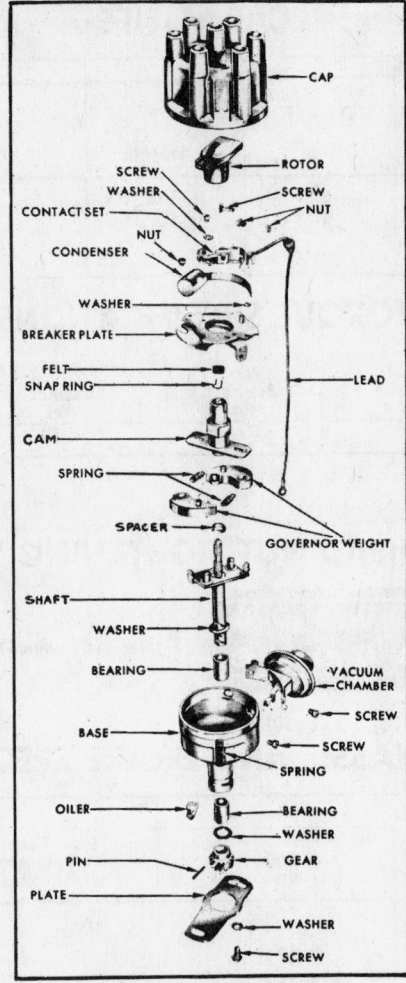

Distributor, Exploded View

3. Turn the rotor to point forward, corresponding to 4 o'clock.
4. Install distributor so that with distributor fully seated on the engine, the gear has spiraled to bring rotor to a 5 o'clock position.
5. Turn the housing until the ignition points are separating and rotor is under #1 cap tower.
6. Install hold-down bolt.
7. Adjust timing to specifications, using a timing light.

ALTERNATOR AND REGULATOR

REFERENCES

Details on Alternator and Regulator can be found in Specifications Table of this section.

General information on Alternator and Regulator repair and trouble shooting can be found in the Unit Repair section.

Removal

To Remove Alternator:
1. Disconnect battery ground cable.

2. Disconnect "BAT" and "FLD" leads from alternator.
3. Remove alternator by removing two mounting bolts and belt tensioner bracket bolt.
   To Reinstall: reverse above.

Never attempt to polarize an alternator, nor short the regulator.

STARTER

REFERENCES

More detailed information on starters will be found in the Unit Repair section, under the heading: "Starters."

Removal

1. Disconnect negative cable at battery.
2. Disconnect starter cable at starter.
3. Remove starter attaching bolts and remove starter and cylinder block seal from beneath the engine.

Install

Reverse above procedure.

INSTRUMENTS

REFERENCES

Thermal type **fuel and temperature gauges** are used on Valiant and Lancer cars.

Both gauges receive a constant voltage supply from a voltage regulator built in the temperature gauge. They are sensitive only to changes in fuel level or temperature.

The terminals on the temperature gauge that houses the constant voltage regulator internally is marked as follows:

"A"—is the output terminal for the controlled voltage from the constant voltage regulator.

"I"—is the 12 volt input voltage terminal to the voltage regulator.

"S"—is the terminal for the connection to the sending unit.

The fuel gauge will have only the controlled voltage terminal "A" and

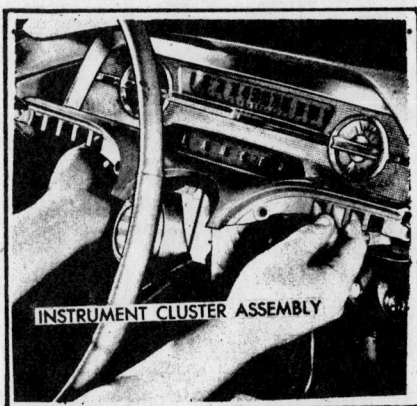

Removing Instrument Cluster

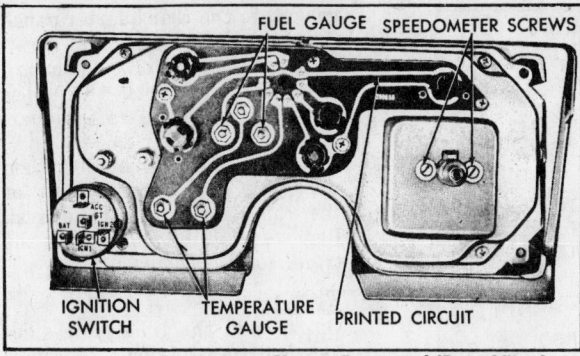

Instrument Cluster Removed (Rear View)

FUEL GAUGE   SPEEDOMETER SCREWS

IGNITION SWITCH   TEMPERATURE GAUGE   PRINTED CIRCUIT

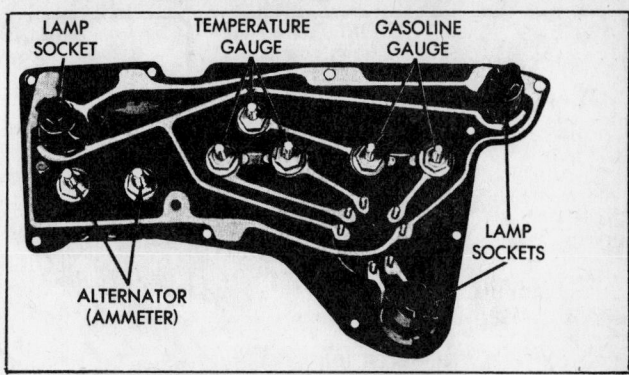

Printed Circuit Board with Instruments

LAMP SOCKET   TEMPERATURE GAUGE   GASOLINE GAUGE

ALTERNATOR (AMMETER)   LAMP SOCKETS

the terminal "S" for the connection to the tank sending unit.

The **oil pressure indicator** lamp is connected between the oil pressure sending unit in the oil pump body and the ignition terminal of the ignition switch. When oil pressure exceeds 8 to 12 psi the contacts open and the light goes out.

More detailed information on instruments may be found in the Unit Repair Section under the heading "Gauges."

SPEEDOMETER

Remove

1. Disconnect negative cable at battery.
2. Remove headlamp switch knob by releasing the spring-loaded retainer on the body of the switch, (knob must be in "IN" position).
3. Remove four screws that hold the instrument cluster and pull the top of the cluster forward.
4. Disconnect speedometer cable at the cluster, also the wire connectors at the instruments.

5. Remove the cluster for bench removal of speedometer head or instruments.

Install

Reverse above procedure.

BRAKES

REFERENCES

Nine inch self energizing hydraulic brakes are used. The front wheels use 2¼" wide lining on primary shoes and 2½" wide lining on secondary shoes. The rear wheels use 2" lining throughout.

The service brakes are operated by a suspended foot pedal. The master cylinder is mounted on the fire wall for easy access. Power brakes are optional and the power unit is located between the brake pedal and the master cylinder. The rear wheel brakes also serve as mechanically operated parking brakes. The parking brake is applied by a foot operated lever and cables to the rear wheel shoes.

Information on brake adjustments, band replacement, bleeding procedure, master and wheel cylinder over-

haul can be found in the Unit Repair section under the heading: "Brakes, Hydraulic."

PARKING BRAKE ADJUST

1. Correctly adjust rear wheel brakes and release parking brake completely.
2. Slack-off on the front cable until the intermediate arm seats on the cross-over stop.
3. Tighten the rear cable adjusting nut until some rear wheel drag is felt.
4. Slack-off on the rear cable adjusting nut until rear wheels just turn freely. Then continue to loosen the rear cable adjusting nut three additional revolutions. Secure the rear cable equalizer in this position with the lock nut on the forward side of the equalizer.
5. Tighten anchor nut on front cable until the intermediate arm is pulled off the cross over stop. Leave 1/16" to 1/8" gap between the arm and the stop with the anchor nut seated in the intermediate arm.
6. Snap the parking brake on and off a few times to double check against dragging of the rear wheels.

FUEL SYSTEM

CARBURETOR

Both Carter and Holley carburetors are used. For details see Unit Repair section "Carburetors."

FUEL PUMP

To test this single action pump, the following steps should be taken:

Pressure Test

1. Insert a "T" fitting between the fuel pump and the carburetor, as illustrated.
2. Connect a 6 inch hose between the "T" fitting and the pressure gauge.

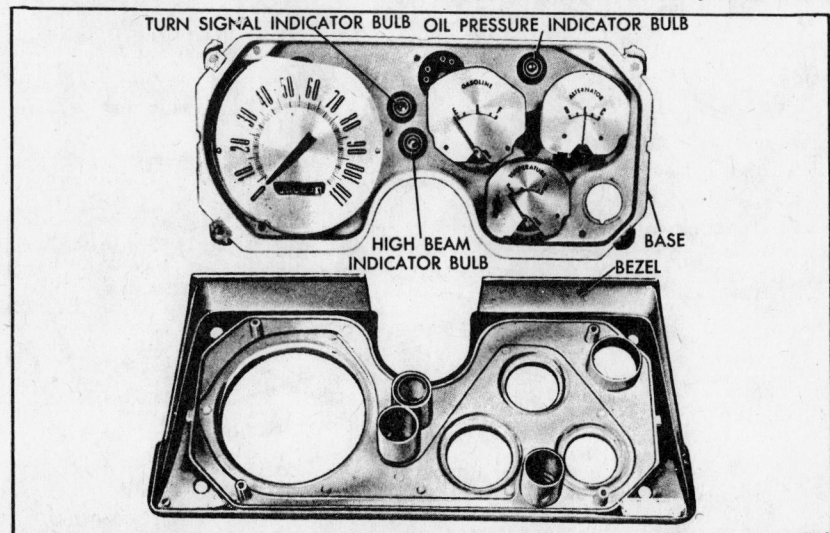

TURN SIGNAL INDICATOR BULB   OIL PRESSURE INDICATOR BULB

HIGH BEAM INDICATOR BULB   BASE BEZEL

Cluster Base with Instruments

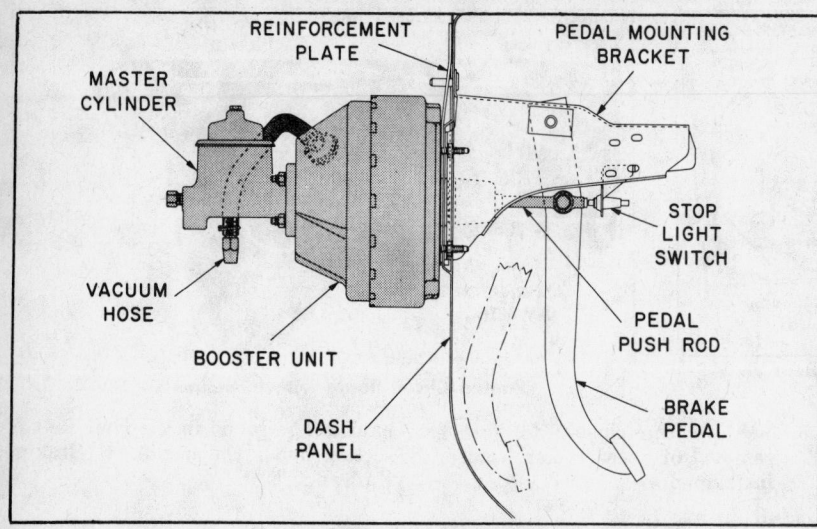

Vacuum-Suspended Power Brake Unit

3. Connect a tachometer to the engine. Start the engine and vent the pump for a few seconds. (If this is not done, the pump will not operate at full capacity and a false reading will result.)
4. Run the engine at 500 RPM, the reading should be 3½ to 5 psi and remain constant or return to zero very slowly, when the engine is stopped. An instant drop to zero indicates a leaky outlet valve. If the pressure is too low, a weak diaphragm main spring or improper assembly of the diaphragm may be the cause. If the pressure is too high, the main spring is too strong.

Vacuum Test

The vacuum test should be made with the fuel line disconnected from the carburetor.
1. Disconnect the inlet line to the fuel pump.
2. Connect a vacuum gauge to the pump inlet fitting.
3. Crank the engine with the starter. There should be a noticeable vacuum present, not alternated with blowback.
4. If blowback is present, the inlet valve is at fault or a new valve body is in order.

Volume Test

The pump should supply one quart of fuel in one minute or less at 500 RPM.

If the fuel pump fails any of the above tests, the pump should be rebuilt or renewed.

FUEL TANK

The 13 gallon fuel tank on both

the conventional and suburban models is located at the rear of the body, under the floor.

The fuel gauge (tank unit) and stand pipe are one unit. The filter on the end of the stand pipe is replaceable. It is quite helpful in preventing water and other foreign matter from entering the fuel pump and carburetor.

When installing a fuel gauge, (tank unit) be sure to push the filter down on the pipe until it is seated.

Remove—Except Suburban

1. Syphon all fuel from tank. Then disconnect the fuel line and the wire to the gauge unit, (right side near top of tank).
2. Disconnect vent tube from the tank at the connector.
3. Remove three attaching screws that hold the filler tube and

gasket, to the rear quarter panel.
4. Grasp the filler tube and twist, at the same time force downward into the tank, until the upper end of the tube clears the quarter panel.
5. Rotate the filler tube 180°, then work the tube carefully out of the tank and dust shield seal. Remove the tube from inside the trunk compartment.

CAUTION:

Do not pull the tube from side-to-side or up-and-down, as rough treatment can cause the soldered sleeve to break its seal to the tank, causing a leak.
6. Remove the nut from the retaining strap "J" bolt. Lower the tank and remove from the car.

Install—Except Suburban

1. Install a new "O" ring in the tank filler tube sleeve. Insert a new gasket in the fuel gauge opening recess, then install gauge in tank.
2. Slide the tank under the car and up into position. Install retaining strap and secure with the nut at the "J" bolt.
3. Lubricate the "O" ring with rubber lube, then slide the filler tube down through the dust seal and into the tank far enough to clear the quarter panel.
4. Rotate the filler tube 180° and align with the quarter panel opening. Install a new gasket over the end of the tube, then carefully work the tube out of the tank and into position against the quarter panel. Anchor tube to quarter panel with attaching screws.

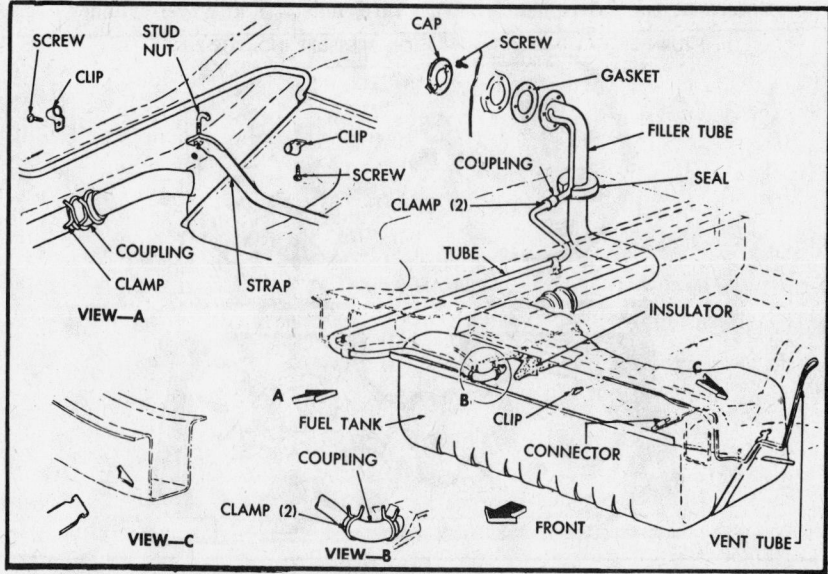

Fig. 1—Fuel Tank Mounting, (Suburban)

5. If the dust shield was disturbed, realign and tighten attaching screws.
6. Reconnect vent tube to the fuel tank connector.
7. Reconnect fuel supply line and the wire lead to the gauge.
8. Refill the tank and check for leaks.

Remove—Suburban

1. Disconnect fuel line and lead wire to the gauge.
2. Disconnect filler vent tube from the tank at "B" in Fig. 1. Disconnect the tank vent tube at the connector.
3. With clamp pliers, slide the clamps that hold the coupling hose to the fuel tank and filler tube "A" in Fig. 1. Slide the coupling along the filler tube until it clears the tank connection.
4. Slide a syphon tube into the tank (through the opening just made) and drain the tank.
5. Remove the nut from the attaching strap "J" bolt and drop the tank.

Install—Suburban

1. Install a new gasket at the gauge opening and snake the gauge into position in the tank. Install lock ring and tighten.
2. Slide the tank under the car and up into position. Install retaining strap and secure with the nut and "J" bolt.
3. Reconnect tank vent tube to the tank connector.
4. Reconnect the filler vent tube at the coupling, secure with clamps.
5. Slide the filler tube coupling hose over the fuel tank tube, then reposition the attaching clamps, using clamp pliers.
6. Reconnect fuel supply line and the wire lead to the gauge.
7. Refill the tank and check for leaks.

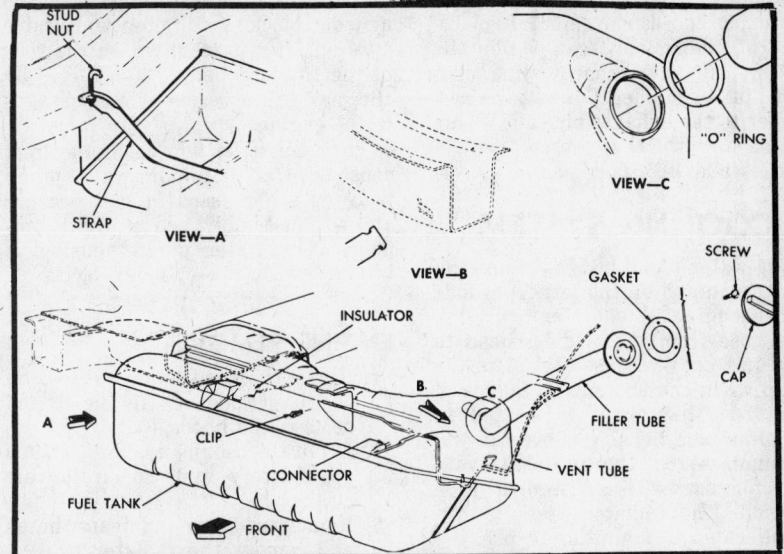

Fuel Tank Mounting, (Except Suburban)

EXHAUST SYSTEM
MANIFOLD
Remove

1. Remove air cleaner.
2. Remove vacuum control tube at carburetor and distributor.
3. Remove fuel line and remove carburetor.
4. Disconnect the exhaust pipe at flange.
5. Remove nuts and washers holding the intake and exhaust manifolds to the cylinder head.
6. Remove the assembly from the head.
7. Remove three bolts holding the intake and exhaust manifolds together.
8. Clean manifold mating and attaching surfaces with a straight edge and feeler gauge. All mating surfaces should be flat and plane within .008".

Install

1. Place a new gasket between intake and exhaust manifolds and install three attaching bolts, **loosely.**
2. With a new gasket in place, position the complete manifold combination on the cylinder head.
3. Install conical washers, (cupped side away from the nut) and nuts. Torque alternately to a final 10 ft. lb.
4. Now torque the three intake-to-exhaust manifold nuts to 15 ft. lb.
5. Connect the exhaust pipe to the manifold flange and torque these two bolts to 30 ft. lb.
6. Install carburetor and make fuel line, vacuum line and throttle linkage connections.
7. Install air cleaner. Start engine and check for intake and exhaust leaks.

MUFFLER AND TAIL PIPE

The exhaust pipe and muffler as produced at assembly is a one piece unit. It is handled in the customary

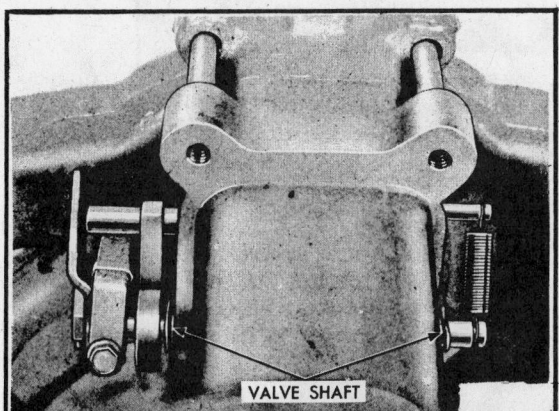

Manifold Heat Control Valve

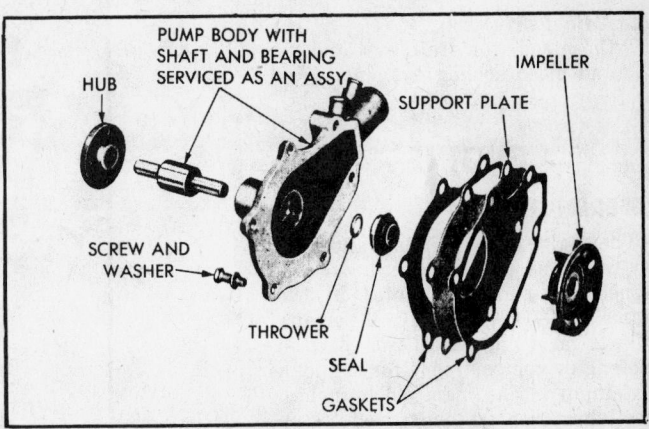

Water Pump, (Exploded View)

way and produces no problems to the experienced mechanic. Replacement of muffler only, can be done by cutting off the exhaust pipe just ahead of the muffler. Connect the new muffler to the exhaust pipe and clamp in place with the present saddle bracket and "U" bolt clamp.

COOLING SYSTEM

The water pump body is aluminum and is mounted on the left front side of the engine. A short external bypass hose from the cylinder head to the pump body returns coolant to the pump when the thermostat is closed. The 180° thermostat is located in the aluminum housing above the water pump. A 160° thermostat is available for use with an alcohol type solution. The radiator pressure cap is calibrated to maintain 14 psi.

WATER PUMP

Remove

1. Drain the cooling system.
2. Loosen the drive belt adjusting strap at the alternator and move alternator toward the engine.
3. Remove the fan, spacer, pulley and belt.
4. Remove the pump inlet hose and the heater hose.
5. Remove clamp from the by-pass hose.
6. Remove water pump body-to-housing bolts and push the pump body down, off the by-pass hose.

Install

1. Place by-pass hose clamp on the hose, then lift the pump up into the hose.
2. Attach pump body to the housing, using the two long bolts above and below the inlet hose. Tighten bolts to 30 ft. lb.
3. Attach the inlet hose and the heater hose.
4. Install drive belt, pulley, spacer and fan.
5. Adjust drive belt.
6. Close radiator drain cock and fill and bleed cooling system.

ENGINE

REFERENCES

The engine used in Valiant and Lancer cars, and the 1963 Dart was designed for and is mounted in the frame at a 30 degree angle. It permits a lower hood line and allows space in the engine compartment for the long aluminum intake manifold branches. The lubrication system consists of an externally mounted rotor type oil pump on the lower right side of the cylinder block. A full flow replaceable type oil filter is mounted on the rear of the oil pump body. Oil is forced by the pump to a series of oil passages in the engine.

The semi-series flow cooling system consists of an aluminum water pump body with a pressed in ball bearing and seal assembly and a plastic impeller. The water pump housing is integral with the cylinder block.

ENGINE REMOVE

1. Scribe the hood hinge outlines on the underside of the hood and remove the hood.
2. Drain the cooling system, remove the battery and carburetor air cleaner.
3. Remove radiator and heater hoses and remove the radiator.
4. Remove the outlet vent pipe from the cylinder head cover.
5. Disconnect fuel lines, linkage and wiring to the engine.
6. Disconnect exhaust pipe at exhaust manifold.
7. Raise car on hoist.
8. If equipped with automatic transmission, drain the converter and the transmission. Remove the oil cooler lines, filler tube and push button cable.
9. Remove the clutch torque shaft, brake cables and rods.
10. Remove the speedometer cable and gear shift rods.
11. Disconnect propeller shaft and tie out of the way.
12. Install an engine support fixture to the rear of the engine.
13. Remove the engine rear support crossmember.
14. Remove transmission mounting bolts from clutch housing.
15. Remove the transmission.
16. Lower the car.
17. Install engine lifting fixture to the engine and attach chain hoist to the fixture eyebolt.

18. Remove the engine support fixture.
19. Remove the engine front mounting bolts.
20. Lift the engine out of the engine compartment and lower it onto a substantial work stand.

ENGINE INSTALL

To install the engine, reverse the above procedure and torque the front engine mounting bolts to 85 ft. lb., the rear ones to 35 ft. lb.

CYLINDER HEAD

The cylinder head is chrome alloy cast iron and is attached to the cast iron cylinder block by 14, 7/16 x 14 bolts.

Remove

1. Drain the cooling system.
2. Remove carburetor air cleaner and fuel lines.
3. Disconnect accelerator linkage.
4. Remove the vacuum line from carburetor to distributor.
5. Carefully disconnect spark plug wires by pulling straight and in line with plug.
6. Disconnect heater hose and clamp holding the by-pass hose.
7. Disconnect the heat indicator sending unit wire.
8. Disconnect exhaust pipe at the exhaust manifold flange.
9. Remove the intake and exhaust manifold and carburetor as an assembly.
10. Remove the outlet vent tube and cylinder head cover.
11. Remove the rocker arms and shaft.
12. Remove the push rods and place them in order (don't mix them up).
13. Remove the head bolts and lift off the cylinder head.
14. Place cylinder head on bench and remove the spark plugs.

LOOSEN BEFORE INSTALLING

Intake Manifold

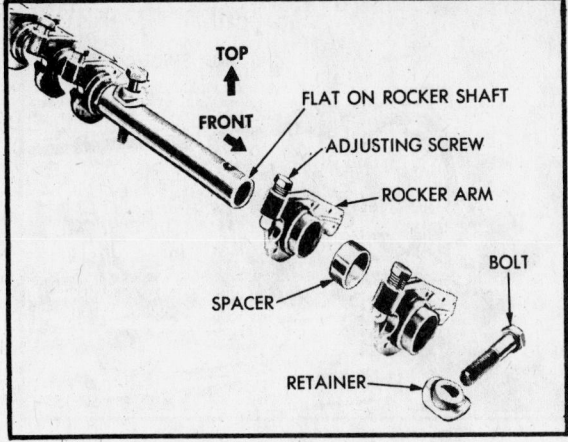

Rocker Arm and Shaft Assembly

Removing Spring and Seal Assembly.

Head Install

1. Clean carbon from the combustion area. Clean all gasket surfaces of both head and cylinder block. Install spark plugs (the aluminum plug shields act as satisfactory gasket material between spark plug body and cylinder head).
2. If there is any cause to suspect leakage, check all surfaces with a straight-edge.
3. Apply a reliable sealer to the new gasket and install the gasket and cylinder head.
4. Install the 14 cylinder head bolts. Starting at the top center, tighten all cylinder head bolts to 65 ft. procedure by loosening, then tightening to 65 ft. lb. final torque.
5. Inspect all push rods for bends or wear. Replace if necessary.
6. Install the push rods, small ends down in the tappets.
7. Install rocker arms and shaft assembly with FLAT on the end of the shaft ON TOP and pointing toward the FRONT of the engine. This is necessary to provide lubrication to the rocker assemblies. Torque the attaching bolts to 30 ft. lb.
8. Loosen the three bolts connecting the intake and exhaust manifolds. (This is necessary to obtain proper alignment.)
9. Install intake and exhaust manifold and carburetor assembly to the cylinder head. Put the cup side of the conical washers against the manifolds, install the attaching nuts and torque to 10 ft. lb.
10. Retighten the three intake-to-exhaust manifold bolts to 15 ft. lb.
11. Connect the heater hose and by-pass hose clamp.
12. Connect the heat indicator sending unit wire, the accelerator linkage and the spark plug wires.
13. Install carburetor-to-distributor vacuum line.
14. Connect exhaust pipe to the exhaust manifold (new gasket, please).
15. Install the fuel line and carburetor air cleaner.
16. Refill the cooling system.
17. Start the engine and let run until operating temperatures have been reached.
18. Adjust valve tappet clearance to .010″ (intake) and .020″ (exhaust). The adjusting screw in the push rod end of the rocker arm should have a minimum of 3 ft. lb. (36 in. lb.) tension as it is turned. If less, replace the adjusting screw and the rocker arm, if necessary.
19. Place the new cylinder head cover gasket in position and install cylinder head cover. Torque attaching nuts to 40 in. lb. (3 1/3 ft. lb.)
20. Install outlet vent tube.

VALVES

Valve guides are not replaceable.

Valve servicing is not unlike other overhead valve engines except for a factory specified difference in the prescribed exhaust valve face angle.

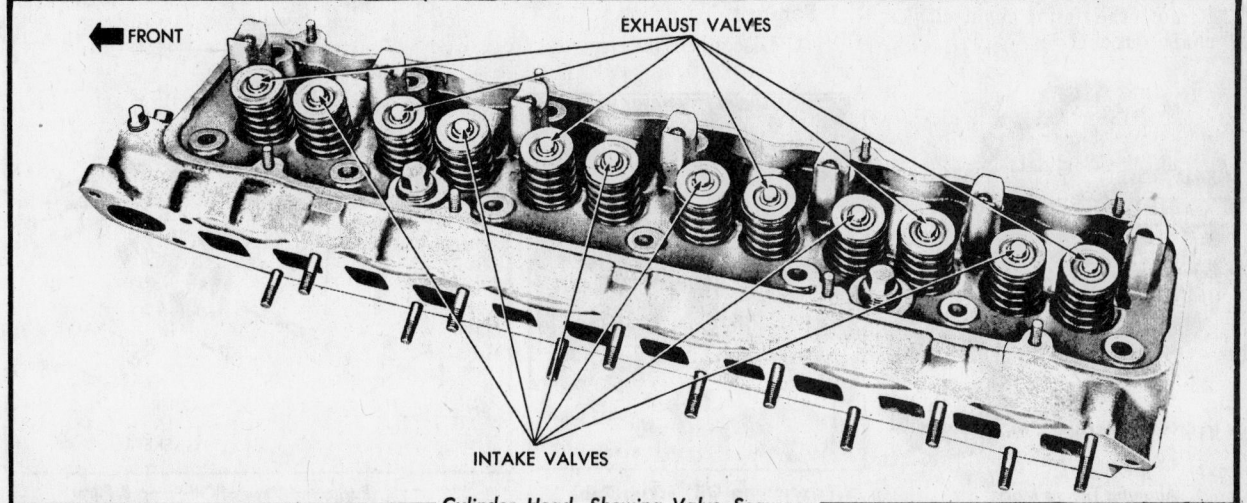

Cylinder Head, Showing Valve Sequence

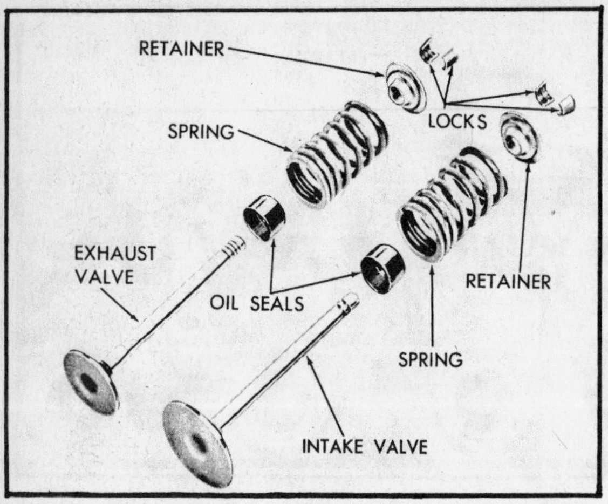

Valve Assembly

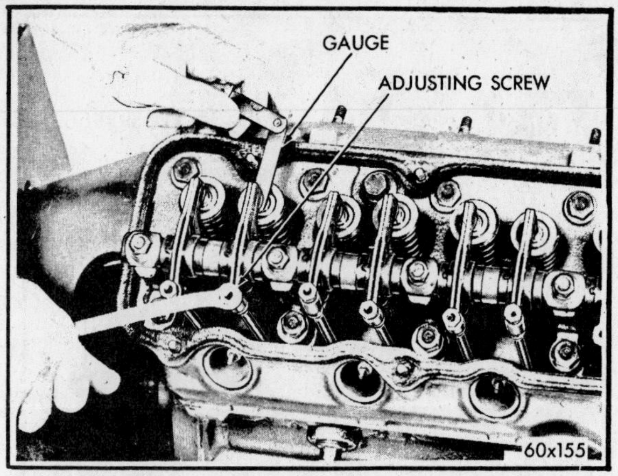

Valve Adjustment

The intake and exhaust valve seats, in the cylinder head, and the intake valve face, have a 45° angle. The exhaust valve face has a 47° angle.

Inspect the remaining valve head margin after the valve has been refaced, and discard any valve with a head margin (unground outer edge thickness) less than 3/64". The width of the intake valve seats should be within 5/64"-3/32" and the width of the exhaust seats should be within 3/64"-1/16".

TIMING CASE

Remove

1. Drain cooling system.
2. Remove radiator and fan.
3. With puller, remove vibration damper.
4. Loosen engine oil pan bolts to allow clearance and remove timing case cover and gasket.
5. Slide crankshaft oil slinger off the front of crankshaft.
6. Remove the camshaft sprocket bolt.
7. Remove the timing chain with camshaft sprocket.

Install

1. Turn crankshaft to line up the timing mark on the crankshaft sprocket with the centerline of camshaft (without the chain). and crankshaft.
3. Align the marks on the crankshaft and camshaft sprockets, using an imaginary center line thru the two shafts.
4. Remove the camshaft sprocket and reinstall with chain.
5. Torque camshaft sprocket to 35 ft. lb.
6. Replace oil slinger (don't forget).
7. Reinstall timing case cover with new gasket and torque to 15 ft. lb. Retighten engine oil pan to 17 ft. lb.
8. Replace vibration damper.
9. Replace radiator and hoses.
10. Refill and bleed cooling system.

ENGINE LUBRICATION

ENGINE OIL PAN

Remove

1. Disconnect battery.
2. Drain oil and cooling system.
3. Disconnect both hoses and other parts to avoid possible damage when raising the engine.
4. Loosen alternator strap and move alternator toward engine.
5. Disconnect exhaust pipe at manifold.
6. Remove steering and idler arm ball joints from center link.
7. Remove two engine support bolts.
8. Jack up front of engine (not under vibration damper) and block in raised position with short pieces of wood at supports.

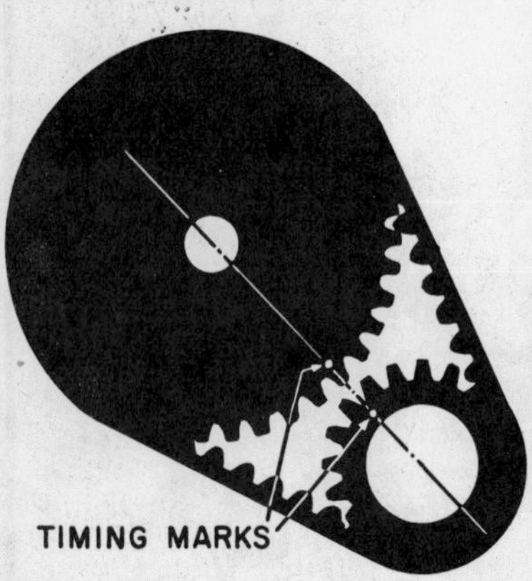

Aligning Timing Marks

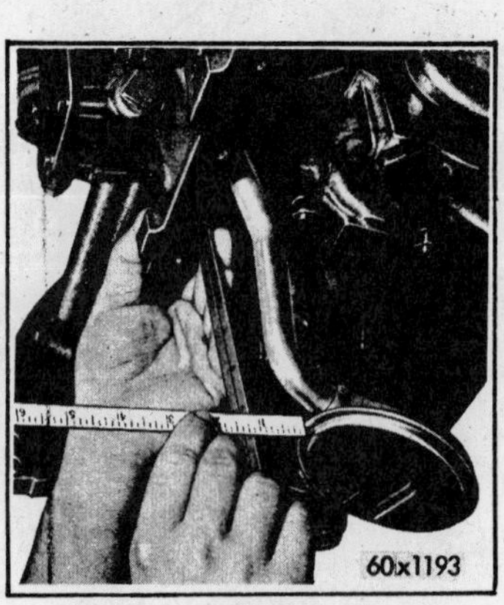

Positioning Oil Pickup Tube

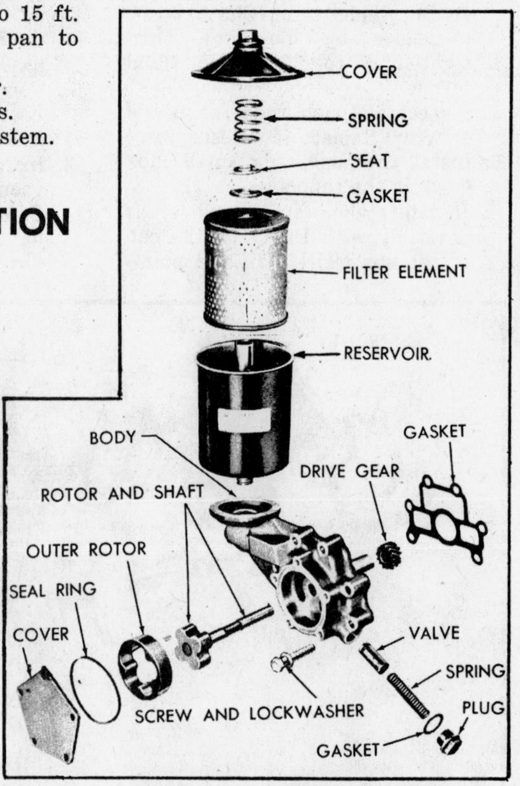

Exploded View of Oil Pump & Filter

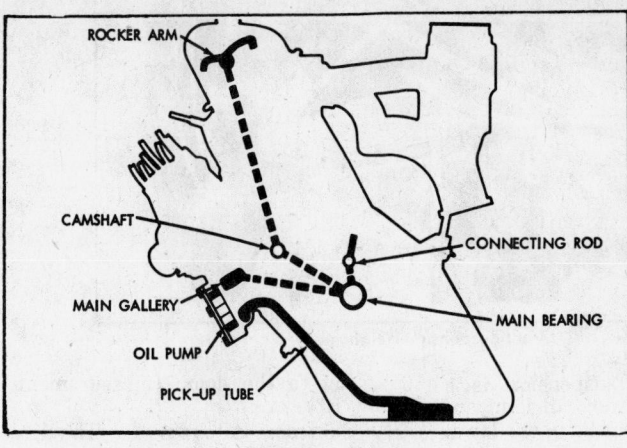

Oil Circuit

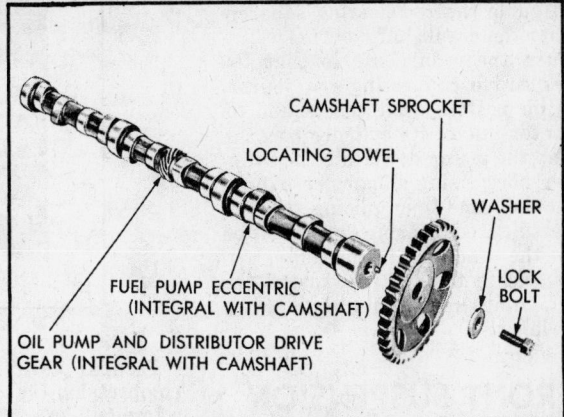

Camshaft and Sprocket Assembly

9. Remove lower and front clutch covers or converter cover plate.
10. Maneuver pan down and forward, lower rear end and remove.
11. Note position of oil screen and pipe, then unscrew the assembly.

Install

Replace oil pan in reverse of removal instructions and torque attaching bolts to 16¾ ft. lb. Torque engine front mounting bolts to 85 ft. lb.

OIL PUMP

The oil pump is an externally mounted rotary type pump. It is attached to the outer, right side of the crankcase and contains an easily accessible by-pass relief valve. The pump is driven, independent of the distributor, by an integral gear of the camshaft.

Remove & Install

1. Drain cooling system and remove top and bottom hoses.
2. Remove engine, front mounting bolts and loosen the rear mount.
3. With proper engine oil pan support, raise the front of the engine sufficiently to allow the oil pump to clear suspension interference (about 2 inches).
4. Remove oil pump attaching bolts and pull the pump and filter assembly from the side of the engine.
5. Replace, in reverse sequence.

Relief Valve Spring Chart

Color	Free Length	Loaded Length	Compression Pounds
Gray (Light)	2.19″	1.60″	11.85 to 12.85
Red (Standard)	2.29″	1.60″	14.85 to 15.85
Brown (Heavy)	2.39″	1.60″	17.90 to 18.90

NOTE: Beginning 1961, a throw-away type filter unit is used.

PISTONS AND CONNECTING RODS

REFERENCES

The pistons are cam ground so that the diameter across the piston at the pin boss is less than its diameter from major to minor thrust faces. This allows for expansion under normal operating conditions. Expansion forces the pin bosses away from each other, and the piston assumes a rounder shape.

Fitting Pistons

The piston and the cylinder wall surfaces must be dry and clean. Clearance between the piston and the cylinder wall is .0005″ to .0015″.

Measurements should be taken at normal room temperature, about 70°F. Measure the piston diameter at the top of the skirt, 90° to the piston pin axis. Measure the cylinder walls half way down the bore, transverse to the length of the engine (measure from right to left hand side of the bore).

Fitting Rings

There are three rings used, two compression and one oil control ring.

Beginning 1963 all iron 6 cyl. engines, oil hole on right.

The ring gap should be between .010″ and .020″ for all rings and is measured with a feeler gauge in the gap, with the ring squarely in the bore, two inches from the bottom. Measure the ring side clearance (between the ring and the top or bottom of the ring land) with a feeler gauge. This clearance should be .0015″-.003″ for the two top rings and .001″-.003″ for the oil control ring.

ROD BEARINGS AND PISTON ASSEMBLIES

Rod bearings are conventional insert type lead-base babbitt on steel shells. They are to be fitted to .0005″-.0015″ clearance.

1. Position the compression ring gaps opposite each other and 90° from the oil control ring gap.
2. Have the oil ring expander gap toward the right (camshaft or distributor side of the engine). Turn the oil ring gap toward the left (manifold) side of the engine.
3. Immerse the piston head and rings in a container of clean engine oil. Compress the rings, taking care not to disturb the position of the rings, and insert the piston and rod assembly into its respective cylinder bore. The notch on top of the piston must point toward the front of the engine. The spit hole, in the rod bearing end of the connecting rod, must point toward the left (manifold side) of the engine for proper cylinder wall and piston lubrication.
4. Protect the connecting rod crankpin journal and the connecting rod bolts, themselves, with a couple of turns of masking tape applied to the threaded end of the rod bearing bolts. This is a worth-while move in the absence of special tools. The angle of this engine requires that some type of guide (personal or mechanical) be used

to guide the rod bearing squarely onto the crankshaft journal.

5. Turn the crankshaft so that the respective connecting rod journal is on bottom dead center and on center line of its cylinder bore.

6. Tap the piston down into the cylinder bore, using a hammer handle. At the same time guiding the connecting rod bearing into position on the crankshaft journal.

7. Lubricate the rod cap, install the attaching nuts and torque to 45 ft. lb.

FRONT SUSPENSION

Torsion-Aire front suspension is similar in principle to that used on other cars of the Chrysler family. The torsion bars are used in the front only and are connected to the lower control arms and anchored to the body under the front floor.

Ball joints are used at the upper and lower ends of the steering knuckles. Cam-type caster and camber adjustment methods are employed. Direct-acting oriflow shock absorbers are attached between the lower control arms and stamped steel towers welded into the body-frame unit.

Radius rods are used on the lower control arms and extend forward to attach to the "K" shaped engine support member. The upper control arm is angled downward toward the rear to reduce nose dive during brake application.

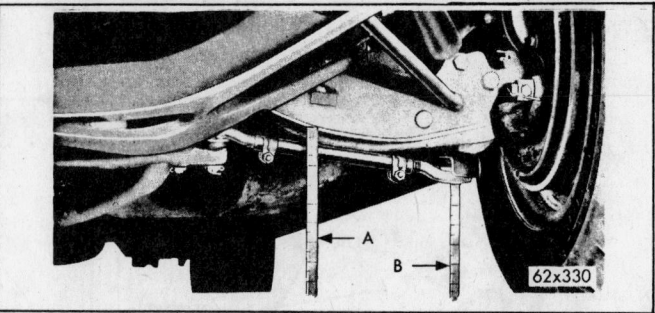

Front Suspension Height

Peculiar to this suspension is a compression-type lower ball joint and a torsion bar adjustment in the lower control arm.

The torsion bar adjustment permits rotating the bar relative to the lower control arm to obtain correct front-end height settings. This adjustment is located at the front end of the bar and permits easy adjustment during wheel alignment operations.

For detailed instructions in repairing and adjusting the front suspension, see the Unit Repair section, "Suspension, Front Repair."

FRONT HEIGHT

Adjustment, Without Gauge

1. Jounce the car and measure from the lower ball joint to the floor, (measurement "A").

2. Measure from the control arm torsion bar spring anchor housing to the floor, (measurement "B").

3. Subtract "A" from "B". The difference should be $1\frac{7}{8}$"$\pm\frac{1}{8}$".

4. Measure the other side in the same way.

5. Adjust, if necessary, by turning the torsion bar adjusting bolt, in to raise or out to lower.

TORSION BAR SPRINGS

Contrary to appearance, the torsion bars are **not** interchangeable from "right" to "left." They are marked with an R or an L, according to their location.

Remove

1. Lift the car by the body only so that the front suspension is free of all load. If the car is to be raised with jacks, place jack under center of "K Member" and raise until suspension is free of all load.

2. Release load from torsion bar by backing off anchor adjusting nuts. Remove the adjusting nut and swivel bolt.

3. Remove the lower control arm strut.

4. Remove the lock spring from the

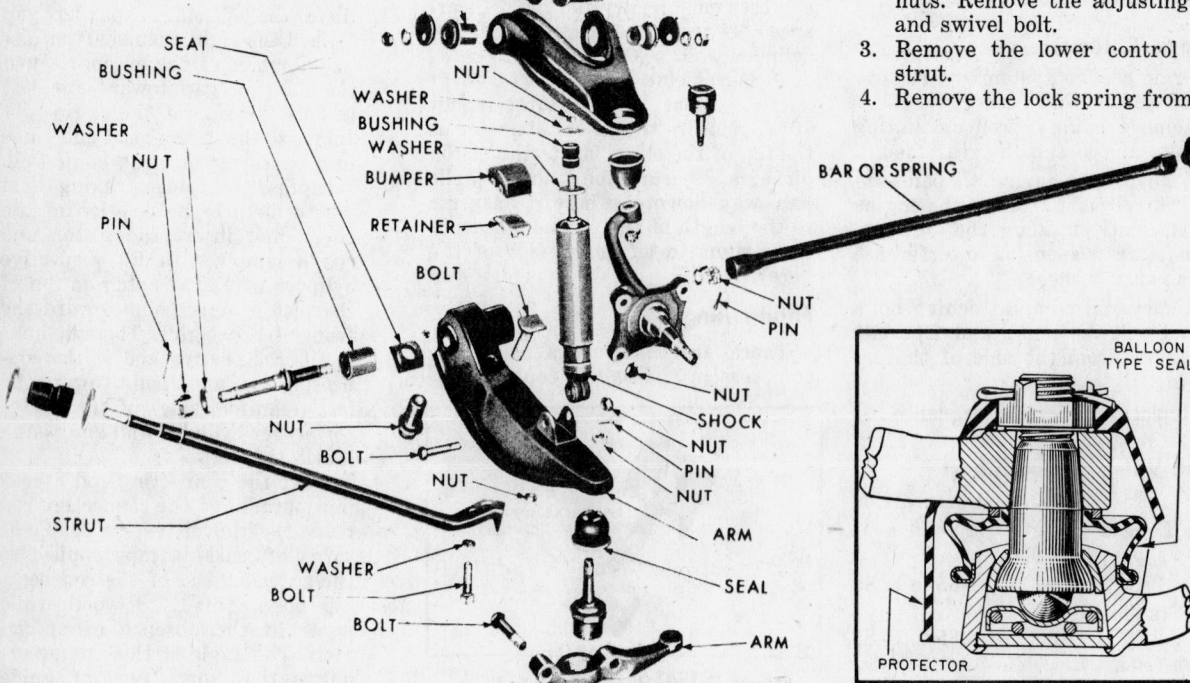

SEAT
BUSHING
WASHER
NUT
PIN
NUT
BOLT
NUT
STRUT
WASHER
BOLT
BOLT

NUT
WASHER
BUSHING
WASHER
BUMPER
RETAINER
BOLT

SHOCK

BAR OR SPRING

NUT
PIN

NUT
SHOCK
NUT
PIN
NUT
ARM
SEAL
ARM

BALLOON TYPE SEAL

PROTECTOR

Front Suspension and Torsion Bar (Exploded View)

Lube-Sealed Ball Joint

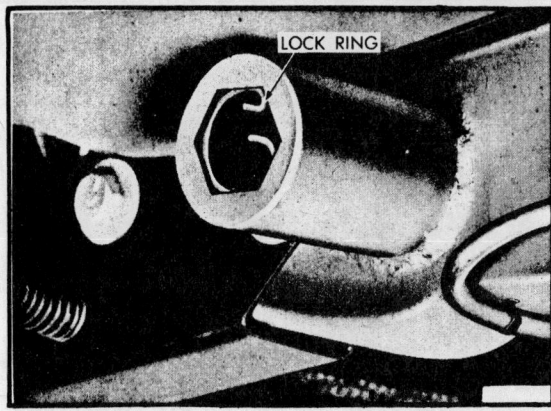

Torsion Bar, Rear Anchor Lock Ring

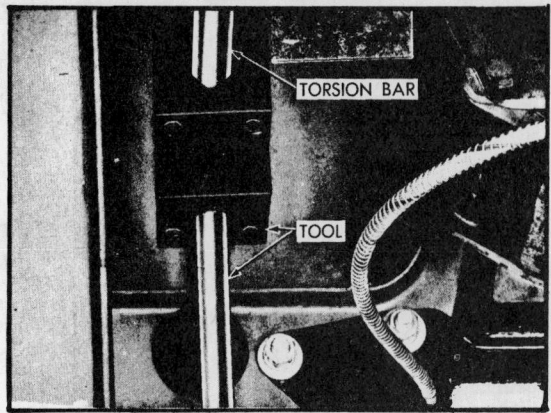

Removing Torsion Bar

rear of torsion bar rear anchor.

5. Install tool #C-3728, or other suitable clamp and remove torsion bar rearward by striking the clamping tool with a hammer. **Do not apply heat to the front or rear anchors. Do not scratch or otherwise mar the skin of the torsion bar during removal or installation.**

6. Remove the clamping tool and slide the rear anchor balloon seal off the front end of the bar.

7. Remove torsion bar by sliding the bar rearward and out through the rear anchor.

Install

1. Clean the hex openings of both front and rear anchors, also clean the male ends of the torsion bar.

2. Feed the torsion bar through the rear anchor.

3. Slide the balloon type seal over the torsion bar, with the large cupped side of the seal facing the rear.

4. Coat both ends of the torsion bar with multi-purpose grease.

5. When starting the bar into the anchor in the lower control arm, position the adjusting arm about 60° below the horizontal plane. This will permit wind-up for future adjustment.

6. Install the lock ring in the rear anchor, then move torsion bar rearward until the bar contacts the lock ring.

7. Position swivel bolt on the control arm and hold in place while installing the adjusting nut and seat. Tighten the adjustment about 10 turns before lowering car to the floor.

8. Pack the annular opening in the rear anchor with multi-purpose grease. Slide the rear anchor balloon type seal into position over the rear anchor until the lip of the seal fits in the groove.

9. Install lower control arm strut.

10. Lower car to the floor and adjust front suspension height.

STEERING

Instructions for the overhaul of the Steering Gear will be found in the Unit Repair section under the headings: "Steering, Manual" or "Steering, Power."

MANUAL STEERING

A worm and recirculating ball type steering gear is used with the manual steering system.

The worm shaft is supported at each end by ball type thrust bearings.

The sector shaft includes an integral sector gear which meshes with helical grooves on the worm shaft ball nut.

The sector shaft is supported and rotates in two needle bearings in the housing and one in the housing cover.

ADJUSTMENTS

There are two adjustments required on this type steering gear. They are the Worm Bearing Pre-Load and the Ball Nut Sector Gear Mesh. The following sequence should be followed.

Worm Bearing Pre-Load

Worm bearing preload is controlled

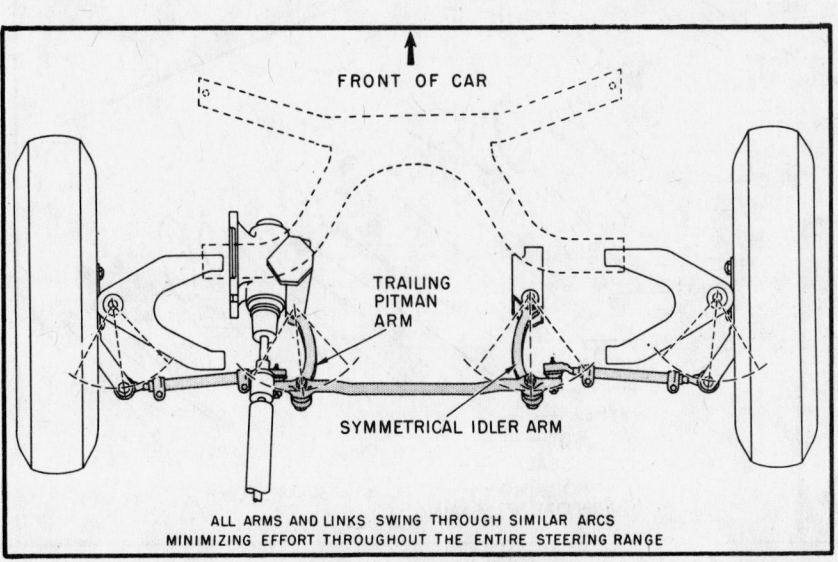

ALL ARMS AND LINKS SWING THROUGH SIMILAR ARCS
MINIMIZING EFFORT THROUGHOUT THE ENTIRE STEERING RANGE

Steering Linkage Arrangement

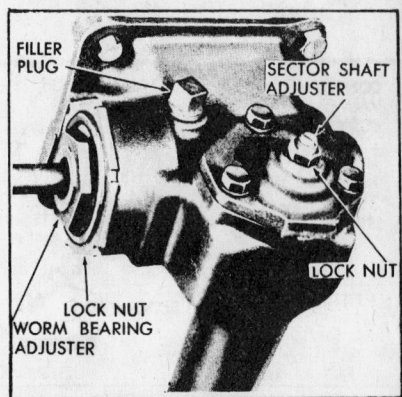

Steering Gear Adjustment Points

VALIANT—LANCER—DART

by the large adjusting nut which threads in the housing.

1. Disconnect the steering gear arm, (Pitman arm) from the sector shaft.
2. Loosen the sector shaft adjusting screw lock nut. Back out the adjusting screw about two turns.
3. Turn the steering wheel two complete rotations from straight ahead.

CAUTION:

Do not turn the steering wheel hard against the stops while the gear is disconnected from the steering linkage. Damage may result.

4. With a scale attached to the rim of the steering wheel, read the required effort necessary to keep the wheel in continuous motion through one revolution. The scale should register about ½ lb. This is worm bearing pre-load.

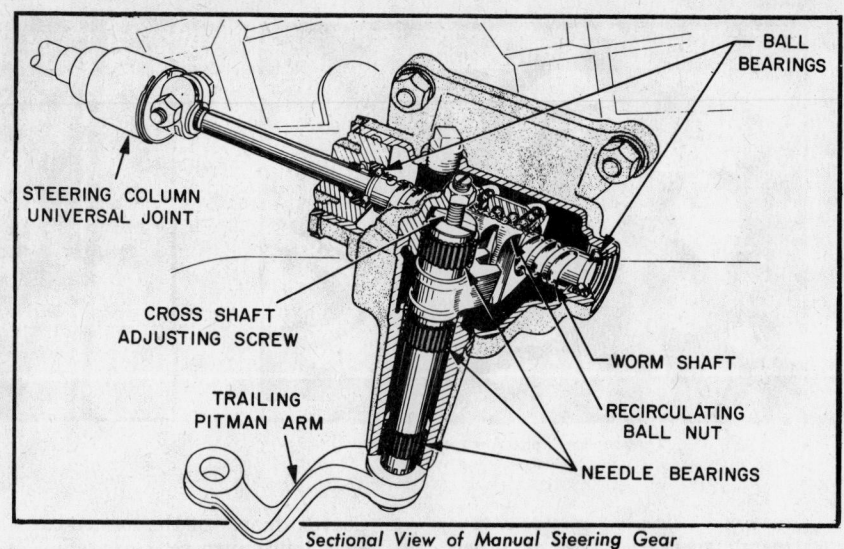

Sectional View of Manual Steering Gear

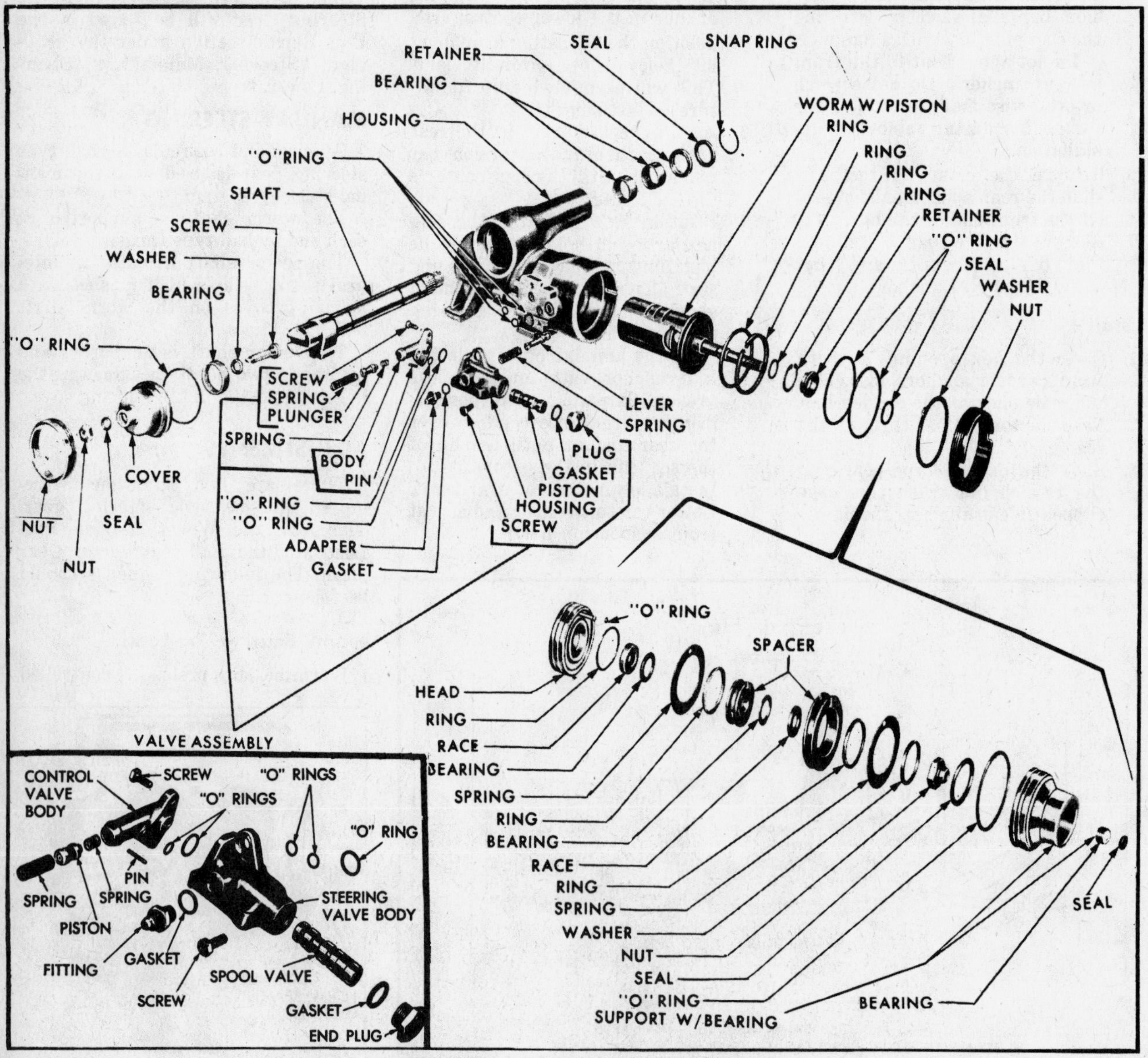

Power Steering Gear Assembly, (Exploded View)

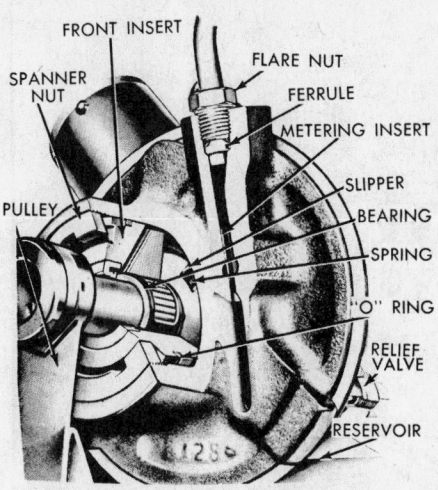

Power Steering Pump

5. Worm bearing pre-load is controlled by tightening or loosening the worm bearing adjusting nut.

6. After the proper pre-load is established, tighten the worm bearing adjuster lock nut.

Ball Nut And Sector Mesh

1. Gently rotate the steering wheel from one extreme to the other while counting the turns. Then turn the wheel back exactly half way, to the center position.

2. Turn the sector shaft adjuster, (Fig. 4) clockwise until all lash has been removed from the gear. Tighten the adjuster lock nut to 40 ft. lb.

3. Turn the steering wheel ½ turn away from center. With the scale attached to the wheel rim, read the effort required to keep the wheel in continuous motion through the straight ahead position. The scale should read about 1¼ lb. This is the steering "High-Spot" load and consists of the sum of the worm bearing pre-load and the gear mesh load.

4. After the adjustments have been completed, align the front wheels in the straight-ahead position. Install the steering arm on the sector shaft and torque the retaining nut to 85 ft. lb.

POWER STEERING

Constant-Control power steering is an option on both Valiant and Lancer models. Hydraulic power is provided by a vane-type, belt-driven pump. A double-groove pump pulley is used. The power steering gear and pump are essentially the same as those used on other Chrysler Corp. cars. Service information may be found in the Unit Repair section under "Steering, Power."

HORN BUTTON AND STEERING COLUMN

Remove & Install

1. Disconnect ground, (neg.) cable from the battery.
2. Press and rotate the horn button ¼ turn counterclockwise and remove the button.
3. Remove three screws and bushings from horn button base and lift out base or horn ring.
4. Disconnect wire from horn switch and remove the switch.
5. Remove steering wheel nut and washer.
6. Position front wheels in straight ahead position. Then pull steering wheel. Remove turn signal switch lever.
7. Disconnect turn signal and horn wires at the multiple connector under instrument panel.
8. Remove clamp bolt and clamp from lower end of column jacket. Remove the column upper clamp.

Steering Column Assembly, (Exploded View)

9. Remove clamp bolt from steering coupling. While lifting the column upward, tap the coupling upward with soft hammer to free it from the worm shaft splines.
10. Slide the column upward through the dash and remove the assembly from the car.

Install in reverse order of removal.

CLUTCH

The clutch is a single dry plate type operated by a pedal suspended under the dash; it is equipped with an assist spring. Both the clutch housing and the transmission extension are die-cast aluminum.

The manual-shift transmission is of special design and standard equipment. Gear changes are accomplished thru a short gearshift lever mounted in the floor, convenient to the driver's right hand. It is connected to the transmission thru a series of links. The rods of the shifter linkage are of large diameter, stiff steel, cadmium plated.

The gearbox proper, is inclined 30° to the left (just opposite the slant of the engine). Access to the gears is thru a stamped steel cover plate in the cast iron gearbox. The selector shafts protrude from the left side of the transmission housing thru bored holes. Blocker-ring synchronizers are used on second and third gears.

No special instructions should be required by the mechanic to remove or replace either clutch or transmission.

REMOVE

1. Drain transmission.
2. Disconnect the propeller shaft, speedometer cable, gear shift rods and parking brake controls.

CAUTION:

Remove speedometer cable with your hand so that housing is not crushed, (pinion comes out with cable).

3. Remove back-up light switch leads, (if so equipped).
4. Install lifting device under engine and raise to support the engine and transmission weight.
5. Remove engine rear support crossmember attaching bolts.
6. With a suitable jack under the transmission, remove the transmission-to-clutch housing bolts.
7. Slide the transmission rearward and down out of the car.
8. Remove the clutch housing pan.
9. Disconnect clutch linkage and retracting spring at the release fork.
10. Remove the fork from the

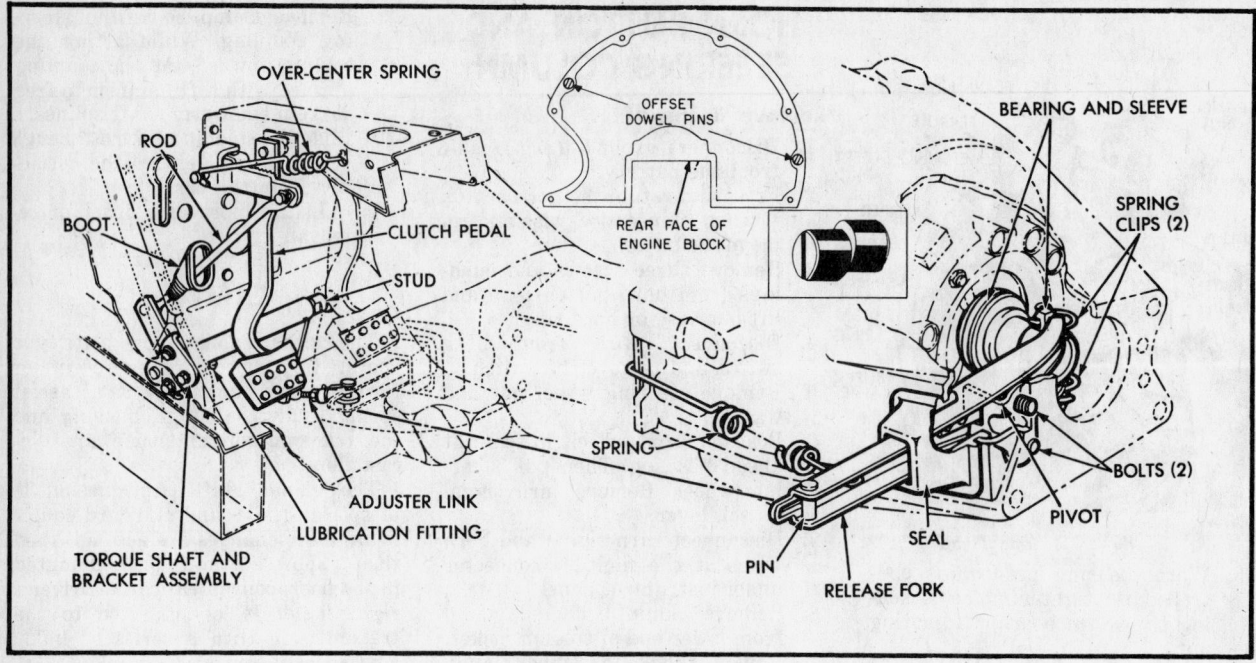

Clutch Pedal and Linkage

through-out bearing assembly.
11. Prick punch the clutch cover and flywheel to assure correct relocation when installing.
12. Remove the six clutch-to-flywheel bolts and remove the clutch cover and driven plate.

INSTALL

Install the clutch in reverse order and adjust clutch linkage.

LINKAGE ADJUST

Adjust the length of the release fork rod until there is 5/32 inch free movement measured at the outer end of the clutch fork. This will produce the one inch free play required at the pedal.

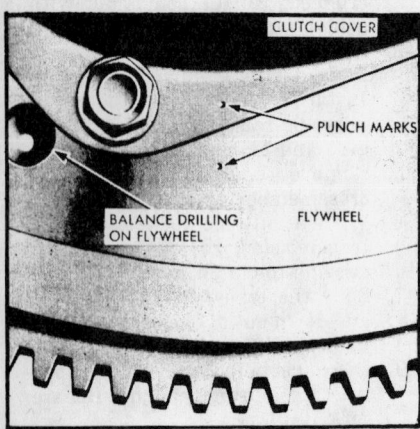

Punch Marks on Clutch Cover and Flywheel

STANDARD TRANSMISSION

DISASSEMBLING THE TRANSMISSION

1. Pull the out-put shaft flange.
2. Remove the bolts and one stud that attach the extension housing to the transmission case. Remove the housing.
3. Remove extension housing oil seal.
4. Remove the transmission case cover.
5. Remove the attaching bolts and remove the main drive pinion bearing retainer. Then grasp the pinion shaft and pull the assembly out of the case.

CAUTION:

Be careful not to bind the inner synchronizer ring on the drive pinion clutch teeth.

6. Remove the snap ring which locks the main drive pinion bearing on the pinion shaft. Remove the bearing washer, press the shaft out of the bearing and remove the oil slinger.
7. Remove the snap ring from the pilot bearing in the end of the drive pinion and remove the 14 rollers.
8. With the transmission in reverse, remove the outer center bearing snap ring, then partially remove the mainshaft.
9. Cock the mainshaft, then remove the clutch sleeve, the outer syn-

chronizer rings, the front inner ring and the 2-3 shift box.
10. Remove clutch gear retaining snap ring and slide the clutch gear off the end of the mainshaft.
11. Slide the second speed gear, stop ring and synchronizer spring off the mainshaft.
12. Remove the low and reverse sliding gear and shift fork, as the mainshaft is completely withdrawn from the case.
13. Check cluster gear end play. End play should be .004" to .012". This measurement will determine thrust washer value at reassembly.
14. Drive the countershaft rearward and out of the case.
15. Lift the gear cluster and thrust washers out of the case. Remove

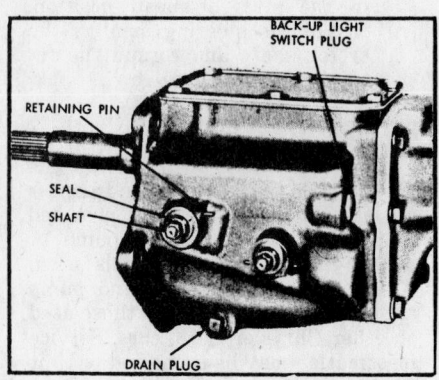

Standard Transmission Assembly

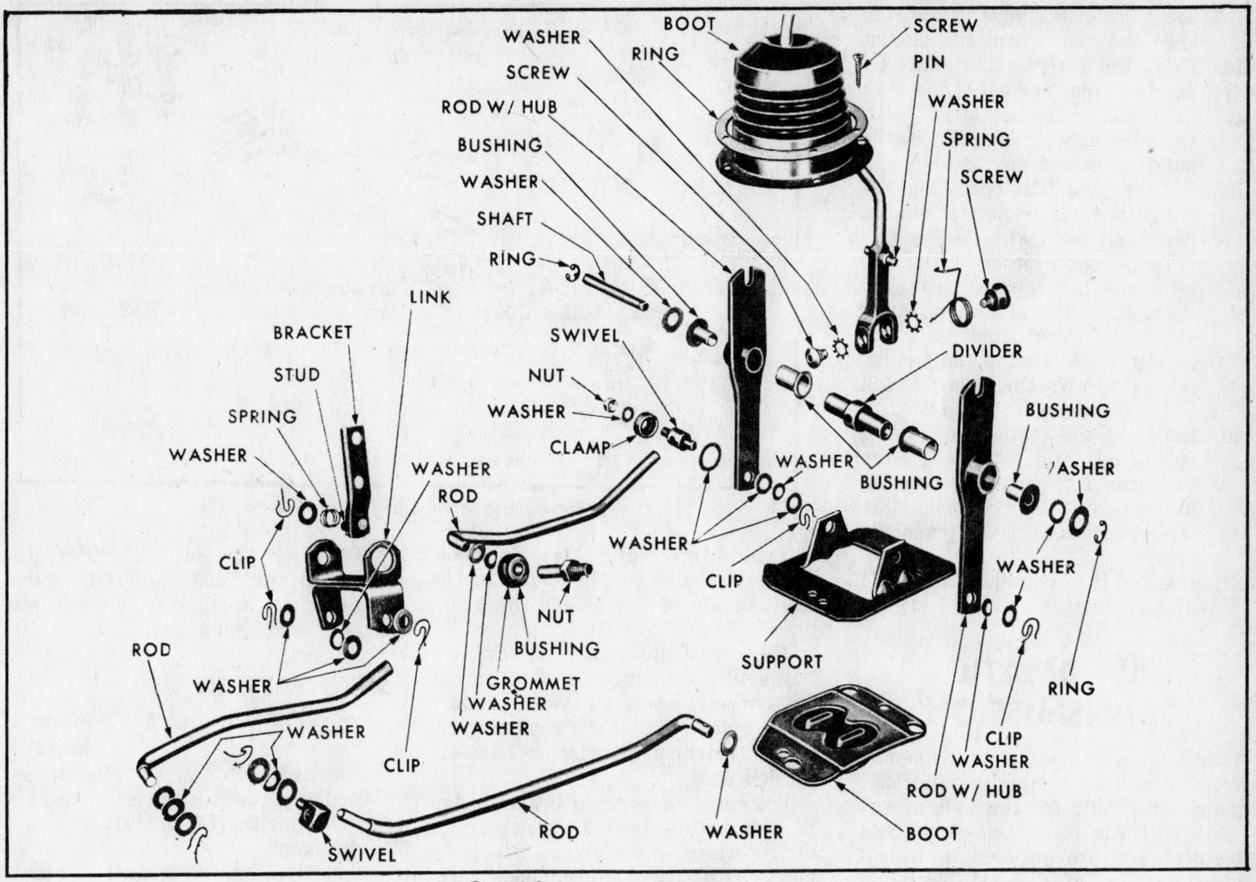

Gearshift Lever Assembly, Exploded View

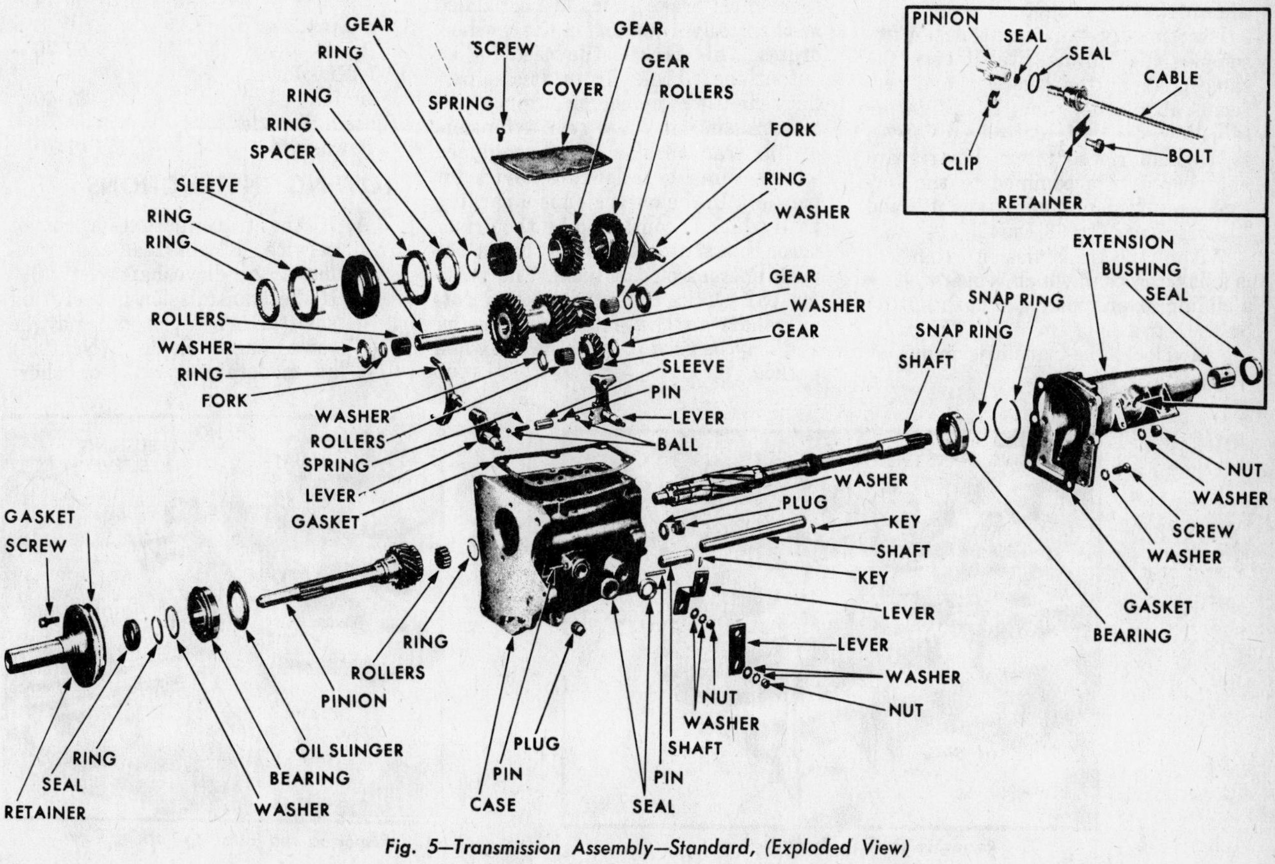

Fig. 5—Transmission Assembly—Standard, (Exploded View)

the needle bearings, (22 each end) and spacer from the cluster.

16. Drive the reverse idler shaft toward the rear and out of the case.

17. Lift the reverse idler gear, thrust washers and 22 needle bearings out of the case.

18. Remove gearshift operating levers from their respective shafts.

19. Drive out tapered retaining pin, (Fig. 5) from either of the two lever shafts, then withdraw the shaft from inside the transmission case. (The detent balls are spring loaded, as the shaft is being withdrawn the balls will fall to the bottom of the case.)

20. Remove the interlock sleeve, spring, pin and both balls from the case. Drive out the remaining tapered pin, then slide the lever shaft out of the transmission.

21. Remove the lever shaft seals and discard them.

AUTOMATIC TRANSMISSION

This 3 speed automatic transmission is a completely new design, fashioned specifically for the Valiant and "Lancer". The torque converter and transmission are enclosed in a one-piece housing of diecast aluminum. The transmission extension is also an aluminum diecasting.

Functionally, this transmission resembles the TorqueFlite. It uses the same push button selection and performs about the same. In design detail, however, it is entirely different. It is smaller, the internal parts are engineered to accommodate the torque requirements of "Valiant" and "Lancer" and "1963 Dart."

Within the transmission extension, is a parking pawl which is operated by a sliding lever under the push-button on the left side of the dash. The parking pawl locks the transmission output shaft.

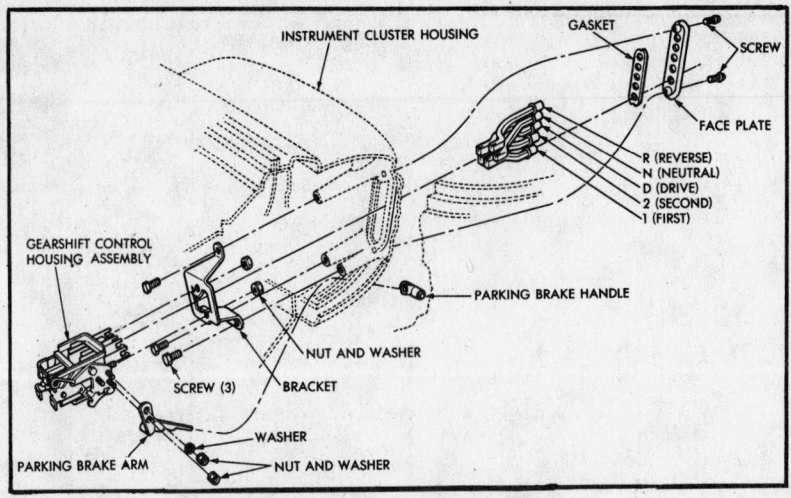

Removing and Installing Gear Selector

General information, trouble shooting and repairs will be found in the Unit Repair section under the heading: Torque Flite (B).

The prime difference between the Torqueflite transmission used on the conventional sized Chrysler product of six cylinders and the compact version is in the transmission rear extension area.

The compact parking brake design is a departure from Chrysler tradition. Parking brake application is no longer through a transmission case-to-propeller shaft brake. Instead, the rear wheel brake shoes are expanded mechanically against the wheel drums. This cancels the need for an output shaft brake drum. It also permits the use of a shorter output shaft and transmission case rear extension.

This transmission is now equipped with a sprag type locking device for parking. In the extension is a parking pawl which is controlled by the driver through a sliding lever just under the push buttons on the dash. The parking pawl locks the transmission output shaft to the extension housing and may be used to hold the car when parked.

These are the essential differences found in the Torqueflite (B) transmission, as applied to Valiant and Lancer, and "1963 Dart."

SHIFT PATTERN

Status		@ Approx. Miles Per Hour
Closed throttle	1-2 upshift	8-11
Closed throttle	2-3 upshift	12-15
Wide open throttle	1-2 upshift	28-43
Wide open throttle	2-3 upshift	60-74
3-2 Kickdown limit		57-70
3-1 Kickdown limit		27-40
Closed throttle downshift		7-10

TOWING INSTRUCTIONS

A. If the transmission is out of service, lift the rear end or remove the driveshaft.

B. If the transmission is operating satisfactorily, the car may be towed safely in "N" (Neutral) at moderate speeds for short

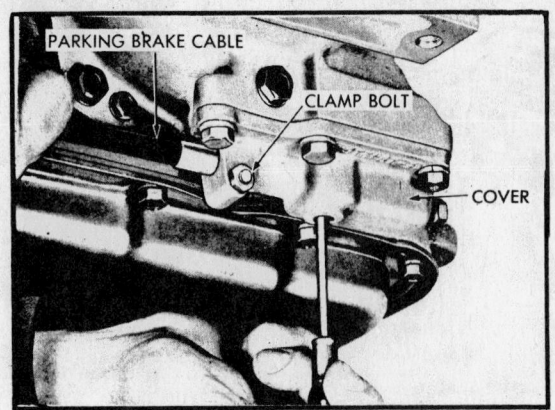

Removing Parking Brake Cable

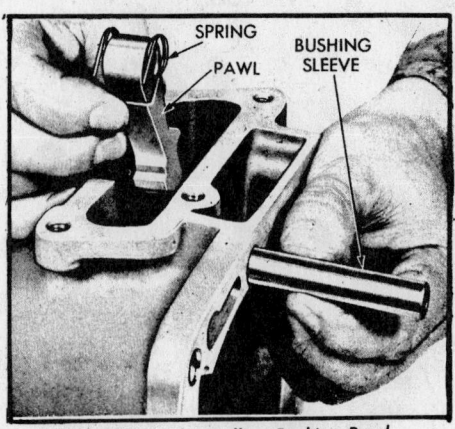

Removing and Installing Parking Pawl

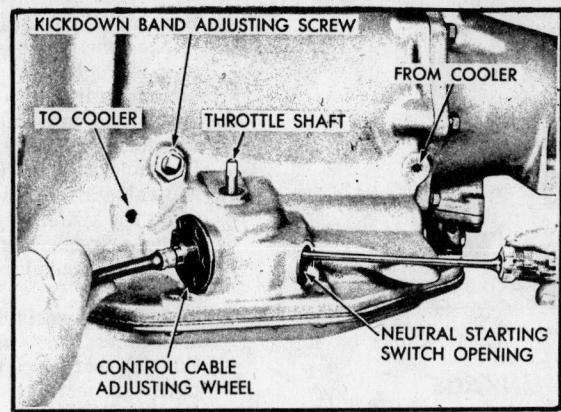

Removing Gearshift Control Cable

distances. For long distance towing (over 100 miles), the driveshaft should be removed.

GEARSHIFT CONTROL UNIT

The transmission is operated from an horizontal dash panel unit (vertical panel on Valiant). The unit consists of five push buttons, identified by "R" (Reverse), "N" (Neutral), "D" (Drive), "2" (Second) and "1" (Low).

Mechanical connection between the gearshift control panel and the transmission manual control valve is obtained through the use of a single push-pull cable. One end of the wire is connected to the cable actuator in the control panel. The other end is attached to the manual control valve lever in the transmission.

Should the "R" button be pushed in while the car speed is above 10 m.p.h., the manual control lever will go to the Neutral position. When the car speed drops below 10 m.p.h., it will be necessary to re-engage the "R" button to attain Reverse.

A back-up light switch (when so equipped) is included in the gearshift control panel. It is operated by the "R" (Reverse) button.

Removal

1. Disconnect one battery cable.
2. Disconnect back-up light switch connectors (if so equipped) at push button control, at the rear of the panel.
3. Remove screws from push button face plate and remove the buttons by pulling them off their slides. Remove lamp bulb.
4. Remove control housing stud nuts (they are now accessible) and remove control cable from the rear of the panel.
5. Remove hairpin lock holding the control cable to the actuator and the screws that hold the cable bracket to the control housing.

Installation

1. Insert end of cable on the actuator and reassemble hairpin clip. Install cable.
2. Carefully guide the unit into position from the rear of the instrument panel and install the attaching stud nuts from the front side of instrument panel.
3. Install lamp bulb in push button control and reinstall push buttons onto actuator slides. Replace the face plate.
4. Connect back-up and push button lamp wires.

PUSH BUTTON LAMP REPLACEMENT

The push button lamp bulb can be replaced by taking the face plate off and removing one or two of the center push buttons.

CONTROL CABLE (TRANS-MISSION END),

Removal

1. Lift car on a hoist and drain about 2 qts. of transmission fluid.
2. Depress "1" (Low) push button to position cable for removal from transmission.
3. Disconnect wire from neutral starting switch and remove switch.
4. Remove push button control cable-to-transmission adjusting wheel lock screw.
5. Insert screwdriver through neutral starting switch opening. Push screwdriver gently against upper projecting portion of the cable lock-spring, and pull outward on the cable to remove cable from adapter and transmission case.

Reinstall

1. Have a helper engage the "R"

button and hold it firmly engaged for the duration of the cable attachment operation.
2. Back the adjusting wheel off on the cable housing (counterclockwise) until 2 or 3 threads are exposed behind the wheel on the guide.
3. Lubricate the cable with transmission fluid. Insert cable in transmission case and push inward on the cable, making sure the lock-spring engages the cable. Adjust cable as outlined in "On-the-Car Adjustments."
4. Refill transmission with automatic transmission fluid (Type "A", Suffix "A") to proper level.

Caution:

While in the process of making adjustments and tests, DO NOT STALL-TEST THE TORQUE CONVERTER. For safety, and to prevent internal damage to the transmission, a wide open throttle stall test should be avoided.

LUBRICATION

Refer to the "CAPACITIES TABLE" of this section.

GEARSHIFT CONTROL CABLE ADJUSTMENT

1. Raise car on hoist. Have a helper hold the "R" button firmly depressed.
2. Remove control cable adjustment wheel lock screw at the left side of transmission.
3. Back the adjustment wheel off on the cable guide until only two or three threads show behind the wheel on the guide.

NOTE: Be sure the adjustment wheel turns freely on the guide. Lubricate the cable guide threads with transmission fluid.

4. Hold the control cable guide centered in the hole of the transmission case and apply only enough inward force (two to three pounds) to bottom the assembly at the reverse detent. While holding the cable bottomed, rotate the adjustment wheel clockwise until it just contacts the case.
5. Turn the wheel clockwise just enough to make the next adjustment hole in the wheel line up with the screw hole in the case.
6. Counting this hole as Number One, keep turning the wheel clockwise until the fifth hole lines up with the screw hole in the case.
7. Install lock screw and torque to 30 to 50 inch pounds.

VALIANT-LANCER-DART

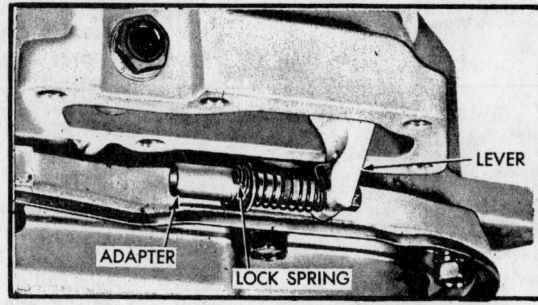

Parking Lock Lever Cable Adapter

NEUTRAL STARTING SWITCH

To properly adjust and test:

1. With the correct cable adjustment certain, depress the "N" button.
2. Raise the car and drain about 2 qts. of transmission fluid.
3. Unscrew the neutral starting switch from the transmission case. Check the alignment of the switch operating lever relative to the switch opening in the case.
4. Place cupped washer and "O" ring over threads of the switch, then screw switch into transmission case a few turns.
5. Hook up a test lamp, one lead to battery current and the other lead to the switch terminal. Further screw the switch into the transmission case until the lamp lights; now seat the switch by turning it an additional 1/3 to ½ turn.

NOTE: The switch must be tight enough to prevent an oil leak. If it isn't, add a thin washer and readjust the switch.

6. Remove test lamp and reconnect the regular wire to the switch.
7. Add fluid to bring transmission to the prescribed level.

THROTTLE LINKAGE ADJUSTMENT

1. With the engine at operating temperature and the carburetor off fast idle cam, adjust engine RPM to 475-500.
2. Loosen lock nut and move the transmission throttle control lever forward until it stops. Then tighten the lock nut securely.
3. Adjust a spirit level protractor to 114 degrees, then place the protractor lengthwise on the flat face of the accelerator pedal.
4. With the car on a level floor, disconnect the accelerator pedal rod and adjust the rod length to center the spirit level bubble. After correct pedal angle is achieved, reconnect the pedal rod.

TRANSMISSION REMOVE

1. Disconnect negative (ground) cable from the battery.
2. Depress "1" (Low) selector button to position control cable for removal from the transmission.
3. Remove the starter motor assembly.
4. Raise the car on a hoist or support it high, with stands.

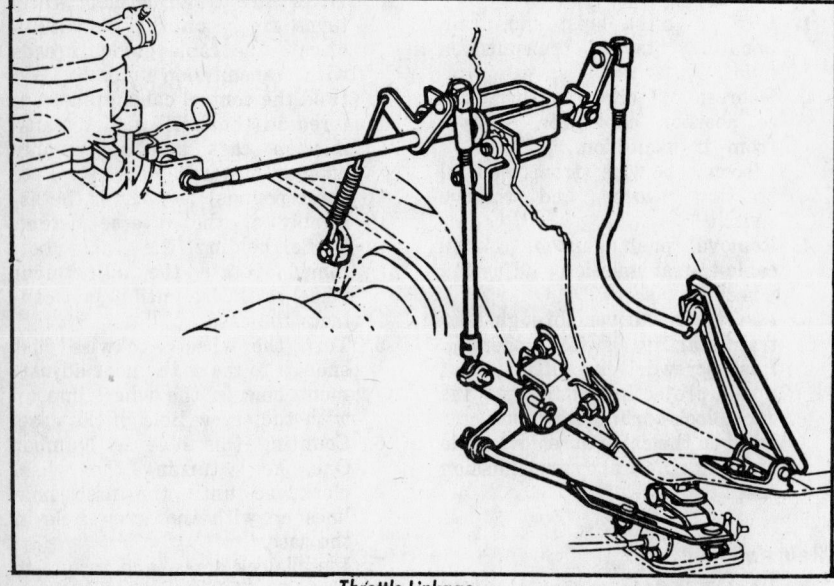

Throttle Linkage

5. Remove cover plate from in front of the converter assembly for access to the converter drain plugs and mounting bolts.
6. Drain the converter and transmission.
7. Disconnect the wire from the neutral starting switch and remove the switch.
8. Remove push button control cable to transmission adjusting plate screw.
9. Insert a screwdriver through the neutral starter switch opening. Push the screwdriver against the upper projecting portion of the cable lock-spring, and pull outward on the cable. This will remove the cable from the adapter and transmission case.
10. Loosen clamp screw and remove throttle link and lever assembly from the throttle shaft.
11. Disconnect oil cooler lines at the transmission and remove oil filler tube.
12. Remove speedometer pinion and sleeve assembly from the transmission.
13. Disconnect front universal joint and secure out of the way.
14. Remove parking brake adjusting nut cover plate and loosen the cable clamp bolt on brake support. Disengage the ball end of the cable from the operating lever and remove cable from the brake support.
15. Remove nut and washers holding the transmission extension housing insulator to the crossmember.
16. Install engine support fixture, tool #C-3487 with adapter #C-3806 and raise the engine slightly.
17. Remove crossmember attaching bolts and lift out crossmember.
18. Place a transmission service jack under the transmission to support the assembly.
19. Mark the converter and driving plate so as to associate their relative positions. Remove the converter-to-driving plate mounting screws. Now attach a small "C" clamp to the edge of the bell housing to keep the converter in place, on the transmission during transmission unit removal.
20. Remove the bell housing retaining bolts. Work the transmission rearward off the engine block dowel pins and to disengage the converter hub from the rear end of the crankshaft.
21. Lower the transmission jack and remove the transmission and converter assembly

TRANSMISSION INSTALL

1. Secure the transmission and con-

verter assembly on a service jack and raise the jack to align the assembly with the engine.

2. Rotate the converter so that the alignment marks of the converter and mounting plate are in register. Carefully work the assembly forward and onto the engine dowels while the con-converter hub enters the crankshaft opening.

3. After the assembly is in position ALL THE WAY, install the bell housing bolts. Torque these bolts to 25-30 ft. lb.

4. Install the driving plate-to-converter bolts and torque to 15-19 ft. lb.

5. Install the crossmember and tighten the attaching bolts securely. Lower the transmission to rest in alignment and on the insulator mounting. Install

mounting washers and nut. Torque to 30-35 ft. lb.

6. Hook up the ball end of the parking brake cable in the brake shoe operating lever and tighten the cable clamp bolt.

7. Install cover plate on back side of parking brake support plate.

8. Hook up the propeller shaft.

9. Install speedometer drive pinion and sleeve.

10. Connect oil cooler lines to the transmission and install oil filler tube.

11. Position throttle lever on transmission throttle shaft and secure with clamp.

NOTE: THROTTLE LINKAGE ADJUSTMENT is covered in the previous section.

12. Insert selector button control cable in the transmission case. Push in on the cable and be sure

the spring lock engages and secures the cable. Install control cable adjusting wheel retaining screw.

13. Install neutral starting switch and connect the wire. Adjust as outlined in "ON-THE-CAR ADJUSTMENTS," in this same section.

14. Install cover plate forward of the converter assembly.

15. Install starter motor and connect up the battery.

16. Refill transmission with automatic transmission fluid, to proper level.

CAUTION. Never exceed torque recommendations. The case is aluminum and may strip threads if exposed to abuse. See UNIT REPAIR SECTION of this manual for suggested aluminum parts repairs, "Thread Inserts."

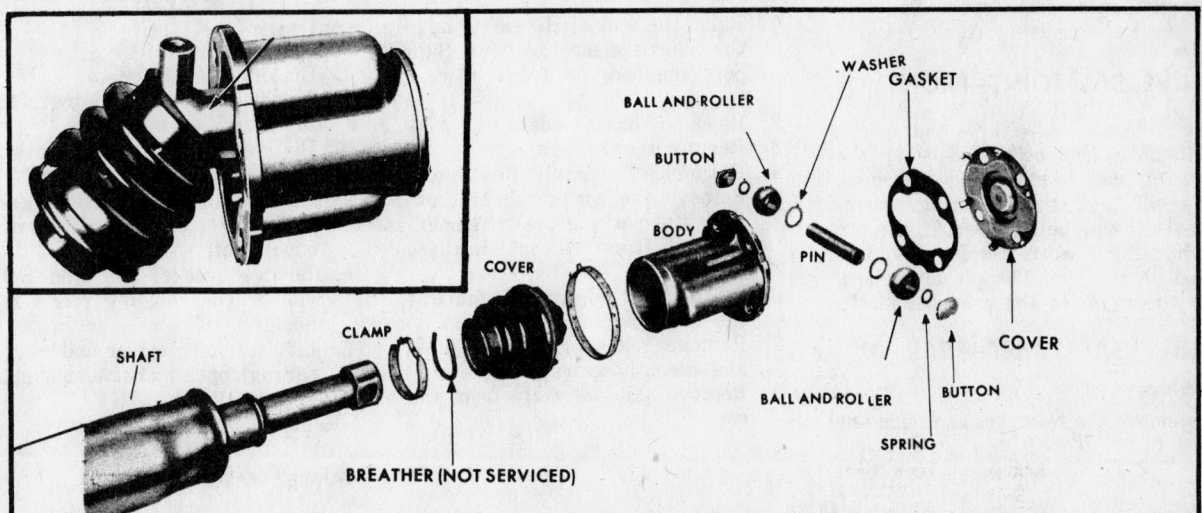

Front Universal Joint

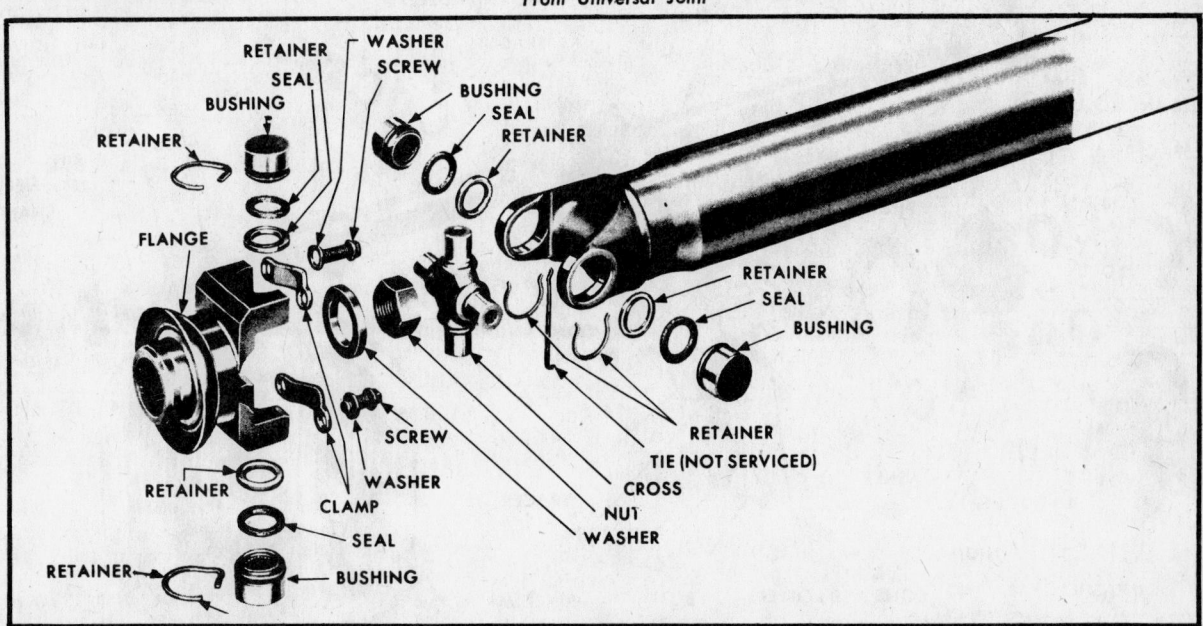

Rear Universal Joint

UNIVERSALS AND PROPELLER SHAFT

The propeller shaft has a ball and trunnion type front universal joint and a cross and roller type rear joint.

All lubrication and service operations on the shaft or joints require removal and disassembly.

PROPELLER SHAFT

Remove And Install

1. Remove both clamps from the pinion yoke and remove the bearings.
2. Remove the front universal joint bolts at the transmission flange.

Note:

To install, reverse above procedure. Do not overtorque the rear universal bearing clamp nuts as distortion may result. The correct torque is 14 ft. lb.

UNIVERSAL JOINT—FRONT

Replace

Remove the boot and slide the housing back to expose the bearings. The ball and needle bearing assemblies can now be removed. If the pin or housing is worn, a press should be used on the pin. The pin **must** be a very tight fit in the propeller shaft.

UNIVERSAL JOINT—REAR

Replace

Remove the retainers and push one roller and bushing assembly out by pressing the opposite side in. The remaining one can be pushed out by using the cross to press it.

REAR AXLE AND SUSPENSION

Due to design, the drive pinion and differential case with drive gear are mounted directly to the center, (carrier) section of the rear axle housing assembly. Access to the drive gears and carrier bearings is obtained through the carrier cover opening. Axle shafts and pinion oil seal can be changed without removal of the assembly from the car. However, the unit should be removed for any other operations.

AXLE ASSEMBLY

Remove

1. Raise the rear of the car to have the wheels clear the floor. Support the body in front of rear springs.
2. Block the brake pedal up.
3. Remove rear wheels.
4. Disconnect hydraulic flex line.
5. Remove the cotter pin and unhook the parking brake rear cable rod from the intermediate arm.
6. Disconnect the propeller shaft at the rear end.
7. Remove rear spring "U" bolts and shock absorbers.
8. Remove axle assembly from the car.

Install

1. Position the rear axle housing spring seats over the spring center bolts.
2. Install "U" bolts and shock absorbers. Torque "U" bolts to 45 ft. lb.
3. Connect parking brake cable at intermediate arm.
4. Connect propeller shaft and torque nuts to 14 ft. lb.
5. Reconnect the brake line or lines.
6. Install brake drums and retainer clips.
7. Install wheels and torque nuts to 55 ft. lb.
8. Remove brake pedal block and bleed brake system.
9. Fill differential with 2 pints of specified compound.
10. Remove support and lower car to the floor.

RADIO

REMOVE

1. Disconnect battery.
2. Remove speaker grille by removing four V-spring clips.
3. Disconnect speaker and antenna and "A" leads.
4. Remove knobs and nuts from mounting studs, and opening cover plate.
5. Remove bracket bolt and Belleville washer holding receiver to housing.
6. Lift rear of receiver and remove through opening between support and speaker.

Reinstall by reversing above.

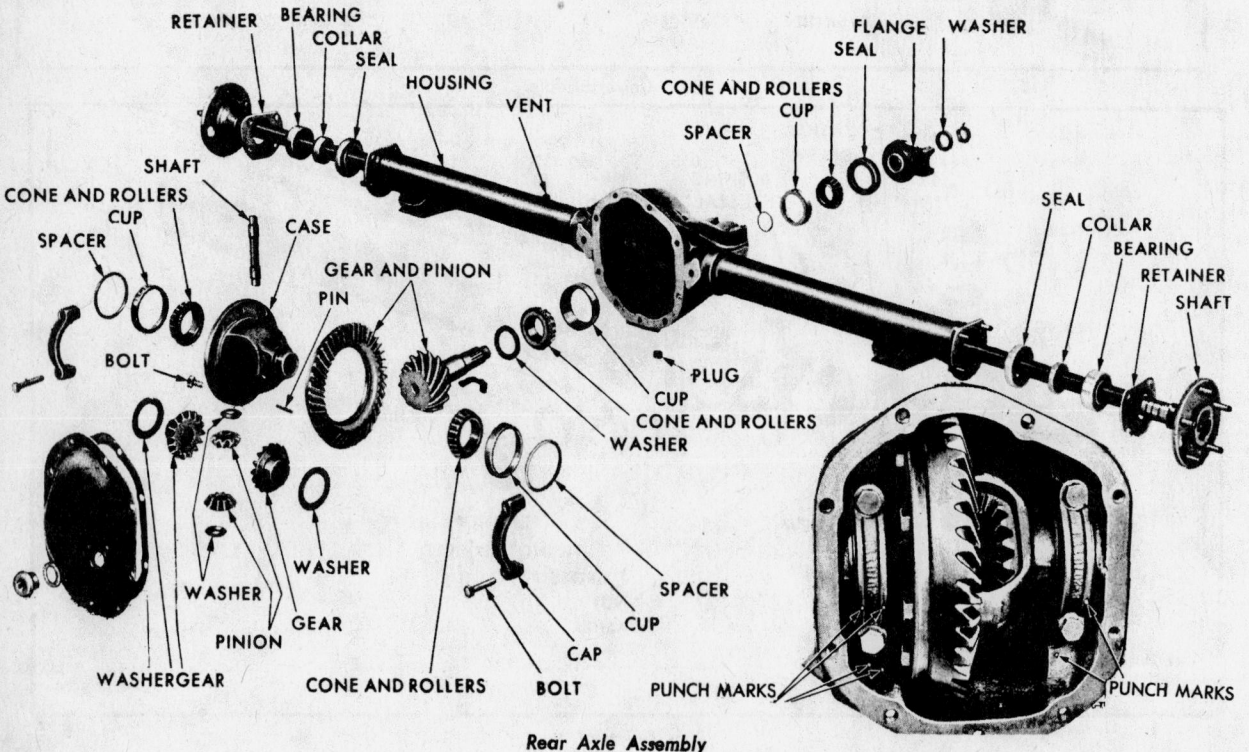

Rear Axle Assembly

Page

AIR CONDITIONING

Service 1092

BRAKES, HYDRAULIC

Brake information 689
Adjustments 938
Bleed brakes 941
Master cylinder service 939

BRAKES, POWER

Power unit overhaul 954
Trouble shooting 954

CLUTCH

Clutch assembly, R & R 698
Clutch pedal, adjust 698

COOLING SYSTEM

Cooling system information 689
Water pump, R & R 689

ELECTRICAL SYSTEM

Distributor, R & R 688
Distributor specifications 685
References 688
Engine 688
Fuses and circuit breakers 685
Gauges 1024
Generator and regulator
   specifications 685
Generator service 1026
Generator specifications 685
Generator trouble shooting chart 1026
Generator service 688
Ignition firing order & timing 683
Ignition timing specifications 684
Starter, R & R 688
Starter specifications 685
Starter systems 1046

ENGINE ASSEMBLY

Cylinder head, R & R 691
Cylinder head tightening 686
Engine diagnosis 1012
Engine firing order & timing 683
Engine identification 682
Engine information 690
Engine assembly, R & R 691
Oil pan, R & R 694
Oil pressure specifications 687
Piston and rod, assembly 695
Piston and rod, R & R 694
Piston specifications 686
Rocker arms & shaft 693

Page

ENGINE ASSEMBLY—continued

Specifications, general, engine .. 687
Specifications, tune-up, engine .. 684
Timing case cover 693
Timing chain, R & R 693
Trouble shooting charts 1012
Tune-up specifications 684
Valve lifters 693
Valve specifications 686
Valves and guides 692

FUEL SYSTEM

Fuel information 688
Carburetors 972
Fuel gauge service 1024
Fuel pump pressure 684
Fuel pump service 1020

INSTRUMENTS

Speedometer, R & R 689

OVERDRIVE

Overdrive disassembly 914
Overdrive, R & R 699
Trouble shooting 915

REAR AXLE AND SUSPENSION

Axle assembly, R & R 701
Axle shaft 918
Axle shaft oil seal 918
Pinion bearings 918
Rear spring, R & R 701
Ring gear & pinion 918
Shock absorbers, R & R 701
Trouble shooting 919

SPECIFICATIONS

Battery 685
Brake cylinder sizes 687
Capacities:
   Axle, rear 685
   Cooling system 685
   Crankcase 685
   Fuel tank 685
   Transmission, automatic ... 685
   Transmission, manual 685
Chassis, general 687
Distributor 685
Engine, general 687
Engine tune-up 684
Fuses and circuit breakers 685
Generator regulators 685
Generators 685
Light bulbs 687
Main bearings 686

Page

SPECIFICATIONS—continued

Model identification 682
Model identification illustrations .. 682
Pistons 686
Quick reference specifications ... 683
Rod bearings 686
Starters 685
Torque wrench 686
Tune-up 684
Valves 686
Wheel alignment 687

STEERING, MANUAL

Adjust gear housing 1052
Steering gear, R & R 698

STEERING, POWER

Pump assembly 1058
Trouble shooting 1081
Unit overhaul 1058

SUSPENSION, FRONT

References 696
Alignment specifications 687
Alignment procedures 1082
Front wheel drives 696
King pins and bushings 1087
Knuckle supports 1087
Shock absorbers 1087
Support arms, pins and bushings 1087

TRANSMISSION, HYDRA-MATIC

Disassembly of transmission 850
Trouble shooting 853

TRANSMISSION, MANUAL SHIFT

Transmission information 698
Disassemble transmission 698
Transmission, R & R 698

TUNE-UP

Procedures 1012
Specifications 684
Engine diagnosis 1012

UNIVERSAL JOINT AND DRIVE SHAFT

Disassemble U joint 701
U joint & drive shaft, R & R 701

WILLYS

YEAR IDENTIFICATION

1954

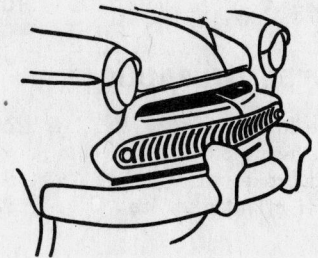

1955

1954–63

ENGINE IDENTIFICATION

WILLYS USES THE SAME NUMBER FOR THE SERIAL NUMBER AND THE ENGINE NUMBER EXCEPT ON THE 1954 ACE, EAGLE AND LARK.

Simplification is the purpose of this manual. It is, therefore, the opinion of the editors of Chilton to identify engine size by referring to the model year and type of engine used, ("F"-head, "L"-head and number of cylinders). This information can be used to determine piston displacement by referring to the "General Engine Specifications." chart.

MODEL IDENTICATION

	C13B—F-4	C15—F-4	CJ6—F-4	DJ3A—L-4	MD—F-4	4-75—F-4	2x4-75—F-4	4x4-75—F-4	6-85A—F-6	4x2—6-226	4x4—6-226	675—L-6	685—F-6	6-226—L-6	FWD-6—226	FWD-F4—134	FC150—F4-134	FC170—L6-226	Tornado 230
1954	X				X	X		X	X		X	X	X	X					
1955	X	X			X	X	X	X	X	X	X	X	X	X					
1956	X	X	X	X	X	X	X	X	X	X	X		X	X					
1957	X	X	X	X	X		X	X		X	X		X	X					
1958	X	X	X	X	X		X	X		X	X				X	X	X	X	
1959		X	X	X	X		X	X		X	X				X	X	X	X	
1960					X		X	X		X	X				X	X	X	X	
1961					X					X	X				X	X	X	X	
1962					X					X	X				X	X	X	X	X
1963										X	X				X	X	X	X	X

QUICK WORKING SPECIFICATIONS

DISTRIBUTOR

Breaker Point Gap

1954-63, All .... .020

Cam Angle

1954-63, All 4 cyl. 40

1954-63, All 6 cyl. 39

SPARK-PLUGS

	Type	Gap
All	A7	.030

IGNITION TIMING

1954-63, All ex. 6-226 ....5B

1958-63 6-226, L Hd. 6 cyl. 4B

GENERATOR & REGULATOR SPECIFICATIONS

YEAR AND SERIES	GENERATOR Field Current In Amperes		REGULATOR		
	6 Volt	12 Volt	Cut-out Closing Voltage	Current Regulator Setting	Voltage Regulator Setting
1954-58 All	1.65	—	6.5	45	7.3
1959-63	—	1.28	12.5	36	14.5±1.(A)

(A) Surrounding temperatures guide this adjustment. Higher temperatures require lower settings and lower temperatures permit higher settings, within limits.

VALVES

Operating Tappet Clearance (When Engine is Cold)

4 cyl. L Hd., Both Valves .... .016

6 cyl. L Hd. ex. 226, Both Valves .... .014

4 & 6 cyl. F Hd., Intake .... .018

4 & 6 cyl. F Hd., Exhaust .... .016

6 cyl. L Hd., 226, Both Valves.. .014

COMPRESSION PRESSURE

1954-57, All 4 cyl. 111

1954-57, All 6 cyl. 145

1958-63, 4 Cyl., L Hd. 110

1958-63, 4 Cyl., F Hd. 125

1958-63, 6 cyl. 135

FRONT WHEEL ALIGNMENT

Caster (Degrees)

1954-56 1

1957-63 3

Camber (Degrees)

1954-56 1

1957-63 ....1½

Toe-In (Inches)

1954-56 ....⅛

1957-63 ....1/16

King Pin Inclination

1954-56 ....8¼

1957-63 ....7½

CAPACITIES

Engine Crankcase (Quarts) (Add 1 quart for new filter)

All 4 cylinder engines 4

All 6 cylinder engines 5

Synchromesh Trans. (Pints) (Add 1 pint for Overdrive)

All 4 W.D. 3

All 2 W.D. ex. 226 ....1½

6-226, 2x4 ....2½

Front Differential (Pints)

All 4 W.D. 2½

Hydramatic Trans. (Pints)

Passenger cars 22

Transfer Case (Pints)

All 4 W.D. 3½

Rear Differential (Pints)

4-63; 6-63; 2 W.D. Sta. Wag. 2

All others 3

Cooling System (Quarts) (Add 1 qt. for Heater)

All others ex. 6-226 10

6-226 11

FIRING ORDER and TIMING

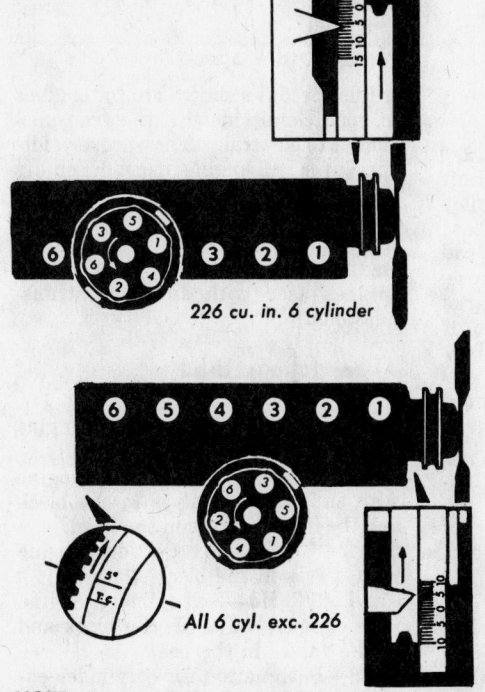

226 cu. in. 6 cylinder

All 6 cyl. exc. 226

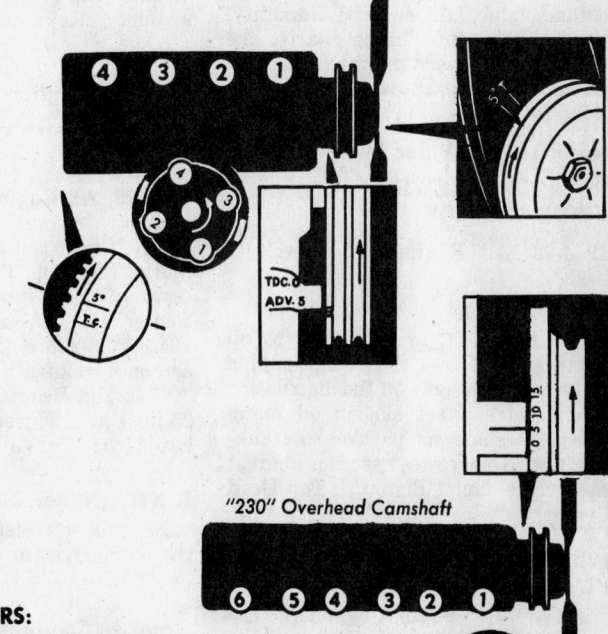

"230" Overhead Camshaft

SPARK OCCURS:

1954 —4 Cyl. "F" Head (134 Cu. In. Engine)—5° BTDC

1954-55—6 Cyl. "F" Head (161 Cu. In. Engine)—5° BTDC

1958-63—6 Cyl. "L" Head (226 Cu. In. Engine)—4° BTDC

1956-63—4 Cyl. "F" Head (134 Cu. In. Engine)—5° BTDC

NOTE:

THESE ARE APPROXIMATE SETTINGS. ENGINE DESIGN, ALTITUDE, TEMPERATURE, FUEL AND ENGINE CONDITION WILL ALL INFLUENCE TIMING. THE DETERMINING FACTOR, LIMITING ADVANCE, WILL STILL BE THE "KNOCK POINT" OF THE INDIVIDUAL ENGINE.

WILLYS

TUNE-UP SPECIFICATIONS

Year Engine Type	Spark Plugs		Distributor (Note 1)				Com- pression Pressure Cranking (Note 3)	Valves				Fuel Pump Pressure	Engine Idle Speed Neutral (Note 4)
	Type	Gap	Cam Angle	Point Gap	Arm Spring Tension	Ignition Timing (Note 2)		Tappet Clearance Cold		Timing			
								Inlet	Exhaust	Inlet Opens			
1954													
4 Cyl., F Head	A7	.030	42	.020	17–20	5B	111	.018	.016	9B		4	550
6 Cyl., L Head (6-226)	A7	.030	39	.020	17–20	4B	145	.014	.014	10B		5	500
6 Cyl., F Head	A7	.030	39	.020	17–20	5B	145	.018	.016	9B		4	600
1955													
6 Cyl., L Head (6-226)	A7	.030	39	.020	17–20	4B	145	.014	.014	10B		5	500
6 Cyl., F Head	A7	.030	39	.020	17–20	5B	145	.018	.016	9B		4	600
1956													
4 Cyl., F Head	A7	.030	42	.020	17–20	5B	111	.018	.016	9B		4	550
6 Cyl., L Head (6-226)	A7	.030	39	.020	17–20	4B	145	.014	.014	10B		5	500
1957													
4 Cyl., F Head	A7	.030	42	.020	17–20	5B	111	.018	.016	9B		4	600
6 Cyl., L Head (6-226)	A7	.030	39	.020	17–20	4B	145	.014	.014	2B		5	550
1958-63													
4 Cyl., L Head	A7	.030	40	.020	17–20	5B	110	.016	.016	9B		3	600
4 Cyl., F Head	A7	.030	40	.020	17–20	5B	125	.016	.016	9B		3	600
6 Cyl., L Head (6-226)	A7	.030	39	.020	17–20	4B	155	.014	.014	2B		5	550
1962-63													
Tornado-230	L-7	.030	38	.020	17–22	5B	150	.006	.008	15B		4½	550

NOTES FOR TUNE-UP SPECIFICATIONS TABLE

Note:

All specifications are standard and should result in satisfactory performance. There are, however, factors that influence these settings, such as fuel octane value, air density, humidity, temperature, etc. Timing charts, like other specifications must be considered as averages, subject to modification.

Note 1: Distributor

ROTATION VIEWED FROM THE TOP

1954-63, All Engines, Counterclockwise.

DRIVE GEAR

1954-63, All Engines: Pinned to oil pump shaft. Note that 6-226 engine has an offset tongue on the distributor shaft. Have offset slot in oil pump extension shaft set parallel to crankshaft with narrowest section nearest the valves. No. 1 Piston at Top Dead Center.

FIRING ORDER AND SPARK PLUG WIRE INSTALLATION

All Willys engine cylinders are numbered from front to back starting with No. 1 cylinder at the front. Using this numbering system:

The FIRING ORDER of the 4 cylinder engines is 1-3-4-2. The spark plug wires go into the 4 cylinder distributor, in the firing order and in a counterclockwise direction.

The FIRING ORDER of the 6 cylinder engines is 1-5-3-6-2-4. The spark plug wires go into the 6 cylinder distributor cap in the firing order and in a counterclockwise direction.

Note 2: Ignition

IGNITION TIMING MARKS AND THEIR LOCATION

1954-63, All Engines ex. 6-226 & 230 Engine: Marks are on crankshaft pulley. Consist of notch on the pulley and a "T" and a "5" on the timing case cover. The "T" being at Top Dead Center. The "55" at 5 degrees before. **1954-63, 6-226 & 230 Engine:** Marks are on crankshaft pulley, consists of "O" at Top Dead Center preceded by 25 lines at 1 degree intervals and followed by 15 lines at 1 degree intervals.

IGNITION RESISTOR

No ballast resistor is required for the 6 volt system used by Willys.

Note 3: Compression Pressure

1954-57 4 cyl.	111 lbs.
1954-57 6 cyl.	145 lbs.
1958-63 L Hd. 4	110 lbs.
1958-63 F Hd. 4	125 lbs.
1958-63 6 cyl.	135 lbs.
1962-63 230	150 lbs.

All cylinders should read alike within 10 pounds. This is more important than the actual reading. Take the readings with all plugs removed, engine at normal operating temperature.

Note 4: Idle Speed

Idle speeds as shown are for engines in good condition with the transmission in Neutral. The proper idle speed for an engine depends on its condition and also on whether or not it has an automatic transmission. Higher idle speeds are required for engines in poor condition and also for engines used with automatic transmissions.

Abbreviations Used

4 cyl. "L" Hd—Four cylinder engine with valves in the block.
4 cyl. "F" Hd—Four cylinder engine with the exhaust valves in the block and the intake valves in the head.
6 cyl. "L" Hd—Six cylinder engine with valves in the block.
6 cyl. "F" Hd—Six cylinder engine with exhaust valves in the block and intake valves in the head.
6-226—Designation for 6 cylinder engine with 226 cubic inch displacement.
Tornado 230 6 cyl. overhead camshaft
TDC—Top Dead Center.

DISTRIBUTOR SPECIFICATIONS, AUTO-LITE

YEAR	MODEL	Auto-Lite Part Number	ROTATION	Cam Angle In Degrees	BREAKER Point Opening (Inch)	BREAKER Arm Spring In Ounces	GOVERNOR CONTROL @ Dist. R.P.M. Advance Starts	GOVERNOR CONTROL @ Dist. R.P.M. Full Advance	VACUUM CONTROL DATA Inches of Vacuum To Start Advance	VACUUM CONTROL DATA Inches of Vacuum For Full Advance	VACUUM CONTROL DATA Max. Adv of Dist. In Degrees
1954-55	4 Cyl. F Head	1AT4204-A	CC	42	.020	17-20	1 @ 425	11 @ 1700	5⅛	13-15	5-7
	6 Cyl. L Head	1AT4206	CC	39	.020	17-20	1 @ 450	9 @ 1672	10	14-16	4-6
	6 Cyl. F Head	1AT4205-A	CC	39	.020	17-20	1 @ 400	9½ @ 1300	5⅛	13-15	5-7
1956	4 Cyl. L Head	1AD4008	CC	42	.020	17-20	1 @ 350	11 @ 1500	None	None	None
	4 Cyl. F Head	1AD4041	CC	42	.020	17-20	1 @ 425	11 @ 1700	None	None	None
	6 Cyl. F Head	1AT4019	CC	39	.020	17-20	1 @ 450	9 @ 1675	10	14-16	4-6
	6 Cyl. F Head	1AT4205-A	CC	39	.020	17-20	1 @ 400	9½ @ 1300	5⅛	13-15	5-7
1957-58	4 Cyl. L Head	1AD4008	CC	42	.020	17-20	1 @ 350	11 @ 1500	None	None	None
	4 Cyl. F Head	1AD4041	CC	42	.020	17-20	1 @ 425	11 @ 1700	None	None	None
	6 Cyl. L Head	1AT4019	CC	39	.020	17-20	1 @ 450	9 @ 1675	None	None	None
1959-63	4 Cyl. F Head	1AT4204-A	CC	42	.020	17-20	1 @ 425	11 @ 1700	None	None	None
	4 Cyl. L Head	1AD4008	CC	42	.020	17-20	1 @ 350	11 @ 1500	None	None	None
	6 Cyl. L Head	1AT4206-B	CC	39	.020	17-20	1 @ 375	7½ @ 1700	None	None	None
1962-63	Tornado 230	1AT4411	CC	38	.020	17-22	1 @ 375	7½ @ 1700	5⅛	15	5

DISTRIBUTOR SPECIFICATIONS, DELCO

YEAR	MODEL	Delco Remy Part Number	ROTATION	Cam Angle In Degrees	Breaker Point Opening (Inch)	Breaker Arm Spring In Ounces	Governor @ Dist. R.P.M. Advance Starts	Governor @ Dist. R.P.M. Full Advance	Vacuum Control Data Inches of Vacuum To Start Advance	Vacuum Control Data Inches of Vacuum For Full Advance	Vacuum Control Data Max. Adv. of Dist. In Degrees
1959-60	4 Cyl. F Head	1112432	CC	30	.20	19-23	1 @ 425	11 @ 1950	None	None	None
	6 Cyl. L Head	1110249	CC	34	.20	19-23	1 @ 375	6 @ 1300	None	None	None

GENERATOR AND REGULATOR SPECIFICATIONS

YEAR	GENERATORS Field Current in Amperes 6 Volts	GENERATORS Field Current in Amperes 12 Volts	GENERATORS Brush Spring Tension	Cut Out Relay Air Gap	Cut Out Relay Closing Voltage	Current and Voltage Regulator Air Gap	REGULATORS Current Regulator Setting	REGULATORS Voltage Regulator Setting
1954-1958, 6 Volt	1.65		44	.033	6.5	.050	45	7.3
1959-63, 12 Volt		1.28	27	.033	12.6	.050	30	14.5
1962-63, Tornado 230		1.65	27	NA	12.3	NA	39	14.4

BATTERY and STARTER SPECIFICATIONS

YEAR	BATTERY Ampere Hour Capacity	BATTERY Volts	BATTERY Group Number	BATTERY Terminal Grounded	STARTERS Lock Test Amps	STARTERS Lock Test Volts	STARTERS Lock Test Torque	STARTERS No-Load Test Amps	STARTERS No-Load Test Volts	STARTERS No-Load Test R.P.M.	Brush Spring Tension
1954-57	100	6	1	Neg.	335	2	6.0	65	5	4300	48
1958, 6 Volt	100	6	1	Neg.	335	2	6.0	65	5	4300	48
1958-63, 12 Volt	50	12	2	Neg.	210	4	5.0	50	10	4400	39
1962-63, Tornado 230	50	12	2	Neg.	405	4	9.0	60	10	4200	36

FUSES AND CIRCUIT BREAKERS

Head, Tail and Instrument Panel Lights:

6 volt: 30 amp. circuit breaker on headlamp switch.

12 volt: 25 amp. circuit breaker on headlamp switch.

Overdrive:

6 volt: SFE 20 fuse on relay mounted on engine side of firewall.

12 volt: SFE 14.

Clock:

6 volt: AGA 2 fuse at clock.

12 volt: Headlamp circuit breaker.

Turn Signal:

6 volt: SFE 14 fuse in line between ignition switch and flasher.

12 volt: Headlamp circuit breaker.

Heater:

6 volt: SFE 14 fuse in line near switch.

12 volt: SFE 9.

Radio:

6 volt: SFE 9 or 14 fuse in line near set.

12 volt: AGC 7½.

CAPACITIES

	ENGINE CRANKCASE Add 1 qt. for New Filter	TRANSMISSIONS MANUAL Add 1 pt. for Overdrive	TRANSMISSIONS HYDRAMATIC Pints	Front Axle Pints	Transfer Case Pints	Rear Axle Pints	Gas Tank Gals.	Cooling System Add 1 qt. for Heater
4 Cyl., 2 Whl. Drive	4	1½	22	------	------	2	15	11
4 Cyl., 4 Whl. Drive	4	3	22	2½	3½	3	15	11
6 Cyl., 2 Whl. Drive exc. 226	5	1½	22	------	------	2	15	11
6 Cyl., 2 Whl. Drive, 226	5	2½	22	------	------	3	15	13
6 Cyl., 4 Whl. Drive	5	3	22	2½	3½	3	15	12
4 Cyl., Forward Control	4	6½	None	3	3½	3	16	22
6 Cyl., Forward Control	5	6½	None	3	3½	3	10	11

VALVE SPECIFICATIONS

ENGINE	Seat In	Seat Ex	Intake Valve Lift Note 1	Exhaust Valve Lift	Valve Spring Pressure Intake	Valve Spring Pressure Exhaust	Stem to Guide Clearance Inlet	Stem to Guide Clearance Exhaust	Stem Diameter Inlet	Stem Diameter Exhaust	Are Valve Guides Replaceable
4 Cyl., L Head (4-63)	45	45	.351	.351	53@2⁷⁄₆₄	53@2⁷⁄₆₄	.0024	.0035	.373	.371	Yes
6 Cyl., L Head (6-63)	45	45	.2843	.3315	51@1⅝	51@1⅝	.0024	.0035	.340	.340	Yes
6 Cyl., L Head (6-73)	45	45	.284	.3315	51@1⅝	51@1⅝	.0024	.0035	.341	.339	Yes
4 Cyl., F Head (4-73, 75)	45	45	.260	.351	73@1²¹⁄₃₂	73@1²¹⁄₃₂	.0014	.0035	.373	.371	Yes
4 Cyl., F Head (134)	45	45	.260	.351	73@1²¹⁄₃₂	73@1²¹⁄₃₂	.0014	.0035	.373	.371	Yes
6 Cyl., F Head (685)	45	45	.260	.300	73@1²¹⁄₃₂	73@1²¹⁄₃₂	.0014	.0035	.373	.340	Yes
6 Cyl., L Head (226)	30	45	.352	.284	51@1⁴³⁄₆₄	51@1⁴³⁄₆₄	.002	.0041	.341	.339	Yes
Tornado, 230	45	45	NA	NA	57@1¼	57@1¼	.002	.0035	.3405	.339	Yes

Note 1: Camshaft Gear Index Marks

All engines exc. 226:
Align marks on camshaft and crankshaft gears nearest each other and in line with shaft centers.

226 engine:
Have ten pins of the chain between the marks on one gear and that of the other.

TORQUE SPECIFICATIONS

	Cylinder Head Bolts	Rod Bearing Bolts	Main Bearing Bolts	Crankshaft Pulley Bolt	Flywheel To Crankshaft Bolts	Intake Manifold Bolts	Exhaust Manifold Bolts
All 4 Cyl.	60–70	35–45	65–75	100–130	35–40	29–35	29–35
All 6 Cyl. exc. 226	60–70	Note 1	65–75	100–130	35–40	29–35	29–35
6 Cyl 226	35–45	40–45	85–95	100–130	35–40	29–35	29–35
Tornado, 230	65–70	40–45	85–95	100–130	85–95	15–20	NA

PISTON AND PIN SPECIFICATIONS

Year and Model	PISTON Skirt Clearance TOP	PISTON Skirt Clearance BOTTOM	PISTON PIN Diameter	Bushing	FIT In Rod	FIT In Piston	Lock
4 Cyl. L Hd.	.0030	.0030	.8119	None	0	.0001-.0003	Clamp
6 Cyl. L Hd.	.0007	.0017	.8592	None	0	.0002	Clamp
4 Cyl. F Hd.	.0030	.0030	.8118	None	0	.0002-.0004	Clamp
6 Cyl. F Hd.	.0021	.0021	.7497	None	0	.0002-.0004	Clamp
Tornado, 230	.0010	.0010	.8592	Yes	.004	.0002	Ring

CRANKSHAFT BEARING JOURNAL SIZES

ENGINE	MAIN BEARING JOURNALS Journal Diameter	Oil Clearance	End Play of Shaft	End Play Held By	CONNECTING ROD BEARING JOURNALS Journal Diameter	Oil Clearance	End Play
4 Cyl., L Head	2.333	.0016	.005	Front	1.9375	.0013	.007
6 Cyl., L Head, exc. 226	2.250	.0014	.004	Front	1.875	.0016	.009
4 Cyl., F Head	2.333	.0022	.005	Front	1.9375	.0014	.007
6 Cyl., F Head	2.250	.0019	.005	Front	1.875	.0013	.007
6 Cyl., L Head, 226	2.375	.0014	.004	Rear	2.0362	.0016	.009
Tornado 230	2.375	.0015	.005	Rear	2.0623	.0015	.007

CYLINDER HEAD NUT TIGHTENING SEQUENCE

4 Cyl. 4-63, L-Head
Tighten to 60-70 ft. lbs.

4 Cyl. 4-73, F4-134, F-Head
Tighten to 60-70 ft. lbs.
Remove carb to tighten
bolt No. 5

6 Cyl. 6-226, L-Head
Tighten to 35-45 ft. lbs.
Do not neglect bolt next to
Distributor Adaptor

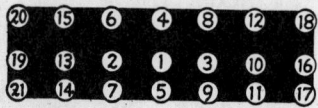

6 Cyl. 6-63, 6-73, L-Head
Tighten to 60-70 ft. lbs.

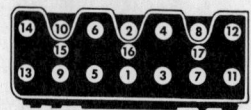

Tornado-230
Tighten to 65-70 ft. lbs.

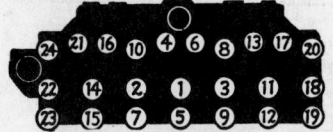

6 Cyl. 685, F-Head
Tighten to 60-70 ft. lbs.

LIGHT BULBS

(C.P. Means Candle Power)

Parking, License:
6 volt, No. 63.
(3 C.P. single contact base.)
12 volt, No. 67 (4 C.P.).

Back-up Lights:
6 Volt, No. 1129.
(21 C.P. single contact base.)

Combination: Tail, Stop and Signal:
6 Volt, No. 1154.
(3 & 21 C.P. double contact indexed base.)
12 volt, No. 1034 (32-4 C.P.).

Combination Front Park and Signal:
6 Volt, No. 1158.
(3 & 21 C.P. double contact base.)
12 volt, No. 1176 (21-6 C.P.).

Headlights:
6 Volt, No. 5040.
(40 & 50 C.P. three contact base.)
12 volt, No. 5400.

Radio Dial:
6 Volt, No. 44.
(25 amps. miniature bayonet base.)
12 volt, No. 1891 (2 C.P.).

Telltales: Headlight, Generator and Oil Pressure:
6 Volt, No. 51.
(2 C.P. miniature bayonet base.)
12 volt, No. 53 (1 C.P.).

Instruments, Clock:
6 Volt, No. 55.
(2 C.P. miniature bayonet base.)
12 volt, No. 57 (2 C.P.).

GENERAL CHASSIS and BRAKE SPECIFICATIONS

YEAR AND MODEL		CHASSIS		BRAKE CYLINDER BORE		
		Overall Length In Inches	Tire Size	Master Cyl. (Inch)	Wheel Cylinder Diameter (Inch) Front	Rear
1954	Station Wagon, 2 W.D.	176¼	6.70x15	1.0	1⅛	1.0
	Station Wagon, 4 W.D.	176¼	6.70x15	1.0	1⅛	1.0
	Passenger Cars, ex. Lark	180¼	5.90x15	1.0	1.0	¾
	Passenger Cars, Lark	180¼	6.40x15	1.0	1⅛	13/16
1955	Station Wagon, 2 W.D.	176¼	6.70x15	1.0	1⅛	1.0
	Station Wagon, 4 W.D.	176¼	6.40x15	1.0	1⅛	1.0
	Passenger Cars, All	184¼	6.40x15	1.0	1⅛	1.0
1956	Station Wagon, 4 W.D.	176¼	6.40x15	1.0	1⅛	1.0
1957-59	Utility Wagon	176¼	7.00x15	1.0	1⅛	1.0
	Truck, 1 Ton Pick Up	182½	7.00x15	1.0	1⅛	1.0
	Universal Jeep, CJ3B	147½	6.00x16	1.0	1⅛	1.0
1960-63	Forward Control FC150	147 5/16	7.00x15	1.0	1⅛	⅞
	FC170	181½	7.00x16	1⅛	1⅛	1.0

GENERAL ENGINE SPECIFICATIONS

Model Engine Type	Bore and Stroke	Number of Main Bearings	Type of Valve Lifter Used	Cubic Inch Displacement	AMA Horsepower	Advertised Horsepower at Stated RPM	Advertised Torque at Stated RPM	Compression Ratio	Oil Pressure At 30 MPH (Note 1)	Cam Shaft Drive
4 Cyl. L. Head	3⅛ x 4⅜	3	Mech. Adj.	134.2	15.63	60 @ 4000	105 @ 2000	6.51	35	Gear
4 Cyl. F. Head	3⅛ x 4⅜	3	Mech. Adj.	134.2	15.63	72 @ 4000	114 @ 2000	7.41	35	Gear
6 Cyl. L. Head	3 x 3½	4	Mech. Adj.	226.2	26.3	115 @ 3650	190 @ 1800	7.31	35	Chain
6 Cyl. F. Head	3⅛ x 3½	4	Mech. Adj.	161.0	23.44	90 @ 4200	135 @ 2000	7.61	35	Gear
Tornado 230	3 11/32 x 4⅜	4	Cam Lever	230.0	26.77	140 @ 4000	210 @ 1750	8.51	50	Chain

NOTES FOR GENERAL ENGINE SPECIFICATIONS TABLE

Note 1: Oil Supply

OIL FILTER TYPE

1954-63 .... Partial flow

ROCKER SHAFT OIL SUPPLY

1954-56, All "F" Heads:

These engines have an external oil line running from the intermediate rear camshaft bearing to a fitting at the top rear of the cylinder head. The oil flows thru the pipe and then thru a drilled passage in the head, into the rocker shaft rear bracket and so into the hollow rocker shaft which has drilled holes to feed each of the rocker arms.

IMPORTANT NOTE: "F" Hd Engine

With this "F" Head engine the oil pressure gauge sending unit is connected at the rear camshaft bearing and the rocker shaft oil supply line is connected at the intermediate rear camshaft bearing. It is possible on some "F" head engines to connect the oil line to the rear camshaft bearing and the pressure gauge sending unit to the intermediate bearing. To avoid this error observe thru the holes in the block left by removal of the pipe and the unit the state of the two camshaft journals. The sending unit should be attached to the grooved journal and the oil supply line should be attached to the drilled journal.

Abbreviations Used

4 cyl. "L" Hd—4 cylinder engine with valves in the block.
6 cyl. "L" Hd—Same as above, but having six cylinders instead of four.
4 cyl. "F" Hd—Engine having four cylinders in a line, exhaust valves in the block and intake valves in the head.
6 cyl. "F" Hd—Same as above, but having six cylinders instead of four.
Tornado-230—O.H. Cam
Mech. Adj.—Solid lifters with adjustable tappets.

FRONT WHEEL ALIGNMENT

YEAR and MODEL	CASTER		CAMBER		Toe In (Inches)	KING PIN INCLINATION (Degrees)	WHEEL PIVOT RATIO	
	Range (Degrees)	Pref. Setting	Range (Degrees)	Pref. Setting			Inner Wheel	Outer Wheel
1954-56, All	½P to 1½P	1P	¾P to 1¾P	1P	⅛	8¼	20	19
1957-63, All	2½P to 3½P	3P	1P to 2P	1½P	1/16	7½	20	19

DISTRIBUTOR

REFERENCES

Detailed information on: distributor drive, direction of distributor rotation; cylinder numbering; firing order; point gap; cam dwell; timing mark location; spark plugs, spark advance; ignition registor location, and idle speed; will be found in the Tune-up Specifications table of this section. Further information on trouble shooting, general tune-up procedures, how to replace ignition wires, how to install points and condensers, how to choose the proper spark plug, and how to adjust timing will be found in the Unit Repair section under the heading: Ignition-Distributors-Tune-up.

REMOVAL

The distributor assembly on all Willys engines is located on the right side of the engine.

To remove it, take off the distributor cap and wire assembly and bend them out of the way. Remove the ignition primary wire from the side of the distributor and take off the vacuum lines to the carburetor. Remove the bolt which holds the distributor down into the block and lift it off the engine.

On all Willys models the drive gear for the distributor is on the oil pump and the distributor is driven by a tongue from the oil pump shaft.

GENERATOR AND REGULATOR

Detailed facts on the generator and the regulator can be found in the Generator and Regulator Specifications Table of this section.

General information on generator and regulator repair and trouble shooting can be found in the Unit Repair section under the heading Generators and Regulators.

GENERATOR POLARITY

Caution: Whenever the circuits to: the generator; the regulator; or the battery have been disconnected it is

best to apply the following procedure:

Before the engine is started momentarily short from the "Bat" to the "Gen" terminals of the regulator with a screwdriver. This gives a momentary surge of current from the battery to the generator and so correctly polarizes the generator with respect to the battery.

Failure to so polarize the generator before starting the engine may severely damage the regulator since reversed polarity causes vibration, arcing and burning of the relay points.

A.C. GENERATOR

Beginning with 1962, an alternating current generator is being made available. The purpose of this unit is to satisfy the increase in electrical loads that have been imposed upon the car battery by modern conditions of traffic and driving patterns.

The A.C. GENERATOR is covered in the Unit Repair section of this manual under "Generators and Regulators."

Caution:

Since the A.C. Generator and regulator are resigned for use on only one polarity system, the following precautions must be observed:

1. The polarity of the battery, generator and regulator must be matched and considered before making any electrical connections in the system.
2. When connecting a booster battery, be sure to connect the negative battery terminals together and the positive battery terminals together.
3. When connecting a charger to the battery, connect the charger positive lead to the battery positive terminal. Connect the charger negative lead to the battery negative terminal.
4. Never operate the A.C. Generator on open circuit. Be sure that all connections in the circuit are clean and tight.
5. Do not short across or ground any of the terminals on the A.C. Generator.
*. Do not attempt to polarize the A.C. Generator.

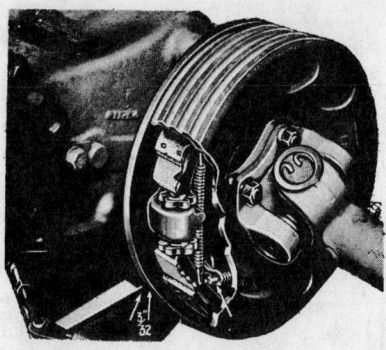

Transmission hand brake

7. Do not use test lamps of more than 12 volts for checking diode continuity.
8. Avoid long soldering times when replacing diodes or transistors. Prolonged heat is damaging to these units.
9. Disconnect the battery ground terminal when servicing any A.C. system. This will prevent the possibility of accidental reversing of polarity.

STARTER, R & R

No problem here. Disconnect battery and starter wires. Remove attaching bolts and lift out starter.

FUEL SYSTEM

FUEL SYSTEM INFORMATION

A chart covering causes of excess fuel consumption will be found in the Unit Repair section under the heading: Fuel Consumption Chart.

Data on capacity of the gas tank will be found in the Capacities Table. Data on correct engine idle speed and fuel pump pressure will be found in the Tune-Up Specifications table. Both the above tables can be found in this section.

General information on fuel pumps and their troubles will be found in the Unit Repair section under the heading: Fuel Pump.

Information covering operation and troubles of the fuel gauge will be found in the Unit Repair section under the heading: Gages.

Detailed information on the carburetor and how to adjust it will be

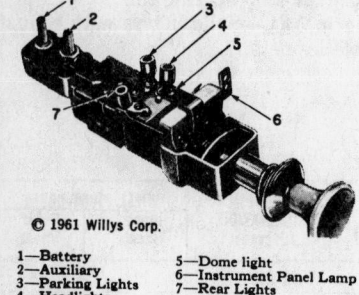

© 1961 Willys Corp.

1—Battery
2—Auxiliary
3—Parking Lights
4—Headlights
5—Dome light
6—Instrument Panel Lamp
7—Rear Lights

Main light switch

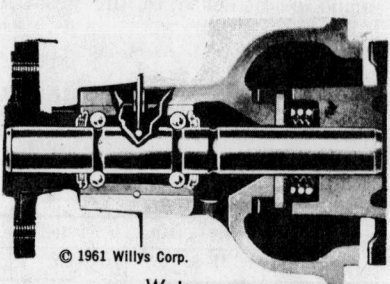

© 1961 Willys Corp.

Water pump

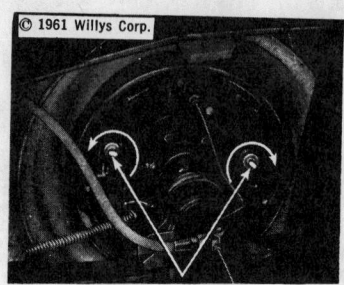

© 1961 Willys Corp.

Brake adjustment

found in the Unit Repair section under the broad heading of the make of carburetor being used on the engine being worked on. Carter, Holley, Rochester and Stromberg carburetors are covered.

Dash pot adjustment can be found in the Unit Repair section under the same heading as that of the automatic transmission used in the car.

BRAKE SYSTEM

BRAKE INFORMATION

Specific information on brake lining sizes can be found in the General Chassis and Brake Specifications Table of this section.

Information on brake adjustments, band replacement, bleeding procedure, master and wheel cylinder overhaul can be found in the Unit Repair section under the heading: Brakes, Hydraulic.

Information on trouble shooting and overhauling power brakes can be found in the Unit Repair section under the heading: Brakes, Power.

Information on the grease seals which may need replacement can be found in the Unit Repair section. The front wheel grease seals under the head: Suspension Front Repair. The rear wheel grease seals under the head: Axles, Rear.

COOLING SYSTEM

COOLING SYSTEM INFORMATION

Detailed information on cooling system capacity can be found in the Capacities Table of this section.

Information on the water temperature gauge can be found in the unit repair section under the heading: Gages.

Caution: Do not run cold water over the outside of pressurized radiators without first removing the radiator cap. When the cap is left on and the cold water hits the hot radiator the steam in the radiator condenses very rapidly and sometimes collapses the top radiator tank. This is most likely to happen if the coolant level is below normal.

REMOVAL OF WATER PUMP

Remove the fan belt and the fan blades and then take out the attaching screws and lift the pump assembly from the front of the block.

It is not necessary to remove the radiator.

INSTRUMENTS

SPEEDOMETER

Removal is done in a conventional manner. No obstructions are in the way. Disconnect cable and remove mounting screws. Lift instrument to bench.

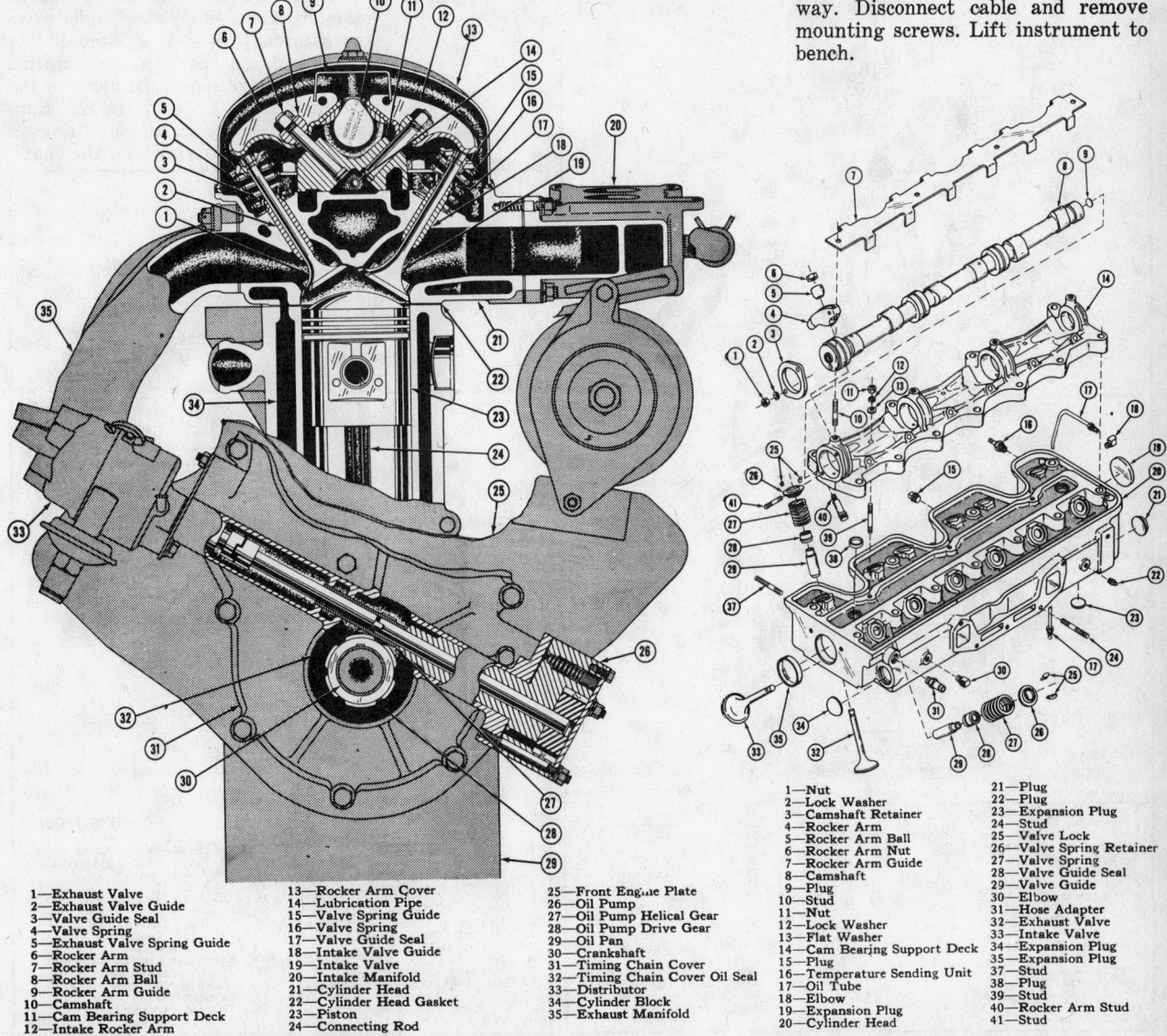

Front Sectional View—Tornado 230

Cylinder Head—Tornado 230

ENGINE ASSEMBLY

REFERENCES

In the specifications tables of this section there are listed all the available facts about the engines. When different size engines are used a note under the General Engine Specifications Table will give an easy means of determining which engine is which.

Engine crankcase capacities are listed in the Capacities Table of this section.

Approved torque wrench readings and head bolt tightening sequences are covered in the Torque Specifications Table of this section.

Information on the engine marking code will be found in the Model Year Identification Table at the start of this section.

Bearings

Detailed information on engine bearings will be found in the Crankshaft Bearing Journal Sizes Table of this section.

Pistons and Pins

Detailed information on pistons and piston pins, together with information on piston, rod and crankshaft relationship for assembly, will be found in the Piston and Pin Specifications Table of this section.

Valves

Detailed information on the valves, the type of valve guide and the location of valve timing marks, can be found in the Valve Specifications Table of this section.

A general discussion of valve clearance and a chart showing how to read pressure and vacuum gauges when using them to diagnose engine troubles will be found in the Unit Repair section under the heading: Tune-Up—Ignition—Distributors. Under the same head will be found a chart on engine trouble shooting.

Valve tappet clearance for each engine is given in the Tune-up Specifications Table of this section.

Starting in 1962

A new engine is available. It is designated TORNADO 230-OHC. It is an overhead—cam type. All valve and valve parts are entirely on the cylinder head, and are removable with the head as an assembly.

The camshaft has only six lobes. Each lobe operates both intake and exhaust valves through rocker arms.

A fully counterbalanced crankshaft is mounted in four main bearings with end play controlled at the rear.

An oil pump mounted outside at the left front, supplies oil under pressure through drilled passages to the main and rod bearings. An external tube carries oil from the block to the cylinder head to lubricate the camshaft and rockers. An oil fitting in front of block spurts oil on the chain.

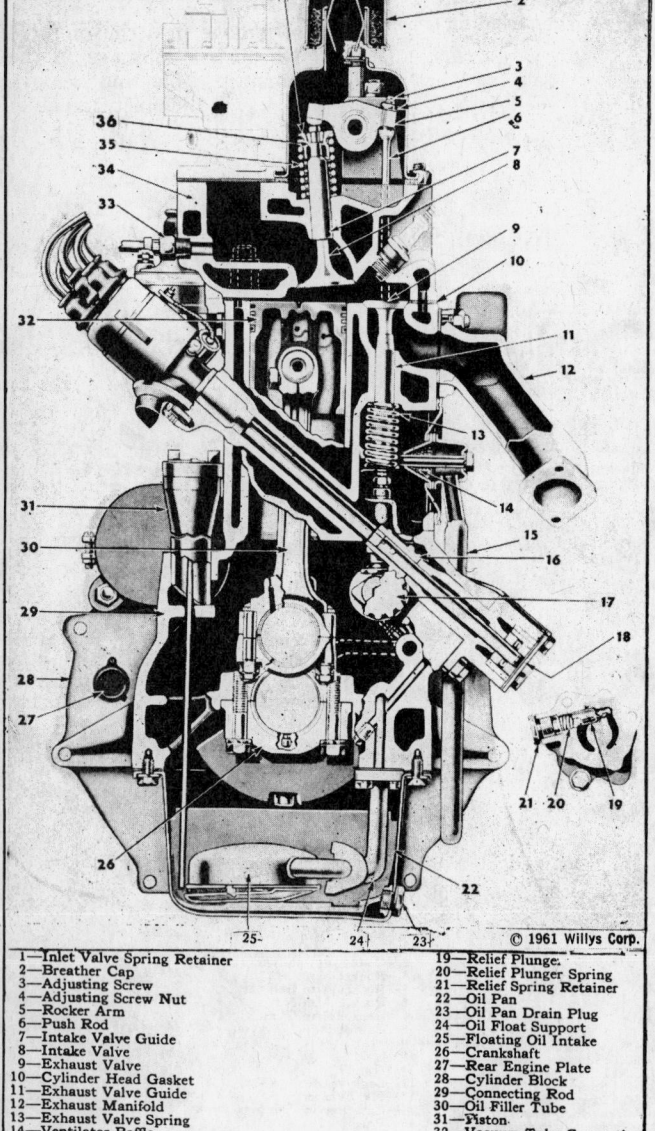

© 1961 Willys Corp.

1—Inlet Valve Spring Retainer
2—Breather Cap
3—Adjusting Screw
4—Adjusting Screw Nut
5—Rocker Arm
6—Push Rod
7—Intake Valve Guide
8—Intake Valve
9—Exhaust Valve
10—Cylinder Head Gasket
11—Exhaust Valve Guide
12—Exhaust Manifold
13—Exhaust Valve Spring
14—Ventilator Baffle
15—Crankcase Ventilator
16—Oil Pump Driven Gear
17—Camshaft
18—Oil Pump
19—Relief Plunger
20—Relief Plunger Spring
21—Relief Spring Retainer
22—Oil Pan
23—Oil Pan Drain Plug
24—Oil Float Support
25—Floating Oil Intake
26—Crankshaft
27—Rear Engine Plate
28—Cylinder Block
29—Connecting Rod
30—Oil Filler Tube
31—Piston
32—Vacuum Tube Connection
33—Cylinder Head
34—Inlet Valve Spring
35—Oil Seal

F4-134 engine—end sectional view

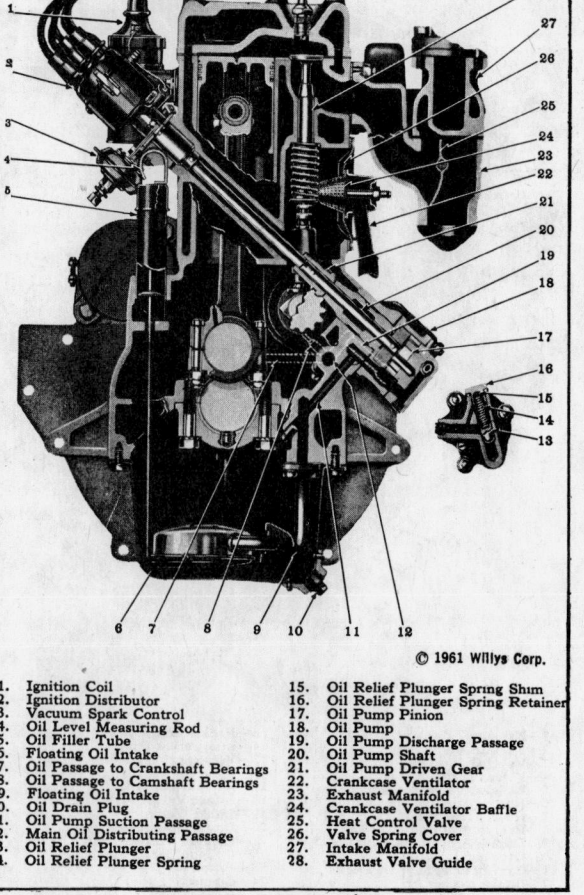

© 1961 Willys Corp.

1. Ignition Coil
2. Ignition Distributor
3. Vacuum Spark Control
4. Oil Level Measuring Rod
5. Oil Filler Tube
6. Floating Oil Intake
7. Oil Passage to Crankshaft Bearings
8. Oil Passage to Camshaft Bearings
9. Floating Oil Intake
10. Oil Drain Plug
11. Oil Pump Suction Passage
12. Main Oil Distributing Passage
13. Oil Relief Plunger
14. Oil Relief Plunger Spring
15. Oil Relief Plunger Spring Shim
16. Oil Relief Plunger Spring Retainer
17. Oil Pump Pinion
18. Oil Pump
19. Oil Pump Discharge Passage
20. Oil Pump Shaft
21. Oil Pump Driven Gear
22. Crankcase Ventilator
23. Exhaust Manifold
24. Crankcase Ventilator Baffle
25. Heat Control Valve
26. Valve Spring Cover
27. Intake Manifold
28. Exhaust Valve Guide

L4, 4-40 engine—end view

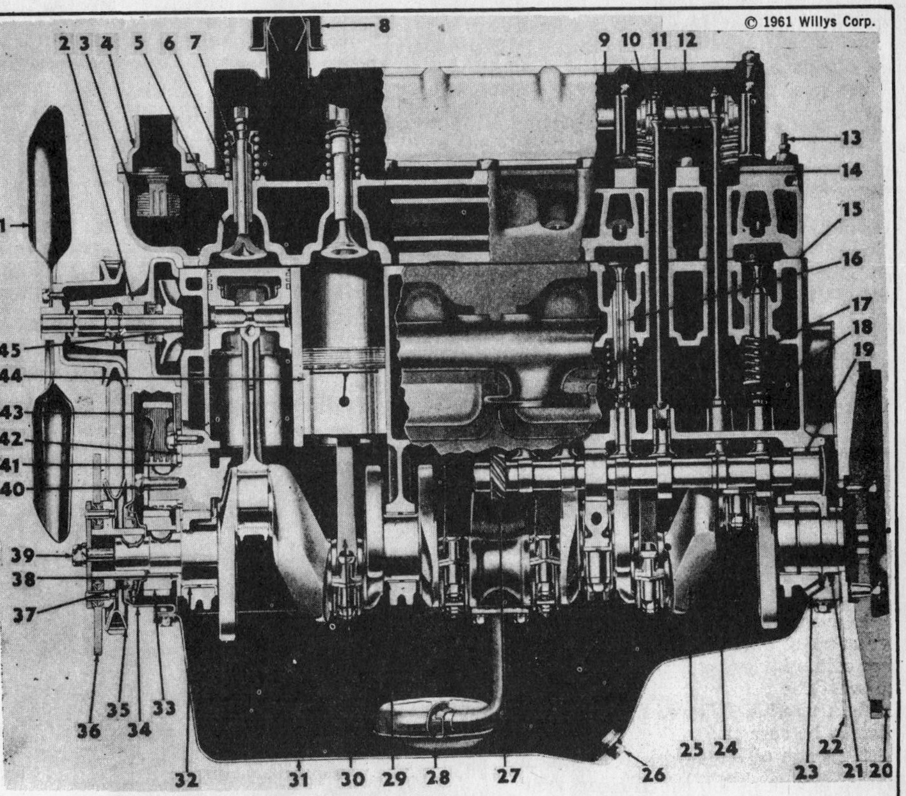

© 1961 Willys Corp.

1—Fan
2—Water Pump
3—Thermostat
4—Water Outlet Fitting
5—Inlet Valve
6—Inlet Valve Spring
7—Inlet Valve Guide
8—Breather Cap
9—Rocker Arm Shaft
10—Rocker Arm
11—Adjusting Screw
12—Rocker Arm Shaft Spring
13—Oil Inlet Tube
14—Push Rod
15—Cylinder Head Gasket
16—Exhaust Valve Guide
17—Exhaust Valve Spring
18—Exhaust Valve Adjusting Screw
19—Camshaft
20—Flywheel
21—Oil Seal
22—Rear Engine Support Plate
23—Oil Return Channel
24—Tappet
25—Crankshaft
26—Oil Pan Drain Plug
27—Oil Pump Drive Gear
28—Floating Oil Intake
29—Connecting Rod Bearing Shell
30—Connecting Rod
31—Oil Pan
32—Crankshaft Main Bearing Shell
33—Crankshaft Gear
34—Timing Gear Cover
35—Fan and Generator Pulley
36—Vibration Damper Disc

37—Oil Seal
38—Front Engine Plate

39—Crankshaft Gear Screw
40—Camshaft Gear Screw

41—Camshaft Thrust Plate Spacer
42—Camshaft Thrust Plate

43—Camshaft Gear
44—Piston

685 engine—side sectional view

ENGINE REMOVAL

It is not necessary to remove the radiator core in order to take an engine out of a Willys car. However, unless some good provision is made to protect the core it is advisable to take it out before attempting to remove the engine.

Remove all attaching parts such as fuel lines, electrical connections, instrument sending units, exhaust lines, etc. The engine is detached at the bell housing, and is lifted out with the transmission supported on a jack.

CYLINDER HEAD

REMOVAL OF CYLINDER HEAD

L Head Engines

Remove the radiator hose and disconnect all fuel lines to the carburetor and fuel pump and all lines and fittings to the carburetor and take off the carburetor.

If the valves are to be worked on, Willys recommends that the manifold be removed at this point. However, if the head is being taken off simply to replace a gasket, then leave the manifold on.

© 1960 Willys Corp.

Removing rocker arm assembly

Remove the bolts which hold the cylinder head to the block and lift off the head.

F Head Engines

Disconnect the radiator hose and remove all lines and rods to the carburetor and take off the carburetor.

Remove the rocker cover and take out the rocker assemblies.

Pull the push rods up through the block, remove the bolts which hold the cylinder head to the block and lift the head off.

Tornado 230 (Timing Chain Cover Not Removed)

1. Disconnect rocker cover vent hose.

2. Remove cover cap nuts, washers and cable brackets from rocker cover studs.

3. Lift off cover and gasket and four seal washers.

4. Install camshaft sprocket tool W-268 on cover studs. Insert hook in sprocket and tighten nut to relieve tension on camshaft.

5. Remove capscrew, lock and flat washer and fuel pump eccentric from camshaft sprocket.

1—Nut
2—Camshaft Sprocket Removal and Installation Tool W-268
3—Camshaft Sprocket

Camshaft Sprocket Tool—Tornado 230

6. Pull sprocket forward from pilot on camshaft. With sprocket still in timing chain release tension on tool W-268 and allow sprocket to rest on bosses in timing chain cover.

Caution: Do not turn engine while Sprocket is removed from camshaft and resting on bosses. This will badly damage the cover. Do not remove sprocket from chain as this will upset camshaft timing. The chain could also be damaged.

7. Disconnect the lubrication line from rear of head and block.
8. Remove three short and eleven long head-bolts and washers and lift off head.

To Reinstall: Be sure all carbon and foreign matter is removed from surfaces and bolt holes.

1. Place head gasket in position. Use no sealer.
2. Carefully place cylinder head on gasket and reverse proceedure of items above. Torque head bolts to 65-70 ft. lbs.

THE VALVE SYSTEM

Two valve systems are available in Willys engines, one the L-Head type and the second the F-Head type. On the F-Head type engines a cylinder head containing intake valve and intake manifold is placed on the standard block.

Service on the exhaust valve is the same on all Willys cars, regardless of the cylinder head. To service the valves it is necessary to remove the cylinder head and the valve chamber cover.

On the Tornado 230 OHC engine the procedures are detailed below.

REMOVAL OF VALVES

All L Head Engines

Remove the cylinder head and the valve chamber cover. **Note:** On some models Willys recommends that the manifold be removed if the valves have to be adjusted.

On some models there is very little space between the side engine pan and the manifolds, others have plenty of room.

Selecting valves in the down position, compress the valve spring, using a good valve spring compressor, and remove the keeper from the bottom of the valve stem.

Release the pressure from the valve spring and pull the valve up to the top of the cylinder block.

If the valve tends to bind on its way through the guide, push it back in again and dissolve the gum and tar from the bottom of the valve stem which prevents it from coming up through the guide.

F Head Engines

On F head engines the exhaust valves are removed in a manner as explained in the above paragraphs. However, the inlet valve is in the cylinder head and is removed on the bench.

Tornado 230 OHC Engines

1. Place head on blocks to provide hand clearance under it.

© 1962 Willys Corp.

1—Valve Spring Compressor Tool W-267
2—Air Hose
3—Rocker Arm Nut
4—Valve Spring
5—Valve Lock
6—Valve Spring Retainer

Valve Spring Tool—Tornado 230

2. Remove valve locks and springs by using tool W-267 assembled on rocker arm stud. (Discard the valve guide seal).

To Reinstall: Always use new guide seals.

1. With head on blocks insert the valves. Apply engine oil to stems.
2. Install seals on stems and push down to seat squarely on guide.
3. Compress spring with tool W-267 and insert retainers and valve locks.

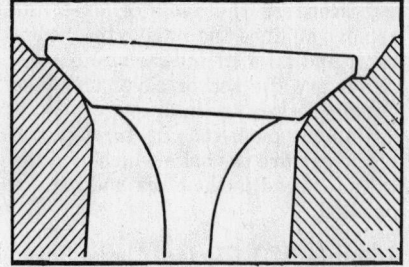

Properly refaced valve seat

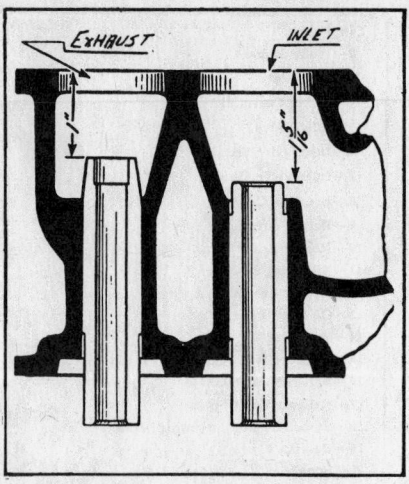

Valve guide installation dimensions

Tornado 230 OHC Engines

To adjust valves in this engine:

If rocker arms are off, install in reverse of removal, as described under "Cylinder Head Remove." Or, if arms have not been removed, proceed as follows:

1. Turn down rocker arm nut but do not tighten.
2. Align each arm on stud and install guide to hold it in place.
3. Adjust the nut to secure .006" clearance on intake valves and .008" on exhaust. Always be sure arm is completely off cam when making the adjustment.

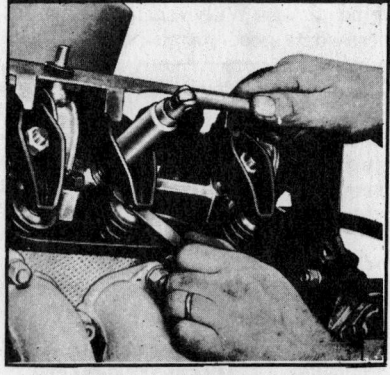

Adjusting valve clearance.

REPLACE VALVE GUIDES

Before removing any valve guide, measure carefully the distance from the top of the block to the top of the guide and see that the new guides are replaced exactly that distance.

It is customary, however, to set the exhaust valve guide up one inch from the top of the cylinder and the inlet guide 1 5/16 inch from the top of the cylinder. The valve guides mounted in the block are pulled through the top of the block and inserted from the top of the block downward. The valve guides in the cylinder head are driven from the combustion chamber out through the top of the head and are inserted from the top of the head down to the combustion chamber.

In all cases it is customary to ream the valve guide to remove any distortion which may have been caused by the driving tool.

VALVE LIFTERS

Valve lifters in all Willys cars are the mushroom type and require removal of the engine and camshaft in order to replace them.

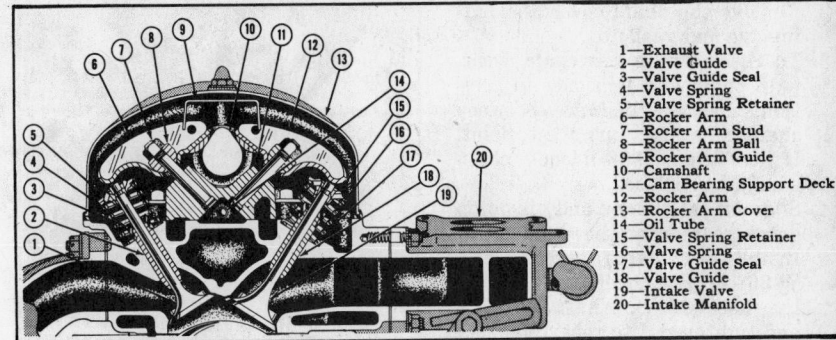

Tornado 230—cutaway valve section

1—Exhaust Valve
2—Valve Guide
3—Valve Guide Seal
4—Valve Spring
5—Valve Spring Retainer
6—Rocker Arm
7—Rocker Arm Stud
8—Rocker Arm Ball
9—Rocker Arm Guide
10—Camshaft
11—Cam Bearing Support Deck
12—Rocker Arm
13—Rocker Arm Cover
14—Oil Tube
15—Valve Spring Retainer
16—Valve Spring
17—Valve Guide Seal
18—Valve Guide
19—Intake Valve
20—Intake Manifold

Valve guide installation dimensions

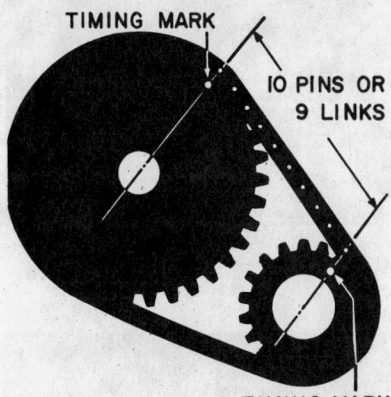

Aligning Timing Marks 6 Cyl. 226 Engine

On the L-Head type valve, the lifter is fitted with a self-locking tappet screw.

Overhead valves are adjusted at the rocker arm.

CAMSHAFT AND BEARINGS INSPECT AND/OR REPLACE

Removal (Head Removed)

1. Lift off rocker arm guide.
2. Turn rocker arms that have no tension parallel with camshaft. Then rotate shaft until more arms are free and turn them parallel.

Continue until all arms are off cams.
3. Remove retainer from front of camshaft bearing deck and pull shaft forward from bearings.
4. By removing three nuts with washers, bearing deck can now be lifted free.

Inspection
1. Clean camshaft thoroughly with solvent. See that all oil passages are clear. Run out of shaft must not exceed .0005". **Check diameter of journals.**
   Front ....1.9975"—1.9965"
   #2 ....1.8725"—1.8715"
   #3 ....1.7475"—1.7465"
   #4 ....1.3725"—1.3715"
2. **Check deck for cracks and distorsions.**
3. **Check diameter of bearing bores.**
   Front ....1.9995"—2.0005"
   #2 ....1.8745"—1.8755"
   #3 ....1.7495"—1.7505"
   #4 ....1.3745"—1.3755"
   Maximum running clearance .004"

Reinstall
1. Place camshaft bearing deck on cylinder head and install nuts and washers and tighten evenly.
2. Lubricate the bearings with engine oil and slide shaft into the bearings from the front, using care not to damage bearings.
3. Secure shaft in place with the retainer plate and nuts and washers.

Aligning Timing Marks all Expect 6 Cyl. 226

TIMING CASE

TIMING CASE COVER REMOVAL

To remove the timing case cover it is nescessary to take off the radiator. The end play in the camshaft is taken up by a spring plunger mounted inside the timing case cover. When replacing the cover make certain that the spring plunger is in its proper position.

TIMING CASE COVER AND CHAIN REMOVAL

Tornado 230 OHC Engine

1. Remove hose from water port on cover. Then remove eight bolts, lock washers and flat washers, and three nuts holding cover to front engine plate.

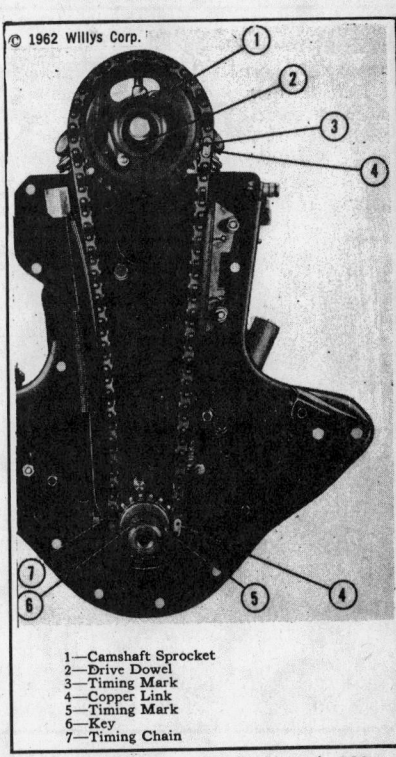

1—Camshaft Sprocket
2—Drive Dowel
3—Timing Mark
4—Copper Link
5—Timing Mark
6—Key
7—Timing Chain

Timing Chain Installed—Tornado 230

2. Remove the chain cover and lifting eye and gaskets.

3. To check for excess chain wear, with chain and tensioner in position, measure distance between chain sides at narrowest point. If less than 3.38 inches chain should be replaced.

4. Slide off oil slinger and oil pump drive gear from the crankshaft.

5. Install the camshaft sprocket tool W-268 on the cover studs. Insert the hook in camshaft sprocket and tighten nut to relieve tension on camshaft.

6. Remove capscrew, lock and flat washer and fuel pump eccentric from sprocket. Pull sprocket forward from pilot on camshaft. Release hook of tool. Slide crankshaft sprocket off crankshaft.

7. Remove pin from top of tensioner and remove the tensioner blade and spring from the lower mounting stud.

8. Remove chain guide bracket from front engine plate.

To Reinstall: Reverse the above. Proper camshaft timing is accomplished by turning No. 1 piston to top of stroke with crankshaft sprocket key up, at 12 o'clock position, and camshaft sprocket dowel down at 6 o'clock position. Both No. 1 intake and exhaust valves should be closed.

ENGINE LUBRICATION
REMOVAL OF OIL PAN

On all Willys models the oil pan is

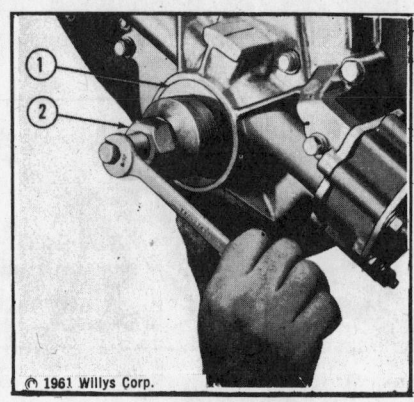

Removing front oil seal

1—Oil Seal
2—W-270 Puller

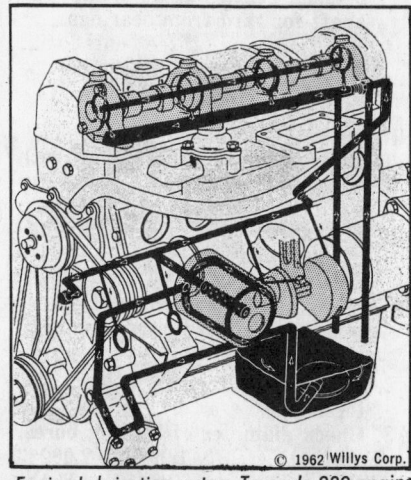

Engine Lubrication system. Tornado 230 engine

simply unbolted and lowered. Spacers are used under the fan belt guard and should be reinstalled in the position from which they were removed.

FRONT CRANKSHAFT OIL SEAL REMOVAL

1. Remove vibration damper.
2. Thread housing of tool W-270 into crankshaft oil seal. Turn tool screw clockwise to force out seal.

To Reinstall: Be sure there are no burrs to damage new seal.

1. Coat outer edge of seal with a good sealing compound and place the seal on shaft with lip toward inside. Drive seal into place with tool W-269.

CONNECTING RODS AND PISTONS
REMOVAL OF ROD AND PISTON ASSEMBLIES

Remove the cylinder head and oil pan and, selecting pistons in the down position, cut the ring ridge from the top of the cylinder with a ring ridge reamer.

If no reamer is available, the ridge can be removed with a good bearing scraper.

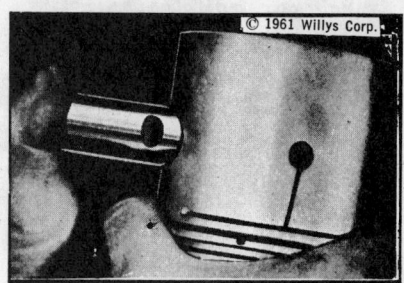

Piston pin fitting

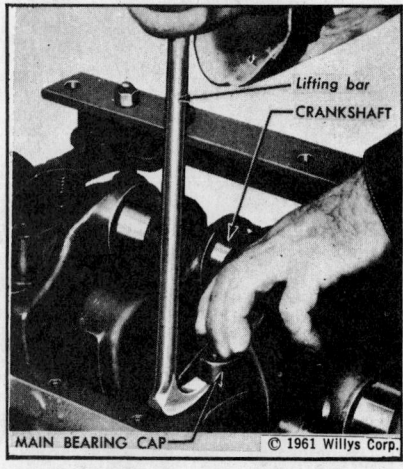

Lifting bar
CRANKSHAFT

MAIN BEARING CAP

Removing main bearing cap

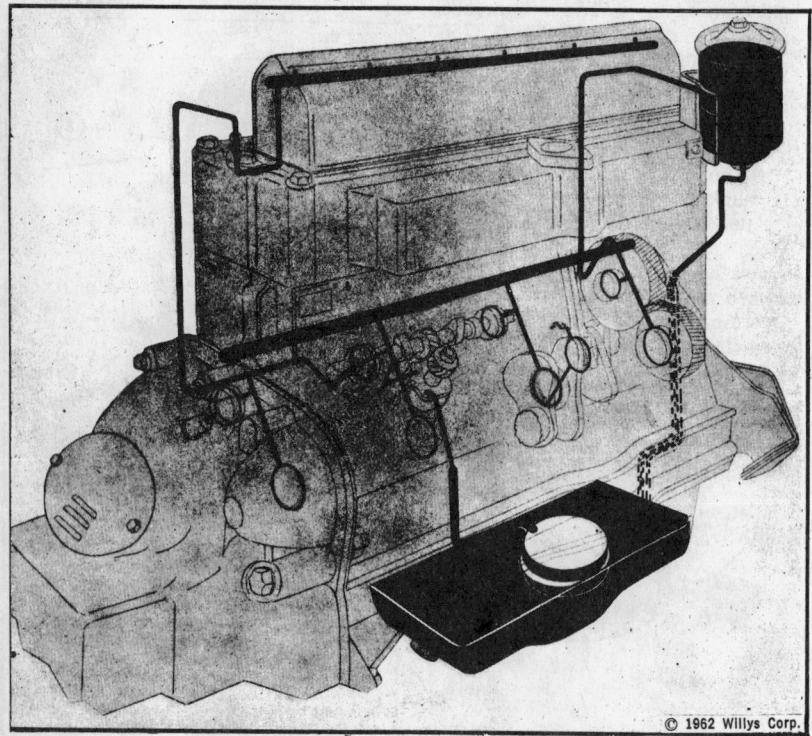

Engine Oil Circulation— 6 Cyl., F-Head

Carefully mark the rod and rod cap on the assembly where the ring ridge has been removed and take off the cap. Push the rod and piston assembly up out of the top of the block.

PISTON AND ROD ASSEMBLIES

Aluminum pistons are used in all Willys models and the wrist pin is locked in the rod. The connecting rod bearings are of the slip-in type and are available in a variety of undersizes.

ASSEMBLING PISTONS TO CONNECTING RODS

The oil spit hole in the connecting rod should be assembled on the side opposite to the T slot in the piston.

ASSEMBLING ROD AND PISTON ASSEMBLIES TO THE ENGINE

When assembling the rod and piston assemblies to the engine, the T slot in the piston should be on the left side of the engine. On all Willys cars

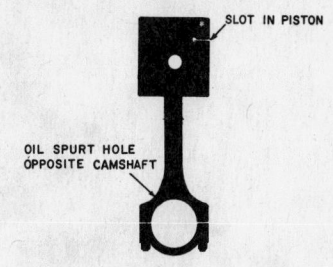

Piston and Rod Installation all except OH Camshaft Engine

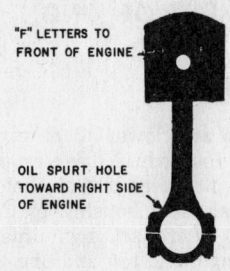

Piston and Rod Installation O.H. Camshaft Engine

this is the valve side. On the 6 cyl. 226 "L" head: Oil spray hole goes toward camshaft.

On all other moders: Oil spray hole goes away from camshaft.

FRONT SUSPENSION

REFERENCES

General instructions covering the front suspension and how to repair and adjust it, together with information on installation of front wheel bearings and grease seals, are given in the Unit Repair section under the heading: Suspension Front Repair.

Definitions of the points of steering geometry are covered in the unit repair section under the heading: Suspension Front Align. This article also covers trouble shooting front end geometry and irregular tire wear.

Figures covering the caster, camber, toe-in, king pin inclination, and turning radius can be found in the Front Wheel Alignment Table of this section.

Wheelbase, tread and tire size figures can be found in the General Chassis and Brake Specifications Table of this section.

FRONT WHEEL DRIVES

On front wheel drive models caster is adjusted by placing shims between the spring pads on the front axle housing and the top of the spring.

This method should only be used where it is necessary to adjust both sides of the car the same amount. In the event the caster reading is low because of sag of the front leaf springs it is advisable to replace the springs rather than use caster wedges. Camber, on front wheel drives, can be adjusted only by bending the axle tube and this certainly is not recommended.

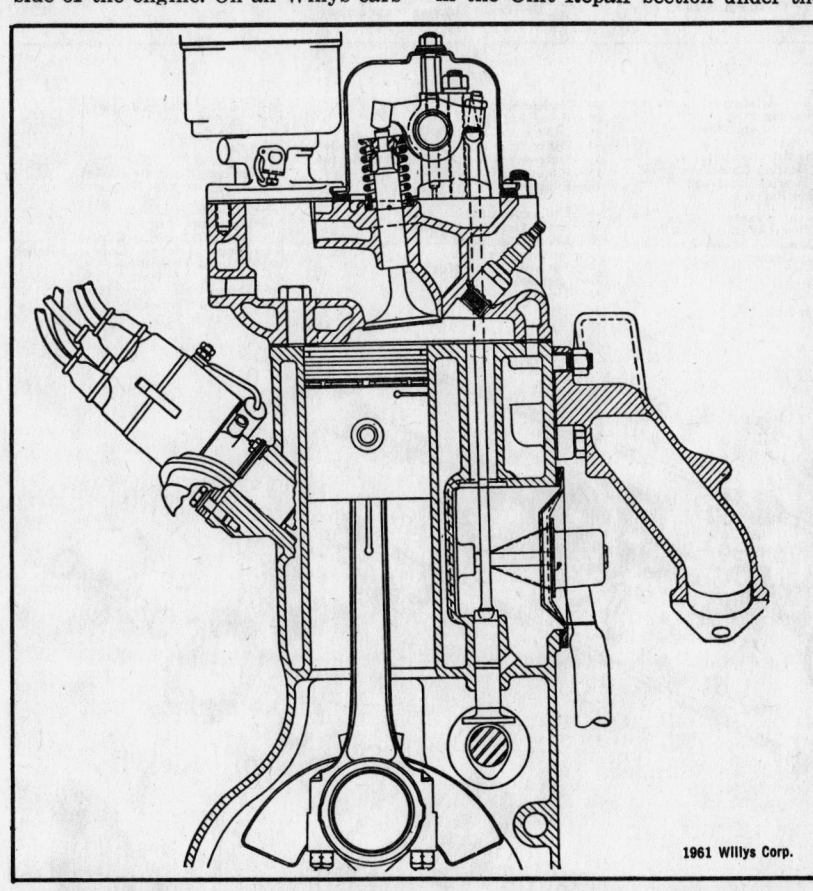

Sectional view of the F-type cylinder head and upper part of four cylinder engine. Note that the block, pistons, rods, and other parts remain interchangeable with the original four-cyl. engine.

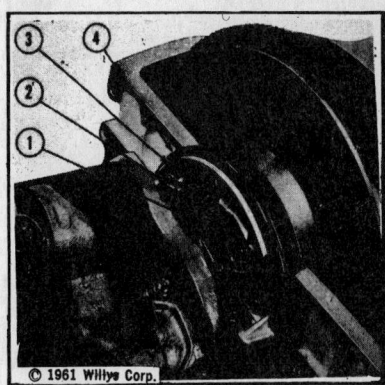

Removing Main Bearing Upper Half with Engine Installed.

1—Rear Main Bearing Cap
2—Bearing Cap Bolt
3—Filler Block
4—Oil Pan Seal

WILLYS

REPLACEMENT OF KING PINS

Four-Wheel Drives

An upper and lower pivot pin is used in the four-wheel drive models. Both upper and lower pins are held to the universal joint housing by four cap screws. There are two tapered roller bearings, one top and one bottom in the axle housing, exactly centered across the neutral point of the constant velocity universal joint. If it is desired to replace the tapered roller bearings, it will be necessary to remove the universal joint outer housing. This involves the wheel and the stationary axle. If the pivot pins only are to be replaced, they can be removed by taking out the four cap screws which hold them to the universal joint housing. Shims are used under the head of the pivot pins to insure zero up and down play in the tapered roller bearings. To remove the pivot pins it is advisable to take off the wheel, brake drum and brake backing plate.

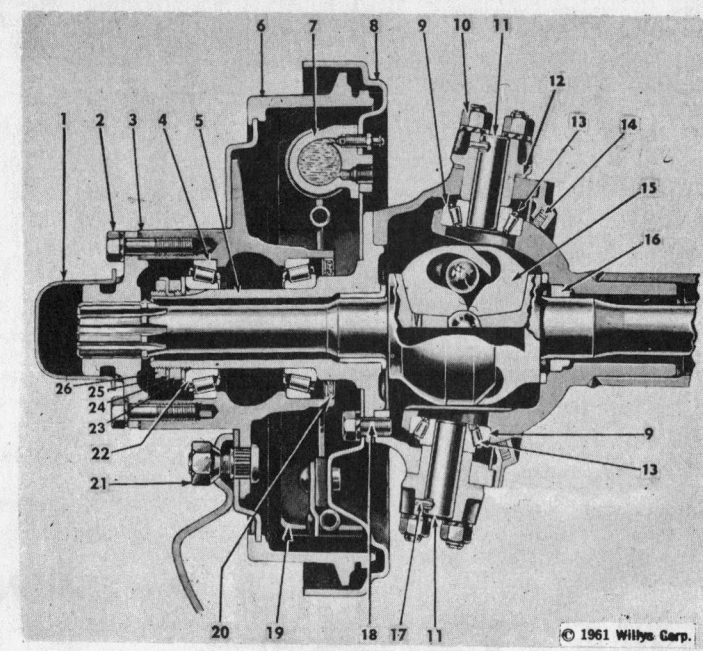

© 1961 Willys Corp.

Front steering knuckle

1—Wheel Hub Cap
2—Driving Flange Cap Screw
3—Axle Shaft Drive Flange Gasket
4—Wheel Bearing Cup
5—Front Wheel Spindle
6—Brake Drum
7—Front Brake Cylinder
8—Brake Backing Plate
9—Pivot Pin Bearing Cap

10—Pivot Pin Bearing Cap Nut
11—Pivot Pin
12—Pivot Bearing Adjusting Shims
13—Pivot Pin Cone and Rollers
14—Steering Knuckle Oil Seal
15—Front Axle Universal Joint
16—Axle Shaft Bushing
17—Pivot Pin Locking Pin
18—Brake Backing Plate Screw

19—Brake Shoe and Lining
20—Hub Oil Seal
21—Wheel Hub Bolt Nut
22—Wheel Bearing Cone and Rollers
23—Wheel Bearing Washer
24—Wheel Bearing Retaining Nut
25—Wheel Adjusting Nut Lock Wash
26—Wheel Bearing Retaining Nut

FRONT AXLE
—4-WHEEL DRIVE MODELS

1—Wheel Bearing Nut
2—Locking Washer
3—Wheel Bearing Washer
4—Wheel Bearing Cup
5—Wheel Bearing Cone and Rollers
6—Wheel Bearing Oil Seal
7—Wheel Spindle
8—Wheel Spindle Bushing
9—Knuckle Housing Filler Plug
10—Knuckle and Arm—Left
11—Adjusting Shims
12—Bearing Cap
13—Lockwasher
14—Bearing Cap Bolt

15—Pinion Huglock Nut
16—Pinion Washer
17—Universal Joint Yoke
18—Pinion Shaft Oil Seal
19—Bearing Oil Slinger
20—Bearing Cone and Rollers
21—Bearing Cup
22—Right Universal Joint and Shaft

23—Knuckle Oil Seal Retainer
24—Front Axle Housing
25—Left Universal Joint and Shaft
26—Axle Shaft Guide
27—Pinion Bearing Adjusting Shims
28—Pinion Shaft Bearing Cup
29—Pinion Shaft Bearing Cone and Rollers
30—Drive Gear and Pinion
31—Side Gear Thrust Washer
32—Pinion Case Thrust Washer
33—Differential Gears
34—Housing Cover Gasket
35—Housing Cover
36—Housing Breather
37—Filler Plug
38—Housing Cover Bolt

39—Lockwasher
40—Retaining Ring
41—Differential Bearing Cup
42—Differential Bearing Cone and Rollers
43—Differential Bearing Adjusting Shims
44—Pinion Shaft Lock Pin
45—Pinion Shaft

46—Differential Case
47—Drive Gear Lock Strap
48—Drive Gear Bolts
49—Steering Tie Rod
50—Tie Rod Clamp Nut
51—Lockwasher
52—Tie Rod Socket Clamp

53—Tie Rod Clamp Screw
54—Tie Rod Socket
55—Dust Cover
56—Washer
57—Tie Rod Stud Nut
58—Steering Knuckle Gasket
59—Universal Joint Thrust Washer

60—Knuckle Stop Bolt
61—Stop Bolt Nut
62—King Pin Bearing Cup
63—King Pin Bearing Cone and Rollers
64—Housing Drain Plug
65—Bearing Cap Bolt
66—Differential Bearing Cap
67—Knuckle Oil Seal

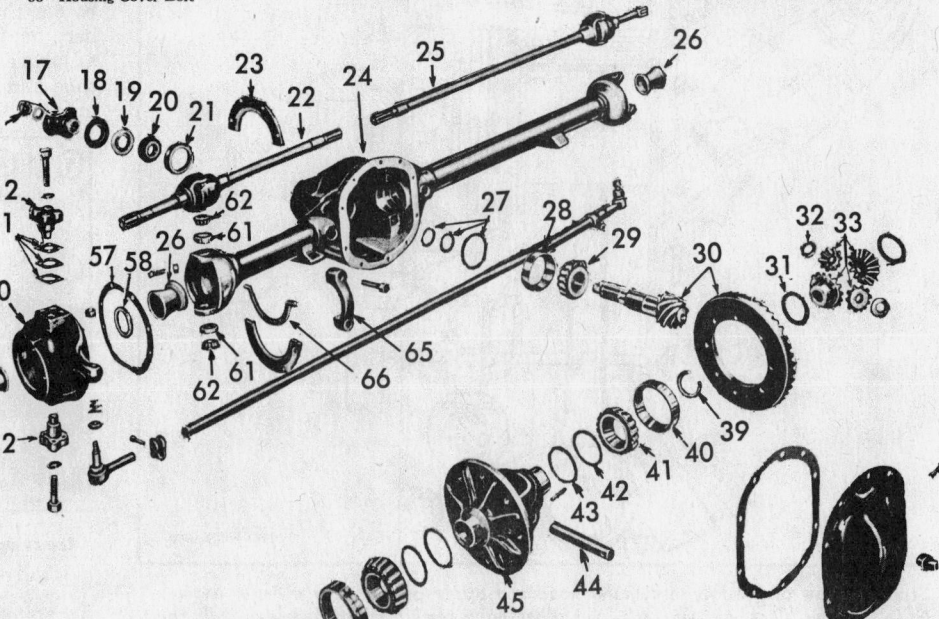

696

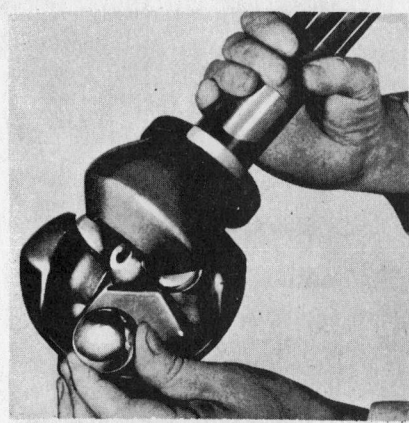

Bendix universal joint balls

UNIVERSAL JOINT— FRONT AXLE

The front axle differential is serviced in exactly the same manner as the rear axle differential, which will be discussed later in this text.

Two types of constant velocity universal joints were used on Willys four-wheel drives. The first was the Bendix type universal joint, the second the Rzeppa type.

Bendix Joint

To disassemble the Bendix joint hold the splined driving axle in a vise and drive out the center ball pin retainer.

Jolt the splined driving axle against a block of wood so that the ball retaining pin will drop through the drilled hole which is lengthwise of the driving axle. Pull the two halves of the joint apart and then bend the joint sharply. Rotate the center ball until the grooved side lines up with a ball raceway, which will permit the adjacent ball to be moved past the center ball and out of the joint. The remaining three driving balls and the center ball will then drop out. Examine the raceways for scoring, scratches or markings.

Note: The driving ball is .875" and is available in .001, .002 and .003 inch under-size and over-size. This permits selective fitting. If the raceways are

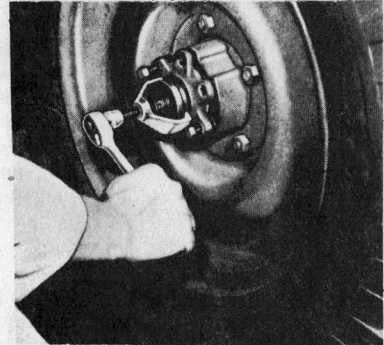

Axle shaft flange puller

free of scores and scratches and the joint has play, select a ball of sufficient over-size to take up the play.

Note: Variation in ball size in any one joint should not be greater than .001 inch.

Rzeppa Joint

Dismantle the Rzeppa joint, remove the three screws which hold the front axle shaft to the joint itself and pull the shaft out of the splined inner race. To take out the axle shaft retainer, remove the retainer ring on the shaft. Push down on the various points of the inner race and cage until the balls can be removed with the help of a small screw driver.

After all the balls have been removed, the inner race and cage can be turned over so the pilot cup is up and then the pilot cup can be taken out.

There are two large elongated holes in the cage. Turn the cage so that the two bosses in the spindle shaft will drop into the elongated holes in the cage and then the cage can be lifted out.

To remove the inner race, turn it so that one of the bosses will drop into an elongated hole in this cage and then shift the race to one side and lift it out.

REPLACEMENT OF TRANSVERSE FRONT SPRING

The transverse front spring used on the independent front suspension on Willys cars can be replaced by supporting the weight of the car on jacks back of the front suspension, removing both bolts from the outer ends of the spring shackles and unbolt the spring from the frame. It is not necessary to detach the shock absorber from the upper suspension arm.

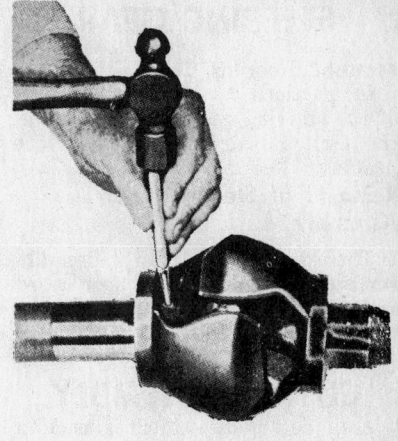

Driving out retainer pin (Bendix joint)

© 1961 Willys Corp.

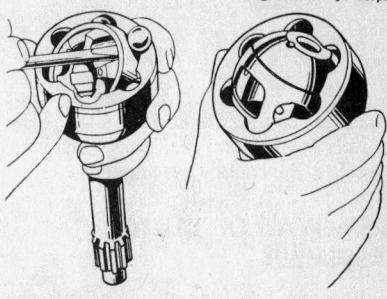

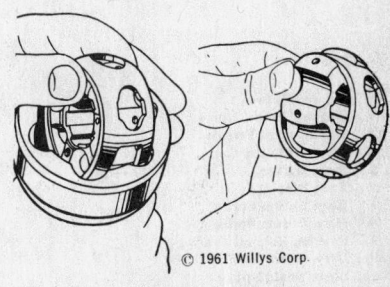

© 1961 Willys Corp.

Disassembly of the Rzeppa joint

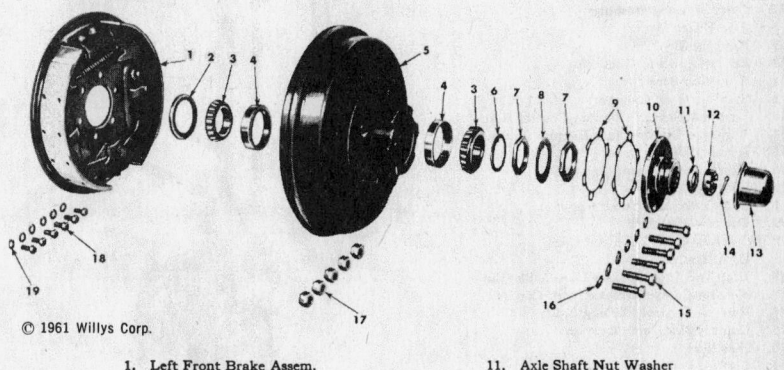

© 1961 Willys Corp.

1. Left Front Brake Assem.	11. Axle Shaft Nut Washer
2. Oil Seal	12. Axle Shaft Nut
3. Bearing Cone and Roller	13. Hub Cap
4. Bearing Cup	14. Cotter Pin
5. Hub and Brake Drum	15. Driving Flange Bolt
6. Bearing Locking Washer	16. Lockwasher
7. Lock Nut	17. Wheel Nut
8. Bearing Nut Locking Washer	18. Backing Plate Bolt
9. Adjusting Shim	19. Lockwasher
10. Driving Flange	

Front wheel drive attaching parts

WILLYS

STEERING GEAR

Manual Steering Gear

Instructions covering the overhaul of the steering gear will be found in the Unit Repair section under the heading: Steering Manual.

Removal of Steering Gear Assembly

The steering gear can be readily removed by removing the floor board and disconnecting the shift levers and the gear mounting bolts.

CLUTCH ASSEMBLY

A single dry disc clutch is used on all Willys models. Except for adjusting the pedal clearance no service is possible on the clutch assembly unless it is removed from the car.

CLUTCH PEDAL ADJUSTMENT

Adjust the clutch linkage so that there is from ¾" to 1" free play of the clutch pedal before the throwout bearing contacts the fingers.

REMOVAL OF CLUTCH ASSEMBLY

Remove the transmission and the clutch housing. Mark the clutch cover and flywheel so that the clutch will be reassembled in the position from which it was removed. Unbolt the clutch from the flywheel and lift off.

REPLACEMENT OF CLUTCH

To replace the clutch, a pilot shaft is needed and if none is available the main drive shaft of the transmission will have to be taken out of the transmission and used as a pilot shaft.

With one hand place the clutch cover assembly and disc into position against the flywheel and with the other hand push the pilot shaft in from the back of the clutch housing so that it engages the center splines of the disc and also the pilot hole in the flywheel.

This will hold the disc in the center position and the bolt can be started in the cover assembly, drawing them up a little at a time so as not to bend or distort the cover assembly.

CLUTCH DISASSEMBLY

Special equipment is required to disassemble and reassemble the pressure plate on all Willys models. Unless this equipment is available it is unwise to attempt to service the pressure plate and cover assembly.

The customary method is to install a new or rebuilt unit.

Clutch service is given in the clutch section of this manual, see index.

SYNCHROMESH TRANSMISSION

TRANSMISSION INFORMATION

Transmission refill capacities will be found in the Capacities Table of this section.

Trouble shooting and repair of overdrive units are covered in the Unit Repair section under the heading Transmission—Overdrive.

REMOVAL OF TRANSMISSION

Remove the floor mat, floor and toe boards. Since it will be necessary to jack up the engine, loosen the radiator mounting bolts so that no undue strain is placed on the radiator. Disconnect all transmission shift rods and jack up the engine, being careful that the fan does not injure the radiator. The engine should be jacked up until the mounting bracket at the rear of the transmission can be removed. Remove the bell housing to engine bolts.

Note: If the aligning bolts are driven in from the rear, reverse them and drive them in from the front, which will hold the motor plate in position and make the bell housing easier to assemble. The transmission can then be lifted off.

DISASSEMBLY OF TRANSMISSION

Mount the transmission in a sturdy vise and remove the cover from the top of the transmission and the shift levers from the side. Remove the bearing housing from the rear of the transmission and slide the main shaft and its gears backward until the main shaft can be cocked somewhat to relieve the second speed gear and low speed gear from their shift levers. Take out the lock rings and slide the gears off the main shaft. After this the main shaft, less its gears, can be slid out the back of the case and the gears can be lifted out through the top.

Drive out the countershaft from the rear of the case and let the cluster gear drop to the bottom. The main drive gear can now be pulled out the front of the transmission.

Inspect the gear teeth for chipping or roughness—replace any bearings which are defective and reassemble in the reverse order of disassembly.

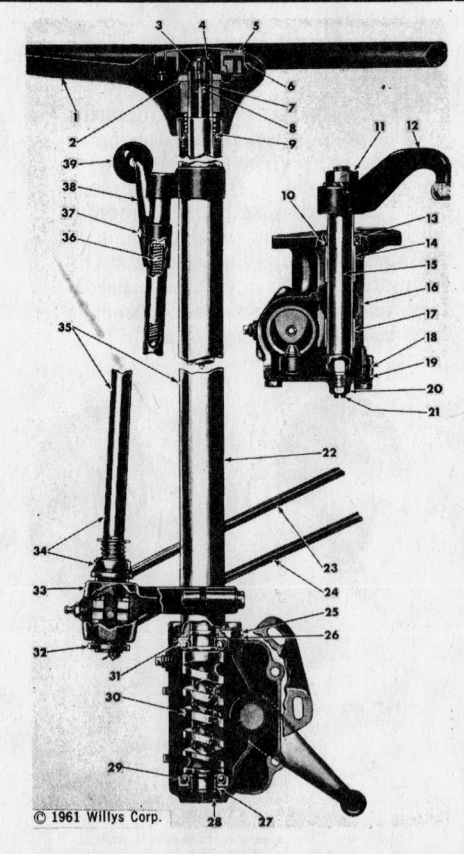

1. Steering Wheel
2. Steering Wheel Nut
3. Horn Button Ferrule
4. Contact Button Cup
5. Horn Button
6. Trim Ring
7. Horn Button Spring
8. Horn Button Spring Cup
9. Steering Column Bearing
10. Lever Shaft Oil Seal
11. Lever Shaft Nut
12. Steering Gear Arm
13. Lever Shaft Oil Seal Gasket
14. Outer Housing Bushing
15. Shaft and Lever
16. Steering Gear Housing
17. Inner Housing Bushing
18. Side Cover Gasket
19. Housing Side Cover
20. Adjusting Screw Lock Nut
21. Adjusting Screw
22. Steering Gear Column
23. Low and Reverse Remote Control Rod
24. High and Intermediate Remote Control Rod
25. Housing Upper Cover
26. Upper Cover Shim
27. Bearing Snap Ring
28. End Cover and Tube
29. Cam Bearing Ball
30. Steering Gear Tube and Cam
31. Cam Bearing Cup
32. High and Intermediate Lever with Clutch
33. Remote Control Bracket with Cap
34. Remote Control Shifting Shaft
35. Control Shaft with Column
36. Bias Spring
37. Control Lever Pin
38. Gear Shift Control Lever
39. Control Lever Ball

© 1961 Willys Corp.

Steering gear

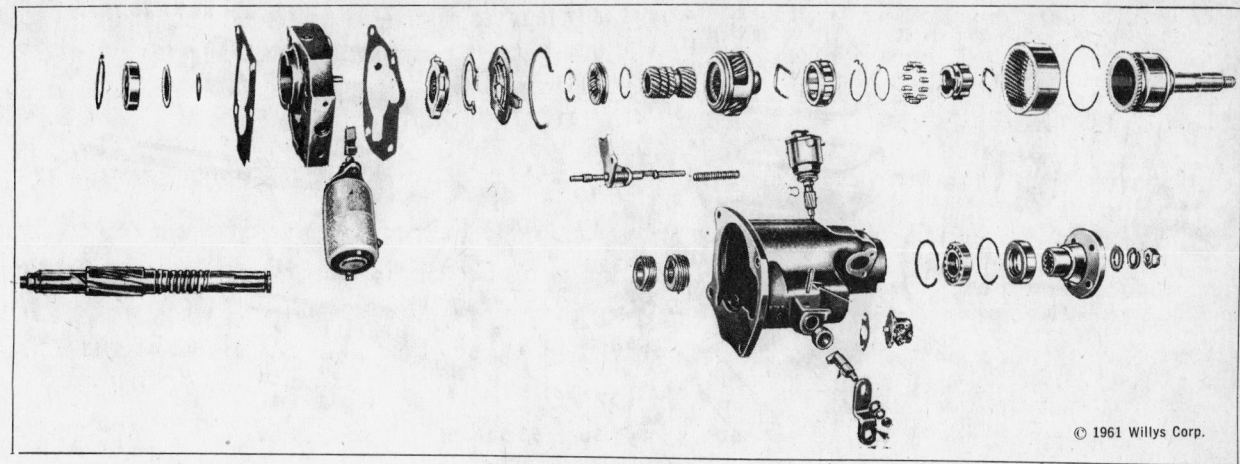

Overdrive—exploded view

OVERDRIVE

The overdrive transmission is disassembled in the same manner as most other overdrives. Drive out the retaining pin which holds the overdrive lockout lever shaft to the side of the overdrive case.

Pull the shaft out of the side of the overdrive case. Remove the universal joint yoke and unbolt the overdrive housing from the adapter plate. (The adapter plate is the thick plate which stands between the transmission case and the overdrive case and contains the solenoid mechanism.) Remove the governor from the back of the overdrive and slide the case and rear main shaft back off the overdrive.

The overdrive unit can now be disassembled by removing the snap rings which hold the free wheeling unit and planetary pinions in place.

Note: The kickdown pawl mechanism is retained to the adapter plate by a large snap ring which can be taken out after the planetary pinions have been removed.

FOUR WHEEL DRIVE TRANSFER CASE

To remove the transfer case from the car it is taken off in one unit with the transmission. To disassemble the transfer case, remove the universal joint, yokes and the brake drum. Take off the lower cover and remove the lock plate which holds the intermediate shaft in the case and drive out the intermediate shaft. The gears and thrust washers will come out the bottim of the case. Take out the rear output bearing cap which will come off with the speedometer gear. Drive against the front end of the main shaft to start the rear bearing from its case and wedge the front bearing from its seat on the shaft. Loosen the snap ring from the front of the shaft and slide it forward on the shaft.

Drive the shaft out through the case and out of the bearing and gears. The bearing gears and snap rings can then be lowered through the bottom of the case. Remove the set screw and the sliding gear shift fork which will allow the shift rod to be removed. Examine all gears for scratches and check the bearings for roughness. The case is assembled in the reverse order of disassembly.

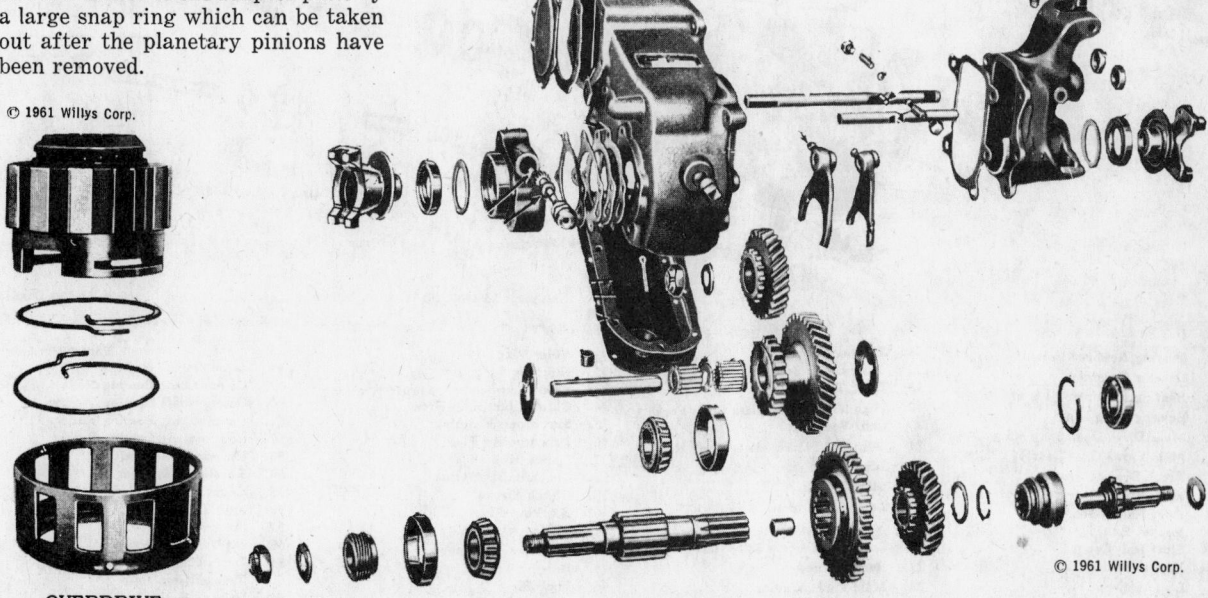

OVERDRIVE FREEWHEELING CAM

Transfer case—4-wheel drive

WILLYS

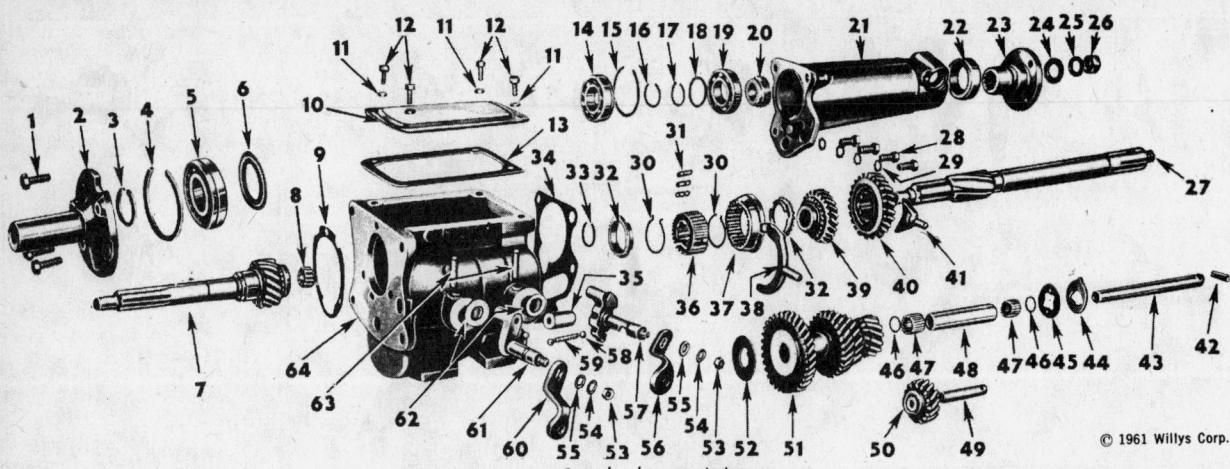

Standard transmission

1—Main Bearing Retainer Bolt
2—Main Bearing Retainer
3—Main Drive Gear Snap Ring
4—Bearing Snap Ring
5—Main Drive Gear Bearing
6—Oil Baffle
7—Main Drive Gear
8—Pilot Bearing Rollers
9—Bearing Retainer Gasket
10—Case Cover
11—Case Cover Bolt Gasket
12—Case Cover Bolt
13—Case Cover Gasket
14—Rear Main Shaft Bearing
15—Rear Bearing Snap Ring
16—Main Shaft Snap Ring

17—Rear Bearing Snap Ring
18—Rear Bearing Washer
19—Rear Main Shaft Bearing
20—Speedometer Drive Gear
21—Rear Bearing Retainer
22—Main Shaft Oil Seal
23—Coupling Flange
24—Main Shaft Washer
25—Main Shaft Nut Lockwasher
26—Main Shaft Nut
27—Main Shaft
28—Rear Bearing Retainer Bolt
29—Retainer Bolt Lockwasher
30—Synchronizer Spring
31—Synchronizer Shifting Plate
32—Blocking Ring

33—Clutch Hub Snap Ring
34—Rear Bearing Retainer Gasket
35—Interlock Sleeve
36—Clutch Hub
37—Clutch Sleeve
38—High and Intermediate Shift Fork
39—Second Speed Gear
40—Low and Reverse Gear
41—Low and Reverse Shift Fork
42—Idler and Countershaft Lock Plate
43—Countershaft
44—Thrust Washer
45—Thrust Washer
46—Countershaft Bearing Shift Spacer
47—Countershaft Bearing Rollers
48—Countershaft Bearing Long Spacer

49—Reverse Idler Gear Shaft
50—Reverse Idler Gear
51—Countershaft Gear
52—Thrust Washer
53—Control Lever to Shaft Nut
54—Lever to Shaft Lockwasher
55—Lever to Shaft Washer
56—Low and Reverse Control Lever
57—Low and Reverse Shift Lever
58—Poppet Ball
59—Poppet Spring
60—High and Intermediate Control Lever
61—High and Intermediate Shift Lever
62—Shift Shaft Oil Seal
63—Shift Lever Shaft Pin
64—Transmission Case

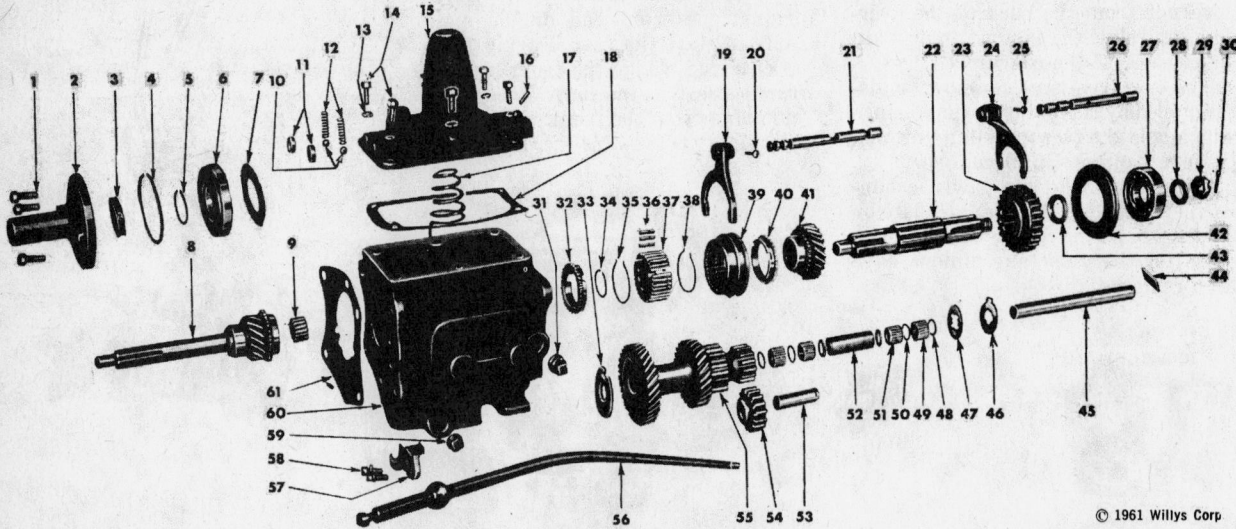

Transmission—4-wheel drive and 473HT

1. Bearing Retainer Bolt
2. Bearing Retainer
3. Bearing Retainer Oil Seal
4. Bearing Snap Ring
5. Main Drive Gear Snap Ring
6. Main Drive Gear Bearing
7. Front Bearing Washer
8. Main Drive Gear
9. Pilot Roller Bearing
10. Poppet Ball
11. Shift Rail Cap
12. Poppet Spring
13. Lockwasher
14. Shift Housing Bolt
15. Shift Housing

16. Interlock Plunger
17. Shift Lever Spring
18. Shift Tower Gasket
19. High and Intermediate Shift Fork
20. Shift Fork Pin
21. High and Intermediate Shift Rail
22. Main Shaft
23. Sliding Gear
24. Low and Reverse Shift Fork
25. Shift Fork Pin
26. Low and Reverse Shift Rail
27. Rear Bearing
28. Main Shaft Washer
29. Main Shaft Nut
30. Cotter Pin

31. Filler Plug
32. Blocking Ring
33. Front Countershaft Thrust Washer
34. Clutch Hub Snap Ring
35. Synchronizer Spring
36. Synchronizer Plate
37. Clutch Hub
38. Synchronizer Spring
39. Clutch Sleeve
40. Blocking Ring
41. Second Speed Gear
42. Rear Bearing Adapter
43. Bearing Spacer
44. Lock Plate
45. Countershaft
46. Rear Countershaft Thrust Washer

47. Rear Countershaft Thrust Washer
48. Countershaft Bearing Washer
49. Countershaft Bearing Rollers
50. Countershaft Bearing Washer
51. Countershaft Bearing Rollers
52. Countershaft Bearing Spacer
53. Reverse Gear Shaft
54. Reverse Idler Gear
55. Countershaft Gear Set
56. Shift Lever
57. Oil Collector
58. Oil Collector Screw
59. Drain Plug
60. Transmission Case
61. Bearing Retainer Gasket

AUTOMATIC TRANSMISSION

For "Transmission Overhaul" and other detailed information, see "Unit Repair Section," "Transmission Group" of this manual.

REAR AXLE AND SUSPENSION

REAR AXLE

Trouble Shooting and Adjustment

General instructions covering the troubles of the rear axle and how to repair and adjust it, together with information on installation of rear axle bearings and grease seals, are given in the unit repair section under the heading: Axles, Rear.

Capacities of the rear axle are given in the Capacities Tables of this section.

The rear axle assembly on all Willys cars is of the shim adjusted type. The front driving axle on four-wheel drive models is serviced in exactly the same manner as the rear driving axle and, as a matter of fact, many of the parts are interchangeable.

Removal of the Rear Axle from the Car

Support the back end of the car on stands on the frame in front of the rear spring. Disconnect the propeller shaft at the rear universal joint companion flange. Disconnect the brake hoses and cables, disconnect the shock absorbers and remove the rear spring shackle.

Now take off the U-bolt nuts which hold the rear spring to the rear axle housing tubes. Lower the springs to the floor and pull out the rear axle assembly from under the vehicle.

Service on the Rear Axle

All service on the rear axle assembly is given in the rear axle section of this manual, see index. This service covers axle shaft end play, the re-

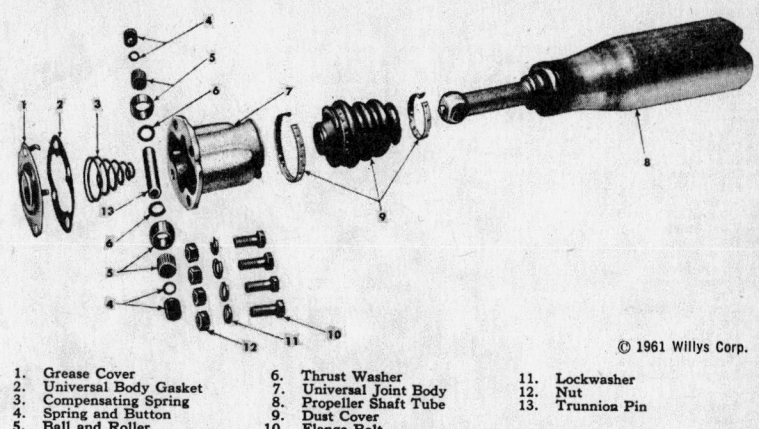

1.	Grease Cover		6.	Thrust Washer	
2.	Universal Body Gasket		7.	Universal Joint Body	
3.	Compensating Spring		8.	Propeller Shaft Tube	
4.	Spring and Button		9.	Dust Cover	
5.	Ball and Roller		10.	Flange Bolt	
			11.	Lockwasher	
			12.	Nut	
			13.	Trunnion Pin	

© 1961 Willys Corp.

Propeller shaft and universal joints—ball and trunnion type

placement of all oil seals and bearings, the replacement and adjustment of the ring gear and pinion.

REAR SPRINGS AND SHOCK ABSORBERS

REAR SUSPENSION

Removal of the Rear Shock Absorbers

The rear shock absorbers are mounted to a single bolt on the U-bolt plate of the rear spring.

Carefully note before removal whether or not the spring center bolt is exactly in the center of the spring. On some models the spring is shorter than at the other.

They are mounted to a bracket on the frame at the top.

Remove the nut from the top and bottom and the shock absorber can be pulled off together with its rubber bushings.

Service on Shock Absorbers

Highly specialized tools and equipment are required to service the shock absorbers, and unless this equipment is available the operation should not be attempted. If the shock absorber is defective, it should be replaced with either a new or rebuilt one.

Replacement of the Rear Spring

Take the weight of the car on jacks on the frame in front of the rear spring and take the bolts and threaded bushings out of the rear spring shackle.

Remove the nut and bolt from the front eye of the spring where it attaches to the frame bracket. Remove the four U bolts which hold the spring to the axle and lower the spring from under the car.

UNIVERSAL JOINTS AND DRIVE LINES

Ball and trunnion type universal joints are used on all models of Willys.

REMOVAL OF THE UNIVERSAL JOINT AND/OR DRIVE SHAFT ASSEMBLY

Remove the bolts which hold the universal joint body to the rear axle companion flange and lower the back end of the drive shaft to the floor.

Repeat the operation on the front end of the drive shaft and the shaft and universal joint assembly can be pulled out from under the car.

On the bench, remove the grease boot from the universal joints and slide the body assembly back on to the propeller shaft.

Remove the ball and needle bearing assemblies and examine the surface of the bearing races.

If the cross pin is to be taken out, an arbor press is required since it is a press fit in the ball end of the drive shaft.

Replace all worn parts with new parts since no adjustment is possible on any universal joint parts.

On reassembly, carefully locate the centering spring and centering buttons.

Install in reverse of the removal procedure.

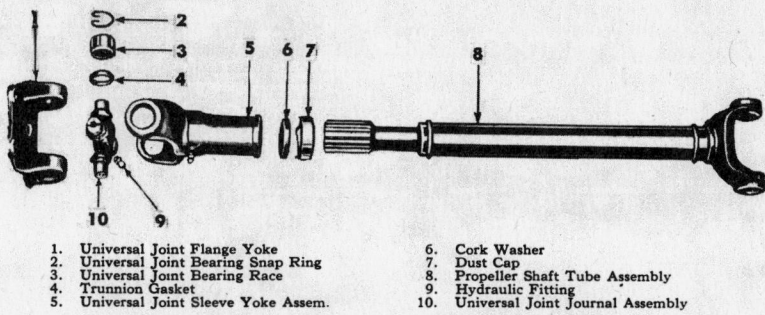

1.	Universal Joint Flange Yoke		6.	Cork Washer
2.	Universal Joint Bearing Snap Ring		7.	Dust Cap
3.	Universal Joint Bearing Race		8.	Propeller Shaft Tube Assembly
4.	Trunnion Gasket		9.	Hydraulic Fitting
5.	Universal Joint Sleeve Yoke Assem.		10.	Universal Joint Journal Assembly

Propeller shaft and universal joints—needle bearing type

WILLYS

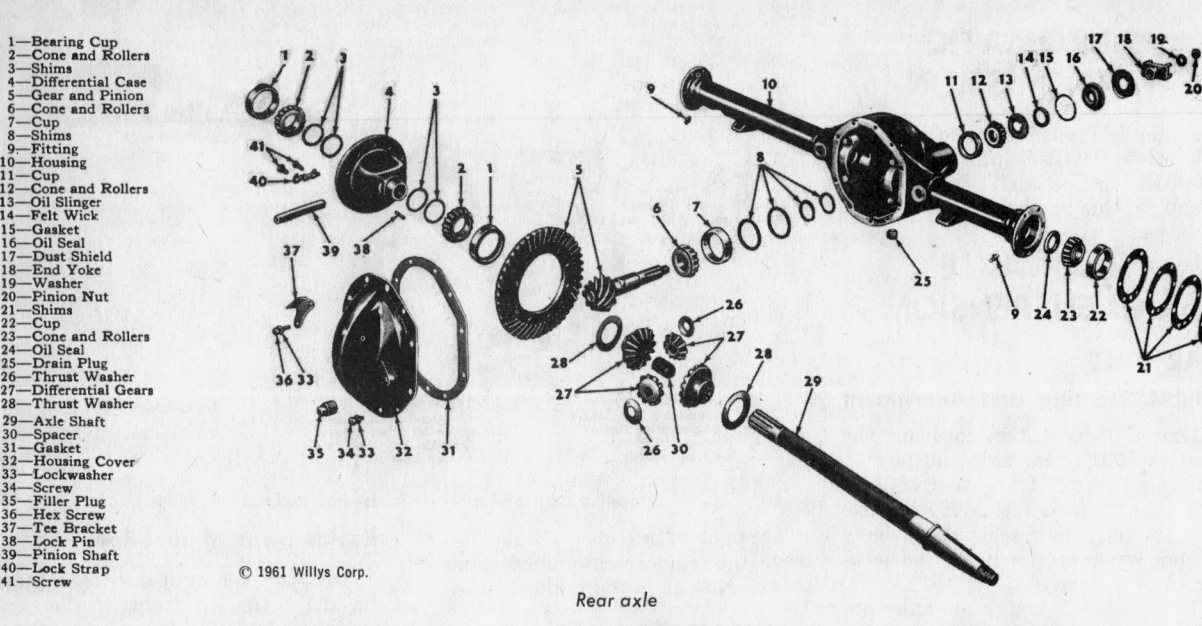

1—Bearing Cup
2—Cone and Rollers
3—Shims
4—Differential Case
5—Gear and Pinion
6—Cone and Rollers
7—Cup
8—Shims
9—Fitting
10—Housing
11—Cup
12—Cone and Rollers
13—Oil Slinger
14—Felt Wick
15—Gasket
16—Oil Seal
17—Dust Shield
18—End Yoke
19—Washer
20—Pinion Nut
21—Shims
22—Cup
23—Cone and Rollers
24—Oil Seal
25—Drain Plug
26—Thrust Washer
27—Differential Gears
28—Thrust Washer
29—Axle Shaft
30—Spacer
31—Gasket
32—Housing Cover
33—Lockwasher
34—Screw
35—Filler Plug
36—Hex Screw
37—Tee Bracket
38—Lock Pin
39—Pinion Shaft
40—Lock Strap
41—Screw

© 1961 Willys Corp.

Rear axle

Spiral Bevel Differential

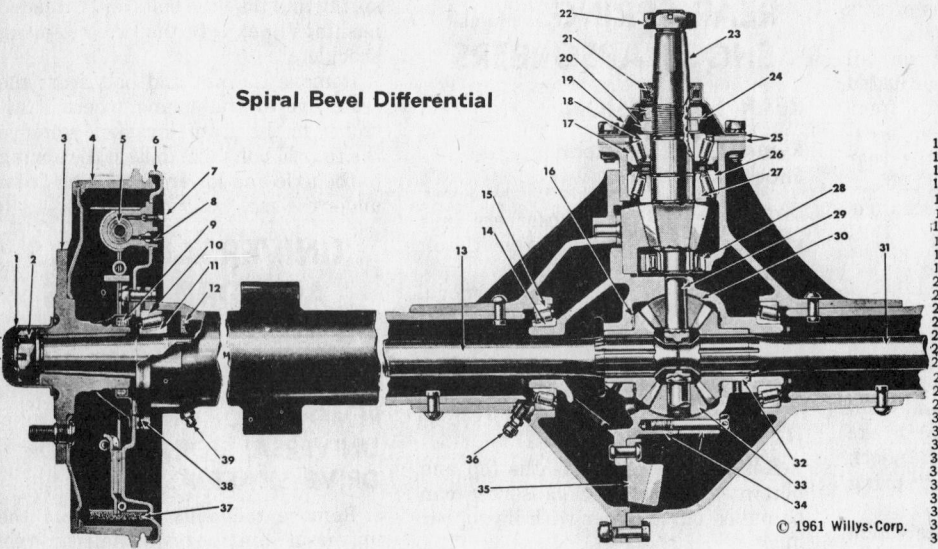

Differential

© 1961 Willys-Corp.

1. Wheel Hub Cap—Left or Right
2. Axle Shaft Nut
3. Wheel Hub
4. Brake Drum
5. Brake Cylinder Assembly—Rear
6. Brake Backing Plate
7. Brake Cylinder Bleeding Screw
8. Brake Hose Connection
9. Axle Shaft Grease Retainer—Outer
10. Axle Shaft Bearing Race
11. Axle Shaft Bearing Cone and Rollers
12. Axle Shaft Grease Retainer—Inner
13. Axle Shaft—Left
14. Differential Bearing Cone and Rollers
15. Differential Bearing Race
16. Differential Side Gear Thrust Washer
17. Pinion Shaft Bearing Race
18. Pinion Shaft Bearing Cone and Rollers
19. Pinion Front Bearing Cover
20. Pinion Front Bearing Adjusting and Lock
21. Pinion Cover Oil Seal
22. Pinion Nut
23. Pinion
24. Pinion Adjusting Nut Lock
25. Pinion Cover Gaskets
26. Pinion Bearing Race
27. Pinion Bearing Cone and Rollers
28. Pinion Rear Bearing
29. Differential Spider
30. Differential Pinion Thrust Washer
31. Axle Shaft Right
32. Differential Side Gear
33. Differential Pinion
34. Differential Case
35. Spiral Bevel Ring Gear
36. Axle Breather
37. Brake Shoe Assembly
38. Axle Shaft Bearing Shim
39. Lubricator

1. Fork and Rod
2. Ball
3. Lever
4. Nut
5. Button and Spring
6. Spring
7. Trunnion and Ball
8. Cup
9. Bearing
10. Snap Ring
11. Plate
12. Gasket
13. Retainer
14. Gasket
15. Gear
16. Oil Seal
17. Oil Seal
18. Oil Sea
19. Gear and Shaft
20. Cup
21. Cone and Roller
22. Shims
23. Spacer
24. Shims
25. Shims
26. Pinion
27. Cone and Roller
28. Cup
29. Shaft
30. Gasket
31. Shims
32. Gasket
33. Gear
34. Shaft
35. Gasket
36. Washer
37. Oil Seal
38. Ball Bearing
39. Gear and Shaft
40. Spacer
41. Gasket
42. Sleeve

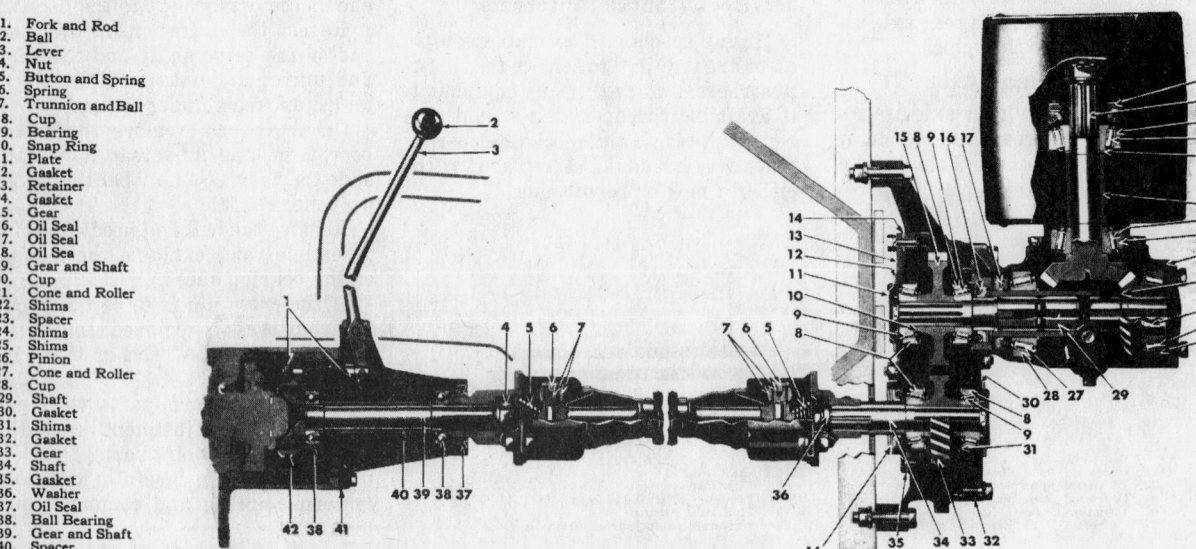

© 1961 Willys Corp.

Power take off

UNIT REPAIR SECTION
and
TRANSMISSION GROUP

UNIT REPAIR SECTION

	PAGE		PAGE		PAGE
Air Conditioning	1092	Fuel Pumps	1021	Thread Inserts	1135
Alignment Troubles	1082	Gauges	1024	Tire Wear Troubles	1082
Alternating Current Generators	1035	Generators and Regulators	1028	Transistor Ignition	1018
Anti Freeze Charts	1096	Generator Trouble Chart	1026	Tune-Up Data (Old Cars)	1106
Axles, Rear	918	Mechanics Data Page	1136	Tune-Up Procedures	1014
Brakes, Hydraulic	938	Starter Systems	1046	Tune-Up, Tractors	1130
Brakes, Power	954	Steering, Manual	1052	Tune-Up Trucks	1111
Carburetors	972	Steering, Power	1058	Truck Transmission Illustrations	1116
Engine Diagnosis	1014	Steering Trouble Chart	1081	Tune-Up Foreign Cars	1098
Engine Trouble Chart	1012	Suspension, Front Align	1082	Wheel Alignment	1082
Fuel Consumption Chart	1020	Suspension, Front Repair	1087		

TRANSMISSION SECTION

	PAGE		PAGE
Transmission Identification Chart	704	Transmission Push-Tow Instructions	1138
Buick Dual Path Transmission	728	TorqueFlite (Type "B") 1960-63 Six and 1962-63 V8	802
Dynaflow Variable Pitch (Twin Turbine)	706	Fordomatic, Merc-o-matic, Turbo-Drive, Flightomatic, Flash-o-matic, Cruise-o-matic—3 Speed	820
Flight Pitch (Triple Turbine)	722	Two Speed Mile-o-matic	838
Powerglide (Type "A") 1953-62	748	Hydramatic—Dual Range	850
(Type "B") 1962-63	758	Hydramatic—Dual Coupling 4 Speed	860
Corvair	224	Hydramatic—3 Speed	886
Turboglide	768	Tempest	646
PowerFlite	778	Studebaker Automatic	906
TorqueFlite (Type "A") 1957-61 V8	788	Overdrive	914

TROUBLE SHOOTING CHARTS
TRANSMISSIONS

	PAGE		PAGE
Buick Dual Path Transmission	729	Fordomatic, Merc-o-matic, Turbo-Drive, Flightomatic, Flash-o-matic, Cruise-o-matic—3 Speed	824
Dynaflow Variable Pitch (Twin Turbine)	708	Two Speed Mile-o-matic	842
Flight Pitch (Triple Turbine)	723	Hydramatic—Dual Range	853
Powerglide (Type "A") 1953-62	749	Hydramatic—Dual Coupling 4 Speed	884
(Type "B") 1962-63	765	Hydramatic—3 Speed	892
Corvair	234	Transmission Push-Tow Instructions	1138
Turboglide	770	Tempest	654
PowerFlite	781	Studebaker Automatic	907
TorqueFlite (Type "A") 1957-61 V8	790	Overdrive	915
TorqueFlite (Type "B") 1960-63 Six and 1962-63 V8	817		

TRANSMISSION IDENTIFICATION CHART

	Chrysler Corp.			Ford Motor Co.											Controlled Coupling Hydra-Matic
	Power-flite	Torque-flite "A"	Torque-flite "B"	Auto-matic	Comet Drive	Cruise-O-Matic	Ford-O-Matic	Ford-O-Matic 2 spd.	Merc-O-Matic	Merc-O-Matic 2 spd.	Mile-O-Matic	Multi-Drive	Turbo-Drive	Twin Range Turbo-Drive	
Page No. →	778	788	802	820	838	820	820	838	820	838	838	820	820	820	860
Buick "A"															
Buick Spcl.															
Cadillac															1956-63
Chevrolet "B"															
Chevy II															
Chrysler "C"	1954-56	1957-61	1962-63												
Comet					1960-63										
Continental													1956-57	1958-63	
Corvair "J"															
Dart "C"	1960-61	1960-61	1960-63												
De Soto "C"	1954-60	1957-61													
Dodge "C"	1954-61	1957-61	1960-63												
Edsel "D"				1958			1959-60		1959-60						
Fairlane								1962-63							
Falcon								1960-63							
Ford "E"						1958-63	1954-57	1959-63							
Lancer			1961-63												
Lincoln													1955-57	1958-63	
Mercury "F"									1954-62	1961-62	1958-63				
Meteor										1962-63					
Oldsmobile															
Olds F-85															
Plymouth "C"	1954-61	1957-61	1960-63												
Pontiac "G"															
Rambler "H"															
Studebaker															
Tempest "J"															
Thunderbird						1958-63	1954-57								
Valiant			1960-63												

A—Buick Flight Pitch uses a "G" on the selector quadrant, whereas Variable Pitch uses an "L".

B—Chevrolet Turboglide uses a "G" on the selector quadrant, whereas Type "A" Powerglide uses an "L". Type "B" Powerglide used only with 327 V-8.

C—Powerflite, single "D" range on gearshift selector. Type "A" Torqueflite, dual "D" range on gearshift selector, used on 1957-61 V-8 models. Type "B" Torqueflite dual "D" range on gearshift selector, used on 1960-61 six cyl. models.

D—Mile-O-Matic used with all engines exc. 352 and 361 V-8's. Dual Power used with 352 and 361 V-8's.

E—Cruise-O-Matic, dual "D" range on selector quadrant. 2 spd. Ford-O-Matic, single "D" range on selector quadrant.

TRANSMISSION IDENTIFICATION CHART

General Motors Corp.											Amer. Motors		Studebaker Corp.		
Dual Path	Dual Range Hydra-Matic	Dyna-flow	Dynaflow Flight Pitch	Dynaflow Variable Pitch	Hydra-Matic 3 spd.	Jetaway Hydra-Matic	Power-glide "A"	Power-glide "B"	Strato-Flight Hydra-Matic	Turbo-glide	Flash-away	Flash-O-Matic	Stude-baker Automatic	Flight-O-Matic	
728	850	706	722	706	886	860	748	758	860	768	850	820	906	820	
		1954	1958-59	1955-63											Buick
1961-63															Buick Spcl.
	1954-55														Cadillac
							1954-62	1962-63		1957-61					Chevrolet
								1962-63							Chevy II
															Chrysler
															Comet
															Continental
															Corvair
															Dart
															De Soto
															Dodge
															Edsel
															Fairlane
															Falcon
															Ford
															Lancer
	1954														Lincoln
															Mercury
															Meteor
	1954-55				1961-63	1956-60									Oldsmobile
			1961-63												Olds F-85
															Plymouth
	1954-55				1961-63				1956-63						Pontiac
	1954-57										1957	1957-63			Rambler
													1954-55	1955-63	Studebaker
															Tempest
															Thunderbird
															Valiant

F—Multi-Drive, dual "D" range on selector quadrant. 2 spd. Merc-O-Matic, one piece, aluminum case and bell housing.
3 spd. Merc-O-Matic, two piece, cast iron case and bell housing.

G—3 spd. Hydramatic, used on all models exc. Bonneville and Star Chief.
4 spd. Hydramatic, used on Bonneville and Star Chief models.

H—Hydramatic, used on early production 1957 6 cyl.
Flash-O-Matic, used on late production 1957 6 cyl.
Flashaway, used on 1957 V-8 models.

J—Due to transaxle construction, see car sections.

BUICK AUTOMATIC TRANSMISSIONS

DYNAFLOW AND VARIABLE PITCH DYNAFLOW TRANSMISSION
1954-63

GENERAL INFORMATION

DRAINING AND REFILLING PROCEDURE

Have transmission hot. (Drive for 20 miles in real or simulated traffic.)

Failure to have the transmission hot before draining may result in an accumulation of harmful deposits inside the transmission.

Remove plug from transmission oil pan to drain it. Fig. 1.

Remove six bolts and bell housing lower front pan. Fig. 1.

Turn flywheel until a drain plug shows in its forward face. Fig 2. Loosen this drain plug to act as an air vent and turn flywheel until the diametrically opposite plug is down.

Remove this second drain plug to drain the converter. Fig. 2.

Fig. 1—View of Dynaflow from under the car showing transmission oil pan drain plug

Note: Do not disturb the Accumulator plugs the locations of which are shown in Fig. 1.

Replace the transmission oil pan plug and tighten to 30-35 ft lbs.

Replace the two converter drain

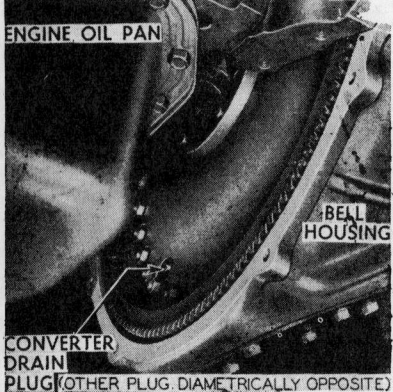

Fig. 2—Location of converter drain plugs

plugs and tighten securely. Replace the bell housing lower front pan.

Capacities vary with different models.

Install 3 quarts of fluid and start the engine. (Hand lever in Park.)

Then add 5½ quarts and check the level. Add more as needed to bring to full mark.

Warm up transmission and check that level remains at full.

<u>Note:</u> Never overfill the transmission as it will permit the planetary gear set to aerate the oil and cause malfunctioning of the valves. If the fluid level drops below "Add Oil" point when warm and idling in Park the transmission will overheat with resultant serious damage to the clutch plates and valving.

OIL REQUIREMENTS

Measure oil with Dynaflow hot and engine idling; hand lever at Park.

Use a good grade of automatic transmission fluid.

Oil should be changed every 25,000

GAGE ROD

In engine compartment just in front of fire wall on right side.
Quantity between add oil and full on gage rod ____1 pt.

TOWING THE CAR

When necessary to tow a Dynaflow car the shift lever **Must** be in the **neutral** position. If the car is damaged so that it is impossible to place the Dynaflow in the neutral position the drive shaft should be disconnected or the car picked up by the rear axle and towed on its front wheels with the steering wheel tied down.

STARTING ENGINE WITHOUT USE OF STARTER

To start the engine by rolling the car always push rather than tow so that, when the engine starts, the car can accelerate without crashing the tow car.

Hold control lever at Neutral until car reaches a speed of 15 mph then shift into Low. Continue to increase car speed. Engine should crank at about 25 mph when oil pressure from the rear oil pump will have increased sufficiently to actuate the transmission. Return lever to Neutral for engine warm up.

BAND ADJUSTMENT

Procedure for adjusting either band as follows: (This applies on early

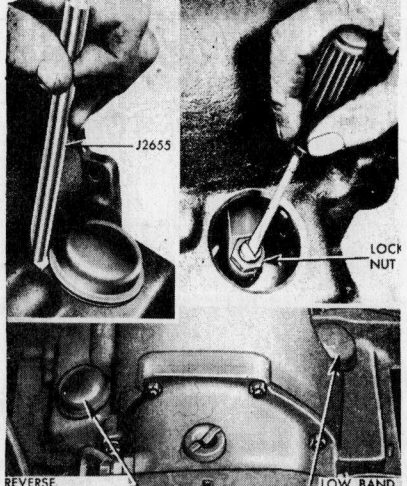

Fig. 3—Adjusting bands

models that have holes in the floor pan. On later models no holes are provided. Although holes can be cut in the pan. Buick feels that if the bands need to be tightened they also need to be replaced.)

Remove front floor mat, insulation pad, transmission opening pan, from the floor of the front compartment.

Remove the band adjusting covers

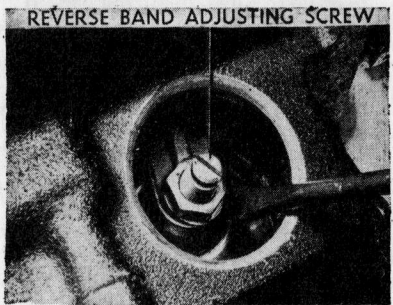

Fig. 4—Feeling for little play

and gaskets using an offset screw driver to pry them off. Fig. 3.

Loosen lock nut and turn adjusting screw clockwise until resistance is felt indicating contact of band with drum.

Pry up on lock nut with screw driver and turn screw counterclockwise until a little play between drum and band can be felt by wiggling the screw driver. Fig. 4.

Now unscrew adjusting screws six full turns. Snug up lock nut being sure screw has not turned.

Replace covers using new gaskets.

Replace floor pan, pad and mat.

For models without removable floor pans drill four inch holes in the floor over the two band adjusting screw covers, Fig. 5, and proceed as above.

Dynaflow and Variable Pitch Dynaflow

CHECKING PROCEDURE FOR TROUBLES

CHECK OIL LEVEL FIRST

Note: Transmission must be hot. That is at operating Temperature.

To warm up transmission drive car at least 20 miles with frequent stops as in heavy traffic.

ROAD TEST

Test Operation in Direct Drive, Low and Reverse.

Check operation during shifts from Low to Drive under load.

Improper operation in more than one range indicates need for control linkage adjustment.

Check for creep in Neutral, Drive, Reverse and Low.

In Drive but held by the brake snap accelerate motor to 1400 rpm and release accelerator.

If it returns to idle too slowly or if it returns to idle too fast and stalls.

Readjust the throttle and dash pot linkage.

OIL LEAKS

If unit is using more than a pint per 1000 miles check all over for leaks.

Check especially these points:

Oil pan.

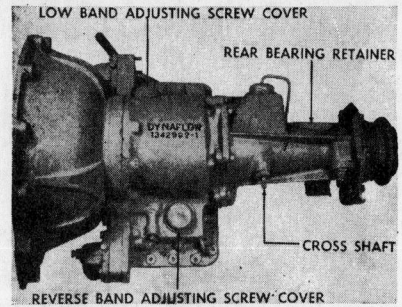

Fig. 5—Location of band covers

Reactor flange.

Front oil pump (insert long roll of paper through hand hole toward the pump. Oil should not show on paper).

The band adjustment covers.

Rear bearing retainer.

Filler pipe.

Primary pump cover (hold a piece of paper between flywheel and bell housing. Oil should not show on paper).

The accumulators. These can be removed while transmission is in the car. If leak is at cap remove and coat with No. 3 Permatex and reinstall.

If leak is at body remove and check for warp and porosity, replace using new gasket.

Check engine and transmission mountings for misalignment of transmission.

Tightness of bolts.
Condition of pads.
Signs of having been hit.

OIL PRESSURE TEST POINT LOCATIONS

SEE FIG. 8

Stator Pressure Test Point. On the left side of the Reactor Flange Assembly near the High Accumulator.

Front Pump Pressure Test Point. On the left side of the transmission just behind the Reaction Flange.

Rear Pump Pressure Test Point. Under the Rear Bearing Retainer where it is fastened to the transmission case.

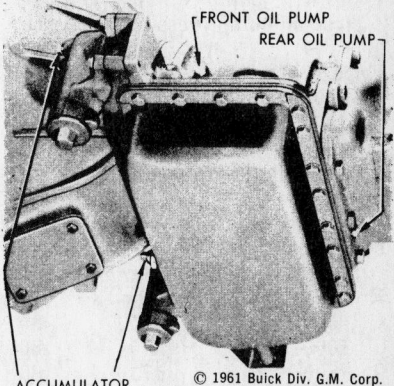

© 1961 Buick Div. G.M. Corp.

Fig. 8—Gauge connections for oil pressure tests

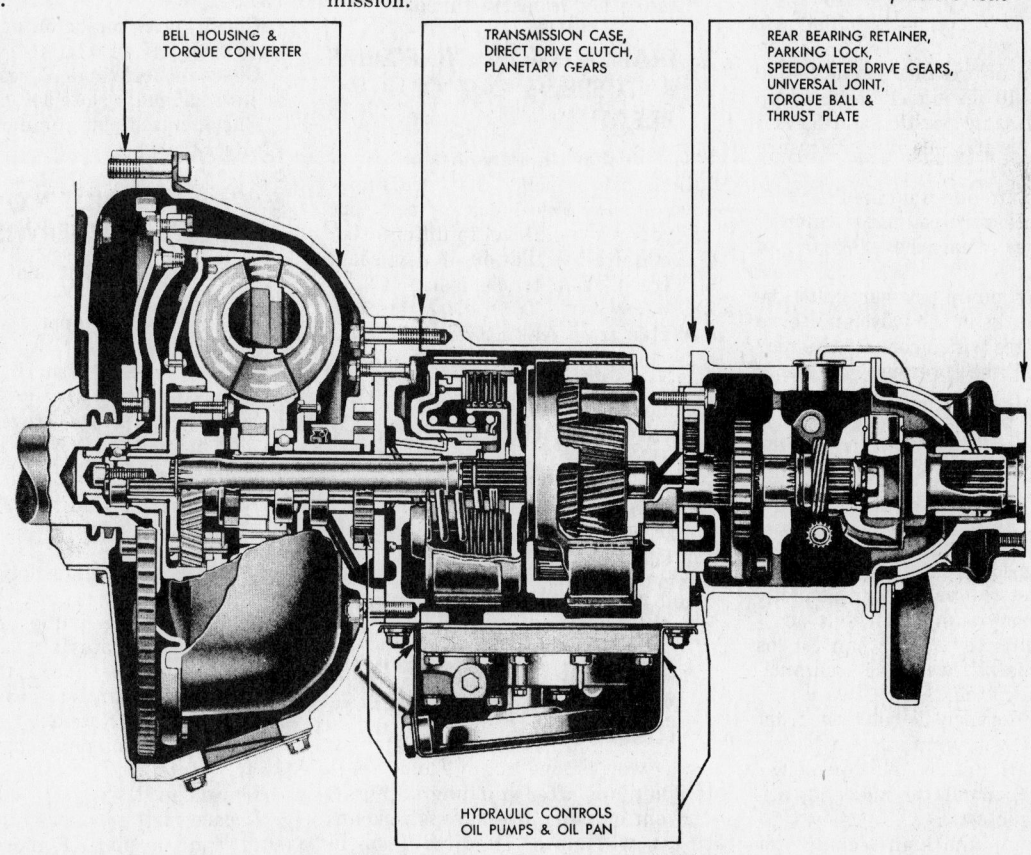

Fig. 9—Principal sections of the Dynaflow transmission

High Accumulator Test Point. On upper front edge of the left hand Accumulator.

Low Accumulator Test Point. On upper front edge of the right hand Accumulator.

OIL PRESSURE SPECIFICATIONS

Front oil pump pressure should be:

Eng. RPM	Low	Drive	Reverse
	Lever-Positions		
500	120	90	120
1000	180	90	...
1800	180	90	...

Front pump should cut out at 2500 rpm. Indicated by pressure drop to 20 lbs as Rear pump cuts in.

Rear oil pump pressure should be:

Eng. RPM	Low	Drive
	Lever-Positions	
500	90	90
1000	180	90
1800	180	90

Accumulators. Check low accumulator with lever in Low. Check high accumulator with lever in Drive. Pressure should be:

Eng. RPM	Low	High
	Accumulators	
500	115	80
1000	175	85
1800	175	85

Stator pressure with lever in Drive:

Eng. RPM	Stator Pressure
500	10
1000	70
1800	75

Accumulator pressure should not be more than 10 lbs under front pump pressure at same position and RPM.

Low or erratic oil pump pressure indicates:

Air leak into pump intake line.

Faulty pressure regulator valve.

Excessive clearance (Wear in pumps).

Low rear pump pressure may be caused by leaks in the valve and servo body passages which connect the rear pump with the pressure regulator valve.

Note: If pressure of one pump is low but pressure of other is OK the intake line and pressure valve are not at fault as both pumps use the same unit.

Very low accumulator pressure may be caused by external or internal leakage past the valve body gasket.

When front and high accumulator differ by more than 10 lbs there is a leak between the accumulator and the clutch.

When difference is between front pump and low accumulator the leak is between accumulator and Low servo.

Or else accumulator metering orifice is obstructed.

Front pump and high accumulator pressures should be checked before testing the stator pressure because the stator operating pressure is taken from the clutch apply pressure in the high accumulator. If the high accumulator pressure is low it is due to a leak in either the high accumulator or the stator control valve. To determine which disconnect the stator control valve operating rod and manually raise the stator control valve to the stop. If the high accumulator pressure remains the same the leak is at the high accumulator gasket. If the high accumulator pressure rises the leak is in the stator control valve.

TROUBLE SHOOTING CHART

Note: 1: Items marked NOTE 1 require removal of Transmission for repairs.

Note 2: Items marked NOTE 2 can be done with Dynaflow in car.

(Causes are listed in descending order of probability)

1. ENGINE STALLS WHILE DECELERATING CAR WITH BRAKE APPLIED

Improper adjustment of throttle dash pot.

Engine not properly tuned.

2. TRANSMISSION OIL FOAMS AND SPEWS OUT OF BREATHER

Too much oil in transmission.

Defective propeller shaft seals may have let rear axle lubricant come in. Check for low oil level in differential. Will require installation of new seals and fresh oil in transmission. (Note 2).

Water from leaking oil cooler has come in. Check for oil in the engine radiator. Requires new cooler and fresh oil. (Note 2).

Air is being sucked in and churned into the oil.

Air leak at rear oil pump gasket. (Note 2).

Excesssive clearance between output shaft journal and rear bearing retainer bushing. (Note 2).

Wrong kind of oil in transmission.

3. CAR WILL NOT MOVE IN ANY RANGE REAR WHEELS TURN FREELY

Car won't move in any range for 1 to 8 minutes after standing all night.

Front oil pump pressure is zero until car will move. Requires removal and inspection of front oil pump and if condition has existed for some time the clutch and bands should be inspected for signs of excessive wear. (Note 1).

Car will not move in any range after backing up.

Air is leaking into pump suction line. Remove oil pan and check oil intake pipe and contact with seal ring in servo body assembly. (Note 2).

Front oil pump is worn. Check clearances of pump. (Note 1).

Air is leaking in at rear oil pump gasket. (Note 2).

4. CAR WILL NOT MOVE IN ANY RANGE REAR WHEELS LOCKED

Parking lock engaged due to maladjusted controls.

Broken part in rear axle.

Broken part in transmission. (Note 1).

5. CAR WILL NOT MOVE IN DRIVE, OTHERWISE O.K.

Pressures at front pump and high accumulator are OK. Remove and inspect clutch assembly. (Note 1).

High accumulator pressure is low.

Check accumulator body gasket for internal leaks. (Note 1).

Check reactor shaft flange gasket. (Note 1).

Check clutch piston outer seal (rubber ring). (Note 1).

Check oil seal rings on reactor shaft at its rear end. (Note 1).

Check clutch piston inner seal ring. (Note 1).

6. CAR WILL NOT MOVE IN REVERSE, OTHERWISE O.K.

Reverse servo is not working. (Note 2).

Band is improperly adjusted. (Note 2).

Band operating strut has dropped out of place. (Note 2).

Obsolete type of reverse band anchor has broken. (Note 1).

7. EXCESSIVE SLIP IN ALL RANGES

If condition appears only after operation in reverse.

Check front oil pump pressure. If it is low it indicates air leakage into pump suction line. (Note 2).

Inspect for air leaks at rear oil pump gaskets. (Note 2).

Inspect front oil pump and cover for wear. (Note 1).

Low oil level.

If case history shows high oil consumption (a pint or more in 1000 miles) and there are no indications of oil leakage around the outside of the transmission, check the lubricant level in the differential which if high indicates leakage past the propeller shaft spline seal. Disconnect propeller shaft at torque ball and renew the seal. Be sure to drain and refill the differential and discard the lubricant which was diluted with oil from the transmission.

Manual control linkage improperly adjusted.

Operation in reverse has no effect on the condition but front oil pump pressure is low.

Remove and inspect the pressure regulator valve and all the valve and servo body assembly gaskets. (Note 2).

Check front oil pump for wear. Check pump cover and reactor shaft flange gaskets for leaks. (Note 1).

Primary pump hub may be worn hour-glass shaped. (Note 1).

8. EXCESSIVE SLIP IN DIRECT DRIVE ONLY

Manual control linkage improperly adjusted.

Leak at high accumulator gasket indicated by low pressure reading at this point. (Note 2).

Stuck clutch piston check ball. Remove clutch assembly and check the plates, the seal rings and the piston itself. (Note 1).

9. EXCESSIVE SLIP IN LOW ONLY

Manual control linkage improperly adjusted.

Low band improperly adjusted. (Note 2).

Band worn. (Note 1).

Drum scored. (Note 1).

Low pressure at low accumulator.

Leak at low accumulator body gasket. (Note 1).

Leaks at valve and servo body assembly gaskets. (Note 2).

Defective low servo piston seal. (Note 2).

10. EXCESSIVE SLIP IN REVERSE ONLY

Manual control linkage improperly adjusted.

Reverse band not functioning or improperly adjusted. (Note 2).

Strut out of place. (Note 2).

Anchor broken. (Note 1.)

Worn or scored band. (Note 1).

Ring gear worn or scored. (Note 1).

Low front oil pump pressure.

Leaks at valve and servo body assembly gaskets. (Note 2).

Defective reverse servo piston seal. (Note 2).

11. CAR CREEPS FORWARD IN NEUTRAL

Manual control linkage improperly adjusted.

Low servo piston or anchor sticking. (Note 2).

Sticking, warped or improperly assembled clutch plates. Dished plates must all face same way. (Note 1).

Check balls for release of clutch pressure not working properly. (Note 1).

12. CAR CREEPS FORWARD IN REVERSE OR BACKWARD IN LOW

Manual control linkage improperly adjusted.

13. SHIFT FROM LOW TO DIRECT DRIVE ABNORMALLY ROUGH OR SLIP OCCURS

If high accumulator pressure is low. Check high accumulator body gasket for leakage. (Note 1).

Check for sticking accumulator piston. Top land of piston must be fully visible through top port in the body. (Note 1).

Check for leaks in the valve and servo body assembly gaskets. (Note 2.)

Low band improperly adjusted. (Note 2).

Binding or worn clutch plates. (Note 1).

Fig. 10—High Accumulator Parts Starting 1955

14. EXCESSIVE CHATTER OR CLUNK WHEN STARTING IN LOW OR REVERSE

Note: A very slight chatter just as car starts to move in reverse which disappears as car gets moving is normal. A slight clunk when shifting into Low or Reverse is also normal.

Check engine and transmission mountings for tightness. Inspect for broken rubber thrust pad at transmission mounting.

Low or Reverse band improperly adjusted. (Note 2).

Check clutch for sticking, warped, or improperly assembled clutch plates. (Note 1).

Inspect for excessive wear of reverse ring gear bushing and for foreign matter in the needle bearings of the planetary assembly. (Note 1).

15. HARD SHIFTING OUT OF PARKING

Transmission shift rod is binding in the shift idler lever.

Remove any burrs with a file.

Distorted idler lever should be replaced with a new one.

16. NOISES IN THE TRANSMISSION

HUM or low whine in any gear is normal.

A BUZZING NOISE.

Low oil level.

Front pump delivery check valve caught on edge of gasket. (Note 2).

Excessive clearance of pressure regulator valve necessitating replacement of the valve. (Note 2).

A clicking noise in all ranges.

Foreign object in converter. (Note 1).

Improper manual control adjustment permitting parking lock pawl to contact ratchet wheel.

ABNORMAL HUM or whine which occurs in all ranges.

Due to worn front oil pump or improperly installed front pump driving gear. Check for low front oil pump pressure. (Note 1).

Wear in the planetary assembly especially if noise is not so apparent in Drive. (Note 1).

SQUEALING or screeching or howling immediately following transmission overhaul indicates that front pump driving gear is in backwards. This condition must be corrected without further operation of the transmission or serious damage will be done to the unit. Note 1).

WHISTLING during slow acceleration in all gears together with poor performance.

Converter is not being filled with oil. Check for restrictions in the passages in the valve and servo body assembly. (Note 2).

Check passages in the reactor shaft flange. (Note 1).

Thin, weak, or bent or cracked turbine blades which vibrate under load. Turbine must be replaced. (Note 1).

17. TRANSMISSION WORKS WHEN COLD AND DOES NOT WHEN HOT

The seal between the oil suction tube and the valve body is defective and should be replaced. As it is possible to install the oil suction tube with its slant in the wrong direction be careful to have the slant toward the drain plug.

Note: On late models there is a ball check valve in the front oil pump intake line. A small bit of dirt can hold the ball off its seat and permit the front pump to lose its prime.

18. FRONT OIL PUMP CHEWS UP MOUNTING PLATE

This occurs on models using a plug to hold the converter to the input shaft. Put shims between the plug and converter. Converter should turn freely after addition of the shims.

Note 1—Items marked Note 1 require removal of transmission for repairs.

Note 2—Items marked Note 2 can be done with the Dynaflow in the car.

OIL COOLER

SEE FIG. 11

If the oil cooler leaks water into the transmission the heat developed by the torque converter in extended traffic operation is sufficient to turn the water into steam. The steam will force the fluid out the transmission breather. If the oil loss it not detected in time the converter will be ruined.

It is therefore recommended that the cooler be tested from time to time. To test the cooler after it has been removed from the car: Block off one oil line fitting and apply not over ten pounds of air pressure to the other fitting. Submerge the cooler in hot water. Air bubbles or oil coming from the water connections of the cooler will indicate that the cooler is bad.

If the cooler leaks plug up the water connections to the radiator and run a line from one oil connection to the other on the transmission.

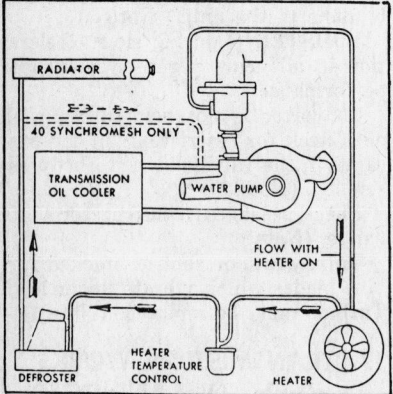

Fig. 11—Hose connections

Jack up the rear end of the car as high as possible. Install cooling system cleaning compound in the radia-

tor. Set the hand lever in Drive and run the engine until its temperature indicator has been near to 212 Deg. F. for at least 15 minutes.

Drain the radiator, the transmission, and the converter. Install a new cooler and reconnect the water and oil lines. Put about five quarts of Type A fluid in the transmission and clean water in the radiator. Again run the engine with the hand lever in Drive the rear wheels spinning free of the ground until the engine temperature is close to 212 Deg. F.

Drain the transmission and the radiator again. Install the proper fluids in the full amounts and road test the car. Pay particular attention to whether oil spews out the transmission breather when the engine is turned off after the test run. If it does it is an indication that there is an emulsion of oil and water which was not removed from the transmission by the draining and flushing operations. In which case it may be possible to clear the trouble by removing and cleaning the rear bearing retainer. If this is not successful the transmission will have to be disassembled and cleaned.

FRONT OIL PUMP FAILURE

SEE FIGS. 12, 13, 14 & 15 ALSO TROUBLE NO. 18

When the front oil pump or its oil seal fails, it is necessary that the runout of the primary pump hub be checked. The runout of this hub is dependent on the flatness of the primary pump locating face of the flywheel. It is best therefore to check the runout of the flywheel first.

To do this make a set-up similar to that shown in Fig. 12. Runout of the flywheel face should not exceed .008" FULL INDICATOR READING. If the runout is greater, try tapping the high side with a lead mallet. Should this fail to bring about a correct reading, then a new flywheel must be installed. Do not neglect to check for burrs at the attaching bolt holes which might be the cause of the runout. Be sure to hold crankshaft end play in toward the front.

When the runout of the flywheel has been brought within the limit, then install the primary pump to it, using the 3 or 6 flywheel attaching bolts and tightening to 25-30 ft-lbs. Install also the bell housing, fastening it tightly in place.

Using a set-up like that shown in Fig. 13, check the runout of the primary pump hub. It must not exceed .012" FULL INDICATOR READING. If the runout is greater, then unbolt the primary pump and revolve its po-

sition on the flywheel 180 degrees; refasten it and recheck the runout. If the figure is still too large, the primary pump will have to be replaced. The runout of the new pump hub will have to be checked in the same manner. If the runout of the primary pump hub is within the limit, make set-ups similar to those shown in Figs. 14 and 15. Runout of the rear face of the bell housing with reference to the primary pump hub must not exceed .005" FULL INDICATOR READING, while that of the pilot hole must not exceed .004" FULL INDICATOR READING. Clamp only to the driving lug as shown.

If either of these figures is exceeded, it will be necessary to replace or relocate the bell housing.

Note A. The front oil pump seal and the oil pump itself cannot tolerate runouts greater than those given for any appreciable length of time.

Note B. There is a tendency for the primary pump hub to wear into an hour-glass shape. This condition is easily found with a straight edge and requires that the primary pump be replaced with a new one.

ALIGNMENT TOLERANCES

Flywheel runout .....008" F.I.R.*
Face of bell housing at 3¾" radius from pump hub ....005" F.I.R.*
Bell housing hole from pump hub ....004" F.I.R.*
Primary pump hub runout ....012" F.I.R.*
Reactor shaft flange out-of-true of face ..002" F.I.R.*
Front face of transmission case out-of-true 002" F.I.R.*
*F.I.R.—Full Indicator Reading.

TORQUE SPECIFICATIONS (IN. FT. LBS.)

½-20 Nuts ....20-25 ft lbs
½-20 Bolts 30-35
7/16-14 Bolts 45-55
7/16-20 Nuts 15.20
⅜-16 Bolts entering the Transmission case ...35.40
⅜-16 Bolts entering the rear bearing retainer .30-35
⅜-24 Nuts 10-15
5/16-18 Bolts at the hand hole covers.....15-20
the servo body 15-20
the oil cooler 15-20
the control detent .15-20
at the accumulators 20-25
at the rear oil pump 25-30
5/16-24 Bolts and nuts at the oil pan 15-18
at the accumulators 20-25

Dynaflow and Variable Pitch Dynaflow

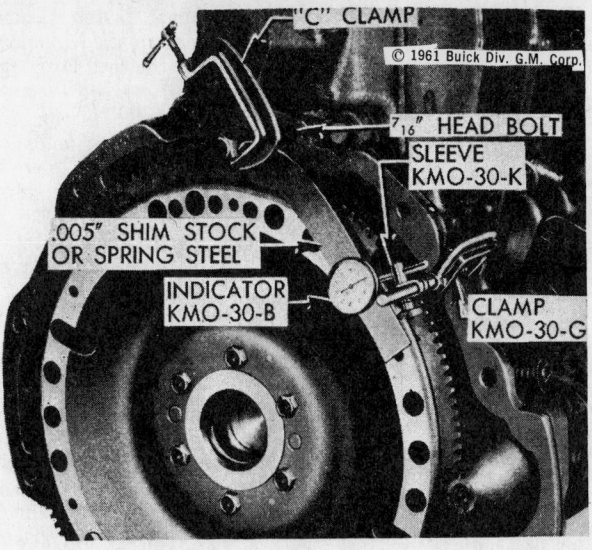

Fig. 12—Checking Runout of Flywheel

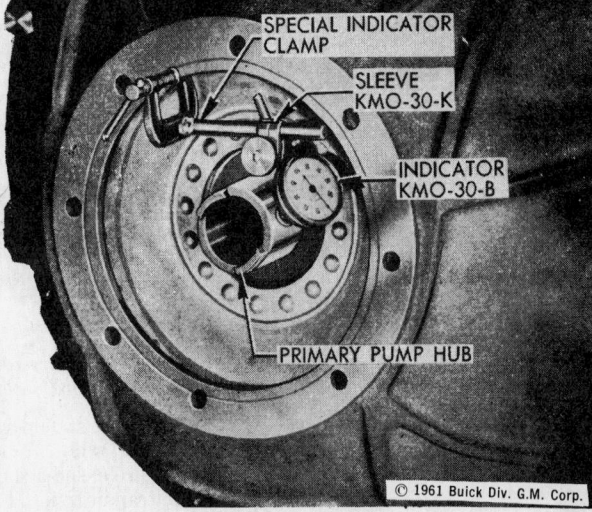

Fig. 13—Checking Runout of Primary Pump Hub

all others 25-30
¼-20 Bolts 11-15
¼-28 Bolts and nuts . . .11-15
1⅛-12 Plugs and seats .20.25
1⅜-12 Accumulator caps
. 40-50
1/5-16-16 sleeve 20.25
⅝-18 Plug 20-25
18 mm Plug 30-35

MATCH POINTS

Items which must be match marked to assure that they are reassembled in the same relative positions they occupied before disassembly.
Flywheel to Primary Pump.
Primary Pump to Cover.
Front portion of Planetary Carrier to rear portion.
Faces of the inner and outer Oil Pump gears to the pump covers.
Rear Oil Pump Body to Case.
Rear Oil Pump Cover to Case.
Flanges of the Bands to Case.

DISASSEMBLY

Before starting to take the transmission apart clean it thoroughly. In the process of disassembly be careful to note the condition of all gaskets as quite often the only clue to trouble is the appearance of a connecting gasket which will clearly show if a good seal existed. No part of the assembly is a force fit. Use a SOFT hammer if any tapping is required.

The relative position of adjacent parts can usually be determined by their wear patterns. There is therefore no need to mark any parts save those mentioned in General Information under Match Marks. The same information is repeated when necessary in the text.

The High and Low accumulators are marked H and L on their caps but they could be mounted one in place of the other so mechanics usually mark the bottom and the adjacent reactor shaft flange of the High accumulator.

REMOVAL OF OIL PAN, VALVE AND SERVO BODY ASSEMBLY

Note: Removal of these units can be accomplished by this same procedure while transmission is still in the car.

Remove oil pan and gasket.

Remove oil screen from suction pipe if it did not come off with oil pan.

Disconnect valve control rod from lever by pushing with a screwdriver to disengage spring loaded socket. See Fig. 16.

Do not loosen or remove the Three Castellated Nuts holding the valve body to the servo body. Fig. 17. Remove the bolts and lockwashers holding the assembly to the transmission case. This includes the one bolt requiring an allen head wrench that is on some models. Tap the assembly

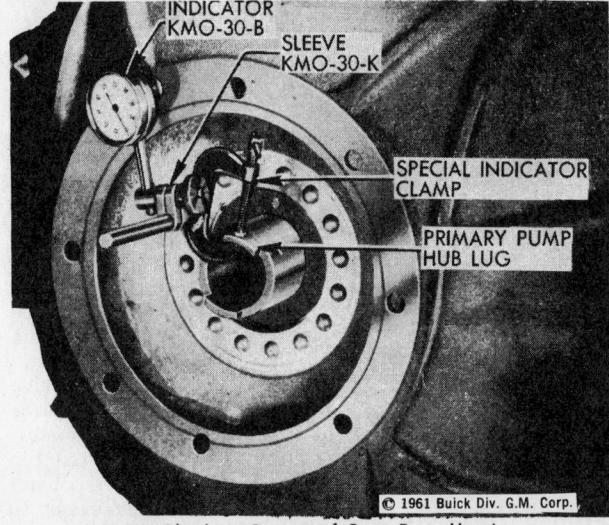

Fig. 14—Checking Runout of Rear Face Housing

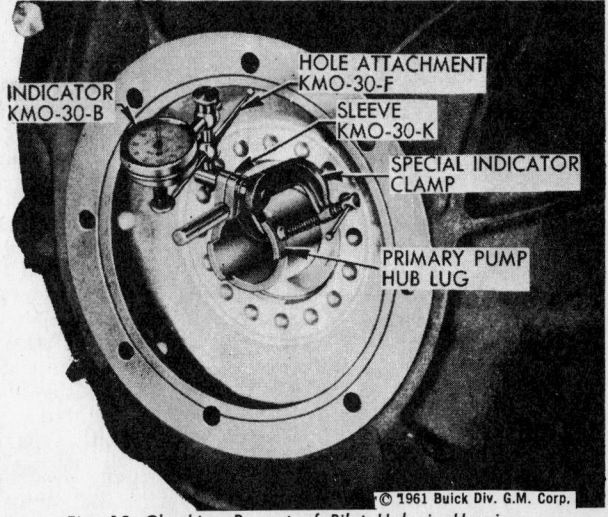

Fig. 15—Checking Runout of Pilot Hole in Housing

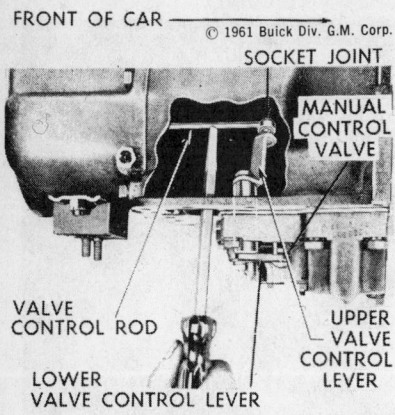

FRONT OF CAR ———
© 1961 Buick Div. G.M. Corp.
SOCKET JOINT
MANUAL CONTROL VALVE
VALVE CONTROL ROD
UPPER VALVE CONTROL LEVER
LOWER VALVE CONTROL LEVER

Fig. 16—Disconnecting Valve Control Rod

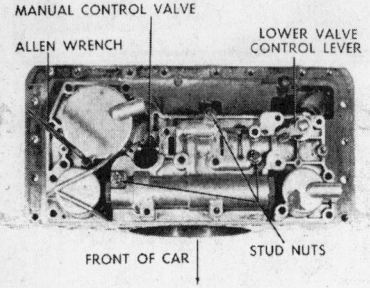

MANUAL CONTROL VALVE
ALLEN WRENCH
LOWER VALVE CONTROL LEVER
FRONT OF CAR
STUD NUTS

Fig. 17—Studs holding valve body to servo

lightly with a soft hammer to loosen the gasket between the servo body and the transmission case. Align upper lever to clear the case by pushing shift control valve and lower lever inward. Fig. 18.

FACING TOWARD FRONT OF CAR
© 1961 Buick Div. G.M. Corp.

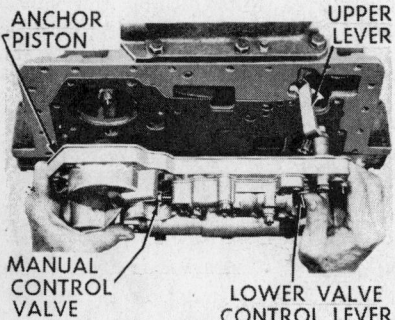

ANCHOR PISTON
UPPER LEVER
MANUAL CONTROL VALVE
LOWER VALVE CONTROL LEVER

Fig. 18—Removing valve and servo body assembly

The low band anchor piston will fall out as the assembly is removed if work is being done at the bench. If transmission is still in the car the piston will remain in the assembly.

Note: The slotted end of the control valve is likely to be sharp enough to cut the hand.

There is a piece of square metal interposed between the end of the reverse band and the operating lever.

© 1961 Buick Div. G.M. Corp.
STRUT
LEVER

Fig. 19—Removing reverse band operating strut

This strut should be removed if transmission is on the bench to prevent its being released accidentally to fall into the transmission. Fig. 19.

OVERHAUL OF VALVE AND SERVO BODY ASSEMBLY

There is nothing particular about the disassembly of the valve and servo assembly once it is off the transmission. The pictures show the component parts. See Fig. 20. Exercise care not to bend the spacer plate that fits onto the servo body. Fig. 21.

Thoroughly wash valve and servo springs push on it. Note also that there are two springs on the reverse servo piston assembly. Watch out for small check ball in reverse servo feed channel in servo body. When removing pressure regulator valve plugs be careful of spring pressure.

Thoroughly wash valve and servo bodies with clean solvent, blow out all passages. Inspect for cracks, signs of leakage on gaskets, scores on pistons and cylinders. The shoulders of the valves should be sharp and square. Check valves on surface plate and replace if bent. Worn or damaged piston seals should be replaced. Make sure the lip of the seal fits over the smaller diameter land. Fig. 22.

Clean and check oil screen for cracks or holes that might pass dirt.

ASSEMBLY OF SERVO BODY

Oil and install the low and reverse servo piston assemblies. Fig. 24. To avoid curling or damaging edge of piston seal, start each piston into cylinder at an angle then turn piston slightly as it is straightened and pushed into cylinder. Fig. 24.

Check that pistons move freely.

Install low band anchor piston, spring and shims in servo body. Fig. 25.

Install the smallest piston return spring with small end in groove in low servo piston. Install the two large return springs with the large ends in grooves in reverse servo piston. Install spring seats on upper ends of springs. Fig. 24.

Place check ball in reverse servo feed channel. Fig. 24.

Install a new spacer plate gasket and place spacer plate in position over spring seats. Be careful not to distort plate while holding it against spring pressure. Tighten screws uniformly.

Check that plate does not interfere with movement of low band anchor piston. Fig. 26. If it should, then loosen spacer plate screws and tap plate slightly in a direction to provide clearance for anchor. When screws are tight and anchor moves freely check that clearance from surface of spacer plate to top surface of top land of anchor is .080" to .090". Fig. 27. This distance is obtained by adding or subtracting shims from between spring and inside end of anchor. Fig. 25.

Insert valve operating lower lever shaft through bearing in servo body. With lower lever pointing to low servo cylinder install upper lever so that it points to reverse servo cylinder. Tighten to 5-7 ft lbs. Fig. 28.

ASSEMBLY OF VALVE BODY

Place front pump delivery check valve spring in body with large end down and place check valve on spring with ridged side up. See Figs. 29 and 30.

Install valve body plate and a new gasket making sure that check valve is seated against plate and is not caught under gasket.

Place the pressure regulator spring seat on the inner spring, then install spring seat, inner and outer springs and the large plug in valve body. Tighten plug to 20-25 ft lbs torque. Fig. 29.

See that oil orifice in pressure regulator valve and end land is clear, then install valve with this land outward. Install small pressure regulator plug and tighten to 20-25 ft lbs torque. Fig. 29.

Install shift control valve with slotted end on same end of valve body as the large pressure regulator plug.

Install rear pump delivery check valve in its seat in servo body ridged face inward and place valve spring on valve with large end out. Fig. 30.

Install a new gasket and the valve assembly on the servo body using care to keep pump delivery check valve spring below the gasket. Install the three castellated nuts with plain washers Fig. 17 and tighten evenly to 11-15 ft lbs.

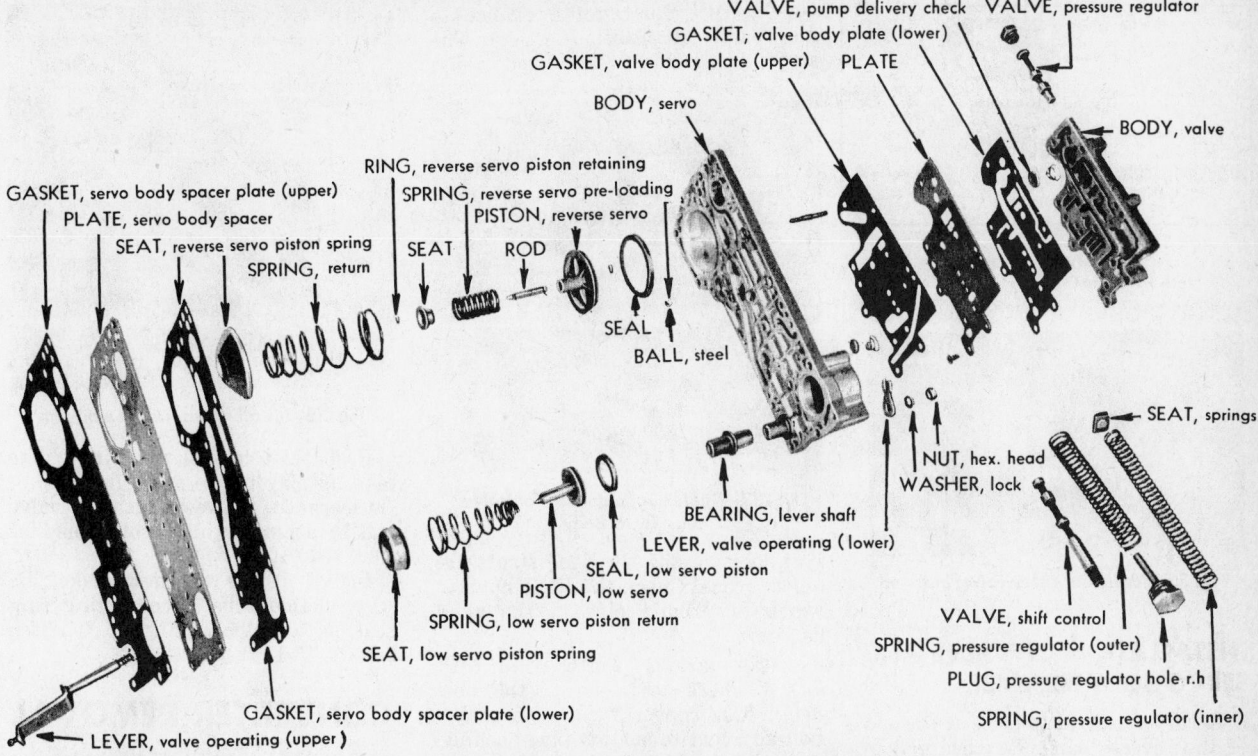

VALVE, pump delivery check   VALVE, pressure regulator
GASKET, valve body plate (lower)
GASKET, valve body plate (upper)   PLATE
BODY, servo
BODY, valve

GASKET, servo body spacer plate (upper)
PLATE, servo body spacer
SEAT, reverse servo piston spring
SPRING, return

RING, reverse servo piston retaining
SPRING, reverse servo pre-loading
PISTON, reverse servo
SEAT   ROD

SEAL
BALL, steel

SEAT, springs

NUT, hex. head
WASHER, lock

BEARING, lever shaft
LEVER, valve operating (lower)

SEAL, low servo piston
PISTON, low servo
SPRING, low servo piston return
SEAT, low servo piston spring

VALVE, shift control
SPRING, pressure regulator (outer)
PLUG, pressure regulator hole r.h
SPRING, pressure regulator (inner)

GASKET, servo body spacer plate (lower)

LEVER, valve operating (upper)

Fig. 20—Exploded View of Typical Valve and Servo Body Assembly

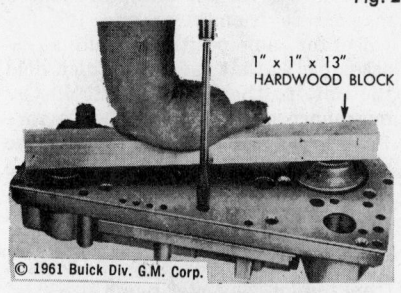

1" x 1" x 13"
HARDWOOD BLOCK

© 1961 Buick Div. G.M. Corp.

Fig. 21—Hold springs compressed with block of wood

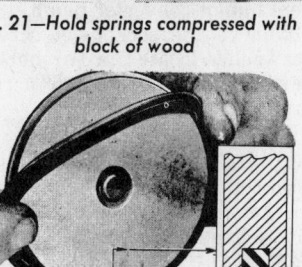

© 1961 Buick Div. G.M. Corp.

Fig. 22—Installing servo piston seal

Fig. 23—Lay-out of servo assembly

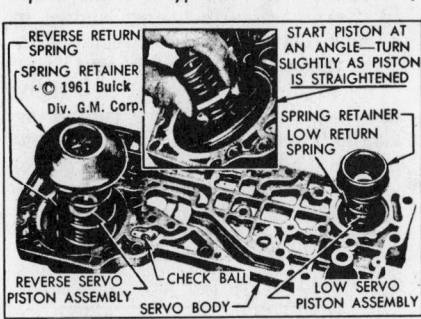

REVERSE RETURN SPRING
SPRING RETAINER
© 1961 Buick Div. G.M. Corp.

START PISTON AT AN ANGLE—TURN SLIGHTLY AS PISTON IS STRAIGHTENED
SPRING RETAINER LOW RETURN SPRING

REVERSE SERVO PISTON ASSEMBLY   CHECK BALL   SERVO BODY   LOW SERVO PISTON ASSEMBLY

Fig. 24—Installing servo pistons be sure to install check ball in reverse servo feed channel

Fig. 25—Lay-out of low band anchor piston

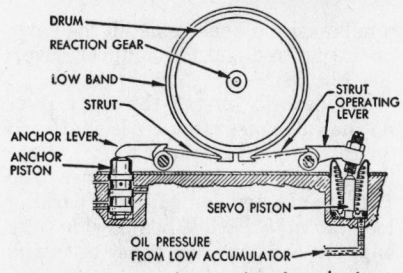

DRUM
REACTION GEAR
LOW BAND
STRUT
ANCHOR LEVER
ANCHOR PISTON
SERVO PISTON
STRUT OPERATING LEVER
OIL PRESSURE FROM LOW ACCUMULATOR

Fig. 26—Section thru low band mechanism

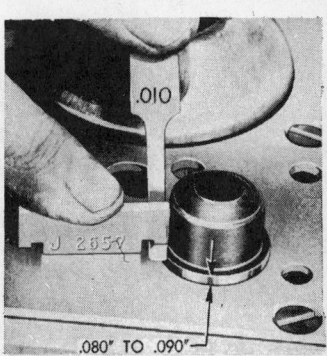

.010
J 2654
.080" TO .090"

Fig. 27—Checking clearance of anchor piston. Can be done with depth gauge

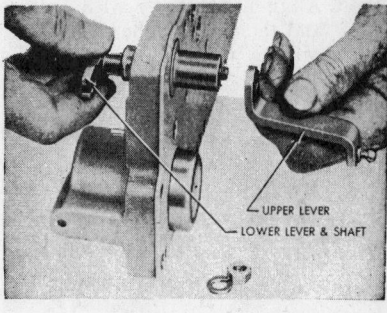

UPPER LEVER
LOWER LEVER & SHAFT

Fig. 28—Installing valve control levers

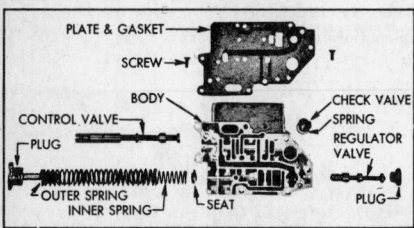

Fig. 29—Layout of valve body
Note front pump delivery check valve

Fig. 30—Position of check valves installed

INSTALLATION OF VALVE AND SERVO BODY ASSEMBLY

Return the strut to place at the end of the reverse band. Rounded end to band. If transmission is on the bench be careful not to disturb the band levers or the strut will fall into the transmission. Fig. 31.

Fig. 31—Valve and Servo Body ready to install

Use a new gasket between servo body spacer plate and transmission case. Align upper lever with hole in case and holding anchor piston in place with a finger install assembly on case being careful the low and re-

Fig. 32—Valve and Servo Body being installed

verse struts don't get a chance to move out of place. Fig. 32. The assembly should fit on flat and easily,

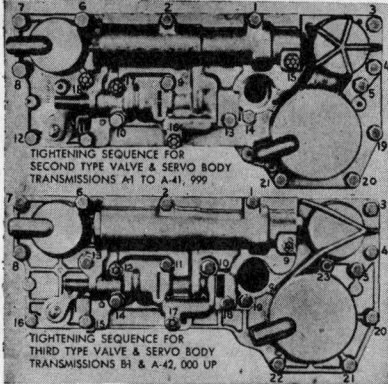

Fig. 33—Tightening Sequence for Valve and Servo Body

if it does not the law band struts are out of place. Check the little notches which fit around pins in the band flanges.

Install various length bolts with lock washers according to the hole depth. Use copper washer on center bolt adjacent to suction pipe opening.

Tighten all bolts to 5 ft lbs torque in the numerical sequence shown in Fig. 33. The variation between models is in the number of bolts used.

When all bolts are tight to 5 ft lbs then repeat the sequence tightening all the bolts to 15 lbs. When tightening those adjacent to the shift control valve operate the valve to make certain that it is not binding.

Using a pair of lock ring pliers or

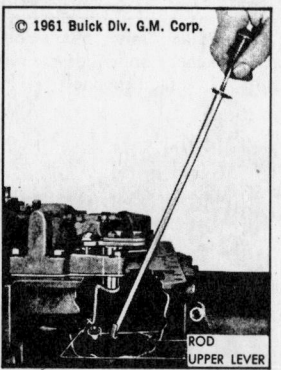

Fig. 34—Reconnecting Valve Control Rod

similar strong hook reinstall the valve operating rod onto the upper lever. See Fig. 34.

Temporarily install the shift lever on the valve operating cross shaft and operate the valve linkage to make sure it works freely. Move lever forward so that the pawl will engage the parking lock ratchet wheel. When pawl is fully engaged the pawl lock must be in full contact with the pawl.

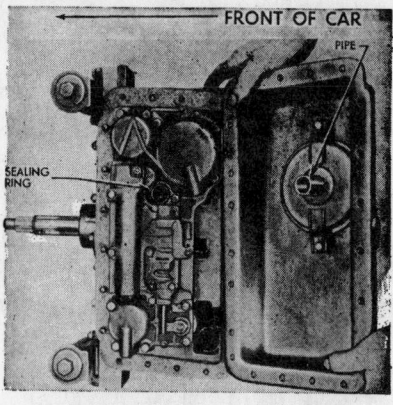

Fig. 35—Installing transmission oil pan

Push shift control valve inward to take up play in the valve linkage.

Clearance between control valve and stop pin at this point should be .030"-.040".

Install oil pan with new gasket. Be sure suction tube is contacting ring seal on valve body. Fig. 35. Tighten bolts to 15-18 ft lbs.

CONVERTER REMOVAL

Be sure cover and pump are match marked to themselves and the flywheel for same position mating at reassembly so that the bolts which held the unit to the flywheel will not by mischance coincide with the balance weights located on the pump rim. The bolts won't be long enough and the unit might be out of balance.

1954 Models

Remove large hex plug and gasket from hub of converter pump cover.

Remove the socket set screw and lockwasher located in the hub, using an Allen head wrench 5/16" across the flats. Fig. 42.

Remove all nuts, plain washers, and bolts attaching the cover to the pump. A punch can be inserted through the bell housing hand hole into a drive bolt to keep the converter from turning.

Remove cover from pump, tapping or prying against the edge to loosen it. Check the "O" ring seal for damage and evidence of leakage before removing it from the cover.

Remove bronze thrust washer from turbine hub. This is also a clearance washer marked either 5, 6, or 7. Do not mix it with others as it is important that it, or a similar one if this one is worn, be between the turbine assembly and the cover to hold the clearance between the ring-gear-hub-and-disc assembly and the turbine front cover to .002"-.010".

Insert screwdriver into a hole in first turbine disk to aid in removing

Dynaflow and Variable Pitch Dynaflow

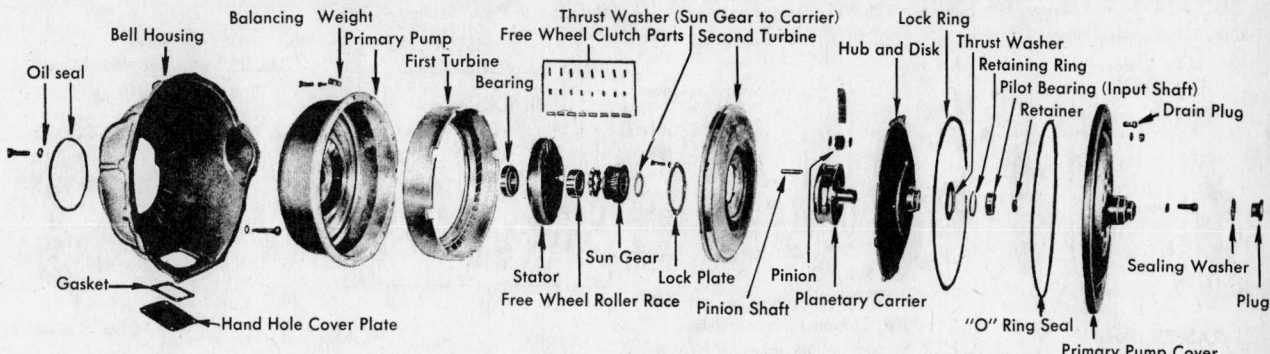

Fig. 37—Exploded view of converter assembly 1954 models.
Front of the car is to the right.

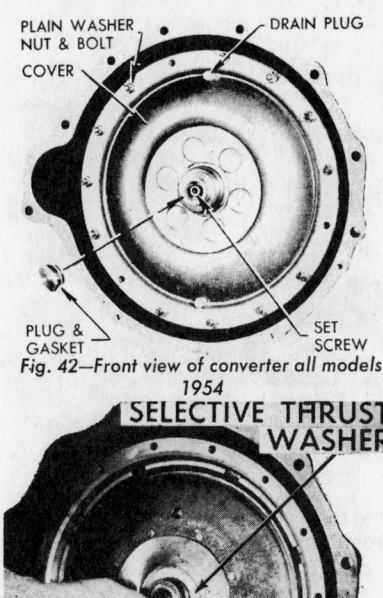

Fig. 42—Front view of converter all models
1954

SELECTIVE THRUST WASHER

Fig. 43—Removing turbine assembly
all models 1954

the twin turbine assembly from the input shaft. Push inward on the shaft to avoid withdrawing it. Fig. 43.

Remove retaining ring from groove in input shaft using snap ring pliers.

Remove bronze thrust washer and slide sun gear off the shaft.

Remove retaining ring from groove in reactor shaft and slide the convert-er stator, free wheel roller face, and stator ball bearing, from the reactor shaft as a unit.

All Models Starting with 1955 Production

Pull the converted pump forward from the reactor shaft and immediately check for evidence of oil leakage.

Radial streaks of fresh oil on back of pump and fresh oil streaks on face of front oil pump indicate leakage past the primary pump oil seal.

The procedure for the removal of this converter is essentially the same as that given for the removal of the 1954 converter.

The converter cover is a solid piece so that there is no socket set screw and washer to remove from the cover hub. Instead there is a bolt in the end of the input shaft which becomes visible after removal of the converter cover. This bolt holds in place a lock washer, a retaining washer, and a selective thrust washer. This thrust washer is the one which governs input shaft endplay. The washer is selected to hold the endplay between .002" and .009".

When the bolt and associated parts have been removed the turbine assembly can be slid off the input shaft.

When the turbine assembly and the converter sun gear have been removed slide a cylinder of thin shim stock into the hub of the variable pitch stator so as to hold the stator free wheel rollers in released position. Reach behind the stator assembly and hold the spacing and thrust washers which ride be-tween the stator and the converter primary pump into contact with the stator assembly. Slide the assembly off the end of the input shaft. Lay the stator assembly on the bench front face down. The thrust washer at the rear of the stator assembly is the one which governs the clearance between the turbine assembly and the convert-er cover. This thrust washer is select-ed to hold the clearance between .004" and .007".

Input Shaft Support Bushing and Lock Ring "Caution"

SEE FIG. 48

In the front end of the reactor shaft there is a support bushing for the input shaft. Just in front of the end of the reactor shaft there is a lock ring installed on the input shaft.

If this lock ring is not removed before any attempt is made to remove the reaction flange from the transmission the lock ring on the input shaft will slide thru the support bushing and lodge in the lock ring groove in the reactor shaft which holds the rear end of the support bushing in place.

This will effectively prevent any further disassembly or assembly, of the input shaft and the reaction shaft flange assembly, rendering it necessary to destroy one of the parts to get them apart.

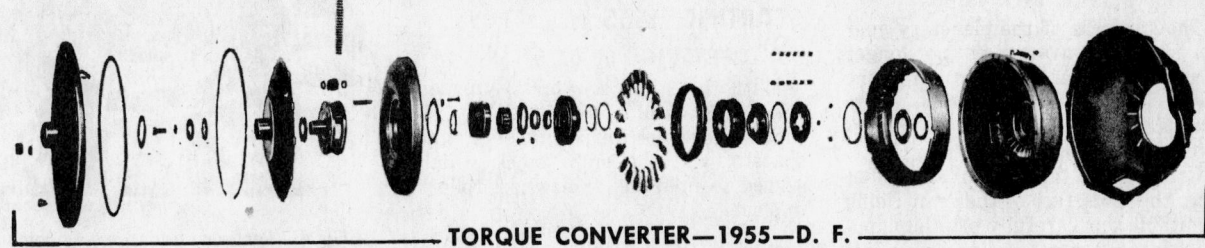

TORQUE CONVERTER—1955—D. F.

Fig. 44—Exploded view of Dynaflow Torque Converter with variable pitch stator starting 1955 production

BUICK AUTOMATIC TRANSMISSIONS

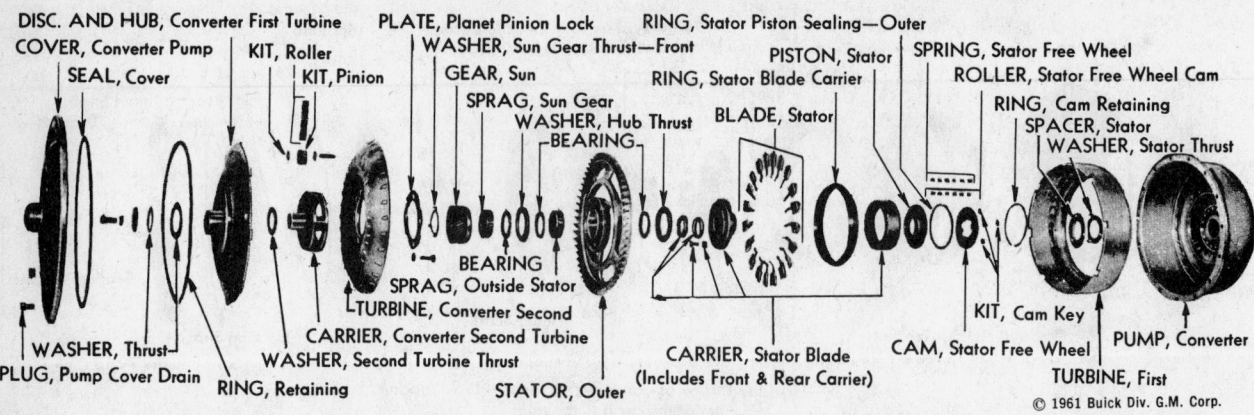

DISC. AND HUB, Converter First Turbine
COVER, Converter Pump
SEAL, Cover
KIT, Roller
KIT, Pinion
PLATE, Planet Pinion Lock
WASHER, Sun Gear Thrust—Front
GEAR, Sun
SPRAG, Sun Gear
WASHER, Hub Thrust
BEARING
RING, Stator Piston Sealing—Outer
PISTON, Stator
RING, Stator Blade Carrier
BLADE, Stator
SPRING, Stator Free Wheel
ROLLER, Stator Free Wheel Cam
RING, Cam Retaining
SPACER, Stator
WASHER, Stator Thrust

WASHER, Thrust
PLUG, Pump Cover Drain
RING, Retaining
BEARING
SPRAG, Outside Stator
TURBINE, Converter Second
CARRIER, Converter Second Turbine
WASHER, Second Turbine Thrust
STATOR, Outer
CARRIER, Stator Blade
(Includes Front & Rear Carrier)
KIT, Cam Key
CAM, Stator Free Wheel
PUMP, Converter
TURBINE, First

© 1961 Buick Div. G.M. Corp.

Fig. 45—Exploded view of Torque Converter with variable pitch stator starting with 1955 production

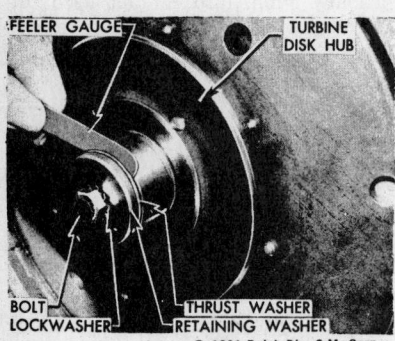

Fig. 46—Checking input shaft end play starting with 1955 production

Fig. 48—Remove input shaft snap ring starting with 1955 production or else it will catch in the groove inside the reactor shaft behind the input shaft bushing.

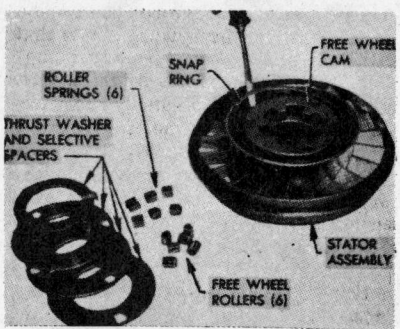

Fig. 50—Removing stator free wheel cam from rear face of variable pitch stator. Starting with 1955 production.

Fig. 47—Removing variable pitch stator starting with 1955 production

Fig. 49—Converter sun gear parts starting with 1955 production. Front of car is to the left. Note that the shoulder of the sprag clutch goes toward the rear. If assembled with shoulder to the front the car will not accelerate

DISASSEMBLY OF THE CONVERTER SUN GEAR STARTING 1955

SEE FIG. 49

The sun gear of the planetary gear set in the converter is no longer carried on a forward extension of the stator but instead is carried on its own free-wheeling clutch on the reactor shaft.

Remove the tanged thrust washer from the front face of the gear. Using a suitable tool carefully pry the flanged thrust washer from the rear face of the gear. Remove the free wheeling

sprag clutch from inside the gear.

DISASSEMBLY OF THE VARIABLE PITCH STATOR STARTING 1955

SEE FIGS. 50, 51, 52, 53

With the stator assembly lying on the bench with its rear face up, remove the steel thrust washer, the spacers, and the shim stock which served to hold the free wheel rollers in place.

Remove the six free wheel rollers and the six square shaped springs.

Pry the free wheel cam retaining ring from its groove. Remove the three driving keys and the cam.

Turn the stator assembly over and using a figure-eight-type screw driver remove the five special screws and lock washers holding the front half of the stator vane support to the rear half. Fig. 51. Separate the two halves but do not pry them apart. Their mating surfaces are a lapped fit. Note the locating dowel pins between the

Fig. 51—Removing stator vane support screws from front face of variable pitch stator. Starting with 1955 production

716

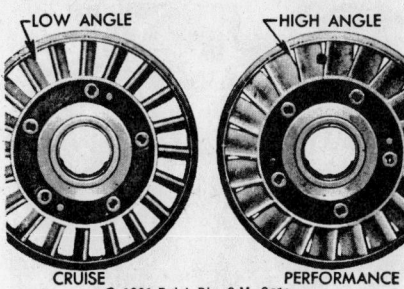

CRUISE   © 1961 Buick Div. G.M. Corp.   PERFORMANCE

Fig. 52—Front view of variable pitch stator starting with 1955 production

halves which prevent use of any twisting force. Fig. 53.

Remove the snap ring and the thrust washer which retain the stator vane crack pins in contact with the stator piston. Now lift the stator vane carrying ring and the vanes from the rear portions of the vane support as

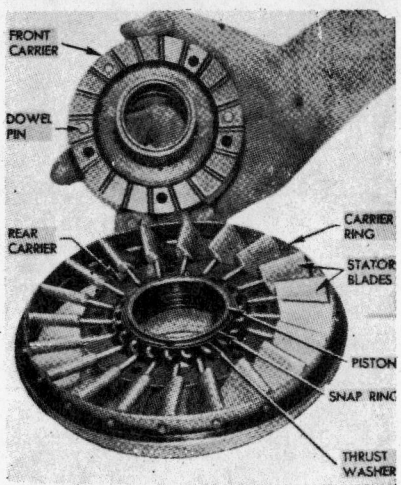

Fig. 53—Removing front portion of Stator Vane Support (Front Carrier). Starting 1955 production.

a unit. Remove the stator piston from the rear vane support.

ASSEMBLY OF THE VARIABLE PITCH STATOR STARTING 1955

SEE FIGS. 52, 53, 54

Intall the stator piston into the rear face of the rear half of the stator support. Check that the oil seal ring is in place and that the piston moves easily. Slightly tilting the piston as it enters the bore makes assembly easier.

Place a small block of wood on the bench and lay the rear face of the rear half of the stator support upon it so that the piston sticks out slightly through the front.

Place the stator blade (vane) carrier ring on the bench with the perforated edge of the ring up. Insert the vanes in the ring with the cranks pointing to the left of center and the cavity side up. When all are in place

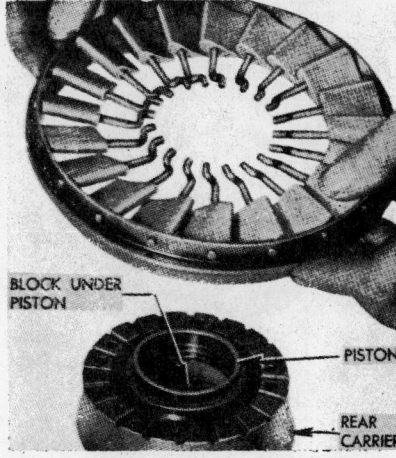

Fig. 54—Installing Vane support Ring and Blades or rear Vane Support (Rear Carrier). Starting 1955 production.

they should be lying in the nearly closed high angle (performance) position. Fig. 52.

Install the ring and vane assembly onto the rear half of the stator carrier so that the cranks are in place in the carrier grooves. Fig. 54. Install the thrust washer and the lock ring onto the protruding edge of the piston so that the cranks are held in position.

Being careful that the mating surfaces of the two portions of the stator carrier are clean and free of burrs, align the dowel pins and install the front portion onto the rear portion so that the screw holes line up and the cranks are nicely placed in the grooves. Using the special figure-eight-type screw driver, tighten the screws (equipped with star lock washers) evenly. A torque wrench rig is recommended. If the tightening is uneven, trouble may result.

Check the assembly for smooth operation, being careful that the vanes move through their full seventy-five degree arc without binding.

Install the stator free wheel cam, the three driving keys and the snap ring retainer in the rear face of the rear portion of the stator support.

Check that the free wheel springs are all the same height and install them and the rollers into place in the cam. Install a cylinder of thin shim stock to hold the rollers in place during installation on the reactor shaft.

ASSEMBLY AND INSTALLATION OF THE TORQUE CONVERTER TYPICAL OF ALL MODELS

Install front oil pump seal ring around the pump body. Install the bell housing using lock washers. Sparingly coat threads of the lower right side

bolt with Permatex No. 3 as this bolt hole runs into the transmission case. Tighten to 35-40 ft. lbs.

At this point go through the procedure to determine the clearance between the converter cover and the turbine assembly.

A special gauge is required for this operation. The instructions that come with the gauge give details of the procedure, the clearance should be .017″ to .030″.

Install the converter primary pump on the reactor shaft, being careful that the front oil pump drive lugs on the hub of the primary pump properly engage the drive tangs of the front oil pump drive gear. Hold the spacer washers and the thrust washer against the rear face of the stator assembly and install the stator assembly onto the reactor shaft. Be certain that the thrust washer and the spacers remain in position until the stator assembly is firmly seated into place. Remove the thin shim stock cylinder which held the free wheel rollers in place.

Install the converter sun gear assembly, checking to be sure that it will turn clockwise and lock against turning counterclockwise.

Check that the input shaft snap ring is in place and install the turbine assembly. Note that the clearance between the first turbine hub and the selective thrust washer should run .002 to .009 inches. This thrust washer is marked 6 or 7. Fig. 46.

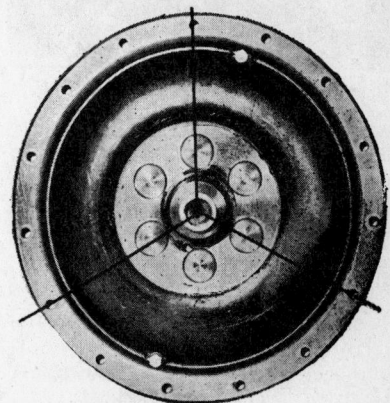

Fig. 55—Showing location of drive holes in Converter Cover

Looking at the front face of the converter cover, select three bolt holes that are aligned with the center of the hub and one of the counterbored recesses adjacent to the hub. Mark these holes with an X as they are to be used to hold the converter to the flywheel. Fig. 55. Note that if the cover, the body (primary pump) of the converter, and the flywheel, were match marked at disassembly the selection of the drive bolt holes will occur automatically.

BUICK AUTOMATIC TRANSMISSIONS

Install a new "O" ring seal on the cover. Be careful that it has an even tension all around and is not twisted.

Grease the bronze thrust washer so it will adhere and place it in the recess in the cover. Install the cover on the converter body, being careful that the selected drive bolt holes are not aligned with any hole in the rim of the body to which a balance weight is already attached.

Install the bolts with plain washers and special nuts in all but the three selected driving bolt holes. Insert an 11/32 in. drill through a bolt hole to align the lot. Tighten the bolts to 5

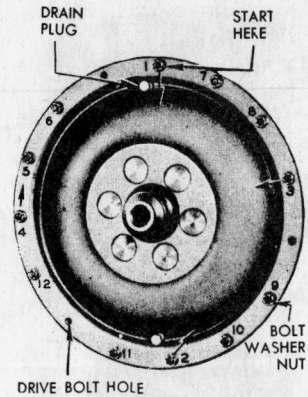

Fig. 56—Converter Cover Tightening Sequence

Fig. 57—Hold reverse band with screw driver while tightening input shaft retaining screw to 25-30 ft. lbs. 1954 models only

ft. lbs. in the sequence shown (see Fig. 56) and then tighten all to 25-30 ft. lbs. in the same sequence. When tightening the bolts insert the blade of a wide bladed screw driver between the plate side of each bolt head and the body in order to prevent the bolt corners from digging into the primary pump casting and so giving a false indication of tightness.

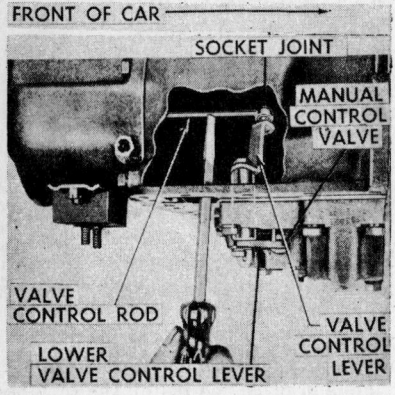

Fig. 58—Disconnecting Valve Control Rod. Typical of all models.

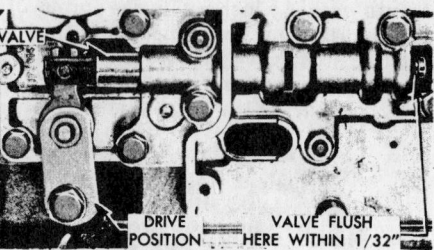

Fig. 61—Position of Manual Control Valve when in Drive Range. Starting with 1955 production.

Fig. 59—Rear Oil Pump tightening sequence typical of all models. Tighten to 25-30 ft. lbs. Note pump to case match marks.

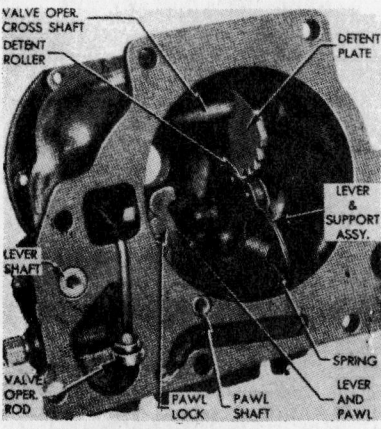

Fig. 60—Rear Bearing Retainer starting with 1955 production.

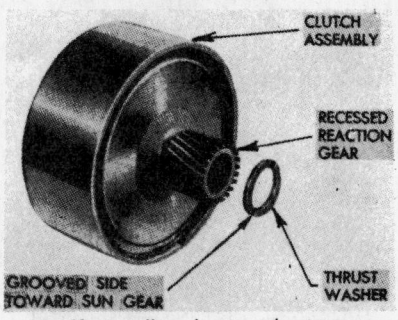

Fig. 62—Installing thrust washer in recess of reaction gear (Low Sun Gear) Starting with 1955 production. This washer holds input shaft end play to .020"-.034" to reduce "clunk."

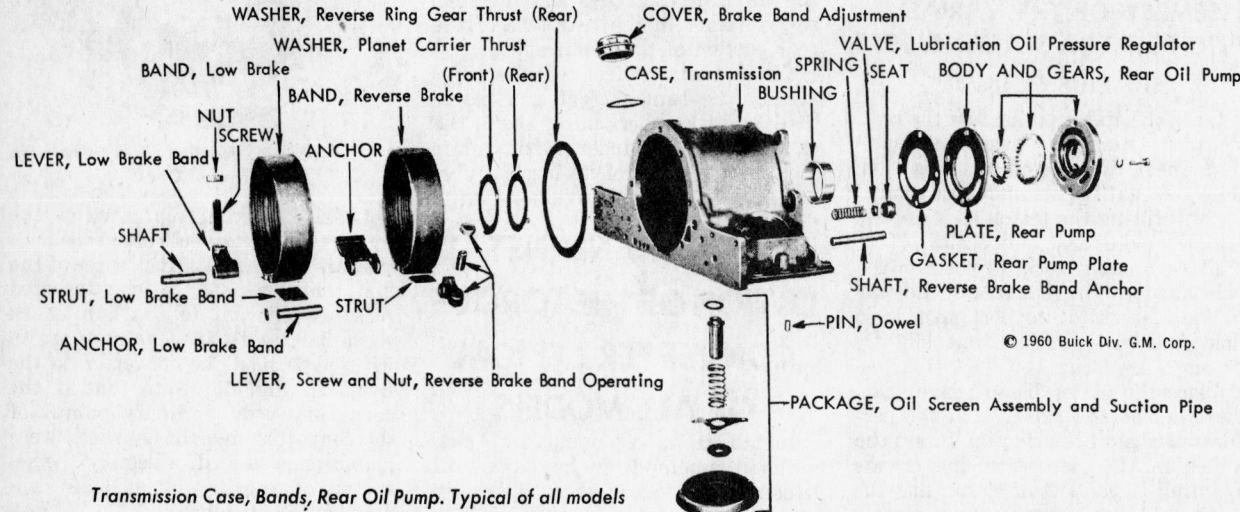

Transmission Case, Bands, Rear Oil Pump. Typical of all models

Dynaflow and Variable Pitch Dynaflow

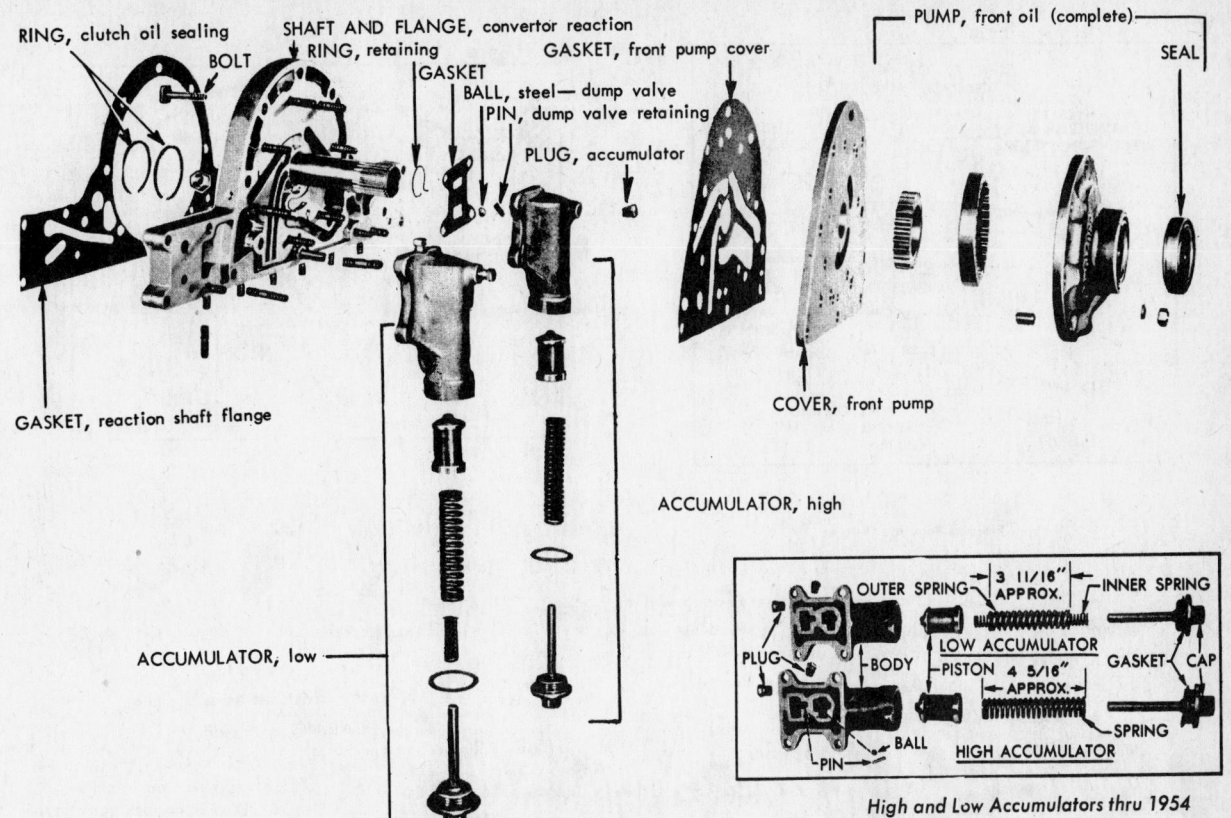

RING, clutch oil sealing
BOLT
SHAFT AND FLANGE, convertor reaction
RING, retaining
GASKET
BALL, steel— dump valve
PIN, dump valve retaining
PLUG, accumulator
GASKET, front pump cover
PUMP, front oil (complete)
SEAL

GASKET, reaction shaft flange

COVER, front pump

ACCUMULATOR, high

ACCUMULATOR, low

OUTER SPRING
3 11/16" APPROX.
INNER SPRING
PLUG
BODY
LOW ACCUMULATOR
PISTON 4 5/16" APPROX.
GASKET CAP
BALL
PIN
SPRING
HIGH ACCUMULATOR

High and Low Accumulators thru 1954

Front Pump, Accumulators, Reactor Shaft and Flange assembly thru 1954

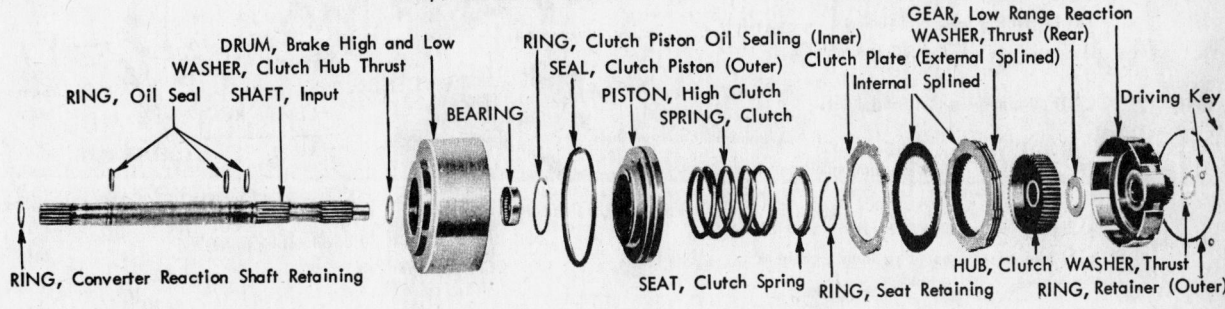

DRUM, Brake High and Low
WASHER, Clutch Hub Thrust
RING, Oil Seal SHAFT, Input
BEARING
RING, Clutch Piston Oil Sealing (Inner)
SEAL, Clutch Piston (Outer)
PISTON, High Clutch
SPRING, Clutch
GEAR, Low Range Reaction
WASHER, Thrust (Rear)
Clutch Plate (External Splined)
Internal Splined
Driving Key

RING, Converter Reaction Shaft Retaining
SEAT, Clutch Spring
RING, Seat Retaining
HUB, Clutch WASHER, Thrust
RING, Retainer (Outer)

Input Shaft and Clutch Assembly starting with 1955 production.

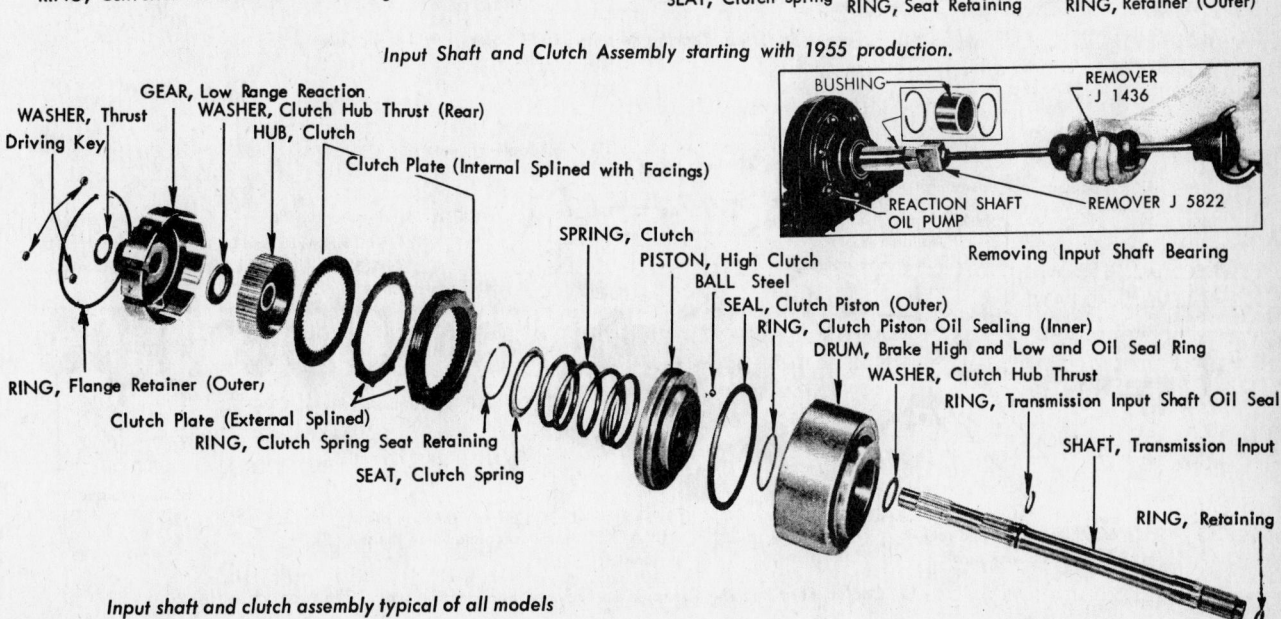

WASHER, Thrust
Driving Key
GEAR, Low Range Reaction
WASHER, Clutch Hub Thrust (Rear)
HUB, Clutch
Clutch Plate (Internal Splined with Facings)

RING, Flange Retainer (Outer)
Clutch Plate (External Splined)
RING, Clutch Spring Seat Retaining
SEAT, Clutch Spring

SPRING, Clutch
PISTON, High Clutch
BALL Steel
SEAL, Clutch Piston (Outer)
RING, Clutch Piston Oil Sealing (Inner)
DRUM, Brake High and Low and Oil Seal Ring
WASHER, Clutch Hub Thrust
RING, Transmission Input Shaft Oil Seal
SHAFT, Transmission Input
RING, Retaining

BUSHING
REMOVER J 1436
REACTION SHAFT OIL PUMP
REMOVER J 5822

Removing Input Shaft Bearing

Input shaft and clutch assembly typical of all models

719

BUICK AUTOMATIC TRANSMISSIONS

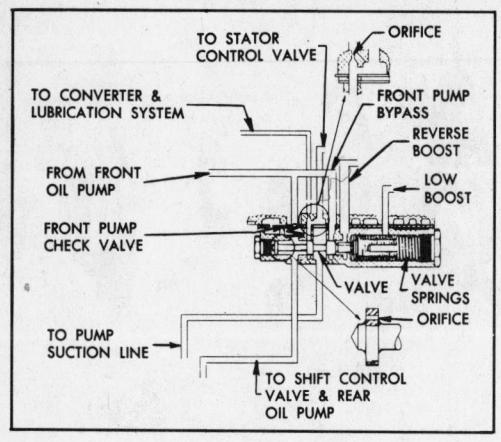

Oil Pump Pressure Regulator Valve

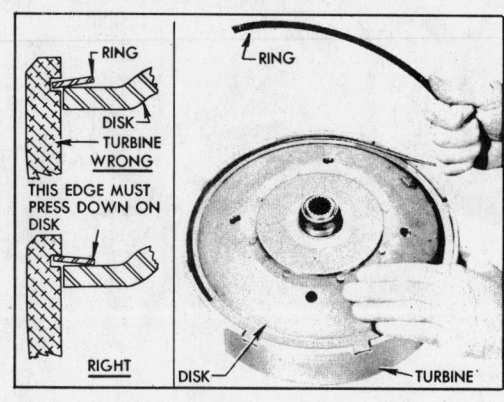

Installing Disk Retaining Ring

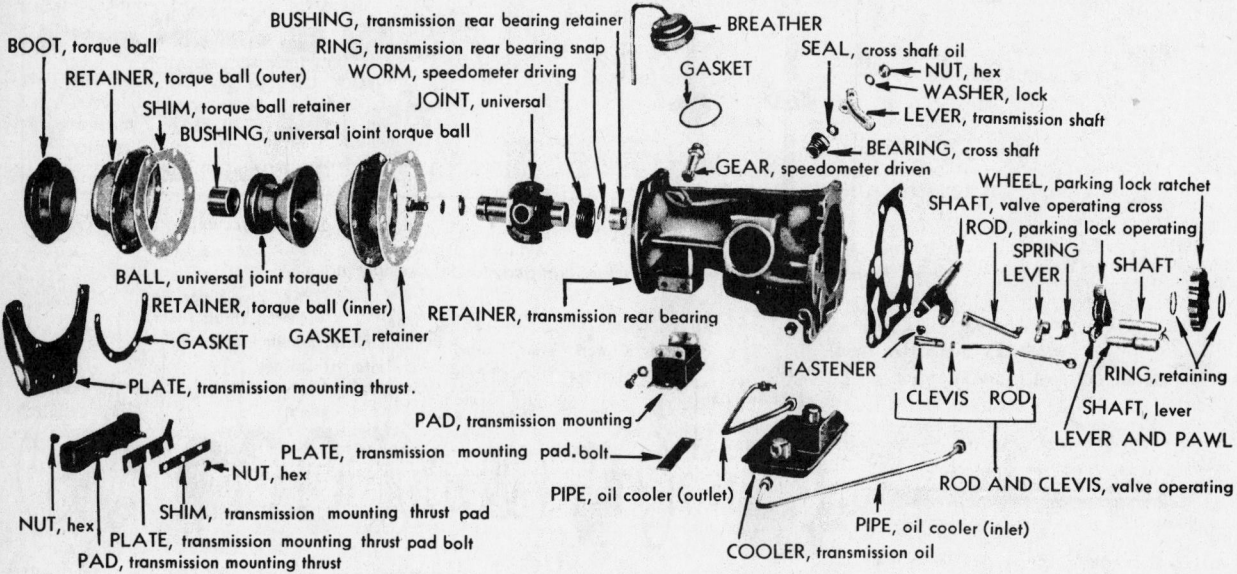

Torque Ball, Rear Bearing Retainer, Oil Cooler. 1954 models

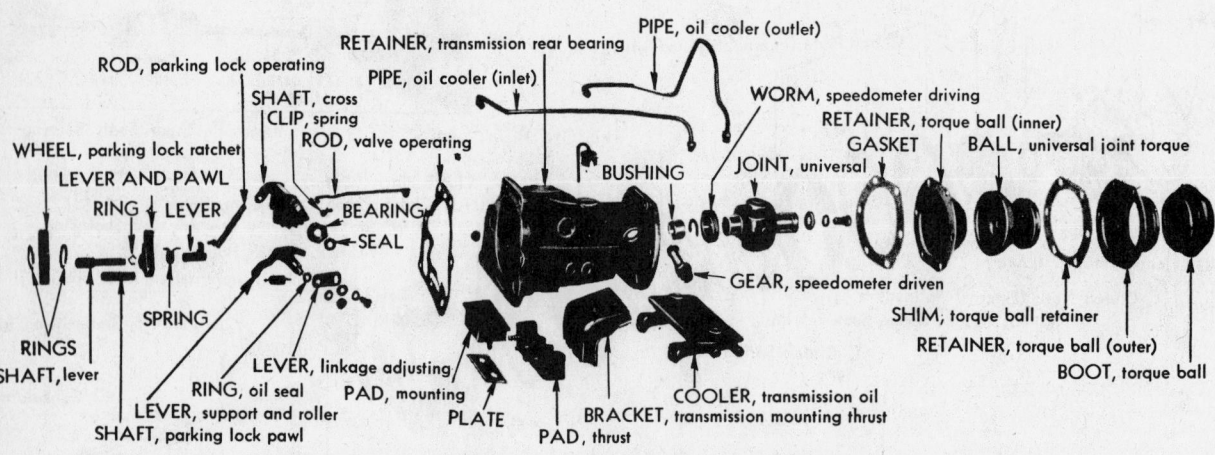

Oil Cooler, Rear Bearing Retainer and Torque Ball starting with 1955 production.

Dynaflow and Variable Pitch Dynaflow

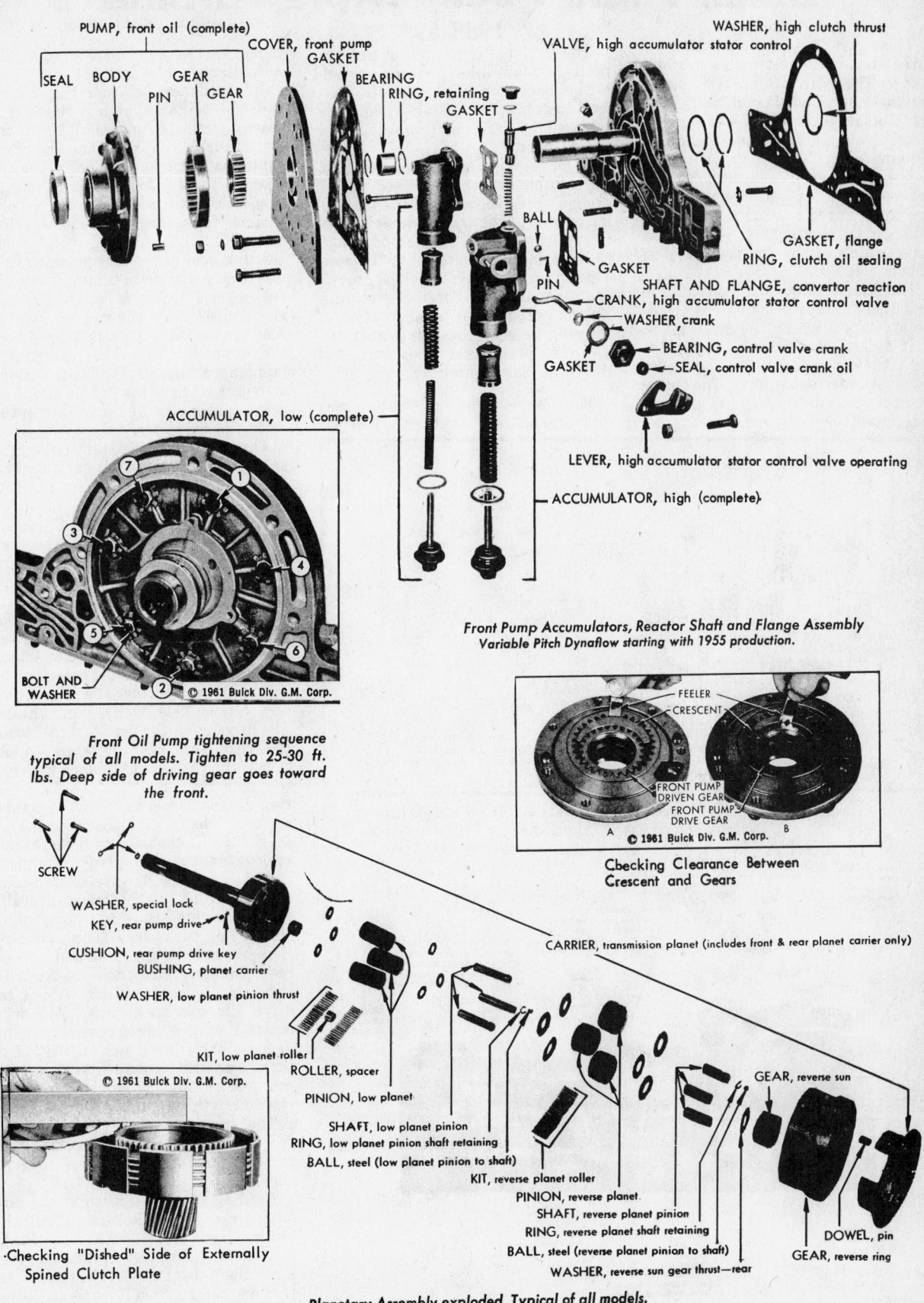

PUMP, front oil (complete)

SEAL   BODY   GEAR   GEAR
PIN

COVER, front pump
GASKET
BEARING
RING, retaining
GASKET

VALVE, high accumulator stator control

WASHER, high clutch thrust

GASKET, flange
RING, clutch oil sealing

BALL
PIN
GASKET

SHAFT AND FLANGE, convertor reaction
CRANK, high accumulator stator control valve
WASHER, crank
BEARING, control valve crank
GASKET
SEAL, control valve crank oil

ACCUMULATOR, low (complete)

LEVER, high accumulator stator control valve operating

ACCUMULATOR, high (complete)

BOLT AND WASHER

© 1961 Buick Div. G.M. Corp.

Front Oil Pump tightening sequence typical of all models. Tighten to 25-30 ft. lbs. Deep side of driving gear goes toward the front.

Front Pump Accumulators, Reactor Shaft and Flange Assembly Variable Pitch Dynaflow starting with 1955 production.

FEELER
CRESCENT

FRONT PUMP DRIVEN GEAR
FRONT PUMP DRIVE GEAR

A   © 1961 Buick Div. G.M. Corp.   B

Checking Clearance Between Crescent and Gears

SCREW

WASHER, special lock
KEY, rear pump drive
CUSHION, rear pump drive key
BUSHING, planet carrier
WASHER, low planet pinion thrust

CARRIER, transmission planet (includes front & rear planet carrier only)

KIT, low planet roller
ROLLER, spacer
PINION, low planet
SHAFT, low planet pinion
RING, low planet pinion shaft retaining
BALL, steel (low planet pinion to shaft)
KIT, reverse planet roller
PINION, reverse planet
SHAFT, reverse planet pinion
RING, reverse planet shaft retaining
BALL, steel (reverse planet pinion to shaft)
WASHER, reverse sun gear thrust—rear

GEAR, reverse sun

DOWEL, pin
GEAR, reverse ring

© 1961 Buick Div. G.M. Corp.

·Checking "Dished" Side of Externally Spined Clutch Plate

Planetary Assembly exploded. Typical of all models.

721

BUICK AUTOMATIC TRANSMISSIONS
Buick Flight Pitch—Triple Turbine
1958-59

This transmission uses an improved three stage converter with a variable stator. The gear box has two planetary gear sets and six clutches. (Four disc clutches and two one-way (sprag) clutches called free wheeling clutches.) Fig. 1.

The three turbines in the converter are splined to separate shafts and are so arranged that as each turbine takes over the load the planetary drive train used by the previous turbine is released.

The transmission is remarkable in that there is provided a special Grade Retarder position on the quadrant so that as the rear wheels attempt to drive the converter, the converter resists with increasing force. The Grade Retarder may be engaged at any engine speed below 45 mph.

The variable pitch stator has two positions: low angle for economy and normal operation; high angle for fast acceleration. The high angle is achieved by pushing the accelerator to the floor.

In all forward operations the Neutral Clutch and the Forward Clutch are engaged. The one to lock the pinion carrier of the front gear set to the third turbine shaft. The second to lock the two one-way clutches to the case. These two one-way clutches provide the reaction force for the gear sets. The one prevents reverse rotation of the ring gear of the rear planet set. The other prevents reverse rotation of the front planet sun gear.

The pinion carriers of the two gear sets are splined together. The rear pinion carrier is also fastened to the output shaft. Fig. 1.

In the Grade Retarder Fig. 2 position the Neutral Clutch is released to disengage the output shaft from the third turbine shaft. The Forward Clutch is disengaged to allow the sun gear of the front gear set to idle as it pleases, which releases the second turbine from torque. The Grade Retarder Clutch is engaged which holds the ring gear of the rear planetary set stationary. The drive coming from the rear wheels turns the rear pinion carrier and so forces the sun gear of the rear set to turn. This in turn drives the first turbine. The consequent pumping action of the first turbine attempts to drive the engine and in so doing causes a lot of turbulence in the oil in the converter.

The oil is thus heated and the heat is then absorbed by the car's cooling system thru the oil cooler in the bottom of the radiator.

In Reverse, the Forward Clutch is disengaged which permits the two one-way clutches to lock the front planet sun gear to the rear planet ring gear in so far as reverse rotation is concerned. The Reverse Clutch locks the ring gear of the front planet set to the case. The power flow under these conditions is easiest explained in this manner: Consider the rear planetary carrier held by the rear wheels. The drive from the first turbine turns the rear sun gear forward which causes the rear planet pinions to drive the rear ring gear backwards. This ring gear is locked to the front planet sun gear when it turns backwards and so the front planet sun gear turns backwards. The front planet ring gear is locked by the Reverse Clutch and so the front planet pinions walk around carrying the front planet pinion carrier backwards. The two carriers are splined together and so the rear planet carrier turns backwards carrying the output shaft with it to drive the car backwards. You will notice that this arrangement results in some drive being put on the third turbine as the Neutral Clutch is still engaged locking the front planet carrier to the third turbine shaft.

The arrangement of the hand control positions is such that rocking the car to get it out of snow or mud is very easy.

Reading from left to right the positions are: Park; Reverse; Neutral; Drive; Grade Retarder. For the Park and Grade Retarder positions the lever must be raised. The result is that one can go from Reverse to Drive and back by just moving the lever back and forth between the gate

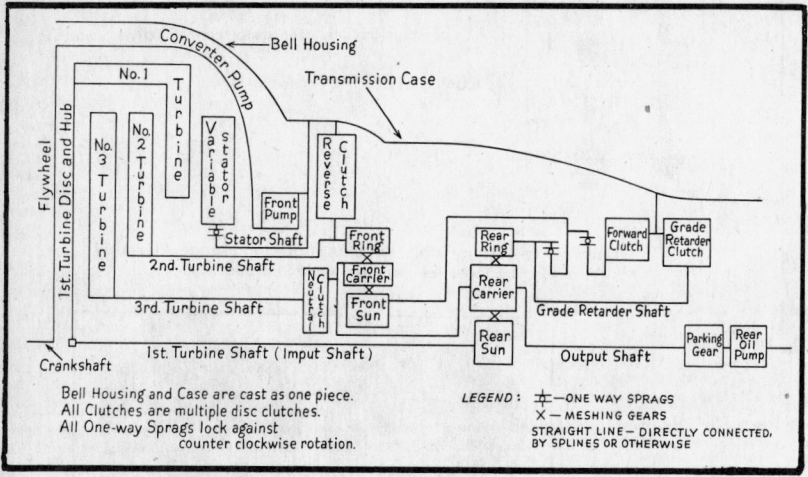

Fig. 1—Schematic diagram showing connections of mechanical units in Flight Pitch Dynaflow starting with 1958 production

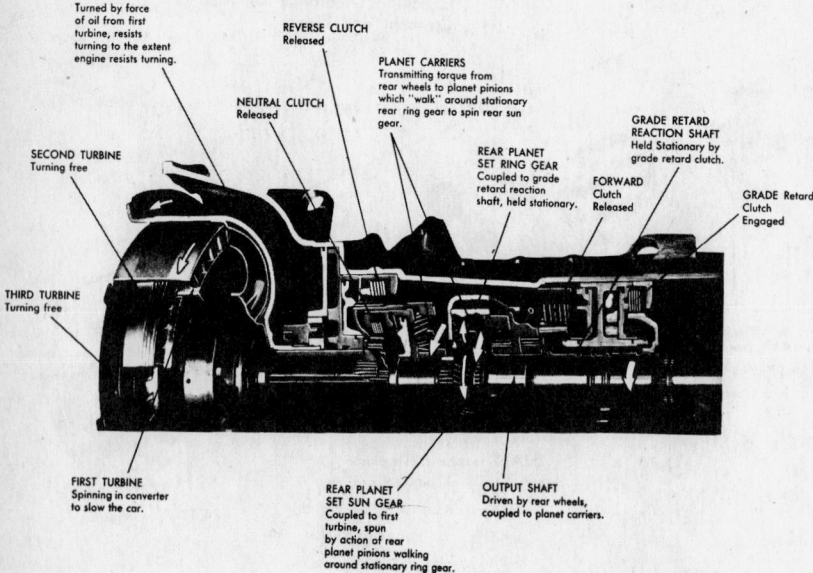

Fig. 2—Operation of Flight Pitch Dynaflow in Hill Retarder Range

limits.

The Park position provides a positive mechanical lock that will hold the car on the steepest grades.

There is a Neutral Safety Switch located at the base of the steering column which prevents operation of the starter unless the hand lever is at either Park or Neutral.

GENERAL INFORMATION

Identification Number

A number is stamped on the lower side of the transmission case directly forward of the left front corner of the oil pan. This number is the clue to any changes in the transmission and should be used when ordering parts.

Fluid Capacity

To refill after overhaul.... 25 pints
To refill after draining.... 24 pints

Checking Fluid Level

Check fluid level with transmission at operating temperature, hand lever at Neutral, engine idling.

Fluid Gauge Rod

Amount between Low and Full marks
.... 1 pint

Fluid Change Interval

Drain and refill every 25,000 miles, oftener if in severe service.

Fluid Type

Use a good grade of Automatic Transmission Fluid. Type A-"AQ-ATF."

Fluid Draining Procedure

Have engine at operating temperature. Remove converter housing cover. Turn flywheel to bring a converter drain plug in view. Loosen this drain plug to provide air vent. Turn flywheel to bring opposite drain plug down. Remove this drain plug to drain converter. Remove transmission filler tube at transmission oil pan to drain transmission case.

Refill Procedure

Install and tighten converter drain plugs. Reconnect and tighten oil filler pipe to transmission case.

Pour four quarts of a good grade of Automatic Transmission Fluid thru the filler pipe. Pour slowly to allow trapped air to escape.

With rear wheels off the ground, put hand lever at "D" and with engine idling add eight more quarts.

Move hand lever to Neutral. Return

rear wheels to the ground. Check the fluid level and adjust as required.

Band Adjustment

This transmission does not have any bands. No bands at all.

Pushing Car to Start Engine

Place shift control lever in Neutral. When car is going 30 m.p.h. move hand lever to "G" (Grade Retard) and engine should turn. It is safer to push a car with an automatic transmission than it is to tow it.

Towing

Car should not be towed with rear wheels on ground if transmission cannot be placed in Neutral. It can be towed with rear wheels on ground if transmission is in Neutral but speed should not exceed 35 m.p.h.

Grade Retard Note

Do not use this position above 45 m.p.h. Do not accelerate in this range.

Rear Oil Pump Note

The rear oil pump on this transmission is attached to the rear extension.

TROUBLE DIAGNOSIS

Road Test Note

Car should be at operating temperature for road tests.

Variable Pitch Stator Test

Car running in "D" range, depress accelerator pedal. As it passes halfway mark engine speed should increase and increased pick-up should be felt. This proves vanes are moving.

Grade Retard Clutch Test

Shift to "G" range at speed below 45 m.p.h. but above 15 m.p.h. A definite and immediate braking action should be felt.

Neutral Test

Little or no creep should be evident.

Other Ranges Test

Should be no abnormal creep in any of the driving ranges.

Linkage Test

With hand lever at "D" and car held with brakes, snap the throttle to get engine speed-up to about 1400 r.p.m.

If on immediate release of pedal the engine returns to idle too slowly or rolls unevenly, the throttle and dashpot linkage requires adjustment. See article on Variable Pitch Dynaflow.

TROUBLE CHART

Engine Stalls While Decelerating Car with Brakes Applied

1. Improper adjustment of throttle dashpot.
2. Engine not properly tuned.

Transmission Oil Foams and Spews Out of Breather Pipe or Filler Pipe

1. Transmission overfilled.

If transmission is overfilled, check for blackened condition of oil, indicating leakage of rear axle lubricant into transmission due to defective propeller shaft seals. Check for low oil level in rear axle housing. Correct cause of leakage and completely drain and refill transmission.

2. Water in transmission.

Indicated by overfilled condition and caramel color of transmission oil. Water in transmission usually comes from a leaking oil cooler. In this case there may be excessive oil accumulation in top tank of the engine radiator. Correct the cause of leakage, and completely drain, flush with 10W oil, then drain and refill transmission with a good grade of Automatic Transmission Fluid.

Car Will Not Move in Any Range— Rear Wheels Free

1. If car will not move for 1 to 8 minutes after standing over night, park car for several hours with engine stopped. Start engine and check front oil pump pressure. A zero reading until such time as car will move indicates that front pump loses its prime due to excessive clearances. Inspect front pump. If condition has existed for some time it is advisable to inspect clutches for excessive wear due to slippage at low apply pressure.

2. Excessively worn neutral clutch plates.

Car Will Not Move in D Only

1. Reverse clutch assembly sticking in applied position.
2. Forward clutch inoperative or excessively worn.

Car Will Not Move in Reverse Only

1. Forward clutch not releasing.
2. Reverse clutch inoperative or excessively worn.

Excessive Slip in All Ranges

1. Low oil level.
2. Manual control linkage improperly adjusted.
3. Neutral clutch worn or damaged.
4. Faulty free wheeling (sprag)

clutches.

5. Forward clutch slipping.

Excessive Slip in Reverse Only

1. Manual control linkage improperly adjusted.

2. Faulty front free wheeling (sprag) clutch.

3. Reverse clutch slipping.

Car Creeps Forward in Neutral

1. Manual control linkage improperly adjusted.

2. Forward and reverse clutches slipping.

3. Inoperative free wheeling (sprag) clutches.

4. Stator control linkage improperly adjusted.

Excessive Slip in D Only

1. Manual control linkage improperly adjusted.

2. Neutral clutch or forward clutch not releasing.

3. Foreign material collected behind neutral clutch piston.

No Brake Action in G Range

1. Inoperative Grade Retard clutch.

2. Excessive worn clutch plates.

3. Manual control linkage improperly adjusted.

Car Slips at Speeds Above 40 MPH

1. Defective neutral clutch.

2. Stator control linkage improperly adjusted.

LOCATION OF NEEDLE BEARINGS, NEEDLE BEARING RACES, THRUST WASHERS

Please note that the difference between the specified items is not easily determined but can be measured. To install the wrong one would injure the transmission. First item of each Group is nearest front of car. Last item is to the rear.

1. BETWEEN CONVERTER COVER AND 1ST TURBINE HUB DISC.

Selected race—Needle bearing 1¾ x 2½—Selected race. The Races are selected to hold clearance between hub and cover to .004-.007. A special gauge is required.

2. BELOW NUT FASTENING 1ST TURBINE HUB DISC TO 1ST TURBINE (INPUT) SHAFT.

One special cupped washer.

3. BETWEEN 1ST TURBINE HUB DISC AND FRONT FACE OF 3RD TURBINE.

Bronze thrust washer .080 thick.

4. BETWEEN 3RD and 2ND TURBINES.

Flanged race (flange to rear)—Needle bearing 1¾ x 2½—plain race .030 thick.

5. BETWEEN 2ND TURBINE AND VARIABLE PITCH STATOR.

Flanged race (flange to the rear)—Needle bearing 1¾ x 2½—Plain race .050 thick.

6. BETWEEN VARIABLE PITCH STATOR AND CONVERTER PUMP.

Plain race—Needle bearing 2¼ x 3. No rear race.

7. BETWEEN STATOR REACTION SHAFT AND FRONT RING GEAR ASSEMBLY.

Front race (press fit in stator shaft)—Needle bearing 1¾ x 2½—Flanged race (flange to rear).

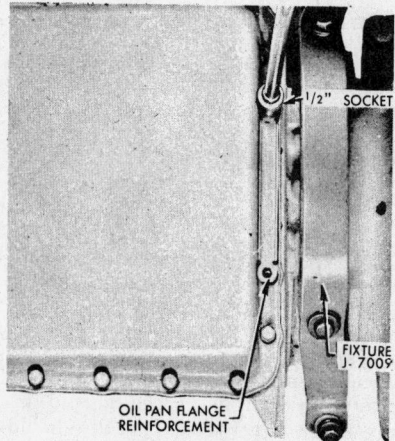

Oil Pan Removal. Flight Pitch Dynaflow 1958-59

Oil Screen Removal. Flight Pitch Dynaflow 1958-59

8. BETWEEN FRONT RING GEAR CARRIER AND NEUTRAL CLUTCH HUB.

Caged needle bearing held with snap ring.

9. BETWEEN NEUTRAL CLUTCH HUB AND FRONT CARRIER.

Tanged thrust washer.

10. BETWEEN FRONT CARRIER AND FRONT SUN GEAR.

Plain race—Needle bearing 1¾ x 2½. No rear race.

11. BETWEEN FRONT SUN GEAR AND REAR CARRIER.

Plain race—Needle bearing 2 x 2¾—plain race.

12. BETWEEN REAR CARRIER AND FRONT OF REAR SUN GEAR.

A tanged thrust washer.

13. BETWEEN REAR CARRIER AND REAR OF REAR SUN GEAR.

A thrust ring.

14. BETWEEN REAR SUN GEAR AND OUTPUT SHAFT.

Needle bearing 13/16 x 1⅞.

15. BETWEEN OUTPUT SHAFT AND REAR RING GEAR.

Needle bearing 1¾ x 2½.

16. BETWEEN REAR SPRAG INNER RACE AND GRADE RETARD SHAFT SNAP RING.

Thrust washer—spacer.

17. BETWEEN GRADE RETARD CLUTCH HUB AND PARKING GEAR.

Plain race—Needle bearing 1½ x 2-3/16—Plain race.

18. BETWEEN REAR BEARING AND SHOULDER OF OUTPUT SHAFT.

One spacer—2 shims—these are selected to hold output shaft end clearance to .015-.035.

Reaction shaft oil rings.

Buick Flight Pitch—Triple Turbine

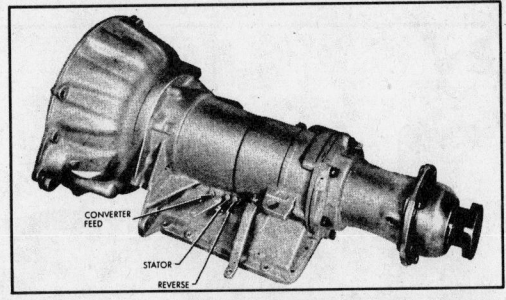

Oil pressure check points, right side

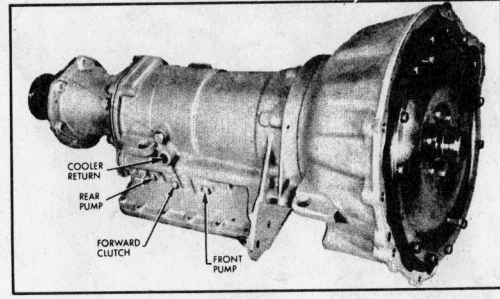

Oil pressure check points, left side

Valve body removal. Note special washer on stator control stop bolt

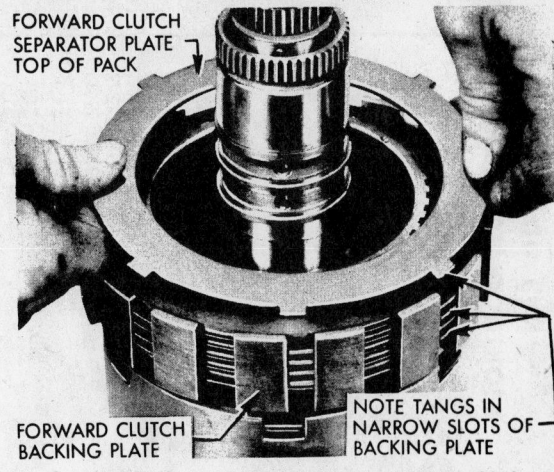

FORWARD CLUTCH SEPARATOR PLATE TOP OF PACK

FORWARD CLUTCH BACKING PLATE

NOTE TANGS IN NARROW SLOTS OF BACKING PLATE

It is very important to have a friction plate assembled next to the backing plate and a separator plate on top

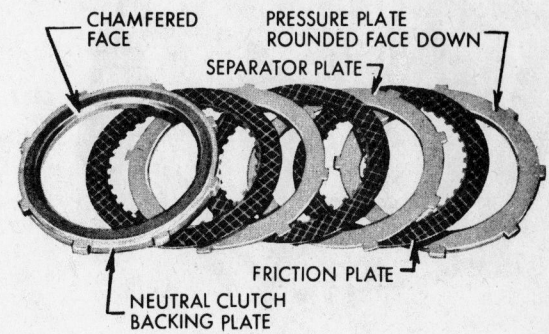

CHAMFERED FACE

PRESSURE PLATE ROUNDED FACE DOWN

SEPARATOR PLATE

FRICTION PLATE

NEUTRAL CLUTCH BACKING PLATE

Layout of clutch plates

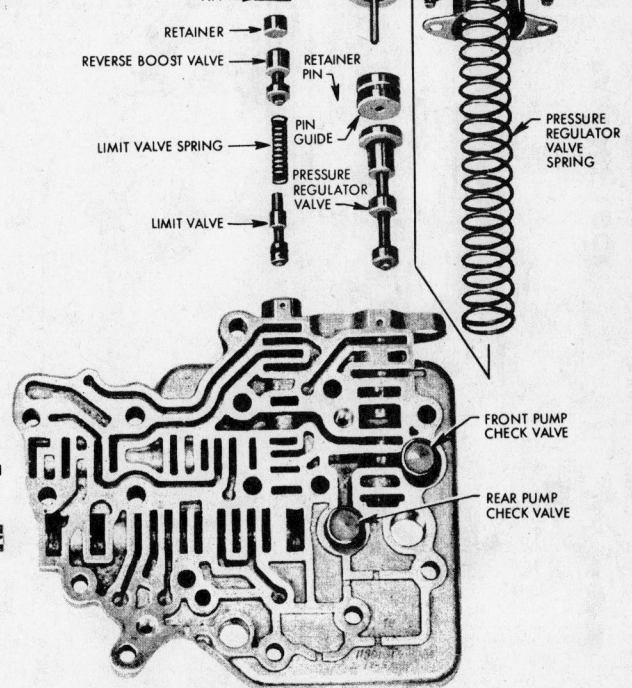

Exploded view of valve body

BUICK AUTOMATIC TRANSMISSIONS

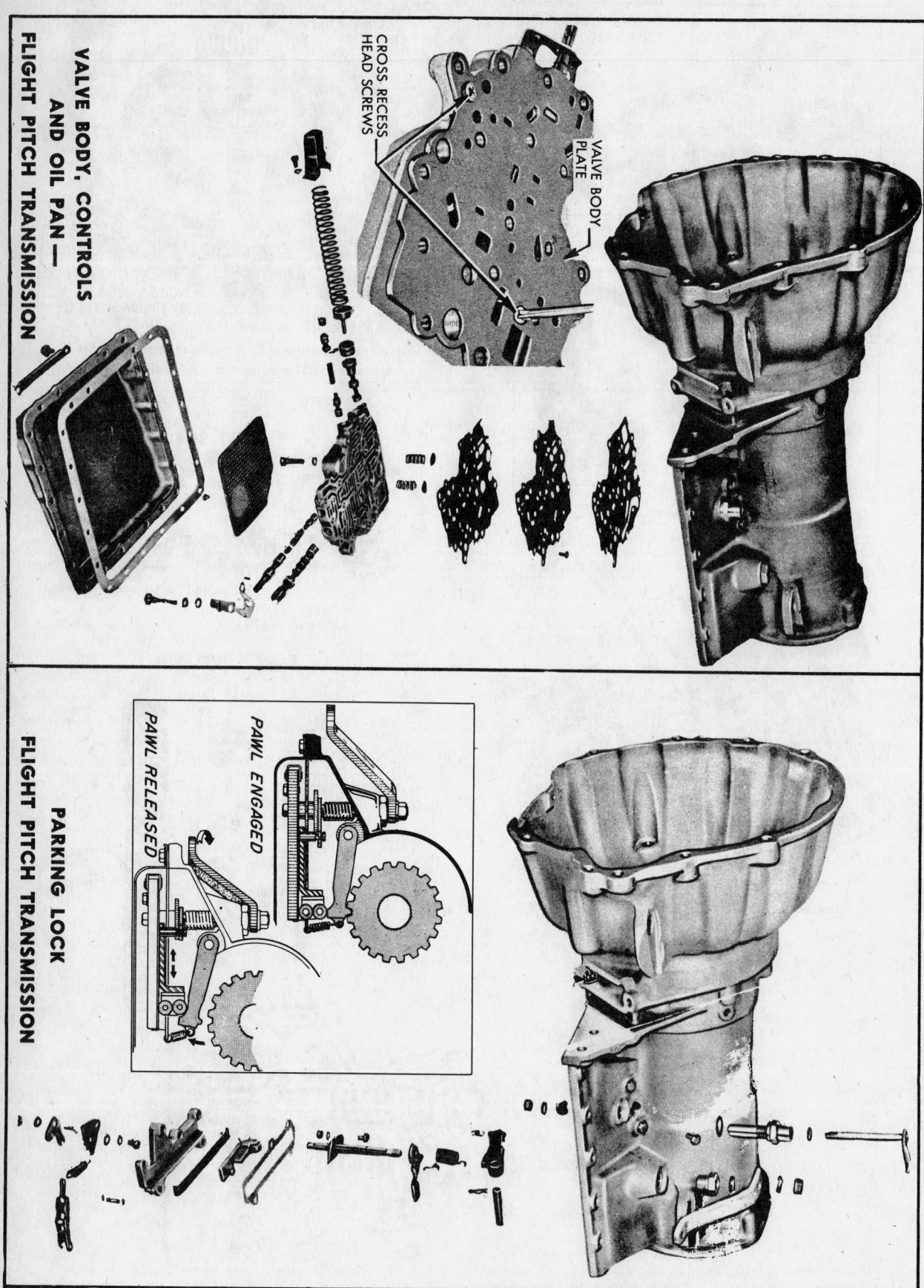

VALVE BODY, CONTROLS AND OIL PAN—
FLIGHT PITCH TRANSMISSION

CROSS RECESS HEAD SCREWS

VALVE BODY PLATE

PARKING LOCK
FLIGHT PITCH TRANSMISSION

PAWL RELEASED

PAWL ENGAGED

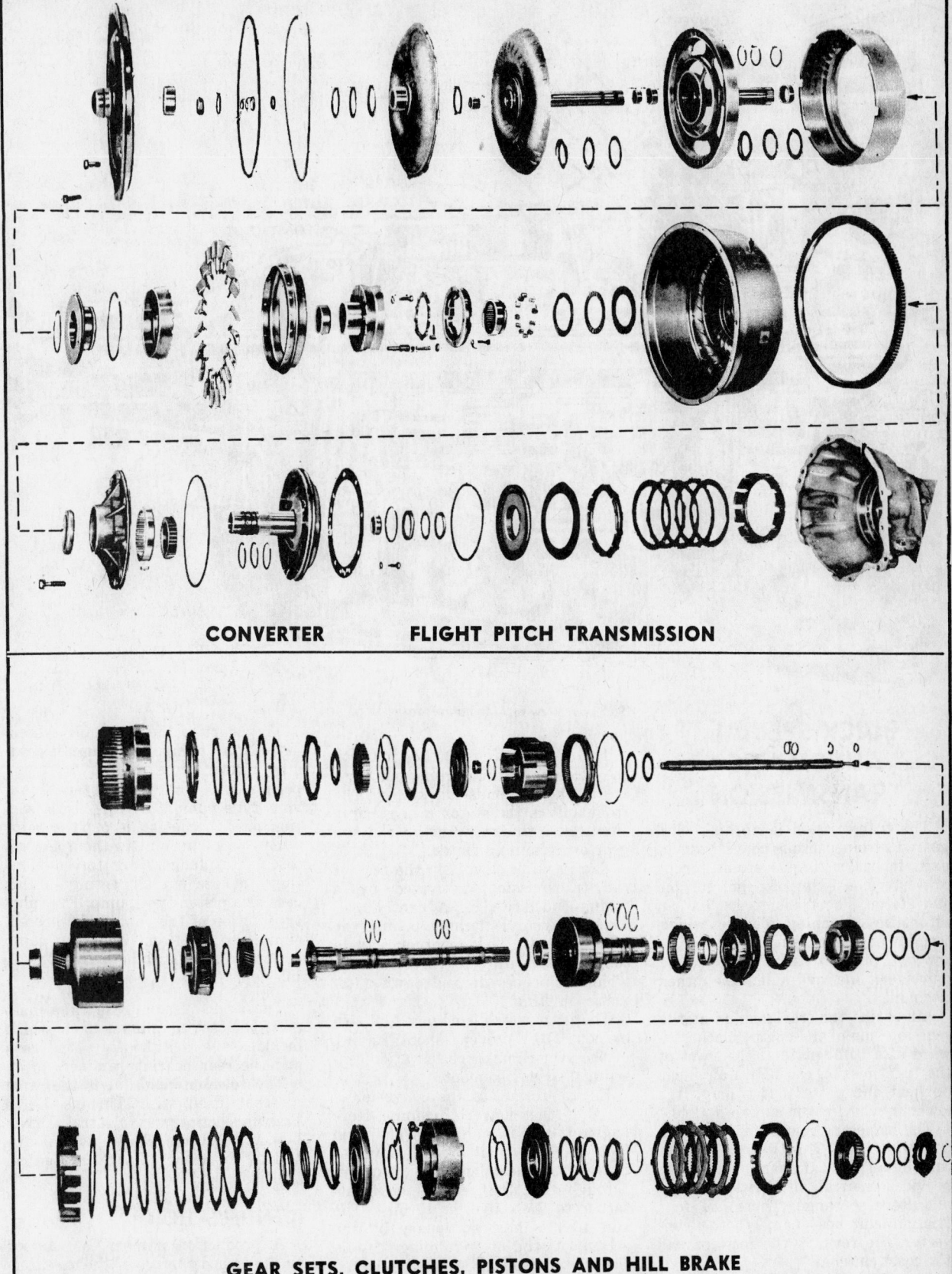

CONVERTER   FLIGHT PITCH TRANSMISSION

**GEAR SETS, CLUTCHES, PISTONS AND HILL BRAKE
FLIGHT PITCH TRANSMISSION**

BUICK AUTOMATIC TRANSMISSIONS

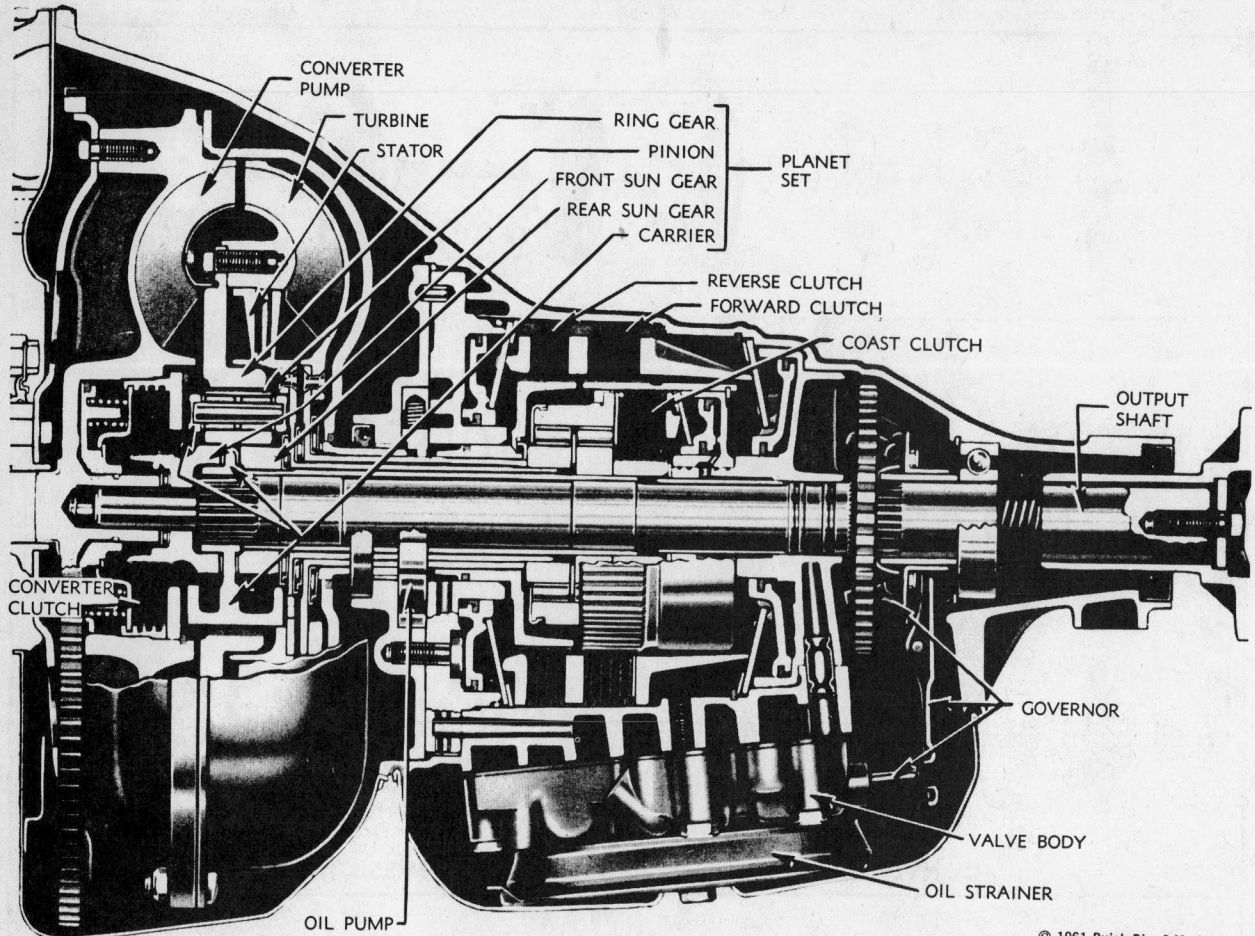

CONVERTER PUMP — TURBINE — STATOR — RING GEAR — PINION — FRONT SUN GEAR — REAR SUN GEAR — CARRIER — PLANET SET — REVERSE CLUTCH — FORWARD CLUTCH — COAST CLUTCH — OUTPUT SHAFT — CONVERTER CLUTCH — GOVERNOR — VALVE BODY — OIL STRAINER — OIL PUMP

Sectional View of Automatic Transmission.

© 1961 Buick Div. G.M. Corp.

BUICK SPECIAL AUTOMATIC TRANSMISSION

The transmission is an air-cooled, geared turbine, torque converter type unit. It has a three element torque converter consisting of pump, turbine and stator. The transmission has an automatic clutching device which permits engine output torque to follow two parallel paths through the converter, one hydraulic, the other mechanical.

Air enters the transmission at the rear top side of the engine block, forward of a baffle plate at the front of the transmission case. This air picks up heat and passes out through the lower flywheel cover at two outlets.

The planetary gear set is located in the converter. This gear set takes care of all the car manipulations. It provides Neutral, all Forward speeds and Reverse range. There are four friction clutches—namely: the converter, the reverse, the forward and the coast clutches.

The transmission has only one pump. This pump is driven off the engine through the converter pump

housing.

The over-running clutches for both the stator and the turbine sun gear are in the transmission proper. The front unit is the stator over-running clutch and the rear unit is the sun gear over-running clutch.

The Parking pawl is in the rear of the transmission, activated by a spring-loaded wedge. A centrifugal-type governor is located behind the parking pawl. The governor acts in conjunction with the throttle valve which influences up and down automatic shifting.

The coast clutch is engaged in park or neutral to prevent shock loading of the over-running clutch after centrifugal disengagement.

Engine torque to the converter is through the converter pump. Here engine torque is multiplied. The ratio is 2.4:1. The ouput of the converter is fed to the planetary gear set through the ring gear which is attached to the converter turbine. The sun gear is held stationary by the action of the over-running clutch. Torque multiplication of the planetary gear set is 1.58:1. The overall transmission torque ratio at stall is 3.8:1.

The heart of the hydraulic system is the front pump. This pump is actually a two stage affair. The outer periphery of the plungers act like a vane-type pump. There is also a suction port to the inside of the rotor which picks up oil. As the rotor rotates, the plungers are forced in so they squeeze out oil, acting in this case as a piston-type pump. The vane-type action of the pump is by-passed, similar to the front and rear pump action on the Turbine Drive Transmission.

The transmission case is a one-piece die-cast aluminum part, which includes the bell housing, the case and the rear bearing retainer.

The selector quadrant is the same as that used with Turbine Drive Transmission: Park, Neutral, Drive, Low and Reverse. The engine may be started in either Park or Neutral positions.

IDENTIFICATION

A production number is stamped on the raised surface of the case, forward of the oil pan, left side. This marking consists of a letter followed by one or more digits. Since this marking furnishes the key to construction and parts interchangiblity, this identification should be used when ordering part or discussing the unit.

FLUID

Capacity

12 pints

Quantity Marked on Dip Stick

1 pint graduations

Fluid Type

A.T. fluid type A, suffix A

Fluid Change Period

25,000 miles

ROAD TEST

With linkage correctly adjusted and car at normal operating temperature, take the car on the road. Observe general performance of transmission and check for abnormal noise.

Accelerate from a dead stop with accelerator down just to the detent. Up-shift should occur smoothly at between 40 and 45 M.P.H. If up-shift occurs at speeds other than those specified, refer to table of "trouble and possible causes."

TROUBLE SHOOTING CHART

TROUBLE	POSSIBLE CAUSE
Upshift at too low speed	Governor valve out of adjustment or sticking. Shift valve or regulator sticking. Throttle valve pressure low—
Upshift at too high speed	worn or broken spring or sticking valve. Governor valve not adjusted properly or sticking. Shift valve and regulator sticking. Throttle valve pressure too high—valve sticking.
Slow engagement of converter clutch	Converter pressure regulator valve sticking, lowering pressure too slow.
Fast engagement of converter clutch	Converter charging pressure too low, converter pressure regulator valve sticking.

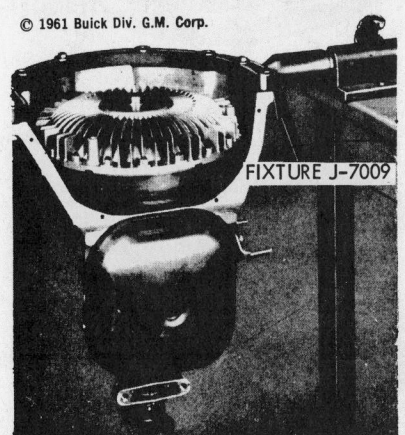

© 1961 Buick Div. G.M. Corp.

FIXTURE J-7009

Assembly in Holding Fixture.

© 1961 Buick Div. G.M. Corp.

SCREWDRIVER

SLOT

Removing Converter Pump.

1. Attach the transmission assembly to a holding fixture.
2. Remove converter pump to housing bolts and nuts.
3. Raise transmission to horizontal position. Provide a pail or other suitable container to catch the oil that drains from the conver-

CONVERTER AND GEAR SET:

REMOVE AND DISASSEMBLE

ter. Pry converter pump away from housing by using screwdriver in slots provided.
4. Remove converter pump and converter clutch assembly and allow to drain.
5. Remove front sun gear, needle thrust bearing, and two select fit thrust bearing races.
6. Slide planet carrier assembly out of ring gear and place on clean working surface.
7. Separate front and rear tanged thrust washers from planet carrier assembly. Check planet pinions for scoring, imbedded metal or looseness on the shaft. Worn or loose pinions require replacement of the carrier assembly. Imbedded metal may be picked out with a small screwdriver.
8. With transmission in a vertical position, remove rear sun gear and needle thrust bearing.
9. Lift turbine and stator assembly and turbine needle thrust bearing out of housing.
10. Lift converter pump housing out of transmission and set housing hub through hole in bench. To save space and for convenience while inspecting and gauging the converter, set the turbine and stator assembly and rear sun gear in the pump housing for the present.
11. Remove rear sun gear and needle thrust bearing from bench assembly. Check gear for scoring or other damage. Check babbitted inner surfaces of gear shaft. If babbitt is chipped or flared off,

© 1961 Buick Div. G.M. Corp.

CONVERTER PUMP AND CONVERTER CLUTCH ASSY.

Separating Converter Pump.

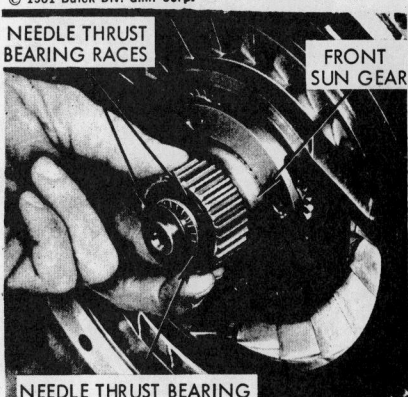

© 1961 Buick Div. G.M. Corp.

NEEDLE THRUST BEARING RACES

FRONT SUN GEAR

NEEDLE THRUST BEARING

Removing Sun Gear, Bearing and Thrust Race

rear sun gear must be replaced. Check needle thrust bearing for looseness or wear.
12. With ½" wrench, remove the three ring gear-to-turbine attaching bolts.
13. Lift ring gear off turbine. Examine ring gear for wear or

other damage.

14. Lift stator and needle thrust bearing out of turbine. Check stator for chipped or damaged vanes. Check babbitted inner surface of stator shaft. If babbitt is chipped or flaked off, the stator must be replaced. Check needle bearing for wear or looseness.

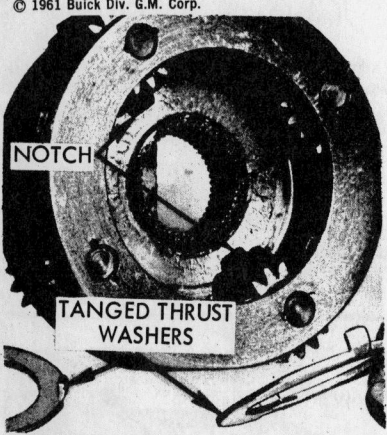

© 1961 Buick Div. G.M. Corp.

Planet Carrier with Tanged Thrust Washers.

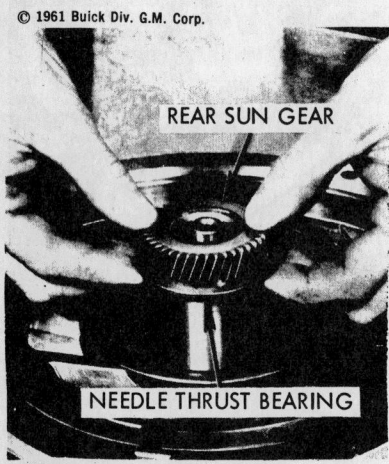

© 1961 Buick Div. G.M. Corp.

Removing Sun Gear and Needle Thrust.

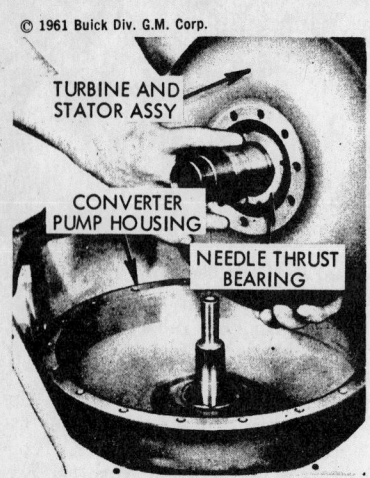

© 1961 Buick Div. G.M. Corp.

Removing Turbine and Stator with Thrust.

15. Lift turbine and needle thrust bearing out of converter pump cover. Examine all parts for chips, cracks, scores or other damage. Any imperfect parts must be replaced.

ASSEMBLE FOR CLEARANCE CHECK

1. Set converter pump housing hub through a hole in the work bench. Place turbine and needle thrust bearing that will be used at final assembly in the pump housing.
2. Set stator and needle thrust bearing that will be used in final assembly in the turbine.
3. Set ring gear in place on the turbine. Bolt holes are unevenly spaced, error in reassembly location is impossible.
4. Install ring gear to turbine bolts and torque to 15-20 ft. lb.
5. Set sun gear and needle thrust bearing in place.
6. Install tanged thrust washers in front and rear of planet carrier. Tangs in washers must engage notches in carrier.
7. Set carrier assembly with tanged thrust washers in place on rear sun gear. **Note:** Deep side of carrier assembly toward rear sun gear.
8. Examine front sun gear for wear or other damage. Be sure tanged washer is in place on forward side of planet carrier. Set front sun gear in place on planet carrier.
9. Set needle thrust bearing that will be used in final assembly and two select fit bearing races in place on top of front sun gear.
10. Set converter clearance gauge, tool #J-9157, on pump housing with longer legs "down" on housing. Loosen thumb screw and push plunger down to bear

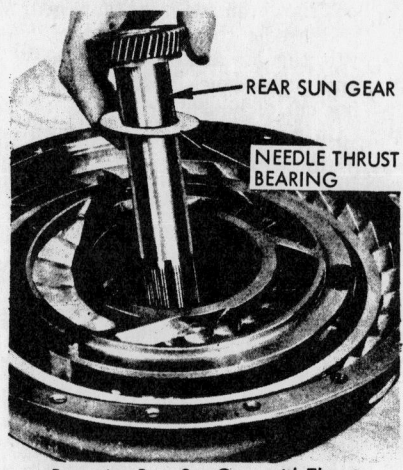

© 1961 Buick Div. G.M. Corp.

Removing Rear Sun Gear with Thrust.

on needle thrust bearing and races. Tighten thumb screw.

11. Turn gauge J-9157 over (short legs down) and place on converter pump. Assemble dial indicator to post with indicator bearing on plunger. "Zero" the indicator. Loosen the plunger thumb screw

© 1961 Buick Div. G.M. Corp.

Removing and Installing Ring Gear at Turbine.

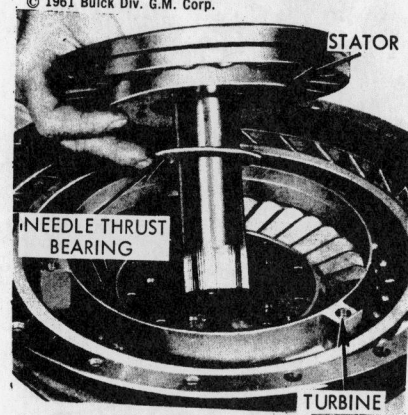

© 1961 Buick Div. G.M. Corp.

Removing and Installing Stator and Thrust at Turbine.

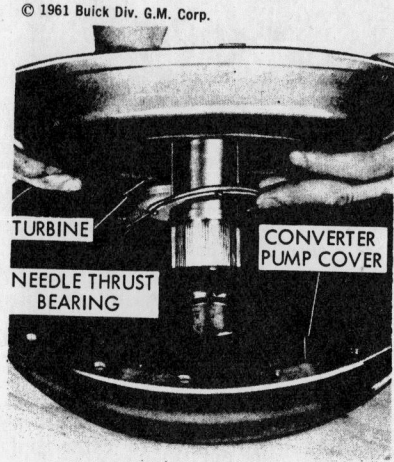

© 1961 Buick Div. G.M. Corp.

Assemble Converter for Clearance Check.

and observe the indicator reading.

Note: If, when the gauge is set in place on converter pump, the plunger holds the gauge up so the legs do not rest on the pump rim, indicator reading when thumb screw is released will be in compression, not clearance.

© 1961 Buick Div. G.M. Corp.

Installing Rear Sun Gear and Thrust

© 1961 Buick Div. G.M. Corp.

Installing Tanged Washers in Planet Carrier.

© 1961 Buick Div. G.M. Corp.

Installing Carrier with Thrusts in Rear Sun Gear.

If plunger drops when thumb screw is released, indicator reading will be in clearance, not compression.

Select needle thrust bearing rales to provide .010″ clearance to .005″ compression.

CONVERTER PUMP AND CLUTCH

DISASSEMBLE

1. Pry converter clutch housing retaining ring out of groove in the pump.
2. Lift converter clutch housing out of converter pump.
3. Remove clutch pack.
4. Remove converter clutch piston and apply-plate, (using pliers). Examine apply-plate for scoring or wear. Check piston bore in converter pump for scoring or pitting. Check inner bore of piston for wear or scoring.

Note: Piston and apply-plate is serviced as an assembly only.

5. Unhook, expand and remove converter clutch piston inner ring. Check for wear or scoring.
6. Remove and examine converter clutch outer piston ring.
7. Examine all parts for wear or other damage and replace as necessary.

ASSEMBLE

1. Examine converter pump for damaged vanes. Check for damaged or loose pump ring. Expand and install converter inner piston ring and hook the ends.
2. Position the clutch outer piston ring squarely in lower part of bore, (about ¼″ from the bottom). Measure ring gap with feeler gauge. Gap must be between .002″ and .007″. If gap is too little, file the ring. If gap is too large, replace the ring.
3. Install outer piston ring on converter clutch piston and apply-plate assembly.
4. Lubricate and push piston and apply-plate assembly into bore of converter pump.

Note: A chamfer in the bore assists in entering the ring in the bore.

5. Examine and measure converter clutch friction plates for wear, or burning. New plates are .079″-.084″ thick. Plates worn below .074″ should be replaced.
6. Dip a friction plate in transmission fluid and install in converter clutch housing.
7. Check a separator plate for "dish" with a straight-edge. All separator plates must be installed with the "dish" the same way.

© 1961 Buick Div. G.M. Corp.

Installing Front Sun Gear in Carrier

© 1961 Buick Div. G.M. Corp.

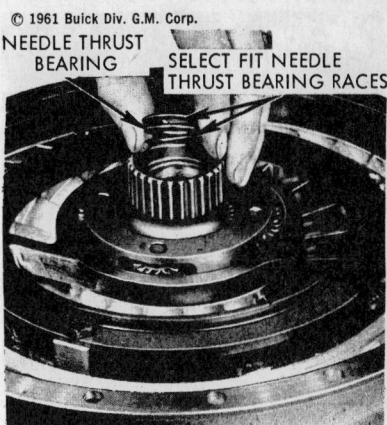

Installing Thrusts on Top of Front Sun Gear

© 1961 Buick Div. G.M. Corp.

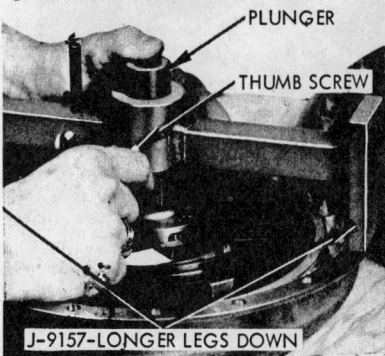

Measuring Converter Clearance.

© 1961 Buick Div. G.M. Corp.

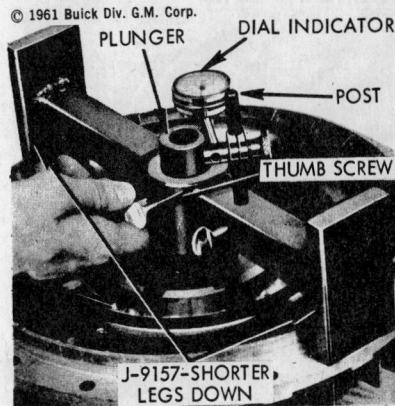

Measuring Converter Compression.

© 1961 Buick Div. G.M. Corp.

CONVERTER CLUTCH HOUSING

Removing Converter Clutch Housing.

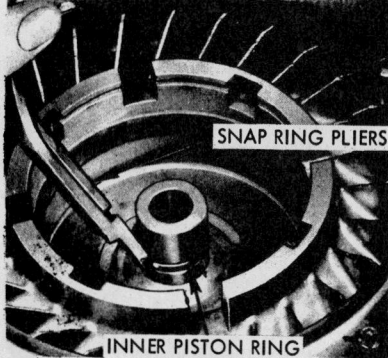

© 1961 Buick Div. G.M. Corp.

SNAP RING PLIERS

INNER PISTON RING

Removing and Installing Inner Ring.

© 1961 Buick Div. G.M. Corp.

APPLY PLATE

CONVERTER CLUTCH PISTON

Removing Converter Clutch Piston and Apply Plate.

© 1961 Buick Div. G.M. Corp.

OUTER PISTON RING

PISTON AND APPLY PLATE ASSY.

Removing and Installing Piston Outer Ring.

Continue alternately installing a lubed friction plate and a separator plate until four friction and three separator plates have been installed.

8. Rotate piston apply-plate so tangs of apply-plate are centered in openings of converter pump.

9. Lower the converter clutch housing and clutch pack assembly into the converter pump. Hold the clutch plates together with the fingers until the assembly is properly aligned. The long tangs of the housing must engage openings in the converter pump.

10. Install housing retaining ring over converter clutch housing in groove of converter pump. Seat the lock ring securely into the groove with a drift.

FRONT TRANSMISSION PUMP:

REMOVE

1. Remove bolts with special sealing lockwashers, with ½" socket wrench.

2. Lift pump body, with hand and pliers, clear of the case.

3. Lift pump assembly out of the case. Reverse clutch hub usually comes out with the pump. (Set reverse clutch hub aside.)

Note: A tanged thrust washer may be stuck on top of the stator overrunning clutch rale. It should be placed in the rear of the reverse clutch hub.

DISASSEMBLE

1. Blow the reverse clutch piston from the reverse clutch housing with compressed air.

2. Check clutch piston inner and outer seals for wear or other damage. If necessary to replace, remove the seals.

3. Remove and discard the oil pump body-to-case seal.

4. Remove reverse clutch piston housing-to-oil pump bolts.

5. Lift reverse clutch piston housing off the oil pump.

Note: Slipper sealing rings may stick to reverse clutch piston housing and be removed with the hosuing.

6. With a dial indicator mounted and "zeroed" on the oil pump body, shift the indicator plunger to bear on oil pump slippers one at a time. Slippers should be from .001" to .0028" below surface of oil pump body.

7. Then shift the plunger to rest on the rotor. Rotor should be from .001" to .0028" below oil pump body.

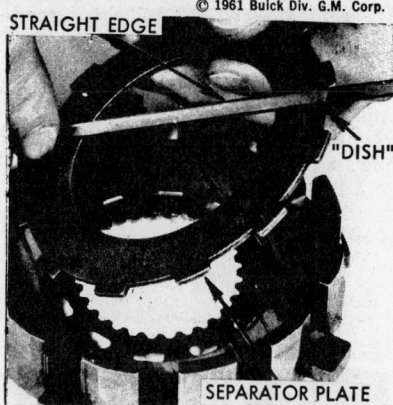

© 1961 Buick Div. G.M. Corp.

STRAIGHT EDGE

"DISH"

SEPARATOR PLATE

Checking Separator Plate.

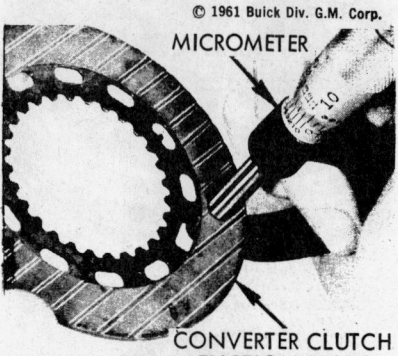

© 1961 Buick Div. G.M. Corp.

MICROMETER

CONVERTER CLUTCH FRICTION PLATE

Measuring Converter Clutch Plates.

© 1961 Buick Div. G.M. Corp.

PISTON AND APPLY PLATE ASSY.

Installing Piston and Apply Plate.

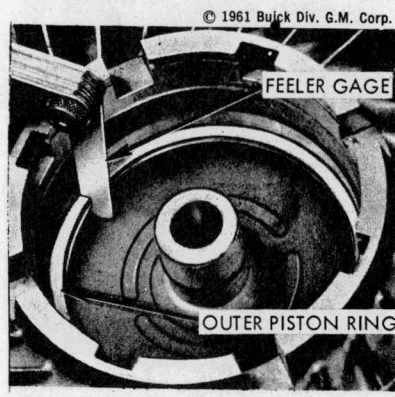

© 1961 Buick Div. G.M. Corp.

FEELER GAGE

OUTER PISTON RING

Checking Piston Outer Ring Gap.

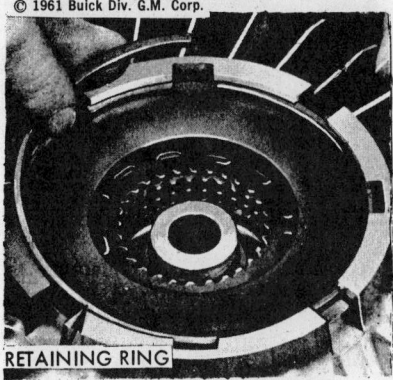

© 1961 Buick Div. G.M. Corp.

TANGS CENTERED IN OPENINGS

Locating Tangs.

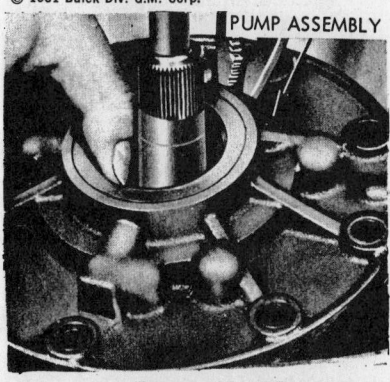

© 1961 Buick Div. G.M. Corp.

RETAINING RING

Installing Clutch Retainer.

© 1961 Buick Div. G.M. Corp.

PUMP ASSEMBLY

Removing Front Pump.

© 1961 Buick Div. G.M. Corp.

LONG TANGS IN OPENINGS

Installing Clutch Housing and Pack in Conver

8. Examine bushings; if worn or scored, remove rotor, slippers, springs and pins and replace bushings and seal with proper tools.

ASSEMBLE

1. Examine rotor, slippers, springs and pins for wear or other damage and replace where necessary. Install rotor with driving tangs "up" as shown in figure. Install slippers and springs as shown.
2. Install sealing pins. Lubricate the assembly with automatic transmission fluid.
3. Set severe clutch piston housing squarely in place on the pump body. Dowel pins are unevenly spaced so assembly is possible in only one position.
4. Install reverse clutch piston housing to pump body bolts and torque alternately and evenly to 15 to 20 ft. lb.
5. Install new oil pump body-to-transmission case sealing ring.
6. Install reverse clutch piston inner seal with lip toward front of piston.
7. Install reverse clutch piston outer seal with lip toward front of piston.
8. Lubricate seals and install piston in the housing using a loop of smooth wire to start the lips of the seals into the bore.

Note: The inner seal lip should be started first. A satisfactory lip starting tool can be made by crimping a loop of .020" music wire in a piece of copper tubing.

REVERSE CLUTCH COMPONENTS

REMOVE AND INSPECT

1. Remove lever assembling ring and apply levers. Check levers for wear or distortion: Lift out reverse clutch hub, select fit thrust washer on the front side and tanged thrust washer on the rear.

Note: Reverse clutch hub and thrust washers may have been removed with pump.

2. Remove reverse clutch hub oil ring. Examine ring for wear. Remove select fit thrust washer. Examine washer and hub for wear or other damage.
3. Remove tanged thrust washer at rear of clutch hub.
4. Remove bellville, (dished) reverse clutch release spring.
5. Remove reverse clutch pressure plate. Check for plate wear.
6. Remove reverse clutch pack. Examine for wear, burning and

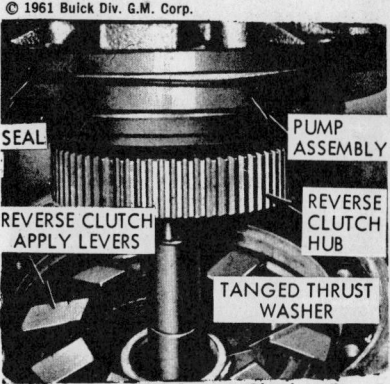

© 1961 Buick Div. G.M. Corp.

SEAL   **PUMP ASSEMBLY**

REVERSE CLUTCH APPLY LEVERS   **REVERSE CLUTCH HUB**

TANGED THRUST WASHER

Lifting Pump with Reverse Clutch Hub.

© 1961 Buick Div. G.M. Corp.

REVERSE CLUTCH PISTON

REVERSE CLUTCH PISTON APPLY HOLE

AIR HOSE NOZZLE

Disassembling Reverse Clutch.

© 1961 Buick Div. G.M. Corp.

OIL PUMP BODY

OIL PUMP BODY TO CASE SEAL

Oil Pump Body to Case Seal.

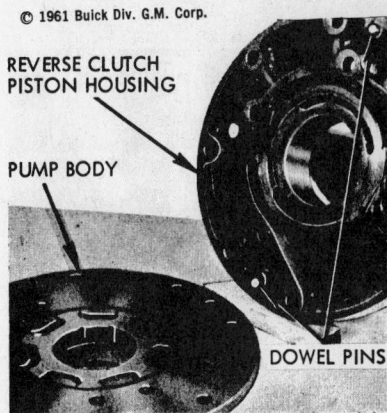

© 1961 Buick Div. G.M. Corp.

REVERSE CLUTCH PISTON HOUSING

PUMP BODY

DOWEL PINS

Removing Reverse Clutch Piston Housing.

Mounting Dial Indicator on Pump.

.001" TO .0028" BELOW PUMP BODY

Measuring Oil Pump Body Slippers.

ROTOR - .001" TO .0028" BELOW PUMP BODY

Measuring Oil Pump Rotor to Body.

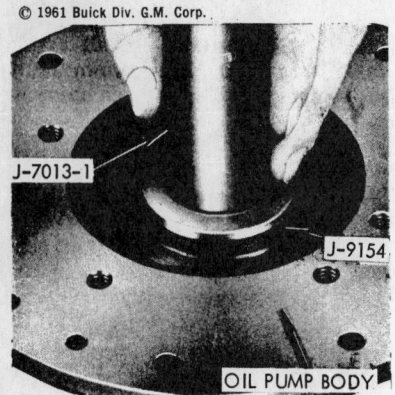

Checking Bushing for Wear and Score.

scoring.

7. Measure thickness of friction plates. New Friction plates are .079"-.084" thick. Plates worn below .074" should be replaced.

COAST AND OVERRUNNING CLUTCH ASSEMBLY:

FORWARD CLUTCH PACK, RELEASE SPRING AND APPLY LEVERS

REMOVE

1. Remove forward and reverse clutch anchor.
2. Rotate forward and reverse clutch backing plate to disengage lugs from slots in case. Remove backing plate. Examine plate for wear or scoring.
3. Grasp overrunning clutch cam and roller retainer and lift complete coast-clutch, overrunning-clutch and forward-clutch pack out of transmission.

Note: The rear externally splined clutch plate will remain in the transmission on forward clutch pressure plate. Remove remaining plate and place with forward clutch pack.

4. Lift forward clutch pack off the coast-clutch housing. Examine plates for wear.

Installing New Pump Bushing.

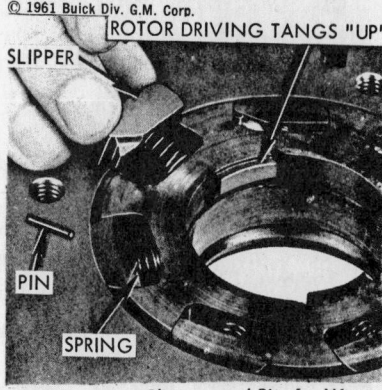

Checking Rotor, Slippers and Pins for Wear.

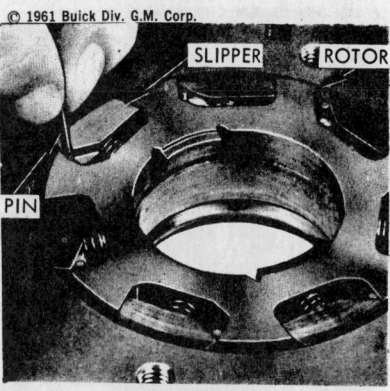

Installing Sealing Pins.

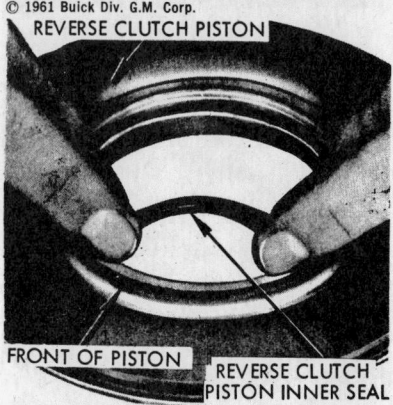

Installing Reverse Clutch Piston Inner Seal.

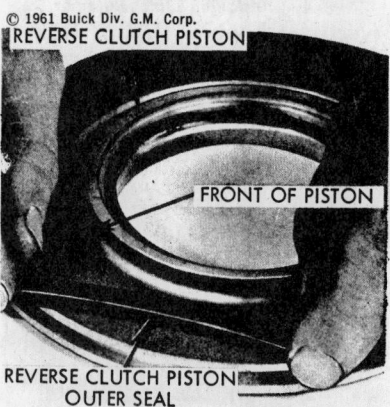

Installing Reverse Clutch Piston Outer Seal.

Installing Reverse Clutch Piston.

APPLY LEVERS

ASSEMBLING RING

Removing Apply Levers and Ring.

REVERSE CLUTCH HUB

HOOKED OIL RING

SELECT FIT THRUST WASHER

Removing Reverse Clutch Hub Oil Ring.

REVERSE CLUTCH RELEASE SPRING

Removing Reverse Clutch Release Spring.

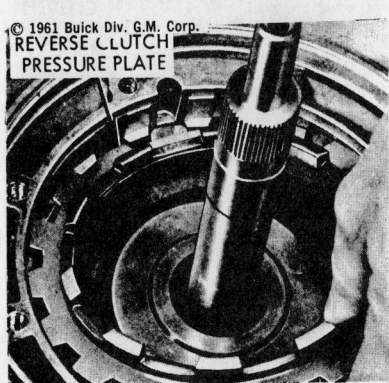

REVERSE CLUTCH PRESSURE PLATE

Removing Reverse Clutch Pressure Plate.

5. Measure forward clutch friction plates. When new the friction plates measure .079" to .084" thick. Renew any plates worn below .074" thickness.
6. Remove forward clutch pressure plate. Examine for cracks, heat discoloration or worn spots where levers contact plate.
7. Pry forward clutch release spring retaining ring out of groove in case. Remove the retaining ring.
8. Remove bellville, (dished) forward clutch release spring.
9. Remove forward clutch apply levers. Check levers for wear or bending.

COAST AND OVERRUNNING CLUTCH

DISMANTLE

1. Place the coast and overrunning clutch assembly in a compression tool. Provide support that will permit the assembly to rest on the lower edge of the coast clutch housing. Compress the tool to relieve pressure on the coast clutch cylinder-to-housing retaining ring. Pry lock ring out of groove in the housing.
2. Gradually release pressure on the compression tool and lift the coast clutch piston and cylinder out of the housing with the aid of pliers.
3. Check piston inner and outer seals for wear or other damage.
4. Remove coast clutch hub to coast clutch support thrust washer.
5. Remove coast clutch apply levers and clutch release spring.
6. Remove pressure plate.
7. Remove clutch pack and hub.
8. Check all parts for wear or other damage and mike the friction plates. Proper thickness is .079" to .084". Plates worn thinner than .074" should be replaced.
9. Pry cam retaining ring out of the groove and remove it.
10. Tilt clutch housing and remove the clutch backing plate and overrunning clutch assembly.

REVERSE CLUTCH PACK

Remove Reverse Clutch Pack.

FORWARD AND REVERSE CLUTCH ANCHOR

Remove Forward and Reverse Clutch Anchor.

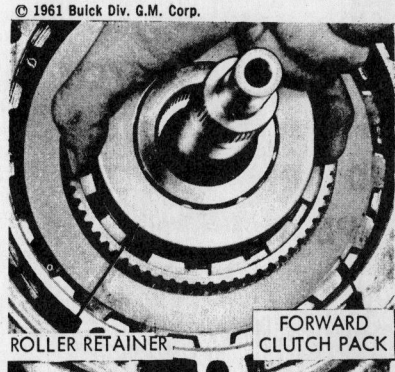

FORWARD AND REVERSE CLUTCH BACKING PLATE

Releasing Forward and Reverse Clutch Lugs.

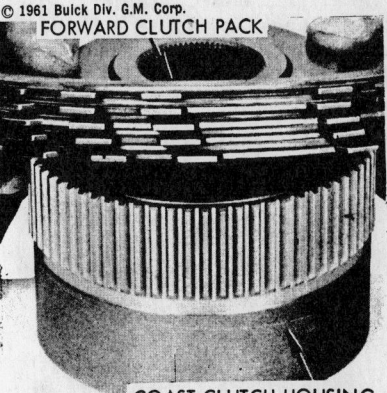

ROLLER RETAINER

FORWARD CLUTCH PACK

Removing Forward Clutch with Coast Clutch.

FORWARD CLUTCH PACK

COAST CLUTCH HOUSING

Removing Forward Clutch Pack.

BUICK AUTOMATIC TRANSMISSIONS

FORWARD CLUTCH PISTON

APPLY LEVERS COAST CLUTCH SUPPORT

Removing Front Clutch Pressure Plate.

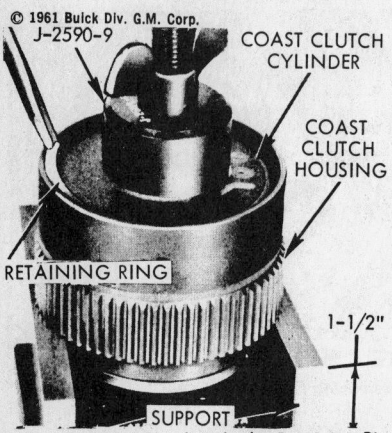

FORWARD CLUTCH PRESSURE PLATE

Removing Front Clutch Apply Levers.

J-2590-9

COAST CLUTCH CYLINDER

COAST CLUTCH HOUSING

RETAINING RING

1-1/2"

SUPPORT

Removing Coast Clutch Cylinder Retaining Ring.

COAST CLUTCH CYLINDER AND PISTON ASSEMBLY

COAST CLUTCH HOUSING

Removing Coast Clutch Piston and Cylinder.

---

11. Pull rear sun gear race out of the cam assembly. Rollers and springs will fall out.
12. Remove roller thrust washer.
13. Pull stator race out of cam. Rollers and springs will fall out.
Note: If cam must be replaced, drive off roller retainer and stake in place on new cam.

COAST AND OVERRUNNING CLUTCH

ASSEMBLE

1. Clean and examine all parts and lay them out on a thoroughly clean surface prior to assembly.
2. Place stator race inside cam. Assemble rollers and springs as illustrated.
Note: Stator race has larger splined I.D. than rear sun gear race.
3. Lubricate and install thrust washer on stator race.
4. Set rear sun gear cam in place on thrust washer. Assemble rollers and springs as shown.
5. Install cam and race assembly in coast clutch housing. Rotate cam assembly so lugs on cam engage notches in coast clutch housing.
6. Set assembly on blocks or other support that will permit the

COAST CLUTCH PISTON COAST CLUTCH CYLINDER

Removing Piston from Cylinder.

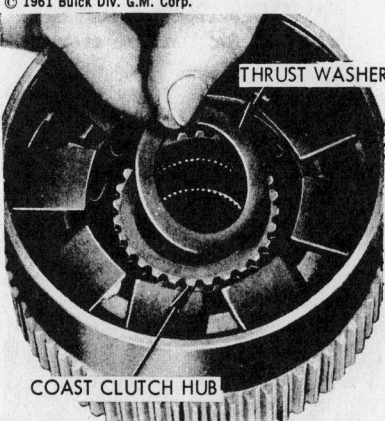

THRUST WASHER

COAST CLUTCH HUB

Removing Coast Clutch Thrust Washer.

APPLY LEVERS

Removing Coast Clutch Apply Levers.

COAST CLUTCH RELEASE SPRING

Removing Coast Clutch Release Spring.

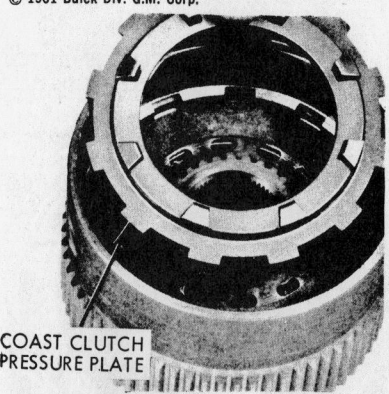

COAST CLUTCH PRESSURE PLATE

Removing Coast Clutch Pressure Plate.

COAST CLUTCH HOUSING

COAST CLUTCH PACK

COAST CLUTCH HUB

Removing Coast Clutch Pack.

lower edge of the clutch housing to carry the load.

7. Install clutch backing plate on cam and race assembly.

8. Install retaining ring in groove of coast-clutch housing above baking plate.

9. Set coast clutch hub in place on rear sun gear race.

10. Lubricate a coast-clutch friction plate with A.T. fluid and install on backing plate with splines engaged with hub splines.

11. Check a coast-clutch separator plate for "dish" with a straight edge. Note the direction of "dish" and continue alternately to install a lubed friction plate, then a seperator plate until five friction plates and four separator plates have been installed.

12. Install pressure plate on top of last friction plate. Engage lugs in notches of clutch housing.

13. Install bellville (dished) clutch release spring on the pressure plate with inner edge of spring "UP."

14. Install apply levers, concave edge "IN", between the lugs of the pressure plate and flat on the release spring. Apply a small daub of clean chassis lube on each lever to hold it in place.

15. Set thrust washer in place on top of coast-clutch hub.

COAST CLUTCH BACKING PLATE — RETAINING RING

Removing Cam Retaining Ring.

CAM ASSY — SUN GEAR RACE — COAST CLUTCH BACKING PLATE

Removing Backing Plate and Overrunning Clutch.

16. Install inner and outer piston seals with lips toward the rear of the piston.

17. Lubricate seals and install piston in bore of clutch cylinder. Use a loop of piano wire to start the lips of the seals into the bore.

   Note: Start the inner seal first.

18. Make sure thrust washer and all apply levers are in place. Install cylinder and piston assembly squarely in bore of clutch housing.

19. Place the coast and overrunning clutch assembly in a compression tool. Compress the tool to a point where the piston cylinder retainer groove in the clutch housing is exposed. Install and secure retaining ring in the clutch housing groove. Remove the compression tool.

20. Insert rear sun gear in sun gear race. Revolve sun gear, as illustrated, to check for binding or drag on the coast-clutch. Excessive drag may indicate "dished" separator plates all not stacked the same way, or that foreign material is present. Correct if necessary. The sun gear overrunning clutch should not permit rotation opposite arrow direction.

THRUST WASHER — STATOR RACE

Removing Roller Thrust.

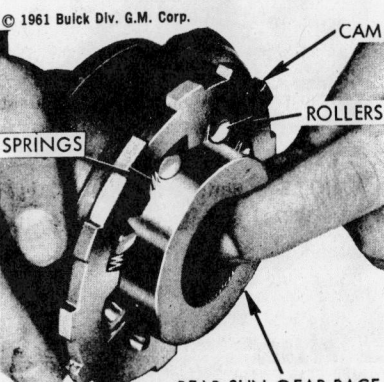

CAM — ROLLERS — SPRINGS — REAR SUN GEAR RACE

Removing Rear Sun Gear from Clutch Cam.

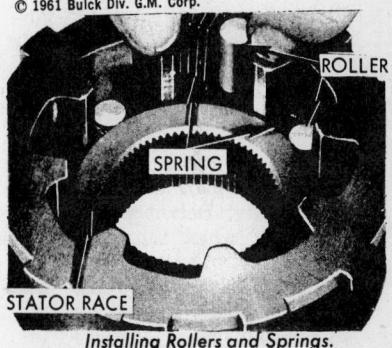

ROLLER — SPRING — STATOR RACE

Installing Rollers and Springs.

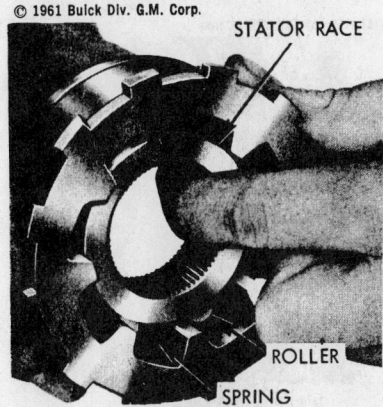

STATOR RACE — ROLLER — SPRING

Removing Stator Race.

COAST CLUTCH BACKING PLATE — CAM AND RACE ASSY — COAST CLUTCH HOUSING — 1-1/2"

Installing Race.

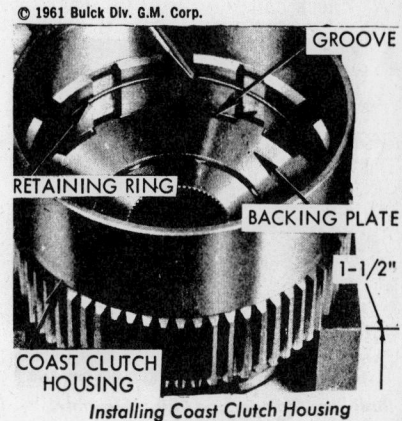

GROOVE — RETAINING RING — BACKING PLATE — 1-1/2" — COAST CLUTCH HOUSING

Installing Coast Clutch Housing Retaining Ring.

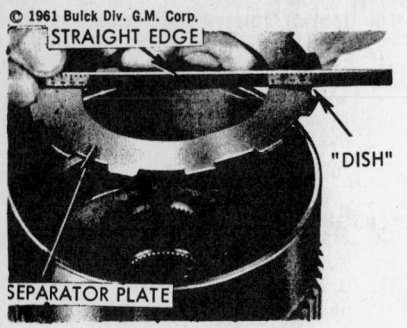

Checking Separator Plates.

OIL PAN AND VALVE BODY:

REMOVE

1. Remove oil pan bolt and gasket with a 1/2" socket wrench. Remove oil pan and seal.
2. Remove strainer strap bolts with a 7/16" wrench. Remove strap, strainer and strainer "O" ring.
3. Use needle nose pliers to remove parking lock pawl disengaging spring.
4. Remove remaining valve body attaching bolts. Remove valve body assembly.

Note: Take care, some of the valves can fall out.

DISASSEMBLE

1. Remove range selector and governor valve. Tilt the valve body to remove governor valve pin.
2. Remove throttle detent valve and throttle pressure regulator valve spring.
3. Remove two screws attaching valve body plate and gaskets to valve body. Detent poppet may slide out when screws are removed.
4. Remove valve body plate and gaskets. Check gaskets for leakage or damage.
5. Remove selector lever detent poppet and spring. Then remove check ball.

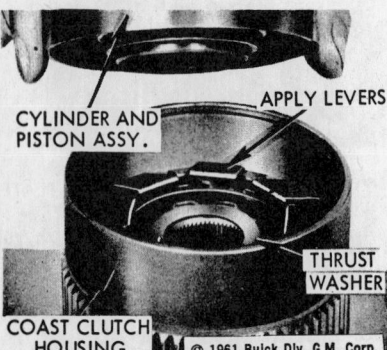

Installing Cylinder and Piston Assembly.

6. Remove pressure regulator valve stop.
7. Tilt valve body and remove throttle pressure regulator valve.
8. Press in on governor valve sleeve to release spring pressure on retainer. Invert valve body to allow removal of retainer. Remove sleeve and second stage governor valve spring.
9. Tilt valve body and remove second stage governor valve.
10. Remove two screws attaching oil gauge rod guide to the valve body. Remove the guide. Firmly hold valve retaining plate and remove the two screws holding the plate to the valve body. Release the plate carefully against pressure of three springs behind the plate. Remove plate and gasket.
11. Tilt valve body and remove the valves, sleeves and springs. Clean all the parts and the valve body in clean solvent. Inspect valves and valve body for wear or damage. Be sure the small holes in the converter pressure regulator, governor, and throttle pressure regulator valves are clear. Also be sure of the .032" hole in the valve body plate. Thoroughly dry the valve body and parts

Installing Clutch Release Spring.

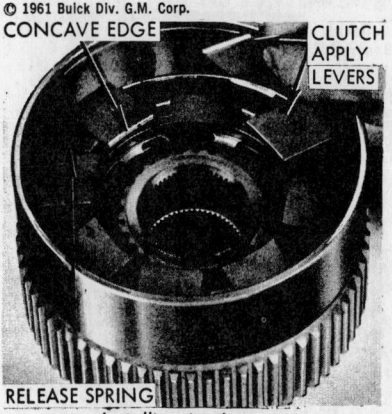

Installing Apply Levers.

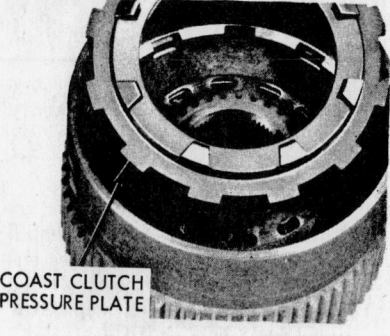

Installing Pressure Plate.

with a clean, dry, air blast. All valves must be free to move of their own weight.

REASSEMBLE

1. Begin the reassembly of valve body by installing the converter pressure regulator, shift and main line pressure regulator valves, sleeves and springs according to the exploded view. Use new valve plate-to-body gasket. Install plate and oil gauge rod guide. Install and tighten screws.
2. Install throttle pressure regulator valve. Tilt valve body so valve slides to the bottom of the bore.
3. With throttle pressure regulator valve at the bottom of it's bore, install throttle pressure regulator valve stop.
4. Install second stage governor valve.
5. Install second stage governor valve spring, sleeve and retainer. Press in on sleeve and install retainer through valve body in wide slot of sleeve.
6. Install check ball.
7. Install detent poppet and spring.
8. With new gaskets, one on each side of the valve body plate, position plate on valve body.

Note: It will be necessary to depress the detent poppet to permit

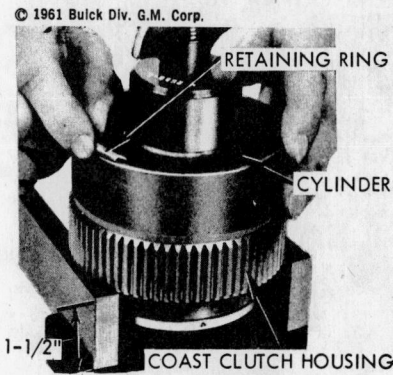

Installing Retaining Ring.

OIL PAN   1/2" SOCKET

SEAL

Removing Oil Pan.

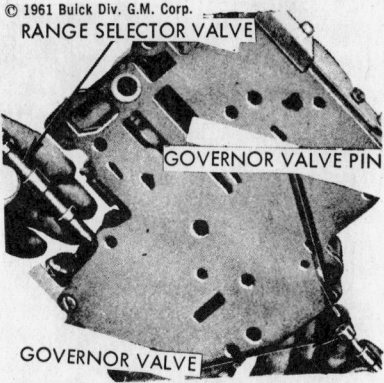

RANGE SELECTOR VALVE

GOVERNOR VALVE PIN

GOVERNOR VALVE

Governor Valve and Pin.

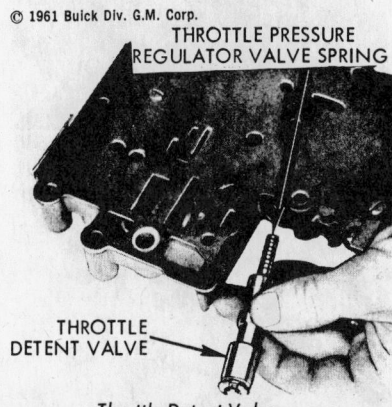

THROTTLE PRESSURE REGULATOR VALVE SPRING

THROTTLE DETENT VALVE

Throttle Detent Valve.

PLATE   GASKETS

DETENT POPPET

Valve Body Plate and Gasket.

plate attaching screws to be started.

Both inner and outer service gaskets are the same, while inner and outer production gaskets are not. Always use two new **service** gaskets when reassembling the valve body.

9. With the detent poppet in place, install the plate attaching screws. Do not over-tighten as the gasket may be damaged.
10. Install throttle detent valve and throttle pressure regulator valve spring.
11. Install range selector valve, governor valve and pin.

<u>Note:</u> If coast clutch support is to be removed, set valve body aside for the present. Refer to text covering "Valve Body, Replace."

COMPANION FLANGE AND SEAL:

REMOVE

1. Engage the parking lock pawl and remove the companion flange attaching bolt (5/8" socket). Tap flange off the output shaft.
2. Pry the old seal out of the case.

<u>Note:</u> This operation may be performed with the transmission in the car by using care to avoid spline damage to the output shaft.

INSTALL

1. With a good sealing compound applied to the outer metal circumference of the seal, enter the seal in place in the transmission.
2. With an appropriate tool, tap the seal into the bottom of the transmission case bore.
3. Engage parking lock pawl. Lubricate companion flange and tap it into place on the output shaft.
4. Install attaching bolt and torque to 45-55 ft. lb.

OUTPUT SHAFT, COAST CLUTCH SUPPORT, FORWARD CLUTCH PISTON, PARKING LOCK RATCHET WHEEL AND GOVERNOR ASSEMBLY:

REMOVE THE ASSEMBLY AS A UNIT

1. Remove the companion flange. Use tool #J-6586, or other suitable puller, to remove three adapter sleeves and retainer out of the transmission case and coast clutch support. Discard the "O" rings.

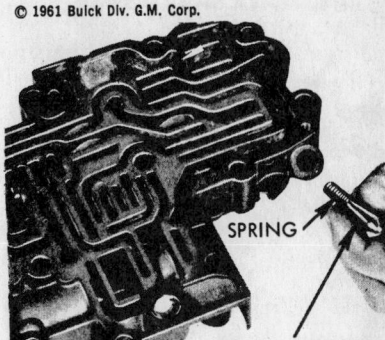

SPRING

DETENT POPPET

Selector Detent Poppet.

CHECK BALL

Poppet Detent Check Ball.

THROTTLE PRESSURE REGULATOR VALVE STOP

Pressure Regulator Valve Stop.

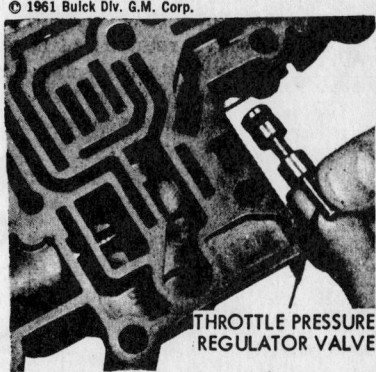

THROTTLE PRESSURE REGULATOR VALVE

Pressure Regulator Valve.

BUICK AUTOMATIC TRANSMISSIONS

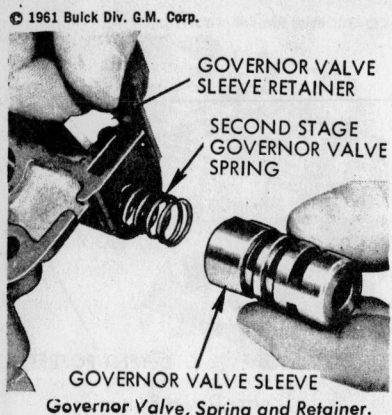

GOVERNOR VALVE
SLEEVE RETAINER

SECOND STAGE
GOVERNOR VALVE
SPRING

GOVERNOR VALVE SLEEVE

Governor Valve, Spring and Retainer.

SCREWS

DETENT POPPET

Proper Tightening of Plate and Gasket.

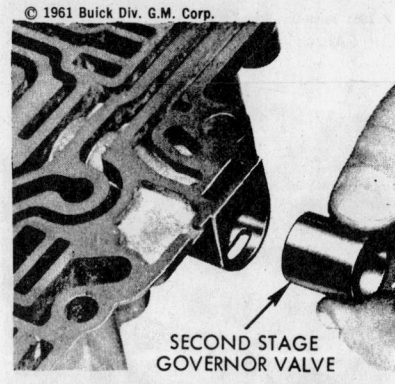

SECOND STAGE
GOVERNOR VALVE

Second Stage Governor Valve.

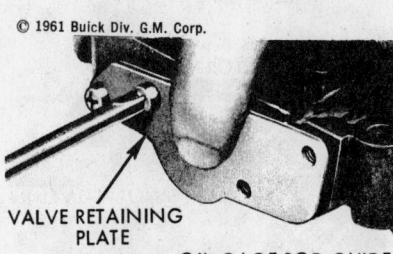

VALVE RETAINING
PLATE

OIL GAGE ROD GUIDE

Valve Retaining Plate.

2. Pull output shaft forward to remove shaft, coast clutch support, parking lock ratchet wheel and governor as an assembly. Speedometer gear will be pulled off the output shaft as the shaft is pulled through the rear bearing. Remove gear through companion flange seal.

DISASSEMBLE ABOVE UNIT

1. Slide governor lever actuating sleeve, needle thrust bearing, thrust bearing race and parking lock ratchet wheel spacer off rear of output shaft. Examine all parts for wear or other damage.
2. Slide governor weight and retainer assembly off rear of output shaft. Check roll-pins for looseness in weights.
3. Slide coast clutch support and forward clutch piston assembly off forward end of output shaft.
4. Examine two hooked oil rings on output shaft just forward of parking lock ratchet wheel. If worn or scored, unhook, expand and remove the rings.

5. If parking lock ratchet wheel is worn or broken, remove the retaining ring on the output shaft and slide the wheel forward and off the shaft.

Assemble—Ratchet Wheel and Output Shaft

1. Install ratchet wheel on output shaft with spline chamfer toward rear of shaft.
2. Position ratchet wheel rearward on output shaft splines. Expand and install lock ring solidly in groove of output shaft.
3. Expand and install two hooked oil rings in grooves of output shaft.

Disassemble—Coast Clutch Support and Forward Clutch Piston

1. Cover the assembly with lint free material to protect against oil spatter. Then direct com-

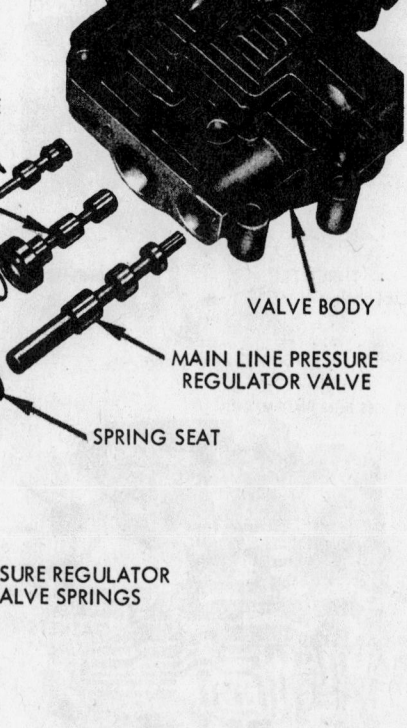

CONVERTER PRESSURE
REGULATOR VALVE

SHIFT VALVE

SPRING

SHIFT VALVE SPRING

SHIFT REGULATOR
VALVE SLEEVE

SHIFT REGULATOR VALVE

VALVE RETAINING
PLATE GASKET

VALVE RETAINING PLATE

VALVE BODY

MAIN LINE PRESSURE
REGULATOR VALVE

SPRING SEAT

PRESSURE REGULATOR
VALVE SPRINGS

OIL GAGE
ROD GUIDE

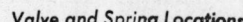

Valve and Spring Locations.

pressed air into center oil transfer sleeve hole to remove forward clutch piston from coast clutch support.

2. Examine two hooked oil rings on coast clutch support. If worn or damaged, remove the rings. Examine inner bore of support where output shaft oil rings contact support for wear or scoring.

3. Examine inner and outer forward clutch piston seals. If worn or damaged remove the seals.

Reassemble—Coast Clutch Support and Forward Clutch Piston

1. Install and hook ends of oil rings on coast clutch support.

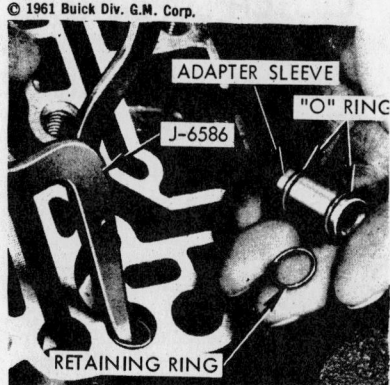

Companion Flange Adaptor Sleeves.

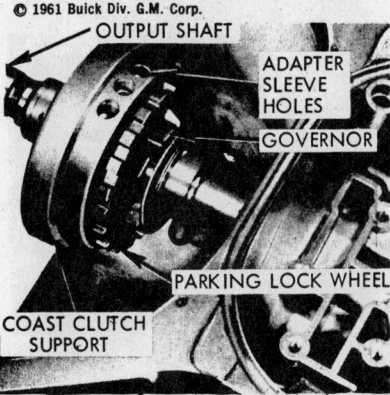

Output Shaft with Governor and Parking Lock.

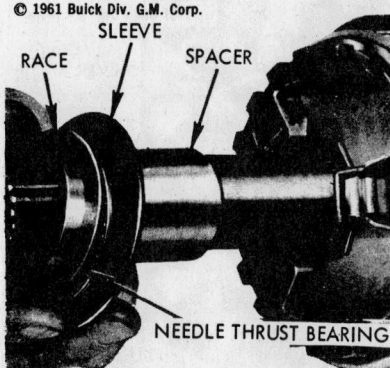

Output Shaft Thrust Bearing.

2. Install forward clutch piston outer seal on piston, (lip of seal toward rear of piston).

3. Install forward clutch piston inner seal, (lip of seal toward rear of piston).

4. Lubricate seals and install forward clutch piston in coast clutch support. A loop of smooth steel wire may be used as an aid in starting the seal lip into the piston bore.

Note: Start inner seal lip first.

Reassemble—Output Shaft, Coast Clutch Support, Forward Clutch Piston, Parking Lock Ratchet Wheel and Governor Assembly

1. Lubricate oil rings and slide coast clutch support and forward clutch piston assembly on the output shaft.

2. Slide governor weight retainer and governor weight assembly on rear of output shaft. Be certain weights and retainers are positioned as illustrated. Inner tangs of retainers must be inside the openings of parking lock ratchet wheel. Forward end of the weights must also be inside openings of wheel.

3. Lubricate needle thrust bearing and slide spacer, sleeve, needle thrust bearing and race on rear of output shaft. Position against governor weights.

GOVERNOR LEVER AND PIN:

REMOVE AND REPLACE

1. If lever is damaged or the pin hole is badly worn, remove pin retaining plug in side of transmission case. Slide pin out of the case and lever. Replace parts as necessary. Install pin through the case and lever. Install retaining plug.

TRANSMISSION REAR BEARING:

REMOVE

1. Remove governor lever and pin. If bearing is defective, pry bearing lock out of groove in case.

2. Drive bearing out of case using a drift inserted from the rear.

INSTALL

1. Drive new bearing squarely into case with special tool #J-9164 or other suitable driver.

2. Start one end of bearing lock into groove above bearing. Form

a ramp with a screwdriver inserted between case and lock. Push lock down the ramp and into groove with second screwdriver.

RANGE SELECTOR LEVERS AND SHAFT, THROTTLE VALVE CONTROL LEVERS AND SHAFT AND PARKING LOCK ACTUATOR:

Remove—Inner Throttle Valve Control Lever

1. Use clutch head screwdriver and 7/16″ wrench to remove screw

Governor Weight and Retainer.

Forward Clutch Assy.

Oil Rings on Output Shaft.

and nut that hold the inner throttle valve control lever to the shaft.

2. Slide inner lever off shaft and remove. Slide outer lever and shaft out of range-selector shaft. Check "O" ring, if damaged remove the "O" ring.

Remove—Range Selector Levers and Shaft and Parking Lock Actuator

1. Use clutch head screwdriver and 7/16" wrench to remove screw and nut that hold the range selector inner lever to the shaft.

2. Slide range selector inner lever off selector shaft. Remove inner lever and parking lock actuator assembly. If actuator or inner selector lever requires replacement, snap off actuator retainer and assemble new parts as necessary. Check shaft "O" ring and replace if necessary.

Install—Range Selector Levers and Shaft

1. Install and lubricate "O" ring. Slide shaft through case and carefully align splines on shaft and inner lever. Hold outer lever and shaft "in" against case and push inner lever completely on shaft.

© 1961 Buick Div. G.M. Corp.

HOOKED OIL RINGS

PARKING LOCK RATCHET WHEEL

Oil Rings on Output Shaft.

© 1961 Buick Div. G.M. Corp.

FORWARD CLUTCH PISTON

COAST CLUTCH SUPPORT

AIR NOZZLE

Coast Clutch Support and Forward Clutch Piston.

2. Install and tighten the attaching screw and nut.

Install—Throttle Valve Control Levers and Shaft

1. Assemble special washer and "O" ring on throttle control lever shaft. Lubricate the "O" ring. Slide the shaft into the range selector shaft.

2. Carefully align splines on shaft with splines on inner lever. Press lever on shaft completely. Install and tighten clutch head screw and nut.

OUTPUT SHAFT, COAST CLUTCH SUPPORT, FORWARD CLUTCH PISTON, PARKING LOCK RATCHET WHEEL AND GOVERNOR ASSEMBLY:

INSTALL THE ASSEMBLY AS A UNIT

1. Lubricate the coast clutch support O.D. and position the support so the oil holes are "up." Hold the governor assembly in

© 1961 Buick Div. G.M. Corp.

HOOKED OIL RINGS

COAST CLUTCH SUPPORT

Coast Clutch Support Oil Ring.

© 1960 Buick Div. G.M. Corp.

REAR OF PISTON

PISTON INNER SEAL

CLUTCH PISTON

Forward Clutch Piston—Inner Seal.

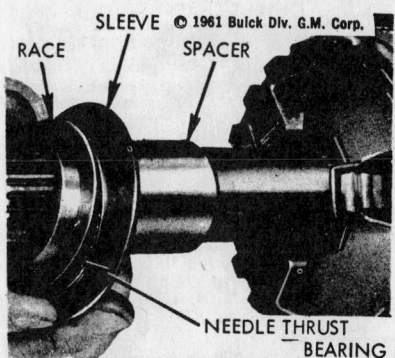

RACE   SLEEVE © 1961 Buick Div. G.M. Corp.   SPACER

NEEDLE THRUST BEARING

Thrust Bearing Arrangement.

REAR OF PISTON © 1961 Buick Div. G.M. Corp.

PISTON OUTER SEAL

FORWARD CLUTCH PISTON

Forward Clutch Piston—Outer Seal.

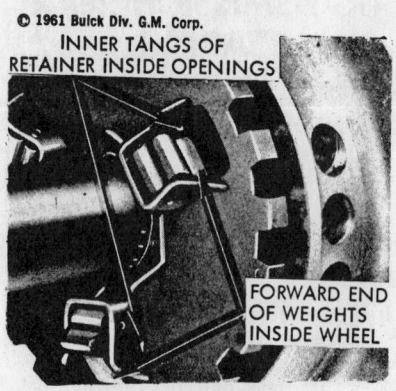

© 1961 Buick Div. G.M. Corp.

INNER TANGS OF RETAINER INSIDE OPENINGS

FORWARD END OF WEIGHTS INSIDE WHEEL

Governor Weight Plan.

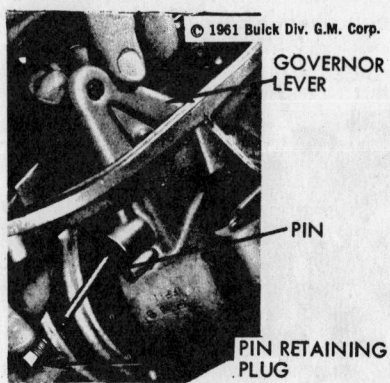

© 1961 Buick Div. G.M. Corp.

GOVERNOR LEVER

PIN

PIN RETAINING PLUG

Governor Lever Replacement.

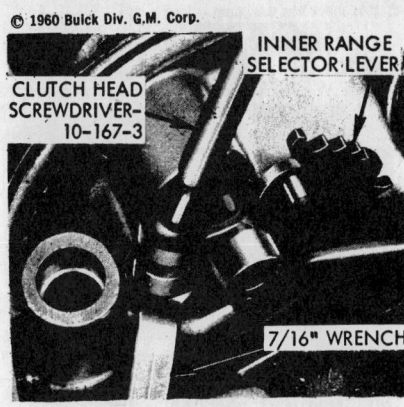

© 1960 Buick Div. G.M. Corp.

CLUTCH HEAD
SCREWDRIVER-
10-167-3

INNER RANGE
SELECTOR LEVER

7/16" WRENCH

A Screw and Nut Clamp Inner Lever to Shaft.

position against parking lock wheel and start rear of shaft through bearing. Ease the assembly into position. If parking lock pawl is installed, hold it "up" out of the way to permit assembly to move freely into case.

When correctly positioned in case, the coast clutch support oil holes will line up with oil transfer holes in the case. If necessary to rotate the support, insert a smooth punch through the oil transfer holes in the case to rotate the support. Use good mechanical care to avoid nicking or denting either the support or the case.

2. Be certain holes in support and case line up. Lubricate and install oil transfer sleeves and "O" rings, and the retainers. Retainers should be positioned flat against the sleeves.
3. Lubricate liberally with chassis lube to avoid damage to seal and install speedometer driving gear on output shaft. Install companion flange.

COAST AND OVERRUNNING CLUTCH ASSEMBLY:

© 1961 Buick Div. G.M. Corp.

SPEEDOMETER
DRIVING GEAR

SEAL

OUTPUT SHAFT

Speedometer Driving Gear.

FORWARD CLUTCH PACK, RELEASE SPRING AND APPLY LEVERS INSTALL

1. With transmission in vertical position, install forward clutch apply levers.
2. Install forward clutch release spring flat on levers, (inner edge of spring "down").
3. Install release spring retainer solidly in groove of case.

Note: The release spring may move to one side and prevent easy installation of retaining ring. Center the

© 1961 Buick Div. G.M. Corp.

Carefully Install Coast and Overrunning Clutch.

© 1961 Buick Div. G.M. Corp.

BACKING PLATE LUGS
ENGAGE LUGS ON CASE

FORWARD AND REVERSE
CLUTCH BACKING PLATE

Top the Clutch Pack with Backing Plate.

spring as necessary to install the ring fully into the groove. Be certain the retaining ring is in the groove all the way around.

4. Set forward clutch pressure plate in place on apply levers. Take care to position wide space between lugs toward top of case for installation of anchor later.
5. Set coast and overrunning clutch assembly in place on coast clutch support.
6. Check a forward clutch separator plate (no notches on lugs) for "dish." Note direction of "dish" and install it on forward clutch pressure plate. Take care

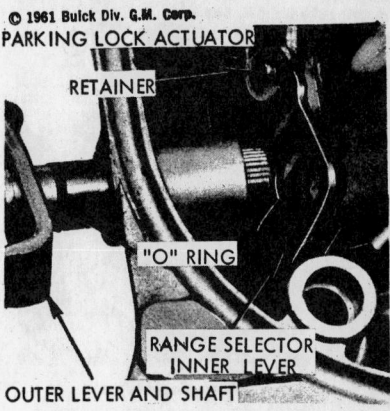

© 1961 Buick Div. G.M. Corp.

PARKING LOCK ACTUATOR

RETAINER

"O" RING

RANGE SELECTOR
INNER LEVER

OUTER LEVER AND SHAFT

Shaft and Lever Mounting Plan.

to position the wide space between lugs toward top of case for installation of anchor later.

7. Lubricate a clutch friction plate with automatic transmission oil. Install over coast clutch housing by engaging splines of plate with splines of coast clutch housing. Continue to alternately install a separator plate and a lubricated friction plate unit five separator plates, (all "dished" the same way) and five friction plates have been installed.

Note: All separator plates must be installed with the wide space between lugs toward the top of the case to permit the installation of the anchor later.

8. Install forward and reverse clutch backing plate on top of forward clutch pack. Rotate backing plate so lugs on backing plate engage lugs in case.

Note: The backing plate should require no force to install if the forward clutch pack has been correctly installed.

9. Install forward and reverse clutch anchor in slot at top of case.

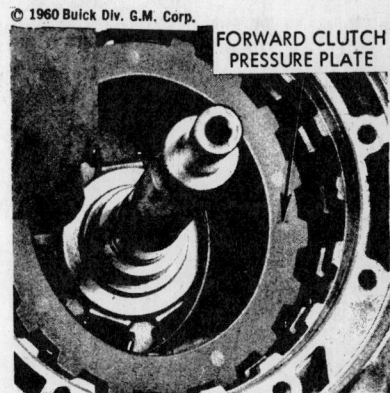

© 1960 Buick Div. G.M. Corp.

FORWARD CLUTCH
PRESSURE PLATE

Note Large Opening Between Top Lugs.

FORWARD AND REVERSE CLUTCH ANCHOR

Clutch Pack Anchor.

REVERSE CLUTCH COMPONENTS AND OIL PUMP

INSTALL

1. Be sure tanged thrust washer is in place at rear of reverse clutch hub.
2. Set reverse clutch hub in place on overrunning clutch assembly.
3. Lubricate and install a reverse clutch friction plate on forward and reverse clutch backing plate by engaging splines on hub with splines on plate.
4. Check a reverse clutch separator plate (notch in tangs) for "dish." Note direction of "dish" and install separator plate above friction plate. Install plate with wide space between lugs toward top of transmission to clear anchor. Continue to build clutch pack with alternate friction and separator plates until four friction and three separator plates have been installed. All separator plates must be installed with "dish" the same way.
5. Reverse clutch pressure plates are supplied in two thicknesses. If a new pressure plate is to be installed, "mike" the old plate at an unworn spot, (near the end of a lug). The new plate to be

PRESSURE PLATE — RELEASE SPRING

ASSEMBLING RING

Release and Assembling Ring.

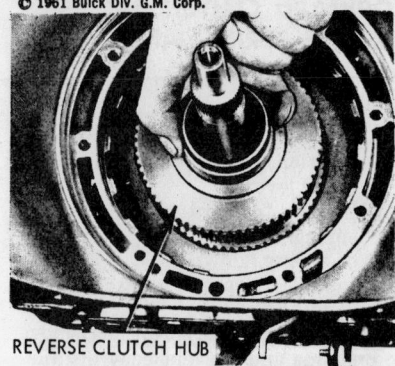

REVERSE CLUTCH HUB

Slip the Reverse Clutch Hub in Place.

THUMB SCREW

J-9167

PLUNGER

OIL PUMP-REVERSE CLUTCH PISTON HOUSING ASSY

Set Up Special Gauging Tool.

installed must be the same thickness or the reverse clutch pack clearance will be affected. Install pressure plate over top friction plate with wide space between lugs toward top of transmission for anchor clearance.

6. Install release spring and assembling ring over pressure plate.
   Note: Center edge of release spring "up."
   Note: Do not install apply levers until hub clearance has been checked and thrust washer (between reverse clutch hub and reverse clutch piston housing) has been selected.
7. Set gauge #J-9167 on oil pump—reverse clutch piston housing assembly with gauge bearing firmly on center hub of reverse clutch piston housing. Loosen thumb screw and allow plunger to bear on gasket surface of oil pump assembly. Tighten the thumb screw.
8. Install new oil pump gasket over 5/16" x 18 guide pins in case. Place a select fit reverse clutch hub to reverse clutch piston housing thrust washer in position on the hub. Set gauge # J-9167 over reverse clutch hub with ends of gauge resting squarely on gasket. Check clearance between end of plunger and

select fit thrust washer with .006" and .035" feeler gauges. If the .006" feeler will not fit between the plunger and the washer, select one size thinner washer. If the .035" feeler will fit between the plunger and the washer, select one size thicker washer.

9. Install reverse clutch apply levers in notches of pressure plate, flat on release spring and with lever ends under the assembling ring. Push assembling ring down on levers to hold them in place. Chassis lube daubed on levers will help keep them in place.
10. Lubricate thrust washer and oil pump body to case seal. Line up bolt holes with guide pins and lower pump into place.
11. Install and tighten at least three oil pump body to case bolts.
12. Insert a .029" feeler gauge through the case between a reverse clutch friction plate and a separator plate. A .029" feeler should "go" and a .051" feeler should "not go."

If the pack clearance is less than .030", it may be due to incorrect pressure plate thickness, separator plates not all "dished" the same way or apply levers incorrectly installed and binding on the piston. If pack clearance is more than .050" it may be due to incorrect pressure plate thickness or excessively worn fric-

GASKET

SELECT FIT THRUST WASHER

FEELER

PLUNGER

J-9167

Measure for Select Fit Washers

REVERSE CLUTCH APPLY LEVERS

RELEASE SPRING

ASSEMBLING RING

Install Apply Levers.

Install Attaching Nuts.

tion or separator plates.

13. If reverse clutch pack clearance is satisfactory, remove guide pins, install remaining special bolts and captive sealing lock washers. Torque the bolts alternately and evenly to 20-24 ft. lb.

VALVE BODY:

INSTALL

1. Be sure the surface of the case and valve body are clean. Set valve body assembly in place and engage pin or range selector inner lever with groove of selector valve.
2. Install parking lock pawl disengaging spring.
3. Install seven ¼" x 20 attaching bolts 1⅞" long in the valve body and torque, in the sequence illustrated, to 100 inch pounds.
4. Insert a .025" feeler, (special tool #J-9153) between the forward edge of rear land of governor valve and valve sleeve.

   Hold governor lever rearward and valve forward against feeler. Adjust screw so screw just touches the end of the valve with valve held "in" against feeler. Then remove the feeler.
5. Use a new "O" ring on oil strainer and set strainer in place on

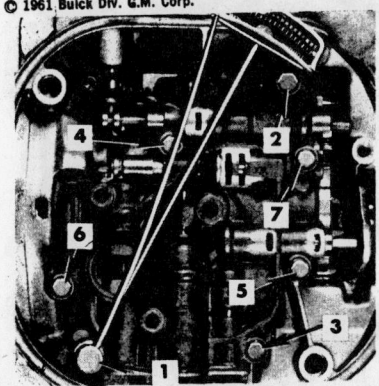

Torque the Valve Body.

Lower Pump into Place.

valve body.

6. Install strainer strap and two ¼" x 20 x 2½" bolts. Now torque the three bolts indicated in the illustration to 100 inch lb.

PARKING LOCK PAWL:

Note: This operation can be performed with the transmission in the car.

REMOVE

1. Remove oil pan. Lift off parking lock pawl disengaging spring with needle nose pliers.
2. Remove parking lock bracket to

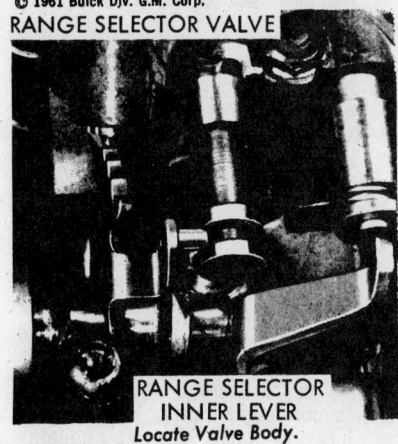

Check Pack Clearance.

RANGE SELECTOR VALVE

Locate Valve Body.

Torque Strainer Attaching Bolts.

case bolts (½" wrench). Remove the bracket.

3. With a small punch, drive the pawl shaft pin out of the case.
4. Pull parking lock pawl shaft and "O" ring out of the case. Remove pawl.

INSTALL

1. Slip a new "O" ring on the parking lock pawl shaft and lube it. Align pawl with shaft and install shaft with slot lined up with hole in case. Install the roll pin.
2. Install parking lock bracket but do not tighten bolts.
3. Shift transmission selector lever to park position. Turn output shaft so pawl engages the lock wheel. Tighten parking lock bracket bolts. Move selector to neutral and back to parking position. Check freedom of travel between park and neutral ranges. If a bind exists, use .001" shim stock under one or both bracket bolts. Torque to 15-20 ft. lb.
4. Install parking lock pawl disengaging spring.

OIL PAN:

INSTALL

1. Assemble new seal to oil pan and set oil pan in place.
2. Assemble new seal on bolt and install bolt. Torque to 15-20 ft.

Adjust Governor Valve.

VALVE BODY

SPRING

PARKING LOCK PAWL

Parking Lock Spring.

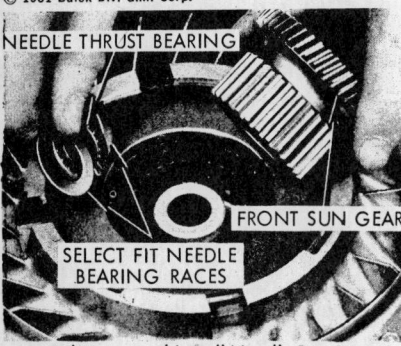

NEEDLE THRUST BEARING

FRONT SUN GEAR

SELECT FIT NEEDLE BEARING RACES

Lubricate and Install Needle Bearing.

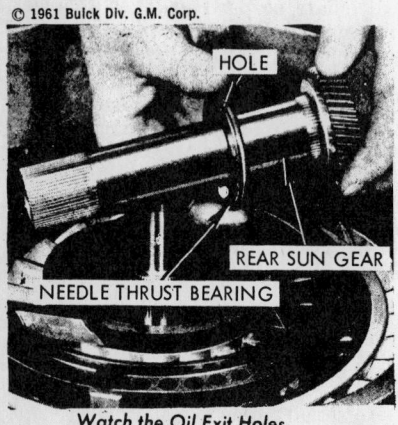

HOLE

REAR SUN GEAR

NEEDLE THRUST BEARING

Watch the Oil Exit Holes.

TURBINE AND STATOR ASSY

CONVERTER PUMP HOUSING

NEEDLE THRUST BEARING

Hold Needle Bearing and Washers with Grease.

CONVERTER AND GEAR SET:

INSTALL

1. Set converter pump housing assembling tool #J-9199 over the output shaft. The tool centers the converter pump housing so housing hub does not damage seal during installation. Lube hub of pump housing and install carefully. Rotate housing to engage lugs on pump with slots of converter pump housing hub. Then remove the tool.

2. Use clean chassis lube to hold the caged needle thrust bearing to rear of turbine, as illustrated. Oil exit holes are to the rear.

3. Set stator and turbine assembly into pump housing carefully to avoid damage to splines. Rotate turbine and stator to engage splines. The stator and turbine will drop into place when the splines are lined up.

4. Assemble caged needle thrust bearing to rear of rear sun gear. Oil exit holes to the rear.

5. Lubricate sun gear shaft inside and out. Slide sun gear and needle bearing into place. Rotate the gear to engage splines.

Note: Two sets of splines must be engaged, (sun gear race and coast clutch hub). Do not force the gear as spline damage may result.

6. Set planet carrier over rear sun gear with tanged thrust washers in place, front and rear. Deeper pocket of carrier "down" toward rear sun gear and splined portion "up."

7. Assemble new converter pump oil seal to pump. The seal is square, in section, and must not be twisted.

8. Lubricate and assemble needle thrust bearing and two select fit bearing races into front sun gear. Retain with chassis lube.

9. Engage splines on sun gear hub friction plates. Rotate gear while with splines of converter clutch pressing down very lightly till all splines are engaged.

10. Hold front sun gear in place with long screwdriver while positioning converter pump against pump housing. Rotate the assembly very slightly to mesh the front sun gear with the planet pinions. When gears are in mesh, push converter pump into converter housing and pull housing toward pump.

11. Before installing pump housing to converter pump bolts, check locating hole through housing

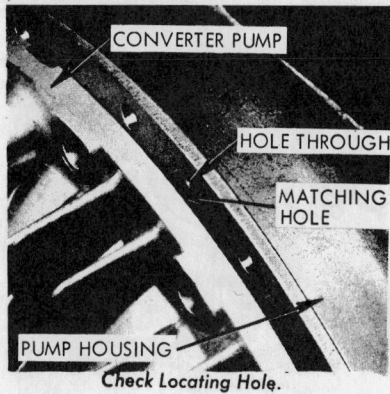

CONVERTER PUMP

HOLE THROUGH

MATCHING HOLE

PUMP HOUSING

Check Locating Hole.

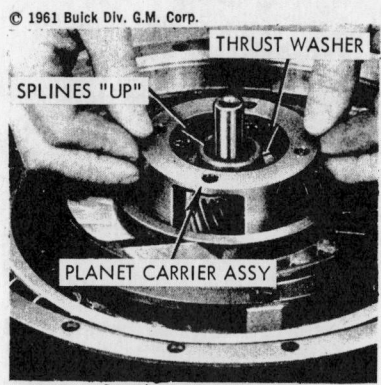

REAR SUN GEAR

NEEDLE THRUST BEARING

Slide Sun Gear and Needle Bearing into Place

THRUST WASHER

SPLINES "UP"

PLANET CARRIER ASSY

Set Planet Carrier in Place.

PARKING LOCK PAWL

PARKING LOCK PAWL SHAFT

"O" RING

Align Pawl with Shaft.

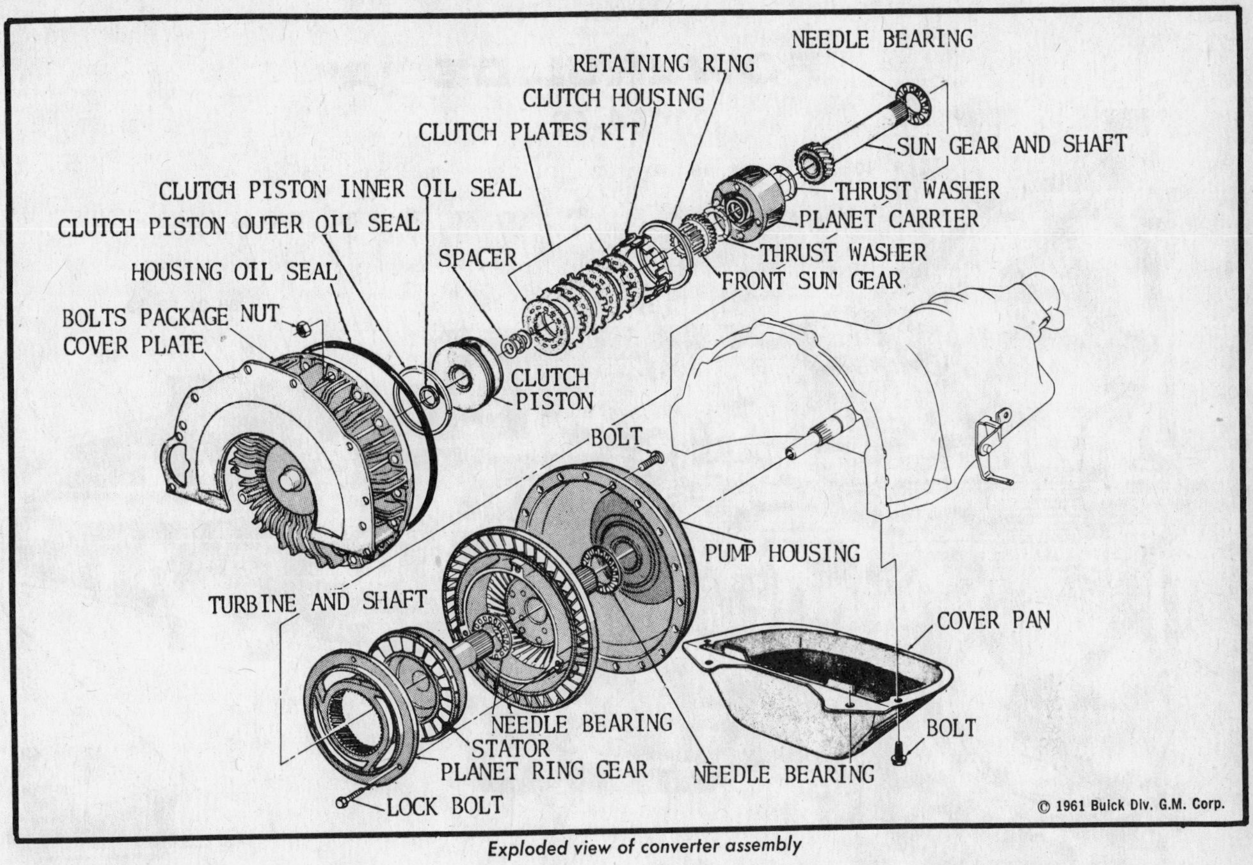

NEEDLE BEARING
RETAINING RING
CLUTCH HOUSING
CLUTCH PLATES KIT
SUN GEAR AND SHAFT
CLUTCH PISTON INNER OIL SEAL
THRUST WASHER
CLUTCH PISTON OUTER OIL SEAL
PLANET CARRIER
SPACER
THRUST WASHER
HOUSING OIL SEAL
FRONT SUN GEAR
BOLTS PACKAGE NUT
COVER PLATE
CLUTCH
PISTON
BOLT
PUMP HOUSING
TURBINE AND SHAFT
COVER PAN
NEEDLE BEARING
BOLT
STATOR
PLANET RING GEAR
NEEDLE BEARING
LOCK BOLT
© 1961 Buick Div. G.M. Corp.
Exploded view of converter assembly

© 1961 Buick Div. G.M. Corp.

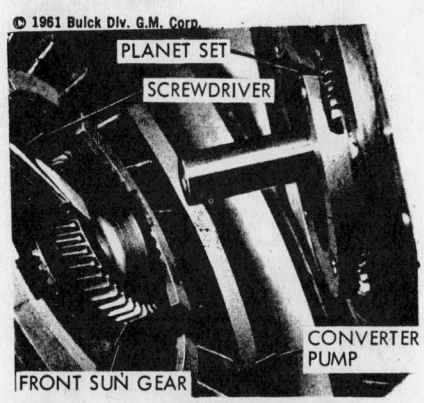

PLANET SET
SCREWDRIVER
CONVERTER
PUMP
FRONT SUN GEAR
Hold Sun Gear in Place.

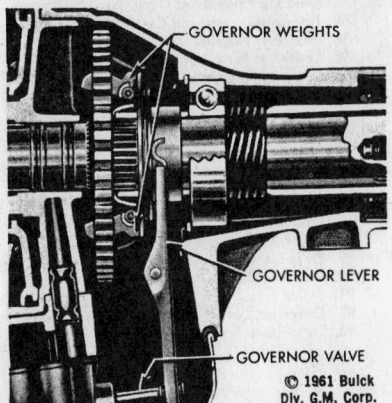

GOVERNOR WEIGHTS
GOVERNOR LEVER
GOVERNOR VALVE
© 1961 Buick
Div. G.M. Corp.
Governor Weights, Lever, and Valve

and matching hole part way through converter pump flange. These holes must line up to preserve balance of the assembly.

12. Set transmission in vertical position. Install and tighten special nuts and bolts alternately and evenly to 15-20 ft. lb. Wire or otherwise secure converter to case before removing the converter and transmission assembly from the fixture.

SPEEDOMETER DRIVEN GEAR SLEEVE AND "O" RING:

REMOVE

1. Remove bolt attaching speedometer driven gear sleeve retainer to case. Remove retainer.
2. Slide driven gear sleeve, gear, and "O" ring out of case. Check "O" ring for damage. Replace if necessary.

<u>Note:</u> The plastic gear and shaft are not retained in the sleeve. If replacement of gear is necessary, slide gear and shaft out of the sleeve.

INSTALL

Install by reversing above procedure.

© 1961 Buick Div. G.M. Corp.

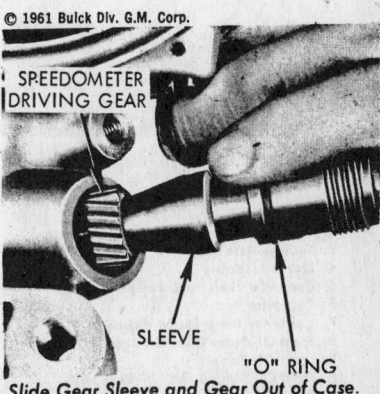

SPEEDOMETER
DRIVING GEAR
SLEEVE
"O" RING
Slide Gear Sleeve and Gear Out of Case.

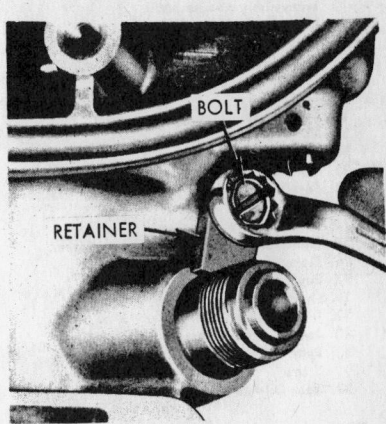

BOLT
RETAINER
Remove the Bolt

POWERGLIDE "A"
1954-62

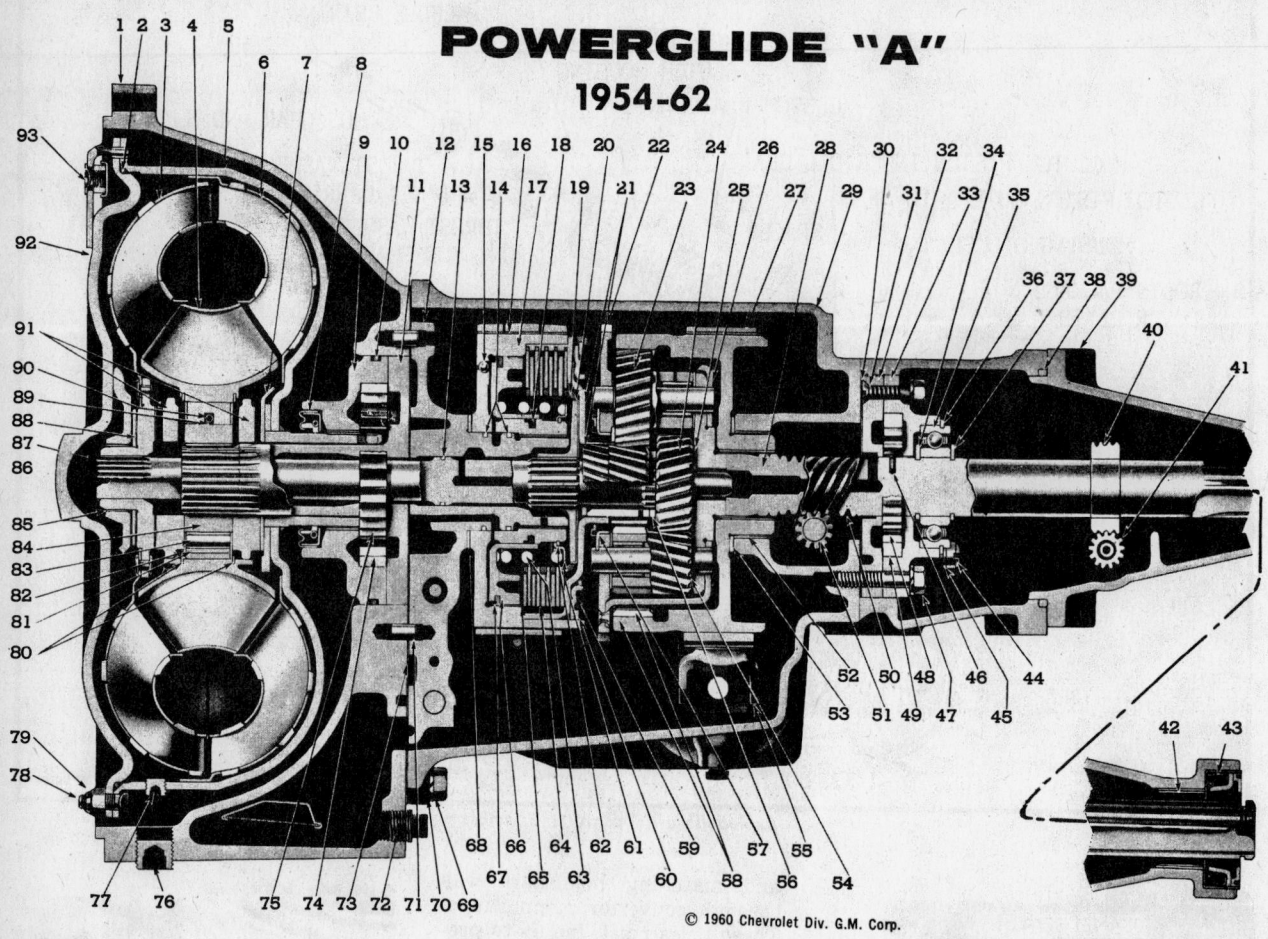

Fig. 1—Cutaway View of Powerglide Transmission 1955 thru 1957 (Typical 1954 thru 1962)

© 1960 Chevrolet Div. G.M. Corp.

1. Transmission Housing
2. Converter Cover "O" Ring Seal
3. Turbine Assembly
4. Stator Assembly
5. Converter Housing & Pump Assembly
6. Converter Pump
7. Converter Pump Thrust Washer
8. Front Oil Pump Body Oil Seal
9. Front Oil Pump Body
10. Front Oil Pump Body "O" Ring Seal
11. Stator Support
12. Transmission Valve Body
13. Input Shaft Oil Seal Ring
14. Clutch Drum Oil Seal Rings
15. Clutch Relief Valve Ball
16. Low Brake Band
17. Clutch Drum
18. Clutch Piston Inner Seal
19. Clutch Hub
20. Clutch Hub Thrust Washer
21. Low Sun Gear & Clutch Flange Assembly
22. Parking Lock Gear
23. Planet Short Pinion
24. Planet Reverse Sun Gear
25. Planet Reverse Sun Gear Thrust Washer
26. Planet Carrier
27. Reverse Brake Band
28. Output Shaft
29. Transmission Case
30. Rear Oil Pump Gasket
31. Rear Oil Pump Cover to Body Attaching Screw
32. Rear Oil Pump Cover

33. Rear Oil Pump Body
34. Rear Bearing Locating Front Snap Ring
35. Transmission Rear Bearing Assembly
36. Transmission Rear Bearing Retainer
37. Rear Bearing Locating Rear Snap Ring
38. Transmission Extension "O" Ring Seal
39. Transmission Extension
40. Speedometer Drive Gear
41. Speedometer Driven Gear
42. Transmission Extension Bushing
43. Transmission Extension Oil Seal
44. Transmission Rear Bearing Retainer Screw
45. Transmission Rear Bearing Retainer Screw Lockwasher
46. Rear Oil Pump Drive Gear Drive Pin
47. Rear Oil Pump Assembly Attaching Screw
48. Rear Oil Pump Drive Gear
49. Rear Oil Pump Driven Gear
50. Governor Drive Gear
51. Governor Driven Gear
52. Transmission Case Bushing
53. Reverse Drum Thrust Washer
54. Planet Long Pinion
55. Reverse Band Lever & Link Assembly
56. Low Sun Gear Thrust Washer
57. Planet Pinion Shaft Lock Plate
58. Reverse Drum & Ring Gear
59. Clutch Flange Retainer
60. Clutch Flange Retainer Ring
61. Clutch Spring Seat
62. Clutch Spring Snap Ring
63. Clutch Spring
64. Clutch Drive Plates

65. Clutch Driven Plates
66. Clutch Piston
67. Clutch Piston Outer Seal
68. Clutch Drum Thrust Washer
69. Converter Housing to Transmission Case Attaching Screw
70. Converter Housing to Transmission Case Attaching Screw Lockwasher
71. Converter Housing Dowel Pin
72. Transmission Housing Drain Plug
73. Transmission Case Gasket
74. Front Oil Pump Driven Gear
75. Front Oil Pump Drive Gear
76. Transmission Housing Converter Drain Plug
77. Converter Housing Drain Plug
78. Converter Pump Housing Bolt
79. Converter Pump Housing Nut
80. Over-run Cam Retaining Rings
81. Over-run Cam Thrust Washer
82. Over-run Cam Roller & Spring Retainer
83. Over-run Cam Roller
84. Stator Race
85. Converter Cover Hub Bushing
86. Input Shaft Stop Ring
87. Input Shaft
88. Turbine Thrust Washer
89. Over-run Cam Roller Guide
90. Over-run Cam Roller Spring
91. Stator Thrust Washers
92. Converter Cover Assembly
93. Flywheel to Transmission Anchor Nut

The type "A" transmission is identified by a cast iron case. It uses a 3-element converter. The clutch plates are waved in place of dished, except 1958, which used dished steel plates. These plates are identified by an "O" and must be stacked in one direction.

GENERAL INFORMATION

OIL LEVEL CHECK

Check the level every 1000 miles, with transmission at operating temperature and the selector in neutral. With engine idling oil should not be above the "full" mark and added to when below the "add 1 quart" mark.

Be careful not to overfill, to avoid aerating and foaming.

OIL CHANGE SCHEDULE

Thru 1957 change every 25,000 miles. Starting with 1958 do not change except at overhaul. Capacity Chart in Car Section shows proper quantities.

DRAIN AND REFILL PROCEDURE

With engine at operating temperature, remove plug at rear of transmission. (No converter drain plug is provided after 1953). To refill replace plug and with engine idling, add 4½ quarts of approved type "A" fluid. Continue idling until oil is hot and recheck level as above.

Now is a good time for visual inspection of cooler core and lines for leaks and proper heat flow.

TOWING THE CAR

When the hand lever is in Neutral the car may be towed. When the rear wheels are on the ground Neutral is the ONLY position that can be used for towing.

Speed in Tow should never exceed 45 mph.

To place the transmission in Neutral when the hand lever is inoperative:

1. Remove the cotter pin and disconnect the long control rod at the bell crank on the left side of the transmission case.

2. Push the bell crank as far rearward as it will go. (This will be Reverse.) Now move it forward to the third detent which will be Neutral. Naturally if the Transmission is locked up the car must not be moved on its rear wheels unless the drive shaft is disconnected at the universal joint.

BAND ADJUSTMENT

REVERSE BAND

The adjustment screw for the reverse band is hidden behind the Servo Cover on the right side of the case. On Convertibles the clearance around the transmission is so small that the factory recommends removal of the transmission from the car before attempting to remove the servo cover. On all other models the cover can be removed without disturbing the transmission.

Remove the vacuum line connection from the intake manifold at the modulator. Unbolt and remove the modulator assembly. Be sure to counteract the modulator diaphragm spring while releasing the cover attaching bolts and be careful not to drop parts. The hydraulic plunger in the modulator body behind the diaphragm must be handled very carefully. See Fig. 2.

After removal of the modulator remove the remaining servo cover to transmission case bolts. Be careful to maintain pressure on the cover to counteract the force of the servo and the valve springs.

Do not remove the servo pistons while the transmission is in the car for to do so will permit the band struts to drop down into the transmission case. See Fig. 2.

© 1960 Chevrolet Div. G.M. Corp.

Fig. 2—Reverse Band Section

Release the reverse band adjusting screw lock nut and tighten the adjusting screw up snug. From up snug back the adjusting screw out two and three-quarters turns. Tighten the lock nut to 20-25 ft lbs.
Starting with 1959 tighten reverse band adjusting screw to 5 to 7 gt. lbs. and back off 2½ turns.
Reinstall the servo cover and the modulator.

LOW BAND ADJUSTMENT

The low band adjusting screw is hidden under a protective cap on the left side of the transmission case. Working under the car remove the cover to expose the adjusting screw and the lock nut. See Fig. 3.

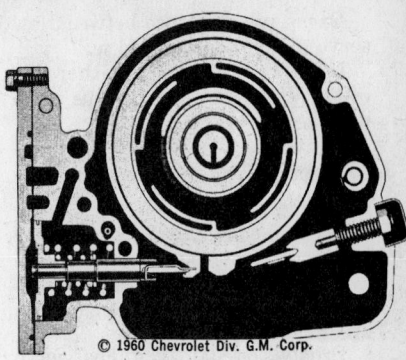

© 1960 Chevrolet Div. G.M. Corp.

Fig. 3—Low Band Section

Tighten the adjusting screw to 5 to 7 ft. lbs. and back off exactly four turns. Tighten lock nut to 20-25 ft. lbs.

In 1958 two types of low servos were used. See Fig. 3. The early type differed in that no cushion spring was used under the piston. Back this type off three turns.

Types can be identified by observing that the pin extends thru the piston on those having the cushion spring.

TROUBLE SHOOTING CHART

Always check oil level, Linkage and Engine Idle before any other checks.

1. Excessive Slip in All Ranges

Shown by high engine speed for relative car speed, poor acceleration, engine races at turns.
This trouble can be caused by:
Low Oil Level, Improper Linkage Adjustment or Pumps Sucking Air due to: Oil Suction Pipe Split or not seating properly. Oil Suction Screen coated with lint or dirt.
Front Pump worn or scored.
Damaged valve body gasket, warped mating surfaces between pump and valve body, porous valve body.
Stuck Regulator Valve. Free Wheeling Cam Rollers on the Stators or the Secondary Pump Improperly assembled.
Note: Chevrolet does not recommend any Stall Speed Tests.

2. Excessive Slip in Drive Range

This trouble can be caused by:
Improper Linkage Adjustment. Worn or burned Clutch Plates due to: Extended operation with low oil level. Damaged or improperly installed clutch piston seals. Restricted Orifice in Cltuch Hyradulic Circuit. Damaged Clutch Release Valve. Clutch drum oil seals leaking.

Excessive clearance between low servo piston shaft and case.

Leak in the gaskets on either side of the Valve Body or a porous valve body.

3. Excessive Slip in Low Range

Can be caused by:

Improper linkage adjustment, or improper low band adjustment.

Accumulator Valve stuck.

Modulator lever or piston is stuck.

Broken or damaged low servo ring.

Leaks at the gaskets on either side of the Valve Body or the Servo Cover to Case gasket.

Clutch Drum Worn smooth.

4. Excessive Slip in Reverse

Can be caused by:

Improper Linkage adjustment, or improper Reverse band adjustment.

Broken reverse band. Bent strut or stretched link assembly.

No pressure in the lines due to: Accumulator Valve stuck, Modulator lever stuck, or Modulator Piston stuck. Broken or damaged reverse servo piston ring. Leaks at the gaskets on either side of the valve body. Step in manual valve body bore causing leakage to sump.

5. Car Creeps Forward with Hand Lever in Neutral

This trouble can be caused by:

Improper linkage adjustment, or Low band adjusted too tight.

Clutch inoperative (shown by car stalling in low and reverse) due to: Clutch Vent valve Stuck Closed. Plates improperly Assembled. All the dished plates must face the same way, toward the rear.

Leak between valve and housing. Control lever unhooked from manual valve inside the transmission. To prove: Drain the case, unfasten the left sump plate and look.

6. Car Creeps Forward with Hand Lever in Reverse

This trouble can be caused by improper linkage adjustment.

7. Car Creeps Backward with Hand Lever in Low

This trouble can be caused by improper linkage adjustment.

8. Car Will Not Move; Rear Wheels Locked

This trouble can be caused by:

Emergency brake applied, parking lock pawl engaged, broken part

in transmission or broken part in differential.

9. Car Will Not Move After Long Reverse; Rear Wheels Free

This trouble can be caused by:

Leak at Rear Pump gasket allowing air into the suction lines so that Front Pump loses prime.

10. Shift from Low to Drive Abnormally Rough with Car in Motion

This trouble can be caused by:

Improper low band adjustment.

Clutch plates worn or binding in clutch flange or drum.

Modulator lever or Piston stuck.

Accumulator dump valve inoperative.

Leak in Modulator Vacuum Line.

11. Engine Speeds Up When Shifting from Low to Drive With Car in Motion

This trouble can be caused by:

Low oil level.

Improper low band adjustment.

Weak Modulator Spring.

Clutch plates glazed, worn or binding.

Restricted orifice in clutch hydraulic circuit.

12. Shift from Drive to Low Abnormally Rough

This trouble can be caused by:

Improper low band adjustment.

Modulator lever or piston stuck.

Accumulator Piston stuck closed.

13. Shift from Neutral to Reverse Abnormally Rough

This trouble can be caused by:

Idling speed too high.

Modulator lever or Piston stuck.

Accumulator valve stuck.

Improper Reserve Band adjustment.

Excessive End clearance in the Transmission.

Torque tube held too tightly at the Ball joint. To correct add more shims.

14. Chatter When Starting in Low

This trouble can be caused by:

Improper low band adjustment.

Malfunctioning Clutch due to: Distorted plates, sticking clutch piston or sticking clutch vent valve.

Worn low drum or band.

15. Chatter When Starting in Drive

This trouble can be caused by:

Improper reverse band adjustment, improper low band adjustment, worn bands, or drums.

16. Chatter When Starting in Reverse

This trouble can be caused by:

Improper reverse band adjustment, worn reverse band or drum, transmission case rear bushing worn or damaged, or reverse ring gear bushing worn or damaged.

17. Drag in Reverse or Jerky Reverse

This trouble can be caused by:

Improper low band adjustment.

Malfunctioning clutch due to: Plates improperly assembled. Plates binding in flange or hub. Stuck Piston. Stuck Vent Valve.

18. Excessive Fuel Consumption

This trouble can be caused by:

Secondary Pump locked to hub of Primary Pump due to improperly assembled free wheel Clutch. Free wheeling clutches of Stators improperly assembled. Clutch vent valve stuck open.

19. Excessive Oil Consumption

This trouble can be caused by:

External leakage at pressure checking points, side covers, or the converter housing.

External leakage at universal ball joint seal.

External leakage at front of flywheel housing. To check; remove plug at bottom of converter housing. If there is an oil pool it will be necessary to check;

The primary pump "O" ring seals, the front pump oil seal, "O" ring, and drain. The turbine bolt "O" ring, and for sand holes in case running from sump to housing.

External leakage at oil cooler connections.

Internal leakage at propeller shaft oil seal. To prove: Check differential lubricant level. If it is too high renew the oil seal and the differential lubricant.

Modulator diaphragm leaking. To prove: Put a glass bowled gasoline filter in the modulator vacuum line at the manifold. When motor is running, if diaphragm is leaking, oil will appear in the filter bowl.

Aerated oil being forced out of the filter tube due to: Oil level too high. Split in suction pipe, damaged suction pipe seal, ears on suction pipe bent, or bore for suction pipe in the housing too deep for proper compression of the seal. Sand holes in suction passages of the housing, the case, or the valve body.

Water in the oil due to faulty oil cooler.

20. Noises

These can be classified as:

Ringing noises in the converter due to:
Low oil level, low oil pressure in the converter, or to aerated oil.

Buzzing noise due to:
Low oil level, malfunctioning of the pumps, or to vibration of the lubrication by-pass valve.

Whining noise due to:
Worn planetary gear teeth, worn pump gears or to worn pump bushings.

Groaning noise.
Audible only at low speeds or when standing when transmission is hot. Usually caused by pulsation of the thermostat valve ball. Disregard it.

Clicking noise.
May be due to improperly adjusted manual linkage permitting the parking lock pawl to contact the rachet gear.

21. Difficulty in Shifting Between Drive and Low Either Way

This trouble can be caused by:
Improperly drilled clutch feed orifice in the valve body.

22. Slipping and Chatter in Low Range

This trouble can be caused by:
A loose or broken low servo piston ring.

23. Unable to Shift into Reverse with Engine Running

This trouble can be caused by the accumulator snap ring being out of place. This permits the accumulator valve to contact the parking lock lever shaft assembly at the clamp nut, so blocking the shift.

24. Car Will Not Move in Drive—Engine Races—Rear Wheels Are Free—Transmission Is Hot

This trouble can be caused by:
Over expansion of the clutch

parts due to excessive heat caused by:
Low coolant level, bad oil cooler, dragging low band, or defective transmission thermostat.

25. Squawk or Grunt on Upshift

This trouble can be caused by:
Improperly nested clutch driven plates. With the "O" marking on all driven plates facing in same direction they should be properly stacked. Sometimes the plates are not correctly marked. The correct stacking can be verified by stacking the driven plates together before combining them with the drive plates.

When the clutch driven plates are correctly stacked they nest together tightly and any error will appear as intermittent openings between adjacent plates. The offending plate can then be turned over and will be well.

It is well to note that the driven plates for 1958 are all the same thickness.

Never mix past model plates in the 1958 clutch stack.

BASIC PRESSURE CHECKS

With transmission at normal operating temperature connect gauge at low servo apply (Fig. 8), clutch release side of low servo (Fig. 7), throttle valve and governor test points (Fig. 6). The gauges should be in car away from driver's feet, with lines along steering jacket, past the jacket seal.

Wide open throttle upshift 82-90 psi with V-8 and 68-74 psi with 6-cylinder.

After up-shift pressure on low servo supply and high clutch should be alike. If pressures are alike and slippage is felt mechanical trouble in clutch is indicated. Leakage in high

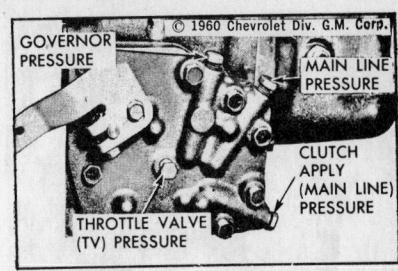

Fig. 6—Oil Pressure Check Points

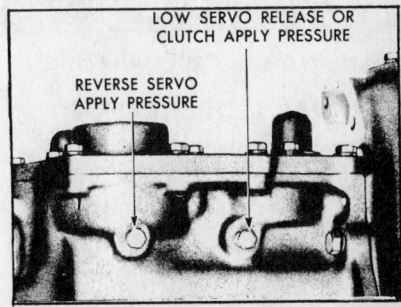

Fig. 7—Oil Pressure Check Points

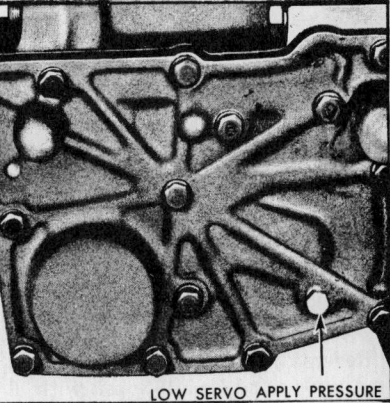

Fig. 8—Oil Pressure Check Points 1955-57

clutch line between low and drive valve body and high clutch is indicated if pressures vary more than 5 psi.

IDLE PRESSURE IN "DRIVE" RANGE

Low servo apply, 60-71 psi with V-8 and 55-65 psi with 6-cylinder.

Car Speed	Governor Pressure
5 mph	2-4 psi
10 mph	8½-13 psi
15 mph	21-27½ psi
20 mph	31½-34½ psi
25 mph	35½-40 psi
30 mph	41-46 psi
35 mph	47½-53½ psi
40 mph	55-62 psi
45 mph	63½-71½ psi
50 mph	73½-82 psi
55 mph	84-93½ psi
60 mph	95½-106 psi

Fig. 4—Governor Pressure Graph 1955-57

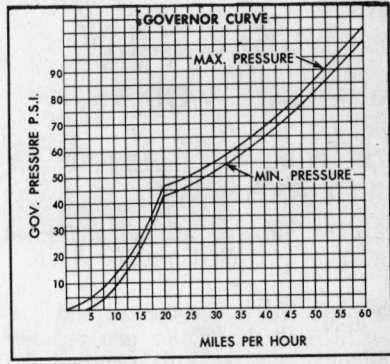

Fig. 5—Governor Pressure Chart 1958-62

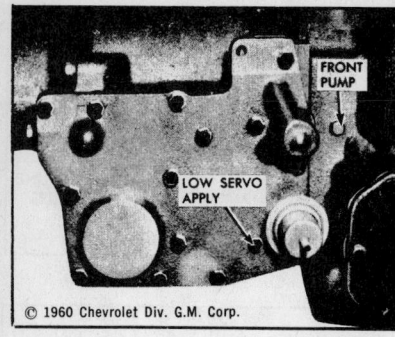

Fig. 9—Oil Pressure Check Points 1958-62

MANUAL "LOW" RANGE

Low servo apply at 1000 rpm, 114-127 psi with V-8 and 70-80 psi with 6-cylinder.

DRIVE RANGE COAST PRESSURE

Coasting in drive at 20-25 mph, low servo apply pressure 47-53 psi with either engine.

THROTTLE VALVE AND GOVERNOR

Throttle valve pressure varies with accelerator position, 0-63 psi with V-8 and 0-50 with 6-cylinder. Governor pressure is relative to car speed and can be checked by referring to Fig. 4 and Fig. 5.

REVERSE PRESSURE

With brakes applied and lever in "Reverse" at 1000 rpm, 240-275 psi with V-8 and 167-191 psi with 6-cylinder.

Match Points

The following points should be marked on disassembly.
Flywheel to Primary Pump Cover
Primary Pump Cover to Primary Pump
Pinion Shaft to Pinion Carrier
Front Portion of Carrier to Rear Portion of Carrier
Bands to Case

DISASSEMBLY ALL MODELS

OIL PUMP SUCTION PIPE AND SCREEN

(This operation can be performed with the transmission still in the car.)

Unbolt the right side cover of the bell housing. Remove cover and gasket. Unbolt the suction pipe retainer and lift out the pipe retainer and screen.

Wash the assembly in solvent. Blow with compressed air to dry.

Reverse removal procedure to replace. Use a new seal on the pipe ahead of the retainer. Install in the cover a new "O" ring seal for the filler tube. Use a new cover to case gasket.

TRANSMISSION THROTTLE VALVE

(This operation can be performed with the transmission still in the car.)

Unbolt the left side cover and remove the cover and throttle valve as an assembly, Fig. 10. Remove cover to case gasket. Do not unbolt the outer lever as it acts to hold the inner lever in place on the assembly.

Note: If it becomes necessary to disassemble the throttle valve, be careful not to disturb the adjustment. It is preset to 62 psi (plus or minus 1 psi) at the factory.

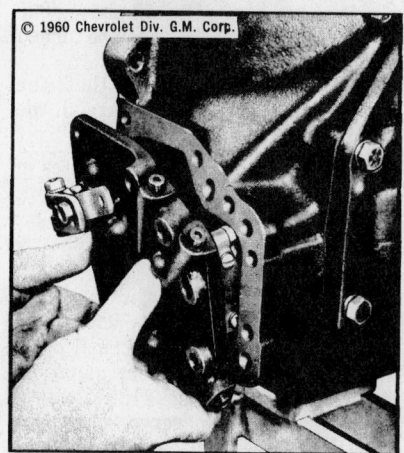

Fig. 10—Removal of Throttle Valve Assembly

It is more than likely that trouble with this assembly can be cleared by a thorough cleaning.

Remove the low-and-drive-valve-body to side cover attaching bolts and lock-washers. Remove the throttle valve outer lever and catch the inner lever and shaft seal.

Hold the low and drive valve body in one hand and with a soft faced hammer tap on the inner side of the side cover until it is free of the locating pins.

Caution: Exert pressure on the detent valve when separating valve body from the cover to keep the parts from falling out. A clip can easily be made that retains the detent valve in its bore during disassembly and assembly to cover.

If during disassembly a new detent valve, throttle valve, or spring, is installed the throttle valve inner lever should be adjusted.

Hold the lever so it just contacts the face of the detent valve. Turn the adjusting screw "A" until it touches the

flat surface of the lever's step, Fig. 11. Back off one complete turn and tighten the adjusting screw lock.

If there is a screw in the lower end of the throttle valve inner lever, hold the lever as described above and turn this lower screw in to touch the thread of the adjusting screw.

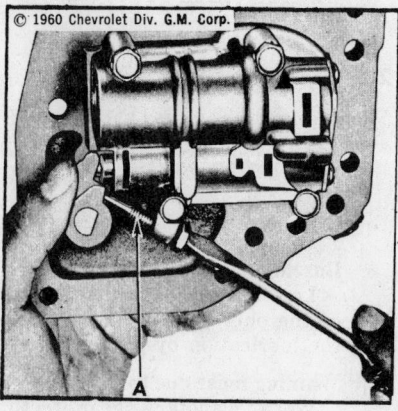

Fig. 11—Setting of Throttle Valve Inner Lever Adjustment

THE MODULATOR AND SERVO COVER ASSEMBLY

(This operation can be performed with the Powerglide in the car.)

Remove the vacuum line connection from the carburetor at the modulator.

Unbolt and remove the modulator assembly from the right front side of the transmission case.

Be sure to counteract the modulator diaphragm spring while releasing the cover attaching bolts and be careful not to drop the parts.

The hydraulic plunger and body in the modulator body behind the diaphragm must be handled very carefully.

Remove the remaining servo cover to transmission case bolts. Be careful to push in on the cover to counteract the force of the servo and valve springs or else the cover may break.

Remove reverse servo spring, pressure regulator springs, and pressure regulator valve.

Do not remove the servo pistons with Powerglide in the car.

Before replacing the servo cover check the adjustment of the reverse band.

If transmission is on the bench, tighten adjusting screw until no end play can be felt by push-pull motion on the reverse servo piston assembly, yet reverse ring gear unit turns freely by hand. Then back off 1/8 to 1/4 turn and tighten lock nut to 20-25 ft lbs.

If tranmission is in the car, tighten the adjusting screw all the way, then back off 2¾ turns and tighten lock nut to 20-25 ft lbs.

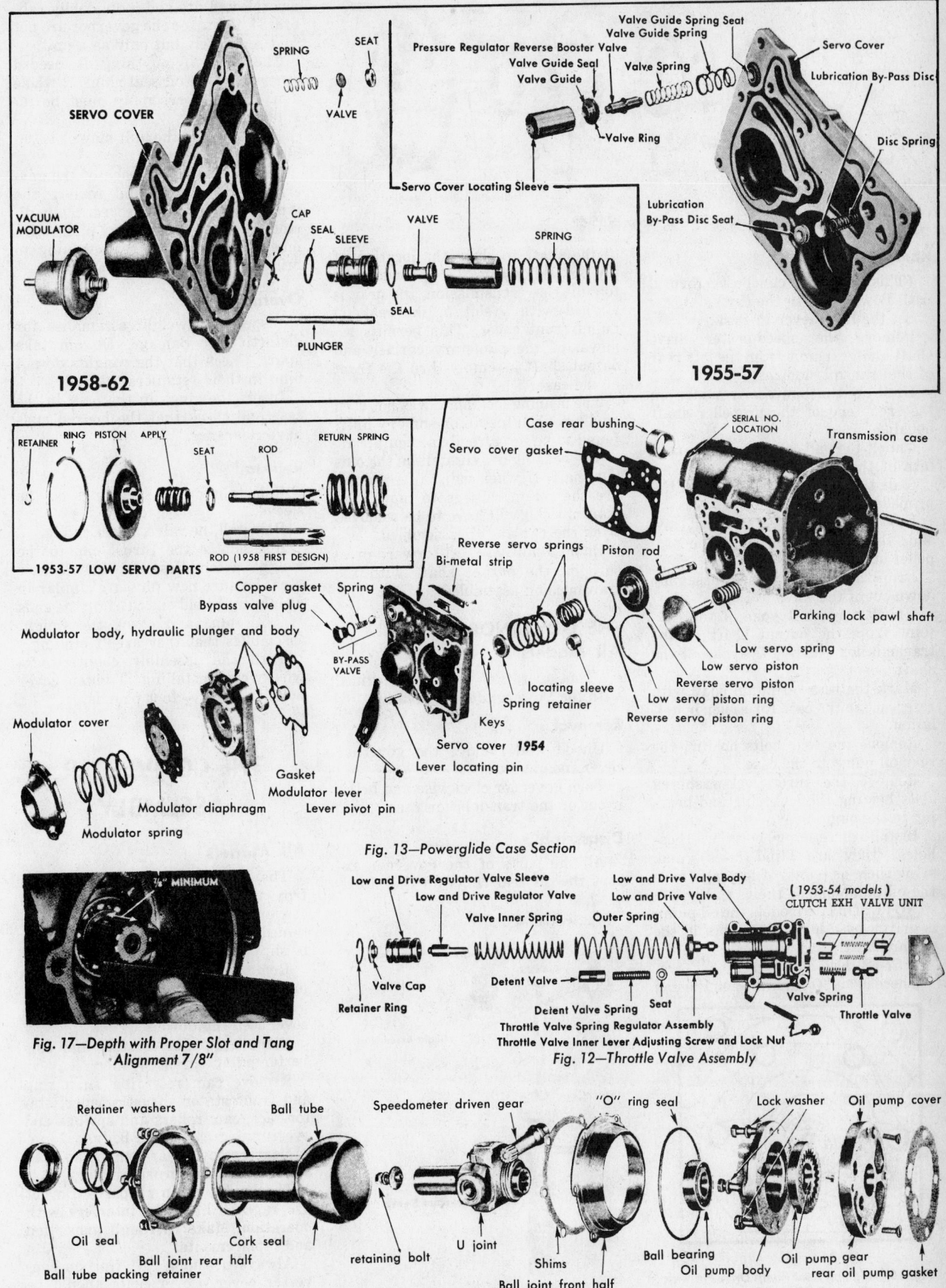

1958-62

1955-57

-1953-57 LOW SERVO PARTS-

ROD (1958 FIRST DESIGN)

BY-PASS VALVE

Fig. 13—Powerglide Case Section

Fig. 17—Depth with Proper Slot and Tang
Alignment 7/8"

Fig. 12—Throttle Valve Assembly

Fig. 14—Powerglide Rear Pump 1954

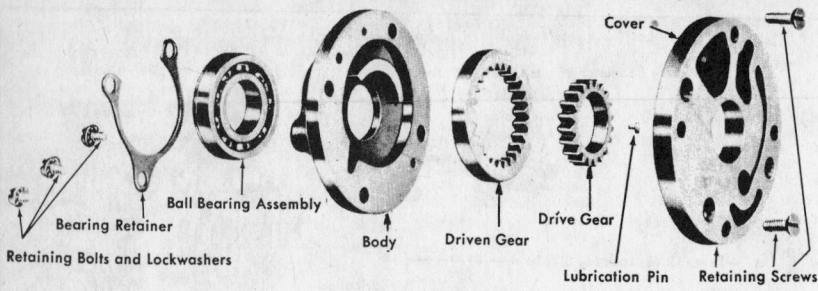

Fig. 15—Rear Pump 1955-62

REAR OIL PUMP

(This operation can be performed with Powerglide in the car.)

Set the hand lever in Park.

Remove the speedometer drive shaft and gear unit from the left rear of the transmission case.

Unscrew the ball seal retainer on the front end of the propeller shaft housing.

Unbolt the ball collar from the rear face of the transmission case.

Slide the ball assembly back on the propeller shaft housing.

Unfasten the universal joint and slide the rear yoke back on the propeller shaft.

Drop the propeller shaft assembly down out of the way.

Unbolt the front yoke of the "U" joint from the output shaft of the transmission and pull the yoke off the shaft.

Mark the rear oil pump body with reference to the case for easier installation.

Remove the four bolts holding the rear oil pump to the case.

Remove the three lock-washered bolts holding the lock ring and bearing in the pump body.

Install three long bolts in these holes (they are blind holes) and, using them as points of leverage, ease the oil pump out of the case, Fig. 15.

NOTE: On late models the oil pump is driven by a loose fitting pin in the output shaft.

1957-62, Figs. 16 & 17.

There is an "O" stamped on the end

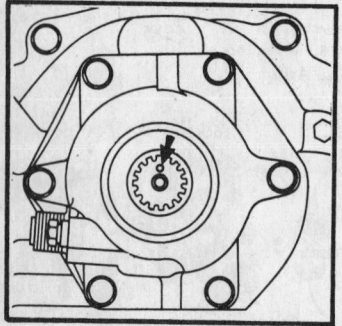

Fig. 16—Aligning Rear Pump Drive Pin with Slot in Oil Pump Cover

754

of the shaft to show the location of the pin. When this "O" is toward the top of the transmission the pin is aligned with a slot in the rear oil pump front cover. This permits removal of the planetary carrier and output shaft assembly thru the front of the case.

The bearing lock plate was not used on all models. Install one on any units found to be not already so equipped.

The bearing is a tight fit on the output shaft. If when using this procedure the pump refuses to move, the transmission will have to be removed from the car and disassembled.

On no condition exert forward pressure on the output shaft with the transmission assembled.

THE GOVERNOR ASSEMBLY
All Models

(This operation can be performed with the Powerglide in the car.)

Removal

Unbolt and remove the governor cover and gasket.

Turn governor clockwise and bring it out of the transmission case.

Disassembly

All the parts of the governor except the oil seal rings on the sleeve

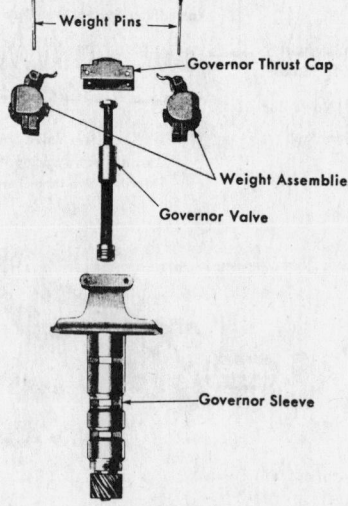

Fig. 18—Governor

are selected fits and individually calibrated. Parts for the governor are not sold separately but only as a unit.

Therefore if anything is needed other than the oil seal rings, a whole new governor assembly must be installed.

For cleaning, the unit may be taken apart.

Cut off one end of each of the governor weight pins and remove the pins. Measure and record their diameter, for the same gage piano wire must be used when reassembling to preserve the unit's calibration.

Overhaul

Inspect the weight assemblies for distortion or damage. Do not take apart. Check that the weights do not bind in their retainers.

Insert the rings in the bore in the case and check that the hooked ends have clearance.

Reinstall

Reinstall the oil seal rings on the sleeve.

Reinstall the valve, wider end in.

Reassemble the thrust cap to the weight assemblies and install new pins. Be sure new pins are similar in weight to the old ones. Crimp the ends of both pins and check the weight assemblies that they aren't binding.

Turn the assembly counterclockwise when installing. Tighten cover bolts to 6½-8½ foot pounds.

THE CONVERTER ASSEMBLY

All Models

The Powerglide must be removed from the car for this operation. The converter assembly is no longer retained to the reactor shaft and may be slipped off the input shaft as a unit.

Remove the primary pump retaining cover to the primary pump.

With a small punch drive out the cover locating dowels.

Remove turbine, stator, and converter pump thrust washer.

Remove cam retaining snap ring and front stator thrust washer, stator race, cam rollers and springs and overrunning cam from body.

Next remove rear cam snap ring and rear stator thrust washer.

Thoroughly clean all parts. Do not use rags as lint may interfere with operation. Make thorough inspection and replacements.

Always use new "O" ring on converter cover. Cover bolts should be tightened to 15-20 ft. lbs.

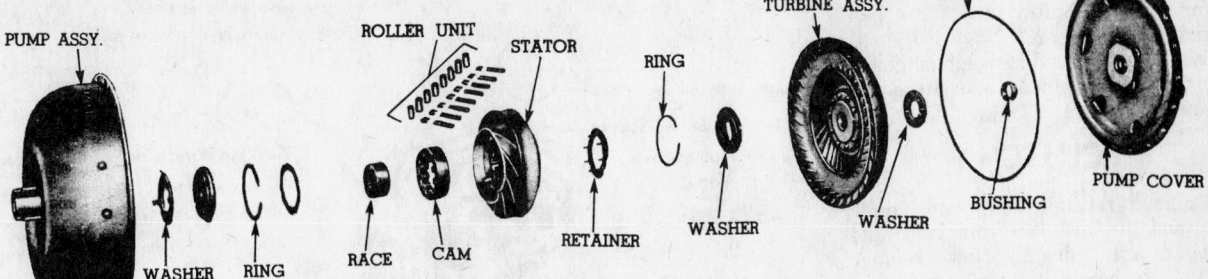

PUMP ASSY.   ROLLER UNIT   STATOR   RING   TURBINE ASSY.   SEAL   PUMP COVER

WASHER   RING   RACE   CAM   RETAINER   WASHER   WASHER   BUSHING

Fig. 20—Powerglide Converter (Typical 1954-62)

To check that converter assembly is properly installed, measure, as shown in Fig. 22, the distance from the machined front face of the bell housing to the front surface of a converter drive lug. The distance should be no more than 9/16″. Temporarily fasten the converter to the bell housing so it won't fall out of place. Fig. 21.

BELL HOUSING, ALL MODELS

REMOVAL

Remove the transmission from the car.

Remove the converter assembly from the transmission.

Remove the oil screen, the modulator assembly, the servo cover assembly and the throttle valve assembly.

Be sure that the pressure regulator valve is out of the case and safely put out of the way.

Remove the low band adjusting screw cover, loosen the lock nut and tighten the adjusting screw to hold the clutch assembly in place. A 1/4″ Allen wrench is required for this operation.

Remove the one bolt running from the inside of the bell housing into the transmission case. Fig. 23.

Remove the transmission case to bell housing bolts and lock washers.

Carefully separate the bell housing from the transmission case.

Note that there are two (2) gaskets, one between the bell housing, the valve body, and the transmission case, and another smaller crescent moon shaped one between the valve body and the case. Fig. 24.

Note that there is a bronze thrust washer on the oil delivery sleeve of the valve body to intervene between the clutch assembly and the valve body.

On late models this thrust washer is the one controlling transmission endplay.

REINSTALL BELL HOUSING

On 1954 models, index manual valve inner lever in bell housing with the manual valve so valve extends 1½″. This is reverse position. On the 1955-57 models the valve should extend 1¹¹⁄₁₆″ in the reverse position. Starting with 1958 it should extend 1¹¹⁄₁₆″ in the low position.

Install new crescent valve body to case gasket.

Raise the manual valve outer lever to top detent position, which is reverse.

The connecting lever inside the case is called the reaction lever. It is now set to engage the inner lever in the bell housing. The fact that they properly engage can be observed through the opening occupied by the throttle valve assembly.

VALVE BODY AND FRONT OIL PUMP ASSEMBLY, ALL MODELS

With the transmission out of the car and lying on the bench remove the manual control valve and wrap it in protective material.

Remove the bolts and lock-washers attaching the valve body to the bell housing and the front pump.

Remove the valve body and its gasket. Wrap the valve body so it is protected.

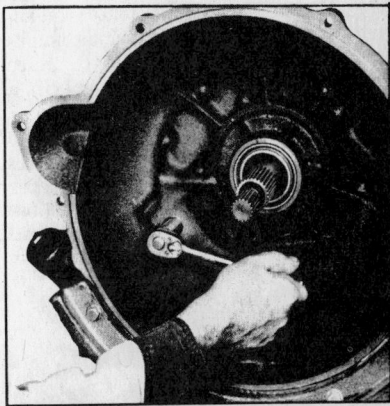

Fig. 23—Bolt to Transmission Case Inside Bell Housing

Fig. 21—Converter Holding Tool

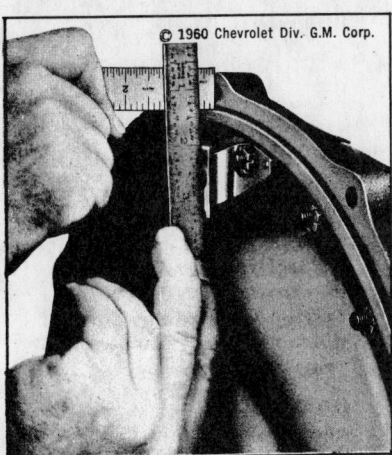

Fig. 22—Distance Not Over 9/16″

Fig. 24—Crescent Shaped Gasket Between Valve Body and Transmission Case

755

Drive the front oil pump and reactor shaft assembly out of the bell housing to the rear.

With oil pumps disassembled check for galling or scoring and check for proper clearances

CLUTCH

Remove retainer ring and flange retainer. Remove low sun gear and flange from drum. Now remove thrust washer hub and plates.

Compress spring to remove snap ring and slowly release seat and spring.

Rap the drum sharply on block of wood to remove piston.

Carefully inspect both seals, piston, drum, bushings and plates. Be sure the relief valve ball is free and that it seats properly.

In reassembling coat all parts with transmission oil to prevent sticking and scoring.

When installing plates start with a steel plate. The three, thick .090" plates must be in center of pack.

REASSEMBLY

As planetary parts, with clutch, drums and bands are reassembled, check clearances as indicated in Figs. 37 and 38. Fig. 37 illustrates measuring sun gear depth. Various thickness washers are available to place in front of clutch drum to obtain a clearance of .007" to .035".

Fig. 38 illustrates measuring to obtain clearance between low and reverse sun gears. Select proper washer to obtain clearance of .025" to .050".

© 1960 Chevrolet Div. G.M. Corp.

Fig. 39—Installing Parking Lock Pawl Spring

© 1960 Chevrolet Div. G.M. Corp.

Fig. 37—Measuring Sun Gear Depth

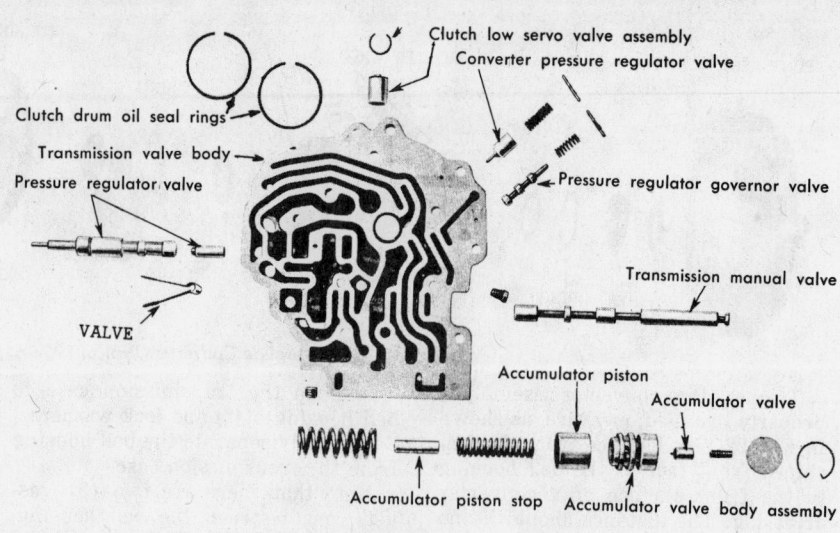

Fig. 25—Powerglide Valve Lay Out 1954

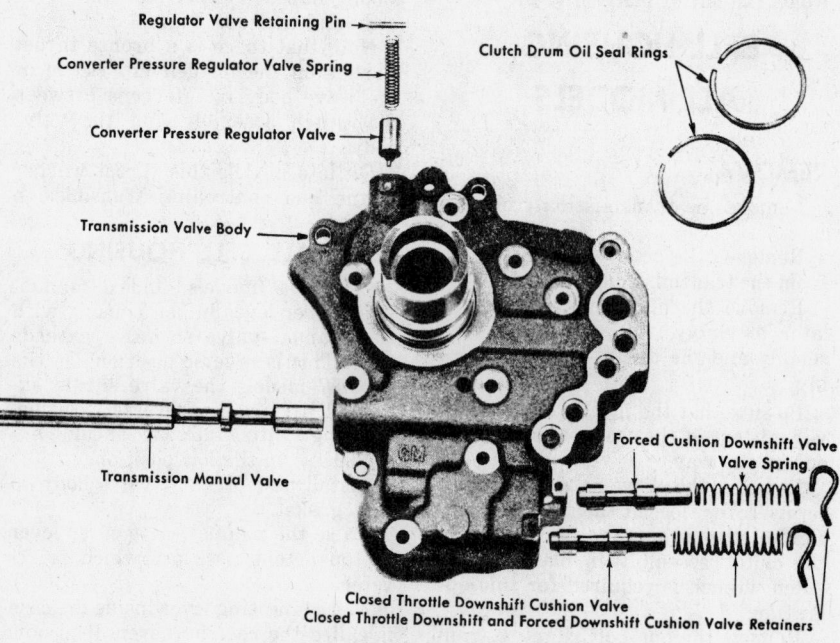

Fig. 26—Powerglide Valve Lay Out 1955-57

© 1960 Chevrolet Div. G.M. Corp.

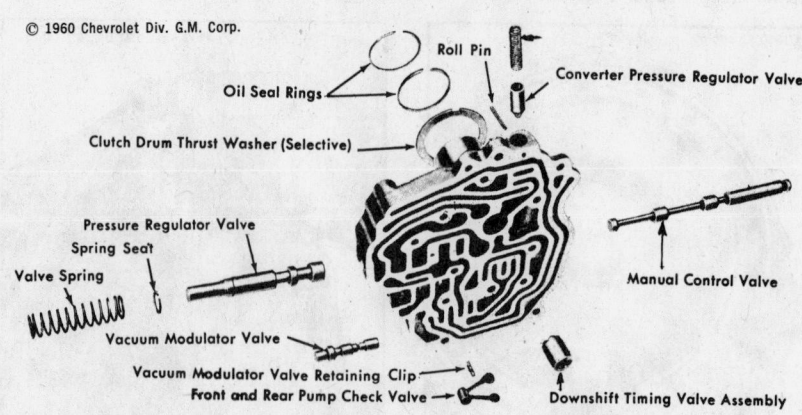

Fig. 27—Powerglide Valve Lay Out 1958-62

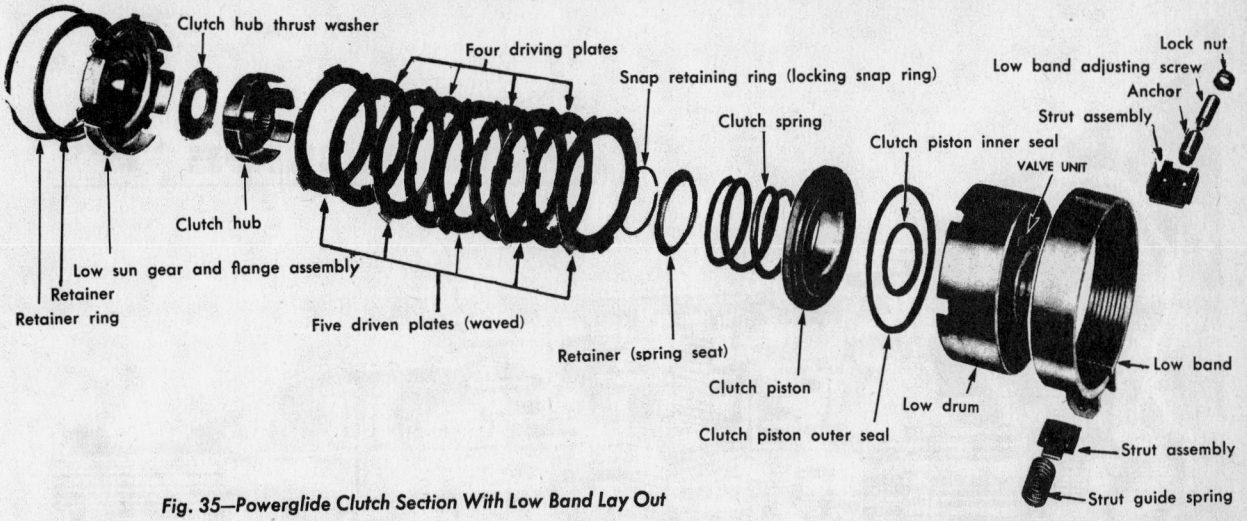

Clutch hub thrust washer

Four driving plates

Snap retaining ring (locking snap ring)

Clutch spring

Clutch piston inner seal

Lock nut

Low band adjusting screw

Anchor

Strut assembly

VALVE UNIT

Clutch hub

Low sun gear and flange assembly

Retainer

Retainer ring

Five driven plates (waved)

Retainer (spring seat)

Clutch piston

Clutch piston outer seal

Low drum

Low band

Strut assembly

Strut guide spring

Fig. 35—Powerglide Clutch Section With Low Band Lay Out

Stator Support

PLUG

Driven Gear

Drive Gear

Pump Body

"O" Ring Seal

Oil Seal

Fig. 29—Front Oil Pump Typical 1955-61

© 1960 Chevrolet Div. G.M. Corp.

Fig. 38—Measuring Low to Reverse Sun Gear Clearance

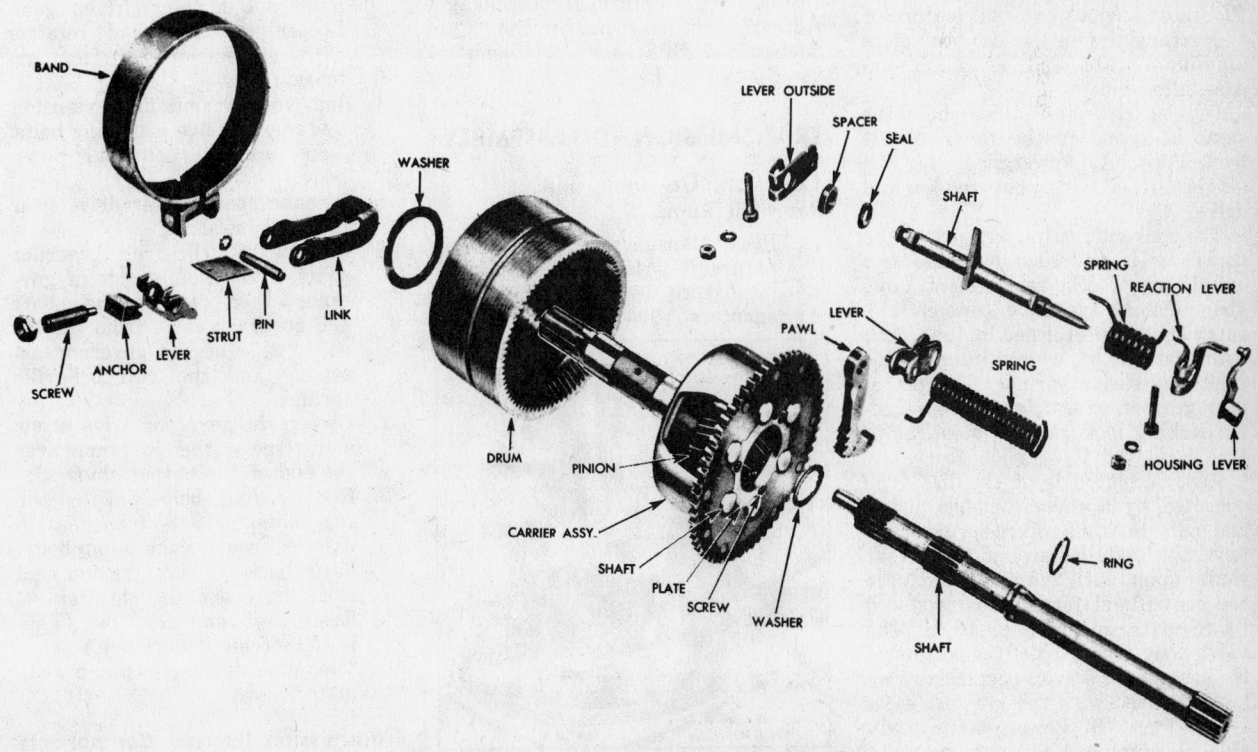

BAND

WASHER

LEVER OUTSIDE

SPACER

SEAL

SHAFT

SPRING

REACTION LEVER

SCREW

ANCHOR

LEVER

STRUT

PIN

LINK

PAWL

LEVER

SPRING

HOUSING LEVER

DRUM

PINION

CARRIER ASSY.

SHAFT

PLATE

SCREW

WASHER

SHAFT

RING

SHAFT

Fig. 36—Planetary Section with Reverse Band Lay Out

CHEVROLET AUTOMATIC TRANSMISSIONS

POWERGLIDE "B"

Aluminum Powerglide—Cross Sectional View—4 Cylinder shown, Typical of All Models.

GENERAL DESCRIPTION

The Type "B" Powerglide transmission is a modified version of the earlier Type "A" Powerglide. Its first appearance was in 1962 production. The most obvious external feature of this transmission is its one piece aluminum case and an aluminum case extension.

Driving characteristics remain the same as found in the familiar cast iron, Type "A" Powerglide with the single shift occurring between low and drive.

The conventionally arranged torque converter is a welded unit and can only be serviced by replacement. Low, (band clutch) and drive, (disc clutch) functions are performed by the clutch drum assembly which incorporates multiple release springs. The planetary gearset, except for the redesigned parking lock gear, is identical to the Type "A" Powerglide gearset.

Reverse clutch is of the disc type operated by a reverse clutch piston and using multiple return springs. The governor, installed around the output shaft, spins with the shaft and uses the centrifugal forces thus produced to regulate governor pressure. The valve body is located at the bottom of the case where service operations may be performed with the greatest ease.

The Type "B" Powerglide is available (beginning 1962) on Chevrolet models powered with the 327 cu. in.

V-8 engine. The Type "B" Powerglide is also optional equipment (with slight torque requirement modifications) on all "Chevy II" models.

Note: "Transmission Remove and Install" and "Transmission Linkage Adjust" will be found in the "Car Section" of this book, pertinent to the car involved.

TRANSMISSION, DISASSEMBLY

Extension, Governor and Rear Oil Pump

1. Place transmission in a holding fixture if possible. Special holding fixture, Tool #J-3289-01 and adapters J-9506 are available on

© 1961 G.M. Corp.

Removing Governor Valve and Shaft.

special order through Chevrolet car dealers.

2. Remove converter holding tool, then lift off the converter.
3. If replacement is necessary, remove speedometer driven gear. Loosen capscrew and retainer clip and remove gear from extension.
4. Remove transmission extension by removing five attaching bolts. Note seal ring on rear pump body.
5. Remove speedometer drive gear from output shaft.
6. Remove "C" clip from governor shaft of the weight side of governor, then remove the shaft and governor valve from the opposite side of the governor assembly and the two belleville springs.
7. Loosen the governor drive screw and remove the governor over the end of the output shaft.
8. Remove four bolts holding the rear oil pump to the transmission case and remove the pump body, drain back baffle, extension seal ring, drive and driven gears.
9. Remove oil pump drive pin. **(This is of extreme importance.)**
10. Then remove the rear pump wear plate.

Transmission Internal Components

11. Rotate holding fixture, or turn

Removing Rear Oil Pump Drive Pin.

the transmission, until the front end is pointing up. Then remove the seven front oil pump bolts. (The bolt holes are of unequal spacing to prevent incorrect location upon installation.)

12. Remove the front oil pump and stator shaft assembly and the selective fit thrust washer using inertia puller, Tool #J-6565 or substitute.

13. Release tension on the low band adjustment, then with transmission horizontal, grasp the transmission input shaft and carefully work it and the clutch drum out of the case. The low sun gear thrust washer will probably remain in the planet carrier.

14. The low brake band and struts may now be removed.

15. Be sure that the rear pump drive pin has been removed, then remove the planet carrier and the output shaft thrust caged bearing from the front of the transmission.

16. Remove reverse ring gear if it did not come out with the planet carrier.

17. With a large screwdriver, remove the reverse clutch pack retainer ring and lift out the reverse clutch plates and the cushion spring.

Applying Air Pressure to Remove Rear Piston.

18. Install Tool #J-9542 through rear bore of the case with the flat plate on the rear face of the case and turn down wing nut to compress the rear piston spring retainer and springs. Then remove the snap ring.

19. Remove the compression tool, the reverse piston spring retainer, and the 17 piston return springs.

20. Remove the rear piston by applying air pressure to the reverse port in the rear of the transmission case. Remove inner and outer seals.

21. Remove the three servo cover bolts, servo cover, piston and spring.

Oil Pan and Valve Body

Note: The oil pan and valve body may be serviced without removing the extension and internal components covered in the preceding steps.

22. Rotate the transmission until the unit is upside down (oil pan on top). Remove oil pan attaching bolts and oil pan.

23. Remove vacuum modulator and gasket, and vacuum modulator valve.

24. Remove two bolts holding the detent guide plate to the valve body and the transmission case. Remove the guide plate and the range selector detent roller spring.

25. Remove the remaining valve body-to-transmission case attaching bolts and lift off the valve body and gasket. Disengage the servo apply tube from the transmission case as the valve body is removed.

26. If necessary, the TV, shift and parking actuator levers and the parking pawl and bracket may be removed.

OVERHAULING
UNIT ASSEMBLIES

CONVERTER AND STATOR

The converter is a welded assembly and no internal repairs are possible.

FRONT PUMP

Seal Replacement

If the front pump seal requires replacement, remove the pump from the transmission, pry out and replace the seal. Drive new seal into place. Then, if no further work is needed on the front pump, reinstall it in the case. (The outer edge of the seal should be coated with non-hardening sealer before installing.)

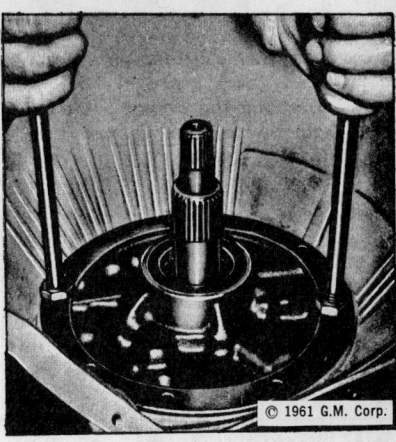

Removing Front Pump.

Disassembly

1. Remove pump cover-to-body attaching bolts and remove the cover.

2. Remove pump gears from body.

3. Remove rubber seal from pump body.

Assembly

1. Remove the input shaft, clutch drum, low band and struts as outlined under "Transmission Disassembly."

2. Install downshift timing valve, conical end out, into place in the pump cover.

3. Lubricate the drive and driven gears and install them in the pump body.

4. Set pump cover in place over the body and loosely install two attaching bolts.

5. Place pump assembly, less the rubber seal ring, upside down into the pump bore of the case. Install remaining attaching bolts and torque to 15-20 ft. lbs.

6. Remove pump assembly from case bore. Replace the clutch drum and input shaft, low band and struts as described under "Transmission Assemble."

7. Renew rubber seal ring in its groove in the pump body and install the pump assembly in place in the case bore, using a new gasket. Be sure that the selective fit thrust washer is in place.

8. Install attaching bolts. (Use new bolt "O" rings if necessary.)

Removing Clutch Drum and Input Shaft.

CHEVROLET AUTOMATIC TRANSMISSIONS

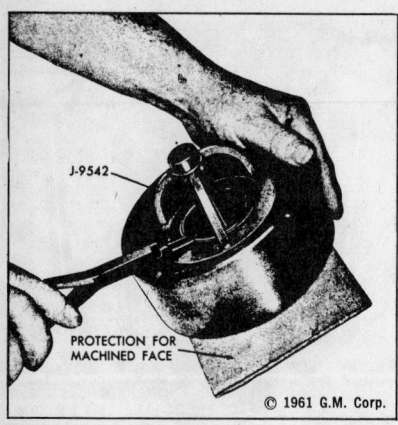

Removing Clutch Spring Retainer Snap Ring.

REAR PUMP

The rear pump is removed and disassembled as described in the "Transmission Disassembly" procedures earlier in this section. Assembly of the rear pump is described in the "Transmission Assemble" procedures later in this section.

CLUTCH DRUM

Disassembly

1. Remove retainer ring and low sun gear and clutch flange assembly from the clutch drum.
2. Remove the hub rear thrust washer.
3. Lift out clutch hub, then remove clutch pack and hub front thrust washer. **Note the number and sequence of plates.**
4. Remove spring retainer with Tool #J-9542, or, if using a press, use Tool #J-5133 and J-7782 adapter ring. Compress the springs enough to permit removal of the retainer snap ring. Then, releasing pressure on the springs, remove retainer and the 24 springs.
5. Lift up on the piston with a twisting motion to remove it from the drum, then remove inner and outer seals.

Clutch Drum Bushing Replacement

If replacing drum bushing, carefully press out the old bushing. Then **press**, (don't hammer) the new bushing into place from the machined face side of the drum. Press only far enough to bring the bushing flush with the clutch drum. Do not force the tool against the clutch drum machined face.

Assembly

1. Install new piston inner seal in hub of clutch drum with seal lip toward front of transmission.
2. Install new piston seal in clutch piston. Seal lips must be pointed toward the clutch drum, (front of transmission). Lubricate the seals and install piston in clutch drum with a twisting motion.
3. Place 24 springs in position on the piston, then place the retainer on the springs.
4. Using the same tools as those used in disassembly, depress the retainer plate and springs enough to permit installation of the spring retainer snap ring in its groove on the clutch drum hub.
5. Install the hub front washer with its lip toward the clutch drum, then install the clutch hub.
6. Install the steel reaction plates and drive (faced) plates beginning with a steel reaction plate.

Note: The number and sequence of plates varies with the power and

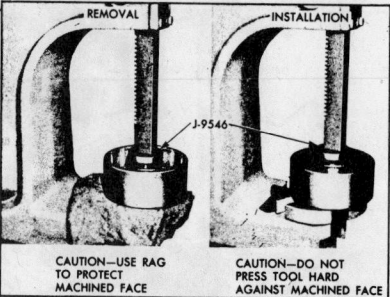

Removing and Installing Clutch Drum Bushing.

torque requirements of the car model involved.

7. Install the rear hub thrust washer with its flange toward the low sun gear, then install the low sun gear and flange assembly and secure with retaining ring. When installed, the openings in the retainer ring should be adjacent to one of the lands of the clutch drum.
8. Check the assembly by turning the clutch hub to be sure it is free to rotate.

LOW BAND

Due to band design and transmission characteristics, this band should require very little attention. However, while the transmission is disassembled the band should be thoroughly cleaned, then replaced if any trace of wear or damage is found.

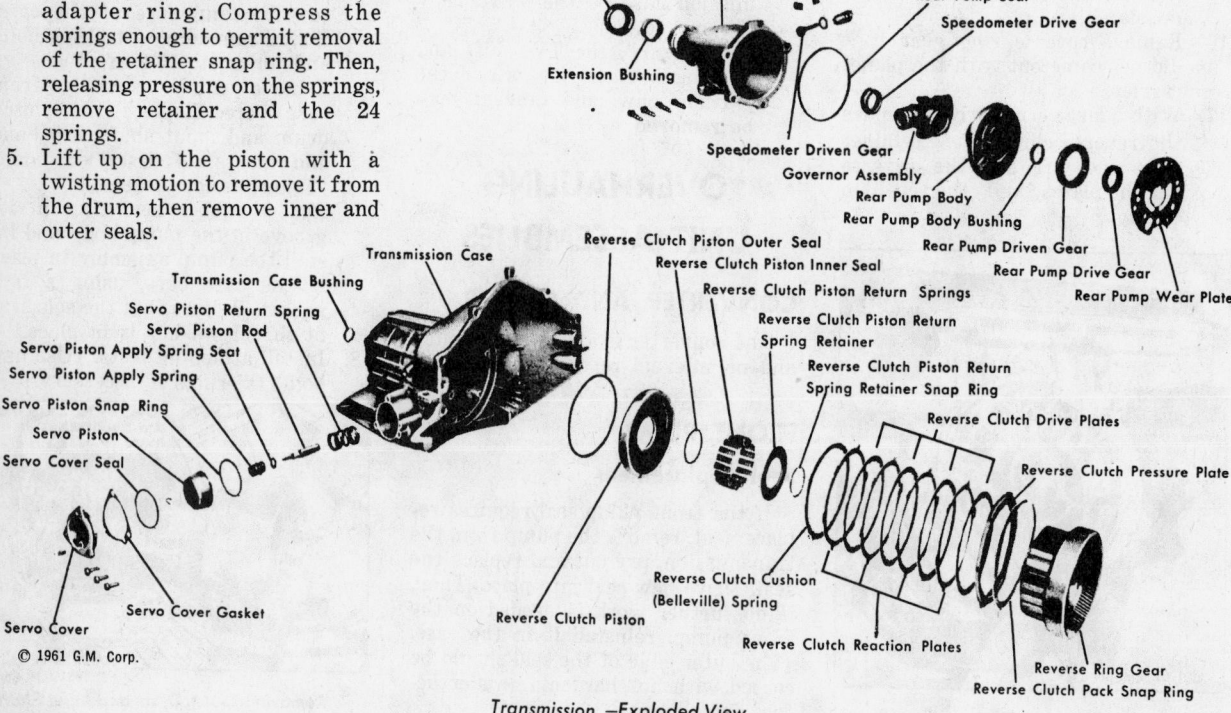

Transmission —Exploded View.

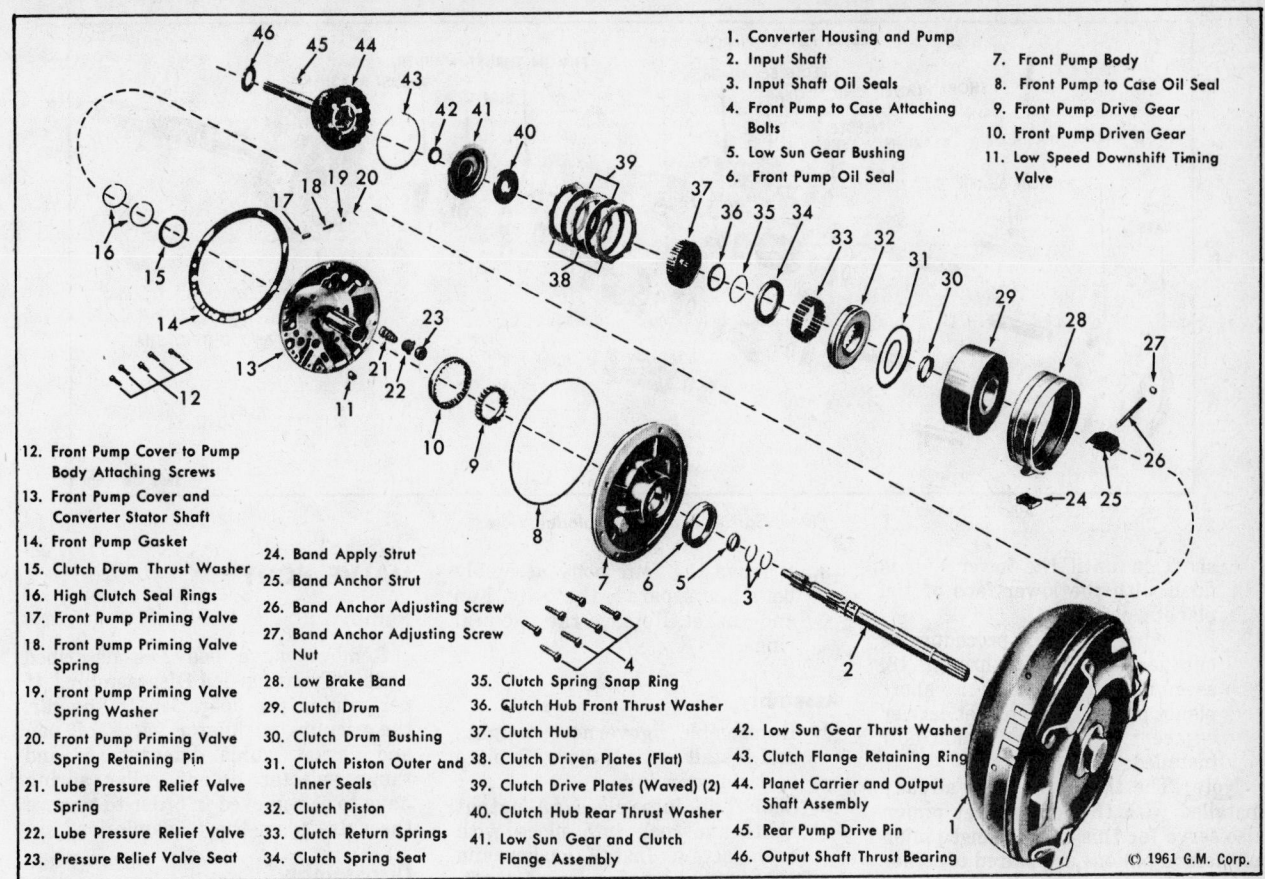

1. Converter Housing and Pump
2. Input Shaft
3. Input Shaft Oil Seals
4. Front Pump to Case Attaching Bolts
5. Low Sun Gear Bushing
6. Front Pump Oil Seal
7. Front Pump Body
8. Front Pump to Case Oil Seal
9. Front Pump Drive Gear
10. Front Pump Driven Gear
11. Low Speed Downshift Timing Valve

12. Front Pump Cover to Pump Body Attaching Screws
13. Front Pump Cover and Converter Stator Shaft
14. Front Pump Gasket
15. Clutch Drum Thrust Washer
16. High Clutch Seal Rings
17. Front Pump Priming Valve
18. Front Pump Priming Valve Spring
19. Front Pump Priming Valve Spring Washer
20. Front Pump Priming Valve Spring Retaining Pin
21. Lube Pressure Relief Valve Spring
22. Lube Pressure Relief Valve
23. Pressure Relief Valve Seat

24. Band Apply Strut
25. Band Anchor Strut
26. Band Anchor Adjusting Screw
27. Band Anchor Adjusting Screw Nut
28. Low Brake Band
29. Clutch Drum
30. Clutch Drum Bushing
31. Clutch Piston Outer and Inner Seals
32. Clutch Piston
33. Clutch Return Springs
34. Clutch Spring Seat

35. Clutch Spring Snap Ring
36. Clutch Hub Front Thrust Washer
37. Clutch Hub
38. Clutch Driven Plates (Flat)
39. Clutch Drive Plates (Waved) (2)
40. Clutch Hub Rear Thrust Washer
41. Low Sun Gear and Clutch Flange Assembly

42. Low Sun Gear Thrust Washer
43. Clutch Flange Retaining Ring
44. Planet Carrier and Output Shaft Assembly
45. Rear Pump Drive Pin
46. Output Shaft Thrust Bearing

© 1961 G.M. Corp.

Internal Mechanism—Exploded View.

PLANET ASSEMBLY AND INPUT SHAFT

If during inspection, any component of the above assembly shows evidence of excessive wear or other damage, the planet assembly should be renewed as a unit or overhauled by the following procedure. (End play of planet gears in the planet carrier should be .006"-.030".)

Repairs

1. Place the planet carrier assembly in a padded vise so that the front (parking lock gear end) of the assembly is up.
2. Using a prick punch, mark each pinion shaft and the carrier assembly so that when reassembling, each shaft will be returned to its original location.
3. Remove pinion shaft lock plate screws and rotate plate counterclockwise enough to remove it.
4. Starting with a short planet pinion, drive the lower end of the pinion shaft up until the shaft is above the press fit area of the output shaft flange. Feed dummy shaft J-4599 into the short planet pinion from the lower end, pushing the planet pinion shaft ahead of it until the tool is centered in the pinion and the pinion shaft is removed.

Note: Planet pinion remover and replacer Tool #J-4599 (dummy shaft) comes in two pieces, both alike. Only one is used when removing planet pinion; two, however, must be used when assembling.

5. Remove short planet pinion.
6. Remove J-4599, needle bearings and bearing spacers from short pinion.

Note: Twenty needle bearings are used in each end of each gear and are separated by a bearing spacer in the center.

7. By following steps 4, 5, and 6, remove the adjacent long planet pinion that was paired by thrust washers to the short pinion now removed.
8. Remove upper and lower thrust washers.
9. Remove and disassemble remaining planet pinions, in pairs, as above.
10. Remove input sun gear and thrust washer.
11. Wash all parts in solvent and blow dry, then inspect.
12. Inspect input shaft bushing in base of output shaft. If damaged, it may be removed by threading Tool #J-9534 into the bushing and pulling the bushing by using slide hammer J-6585. New bearing can be installed by using pilot

end of input shaft as press tool.
13. Using dummy shaft, assemble needle bearings and spacer (20 rollers in each end) in one of the long planet pinions. Use petrolatum to aid in holding the rollers in position.
14. Position long planet gear, with dummy shaft centered in the pinion and with thrust washers at each end, in the planet carrier. Oil grooves on thrust washers must be toward the gears.

Note: Long pinions are located opposite the closed portions of the carrier and short pinions are located in the openings.

15. Feed the second dummy shaft (J-4599) in from the top, picking up the upper thrust washer and the pinion and pushing the already installed dummy shaft out the lower end. As the first dummy is pushed down, be sure that it picks up the lower thrust washer.
16. Select the correct pinion shaft, as marked in step 2, lubricate the shaft and install it from the top, pushing the assembling tools (dummys) ahead of it.
17. Turn the pinion shaft so that the slot or groove at the upper end faces the center of the assembly.
18. With a brass drift, drive the

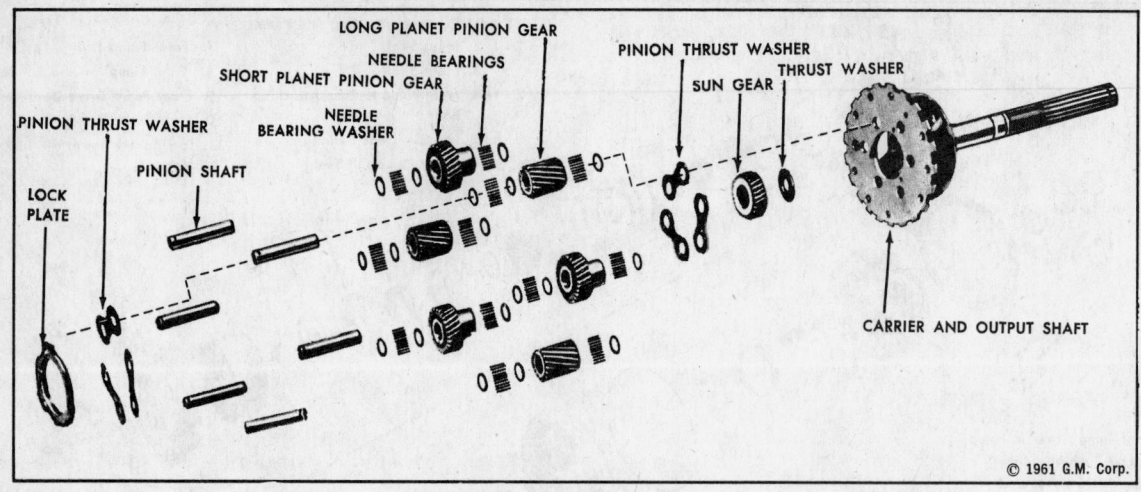

Planet Carrier Assembly Exploded View.

shaft in until the lower end is flush with the lower face of the planet carrier.

19. Following the same procedure as outlined in steps 13 through 18, assemble and install a short planet pinion in the planet carrier adjacent to the long pinion now installed.

Note: The thrust washers already installed with the long planet pinion also serve for this short planet pinion as the two pinions are paired together on one set of thrust washers.

20. Install the input sun gear thrust washer and install the input sun gear.
21. Assemble and install the remaining planet pinions, in pairs, as previously explained.
22. Check end clearance of planet gears. This clearance should be .006"-.030".
23. Place the shaft lock plate in position. Then, with the extended portions of the lock plate aligned with slots in the planet pinion shafts, rotate the lock plate clockwise until the three attaching screw holes are accessible.
24. Install lock plate attaching screws and torque to 2½-3 ft. lbs.

GOVERNOR

The governor assembly is a factory balanced unit. If body replacement is needed, the two sections must be replaced as a unit.

Disassembly

Note: The governor valve and shaft were removed in step 6 of "Removal" procedures.

1. Remove the outer weight by sliding toward center of body.
2. Remove smaller inner weight retaining snap ring and remove inner weight and spring.

3. Remove the four body assembly bolts and separate the body, hub and gasket. Remove the two seal rings.

Assembly

1. Reassemble governor weights and install in body bore. Replace seal rings on hub.
2. Slide hub into place on output shaft and lock into place with drive screw. Install gasket and governor body over output shaft, install governor shaft, line up properly with output shaft and install body attaching bolts. Torque bolts to 6 to 8 ft. lbs.
3. Check governor weight for free fit in body after the four attaching bolts are torqued. If the weight sticks or binds, loosen the bolts and retorque.

VALVE BODY

Remove

Remove valve body as described under "Transmission Disassembly." If performing the operation on the car, the vacuum modulator valve, oil pan and gasket, guide detent plate and range selector detent roller spring have to be removed in order to remove the valve from the transmission.

Disassembly

1. Remove manual valve, suction screen and gasket.
2. Remove cover bolts, then remove lower valve body and transfer plate from upper valve body. Discard gaskets.
3. Remove the front and rear pump check valves and springs.
4. From the upper valve body, re-

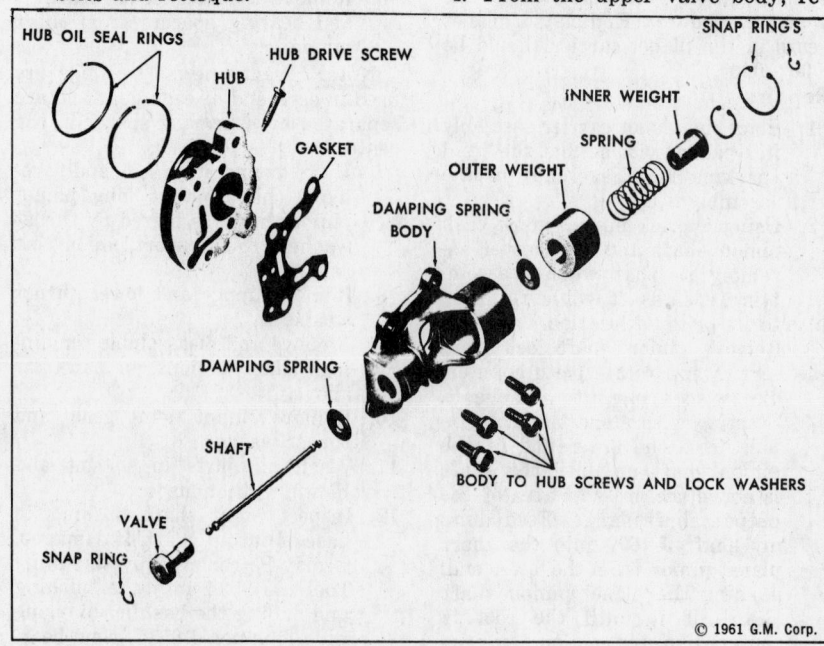

Governor—Exploded View.

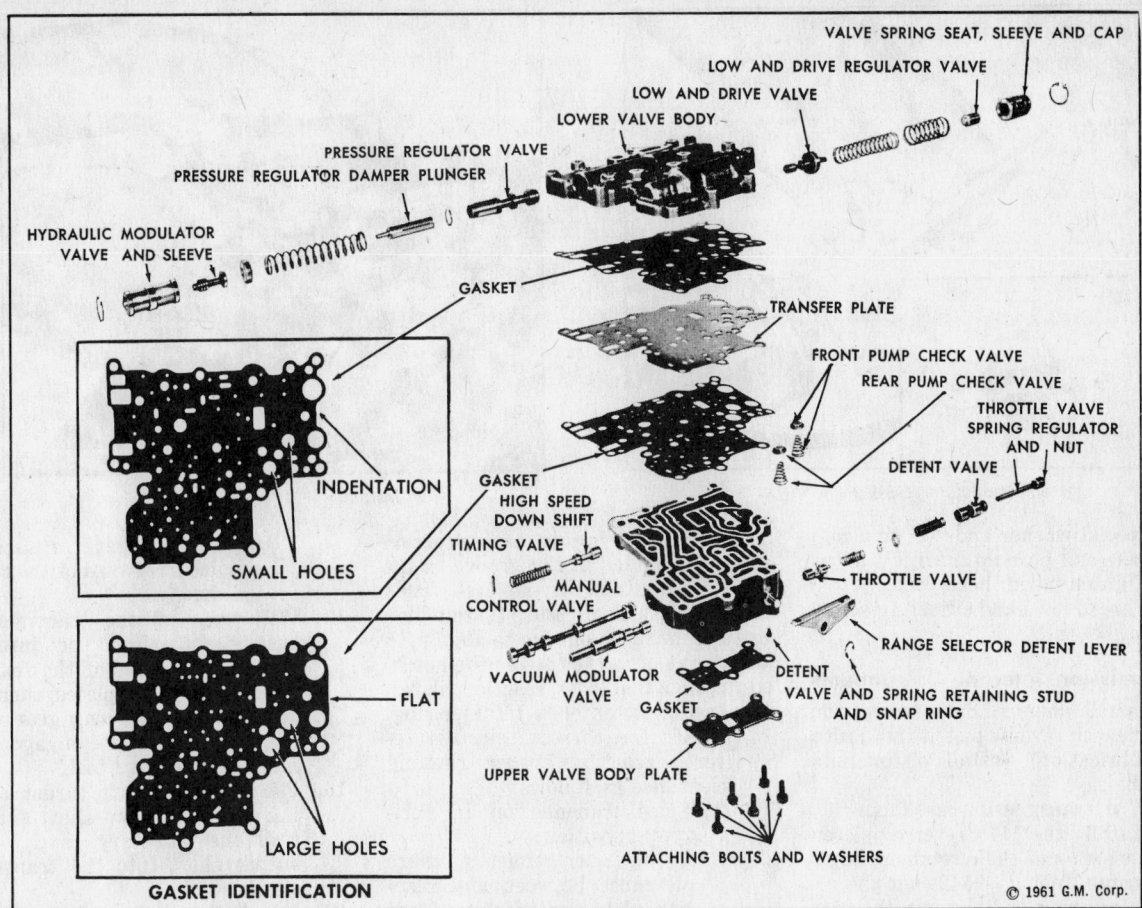

LOW AND DRIVE REGULATOR VALVE — VALVE SPRING SEAT, SLEEVE AND CAP

LOW AND DRIVE VALVE

LOWER VALVE BODY

PRESSURE REGULATOR VALVE

PRESSURE REGULATOR DAMPER PLUNGER

HYDRAULIC MODULATOR VALVE AND SLEEVE

GASKET

TRANSFER PLATE

INDENTATION

SMALL HOLES

FRONT PUMP CHECK VALVE

REAR PUMP CHECK VALVE

THROTTLE VALVE SPRING REGULATOR AND NUT

DETENT VALVE

GASKET HIGH SPEED DOWN SHIFT

TIMING VALVE

MANUAL CONTROL VALVE

THROTTLE VALVE

VACUUM MODULATOR VALVE

RANGE SELECTOR DETENT LEVER

DETENT VALVE AND SPRING RETAINING STUD AND SNAP RING

GASKET

FLAT

UPPER VALVE BODY PLATE

ATTACHING BOLTS AND WASHERS

LARGE HOLES

GASKET IDENTIFICATION

© 1961 G.M. Corp.

Valve Body—Exploded View.

move the TV and detent valves and the downshift timing valve as follows:

A. TV and Detent Valve—Remove the retaining pin by wedging a thin screwdriver between its head and the valve body, then remove the detent valve assembly and throttle spring. Tilt valve body to allow the throttle valve to fall out. If necessary, remove the "C" clip and disassemble the detent valve assembly.

Note: Do not change adjustment of hex nut on the detent valve assembly. This is a factory setting and should not normally be changed. However, some adjustment is possible if desired. See "Throttle Valve Adjustment," in later text.

B. Downshift Timing Valve—Drive out the roll pin, remove valve spring and downshift timing valve.

5. From the lower valve body, remove the low-drive shift valve and the pressure regulator valve as follows:

A. Low-Drive Shift Valve—Remove the snap ring and tilt valve body to remove low-drive regulator valve sleeve

and valve assembly, valve spring seat, valve springs and the shifter valve.

B. Pressure Regulator Valve—Remove the snap ring, then tilt valve body to remove the hydraulic modulator valve sleeve and valve, pressure regulator valve spring seat, spring, damper valve, spring seat and valve.

Assembly

1. Replace valve components in proper bores, reversing the steps of disassembly outlined above.
2. Place front and rear pump check valves and springs into place in upper valve body and install the gasket and transfer plate.
3. Install lower valve body and gasket and install fifteen $1\frac{3}{8}$" attaching bolts. Torque to 8 to 11 ft. lbs.
4. Install valve body onto transmission as outlined under "Transmission, Assembly" in later text.

VACUUM MODULATOR

The vacuum modulator is mounted on the left rear of the transmission and can be serviced from beneath the car.

Remove

1. Remove vacuum line at the modulator.
2. Unscrew the modulator from the transmission with a thin 1" tappet type wrench.
3. Remove vacuum modulator valve.

Install

Reverse above procedure.

TRANSMISSION, ASSEMBLY

Note: If removed, assemble manual linkage to case as described in steps 1-7.

1. Install parking lock pawl and shaft and insert a new roll pin (or "E" ring, whichever the case may be).
2. Install parking lock pawl pullback spring over its boss to rear of pawl. The short leg of the spring should locate in the hole in the pawl.
3. Install parking pawl reaction bracket with its two bolts.
4. Fit the actuator assembly between the parking pawl and the bracket.
5. Insert outer shift lever into the case.
6. Insert outer TV lever and shaft

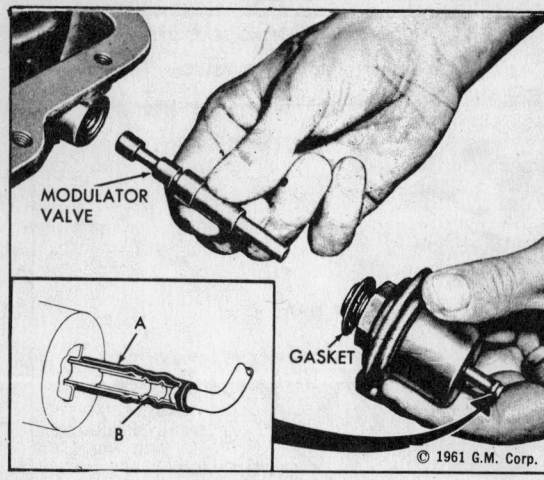

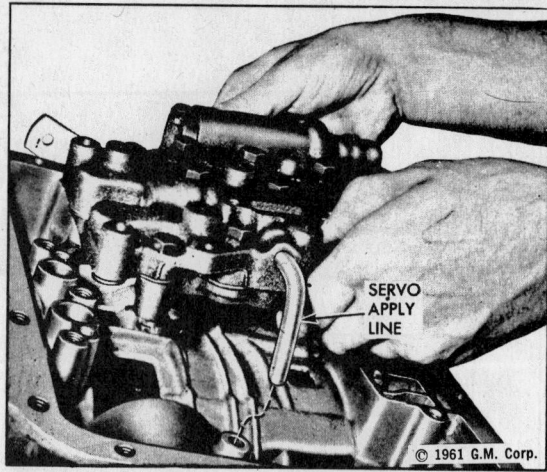

Vacuum Modulator, Gasket and Valve.

Installing   Valve Body

special washer and "O" ring into case and pick up inner TV lever. Tighten allen head lock.

7. Thread low band adjusting screw into case.

Transmission Internal Components

8. Install inner and outer rear piston seals on reverse piston and, (with lubrication) install piston into the case.

9. With transmission case facing up, install the 17 reverse piston springs and their retainer ring.

10. Install Tool #J-9542 over the retainer ring and through the rear bore of the case. With the flat plate on the rear face of the case, turn down on the wing nut to compress the return springs to allow the retaining ring snap ring to be installed. Remove the compressor.

11. Install the large belleville spring, small end down.

12. Lubricate and install reverse clutch pack beginning with a reaction spacer plate and alternating with the faced plates until all plates are installed.

Note: The number and sequence of plates varies with the power and torque requirements of the car model involved.

The notched lug on each reaction plate is installed in the groove at the 7 o'clock position in the case. Then install the thick pressure plate which has a "dimple" in one lug to align with the same slot in the case as the notched lugs on the other reaction plates.

13. Install clutch plate retainer ring.

14. Check for correct selective reverse reaction spacer running clearance as follows:

A. Place transmission in horizontal position.

B. Using feeler gauges, measure clearance between any reaction plate and adjacent faced plate. (Because the faced plate is waved, it is necessary to slide the guage in an arc of several inches to get an average reading.)

C. If the correct selective spacer is installed, gauge measurement will be .012" to .030" in transmissions used with the 4-cylinder engine and .016" to .040" in transmissions built for higher torque requirements.

D. If clearance is not within limits, remove the clutch pack and install a thicker or thin-

ner selective reverse plate, as required, forward of the cushion spring.

15. With rear of the transmission case down, align the internal lands and grooves of the reverse clutch pack faced plates, then engage the reverse ring gear with these plates. This engagement must be made by "feel."

16. Place output shaft thrust bearing over the output shaft and install the planetary carrier and output shaft into the transmission case.

17. Install the low sun gear thrust washer on the sun gear in the planetary gear set with the flange of the thrust washer toward the front of the transmission.

18. With transmission in horizontal position, the two input shaft seal rings should be in place on the shaft. Install clutch drum (ma-

Installing Reverse Piston.

Installing Gearset.

Installing Clutch Plates.

chined face first) onto the input shaft and install the low sun gear bushing against shoulder on shaft.

19. Install clutch drum and input shaft assembly into case, aligning thrust washer on input shaft and indexing low sun gear with the short pinions on the planet carrier.

20. Remove rubber seal ring from the front pump body and install front pump and gasket and selective fit thrust washer into case. Install pump-to-case bolts.

21. To check for correct thickness of the selective fit thrust washer, move transmission so that output shaft points down and proceed as follows:
   A. Mount a dial indicator so that the indicator plunger is resting on the end of the input shaft (J-5492 may be used as a support for the indicator.) Zero the indicator.
   B. Push up on the output shaft and watch the total dial movement.
   C. The indicator should read .030" to .054". If reading is not within limits, remove front pump, change to a thicker or thinner selective thrust washer. Repeat above checking procedure.

Note: Washers are available in thicknesses of .061", .078", .090" and .106".

22. Install servo piston, piston ring, and spring into the servo bore. Then, using a new gasket and "O" ring, install the servo cover.

23. Remove front pump and selective fit washer from the case, and install the low brake band, anchor and apply struts into the case. Tighten the low band adjusting screw enough to prevent struts from falling out of case.

24. Place the seal ring in the groove around front pump body and the two seal rings on the pump cover extension. Install the pump, gasket and thrust washer into the case. Install all pump bolts and torque bolts to 13 to 17 ft. lbs.

Extension, Governor and Rear Oil Pump

25. Turn transmission so that output shaft points upward. Install rear pump wear plate, drive pin, and drive gear, indexing gear to drive pin.

26. Install rear pump body and driven gear, drain back baffle and pump-to-case attaching bolts.

27. Install governor over output shaft. Install governor shaft and valve, two belleville washers, and

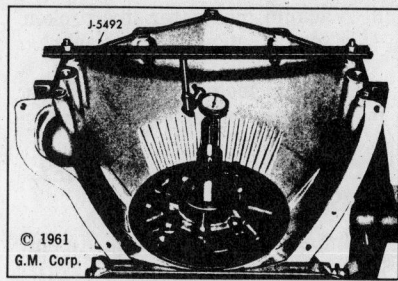

Checking Endplay for Proper Thrust

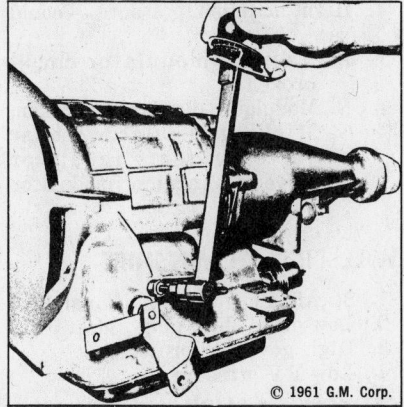

Low Band Adjustment.

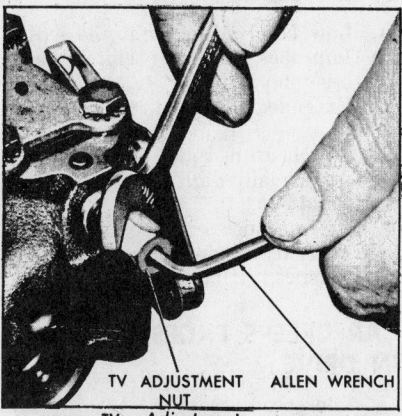

TV Adjustment.

Installing Detent Guide Plate

retaining "C" clips. Center shaft in output shaft bore and tighten governor drive screw.

28. Install speedometer drive gear onto output shaft

29. Place extension seal ring over rear pump body and install trans-

mission extension and five retaining bolts.

30. If removed, replace speedometer driven gear.

Oil Pan and Valve Body

31. With transmission upside down, the manual linkage installed, and the selector lever detent roller installed, install the valve body with a new gasket. (Carefully guide the servo apply line into its boss in the case as the valve is set in place.) Install six mounting bolts and the range selector detent roller spring.

32. Install the guide plate. Install attaching bolts.

33. Install vacuum modulator valve, the vacuum modulator and the gasket.

34. Install oil pan, using a new gasket, then the pan attaching bolts.

35. Install the converter and safety holding strap J-5949 or a suitable substitute.

Low Band Adjustment

Tighten the low servo adjusting screw to 40 inch pounds. The input and output shaft must be rotated simultaneously to properly center the low band on the clutch drum. Then back off four complete turns, and tighten the lock nut.

Caution: The amount of back-off is very critical. Back off exactly 4 turns.

Throttle Valve Adjustment

No provision is made for checking TV pressures. However, if operation of the transmission is such that some adjustment of the TV is indicated, pressures may be raised or lowered by adjusting the position of the jam nut on the throttle valve assembly. To raise TV pressure 3 PSI, backoff the jam nut one full turn.

Conversely, tightening the jam nut one full turn, lowers TV pressure 3 PSI. A difference of 3 PSI in TV pressure will cause a change of about 2 to 3 MPH in the wide open throttle upshift point. The end of the TV adjusting screw has an Allen head so the screw may be held stationary while the jam nut is locked.

Note: Use care in changing this adjustment as no pressure tap is provided to check TV pressure.

DIAGNOSIS GUIDE

NO DRIVE IN ANY SELECTOR POSITION:

1. Low oil level.
2. Clogged oil screen.
3. Bad pressure regulator valve.
4. Bad front pump.
5. Input shaft broken.
6. Front pump priming valve stuck.

CHEVROLET AUTOMATIC TRANSMISSIONS

ENGINE SPEED FLARES ON STANDSTILL, ACTS LIKE CLUTCH SLIPPING

1. Low band partially applied — could be:
   A. Low oil level.
   B. Clogged oil screen.
   C. Improper band adjustment.
   D. Servo apply passage blocked.
   E. Servo piston ring broken.
   F. Band facing worn.
   G. Low band apply linkage broken.
   H. Converter stator not holding.

ENGINE RUN-AWAY ON UPSHIFTS

1. Low oil level.
2. Improper band adjustment.
3. Clogged oil screen.
4. High clutch partially applied.
5. High clutch plates worn.
6. High clutch seal leak.
7. High clutch piston stuck.
8. High clutch drum relief ball not seating.
9. Vacuum modulator line blocked.

TRANSMISSION WILL NOT UPSHIFT

1. Low band not releasing—could be:
   A. Stuck low-drive valve.
   B. Defective governor.
   C. No rear pump output.
   D. Throttle valve stuck or maladjusted.
   E. Improperly adjusted manual valve lever.

UPSHIFT, HARSH

1. Improper carburetor-to-transmission T V rod adjustment.
2. Incorrect low band adjustment.

3. Vacuum modulator line broken.
4. Vacuum modulator diaphragm leaks.
5. Vacuum modulator valve stuck.
6. Hydraulic modulator valve stuck.

DECELERATION DOWNSHIFT, HARSH

1. Improper low band adjustment.
2. High engine idle speed.
3. Downshift timing valve malfunction.
4. High mainline pressure — could be:
   A. Vacuum modulator circuit broken.
   B. Modulator diaphragm broken.
   C. Sticking regulator booster valve, pressure regulator valve or vacuum modulator valve.

WILL NOT DOWNSHIFT

1. Sticking low-drive shift valve.
2. Low-drive shift plug stuck.
3. High governor pressure.
4. Low T V pressure.

CLUTCH FAILURE, BURNT PLATES

1. Low band adjustment too loose.
2. Improper order of clutch pack assembly.
3. Extended operation with low oil level.
4. Clutch drum relief ball stuck.
5. Abnormally high speed upshift— could be:
   A. Improper governor action.
   B. Transmission operated at high speed in manual "Low."

CAR CREEPS EXCESSIVELY IN DRIVE

1. Idle speed too high.

CAR CREEPS IN "NEUTRAL"

1. Incorrect manual valve lever adjustment.
2. High clutch or low band not released.

NO DRIVE IN REVERSE

1. Incorrect manual valve lever adjustment.
2. Reverse clutch piston stuck.
3. Reverse clutch plates worn out.
4. Reverse clutch leaking excessively.
5. Blocked reverse clutch apply orifice.

IMPROPER SHIFT POINTS

1. Incorrectly adjusted carburetor-to-transmission linkage.
2. Incorrectly adjusted throttle valve.
3. Bad governor.
4. Rear pump priming valve stuck.

UNABLE TO PUSH-START CAR

1. Rear pump drive gear not engaged with drive pin on output shaft.
2. Drive pin sheared off.
3. Rear pump priming valve not sealing.

OIL LEAKS

1. Transmission case and extension —could be:
   A. Extension oil seal.
   B. Shifter shaft oil seal.
   C. Speedometer driven gear fitting.
   D. Pressure taps.
   E. Oil cooler pipe connections.
   F. Vacuum modulator. A very smoky exhaust with low transmission oil level may be

POWERGLIDE SHIFT POINTS

Engine	Passenger Car				Corvette	
	327*		327 High Perf.**		327*	
Throttle Position	Up	Down	Up	Down	Up	Down
Closed	14-16	11.5-15	12-15	10.5-14	12-15	11-14
Detent Touch	48-58	17-25	49-60	16-25	50-62	16-26
Through Detent	59-65	55-63	59-66	56-63	61-68	58-65

* 3.08:1 Axle   ** 3.36:1 Axle

ENGINE	L-4		L-6	
Throttle Position	Up	Down	Up	Down
Closed	10-13	9-12	12-15	10-13
Detent Touch	34-43	18-27	38-47	19-30
Through Detent	42-48	39-46	47-53	43-50

caused by a ruptured vacuum modulator diaphragm.
2. Transmission oil pan gasket.
3. Converter cover pan—could be:
   A. Front pump attaching bolts.
   B. Front pump seal ring.
   C. Front pump oil seal.
   D. Oil drain in front pump plugged.
   E. Porosity in transmission case.

OIL FORCED OUT OF FILLER TUBE

1. Oil level too high.
2. Water in the oil.
3. Leak in pump suction circuits.

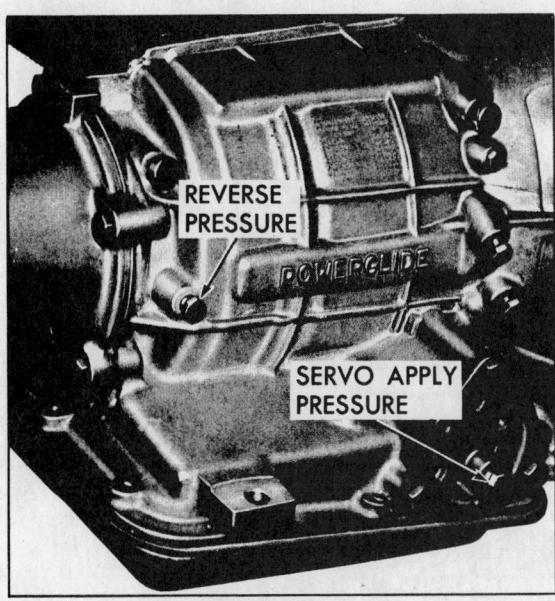

Pressure Test Plugs

VACUUM	LOW SERVO APPLY (MAINLINE) PRESSURE	
	L-4 Engine	L-6 Engine
16" Hg.	61-69	62-73
10" Hg.	78-86	85-95

Checking Driven Gear to Pump Body Clearance

Checking Gear End Clearance

Driven Gear to Crescent Clearance

Checking Pump Body Bushing to Converter Pump Hub Clearance

TURBOGLIDE

1957-61

© 1960 Chevrolet Div. G.M. Corp.

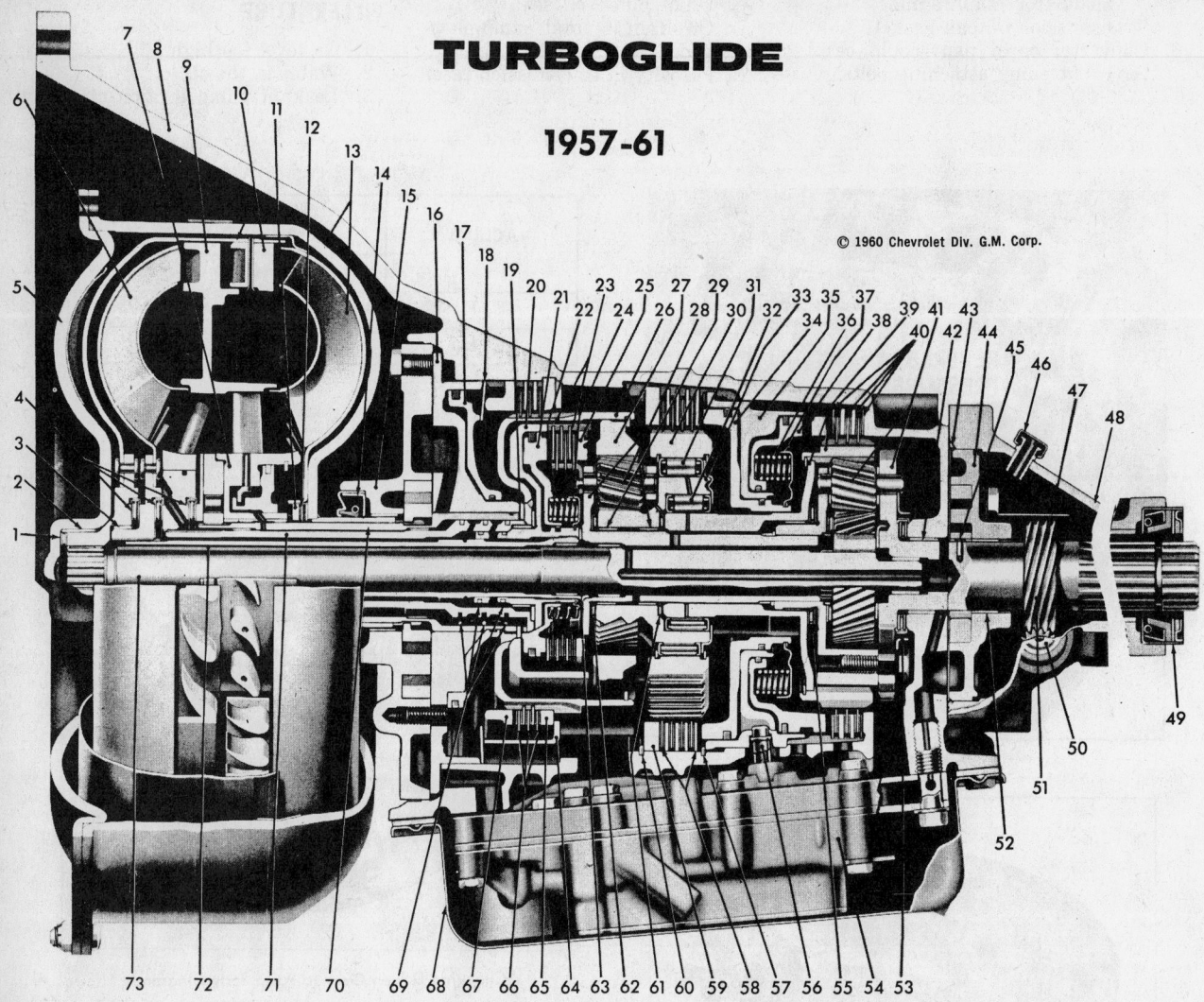

Fig. 1—Turboglide Transmission—Cross Sectional View

1. Needle Bearing and Races
2. Converter Cover Hub Bushing
3. First Turbine Hub Bushing (Serviced)
4. Caged Needle Bearings
5. Converter Cover (Serviced as an Assembly with Item 7)
6. Third Turbine Assembly
7. Stator Assembly
8. Transmission Case
9. Second Turbine Assembly
10. First Turbine Assembly
11. Stator Rear Thrust Pad
12. Needle Bearing and Race
13. Converter Pump (Serviced as an Assembly with Item 4)
14. Front Pump Oil Seal
15. Front Pump Assembly
16. Front Pump Cover (Stator Support)
17. Reverse Piston
18. Reverse Piston Spring
19. Thruster Washer (Selective)
20. Neutral Clutch Hub
21. Neutral Clutch Piston
22. Neutral Clutch Piston Return Spring (16)
23. Neutral Clutch Drive Plates (3) and Driven Plates (3)
24. Neutral Clutch Piston Return Spring Retainer
25. Neutral Clutch Rear Drive Plate
26. Front Ring Gear Hub

27. Front Ring Gear
28. Front Planet Carrier Assembly
29. Front Sun Gear Front Bushings (Serviced)
30. Forward Clutch Freewheel Sprag Race
31. Forward Clutch Freewheel Sprag (Outer Sprag)
32. Rear Ring Gear Freewheel Sprag (Inner Sprag)
33. Front Sun Gear
34. Forward Piston
35. Forward and Brake Piston Support
36. Forward and Brake Piston Return Spring
37. Forward and Brake Piston Return Spring Seat
38. Brake Piston
39. Rear Ring Gear Assembly
40. Brake Drive Plates (3) and Reactor Plates (2 Inner and 2 Outer)
41. Rear Planet Carrier Assembly (includes Output Shaft)
42. Transmission Case Bushing (Serviced)
43. Rear Oil Pump Gear Spacer
44. Rear Oil Pump Assembly
45. Rear Oil Pump Drive Pin
46. Vent Assembly
47. Oil Deflector
48. Transmission Extension
49. Oil Seal Assembly
50. Speedometer Driven Gear

51. Speedometer Drive Gear
52. Rear Oil Pump Bushing (Serviced)
53. Needle Thrust Bearing Assembly
54. Valve Body Assembly
55. Needle Bearing Assembly
56. Oil Pressure Tube (2)
57. Retainer Ring
58. Forward Clutch Drive Plates (4) and Reaction Plates (4)
59. Forward Clutch Pressure Plate
60. Retainer Ring
61. Needle Bearing Assembly
62. Needle Bearing Assembly and Race
63. Front Planet Carrier Thrust Washer
64. Reverse Clutch Reaction Insert
65. Reverse Rear Pressure Plate
66. Reverse Drive Plates (3) and Reaction Plates (2)
67. Reverse Front Pressure Plate (Selective)
68. Oil Pan
69. Oil Seal Rings
70. Stator Support Shaft (Part of Stator Support)
71. Second Turbine Shaft (Part of Front Ring Gear Hub)
72. Third Turbine Shaft (Part of Neutral Clutch Hub)
73. First Turbine Shaft (Part of First Turbine Assembly)

TURBOGLIDE TRANS-
MISSION
1957-61

Beginning 1959 some changes have been made in Turbo-Glide design. In function however, the unit is identical to that used in 1957 and 1958.

All manually controlled clutches are now of the multiple plate type. Cone clutches have been discontinued at the reverse and forward clutch locations. The plate-type grade retarder and neutral clutch units brought out in the previous year's design remain basically unchanged.

A five spoke converter became effective in late 1958 production. In addition the 1959 design includes a second turbine shaft of heavier construction, and a bushing to prevent interference between the second turbine shaft and the stator shaft bore.

The radial needle bearings and races used at the first turbine hub in the converter have been replaced by a solid bearing.

Changes in the valve body include the elimination of the body reinforcing straps, accumulator passage plug, and the two check valves in the modulating oil circuit. Other changes include the adding of a second spring and spring cap between the pressure regulator valve and the hydraulic modulator valve, and the replacement of two springs that were used with the hydraulic modulator accumulator by one short, heavy spring.

The front planetary set now consists of six planet gears instead of three. The front planetary set is no longer serviceable except as a unit. However, components for the rear planetary set are still available.

GENERAL
INFORMATION

CHECKING FLUID LEVEL

The fluid level should be checked every 1000 miles. The engine should be idling. The temperature gauge should indicate that the car is at normal operating temperature as the oil in the transmission must be HOT to give a correct reading. The hand lever should be at "D."

Remove the oil level dipstick from the transmission fill tube on the right rear side of the engine. The level should be AT the "Full" mark. Add fluid only if the level is below. Never overfill the transmission as the resultant aeration of the oil by the planetary gears will impair the proper operation of the clutches. If the level is consistently low be sure to find the

leak. The transmission can be quickly ruined by the high temperatures resulting from insufficient fluid.

DRAINING AND REFILLING

Note: The converter has no drain plugs. Start engine and run with brake set and hand lever at "D" until transmission is HOT. Shut off the engine and remove the drain plug from the front end of the transmission oil pan.

When draining is completed reinstall the plug and pour 3½ quarts of fluid into the transmission.

Start the engine and allow to idle with hand lever at "D." When transmission is up to operating temperature check that level is at "Full" mark.

Starting with 1958 production, periodic draining is not required.

REFILLING AFTER OVERHAUL

Total capacity of the transmission is 9½ quarts. Use a good grade of automatic transmission fluid.

Pour in 5 quarts and start engine. Slowly add 4 more quarts while engine idles with hand lever at "N."

When transmission has reached operating temperature move hand lever to "D" and check the level. Add sufficient fluid to bring the level to the "Full" mark.

FLUID TEMPERATURE

There is a thermal by-pass valve fastened to the right front side of the transmission case. Fluid flows from the converter thru the by-pass valve to the transmission lubricating system and the sump. When the temperature of the fluid reaches 180 deg F. the valve routes it to the oil cooler in the bottom of the radiator. The fluid flows thru the cooler and back to the by-pass valve and so into the lubricating system and the sump.

OIL COOLER

Whenever any work is done on the transmission be sure to check the oil cooler. It is possible for sludge to choke the cooler or the lines. The resultant rise in temperature can raise the fluid level causing aeration of the oil and malfunction of the controls. Fluid can also be lost out the filler tube or the breather on the rear extension as a result of the transmission being overheated. Loss of fluid can result in failure of the oil seals at the front and rear ends of the transmission.

PUSHING THE CAR TO
START THE ENGINE

Place hand lever at "N." When car

reaches 25-30 mph turn ignition key to "On" and move the hand lever to "Hr" (Hill Retarder). Starting with 1958 "Gr" (Grade Retarder) is used in place of the former "Hr." At this speed the first turbine is spinning fast enough to turn the engine and the rear oil pump has developed enough pressure to operate the transmission. Car must be pushed to start because if towed it may accelerate into the tow car when the engine starts.

TOWING THE CAR

A car equipped with Turboglide transmission can only be towed on its rear wheels when the hand lever is in Neutral "N" position. It should not be towed in excess of 30 mph.

If the hand lever cannot be put in Neutral the rear wheels must be off the ground or the drive shaft disconnected from the transmission before it can be towed.

CHECKING OPERATION
OF UNITS WITH AIR
PRESSURE SEE FIG. 2

Use air at 100 lbs pressure. Drain the transmission oil pan and remove the pan, the screen and the oil body. Leave the little tubes that connect the valve body to the Forward and Grade Retarder clutches, see Fig. 2. If tests are made with transmission on the bench be sure to clamp the converter into place to prevent air pressure blowing it off.

REVERSE CLUTCH

Apply air to the reverse clutch port and check that the reverse cone moves rearward. If the cone does not move check into the position of the front pump-to-transmission case gasket. Check also that the reverse piston is not cocked or stuck. If air leaks are heard the gasket may be defective or the reverse piston seals have been damaged.

STATOR PISTON

Apply air to the stator piston port and listen for air leaks. Leakage at this point may be due to the front pump-to-transmission case gasket, broken or warped seal rings on the second turbine shaft, defective stator piston seal or damage to the brass seal on the inside diameter of the stator support. The last mentioned seal is not available separately so that if it is damaged the stator support assembly must be replaced.

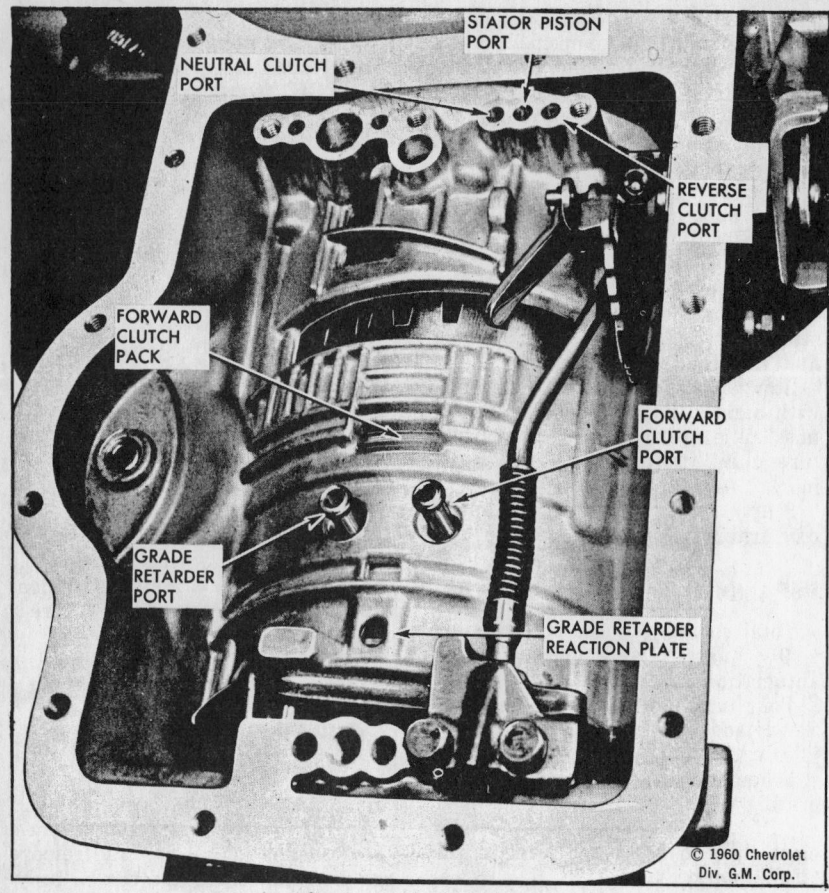

STATOR PISTON PORT

NEUTRAL CLUTCH PORT

REVERSE CLUTCH PORT

FORWARD CLUTCH PACK

FORWARD CLUTCH PORT

GRADE RETARDER PORT

GRADE RETARDER REACTION PLATE

© 1960 Chevrolet Div. G.M. Corp.

Fig. 2—Air Check Apply Points

NEUTRAL CLUTCH

Apply air pressure to the neutral clutch port. Listen for application of the clutch. If nothing is heard the front pump-to-transmission case gasket may be blocking the passages or the clutch piston may be stuck. Leakage noise can be due to the gasket, broken seal rings on the 2nd or 3rd turbine shafts, defective seals on the clutch piston, defective brass seal on the inside diameter of the second turbine shaft. If the last named seal is faulty the front ring gear hub and shaft assembly must be replaced.

FORWARD CLUTCH

Apply air to the little tube leading to the forward cone clutch. Check that the clutch applies. A blockage of the oil feed orifice in the forward and brake piston support, or cocked piston "O" rings can prevent clutch application. Leakage can be due to damaged seals: on the oil pressure tube in the forward clutch port; or on the piston itself.

GRADE RETARDER CLUTCH

Apply air to the little tube leading to the Grade Retarder clutch. Check for the movement of the clutch reaction plate which should occur as the brake plates are forced against it. If no movement, the orifice in the piston support is blocked or the seals on the Forward and Grade Retarded clutches are cocked.

Leakage can be due to damaged "O" ring seals on the tube or the piston.

TROUBLE SHOOTING CHART

TROUBLE: NO DRIVE IN ANY POSITION

Possible Cause: Front Pump Assembled Backwards

Remedy: Remove transmission from car and overhaul front pump.

TROUBLE: DRIVE ON "HR" OR "GR" POSITION ONLY

Possible Cause: One-Way Clutches Assembled Backwards

Remedy: Remove transmission from car and overhaul one-way clutches.

TROUBLE: DRIVE IN "HR" OR "GR" AND—REVERSE ONLY

Possible Causes: Front Sun Gear One-Way Clutch Installed Wrong or Severe Leakage in Forward and Neutral Cone Clutch Circuit

Remedy: Remove transmission from car and check the one-way clutch and the cone clutch fluid passages.

TROUBLE: HILL OR GRADE RETARD APPLIES TOO FAST

Possible Cause: Vacuum Line To Vacuum Diaphragm Valve Disconnected

Remedy: Reinstall vacuum line.

TROUBLE: NO REVERSE, POOR PERFORMANCE AT LOW SPEED, "HR" OR "GR" NORMAL

Possible Cause: Rear Planet Ring Gear One-Way Clutch Installed Wrong

Remedy: Remove transmission from car and check inner one of the two one-way clutches.

TROUBLE: CAR CREEPS IN NEUTRAL, REVERSE OK

Possible Cause: Neutral Cone Clutch Not Releasing

Remedy: Remove and overhaul transmission.

TROUBLE: CAR DRIVES IN NEUTRAL. REVERSE WON'T WORK

Possible Cause: Forward Cone Clutch Not Releasing

Remedy: Remove and overhaul transmission.

TROUBLE: CANNOT ACHIEVE CHANGE OF STATOR ANGLE

Possible Cause No. 1: Stator-Throttle Linkage Maladjusted

Remedy: Apply procedure in paragraph headed "Throttle Linkage" in car section, headed Adjustments.

Possible Cause No. 2: Leakage Inside the Transmission Resulting In Low Pressure Within The Converter

Remedy: Remove and overhaul transmission.

TROUBLE: UNABLE TO PUSH START

Possible Cause: Rear Oil Pump Drive Pin Broken Or Missing

Remedy: Rear oil pump can be removed without taking transmission out of car. Follow, procedure under general heading Disassembly, in the paragraph covering the rear extension.

TROUBLE: SLIPPAGE DURING FULL THROTTLE STARTS

Probable Causes: Internal Leakage, Cone Clutch Pistons Sticking, Cone Clutch Facings Worn

Remedy: Remove and overhaul transmission.

TROUBLE: HILL OR GRADE RETARD SLOW TO APPLY

Possible Cause No. 1: Manual Control Maladjusted

Remedy: Apply procedure in paragraph headed "Manual Linkage" in car section headed Adjustments.

Possible Causes 2 and 3: Leakage Within The Transmission or Stuck Cone Clutch Pistons. Note That If Neutral Cone Clutch Sticks on During Hill or Grade Retard The Multiple Disc Clutch Is Quickly Damaged

Remedy: Remove and overhaul transmission.

TROUBLE: DRIVES IN REVERSE ONLY

Possible Cause: Reverse Cone Clutch Not Disengaged

Remedy: Remove and overhaul transmission.

TROUBLE: SHIFTS FROM STANDSTILL TOO SLOW

Possible Cause No. 1: Manual Control Maladjusted

Remedy: See car section headed Adjustments. Apply paragraph headed Manual Control.

Possible Causes Nos. 2 and 3: Neutral Accumulator Piston Stuck Closed, Leakage in Hydraulic System

Remedy: Remove and overhaul valve body and transmission.

TROUBLE: SHIFTS FROM STANDSTILL TOO FAST

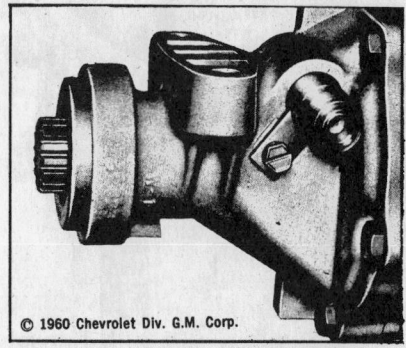

© 1960 Chevrolet Div. G.M. Corp.

Fig. 3—Speedometer Driven Gear and Extension

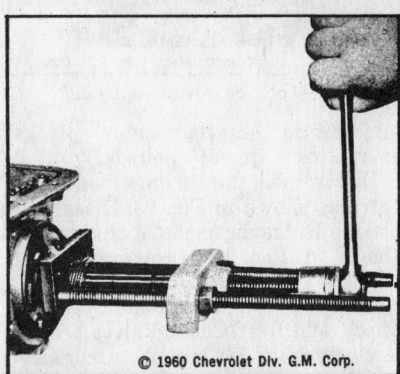

© 1960 Chevrolet Div. G.M. Corp.

Fig. 4—Removal of Speedometer Drive Gear from Output Shaft

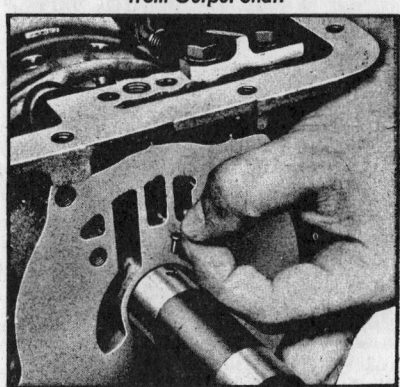

Fig. 5—Removal and Installation of Rear Oil Pump Gear Drive Pin

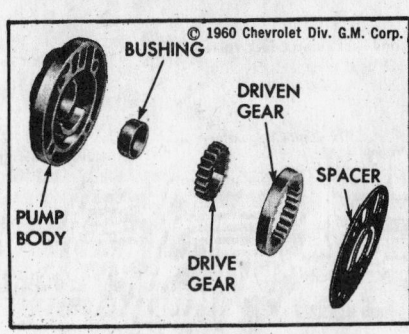

© 1960 Chevrolet Div. G.M. Corp.

Fig. 6—Rear Oil Pump Lay Out

Possible Cause: Neutral Accumulator Piston Stuck Open

Remedy: Remove and overhaul valve body.

DISASSEMBLY, OVER-HAUL AND ASSEMBLY

PARTS THAT CAN BE REMOVED WITH TRANSMISSION IN THE CAR

SPEEDOMETER DRIVEN GEAR (FIG. 3)

Located on left rear of rear extension. Remove cap screw and retainer which will release the pinion.

REAR EXTENSION

Remove the five cap screws retaining the rear extension to the case and remove the extension. Note square seal ring on rear oil pump body. The bushing in the rear extension is not serviced separately. The rear oil seal is replaceable. If the output shaft is not concentric to the seal remove the extension and tap the rear oil pump slightly.

REAR OIL PUMP (FIGS. 4, 5, 6)

Using a puller, remove the speedometer drive gear from the output shaft. Unscrew four bolts and so release the rear oil pump body from the case.

Remove the oil pump gears, being careful to catch the pump drive pin which will fall out of its hole in the shaft when the drive gear is removed.

Wash the oil pump parts and blow out the passages. Check the clearances. Driven gear to body should be .0025-.0055 inch. Drive gear to cres cent .003-.009 inch. Faces of gears to face of body .003-.009 inch.

A precision-type bushing is available to replace the rear pump body bushing. Cut the old bushing out. Press the new one in from the front face of the pump so that it is flush with surface of gear chamber. Bushing does not require reaming.

Oil the gears with Type A fluid before installing. Install the drive gear pin and install the pump, being careful that pin aligns with slot in drive gear. Refasten pump to case with four bolts. Note that if this operation is performed with transmission out of car the converter must be installed before the rear pump bolts are tightened. Reinstall speedometer drive gear and rear extension.

OIL PAN

Remove oil pan screws to release the oil pan and gasket.

VALVE BODIES (FIGS. 7 THRU 13)

Remove four bolts and parking lock spring clip to release the valve body assembly and two gaskets. Note that these bolts are of two different sizes and that one has a drilled oil passage. The one with the oil passage is the rear one. Fig. 7.

Removal of the valve assembly exposes two oil transfer tubes equipped with "O" seal rings. The two tubes are identical and interchangeable. Fig. 8.

Remove one screw to release the oil screen. Remove two screws to release vacuum modulator valve and gasket.

Remove nine screws to release the ditch plate (upper portion of assembly) and its gasket from the transfer plate; and the main valve body (lower portion of assembly) and its gasket from the transfer plate. Fig. 10.

Carefully hold the hydraulic modulator valve assembly to the main valve body to counter the thrust of the pressure regulator valve spring while removing the two bolts that hold it to the body.

Hold the hydraulic modulator valve in a vise as shown in Fig. 9 while removing the accumulator valve retain-

ATTACHING BOLTS

HOLLOW BOLT

PARKING PAWL SPRING

© 1960 Chevrolet Div. G.M. Corp.

Fig. 7—Location of Valve Body Bolts

ing ring as the accumulator springs exert a pressure of 90 pounds.

Disassemble the vacuum modulator valve as shown in Fig. 10. Disassemble the hydraulic modulator valve as shown in Fig. 11. Disassemble the main valve body as shown in Fig. 12. Note that the Lube-Relief, Front-Check, and Rear-Check Valves are interchangeable. Do not lose accumulator check valve from ditch plate. Re-

move the seven oil passage pipe plugs shown in Fig. 13.

Clean all the parts. Check the springs for distortion; the bodies for cracks; the passages for cleanliness; the valves for burrs and scuff marks.

Reverse the procedure to reinstall and assemble. Be careful not to interchange the hydraulic accumulator outer spring, which is $3\frac{1}{4}$ inches long and heavy, with the pressure regulator valve spring, which is shorter and lighter.

Note that the accumulator check valve spring (not illustrated) is the lightest coil spring in the assembly; the valve itself has a hole in the center and the two are installed in a hole in the ditch plate. Note that the center bolt hole in the valve body receives bolts from both sides: one a short one from the ditch plate; the other the bolt which holds the oil screen. Failure to note this fact will prevent proper installation of the oil pan. The bolt is not illustrated. Tighten bolts to 8-10 ft. lbs. Be careful to tighten them evenly. Note long bolt used as shown in Fig. 13.

Make sure the "O" rings shown in Fig. 8 are seated in the case. Install the front and rear valve assembly gaskets. Install the valve assembly to

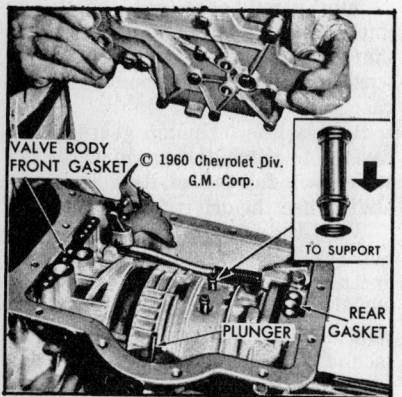

VALVE BODY FRONT GASKET © 1960 Chevrolet Div. G.M. Corp.

TO SUPPORT

PLUNGER

REAR GASKET

Fig. 8—Oil Tube and Gasket Location from Valve Body to Clutches

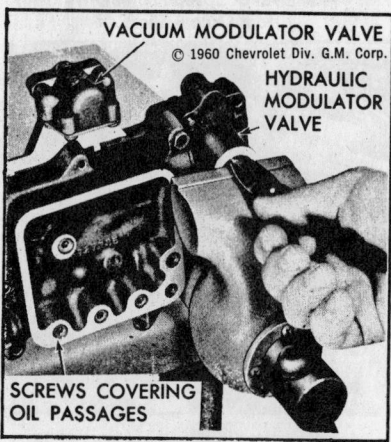

VACUUM MODULATOR VALVE
© 1960 Chevrolet Div. G.M. Corp.

HYDRAULIC MODULATOR VALVE

SCREWS COVERING OIL PASSAGES

Fig. 9—Removal and Installation of Accumulator Valve Retaining Ring

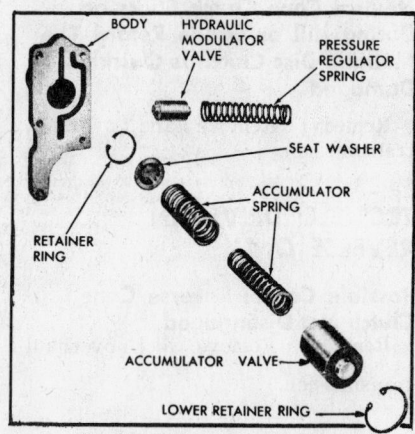

BODY

HYDRAULIC MODULATOR VALVE

PRESSURE REGULATOR SPRING

SEAT WASHER

ACCUMULATOR SPRING

RETAINER RING

ACCUMULATOR VALVE

LOWER RETAINER RING

Fig. 11—Hydraulic Modulator Valve

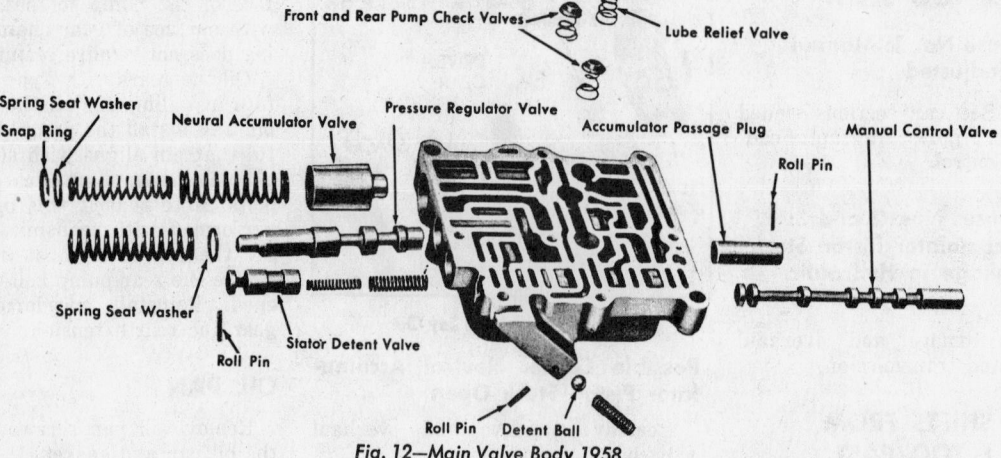

Front and Rear Pump Check Valves

Lube Relief Valve

Spring Seat Washer

Snap Ring

Neutral Accumulator Valve

Pressure Regulator Valve

Accumulator Passage Plug

Roll Pin

Manual Control Valve

Spring Seat Washer

Roll Pin

Stator Detent Valve

Roll Pin

Detent Ball

Fig. 12—Main Valve Body 1958

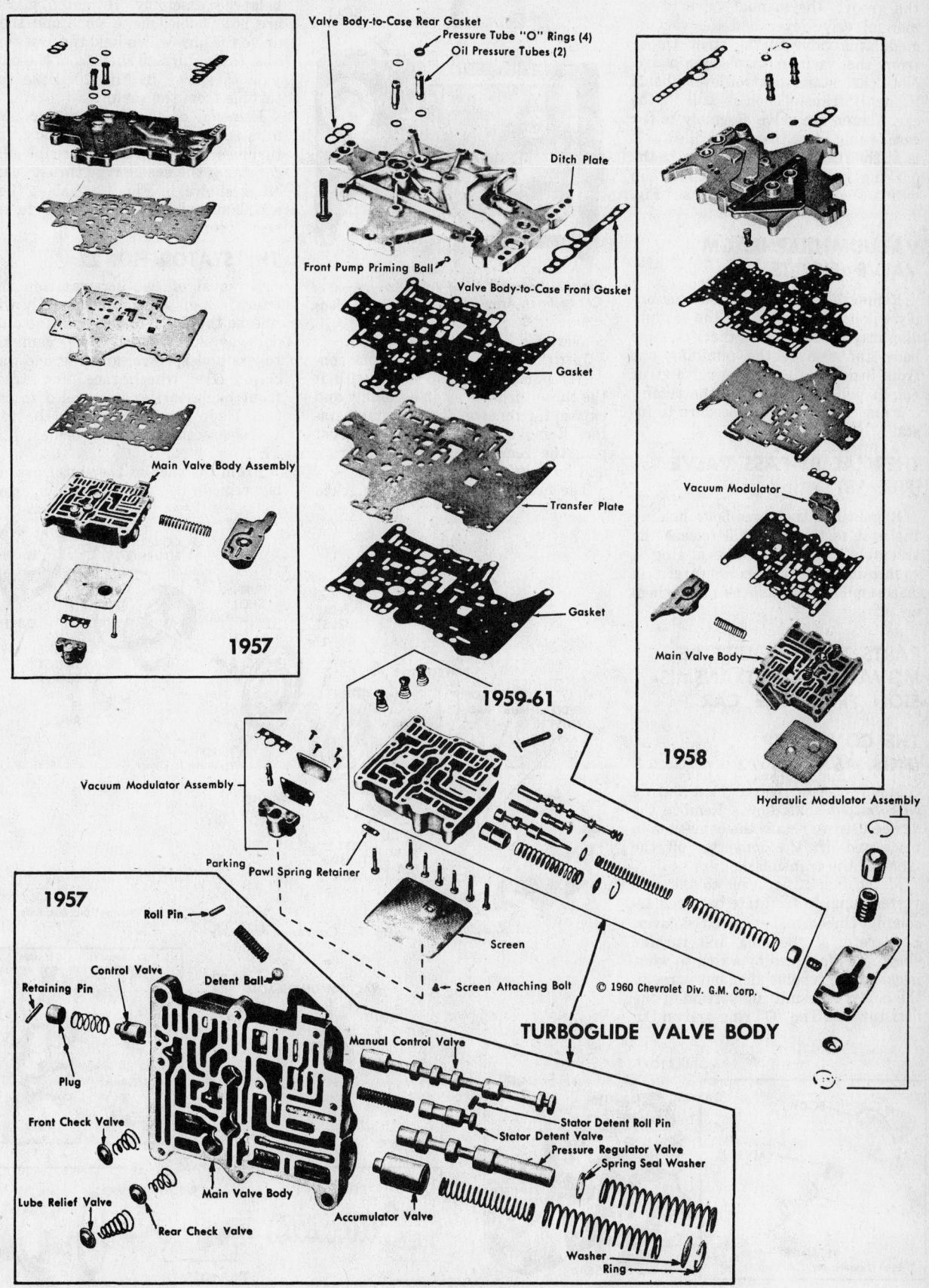

Valve Body-to-Case Rear Gasket
Pressure Tube "O" Rings (4)
Oil Pressure Tubes (2)

Ditch Plate

Front Pump Priming Ball

Valve Body-to-Case Front Gasket

Gasket

Transfer Plate

Gasket

Main Valve Body Assembly

1957

Vacuum Modulator

Main Valve Body

1958

1959-61

Vacuum Modulator Assembly

Parking Pawl Spring Retainer

Screen

Screen Attaching Bolt

© 1960 Chevrolet Div. G.M. Corp.

Hydraulic Modulator Assembly

TURBOGLIDE VALVE BODY

1957

Roll Pin

Retaining Pin

Control Valve

Detent Ball

Plug

Manual Control Valve

Front Check Valve

Stator Detent Roll Pin
Stator Detent Valve
Pressure Regulator Valve
Spring Seal Washer

Lube Relief Valve

Main Valve Body

Accumulator Valve

Rear Check Valve

Washer

Ring

Fig. 10—Turboglide Valve Body

the case guiding the dedent plate into the groove, the manual valve to the manual valve lever and the vacuum modulator valve to the strut (pipe) from the vacuum diaphragm valve. Note that stator control lever should be up if transmission is still in the car. Fasten the valve assembly to the case, being sure that the drilled bolt is at the rear. Index the spring in the parking lock pawl and attach to clip on main valve body rear bolt, see Fig. 7.

VACUUM DIAPHRAGM VALVE (FIG. 15)

Removal of the valve body assembly will permit removal of the vacuum diaphragm valve. Hold the VD valve body and remove the retaining nut from inside the case. The valve strut (pipe) will come off with the retaining nut. Reverse the procedure to install.

THERMAL BY-PASS VALVE (FIG. 15)

Removal of the three bolts holding the unit to the case will release the assembly. Note that the seal ring is square in cross section. Be careful in disassembling the unit as the springs are strong.

PARTS THAT REQUIRE RE-MOVAL OF THE TRANSMIS-SION FROM THE CAR

THE CONVERTER (FIGS. 16 THRU 22)

Mount the converter in a fixture with output shaft down. Remove the device used to retain the converter in place and lift the converter off the front of the transmission.

Match mark the cover to the converter pump to facilitate balanced assembly. Unbolt and remove the cover. Be careful of the long first turbine shaft; it is fastened by a ring to what is called the turbine shell but is really the power transmitting portion of the first turbine. The "O" ring seal on the

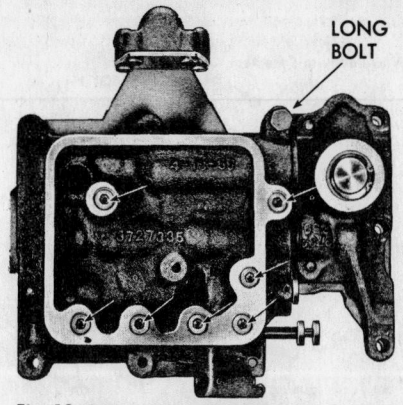

Fig. 13—Bottom View of Valve Body. Front of Car to Right. Arrows Show Oil Passage Plugs.

converter cover must be renewed.

Lift the turbine shell from the converter pump. This will bring with it the three turbines as an assembly and expose for removal the two stage stator. Remove the stator, the thrust pad, the rear needle thrust bearing and its race.

The first turbine is match marked

to the turbine shell as this is also a balanced assembly. If match marks are not visible, make some and then drive the pins which hold the first turbine to the turbine shell from the outside as shown in Fig. 20. Ease the turbine from the shell.

Removal of the first turbine permits removal of the second and third turbines without further trouble. Be careful of the needle type thrust bearings shown in Fig. 16. Unless they are damaged there is no need to remove them.

THE STATOR FIG. 22

Removal of five screws from the front face of the stator assembly will release the front thrust pad, the only one-way clutch (free wheel) cam, six rollers and springs, and the one-way clutch (free wheel) race. The stator front blade carrier is doweled to the rear blade carrier. Separate the two to release the 20 stator blades. Fig. 17.

From the back of the stator assembly remove the piston retaining ring

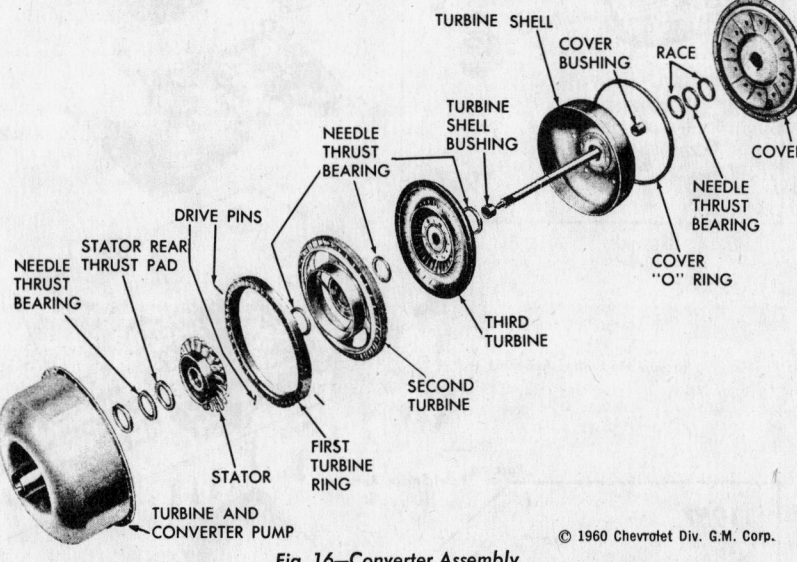

Fig. 16—Converter Assembly

© 1960 Chevrolet Div. G.M. Corp.

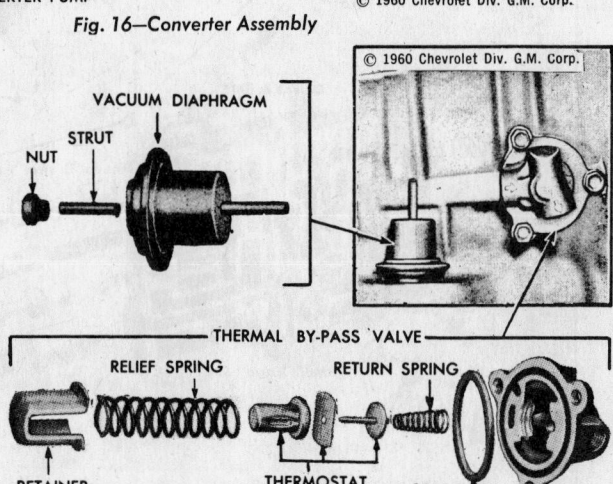

Fig. 14—By-Pass Valve and Vacuum Modulator 1958-61

Fig. 15—By-Pass Valve and Vacuum Diaphgram Valve 1957

© 1960 Chevrolet Div. G.M. Corp.

and the piston. The "O" ring seal on the OD of the piston must be removed. Be careful not to damage the cast iron seal on the piston.

Wash the parts in clean solvent and check for loose vanes, galls, scores and such on all bearing surfaces. Check the free wheel springs for distortion. The bushings in the cover and the turbine shell are replaceable and do not require reaming.

Reverse the procedure to reassemble.

The sharp edges of the stator blades should point toward the rear of the car; that is, toward the piston.

Install the needle thrust bearings in the three turbines. They are interchangeable. A press may be used on the outer edge of the bearings.

Install the third turbine in turbine shell with vanes up. Install second turbine in turbine shell with flange up. Align the balance marks and install the first turbine inner ring with inner flat surface facing up in shell. See Fig. 19.

Locate the three drive pins in shell with their respective holes in the first turbine ring, using a small drift and complete installation of pins with a small "C" clamp as shown in Fig. 21.

Install the stator assembly; the bolts go to the front of the car.

Align the match marks and install the converter pump over the shell on-

to the converter cover.

In fastening the cover to the converter pump tighten every third bolt to 8-12 ft. lbs. Then tighten the remainder to 8-12 ft. lbs. Then tighten all to 18 ft. lbs. in rotation.

INSTALL CONVERTER

Install the converter assembly onto the front of the transmission so that the oil seal rings on the second turbine shaft are not damaged and the drive groove of the converter pump hub engages the tang of the front oil pump drive gear. Turn the converter assembly so as to align the splines of the shafts. When properly installed the converter is at least ¾ inch below the surface of the forward edge of the transmission housing. Install the converter holding tool. **Note that converter must be in place before rear pump can be bolted to the case.** The clearance thrust washer on this transmission is located between the front oil pump and the thrust surface of the front planetary ring gear.

FRONT OIL PUMP (FIGS. 23 THRU 28)

Removal of seven various sized cap

screws will permit removal of the front oil pump. Note location of the screws to permit easier assembly. The pump body has two threaded holes to permit the use of pullers. The pump assembly includes the stator support, the reverse cone clutch piston, and an "O" ring seal of square cross section. There is a gasket between the rear face of the stator support and the front face of the case.

In disassembling, use air pressure to move the reverse cone clutch piston from the rear of the stator support, being careful not to damage the piston inner seal ring. Removal of the reverse clutch piston permits removal of the five stator support to pump body bolts and so separation of the pump from the support. Mark the pump gears so the same faces will be up when assembled.

Oil the parts and reverse the procedure to reassemble. The lug on the drive gear goes toward the converter. In fastening the stator support to the front oil pump body the stator sup-

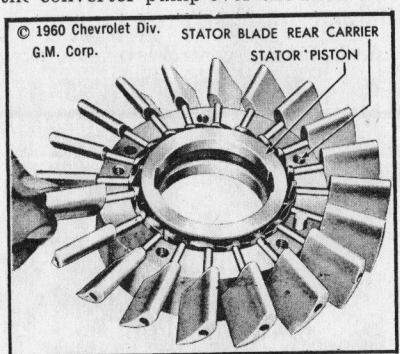

Fig. 17—Installing Stator Blades

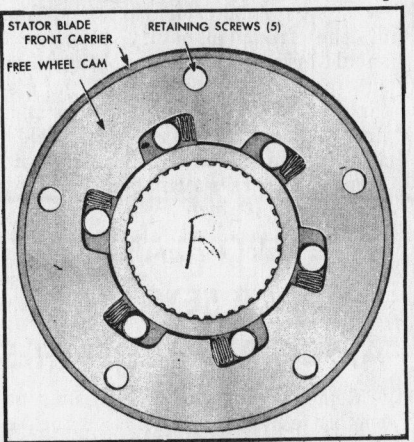

Fig. 18—Stator Cam Showing Location of Balls and Springs

Fig. 20—Removing First Turbine Drive Pins From Shell

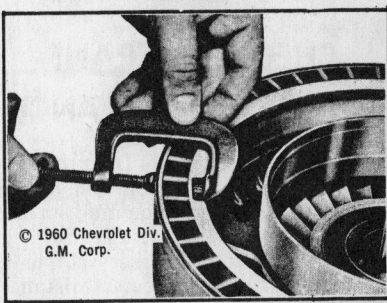

Fig. 21—Installing First Turbine Drive Pins Into Shell

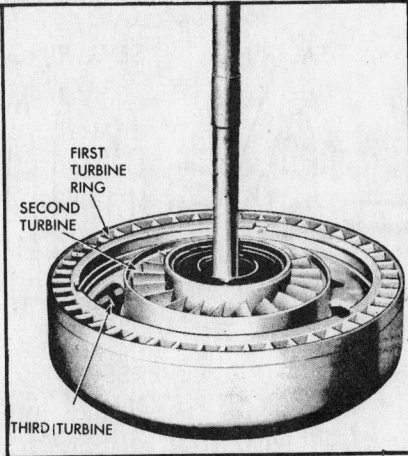

Fig. 19—View of Three Turbines Installed in Turbine Shell

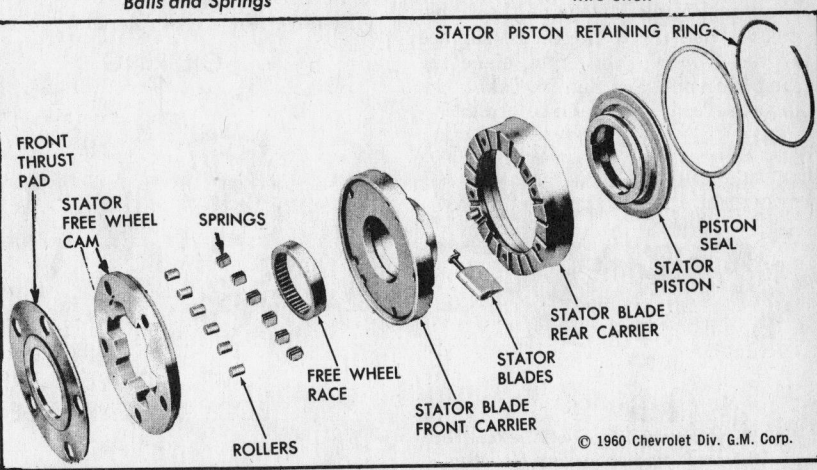

Fig. 22—Two-Stage Stator Assembly, Front of Car to Left

Fig. 24—Removing Front Oil Pump and Stator Support

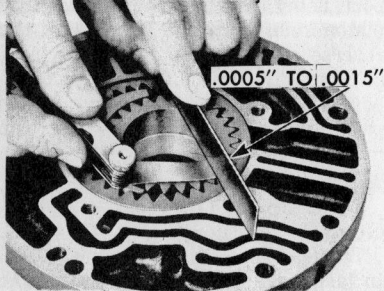

Fig. 26A—Checking Gear End Clearance

Fig. 25—Checking Driven Gear to Oil Pump Body

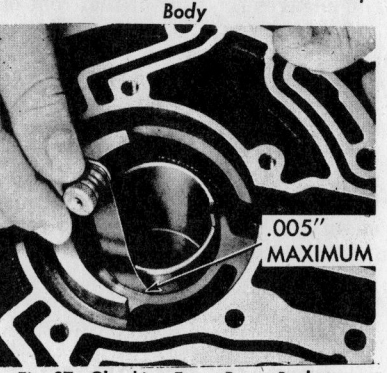

Fig. 27—Checking Front Pump Body to Converter Hub Clearance

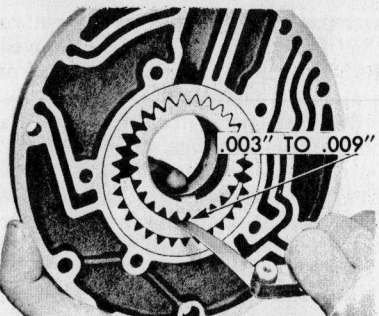

Fig. 26—Checking Either Gear to Crescent

Fig. 28—Aligning Stator Support to Pump Body

port shaft must be concentric to the pump body bushing and the front oil seal. A sleeve can be used or the oil pump body hub can be used as the locating sleeve. Tighten the support to body bolts evenly to 15-18 ft. lbs.

Before installing the front oil pump onto the transmission case the size of the transmission clearance thrust washer should be checked.

CHECKING TRANS-MISSION CLEARANCE

Measure the distance from the rear face of the rear hub of the stator shaft support to the mounting surface of the stator-pump assembly. See Fig. 29. Take reading at several points around and record greatest distance. Call this amount "A."

Measure the distance from the oil pump mounting surface on the transmission housing to the thrust surface at the front of the front planetary ring gear hub. See Fig. 30. Take reading at several places and record great-

est distance. Call this amount "B."

The thrust washer which is selected to sit on the front thrust surface of the front planetary ring gear should bring the distance obtained by subtracting distance "A" from distance "B" to within the clearance limits of .008 inch to .028 inch. Select a thrust washer to do this. There are three thicknesses available: .068 inch, .085 inch, .103 inch.

THE TWO PLANETARY GEAR SETS AND ASSOCIATED CLUTCHES

Removal of the front oil pump assembly exposes the cone of the reverse cone clutch still in the case. Remove the cone.

Remove the front planetary gear

set which includes: the neutral cone clutch, the two one-way clutches, and the second and third turbine shafts.

ASSEMBLY

After installing parking pawl, shaft, manual control lever into pawl

Fig. 30—Measuring Distance "B"—Thrust Face of Front Ring Gear to Front Pump Mounting Surface on Case

Fig. 29—Measuring Distance "A"—Rear Face of Front Pump Hub to Pump Mounting Surface

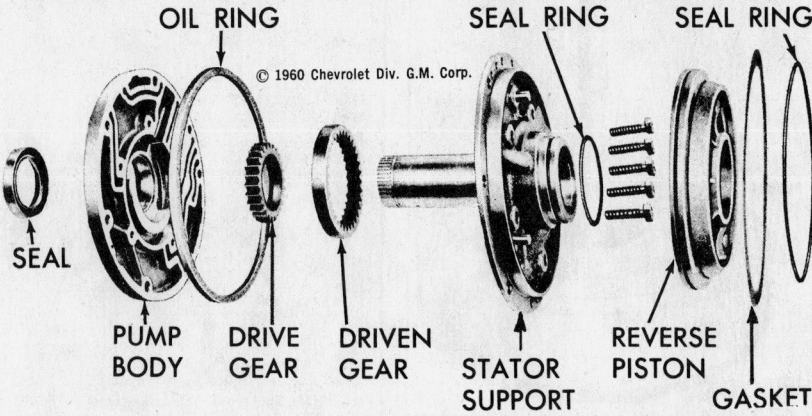

© 1960 Chevrolet Div. G.M. Corp.

Fig. 23—Front Oil Pump With Stator Support and Reverse Cone Clutch Piston

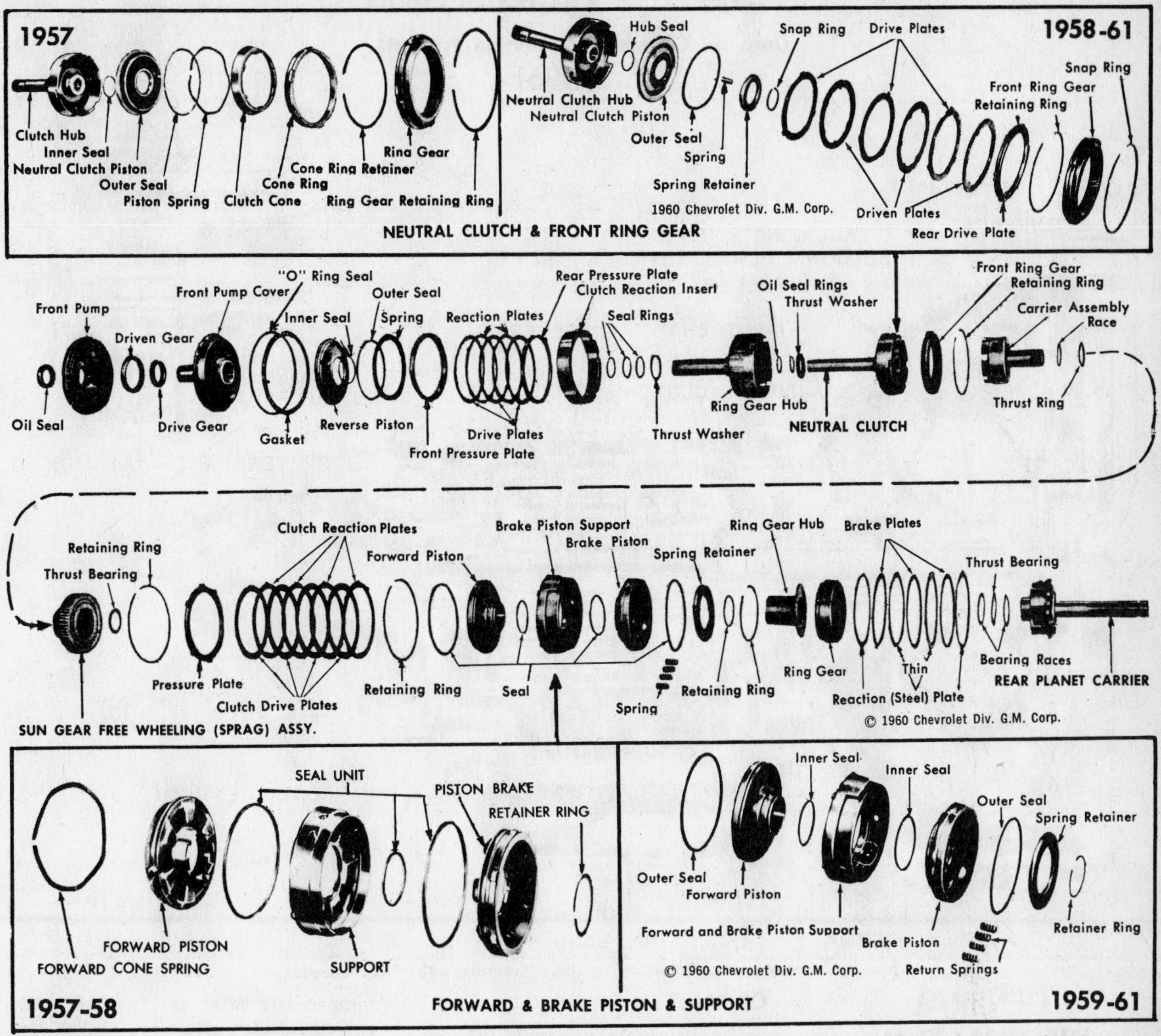

1957

Clutch Hub
Inner Seal
Neutral Clutch Piston
Outer Seal
Piston Spring
Clutch Cone
Cone Ring
Cone Ring Retainer
Ring Gear
Ring Gear Retaining Ring

1958-61

Hub Seal
Neutral Clutch Hub
Neutral Clutch Piston
Outer Seal
Spring
Spring Retainer
1960 Chevrolet Div. G.M. Corp.
Snap Ring
Drive Plates
Driven Plates
Rear Drive Plate
Front Ring Gear Retaining Ring
Snap Ring

NEUTRAL CLUTCH & FRONT RING GEAR

Front Pump
Oil Seal
Driven Gear
Drive Gear
Front Pump Cover
"O" Ring Seal
Inner Seal
Gasket
Reverse Piston
Outer Seal
Spring
Reaction Plates
Drive Plates
Front Pressure Plate
Rear Pressure Plate
Clutch Reaction Insert
Seal Rings
Thrust Washer
Oil Seal Rings
Thrust Washer
Ring Gear Hub
Front Ring Gear Retaining Ring
Carrier Assembly Race
Thrust Ring

NEUTRAL CLUTCH

Retaining Ring
Thrust Bearing
Pressure Plate
Clutch Drive Plates
Clutch Reaction Plates
Forward Piston
Retaining Ring
Seal
Spring
Brake Piston Support
Brake Piston
Spring Retainer
Retaining Ring
Ring Gear Hub
Ring Gear
Reaction (Steel) Plate
Brake Plates
Thin
Thrust Bearing
Bearing Races

SUN GEAR FREE WHEELING (SPRAG) ASSY.

© 1960 Chevrolet Div. G.M. Corp.

REAR PLANET CARRIER

1957-58

FORWARD CONE SPRING
FORWARD PISTON
SEAL UNIT
SUPPORT
PISTON BRAKE
RETAINER RING

FORWARD & BRAKE PISTON & SUPPORT

1959-61

Outer Seal
Forward Piston
Inner Seal
Forward and Brake Piston Support
Inner Seal
Brake Piston
Return Springs
Outer Seal
Spring Retainer
Retainer Ring

© 1960 Chevrolet Div. G.M. Corp.

Fig. 37—Internal Components—Exploded View, with Inserts Showing Neutral Clutch and Front Ring Gear, and Forward Piston and Brake Piston and Support

lock rod, install stator lever, detent plate, and parking lever bracket.

Now assemble parts, following layout shown in Fig. 37, noting differences shown between 1957-58 clutches and 1959-61 clutches. Note the proper sprag assembly shown in Fig. 36.

NOTE: Sprags are assembled correctly if units will slip while holding outer cam stationary and turning sun gear clockwise as viewed from front (direction of stamped arrows). Also check that both sprags hold while twisting counterclockwise.

As parts are assembled be sure they are lubricated with transmission oil to prevent scuffing and galling.

It is important that transmission be in a vertical position with front end up to avoid damage to seal rings.

CHECKING CLEARANCES—1959-61

Measure clearance at reverse front-pressure-plate and the adjoining faced plate, noting that the clutch pack is not compressed when inserting the feeler gauge. This clearance should be .025"-.050". Three sizes of reverse pressure plates are available to control this clearance.

Measure main assembly clearance by mounting dial gauge against neutral clutch hub and by raising output shaft. Read movement on gauge.

Select proper thrust washer to obtain play of .008"-.028". Three washer thicknesses are available.

After installing converter check that converter shaft engages the pump lugs. It should be ¾" from front of case to front of converter.

Fig. 33—Removing Forward Cone Clutch Retaining Ring

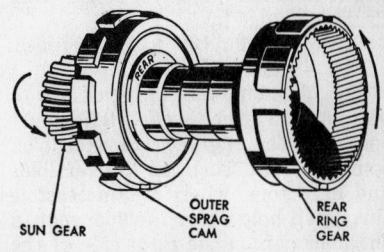

SUN GEAR
OUTER SPRAG CAM
REAR RING GEAR

Fig. 36—Correct Installation of Sprags Showing Proper Rotation

CHRYSLER AUTOMATIC TRANSMISSIONS
POWERFLITE TRANSMISSION
Used on Chrysler Corporation Products
Thru 1961

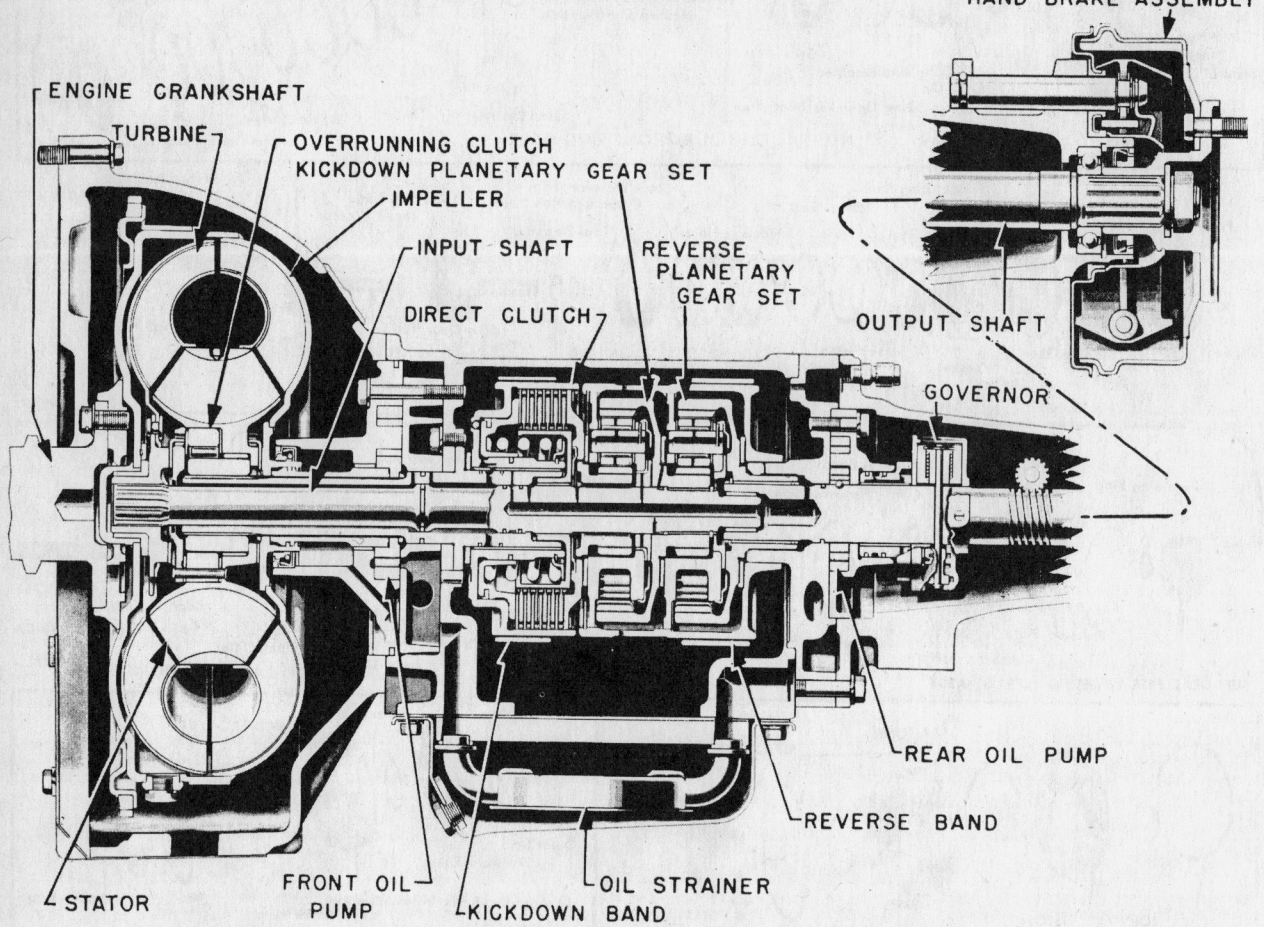

Fig. 1—Cutaway view of Powerflite Transmission starting with 1954 production.

GENERAL INFORMATION

FLUID REQUIREMENTS

Check the fluid level every 1,000 miles.

Measure the fluid with the engine at operating temperature and idling at 475-500 rpm. Have the hand lever at Neutral, after having moved the shift lever through all the positions so as to fill all the servos.

Use a good grade of Automatic Transmission Fluid.

Change the fluid every 20,000 miles.

The filler pipe and dip stick are to be found at the lower right hand corner of the engine block except on some models, such as convertibles and hard tops, where it is accessible through a hole under the floor mat in the floor pan on the right side of the tunnel.

Fluid should be at the full mark, no more, a little less is OK.

CAPACITY

Capacity after overhaul: 12½ qts.
Capacity after draining: 11 qts.

CHECKING OIL LEVEL

The oil level should be checked every 1,000 miles but be very careful not to overfill the transmission as excess oil will blow out onto the exhaust pipe and result in a lot of smoke.

When the Transmission Is Cold

Start the engine, set the hand brake firmly, move the hand lever through all positions, allowing sufficient time for the servos and converter to fill completely. Place the hand lever at Neutral and check the oil level with the engine idling. The level should not be more than one-half inch above the low mark, and it should not be below the low mark on the dip stick.

When the Transmission Is At Operating Temperature

The Transmission is at operating temperature after the car has been driven until the engine has reached its normal operating temperature.

Place the hand lever at Neutral and check the level with the engine idling. The oil level should not be above the Full mark on the dipstick; a little less is OK.

DRAINING TRANSMISSION

Remove the drain plug from the left front lower corner of the transmission oil pan. If no drain plug, remove nut holding filler tube to trans. oil pan.

Remove the access plate from the bottom of the torque converter bell housing. Rotate the converter until the drain plug, which is to the rear of the starter ring gear, points down. Remove the plug and drain the fluid. Tighten the oil pan drain plug to 20-25 ft lbs., the converter drain plug to 45-50 ft lbs.

Pour in 5 quarts of Type A fluid and run the engine for two minutes with the hand lever at Neutral. Pour in six more quarts and allow engine to idle

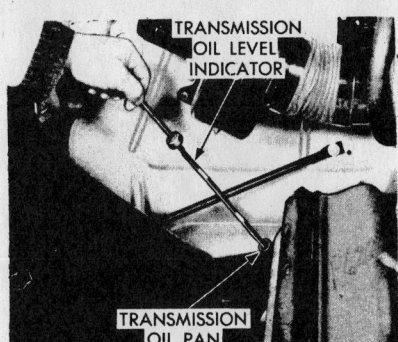

Fig. 2—Check the oil level with engine idling and hand lever at Neutral

until it reaches operating temperature. Move the hand lever to all the positions in order to fill the servos and return it to Neutral. Measure the level and add more fluid or drain some to bring the level to the full mark. Do not overfill the transmission.

TORQUE SPECIFICATIONS

	Ft. Lbs.
"U" Joint Flange Nut	140-160
Governor Locating Screw	3½-4
Oil Pan Drain Plug	20-25
Oil Pan Filler Tube Nut	35-40
Speedometer Pinion Nut	40-45
Converter Drain Plug	45-50
Oil Cooler Fittings	5-7
Reactor Shaft Screw	10-15
Transmission Case to Bell Housing	45-50
Crossmember to Frame	50-55
Insulator to Crossmember	30-35

STARTING THE CAR WITHOUT THE USE OF THE STARTER

Always push the car to start the engine when the starter is not working. Towing the car is dangerous as the towed car is likely to ram the towing car. Turn on the ignition switch. Have the car pushed with the hand lever held at Neutral. When the speed of the car reaches 25 mph or more move the hand lever to Low. The engine should turn over.

TOWING THE CAR

When the transmission is in Neutral the car may be towed indefinitely at moderate speeds. There would result definite damage to the transmission were the car to be towed with the manual control valve in any other position. If the transmission has been damaged do not tow the car with the rear wheels on the ground but if this is impractical disconnect the drive shaft from the transmission.

BAND ADJUSTMENT

FRONT BAND

The low (kickdown) band is the one nearest the engine. The band adjusting screw is on the left side of the case just forward of the manual and throttle control levers.

Using a box wrench from under the car loosen the adjusting screw lock nut and back it off the screw a bit so that the adjusting screw is loose and turns freely. Now tighten the adjusting screw in, clockwise, to 5-6 ft lbs. (60-72 inch pounds). Next back the screw out exactly 2¾ (Chrysler and DeSoto), 3 (Dodge and Plymouth) full turns (revolutions). Hold the screw and tighten the lock nut to 35-40 ft lbs.

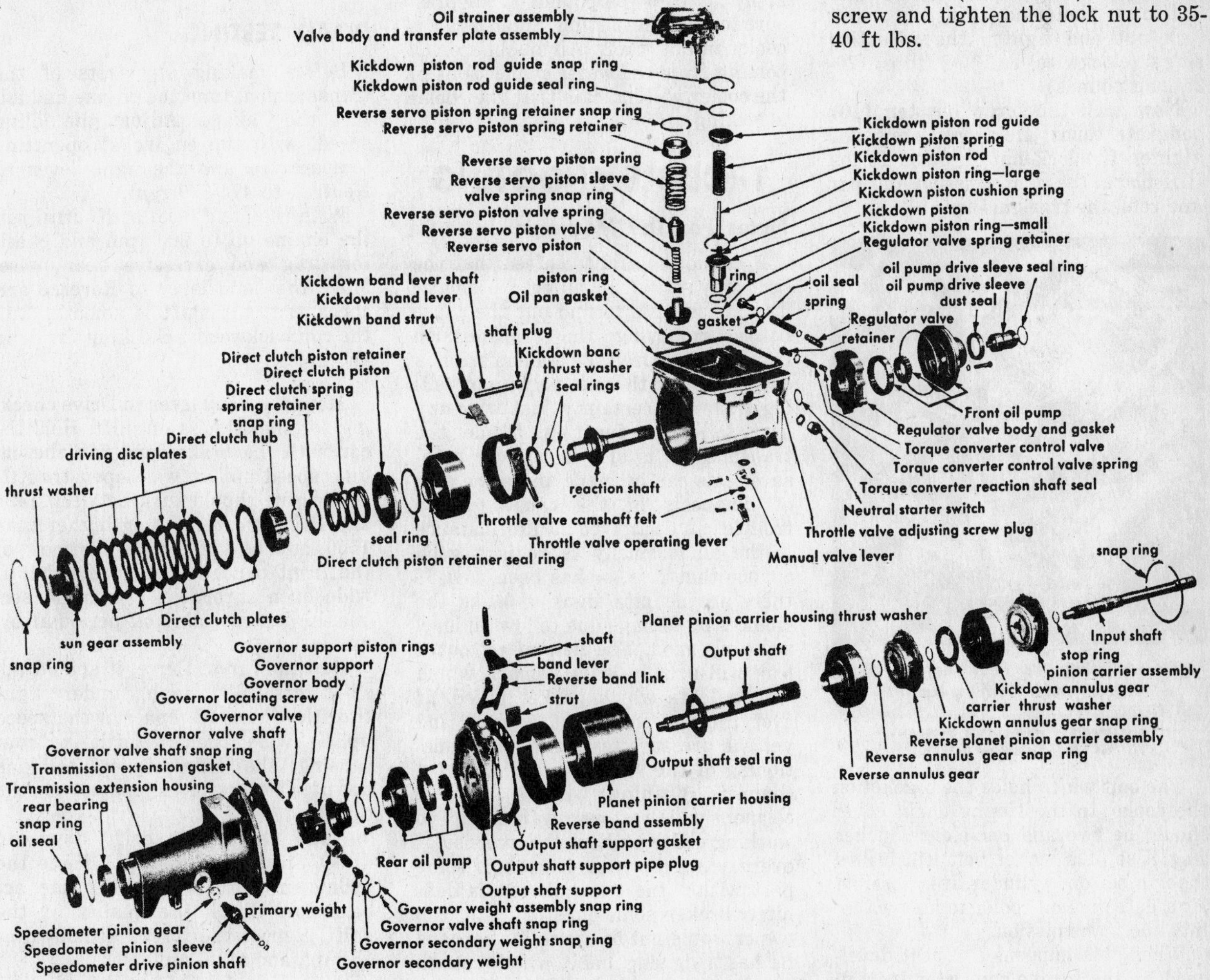

Oil strainer assembly
Valve body and transfer plate assembly
Kickdown piston rod guide snap ring
Kickdown piston rod guide seal ring
Reverse servo piston spring retainer snap ring
Reverse servo piston spring retainer
Reverse servo piston spring
Reverse servo piston sleeve
valve spring snap ring
Reverse servo piston valve spring
Reverse servo piston valve
Reverse servo piston
Kickdown band lever shaft
Kickdown band lever
Kickdown band strut
Direct clutch piston retainer
Direct clutch piston
Direct clutch spring
spring retainer
snap ring
Direct clutch hub
driving disc plates
thrust washer
piston ring
Oil pan gasket
shaft plug
Kickdown band
thrust washer
seal rings
ring
oil seal
spring
gasket
Kickdown piston rod guide
Kickdown piston spring
Kickdown piston rod
Kickdown piston ring—large
Kickdown piston cushion spring
Kickdown piston
Kickdown piston ring—small
Regulator valve spring retainer
oil pump drive sleeve seal ring
oil pump drive sleeve
dust seal
Regulator valve retainer
Front oil pump
Regulator valve body and gasket
Torque converter control valve
Torque converter control valve spring
Torque converter reaction shaft seal
reaction shaft
Throttle valve camshaft felt
Throttle valve operating lever
Direct clutch piston retainer seal ring
seal ring
Manual valve lever
Neutral starter switch
Throttle valve adjusting screw plug
sun gear assembly
snap ring
Direct clutch plates
Governor support piston rings
Governor support
Governor body
Governor locating screw
Governor valve
Governor valve shaft
Governor valve shaft snap ring
Transmission extension gasket
Transmission extension housing
rear bearing
snap ring
oil seal
Speedometer pinion gear
Speedometer pinion sleeve
Speedometer drive pinion shaft
primary weight
Rear oil pump
Governor weight assembly snap ring
Governor valve shaft snap ring
Governor secondary weight snap ring
Governor secondary weight
shaft
band lever
Reverse band link
strut
Output shaft
Output shaft seal ring
Planet pinion carrier housing
Reverse band assembly
Output shaft support gasket
Output shaft support pipe plug
Output shaft support
Planet pinion carrier housing thrust washer
snap ring
Input shaft
stop ring
pinion carrier assembly
Kickdown annulus gear
Kickdown annulus gear thrust washer
Kickdown annulus gear snap ring
Reverse planet pinion carrier assembly
Reverse annulus gear snap ring
Reverse annulus gear

Fig. 3—Exploded view of Powerflite Transmission starting with 1954 production.

CHRYSLER AUTOMATIC TRANSMISSIONS

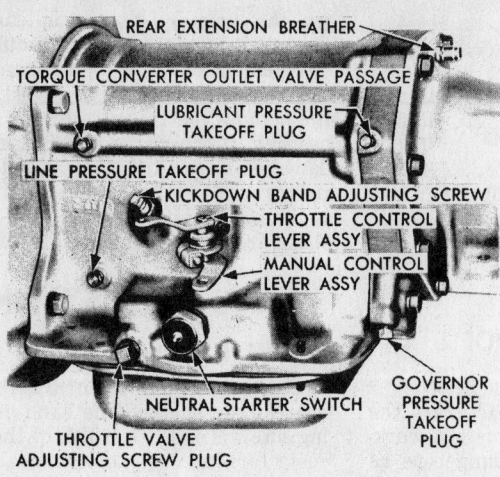

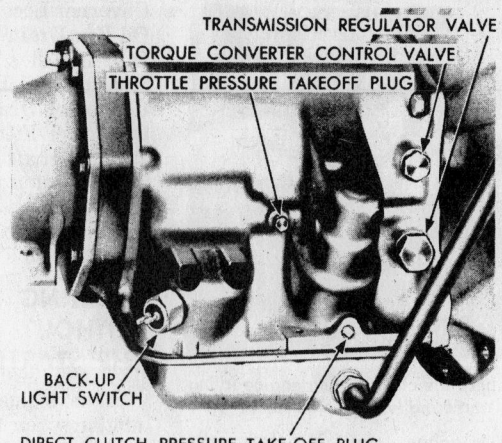

Fig. 4—View Showing Left Side of Transmission

Fig. 5—View Showing Right Side of Transmission

REAR BAND

The rear (reverse) band adjusting screw is in the bottom right rear corner of the case. It is a part of the rear servo linkage.

Drain the transmission and remove the oil pan.

Loosen the band adjusting screw lock nut and tighten the adjusting screw (clockwise) to 1¾-2 ft lbs. (20-25 inch pounds).

Now back the screw out ten (10) complete turns. Hold the screw and tighten the lock nut to 30-35 ft lbs.

Replace the transmission oil pan and refill the transmission.

Fig. 6—Adjusting the Rear (Reverse) Band from underneath the car.

OIL COOLER

The bolt which holds the bracket on the cooler to the timing chain cover should be two and one-eighth inches long. Use of a longer bolt will injure the number one cylinder. It is possible for a defective oil cooler to leak water into the transmission.

When this happens the heat developed by the torque converter is sufficient to turn the water into steam.

The steam will force the fluid out of the transmission breather. If the oil loss is not detected in time the converter will be ruined.

To test the cooler, remove it from the car and block off one oil line fitting with a one-eighth inch plug and apply not over ten pounds of air pressure to the other fitting. Submerge the cooler in hot water. Air bubbles or oil coming from the water connections of the cooler will indicate that the cooler is leaking.

TROUBLE SHOOTING

Notes For The Mechanic

It cannot be said too often that the best way to fix an ailing Automatic Transmission is to find out the cause before removing the transmission from the car. Once the transmission is out of the car there is no way of telling with any certainty just why any part failed to function. While the transmission is still in the car pressure tests can be made and some sort of diagnosis of the cause of the trouble can be arrived at. For instance if the oil is smelly there is a good chance that it is, or has been, low. If there are definite signs of leaks the chances of damage due to low oil level are very good. The flow of oil out a leak will usually leave a mark which will indicate which gasket failed. If everything seems tight enough and yet the pressure tests show malfunctioning of the valves it can be that a complete flushing with a suitable cleaner will restore everything to working order without the expense of overhauling the transmission. If some part within the transmission is definitely broken some questioning of the owner would not be amiss for perhaps he has a driving habit which caused the breakage; like shifting into reverse with the car moving forward at

more than 5 mph., or shifting into Low at speeds above 45 mph. In theory an automatic transmission has less chance to develop trouble than a conventional transmission. Trouble is more likely to originate in a defective operator than in a defective part.

ROAD TESTING

Before making any tests of the transmission, tune the engine and adjust the linkage. Adjust the idling speed, with the engine at operating temperature and the hand lever at Neutral, to 475-500 rpm.

With the hand lever at Neutral run the engine up to 800 rpm and check for drag and excessive gear noise. Move the hand lever to Reverse and check that the shift is smooth. Run the car backwards, checking for drag and noise.

Move the hand lever to Drive checking for smoothness of shift. Hold the car with the brakes and run the engine speed up. At wide open throttle the engine should turn between 1450 and 1550 rpm. A reading higher than 1550 could be due to maladjustment of the front band. **Note:** Do not run at wide open throttle for over 30 seconds. Allow a cooling off period afterwards.

Run the car in Drive, it should upshift at 15-20 mph. under light throttle. From 15 mph run the speed up to wide open throttle without causing the transmission to kick down. Check for slippage of the clutch.

Allow the car to drift down in direct drive to 15-20 mph. Force the kickdown shift by flooring the accelerator. Check the quality of the shift. Repeat the forced kickdown at 35 mph and at 45 mph.

Slow down to 40-50 mph and move the hand lever to Low. The transmission should downshift. Check for noise. Move the lever back to Drive at 20 mph, the transmission should upshift. Coast to a stop and check the downshift which should occur at 10-12 mph.

SHIFT PATTERN SUMMARY

Upshift	V8	6
Light Throttle	15-20 mph	13-18mph
Wide Open Throttle	60-75 mph	49-63mph
Downshift		
Light Throttle	10-12 mph	9-11 mph
Wide Open Throttle	10-14 mph	9-13 mph
Kickdown Limit	45-60 mph	34-48 mph

PRESSURE TESTS

Line Pressure

Remove the 1/8 in. pipe plug from the line pressure test point (take-off) on the lower left front end of the case. Install a pressure gage. See Fig. 4.

With the rear wheels free to turn, the hand lever at Reverse, and the engine turning at 1600 rpm, the pressure should be 225-275 psi.

With the hand lever in Neutral, the engine turning at 800 rpm the pressure should be 85-90 psi.

With the brakes holding the car, the hand lever in Drive, and the engine turning at 800 rpm, the pressure should be 85-90 psi.

With the brakes holding the car, the hand lever in Low, and the engine turning at 800 rpm, the pressure should be 85 to 95 psi.

If these pressures are not found the cause may be:

Oil Level Too High or too Low.
Defective Regulator Valve Spring.
Clogged Oil Strainer.
Leaks in the Hydraulic System.
The manual or throttle valve stuck.
The front servo stuck.
The rear servo stuck.
Defective front pump.

Governor Pressure

Remove the one-eighth inch pipe plug from the governor pressure take-off (test) point on the lower left front end of the rear extension and connect in a pressure gage. See Fig. 4. Put the hand lever at Drive. Jack up the rear wheels so that they are free to turn. Start the engine. Gradually depress the accelerator. When the speedometer reads 14-17 mph on V8's or 12-14 mph on 6's the pressure should be 15 psi. When the speedometer reads 24-27 mph on either V8's or 6's the pressure should be 45 psi. When the speedometer reads 58-65 mph on V8's or 46-53 on 6's the pressure should be 60 psi. If these pressures are not found, the trouble may be due to: leaks at the valve body mating surface or the gasket between the rear extension and the case, a defective governor or rear oil pump.

Clutch Pressure

Starting with Powerflite Transmission No. 78758-E there is provided at the bottom of the Kick-Down Servo (right side of case) a pressure take-off plug which will permit checking of oil pressure in the multiple disc clutch circuit.

Should the pressure found at this new take off point be more than ten pounds below the pressure take-off plug (left side of transmission) the seal rings in the multiple disc clutch circuit are defective.

TROUBLE SHOOTING CHART

Items Marked "X" Can Be Serviced Without Removing The Transmission From The Vehicle

POOR SHIFT QUALITY

Such As:

Harsh Shifting, Runaway on Shifting, Shudder During Shift.

Can Be Due To:

Maladjusted bands X, maladjusted manual controls X, low oil level X, defective servos X, defective shift valve spring X.

IMPROPER RESPONSE TO SHIFT LEVER POSITION

Such As:

No Detent Feel, Detent and Pointer Not in Agreement, Car Moves Forward or Back While in Neutral, Car Will Not Move Although Wheels Are Free.

Can Be Due To:

Maladjusted manual control X, improperly adjusted bands X, leak between the valve bodies X, defective shift valve spring X, defective servos X, low oil level X, clogged oil pump intake screen X, regulator valve stuck X, multiple disc clutch not functioning correctly, front oil pump leaking or worn.

"R" PUSH BUTTON WILL NOT GO IN AND STAY

Try With Engine Off

If OK then the trouble is in the governor valve. Remove governor pressure test plug (See Fig. 4) and with short blasts of air attempt to free valve.

EXCESSIVE SLIPPAGE

Such As:

Slip in all ranges, slip in only one range.

Can Be Due To:

Low oil level X, stuck regulator valve X, stuck converter control valve X, leak between the valve bodies X, leaking valve body and cover plug X, leaking shuttle valve plug X, maladjusted bands X, servos stuck X, front oil pump sleeve incorrectly installed or pump itself defective, multiple disc clutch not working correctly.

INCORRECT SHIFT PATTERN

Such As:

No upshift, Pattern Too Low, Pattern Too High, Pattern Erratic.

Can Be Due To:

Low oil level X, incorrect linkage adjustment X, leak between the valve bodies X, defective governor valve regulator valve defective X, shift valve spring defective X, defective throttle valve X, malfunctioning rear pump, leaking rear extension gaskets, clutch check valve stuck.

NOISES

Such As:

Grating, Buzzing, Rubbing, Whistling, Grinding.

Can Be Due To:

Speedometer pinion improperly installed X, converter control valve

Trouble Chart—con'd

stuck X, low oil level X, rear bearing snap ring broken, front oil pump drive sleeve or pinion improperly installed, front oil pump worn, thrust washers improperly installed, low sun gear snap ring broken, rear oil pump worn.

MISCELLANEOUS TROUBLES

STARTER WON'T ENERGIZE

Gearshift linkage needs adjustment X.

Neutral starter switch defective X

Manual valve lever needs adjustment X

HARD TO SHIFT INTO NEUTRAL

Neutral starter switch defective X

HARD TO SHIFT INTO REVERSE

Back-up switch defective X

ACCELERATOR PEDAL STICKS AT CLOSED THROTTLE POSITION

Throttle linkage needs adjusting X

Throttle valve needs adjusting X

HARD TO FILL TRANSMISSION

Breather on rear extension is plugged X Fig. 4.

Rear extension to case gaskets improperly placed

OIL FOAMS FROM FILL PIPE

Oil level too high X

Breather on rear extension plugged X

Rear extension to case gaskets improperly placed

Water has gotten into transmission from oil cooler; drain and flush transmission, install new cooler X

TRANSMISSION OVERHEATS

Kickdown band needs adjusting X
Converter control valve is stuck X
Reverse band needs adjustment X
Reverse servo defective X
Regulator body mating surfaces are leaking X
Rear pump assembly worn X
Plugged lubrication holes
Kickdown sun gear snap ring broken
Clutch spring retaining snap ring broken
Clutch discs, plates sticking
Thrust washers improperly placed

IMPOSSIBLE TO PUSH CAR TO START THE ENGINE

Rear extension to case gaskets leaking

Rear pump assembly worn

DISASSEMBLY OF UNITS

VALVE BODY AND TRANSFER PLATE ASSEMBLY

This procedure does not require that the transmission be removed from the car.

Drain the transmission and remove the oil pan. Disconnect the throttle and manual control rods at the levers on the left side of the transmission case. Loosen the lock screws and remove the levers. Unbolt the oil strainer and remove it. Remove the five transfer plate retaining screws and remove the valve body and transfer plate assembly.

FRONT OIL PUMP

The transmission must be out of the car for this operation.

Remove the transmission regulator valve spring retainer, spring, gasket, and the regulator valve. Remove the

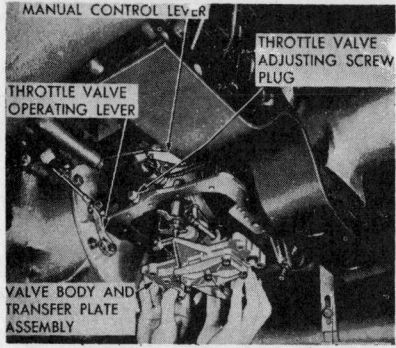

Fig. 7—Removing Valve Body and Transfer Plate Assembly

Fig. 8—Do not use a vise to hold the Valve Body and Transfer Plate Assembly. Use equivalent of holding tool shown

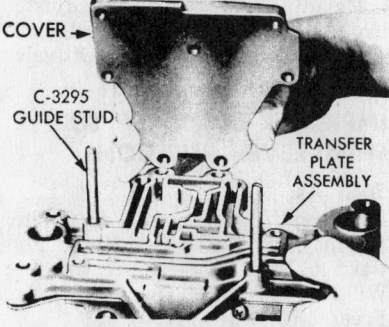

Fig. 9—Remove Transfer Plate Cover

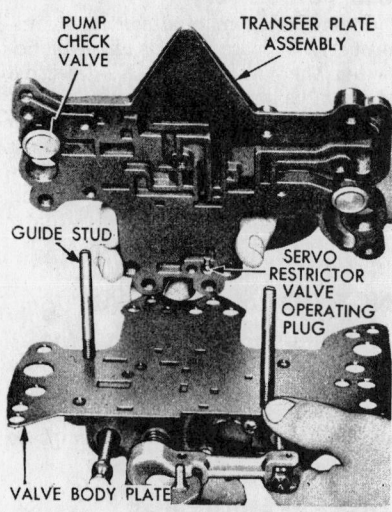

Fig. 11—Remove Transfer Plate Assembly

converter control valve spring retainer, spring, gasket, and the control valve. To remove these valves when the transmission is still in the car insert a piece of welding rod in the end of the valve.

Remove the seven front oil pump body to transmission case bolts and washers. Note that the washers are made of soft metal and should be replaced by new ones at assembly as they act to seal the assembly.

Use a puller and guide pins as shown in the cut to pull the oil pump assembly from the front of the case. The pump body has threaded holes for installation of the puller.

REGULATOR VALVE BODY

The transmission must be out of the car for this operation.

The regulator valve body is just behind the front oil pump body. Use the two threaded holes in the body and the puller and guide pins as shown in the cut. Pull the regulator valve body off the reaction shaft.

The regulator valve body is made of aluminum and should be handled carefully. Clean the body and the two regulator valves in solvent. Check that the valves will fall freely in their bores when all the parts are clean and dry. If the regulator valve should have a slight nick it can be removed by using a surface plate and crocus cloth. Be sure all the oil passages are clean.

TRANSMISSION OUTPUT SHAFT REAR BEARING OIL SEAL

This procedure for the renewal of the rear extension oil seal does not require that the transmission be removed from the car.

Disconnect the front "U" joint and tie the propeller shaft off to one side. Apply the hand brake and remove the propeller shaft flange nut, shakeproof washer and flat washer. When reinstalling the nut tighten to 175 ft lbs.

Use a puller to remove the flange and drum assembly. Remove the small brake support grease shield spring. Remove the brake support grease shield.

Be careful not to damage the neoprene sealing surface at the bottom of the shield.

Using a puller remove the rear bearing oil seal.

TRANSMISSION REAR EXTENSION

The transmission must be out of the car for this operation.

Remove the speedometer drive

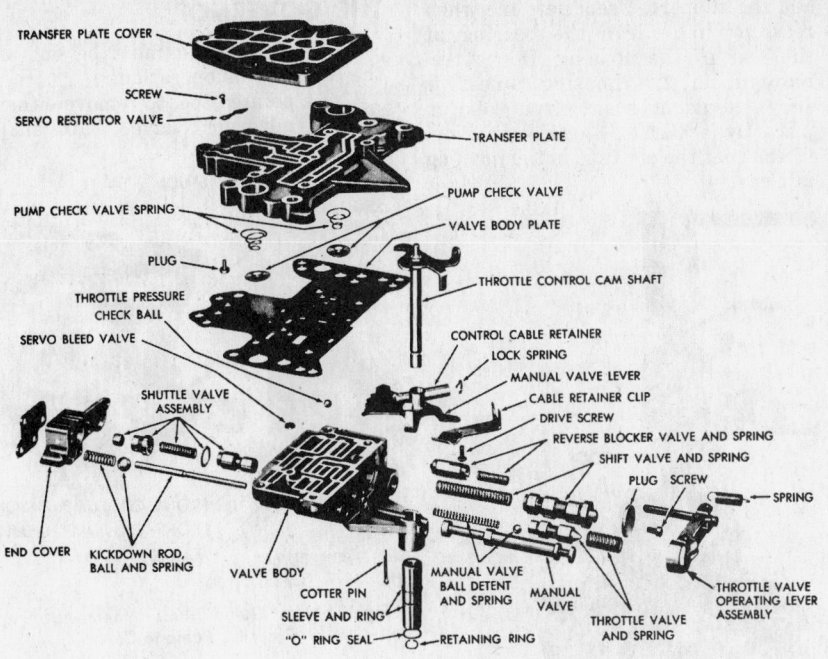

Fig. 10—Exploded View of Valve Body: 1956-61. Typical of 1953-55 Except for the Reverse Blocker Valve.

TRANSFER PLATE COVER
SCREW
SERVO RESTRICTOR VALVE
TRANSFER PLATE
PUMP CHECK VALVE SPRING
PUMP CHECK VALVE
PLUG
VALVE BODY PLATE
THROTTLE PRESSURE CHECK BALL
THROTTLE CONTROL CAM SHAFT
SERVO BLEED VALVE
CONTROL CABLE RETAINER
LOCK SPRING
MANUAL VALVE LEVER
SHUTTLE VALVE ASSEMBLY
CABLE RETAINER CLIP
DRIVE SCREW
REVERSE BLOCKER VALVE AND SPRING
SHIFT VALVE AND SPRING
PLUG SCREW
SPRING
END COVER
KICKDOWN ROD, BALL AND SPRING
VALVE BODY
COTTER PIN
SLEEVE AND RING
"O" RING SEAL
RETAINING RING
MANUAL VALVE BALL DETENT AND SPRING
MANUAL VALVE
THROTTLE VALVE AND SPRING
THROTTLE VALVE OPERATING LEVER ASSEMBLY

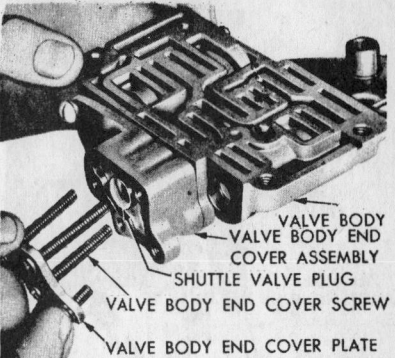

Fig. 16—Removing Valve Body End Cover Plate

VALVE BODY
VALVE BODY END COVER ASSEMBLY
SHUTTLE VALVE PLUG
VALVE BODY END COVER SCREW
VALVE BODY END COVER PLATE

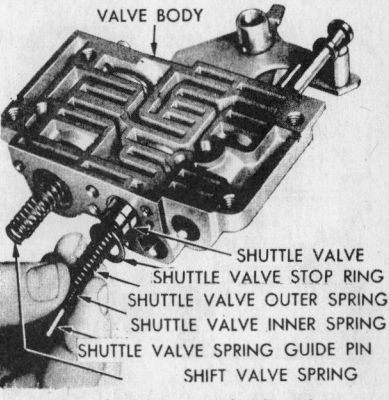

Fig. 17—Removing Shuttle Valve

VALVE BODY
SHUTTLE VALVE
SHUTTLE VALVE STOP RING
SHUTTLE VALVE OUTER SPRING
SHUTTLE VALVE INNER SPRING
SHUTTLE VALVE SPRING GUIDE PIN
SHIFT VALVE SPRING

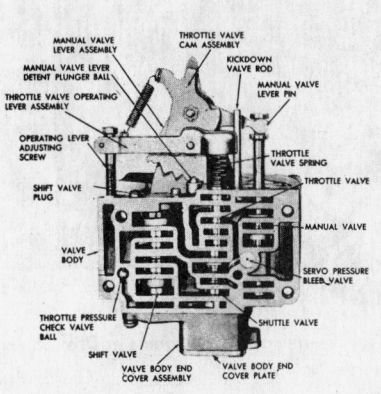

Fig. 12—Valve Body Assembly. 1953-55

MANUAL VALVE LEVER ASSEMBLY
THROTTLE VALVE CAM ASSEMBLY
MANUAL VALVE LEVER DETENT PLUNGER BALL
KICKDOWN VALVE ROD
THROTTLE VALVE OPERATING LEVER ASSEMBLY
MANUAL VALVE LEVER PIN
OPERATING LEVER ADJUSTING SCREW
THROTTLE VALVE SPRING
THROTTLE VALVE
SHIFT VALVE PLUG
MANUAL VALVE
VALVE BODY
SERVO PRESSURE BLEED VALVE
THROTTLE PRESSURE CHECK VALVE BALL
SHUTTLE VALVE
SHIFT VALVE
VALVE BODY END COVER ASSEMBLY
VALVE BODY END COVER PLATE

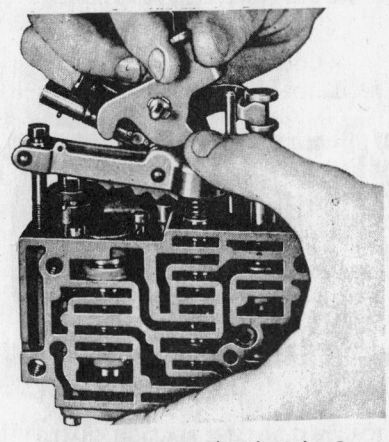

Fig. 14—Removing Throttle Valve Cam Assembly

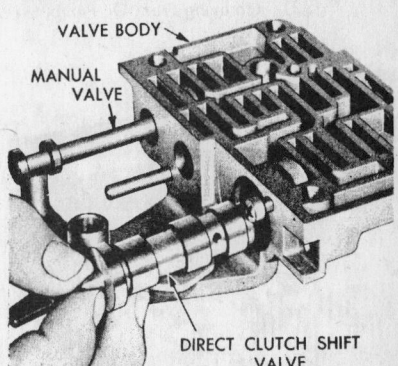

Fig. 18—Remove the Direct Clutch Shift Valve

VALVE BODY
MANUAL VALVE
DIRECT CLUTCH SHIFT VALVE

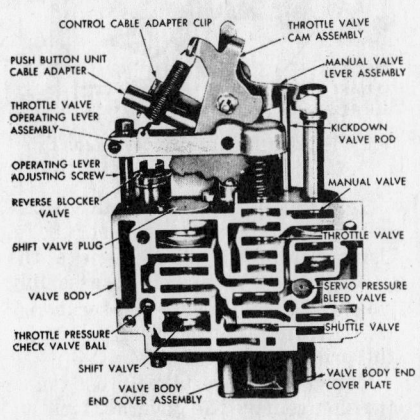

Fig. 13—Valve Body Assembly. 1956-61

CONTROL CABLE ADAPTER CLIP
THROTTLE VALVE CAM ASSEMBLY
PUSH BUTTON UNIT CABLE ADAPTER
MANUAL VALVE LEVER ASSEMBLY
THROTTLE VALVE OPERATING LEVER ASSEMBLY
KICKDOWN VALVE ROD
OPERATING LEVER ADJUSTING SCREW
MANUAL VALVE
REVERSE BLOCKER VALVE
THROTTLE VALVE
SHIFT VALVE PLUG
VALVE BODY
SERVO PRESSURE BLEED VALVE
THROTTLE PRESSURE CHECK VALVE BALL
SHUTTLE VALVE
SHIFT VALVE
VALVE BODY END COVER ASSEMBLY
VALVE BODY END COVER PLATE

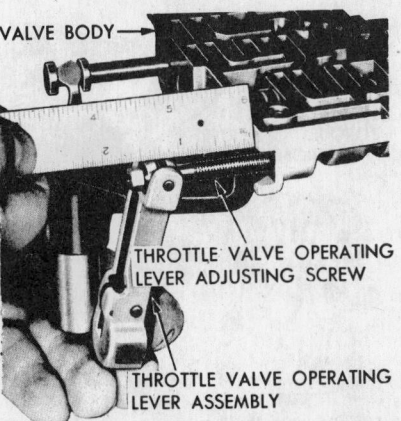

Fig. 15—Distance from Edge of Body to

VALVE BODY
THROTTLE VALVE OPERATING LEVER ADJUSTING SCREW
THROTTLE VALVE OPERATING LEVER ASSEMBLY

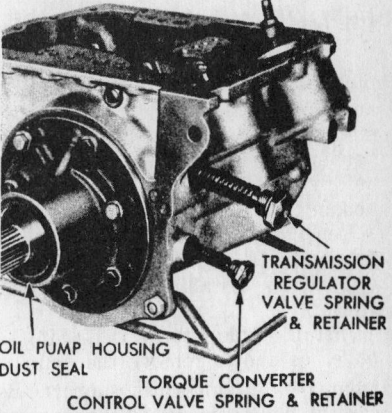

Fig. 19—Remove the Retainers to Release the Springs and Valves

TRANSMISSION REGULATOR VALVE SPRING & RETAINER
OIL PUMP HOUSING DUST SEAL
TORQUE CONVERTER CONTROL VALVE SPRING & RETAINER

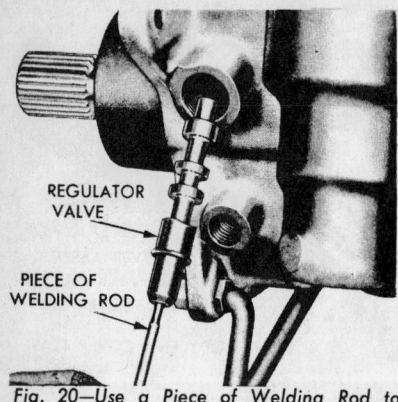

REGULATOR VALVE

PIECE OF WELDING ROD

Fig. 20—Use a Piece of Welding Rod to Hook the Regulator Valve From the Case

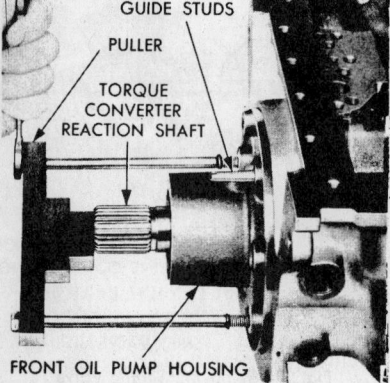

GUIDE STUDS

PULLER

TORQUE CONVERTER REACTION SHAFT

FRONT OIL PUMP HOUSING

Fig. 21—Removing Front Oil Pump

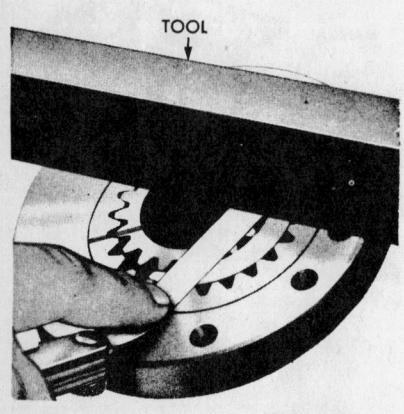

TOOL

Fig. 22—Use Straight Edge of Check End Clearance Limits .001 in.-.003 in.

pinion gear. The gear is made of nylon and will be damaged if an attempt is made to remove the rear extension housing from the transmission case before removing the pinion from the housing.

Remove the seven transmission extension to case screws and lockwashers. When installing tighten to 25 ft lbs.

Install guide studs and using a puller as shown remove the housing from the output shaft support. Be careful not to injure the aluminum governor housing on the output shaft. Note the gasket between the housing

and the support. Use a new one when reassembling. Clean the bearing at the rear of the housing. Do not remove from the housing unless it shows signs of wear. It is held in place by a beveled edge snap ring. Check that the air vent in the housing is clear.

TOOL

FRONT OIL PUMP HOUSING

Fig. 23—Use Driver to Install New Oil Seal and Dust Seal in Front Pump Housing

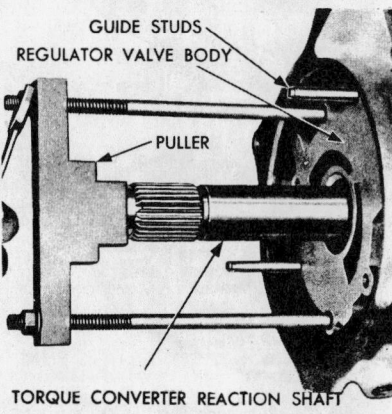

GUIDE STUDS

REGULATOR VALVE BODY

PULLER

TORQUE CONVERTER REACTION SHAFT

Fig. 24—Use a Puller to Remove Front (Regulator) Valve Body From Front of Transmission Case

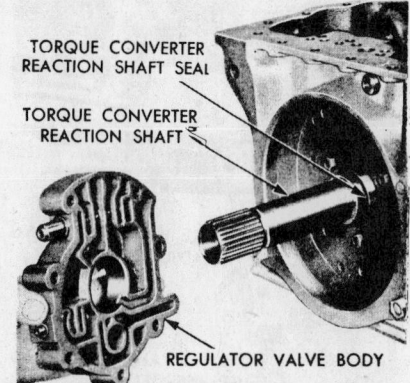

TORQUE CONVERTER REACTION SHAFT SEAL

TORQUE CONVERTER REACTION SHAFT

REGULATOR VALVE BODY

Fig. 25—Installing Front (Regulator) Valve Body. Note Neoprene Seal

THE GOVERNOR

The transmission must be out of the car for this operation.

Use a pointed tool to remove either of the governor valve shaft snap rings.

GUIDE STUDS

REGULATOR VALVE BODY

TORQUE CONVERTER REACTION SHAFT

FRONT OIL PUMP PINION

FRONT OIL PUMP GEAR

MARKS

FRONT OIL PUMP HOUSING SEAL

Fig. 26—Use Guide Studs When Installing Front Oil Pump to Case

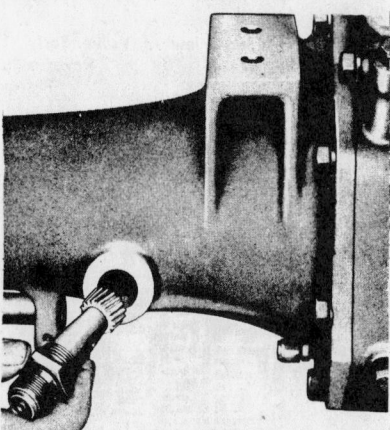

Fig. 27—Removing Speedometer Drive Pinion

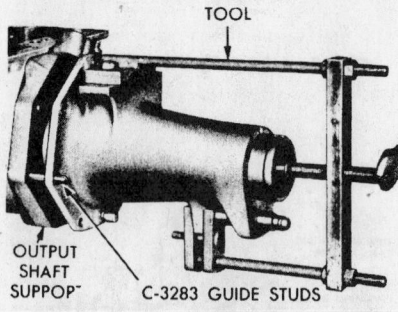

TOOL

OUTPUT SHAFT SUPPORT

C-3283 GUIDE STUDS

Fig. 28—Using Puller to Remove Rear Extension from the Case

Remove the governor valve shaft and valve from the governor body. Using snap ring pliers remove the governor primary weight assembly ring which will release the secondary weight, and the spring from inside the primary weight.

Being very careful not to damage the slot, remove the governor locating screw and slide the governor body

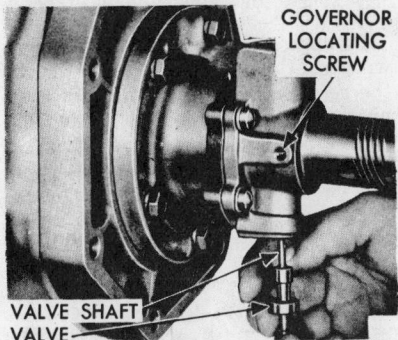

Fig. 29—Removing a Governor Valve Shaft Snap Ring

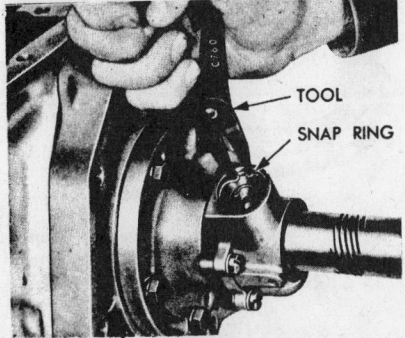

GOVERNOR LOCATING SCREW

VALVE SHAFT VALVE

Fig. 30—Removing Governor Valve and Shaft

and support from the output shaft. retaining ring, and the governor primary weight assembly.

Hold the secondary weight against its spring load and remove the snap

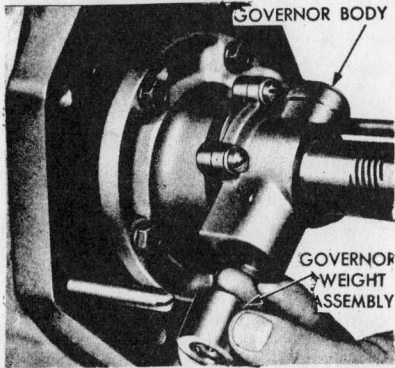

TOOL

SNAP RING

Fig. 31—Remove Primary Weight Retaining Ring

GOVERNOR BODY

GOVERNOR WEIGHT ASSEMBLY

Fig. 32—Remove Governor Primary Weight Assembly

OUTPUT SHAFT SUPPORT
REAR OIL PUMP HOUSING
GOVERNOR BODY SUPPORT
GOVERNOR BODY

GOVERNOR SUPPORT PISTON RINGS

Fig. 33—Slide Governor Body and Support Assembly from the Output Shaft

Remove the four screws and lock-washers holding the governor body to the governor support.

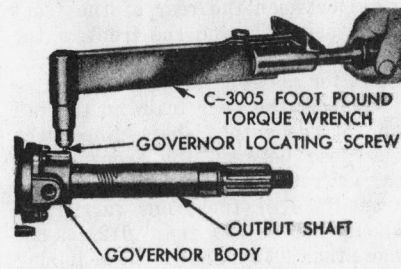

C–3005 FOOT POUND TORQUE WRENCH
GOVERNOR LOCATING SCREW

OUTPUT SHAFT
GOVERNOR BODY

Fig. 34—Tighten Governor Locating Screw to 4-5 ft. lbs.

THE REAR OIL PUMP

The transmission must be out of the car for this operation.

Remove the five rear oil pump to output shaft support screws and lock-washers. Remove the oil pump housing and driven gear. Mark the forward face of the gear with prussian blue or equivalent.

Remove the rear oil pump pinion (driving gear) and mark its forward surface with prussian blue. Do not lose the oil pump pinion drive ball.

Reverse the procedure to reinstall.

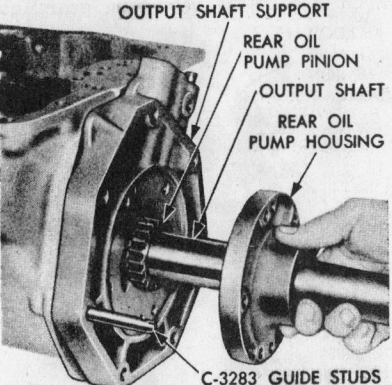

OUTPUT SHAFT SUPPORT
REAR OIL PUMP PINION
OUTPUT SHAFT
REAR OIL PUMP HOUSING

C–3283 GUIDE STUDS

Fig. 35—Removing Rear Oil Pump Body (Housing)

REAR OIL PUMP PINION BALL
OIL PUMP PINION KEYWAY

REAR OIL PUMP PINION

Fig. 36—Remove Rear Oil Pump Pinion (Drive Gear)

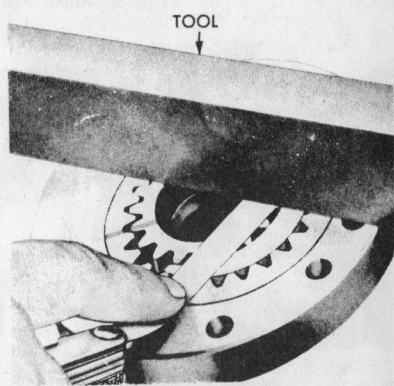

TOOL

Fig. 37—Using Straight Edge to Check End Clearance. Limits: .0012" to .0022"

Be sure that the gears have the same faces forward that they had when removed. Note that there are two extra holes in the rear oil pump housing which act as vents for the transmission case. Make definitely sure that you do not install screws into these vent holes. Tighten the five attaching screws and lockwashers to 15 ft lbs. Turn the output shaft and so be sure the oil pump gears are free to rotate.

TRANSMISSION GEAR TRAIN

The transmission must be out of the car for this operation. The rear extension and the rear oil pump must also have been removed.

Remove the one remaining screw and washer which holds the transmission output shaft support to the transmission case. With one hand, work the output shaft up and down while at the same time pushing backward on the front end of the input shaft with the other hand. With luck the support will loosen from the case and the whole gear train can be slid out the rear of the case. If the support cannot be loosened by the up and down movement, install one of the oil pan screws into the lower edge of the case and using the bolt as a fulcrum

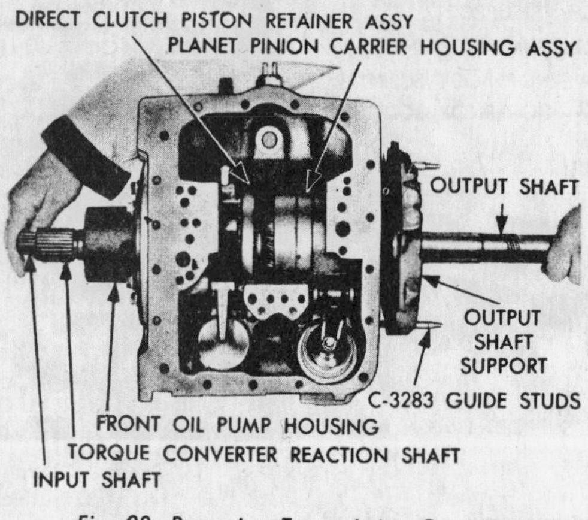

Fig. 38—Removing Transmission Gear Train

DIRECT CLUTCH PISTON RETAINER ASSY
PLANET PINION CARRIER HOUSING ASSY
OUTPUT SHAFT
OUTPUT SHAFT SUPPORT
C-3283 GUIDE STUDS
FRONT OIL PUMP HOUSING
TORQUE CONVERTER REACTION SHAFT
INPUT SHAFT

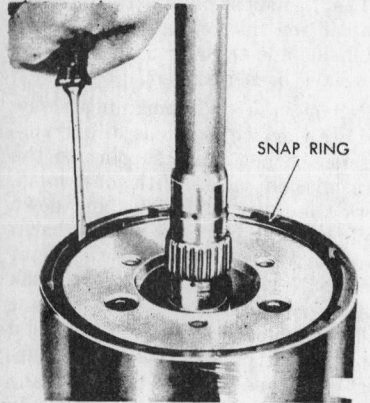

OUTPUT SHAFT SUPPORT
OIL PAN SCREW

Fig. 39—Prying Support Loose From Case

pry the support from the case.

The front drum assembly called the Direct Clutch Piston Retainer in the cuts, will in all probability remain in place on the inner end of the reaction shaft. Removal of the front drum assembly from the shaft end will reveal the selective thrust washer which controls the end play of the gear train. The selection of the proper thickness of washer is described in the paragraph on Transmission End

Clearance. Inspect the thrust washer for cracks, burrs, and wear, then mark for identification at assembly.

Remove the thrust washer which rides between the rear of the front drum assembly and the front of the kickdown (front) planet carrier. Mark for easier assembly.

Support the gear train on the tail end of the output shaft. Check the clearance between the front pinion carrier retaining snap ring and the front face of the front carrier. It should not be less than .012 in. nor more than .038 in. Mark the snap ring for identification at assembly.

Removal of the snap ring will permit removal of the input shaft, the kickdown (front) planet pinion carrier, and the front planet ring gear, together with the thrust washer which separates this planet set from the rear planet set. Mark the thrust washer for easy assembly.

Removal of the snap ring which holds the rear (reverse) planet pinion carrier in the rear drum (carrier housing) will permit removal of the rear planet carrier from the planet pinion carrier housing (rear drum).

Remove the output shaft and the rear planet ring gear assembly from the rear drum. Remove and mark the thrust washer which goes between the rear face of the rear ring gear and

the inside face of the rear drum.

Remove the rear drum (planet pinion carrier housing) from the output shaft support.

DIRECT DRIVE CLUTCH

After removal of drive train, remove kick down sun gear snap ring. Scribe mark for location in reassembly. Lift out sun gear. Inspect for foreign material in oil passages and clean. Turn over the container and drop out the steel plates and driving disc.

Note position of plates and discs as they must be reassembled in same sequence.

Compress the direct clutch spring with tool C-3533 or C-3302 and release the retaining snap ring. Release compressor tool and remove snap ring, spring retainer and spring. Now remove piston. Inspect piston bushing and check valve. Be sure check valve is free. Bushing is not serviced separately. If bad a new piston is required.

REVERSE PLANET PINION CARRIER ASSY
HOUSING

Fig. 42—Remove Rear (Reverse) Planet Carrier Assembly. Note that starting March, '56 aluminum carrier is used

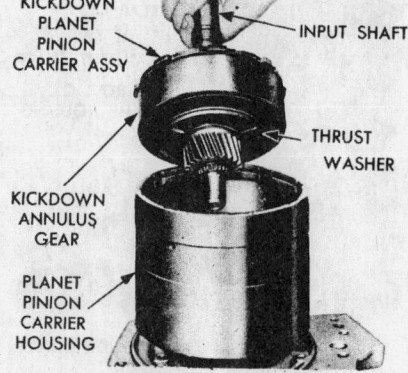

KICKDOWN PLANET PINION CARRIER ASSY
INPUT SHAFT
THRUST WASHER
KICKDOWN ANNULUS GEAR
PLANET PINION CARRIER HOUSING

Fig. 40—Remove Front (Kickdown) Planet Carrier Retaining Snap Ring

SNAP RING

Fig. 41—Remove Front (Kickdown) Planet Carrier Assembly

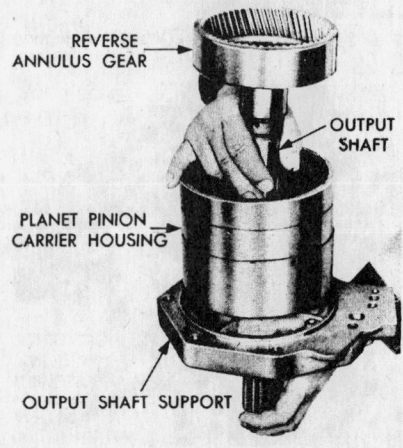

REVERSE ANNULUS GEAR
OUTPUT SHAFT
PLANET PINION CARRIER HOUSING
OUTPUT SHAFT SUPPORT

Fig. 43—Remove Rear (Reverse) Planet Ring Gear

TRANSMISSION END CLEARANCE

End play of the transmission gear train can be measured with the transmission still in place in the car.

Remove the transmission oil pan and the valve body assembly.

Check the transmission end clearance with an indicator or with a feeler gauge. Pry the multiple disc clutch front drum assembly to the rear. Remove the pry and measure the clearance between the front and the rear drum.

It should not be less than .026 in.

Put a screw driver between the front and the rear drums and pry the front drum forward. Remove the driver.

Measure the clearance between the front and the rear drum, it should not be more than .052 in.

If the clearance as measured is more than .052 in. it will be necessary to remove the transmission from the car and disassemble it in order to replace the selective thrust washer. The selective thrust washer is the thrust washer between the front face of the clutch assembly and the rear face of the reaction shaft retainer. It is made of fiber and does not show in any picture. The thrust washer is available in three thicknesses: .078-.080; .095-.097; .112-.114.

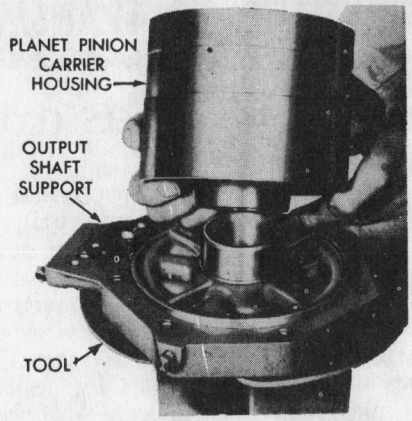

Fig. 44—Remove Rear Drum (Planet Carrier Housing) from Output Shaft Support

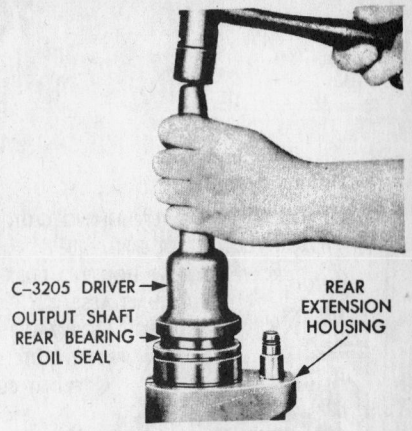

Installation of Output Shaft Oil Seal

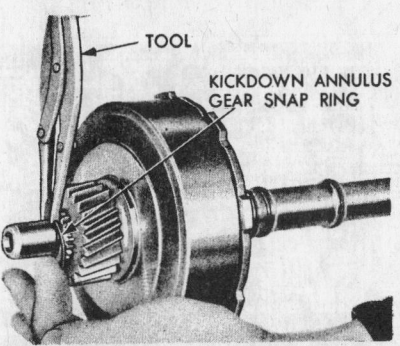

Fig. 45—Remove Snap Ring Holding Front (Kickdown) Ring Gear to Input Shaft

Removing Direct Clutch Assembly

Checking Transmission End Clearance

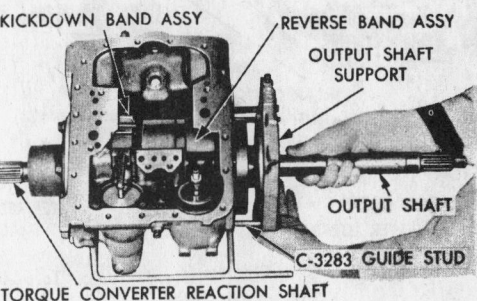

Installation of Power Train in Transmission

Removal of Output Shaft Support, Extension, Handbrake Assy.
and Pinion Carrier Housing as an Assembly

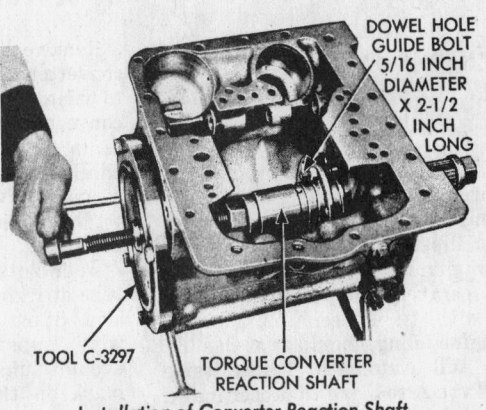

Installation of Converter Reaction Shaft

CHRYSLER AUTOMATIC TRANSMISSIONS

TORQUEFLITE V8 TRANSMISSION
Used on Chrysler Corporation Products

1957-61 V-8 MODELS (TYPE A)

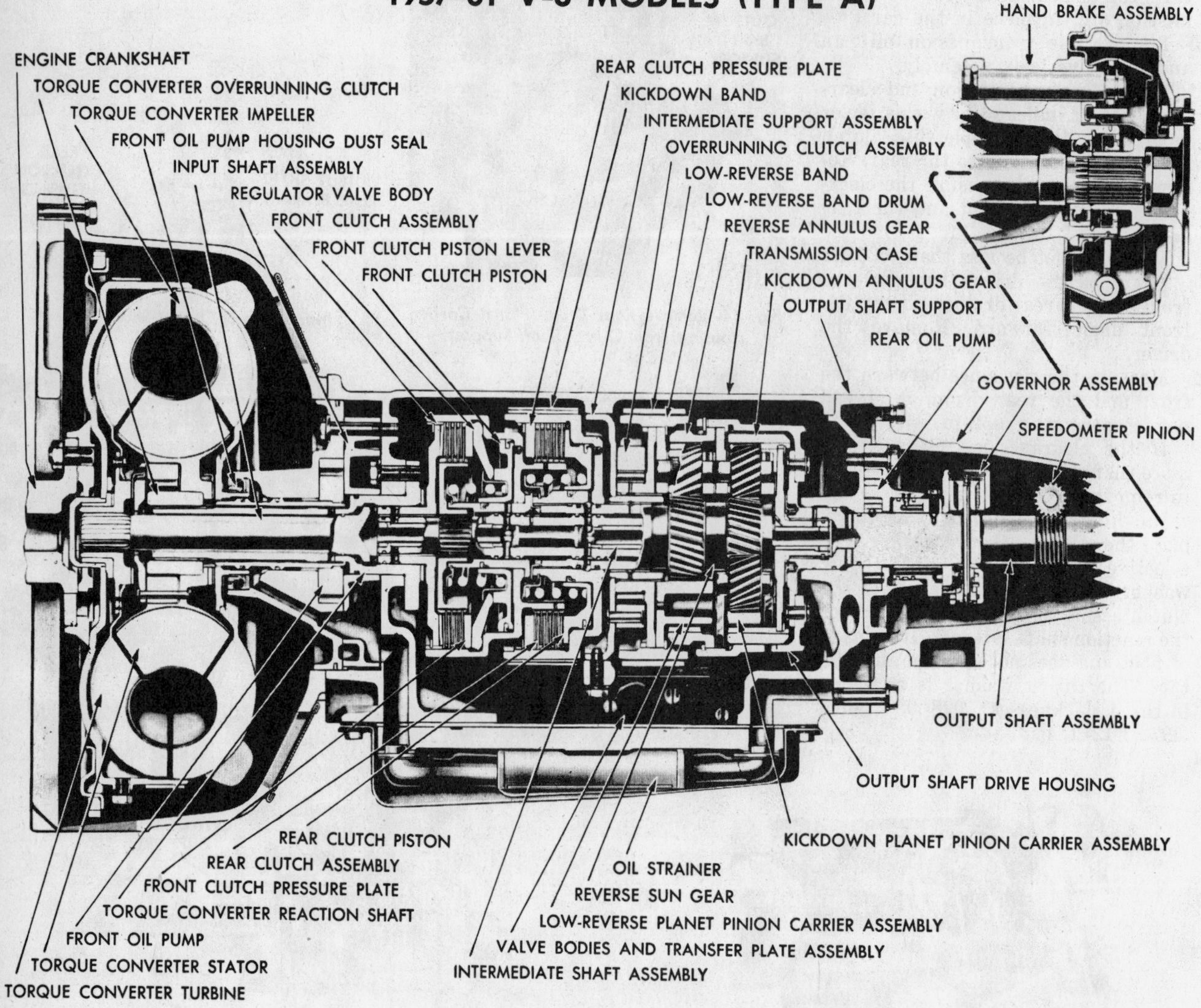

HAND BRAKE ASSEMBLY

ENGINE CRANKSHAFT
TORQUE CONVERTER OVERRUNNING CLUTCH
TORQUE CONVERTER IMPELLER
FRONT OIL PUMP HOUSING DUST SEAL
INPUT SHAFT ASSEMBLY
REGULATOR VALVE BODY
FRONT CLUTCH ASSEMBLY
FRONT CLUTCH PISTON LEVER
FRONT CLUTCH PISTON

REAR CLUTCH PRESSURE PLATE
KICKDOWN BAND
INTERMEDIATE SUPPORT ASSEMBLY
OVERRUNNING CLUTCH ASSEMBLY
LOW-REVERSE BAND
LOW-REVERSE BAND DRUM
REVERSE ANNULUS GEAR
TRANSMISSION CASE
KICKDOWN ANNULUS GEAR
OUTPUT SHAFT SUPPORT
REAR OIL PUMP

GOVERNOR ASSEMBLY
SPEEDOMETER PINION

OUTPUT SHAFT ASSEMBLY
OUTPUT SHAFT DRIVE HOUSING
KICKDOWN PLANET PINION CARRIER ASSEMBLY

REAR CLUTCH PISTON
REAR CLUTCH ASSEMBLY
FRONT CLUTCH PRESSURE PLATE
TORQUE CONVERTER REACTION SHAFT
FRONT OIL PUMP
TORQUE CONVERTER STATOR
TORQUE CONVERTER TURBINE

OIL STRAINER
REVERSE SUN GEAR
LOW-REVERSE PLANET PINION CARRIER ASSEMBLY
VALVE BODIES AND TRANSFER PLATE ASSEMBLY
INTERMEDIATE SHAFT ASSEMBLY

Fig. 1—Typical TorqueFlite Transmission and Torque Converter

GENERAL INFORMATION

CHECK THE FLUID LEVEL EVERY 1,000 MILES

If the transmission is at room temperature, having engine idling and transmission in Neutral, the "L" mark on the dipstick is then the correct level. Fig. 2. However, if transmission is at operating temperature, the oil level, with transmission in Neutral and engine idling, should be at the "F" mark. Add Automatic Transmission Fluid Type A to bring to proper mark. Be careful not to overfill.

DRAIN AND REFILL EVERY 20,000 MILES, OFTENER IN SEVERE SERVICE

Remove plate from bottom of torque converter housing and turn converter to bring drain plug into reach. Remove converter drain plug and transmission drain plug. When reinstalling plugs check that gaskets are good. Tighten torque converter drain plug to 50 ft. lbs. Tighten oil pan drain plug to 25 ft. lbs.

Pour 5 qts of Type A fluid thru filler tube at right of engine into transmission. Start engine and while it idles with transmission in Neutral add enough fluid to bring level to the "L" mark on the dipstick. This will be about 3 qts. Shift transmission thru

all ranges and recheck that level is at "L" mark.

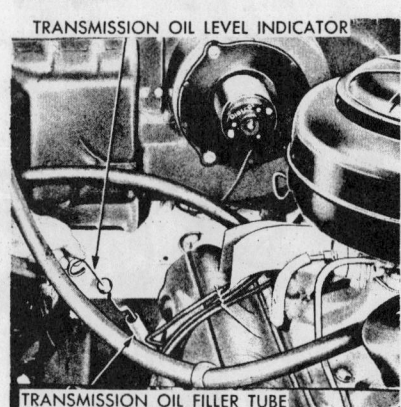

TRANSMISSION OIL LEVEL INDICATOR

TRANSMISSION OIL FILLER TUBE

Fig. 2—Oil level indicator. Total capacity is about 8 quarts

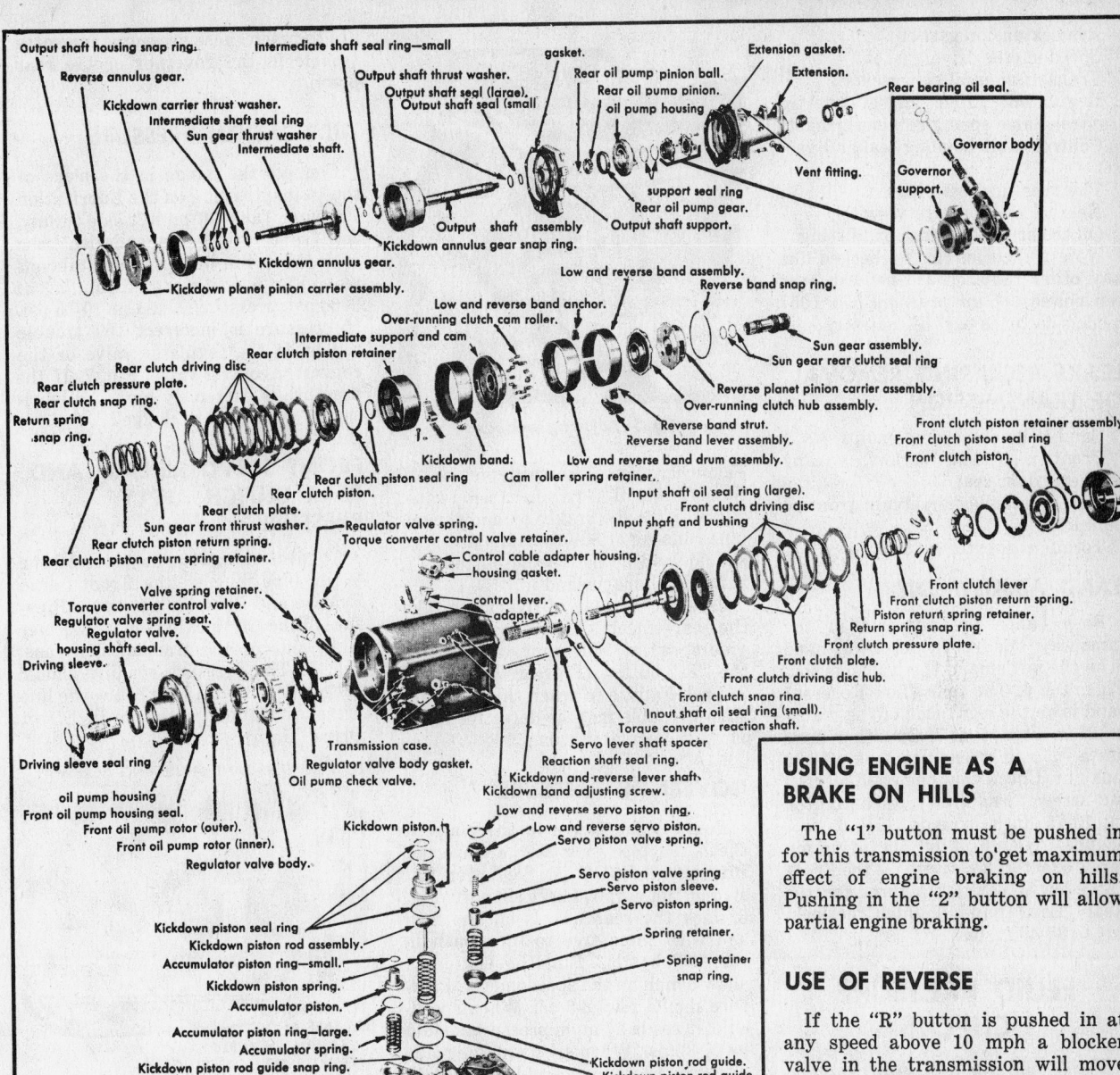

Fig. 3—Exploded View of TorqueFlite Transmission

COLD WEATHER OPERATION

If weather temperatures are low enough to require 5W oil in the engine the Type A fluid in the transmission may be diluted with one quart of kerosene. Drain 1 qt. from transmission and then add kerosene. Check level.

When weather gets warmer, the kerosene will evaporate and the level can be kept constant by adding Type A fluid as required.

STARTING THE ENGINE WITHOUT USE OF THE STARTER

Push the car to start it. Towing a car with an automatic transmission to start the engine is likely to result in the towed car ramming the towing car.

With the "1" button pushed in, push the car. At a speed above 15 mph the transmission will operate and the engine will turn.

TOWING CAR EQUIPPED WITH TORQUE-FLITE

If transmission is undamaged and can be placed in Neutral the car can be towed at moderate speed. Chrysler says that distance towed with transmission turning should not exceed 100 miles.

USING ENGINE AS A BRAKE ON HILLS

The "1" button must be pushed in for this transmission to get maximum effect of engine braking on hills. Pushing in the "2" button will allow partial engine braking.

USE OF REVERSE

If the "R" button is pushed in at any speed above 10 mph a blocker valve in the transmission will move the manual control to Neutral. When the car speed drops below 10 mph the "R" button must be pushed in again.

Note on Disassembly and Repair

There are many points of similarity in construction and design between the TorqueFlite Transmission and the PowerFlite Transmission. While the parts are not interchangeable the procedures for repair are often the same. Any specific items not covered in this article will be found adequately covered in the article on the PowerFlite Transmission.

CHECKING FOR OIL LEAKS

LEAKS REPAIRED WITHOUT REMOVING TRANSMISSION

Rear bearing oil seal

Rear extension gasket
Speedometer drive gasket
Transmission oil pan gasket
Regulator Valve and Converter
Control Valve spring-retainer gaskets
Control cable housing seal and gasket
The pressure test plugs
Neutral starter safety switch
Oil cooler and its lines and fittings
Note: Oil cooler can be checked like any other radiator. Do not use over ten pounds of air pressure. On 1957 models cooler is part of radiator.

LEAKS REQUIRING REMOVAL OF TRANSMISSION

Sand holes in case or pumps
Front oil pump screws, sealing washers, dust seal
Seal on outside diameter of front oil pump
Torque converter seals

BAND ADJUSTMENT

Both bands are adjusted in the same way. The front (kickdown) band is on the left side of the transmission. Figs. 4 & 6. The rear (Low-Reverse) band is on the right side of the transmission. Figs. 5 & 7. On either band use a ¾ inch wrench to back off the lock nut. Check that the band adjusting screw turns freely, then tighten to 70-75 inch pounds (5½-6 foot pounds). Now back off the adjusting screw exactly: 3½ turns for the Front (Kickdown) band; 2¼ turns for the Rear (Low) Band. Tighten the lock-nut to 35-40 ft. lbs.

FLUID PRESSURE CHECKS

Use a fluid pressure gauge capable of measuring from 0 to 300 psi.

LINE PRESSURE

Connect the gauge in place of the ⅛ in. pipe plug at the Line Pressure

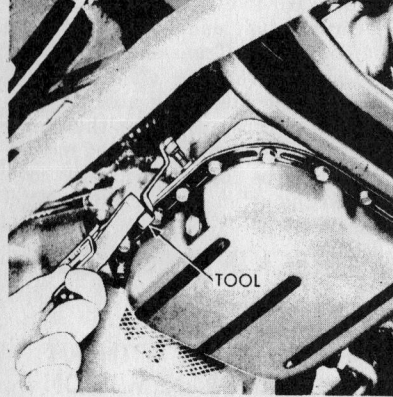

Fig. 4—Adjusting front band

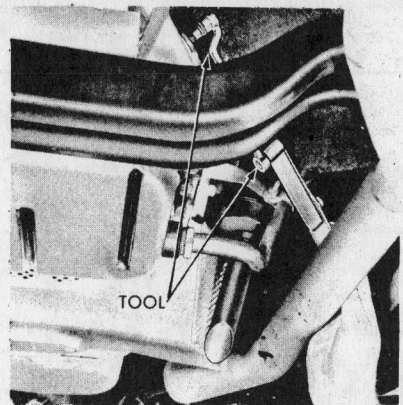

Fig. 5—Adjusting rear band

Take-Off on the forward portion of the left side of the transmission case. Fig. 6. With the brakes on and the engine running at 800 rpm, the pressure should read 90 psi as the buttons: 1, 2, D and N are pushed in.

Jack up the rear of the car to take the rear wheels off the floor. Set engine speed at 1600 rpm and push in the "R" button. Pressure should be 225 psi. Failure to reach this pressure shows trouble may be defective front pump or regulator valve.

GOVERNOR PRESSURE

Connect the gauge in the place of the ⅛ in. pipe plug at the Governor Pressure Take-Off on the lower left side of the output shaft support. Fig. 6. Jack the rear wheels off the floor and with them free to turn push in the "D" button. Run the engine to show 8 mph on the speedometer. Pressure should read 2-3 psi. When speedometer reads 27 mph, pressure should be 27-32 psi. When speedometer reads 38 mph, pressure should read 44-47 psi. When speedometer reads 75 mph, pressure should read 75-82 psi. Fail-

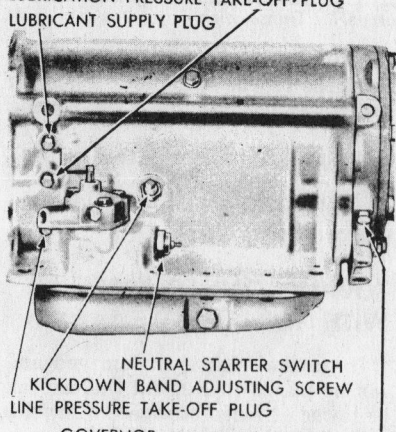

LUBRICATION PRESSURE TAKE-OFF PLUG
LUBRICANT SUPPLY PLUG

NEUTRAL STARTER SWITCH
KICKDOWN BAND ADJUSTING SCREW
LINE PRESSURE TAKE-OFF PLUG
GOVERNOR PRESSURE TAKE-OFF PLUG

Fig. 6—View of left side of transmission

ure to reach these pressures indicates trouble in the governor or the rear pump.

LUBRICATION PRESSURE

Connect the gauge in the place of the ⅛ in. pipe plug on the Lubrication Pressure Take-Off on left side toward the front of the transmission case just above the line pressure take-off plug. Fig. 6. With engine running at 800 rpm, pressure should be 10-30 psi. If pressure is incorrect the trouble can be in the regulator valve or the converter control valve. Fig. 7. If the pressure is extremely high the lubrication passages are clogged.

FRONT SERVO RELEASE AND REAR CLUTCH APPLY PRESSURE

Connect the gauge in place of the ⅛ in. pipe plug on the Front Servo Release and Rear Clutch Apply Pressure Take-Off located on the lower right side of the transmission case. Fig. 7. The pressure reading should not be more than 15 psi below the line pressure reading with car in Direct Drive (High).

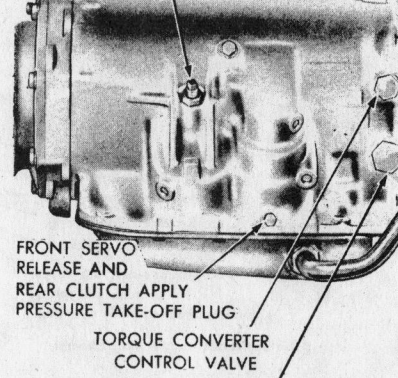

LOW-REVERSE BAND ADJUSTING SCREW

FRONT SERVO
RELEASE AND
REAR CLUTCH APPLY
PRESSURE TAKE-OFF PLUG
TORQUE CONVERTER
CONTROL VALVE
TRANSMISSION REGULATOR VALVE

Fig. 7—View of right side of transmission

TROUBLE SHOOTING CHART

Always check oil level, linkage adjustment, control cable adjustment and engine idle before any other checks.

Note: Items marked "X" require removal of unit from car for servicing.

TROUBLE: HARSH SHIFTING, N TO D, N TO R.

Possible Cause No. 1: Internal Leaks.

Remedy: Pinpoint trouble. See paragraph on "Fluid Pressure Checks."

Possible Cause No. 2: Loose Rear Band.

Remedy: See par. "Band Adjustment."

Possible Cause No. 3: Idle Speed Too High.

Remedy: Adjust idle speed to 475-500 rpm.

Possible Cause No. 4: Rear Servo or Accumulator Stuck.

Remedy: Apply par. on "Air Pressure Checks" to pinpoint trouble.

Possible Cause No. 5: Front or Rear Clutches Sticking. "X"

Remedy: Clean and inspect drive hub, discs, plates, return spring and piston.

TROUBLE: SHIFT FROM NEUTRAL TO DRIVE DELAYED.

Possible Cause No. 1: Incorrect Oil Level.

Remedy: Check that oil level is at "L" mark when transmission is at room temperature.

Possible Cause No. 2: Defective Fluid Pressure.

Remedy: Apply par. on "Fluid Pressure Checks" to pinpoint trouble.

Possible Cause No. 3: Valve Body Improperly Installed or Loose. Accumulator Piston Rings Broken or Cover Loose.

Remedy: Remove oil pan and check that valve body and mating surfaces are smooth and clean. Check movement of valves. Tighten bolts to 14-16 ft. lbs. See paragraphs on "Removal Of Valve Body," "Removal of Accumulator," "Fluid Pressure Checks."

Possible Cause No. 4: Front Pump Drive Sleeve Seal Rings Broken. "X"

Remedy: Check clearance of drive sleeve and pump gears. Check drive sleeve seal rings. See par. "Front Pump Removal."

Possible Cause No. 5: Front Clutch Defective. "X"

Remedy: Check fluid circuits to the clutch for leaks and the unit for wear and broken parts.

TROUBLE: ERRATIC SHIFTING. RUNAWAY ON UPSHIFT AND 3-2 KICKDOWN. HARSH UPSHIFT AND 3-2 KICKDOWN. NO UPSHIFT, NO DOWNSHIFT, NO KICKDOWNS.

Possible Cause No. 1: Incorrect Oil Level. Incorrect: Throttle Linkage Adjustment, Manual Control Adjustment, Fluid Pressure.

Remedy: Check over items and correct as necessary.

Possible Cause No. 2: Front Band Requires Adjustment.

Remedy: See par. "Band Adjustment."

Possible Cause No. 3: Regulator Valve Spring Defective.

Remedy: Remove regulator valve spring retainer (fig. 7) and remove spring and valve. Check for stuck or scratched valve and defective spring. When reinstalling tighten retainer to 45-50 ft. lbs.

Possible Cause No. 4: Output Shaft Rear Bearing Snap Ring Distorted or Improperly Installed.

Remedy: See par. "Rear Extension and Output Shaft Bearing."

Possible Cause No. 5: Front Servo or Linkage Defective. Accumulator Defective. Loose Valve Body.

Remedy: See par. "Air Pressure Checks."

Possible Cause No. 6: Air Leaks at Oil Screen or Suction Tubes.

Remedy: Remove oil pan and check units.

Possible Cause No. 7: Governor Sticking.

Remedy: Remove governor pressure test (take-off) plug and with short blasts of air attempt to cause governor weights to move. If this does not work see par. "Rear Extension and Output Shaft Bearing."

Possible Cause No. 8: Leaks at Front Pump Drive Sleeve. "X"

Remedy: Check seal rings on drive sleeve.

Possible Cause No. 9: Rear Clutch Defective. "X"

Remedy: Overhaul rear clutch.

Possible Cause No. 10: Over Running Clutch Defective. "X"

Remedy: Overhaul over running clutch.

TROUBLE: CAR DRIVES IN NEUTRAL.

Possible Cause No. 1: Manual Control Cable Improperly Adjusted.

Remedy: See par. "Manual Control Cable Adjustment," in car section.

Possible Cause No. 2: Loose Valve Body Bolts.

Remedy: Tighten bolts evenly to 5 ft. lbs.

Possible Cause No. 3: Defective Front Clutch. "X"

Remedy: Overhaul front clutch.

TROUBLE: SLIPS IN FORWARD DRIVE POSITIONS.

Possible Cause No. 1: Incorrect Oil Level.

Remedy: Check that oil level is at "L" mark when transmission is at room temperature.

Possible Cause No. 2: Internal Leaks.

Remedy: See par. "Fluid Pressure Checks."

Possible Cause No. 3: Valve Body Improperly Installed or Loose. Accumulator Defective.

Remedy: Remove oil pan and check that valve body and mating surfaces are smooth and clean. Check movement of valves. Tighten bolts to 14-16 ft. lbs. Check accumulator piston rings and accumulator cover. See paragraphs on "Removal of Valve Body," "Removal of Accumulator" and "Fluid Pressure Checks."

Possible Cause No. 4: Defective Regulator Valve Body or Gasket. "X"

Remedy: Inspect pump housing side of valve body for scratches and scores. Check uniformity of gasket.

Possible Cause No. 5: Defective Clutches. "X"

Remedy: Locate defective unit and overhaul.

TROUBLE: SLIPS IN L-R ONLY.

Possible Cause No. 1: Loose Rear Band.

Remedy: See par. "Band Adjustment."

Possible Cause No. 2: Internal Leaks.

Remedy: See par. "Fluid Pressure Checks."

Possible Cause No. 3: Rear Servo Stuck.

Remedy: See par. "Air Pressure Checks."

Possible Cause No. 4: Loose Valve Body Bolts.

Remedy: Tighten bolts evenly to 5 ft. lbs.

Possible Cause No. 5: Defective Regulator Valve Body or Gasket. "X"

Remedy: Inspect pump housing side of valve body for scratches and scores. Check uniformity of gasket.

TROUBLE: SLIPS IN ALL POSITIONS. NO DRIVE IN ANY POSITION.

Possible Cause No. 1: Incorrect Oil Level.

Remedy: Check that level is at "L" mark when transmission is at room temperature.

Possible Cause No. 2: Internal Leaks.

Remedy: See par. "Fluid Pressure Checks."

Possible Cause No. 3: Defective Regulator Valve Spring.

Remedy: Remove regulator valve spring retainer (fig. 7) and remove spring and valve. Check for stuck or scratched valve and defective spring. When reinstalling tighten retainer to 45-50 ft. lbs.

Possible Cause No. 4: Loose Valve Body.

Remedy: Tighten bolts evenly to 5 ft. lbs.

Possible Cause No. 5: Leaks at Front Pump Drive Sleeve. "X"

Remedy: Check seal rings on drive sleeve.

Possible Cause No. 6: Defective Regulator Valve Body or Gasket. "X"

Remedy: Inspect pump housing side of valve body for scratches or scores. Check uniformity of gasket.

TROUBLE: NO DRIVE IN FORWARD POSITIONS.

Possible Cause No. 1: Internal Leaks.

Remedy: See par. "Fluid Pressure Checks."

Possible Cause No. 2: Loose Front Band.

Remedy: See par. "Band Adjustment."

Possible Cause No. 3: Front Servo or Accumulator Stuck.

Remedy: Apply par. "Air Pressure Checks" to pinpoint trouble.

Possible Cause No. 4: Loose Valve Body.

Remedy: Tighten bolts evenly to 5 ft. lbs.

Possible Cause No. 5: Defective Clutches. "X"

Remedy: Locate defective unit and overhaul.

TROUBLE: NO DRIVE IN REVERSE.

Possible Cause No. 1: Internal Leaks.

Remedy: See par. on "Fluid Pressure Checks."

Possible Cause No. 2: Loose Rear Band.

Remedy: See par. "Band Adjustment."

Possible Cause No. 3: Rear Servo Stuck.

Remedy: See par. "Air Pressure Checks."

Possible Cause No. 4: Rear Clutch Defective. "X"

Remedy: Overhaul unit.

TROUBLE: TRANSMISSION DRAGS OR LOCKS UP

**1: Possible Cause
Maladjusted Bands Or Hand Brake**

Remedy: See paragraph on "Band Adjustment." Check hand brake for drag.

**2: Possible Cause
Inoperative Or Sticking Servos**

Remedy: Remove oil pan and check units.

**3: Possible Cause
Clutches Or Gear Sets Worn "X"**

Remedy: Disassemble transmission and overhaul.

TROUBLE: GRATING AND/OR SCRAPING NOISES

**1: Possible Cause
Dragging Hand Brake**

Remedy: Adjust hand brake. Clearance between shoes and drum when released should be .015 to .020 inches. Remove adjusting screw cover plate and turn adjusting screw to give slight drag on drum. Back off screw one notch from this point to give at least .010 inch clearance. Be sure two raised shoulders on adjusting nut are seated in grooves on adjusting sleeve. Do not attempt to adjust brake by adjusting cable.

**2: Possible Cause
Output Shaft Rear Bearing Worn. Governor Or Rear Pump Worn**

Remedy: See paragraph on "Removal of Rear Extension."

**3: Possible Cause
Front Pump Drive Sleeve Worn "X"**

Remedy: See paragraph on "Front Pump Removal."

**4: Possible Cause
Malfunctioning of the Hydraulic Clutches or the Planetary Gear Set**

Remedy: Disassemble and overhaul transmission.

TROUBLE: BUZZING NOISES

**1: Possible Cause
Low Fluid Level**

Remedy: Check fluid level.

**2: Possible Cause
Stuck Converter Or Regulator Control Valve**

Remedy: Remove and inspect for stuck valves or collapsed springs.

**3: Possible Cause
Malfunction Of Or Dirt In Valve Body**

Remedy: See paragraph on "Removal of Valve Body."

TROUBLE: OIL FOAMS OUT FILLER TUBE

**1: Possible Cause
Transmission Overfilled Allowing Aeration Of Oil Which Increases Volume and Causes Foaming. Vent Hole In Top Of Rear Extension Clogged. Oil Cooler Leaking**

Remedy: Check level with transmission cold. It should not be above the "L" mark. Check vent hole in top of rear extension, be sure it is open. Check on transmissions equipped with a cooler that the water has not leaked into the oil. If this has happened, install new cooler and lines. Disconnect lines at left of transmission and install plugs in cooler line attaching holes in the case. Drain fluid. Install new fluid, run car in traffic until transmission is hot. Drain fluid while hot. Install new fluid, remove plugs from cooler line attaching holes at transmission and reconnect cooler lines to transmission. Purpose of all this is to remove, if possible, the sludge which was formed when water got into the transmission. The high temperature tends to break the sludge up. SAE 10W engine oil can be used with 1 quart of kerosene for the flushing operation. Bear in mind that in warm weather an automatic transmission which is normally equipped with an oil cooler will get very hot in a short run if the cooler is disconnected as this procedure requires. While it is necessary that the transmission be run until it is hot it is not recommended that it get hotter than say 212-225 degrees Fahrenheit.

If there definitely was water in the transmission fluid and if this flushing procedure fails to stop the fluid foaming from the fill pipe it will be necessary to remove: the oil pan and clean it and the screen; the rear extension and clean it and the passages from it into the case; the rear oil pump and output shaft support assembly and clean it.

2: Possible Cause
Regulator and Converter Control Valves Sticking
Remedy: See Fig. 7. Remove and clean the valves.

3: Possible Cause
Obstruction in the Filler Tube
Remedy: Unfasten filler tube from transmission and clean the tube. When reinstalling tighten filler tube nut to 40 ft. lbs.

4: Possible Cause
Air Leaks In Pump Suction Tube Or Strainer
Remedy: Remove oil pan and check units.

5: Possible Cause
Front Pump Drive Sleeve Or Regulator Valve Body Leaking "X"
Remedy: See paragraph on "Removal of Front Pump."

TROUBLE: TRANSMISSION OVERHEATS

1: Possible Cause
Low Fluid Level
Remedy: Check fluid level with transmission cold. It should be at "L" mark on dipstick. Check transmission for oil leaks.

2: Possible Cause
Improperly Adjusted Bands
Remedy: See paragraph on "Band Adjustment."

3: Possible Cause
Dragging Hand Brake
Remedy: See "Remedy for possible cause No. 1" under "Grating and Scraping Noises."

4: Possible Cause
Sticking Regulator Or Converter Control Valve
Remedy: See Fig. 7. Remove and clean valves.

5: Possible Cause
Plugged Fluid Cooler Lines
Remedy: Check that fluid is flowing to and from the cooler by feeling the lines, one should be cooler than the other.

6: Possible Cause
Rear Pump Not Operating
Remedy: See paragraph on "Removal of Rear Pump."

7: Possible Cause
Front Pump Not Operating Correctly "X"
Remedy: See paragraph on "Removal of Front Pump."

8: Possible Cause
Clutches Sticking "X"
Remedy: Disassemble and overhaul transmission.

TROUBLE: ENGINE WILL NOT TURN WHEN CAR IS PUSHED WITH BUTTON "1" IN AT SPEED OF 15 MPH

1: Possible Cause
Obstruction In Fluid System
Remedy: Pinpoint trouble by procedure in paragraph on "Fluid Pressure Checks."

2: Possible Cause
Rear Band Improperly Adjusted
Remedy: See paragraph on "Band Adjustment."

3: Possible Cause
Rear Servo Not Working
Remedy: Overhaul Rear Servo.

4: Possible Cause
Leaks At Valve Body
Remedy: See paragraph on "Valve Body Removal."

5: Possible Cause
Rear Pump Inoperative
Remedy: See paragraph on "Removal of Rear Pump."

TROUBLE: STARTER WON'T WORK ALTHOUGH "N" BUTTON IS IN

1: Possible Cause
Maladjustment On Manual Control Cable Or Defective Neutral Safety Switch
Remedy: See paragraph on "Adjustment of Manual Control Cable." Remove switch and check wiring and switch with a test light.

TROUBLE WITH PUSH BUTTON CONTROL

Details of Procedures for Next Six Items Will be Found in Car Section.

TROUBLE: LOW (1) BUTTON REQUIRES TOO MUCH PRESSURE TO LOCK

Cause: Maladjustment of the Manual Control
Remedy: Apply procedure in paragraph on "Manual Control Cable Adjustment."

TROUBLE: CLUNKING NOISE AS A BUTTON COMES OUT

Cause: Rubber Bumper in Dash Unit Missing or Worn
Remedy: Apply procedure in paragraph on "Removing Push Button Unit from Dash," and renew bumper.

TROUBLE: PUSH BUTTON FAILS TO COME OUT

Cause: Broken or Defective Button Return Spring
Remedy: Apply procedure in paragraph on "Removing Push Button Unit from Dash," and renew the spring.

TROUBLE: PUSH BUTTON WILL NOT STAY IN

Cause: Operating Slide Defective
Remedy: Apply procedure in paragraph on "Removing Push Button Unit from Dash," and renew operating slide.

TROUBLE: PUSH BUTTON BINDS

1: Cause
Operating Slides Warped
Remedy: Apply procedure in paragraph on "Removing Push Button Unit from Dash," and renew slides.

2: Cause
Push Buttons Not Centered In Bezel
Remedy: Center bezel on buttons.

3: Cause
Push Button Light Wire Interfering
Remedy: Apply procedure in paragraph on "Removing Push Button Dash Unit," and adjust light wire.

4: Cause
Felt Under Bezel Interfering
Remedy: Insert a .005 inch feeler gauge between the side of the button and the bezel. Gently move the feeler in and out to smooth down the felt and so relieve the binding. Should it become necessary to replace or reglue felt mask, note location of present glue spots. Diameter of glue spots should not exceed 3/8 inch.

TROUBLE: PUSH BUTTON LOOSE

Cause: Tangs Of Slider Not Tightly Seated In Plastic Button

CHRYSLER AUTOMATIC TRANSMISSIONS

Remedy: Remove bezel and using a small screwdriver force tangs of slide deeper into recess in plastic button.

AIR PRESSURE CHECKS (Fig. 8)

1. The Front Clutch Passage

Located slightly toward the center of the transmission from the accumulator. Listen for dull thud to indicate clutch is operating.

2. The Rear Clutch Passage

Located near center of rear edge of transmission. Listen for dull thud to indicate rear clutch is operating.

3. Kickdown (Front) Servo Line Apply Passage

Located toward center of case and to the front of the servo. Observe operation of servo, linkage and front band.

4. Kickdown (Front) Servo Throttle-Compensated Apply Passage

Located toward center of case and to rear of servo. Observe operation of servo.

5. Low-Reverse (Rear) Servo Apply Passage

Located toward center of case and to the front of the servo. Observe operation of the servo, the linkage, the rear band.

6. Line Pressure To Governor Passage

Located in left rear corner of transmission case lower surface. Rotate the propeller shaft slightly. Listen for a click to indicate that flyweight has operated.

PARTS THAT CAN BE REMOVED WITH TRANSMISSION IN THE CAR

SPEEDOMETER PINION

Located on left side of rear extension.

Disconnect speedometer cable and sheath from the drive pinion and sleeve assembly. Unscrew pinion and sleeve assembly from the extension. When reinstalling, tighten pinion and sleeve assembly to 45 ft. lbs. before reconnecting cable and sheath.

NEUTRAL SAFETY (STARTER) SWITCH

Located on left side of transmis-

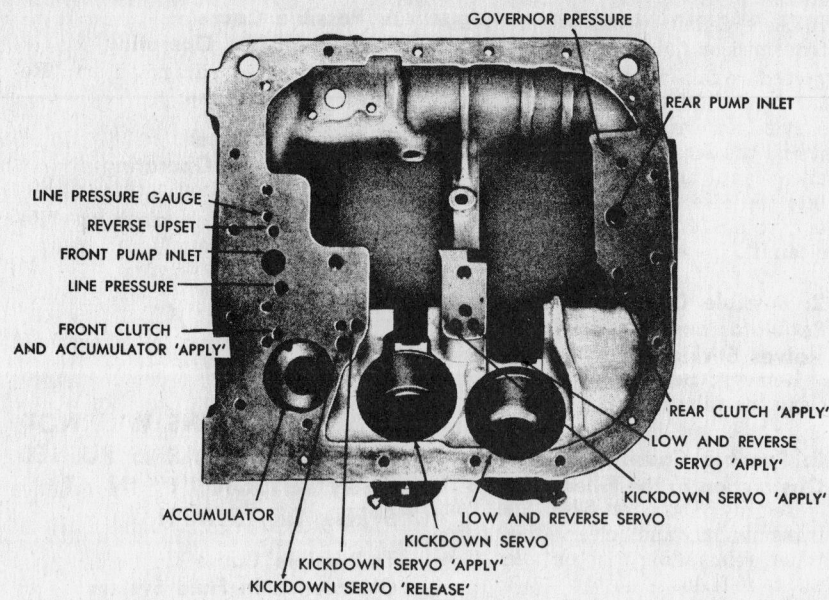

Fig. 8—Use air pressure on passages shown to check operation of units

sion. It is screwed into the manual control cable housing. Two quarts of fluid should be drained from the transmission before the switch is removed from the control cable housing. Note that the switch uses a gasket. Tighten to 15-20 ft. lbs. Do not neglect to refill transmission to proper level.

VALVE BODIES AND TRANSFER PLATE ASSEMBLY

Push in button marked "1." Remove oil pan. Disconnect throttle rod from throttle lever at transmission; be careful not to change adjustment. Loosen the screw holding transmission throttle lever and remove the lever. Clean up control cable housing and remove flat washer and felt seal from throttle lever shaft. Remove clip screw, lock washer and clip holding control cable sheath to housing. Remove plug in side of housing and working thru this opening with a screwdriver release the spring lock and pull the cable free. Now use screwdriver to push the manual control lever rearward to the last detent which is reverse. Remove the three screws and dished washers to release control cable housing and gasket. Note that the manual valve is located on its shaft just 7/32 in. above surface to which housing was attached. Loosen clamp screw and slide lever from shaft.

Remove the two front pump suction elbow screws and dished washers. Note that the dish is always away from the head. Remove oil strainer assembly.

The accumulator is spring loaded. Use care when removing the three

screws and removing the accumulator cover and spring.

Unscrew five transfer plate bolts and dished washers and so remove valve bodies and transfer plate assembly.

FRONT (KICKDOWN) SERVO PISTON

After the valve bodies and the transfer plate assembly have been removed, the front band adjusting screw should be loosened to permit removal of the front band anchor and strut. A special tool is now required to compress the servo piston into its bore so that the snap ring can be removed. Removal of the snap ring permits removal of the piston rod guide, piston spring, piston rod and the piston. Fig. 20.

Inspect riveting of piston rod, inspect guide contacting surface for nicks or burrs. Check that seal ring turns freely in groove. Inspect the three rings, two are interlocking, on the piston for wear and broken locks. They should turn freely in their grooves. It is not necessary to remove rings. Check surface of the piston for surface smoothness. Check the spring and snap ring for distortion.

ACCUMULATOR PISTON

Remove valve bodies and transfer plate assemblies. Using pliers, remove accumulator piston from transmission case. Figs. 22 and 23.

Lubricate seal rings and place accumulator piston into position. Compress outer seal ring and tap lightly into transmission case. Install valve bodies and transfer plate assemblies.

OUTPUT SHAFT REAR BEARING OIL SEAL

Disconnect the front universal joint. Apply the hand brake and remove the propeller shaft flange nut and dished washer. Release hand brake and install puller (if necessary). Remove the propeller shaft flange and brake drum assembly. Remove the transmission brake support grease shield spring (small one). Remove brake support grease shield from extension. If screwdriver or sharp instrument is used in performing this operation, care must be exercised not to damage the neoprene sealing surface at bottom of shield. Install puller, and remove the transmission output shaft rear bearing oil seal.

Using driver, install new output shaft rear bearing oil seal (metal portion of seal facing in) until driver bottoms on extension. Install brake support grease shield on extension. Indent on grease shield must match groove in extension for correct positioning. Also, shield must be located on extension far enough to permit installation of spring. Install brake

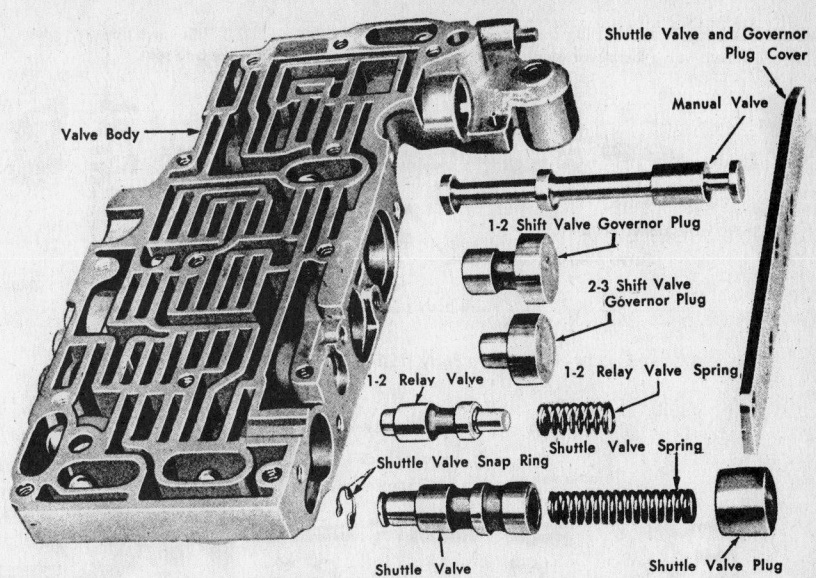

Fig. 11—Valve Body. 1960-61. *Shuttle and Relay Valve Side.*

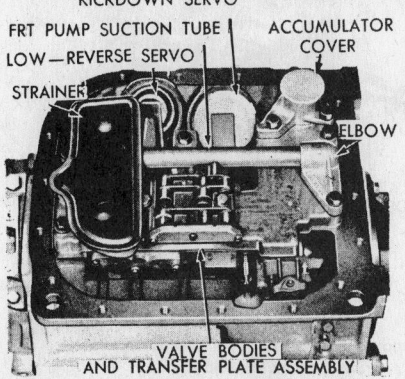

Fig. 9—Strainer and valve bodies installed

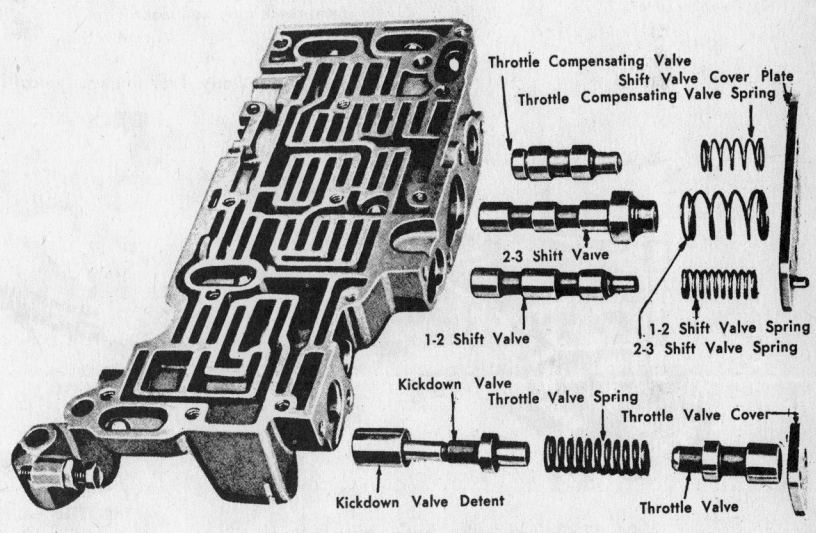

Fig. 12—Valve Body. 1960-61. *Shift and Throttle Valve Side.*

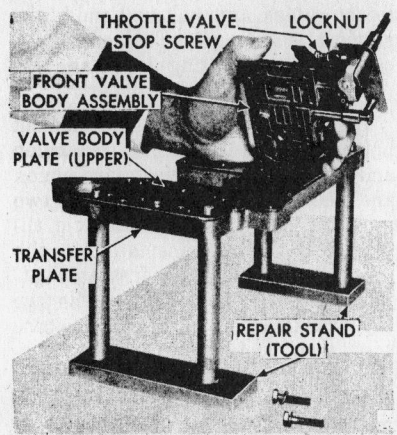

Fig. 10—Removal of front valve body

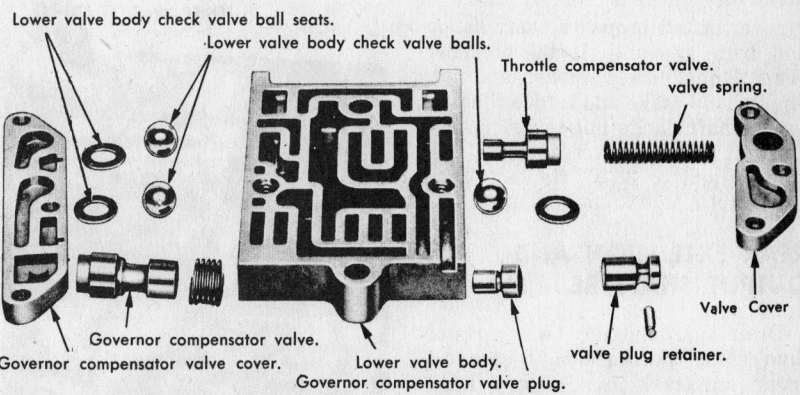

Fig. 13—Lower Valve Body. 1957. Shown. Typical 1958-61. Note that the Governor Compensator Valve was Discontinued After Trans. No. 633519 During 1957.

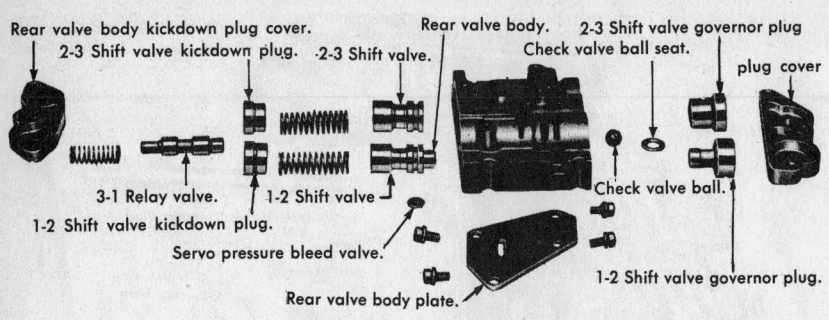

Rear valve body kickdown plug cover.
2-3 Shift valve kickdown plug.
-2-3 Shift valve.
3-1 Relay valve.
1-2 Shift valve kickdown plug.
1-2 Shift valve
Servo pressure bleed valve.
Rear valve body plate.
Rear valve body.
2-3 Shift valve governor plug
Check valve ball seat.
plug cover
Check valve ball.
1-2 Shift valve governor plug.

Fig. 14—Rear Valve Body, 1957 Shown. Typical 1958-61

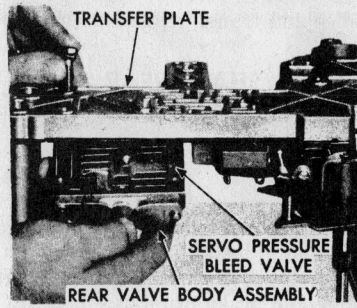

TRANSFER PLATE

SERVO PRESSURE
BLEED VALVE

REAR VALVE BODY ASSEMBLY

Fig. 15—Removal of rear valve body

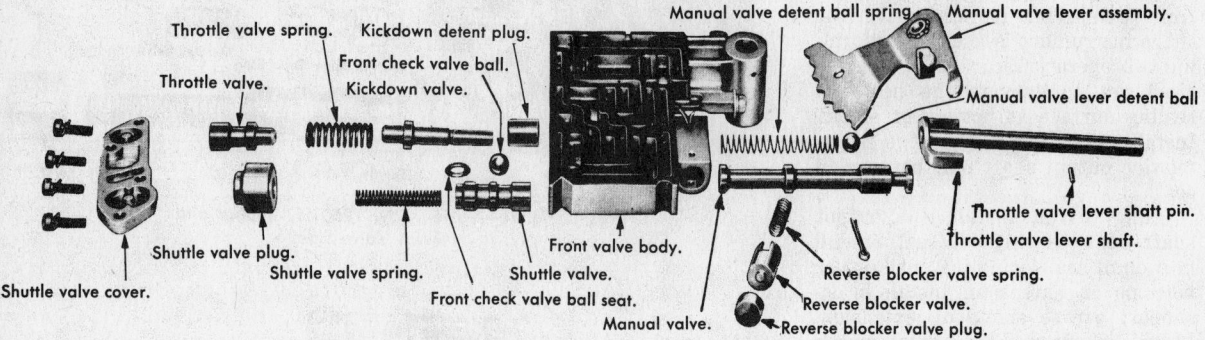

Throttle valve spring.
Throttle valve.
Kickdown detent plug.
Front check valve ball.
Kickdown valve.
Manual valve detent ball spring
Manual valve lever assembly.
Manual valve lever detent ball
Throttle valve lever shaft pin.
Throttle valve lever shaft.
Reverse blocker valve spring.
Reverse blocker valve.
Reverse blocker valve plug.
Shuttle valve cover.
Shuttle valve plug.
Shuttle valve spring.
Shuttle valve.
Front valve body.
Front check valve ball seat.
Manual valve.

Fig. 16—Front Valve Body. 1957 Shown. Typical 1958-61

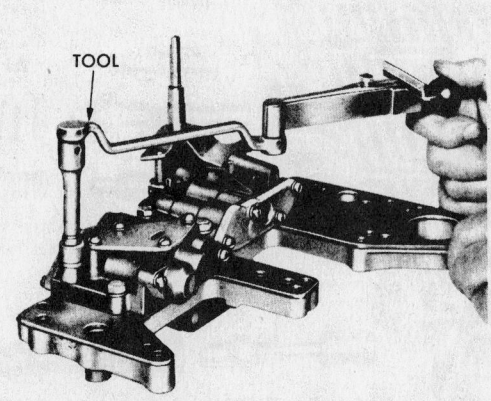

TOOL

*Fig. 17—Tighten valve body screws to
50-60 inch pounds (4-5 ft. lbs.)*

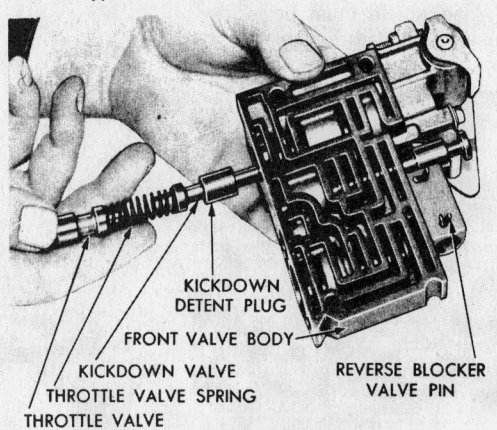

KICKDOWN
DETENT PLUG
FRONT VALVE BODY
KICKDOWN VALVE
THROTTLE VALVE SPRING
THROTTLE VALVE
REVERSE BLOCKER
VALVE PIN

*Fig. 18—Removal of throttle and kickdown
valves from front valve body*

support grease shield spring (opening in spring toward adjusting sleeve). Make sure spring is properly seated in groove. Install propeller shaft flange and drum assembly. Install propeller shaft flange, dished washer, and nut. Apply hand brake and torque the propeller shaft flange nut to 200 ft. lbs. Connect front universal joint and torque nuts to 33-37 ft. lbs. Check fluid level.

REAR EXTENSION AND OUTPUT SHAFT BEARING

Drain approximately two quarts of fluid from transmission. Disconnect front universal joint. Apply hand brake and remove propeller shaft flange nut and dished washer. Release

hand brake and using puller (if necessary), remove the propeller shaft

TOOL   SNAP RING

*Fig. 20—Removal of Kickdown-Piston-Rod-
Guide retaining Snap Ring*

flange and drum assembly. Remove brake adjusting screw cover plate and loosen cable clamp bolt on hand brake support. Disengage the ball end of the cable from operating lever and remove cable from brake support.

Disconnect speedometer cable and housing at transmission extension and remove speedometer drive pinion and sleeve assembly. Remove the two nuts and lock washers that hold engine rear support insulator to the crossmember, leaving insulator attached to extension. Remove the two top transmission extension to case screws and lock washers. Using suitable jack and extreme care (to prevent damage to oil pan), raise transmission sufficiently for insulator on extension to clear crossmember. Re-

Fig. 21—Removal of Kickown-Piston Spring

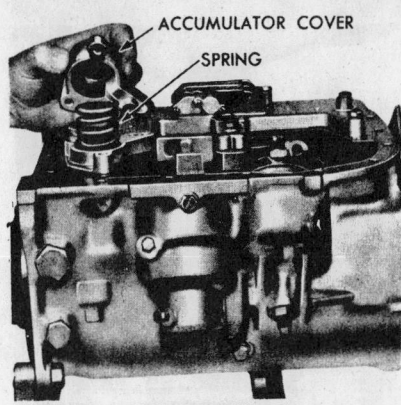

Fig. 22—Removal of Accumulator Cover

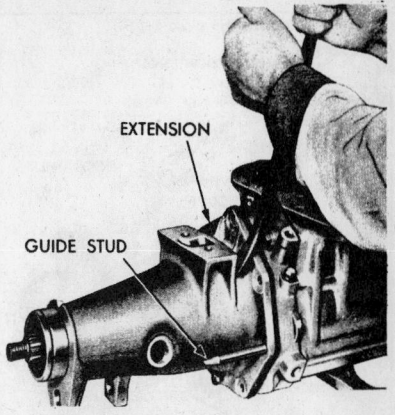

Fig. 25—Pry against output housing support screw to remove rear extension

move four of the remaining extension to case screws and lock washers and install guide studs.

Due to interference of the insulator, it will be necessary to remove the bottom extension to case screw with the extension; that is, back screw out as far as possible and slide extension back and continue loosening of screw. <u>Caution:</u> Do not remove the one output shaft support to transmission case screw.

Remove extension and hand brake as one assembly. Remove extension gasket. If care is used, it is not necessary to remove hand brake support and shoe assemblies from extension to replace output shaft rear bearing.

Inspect extension for cracks in casting and remove burrs from gasket surface. Inspect vent in top of extension. It must be clear of dirt, undercoating, and such. Besides allowing air to enter as transmission is drained this vent takes care of fumes and oil expansion due to heat. Clean the output shaft rear bearing with compressed air but do not spin it. If bearing is rough, remove the oil seal and then the bearing snap ring. Note that snap ring has a beveled edge. Drive bearing out the rear of the extension. When new bearing is properly seated install the snap ring. It should be firmly seated in its groove with bevel side out.

With guide studs installed in transmission case, install a new extension gasket over guide studs and into position against output shaft support. Do not use sealing material on gasket. Using extreme care, place extension and hand brake assembly over output shaft and on guide studs. Due to interference of the insulator, it will be necessary to start the bottom extension to case screw as the extension is pushed into position against support. Do not attempt to pull extension in with the aid of screws; otherwise, damage to extension may result. The propeller shaft flange and drum as-

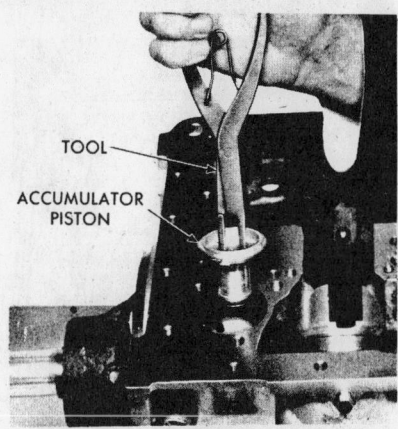

Fig. 23—Removal of accumulator piston

Fig. 24—Removal of speedometer drive pinion from rear extension

sembly may be used to force bearing in extension on output shaft. Do not use hammer.

Remove guide studs and install the six remaining extension to case screws and lock washers. Draw down evenly and tighten from 25 ft. lbs. After screws have been properly torqued, turn output shaft to make sure it turns freely. Lower transmission and at the same time align mounting studs in insulator with

holes in crossmember. Install the two nuts and lock washers that hold the rear engine support insulator and torque from 30-35 ft. lbs. Engage ball end of hand brake cable in operating lever and tighten cable clamp bolt. Apply hand brake and tighten Universal Joint Flange Nut to 200 ft. lbs. Install adjusting screw cover plate on hand brake support. Connect front universal joint and torque nuts from 33-37 ft. lbs. Install speedometer pinion and sleeve assembly. Torque from 40-45 ft. lbs. and connect speedometer cable housing. Refill transmission to proper level with a good grade of Automatic Transmission Fluid.

GOVERNOR

Refer to Extension Removal. Using a screwdriver, remove the governor valve shaft snap ring (small) from the weight assembly end. Fig. 27. Remove governor valve shaft and valve from governor body assembly. Fig. 28. Using pliers, remove governor weight assembly snap ring (large) and remove governor weight assembly from governor body. Figs. 29 and 30.

The primary cause of governor operating failures is due to improper operation of governor valve which may be sticking in housing or travel restricted by chips or other foreign matter. If inspection reveals that it is necessary for further governor servicing, then remove governor support locating screw, using a 5/16 in. socket, and remove governor and support assembly from rear oil pump housing. Fig. 31. Normal servicing does not require removal of the governor body from the governor support. If condition warrants removal of governor body from governor support, when reassembling, do not tighten governor body screws until governor body support is located on output shaft.

Inspect all parts for burrs and wear.

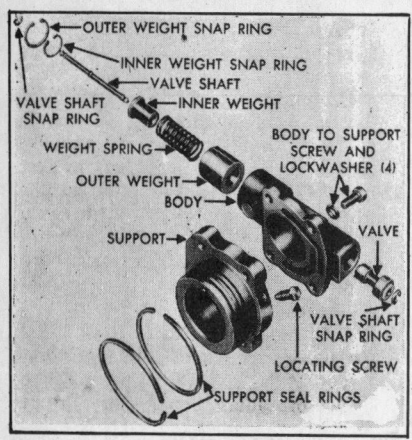

Fig. 26—Exploded view of governor

Fig. 27—Removal of governor valve-shaft snap ring

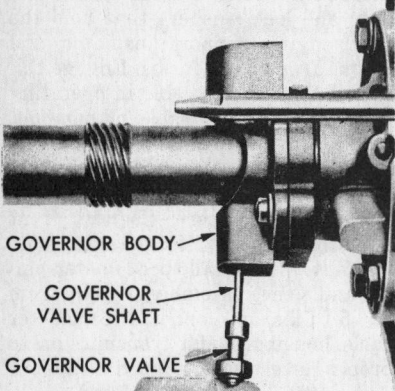

Fig. 28—Removing Governor Valve and Shaft Assembly

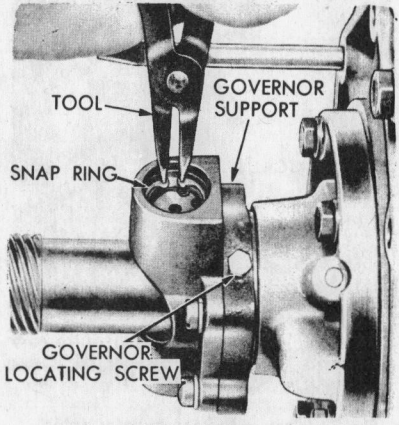

Fig. 29—Remove large snap ring to release governor weight

Fig. 30—Removal of governor weight

Fig. 31—Remove locating screw to release governor assembly

Inspect oil passages; they should be clean. Valves and weights should move freely.

Slide governor body and support assembly into position in rear oil pump housing. Using extreme care, compress governor support seal rings as support enters oil pump housing. Do not force. Align locating hole in output shaft to locating screw hole in governor support and install screw. Torque from 5-7 ft. lbs. Holes can be aligned by turning output shaft and holding governor body.

If governor body has been removed and reinstalled, torque the four governor body screws from 6-8 ft. lbs. Place governor weight assembly (secondary weight snap ring facing out) into governor body; and using pliers install snap ring. Make sure snap ring seats properly. With the governor

valve (small end up) on governor valve shaft, slide shaft into governor body through the output shaft and governor weight assembly; at the same time, position valve into body. Install the governor valve shaft snap ring. Replace snap ring if distorted. After snap ring installation, apply sufficient pressure to both ends of valve shaft to force snap rings to outer portion of snap ring grooves. Check operation of governor weight assembly and valve by turning output shaft. Both should fall freely in body. Install transmission extension.

REAR OIL PUMP

Apply paragraphs on "Rear Extension" and "Governor." Then remove the five rear oil pump housing to output shaft support screws and dished washers, and install guide studs. Remove pump housing, gear, and governor assembly from output shaft. Fig. 33.

Use Prussian blue and mark both pump gears in relation to pump housing face. Fig. 35. Do not use scribe. Oil pump pinion is keyed to output shaft by a small ball. Fig. 34. Use care when removing pinion so as not to lose ball. Remove output shaft support. Fig. 36.

FRONT PUMP DRIVE SLEEVE

Removal of the transmission permits removal of the front pump drive sleeve. It slips out of the front pump housing. Fig. 37. Inspect the neoprene seal ring for nicks, deterioration, hardness. Inspect the interlocking seal ring for wear or broken locks; check that it turns freely in the groove. Check the driving lugs at each end for excessive wear. Check bearing surface for nicks, burrs, scratches.

FRONT OIL PUMP

Remove the Transmission Regulator and Converter Control Valves.

Remove the seven front oil pump to transmission case screws and washers. The washers are made of aluminum and should be discarded if distorted. Tap pump housing gently with a plastic hammer and so remove front pump from transmission case. Fig. 38. Mark the pump gears with Prussian blue (do not scribe) so that they may be reassembled with the same faces out. Fig. 39.

Inspect the dust shield in the front of the pump housing and if need be drive the seal out the front. Put metal portion of new seal down on front of pump and drive on new seal until it bottoms.

Inspect inner surface of housing that contacts the seal rings of the

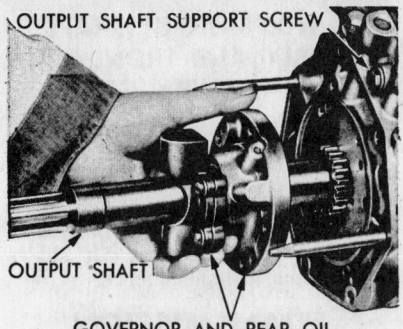

OUTPUT SHAFT SUPPORT SCREW

OUTPUT SHAFT

GOVERNOR AND REAR OIL
PUMP HOUSING ASSEMBLIES

Fig. 33—Removing rear oil pump

REAR OIL PUMP PINION BALL
REAR OIL PUMP
PINION KEYWAY

REAR OIL PUMP PINION

Fig. 34—Removal of rear oil pump drive
pinion

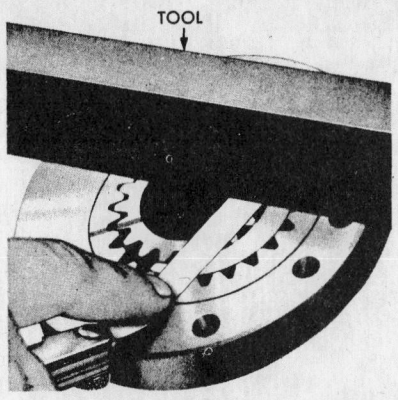

TOOL

Fig. 35—End clearance of gears should be
.0010"-.0025". Note markings on gear faces

Fig. 36—Removal of output shaft support

Fig. 37—Removal of front oil pump
drive sleeve

FRONT OIL PUMP HOUSING

Fig. 38—Removal of front pump

drive sleeve. Surface should be smooth. If bushing in housing is worn, replace housing assembly. Bushing is not sold separately.

Check the oil pump gears for scratches or grooving. Check that passages in housing are free and clear.

Using a straight edge and feeler gauge, check that clearance is .0010 to .0025 inch. If clearance between lobes is greater than .010 inch, or the clearance between outer edge of outer gear and housing is greater than .010 inch, the gears or pump housing should be renewed.

Replace the gears in the housing as marked at disassembly; that is, be sure counterbore in pinion gear faces front of car.

Check the outer "O" ring seal on the pump body for nicks or deterioration. With inner and outer seals lubricated and pump gears is position, place oil pump housing over guide pins as shown in Fig. 39. Start five of the screws with aluminum washers and draw the housing down evenly until it is seated in transmission case. Remove guide pins, install the two remaining screws and washers and tighten all evenly to 14-16 ft. lbs.

Lubricate and install the front pump drive sleeve bearing surface

first. See Fig. 37. Turn sleeve to check that oil pump gears turn freely.

REGULATOR VALVE BODY

Remove the front pump, the torque converter control valve, and the transmission regulator valve.

Install guide pins thru valve body into case and, using threaded holes provided in valve body, thread in two screws and use as handles to pull valve body from the case. Fig. 40. The valve body is made of aluminum and must be carefully handled. Removal of the body permits removal of regulator valve body to transmission case gasket.

Clean the valve body and valves in solvent and dry with compressed air. Check that valves move freely in their bores. Fig. 41.

The inner bore of the valve body must be smooth where it contacts the neoprene seal on the reaction shaft. The reaction shaft is a force fit in the transmission case and unless the splines are worn there is no need to mess with it.

If it does have to be pressed out, use heat lamps to heat transmission case to 170-190 deg. F. before attempting to reinstall.

Be sure that guide pins are in place and then install regulator valve body

gasket into position against the transmission case. Check that neoprene seal ring is properly positioned on reaction shaft. Install valve body.

POWER TRAIN UNITS

There are three power train units in the transmission; these are numbered 1, 2 and 3 with No. 1 the rearmost but first-out unit. The units are removed, disassembled, and assembled in the order of 1, 2, 3. Installation in the transmission goes in the order of 3, 2, 1.

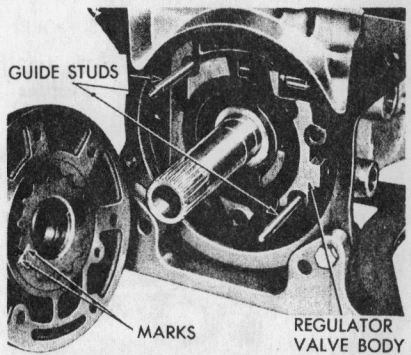

GUIDE STUDS

MARKS

REGULATOR
VALVE BODY

Fig. 39—Installing front oil pump. Note
match marks. Counterbore in pinion goes
toward front of car

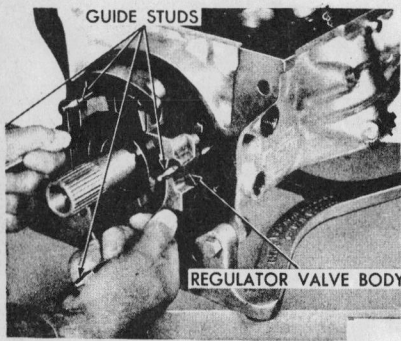

Fig. 40—Removal of regulator valve body

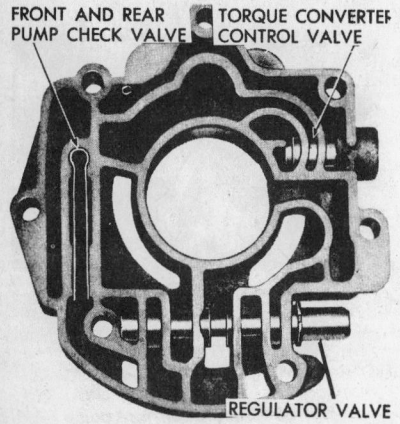

Fig. 41—Rear view of regulator valve body

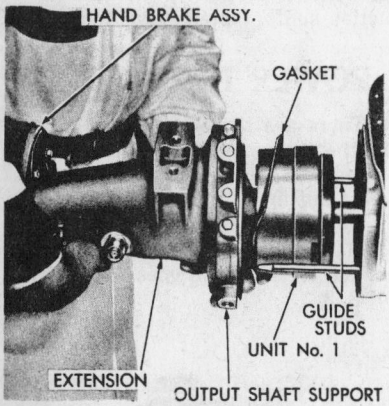

Fig. 42—Removing unit No. 1 complete with hand brake and rear extension assemblies

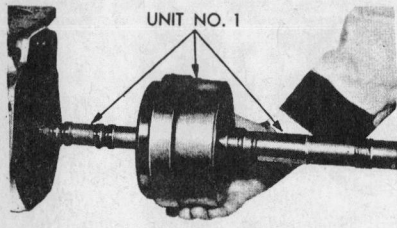

Fig. 43—Removal of power train unit No. 1 thru rear of case

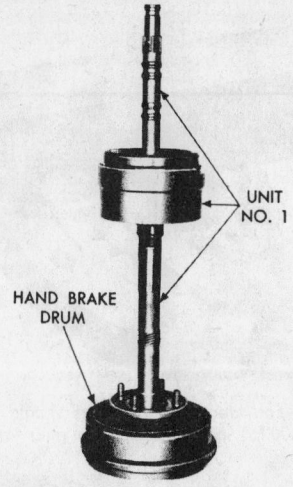

Fig. 44—Showing use of hand-brake drum as holding fixture for unit No. 1

UNIT NO. 1: OUTPUT SHAFT, KICKDOWN (2nd SPEED) PLANET PINION CARRIER, INTERMEDIATE SHAFT

Unit No. 1 is easily removed after removal of rear extension, governor and rear oil pump as covered earlier in this section.

Remove Unit No. 1 by sliding unit out rear of transmission case. Support assembly as much as possible to prevent damage to seal rings on intermediate shaft. Fig. 43. The unit can also be removed as one piece with the rear extension as can be seen in Fig. 42.

Use the hand brake drum and the front half of the front universal joint as a holding fixture. See Fig. 44.

UNIT: NO. 2: LOW-REVERSE, ALSO KICKDOWN, SUN GEAR ASSEMBLY; LOW-REVERSE PLANETARY GEAR SET; OVER-RUNNING (FREE WHEELING) CLUTCH

ASSEMBLY; AND REAR CLUTCH ASSEMBLY GROUP

Loosen both front and rear band adjusting screw lock nuts and back the screws out about three turns. Remove the three intermediate-support locating screws and lock washers. Two are outside the case. One is inside. Match mark intermediate support to the inside locating screw hole to facilitate reassembly. Figs. 48 and 53.

Keeping unit centered and holding front clutch assembly forward, remove Unit No. 2 from case. See Fig. 47. Fig. 49, shows rear clutch group sequence.

UNIT NO. 3: INPUT SHAFT ASSEMBLY AND FRONT CLUTCH ASSEMBLY GROUP

Keep unit centered as much as possible and remove from transmission case. Fig. 50. Be careful to prevent the seal rings on the input shaft gouging the aluminum sealing surface in the reaction shaft. Fig. 51, shows front clutch group sequence.

TRANSMISSION END PLAY

The end clearance of the front clutch assembly is critical in that too much will result in a clunking noise while too little will damage the thrust washers and clutches. The end play can be checked with the transmission in the car.

The fibre input shaft thrust washer in Fig. 51 is the control thrust washer for end play in the transmission. The required thickness of this washer is determined both before disassembly of the transmission and after reassembly.

Install a dial indicator as shown Fig. 50. Pry the front clutch forward by inserting a screwdriver between the front and rear clutch assemblies. While so holding front clutch forward, set dial indicator on zero. Now pry the front clutch assembly toward the rear and take indicator reading. The reading should be between .020 in. and .050 in. If the clearance is not within limits the transmission must be removed from the car and the input-shaft to trogue-converter reaction-shaft thrust washer changed. Measure the thickness of the old washer and select a thicker or thinner one to give the correct clearance. There are three available: Natural color — .115-.117; black — .097.-.099; red—.078-.080.

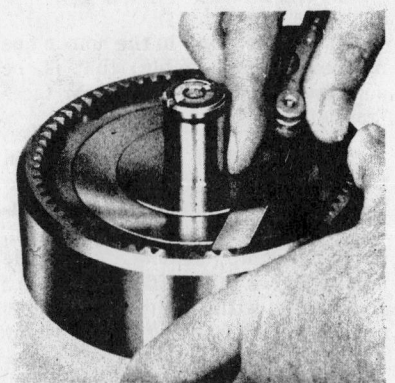

Fig. 45—Clearance between snap ring and intermediate shaft assembly should be as near zero as possible

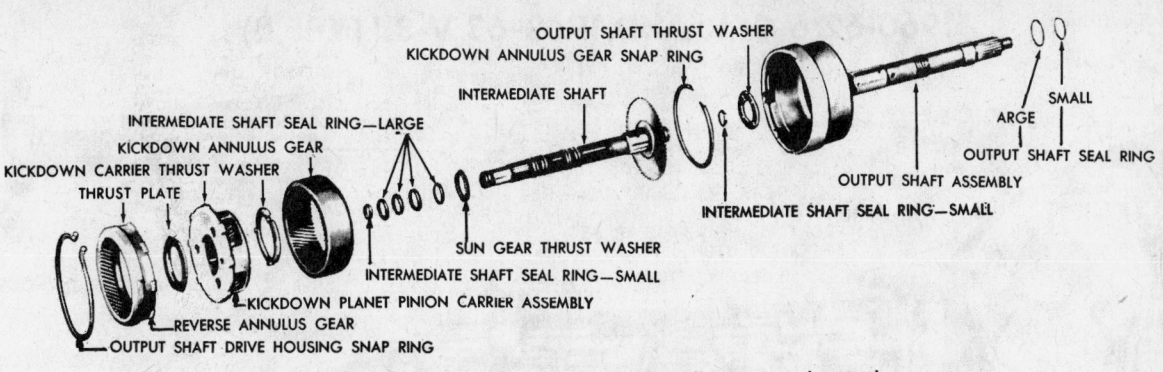

Fig. 46—Exploded view of unit No. 1. Note that "G", the roller type washer, is the sun gear rear thrust washer

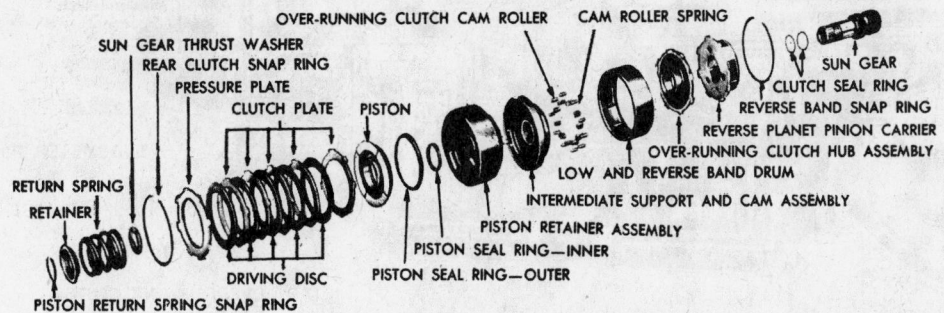

Fig. 49—Exploded view of unit No. 2.

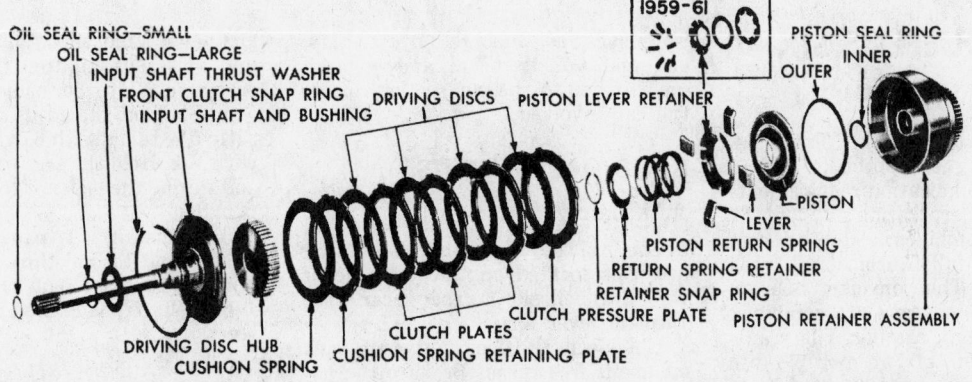

Fig. 51—Exploded view of unit No. 3. Note that fibre thrust washer controls front clutch end play

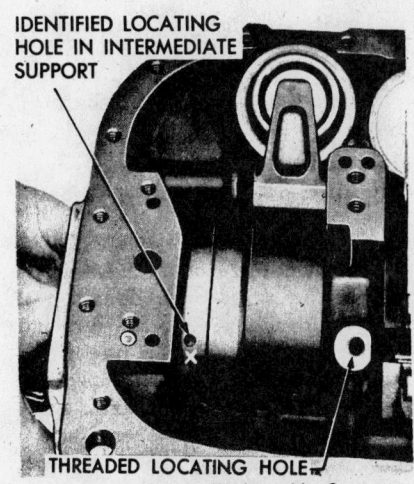

IDENTIFIED LOCATING HOLE IN INTERMEDIATE SUPPORT

THREADED LOCATING HOLE

Fig. 53—Installing unit No. 2

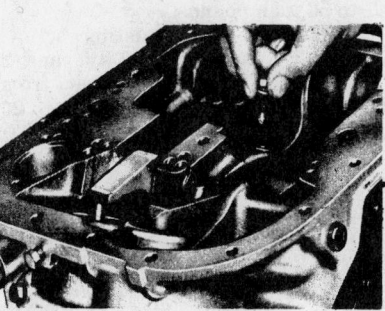

Fig. 48—Match mark intermediate support to locating screw hole for easier installation of Unit No. 2

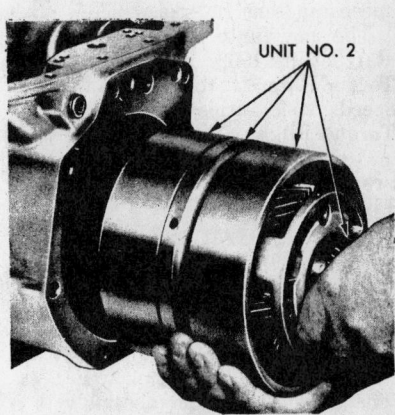

UNIT NO. 2

Fig. 47—Removal of power train unit No. 2 thru rear of case

1960-62 6 CYL. AND 1962-63 V-8 (TYPE B)

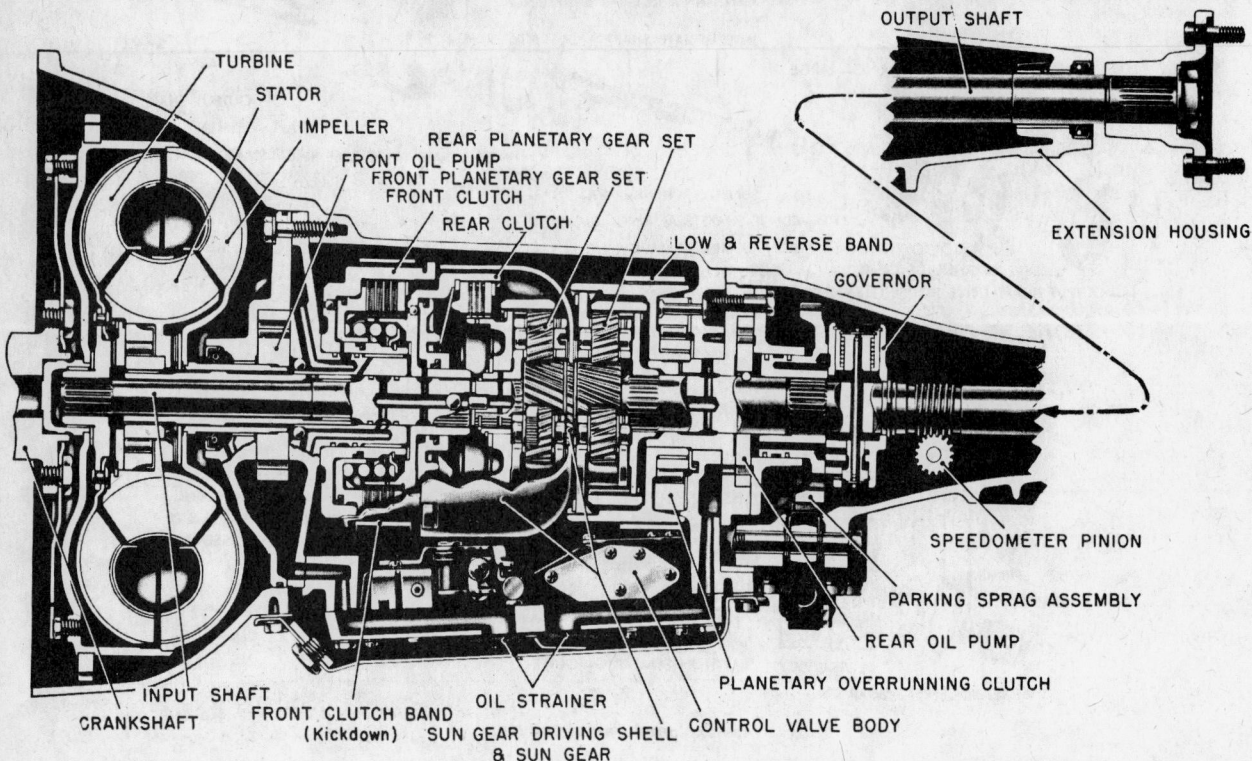

Fig. 1—Sectional View of Torqueflite Six Transmission

TORQUEFLITE SIX TRANSMISSION

The TorqueFlite Six Transmission was designed especially to balance the car-application requirements of Chrysler Corporation's "Slant 6" engine. It combines a torque converter with a fully automatic 3-speed gear system. The converter housing and transmission case are combined in one aluminum casting. The transmission consists of two multiple disc clutches, an overrunning clutch, two servos and bands, and two planetary gear sets to provide three forward speeds and one reverse.

The new automatic transmission, starting in 1962, is similar to the Torque Flite Six. It has three forward speeds with ratios the same as the Torque Flight Six.

Adjustments and repair methods are similar to those of the Torque Flight Six.

The torque converter is driven by the crankshaft, through a bolted-on, flexible driving plate. Cooling of the converter-transmission assembly is controlled by circulating the transmission fluid through a cooler core located in the radiator lower tank. The torque converter assembly is a sealed unit, impractical to service in the field except for cleaning.

For information relative to application, such as, linkage adjustments, etc. and unit removal and replacement, refer to the car section, under the car involved.

BAND ADJUSTMENTS

A. Kickdown Band

The kickdown band adjusting screw is located on the left side of the transmission case near the throttle lever shaft.

1. Loosen the lock nut and back off about five turns. Be sure the adjusting screw is free in the case.

2. Using wrench, tool #C-3380 with adapter #C-3790, or similar tools, torque the adjusting screw to 47 to 50 inch pounds.

3. Back off the adjusting screw, exactly $2\frac{1}{8}$ turns with 6 cyl. and 2 turns with V-8. Hold the screw from turning and torque the lock nut to 20 to 25 foot pounds.

B. Low & Reverse Band

Access to the low and reverse band requires oil pan removal, Fig. 3.

1. Raise the car, drain transmission and remove the transmission oil pan.

2. Loosen the band adjusting screw lock nut and back off the nut about five turns. Be sure the adjusting screw turns freely in the lever.

3. With the same tools as used in

kickdown band adjustment (#C-3380 and #C-3790), tighten the adjusting screw to 47 to 50 inch pounds.

4. Back off the adjusting screw exactly $5\frac{1}{4}$ turns with 6 cyl. and 3 turns with V-8. Hold the screw from turning and torque the lock nut to 20 to 25 foot pounds.

5. Reinstall oil pan, using new gasket and torque the pan attaching bolts to 13 to 17 foot pounds.

6. Refill transmission to prescribed level.

FLUID LEAKS

Some leaks that can normallly be corrected WITHOUT TRANSMISSION REMOVAL are:

1. Transmission output shaft oil seal.
2. Extension housing gasket.
3. Speedometer pinion seal and cable seal.
4. Oil filler tube seal.
5. Oil pan gasket and drain plug.
6. Gearshift control cable seal.
7. Throttle shaft seal.
8. Neutral starting switch seal.
9. Oil cooler line fittings and pressure take-off plugs.

Oil found inside the converter housing should be positively identified as transmission oil before any major transmission work is performed; it could be engine oil.

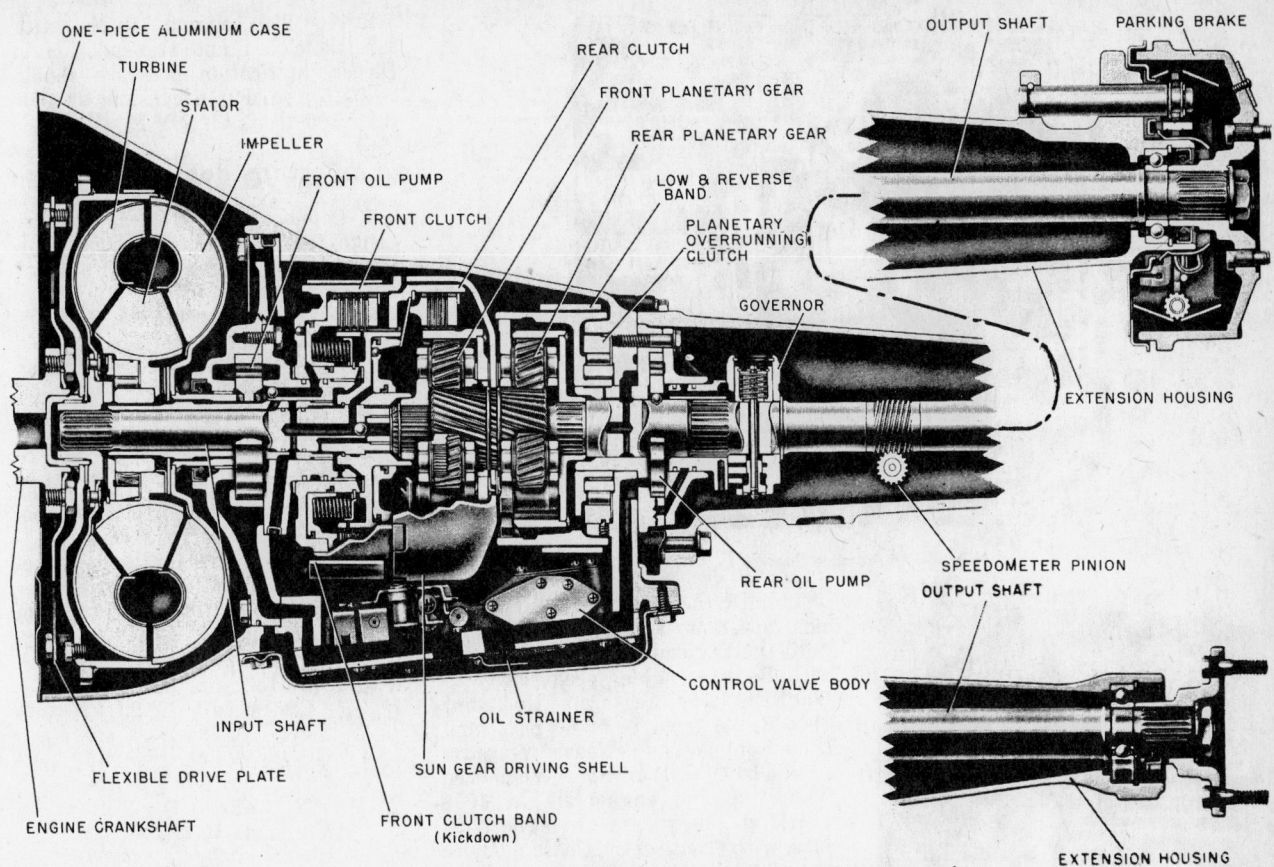

ONE-PIECE ALUMINUM CASE
TURBINE
STATOR
IMPELLER
FRONT OIL PUMP
FRONT CLUTCH

REAR CLUTCH
FRONT PLANETARY GEAR
REAR PLANETARY GEAR
LOW & REVERSE BAND
PLANETARY OVERRUNNING CLUTCH
GOVERNOR

OUTPUT SHAFT
PARKING BRAKE

EXTENSION HOUSING

REAR OIL PUMP
SPEEDOMETER PINION
OUTPUT SHAFT

INPUT SHAFT
OIL STRAINER
CONTROL VALVE BODY

FLEXIBLE DRIVE PLATE
SUN GEAR DRIVING SHELL

ENGINE CRANKSHAFT
FRONT CLUTCH BAND (Kickdown)

EXTENSION HOUSING

Fig. 2—Sectional View of Torqueflite Transmission. Starting with 1962 production.

LEAKS REQUIRING TRANSMISSION REMOVAL

1. Fractures or sand holes in transmission case.
2. Sand hole or fracture in front oil pump.
3. Front pump housing retaining screws or damaged sealing washers.
4. Front oil pump housing seal (on outside diameter of pump housing).
5. Converter assembly and impeller shaft oil seal (located in front pump housing).

TESTS

AIR PRESSURE CHECKS

The front clutch, rear clutch, kickdown servo and low and reverse servo may be checked with air pressure, after the valve body assembly has been removed.

To make air pressure checks proceed as follows:

CAUTION: Compressed air used must be free of dirt and moisture.

A. Front Clutch

Apply air pressure to the front clutch "apply" passage and listen for a dull "thud." This will indicate operation of the front clutch. Hold the air pressure on at this point for a few

seconds and check for excessive oil leaks.

B. Rear Clutch

Apply air pressure to the rear clutch "apply" passage and proceed in an identical manner as that described in the previous paragraph, (Front Clutch).

C. Kickdown Servo

Air pressure applied to the kickdown servo "apply" passage should tighten the front band. Spring tension should be sufficient to release the band.

D. Low and Reverse Servo

Direct air pressure into the low and reverse servo "apply" passage. Response of the servo will result in a tightening of the rear band. Spring tension should be enough to release the band.

If clutches and servos operate properly, that is, no upshift or erratic shift conditions exist, it indicates that trouble exists in the control valve body assembly.

E. Governor

Governor action troubles can usually be found during a road test or pressure test.

HYDRAULIC CONTROL PRESSURE CHECKS

A. LINE PRESSURE AND FRONT SERVO RELEASE PRESSURE

LOW AND REVERSE BAND ADJUSTING SCREW
BOLTS (10)
CABLE ADAPTER NUT
LINE PRESSURE ADJUSTMENT SCREW

Fig. 3—Bottom View of Transmission —Pan Removed.

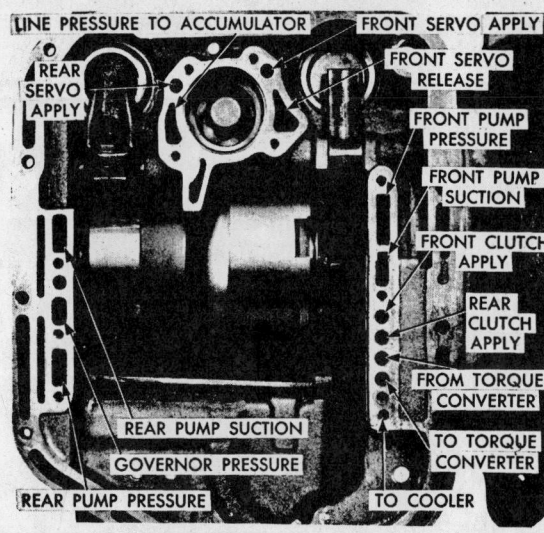

Fig. 4—Air Pressure Checks.

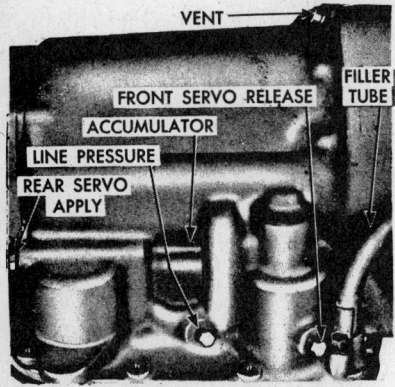

Fig. 5—Pressure Test Locations (Right Side of Case).

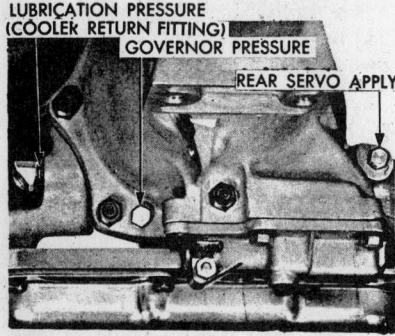

Fig. 6—Pressure Test Locations (Rear of Case).

NOTE: These pressure checks must be made in the "D" position with the rear wheels free to turn. The transmission fluid must be at operating temperature (150° F. to 200° F.).

1. Install an engine tachometer, then raise the car on a hoist and locate the tachometer so it can be read from under the car.

2. Connect two 0-100 p.s.i pressure gauges (tool #C-3292 or other good gauges) to pressure take-off points at the top of the accumulator and at the front servo release.

3. With the selector in "D" position, speed up the engine gradually until the transmission shifts into Direct. Reduce engine speed slowly to 800 RPM. Line pressure at this point (800 RPM) must be 52-60 p.s.i., and the front servo release pressure should be 45 p.s.i. or more. When used with V-8, and engine set at 1000 R.P.M. the line pressure must be 54-60 p.s.i. with front servo release no more than 3 p.s.i. drop.

4. Disconnect linkage from the transmission throttle lever and hold the lever at the detent position. Increase engine speed to 3500 RPM with transmission in Direct; the line pressure should be 90-96 p.s.i and the front servo release pressure should be 80 p.s.i. or more.

NOTE: The transmission should not be operated with engine speeds above 1500 RPM without opening the transmission throttle lever.

If line pressure is not as above, adjust the pressure as outlined under the heading: HYDRAULIC CONTROL PRESSURE ADJUSTMENTS—"Line Pressure."

NOTE: Do not adjust line pressure to correct reading at 3500 RPM.

If front servo release pressures are less than specified, and line pressures are within limits, there is excessive leakage in the front clutch and/or front servo circuits.

LUBRICATION PRESSURES

A lubrication pressure check should be made at the same time that line pressure and front servo release pressures are checked.

1. Install a "Tee" fitting between the cooler return line fitting and the fitting hole in the transmission case at the rear left side of the transmission. Connect a 0-100 p.s.i pressure gauge to the "Tee" fitting.

2. At 800 engine RPM, with throttle closed and transmission in Direct, lubrication pressure should be 5-25 p.s.i. For 6 cyl. and at 1000 R.P.M., 5-15 p.s.i. for V-8.

REAR SERVO APPLY PRESSURE

1. Connect a 0-300 p.s.i. pressure gauge, tool #C-3293 or its equivalent, to the apply pressure take-off point at the rear servo.

2. With the control in the "R" position and the engine running at 1600 RPM the reverse servo apply pressure should be 230-280 p.s.i.

GOVERNOR PRESSURE

1. Connect a 0-100 p.s.i. gauge (same as the one used for line pressure and front servo release pressure) to the governor pressure take-off point. This location is at the lower left rear corner of the extension mounting flange.

2. Governor pressure should fall within the following limits:

Car Speed	P.S.I. Pressure
6 cyl. 16-19	15
6 cyl. 29-39	45
6 cyl. 59-69	75
V-8 18-23	15
V-8 41-55	50
V-8 60-72	65

Pressure should change smoothly with car speeds.

If governor pressures are incorrect at the prescribed speeds, the governor valve and/or weights are probably sticking.

HYDRAULIC CONTROL PRESSURE ADJUSTMENTS

A. LINE PRESSURE

If line pressure is incorrect, it will be necessary to remove the valve body assembly to perform the adjustment.

The standard adjustment is 1 25/64", measured from the valve body to the inner edge of the adjusting nut. Fig. 7. For the 6 cyl. and 15/16" for the V-8. However, the adjustment can be slightly changed to obtain the desired line pressure.

One complete turn of the adjusting screw (Allen screw) changes closed throttle line pressure about 1⅔ p.s.i. Turing the screw counterclockwise increases pressure, clockwise decreases pressure.

B. THROTTLE PRESSURE

Because throttle pressures cannot be checked, exact adjustments should be checked and made correct whenever the valve body is disturbed or when the occasion arises.

1. Remove the valve body assembly, as outlined in a succeeding coverage entitled, VALVE BODY ASSEMBLY AND ACCUMULATOR PISTON—"Removal."

2. Loosen throttle lever stop screw lock nut and back off the screw about five turns (Fig. 8).

3. Insert gauge pin of tool #C-3763 between the throttle lever cam and the kickdown valve.

4. Push in on the tool and compress the kickdown valve against its spring so that the throttle valve is completely bottomed inside the valve body.

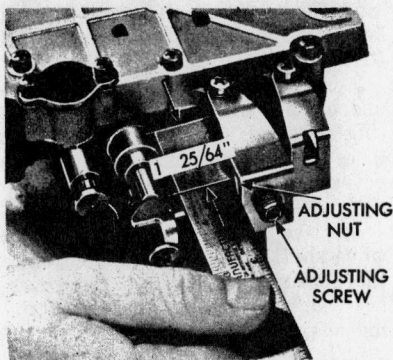

Fig. 7—Line Pressure Adjustment.

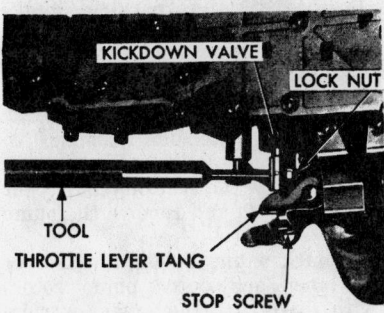

Fig. 8—Throttle Pressure Adjustment.

5. As the spring is being compressed, finger tighten the throttle lever stop screw against the throttle lever tang with the lever cam touching the tool and the throttle valve bottomed. (Be sure the adjustment is made with the spring fully compressed and the valve bottomed in the valve body.)

6. Remove the tool and secure the stop screw lock nut.

SERVICE OPERATIONS WITH TRANSMISSION IN THE CAR

Some sub-assemblies can be removed for repairs without removing

the transmission from the car. "DETAILED RECONDITIONING OF SUB-ASSEMBLIES," is covered further in the text.

SPEEDOMETER PINION
Removal and Installation

1. Remove screw and retainer holding the cable to the extension housing. Carefully work the pinion and sleeve out of the housing (Fig. 9).

2. Replace the pinion and/or oil seal by prying the clip off the pinion and slide the pinion and seal assembly off the cable.

3. If transmission fluid is found in the cable housing, replace the seal inside the pinion bore, then slide the pinion over the end of the cable and secure it with the spring clip.

4. To install, push the pinion and sleeve into the extension housing as far as possible, then install the retainer screw. Torque the screw to 35-54 inch pounds.

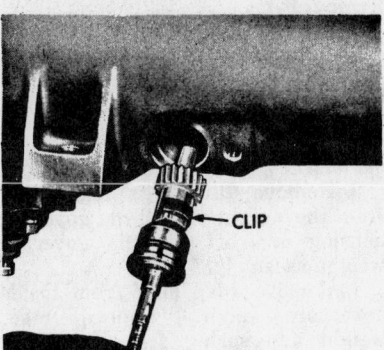

Fig. 9—Removing or Installing Speedometer Pinion.

PARKING BRAKE ASSEMBLY, (BRAKE DRUM TYPE)
Removal

1. Disconnect propeller shaft at the parking brake drum flange.

2. Hold drum from turning with tool #C-3281, or similar holding device, and remove retaining nut and washer.

3. Pull the drum flange assembly with tool #C-452 or satisfactory substitute.

4. Remove the brake shoe adjusting nut cover plate and loosen the cable guide clamp bolt on the brake support. Disconnect the ball end of the cable from the operating lever and remove the cable from the support.

5. Remove the grease shield spring and the grease shield. Don't damage the neoprene seal at the bottom of the shield.

6. With a suitable drift, remove the lock pin that secures the brake

shoe anchor pin in the front lug of the extension housing.

7. Slide the remainder of the brake assembly with the anchor pin from the extension housing.

8. Remove neoprene spacer and steel sleeve from the back of the brake support plate.

Installation

1. Replace neoprene spacer on the back of the brake suport plate with steel sleeve in the center of the support.

2. Locate the brake assembly and anchor pin on the end of extension, make sure the spacer sleeve remains in the center of the support. Align anchor pin hole with the hole in the front lug and install lock pin.

3. Install grease shield, (align the flat of the shield with the flat of the extension housing). Install shield retaining spring, with the spring opening toward the brake shoe adjusting nut. Spring must be seated in the groove.

4. Slide the shoe return spring behind the grease shield spring and hook into position.

5. Engage the ball end of the brake cable in the shoe operating lever and tighten cable clamp bolt.

6. Install cover plate on back side of parking brake support plate.

7. Install brake drum and flange assembly, washer and nut. Torque the nut to 175 ft. lb.

8. Reconnect the propeller shaft.

OUTPUT SHAFT OIL SEAL
Removal

1. Remove parking brake assembly (brake drum type).

2. Screw tapered tool #C-3753, or satisfactory substitute, into the seal, then tighten the screw of the tool to remove seal.

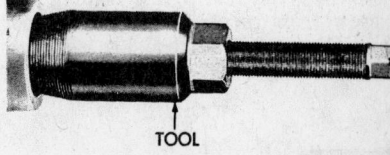

Fig. 10—Removing Output Shaft Oil Seal.

Installation

1. Slide protector sleeve, tool #C-3768, over the output shaft splines, or tape on a thin sleeve of shim stock. Drive in the new lubricated seal (lip side in) with tool #C-3754 or reasonable substitute (Fig. 11).

2. Install the parking brake assembly (brake drum type) and connect the propeller shaft.

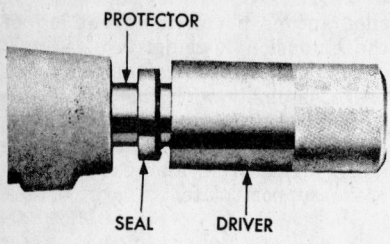

Fig. 11—Installing Output Shaft Oil Seal.

EXTENSION HOUSING
Removal

1. Remove the speedometer drive pinion and sleeve assembly.
2. Disconnect front universal joint at companion flange. Disconnect parking brake cable (brake drum type).
3. Drain about two quarts of fluid from the transmission.
4. Remove attaching nut and washers from the extension housing insulator-to-crossmember.
5. Using a suitable jack (or engine supporting fixture) raise the transmission slightly to clear the crossmember. Remove crossmember attaching bolts and remove the crossmember.
6. Remove extension housing-to-transmission bolts and break housing loose from the transmission with a soft mallet. Lift off extension housing.
7. Remove parking brake assembly (brake drum type).

EXTENSION HOUSING BUSHING REPLACEMENT

1. Press or drive out the bushing.
2. Slide a new bushing over the ground end of tool #C-3751 (or substitute), then drive the bushing into the housing with the tool. Be sure the bushing oil hole lines up with the housing slot.
3. Install the cup on the tool followed by the nut. While holding the screw from turning, tighten the tool nut to draw the burnisher through the bushing (Fig. 13).

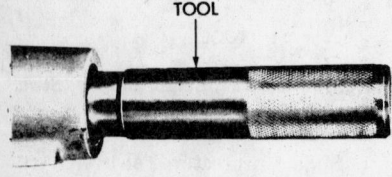

Fig. 12—Removing Extension Housing Bushing.

Installation

1. Install parking brake assembly on the extension housing.
2. Using a new gasket, slide the

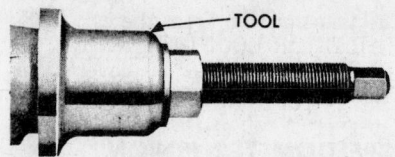

Fig. 13—Installing Extension Housing Bushing.

housing into place and install retaining bolts and washers. Torque bolts to 25-30 ft. lb.
3. Install crossmember and tighten bolts securely.
4. Lower the transmission to rest on the crossmember. Install the mounting washers and nut and torque the nut to 30-35 ft. lb.
5. Hook up the propeller shaft at the front end and connect the parking brake cable.
6. Install speedometer drive pinion and sleeve.
7. Add transmission fluid to correct level.

GOVERNOR
Removal

1. Remove extension housing.
2. With a screwdriver, carefully pry the snap ring from the weight end of governor valve shaft (Fig. 14). Slide the valve and shaft assembly out of the governor housing.
3. Remove the large snap ring from the weight end of the governor housing and lift out the governor weight assembly.
4. Remove snap ring from inside governor weight, remove inner weight and spring from the outer weight.
5. Remove the snap ring from behind the governor housing, then slide the governor housing and support assembly off the output shaft. If necessary, remove the four screws and separate the governor housing from the support.

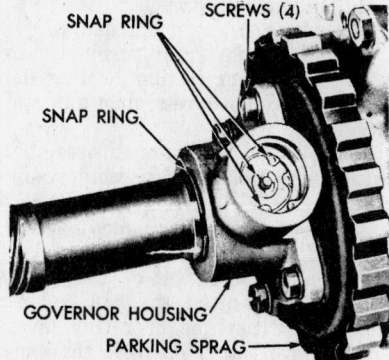

Fig. 14—Governor Shaft and Weight Snap Rings.

Cleaning and Inspection

The primary cause of governor operating trouble is sticking of the

valve or weights. This is brought about by dirt or rough surfaces. Thoroughly clean and blow dry all of the governor parts, crocus cloth any burrs or rough bearing surfaces and clean some more. If all moving parts are clean and operating freely, the governor may be reassembled.

Installation

1. Assemble the governor housing to the support, then finger-tighten the screws. Be sure the oil passage of the governor housing aligns with the passage in the support.
2. Align the master spline of the support with the master spline on the output shaft and slide the assembly into place. Install the snap ring behind the governor housing. Torque housing-to-support screws to 6-8 ft. lb.
3. Assemble the governor weights and spring, make secure with snap ring inside of large governor weight. Place the weight assembly in the governor housing and install snap ring.
4. Place the governor valve on the valve shaft, insert the assembly into the housing and through the governor weights. Install the shaft retaining snap ring.
5. Install the extension housing and parking brake. Hook up the propeller shaft.
6. Connect the parking brake cable.

REAR OIL PUMP
Removal

1. Remove extension housing.
2. Remove governor and support.
3. Unscrew the rear oil pump cover retaining bolts and remove the pump cover.
4. Mark a line across the face of the inner and outer pump rotors (with dye) that they may be reinstalled in the same relation to each other.

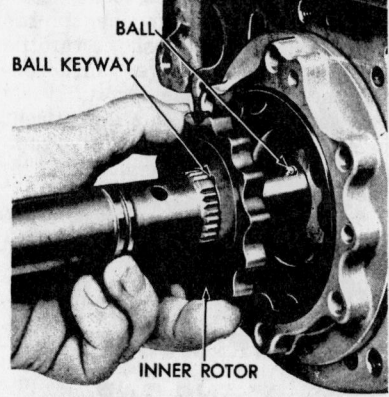

Fig. 15—Removing or Installing Rear Oil Pump Inner Rotor.

5. Slide off the inner rotor, (DON'T DROP THE SMALL DRIVING BALL). Remove the outer rotor from the pump body.

NOTE: If replacement of the pump body is necessary, the transmission must be dismantled to allow driving out the pump body (rearward) with a wood block.

Inspection

Clean and blow dry all pump parts and examine contacting surfaces for evidence of wear, burrs or other damage. With the parts cleaned and reassembled, place a straight edge across the face of the rotors and pump body. With a feeler gauge, check clearance between the straight edge and the face of the rotors. Clearance limits are .001"-.0025" (Fig. 16).

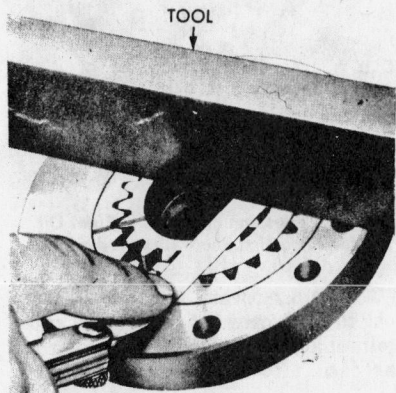

Fig. 16—Checking Oil Pump Rotor Clearance.

Installation

1. Place the outer rotor in the pump body.
2. Rotate the output shaft so that the inner rotor driving ball (or ball key) pocket is up. Drop the ball in the pocket and slide the inner rotor on the output shaft in alignment with the ball.
3. Position the outer rotor to align its dye mark with the mark on the inner rotor and mesh them.
4. Install the pump cover with the attaching bolts turned in a few threads. Slide the aligning fixture, too #C-3762 all the way in until it bottoms against the rotor. Torque the cover attaching bolts to 14-16 ft. lb.
5. Install the governor and support.
6. Install extension housing, brake assembly and hook up the propeller shaft.
7. Connect the parking brake cable (brake drum type).

NEUTRAL STARTING SWITCH
Removal

1. Drain about two qts. of trans-

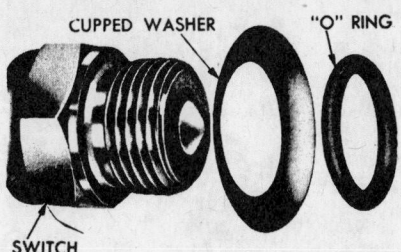

Fig. 17—Neutral Starting Switch (Disassembled).

mission fluid.
2. Disconnect wire from switch and unscrew switch from transmission case.

Installation and Test

1. With the proper control cable adjustment assured and the "N" selector depressed, make sure the switch operating lever is aligned in the center of the switch opening in the case.
2. Place the cupped washer and "O" ring over the threads of the switch. Screw the switch into the transmission case a few turns.
3. Connect one lead of a test lamp to battery current and the other lead to the switch terminal. Screw into the transmission case until the lamp lights. Now tighten the switch an additional 1/3 to 1/2 turn.

NOTE: The switch must be tight enough to prevent oil leaks. If not, add a thin washer and readjust the switch.
4. Remove test lamp and reattach the regular wire to the switch.
5. Bring transmission fluid to correct level.

VALVE BODY ASSEMBLY AND ACCUMULATOR PISTON
Removal

1. Remove the plug and drain all

of the fluid from the transmission.
2. Remove the oil pan and gasket.
3. Loosen the clamp bolt and lift the throttle lever, washer and seal off the transmission throttle lever shaft.
4. Shift the manual control into "1" (Low) position to expose the nut holding the cable adapter to the manual lever. Remove the nut and disengage the adapter from the lever.
5. With a drain pan under the transmission, remove the ten (10) hex-head valve body to transmission case bolts. Hold the valve body in position while removing bolts.
6. Lower the valve body assembly. Be careful not to cock the throttle lever shaft in the case hole or lose the accumulator spring.
7. Insert tool #C-434 inside the accumulator piston and remove the piston from the transmission case. Inspect the piston assembly for scoring, broken rings and wear. Replace as required.

NOTE: Servicing the valve body is outlined later in the text.

Installation

1. All mating surfaces must be clean and free of burrs.
2. Install accumulator piston in the transmission case.
3. Position accumulator spring on the valve body.
4. Position the valve body assembly into place in the transmission and start all the retaining bolts.
5. Snug the bolts down evenly then torque to 55 inch pounds.
6. Connect the control cable adapter to the manual lever and install retaining nut.
7. Install seal, flat washer and throttle lever on the throttle shaft. Tighten the clamp bolt.
8. Install clean oil pan with new gasket.
9. Add fluid to correct level.

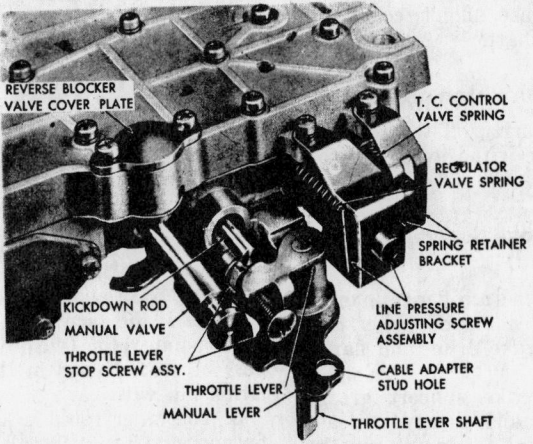

Regulator and conveter control valves assembled view

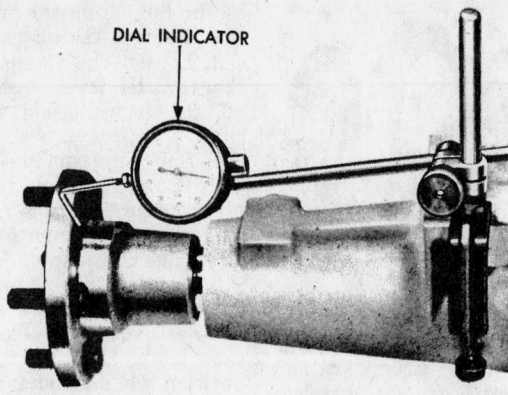

Fig. 19—Checking Drive End Play.

DETAILED UNIT RECONDITIONING

The following reconditioning data cover the removal, disassembly, inspection, repair, assembly and installation procedures for each sub-assembly in detail.

NOTE: In the event that any part has failed in the transmission, the converter should be thoroughly flushed to insure the removal of fine particles that may cause damage to the reconditioned transmission.

(A) Oil Pan

1. Secure transmission in a repair stand.
2. Unscrew attaching bolts and remove oil pan and gasket.

(B) Valve Body Assembly

1. Unscrew nut and remove control cable adapter from valve body manual lever.
2. Remove (10) hex-head valve body-to-transmission case bolts (Fig. 3). (Hold the valve body in position while removing bolts.)
3. Lift the valve body out of the transmission case, don't cock the throttle lever shaft.

(C) Accumulator Piston and Spring

1. Lift the spring off the accumulator piston and withdraw the piston from the case.

(D) Parking Brake Assembly (If So Equipped)

1. Hold brake drum flange and remove attaching nut and washer.
2. Remove brake drum and flange assembly.
3. Remove brake support grease shield spring, and remove grease shield. Be careful not to damage the neoprene seal surface at the bottom of the shield.

4. Remove the lock pin that secures the brake shoe anchor pin in the the front lug of the extension housing.
5. Slide the balance of the brake mechanism with the anchor pin from the housing.
6. Remove neoprene spacer and steel sleeve from the rear of the brake support plate.

(E) Check Drive Train End Play

1. With a dial indicator attached to the extension housing and the plunger seated on the end of the output shaft.
2. Pry the output shaft out and tap it in to register the extreme shaft end play.
3. Record this reading for possible future use upon reassembling. End play readings should be .024" to .062".

(F) Remove Extension Housing

1. Remove attaching bolts and lift off extension housing.

(G) Governor and Support

1. Remove the snap ring from the weight end of the governor valve shaft (Fig. 14). Slide the valve and shaft assembly out of the governor housing.
2. Remove the snap ring from behind the governor housing, then slide the governor housing and support off the output shaft.

(H) Rear Oil Pump

1. Unscrew the rear oil pump cover retaining bolts and remove the cover.
2. Mark the face of the inner and outer pump rotor (with dye) so they may be reassembled in the same relationship with each other.
3. The inner rotor is keyed to the output shaft by a small ball (don't loose the ball). Remove outer rotor from pump body.

NOTE: If the rear oil pump body is to be replaced, drive it rearward out of the case (with a wood block) after the transmission case has been stripped.

(I) Front Oil Pump and Reaction Shaft Support

1. Remove front pump housing retaining bolts.
2. Attach a tool to the pump housing flange, using the 11 and 4 o'clock hole locations (Fig. 20).

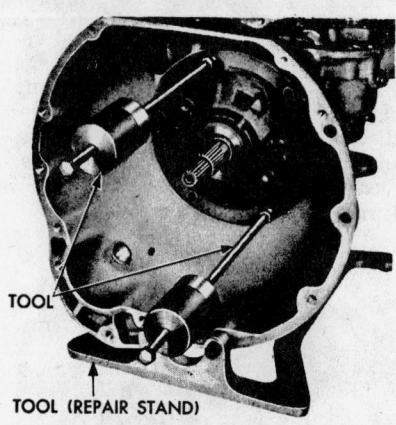

Fig. 20—Removing or Installing Front Oil Pump and Reaction Shaft Support Assembly.

3. Bump outward evenly with the tool to withdraw oil pump and reaction shaft support assembly from the case.

(J) Front Band and Front Clutch

1. Loosen the front band adjuster, remove the head strut and slide the band out of the case.
2. Slide the front clutch assembly out of the case.

(K) Input Shaft and Rear Clutch

1. Grasp the input shaft and slide the shaft and rear clutch assembly out of the case.

NOTE: Don't lose the thrust washer located between the rear end of the input shaft and the fore end of the output shaft.

(L) Planetary Gear Assemblies, Sun Gear, Driving Shell, Low and Reverse Drum

1. While hand-supporting the output shaft and driving shell, carefully slide the assembly forward and out of the case.

(M) Rear Band

1. Loosen rear band adjuster, remove the band strut and remove the band from the case.

(N) Overrunning Clutch

1. Notice the established position of the overrunning clutch rollers and springs before disassembly, to assure correct assembly.

2. Slide out the clutch hub and remove rollers and springs.

3. Remove low and reverse drum thrust washer from inside the overrunning clutch case.

(O) Kickdown Servo

1. Remove snap ring holding the piston rod guide in the case.

2. Remove the rod guide, spring and piston rod from the case. Don't damage the piston rod or guide during removal.

3. Use tool to withdraw piston from the transmission case.

(P) Low and Reverse Servo

1. Using a suitable tool, depress the piston spring retainer and remove the snap ring.

2. Remove the spring retainer, spring and servo piston and plug assembly from the case.

FLUSHING THE
TORQUE CONVERTER

1. Reinstall the converter assembly to the crankshaft mounting plate. Remove one drain plug and empty the converter of transmission fluid.

2. Insert a screwdriver into the converter and turn the stator hub (large splined hub) counterclockwise until one of the 1/8" x 3/8" slots of this assembly is visible at the top. A second opening directly below provides an ample opening for the kerosene flush (if poured slowly).

3. Slowly pour 2 qts. of new, clean kerosene into the torque converter. Wipe dry and close the hub opening with masking tape.

4. Disconnect the coil wire, then rotate the converter for about 10 seconds by cranking the engine.

5. Drain the converter and repeat the operation at least once, but as many times as is required to thoroughly flush ALL of the flakes and dirt from the unit.

6. Now, with both plugs removed, rotate the converter several times; this should further remove pocketed solvent and dirt. Replace the plugs and remove the converter assembly from its mounting plate.

Before removing any of the transmission sub-assemblies, thoroughly clean the exterior of the unit, preferably by steam. When disassembling, each part should be washed in a suitable solvent, and either set aside to drain or dried with compressed air. DO NOT WIPE WITH SHOP TOWELS. All of the transmission parts require extremely careful handling to avoid nicks and other damage to the accurately machined surfaces.

RECONDITIONING OF
SUB-ASSEMBLIES

The following procedures cover the disassembly, inspection, repair and assembly of each sub-assembly as removed from the transmission.

The use of crocus cloth is permissible but not encouraged as extreme care must be used to avoid rounding off sharp edges of valves. The edge portion of valve body and valves is very important to proper functioning. NOTE: Use all new seals and gaskets and coat each part with automatic transmission fluid, Type "A", Suffix "A", during assembly.

VALVE BODY
(A) Disassembly

NOTE: This area is extremely critical to distortion. Never clamp any portion of the valve body or transfer plate in a vise. Clean with new solvent and dry with compressed air. Start all valves into their respective chambers with a twisting motion and well lubricated with automatic transmission fluid.

1. With the valve body on a clean repair stand (Fig. 21), remove (3) attaching screws and the oil screen.

2. Hold the spring retainer bracket against spring tension, remove the (3) bracket retaining screws (Fig. 22).

3. Remove spring bracket, torque converter valve spring, and the regulator valve spring with line pressure adjusting screw assembly.
NOTE: DO NOT ALTER THE SETTING OF THE LINE PRESSURE ADJUSTING SCREW AND NUT. THE NUT HAS AN INTERFER-

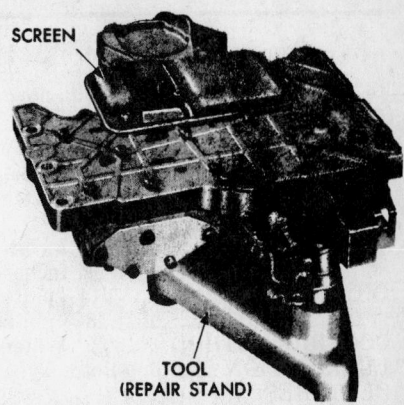

Fig. 21—Removing or Installing Oil Screen.

ENCE THREAD AND DOES NOT TURN EASILY ON THE SCREW.

4. Slide the regulator valve and spring retainer ring out of the valve body. Slide torque converter control valve out of the valve body.

5. Remove the (14) transfer plate retaining screws. Lift the transfer plate and steel plate assembly off the valve body.

6. Invert the transfer plate assembly and remove the stiffener plate. Remove the remaining screws securing the steel plate to the transfer plate, and lift off the steel plate (Fig. 23). Remove rear pump check valve and spring.

7. Remove reverse blocker valve cover and lift out spring and valve.

8. Make a notation, locating the (6) steel balls in the valve body (one of them is larger than the other five and is in the larger chamber). Remove the steel balls, front pump check valve and spring (Fig. 24).

9. Invert valve body and lay it on clean paper. Remove "E"-clip from the throttle lever shaft (Fig. 25). While holding manual lever detent ball and spring in their bore with tool #C-3765, or similar tool, slide manual lever off the throttle shaft. Remove detent ball and spring.

10. Remove manual valve from

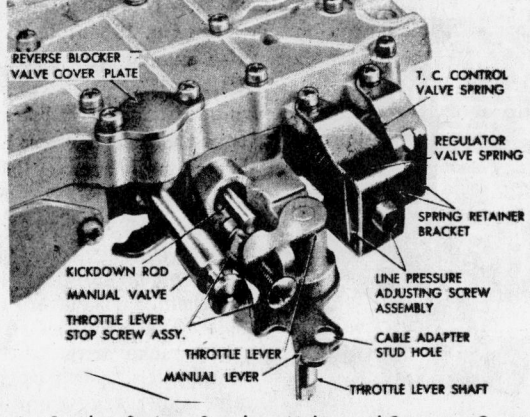

Fig. 22—Spring Bracket, Springs, Regulator Valve, and Converter Control Valve (Assembled View).

TORQUEFLITE (B)
SPECIFICATIONS

TYPE
......Automatic 3-Speed with Torque
Converter
CONVERTER DIAMETER
.... □ 10¾ inches
.... △ 11¾ inches
OIL CAPACITY .... □ 14 pints
.... △ 18½ pints
COOLING METHOD ....Water
LUBRICATION .....Pump-Rotor Type
CLUTCHES
    Number of Front Plates (Steel) ..4
    Numper of Front Discs (Lined) ..4
    Number of Rear Plates (Steel) □ 2
                                    △ 3
    Number of Rear Discs (Lined) 4
FRONT & REAR PUMPS
    Type ....Gear (Rotary)
    End Clearance ....001″ to .0025″
DRIVE TRAIN END PLAY
    .... □ .024″ to .062″
    .... △ .030″ to .070″
CLUTCH PLATE CLEARANCE
    Front Clutch .... □ .056″ to .104″
    .... △ .024″ to .123″

Rear Clutch .... □ .018″ to .036″
.... △ .026″ to .054″
SNAP RINGS
    Front & Rear Clutches, Rear Snap
    Ring (Selective) ....060″ to .062″
    ....068″ to .070″
    ....074″ to .076″
    ....076″ to .078″
    Output Shaft Bearing .086″ to .088″
THRUST WASHERS (With Slant-6)
    Output to Input Shaft
    ....052″ to .054″—Natural
    ....068″ to .070″—Red
    ....083″ to .085″—Black
    Sun Gear Driving
    Shell ....060″ to .062″
    Driving Shell
    (Steel) ....034″ to .036″
    Overrunning Clutch
    Race ....060″ to .062″
    Kickdown Annulus
    Support ....121″ to .125″
    Front to Rear
    Clutch ....043″ to .045″
    Front Clutch to Reaction Shaft

Support....................043″ to .045″
THRUST WASHERS (with V-8)
    Reaction Shaft Support to Front
    Clutch Retainer
    ....043″ to .045″—Natural
    ....061″ to .063″—Green
    ....084″ to .086″—Red
    Output to Input
    Shaft ....062″ to .064″
    Sun Gear Driving Shell Thrust
    Plate (Steel) ....034″ to .036″
    Rear Planetary Gear to
    Driving Shell ....062″ to .064″
    Front Planetary Gear to Annulus
    Gear Support ....062″ to .064″
    Front Annulus Gear Support to
    Driving Shell ....062″ to .064″
    Front Clutch Piston Retainer to
    Rear Clutch Piston Retainer.
    ....061″ to .063″—Green
NOTE: □—Torqueflight (B) used
            with slant-6 engine.
        △—Torqueflight (B) used
            with V-8 engine.

---

valve body.

11. Remove throttle lever and shaft from body.

12. Remove shuttle valve cover plate. Remove "E"-clip from the exposed end of shuttle valve (Fig. 26).

13. Remove throttle lever stop screw, being careful not to disturb the setting.

14. Remove kickdown detent, kickdown valve, throttle valve spring and throttle valve (Fig. 27).

15. Remove governor plug and end plate. Tip up the valve body to allow the shuttle valve throttle plug, spring, shuttle valve and the shift valve governor plugs to slide out into your hand.
NOTE: The 1-2 shift valve plug has a longer stem.

16. Remove the shift valve end

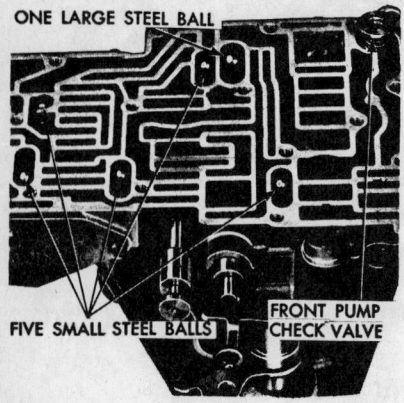

Fig. 24—Front Pump Check Valve and Steel Ball Locations.

ONE LARGE STEEL BALL
FIVE SMALL STEEL BALLS
FRONT PUMP CHECK VALVE

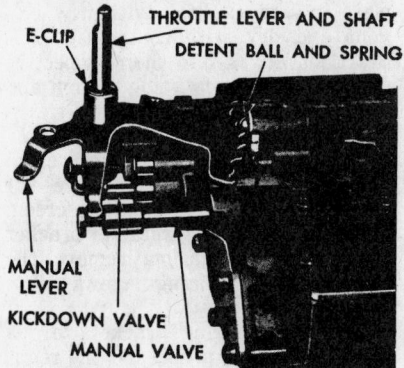

E-CLIP
THROTTLE LEVER AND SHAFT
DETENT BALL AND SPRING
MANUAL LEVER
KICKDOWN VALVE
MANUAL VALVE

Fig. 25—Manual Lever, Detent Ball and Spring, Throttle Lever and Shaft, Manual Valve, and Kickdown Valve (Assembled View).

plate and slide out the (2) springs and valves (Fig. 28).

17. Remove the regulator valve end plate. Slide the regulator valve line pressure plug, sleeve, and the regulator valve throttle pressure plug out of the body.

(B) Cleaning and Inspection

Inspect all components for scores, loose or bent levers, burrs and warping. Don't straighten bent levers; renew them. Loose levers may be silver soldered at the shaft. Burrs and minor nicks may be carefully removed with crocus cloth. Check for valve body warping or distortion with a surface plate (plate glass will do) and a feeler gauge. DO NOT AT-

TEMPT TO SERVICE A DISTORTED PLATE OR VALVE BODY, THIS IS A VERY CRITICAL AREA. Check all springs for distortion or fatigue. Check valves for scores and freedom of movement in the bores, they should fall of their own weight, in and out of the bore. The front and rear pump check valves are provided with a controlled leakage path. This assures that the rear pump remains primed.

(C) Assembly

1. Insert the rear pump check valve and spring in the transfer plate. Position the steel plate on the transfer plate, hold the rear pump check valve in its bore with a thin steel scale and install (4) steel plate

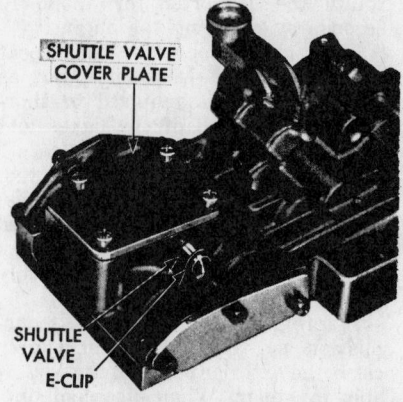

SHUTTLE VALVE COVER PLATE
SHUTTLE VALVE
E-CLIP

Fig. 26—Shuttle Valve Cover, Shuttle Valve and Retaining E-Clip (Assembled View).

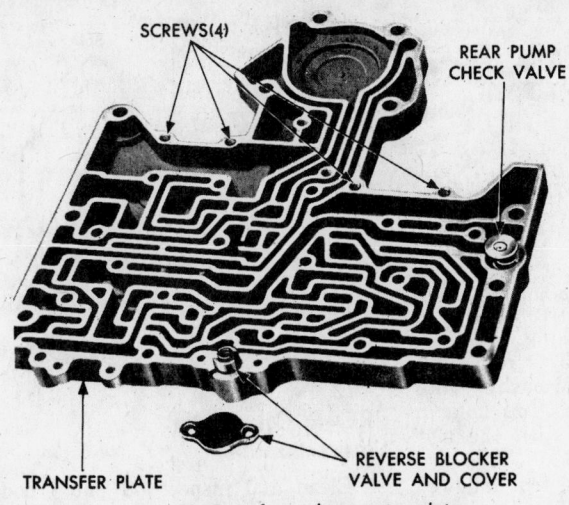

Fig. 23—Transfer and separator plate.

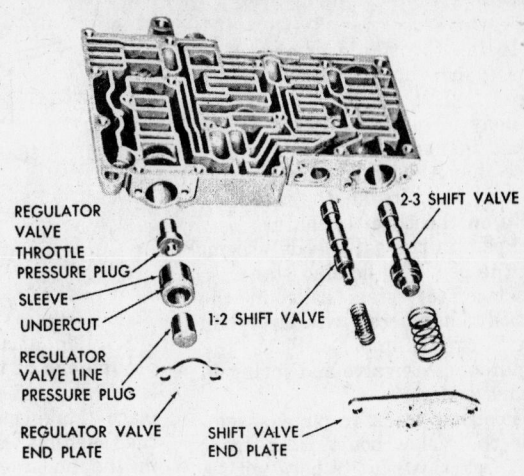

Fig. 27—Valve Body—Shift Valve Side (Exploded View).

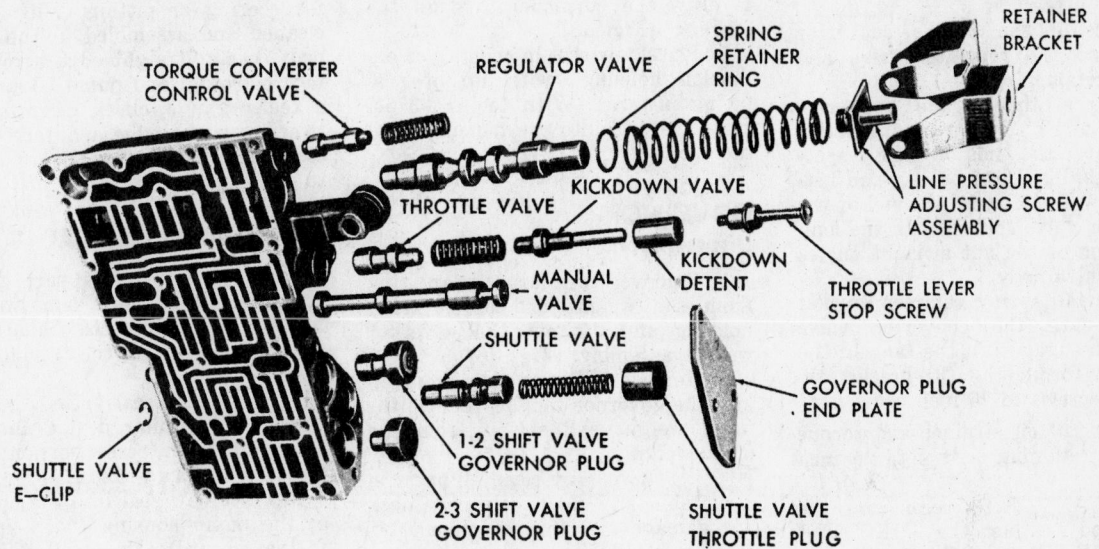

Fig. 28—Valve Body—Lever Side (Exploded View).

to transfer plate retaining screws. Torque these screws evenly to 25 inch pounds. Check rear pump check valve for free movement in the transfer plate. Install stiffener plate and tighten retaining screw to 25 inch pounds.

2. Turn transfer plate over and install reverse blocker valve spring and valve. Rotate valve until it seats through the steel plate. Hold the valve down and install blocker valve cover plate. Torque the (2) retaining screws to 25 inch pounds.

3. Insert the 1-2 and 2-3 shift valve governor plugs in their respective bores. Install shuttle valve, valve spring and shuttle valve throttle plug. Install governor plug end plate and torque the (4) retaining screws to 25 inch pounds.

4. Install "E"-clip on end of shuttle valve. Install shuttle valve cover plate and torque the (4) retaining screws to 25 inch pounds.

5. Install the 1-2 and 2-3 shift valves and springs. Install shift valve and plate and torque the three retaining screws to 25 inch pounds.

6. Insert regulator valve throttle pressure plug, sleeve (with the undercut on the sleeve toward the end plate), and the line pressure plug. Install regulator valve end plate and

7. Insert throttle valve and spring. Slide the kickdown detent on kickdown valve (with counterbore side of detent toward valve), then insert the assembly in the valve body.

8. Install throttle lever stop screw and tighten lock nut finger tight.

9. Insert manual valve in the valve

torque the (2) retaining screws to 25 inch pounds.

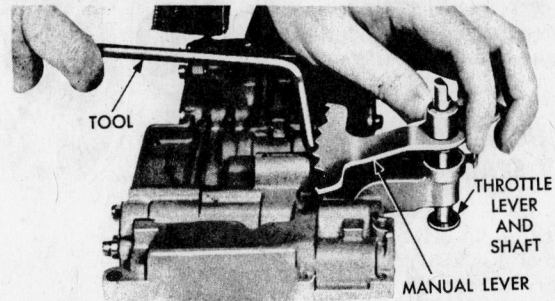

Fig. 29—Installing Detent Ball, Spring, and Manual Lever.

body.

10. Install throttle lever and shaft on the valve body. Insert detent spring and ball in its bore of the valve body. Depress ball and spring and slide manual lever over throttle shaft so that it engages manual valve and detent ball. Install the retaining "E"-clip on the throttle shaft.

11. Position the valve body assembly on the bench or holding stand.

12. Place (6) steel balls in the valve body chambers (with large ball in the large chamber). Place the front pump check valve and spring in the valve body.

13. Position transfer plate assembly on the valve body. Hold front pump check valve in its bore with a thin steel scale. Install the (14) retaining screws, starting at the center and working outward, torque screws to 25 inch pounds.

14. Install the torque converter valve and the regulator valve and spring retainer ring.

15. Place the torque converter valve spring and the regulator valve spring over the ends of their respective valves. Place line pressure adjusting screw assembly on the end of the regulator valve spring, with the long dimension of the nut at right angles to the valve body.

16. Install spring retainer bracket (make sure the converter valve spring is engaged on the tang in the bracket. Torque the (3) bracket retaining screws to 25 inch pounds.

17. Install oil strainer and torque the (3) retaining screws to 25 inch pounds.
IMPORTANT: After reconditioning the valve body, adjust the THROTTLE and LINE PRESSURE as outlined in the car section of this manual. However, if line pressure was satisfactory before disassembly, do not change this adjustment.

ACCUMULATOR PISTON AND SPRING

Inspect both seal rings (2) for wear and freedom in the piston grooves. Check the piston for scores, burrs, nicks and wear. Check the piston bore for corresponding damage and check piston spring for distortion and fatigue. Replace parts as required.

EXTENSION HOUSING BUSHING AND OIL SEAL
Replacement:

1. Press or carefully drive out the bushing with tool #C-3755 or reasonable substitute.
2. Drive out the oil seal with a long blunt drift.

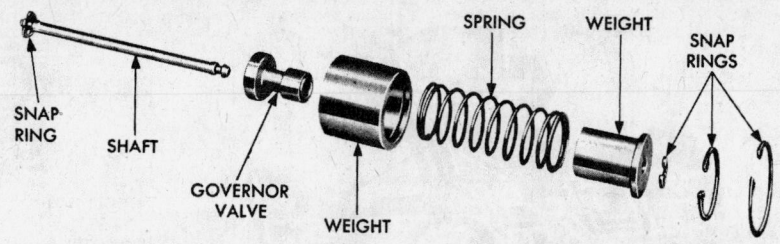

Fig. 30—Governor Valve, Weights, Spring, and Shaft (Exploded View).

3. Slide a new bushing over the ground end of tool #C-3751 or a similar device and press the bushing into place. Make sure of the oil hole in the bushing aligning with the slot in the housing.

4. Install cup on the tool followed by the nut. While holding the screw from turning, tighten the tool nut to draw the burnisher through the bushing (Fig. 13).

5. Place new seal in opening of extension housing (with lip of seal facing inward). With tool #C-3754, drive the seal into the housing until the tool bottoms (Fig. 11).

GOVERNOR
Disassembly:

1. Remove the large snap ring from the weight end of governor housing and lift out the governor weight assembly (Fig. 30)
2. Remove the snap ring from inside the governor weight, remove the inner weight and spring from the outer weight.
NOTE: Thoroughly clean all parts in a suitable and clean solvent. Check for damage and free movement before assembly.

Assembly:

1. Assemble the governor weights and spring, then secure with snap ring inside of large governor weight (Fig. 30).
2. Place the weight assembly in

the governor housing and install snap ring.

REAR OIL PUMP
Inspection:

Clean and inspect oil pump body and cover for wear, gouging or any other type of damage. Inspect rotors for scoring or pitting. With rotors cleaned and assembled in the pump body, use a straight edge across the face of rotors and pump body. With a feeler gauge, check clearance between straight edge and face of rotors. Clearance limits should be .001" to .0025" (Fig. 16).

FRONT PUMP OIL SEAL

Replacement of this part can be accomplished without removing the front pump and reaction shaft support assembly from the transmission case.
1. Screw a seal remover, tool #C-3758 or similar device, into the seal. Tighten the screw portion of the tool to withdraw the seal.
2. Place new seal into the opening of the pump housing (with lip side facing inward). Use tool #3757 or other satisfactory seal driver to locate the seal in the housing.

FRONT PUMP AND REACTION SHAFT SUPPORT
Disassembly:

Figure 31 shows the front oil

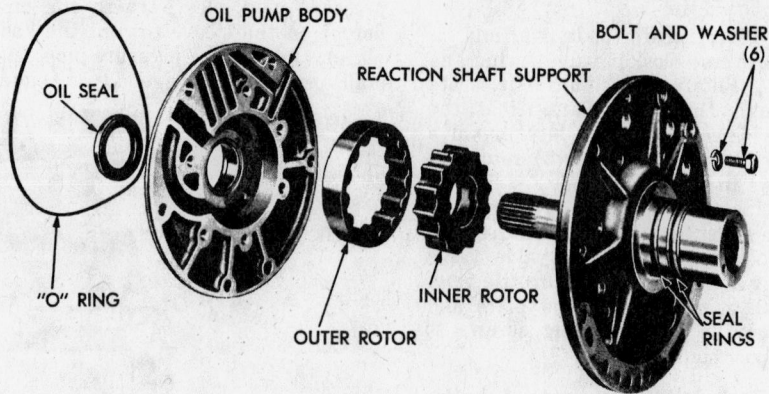

Fig. 31—Front Oil Pump and Reaction Shaft Support (Exploded View).

pump and reaction shaft support disassembled.

1. Remove bolts from rear side of reaction shaft support and lift support off the pump.

2. Dye-spot the face of the inner and outer rotors so they may be reinstalled in their original relationship, then remove the rotors.

3. Remove the rubber seal ring from front pump body flange.

4. Drive out the oil seal with blunt punch.

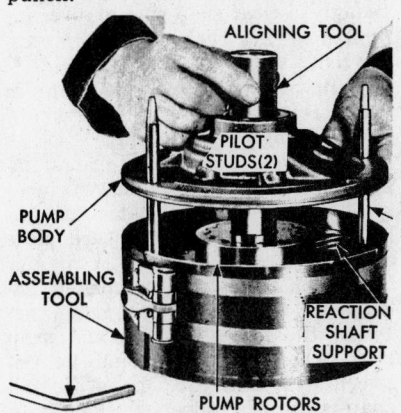

Fig. 32—Assembling Front Pump and Reaction Shaft Support.

Inspection:

Clean and inspect interlocking seal rings on the reaction shaft support for wear or broken interlocks, be sure they turn freely in their grooves. Check all machined surfaces of pump body and reaction shaft support for scuff marks and burrs. Inspect pump rotors for scores and pits. With rotors clean and installed in the pump body, use a straight edge across the face of the rotors and pump body. With a feeler gauge, check straight edge to rotor face clearance. Limits should be from .001" to .0025".

Assembly:

1. Place reaction shaft support in assembling tool #C-3759 and place it on the bench with the support hub resting on the bench (Fig 32). Screw (2) pilot studs, tool #C-3283 or satisfactory substitutes, into threaded holes of reaction shaft support flange (Fig. 20).

2. Assemble rotors with dye marks aligned, place rotors in center of the support. THE TWO DRIVING LUGS INSIDE ROTOR MUST BE NEXT TO THE FACE OF THE REACTION SHAFT SUPPORT.

3. Lower pump body over pilot studs, insert tool #C-3756 or substiture through pump body and engage pump inner rotor. Turn the rotors with the tool to enter rotors in pump body. With the pump body firmly against the reaction shaft support, tighten ring squeezer or clamping tool securely.

4. Invert the front pump and reaction shaft suport assembly with the clamping tool intact. Install support to pump body bolts and torque to 14-16 foot pounds. Remove clamping tool, pilot studs and rotor aligning studs.

5. Insert new oil seal in opening of front oil pump housing (with lip of seal facing inward). With tool #C-3757 or other suitable device, drive seal into housing.

FRONT CLUTCH
Disassembly:

Exploded view of front clutch assembly is given in Fig. 33.

1. With screwdriver or pick, remove large snap ring holding the pressure plate in the clutch piston retainer. Lift pressure plate and clutch plates out of the retainer.

2. Install compressor, tool #C-3575 or similar tool, over piston spring retainer (Fig. 34). Compress spring and remove snap ring, then slowly release tool until the spring retainer is free of the hub. Remove the compressor, retainer and spring.

3. Turn the clutch retainer upside down and bump on a wooden block to remove the piston. Remove seal rings from the piston and clutch retainer hub.

Inspection:

Inspect clutch discs for evidence of burning, glazing and flaking. A general method of determining clutch plate breakdown is to scratch the lined surface of the plate with a finger nail, if material collects under the nail, replace all driving discs. Check driving splines for wear or burrs. Inspect steel plates and pressure plate surfaces for discolor, scuffing or damaged driving lugs, replace if necessary.

Check steel plate lug grooves in clutch retainer for smooth surfaes, plate travel must be free. Inspect band contacting surface of clutch retainer, be sure the ball moves freely.

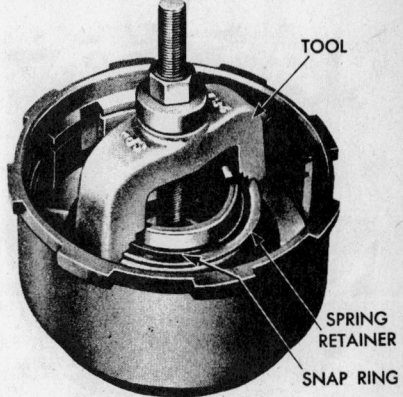

Fig. 34—Removing or Installing Front Clutch Spring Retainer Snap Ring.

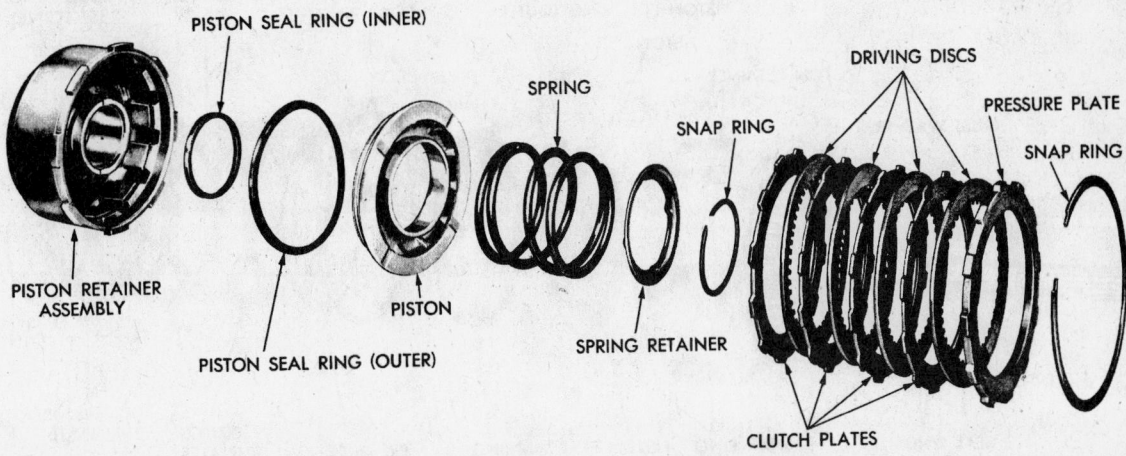

Fig. 33—Front Clutch Assembly (Exploded View).

Check seal ring surfaces in clutch retainer for scratches or nicks, light annular scratches will not interfere with the sealing of neoprene rings.

Inspect inside bore of piston for score marks; if light, polish with crocus cloth. Check seal ring grooves for nicks and burrs. Inspect neoprene seal rings for deterioration, wear and hardness. Check piston spring, retainer and snap ring for distortion and fatigue.

Assembly:

1. Lubricate and install inner seal ring on hub of clutch retainer. Be sure that lip of seal faces down and is properly seated in the groove.

2. Lubricate and install outer seal ring on clutch piston, with lip of seal toward the bottom of the clutch retainer. Place piston assembly in retainer and, with a twisting motion, seat the piston in the bottom of the retainer.

3. Place spring on the piston hub and position spring retainer and snap ring on spring. Compress spring with tool #C-3575 or suitable ring compresser, and seat snap ring in the

hub groove. Remove compressor.

4. Lubricate all clutch plates, install a steel plate followed by a lined plate until all plates are installed. Install the pressure plate and snap ring. Be sure the snap ring is correctly seated.

5. With front clutch assembled, insert a feeler gauge between the pressure plate and snap ring (Fig. 35). The clearance should be .056" to .104". If not, install a snap ring of proper thickness to result in the specified clearance.
NOTE: Snap rings are the same as those used in the rear clutch and are available in sizes of .060"-.062", .068"-.070" and .076"-.078" thicknesses, see previous chart.

REAR CLUTCH
Disassembly:

Exploded view of rear clutch assembly is given in Fig. 36.
1. With a small screwdriver or pick, remove the large snap ring that secures the pressure plate in the clutch piston retainer. Lift the pressure plate, clutch plates, and inner pressure plate out of the retainer.

2. Install tool #C-3760 or other suitable compressor over the piston spring. Compress spring just enough to clear the snap ring, then remove the snap ring.

3. Remove compressor tool and piston spring. Turn clutch retainer assembly upside down and bump on a wood block to remove the piston. Remove seal rings from the piston.

Inspection:

Inspect driving discs for indication of damage, handle as previously outlined under front clutch inspection.

Assembly:

1. Lubricate and install inner and

outer seal rings on the clutch piston. Be sure the lip of seals face toward the head of the clutch retainer and are properly seated in the piston grooves.

2. Place piston assembly in retainer and, with a twisting motion, seat piston in bottom of retainer.

3. Place spring over piston with outer edge of spring positioned below snap ring grooves. Install tool #C-3760 or substitute, as in disassembly, and compress spring just enough to clear snap ring groove. Install snap ring, then remove compressor tool.

4. Install inner pressure plate in clutch retainer with raised portion of plate resting on the spring.

5. Lubricate all clutch plates, install one lined plate followed by a steel plate until all plates are installed. Install outer pressure plate and snap ring.

6. With rear clutch completely assembled, insert a feeler gauge between the pressure plate and snap ring. The clearance should be between .018" and .036". If not, install snap ring of proper thickness to obtain the required clearance.
NOTE: Rear clutch plate clearance is very important in obtaining satisfactory clutch performance. Clearance is influenced by the use of various thickness outer snap rings. Snap rings are available in .060"-.062", .068"-.070" and .076"-.078" thicknesses, see previous chart.

PLANETARY GEAR ASSEMBLIES, SUN GEAR DRIVING SHELL, LOW AND REVERSE DRUM
Disassembly:

Refer to Fig. 37 for assembly and disassembly of these units.
1. Remove thrust washer from forward end of output shaft.

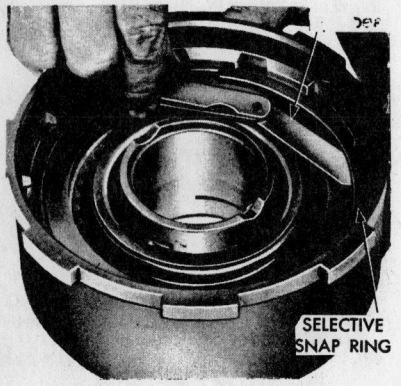

SELECTIVE SNAP RING

Fig. 35—Checking Front Clutch Plate Clearance.

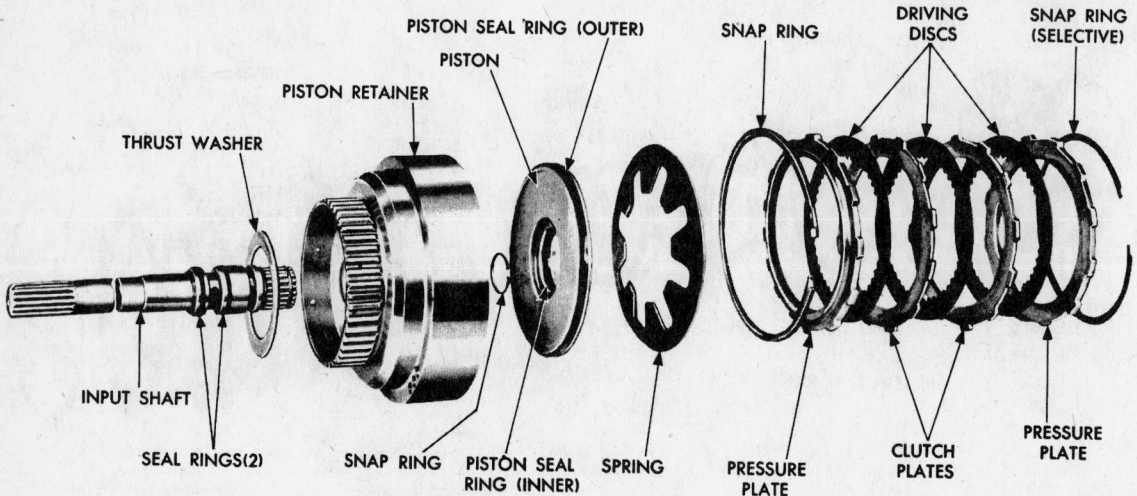

THRUST WASHER · INPUT SHAFT · SEAL RINGS(2) · PISTON RETAINER · PISTON · PISTON SEAL RING (OUTER) · SNAP RING · PISTON SEAL RING (INNER) · SPRING · PRESSURE PLATE · SNAP RING · DRIVING DISCS · CLUTCH PLATES · PRESSURE PLATE · SNAP RING (SELECTIVE)

Fig 36—Rear Clutch Assembly (Exploded View).

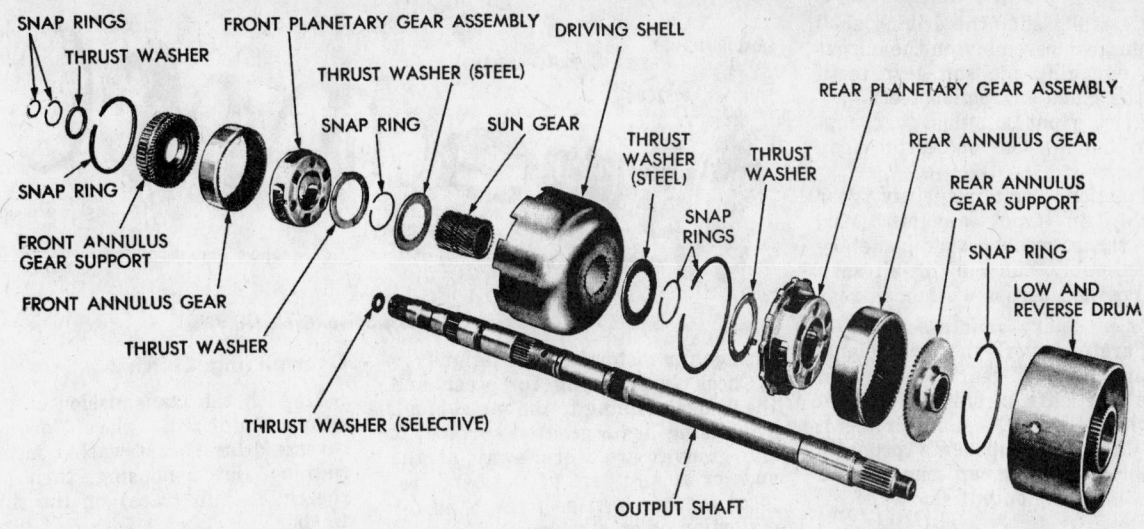

Fig. 37—Planetary Gear Assemblies, Sun Gear, Driving Shell, Low and Reverse Drum, and Output Shaft (Exploded View).

2. Remove snap ring from forward end of output shaft, then slide front planetary assembly off the shaft.

3. Remove snap ring and thrust washer from forward hub of front planetary gear assembly, slide front annulus gear and support off the planetary gear set. Remove thrust washer from rear side of planetary gear set. If necessary, remove snap ring from front of annulus gear (ring gear), to separate the support from annulus gear.

4. Slide the sun gear, driving shell, rear planetary assembly with low and reverse drum off the output shaft.

5. Lift sun gear and driving shell off the rear planetary assembly. Remove snap ring and steel washer from sun gear (rear side of driving shell). Slide sun gear out of driving shell, and remove snap ring and steel washer from opposite end of sun gear if necessary.

6. Remove thrust washer from forward side of rear planetary assembly. Remove snap ring from front side of low and reverse drum, then slide rear planetary assembly out of the drum. If necessary, remove snap ring from rear of annulus gear to separate the support from the annulus gear.

Inspection:

Inspect bearing surfaces on the output shaft for burrs or other damage. Light scratches or burrs may be polished out with crocus cloth or a fine stone. Check speedometer drive gear for damage and make sure all oil passages are clear.

Check bushings in the sun gear for wear or scores, replace sun gear assembly if bushings show wear or other damage. Inspect all thrust washers for wear and scores, replace

Fig. 38—Overrunning Clutch Assembled.

if necessary. Check lock rings for distortion and fatigue. Inspect annulus gear and driving gear teeth for damage. Inspect planetary gear carrier for cracks and the pinions for broken or worn gear teeth.

Assembly:

1. Locate the rear annulus gear support in the annulus gear and install snap ring.

2. Position the rear planetary gear assembly in the rear annulus gear, slide the assembly into low and reverse drum. Put thrust washer on the front side of the planetary gear assembly.

3. Insert output shaft in the rear opening of the drum. Carefully work the shaft through the annulus gear support and planetary gear assembly. Make sure the shaft splines are fully engaged in the splines of the annulus gear support.

4. Install steel washer and snap ring on the shortest end of the sun

gear. Insert sun gear through front side of the driving shell, install rear steel washer and snap ring. (THE LONGER END OF THE SUN GEAR MUST BE TOWARD THE REAR, EXTENDING OUT OF THE DRIVING SHELL).

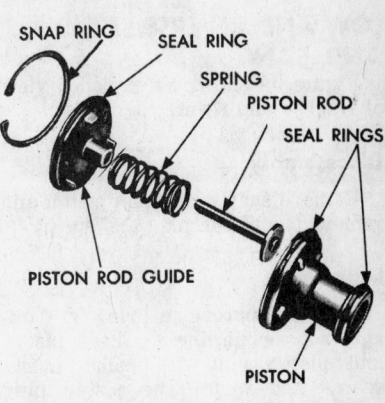

Fig. 39—Kickdown Servo (Exploded View).

5. Carefully slide the driving shell and sun gear assembly on the output shaft, engaging the sun gear teeth with the planetary pinion teeth.

6. Place front annulus gear support in annulus gear and install snap ring.

7. Position front planetary gear assembly in front annulus gear, place thrust washer over planetary gear assembly hub and install snap ring. Position thrust washer on rear side of planetary gear assembly.

8. Carefully work the front planetary and annulus gear assembly on the output shaft, meshing the planetary pinions with the sun gear teeth.

9. With all components properly assembled, install snap ring on the front end of the output shaft.

OVERRUNNING CLUTCH
Inspection:

Inspect clutch rollers for smooth round surfaces, they must be free of flat spots, chipped edges and flaking. Inspect roller contacting surfaces on both cam and race for pock marks and roller wear-marks. Check springs for distortion and fatigue and inspect low and reverse drum thrust.

KICKDOWN SERVO AND BAND
Inspection:

Figure 39 shows an exploded view of the kickdown servo.

Inspect piston and guide seal rings for wear, and be sure of their freedom in grooves. It is not necessary to remove seal rings unless conditions warrant. Inspect piston for scores, burrs or other damage. Check fit of guide on piston rod. Check piston for distortion and fatigue. Inspect band lining for wear and fit of lining material to the metal band. This lining is grooved; if grooves are not still visible at the ends or any part of the band, replace the band. Inspect band for distortion or cracked ends.

LOW AND REVERSE SERVO AND BAND

Figure 40 shows an exploded view of the low and reverse servo.

Disassembly:

Remove snap ring from piston and remove the piston plug and spring.

Inspection:

Inspect neoprene seal ring for damage, rot, or hardness. Check piston and piston plug for nicks, burrs, scores and wear. The piston plug must operate freely in the piston. Check the piston bore in the case for scores or other damage. Examine

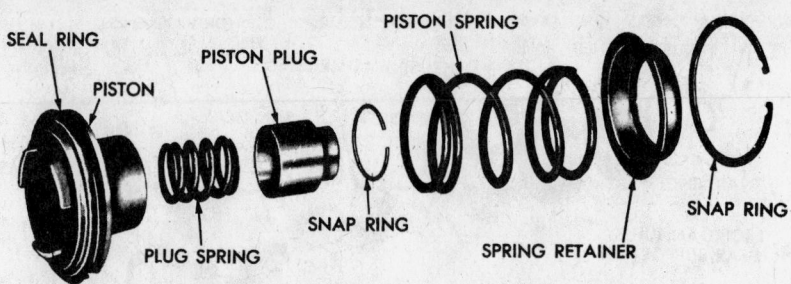

Fig .40—Low and Reverse Servo (Exploded View).

springs for distortion and fatigue.

Check band lining for wear and the fit of the lining to the metal band. This lining has a grooved surface; if the grooves are worn away at the ends or at any part of the band, replace the band. Inspect the band for distortion or cracked ends.

Assembly:

Lubricate and insert the piston plug and spring in the piston, and secure with the snap ring.

INSTALLATION OF SUB-ASSEMBLIES

The following assembly procedures given here include the installation of sub-assemblies in the transmission case and adjusting the drive train end play. DO NOT USE FORCE TO ASSEMBLE ANY OF THE MATING PARTS. Always use new gaskets during the assembly operations.

NOTE: Use only automatic transmission fluid, Type "A", Suffix "A", or fluid of equivalent chemical structure, to lubricate these automatic transmission parts during or after assembly.

Rear Oil Pump Body

The following procedures should be followed closely when installing a new rear pump body or reinstalling the original pump body to prevent pump body distortion.

1. Cut a piece of .002" to .003" thick wrapping paper, slightly smaller than the outside diameter of the outer rotor, to use as a shim during installation.

2. Chill the pump body to an approximate zero temperature in a deep freeze or with dry ice.

3. Quickly place pump body in the case, and install inner and outer rotors. Smear a daub of grease on the face of the rotors and center the paper shim on face of rotors, then install pump cover and tighten retaining bolts firmly.

4. After the pump body has warmed to room temperature, remove the pump cover, paper shim and rotors.

Overrunning Clutch

1. With the transmission case positioned upright, place low and reverse drum thrust washer in overrunning clutch housing, then place the clutch hub (race) on the thrust washer.

2. Install springs and rollers as shown in illustration.

Low and Reverse Servo and Band

1. Carefully work servo piston assembly into the case with a twisting motion. Place spring, retainer and snap ring over the piston.

2. Using the screw portion of tool C-3322 or suitable substitute, depress the spring and install the snap ring.

3. Position rear band in the case, install the short strut, then connect the long lever and strut to the band. Screw in band adjuster just enough to hold struts in place.

Kickdown Servo

1. Carefully insert servo piston into case bore. Install piston rod, spring and guide. Depress guide and install snap ring.

Planetary Gear Assemblies, Sun Gear, Driving Shell, Low and Reverse Drum

1. While supporting the assembly in the case, insert output shaft through the overrunning clutch hub. Carefully work the assembly rearward, engaging the drum splines with splines of the overrunning clutch hub.

CAUTION: Be careful not to damage the ground surfaces on the output shaft during installation.

2. Apply a daub of grease to the selective thrust washer and install washer on the front end of the output shaft.

NOTE: If the drive train end play was not within specifications (.024"-.062") when checked (in text entitled "Checking Drive Train End Play"), replace the thrust washer with one of proper thickness. The following selective washers are available, see previous chart.

Input Shaft and Rear Clutch

1. Turn transmission in an upright position with the output shaft pointing downward.

2. Align the rear clutch plate inner splines, lower the input shaft and clutch assembly into position in the case.

3. Carefully work the clutch assembly in a circular motion to engage the clutch splines over the splines of the kickdown annulus gear support.

4. Daub one side of the fiber thrust washer with heavy grease, then position washer in the recess on the front face of the rear clutch retainer.

Front Clutch

1. Align the front clutch plate inner splines, lower the clutch assembly into position in the case.

2. Carefully work the clutch assembly in a circular motion to engage clutch splines over splines of the rear clutch piston retainer. Be sure the front clutch driving lugs are fully engaged in the slots in the driving shell.

Front Band

1. Slide the band over the front clutch assembly.

2. Install band strut, screw in the adjuster just enough to hold the band in place.

Front Oil Pump and Reaction Shaft Support

1. Screw (2) pilot studs in front pump opening in the case.

2. Place a new rubber seal ring in groove on outer flange of pump. Be sure the seal ring is not twisted.

3. Insert aligning tool C-3756 through the pump body and engage with the inner rotor.

4. Install the assembly in the case, tap lightly with a soft mallet if necessary. Install four bolts, remove pilot studs and install remaining bolts and pull down evenly, then torque the bolts to 14-16 ft. lb.

5. Rotate the pump rotors with tool C-3759 or substitute, until the two small holes in the handle of the tool are vertical. This is to locate the inner rotor so the converter impeller shaft will engage the inner rotor lugs during installation.

Rear Oil Pump

1. Place outer rotor in pump body.

2. Turn output shaft so the inner rotor driving ball pocket is facing up. Install the ball and slide the inner rotor onto the output shaft and in alignment with the ball.

3. Position the outer rotor so the

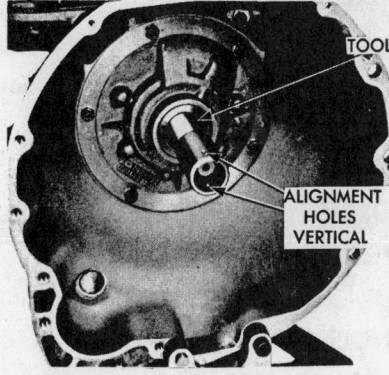

Fig. 41—Aligning Front Pump Rotors.

dye marks will be aligned, then push the inner rotor in mesh with the outer rotor (Fig. 41).

4. Install the pump cover with the retaining bolts threaded in a few turns. Slide aligning sleeve, tool #C-3762, all the way in until it bottoms against the rotors. Torque the cover bolts evenly to 14-16 ft. lb.

Governor

1. Align the master spline of the governor support with the master spline on the output shaft and slide the assembly into place. Install snap ring behind the governor housing. Torque housing-to-support screws to 6-8 ft. lb.

2. Place the governor valve on the valve shaft, insert the assembly into the housing and through the governor weights. Install the valve shaft retaining snap ring.

Extension Housing and Parking Brake, If So Equipped

1. Using a new gasket, carefully slide the extension into place. Install the retaining bolts and washers, torque the bolts to 25-30 ft. lb.

IMPORTANT AT THIS POINT:

Recheck the drive train end play as previously described in this text, correct if necessary.

2. Place neoprene spacer in position on back of brake support plate with steel sleeve in the center of support.

3. Position brake assembly and anchor pin on end of extension, be sure spacer sleeve remains in center of support. Align anchor pin hole with hole in front lug and install lock pin.

4. Install grease shield, with flat on the shield aligned with flat on extension housing. Install grease shield retainer spring with opening of spring toward brake shoe adjusting nut. Be sure the spring is properly seated in the groove.

5. Slide the brake shoe return spring behind the grease shield spring and hook it into position.

6. Install the brake drum and flange assembly, washer and nut. Torque the nut to 175 ft. lb.

TROUBLE SHOOTING

OIL BACKS OUT FILLER TUBE

Probable Causes:

1. High oil level, foaming.
2. Clogged vent hole.
3. Stuck converter valve.
4. Front or rear pumps sucking air.
5. Water in the oil.
6. Band or clutch failure, causing lining debris to stick valves in valve body.

HARSH "N"-"D" OR "N"-"R" SHIFTS

Probable Causes:

1. High engine RPM.
2. Poor throttle linkage adjustment.
3. Line pressure incorrect.

LIGHT THROTTLE SHIFT POINTS HIGH AND/OR HARSH

Probable Causes:

1. Poor throttle linkage adjustment.
2. Throttle pressure adjustment in valve body.
3. Clogged valve body or governor.
4. Damaged throttle valve operating lever.

1-2 LIGHT THROTTLE SHIFT BUMP

Probable Causes:

1. Poor throttle linkage adjustment.
2. Throttle pressure adjustment in valve body.
3. Stuck rings on kickdown piston or accumulator piston.

2-3 UPSHIFT AND 3-2 KICKDOWN HARSH

Probable Causes:

1. Poor throttle linkage adjustment.
2. Kickdown band adjustment too high.
3. Engine not properly tuned.

3-1 DOWNSHIFT ABOVE 20 M.P.H.

Probable Causes:

1. Governor valve stuck.
2. 1-2 shift valve stuck.
3. Line pressure or throttle pressure adjusted too high.

2-3 UPSHIFT AND 3-2 KICKDOWN SLIPPAGE

Probable Causes:
1. Poor throttle linkage adjustment.
2. Push button cable adjustment.
3. Kickdown band adjustment loose.
4. Stuck rings on kickdown piston.
5. Low oil level.
6. Excessive ring clearance on kickdown piston or on input shaft or broken oil ring on input shaft.
7. Stuck shuttle valve or plug.
8. Damaged throttle valve operating lever.

NO DOWNSHIFT AT STOP

Probable Causes:
1. Stuck governor valve.
2. Stuck 1-2 shift valve.

ERRATIC SHIFTS

Probable Causes:
1. Oil level incorrect.
2. Cable adjustment.
3. Sticking valves.
4. Stuck rings on kickdown piston.
5. Sticking governor valve.
6. Throttle pressure adjustment screw loose or lever bent.

1-3 UPSHIFT

Probable Causes:
1. Governor valve stuck.
2. 2-3 shift valve sticking.
3. Throttle pressure adjustment.
4. Kickdown band too lose or damaged.

NO SHIFTS

Probable Causes:
1. Control cable disconnected.
2. Not enough fluid.
3. Broken front pump or drive sleeve.
4. Clogged oil passage.
5. Clogged valve body.

NO DRIVE IN ANY GEAR

Probable Causes:
1. Not enough oil.
2. Manual lever disconnected.
3. Broken front pump drive.
4. Stuck regulator valve (no line pressure).

NO REVERSE

Probable Causes:
1. Governor valve stuck.
2. Stuck reverse blocker valve.
3. Control cable adjustment.

NO WIDE OPEN THROTTLE UPSHIFTS

(LIGHT THROTTLE UPSHIFT O.K.)

Probable Causes:
1. Throttle pressure adjustment.
2. Throttle linkage adjustment.
3. Excessive line pressure, (must not exceed 98 PSI at 3000 RPM).
4. Poor engine performance.
5. Governor malfunction.

DRIVES IN NEUTRAL

Probable Causes:
1. Cable adjustment incorrect.

NOISES

Noises which seem to originate in the transmission, may be caused by other items of equipment. The generator, water pump, power steering pump, exhaust line, rear axle or a wheel bearing my cause a disturbance that could be misleading. Use extreme care in diagnosis to prevent needless cost and embarrassment.

FRONT PUMP NOISE

Probable Causes:
1. Converter housing runout.
2. Imperfect pump gears.
3. Worn bushing in front pump and reaction shaft support.
4. Damaged front pump drive sleeve.

PARKING SPRAG NOISE

Probable Causes:
1. Improper adjustment.

FRONT CLUTCH NOISE

Probable Causes:
1. Squealing noise on heavy throttle breakaway indicates a failing front clutch.

WHINE IN 1st & 2nd ONLY

Probable Causes:
1. Damaged gear teeth.
2. Damaged thrust washer at sun gear driving shell.

GOVERNOR BUZZ

Probable Causes:
1. Not enough oil.
2. Governor assembly.

ROAD TESTING

NEUTRAL

Engage "N" button (car should not creep). Increase engine RPM to 1500, there should be no indication of car movement. If movement is evident, check push button cable adjustment.

NEUTRAL TO DRIVE—

NEUTRAL TO REVERSE

With engine at normal idle speed, shift the transmission from "N" to "D" and "N" to "R" several times. The shift should occur quickly and smoothly. With light throttle opening, shift from "D" to "R" and "R" to "D". Shifts should occur immediately.

SHIFT QUALITY—DRIVE

With very light throttle opening, gradually increase car speed to 25 MPH. At car speed of about 7-11 MPH, the 1-2 shift should occur. A light bump is normal but, if the shift is harsh or has a delayed feeling (with a bump as the shift is completed), the throttle linkage may be improperly adjustde. At 10-14 MPH, the 2-3 shift should occur. The shift should not be harsh and there should be no indication of engine runaway.

Quality of the 2-3 shift is also affected by throttle linkage adjustment. Shifts at half throttle opening should be very smooth. Normal shifts near wide open throttle position may be firm to sharp, but there should be no indication of engine runaway.

3-2 AND 3-1 KICKDOWN

Check 3-2 kickdown at 50-60 MPH with fully depressed accelerator pedal. Check 3-1 kickdown at 25-30 MPH. Kickdowns should be firm but smooth, with no indication of excessive runaway.

3-1 CLOSED THROTTLE DOWNSHIFT

The transmission should downshift at about 6-10 MPH at closed throttle. The downshift is from direct drive ratio to first gear, without going through second. Downshift cannot be felt, however, if downshift has not occured, car performance will be sluggish when accelerated.

SELECTIVE LOW & SECOND

With car in "D", at a speed of 45 mph., push in the #2 button. The transmission should downshift smoothly to second gear. Reduce speed to 20 mph. and push in #1 button. Car should downshift to low gear.

With #1 button engaged, bring car to full stop, then accelerate to 35 mph., transmission should not upshift.

Bring car to full stop and engage #2 button. With light throttle opening, increase car speed to 20 mph., transmission should upshift to second gear at 7-11 mph.

REVERSE

With idled engine, shift from "N" to "R". Transmission should shift into reverse smoothly. Try several quick, light throttle accelerations for rear band or front clutch slippage.

TROUBLE CHECK WHILE ROAD TESTING

Front Clutch Slippage

With vehicle standing still, engage "D" button. after the front clutch has been fully engaged, accelerate quickly to ¾ throttle. If engine speed in- creases rapidly but vehicle response is slow, the clutch is not holding. (Se- vere clutch slippage is often accom- panied by a squealing noise.)

Rear Clutch Slippage

Rear clutch slippage can be difficult to diagnose. If the rear clutch can be made to slip by heavy throttle ac- celeration while upshifted, the clutch pack will probably be near complete failure. Prolonged operation of the vehicle when there is slippage during the 2-3 upshift will fail the clutch. Slippage and subsequent failure of the clutch may be due to leakage and low hydraulic pressure that exists only during the shift. It may not be apparent by measuring rear clutch pressure after the upshift.

Slippage in Reverse

In reverse, the front clutch and rear band are applied. If the trans- mission operates normally in "D" range but slips in reverse, reverse band adjustment should be checked first. If this adjustment is correct, check the following items in sequence:
Push button cable adjustment.
Line pressure.
Rear servo pressure.

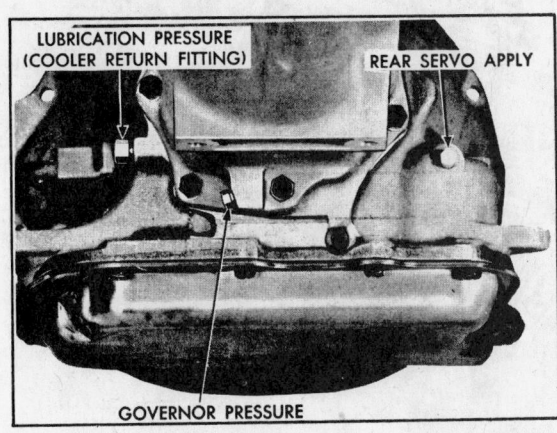

Pressure test locations

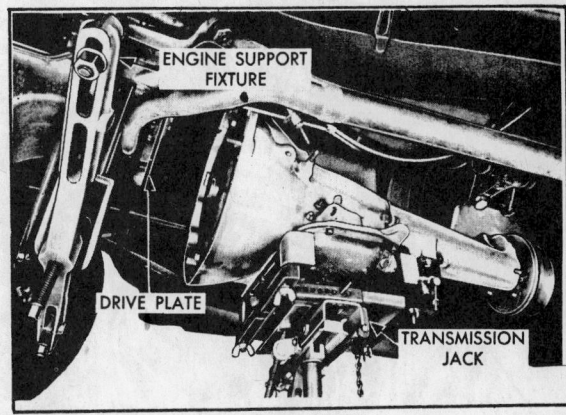

Removing or installing transmission and converter assembly

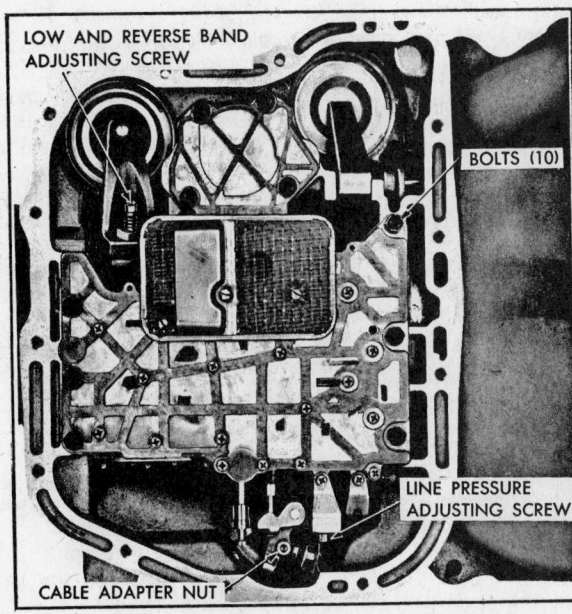

Bottom view of transmission (pan removed)

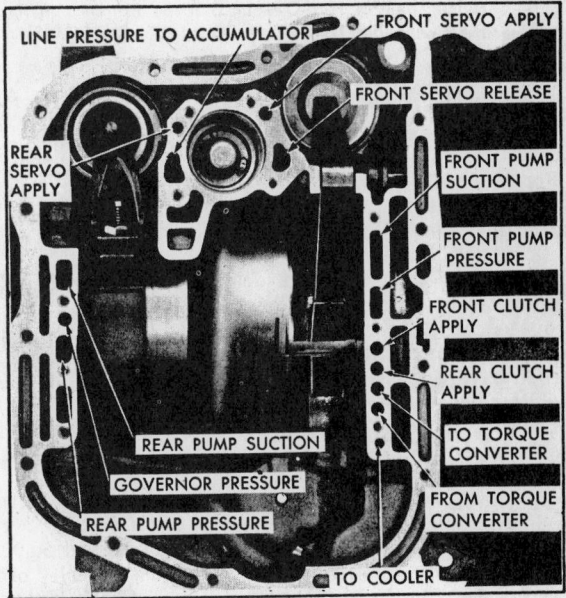

Air pressure tests

AUTOMATIC TRANSMISSION

AUTOMATIC TRANSMISSION AS USED ON FORD (FORDOMATIC), MERCURY (MERC-O-MATIC) LINCOLN AND CONTINENTAL (TURBO-DRIVE), STUDEBAKER (FLIGHTOMATIC), RAMBLER (FLASH-O-MATIC), EDSEL (AUTOMATIC), AND (WITH NEW VALVING AND A NEW ONE-WAY CLUTCH) THE "HIGH PERFORMANCE" 3-SPEED TRANSMISSION (CRUISE-O-MATIC)

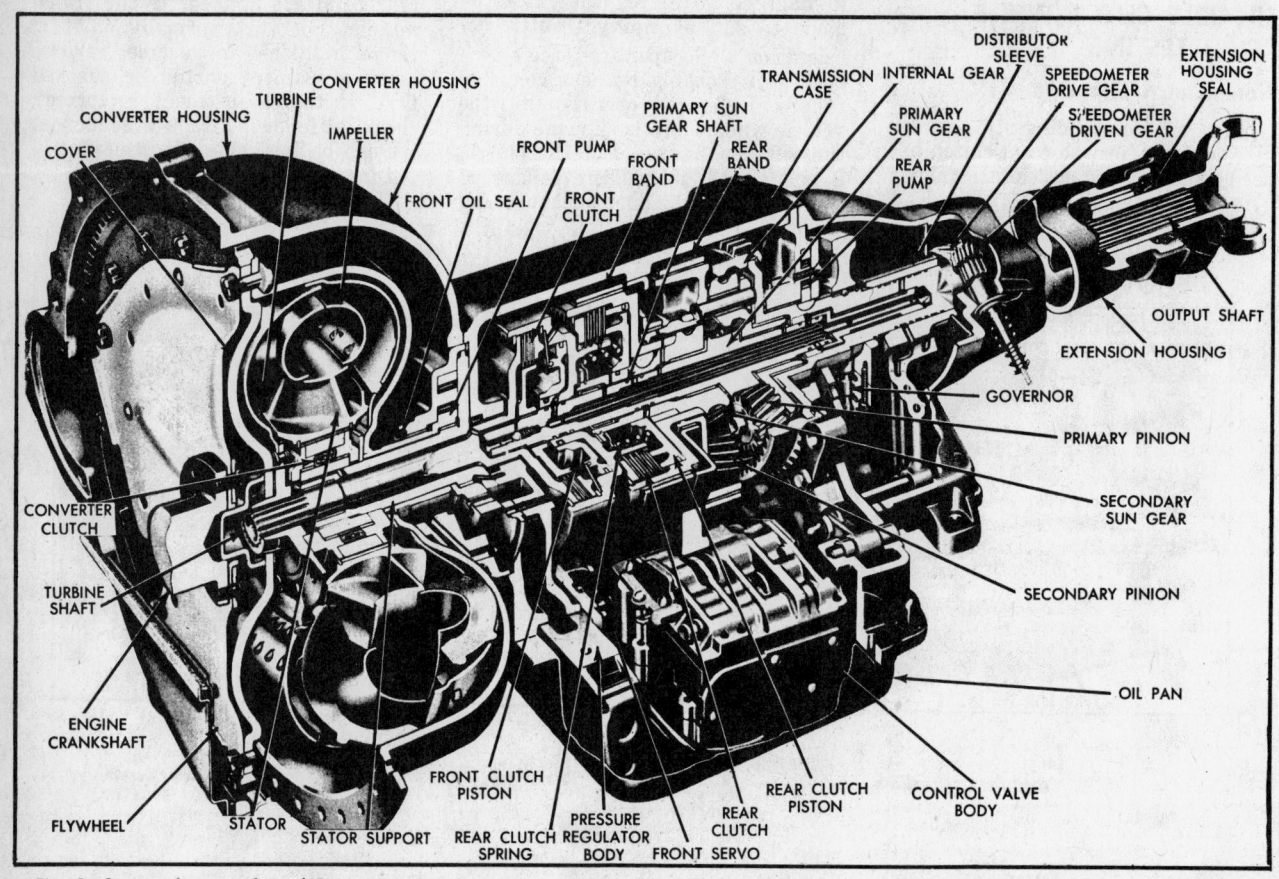

Fig. 1—Sectional view of Ford-O-Matic 3 speed transmission thru 1959, also typical Mercury (Merc-O-Matic), Edsel ,Automatic, 1958), Lincoln & Continental (Turbo-Drive, thru 1957), Rambler (Flash-O-Matic, thru 1958), and Studebaker (Flight-O-Matic) exc. OHV-6.

GENERAL INFORMATION

Ford's new Cruise-O-Matic transmission, introduced in 1958, is essentially the same as earlier Ford-O-Matic models. It differs only in clutch and hydraulic control system design and operation. This transmission is also used on Mercury (multi-drive), Lincoln & Continental (twin range turbo drive), Edsel (dual power), and Rambler (flash-o-matic).

Cruise-O-Matic is equipped with a sprag clutch which is incorporated in the pinion carrier (Fig. 54). This sprag clutch, by holding the planet carrier stationary, provides the transmission with an additional manually selected driving range.

Differences in Ford-O-Matic and Cruise-O-Matic control valves are shown in figures 17 thru 21.

The Cruise-O-Matic transmission for 1961 is equipped with vacuum throttle valve controls. By improving the method by which the accelerator setting is relayed to the transmission it provides smoother shifting, and more accurate response to the driver's foot pressure.

This new system eliminates periodic adjustment since the shift quality and timing are built into the transmission, independent of any external adjustments.

CHECKING FLUID LEVEL— ALL MODELS

Check fluid level every 1,000 miles.

Drain and refill beteween 15,000 miles and 25,000 miles, depending on the severity of use.

Check the level when engine is at operating temperature. Have hand lever at neutral and engine idling.

On some models the dipstick is under the front floor mat to the right of center. On other models it is in the right rear corner of the engine compartment.

Remove the dipstick. The level should be at the F mark. Add or drain fluid to make it so. Do not overfill as then the planetary gears will aerate the fluid and cause trouble. Average total capacity is 10 quarts.

Use a good grade of automatic transmission fluid.

DRAINING PROCEDURE

Remove the plate on the lower front face of the bell housing.

Remove a converter drain plug. Rotate the converter 180 deg. and remove the other drain plug.

The drain plugs are located on a smaller circle than that of the primary pump attaching bolts.

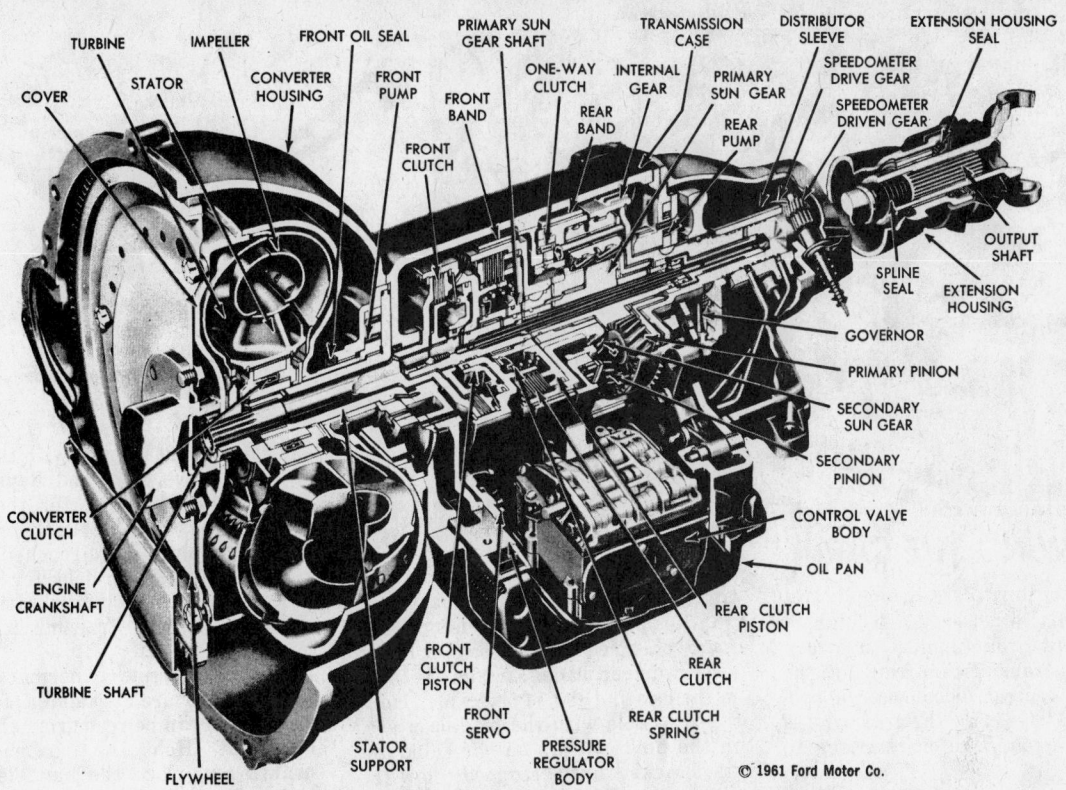

TURBINE IMPELLER FRONT OIL SEAL PRIMARY SUN GEAR SHAFT TRANSMISSION CASE DISTRIBUTOR SLEEVE EXTENSION HOUSING SEAL

STATOR CONVERTER HOUSING FRONT PUMP ONE-WAY CLUTCH INTERNAL GEAR PRIMARY SUN GEAR SPEEDOMETER DRIVE GEAR

COVER FRONT BAND REAR BAND REAR PUMP SPEEDOMETER DRIVEN GEAR

FRONT CLUTCH OUTPUT SHAFT

SPLINE SEAL EXTENSION HOUSING

GOVERNOR

PRIMARY PINION

SECONDARY SUN GEAR

SECONDARY PINION

CONTROL VALVE BODY

CONVERTER CLUTCH OIL PAN

ENGINE CRANKSHAFT REAR CLUTCH PISTON

REAR CLUTCH

TURBINE SHAFT

FRONT CLUTCH PISTON FRONT SERVO REAR CLUTCH SPRING

STATOR SUPPORT PRESSURE REGULATOR BODY

FLYWHEEL © 1961 Ford Motor Co.

*Fig. 2—Sectional view of Ford Cruise-O-Matic transmission 1958-63,
also typical Mercury (Multi-Drive), Edsel (Dual Power 1959-60) Lincoln
& Continental (Twin Range Turbo Drive) and Rambler (Flash-O-Matic,
1959-63) Studebaker OHV-6*

Remove the plug from the forward edge of the transmission oil pan. On some models the transmission case drain plug is on the right side of the pan.

Note: On models equipped with underhood filler tube the tube connects to the drain hole. Loosen the hex nut and move the filler tube away from the drain hole, to drain the case.

When reinstalling the drain plugs: Tighten the transmission case drain plug to 20-25 ft. lbs. Tighten the converter drain plugs to 15-25 ft. lbs. Add 5 qts. of fluid.

Run the engine at idle for two minutes then add 4 more quarts. Let transmission idle until it comes up to normal temperature. Move the hand lever to all the positions so that all the valves are full. Return hand lever to Park and check that level is at the full mark.

COOLING AND SEALS

If the oil seals suddenly give way the trouble may be due to overheating of the transmission. Be sure to clean out the air intake, on air cooled models. Be sure to clean the lines and cooler on water cooled models.

BAND ADJUSTMENT

Note: The use of two special wrenches (which release at 10 in. lb.) is recommended for these operations. Adjust the bands every 15,000 miles.

FRONT BAND

Drain the transmission and remove the oil pan.

Insert a $\frac{1}{4}$" gage block between the front servo piston's stem and the band actuating lever. Fig. 3.

Loosen the adjusting screw lock nut and tighten the screw to 10 in. lb. Back off and retighten if necessary to be certain that the screw is as near to being exactly 10 in. lb. tight as is possible.

Back the adjusting screw off exactly one turn and tighten the lock nut to 20-25 ft. lb.

Remove the gage block. Replace oil pan, add new fluid.

REAR BAND

Remove the cover plate in the right front floor of the front compartment.

Loosen the lock nut and tighten the adjusting screw to exactly 10 ft. lb. Fig. 4.

Back off and retighten if necessary to be certain the screw is as near to being exactly 10 ft. lb. tight as is possible.

Back the screw off exactly one and one-half (1½) turns.

Tighten the lock nut to 35-40 ft. lb. Replace cover plate.

© 1961 Ford Motor Co.

TOOL 7225-C13-B

Fig. 3—Adjusting front band

AUTOMATIC TRANSMISSION

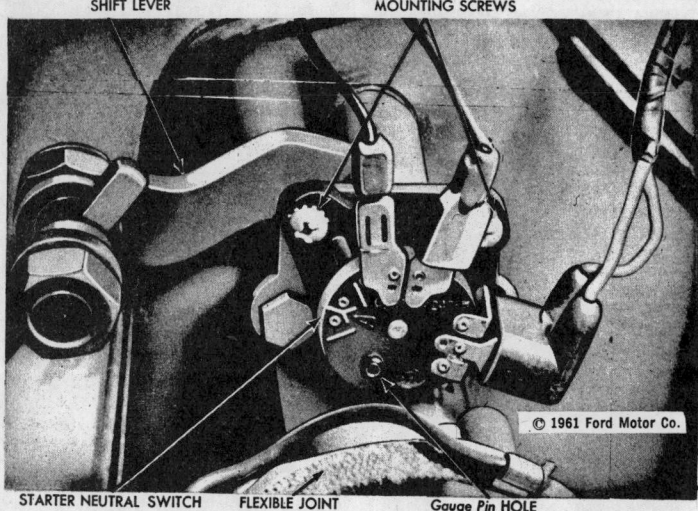

SHIFT LEVER   MOUNTING SCREWS

© 1961 Ford Motor Co.

STARTER NEUTRAL SWITCH   FLEXIBLE JOINT   *Gauge Pin* HOLE

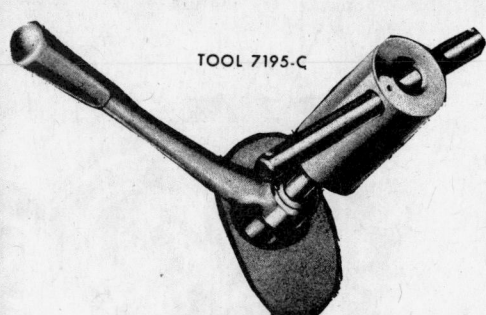

TOOL 7195-C

Fig. 4—Adjusting rear band

TOWING THE CAR

For short tows place the hand lever in Neutral. Do not exceed 40 mph.

For trips over 12 miles or whenever the transmission can not be placed in Neutral, disconnect the propeller shaft or raise the rear wheels from the ground before starting to move the car.

STARTING THE CAR WITHOUT USE OF THE STARTER

<u>Caution:</u> Never tow the car to start. As with all cars equipped with automatic transmissions the engine will pick up very quickly and the towed car is likely to hit the towing car before the brakes can be applied.

Turn on the ignition and hold the hand lever at Neutral until the car has attained a speed of 20 mph or more.

Now move the hand lever to Low and the engine will turn.

Note on Edsel with Tele-Touch Control

Hold in Neutral until 30mph is reached, then push button marked Dr.

DASH MOUNTED PUSH BUTTON MANUAL CONTROL

Remove the pipe plug from the left side of the case near the levers. Disconnect the park release cable and clamp at the transmission. **Note:** The park release cable must be disconnected before the manual control cable can be worked on.

Loosen the screw which holds the manual control cable bracket to the transmission case.

Hold the push button marked "D"

all the way in.

Move the cable bracket at the transmission down as far as it will go. Reach thru the opening (formerly occupied by the pipe plug) with a screwdriver blade. Engage the blade in the locating slot of the cable. Holding the cable with the blade centered in the hole, pull up on the cable and its bracket until stopped, now retighten the bracket screw to 18-22 ft. lbs. Remove the screwdriver, replace the pipe plug and check the operation of the push buttons.

Now proceed to adjust the park release cable.

Hold the PARK BAR depressed. Replace the park release cable and clamp. Turn the lever clockwise to its stop. Remove cable slack by adjusting the cable sheath forward or back thru the clamp. Check that the parking pawl is engaged. Do the checking by jacking up a rear wheel and trying to turn it. If the parking pawl is engaged the wheel will not turn. Hold the assemby so and tighten the cable clamp. <u>Note:</u> There is a gauge available to control the position of the lever. The tolerance is pretty small and that is why the above check should be made if the gauge is not available.

Now release the parking bar on the dash and check that the parking pawl is released. If not, release the cable clamp and move the cable and sheath ⅛ inch forward. Refasten and recheck that PARK is engaged when bar is pushed in.

TROUBLE SHOOTING

PRELIMINARY CHECKS

Check the fluid level, the idling speed, the operation of the dashpot, the throttle and manual linkages, and then apply the stall test.

STALL TEST

The stall test is made with the hand lever in Drive, Low and Reverse, to find whether the converter, the bands and clutches are working properly. The high engine RPM reached in this test should not be held for over 5 seconds at a time or overheating and damage to the transmission will result.

Have the engine at normal operating temperature. Attach a tachometer which can be read from the driver's seat. Hold the car with the brakes and place the hand lever at Drive. Press the accelerator down until the detent is reached. Do not go thru the detent or the transmission will shift to low.

The stall spead RPM point at which engine RPM's do not increase should agree with the table.

Model		Stall Speed RPM
Ford	6	1370-1570
Ford	V8	1530-1730
Lincoln	312	1530-1730
Mercury	383	1640-1840
Mercury	430	1690-1890
Rambler	10	1400
Rambler	20	1575
Rambler	80	1600
Studebaker	G—LH-6	1250-1400
Studebaker	G—OHV-6	1500-1600
Studebaker	B	1550-1650
Studebaker	H	1750-1850

Readings below those given usually mean that the stator one-way clutch in the convertor is not working correctly.

A road test will help to pinpoint just what is wrong with the stator clutch. If the stall RPM's are 300 to 400 below those in the table, and: The car has very poor acceleration, although able to cruise properly. The stator clutch is slipping. Check the stator clutch springs and races for flat spots and wear.

The car will not cruise properly and acceleration is very poor. The stator clutch is in backwards.

CONTINENTAL
EDSEL
FORD
LINCOLN
MERCURY
RAMBLER
STUDEBAKER

The Rambler and Studebaker Torque Converters are only serviced as assemblies. They are sealed units.

If the stall test RPM's were correct and the car's acceleration is OK but it drags at cruising speeds, the stator has seized. Check the races for scores.

Readings higher than those given in the table indicate slipping bands or clutches inside the transmission. In Drive, these could be the Front Band or Front Clutch.

Move the hand lever to Low and again push down on the accelerator. If the stall speed is high, the Front Clutch is slipping. If there was slipping in Drive but there is none in Low, the Front Band is at fault.

Move the hand lever to Reverse and again depress the accelerator. Readings above those given in the table indicate slippage of the Rear Clutch.

If slippage is evident only in Low and Reverse, the Rear Band is slipping.

AIR PRESSURE CHECKS

In case of No Drive in one or more ranges or erratic shifting, the items at fault can be determined by using air pressure on the indicated passages.

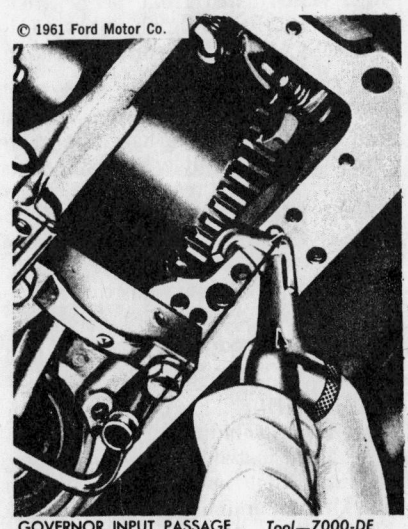

GOVERNOR INPUT PASSAGE   Tool—7000-DE

Fig. 5—Front Clutch and Governor passage

Drain the transmission and remove the oil pan and the control valve assembly. Have a rag handy to protect you from the oil spray.

FRONT CLUTCH

Apply sufficient air pressure to the front clutch input passage. Fig. 4. A dull thud can be heard when the clutch piston moves. Check also for leaks.

GOVERNOR

Remove the governor inspection cover from the extension housing. Apply air to the front clutch input passage. Fig. 5. Listen for a sharp click and watch to see if the governor valve snaps inward as it should.

REAR CLUTCH INPUT PASSAGE   Tool   © 1961 Ford Motor Co.

Fig. 6—Rear Clutch Apply Passage

REAR CLUTCH

Apply air to the rear clutch passage Fig. 6 and listen for the dull thud that will indicate that the rear clutch piston has moved. Listen also for leaks.

FRONT SERVO

Apply air pressure to the front servo apply tube Fig. 7 and note if front band tightens. Shift the air to the front servo release tube which is next to the apply tube and watch band release.

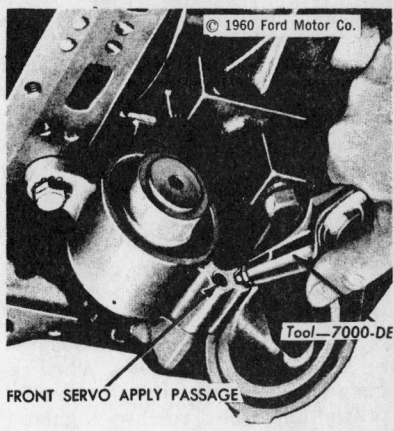

© 1960 Ford Motor Co.

Tool—7000-DE

FRONT SERVO APPLY PASSAGE

Fig. 7—Front Servo Apply Tube

© 1961 Ford Motor Co.

REAR SERVO APPLY PASSAGE

TOOL 7000-DE

Fig. 8—Rear Servo Apply Passage

TABLE SHOWING PRESSURE RANGES

Make and Model		Idle All	Engine Speed and Selector Lever Position		
			1000 RPM DR	Stall DR	R
Ford	223	49-63 psi	80-85 psi	124-155 psi	173-195 psi
Products	272	51-69 psi	80-85 psi	133-165 psi	181-205 psi
	292	51-69 psi	80-85 psi	133-165 psi	181-205 psi
312, 332, 361, 410		55-70 psi	80-85 psi	194-216 psi	194-216 psi
Rambler		50-80 psi	80-85 psi	130-175 psi	170-190 psi
Studebaker		50-80 psi	80-85 psi	130-175 psi	170-190 psi

AUTOMATIC TRANSMISSION

REAR SERVO

Apply air pressure into the rear servo apply passage. The rear band should tighten around the drum.

Conclusions

If the operation of the servos and clutches is normal with air pressure the No-Drive condition is due to the control valve and pressure regulator valve assemblies which should be disassembled, cleaned and inspected.

If operation of the clutches is not normal; that is, if both clutches apply from one passage or if one fails to move, the aluminum sleeve (bushing) in the output shaft is out of position or badly worn. Fig. 10.

Use air pressure to check the passages in the sleeve and shaft and also check the passages in the primary sun gear shaft.

If the passages in the two shafts and the sleeve are clean, remove the clutch assemblies, clean and inspect the parts.

Erratic operation can also be caused by loose valve body screws. When reinstalling the valve body be careful to tighten: the pressure regulator valve to case bolts to 17-22 ft. lbs.; the pressure regulator valve cover screws to 20-30 in. lbs. The control valve body screws to 20-30 in. lbs.; the 1/4-20 capscrew (lower to upper valve body) to 4-6 ft. lbs.; control valve body to case bolts to 8-10 ft. lbs.

TROUBLE SHOOTING CHART

Trouble: Severe Engagement in All Ranges

PROBABLE CAUSES: Idle speed too high. Throttle linkage out of adjustment, rear band out of adjustment.

REMEDY: Adjust the idle speed. Adjust the throttle linkage. Tighten the rear band. If these fail to clear the trouble run the pressure check detailed under throttle linkage adjustment. If the pressures are low or erratic remove and overhaul the valve body.

Trouble: The Shift from Intermediate to High Occurs at too High or Low a Speed or Erratically

PROBABLE CAUSES: Low fluid level. Maladjusted manual and throttle linkage. Governor weight sticking.

REMEDY: Check the fluid level. Readjust the manual and throttle linkage. The pressure check portion of the throttle adjustment procedure should give some clue as to the specific item after which application of the air pressure check should pinpoint the item.

Trouble: Shift from Intermediate to High is too Severe, or Engine Overspeeds during Shift

PROBABLE CAUSES: Maladjusted throttle linkage. Maladjusted front band. Sticking valves or front servo.

REMEDY: Readjust the throttle linkage, overhaul the control valve and the pressure regulator valve. Remove, clean and reassemble the front servo. Readjust the front band.

Trouble: Shift from Intermediate to High Does Not Take Place

PROBABLE CAUSES: Governor stuck. Valve body dirty. Rear clutch sticking. Leakage at the valve body. Aluminum sleeve in output shaft has turned out of position.

REMEDY: Perform the air pressure check to find the unit at fault.

Trouble: Shift from High to Intermediate cannot be Forced (No Forced Downshift)

PROBABLE CAUSES: Malad-justed throttle linkage. Sticking valves. Throttle valve stop inside transmission requires adjustment.

REMEDY: Apply the full procedure for throttle linkage adjustment.

Trouble: Shift from High to Intermediate with Throttle Closed is too Severe

PROBABLE CAUSES: Improper engine idle speed. Maladjusted throttle linkage. Sticking valves in valve body.

REMEDY: Apply the full procedure for throttle linkage adjustment. Remove and overhaul the valve body.

Trouble: Excessive Creeping when in Drive

PROBABLE CAUSE: Engine idle speed too high.

REMEDY: Adjust engine idle speed to 425-450 with hand lever at Drive.

Trouble: Slippage or Chatter in Intermediate

PROBABLE CAUSES: Wrong fluid level. Maladjusted throttle linkage. Maladjusted front band. Sticking valves. Front clutch not working correctly. Leaks in hydraulic system.

REMEDY: Check the fluid level. Adjust the throttle linkage. Adjust the front band. Overhaul the valve body. If the trouble persists apply the air pressure tests to find if the trouble is due to leaks or to malfunction of the front clutch. Overhaul of the front clutch will require removal of the transmission from the car.

Trouble: Slippage or Chatter in Low or Reverse

PROBABLE CAUSES: Wrong fluid level. Maladjusted throttle linkage. Maladjusted rear band. Sticking valves. Front or rear clutches not working. Aluminum sleeve in output shaft has turned.

REMEDY: Check the fluid level. Apply the full procedure for adjusting the throttle linkage. Adjust the rear band. Overhaul the valve body. If the trouble persists apply to air pressure checks to see which clutch is at fault or if the trouble is due to the aluminum sleeve in the output shaft. Fig. 10. This sleeve is available as a spare part. Design of the sleeve varies from year to year so be sure the new one matches the old. The transmission must be out of the car for clutch removal.

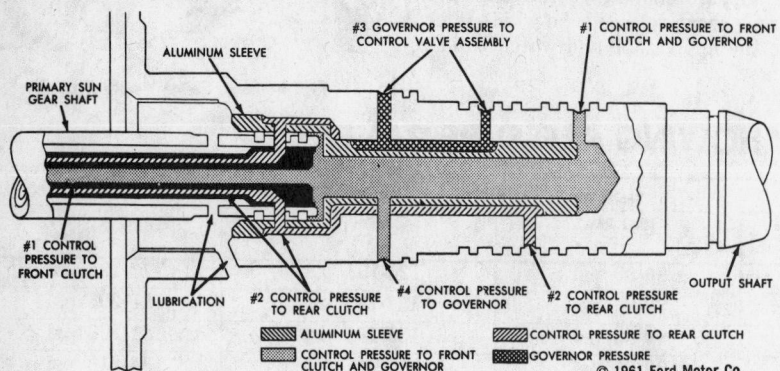

Fig. 10—Cutaway view of front end of Output Shaft showing destination of passages in replaceable aluminum bushing (sleeve)

© 1961 Ford Motor Co.

Trouble: Will Not Move in Drive. Other Ranges OK

PROBABLE CAUSES: Maladjusted front band, sticking valves, malfunctioning front clutch. Leaks in the hydraulic system. Aluminum sleeve in output shaft is out of position.

REMEDY: Adjust the front band. Overhaul the valve body. Apply air pressure tests to determine if the sleeve or the clutch is at fault. Overhaul of the clutch requires removal of the transmission from the car.

Trouble: Will Not Move in Reverse. Will Not Move in Low Only.

PROBABLE CAUSES: Maladjusted rear band. Maladjusted manual control linkage. Stuck valves. Malfunctioning rear servo or clutch. Aluminum sleeve in output shaft has shifted.

REMEDY: Adjust rear band. Adjust manual control linkage. Overhaul valve body. Use air pressure to check operation of the servo and clutch. It will be necessary to remove the transmission to overhaul the clutch.

Trouble: No Drive in Any Range

PROBABLE CAUSES: Improper fluid level. Maladjusted manual linkage. Malfunctioning fluid system. Rear band or servo inoperative. Converter not working.

REMEDY: Correct the fluid level. Adjust the manual linkage. Apply the fluid pressure checks outlined in the second part of the throttle linkage adjustment procedure. Apply the air pressure checks. Check engine stall speed to diagnose trouble in converter.

Trouble: Locks Up in Drive

PROBABLE CAUSES: Maladjusted manual linkage. Maladjusted rear band. Rear servo stuck. Front servo stuck. Rear clutch not working, hydraulic system leaking. Parking linkage out of adjustment.

REMEDY: Readjust the manual linkage, being careful to check operation of the parking lock. Readjust the rear band. Use the air pressure check procedure to find which item is stuck or leaking.

Trouble: Locks Up in Reverse

PROBABLE CAUSES: Maladjusted front band. Inoperative front servo or front clutch. Leakage in the hydraulic system. Parking linkage out of adjustment.

REMEDY: Readjust the front band and check operation of the manual linkage. Use the air pressure check procedure to find the leaks and inoperative assemblies. Clean the control valve assembly.

Trouble: Locks Up in Low

PROBABLE CAUSES: Maladjusted front band. Inoperative front servo or rear clutch. Stuck or leaking valves.

REMEDY: Adjust the front band. Overhaul the valve body. Use air pressure check procedure to find inoperative assemblies.

Trouble: Unable to Start Engine by Pushing

PROBABLE CAUSES: Low fluid level. Maladjusted manual linkage. Pressure regulator valve sticking. Rear pump inoperative. Leaks in hydraulic system.

REMEDY: Check and correct fluid level. Readjust manual linkage. Remove and overhaul valve body. Remove rear extension and check over rear pump. Use air pressure to find leaks in hydraulic system.

Trouble: Transmission Overheats

PROBABLE CAUSES: Oil cooler or lines stopped up. Air passages to converter housing plugged. Pressure regulator valve stuck. Stator clutch stuck.

REMEDY: Check over oil cooler and lines. Clean the air passages to the converter. Remove and clean the pressure regulator valve assembly. Use the stall test procedure to check condition of stator clutch.

Trouble: Engine Runaway on Forced Downshift

PROBABLE CAUSES: Maladjusted front band or inoperative front servo. Leaks in hydraulic system or sticking valves in valve body.

REMEDY: Readjust front band. Use air pressure check procedure to pinpoint leaks and inoperative assemblies. Overhaul valve body.

Trouble: No 2-1 Downshift

PROBABLE CAUSES: Maladjusted throttle linkage. Dirt in valve body. Inoperative rear servo.

REMEDY: Adjust the throttle linkage. Overhaul the valve body assembly. Use air pressure to check operation of rear servo.

CONTINENTAL
EDSEL
FORD
LINCOLN
MERCURY
RAMBLER
STUDEBAKER

Trouble: Car Will Not Accelerate Properly. Will Not Get out of its Own Way

PROBABLE CAUSE: Stator clutch in converter is inoperative.

REMEDY: Use Stall Test procedure to check operation of stator clutch. Transmission must be removed from the car for overhaul of the stator clutch.

Trouble: Noise in Neutral

PROBABLE CAUSES: Pressure regulator valve not working correctly. Engine crankshaft end play excessive. Front clutch defective. Front oil pump not correctly assembled.

REMEDY: Overhaul the pressure regulator valve. Use the air pressure check procedure to investigate the front clutch. Remove transmission from car and overhaul front pump and check crankshaft end play.

Trouble: Noise when Hand Lever is Moved to Drive, Low or Reverse

PROBABLE CAUSES: Pressure regulator valve defective. Planetary gearing worn. Front or rear clutches defective. Front pump defective.

REMEDY: Overhaul pressure regulator valve. Remove transmission from car and overhaul the planetary assemblies, the clutches and the front oil pump.

Trouble: Noise when Hand Lever is at Park

PROBABLE CAUSES: Defective pressure regulator valve. Defective front pump.

REMEDY: Overhaul pressure regulator valve assembly. If this does not cure trouble remove transmission from the car and overhaul the front pump.

Trouble: Noise when Car is Coasting at 30 to 20 mph with Hand Lever in Neutral and Engine Off

PROBABLE CAUSE: Defective rear pump.

REMEDY: Take off rear extension and overhaul rear pump.

LEAKS

The following troubles are classified as Leaks. The easiest way to pinpoint a leak is to introduce an aniline dye into the transmission. Add about ½ teaspoon of dye powder to a half pint of fluid and pour into transmission. Should the transmission air vent on the right side of the case become clogged, there will be generalized leakage and it will be difficult to fill the transmission.

Leaks at Converter Housing

PROBABLE CAUSES: Converter drain plugs. Converter cover bolts. Engine crankshaft rear oil seal. Defective converter cover seal. Defective front pump oil seal. Defective converter hub seal. Defective front oil pump to case gasket.

REMEDY: Remove the two converter drain plugs and coat the threads with No. 3 Permatex. Reinstall the plugs and tighten to 15-20 ft. lbs. Do not tighten the converter cover bolts while transmission is hot. When converter is cool tighten the cover bolts to 25-28 ft. lbs. If use of the dye traces proves that the leak is coming from the pump or converter, remove the transmission and replace the defective seals and gaskets.

Leak at Transmission Oil Pan

PROBABLE CAUSES: Oil pan bolts loose. Defective oil pan gasket. Distorted oil pan. Loose drain plug or filler connection.

REMEDY: Tighten the drain plug and the filler tube. Tighten the oil pan bolts to 10-13 ft lbs. If this is not effective, remove the pan and inspect for distortion, possibly caused by supporting the transmission on the oil pan instead of a cradle. If oil pan is OK install new gasket.

Leak at Left Side of Transmission Case

PROBABLE SOURCES: Manual and throttle lever shafts seals. Throttle pressure take-off plug in side of case. Center support bolt lock washer.

REMEDY: Replace seals. Put sealer on pressure take-off plug. Tighten support bolt.

Leaking at Right Side of Transmission Case

PROBABLE SOURCES: ⅛ inch pipe plug. Center support bolt lock washer. Loose oil cooler connections.

REMEDY: Put sealer on pipe plug and tighten to 10-15 ft lbs torque. Renew center support bolt lock washer. Check tightness of oil cooler with 5 pounds of air pressure. Coolers which do not hold this pressure are defective. Replace a defective cooler line or fitting.

Leakage at Front or Rear of Extension Housing

PROBABLE SOURCES: Extension housing to case gasket or lock washers. Governor inspection hole cover gasket. Extension housing rear oil seal. Speedometer driven-gear adapter seal.

REMEDY: Renew extension to case gasket and the lock washers. Note that prongs of washers must be away from case. Renew the cover gasket, the rear oil seal, the adapter seal as required.

HYDRAULIC SYSTEM TESTS WITH TRANSMISSION ON THE BENCH

After a transmission has been overhauled it can be tested on the bench to see if all is well.

Install a plug on the oil pan filler hole. Pour 4 quarts of Type A fluid into the transmission thru the speedometer gear opening.

Remove the ⅛ inch pipe plug at the pressure take off on the side of the transmission case. In order to bleed the pump of air turn the front pump drive gear at 75-100 rpm in a clockwise direction until a regular flow of transmission fluid leaves the hole.

Attach a pressure gauge to the pressure take off hole. Again turning the front pump drive gear clockwise at 75 to 100 rpm, carefully note the pressure.

The manual valve lever should be set in the Drive position, which is the second detent from the bottom.

THE PRESSURE SHOULD BE:
49 to 63 For the 6 Cyl.;
51 to 69 For the Smaller V8's;
55 to 70 for Larger V8's.

While turning the pump drive gear fast enough to maintain this pressure, push the throttle valve lever down slowly and note that a pressure rise is obtained. If the pressure drops the throttle system is leaking. The cause of low pressure is seldom due to trouble with the valves. It is more likely some leakage in a passage or a sub-assembly. Normal pressure during this test indicates that normal pressure will be reached when the transmission is back on the car. When on the bench, although the rpm's are low, the fluid is cold, whereas during operation on the car the rpm's are high and the fluid is hot. Hand cranking is advised for this test. The pressure should be the same for all positions of the manual valve lever with the throttle lever in the closed position.

If pressure is low only when manual valve lever is in Reverse, then the rear clutch apply system is at fault.

If pressure is low only when manual valve lever is in Low or Drive, the front clutch and governor apply system is at fault.

If pressure is normal only when manual valve lever is in Drive or Neutral, the rear servo apply and front servo release systems are at fault.

If pressure is normal only when manual valve lever is in Neutral, the front servo apply system is at fault.

DISASSEMBLY OF TRANSMISSION

THE GOVERNOR

This operation can be done without removing the transmission from the car.

Remove the governor inspection cover from the right side of the extension housing Fig. 13 and rotate the drive shaft until the governor appears in the opening. Remove the two screws securing the governor body to the counterweight sleeve. Be careful not to drop the bolts or the valve into the extension housing.

Remove two screws and remove the side plate. Check that the governor valve is not scored and moves freely in its bore. Blow out the passages. Check all over for burrs.

Reverse the procedure to reinstall. Be sure that the passages in the sleeve and body are aligned. The governor counterweight can only be removed when the transmission is out of the car.

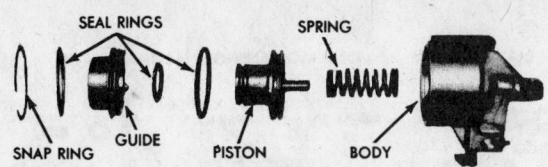

Fig. 14—Exploded view of Front Servo, Typical Ford (Ford-O-Matic), Mercury (Merc-O-Matic), Edsel (Automatic), Lincoln & Continental (Turbo Drive), Rambler (Flash-O-Matic) Studebaker (Flight-O-Matic).

CONTINENTAL EDSEL FORD LINCOLN MERCURY RAMBLER STUDEBAKER

THE FRONT SERVO

This operation can be done without removing the transmission from the car.

Drain the transmission case and remove the oil pan. Remove the lubrication tube. Loosen the control valve body attaching bolts. Remove the front servo attaching bolt and, holding the front band strut in place with the fingers, remove the servo.

Apply pressure to the servo piston and remove the guide retaining snap ring. Remove the piston and guide from the servo body. Remove the spring from the body and the guide from the piston. Fig. 14 & 15.

Inspect the body for cracks, the piston for scores, the actuating lever for free movement, and the spring for distortion.

Reverse the procedure to assemble and install. Use new seal rings on the piston and the guide.

© 1961 Ford Motor Co.

ATTACHING SCREWS   GOVERNOR BODY

Fig. 13—Remove inspection plate from rear extension

With the oil pan off and the lubrication tube out, remove the servo attaching bolts. Hold the rear band struts in place and remove the rear servo.

Drive the servo actuating lever shaft retaining pin out with a 1/8 in. punch and remove the shaft and lever. Push in on the spring retainer and remove the retainer snap ring. Release the pressure slowly and remove the retainer and the spring. Use air pressure to force the piston out of its bore. Fig. 16.

Inspect the servo body for cracks and the piston for scores. Check the lever and shaft for wear. Check the spring for distortion. Blow out the passages.

Reverse the procedure to assemble.

THE REAR SERVO

This operation can be done without removing the transmission from the car.

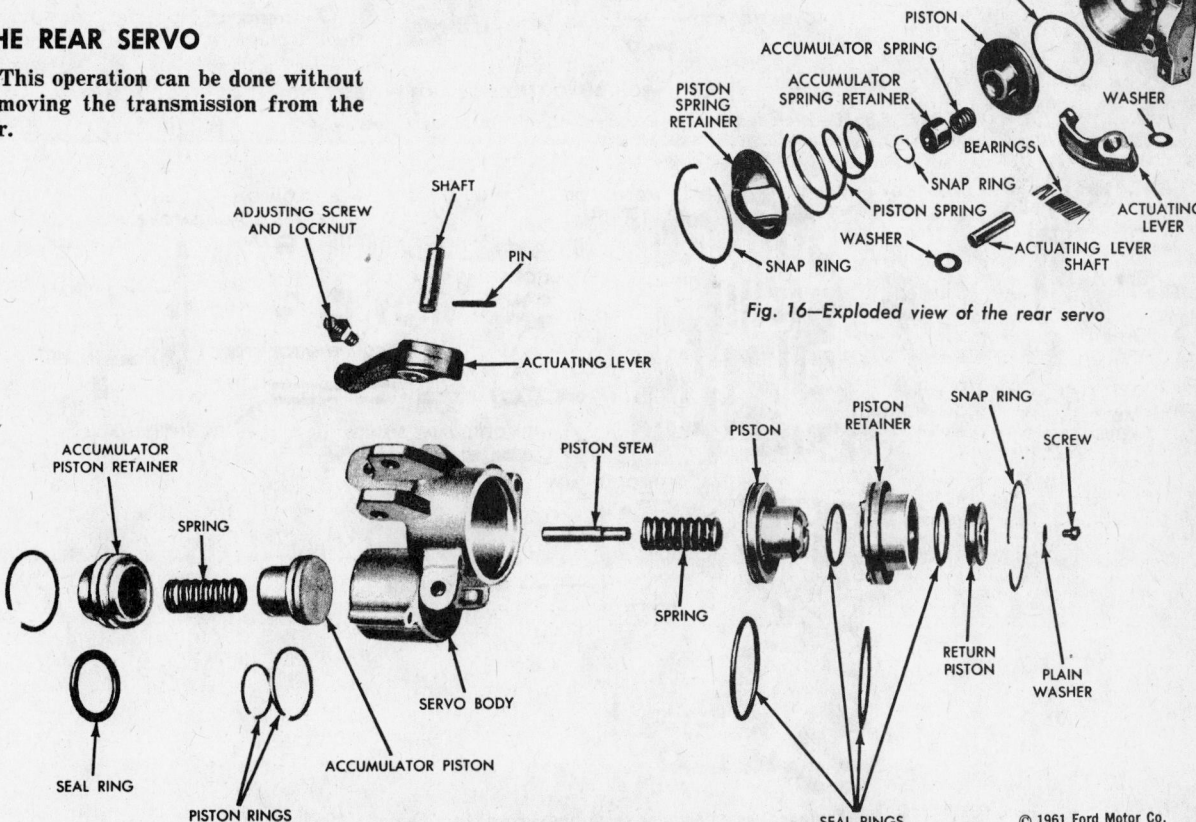

© 1960 Ford Motor Co.

Fig. 16—Exploded view of the rear servo

Fig. 15—Exploded view of front servo, typical Ford (Cruise-O-Matic), Mercury (Multi-Drive), Edsel (Dual Power) Lincoln & Continental (Twin Range Turbo Drive).

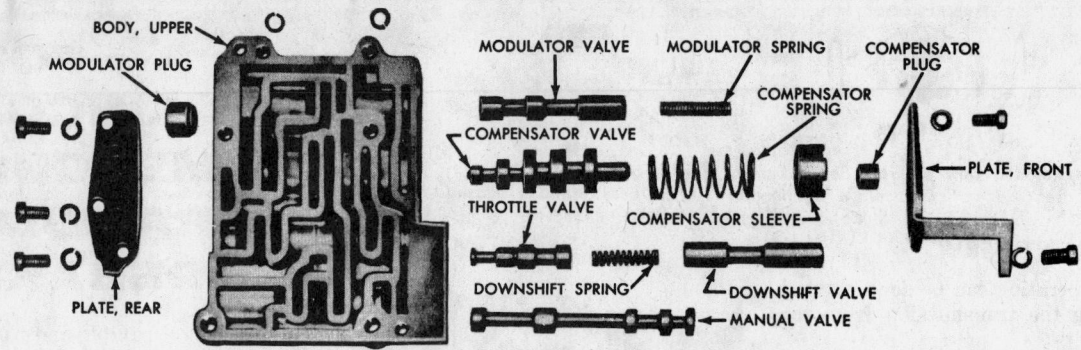

Fig. 17—Exploded view of upper valve body, all models, thru 1954

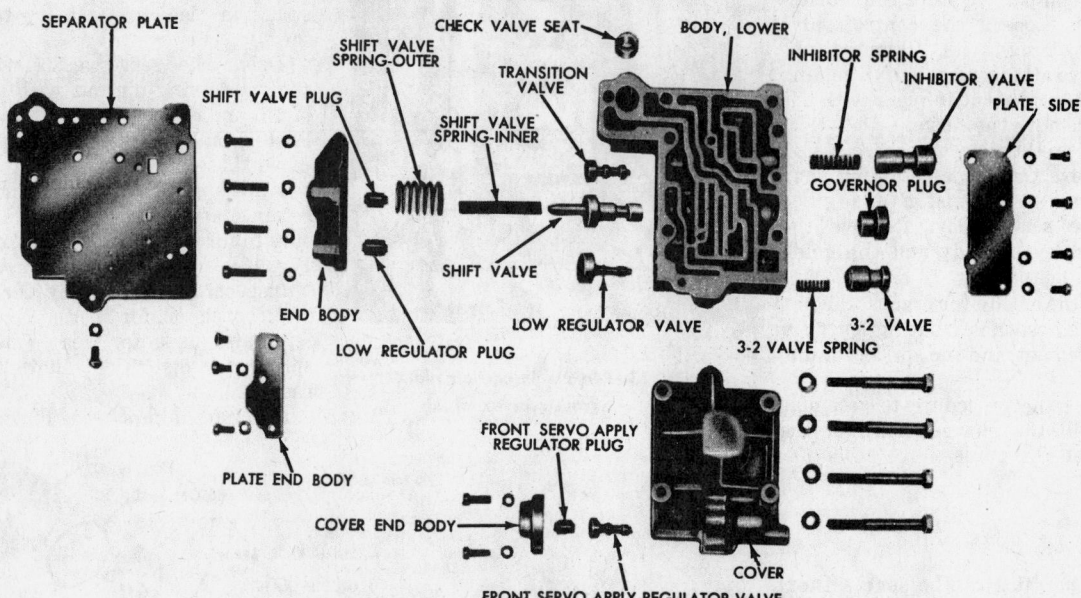

Fig. 18—Exploded view of lower valve body, all models, thru 1954

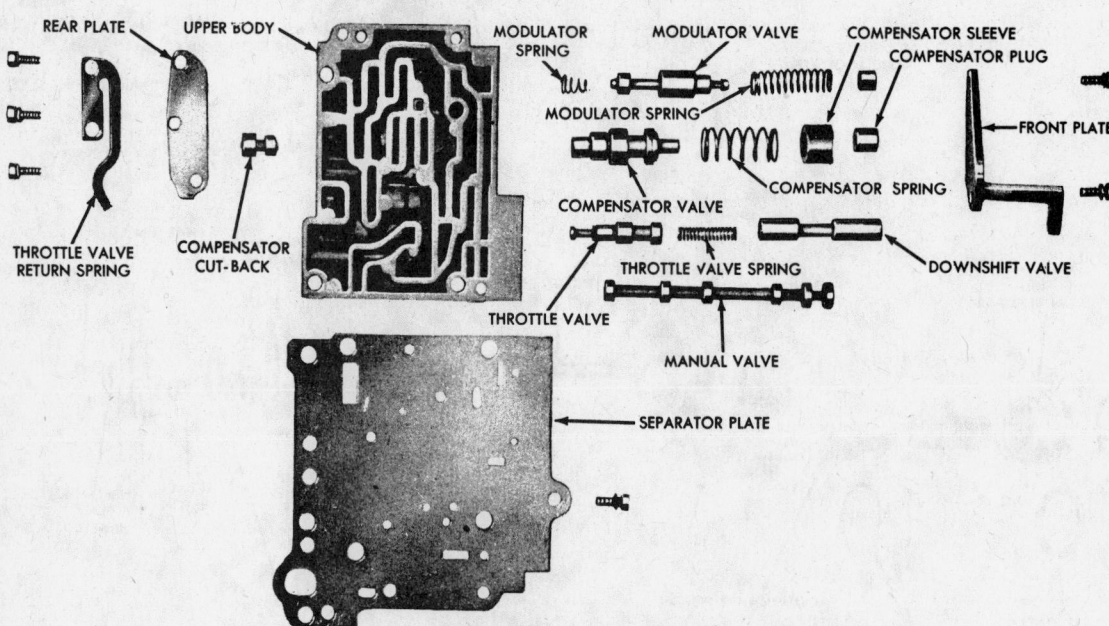

Fig. 19—Exploded view of upper valve body, Ford (Ford-O-Matic, 1955 -59), Mercury (Merc-O-Matic, 1955-61), Lincoln & Continental, (Turbo Drive, 1955-58), and Edsel (Automatic, 1958)

CONTINENTAL
EDSEL
FORD
LINCOLN
MERCURY
RAMBLER
STUDEBAKER

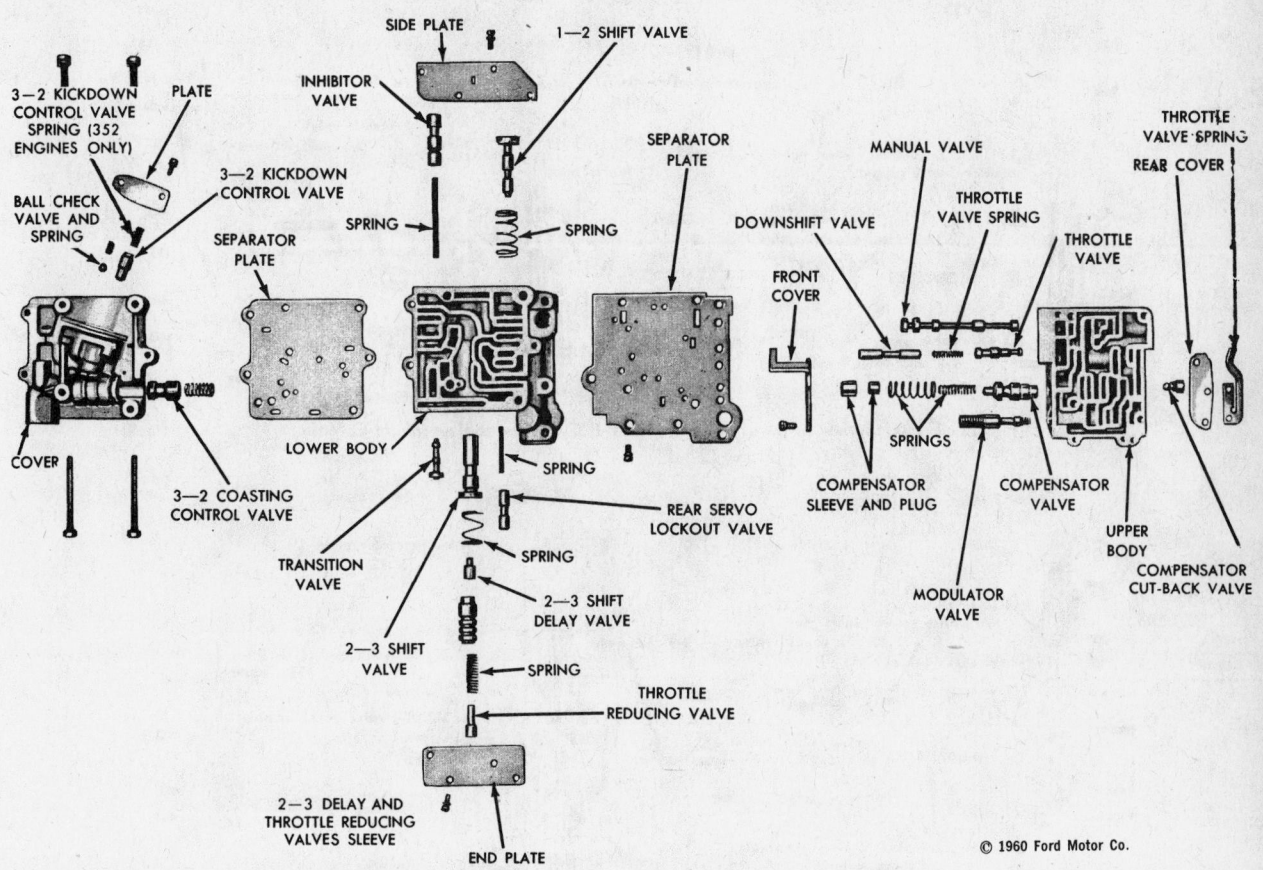

Fig. 24—Exploded view of upper valve body—Six & V-8 Cyl., Studebaker (Flight-O-Matic)

© 1960 Ford Motor Co.

Fig. 21—Exploded view of valve body assembly—Ford (Cruise-O-Matic
1958-63), Lincoln & Continental (Twin Range Turbo Drive, 1958-63),
Edsel (Dual Power, 1959-60), and Rambler (Flash-O-Matic 1958-63)

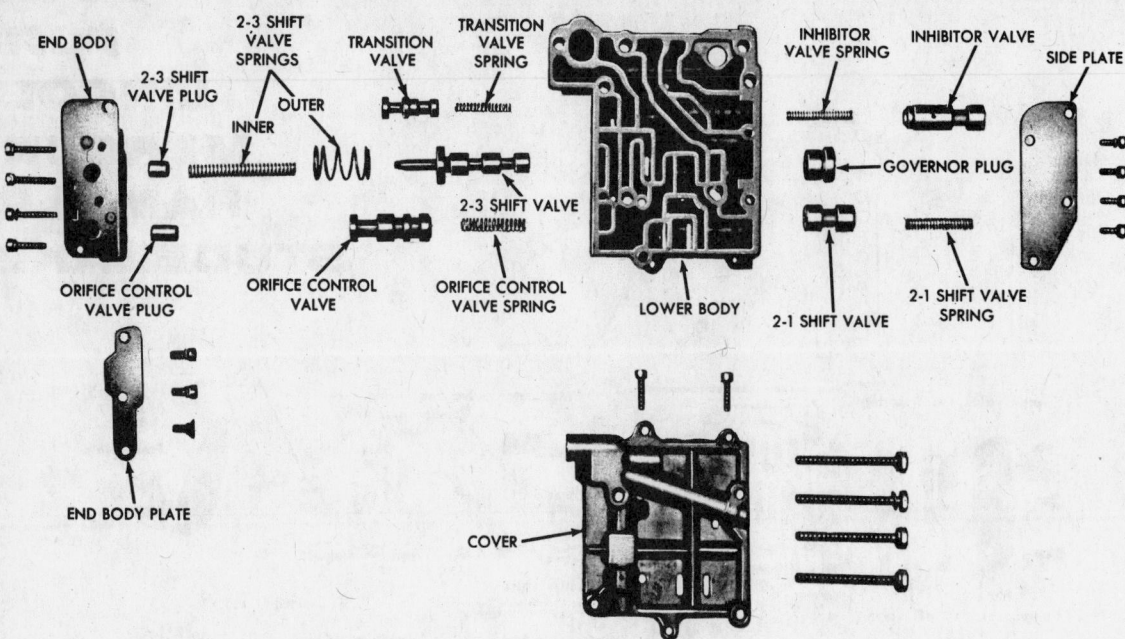

Fig. 20—Exploded view of lower valve body—Ford (Ford-O-Matic, 1955-59), Mercury (Merc-O-Matic, 1955-61), Lincoln & Continental (Turbo-Drive, 1955-58), and Edsel (Automatic, 1958)

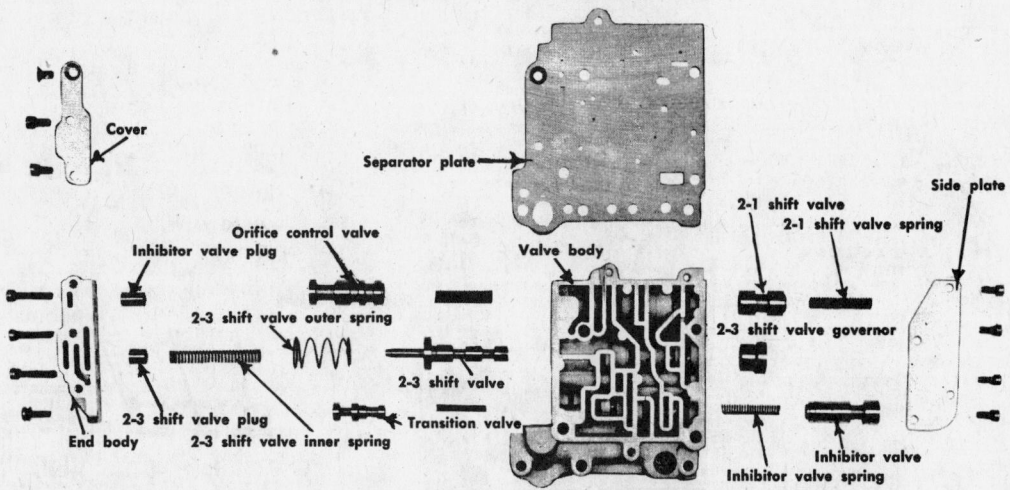

Fig. 22—Exploded view of lower valve body—V-8 Cyl., Studebaker (Flight-O-Matic)

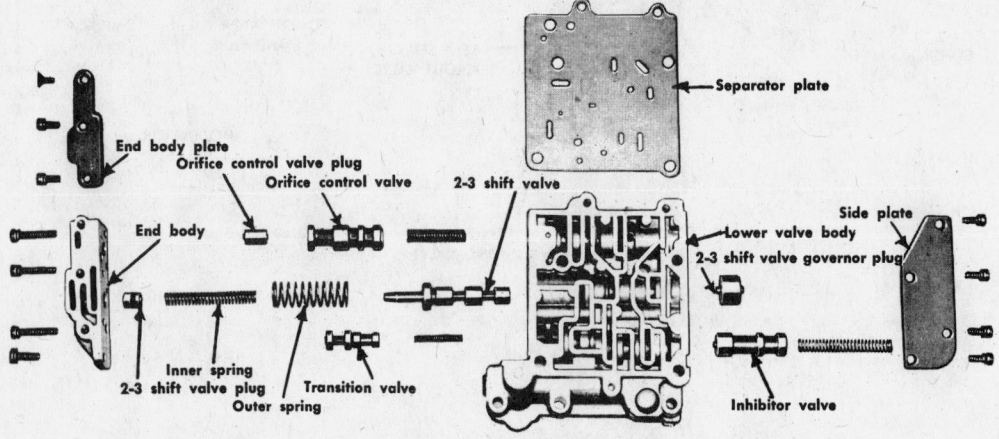

Fig. 23—Exploded view of lower valve body—Six Cyl., Studebaker (Flight-O-Matic)

CONTINENTAL
EDSEL
FORD
LINCOLN
MERCURY
RAMBLER
STUDEBAKER

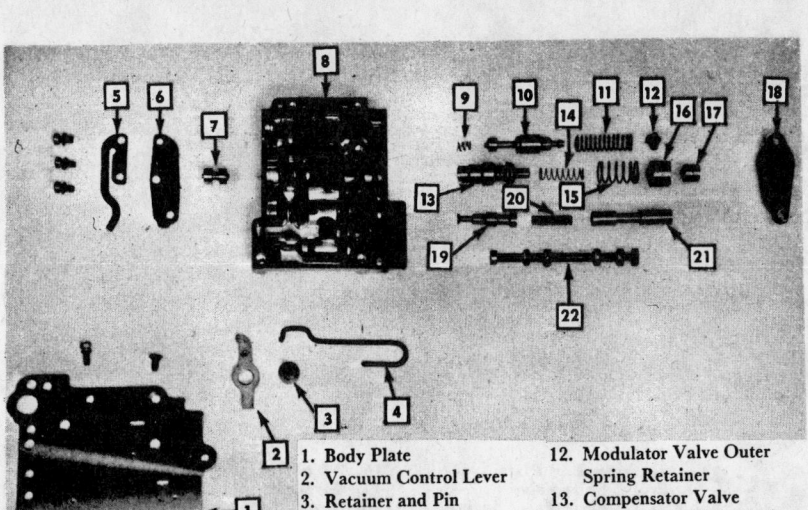

1. Body Plate
2. Vacuum Control Lever
3. Retainer and Pin
4. Lever Hook
5. Throttle Valve Return Spring
6. Rear Plate
7. Compensator Cut-off Valve
8. Upper Body
9. Modulator Valve Spring, Inner
10. Modulator Valve
11. Modulator Valve Spring, Outer
12. Modulator Valve Outer Spring Retainer
13. Compensator Valve
14. Compensator Valve Spring, Inner
15. Compensator Valve Spring, Outer
16. Compensator Valve Sleeve
17. Compensator Valve Plug
18. Front Plate
19. Throttle Valve
20. Throttle Valve Spring
21. Downshift Valve
22. Manual Valve

Fig. 27—Exploded view of upper valve body—All Rambler models with out sprag clutch (Flash-O-Matic)

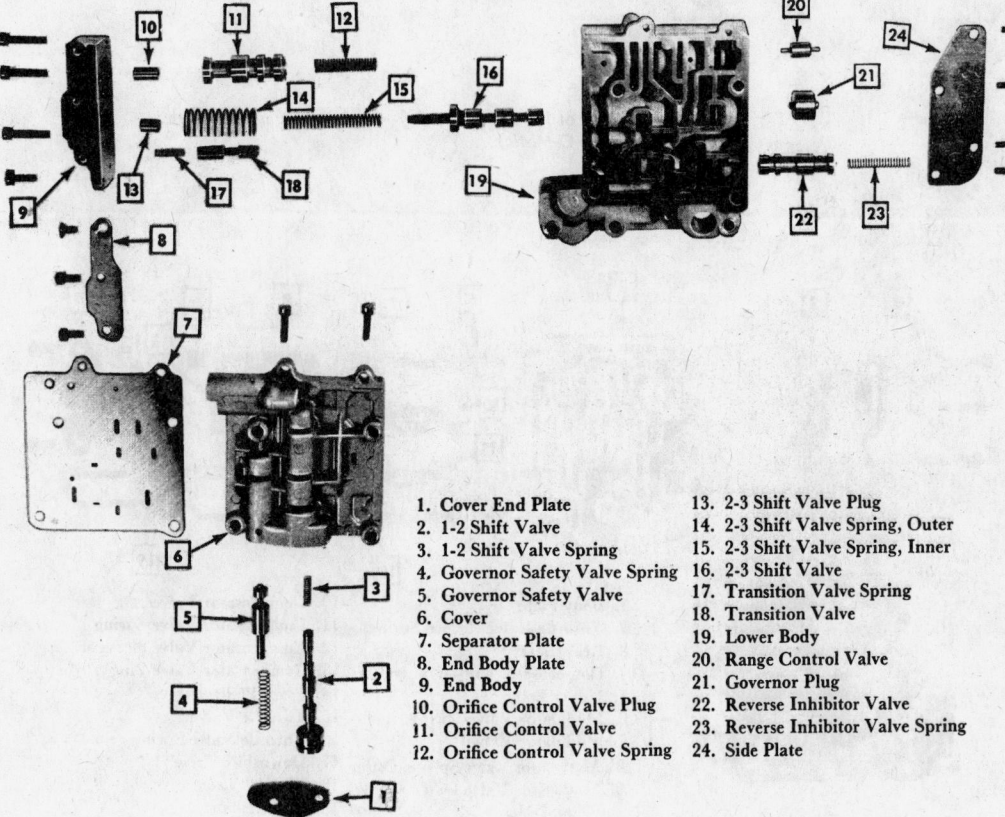

1. Cover End Plate
2. 1-2 Shift Valve
3. 1-2 Shift Valve Spring
4. Governor Safety Valve Spring
5. Governor Safety Valve
6. Cover
7. Separator Plate
8. End Body Plate
9. End Body
10. Orifice Control Valve Plug
11. Orifice Control Valve
12. Orifice Control Valve Spring
13. 2-3 Shift Valve Plug
14. 2-3 Shift Valve Spring, Outer
15. 2-3 Shift Valve Spring, Inner
16. 2-3 Shift Valve
17. Transition Valve Spring
18. Transition Valve
19. Lower Body
20. Range Control Valve
21. Governor Plug
22. Reverse Inhibitor Valve
23. Reverse Inhibitor Valve Spring
24. Side Plate

Fig. 26—Exploded view of lower valve body—All Rambler models with sprag clutch (Flash-O-Matic)

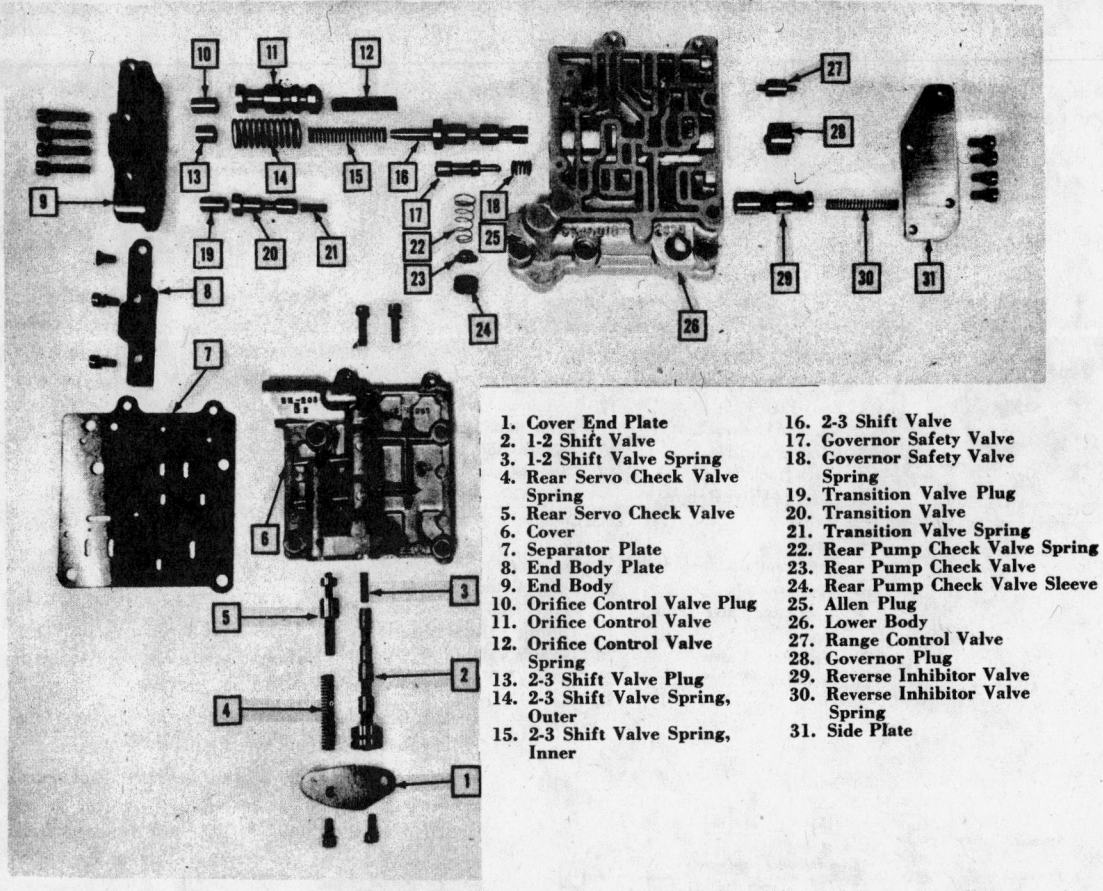

Fig. 25—Exploded view of lower valve body—All Rambler models with out sprag clutch (Flash-O-Matic)

1. Cover End Plate
2. 1-2 Shift Valve
3. 1-2 Shift Valve Spring
4. Rear Servo Check Valve Spring
5. Rear Servo Check Valve
6. Cover
7. Separator Plate
8. End Body Plate
9. End Body
10. Orifice Control Valve Plug
11. Orifice Control Valve
12. Orifice Control Valve Spring
13. 2-3 Shift Valve Plug
14. 2-3 Shift Valve Spring, Outer
15. 2-3 Shift Valve Spring, Inner
16. 2-3 Shift Valve
17. Governor Safety Valve
18. Governor Safety Valve Spring
19. Transition Valve Plug
20. Transition Valve
21. Transition Valve Spring
22. Rear Pump Check Valve Spring
23. Rear Pump Check Valve
24. Rear Pump Check Valve Sleeve
25. Allen Plug
26. Lower Body
27. Range Control Valve
28. Governor Plug
29. Reverse Inhibitor Valve
30. Reverse Inhibitor Valve Spring
31. Side Plate

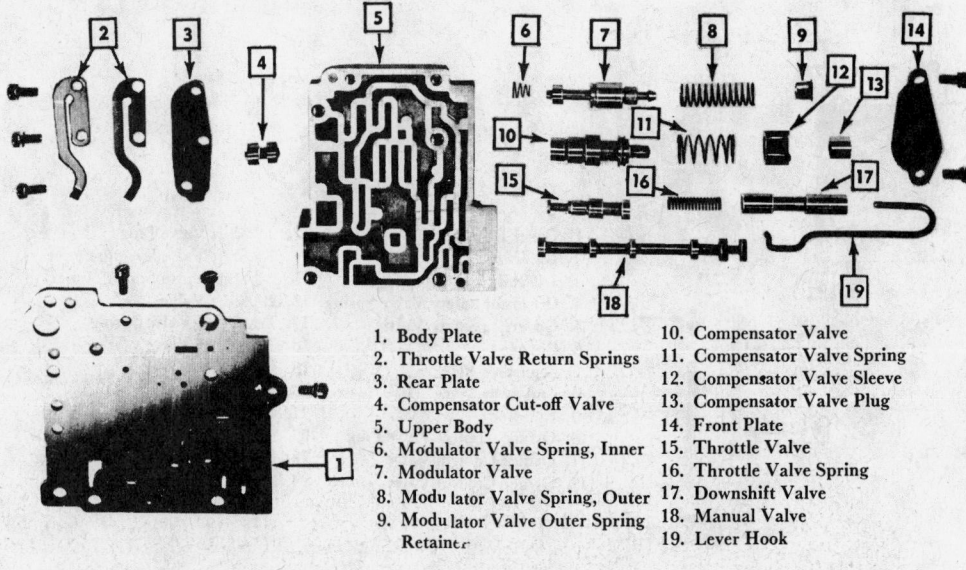

1. Body Plate
2. Throttle Valve Return Springs
3. Rear Plate
4. Compensator Cut-off Valve
5. Upper Body
6. Modulator Valve Spring, Inner
7. Modulator Valve
8. Modulator Valve Spring, Outer
9. Modulator Valve Outer Spring Retainer
10. Compensator Valve
11. Compensator Valve Spring
12. Compensator Valve Sleeve
13. Compensator Valve Plug
14. Front Plate
15. Throttle Valve
16. Throttle Valve Spring
17. Downshift Valve
18. Manual Valve
19. Lever Hook

Fig. 28—Exploded view of upper valve body—All Rambler models with sprag clutch (Flash-O-Matic)

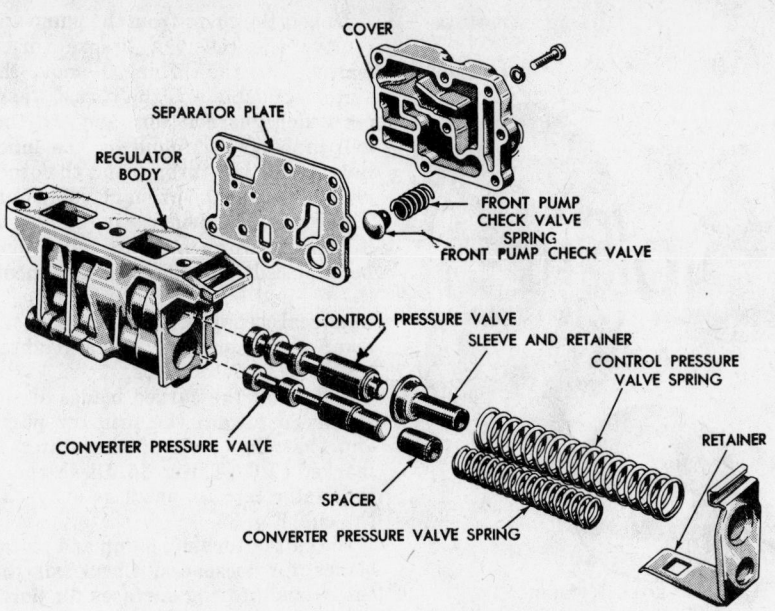

Fig. 30—Pressure Regulator starting 1955 production

1. 2-3 SHIFT-OUTER
2. COMPENSATOR
3. MODULATOR
4. 2-3 SHIFT-INNER
5. ORIFICE CONTROL
6. 2-1 SHIFT
7. LOW INHIBITOR
8. DOWNSHIFT
9. TRANSITION
10. MODULATOR-AUXILIARY

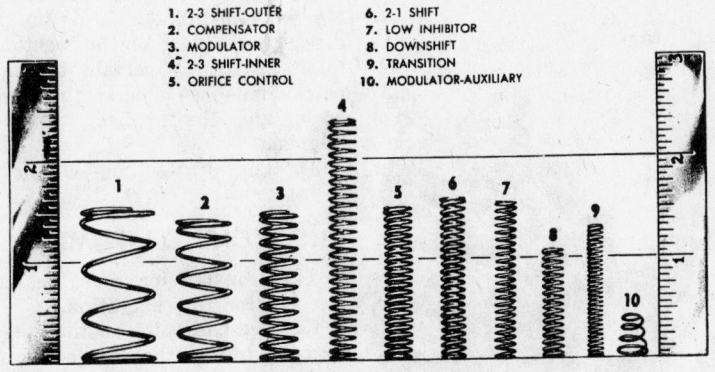

Fig. 31—Valve Body Spring Identification

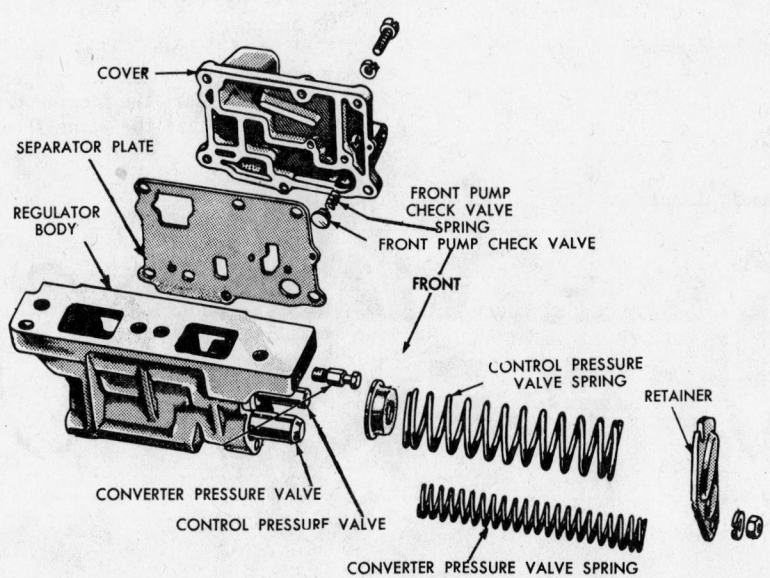

Fig. 29—Pressure Regulator thru 1954

CONTINENTAL
EDSEL
FORD
LINCOLN
MERCURY
RAMBLER
STUDEBAKER

CONTROL VALVE ASSEMBLIES

This operation can be done without removing the transmission from the car.

Caution: Have the hand lever at neutral for this operation.

With the oil pan off and the lubrication tube out. Remove the compensator pressure tube and the control pressure tube from the control valve body and the regulator valve body. Loosen the front servo attaching bolt a few turns.

Remove the control valve body to case bolts and remove the body by disengaging the tubes to the front servo.

Extra care should be lavished on this assembly. Use a clean towel over the bench while separating the assembly into its three major parts; the upper body, the lower body, and a lower body cover.

Remove the manual control valve and separate the parts of the upper body as shown in the cut.

Remove the separator plate and disassemble the lower body as shown in the cut.

Be careful when removing the end and side plates of these portions as many of the valves are spring loaded.

Inspect the parts for fit and signs of damage. Inspect the mating surfaces for burrs and flatness.

In reassembling be careful about tightening the separator plate screws

Fig. 32—Pull converter straight out

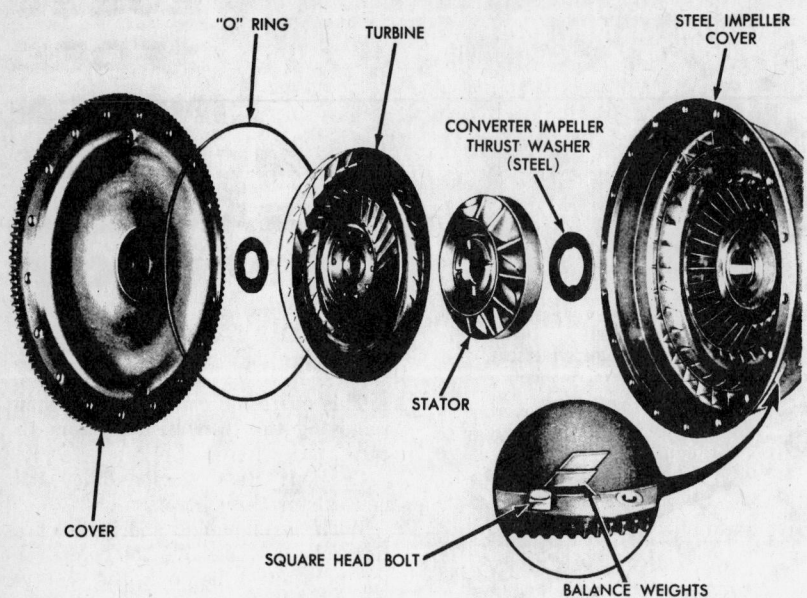

Fig. 33—Exploded view of cenverter assembly

as excessive tightening could cause the valves to bind in their bores.

Tighten the lower body cover bolts to 4-6 ft lbs.

Reverse the procedure to reassemble and install.

Index the servo tubes with the holes in the front servo assembly while pushing in on the throttle valve so that it will clear the case. Be sure that the manual control valve indexes with the detent.

The large control pressure tube and the small compensator pressure tube connect the control and regulator valve bodies.

Tighten the attaching bolts to 8-10 ft lbs. Tighten the front servo bolt to 35-40 ft lbs.

Readjust the manual and throttle valve controls.

THE CONVERTER

The transmission must be removed from the car for this operation.

The Rambler and Studebaker Torque Converters are only serviced as assemblies. They are sealed units.

Make sure that the primary pump cover is match marked to the primary pump for balanced reassembly. Note that the bolts holding the cover to the pump are special equally weighted bolts and should not be used elsewhere.

Remove the wedges which prevented the converter from falling out of the bell housing during removal from the car. Grasp the converter with both hands and pull straight out. Do not twist the assembly as you pull, else you will damage the front oil seal.

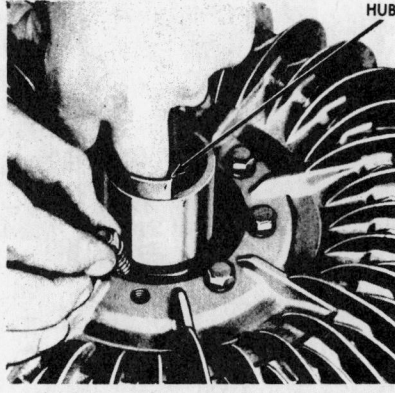

Fig. 34—Replacing primary pump hub

Unbolt the cover from the pump and remove the cover, a bronze thrust washer, and the turbine. Remove the stator assembly and the thrust washers which guard it fore and aft. One will probably be found on the inner hub face of the turbine and the other on the front of the primary pump hub.

Examine the primary pump hub, if it appears worn or damaged it may be replaced. Fig. 34. Simply unbolt the old and bolt on the new, using a new seal between the hub and the body of the primary pump. Tighten the bolts to 8-10 ft lbs.

Note that the curved blades of the stator go toward the primary pump and that the front of the stator is marked FRONT. Fig. 35. Disassemble the stator into its parts as shown in the cut. Fig. 35.

Check the turbine, pump and stator blades for looseness. Check all the thrust and bearing surfaces for burrs and wear. Check the sprag assembly for broken or worn parts.

Reverse the procedure to reassemble and reinstall. Assemble the parts directly into place on the reactor and input shafts. Be certain the match marks made at disassembly on the cover and the primary pump are aligned.

Tighten the attaching bolts to 25-28 ft lbs.

THE FRONT OIL PUMP

The transmission must be out of the car for this operation.

Remove the bolts holding the bell housing to the transmission case and remove the housing. Fig. 36.

Unbolt the front oil pump assembly and remove it from the front of the case. Fig. 37. If the pump does not come off easily, tap it lightly with a plastic hammer.

Unbolt and remove the reactor shaft and rear plate assembly from the pump body. Mark the faces of the pump gears so that the same faces

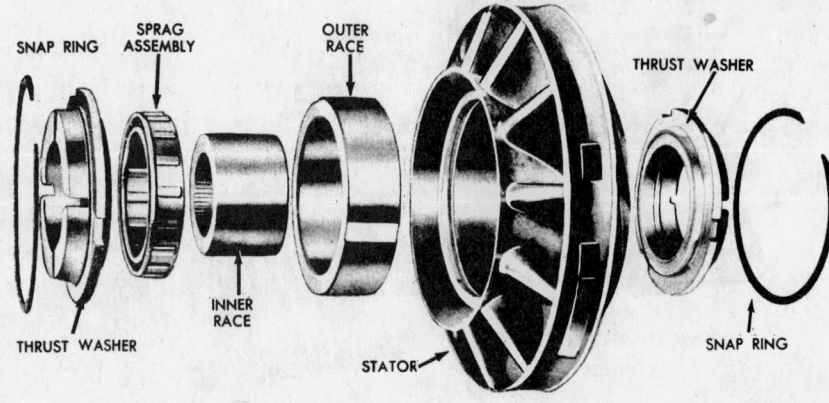

Fig. 35—Stator assembly disassembled

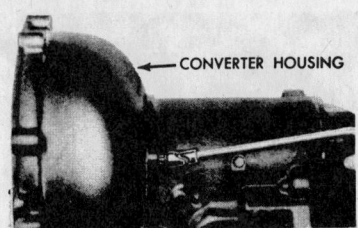

Fig. 36—Unbolt bell housing from case

GASKET   FRONT PUMP

Fig. 37—Remove front oil pump

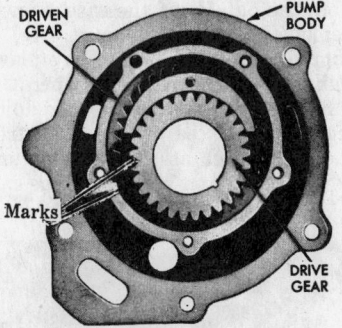

DRIVEN GEAR   PUMP BODY

Marks

DRIVE GEAR

Fig. 38—Mark the gear faces

will be up at reassembly. Use prussian blue. Do not scratch or punch mark the gears. Fig. 38.

Separate the parts as shown in the cut. Fig. 43.

Inspect the oil seal in the pump body and replace if it shows signs of wear. Coat the outside diameter of the seal with permatex No. 3 prior to installation. Check the machined surfaces of the pump parts for burrs. Blow out the oil passages in the reactor shaft assembly and look it over for signs of wear, especially the inner bushing.

Reverse the procedure to reassemble and reinstall. Use a sew gasket between the pump rear plate and the transmission case. Note that there is counterbore. Tighten the four attaching bolts to 17-22 ft lbs.

THE EXTENSION HOUSING

The transmission must be out of the car for this operation.

Unbolt and remove the extension housing, being careful to support the housing so that its weight does not concentrate on the rear oil seal and ruin the seal as the housing passes over the splines of the output shaft.

Inspect the housing for cracks. Check all machined surfaces for burrs. Check the rear oil seal and replace if necessary. Position the felt side of the seal to the rear. Remove the governor cover plate and check the gasket. Check the fluid baffle for a tight fit in the housing.

Reverse the procedure to reinstall. Tighten the attaching bolts to 28-33 ft lbs.

THE REAR OIL PUMP AND OUTPUT SHAFT

The transmission must be out of the car for this operation.

Remove the snap ring and the speedometer drive gear from the output shaft. Do not lose the ball which keys the gear to the shaft. Fig. 39.

Unbolt and remove the fluid distrubutor body and its three delivery tubes. Slide the fluid distributor sleeve off the output shaft.

Remove the snap ring and slide the governor body and counterweighted sleeve assembly from the shaft. Fig. 40. Do not lose the ball which keys the sleeve to the shaft. Do not damage the oil seal rings. Pull the rear oil pump discharge tube out of the case. Fig. 41.

Unbolt and remove the rear oil pump and its drive key. Remove the bronze thrust washer which rides between the rear pump and the ring gear. Remove the output shaft and ring gear assembly.

CONTINENTAL
EDSEL
FORD
LINCOLN
MERCURY
RAMBLER
STUDEBAKER

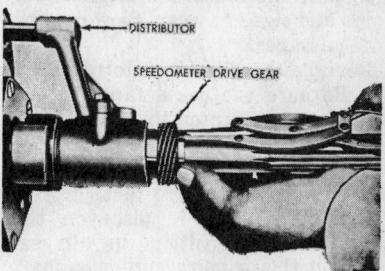

DISTRIBUTOR

SPEEDOMETER DRIVE GEAR

Fig. 39—Remove snap ring to release speedometer drive gear

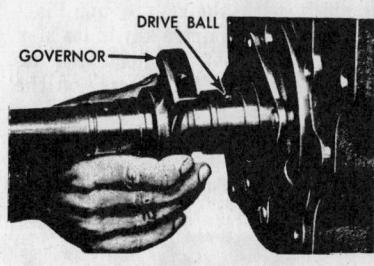

DRIVE BALL

GOVERNOR

Fig. 40—Slide governor assembly from shaft, note the drive balls

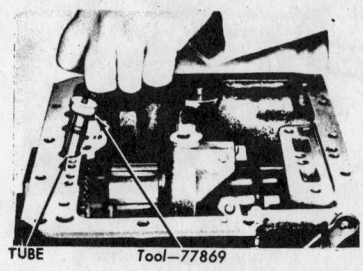

TUBE   Tool—77869

Fig. 41—Remove rear oil pump discharge tube

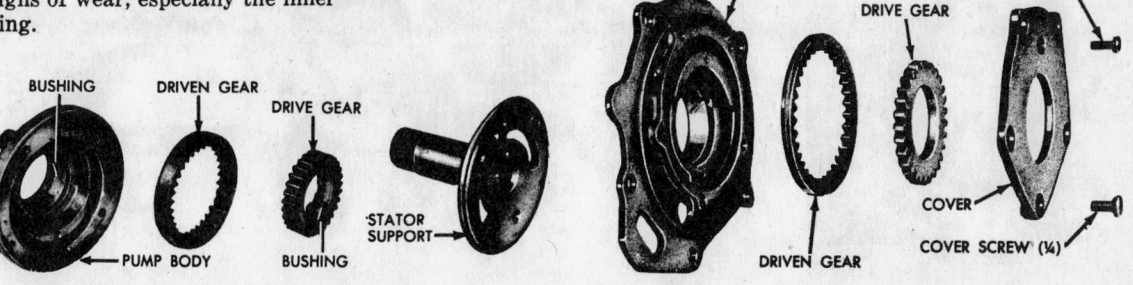

BUSHING   DRIVEN GEAR   DRIVE GEAR

PUMP BODY   BUSHING   STATOR SUPPORT

Fig. 42—Rear pump disassembled

PUMP BODY   DRIVE GEAR   COVER SCREW (No. 10-24)

DRIVEN GEAR   COVER   COVER SCREW (¼)

Fig. 43—Front pump disassembled

<u>Note:</u> The washer left on the rear hub of the planetary carrier is the selective thrust washer.

Remove the screws and lockwashers which secure the rear pump cover to the pump body and remove the cover. Using prussian blue, mark the faces of the pump gears so that they can be assembled with the same faces up. Do not scratch or injure the gears.

Disassemble the pump as shown in the cut. Fig. 42.

Inspect the machined surfaces for burrs and signs of wear. Blow out the fluid passages.

Reverse the procedure to reassemble. Be sure the same faces of the gears are up. Tighten the pump cover screws to 7-8 ft lbs.

Install the output shaft and ring gear assembly. Be sure the Selective Thrust Washer is in place on the pinion carrier. Position the oil seal rings on the primary sun gear shaft with the gaps up to prevent breakage as the output shaft slides into place.

Position the seal rings on the output shaft with their gaps up. Place the rear oil pump drive key in its slot. Install the thrust washer with its tangs indexed with the bosses on the pump body. The bronze side up.

Using care that the keyway in the pump drive gear and the key on the output shaft are aligned, install the

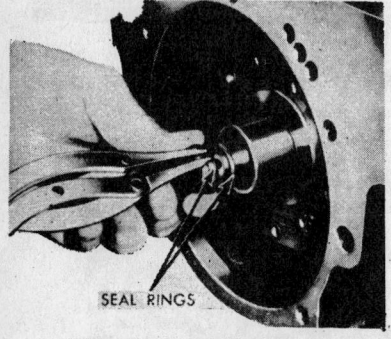

Fig. 44—Remove seal rings from rear end of primary sun gear shaft

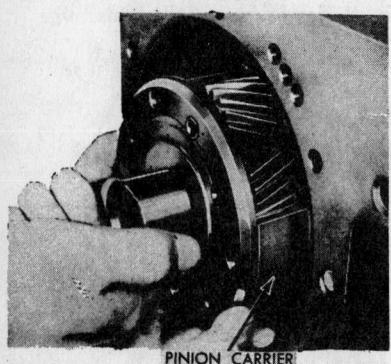

Fig. 45—Remove planetary pinion carrier from case

rear pump with a new gasket fore and aft.

Use fluid to retain the governor drive ball in its pocket and install the governor assembly. The governor body plate goes toward the front of the car. Install the snap ring.

Install the distributor sleeve chamfered end first. Use fluid to ease the sleeve into place. Index the fluid passages in the fluid distributor with those in the sleeve. Enter the tubes into their hole in the case up to the spacer on the center tube and refasten the distributor body to the sleeve. Tighten to 8-10 ft lbs.

Use fluid to retain the speedometer drive ball in its pocket in the shaft and install the speedometer drive gear so that the ball and drive slot index. Install the snap ring.

Install a new seal ring on the rear pump discharge tube and install the tube into the case.

THE PLANETARY CARRIER

The transmission must be out of the car for this operation.

Remove the two seal rings from the primary sun gear shaft.

<u>Note:</u> The hook type seal rings used throughout the transmission are easily broken, so that care must be the guiding light in all dealings with them. Cocking and twisting of the parts during removal and installation is the biggest cause of breakage.

Remove the selective thrust washer from the rear of the planetary carrier.

Remove the planetary pinion carrier. Fig. 45.

The planetary carrier is replaced as an assembly. Parts for it are not available separately.

THE FRONT AND REAR CLUTCHES

The transmission must be out of the car for this operation.

Remove the bronze thrust washer from the primary sun gear shaft. Fig.

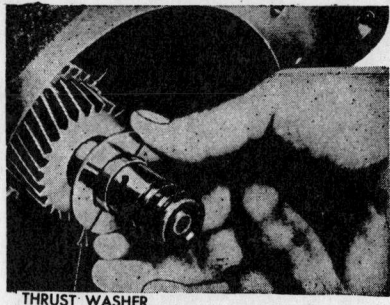

Fig. 46—Remove primary sun gear rear thrust washer

46. This thrust washer rides the shaft between the primary sun gear and the front thrust surface of the planetary carrier.

Mark the rear band with reference to the side of the case so that it can be reinstalled to the same position. A new band is not sensitive to position. Remove the rear band.

Remove the center support special bolts (one on each side of the case) from the outside of the case. Fig. 47. Remove the center support. Fig. 48. Tapping the input shaft with a plastic hammer will facilitate this operation.

Being very careful that they do not become separated, remove the front and rear clutch assemblies as a unit. Remove the front band from the case.

Fig. 47—Remove Center Support Bolts

Fig: 48—Install indicator to contact front end of Input Shaft

CHECKING TRANSMISSION END PLAY

Transmission must be removed from the car for this operation.

This operation is used to determine the thickness of the selective thrust washer which rides the hub of the planetary carrier between the carrier and the ring gear.

Tool—77067   Tool—7657

Fig. 49—Pry between front clutch and case to force gear train to the rear

REAR

Fig. 50—Pry between ring gear and case to force gear train to the front

Mount an indicator in some manner similar to that shown in the cut Fig. 49 so that it contacts the front end of the input (turbine) shaft. Pry between the front clutch and the front of the case so as to force the planetary gear train as far rearward as it will go. Fig. 50. While holding the train so, set the indicator to read zero.

Now pry between the rear of the case and the rear face of the ring gear. Fig. 50. The indicator should show an end play of the input shaft of between .010″ and .029″ F. I. R.

As mentioned above the selective thrust washer which controls this end play is located at the rear of the planetary carrier. Fig. 52. It bears against the inner front face of the ring gear.

In order to correct any variation between the recommended limits and those found it is necessary to disassemble the transmission. Therefore record at this point the amount of end play as found whether over or under the limits.

Measure the thickness of the washer with a micrometer and select a washer that is thicker or thinner as need be to bring the end play within the designated limits.

There for four thicknesses of thrust washers available from the factory: .061″-.063″, .067″-.069″, .074″-.076″, and .081″-.083″.

Reassemble the transmission and check that the end play is within the limits, .010″-.029″. Note that if the end play is too little the parts of the gear train will wear out very rapidly and if the end play is too great there will be considerable noise as the gear train clunks from one end of the case to the other.

CONTINENTAL EDSEL FORD LINCOLN MERCURY RAMBLER STUDEBAKER

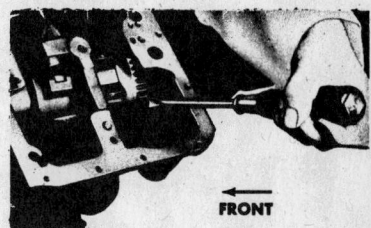

FRONT

Fig. 51—Install Selective Thrust Washer onto Rear Hub of Planetary Carrier

SELECTIVE WASHER

Fig. 52—Remove Center Support

GOVERNOR DRIVE BALL POCKET

OUTPUT SHAFT ALUMINUM SLEEVE

180°

TEAR DROP

Fig. 53—Correct position of Output Shaft Bushing All Models

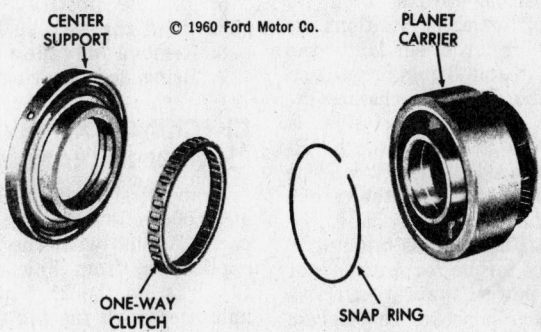

CENTER SUPPORT   © 1960 Ford Motor Co.   PLANET CARRIER

ONE-WAY CLUTCH   SNAP RING

Fig. 54—Cruise-O-Matic One-Way Sprag Clutch. Front of car is to the left. When installed Sprag assembly should turn with Pinion Carrier when carrier is turned counter-clockwise as viewed from the rear. Flanged side of cage rings go to the rear

FORDOMATIC-2 SPEED AUTOMATIC-MILEOMATIC

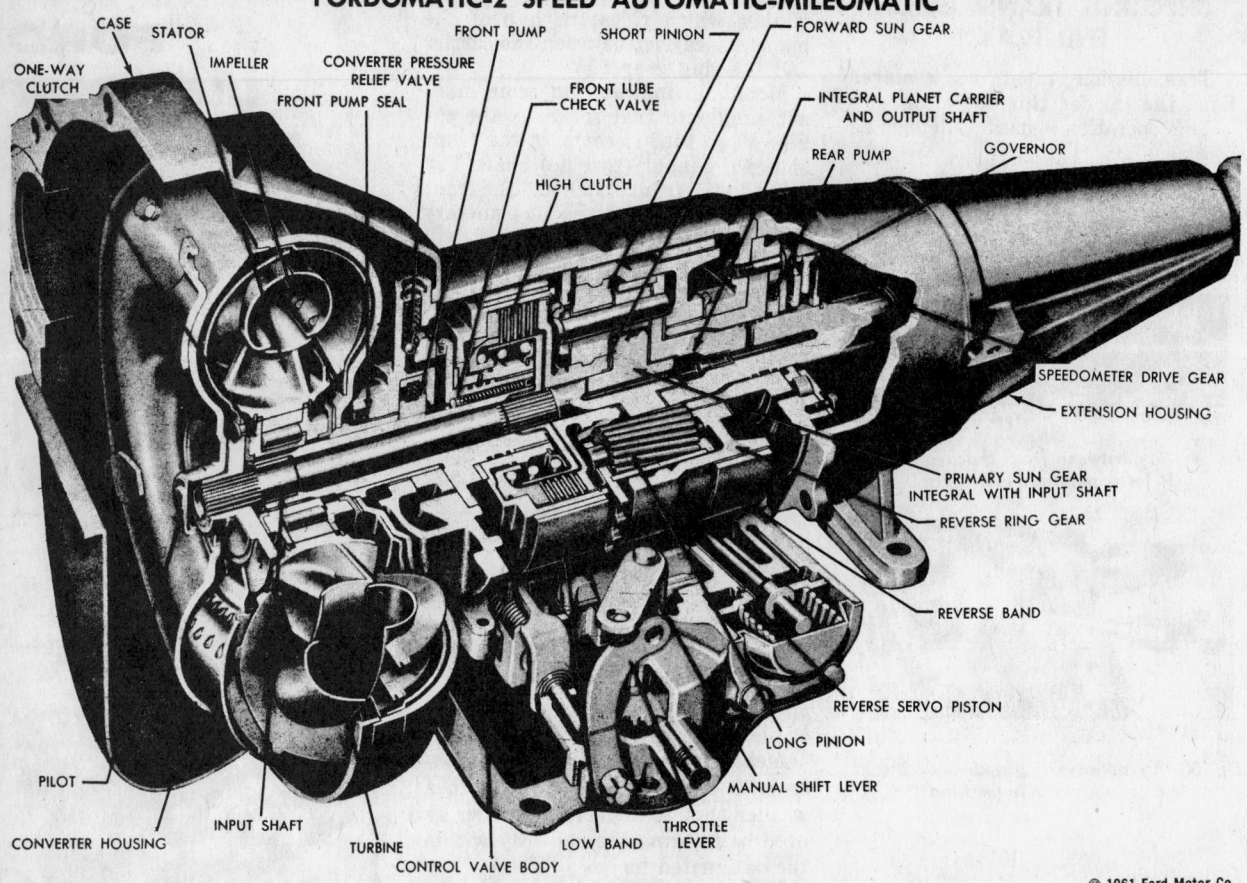

Fig. 1—Sectional View of Transmission Assembly

© 1961 Ford Motor Co.

Beginning with 1959 Ford produced a 2 speed automatic transmission.

It is equipped with a low gear and high gear in the forward range, and, of course, reverse. Automatic shifts are provided from low to high and from high to low. There are two bands, low and reverse and only one clutch.

There is no intermediate speed as in previous 3 speed automatic transmissions of Ford manufacture, nor does it provide an alternate driving range like Cruise-o-matic with its "D1" and "D2" selector positions.

This transmission is similar to the 3 speed version and should present no problem to the skilled mechanic.

The same basic transmission is available in Ford, Mercury, Edsel, Falcon and Comet with variations. The prime differences being in the torque converter, the valve body and the clutch plates. Each unit is tailored to accomplish the torque requirements of its peculiar power application. It is therefore necessary to be specific about the car model and engine used when ordering any replacement parts.

Identification of the various transmissions can be made by the prefix and number of the transmission, stamped into the right side of the unit case near the filler tube fitting.

SERVICE INFORMATION

Check oil at 1,000 mile intervals unless some abnormal condition requires a more frequent check.

1. Car on level.
2. Engine at normal operating temperature and idle speed.
3. Shift the selector thru all positions, then place the lever in "P."
4. Clean all dirt from around top of dipstick and dipstick tube opening.
5. Remove dipstick, wipe dry and push it all the way back into tube.
6. Remove and take a level reading.
7. Bring to operating level.

CHECKING OIL LEVEL
CHANGING TRANSMISSION OIL

Transmission oil should be changed at 24,000 mile intervals. The refill capacity varies with the transmission application, from Falcon or Comet's 14½ pts. to the 21 pint capacity of unit used with the big engines.

1. Remove the cover from the lower, front side of the converter housing.
2. Remove one of the converter drain plugs.
3. Rotate the converter a half turn and remove the other drain plug.

4. Remove the plug from the transmission oil pan and let drain.
5. Remove and THOROUGHLY clean the oil pan, screen and any accessible surfaces that might catch and hold sediment. (Unless extreme care is used at this time the small particles of dirt that lay dormant and harmless, will be disturbed and put into circulation resulting in the final state of the transmission being worse than the first.)
6. Replace the gasket on the oil pan and install the screen and pan on the transmission.
7. Install both drain plugs in the converter, tighten them to 15 to 25 ft. lb.
8. Install the converter housing cover.
9. Pour in 8 pts. of the recommended transmission oil and run the engine at IDLE speed for about 2 minutes.
10. Add the difference in oil quantity to arrive at the recommended capacity and run the engine at fast idle until normal operating temperatures prevail. (DO NOT RACE THE ENGINE.)
11. Shift the selector thru all positions. Place lever in "P" and check oil level. Bring to level.

ENGINE IDLE SPEED ADJUSTMENT

1. Apply the parking brake and place the selector lever at "N."
2. Run the engine at normal idle.

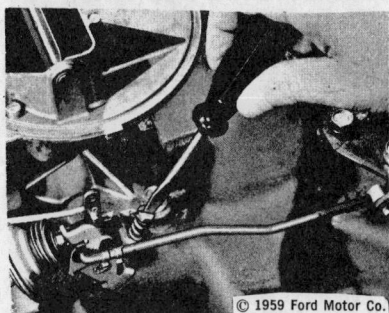

Fig. 2—Engine Idle Speed Adjustment

(THE ENGINE MUST BE AT OPERATING TEMPERATURE.)

3. With a tachometer hooked up, adjust the engine idle to specified RPM. Check this setting in the "D" position also; it may be necessary to slightly alter the idle speed at "N" to obtain satisfactory idle speed at "D".

It may be that the anti-stall dashpot interferes with the throttle closing. If so, adjust the dashpot clearance so that the correct idle can be obtained.

Fig. 8—Low Band Adjustment

BAND ADJUSTMENTS

Both bands should be adjusted after the first 1,000 miles of car operation and at subsequent 24,000 mile intervals.

LOW—FRONT BAND

A special tool (T59P-77370-A, or its equivalent) is essential for making this adjustment. It is equipped with a slip or click device for determining 10 ft. lb.

The front band (low gear) can be adjusted from outside of the case (left front).

1. Loosen the lock nuts several turns.
2. Turn the adjusting screw clockwise (in) until 10 ft. lb. has been reached.

Fig. 12—Reverse Band Adjustment

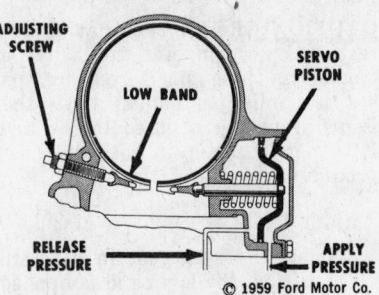

Fig. 13—Low Band and Servo

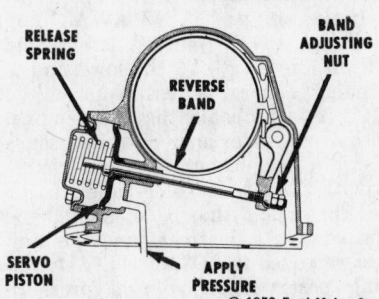

Fig. 14—Reverse Band and Servo

3. Back off (counterclockwise) on the adjusting screw exactly 2 turns.
4. Hold the adjusting screw in this position, and tighten the locknut to 35-40 ft. lb.

REVERSE—REAR BAND

Special tools (T59P-77423-A and T59P-77409-A, or their equivalents) are essential for making this adjustment. T59P-77423 is a torque wrench that clicks and overruns at 4 ft. lb. T59P-77409-A is a holding tool and thickness gauge.

1. Drain the transmission oil (not the converter).
2. Remove and thoroughly clean the oil pan and screen.
3. Place the special holding tool on the rear servo piston rod so that the two sets of forks straddle the band-

apply lever. The inner fork must engage the flat on the servo piston rod. The outer fork is also a thickness gauge, or spacer, and must be inserted between the piston rod seat and the adjusting nut.

4. Loosen the rear servo piston rod locknut and adjusting nut.
5. Back off the piston rod locknut so that the tool can engage the adjusting nut. Tighten the adjusting nut to 4 ft. lb. (or until the tool clicks).
6. Back off the adjustment exactly two turns.
7. Keep the adjusting nut from turning by withdrawing the forked tool about 1/2 inch away from the piston rod. The tool is machined with a special slot and at this position will keep the adjusting nut from turning. Tighten the locknut to 15-18 ft. lb. and remove the special forked tool from the servo piston rod.
8. Replace the oil screen, oil pan and drain plug.
9. Refill the transmission to capacity with new or thoroughly filtered oil. (Follow "CHANGING TRANSMISSION OIL" procedures as previously described.)

THINGS TO CHECK FIRST

The following items should be considered before any major work is performed or any commitments made for repair cost.

1. Check the oil level and smell it.
2. Check for oil leaks. They may occur at any of the following places:
   A. Front oil seal.

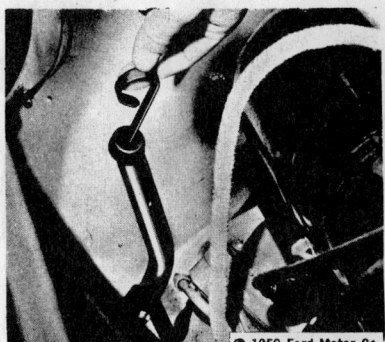

Fig. 15—Check Oil Level

B. Rear oil seal.

C. Speedometer cable connection.

D. Governor inspection plate gasket.

E. Oil pan gasket.

F. Oil filler tube connection.

G. Oil cooler lines and connections on Ford and Edsel. (Falcon and Comet use air cooled converters.)

H. Engine coolant in radiator for evidence of cooler core leak. This may require replacement of engine radiator (the cooler core is part of the radiator).

I. Throttle lever and manual lever shaft seals.

J. Low and reverse servo cover seals.

K. Oil leaking from the converter drain plugs.

CAUTION: Oil dripping from the converter housing may be engine oil leaking past the rear main bearing or from the engine oil gallery plugs. A positive way to determine the source of a converter housing leak is to add color to the transmission oil. Premix one level teaspoon of powdered oil-soluble aniline dye to each pint of transmission oil. This solution is harmless to the transmission and will isolate transmission leaks that may have been incorrectly diagnosed as engine oil leaks or vice versa. It will also accent any leak that may exist in the oil cooler core by showing color in the engine coolant.

Other checks that should be made prior to major operations are: Engine idle speed, throttle linkage, anti-stall dashpot clearance and manual linkage conditions and adjustments.

STALL TEST

1. Run the engine at fast idle with the selector at "N" until normal operating temperature is reached.

2. Attach a tachometer to the engine so that it can be read from the driver's seat.

3. Apply both brakes firmly.

4. Shift selector lever to "D", "L" or "R".

5. With constant pressure, push the accelerator pedal to the floor. Watch the tachometer reading. If the reading exceeds the high limit, or engine runaway is apparent, release the pedal immediately to prevent damage. FIVE SECONDS IS THE MAXIMUM TIME TO HOLD THE THROTTLE OPEN. Between stall tests, in the various positions, run the car for at least two minutes in the neutral position at high idle. This will help cool the transmission between tests.

STALL SPEED CHART

Engine Size-cu. in.	Stall Speed
223	1370-1570 RPM
292-260	1590-1790 RPM
332-352-390	1625-1845 RPM
144-170	1740-1940 RPM

CAUTION: Remember that a stall test does not pinpoint the source of trouble, as the engine torque converter, transmission bands and other items are being exposed to the test. It is merely a step in good diagnosis procedure.

BAND CHECK

During the stall test in "D" and "L" position, the low band is applied. When the test is made in "R", the reverse band is applied.

If the engine "RUNS AWAY", on stall test, in "D" or "L", but is held within limits in "R", the low band is slipping. Since the test is normal in "R", it is probable that the engine, torque converter and control pressure also are normal but that the trouble is with the low servo or band. If this be the case, the band should be checked for adjustment and the stall test repeated in "D" and "L". If slipping persists, hook up a pressure gauge to the transmission and do a control pressure check before inspecting the servo and band.

If the engine RUNS AWAY in the "R" position, but holds within limits in "D" and "L", the reverse band is slipping. This is a logical reasoning but because of the labor required to

adjust the reverse band, make a control pressure check before pulling the oil pan.

The transmission clutch plates (high gear) cannot be stall-tested because 14 m.p.h. road speed is required to effect clutch application.

CONVERTER OPERATION CHECK

During a stall test, the stator one-way clutch locks the stator against counterclockwise rotation. If the stator clutch fails to lock properly, the converter will offer greater resistance to rotation.

If the above condition is present, maximum RPM during a stall test will be about 1200. However, a thorough road test should be made before replacing the converter. Failure of the stator clutch to LOCK during stall test will cause acceleration up to 30 m.p.h. to be very slow. Above 30 m.p.h., acceleration will be almost normal and performance at steady speeds above 30 m.p.h. will be normal. If the stator clutch fails to UNLOCK during stall test, operation will appear to be normal but maximum road speed will be about 50 m.p.h.

If either of these conditions is found, the converter must be replaced as a unit. Components are not available for service.

CONTROL PRESSURE CHECKS

When minor checks have been made with no apparent success, control pressures should be examined. An opening and 1/8" pipe plug is available on the left side of the case, forward and just above the low band adjusting screw for a pressure gauge connection.

A gauge installed here will register the pressure between the front pump and the front pump check valve. This pressure is influenced by the control pressure regulator valve and IS transmission control pressure. Hook up the gauge so that it can be read from the driver's seat. (SEE CHART.)

CONTROL PRESSURE LIMITS

Both brakes should be securely set. These readings are taken with both

Fig. 17—Some Possible Seepage Points

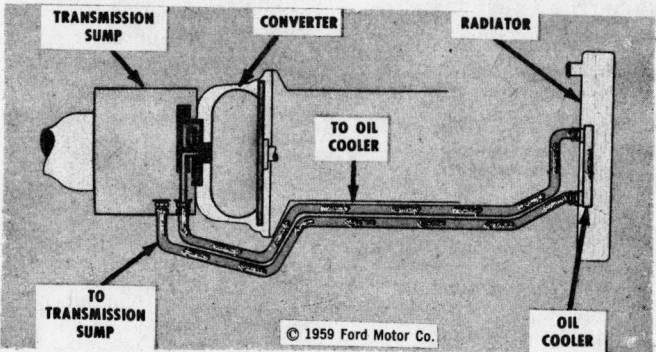

Fig. 16—Coolant Flow, Ford, Mercury and Edsel

rear wheels stopped so that the front pump only is supplying pressure. Pump operation is quite critical in this transmission as the oil to the governor is supplied entirely by the rear pump. The same pressure gauge hook-up is used for checking the performance of the rear pump. During a road test, the gauge reading should drop from about 80 p.s.i. to 5 lb. or less, when reaching approximately 50 m.p.h. This sudden drop in pressure is normal and indicates that the rear pump has taken over the COMPLETE job of supplying oil pressure within the transmission. If this sudden pressure drop does not occur, either the rear pump or the front pump check valve is at fault.

CAUTION: This test should be made on the road and NOT on a jack or stands for various reasons. One being the possibility of doing harm to the differential, in the case of the equalock or other positive traction differentials.

CONTROL PRESSURE RISE

In "D" or "L" selector lever positions, control pressure should rise from 46-56 p.s.i., at idle to 170-205 p.s.i. at full throttle (stall).

If this rise does not occur, there are four probable causes: Throttle linkage, throttle and compensator pressures, pump pumping capacity, and excessive leakage.

Check the control pressure with the selector at "R". In the "R" position, control pressure is regulated entirely by the control pressure regulator valve and its spring. In "R", the control pressure degree does not depend on throttle linkage, throttle pressure or compensator pressure. If, therefore, control pressure is normal in reverse, pump capacity and leakage in the main hydraulic system (upstream or before the manual valve) is not offensive and can be considered okay. Absence of pressure rise in "D" and "L" is probably due to throttle linkage, throttle and compensator pressure or leakage downstream or after the manual valve.

To check operation of the throttle linkage, proceed as follows:

1. Disconnect the throttle control rod from the accelerator shaft and lever at the clevis.
2. Place the selector lever in "P" position.
3. Adjust engine RPM to 1,000.
4. Push down on throttle control rod and watch the pressure gauge. Control pressure should rise to 170-205 p.s.i. If it does, pump capacity, main system leakage, throttle and compensator pressures, and the throttle linkage are okay. The trouble is probably due to leakage in the low servo-apply system.

If the pressure does not rise when the throttle control rod is moved downward, check the following. Raise and lower the throttle rod, feeling for the compression of the throttle valve spring as the rod moves downward. Also check for loose throttle levers on the shaft by pushing the rod down firmly against the stop inside the transmission.

AIR PRESSURE CHECKS

In some instances the trouble can be located by draining the oil and removing the oil pan and valve body and substituting air pressure in selective order from unit to unit.

COMET FALCON FAIRLANE FORD MERCURY METEOR

FRONT SERVO

Direct air pressure into the front servo apply passage. This should tighten the low band around the drum. The moment the air pressure is released the servo return spring should release the band. Also, apply air to the same passage and listen for excessive leakage.

REAR SERVO

Air test the same as front servo.

CLUTCH

Direct air pressure into the clutch apply passage. A dull "thud" should be heard when the clutch piston is forced against the plates.

NOTE: If the bands or clutch fail to respond to the air application, dismantle and repair the transmission. It is recommended that a soft tipped hose nozzle be used for the air check to insure against air leaks.

NO DRIVE IN ANY RANGE

When requested to diagnose a NO DRIVE condition, take the following steps:

1. **Determine whether the engine is running under load or without load.**

If the engine is running under load, the transmission is actually locked up, and the converter turbine is at stall. If the engine is running without load the converter or transmission is actually in neutral.

2. **To find whether the converter or transmission is at fault.**

SHUT OFF THE ENGINE and tighten the low band adjusting screw to about 25 ft. lb. torque. This will put the transmission in low gear, without hydraulic assistance.

3. **Be sure both brakes are securely set.**

4. **Now slowly release the brakes and advance the throttle.**

If the car now moves forward as though normal, the converter is probably okay, it is reasonable to assume that the trouble is in the transmission.

CAUTION: Do not, in any case, drive the car for even a short distance in this condition. This operation is for trouble shooting and not as a substitute for a tow job. There may be no oil in the transmission lubrication system.

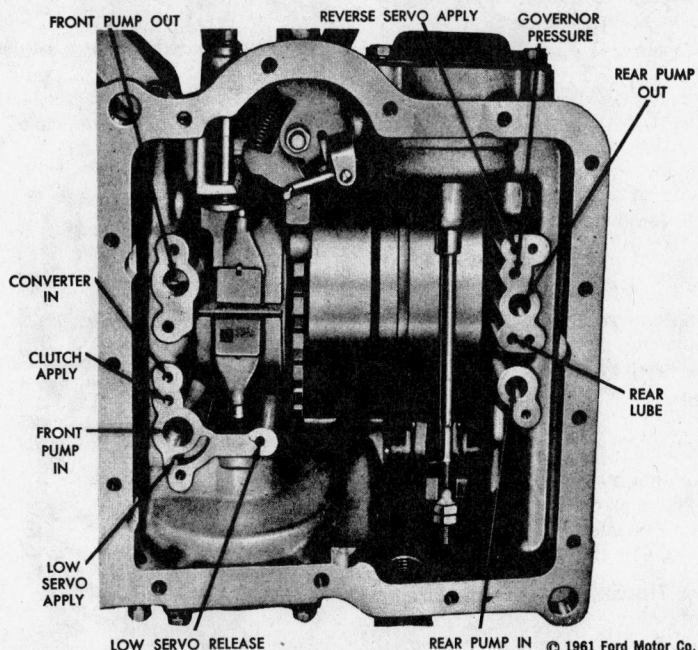

FRONT PUMP OUT   REVERSE SERVO APPLY   GOVERNOR PRESSURE

REAR PUMP OUT

CONVERTER IN

CLUTCH APPLY

FRONT PUMP IN

REAR LUBE

LOW SERVO APPLY

LOW SERVO RELEASE   REAR PUMP IN   © 1961 Ford Motor Co.

Fig. 18—Air Pressure Check Openings

AUTOMATIC TRANSMISSION

TROUBLE SHOOTING CHARTS

ITEMS MARKED (*), REQUIRE TRANSMISSION REMOVAL

Trouble: Grab or Harsh Engagement in "D", "L" and "R" Positions

CHECK

1. Engine idle speed
2. Throttle linkage

Trouble: Slip or Chatter in "D" or "L" Positions

CHECK

1. Oil level
2. Throttle linkage
3. Control pressure
4. Low band adjustment
5. Air pressure
6. Engine or transmission mounts
7. Low servo and band*
8. Leakage in low servo apply circuit*

Trouble: Slip or Chatter in "R" Position

CHECK

1. Oil level
2. Throttle linkage
3. Control pressure
4. Reverse band adjustment
5. Air pressure
6. Engine or transmission mounts
7. Reverse servo and band*
8. Leakage in reverse servo apply circuit*

Trouble: Creeps Excessively in "D" Position

CHECK

1. Engine idle speed
2. Oil viscosity

Trouble: Engine Overspeeds Between 1 & 2 Shift

CHECK

1. Oil level
2. Throttle linkage
3. Oil odor for evidence of burned plates
4. Control pressure
5. Low band adjustment
6. Air pressure
7. Control valve body
8. Leakage in clutch apply or low servo release circuit*
9. High clutch mechanism*
10. Planetary gears*

Trouble: Momentary Lock-up During 1-2 Shift

CHECK

1. Oil level
2. Throttle linkage
3. Control pressure
4. Low band adjustment

5. Low servo and band*
6. High clutch mechanism*
7. Low servo piston return spring*

Trouble: Severe 2-1 Shift During Coast-Down

CHECK

1. Engine idle speed
2. Throttle linkage
3. Control valve body
4. Control pressure

Trouble: No 1-2 Shift in "D" Position
CHECK

1. Oil level
2. Oil viscosity
3. Oil odor for evidence of burned plates
4. Throttle linkage
5. Manual linkage
6. Governor
7. Leakage in control pressure main circuit*
8. High clutch*
9. Low servo and band*

Trouble: Delayed 1-2 Shift

CHECK

1. Throttle linkage
2. Governor
3. Leakage in control pressure main circuit*

Trouble: Slips Continuously After 1-2 Shift

CHECK

1. Oil odor for evidence of burned plates
2. Oil level
3. Throttle linkage
4. Control pressure
5. Air pressure
6. High clutch plates*
7. Leakage in clutch apply or low servo release*

Trouble: No 2-1 Kick-Down

CHECK

1. Throttle linkage
2. Control valve body
3. Leakage in control pressure main circuit*

Trouble: No 2-1 Shift During Coast-Down

CHECK

1. Control valve body
2. Governor

Trouble: Oil Loss Thru Filler Tube or Vent

CHECK

1. For engine coolant and transmission oil contamination
2. Transmission external vent
3. Fluid aeration check

Trouble: Transmission Overheats
CHECK

1. Control pressure
2. Cooler flow check

Trouble: Acceleration Normal, but Maximum Speed is About 45 m.p.h.

CHECK

1. Converter one-way clutch*

Trouble: Acceleration Poor, but Performance Above 30 m.p.h., with Steady Throttle, Normal

CHECK

1. Converter one-way clutch*

Trouble: Engine Won't Start by Pushing

CHECK

1. Oil level
2. Manual linkage
3. Control valve body
4. Rear pump*
5. Leakage in control pressure main circuit*

Trouble: Parking Lock Does Not Hold, or Binds

CHECK

1. Manual linkage
2. Parking linkage or pawl*

TORQUE CONVERTER

The torque converter is a combination hydraulic torque multiplier and fluid coupling. The sectional views illustrate the difference between the water cooled converter used in Ford, and Edsel, and the air cooled version of the smaller power trains, Falcon and Comet. This converter is impractical to service in the field and must be replaced as a unit. Checks and limits are identical to those used with Cruis-O-Matic.

THROTTLE LEVER ADJUSTMENT—ALL MODELS, PRESSURE METHOD

1. Apply parking brake securely.
2. Raise car on a hoist, and remove the 1/8" pipe plug from the left hand side of the transmission case.

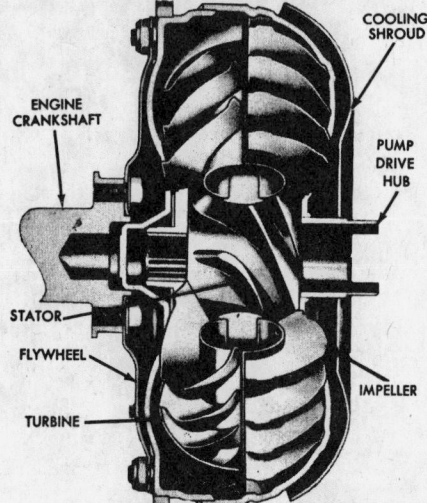

© 1961 Ford Motor Co.

Fig. 20—Air-Cooled Torque Converter

COMET
FALCON
FAIRLANE
FORD
MERCURY
METEOR

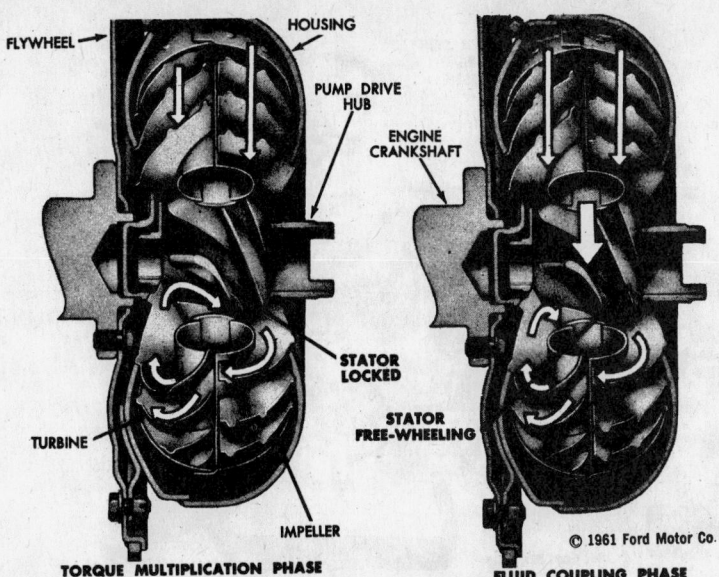

FLYWHEEL

HOUSING

PUMP DRIVE HUB

ENGINE CRANKSHAFT

STATOR LOCKED

TURBINE

STATOR FREE-WHEELING

IMPELLER

© 1961 Ford Motor Co.

TORQUE MULTIPLICATION PHASE

FLUID COUPLING PHASE

Water-Cooled Torque Converter

© 1959 Ford Motor Co.

Fig. 19—One-Way Clutch Check

3. Hook up a pressure gauge.

4. Lower the car to the floor.

5. Place the gauge so it can be read from the driver's seat and connect a tachometer to the engine.

6. Shift the selector lever to "D" position.

7. Apply service brakes. Increase engine speed to 1,000 R.P.M. (1,200 for Falcon and Comet). Note gauge reading. Pressure should be within limits shown in the following chart. If pressure is not within limits, adjust throttle control rod until correct reading is obtained.

ble other than throttle linkage adjustment is indicated. (Refer to Control Pressure Charts.)

8. Secure throttle rod clevis to the linkage and tighten the locknut to maintain the adjustment.

9. Check pressure adjustments at idle and stall speeds. Acceptable limits for idle and stall conditions are shown in the Control Pressure Limit Charts.

4. Remove six bolts that hold the valve body to the transmission case and remove the valve body assembly. (Fig. 23)

TRANSMISSION END PLAY CHECK

1. Mount a dial indicator on the transmission case, contacting the end of the primary sun gear (turbine) shaft. (Fig. 24).

2. Slip the front universal joint yoke on the output shaft spline to align the output shaft in the housing.

3. Pry the reverse ring gear forward. Set the dial indicator at zero.

4. Now pry the clutch drum to the rear. Record the end play in the shaft. End play should be from .020″ to .040″.

5. Remove the indicator and the aligning yoke.

CONTROL PRESSURE LIMITS

Engine Speed	Position	PSI
MERCURY-FORD & EDSEL		
Idle	All	46-56
1000 R.P.M.	D	77-84
Stall	D, L, R	170-192
FALCON-FAIRLANE		
Idle	All	46-56
1200 R.P.M.	D	78-82
Stall	D, L, R	170-192
COMET-METEOR		
Idle	All	40-48
1200 R.P.M.	D	55-60
Stall	D, L, R	135-155

From the preliminary adjustment, (in the Car Section of this manual) the rod may be lengthened or shortened by 2½ turns. If control pressures cannot be brought within limits, trou-

TRANSMISSION OVERHAUL

After removal of the transmission from the car and before dismantling any portion of the unit, **do yourself a favor and clean the entire outside of the transmission case.**

REMOVAL OF OIL PAN AND VALVE BODY

1. Remove converter and vent tube. Secure transmission in some type of transmission holder or stand.

2. Remove oil pan.

3. Remove oil screen holding clip, then remove screen.

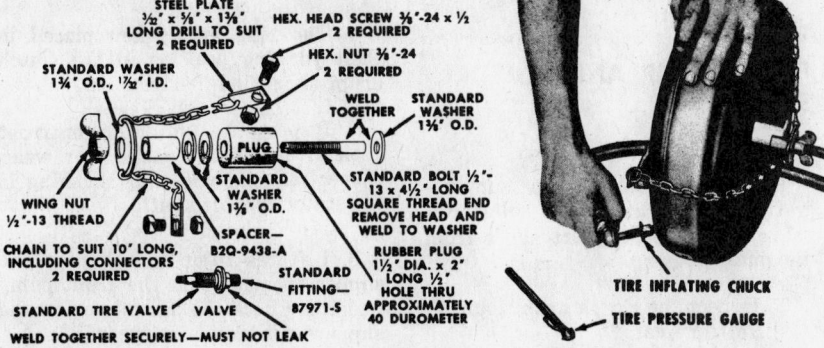

STEEL PLATE ½″ x ⅝″ x 1⅜″ LONG DRILL TO SUIT 2 REQUIRED

HEX. HEAD SCREW ⅜″-24 x ½ 2 REQUIRED

HEX. NUT ⅜″-24 2 REQUIRED

STANDARD WASHER 1¾″ O.D. 1½₂″ I.D.

WELD TOGETHER

STANDARD WASHER 1⅜″ O.D.

PLUG

WING NUT ½″-13 THREAD

STANDARD WASHER 1⅜″ O.D.

STANDARD BOLT ½″-13 x 4½″ LONG SQUARE THREAD END REMOVE HEAD AND WELD TO WASHER

SPACER— B2Q-9438-A

CHAIN TO SUIT 10″ LONG, INCLUDING CONNECTORS 2 REQUIRED

STANDARD FITTING— 87971-S

RUBBER PLUG 1½″ DIA. x 2″ LONG ½″ HOLE THRU APPROXIMATELY 40 DUROMETER

STANDARD TIRE VALVE

VALVE

WELD TOGETHER SECURELY—MUST NOT LEAK

TIRE INFLATING CHUCK

TIRE PRESSURE GAUGE

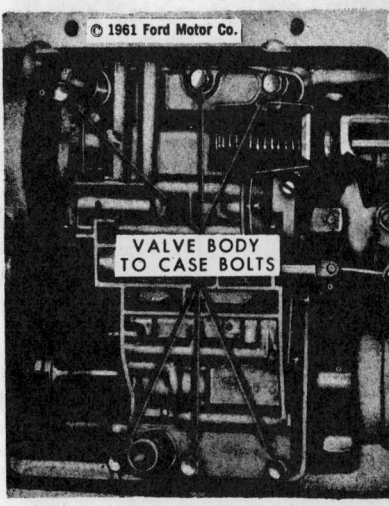

© 1961 Ford Motor Co.

VALVE BODY TO CASE BOLTS

Fig. 23—Control Valve Body Mounted on Transmission

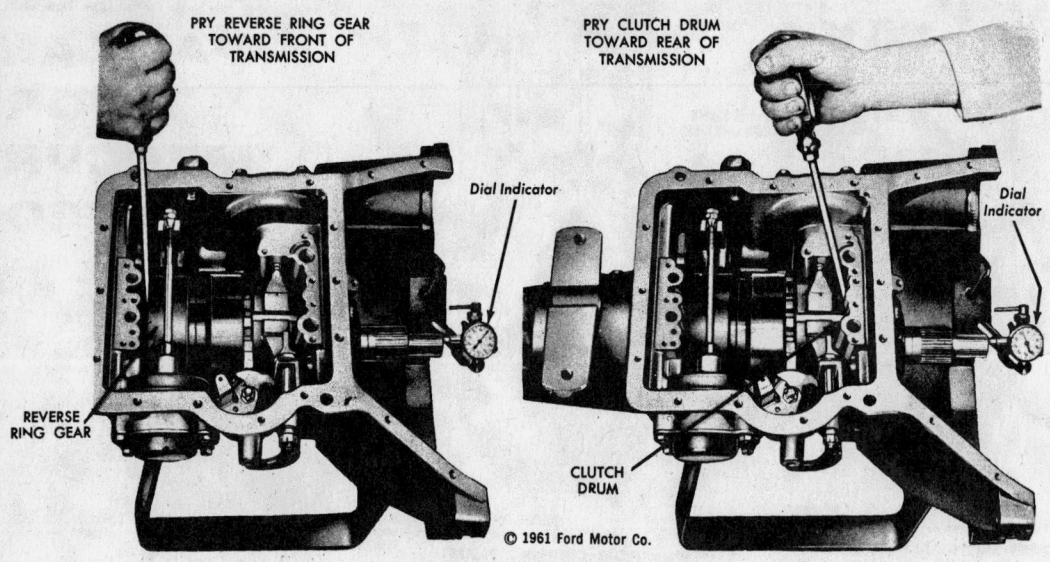

PRY REVERSE RING GEAR TOWARD FRONT OF TRANSMISSION

PRY CLUTCH DRUM TOWARD REAR OF TRANSMISSION

Dial Indicator

Dial Indicator

REVERSE RING GEAR

CLUTCH DRUM

© 1961 Ford Motor Co.

Fig. 24—Transmission End Play Check

REMOVAL OF CASE AND EXTENSION HOUSING PARTS

1. If extension housing bushing or seal is to be replaced, use special replacing tools.

2. Remove five extension housing to case bolts and lift off extension housing.

3. Remove the governor and governor drive ball, (Fig. 25).

4. Remove seven front pump attaching bolts. Remove front pump and stator support assembly.

5. Loosen the low band adjusting screw. Remove low band struts. Remove seal ring from the primary sun gear, (turbine) shaft and remove the clutch drum. Now, remove the low band.

6. Pull on the primary sun gear shaft and remove the integral pinion carrier and output shaft from the case. Rotate the assembly so the reverse gear can separate from the short pinions and stay in the case.

7. Remove the governor pressure seal rings from the output shaft. (These two metallic rings are located at the governor location on the output shaft.)

8. Place the integral output shaft and pinion carrier assembly in a bench fixture similar to that shown in Fig. 26.

9. Remove the reverse ring gear and ring gear rear thrust washer from the case.

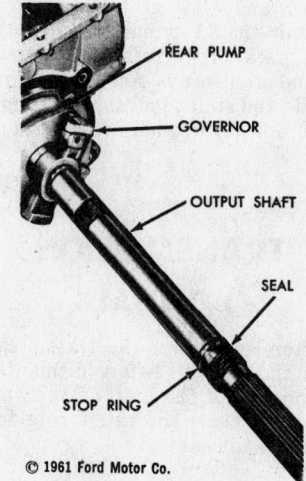

REAR PUMP

GOVERNOR

OUTPUT SHAFT

SEAL

STOP RING

© 1961 Ford Motor Co.

Fig. 25—Output Shaft, Governor, and Spline Seal

10. Remove four rear pump attaching bolts and remove the rear pump from the case.

11. Remove the reverse band and band strut from the case.

FRONT PUMP AND STATOR SUPPORT

1. Remove the five stator support-to-front pump attaching bolts. Remove the stator support shaft from the pump housing.

2. Inspect the clutch drum journal, (Fig.27) for wear.

© 1961 Ford Motor Co.

Tool— T59P-77059-B

PINION PIN RETAINER

Tool— T59P-77059-B

D1176-A

Fig. 26—Output Shaft Mounted in Holding Fixture

3. Check side clearance between the clutch. Apply pressure seal rings and their grooves in the stator support. These clearances should be .0035″ to .0045″.

4. The ring gap, when placed in their running position in the clutch drum should be .002″ to .009″.

5. Inspect the clutch drum front (selective) thrust washer for wear. Inspect the turbine shaft bushing in the stator support shaft.

6. Lift the rotor and slippers and slipper springs from the front pump housing. Check the pump housing and slippers for excessive wear.

COMET
FALCON
FAIRLANE
FORD
MERCURY
METEOR

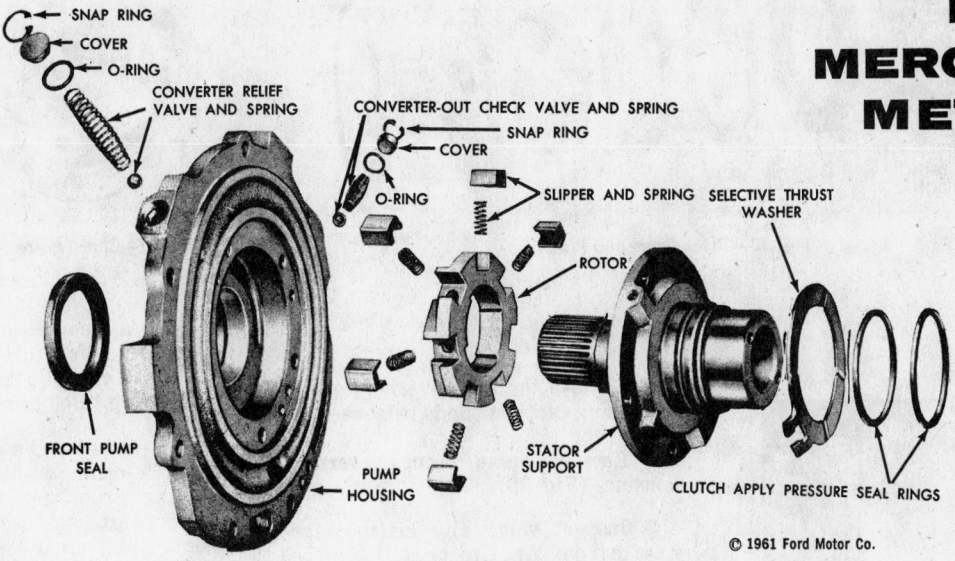

Fig. 27—Front Pump and Stator Support

7. The converter pressure relief valve and converter out check valve may be removed from the pump housing, (Fig. 27).

8. Inspect the pump bushing and seal.

9. To assemble the front pump, place the rotor in the pump housing, flat side up.

10. When installing the slippers and slipper springs, make sure each spring bottoms in the holes of both slipper and rotor.

11. Place stator support in the pump housing and install the five bolts. Torque the bolts to 12-15 foot pounds.

12. Check the pump for freedom of rotation by placing it on the converter pump drive hub in normal running position and turning the pump housing.

REAR PUMP

1. Remove the screws that hold the rear pump cover plate to the housing. Remove the plate.

2. Remove the rotor, slippers and springs.

3. Inspect all surfaces for wear or damage.

4. Install the governor pressure seal rings in the pump housing and check the ring gap. Tolerance is .001″ to .006″.

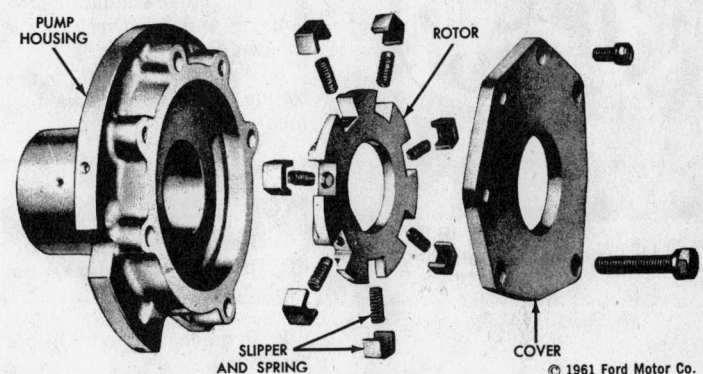

Fig. 28—Rear Pump—Disassembled

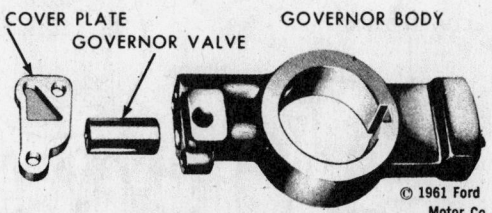

Fig. 29—Governor—Disassembled

5. Check governor pressure orifice for obstruction and size. Hole should be .063″.

6. Inspect all components for wear or damage. The slippers, housing and rotor must be replaced as a matched assembly. The springs, however, may be replaced as a set.

7. Assemble the pump, as illustrated in Fig. 28.

8. Install pump cover and torque the screws to 4 to 5 foot pounds.

9. Install the pump on the output shaft in its normal operating position and check for free rotation.

NOTE: Before removing the pump from the output shaft, make sure the flat surface of the pump rotor I.D. is toward the bottom of the pump housing.

845

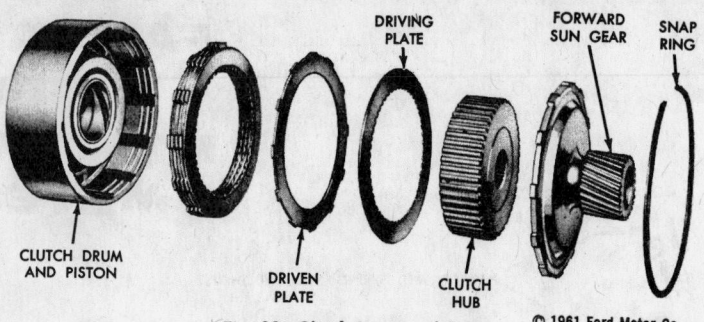

CLUTCH DRUM AND PISTON · DRIVEN PLATE · DRIVING PLATE · CLUTCH HUB · FORWARD SUN GEAR · SNAP RING

Fig. 30—Clutch Drum and Piston © 1961 Ford Motor Co.

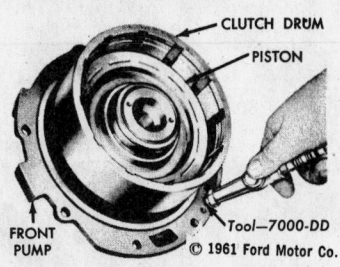

CLUTCH DRUM · PISTON · FRONT PUMP · Tool—7000-DD © 1961 Ford Motor Co.

Fig. 32—Clutch Piston Removal

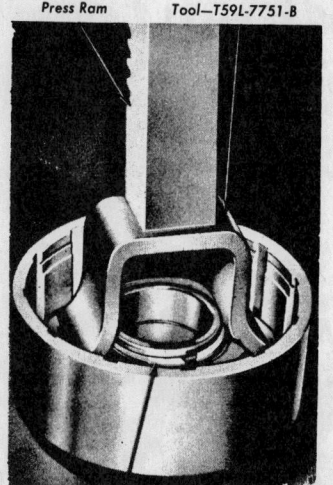

Press Ram · Tool—T59L-7751-B

SNAP RING © 1961 Ford Motor Co.

Fig. 31—Clutch Spring Snap Ring—Removal or Installation

GOVERNOR

1. Remove the two governor cover-to-housing screws and remove the plate.

2. Remove valve from governor housing, (Fig. 29).

3. Inspect valve and housing for wear and damage. Crocus cloth may be used for polishing but avoid rounding the sharp edges of the valve.

4. The valve should fit freely in the housing and fall through the bore of its own weight.

5. Assemble the governor and torque the plate screws to 20 to 30 inch pounds.

HIGH CLUTCH

1. Remove the large snap ring and lift the gear and flange out of the drum, (Fig. 30).

2. Remove the clutch plates and clutch hub.

3. With a compression tool, (Fig. 31) on the clutch piston spring retainer, apply enough pressure to allow the snap ring to be removed.

4. The piston can be removed from the clutch drum with air pressure. Place the drum on the assembled stator support shaft and front pump housing. Apply air pressure as shown in Fig. 32.

5. Remove outer seal from piston and the inner seal from the drum, (Fig. 33).

6. Check all components for wear and damage.

NOTE: If clutch plates are to be reused, DO NOT USE A DETERGENT or CAUSTIC TYPE CLEANING SOLUTION. None of the plates should show any degree of dish. They must be flat.

7. Inspect clutch piston ball check for freedom and proper seating. The ball check must be unobstructed and measure .039″ to .043″.

8. Install a new piston inner seal in the clutch drum and an outer seal on the piston. Lubricate and install the piston in the clutch drum.

9. Locate the piston return spring and spring retainer on the piston. Place the compression tool in the clutch drum and compress the spring. Install the retainer snap ring.

10. Install the drive and driven plates alternately in the clutch drum, starting with a steel plate next to the piston.

NOTE:
PBZ Model, Air Cooled .... 4 Plates
PBP Model, Water Cooled, 223 cu. in. "6" .... 6 Plates
PBR Model, Water Cooled, 292 cu. in. V-8 .... 8 Plates
PBS Model, Water Cooled, 352 cu. in. V-8 ....10 Plates

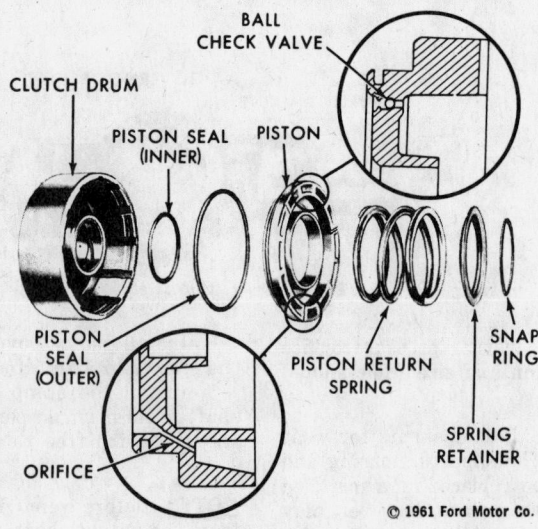

CLUTCH DRUM · PISTON SEAL (INNER) · PISTON · BALL CHECK VALVE · PISTON SEAL (OUTER) · PISTON RETURN SPRING · SNAP RING · SPRING RETAINER · ORIFICE

© 1961 Ford Motor Co.

Fig. 33—Clutch Drum and Piston

11. The last plate in the pack, (top of the pack) should be a non-metallic drive plate.

12. After the plates, install the clutch hub.

13. Install the integral forward sun gear and flange in the clutch drum, and install the snap ring.

CONTROL VALVE BODY

Five different control valve bodies are used, depending upon the torque requirements of the car involved and the application. The valve bodies are marked and can be identified by a number stamped on the lower valve body at the left hand front corner.

Illustrations 34 through 39 show the control valve body and components and their relationship. The Control Valve Body Spring Identification Charts will help in recognizing spring fatigue or other reasons for spring identification and replacement.

PLANETARY SYSTEM

The pinion carrier assembly is the same on all Two Speed Fordomatic models.

1. Mark the pinion shafts to help in reassembly in the same locations.

2. Take the retainer ring screws out of the pinion carrier. Turn the retainer counterclockwise until the shafts are unlocked, (Fig. 26).

3. Force a short pinion up with a dummy shaft, (Fig. 40) until the dummy clears the top of the gear spacer. Now, remove the short pinion and its upper and lower washers and needle bearings out the pinion carrier window. Hold the needle bearings in place in the short pinion by pushing the dummy out with the removed shaft.

4. Remove the two remaining short pinion assemblies in the same manner.

5. Remove the integral primary sun gear and shaft, (Fig. 41).

6. With a dummy shaft, push a long pinion shaft up until the dummy just clears the pinion carrier bottom plate, (Fig. 43). Remove the long pinion gear assembly in the same manner as the short pinion assembly, with the aid of a dummy.

7. Remove the two remaining long pinion assemblies in the same manner.

LOW SERVO

1. Remove two low servo cover bolts and install a tool as in Fig. 44, and apply pressure.

COMET
FALCON
FAIRLANE
FORD
MERCURY
METEOR

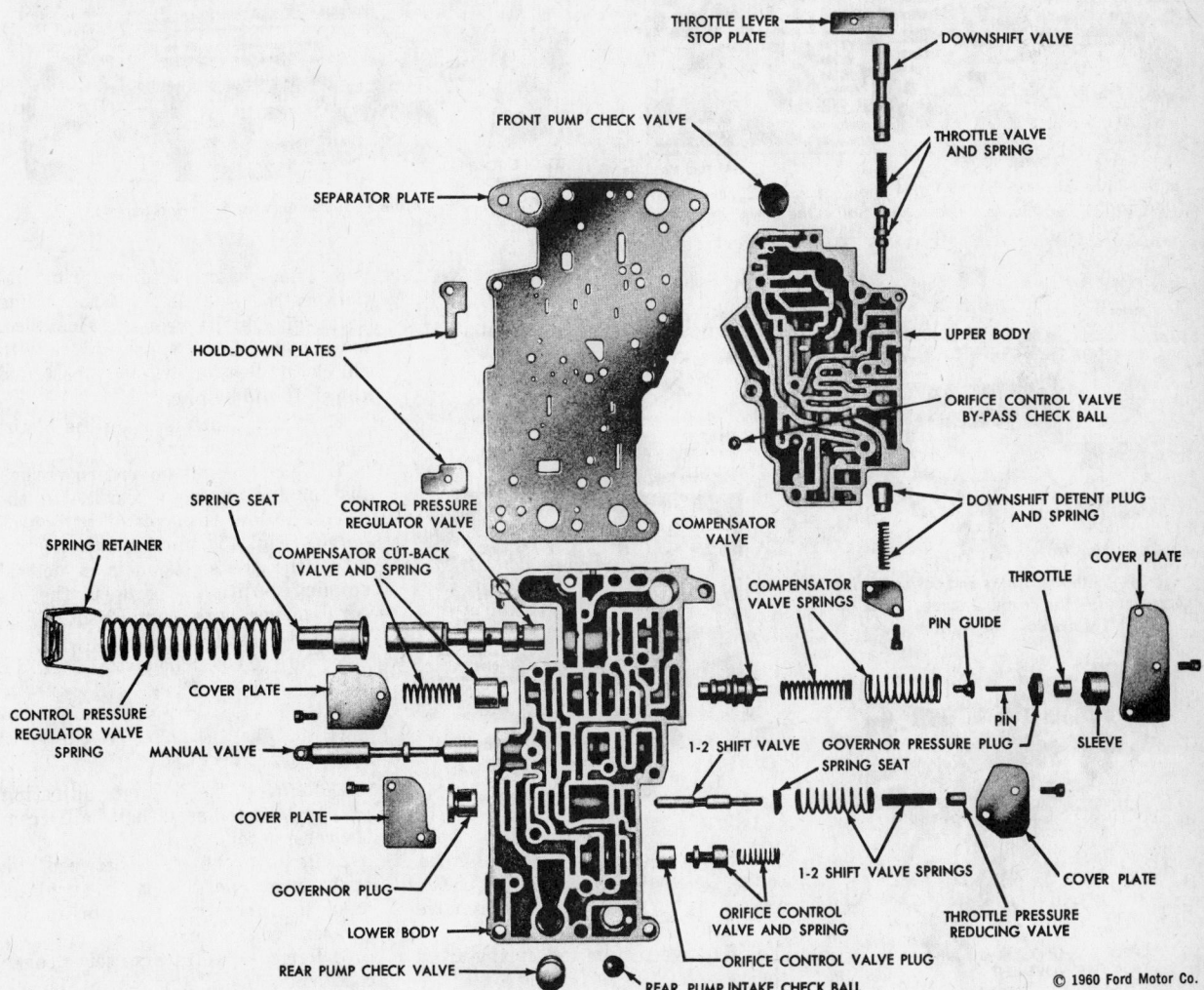

© 1960 Ford Motor Co.

Fig. 34—Control Valve Body—Disassembled

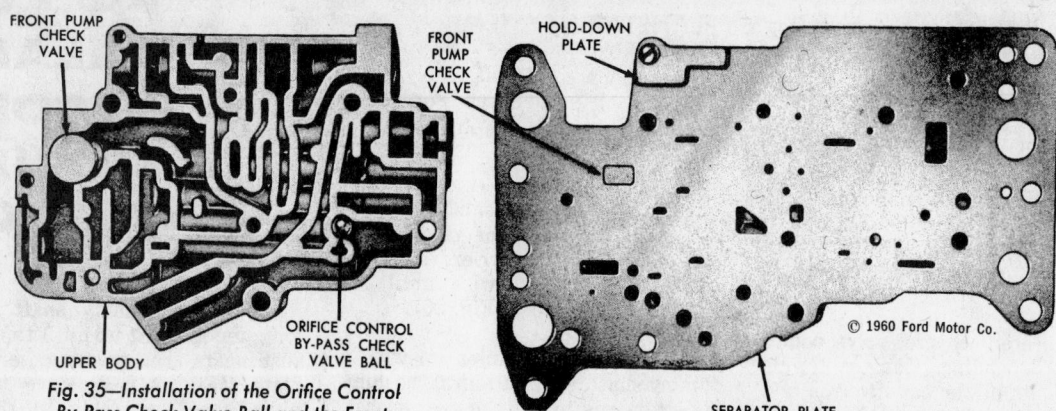

Fig. 35—Installation of the Orifice Control By-Pass Check Valve Ball and the Front Pump Check Valve

Fig. 36—The Hold-Down Plate and Screw are Used to Position the Separator Plate on the Upper Body

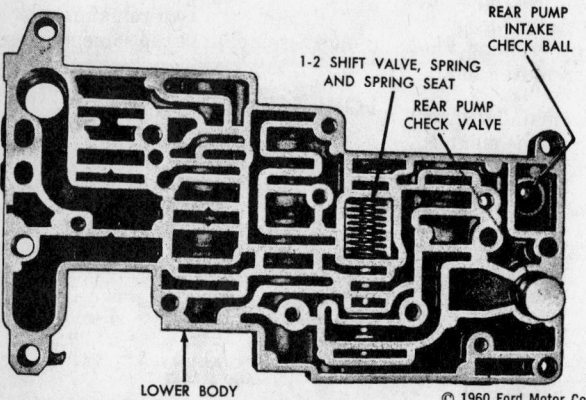

Fig. 37—Installation of the 1-2 Valve, the Rear Pump Check Valve and Spring Rear Pump Intake Check Ball in the Lower Body

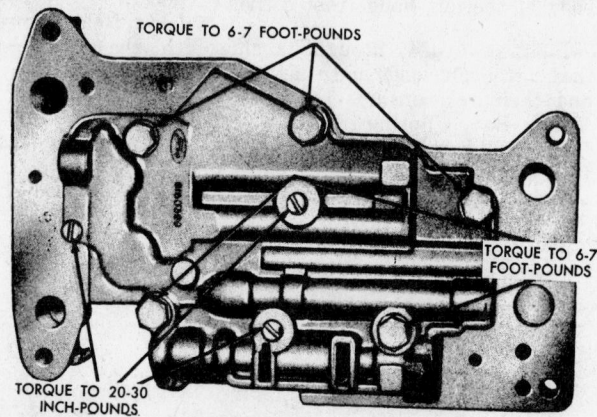

Fig. 38—Torque Requirements for Bolts and Screws

Fig. 39—With the Upper and Lower Bodies Assembled at the Proper Torque, Check the 1-2 Valve for Free Movement

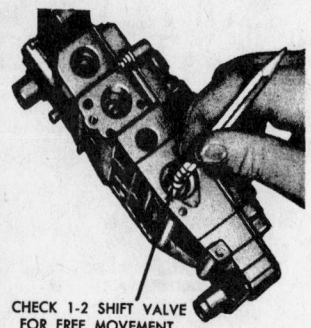

Fig. 40—Short Pinion Removal or Installation

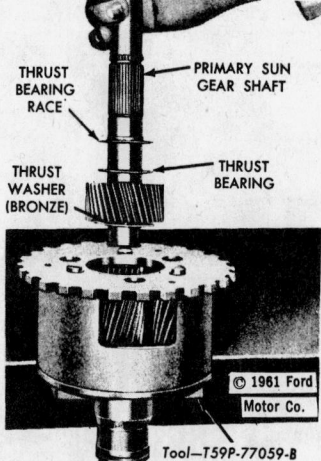

Fig. 41—Primary Sun Gear Removal or Installation

2. Remove the remaining cover bolts. Gradually release the piston return spring tension, then remove cover and seal.

3. Remove piston and spring from the case.

4. Inspect piston and bore for damage.

5. This piston return spring influences the 1—2 shift. If the spring is fatigued or the wrong one installed, low band release synchronism with clutch application will be upset and the shift will be rough.

6. Install a new seal on the piston and one on the cover.

7. Place the piston return spring, piston, and cover in position in the case. The low servo piston ball check valve, (Fig. 45) must be at the top, when the transmission is in normal running position. Compress the return spring with compressor, (Fig. 44) and install the cover.

8. Torque cover bolts to 12—15 ft. lb.

REVERSE SERVO

1. Remove the locknut, adjusting nut, and the rod seat (half-ball) from the reverse servo rod.

2. Remove the strut between the apply lever and the band. Turn the band to unhook it from its anchor and remove the band.

3. Remove two reverse servo cover case bolts. Install tool, as in Fig. 46, apply pressure and remove remaining bolts.

COMET
FALCON
FAIRLANE
FORD
MERCURY
METEOR

4. Back off the tool to relieve spring tension, remove cover, cover seal, piston, spring and piston rod.

5. Apply air pressure at the reverse servo apply passage in the case, (Fig. 18). This will force the piston out of the case.

6. Remove the piston outerseal.

7. Inspect the components.

8. Install a new seal on the piston. Lubricate and install the piston in the case. Insert the piston rod through the servo and into the case.

9. Place a new seal on the servo cover.

10. Place the return spring against the piston and the cover against the spring.

11. With the tool, (Fig. 46) compress the spring and install cover bolts.

12. Remove the tool, install remaining bolts and torque all cover bolts to 12 to 15 ft. lb.

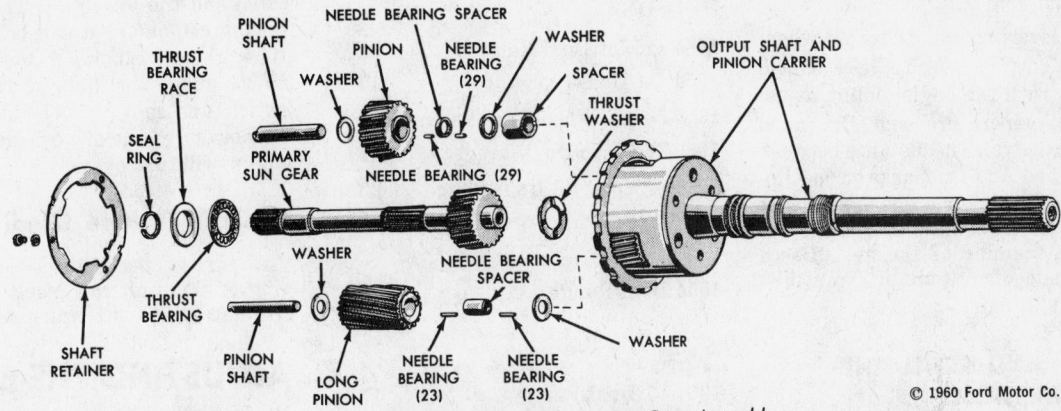

Fig. 42—Pinion Carrier and Primary Sun Gear Assembly

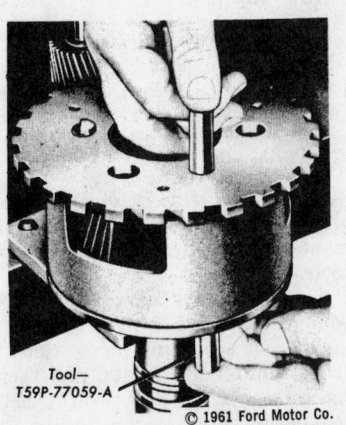

Fig. 43—Long Pinion Removal or Installation

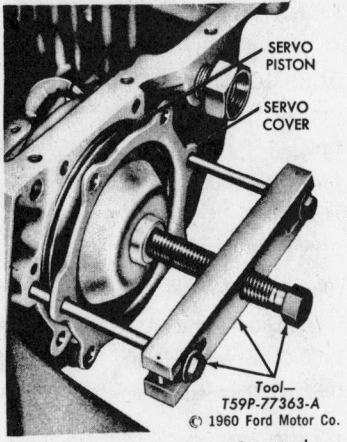

Fig. 44—Low Servo Cover Removal or Installation

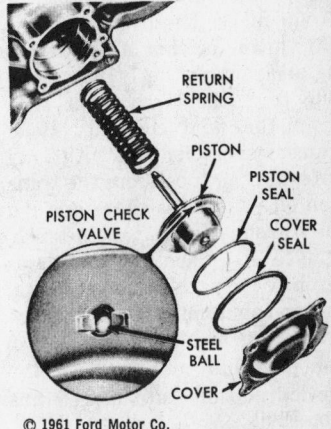

Fig. 45—Low Servo—Disassembled

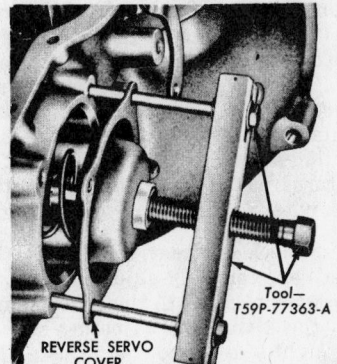

Fig. 46—Reverse Servo Cover Removal or Installation

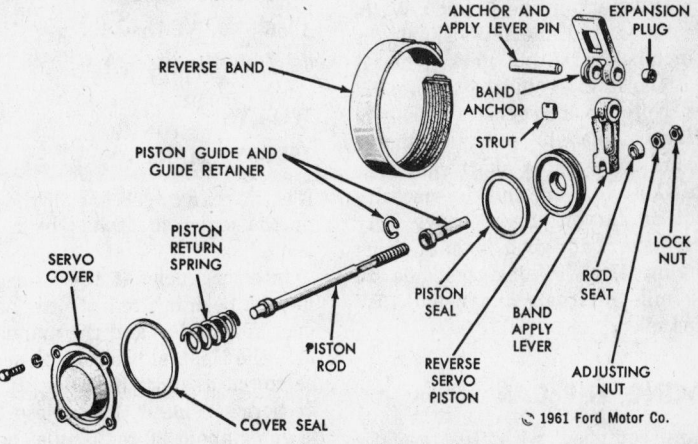

Fig. 47—Reverse Servo Piston and Band Apply Linkage

849

HYDRAMATIC TRANSMISSIONS

GENERAL INFORMATION APPLICABLE TO ALL MODELS

Corvair and Tempest Transmission Procedures will be found in the car section.

CHECKING HYDRAMATIC FLUID LEVEL

Fluid level should be checked whenever the car is greased. Check should be made with the engine idling at operating temperature and the hand lever at Neutral. The distance between the Full and Add-Oil marks on the dipstick represents about one pint. Do not overfill the transmission as this will result in foaming of the fluid. Use a good grade of Automatic Transmission Fluid.

DRAIN AND REFILL THE TRANSMISSION

The fluid should be drained every 25,000 miles. Remove the inspection plate in the bottom of the Bell Housing and remove the 7/16ths inch pipe plug from the torus cover so as to drain the fluid coupling. Hold the transmission filler tube with a rag and unfasten the tube from the transmission oil pan unless there is a plug in the transmission oil pan, in which case remove it. When all the fluid has drained from the fluid coupling and the transmission oil pan, replace the drain plug and the filler tube or oil pan plug and pour in 8 quarts of a good grade of Automatic Transmission Fluid.

Now with the engine running add fluid to bring the level within 1/4" of the full mark on the dipstick. When the fluid is cold the level should be 1/4 inch below the full mark. When it is hot the level should be at the full mark. **Note:** In emergencies SAE 10W Engine Oil may be used but should only be left in for a short run. It is more likely to foam and the viscosity is not as durable. Some heavy duty users have had good results from changing the draining schedule to 3,000 mile intervals and using 10W engine oil.

TOWING THE CAR

Cars equipped with Hydra-matic transmissions should not be towed un-

APPROXIMATE TOTAL NUMBER OF PINTS TO REFILL HYDRA-MATIC AFTER DRAINING

CAR	PINTS
CADILLAC	
1954-55 Dual-Range	22
1956 Dual-Coupling	23
1957-63 Dual-Coupling	22
HUDSON	
1954 ex. Jet Dual-Range	22
1954 Jet Dual-Range	17
1955-56 ex. Wasp Dual-Range	22
1955-56 Wasp Dual-Range	17
1956-57 Spcl. V8 Dual-Range	23
LINCOLN	
1954 Dual-Range	22
NASH	
1954-55 Dual-Range	17
1956-57, 6 Cyl. Dual-Range	17
1957, V8 Dual-Range	23
OLDSMOBILE	
1954-55 Dual-Range	20
1956-60, Jet-A-Way	22
1961-63, 3 speed	18½
PONTIAC	
1954 Dual-Range	22
1955- Dual-Range	19
1956-63, Strato-Flight	18½
1961-63, 3 speed	18½
RAMBLER	
1954-55 Dual-Range	17
1956-57 6 Cyl. Dual-Range	17
1957, V8 Dual-Range	23
WILLYS	
1954-55 Dual-Range	22

less the rear wheels are off the ground or the drive shaft has been disconnected.

In emergencies if the transmission has not been injured, the car has gone over 2500 miles, and the manual lever is in the Neutral position, the car may be towed a short distance. It should be borne in mind that unless the car is going about 20 to 25 miles per hour the rear pump does not have enough capacity to properly lubricate the transmission. From this fact comes the advice that to tow one of these cars with the transmission turning will undoubtedly damage it.

STARTING ENGINE WITHOUT USE OF STARTER

Put the hand lever in Neutral. Have another car push from behind. (Never tow to start; the engine will catch and the towed car will ram the towing car before it can be stopped.) When the car is being pushed at about 20-25 miles per hour turn on the switch and move the hand lever to Low or one of the drive positions. The engine will turn over.

COOLER (Where Used)

Be sure to check the oil cooler. Clogging of this unit can result in extensive damage to the transmission.

ADJUSTING THE BANDS

DUAL-RANGE MODELS Thru 1954

On these models there are two screws on the left side of the case just above the side cover. The front band adjustment screw is to the front and the rear band adjusting screw is to the rear.

Perfect adjustment requires special gages but a quite serviceable adjustment can be done without special tools.

The basic idea of this system of band adjustment is to determine the number of adjusting screw turns between full on and full off and then to tighten the bands just two-thirds that number of turns.

Place the transmission in Low Range 1st speed. Now with the motor running and the brakes full on adjust the two bands until they are tight. Next shift the transmission into neutral. Count the number of turns required to tighten bands so they just contact the drums. Loosen the adjusting screws exactly 1/3 the number of turns just counted and tighten the lock nuts.

To check in order to be sure the bands are correctly adjusted: Return the transmisssion to the Drive range and check that the adjusting screws are tight and cannot be adjusted by hand, then put the transmission in Neutral and check that the adjusting screws are loose. If all is well retighten the lock nuts.

DUAL RANGE MODELS
Starting 1955

These models have only one external band adjusting screw. It is behind the pressure takeoff point on the left side of the case above the levers. It is for the rear band. Adjustment of the front band cannot be made without the special gauge which can only be used after the transmission oil pan has been removed.

The rear band can be adjusted in this manner: With the engine running and the hand brake set put the manual control level in Low Range. Now loosen the adjusting screw quite a bit and then slowly screw it in until it starts to contact the drum. You can feel it. The band is now too loose. Now put the hand lever in Neutral and then while carefully counting the turns tighten the screw until the band contacts the drum. Turn the screw back out from this counted-to position one-third the number of turns made to get it there. This will be an approximately correct position. Check by moving the hand lever again to Low and noting that the adjusting screw is tight and then returning to Neutral to note that it is loose. These things being so, tighten the lock nut.

TESTING THE DUAL-RANGE HYDRAMATIC

Before any testing or diagnosis is attempted, fluid level must be checked and brought to the proper level. An excessive amount of fluid or insufficient fluid can cause slipping, jerking, erratic shifting, etc.

Before road testing to check for high shift speeds, slipping, or no drive, either forward or reverse, make a stall test to check transmission and engine performance.

STALL TEST

A "stall" or torque test should be made to determine engine and transmission performance. This test must be used with moderation because considerable strain is exerted on the drive line, differential gears and axles. To perform "stall test" proceed as follows:

1. Start engine and warm up to operating temperature.
2. Connect electric tachometer.
3. Set hand brake lever tightly and apply foot brake firmly.
4. Place shift control lever in DR position.
5. Depress accelerator pedal to floor.

Action here has placed transmission in first speed. Brakes are applied, therefore the car cannot move. Opening the throttle and speeding up the engine is comparable to slipping a mechanical clutch, as the driving torus is turning and trying to turn the driven torus which is held stationary by the transmission being in first speed and brakes locked.

The engine will speed up until the friction created between the torus members equals the power output on the engine. Engine efficiency will be noted by its stall RPM which should be between 1750 and 1900 RPM.

If engine RPM is less than 1750 the engine is in need of a tune-up.

If engine continues to speed up to, or above 2200 RPM, it indicates that bands are not holding properly or that there is slippage in fluid coupling due to damaged torus members.

CAUTION: EXTREME CARE MUST BE USED IN MAKING THIS TEST. NEVER HOLD THROTTLE OPEN MORE THAN ONE MINUTE. IF ENGINE SPEEDS UP TO 2000 RPM, CLOSE THROTTLE IMMEDIATELY TO AVOID POSSIBLE DAMAGE TO TRANSMISSION.

6. To check for a cause of slipping, place selector lever in R and test again. In reverse the front band and reverse cone clutch are applied. Slippage in this test indicates front band or reverse cone clutch slippage.

TORUS CHECK VALVE TEST

A missing torus check valve or torus check valve stuck open, will cause the engine to speed up excessively when starting away after the car has been standing for a short time.

Determine the effectiveness of the torus check valve and pump relief valve by checking the rate at which fluid drains back from the coupling into the transmission.

1. Set hand brake lever tightly.
2. See that fluid is at the "Full" mark on the indicator.
3. After level has been checked, shut off engine and wait 10 minutes. Recheck fluid level with engine shut off. If after 10 minutes, the fluid level in the transmission has not raised more than 1/2 inch, the check valve and relief valve are operating satisfactorily. Should oil level be raised more than 1/2", the check valve or relief valve is not operating satisfactorily and should be replaced.

FLUID PRESSURE TESTS —DUAL-RANGE

Fluid Pressure With Car At Rest

Install a pressure gauge on the transmission at the line pressure test point.

Start engine and operate for several minutes to warm transmission oil to normal operating temperature, (approx. 175° F.).

When transmission is thoroughly warm, check pressure in all ranges. Pressure should be at least 50 lbs. in N, in both DR ranges, and in LO, with a maximum variation of 10 lbs. between ranges. Pressure may be higher in reverse.

Fluid Pressure Car Coasting

Make closed throttle pressure road test as follows:

Drive car at a speed of over 30 MPH in 4th speed.

Release accelerator and check pressure gauge reading as car speed drops to exactly 30 MPH. Pressure should be between 64 and 72 lbs.

Fluid Pressure Car Accelerating

Make full throttle pressure road test as follows:

With car operating at approximately 25 MPH in 4th speed, press accelerator pedal to detent without going into a forced downshift.

Check pressure as car speed reaches exactly 30 MPH. Gauge should read 101-109 lbs.

Fluid Pressure Car Reversing

Check pressure in reverse as follows:

Stop car and set hand brake firmly. Place selector lever in R, apply foot brake and open accelerator to half throttle. Pressure should increase to 145 to 185 lbs.

ROAD TEST—DUAL-RANGE

Diagnosis of malfunctions can frequently be aided by noting oil pressure under all operating conditions while driving on the road.

A predetermined test route should be established to save time and permit comparison of different cars over the same route. Where possible the route should be laid out to include a hilly section to test for open throttle upshift, slippage and throttle downshifts, a level section for testing upshift points and a quiet section for testing for noise. When a chassis dynamometer is available, it may be used as a substitute for the road test.

If possible a pressure gauge should be installed and pressure should be checked in all speeds while car is being operated on road.

Shift speeds should be checked and abnormal operating conditions should be noted during road test.

HYDRAMATIC TRANSMISSIONS

TESTING DUAL-RANGE WITH AIR PRESSURE

The following procedure outlines a method of testing a Hydramatic transmission in the car by use of air pressure applied with a special gun to the transmission case passages which are reached after removing the control valve body and reverse clutch pipe. While primarily designed to allow checking before removing the transmission from the car, the procedure applies equally well to checking a transmission assembly on the bench.

TEST PROCEDURE USING AIR PRESSURE

Remove bottom pan (after draining oil), oil screen, side cover, pressure regulator reverse oil pipe, parking pawl return spring, control valve assembly, and reverse clutch pipe. Using an air hose connected to approximately 80 lbs. per sq. in. air pressure, and referring to the oil passage identification illustration, carefully check each passage in sequence, observing operation of unit actuated and presence of any unusual leakage.

FRONT CLUTCH APPLY

Air pressure applied into FRONT CLUTCH passage should actuate front clutch. As pressure is intermittently applied, movement of the clutch piston should be audible and, in most cases, can be felt by holding front drum firmly with free hand.

If an unusual amount of air is escaping around oil delivery sleeve area, another check at this point must be made after servos are removed to observe more clearly the exact point of leakage.

If a fog of oil is emitted from inside of front unit drum assembly accompanied by the escape of a great amount of air, leak is probably due to a faulty front clutch annular piston seal.

Leakage from any other drilled passages inside of transmission case, while pressure is applied in FRONT CLUTCH passage, is an indication of a faulty transmission case or oil delivery sleeve allowing pressure to "short circuit" between passages.

FRONT BAND APPLY

Air pressure applied into FRONT BAND APPLY passage should actuate front servo and apply band with no unusual escape of air. A small amount of leakage is permissible between front servo valve body and servo body, and between servo body and transmission case.

It is also normal for a small amount of air to escape past line plug in servo body. A little air will also be noted escaping from FRONT BAND RELEASE, COMPENSATOR and GOVERNOR passages. Leaks from any of these passages should not be a direct blow-by, however, but only that amount which would escape past ring gaps or around 4-3 downshift valve.

FRONT BAND RELEASE

Air pressure applied into FRONT BAND RELEASE passage will not actuate servo because apply piston is held in released position by retracting spring. However, there should be no unusual escape of air between servo body and transmission case or around joint between servo band release cylinder and servo body, except that which would normally leak past servo

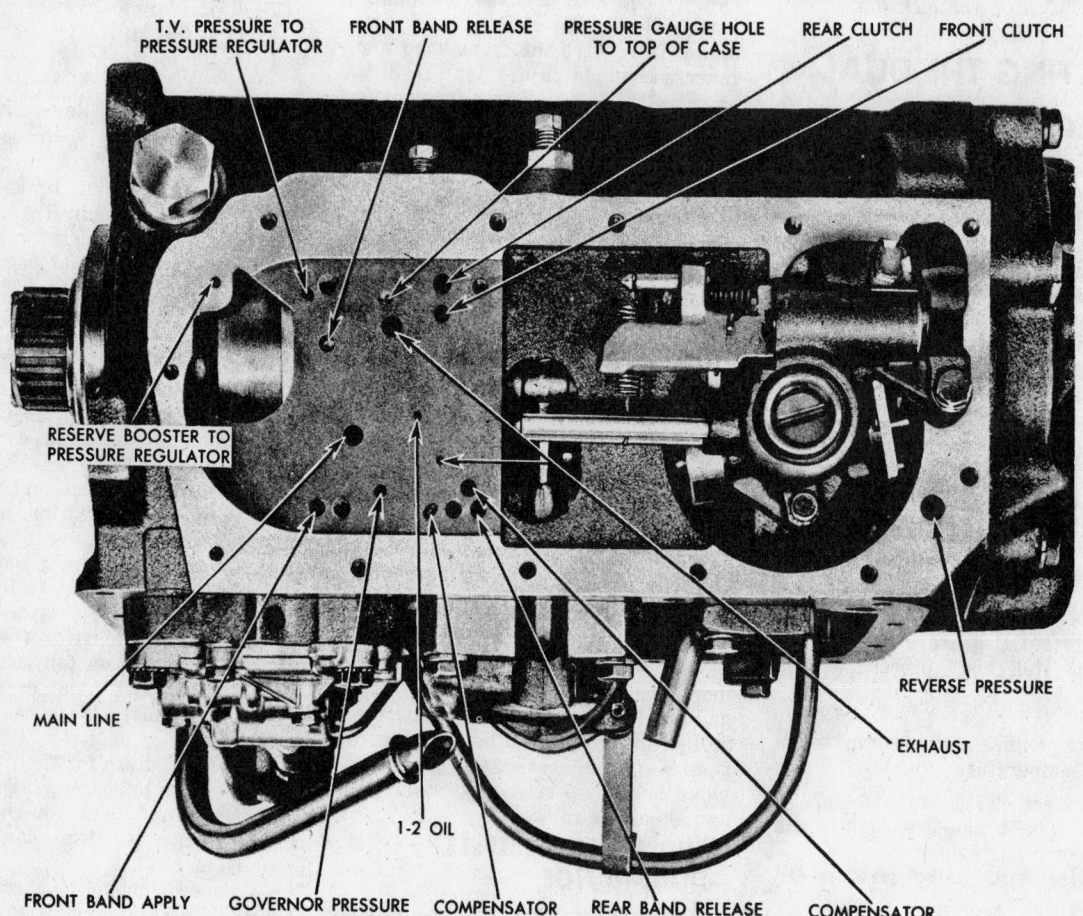

Fig. 3—Dual-Range Hydramatic Air Pressure Check Points

release piston ring gap. A small leak may also be detected at FRONT BAND APPLY and COMPENSATOR passages due to normal leakage past ring gaps.

GOVERNOR

When air pressure is applied into the GOVERNOR passage no air should escape between servo body and transmission case or from any other passages on side of case except a very small amount from FRONT BAND APPLY and COMPENSATOR passages.

REAR BAND RELEASE

Air pressure applied into REAR BAND RELEASE passage should release rear servo and band. A small amount of air will escape through piston ring gaps, but this would not indicate enough leakage to impair normal servo operation. See that no appreciable amount of air escapes between servo body and case. A very small amount of air may be emitted from COMPENSATOR passage, but there should be no leaking from any other passage.

REAR CLUTCH

Air pressure applied into REAR CLUTCH passage should actuate rear clutch. As pressure is intermittently applied, movement of the clutch piston should be audible and, in most cases, can be felt by holding rear drum firmly with free hand.

If an unusual amount of air is escaping around oil delivery sleeve area, another check at this point must be made after servos are removed to observe more clearly exact point of leakage.

If a fog of oil is emitted from inside rear unit drum assembly, accompanied by escape of a large amount of air, leak is probably due to a faulty rear clutch annular piston seal.

Leakage from any other drilled passage in side of transmission case while pressure is applied in rear clutch passage is an indication of faulty transmission case or oil delivery sleeve allowing pressure to "short circuit" between passages.

COMPENSATOR—FRONT SERVO

Air pressure applied into front servo compensator passage should actuate front servo to apply front band. No appreciable amount of air should escape from the front servo, or any

other passages on side of case except that which might escape through piston ring gaps.

COMPENSATOR—REAR SERVO

Air pressure applied into rear servo compensator passage should actuate rear servo to tighten rear band which is applied by spring pressure. Some leakage will be noted at exhaust hole on bottom side of rear servo body due to normal leakage past ring gaps. No appreciable amount of air should escape from the rear servo or any other passages on the side of the case except that which might escape through piston ring gaps. Also the 4-3 valve in the front servo will be actuated by the air applied in the rear servo.

MAIN LINE

Pressure directed in MAIN LINE passage should be an open blow-by due to the fact that the main line exhaust valve is in the exhaust position.

LINE PRESSURE

Air pressure applied into pressure gauge hole passage should produce no leak whatever if plug is in place.

Observe other passages for escaping air indicating interconnecting passages due to faulty case.

EXHAUST PASSAGES

Air pressure applied into EXHAUST passages should be a complete blow-by to inside of transmission case. Visually inspect hole to be sure that it is completely open for its full diameter to the inside of the case. A partial obstruction of EXHAUST passage can cause poor shift conditions.

REVERSE

Air pressure applied into REVERSE passage should actuate the reverse cone clutch with no unusual escape of air. As pressure is intermittently applied, movement of the reverse internal gear can be felt and seen as the cone clutch is applied and released.

REVERSE BOOSTER AND THROTTLE VALVE

Air pressure applied first to REVERSE BOOSTER passage should be heard to actuate reverse booster plug. Some leakage will be heard, but there should be no direct blow-by. Pressure applied to THROTTLE VALVE pas-

sage after actuating reverse booster should be heard to actuate throttle valve plug. Some leakage will be heard but there should be no direct blow-by.

1-2 OIL

Air pressure applied at 1-2 OIL passage should actuate the rear servo exhaust valve. A very slight leak past the exhaust valve will result in slight leak at REAR BAND RELEASE passage and at the hole in the accumulator body at the end of the exhaust valve bore.

DUAL-RANGE TROUBLE SHOOTING CHART

Items ending with X require removal of the transmission from the car.

1. SHIFTS OCCUR AT TOO HIGH OR TOO LOW A SPEED

This trouble may be caused by:
Improper linkage adjustment.
Malfunctioning governor.
Sticking control valve.

2. SHIFTS ARE ERRATIC

This trouble may be due to:
Improper linkage adjustment.
Sticking control valve.
Leaks in the hydraulic system. X
Malfunctioning governor.

3. SHIFT HUNTING

This trouble may be due to:
Improper linkage adjustment.
Compensator valve in control valve assembly not working.

4. MISSES ONE OR MORE SHIFTS

This trouble may be due to:
Sticking valves in the control valve assembly.
Sticking governor valve.
Front band not holding.

5. NO SHIFT STAYS IN SAME GEAR OR SHIFTS VIOLENTLY

This trouble may be due to:
Improper linkage adjustment.
Sticking valves in control valve assembly.
Weak pressure regulator valve spring.

6. CAR LUNGES FORWARD WHEN SHIFTING FROM NEUTRAL TO DRIVE. CLUNK NOISE APPARENT

This trouble may be due to:
Broken rear servo check valve or check valve spring.

7. EXCESSIVE SLIP WHEN STARTING FROM STAND-STILL

This trouble may be due to:
Torus check valve missing or stuck. X
Front pump relief valve stuck.

8. SELECTOR LEVER STUCK IN REVERSE

This trouble may be due to:
Damaged parking pawl. X
Rough detent plunger.

9. SELECTOR LEVER WON'T GO INTO REVERSE

This trouble may be due to:
Governor G-1 valve stuck open.
Damaged parking assembly. X

10. IMPROPER THROTTLE DOWNSHIFTS

These troubles may be due to:
Maladjusted linkage.
Leaks in the hydraulic system allowing loss of oil pressure. X.
Sticking valves in valve body.
Sticking valves in Governor.
Defective front pump. X
4-3 Valve not working.
Rear servo piston sticking.
Rear servo to accumulator gasket improperly installed.

11. EXCESSIVE CREEPING

This trouble may be due to:
Improper engine idling speed.
Leaking annular piston seal rings in the front or rear units. X

12. CAR WILL NOT MOVE IN ANY RANGE OR THERE IS EXCESSIVE SLIP

This trouble may be due to:
Incorrect oil level.
Improperly adjusted linkage.
Lack of oil pressure. X
Improperly adjusted bands.
Malfunctioning front pump. X
Valves in control valve assembly sticking.
Front servo not working properly.
Rear servo not working properly.
Loose or damaged valves in the fluid coupling. X
Leaking seals in the front unit. X
Leaking seals in the rear unit. X
Leaks in the hydraulic system. X

13. JUMPS OUT OF REVERSE

This trouble may be due to:
Manual linkage improperly adjusted.
Reverse unit not functioning correctly. X
Damaged side cover.

14. TRIES TO REVERSE WHILE IN DRIVE OR LOW

This trouble may be due to:
Oil leaking past an improperly fitted front servo exhaust valve.
Damaged front servo exhaust body plate.
Damaged detent retainer spacer permitting oil to leak from end of double transition valve.

15. DRIVES IN REVERSE ONLY

This trouble may be due to:
Improperly adjusted linkage.
Defective Reverse unit. X
Manual detent lever loose on shaft.
Broken rear band. X

16. NOISES

LOW PRESSURE RATTLE IN FRONT PUMP

Trouble—Low pressure rattle in front pump can be heard as a light rattle or buzz when "floating" in high, from 35 miles per hour down to about 24 to 22 m.p.h. (most critical period). At this point it cuts off cleanly and is not apparent at lower speeds.

Remedy—If a new regulator valve body does not eliminate the rattle, when installed, the pump gears should be replaced.

HIGH PRESSURE WHINE IN FRONT PUMP

Trouble—High pressure whine in front can be heard as a growl or howl when the car is standing still, in neutral. Note approximate speed at which engine is running, then drive car at approximately 30 to 35 mph, or at speed above which the rear pump takes over high pressure load. Throw manual lever into neutral and bring engine speed up to point where noise was heard when standing still. If whine or growl is not apparent, then a front pump high pressure noise exists. This front pump high pressure whine or growl is apparent only up to point when rear pump takes over high pressure load.

Remedy—Examine pump gears for wear or dirty condition. If this condition exists, clean or replace parts affected.

REAR PUMP AND DRIVE, NOISY

Trouble—To detect rear pump noise, drive car at 25-35 mph, shift into neutral, shut off engine and allow car to coast through range. Then listen for a clicking noise or a light knock. This is most usually caused by nicked teeth.

Drive gear noise can be heard at any time and sounds like a low axle growl heard on drive, coast and torque changeover. It usually peaks at 28-32 mph.

Remedy—Replace the rear pump.

LOOSE TORUS NUT

Trouble—This causes a scraping sound on initial start or stop until driven member catches up to speed of driving member in fourth gear.

Remedy—Tighten torus nut to 50-60 foot pounds torque and lock with lock plate.

DUAL-RANGE MECHANICAL DETAIL

REMOVE FLUID COUPLING—DUAL-RANGE

Straighten lock plate and remove lock nut at front of mainshaft.

Slide the driven torus member forward off the shaft. There is a torus check valve and spring between the driven torus and the drive torus. It may or may not be held to the driven torus with two bolts. Now remove the snap ring from the intermediate shaft just forward of the driving torus Fig. 2 and slide the torus forward off the shafts. Fig 3.

Remove the torus cover by pulling it gently from the front oil pump oil seal. Be careful of the oil ring inside the front pump cover. Remove the

Fig. 2—Remove Driving Torus Snap Ring Dual-Range

four bolts holding the flywheel housing to the case and remove the housing. See Fig. 4.

Fig. 3—Remove Driving Torus –Dual-Range

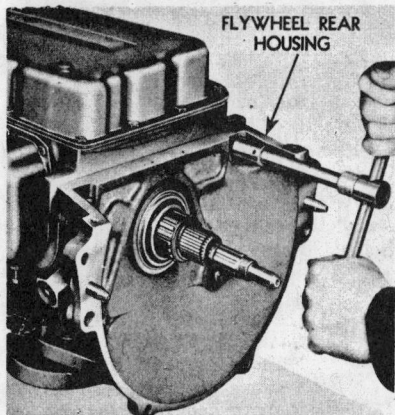

Fig. 4—Unbolting flywheel housing —Dual-Range

REMOVE VALVE BODY, GOVERNOR, REAR OIL PUMP AND SERVOS—DUAL-RANGE

This can be done with unit in the car.

Unbolt and remove the oil pan.

Unbolt and remove the side cover. Note that these bolts use copper washers in addition to lock washers. Loosen rear band adjusting screw. Remove the oil pipe running from the valve body to the pressure regulator valve. Using the manual valve lever as a wrench turn the manual valve control shaft to put the valve in "Lo" position (next to last detent counterclockwise).

Remove four valve body to case attaching screws and slide the valve body from the oil pipes. Fig 6.

Unhook the parking brake release spring from the inside one of the two governor pipes and remove the two governor pipes and reverse clutch pipe.

Remove the parking pawl support bolt and position the pawl down. Straighten the special lock on the

lower bolt and remove the two bolts holding the parking brake bracket. Remove the bracket and governor sleeve assembly. Do not lose the roller from the parking brake pawl crank.

Unscrew the pressure regulator valve while holding in against the spring pressure. Remove the valve as an assembly. The design of this valve has varied considerably from year to year so do not lose any of its parts.

Remove the intake screen from the

Fig. 6—Removing valve body from transmission case—Dual-Range

rear and front pump intake pipes and remove the front intake pipe.

Loosen the front band adjusting screw. This can be the forward of the two screws on the outside of the case or (staring with 1954 models) it is the notched affair on the front servo, see Fig. 8.

Remove the bolts holding the front servo, rear servo and rear pump and governor assembly to the case.

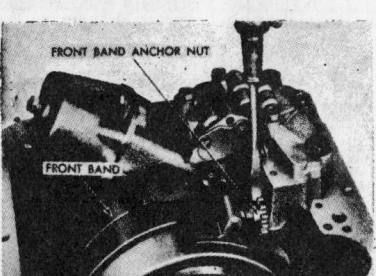

Fig. 8—Front Band Adjusting Screw starting with 1954—Dual-Range Models

REMOVE FRONT PUMP —DUAL-RANGE

Unit must be out of car for this and all other removal operations.

Remove driving torus rear snap ring from the intermediate shaft and then remove the steel and bronze thrust washers. See Fig. 9. These washers should be tied together and kept separate for return to this location.

Remove front pump to case screws and the pump locating washer. Remove the front pump and front unit internal ring gear (called front unit

drive gear in some of the pictures) from the case. Tap on rear of gear with a brass drift if the assembly sticks in the case.

Fig. 9—Removing driving torus rear snap ring and thrust washers—Dual-Range

Fig. 10—Indicator setup to check end play of transmission. Mainshaft. Should be .004-.018 Dual-Range Models

CHECKING TRANSMISSION END PLAY—DUAL-RANGE

Insert a screwdriver between the rear of the front drum and the center bearing support to hold the front drum forward.

Now using a setup as shown in Fig. 10 or some equivalent, move the mainshaft which is the center one of the two shafts in and out. Do not force; the idea is to measure the float of the shaft.

A pair of pliers and a rag can be used to grip the mainshaft and move it in place of the tool shown. The end play of the mainshaft should be between .004 in. and .018 in. Record the end play so that the selective washer which is located between the rear end of the mainshaft and the front of the rear unit planet carrier can be changed to bring the float within the limits. If the float is too little the transmission may jam up. If it is too great the transmission will be noisy.

REMOVAL OF REVERSE ASSEMBLY TOGETHER WITH THE MAIN AND OUTPUT SHAFTS—

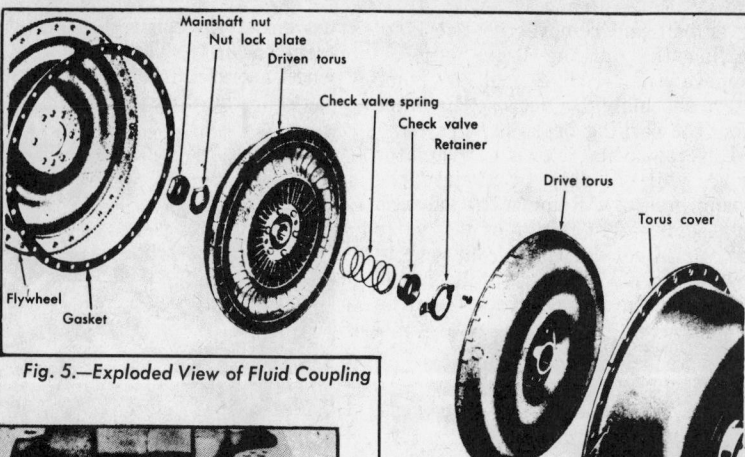

Fig. 5.—Exploded View of Fluid Coupling

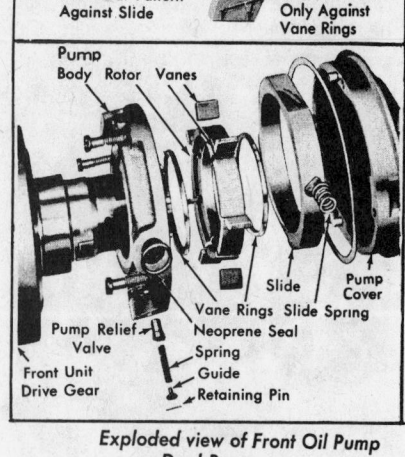

Exploded view of Front Oil Pump
—Dual-Range

Fig. 11—Rear clutch hub retainer bracket
installed

Remove rear bearing retainer oil seal.

Hold the rear drum with a screwdriver and remove the screws holding the reverse-drive-flange-reverse-sun-gear assembly to the rear unit drum.

Put a screwdriver at an angle between the front of the rear drum and the center bearing support to hold the rear drum in place.

Unbolt the rear-bearing-reverse-unit assembly from the case and remove the rear extension complete with reverse unit, output shaft and mainshaft.

Do not lose the stationary cone lock key.

Separate the mainshaft from the output shaft. Be sure to secure and set aside the selective thrust washer which may stick to the mainshaft or remain in the counterbore in the forward inner face of the rear unit planetary carrier.

Remove also the bronze thrust washer from the rear clutch hub. Install a clamp as shown to keep the rear clutch hub in place. Fig. 11.

REMOVE FRONT AND REAR UNITS—DUAL-RANGE

Bend down the locks and remove the two center bearing bolts and lock plates.

Remove rear band release spring and the rear band and strut assembly from the rear unit.

Install a wire or spring to keep the front band wrapped around the front drum and remove the two drums complete with the intermediate shaft.

DISASSEMBLE THE FRONT AND REAR UNITS—DUAL-RANGE

Support the assembly on the forward end of the intermediate shaft.

Remove the snap ring from the intermediate shaft just behind the rear unit clutch hub and lift the rear unit from the intermediate shaft. Remove thrust washer and snap ring from

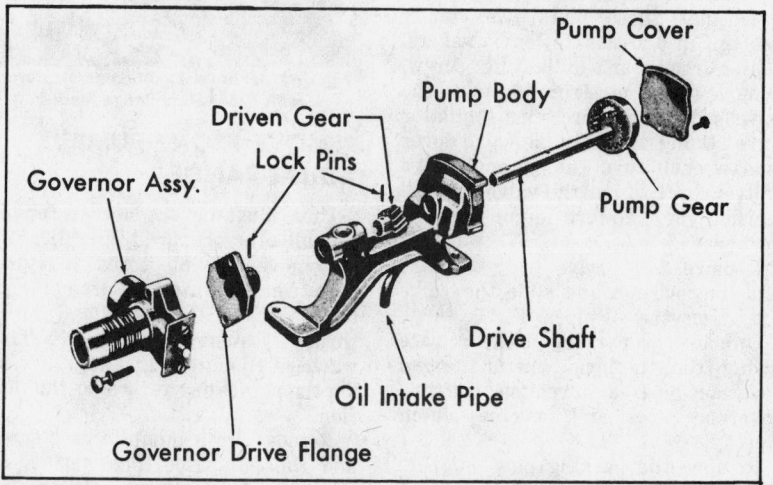

Exploded view of Reverse Blocker Assembly—Dual-Range

Exploded view Rear Oil Pump and Governor—Dual-Range

rear of oil delivery sleeve (center bearing).

Remove the oil delivery sleeve from the intermediate shaft.

Remove the snap ring from behind the front unit sun gear. Be careful not to scratch the intermediate shaft bearing surface while removing the ring.

Remove six inner and six outer clutch release springs and pins.

Remove the clutch plates being careful to count them. 1954-55 models had eight of each.

Remove front unit assembly from the shaft. Reach in and remove the thrust washers from the rear face of the front unit sun gear. Tie these two together as they must be kept separate for return to the location.

DISASSEMBLY OF THE FRONT UNIT—DUAL-RANGE

Use a press to compress the front clutch springs to permit removal of

the clutch drum snap ring. This will permit disassembly of the unit. The number of plates varies.

DISASSEMBLY OF THE REAR UNIT—DUAL-RANGE

Remove rear clutch hub and bronze thrust washer that is in front of it. Place rear unit in a press and remove the clutch drum retaining snap ring.

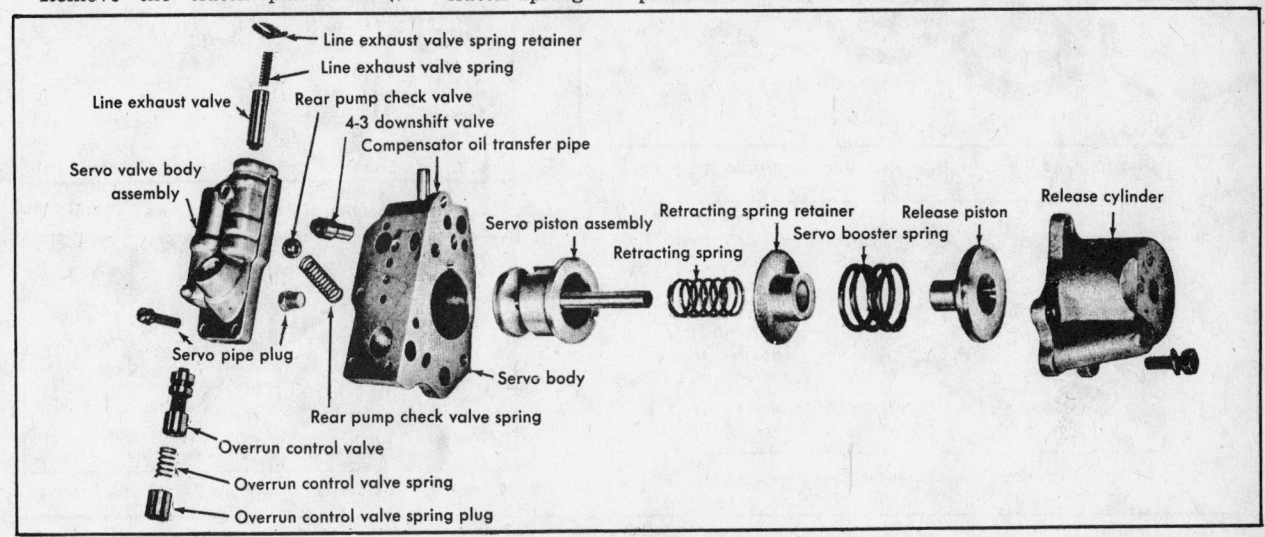

Front Servo Assembly, Thru 1954, Dual-Range

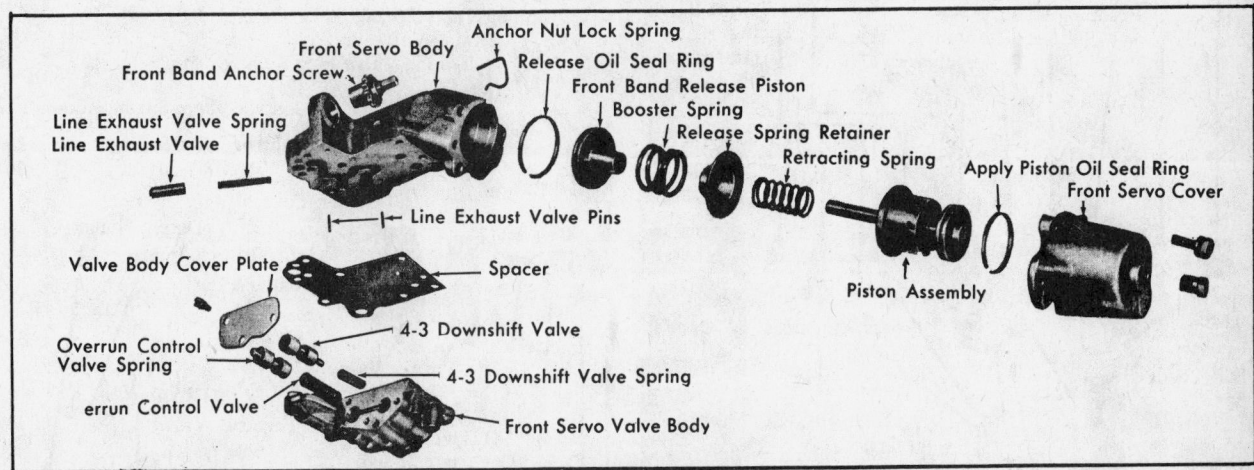

Front Servo Assembly, 55-56—Dual-Range

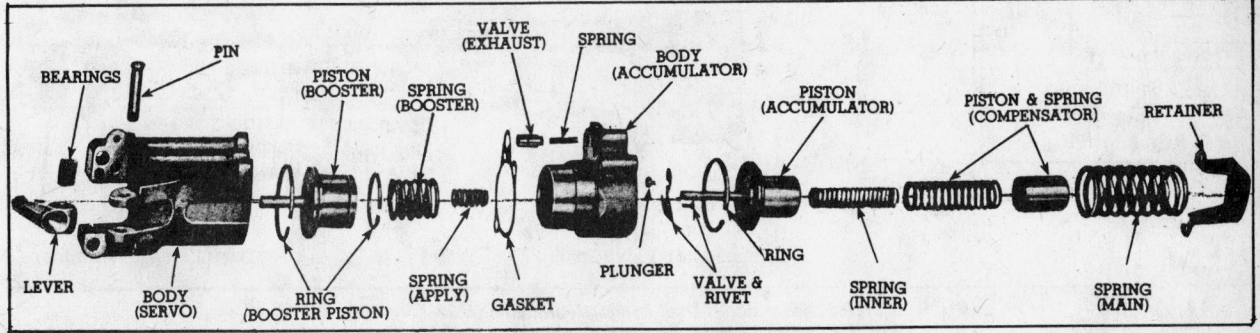

Rear Servo Assembly—Dual-Range

HYDRAMATIC TRANSMISSIONS

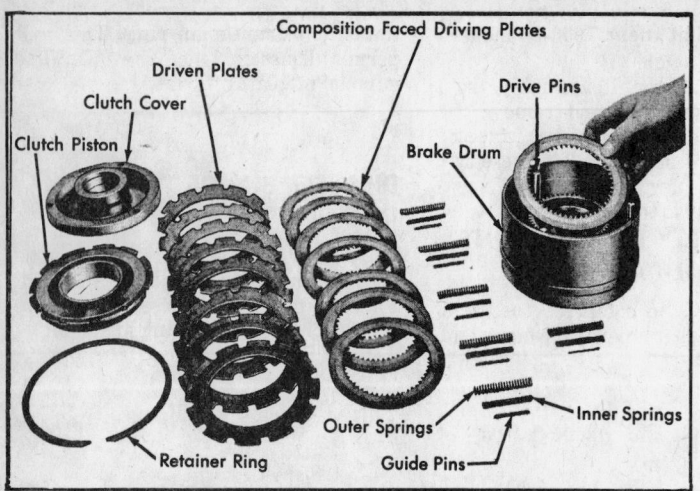

Disassembled View of Typical Rear Unit—Dual-Range

Composition Faced Driving Plates
Driven Plates
Clutch Cover
Clutch Piston
Drive Pins
Brake Drum
Inner Springs
Outer Springs
Guide Pins
Retainer Ring

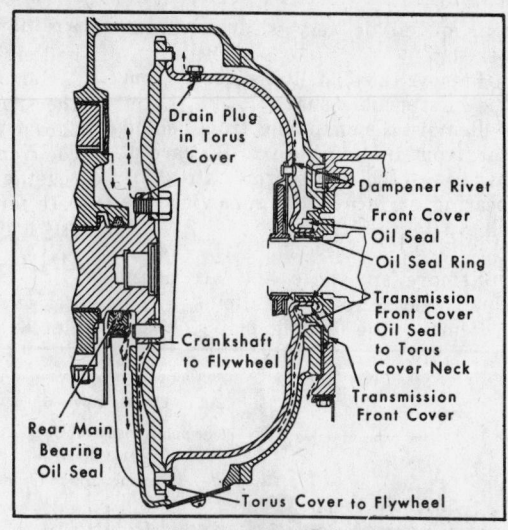

Location of Possible Oil Leaks

Drain Plug in Torus Cover
Dampener Rivet
Front Cover Oil Seal
Oil Seal Ring
Transmission Front Cover Oil Seal to Torus Cover Neck
Transmission Front Cover
Crankshaft to Flywheel
Rear Main Bearing Oil Seal
Torus Cover to Flywheel

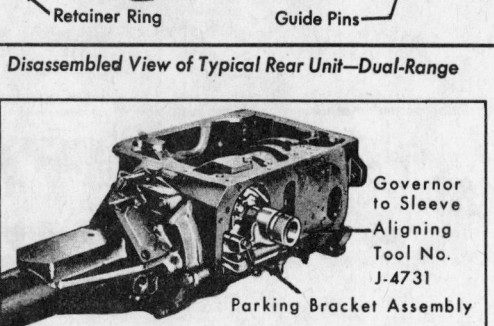

Checking Governor Sleeve Clearance

Governor to Sleeve Aligning Tool No. J-4731
Parking Bracket Assembly

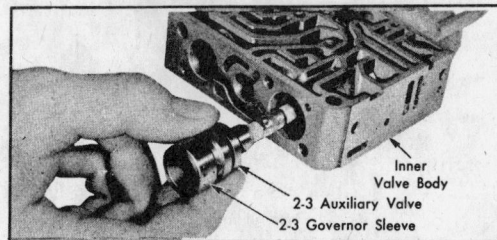

Removing 2-3 Governor Sleeve and 2-3 Auxiliary Valve

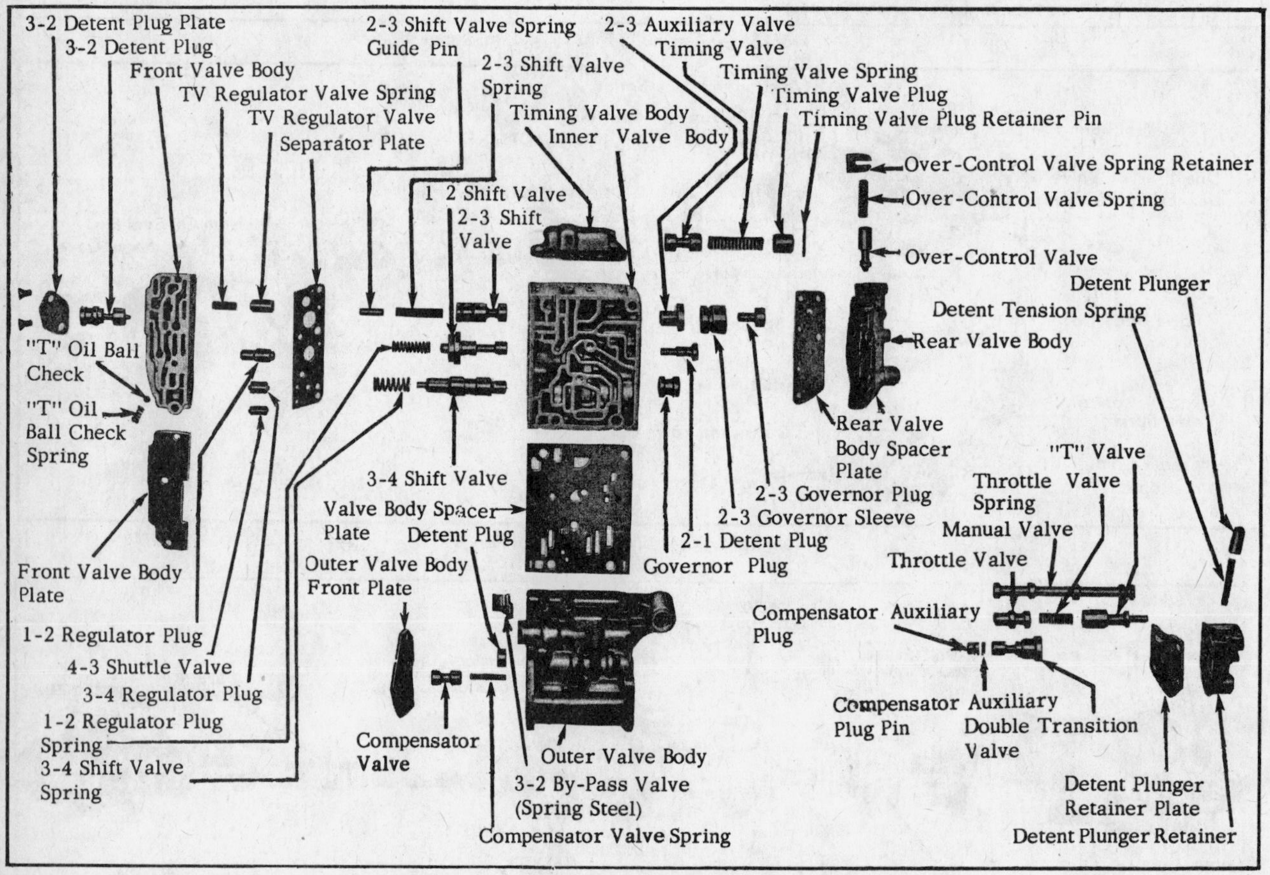

Inner Valve Body
2-3 Auxiliary Valve
2-3 Governor Sleeve

3-2 Detent Plug Plate
3-2 Detent Plug
Front Valve Body
TV Regulator Valve Spring
TV Regulator Valve
Separator Plate
2-3 Shift Valve Spring
Guide Pin
2-3 Shift Valve Spring
Timing Valve Body
Inner Valve Body
2-3 Auxiliary Valve
Timing Valve
Timing Valve Spring
Timing Valve Plug
Timing Valve Plug Retainer Pin
Over-Control Valve Spring Retainer
Over-Control Valve Spring
Over-Control Valve
Detent Plunger
Detent Tension Spring
Rear Valve Body
1 2 Shift Valve
2-3 Shift Valve
"T" Oil Ball Check
"T" Oil Ball Check Spring
Front Valve Body Plate
1-2 Regulator Plug
4-3 Shuttle Valve
3-4 Regulator Plug
1-2 Regulator Plug Spring
3-4 Shift Valve Spring
3-4 Shift Valve
Valve Body Spacer Plate
Detent Plug
Outer Valve Body Front Plate
Compensator Valve
Outer Valve Body
3-2 By-Pass Valve (Spring Steel)
Compensator Valve Spring
Governor Plug
2-1 Detent Plug
2-3 Governor Plug
2-3 Governor Sleeve
Rear Valve Body Spacer Plate
Compensator Auxiliary Plug
Compensator Auxiliary Plug Pin
"T" Valve
Throttle Valve Spring
Manual Valve
Throttle Valve
Double Transition Valve
Detent Plunger Retainer Plate
Detent Plunger Retainer

Typical Valve Body, Dual-Range Hydramatic (Model Variation Requires this Picture Be Used for Parts Identification Only).

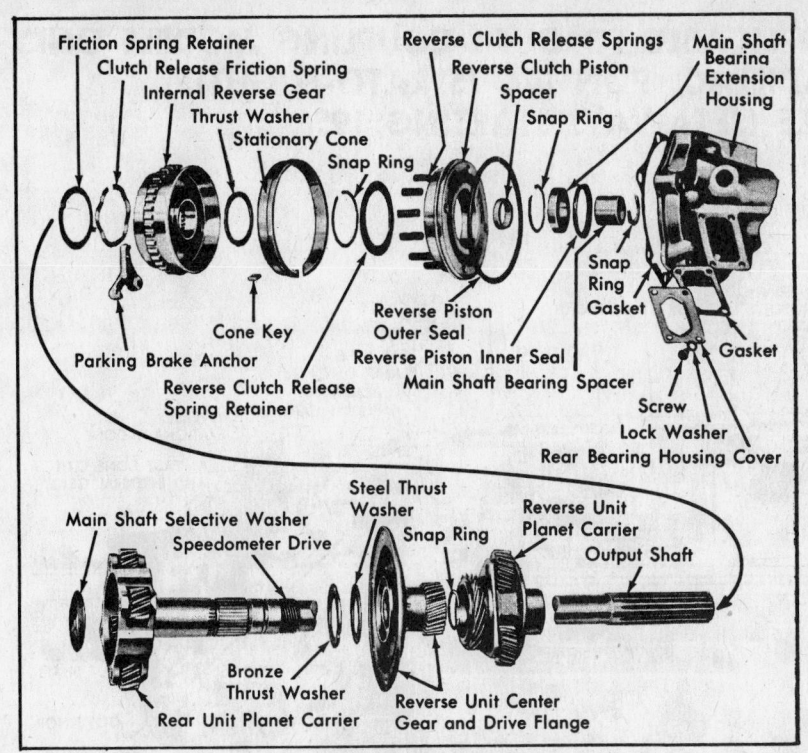

Upper Left Diagram Labels

Friction Spring Retainer
Clutch Release Friction Spring
Internal Reverse Gear
Thrust Washer
Stationary Cone
Snap Ring
Reverse Clutch Release Springs
Reverse Clutch Piston
Spacer
Snap Ring
Main Shaft Bearing Extension Housing

Cone Key
Parking Brake Anchor
Reverse Clutch Release Spring Retainer
Reverse Piston Outer Seal
Reverse Piston Inner Seal
Main Shaft Bearing Spacer
Snap Ring Gasket
Gasket
Screw
Lock Washer
Rear Bearing Housing Cover

Main Shaft Selective Washer
Speedometer Drive
Steel Thrust Washer
Snap Ring
Reverse Unit Planet Carrier
Output Shaft

Bronze Thrust Washer
Rear Unit Planet Carrier
Reverse Unit Center Gear and Drive Flange

Output Shaft and Reverse Unit—Disassembled

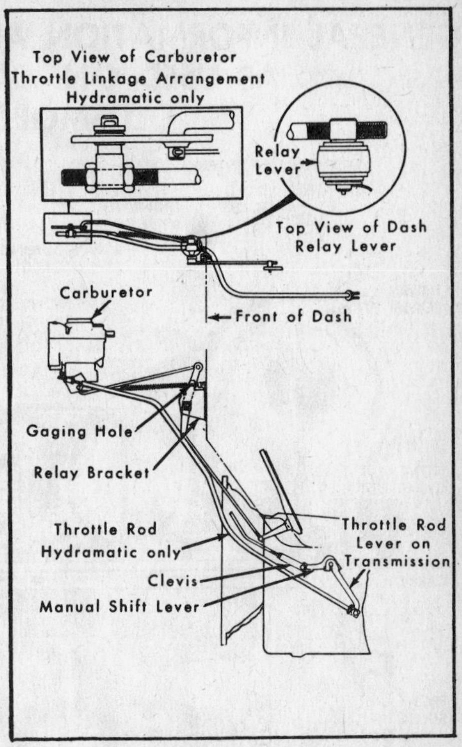

Upper Right Diagram Labels

Top View of Carburetor Throttle Linkage Arrangement Hydramatic only
Relay Lever
Top View of Dash Relay Lever
Carburetor
Front of Dash
Gaging Hole
Relay Bracket
Throttle Rod Hydramatic only
Clevis
Manual Shift Lever
Throttle Rod Lever on Transmission

Manual and Throttle Control Linkage

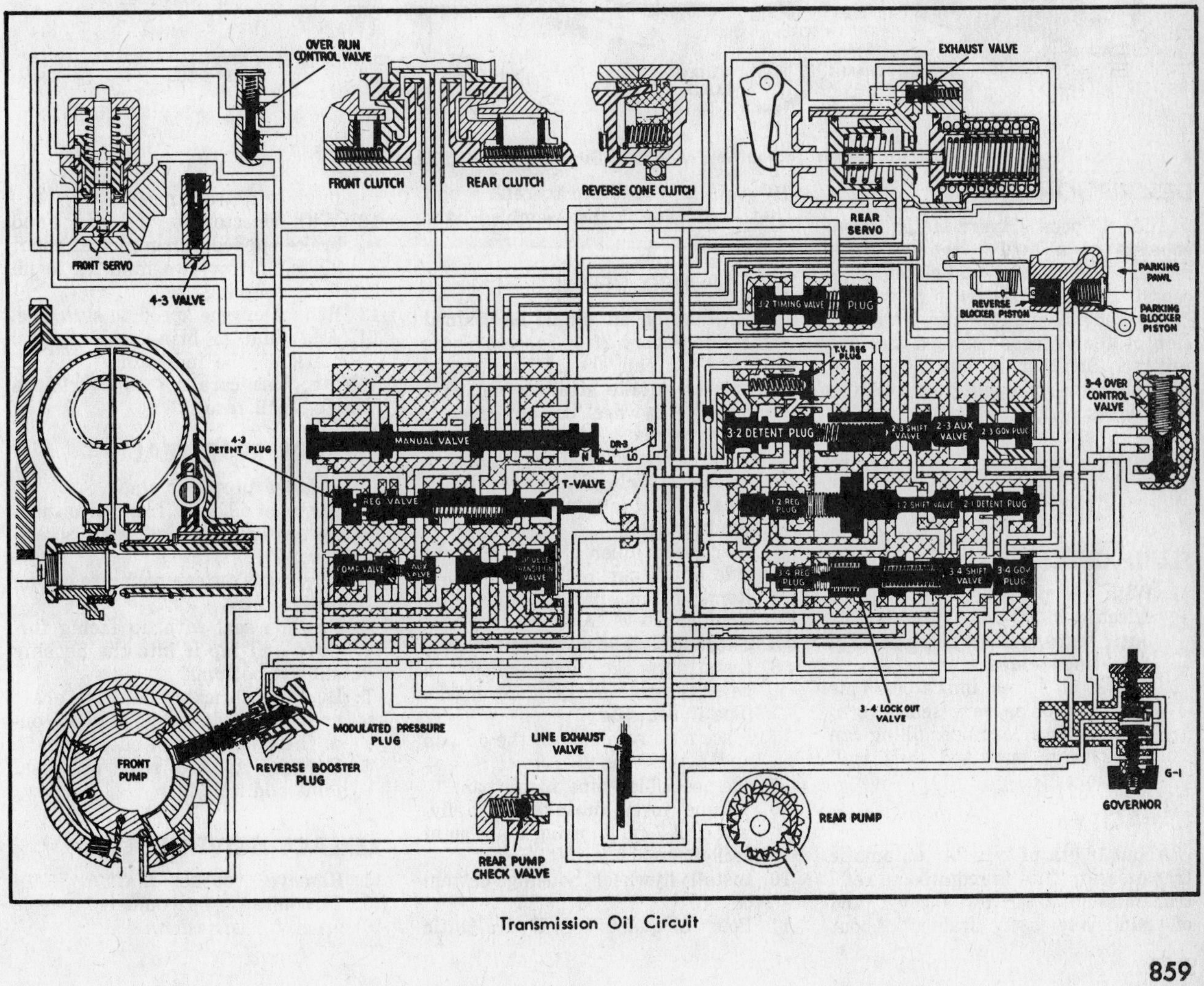

Lower Diagram Labels

OVER RUN CONTROL VALVE
EXHAUST VALVE
FRONT CLUTCH
REAR CLUTCH
REVERSE CONE CLUTCH
REAR SERVO
FRONT SERVO
4-3 VALVE
PARKING PAWL
REVERSE BLOCKER PISTON
PARKING BLOCKER PISTON
1-2 TIMING VALVE
PLUG
3-2 DETENT PLUG
2-3 SHIFT VALVE
2-3 AUX VALVE
2-3 GOV PLUG
3-4 OVER CONTROL VALVE
4-3 DETENT PLUG
MANUAL VALVE
REG VALVE
T-VALVE
1-2 REG PLUG
1-2 SHIFT VALVE
2-1 DETENT PLUG
COMP VALVE
AUX VALVE
REVERSE TRANSITION VALVE
3-4 REG PLUG
3-4 SHIFT VALVE
3-4 GOV PLUG
FRONT PUMP
MODULATED PRESSURE PLUG
REVERSE BOOSTER PLUG
LINE EXHAUST VALVE
3-4 LOCK OUT VALVE
REAR PUMP
GOVERNOR
REAR PUMP CHECK VALVE

Transmission Oil Circuit

GENERAL INFORMATION APPLICABLE TO DUAL-COUPLING MODELS ONLY AS USED ON: CADILLAC, PONTIAC (STRATO-FLIGHT), OLDSMOBILE (JETAWAY) STARTING 1956

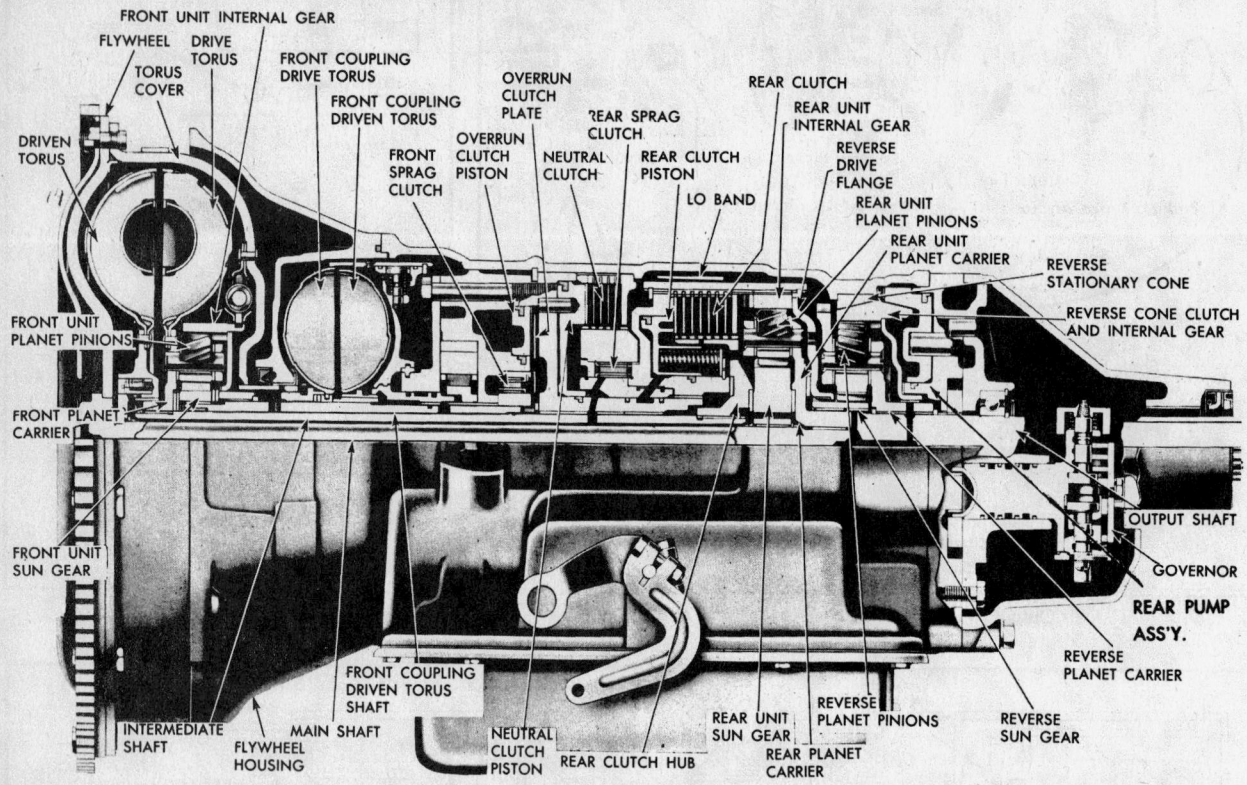

Cross Section View of 1956-58 Dual-Coupling Hydramatic

DESCRIPTION

The 4-Speed Hydra-Matic drive consists of a fluid coupling, which replaces the conventional clutch. This coupling is combined with a hydraulically controlled automatic transmission of four speeds forward and one reverse. Shifting is automatic and controlled by road requirements plus the wishes of the driver.

MINOR MAINTENANCE OPERATIONS

FLUID CHECK

1. With car parked on level, place selector in "Park." Run engine until transmission is at normal operating temperature.
2. Check oil level indicator. This transmission is very sensitive to oil level. Over or under filling can cause valve buzz and shift malfunctions.

CAPACITY

About 10 qts. of type "A" automatic transmission fluid is required to refill transmission after torus cover and oil pan have been drained. About 10½ qts. are required to refill a unit that has been disassembled and rebuilt.

DRAIN AND REFILL

Transmission oil should be drained and refilled every 25,000 miles. To do this, the oil pan should be dropped and the oil intake strainer replaced.

1. Remove flywheel bottom cover.
2. Remove hex head pipe plug from torus cover, use a six-point socket on this soft plug. A regular twelve point socket is very likely to ruin the hex head.
3. Disconnect filler pipe from right side of oil pan.
4. Remove oil pan, discard oil strainer.
5. Thoroughly clean oil pan.
6. Install new strainer and use a new "O" ring on the pump intake pipe if necessary.
7. Place a new gasket on the oil pan and attach the pan.
8. Connect filler pipe to oil pan.
9. Torque torus drain plug to flywheel. 6-7 ft. lb. **using a six-point socket wrench.**
10. Install flywheel housing bottom cover.
11. Pour 8 quarts of Hydra-Matic fluid into transmission.
12. With selector in "P" and hand brake applied, run engine at about 20 m.p.h. for two minutes to fill fluid coupling.
13. Reduce engine speed to slow idle.
14. Add fluid to bring level to full mark on the indicator.

Note: Use care not to overfill as foaming will result.

REPLACE REAR SEAL

1. Remove propeller shaft.
2. Remove oil seal from transmission rear extension with screwdriver.
3. Apply gasket compound to casing of new seal.
4. Position seal with lip facing forward and tap it into the housing until it bottoms.
5. Lightly lubricate the drive shaft yoke and slide propeller shaft onto the transmission output shaft.
6. Connect up the rear universal joint and lock.

REPLACE GOVERNOR

1. Remove propeller shaft.
2. Disconnect speedometer cable from transmission.

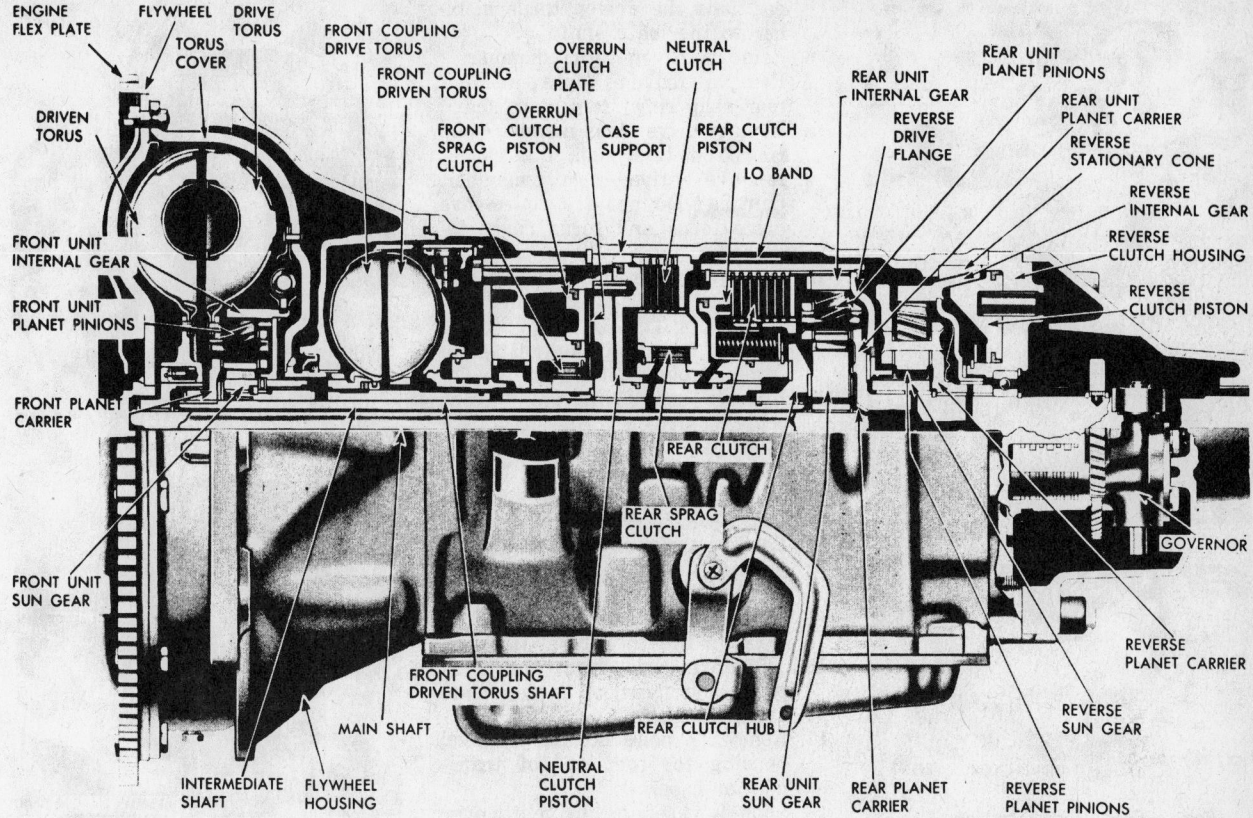

ENGINE FLEX PLATE · FLYWHEEL · DRIVE TORUS · TORUS COVER · FRONT COUPLING DRIVE TORUS · FRONT COUPLING DRIVEN TORUS · OVERRUN CLUTCH PLATE · NEUTRAL CLUTCH · REAR UNIT INTERNAL GEAR · REAR UNIT PLANET PINIONS · REAR UNIT PLANET CARRIER · REVERSE DRIVE FLANGE · REVERSE STATIONARY CONE · REVERSE INTERNAL GEAR · REVERSE CLUTCH HOUSING · REVERSE CLUTCH PISTON · DRIVEN TORUS · FRONT SPRAG CLUTCH · OVERRUN CLUTCH PISTON · CASE SUPPORT · REAR CLUTCH PISTON · LO BAND · FRONT UNIT INTERNAL GEAR · FRONT UNIT PLANET PINIONS · FRONT PLANET CARRIER · REAR CLUTCH · REAR SPRAG CLUTCH · GOVERNOR · FRONT UNIT SUN GEAR · REVERSE PLANET CARRIER · REVERSE SUN GEAR · INTERMEDIATE SHAFT · FLYWHEEL HOUSING · MAIN SHAFT · FRONT COUPLING DRIVEN TORUS SHAFT · REAR CLUTCH HUB · NEUTRAL CLUTCH PISTON · REAR UNIT SUN GEAR · REAR PLANET CARRIER · REVERSE PLANET PINIONS

© 1959 Pontiac Div. G.M. Corp.

Cross Section View of 1959-61 Dual-Coupling Hydramatic

3. Remove two rear mount support-to-crossmember nuts.
4. Place jack under transmission and raise studs above the crossmember.
5. Remove brake cable guide rod and return spring from crossmember.
6. Remove two bolts from each end of the frame crossmember and remove crossmember.
7. Lower rear of transmission and remove eight rear bearing retainer to reverse piston housing attaching screws and washers.
8. Remove breather pipe.
9. Withdraw rear bearing retainer and gasket and discard the gasket.
10. Remove and replace the governor.
11. Place a new gasket on the reverse piston housing with petrolatum.
12. Locate rear bearing retainer over end of output shaft and secure to reverse piston housing and case with eight attaching screws and washers.
13. Raise transmission and install frame crossmember. Attach with 2 bolts at each end.
14. Lower transmission while piloting the rear mount studs into holes in crossmember. Install nuts on studs.
15. Connect speedometer cable.
16. Install breather pipe.

17. Reinstall propeller shaft.

REPLACE PARKING BRAKE LINKAGE AND INSIDE DETENT AND THROTTLE CONTROL LEVERS

The parking brake links, lever, bracket and lever spring can be replaced without disturbing the rear extension housing.

After removing oil pan and screen, remove all control valve assembly attaching screws and allow valve body to hang. Letting the body hang permits the inside detent and throttle levers to be rotated to allow the parking brake bracket and spring to slide off the shaft. It also provides clearance for removing the inside detent and throttle control lever.

When reassembling be sure to engage parking brake bracket properly in parking brake lever and detent lever. Position throttle control lever between stop and stem of TV plunger and engage pin of detent lever in manual valve.

If parking pawl is to be replaced, it will be necessary to remove the rear bearing retainer and reverse clutch housing so that the reverse clutch housing can be removed to expose the parking pawl shaft for removal.

REPLACE CONTROL VALVE ASSEMBLY AND SERVO AND ACCUMULATOR ASSEMBLY

The servo and accumulator assembly can be removed without disturbing the control valve assembly. However, when removing the control valve assembly it is first necessary to remove the servo and accumulator assembly.

REPLACE PRESSURE REGULATOR ASSEMBLY

When replacing the pressure regulator be sure to tighten it to 5 ft. lb. torque.

REMOVAL OF UNITS FROM CASE

TORUS MEMBERS AND FLYWHEEL HOUSING

1. Remove cooler strap attaching bolt and strap.
2. Remove oil cooler sleeve assemblies, "O" rings, and sleeve seals.
3. Remove torus cover-to-flywheel attaching nuts and remove flywheel.
4. Remove square torus cover to flywheel seal.
5. Remove Truarc snap ring which

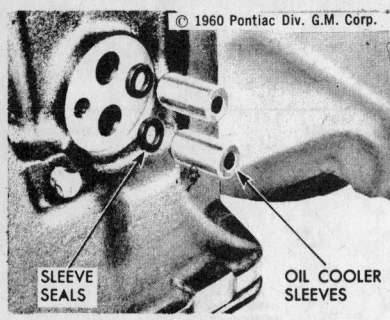

SLEEVE SEALS · OIL COOLER SLEEVES

Cooler Sleeves and Seals

J-4880 · DRIVEN TORUS

© 1960 Pontiac Div. G.M. Corp. · DRIVEN TORUS FRONT SNAP RING

Remove Driven Torus Front Snap Ring

J-4880 · DRIVE TORUS SNAP RING

© 1960 Pontiac Div. G.M. Corp. · DRIVEN TORUS REAR SNAP RING

Remove Driven Torus Rear Snap Ring

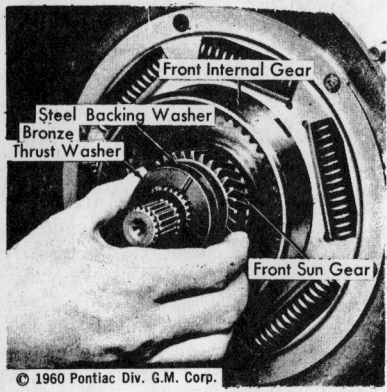

Front Internal Gear · Steel Backing Washer · Bronze Thrust Washer · Front Sun Gear

© 1960 Pontiac Div. G.M. Corp.

Torus Hub Thrust Washers

positions the driven torus member to the main shaft.

6. Remove driven torus member.
7. Remove driven torus member rear snap ring from main shaft.
8. Remove drive torus member snap ring from intermediate shaft.
9. Remove drive torus member. **Caution:** Do not try to remove drive torus and torus cover together.
10. Remove bronze thrust washer and steel selective spacer from torus hub.
11. Remove front unit sun gear from front coupling torus shaft.
12. Remove snap ring from front coupling driven torus shaft.
13. Withdraw front unit internal gear together with steel thrust washer, needle bearing and second steel thrust washer.
14. Remove torus cover assembly by pulling out with even pressure.
15. Install seal protector (tool) over intermediate shaft.
16. Remove breather pipe and clip.
16A. Remove nuts from six torus cover and flywheel to flex plate attaching bolts.
17. Remove 6 bolts holding flywheel housing to front end of transmission case.
18. Slide flywheel housing gently over the seal protector and away from the case.
19. Remove seal protector.
20. Remove housing-to-case square seal from rear side of housing.
21. Remove front unit coupling assembly from case.

CHECK MAIN SHAFT END PLAY

Note: The result of taking this measurement will be used later to determine the proper rear unit selective thrust washer to use.

1. Install collar of end play checking fixture, J-6127 on intermediate shaft and secure in position by installing Truarc snap ring. Attach the fixture of the indicator tool, J-6127 to collar by threading the collar tightly into the fixture.
2. Install dial indicator support J-6126.
3. Install J-8001 dial indicator.
4. Move main shaft back and forth to check end play of main shaft. Be sure to get only free main shaft end play. Applied force will give inaccurate reading.
5. Record the amount of end play.
6. Remove dial indicator, support, and end play checking fixture.

OIL PAN, STRAINER AND INTAKE PIPE

1. Remove oil pan attaching screws.
2. Remove oil pan and discard the

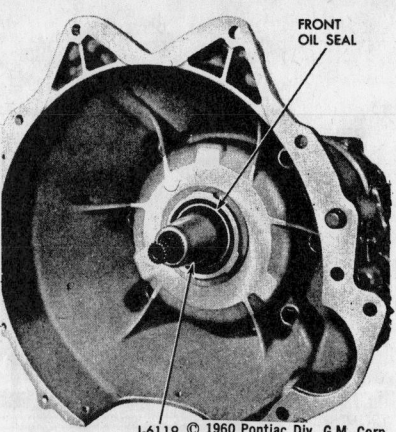

FRONT OIL SEAL

J-6119 © 1960 Pontiac Div. G.M. Corp.

Front Seal Protector

FRONT OIL SEAL

© 1960 Pontiac Div. G.M. Corp.

Front Unit Coupling

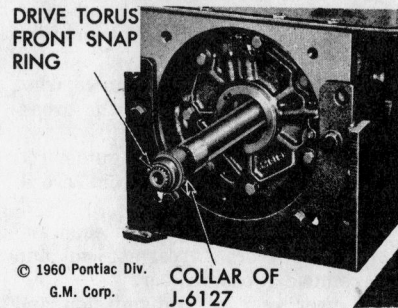

DRIVE TORUS FRONT SNAP RING

© 1960 Pontiac Div. G.M. Corp. · COLLAR OF J-6127

Indicator Collar in Place

J-6126 · J-6127 © 1960 Pontiac Div. G.M. Corp. · KMO-30

Measure Mainshaft End Play

gasket.

3. Loosen accumulator attaching bolt retaining the intake pipe clip. Pull oil strainer and intake pipe away from attaching clip. Remove intake pipe and strainer.
4. Withdraw intake pipe from

strainer.

5. Remove "O" rings from pump and strainer.

SERVO AND ACCUMULATOR AND CONTROL VALVE

1. Remove two bolts holding accumulator and servo assembly to case. **Note:** There is some spring tension under the servo.
2. Remove servo and accumulator assembly.
3. Remove servo spring.
4. Remove five control valve assembly to case attaching bolts.
5. Remove control valve assembly from transmission and at the same time, remove manual valve.

PUMP AND OVERRUN CLUTCH

1. Remove pump locking screw from control valve case pad.
2. Remove pressure regulator plug from side of the case and withdraw regulator spring and valve using snap ring pliers.
3. Remove three pump to case support washer head attaching screws.
4. Withdraw pump assembly from case using pullers J-6125 if necessary. Two of the pump cover to pump body attaching screws must be removed to attach the pullers.
5. Remove small "O" ring from rear clutch apply hole.
6. Remove overrun clutch release spring.
   Note: Spring may have remained in the pump.
7. Remove front sprag inner race if it remained on the intermediate shaft.
8. Remove overrun clutch plate and bronze thrust washer.
9. Back retainer screw out of retainer J-6135, then slide retainer onto intermediate shaft against center case support and lock it securely.

CASE SUPPORT, NEUTRAL CLUTCH AND REAR UNIT

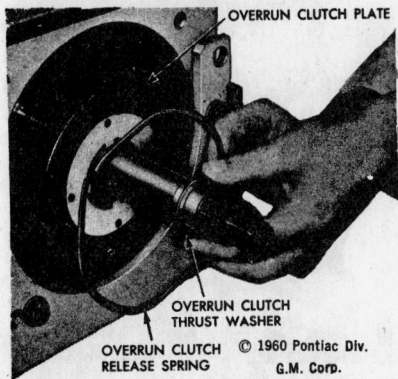

Overrun Clutch Plate and Spring

© 1960 Pontiac Div. G.M. Corp.
PUMP LOCK SCREW

Front Pump Lock Screw

PUMP

J-6125 © 1960 Pontiac Div. G.M. Corp.

Remove Front Pump

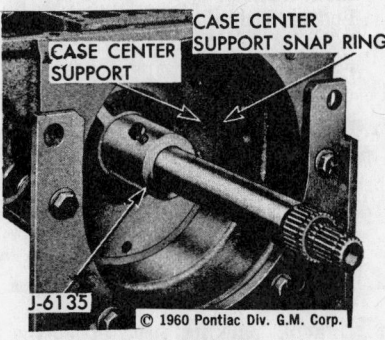

CASE CENTER SUPPORT SNAP RING
CASE CENTER SUPPORT

J-6135 © 1960 Pontiac Div. G.M. Corp.

Rear Unit Clutch Retainer

1. Remove speedometer driven gear from rear bearing retainer.
2. If rear oil seal is to be replaced, remove seal with screw driver.
3. Remove remaining rear bearing retainer to reverse clutch piston housing screws.
4. Remove rear bearing retainer and gasket and discard the gasket. Tap housing toward rear to loosen.
5. Remove cylindrical screen from governor feed line.
6. Pull governor out of reverse clutch piston housing.
7. Remove governor drive gear retaining ring, governor drive gear, drive gear key and second retaining snap ring.
8. Remove rear bearing snap ring from output shaft.
9. Remove center support to case

snap ring with a screw driver.
10. Tap rear end of output shaft with soft hammer to free shaft from rear bearing inner race.
    Caution: Be sure parking brake pawl is not engaged.
11. Slide rear unit, neutral clutch, and case center support assembly out of front end of case.
12. Remove reverse clutch release spring from output shaft.
13. Remove reverse planet carrier from output shaft.
14. Rest rear unit, neutral clutch, and case support assembly in holding fixture J-6116, output shaft down.
15. Remove neutral clutch drum locating key from transmission case.

REAR EXTENSION AND REAR OIL PUMP REMOVAL— DUAL-COUPLING

1956-58 ONLY

Remove cap screws and lock washers and rear extension housing.

Remove gasket and lift off governor assembly. Unfasten holding clamp and remove transmission breather oipe. Speedometer drive gear may be a push fit on output shaft; if so, use puller to remove.

Remove rear bearing snap ring from output shaft.

Remove two opposite rear pump screws and install the two small slide hammers.

Remove pump locating screw and screw next to dowel pin.

Remove rear-pump and reverse-clutch-piston assembly out of case and remove the gasket.

REVERSE PARTS

1. Place transmission in a vertical position with reverse piston housing up.
2. Remove reverse clutch piston housing attaching screw and lift housing from case.
3. Remove and discard gasket.
4. Remove governor feed screen.

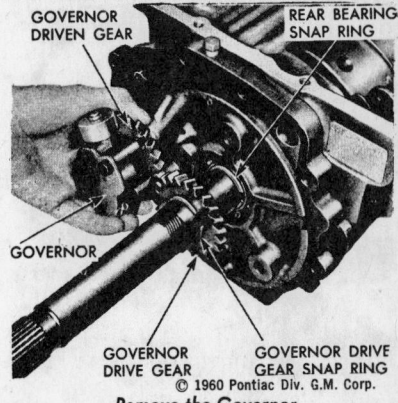

GOVERNOR DRIVEN GEAR
REAR BEARING SNAP RING
GOVERNOR
GOVERNOR DRIVE GEAR
GOVERNOR DRIVE GEAR SNAP RING
© 1960 Pontiac Div. G.M. Corp.

Remove the Governor

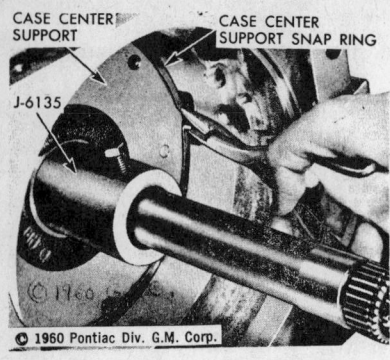

Remove Snap Ring from Center Support

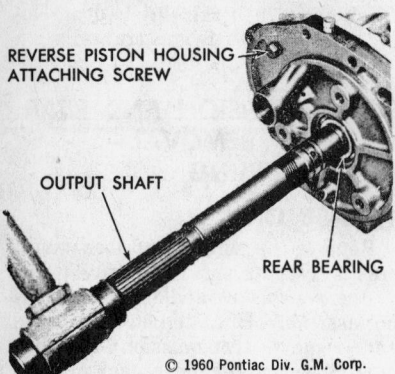

Freeing the Output Shaft

Lift Out the Rear Unit

Reverse Planet Carrier

5. Remove reverse internal gear thrust washer and internal gear from case.
6. Remove reverse stationary cone from the case with the fingers. **Note:** Stationary cone is brittle, the use of tools on this part may break it.
7. Remove reverse stationary cone key. If key sticks, tap it out with ⅜" brass rod thru key hole in bottom of case.
8. Turn transmission to horizontal position.

LOW BAND

1. Unhook band end from anchor inside of case.
2. With band unhooked, rotate it to horizontal position in the case.
3. Turn band so that ends are facing rear of case and remove from front of case.

INSIDE DETENT AND THROTTLE LEVERS

Don't remove these parts unless they are to be renewed.
1. Loosen inner T.V. lever to T.V. shaft clamp screw.
2. Remove inside T.V. lever. Withdraw outside T.V. lever, shaft, and "O" seal ring from case. Discard the seal.
3. Loosen inside detent lever screw.
4. Withdraw outer shift lever, shaft, washer, and seal ring from case. Remove inside detent lever.

PARKING PAWL AND LINKAGE

Don't remove these parts unless they are to be renewed.
1. Remove parking pawl pin from transmission case with a ⅛" brass rod and hammer.
2. Remove parking pawl spacer washer.
3. Unhook parking bracket spring from lever.
4. Remove bracket and spring from parking brake pin.
5. Rotate parking lever and pawl and remove from parking brake pin.

DISASSEMBLY AND ASSEMBLY OF UNIT

Clean all parts thoroughly and dry with compressed air. Do not wipe with rags.

CASE SUPPORT, NEUTRAL CLUTCH AND REAR UNIT

Disassembly

1. Remove rear unit clutch retainer, J-6135.
2. Remove hook-type oil ring from intermediate shaft.
3. Remove case center support and

Clutch Units in Holding Fixture

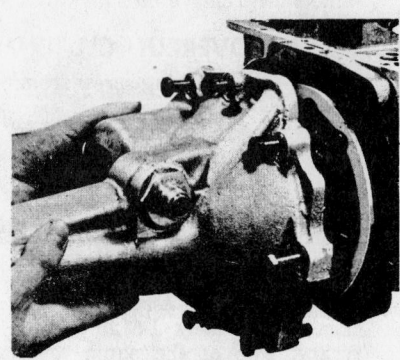

Removing Extension Housing

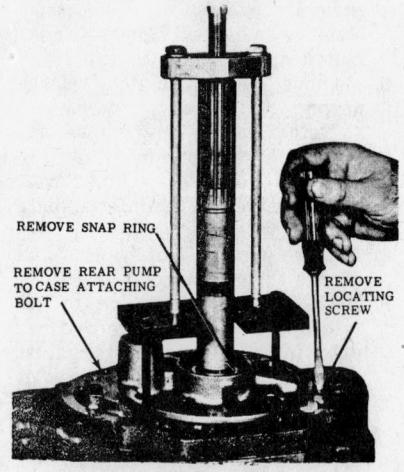

Removing Rear Pump

Removing Reverse Piston Housing

neutral clutch piston assembly from intermediate shaft.

4. Remove two oil rings from case support hub and remove neutral clutch piston. Turn case support over and tap on bench to remove piston. Remove seals from piston and hub of case center support.

5. Remove neutral clutch drum assembly.

6. Remove large snap ring from rear drum with screwdriver.

7. Lift rear clutch cylinder and sprag assembly over intermediate shaft.

8. Remove intermediate shaft and clutch hub.

Note: The rear clutch hub may be removed from the intermediate shaft, if replacement of shaft or hub is necessary, by removing snap ring retaining hub on shaft.

9. Remove clutch hub front thrust washer from clutch hub.

10. Remove main shaft and rear sun gear assembly from rear unit. Remove clutch hub thrust washer from sun gear.

11. Remove seven steel and seven composition clutch plates.

12. Remove needle bearing and retainer from counterbore of output shaft.

13. Remove rear unit drum and output shaft assembly from holding fixture and rest on bench with output shaft end up.

14. Remove large snap ring holding reverse drive flange in rear unit drum.

15. Lift output shaft and reverse drive flange assembly out of rear drum.

16. Remove internal gear and plate together from rear unit drum by tapping backing plate with a soft hammer.

Note: Mark the internal gear so that upon reassembly balance can be maintained by assembling in the original position.

17. Remove snap ring from output shaft.

18. Remove reverse drive flange and sun gear assembly from output shaft.

19. Remove selective washer from reverse drive flange or output shaft.

20. Remove spiral snap ring from rear unit sprag outer race.

21. Remove outer race, sprag, and retainer by rotating counterclockwise and pulling upward.

22. Remove rear unit sprag retainer and sprag from outer race.

Caution: Don't dismantle sprag assembly.

23. Disassemble rear unit clutch piston assembly as follows:

   A. Place stud J-6129 on the bench.

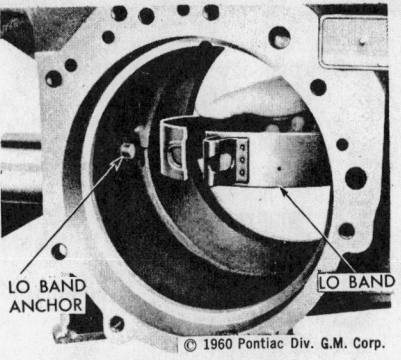

Low Band and Anchor

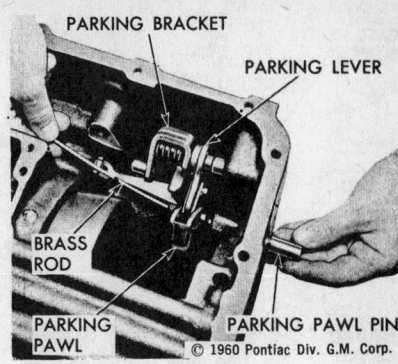

Parking Pawl

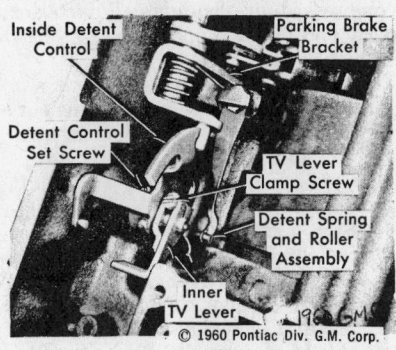

Parking Linkage

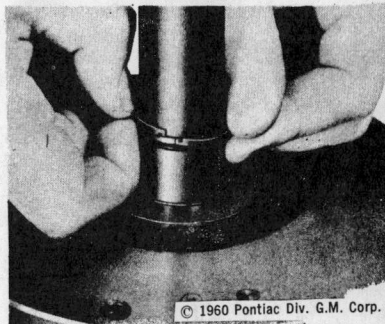

Remove Oil Ring from Intermediate Shaft

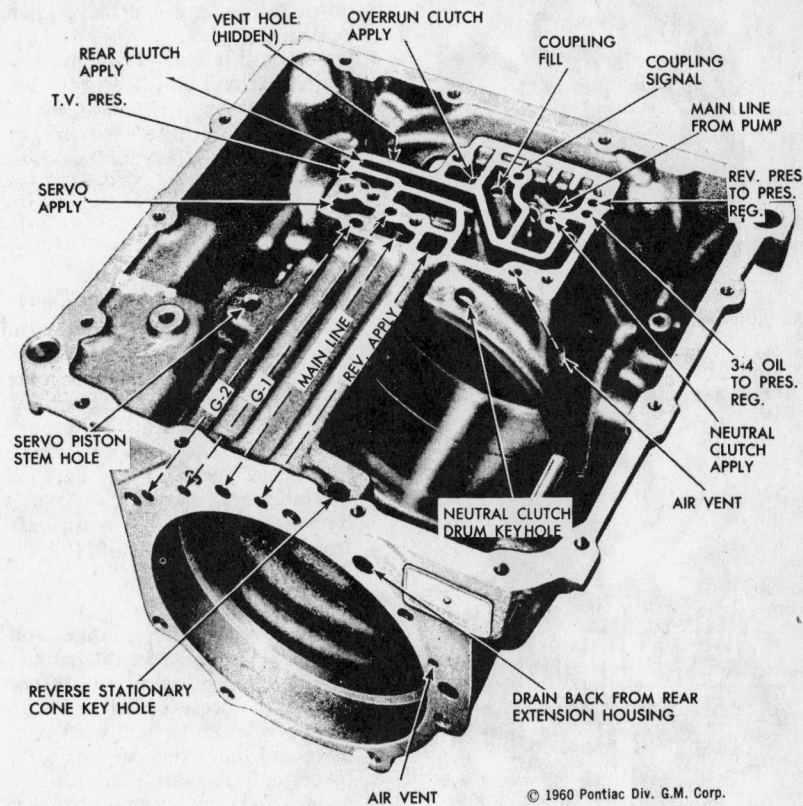

Passages in the Case

B. Lower cylinder and piston assembly over the stud, spring end up. Set spring compressor J-4670 on top of spring retainer and start nut on stud J-6129.

Note: If compressor J-4670 has no hole in the middle, drill a

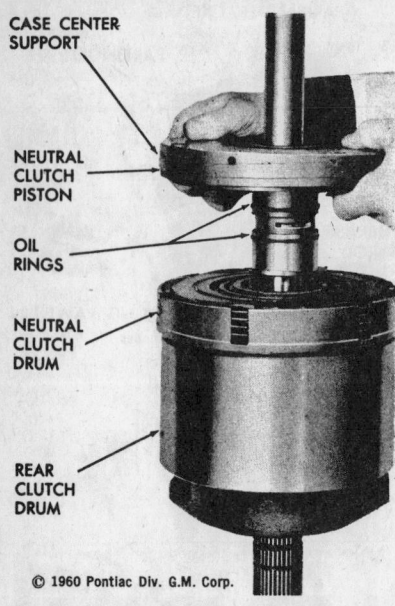

CASE CENTER SUPPORT

NEUTRAL CLUTCH PISTON

OIL RINGS

NEUTRAL CLUTCH DRUM

REAR CLUTCH DRUM

© 1960 Pontiac Div. G.M. Corp.

Case Support and Neutral Clutch Piston

© 1960 Pontiac Div. G.M. Corp.

Rear Clutch Cylinder and Sprag Assembly

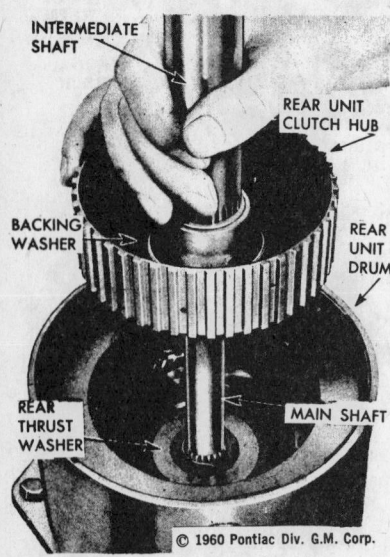

INTERMEDIATE SHAFT

REAR UNIT CLUTCH HUB

BACKING WASHER

REAR UNIT DRUM

REAR THRUST WASHER

MAIN SHAFT

© 1960 Pontiac Div. G.M. Corp.

Clutch Hub

7/16″ hole so that stud J-6129 can be inserted thru it.

C. Turn down on J-6129 to compress clutch springs.

D. Remove snap ring.

E. Release compression, then remove tool and spring retainer from clutch springs.

F. Remove eight release springs.

G. Remove rear clutch piston from cylinder.

H. Remove seals from piston and hub.

Inspection

Clean all parts thoroughly with suitable solvent, then blow dry with compressed air. Examine all parts for wear and damage and replace as necessary.

Measure end play of rear unit sun gear on mainshaft and determine correct selective washer to use in rear unit as follows:

1. Clamp sun gear and mainshaft assembly in holding fixture J-6116 using "C" clamp and dial indicator J-8001. Gear must be firmly clamped on both sides so it cannot give.

2. Set dial indicator stem to contact end of mainshaft.

3. Move mainshaft straight up and down to measure end play. Then record end play.

4. Subtract this end play from the mainshaft end play (recorded before the transmission was disassembled). The difference will be the actual end play of the rear unit and should be .004″-.013″.

   EXAMPLE:
   Mainshaft end play ...... .021″
   Rear unit sun gear
   end play .... .012″
   Rear unit end play ...... .009″

   If rear unit end play is beyond the limits of .004″-.013″, select the reverse drive flange to rear unit planet carrier thrust washer which will produce the proper end play as shown in the Front Unit Selective Spacer Chart of assembly instructions.

5. Remove sun gear and mainshaft from holding fixture J-6119.

Assembly

1. With reverse drive flange and sun gear held, drive flange up, install proper selective thrust washer in recess of drive flange. Use petrolatum to hold washer in place and index lugs in flange.

2. Insert output shaft though drive flange and sun gear until carrier bottoms on selective thrust washer.

3. Holding drive flange and sun gear tightly against carrier to keep selective washer secure, set output shaft and carrier on bench

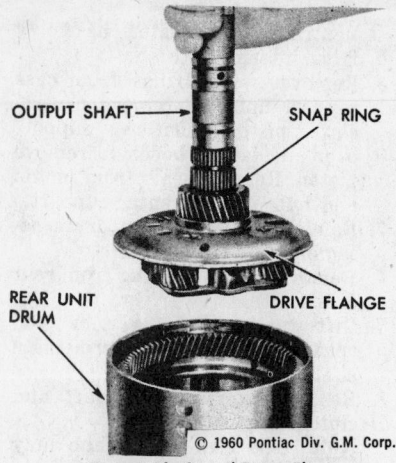

OUTPUT SHAFT

SNAP RING

REAR UNIT DRUM

DRIVE FLANGE

© 1960 Pontiac Div. G.M. Corp.

Output Shaft and Drive Flange

INSERT SMALL SCREWDRIVER IN THIS HOLE TO START REMOVAL OF SNAP RING

SPRAG RETAINER

REAR SPRAG OUTER RACE

© 1960 Pontiac Div. G.M. Corp.

Remove Snap Ring

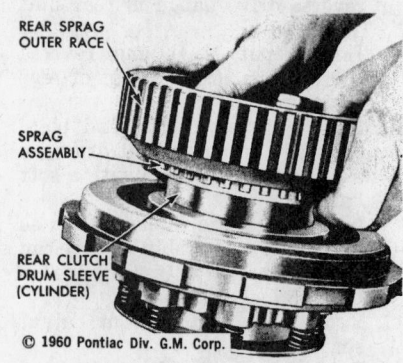

REAR SPRAG OUTER RACE

SPRAG ASSEMBLY

REAR CLUTCH DRUM SLEEVE (CYLINDER)

© 1960 Pontiac Div. G.M. Corp.

Remove Rear Unit Sprag Assembly

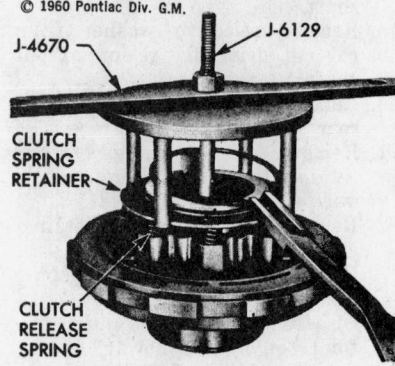

© 1960 Pontiac Div. G.M.

J-4670

J-6129

CLUTCH SPRING RETAINER

CLUTCH RELEASE SPRING

Rear Unit Clutch Spring Snap Ring

CLAMP SECURELY
BOTH SIDES

© 1960 Pontiac Div. G.M. Corp.

Measure End Play of Rear Unit Sun Gear
on Mainshaft

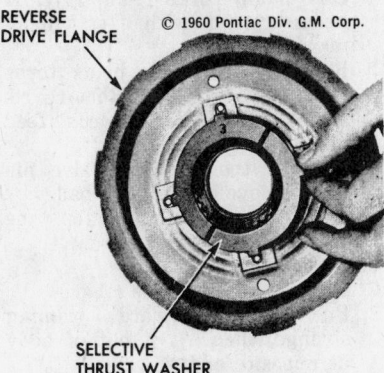

REVERSE
DRIVE FLANGE

© 1960 Pontiac Div. G.M. Corp.

SELECTIVE
THRUST WASHER

Locating Selective Washer

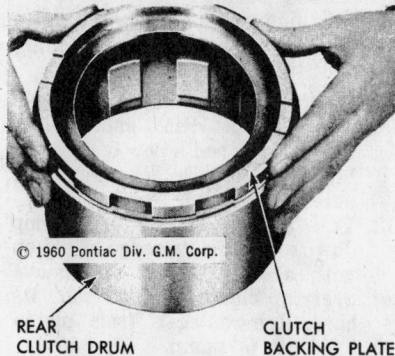

© 1960 Pontiac Div. G.M. Corp.

REAR
CLUTCH DRUM

CLUTCH
BACKING PLATE

Installing the Rear Unit Clutch Backing Plate

on the carrier end.

4. Install reverse planet carrier front snap ring on output shaft.
5. Insert reverse drive flange retainer J-6120 between snap ring and flange to prevent selective washer from dropping out of position.
6. Set rear unit drum on bench with long undercuts on lugs up (or with internal gear up if it was not removed).
7. Install clutch backing plate, flat surface down. Align lugs of plate with slots of rear drum and tap the plate into place against the spline shoulder in drum.
8. Tap rear unit internal gear into place against clutch backing plate. **Note:** If the old gear is being reinstalled, note mark made or gear at time of disassembly and align it accordingly.
9. Install output shaft and reverse drive flange assembly in rear unit drum and secure with large snap ring.
10. Rest rear unit assembly on holding fixture J-6116 with output shaft down. As unit is lowered, lift up on drum and remove retainer J-6120.
11. Position needle bearing and retainer in counterbore of output shaft and retain with petrolatum.

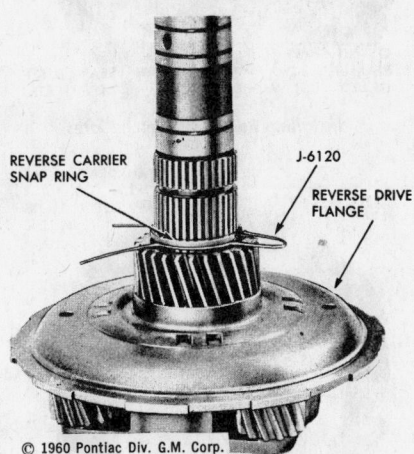

REVERSE CARRIER
SNAP RING

J-6120

REVERSE DRIVE
FLANGE

© 1960 Pontiac Div. G.M. Corp.

Reverse Drive Flange Retainer Tool

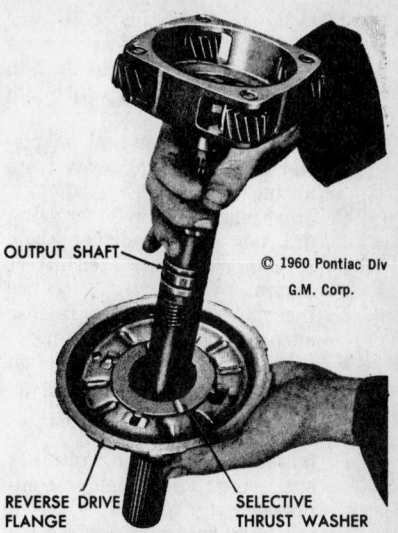

OUTPUT SHAFT

© 1960 Pontiac Div
G.M. Corp.

REVERSE DRIVE
FLANGE

SELECTIVE
THRUST WASHER

Assemble Reverse Drive Flange
to Output Shaft

12. Dip seven steel plates and seven composition plates in Hydra-Matic oil and alternately install them in rear unit drum. Start with the drive (composition) plate and finish with a driven (steel) plate. Assemble driven plates with lugs registering in rear unit drum slots and so that the .030" wide slots in the driven plate lugs are all in line.
13. Install mainshaft and sun gear assembly into output shaft in rear unit, meshing sun gear with planet pinions of output shaft.
14. Assemble rear unit clutch hub to rear end of intermediate shaft if it was removed. The open side of the hub goes toward front end of shaft on end with longest spline and long machined surface.
15. Apply petrolatum to two bronze thrust washers and backing washer. Then affix small diameter washer to rear side and large washer to front side of clutch hub. Place backing washer, flange up, on the large thrust washer.
16. Lower intermediate shaft and clutch hub with thrust washers into rear drum.

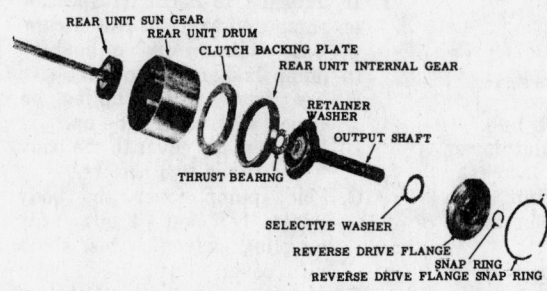

REAR UNIT SUN GEAR
REAR UNIT DRUM
CLUTCH BACKING PLATE
REAR UNIT INTERNAL GEAR
RETAINER
WASHER
OUTPUT SHAFT
THRUST BEARING
SELECTIVE WASHER
REVERSE DRIVE FLANGE
SNAP RING
REVERSE DRIVE FLANGE SNAP RING

Exploded view of Mainshaft, Rear Unit Drum
and Output Shaft—Dual-Coupling

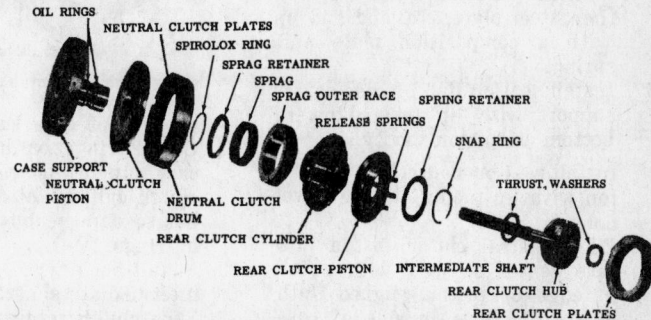

OIL RINGS
NEUTRAL CLUTCH PLATES
SPIROLOX RING
SPRAG RETAINER
SPRAG
SPRAG OUTER RACE
RELEASE SPRINGS
SPRING RETAINER
SNAP RING
THRUST WASHERS
CASE SUPPORT
NEUTRAL CLUTCH
PISTON
NEUTRAL CLUTCH
DRUM
REAR CLUTCH CYLINDER
REAR CLUTCH PISTON
INTERMEDIATE SHAFT
REAR CLUTCH HUB
REAR CLUTCH PLATES

Exploded view of Neutral Clutch and Intermediate
Shaft Assemblies—Dual-Coupling

17. Install rear clutch piston in rear clutch cylinder as follows:
   A. Install new inner seal on hub of clutch cylinder with lip down.
   B. Install new outer seal on piston with lip facing away from spring bore side.
   C. Start piston into cylinder using flat side of screwdriver blade to compress seal. Then insert piston.
   D. Insert eight clutch release springs in bores of piston.
   E. Place spring retainer on springs with tangs facing up. Compress springs using tools J-4670 and J-6129.
   F. Install release spring retainer snap ring. Then remove compressor.
18. Install rear sprag in outer race with shoulder side of sprag on counterbored side of outer race.
19. Lower sprag and outer race on rear unit inner race (rear clutch cylinder).
   Note: Push sprag part way down through outer race while rotating sprag counterclockwise to help in assembly.
20. Install sprag retainer in rear unit outer race with large O.D. up. Push retainer down to expose snap ring groove.
21. Install spiral snap ring on rear sprag inner race.
22. Apply petrolatum to clutch hub front thrust washer race and install, flange first, onto release spring side of cylinder.
23. Lower rear unit cylinder and sprag assembly over end of intermediate shaft and into rear clutch drum, sprag side up.
24. Secure cylinder and sprag assembly to rear unit drum with large snap ring.
25. Install neutral clutch drum on rear unit with driven clutch plate lug slots up.
26. Dip five composition and four steel clutch plates in Hydra-Matic fluid. Install plates alternately using a release spring between steel plates. Start with a composition plate and release spring then steel plate, etc. and end up with a composition plate and spring.
27. Install seal on hub of case center support with lip facing toward bottom of piston cavity.
28. Install seal on neutral clutch piston with lip facing side of dowel holes.
29. Pilot neutral clutch piston into case center support with notch in edge of piston aligned with lock screw hole in side of case center support.
30. Install two oil rings in ring

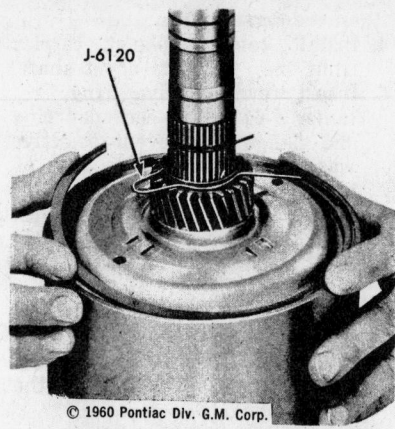

© 1960 Pontiac Div. G.M. Corp.

Installing the Output Shaft and Reverse Drive Flange Ring

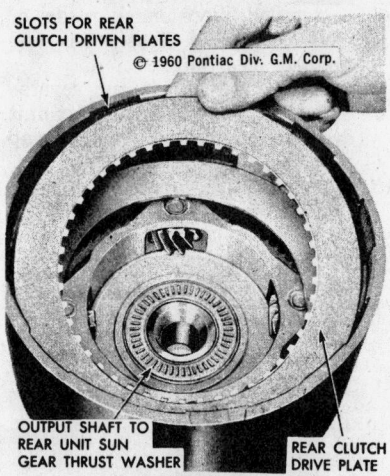

SLOTS FOR REAR CLUTCH DRIVEN PLATES

© 1960 Pontiac Div. G.M. Corp.

OUTPUT SHAFT TO REAR UNIT SUN GEAR THRUST WASHER

REAR CLUTCH DRIVE PLATE

Installing Rear Unit Clutch Plates

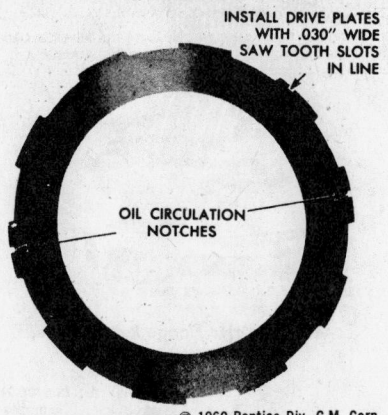

INSTALL DRIVE PLATES WITH .030" WIDE SAW TOOTH SLOTS IN LINE

OIL CIRCULATION NOTCHES

© 1960 Pontiac Div. G.M. Corp.

Keep the Saw Tooth Slots in Line

grooves of case support hub.
31. Center rings on hub and lower case support assembly into rear clutch cylinder of rear unit so as not to damage bushing or break oil rings.
32. Install hook type oil seal ring on intermediate shaft.
33. Slide clutch retainer J-6135 over end of intermediate shaft screw end up, apply pressure to com-

press clutch release springs, and tighten lock bolt.
34. Rotate case center support so that the right hand edge of cup plug in the center support is aligned with left edge of the first neutral clutch plate slot to the right of neutral clutch drum key slot.
   Note: This alignment must be accurate so as to insure alignment of oil passage between pump and case.
35. Mark the rear drum to indicate alignment of neutral clutch drum key slot.

PUMP AND OVERRUN CLUTCH
Disassembly

1. Remove four pump cover to body attaching screws.
2. Lift pump cover from body. If necessary tap with a soft hammer.
3. Remove pin which holds torus feed valve retainer. Remove retainer, spring and torus feed valve.
4. Remove cooler check valve pin and remove spring and ball.
5. Remove pump rotor and top vane ring.
6. Remove seven vanes.
7. Remove bottom vane ring.
8. Push slide toward priming springs, then lift it out of body at opposite end.
9. Remove inner and outer pump priming springs.
10. Turn pump over and remove sprag inner race, and spiral retaining ring using small screwdriver.
11. Remove sprag assembly from pump. Do not disassemble sprag. If it is damaged a new one should be used. **Note:** Do not remove the outer race.
12. Turn piston (rear) side of pump down and tap outer edge of piston with a soft hammer to remove overrun clutch piston from its bore. Remove seals from piston and hub in pump.

Inspection

1. In addition to normal inspection of pump and overrun clutch components, measure wear of bushing in pump body as follows:
   A. Set front unit coupling on bench with cover side up.
   B. Fasten pump cover to the body with one or two screws.
   C. Place pump cover and body assembly over front unit coupling driven torus shaft with cover down.
   D. Measure clearance between driven torus shaft and pump housing at point in pump body illustration using ½" wide

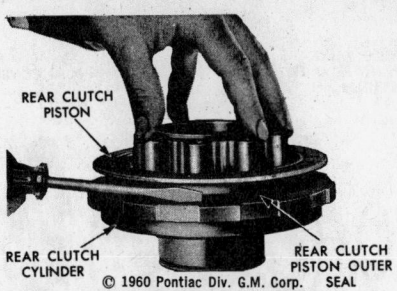

Rear Clutch Piston into Cylinder

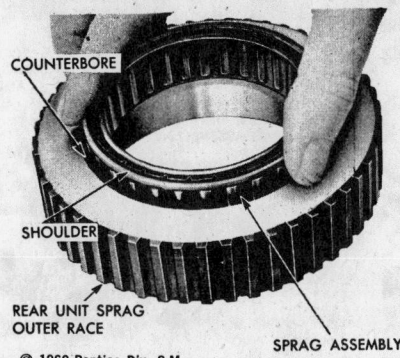

Rear Unit Sprag and Outer Race

Install Sprag and Outer Race on Inner Race

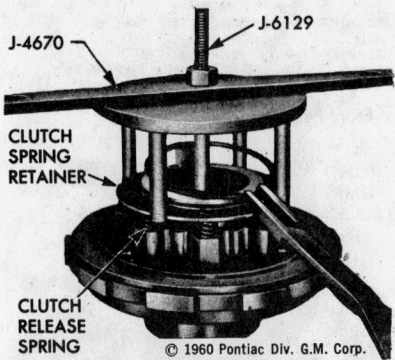

Installing Rear Clutch Release Spring Snap Ring

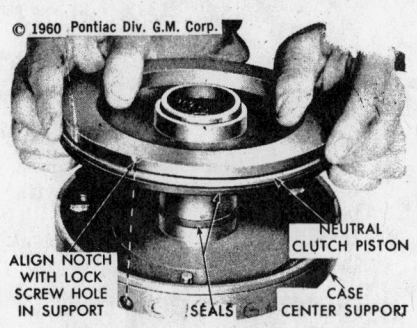

Neutral Clutch Piston

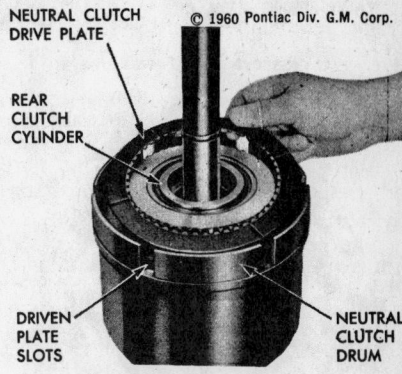

Neutral Clutch Plates

feeler blade. (Thrust of the shaft against the bushing is taken at this point). Clearance must not be more than .003″. If a .004″ gauge can be inserted between the shaft and the bushing, the pump and the driven torus member of the front unit must be replaced. **Note:** Bushing should be flush with rear side of pump and it should project slightly from front side.

2. Inspect overrun clutch release spring to see that it has five equally spaced waves about ¼″ deep.

Assembly

1. Insert inner and outer priming springs in the recess in the pump body.

2. Position pump slide in pump body toward priming springs. Compress priming springs with slide until it drops into pocket of pump. Work slide into position.

3. Insert torus feed valve in large bore on side of pump opposite priming springs with the long land entering first.

4. Install valve spring, retainer and valve retaining pin. Check freedom of valve by removing the slide.

5. Insert oil cooler check ball in oil cooler passage nearest to dowel. Then install check ball spring and spring retaining pin.

6. Lay a vane ring in the pump body, locating it concentrically with the slide bore.

7. Install rotor in pump cavity with drive slots up.

8. Install seven vanes in rotor with polished areas toward vane rings.

9. Install second vane ring on top of rotor. Check for free rotation of rotor.

10. Total clearance between vanes and slide, with vane rings installed, should be .000″-.003″. with vanes contacting slide on one side, clearance should not exceed .003″ on opposite side.

11. Attach front cover to pump body with four screws. Tighten to 15-18 lb. ft. **Note:** Short screw goes in hole nearest top of pump.

12. Install overrun clutch seal in hub of pump body with lip facing toward bottom of piston bore.

13. Install outer seal on overrun

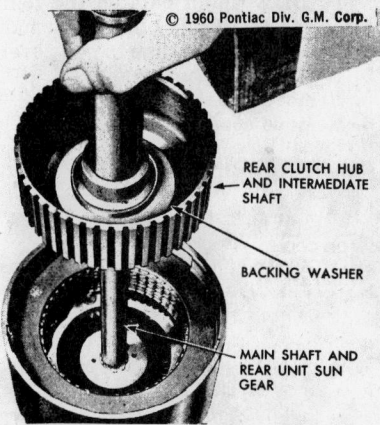

Install Shaft and Hub into Plates

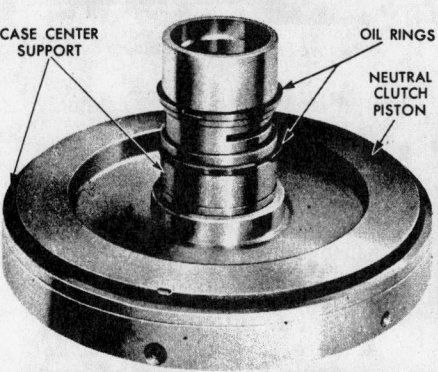

Case Support and Rings

Install Rear Unit Sprag Retainer Snap Ring

869

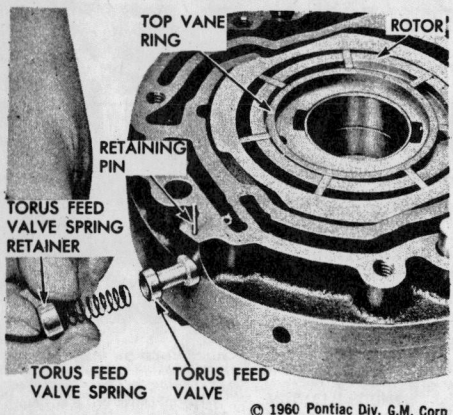

Remove Torus Feed Valve

© 1960 Pontiac Div. G.M. Corp

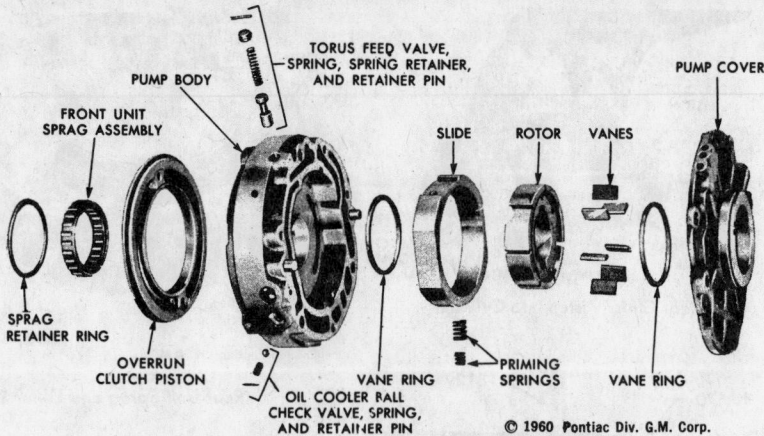

Exploded view of Front Pump—Dual-Coupling

© 1960 Pontiac Div. G.M. Corp.

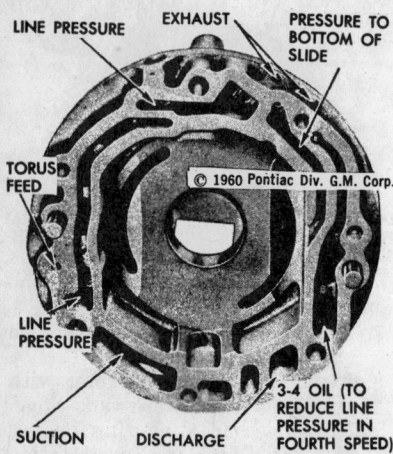

© 1960 Pontiac Div. G.M. Corp.

Pump Body Passages (Front Side)

clutch piston with lip facing side. with dowel holes.

14. Install overrun clutch piston in pump body.
15. Install sprag into rear of pump, shoulder side up. Rotate sprag counterclockwise while installing it.
16. Secure sprag with spiral snap ring.
17. Install sprag inner race into sprag with lug side up. Inner race must be free to rotate counterclockwise from top.
18. Place overrun clutch plate on top of piston, indexing drive lugs with sprag inner race. Stick clutch plate in place with petrolatum.
19. Put petrolatum on thrust washer and place washer on sprag in-

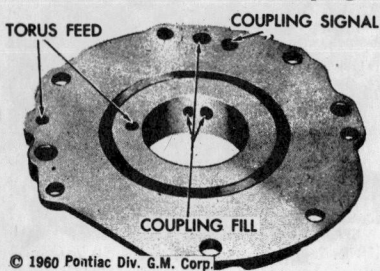

© 1960 Pontiac Div. G.M. Corp.

Pump Cover

ner race with drive lugs down and indexed with sprag outer race.

20. Position clutch release spring on top of piston and retain with petrolatum.
21. Install pump intake "O" ring seal in pump body.

FRONT UNIT COUPLING

Disassembly

To maintain balance, it is important that the coupling cover be installed in it's original position.

Scribe parts in this area so that during reassembly, all parts may be relocated as they were, including the gap in the snap ring.

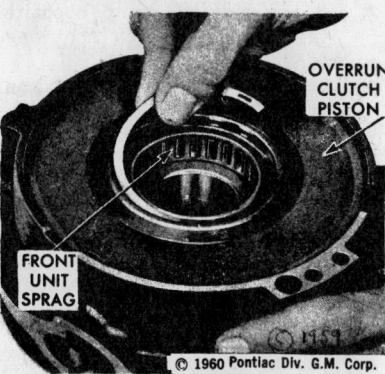

© 1960 Pontiac Div. G.M. Corp.

Remove Front Sprag Retaining Ring

1. Rest front unit coupling assembly in holding fixture J-6116.
2. Remove large snap ring retaining coupling cover to drive torus shell.
3. Install two coupling exhaust valve retainers J-6122 to hold exhaust valves in position when removing the cover.
4. Remove cover from coupling using remover J-6121 as follows:
   A. Place the cross piece of remover J-6121 on end of torus shaft with end of shaft extended in counterbore on underside of tool.

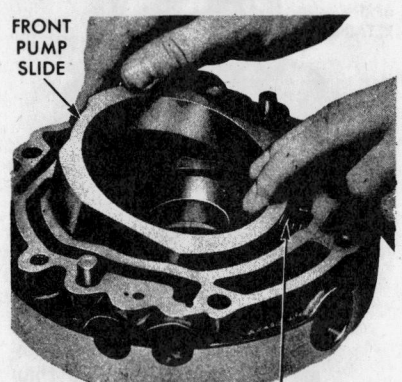

© 1960 Pontiac Div. G.M. Corp.

Remove Pump Slide

   B. Screw stud at end of each leg into holes in coupling cover until they bottom. (Nuts on the studs should be backed off so they will not contact the cross piece.)
   C. Insert long stud of J-6121 through coupling and cross piece. Index bottom end with hole in clutch unit holding fixture so it cannot turn. Install washer and nut on upper end and tighten securely.
   D. Draw up on nuts on the four studs evenly and a small amount at a time to pull cover out of the unit.
5. Remove the tool.
6. Remove coupling cover.

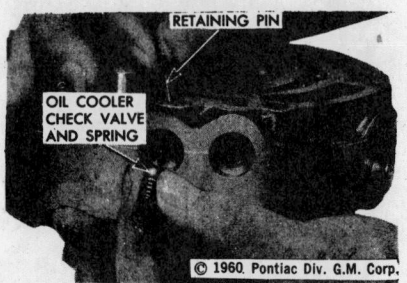

© 1960 Pontiac Div. G.M. Corp.

Remove Oil Cooler Check Valve

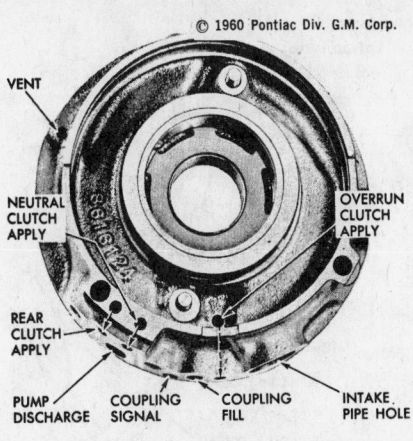

Pump Body Passages (Rear Side)

Labels: VENT, NEUTRAL CLUTCH APPLY, OVERRUN CLUTCH APPLY, REAR CLUTCH APPLY, PUMP DISCHARGE, COUPLING SIGNAL, COUPLING FILL, INTAKE PIPE HOLE

© 1960 Pontiac Div. G.M. Corp.

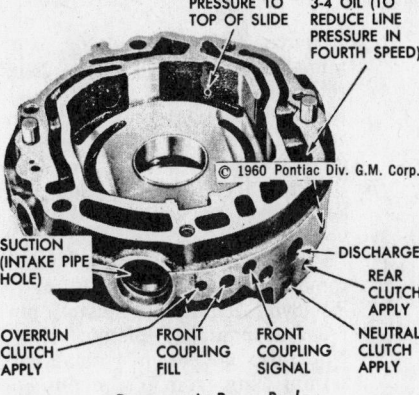

Passages in Pump Body

Labels: PRESSURE TO TOP OF SLIDE, 3-4 OIL (TO REDUCE LINE PRESSURE IN FOURTH SPEED), SUCTION (INTAKE PIPE HOLE), DISCHARGE, REAR CLUTCH APPLY, OVERRUN CLUTCH APPLY, FRONT COUPLING FILL, FRONT COUPLING SIGNAL, NEUTRAL CLUTCH APPLY

© 1960 Pontiac Div. G.M. Corp.

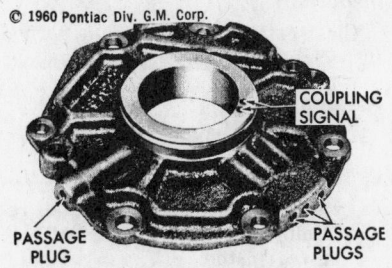

Passages in Pump Cover

Labels: COUPLING SIGNAL, PASSAGE PLUG, PASSAGE PLUGS

© 1960 Pontiac Div. G.M. Corp.

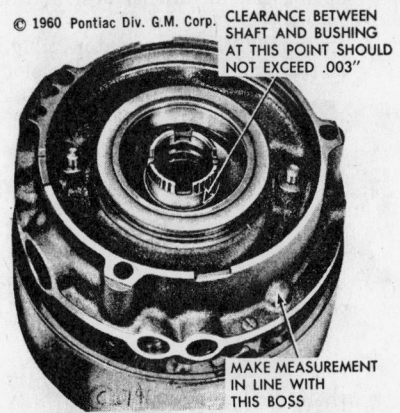

Measure Bushing Wear in Pump Body

Labels: CLEARANCE BETWEEN SHAFT AND BUSHING AT THIS POINT SHOULD NOT EXCEED .003", MAKE MEASUREMENT IN LINE WITH THIS BOSS

© 1960 Pontiac Div. G.M. Corp.

7. While holding fingers over valves so they will not pop out, remove coupling exhaust valve retainers J-6122 and exhaust valves and springs from cover. Remove and discard seal rings from outer diameter of cover.

8. Remove driven torus member by pulling up on shaft, and remove bronze and steel thrust washers.

9. Remove drive torus member from holding fixture.

Inspection

Clean and make normal inspection for wear and other damage. Make sure that the signal oil passages are clear and that the passage plugs are in place.

Assembly

1. Place drive torus in holding fixture J-6116 with hub down.

2. Install steel, then bronze thrust washer in drive torus member.

3. With oil rings in place on driven torus shaft, install driven torus into drive torus.

4. Install two new torus cover square ring seals. Apply petrolatum to lubricate the seals for inserting cover into drive torus.

5. Install springs and coupling exhaust valves in cover and install valve retainers J-6122.

6. Insert cover into drive torus shell indexing #1 exhaust valve (or mark made during disassembly) with mark on drive torus shell. The cover will be secure when the snap ring groove in torus shell shows evenly above the cover.

7. Remove the two retainers J-6122 from the cover.

8. Install snap ring to retain torus cover in drive torus shell with gap in snap ring aligned with #1 exhaust valve.
   Note: Cover, shell, and gap in snap ring must be replaced in original locations to maintain balance of the unit.

REVERSE CLUTCH PISTON HOUSING

Disassembly

1. Remove large snap ring retaining wave type reverse piston release spring and retainer.

2. Remove retainer and release spring.

3. Lift reverse piston from reverse clutch piston housing.

4. Remove bearing to housing snap ring.

5. Tap bearing out of housing.

Inspection

Clean components and make normal inspection. In addition, check that the reverse piston release spring has five

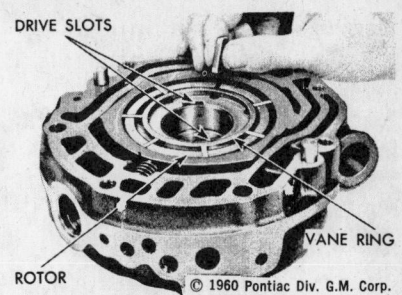

Installing Vanes in Rotor

Labels: DRIVE SLOTS, VANE RING, ROTOR

© 1960 Pontiac Div. G.M. Corp.

Install Front Sprag in Hub of Pump

© 1960 Pontiac Div. G.M. Corp.

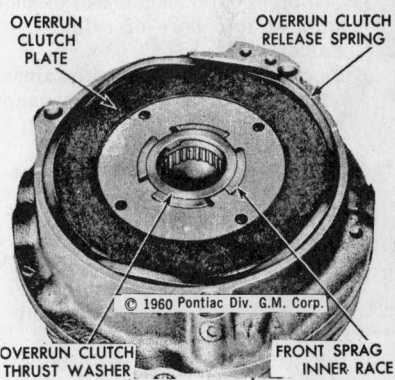

Overrun Clutch Parts Installed

Labels: OVERRUN CLUTCH PLATE, OVERRUN CLUTCH RELEASE SPRING, OVERRUN CLUTCH THRUST WASHER, FRONT SPRAG INNER RACE

© 1960 Pontiac Div. G.M. Corp.

Remove the Coupling Cover

Labels: J-6121, J-6122, COVER, J-6122, DRIVE TORUS, J-6116

© G.M.C.—1960

REVERSE PLANET

REVERSE CLUTCH RELEASE SPRING

STATIONARY CONE

INTERNAL GEAR

FIBER THRUST WASHER

Driving Torus Assembly

Driven Torus Assembly

Oil Seal Ring (Torus Hubs)

Oil Ring Seal (Coupling Cover to Driving Torus)

Exhaust Valve

Exhaust Valve Spring

Steel Thrust Backing Washer

Bronze Thrust Washer

Oil Seal Ring (Driven Torus Hub)

Coupling Cover

Oil Seal Rings (Coupling Cover to Front Pump)

Snap Ring (Coupling Cover to Driving Torus)

Exploded view of Reverse Unit

Second Fluid Coupling—Dual-Coupling Models

equally spaced, ¼″ deep waves.

Assembly

1. Place tool J-7577 over inner hub of reverse piston housing.
2. Lower reverse piston over tool, rotating it to engage dowel pins.
3. Compress outer piston seal to and enter it into bore of cylinder.
4. Remove tool J-7577.
5. Place release spring and retainer on piston and install large snap ring.
Note: Rear bearing will be installed after piston housing is attached to transmission.

GOVERNOR

Disassembly

1. Remove two cover-to-governor driven gear attaching bolts.
2. Remove cover plate, G-2 bushing retaining pin, G-2 bushing and plunger assembly, and bushing stop washer.
3. Remove G-2 plunger from bushing.
4. Remove four governor oil rings.
5. Remove governor driven gear if necessary.

Inspection

Clean components and make normal inspection for wear or other damage.

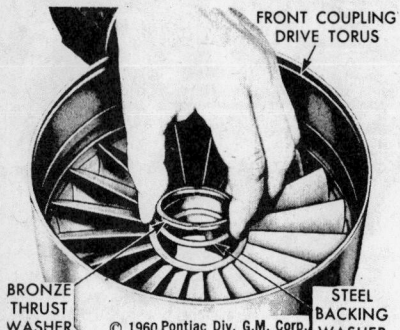

FRONT COUPLING DRIVE TORUS

BRONZE THRUST WASHER

STEEL BACKING WASHER

© 1960 Pontiac Div. G.M. Corp.

Install Thrust Washers in Drive Torus

Assembly

1. Insert G-2 bushing stop washer into body.
2. Install G-2 (secondary) plunger into bushing.
3. Install G-2 bushing and plunger assembly into the governor body.
4. Rotate bushing to align recess in bushing to accept retaining pin and install pin.
5. If governor driven gear was removed, install it over governor tower and roll the pin.
6. Attach governor cover plate-to-

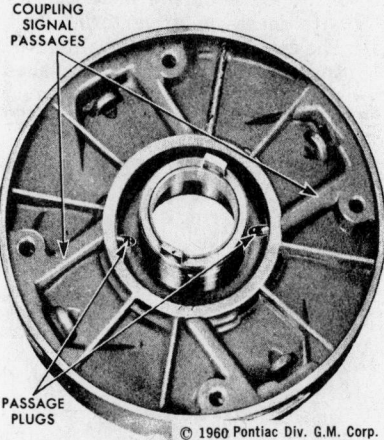

COUPLING SIGNAL PASSAGES

PASSAGE PLUGS

© 1960 Pontiac Div. G.M. Corp.

Plug in Exhaust Valve Signal oil Passages, Coupling Cover

body with two screws entering the driven gear. Overhang of plate must be toward G-2 weight.
7. Install four governor oil rings.

SERVO AND ACCUMULATOR

Disassembly

1. Remove servo piston from servo body.
2. Remove cover attaching screws. Then remove cover and discard gasket.

3. Remove T.V. accumulator stop pin and accumulator valve plug retainer.
4. Remove plug, accumulator valve, spring, and T.V. accumulator plug.
5. Remove accumulator piston and spring from accumulator and servo body.
6. Compress accumulator spring and remove retaining washer.
7. Remove accumulator piston pin from accumulator piston.
Note: Do not remove small retaining ring from piston pin.
8. Remove oil seal ring from accumulator piston.

Inspection

Clean components and make normal inspection for wear or other damage.

Assembly

1. Install oil ring on accumulator piston.
2. Assemble accumulator piston stem in piston with the small retaining ring toward the flat side of the piston.
3. Place accumulator spring over stem end of piston, compress spring and install spring retaining washer.
4. Install T.V. accumulator plug, slotted end last and align the slot

J-6122

© 1960 Pontiac Div. G.M. Corp.

Install Torus Cover into Drive Torus Shell

in plug with vent passage.

5. Install accumulator valve spring in accumulator valve and install valve and valve spring, spring end first, into the bore.

6. Insert accumulator valve plug into bore.

7. Install T.V. accumulator plug stop pin into vent passage and slot in plug.

8. Install plug retainer in body and in groove in the plug.

9. Install accumulator piston assembly in accumulator.

10. Attach accumulator gasket and cover with five screws.

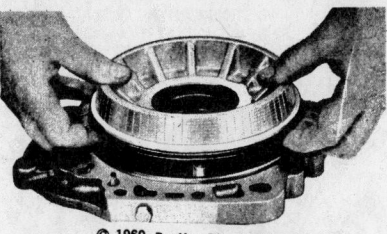

© 1960 Pontiac Div. G.M. Corp.

Remove Piston from Reverse Clutch Housing

1. Remove three screws holding the shift valve to the channel plate and remove the shift valve group.

2. Remove two screws holding the clutch valve group to channel plate and remove clutch valve group.

3. Remove channel plate to valve body spacer plate.

4. Remove three screws holding the manual valve group to channel plate and remove this group.

5. Remove channel plate to case spacer plate.

6. Remove the coupling fill thermostat from the channel plate.

CLUTCH VALVE

Disassemble

1. Remove three screws holding the clutch valve body front plate and remove the plate.

2. Remove transition valve and spring.

3. Remove coupling signal valve, coupling valve, valve spring, and plug from the clutch valve body.

4. Remove two screws holding the clutch body rear plate and remove the plate and oil screen retaining clip.

5. Remove inner and outer limit valve springs.

6. Remove limit valve spring washer and limit valve.

Inspection

Clean components and make normal inspection for wear or other damage.

Assembly

1. Install limit valve, stem end out.

2. Install limit valve washer, inner spring and outer spring.

3. Attach rear plate and retainer clip to clutch body with one screw thru the clip. Leave this screw loose.

4. Rotate plate over the limit valve springs while holding springs compressed and install the remaining screw. Now tighten both screws.

5. Insert coupling valve plug, spring, coupling valve and coupling signal valve in valve body.

6. Insert spring in transition valve, then instal the transition valve and spring, spring first, into the clutch body.

7. Attach clutch body front cover with three attaching screws.

J-7577

© 1960 Pontiac Div. G.M. Corp.

Installing Reverse Piston in Housing

SHIFT VALVE

Disassemble

1. Remove neutral clutch by-pass valve from shift valve body.

2. Remove two screws holding the regulator body cover and remove the cover.

3. Remove three screws holding the regulator body. Remove regulator body, end plate, and two T.V. valve plugs together.

4. Remove the 2-3 and 3-4 T.V. valve plugs from the regulator body.

5. Remove the neutral clutch spring, 2-3 shift valve spring, 2-3 T.V. spring, and the 3-4 shift valve spring from the shift body.

6. Remove the neutral clutch regu-

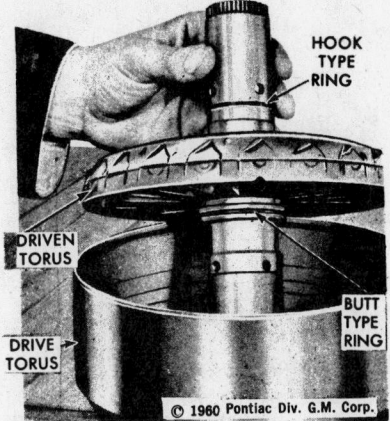

HOOK TYPE RING

DRIVEN TORUS

DRIVE TORUS

BUTT TYPE RING

© 1960 Pontiac Div. G.M. Corp.

Install Driven Torus into Drive Torus

CONTROL VALVE ASSEMBLY

Disassembly of Components

The complete control valve body consists of three individual groups and two spacer plates connected to a channel plate. In the disassembly and assembly procedure each individual group should be removed from the complete valve body, disassembled, cleaned and inspected, and assembled before proceeding to the next group. The names of these individual groups are:

    A. Clutch valve.
    B. Shift valve.
    C. Manual valve.

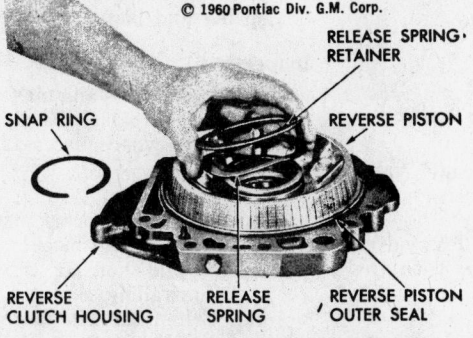

© 1960 Pontiac Div. G.M. Corp.

RELEASE SPRING RETAINER

SNAP RING

REVERSE PISTON

REVERSE CLUTCH HOUSING

RELEASE SPRING

REVERSE PISTON OUTER SEAL

Remove Snap Ring, Reverse Piston Release Spring and Retainer

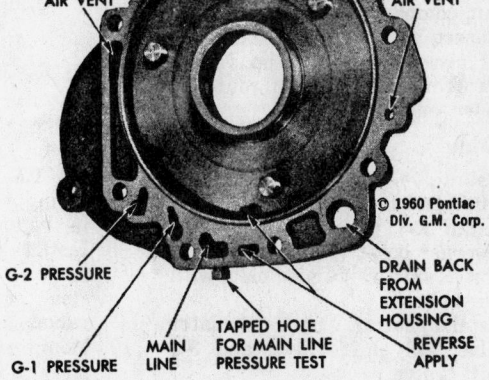

AIR VENT

AIR VENT

© 1960 Pontiac Div. G.M. Corp.

G-2 PRESSURE

DRAIN BACK FROM EXTENSION HOUSING

G-1 PRESSURE

MAIN LINE

TAPPED HOLE FOR MAIN LINE PRESSURE TEST

REVERSE APPLY

Reverse Clutch Piston Housing Passages

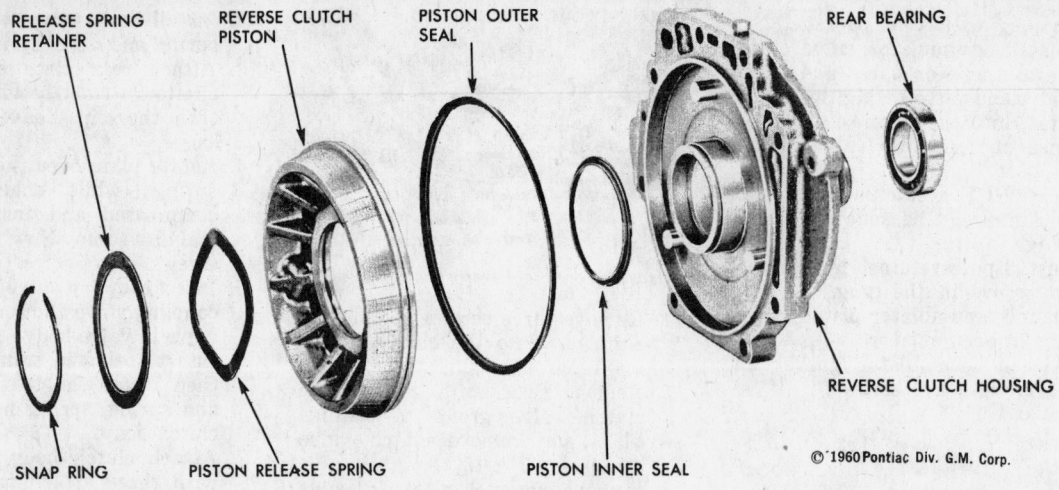

RELEASE SPRING RETAINER • REVERSE CLUTCH PISTON • PISTON OUTER SEAL • REAR BEARING

SNAP RING • PISTON RELEASE SPRING • PISTON INNER SEAL • REVERSE CLUTCH HOUSING

© 1960 Pontiac Div. G.M. Corp.

Reverse Clutch Piston, Housing and Parts

Rear Pump Cover • By-Pass Valves • Pump Driven Gear • Pump Drive Gear

Governor Drive Clip

Snap Ring

Ball Bearing Assembly

Oil Seal

Reverse Clutch Piston

Rear Pump Body

Rear Pump Gasket

Exploded View of Rear Oil Pump

lator valve, 2-3 shift valve, and the 3-4 shift valve.

7. Remove four screws holding the shift valve body plate and remove the plate.

8. Remove governor boost valve, 2-3 governor valve, and the 3-4 governor valve.

Inspection

Clean components and make normal inspection for wear or other damage. If necessary to free up valves, refrain from abrading or rounding the valve edges.

Assembly

1. Install 3-4 governor valve with round end facing out.
2. Install 2-3 governor valve and governor boost valve.
3. Attach shift valve body plate with four screws.
4. Install neutral clutch regulator valve, 2-3 shift valve, and 3-4 shift valve.
5. Insert neutral clutch valve spring,

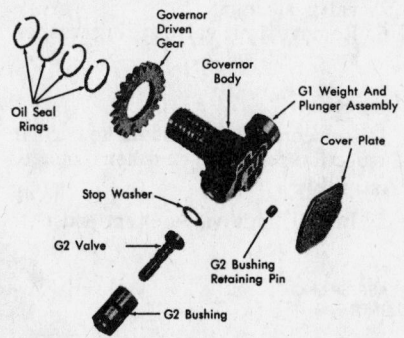

Governor Driven Gear

Governor Body

G1 Weight And Plunger Assembly

Cover Plate

Oil Seal Rings

Stop Washer

G2 Valve

G2 Bushing Retaining Pin

G2 Bushing

Exploded view of Governor Assembly

2-3 T.V. spring, 2-3 shift valve spring, and 3-4 shift valve spring in the shift valve body.

6. Install the 2-3 and 3-4 T.V. valves in the regulator body, with the small ends toward the shift valves.

7. Mount regulator valve body and plate to valve body using the one plate attaching screw.

8. Align and secure the regulator body to shift valve body with two screws.

9. Attach the regulator body cover.

10. Install neutral clutch by-pass valve in shift valve body.

MANUAL VALVE

Disassembly

1. Remove two screws holding the T.V. lever stop and remove stop. **Note:** Do not tamper with the factory adjusted T.V. stop adjusting screw.

2. Remove detent valve.

3. Remove T.V. plunger and guide. Then separate the plunger from the guide.

4. Remove T.V. spring.

5. Remove detent spring.

6. Remove throttle valve.

7. Remove thermostatic element retaining clip and the element. **Note:** The small thermostatic element adjusting screw is preset at the factory.

8. Clip one end of the reverse blocker piston retaining pin.

9. While holding thumb over the reverse blocker piston bore, remove retaining pin.

10. Remove reverse blocker piston spring and piston.

Inspection

Clean components and make normal inspection for wear or other damage. Renew parts where necessary.

Assembly

1. Install reverse blocker piston.

2. Insert reverse blocker piston spring and hold it compressed while installing a new retaining pin. Crimp the pin to secure it.

3. Install T.V. thermostatic element and clip.

4. Install throttle valve, with the

Accumulator Piston Installed in Accumulator Body

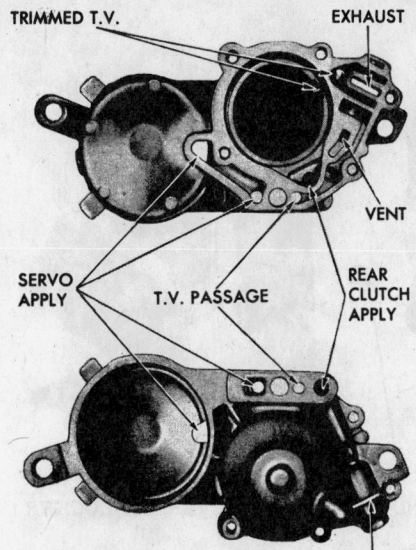

Passages in Servo and Accumulator

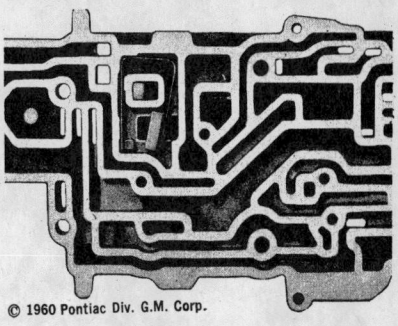

Coupling Fill Thermostat Installed

large land first, into the manual body.

5. Insert T.V. spring in the T.V. bore.
6. Install detent valve spring in detent bore.
7. Install detent valve, long land last, in the detent bore.
8. Insert T.V. plunger in the guide and install both parts into the T.V. bore.
9. Attach the T.V. lever stop.

Assembly of Components

1. Place the coupling fill thermostat element in the channel plate.
2. Lay channel plate to case spacer over channel plate and coupling fill element.
3. Place manual valve body assembly over channel plate to case spacer and attach with three screws. Leave screws one turn loose.
4. Turn assembly over and position the channel plate to valve body spacer.
5. Lay the shift valve body in place opposite the manual body and secure with three screws. Leave screws loose.
6. Attach clutch valve body in place

with two screws, leaving screws loose.
7. Use five valve body to case attaching bolts as guides through valve bodies and tighten the shift valve and clutch valve body attaching screws.
8. Remove the five bolts as guides.
9. Turn assembly over and tighten three manual valve body screws.

FLYWHEEL HOUSING OIL SEAL

Remove

Drive the seal out of the housing by inserting a blunt punch thru housing oil drain back hole.

Replacement

1. Apply light coat of sealer on the outside edge of the seal casing and place it in the bore of the housing, lip down.

2. Tap seal into place with tool J-7026 or suitable drift.
3. Stake seal at three housing reinforcement bosses.

PRESSURE REGULATOR

Disassembly

1. Remove pressure regulator valve stop plug.
2. Remove reverse booster plug.
3. Remove seal from pressure regulator plug.

Assembly

1. Install new "O" ring on pressure regulator plug.
2. Apply a small bit of petrolatum to the bore of the pressure regulator plug and the reverse booster plug to hold parts after assembly.
3. Install reverse booster plug in pressure regulator sleeve.
4. Install pressure regulator valve stop in reverse booster plug.

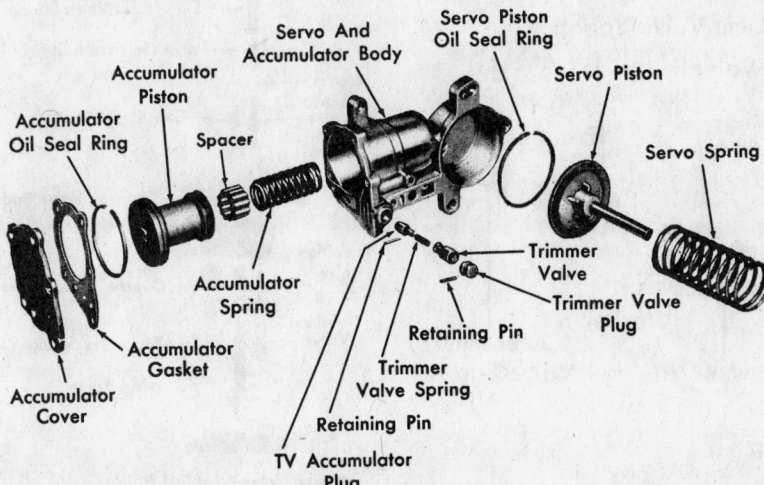

Exploded View of Overrun Band Servo and Accumulator—1956-58, 1959 Early

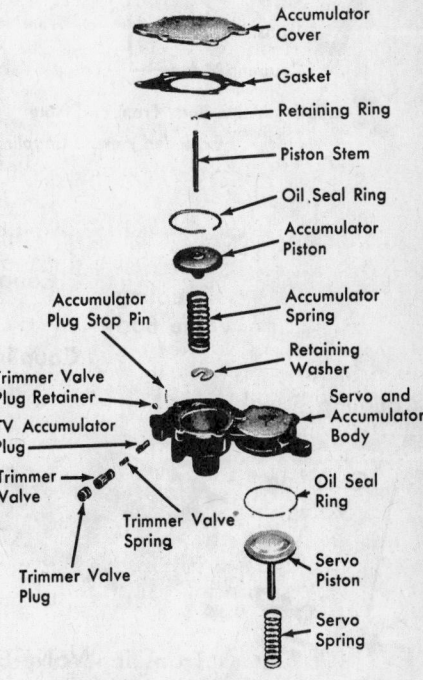

Exploded View of Overrun Band Servo and Accumulator—1959 Late, 1960

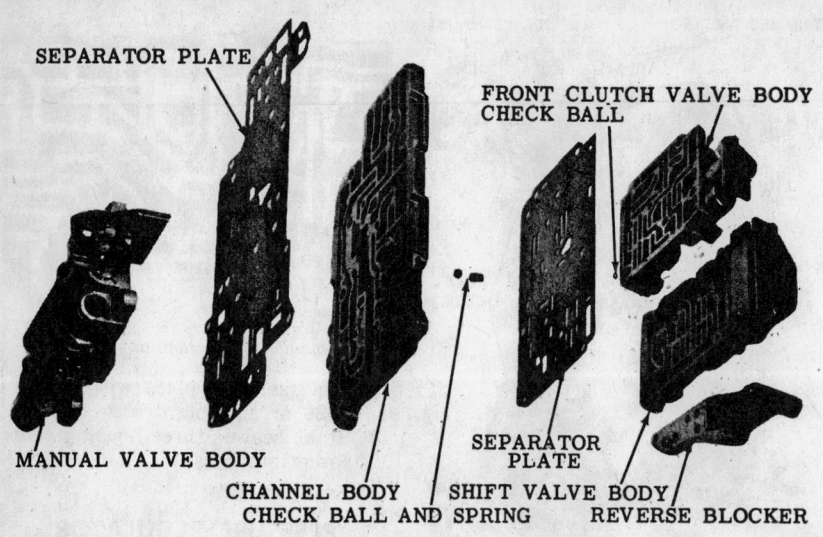

SEPARATOR PLATE

FRONT CLUTCH VALVE BODY
CHECK BALL

MANUAL VALVE BODY

CHANNEL BODY
CHECK BALL AND SPRING

SEPARATOR
PLATE

SHIFT VALVE
BODY

REVERSE BLOCKER

Dual-Coupling Valve Body Assembly, Typical 1956-59

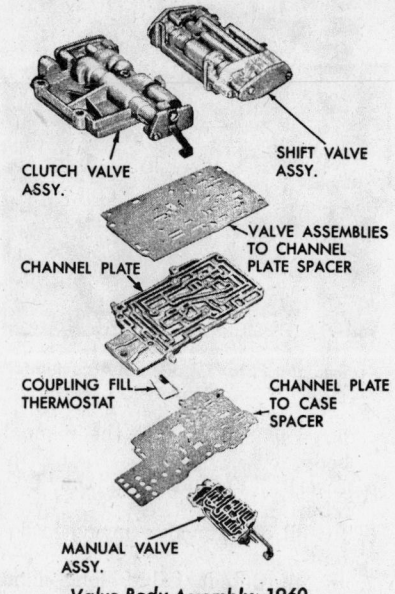

CLUTCH VALVE
ASSY.

SHIFT VALVE
ASSY.

VALVE ASSEMBLIES
TO CHANNEL
PLATE SPACER

CHANNEL PLATE

COUPLING FILL
THERMOSTAT

CHANNEL PLATE
TO CASE
SPACER

MANUAL VALVE
ASSY.

Valve Body Assembly, 1960

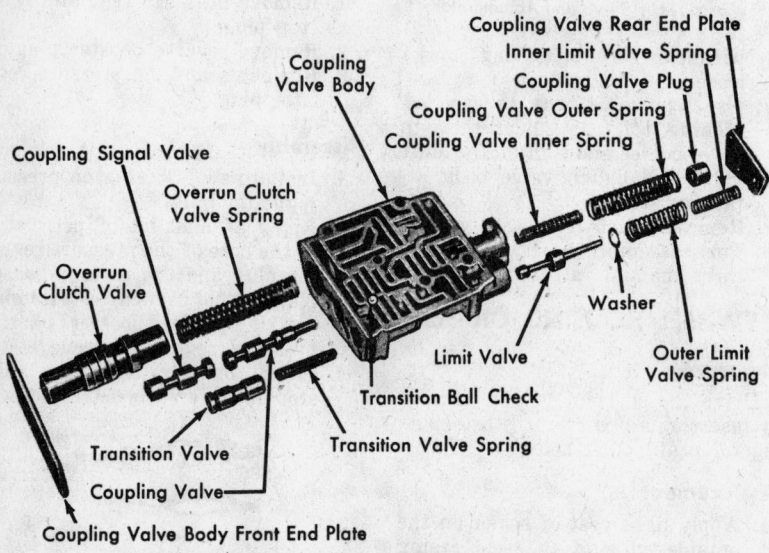

Coupling Valve Rear End Plate
Inner Limit Valve Spring
Coupling Valve Plug
Coupling Valve Outer Spring
Coupling Valve Inner Spring

Coupling
Valve Body

Coupling Signal Valve

Overrun Clutch
Valve Spring

Overrun
Clutch Valve

Washer

Limit Valve

Outer Limit
Valve Spring

Transition Valve

Transition Ball Check

Transition Valve Spring

Coupling Valve

Coupling Valve Body Front End Plate

Exploded View of Coupling Valve Body, 1957

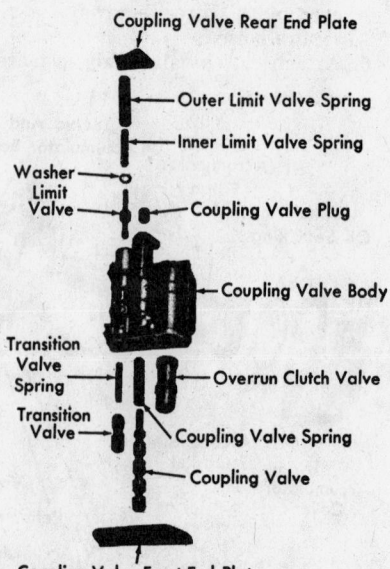

BLOCKER
PISTON PIN

REVERSE
BLOCKER BODY

DETENT PLUNGER
RETAINER

REVERSE
BLOCKER
PISTON

DETENT
PLUNGER
SPRING

DETENT PLUNGER

REVERSE BLOCKER
PISTON SPRING

Reverse Blocker Body— 1956-59

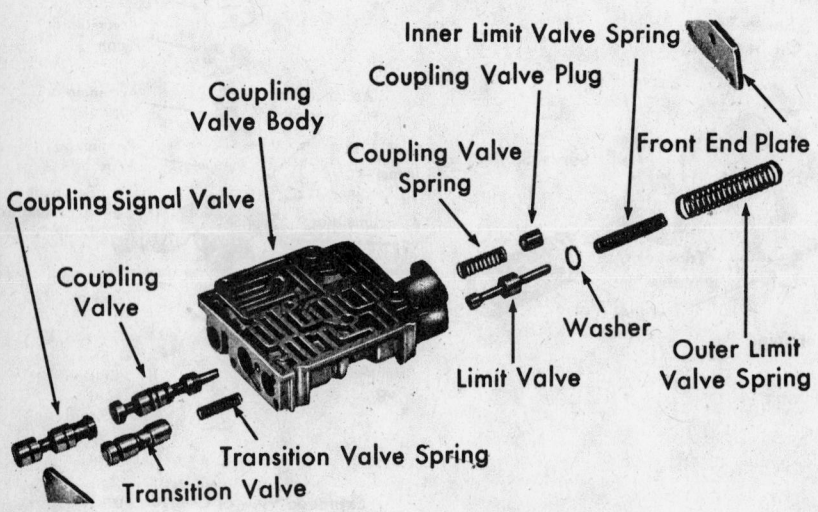

Inner Limit Valve Spring

Coupling Valve Plug

Coupling
Valve Body

Coupling Valve
Spring

Front End Plate

Coupling Signal Valve

Coupling
Valve

Washer

Limit Valve

Outer Limit
Valve Spring

Transition Valve Spring

Transition Valve

Exploded View of Coupling Valve Body, 1958-60

Coupling Valve Rear End Plate

Outer Limit Valve Spring

Inner Limit Valve Spring

Washer
Limit
Valve

Coupling Valve Plug

Coupling Valve Body

Transition
Valve
Spring

Overrun Clutch Valve

Transition
Valve

Coupling Valve Spring

Coupling Valve

Coupling Valve Front End Plate

Exploded View of Coupling Valve Body, 1956

DRIVEN TORUS MEMBER CHECK VALVE

Disassembly

1. Hold finger over check valve bore and remove the cotter pin.
2. Invert torus member and tap the case lightly to dislodge and remove the valve and spring.

Assembly

1. Install spring in torus check valve.
2. Install spring and check valve into torus member. Be sure valve fully seats in the bore.
3. Install cotter pin to hold valve and spring in place.

INSTALLATION OF UNITS INTO THE CASE

DETENT SPRING AND ROLLER

1. Place detent spring and roller assembly on the mounting pad in the case and start attaching bolt

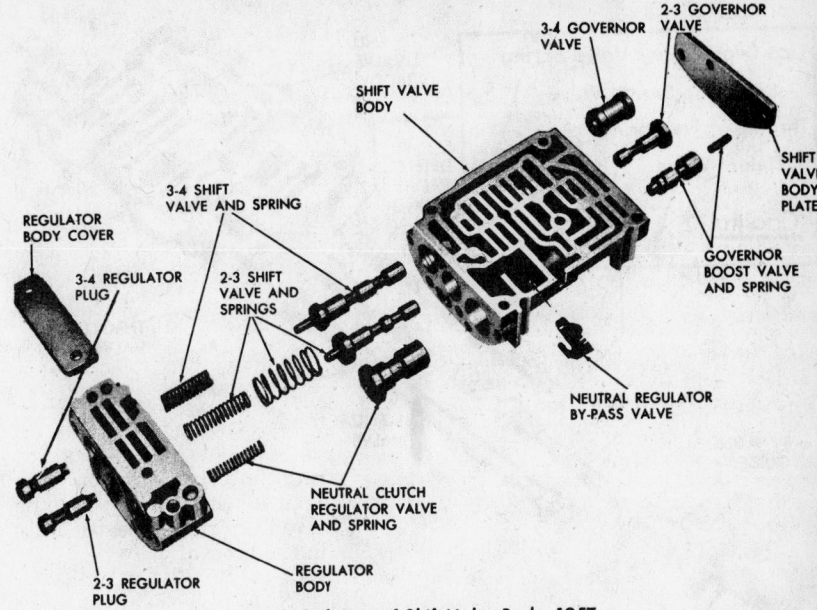

Exploded View of Shift Valve Body, 1957

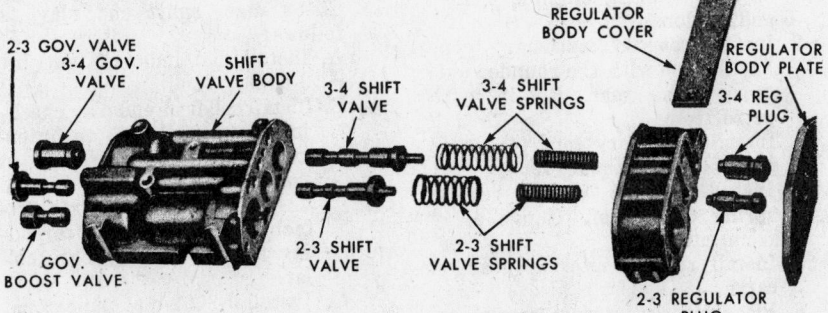

Exploded View of Shift Valve Body, 1956

into tapped hole.
2. While holding inside detent lever in position in the case to act as a guide center the roller in the detent. Install and torque attaching bolt to 15-18 lb. ft.
3. Bend lock tab of retaining clip against bolt head.

PARKING BRAKE LINKAGE

1. Place parking pawl pin spacer in recess in the case.
2. Position parking brake pawl and brake lever assembly in case with brake lever on pivot in the case. Locate pawl at pawl pin hole and insert pin thru case, pawl and spacer until shaft bottoms.
3. Position parking brake lever spring in bracket, long end toward the rear. Slide bracket and spring onto pivot shaft with short end of spring under parking brake bracket. Hook long end of spring under parking brake lever.

INSIDE DETENT AND THROTTLE LEVERS

1. Install new "O" ring on manual lever shaft.
2. Place detent lever in position against detent roller so that dowel

pin on parking brake bracket is between the lever and outside of case.
3. Insert the manual lever shaft thru side of case, align serrations and slide the lever onto the shaft.
4. Tighten set screw while holding lever in place.
5. Install new "O" ring on T.V. lever shaft.
6. Insert T.V. shaft thru manual lever shaft.
7. Install inside T.V. lever on T.V. shaft, lever facing out.
8. With a .010" feeler as a spacer, press the T.V. lever onto the shaft as far as possible and tighten the lock screw to 10-12 lb. ft. torque.

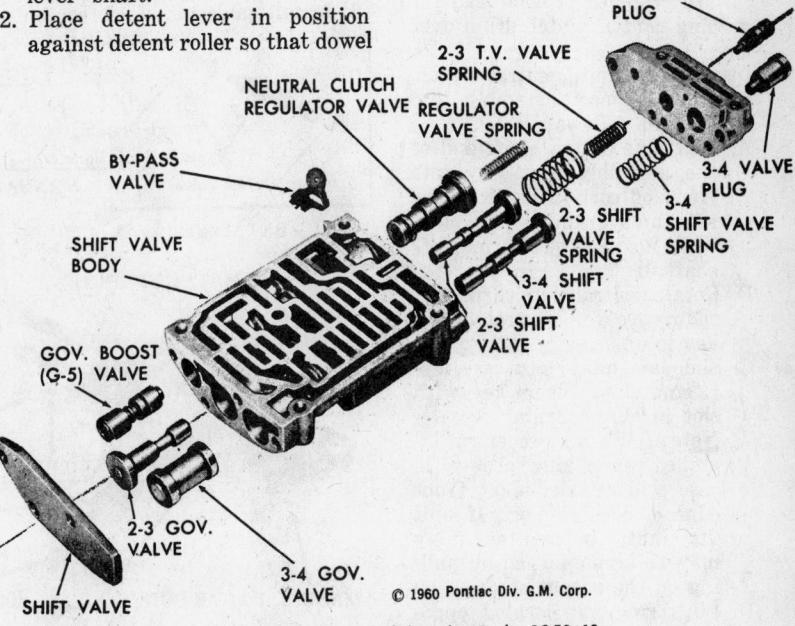

© 1960 Pontiac Div. G.M. Corp.

Exploded View of Shift Valve Body, 1958-60

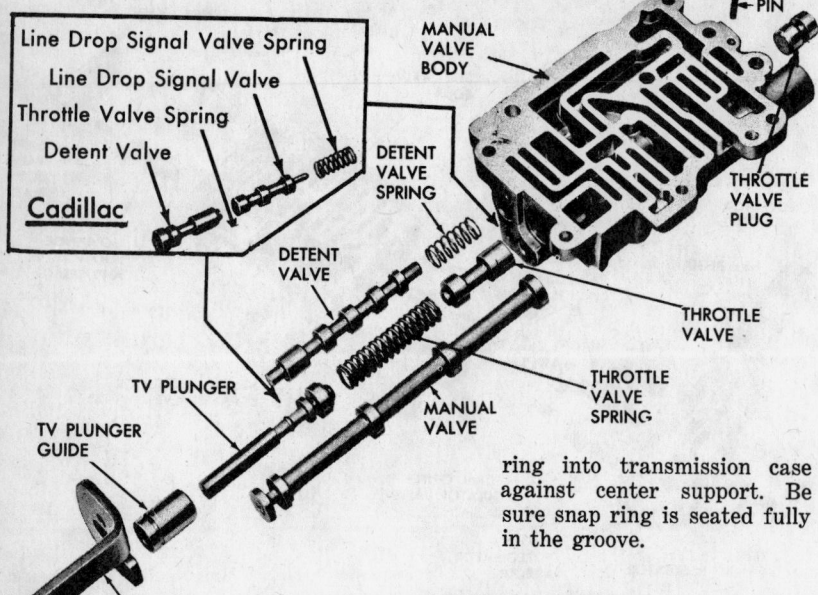

Manual Valve Body, 1956-57

Line Drop Signal Valve Spring
Line Drop Signal Valve
Throttle Valve Spring
Detent Valve
Cadillac
MANUAL VALVE BODY
PIN
DETENT VALVE SPRING
THROTTLE VALVE PLUG
DETENT VALVE
THROTTLE VALVE
TV PLUNGER
MANUAL VALVE
THROTTLE VALVE SPRING
TV PLUNGER GUIDE
TV LEVER STOP

"LO" BAND

1. Install LO band thru front end of transmission case with the band ends facing rearward in a horizontal position.
2. Twist band and position band end on anchor in the case.

REAR UNIT, NEUTRAL CLUTCH AND CASE SUPPORT

1. Install neutral clutch key in case using petrolatum to hold it in place. Place the rounded side toward front to provide lead for guiding neutral clutch drum over key.
2. Install rear unit, neutral clutch, and case support assembly into the case as follows:
   A. Start the output shaft end of the assembly part way into front of case. Then rest the rear unit drum on the case, while holding the intermediate shaft.
   B. Rotate neutral clutch drum until groove for neutral clutch key is up.
   C. Slide assembly into case, engaging clutch drum key with slot in clutch drum.
   Note: When properly installed, snap ring groove in case will be visible at front edge of case support. If unit fits tightly in case, assembly may be accomplished by pulling on the output shaft.
   D. With ring gap located opposite oil passages, slide snap ring into transmission case against center support. Be sure snap ring is seated fully in the groove.

REVERSE PARTS

1. Install reverse planet carrier on output shaft, aligning splines and pinions.
2. Install reverse stationary cone key in case with the rounded side toward the rear. Retain with petrolatum.
3. Install stationary cone, (be sure cone aligns with key).
4. Install reverse clutch release spring on carrier, (tangs away from carrier).
5. Install reverse internal gear on carrier.
6. Place reverse internal gear to reverse clutch housing hub thrust washer against internal gear.
7. Affix a new gasket to the reverse clutch housing with petrolatum.
8. Install governor feed screen in reverse clutch housing governor feed line.
9. Slide housing over end of output shaft and secure to transmission case with one bolt.
10. Remove rear unit clutch retainer J-6135 from intermediate shaft.
11. Drive rear bearing over output shaft using bearing installer J-6133-A until the snap ring groove on the shaft is exposed behind the rear bearing.
    Note: If bearing is a slip fit on output shaft, slide snap ring over shaft against bearing, pull shaft rearward and push snap ring into groove. However, if snap ring will not seat into groove, rotate unit to position the output shaft down, then drive the snap ring into place with installer J-6133-A.
12. After snap ring is installed in groove of output shaft, install bearing retaining snap ring in reverse clutch housing.
13. Attach extension housing to transmission case with bolt at each long ear.
14. Check main shaft end play as follows:
    A. Install dial indicator support J-6126.
    B. Install collar of end play checking fixture J-6127 on intermediate shaft and secure in position by installing Truarc snap ring on main shaft. Attach fixture to collar by threading fixture securely onto collar.
    C. Install J-8001 dial indicator.
    D. Move main shaft back and forth to check end play of main shaft.

Note: Be sure to register **only free** mainshaft end play.

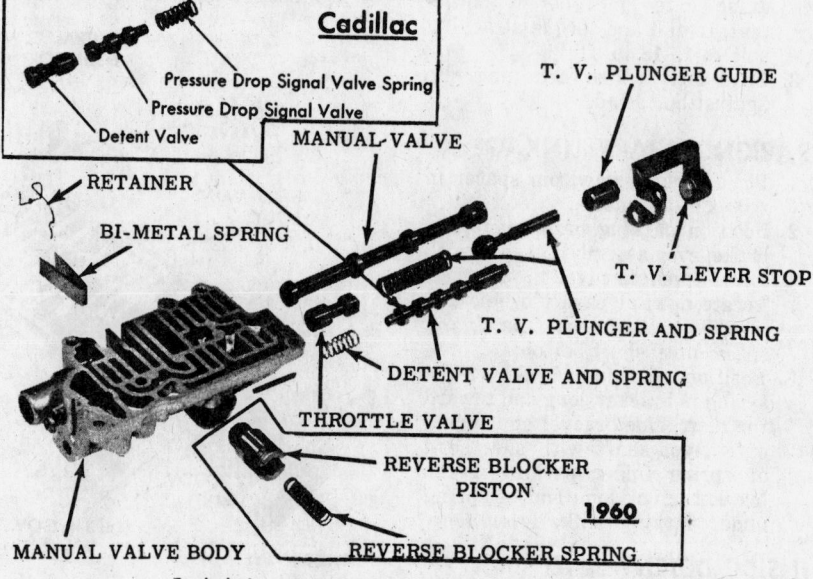

Cadillac
Pressure Drop Signal Valve Spring
Pressure Drop Signal Valve
Detent Valve
MANUAL VALVE
T. V. PLUNGER GUIDE
RETAINER
BI-METAL SPRING
T. V. LEVER STOP
T. V. PLUNGER AND SPRING
DETENT VALVE AND SPRING
THROTTLE VALVE
REVERSE BLOCKER PISTON
1960
MANUAL VALVE BODY
REVERSE BLOCKER SPRING

Exploded View of Manual Valve Body, 1958-60

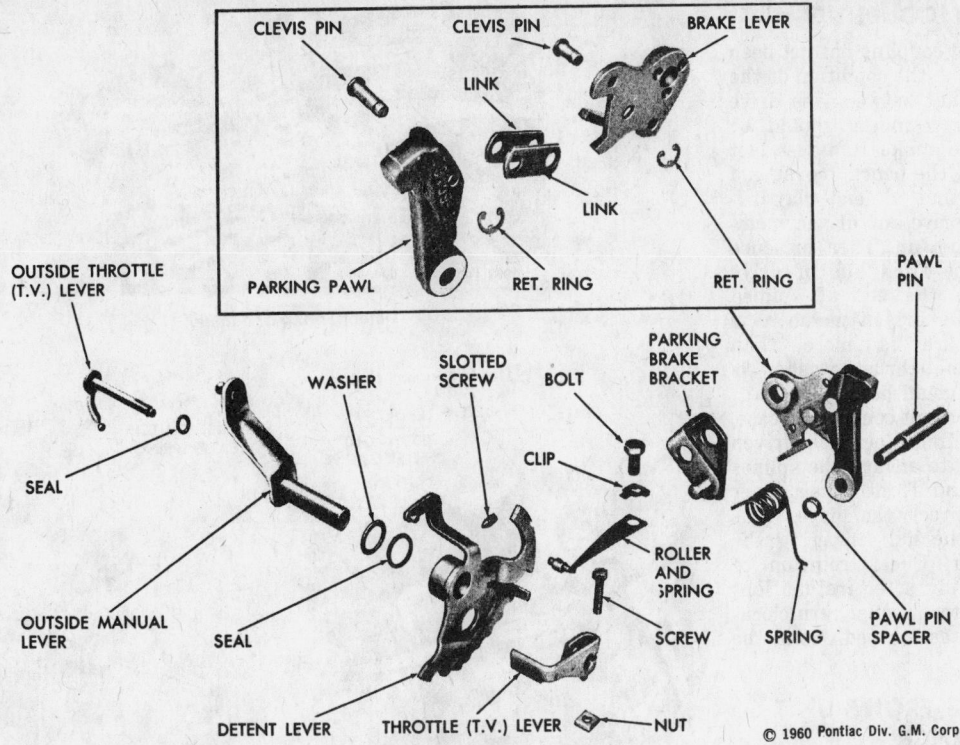

Parking Brake Parts

© 1960 Pontiac Div. G.M. Corp.

Subtract end play of rear unit sun gear on mainshaft from mainshaft end play. The difference is the actual end play of the rear unit. It should be .004"-.013". If reading is outside these limits it will be necessary to remove and disassemble the clutch unit so that the correct thrust washer (as selected from the selective spacer chart illustration), can be installed between the rear unit planet carrier and the reverse drive flange.

E. Remove end play checking tool.
15. Remove extension housing.
16. Install governor drive gear front retaining snap ring.
17. Install governor drive gear key in output shaft.
18. Slide governor drive gear on output shaft, locating slot in gear over key.
19. Install second snap ring to retain governor drive gear.
20. Install governor in reverse clutch housing as follows:
   A. Align gaps of rings in up positions.
   B. Compress rings by hand and work governor into bore in reverse clutch housing.
21. Affix gasket to reverse clutch housing with petrolatum and slide extension housing over output shaft against reverse clutch housing.
22. Turn seven extension housing bolts into case finger tight.

23. Torque all bolts to 25 lb. ft.
24. If rear seal was removed; coat outer edge of seal casing with gasket cement and drive new seal into housing with installer J-5154 A or substitute.
25. Install speedometer driven gear assembly.

PUMP AND OVERRUN CLUTCH

1. Screw two studs from tool J-6121. into two of the three 3/8"x16 tapped holes in the case center

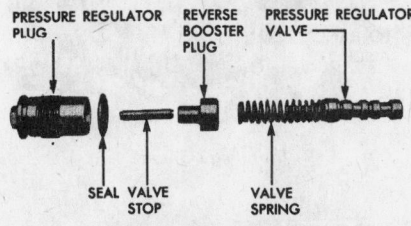

PRESSURE REGULATOR PLUG | REVERSE BOOSTER PLUG | PRESSURE REGULATOR VALVE

SEAL VALVE STOP | VALVE SPRING

Pressure Regulator Parts

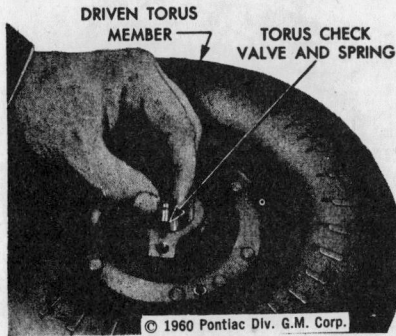

DRIVEN TORUS MEMBER | TORUS CHECK VALVE AND SPRING

© 1960 Pontiac Div. G.M. Corp.

Torus Check Valve

support.
2. Install the small "O" ring in the rear clutch apply hole in the pump.
3. Pilot pump and overrun clutch assembly over the intermediate shaft and studs, making sure intake pipe holes in pump and case are aligned.
4. Secure pump to case with one screw. Then remove two pilot studs and install remaining two screws.
5. Tighten all three screws, then back off 1/4 turn.
6. Apply air pressure in neutral clutch apply hole to position case center support against the snap ring. With air pressure applied, tighten pump locking screw to 25 lb. ft. torque. Then tighten the pump to case support screws to 25 lb. ft. torque.
7. Recheck pump cover screws to insure proper tightening.
8. The overrun clutch, neutral clutch and rear clutch should be checked for proper operation with compressed air in the specific air check holes.

PRESSURE REGULATOR

1. With spring assembled to pressure regulator valve, install valve and spring in case.
2. Install pressure regulator plug assembly and torque to 5 lb. ft.

Detent Spring and Roller

FRONT UNIT COUPLING

1. If front unit coupling has not been disassembled, the condition of the thrust washer between the drive and driven members should be checked. To make this test, set the unit on the bench (cover end down) so that all end play between the drive and driven members is taken up. Then measure the distance from hub of drive member to the end of splined shaft of the driven member. If this measure is more than 1-47/64" the thrust washer is worn and should be replaced.

2. Install front unit coupling in case, cover end first. Rock the driven torus shaft to engage the splines on shaft and front sprag inner race. Then rock the drive torus to insure the hub engaging the pump rotor. Check rotation of front coupling after installation; the driven torus must turn clockwise only, as viewed from the front.

TO MEASURE FRONT UNIT END CLEARANCE

To control front unit end play a selective spacer is used between the front unit sun gear and the bronze drive torus thrust washer.

The following method describes a way to determine the correct selective spacer to give a .020"-.035" front unit end clearance.

1. Turn transmission to the vertical position with the mainshaft up.
2. Install front unit internal gear.
3. Install black steel thrust washer, needle bearing, and second (bright) steel washer in recess of hub of internal gear.
4. Install snap ring in groove of driven torus shaft.
5. Slide front unit sun gear onto shaft of driven torus.
6. Lay a #1 (.046") steel selective washer against the sun gear followed by a bronze thrust washer.
7. Install drive torus snap ring in groove on intermediate shaft next to bronze washer.
8. Push intermediate shaft and sun gear firmly to rear of transmission to make sure all end play is taken up.
9. Push snap ring down against rear of groove and carefully measure clearance between the snap ring and the bronze thrust washer with a feeler gauge.
10. Compare this measurement with the selective spacer chart to determine the correct spacer washer to use.

Example:

If the feeler gauge measure-

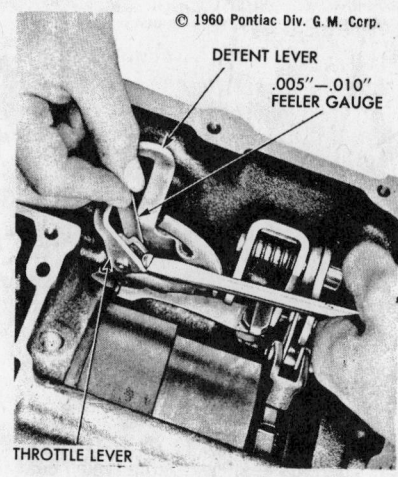

Installing Inside T.V. Lever

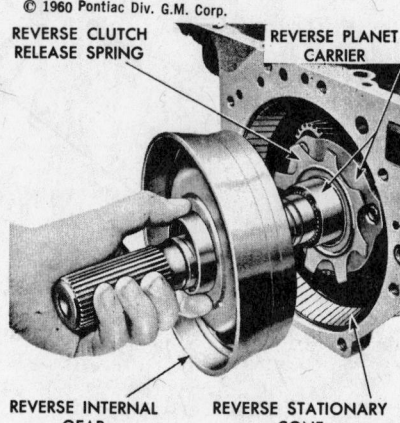

Reverse Internal Gear

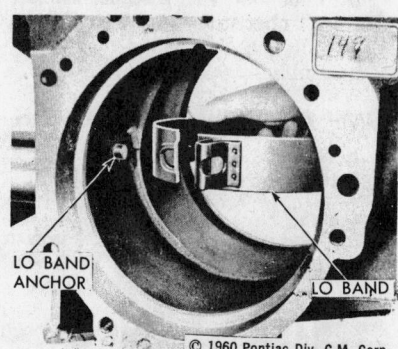

Installing LO Band

Reverse Planet Carrier

Alignment of Center Support in Case

Reverse Clutch Housing

ment is .067", a #4 (.084"-086") washer must be used to obtain the desired clearance of .020"-.035". This is determined by adding the mean thickness (.046") of #1 washer to gauge reading giving total thickness of .113". Then subtract thickness of #4 washer (.085); this results in .028" which is within desirable clearance.

11. Remove snap ring, sun gear with bronze washer and steel selective spacer, snap ring, and internal gear with steel spacers and roller thrust bearing.
12. Remove front unit coupling.

CONTROL VALVE ASSEMBLY, AND SERVO-AND-ACCUMULATOR

1. Turn the transmission to the horizontal position.
2. Attach control valve assembly to transmission with five attaching screws.

Note: Position the detent lever so that pin indexes with the manual valve. The dowel pin must index with the hole in the transmission case.

3. Install new "O" rings in the screen and pump if they were not previously installed.
4. Lay the servo-and-accumulator assembly with servo release spring in position and attach to the case with two bolts.
5. Insert the intake pipe (dimple end) into the screen. Be careful not to cut the "O" ring.
6. Insert the other end of the pipe in the pump and align the screen with the retaining clip on clutch with valve body.
7. Rotate the pipe retaining clip over the pipe and tighten the long servo attaching bolt.

INSTALL INTAKE PIPE, STRAINER AND OIL PAN

1. Install intake pipe and secure it with clip and valve body attaching screw.
2. Install oil screen on intake pipe and screen retaining clip.
3. Install oil pan with new gasket

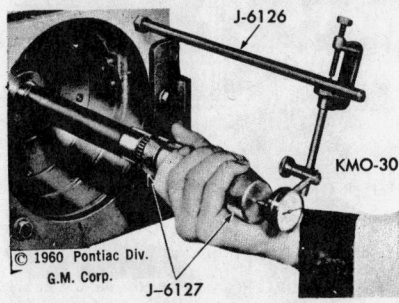

Check Mainshaft End Play

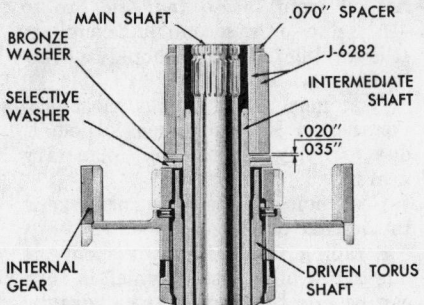

SELECTIVE WASHER IDENTIFICATION

NO.	THICKNESS	NO.	THICKNESS
1	.045"-.047"	7	.123"-.125"
2	.058"-.060"	8	.136"-.138"
3	.071"-.073"	9	.145"-.151"
4	.084"-.086"	10	.162"-.164"
5	.097"-.099"	11	.175"-.177"
6	.110"-.112"		

© 1960 Pontiac Div. G.M. Co.

Front Unit Selective Spacer Chart

and secure with attaching screws.

INSTALL FLYWHEEL HOUSING AND TORUS MEMBERS

1. If a holding fixture is used, remove fixture and place the unit on the bench in a horizontal position with pan down.
2. Install front unit coupling, turning the driven torus counterclockwise to engage shaft splines with splines of front sprag inner race. Also rotate coupling to permit lugs to engage pump rotor.
3. Place protector J-6119 over intermediate shaft.
4. Lay new flywheel housing-to-case "O" ring in groove provided in housing.
5. Pilot flywheel housing into position against case and secure with six bolts. Torque to 40-50 lb. ft.
6. Remove protector J-6119 and apply a coat of Hydra-Matic oil to hub of torus cover.
7. Slide torus cover into place. Be careful of flywheel housing oil seal.
8. Install front unit internal gear in torus cover. Make sure lugs of gear engage those of the front coupling drive torus.
9. Install (black) steel thrust washer, needle bearing and second (bright) steel thrust washer in internal gear.
10. Secure needle bearing and washers by installing snap ring in groove of front coupling driven torus shaft.
11. Install sun gear with recess side facing toward the needle bearing.
12. Install selective washer as previously determined by front unit end clearance check.
13. Place bronze washer against selective washer.

14. Install drive torus member in intermediate shaft, indexing front unit planet carrier with sun, gear and internal gear.
15. Secure drive torus to intermediate shaft with snap ring.
16. Install driven torus rear snap ring on the mainshaft.
17. Install driven torus member on mainshaft and secure with snap ring.
18. Install "O" ring seal on the flywheel and position flywheel against torus cover, indexing with dowels.

Note: The flywheel can be installed in only one position as the dowels are of different sizes.

19. Install six flywheel-to-torus cover nuts, leaving nuts off every second bolt. Torque nuts to 15-20 lb. ft. The remaining six bolts are used to attach the flywheel and torus cover to the engine flex plate.

INSTALL OIL COOLER SLEEVES AND T.V. PIPE PLUG

1. Assemble sleeve seals and "O" rings on oil cooler sleeves.
2. Insert sleeves in case, seal end first, and bolt strap to case.
3. Install pipe plug in T.V. pressure take-off tapped hole on right side of case if previously removed.

DIAGNOSIS OF NOISES DUAL-COUPLING

Gear noise in Park, Neutral, Drive, Reverse, in 1st and 3rd, is due to noisy planetary gears in the front unit.

Gear noise in Park, Neutral, Reverse, in 1st and 2nd, is due to noisy planetary gears in the rear unit. Abnormal whine in all ranges, car standing still, especially when cold, is due to the front pump. Check the "O" ring seals on the front pump intake pipe and on the cooler adapter sleeves.

Abnormal whine in all ranges, car in motion, is due to the rear pump.

Abnormal whine during shift with

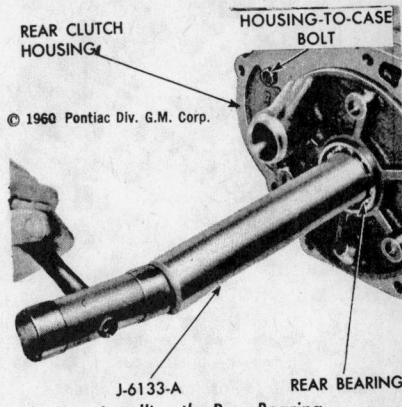

Installing the Rear Bearing

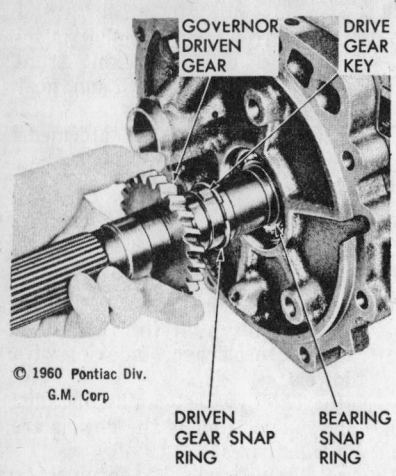

© 1960 Pontiac Div.
G.M. Corp

GOVERNOR DRIVEN GEAR
DRIVE GEAR KEY
DRIVEN GEAR SNAP RING
BEARING SNAP RING

Install Governor Drive Gear

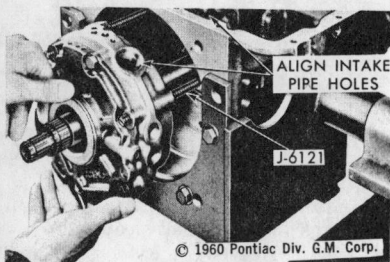

ALIGN INTAKE PIPE HOLES
J-6121
© 1960 Pontiac Div. G.M. Corp.

Install the Pump

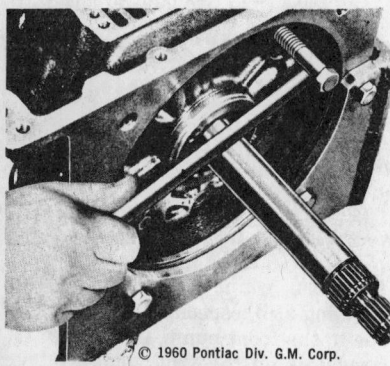

© 1960 Pontiac Div. G.M. Corp.

Rotating Pump and Case Center Support

J-8124-01
© 1960 Pontiac Div. G.M. Corp.

Applying Air to Position Case Center Support

hot oil from 1st to 2nd, and 3rd to 4th, is due to the second fluid coupling. It is leaking badly and should be overhauled.

Gear noise in all ranges, most pronounced in Reverse when loaded, is due to noisy reverse unit planetary gears.

Gear noise in Reverse only is due to the rear pump gears.

Scraping noise in Reverse only is due to low oil pressure, which in turn can be due to leaks in the hydraulic system or malfunction of the pressure regulator valve.

Clicking or buzzing noise when car is in Neutral or in motion is due to: the pressure regulator valve, the speedometer gear, low oil level, governor or coupling valve.

Rattle or buzz under light load in 3rd or 4th is due to the torus cover dampener springs.

Vibration is due to an out of balance unit: the flywheel, the 1st fluid drive unit cover, the front unit assem-

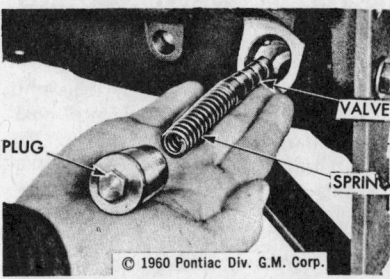

PLUG
VALVE
SPRING
© 1960 Pontiac Div. G.M. Corp.

Install Pressure Regulator

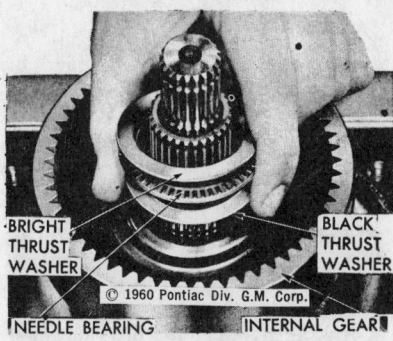

BRIGHT THRUST WASHER
BLACK THRUST WASHER
© 1960 Pontiac Div. G.M. Corp.
NEEDLE BEARING
INTERNAL GEAR

Install Internal Gear, Needle Bearing and Washers

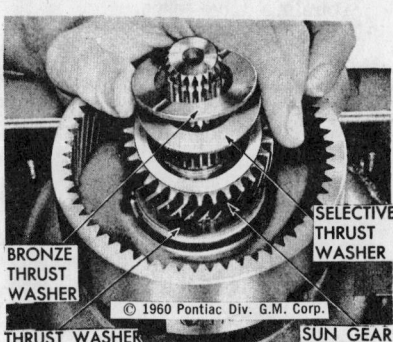

SELECTIVE THRUST WASHER
BRONZE THRUST WASHER
© 1960 Pontiac Div. G.M. Corp.
THRUST WASHER
SUN GEAR

Install Sun Gear and Washers for Clearance Check

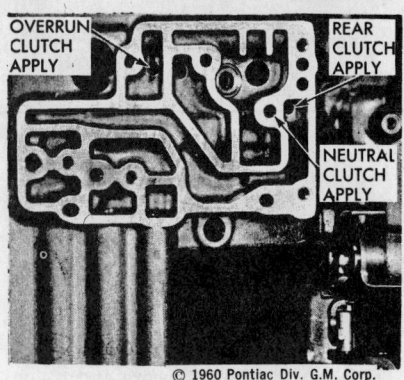

OVERRUN CLUTCH APPLY
REAR CLUTCH APPLY
NEUTRAL CLUTCH APPLY
© 1960 Pontiac Div. G.M. Corp.

Air Check Holes

© 1960 Pontiac Div. G.M. Corp.

Install Servo and Accumulator

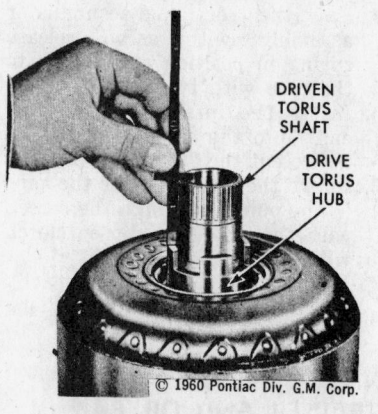

DRIVEN TORUS SHAFT
DRIVE TORUS HUB
© 1960 Pontiac Div. G.M. Corp.

Measure Wear of Coupling Thrust Washer

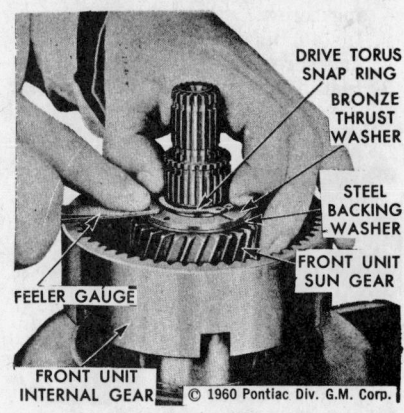

DRIVE TORUS SNAP RING
BRONZE THRUST WASHER
STEEL BACKING WASHER
FRONT UNIT SUN GEAR
FEELER GAUGE
FRONT UNIT INTERNAL GEAR
© 1960 Pontiac Div. G.M. Corp.

Measure Front Unit End Clearance

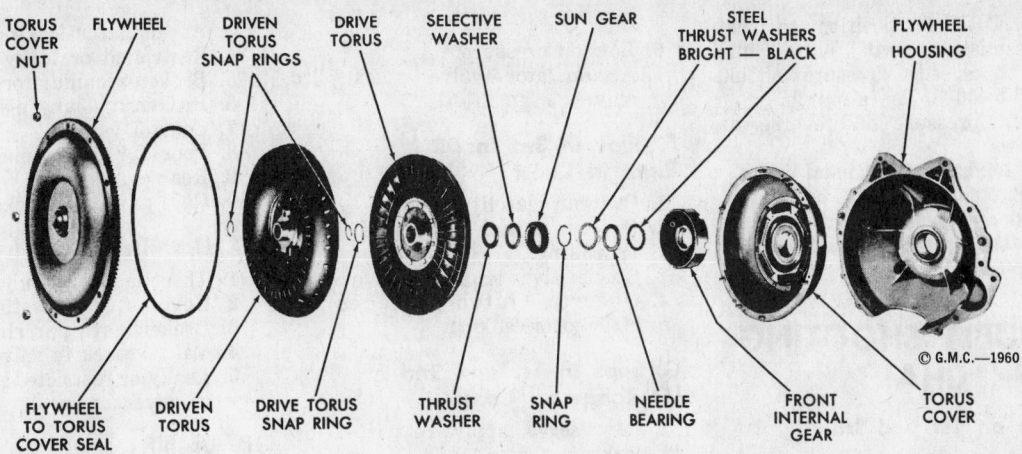

Flywheel Housing and Torus Parts

Labels (top row, left to right): TORUS COVER NUT, FLYWHEEL, DRIVEN TORUS SNAP RINGS, DRIVE TORUS, SELECTIVE WASHER, SUN GEAR, STEEL THRUST WASHERS BRIGHT — BLACK, FLYWHEEL HOUSING

Labels (bottom row, left to right): FLYWHEEL TO TORUS COVER SEAL, DRIVEN TORUS, DRIVE TORUS SNAP RING, THRUST WASHER, SNAP RING, NEEDLE BEARING, FRONT INTERNAL GEAR, TORUS COVER

© G.M.C.—1960

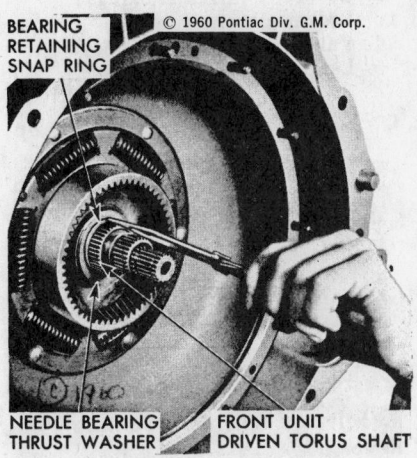

BEARING RETAINING SNAP RING
© 1960 Pontiac Div. G.M. Corp.
NEEDLE BEARING THRUST WASHER — FRONT UNIT DRIVEN TORUS SHAFT

Bearing Retaining Snap Ring

J-4880
© 1960 Pontiac Div. G.M. Corp.
DRIVEN TORUS SNAP RING
DRIVEN TORUS REAR SNAP RING

Driven Torus Rear Snap Ring

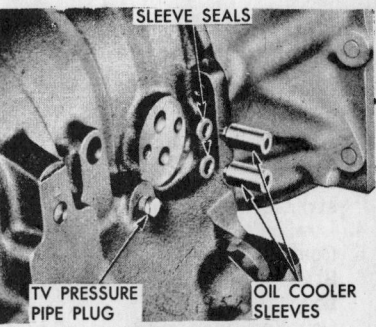

SLEEVE SEALS
TV PRESSURE PIPE PLUG — OIL COOLER SLEEVES
© 1960 Pontiac Div. G.M. Corp.

Oil Cooler Sleeves and Seals

bly, the rear unit brake drum.

Excessive vibration at an engine speed of 2800 to 3500 rpm is indicative of runout. Check the runout of the flexplate first; it should not exceed .010 F.I.R. The clearance between the flywheel and the flexplate should be even all around.

PARTS THAT CAN BE REMOVED WITH TRANSMISSION IN PLACE IN THE CAR

Oil Pan
Control Valve Body and Valves
Accumulator and Servo
Pressure Regulator Valve
Speedometer Drive Gear
Oil Cooler
Extension Housing
Governor
Parking Brake Bracket
Rear Oil Seal
Rear Pump
Reverse Unit, including stationary cone, piston, planet carrier, internal ring gear.

TESTING AND TROUBLE CHECKS

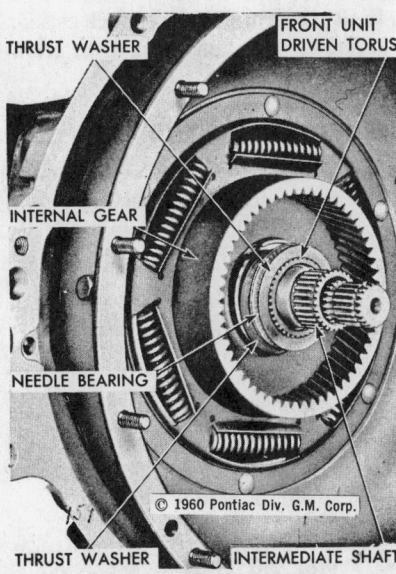

THRUST WASHER — FRONT UNIT DRIVEN TORUS
INTERNAL GEAR
NEEDLE BEARING
THRUST WASHER — INTERMEDIATE SHAFT
© 1960 Pontiac Div. G.M. Corp.

Install Front Unit Gear Bearing and Thrust Washer

OIL PRESSURE TEST

1. Connect oil pressure gauge to take-off hole at bottom of reverse clutch housing.
2. Run engine a few minutes to warm transmission to operating temperature.
3. Read pressure in all ranges. Pressure should be 50 lb. minimum in P, N, both DR ranges and L with a maximum variation of 10 lbs. between ranges, but may be higher in reverse.
4. Road test car in DR right position at about 25 mph. Pressure should be 90-100 Psi.

Note: Pressure at any speed is constant regardless of throttle position.

5. While driving at 25 mph, shift

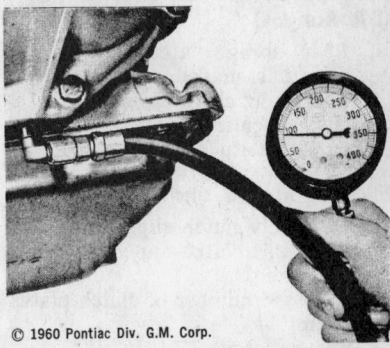

© 1960 Pontiac Div. G.M. Corp.

Gauge Hook-up for Oil Pressure Test

into DR left position so that transmission will shift into fourth speed. Pressure should drop to 60-70 Psi in fourth.

6. Check pressure in reverse as follows:
   A. Stop car and set hand brake.
   B. Put selector in R, apply foot brake and open accelerator to half throttle. Pressure should increase to 150-200 lbs.

TROUBLE SHOOTING CHART

A. Slips on 1st and 3rd

1. Front sprag clutch slipping.
2. Front sprag clutch broken.

B. Slips in or Misses 2nd and 4th

1. Front unit torus cover exhaust valves stuck.
2. Front unit torus feed restricted or leaking.
3. Front unit torus cover signal restricted or leaking.
4. Low oil pressure.
5. Coupling valve stuck.
6. Sticking valves or dirt in valve body.
7. Coupling snap ring out of place or broken.
8. Limit valve.
9. Coupling valve restricted or leaking.
10. Front unit torus vanes damaged.

C. Slips in All DR Ranges

1. Manual linkage.
2. Neutral clutch slipping.
3. Neutral clutch apply restricted or leaking.
4. Wrong number of neutral clutch plates used.
5. Low oil pressure.
6. Control valve.
7. Torus members (check valve).
8. Intake pipe sucking air.
9. Pressure regulator valve stuck in pump.
10. Pump slide stuck.

D. Slips in 1st and 2nd (DR Ranges)

1. Rear sprag clutch slipping or poorly assembled.
2. Rear strag clutch broken.
3. Neutral clutch burned, restricted or piston stuck.

E. Slips in 3rd and 4th

1. Rear unit clutch slipping.
2. Rear unit clutch apply restricted or leaking.
3. Incorrect number of clutch plates (rear).
4. Accumulator.
5. Center support, leak at 2-3 passage.
6. Low oil pressure.
7. Accumulator valve stuck, 3rd only.

F. Slips in 3rd in DR Right in Coast

1. Overrun clutch slipping.
2. Overrun clutch apply restricted or leaking.
3. Stuck valves or dirt in valve body.
4. Overrun clutch passages restricted or leaking.

G. Slips in 1st and 2nd in LO Range on Coast

1. Low servo apply restricted or leaking.
2. Low band not anchored or broken.
3. Low servo piston binding.
4. Low band facing worn or loose.
5. Anchor dowel missing or loose.

H. No Drive in DR Range

1. Manual linkage poorly adjusted.
2. Manual valve not engaged with drive pin.
3. Low oil pressure.
4. Pressure regulator stuck
5. Pump intake pipe leak.
6. Front sprag broken or incorrectly installed.
7. Rear sprag broken.
8. Front sprag inner race broken.
9. Rear sprag outer race broken.
10. Neutral clutch slipping.
11. Neutral clutch piston.
12. Control valve or faulty pump.

I. Erratic or No Upshift

1. Governor valves stuck.
2. Broken governor rings.
3. Sticking valves in valve body.
4. G-2 bushing turned.

J. Shift Misses 2nd

1. Governor boost valve stuck closed.
2. Transition valve stuck away from plate.
3. Sticking valves in valve body.
4. Sticking governor.

K. Shift Misses 3rd or 2-4-3

1. Transition valve sticking.
2. Sticking valves in valve body.
3. T.V. adjustment too long.
4. Rear clutch.
5. Transition valve spring.

L. Locks Up in 2nd and 4th

1. Front sprag clutch broken or reversed.
2. Overrun clutch applied or stuck.

M. Locks Up in 3rd and 4th

1. Rear sprag clutch broken.
2. Low band not releasing.

N. Rough 2-3 Shift

1. Accumulator valve stuck.
2. Accumulator piston stuck.

3. Accumulator leaking.
4. Restricted or leaky oil passages.
5. Broken accumulator spring.
6. Broken or leaky piston rings.
7. Control valve.
8. Poor T.V. adjustment.
9. Rear clutch pack.
10. Case passages blocked or leaking.

O. Upshifts High

1. Throttle linkage short.
2. Governor valves sticking.
3. Broken governor rings.
4. Valves stuck in valve body.
5. Leaky or restricted main line feed to governor.

P. Upshifts Low

1. Throttle linkage long.
2. Governor valves sticking.
3. Broken governor rings.
4. Valves stuck in valve body.
5. Leaking T.V. oil.

Q. No Reverse, Slips or Locks Up

1. Manual linkage poorly adjusted.
2. Manual valve not engaged with drive pin.
3. Reverse piston apply restricted or leaky.
4. Low oil pressure.
5. Pressure regulator.
6. Neutral clutch not releasing.
7. Restriction at neutral clutch exhaust port on manual body.

R. Selector Will Not Go Into Reverse

1. Governor valves sticking.
2. Broken governor rings.
3. Reverse blocker piston stuck.
4. Manual linkage interference.

S. Reverse Drive in Neutral

1. Reverse stationary cone sticking.

T. Delayed 1-2 Shift

1. Coupling valve sticking.
2. Governor boost valve sticking.
3. G-1 valve sticking.
4. Incorrect spring on coupling valve..

U. Drive in LO Range Only

1. Rear sprag broken.
2. Neutral clutch not applying.

V. No Kick-Down 4-3 or 3-2

1. Control valve.
2. Linkage poorly adjusted.

W. 2-3 Runaway or 2-1-3

1. 2-3 passage in center bearing support.
2. Plug out of accumulator.
3. Rear clutch slipping.
4. Transition valve in valve body not working.
5. Valve body passages, 2-3 circuit.

DUAL COUPLING

X. Will Not Park
1. Parking linkage broken.
2. Interference, parking mechanical.
3. Linkage manual.
4. Parking pawl.

Y. Starts in 2nd Speed

1. Valves sticking.
2. Governor sticking.
3. Governor boost valve stuck.

Z. Drives Forward in Reverse and Neutral

1. Neutral clutch piston stuck in on position.

Z-1. Drives Forward Before Backing Up, With Selector in Reverse

1. G-2 plunger stuck in outward position.
2. Restricted oil release passage.

UPSHIFTS

Shift	Left Drive Range		Right Drive Range		Lo Range	
	Minimum Throttle	Full Throttle	Minimum Throttle	Full Throttle	Minimum Throttle	Full Throttle
1-2	5-9	11-15	5-9	11-15	4-9	11-15
2-3	11-15	39-43	11-15	39-43	—	47-54
3-4	21-25	65-75	—	74-80	—	74-80

DOWNSHIFTS

Shift	Left Drive Range		Right Drive Range		Lo Range	
	Closed Throttle	Full Throttle Forced	Closed Throttle	Full Throttle Forced	Closed Throttle	Full Throttle Forced
4-3	18-15*	70-33	74-68	74-28	70-60	70-28
3-2	10-6*	25-14	10-6	25-14	48-44	48-44
2-1	8-3*	12-3	8-3*	12-3	8-3	12-3

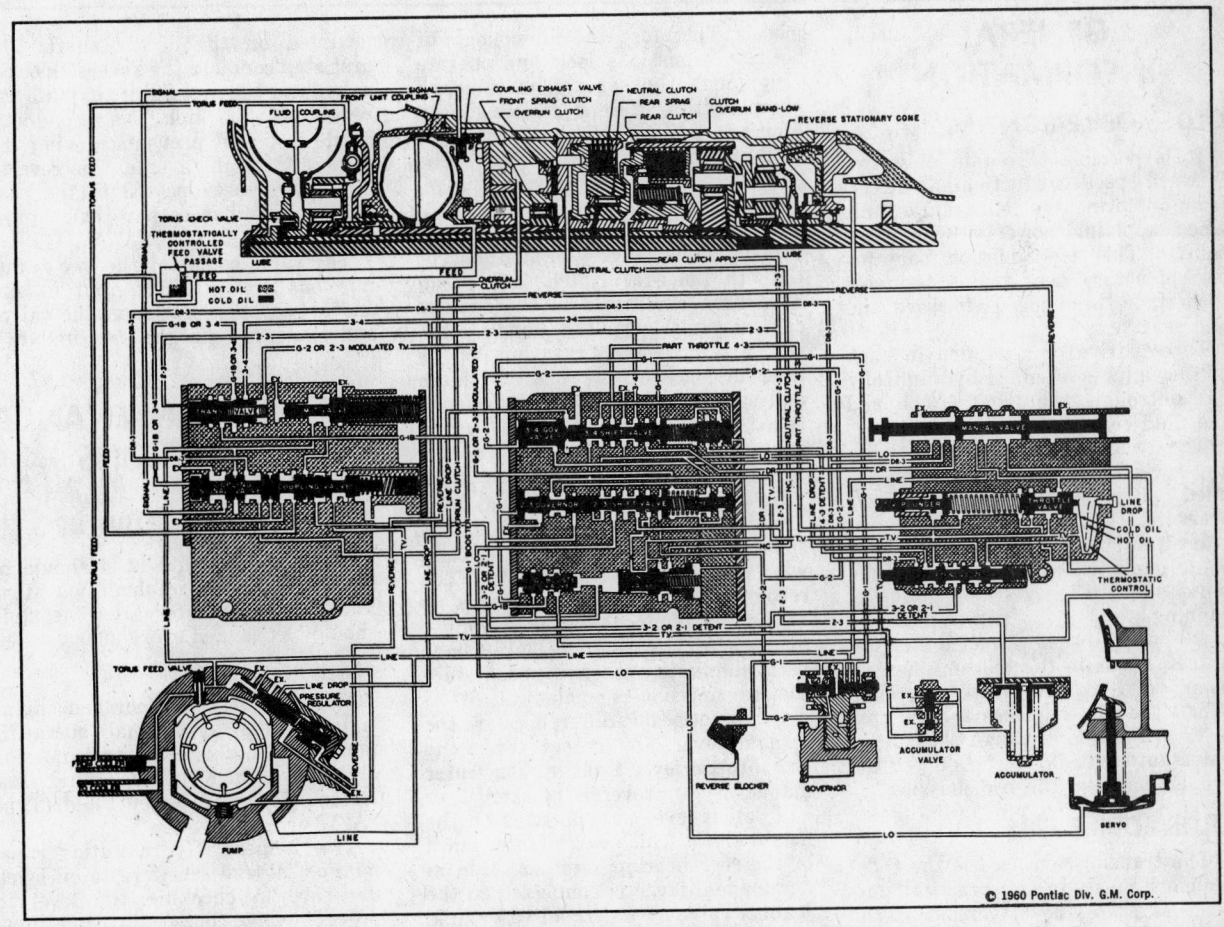

© 1960 Pontiac Div. G.M. Corp.

Schematic Oil Circuit Diagram

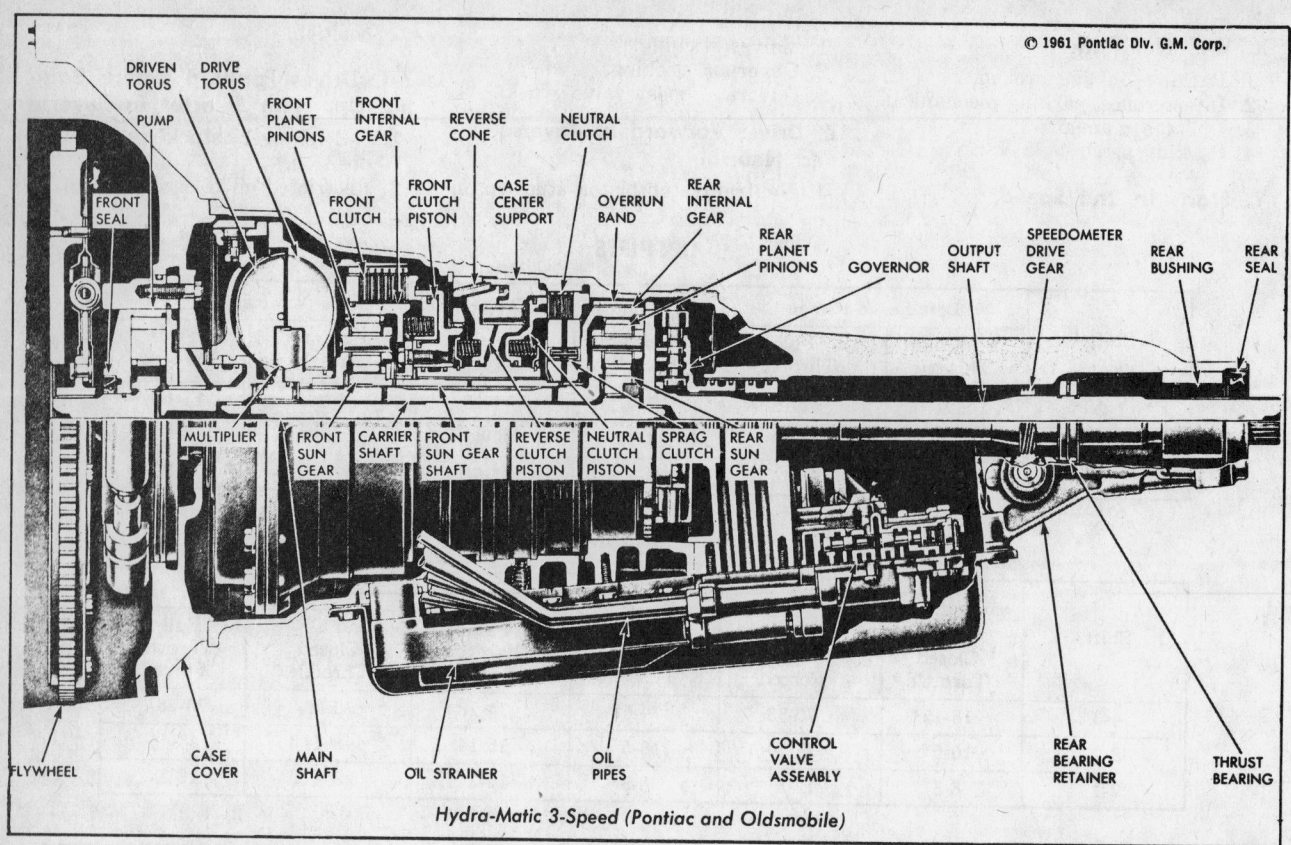

© 1961 Pontiac Div. G.M. Corp.

Labels on diagram (clockwise/left to right): DRIVEN TORUS, DRIVE TORUS, FRONT PLANET PINIONS, FRONT INTERNAL GEAR, REVERSE CONE, NEUTRAL CLUTCH, PUMP, FRONT SEAL, FRONT CLUTCH, FRONT CLUTCH PISTON, CASE CENTER SUPPORT, OVERRUN BAND, REAR INTERNAL GEAR, REAR PLANET PINIONS, GOVERNOR, OUTPUT SHAFT, SPEEDOMETER DRIVE GEAR, REAR BUSHING, REAR SEAL, MULTIPLIER, FRONT SUN GEAR, CARRIER SHAFT, FRONT SUN GEAR SHAFT, REVERSE CLUTCH PISTON, NEUTRAL CLUTCH PISTON, SPRAG CLUTCH, REAR SUN GEAR, FLYWHEEL, CASE COVER, MAIN SHAFT, OIL STRAINER, OIL PIPES, CONTROL VALVE ASSEMBLY, REAR BEARING RETAINER, THRUST BEARING

Hydra-Matic 3-Speed (Pontiac and Oldsmobile)

GENERAL INFORMATION

OLDSMOBILE-PONTIAC

It is possible to obtain only two forward speeds, reduction and direct, from one planetary gear train or unit when applying power at the same source. This transmission contains two planetary gear trains arranged to provide three speeds forward and one reverse.

Direct drive or reduction in each of the units is obtained hydraulically by controlling the front clutch and the fluid coupling.

The overrun band, neutral clutch and reverse cone clutch are also applied, when necessary, by hydraulic pressure.

Hydraulic pressure is maintained by a pump which is driven by the input shaft whenever the engine is running.

Oil pressure is directed to the proper places in the transmission by means of a control valve assembly. When the driver places the selector lever in the desired range, the control valve automatically directs oil to the proper places in the transmission.

OLDSMOBILE F-85

The transmission used in the Oldsmobile F-85 is, for all practical purposes, a scaled down version of the one used in the larger Oldsmobile

models. Therefore, the components of both transmissions look and operate very much the same. The same oil pump, with different coupling feed limit and pressure regulator valves, is used in both transmissions. (The pump, less valves, are interchangeable.)

The assembly of parts in the two transmissions is very similar except that the neutral clutch and sprag have been eliminated in the smaller car transmissions. The band (overrun band in the large transmission) is used in place of the neutral clutch and sprag to obtain first and second speed reduction in drive and super range and first speed reduction in low range.

To make up for the additional work load, the band is wider with a double split which makes it a triple band with greater holding ability. The recommended adjustment interval is at the time of oil change, 26,000 miles.

The neutral clutch and sprag have been eliminated to save space since the transmission is smaller.

Other noticeable differences are the manual lever, the detent lever and the throttle lever linkage. The outer manual lever, reverse blocker lever and detent lever are mounted on the detent shaft, which extends the width of the rear bearing retainer. The inner manual lever is connected to the manual valve by a manual valve link.

The reverse blocker lever is

mounted on the detent shaft. The first step contacts the reverse blocker valve and prevents shifting into reverse above 5-7 mph. The second step is the stop that prevents moving the linkage through reverse. The reverse blocker valve is located in the rear bearing retainer rather than in the valve body.

The valve bodies of the two transmissions are quite different in size and appearance. However, the valves and oil control circuits are similar.

MINOR MAINTENANCE OPERATIONS

TRANSMISSION FLUID

Transmission fluid level should be checked with the transmission warm at 2,000 mile intervals. The fluid should be changed every 26,000 miles.

Check Level

With car on level floor and engine running idle at normal operating temperature, check the transmission dipstick. When adding fluid use Automatic Transmission Fluid (Type "A").

The 3-Speed Hydra-Matic transmission is very sensitive to oil level, use care in checking the level to prevent valve buzz, shift malfunctions and possible damage.

CAPACITY, DRAIN AND REFILL

Capacity

About 4¼ qts. of fluid are required to refill the transmission after oil has been drained.

When unit has been disassembled and rebuilt, about 8½ qts. will be needed to refill.

Drain and Refill

At 26,000 mile intervals the following procedure is recommended:

1. Disconnect filler pipe from right side of transmission and drain fluid.
2. Remove oil pan and strainer.
3. Thoroughly clean oil pan.
4. Install strainer using new pump intake pipe "O" ring if necessary.
5. Place new gasket on oil pan with petrolatum.
6. Install oil pan, tighten attaching screws securely.
7. Connect filler pipe to oil pan.
8. Remove oil level dipstick and clean it.
9. If only the oil pan has been removed, pour 4 qts. of fluid into the transmission. If the valve body has also been removed, use 5 qts. After a complete overhaul, 8 qts. are required.
10. Start the engine and let it idle, (carburetor off fast idle cam). Place selector lever in P position and apply the hand brake.
11. With transmission warm (about

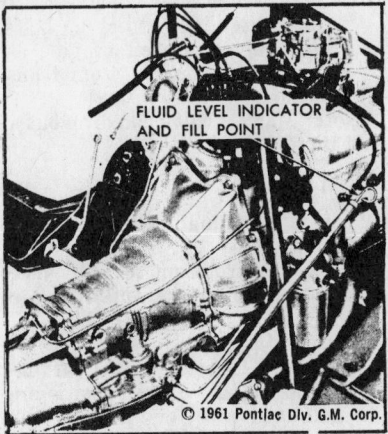

FLUID LEVEL INDICATOR AND FILL POINT

© 1961 Pontiac Div. G.M. Corp.

Location of dipstick

150°F), add fluid to bring level to full mark on indicator.
12. Replace oil level indicator and stop engine.

PRESSURE REGULATOR VALVE

Remove

1. Remove left hand inspection cover on case cover.
2. With a ¾" socket remove regulator valve plug, stop, spring and valve from pump body.

Install

1. Replace "O" ring on plug, if necessary.
2. Place valve plug in ¾" socket equipped with speed handle.

3. Place the line boost plug in the valve plug, (hollow end facing out). Then set the valve stop on top of the plug. See "Line Boost Plug" information, following this paragraph.
4. With the spring attached to the regulator valve, place the spring through the plug stop and into the plug. The assembly is now in order to be installed in the pump.
5. Feed the assembly through the inspection hole and into the pump. A little maneuvering may be necessary to get the valve and plug stop into their bores. Torque plug to 15-20 ft. lb.
6. Replace inspection cover.

LINE BOOST PLUG

These plugs are supplied in three different bore depths which provide different line boost pressures.

The plugs are distinguished by either a plain side, a ring, or a groove on the side of the cap at the end of the plug. The plain side plug creates normal pressure, the ring plug a higher pressure and the groove plug creates the highest pressure.

If replacement of a plug is necessary, the same size should be used unless a pressure test shows otherwise.

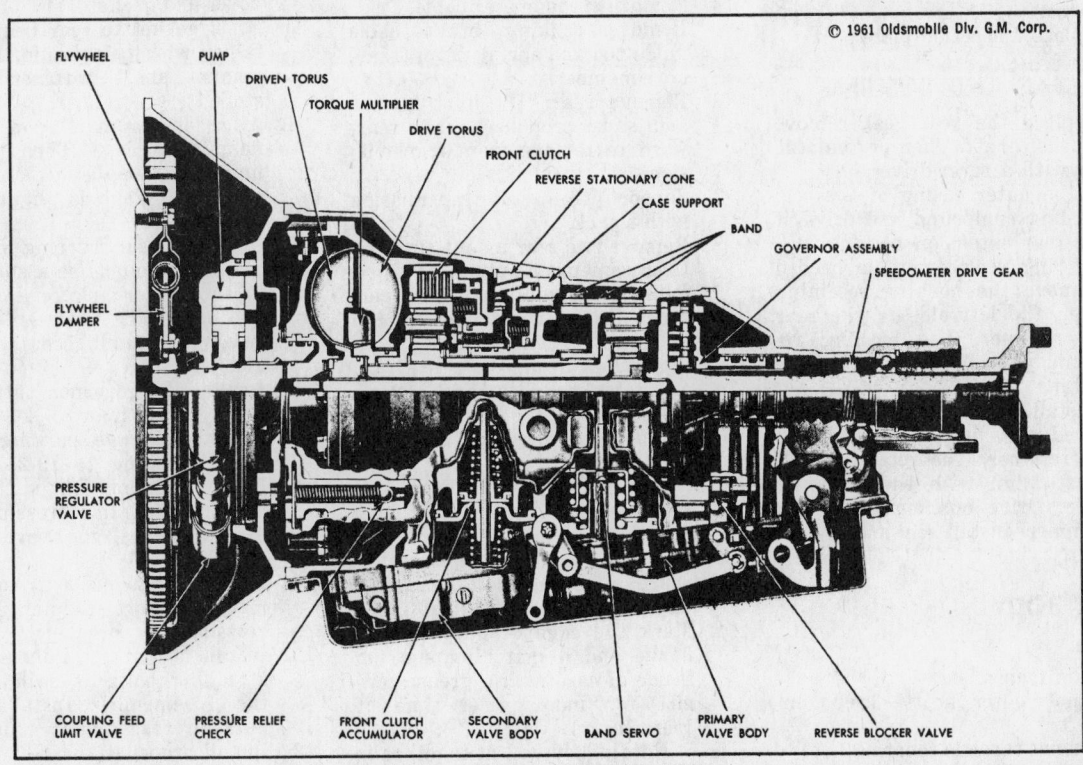

© 1961 Oldsmobile Div. G.M. Corp.

FLYWHEEL — PUMP — DRIVEN TORUS — TORQUE MULTIPLIER — DRIVE TORUS — FRONT CLUTCH — REVERSE STATIONARY CONE — CASE SUPPORT — BAND — GOVERNOR ASSEMBLY — SPEEDOMETER DRIVE GEAR

FLYWHEEL DAMPER

PRESSURE REGULATOR VALVE

COUPLING FEED LIMIT VALVE — PRESSURE RELIEF CHECK — FRONT CLUTCH ACCUMULATOR — SECONDARY VALVE BODY — BAND SERVO — PRIMARY VALVE BODY — REVERSE BLOCKER VALVE

Hydra-Matic 3-Speed (Oldsmobile F-85)

Check Boost Pressure

1. Disconnect control rod to T.V. outside lever.
2. Secure the T.V. lever in the full T.V. position with a length of wire.
3. Install oil pressure gauge in upper of the two test holes in rear bearing retainer.
4. Start the engine and run at 1500 R.P.M. in "P" position. Main line pressure should be 176-183 psi.
5. Change line boost plug if necessary to get correct pressure.

COUPLING FEED LIMIT VALVE

Remove

1. Remove inspection plate on right hand side of case cover.
2. Coupling feed valve plug is located in the lower portion of the pump and may be removed with a ³/₄" socket.
3. The valve plug and pin will come out with the socket. It may be necessary to use long nose pliers to remove the spring and valve.

Install

1. Carefully insert the spring and valves (together) into pump.
2. Replace "O" ring on plug, if necessary.
3. Place valve plug into wrench socket and place pin into plug.
4. Insert plug and pin through the inspection hole and, with the pin in the center of the spring, screw plug into pump. Torque to 15-20 ft. lbs.
5. Replace inspection plate.

REAR SEAL AND BUSHING

To replace the rear seal, remove the propeller shaft. Then pry out the old seal with a screwdriver.

Coat the outer casing of the seal with sealing compound and drive it into the rear extension housing.

If bushing replacement is needed also, remove the bushing retaining bolt from the left side of the rear bearing retainer. Use bushing remover and slide hammer to remove the bushing.

To install the bushing, install it, chamfered end first, into the rear bearing retainer. The retaining bolt slot must align with the retaining bolt hole. Drive bushing in with a soft hammer. Install seal and propeller shaft.

VALVE BODY

Remove

1. Drain transmission.
2. Remove outer throttle lever from shaft.
3. Remove throttle lever seal.
4. Remove oil pan and gasket.
5. Remove five valve body-to-rear bearing retainer attaching bolts.
6. Slide valve body off of pipe assembly and remove from transmission.

Note: Manual valve can drop out at this time.

Install

1. Install manual valve in valve body.
2. Apply petrolatum to valve body pipe ports to prevent injury to "O" rings during assembly.
3. Install valve body into place by guiding throttle shaft through its opening. Then positioning manual valve on pick-up pin, (detent lever). Guide valve body over pipe assembly and slide forward to seat seals. Attach with five bolts.
4. Install throttle shaft seal over throttle shaft and into case.
5. Install oil pan with new gasket. Torque to 12-15 ft. lbs.
6. Install oil filler pipe.
7. Refill transmission.

GOVERNOR

Remove

1. Hoist car, remove filler tube and drain transmission.
2. Remove transmission oil pan.
3. Remove T.V. lower control arm from the outside lever. Remove T.V. outside lever and gearshift control lower rod from outside shift lever.
4. Remove speedometer cable.
5. Remove parking brake cable guide rod and spring from frame crossmember.
6. Remove rear "U" joint clamps and slide propeller shaft rearward to remove from transmission.
7. Support front of transmission with a jack.
8. Remove two rear mount support-to-crossmember nuts.
9. Remove attaching bolts from each end of crossmember and remove the retaining clamp from the rubber insulator.
10. Raise jack slightly and remove crossmember.
11. Remove control valve assembly, (5 bolts).
12. Lower transmission to remove breather pipe clamp. Pull pipe out of its bore.
13. Remove 4 governor and output shaft attaching bolts, through the rear bearing retainer.
14. Mark the edge of output shaft flange and a matching spot on inside of case with a grease pencil, (for indexing at time of reassembly).

    Note: They will fit together in one position only. Do not rotate the carrier after removing the output shaft as reference marks will loose their value.
15. Remove rear bearing retainer-to-case attaching bolts, (2 are inside) and slide retainer rearward, away from the transmission.
16. Remove rear bearing retainer cover (4 bolts).
17. Reach through access hole with 90° snap ring pliers and unseat the snap ring from the output shaft.
18. Remove output shaft from front of retainer. Be careful not to bump the inner sleeve of the rear bearing retainer with the speedometer gear while removing the shaft.
19. Press speedometer drive gear off of the shaft.
20. Remove the governor.

Install

1. Place governor and gasket on output shaft.
2. Drive speedometer gear onto output shaft. Rear side of drive gear should be 6-9/32" from end of shaft.
3. Place snap ring through the access hole in the rear bearing retainer and slide over end of output shaft as it is carefully installed into the retainer. Seat snap ring in grooves against thrust bearing race.
4. Install rear bearing retainer cover and gasket.
5. Stick gasket to rear bearing retainer with petrolatum. Be sure manual shaft retainer is installed.
6. Align index marks on output flange and case. Then position unit on case being sure that parking linkage is aligned with manual lever.
7. Install 8 rear bearing retainer attaching bolts. Use a short bolt in the center hole on each side and one inside the rear bearing retainer. Install breather pipe and clip.
8. Install 4 governor attaching bolts. Hold manual lever forward to engage parking brake while torquing to 19-23 ft. lb.
9. Raise transmission with jack and install frame crossmember, (brake cables go above crossmember).
10. Lower transmission so rear mount support studs engage the crossmember bracket.
11. Install insulator retainers and 2 attaching bolts at each end of the crossmember. Install 2 stud nuts on rear mount support.
12. Install propeller shaft by sliding over the output shaft and install-

ing the "U" joint. Bend locking clips.

13. Install control valve body by putting T.V. lever shaft through its seal and positioning the manual valve on its control pin. Slide the body forward onto the pipe assembly.
14. Install 5 attaching bolts and torque to 6-8 ft. lbs.
15. Install oil pan and new gasket.
16. Install outside T.V. lever.
17. Install T.V. control rod.
18. Install gear selector lower control rod.
19. Hook up speedometer cable.
20. Install oil filler pipe.
21. Install brake cable guide and return spring.
22. Refill transmission to level.

PARKING LINKAGE

Parking linkage may be removed by following steps 1 through 17 of "Governor Removal" instructions. Then push parking pawl pin from the case. Remove pin and the pawl pin spacer from the case. The remaining linkage may then be removed as a unit from the rear of the case.

To install parking linkage, reverse removal procedure.

Band Adjustment, F-85

(Recommended at 26,000 mile oil change)
1. Drain oil and remove pan.
2. Remove oil screen.
3. Loosen adjusting screw lock nut.
4. Use an inch pound torque wrench to tighten the adjusting screw to 20 in. lbs.
5. Then loosen the screw, two complete turns and hold it while jamming the lock nut.
6. Install oil screen, gasket and oil pan.
7. Pour in about 5 qts. Hydra-Matic oil.
8. Start engine, run for a minute, then bring transmission oil to level.

Throttle Stop Adjustment, F-85

See Oldsmobile F-85, car section.

SERVO AND ACCUMULATOR
Remove

1. Remove oil filler pipe and drain transmission.
2. Remove the oil pan and strainer.
3. Remove compensator valve body, (three attaching screws and one bolt).
4. Remove remaining cover attaching bolts and remove the cover.
   Note: Hold the cover against the possibility of dropping the servo piston. The accumulator lower spring and possibly the case center support springs will be removed with the cover.
5. Use the accumulator pin to remove both accumulator pistons and the remaining spring.
6. Remove the case support seal springs and seals if they did not previously fall free.

Install

1. It is necessary to use a temporary retainer to hold the servo piston in place while the cover is being installed. A rectangular piece of stiff sheet metal can be cut so it will hold the servo piston in its bore when bolted to the right rear oil pan bolt hole.
2. Place upper accumulator piston on piston pin and place tapered spring over the pin with the large end of the spring against piston. The piston seal facing away from the spring.
3. Install tapered spring, pin and upper piston into case with small end of spring up. Hold these parts in case and install lower accumulator piston, pocket side down.
4. Screw the ends of the case center support seal springs into the seals far enough to secure them. Then install the seals into the case so the springs are suspended below them. Petrolatum will help hold the seals and springs in place.
5. Place servo return spring over servo pin and install assembly in case. Retain it in its bore using the afore mentioned plate bolted to an oil pan hole.
6. Place remaining accumulator spring in position over the accumulator pin. Hold in place while installing servo and accumulator cover. Attach cover with 3 bolts and leave just loose enough to move the servo retaining tool. Make sure the three seal springs enter the case straight.
7. Remove servo retaining tool and install remaining cover bolts, except the strainer attaching bolt. Torque to 6-8 ft. lbs.
8. Install compensator.

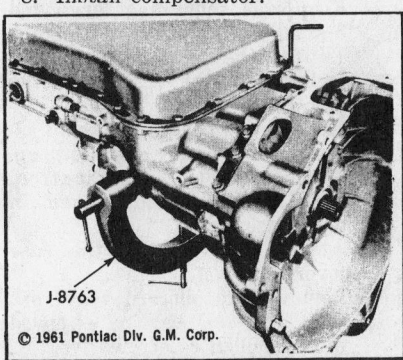

Transmission holding fixture

9. Install oil strainer.
10. Install oil pan with new gasket.
11. Install filler tube and refill transmission to level.

DISASSEMBLY OF TRANSMISSION BY UNITS
CONTROL VALVE, SERVO, AND ACCUMULATOR

1. Attach transmission to holding fixture. Do not over tighten in fixture as distortion may occur.
2. Remove outer shift lever and T.V. lever.
3. Arrange holding fixture so that the bottom of the transmission is up.
4. Remove 21 oil pan attaching screws.
5. Remove oil pan and gasket.
6. Remove bolt and remove strainer.
7. If necessary remove oil strainer-to-case "O" ring with small screwdriver.
8. Pry throttle shaft seal from side of rear bearing retainer with small screwdriver.
9. Remove five control valve assembly attaching bolts and care-

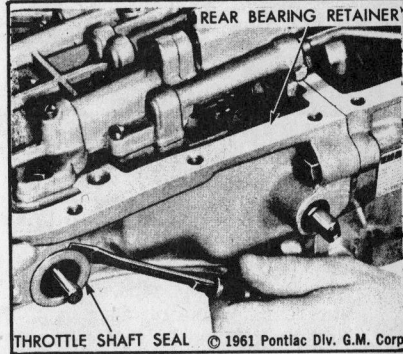

Removing throttle shaft seal

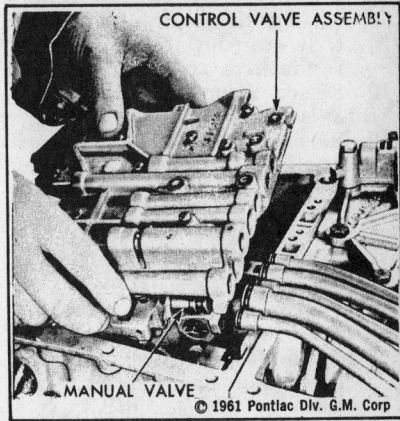

Removing compensator valve body

889

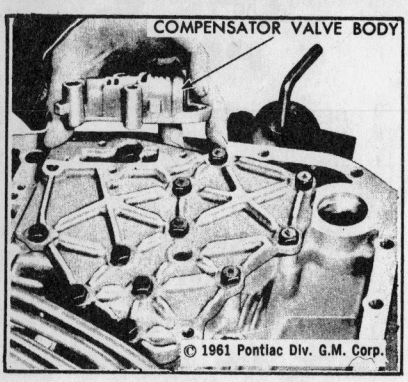

Removing Compensator Valve Body

Case center support seals

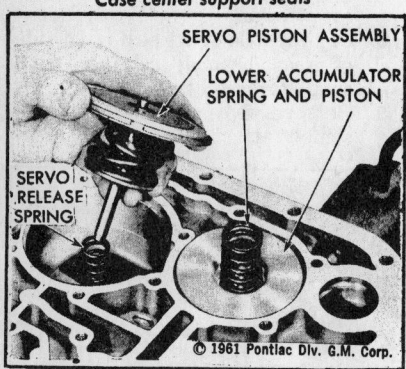

Removing servo piston

fully remove control valve assembly from the pipe assembly and rear bearing retainer.

10. Remove manual valve from control valve assembly.
11. Remove 1 bolt and 3 screws holding the compensator valve body assembly to the servo and accumulator cover.
12. Remove compensator valve body assembly.
13. Remove 12 remaining servo and accumulator cover attaching bolts.
14. Remove servo and accumulator cover and gasket.
15. Remove 3 case center support springs and seals.
16. Remove servo piston assembly from the bore in the case.
17. Remove servo release spring and lower accumulator spring.
18. Remove lower accumulator piston.

19. Remove lower accumulator piston pin and, using the stem of the accumulator pin as a tool, remove the upper accumulator piston.
20. Remove upper accumulator spring.
21. Remove the ring and seal from the lower and upper accumulator pistons.
   Note: If transmission is to be completely disassembled, measure front unit end travel as follows:

Front End Play Check

A. Remove one case cover attaching bolt and install dial indicator as illustrated.
B. Assemble end play adapter on input shaft of the torus cover.
C. Position the dial indicator and set the dial plunger with its end on the end of the end play adaptor.
D. Position a screwdriver through the case, behind the flange on the output shaft.
E. Gently pry forward on output shaft to position the units forward.
F. Zero the dial indicator. Then push the units rearward and read the gauge.
G. End play should be .006" to .018". If it is not, examine the thrust bearing and washers when removing units from the case to determine the cause of excess.
22. Remove the pipe assembly attaching bolt and seal from side of the transmission case cover.
23. Withdraw the pipe assembly and seals from the transmission. Multiple seals may have remained in the transmission.

REAR BEARING RETAINER

See, "Rear Seal and Bushing" replacement under "Minor Maintenance Operations" earlier in this coverage.

CASE COVER, PUMP, AND TORUS COVER

1. Remove 5 remaining large and 3 small case cover-to-case bolts. Two of the small bolts are attached from the case side of the case cover.
2. Remove the cover and pump assembly by lifting straight up. Remove thrust bearing race from torus cover if it did not remain with case cover.
3. Remove and discard the case cover gasket.
4. Remove and discard the front seal. The seal can be removed with a punch or screwdriver.
   Note: If difficulty is encoun-

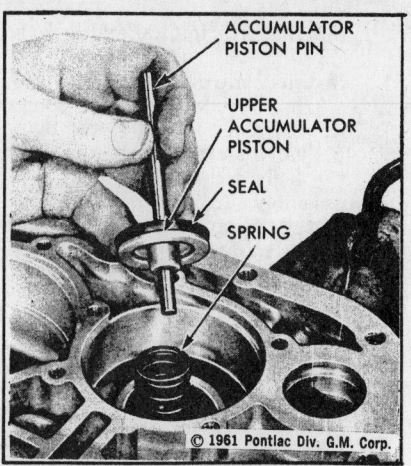

Accumulator piston

Check front unit end play

Pry out front seal

tered, the case cover can be replaced. It is held by two attaching bolts.
5. Remove 12 torus cover attaching bolts.
6. Remove torus cover by lifting straight up on the input shaft. Discard the gasket.
7. Remove race, thrust bearing, and

Remove torus cover bolts

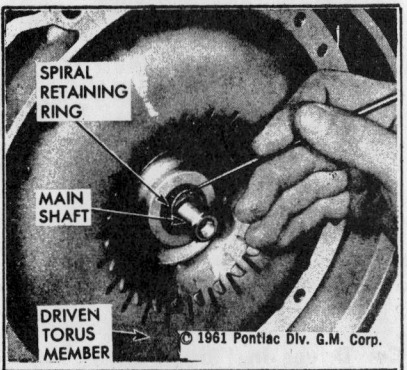

SPIRAL RETAINING RING

MAIN SHAFT

DRIVEN TORUS MEMBER

Remove mainshaft spiral spring

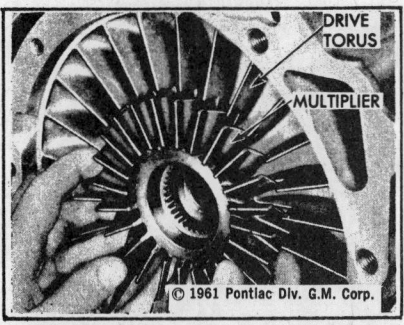

DRIVE TORUS

MULTIPLIER

Remove multiplier and drive torus

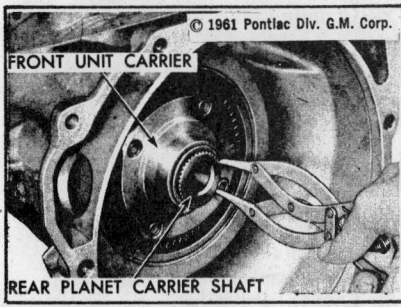

FRONT UNIT CARRIER

REAR PLANET CARRIER SHAFT

Remove front unit carrier snap ring

race from either torus cover or torus member. (Parts may have remained with either unit.)

8. Rotate transmission to horizontal position with bottom up.

TORUS, FRONT UNIT, AND REAR UNIT

1. Remove spiral snap ring that locks the driven torus member to the main shaft.
2. Push main shaft through driven torus member and remove driven torus member.
3. Remove race, thrust bearing and race from drive torus member.
4. Remove mainshaft and sun gear from the rear of the transmission.
5. Remove bearing and race from the rear carrier.
6. Remove sun gear from mainshaft by pushing toward splined end of shaft.
7. Remove the drive torus member and torque multiplier as a unit, from front of transmission.
8. Remove torque multiplier by pushing from rear of the drive torus member.
9. If necessary, remove oil seal rings from driven torus member and torque multiplier.
10. Remove front carrier to carrier shaft snap ring.
11. Remove the front unit carrier assembly.
12. Remove race, thrust bearing and race.
13. Remove the rear carrier and shaft assembly from the rear of the transmission.
14. Remove the roller thrust bearing, and the race from the rear unit carrier assembly.
15. From the rear of the transmission, remove the rear internal gear to front sun gear shaft snap ring.
16. Remove the rear unit internal gear and sprag assembly including retainer. Make sure parking pawl is disengaged.
17. Turn the transmission to vertical position, with the front up.
    <u>Caution:</u> Transmission parts are now loose and can drop out if the case is handled otherwise.
18. Remove the front unit sun gear assembly, race, roller thrust bearing and race.
19. Remove the front unit internal gear and clutch assembly from front of transmission.
20. Remove bronze thrust washer from the front unit clutch drum.

REVERSE CLUTCH AND CASE CENTER SUPPORT

1. Remove the reverse stationary cone to case snap ring.
2. With special puller #J-8768, remove the reverse cone and reverse stationary cone. Position the tool under lugs of reverse cone and pull upward.
3. Remove the reverse stationary cone key from the case.

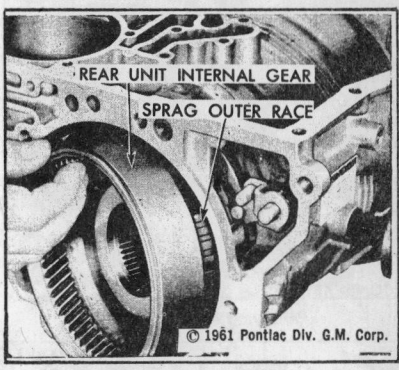

REAR UNIT INTERNAL GEAR

SPRAG OUTER RACE

Rear internal gear

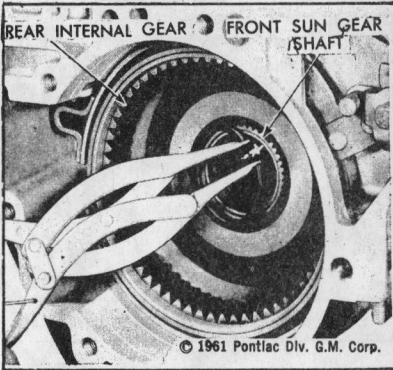

REAR INTERNAL GEAR

FRONT SUN GEAR SHAFT

Rear internal gear snap ring

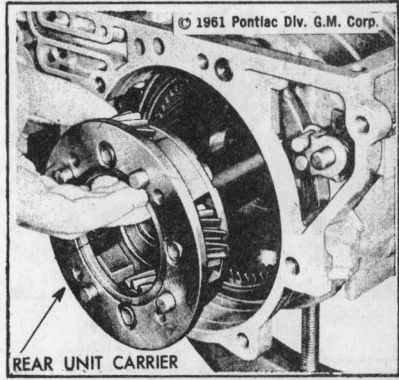

REAR UNIT CARRIER

Remove rear unit carrier

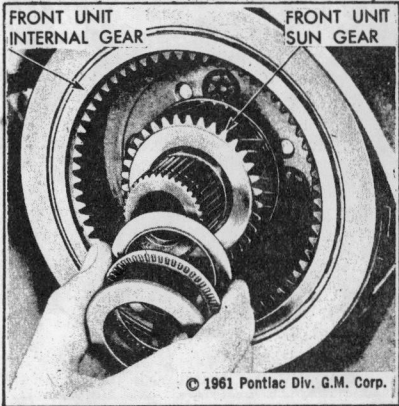

FRONT UNIT INTERNAL GEAR

FRONT UNIT SUN GEAR

Front sun gear to carrier thrust bearing and races

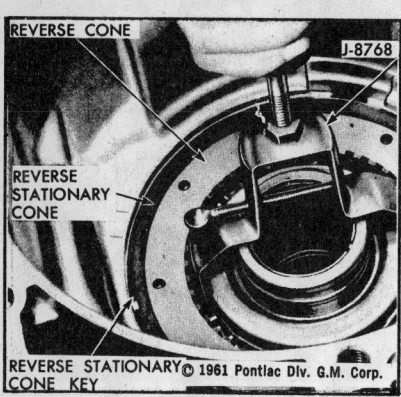

Removing reverse cone

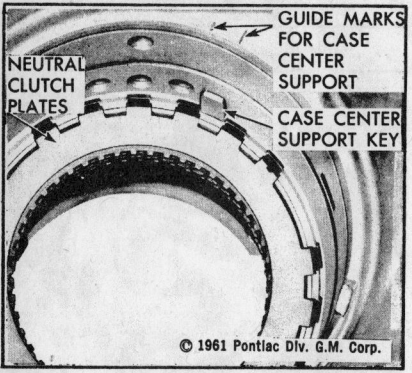

clutch plates and case center support key

Removing parking linkage

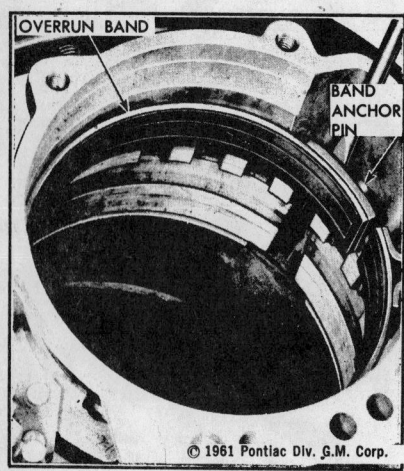

Removing overrun band from anchor pin in case

4. Remove the reverse and neutral piston and support assembly.
5. Remove the case center support key from the transmission case.
6. Remove neutral clutch plates (4 drive-composition and 4 driven-steel) and clutch backing plate from the transmission case.
7. Now turn the transmission to the vertical position with the rear end up.
8. Remove the band assembly by unhooking from the anchor and lifting upward.

PARKING LINKAGE

1. Remove parking pawl pin from the case.
2. Remove parking linkage assembly from case by lifting the parking bracket shaft and entire assembly out of the hole in the rear of the case.
3. Remove parking pawl spacer from case.

DIAGNOSIS AND TESTING GUIDE

The following guide is prepared as an aid, and not a substitute for a good understanding of the principles of operation.

<u>Caution:</u> Do not stall test transmission under any conditions.

PRESSURE TEST

While road testing, a transmission oil pressure gauge should be connected to the upper of the two test holes on the left-hand side of the rear bearing retainer and the pressure checked as follows:

With the selector in "Right Drive" and the road speed at 25 mph, the transmission should be in 2nd speed and the oil pressure between 98.6 and 111.4 pounds.

TROUBLE SHOOTING CHART

Low Oil Pressure
Caused By:
1. Oil Level—Low.
2. Boost Plug—Wrong—Stuck.
3. Pressure Regulator Valve
4. Strainer Blocked.
5. "O" Ring Leaking.
6. Manual Valve—Misaligned.
7. Foaming or Cavitation.
8. Internal Leak.
9. Control Valve Stuck.
10. Front Pump—Slide Stuck—Low Output.

High Oil Pressure
Caused By:

1. Pressure Regulator Valve—Stuck.
2. Boost Plug—Wrong—Stuck.
3. Manual Valve—Misaligned.
4. Control Valve—Stuck.
5. Front Pump—Slide Stuck—High Output.

DIAGNOSIS

No Drive in Drive Range
1. Neutral Clutch.
2. Sprag Assembly—Or Race.
3. Coupling.
4. Low Oil Level.
5. Low Oil Pressure.
6. Passage Restricted.
7. Internal Leak.
8. Linkage—Manual.
9. Control Valve Assembly.
10. Reverse Cone Sticking.

Car Moves in Neutral
1. Neutral Clutch.
2. Linkage—Manual.

No Reverse
1. Linkage—Manual.
2. Low Pressure.
3. Reverse Cone Clutch.
4. Restricted Passage.
5. Neutral Clutch.

Car Drives in "Right Drive" or "Low" Only
1. Sprag Assembly.
2. Neutral Clutch.

Forward Drive in Reverse
1. Manual Linkage.
2. Neutral Clutch.

Reverse Drive in Neutral
1. Reverse Cone Clutch.

Car Drives in Second and Third Only
1. Control Valve Assembly.

Car Drives in First and Third Only
1. Control Valve Assembly.
2. Coupling.

Car Drives in First and Second Only
1. Governor.
2. Control Valve Assembly.

Slipping 1-2 Shift
1. Front Clutch.
2. Control Valve Assembly.
3. Accumulator.
4. Compensator Body Assembly.
5. Low Oil Pressure.
6. T.V. Linkage.
7. 1-2 Oil Passages.

Slipping 2-3 Shift
1. Coupling.
2. Control Valve Assembly.
3. Front Clutch.

UPSHIFTS

Shift	Left Drive Range		Right Drive Range		Lo Range	
	Minimum Throttle	Full Throttle	Minimum Throttle	Full Throttle	Minimum Throttle	Full Throttle
1-2	14-18	33-40	14-18	33-40	No Shift Possible	
2-3	18-23	76-89	—	76-89	—	76-89

DOWNSHIFTS

Shift	Left Drive Range		Right Drive Range		Lo Range	
	Closed Throttle	Full Throttle Forced	Closed Throttle	Full Throttle Forced	Closed Throttle	Full Throttle Forced
3-2	20-15*	84-68	84-72	84-72	84-72	84-72
2-1	16-13*	29-25	16-13	29-25	52-46	52-46

Shift speed chart

Slipping in All Ranges
1. Low Oil Pressure.

Rough 1-2 Shift
1. Accumulator.
2. Compensation Body.
3. Front Clutch.
4. Front Clutch Passage.
5. Control Valve Assembly.
6. T.V. Linkage.
7. Coupling.

Erratic Shifts
1. Governor Assembly.
2. Control Valve Assembly.

High or Low Shifts
1. T.V. Linkage (Short-High Up-shifts)—(Long-Low Upshifts).
2. Control Valve Assembly.
3. Governor.
4. T.V. Lever.
5. Governor Oil Passage.
6. T.V. Pressure.
7. Line Pressure.

No Engine Breaking, Intermediate or Low Range
1. Overrun Band.
2. Overrun Servo.

No Part Throttle or Detent Downshifts
1. T.V. Linkage.
2. Control Valve Assembly.
3. Accelerator Travel.
4. Governor.

Selector Lever Will Not Go Into "Reverse"
1. Manual Linkage.
2. Reverse Blocker Valve.
3. Governor.

Selector Lever Will Not Go Into "Park"
1. Parking Linkage.
2. Manual Linkage.

DISASSEMBLY AND ASSEMBLY OF UNITS
CASE COVER AND PUMP

Disassemble
1. Loosen 6 case cover-to-pump bolts.

2. Support cover so the pump is clear of the bench. Tap heads of bolts with hammer to dislodge pump.
3. Remove the bolts and remove the pump.
4. Remove 2 hook type oil seal rings from the case cover.
5. Remove race, thrust bearing and selective washer from case cover.
6. Remove 2 screws (case cover-to-cooler control valve) and remove cooler control valve assembly and gasket. Do not disassemble

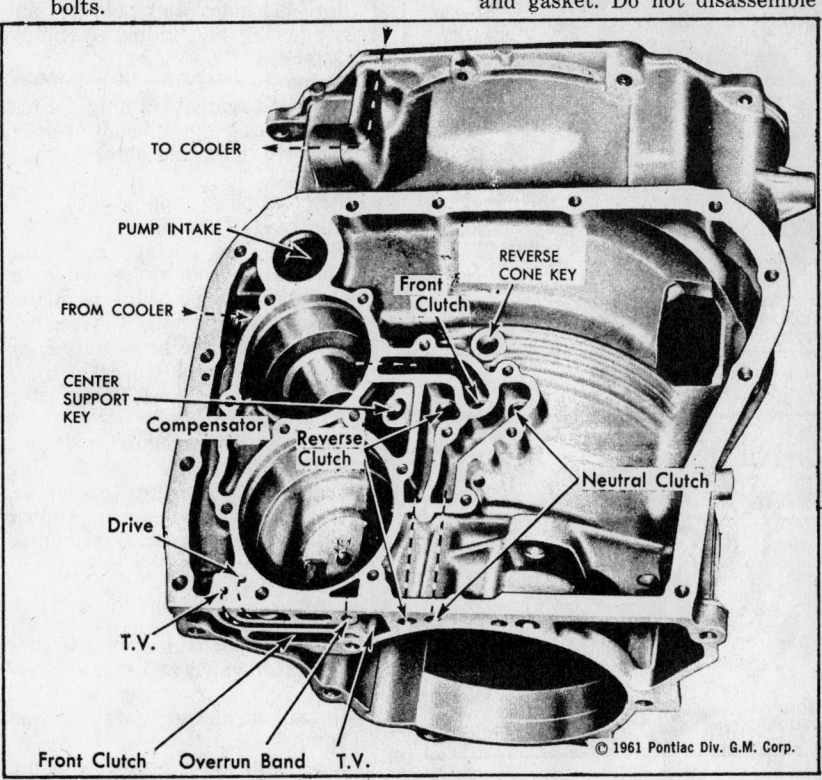

TO COOLER

PUMP INTAKE

FROM COOLER

CENTER SUPPORT KEY

Compensator

Drive

Reverse Clutch

Front Clutch

REVERSE CONE KEY

Neutral Clutch

T.V.

Front Clutch   Overrun Band   T.V.

© 1961 Pontiac Div. G.M. Corp.

Case passages

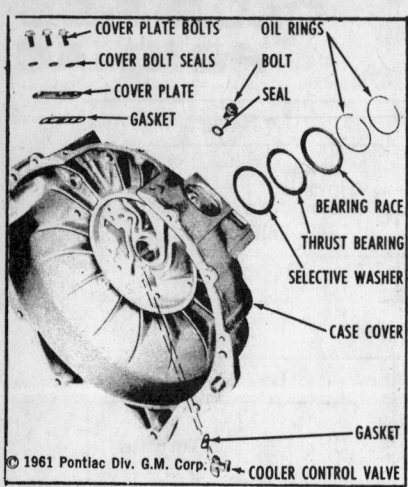

Case cover—exploded

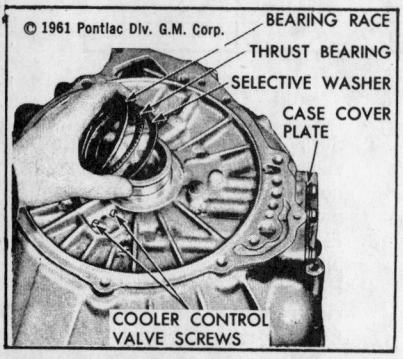

Case cover thrust bearing and selective washer

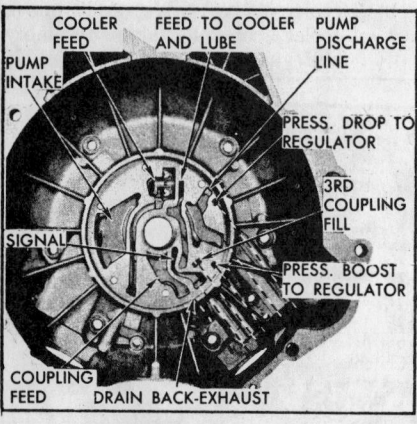

Case cover oil passages

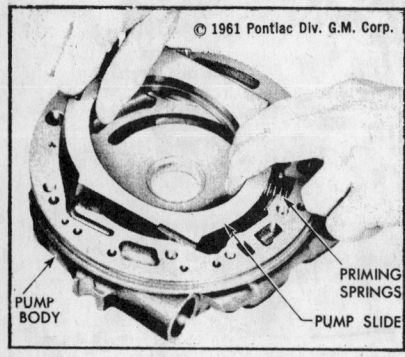

Removing pump slide

cooler control valve assembly.

7. Remove 3 case cover plate-to-case cover bolts and seals.
8. Remove case cover plate and gasket.
9. Remove the remaining bolt and seal in the case cover.

Assemble

1. Install case cover plate and gasket with 3 bolts and seal washers. Torque to 18-20 ft. lb.
2. Install remaining bolt and seal washer in case cover. Torque to 18-20 ft. lb.
3. Attach cooler control valve assembly and gasket with 2 screws. Torque to 2½-3½ ft. lb.
4. Install selective washer over tower of case cover.
5. Install thrust bearing and cupped race with cup side over bearing on case cover.
6. Install 2 hook type oil seal rings on tower.

Note: Pump to case cover in later text, see ("Assemble Pump to Case Cover").

PUMP

Disassemble

1. Remove pump-to-cover seal ("O" ring).
2. Remove pump cover attaching screw.
3. Remove cover from pump over roll pin, (do not pry to remove).
4. Remove top vane guide ring, rotor, 11 vanes and bottom vane guide ring. See "Pump Assembly, Exploded Illustration."
5. Remove pump slide by compressing slide against priming springs and cocking the slide out of body.
6. Remove inner and outer priming springs.
7. Remove the coupling feed limit plug and "O" ring.
8. Remove the spring, guide pin and valve from the same bore.
9. Remove the pressure regulator plug assembly and "O" ring.
10. Remove the line boost plug from the regulator plug.
11. Remove line boost plug stop from pump.
12. Remove the regulator valve spring and valve by inserting snap ring pliers into the spring.
13. If necessary, remove rubber cushion from pressure regulator valve.

Assemble

1. Install new cushion on pressure regulator valve and install pressure regulator spring on valve.
2. Install valve and spring in the pump.
3. Install regulator stop into pump over spring.

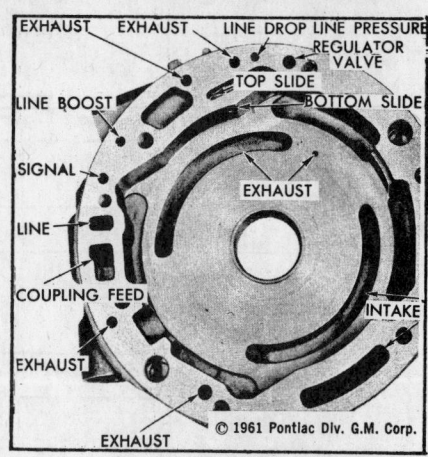

Pump body oil passages

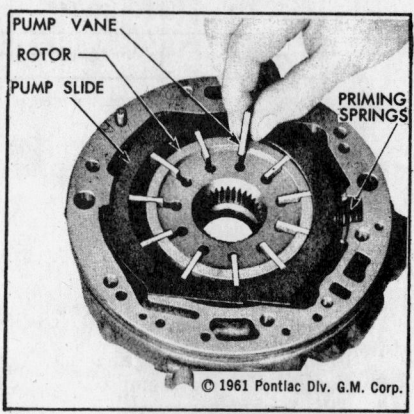

Pump vanes

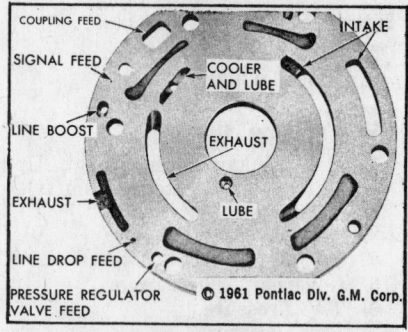

Pump cover passages

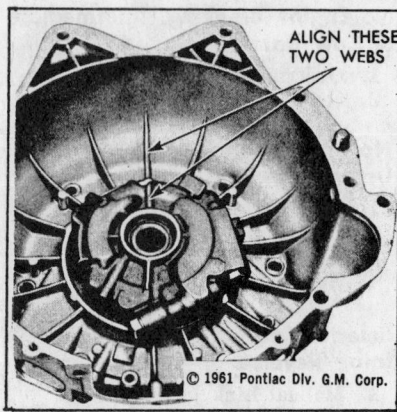

Align pump in case cover

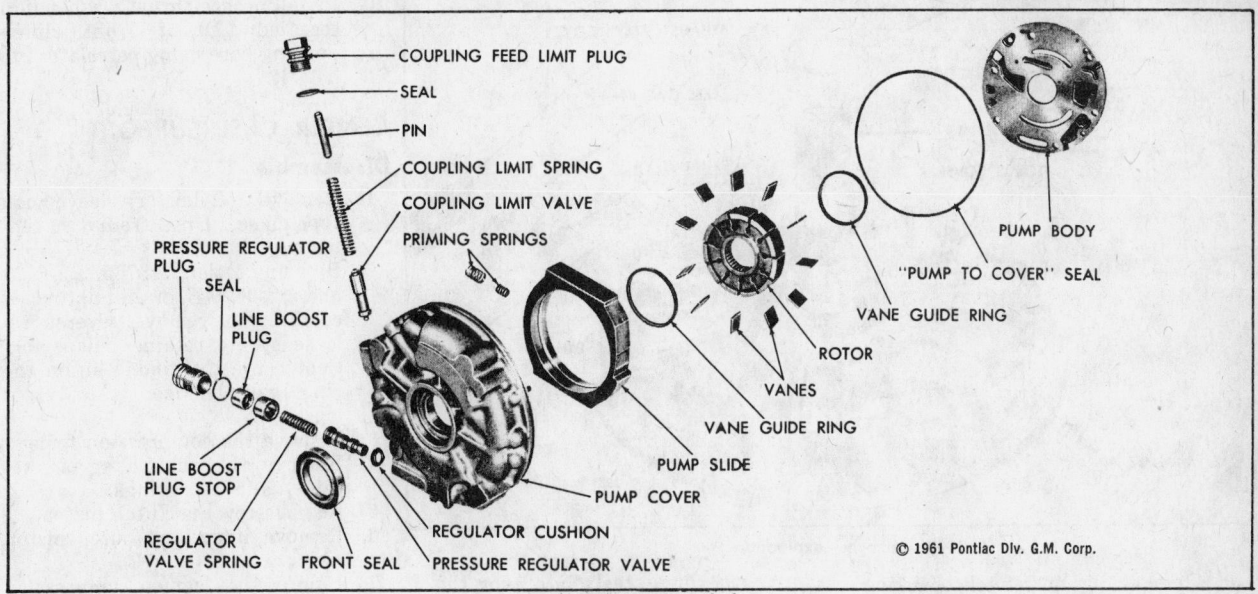

COUPLING FEED LIMIT PLUG — SEAL — PIN — COUPLING LIMIT SPRING — COUPLING LIMIT VALVE — PRIMING SPRINGS — PRESSURE REGULATOR PLUG — SEAL — LINE BOOST PLUG — LINE BOOST PLUG STOP — REGULATOR VALVE SPRING — FRONT SEAL — REGULATOR CUSHION — PRESSURE REGULATOR VALVE — PUMP COVER — PUMP SLIDE — VANE GUIDE RING — VANES — ROTOR — VANE GUIDE RING — "PUMP TO COVER" SEAL — PUMP BODY

© 1961 Pontiac Div. G.M. Corp.

4. Install new "O" ring on pressure regulator plug.
5. Install line boost plug into regulator plug, cup side out.
6. Install plug assembly into pump. Torque to 15-20 ft. lbs.
7. Install coupling limit valve, spring and pin into pump.
8. Install new "O" ring on coupling feed limit valve plug.
9. Install feed limit valve plug into pump. Torque to 15-20 ft. lbs.
10. Install inner and outer priming springs into pump body.
11. Assemble slide into pump body by compressing slide against springs until slide can be fully installed into pump.
12. Install bottom guide ring into pump.
13. Install pump rotor (shoulder side down) into pump pocket over guide ring.
14. Install 11 vanes into rotor. Insert them so the ring wear pattern on the edge of the vane is against the guide ring.
15. Install top guide ring on rotor.
16. Install pump cover over roll pin and secure with screw. Torque to 6-8 ft. lbs.
17. Install new pump-to-cover "O" ring.

Assemble Pump to Case Cover

1. With case cover, (open side up) lay pump in its recess with coupling feed limit plug and pressure regulator plug facing their access holes.
2. Align the top pump web with the case cover web, as illustrated. Start one pump attaching bolt from under side of cover as an aligning guide. Then push pump

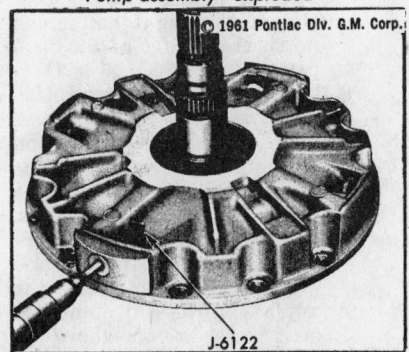

© 1961 Pontiac Div. G.M. Corp.

Pump assembly—exploded

J-6122

Exhaust valve cover

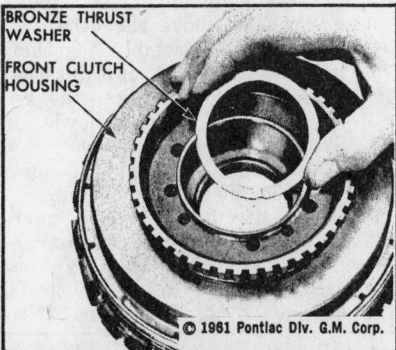

BRONZE THRUST WASHER
FRONT CLUTCH HOUSING

© 1961 Pontiac Div. G.M. Corp.

Thrust washers in front clutch housing

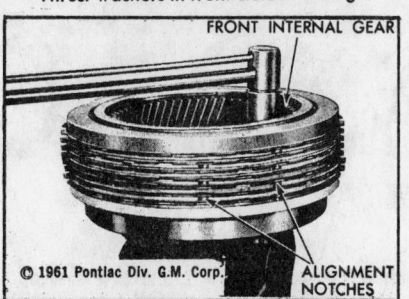

FRONT INTERNAL GEAR

© 1961 Pontiac Div. G.M. Corp.

ALIGNMENT NOTCHES

Torquing front clutch bolts

to bottom of its recess in the cover.
3. Install 6 case cover-to-pump bolts and torque to 15-18 ft. lbs.

TORUS COVER

Disassemble

1. Remove 2 hook type oil rings from the input shaft.
2. Remove torus exhaust valve cover screw with a clutch head socket.
3. Remove exhaust valve cover, steel gasket, valve and spring.
4. Repeat operation for second exhaust valve.

Assemble

1. Install exhaust valve and spring.
2. Install exhaust valve retaining tool #J-6122 or an equivalent.
3. Install cover and new gasket. Secure with screw and torque with a clutch head socket to 19-23 ft. lbs.
4. Repeat for second exhaust valve.
5. Install 2 hook type oil rings on input shaft.

FRONT CLUTCH

Disassemble

1. Remove bronze thrust washer from front clutch assembly.
2. Install the assembly in a padded vise with the internal gear "UP" and vise engaging large teeth on opposite side of assembly.
3. Remove 4 front internal gear-to-clutch housing bolts.
4. Gently tap a dowel pin with a drift to remove front internal gear from clutch housing. The housing is spring loaded.
5. Remove from internal gear.

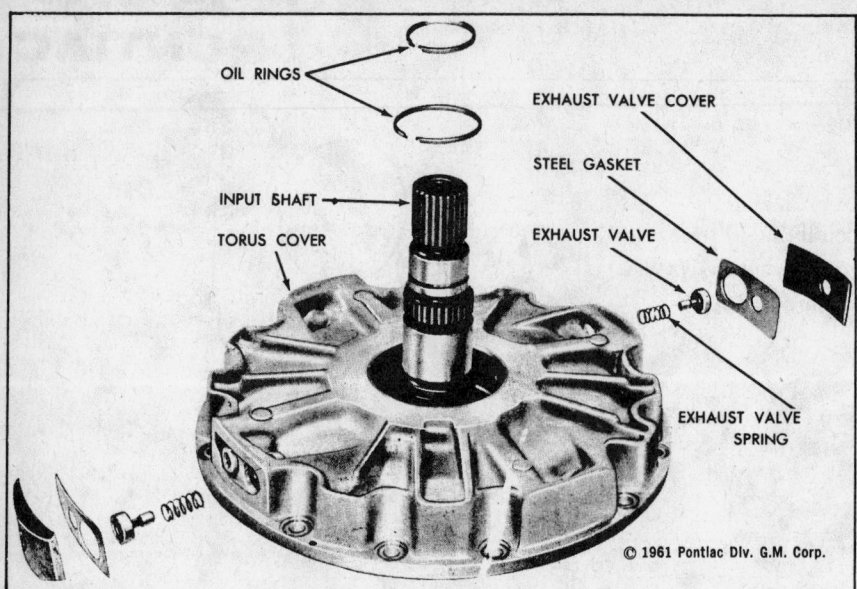

Torus cover—exploded

OIL RINGS

INPUT SHAFT

TORUS COVER

EXHAUST VALVE COVER

STEEL GASKET

EXHAUST VALVE

EXHAUST VALVE SPRING

© 1961 Pontiac Div. G.M. Corp.

check for freedom of bottom steel clutch plate.

10. Install bronze thrust washer into recessed I.D. of front clutch housing bore using petrolatum to hold it.

CENTER CASE SUPPORT

Disassemble

1. Remove 2 oil delivery sleeve hook type oil seal rings from case center support.
2. By using tools #J-8765, #J-6129 and #J-4670-B, or an improvised compressor, remove reverse release spring retainer snap ring. Center the tool and position the ring gap between compressor legs.
3. Remove the compression tools.
4. Remove the release spring retainer and 12 springs.
5. Remove reverse clutch piston.
6. Remove inner and outer piston rings.
7. Using the same compression tools, remove neutral clutch release spring retainer snap ring. Center tool and position ring gap between tool legs.
8. Remove compression tools.
9. Remove clutch spring retainer.
10. Remove 16 neutral clutch springs.
    Note: Do not mix neutral clutch springs with reverse springs.
11. Remove neutral clutch piston.
12. Remove inner and outer neutral clutch seal rings.

Assemble

1. Install new inner and outer neutral clutch seals with lip of seal away from spring pockets.
2. Install inner spring protector, #J-8766 over the neutral clutch inner hub.
3. Install neutral clutch piston, (use care in depressing seal lip.)
4. Remove seal protector.
5. Install 16 release springs.
6. Install neutral clutch spring retainer over release springs.
7. Using tools #J-8761, #J-6129 and #J-4670-B, compress neu-

6. Remove front clutch backing plate.
7. Remove 7 drive and 7 driven plates.
8. Remove 20 release springs.
9. Remove front clutch piston from housing.
10. Remove seal from piston, discard seal.
11. Remove clutch inner piston seal from . clutch housing, discard seal.

Assemble

1. Install new inner piston seal on front clutch housing with seal lip facing away from spring pockets.
3. Install clutch piston in the housing. Use care to prevent piston seal damage.
4. Install the 20 release springs.
5. Install front clutch backing plate on front internal gear with the undercut facing the flange on the internal gear.
6. Install 7 composition and 7 steel plates alternately over the front internal gear. Start with a composition plate.
   A. Place a composition plate and

the first steel plate over the internal gear. Notice the location of the slight half moon notch in the edge of the steel plate.
   B. Install another composition plate and the second steel plate so that the half moon is located 2 drive lugs on the internal gear away from the notch in the first steel plate.
   C. Continue to alternatively install the composition and steel plates so that the notches in the odd numbered steel plates are one above the other and the notches in the even numbered steel plates are one above the other.
7. Holding the assembly together, position the front unit internal gear (with plates) on the release springs, aligning dowls.
8. Secure entire assembly in a padded vise, engaging the large teeth on the clutch housing.
9. Install 4 front unit internal gear-to-clutch housing bolts. Alternatively tighten the bolts to properly seat the gear on the dowls. Torque to 22-27 ft. lbs. Then

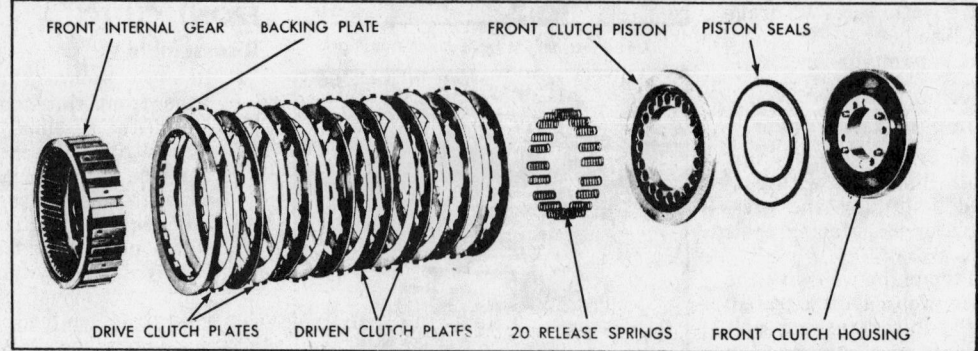

FRONT INTERNAL GEAR

BACKING PLATE

FRONT CLUTCH PISTON

PISTON SEALS

DRIVE CLUTCH PLATES

DRIVEN CLUTCH PLATES

20 RELEASE SPRINGS

FRONT CLUTCH HOUSING

Front clutch—exploded

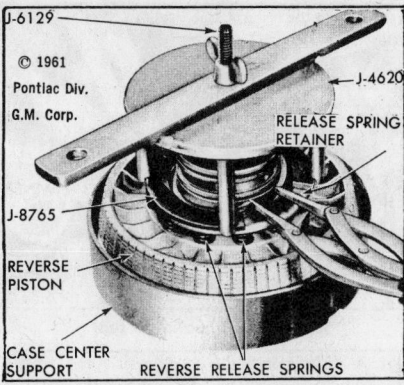

Removing reverse release spring snap ring

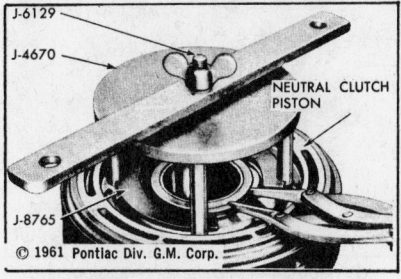

Removing neutral clutch spring snap ring

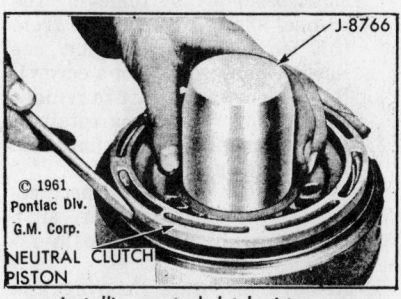

Installing neutral clutch piston

Installing reverse clutch piston

tral clutch release springs and install retainer snap ring.

8. Remove compressor.
9. Install inner seal protector over oil delivery sleeve.
10. Install outer seal protector, #J-8767 into case center support.
11. Install new inner and outer piston seal rings on reverse piston, (lip of seals facing dowel pin holes in piston).
12. Install reverse piston, align the piston to index with dowel pins.
13. Remove tool.
14. Install 12 piston springs.
15. Install piston spring retainer.
16. Lay snap ring on top of tower. Using tools, compress the release springs.
17. Install piston spring retainer snap ring.
18. Remove compressor.
19. Be sure all springs are in their pockets.
20. Install 2 hook type oil seal rings on oil delivery sleeve.

REAR INTERNAL GEAR AND SPRAG

Disassemble

1. Remove sprag retainer.
2. Remove sprag outer race.
3. Remove sprag and bushing assembly from internal gear.

Assemble

1. Place one bronze bushing over inner race of internal gear, (cup side up).
2. Place sprag assembly into sprag outer race.
3. With shoulder side of sprag up, start sprag and outer race over the gear.
4. Slide sprag and outer race down against internal gear.

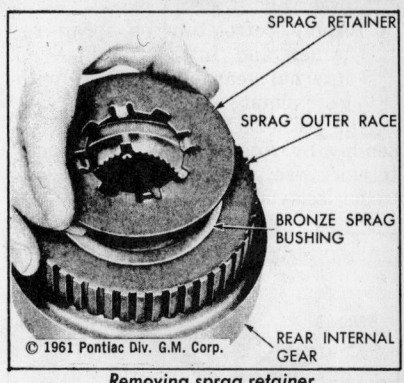

Removing sprag retainer

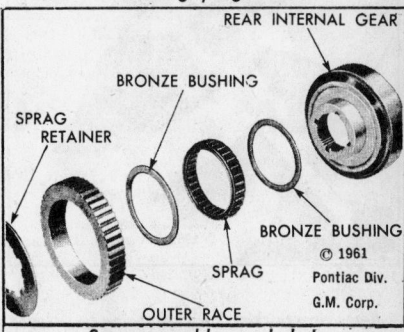

Sprag assembly—exploded

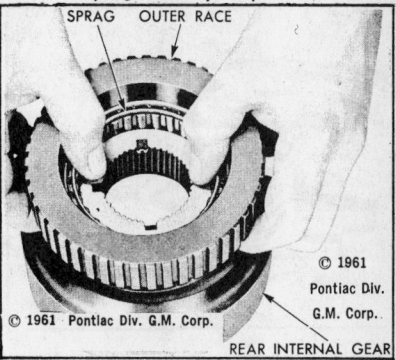

Installing sprag outer race

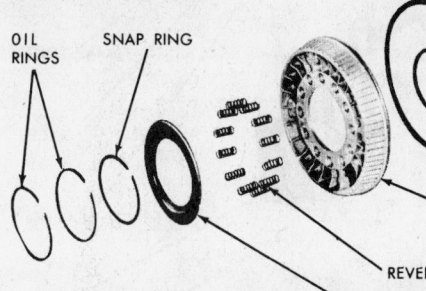

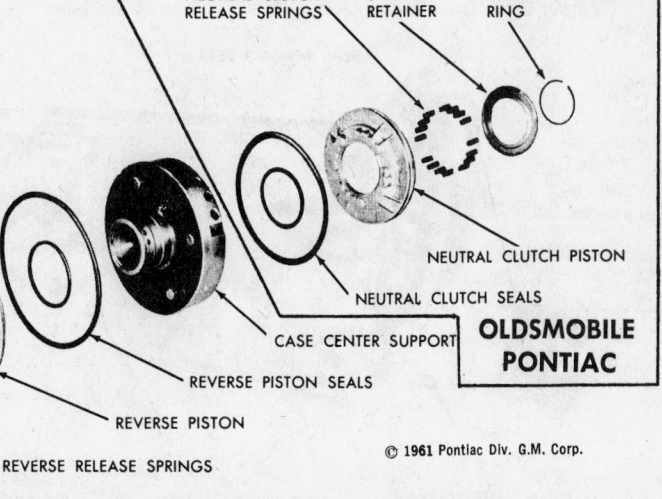

Case center support—exploded

5. Install second bronze bushing, (cup side down) against sprag assembly.
6. Apply petrolatum on sprag retainer and install retainer on internal gear. Align tangs with gear slots.

Note: Check for proper sprag assembly by rotating outer race counterclockwise. Outer race should not turn clockwise.

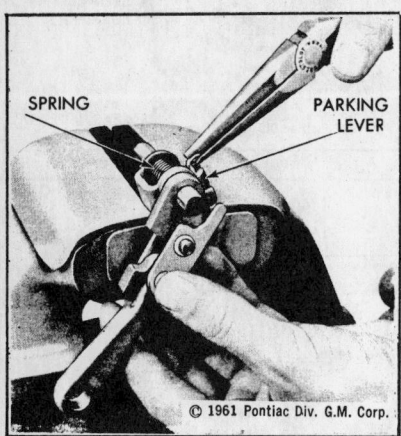

Removing parking bracket spring from lever

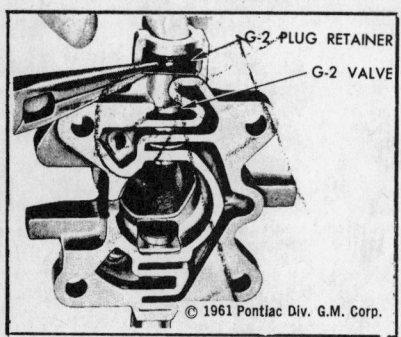

Removing G-2 plug retainer

GOVERNOR

Disassemble

1. Compress finger of G-2 plug retainer and remove.
2. Remove plug and G-2 valve.
3. Remove 4 governor hook-type oil seal rings from governor tower.

Assemble

Reverse above procedure.

PARKING LINKAGE

Disassemble

1. Install assembly in a vise using the dowel pin to hold the unit.
2. Lift hook end of bracket spring off parking lever and disassemble parts.

Assemble

Assemble in reverse order. Refer to exploded view of "Parking Brake Assembly."

REAR BEARING RETAINER

Disassemble

1. Remove inside detent lever and

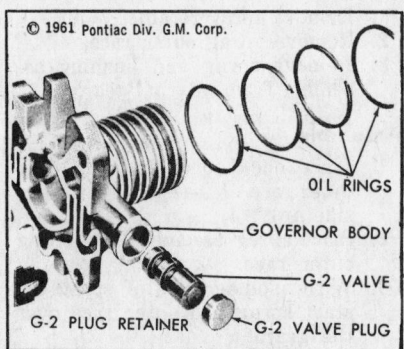

Governor—exploded

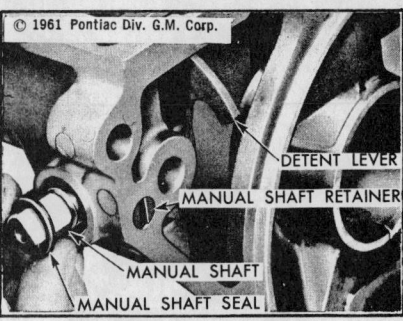

Removing manual shaft seal

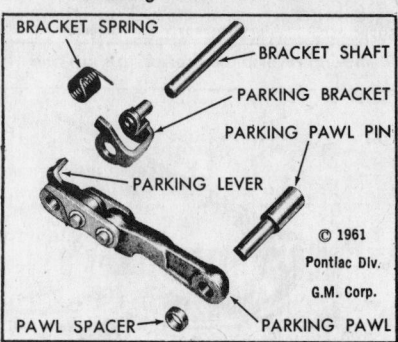

Parking linkage assembly—exploded

shaft assembly by removing the manual shaft retaining pin from the rear bearing retainer, see illustration (this is not a screw).
2. Rotate lever and shaft to remove them from the bearing retainer.
3. Remove manual valve shaft seal from bore in retainer.
4. Remove rear thrust bearing race-to-rear bearing retainer snap ring through access hole in retainer.
5. Remove rear race, bearing and front race from rear bearing retainer.

Assemble

1. Install race, thrust bearing, and race into rear bearing retainer.

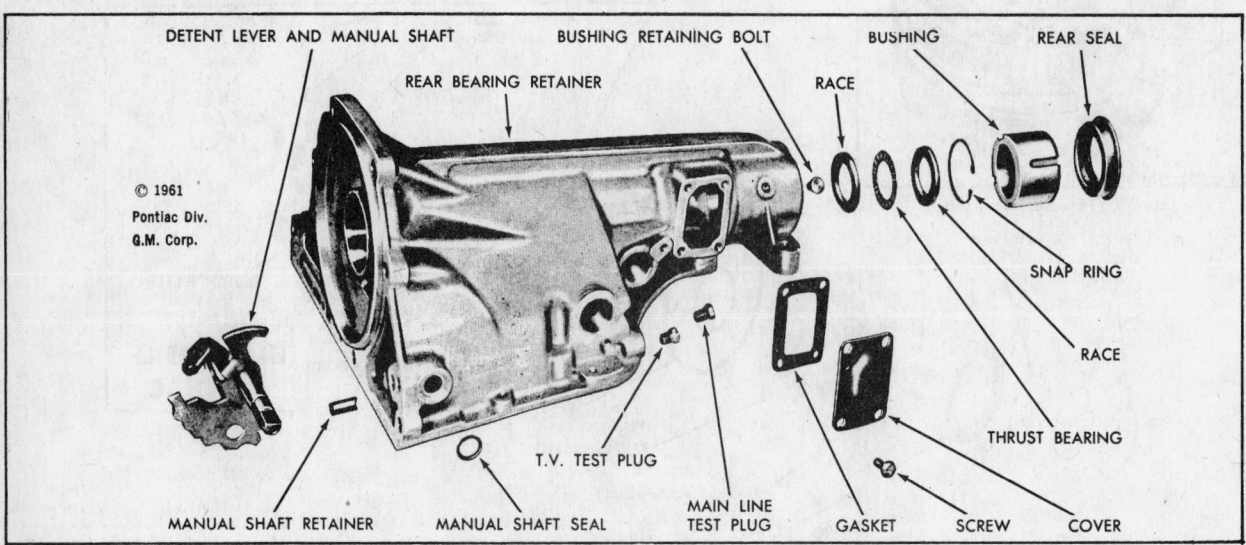

Rear bearing retainer exploded (Pontiac and Oldsmobile)

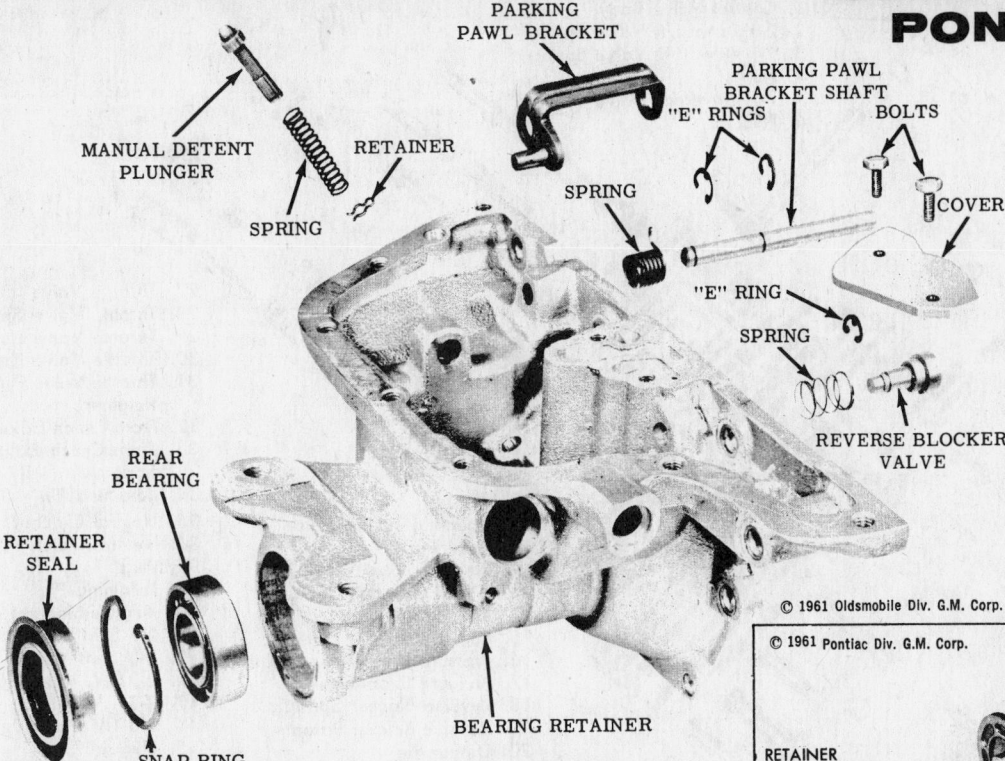

PARKING PAWL BRACKET

MANUAL DETENT PLUNGER

RETAINER

SPRING

PARKING PAWL BRACKET SHAFT

"E" RINGS

BOLTS

SPRING

COVER

"E" RING

SPRING

REVERSE BLOCKER VALVE

REAR BEARING

RETAINER SEAL

SNAP RING

BEARING RETAINER

© 1961 Oldsmobile Div. G.M. Corp.

Rear Bearing Retainer—Exploded (F-85)

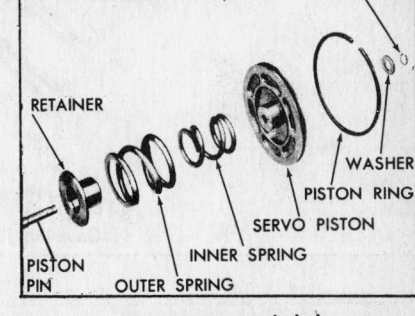

© 1961 Pontiac Div. G.M. Corp.

SNAP RING

RETAINER

WASHER

PISTON RING

SERVO PISTON

INNER SPRING

PISTON PIN

OUTER SPRING

Servo piston—exploded

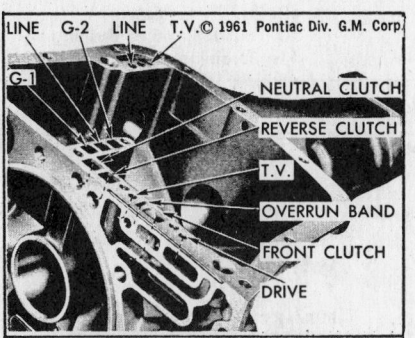

LINE   G-2   LINE   T.V. © 1961 Pontiac Div. G.M. Corp.

G-1

NEUTRAL CLUTCH

REVERSE CLUTCH

T.V.

OVERRUN BAND

FRONT CLUTCH

DRIVE

Rear bearing retainer passages

INNER SPRING

OUTER SPRING

7/16" SOCKET

© 1961 Pontiac Div. G.M. Corp.

SNAP RING

SERVO PISTON

PISTON RING

Removing snap ring from servo piston pin

2. Install snap ring, concave side towards the rear, (identification away from race) and align ear on snap ring with top slot in retainer.

3. Install bushing and sleeve, chamfered end first. Align short slot

in bushing with retaining bolt hole in bearing retainer.

4. Install bushing retaining bolt and torque to 12-15 ft. lbs.

5. Install inside detent lever and shaft assembly.

6. Install detent shaft retainer into hole in rear housing. Align key with annular groove in detent shaft.

7. Install new manual shaft seal, (grooved side toward retainer) over detent shaft.

SERVO AND ACCUMULATOR PISTONS

Disassemble

1. Place a 7/16" deep socket over the long end of the servo piston pin.

2. Position a "U" shaped spacer against the piston end of the piston and place the socket, piston assembly and "U" shaped spacer between the jaws of a vise.

3. Tighten the vise enough to remove the snap ring.

4. Remove the servo piston-to-piston pin snap ring and washer.

5. Remove piston assembly from vise.

6. Remove servo piston, springs and retainer.

7. Remove the lip seal from the upper accumulator piston.

Assemble

Reverse disassembly procedure.

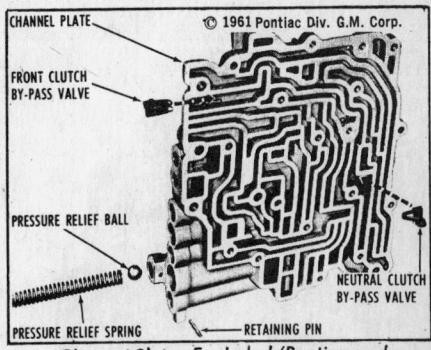

CHANNEL PLATE

© 1961 Pontiac Div. G.M. Corp.

FRONT CLUTCH BY-PASS VALVE

PRESSURE RELIEF BALL

PRESSURE RELIEF SPRING

NEUTRAL CLUTCH BY-PASS VALVE

RETAINING PIN

Channel Plate—Exploded (Pontiac and Oldsmobile)

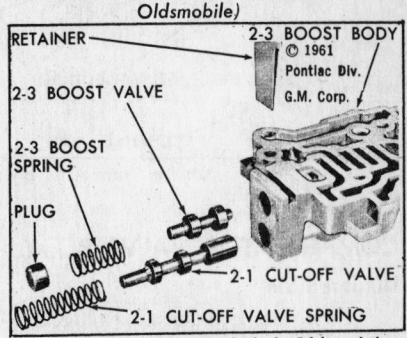

RETAINER

2-3 BOOST BODY

© 1961 Pontiac Div. G.M. Corp.

2-3 BOOST VALVE

2-3 BOOST SPRING

PLUG

2-1 CUT-OFF VALVE

2-1 CUT-OFF VALVE SPRING

2-3 Boost Body—Exploded (Oldsmobile and Pontiac)

899

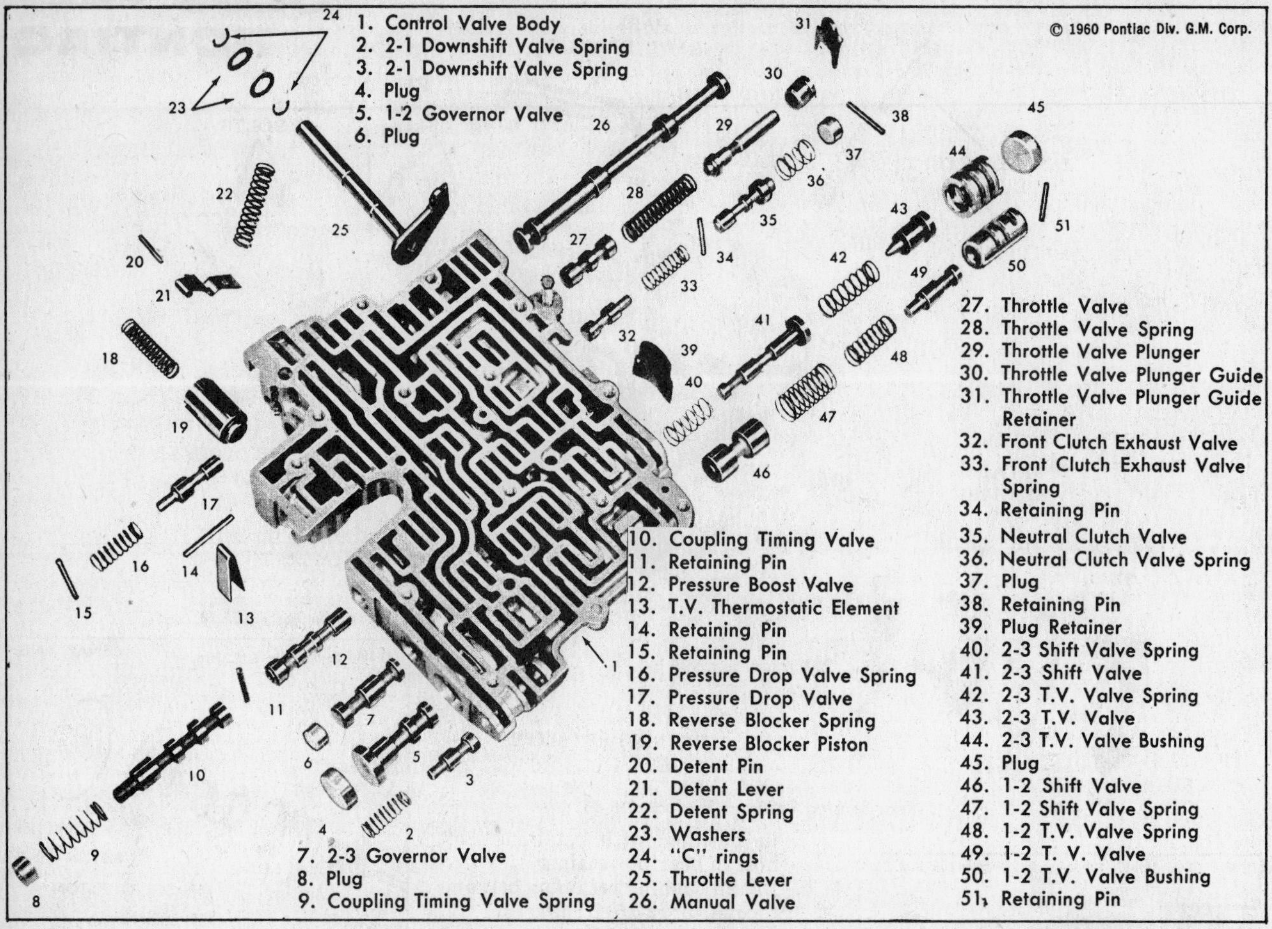

© 1960 Pontiac Div. G.M. Corp.
1. Control Valve Body
2. 2-1 Downshift Valve Spring
3. 2-1 Downshift Valve Spring
4. Plug
5. 1-2 Governor Valve
6. Plug
7. 2-3 Governor Valve
8. Plug
9. Coupling Timing Valve Spring
10. Coupling Timing Valve
11. Retaining Pin
12. Pressure Boost Valve
13. T.V. Thermostatic Element
14. Retaining Pin
15. Retaining Pin
16. Pressure Drop Valve Spring
17. Pressure Drop Valve
18. Reverse Blocker Spring
19. Reverse Blocker Piston
20. Detent Pin
21. Detent Lever
22. Detent Spring
23. Washers
24. "C" rings
25. Throttle Lever
26. Manual Valve
27. Throttle Valve
28. Throttle Valve Spring
29. Throttle Valve Plunger
30. Throttle Valve Plunger Guide
31. Throttle Valve Plunger Guide Retainer
32. Front Clutch Exhaust Valve
33. Front Clutch Exhaust Valve Spring
34. Retaining Pin
35. Neutral Clutch Valve
36. Neutral Clutch Valve Spring
37. Plug
38. Retaining Pin
39. Plug Retainer
40. 2-3 Shift Valve Spring
41. 2-3 Shift Valve
42. 2-3 T.V. Valve Spring
43. 2-3 T.V. Valve
44. 2-3 T.V. Valve Bushing
45. Plug
46. 1-2 Shift Valve
47. 1-2 Shift Valve Spring
48. 1-2 T.V. Valve Spring
49. 1-2 T. V. Valve
50. 1-2 T.V. Valve Bushing
51. Retaining Pin

Control Valve Assembly—Exploded (Pontiac and Oldsmobile)

© 1961 Pontiac Div. G.M. Corp.
FRONT CLUTCH BY-PASS VALVE
T.V. THERMOSTATIC ELEMENT
2-3 BOOST BODY
CHECK BALLS
SPACER
VALVE BODY
CHECK BALLS
SPACER
NEUTRAL CLUTCH BY-PASS VALVE
CHANNEL PLATE

Control Valve Assembly (Pontiac and Oldsmobile)

SECONDARY VALVE BODY
PRIMARY VALVE BODY
CHANNEL PLATE TO VALVE BODY SPACER
CHANNEL PLATE
VALVE BODY TO CASE SPACER PLATE
© 1961 Oldsmobile Div. G.M. Corp

Control Valve Assembly (Oldsmobile F-85)

COMPENSATOR VALVE BODY

Disassemble

1. Compress compensator plug and remove retaining pin.
2. Remove compensator plug.
3. Remove secondary compensator valve and spring.
4. Remove primary compensator valve and spring.

Assemble

Assemble in reverse order of disassembly.

CONTROL VALVE

Disassemble 2-3 Boost Body

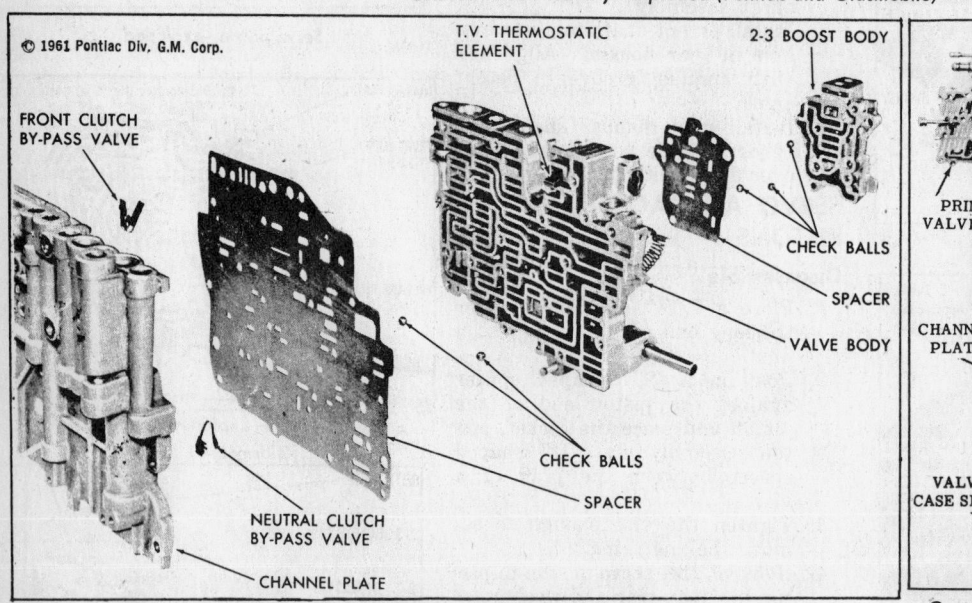

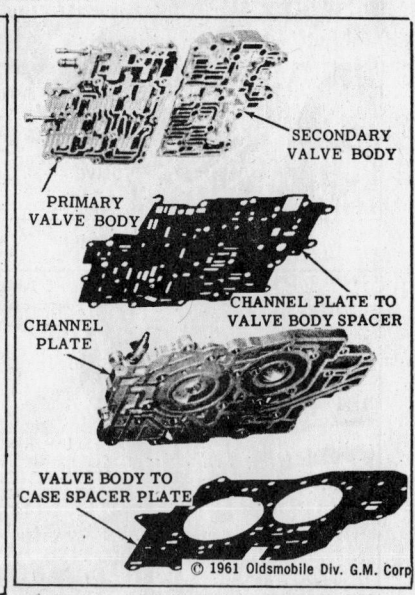

1. Remove the 2-3 boost body by removing 4 attaching screws. (One screw is mounted on the channel plate side of the body.) **Caution:** This body contains 3 loose check balls, **don't lose them.**
2. Remove the balls and channel spacer plate.
3. Remove the retainer from the 2-3 boost body. Retainer is under spring pressure.
4. Remove the 2-1 cut off valve and spring.
5. Remove the 2-3 boost plug, spring, and valve.

Assemble

Assemble in reverse order of disassembly.

CONTROL VALVE BODY

Disassemble

1. Remove channel plate from valve body by removing 2 screws from valve body side and 13 screws from the plate side.
2. Remove neutral clutch by-pass valve from cored side of channel plate.
3. Remove front clutch by-pass valve from channel plate.
4. If necessary to remove pressure relief ball and spring:
   A. Turn channel plate over to casting side and remove retaining pin. (The pin is under extreme pressure.)
   B. Remove pressure relief spring.
   C. Remove pressure relief ball.
   D. Assemble relief ball, spring and retaining pin into channel plate.
5. Install neutral clutch by-pass valve and front clutch by-pass valve into channel plate.

   Set the assembled channel plate aside and continue with disassembly.
6. Remove the channel plate-to-valve body spacer.
7. Remove 2 check balls and T.V. thermostatic element.
8. Remove T.V. plunger guide retainer in the cored passage near T.V. adjusting screw. Position control valve assembly with the cored side up and T.V. lever at the top right hand side.
9. Remove multiple valve plug retainer from the lower left hand corner. Plugs are under spring tension.
10. Remove the 2-1 downshift spring and valve from the lowest bore.
11. Remove valve bore plug by threading a valve body attaching screw into the plug, and sliding the plug out from the adjacent bore.
12. Remove the 1-2 governor valve from the same bore.
13. Remove valve bore plug from the adjacent bore.
14. Remove 2-3 governor valve from the same bore.
15. Remove the valve bore plug from the next adjacent bore.
16. Remove the coupling timing valve spring and valve from the same bore.
17. Remove pressure boost valve retaining pin from the center of the cored side of the valve body in the same bore.
18. Remove pressure boost valve from the same bore.
19. On the opposite side of the valve body, start with the lower bore and remove the retaining pin.
20. Remove the 1-2 T.V. bushing and valve from the same bore.
21. Remove the 1-2 T.V. and shift valve springs. Then remove the 1-2 shift valve.
22. Remove the valve bore plug retainer and plug, while holding finger over plug. Plug is under spring pressure from adjacent bore.
23. Remove 2-3 T.V. valve, spring and bushing from same bore.
24. Remove 2-3 shift valve spring, same bore.
25. Remove the retaining pin and valve bore plug from the fourth bore.
26. Remove the neutral clutch valve and valve spring.
27. Remove the front clutch exhaust valve retaining pin. Pin is under

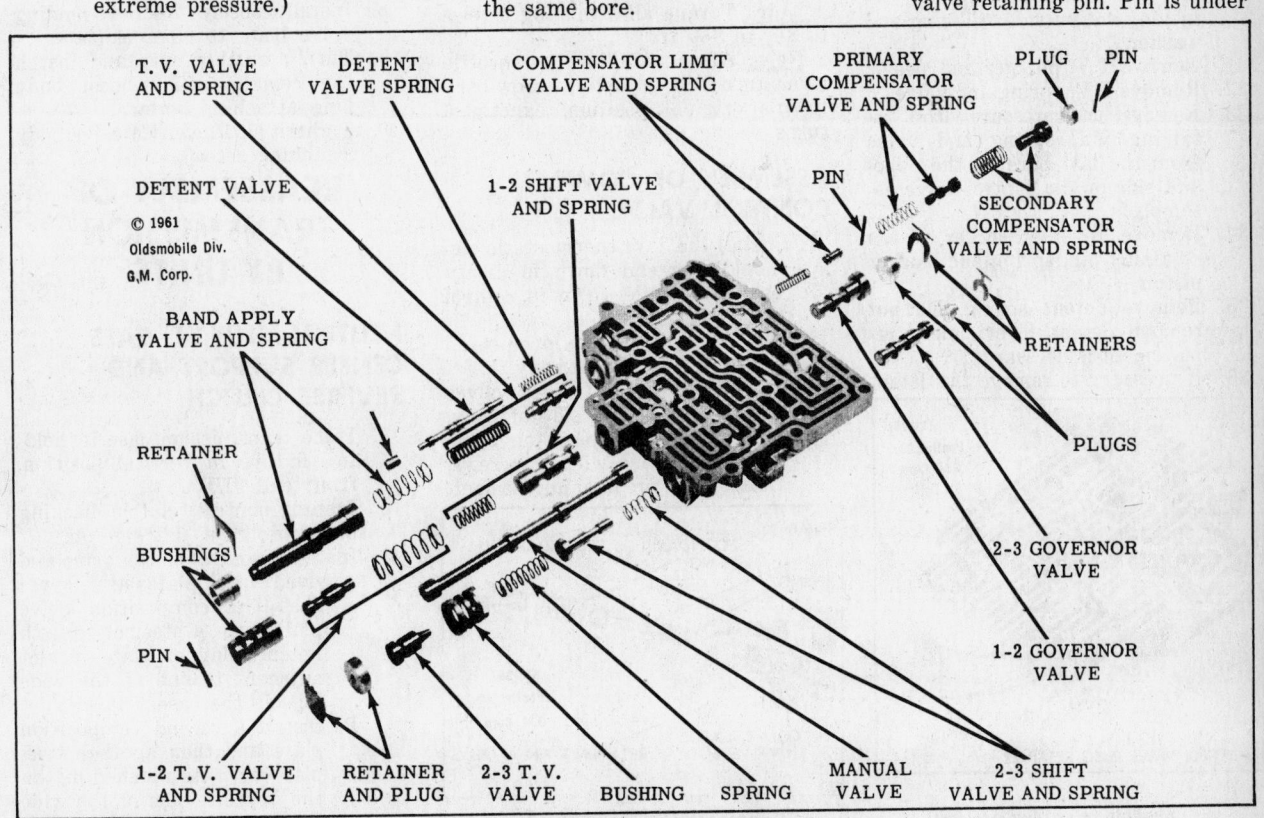

T.V. VALVE AND SPRING   DETENT VALVE SPRING   COMPENSATOR LIMIT VALVE AND SPRING   PRIMARY COMPENSATOR VALVE AND SPRING   PLUG   PIN

DETENT VALVE

© 1961
Oldsmobile Div.
G.M. Corp.

1-2 SHIFT VALVE AND SPRING   PIN

SECONDARY COMPENSATOR VALVE AND SPRING

BAND APPLY VALVE AND SPRING

RETAINERS

RETAINER

PLUGS

BUSHINGS

2-3 GOVERNOR VALVE

PIN

1-2 GOVERNOR VALVE

1-2 T.V. VALVE AND SPRING   RETAINER AND PLUG   2-3 T.V. VALVE   BUSHING   SPRING   MANUAL VALVE   2-3 SHIFT VALVE AND SPRING

Primary Valve Body (Oldsmobile F-85)

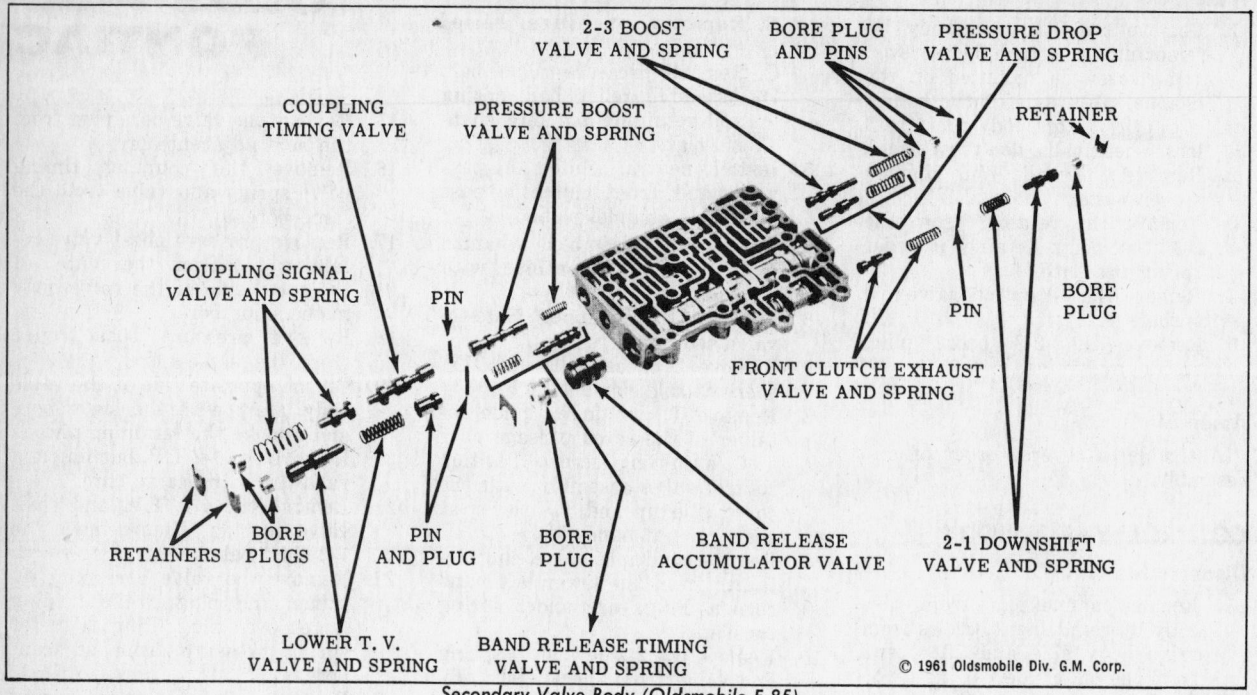

Secondary Valve Body (Oldsmobile F-85)

© 1961 Oldsmobile Div. G.M. Corp.

pressure. Unload pressure from the uncored side with a small screwdriver to remove pin.

28. Remove front clutch valve and spring.
29. Mark T.V. adjustment screw and **loosen exactly 5 turns.**
30. Turn valve body over and remove the throttle lever by removing the outside "C" ring and washer.
31. Remove T.V. plunger and sleeve.
32. Remove T.V. spring and valve.
33. Remove the pressure drop retaining pin, spring and valve from the last bore on the opposite side of the control valve assembly.
34. Remove reverse blocker piston retaining pin, spring and blocker piston.
35. Remove detent spring. Do not remove detent lever unless replacement is necssary.
36. If ncessary to remove the detent

lever, tap the retainer pin through the lever with a small punch. Remove detent lever and pin from valve body.

Assemble

Assemble by reversal of disassembly procedure.

Note: Torque all attaching screws to 2½ to 3½ ft. lbs.

Note: After installing the throttle lever, turn T.V. adjusting screw back to it's original position, exactly 5 turns.

ASSEMBLY OF COMPLETE CONTROL VALVE

1. Install the T.V. thermostatic element open end down in cavity behind throttle valve in control valve body.
2. Position spacer plate over cored side of control valve body.
3. Install small 2 ball check valves into place in cored side of body.
4. Position channel plate on valve body and attach with 13 screws. Leave loose for final adjustment.

5. Turn control valve assembly over and install 3 ball check valves into pockets.
6. Place 2-3 boost valve body spacer on valve body.
7. Place 2-3 boost body on spacer plate and install 3 attaching screws, (don't tighten screws).
8. Install (loosely) 2 screws holding valve body to channel plate.
9. Turn assembly over and install the remaining 2-3 boost body long attaching screw.
10. Tighten all 19 control valve body attaching screws.

REASSEMBLY OF TRANSMISSION BY UNITS

NEUTRAL CLUTCH, CASE CENTER SUPPORT AND REVERSE CLUTCH

1. Place transmission case in holding fixture in vertical position, front end "UP".
2. Install neutral clutch backing plate into case, flat side up.
3. Install a neutral clutch drive and 4 driven clutch plates as follows:
   A. Install a composition drive plate then a steel plate with notched lug of plate in slot adjacent to one of the wide lugs in the case.
   B. Install a second composition plate and then another steel plate with its notched lug on the opposite side of the wide case lug from the first. This

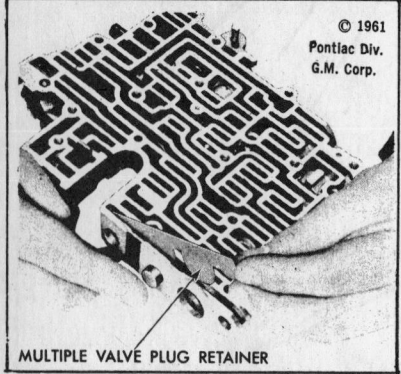

MULTIPLE VALVE PLUG RETAINER

© 1961 Pontiac Div. G.M. Corp.

Multiple valve plug retainer

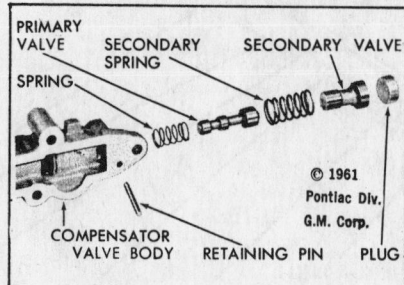

PRIMARY VALVE
SECONDARY SPRING
SECONDARY VALVE
SPRING
© 1961 Pontiac Div. G.M. Corp.
COMPENSATOR VALVE BODY
RETAINING PIN
PLUG

Compensator valve—exploded

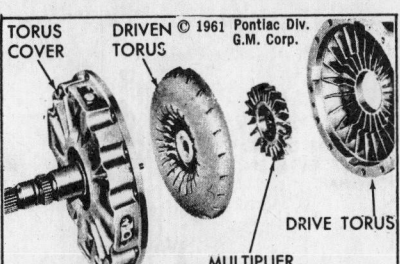

Torus Assembly—exploded

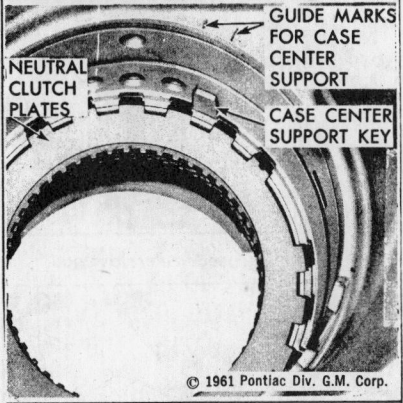

Neutral clutch plates

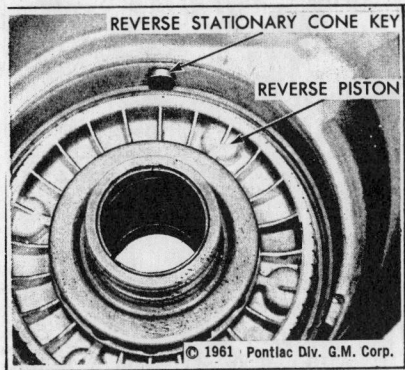

Reverse piston in case

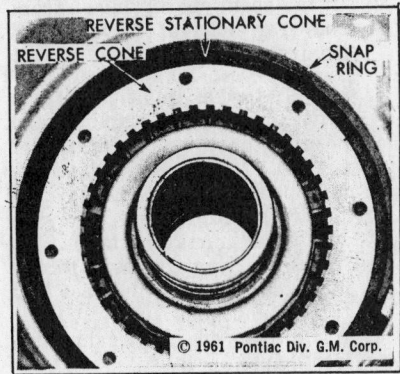

Reverse cone in case

arrangement is necessary to avoid nestiing of the clutch pack.

C. Alternately, install composition and steel plates so that notches on the the first and third steel plates are on one side of a wide lug and the second and fourth steel plate notches are on the opposite side.

4. Install long case center support key with longer lip toward front of case. Hold in place with petrolatum.

5. Mark case to indicate sides of key to help in alignment for installation of case center support.

6. Install neutral and reverse clutch assembly (case center support) into case, aligning support key into key way. Make sure oil rings did not come unhooked during installation.

7. Install reverse stationary cone key into case, rounded side toward front of case.

8. Install reverse cone (steel) into case cover reverse piston.

9. Install reverse stationary cone (plastic) in case, aligning stationary cone key with key way in cone, tapping into place if required.

10. Install large reverse cone snap ring into snap ring groove in case with flat ends of snap ring "UP", and ring gap at open segment of ring groove.

11. Reposition transmission, rear end "UP", and install overrun band over anchor in case.

12. Install rear unit internal gear, sprag assembly and sprag retainer into case, aligning neutral clutch plates with sprag outer race. Be sure sprag retainer bottoms in place.

13. Reposition transmission, "Bottom up."

FRONT UNIT AND REAR UNIT

1. Install front clutch assembly into front of transmission engaging teeth in front clutch hub with reverse cone. Be sure bronze washer is positioned in the counterbore of front clutch drum.

2. Install thick bearing race, thrust bearing, thin cupped bearing race on front sun gear and shaft assembly.

3. Install front sun gear and shaft assembly through case center support. Align the splines of sun gear shaft with rear internal gear and cutaway splines with sprag retainer.
   Note: Hold rear unit internal gear forward during this operation.

4. Install front sun gear shaft-to-rear unit internal gear snap ring.

5. Install bearing race (flange up) and bearing on rear planet carrier. Hold in place with petrolatum.

6. Install rear planet carrier through front unit sun gear

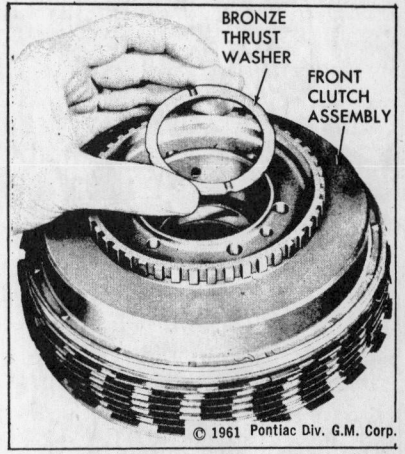

Thrust washer in front clutch

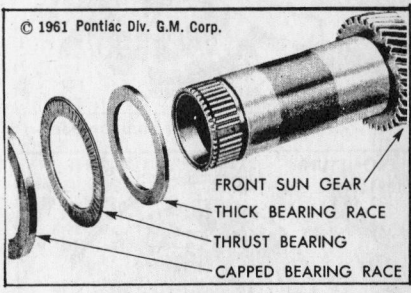

Front sun gear

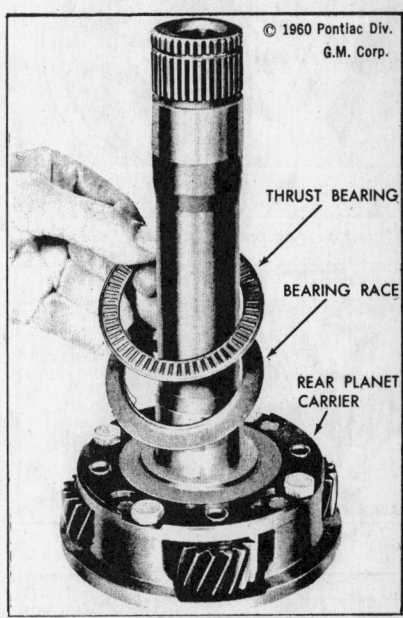

Thrust bearing plan on rear planet carrier

shaft from rear of transmission.

7. Install front carrier thrust bearing race onto rear carrier shaft, inner flange out.

8. Install front carrier thrust bearing.

9. Install bearing race, outer flange "IN".

10. Holding the rear planet carrier

903

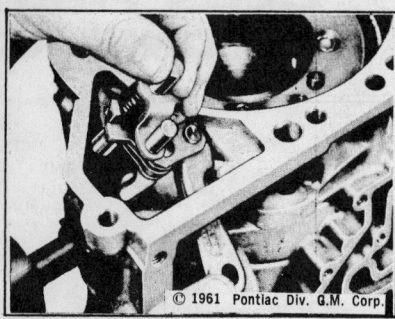

Installing parking linkage in case

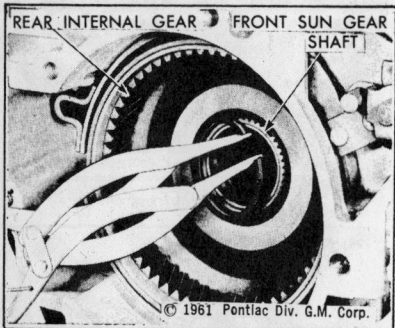

Installing snap ring on front sun gear

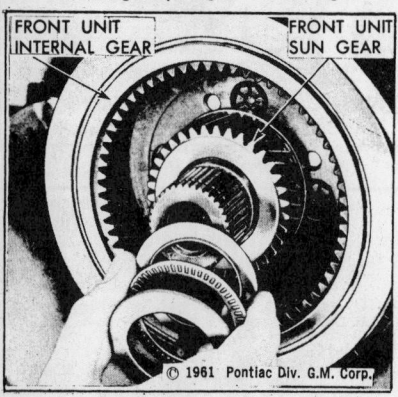

Thrust bearing and races on front sun gear

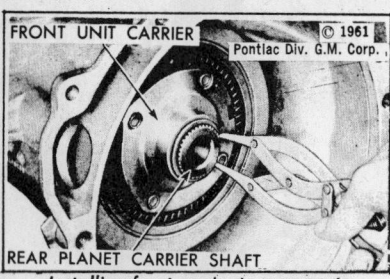

Installing front carrier to rear carrier shaft snap ring

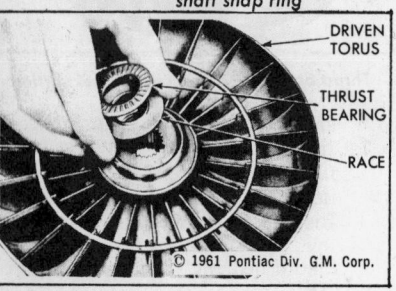

Thrust bearing in driven torus

forward, install front carrier.

11. Install front carrier-to-rear planet carrier shaft snap ring.
12. Reposition transmission, rear end "UP".

PARKING LINKAGE

1. Install pawl spacer in case.
2. Install parking assembly, parking pawl first, through opening in rear of case.
3. Install pawl pin into case, through pawl and spacer.
4. Push parking bracket to bottom of bore.
5. Move pawl to its disengaged position.

OUTPUT SHAFT AND GOVERNOR

1. Install rear unit sun gear-to-rear carrier bearing race into rear carrier, flange up. Hold with petrolatum.
2. Install thrust bearing into bearing race.
3. Assemble rear unit sun gear-to-mainshaft and install through rear carrier.
4. Install gasket and governor on output shaft.
5. Install speedometer drive gear. Drive the gear on until rear side of gear is 6-9/32" from end of output shaft.
6. Install output shaft to rear carrier assembly using alignment marks.
7. Engage parking pawl.
8. Install 4 governor attaching bolts. Torque to 19-23 ft. lbs.
9. Install snap ring on front output shaft groove.

REAR BEARING RETAINER

1. Install rear bearing retainer gasket on bearing retainer with petrolatum.
2. Start bearing retainer down over output shaft and install output shaft snap ring through access hole and over end of output shaft while retainer is lowered over governor.
3. Align parking linkage pin and manual detent lever as bearing retainer is aligned with dowel pin in case.
4. Seat rear bearing snap ring.
5. Install 2 short rear bearing-to-case bolts and center location on each side. Install the remaining short bolt inside the bearing retainer. Install 5 remaining long bolts. Torque all bolts 20-25 ft. lbs.
6. Install new rear seal.
7. Install rear bearing retainer cover plate and gasket with 4 bolts.
8. Reposition transmission, "Front

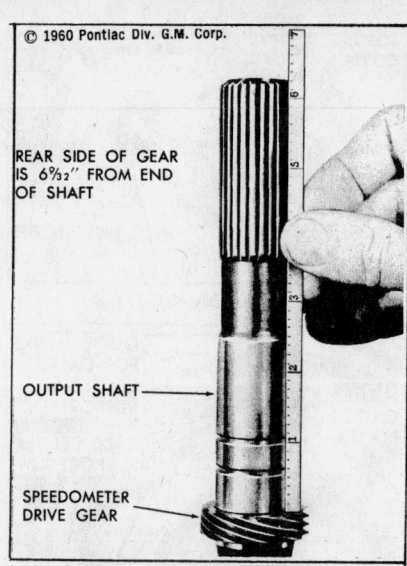

Locating speedometer drive gear

REAR SIDE OF GEAR IS 6⁹⁄₃₂" FROM END OF SHAFT

OUTPUT SHAFT

SPEEDOMETER DRIVE GEAR

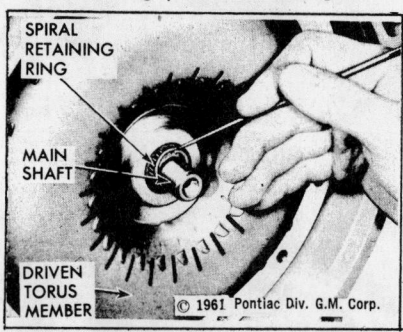

SPIRAL RETAINING RING

MAIN SHAFT

DRIVEN TORUS MEMBER

Install spiral retaining spring

end up."

TORUS

1. Install front unit drive torus aligning front unit clutch plates with drive slots in drive torus.
2. Install hook type oil ring on torque multiplier hub.
3. Install hook type oil ring on front and rear hubs of driven torus member.
4. Install torque multiplier into drive torus aligning splines and position torque multiplier so that the I.D. of the hub of the torque multiplier is flush with the planet carrier shaft. A light tap with soft hammer may be needed.
5. Install driven torus-to-torque multiplier rear bearing race into torque multiplier.
6. Install flanged race, flange up, into driven torus.
7. Install bearing into flange race, hold with petrolatum.
8. Install driven torus member over main shaft.
9. Reposition transmission just 90° so bottom is "UP" (Don't go further, parts will fall out).
10. While moving main shaft forward, install driven torus-to-main shaft spiral retaining ring.

© 1961 Pontiac Div. G.M. Corp.

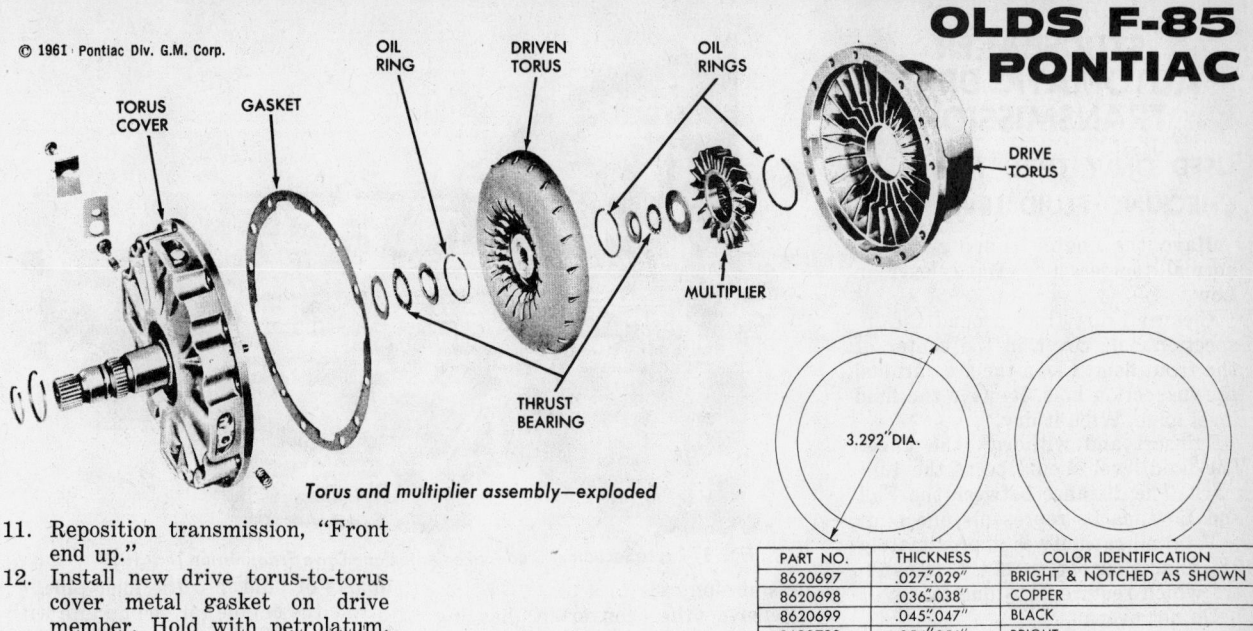

Torus and multiplier assembly—exploded

PART NO.	THICKNESS	COLOR IDENTIFICATION
8620697	.027″-.029″	BRIGHT & NOTCHED AS SHOWN
8620698	.036″-.038″	COPPER
8620699	.045″-.047″	BLACK
8620700	.054″-.056″	BRIGHT

Table of selective washers

11. Reposition transmission, "Front end up."
12. Install new drive torus-to-torus cover metal gasket on drive member. Hold with petrolatum.
13. Install flat bearing race.
14. Install bearing into flanged race.
15. Install bearing and flanged race into torus cover, flange down.
16. Install torus cover-to-drive torus member, aligning the dowel pins.
17. Install 12 torus cover-to-drive torus bolts and torque to 17-20 ft. lbs.

CASE COVER

1. With a new gasket in place, install case cover and pump assembly on transmission case.
2. Install 5 large case cover-to-case bolts (leave one hole to install dial indicator support. Torque to 30-35 ft. lbs. of the 3 small attaching bolts, the one long bolt is attached from the front of the cover. The 2 remaining cover bolts are installed from the rear of the case cover. Torque 3 short bolts 15-18 ft. lbs.
3. Rotate transmission so front end is "UP."
4. Install front seal, rubber lip down. Rotate transmission back to "Bottom Up" position.

Front Unit End Play Check

A. Rotate transmission, "Bottom Up."
B. Install dial indicator into the open bolt hole in transmission case.
C. Assemble end play adapter on input shaft of torus cover.
D. Clamp dial indicator on support and index the indicator with the end of the end play adapter.
E. Position a screwdriver through the case, behind the flange on the output shaft.
F. Gently pry forward on the shaft to position units in extreme forward position.

G. Zero the indicator. Then push the shaft and units rearward and read the gauge.
H. End play should be .006″ to .018″.
Note: If end play is not within limits, remove case cover and install proper thrust washers between case cover and torus cover to produce .006″ to .018″. Replace cover and recheck end play.
I. Remove tools.
J. Install remaining cover-to-case attaching bolt and torque to 30-35 ft. lb.

VALVE BODY AND OIL PAN

1. Install manual valve in valve body.
2. Lubricate the pipe ports and install valve body assembly to rear bearing retainer, guiding T.V. shaft through opening in rear bearing retainer and position manual valve on pick up pin. Position pipe assembly to index with pipe ports in valve body and move forward to seat pipe seals. Secure valve body assembly with 5 bolts. Torque to 6-8 ft. lbs.
3. Install throttle shaft seal over T.V. shaft into case.
4. Install a case-to-strainer neck "O" ring in case bore.
5. Install strainer with neck in case bore. Secure strainer in position with accumulator attaching bolt. Torque to 6-8 ft. lbs.
6. Install oil pan, with new gasket. Secure with 21 bolts, torque to 12-15 ft. lbs.
7. Install outer shift lever and T.V. lever.
8. Install speedometer driven gear.

SERVO AND ACCUMULATOR

1. Install accumulator pin into case.
2. Install upper accumulator spring, small end first.
3. Install new piston seal with lip of seal facing flat side of piston.
4. Install upper piston with lip of seal facing away from tapered spring.
5. Install lower accumulator piston ring on piston.
6. Install lower piston over pin with spring pocket facing out.
7. Install lower accumulator spring into spring pocket.
8. Install servo release spring.
9. Install servo piston assembly, stem first.
10. Install 3 case center support-to-case seals and springs, seals down.
11. Install servo and accumulator gasket on servo and accumulator cover.
12. Install servo cover. Use 4 bolts to locate the cover, then align the springs. Then install all the cover bolts and torque to 6-8 ft. lbs.
13. Install 8 servo and accumulator cover bolts. Torque to 6-8 ft. lbs.
14. Install compensator body assembly on accumlator cover with 3 screws and 1 bolt. Torque screws to 2½-3½ ft. lb. and the bolt to 6-8 ft. lbs.
15. Install seals on both ends of pipe assembly.
16. Install pipe assembly, fixed end first, into case cover through case opening.
17. Install seal and washer on pipe assembly attaching bolt, then install bolt-to-pipe assembly from from front side of case cover.

STUDEBAKER AUTOMATIC DRIVE

STUDEBAKER AUTOMATIC DRIVE TRANSMISSION

USED ONLY THRU 1955
CHECKING FLUID LEVEL

Have the engine running and at normal temperature. Hand lever in Low.

Clean all dirt from around the inspection hole cover in the center of the front floor. Clean the area around the inspection hole. Remove the fluid level gage. Wipe it dry.

Reinsert and withdraw the gage. The fluid level should be at the Full mark. The distance between the Full and Low marks represents one pint.

Total oil capacity is approximately 9½ quarts except on 17A Commanders which require 11½ quarts.

Do not overfill.

FLUID CHANGE INTERVAL

Change fluid every 15,000 miles or every year whichever is first.

Use a good grade of Automatic Transmission Fluid.

DRAINING PROCEDURE

Have the car level and set the hand brake. Idle the engine with the hand lever at Low until normal operating temperature has been reached.

Stop the engine, remove the inspection hole cover. Clean the area around the inspection hole and remove the dip stick.

Remove the transmission oil pan drain plug and catch the oil from the

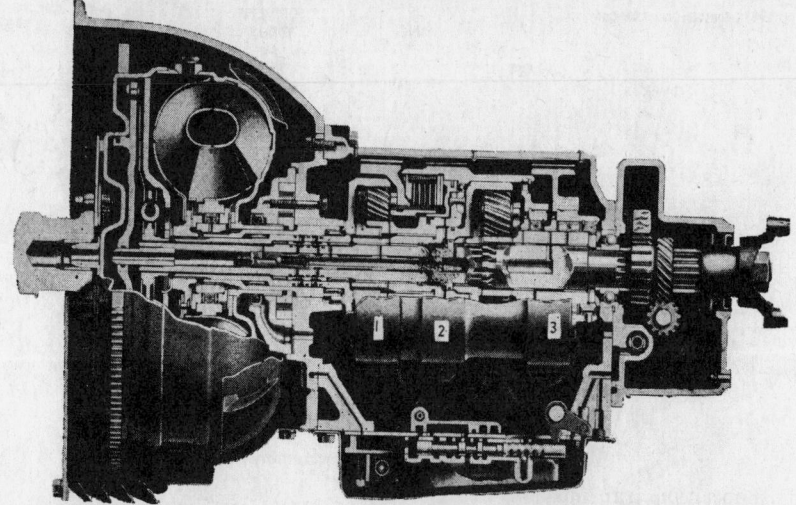

Fig. 1—Cross Section of Studebaker Automatic Drive Transmission Thru 1955

transmission case in a pan.

Remove the converter housing cover.

Note: This converter has only one drain plug. The other plug is not a plug at all, it is a balancing weight. Figs. 5 & 6.

Rotate the converter until the drain plug is down and remove it.

In order for the converter to drain properly air must get into it. It is therefore necessary to remove the pipe plug in the No. 1 servo as shown. Fig. 4. The plug has two possible locations but there is no choice on any particular No. 1 servo body. Catch the oil as it flows from the converter drain.

Replace the drain plugs. Pour 5

quarts of fluid into the filler pipe.

Idle the engine for one minute with the hand lever at Low. Then still idling in Low pour in three more quarts of fluid. Move the lever through the different positions. Return it to Low and check the level. Add more fluid, enough to bring the level to Full. Do not overfill.

BAND ADJUSTMENT

The bands are adjustable without disturbing the transmission. The adjusting screw for the No. 1 band is the forward screw in the 2-3 servo casting. The adjusting screw of the No. 2 band is the rearward screw in the No. 1 servo casting. The adjustment screw for the No. 3 band is behind the manual valve control lever.

TO ADJUST ANY BAND

Loosen and back off the lock nut on the adjusting screw of the band to be adjusted a way.

Using a short wrench turn the adjusting screw in until it is snug. Back the screw off 4 (four) complete turns. Hold it so and tighten the lock nut.

IDLING SPEED ADJUSTMENT

The idling speed should be adjusted to 500-550 rpm with the engine warm and the choke wide open.

TOWING THE CAR

Never tow a car with automatic drive at any speed over 30 mph.

With the transmission in Neutral the car can be towed indefinitely—at speeds below 30 mph—without harm to the transmission.

If the hand control lever cannot be used to put the car in Neutral disconnect the rod at the valve control lever on the transmission.

The valve control lever is the forward one of the two levers at the left rear of the transmission. Move the lever counterclockwise until it stops then move it clockwise one detent.

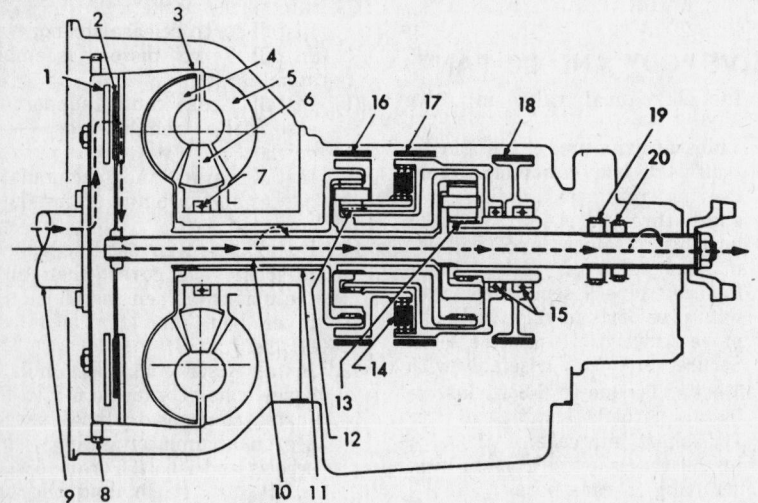

Fig. 2—Power Flow in Drive Position—Direct

1. D. D. clutch piston
2. D. D. clutch
3. Torque converter
4. Turbine
5. Impeller
6. Stator
7. Free wheel unit
8. Starter gear
9. Crankshaft
10. Main shaft
11. Front ring gear
12. Front planetary set
13. Rear planetary set
14. Multiple disc clutch
15. Free wheel unit
16. Reverse band
17. Low band
18. Forward band (applied)
19. Parking brake gear
20. Drive gear for rear pump, governor, and speedometer

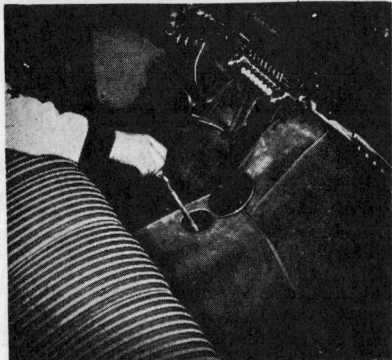

Fig. 3—Removing Fluid Level Gage

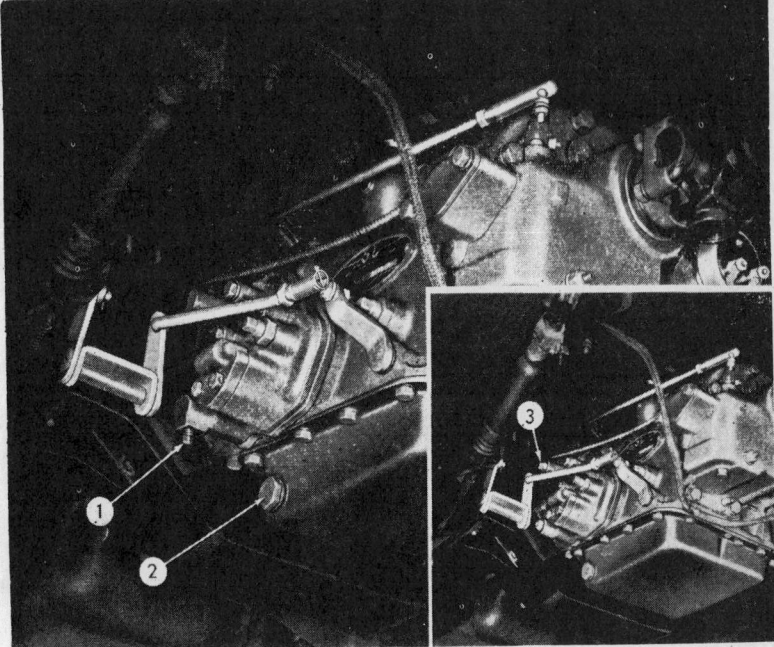

1. Converter air vent to facilitate draining. Type 1
2. Transmission oil pan drain plug
3. Converter air vent. Type 2

Fig. 4—Location of Transmission Drain Plug and the two possible locations of the Converter Air Vent used when draining it

Fig. 5—Torque Converter Assembly Showing Attaching Bolts and Pilot. Arrow points to weight which balances drain plug on opposite side

This will be Neutral position. There is no need to fasten the lever—the detent will hold it firmly. In Neutral position the lever is directly in front of the No. 3 band adjusting screw.

If the transmission has been damaged disconnect the drive shaft.

STARTING THE CAR WITHOUT USE OF THE STARTER

Caution: Never tow the car to start it. The engine might pick up very quickly and the towed car is very likely to hit the towing car before the brakes can stop it.

Turn the ignition switch on. Depress and release the accelerator pedal once to squirt a little gas in the intake manifold. Move the hand lever to Neutral position. Have the car pushed. When it has reached a speed of 20 to 30 mph move the hand lever to Drive or Low, depending on road conditions, and the engine will turn.

TROUBLE SHOOTING CHART
Items Ending With An X Require Removal of the Transmission To Correct

1. Transmission Fluid Foams Out

This trouble is probably due to:
Too high a fluid level which permits the planet gears to aerate the fluid.

2. Car Will Not Move in Any Range—Rear Wheels Turn Freely

This trouble may be due to:
Worn or misadjusted bands. X
Maladjusted controls.
Fluid level too low.

Defective pressure regulator.
Leaks in the hydraulic system. X
Defective front oil pump. X
Defective converter. X

3. Car Will Not Move in Any Range—Rear Wheels Locked

This trouble can be due to:
Maladjusted controls.
Broken part in transmission or differential. X
Solenoid of anti-creep grounded.

4. Excessive Slip Below 25 MPH in All Ranges

This trouble can be due to:
Low front pump pressure. X
Broken fins in the converter. (This will be audible and requires replacement of the converter.) X

5. Excessive Slip in Intermediate
This trouble can be due to:
No. 3 band worn out. X

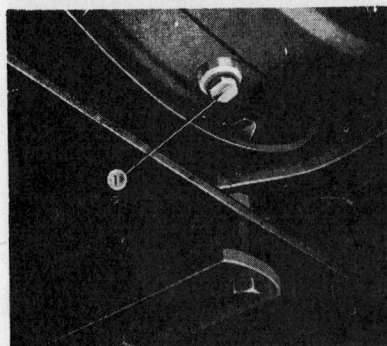

Fig. 6—Arrow No. 1 points to the Converter Drain Plug

1. Test point for No. 3 servo
2. Test point for No. 2 servo
3. Adjusting screw for No. 1 band.

Fig. 7—View of 2-3 Servo Casting Showing No. 1 Band Adjusting Screw on Right Side of Case

1. No. 3 band adjusting screw
2. No. 2 band adjusting screw
3. Test point for No. 1 servo

Fig. 8—View of Left Side Transmission Case Showing Adjusting Screws for No. 2 and No. 3 Bands

Incorrect adjustment of the No. 3 band.

Sprag type free wheeling clutch in No. 3 drum not holding (in which case there should be slippage in Low and the hill holder will slip). X

Stuck No. 3 servo.

6. Excessive Slip in Reverse

This trouble can be due to:

No. 1 band worn out. X

Incorrect adjustment of the No. 1 band.

Stuck No. 1 servo.

Sprag type free wheeling clutch in No. 2 drum not holding (in which case hill holder won't work). X

7. Excessive Slip in Low

This trouble can be due to:

No. 2 band worn out. X

Incorrect adjustment of the No. 2 band.

Stuck No. 2 servo.

8. Slip During Acceleration in Drive Position and Hill Holder Does Not Work

This trouble can be due to:

Defective multiple disk clutch. X

Worn facings on the plates. X

Blocked oil passages. X

Stuck clutch piston. X

Two spring retainer plates in the clutch interchanged. X

9. Fails to Shift to Direct Drive or Slips After the Single Plate Clutch Is Engaged

This trouble can be due to:

Improper governor valve operation.

Converter pressure too high.

Single plate clutch defective. X

Oil seal rings on main shaft broken. X

10. Engine Cannot Be Turned by Pushing Car

This trouble can be due to:

A malfunction of the rear pump.

11. Engine Labors or Stalls When Hand Lever Is Moved to Direct Drive

This trouble can be due to:

Improper linkage adjustment.

Something wrong with the governor valve.

Broken oil seal rings on the main shaft. X

12. The Engine Shudders or Stalls When the Car Is Stopped with Hand Lever at Drive Position

This trouble is due to:

The single plate clutch in the converter failing to release. X

Improperly adjusted controls.

Improper governor operation.

Broken oil seal rings on the main shaft. X

13. Transmission Will Not Kick Down at All or Does So at Wrong Speed

This trouble can be due to:

Improperly adjusted controls.

Oil level too high.

Governor adjusting screw at tail of transmission assembly requires adjustment.

14. Reverse Interlock Fails to Function

This trouble can be due to:

Inoperative rear pump.

Defective interlock valve.

15. Parking Lock Interlock Fails to Operate

This trouble can be due to:

Inoperative rear pump.

16. Engine Works Hard and Car Performs Badly in All Positions Except Reverse

This trouble can be caused by:

A dragging No. 1 band.

Leaks in the hydraulic system.

No. 1 servo piston stuck.

17. Car Runs Fine in Low but Performs Badly in All Other Ranges

This trouble can be caused by:

A dragging No. 2 band.

Leaks in the hydraulic valve system.

No. 2 servo piston stuck.

18. Poor Performance in Reverse

This trouble can be due to:

The No. 3 band dragging.

Leaks in the hydraulic system.

No. 3 servo piston stuck.

19. Poor Performance in All Ranges Except Drive

This trouble can be due to:

The multiple disc clutch dragging. X

20. Normal Operation at Low Speeds—Transmission Overheats in Direct Drive

This trouble is due to:

Stator free wheel unit in the converter sticking. Replace the converter. X

21. Normal Operation with Single Plate Clutch Engaged, Poor Performance Otherwise. Stall Speed Below Normal

This trouble is due to:

Stator free wheel unit in the converter slipping. Stall speed should be about 1500 rpm. If it is not, replace the converter. X

22. Transmission Noisy When Car Is Standing Still and Hand Lever Is at Drive, Low or Reverse

This trouble can be due to:

Low fluid level.

Fluid intake screen clogged.

Damaged front pump drive. X

Worn front pump. X

Air leaks in lines to front pump. X

Loose direct drive clutch backing plate. X

23. Transmission Is Noisy When

Car is Going Forward

This trouble can be due to:

Worn rear pump. X

Worn speedometer drive gear.

Worn gears in the planet sets. X

Damaged governor assembly.

Defective converter. X

MECHANICAL DETAIL

Torque Specifications

	Ft Lb
Case to bell housing	35-40
Bell housing to engine	28-32
Converter to drive plate	23-28
Universal joint flange nut	60-80
Band adjusting screw lock nut	40-50
Oil pan drain plug	35-45
Rear extension to case	28-33
Valve block to case	10-13

CONVERTER REMOVAL

With transmission out of car, converter can be unbolted from crankshaft plate and lowered. The converter is a welded assembly. It cannot be repaired in the field.

CONVERTER INSTALLATION

When reinstalling the converter bolt it to flywheel flange. Using aligning tool J-4283 to get splines in position and with oil tube in front end of main shaft, Fig. 9, slide the transmission into place.

When in place the converter is well within the bell housing and turns freely with no noise.

Fig. 9—Install Oil Tube in Front End of Main Shaft. Tapered End Out

FRONT OIL PUMP REMOVAL

The transmission must be out of the car for this operation.

Unbolt the stator reactor shaft (called the collector ring) and front oil pump assembly from the transmission case. Fig. 10. Fasten the front-planet-ring-gear-shaft to the main shaft so that when the collector-ring-oil-pump-assembly is slid forward the ring gear does not also come forward and allow the ring-gear-to-front-planet-carrier-thrust-washer to drop out of place. Fig. 11. The front oil pump is held to the collector ring by bolts from the rear side.

The bolts holding the collector ring to the transmission case and the bolts which hold the pump to the ring are of different lengths but the difference is hard to note and a lot of assembly time will be saved if the attaching bolts of these and other units in the

Fig. 10—Arrows Indicate Bolts Holding Collector Ring to Case

transmission are kept separate one from the other.

There is a tanged thrust washer which fits between the collector ring and the front planet ring gear. There is one long special bolt which with four other special bolts serves to hold the oil pump to the collector ring. Fig. 12.

Fig. 11—Block Shaft of Front Planet Ring Gear Against Main Shaft So That Gear Does Not Come Off with Front Pump. Assembly No. 1 is a rubber band. No. 2 is a block that fits the groove in the main shaft.

FRONT OIL PUMP DISASSEMBLY

Note that there is a large "O" ring seal between the rear face of the pump and front face of the collector ring. Note also the small "O" ring seal in the oil drain hole in the rear face of the pump. Fig. 13. This hole drains the front oil seal through the boss cast in the front face of the pump. When the pump assembly is reinstalled onto the transmission case this boss helps to locate the collector ring passages with those in the case. The assembly is installed so that the boss points down toward the bottom of the transmission.

FRONT OIL PUMP INSTALLATION

Reverse the removal procedure to reinstall. The thrust washer which goes between the collector ring and the front face of the front planet ring gear is the selective thrust washer for the transmission. Fig. 12. Should this washer require renewal be sure the replacement carries the same code number. There should be very little end play of the front planet ring gear shaft when the front pump assembly is fastened in place.

Fig. 12—Rear Face of Collector Ring. Note special bolt which locates front oil pump, and notched thrust washer, which is the selected, numbered thrust washer controlling End Play of the front ring gear shaft

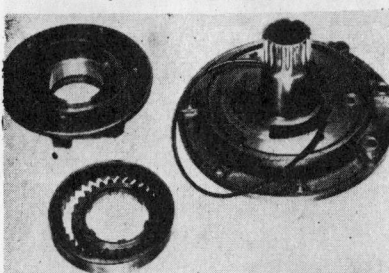

Fig. 13—Front Oil Pump Disassembled

VALVE BODY REMOVAL

The valve body can be removed from the transmission without removing the transmission from the car. Drain the converter and the

Fig. 14—Arrows Point to Bolts Holding Valve Block to Case

transmission. Remove fourteen bolts to release the oil pan.

Remove the seven screws which retain the valve block assembly to the case. Fig. 14. Note that the lever which moves the manual control valve rides toward the inside of the operating slot in the valve.

When removing the assembly from the case do not touch the manual control valve. This valve has a detent ball and spring to keep it in position. If the valve is accidentally pushed into the valve body the detent ball is likely to engage the operating slot. Fig. 15. The operating slot has square, sharp edges which effectively prevent any further movement of the valve. Should this happen it will be necessary to drill a small hole in the casting as shown in Fig. 16.

VALVE BODY DISASSEMBLY

The valve body has two main parts separated by a base plate. To the upper side of the base plate is fastened a casting containing the converter valve and the reverse interlock valve assemblies.

Reach into the hole (Fig. 16) with a pick and force the ball down into the cavity against its spring so that the valve can be turned to put its round side nearest the ball. (Use pliers on the end nearest the operating slot.)

1. Manual Valve (note operating slot)
2. Detent Ball
3. Detent Spring
4. Detent Cavity

Fig. 15—Showing Relation of Detent Ball to Manual Valve

Fig. 16—Arrow Points to Hole Drilled in Detent Cavity so that Detent Ball Could Be Pushed Down and Manual Valve Released

Then push the valve out of the body toward the end away from the detent.

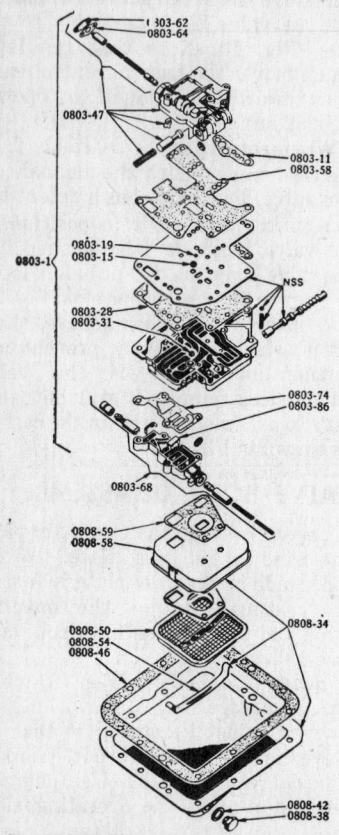

Fig. 17—Exploded view of Valve Block Assembly Showing Studebaker Numbers

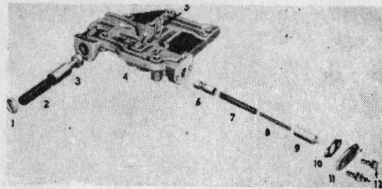

1. Retainer
2. Spring
3. Reverse interlock valve piston
4. Upper casting
5. Stop plate
6. Converter valve piston
7. Outer spring
8. Inner spring
9. Converter valve compensating piston
10. Gasket
11. Cover plate
12. Cover plate screw

Fig. 18—Upper Casting of Valve Block Assembly Disassembled

REAR EXTENSION REMOVAL

The separate casting at the rear of the transmission is called the rear extension. It houses the governor and the governor drive, together with the speedometer and rear oil pump drives, and the parking brake. The rear extension can be removed without removing the transmission from the car.

Disconnect the drive shaft at the

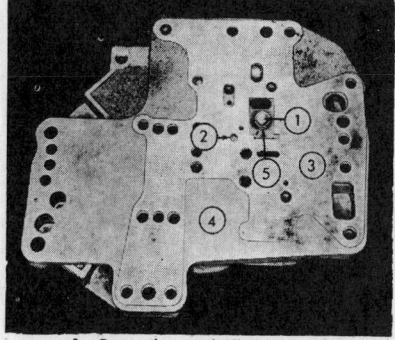

1. Rear oil pump ball check valve
2. Converter ball check
3. Upper casting gasket
4. Base plate
5. Ball check seat in base plate

Fig. 19—Remove gasket and two Ball Checks from Base Plate

Fig. 20—Remove Base Plate from Lower Portion of Valve Body

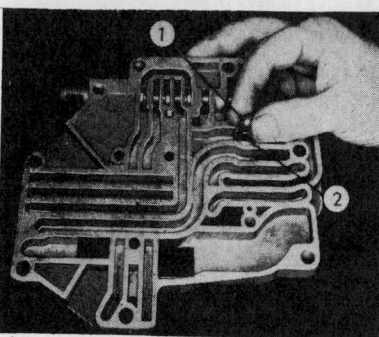

1. Front pump ball check valve
2. Check valve seat

Fig. 21—Remove Front Oil Pump Ball Check Valve from Power Portion of Valve Body

front "U" joint and, holding the transmission main shaft with the parking brake, remove the "U" joint front yoke. Disconnect the hand shift rod from the manual valve control lever. Disconnect the throttle rod from the governor control lever. Disconnect the speedometer cable. Disconnect the wires from the No. 2 Anti-Creep switch.

If the transmission is still in the car provide a pan to catch the fluid that may be trapped in the extension.

Unfasten six bolts and remove the rear extension from the case.

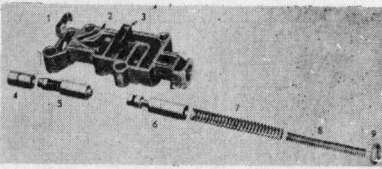

1. Retainer
2. Oil pump relief valve body
3. Screen (not on all models)
4. Front oil pump relief valve piston sleeve.
5. Front oil pump relief valve pistons and spring
6. Rear oil pump relief valve piston
7. Outer spring
8. Inner spring
9. Retainer

Fig. 22—Front and Rear Oil Pump Relief Valve Body Disassembled

REAR EXTENSION OVERHAUL

There are two types of governor assemblies. Those for the Champions and for late model Commanders do not have the direct drive (single plate) clutch lock. This lock prevents dropping out of direct drive unless the accelerator is floored. Champions and late model Commanders can downshift from direct drive to intermediate at any speed between 20 and 30 mph.

Check the governor parts for ease of operation. There should not be more than .030 in. free play of the governor valve fork on the governor collar. Fig. 23.

Check the hydraulic detent piston in the governor valve sleeve. The stepped end of the detent goes in first. Fig. 24.

Note that the parking interlock piston spring is installed ahead of the piston (Fig. 25) while the governor control detent piston goes in pointed end first ahead of the spring. Fig. 26.

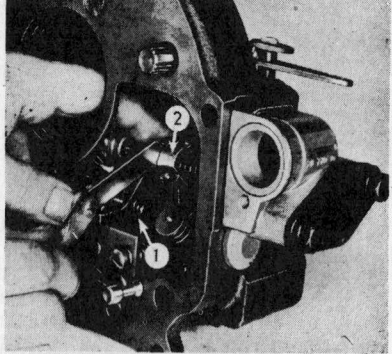

Fig. 23—Checking free play of No. 1 the Governor Fork on No. 2 the Governor Collar

REAR EXTENSION INSTALLATION

Reverse the removal procedure to reinstall. The passages in the case and those in the gasket and the extension must be carefully alined.

Fig. 24—Checking the Hydraulic Detent Piston (No. 1) in the Governor Valve Sleeve

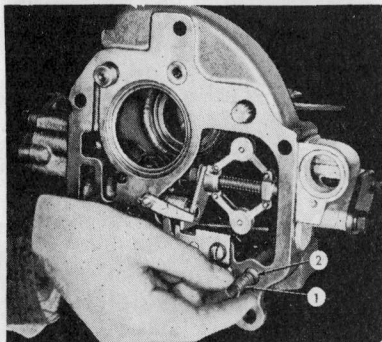

Fig. 25—Install the Parking Interlock Piston Spring (No. 2) ahead of the Piston (No. 1)

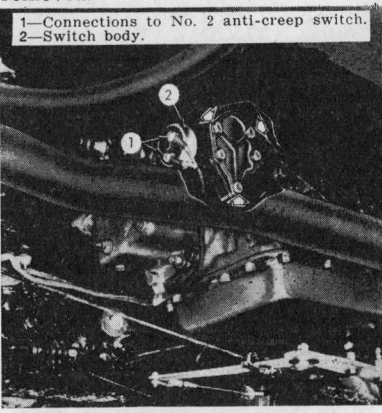

Fig. 26—Install the Governor Control Detent Piston (No. 2) ahead of the Spring (No. 1)

REAR OIL PUMP OVERHAUL

Three screws hold the rear oil pump housing and cover to the rear extension. Fig. 27. Although the pump on some models can be removed without first removing the rear extension from the transmission, the easiest way is to remove the rear extension first.

Remove the No. 2 Anti-Creep switch from the body of the rear oil pump and check that the hole is clear.

The rear oil pump is a spur gear pump and is serviced as an assembly. The pump cover gasket can be renewed. Two screws hold the pump cover to the pump body. The thickness of the pump cover gaskets is critical. The gaskets come in colors for easy identification. Red gaskets are .002 in. thick. Green and clear gaskets are .003 in. thick. Blue gas-

kets are .005 in. thick. Always use a gasket of the same thickness as that removed.

1—Connections to No. 2 anti-creep switch.
2—Switch body.

Fig. 27—Arrows Point to Bolts Holding Rear Pump to Extension

GEAR TRAIN REMOVAL AND DISASSEMBLY

The transmission must be out of the car for this operation. Remove the rear extension, the front oil pump and the valve body.

1. Narrow spacer   2. Parking lock ratchet gear
3. Governor drive gear   4. Wide spacer

Fig. 28—Sequence of Installation of Gears on Tail of Main Shaft

Fig. 29—Removing Gear Train Assembly thru Front of Transmission Case

← FRONT OF CAR

Fig. 30—Transmission Gear Train Assembly Distance between the end of the front planet ring gear shaft and front end of the main shaft, as indicated by the lines, should be 1 3/16" when assembled. Note drum assemblies 1, 2, and 3

The gear train consists of a main shaft and three drum assemblies. The main shaft runs from the direct drive, single plate clutch in the converter, all the way through the transmission

case to the "U" joint. The three drum assemblies ride on the main shaft. To remove the gear train from the transmission case, tap the rear end of the mainshaft with a soft hammer to re-

Fig. 31—Removing Front Planet Ring Gear Numbers indicate drum assemblies starting from the front of car

1. Toothed thrust washer
2. Rear planet ring gear shaft
3. Front face of front planet pinion carrier

Fig. 32—Looking Into Front of No. 1 Drum Assembly Note thrust washer. Steel face goes toward back

Fig. 33—Removing the No. 1 Drum Assembly over front end of mainshaft

Fig. 34—Looking Into Rear of No. 1 Drum Assembly. No. 1 is a notched thrust washer. Its steel face goes toward the rear. No. 2 is the rear of the front planet pinion carrier

Fig. 35—Remove the Bearing Spacer and the No. 3 Drum over rear end of mainshaft

Fig. 36—Exploded View of No. 3 Drum. The Face of the sprag cage with an arrow on it goes in first. Front of car is to the left. Note spacer dowel

Fig. 37—Removing the Spacer and Thrust Washer from Rear of Rear Planet Sun Gear. Steel Face of Washer Goes to the Rear

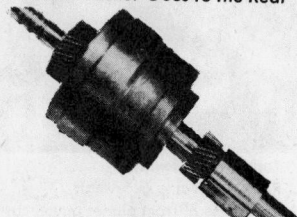

Fig. 38—Removing Rear Planet Sun Gear over rear end of mainshaft. Note length of gear shaft

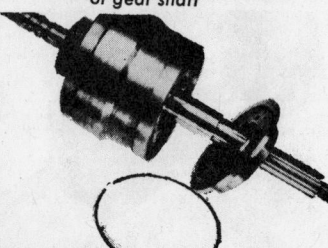

Fig. 39—Remove Lock Plate from Rear of No. 2 Drum and over rear end of mainshaft

Fig. 40—Disassembly of No. 2 Drum Lock Plate. The face of the sprag cage with an arrow on it goes in last. Front of car is to the left

Fig. 41—Removing No. 2 Drum Over Front End of Main Shaft

lease it from the rear bearing and remove the gear train through the front of the case as a unit. Fig. 29.

In this discussion the drum assemblies are referred to as number 1, 2, or 3, counting from the front of the transmission to the rear. Fig. 30. The No. 1 drum at the front end of the transmission is involved in reverse operation. The No. 2 drum (the middle drum) is for operation in low. The No. 3 drum (the farthest to the rear) is involved in all forward speeds.

The No. 1 drum contains the front planet gear set. The No. 2 drum contains the multiple disc clutch, the rear planet gear set and a sprag-type free wheeling clutch for reverse operation. The No. 3 drum contains a sprag-type free wheeling clutch which functions in all forward operation and in addition acts with the sprag clutch in the No. 2 drum to provide the No-Roll feature of the transmission in intermediate gear.

The drum assemblies can be removed from their position on the main shaft with little trouble.

INSTALLING THE SPRAG (ONE-WAY) CLUTCHES

In assembling the sprag clutch into the lock plate of the No. 2 drum the arrow on the sprag cage goes up. This sprag clutch locks onto the shaft of the rear-planet-sun-gear when the No. 2 drum is turned counterclockwise as viewed from the front of the car.

In assembling the sprag clutch into the No. 3 drum the arrow on the sprag cage goes down. This sprag clutch locks onto the shaft of the rear-planet-sun-gear when the rear-planet-sun-gear turns counterclockwise as viewed from the front.

MULTIPLE DISC CLUTCH

The gear train must be out of the transmission and disassembled before this procedure applies.

The multiple disc clutch is in the forward part of the No. 2 drum. Use a set up such as that shown Fig. 45 and put pressure on the plate which holds the clutch springs in place. Use sufficient pressure to permit removal of the lock ring.

Mark the top face of the spring retainer plate with the word TOP so that at assembly it will be easy to know that this is the top plate and this the top surface of it. Remove the plate and the springs. If the clutch has a centrifugal check valve, only twelve springs are used; eighteen springs are used if there is no check valve. The pattern for spring replacement is shown in Fig. 46.

Remove the clutch plates. On Commanders there are 5 externally splined and dished steel plates and 4 internally splined and lined plates. On Champions there are 4 of the steel plates

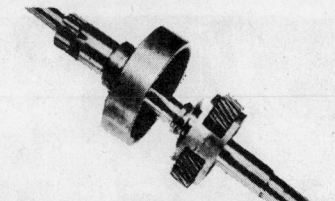

Fig. 42—Remove Rear Planet Ring Gear over front end of Main Shaft. Note plain thrust washer, steel face goes to the rear. Rear planet pinion carrier is locked to the main shaft

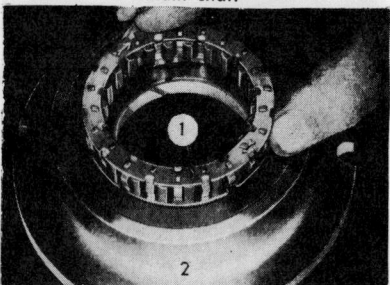

Fig. 43—Install Sprag Cage in Lock Plate of No. 2 Drum with Arrows Up. No. 1 is the sprag clutch and No. 2 is the lock plate of No. 2 Drum

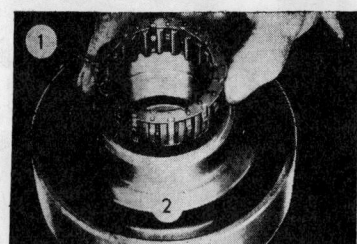

Fig. 44—Install Sprag Cage in No. 3 Drum with Arrows Down. No. 1 is the sprag clutch and No. 2 is the No. 3 Drum

Fig. 45—Putting Pressure on Clutch Release Spring Top Retainer Plate so as to be Able to Remove the Lock Ring

1. No. 2 drum
2. Piston inner seal
3. Clutch piston
4. Bottom spring retainer plate
5. Steel plates
6. Lined plates
7. Clutch springs
8. Top spring retainer plate
9. Lock ring

Fig. 47—Exploded View of Multiple Disc Clutch Used on Champion Models

Fig. 46—Pattern for Clutch Spring Replacement. Arrows indicate locations when 12 springs are used. Springs show location when 18 springs are used

Fig. 48—Layout of Parts of Multiple Disc Clutch Used on Commander Models

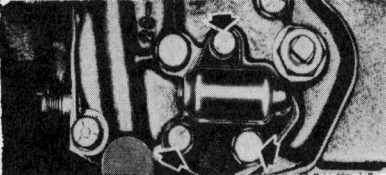

Fig. 50—Arrows Point to Bolts Holding Reverse Shuttle Valve Assembly to No. 1 Servo Body on left front

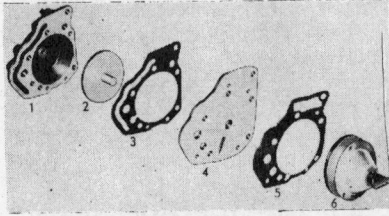

1. No. 1 servo body
2. Outer piston
3. Gasket body to plate
4. Body plate
5. Gasket body plate to case
6. Inner piston assembly.

Fig. 51—Exploded View of No. 1 Servo

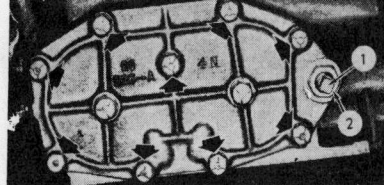

Fig. 52—Remove Bolts indicated by Arrows to Release the 2-3 Servo Casting from right rear corner of case

and 3 of the lined plates. In either case the dish must be in the same direction for all the steel plates. Check the amount of the "dish." It should be no more than .010 in.

Mark the top face of the bottom spring retainer plate with the word BOTTOM so that at reassembly the plate can be reinstalled in the proper position. The precaution of marking the two spring retainer plates is necessary because it is possible to interchange them. The bad results of doing so will not be noticeable until the transmission is back in the car.

The clutch piston should now be removed. Use some nails about as thick as the splines are deep to keep the piston seal from catching on the splines. Bend the end of a small screw driver at right angles to form a short hook and use this to work the piston seal into its groove first on one side and then on the other so that the piston can be withdrawn. The piston seal is made of either rubber or steel. The steel one is preferable. Note that the inner clutch piston seal is in a groove in the drum.

Coat all the parts well with transmission fluid and reverse the disassembly procedure to reassemble. Note that when installing the piston it is likely to hang up on the inner seal. Use the small screw driver hook to work the piston and the outer seal down into place. Check that it is truly in place with the little hook.

The bottom clutch spring retainer plate goes in splined end down. Be sure that the top spring retainer plate is properly indexed with the bottom spring retainer plate. Install the springs in the pattern shown in Fig. 46.

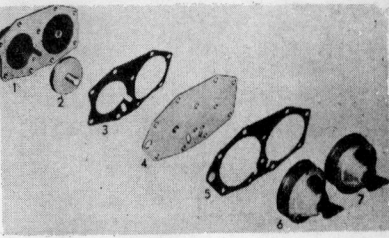

1. 2-3 servo casting
2. No. 2 servo outer piston (Commanders only)
3. Gasket casting to plate
4. Body plate
5. Gasket plate to case
6. No. 2 servo inner piston assembly
7. No. 3 servo piston assembly

Fig. 53—Exploded View of No. 2 and No. 3 Servos

BAND RENEWAL

The bands can only be renewed after the gear train has been removed from the case. Do not distort the bands to remove them. Be sure that the guide strip which holds the bands in position at the top of the case is firmly riveted to the case.

The No. 1 band (reverse) is thicker than the other two. The bands for No. 2 and No. 3 are identical. Install the bands so that the offset pins at the flanges are toward the respective servo pistons. Make sure that the pins are engaged in the notches provided. Check that the bands are properly positioned in the guide strap.

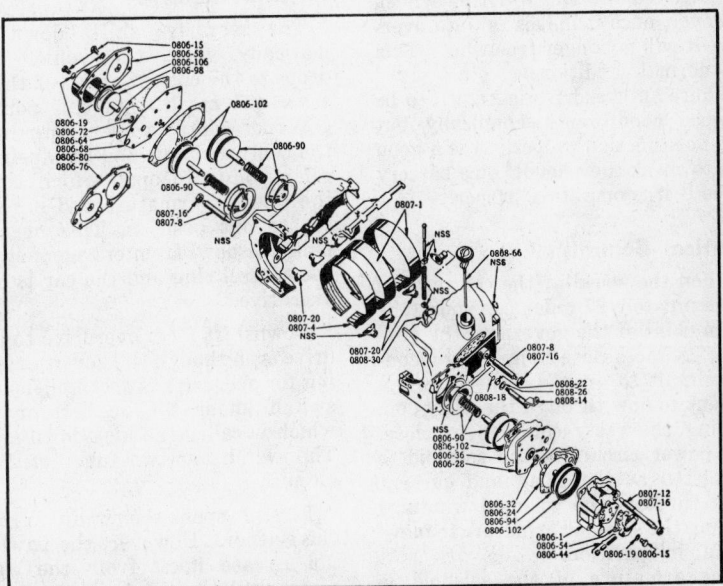

Fig. 49—Exploded View of Bands and Servos. Studebaker Numbers Shown

OVERDRIVE TRANSMISSION

OVERDRIVE ASSEMBLY

OPERATION OF THE OVERDRIVE

Mechanical Controls

An overdrive is designed so that when the instrument panel control knob is in the "in" position (overdrive functioning) the final drive is through a free wheeling clutch so that any time the car speed is greater than that of the engine free-wheeling takes place. However, if the car speed is greater than 27 m.p.h. the solenoid will act to lock the sun gear so that free-wheeling cannot occur.

Locking the sun gear causes the planetary pinions of the overdrive to rotate the internal ring gear at a greater speed than that of the input shaft. The increase of output over input speed is approximately 7:10. That is, for every .7 of a revolution of the input shaft the output makes a complete revolution.

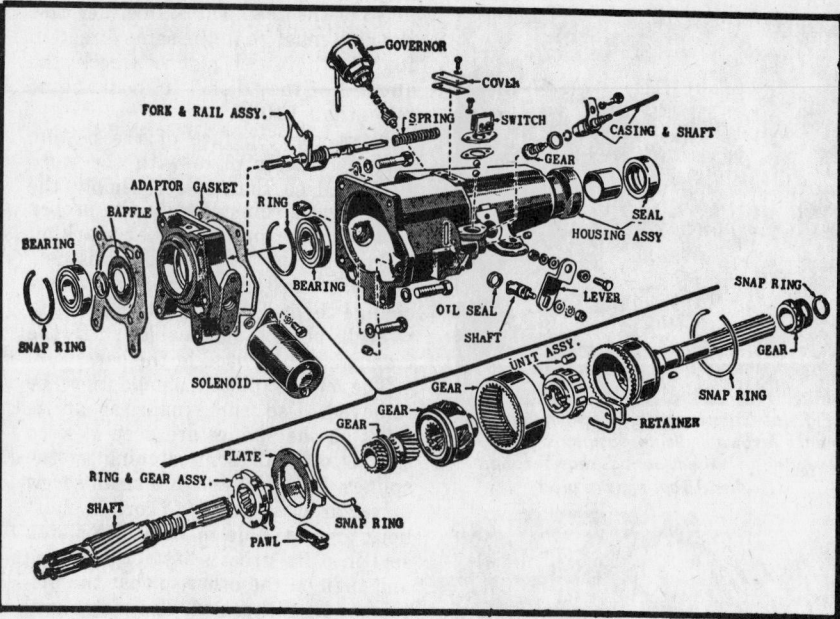

Overdrive assembly, Ford Installation Shown

When the dash control is pulled out, the shift rail is moved to the rear position. This causes the shifter fork to move the sun gear into engagement with the planet carrier, thus locking the two together. As a result the planetary gear set is locked and the output shaft rotates with the input shaft.

If the dash control is "in," and the manual gear shift lever is moved to reverse, the shift rail of the overdrive is moved to the rear by a cam on the transmission reverse gear fork. Thus the overdrive is automatically locked out when in reverse.

When the overdrive is operative but not engaged the car will free wheel. However, once it moves up into overdrive it will no longer free wheel. This is a normal condition.

Where an overdrive is known to be in good condition mechanically but does not function properly it is a good idea to check the solenoid on a battery to see if it is operating properly.

Electrical Controls

When the speed of the car reaches approximately 27 miles per hour (the cut in point of the governor) the governor contacts close completing a control circuit to ground. This causes a current to flow through the relay coil, causing the relay contacts to close. The power circuit to the solenoid is completed at the relay and current flows through the solenoid windings causing the solenoid armature to move to the "in" position.

The armature of the solenoid is moved by two coils, a "holding" coil and a "traction" coil. When the armature moves in, it automatically disconnects the "traction" coil and remains in position due to the "holding" coil which is lighter and takes less current.

The movement of the armature is conveyed to the pawl, which is to block the sun gear by a spring, so that the pawl is not forced into engagement but sits there waiting its chance to enter the notch in the sun gear control plate. This chance comes when the driver eases up on the accelerator momentarily, thus permitting the pawl to nudge the balk ring out of its way and engage the control plate. As soon as the pawl has engaged the plate the car is in overdrive.

The overdrive shifts down automatically when the vehicle speed drops to the cut-out speed of the governor (21 m.p.h.). At this point the governor contacts open, interrupting the control circuit and so causing the relay points to open which releases the solenoid armature and it returns to the out position. This of course pulls the pawl from engagement with the control ring and the car is out of overdrive.

Downshift from overdrive to direct drive even though the governor is calling for overdrive is accomplished by a switch under the accelerator pedal which is called the kick-down switch. The switch has two functions in the circuit:

First, it opens the circuit to release the solenoid. However, the pawl cannot release itself from the control plate until the driving torque is removed.

Second, it momentarily grounds out the engine ignition circuit. This shorting out is for about one-half revolution of the crankshaft but it is enough to release the torque on the pawl so that it can retract and so put the car in direct drive for faster acceleration.

This ability of the kick-down switch to ground out the ignition is controlled by another set of contacts in the solenoid which restores the ignition as soon as the solenoid armature has returned to the out position.

On early models there is a "rail switch" (reverse lock-out switch) which locks out the governor circuit when the dash control is in the out position. This rail switch is actuated by the shift rail. On later models the movement of the shift rail accomplishes the same thing mechanically by moving the control plate so that the pawl cannot engage it.

SERVICING THE OVERDRIVE

The overdrive gets its oil supply from the regular transmission and so the standard transmission of a car equipped with an overdrive requires an extra pint of lubricant to fill it. The overdrive has its own drain plug.

Some models also have a separate fill plug thru which the extra pint should be installed when transmission plus overdrive assembly has been drained. One must remove the transmission and overdrive assembly from the car in order to be able to do any mechanical work on the overdrive.

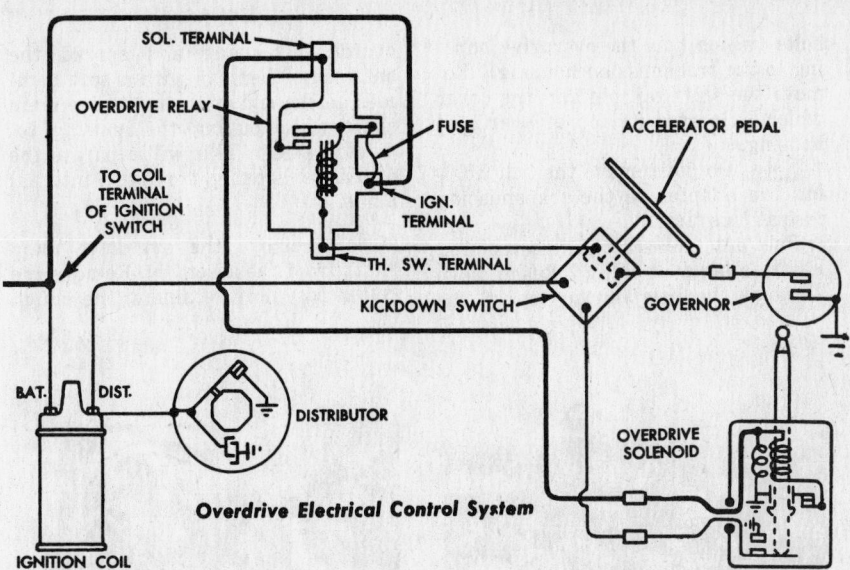

Overdrive Electrical Control System

Schematic Wiring Diagram of Typical Overdrive Installation. The lockout switch is not always used.

TROUBLE SHOOTING CHART

Trouble: Overdrive Does Not Engage

Remedy No. 1: Check that the control lever on the unit moves as far in each direction as it should and that hand control on dash has ¼ inch free travel before lever moves.

Remedy No. 2: Be sure that fuse on relay has not burnt out.

Remedy No. 3: With ignition on, connect test lamp from fuse clip to ground. If lamp does not light replace wire from switch to relay.

Remedy No. 4: Connect test lamp between K.D. switch terminal on relay and ground. If relay does not "click" replace it.

Remedy No. 5: Disconnect wire from solenoid terminal on relay. Connect test lamp between this solenoid terminal and ground. Ground K.D. switch terminal on relay. If lamp does not light replace the relay.

Remedy No. 6: Disconnect the wire from the relay at the solenoid. Connect test lamp between end of wire and ground. Ground the kickdown switch terminal on the relay. If lamp does not light replace the wire from relay to solenoid.

Remedy No. 7: Ground kickdown switch terminal on the relay. Solenoid should click; if it does not; replace the solenoid.

Remedy No. 8: Operate kickdown switch several times to be sure it is not sticking. Ground each "A" terminal on the switch in turn. Solenoid should click when one terminal is grounded; if it does not, replace kickdown switch.

Remedy No. 9: The purpose of this test is to determine if there is an open circuit between the solenoid and the governor. If the solenoid clicks when "A1" is grounded, the circuit from the switch to the solenoid is OK. Next ground the "A2" terminal. If the solenoid again clicks the switch is OK. Now ground the governor terminal at the governor. The solenoid should click. If it does not, the wire to the switch is defective.

Trouble: Overdrive Does Not Release

Remedy No. 1: With control pushed "IN" turn ignition key "ON." If a click is heard in the overdrive relay the trouble is electrical; if no click the trouble is mechanical and unit must be removed and overhauled.

Remedy No. 2: Disconnect wire at governor. If overdrive then releases replace governor.

Remedy No. 3: Disconnect wire from governor at kickdown switch. If overdrive then releases, the wire is grounded.

Remedy No. 4: Disconnect wire from relay and wire from governor at the kickdown switch. If the overdrive then releases replace the kickdown switch.

Remedy No. 5: Disconnect wire from kickdown switch at the relay. If overdrive then releases replace the wire; it is grounded.

Remedy No. 6: Disconnect wire from solenoid at the relay. If overdrive then releases replace the relay.

Remedy No. 7: Unfasten the screws holding the solenoid to the case. If the solenoid can be pulled out without turning it then the little pin which normally prevents the solenoid plunger from turning has been sheared or omitted. It will be necessary to assemble the solenoid correctly. If it can be withdrawn ½ inch without being turned the solenoid is defective and should be replaced.

Trouble: Overdrive Does Not Kick Down

Remedy No. 1: With engine running, ground the kickdown switch terminal on the solenoid. If engine stops, replace solenoid.

Remedy No. 2: With engine running, depress the kickdown switch and ground each of the "B" terminals in turn. If engine dies, all is well. If engine does not die when one terminal is grounded, replace the kickdown switch. If engine does not die no matter what, replace the wire from the switch to the coil.

Remedy No. 3: Ground the governor terminal at the governor. This should cause the solenoid to click on. Now operate the kickdown switch. This should cause a second click as the solenoid releases. If there is no second click the kickdown switch is defective.

Trouble: Engine Stops When Kickdown Switch Is Depressed

Remedy: With engine running, disconnect wire from kickdown switch at solenoid. Operate kickdown switch. If engine does not stop, replace the solenoid. If engine does stop, replace the wire.

Trouble: Car Will Not Move Unless Overdrive Is Locked Out Acts like Slipping Clutch

Remedy: Remove unit and overhaul free wheel mechanism.

Trouble: Stays in Overdrive When Hand Control Is Positioned to Lock It Out of Overdrive

Remedy: Check hand control. Lever on unit must move from stop to stop. If all is well there, the shift rail is binding. Remove and overhaul.

Trouble: Does Not Reverse Unless Locked Out

Remedy: Check operation of gear shift mechanism on transmission. The shift rail in the overdrive is not being moved by reverse fork.

OVERDRIVE TRANSMISSION

OVERDRIVE DISASSEMBLY

First, remove the lock-out switch, if present. (The lock-out switch is located toward the rear of the overdrive on the left side) and then turn over the assembly to permit the two steel balls under the switch to drop out.

Take off the governor assembly and then remove the overdrive housing bolts (which hold the overdrive housing to the transmission housing). Remove the shift rail pin and the cover which is located on top of overdrive housing.

<u>Note:</u> Do not remove the bolt holding the adapter to the transmission case at this time.

Pull out the shift rail lever and shaft as far as it will go. Reach down through the hole in the top of the overdrive housing and spread the snap ring, then tap with a soft hammer on the end of the overdrive main shaft while pulling the housing toward the rear. This will separate the overdrive housing from the internal parts.

Now remove the overdrive main shaft from the assembly. Remove the clutch assembly retainers, the clutch

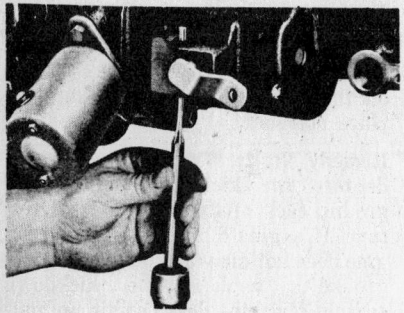
Fig. 1—Removing Shift Lever Lock Pin

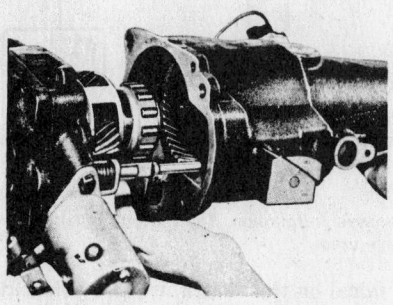
Fig. 2—Removing Overdrive Case

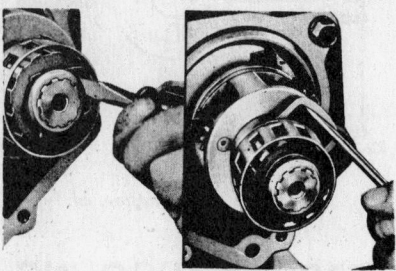
Fig. 3—Removing Pinion Cage Lock Rings

Fig. 4—Removing Sun Gear

Fig. 5—Removing Balk Ring Cover Lock

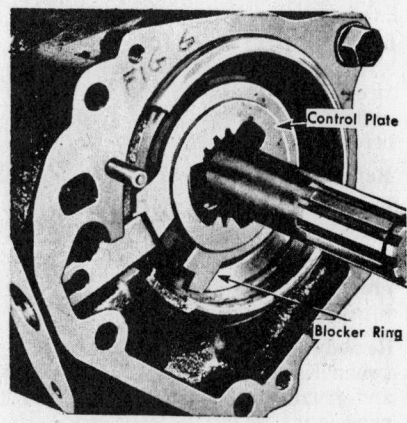
Fig. 6—Removing Balk Ring Cover

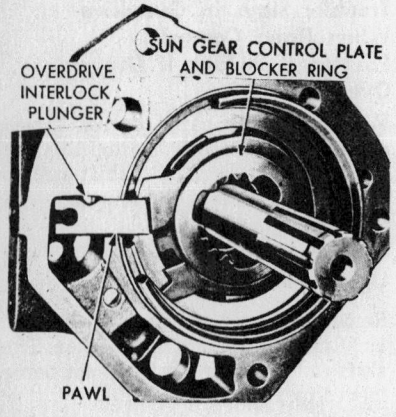
Fig. 7—Removing Sun Gear Plate

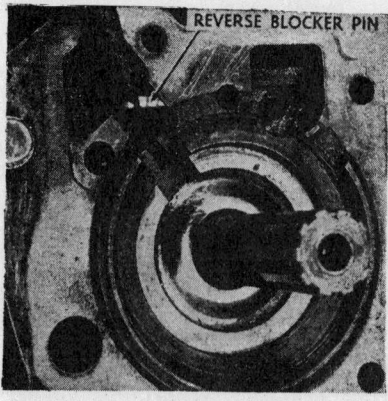
Fig. 8—Removing Reverse Blocker Pin

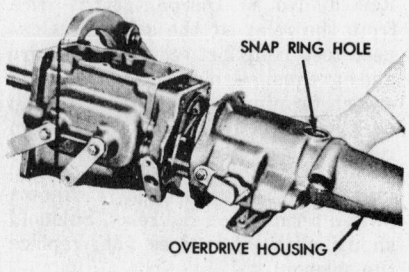
Fig. 9—Mainshaft Lock Ring Location

916

and planetary gear assemblies and the sun gear and shift rail. These all will come off as a unit, after the retainer is raised to permit sliding them off the shaft.

TRANSMISSION OVERDRIVE

Inspection After Disassembly

If the overdrive has a history of noisy gears examine the sun gear, ring gear, and planetary pinions for scratches, nicks, burrs or roughness. If any are found it will be necessary to replace the defective gears.

If the overdrive has a history of slipping in normal drive (not overdrive) examine the free wheeling rollers and the roller cage for roughness or pits.

If the free wheeling rollers have little depressions worn in the free wheeling cam it will be necessary to replace both the cam and the free wheeling rollers.

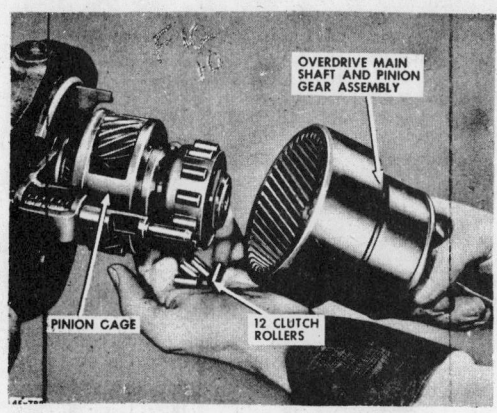

Fig. 10—Removing Mainshaft Assembly

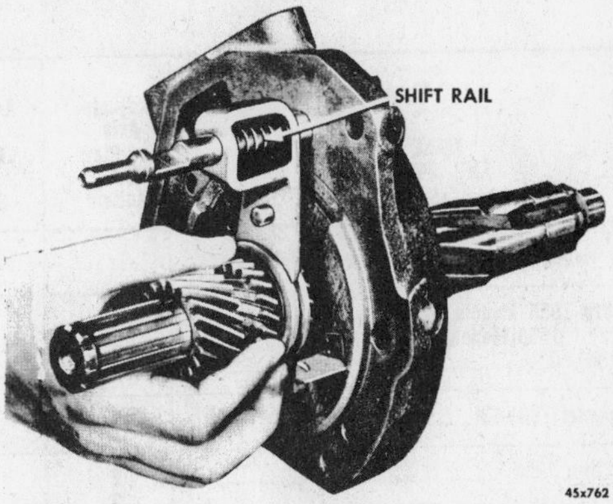

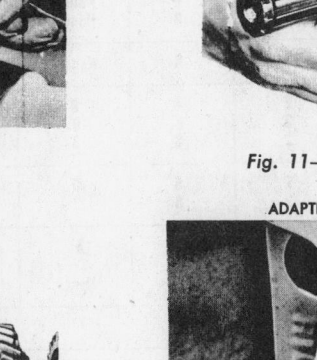

Fig. 11—Installing Shift Rail and Sun Gear

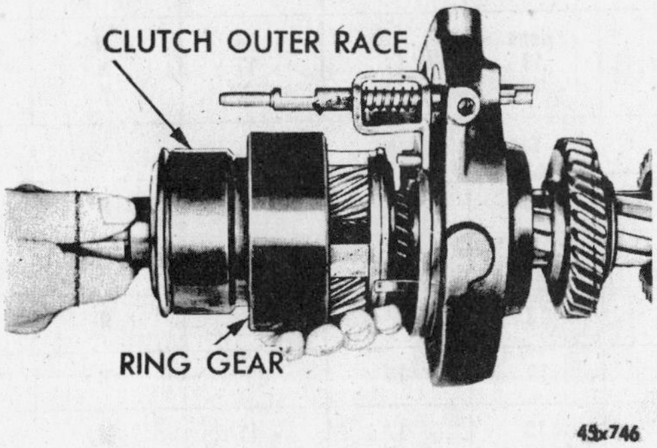

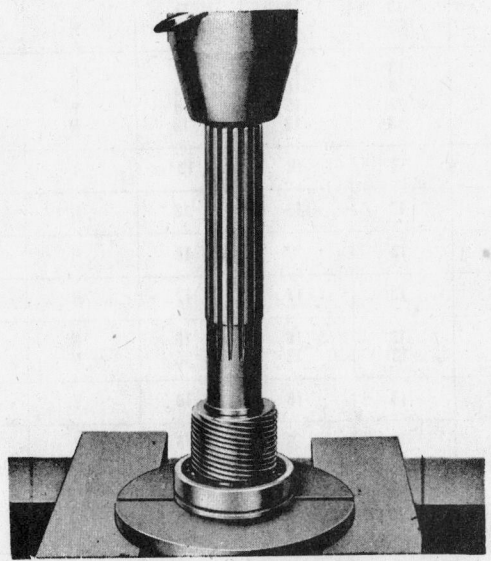

Fig. 12—Installing Clutch Outer Race

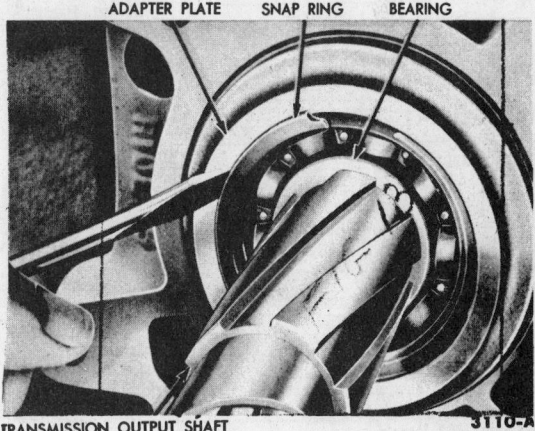

Fig. 13—Removing Output Shaft

Fig. 14—Removing Speedometer Drive Gear

Fig. 15—Installing Rollers

Rear Axle Service Procedure Index

Numbers in columns refer to Section numbers in text. Thus, Section 2 describes methods of adjusting axle end play on Cadillacs, some Fords & Mercurys, Oldsmobile and Pontiac.

MAKE AND MODEL	Adjust Axle End Play (See Section)	Install Axle Shaft and/or Bearing (See Section)	Install Axle Outer Oil Seal (See Section)	Install Axle Inner Oil Seal (See Section)	Install Pinion and Ring Gear (See Section)	Install Pinion Bearing (See Section)	Cover Removable? N—No Y—Yes	Carrier Removable? N—No Y—Yes
For Non-Slip Differentials. See Section 26.								
Buick thru 1955 Models	1	5	8	13	14	14	Y	Y
1956 thru 1960 Models	2	6	None	None	15	15	N	Y
Buick 1961-63	2	6	None	13	16	16	N	Y
Buick Special 1961-63	2	6	None	13	18	18	Y	N
Cadillac thru 1960	2	6	9	13	15	15	N	Y
Cadillac 1961-63	2	6	9	None	15	15	N	Y
Cadillac-Commercial 1961-63	2	6	9	13	15	15	N	Y
Chevrolet thru 1954 Models	1	5	10	None	14	14	Y	Y
1955 thru 1963 Models	2	6	9	None	16	16	N	Y
Chevy II 1962-63	2	6	9	None	16	16	N	Y
Chrysler thru 1963 Models	3	7	12	13	17	17	N	Y
Comet—All Models	2	6	None	13	20	20	Y	N
Corvair 1961-63			See Car Section					
De Soto thru 1961 Models	3	7	12	13	17	17	N	Y
Dodge-Dart thru 1963 Models	3	7	12	13	17	17	N	Y
Fairlane 1962-63	2	6	None	13	19	19	N	Y
Falcon—All Models	2	6	None	13	20	20	N	Y
Ford thru 1956 Passenger	2	6	9	13	17	17	N	Y
Station Wagons thru 1956	2	6	9	13	18	18	Y	N
1957 thru 1963 Models	2	6	None	13	19	19	Y	N
Lincoln thru 1956 Models	2	6	9	13	18	18	Y	N
1957 thru 1963 Models	2	6	None	13	19	19	N	Y
Mercury thru 1954 Models	2	6	9	13	17	17	N	Y
1955 thru 1956 Models	2	6	9	13	18	18	Y	N
Station Wagons	2	6	9	13	18	18	Y	N
1957 thru 1963 Models	2	6	None	13	19	19	N	Y
Meteor 1962-63	2	6	None	13	19	19	Y	N
Oldsmobile thru 1963 Models	2	6	9	13	16	16	N	Y
Oldsmobile F-85 1961-63	2	6	None	13	18	18	N	Y
Plymouth thru 1963 Models	3	7	12	13	17	17	N	Y
Pontiac thru 1955 Models	2	6	9	13	16	16	N	Y
1956 thru 1963 Models	2	6	None	13	16	16	N	Y
Rambler—All Models	3	7	11	13	18	18	Y	N
Studebaker—All models	3	7	11	13	18	18	Y	N
Tempest 1961-63			See Car Section					
Valiant-Lancer—All	2	6	None	13	18	18	Y	N
Willys—All Models	3	7	11	13	18	18	Y	N

TROUBLE SHOOTING

As long as gears are used to drive rear axles, some noise can be expected in this area. All the service man can do is to keep this noise at an acceptable low level. However in some cases, axle noise is the result of worn or damaged parts. This condition, if carefully studied, can aid in diagnosis and preventive maintenance.

A road test is necessary to assess the degree of noise and trace its cause. Before testing be sure that the unit is filled to correct level with the proper lubricant. Also check tire pressures and tread conditions. Tire noise can cause a very misleading kind of differential-type sound. The rear axle and lubricant must be at normal operating temperature.

With the car stopped and the transmission in neutral, run the engine at various speeds and under different conditions of acceleration. If the noise persists under these circumstances its origin is obviously elsewhere.

To isolate tire noise from similar sounds a test on several different road surfaces should help pinpoint the trouble. Smooth asphalt or black-top roads reduce tire noise to a minimum. Tire noise may also be modified by cross switching the tires to reverse their direction of rotation. Some snow treads are quite noisy and cause sounds similar to gear or bearing faults.

A defective wheel bearing is usually audible (depending upon the degree of failure) when the car is coasting at low speeds.

After all other possible causes of noise have been checked, road-test the rear axle under all five conditions—drive, cruise, float, coast and decelerate. Only when convinced that the sound is objectionable and of rear axle origin, should the axle unit be removed, disassembled and the parts examined for damage.

ADJUST AXLE SHAFT END PLAY

SECTION 1

BUICK—All Models thru 1955
CHEVROLET—All Models thru 1954

On these models the end play of the axle shaft is controlled by the thickness of the spacer on the differential pin in the center of the rear axle assembly. The inner ends of the axle shaft butt against this spacer block. If too much end play exists, it is necessary to install an oversized spacer block to take up the play.

A sealed radial ball bearing is used at the outer end of the axle shaft and, unless it is absolutely necessary because of noises on turns and so forth, to reduce the axle shaft end play to its desired minimum, it is advisable to put up with some end play in the axle shaft rather than go through the involved procedure of correcting it.

In other words, the job should be done only if it is absolutely essential that it be done, since opening the rear axle always leaves a chance of dust, dirt and grit getting into the ring gear and pinion case and thus eventually destroying the mesh of the ring gear and pinion.

The procedure for taking out the end play is as follows: Support the rear axle assembly on a jack, drain the oil from the housing and remove the cover. Carefully scrape the gasket from the cover and rear axle housing and install a new one when the cover is replaced.

Turn the ring gear until the screw which holds the differential pinion pin in place is accessible and remove the screw.

After the screw is removed push the pin out of the differential and remove the spacer block. See fig. 2.

Replace the spacer block with a thicker one to take up the end play, insert it into place and push the pin back into place being careful to line up the hole for the locking screw. Check the end play between the butt of the axle and the spacer block with a feeler gage. See fig. 1. Replace the locking screw and cover assembly. Fill to the proper level with the correct grade of lubricant.

Fig. 1—Checking axle shaft end play, using a feeler gage (Section 1)

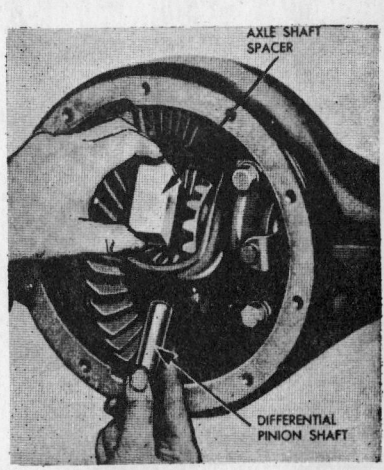

AXLE SHAFT SPACER

DIFFERENTIAL PINION SHAFT

Fig. 2—Replacing axle shaft spacer with one of a greater thickness (Section 1)

ADJUST AXLE SHAFT END PLAY

SECTION 2

BUICK—1956-63
BUICK SPECIAL—1961-63
CADILLAC—All Models
CHEVROLET—1955-63
Models
CHEVY II—All Models
EDSEL—All Models
FAIRLANE—All Models
FALCON-COMET—All Models
FORD—All Models
LINCOLN—All Models
MERCURY—All Models
METEOR—All Models
OLDSMOBILE—All Models
PONTIAC—All Models
VALIANT-LANCER—All
Models

On this construction, the axle bearing is held in place by pressure from the backing plate. The bearing, a radial ball bearing, is held to the axle shaft by a shrunk on ring. If end play exists in this construction,

either the bearing is loose on the shaft, the bearing retainer has moved on the shaft, or the backing plate is bent where it retains the bearing in the housing.

To correct this condition, see axle shaft and/or bearing replace.

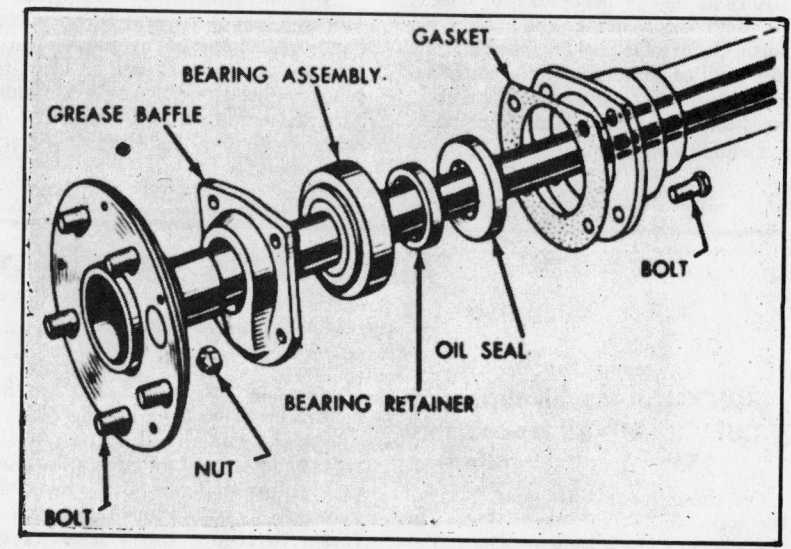

Fig. 3—Axle Shaft, Bearing, and Oil Seals

ADJUST AXLE SHAFT END PLAY

SECTION 3

CHRYSLER—All Models
DE SOTO—All Models
DODGE-DART—All Models
FRAZER—All Models
HENRY J—All Models
HUDSON—Late 1952 thru
1956
KAISER—All Models
NASH—All Models
PACKARD—All Models
PLYMOUTH—All Models
RAMBLER—All Models
STUDEBAKER—All Models
WILLYS—All Models

On this construction, the adjustment for axle shaft end play is actually the adjustment of the tapered roller axle bearing. Because it is an adjustment of the bearing, it should

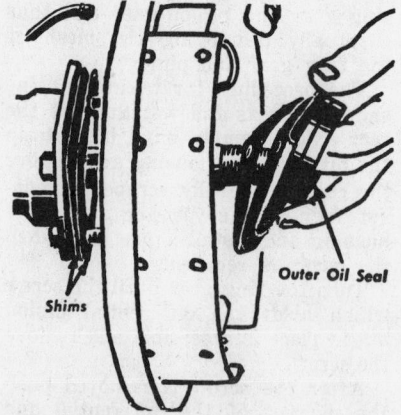

Fig. 4—Adjusting axle shaft end play (Section 3)

be done carefully.

Jack up the back of the car and set both sides of the rear axle on stands. Remove the wheel and, using a puller, pull off the brake drum and hub assembly.

Since these are all taper axles it is

recommended that a pressure type wheel puller be used rather than a knock-off type.

Do not use a knock-off type puller. The knock-off type puller may shatter the axle thrust block, axle bearings or axle threads.

After the hub and drum assembly is removed, disconnect the brake line where it enters the wheel cylinder at the backing plate.

Remove the bolts which hold the backing plate to the axle tube.

It is not necessary to disturb the setting of the brakes in any way. However, it will be necessary to disconnect the brake cable on models which use the rear brake shoes for the hand brake.

To give the axle shaft less end play, remove one or more of the shims which will be found in back of the backing plate, between the backing plate and the axle tube flange. See fig. 4.

ADJUST AXLE SHAFT END PLAY — continued

To increase the axle shaft end play, add shims at this point.

On models fitted with an outer oil seal it is always a good idea to install a new oil seal when this job is being done.

Rebolt the backing plate, reconnect the brake lines, install the hub and drum assembly, install the wheel and bleed the brakes. After complet-ing the assembly recheck to make sure that the shaft now has the correct end play. On these models end play should be between .012 and .020 inch.

REPLACE AXLE SHAFT AND/OR BEARING

SECTION 5

BUICK—All Models thru 1955
CHEVROLET—All Models to 1954

To replace the axle shaft and/or bearings on this model, jack up the back of the car and place a stand jack under both rear axles.

Drain the oil from the differential and remove the differential cover. Scrape the gasket from the cover and the housing. Install a new gasket the brake drum. The brake drum is held by the same bolts which hold the wheel in place. There are usually two additional screws to retain the brake drum to the axle flange after the wheel has been removed.

At the differential, remove the differential pin lock screw. Push the differential pin out which will release the spacer between the inner ends of the two axle shafts. Lift the spacer out. See fig. 2.

Push inward on the axle shaft and remove the C washer which retains the inner end of the axle shaft to the side gear. With the C washer removed the axle can be pulled out of the housing.

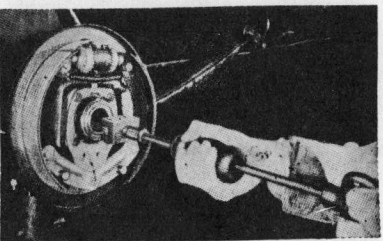

Fig. 5—Removing rear axle shaft bearing from housing using an inertia type puller

In some few instances the axle may tend to freeze to the bearing. However, a few jolts will generally remove it.

The axle shaft is supposed to come out leaving the bearing in the housing.

The bearing is removed from the housing with an inertia type puller. See fig. 5.

To replace the bearing it must be driven back into the housing using a special bearing driving tool or a tool which will drive against the outer rim of the bearing and not the inner ring. Do not attempt to replace this type of bearing by tapping with a hammer on the outside rim. This generally shortens the life of the bearing and makes the job a waste of time.

Install the new bearing in the housing and put in the new axle shaft. Push the axle shaft in past the center and put the C washer in place. Pull the axle shaft out until the C washer goes down into the groove in the differential side gear. Install the spacer and push the pinion pin into the differential, securing it with the lock screw.

With a feeler gauge check the clearance between the spacer and the end of the axle shaft to make sure that the new axle shaft has the proper end play. See fig. 1.

If the clearance at this point is excessive, an oversized spacer block will have to be installed as explained in section 1.

Remount the hub and drum assembly and the wheel, install the rear axle cover and put in new rear axle fluid.

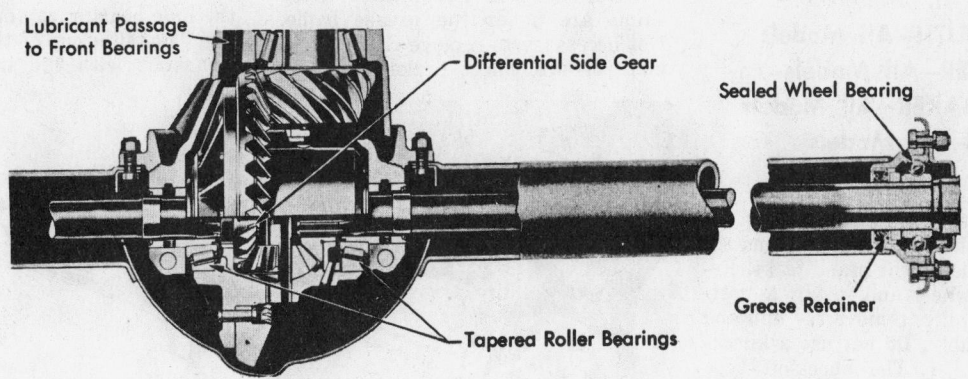

Fig. 6—Cross sectional view. Differential and Tapered Axle

AXLES REAR

REPLACE AXLE SHAFT AND/OR BEARING

SECTION 6

BUICK—1956-63
BUICK SPECIAL—1961-63
CADILLAC—All Models
CHEVROLET—1955-63
CHEVY II—All Models
EDSEL—All Models
FAIRLANE—All Models
FALCON-COMET—All Models
FORD—All Models
LINCOLN—All Models
MERCURY—All Models
METEOR—All Models
OLDSMOBILE—All Models
OLDSMOBILE F-85—All Models
PONTIAC—All Models
VALIANT-LANCER—1961-63

Note: The 1956-61 Pontiac axle bearing has a built-in oil seal, the only oil seal used on the axle.

Note: 1956 Buick 70 models, the right axle shaft drives an oil pump inside the differential. Use care replacing the axle so as not to damage the pump.

This type of construction uses a flange type axle having a pressed-on bearing held in place by a shrunk-on retaining ring. To remove the axle shaft and/or bearing, jack up the rear of the car and place it on stand jacks. Remove the wheel and the brake drum. The drum will come off readily since the flange type axle is used and the drum is retained by two small screws after the wheel has been removed. Working back of the axle flange, remove the bolt which holds the grease baffle plate and the backing plate to the axle tube.

After the axle retainer plate bolts have been taken out, the axle shaft can then be pulled out of the housing.

Generally, an inertia type puller will be required to jolt the axle out of the housing since the bearing is a reasonably tight fit in the housing.

Most of the car companies listed above service the axle with bearing retainer ring and axle retainer plate in place.

However, if it is desired to replace the bearing only, crack the retaining ring, being careful to protect the eyes since the retaining ring is hard and may chip.

Press the retaining ring and bearing off the long end of the shaft. Install the new bearing by pressing it from the long end of the shaft up to the flange and then, using a hot retaining ring, press the retaining ring into place quickly so that it will shrink in place. If the end of the axle shaft is packed in dry ice it will shrink two or three thousandths, which sometimes helps.

Since it is necessary to press these parts on from the long end of the axle shaft, a very deep throated press is required, and because the retaining ring must be put on hot, the work should be carried out very quickly.

Generally speaking, it is recommended that the new axle bearing and retainer plate assembly be used whenever it is necessary to install a new axle shaft and/or bearing.

Install the new shaft and bearing assembly into the axle housing and, using a heavy hammer but short blows, jolt the axle, setting the bearing into the housing.

When the bearing is firmly seated, bolt up the axle retainer plate, install the drum and wheel assembly.

REPLACE AXLE SHAFT AND/OR BEARING

SECTION 7

CHRYSLER—All Models
DE SOTO—All Models
DODGE-DART—All Models
HUDSON—All Models
HUDSON JET—All Models
NASH—All Models
PLYMOUTH—All Models
RAMBLER—All Models
STUDEBAKER—All Models
WILLYS—All Models

This construction uses a taper axle and a tapered roller bearing.

Jack up the rear of the car and set the rear axle on the stand jacks. Remove the wheel and, using a pressure type puller, remove the hub and drum assembly. **Do not use a knock-off type puller.** The knock-off type puller may shatter the axle thrust block, axle bearings or axle threads.

Disconnect the brake tube and the hand brake cables on those models which use the rear shoes for the hand brake.

Remove the bolts which retain the backing plate to the rear axle flange, being careful not to lose the shims in back of the backing plate which control the axle end play. (On Hudson and Hudson Jet models these shims are under the grease baffle. Not necessary to remove the backing plate or disconnect brakes.) It will probably be necessary to jolt the axle shaft out of the housing. This may be done by removing the key from the taper axle, temporarily reinstalling the hub and drum assembly and running the axle nut up about three or four threads. The hub and drum assembly can then be used to jolt the axle bearing cup out of the housing. The outer cup of the bearing will come out with the shaft and cone.

Fig. 7—Removing bearing cone from rear axle shaft using screw type puller

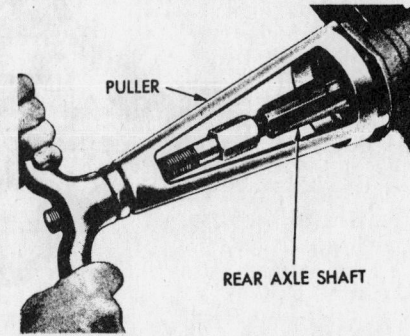

Fig. 8—Removing rear axle shaft and bearing using screw type puller

REPLACE AXLE SHAFT AND/OR BEARING—continued

The bearing cone is pressed off the short end of the axle shaft and pressed on in the same manner. See fig. 7.

Press the new bearing on the axle shaft and install the axle shaft in the housing. Put the bearing cup in place, using a bearing cup driver. Do not attempt to put the bearing in by driving with a hammer against the rim of the cup since this may easily damage the cup.

Reinstall the shims and the backing plate and immediately check the axle shaft for end play.

See section 3 for end play on this type of axle.

Reinstall the hub and drum, the wheel and then bleed the brakes.

REPLACE AXLE OUTER OIL SEAL

SECTION 8

BUICK—All Models thru 1955

In order to replace the outer oil seal on Buick cars it is necessary to remove the axle shaft. Follow the instructions in section 5. Replace axle shaft and/or bearing—for instructions on removing the axle shaft.

After the axle shaft is taken out of the housing, the new oil seal can be inserted first and then the axle shaft is replaced into the housing.

All of the procedure is exactly the same as that given in section 5 to replace an axle shaft and/or bearing.

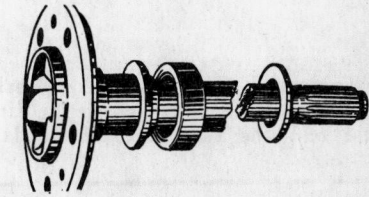

Fig. 9—Rear axle shaft showing arrangement of oil seals

REPLACE AXLE OUTER OIL SEAL

SECTION 9

CADILLAC—All Models
CHEVROLET—1955-63 Models
CHEVY II—All Models
FORD—1950 thru 1956 Passenger Cars and Station Wagons
LINCOLN—1950 thru 1956
MERCURY—1950 thru 1956
OLDSMOBILE—All Models

PONTIAC—All Models thru 1955

On these models an outer oil seal is included in the bearing. There is a drain plate which tends to drain away whatever lubricant gets past the bearing to the inside of the backing plate. Cadillac however, uses a synthetic "O" ring seal recessed into the outer diameter of the axle bearing race. Chevrolet uses an inner and outer oil seal on the bearing.

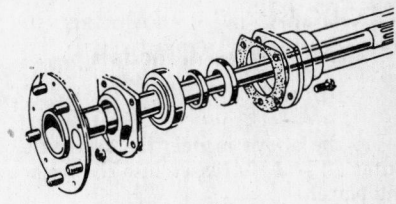

Fig. 10—

REPLACE AXLE OUTER OIL SEAL

SECTION 10

CHEVROLET—All Models thru 1954

Jack up the back of the car and remove the axle shaft as explained in section 5. As also explained in section 5, the axle outer bearing is pulled out of the housing with an inertia puller. When this bearing is pulled out the outer oil seal comes out with it.

Therefore, the procedure to replace the outer oil seal is exactly the same as that given in section 5 for replacing an axle shaft and/or bearing.

Fig. 11—Replacing rear axle shaft bearing or oil seal

REPLACE AXLE OUTER OIL SEAL

SECTION 11

HUDSON—All Models
HUDSON JET—All Models
NASH—All Models
RAMBLER—All Models
STUDEBAKER—All Models
WILLYS—All Models

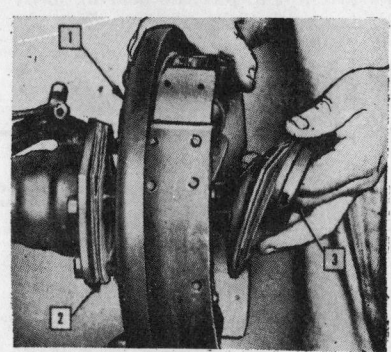

Fig. 12—
1. Support Plate
2. Shims
3. Oil Seals

To remove the outer axle oil seal on the above models, jack up the car and rest the rear axle on stands.

Remove the wheel and, using a puller, remove the hub and drum assembly. The bolts which retain the backing plate to the rear axle tubes also hold the axle outer oil seal in place.

Remove these bolts and lift off the oil seal, being careful not to disturb the shims which govern the axle shaft end play. On these models, except Hudson and Jet, the shims are back of the backing plate. On Hudson and Jet models the shims are back of the grease seal retainer.

Clean up the backing plate and install a new oil seal.

Replace the hub and drum assembly and the wheels.

REPLACE AXLE OUTER OIL SEAL

SECTION 12

CHRYSLER—All Models
DE SOTO—All Models
DODGE-DART—All Models
PLYMOUTH—All Models

On the above models the rear axle outer oil seal is pressed into the backing plate.

To replace it, jack up the car and set the rear axle on stands. Remove the wheels and the hub and drum assemblies. A puller is required to remove the hub and drum assemblies since this is a tapered axle.

Disconnect the brake lines and remove the bolts which hold the backing plate to the rear axle tube. Remove the backing plate, being careful not to lose the shims in back of the backing plate which control the axle end play.

Drive the old oil seal out of the

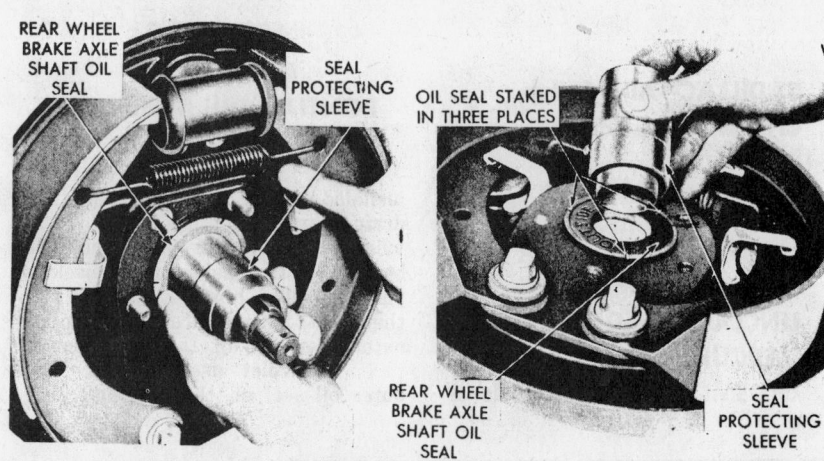

Fig. 13—Removing or installing rear brake support plate using seal protecting sleeve

backing plate and press a new one into place.

Guide the backing plate carefully back onto the axle tube so as not to damage the oil seal against the axle

shaft.

Button up the backing plate and reconnect the brake lines. Install the hub and drum assemblies and the wheels and bleed the brakes.

REPLACE AXLE INNER OIL SEAL

SECTION 13

ALL MAKES—ALL MODELS

The inner oil seal is contained on the inside of the bearing in the axle tube on all American cars except those noted in index.

Take out the axle shaft as outlined in the paragraphs devoted to axle shafts for the car on which you are working. After the axle shaft, bearing and outer oil seal have been removed, reach into the housing with

an inertia type puller and pull out the inner oil seal.

The new oil seal is driven by its rim into the housing. Install the bearing, outer oil seal and axle shaft, replace the hub and drum assemblies and the wheels.

INSTALL RING AND PINION GEAR AND/OR PINION BEARINGS

SECTION 14

BUICK—1954-55
CHEVROLET—1954 Models

Keep in mind that the installation of a ring gear and pinion or pinion bearings is a very critical job. Care, cleanliness and patient workmanship are essential if the new gears and/or bearings are to function quietly and well.

While the job can be done with the rear axle assembly under the car, it is much simpler to perform the critical work with the entire rear axle assembly removed.

Support the vehicle on stand jacks at the frame in front of the rear axle "kick up" and place a roller jack under the center of the rear axle. Drain the lubricant from the axle housing.

Disconnect the hand brake cable and the brake hydraulic line at the "T" fitting, disconnect the shock absorbers and remove the bolt from the universal joint ball at the front end of the torque tube.

On Buick, remove the bolts which hold the coil springs to their seat at the rear of axle housing; some of these bolts have left hand threads.

On Chevrolet, remove the rear spring "U" bolt nuts from the spring seat on the axle tube and disconnect the rear shackles, lower the back end of the springs to the floor.

Roll the rear axle assembly out from under the car and remove both axleshafts as outlined in paragraph "Axle Shaft and/or Bearing Replace" earlier in this text.

Carefully scrape the gasket surface on the axle housing until it is clean and smooth for a new gasket.

Remove the bolts which hold the side bearing lock plates to the bearing caps and turn both adjusting cages (they have right hand threads) to relieve the pressure from the bearings. Note: If the cages are difficult to turn, loosen the bearing pedestal cap bolts just slightly to relieve the cramping on the bearing cage.

With the cages loose, remove the four pedestal cap bolts and take off the caps. Lift out the differential as-

sembly and remove to a bench. Note: Chevrolet ring gears are bolted to the differential case, Buick ring gears are riveted to the case.

Installation of a new ring gear on a differential case should be farmed out to a shop specializing in such work as the case must be trued up to have a maximum runout of .003 full indicator reading at the ring gear seat before attaching a new ring gear.

If necessary, the side bearings can be pulled off using a hooked type bearing puller, and new ones pressed on.

Pinion Removal

Loosen the jam nuts and remove the pinion spacer taper screws located at the outside of the pinion housing. Using a soft lead or brass hammer, tap the front end of the driveshaft toward the rear, forcing the pinion out the rear of the housing. The pinion nut was left intact and so the pinion comes out complete with all its bearings and spacer.

Shop note: Buick recommends using

PINION SETTING TABLE FOR GAUGE J 681-A															
PINIONS MARKED "O" USE THE NOMINAL MICROMETER READING OF .317															
Pinion Marking (—)	—1	—2	—3	—4	—5	—6	—7	—8	—9	—10	—11	—12	—13	—14	—15
1953–55 Micrometer Reading	.318	.319	.320	.321	.322	.323	.324	.325	.326	.327	.328	.329	.330	.331	.332
1953–55 Micrometer Reading	.316	.315	.314	.313	.312	.311	.310	.309	.308	.307	.306	.305	.304	.303	.302

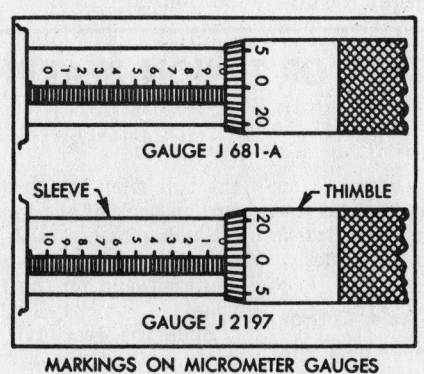

MARKINGS ON MICROMETER GAUGES

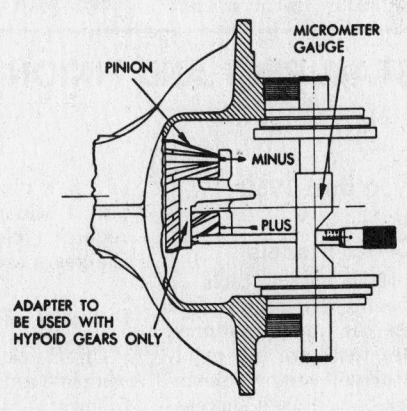

PINION SETTING TABLE FOR GAUGE J 2197															
PINIONS MARKED "O" USE THE NOMINAL MICROMETER READING OF .864															
Pinion Marking (—)	—1	—2	—3	—4	—5	—6	—7	—8	—9	—10	—11	—12	—13	—14	—15
1953–55 Micrometer Reading	.863	.862	.861	.860	.859	.858	.857	.856	.855	.854	.853	.852	.851	.850	.849
1953–55 Micrometer Reading	.865	.866	.867	.868	.869	.870	.871	.872	.873	.874	.875	.876	.877	.878	.879

Fig. 14

a special pinion puller rather than tapping the driveshaft on rears having ratios numerically higher than 4.1 to 1. On Buick rears with 3.9 to 1 ratio pullers cannot be used and the pinion must be driven out.

With the pinion and driveshaft out of the case, reach into the case and very carefully remove the shims which will be found in the front shoulder of the pinion housing. These shims are located between the outer race of the double row ball bearing and the front shoulder of the housing. Carefully clean and mike each shim and make a note of the thickness of each shim and the total thickness.

On the bench, center drill and drive out the pin which holds the driveshaft to the pinion shaft and separate the pinion from the driveshaft. Pry or drive up the staked portion of the pinion shaft and remove the pinion nut. Remove the oil seal (some Buicks), the double row ball bearing, the spacer and the bearing lock ring (some Chevrolets) and the roller bearing if it is to be replaced or the pinion is to be replaced.

Reassembly of Pinion

Install the roller bearing (and lock ring on some Chevrolets), the spacer with its taper side toward the ring gear, the double row ball bearings (and oil seal on some Buicks) and the pinion nut. Hold the pinion in a vise, gripping it at the spline end rather than at the gear end and securely tighten the pinion nut and stake it into place. Install the pinion on the driveshaft and secure with a new

rivet. The pinion and driveshaft are now ready for assembly into the housing.

Pinion Shim Selection—Buick

Buick pinions are marked with a (code) numbering intended for use with pinion depth micrometer No. J-681A or J-2197. Pinion shim selection charts for use with this gauge are given in Fig. 14.

Where micrometer depth gauges are not available, start selecting shims by comparing the marks on the old pinion with the marks on the new one. See section 25.

Pinion Shim Selection—Chevrolet

On 1954 Chevrolets one .018 shim is used as a starting point. The final selection of shims is governed by the gear mesh pattern which will be discussed later. See "Pinion Mesh Markings," Section 25.

Reinstallation

Assemble the selected shims into a pack and install the shims carefully into the housing.

Install the pinion into the carrier. Note: On Chevrolet the spacer tends to drop off to one side, making it somewhat difficult to engage the taper lock screws with the taper on the spacer. It sometimes helps to stand the whole housing on end so that the spacer "falls" against the bearing, making it somewhat easier to set the taper screws.

Tighten the taper locking screws to approximately 30 ft. lbs. torque and secure with a jam nut. Install the dif-

ferential assembly and the adjusting cages and tentatively install the bearing pedestal caps.

Before tightening the pedestal caps make sure the threads of the adjusting cages are properly meshed. This can be done by rocking the adjusting cage back and forth as the cap bolts are tightened. Failure to do this may result in damage to the cage and/or pedestal threads.

Now turn the bearing adjusting cage on the ring gear side until there is zero lash in the gears. It pays to repeat this adjustment two or three times very carefully to be sure the gear is adjusted to exactly zero lash without preload. On the opposite side of the ring gear turn the cage until there is zero play in the bearings. Repeat this two or three times to be sure that there is zero play. Now turn that cage two notches tight (preload). This will not only preload the bearing, but will provide backlash in the gears which should be .008 to .012 inch. If less than above, back off the cage on the ring gear side and tighten the cage opposite the ring gear one notch each and recheck. If it is more than .012 inch, tighten the ring gear side and loosen the opposite side one notch and recheck. Finally, tighten and secure the pedestal cap bolts and install the adjusting cage lock.

Check Gear Tooth Contact

Even when shims have been selected from a chart or selected for the use of a micrometer depth gauge it pays to check gear tooth contact pattern. See "Pinion Mesh Markings." Section 25.

INSTALL RING AND PINION GEAR AND/OR PINION BEARINGS

SECTION 15

BUICK—1956 thru 1960 Models
CADILLAC—All Models

Caution: Certain special tools or suitable substitutes are required to properly service the above captioned models. If these tools are not available the operator will require phenomenal good luck to complete successful service.

Note: Cadillac Division does not recommend servicing the internal parts of the rear axle assembly. If damaged, they believe a complete new carrier assembly should be installed. For this reason Cadillac does not supply gears or pinions for their axle assemblies.

Keep in mind that the installation

of a new pinion and ring gear and/or pinion bearings is a very critical job requiring cleanliness and patience if the gears are to run well and quietly.

Removal of the Rear Axle Carrier

On Buick models, thru 1960 the complete axle assembly is removed as follows:

Jack up the car and place stand jacks at the frame in front of the rear axle. Disconnect the hand brake cable at the equalizer and at the frame clips, the hydraulic lines at the "T" fitting, the stabilizer bar at the rear axle and the springs and shock absorbers at their lower ends.

Loosen the flange bolts at the universal joint torque ball and remove

the bolt from the torque tube flange just in back of the torque ball.

Guide pins are used in place of two of the bolts to help pilot the driveshaft off and on the universal joint yoke.

Slide the rear axle assembly out from under the car to a convenient work place, on its own wheels if the car is high enough, otherwise on a roller jack with the wheels removed. Remove the bolts from the torque tube and driveshaft.

Cadillac Carrier Replacement

On Cadillac models, jack up the car and support it at the rear axle housing, both sides. Remove both wheel and drum assemblies. Remove the bolts which hold the backing plate and dust shield to the axle tube flange. These bolts can be reached with an end or box wrench back of the axle shaft flange.

Attach an inertia type puller to the axle shaft flange and jolt both axle shafts out of the housing, being careful not to damage the inner oil seal as the axle is removed.

From under the car split the rear universal joint. Note: On some limousine and 7 passenger models a jack shaft is used. On these models disconnect the jack shaft flange at the frame to release the rear universal joint.

Remove the bolts which hold the differential carrier assembly to the axle housing and remove the carrier assembly to the bench.

Disassembly of Carrier

See Fig. 15.

Secure the carrier in a vise with the ring gear side up. (On Buick Series 70, 1956, remove the oil pump from the right pedestal.)

Remove the pedestal pinch bolts and drive a thin wedge into the pedestal slot to spread the pedestal slightly. Caution: Do not spread the pedestal too much. The bearing support sleeve tends to be tight in the bearing, not the pedestal. Therefore, just a slight spread to relieve the pressure is sufficient. If the wedge is forced in too tightly the carrier can be strained beyond recovery and rendered useless.

A special inertia type (sliding weight) puller is used to jolt the bearing support sleeves out of the side bearings and pedestal.

With the bearing support sleeves out of the assembly a special carrier spreader or suitable substitute is used to spread the pedestals apart and relieve the preload pressure from the side bearings. Caution: Spread the pedestal just enough to get the differential out of the carrier. Spreading too much could easily make the carrier unfit for use.

Mike the shims found at the side bearings and make a note of their thickness.

Remove the nut from the front of the pinion shaft. Some Buicks are staked. (On Cadillac remove the U joint flange and spacer washer.)

Using a soft (lead or brass) hammer, tap the pinion out the rear of the carrier. The rear bearing cone and rolls will come out with the pinion. The spacer (long crumple type on Cadillac—thick washer type on Buick) might come out with the pinion, but if it doesn't, fish it out of the housing after the pinion is removed.

Pull the oil seal out of the front of the case and lift out the front bearing cone and rolls.

The case will now contain the front and rear bearing outer races. The front race can be pulled or driven out the front of the case and the rear race out the rear of the case.

Using a hooked type bearing race puller, remove the rear bearing cone and rolls from the pinion, being careful not to damage the shim which will be found back of this bearing. This shim controls pinion depth.

Pinion Shim Selection

Since the Cadillac Division does not recommend servicing the rear axle differential assembly or ring gear and pinion, the only possible selection on Cadillac is to use a shim having the same thickness as the one found on the pinion, at least for a starting point.

Buick pinions are marked with a + (plus) or — (minus) followed by a number. This marking is intended for use with pinion setting gauge #J-5647 upon which is attached dial indicator #KMO-30-B and adapters (2) #J-5647-17. Instructions explaining the somewhat involved procedure required to use this gauging device are packed with the gauge. Unless this special gauging equipment is available, the code number has no practical use.

On the above captioned Buick models pinions having the same code marking do not necessarily use the same thickness shim.

Where special gauging equipment

is not available, the pinion depth (proper shim selection) can be determined by trial and error using gear mesh markings as a standard. See "Pinion Mesh Markings," Section 25.

Assembly of Pinion

As a starting point, use a shim having the same thickness as the old shim. Install the shim on the pinion and then press the bearing cone and rolls onto the shaft, seating solidly against the shim.

Install bearing races into the housing if they were removed.

Place the pinion into the housing and install the front bearing. Do not install the spacer at this time since this is a test run only. (On Cadillac install the U joint yoke and washer.) Start the pinion shaft nut onto the pinion and run it up until the bearings are preloaded to about 5 in. lbs. That is, tighten the pinion nut until about 5 in. lbs. torque is required to turn the pinion. This is not the final preload but is sufficient to establish gear tooth contact markings.

If the differential side bearing races were removed, reinstall them, seating each firmly in the case.

Attach the pedestal spreading device to the carrier and spread the pedestals just barely enough to slide the differential and its bearings into the carrier, using the same thickness of shims which were found at each side when the case was disassembled.

Drive a wedge into the pedestal slot to open it just barely enough to tentatively install the bearing sleeves,, seating each firmly in its bearing. Remove the spreading fixture and before removing the wedges from the pedestal again firmly seat the mounting sleeves.

Note: On Buick, the tapered end of the mounting sleeve goes into the bearing.

Remove the wedges and paint the ring gear teeth with red or white lead and, while "braking" the ring gear with a piece of wood, have a helper turn the pinion shaft in a clockwise direction (forward) and note the mesh markings made on the white lead. See "Pinion Mesh Markings," Section 25.

If different thickness shims (as indicated by the mesh markings) are required, the carrier will have to be completely disassembled, the shim changed, reassembled and another gear mesh marking noted until desirable markings are obtained.

When final shims have been selected, remove the pinion nut (the U joint flange on Cadillac) and the front bearing cone.

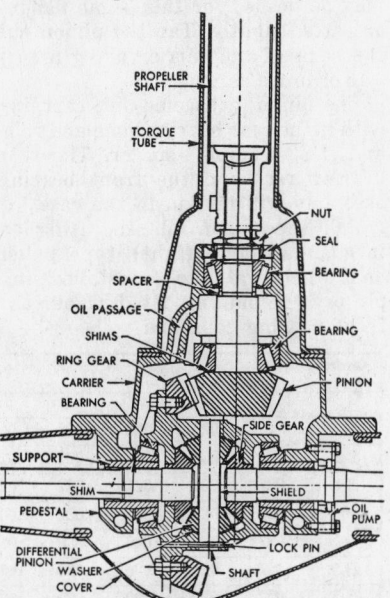

PROPELLER SHAFT

TORQUE TUBE

NUT

SEAL

BEARING

SPACER

BEARING

OIL PASSAGE

SHIMS

RING GEAR

PINION

CARRIER

BEARING

SIDE GEAR

SUPPORT

SHIM

SHIELD

PEDESTAL

OIL PUMP

DIFFERENTIAL PINION

LOCK PIN

WASHER

SHAFT

COVER

Fig. 15—Cross Section View of the 1956 Buick Rear Axle

INSTALL RING AND PINION GEAR AND/OR PINION BEARINGS — continued

Pinion Bearing Preload

On Cadillac, install the long "crumple" spacer, the bearing cone, the oil seal, the U joint yoke and nut. Tighten the nut until the spacer starts to "crumple" and keep tightening until 25 to 35 in. lbs. torque are required to turn the pinion. Stake the nut in this position.

On Buick, install the bearing spacer (preload) washer, the bearing cone, but not the oil seal until preload has been established. Install the nut and tighten it.

Since the proper bearing preload spacer has not yet been established, tighten the nut carefully and keep checking to see if the pinion is being preloaded. If the pinion preloads to 30 in. lbs. torque (to turn the pinion) before the pinion nut is tightened to 80 ft. lbs., the pinion spacer washer is too thin; remove the nut and bearing and install a thicker one and try again.

If the pinion nut can be tightened to 80 ft. lbs. torque and the pinion preload requires less than 20 in. lbs. to turn the pinion, the spacer is too thick; remove the nut and bearing, install a thinner shim and try again.

The proper thickness shim will produce 20 to 30 in. lbs. preload on the pinion with the pinion nut tightened to 80 ft. lbs. Once established, remove the nut, install the oil seal, reinstall the nut and tighten to 80 ft. lbs. and stake into position.

With a well lubricated oil seal in place not more than 40 in. lbs. torque should be required to turn the pinion.

Reinstall the carrier into the housing and the vehicle, reversing the procedure which removed it.

INSTALL RING AND PINION GEAR AND/OR PINION BEARINGS

SECTION 16

BUICK—1961-63
CHEVROLET—1955-63
CHEVY II—All Models
OLDSMOBILE—thru 1963,
    Except F-85
PONTIAC—thru 1963

Keep in mind that service on the ring gear and pinion requires careful, clean, patient workmanship and it may be necessary to disassemble the carrier three or four times before correct positioning of the pinion and ring gear is accomplished.

Removal and Disassembly of Carrier

Jack up the car and support it with stand jacks at the frame in front of the "kick up" and drain the lubricant from the rear.

Remove both axle shafts as explained in paragraph on "Axle Shaft and/or Bearing Replace."

Disconnect the rear universal joint and let the back end of the drive shaft rest on any kind of a support out of the way. Remove the bolts which hold the carrier to the front face of the axle housing and slide the carrier out from under the car. Remove the carrier to a convenient work place.

Clean up the carrier and remove the lock plates from the side bearing adjusting cages. Loosen the 4 pedestal cap bolts just enough to permit backing off the adjusting cages. The cages have right hand threads.

Now remove the 4 cap bolts and both caps and lift off the differential and bearings. If the ring gear is to be replaced, unbolt it from the case at this time.

Note: Before installing a new ring gear, the ring gear seat on the case should be trued up to .003 inch maximum runout. The existing runout can be checked with a dial indicator by mounting the case into the differential carrier with its bearing in place.

However, this is only good to check the ring gear seat. If truing up is required it will have to be done in a lathe or suitable case turning equipment.

When truing up the ring gear mounting face keep in mind that the face and shoulder must be true with the differential running in its own bearings.

Pinion Removal

Remove the pinion shaft nut (they are sometimes staked into place) and pull off the U joint flange. A puller may be needed for this, some flanges are fitted tightly. Tap the pinion out the back of the carrier using a soft lead or brass hammer.

The pinion will come out, carrying with it the rear bearing cone and rolls and the "crumple" spacer. The rear bearing race and the front bearing assembly will remain in the case.

Pull the pinion oil seal using an inertia (sliding weight) type puller or if a new seal is to be installed simply pry the old one out. Lift out the front bearing cone and rolls.

The housing now contains the front and rear bearing races. If new bearings are to be installed, drive the rear bearing race out the back of the case and the front race out the front of the case.

Note: The pinion shim on Olds and Pontiac is in front of the rear bearing race.

Clean up the housing and install new races using a bearing race driver or if a driver is not available a brass drift, tapping gently around the rim of the race so as not to cock it in the housing. Seat both new races firmly against the shoulders (against the shims on Olds and Pontiac) of the housing. The housing is now ready for reassembly.

Pinion Shim Selection

Chevrolet 1955 model pinions are marked with a + (plus) or = (minus) followed by a number. The gasket face of the carrier is marked S or D followed by a number. S indicates Shallow, D indicates Deep and the mark means that the carrier bearing shoulder is Shallow or Deep the amount indicated by the number (in thousandths of an inch).

1956-58 Chevrolet pinions are marked with a code number in a circle. This code number is intended for

Carrier Markings	PINION MARKINGS										
	-5	-4	-3	-2	-1	0	+1	+2	+3	+4	+5
S-3		.024	.024	.024	.027	.027	.027	.030	.030	.030	.033
S-2	.024	.024	.024	.027	.027	.027	.030	.030	.030	.033	.033
S-1	.024	.024	.027	.027	.027	.030	.030	.030	.033	.033	.033
0	.024	.027	.027	.027	.030	.030	.030	.033	.033	.033	.036
D-1	.027	.027	.027	.030	.030	.030	.033	.033	.033	.036	.036
D-2	.027	.027	.030	.030	.030	.033	.033	.033	.036	.036	.036
D-3	.027	.030	.030	.030	.033	.033	.033	.036	.036	.036	

Fig. 16—Chevrolet shim chart—1955

INSTALL RING AND PINION GEAR AND/OR PINION BEARINGS — continued

use with pinion setting gauge fixture #J 6266 on which is attached dial indicator #KMO-30. The code number on the pinion is written down, the reading on the dial indicator is written under it and subtracted from it. The difference is the thickness of shims required.

If the special fixture is not available, a very close to accurate shim thickness can be determined by comparing the markings on the old pinion with the marking on the new pinion.

Where the new pinion code number is higher than the old pinion code number—add shims to equal the difference.

When the new pinion code number is lower than the old pinion code number—subtract shims to equal the difference.

Example:

Old pinion	New pinion	Change Shim pack
42	45	add .003 in.
45	41	remove .004 in.
51	45	remove .006 in.

Accompanying this text is a chart, Fig. 16, showing the correct starting shim for each pinion-carrier marking for 1955 models. Zero or no mark at all on the pinion and/or carrier indicates nominal size and is indicated in the zero column of the chart. If new pinion bearings are to be used, see "Shim Pack Selection for New Pinion Bearings," Section 22.

Installation of Pinion and Ring Gear

On Chevrolet install the shim or the pinion with the tangs toward the pinion face and press on the rear bearing cone and rolls. On Olds and Pontiac the shim is in front of the rear bearing race.

Insert the pinion into the carrier and install the front bearing cone and rolls and the U joint flange but do not install the "crumple" spacer nor the oil seal until final setting is assured.

Run the pinion nut up and tighten until 10 to 15 inch pounds torque is required to turn the pinion. This is not the final setting but will serve to check the tooth contact markings.

Install the differential assembly with its new ring gear and bearings and turn up the adjusting cage on the ring gear side until there is zero lash in the gears. Back off on the adjuster and again turn it up to be sure there is exactly zero backlash—sort of sneak up on the adjustment.

Now turn up the cage on the side opposite the ring gear until there is zero clearance in the side bearings—sneak up on this adjustment also. Now tighten it one notch past zero which will preload the side bearings slightly and develop a little backlash between the gears.

The rear is now set up well enough to get a mesh marking. See "Pinion Mesh Markings," Section 25.

When the markings are satisfactory remove the pinion gear nut, the U joint flange and the front bearing cone and insert a new spacer.

Replace the bearing cone and rolls and drive in a new oil seal assembly using a bearing driver or by tapping gently around its rim. Install the U joint yoke and the pinion nut.

Tighten the pinion nut and continue tightening until 15 to 25 inch pounds torque are required to turn the pinion. The new spacer will "crumple" somewhat as the nut is being tightened.

Stake the nut in this position. Install the differential side bearing lock plates, securely tighten the pedestal nuts and reinstall the carrier in the car using a new gasket.

Fill the rear with suitable lubricant.

INSTALL RING AND PINION GEAR AND/OR PINION BEARINGS

SECTION 17

CHRYSLER—All Models

DE SOTO—All Models

DODGE-DART—All Models

FORD—thru 1956 Exc. Station Wagons

MERCURY—1954 Exc. Station Wagons

PLYMOUTH—All Models

Keep in mind that the job of installing a ring and pinion gear and/or pinion bearing is one that requires careful, patient, clean workmanship. It may be necessary to disassemble the rear two or three times before the correct pinion shims have been decided.

Removal from Car

Jack up the back of the car and support it with stand jacks on the frame in front of the rear axle "kick up." Drain the lubricant from the rear and remove both axle shafts as outlined under Axle Shaft and/or Bearing Removal.

Split the rear universal joint and let the back end of the driveshaft down toward the floor. Remove the bolts which hold the carrier to the rear axle housing and lift the carrier out from under the vehicle and remove to a bench where it can be mounted conveniently. Carefully scrape the gasket from the mounting flange of the carrier and the mounting face of the axle housing.

With the carrier mounted firmly on the bench, remove the pinion shaft nut (some of these are staked on, others held with cotter pins). Pull off the universal joint flange. A puller or suitable substitute may be required since some of the flanges fit rather tightly on the pinion splines.

Remove the differential side bearing adjusting cage lock plates and back off slightly on the adjusting cages to relieve the pressure and then take out the four pedestal cap bolts, lift off the pedestal and take out the differential assembly with its ring gear and bearings.

Tap the pinion shaft toward the rear and out of the housing. It will carry with it the rear bearing cone and rolls and the bearing spacer (on those models which have a spacer).

Remove the pinion oil seal. Since a new oil seal should be installed, simply pry the old one out, which will of course damage it beyond reusing. Lift out the front bearing cone and rolls.

The pinion housing will now contain the front and rear bearing races and if the new ones are to be installed the front race is driven out the front of the case and the rear race out the rear of the case. Bearing drivers are used for this purpose, but if a suitable size bearing driver is not available the race can be driven out by tapping gently around its rim. Be sure to tap gently since a heavy blow may cock the race and render it very difficult to remove and also may cause the race to cut or scar the bearing seat in the housing and render the entire housing useless.

Thoroughly clean up the housing. Install the new bearing races by driving at their rim and seat them firmly in the housing.

If new differential side bearings

INSTALL RING AND PINION GEAR AND/OR PINION BEARINGS — continued

are to be used they are installed at this time. A hook type bearing cone puller is required to take off the differential side bearings. Attempting to jar or jolt the side bearings off the differential generally results in damaging it beyond use.

Install new differential side bearing cones, seating them firmly on the differential.

Remove the pinion rear bearing cone from the pinion shaft, being careful not to damage the shim which will be found behind the bearing. Carefully preserve or measure the thickness of the shim, making a note of the measurement.

Pinion Depth Control
Shim Selection

On Plymouth, Dodge, DeSoto, Chrysler, Ford thru 1956 (except Ford station wagons) and 1954 Mercury the pinions are marked with a + (plus) or a — (minus) followed by a number. This code marking is intended for use with special pinion depth gauges.

Gauge #C758 A for Chrysler
Gauge #C758 B for DeSoto and Dodge
Gauge #758 C for Plymouth
Gauge #4610 A or P for Ford
Gauge #4610 CC for Mercury

If these special tools are not available, the proper shim thickness can be determined by comparing the code number on the old pinion with the code on the new one. See "Shim Pack Selection by Pinion Code Markings."

Insert the shims selected from the chart onto the pinion so that they bottom on the shoulder of the pinion Press on the rear bearing and place the spacer on the pinion shaft, but not the shims found in front of the spacer. These are bearing preload shims and at this time they will not be needed since this is a check to determine whether or not the proper pinion depth shims are being used.

Install the pinion in the housing and insert the front bearing cone and rolls. Install the universal joint flange

and pinion nut, but at this time do not put in the oil seal.

Hold the universal joint flange and slowly and very carefully tighten the pinion nut until from 8 to 12 in. lbs. are required to turn the pinion. This is not the final preload but will do for the test.

Install the differential case and bearing caps and tighten up the adjusting cage on the ring gear side until there is zero play between the ring gear and the pinion. Now tighten the cage on the side opposite the gear until there is zero play in the bearings. When the zero point has been reached turn the cage one notch further to put a preload on the pinion side bearings. These two adjustments are critical and should be done with extreme care.

Now refer to "Pinion Mesh Markings," Section 25.

When proper markings have been obtained remove the pinion shaft nut and take off the pinion shaft flange. Pull out the front bearing and insert shims on the pinion in back of the front bearing cone. Reinstall the cone and the universal joint flange and nut, but not the oil seal.

Tighten up the nut, being careful in checking how much pressure is required to turn the pinion shaft while tightening the nut.

The object is to arrive at between 15 and 25 in. lbs. pressure to turn the pinion shaft when the nut has been run up to 200 ft. lbs. torque.

If it is found when the nut is run up to 200 ft. lbs. torque it requires less than 15 in. lbs. to turn the pinion, then the flange and bearing will have to be removed and a thin shim removed.

Rearrange the pack so that .001 less shims are used.

Keep repeating until 15-25 in. lbs. are required to turn the pinion. At this point, remove the pinion nut and the universal joint flange, install a new pinion oil seal, replace the universal joint yoke and the pinion nut and run the nut up to 200-250 ft. lbs. torque and stake it in this position.

Recheck at the ring gear to make sure that the backlash of the gears is between .006 and .010 inch measured at the rim of the ring gear. Securely tighten the bearing pedestal caps and install the adjusting cage lock plates. Install the carrier in the housing using a new gasket, secure, fill with lubricant and recouple the rear universal joint.

Chrysler and DeSoto
Drum or Barrel
Type Differential Cases

Some of the Chrysler New Yorker, Saratoga and Imperial models and some DeSoto models, together with their station wagons, are fitted with a drum type differential case. If the differential pinions and/or the axle side gears are to be removed or serviced this case must be disassembled.

In order to disassemble the pinions and/or the left side axle gear the end plate on the right side of the differential case must be removed. Note: To take out the differential pinion cross pin it is necessary to remove the ring gear.

A dowel pin is used on the periphery of the differential case to prevent the end plate from turning once it is screwed into its proper position. This can be located readily and it must be drilled out.

Once the pin is drilled out the differential case can be clamped in any type of holding device, such as a vise with well padded jaws and a spanner type wrench can be used to unscrew the right side case cap. This cap is very difficult to unscrew and does require quite a little bit of effort and patience.

It is screwed in on a right hand thread and is a fairly tight fit.

The only way to disassemble it is to unscrew this cap regardless of the effort required.

On all Chrysler, DeSoto, Dodge and Plymouth rear axles the ring gear must be removed in order to drive out the differential pinion pin.

INSTALL RING AND PINION GEAR AND/OR PINION BEARINGS

BUICK SPECIAL—All Models

FORD—All Station Wagons thru 1956

HUDSON—All Models

LINCOLN—All Models

MERCURY—1955-56 Models and all Station Wagons

SECTION 18

NASH—All Models

OLDSMOBILE F-85

RAMBLER

STUDEBAKER—All Models

VALIANT-LANCER—All Models

WILLYS—All Models

The above captioned models are all equipped with an integral housing type rear axle assembly. On this type axle all adjustments, pinion depth, pinion bearing preload, differential bearing preload, ring and pinion backlash are controlled and adjusted

INSTALL RING AND PINION GEAR AND/OR PINION BEARINGS — continued

by means of shims. There are no screw adjusters.

Patience and careful workmanship are needed to service this type rear since to change a differential side bearing shim requires partial disassembly of the rear and to change a pinion bearing shim requires complete disassembly.

While it is possible to remove the ring gear and pinion with the axle assembly under the car, the job can be done more quickly and accurately on the bench.

Jack up the car and support it with stand jacks at the frame in front of the rear axle "kick up." Drain the lubricant. On Buick Special beginning 1961, R. & R. differential housing assembly, see car section.

Disconnect the hydraulic brake lines and the hand brake cables. Detach the shock absorbers and the sway or track bar. Split the rear universal joint. Remove the nuts from the spring U bolts and detach the rear spring shackle. Lower the back end of the spring to the floor. Slide the rear axle assembly out from under the vehicle. Note: If the wheels are removed first, very little clearance is needed to get the assembly out from under the car.

Set the assembly up in a convenient workplace (two stand jacks make a good holding fixture). Remove the cover and scrape the gasket surface clean ready for a new gasket. Remove both axle shafts as explained under "Axle Shaft and/or Bearing Renew."

Remove the four pedestal cap bolts and lift off the caps.

The differential side bearings are fitted to preload which "spreads" the pedestals approximately .010 in. If a special pedestal spreading fixture is available, attach it to the housing and spread the pedestals just barely enough to pull the differential assembly out of the housing. DO NOT OVERSPREAD.

If a special spreading fixture is not available, pry the differential out of the case using two pry bars. Place a piece of wood on the gasket surface of the housing so as to avoid nicking the surface with the pry bar.

If new pinion bearings only are to be installed, clean up the differential and its bearings, being careful not to get grit or sludge into the bearings and set the differential off to one side, ready to be reinstalled. If the rear had been running satisfactorily before the pinion bearings failed, the differential adjusting shims, located behind the side bearing cones, will be the correct ones for that ring gear.

If a new ring gear and pinion and/

or new differential side bearings are to be installed, pull both side bearings off the differential and very carefully "mike" the thickness of the shims. Make a note of the total thickness of each shim pacck. This is very important.

Replace Ring Gear

Ring gears on all of the above captioned models are bolted to the case. Remove the bolts and lockplates and tap off the ring gear. Before installing the new ring gear, the case should be set up in its own bearings (in the axle housing if necessary and the ring gear mounting face on the differential checked for run-out with a dial indicator. Maximum runout should not exceed .003 in. full indicator reading. If a dial indicator (or suitable substitute) is not available, attaching the ring gear should be farmed out to a shop which specializes in and has the proper equipment for this particular job. Runout in excess of .003 in. will almost invariably result in noisy gear operation.

Removal of Pinion

Remove the nut from the front end of the pinion shaft. (Pinion nuts are tightened to 150-00 ft. lb. torque and they are usually staked in place so that quite a lot of force is needed to remove them.) Pull off the universal joint flange. It may be necessary to get the flange off since some of these flanges fit rather tightly.

If a flange pulling device is not available, take a large brass (or other soft metal) punch and drive the pinion shaft to the rear. On very tight flanges, driving the pinion shaft can result in damage to the front bearing, but if new bearings are to be installed this will not matter.

Drive the pinion out the back of the case. It will carry with it the rear bearing cone and, very likely, the small (bearing preload) adjusting shims. Whether shims come out with the pinion or not, look into the case to make sure none of the shims are lying in the case. Sometimes part of the shim pack sticks to the front bearing and it is very important to measure the total thickness of the shim pack. Make a note of the total thickness.

With the pinion on the bench, pull off the rear bearing cone and "mike" the total thickness of the shim pack which will be found in back of the bearing (between the bearing and the gear). The case now contains the front and rear bearing races. Note: If no shims are found between the bearing cone and the gear shoulder, they will

be found in front of the rear bearing race (between the race and the depth face in the housing).

If a bearing race driver is not available, remove the races by tapping gently around the rim of the race. Do not tap too hard or the race may cock in the housing and bind very tightly. The rear race comes out the back of the case (see note above) and the front race out the front. Clean up the housing ready for reassembly.

Pinion Marking

On the above captioned models the pinion is marked with a plus or minus mark followed by a number. This mark is intended for use with special pinion depth micrometer gauges.

If pinion depth micrometer gauges are not available, the correct shim pack may be ascertained by adjusting the thickness to compensate first for the new pinion, and second, for the bearings. See "Shim Pack Selection for New Bearings." Section 22 and "Shim Pack Selection by Pinion Depth Marking," Section 21. Take the shims selected from the chart and place them on the pinion shaft (or in front of the rear bearing race, depending on which rear is being worked on) and install the pinion bearing.

Insert the pinion into the housing with its spacer in place, but without the bearing preload shims. Do not install the oil seal at this time. Install the front bearing cone and the universal joint flange and pinion nut.

Tighten up the pinion nut while very carefully measuring the amount of force required to turn the pinion shaft. Keep tightening the nut until from 10 to 15 in. lbs. are required to turn the pinion shaft. This preload will be fine for checking the pinion mesh markings. However, this is not the final preload. Insert the differential into the carrier and select shims for it according to "Differential Side Bearing Shim Selection," Section 23.

Now check the pinion mesh markings as shown in Section 25.

When the proper shims have been selected, remove the universal joint flange and bearing and insert shims in back of the bearing, replace the bearing and the universal joint flange and start tightening the pinion nut.

While tightening the pinion nut, check the amount of force required to turn the pinion. This should be done carefully since there is the possibility that there is insufficient number of shims being used on this test and damage to the bearings could result if the nut is pulled up too tightly.

Keep adding shims until from 15

to 20 in. lbs. force is required to turn the pinion shaft with the pinion nut pulled up to 200-250 ft. lbs.

When this point has been reached

remove the pinion nut, remove the universal joint flange, install the oil seal, reinstall the universal joint

flange and the pinion nut and secure to 200-250 ft. lbs. torque.

Reinstall on the vehicle and fill with lubricant.

INSTALL RING AND PINION GEAR AND/OR PINION BEARINGS

SECTION 19

EDSEL—All Models
FAIRLANE—All Models
FORD—1957-63 Models
MERCURY—1957-63 Models
METEOR—All Models

This construction uses a removable pinion bearing housing in addition to the removable carrier assembly.

Pinion depth is controlled by shims placed between the carrier housing and the pinion bearing housing.

Disassembly of the Carrier

Support the car on stand jacks at the rear axle, remove both axle shafts as outlined under axle shaft and/or bearing for this model, split the rear universal joint and either lower the driveshaft to the floor or tie it up out of the way.

Remove the bolts which hold the carrier assembly to the rear axle housing and remove the carrier assembly from the vehicle to the workbench.

On the bench, remove the bolts which hold the pinion bearing housing to the carrier housing and carefully slide the two apart. The front end of the pinion is mounted in a pilot bearing, making it necessary to pull the assembly loose in a straight line.

There is a shim (in addition to the O ring oil seal) used between the pinion bearing housing and the carrier housing. Be careful not to damage this shim since it controls the depth of the pinion. Instead, mike it carefully and make a note of its thickness.

Remove the nut which holds the universal joint flange to the pinion shaft and pull off the universal joint flange.

Press the pinion shaft out through the pinion bearing carrier. This will leave the front bearing cone in the carrier housing, but the rear bearing cone will come out with the pinion.

On the carrier, just barely loosen the four pedestal cap screws so that the differential side bearing adjusting cages can be backed off relieving the preload. Once the preload is relieved, remove the four cap screws, take off the caps, lift out the bearing adjusting cages and lift out the differential case with its ring gear.

Cap screws are used to hold the ring gear to the differential case and these cap screws also hold the case together.

Carefully mark the relative position of the two halves of the case before removing the bolts.

Before installing a new ring gear the case should be checked while running on its own bearings for runout for the mounting face of the ring gear.

The maximum runout should not exceed .003 inch full indicator reading.

Install the new ring gear on the differential case.

If new bearings are to be installed on the differential side they should be installed at this time. No shims are necessary on these bearings since there are screw-type cages provided to adjust for backlash and ring gear mesh.

Installation of Pinion Gear

Remove the old bearing from the pinion or install a new bearing on the new pinion. Install the bearing race in the pinion carrier by driving the race at its rim. If a bearing race driver is not available it should be tapped around the rim very gently and carefully so as not to cock the race in the housing.

Slide the pinion gear and its bearing into the back of the housing and then install the bearing spacer. Install the front bearing cone, the oil slinger and seal and the universal joint flange.

Now hold the flange in a vise and tighten the pinion shaft nut until the torque required to turn the pinion shaft is 8-12 inch pounds if the old bearings are being used, or 17-27 inch pounds if new bearings are being used.

This should be done with extreme care. As the pinion shaft nut is being tightened keep rotating the pinion frequently to allow the bearing to seat and also to check the preload.

Pinion Shim Selection

There are two marks on the pinion gear: one, the matched gear set marking (this same number will also be on the ring gear); the other, the shim adjustment required for that particular pinion.

This number will be preceded by either a plus or a minus. If no number is found other than the gear matching number, the pinion is presumed to be zero or nominal setting.

Nominal setting requires a .015 inch shim.

A minus mark on the pinion indicates the pinion should move closer to the ring gear by the number of thousandths indicated by the number, for instance, a minus five indicates that the pinion must be moved in .005 inch closer to the ring gear than the nominal setting.

A plus sign indicates that the pinion gear is moved further away from the ring gear (requires more shims).

Compare the marks on the original pinion with the mark on the new pinion to determine how the original shim should be modified. Example: original shim .015, original pinion −1, new pinion +1.

The new pinion then requires .002 inch thicker shim; therefore, since the old shim was .015 the new one will be 0.17.

If the new pinion has the same mark as the old pinion, the old shim can be reused. When the proper shim has been selected, install the pinion carrier housing onto the differential housing.

Installation of Differential

Install the differential and its bearings and caps into the carrier and manually slide the ring gear over until it comes into solid mesh with the pinion. Snug up the pedestal cap screws.

On the ring gear side, tighten the bearing adjusting cage until there is zero lash between the ring and pinion gear. Now tighten the adjusting cage on the side opposite the ring gear until there is zero clearance in the bearing and then tighten it one more notch.

Check the backlash between the ring gear and pinion. The backlash for new gears is .004 to .009. If the lash is too great the ring gear should be

INSTALL RING AND PINION GEAR AND/OR PINION BEARINGS — continued

shifted over by readjusting the cages to provide the proper backlash.

Secure the pedestal cap bolts to 75-80 ft. lbs. torque.

It's a good idea to measure backlash in several different places since this is a good indication of runout. If the measurements vary more than .003 inch between any two places there is excessive runout in the gears or their mountings which must be corrected to obtain a satisfactory operation.

When making final settings on the adjusting cages always make the final setting in a tightening direction.

When the assembly is completed, check the gear mesh markings and compare them with those given in Section 24.

INSTALL RING AND PINION GEAR AND/OR PINION BEARINGS

SECTION 20

FALCON-COMET—All Models

There are four different axle housings and three types of differential case used in this rear end construction. The design change depends upon car model and engine size, therefore, the model-year identification plate should be used to identify correct model and gear ratio when ordering replacement parts.

The rear axle assembly uses an integral-type housing. The axle shafts are held in the housing by ball bearings and a bearing retaining plate at the axle housing outer ends.

The differential assembly is mounted on two opposed tapered roller bearings. The bearings support and position the differential between two pedestals and spanner adjustable caps. Differential bearing preload and drive gear backlash is controlled by the thrust of these large pedestal nuts against the differential side bearing cups.

The drive pinion assembly is mounted on two opposed tapered roller bearings. Pinion bearing preload is adjusted by a collapsible spacer on the pinion shaft. Pinion and ring gear tooth contact is adjusted by shims between the rear bearing cone and pinion gear. Gear ratio is stamped on a metal tag attached to the differential case inspection cover. This axle is not equipped with a lubricant drain.

Rear Axle Housing Assembly, Remove

1. Raise car and support it on the underbody.
2. Loosen the differential carrier inspection cover, drain and discard lubricant.
3. Disconnect drive shaft at rear "U" joint.
4. Disconnect rear shock absorbers at axle.
5. Remove both rear axle shafts.
6. Separate brake "T" from rear axle housing and separate hydraulic brake line from its retaining clip on axle housing.
7. Disconnect both rear brake backing plates from the axle housing and wire them out of the way.

8. Support the axle housing on a jack, then remove spring "U" bolts and plates.
9. Lower axle housing and remove it from under the car.

Rear Axle Housing Assembly, Install

1. Raise the axle housing up into position and install spring "U" bolts and plates. Torque spring "U" bolt nuts to 13-20 ft. lbs.
2. Attach brake backing plates. Use new gaskets on each side of the backing plates.
3. Install axle shafts, brake drums and wheels.
4. Attach brake line "T" fitting to the axle housing, and fasten the hydraulic brake line in its retainer on the housing.
5. Raise the axle housing and connect the shock absorbers.
6. Connect drive shaft at rear "U" joint.
7. Clean inspection cover and axle housing. Apply sealer to both sides of inspection cover gasket. Daub cover attaching screw threads with antiseize compound. Attach inspection cover and torque screws to 15-20 ft. lbs.
8. Fill axle to level with proper lubricant.

Differential Case and Drive Pinion, Remove and Disassemble

With the axle assembly out of the car and the inspection cover removed:
1. Remove the differential side bearing adjusting nut locks.
2. Mark the differential bearing caps, adjusting nuts and case for relative identity during reassembly.
3. Remove differential bearing pedestal cap bolts and caps.
4. Remove differential case and bearing cups.
5. Remove ring gear attaching bolts. Separate ring gear from differential case with a soft-faced hammer.
6. Drive out the differential pinion shaft retaining pin with a punch.

7. Use a drift to drive out the differential pinion shaft. Remove the gears and thrust washers.
8. Hold the drive pinion flange and remove pinion nut and flat washer.
9. With a soft-faced hammer, drive the pinion out of the front bearing cone and remove it through the rear of the carrier casting.
10. Remove and replace damaged bearings and bearing cups as required. Special pullers are needed except for the differential side bearing cups.

Drive Pinion Shim Selection

Pinion bore dimension tolerances and operating positions of the gears present the need for various shim thicknesses between the pinion rear bearing cone and the pinion gear. When the shim thickness is decreased, the pinion is moved away from the ring gear. The reverse is true when shim thickness is increased, the pinion is moved closer to the ring gear. Shims are available in thicknesses of 0.008" thru 0.024" in increments of 0.001".

If a new ring gear and pinion set is to be installed, refer to the pinion gear end marking for plus(+) or minus(−) signs followed by a number.

To select the correct shim thickness required for proper installation of a new pinion gear, perform the following steps:
1. Mike the thickness of the original shim pack.
2. Refer to "Shim Thickness Table." Note the shim adjustment number on both the old and new pinion. Observe the amount of change shown in the table under "New Pinion Marking" and in line with "Old Pinion Marking." Note the reading. Add or subtract the reading obtained from that of the original shim pack and note the result.
3. To the above result, add or subtract the shim thickness correction indicated during the gear tooth

INSTALL RING AND PINION GEAR AND/OR PINION BEARINGS — continued

contact pattern check. This final result is the shim thickness required for installation of the new drive pinion.

Drive Pinion Assembly and Installation

1. Place the shim and pinion bearing cone on the pinion shaft. Press the bearing and shim firmly against the pinion shaft shoulder.
2. Put a new pinion bearing preload spacer on the pinion shaft. If the unit uses a long spacer, be sure the large diameter end of the spacer is against the pinion rear bearing inner race.
3. Lubricate the pinion rear bearing with axle lubricant.
4. Lubricate the pinion front bearing cone and place it in the housing.
5. Coat the outer edge of a new oil seal with oil resistant sealer and install it into the carrier casting.
6. Insert the drive pinion shaft flange into the oil seal and hold it firmly against the pinion front bearing cone. From the rear of the carrier casting, insert the pinion shaft into the flange.
7. Place the flat washer and nut on the pinion shaft. Use a holding tool on the flange and tighten the shaft nut. As the nut is tightened the pinion shaft is pulled into the front bearing cone and into the flange. Continue this tightening action, reducing end play, until the bearing cone and flange have bottomed on the collapsible spacer (no end play). From this point on, tighten the nut very slowly as the preload sleeve is being collapsed. A minimum torque of 140 ft. lbs. is required.

Caution: If the nut is overtorqued to exceed the limits, the pinion shaft must be removed and a new collapsible sleeve installed. Do not decrease the preload by loosening the pinion shaft nut.

8. As soon as there is preload on the bearings, turn the pinion shaft in both directions a few times to seat

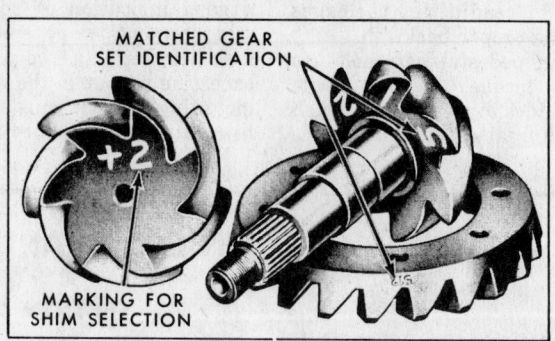

MATCHED GEAR SET IDENTIFICATION

+2

MARKING FOR SHIM SELECTION

the bearings.

9. Adjust pinion preload on used bearings to 10-16 inch pounds torque. On new bearings, to 17-27 inch pounds.

Differential Case Assemble and Install

1. Lubricate all differential parts with axle lubricant, before they are installed in the case.
2. Place side gears and thrust washers in case.
3. Place the two pinion gears and thrust washers exactly opposite each other in the case openings and in mesh with the side gears.
4. Turn the pinions and thrust washers until the holes in the pinion gears align with the pinion shaft holes in the case.
5. Start the pinion shaft into the differential case. Align the shaft retaining pin hole with the pin hole in the case. Drive the shaft into place and install the pinion shaft retaining pin.
6. Place the drive gear on the differential case and install attaching bolts. Torque the bolts to 40-50 ft. lbs.
7. Press differential bearing cones onto the differential assembly.
8. Lubricate the bearing bores of the pedestals, place the cups on the bearings and set the case assembly in the carrier casting.
9. Position the differential case in the bores until a slight amount of backlash is felt between the gear

teeth. Hold differential in place.

10. Set adjusting nuts in the bores so that they just contact the bearing cups.
11. Match up and place the bearing caps on their respective pedestals.
12. Install bearing cap bolts. While tightening the bolts, turn the adjusting nut with an adjusting nut spanner wrench.
13. If the adjusting nuts bind as the pedestal caps are tightened, remove the caps and inspect the caps and nuts for cross-threading or other damage. When satisfied that the nuts are correctly seated in the pedestals and caps, tighten the cap bolts. Now loosen the cap bolts, then torque them to 5 ft. lbs.
14. Loosen the right hand adjusting nut until it is away from the cup. Tighten the left-hand nut until the ring gear is just fully meshed with the pinion with no back lash.
15. Loosen the left-hand adjusting nut 1—1½ notches. Tighten the right-hand adjusting nut to the specified 2½—3 notches beyond the point where it first contacts the bearing cup. As preload is applied from the right-hand side, the ring gear is moved away from the pinion and usually results in correct backlash. Backlash should be 0.008″—0.012″.
16. Torque differential cap bolts to 40-50 ft. lbs. Measure pinion-to-ring gear backlash at several

Old Pinion Marking	New Pinion Marking								
	−4	−3	−2	−1	0	+1	+2	+3	+4
+4	+0.008	+0.007	+0.006	+0.005	+0.004	+0.003	+0.002	+0.001	0
+3	+0.007	+0.006	+0.005	+0.004	+0.003	+0.002	+0.001	0	−0.001
+2	+0.006	+0.005	+0.004	+0.003	+0.002	+0.001	0	−0.001	−0.002
+1	+0.005	+0.004	+0.003	+0.002	+0.001	0	−0.001	−0.002	−0.003
0	+0.004	+0.003	+0.002	+0.001	0	−0.001	−0.002	−0.003	−0.004
−1	+0.003	+0.002	+0.001	0	−0.001	−0.002	−0.003	−0.004	−0.005
−2	+0.002	+0.001	0	−0.001	−0.002	−0.003	−0.004	−0.005	−0.006
−3	+0.001	0	−0.001	−0.002	−0.003	−0.004	−0.005	−0.006	−0.007
−4	0	−0.001	−0.002	−0.003	−0.004	−0.005	−0.006	−0.007	−0.008

INSTALL RING AND PINION GEAR AND/OR PINION BEARINGS — continued

points around the ring gear to check runout. Runout should not

exceed 0.002".
17. Run a gear tooth contact pattern

check as outlined in section 26 of this axle group.

SHIM PACK SELECTION BY PINION CODE MARKINGS

SECTION 21

The following method of checking pinion depth marking does not apply to the markings on Buick models starting in 1956.

There are several marks on most pinions, usually the part number, the number indicating a matched gear set, and the pinion depth code mark. The pinion depth code mark can be identified easily because it is usually etched rather than stamped and is almost always etched on the rear face of the tooth itself rather than the body or hub of the gear. In almost all cases a plus or minus symbol is etched rather than stamped and is almost always etched on the rear face of the tooth itself rather than the body or hub gear. In almost all cases a plus or minus symbol is etched on one gear tooth and the number is etched on the next tooth. If neither a plus or minus sign nor a number is found, the marking is presumed to be zero.

A plus sign indicates there is too much metal on the pinion (uses less shims; a minus sign indicates too little metal on the gear (uses more shims). The number states how many thousandths too much or too little.

If possible, secure a pinion from the parts department having the same markings as the old one and no change

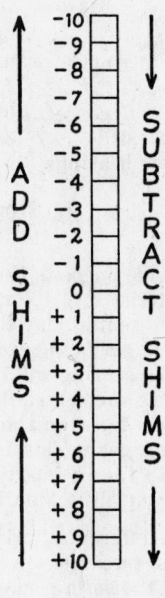

Fig. 18

in shims will be necessary to compensate for pinion depth. It may be necessary, however, to adjust the shim pack thickness to compensate for new bearings.

For a pinion having different markings from the old one, refer to the chart which shows how much shim thickness should be added to or subtracted from the original shim pack.

Using the chart, start at the number on the chart between the old pinion mark and the new pinion mark. The chart shows that if you count toward the bottom the shim pack is decreased; toward the top increases the shim pack.

For example:

An old pinion has −5 etched on the tooth. The new pinion has +3 etched on the tooth. The shim pack has .038 in. total thickness. On the chart above, starting with −5 (the old pinion mark) count to +3 (the mark on the new pinion) —8 blocks or .008 in. to be subtracted from the shim pack. The original pack had .038 in., subtract .008 in., new pack will have .030 in. shim thickness.

CAUTION: Keep in mind that the shim adjustment just made is to compensate for the manufacturing difference between the old and new pinion. It probably will be necessary to compensate further if new bearings are going to be used.

SHIM PACK SELECTION FOR NEW BEARINGS

SECTION 22

The standard manufacturing tolerance on the total width of a tapered roller bearing can be as much as .008 in. Therefore, in order to make proper allowances for possible differences between the old and new bearings it is necessary to know the total width of both the old and the new bearing.

On the old bearing, remove the cone from the pinion and the outer race from the housing. Assemble the bearing on the bench and place a machinist parallel bar across the outer race and then, using micrometers, measure from the face of the inner cone to the face of the parallel bar. Sub-

tract the thickness of the parallel bar. The difference will be the total width of the bearing. Make a note of this figure. Do the same with the new bearing and make a note of the figure. The difference between the width of the old and new bearing will be the amount of shims which will have to be changed to accommodate the new bearing.

If the new bearing is thinner, add the shims to the pack. If the new bearing is thicker, subtract the shims from the pack. Example:

Old bearing measures	1.495 in. across
Parallel measures	.500 the parallel
Old bearing is	.995 in.
New bearing measures	1.499 in. across
Parallel measures	.500 the parallel
New bearing is	.999 in. wide
New bearing	.999
Old bearing	.995
Difference	.004 in.

Remove .004 in. from the shim pack because the new bearing is thicker than the old bearing.

DIFFERENTIAL SIDE BEARING SHIM SELECTION

SECTION 23

When selecting shim pack thickness for differential side bearings, keep in mind that the bearings are preloaded a sufficient amount to "spread" the pedestals approximately .010 in. This means that the final shim packs make the differential .010 in. wider than the space where it must fit. Remove both differential side bearings and carefully mike the shim packs found behind each bearing. Make a note of the thickness of each pack and also the total thickness of both packs. Refer to section "Shim Pack Selection for New Bearing" and alter the total shim pack to compensate for the new bearings.

In the above example .085 in. shim thickness will be required to set the differential up with proper preload. It remains then to decide how many on the ring gear side, how many on the side opposite the ring gear.

Press the bearing cones on to the differential without any shims. Make sure the bearing cones are seated firmly against the shoulder.

Slip the races over the bearing cones and install the differential into the carrier but do not install the pedestal caps. Using two screwdrivers or two putty knives, pry against the outer race of the bearing is on the ring side, forcing the ring gear into mesh with the pinion. Pry until there is zero lash between the ring gear and pinion. CAUTION: Be sure the bearing on the side opposite the ring gear is fully entered into its race, otherwise the differential may tend to cock slightly, giving a false reading. To insure that the bearing will be firmly in its race, some shops install the pedestal cap finger tight on the side opposite the ring gear. This offers some resistance to the pry bars and keeps the bearing firmly seated in its race.

With the differential pried over until there is zero lash in the gears, select from the shim pack a combination of shims which will just take up the space between which will just take up the space between the outer race and the shoulder in the carrier on the

Example:

Shim pack on ring gear side	.038 in.
Shim pack opposite ring gear	.045 in.
Total	.083 in.
Required adjustment for bearings	
Ring gear side	.005 added
Side opposite ring gear	.003 removed
Net difference	.002 in.
Old shim pack	.083 in.
Add for new bearings	.002 added
New shim pack total	.085

ring gear side. The shims are too small, of course, to fit all around the race at the same time, but the selection can be rolled around in the space to be sure they fit tightly all the way around.

This group of shims will be just about right for the ring gear side of the differential.

Remove the differential, pull off the bearing cone on the ring gear side and install the group of shims just selected on the differential and reinstall the bearing, pressing it firmly against the shim pack.

The balance of the shims go behind the bearing cone on the side opposite the ring gear. Remove that bearing, install the shims and reinstall the bearing, seating it firmly also.

As stated in the first section, the differential assembly is now .010 in. wider than the space into which it must fit. If a spreader is available, spread the carrier just barely enough to slip the differential into place. If a spreader is not available, start the assembly into the carrier by cocking the outer races slightly so that their edges will enter into the carrier bearing seats and then press the differential into the carrier. Quite a bit of force is needed since pressing the differential "spreads" the carrier something more than .010 in.

Install the pedestal caps and secure.

SHIM COMBINATION CHART

SECTION 24

Most bearing manufacturers supply, for each of their bearings, shims in .005 in., 007 in. and .020 in. thickness. Using combinations of the above three shims the following shim packs can be obtained:

Required thickness	Shim combinations		
.005	(1) .005		
.007	(1) .007		
.010	(2) .005		
.012	(1) .005	(1) .007	
.014	(2) .007		
.015	(3) .005		
.017	(2) .005	(1) .007	
.019	(1) .005	(2) .007	
.020	(1) .020		
.021	(3) .007		
.022	(3) .005	(1) .007	
.024	(2) .005	(2) .007	

Required thickness	Shim combinations		
.025	(1) .005	(1) .020	
.025	(1)1005	(3) .007	
.027	(1) .007	(1) .020	
.028	(4) .007		
.029	(3) .005	(2) .007	
.030	(2) .005	(1) .020	
.031	(2) .005	(3) .007	
.032	(1) .020	(1) .007	(1) .005
.033	(1) .005	(2) .007	
.034	(1) .020	(2) .007	
.035	(1) .020	(3) .005	

The above sample list can be continued in increments of .001 in. to any desired pack thickness.

DRIVE SIDE

MOVE PINION TOWARDS
REAR OF CAR

COAST SIDE   DRIVE SIDE

MOVE RING GEAR
CLOSER TO PINION

COAST SIDE

MOVE PINION TOWARDS
FRONT OF CAR

TOE END OF TOOTH

HEEL END OF TOOTH

CORRECT MESH MARKINGS

MOVE RING GEAR
AWAY FROM PINION

PINION MESH MARKINGS
SECTION 25

The following method of determining the relative position of the ring gear and pinion and whether or not they are in proper mesh will prove satisfactory for all pinion and ring gears and should be followed by a final check even when the pinion depth has been determined by special micrometers. Assemble the pinion into the housing without preload and tighten up the pinion nut until a preload of about ten inch pounds is developed on the bearings to insure that they are completely free of end play.

This of course is not the final bearing preload setting but is a good one for checking the pinion mesh markings.

Install the differential assembly and adjust it to provide from .004 to .008

inch back lash of the ring gear measured at the rim of the ring gear.

Paint five or six of the ring gear teeth with red or white lead and, while the helper brakes the ring gear with a piece of wood, slowly turn the pinion until the ring gear makes at least one full revolution. The mesh of the pinion with the ring gear will be indicated as a mark in the red lead on the ring gear teeth. Compare this mark with the accompanying photographs. The caption on each photograph explains whether the mark indicates the pinion is too deep or too shallow, the ring gear too close or too far away.

The center photograph shows a proper marking.

When the marking is found to be improper it is customary to make trial changes in increment of .005 or .007 inch. In changing the shim .005-.007 inch throws the marking from say too deep to too shallow, obviously the selection is about half way between.

If after changing this increment of shims the mark still indicates that more must be changed, it is advisable to continue changing in the same increments, that is .005 to .007 inch.

While considerable time is generally required to disassemble the rear, press off the bearings, change the shims, press the bearing back on and reassemble the rear; this is still the only positive method of determining if the rear will operate quietly after it is finally installed on the vehicle.

IMPROVED TRACTION DIFFERENTIALS
SECTION 26

The principal distinction between any of the improved traction differentials and the conventional type units is the incorporation of a wheel drive control device. It directs extra pulling power to the car's rear wheel with the most traction, therefore, a decided advantage to the driver when operating in snow, ice or mud.

This control is accomplished, automatically, through the use of special axle gears that are part of either a cone or disc friction driving system. The clutching mechanism is actuated through the wedging motion of two beveled differential cross pins working on ramps.

The system is entirely automatic and requires no adjustment or attention, except care in the selection of lubricants. It is important that the

car manufacturer's recommendations be followed in this respect as chattering and damage can result from using improper compounds.

It is most important that correct identification of these units be made if successful maintenance procedures be followed. Therefore, a close examination of the differential carrier or the rear axle housing is in order. Most car makers furnish an identification tag, attached to the unit for this purpose as the outward appearance is generally similar. A rule-of-thumb way to distinguish between the standard and the controlled slip type unit is:

1. Raise both wheels off the ground.
2. With the parking brake off, turn one wheel forward (by hand) and

note the direction of rotation of the other wheel.

3. If the other wheel turns in the same direction as the one being turned, the rear axle is of the improved type.

4. If the other wheel turns in the opposite direction, the axle is of standard design.

CAUTION:

Non-slip differentials can create a problem in balancing rear tire or rear wheel assemblies. Balancing procedures that require one of the rear wheels to be raised and spun is hazardous since any abnormal friction will cause torque transfer to the stationary wheel resulting in movement of the vehicle.

BRAKE TYPE INDEX

MAKE	MODEL		SECTION	MAKE	MODEL		SECTION
BUICK				LINCOLN—CONTINENTAL			
	1954-60		2		1954-55	Front	11
	1961-62		3			Rear	2
	1963		10		1956-58		3
BUICK SPECIAL					1959-63		7
	1961-62		3	MERCURY			
	1963		10		1954-55	Front	11
CADILLAC						Rear	2
	1954-55		1		1956-57		3
	1956		2		1958-63		7
	1957-59	Front	8	OLDSMOBILE			
	1957-60	Rear	2		1954-58		1
	1960	Front	9		1959-61		3
	1961-63		10		1962-63		10
CHEVROLET	1954		2	OLDS F-85			
	1955-62		3		1961-62		6
	1963		10		1963		10
CHEVY II				PLYMOUTH			
	1962		3		1954-56	Front	15
	1963		10			Rear	16
CHRYSLER					1957-61		17
	1954-55	Front	15		1962-63		7
		Rear	16	PONTIAC			
	1956-62		17		1954-60		1
	1963		7		1961-63	Front	1
CORVAIR						Rear	3
	1960-62		4	RAMBLER			
	1963		10		1954-58	Six	13
CORVETTE					1958-61	Six	14
	1955-63		3		1958-59	American	14
DESOTO					1960-63	American	5
	1954-55	Front	15		1958-63	Ambassador	7
		Rear	16		1958-61	V-8	3
	1956-61		17		1962-63	Six & V-8	7
DODGE				STUDEBAKER			
	1954-56	Front	15		1954-62		14
		Rear	16		1963		7
	1957-61		17		1963	Avanti	*
	1961-63		7	TEMPEST			
FAIRLANE—METEOR					1961-62		6
	1962-63		7		1963		10
FALCON—COMET				VALIANT—LANCER			
	1960-62		5		1960-61		5
	1963		7		1962-63		3
FORD				WILLYS			
	1954	Front	11		1954-63		13
	1955	Front	12				
	1954-55	Rear	2				
	1956-60		3				
	1961-63		7				

* SEE CAR SECTION

HYDRAULIC SYSTEMS
WHEEL CYLINDERS

There are two general types of wheel cylinders, Single piston and Double piston. The double piston type, is divided into Step bored and Straight bored. Single piston wheel cylinders are used on Chrysler Lockhead brakes having two forward shoes. The purpose of step boring wheel cylinders is to get greater pressure on the forward shoe. For this reason, the larger bore is towards the forward shoe.

No fluid whatever should leak from a wheel cylinder. The slightest leak, just enough to dampen the dust boot is too much, if a cylinder is only suspected of leaking it must be serviced or replaced.

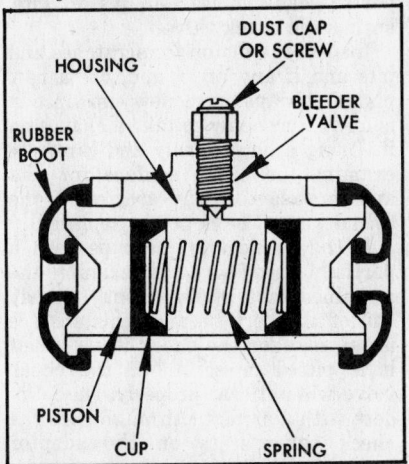

Typical straight bore wheel cylinder

Service on Wheel Cylinders

Jack up the car and remove the wheel and drum assembly from the brake to be serviced. Remove the brake shoe assemblies from the backing plate. At this point it is a good idea to thoroughly clean up the backing plate and the outside of the wheel cylinder before taking it off the backing plate.

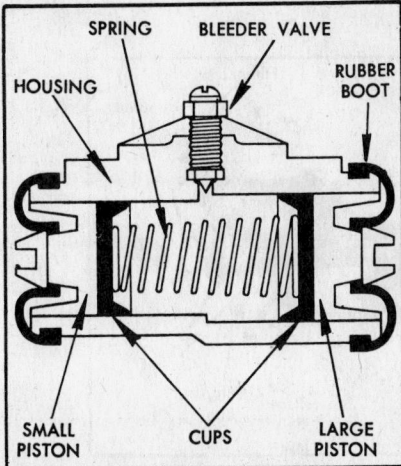

Typical step-bore wheel cylinder

ing plate.

Disconnect the hydraulic line. The flexible line on the front brakes is disconnected first where it joins to the metal line at the frame bracket. With a wrench, hold the end of the flexible line from turning and with another wrench, turn the compression nut on the metal line in a counter clockwise direction to disconnect. Now, using a wrench right at the wheel cylinder, take off the flexible line. Do not twist up the flexible line since this probably will damage it too much for further use. The line at the rear brakes is usually a metal line right up to the wheel cylinder and the compression nut is screwed right into the cylinder fitting.

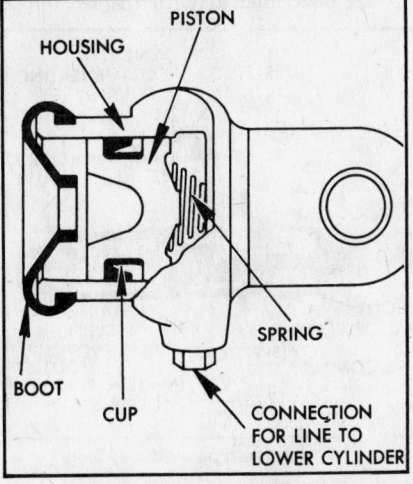

Typical single piston wheel cylinder

After the line is disconnected, remove the mounting bolts which hold the wheel cylinder to the backing plate.

On Lockheed brakes having two forward shoes the flexible line goes to the top cylinder only. A rigid line is used on the brake side of the backing plate to connect the top cylinder to the bottom cylinder.

Remove the boots from the cylinder and then take out the pistons and cups. If there are any scratches lengthwise of the piston on the outside diameter there are very likely matching scratches on the inside of the cylinder and it will be necessary to either replace the cylinder or have it honed.

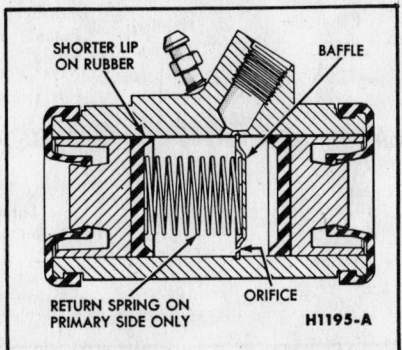

Typical baffle type wheel cylinder

In any case, thoroughly clean up the cylinder and, holding it up to the light, examine the inside surface for roughness or pits, examine it slowly and carefully since it is vital that the inside surface be perfectly smooth and regular. The reflected light pattern on the inside surface should be uninterrupted. If any defects are found the cylinder must be honed or replaced.

Mount the spring, cups, pistons and boots into the wheel cylinder, dipping each part in clean brake fluid before putting it into the cylinder. Put a wheel cylinder clamp on the cylinder to hold the pistons in place and mount the cylinder onto the backing plate. Connect up the lines and mount the brake shoes, drum and wheel.

MASTER CYLINDERS

The following text does not apply to cars fitted with Bendix Power Brakes. Cars fitted with Kelsey Hayes Power Brakes have Master cylinders which are only slightly modified conventional units.

Conventional Piston Type

For the purpose of servicing the master cylinder itself, (not removing it from the car) there are two types of master cylinders. First, the type with a straight through bore and second, the type with a partially closed bore. That is, the casting is made to take a standard line fitting at its front end, whereas the straight through bore type has a large adapter fitting at its front end to accommodate the line fitting.

Displacement Type Master Cylinders

Some cars use a master cylinder having a displacement piston (or rod) which does not contact the master cylinder bore. A primary and secondary cup are used but these are mounted in the master cylinder body and sealed around the outside diameter of the long piston. The master cylinder is made in two pieces: the forward piece, known as the cylinder nose and insert, contains the stoplight switch and the copper line takeoffs and in its back end the primary cup, piston bearing and sealing "O" ring.

The rear portion of the casting contains the reservoir into which is placed the secondary cup and the secondary cup retainer. There are two holes drilled in the front nose of the displacement piston. These two holes are arranged to come out the outside diameter of the piston, back a little

HYDRAULIC BRAKES

further so that they will index with the reservoir and allow for compensation of the master cylinder each time the brakes are released.

Dual Type Master Cylinders

Two types of Dual Master cylinders are used in some cars, starting in 1962. The rear reservoir supplies the front brakes and the front reservoir supplies the rear brakes. The Moraine type has the two reservoirs completely separated. The Bendix type are only partially separated.

Servicing the Displacement Type Master Cylinder

Remove the unit from the car and clean the outside of the cylinder thoroughly so that no grit gets into the working parts while it is being disassembled. Place the master cylinder in a vise with the push rod up, remove the boot and the retaining ring and the guide bumper washer. This will permit pulling the push rod and piston from the body. Remove the return spring, retainer and piston washer. To disassemble the push rod from the piston, insert the piston into a 9/16 in. inside diameter washer and support the washer in the jaws of a vise. <u>Caution:</u> Protect the piston from the jaws of the vise since it cannot have scratches or marks. Do not clamp the piston, simply let the washer lay on the top of the jaws of the vise and strike the push rod with a soft headed mallet to drive the piston

out of the piston guide.

Turn the cylinder upside down and remove the three bolts which hold the cylinder nose and insert to the main reservoir casting, separate the two parts and from the hydraulic cylinder remove the primary cup insert, primary cup and primary cup spacer. From the body remove the primary cup washer "O" ring, the bearing, the secondary cup retainer, the secondary cup expander, the secondary cup and secondary cup support. Discard these parts since they must be replaced new.

Inspect the bore of the nose piece for rust or dirt and if any is found clean it up. Scratches mean nothing in the bore of the nose piece since the piston does not contact the bore.

Pay particular attention to the out-

FILLER PLUG
VENT COMPENSATING PORT
INTAKE PORT
FLUID RESERVOIR
PUSH ROD
CHECK VALVE
BOOT
STOP PLATE
SECONDARY CUP
(B) PISTON
PRIMARY CUP
CYLINDER PROPER OUTLET
PISTON RETURN SPRING

Typical piston type master cylinder

side diameter of the piston rod; it must be free of nicks and scratches since this is the surface which seals against the primary and secondary cup. The surface must be smooth and free from pits, scores, rust or dirt.

Refer to the accompanying exploded illustration for the order in which the parts are reassembled.

Servicing the Conventional Master Cylinder

Remove the cylinder from the car and, before taking it apart, thoroughly clean up the outside of the casting to eliminate the possibility of getting grit or dirt into the cylinder. To take the cylinder apart, first remove the boot from the cylinder then take out the lock wire from the end of the cylinder releasing the internal parts. Take the washer, piston, cup, spring and check valve.

Inspect the piston for scratches and pits and if any are found, use a new piston. Always use a new cup since it is unwise economy to take a chance on it. Using a light slowly and carefully examine the inside surface for pits and scratches. If any are found, the cylinder must be honed or replaced.

If the cylinder is the type with a partially closed bore, also examine the machined face at the front (closed) end of the bore because this surface is the seat for the check valve and if it is pitted or scratched the check valve will not seat properly. On cylinders with a straight through bore the check valve seats on the adaptor

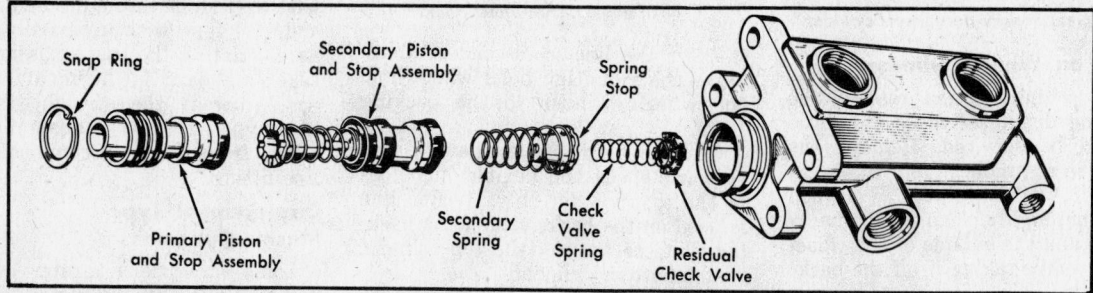

Snap Ring
Secondary Piston and Stop Assembly
Spring Stop
Primary Piston and Stop Assembly
Secondary Spring
Check Valve Spring
Residual Check Valve

Bendix dual type master cylinder

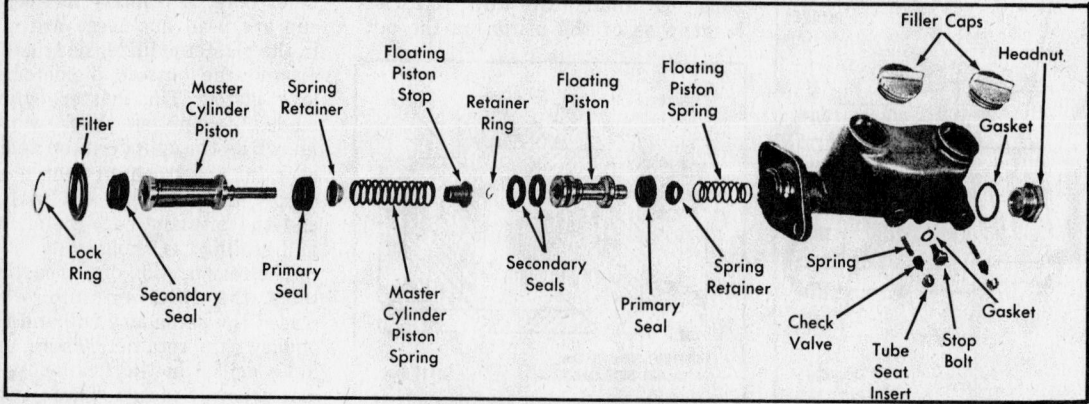

Filter
Master Cylinder Piston
Spring Retainer
Floating Piston Stop
Retainer Ring
Floating Piston
Floating Piston Spring
Filler Caps
Headnut
Gasket
Lock Ring
Secondary Seal
Primary Seal
Master Cylinder Piston Spring
Secondary Seals
Primary Seal
Spring Retainer
Spring
Check Valve
Tube Seat Insert
Stop Bolt
Gasket

Moraine dual type master cylinder

fitting in the front of the cylinder. This fitting can be removed to inspect the check valve surface.

To reassemble the cylinder first dip each part in clean brake fluid and then put in the check valve, the spring, the cup, piston, washer and lock ring. Except for those cylinders where the push rod and washer are assembled under the lock ring, the boot is first attached to the push rod and, after the cylinder is mounted on the car, the big end is attached to the cylinder and secured.

Servicing the Dual Master Cylinder

Service is similar to that of the conventional master cylinder. Failure of one section will not necessarily cause any trouble with the other.

After removing from car and thoroughly cleaning, remove snap ring, primary and secondary pistons and stops. The springs and check valves can now be removed. Again, follow cleaning, inspection and assembly procedures as with the conventional types.

BLEEDING BRAKES

Brake fluid is for all practical purposes non-compressible, the inclusion of even small amounts of air will cause the brake to feel soft, spongy and rubbery since the fluid under pressure will compress the air if it is anywhere in the system.

Therefore, if the brakes are spongy or rubbery it is usually a good idea to bleed the system immediately.

The purpose of bleeding brakes is to

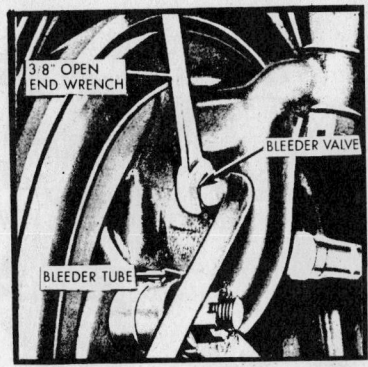

Bleeding brakes

expell all of the entrapped air from the hydraulic system. Cleaning and flushing the system is a much bigger job although it includes bleeding.

Bleeding is not considered a service adjustment since it in no way affects the actual adjustment of the brakes.

Exclusive of pressure bleeding and flushing, there are two methods in common use to bleed brakes, the first is sometimes called the Safety Method, the second is generally referred to as Bleeding Out.

Safety Method of Bleeding Brakes

The advantage of this method is that it requires only one man and it is cleaner. Proceed as follows: Clean off the bleeder screw at each wheel. (Note: Lockhead Brakes with two wheel cylinders and two forward shoes have two bleeder screws at each front wheel, one at each wheel cyl-

inder.)

Attach a hose to the bleeder screw. (Note: Special hoses are made for this purpose), place the end of the hose in a jar which has been filled with fluid, preferably brake fluid but any liquid even water will do. Make sure the end of the hose is down in the fluid. The idea is to prevent air from backing up into the cylinder. Now fill the master cylinder.

Open the bleeder screw about 1/4 turn and then depress the brake pedal slowly all the way to the floor, hold it there for about one second and then very slowly let it come up. Air being ejected from the system will appear as bubbles in the bleeder jar. Repeat until no more bubbles appear in the jar while the pedal is being depressed. CAUTION: Refill the master cylinder when the pedal has been depressed three times.

Close the bleeder screw and remove the bleeder hose. Repeat at all bleeder screws. Do not reuse the fluid in the bleeder jar.

To bleed with a pressure bleeder, be sure all dirt is away from the cylinder cap. Connect bleeder and apply pressure as specified by equipment maker. Proceed from wheel to wheel until all air is expelled.

On dual type master cylinders, the Moraine type has reservoirs separated and either section can be bled separately. On Bendix type there is a vent between reservoirs. In this type it is necessary to cap one section with a solid cap to prevent fluid and pressure loss through the cap vent hole.

ADJUSTMENT PROCEDURES

BENDIX BRAKES WITH ECCENTRIC ANCHORS

Section 1.

These are hydraulically actuated two shoe brakes which have a certain amount of self-energy in either direction.

The two shoes are arranged on the backing plate so they bear against (but are not attached to) the anchor pin which is located at the top of the

backing plate. The lower end of the shoes are linked together by an adjustable sleeve known as a star wheel. The shoes are held to the star wheel by a spring which also acts as a detent on the star wheel.

Minor or Service Adjustment

The minor or service adjustment is used to compensate for normal lining wear. Jack up the car and remove one wheel and drum assembly to inspect the brakes. If all is okay replace the wheel and drum assembly.

Remove the plug from the adjusting hole cover at the lower edge of the backing plate. Working through the slot in the backing plate, expand the shoes by prying the star wheel adjuster with the special brake tool or a bent screwdriver (handle of the tool moves toward the axle to expand the shoes). Keep prying at the star wheel until the shoes are very tight against the drum and it is impossible to turn the wheel. Now retract the

shoes by prying the star wheel in the opposite direction until the wheels are just free. Replace the plug in adjusting slot. Repeat at all four wheels. Road test the car.

Major or Complete Adjustment

The major or complete adjustment is performed when new linings have

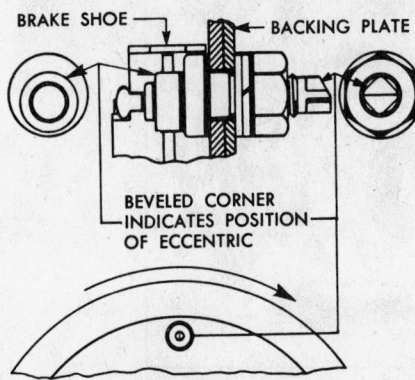

Bendix eccentric anchor

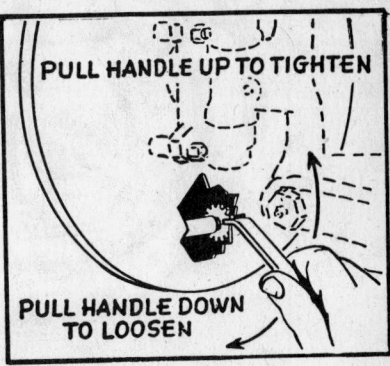

Adjusting star wheel

HYDRAULIC BRAKES

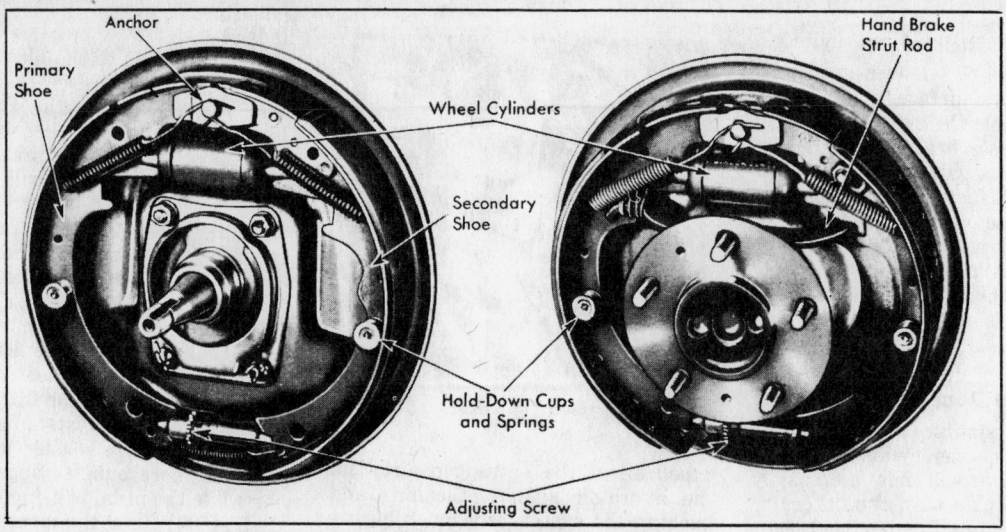

Bendix with eccentric type anchor

been installed or when there is brake difficulty which cannot be overcome by a minor adjustment.

Jack up the car and remove one wheel and drum assembly to inspect the lining. If all is okay replace the drum only but leave the wheel off. Remove the other three wheels, but leave the drums in place. Notice that each drum is provided with a slot for a feeler gauge.

Remove the cover from the star wheel adjusting slot and pry the star wheel handle of the tool toward the axle, until the brakes drag very lightly. Now loosen the jam nut on the anchor. This is the large nut located at the top of the backing plate.

Turn the drum until the feeler gauge slot is between one and one-half inches away from the heel end of the secondary shoe and insert a .010 inch feeler gauge between the

lining and the drum at this point. Now turn the eccentric anchor until the feeler gauge is just gripped. Holding the eccentric anchor at this point securely tighten the anchor jam nut.

Go back to the star wheel slot and turn the star wheel handle of the tool towards the axle until the shoes are very tight against the drum and then slowly back off until the shoes are just free. Repeat this procedure at all four wheels and then replace the wheels.

Road test the car.

Hand Brake Adjustments

The hand brake adjustment on these brakes is usually done in conjunction with the service brake adjustment since the procedure for adjusting the hand brake requires that the first part of a minor service adjustment be performed on the rear

wheels.

The procedure is as follows: Make sure the cables are not binding in the conduit then remove the plug from the adjusting slot at the lower edge of the backing plate on both rear wheels.

Expand the brake shoes by prying the adjusting star wheel, handle of the tool towards the axle until the shoes are very tight against the drum.

Do this at both rear wheels and then back off on the star wheel adjuster (handle of the tool away from the axle) until the back wheels are just free of drag.

Disconnect hand brake cable at cross shaft or equalizer bar. Pull all slack from cables and adjust cable to a snug tightness and reconnect. Test by turning both rear wheels to be sure no drag has been created.

Section 2.   BENDIX BRAKES WITH SLIDING ANCHORS

The arrangement of these brakes is exactly the same as that given for Bendix brakes with eccentric anchors, the only difference being that on these brakes the anchor is not eccentric and there is no feeler gauge slot in the

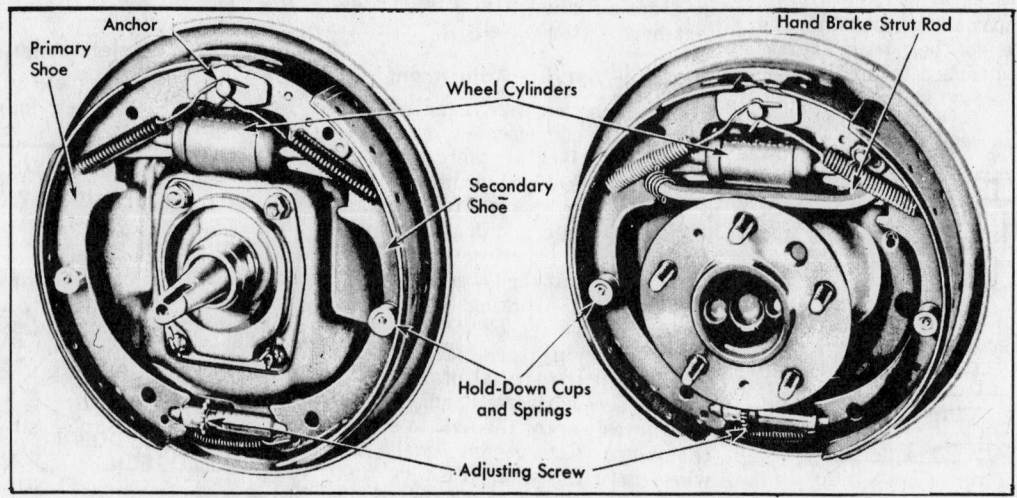

Bendix with sliding anchor

drum, except Cadillac.

Starting 1957, Cadillac has adjusting slots in drum.

Minor or Service Adjustment

This is same as in Section 1.

Major or Complete Adjustment

This should always be done after reline or when a hard-to-overcome difficulty is met.

Jack up car and remove all wheels. Remove at least one drum and inspect drum, lining, cylinder, etc. Then re-

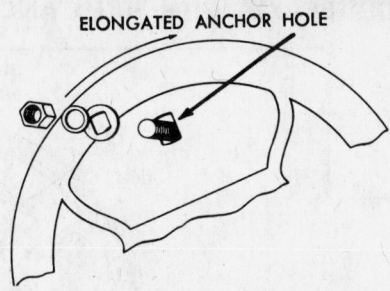

ELONGATED ANCHOR HOLE

Bendix sliding anchor

install drum.

Turn adjusting star wheel until shoes are **tight** against drum. Loosen anchor jam nut to allow shoes to center in drum. To assist centering, tap anchor nut lightly. After shoes are centered tighten jam nut.

Back off star wheels until the wheels are just free.

Road test car.

Hand Brake Adjustment

Proceed as described in Section 1.

Section 3.

BENDIX BRAKES WITH FIXED ANCHORS

These are hydraulically actuated two-shoe brakes which have a certain amount of self-energy in either direction and in appearance the shoes look to be the same as the Bendix brakes with eccentric anchors and Bendix brakes with sliding anchors.

The difference is that on the fixed anchor brake and the Self-Centering anchor brake no adjustment whatever is provided for the anchor.

Adjustments

Both minor and major adjustments are made as in Section 1, except that, because of the fixed anchor the centering of the shoes is omitted. **Note:** 1960 Ford, L.R. star wheel turns in opposite direction to adjust.

The parking brake is also adjusted as in Section 1.

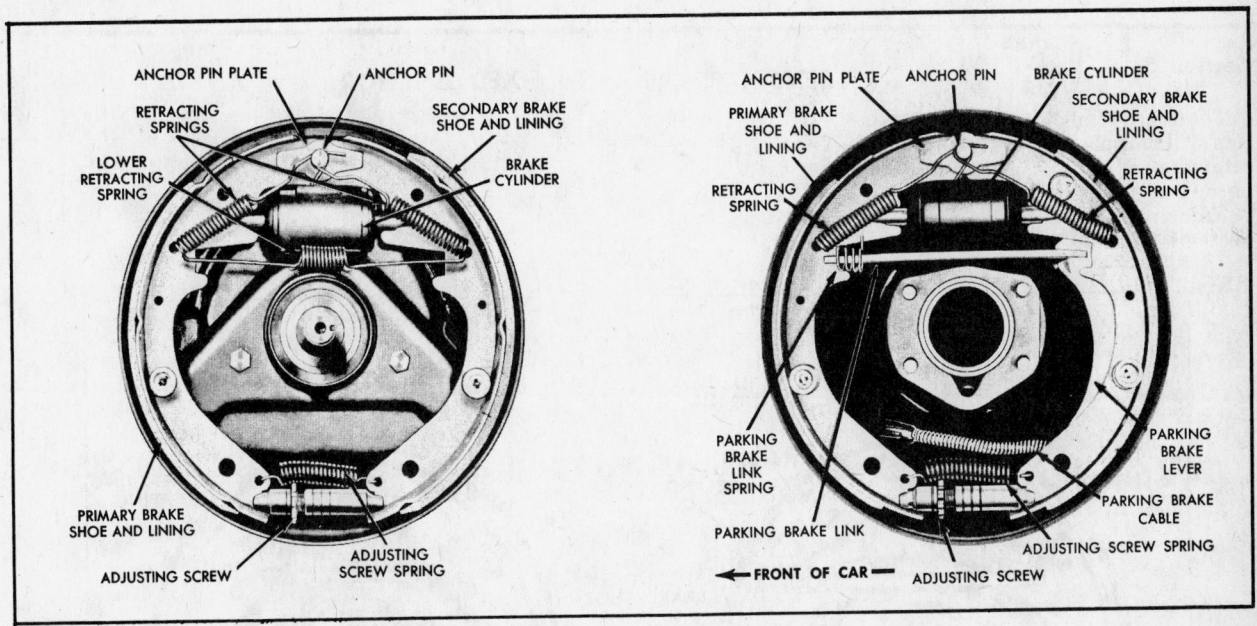

Bendix with fixed anchor

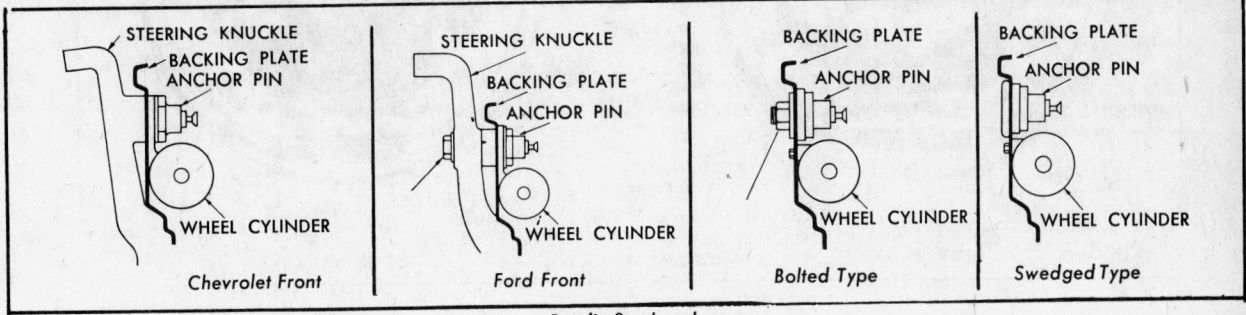

Bendix fixed anchors

HYDRAULIC BRAKES

Section 4.

BENDIX BRAKES WITH FIXED ANCHORS

These are the same as in Section 3 except for minor spring changes, see illustrations. Adjustments are the same as for Section 1 and 3.

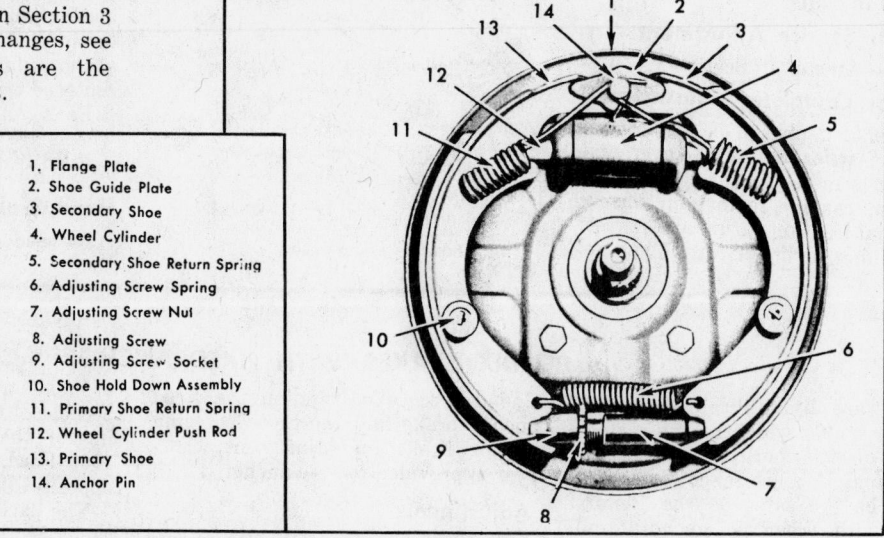

1. Flange Plate
2. Shoe Guide Plate
3. Secondary Shoe
4. Wheel Cylinder
5. Secondary Shoe Return Spring
6. Adjusting Screw Spring
7. Adjusting Screw Nut
8. Adjusting Screw
9. Adjusting Screw Socket
10. Shoe Hold Down Assembly
11. Primary Shoe Return Spring
12. Wheel Cylinder Push Rod
13. Primary Shoe
14. Anchor Pin

Bendix with fixed anchor

Section 5.

BENDIX BRAKE WITH FIXED ANCHOR

These are similar to those in Section 3. Principle changes are in shoe retainers and springs, and the lack of an anchor pin plate, see illustration.

Adjustments are the same as in Sections 1 and 3.

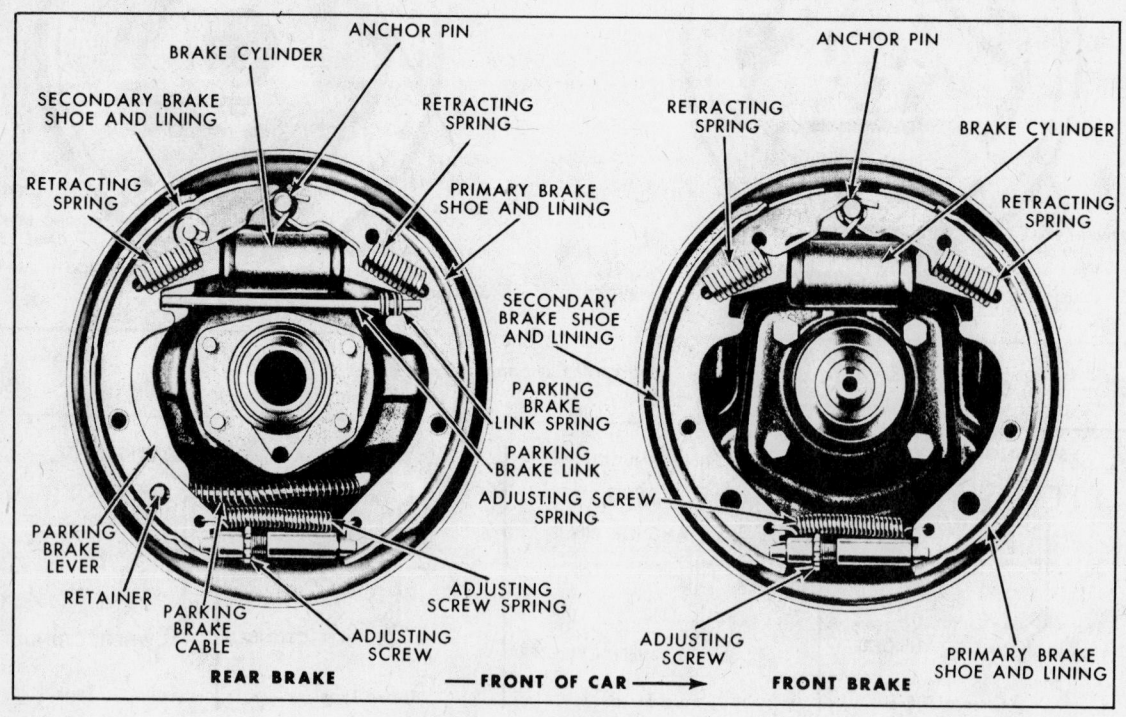

Bendix with fixed anchor

Section 6.

BENDIX BRAKE WITH FIXED ANCHOR

These are similar to those in Section 3. Principle changes are in shoe retainers and springs, see illusrations.

Adjustments are the same as in Sections 1 and 3.

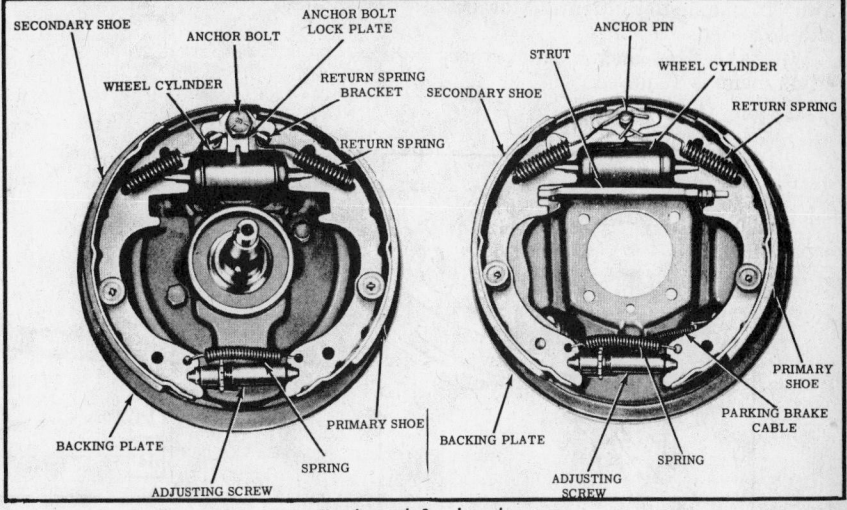

Bendix with fixed anchor

Section 7.

BENDIX BRAKE WITH FIXED ANCHOR AND SELF ADJUSTER

These brakes are very similar to the brakes common to the Bendix with fixed anchors in Section 3, but with a self adjusting feature.

The self adjuster continuously maintains the proper operating clearance between the lining and drums by making small amounts of adjustment gradually as lining wears. When brakes are applied while backing car the lever engages the star wheel

whenever the lining to drum clearance is too great. With the reverse brake application under these conditions the star adjuster is moved one notch at a time until proper clearance is obtained.

Note: On Rambler series 10 cars only, with self-adjusters, this action is accomplished on forward stops rather than reverse.

The self adjusting parts consist of a shoe guide plate, cable, cable guide, lever with pivot hook and a star wheel and pivot assembly. See illustration.

Manual adjustment can be made through the backing plate slot by using a screw driver or special adjusting tool. An ice pick or narrow screw driver should also be inserted to raise the lever from the star wheel.

Star wheel rotation is opposite to

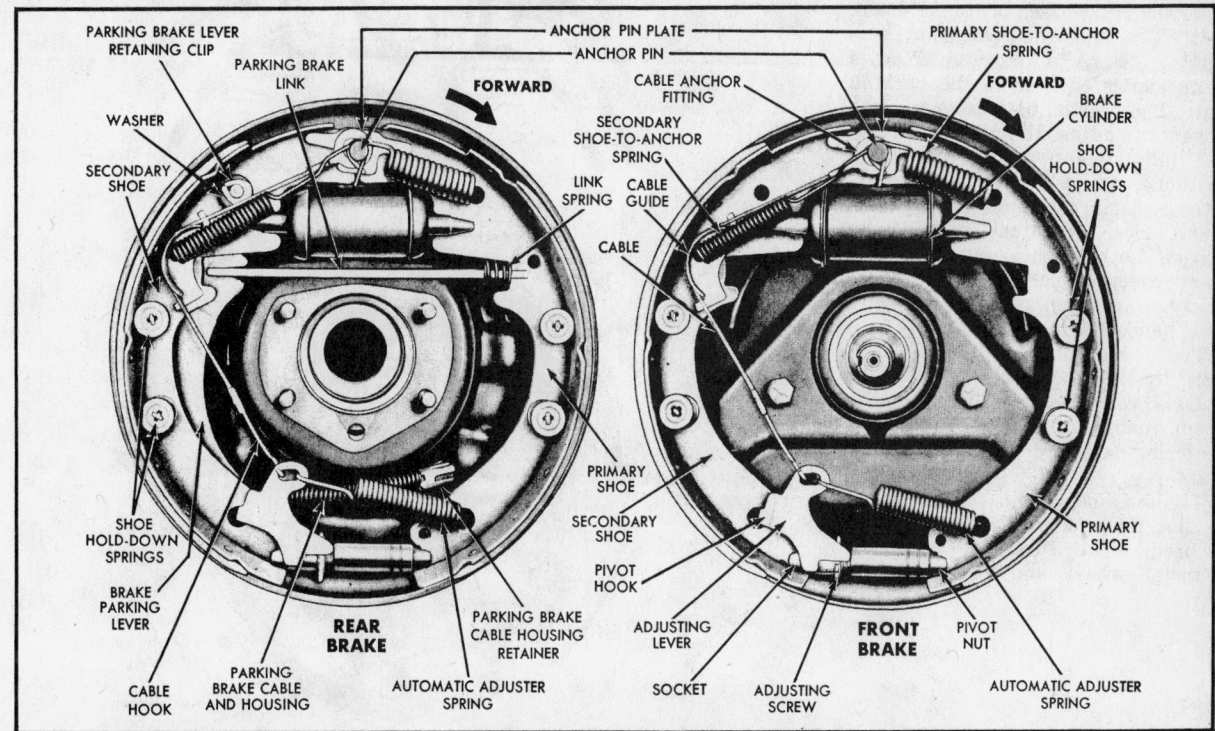

Bendix with fixed anchor—self adjusting

that of non-self adjusting brakes. That is, the tool is inserted and pried away from axle to tighten and toward axle to loosen.

With the fixed anchor no further adjustment is required.

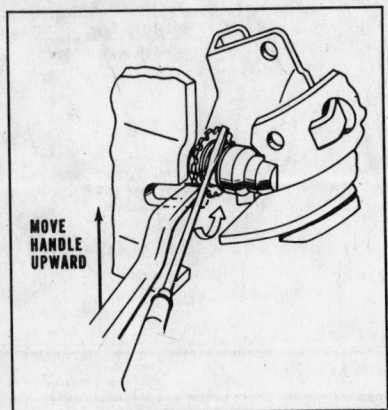

Push the Self Adjusting Lever out of the way with a small screw driver or ice pick to back off star wheel

Self adjuster method

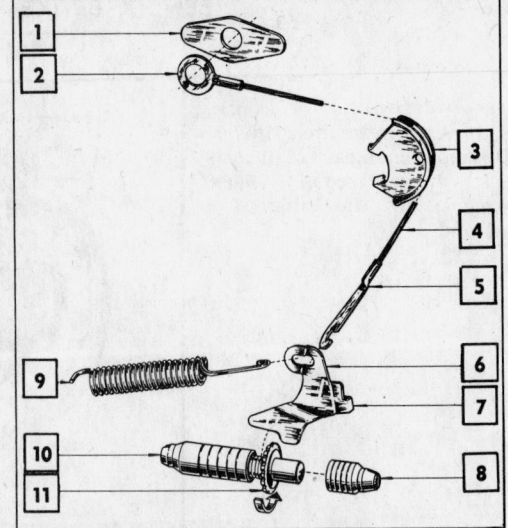

1. Shoe Guide Plate	7. Pivot Hook
1. Cable Anchor Fitting	8. Socket
3. Cable Guide	9. Spring — Automatic Adjuster
4. Cable	10. Pivot Nut
5. Cable Hook	11. Adjusting Screw
6. Lever	

Self adjusting brake components

Section 8. **BENDIX BRAKE WITH TWO-POINT ADJUSTABLE ANCHOR**

This brake is similar to that in Section 3, except that it has a two point solid forged anchor assembly which pivots as a unit to raise or lower the brake assembly in the drum. Bolt "B" acts as the pivot point, permitting bolt "A" to move up or down in an elongated hole in the backing plate. The nuts on both bolts must be loosened to adjust this type of anchor.

All adjustments are the same as in Section 1, except the anchors. Always, after replacing shoes or if anchor is found loose, readjust as follows: Loosen both anchor nuts. Tighten star wheel adjustment to produce heavy drag when turnig drum with both hands.

Tap anchor pin "A" (see illustration) to allow shoes to center in drum. If this centering changes drag on drum, readjust star wheel and repeat centering, until drag remains constant.

Tighten anchor pin nuts to 60-80 ft. lbs. Back off star wheel adjuster to produce free turning drum.

Install wheels and road test.

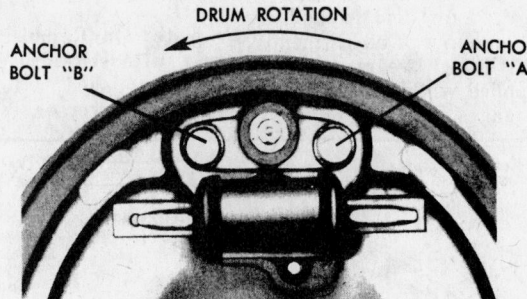

Two-point anchor location

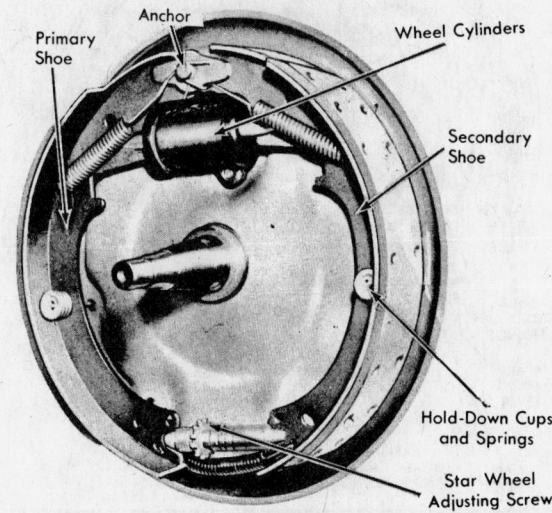

Bendix with two-point adjustable anchor

Section 9.   BENDIX BRAKE WITH TWO-POINT ANCHOR AND SELF ADJUSTER

This brake is a combination of previously described types.

Shoes are self adjusting and procedures are described in Section 7.

Anchors are adjustable and procedures are described in Section 8.

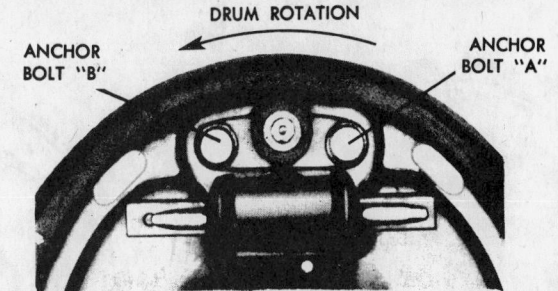

Two point anchor location

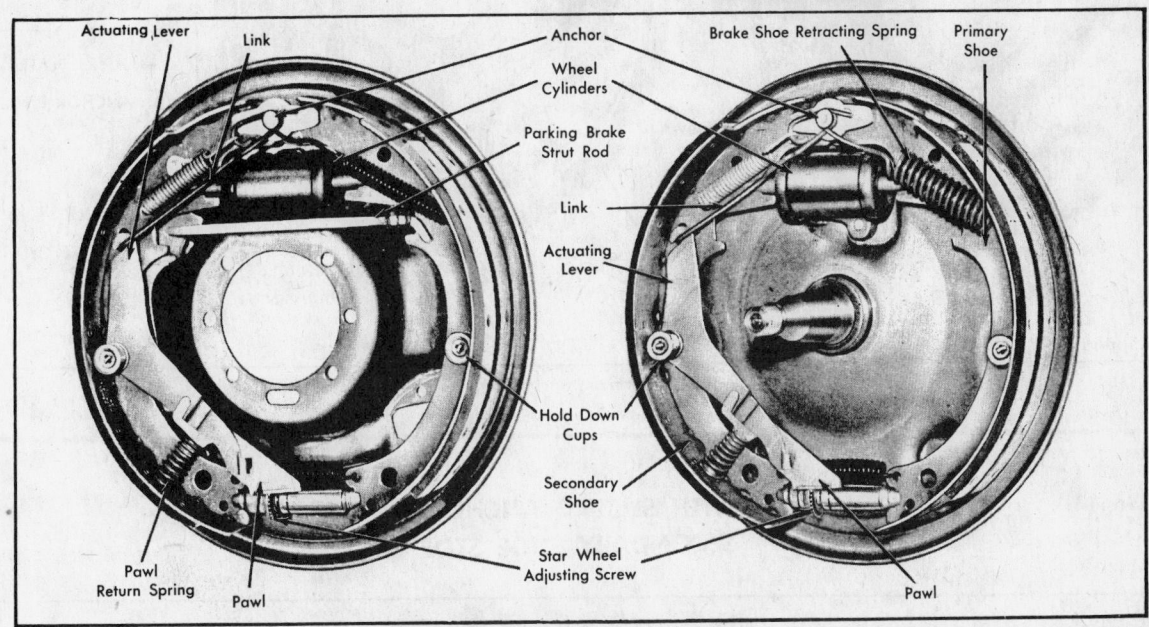

Bendix two-point anchor and self adjusting

Section 10.   BENDIX BRAKE WITH FIXED ANCHOR AND SELF ADJUSTER

All procedures with this brake are the same as in Section 7.

The difference is structural (see illustration). Self adjusting is accomplished through an actuating link and adjusting lever contacting the star wheel adjuster. It is operated when brakes are applied while moving car in reverse.

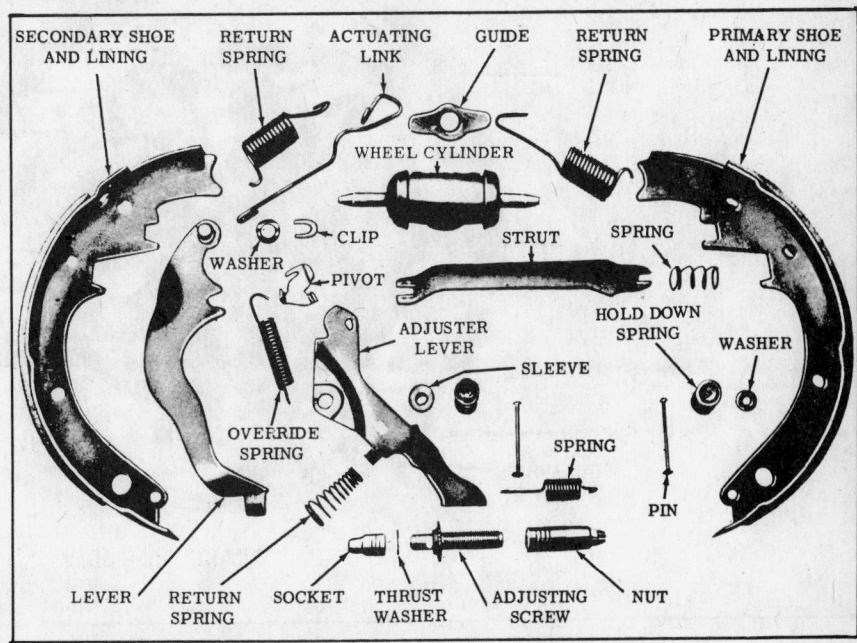

Self adjusting brake components

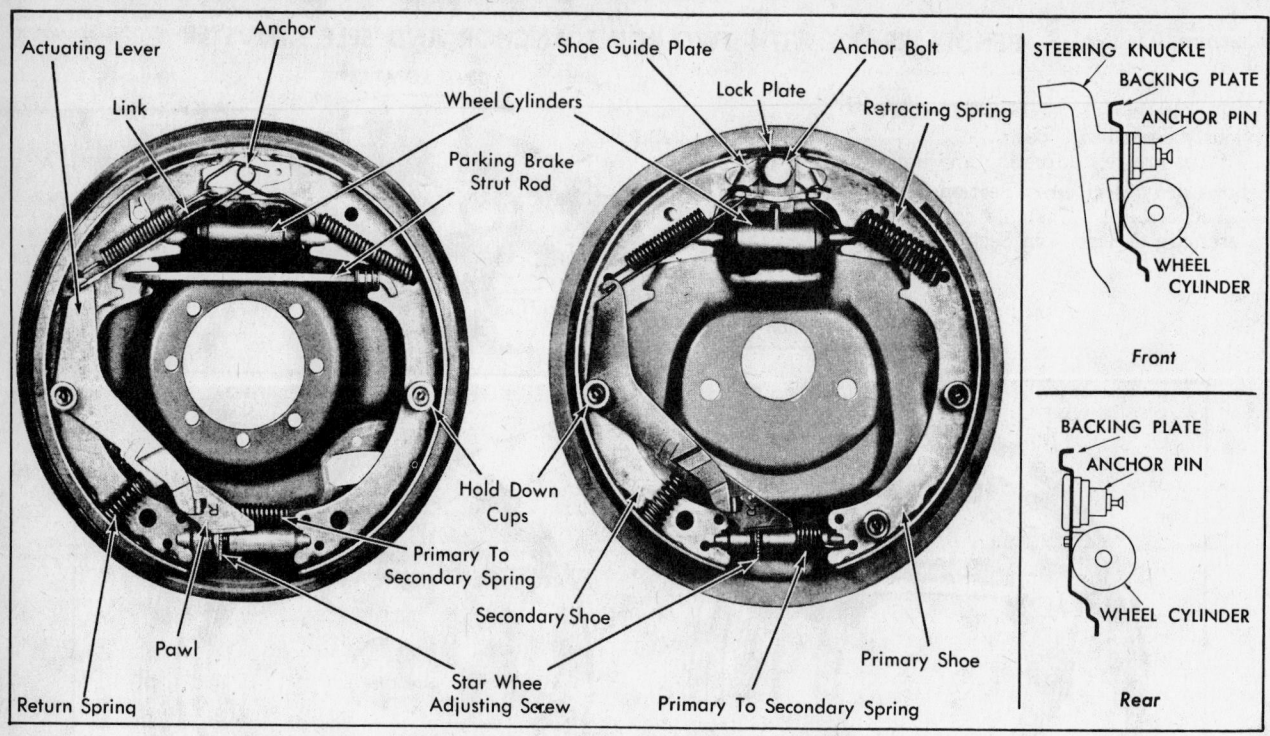

Bendix with fixed anchor—self adjusting

Section 11. **BENDIX BRAKE WITH SLIDING ANCHOR AND ECCENTRIC
SECONDARY SHOE STOP**

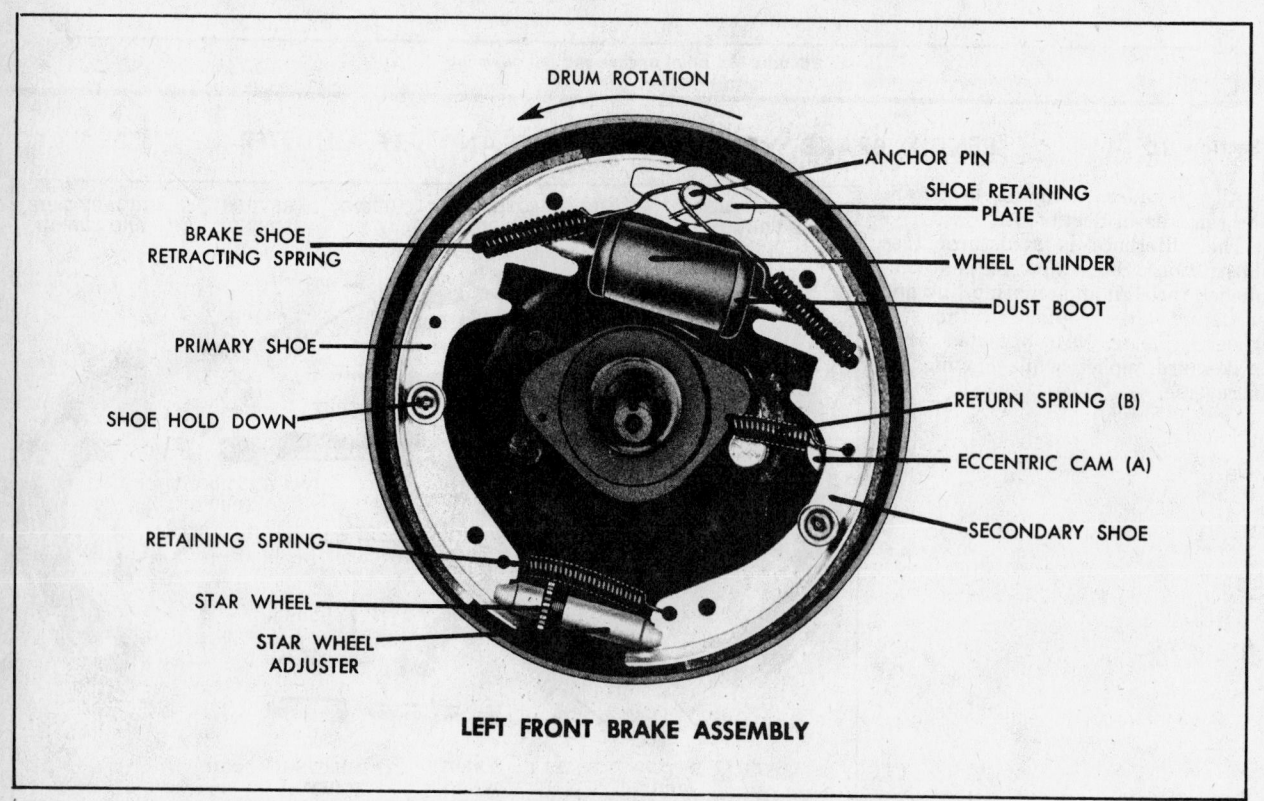

LEFT FRONT BRAKE ASSEMBLY

Bendix with sliding anchor and secondary cam

These brakes are two shoe type with backing plate so designed that wheel cylinder and sliding anchor are approximately 3″ to the rear of vertical to allow clearance from the front wheel suspension ball joint. To prevent the secondary shoe from dragging due to this change a short return spring (B) and eccentric cam (A) were added.

Minor or Service Adjustment

Jack up car. Expand shoes by turning star wheel until drum can be merely moved with both hands, back off adjustment till wheel turns just freely. Loosen lock nut on eccentric (A) and turn eccentric in direction of forward rotation until drag is felt then back off eccentric until wheel is free. Tighten lock nut. Make sure eccentric does not turn while locking nut.

<u>Note:</u> 1955 Lincoln and Mercury front brakes have no eccentric lock nut. The eccentric is spring loaded.

Major or Complete Adjustment

Follow procedure as in Section 2.

Parking Brake Adjustment

Follow procedure as in Section 1.

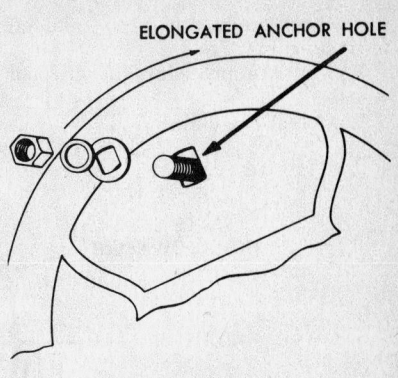

ELONGATED ANCHOR HOLE

Bendix sliding anchor

Section 12.

BENDIX BRAKE WITH SLIDING ANCHOR AND ECCENTRIC PRIMARY SHOE STOP

These brakes are same as Section 11, except the eccentric cam (A) operates on the primary rather than the secondary shoe. (See Illustration).

All adjustments are the same as Section 11.

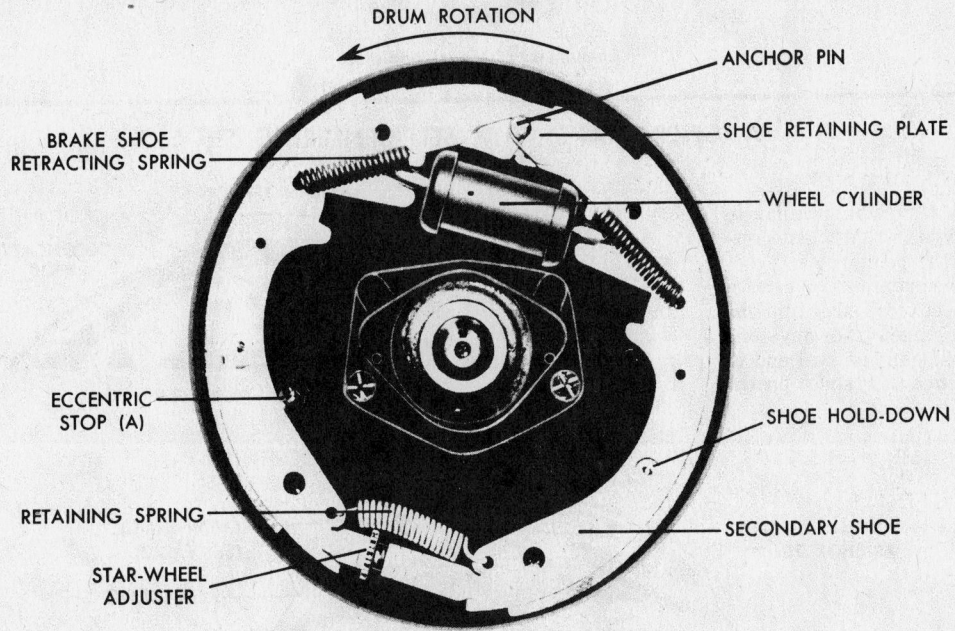

DRUM ROTATION

ANCHOR PIN

SHOE RETAINING PLATE

WHEEL CYLINDER

BRAKE SHOE RETRACTING SPRING

ECCENTRIC STOP (A)

SHOE HOLD-DOWN

RETAINING SPRING

SECONDARY SHOE

STAR-WHEEL ADJUSTER

LEFT FRONT BRAKE ASSEMBLY

Bendix with sliding anchor and primary cam

Section 13.

BENDIX BRAKE WITH SELF- CENTERING SHOES

This brake is completely different from and should not be confused with those listed above. On Bendix self-centering brakes, two shoes hydraulically actuated which are not connected together are used.

Instead of being connected with the usual star wheel adjuster at the bottom of the backing plate, these brakes are fitted with a thrust block against which the shoes bear. However, the shoes are not attached to this block, they simply bear against it so that each time the brakes are applied the shoe automatically centers itself for each application.

Adjustment Procedure

Only one adjustment is provided for each shoe on this contruction.
Proceed as follows:
Jack up the car and remove one wheel and drum assembly and inspect the linings, drum and wheel cylinder.

If everything is okay replace the wheel and drum assembly. Now on the forward shoe, loosen the jamb nut and turn the eccentric adjuster, which will be found near the forward edge of the backing plate, in the direction of forward wheel rotation until the shoe binds heavily against the drum. Now back off until the wheel is just barely free. Now turn the reverse shoe adjuster, located at the back edge of the backing plate, in a direction of rearward wheel rotation until

HYDRAULIC BRAKES

the wheel binds and then take off until it is just free.

Repeat the procedure at all four wheels.

Road test the car.

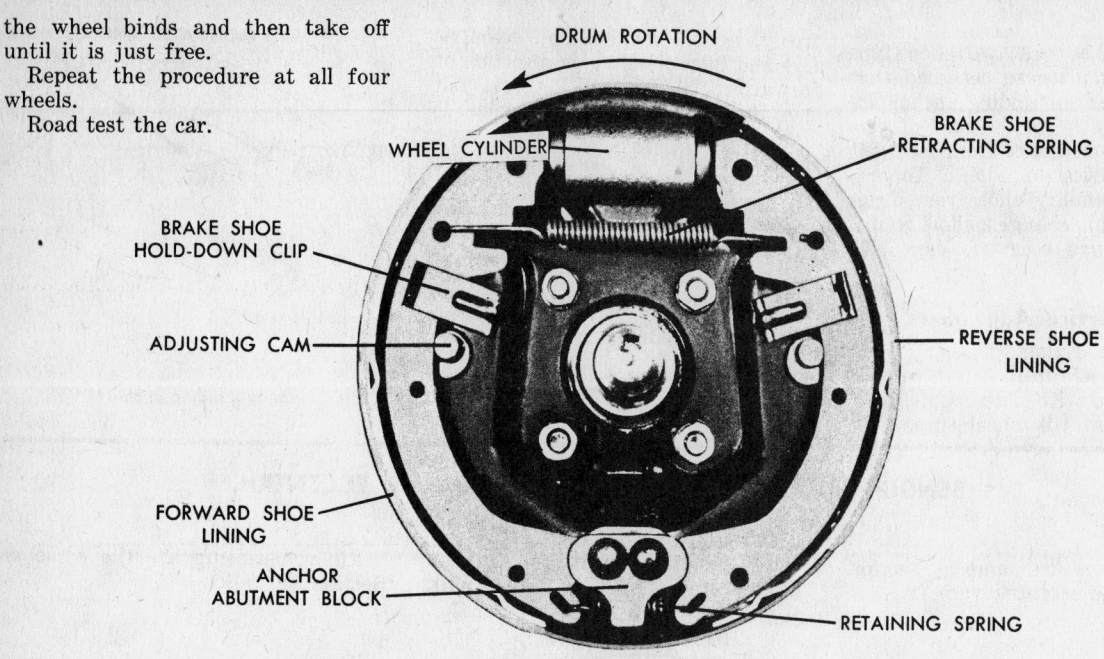

Bendix with self-centering shoes

Section 14.

WAGNER BRAKE WITH SELF-CENTERING SHOES

This brake is somewhat similar to the duo-servo type in that when pressure is applied the primary shoe contacts first and the drum motion carries it against the secondary shoe and the assembly on against the keystone shaped anchor block. The heel end of the secondary shoe now slides on the

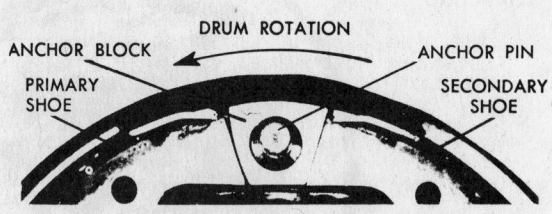

Wagner self-centering anchor

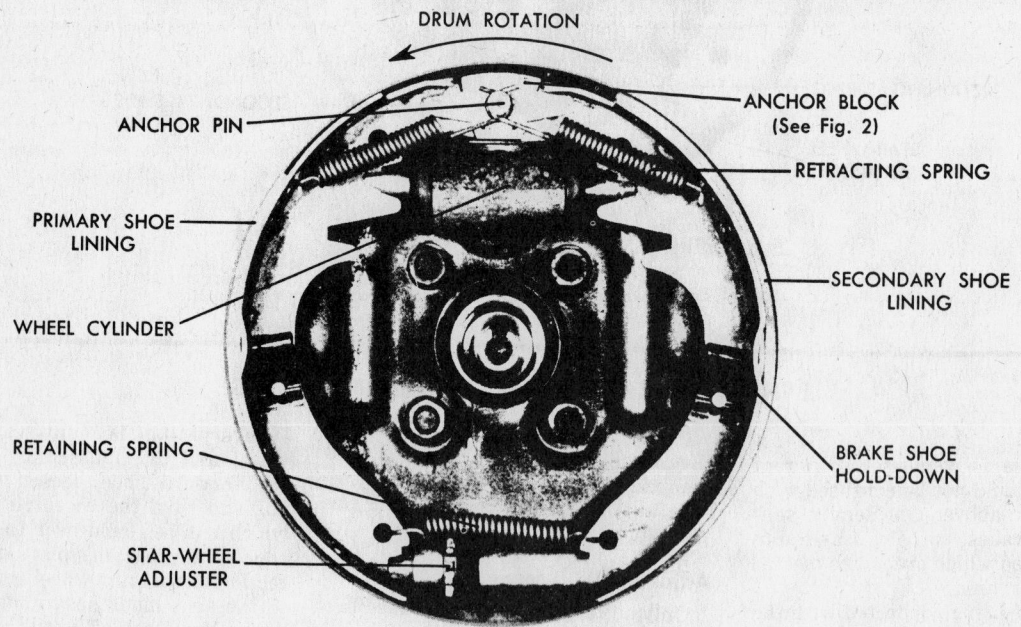

LEFT FRONT BRAKE ASSEMBLY

Wagner with self-centering shoes

anchor block and the assembly centers itself in the drum.

Adjustments

Jack up car. Be sure parking brake cables do not hold rear shoes off of anchor. Adjust the star wheel until the shoes are tight in the drum. Press the brake pedal a few times to be sure shoes have centered, then try star wheel to be sure shoes are fully expanded. Back off star wheel until wheels are free.

Be sure that anchor block is free to rotate on anchor pin and that the curved side (see illustration) is toward front of car. Anchor pin must not move in backing plate.

Parking Brake Adjustment

This procedure is same as in Section 1.

Section 15.   WAGNER LOCKHEED WITH TWO SINGLE CYLINDERS

This type brake uses two single wheel cylinders, one at the toe of each shoe. This gives both shoes a self-wrapping action when applied in forward motion.

Minor or Service Adjustment

Jack up car. Expand shoes by turning cams away from the top until a heavy drag is produced. Then back off slowly until wheel is free. This adjustment is made at both shoes on each wheel.

Major or Complete Adjustment

With drums removed install brake gauge or spindle grinder. Back off adjusting cams. Check arrows on anchor posts and make sure they point to adjacent wheel cylinder. Adjust cams so that center of shoe is just touching gauge.

Turn anchor pin (see illustration) until .007" clearance is obtained at both ends of each shoe, and at each wheel.

Road test car.

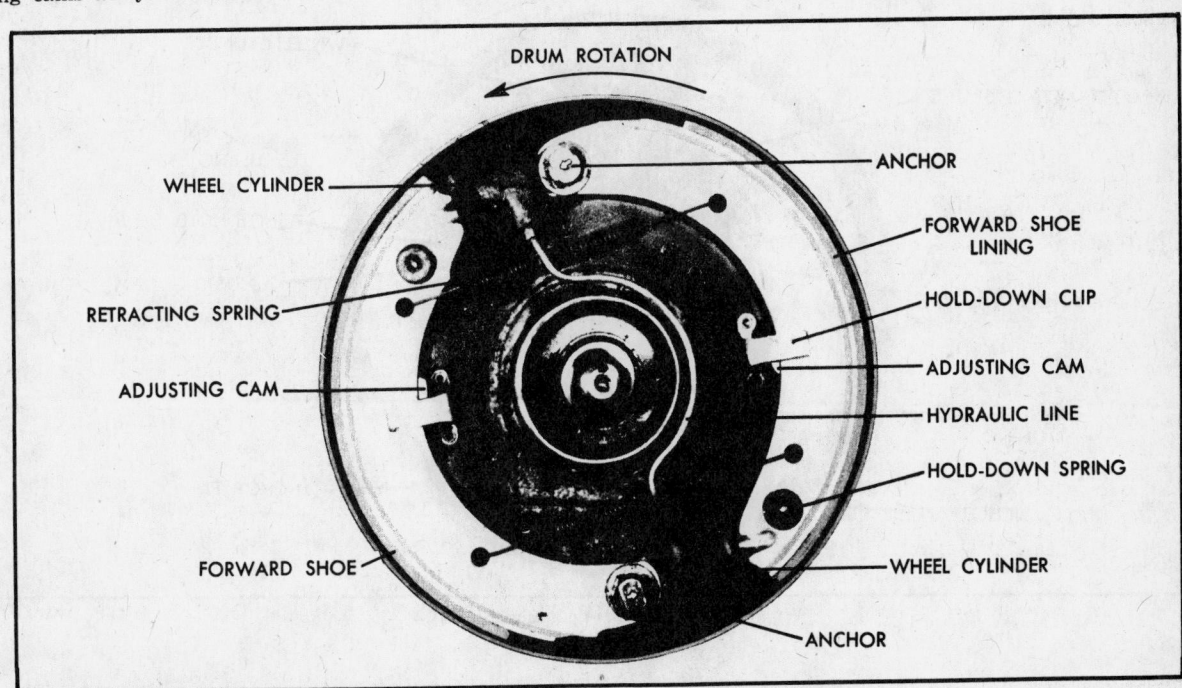

DRUM ROTATION

WHEEL CYLINDER

RETRACTING SPRING

ADJUSTING CAM

FORWARD SHOE

ANCHOR

FORWARD SHOE LINING

HOLD-DOWN CLIP

ADJUSTING CAM

HYDRAULIC LINE

HOLD-DOWN SPRING

WHEEL CYLINDER

ANCHOR

Wagner Lockheed with 2 single end cylinders

DRUM ROTATION

Anchor location with single end cylinders

HYDRAULIC BRAKES

WAGNER LOCKHEED WITH ADJUSTABLE ANCHORS

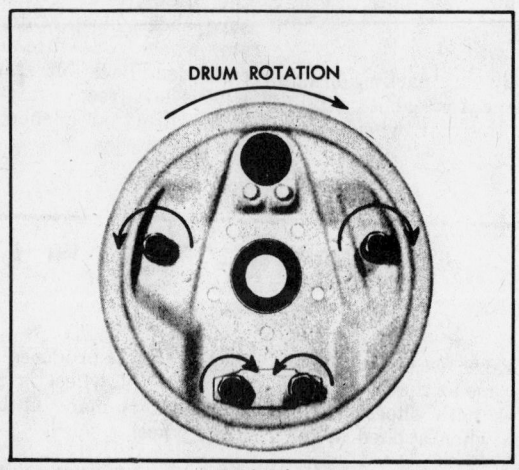

DRUM ROTATION

Anchor location

This brake has one double-end wheel cylinder. In some early models the cylinder was step-bored to control a pressure differential.

Adjustments are similar to those shown in Section 15.

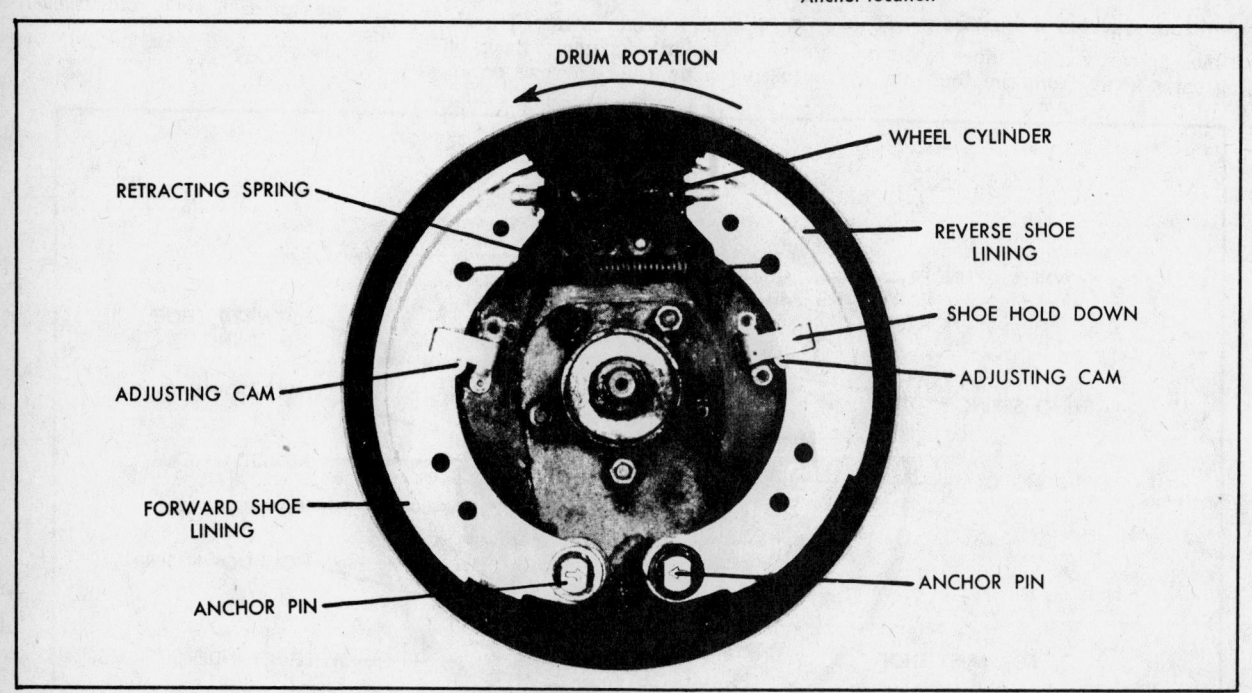

DRUM ROTATION

RETRACTING SPRING

WHEEL CYLINDER

REVERSE SHOE LINING

SHOE HOLD DOWN

ADJUSTING CAM

ADJUSTING CAM

FORWARD SHOE LINING

ANCHOR PIN

ANCHOR PIN

Wagner Lockheed with adjustable anchors

Section 17.   CHRYSLER TOTAL CONTACT

The front brakes are of the two single cylinder type, one at the toe of each shoe. This gives both shoes a self-wrapping action when applied in forward motion. The rear brake is the double end cylinder operating on the tops or toes of the two shoes. The anchors are fixed.

Adjustment

Jack up car. Adjust front brake shoes by rotating eccentrics in direction of forward drum rotation (see illustration). Adjust rear brake shoes by turning eccentrics away from the top.

Turn eccentrics until shoe have heavy drag. Then loosen just enough to make drums turn freely.

No anchor adjustments can be made.

LEFT FRONT
RIGHT FRONT
LEFT REAR
RIGHT REAR
BACKING PLATE SIDE

Rotation of adjustment eccentrics

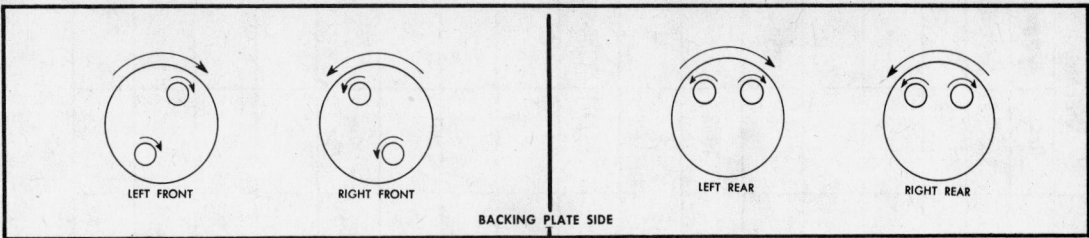

UPPER CYLINDER ASSEMBLY
ANCHOR
ADJUSTING CAM
SHOE AND LINING
DUST SHIELD
SHOE RETURN SPRING
SHOE RETAINER
SUPPORT
SHOE RETURN SPRING
ADJUSTING CAM
SHOE RETAINER
CONNECTING TUBE
ANCHOR
LOWER CYLINDER ASSEMBLY
FRONT
59x138
CYLINDER ASSEMBLY
ADJUSTING CAMS
SHOE RETURN SPRINGS
DUST SHIELD
SHOE RETAINERS
SUPPORT
ANCHORS
SHOE AND LINING
REAR

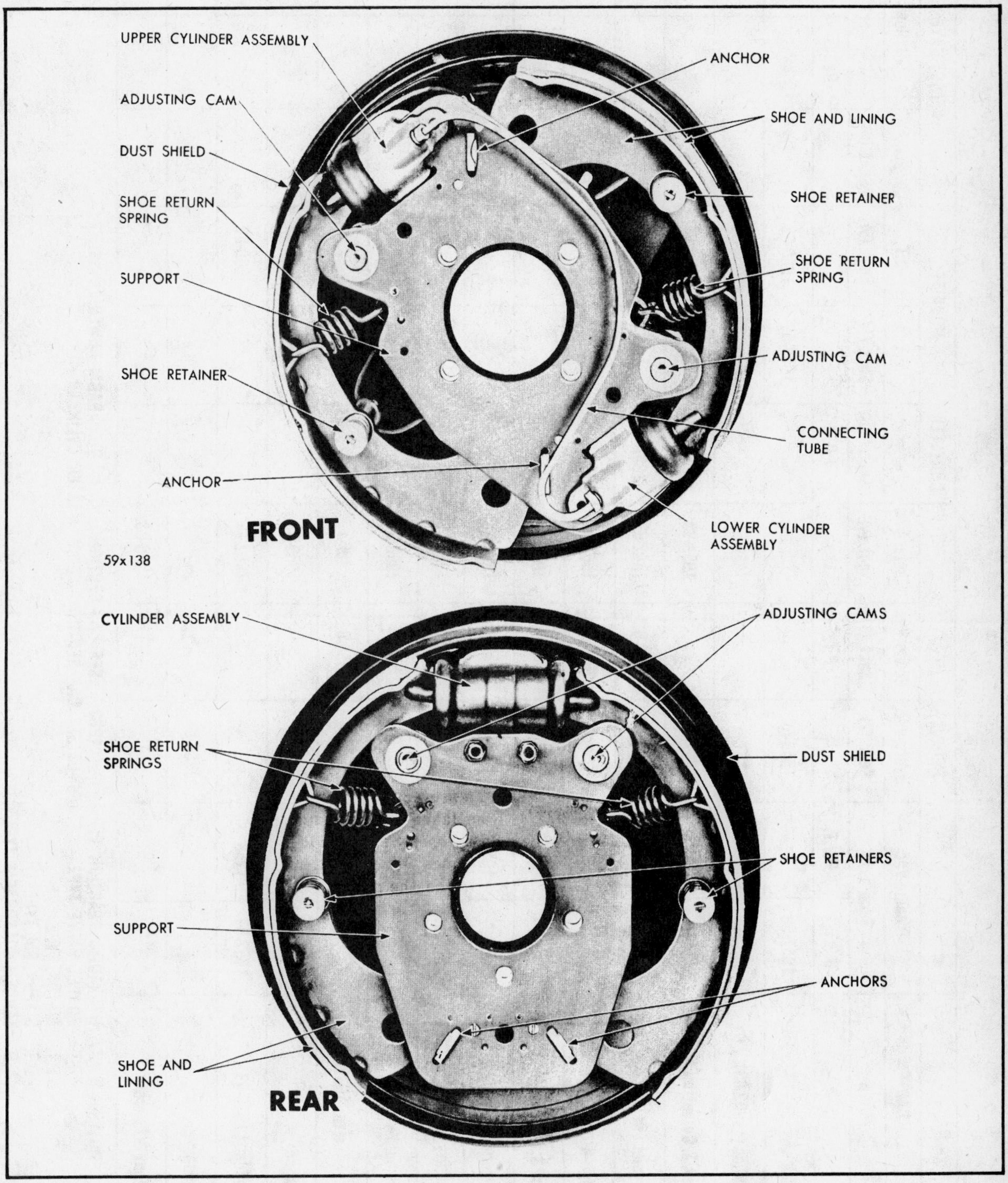

Chrysler total contact

POWER BRAKES

CAR MAKE	BENDIX Treadle-Vac Sect. (1) H.R.T.	BENDIX Treadle-Vac Sect. (1) P.V.T.	BENDIX Hydro-Vac Sect. (2)	BENDIX Power-Vac Sect. (3) P.I.	BENDIX Master-Vac Sect. (4)	CHRYSLER Sect. (10) T.D.	MORAINE P.T. Sect. (1)	MORAINE D.T. Sect. (5)	KELSEY-HAYES D.T. Sect. (9)	KELSEY-HAYES Bellows Type Sect. (7) Round	KELSEY-HAYES Bellows Type Sect. (7) Oval	MIDLAND Ross Sect. (6)	MIDLAND Hy Power Sect. (8)
Buick	1957-59		1955-59				1957-59	1960-63					
Cadillac (*1962-63)		1956 & 58	1957		1959-63		1956 & 58	1959-63					1954
Chev. & Corvette Chevy II	1958	1955-56	1957		1959-63		1958	1959-63					
Chrysler (■ 1962)				1956-62	1962-63	1962			1955		1956-62	1963	
Dodge & DeSoto (■ 1962)				1956-62	1962-63	1962			1955		1956-62	1963	
Ford & T. Bird					1959-62					1956-60		1961-63	1954-55
Lincoln & Continental		1954-59			1961-63								
Mercury		1954-56			1959-63								
Oldsmobile	1957-59	1956			1960-63		1956-59	1960-63					
Plymouth (■ 1962)				1956-62	1963	1962			1955		1956-62	1963	
Pontiac	1957-58	1954-56			1959-63		1956-58	1959-62					
Rambler *1962-63	1957-59	1956			1962-63			1960-62					
Studebaker			1956-63		1961-63								
Valiant & Lancer					1960-63								

NOTES: H.R.T. HYDRAULIC REACTION TYPE   ■ 1962   SEE CAR SECTION — DUAL DIAPHRAGM POWER CYLINDER
P.V.T. POPPET VALVE TYPE   * 1962-63   SEE CAR SECTION — DUAL MASTER CYLINDER
P.I. PISTON TYPE
D.I. DIAPHRAGM TYPE
T.D. TANDEM DIAPHRAGM TYPE

MORAINE POWER BRAKE
BENDIX TREADLE-VAC POWER BRAKES

There are two basic types of Bendix Treadle-Vac, the Hydraulic Reaction Type and the Poppet Valve Type. Introduced in 1957, the Hydraulic Reaction Type differs from other Treadle-Vac units only in the inner control mechanism. The Hydraulic Reaction Type employs a mechanical control valve, while in the Poppet Valve Type the control valve is intergral with the vacuum power piston.

The Treadle-Vac is a self contained unit in which the master cylinder of the regular hydraulic system is part of the unit. It is therefore called an adjacent type unit. It is worthy to note that this unit is an atmospheric balanced unit in which, when the brakes are not applied, there is atmospheric pressure on both sides of the piston.

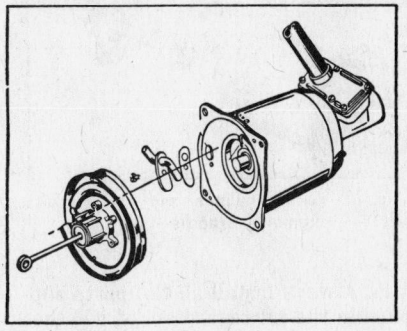

Fig. 7—Vacuum piston and valve removal. Treadle-Vac

Moraine power brakes are similar from the standpoint of service and trouble shooting procedure.

The other unit is known as the Bendix Hydro-Vac. It is a unit which can be mounted anywhere on the car and so uses a slave cylinder which makes it a remote type unit. This is a vacuum balanced unit in which when the brakes are not applied there is vacuum on both sides of the piston. Section 2.

Treadle-Vac Removal

Disconnect the hydraulic line at the hydraulic cylinder and tie it up so that all the fluid does not run out. Discon-

nect the vacuum line at the unit. Remove the brake pedal pivot pin and tip the upper end of the pedal back to expose the push rod pivot pin under the pedal pad.

Remove the brake pedal and the accelerator pedal. Fold back the carpet. Unfasten the steering column grommet and slide it up the column.

Remove steering column cover plate to toe pan screws and remove the cover plate and the power brake unit as an assembly.

Remove four bolts to release the unit from the plate.

Reverse the procedure to reinstall.

Be careful not to pull on the push rod as push rod could thereby be pulled out of the plunger which is inside the assembly.

Fig. 8—Sleeve valve and vacuum hose removal. Treadle-Vac

Fig. 6—End plate removal. Treadle-Vac

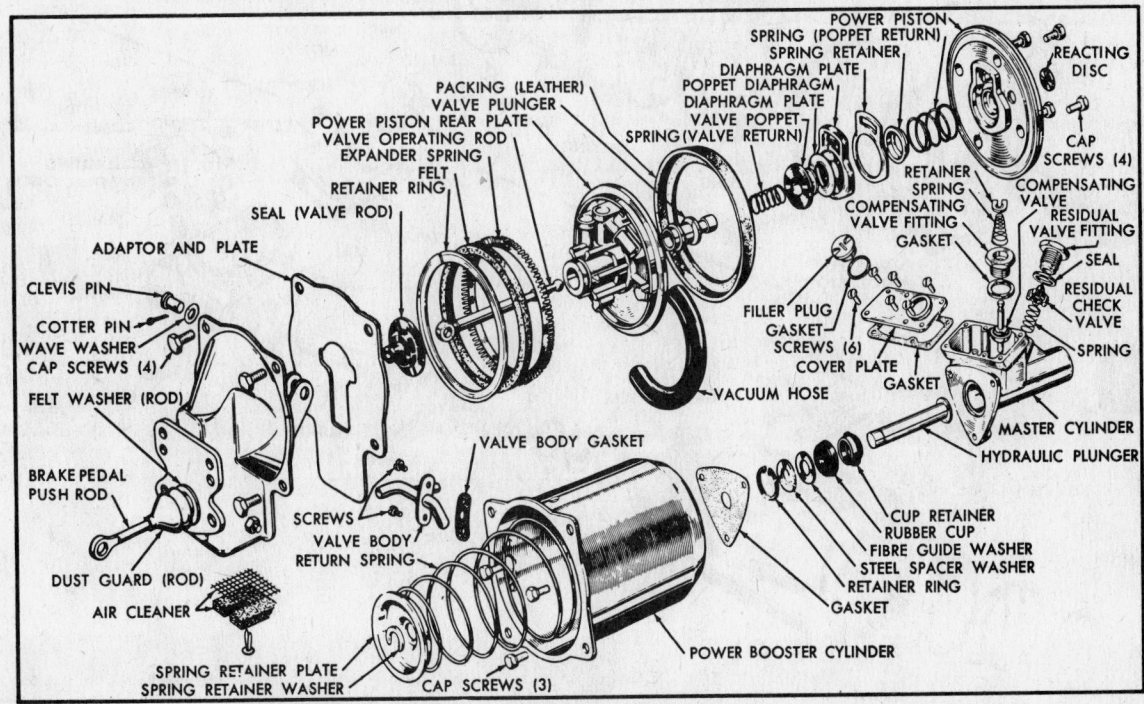

POWER PISTON
SPRING (POPPET RETURN)
SPRING RETAINER
DIAPHRAGM PLATE
POPPET DIAPHRAGM
DIAPHRAGM PLATE
VALVE POPPET
SPRING (VALVE RETURN)
PACKING (LEATHER)
VALVE PLUNGER
POWER PISTON REAR PLATE
VALVE OPERATING ROD
EXPANDER SPRING
FELT
RETAINER RING
SEAL (VALVE ROD)
ADAPTOR AND PLATE
CLEVIS PIN
COTTER PIN
WAVE WASHER
CAP SCREWS (4)
FELT WASHER (ROD)
BRAKE PEDAL PUSH ROD
DUST GUARD (ROD)
AIR CLEANER
SPRING RETAINER PLATE
SPRING RETAINER WASHER
CAP SCREWS (3)
SCREWS
VALVE BODY
RETURN SPRING
VALVE BODY GASKET
VACUUM HOSE
FILLER PLUG
GASKET
SCREWS (6)
COVER PLATE
GASKET
COMPENSATING VALVE FITTING GASKET
RETAINER SPRING
REACTING DISC
CAP SCREWS (4)
COMPENSATING VALVE
RESIDUAL VALVE FITTING
SEAL
RESIDUAL CHECK VALVE
SPRING
MASTER CYLINDER
HYDRAULIC PLUNGER
CUP RETAINER
RUBBER CUP
FIBRE GUIDE WASHER
STEEL SPACER WASHER
RETAINER RING
GASKET
POWER BOOSTER CYLINDER

Exploded View of Treadle-Vac Unit (Hydraulic Reaction Type).

Fig. 9—Vacuum piston return spring and retainer removal. Treadle-Vac

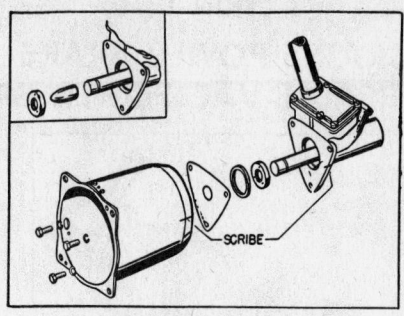

Fig. 10—Vacuum cylinder and leather seal removal. Treadle-Vac

Fig. 11—Seal, hydraulic plunger and compensating valve removal. Treadle-Vac

Bleeding the Treadle-Vac

Bleed the brakes in the normal manner. This unit does not have any bleed screws. Fill to within 1/4 in. of top.

Overhaul of Treadle-Vac Unit

Repair parts for the unit come in kits. Always install all the parts supplied in the kit regardless of whether is appears necessary.

The pictures, Figs. 6 thru 15, give the order of disassembly. There is nothing very difficult involved. Be sure to keep the parts clean as any sign of grease will interfere with the operation of the rubber seals. Be sure

to scribe across the vacuum cylinder and the hydraulic cylinder to facilitate assembly to the same position. Do the same thing to show assembly position of the cover and the hydraulic cylinder. Use alcohol to clean the parts. Be sure that no fluid gets on the valve assembly. Inspect all parts for damage and excessive wear. Re-

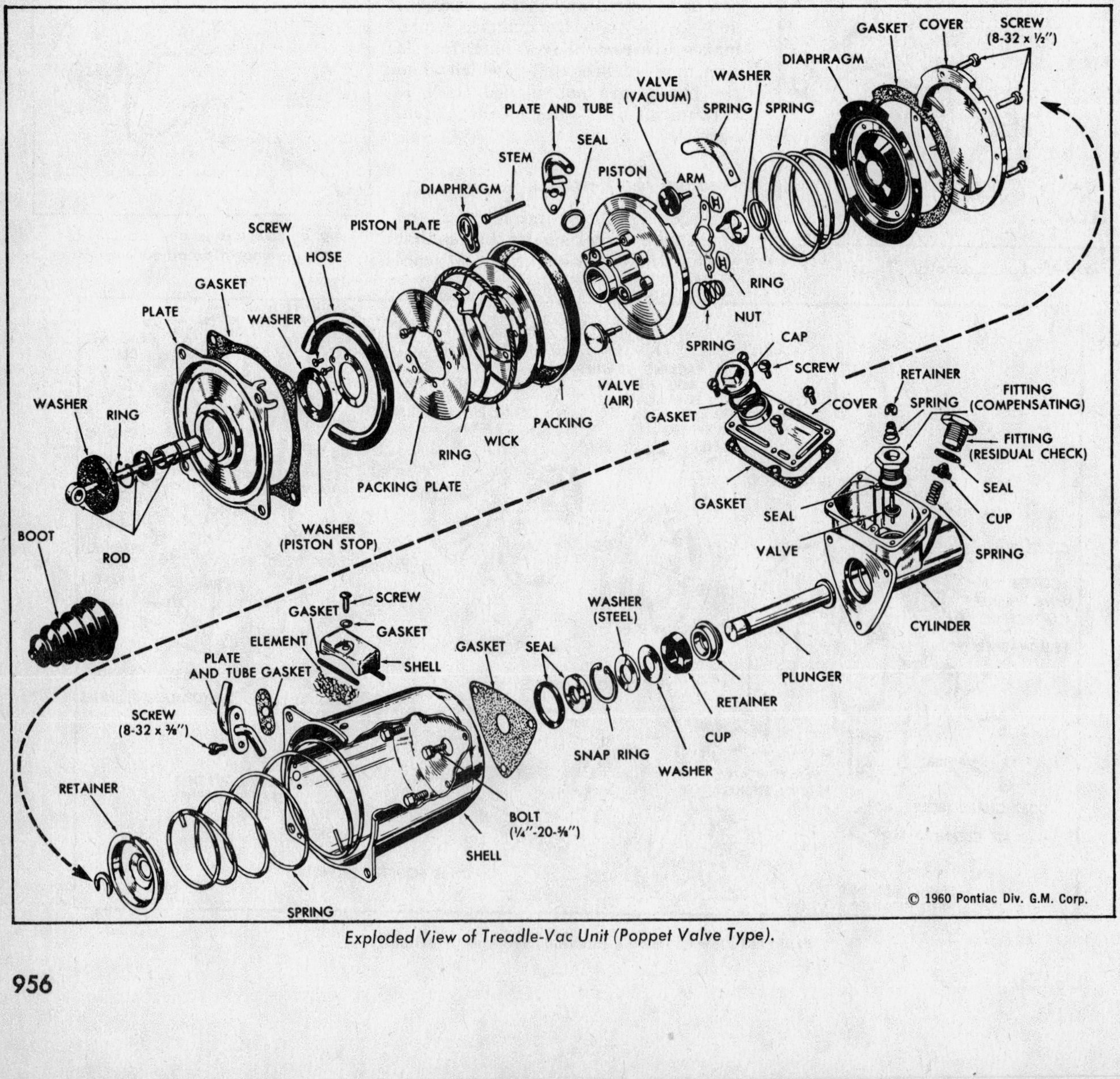

© 1960 Pontiac Div. G.M. Corp.

Exploded View of Treadle-Vac Unit (Poppet Valve Type).

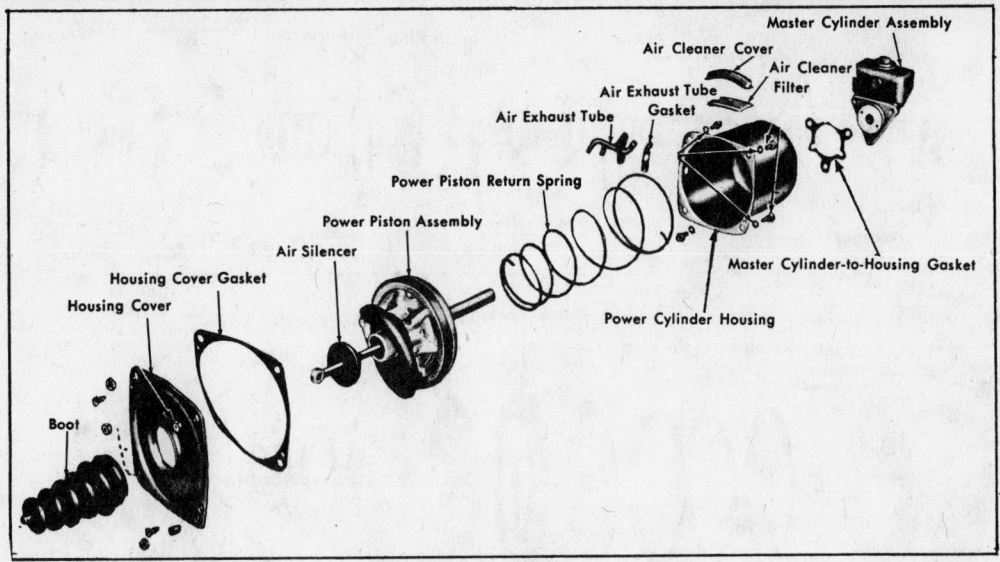

Exploded View of Moraine Piston Type Unit.

place if need be. If the inside of the vacuum cylinder is rusted or corroded it can be cleaned up with steel wool or emery cloth but be sure to remove all traces of the abrasive. If it is scored it must be replaced. Replace the hydraulic plunger if it is rusted or scored.

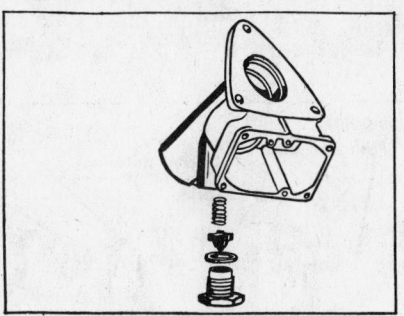

Fig. 12—Residual check valve removal. Treadle-Vac

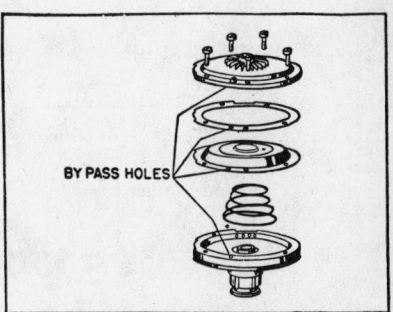

Fig. 13—Diaphragm cover and valve spring removal. Treadle-Vac

SECTION 2

BENDIX HYDROVAC

The Bendix Hydrovac is a unit which can be mounted anywhere on the vehicle because it contains its own slave cylinder. Such a unit is referred to as "Remote type."

The power piston is vacuum balanced which means that when the unit is at rest, brakes released there is vacuum on both sides of the piston.

Bleeding the Hydrovac System

The hydrovac unit must be bled before the wheel cylinders. The unit has two bleed points.

The entire operation must be performed with the engine shut off and no vacuum in the power system.

Remove the filler plug from the brake master cylinder and fill it with hydraulic brake fluid. Attach a bleeder drain hose to the bleeder valve screw on the side of the control valve housing on the hydrovac unit. Keep the end of the hose below the surface of the fluid in the drain jar. Loosen

the valve one-half to three-quarters of a turn. Depress the brake pedal slowly by hand to expel air: When the pedal reaches the toe board close the bleeder valve before releasing the pedal. Repeat the procedure until no more bubbles appear at the end of the drain tube and the stream is a solid fluid mass. Tighten the bleeder valve and remove the drain hose. Note that during the operation the master cylinder must be kept full of fluid.

Now repeat the operation at the bleeder valve on the outlet to the wheel cylinders at the end of the hydraulic cylinder of the unit.

The remainder of the bleeding procedure is the same as for all hydraulic brakes.

Maintenance of the Hydrovac

The seals on the vacuum piston are made of leather and so require lubrication with a special power brake cylinder oil. If this oil is not available

some pure neats foot oil, obtainable from drugstores, can be used instead. One ounce of the special oil or neats foot oil should be introduced into the vacuum cylinder every six months through the lubrication plug provided in the end of the cylinder.

Hydrovac Removal

Remove vacuum line, brake fluid lines to the wheel cylinders and the master cylinder, and the air cleaner hose at the hydrovac unit. Remove the two nuts and one bolt which attach the unit to its mounting bracket.

Reverse procedure to reinstall. Fill the vacuum cylinder with vacuum cylinder oil to the level of the lubrication plug. Bleed the system.

Hydrovac Disassembly

Remove both bleeder screws, hold hexagonal head of the slave cylinder in a vise, loosen locknut on cylinder and unscrew it from the endplate.

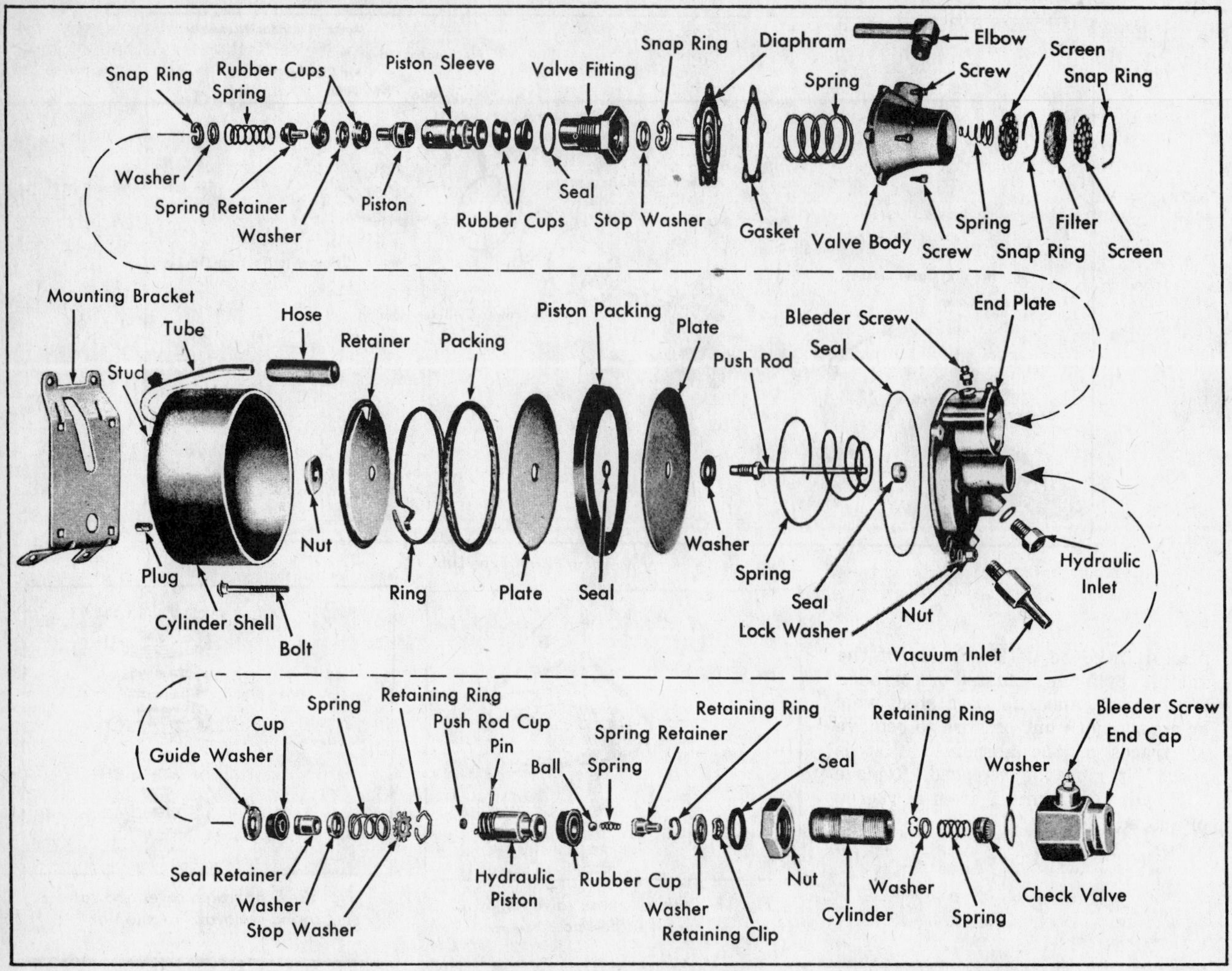

Snap Ring — Rubber Cups — Piston Sleeve — Valve Fitting — Snap Ring — Diaphram — Elbow — Screen — Snap Ring
Spring — Screw — Screen
Washer — Spring
Spring Retainer — Piston — Seal — Stop Washer — Gasket — Valve Body — Screw — Snap Ring — Filter — Screen
Washer — Rubber Cups

Mounting Bracket — Hose — Retainer — Packing — Piston Packing — Plate — Bleeder Screw — End Plate
Tube — Push Rod — Seal
Stud — Hydraulic Inlet
Plug — Nut — Washer — Spring — Seal — Nut
Cylinder Shell — Ring — Plate — Seal — Lock Washer — Vacuum Inlet
Bolt

Cup — Spring — Retaining Ring — Retaining Ring — Retaining Ring — Bleeder Screw
Guide Washer — Push Rod Cup — Spring Retainer — End Cap
Pin — Ball — Spring — Seal — Washer
Seal Retainer — Hydraulic Piston — Rubber Cup — Nut — Washer — Check Valve
Washer — Washer — Cylinder — Spring
Stop Washer — Retaining Clip

Exploded View of Hydro-Vac Unit.

Loosen hose connection on the external tube and slide hose along tube. Remove the four nuts which hold the end plate to the vacuum cylinder and lift off the end plate with the piston assembly attached. Press end plate down on vacuum piston rod until hydraulic piston protrudes from the front of the plate. Remove the push rod to hydraulic piston connecting pin. Remove hydraulic piston, pull out the vacuum piston, rod and return spring from the endplate. Use a one and one-eighth inch wrench to unscrew the end cap from the slave cylinder. Take out five screws attaching control valve assembly to the end plate. Use a one and one-eighth inch wrench to remove the control valve hydraulic cylinder from the end plate.

Fig. 18—Using pilot screws to assemble control valve diaphragm. Hydrovac

Hydrovac Reassembly

It is good practice when overhauling a hydrovac unit to replace all rubber parts and to make sure all parts are kept clean. All rubber parts should be dipped in brake fluid before assembly. Reverse the procedure to reassemble.

Be careful in assembling the control valve diaphragm and poppet valve assembly to use three 8-32x7 inch guide screws so as not to tear the diaphragm, see Fig. 18. When assembling the hydraulic piston into the slave cylinder be sure to push the piston into the outer end until it protrudes from the inner end. Otherwise the rubber cup will be damaged.

This power brake unit is connected to the brake pedal linkage, not directly to the master cylinder.

Mechanical contact between the power unit and brake linkage exists only when the power unit is helping in a brake application. If there is a loss of engine vacuum, the brake

SECTION 3

BENDIX, POWER–VAC
(ROUND OR OVAL TYPE)

pedal is free to work independent of the power unit to apply the brakes in the conventional way.

Testing the Power Brake

1. Remove screw plug from mounting ring and connect the test fitting, hose and vacuum gauge at this point.
2. With brakes in the released position, start the engine and allow it to idle, while watching the

POWER BRAKES

vacuum gauge. (A zero reading shows that the power unit is fully released.) A gauge reading of 1 to 16 inches or more indicates that the power unit is not releasing properly. This may be due to a faulty pedal adjustment or poor power unit operation.

3. Depress the pedal slowly and watch the vacuum gauge reading. (A gauge reading of 1 to 16 inches or more, depending upon pedal pressure applied, indicates that the power unit is operating.) A zero reading indicates faulty power unit operation, restriction in the vacuum supply, or the brake pedal requires corrective service. **Note:** Before proceeding with correction, determine if the source of vacuum is satisfactory.

Alternative:

4. If a vacuum gauge is not handy, depress the pedal several times to deplete any vacuum in the system.

5. Hold the pedal depressed while starting the engine. As soon as the engine starts, the pedal will fall away under the pressure applied.

6. Shut off the engine, depress the pedal a few times. There should be a noticeable increase in the effort required to depress the pedal a given distance as the vacuum in the system is depleted.

7. If there is no noticeable difference in the pedal effort with or without the engine running, check for a restriction in vacuum supply, air cleaner, incorrect pedal adjustment or faulty power unit operation.

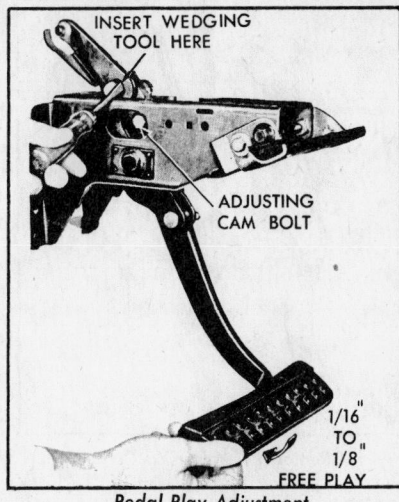
Pedal Play Adjustment

8. Disconnect the vacuum hose from the power unit and place a finger over the end of the hose. A high vacuum indicates that vacuum is being applied to the unit. If no vacuum is present at the end of the cylinder end of the vacuum hose, a restriction in the vacuum supply is present and should be corrected.

9. If vacuum is being supplied to the unit, check pedal linkage adjustment. If all adjustments have been made and the unit still fails to work properly, remove and overhaul the unit.

Pedal Free Play, Adjust

A free play adjustment should be made at no vacuum, engine not running. Apply the brakes a few times to exhaust all vacuum. Insert a screw-driver between the trigger pivot and the rear side of the hole in the power brake lever, forcing the brake pedal and power lever apart.

Check free play with screwdriver in this position by pressing lightly at the pad end of the pedal. This will give a true free play measurement between master cylinder piston and push rod. Free play should be 1/16"—1/8". If free play is incorrect, lengthen or shorten the master cylinder push rod accordingly. If the trigger pivot and power brake lever are not wedged apart, a false reading will result.

Trigger Adjustment

After pedal free play is correctly set, a final check should be made to assure maximum performance of booster.

A slight **clockwise** rotation of the adjusting cam **will speed up a slow pedal return.**

A slight **counterclockwise** rotation of the adjusting cam **will eliminate a time lag** during a fast brake application.

Removing the Power Brake

1. Insert a wooden block between the power lever and the bracket.
2. Scratch alignment marks across the power unit adjacent to the vacuum test port, and across the mounting bracket and between the mounting bracket and the fire wall.
3. Disconnect the vacuum hose at the power unit.
4. Remove master cylinder push rod eye bolt from pedal.
5. Remove stop light switch wires and master cylinder brake tube from master cylinder.

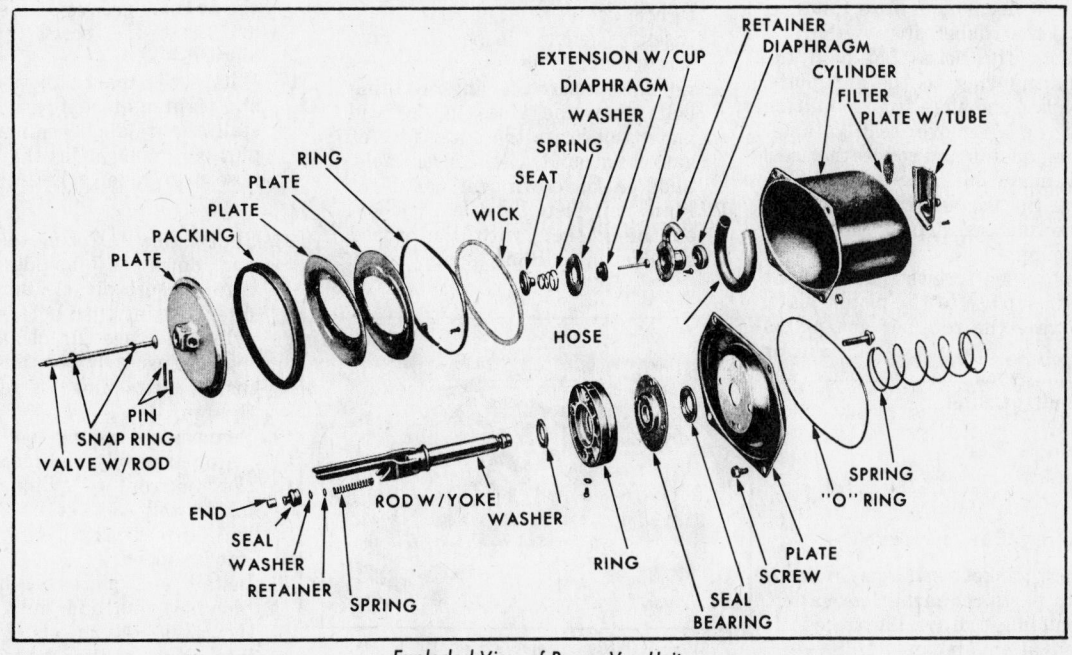
Exploded View of Power-Vac Unit.

6. Remove master cylinder.
7. Remove the bolts that attach the power unit mounting bracket to the fire wall. Slide unit and bracket straight out from fire wall and out of engine compartment.

Disassemble Power Brake

1. Scribe a mark across the flange of the cylinder end plate, and remove attaching nuts and bolts. Slide vacuum piston out of the cylinder. Reach inside and slide the vacuum hose off the air cleaner tube. Then remove the cylinder end plate "O" ring.
2. Remove air cleaner attaching screws, disengage air cleaner and filter from the cylinder.
3. Remove hose from vacuum tube. Remove balancing pin diaphragm from the end of pin housing. Remove balancing pin.
4. Remove tube and housing attaching screws, then separate housing from piston.
5. Remove valve retaining plate from diaphragm. Remove the spring, then peel diaphragm from valve.
6. Pry the nylon button from the end of the valve shaft, then slide the valve rod seal from end of rod.
7. Remove the snap ring that holds the valve rod in the piston.
8. Slide the valve rod washer and spring off end of rod. Slide valve rod out of piston.
9. Drive out the piston rod retaining pins, using a 3/16" drift. Then remove piston from rod.
10. Remove return spring, slide piston rod out from end plate, and remove the rubber stop washer.
11. Remove the bolts that hold the mounting ring to the end plate. Separate end plate from mounting ring and remove seal retainer spring, piston and rod leather seal and mounting ring gasket. Remove the vacuum inspection port screw and gasket from the mounting ring.
12. Remove the screws that hold the retainer plate to the piston plate. Separate the retainer and piston plate, remove the expander spring, wick, packing plate and leather packing.

Assembling Power Brake

Use new gaskets and apply silicone grease to parts requiring lubrication. An assembling tool (as illustrated) is a big help at this point.

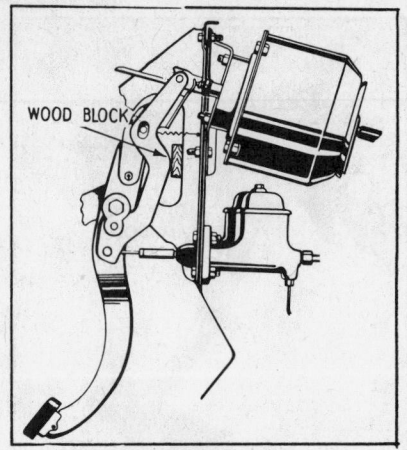

Removal of Power-Vac Unit.

1. Place piston in assembling tool with the threaded holes in the piston facing up.
2. Place leather packing on the piston with the lip side up. Place packing retainer plate on the packing, raised portion side up, and the holes in the plate aligned with those in the piston.
3. Coil the cotton wick inside the packing lip and cup to the required length. Remove the wick and dip in vacuum cylinder oil. Let excess oil drip off then install in packing.
4. Install expander spring inside of wicking with the gripper points next to the wicking. Engage the notch at the loop end of spring with the hook at the opposite end.
5. Install expander spring retainer plate, and align the holes in the plate with the threaded holes in the piston plate. Install screw and tighten.
6. Insert vacuum inspection port screw and gasket into the mounting ring. Insert the ring retaining bolts thru the holes in the end plate. Lubricate the outer face of gasket around the center hole. Slide gasket down over bolts.
7. Place new piston rod leather seal on the gasket, with the raised shoulder up. Slide spring over

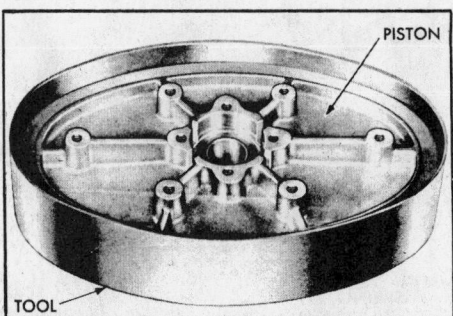

Piston Assembling Tool

shoulder and seat against seal. Center the seal and spring.
8. Coat the bearing surface of the mounting ring with grease, and side mounting ring down over bolts until threads are contacted. Tighten bolts.
9. Slide the rubber stop washer over the piston rod and up against the steel washer. Insert the rod thru leather seal in end plate. Install piston spring over piston rod and down against end plate.
10. Slide the vacuum piston on piston rod and up against the shoulder. Install the retaining pins.
11. Slide valve rod thru the center of the piston and piston rod until the end of the rod protrudes. Slide the valve rod spring and retainer washer over end of rod.
12. Compress the spring, then install the snap ring in the groove of the valve rod.
13. Install the valve rod seal over the end of the valve rod and piston rod.
14. Slide the small diameter of the valve diaphragm over the small shoulder on the valve.
15. Compress the diaphragm enough to permit the valve spring to be installed and down against the valve plate. While holding the diaphragm compressed, install the retainer plate. Seat evenly on the diaphragm.

16. Center the valve and retainer plate on the piston. Place the vacuum tube and pin housing on the retainer plate, be sure that the bead of the diaphragm is in the angular groove of the housing and that the screw holes are aligned.
17. With scribe marks aligned, install and tighten attaching screws. Install the balancing pin and diaphragm, and slide the vacuum hose over tube of housing.

18. Slide a new "O" ring over piston and down on shoulder of end plate. Insert air cleaner tube of filter housing thru hole in vacuum cylinder. Place air cleaner housing against cylinder, align holes, install attaching screws and tighten.
19. Remove assembling tool from the piston assembly and place in position in front of cylinder. Reach inside and connect vacuum hose with air cleaner tube. Slide piston into cylinder.
20. Install end plate-to-cylinder attaching bolts and nuts. Tighten securely. Return air filter hair into place in filter housing.

SECTION 4
BENDIX, MASTER–VAC

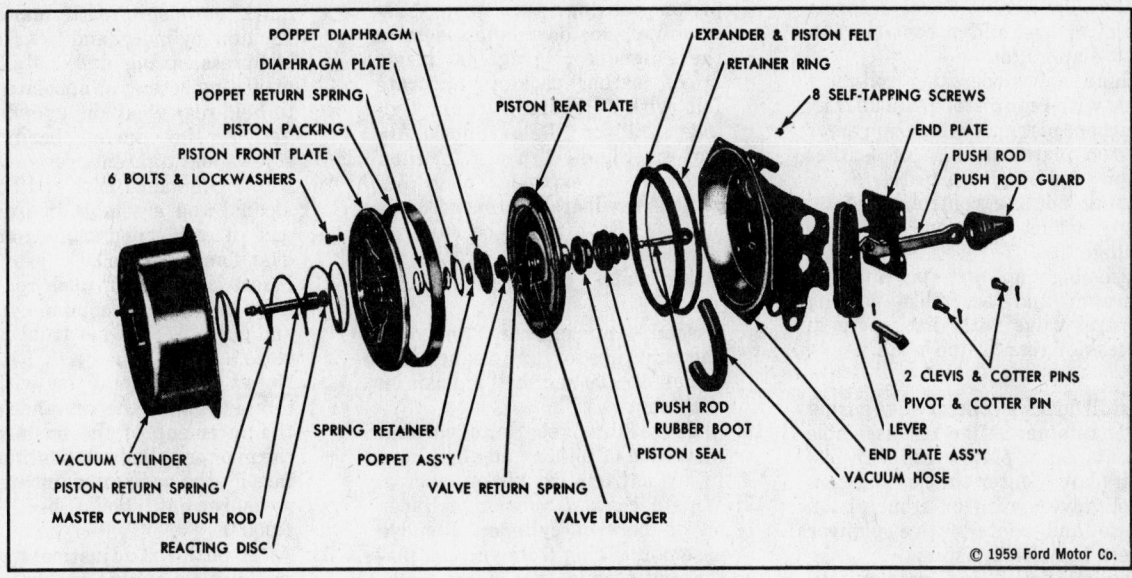

POPPET DIAPHRAGM
DIAPHRAGM PLATE
POPPET RETURN SPRING
PISTON PACKING
PISTON FRONT PLATE
6 BOLTS & LOCKWASHERS

PISTON REAR PLATE

EXPANDER & PISTON FELT
RETAINER RING
8 SELF-TAPPING SCREWS
END PLATE
PUSH ROD
PUSH ROD GUARD

VACUUM CYLINDER
PISTON RETURN SPRING
MASTER CYLINDER PUSH ROD
REACTING DISC

SPRING RETAINER
POPPET ASS'Y
VALVE RETURN SPRING
VALVE PLUNGER

PUSH ROD
RUBBER BOOT
PISTON SEAL

2 CLEVIS & COTTER PINS
PIVOT & COTTER PIN
LEVER
END PLATE ASS'Y
VACUUM HOSE

© 1959 Ford Motor Co.

Remove the Assembly

1. Disconnect clevis at brake pedal-to-push rod.
2. Remove vacuum hoses from power cylinder.
3. Disconnect hydraulic line from master cylinder.
4. Remove the 4 attaching nuts and lock washers holding the unit to the firewall. Remove the power brake unit.

Disassemble

1. Remove 4 master cylinder-to-vacuum cylinder attaching nuts and washers.
2. Separate master cylinder from vacuum cylinder, then remove the rubber seal from the outer groove at end of master cylinder.
3. Remove the push rod from the power section. (Do not disturb adjusting screw.)
4. Remove push rod boot and valve operating rod.
5. Scribe alignment marks across the rear shell and vacuum cylinder. Remove all but two of the end plate attaching screws (opposite each other). Hold down on the rear shell while removing the two remaining screws to prevent the piston return spring from expanding, uncontrolled.
6. Scribe a mark across the face of the piston to index the mark on the rear shell and remove rear shell with vacuum piston and piston return spring.
7. Remove vacuum hose from vacuum piston and from vacuum tube on inside of rear shell. Separate rear shell from vacuum piston.

8. Remove air cleaner and vacuum tube assembly, and air filter from the rear shell.
9. Spring the felt retaining ring enough to disengage ring from grooves in bosses on rear piston plate.
10. Remove piston felt and expander ring from piston assembly.
11. Remove six piston plate attaching screws and separate front piston plate and piston packing from piston plate.
12. Remove valve return spring, floating control valve and diaphragm assembly, valve spring and diaphragm plate. Separate floating control valve spring retainer and control valve diaphragm from control valve.
13. Remove rubber reaction disc and shim (if present) from front piston plate.
Note: Do not remove the valve operating rod and valve plunger from the rear piston plate unless it is necessary to replace bad parts. Normally the next two steps can be omitted.
14. When it is necessary to replace the valve operating rod or valve plunger, remove valve rod seal from groove in piston plate and pull seal over end of rod.
15. Hold piston with valve plunger side down and inject alcohol in valve plunger thru opening around valve rod. This will wet the rubber lock in the plunger, then drive or pry valve plunger off the valve rod.
Note: If master cylinder is not to be rebuilt, omit steps 16-19.
16. Remove snap ring from groove in

base at end of master cylinder.
17. Remove piston assembly, primary cup, retainer spring, and check valve from master cylinder.
18. Remove filler cap and gasket from master cylinder body.
19. Remove secondary cup from master cylinder piston.

Cleaning Note

After disassembly, cleaning of all metal parts in "Bendix Metalclene" or satisfactory commercial cleaner solvent is recommended. Use only alcohol or "Declene" on rubber parts or parts containing rubber. After cleaning and drying, metal parts should be rewashed in clean alcohol or "Declene" before assembly.

Assembly

Steps 1-5 apply to a completely disassembled master cylinder. Otherwise, omit steps 1 thru 5.
1. Coat bore of master cylinder with brake fluid.
2. Dip secondary cup in brake fluid and install on master cylinder piston.
3. Dip other piston parts in brake fluid and assemble the piston. Install piston.
4. Install snap ring in groove of cylinder.
5. Use new gasket and install filler cap.
6. Assemble valve rod seal on rod and insert valve rod through the piston. Dip valve plunger in alcohol and assemble to ball end of valve rod. Be sure ball end of rod is locked in place in plunger.

7. Assemble floating control valve diaphragm over end of floating control valve. Be sure diaphragm is in recess of floating control valve. Press control valve spring retainer over end of control valve and diaphragm.

8. Clamp valve operating rod in a vise with rear piston plate up. Lay leather piston packing on rear piston plate with lip of leather over edge of piston plate.

9. Install floating control valve return spring over end of valve plunger.

10. Assemble diaphragm plate to diaphragm and assemble floating control valve with diaphragm in recess of rear piston plate.

11. Install floating control valve spring over retainer. Align and assemble front piston plate with rear piston plate. Center the floating control valve spring on front piston plate and center valve plunger stem in hole of piston.

12. Holding front and rear piston plates together, loosely install six piston plate cap screws.

13. Install shim and rubber reaction disc in recess at center of front piston plate.

Note: A piston assembling ring (tool #J-7780) is handy in assembling the piston.

14. Place the assembling tool over piston packing, turn piston assembly upside down and assemble the expander ring against inside lip of leather packing. Saturate felt with "Bendix Vacuum Cylinder Oil" or "Delco Shock Absorber Fluid—Type A," then assemble in expander ring. Assemble retainer ring over bosses on rear piston plate; be sure retainer is anchored in grooves of piston plate.

15. Assemble air cleaner filter over vacuum tube of air cleaner and attach air cleaner shell in position with screws.

16. Slide vacuum hose onto vacuum inlet tube of piston and align hose to lay flat against piston.

17. Wipe a coat of vacuum cylinder oil on bore of cylinder. Remove assembling ring from vacuum piston and coat leather piston packing with vacuum cylinder oil.

18. Install rear shell over end of valve operating rod and attach vacuum hose to tube end on each side of end plate.

19. Center small diameter end of piston return spring in vacuum cylinder. Center large diameter of spring on piston. Check alignment mark on piston with marks on vacuum cylinder and rear shell, compress spring and install two attaching screws at opposite sides to hold rear shell and cylinder together. Now install balance of screws and tighten screws evenly.

20. Dip small end of push rod boot in alcohol and assemble guard over end of valve operating rod and over flange of shell.

21. Insert large end of push rod thru hole in end of vacuum cylinder and guide into hole of front piston plate.

Note: Before going on with assembly, check the distance from the outer end of the push-rod to the master cylinder mounting surface on the vacuum cylinder. This measurement should be 1.195"-1.200".

22. After push-rod adjustment is correct, replace rubber seal in groove on master cylinder body.

23. Assemble master cylinder to the vacuum cylinder at four studs. Replace lock washers and nut and securely tighten.

SECTION 5
MORAINE— DIAPHRAGM TYPE

Remove the Assembly

1. Disconnect clevis at brake pedal assembly.
2. Remove vacuum hoses from power brake unit.
3. Disconnect hydraulic line from master cylinder.
4. Remove the four nuts and lock washers holding the unit to the firewall. Lift out the power brake unit.
5. Remove the cotter pin, clevis pin and washer from the end of the brake pedal push rod.
6. Remove the cotter pin, clevis pin and washer from the end of the power brake operating rod. Remove the wave washer.
7. Remove the cotter pin, then tap out the pivot pin. Remove two operating levers and the pivot collar.

Disassembling Vacuum Unit

1. Place the power unit in a vise with push rod up. With the unit firmly clamped by the fluid reservoir, position a bar on the rear shell so as to provide leverage to rotate the rear shell counterclockwise. This will separate the rear shell from the front shell.
2. Now lift the power piston assembly and the rear shell from the unit.

3. Remove the piston return spring from the front shell.
4. Pull the push rod through the boot and remove the exhaust hose from the exhaust tube on the rear shell.
5. Re-position the master cylinder assembly in the vise to allow the removal of the front shell from the master cylinder.
6. Remove four attaching nuts and lock washers, then separate master cylinder from the shell assembly, and count the in-between shims.
7. Remove screw, cover and air filter element from the rear shell assembly.
8. Remove two screws from the exhaust tube bracket and free the exhaust tube assembly.
9. Loosen the four 1/4" screws in the power piston assembly. With master cylinder piston up, remove the four screws and lift the master cylinder piston, piston diaphragm plate and power piston diaphragm from the power piston assembly.
10. Remove the three reaction levers and the air valve reaction plate. Remove the floating control valve

return spring and power piston seal ring.

11. Turn the power piston over, release the exhaust hose clamp and remove the exhaust hose from the piston assembly, then remove the air valve boot.

12. Push the air valve and push rod assembly thru the power piston and remove the floating control valve and diaphragm assembly.

13. Separate the floating control valve and diaphragm from the push rod.

14. Remove the spring retainer from the floating control valve and diaphragm. Remove the reaction diaphragm retainer from under the lip of the diaphragm and remove the diaphragm from the floating control valve. The reaction diaphragm support plate can now be lifted from the control valve.

15. Remove the power piston diaphragm from the piston diaphragm plate.

16. Remove the retaining ring from the master cylinder piston. Remove the reaction lever plate from master cylinder piston and press the piston assembly thru the piston diaphragm plate.

17. Remove the retaining ring from the master cylinder piston. Remove the reaction lever plate from

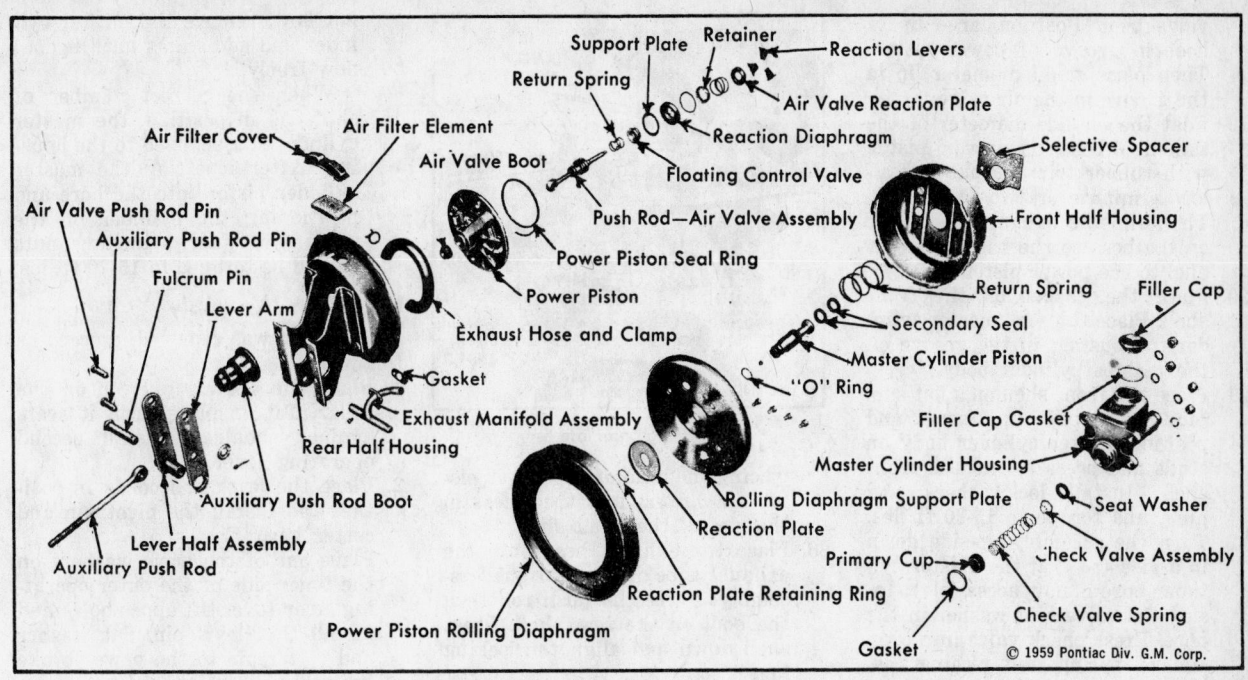

Exploded View of Moraine Diaphragm Type Unit.

the master cylinder piston and press the master cylinder piston assembly thru the piston diaphragm plate.

18. Remove the master cylinder piston "O" ring, two secondary seals and the small rubber bumper from the piston.

Cleaning Note

Use "Declene" or fresh brake fluid to clean all parts thoroughly. Soak in the fluid and use hair brush to dislodge all foreign matter. Use compressed air on all orifices and valve holes, then air dry.

The use of gasoline, kerosene or any other mineral cleaner will react on rubber parts. Lubricate with brake fluid only.

Assembly

1. Position the filter element and the air filter cover over two holes in the rear housing.
2. Inspect the exhaust tube assembly for damage. Insert the tube (with new gasket), in the rear housing and install two screws.
3. Insert the small rubber bumper in the counter-bore of the master cylinder piston. Place two secondary seals in grooves of master cylinder piston with lips toward the small drilled holes in the end of the piston.
4. Install the "O" ring into the second groove from the counterbored end of the master cylinder piston. Lubricate with silicone grease and insert piston into the piston diaphragm plate, from the flange side.

5. Place reaction lever plate (with raised rim away from piston diaphragm plate) over piston and install snap ring in the groove.
6. Set the assembly aside for the moment.
7. Place the reaction diaphragm support plate over the hub of floating control valve. Assemble reaction diaphragm over flanged hub of control valve so that the flange fits into the groove on the inside diameter of the diaphragm.
8. Insert diaphragm retainer under the lip of the diaphragm and place the floating control valve spring retainer over the reaction diaphragm hub. The six small rubber bumpers must be positioned in the spring retainer.
9. Place power piston in vise with the flat surface up. (Do not clamp.)
10. Insert the push rod end of the air valve push rod into the piston and press down into the piston to seat the air valve.
11. Wipe a light film of silicone grease on the outer diameter of reaction diaphragm.
12. Place the floating control valve and diaphragm assembly down over the air valve and press the outer edge of the reaction diaphragm into position in the power piston.
13. Place the air valve return spring inside the floating control valve to seat on the air valve. Place the floating control valve spring to seat on the flange of the spring retainer. Position the air valve reaction plate over the air valve

so the low center portion rests on the inner spring (air valve return spring). The outer spring (floating control valve spring) will also be in a position to engage the reaction lever plate.
14. Position the ears of the reaction levers in the machined locations in the power piston and rest the small ends on the reaction lever plate. Insert seal ring into the inner groove on the flat surface of the power piston face.
15. Pull the skirt of the power piston diaphragm down over the piston and place the bead on the inner diameter of the diaphragm in the outer groove of the power piston face so the bumpers are toward the piston.
16. The master cylinder piston and piston diaphragm plate are positioned over the power piston diaphragm and the lugs on the plate are aligned with the depressions in the power piston.
17. The snap ring on the master cylinder piston must be rotated to position the lobes between the reaction levers. The ears of the reaction levers must stay in place in the machined seats on the power piston as the diaphragm plate contacts the power piston face. The position of the bead and levers must be correct as the support plate is finally positioned and the four 1/4" screws tightened thru the support plate and into the power piston. Torque to 65-85 in. lbs.
18. Turn power piston assembly upside down to assemble the air

valve boot. Position large lip of boot in groove of power piston. Then place small diameter lip in the groove in the air valve.

19. Coat the outside diameter of the tube-like boss on power piston with rubber trim cement and allow a minute or two to air dry. Then slip the exhaust hose fully on the boss so the hose lays parallel to the power piston.

20. Place the gasket on the front shell. Place the seal, master cylinder to housing, in the groove on the master cylinder body.

21. Place the front shell on a flat surface with studs up. Insert and position master cylinder body on studs and press it into the front shell. Install lockwashers and nuts, and torque to 15-20 ft. lbs.

22. Turn the assembly up-side down in a vise (so that the master cylinder bore is now accessible). Insert the valve seat washer in the bore. Press check valve into open end of spring and retainer assembly, and position in the bore with the check valve against the valve seat washer. Dip the primary cup into clean brake fluid and insert it into the bore with lips over the spring and retainer.

23. Work the groove of the push rod boot into position in the center hole of the rear shell.

24. Place the return spring over the flange in the center of the front shell. Place the power piston over the front shell and insert the master cylinder piston thru the return spring into the master cylinder bore.

25. Press the power piston assembly down and hold it in position while

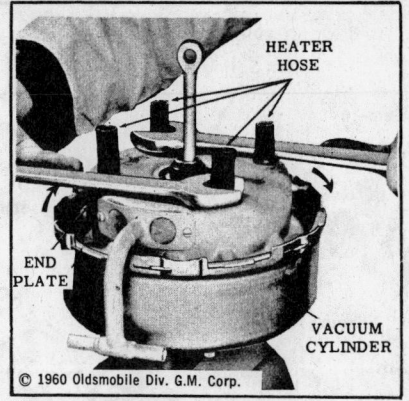

© 1960 Oldsmobile Div. G.M. Corp.

Installing End Plate.

placing the bead of the power piston diaphragm into the recess in the rim of the front shell.

26. Place the exhaust hose onto the exhaust tube of the rear shell assembly. Force the push rod thru the boot on the rear shell. Press shell down and align the locking lugs.

Note:

The following gauging operation is necessary only after structural parts have been replaced. It is also necessary if the exact number of shims removed at disassembly are not known.

27. Torque master cylinder nuts to 15-20 ft. lbs. and remove the filler cap. With the brake cylinder in the released position, force air into the hydraulic outlet of the master cylinder. If air passes freely thru the compensating port (the smaller of the two holes in the bottom of the master cylinder reservoir), shimming can be considered satisfactory. If air does

not flow, remove the master cylinder and add shims until it does flow freely.

When the correct number of shims is in position, the master cylinder is assembled to the housing. After inserting the master cylinder piston into the bore and positioning the cylinder on the studs, the four attaching nuts should be torqued to 15-20 ft. lbs.

Install the Assembly

If linkage was removed, proceed as follows:

1. Place one operating lever on the collar. Tap in place until it seats against shoulder. Install second operating lever.

2. Place the lever and collar in position and install the pivot pin and cotter key.

3. Place one of the wave washers on the inner side of the outer operating lever (over the upper hole) and install the clevis pin, flat washer and cotter pin to the power brake assembly operating rod.

4. Place the remaining wave washer on the inner side of the outer operating lever (over the middle hole) and install the clevis pin, flat washer and cotter key to the brake pedal push rod.

5. Mount the power brake assembly in place and install the four attaching nuts and lock washers.

6. Hook up the hydraulic line to the master cylinder.

7. Attach the vacuum lines to the power unit.

8. Attach the push rod clevis to the brake pedal assembly. Adjust pedal height by means of clevis on brake pedal push rod at the pedal.

SECTION 6

MIDLAND-ROSS

The self-contained booster assembly is mounted on the engine side of the fire wall. It is connected directly to the brake pedal. This booster is not equipped with a separate vacuum tank.

The master cylinder is attached to the forward side of the booster. The balance of the hydraulic brake system is identical to other standard service brakes.

Booster Removal

1. From inside the car, remove the horseshoe-type retainer holding the booster push rod link on the brake pedal pin. Then slide the link off the pin.

2. Disconnect wires from the stop light switch.

3. Disconnect hydraulic line at master cylinder.

4. Disconnect manifold vacuum hose

from the booster. If car is equipped with a transmission vacuum throttle valve hose, remove this hose.

5. Remove nuts and washers from booster bracket mounting studs on fire wall. Then pull booster and bracket assembly off the studs, sliding the push rod link out of the hole in the panel.

Booster Repairs

1. Separate master cylinder from booster body.

2. Remove air filter cover and hub and the filter from the booster body.

3. Remove the vacuum manifold mounting bolt, manifold, gaskets and vacuum check valve from the booster body.

4. Disconnect the valve operating rod from the lever by removing

its retaining clip, washers, and pilot pin.

5. Disconnect the lever from the booster end plate brackets by removing its retaining clip, washers, and pivot pin.

6. Remove two brackets from the end plate.

7. Remove the rubber boot from the valve operating rod.

8. **To remove the bellows, control valve, and diaphragm assemblies,** remove large "C" ring that holds the rear seal adapter assembly on the booster end plate.

9. Scribe matching lines on the booster body and the end plate. Then remove the ten retaining screws. Tap the outside of the plate with a soft hammer and separate the plate from the booster body.

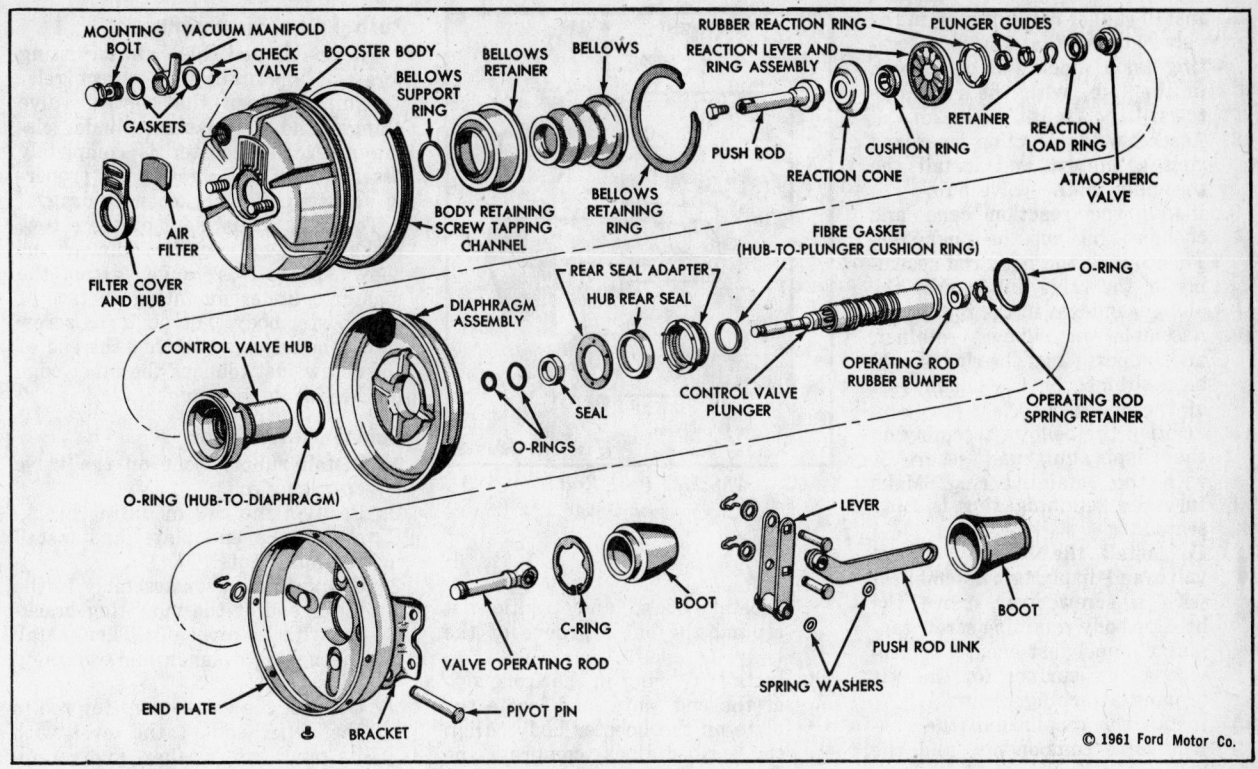

Disassembled View of Booster

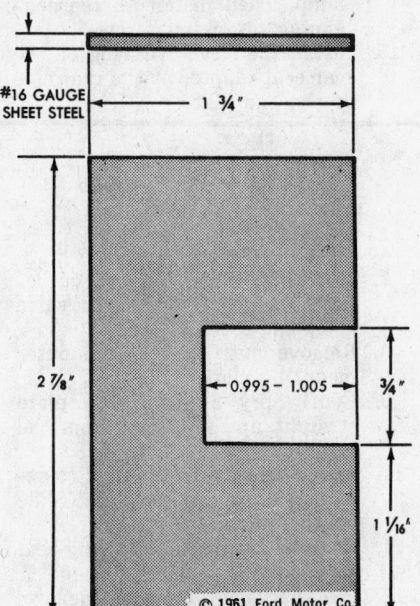

Push Rod Gauge

10. Push the bellows assembly into the vacuum chamber and remove the bellows, control valve, and diaphragm as an assembly from the booster body.
11. Remove the outer "O" ring from the control valve hub.
12. **To disassemble the bellows, push rod, and control valve assemblies,** remove the large bellows retaining ring, bellows, bellows retainer, and support ring from the diaphragm and valve assembly.
13. Remove the retainer and support ring from the bellows.
14. Remove push rod assembly, the reaction lever and ring assembly, and the rubber reaction ring from the control valve hub.
15. Remove the reaction cone and cushion ring from the push rod assembly. Then disassemble the reaction levers from the ring.
16. Remove the two plastic plunger guides from the control valve plunger. Then remove the retainer that holds the reaction load ring and atmospheric valve on the control valve hub.
17. Slide the reaction load ring and atmospheric valve from the control valve hub.
18. Separate the control valve hub and the plunger assembly from the diaphragm by sliding the plunger and rear seal adapter from the rear of the hub. Then remove the hub outer "O" ring from the front side of the diaphragm.

19. **To disassemble the control valve plunger,** remove the hub rear seal adapter from the valve plunger assembly, and remove the seal from the adapter.
20. Remove the "O" rings, the seal, and the fiber gaskets from the plunger.
21. If the plunger assembly needs to be replaced, hold the plunger and pull out the valve operating rod with pliers. Do not separate the

operating rod and plunger unless the plunger is to be replaced.

Assembling

1. If valve operating rod was removed for replacement of plunger, install a new rubber bumper and spring retainer on the rod before installing it on the replacement plunger. Then push the rod firmly until it bottoms in the plunger.
2. Install fiber gaskets, plunger seal, and the two "O" rings on the plunger assembly.
3. Install the valve hub rear seal in the adapter assembly with the sealing lip toward the rear. Then slide the adapter assembly onto the plunger with the small diameter end of the hub toward the rear.
4. **To assemble the control valve, push rod, and bellows assemblies,** install the hub outer "O" ring. Then install the plunger with the seal adapter and the hub on the diaphragm. To do this, hold the hub on the front side of the diaphragm, and insert the plunger assembly in the hub from the rear side of the diaphragm.
5. Install atmospheric valve and then the reaction load ring on the plunger and hub. Compress the valve spring, and install the load ring retainer in the groove of the plunger.
6. Install two plastic plunger guides in their grooves on the plunger.

7. Install rubber reaction ring in the valve hub so that the ring locating knob indexes in the notch in the hub, with the ring tips toward the front.

8. Assemble the reaction lever and ring assembly, and install the assembly in the valve hub.

9. Install the reaction cone and cushion ring on the push rod. Then install the push rod assembly on the valve hub so that the plunger indexes in the rod.

10. Assemble the bellows, retainer, and support ring. The ring should be positioned on the middle fold of the bellows.

11. Position the bellows assembly on the diaphragm, and secure it with the retaining ring. Make sure the retaining ring is fully seated.

12. **To install the bellows, control valve, and diaphragm assemblies;** with a screwdriver, move the booster body retaining screw tapping channel just enough to provide a new surface for the self tapping attaching screws.

13. Install the diaphragm, the control valve components, and the bellows as an assembly in the booster body. (Be sure the lip of the diaphragm is evenly positioned on the retaining radius of the booster body.) Pull the front lip of the bellows through the

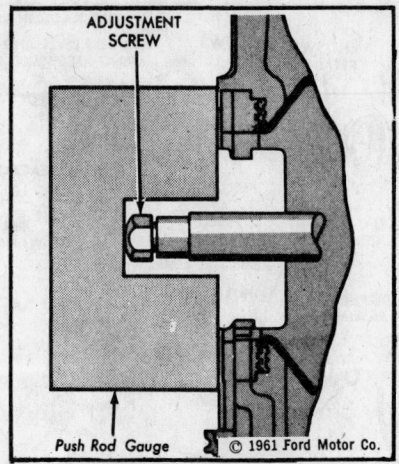

Checking Push Rod Screw with Gauge

booster body, and position it around the outer groove of the body.

14. Install "O" ring in the front side of the end plate, and locate the plate on the booster body. Align the scribed lines, compress the two assemblies together with a clamp. Then install all ten self-tapping attaching screws.

15. Install the large "C" ring on the rear seal adapter at the rear side of the end plate.

Push Rod Adjustment

The push rod has an adjusting screw to maintain the correct relationship between the control valve plunger and the master cylinder piston after the booster is completely assembled. If this screw is not properly adjusted, the brakes may drag.

To check adjustment of the screw, make a gauge to the dimensions shown. Place this gauge against the master cylinder mounting surface of the booster body. The push rod screw should be adjusted so that the end of the screw just touches the inner edge of the slot in the gauge.

Booster Installation

1. Install rubber boot on the valve operating rod.

2. Position the two mounting brackets on the end plate, and install retaining nuts.

3. Connect the lever assembly to the lower end of the mounting brackets with its pivot pin. Then install the spring washer and retaining clip.

4. Connect the valve operating rod to the upper end of the lever with its pivot pin, washer, and retaining clip.

5. Install the vacuum check valve, the vacuum manifold, the two gaskets, and the mounting bolt. Torque the mounting bolt to 8-10 ft. lbs.

SECTION 7
KELSEY-HAYES
BELLOWS TYPE

Remove the Assembly

1. Use a pedal depressor. Depress the pedal to prevent trigger arm from extending beyond the bracket limits. If the pedal linkage is permitted to extend thru the hole in the firewall, the trigger arm may be damaged.

2. Disconnect the vacuum hose at power vent.

3. Remove master cylinder power unit and bracket assembly nuts and lock washers.

4. Withdraw the unit from the firewall. Don't loose the nylon bushing at the pedal linkage cross pin.

Disassembly

1. Remove mounting plate-to-unit attaching nuts.

2. Slide plate off and away from unit.

3. Remove mounting plate "O" ring.

4. With an Allen wrench, back out two set screws enough to permit removal of yoke.

5. Slide yoke off end of guide and away from unit.

6. Remove rubber stop seal washer.

7. Lift valve operating rod out of unit, remove, and discard valve operating rod button seal.

8. Remove nuts that attach outer mounting plate.

9. Gently pry and lift the plate straight up and away from the unit.

10. Compress bellows by hand to expose the guide bearing. Slide bearing off end of guide.

11. Remove and discard bearing seal from outside bearing.

12. Peel back outer lip of bellows from around inner mounting plate.

13. Remove plate and lift out return spring and return spring retainer.

14. Remove bolts and lockwashers that attach valve cover to valve. Lift off cover.

15. Remove and discard "O" ring from valve cover.

16. Remove air valve spring from center of valve.

17. Remove air filter and hook the air valve out of the housing with a small bent wire, (paper clip).

18. Place valve housing end down on bench. Remove bellows from valve by peeling back outer lip of bellows.

19. Lift bellows up, away from valve.

20. Remove guide-to-valve body bolts and lift off guide to expose vacuum valve, valve spring and seals.

21. Remove seals, then lift out vacuum valve and retainer.

22. Remove valve housing-to-guide seal.

23. Insert valve housing and remove air valve seal from its groove in the valve body.

Assembly

Lubricate all seals and "O" rings with silicone grease before installation.

1. Insert new air valve seal into bore of valve housing (with lips of seal facing out).

2. Position new vacuum valve in retainer.

3. Invert valve housing and install vacuum valve and retainer in housing.

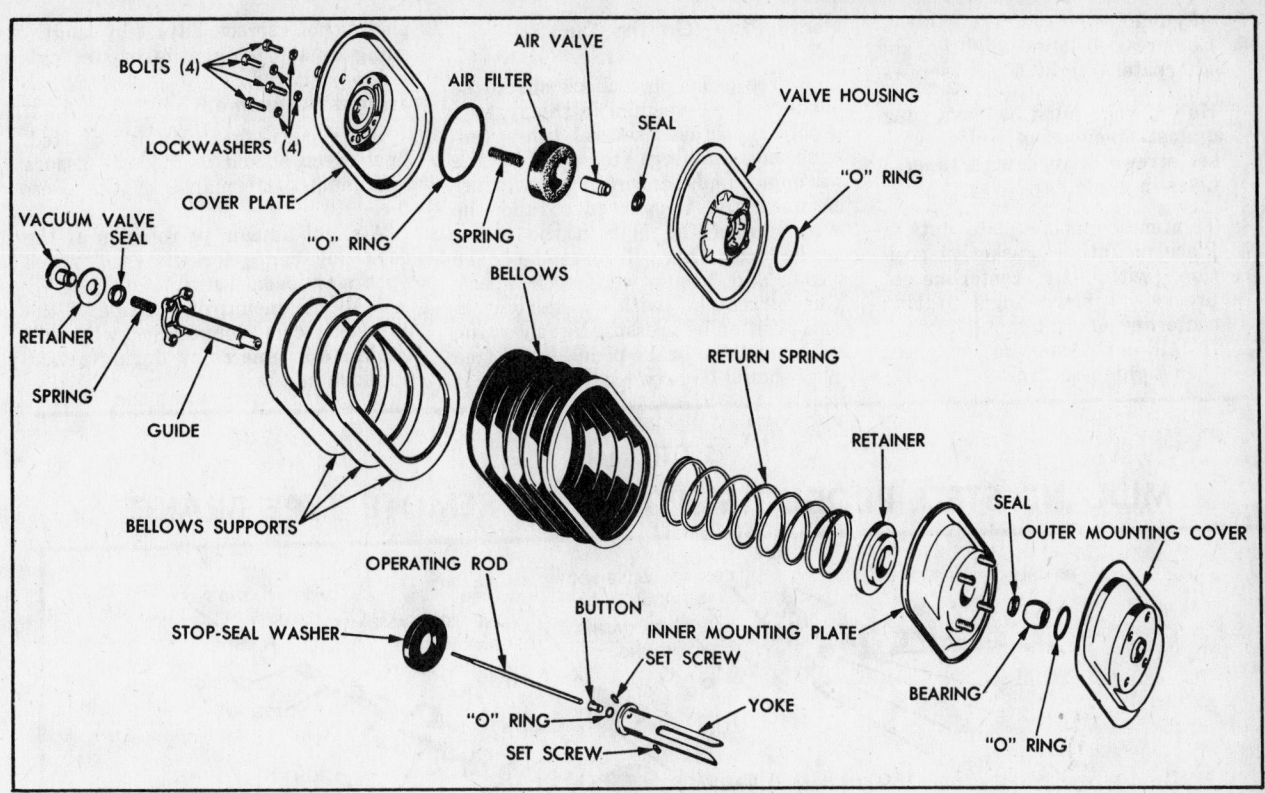

BOLTS (4)
LOCKWASHERS (4)
COVER PLATE
VACUUM VALVE SEAL
RETAINER
SPRING
GUIDE
BELLOWS SUPPORTS
STOP-SEAL WASHER
OPERATING ROD
"O" RING
SET SCREW
AIR VALVE
AIR FILTER
"O" RING
SPRING
SEAL
VALVE HOUSING
"O" RING
BELLOWS
RETURN SPRING
RETAINER
SEAL
OUTER MOUNTING COVER
BUTTON
INNER MOUNTING PLATE
SET SCREW
YOKE
BEARING
"O" RING

Exploded View of Kelsey-Hayes Bellows Type Unit.

4. Press down firmly on retainer to snap it in place.
5. Position new valve housing to guide seal in groove provided.
6. Install new vacuum valve seal in bore guide, (lip of seal toward bottom of bore).
7. Install vacuum valve spring in center of valve.
8. Position guide over vacuum valve, lining up bolt in guide with bolt holes in valve body.
9. Lower guide down against valve body. Be certain that the tapered portion of valve enters seal evenly.
10. Press down on guide to seal and install bolts and lockwashers. Tighten bolts evenly.
11. If new bellows are being installed, position supports in bellows.
12. Using holding fixture (made from 3" length of 4" pipe) to support guide and valve assembly in upright position, install the bellows. Be sure arrows on edge of bellows and housing are aligned.
13. With assembly in holding fixture, wipe the outer surface of the air valve with silicone grease and insert the small end into bore of housing.
14. Use finger pressure to test for free movement of valve against vacuum valve spring.
15. Install air valve spring in recess in air valve and air filter.
16. Install new valve housing cover

"O" ring on shoulder provided on valve body hub.
17. Position valve body cover over valve housing, with notch in edge of cover matching arrow on bellows. Be sure air valve spring rests on dimple in center of cover.
18. Press cover down evenly over valve housing to seat over "O" ring, install bolts, then tighten securely.
19. Remove assembly from holding fixture and invert unit.
20. Wipe guide lightly with silicone grease and install return spring.
21. Position spring evenly around hub of valve housing and guide.
22. Place spring retainer and inner mounting plate over spring, (be sure the arrow marks on the plate are in line with the arrow on the edge of the bellows).
23. Compress return spring and fold bellows lip over edge of plate.
24. Install new guide bearing seal in groove inside bearing bore.
25. Seat the seal snugly in the bearing.
26. Lubricate inside of bearing with silicone grease and slide it over guide, while compressing the bellows. **Bearing to be installed with lip of seal facing out.**
27. Push bearing down over guide and into pocket of plate.
28. Release bellows and the bearing will ride up guide with plate into position.
29. Install bearing to mounting plate

"O" ring and lower outer mounting plate down on assembly.
30. Install nuts and draw down finger tight.
31. Slide new valve operating rod seal ring over nylon bumper on end of rod and into groove.
32. Install rod in center of guide.
33. Press on end of rod to test for free operation or movement of air and vacuum vanes. A two-step movement should be felt when rod is depressed and released fully.
34. Place new stop seal washer in position and install yoke on end

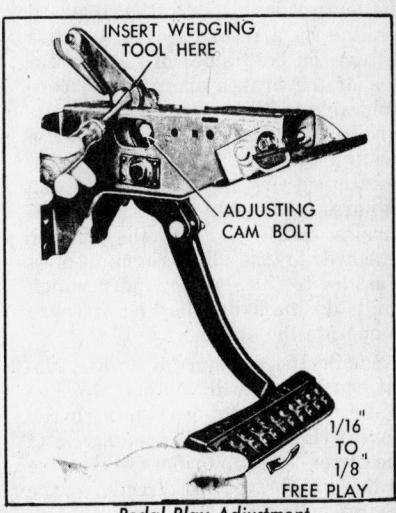

INSERT WEDGING TOOL HERE
ADJUSTING CAM BOLT
1/16" TO 1/8"
FREE PLAY

Pedal Play Adjustment

of guide.

35. Compress bellows slightly and alternately tighten set screws.

Hub of yoke must be down snug against shoulder of guide, with set screws aligned with tapered holes in guide.

36. Tighten mounting plate nuts.
37. Place mounting bracket in position, with long centerline of bracket at right angle to long centerline of unit section.
38. Install nuts and lockwashers, then tighten securely.

Pedal Play (On the Car)

A free pedal play check should be made with no vacuum in the system. Apply the brakes several times (engine not running) to exhaust the vacuum supply. Insert a screwdriver between the trigger pivot and the rear side of the hole in the power brake lever. This will force the brake pedal and the power lever apart. Check free play with screwdriver in this position by pressing lightly at the pad end of the brake pedal. Pedal free play should be between 1/16"-1/8". If

play is not correct, adjust by lengthening or shortening the master cylinder push rod.

Trigger Adjustment

After pedal free play is adjusted, final check should be made to assure maximum performance of the booster.

A slight amount of rotation of the adjusting cam, **clockwise** will speed up a **slow pedal return.**

A slight amount of rotation of the adjusting cam, **counterclockwise** will **eliminate a time delay** during a fast application.

SECTION 8
MIDLAND STEEL PRODUCTS HY-POWER REMOTE TYPE BRAKES

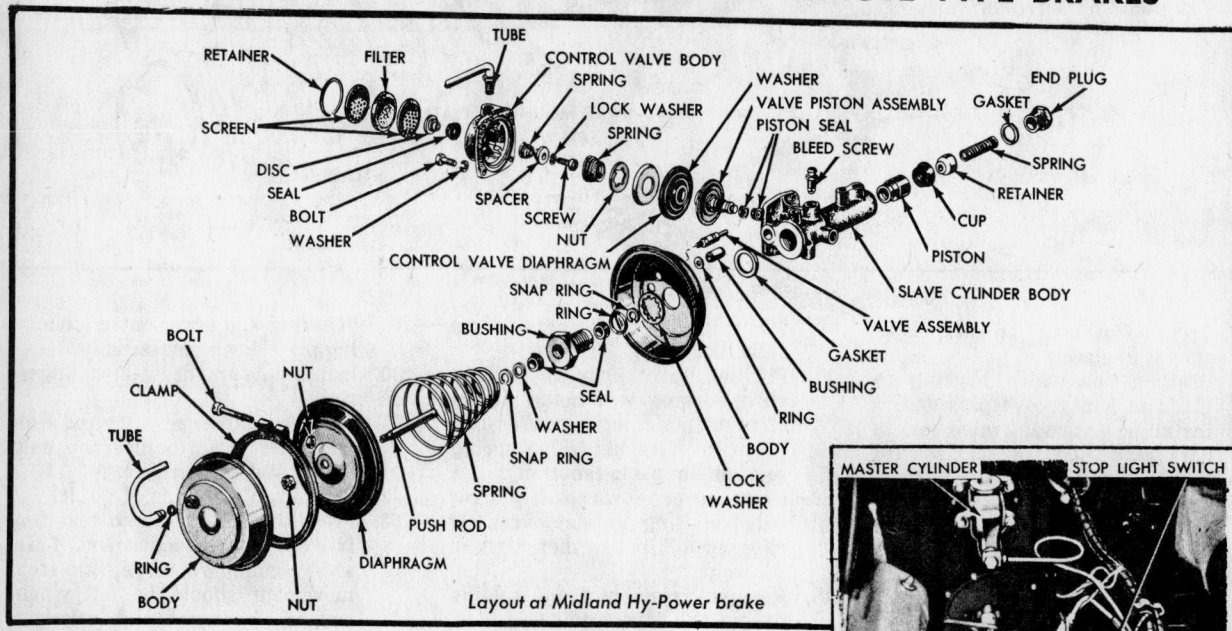

Layout at Midland Hy-Power brake

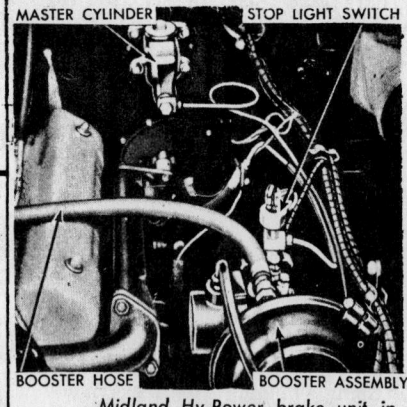

Midland Hy-Power brake unit installed. Ford installation shown

Operation

In operation this unit is known as a vacuum suspended system in that the diaphragm is held in the released position by a return spring and has vacuum on both sides of it. Application of the brakes operates the control valve to allow atmospheric pressure to enter the front portion of the vacuum cylinder. With vacuum still maintained on the rear side of the diaphragm the air forces the diaphragm to the rear and the plunger attached to the diaphragm applies pressure to the slave cylinder which builds up the hydraulic line pressure to operate the brakes.

Should the vacuum fail to be present, the brakes will still operate. The brake fluid will by-pass through the slave cylinder piston openings and the piston and cup orifices so that the brakes will be applied directly by the master cylinder.

Checking Operation of the System

POWER UNIT OPERATION TEST

Having the engine turned off, apply the brakes several times to eliminate all vacuum from the system. Now apply the brakes and while holding the pedal steady in that position start the engine. The pedal should move away from the foot or at least require less pressure to hold it in position. This indicates that the power system is working.

CHECKING FOR LEAKS

With the engine running, depress the brake pedal all the way. Hold the pedal in this position for one minute. Any downward movement of the pedal during this time indicates a brake fluid leak. Any kickback of the pedal indicates a vacuum leak.

CHECKING ENGINE VACUUM

Connect a vacuum gage between the power unit and the check valve. (The check valve is on the unit.) Run the engine at idle speed and check the reading on the vacuum gage. The gage should read between 18 and 21 inches of vacuum. Stop the engine and note the rate of vacuum drop. If the vacuum drops more than one inch in fifteen seconds the check valve is leaking. If the vacuum did not reach 18 inches or is unsteady, an engine tune up is needed.

Removal and Installation

Apply the brakes several times to eliminate any residual vacuum. Disconnect the hydraulic lines at the unit. Disconnect the vacuum line at the unit. Disconnect the stop light wires at the switch. Unbolt the unit from the mounting bracket.

Remove the clamp ring, the front section of the booster chamber, and the diaphragm-pressure plate assembly together with the return spring.

Unscrew the bushing in the back of the rear section of the booster chamber and remove the section from the slave cylinder body. Remove the plug in the rear end of the slave cylinder body and then remove the gasket, the spring, the retainer, the cup, and the piston from the body.

Remove the inner and outer seals from the control valve shaft. Remove the control valve disc seal from the diaphragm assembly. Remove the snap ring and so release the air cleaner.

Remove the screw and lockwasher that hold the control valve disc in place, then remove the disc, seal, spacer, and spring from the control valve body.

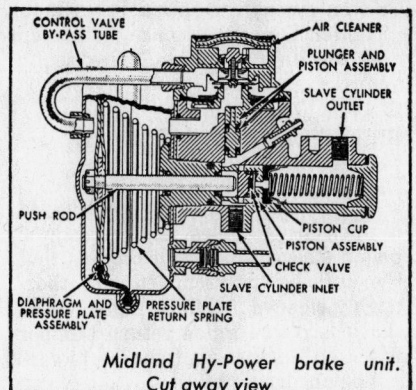

CONTROL VALVE BY-PASS TUBE / AIR CLEANER / PLUNGER AND PISTON ASSEMBLY / SLAVE CYLINDER OUTLET / PUSH ROD / PISTON CUP / PISTON ASSEMBLY / CHECK VALVE / SLAVE CYLINDER INLET / DIAPHRAGM AND PRESSURE PLATE ASSEMBLY / PRESSURE PLATE RETURN SPRING

Midland Hy-Power brake unit. Cut away view

Remove the seal from the inner end of the push rod bushing and then the seal from the outer end. Remove the seal from the slave cylinder end plug. Remove the check valve and spring from the slave piston.

Wash all the metal parts in brake fluid. Wipe them with clean rags and use air to blow out the passage ways. Replace the push rod if it is rough or

damaged, also replace the slave cylinder if it or the control valve plunger is worn or corroded. If the control valve seat is damaged replace the control valve body.

Renew all the cups, seals, and springs, and the control valve diaphragm. These parts all come in the repair kit.

Reverse the procedure to assemble.

Reverse the procedure to install. Bleed all the lines, not forgetting the bleed screw on the unit.

Disassembly, Inspection, and Assembly

Remove the control valve by-pass tube which runs from the front face of the vacuum chamber to the control valve. Punch mark the valve body and the slave body so they will match at reassembly. Unbolt the control valve from the slave cylinder. Remove the control valve body, diaphragm spring, and the control valve piston and diaphragm assembly from the slave cylinder body.

Mark both halves of the booster chamber so they can be reassembled to their original positions.

SECTION 9

KELSEY–HAYES, DIAPHRAGM TYPE

This unit is used on all 1955 Chrysler, DeSoto, Dodge, and Plymouth cars. It is a vacuum suspended unit and its theory of operation is the same as that outlined in the section on Kelsey-Hayes Power Brakes. It should be noted, however, that this is an adjacent type brake using a diaphragm in conjunction with the piston.

The unit has a built-in pedal return spring and a pedal return stop so that the brake pedal does not have to be adjusted for any free play. The pedal height and travel are determined by the combined length of the push rod and the push rod end (which is adjustable).

When the brake pedal is depressed the push rod is moved into the unit and in doing so, actuates the valves which seal off the rearmost portion of the unit from the vacuum while maintaining vacuum in the forward portion. The valves are located in the center of the power piston which is in turn the center of the diaphragm.

Further movement of the pedal admits atmospheric pressure into the rearmost portion which causes the piston diaphragm assembly to move forward into the vacuumized forward portion. This movement forces the

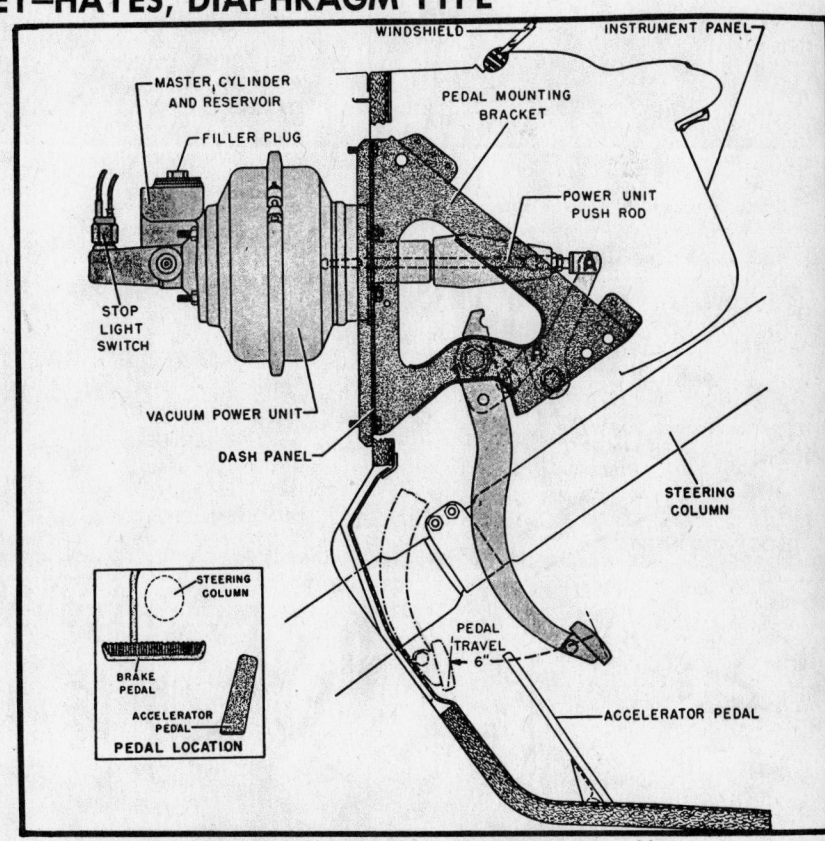

WINDSHIELD / INSTRUMENT PANEL / MASTER CYLINDER AND RESERVOIR / PEDAL MOUNTING BRACKET / FILLER PLUG / POWER UNIT PUSH ROD / STOP LIGHT SWITCH / VACUUM POWER UNIT / DASH PANEL / STEERING COLUMN / PEDAL TRAVEL 6" / ACCELERATOR PEDAL

STEERING COLUMN / BRAKE PEDAL / ACCELERATOR PEDAL / **PEDAL LOCATION**

Fig. 41—Suspended brake pedal and brake booster assembly PowerFlite-equipped cars

piston into the hydraulic cylinder thus displacing fluid and applying the brakes. In the center of the piston is a reaction rod which relays the brake fluid pressure back to the push rod in direct proportion to the force applied by the unit to the brakes. This lets the driver have the feel of applying the brakes and so gives him complete control of their operation.

Trouble Shooting the Chrysler Adjacent Type Unit

PEDAL FAILS TO RETURN PROPERLY

This trouble can be due to damaged nylon bushings in the pedal hub or to the hub being thicker than the spacer so that the bushings are pinched. Replace the bushings if they are damaged or grind off the excess thickness of the pedal hub if the bushings are pinched.

BRAKE SYSTEM LOSES FLUID

This trouble may be due to loose connections in the hydraulic system or a loose stop light switch or worn or damaged sealing cups where the

piston enters the hydraulic cylinder. Tighten the connections or disassemble the unit and install new sealing cups.

BRAKES DO NOT RELEASE PROPERLY

This trouble can be due to plugged compensating holes in the power piston sleeve which will require that the unit be disassembled and thoroughly cleaned; while doing so check that the piston guide return bumper is not so thick so that the ports cannot be uncovered by the piston. It can also be due to broken springs in the valve assembly which must be replaced. It can also be due to lack of lubrication on the air valve "O" ring seal which requires silicone grease. It can also be due to a missing or loose inspection screw. **Note:** The inspection screw and gasket are installed into a hole which is necessary for testing purposes during manufacture. The screw is a 10/32 and is located in the upper front face of the forward portion of the unit. Lack of the screw can also result in touchy, grabby brakes. It can also be due to misplace-

ment of the air cleaner cover so that it is not concentric with the power piston guide sleeve, with the result that there is interference between the nylon bushing in the cover and the pedal push rod. To remedy this condition loosen the power unit mounting stud nuts and move the air cleaner cover assembly until the retainer sleeve is concentric with the guide sleeve.

POWER UNIT DOES NOT SEEM TO WORK

Test that the unit is operating by applying the brakes several times to remove all traces of residual vacuum and then hold the brakes on while starting the engine. If the unit is operating the vacuum will cause the pedal to move forward.

If the test shows that the unit is not working correctly the trouble can be in the vacuum line to the unit, or at the manifold, or in the vacuum check valve on the unit. Check over the parts mentioned and replace those that are faulty. The air cleaner can be plugged which will require installation of a new air cleaner on the unit. There may be dirt on the air valve assembly in the piston which will re-

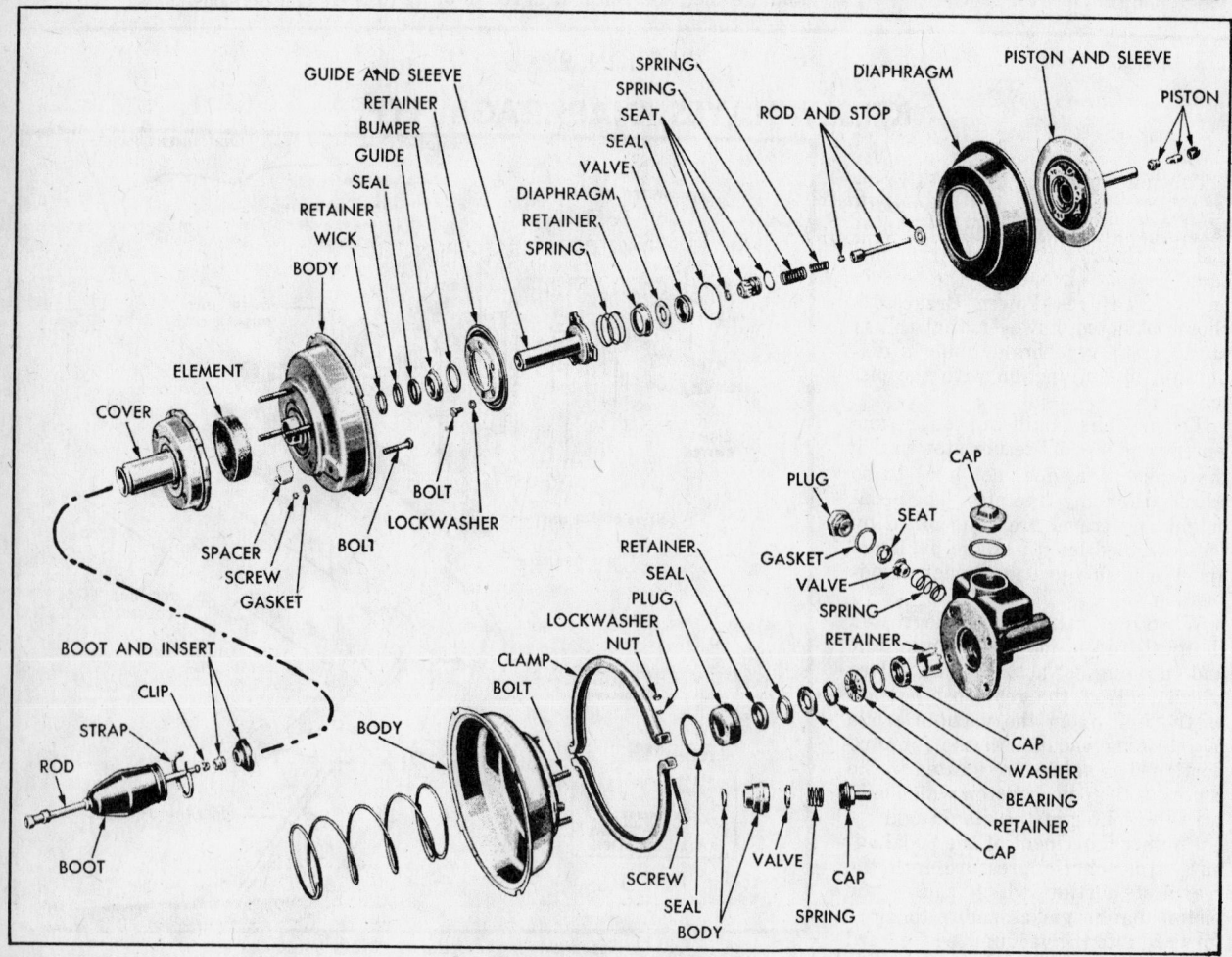

Fig. 43—Power unit operating parts

quire disassembly and cleaning of the unit. Replace all the parts supplied in the repair kit. The trouble can also be due to a damaged seal where the piston enters the hydraulic cylinder. A new seal comes with the repair kit.

LOSS OF PEDAL

This trouble is more than likely due to dirt between the lip of the seal and the cylinder bore. Be sure to clean the unit and then install new seals as supplied in the repair kit.

Removal and Installation of the Chrysler Adjacent Type Unit

Clean all dirt from the hydraulic cylinder and the filler plug. Discon-nect the brake hydraulic line at the cylinder and tie up out of the way to prevent loss of fluid. Disconnect the stop light wires. Disconnect the push rod from the pedal linkage. Remove the stud nuts holding the unit to the dash panel and remove the unit from the car. Reverse the procedure to install. After the unit has been refastened to the dash adjust the end of the push rod so that the distance from the dash panel to the center of the push rod clevis is 8 57/64th inches. Connect the clevis to the pedal arm. Connect the hydraulic line to the outlet on the side of the cylinder. Connect the vacuum line from the intake manifold to the vacuum check valve on the forward portion of the unit.

Reinstall the stop light wires and refill the master cylinder. Then bleed the brakes.

Bleeding the Chrysler Adjacent Type Unit

Start the bleeding procedure at the bleeder screw just forward of the filler plug on top of the hydraulic cylinder. Next do the four wheel cylinders. When the fluid runs clear at all points start the engine, pump the brake several times, and rebleed the system. After bleeding is completed check for leaks in the system, while holding the brakes hard on with the engine running. After bleeding the system fill the reservoir no higher than one-eighth inch below the cap.

SECTION 10

CHRYSLER
DIAPHRAGM TYPE

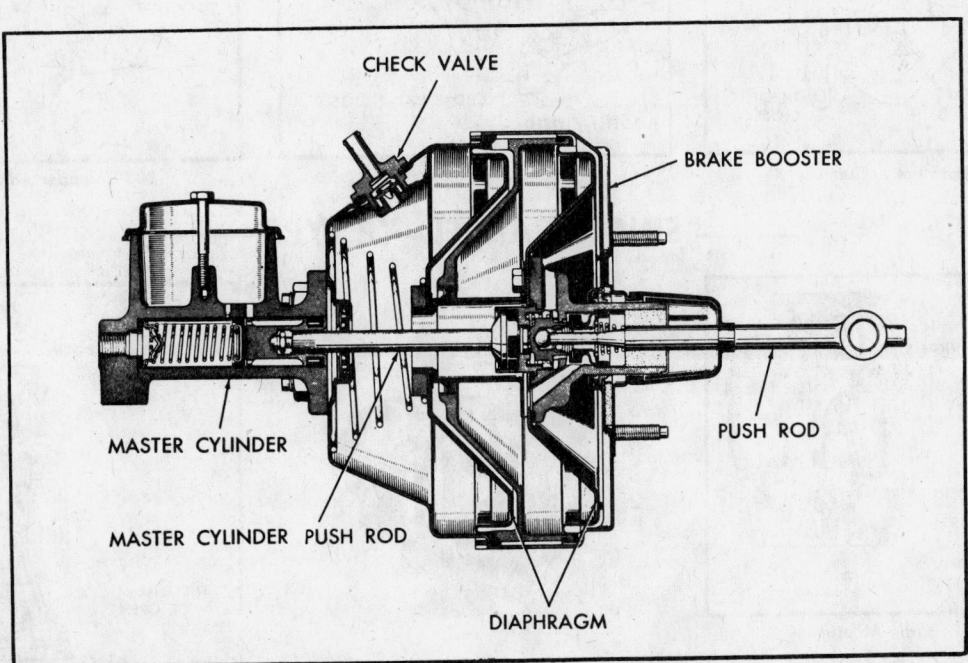

Cut away view of brake booster and master cylinder

Starting in 1962 with some Chrysler Products a new power brake unit is used. It features a direct pedal connection to a vacuum unit mounted on the fire wall with the master cylinder directly mounted to booster.

The booster chamber contains two diaphragms and is under constant engine vacuum. When brakes are applied the control valve is opened to allow atmospheric pressure behind both diaphragms. This provide the power boost to the master cylinder.

This vacuum-suspended system pro-vides reserve against fade. Pedal linkages are eliminated, no additional vacuum storage tanks are needed.

Removal of Unit

1. Remove bolt attaching pedal to push rod.
2. Disconnect fluid line from master cylinder.
3. Disconnect vacuum line from check valve.
4. Remove four attaching nuts and washers under dash.
5. Pull booster and cylinder assembly forward from support bracket.
6. Remove four nuts and washers holding master cylinder to booster and remove cylinder.

To Reinstall

Reverse the above procedure.

Note: Do not attempt to disassemble the booster it is serviced only by the Manufacturer's Service Station.

CARTER CARBURETOR

SINGLE-BARREL–BBS TYPE

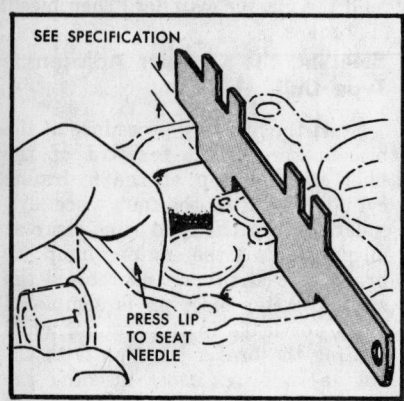

BBS Float Adjustment

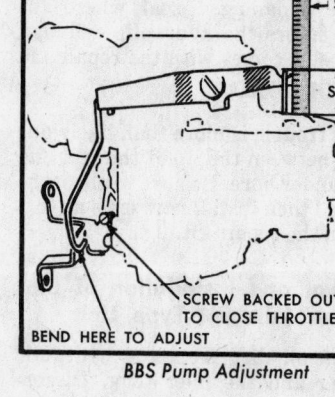

BBS Pump Adjustment

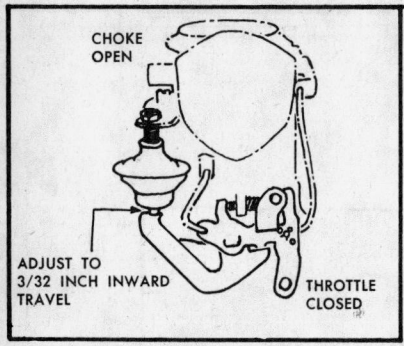

BBS Dash Pot Adjustment

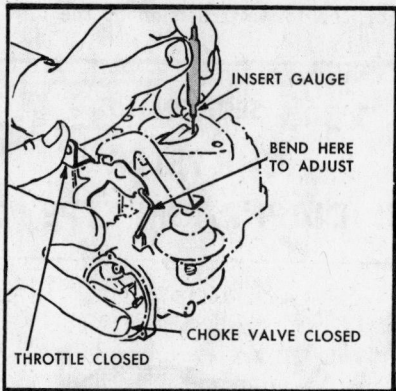

BBS Fast Idle Adjustment

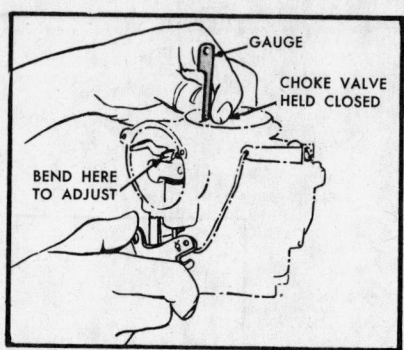

BBS Unloader Adjustment

SINGLE-BARREL –YF TYPE

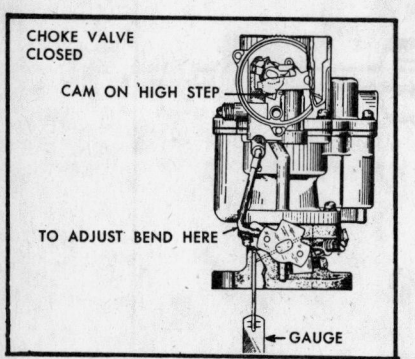

YF Fast Idle Adjustment

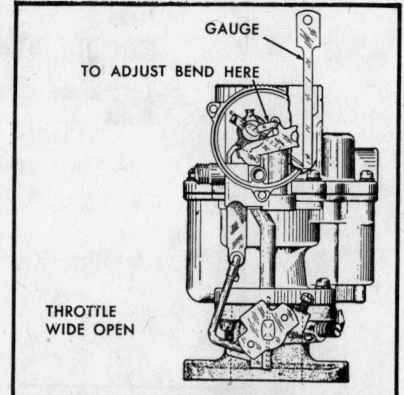

YF Unloader Adjustment

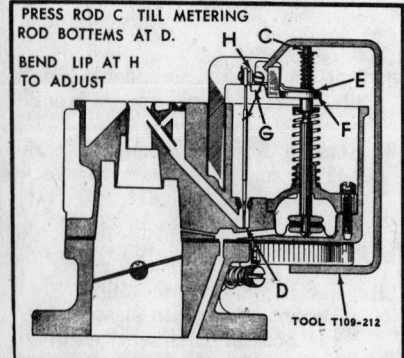

YF Metering Rod Adjustment

YF Float Level Adjustment

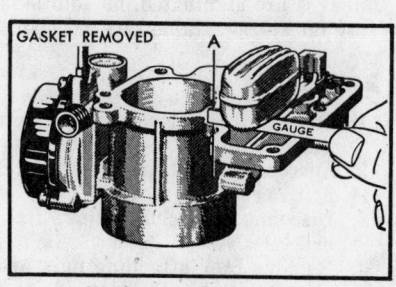

YF Float Drop Adjustment

SINGLE-BARREL—AS TYPE

AS Float Adjustment (early models)

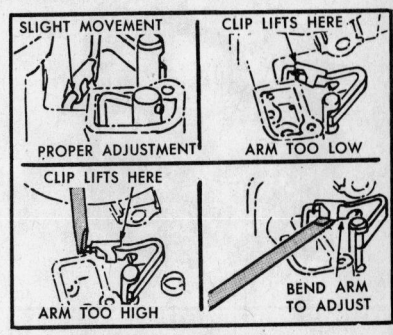

AS Metering Rod Adjustment

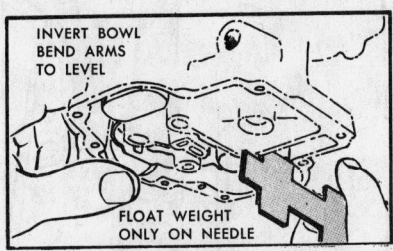

A\S Float Adjustment (late models)

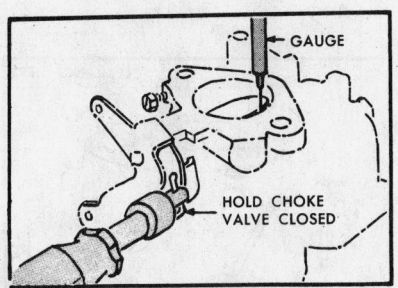

AS Fast Idle Adjustment

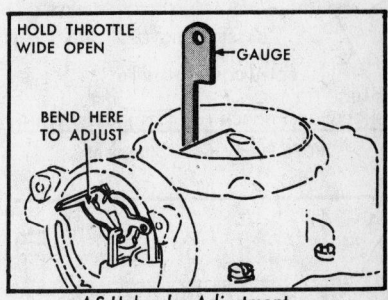

AS Unloader Adjustment

———TWO-BARREL TYPE — BBD TYPE———

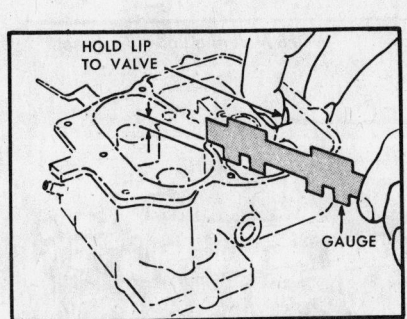

BBD Float Adjustment

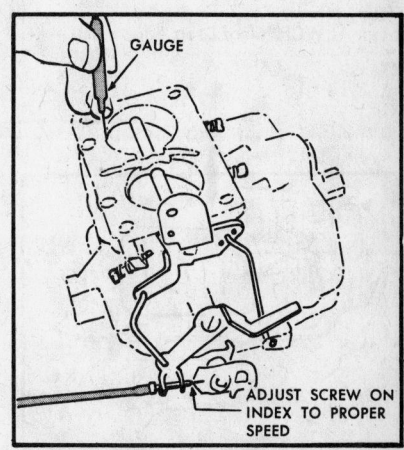

BBD Fast Idle Adjustment

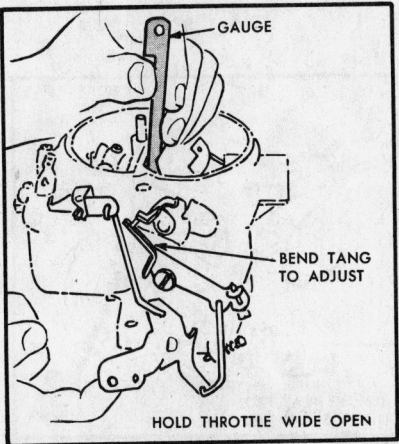

BBD Unloader Adjustment

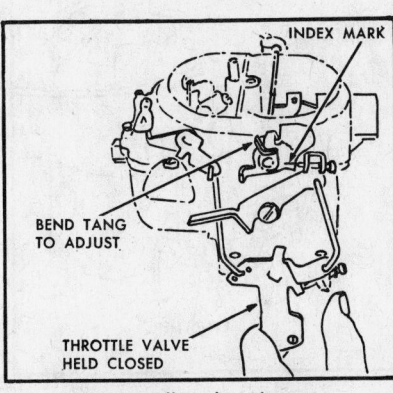

BBD Fast Idle Index Alignment

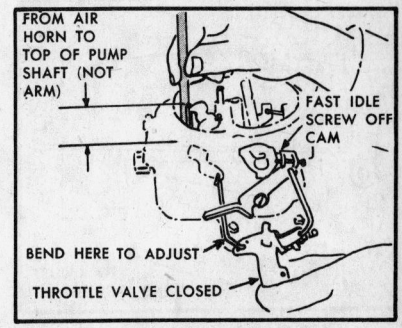

BBD Pump Adjustment

CARTER CARBURETOR

FOUR-BARREL — WCFB TYPE

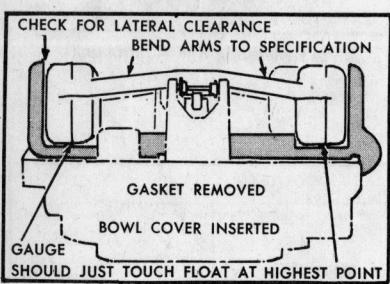

WCFB Float Level Adjustment

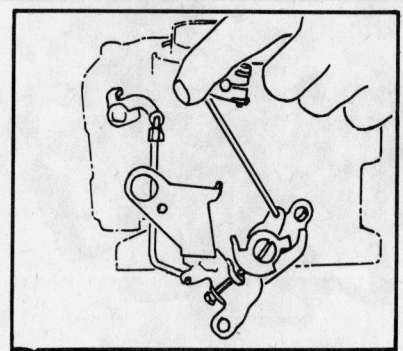

WCFB Fast Idle Adjustment

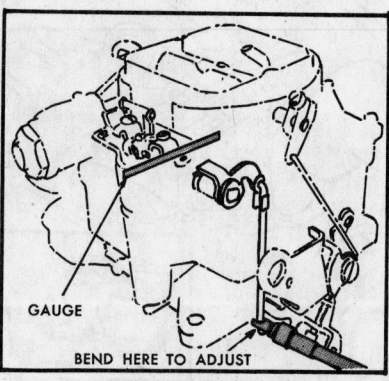

WCFB Pump Adjustment

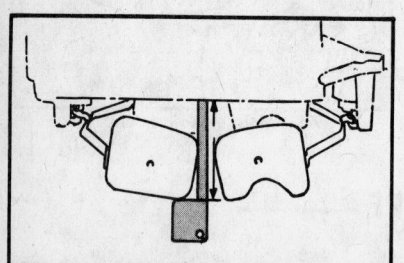

WCFB Float Drop Adjustment

WCFB Unloader Adjustment

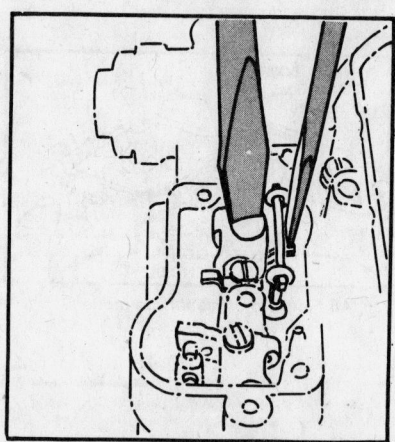

WCFB Metering Rod Adjustment

— FOUR-BARREL — AFB TYPE —

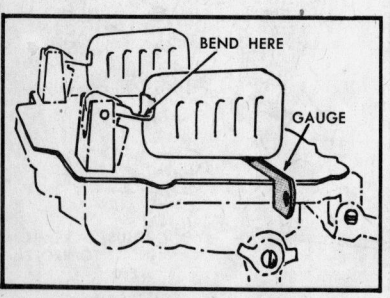

AFB Float Level Adjustment

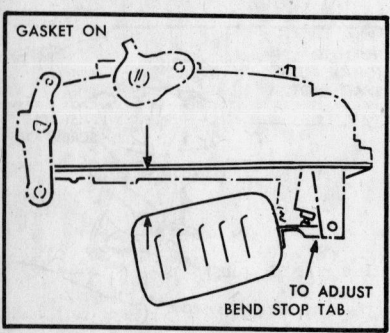

AFB Float Drop Adjustment

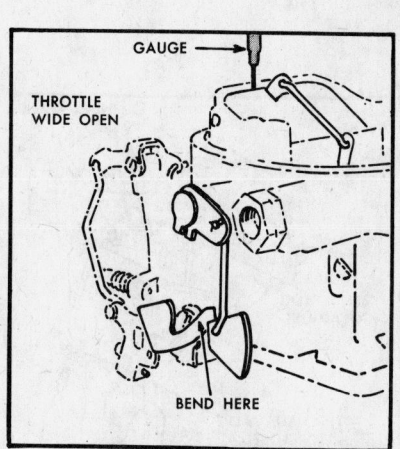

AFB Unloader Adjustment

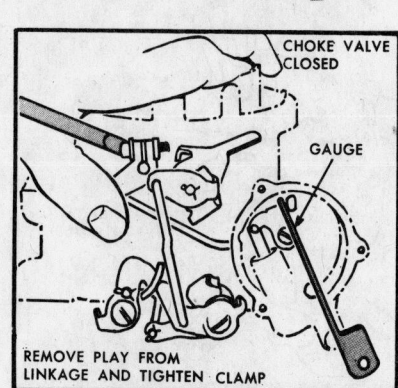

AFB Choke Piston Lever Adjustment

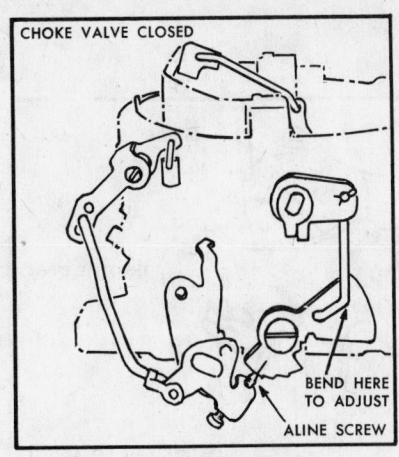

AFB Fast Idle Linkage Adjustment

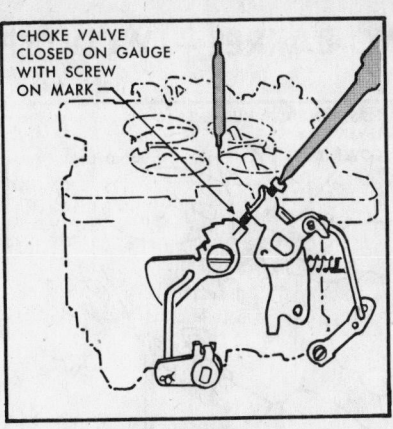

AFB Fast Idle Throttle Adjustment

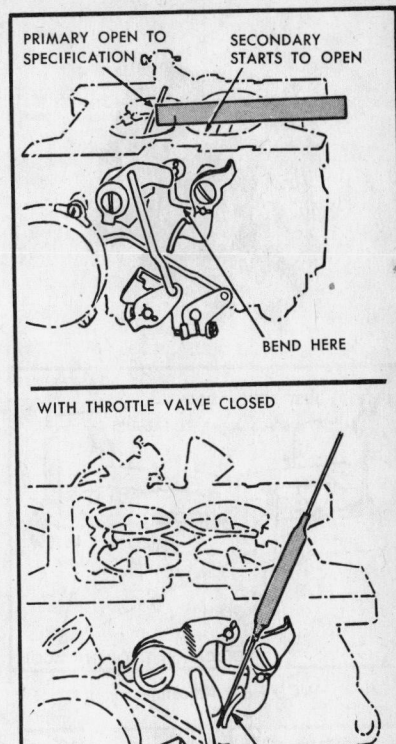

AFB Dash Pot Adjustment

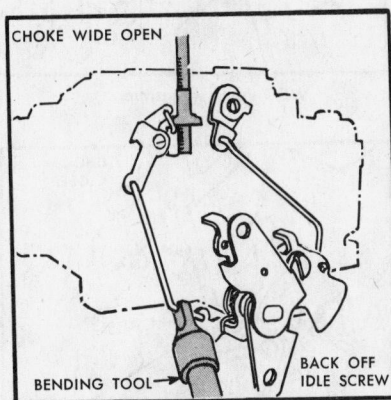

AFB Pump Adjustment

AFB Secondary Throttle Adjustment

TWO-BARREL — WGD TYPE

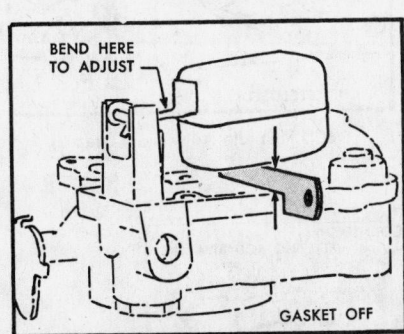

WGD Float Adjustment

WGD Pump Adjustment

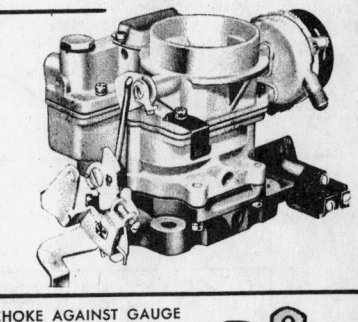

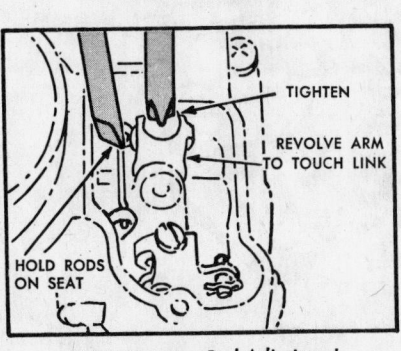

WGD Metering Rod Adjustment

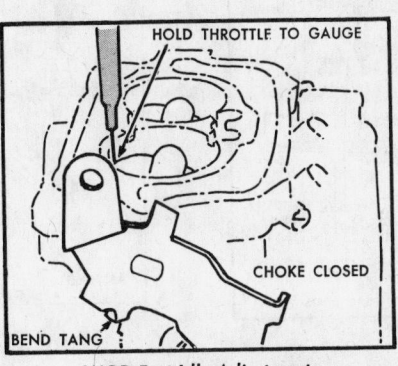

WGD Fast Idle Adjustment

WGD Unloader Adjustment

CARTER CARBURETOR

TWO-BARREL — WCD TYPE

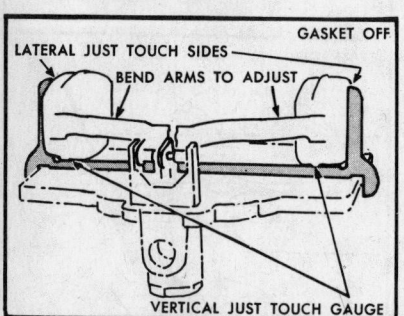

WCD Pump Adjustment

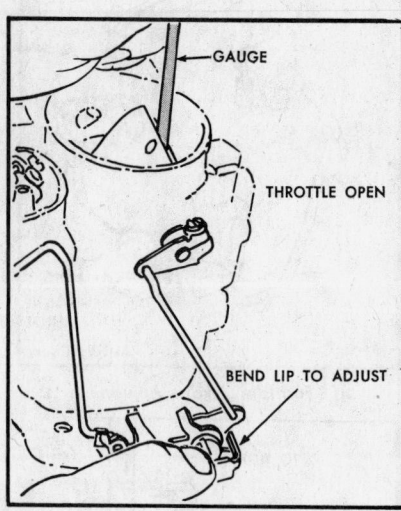

WCD Unloader Adjustment

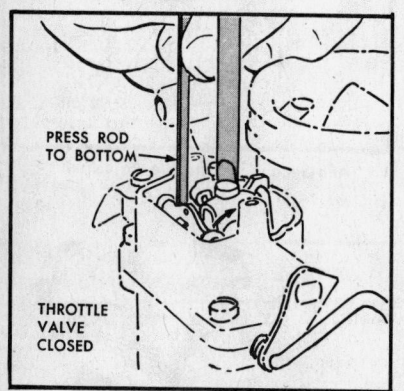

WCD Float Adjustment

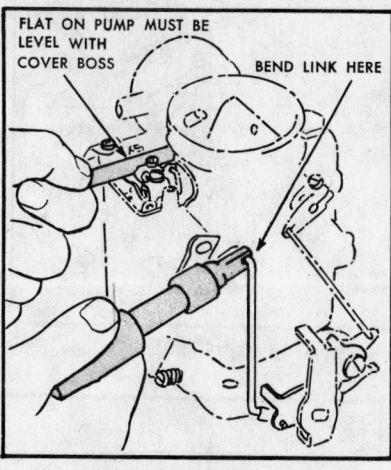

WCD Metering Rod Adjustment

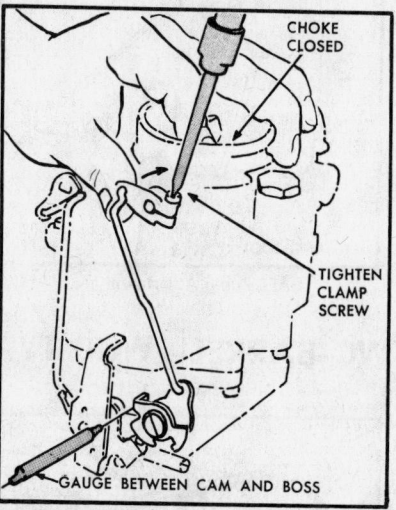

WCD Fast Idle Adjustment (step 1)

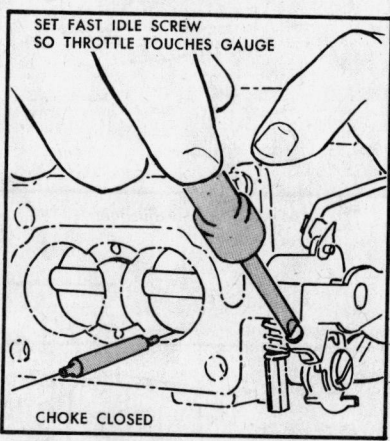

WCD Fast Idle Adjustment (step 2)

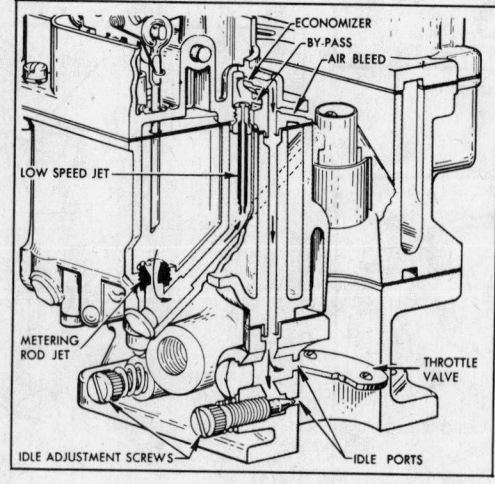

Low Speed System

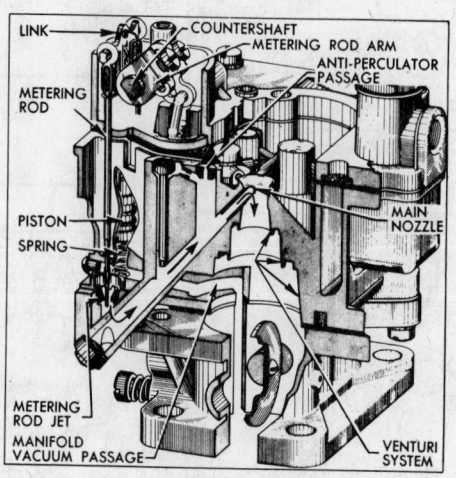

High Speed and Power Systems

CARTER CARBURETORS

YEAR	MODEL OR TYPE	FLOAT LEVEL		FLOAT DROP		Pump Travel Setting	CHOKE SETTING		ON THE CAR ADJUSTMENTS			
		Prim.	Sec.	Prim.	Sec.		Unloader	Housing	Idle Screw Turns Open	Idle Speed	Fast Idle Speed	Dashpot Plunger Clearance

BUICK

1953	WCD-2081S	15/64	....	....	....	17/64	3/16	INDEX	1	N-450	1650	.030
1953	WCFB-2053S	3/32	3/16	5/8	11/16	9/32	3/16	INDEX	1¼	N-450	1650	.030
1953-4	WCD-2017S	15/64	....	....	....	17/64	3/16	INDEX	1	N-450	1650	.030
1954	WCFB-2082S	1/8	3/16	5/8	11/16	(1)	11/64	INDEX	½-1½	N-450	1650	.030
1955	WCD-2079S	3/8	....	....	....	17/64	3/16	INDEX	1	N-450	1650	.030
1955	WCFB-2197S	3/32	3/16	19/32	11/16	(1)	11/64	INDEX	1¼	N-450	1650	.030
1956	WGD-2378S	1/4	....	....	....	(1)	5/32	INDEX	¼-1¼	N-450	1650	.030
1956	WGD-2400S	1/4	....	....	....	(1)	5/32	INDEX	1	N-450	1650	.030
1956	WCFB-2347S	3/16	3/16	11/16	11/16	(1)	5/32	1-LEAN	1¼	N-450	1650	.030
1957	WGD-2529S	17/64	....	....	....	(1)	9/64	1-LEAN	1	N-485	1500	.000
1957	WGD-2536S	17/64	....	....	....	(1)	11/64	INDEX	1	N-485	1500	.000
1957	AFB-2507S	7/32	7/32	23/32	23/32	33/64	3/16	INDEX	1¼	N-485	1500	.000
1958	WGD—ALL	1/4	....	....	....	(1)	3/16	1-LEAN	1½	N-485	1500	.000
1958	AFB-2800S	7/32	7/32	23/32	23/32	33/64	3/16	1-RICH	1¼	N-485	1500	.000
1959	WGD—ALL	1/4	....	....	....	(1)	3/16	1-LEAN	1½	N-485	1500	.000
1959	AFB-2877-40	7/32	7/32	23/32	23/32	33/64	3/16	1-RICH	1¼	N-485	1500	.000
1960	WGD—ALL	1/4	....	....	....	(1)	7/32	INDEX	1½	N-485	1500	.000
1960	AFB—ALL	7/32	7/32	3/4	3/4	1/2	3/16	1-RICH	1½	N-485	1500	.000
1961	AFB—ALL	7/32	7/32	23/32	23/32	7/16	7/32	INDEX	1¾	N-500	625*	.000
1962	AFB—ALL	7/32	7/32	3/4	3/4	7/16	3/16	INDEX	1½	N-500	625*	.000
1963	AFB—ALL	7/32	7/32	3/4	3/4	7/16	3/16	INDEX	1½	N-500	625*	.000

(1)—Set pump arm parallel. *—With screw on bottom step of cam. N—Neutral.

CADILLAC

1953	WCFB-2119S-A	1/8	3/16	5/8	11/16	(1)	3/16	INDEX	1¼	D-400	1700	(3)
1953	WCB-2088S	1/8	3/16	5/8	11/16	(1)	3/16	INDEX	1¼	D-400	1700	(3)
1953	WCFB-2005S-A	1/8	3/16	5/8	11/16	(1)	3/16	INDEX	1½-2	D-400	1700	......
1953	WCFB-2072S	1/8	3/16	5/8	11/16	(1)	3/16	INDEX	1½-2	D-400	1700	......
1953-4	WCFB-2143S	1/8	3/16	5/8	11/16	(1)	3/16	INDEX	½-1½	D-400	1700	(3)
1954	WCFB-2109-10S	1/8	3/16	5/8	11/16	(1)	3/16	INDEX	½-1½	D-400	1700	......
1955	WCFB—ALL	1/8	3/16	5/8	11/16	(1)	13/64	1-LEAN	½-1½	D-400	1700	......
1956	WCFB-2543-4-5S	1/8	3/16	5/8	11/16	(1)	13/64	1-LEAN	1½	D-400	1700	(3)
1956	WCFB-2333S-A	1/8	3/16	5/8	11/16	(1)	13/64	1-LEAN	2-2½	D-400	1700	(3)
1956	WCFB-2334S-A	1/8	3/16	5/8	11/16	(1)	13/64	1-LEAN	2-2½	D-400	1700	(3)
1956	WCFB-2370S-A	1/8	3/16	5/8	11/16	(1)	13/64	1-LEAN	2-2½	D-400	1700	(3)
1956	WCFB-2371S	1/8	3/16	5/8	11/16	(1)	13/64	INDEX	1¼	D-400	1700	(3)
1956	WCFB-2372S	1/8	3/16	5/8	11/16	(1)	13/64	INDEX	1¼	D-400	1700	(3)
1956	WCFB-2373S	1/8	3/16	5/8	11/16	(1)	13/64	INDEX	1¼	D-400	1700	(3)
1957-8	AFB—ALL	5/16	5/16	23/32	23/32	15/32	9/32	INDEX	1½	D-400	1750	(3)
1957	WCFB—ALL	1/8	1/4	5/8	3/4	(2)	13/64	INDEX	1¼	D-400	1750	(3)
1959-60	AFB-2814S	5/16	5/16	23/32	23/32	15/32	9/32	INDEX	1½-2½	D-450	1725	(3)
1961	AFB	3/8	3/8	13/16	13/16	15/32	9/32	1-RICH	¾-2½	D-480	1725	(3)
1962	AFB	3/8	3/8	13/16	13/16	15/32	9/32	1-RICH	¾-2½	D-480	1725	(3)
1963	AFB	3/8	3/8	13/16	13/16	15/32	9/32	1-RICH	¾-2½	D-480	1725	(3)

(1)—Pump arm parallel, link in outer hole.

(2)—Pump arm parallel, link in inner hole.

(3)—By trial.

D—Drive.

CHEVROLET

1955	WCFB-2351S	1/8	1/4	5/8	3/4	(1)	3/16	2-LEAN	½-1	N-450	1600-1800	......
1955	WCFB-2218S	1/8	1/4	5/8	3/4	(1)	3/16	INDEX	½-1	N-450	1600-1800	......
1956	WGD-2286S	1/4	......	......	......	(1)	7/32	INDEX	1½	N-450	1600-1800	......
1956	WCFB-2362S	1/8	1/4	5/8	3/4	(1)	3/16	INDEX	½-1	N-450	1600-1800	......
1956	WCFB-2419S	1/8	1/4	5/8	3/4	(1)	......	......	½-1	N-450	......	......
1956	WCFB-2366SA	1/8	1/4	5/8	3/4	(1)	3/16	INDEX	½-1	N-450	1600-1800	......
1957	WCFB-2505SA	1/8	1/4	5/8	3/4	(1)	3/16	INDEX	1¼	N-450	1600-1800	.060
1957	WCFB-2555S	1/8	1/4	5/8	3/4	(1)	3/16	INDEX	1¼	N-450	1600-1800	.060
1957	WCFB-2626S	1/8	1/4	5/8	3/4	(1)	......	......	½-1	N-450	......	......
1957	WCFB-2627S	1/8	1/4	5/8	3/4	(1)	1/8	INDEX	½-1	N-450	1600-1800	.060
1957	WCFB-2655S	1/8	1/4	5/8	3/4	(1)	3/16	INDEX	½-1½	N-450	1600-1800	.060
1958	WCFB—ALL	1/8	1/4	5/8	3/4	(1)	3/16	INDEX	½-1	N-450	1600-1800	.060
1959-62	WCFB—ALL	3/32	9/32	2	2	(1)	3/16	INDEX	½-2	N-450	1700	(2)
1963	WCFB—ALL	3/32	9/32	2	2	(1)	3/16	INDEX	½-2	N-450	1700	(2)
1961	AFB—ALL	7/32	7/32	23/32	23/32	33/64	1/4	INDEX	½-2	N-450	1600-1800	.060
1962	AFB—3270S	7/32	7/32	23/32	23/32	33/64	1/4	1-RICH	¼-1½	......	......	......
1963	AFB—3270S	7/32	7/32	23/32	23/32	33/64	1/4	1-RICH	¼-1½	......	......	......

(1)—Set pump arm parallel. (2)—By trial. N—Neutral.

CARTER CARBURETORS

YEAR	MODEL OR TYPE	FLOAT LEVEL		FLOAT DROP		Pump Travel Setting	CHOKE SETTING		ON THE CAR ADJUSTMENTS			
		Prim.	Sec.	Prim.	Sec.		Unloader	Housing	Idle Screw Turns Open	Idle Speed	Fast Idle Speed	Dashpot Plunger Clearance
CHEVY II												
1963	4 Cyl-YF-Std.	3/8	......	13/16	......	......	......	......	1½	......	......	......
	4 Cyl-YF-PG	3/8	......	13/16	......	......	......	......	1½	......	......	......
CHRYSLER IMPERIAL												
1953–54	WCD-2039SA	11/64	......	......	......	17/64	7/32	INDEX	½–1	N-475	.019	3/64
1954	BB-EB91	5/64	......	......	......	(2)	5/32	INDEX	1	N-475	.017	(3)
1954	WCFB-2041S	1/8	1/4	5/8	3/4	(1)	3/16	INDEX	1½	N-475	.015	......
1955	BBD-2162SAB	7/32	......	......	......	54/64	1/4	INDEX	1	N-475	.017	1/16
1955	BBD-2180SAB	7/32	......	......	......	54/64	1/4	INDEX	1	N-475	.017	......
1955	WCFB-2317S	7/32	11/32	23/32	27/32	(1)	3/16	INDEX	1	N-600	.008	......
1955	WCFB-2126S	1/8	3/16	5/8	11/16	(1)	3/16	INDEX	1½	N-500	.018	......
1956	BBD-2312S	1/4	......	......	......	31/32	3/16	INDEX	1	N-500	.020	1/16
1956	BBD-2313S	1/4	......	......	......	31/32	3/16	1-RICH	1	N-500	.020	1/16
1956	WCFB-2367-14	5/32	7/32	23/32	23/32	(1)	3/16	1-RICH	1–1½	N-500	.012	......
1956	WCFB-2444-45	7/32	11/32	23/32	27/32	(1)	3/16	INDEX	1	N-600	.008	......
1957	AFB—ALL	1/4	5/32	23/32	23/32	7/16	1/4	1-RICH	1–1½	N-500	1400	......
1957	WCFB—ALL	5/32	9/32	21/32	25/32	(1)	15/64	1-RICH	1–1½	N-500	1375	......
1957	BBD-2527S	9/32	......	......	......	11/32	3/16	1-RICH	½–1½	N-500	1325	......
1958	AFB—ALL	7/32	7/32	23/32	23/32	7/32	1/4	1-RICH	1	N-500	1375	......
1958	WCFB-2741S	9/32	11/32	23/32	23/32	(1)	......		1½	N-650	NONE	......
1958	WCFB-2742S	9/32	11/32	23/32	23/32	(1)	1/8	1-RICH	1½	N-650	1450	......
1959	AFB-2797S	7/32	7/32	23/32	23/32	7/16	1/4	INDEX	1½	N-500	1400	......
1959	BBD—ALL	5/16	......	......	......	1	15/64	INDEX	1–2	N-500	1400	......
1960	BBD-2924S	9/32	......	......	......	1	1/4	INDEX	1	N-500	1400	......
1960–61	AFB-2903S	9/32	9/32	23/32	23/32	27/64	1/4	1-RICH	½–1	N-500	1750	.010
1960–61	AFB—Others	7/32	7/32	23/32	23/32	7/16	1/4	2-RICH	½–2	N-500	1750	......
1960–61	BBD-2923SA	9/32	......	......	......	1	1/4	INDEX	½–1½	N-500	1400	......
1961	BBD-3132S	9/32	......	......	......	1	1/4	INDEX	1	N-500	1400	......
1962	AFB—3251S—Imp.	7/32	7/32	3/4	3/4	7/16	1/4	2-RICH	1–2	N-500	1800	......
	AFB—3256S	9/32	9/32	3/4	3/4	7/16	1/4	2-RICH	1–2	N-500	1800	......
	AFB—3258S—Front	9/32	9/32	3/4	3/4	7/16	1/4	......	1–2	N-650	......	......
	AFB—3259S—Rear	7/32	7/32	3/4	3/4	7/16	1/4	1-RICH	1–2	N-650	1400	......
	BBD—3245S*	9/32	......	......	......	1	1/4	INDEX	1	N-500	1400	......
	BBD—3244S	9/32	......	......	......	1	1/4	INDEX	1	N-500	1400	......
1963	BBD—ALL	1/4	......	......	......	1	1/4	2-RICH	3/4	500	1400	......
1963	AFB—ALL	7/32	7/32	3/4	3/4	......	3/8	2-RICH	1–2	500	1800	......

(1)—Set pump arm parallel. (2)—Shaft right angle to arm. (3)—By trial. N—Neutral.

(*)—Used with closed crankcase vent system.

DESOTO

YEAR	MODEL OR TYPE	Float Level Prim.	Float Level Sec.	Float Drop Prim.	Float Drop Sec.	Pump Travel Setting	Choke Unloader	Choke Housing	Idle Screw Turns Open	Idle Speed	Fast Idle Speed	Dashpot Plunger Clearance
1953–54	BBD-2250S	7/32	......	......	......	1	1/4	INDEX	1	N-475	.017	1/16
1954	BB-E9B1	5/64	......	......	......	(2)	5/32	INDEX	½–1½	N-475	.017	(3)
1954	BBD-2030-70S	7/32	......	......	......	57/64	1/4	INDEX	1	N-475	.017	1/16
1954	BBD—Others	7/32	......	......	......	57/64	1/4	INDEX	1	N-475	.017	......
1955	WCFB-2210S	1/8	3/16	5/8	11/16	(1)	3/16	INDEX	1½	N-475	.018	......
1955	BBD-2178SA	7/32	......	......	......	1	1/4	INDEX	1	N-475	.017	1/16
1955	BBD—Others	7/32	......	......	......	1	1/4	INDEX	1	N-475	.017	......
1956	WCFB-2311SA	5/32	7/32	21/32	23/32	(1)	3/16	1-RICH	1½	N-500	1350	......
1956	WCFB—Others	7/32	11/32	23/32	27/32	(1)	11/64	INDEX	1	N-500	1350	......
1956	BBD—ALL	1/4	......	......	......	11/32	3/16	INDEX	½–1½	N-500	.015	1/16
1957	WCFB-2532S	7/32	9/32	23/32	25/32	(1)	15/64	INDEX	½–1½	N-500	1350	......
1957	WCFB-2588S	5/32	9/32	23/32	25/32	(1)	15/64	1-RICH	½–1½	N-500	1325	......
1957	BBD-2522S-A-B	9/32	......	......	......	11/32	1/4	1-RICH	½–1½	N-500	1325	......
1958	AFB-2823S	5/16	5/16	23/32	23/32	7/16	1/4	INDEX	1–2	N-500	1400	......
1958	AFB-2642S	5/16	5/16	23/32	23/32	7/16	1/4	2-RICH	1–2	N-500	1400	......
1958	AFB-2373S	7/32	7/32	23/32	23/32	7/16	1/4	2-RICH	1–2	N-500	1400	......
1958	BBD—ALL	5/16	......	......	......	1	15/64	INDEX	1	N-500	1400	......
1959	AFB-2794S	7/32	7/32	23/32	23/32	7/16	1/4	INDEX	½–2	N-500	1400	......
1959	BBD-2924S	9/32	......	......	......	1	1/4	INDEX	½–1½	N-500	1400	......
1959	BBD—Others	5/16	......	......	......	1	15/64	INDEX	½–1	N-500	1400	......
1960–61	AFB-2950S	7/32	7/32	3/4	3/4	7/16	1/4	2-RICH	1–2	N-500	1800	......
1960–61	AFB-2903S	9/32	9/32	23/32	23/32	27/64	1/4	1-RICH	1	N-500	1800	.010
1960–61	AFB-2927-68	7/32	7/32	23/32	23/32	7/16	1/4	2-RICH	1	N-500	1800	......
1960–61	BBD-2923-A	9/32	......	......	......	1	1/4	INDEX	½–1½	N-500	1400	......

(1)—Set pump arm parallel. (2)—Shaft right angle to arm. (3)—By trial. N—Neutral.

YEAR	MODEL OR TYPE	FLOAT LEVEL		FLOAT DROP		Pump Travel Setting	CHOKE SETTING		ON THE CAR ADJUSTMENTS			
		Prim.	Sec.	Prim.	Sec.		Unloader	Housing	Idle Screw Turns Open	Idle Speed	Fast Idle Speed	Dashpot Plunger Clearance

CORVAIR

YEAR	MODEL OR TYPE	Prim.	Sec.	Prim.	Sec.	Pump	Unloader	Housing	Idle Screw	Idle Speed	Fast Idle	Dashpot
1962 Late	YH—ALL	5/8	.....	2 3/8	.....	INDEX	7/16	1-LEAN	.....	850	(1)	.....
1963	YH—ALL	5/8	.....	2 3/8	.....	INDEX	7/16	1-LEAN	.....	850	(1)	.....

(1)—.030 clearance at choke valve—set on highest step.

DODGE-DART

YEAR	MODEL OR TYPE	Prim.	Sec.	Prim.	Sec.	Pump	Unloader	Housing	Idle Screw	Idle Speed	Fast Idle	Dashpot
1953	BB—ALL	5/64	.....						1/2-1 1/2	N-475	.....	(3)
1954	WCFB-2191S	1/8	3/16	5/8	11/16	(1)	3/16	3-LEAN	1 1/2	N-475	.015	
1954	BB-E9U1	1/16				(2)			1/2-1 1/2	N-475	.....	(3)
1954	BB—Others	5/64				(2)			1/2-1 1/2	N-475		
1955	WCFB—ALL	1/8	3/16	5/8	11/16	(1)	3/16	INDEX	1/2-1 1/2	N-475	.012	
1956	WCFB-2303-2443	7/32	9/32	23/32	25/32	(1)	11/64	1-RICH	1/2-1 1/2	N-475	.012	
1956	WCFB-2432-2474	1/8	3/16	5/8	11/16	(1)	11/64	INDEX	1/2-1 1/2	N-475	.012	
1957	WCFB—ALL	7/32	9/32	23/32	25/32	(1)	15/64	INDEX	1/2-1 1/2	N-475	1375	
1958	AFB-2642S	3/16	3/16	23/32	23/32	7/16	1/4	2-RICH	1	N-475	1375	
1958	WCFB-2660S	7/32	9/32	23/32	23/32	(1)	11/64	INDEX	1/2-1 1/2	N-475	1375	
1959	AFB—ALL	7/32	7/32	23/32	23/32	7/16	1/4	INDEX	1 1/2	N-475	1400	
1959	BBD—ALL	9/32	.....			1	15/64	INDEX	1	N-475	1400	
1959	BBS—ALL	7/32	.....			27/32	9/64	INDEX	1/2-1 1/2	N-475	1300	
1960-61	AFB-2903S	9/32	9/32	3/4	3/4	1/4	1/4	1-RICH	1 1/2	N-700	1800	.010
1960	AFB—Others	7/32	7/32	3/4	3/4	7/16	1/4	INDEX	1-2	N-500	1250	
1960	BBS—ALL	7/16	.....			27/32	9/64	INDEX	1	N-500	1300	
1960-61	BBD—ALL	7/16	.....			1	15/64	INDEX	1	N-500	1400	
1961	BBS—ALL	7/32	.....			27/32	3/16	INDEX	1	N-500	1600	
1961	BBD-3132S	9/32	.....			1	1/4	INDEX	1	N-500	1400	
1961	AFB-2968-3133-52	7/32	7/32	9/16	9/16	7/16	1/4	2-RICH	1 1/2	N-550	1800	
1961	AFB-3105-40	7/32	7/32	9/16	9/16	7/16	1/4	INDEX	1 1/2	N-550	1700	
1961	AFB-3103-06-31	7/32	7/32	9/16	9/16	7/16	1/4	INDEX	1 1/2	N-550	1800	
1962	AFB—ALL	7/32	7/32	9/16	9/16	7/16	1/4	2-RICH	1 1/2	N-550	1800	
	BBS—ALL	7/32	.....			27/32	3/16	INDEX	1	N-550	1400	
	BBD—ALL	9/32	.....			5/64	1/4	INDEX			1400	
1963	AFB—ALL	7/32	7/32	3/4	3/4	7/16	3/8		1 1/2	500	2100	
	BBS—ALL	7/32	.....				3/16	4-RICH	1	550	1400	
	BBD—ALL	1/4	.....			5/64	1/4	INDEX	1	500	1400	

(1)—Set pump arm parallel.　(2)—Shaft right angle to arm.　N—Neutral.　(3)—By trial.

FORD-THUNDERBIRD

YEAR	MODEL OR TYPE	Prim.	Sec.	Prim.	Sec.	Pump	Unloader	Housing	Idle Screw	Idle Speed	Fast Idle	Dashpot
1957	AFB-2441S	3/16	3/16	23/32	23/32	11/32	1/8	INDEX	1 1/2-2 1/2	N-485	550	7/16
1958	AFB-2640S-AC	3/16	3/16	23/32	23/32	17/32	1/8	INDEX	1 1/2-2 1/2	N-485	550	7/16
1959	AFB-2853S	5/16	5/16	23/32	23/32	15/32	1/8	INDEX	1/2-1 1/2	N-500	650	7/16
1960	AFB-2992S	3/16	3/16	23/32	23/32	15/32	1/8	INDEX	1/2-1 1/2	N-485	625	7/16

N—Neutral.

LINCOLN-CONTINENTAL

YEAR	MODEL OR TYPE	Prim.	Sec.	Prim.	Sec.	Pump	Unloader	Housing	Idle Screw	Idle Speed	Fast Idle	Dashpot
1957	WCFB-2404S-A	1/16	3/16	9/16	11/16	(1)	1/8	1-RICH	1/2-1 1/2	D-465	800	1/16
1959	AFB-2853S	3/16	3/16	23/32	23/32	17/32	1/8	INDEX	1 1/2-2 1/2	D-450	550	7/16
1960	ABD-2965S-A	1/4	.....			7/16	1/8	1-LEAN	1 1/2	D-465	625	.075
1961	ABD-3149S	5/16	.....			17/32	1/8	INDEX	1-1 1/2	D-465	650	0.105
1962	ABD	5/16	.....			17/32	1/8	1-RICH	1-1 1/2	D-465	650	0.105
1963	AFB	3/16	3/16			17/32	.....	1-RICH	1 1/2	465	(1)	7/16

(1)—.026 clearance at choke valve—set on high step.

(1)—Set Pump arm parallel.

D—Drive.

MERCURY

YEAR	MODEL OR TYPE	Prim.	Sec.	Prim.	Sec.	Pump	Unloader	Housing	Idle Screw	Idle Speed	Fast Idle	Dashpot
1957	AFB-2441S-A	5/32	5/32	23/32	23/32	15/32	.067	1-RICH	1/2-1 1/2	D-450	1900*	7/16
1959	AFB-2853S	3/16	3/16	23/32	23/32	17/32	1/8	INDEX	1 1/2-2 1/2	D-450	550▲	7/16
1960	ABD-2965S	1/4	.....			7/16	1/8	1-LEAN	1 1/2	D-450	625▲	7/16

D—Drive.

*—On high cam.

▲—On low cam.

CARTER CARBURETORS

YEAR	MODEL OR TYPE	FLOAT LEVEL		FLOAT DROP		Pump Travel Setting	CHOKE SETTING		ON THE CAR ADJUSTMENTS			
		Prim.	Sec.	Prim.	Sec.		Unloader	Housing	Idle Screw Turns Open	Idle Speed	Fast Idle Speed	Dashpot Plunger Clearance

OLDSMOBILE

YEAR	MODEL OR TYPE	Prim.	Sec.	Prim.	Sec.	Pump Travel	Unloader	Housing	Idle Screw	Idle Speed	Fast Idle	Dashpot
1953	WGD—ALL	1/4	....	....	....	(1)	1/4	INDEX	1	N-425	.020	.....
1953	WCFB-2016S	3/16	3/16	1/2	1/2	(1)	3/16	INDEX	1 3/4–2 3/4	N-425	.020	.....
1953	WCFB-2080S	3/16	3/16	11/16	11/16	(1)	3/16	INDEX	1 3/4–2 3/4	N-425	.020	.....
1954	WGD-2058S	1/4	....	....	....	(1)	7/32	INDEX	2	N-450	.020	.....
1954	WCFB-2059S	1/4	1/4	3/4	3/4	(1)	3/16	INDEX	1 1/2	N-450	.015	.....
1955	WCFB-2246S	3/16	3/16	11/16	11/16	(1)	3/16	INDEX	1 1/2	N-450	.015	.....

(1)—Set pump arm. parallel. N—Neutral.

PLYMOUTH

YEAR	MODEL OR TYPE	Prim.	Sec.	Prim.	Sec.	Pump Travel	Unloader	Housing	Idle Screw	Idle Speed	Fast Idle	Dashpot
1953	BB-D6P1, 2	5/64	....	....	....	11/32	....	....	1/2–1 1/2	N-475	....	2 1/2*
1953	BB-Others	5/64	....	....	....	11/32	....	....	1/2–1 1/2	N-475	....	.....
1954	BBS-994S, A	7/32	....	....	....	27/32	9/64	INDEX	1/2–1 1/2	N-475	.021	2 1/2*
1954	BBS—Others	7/32	....	....	....	27/32	9/64	INDEX	1/2–1 1/2	N-475	.021	.....
1954-55	BBS-2203S	7/32	....	....	....	51/64	9/64	INDEX	1/2–1 1/2	N-475	.021	.....
1954-55	BBS-2215S	7/32	....	....	....	49/64	9/64	INDEX	1/2–1 1/2	N-475	.021	.....
1954-55	BBS-2062-3S	7/32	....	....	....	27/32	9/64	INDEX	1/2–1 1/2	N-475	.024	.....
1955	WCFB-2253S	1/8	3/16	5/8	11/16	(1)	3/16	INDEX	1/2–1 1/2	N-500	.012	.....
1955	BBD-2262S	7/32	....	....	....	29/32	1/4	INDEX	1/2–1 1/2	N-500	.011	.....
1955	BBD-2151-4S	7/32	....	....	....	29/32	1/4	INDEX	1/2–1 1/2	N-500	.011	.....
1955	BBD-2155S	7/32	....	....	....	29/32	1/4	INDEX	1/2–1 1/2	N-500	.011	1/16*
1956	WCFB-2442S	7/32	9/32	23/32	25/32	(1)	11/64	INDEX	1 1/2	N-500	.015	.....
1956	BBS-2293-4S	7/32	....	....	....	27/32	9/64	INDEX	1/2–1 1/2	N-500	.018	.....
1956	BBS-2295S	7/32	....	....	....	27/32	9/64	INDEX	1/2–1 1/2	N-500	.018	3/32
1956	BBD-2407-8S	1/4	....	....	....	1 1/32	3/16	INDEX	1/2–1 1/2	N-500	.020	.....
1956	BBD-2422-3S	7/32	....	....	....	1	1/4	INDEX	1/2–1 1/2	N-500	.018	.....
1956	BBD-2424S	7/32	....	....	....	1	1/4	INDEX	1/2–1 1/2	N-500	.018	1/16
1957	BBD-2512-3-4SA	9/32	....	....	....	1 1/32	1/4	INDEX	1/4–1 1/4	N-500	1450	.....
1957	BBD-2567-8S	7/32	....	....	....	27/32	9/64	INDEX	1/2–1 1/2	N-500	.018	.....
1957	BBD-2569-S	7/32	....	....	....	27/32	9/64	INDEX	1/2–1 1/2	N-500	.018	1/16
1957	WCFB-2530S	7/32	9/32	23/32	25/32	(1)	11/64	INDEX	1/2–1 1/2	N-500	.010	.....
1958	BBD-2644-5-6S	9/32	....	....	....	1 1/32	1/4	INDEX	1/4–1 1/4	N-500	1400	.....
1958	BBD-2641-2744S	(2)	(2)	23/32	23/32	7/16	1/4	2-RICH	1/4–1 3/4	N-500	1400	.....
1958	BBD-2652-3S	(3)	(3)	23/32	23/32	7/16	....	....	1/4–1 1/2	N-650	1450	.....
1958	AFB-2812-S	7/32	7/32	23/32	23/32	7/16	1/4	INDEX	1/4–1 3/4	N-500	1400	.....
1958	AFB-2813-S	7/32	7/32	23/32	23/32	7/16	1/4	2-RICH	1/4–1 1/2	N-500	1400	.....
1959	BBD—ALL	9/32	....	....	....	1 1/8	1/4	INDEX	1/4–1 1/2	N-500	1400	.....
1959	BBS—ALL	7/32	....	....	....	27/32	9/64	INDEX	1/2–1 3/4	N-475	1400	3/32
1960	BBS-2985-6S	7/32	....	....	....	27/32	11/64	INDEX	1/2–1 1/2	N-500	1300	.....
1960	BBD-2921-2S	9/32	....	....	....	1 1/8	1/4	INDEX	1/4–1 1/2	N-500	1400	.....
1960	AFB-2969-70S	7/32	7/32	3/4	3/4	7/16	1/4	INDEX	1/4–1 3/4	N-500	1800	.....
1960	AFB-2903S	9/32	9/32	3/4	3/4	1/4	1/4	1-RICH	1–2	N-750	1550	(4)
1960	AFB-2925S	7/32	7/32	23/32	23/32	7/16	1/4	1-RICH	1 1/4–2 3/4	N-500	1800	.....
1961	BBS-3097S	7/32	....	....	....	3/4	3/16	INDEX	1	N-550	1600–1800	.....
1961	BBS-3098-3128S	7/32	....	....	....	27/32	3/16	INDEX	1	N-500	1600–1800	.....
1961	BBS-3129S	7/32	....	....	....	3/4	3/16	INDEX	1	N-500	1600–1800	.....
1961	BBD-2921-2S	9/32	....	....	....	5/64	1/4	INDEX	1	N-500	1400	.....
1961	AFB-2903S	9/32	9/32	9/16	9/16	1/4	1/4	1-RICH	1 1/2	N-750	1500	(4)
1961	AFB-3131S	7/32	7/32	9/16	9/16	7/16	1/4	INDEX	1 1/2	N-500	1800	.....
1961	AFB-3133S	7/32	7/32	9/16	9/16	7/16	1/4	2-RICH	1 1/2	N-500	1800	.....
1961	AFB-3105-3140S	7/32	7/32	9/16	9/16	7/16	1/4	INDEX	1 1/2	N-500	1700	.....
1961	AFB-3103-6S	7/32	7/32	9/16	9/16	7/16	1/4	INDEX	1 1/2	N-500	1800	.....
1962	BBS-3231S, 3232S	7/32	....	....	....	27/32	3/16	INDEX	1	N-500	1400	.....
1962	BBD-3240S	9/32	....	....	....	5/64	1/4	INDEX	1	N-500	1400	.....
1962	BBD-3241S	9/32	....	....	....	5/64	1/4	INDEX	1	N-500	1400	.....
1962	AFB-3247S	7/32	7/32	9/16	9/16	7/16	1/4	2-RICH	1 1/2	N-500	1800	.....
1962	AFB-3249S	7/32	7/32	9/16	9/16	7/16	1/4	2-RICH	1 1/2	N-500	1800	.....
1962	AFB-3252S	7/32	7/32	9/16	9/16	7/16	1/4	2-RICH	1 1/2	N-500	1700	.....
1962	AFB-3253S	7/32	7/32	9/16	9/16	7/16	1/4	2-RICH	1 1/2	N-500	1800	.....
1962	AFB-3257S	7/32	7/32	9/16	9/16	7/16	1/4	2-RICH	1 1/2	N-500	1700	.....
1963	BBS-ALL	7/32	....	....	....	27/32	3/16	4-RICH	1	550	1400	.....
1963	BBD-3475S	1/4	....	....	....	1	1/4	2-RICH	3/4	500	1400	.....
1963	BBD-OTHERS	1/4	....	....	....	....	1/4	INDEX	1	500	1400	.....
1963	AFB-ALL	7/32	7/32	3/4	3/4	7/16	3/8	INDEX	1 1/2	500	2100	.....

(1)—Set pump arm parallel. (3)—Ribbed 9/32, plain 3/8. N—Neutral.
(2)—Ribbed 7/32, plain, 1/4. (4)—By trial. *—Turns off of seat.

YEAR	MODEL OR TYPE	FLOAT LEVEL		FLOAT DROP		Pump Travel Setting	CHOKE SETTING		Idle Screw Turns Open	Idle Speed	Fast Idle Speed	Dashpot Plunger Clearance
		Prim.	Sec.	Prim.	Sec.		Unloader	Housing				
PONTIAC												
1953	WCD-2010S	5/32				(1)	9/64	INDEX	1/2–11/2	N-475		.026
1953–54	WCD-2122S	3/16				(1)	1/8	INDEX	3/4–13/4	N-475		.040
1955	WGD-2182-S-A-B	7/32				(1)	5/32	1-RICH	11/4–21/4	N-475		.026
1955	WGD-2207-S-B	7/32				(1)	5/32	1-LEAN	1/2–11/2	N-475		.026
1955	WCFB—ALL	3/16	3/16	11/16	11/16	(1)	1/8	INDEX	3/4–13/4	N-475		.018
1956	WGD-2359S	15/64				(1)	1/8	INDEX	11/4–21/4	N-475		.030
1956	WCFB-2364-S-A	3/16	3/16	11/16	11/16	(1)	1/8	1-RICH	11/4–21/4	N-475		.030
1957	AFB-2506S	17/64	17/64	3/4	3/4	33/64	1/8	INDEX	1–2	N-475	1900	
1958	AFB-2740S	21/64	21/64	23/32	23/32	33/64	1/8	1-RICH	1/2–2	N-500	1900	
1958	AFB-2751S	9/32	9/32	23/32	23/32	33/64	1/8	INDEX	1/2–2	N-500	1900	
1958	AFB-2767-S-A	21/64	21/64	23/32	23/32	33/64	1/8	1-RICH	1/2–2	N-500	2200	1/8
1958	AFB-2768-S-A	9/32	9/32	23/32	23/32	33/64	1/8	1-RICH	1/2–2	N-500	2200	
1959	AFB-2819-S	21/64	21/64	23/32	23/32	33/64	1/8	1-RICH	1/2–2	N-550	2200	3/32
1959	AFB-2820-S	9/32	9/32	23/32	23/32	33/64	5/32	1-RICH	1/2–2	N-550	2200	
1960	AFB-2975-S	21/64	21/64	23/32	23/32	33/64	5/32	1-RICH	1/2–2	N-550	2200	
1960	AFB-2976-S	21/64	21/64	23/32	23/32	33/64	5/32	1-RICH	1/2–2	N-550	2200	3/32
1961	AFB—ALL	21/64	21/64	23/64	23/64	5/16	5/32	1-RICH	1/2–2	N-550	2200	15/16
1962	AFB—ALL	21/64	21/64	23/64	23/64	5/16	5/32	1-RICH	1/2–2	N-550	2200	15/16
1963	AFB—ALL	21/64	21/64	23/64	23/64	5/16	5/32	1-RICH	1/2–2	N-550	2200	15/16

(1)—Set pump arm parallel.

RAMBLER-HUDSON-NASH

YEAR	MODEL OR TYPE	FLOAT LEVEL		FLOAT DROP		Pump Travel Setting	CHOKE SETTING		Idle Screw Turns Open	Idle Speed	Fast Idle Speed	Dashpot Plunger Clearance
		Prim.	Sec.	Prim.	Sec.		Unloader	Housing				
1955–56	WGD-2231S	3/16				(1)	3/16	1-RICH	1/2–11/2	N-475		.030
1955–56	WCD-2061S	5/32				(1)	11/64	INDEX	1/2–11/2	N-550		.026
1955–60	YF-2014S	1/2				(1)	9/32	1-LEAN	1/2–11/2	N-550		.054
1957	WFCB-2593S-A	1/8	3/16	5/8	11/16	(1)	9/32	INDEX	3/4–13/4	N-500		.023
1957–60	AS-2748S	1/4				(1)	3/16	2-RICH	1/2–11/2	N-500		.030
1957–60	WCD-2586S	5/32				(1)	3/16	INDEX	1/2–11/2	N-500		.020
1957–60	WGD-2352S-A	7/32				(1)	3/16	INDEX	1–2	N-500		.023
1958–60	YF-2757-S	1/2					9/32	1-LEAN	1/2–11/2	N-500		.054
1961	WCD-3170S	5/32				(1)	3/16	INDEX	1/2–11/2	N-500		.020
1961	AS-3169S	1/4				(1)	1/8	INDEX	1/4–11/4	N-500		.035
1962	AS-3206S	5/32				(1)	1/8	INDEX	1/4–11/4	N-500		.035
1962	WCD-3322S	5/32		5/8		(1)	3/16	INDEX	1/4–11/4	N-500		
1962	YF-2014S	1/2				(1)	9/32	1-LEAN	1/2–11/2	N-500		1/8
1963	AS-3206-8	5/32				(1)	1/8	INDEX	1/4–11/4	N-500		.035
1963	WCD-3322S	5/32		5/8		(1)	3/16	INDEX	1/4–11/4	N-500		
1963	YF-2014S	1/2				(1)	9/32	1-LEAN	1/2–11/2	N-500		1/8

(1)—Set pump arm parallel.

STUDEBAKER

YEAR	MODEL OR TYPE	FLOAT LEVEL		FLOAT DROP		Pump Travel Setting	CHOKE SETTING		Idle Screw Turns Open	Idle Speed	Fast Idle Speed	Dashpot Plunger Clearance
		Prim.	Sec.	Prim.	Sec.		Unloader	Housing				
1953	WE-989-S-A	3/8				7/32	3/16	1-LEAN	1/2–11/2	N-550		.046
1953–56	WE-2108-2190S	3/8				7/32	3/16	1-LEAN	1/2–11/2	N-550		.046
1955	WCFB-2330S	3/16	3/16	11/16	11/16	(1)	1/8	1-RICH	1/2–11/2	N-550		.020
1955–56	WCFB-2214-19S	3/16	3/16	11/16	11/16	(1)	1/8	1-RICH	1/2–11/2	N-550		.024
1956	WCFB-2394S	1/8	3/16	5/8	11/16	(1)	9/32	INDEX	3/4–13/4	N-450		.023
1957	BBR1-2724S	5/64				1/2			1/2–11/2	N-550		
1957	WE-2417S	3/8				7/32	3/16	1-LEAN	1/2–11/2	N-550		.046
1958	BBR1-2764S	5/64				1/2			1/2–11/2	N-550		
1958	BBR1-2808S	1/8				7/32			1/2–11/2	N-550		
1958–61	WCFB-2574-5S	3/16	3/16	11/16	11/16		1/8	1-RICH	1/2–11/2	N-550		.024
1959	AS-2876-S	1/4				(2)	3/16	INDEX	1/4–13/4	N-550		.024
1960–61	AS—ALL	1/4				(2)	3/16	1-RICH	1/4–11/2	N-550		.065
1962	AS-3370S, 3372S	1/4				(2)	3/16	1-RICH	1/4–11/2	N-550	2700	
1963	6 Cyl. RBS-3538S	15/32				**	5/32	INDEX	1/2–11/2	575		
1963	V8—ALL—AFB	9/32		23/32		27/64	5/32	INDEX	1–11/2	650		

(1)—Set pump arm parallel. **—Not adjustable. (2)—Set link arm parallel.

VALIANT-LANCER—1963 DART

YEAR	MODEL OR TYPE	FLOAT LEVEL		FLOAT DROP		Pump Travel Setting	CHOKE SETTING		Idle Screw Turns Open	Idle Speed	Fast Idle Speed	Dashpot Plunger Clearance
		Prim.	Sec.	Prim.	Sec.		Unloader	Housing				
1960	BBS—ALL	7/32				27/32	9/64	INDEX	1/2–11/2	N-550	(1)	
1961	BBS—ALL	7/32				27/32	3/16	INDEX	1	N-550	1600–1800	
1962	BBS-3231S	7/32				27/32	3/16	INDEX	1	N-550	1300	
1962	BBS-3232S	7/32				27/32	3/16	INDEX	1	N-550	1400	
1962	BBS-3235S	7/32				27/32	3/16	INDEX	1	N-550	(2)	
1963	BBS-3462S	7/32				27/32	3/16	4-RICH	1	550	1500	
1963	BBS-3463S	7/32				27/32	3/16	4-RICH	1	550	1400	

(1)—On mark. (2)—Standard transmission, 1300; automatic transmission, 1400. **—Not adjustable.

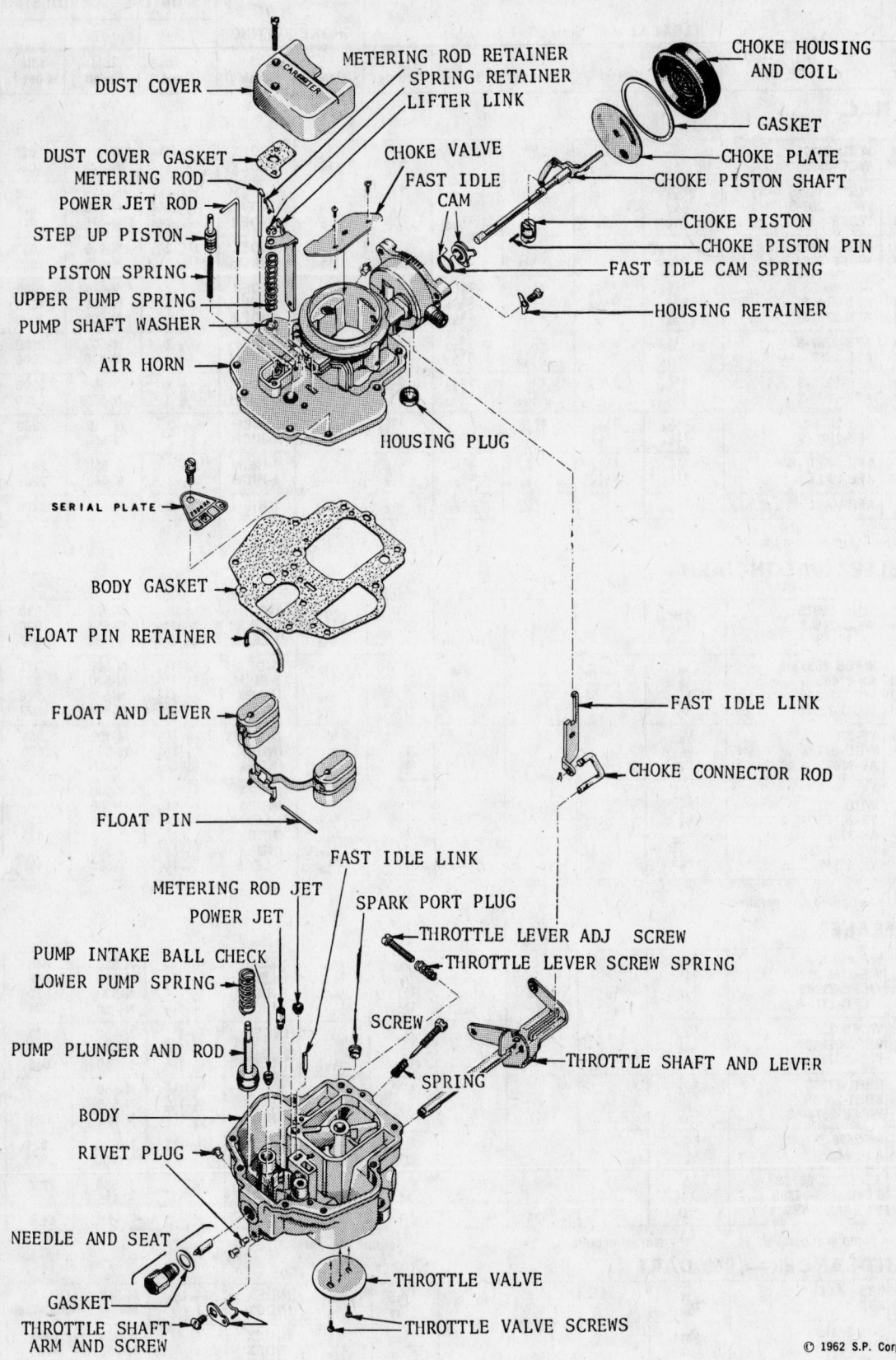

Carter— AS single barrel (typical)

© 1962 S.P. Corp.

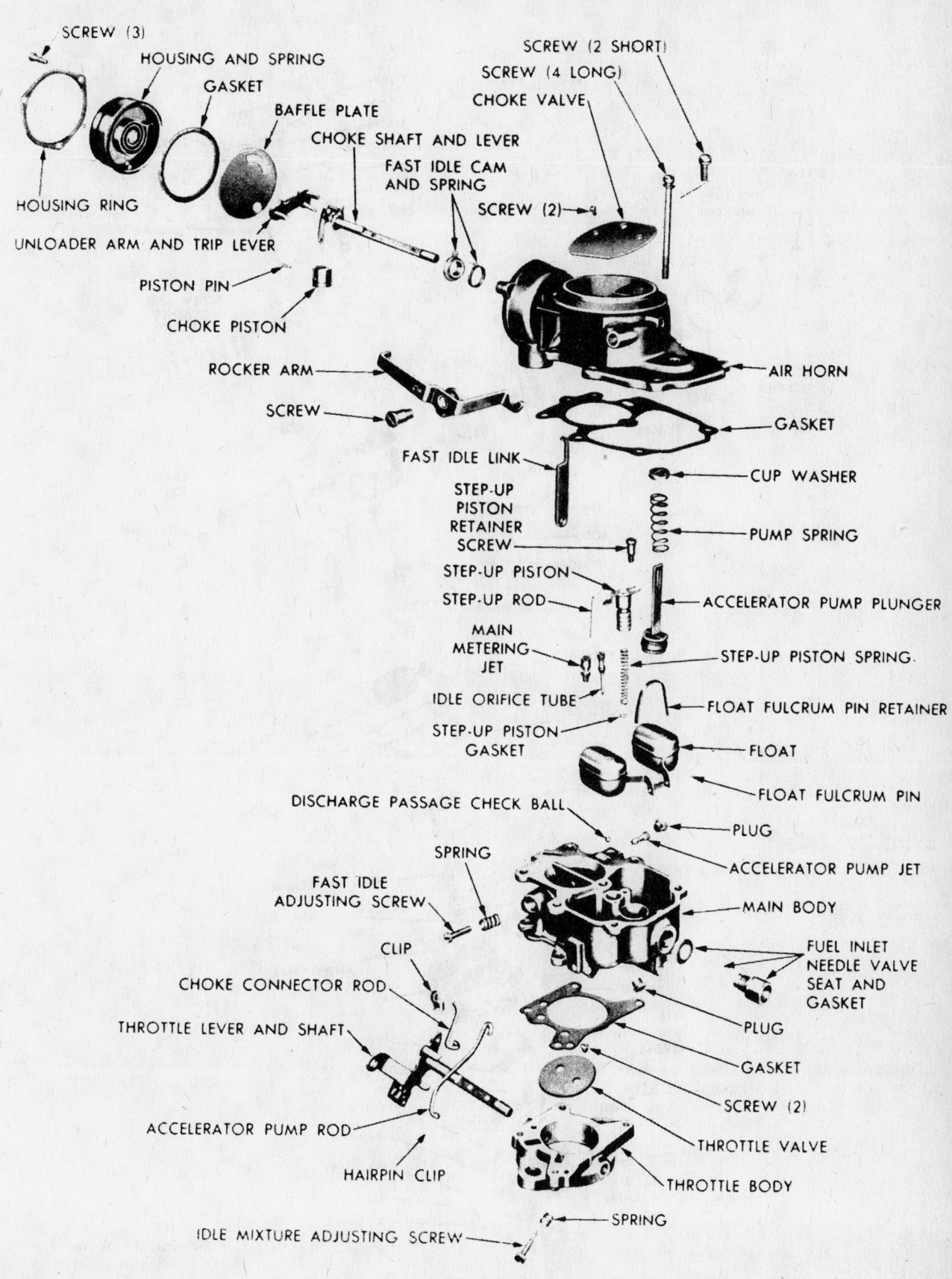

SCREW (3)

HOUSING AND SPRING

GASKET

BAFFLE PLATE

CHOKE SHAFT AND LEVER

FAST IDLE CAM AND SPRING

HOUSING RING

UNLOADER ARM AND TRIP LEVER

PISTON PIN

CHOKE PISTON

SCREW (2 SHORT)

SCREW (4 LONG)

CHOKE VALVE

SCREW (2)

ROCKER ARM

SCREW

FAST IDLE LINK

STEP-UP PISTON RETAINER SCREW

STEP-UP PISTON

STEP-UP ROD

MAIN METERING JET

IDLE ORIFICE TUBE

STEP-UP PISTON GASKET

DISCHARGE PASSAGE CHECK BALL

SPRING

FAST IDLE ADJUSTING SCREW

CLIP

CHOKE CONNECTOR ROD

THROTTLE LEVER AND SHAFT

ACCELERATOR PUMP ROD

HAIRPIN CLIP

IDLE MIXTURE ADJUSTING SCREW

AIR HORN

GASKET

CUP WASHER

PUMP SPRING

ACCELERATOR PUMP PLUNGER

STEP-UP PISTON SPRING.

FLOAT FULCRUM PIN RETAINER

FLOAT

FLOAT FULCRUM PIN

PLUG

ACCELERATOR PUMP JET

MAIN BODY

FUEL INLET NEEDLE VALVE SEAT AND GASKET

PLUG

GASKET

SCREW (2)

THROTTLE VALVE

THROTTLE BODY

SPRING

Carter—BBS single barrel (typical)

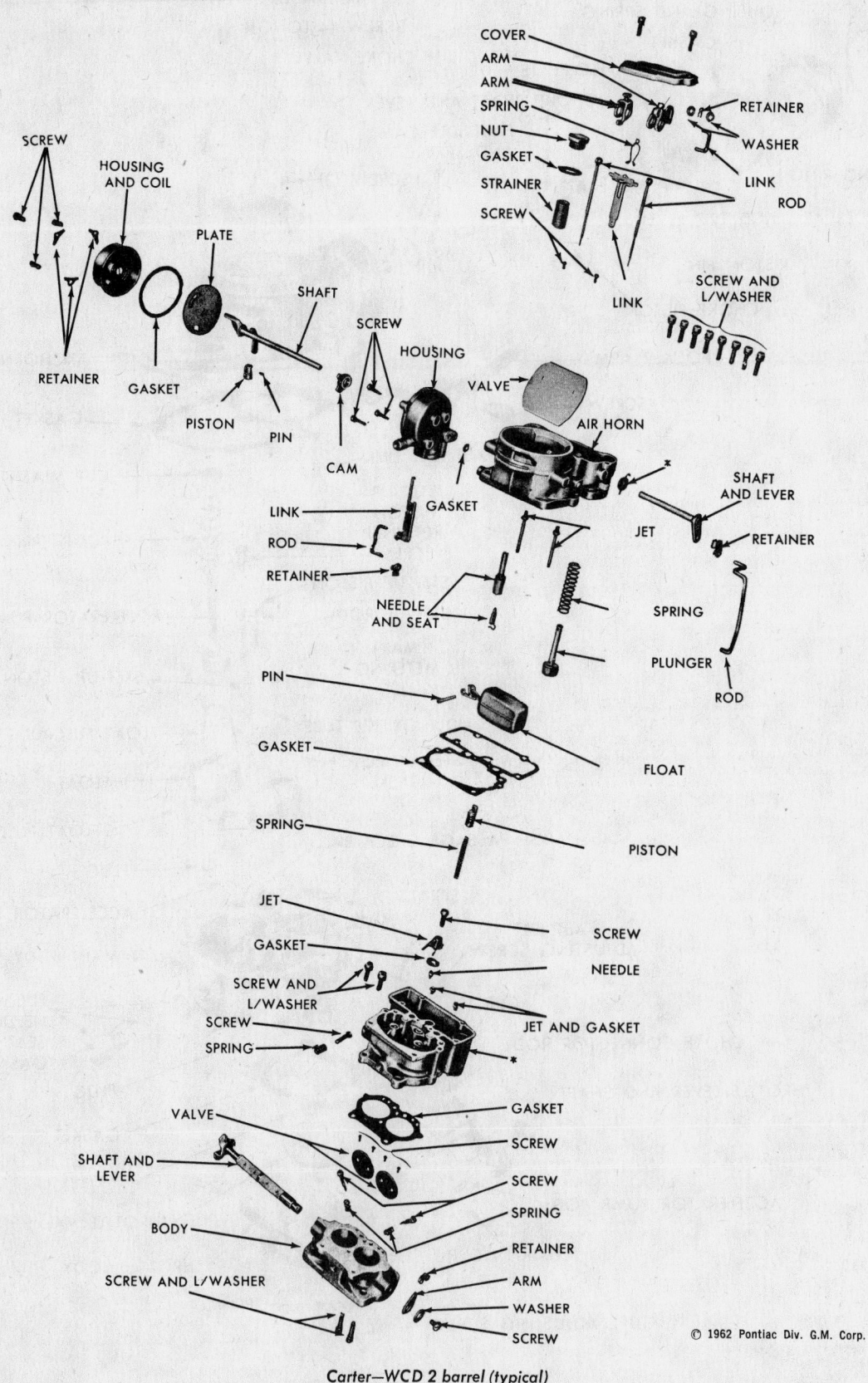

SCREW

HOUSING
AND COIL

PLATE

SHAFT

SCREW

HOUSING

VALVE

AIR HORN

RETAINER

GASKET

PISTON

PIN

CAM

LINK

GASKET

ROD

RETAINER

NEEDLE
AND SEAT

PIN

GASKET

SPRING

JET

GASKET

SCREW AND
L/WASHER

SCREW

SPRING

VALVE

SHAFT AND
LEVER

BODY

SCREW AND L/WASHER

COVER
ARM
ARM
SPRING
NUT
GASKET
STRAINER
SCREW

RETAINER
WASHER
LINK
ROD

LINK

SCREW AND
L/WASHER

SHAFT
AND LEVER

JET

RETAINER

SPRING

PLUNGER

ROD

FLOAT

PISTON

SCREW

NEEDLE

JET AND GASKET

GASKET
SCREW
SCREW
SPRING
RETAINER
ARM
WASHER
SCREW

Carter—WCD 2 barrel (typical)

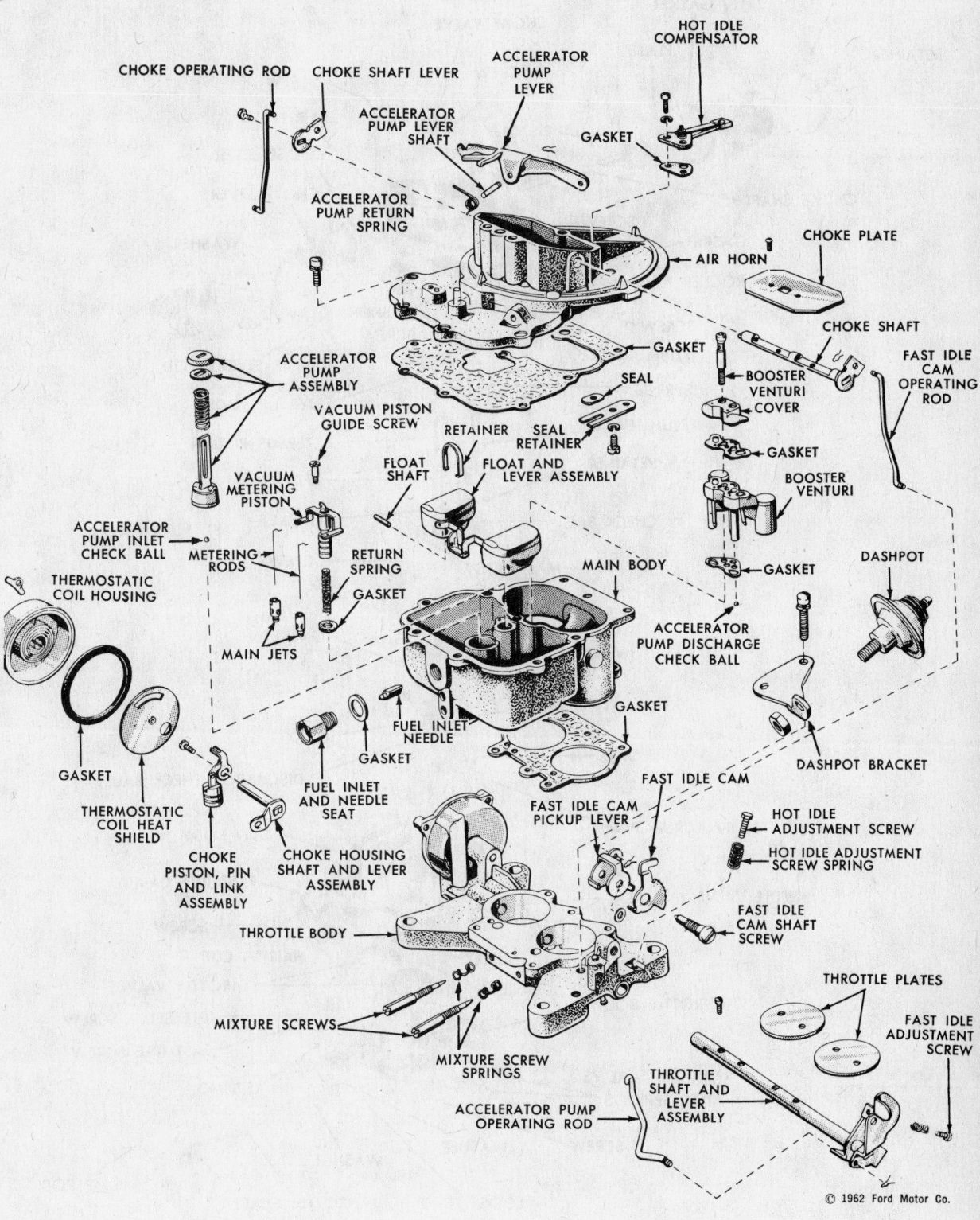

CHOKE OPERATING ROD

CHOKE SHAFT LEVER

ACCELERATOR PUMP LEVER

HOT IDLE COMPENSATOR

ACCELERATOR PUMP LEVER SHAFT

GASKET

ACCELERATOR PUMP RETURN SPRING

AIR HORN

CHOKE PLATE

CHOKE SHAFT

ACCELERATOR PUMP ASSEMBLY

GASKET

BOOSTER VENTURI COVER

FAST IDLE CAM OPERATING ROD

VACUUM PISTON GUIDE SCREW

SEAL

FLOAT SHAFT

RETAINER

SEAL RETAINER

VACUUM METERING PISTON

FLOAT AND LEVER ASSEMBLY

GASKET

BOOSTER VENTURI

ACCELERATOR PUMP INLET CHECK BALL

METERING RODS

RETURN SPRING

MAIN BODY

DASHPOT

THERMOSTATIC COIL HOUSING

GASKET

ACCELERATOR PUMP DISCHARGE CHECK BALL

ACCELERATOR PUMP INLET CHECK BALL

MAIN JETS

GASKET

THERMOSTATIC COIL HEAT SHIELD

FUEL INLET NEEDLE

GASKET

CHOKE PISTON, PIN AND LINK ASSEMBLY

FUEL INLET AND NEEDLE SEAT

GASKET

CHOKE HOUSING SHAFT AND LEVER ASSEMBLY

FAST IDLE CAM

DASHPOT BRACKET

FAST IDLE CAM PICKUP LEVER

HOT IDLE ADJUSTMENT SCREW

HOT IDLE ADJUSTMENT SCREW SPRING

THROTTLE BODY

FAST IDLE CAM SHAFT SCREW

THROTTLE PLATES

FAST IDLE ADJUSTMENT SCREW

MIXTURE SCREWS

MIXTURE SCREW SPRINGS

THROTTLE SHAFT AND LEVER ASSEMBLY

ACCELERATOR PUMP OPERATING ROD

© 1962 Ford Motor Co.

Carter—ABD 2 barrel (typical)

CARTER CARBURETORS

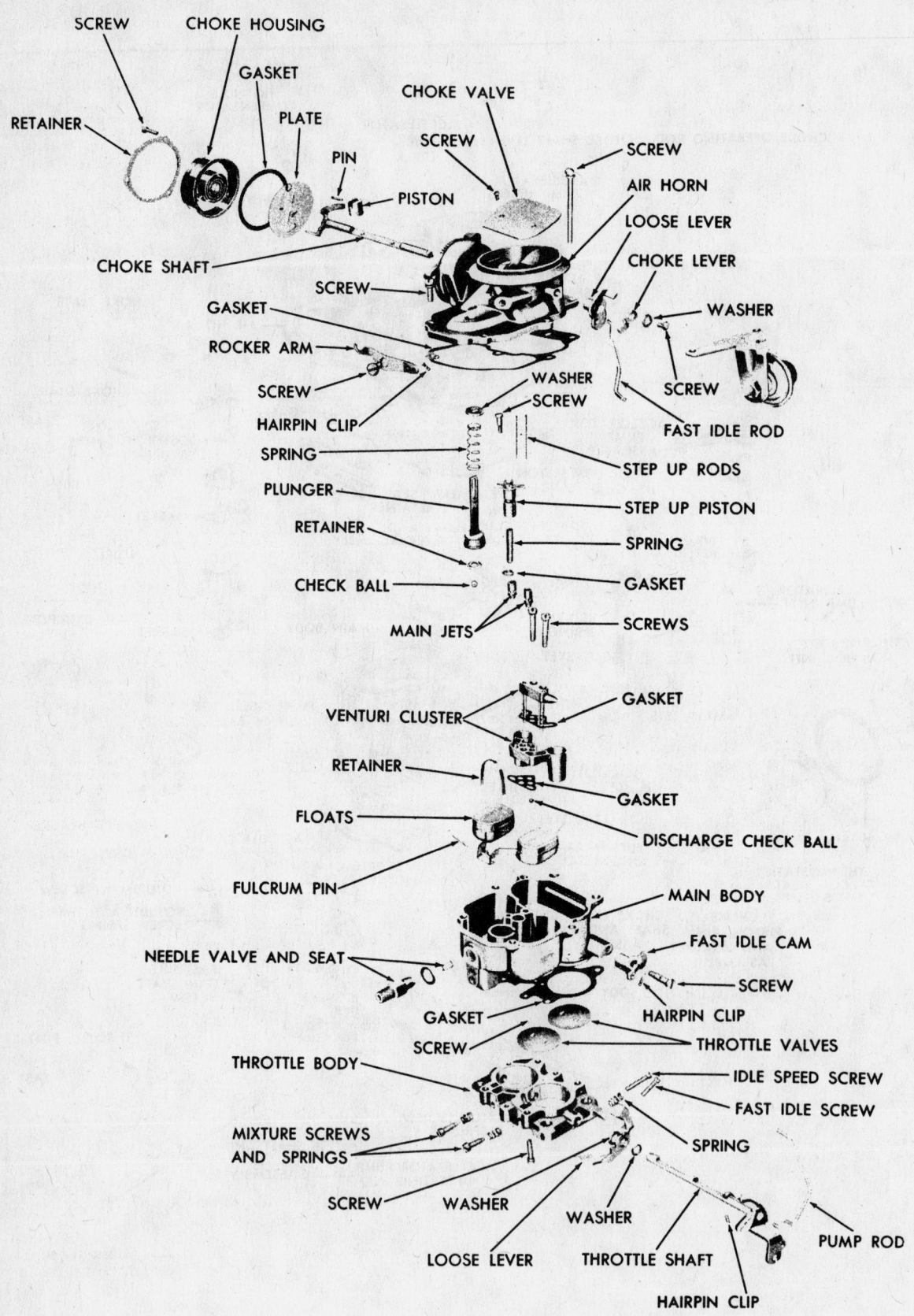

Carter—BBD 2 barrel (typical)

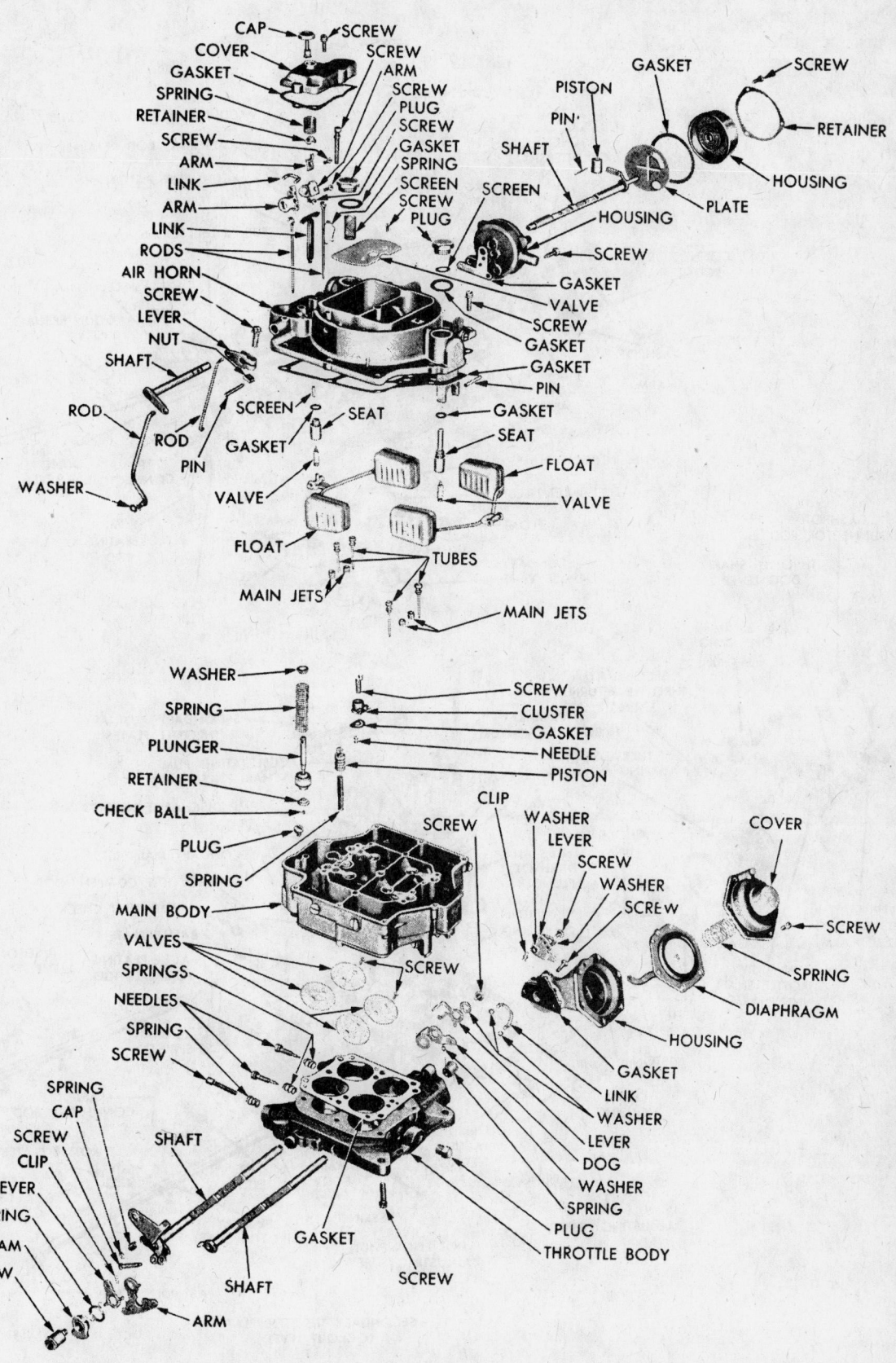

CAP — SCREW
COVER — SCREW
GASKET — ARM
SPRING — SCREW
RETAINER — PLUG
SCREW — SCREW
ARM — GASKET
LINK — SPRING
ARM — SCREEN
LINK — SCREW
RODS — PLUG
AIR HORN
SCREW
LEVER
NUT
SHAFT
ROD
ROD
WASHER
SCREEN — SEAT
GASKET
VALVE
FLOAT
MAIN JETS
PIN

PISTON — GASKET — SCREW
PIN — RETAINER
SHAFT — HOUSING
SCREEN — PLATE
HOUSING
SCREW
GASKET
VALVE
SCREW
GASKET
GASKET
PIN
GASKET
SEAT
FLOAT
VALVE
TUBES
MAIN JETS

WASHER — SCREW
SPRING — CLUSTER
PLUNGER — GASKET
RETAINER — NEEDLE
CHECK BALL — PISTON
PLUG
SPRING — CLIP
MAIN BODY — SCREW
VALVES — WASHER — COVER
SPRINGS — LEVER
NEEDLES — SCREW — SCREW
SPRING — WASHER — SPRING
SCREW — SCREW — DIAPHRAGM
SPRING — SCREW — HOUSING
CAP — GASKET
SCREW — LINK
CLIP — WASHER
LEVER — LEVER
SPRING — DOG
CAM — SHAFT — WASHER
SCREW — SPRING
SHAFT — PLUG
GASKET — THROTTLE BODY
ARM — SCREW

Carter—WCFB 4 barrel (typical)

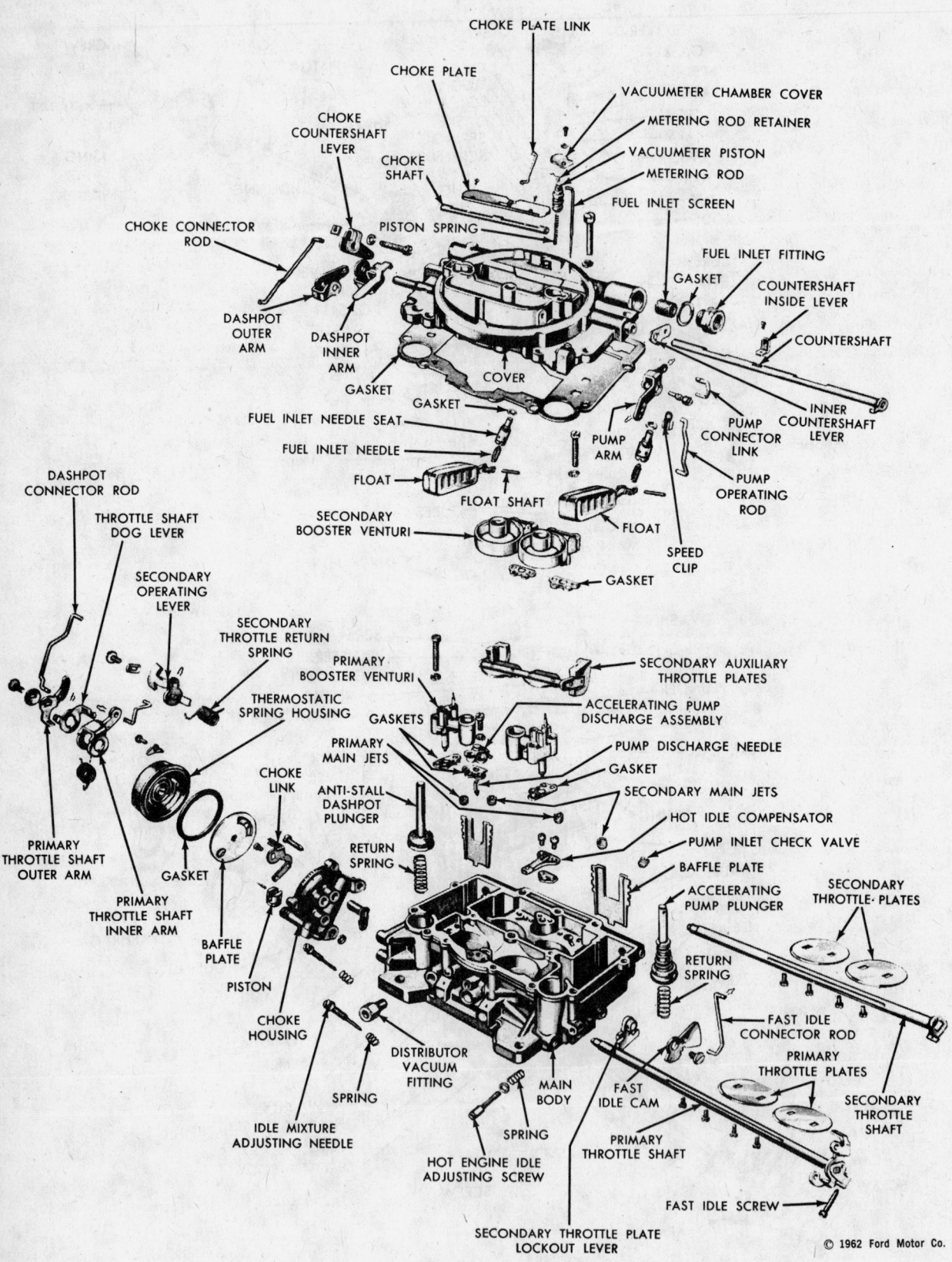

CHOKE PLATE LINK

CHOKE PLATE

VACUUMETER CHAMBER COVER

METERING ROD RETAINER

VACUUMETER PISTON

METERING ROD

FUEL INLET SCREEN

CHOKE COUNTERSHAFT LEVER

CHOKE SHAFT

FUEL INLET FITTING

CHOKE CONNECTOR ROD

PISTON SPRING

GASKET

COUNTERSHAFT INSIDE LEVER

COUNTERSHAFT

DASHPOT OUTER ARM

DASHPOT INNER ARM

COVER

INNER COUNTERSHAFT LEVER

GASKET

GASKET

PUMP CONNECTOR LINK

FUEL INLET NEEDLE SEAT

PUMP ARM

FUEL INLET NEEDLE

PUMP OPERATING ROD

DASHPOT CONNECTOR ROD

FLOAT

FLOAT SHAFT

FLOAT

THROTTLE SHAFT DOG LEVER

SECONDARY BOOSTER VENTURI

SPEED CLIP

SECONDARY OPERATING LEVER

GASKET

SECONDARY THROTTLE RETURN SPRING

PRIMARY BOOSTER VENTURI

SECONDARY AUXILIARY THROTTLE PLATES

THERMOSTATIC SPRING HOUSING

GASKETS

ACCELERATING PUMP DISCHARGE ASSEMBLY

PRIMARY MAIN JETS

PUMP DISCHARGE NEEDLE

CHOKE LINK

GASKET

ANTI-STALL DASHPOT PLUNGER

SECONDARY MAIN JETS

PRIMARY THROTTLE SHAFT OUTER ARM

HOT IDLE COMPENSATOR

GASKET

RETURN SPRING

PUMP INLET CHECK VALVE

PRIMARY THROTTLE SHAFT INNER ARM

BAFFLE PLATE

ACCELERATING PUMP PLUNGER

SECONDARY THROTTLE PLATES

BAFFLE PLATE

PISTON

RETURN SPRING

CHOKE HOUSING

FAST IDLE CONNECTOR ROD

DISTRIBUTOR VACUUM FITTING

PRIMARY THROTTLE PLATES

SPRING

MAIN BODY

FAST IDLE CAM

SECONDARY THROTTLE SHAFT

IDLE MIXTURE ADJUSTING NEEDLE

SPRING

PRIMARY THROTTLE SHAFT

HOT ENGINE IDLE ADJUSTING SCREW

FAST IDLE SCREW

SECONDARY THROTTLE PLATE LOCKOUT LEVER

© 1962 Ford Motor Co.

Carter—AFB 4 barrel (typical)

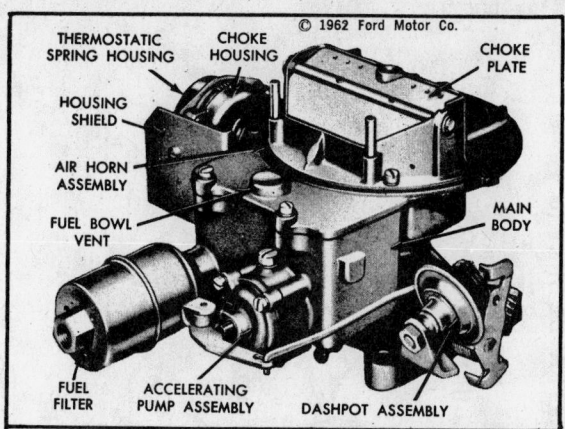

Ford Dual Carburetor

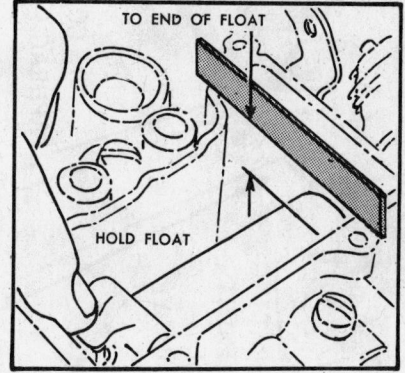

Ford Two- and Four-Barrel Float Setting

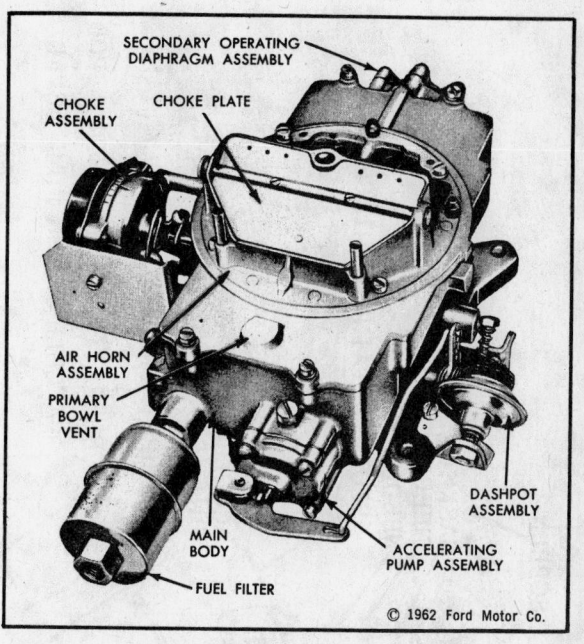

Ford Four-Barrel Carburetor

YEAR	MODEL OR TYPE	Float Level	Fuel Level	Fast Idle Cam	Pump Travel Setting	Choke Setting	ON THE CAR ADJUSTMENTS			
							Idle Screw Turns Open	Idle Speed	Fast Idle Speed	Dashpot Plunger Clearance
FORD										
1957	2-Barrel	1/2	1	(6)	(5)	INDEX	1	500	(7)	.055
1957	4-Barrel	9/16	1	(6)	(5)	INDEX	1	500	(7)	.055
1958	2-Barrel	7/16	29/32	(6)	(8)	INDEX	1½	500	(7)	.075
1958	4-Barrel	7/16	29/32	(6)	(9)	INDEX	1½	500	(7)	.075
1959	2-Barrel	7/16	29/32	(6)	(9)	INDEX	1½	500	(7)	.045
1959	4-Barrel	7/16	29/32	(6)	(9)	INDEX	1½	500	(7)	.045
1960	2-Barrel(1)	7/16	29/32	.030	(5)	2-RICH	1½	500	1800	.075
1960	2-Barrel(3)	7/16	29/32	.030	(5)	3-LEAN	1½	500	1800	.075
1960	4-Barrel	7/16	29/32	.030	(5)	3-LEAN	1½	500	1800	.075
1961	2-Barrel(1)	29/64	29/32	.040	(5)	INDEX	1½	475	1500	.075
1961	2-Barrel(2)	29/64	29/32	.040	(5)	2-LEAN	1½	475	1700	.075
1961	2-Barrel(3)	29/64	29/32	.040	(5)	INDEX	1½	525	1500	.075
1961	2-Barrel(4)	29/64	29/32	.040	(5)	2-LEAN	1½	525	1700	.075
1961	4-Barrel	21/32	29/32	.040	(5)	2-LEAN	1–1½	600	1600	.075
1962	2-Barrel(1) 292 Std.	21/32	......	.040	(5)	INDEX	1–1½	475	1500	......
1962	2-Barrel(2) 292 A.T.	21/32	......	.040	(5)	INDEX	1–1½	475	1700	.075
1962	2-Barrel(3) 352 Std.	21/32	......	.040	(5)	INDEX	1–1½	525	1500	
1962	2-Barrel(3) 352 A.T.	21/32	......	.040	(5)	2-LEAN	1–1½	525	1700	.075
1962	4-Barrel A.T.	21/32	......	.040	(5)	2-LEAN	1–1½	600	1600	.075
1963	2-Barrel(3) 352 Std.	21/32	......	.040	(5)	INDEX	1–1½	525	1500	......
1963	2-Barrel(4) 352 A.T.	21/32	......	.040	(5)	2-LEAN	1–1½	525	1700	.075
1963	4-Barrel A.T.	21/32	......	.040	(5)	2-LEAN	1–1½	600	1600	.075
1963	1-Barrel	15/16		.040	......	INDEX	1½	550	1600	.075

2-Barrel (1)—On 292 cu. in.   2-Barrel (3)—On 352 cu. in.
2-Barrel (2)—On 292 cu. in. A. T.   2-Barrel (4)—On 352 cu. in. A.T.
(5)—Install pump rod in top hole for winter and second hole from bottom for summer.

(6)—Adjust bellcrank to 2nd fastest cam.
(7)—Screw just touches lowest step on cam. Set ¼ to ½ turn less.
(8)—Insert in bottom hole.
(9)—By trial.

FORD CARBURETORS

(STARTING WITH 1963 PRODUCTION)

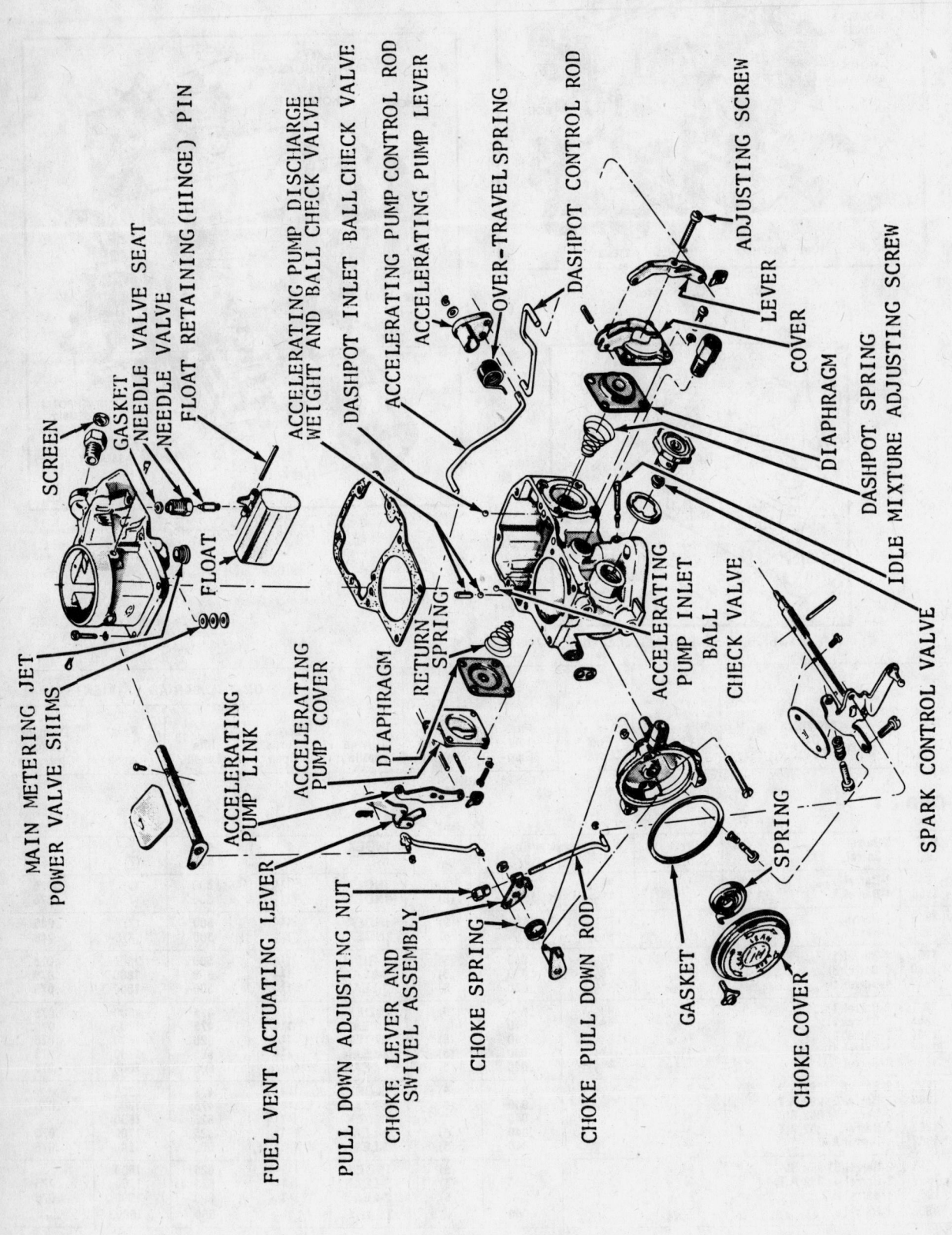

Ford—Single barrel (typical)

990

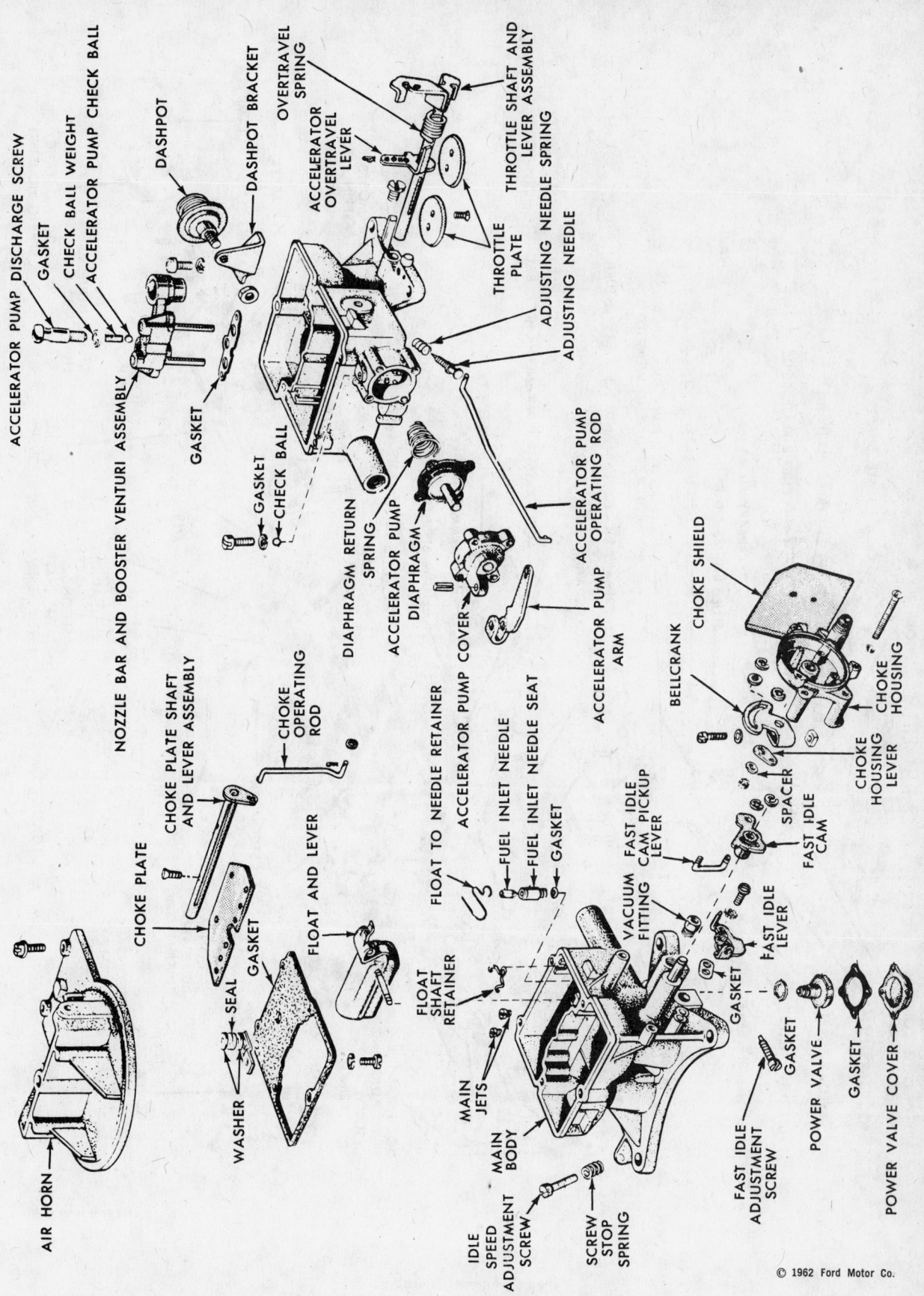

ACCELERATOR PUMP DISCHARGE SCREW

GASKET

CHECK BALL WEIGHT

ACCELERATOR PUMP CHECK BALL

DASHPOT

DASHPOT BRACKET

OVERTRAVEL SPRING

ACCELERATOR OVERTRAVEL LEVER

THROTTLE SHAFT AND LEVER ASSEMBLY

ADJUSTING NEEDLE SPRING

THROTTLE PLATE

ADJUSTING NEEDLE

ADJUSTING NEEDLE

NOZZLE BAR AND BOOSTER VENTURI ASSEMBLY

GASKET

GASKET

CHECK BALL

DIAPHRAGM RETURN SPRING

ACCELERATOR PUMP DIAPHRAGM

ACCELERATOR PUMP COVER

ACCELERATOR PUMP OPERATING ROD

ACCELERATOR PUMP ARM

CHOKE SHIELD

BELLCRANK

CHOKE HOUSING

CHOKE HOUSING LEVER

CHOKE HOUSING

CHOKE PLATE SHAFT AND LEVER ASSEMBLY

CHOKE OPERATING ROD

CHOKE PLATE

FLOAT TO NEEDLE RETAINER

ACCELERATOR PUMP NEEDLE SEAT

FUEL INLET NEEDLE

FUEL INLET NEEDLE SEAT

GASKET

VACUUM FAST IDLE CAM PICKUP LEVER

FAST IDLE CAM

SPACER

FAST IDLE LEVER

FLOAT AND LEVER

SEAL

GASKET

FLOAT SHAFT RETAINER

GASKET

WASHER

AIR HORN

MAIN JETS

MAIN BODY

IDLE SPEED ADJUSTMENT SCREW

SCREW STOP SPRING

FAST IDLE ADJUSTMENT SCREW

GASKET

POWER VALVE

GASKET

POWER VALVE COVER

© 1962 Ford Motor Co.

Ford—2 barrel (typical)

FORD CARBURETORS

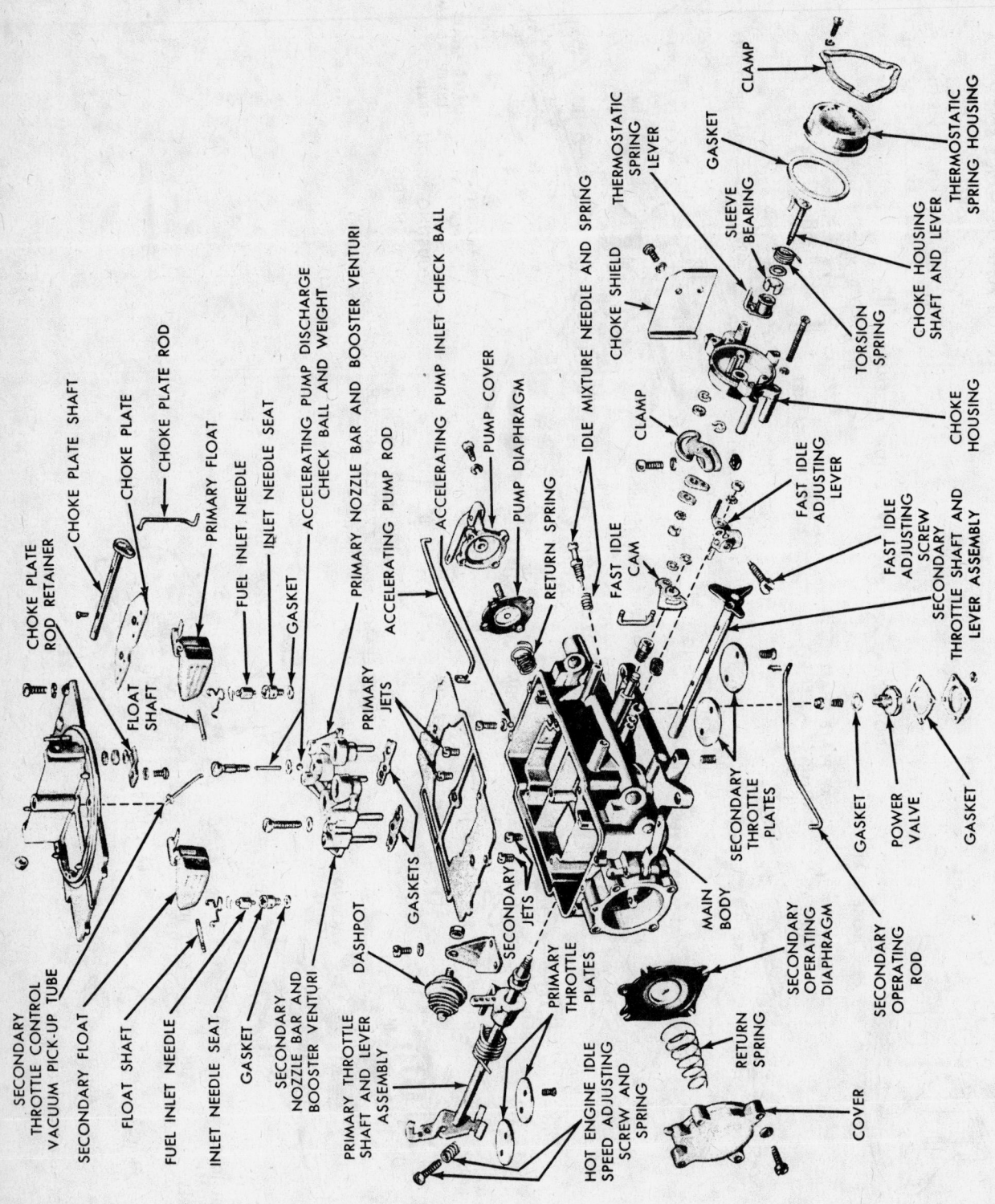

Ford—4 barrel (typical)

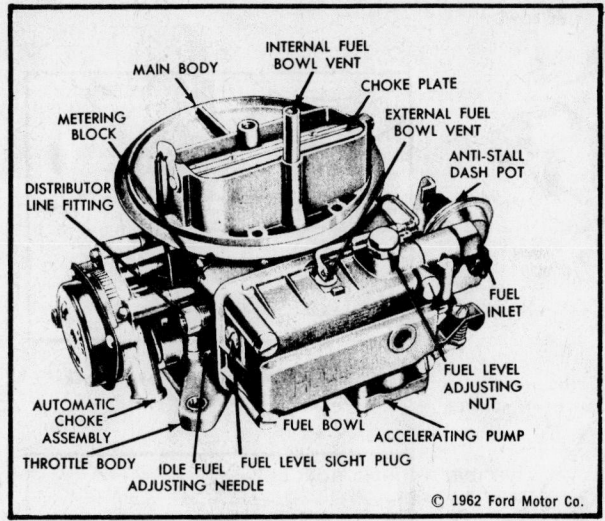

Holley Dual Carburetor

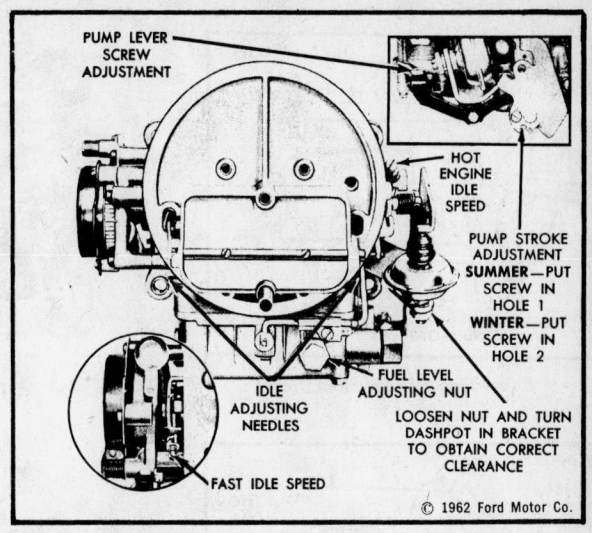

Holley Dual Carburetor Idle Adjustment

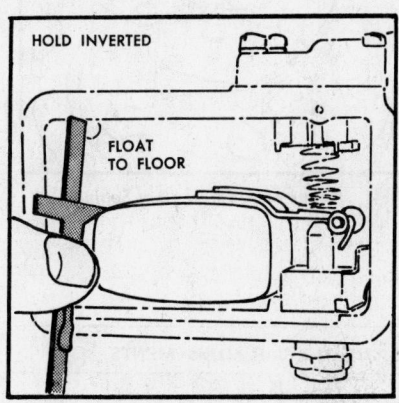

Holley Two- and Four-Barrel Float Adjustment

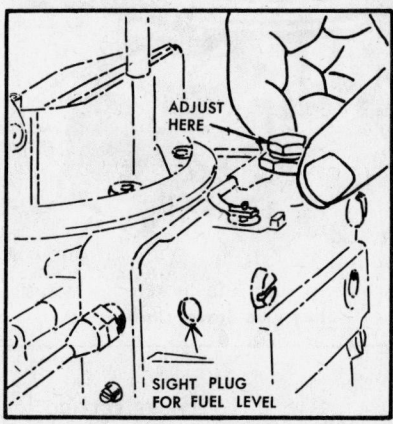

Holley Two- and Four-Barrel Fuel Level Adjustment

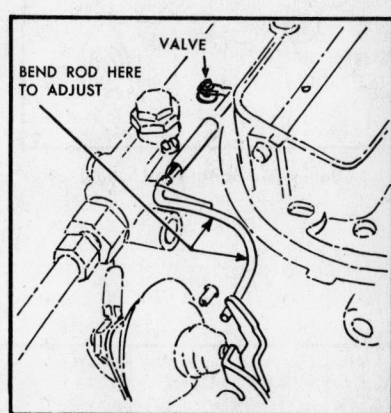

Holley Dual Bowl Vent Adjustment

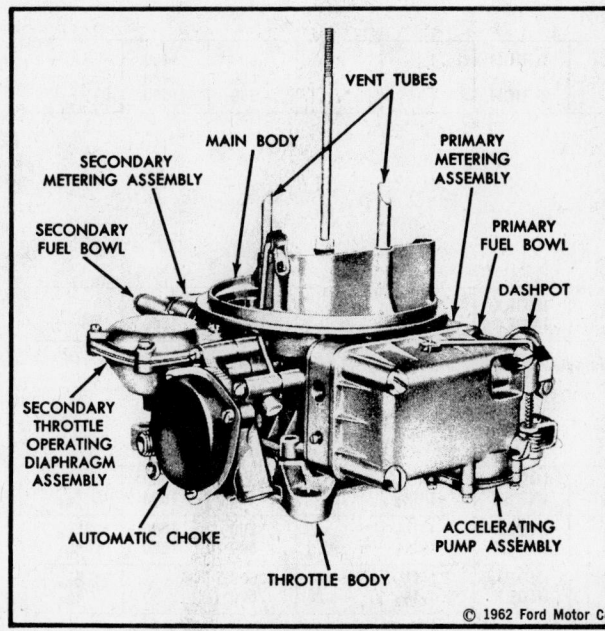

Holley Four-Barrel Carburetor

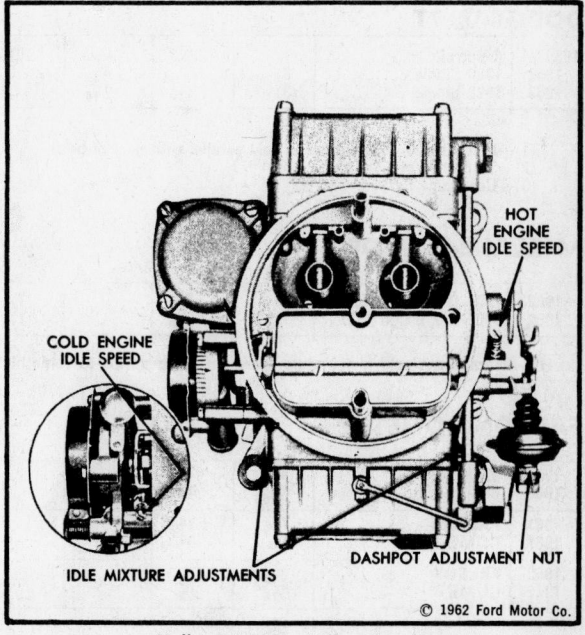

Holley Four-Barrel Idle Adjustment

HOLLEY CARBURETORS

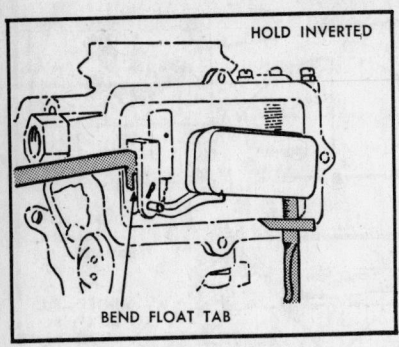

Holley Single Barrel Float, Drop

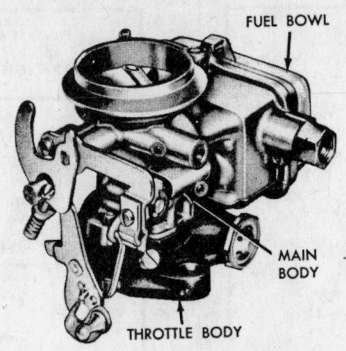

Holley Single-Barrel Carburetor

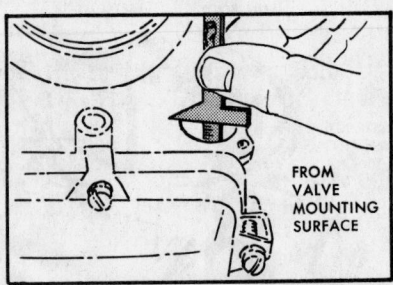

Holley Single-Barrel Fuel Level Check

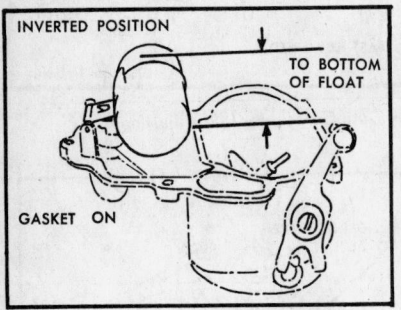

Holley Two-Barrel Float Setting

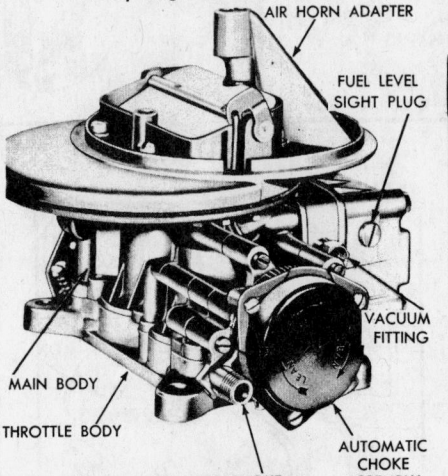

Holley Two-Barrel Carburetor

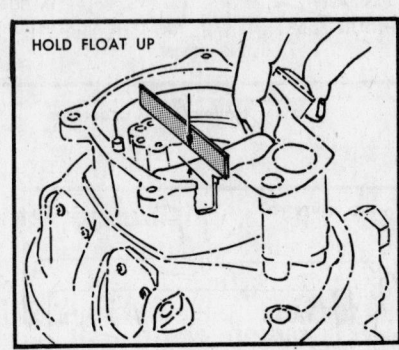

Holley Four-Barrel Float Setting

| YEAR | MODEL OR TYPE | Float Level (4) | Fuel Level (4) | Bowl Vent Valve | Pump Travel Setting | CHOKE SETTING | | ON THE CAR ADJUSTMENTS | | | | |
						Unloader	Housing	Idle Screw Turns Out	Air Bypass Turns Open	Idle Speed	Fast Idle Speed	Dashpot Plunger Clearance

DODGE-DART

1960-61	4-Barrel	(1)	(2)	.060	.015	1/16	1-RICH	1	1	500	1400	......
1962	1920-Single	(3)	11/16	3/32	......	......		1	......	550	1350	......
1963	1920-Single	(3)	11/16	1/16	......	......	2-RICH	1	......	550	1500	......

(1)—Invert bowl.—Set bottom of float parallel with floor of bowl.
(2)—To bottom of sight plug.
(3)—Use gauge C-3903.

FAIRLANE-METEOR

1962	1909-170-6 Cyl. Std.	5/16	7/32	......	(1)	9/32	INDEX	1-1½	......	500	1500	......
1962	1909-170, 6 Cyl. A.T.	5/16	7/32	......	(1)	9/32	INDEX	1-1½	......	500	1800	......

(1)—Average and cold temperature operation—long stroke, extreme high temp.—short stroke.

FALCON-COMET

1960	FALCON	11/64	23/32	......	......	1/4	INDEX	1-1½	......	500	1600	5/64
1960	COMET	11/64	23/32	......	......	1/4	INDEX	1-1½	......	500	1600	9/64
1961	FALCON	11/64	23/32	......	......	1/4	INDEX	1-1½	......	500	1600	9/64
1961	COMET	11/64	23/32	......	......	1/4	INDEX	1-1½	......	500	1600	9/64
1962	FALCON	5/16	1/2	......	......	17/64	INDEX	1-1½	......	500	......	9/64
1962	COMET	5/16	1/2	......	......	17/64	INDEX	1-1½	......	500	......	9/64

YEAR	MODEL OR TYPE	Float Level (4)	Fuel Level (4)	Bowl Vent Valve	Pump Travel Setting	CHOKE SETTING		ON THE CAR ADJUSTMENTS				
						Unloader	Housing	Idle Screw Turns Out	Air Bypass Turns Open	Idle Speed	Fast Idle Speed	Dashpot Plunger Clearance

FORD-EDSEL-THUNDERBIRD

YEAR	MODEL OR TYPE	Float Level (4)	Fuel Level (4)	Bowl Vent Valve	Pump Travel Setting	Unloader	Housing	Idle Screw Turns Out	Air Bypass Turns Open	Idle Speed	Fast Idle Speed	Dashpot Plunger Clearance
1953–55	Single	5/16	11/16	......	......	......	......	1 1/2	......	500	(1)	.055
1953–55	2-Barrel	1 9/32	5/8	......	......	......	......	1 1/2	......	500	(1)	.055
1955–56	4-Barrel	1/4	1/2	......	......	......	......	1 1/4	......	500	(1)	.055
1956–57	Single	5/16	11/16	......	......	......	......	1 1/2	......	500	......	.055
1956	2-Barrel	1 1/2	11/16	......	......	......	......	1 1/2	......	500	(1)	.055
1957	2-Barrel	3/4	1/2	1/16	.015	......	INDEX	1	......	500	(2)	.055
1957	4-Barrel	13/16–3/4	(3)	1/16	.015	......	INDEX	1	......	500	(2)	.055
1958–59	Single	3/16	11/16	......	......	......	......	3/4–1 3/4	......	500	......	.055
1958	2-Barrel	3/4	(3)	1/16	.015	......	1-RICH	3/4–1 3/4	......	500	(2)	.055
1958	4-Barrel	5/16	(3)	......	15/32	.067	INDEX	1/2–1 1/2	......	500	.010	7/16
1959	2-Barrel	7/8	(3)	.060	.015	......	1-RICH	3/4–1 3/4	......	500	.007	.042
1960–61	Single	3/16	11/16	......	......	......	......	1–1 1/2	......	485	......	.075
1962	Single	3/16	7/16	......	......	......	......	1–1 1/2	......	485	......	.075
1962	Six	13/64	11/16	......	......	......	......	1–1 1/2	......	485	......	.075
1962	V-8	(A)	(3)	.060	.015	3/16	INDEX	1–1 1/2	1	......	.015	.075
1963	V-8	(A)	(3)	.060	.015	3/16	INDEX	1–1 1/2	1	......	.015	.075

(3)—Bottom of sight plug.
(A)—Invert fuel bowl, turn adjusting nut until base of float is parallel with floor of bowl.

LINCOLN-CONTINENTAL

YEAR	MODEL OR TYPE	Float Level (4)	Fuel Level (4)	Bowl Vent Valve	Pump Travel Setting	Unloader	Housing	Idle Screw Turns Out	Air Bypass Turns Open	Idle Speed	Fast Idle Speed	Dashpot Plunger Clearance
1953–54	ALL	1/4	1/2	......	......	......	INDEX	1 1/4	......	460	(1)	......
1955–56	ALL	1/4	1/2	......	......	......	INDEX	1 1/4	......	500	(1)	.055
1958	ALL	11/16–9/16	(3)	1/16	.015	......	1-RICH	1 1/4	......	500	1800	.067

MERCURY

YEAR	MODEL OR TYPE	Float Level (4)	Fuel Level (4)	Bowl Vent Valve	Pump Travel Setting	Unloader	Housing	Idle Screw Turns Out	Air Bypass Turns Open	Idle Speed	Fast Idle Speed	Dashpot Plunger Clearance
1953	2-Barrel	1/4	1/2	......	......	......	INDEX	1 1/2–2	......	500	(1)	.055
1954–56	4-Barrel	1/4	1/2	......	......	......	INDEX	1 1/4	......	500	(1)	.055
1957	4-Barrel	3/4–1/2	(3)	......	......	......	INDEX	1 1/2	......	500	2250	.055
1958	2-Barrel	3/4	(3)	.067	.015	......	INDEX	3/4–1 3/4	......	500	1800	.067
1958	4-Barrel(1)	3/4–1/2	(3)	1/16	.015	......	2-RICH	1 1/2	......	500	1800	.067
1958	4-Barrel(2)	11/16–9/16	(3)	1/16	.015	......	1-RICH	1 1/2	......	500	1800	.067
1959	2-Barrel	11/16	(3)	.067	.015	......	INDEX	3/4–1 3/4	......	500	1925	.055
1960	2-Barrel	7/8	(3)	......	......	......	2-RICH	1–1 1/2	......	525	(1)	.075
1961	Single	13/64	11/16	......	......	......	......	1 1/2	......	525	......	.075
1962	Single	13/64	11/16	......	......	......	......	1 1/2	......	525	......	.075

(1)—Screw just touches lowest cam step.
(2)—1/4 turn less than Note A.
(3)—Bottom of sight plug.
(4)—Two dimensions—Primary and Secondary.
4-Barrel (1)—Used on 383 cu. in. engine.
4-Barrel (2)—Used on 430 cu. in. engine.

PLYMOUTH

YEAR	MODEL OR TYPE	Float Level (4)	Fuel Level (4)	Bowl Vent Valve	Pump Travel Setting	Unloader	Housing	Idle Screw Turns Out	Air Bypass Turns Open	Idle Speed	Fast Idle Speed	Dashpot Plunger Clearance
1962	1920-Single	(1)	11/16	3/32	......	WELL-TYPE		1	......	550	1350	......
1963	1920-Single	(1)	11/16	1/16	......	......	2-RICH	1	......	550	1500	......

(1)—Use gauge C-3903.

RAMBLER

YEAR	MODEL OR TYPE	Float Level (4)	Fuel Level (4)	Bowl Vent Valve	Pump Travel Setting	Unloader	Housing	Idle Screw Turns Out	Air Bypass Turns Open	Idle Speed	Fast Idle Speed	Dashpot Plunger Clearance
1958	4-Barrel	13/16–3/4	(2)	1/16	(3)	......	1-LEAN	1	......	550	(4)	......
1959–60	Single	3/16	23/32	......	......	......	INDEX	1 1/4	......	475	......	......
1959–60	4-Barrel	7/8–11/16	1/2–5/8	.060	(3)	.180	1-LEAN	1	......	550	1700	......
1960	2-Barrel	(5)	(2)	.060	(3)	.180	1-RICH	1	......	550	1700	......
1961	Single—Six	(5)	3/4	......	......	5/16	INDEX	1	......	550	......	......
1961	2-Barrel—V-8, 2300	(5)	(2)	.060	(3)	3/16	1-RICH	1	......	550	1700	3/32
1961	4-Barrel—V-8, 4150	(5)	(2)	.060	(3)	.180	1-LEAN	1	......	550	1700	7/64
1962	Single—1908—Six	(6)	3/4	......	(3)	5/16	INDEX	1	......	550	1700	......
1962	2 Barrel—V-8	(5)	(2)	.060	(3)	3/16	1-RICH	1	......	550	1700	3/32*
1962	4-Barrel—V-8	(5)	(2)	.060	(3)	3/16	1-LEAN	1	......	550	1700	7/64*
1963	Single	(6)	3/4	......	(3)	5/16	INDEX	1	......	550	1700	......
1963	2-Barrel	(5)	(2)	.060	(3)	3/16	1-RICH	1	......	550	1700	3/32*
1963	4-Barrel	(5)	(2)	.060	(3)	3/16	1-LEAN	1	......	550	1700	7/64*

(1)—Two dimensions.—Primary and Secondary.
(2)—To bottom of sight hole.
(3)—Tighten screw 1/4 turn beyond touch point.
(4)—Screw just touches lowest cam.
(5)—Parallel with floor.
(6)—Use gauge J-10231.
*—At curb idle.

VALIANT-LANCER

YEAR	MODEL OR TYPE	Float Level (4)	Fuel Level (4)	Bowl Vent Valve	Pump Travel Setting	Unloader	Housing	Idle Screw Turns Out	Air Bypass Turns Open	Idle Speed	Fast Idle Speed	Dashpot Plunger Clearance
1962	1920-Single	(1)	11/16	3/32	......	WELL-TYPE		1	......	550	1350	......
1963	1920-Single	(1)	11/16	1/16	......	......	2-RICH	1	......	550	1500	......

(1)—Use gauge C-3903.

HOLLEY CARBURETORS

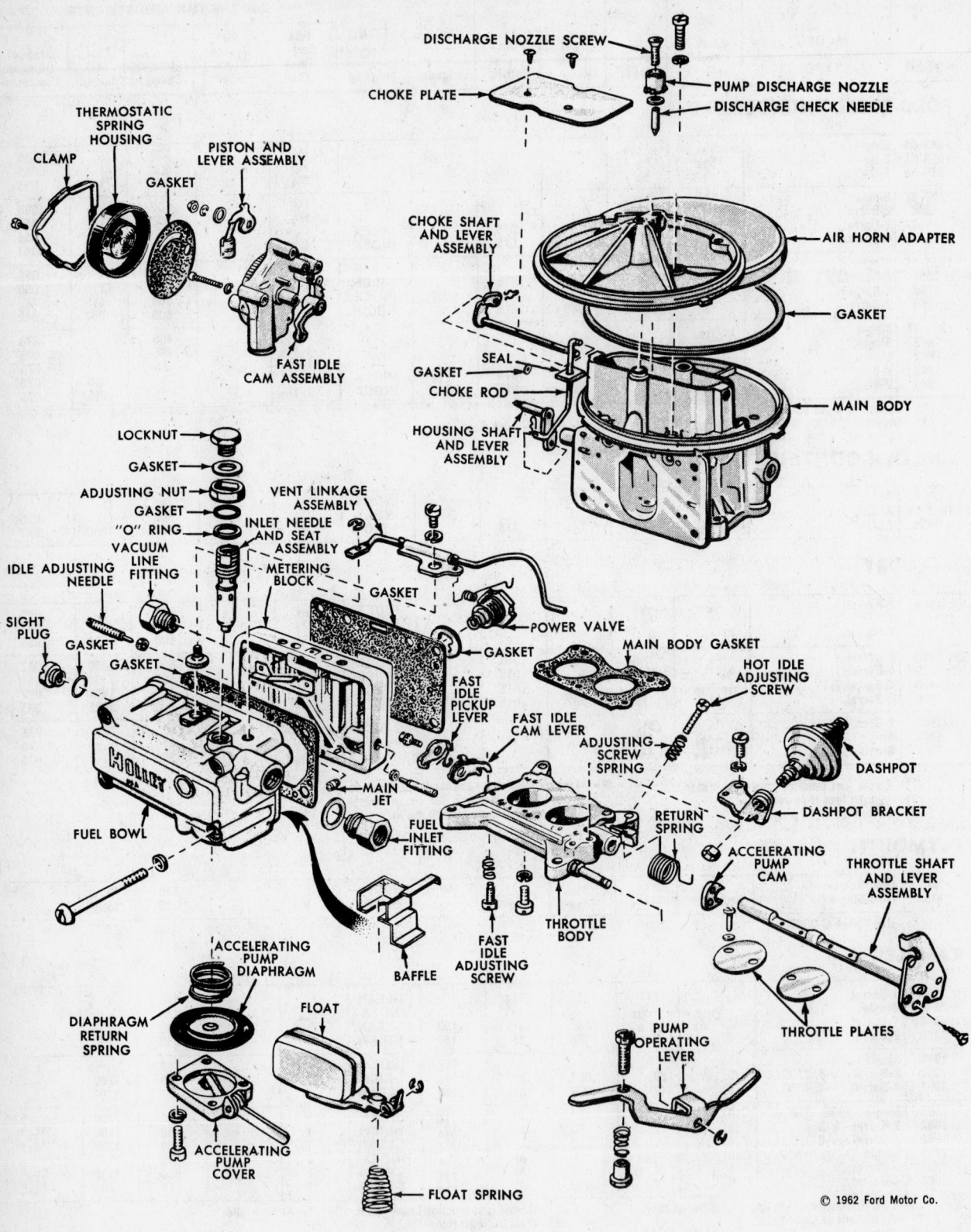

DISCHARGE NOZZLE SCREW

CHOKE PLATE

PUMP DISCHARGE NOZZLE

DISCHARGE CHECK NEEDLE

THERMOSTATIC SPRING HOUSING

CLAMP

GASKET

PISTON AND LEVER ASSEMBLY

FAST IDLE CAM ASSEMBLY

CHOKE SHAFT AND LEVER ASSEMBLY

AIR HORN ADAPTER

GASKET

GASKET
SEAL
CHOKE ROD

HOUSING SHAFT AND LEVER ASSEMBLY

MAIN BODY

LOCKNUT
GASKET
ADJUSTING NUT
GASKET
"O" RING
VACUUM LINE FITTING

VENT LINKAGE ASSEMBLY

IDLE ADJUSTING NEEDLE

INLET NEEDLE AND SEAT ASSEMBLY

METERING BLOCK

GASKET

POWER VALVE

MAIN BODY GASKET

HOT IDLE ADJUSTING SCREW

SIGHT PLUG
GASKET
GASKET

GASKET

FAST IDLE PICKUP LEVER

FAST IDLE CAM LEVER

ADJUSTING SCREW SPRING

DASHPOT

DASHPOT BRACKET

MAIN JET

FUEL INLET FITTING

RETURN SPRING

ACCELERATING PUMP CAM

THROTTLE SHAFT AND LEVER ASSEMBLY

FUEL BOWL

FAST IDLE ADJUSTING SCREW

THROTTLE BODY

THROTTLE PLATES

ACCELERATING PUMP DIAPHRAGM

BAFFLE

FLOAT

PUMP OPERATING LEVER

DIAPHRAGM RETURN SPRING

ACCELERATING PUMP COVER

FLOAT SPRING

© 1962 Ford Motor Co.

Holley—2 barrel (typical)

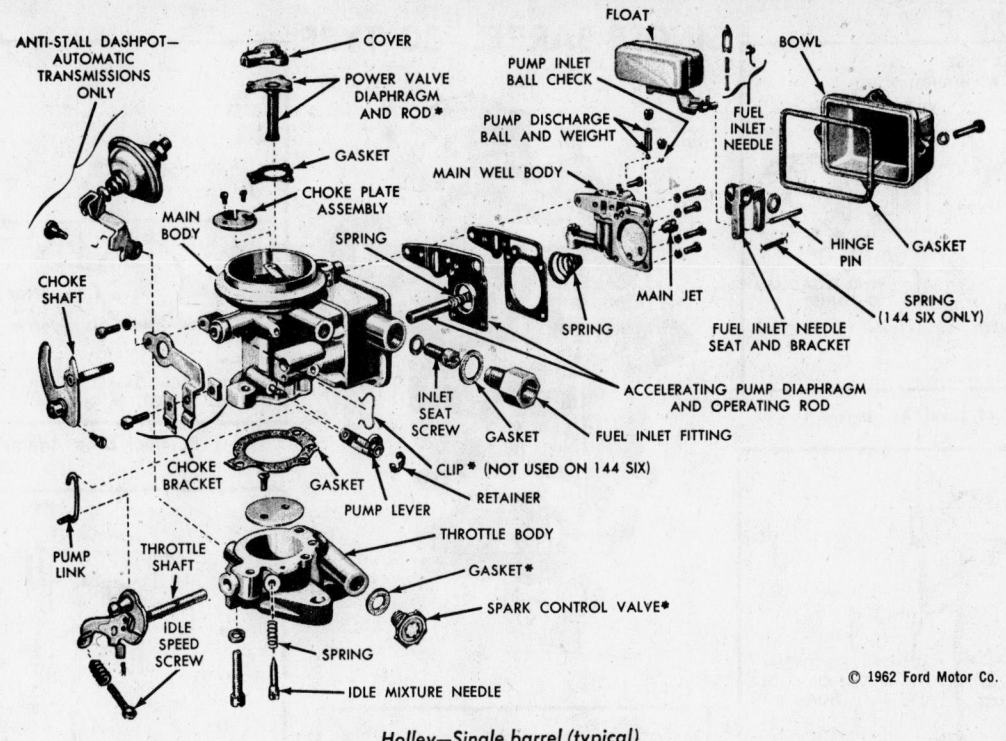

ANTI-STALL DASHPOT—
AUTOMATIC
TRANSMISSIONS
ONLY

COVER

POWER VALVE
DIAPHRAGM
AND ROD *

GASKET

CHOKE PLATE
ASSEMBLY

MAIN BODY

CHOKE SHAFT

SPRING

CHOKE BRACKET

GASKET

PUMP LEVER

PUMP LINK

THROTTLE SHAFT

IDLE SPEED SCREW

SPRING

IDLE MIXTURE NEEDLE

INLET SEAT SCREW

GASKET

FUEL INLET FITTING

CLIP * (NOT USED ON 144 SIX)

RETAINER

THROTTLE BODY

GASKET *

SPARK CONTROL VALVE *

FLOAT

PUMP INLET BALL CHECK

PUMP DISCHARGE BALL AND WEIGHT

MAIN WELL BODY

MAIN JET

SPRING

FUEL INLET NEEDLE SEAT AND BRACKET

ACCELERATING PUMP DIAPHRAGM AND OPERATING ROD

FUEL INLET NEEDLE

BOWL

HINGE PIN

GASKET

SPRING (144 SIX ONLY)

© 1962 Ford Motor Co.

Holley—Single barrel (typical)

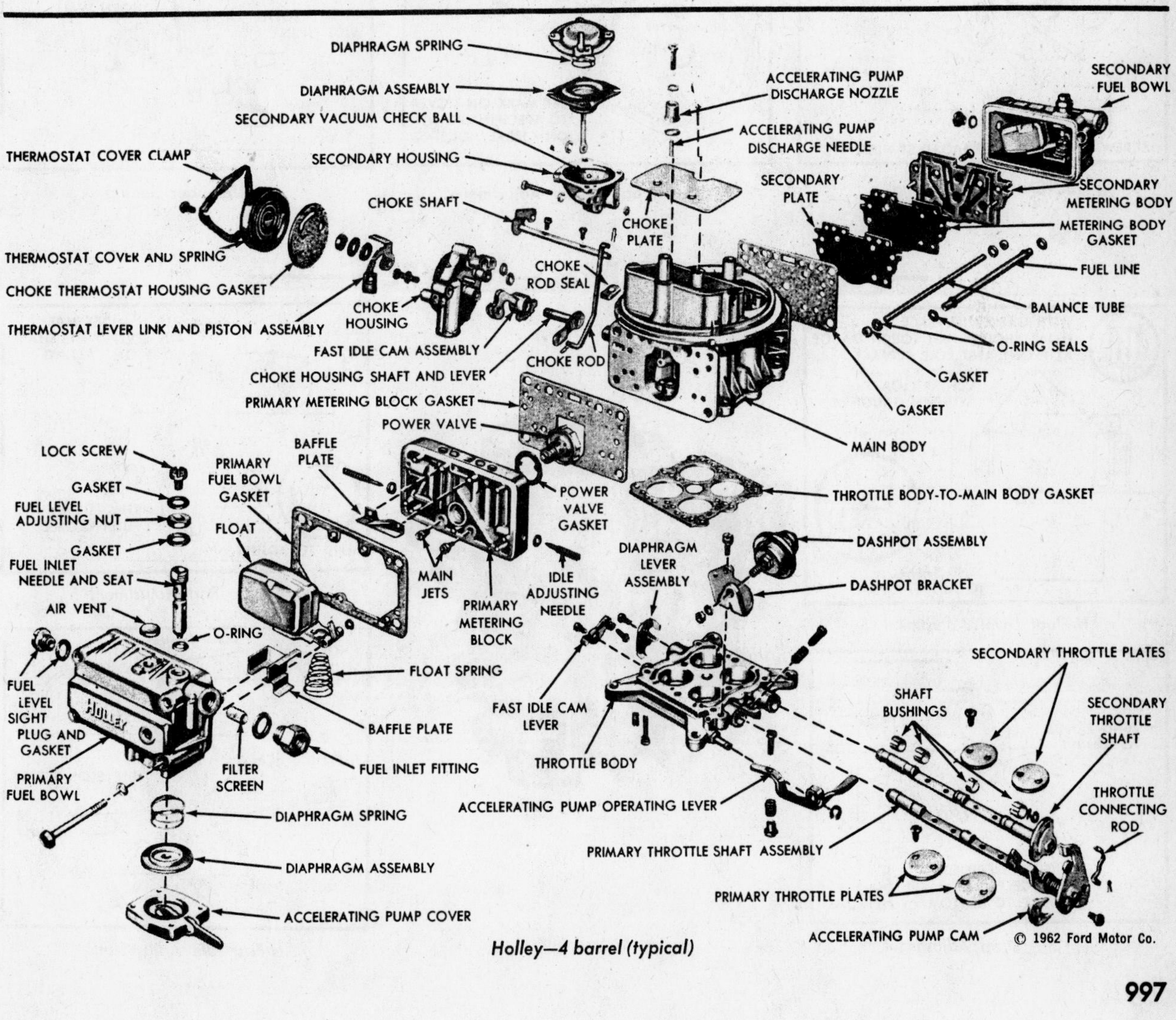

THERMOSTAT COVER CLAMP

THERMOSTAT COVER AND SPRING

CHOKE THERMOSTAT HOUSING GASKET

THERMOSTAT LEVER LINK AND PISTON ASSEMBLY

LOCK SCREW

GASKET

FUEL LEVEL ADJUSTING NUT

GASKET

FUEL INLET NEEDLE AND SEAT

AIR VENT

O-RING

FUEL LEVEL SIGHT PLUG AND GASKET

PRIMARY FUEL BOWL

DIAPHRAGM SPRING

DIAPHRAGM ASSEMBLY

ACCELERATING PUMP COVER

FILTER SCREEN

PRIMARY FUEL BOWL GASKET

FLOAT

FLOAT SPRING

BAFFLE PLATE

FUEL INLET FITTING

DIAPHRAGM SPRING

DIAPHRAGM ASSEMBLY

SECONDARY VACUUM CHECK BALL

SECONDARY HOUSING

CHOKE SHAFT

CHOKE HOUSING

FAST IDLE CAM ASSEMBLY

CHOKE HOUSING SHAFT AND LEVER

PRIMARY METERING BLOCK GASKET

POWER VALVE

BAFFLE PLATE

MAIN JETS

PRIMARY METERING BLOCK

IDLE ADJUSTING NEEDLE

POWER VALVE GASKET

FAST IDLE CAM LEVER

THROTTLE BODY

ACCELERATING PUMP OPERATING LEVER

PRIMARY THROTTLE SHAFT ASSEMBLY

CHOKE PLATE

CHOKE ROD SEAL

CHOKE ROD

ACCELERATING PUMP DISCHARGE NOZZLE

ACCELERATING PUMP DISCHARGE NEEDLE

SECONDARY PLATE

DIAPHRAGM LEVER ASSEMBLY

MAIN BODY

THROTTLE BODY-TO-MAIN BODY GASKET

DASHPOT ASSEMBLY

DASHPOT BRACKET

SHAFT BUSHINGS

PRIMARY THROTTLE PLATES

ACCELERATING PUMP CAM

SECONDARY FUEL BOWL

SECONDARY METERING BODY

METERING BODY GASKET

FUEL LINE

BALANCE TUBE

O-RING SEALS

GASKET

GASKET

SECONDARY THROTTLE PLATES

SECONDARY THROTTLE SHAFT

THROTTLE CONNECTING ROD

© 1962 Ford Motor Co.

Holley—4 barrel (typical)

ROCHESTER CARBURETORS

SINGLE-BARREL – BC TYPE

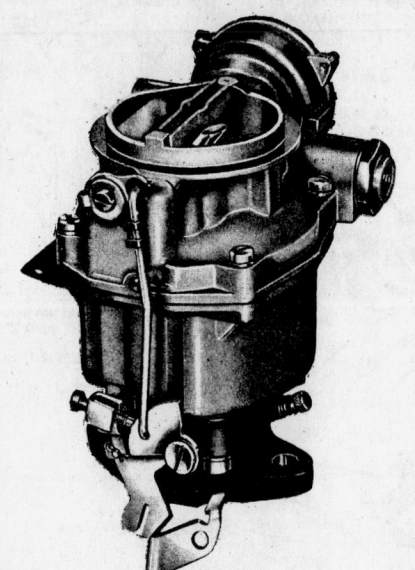

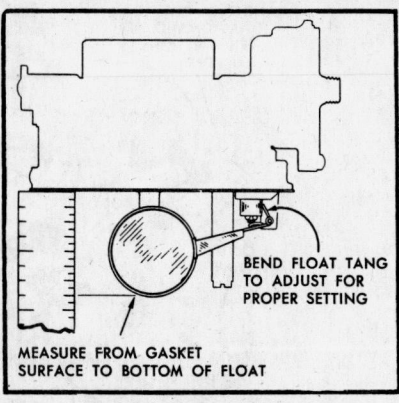

GAUGE SHOULD JUST TOUCH FLOAT AT HIGHEST POINT WITH GASKET IN PLACE

BEND FLOAT ARM TO ADJUST

FLOAT MUST BE CENTERED BETWEEN GAUGE LEGS

BC-Float Level Adjustment

BEND FLOAT TANG TO ADJUST FOR PROPER SETTING

MEASURE FROM GASKET SURFACE TO BOTTOM OF FLOAT

BC-Float Drop Adjustment

BEND ROD TO ADJUST

PLACE GAUGE BETWEEN BOTTOM EDGE OF CHOKE VALVE & AIR HORN WALL

SCREW ON SECOND STEP AGAINST HIGH STEP

BC-Choke Rod Setting

RICH LEAN
GM CARBURETOR
ROCHESTER PRODUCTS
MADE IN USA

SET MARK ON COVER TO SPECIFIED POINT ON CHOKE HOUSING

BC-Automatic Choke Adjustment

WITH THROTTLE VALVE WIDE OPEN

PLACE GAUGE BETWEEN BOTTOM EDGE OF CHOKE VALVE AND AIR HORN WALL

BC-Unloader Setting

SINGLE-BARREL – H TYPE

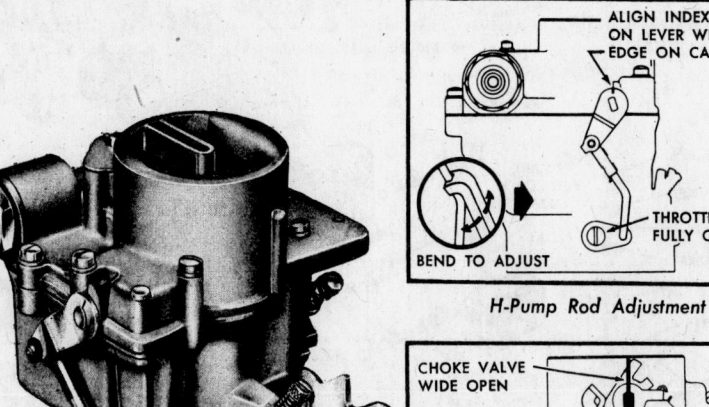

WITH GASKET IN PLACE, FLOAT SHOULD JUST TOUCH GAUGE AT FRONT AND REAR SURFACE

CENTER FLOATS BETWEEN GAUGE LEGS

BEND TANG TO ADJUST

H-Float Level Adjustment

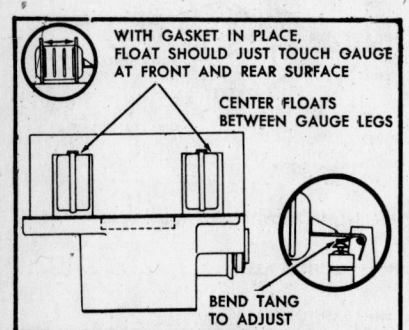

ALIGN INDEX MARK ON LEVER WITH SHARP EDGE ON CASTING

THROTTLE VALVES FULLY CLOSED

BEND TO ADJUST

H-Pump Rod Adjustment

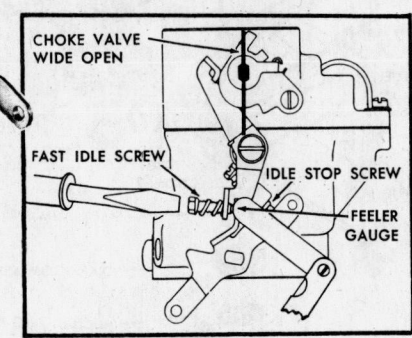

BEND TANGS TO ADJUST

MEASURE SPECIFIED DISTANCE FROM GASKET SURFACE TO BOTTOM OF FLOAT

H-Float Drop Adjustment

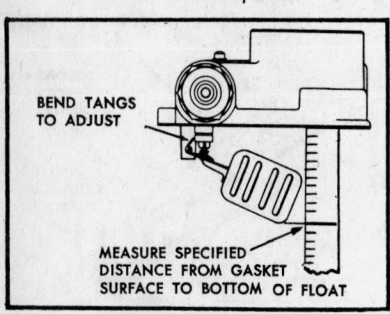

CHOKE VALVE WIDE OPEN

FAST IDLE SCREW

IDLE STOP SCREW

FEELER GAUGE

H-Fast Idle Adjustment

FOUR-BARREL – 4GC TYPE

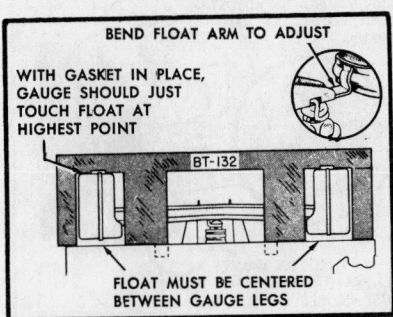

BEND FLOAT ARM TO ADJUST

WITH GASKET IN PLACE, GAUGE SHOULD JUST TOUCH FLOAT AT HIGHEST POINT

BT-132

FLOAT MUST BE CENTERED BETWEEN GAUGE LEGS

4GC-Float Level Adjustment

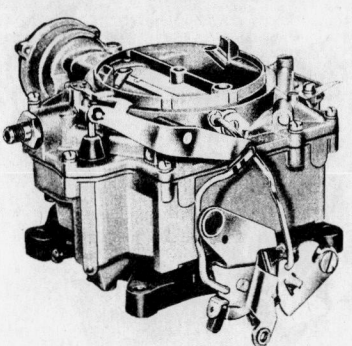

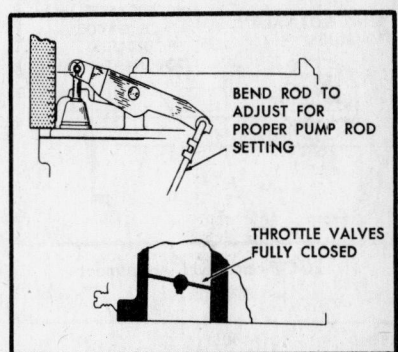

BEND FLOAT TANG TO ADJUST FOR PROPER SETTING

MEASURE FROM GASKET SURFACE TO BOTTOM OF FLOAT

4GC-Float Drop Adjustment

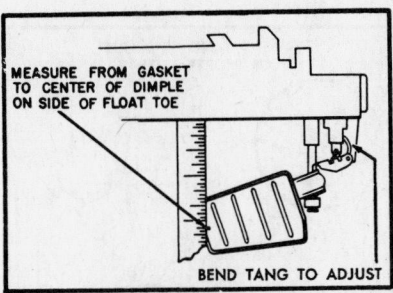

MEASURE FROM GASKET TO CENTER OF DIMPLE ON SIDE OF FLOAT TOE

BEND TANG TO ADJUST

4GC-Float Drop Adjustment

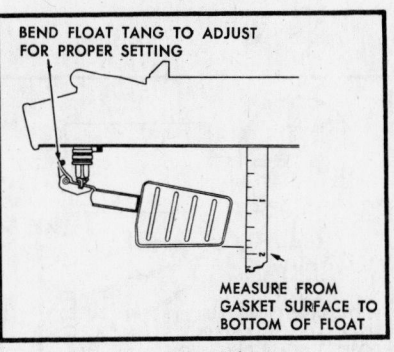

BEND FLOAT TANG TO ADJUST FOR PROPER SETTING

MEASURE FROM GASKET SURFACE TO BOTTOM OF FLOAT

4GC-Float Drop Adjustment

BEND ROD TO ADJUST FOR PROPER PUMP ROD SETTING

THROTTLE VALVES FULLY CLOSED

4GC-Pump Rod Setting

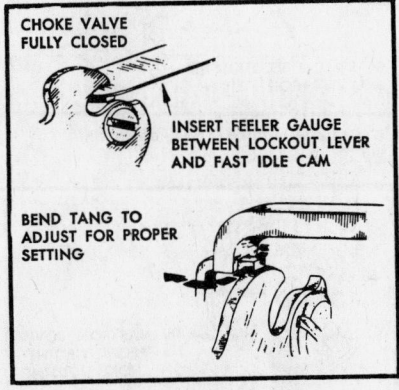

CHOKE VALVE FULLY CLOSED

INSERT FEELER GAUGE BETWEEN LOCKOUT LEVER AND FAST IDLE CAM

BEND TANG TO ADJUST FOR PROPER SETTING

4GC-Secondary Lockout Adjustment

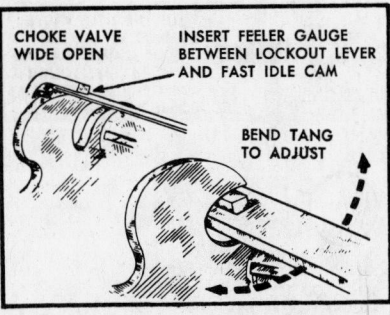

CHOKE VALVE WIDE OPEN

INSERT FEELER GAUGE BETWEEN LOCKOUT LEVER AND FAST IDLE CAM

BEND TANG TO ADJUST

4GC-Secondary Contour Adjustment

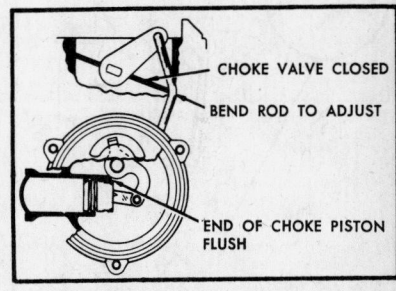

CHOKE VALVE CLOSED

BEND ROD TO ADJUST

END OF CHOKE PISTON FLUSH

4GC-Intermediate Choke Rod Adjustment

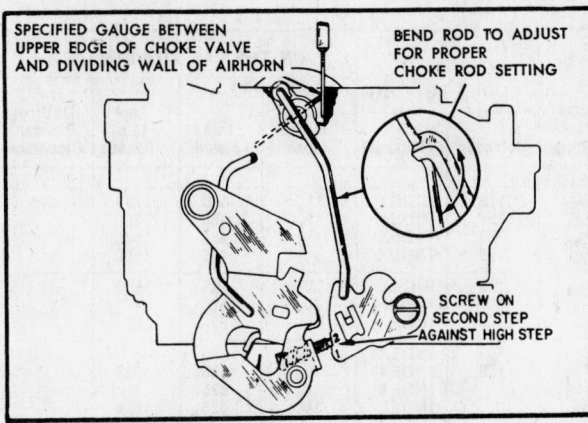

SPECIFIED GAUGE BETWEEN UPPER EDGE OF CHOKE VALVE AND DIVIDING WALL OF AIRHORN

BEND ROD TO ADJUST FOR PROPER CHOKE ROD SETTING

SCREW ON SECOND STEP AGAINST HIGH STEP

4GC-Choke Rod Adjustment

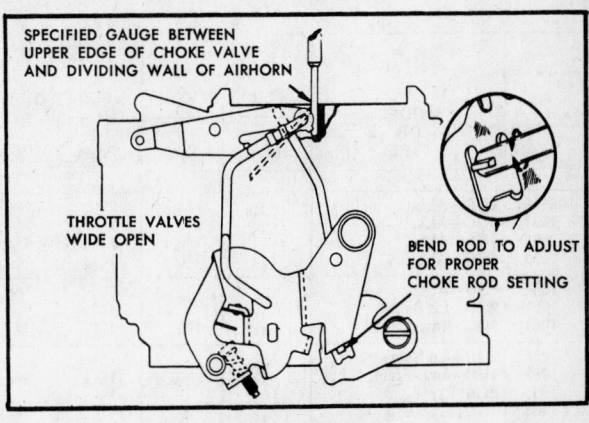

SPECIFIED GAUGE BETWEEN UPPER EDGE OF CHOKE VALVE AND DIVIDING WALL OF AIRHORN

THROTTLE VALVES WIDE OPEN

BEND ROD TO ADJUST FOR PROPER CHOKE ROD SETTING

4GC Unloader Adjustment

ROCHESTER CARBURETORS

TWO-BARREL 2GC TYPE

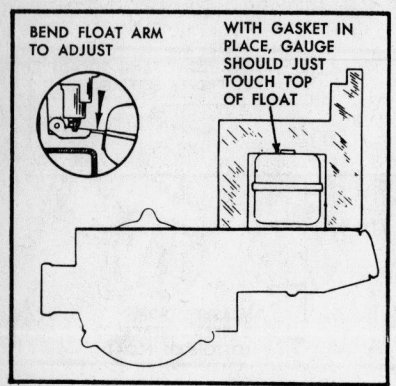

2GC-Float Level Adjustment

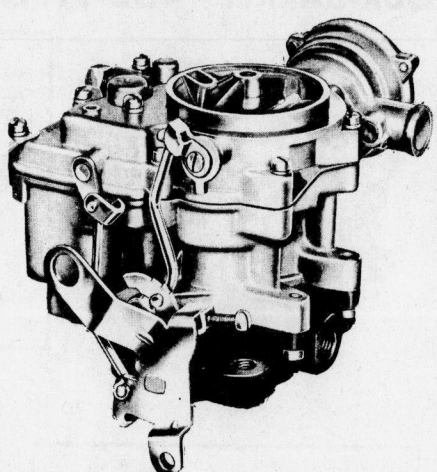

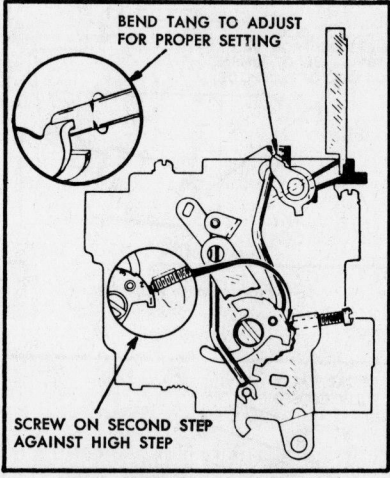

2GC-Idle Vent Adjustment

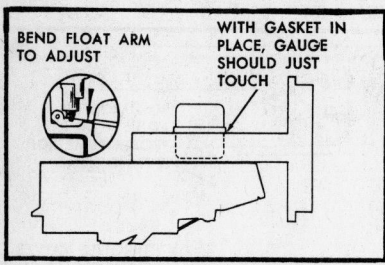

2GC-Float Level Adjustment

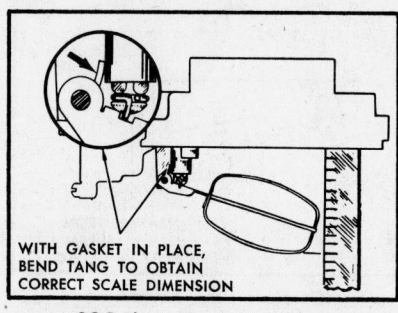

2GC-Float Drop Adjustment

2GC-Choke Rod Adjustment

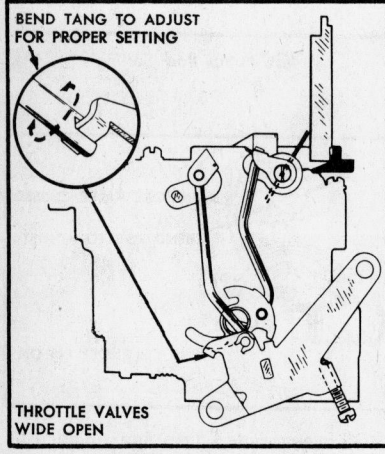

2GC-Unloader Adjustment

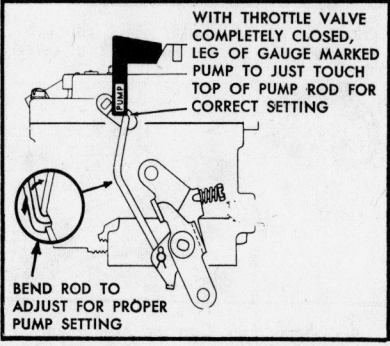

2GC-Pump Rod Adjustment

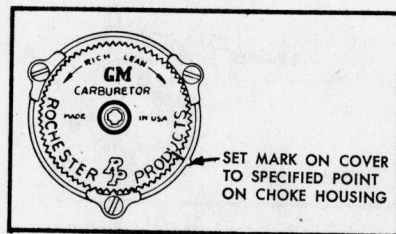

2GC-Automatic Choke Adjustment

YEAR	MODEL OR TYPE	FLOAT LEVEL		FLOAT DROP		Pump Travel Setting	CHOKE SETTING		ON THE CAR ADJUSTMENTS			
		Prim.	Sec.	Prim.	Sec.		Unloader	Housing	Idle Screw Turns Open	Idle Speed	Fast Idle Speed	Dashpot Plunger Clearance
1955–60	4GC—ALL	1 35/64	1 35/64	2 1/4	2 1/4	1 3/32	.115	INDEX	1 1/4	450	1700	.028
1957	4GC—ALL	1 3/8	1 3/8	1 13/16	1 13/16	1 1/64	.129	INDEX	1 1/2	485	1500	(1)
1958	4GC—ALL	1 3/8	1 3/8	1 5/16	1 5/16	1 1/64	.129	INDEX	1 1/2	485	1500	(1)
1959	4GC—ALL	9/32	1 3/8	1 3/64	1 5/16	1 1/64	.129	INDEX	1 1/2	485	1500	(1)
1960	4GC—ALL	9/64	1 3/8	1 3/8	1 5/16	1 1/64	.129	INDEX	1 1/2	485	1500	(1)
1961	2GC—Le Sabre	11/16		1 29/32		1 1/64	.081	1-RICH	1 1/8	525	......	......
1961	4GC—Inv.-Elect.	9/64	1 3/8	1 7/16	1 5/16	1 1/64	.129	INDEX	1 1/2	525	625	......
1962	2GC—Le Sabre	11/16	......	1 29/32	......	1 29/32	1/4	INDEX	1 1/2	525	......	......
1962	4GC—Inv.-Elect.	9/64	9/64	1 7/16	1 5/16	1 1/64	.129	INDEX	1 1/2	525	625	......
1963	2GC	11/16	......	1 29/32	......	1 29/32	1/4	INDEX	1 1/2	525	......	......
1963	4GC	9/64	9/64	1 7/16	1 5/16	1 1/64	1/8	INDEX	1 1/2	525	625	......

(1)—By trial.

YEAR	MODEL OR TYPE	FLOAT LEVEL Prim.	FLOAT LEVEL Sec.	FLOAT DROP Prim.	FLOAT DROP Sec.	Pump Travel Setting	CHOKE SETTING Unloader	CHOKE SETTING Housing	ON THE CAR ADJUSTMENTS: Idle Screws Turn Open	Idle Speed	Fast Idle Speed	Dashpot Plunger Clearance
BUICK SPECIAL												
1961	2GC—ALL	1 17/64	......	1 29/32	......	1 3/32	.157	INDEX	1½	525	650	......
	4GC—ALL	9/64	1 3/8	1 9/16	1 7/16	61/64	.128	INDEX	1½	525	625	......
1962	2GC—V-6	1 17/64	......	1 29/32	......	3/4	.157	INDEX	1½	525	650	......
	2GC—V-8	1 17/64	......	1 29/32	......	1 3/32	.157	INDEX	1½	525	650	......
	4GC	9/64	1 3/8	7/16	5/16	1 29/32	.129	INDEX	1½	525	625	......
1963	2GC—V-6	1 17/64	......	1 29/32	......	3/4	.157	INDEX	1½	525	650	......
	2GC—V-8	1 17/64	......	1 29/32	......	1 3/32	.157	INDEX	1½	525	650	......
	4GC	9/64	1 3/8	1 9/16	1 9/32	61/64	.129	INDEX	1½	525	625	......

CADILLAC

YEAR	MODEL OR TYPE	FLOAT LEVEL Prim.	FLOAT LEVEL Sec.	FLOAT DROP Prim.	FLOAT DROP Sec.	Pump Travel Setting	CHOKE SETTING Unloader	CHOKE SETTING Housing	Idle Screws Turn Open	Idle Speed	Fast Idle Speed	Dashpot Plunger Clearance
1953	4GC—ALL	1 9/16	1 9/16	2 1/4	2 1/4	15/16	.067	1-RICH	1-1¼	450	1700	......
1954	4GC—ALL	1 19/32	1 19/32	2 1/4	2 1/4	61/64	.125	INDEX	1-1¼	450	.026	......
1955	4GC—ALL	1 19/32	1 19/32	2 1/4	2 1/4	63/64	.125	INDEX	1½-2½	450	2000	......
1956	4GC—ALL	1 19/32	1 19/32	2 1/8	2 1/8	63/64	.125	1-RICH	1½-2½	450	.040	(3)
1957	4GC—ALL	1 3/8	1 3/8	1 15/16	1 15/16	15/16	.125	INDEX	1½-2½	470	.020	(3)
1958	4GC—ALL	1 3/8	1 3/8	1 15/16	1 15/16	29/32	.125	INDEX	1½-2½	500	.023	(3)
1958	2GC-(1)*	1 25/64	......	1 29/32	......	15/16	.163	2-RICH	1½	500	1700	(3)
1958	2GC-(2)■	1 25/64	......	1 29/32	......	15/16	......	......	......	......	......	......
1959-60	2GC-(1)*	63/64	......	1 29/32	......	1 3/16	.163	INDEX	1½	500	1700	(3)
1959-60	2GC-(2)■	23/32	......	1 29/32	......	7/8	......	......	......	......	......	......
1959-60	4GC—ALL	9/32	1 3/8	(1)	1 5/16	29/32	.125	1-RICH	1½-2½	500	1700	(3)
1961	4GC	15/64	1 3/8	(2)	1 5/16	29/32	.125	1-RICH	1½-2½	500	1700	(3)
1962	4GC	15/64	1 3/8	Note B	1 5/16	29/32	.125	1-RICH	1½-2½	500	1700	(3)
1963	4GC	15/64	1 3/8	Note B	1 5/16	29/32	.125	1-RICH	1½-2½	500	1700	(3)

(1)—Power Piston up—63/64, Power Piston down—1½.
(2)—Power Piston up—1 3/32, Power Piston down—1½.
(3)—By trial.

*—1958-60—GC2-(1)—Is center carburetor on the three 2-barrel application.
■—GC2-(2)—Are the front and rear carburetors in this application.
Note B—Screw on 2nd step with gauge.

CHEVROLET

YEAR	MODEL OR TYPE	FLOAT LEVEL Prim.	FLOAT LEVEL Sec.	FLOAT DROP Prim.	FLOAT DROP Sec.	Pump Travel Setting	CHOKE SETTING Unloader	CHOKE SETTING Housing	Idle Screws Turn Open	Idle Speed	Fast Idle Speed	Dashpot Plunger Clearance
1953	BC-7004478	1 9/32	......	1 3/4	......	......	.166	INDEX	2½	475	......	......
	BC-7004915	1 9/32		1 3/4			.230	INDEX	2½	475		
1954	BC-7005921	1 9/32	......	1 3/4	......	......	.230	INDEX	2½	475	......	......
	BC-7005922	1 9/32		1 3/4			.230	2-LEAN	2½	475		
1955	2GC—ALL	1 5/32	......	1 29/32		15/16	.360	INDEX	1½	475	......	......
	BC-7007180	1 9/32	......	1 3/4		......	.230	2-LEAN	2½	475	......	......
	BC-7007181	1 9/32	......	1 3/4		......	.230	INDEX	2½	475	......	......
1956	2GC—ALL	1 1/4	......	1 29/32	......	27/64	.360	INDEX	1½	475	......	......
	BC-7009254	1 9/32	......	1 3/4	......	......	.230	2-LEAN	2½	475	......	......
	BC-7009255	1 9/32	......	1 3/4	......	......	.230	INDEX	2½	475	......	......
	4GC-7008737	1 5/8	1 5/8	2 1/4	2 1/4	1 1/16	.235	1-LEAN	1½	500	......	......
1957	2GC—ALL	1 1/4	......	1 29/32	......	57/64	.360	INDEX	1½	475	......	(1)
	4GC—ALL	1 5/8	1 5/8	2 1/4	2 1/4	1 1/16	.235	1-LEAN	1½	500	......	(1)
	BC—ALL	1 9/32	......	1 3/4	......	......	.230	3-LEAN	1½	475	......	......
1958	2GC—ALL	1 29/32	......	57/64	......	57/64	.360	INDEX	1½	475	(A)	(1)
	4GC-7011108	1 5/8	1 11/16	2 1/4	2 1/4	1 1/16	.235	INDEX	1½	500	(A-1)	(1)
	4GC-7012128	1 5/8	1 11/16	2 1/4	2 1/4	1 1/16	.235	1-LEAN	1½	500	(A-1)	(1)
	BC—ALL	1 9/32	......	1 3/4	......	......	.230	INDEX	1½	475	......	......
1959-60	2GC—ALL	1 23/64	......	1 29/32	......	57/64	.230	INDEX	1½	500	......	(1)
	4GC—ALL	1 43/64	2 1/4	1 47/64	2 1/4	1 1/16	.235	INDEX	1¼	500	......	(1)
	BC—ALL	1 9/32	......	1 3/4	......	......	.230	INDEX	1½	475	......	......
	BC-(1)*	1 21/64	......	1 29/32	......	15/16	.360	INDEX	1½	500	......	......
	BC-(2)■	1 27/64	......	1 29/32	......	15/16	......	......	......	......	......	......
1961	BC—ALL	1 9/32	......	1 3/4	......	......	.230	(2)	1½	475	......	......
1961	2GC—ALL	1 23/64	......	1 29/32	......	57/64	.360	(D)	2½	500	......	(3)
1961	4GC—ALL	1 33/64	1 37/64	2 1/4	2 1/4	1 1/16	.235	INDEX	1½	500	......	(3)
1961	GC-(1)*	1 5/16	......	1 29/32	1 29/32	15/16	.360	INDEX	1½	475	......	......
1961	GC-(2)■	1 25/64	......	1 29/32	1 29/32	15/16	......	......	......	......	......	......
1962	BC—ALL	1 9/32	......	1 3/4	......	......	.230	Note C	1½	475	......	......
1962	2GC—ALL	1 23/64	......	1 29/32	......	57/64	.360	(D)	2½	500	......	......
1962	4GC—ALL	1 33/64	1 37/64	2 1/4	2 1/4	1 1/16	.250	INDEX	1½	500	......	(3)
1962	GC-(1)*	1 5/16	......	1 29/32	1 29/32	15/16	.360	INDEX	1½	475	......	(3)
1962	GC-(2)■	1 25/64	......	1 29/32	1 29/32	15/16	......	......	......	......	......	......
1963	BC—ALL	1 9/32	......	1 3/4	......	......	.230	Note C	1½	475	......	......
	2GC—ALL	1 23/64	......	1 29/32	......	57/64	.360	(D)	2½	500	......	......
	4GC—ALL	1 33/64	1 37/64	2 1/4	2 1/4	1 1/16	.250	INDEX	1½	500	......	(3)
	GC-(1)*	1 5/16	......	1 29/32	1 29/32	15/16	.360	INDEX	1½	475	......	(3)
	GC-(2)■	1 25/64	......	1 29/32	1 29/32	15/16	......	......	......	......	......	......

(1)—Turbo-glide only—.060.
(2)—Std. trans. 1-rich; automatic trans. 2-rich.
(3)—By trial.
*—Is center carburetor on the three 2-barrel application.
■—Are the front and rear carburetors with this application.

(C)—Std. trans. 1-rich, automatic trans. index.
(D)—Std. trans. 1-lean, automatic trans. index.
(A)—Screw on 2nd step with gauge.
(A-1)—Set on 2nd step.

ROCHESTER CARBURETORS

YEAR	MODEL OR TYPE	FLOAT LEVEL		FLOAT DROP		Pump Travel Setting	CHOKE SETTING		ON THE CAR ADJUSTMENTS			
		Prim.	Sec.	Prim.	Sec.		Unloader	Housing	Idle Screw Turns Open	Idle Speed	Fast Idle Speed	Dashpot Plunger Clearance

CHEVY II

YEAR	MODEL OR TYPE	Prim.	Sec.	Prim.	Sec.	Pump	Unloader	Housing	Idle Screw	Idle Speed	Fast Idle	Dashpot
1962	4 Cyl-B	19/32	....	1 3/4	....	....	.250	(2)	1½	500	(1)....	....
	6 Cyl-BC	19/32	....	1 3/4	....	....	.350	....	1½	500	(3)	....
1963	6 Cyl.-BC, PG	19/32	....	1 3/4	....	....	.350	....	1½	500	(3)	....
	6 Cyl.-BC, Std	19/32	....	1 3/4	....	....	.350	....	1½	500	(3)	....

(1)—With .035 clearance at choke valve—set on next to high step.

(2)—Std. trans. 1-rich, auto. trans. index.

(3)—With .060 clearance at choke valve—Set on next to high step.

CORVAIR

YEAR	MODEL OR TYPE	Prim.	Sec.	Prim.	Sec.	Pump	Unloader	Housing	Idle Screw	Idle Speed	Fast Idle	Dashpot
1960	H	1 13/64	....	1 3/4	....	INDEX	.250	INDEX	(1)	500	(1)	....
1961	H	1 13/64	....	1 3/4	(1)	INDEX	.250	INDEX	(1)	500	(1)	....
1962	H	1 13/64	....	1 3/4	(1)	INDEX	.250	INDEX	1½	500	(1)	....
1963	H	1 13/64	....	1 3/4	(1)	INDEX	.250	INDEX	1½	500	(1)	....

(1)—See Corvair car section for balancing and linkage adjustments.

OLDSMOBILE

YEAR	MODEL OR TYPE	Prim.	Sec.	Prim.	Sec.	Pump	Unloader	Housing	Idle Screw	Idle Speed	Fast Idle	Dashpot
1953	4GC	1 9/16	1 9/16	2 1/4	2 1/4	1 1/16	.092	INDEX	1½	425	1450	.028
1944-5	4GC	1 5/8	1 5/8	2 1/4	2 1/4	1 1/16	.115	INDEX	1½	425	1450	.028
1955	2GC	19/32	....	1 29/32	....	15/16	.141	INDEX	1½	400	1500	.028
1956	4GC	1 5/8	1 5/8	2 1/4	2 1/4	1 1/16	.115	1-LEAN	1½	425	1450	.020
1956	2GC	1 7/16	....	2	....	3/16	.115	INDEX	1½	425	1650	.028
1957	4GC	1 5/8	1 5/8	2 1/4	2 1/4	1 3/64	.092	INDEX	1½	450	1550	.020
1958	4GC	3/4	1 3/8	1 1/2	15/16	1 3/64	.115	INDEX	1½	460	1550	.020
1958	2GC	1 25/64	....	1 29/64	....	15/16	.140	1-LEAN	1½	460	1550	.050
1959-61	4GC	3/8	3/8	1 1/2	15/16	1 1/64	.115	INDEX	1½	460	1600	.020
1959-61	2GC	1 1/16	....	1 3/4	....	1 7/16	.163	1-RICH	1½-2	550	1900	.050
1962	2GC	1/2	....	1 3/4	....	1 7/16	.150	1-LEAN	1½-2	550	1900	.050
1962	4GC	9/32	1 3/8	1 1/2	15/16	1 1/64	.115	INDEX	1½	460	1600	.020
1962	4GC	9/32	1 3/8	1 1/2	15/16	1 1/64	.115	INDEX	1½	460	1600	.020
1963	4GC	9/32	1 3/8	1 1/2	15/16	1 1/64	.115	INDEX	1½	460	1600	.020
1963	4GC	9/32	1 3/8	1 1/2	1 15/16	1 1/64	.115	INDEX	1½	460	1600	.020

OLDSMOBILE F-85

YEAR	MODEL OR TYPE	Prim.	Sec.	Prim.	Sec.	Pump	Unloader	Housing	Idle Screw	Idle Speed	Fast Idle	Dashpot
1961	2GC	35/64	....	1 29/32	....	59/64	.250	1-LEAN	1½	550	(1)	.020
1962	2GC—Early	35/64	....	1 29/32	....	59/64	.250	INDEX	1½	550	(1)	.020
1962	2GC—Late	25/32	....	1 29/32	....	57/64	.250	INDEX	1½	550	(1)	.020
1963	2GC–Late	25/32	....	1 29/32	....	59/64	.250	INDEX	1½	550	(1)	.020

(1)—Fast idle is automatic with proper curb idle.

ROCHESTER CARBURETORS

PONTIAC

YEAR	MODEL OR TYPE	FLOAT LEVEL Prim.	FLOAT LEVEL Sec.	FLOAT DROP Prim.	FLOAT DROP Sec.	Pump Travel Setting	CHOKE SETTING Unloader	CHOKE SETTING Housing	ON THE CAR ADJUSTMENTS Idle Screws Turn Open	Idle Speed	Fast Idle Speed	Dashpot Plunger Clearance
1955	2GC	1 15/64	......	1 29/32	......	15/64	.163	INDEX	1½	450	......	......
1955	4GC	1 19/32	1 19/32	2¼	1 19/32	1 1/16	.115	INDEX	1½	450	.052(1)	......
1956	2GC	1 15/64	......	1 29/32	......	57/64	.163	INDEX	1½	450	......	......
1956	4GC	1 19/32	1 19/32	2¼	1 19/32	61/64	.115	INDEX	1½	450	.052(1)	......
1957	2GC	1 15/64	......	1 29/32	......	53/64	.163	INDEX	1½	470	.062(1)	......
1957	4GC	1 3/8	1 3/8	1 13/16	1 13/16	1 5/16	.115	INDEX	1½	470	.062(1)	......
1957	2GC-(1)*	1 15/64	......	1 29/32	......	57/64	.163	INDEX	1½	500	.061(1)	......
1957	2GC-(2)■	1 5/16	......	1 29/32	......	1 5/16	......	......	......	......	......	......
1958	2GC	1 1/16	......	1 29/32	......	1 23/64	.163	INDEX	1½	500	.061(1)	......
1958	2GC-(1)*	1 17/64	......	1 29/32	......	57/64	.163	INDEX	1½	500	.061(1)	......
1958	2GC-(2)■	1 13/32	......	1 29/32	......	1 5/16	......	......	......	......	......	......
1959	2GC●	5/8	......	1 29/32	......	1 5/16	.163	INDEX	1½	500	2700	.093
1959	2GC△	11/16	......	1 29/32	......	1 3/16	.163	INDEX	1½	500	......	.093
1959	2GC-(1)*	23/32	......	1 29/32	......	1 3/16	.163	INDEX	1½	500	.056(1)	......
1959	2GC-(2)■	23/32	......	1 29/32	......	55/64	......	......	......	500	......	......
1960	2GC●	5/8	......	1¾	......	1 21/64	.163	INDEX	1½-2½	500	2700	.093
1960	2GC△	11/16	......	1¾	......	1 1/8	.163	INDEX	1½-2½	500	......	.093
1960	2GC-(1)*	23/32	......	1¾	......	55/64	.163	INDEX	1½	500	.056(1)	......
1960	2GC-(2)■	23/32	......	1¾	......	55/64	......	......	......	......	......	......
1961	2GC●	5/8	......	1¾	......	1 21/64	.163	INDEX	1½	500	......	.064
1961	2GC△	11/16	......	1¾	......	1 1/8	.163	INDEX	1½	500	......	.094
1961	2GC-(1)*	23/32	......	1¾	......	1 1/8	.163	INDEX	1½	500	.056(1)	......
1961	2GC-(2)■	23/32	......	1¾	......	55/64	......	......	......	......	......	......
1962	2GC●	5/8	......	1¾	......	1 21/64	.163	INDEX	1½	500	......	.064
1962	2GC△	11/16	......	1¾	......	1 1/8	.163	INDEX	1½	500	......	.094
1962	2GC*	23/32	......	1¾	......	1 1/8	.163	INDEX	1½	500	.056(1)	......
1962	2GC■	23/32	......	1¾	......	55/64	......	......	......	......	......	......
1963	2GC●	5/8	......	1¾	......	1 21/64	.163	INDEX	1½	500	......	.064
1963	2GC△	11/16	......	1¾	......	1 1/8	.163	INDEX	1½	500	......	.094
1963	2GC*	23/32	......	1¾	......	1 1/8	.163	INDEX	1½	500	.056(1)	......
1963	2GC■	23/32	......	1¾	......	55/64	......	INDEX	1½	......	......	......

Note (1)—Set cam on #2 step.
●—2GC—With 1 11/16″ throat.
△—2GC—With 1 7/16″ throat.
*—2GC-(1)—Is center carburetor on three 2-barrel application.
■—2GC-(2)—Are the front and rear carburetors with this application.

TEMPEST

YEAR	MODEL OR TYPE	FLOAT LEVEL Prim.	FLOAT LEVEL Sec.	FLOAT DROP Prim.	FLOAT DROP Sec.	Pump Travel Setting	CHOKE SETTING Unloader	CHOKE SETTING Housing	ON THE CAR ADJUSTMENTS Idle Screws Turn Open	Idle Speed	Fast Idle Speed	Dashpot Plunger Clearance
1961	B & BC	1 9/32	......	1¾	......	......	.161	INDEX	1½	700	......	.064
1961	4GC	1 21/64	1 21/64	1¼	1¼	1 5/16	.152	(2)	1½	700*	(1)	.085
1961	2GC	1 17/64	......	1 29/32	......	1 3/32	.157	INDEX	1½	600	.055	.010
1962	B & BC	1 9/32	......	1¾	......	......	.161	INDEX	1½	700	......	.064
1962	4GC	1 21/64	1 21/64	1¾	1¾	1 5/16	.152	(2)	1½	700*	(1)	.085
1962	4GC	9/64	1 3/8	1 9/16	1 9/32	61/64	.128	(2)	1½	600	(1)	.010
1963	4GC	9/64	1 3/8	1 9/16	1 9/32	61/64	.128	(2)	1½	600	(1)	.010

Note (1)—Auto. Trans. 3000. Std. Trans. 2800.
(2)—Std. trans., index, aut. trans., 1-rich.
*—Auto trans. 600 "DR", std. trans. 700 neutral.

ROCHESTER CARBURETORS

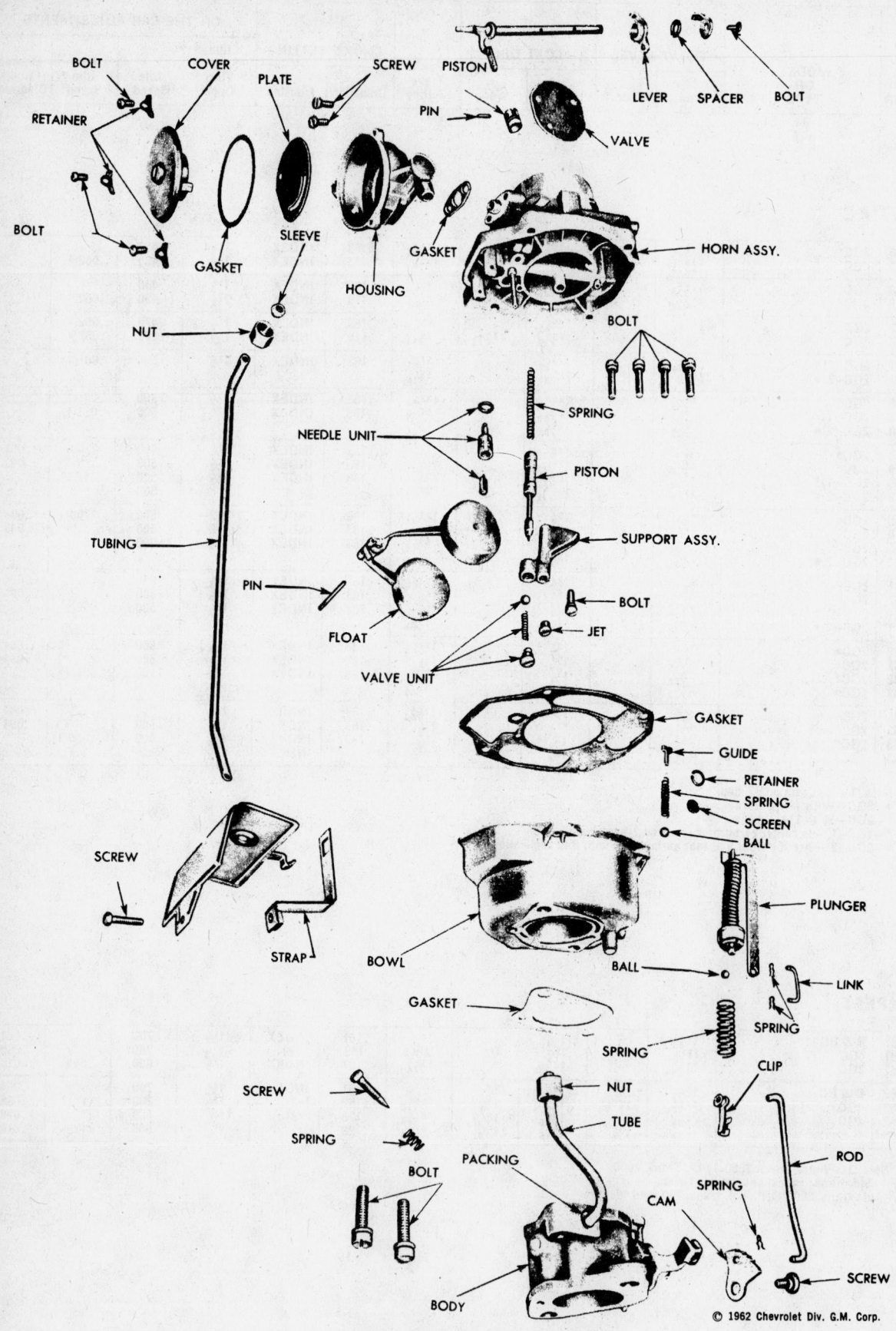

Rochester—BC single barrel (typical)

© 1962 Chevrolet Div. G.M. Corp.

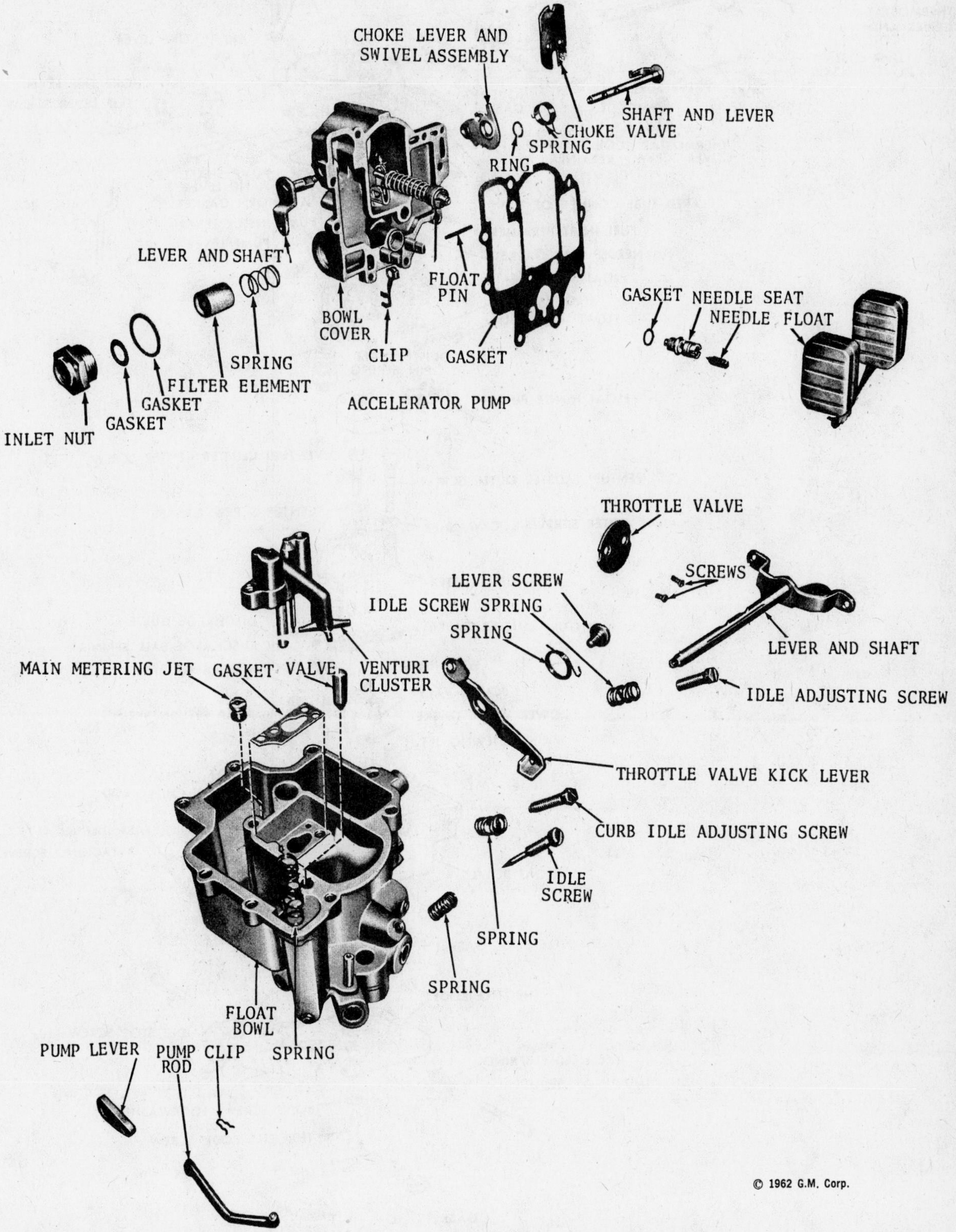

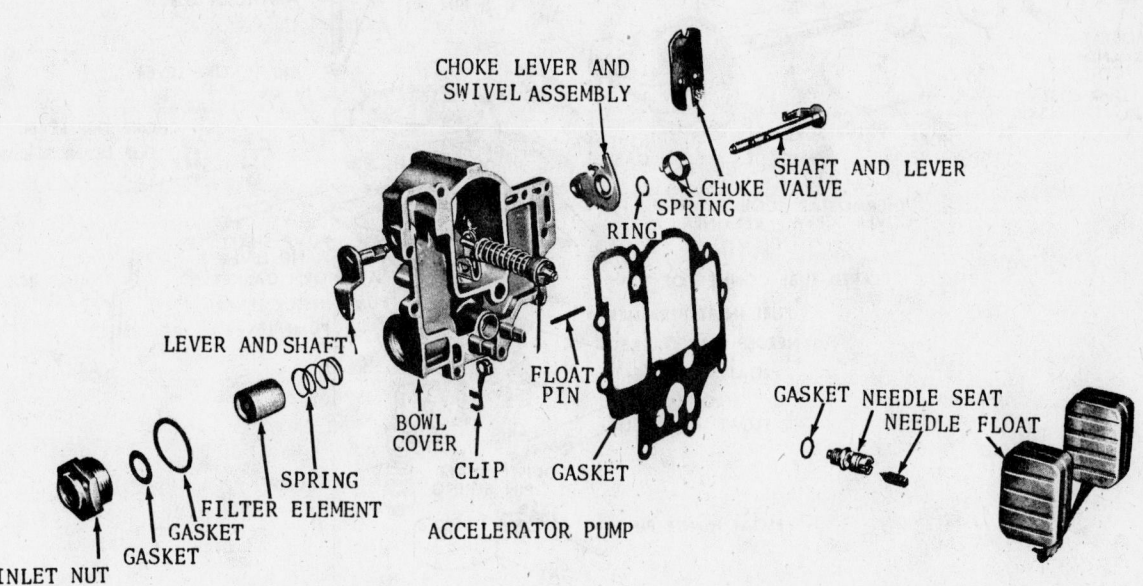

CHOKE LEVER AND
SWIVEL ASSEMBLY

SHAFT AND LEVER

CHOKE VALVE

SPRING

RING

LEVER AND SHAFT

FLOAT
PIN

BOWL
COVER

CLIP

GASKET

SPRING

FILTER ELEMENT

GASKET

GASKET

INLET NUT

ACCELERATOR PUMP

GASKET NEEDLE SEAT
NEEDLE FLOAT

THROTTLE VALVE

LEVER SCREW

SCREWS

IDLE SCREW SPRING

SPRING

LEVER AND SHAFT

MAIN METERING JET GASKET VALVE

VENTURI
CLUSTER

IDLE ADJUSTING SCREW

THROTTLE VALVE KICK LEVER

CURB IDLE ADJUSTING SCREW

IDLE
SCREW

SPRING

SPRING

FLOAT
BOWL

PUMP LEVER PUMP CLIP SPRING
ROD

Rochester—Mod. H single barrel (Corvair)

ROCHESTER CARBURETORS

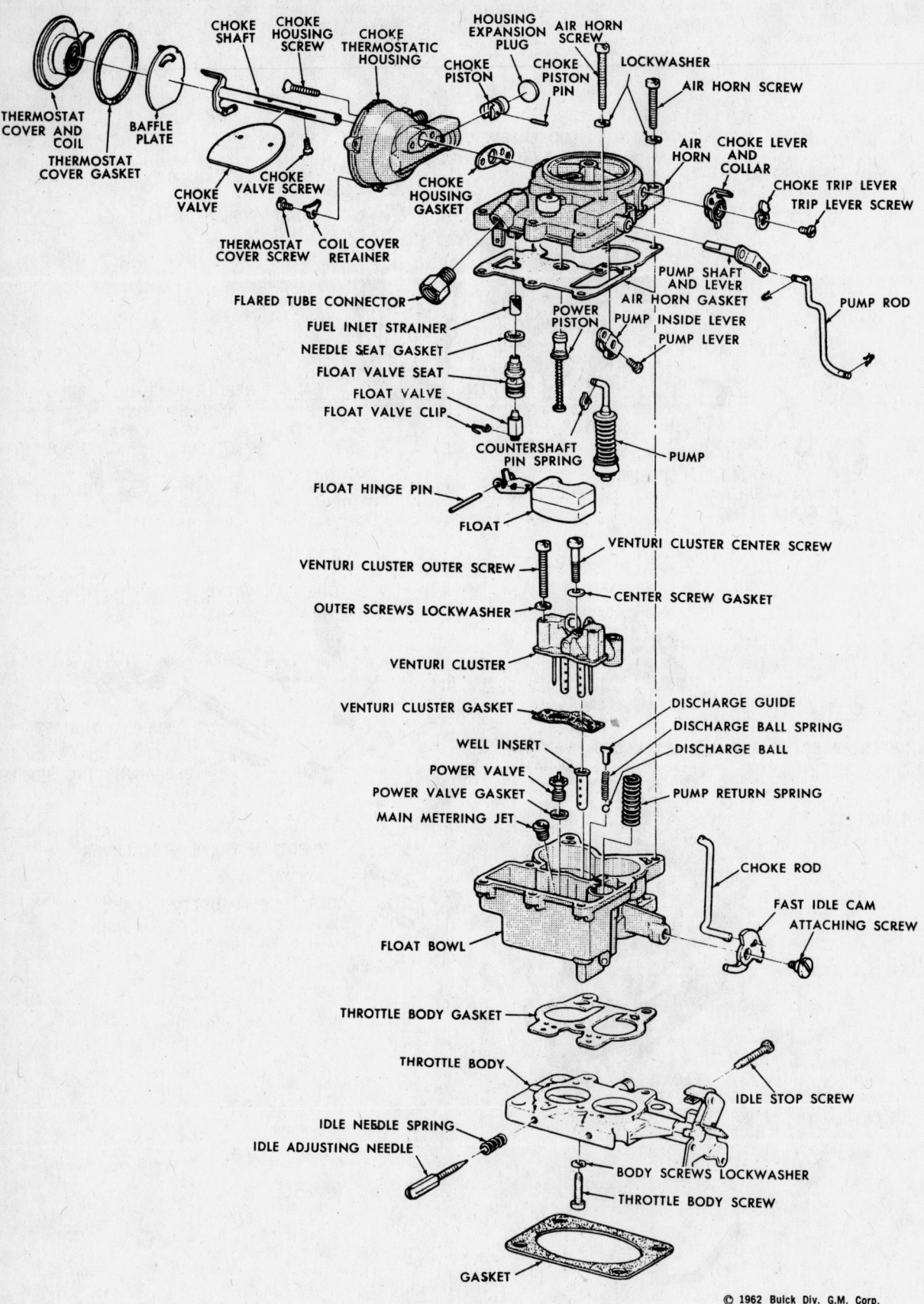

THERMOSTAT COVER AND COIL
THERMOSTAT COVER GASKET
BAFFLE PLATE
CHOKE SHAFT
CHOKE HOUSING SCREW
CHOKE THERMOSTATIC HOUSING
HOUSING EXPANSION PLUG
CHOKE PISTON
CHOKE PISTON PIN
AIR HORN SCREW
LOCKWASHER
AIR HORN SCREW

CHOKE VALVE
CHOKE VALVE SCREW
THERMOSTAT COVER SCREW
COIL COVER RETAINER
CHOKE HOUSING GASKET
AIR HORN
CHOKE LEVER AND COLLAR
CHOKE TRIP LEVER
TRIP LEVER SCREW

FLARED TUBE CONNECTOR
FUEL INLET STRAINER
NEEDLE SEAT GASKET
FLOAT VALVE SEAT
FLOAT VALVE
FLOAT VALVE CLIP
COUNTERSHAFT PIN SPRING
POWER PISTON
PUMP SHAFT AND LEVER
AIR HORN GASKET
PUMP INSIDE LEVER
PUMP LEVER
PUMP ROD
PUMP

FLOAT HINGE PIN
FLOAT

VENTURI CLUSTER CENTER SCREW
VENTURI CLUSTER OUTER SCREW
OUTER SCREWS LOCKWASHER
CENTER SCREW GASKET

VENTURI CLUSTER

VENTURI CLUSTER GASKET
DISCHARGE GUIDE
DISCHARGE BALL SPRING
DISCHARGE BALL
WELL INSERT
POWER VALVE
POWER VALVE GASKET
MAIN METERING JET
PUMP RETURN SPRING

CHOKE ROD
FAST IDLE CAM
ATTACHING SCREW
FLOAT BOWL

THROTTLE BODY GASKET

THROTTLE BODY
IDLE STOP SCREW
IDLE NEEDLE SPRING
IDLE ADJUSTING NEEDLE
BODY SCREWS LOCKWASHER
THROTTLE BODY SCREW

GASKET

© 1962 Buick Div. G.M. Corp.

Rochester—2GC 2 barrel (typical)

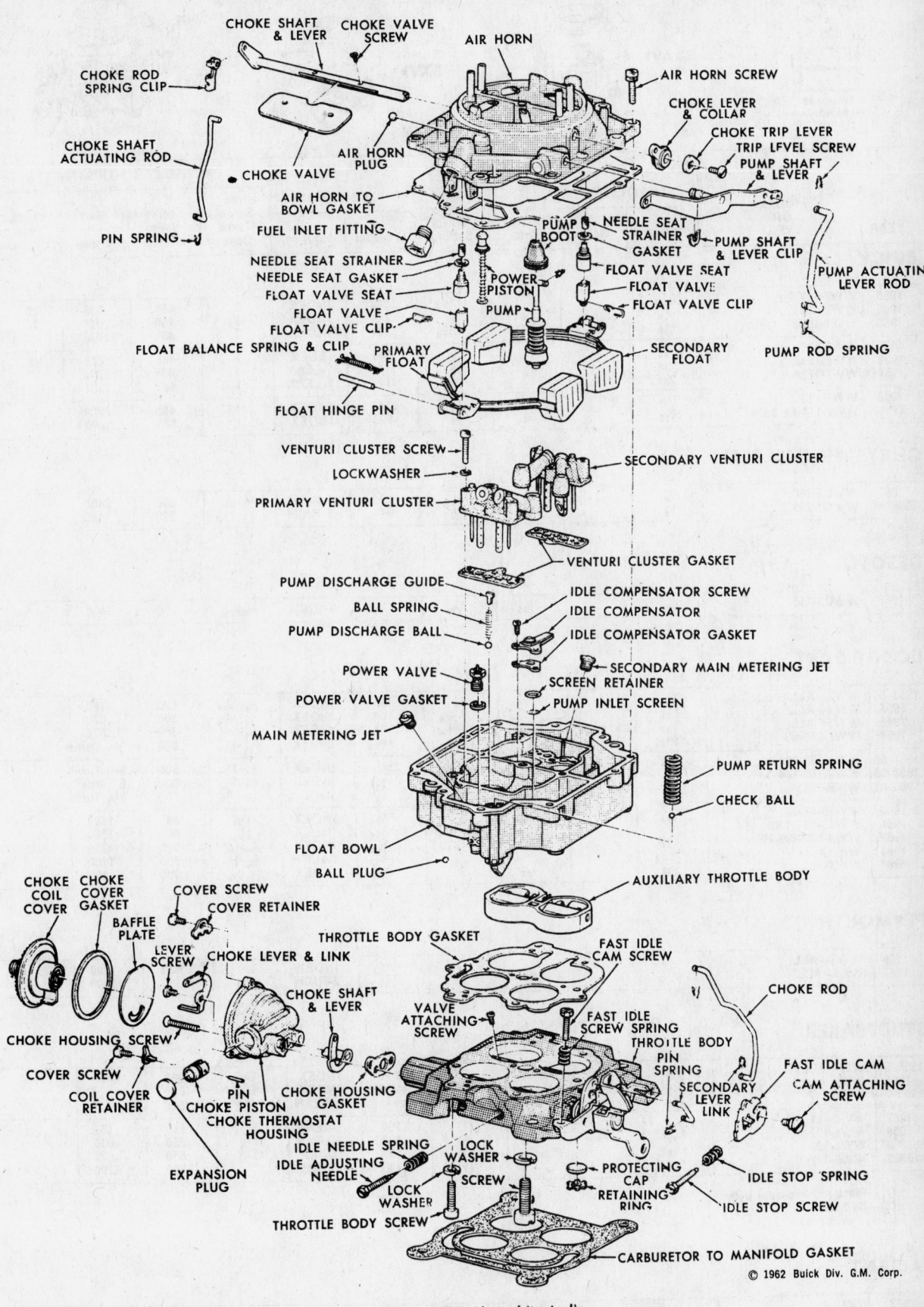

Rochester—4GC 4 barrel (typical)

© 1962 Buick Div. G.M. Corp.

STROMBERG CARBURETORS

I-92

STANDARD CODE NO. TAG

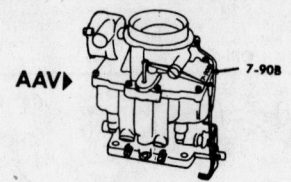

AAV▶ 7-90B   BXV▶ 3-111

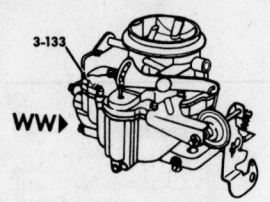

3-133   WW▶

YEAR	MODEL OR TYPE	FLOAT LEVEL		Bowl Vent Drop	Pump Travel Setting	CHOKE SETTING		ON THE CAR ADJUSTMENTS			
		Prim.	Sec.			Unloader	Housing	Idle Screw Turns Open	Idle Speed Neutral	Fast Idle Speed	Dashpot Plunger Clearance
BUICK											
1955	WW7-107	3/16	......	......	15/16	.144	INDEX	1	450	.096	(2)
1956	WW7-103	3/16	......	......	7/8	.144	INDEX	1	450	.076	(2)
1956	WW7-105B	3/16	......	......	15/16	.144	INDEX	1	450	.076	(2)
1957	WW7-106C	7/32	......	......	7/8	.144	INDEX	1	485	.076	(2)
1958	WW7-109B	5/32	......	......	7/8	.144	1-LEAN	1	485	.076	(2)
1959	WW7-112A	5/32	......	......	7/8	.144	1-LEAN	1	485	.204	(2)
1960	WW7-113	5/32	......	......	7/8	.146	INDEX	1	485	.204	(2)
1961	WW7-114 Le Sabre	3/16	......	5/64	7/8	.025	INDEX	1	525	.070	(2)
CHRYSLER IMPERIAL											
1961	WWC3-188	1/8	......	5/64	9/16	1/4	1-RICH	1/2-5/8	500	1400	......
1962-63	WWC3-201	1/8	......	5/64	9/16	15/64	1-RICH	1-1 1/2	500	1400	......
DESOTO											
1961	WWC3-188	1/8	......	5/64	9/16	1/4	1-RICH	1/2-5/8	500	1400	......
DODGE-DART											
1953-54	WW3—ALL	3/16	......	......	3/4	.165	INDEX	3/4-1 1/4	500	.150	......
1955	WW3—ALL	3/16	......	......	15/64	.165	INDEX	3/4-1 1/4	500	.076	......
1956	WW3—ALL	7/32	......	......	15/64	.165	INDEX	3/4-1 1/4	500	.076	......
1957	WW3-149-50	7/32	......	......	19/64	.165	INDEX	3/4-1 1/4	500	5 1/2 Turns	......
1957-59	WW3-159-160	7/32	......	......	7/32	.165	INDEX	3/4-1 1/4	500	5 1/8 Turns	......
1958-59	WW3-163-164	7/32	......	......	19/64	15/64	INDEX	3/4-1 1/4	500	8 Turns	......
1960-61	WW3-188	1/8	......	......	9/16	1/4	1-RICH	1/2-3/4	500	3 1/2 Turns	......
1960	WW15-41-42	7/32	......	3/32	5/16	15/64	INDEX	1 1/4	500	1400	......
1961	WW15-43-44-45	7/32	......	3/32	Automatic	15/64	INDEX	1 1/4	500	1250	......
1962	WW3-198-199-200	7/32	......	5/64	19/64	15/64	INDEX	1 1/4	500	1250	......
1963	WA—ALL	11/32	......	.060	......	11/32	2-RICH	3/4-1	550	1400	......
1963	WW3—ALL	7/32	......	5/64	......	15/64	INDEX	1 1/4	500	1400	......
PLYMOUTH											
1963	WW3—ALL	7/32	......	.060	......	15/64	INDEX	1 1/4	500	1400	......
1963	WA3—ALL	11/32	......	......	......	11/32	2-RICH	3/4-1	550	1400	......
STUDEBAKER											
1953-54	WW—ALL	3/16	......	......	(1)	.244	INDEX	1 3/4	550	.120	......
1955	WW—ALL	3/16	......	......	(1)	.244	INDEX	1 3/4	550	.120	......
1956-7-8	WW6-117	3/16	......	......	(1)	.244	1-LEAN	1 3/4	550	.120	......
1957	WW6-121	7/32	......	......	(1)	.195	1-LEAN	1 3/4	550	.152	......
1958	WW6-122	7/32	......	......	(1)	.195	1-LEAN	1 3/4	550	.030	......
1959-61	WW6-123	3/16	......	......	(1)	.177	INDEX	1 1/4	550	.025	......
1962	WW6-127	3/16	......	......	(1)	.195	INDEX	1 1/4	550	1700	(3)

(1)—Place rod in center hole.
(2)—By trial.
(3)—Two turns.

VALIANT

YEAR	MODEL OR TYPE	Prim.	Sec.	Bowl Vent Drop	Pump Travel Setting	Unloader	Housing	Idle Screw Turns Open	Idle Speed Neutral	Fast Idle Speed	Dashpot Plunger Clearance
1963	WA3—ALL	11/32	......	.060	......	11/32	2-RICH	3/4-1	550	1400	......

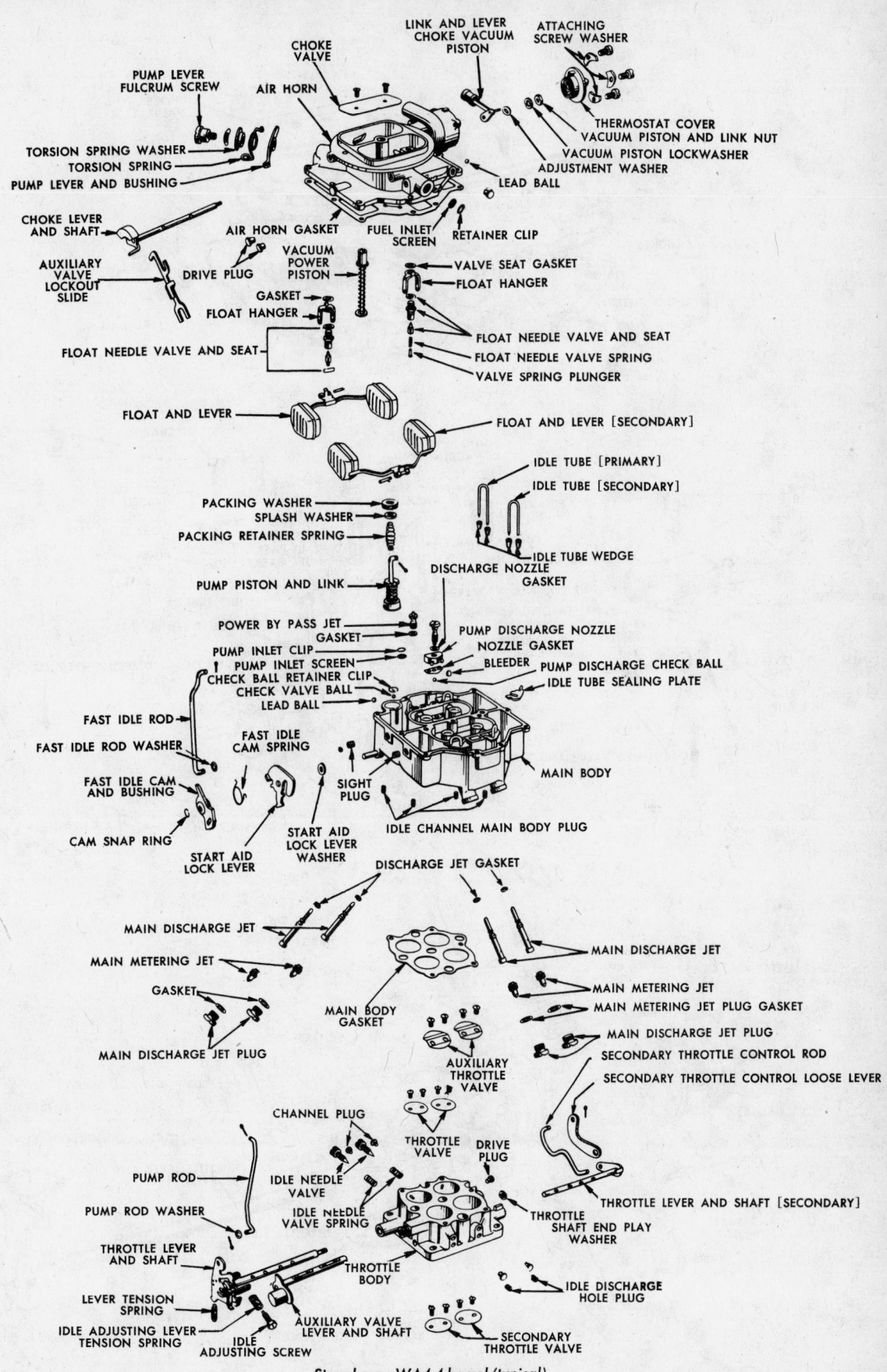

Stromberg—WA4 4 barrel (typical)

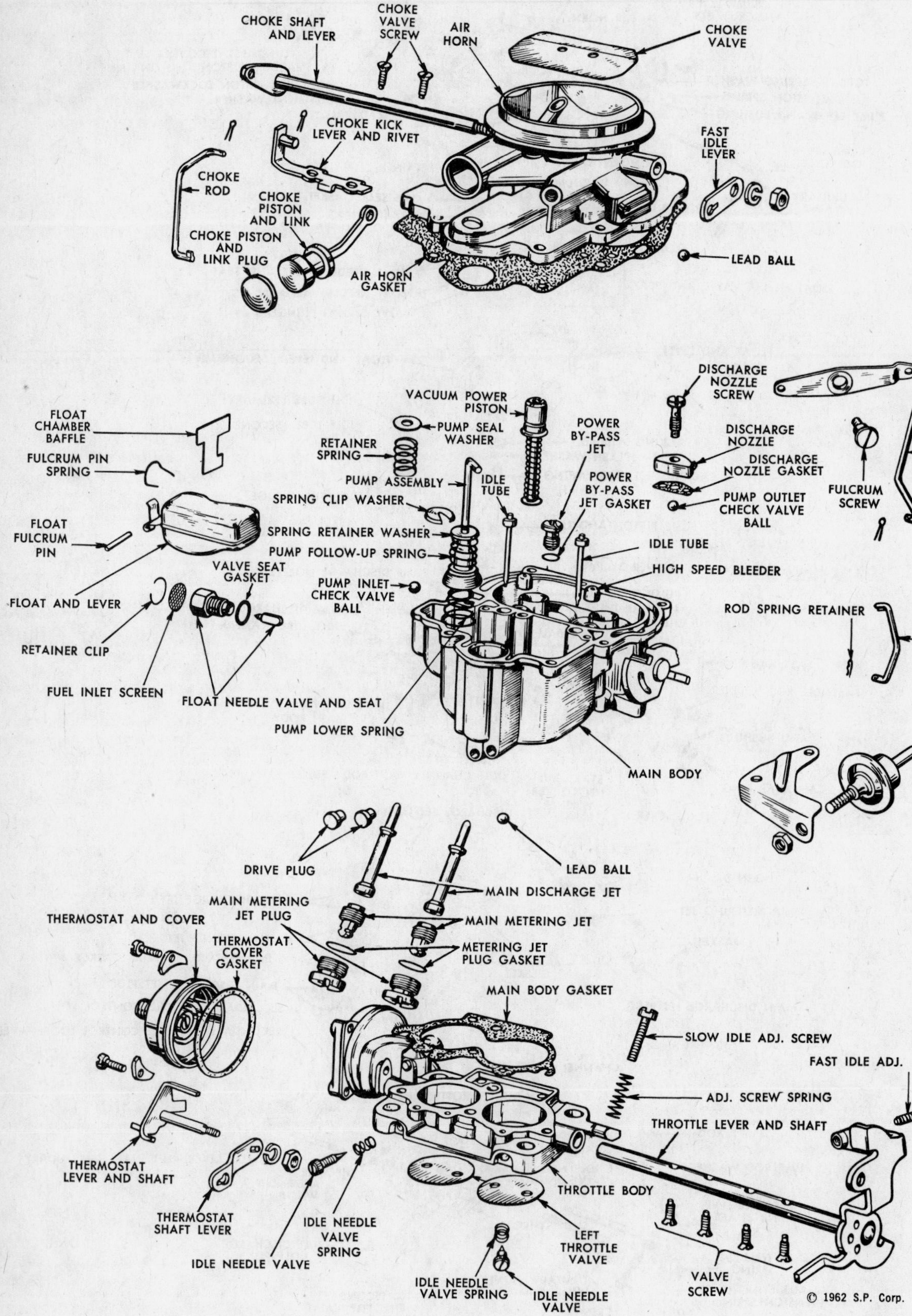

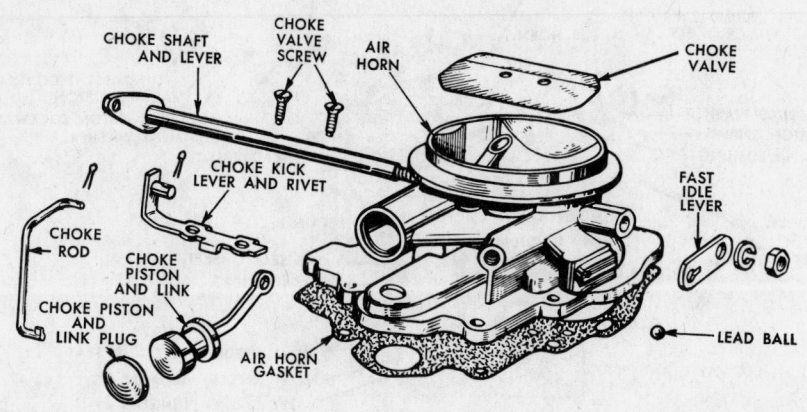

CHOKE SHAFT AND LEVER

CHOKE VALVE SCREW

AIR HORN

CHOKE VALVE

CHOKE KICK LEVER AND RIVET

FAST IDLE LEVER

CHOKE ROD

CHOKE PISTON AND LINK

CHOKE PISTON AND LINK PLUG

AIR HORN GASKET

LEAD BALL

FLOAT CHAMBER BAFFLE

FULCRUM PIN SPRING

FLOAT FULCRUM PIN

FLOAT AND LEVER

RETAINER CLIP

FUEL INLET SCREEN

FLOAT NEEDLE VALVE AND SEAT

PUMP LOWER SPRING

VACUUM POWER PISTON

PUMP SEAL WASHER

RETAINER SPRING

PUMP ASSEMBLY

SPRING CLIP WASHER

SPRING RETAINER WASHER

PUMP FOLLOW-UP SPRING

PUMP INLET CHECK VALVE BALL

VALVE SEAT GASKET

IDLE TUBE

POWER BY-PASS JET

POWER BY-PASS JET GASKET

DISCHARGE NOZZLE SCREW

PUMP LEVER

DISCHARGE NOZZLE

DISCHARGE NOZZLE GASKET

PUMP OUTLET CHECK VALVE BALL

IDLE TUBE

HIGH SPEED BLEEDER

ROD SPRING RETAINER

FULCRUM SCREW

PUMP ROD

FAST IDLE ROD

MAIN BODY

DRIVE PLUG

MAIN DISCHARGE JET

LEAD BALL

THERMOSTAT AND COVER

MAIN METERING JET PLUG

MAIN METERING JET

THERMOSTAT COVER GASKET

METERING JET PLUG GASKET

MAIN BODY GASKET

SLOW IDLE ADJ. SCREW

FAST IDLE ADJ.

ADJ. SCREW SPRING

THROTTLE LEVER AND SHAFT

THERMOSTAT LEVER AND SHAFT

THERMOSTAT SHAFT LEVER

IDLE NEEDLE VALVE SPRING

IDLE NEEDLE VALVE

THROTTLE BODY

LEFT THROTTLE VALVE

IDLE NEEDLE VALVE SPRING

IDLE NEEDLE VALVE

VALVE SCREW

© 1962 S.P. Corp.

Stromberg—WW 2 barrel (typical)

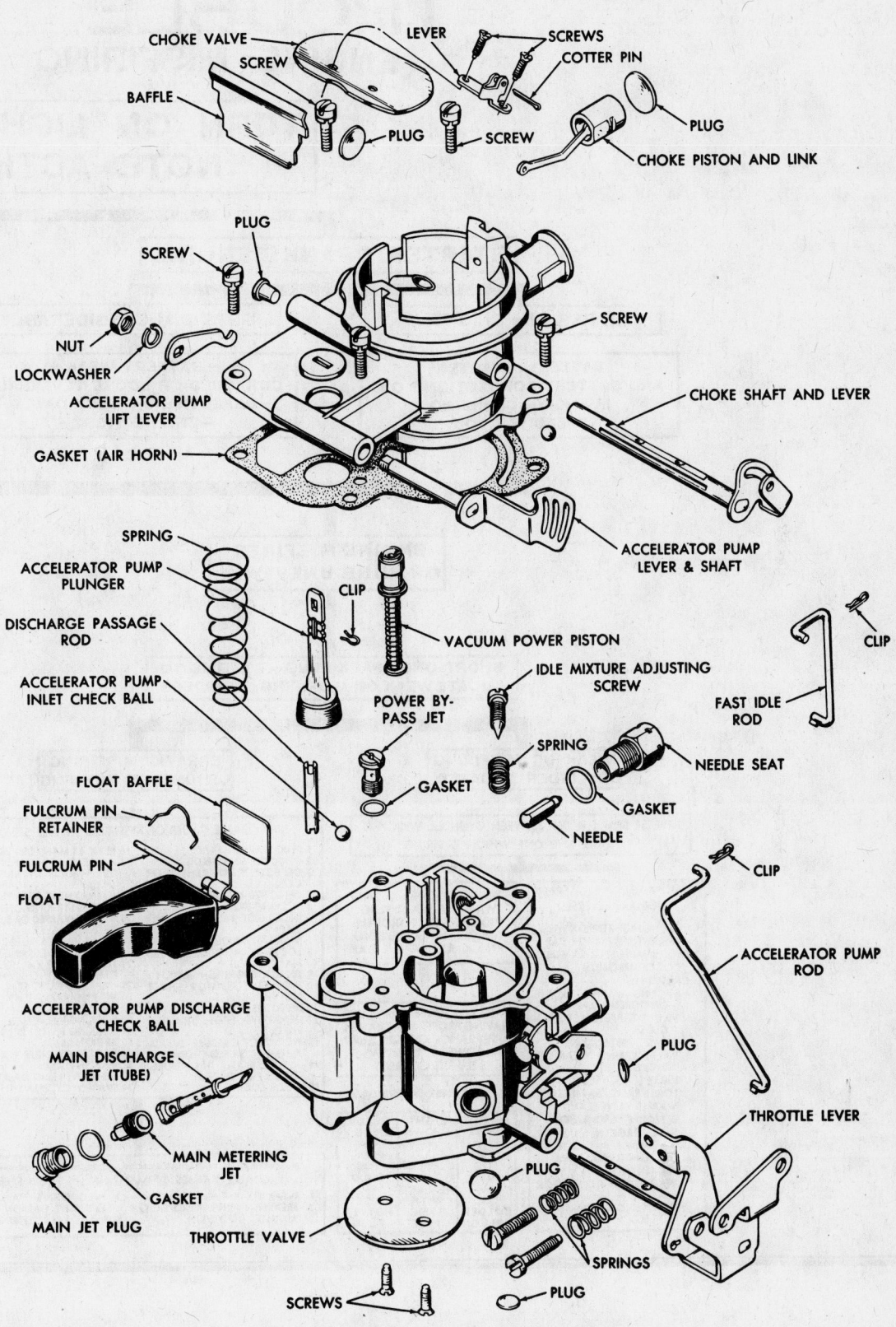

Stromberg—WA3 single barrel (typical)

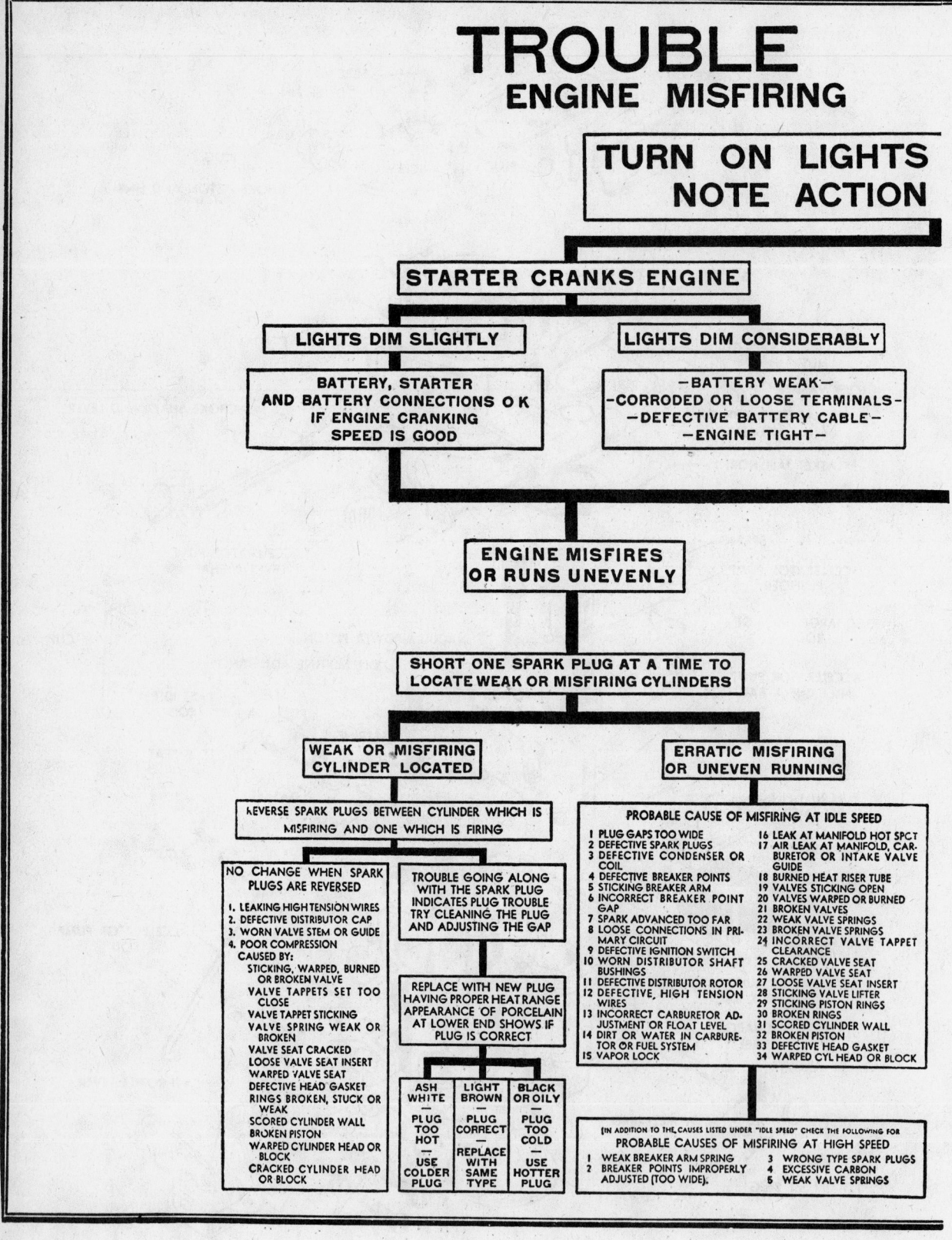

TROUBLE
ENGINE MISFIRING

TURN ON LIGHTS NOTE ACTION

STARTER CRANKS ENGINE

LIGHTS DIM SLIGHTLY

BATTERY, STARTER AND BATTERY CONNECTIONS O K IF ENGINE CRANKING SPEED IS GOOD

LIGHTS DIM CONSIDERABLY

—BATTERY WEAK—
—CORRODED OR LOOSE TERMINALS—
—DEFECTIVE BATTERY CABLE—
—ENGINE TIGHT—

ENGINE MISFIRES OR RUNS UNEVENLY

SHORT ONE SPARK PLUG AT A TIME TO LOCATE WEAK OR MISFIRING CYLINDERS

WEAK OR MISFIRING CYLINDER LOCATED

ERRATIC MISFIRING OR UNEVEN RUNNING

REVERSE SPARK PLUGS BETWEEN CYLINDER WHICH IS MISFIRING AND ONE WHICH IS FIRING

NO CHANGE WHEN SPARK PLUGS ARE REVERSED

1. LEAKING HIGH TENSION WIRES
2. DEFECTIVE DISTRIBUTOR CAP
3. WORN VALVE STEM OR GUIDE
4. POOR COMPRESSION
CAUSED BY:
   STICKING, WARPED, BURNED OR BROKEN VALVE
   VALVE TAPPETS SET TOO CLOSE
   VALVE TAPPET STICKING
   VALVE SPRING WEAK OR BROKEN
   VALVE SEAT CRACKED
   LOOSE VALVE SEAT INSERT
   WARPED VALVE SEAT
   DEFECTIVE HEAD GASKET
   RINGS BROKEN, STUCK OR WEAK
   SCORED CYLINDER WALL
   BROKEN PISTON
   WARPED CYLINDER HEAD OR BLOCK
   CRACKED CYLINDER HEAD OR BLOCK

TROUBLE GOING ALONG WITH THE SPARK PLUG INDICATES PLUG TROUBLE TRY CLEANING THE PLUG AND ADJUSTING THE GAP

REPLACE WITH NEW PLUG HAVING PROPER HEAT RANGE APPEARANCE OF PORCELAIN AT LOWER END SHOWS IF PLUG IS CORRECT

ASH WHITE	LIGHT BROWN	BLACK OR OILY
PLUG TOO HOT	PLUG CORRECT	PLUG TOO COLD
—	—	—
USE COLDER PLUG	REPLACE WITH SAME TYPE	USE HOTTER PLUG

PROBABLE CAUSE OF MISFIRING AT IDLE SPEED

1. PLUG GAPS TOO WIDE
2. DEFECTIVE SPARK PLUGS
3. DEFECTIVE CONDENSER OR COIL
4. DEFECTIVE BREAKER POINTS
5. STICKING BREAKER ARM
6. INCORRECT BREAKER POINT GAP
7. SPARK ADVANCED TOO FAR
8. LOOSE CONNECTIONS IN PRIMARY CIRCUIT
9. DEFECTIVE IGNITION SWITCH
10. WORN DISTRIBUTOR SHAFT BUSHINGS
11. DEFECTIVE DISTRIBUTOR ROTOR
12. DEFECTIVE, HIGH TENSION WIRES
13. INCORRECT CARBURETOR ADJUSTMENT OR FLOAT LEVEL
14. DIRT OR WATER IN CARBURETOR OR FUEL SYSTEM
15. VAPOR LOCK
16. LEAK AT MANIFOLD HOT SPOT
17. AIR LEAK AT MANIFOLD, CARBURETOR OR INTAKE VALVE GUIDE
18. BURNED HEAT RISER TUBE
19. VALVES STICKING OPEN
20. VALVES WARPED OR BURNED
21. BROKEN VALVES
22. WEAK VALVE SPRINGS
23. BROKEN VALVE SPRINGS
24. INCORRECT VALVE TAPPET CLEARANCE
25. CRACKED VALVE SEAT
26. WARPED VALVE SEAT
27. LOOSE VALVE SEAT INSERT
28. STICKING VALVE LIFTER
29. STICKING PISTON RINGS
30. BROKEN RINGS
31. SCORED CYLINDER WALL
32. BROKEN PISTON
33. DEFECTIVE HEAD GASKET
34. WARPED CYL HEAD OR BLOCK

[IN ADDITION TO THE CAUSES LISTED UNDER "IDLE SPEED" CHECK THE FOLLOWING FOR
PROBABLE CAUSES OF MISFIRING AT HIGH SPEED

1. WEAK BREAKER ARM SPRING
2. BREAKER POINTS IMPROPERLY ADJUSTED (TOO WIDE).
3. WRONG TYPE SPARK PLUGS
4. EXCESSIVE CARBON
5. WEAK VALVE SPRINGS

SHOOTING
LACK OF POWER

—TRY STARTER OF LIGHTS

STARTER DOES NOT CRANK ENGINE

LIGHTS STAY BRIGHT

OPEN CIRCUIT AT STARTER SWITCH OR STARTING MOTOR BRUSHES MAY NOT MAKE CONTACT WITH ARMATURE

DIM VERY SLIGHTLY

STARTER MAY NOT ENGAGE WITH ENGINE
———
RESISTANCE AT STARTER OR STARTER SWITCH

VERY DIM OR GO OUT

—BATTERY DISCHARGED—
—POOR BATTERY CONNECTIONS—
—STARTER BINDS OR SHORTED—
—ENGINE TIGHT—

ENGINE LACKS POWER

1 POOR COMPRESSION (SEE CAUSES LISTED UNDER ITEM 4, FIRST COL.)
2 IGNITION IMPROPERLY TIMED
3 IGNITION POINTS NOT PROPERLY SYNCHRONIZED
4 AUTOMATIC ADVANCE NOT OPERATING PROPERLY
5 VACUUM SPARK CONTROL NOT OPERATING PROPERLY
6 INCORRECT CARBURETOR ADJUSTMENT
7 INCORRECT VALVE TIMING
8 VAPOR LOCK
9 CLOGGED MUFFLER
10 DENTED EXHAUST OR TAIL PIPE
11 CLOGGED AIR CLEANER
12 ENGINE OVERHEATING
13 EXCESSIVE INTERNAL ENGINE FRICTION
14 SLIPPING CLUTCH
15 DRAG IN CHASSIS WHICH RETARDS FREE RUNNING OF CAR

ENGINE WILL NOT RUN

REMOVE SPARK PLUG WIRE AND HOLD NEAR ENGINE WHILE CRANKING

WEAK SPARK

1 DIRTY, PITTED OR BURNED POINTS
2 POOR ELECTRICAL CONNECTIONS
3 DEFECTIVE HIGH TENSION WIRES
4 DEFECTIVE COIL
5 DEFECTIVE CONDENSER
6 DEFECTIVE DISTRIBUTOR ROTOR
7 DEFECTIVE DISTRIBUTOR CAP
8 BROKEN ROTOR BRUSH
9 WET COIL, DISTRIBUTOR OR HIGH TENSION WIRES

NO SPARK
AMMETER SHOWS

NO READING

1 POINTS NOT CLOSING
2 POINTS DIRTY, PITTED OR BURNED
3 DEFECTIVE SWITCH
4 OPEN COIL WINDING
5 BROKEN PRIMARY WIRE OR LOOSE CONNECTION

NORMAL READING NEEDLE UNSTEADY

1 HIGH TENSION WIRE FROM COIL TO DISTRIBUTOR OPEN OR GROUNDED
2 DEFECTIVE COIL OR CONDENSER
3 DEFECTIVE ROTOR OR CAP
4 WET COIL DISTRIBUTOR OR HIGH TENSION WIRES

DISCHARGE

1 POINTS NOT OPENING
2 SHORTED CONDENSER
3 GROUNDED CONTACT ARM
4 SHORTED COIL PRIMARY WINDING
5 SHORT OR GROUND IN PRIMARY CIRCUIT

GOOD SPARK

CHECK FUEL SUPPLY

GAS IN CARBURETOR

1 CARBURETOR FLOODED
2 AUTOMATIC OR MANUAL CHOKE NOT OPERATING
3 WATER LEAKING TO CYLINDERS
4 DIRT OR WATER IN CARBURETOR

NO GAS IN CARBURETOR

1 CLOGGED FUEL LINES
2 CLOGGED FUEL FILTER
3 NO VENT IN TANK CAP
4 DEFECTIVE FUEL SUPPLY UNIT
5 AIR LEAK IN LINE FROM TANK

ENGINE DIAGNOSIS

TUNE-UP

The editors of CHILTON consider it unnecessary to outline the fundamentals of engine tune-up to the professional mechanic. Tune-up simply means, returning existing factors to original specifications.

ENGINE DIAGNOSIS, PROFESSIONAL APPROACH

Diagnosing engine problems requires a combination of know-how, mechanical skill and good test equipment. However, testing equipment is only as good as the person operating it.

THE OSCILLOSCOPE

It is a time consuming job to even remove spark plugs from some of the V-8 engines. It is also good logic to test engine components while performing their normal duties under various conditions. The oscilloscope will do this.

While this tool is no cure-all, it does produce a television screen picture of the situation as it exists within the running engine.

This picture can be translated into functions of the engine that are familiar to the average mechanic. When used with other pieces of test equipment, most engine problems can be brought to light and corrected in a very short time.

A good Oscilloscope in the hands of an average mechanic can determine:

1. Compression balance.
2. Condition of spark plugs.
3. Condition of distributor points.
4. Ignition coil or condenser problems.
5. Bad ignition wiring.
6. Distributor point dwell.
7. Cracked distributor cap.
8. Worn or broken rotor.
9. Worn distributer points.
10. Bad secondary wires and terminals.
11. Reversed polarity.
12. Many other items that will become more numerous as the mechanic gains experience with the machine.

It is not possible here to outline the various Oscilloscope hook-ups, as each instrument manufacturer knows the best hook-up for his piece of equipment. Instead, follow the manufacturers instructions.

The following operations depend largely upon the results of the Oscilloscope picture.

COMPRESSION CHECK

Due to the added torque of modern engine starting systems, plus changes in engine camshaft design, it is no longer practical to determine cylinder compression balance by listening to the starter while cranking the engine. For positive cranking pressure readings use a cylinder compression gauge.

Because engine design and other factors influence compression, a pressure test of all of the cylinders in any one engine will furnish a yardstick of comparison for that particular engine only. Therefore there can

Checking Compression

be no table established for compression pressure standards. There must be a compression check and a comparison made on each engine tested.

A. Run the engine until normal temperature has been reached.
B. Carefully remove spark plug wires.
C. Blow foreign matter from spark plug wells. Then loosen plugs one turn.

D. Replace plug wires, start engine and snap throttle open once or twice, (this should clear the engine cylinders of dislodged carbon particles).
E. Stop engine and remove plug wires and spark plugs.
F. Remove carburetor air cleaner or cleaners and, (depending upon intake manifold design) block throttle valve or valves wide open.
G. Hook up starter remote control cable and switch. Then using a compression gauge in the cylinder, crank the engine thru about four strokes. Record the highest gauge pressure for that cylinder.
H. Proceed thru the remaining cylinders in the same manner.
I. Some variation in cylinders is to be expected, however, the difference should not exceed 20 pounds.

POOR COMPRESSION

In the event of poor compression in two adjacent cylinders of a multi-cylinder engine, the probable cause is a blown head gasket between the two offending cylinders. This condition can generally be identified by an identical pressure reading for these two cylinders. The condition can sometimes be spotted by a popping back thru the carburetor.

Low compression may also be the result of a leaky head gasket at a point between the compression chamber and a coolant passage of the water jacket, (on water cooled engines). This will usually affect individual cylinders and will probably manifest itself as excess water in the crankcase. A rusty dipstick or water droplets in the oil filler cap is

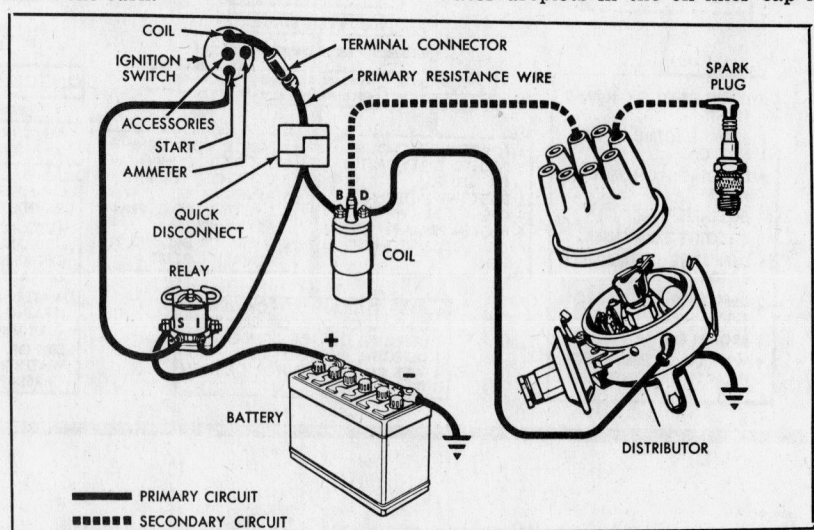

Typical Ignition Circuit

also a pretty good indication of coolant entering the crankcase. A bad coolant leak into the combustion chamber may stop the crankshaft from turning. The coolant hydraulically prevents completion of the compression stroke in the bad cylinder. Any further attempt at cranking the engine, under these conditions, can cause severe damage.

To locate a compression leak, if the cooling system is not involved, pour about a tablespoon full of S A E 30 oil into the combustion chamber. Crank the engine to spread the oil. If the gauge reading is 10 lbs. or Then complete the compression test. more higher than the original reading, bad rings are a probability. If the compression pressure has not been improved, the trouble is apparently valves. However, one other remote possibility would be a crack or hole in the piston head that has been temporarily sealed by the oil.

INTAKE MANIFOLD

Since the power developed by any gas engine can be regulated entirely (within it's limits) by the air it breathes, the fuel induction system performs a very important role.

The intake manifold is a major part of the system and is often overlooked in engine diagnosis and tune-up.

A leaky intake manifold can cause hard starting, poor idling, detonation, burned spark plugs, burned valves, damaged pistons and rings and in some engine designs, plug fouling and high oil consumption. Therefore, wherever feasible, the intake manifold gaskets should be checked for leaks and the manifold attaching bolts or nuts retorqued.

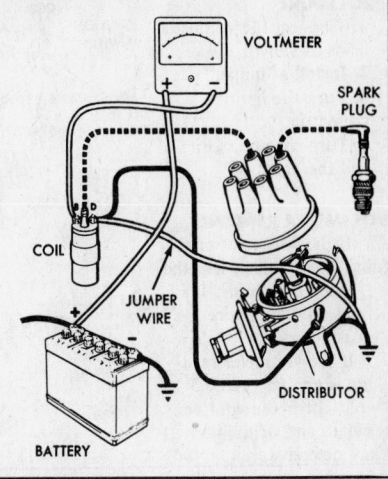

PROCEDURE
1. Connect the voltmeter leads as shown.
2. Install a jumper wire.
3. Turn the ignition switch on.
4. Turn the accessories and the lights off.

VOLTMETER READING
If the voltmeter reading is 6.9 volts or less, the primary circuit from battery to coil is satisfactory.

If the voltmeter reading is greater than 6.9 volts, check:
1. All components in the battery to coil circuit as outlined under "Preliminary Checks."
2. Resistance wire for defects.
3. Relay to ignition switch for defects.

Battery to Coil Test

An intake manifold or carburetor air leak will also show on the Oscilloscope screen as well as an over-rich or extremely lean carburetor mixture.

VACUUM GAUGE

Vacuum studies are an established practice and indicate much to the experienced mechanic. However, due to some intake manifold designs, vacuum gauge hook-ups can be quite difficult and, in some cases the readings, misleading.

SPARK PLUGS

A. Let's not waste time on a plug cleaning job if plug damage is at all obvious. Cracked or blistered porcelains, badly worn electrodes, etc. are certainly good reasons to renew the plugs.

B. If examination and circumstances warrant cleaning, wipe the top of the porcelain clean with a good solvent (preferably carbon tetrachloride). A clean porcelain won't support a short circuit.

C. Clean the electrodes, lower porcelain and inner shell in a good sand blaster.

D. File if necessary, and properly gap the electrodes.

E. Clean and check the plug threads, (dirty threads will influence the torque reading and heat transfer).

F. Use a new gasket on all spark plugs, (except those designed to be used without gaskets) install and torque to specifications.

All spark plugs are designed to operate within a certain heat range. The design is essential to good engine performance and plug life. Be

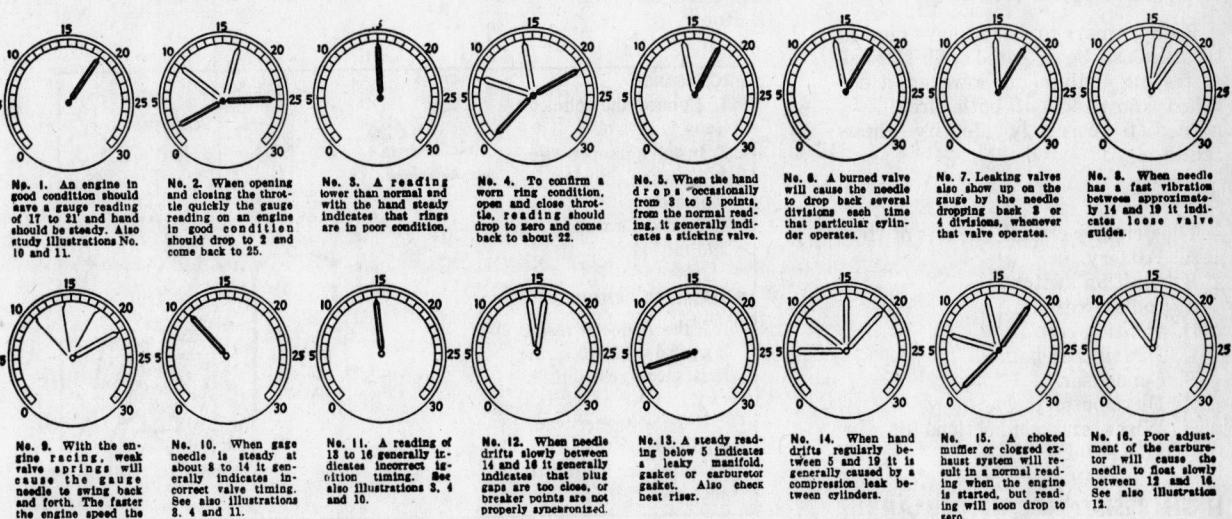

No. 1. An engine in good condition should have a gauge reading of 17 to 21 and hand should be steady. Also study illustrations No. 10 and 11.

No. 2. When opening and closing the throttle quickly the gauge reading on an engine in good condition should drop to 2 and come back to 25.

No. 3. A reading lower than normal and with the hand steady indicates that rings are in poor condition.

No. 4. To confirm a worn ring condition, open and close throttle, reading should drop to zero and come back to about 22.

No. 5. When the hand drops occasionally from 3 to 5 points, from the normal reading, it generally indicates a sticking valve.

No. 6. A burned valve will cause the needle to drop back several divisions each time that particular cylinder operates.

No. 7. Leaking valves also show up on the gauge by the needle dropping back 3 or 4 divisions, whenever that valve operates.

No. 8. When needle has a fast vibration between approximately 14 and 19 it indicates loose valve guides.

No. 9. With the engine racing, weak valve springs will cause the gauge needle to swing back and forth. The faster the engine speed the greater the swing.

No. 10. When gage needle is steady at about 8 to 14 it generally indicates incorrect valve timing.

No. 11. A reading of 15 to 16 generally indicates incorrect ignition timing. See also illustrations 3, 4 and 11.

No. 12. When needle drifts slowly between 14 and 16 it generally indicates that plug gaps are too close, or breaker points are not properly synchronized.

No. 13. A steady reading below 5 indicates a leaky manifold, gasket or carburetor gasket. Also check heat riser.

No. 14. When hand drifts regularly between 5 and 19 it is generally caused by a compression leak between cylinders.

No. 15. A choked muffler or clogged exhaust system will result in a normal reading when the engine is started, but reading will soon drop to zero.

No. 16. Poor adjustment of the carburetor will cause the needle to float slowly between 12 and 16. See also illustration 12.

The above gauge readings are typical of the various engine troubles that can be pinpointed by Vacuum Gauge Checks

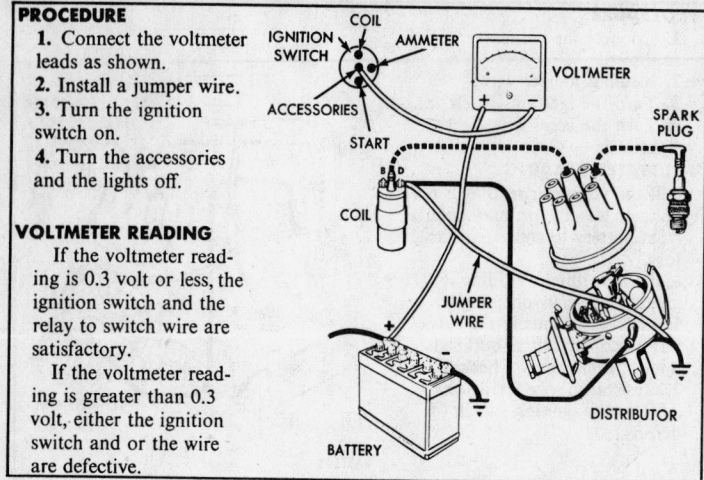

PROCEDURE

1. Connect the voltmeter leads as shown.
2. Install a jumper wire.
3. Turn the ignition switch on.
4. Turn the accessories and the lights off.

VOLTMETER READING

If the voltmeter reading is 0.3 volt or less, the ignition switch and the relay to switch wire are satisfactory.

If the voltmeter reading is greater than 0.3 volt, either the ignition switch and or the wire are defective.

Ignition Switch Test

guided by the manufacturers heat range chart.

DISTRIBUTER POINTS

Check spring tension and distributer point condition. The spring can be tested with a tension scale and replaced if necessary. While a visual inspection of the breaker points is a necessity, more positive proof of their electrical condition can be determined by using modern testing equipment. If points are badly pitted or otherwise damaged, renew them. Only in an emergency or as a temporary measure should distributer points be filed.

While there is ample room, in some cases, to install the new points and condenser with the distributer still in the car, it is easier and a lot more thorough to pull the distributer. See the Car Section for distributer timing

IGNITION CIRCUITS

Both primary and secondary circuit troubles can be detected with the aid of testing equipment, however, a detailed knowledge of both circuits is needed to correctly identify these faults.

PRIMARY

The primary circuit consists of the:
A. Battery.
B. Ignition switch.
C. Ballast resister.
D. Ignition coil.
E. Distributer points.
F. Condenser.
G. Distributer body.
H. Wires and connections of the above units.

HIGH RESISTANCE IN PRIMARY

If the Oscilloscope pattern indicates high resistance in the primary

circuit, a jumper wire used as a bypass at each successive unit in the circuit will locate the troubled spot. A voltmeter will also register voltage drop across any switch or wire comprising the circuit.

DISTRIBUTER TROUBLES

The condition of the points, condenser, breaker plate, cam lobes, distributer shaft or bushings, rotor, distributer cap and wires and the distributer ground will be projected in a pattern on a good Oscilloscope screen. Reconditioning of the distributer body or shaft is extra and will not be included in tune-up.

SECONDARY

The secondary circuit consists of the:
A. Coil.
B. Distributer cap.
C. Rotor.

D. Coil and plug wires.
E. Spark plugs.

If test equipment shows high resistance anywhere in either circuit the trouble must be corrected before proceeding with an intelligent diagnosis or successful tune-up.

While the Oscilloscope will definitely indicate troubles that are present in the running engine, it does not replace the need for experience and the familiar gauges of the trade, such as the voltmeter, ammeter, tachometer, etc.

BATTERY

A. Check physical and chemical condition of battery, (clean up battery and test electrolite with a hydrometer, then add water if necessary).

B. HYDROMETER TEST

Draw electrolite into the hydrometer barrel from the battery and return it a few times to bring the temperature of the hydrometer to that of the electrolite. Then draw just enough electrolite into the hydrometer barrel to float the gauge. A specific gravity reading of 1.275 to 1.285 indicates a fully charged battery. Batteries should give fair per-

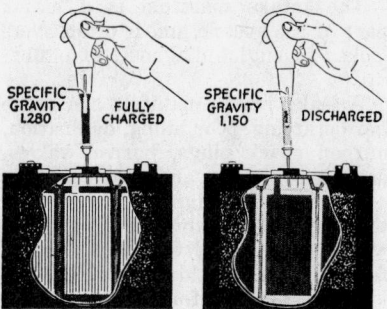

Fully charged   *Discharged*

PROCEDURE

1. Connect the voltmeter leads as shown.
2. Install a jumper wire.
3. Turn the ignition switch on.
4. Turn the accessories and the lights off.

VOLTMETER READING

If the voltmeter reading is 6.6 volts or less, the resistance wire is satisfactory.

If the voltmeter reading is greater than 6.6 volts, replace the resistance wire.

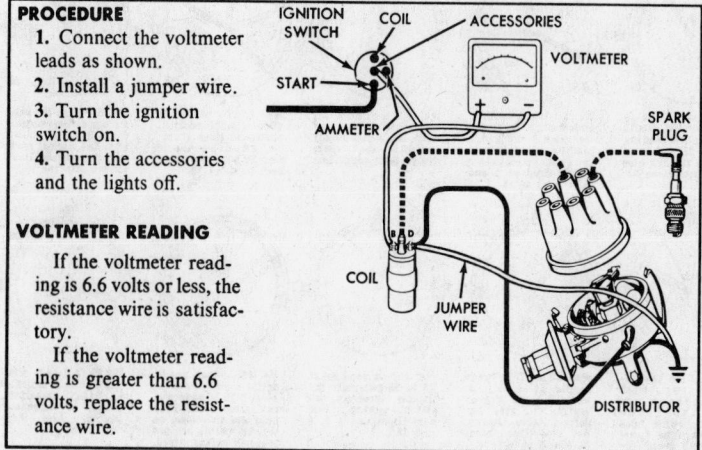

Resistance Wire Test

formance to a minimum gravity reading of 1.230 to 1.240, or about 60% charge. If individual cells show a variation of more than 0.025, replace the battery.

C. CAPACITY TEST, DISCHARGE METHOD

The discharge method of testing is a more decisive way to judge the reaction a battery will have to normal cranking load.

Hook up a high rate discharge tester and a voltmeter to the battery. Adjust the discharge tester to draw twice the ampere-hour rating of the battery for 6 volt batteries, and three times the ampere-hour rating of the battery for 12 volt batteries. The electrolite temperature for the test should be 70°F-90°F.

After applying the specific load for about 15 seconds, measure the terminal voltage of the battery. If the voltage is 4.5 volts or more for a 6 volt battery or 9.0 volts or more for a 12 volt battery, the output capacity of the battery may be considered to be good. However, if the voltage reading is below this value, the battery should be charged or replaced as conditions warrant.

AIR CLEANER

All automotive engines are equipped with some sort of air cleaner and silencer. This device also acts as a flame trap in the event of back-fire. The air cleaner, whether wet or dry type, is designed to furnish the engine with adequate air for maximum performance at top speed. The cleaner can only handle this much air if clean and in good condition. Always follow the manufacturers service instructions as some filtering elements are quite sensitive to rough handling.

The air cleaner is very important to high speed performance and to extended engine life, especially in dusty areas.

FUEL FILTER

There are various types of filters used, the filter and sediment bowl type at the carburetor, the unit type fuel line filter between the fuel pump and carburetor and the filter screen and bowl on the underside of the fuel pump.

Fuel filters should be serviced as tune-up routine, (except the standpipe filter in the gas tank of cars so equipped). The servicing of the gas tank filter is not included in tune-up.

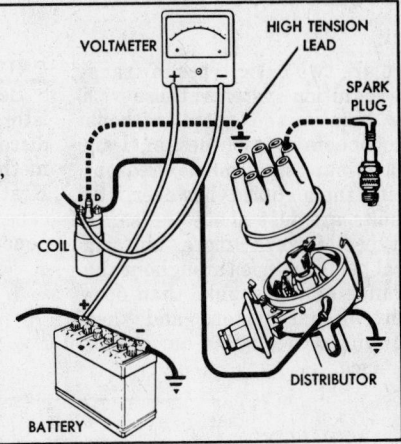

PROCEDURE
1. Connect the voltmeter leads as shown.
2. Disconnect the high tension lead from the distributor cap and ground the lead.
3. Using a remote starter switch, crank the engine while observing the voltage drop.

VOLTMETER READING
If the voltage drop is 0.1 volt or less, the starting ignition circuit is satisfactory.

If the voltage drop is greater than 0.1 volt, clean and tighten terminals in the circuit or replace wiring as necessary.

Starting Ignition Circuit Test

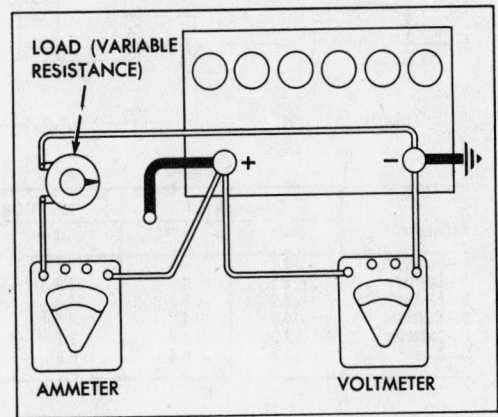

Battery Capacity Test

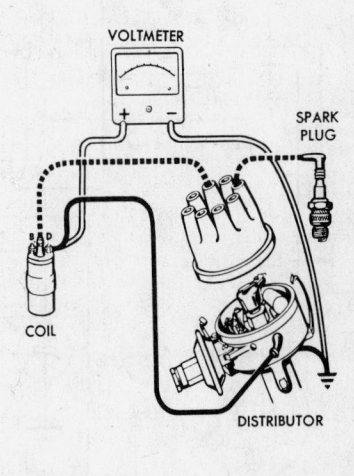

PROCEDURE
1. Connect the voltmeter leads as shown.
2. Turn the ignition switch on.
3. Turn the accessories and the lights off.
4. Close the breaker points.

VOLTMETER READING
If the voltmeter reading is 0.1 volt or less, the primary circuit from coil to ground is satisfactory.

If the voltmeter reading is greater than 0.1 volt, test the voltage drop of each of the following:
1. Coil to distributor primary wire.
2. The moveable breaker point and the breaker plate.
3. The breaker plate and the distributor housing.
4. The distributor housing and engine ground.

Coil to Ground Test

TRANSISTOR IGNITION

There are two basic types of transistorized ignition systems; those with breaker points, and those without. The proponents of each design, I am sure, have many and complex reasons to justify their choice, however, the end results are just about the same. Both types furnish more uniform electrical performance throughout the speed range of the engine, than does the conventional system, and they operate with a negligible amount of maintenance.

CAUTION:

Because we are dealing with transistors and diodes, it is advisable to discontinue some of the previous methods of ignition circuit testing. Heat, shock, or reverse polarity may cause extensive damage to the components of the system.

BREAKER POINT TYPE

Trouble Checks

1. Check for the existence and approximate quality of spark by pulling the coil-to-distributor wire out of the distributor cap. With ignition switch "on" and the loose end of this wire held about 1/4" from the engine block, crank the engine. This should produce a good, strong spark.
2. Reconnect the high tension coil wire to the distributor cap and make a similar test at the spark plugs. A good spark at the plugs

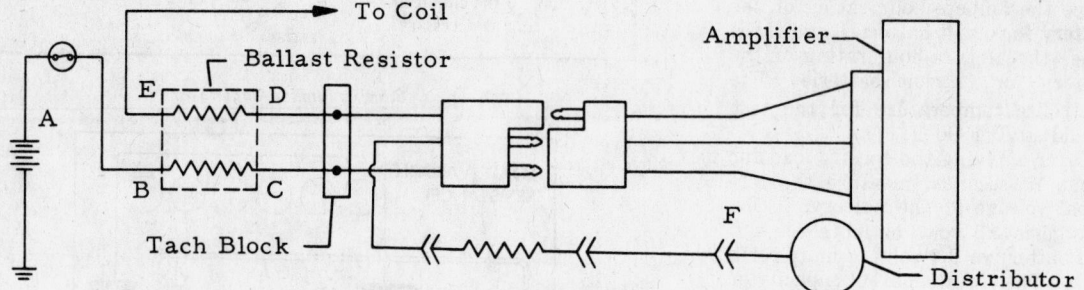

Reference	Cranking R.P.M.		Idle (700 R.P.M.)		Normal (1500 R.P.M.)	
	Volts	Amps	Volts	Amps	Volts	Amps
A—Battery	10.4	—	13.2	—	14.7	—
B—Emitter	9.5	4.6	13.0	5.6	14.0	12.5
C—Emitter	8.0	4.6	11.2	5.6	10.0	12.5
D—Collecter	4.0	4.2	4.6	5.0	9.5	12.0
E—Collecter	2.0	4.2	2.2	5.0	4.5	12.0
F—Base	4.0	0.4	5.8	0.6	3.5	0.5

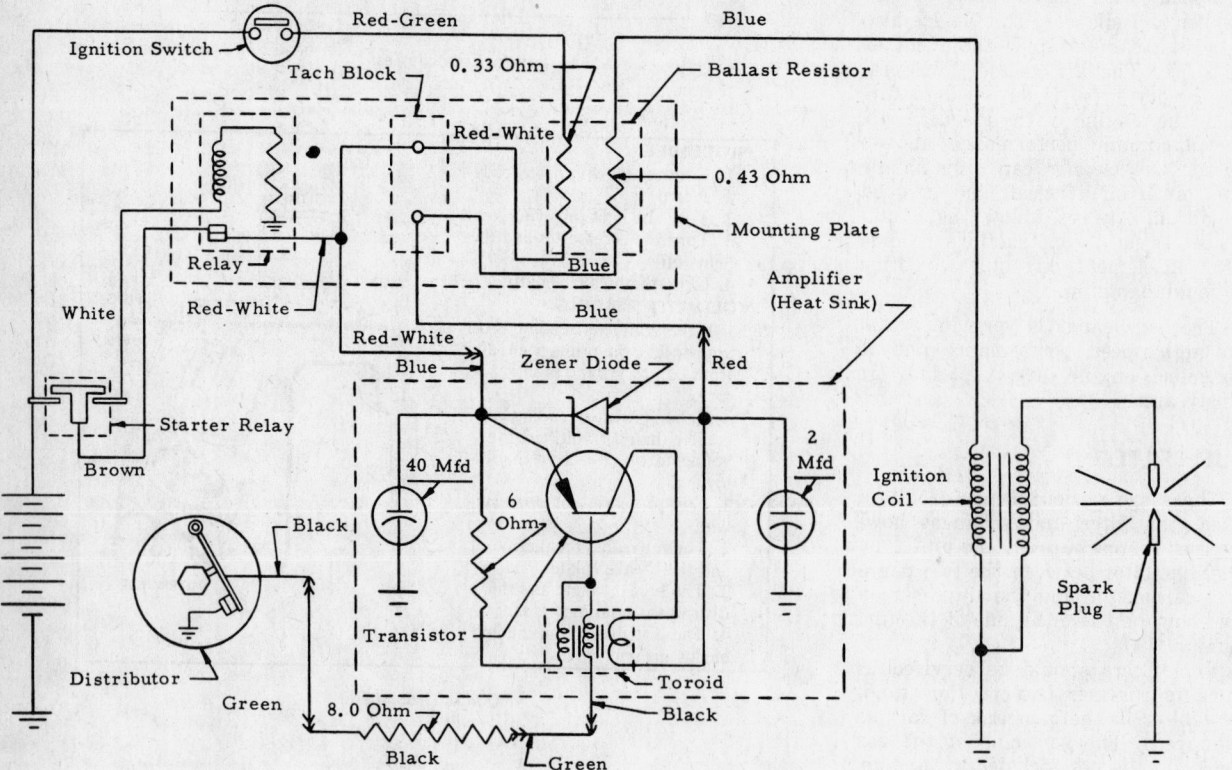

Wiring Diagram - Breaker Point Type

indicates the trouble to be other than ignition output failure.

3. If the spark is weak or non-existent, remove the cover from the mounting plate and connect a dwell meter to the tach. (tachometer) block. Hook up the red lead to the terminal in the red area and the black lead to black.

4. With ignition "on," crank engine and note meter reading. A dwell angle of less than 45° (for an 8 lobe cam) indicates that the transistor is working properly, the trouble is not in this component.

5. A dwell meter reading of "zero" indicates that the breaker points are dirty or not closing and should be replaced or adjusted.

6. A dwell meter reading of 45° (8 lobe cam) indicates the following:
   A. Ignition system is not being supplied with current.
   B. Breaker points are not opening.
   C. Transistor is defective.
   Disconnect the bullet connector from the distributor lead and again crank the engine. A meter reading of "zero" indicates trouble in the breaker points. A meter reading of 45° (8 lobe cam) indicates power source or transistor trouble. To determine which, connect a voltmeter, or test light to the red/green lead terminal of the ballast resistor and crank the engine. A reading of 45° or steady light indicates transistor failure. Replace the amplifier assembly (transistor). Absence of any indication shows an open circuit between the battery and the transistor.

7. A weak spark in steps 1 or 2 indicates a weak ignition coil. Turn ignition off, replace coil, then repeat step 1. Do not attempt to test coil, because its low impedence will cause inaccurate readings.

8. To jump the ignition switch from under the hood, disconnect the ballast resistor-to-ignition switch wire (red with green chaser) at the ballast resistor. Then connect a jumper from the positive battery terminal to the vacated ballast resistor blade terminal. The ignition system will now be supplied with current, if the resistor is not open. Check this provision before going further.

9. The only locations from which to get trouble shooting information are the tach. block terminals, the ballast resistor terminals and the distributor primary bullet connector. By connecting a voltmeter and an ammeter at these points, with a well charged battery and the brown wire disconnected from the cold start relay, cranking amperages and voltages may be obtained which should correspond with the following chart.

Caution:
Do not pierce insulation material to obtain meter readings.

MAGNETIC PULSE TYPE

The Delco-Remy, magnetic pulse, fully transistorized ignition system uses a magnetic pulse distributor (no breaker points). This system switches power electronically rather than with ignition contact points. Instead of the familiar cam and breaker plate assembly, this distributor uses a rotating iron timer core and a magnetic pickup assembly. The magnetic pickup assembly consists of a bearing plate on which are sandwiched a ceramic ring-type permanent magnet, two pole pieces and a pick-up coil. The pole pieces are doughnut shaped steel plates with accurately spaced internal teeth, one tooth for each cylinder of the engine.

A critically important part is the iron timer core. It has a number of equally spaced projections or vanes and is attached to, and rotates with, the distributor shaft.

The transistor control unit, the switchbox of the system, is mounted in an aluminum case and contains 3 transistors, a Zener diode, a condenser and 5 small resistors. The Zener diode is a circuit protection device. Remaining components control and switch ignition-coil current electronically; there are no moving parts in the control unit.

The ignition coil is of standard design except for a special winding. The external primary resistor is a ceramic type, similar to those used on various conventional systems.

The magnetic pulse distributor provides a triggering pulse or signal for the transistor control unit. Within the distributor, a magnetic field through the internal teeth of the upper and lower pole pieces is produced by the permanent magnet between them. As the vanes of the iron timer core on the distributor shaft pass near the pole teeth as the shaft rotates, the magnetic field alternately builds up and collapses. Thus, a voltage pulse is induced in the pick-up coil each time a vane of the iron core passes a tooth on the pole pieces.

Each voltage pulse is conducted to the transistor control unit where it "turns on" the triggering transistor, causing it to "turn off" the switching transistor. This action interrupts the current flow thru the ignition coil primary winding, causing the coil to fire the spark plug. The switching transistor then automatically returns to an "on" condition, permitting coil current to build up for the next firing.

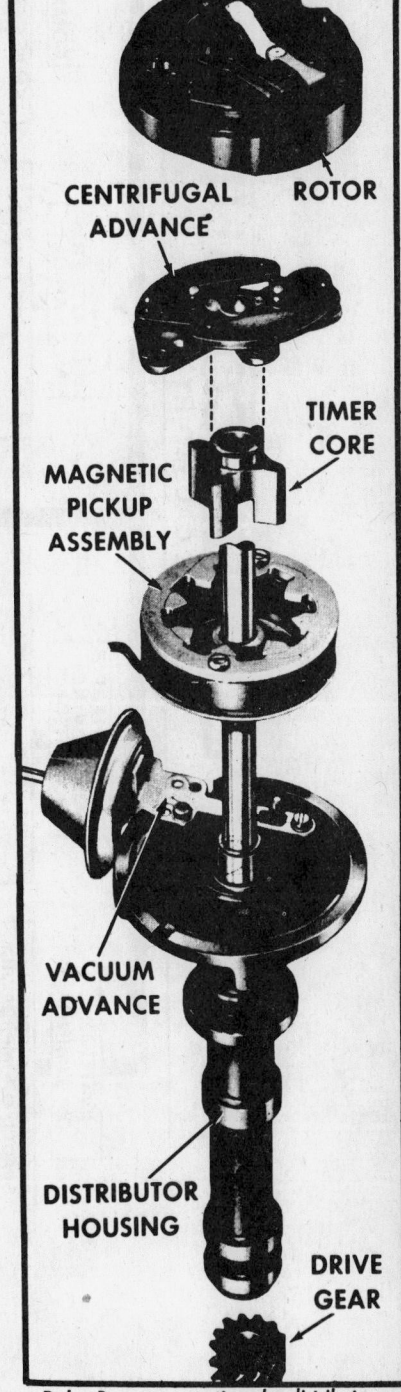

CENTRIFUGAL ADVANCE — ROTOR

TIMER CORE

MAGNETIC PICKUP ASSEMBLY

VACUUM ADVANCE

DISTRIBUTOR HOUSING

DRIVE GEAR

Delco-Remy magnetic pulse distributor

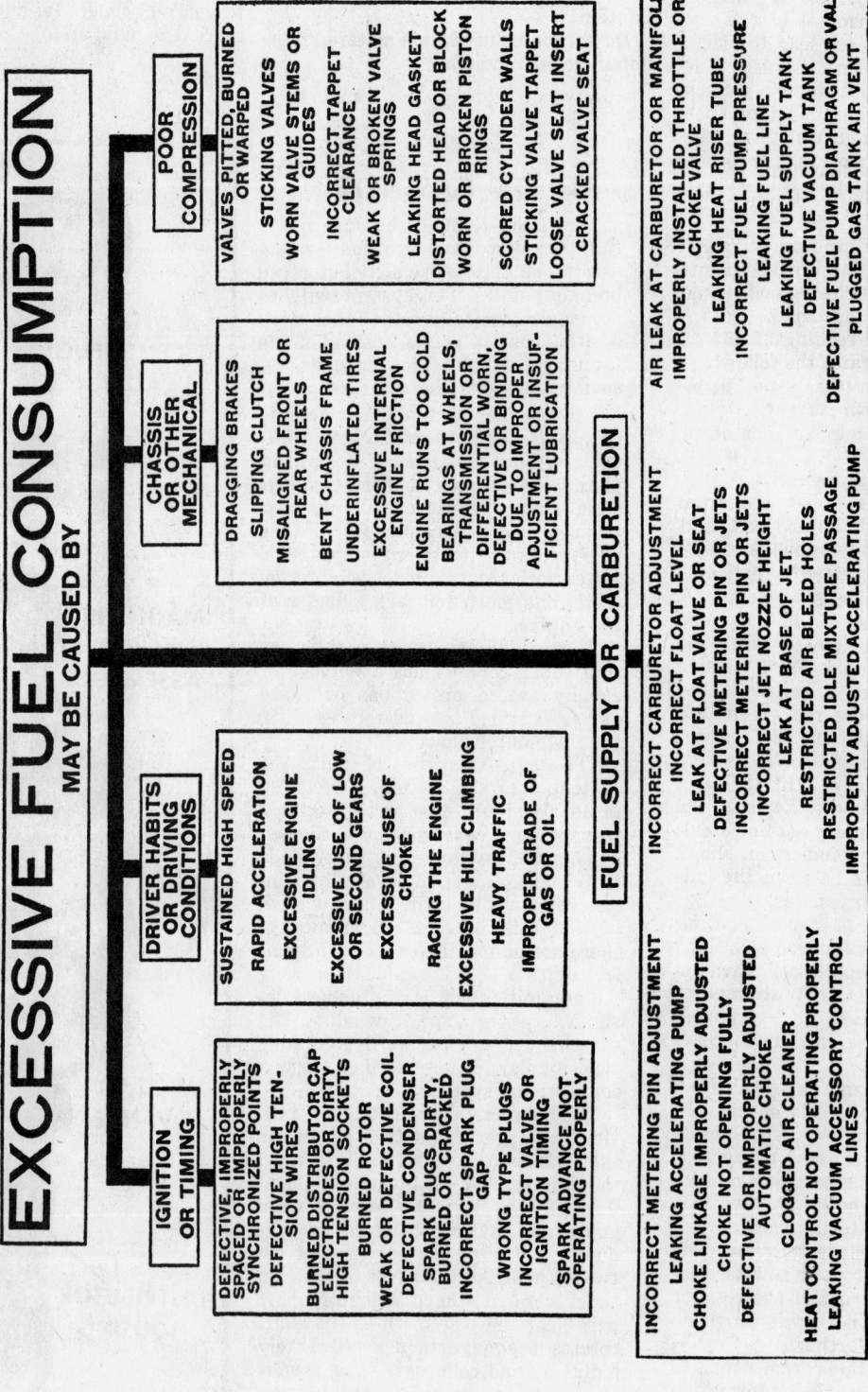

EXCESSIVE FUEL CONSUMPTION

MAY BE CAUSED BY

IGNITION OR TIMING

- DEFECTIVE, IMPROPERLY SPACED OR IMPROPERLY SYNCHRONIZED POINTS
- DEFECTIVE HIGH TENSION WIRES
- BURNED DISTRIBUTOR CAP ELECTRODES OR DIRTY HIGH TENSION SOCKETS
- BURNED ROTOR
- WEAK OR DEFECTIVE COIL
- DEFECTIVE CONDENSER
- SPARK PLUGS DIRTY, BURNED OR CRACKED
- INCORRECT SPARK PLUG GAP
- WRONG TYPE PLUGS
- INCORRECT VALVE OR IGNITION TIMING
- SPARK ADVANCE NOT OPERATING PROPERLY

DRIVER HABITS OR DRIVING CONDITIONS

- SUSTAINED HIGH SPEED
- RAPID ACCELERATION
- EXCESSIVE ENGINE IDLING
- EXCESSIVE USE OF LOW OR SECOND GEARS
- EXCESSIVE USE OF CHOKE
- RACING THE ENGINE
- EXCESSIVE HILL CLIMBING
- HEAVY TRAFFIC
- IMPROPER GRADE OF GAS OR OIL

CHASSIS OR OTHER MECHANICAL

- DRAGGING BRAKES
- SLIPPING CLUTCH
- MISALIGNED FRONT OR REAR WHEELS
- BENT CHASSIS FRAME
- UNDERINFLATED TIRES
- EXCESSIVE INTERNAL ENGINE FRICTION
- ENGINE RUNS TOO COLD
- BEARINGS AT WHEELS, TRANSMISSION OR DIFFERENTIAL WORN, DEFECTIVE OR BINDING DUE TO IMPROPER ADJUSTMENT OR INSUFFICIENT LUBRICATION

POOR COMPRESSION

- VALVES PITTED, BURNED OR WARPED
- STICKING VALVES
- WORN VALVE STEMS OR GUIDES
- INCORRECT TAPPET CLEARANCE
- WEAK OR BROKEN VALVE SPRINGS
- LEAKING HEAD GASKET
- DISTORTED HEAD OR BLOCK
- WORN OR BROKEN PISTON RINGS
- SCORED CYLINDER WALLS
- STICKING VALVE TAPPET
- LOOSE VALVE SEAT INSERT
- CRACKED VALVE SEAT

FUEL SUPPLY OR CARBURETION

- INCORRECT METERING PIN ADJUSTMENT
- LEAKING ACCELERATING PUMP
- CHOKE LINKAGE IMPROPERLY ADJUSTED
- CHOKE NOT OPENING FULLY
- DEFECTIVE OR IMPROPERLY ADJUSTED AUTOMATIC CHOKE
- CLOGGED AIR CLEANER
- HEAT CONTROL NOT OPERATING PROPERLY
- LEAKING VACUUM ACCESSORY CONTROL LINES

- INCORRECT CARBURETOR ADJUSTMENT
- INCORRECT FLOAT LEVEL
- LEAK AT FLOAT VALVE OR SEAT
- DEFECTIVE METERING PIN OR JETS
- INCORRECT METERING PIN OR JETS
- INCORRECT JET NOZZLE HEIGHT
- LEAK AT BASE OF JET
- RESTRICTED AIR BLEED HOLES
- RESTRICTED IDLE MIXTURE PASSAGE
- IMPROPERLY ADJUSTED ACCELERATING PUMP

- AIR LEAK AT CARBURETOR OR MANIFOLD
- IMPROPERLY INSTALLED THROTTLE OR CHOKE VALVE
- LEAKING HEAT RISER TUBE
- INCORRECT FUEL PUMP PRESSURE
- LEAKING FUEL LINE
- LEAKING FUEL SUPPLY TANK
- DEFECTIVE VACUUM TANK
- DEFECTIVE FUEL PUMP DIAPHRAGM OR VALVE
- PLUGGED GAS TANK AIR VENT

MECHANICAL FUEL PUMPS

Operation of the Fuel Pump

The fuel pump is operated by an eccentric which is either part of the camshaft or, in the case of some of the V-8 engines, by an eccentric which is bolted to the front of the camshaft timing gear.

The eccentric moves the fuel pump lever causing the diaphragm to pull downward creating a suction on the intake check valve. This draws gasoline into the closed chamber above the fuel pump diaphragm. When the fuel pump lever reaches the high point of the eccentric the intake check valve, which is loaded with a light spring, closes preventing the gasoline in the diaphragm chamber from returning back into the main fuel line from the gas tank.

As the eccentric continues to turn to its low spot the lever, which is spring loaded, follows the eccentric. The diaphragm which has a pressure spring in back of it forces the fuel trapped in the chamber out of the output side of the fuel pump into the line connected to the carburetor float bowl.

When the float bowl of the carburetor becomes full the gasoline remains in the diaphragm chamber of the fuel pump under spring pressure from the spring under the diaphragm and the linkage idles.

All fuel pumps are connected to their lever by overrunning links which allow the diaphragm to remain stationary until such time as the carburetor float bowl requires more fuel, at which time the spring under the diaphragm will force the fuel out of the diaphragm chamber into the carburetor float bowl.

On all mechanical fuel pumps the fuel is drawn into the fuel pump by mechanical action of the diaphragm and forced out of the fuel pump by the spring only. The mechanical action does not force the gasoline out of the fuel pump. (CONTINUED)

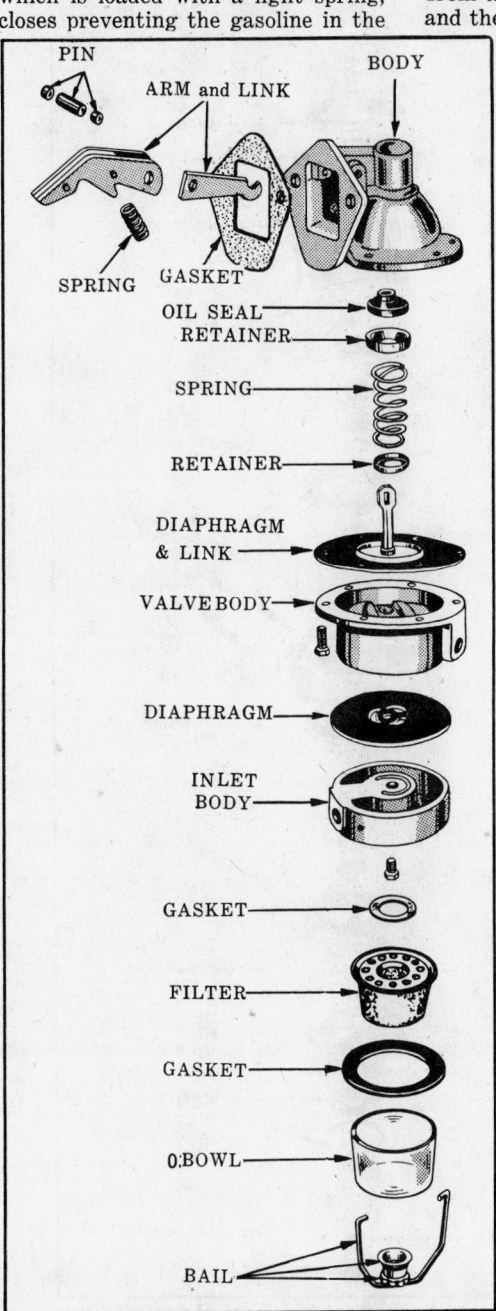

Fuel pump (Exploded view)—A.C.

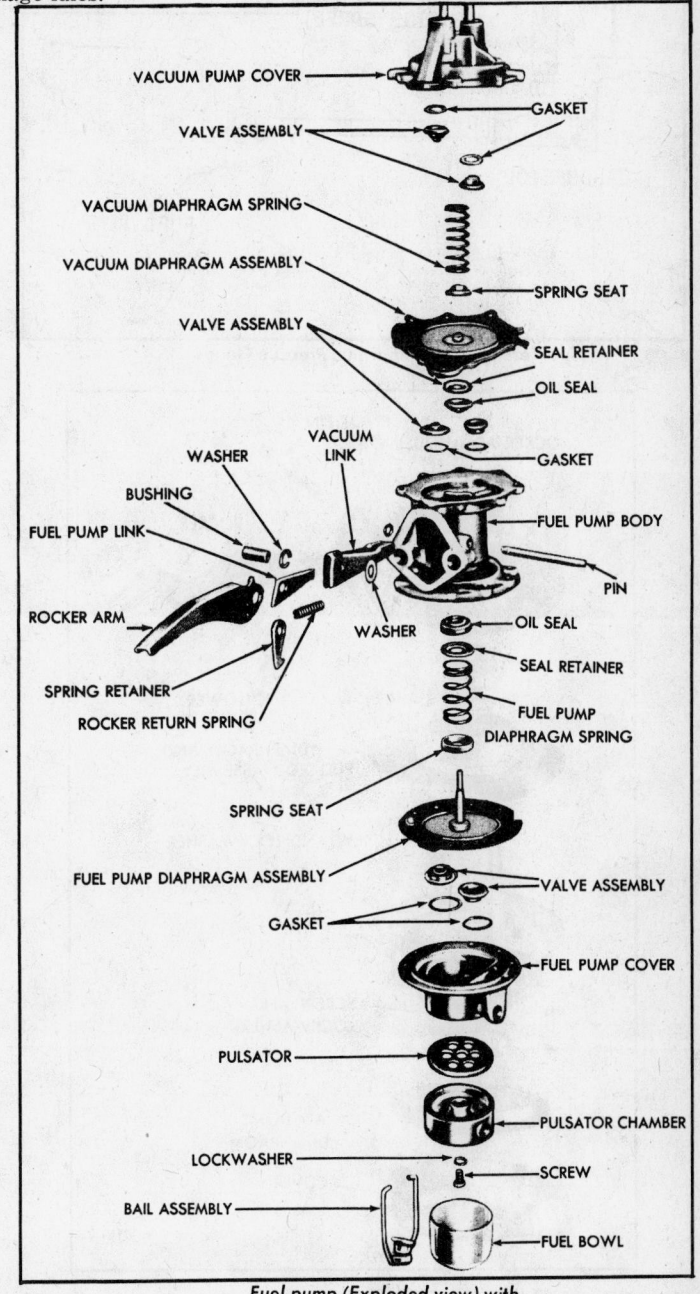

Fuel pump (Exploded view) with vacuum booster—A.C.

FUEL PUMPS

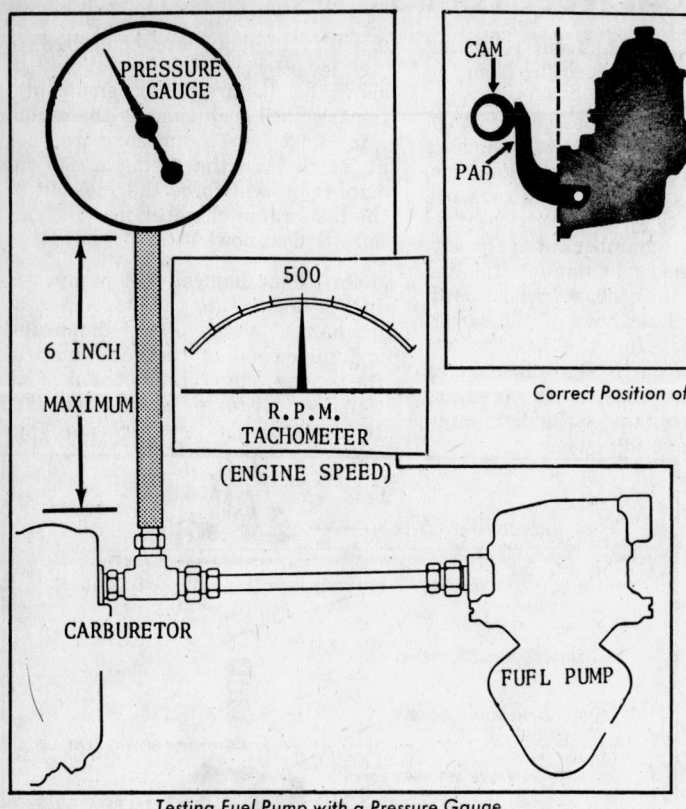

PRESSURE GAUGE

6 INCH MAXIMUM

500

R.P.M. TACHOMETER (ENGINE SPEED)

CARBURETOR

FUFL PUMP

Testing Fuel Pump with a Pressure Gauge

CAM

PAD

PAD

CAM

PAD

CAM

Correct Position of Rocker Arm and Cam on Common Types of Pumps

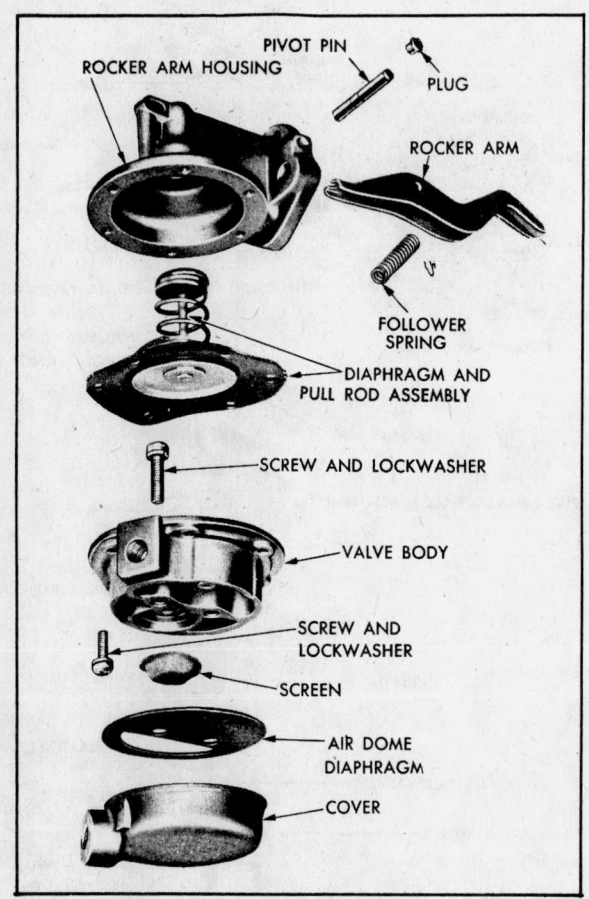

PIVOT PIN

PLUG

ROCKER ARM HOUSING

ROCKER ARM

FOLLOWER SPRING

DIAPHRAGM AND PULL ROD ASSEMBLY

SCREW AND LOCKWASHER

VALVE BODY

SCREW AND LOCKWASHER

SCREEN

AIR DOME DIAPHRAGM

COVER

Fuel pump (Exploded view)—Carter

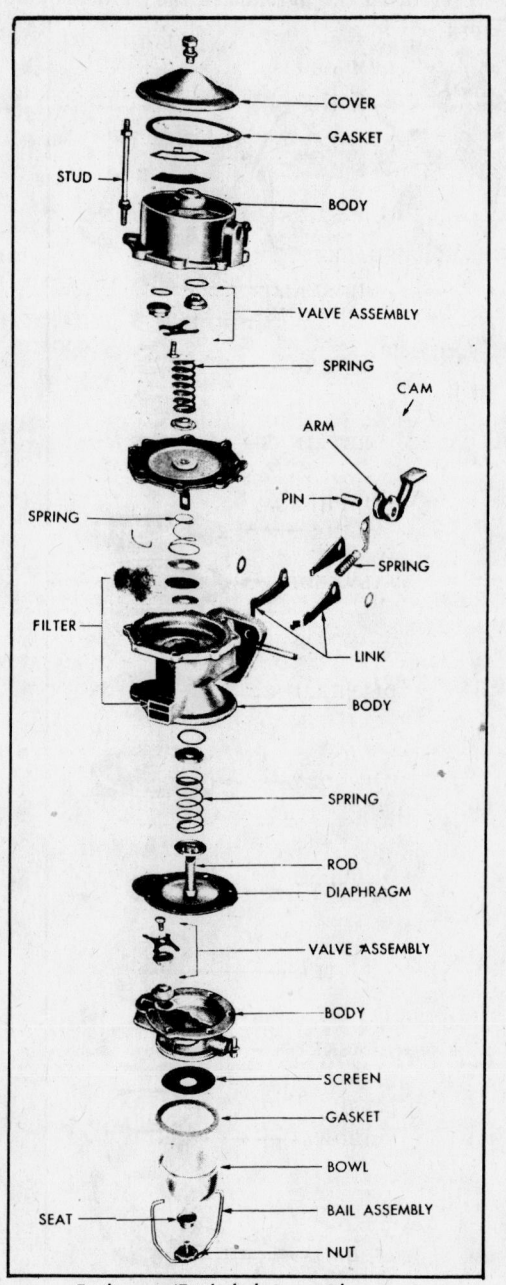

COVER

GASKET

STUD

BODY

VALVE ASSEMBLY

SPRING

CAM

ARM

SPRING

PIN

SPRING

FILTER

LINK

BODY

SPRING

ROD

DIAPHRAGM

VALVE ASSEMBLY

BODY

SCREEN

GASKET

BOWL

SEAT

BAIL ASSEMBLY

NUT

Fuel pump (Exploded view) with vacuum booster—Carter.

Accurate Pressure Tests for Fuel Pumps

Install a low reading pressure gauge with a "T" connection into the fuel pump line at the carburetor. The gauge should be mounted vertically and have a 6 inch "stand pipe." With the engine running, the gauge should read between 3 and 4 pounds. (Exact specifications for fuel pump pressures are given in the specifications table for each car, see index.) If less than 3 pounds, the fault is in the check valves or the diaphragm spring. If the pressure is over 6 pounds, the pump is improperly mounted or the diaphragm spring is too strong or the gasoline is vaporizing due to excess heat.

Fuel Pump Quick Check

If the engine will not run and the fuel pump is suspected, first make certain there is plenty of gasoline in the fuel tank and then examine the filter bowl located either on the fuel pump or at the carburetor to determine if it is full. If the filter bowl is full, disconnect the gasoline line at the carburetor and step on the starter. As the

engine cranks gasoline should spurt out of the fuel line in little spurts every second revolution of the engine.

If fuel spurts out after the engine has turned over several times the fuel pump can be assumed okay.

If gasoline does not spurt out of the open fitting after the engine has cranked over many times, determine if there is any stoppage in the fuel line by disconnecting the fuel line at the input side of the fuel pump and blowing the line clear to make sure that it is not stopped up or restricted in any way.

It is sometimes a good idea that, while the input line is disconnected, to place your finger over the input hole in the fuel pump and again crank the engine and feel that the fuel pump draws against your finger.

Actually, stopped up fuel lines are pretty rare (except frozen lines in very cold weather) and the chances are that the fuel pump is bad if it will not deliver fuel through an open carburetor line.

Fuel Pump Off-Car Check

Hold the thumb tightly against the output side of the pump and then work the lever so that the diaphragm can be felt to move. This will require considerable pressure against the air, pressure will build up against the thumb and the linkage will be felt to move freely since it no longer pulls

springs. As the fuel pump fills up with the diaphragm. The diaphragm is being held down by the fact that the thumb will not let the air out of the diaphragm chamber.

As the thumb is released, air will be felt to hiss out of the chamber. If this happens, the pump may be assumed to be in good condition.

Operation of Combination Pump

A combination pump is a fuel pump with a vacuum pump attached. The method of operation of the vacuum portion is exactly the same as that of the fuel pump only air is pumped instead of gasoline. The input to the pump is from the accessories and the output is to the intake manifold.

Testing the Vacuum Side of Combination Pumps

To make an accurate check of the vacuum pump, disconnect both lines from the vacuum pump and connect a vacuum gauge tightly to the accessory fitting on the pump so that it doesn't leak. With the engine running the gauge should read 10-14 inches of vacuum. Stop the engine, the vacuum gauge should take a little time to run down to zero. If the gauge reads zero just as the engine stops the vacuum check valves are not functioning properly and should be replaced. If the gauge reads less than 10 inches the pump and/or check vales are defective.

Vacuum Side Quick Check

Disconnect the intake side of the vacuum pump and, with the engine running, place your finger over the opening on the intake side and your finger should be drawn tightly against the side of the pump. If this happens, the vacuum unit is functioning properly and, if the accessory units do not function well, they are at fault rather than the vacuum pump itself.

A second check can be made on the vacuum pump to determine if oil is getting past the diaphragm.

To make this check simply disconnect the line between the vacuum pump and the manifold and look in the line to see if there is any oil in it. The slightest trace of oil in this line indicates that the diaphragm is leaking and is drawing oil out of the crankcase of the car.

There have been many instances of engines being completely overhauled to cut down on oil consumption when all that was at fault was the vacuum diaphragm drawing oil from the crankcase and pumping it into the manifold where it is drawn in with the combustible mixture and burned and blown out the exhaust.

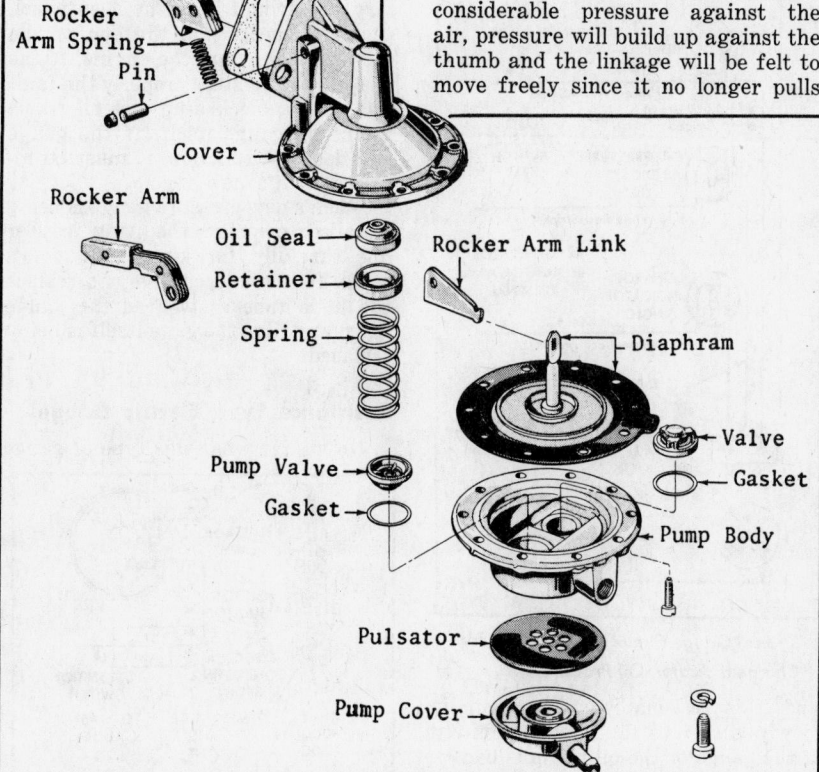

Holley Single Diaphragm Fuel Pump— Exploded View

GAUGES

INSTRUMENT PANEL GAUGES

HOW TO IDENTIFY GAUGES

There are four general types of instrument panel gauges. Bourdon Tube, Resistance type electric, Bi-metal type electric and the Warning Light.

BOURDON TUBE TYPE

This gauge can be distinguished by the small copper tube running from the dash unit to the engine unit. This type of gauge is used to indicate oil pressure or water temperature.

RESISTANCE TYPE ELECTRIC

This gauge can be distinguished from the Bi-metal electric by observation. When the key is turned "ON" the resistance type gauge will "snap" to its position rather than move slowly. There is a single wire connecting the dash unit, called the receiving unit, to the engine or gas tank unit, called the sending unit. This type of gauge is used to indicate oil pressure, water temperature and gasoline supply.

BI-METAL TYPE ELECTRIC

This gauge can be distinguished from the resistance type by observation.

When the key is turned ON the Bi-metal gauge will move slowly to its gauging position.

The Warning Light Type is readily identified by the light. This type of gauge is used to indicate oil pressure and generator operation. Sometimes it is also used to indicate temperature.

TROUBLE SHOOTING GAUGES

Bourdon Tube Types

FOR WATER TEMPERATURE

These gauges cannot be repaired. If the unit does not seem to be working correctly, remove the bulb assembly from the engine, being careful not to kink the small tube.

Place the bulb in boiling water. The dash gauge should respond to show hot. Now substitute cold water. If the gauge follows to read cool, the assembly is OK. If it does not, the whole assembly must be replaced.

FOR OIL PRESSURE

If the oil pressure gauge fails to operate, shut the engine down immediately on the assumption that the

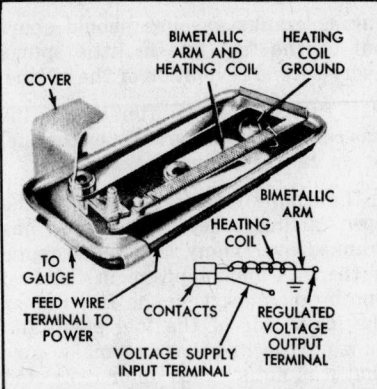

Constant Voltage Regulator.

gauge is accurate and that the oil pump itself has failed. This is the safest thing to do since, if the gauge is functioning properly and there is no oil pressure, the engine will burn up in a few short minutes.

After shutting the engine down, disconnect the tiny oil line from its fitting on the engine block and then start up the engine and see if oil comes out of the hole in which the tube is connected. If oil comes out of this hole in a steady flow, there is actually oil pressure in the engine

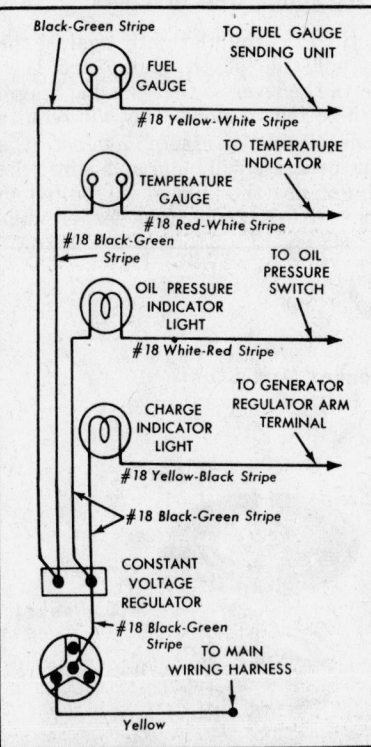

Typical Gauge Circuit (Tel-Tail Light for Charge Indicator, Oil Pressure)

and it is reasonably safe to run it slowly until it is found out definitely if the gauge or the oil pump is bad.

Connect up the tube to the engine and disconnect it at the pressure gauge and again start the engine. See

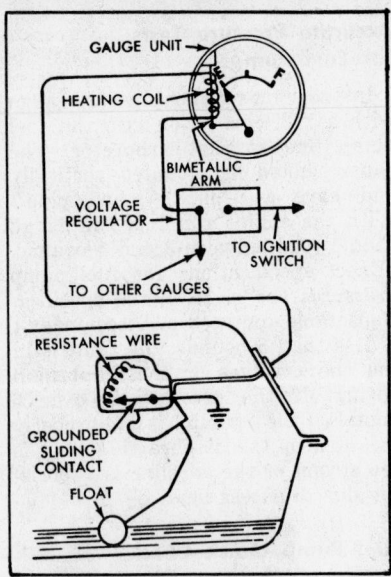

Fuel Gauge Circuit-King Seeley

if oil comes out of the little tube in back of the gauge in a steady but small flow, which would indicate that the oil pump in the engine is functioning and the gauge on the dash is failing to register.

Next, remove the gauge from the dash and make sure the tiny hole in the gauge fitting is open. Prod it with a pin or needle to make sure it is not stopped up or blocked in any way. After being sure the hole is open, reconnect the gauge; it is not necessary to remount it on the dash panel, simply connect it to the end of the tube and again run the engine. If the gauge now registers properly the fault was with a blocked-up metering hole in the oil gauge itself. If the gauge still does not function, it must be replaced with a new one.

When a new pressure gauge is being installed, examine the tiny copper line carefully for kinks and worn spots. It is sound economy to replace the little tube as well as the gauge when any time the gage itself is being replaced.

Resistance Type Electric Gauges

No matter what this type of gauge

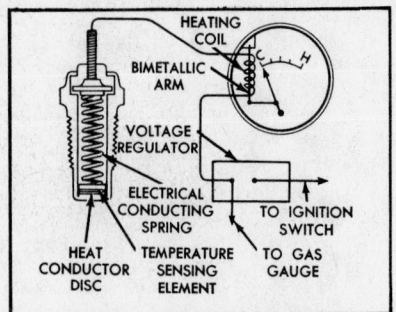

Temperature Gauge Circuit-King Seeley

is used for, the checking procedure is the same, when used to indicate oil pressure the following procedure should be applied first.

GAUGE READS ZERO OIL PRESSURE

If the oil pressure gauge on the dash fails to register, immediately shut the engine down as a safety precaution since the gauge may be reading properly and there may be no oil pressure in the engine. Running the engine without oil pressure will shortly damage it considerably.

In an emergency a quick check can be made by first determining that there is plenty of oil in the engine and then disconnect the wire from the sending unit on the engine and remove the sending unit from its hole in the engine block. Now start the engine and if the pump is operating oil will come out of the mounting hole in a steady flow. If no oil comes out of the hole it means that the oil pump in the engine is not working and should be attended to before any further check is made on the gauges themselves.

GAUGE READS ZERO AT ALL TIMES

Disconnect the wire at the sending unit on the engine (or gas tank) and ground this wire against the frame or engine. If the gauge being tested now reads "full on," replace the sending unit.

If grounding the wire to the sending unit does not cause the gauge to read "full on," then check further by disconnecting at the gauge the wire which runs to the sending unit. Now connect a jumper wire from this terminal and ground the jumper wire right at the dash. If the gauge now reads "full on," the wire leading to the sending unit is broken.

If grounding right at the dash unit does not make the gauge read "full on," check to determine if current is reaching the gauge from the ignition switch. If it is, and the gauge still does not read "full on," the dash unit should be replaced.

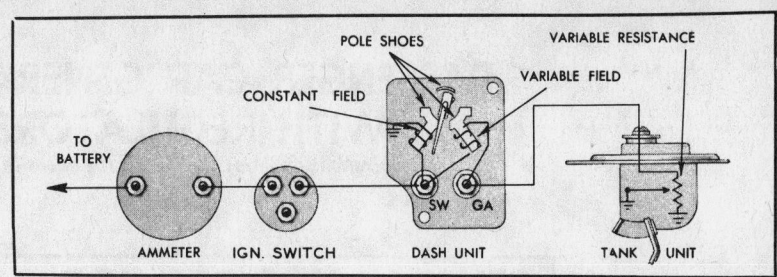

WIRING CIRCUIT OF THE MAGNETIC FUEL GAUGE.

GAUGE READS FULL AT ALL TIMES

Again disconnect the wire from the sending unit and if this causes the gauge to read "full off," the sending unit either on the tank or engine is defective and should be replaced.

If disconnecting the wire from the sending unit has no effect on the gauge, disconnect the wire at the gauge. If it now shows "full off," the wire between the gauge and the sending unit is grounded and the ground should be corrected.

If disconnecting the wire at the gauge does not cause it to read "full off," the dash unit has an internal ground and should be replaced.

GAUGE READS TOO HIGH AT ALL TIMES

By this is meant that the gas tank gauge may read ¾ full when it is known there is only ¼ of a tank full of gas. Or the temperature gauge may read boiling when the operator knows that the temperature is probably not more than 160 degrees.

This condition is generally caused by the wire from the sending unit to the receiving unit being partially grounded.

The only accurate check that can be made for this condition is to use a rheostat in place of the sending unit to determine if the gauge on the dash is in good condition.

If after making certain that there is no partial ground on the wire between the sending and receiving unit, the sending unit should be replaced.

GAUGE READS TOO LOW AT ALL TIMES

This is almost always caused by a high resistance connection in one or more of the wires.

The wire, for instance, to the gauge on the gas tank is usually a bayonet connection and frequently it develops high resistance because of water in the trunk of the car, etc.

To cure a too low reading gauge, clean up all of the connections in the gauge circuit including that of the gauge itself. If this fails to make the gauge read properly, it will have to be checked with the rheostat to determine which of the units is defective.

Bi-Metal Type Electric Temperature Gauge

If the dash gauge reads low temperature at all times even when the engine is known to be warm, check first to find out if the wire from the gauge on the dash to the gauge on the engine block is grounded in some way. If this wire is grounded the gauge will read cold.

An open circuit in this type gauge will cause the gauge to read hot.

To check to see if the instrument on the dash is functioning properly, first ground the wire which goes to the sending unit to the cylinder head. This should cause the gauge to read extreme cold. In fact, it should go all the way down to the stop pin.

To determine if the gauge is operating properly, remove the ground and immediately and quickly the needle should register maximum temperature. If the dash instrument responds to these two tests when the gauge is not functioning properly, the sending unit in the engine block should be replaced.

The Warning Light Type

The light should light when the engine is not running but the switch is turned on. If it does not, try a new bulb. If still no light, check the wire from the light to the ignition switch. If still no light, disconnect the wire at the sending unit and ground it. If the light now lights, the sending unit is faulty.

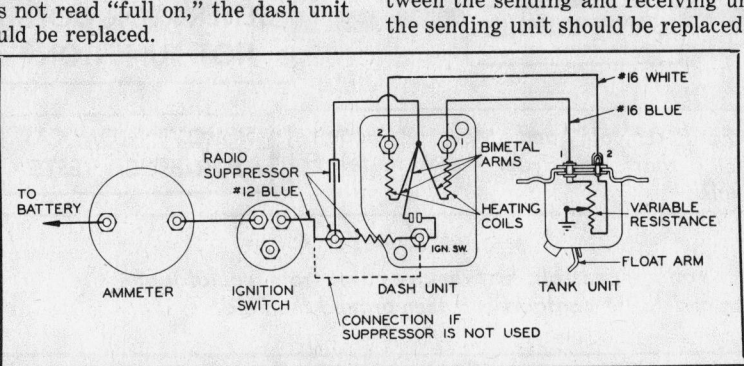

WIRING CIRCUIT OF THE THERMAL FUEL GAUGE.

PASSENGER CAR GENERATORS
WITH REGULATORS
Illustrations for this chart are on the opposite page

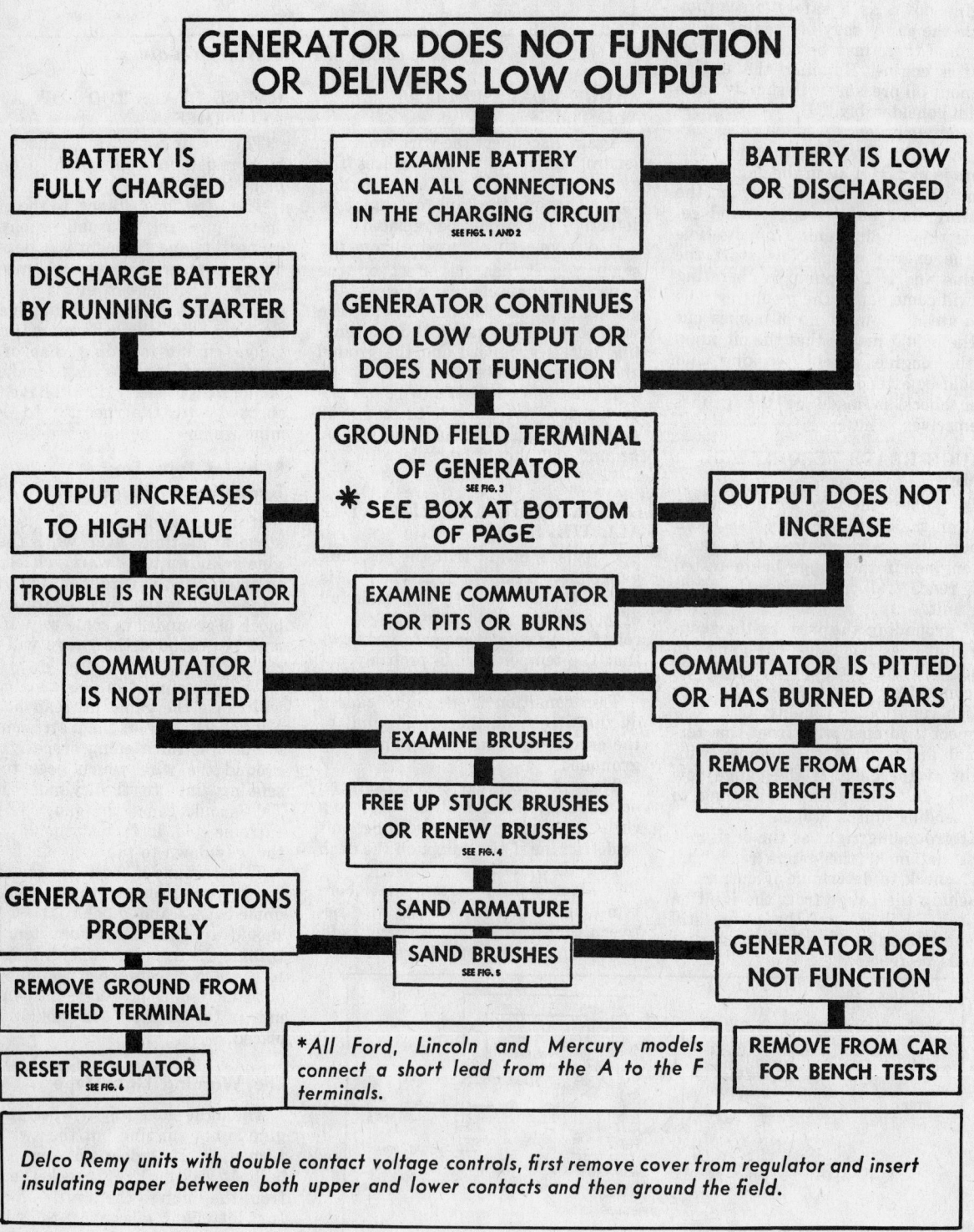

GENERATOR DOES NOT FUNCTION OR DELIVERS LOW OUTPUT

BATTERY IS FULLY CHARGED

EXAMINE BATTERY CLEAN ALL CONNECTIONS IN THE CHARGING CIRCUIT
SEE FIGS. 1 AND 2

BATTERY IS LOW OR DISCHARGED

DISCHARGE BATTERY BY RUNNING STARTER

GENERATOR CONTINUES TOO LOW OUTPUT OR DOES NOT FUNCTION

GROUND FIELD TERMINAL OF GENERATOR
SEE FIG. 3
*** SEE BOX AT BOTTOM OF PAGE**

OUTPUT INCREASES TO HIGH VALUE

OUTPUT DOES NOT INCREASE

TROUBLE IS IN REGULATOR

EXAMINE COMMUTATOR FOR PITS OR BURNS

COMMUTATOR IS NOT PITTED

COMMUTATOR IS PITTED OR HAS BURNED BARS

EXAMINE BRUSHES

REMOVE FROM CAR FOR BENCH TESTS

FREE UP STUCK BRUSHES OR RENEW BRUSHES
SEE FIG. 4

GENERATOR FUNCTIONS PROPERLY

SAND ARMATURE

SAND BRUSHES
SEE FIG. 5

GENERATOR DOES NOT FUNCTION

REMOVE GROUND FROM FIELD TERMINAL

RESET REGULATOR
SEE FIG. 6

All Ford, Lincoln and Mercury models connect a short lead from the A to the F terminals.

REMOVE FROM CAR FOR BENCH TESTS

Delco Remy units with double contact voltage controls, first remove cover from regulator and insert insulating paper between both upper and lower contacts and then ground the field.

DC GENERATORS and REGULATORS

Illustrations on this page apply to chart opposite

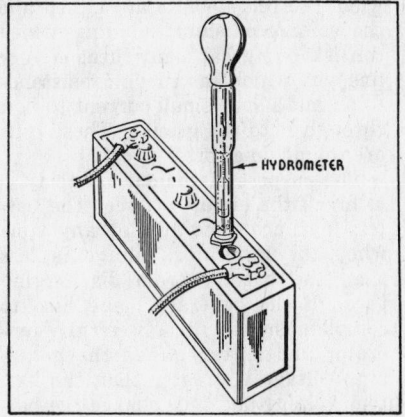

Fig. 1. Test battery with a hydrometer

HYDROMETER

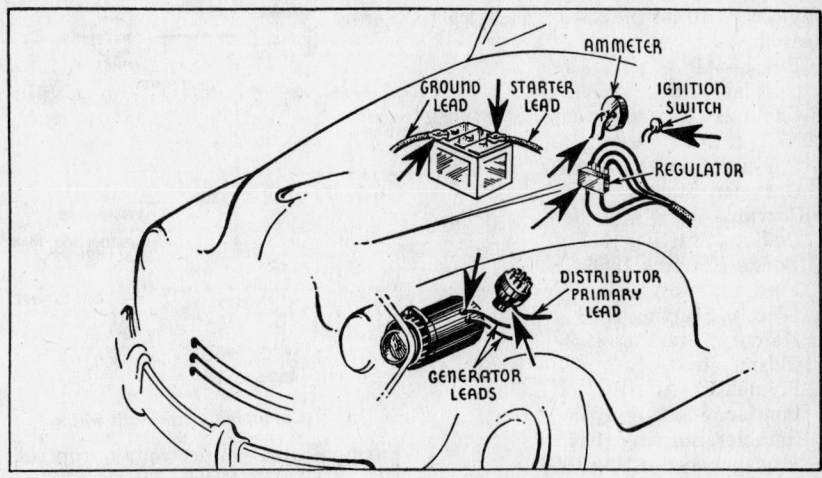

GROUND LEAD STARTER LEAD AMMETER IGNITION SWITCH REGULATOR DISTRIBUTOR PRIMARY LEAD GENERATOR LEADS

Fig. 2—The connections shown in above sketch should be clean and tight

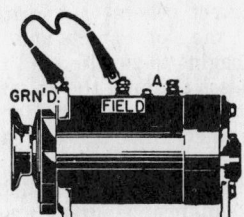

GRN'D. FIELD A

Fig. 3—Grounding "Field Lead Except Ford

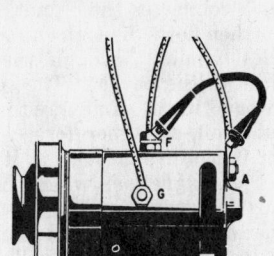

F G A

Fig. 3A—Ford—Connecting Field to "A" Lead

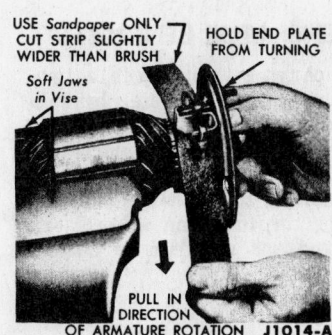

USE Sandpaper ONLY CUT STRIP SLIGHTLY WIDER THAN BRUSH HOLD END PLATE FROM TURNING Soft Jaws in Vise PULL IN DIRECTION OF ARMATURE ROTATION J1014-A

Fig. 5—Sanding brushes—Generator body has been removed to get a better picture, the actual sanding is done with the generator assembled.

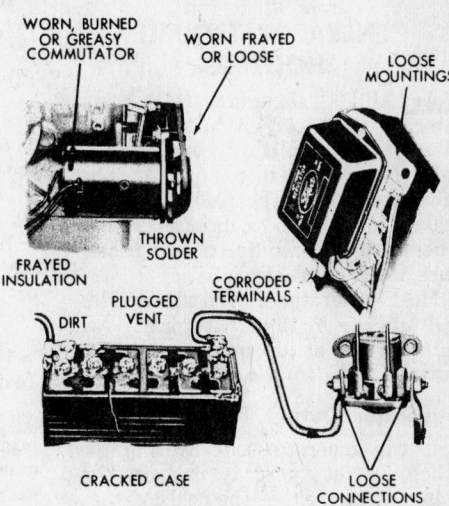

WORN, BURNED OR GREASY COMMUTATOR WORN FRAYED OR LOOSE LOOSE MOUNTINGS FRAYED INSULATION THROWN SOLDER CORRODED TERMINALS DIRT PLUGGED VENT CRACKED CASE LOOSE CONNECTIONS

Visual Inspection of Charging Circuit

Fig. 4—Examine brushes for wear. Above shows a worn brush compared to a new one. Make sure the brush holder does not stick

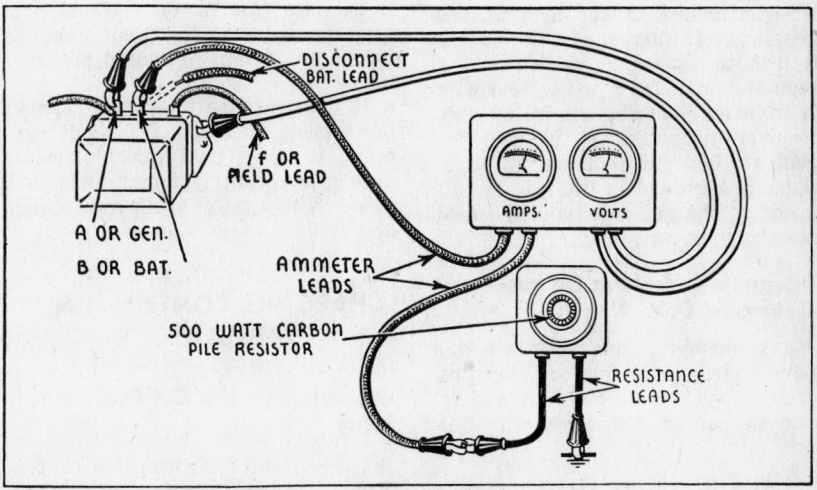

DISCONNECT BAT. LEAD f OR FIELD LEAD A OR GEN. B OR BAT. AMMETER LEADS AMPS. VOLTS 500 WATT CARBON PILE RESISTOR RESISTANCE LEADS

Fig. 6. Meter hook-up to set regulator

DC GENERATORS and REGULATORS

12 VOLT SYSTEMS

The following American built passenger cars utilize the 12-volt electrical system:

Buick—All
Cadillac—All
Chevrolet Passenger cars, Starting 1955
Chrysler Imperials—All
Chrysler, Starting 1956
Corvair—All
De Soto, Starting 1956
Dodge, Starting 1956
Ford, Starting 1956
Lincoln, Starting 1956
Mercury, Starting 1956
Oldsmobile—All
Plymouth—All
Pontiac, Starting 1955
Rambler, Starting 1956
Studebaker, Starting 1956
Tempest—All
Valiant and Lancer—All
Willys, Starting 1959

GENERATOR TROUBLE SHOOTING

Note: All D.C. Generators with regulators used on Ford Products are regulated at the main brush connection to the field coil rather than at the grounded end of the field. This text will refer to the above units as "Ford" where there is a difference of procedure of the unusual regulation.

Most generator electrical troubles fall into one of three categories: (a) Intermittent or low output. (b) Output too high. (c) No Output.

Generator Output Too High

If the generator is delivering too much output there is one or two things wrong, either the field coils are grounded internally, or the regulator is not functioning properly.

Make a quick check by disconnecting the field lead at the generator. This will be the smaller of the two wires attached to the side of the generator. If this causes the output to drop to a very low value then the regulator is at fault or the field wire is grounded somewhere in its harness. If after disconnecting the field the generator output remains too high, there is a ground in the field circuit inside of the generator and the field coil should be replaced.

Intermittent or Low Output—Generator Does Not Function

Accompanying this text is a full page chart of the step by step procedure required to determine and repair the causes of this generator failure.

CAUTION: When D.C. Generators are used with Delco Remy regulators

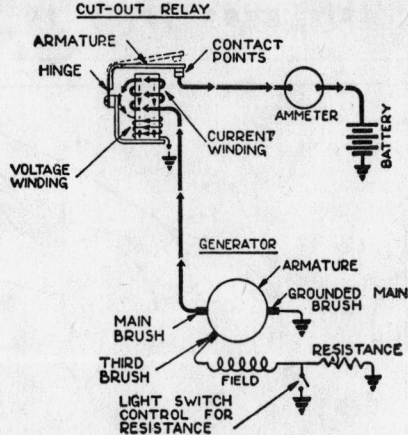

Fig. 1—Cutout relay schematic wiring

having double contact voltage control, DO NOT GROUND THE FIELD LEAD as this may cause the high voltage points in the regulators to burn.

Refer to the box at the bottom of the chart for instructions.

DC GENERATOR BENCH TEST

Accompanying this text is a two-page chart showing the step by step procedure together with the methods of testing and repairing generators on the bench.

By following the lines in the chart, any generator, including a Ford, can be repaired and returned to normal duty.

Test Instruments Required

Commercial test sets are made especially for testing regulators and generators conveniently and easily, however, if a test set is not available, the instruments necessary to test a generator, cutout relay, voltage or current regulator are: A voltmeter with a full scale reading from zero to 10 volts(for 6-volt systems) or zero to 20 volts (for 12-volt systems), an ammeter with a full scale reading from minus 5 amp. to 40 amp. positive,

a ¾ ohm variable resistance capable of carrying 50 amp. (for 6-volt systems) or a 1½ ohm variable resistance (for 12-volt systems). It is well to have also a 1½ ohm 1000 watt variable resistor to test batteries.

CHARGING CONTROL UNITS (REGULATORS)

Operation of the Cut-Out Relay

The cut-out relay consists of two windings—the current or series winding which consists of a few turns of

heavy wire through which all the current output of the generator flows when the relay points are closed and the voltage or shunt winding which consists of a great many turns of very fine wire which has enough resistance to permit a very small current to flow through it to the ground. These coils are wound on a soft iron core.

The purpose of the cut-out relay is to break the circuit between the battery and the generator at any time when the generator voltage is less than the battery from discharging through the generator; and also to complete the circuit between the generator and battery when the generator voltage is greater than the battery voltage and thus charge the battery.

Note: When installing a new relay it is a good precaution to momentarily connect a wire between the generator main lead and the battery lead to insure correct generator polarity.

When the motor starts and the generator begins to function, all the current passes through the shunt coil to ground. As the generator speed increases, the voltage also increases and more and more current passes through the shunt coil until the magnetism obtained is great enough to overcome the pull of the relay contact armature spring. The magnetism in the core closes the contact points which completes the circuit. The current then flows through the current or series winding through the contact points to the battery. The series coil is wound in the same direction as the shunt coil, and, therefore, when current is passing through it, it will add to the magnetism which holds the armature down. See Fig. 1. Should the generator stop or slow to below generating speed, current will begin to flow from the battery to the generator. Reference to Fig. 1 will clearly show that this current will pass through the shunt coil in the same direction as the generator current but in the series coil it will be in the opposite direction. Therefore, magnetism of the series coil will oppose the magnetism of the shunt coil and the resultant magnetic force is not sufficient to hold the armature in its closed position and the contact points will open, breaking the circuit between the battery and the generator.

Refer to cut-out relay data table (in the car section) for correct closing voltage. To test relay attach instruments according to the test set manufacturers instructions. If "made up" instruments are used, attach as shown in Fig. 4.

If test shows that contacts close at too low voltage, increase spring ten-

DC GENERATORS and REGULATORS

Bench Tests—Cont'd

sion on contact armature.

Air gap between armature and core should be from .012 to .017 in. with points closed. Clearance between contacts should be from .015 to .025 in. Exact settings are given in the data tables for each car in the car section.

In the event generator fails to charge battery, make certain that generator itself is functioning properly before making any correction in relay.

Single Contact Voltage Regulators

Voltage control units consist of one or two coils used in conjunction with the cutout relay to limit the output of the generator when the voltage in the charging circuit reaches a predetermined safe maximum. See Fig. 2.

Double Contact Voltage Regulators

Double contact voltage regulators are basically the same as single contact units and serve the same basic functions, that of limiting the output of the generator when the voltage in the circuit reaches a predetermined safe maximum. See Fig. 3.

The upper set of points function in the same manner as single contact regulators but in addition there is a second set of points (designed as the "lower set of points") which operate to short circuit the field coils when the voltage in the circuit continues to gain or increase with the upper set of points working.

Current Regulators

Current regulator units consist of one or two coils used in conjunction with a cutout relay and voltage regulator. Its function is to hold the generator to a maximum safe output. The current relay coils are in series with the generator output.

Adjustment of Regulators

Before doing any work on the regulator, make certain all connections in

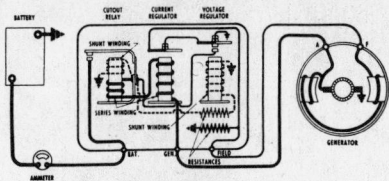

Fig. 3—Circuit diagram of a Delco Remy double contact voltage regulator

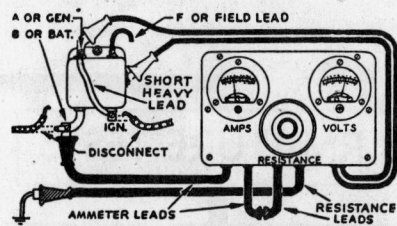

Fig. 4—Made up meter hook-up for resetting voltage and current regulators. If a commercial test set is used, connect according to instructions furnished by manufacturer of test set

the charging circuit are clean and tight. On regulators with three binding posts (Battery, Field and Generator) resistance in the charging circuit will limit the output of the generator before the battery reaches full charge.

Next, make certain the generator itself is functioning properly: See "TROUBLE SHOOTING ON GENERATORS" at the beginning of this section.

When the trouble is definitely placed in the regulator proceed as follows: Remove regulator cover (some Auto-Lite covers are sealed on) and examine contact points for pits and burns. (Single contact voltage and current contact points are the ones which are closed, cutout relay points are open when the generator is not turning. On Delco Remy double contact voltage regulators the double contact will be self evident when the cover is removed.) Thoroughly clean regulator and relay points. **Note:** If points are too badly pitted unit will have to be replaced.

Now check both the current and voltage regulator armature air gap (correct gap is given in the data

tables in the car section).

Gap on both voltage and current unit should be adjusted to the specified clearance with the armature depressed until the points just barely touch. Adjust by moving the stationary points up or down. On some Ford regulators no provision is made to adjust the armature air gap.

Resetting Current or Single Contact Voltage Regulators

Note: The following text does not apply to Delco Remy regulators with double contact voltage control.

Note: If a commercial test set is to be used, follow the instructions given for your test instrument and ignore the meter hook-up given here.

After points are cleaned and gaps properly set, proceed with setting the regulator as follows, regardless of the number of terminals: Disconnect the wire from the "BAT" (Delco) or "B" (Auto-Lite) lug of the generator. (Tape this wire as a precaution against fire.) Connect one side of the test set ammeter to the "BAT" or "B" lug from which the wire was removed. Connect the other side of the ammeter to one side of the variable resistance (¾ ohm max., capable of carrying 50 amp.), the other variable resistance lead to a good clean ground. This hook-up eliminates the battery and charging circuit and causes all the current to pass through the test set resistance.

Connect one side of the voltmeter to the "GEN" (Delco) or "A" (Auto-Lite) lug (do not remove the wire from this lug), the other voltmeter lead to a good ground.

Note: On some commercial test sets the resistance is inserted into the circuit by simply turning the resistance knob to the IN position. Since the internal hook-up and capacity of commercial test sets vary it is wise to apply the meters as recommended by the manufacturer of your own particular test unit.

Now start the motor and run at maximum charge as indicated by the ammeter.

Note: On full current a voltage regulator unit having three elements (relay, current regulator and voltage regulator), the element whose arma-

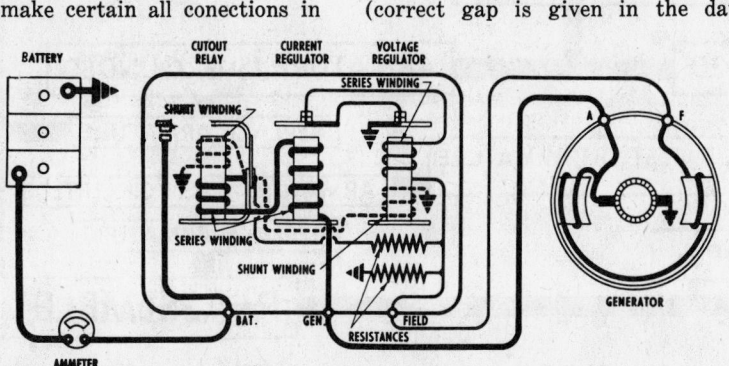

Fig. 2—Circuit diagram of a Delco Remy single contact voltage regulator

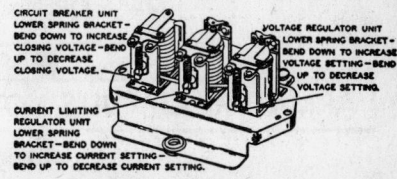

Fig. 5—Auto-Lite 3 element (relay, voltage and current) regulator showing spring, hangers and points of adjustment

DC GENERATORS and REGULATORS

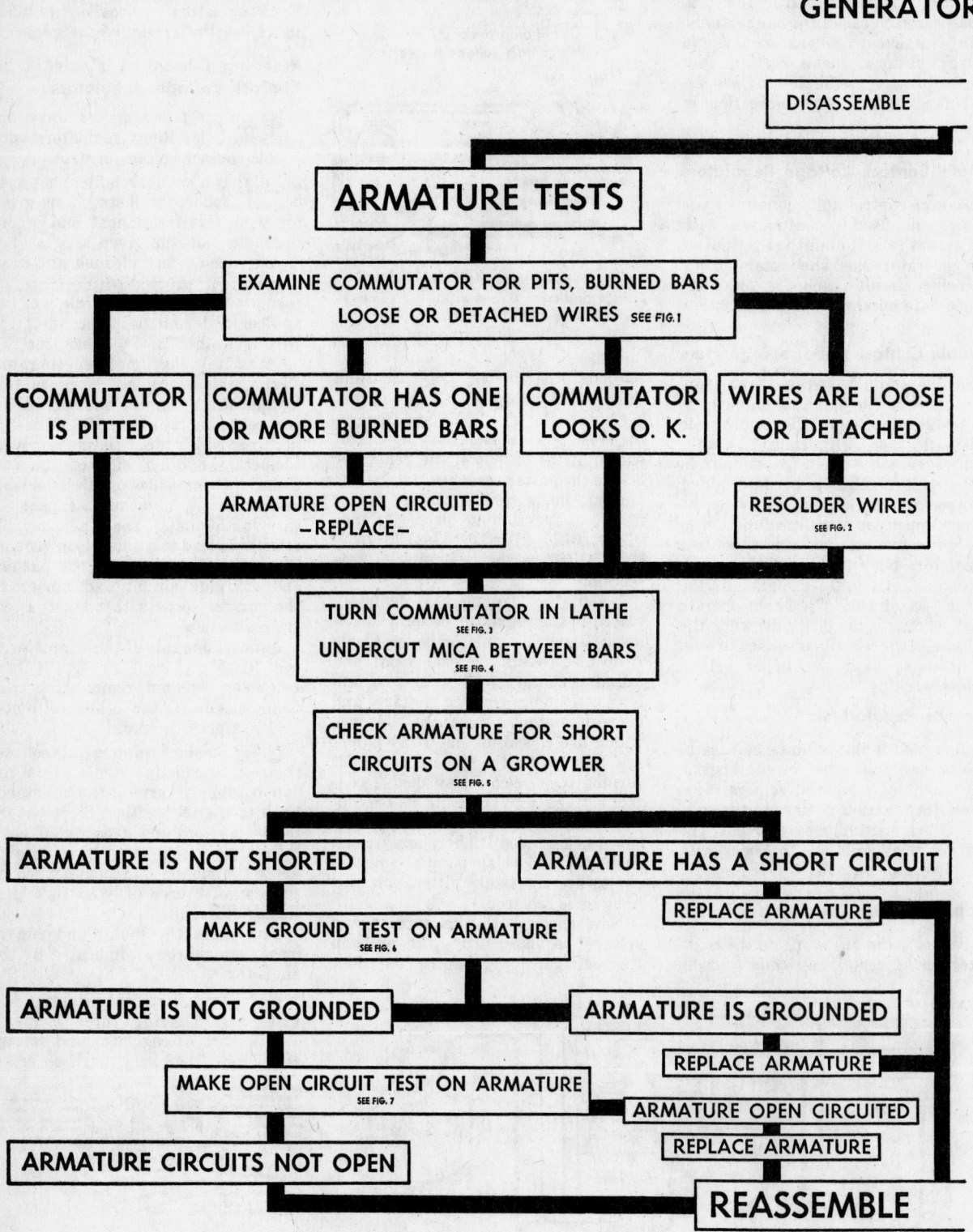

DISASSEMBLE

ARMATURE TESTS

EXAMINE COMMUTATOR FOR PITS, BURNED BARS
LOOSE OR DETACHED WIRES SEE FIG. 1

COMMUTATOR
IS PITTED

COMMUTATOR HAS ONE
OR MORE BURNED BARS

COMMUTATOR
LOOKS O. K.

WIRES ARE LOOSE
OR DETACHED

ARMATURE OPEN CIRCUITED
– REPLACE –

RESOLDER WIRES
SEE FIG. 2

TURN COMMUTATOR IN LATHE
SEE FIG. 3
UNDERCUT MICA BETWEEN BARS
SEE FIG. 4

CHECK ARMATURE FOR SHORT
CIRCUITS ON A GROWLER
SEE FIG. 5

ARMATURE IS NOT SHORTED

ARMATURE HAS A SHORT CIRCUIT

REPLACE ARMATURE

MAKE GROUND TEST ON ARMATURE
SEE FIG. 6

ARMATURE IS NOT GROUNDED

ARMATURE IS GROUNDED

REPLACE ARMATURE

MAKE OPEN CIRCUIT TEST ON ARMATURE
SEE FIG. 7

ARMATURE OPEN CIRCUITED

REPLACE ARMATURE

ARMATURE CIRCUITS NOT OPEN

REASSEMBLE

AND TROUBLE SHOOTING

BENCH TESTS

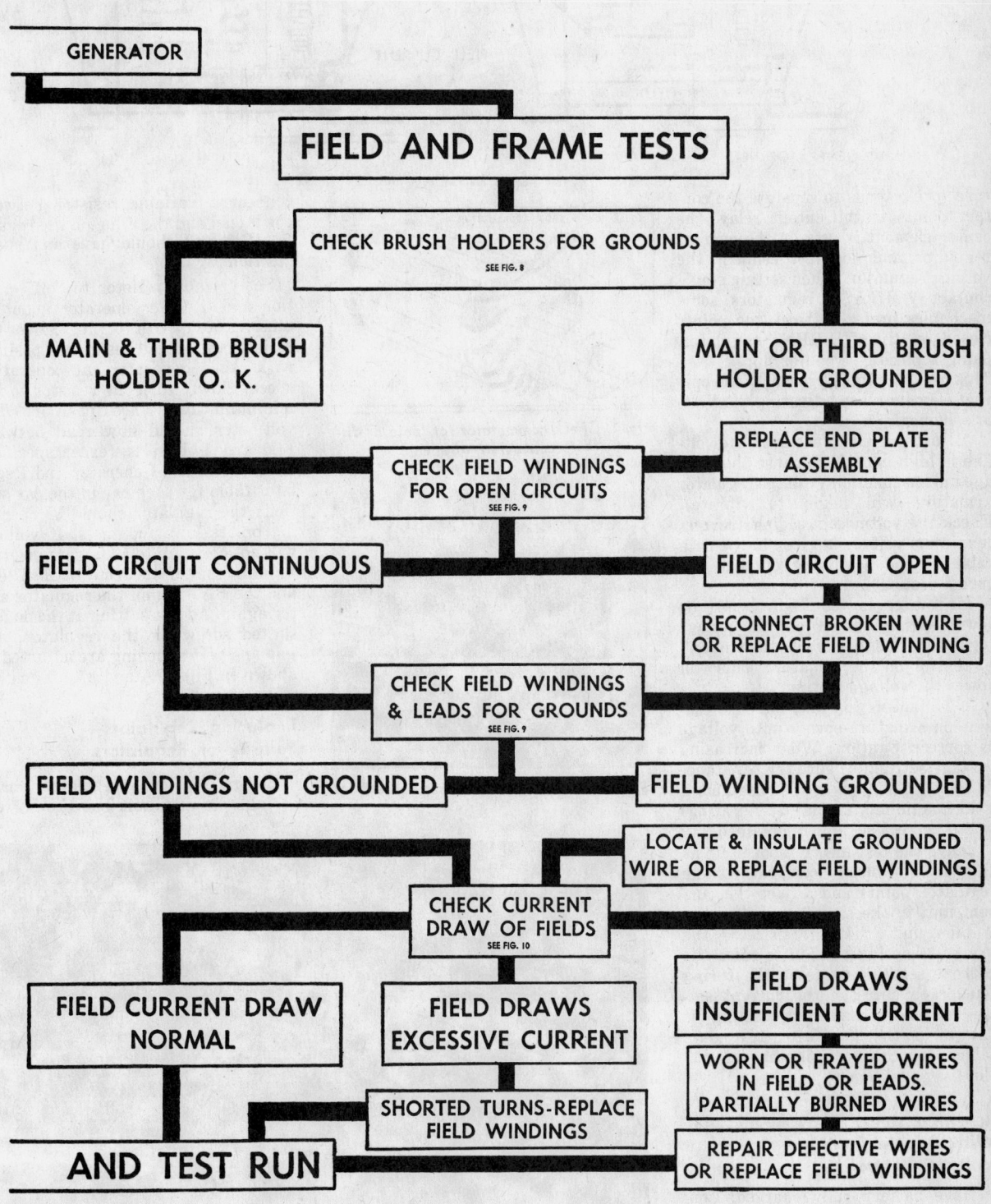

GENERATOR

FIELD AND FRAME TESTS

CHECK BRUSH HOLDERS FOR GROUNDS
SEE FIG. 8

MAIN & THIRD BRUSH HOLDER O. K.

MAIN OR THIRD BRUSH HOLDER GROUNDED

REPLACE END PLATE ASSEMBLY

CHECK FIELD WINDINGS FOR OPEN CIRCUITS
SEE FIG. 9

FIELD CIRCUIT CONTINUOUS

FIELD CIRCUIT OPEN

RECONNECT BROKEN WIRE OR REPLACE FIELD WINDING

CHECK FIELD WINDINGS & LEADS FOR GROUNDS
SEE FIG. 9

FIELD WINDINGS NOT GROUNDED

FIELD WINDING GROUNDED

LOCATE & INSULATE GROUNDED WIRE OR REPLACE FIELD WINDINGS

CHECK CURRENT DRAW OF FIELDS
SEE FIG. 10

FIELD CURRENT DRAW NORMAL

FIELD DRAWS EXCESSIVE CURRENT

FIELD DRAWS INSUFFICIENT CURRENT

WORN OR FRAYED WIRES IN FIELD OR LEADS. PARTIALLY BURNED WIRES

SHORTED TURNS-REPLACE FIELD WINDINGS

REPAIR DEFECTIVE WIRES OR REPLACE FIELD WINDINGS

AND TEST RUN

DC GENERATORS and REGULATORS

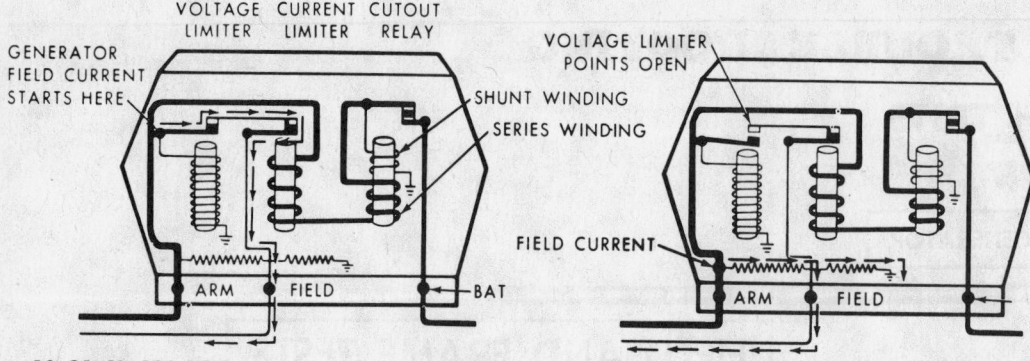

FIELD CURRENT (POINTS CLOSED)

FIELD CURRENT (POINTS OPEN)

VOLTAGE CURRENT CUTOUT
LIMITER LIMITER RELAY

GENERATOR
FIELD CURRENT
STARTS HERE

SHUNT WINDING
SERIES WINDING

VOLTAGE LIMITER
POINTS OPEN

FIELD CURRENT

ARM FIELD BAT

ARM FIELD

TO GENERATOR FIELD

Auto-Lite 3 element regulator

ture spring tends to separate the contact points is the cutout relay, the center element is usually the current regulator and the last element the voltage regulator. When setting single contact VOLTAGE regulators some mechanics prefer to block the points closed on the CURRENT regulator, using a piece of wood or fibre.
This prevents interference by the current element when adjusting the Voltage element.

Adjust the resistance until the voltage is high enough to cause the voltage unit to function (voltage regulator armature will begin to vibrate). Check the voltmeter reading (correct maximum voltage is given in the data table at the beginning of each car model section).

If voltage is too high, bend the lower spring hanger on the voltage regulator so as to decrease the amount of tension on the armature. This will lower the voltage setting.

If voltage is too low, increase tension on armature spring until voltage is correct. <u>Caution:</u> When increasing voltage setting, be sure the resistance is set high enough so that the unit is still functioning (armature vibrating) when correct setting is obtained.

Leave the test meters hooked up as they are and block closed the voltage regulator points and adjust the current unit in the same manner as the voltage unit, that is: Increase the armature spring tension to raise the current setting; decrease the spring tension to decrease the current setting (correct maximum setting is shown in the generator test data tables, for each car, in the car section).

Resetting Delco Remy Regulators With Double Contact Voltage Control

Have battery fully charged. Connect voltmeter from BAT. terminal to ground. Disconnect the F lead and

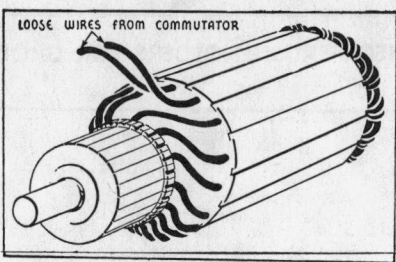

LOOSE WIRES FROM COMMUTATOR

Fig. 1. Check commutator for loose or disconnected wires

Fig. 2. Carefully resolder loose connections

connect a variable resistor between the F lead and the F lug on the regulator. Resistor should have an "open" position.

Set variable resistor to "off" position and operate generator about 15 minutes to warm it up. Move the resistor to the full resistance position with the generator at operating speed. Slowly turn the resistor to the minimum resistance position. The voltmeter should now read between 14.0 and 14.6 volts (exact specifications are in the Generator and Regulator table for each car in the car section) the regulator should be operating on its lower contacts. If voltage will not come up to 14.0 volts insert a ¼ ohm resistor between the BAT lead and the BAT lug on the regulator and try again. Adjust setting at the double slotted screw on the regulator. Air gap and point opening are adjusted as shown in Figs. 7A and 8A.

Replacing Regulators— Polarity of Regulators

Before replacing regulator, make certain the new unit has the correct

Fig. 3. Turn down commutator in lathe

polarity for the battery in the car. That is, do not use a regulator designed to operate with a positive terminal grounded battery on a car which has the negative battery post grounded.

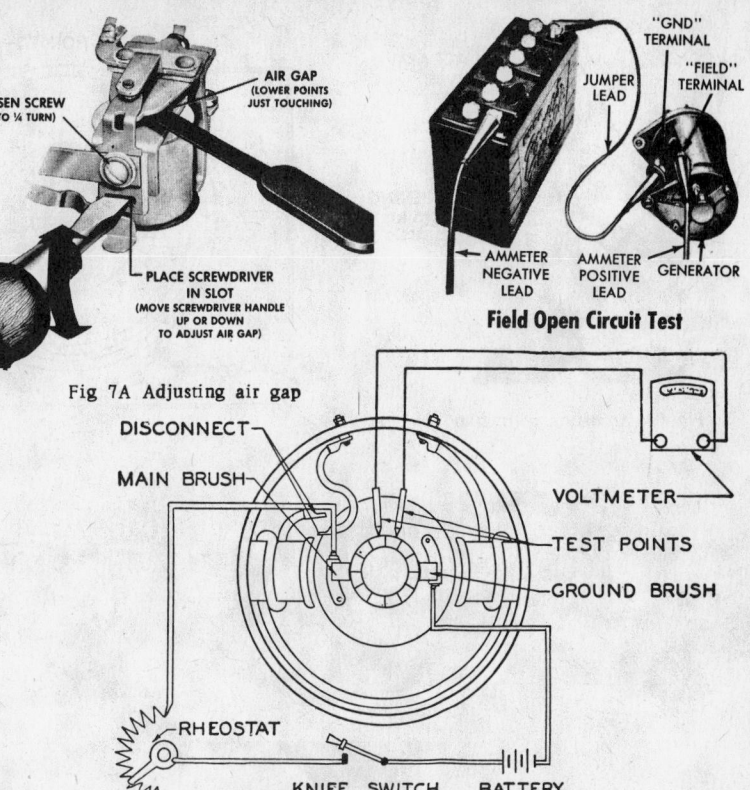

Fig 7A Adjusting air gap

Field Open Circuit Test

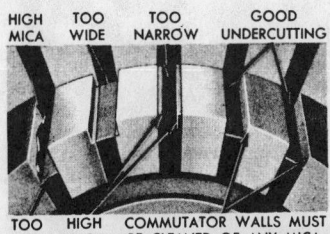

Fig. 4. Mica may be undercut as shown above

Fig. 5. Check armature for short circuits on a growler. To become proficient in the use of a growler, practice with a new armature and also with an armature known to have a short circuit

Fig. 7. Sketch showing armature open circuit test. Rotate slowly and, if an open circuit exists, the meter will show full battery voltage

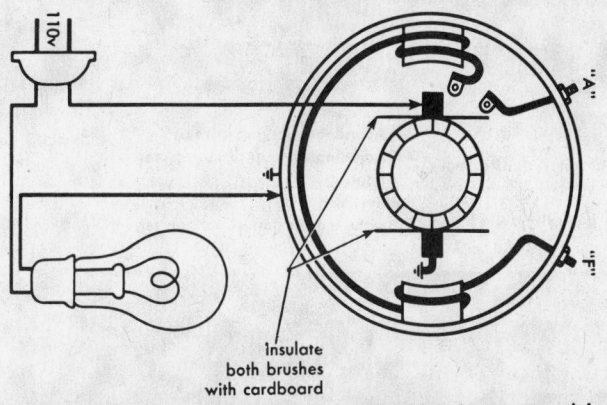

Fig. 8. Test brush holders for grounds. Lamp should light on ground brush only

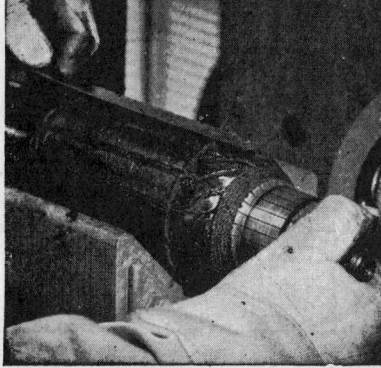

Fig. 6. Armature ground test. Lamp will light if armature is grounded

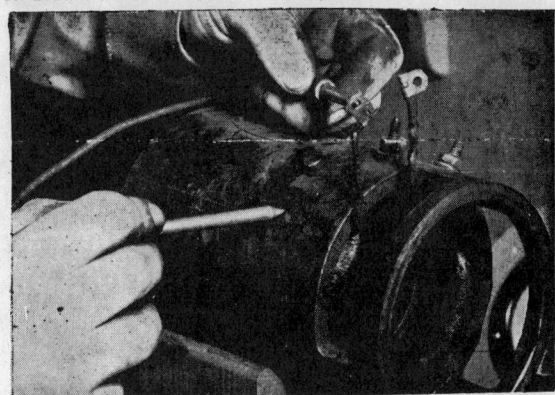

Fig. 9. Field test as shown is for grounds. Lamp should not light. To check for open circuit touch the right hand lead to the other field lead. Lamp should light

DC GENERATORS and REGULATORS

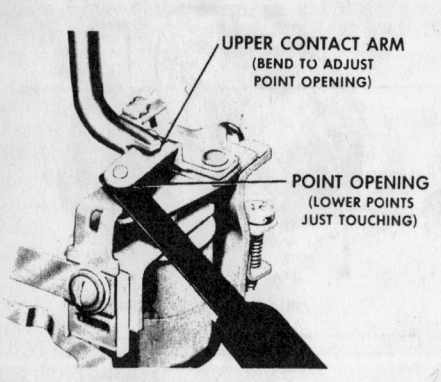

UPPER CONTACT ARM
(BEND TO ADJUST
POINT OPENING)

POINT OPENING
(LOWER POINTS
JUST TOUCHING)

Fig 8A Adjusting point gap

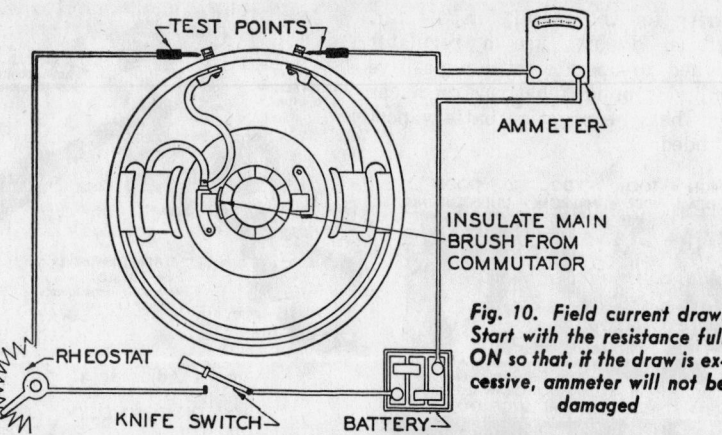

TEST POINTS

AMMETER

INSULATE MAIN
BRUSH FROM
COMMUTATOR

RHEOSTAT

KNIFE SWITCH   BATTERY

*Fig. 10. Field current draw.
Start with the resistance full
ON so that, if the draw is excessive, ammeter will not be
damaged*

Top Row:

1. Front view of an Auto-Lite regulator.

2. Checking air gap of relay.

3. Adjusting point gap of relay.

4. Adjusting air gap of current regulator.

Bottom Row:

5. Adjusting air gap of voltage regulator.

6. Adjusting relay closing voltage.

7. Adjusting current setting.

8. Adjusting voltage setting.

6-7 and 8 are shown off the car for convenient photography. Adjust at point shown with regulator on car, connected to charging generator.

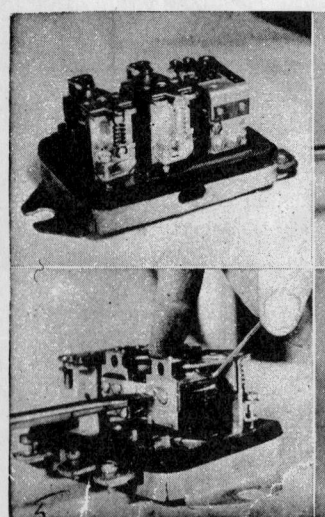

Top Row:

1. Delco-Remy current and voltage regulator.

2. Adjusting air gap.

3. Adjusting relay point gap.

4. Adjusting current regulator air gap.

Bottom Row:

5. Adjusting voltage regulator air gap.

6. Setting relay closing voltage.

7. Adjusting current setting—current regulator.

8. Adjusting voltage setting—voltage regulator.

6-7 and 8 are shown off the car for better photography. Adjust at points shown, with regulator connected to charging generator.

ALTERNATING
CURRENT GENERATORS

Until 1960 production the charging circuits of American made passenger cars were entirely of a direct current nature. Alternating current generators have been in use for some time but their application has usually been reserved to special purpose functions, mainly emergency vehicle equipment.

A quality of the A.C. generator is its ability to generate large amounts of electrical current at low RPM.

Major car manufacturers are now producing automobiles equipped with very efficient alternating current generating systems.

These A.C. generators will be found designated under various names. Prominent among them are Chrysler, Prestolite and Leece-Neville "Alternator" and Delco-Remy "Delcotron." Their function is the same, to supply the current needs of the car's 12-volt D.C. electrical system. To convert this current to usable direct current, diode rectifiers are used.

The chemical make-up of this diode has an ability to permit current to flow through itself in but one direction. Thus, when the diode is connected in a circuit with an A.C. voltage, current will flow in one direction only. These A.C. generating systems employ internal rectifiers that consist of six separate diodes connected together. The rectifier changes the A.C. voltage to D.C. voltage. The D.C. voltage is then acceptable to charge the battery and operate the various electrical units in the car's electrical system.

THE ALTERNATOR BY CHRYSLER

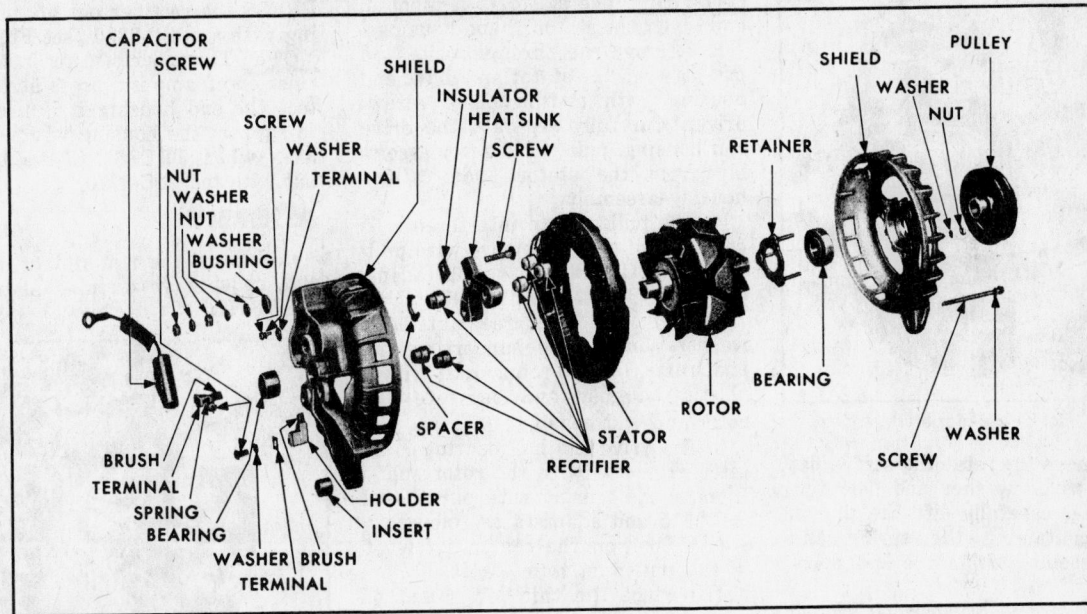

Fig. 1—Alternator, exploded view

The main components of the alternator are two end housings, the stator, the rotor and the rectifiers. The housings are vented at both ends and around the circumference and held together by three, long through-bolts.

The ROTOR consists of a field coil encased between two six-fingered, overlapping sections which are the pole pieces. The rotor produces an effective 12 pole magnetic field. The ends of the coil are connected to slip rings. The battery is connected to the field windings through the brushes and the slip rings.

The rotor shaft is supported at the drive end by a PRE-LUBRICATED BALL BEARING. At the opposite end, the rotor shaft is supported by a PRE-LUBRICATED ROLLER BEARING. In the alternator, A.C. is converted to D.C. current through SIX SILICON DIODE RECTIFIERS. Three of the rectifiers have negative

polarity and are pressed into the die cast aluminum end housing. These rectifiers are in the ground side of the system. The remaining three rectifiers have positive polarity cases and are pressed into a die cast aluminum housing called a HEAT SINK. The heat sink is electrically insulated from the end housing but is of sufficient area to absorb and dissipate the heat from the rectifiers that are pressed into it.

Silicon diode rectifiers have a very high resistance to the flow of electrical current in one direction, but a very low resistance to electrical flow in the opposite direction. Therefore, with the proper polarity, the low resistance permits current to flow from the alternator to the battery. The high resistance prevents current from flowing from the battery to the alternator. Because of the high resistance which does not permit current to flow from the battery back

through the alternator, no circuit breaker is required. An alternating current is transformed by the rectifiers and flows into the battery circuit as direct current.

CAUTION: Always be sure the negative post of the battery only, is connected to ground when installing a battery. A battery that is connected backwards may result in burning out the rectifiers. Do not unduly jar the rectifiers, permanent damage may result.

SPECIFICATIONS

Rotation ....Clockwise at drive end
Voltage 12
Standard Output (Amperes) 35

Heavy Duty Output 40
Brushes (Number) 2
Field Coil Draw ......2.38 amperes minimum to 2.75 amperes maximum at 12 volts or 2.97 amperes

minimum to 3.43 amperes maximum at 15 volts at 70° F. alternator operating temperature at 750 alternator RPM.

Rectifier Resistance ...4 to 10 ohms in the forward direction. Essentially none in reverse direction

Condenser Capacity .. .5 microfarad

DISASSEMBLY

To prevent damage to the brush assemblies (see Fig. 2) they should be removed before proceeding with the disassembly of the alternator. The insulated brush is mounted in a plastic holder that positions the brush vertically against one of the slip rings.

Fig. 2—Insulator brush

1. Remove the retaining screw, flat washer, nylon washer and field terminal and carefully lift the plastic holder containing the spring and brush assembly from the end housing.

2. The ground brush is positioned horizontally against the remaining slip ring and is retained in the holder that is integral with the end housing. Remove the retaining screw and lift the clip, spring and brush assembly from the end housing.

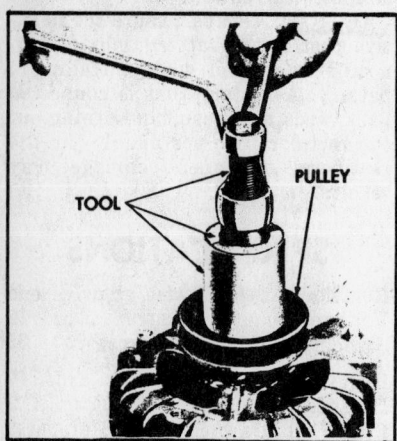

Fig. 3—Removing the pulley

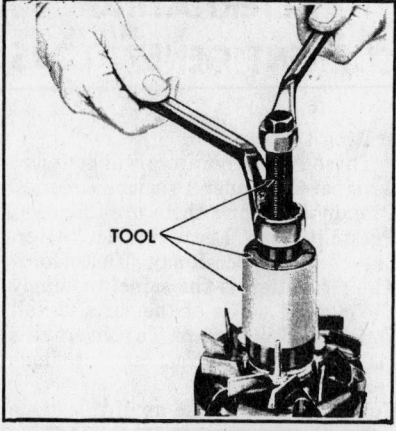

Fig. 4—Pulling bearing from rotor shaft

CAUTION: The stator is laminated, don't burr the stator or end housings.

3. Remove the through bolts and pry between the stator and drive end housing with a thin blade screwdriver. Carefully separate the drive end housing, pulley and rotor assembly from the stator and rectifier housing assembly.

4. The pulley is an interference fit on the rotor shaft. Remove with puller, tool #C-3615 and special adapters, tool SP-3002, (see Fig. 3).

5. Remove the three nuts and washers and, while supporting the end frame, tap the rotor shaft with a plastic hammer and separate the rotor and end housing.

6. The drive end ball bearing is an interference fit with the rotor shaft. Remove the bearing with puller, tool #C-3615 and adapters as follows:
(A) Position the center screw of puller on rotor shaft.
(B) Place the thin lower end of the adapters SP-3375 under the bearing equally spaced and the upper end of the adapters around the center screw.
(C) Hold adapters and center screw in position with the sleeve (see Fig. 4).

CAUTION: Tool sleeve must bottom on bearings, otherwise adapters may be damaged.
(D) Turning center screw clockwise while holding the body of the tool will draw the bearing from the shaft.

NOTE: Further dismantling of the rotor is not advisable, as the remainder of the rotor assembly is not serviced separately.

7. Remove the D.C. output terminal nuts and washers and remove terminal screw and inside capacitor (on units so equipped). (See Fig. 5.)

NOTE: The heat sink (see Fig. 6) is also held in place by the terminal screw.

8. Remove the insulator.

NOTE: Three positive rectifiers are pressed into the heat sink and three negative rectifiers in the end housing. When removing the rectifiers, it is necessary to support the end housing and/or heat sink to prevent damage to these castings. Another caution is in order relative to the diode rectifiers. DON'T SUBJECT THEM TO UNNECESSARY JOLTING. Heavy vibration or shock may ruin them.
(A) Cut rectifier wire at point of crimp.
(B) Support rectifier housing on tool #C-3771.

NOTE: This tool is cut away and slotted to fit over the wires and around the bosses in the housing. Be sure that the bore of the tool completely surrounds the rectifier then PRESS the rectifier out of the housing with tool SP-3380 (see Fig. 7).

NOTE: The roller bearing in the rectifier end frame is a press fit. To protect the end housing it is necessary to support the housing with tool SP-3383 when PRESSING the bearing out with tool #C-3770.

ASSEMBLY

1. Support the heat sink or rectifier end housing on circular plate, tool #SP-3377.

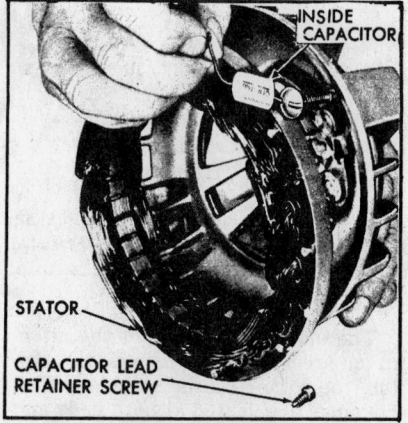

Fig. 5—Inside capacitor

Fig. 6—Heat sink and insulator

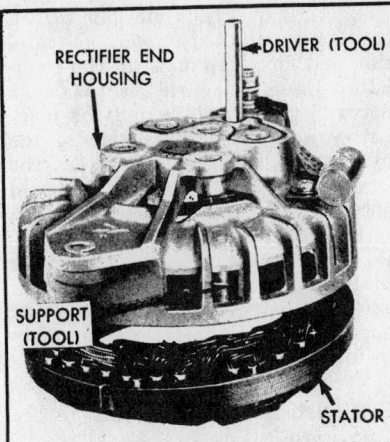

Fig. 7—Removing a rectifier

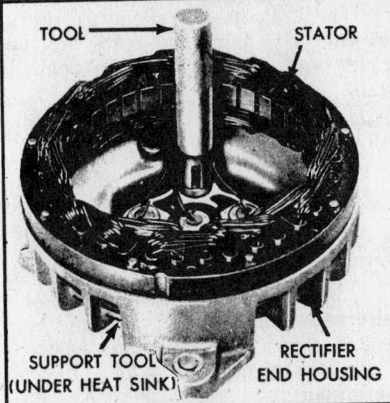

Fig. 8—Installing diode rectifier

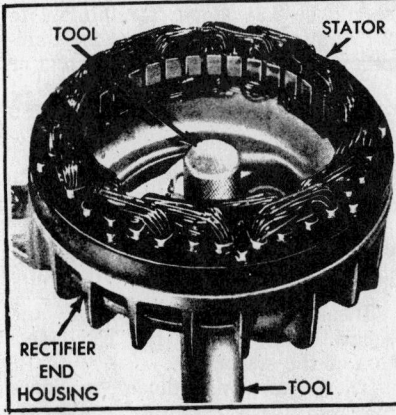

Fig. 9—Installing end frame bearing

2. Check rectifier identification to be sure the correct rectifier is being used. The part numbers are stamped on the case of the rectifier. They are also marked, RED FOR POSITIVE and BLACK FOR NEGATIVE.

3. Start the new rectifier into the casting and press it in with tool #C-3772 (see Fig. 8).

4. Crimp attach the new rectifier wire to the wires disconnected at removal.

5. Support the end housing on tool #SP-3383 so that the notch in the support tool will clear the raised section of the heat sink and press the bearing into position with tool #SP-3381 (see Fig. 9).

NOTE: New bearings are pre-lubricated, additional lubrication is not required.

6. Insert the drive end bearing in the drive end housing and install the bearing plate, washers and nuts to hold the bearing in place.

7. Position the bearing and drive end housing on the rotor shaft and while supporting the base of the rotor shaft, press the bearing and housing in position on the rotor shaft with an arbor press and tool #C-3769 (see Fig. 10).

CAUTION: Be careful that there is no cocking of the bearing at installation; or damage will result. Press the bearing on the rotor shaft until the bearing contacts the shoulder on the rotor shaft.

8. Install pulley on rotor shaft (see Fig. 11). Shaft of rotor must be supported so that all pressing force is on the pulley hub and rotor shaft.

NOTE: Do not exceed 6,800 lbs. pressure. Pulley hub should just contact bearing inner race.

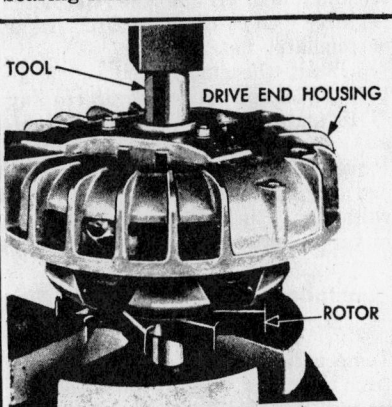

Fig. 10—Installing drive end rrame and bearing on rotor shaft

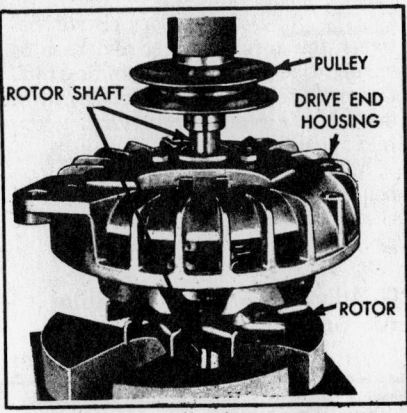

Fig. 11—Installing the pulley

9. Some alternators will be found to have the capacitor mounted internally. Be sure the heat sink insulator is in place.

10. Install the output terminal screw with the capacitor attached through the heat sink and end housing.

11. Install insulating washers, lockwashers and locknuts.

12. Make sure the heat sink and insulator are in place and tighten the locknut.

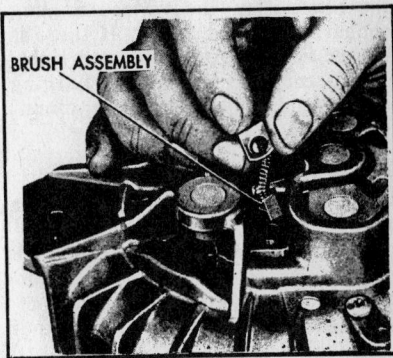

Fig. 12—Installing ground brush

13. Position the stator on the rectifier end housing. Be sure that all of the rectifier connectors and phase leads are free of interference with the rotor fan blades and that the capacitor (internally mounted) lead has clearance.

14. Position the rotor assembly in the rectifier end housing. Align the through bolt holes in the stator with both end housings.

15. Enter stator shaft in the rectifier end housing bearing, compress stator and both end housings MANUALLY and install through bolts, washers and nuts.

16. Install the insulated brush and terminal attaching screw.

17. Install the ground screw and attaching screw (see Fig. 12).

18. Rotate pulley slowly to be sure the rotor fan blades do not hit the rectifier and stator connectors.

TESTING THE ALTERNATOR SYSTEM (IN THE CAR)

With the battery fully charged and in good condition and the engine at normal operating temperature, proceed with tests as follows:

CAUTION: Never ground the field circuit between the alternator and the regulator as this will result in damage to the voltage regulator.

A. Charging Circuit Resistance Test

1. Connect a D.C. ammeter which will read a minimum of 40 amperes in series with the alternator D.C. output

terminal and the D.C. output lead which was disconnected from the alternator.

2. Connect a D.C. voltmeter positive lead to the D.C. output lead that was disconnected from the alternator, and the voltmeter negative lead to the battery positive post.

NOTE: A voltage drop test across each connection will locate any bad connections.

3. Start the engine and adjust the speed to produce 10 amperes from the alternator. The voltage reading should not exceed .2 volt. If there is higher voltage drop, clean and tighten all connections in the charging circuit and recheck charging circuit resistance.

B. Current Output Test

1. Disconnect the field lead at the alternator and the regulator.

2. Install a test D.C. ammeter in series with the alternator D.C. output terminal and the wire disconnected from the alternator D.C. output terminal.

3. Connect a jumper between the D.C. output terminal and the alternator field terminal.

4. Connect a carbon pile rheostat across the battery.

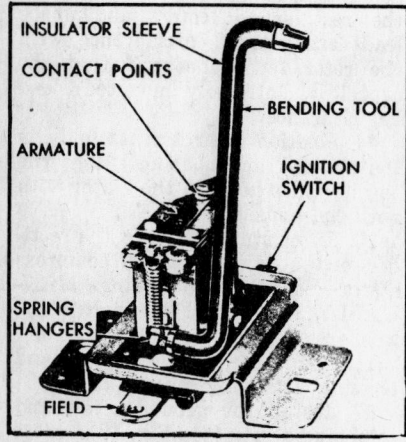

Fig. 13—Adjusting spring tension

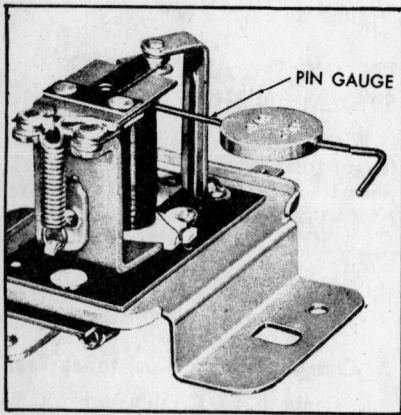

Fig. 14—Checking the air gap

5. Connect a voltmeter positive lead to the alternator D.C. output terminal and ground the voltmeter negative lead to the alternator frame.

6. Hook up a tachometer, start the engine and adjust the speed to 1250 RPM. The current output should be 28 amperes minimum output at 14.6 volts. Adjust engine to 2200 RPM, output should be not less than 33 amperes, at 15 volts. If output is over 40 amperes, a rectifier is open. If output is under 33 amperes, a rectifier is shorted.

C. Voltage Regulator Specifications and Setting Test

Volts 12
Ground Polarity . . . . Negative
Point Gap . . . . .015" ± .001"
Air Gap . . . . .048" to .052"
(Measure gap with gauge touching nylon stops. Points closed with .052" gauge installed. Points open with .048" gauge installed.)

1. Connect an ammeter in series with the alternator output terminal (Bat.) and the wire disconnected from alternator D.C. output terminal.

2. Connect a D.C. voltmeter positive lead to the alternator D.C. output terminal and ground the voltmeter negative lead to the alternator frame or regulator base.

3. Start the engine and adjust to 1400 RPM and an ammeter reading of 10 amperes. Operate for 15 minutes to stabilize the temperature (cover in place). With the alternator and regulator operating, read the voltmeter. The voltage should be as in the following chart:

Operating Voltage—Degrees (F.) Surrounding Temperature

Temperature checked about 2 in. from the cover. There will be a slightly higher voltage at higher engine speeds, however, this must not exceed .7 volts at any temperature range.

CAUTION: Do not short circuit between the spring hanger and base or spring. Use an insulated bending tool. Grounding the spring hanger will damage the regulator (burn the contact spring), see Fig. 13.

Adjust the voltage if required by bending the lower spring hanger of the regulator DOWN to increase voltage, UP to decrease voltage.

D. Adjusting Voltage Regulator Air Gap

Set upper contact gap to get .048"–

.052" air gap. Check air gap with a test lamp connected between the ignition and field terminals on the regulator. Insert the .048" wire gauge between the armature and the magnet core at the hanger side of the nylon stops, see Fig. 14. Press the armature plate down. Contacts should open and test light should go out. Insert the .052" gauge in the same position and depress the armature. Upper contacts should be closed and test lamp should remain lighted. Bend upper contact support as necessary to maintain the air gap adjustment.

E. Adjusting Lower Contact Clearance

Set lower contact gap to .015" (± .001") by bending the lower contact arm. Press the armature down so that the armature rests on the nylon stop and recheck the contact gap.

NOTE: Press down on the armature and not on the contact spring.

BENCH TESTS

A. FIELD CIRCUIT OPEN

1. Disconnect field terminal at the alternator and the voltage regulator.

2. Connect a D.C. ammeter positive lead to the alternator D.C. output terminal.

3. Connect the ammeter negative lead to the alternator field terminal.

The field current draw at 12 volts should be 2.38 amperes minimum to 2.75 amperes maximum or 2.97 amperes minimum to 3.43 at 15 volts or 3.43 amperes maximum at 15 volts at 70° F. alternator operating at 750 RPM.

B. TESTING SILICON DIODE RECTIFIERS WITH OHMMETER

Preferred Method—Rectifiers Open in All Three Phases

Disassemble the alternator and separate the wires at the "Y" connection of the stator.

There are six diode rectifiers mounted in the back of the alternator. Three of them are marked with a plus (+), and three are marked with a negative (−). These marks indicate diode case polarity.

To test, set ohmmeter to its lowest range. If case is marked positive (+), place positive meter probe to case and negative probe to the diode lead. Meter should read between 4 and 10 ohms. Now, reverse leads of ohmmeter, connecting negative meter

Temp. in Degrees	20°	40°	60°	80°	100°	120°	140°
Minimum Setting	13.9 to	13.82 to	13.74 to	13.65 to	13.56 to	13.48 to	13.40 to
Maximum Setting	14.5	14.42	14.34	14.25	14.16	14.08	14.0

probe to positive case and positive meter probe to wire of rectifier. Set meter on a high range. Meter needle should move very little if any (infinite reading). Do this to all three positive diode rectifiers.

The three with negative (—) marks on their cases are checked the same way as above. Only now the negative ohmmeter probe is connected to the case for a reading of 4 to 10 ohms. Reverse leads as above for the other part to test.

If a reading of 4 to 10 ohms is obtained in one direction and no reading (infinity) is read on the ohmmeter in the other direction, diode rectifiers are OK. If either infinity or a low resistance is obtained in both directions on a rectifier, it must be replaced.

If meter reads more than 10 ohms when ohmmeter positive probe is connected to positive on diode, and negative probe to negative, replace diode rectifier.

NOTE: With this test, it is necessary to determine the polarity of the ohmmeter probes. This can be done by connecting the ohmmeter to a D.C. voltmeter. The voltmeter will read up-scale when the positive probe of the ohmmeter is connected to the positive side of the voltmeter and the negative probe of the ohmmeter is connected to the negative side of the voltmeter.

Alternate Method—With a Test Light

Make-up a tester as shown in sketch. Refer to first paragraph of the preferred method. Be sure lead from center of the diode rectifiers are

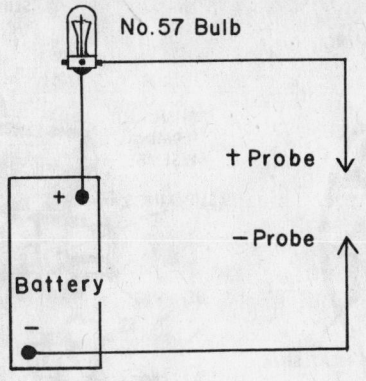

Fig. 15—The test light method

disconnected.

To test rectifiers with positive (+) case, touch positive probe of tester to case and negative (—) probe to lead wire of rectifier. Bulb should light if rectifier is OK. If bulb does not light, replace rectifier.

Now reverse tester probe connections to rectifier. Bulb should not light. If bulb does light, replace rectifier.

For testing negative (—) marked cases, follow above procedure, except that now bulb should light with negative probe of tester touching rectifier case and positive probe touching lead wire.

To Summarize:

Rectifier is OK if the bulb lights when tester probes are connected one way, and does not light when tester connections are reversed.

Rectifier must be replaced if the bulb does not light either way tester is connected. Also, replace rectifier if bulb lights for both ways tester is connected to the diode rectifier.

NOTE: The usual cause of an open or blown diode or rectifier is a defective capacitor or a battery that has been installed in reverse polarity. If the battery is installed properly and the diodes are open, test the capacitor.

Capacitor Capacity (Int. Installed)
.... .158 microfarad, min.
(Ext. Installed) ... .5 microfarad

C. GROUND STATOR

1. Disconnect the diode rectifiers from the stator leads.
2. Test from stator leads to stator core, using a 110 volt test lamp. Replace stator assembly if grounded.

D. LOW OUTPUT

(About 50% output accompanied with a growl-hum caused by a shorted phase or a shorted rectifier.)

Perform operations 1, 2 and 3 (rectifier open in all three phases). If the rectifiers are found to be within specifications, replace the stator assembly.

E. CURRENT OUTPUT TOO HIGH (NO CONTROL) CAUSED BY OPEN RECTIFIER OR OPEN PHASE

Perform operations 1, 2 and 3 (rectifier open in all three phases). If the rectifier tests satisfactorily, inspect the stator connections before replacing the stator.

DELCOTRON BY DELCO-REMY

Though the unit is built to give long periods of trouble-free service, a regular inspection procedure should be followed to enjoy the maximum life that is built into each generator.

INSPECTION

Frequency of inspection is determined by exposure to adverse operating conditions. High speed operation, high temperatures, dust and dirt all increase wear on brushes, slip rings and bearings.

At regular periods, inspect terminals for corrosion and loose connections, and the wiring for frayed insulation. Check mounting bolts for tightness, and the belt for alignment, proper tension and wear. Because of higher load capacity and the higher inertia of the heavy rotor used in A.C. generators, belt tension is more critical. Tension should be adjusted

according to the vehicle manufacturer's recommendations. In most cases this will be slightly greater than for D.C. generators.

NOISY GENERATOR

Noise in a Delcotron may be caused by worn or dirty bearings, loose mounting or a loose drive pulley. In the self-rectifying generator, noise may come from a shorted or open diode.

DISASSEMBLY

After long periods of operation, or at engine overhaul, the generator warrants removal, disassembly and cleaning of all parts. The unit consists of four main components—the two end frames, the stator and the rotor.

1. Remove four thru-bolts.
2. Separate drive end frame and rotor from stator assembly by prying with screw driver. Note that separation is between **stator frame** and **drive end frame**.
3. Place tape over slip ring end frame bearing to seal dirt.
4. Lightly clamp rotor in vise to remove shaft nut. **Do not distort rotor by tightening vise too much.**
5. After nut removal, take off washer, pulley, fan and collar.
6. Separate drive end frame from rotor shaft.

DIODE CHECKS

There are six silicon diodes mounted on the slip ring end frame assembly. Three of these diodes are mounted in the end frame, and three are mounted into a bracket or heat sink which is attached to, but insu-

AC GENERATORS

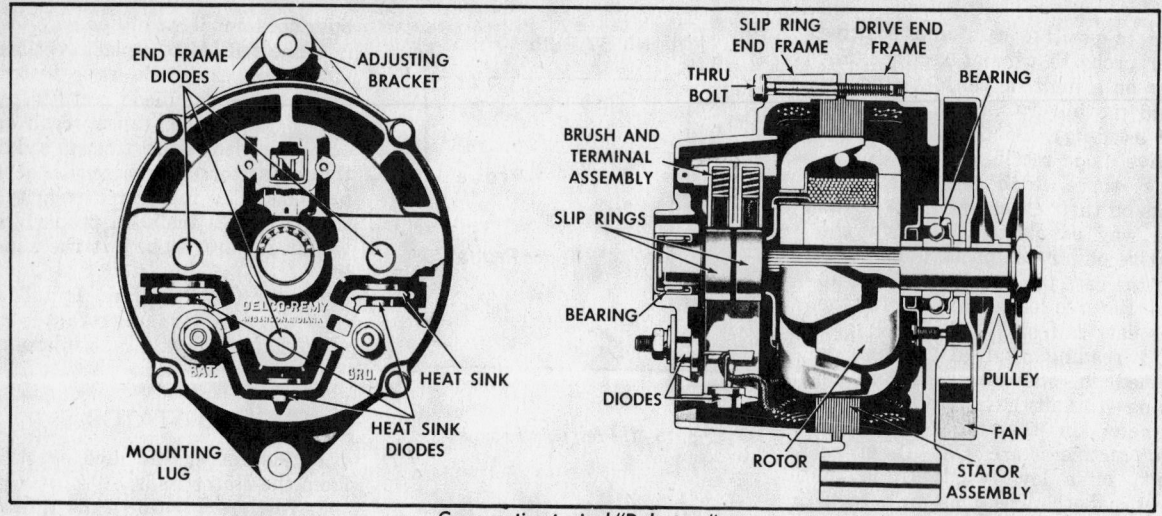

Cross section typical "Delcotron"

lated from the slip ring end frame. The "Bat." terminal on the generator is attached to the insulated heat sink.

All diodes are marked with either a + or − on the hexagonal head, to identify the polarity of the case. On a generator to be used with a negative grounded system, the negative case diodes are mounted into the slip ring end frame and the positive case diodes are mounted into the insulated heat sink. Diodes with a negative

case have positive polarity leads, whereas positive case diodes have negative polarity leads. To further identify these diodes, the negative case diodes have right hand threads and the positive case diodes, left hand threads.

Diodes can be checked for "shorts" or "opens" with an ohmmeter. To check for "shorts", connect the negative lead of the ohmmeter to the negative case of the diode. Connect the positive lead of the ohmmeter to the positive lead of the diode. Reverse the connections for positive case diodes. Ohmmeter readings may vary considerably when checking diodes, but if the reading is below 300 ohms, the diode most likely is faulty and should be replaced. Push and pull on the lead to show up loose connections. Use an ohmmeter scale on which the 300 ohm value can be accurately read. NOTE: The polarity of the ohmmeter leads must be determined. This can be done by connecting the ohmmeter to a D.C. voltmeter. The voltmeter will read up scale when the positive

lead of the ohmmeter is connected to the positive side of the voltmeter, and the ohmmeter negative lead is connected to the negative side of the voltmeter.

To check for an OPEN circuit, connect the negative lead of the ohmmeter to the positive lead of the diode and the positive lead of the ohmmeter to the negative case of the diode. Reverse the connections for positive case diodes. If the ohmmeter reads an infinite resistance (all the way), the diode is open and must be replaced.

REPLACEMENT OF DIODES

To replace a diode that is mounted in the outside frame, use diagonal cutters to clip the leads on each side of the diode lead. Leave about ½" of lead length on each side of the diode lead to match the replacement diode. Remove the defective diode.

Before installing the new diode, lightly coat the threads with silicon grease or light engine oil. Install the

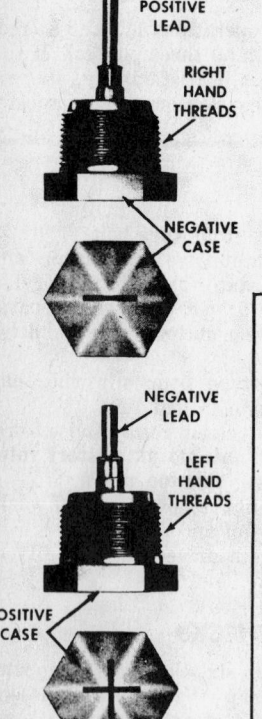

Diode rectifiers

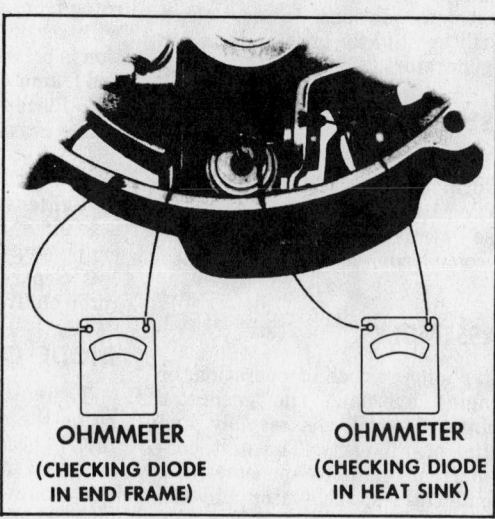

Checking Diodes "Delcotron"

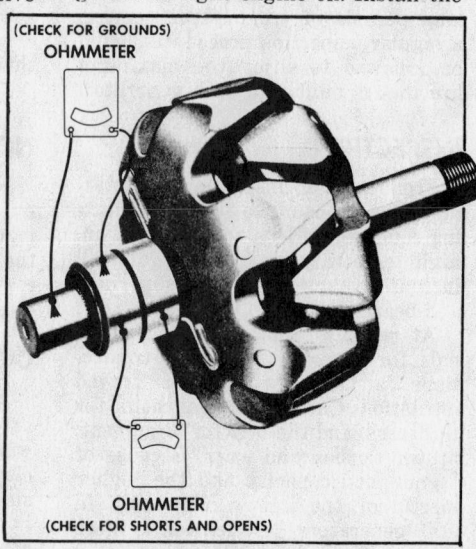

Checking Rotor "Delcotron"

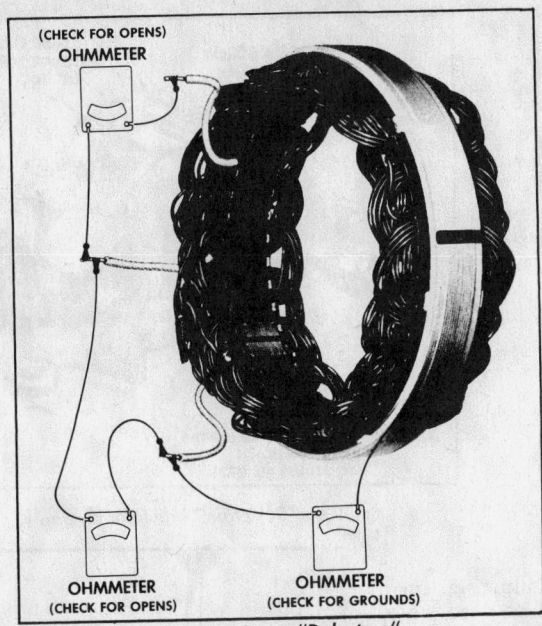

Checking Stator "Delcotron"

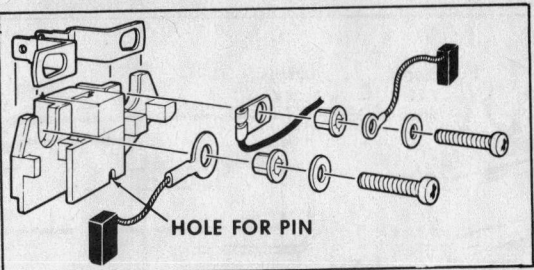

Brush holder assembly "Delcotron"

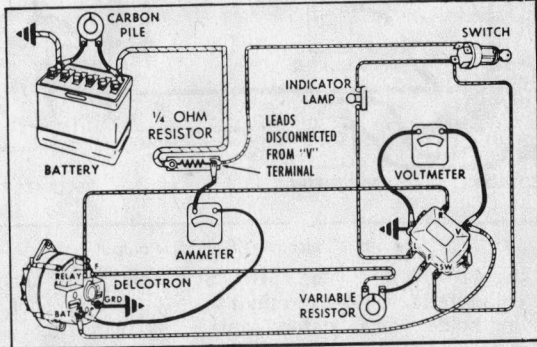

Setting "Delcotron" Regulator (Double Contact)

diode and torque to 200 INCH-POUNDS. Strip about ½ of insulation from the long lead which is connected to the nylon terminal holder, and place over the long lead the insulating sleeve which is supplied with the new diode. Join the ends of the leads of the new diode to the respective leads in the end frame, using the special connectors provided with the new diode. Crimp the connectors tightly over the ends of the wires and solder securely. Then push the sleeve over the soldered connector.

CAUTION: Use only 60% tin, 40% lead solder, or other solder with melting point of 360° F. or above.

To replace a diode mounted in the heat sink, it is necessary to remove the heat sink from the end frame. This is done by clipping, with diagonal cutters, the lead midway between each pair of negative and positive case diodes, removing the nylon terminal holder from the frame

and the leads from the holder, and then removing the "Bat." terminal and the heat sink attaching screws. It is not necessary to clip the long insulated leads attached to the diodes mounted in the outside end frame.

REMEMBER: Negative case diodes have right hand threads, and positive case diodes have left hand threads.

After removing the defective diode, lightly coat the threads of the new diode with lubricant, install, torque and solder as described in above paragraph.

ROTOR CHECKS

The rotor may be checked electrically for grounded, open, or shorted field coils.

To check for GROUNDS, connect a 100-volt test light from either slip ring to the rotor shaft or to the laminations. If the lamp LIGHTS, the

field windings are grounded.

To check for OPENS, connect the leads of a 110-volt test light to each slip ring. If the lamp FAILS TO LIGHT, the windings are open.

The windings are checked for short-circuits by connecting a battery and ammeter in series with the two slip rings. Note the ammeter reading and refer to the chart.

An ammeter reading greater than the specified value, indicates shorted windings. Ohmeter checks are shown in the attached illustration.

Since the field windings are not serviced separately, the rotor assembly must be replaced if the windings are defective.

STATOR CHECKS

Stator windings may be checked for grounded, open, or shorted wind-

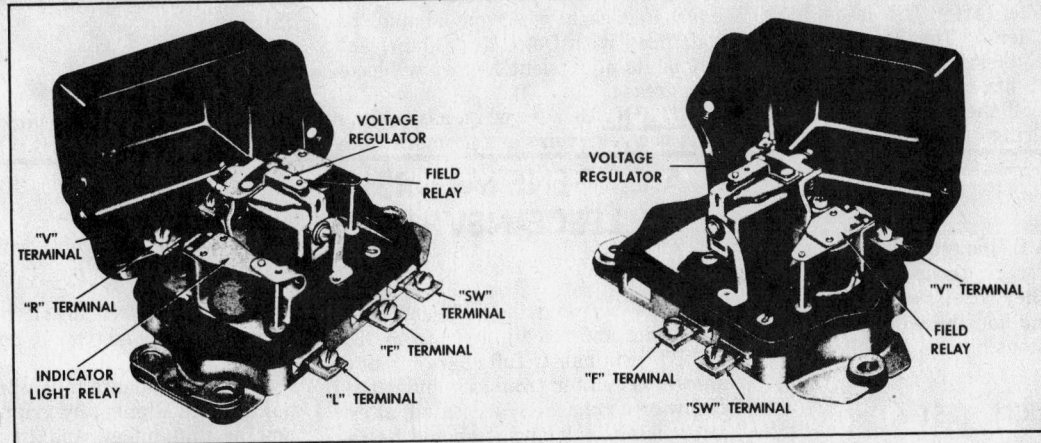

Three-Unit and two unit "Delcotron" Regulators

AC GENERATORS

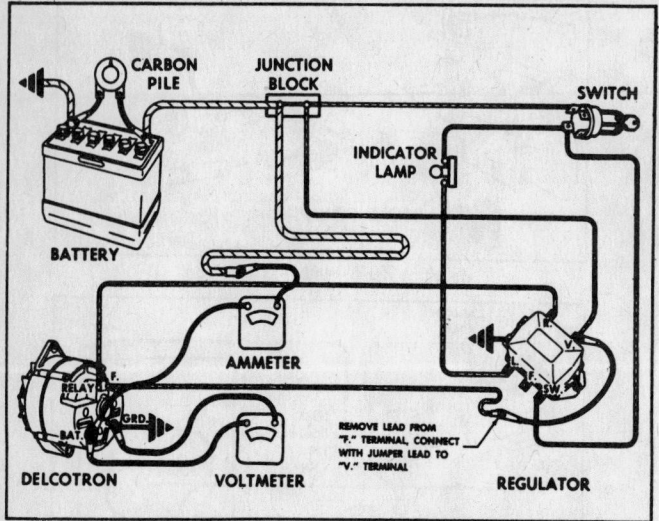

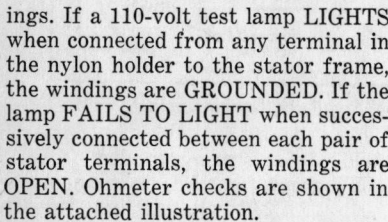

Checking "Delcotron" Regulator output

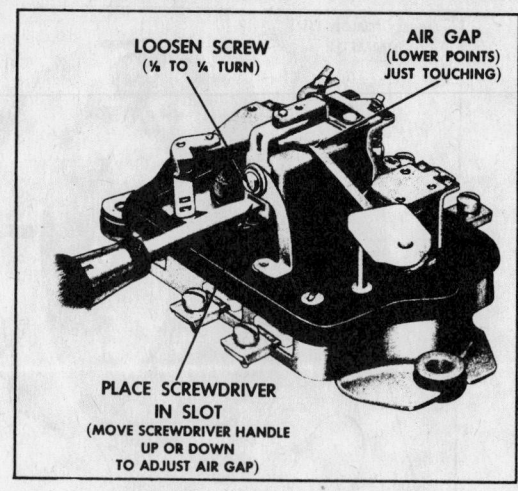

Adjusting "Delcotron" Regulator air gap

ings. If a 110-volt test lamp LIGHTS when connected from any terminal in the nylon holder to the stator frame, the windings are GROUNDED. If the lamp FAILS TO LIGHT when successively connected between each pair of stator terminals, the windings are OPEN. Ohmeter checks are shown in the attached illustration.

A short circuit in the stator windings is difficult to locate without laboratory equipment due to the low resistance of the windings. However, if all other electrical checks are normal and the generator fails to supply the rated output, shorted stator windings are indicated.

SLIP RING SERVICING AND REPLACEMENT

Slip rings which are rough or out-of-round should be trued in a lathe to .001" maximum indicator reading. Remove only enough material to make the rings smooth and round. Finish with 400 grit or finer polishing cloth and blow away all dust.

Slip rings which must be replaced can be removed from the shaft with a gear puller after the leads have been unsoldered. The new assembly should be pressed on with a sleeve which just fits over the shaft; this will apply all the pressure to the inner slip ring collar and prevent

damage to the outer slip ring. Only pure tin solder should be used when reconnecting field leads.

BRUSH REPLACEMENT

The extent of brush wear can be determined by comparison with a new brush. If brushes are worn over half way, they should be replaced.
1. Remove brush holder assembly from end frame by removing two holder assembly screws.
2. Place springs and brushes in the holder and insert straight wire or pin in holes at bottom of holder to retain brushes (See cut).
3. Attach holder assembly onto end frame, keeping parts stack-up as shown.

LUBRICATION

Under normal conditions, the generator should not require lubrication between engine overhaul periods. The grease reservoir in each end frame provides an adequate supply of special lubricant for long periods of operation.

Before reassembly after generator overhaul, each reservoir should be half filled with Delco-Remy lubricant #3 or its equivalent in a slow bleeding grease.
CAUTION: Be sure when assembling that the reservoirs are no more than

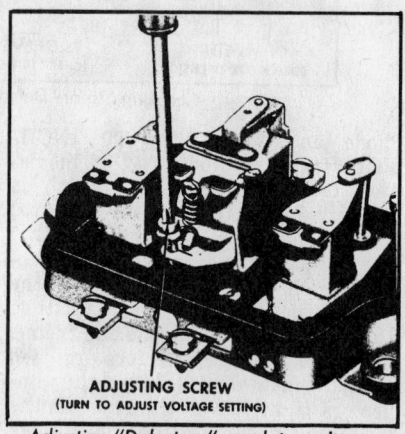

ADJUSTING SCREW
(TURN TO ADJUST VOLTAGE SETTING)

Adjusting "Delcotron" regulator voltage

½ filled. Overfilling will cause the bearings to overheat.

If the bearings are found to be in satisfactory condition, they should be repacked with Delco-Remy grease, as above.
CAUTION: Make sure the sealed side of the slip ring end bearing is away from the grease reservoir and the open side is toward the grease reservoir. Failure to comply with this caution will result in quick bearing failure.

REASSEMBLY

Reassembly is the reverse of disassembly.

A.C. GENERATORS BY LEECE-NEVILLE

These A.C. generators are similar in character to those in preceeding sections. They consist of stator, rotor, slip ring end housing with heat sinks, drive end housing and six silicon rectifiers.

ON VEHICLE TEST

With engine at idle, eliminate the

regulator by removing "F" lead from alternator and place jumper from "F" to "B" terminal. If full charge is now shown, regulator trouble is indicated. If low or no charge is indicated, alternator is at fault and it should be removed from vehicle.

DISASSEMBLY

1. Remove two brush holder assembly screws and remove holder with brushes.
2. Remove shaft nut, preventing pulley from slipping by gripping a fan belt around pulley and in vise. Remove pulley.

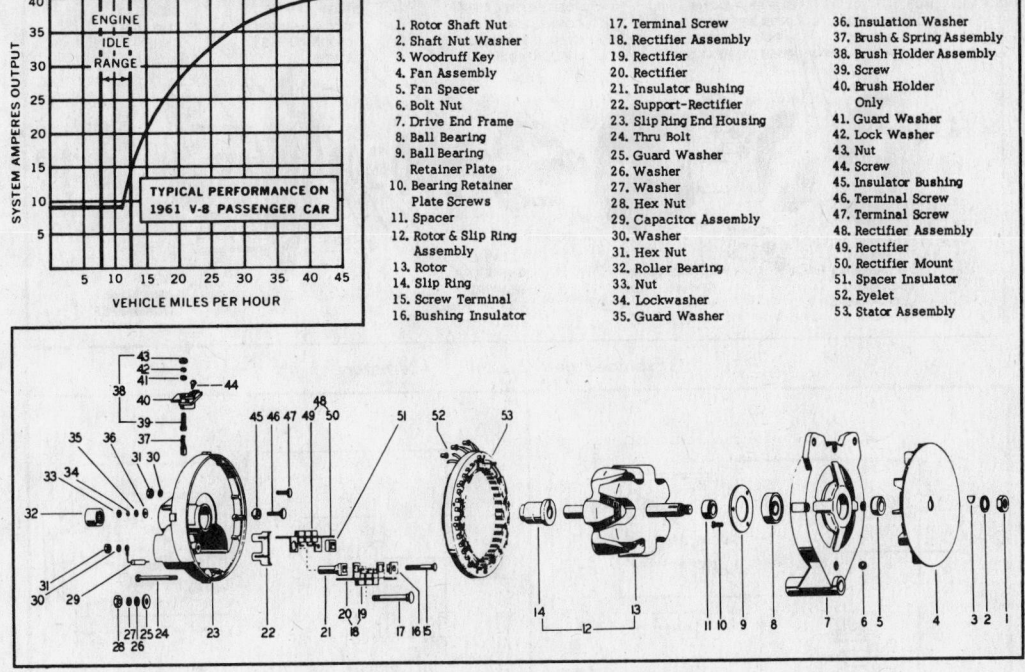

1. Rotor Shaft Nut
2. Shaft Nut Washer
3. Woodruff Key
4. Fan Assembly
5. Fan Spacer
6. Bolt Nut
7. Drive End Frame
8. Ball Bearing
9. Ball Bearing
   Retainer Plate
10. Bearing Retainer
    Plate Screws
11. Spacer
12. Rotor & Slip Ring
    Assembly
13. Rotor
14. Slip Ring
15. Screw Terminal
16. Bushing Insulator

17. Terminal Screw
18. Rectifier Assembly
19. Rectifier
20. Rectifier
21. Insulator Bushing
22. Support-Rectifier
23. Slip Ring End Housing
24. Thru Bolt
25. Guard Washer
26. Washer
27. Washer
28. Hex Nut
29. Capacitor Assembly
30. Washer
31. Hex Nut
32. Roller Bearing
33. Nut
34. Lockwasher
35. Guard Washer

36. Insulation Washer
37. Brush & Spring Assembly
38. Brush Holder Assembly
39. Screw
40. Brush Holder
    Only
41. Guard Washer
42. Lock Washer
43. Nut
44. Screw
45. Insulator Bushing
46. Terminal Screw
47. Terminal Screw
48. Rectifier Assembly
49. Rectifier
50. Rectifier Mount
51. Spacer Insulator
52. Eyelet
53. Stator Assembly

Exploded view "Leece-Neville" Alternator

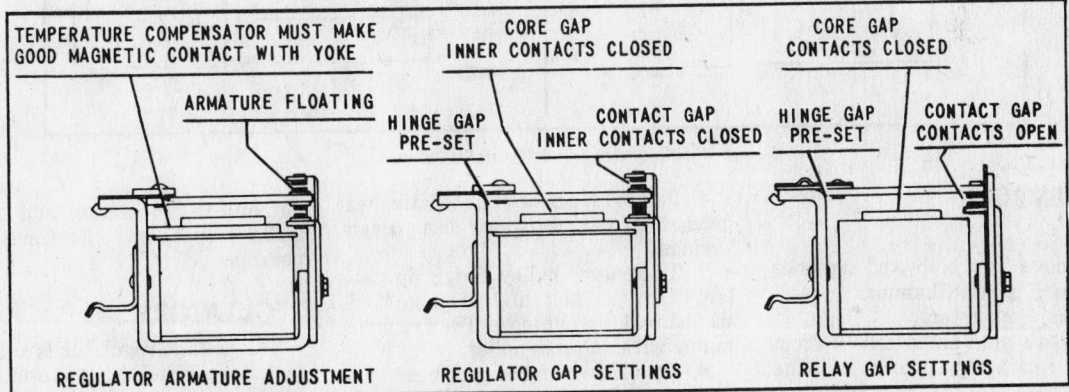

Adjusting "Leece-Neville" Regulator

3. Remove four thru bolts and carefully pry two end housings apart.

4. Place tape over slip ring end housing bearing to keep out dirt.

5. Remove fan, key and spacer and with puller remove drive end housing.

6. Bearings from both housings can be removed after taking off retainer

at drive end or tape from slip ring end.

7. To remove individual rectifier, loosen solder around cell while pressing it out. A piece of asbestos or fiber will help concentrate heat.

TESTS

Test methods are very similar to those shown under Chrysler Alternator and Delco-Remy Delcotron.

REGULATORS

Adjustment points are shown in the accompanying diagrams. For specifications see charts.

A.C. GENERATORS
BY PRESTOLITE
(AUTOLITE)

This is a typical A.C. Generator. It is composed of stator, rotor, slip ring end head, drive end head, with three positive and three negative rectifiers pressed in brackets or heat sinks. The slip ring head is fiitted with a pre-lubricated roller bearing, brush holders and brushes. The drive end is fitted with a pre-lubricated ball bearing.

ON VEHICLE TEST

Alternator

With voltmeter from "A" to ground and ammeter in "A" line to regulator, install jumper from "A" to "F" alternator terminals with field wire disconnected at alternator. At 1750 engine RPM output should be as in the specification table following.

Regulators

Use fully charged battery. With voltmeter connected from regulator "I" to ground and ammeter in "A" line to regulator. With field line connected and jumper removed, run engine at 750 RPM. With system up to normal operating temperature check against specification table following.

AC GENERATORS

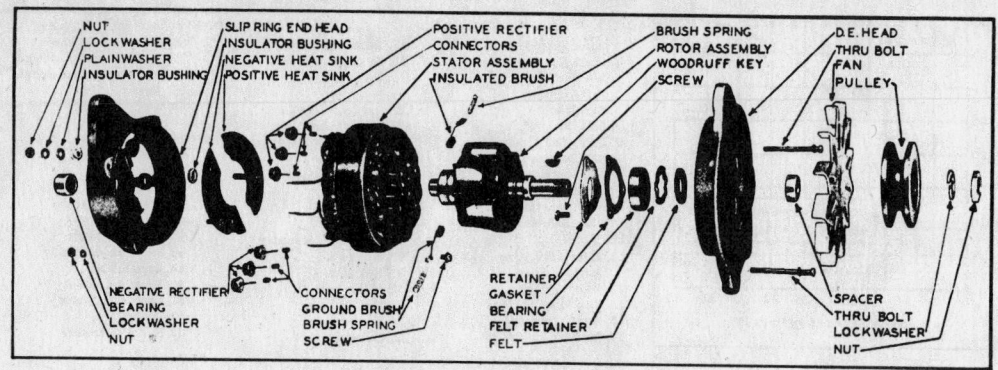

Exploded view "Prestolite" Alternator

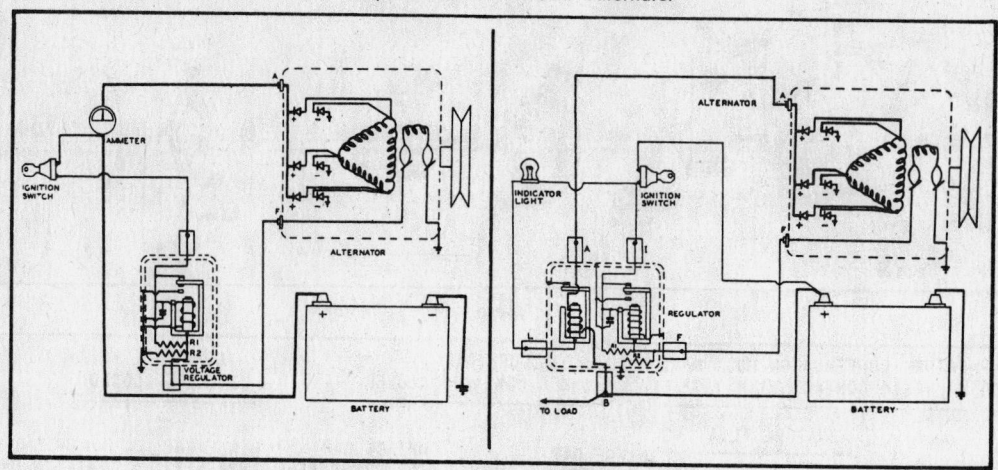

Single and two-unit "Prestolite" circuits

DISASSEMBLY

1. Remove thru bolts and tap ends lightly with plastic hammer to separate ends from rotor.

2. Remove nuts and washers from negative rectifier brackets, and the nuts, washers and insulator bushings from the positive rectifier brackets, and separate the slip ring end head.

3. Remove insulated brush, gripping brass terminal on brush head with pliers and pulling from field terminal insulator.

4. Remove screw that attaches ground brush. Do not lose brush springs.

5. To remove pulley nut, grip pulley with fan belt and vise to hold while breaking nut loose. Then remove pulley with suitable puller.

6. To remove drive end head, remove key, fan and spacer. Then with suitable puller remove head.

7. Remove retaining plate and press out drive end head bearing.

8. The slip end head bearing can be removed with a puller.

9. The rectifiers can now be pressed

out and in. In cutting and crimping leads keep as close to the sleeve as possible.

REGULATORS

The voltage regulator is a dual contact type. Field (F) terminal and ignition (I) terminal are insulated from base. A regulating resistor is conected between these terminals.

To adjust remove the cover, loosen stationary contact support screw and move support up or down. Use following specification tables for settings.

ALTERNATOR
PRESTOLITE (AUTOLITE)

	Model No.		
	ALC 5001	ALD 5001	ALD 5005
Rotation—Clockwise, Drive End	Yes	Yes	Yes
Voltage	12	12	12
Rated Output (Amperes)	45	40	40
Brushes (Number)	2	2	2
Rotor Field Coil Draw (At 70°F) At 10 Volts	2.34—2.43 Amps.	2.32—2.42 Amps.	2.32—2.42 Amps.
Current Output—4200 RPM (Engine Speed 1750 RPM)	42 Amps. 14.2 Volts	38 Amps. 14.2 Volts	38 Amps. 14.2 Volts
Ground Polarity	Negative	Negative	Negative
Control	VR	VR	VR

PRESTOLITE (AUTOLITE)

VOLTAGE REGULATOR

	Model No.		
	VBS 6201A	VBT 6201A	VBS 6201A-1
Volts	12	12	12
Ground Polarity	Negative	Negative	Negative
Point Gap	.010	.010	.010
Air Gap	.034-.038	.034-.038	.034-.038
Relay Air Gap	.015-.020	—	.015-.020
Relay Opening (Amperes)	2.0-2.5	—	2.0-2.5
Relay Closing (Amperes)	1.5 Max.	—	1.5 Max.

Operating Voltage (Upper Contact)
  50°F 80°F 110°F 140°F Tolerance
  14.3 14.1 13.9 13.7 ±.2
		—All Models—	

Voltage Spread (Between upper & lower contact operation)	.1-.3 Volts	.1-.3 Volts	.1-.3 Volts
Capacitor Capacity (Color band indicates ground end)	.1 MFD	.1 MFD	.1 MFD

Resistance
  Rx ....
  R⁹ ....
  VR Winding ....
	10 Ohms.
	20 Ohms.
	52-58 Ohms.
		10 Ohms.
		20 Ohms.
		52-58 Ohms.
			10 Ohms.
			20 Ohms.
			52-58 Ohms.

1600-1800 RPM Alternator Speed, 15 minute warm-up, 10 Amp. load		—All Models—	
3400-3600 RPM Alternator Speed, 15 Amp. load Upper contacts—2-7 Amperes			
Charge rate—lower grounding contacts		—All Models—	
All tests to be made with a fully charged battery		—All Models—	

LEECE-NEVILLE

VOLTAGE SETTING (COVER OFF)

Regulator Number	Relay Closing	Starts to Regulate	Transfer Voltage (max.)	Regulator Operating Voltage Bottom Contact
3532 RA	5.8-6.2	13.9-14.3	14.7	13.9-14.3
3533 RA	5.8-6.2	13.9-14.3	14.7	13.9-14.3
3628 RA	1.9-2.4	14.6-15.2	15.4	14.6-15.2
3629 RA	1.9-2.4	14.6-15.2	15.4	14.6-15.2
3630 RA	1.9-2.4	14.6-15.2	15.4	14.6-15.2
3631 RA	1.9-2.4	14.6-15.2	15.4	14.6-15.2
3687 RA	2.0-2.1	14.2-14.4	14.8	14.2-14.4*

* 3000 RPM Alternator Speed

NOTE: Voltage regulator settings will be approximately one-half volt lower with the cover on. When regulator cover is securely fastened in place and regulator reaches maximum operating temperature voltage will use approximately 2 to 3 tenths. Gaps may be varied above or below to meet settings desired.

AIR GAP AND POINTS SETTINGS

Regulator Number	Voltage Regulator		Relay Element	
	Contact Gap Outer Contacts Open	Core Gap Inner Contacts Closed	Contact Gap Contacts Open	Core Gap Contacts Closed*
3532 RA	.018-.020	.031-.039	.018-.020	.011-.013
3533 RA	.018-.020	.031-.039	.018-.020	.011-.013
3628 RA	.018-.020	.030-.035	.018-.020	.005-.007
3629 RA	.018-.020	.030-.035	.018-.020	.005-.007
3630 RA	.018-.020	.030-.035	.018-.020	.005-.007
3631 RA	.018-.020	.030-.035	.018-.020	.005-.007
3687 RA	.018-.020	.035-.043	.018-.020	.009-.011

* Settings are made with contacts closed and armature held to core.

CAUTION: When checking these regulators for maximum output DO NOT use a jumper from "F" terminal to ground, or "F" terminal to "G" terminal. Doing so will result in burned out jumpers, or fused contacts.

CAR MAKE	CONTROL SWITCH			NEUTRAL SWITCH		STARTER SWITCH				STARTER DRIVE	
	Ignition Switch	Button Neutral	Button Dash	On Transmission	On Column	Magnetic Sec. 1	Solenoid Sec. 2	Relay on Solenoid Sec. 3	Relay and Solenoid Sec. 4	Bendix	Clutch
Buick	1961-63		Note D		1952-63				1952-60		1952-63
Buick Special	1961-63				1961-63		1961-63				1961-63
Cadillac	1952-63				1952-63		1952-63				1952-63
Chevrolet	1953-63		1952		1953-63		1952-63				1952-63
Chevy II	1962-63			Note A			1962-63				1962-63
Chrysler		Note C		1952-63					1952-61		1952-63
Corvair	1960-63			Note A			1960-63				1960-63
DeSoto		Note C		1952-63					1952-61		1952-63
Dodge—Dart		Note C		1952-63			1962-63		1952-61		1952-63
Falcon—Comet	1960-63					1960-63				1960-63	
Fairlane—Meteor	1962-63					1962-63				1962-63	
Ford—Thunderbird	1952-63				1952-63	1952-63				1952-63	
Lincoln	1956-63		1952-55		1952-63	1952-63				1952-63	
Mercury	1954-63		1952-53		1952-63	1952-63				1952-63	
Oldsmobile	1952-63				1952-63		1952-63				1952-63
Oldsmobile F-85	1961-63				1961-63		1961-63				1961-63
Plymouth		Note C		1952-63			1960-63				1952-63
Rambler	1956-61	Notes B & E		None		1954-55		1952-63		1954-55	1956-63
Studebaker	1954-63	Note F			1954-63	1954-63					1954-63
Tempest	1961-63			Note A			1961-63				1961-63
Valiant—Lancer	1960-63			1960-63		1960-61	1962-63				1962-63
Willys	1952-63			None		1952-63				1952-63	

NOTE A:—Located on rear of control lever.
NOTE C:—1957-59 neutral button. 1952-56 & 60-63 ign. switch.
NOTE E:—1954-63 auto. trans. lift shift lever.

NOTE B:—With manual trans. button under clutch pedal.
NOTE D:—1952-60 switch on carburetor.
NOTE F:—1952-54 under clutch pedal.

Terms Used in the Application Table

MAGNETIC Switch. An electrically operated switch whose only function is to make contact for the starter. May be located on the starter, on the engine side of the firewall or on the fender apron.

SOL. (Solenoid). An electrically operated switch whose function is to make electrical contact for the starter, and in addition shift the starter clutch into mesh with the flywheel. No relay is used. Always located on the starter.

SOL AND REL (Solenoid and Relay). A solenoid having a separate relay, the relay being located some distance from the solenoid, usually on the fender apron or the engine side of the firewall. The solenoid is always located on the starter.

SOL-REL (Solenoid-Relay). A solenoid relay combination where the relay is a built-in portion of the solenoid assembly. Always located on **the** starter.

Section 1
Magnetic Switches with a Single Control Terminal and an Internal Ground

All models using this device are fitted with a magnetic switch having an internal ground and a single control terminal. The single control terminal will be much smaller than the two main battery terminals. See fig. 1.

Trouble Shooting Quick Checks

STARTER DOES NOT SPIN

First, check the condition of the battery and make sure the battery terminals are clean and tight.

On cars with automatic transmissions, make sure the transmission shift lever is in Neutral or Park.

To check the magnetic switch, connect the jumper wire from the hot side of the battery to the control terminal on the magnetic switch. If this makes the starter turn the magnetic switch is probably OK and the fault lays in either the control switch or the neutral safety switch and/or their wires.

STARTER TURNS BUT DOES NOT CRANK ENGINE

If the starter spins freely but does not crank the engine, the Bendix drive is either stuck or defective, or the teeth are broken in the flywheel.

STARTER TURNS ENGINE VERY SLUGGISHLY

Refer to this subject later in this text. The test and quick checks are the same for all types of controls.

Magnetic Switches with External Ground, Single Control Terminal

On this device the magnetic coil receives its current from the main battery terminal. The control terminal leads to a ground, usually a button on the dash panel. See fig. 2.

Trouble Shooting Quick Checks

STARTER DOES NOT SPIN

First, check the condition of the battery and the battery terminals. The battery should be up and the terminals clean and tight. Connect a jumper from the single control terminal to ground. If this causes the starter to turn, the magnetic switch is probably OK and the difficulty lays in the ground button on the dash or

MAGNETIC SWITCHES

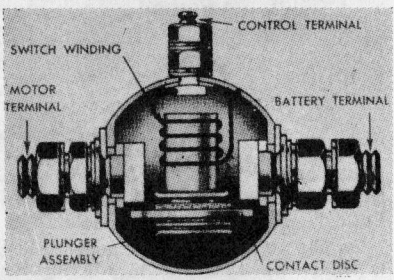

Fig. 1—Schematic diagram of a magnetic switch with a single control terminal and an internal ground

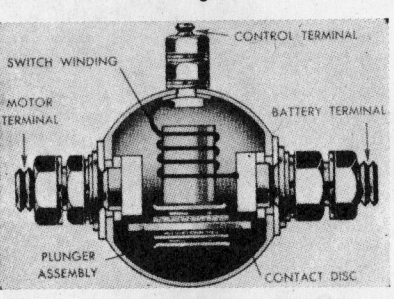

Fig. 2—Schematic diagram of a magnetic switch with a single control terminal and an external ground

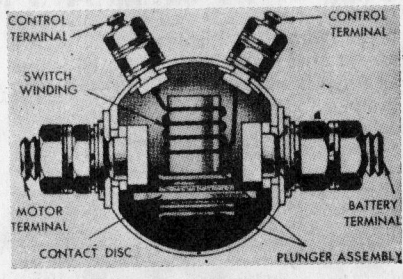

Fig. 3—Schematic diagram of a magnetic switch with two control terminals

the wire leading to it.

If this check fails to spin the starter, the magnetic switch is defective.

STARTER SPINS BUT DOES NOT CRANK ENGINE

Usually caused by jammed or defective Bendix drive or broken teeth in flywheel.

STARTER TURNS ENGINE SLUGGISHLY

Make the tests given later in this text for this trouble. The same quick checks are made for all types of controls.

Magnetic Switches with Two Control Terminals

On this type of magnetic switch current is supplied from the ignition switch (transmission neutral button in 1957) to one of the magnetic switch control terminals. The other control terminal is connected to the transmission neutral safety switch (on the transmission) where it is grounded. See fig. 3.

Trouble Shooting Quick Checks

STARTER DOES NOT TURN

First, check the condition of the battery and its terminals and also make certain the automatic transmission is in Neutral or Park.

Disconnect both control terminals of the magnetic switch and connect one of these terminals with a jumper to the hot side of the battery, the other terminal to ground. If this cranks the engine, the magnetic switch is probably OK and the difficulty lies either in the control switch (ignition switch or neutral safety button) or the neutral safety switch (on transmission).

To determine which, connect up the control wire which goes to the ignition switch and ground the other control terminal. If this causes the engine to crank, the neutral safety switch is at fault. If the engine does not crank, the control switch and/or its wiring is at fault.

If the tests made above fail to crank the engine, the magnetic switch is defective.

STARTER CRANKS ENGINE SLUGGISHLY

Make the tests given later in this text for this condition.

Magnetic Switches with Ignition Resistor By-Pass Terminals

The above captioned switch is used with 12-volt systems. All normally use a magnetic switch with a single control terminal. The second terminal is not a control terminal; it is an ignition resistor by-pass terminal. To trouble shoot this type of switch, simply ignore the ignition terminal and check according to the instructions given for magnetic switches with internal grounds, except Studebaker which is to be tested as for magnetic switches with external grounds.

STARTER SYSTEMS

SOLENOIDS WITHOUT RELAYS

Section 2

This type of starter solenoid is always mounted on the starter, and in addition to making electrical contact for the starter also pulls the starter drive clutch into mesh with the flywheel. See fig. 4.

On the above captioned switch there is one control terminal only on the solenoid. However, except for Chevrolet, all of the models which have 12-volt batteries are fitted with an ignition resistor by-pass terminal on the solenoid. This terminal should not be confused with the control terminal.

The ignition by-pass terminal is usually marked IGN.

Trouble Shooting Quick Checks

STARTER WILL NOT TURN

A quick check of the solenoid can be made by connecting a hopper wire between the hot side of the battery and the control terminal of the solenoid. If this causes the engine to crank, the solenoid may be presumed to be in good condition and the difficulty is in the control switch (usually the ignition switch), the neutral safety switch and/or their wiring.

If the jumper test does not cause the starter to turn the solenoid is defective.

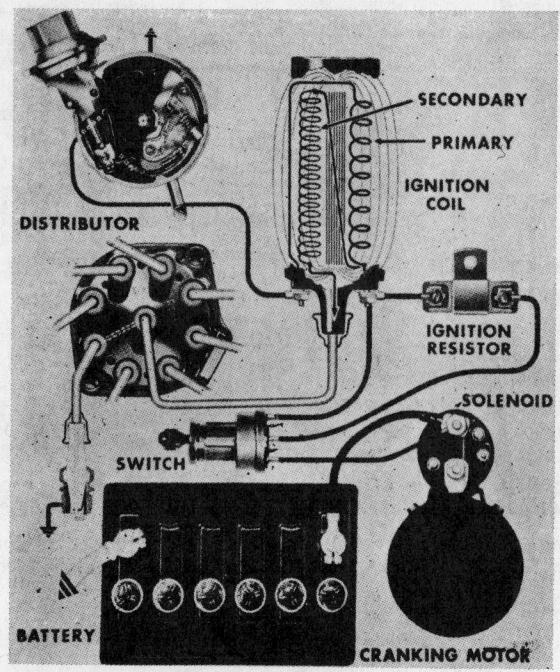

Fig. 4—Wiring diagram showing starter solenoid mounted on cranking motor

STARTER SPINS BUT DOES NOT CRANK THE ENGINE

Check to see if the back end of the solenoid is connected to the starter clutch shift lever. If it is connected and it does shift, the teeth are broken from the flywheel or the starter drive is broken.

STARTER TURNS ENGINE SLUGGISHLY

Make the test given for this subject later in this text.

SOLENOIDS WITH SEPARATE RELAYS

Section 3

The solenoid itself is always mounted on the starter, and in addition to making contact for the starter, it also pulls the starter drive clutch gear into mesh with the flywheel. A single control terminal is used on the solenoid itself. On V8 Buicks with 12-volt systems, there is, in addition to control terminal, an ignition resistor by-pass terminal on the solenoid. This by-pass terminal should not be confused with the control terminal. See fig. 5.

Trouble Shooting Quick Checks

STARTER FAILS TO TURN

First, make sure the battery is up and the battery connections are clean and tight. Check to be sure the automatic transmission is in Neutral.

Connect a jumper lead from the hot side of the battery to the control terminal on the solenoid (on the starter). If this causes the starter to spin, the

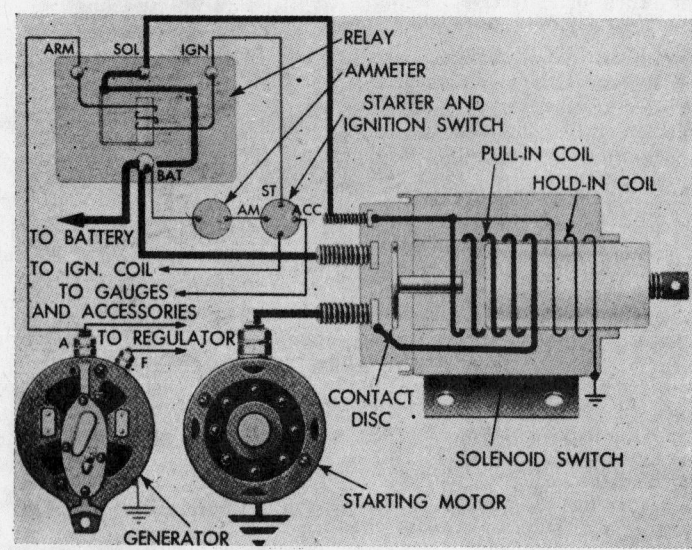

Fig. 5—Pictorial drawing of an Auto-Lite solenoid with a separate relay

SOLENOIDS WITH SEPARATE RELAYS—continued

solenoid is probably OK and the difficulty may lay in the relay. If this does not cause the starter to turn, either the solenoid is defective or the starter drive clutch is jammed. To check for a jammed starter clutch, disconnect the back end of the solenoid from the starter clutch and again make the preceding test. If the starter spins with the linkage disconnected, the clutch mechanism is jammed or defective and the starter should be removed.

QUICK CHECK ON RELAY

Delco (Buick) relays have four terminals which are marked: 1, 2, 3 and 4.

Auto-Lite (Chrysler, De Soto, Dodge) relays have four terminals: One large unmarked terminal, one marked IGN, one SOL, and one ARM.

First, determine if there is current being supplied to the relay by making a momentary short circuit with a screwdriver between ground and the large terminal on Auto-Lite or the No. 1 terminal on Delco. If current is supplied to the relay, this will produce a big fat spark. If there is no current at the terminal, the wire feeding it is broken.

Second, clip a jumper wire from the power terminal just tested to the No. 4 terminal on Delco, or the IGN terminal on Auto-Lite. If this causes the engine to crank the relay is OK, the difficulty is in the control (ignition) Switch and/or the neutral safety and/or their wires.

If the engine still doesn't crank, take a screwdriver and ground the No. 3 terminal (Delco) or the ARM terminal (Auto-Lite). If this causes the engine to crank, the wire is broken between the relay and the

generator armature lead (usually connected to the generator terminal on the generator regulator).

If after making the above test the starter does not function, replace the relay.

STARTER SPINS BUT DOES NOT CRANK THE ENGINE

Solenoid (on starter) linkage is disconnected, or starter drive clutch is defective, or flywheel teeth are broken.

STARTER CRANKS THE ENGINE SLUGGISHLY

See the test for this given separately since the same test applies to all types of starter mechanisms.

SOL-REL-SOLENOIDS WITH BUILT-IN RELAYS

Section 4

These units are always mounted on the starter and are connected through linkage to the starter drive clutch. The relay portion is a square box built into and integral with the front end of the solenoid assembly. See fig. 6.

Trouble Shooting Quick Checks

STARTER DOES NOT TURN

First, remove the cover from the shift linkage on the starter and make sure the linkage isn't binding, check the condition of the battery and its terminals.

Now disconnect the two wires from the control terminals on the relay and connect one of these terminals with a jumper to the hot side of the bat-

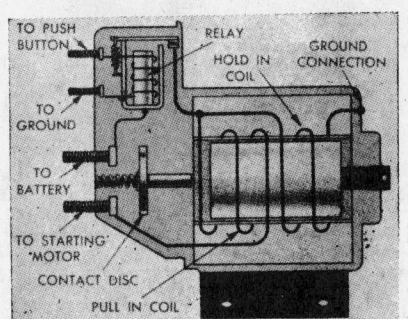

Fig. 6—Pictorial drawing of an Auto-Lite solenoid with a built-in relay

tery, the other terminal to ground. If this does not cause the starter to operate the solenoid relay is defective.

If the starter cranks under this con-

dition, leave the ground wire on and reconnect the other control terminal and try to start it with the ground clip to the ground terminal. If this starts the engine, the wire is broken between the terminal which is temporarily grounded and the generator regulator.

If the second test does not cause the engine to crank, either the control switch or the neutral safety switch and/or their wires are defective.

STARTER SPINS BUT DOES NOT CRANK THE ENGINE

Starter shift linkage is disconnected, starter clutch is defective, or teeth are broken in the flywheel.

STARTER CRANKS SLUGGISHLY

The test for this is given separately in the following paragraphs for all types of starters.

STARTER CRANKS ENGINE SLUGGISHLY

Section 5

First, make sure the battery is fully charged and the battery connections are clean and tight, then check the oil in the crankcase to make certain that it is suitable for the climate, next take a voltage drop reading across the main terminals of the starter main

switch; that is, the starter solenoid or the starter magnetic switch.

Put the volt meter across the two terminals and the meter should read full battery voltage. Start the cranking motor and read the voltage on the engine. The reading should not exceed .5 volt, or in extremely cold weather

.8 volt. If the voltage reading (drop across the terminals) exceeds the above figures there is too much resistance and/or load on the contacts. Remove the starter and check it for loose bearings, poor brush contact, worn brushes, armature rubbing the fields, etc. If the starter is found to be in good condition, replace the switch.

STARTER SYSTEMS

NEUTRAL SAFETY SWITCHES

Section 6

The purpose of the neutral safety switch is to prevent the starter from cranking the engine except when the transmission is in Neutral or Park.

On Chrysler, De Soto, Dodge and Plymouth the neutral safety switch is located on the transmission and it grounds the solenoid or magnetic switch, whichever is used. See fig. 7.

On all other cars the neutral safety switch is located either at the bottom of the steering column where it contacts the shift mechanism or on the steering column underneath the dash.

On most cars the neutral safety switch and the back-up light switch are combined into a single switch mechanism.

On Hudson 1956 and 1957 models with automatic transmission, all Nash models with automatic transmission, and all Rambler models with automatic transmission, the neutral safety switch is the control switch. It is located at the bottom of the steering column and functions by lifting the shift lever. This is the only safety switch used; no other control switch is used.

Trouble Shooting Neutral Safety Switches—Quick Check

If the starter fails to function and the neutral safety switch is to be checked, a hopper can be placed across its terminals. If the starter then func-

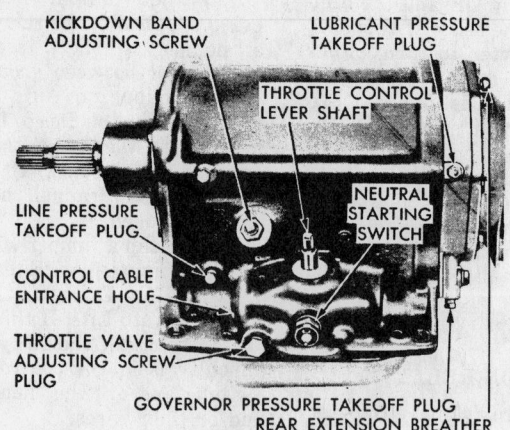

Fig. 7—Location of the neutral safety switch on Chrysler, De Soto, Dodge Dart, Plymouth and Valiant-Lancer

tions the safety switch is known to be defective.

In the case of Chrysler, De Soto, Dodge and Plymouth, the neutral safety switch has one wire. This wire should be grounded to test the neutral safety switch. If the starter works with that wire grounded, the neutral safety switch is defective.

Neutral Safety Switch—Back-Up Light Switch

Where the neutral safety switch is built in combination with the back-up light switch the easiest way to tell which terminals are the back-up light terminals is to take a hopper and jump across every pair of wires. The pair of wires which light the back-up lamps are obviously the back-up light switch wires and should be ignored when testing the neutral safety switch. Once the back-up light wires have been located, simply place your hopper across the other pair of wires to test the neutral safety switch. If the starter functions only when the hopper is placed across these two wires the neutral safety switch is defective or requires adjustment.

Adjustment of neutral safety switches for each of the automatic transmissions is given in the Automatic Transmission Section of this manual.

REDUCTION-GEAR STARTING MOTOR

(CHRYSLER CORPORATION PRODUCTS)

Section 7

Commencing with 1962 production an entirely new starter is used, featuring a built-in reduction gear and positive engagement. It is smaller, lighter and quieter with greater torque at low cranking speeds. There is less current draw under load.

This starter weighs only 15 pounds and has 15% fewer parts. The housing is die-cast aluminum.

With 3.5 to 1 reduction and the starter to ring gear ratio a total of around 45 to 1 is obtained. This higher starter speed emits a high-pitched, high-quality sound.

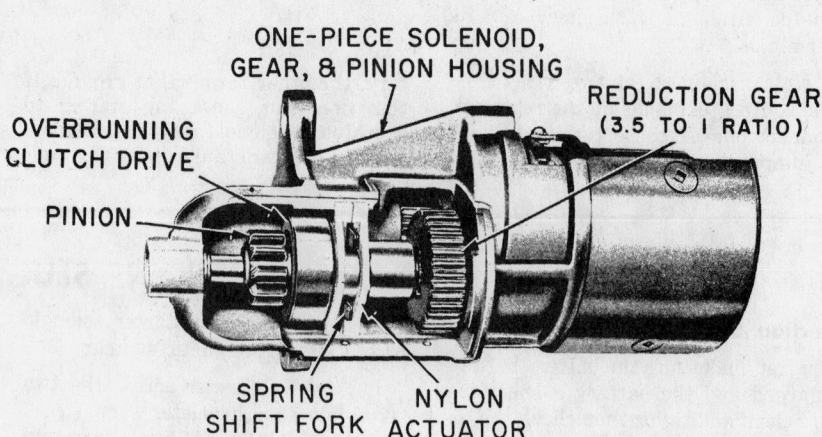

Reduction Gear Starting Motor (Reduction Gear Side)

The positive shift solenoid is enclosed in the starter housing and is energized through the ignition switch. When ignition switch is turned to "start" the solenoid plunger engages drive gear thru a shifting fork. At the completion of travel the plunger closes a switch to revolve the starter.

The tension of the spring type shifting prevents a butt-tooth lock up and motor will not start before total shift.

An overrunning clutch prevents motor damage if key is held on after engine starts.

No lubrication is required due to Oilite bearings.

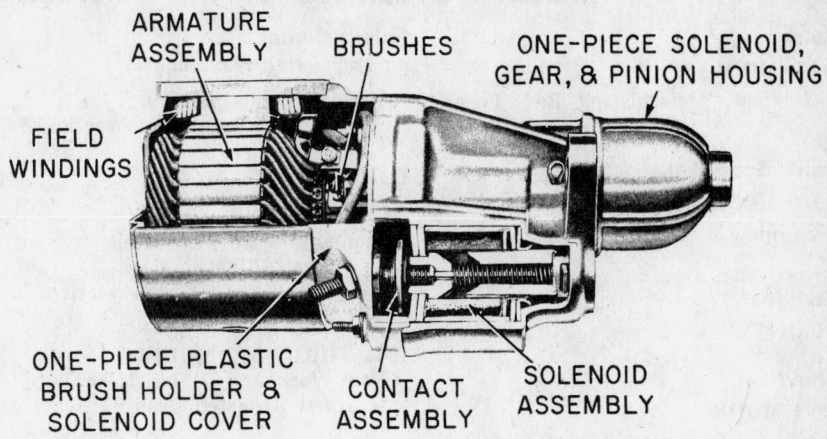

ARMATURE ASSEMBLY — BRUSHES — ONE-PIECE SOLENOID, GEAR, & PINION HOUSING

FIELD WINDINGS

ONE-PIECE PLASTIC BRUSH HOLDER & SOLENOID COVER — CONTACT ASSEMBLY — SOLENOID ASSEMBLY

Reduction Gear Starting Motor (Solenoid Side)

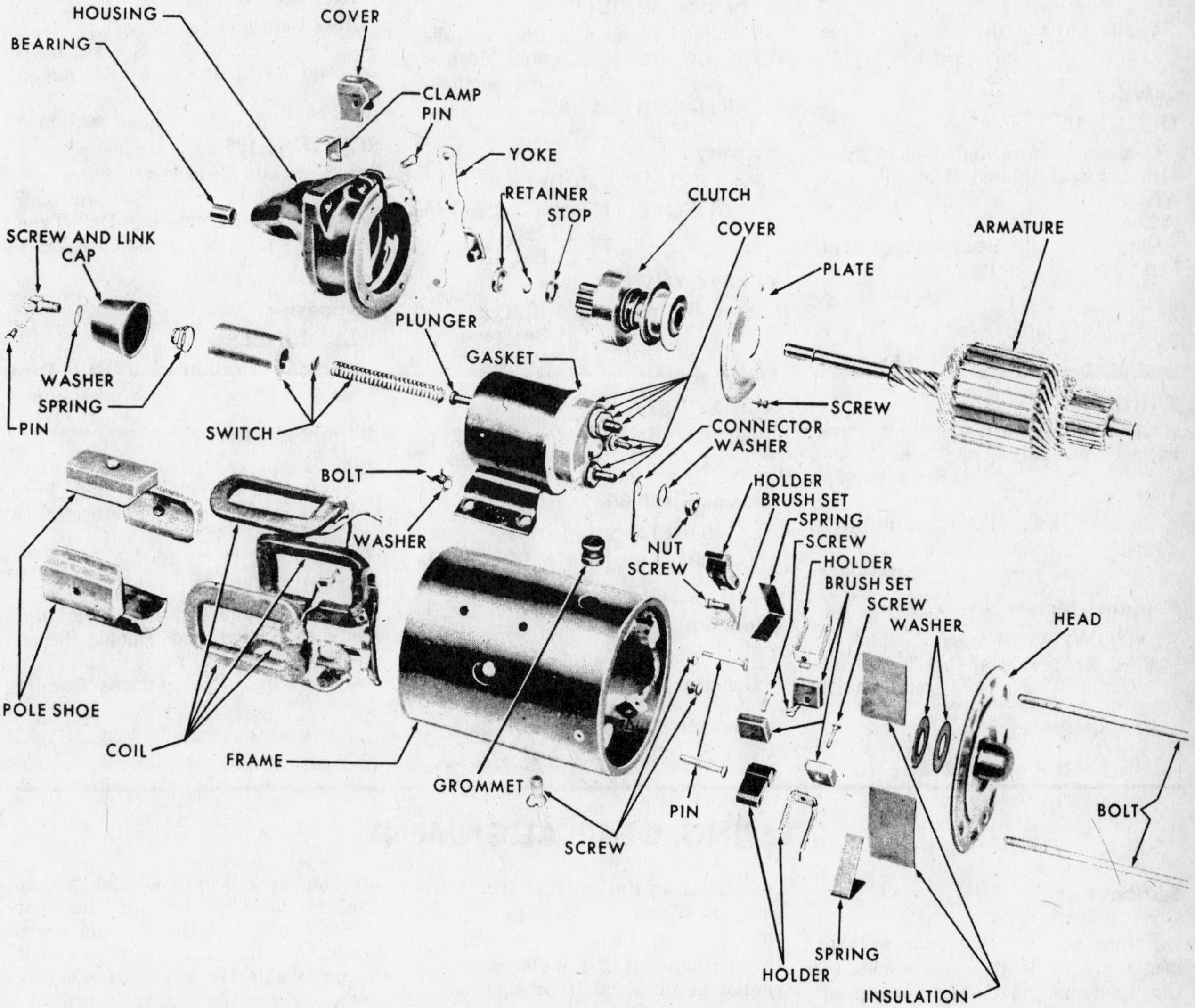

HOUSING — COVER
BEARING — CLAMP PIN
YOKE
RETAINER STOP — CLUTCH COVER — PLATE — ARMATURE
SCREW AND LINK CAP
WASHER SPRING — PLUNGER
PIN — GASKET — SCREW
SWITCH — CONNECTOR WASHER
BOLT — NUT SCREW — HOLDER BRUSH SET — SPRING — SCREW — HOLDER BRUSH SET SCREW WASHER — HEAD
WASHER
POLE SHOE
COIL — FRAME
GROMMET — PIN — SCREW — HOLDER — SPRING — INSULATION — BOLT

Exploded view starting motor and solenoid

MANUAL STEERING GEAR APPLICATION CHART

Buick
ALL MODELS
Saginaw Recirculating Ball Type
See section 4

Buick Special
ALL MODELS
Saginaw Recirculating Ball Type
See section 4

Cadillac
STARTING 1954*

Chevrolet
1954 MODELS
Saginaw with Screw Adjusted Mesh
See section 6
STARTING WITH 1955
Saginaw Recirculating Ball Type
See section 4

Chevy II
ALL MODELS
Saginaw Recirculating Ball Type
See section 4

Chrysler
THRU 1961
Gemmer Worm and Roller Type
with Screw Adjusted Mesh
See section 2
1962-63
Chrysler Built Recirculating Ball
Type
See section 8

Dodge—Dart
THRU 1961
Gemmer Worm and Roller Type
with Screw Adjusted Mesh
See section 2
1962-63
Chrysler Built Recirculating Ball
Type
See section 8

Fairlane—Meteor
STARTING WITH 1962
Ford Recirculating Ball Type
See section 3

Falcon-Comet
STARTING WITH 1960
Ford Recirculating Ball Type
See section 3

De Soto
ALL MODELS
Gemmer Worm and Roller Type
with Screw Adjusted Mesh
See section 2

Ford
1954 THRU 1957 MODELS
Ford Worm and Double Roller Type
with Screw Adjusted Mesh
See section 2
STARTING WITH 1958
Saginaw Recirculating Ball Type
Gear
See section 3

Lincoln
Thru 1956 MODELS
Gemmer Worm and Double Roller
Type with Screw Adjusted Mesh
See section 2
STARTING WITH 1957*

Mercury
1954 THRU 1957 MODELS
Ford Worm and Double Roller Type
with Screw Adjusted Mesh
See section 2
STARTING WITH 1958
Ford Recirculating Ball Type
See section 3

Oldsmobile
ALL MODELS
Saginaw Recirculating Ball Type
See section 4

Oldsmobile F-85
ALL MODELS
Saginaw Recirculating Ball Type
See section 4

Plymouth
THRU 1961
Gemmer Worm and Double Roller

Manual Steering Not Available

Type with Screw Adjusted Mesh
See section 2
1962-63
Chrysler Built Recirculating Ball
Type
See section 8

Pontiac
1954 MODELS
Saginaw with Eccentric Cage Adjuster
See section 5
STARTING WITH 1955
Saginaw Recirculating Ball Type
See section 4

Rambler
ALL MODELS
Gemmer Worm and Double Roller
Type with Screw Adjusted Mesh
See section 2

Studebaker
THRU 1960
Ross Cam and Lever
See section 7
or Saginaw with Screw Adjusted
Mesh
See section 6
STARTING 1961
Ross Cam and Twin Lever
See section 7
or Saginaw Recirculating Ball Type
See section 4

Tempest
ALL MODELS
Saginaw Recirculating Ball Type
See section 4

Valiant—Lancer
1960-63
Saginaw Recirculating Ball Type
See section 4

Willys
ALL MODELS
Ross Cam and Twin Lever on Some
Gemmer Worm and Double Roller
Tooth on Some
See sections 7 and 2

STEERING GEAR ALIGNMENT

Section 1

Before any steering gear adjustments are made it is recommended that the front end of the car be raised and a thorough inspection be made for stiffness or lost motion in the steering gear, steering linkage and front suspension. Worn or damaged parts should be replaced, since a satisfactory adjustment of the steering gear cannot be obtained if bent or badly worn parts exist.

It is also very important that the steering gear be properly aligned in the car. Misalignment of the gear places a stress on the steering worm shaft, therefore a proper adjustment is improbable. To align the steering gear, loosen the steering gear to frame mounting bolts to permit the gear to align itself. Check the steering gear to frame mounting seat, if there is a gap at any of the mounting bolts, proper alignment may be obtained by placing shims where excessiv gap appears. Tighten the steering gear to frame bolts. Alignment of the gear in the car is very important and should be done carefully so that a satisfactory trouble free gear adjustment may be obtained.

GEMMER WORM AND DOUBLE ROLLER TOOTH TYPE WITH SCREW ADJUSTED MESH

FORD WORM AND ROLLER TOOTH TYPE WITH SCREW ADJUSTED MESH

Section 2

Worm Bearing Adjustment

Refer to the section 1 on steering gear alignment. After steering gear has been aligned in car and an inspection of the steering linkage and front suspension completed, proceed to adjust the worm bearings as follows.

Disconnect the steering linkage from the pitman arm. Remove the cross shaft adjusting screw lock nut, disengage the adjusting screw lock plate and back out the adjusting screw. See Fig. 1. Turn the steering wheel to the extreme right or left up 1/8 of a turn. This is necessary so that the worm and roller are not on the high spot. Attach a pull spring scale on the rim of the steering wheel at the spoke. The pull required to turn the steering wheel should be approximately one pound as indicated on the spring scale. If the pull required to turn the steering wheel is less than 1/2 pound, loosen or remove the four cap screws in the lower end plate of the gear box, carefully separate the shims. See Fig. 2. Clip and remove one at a time, tighten cap screws each

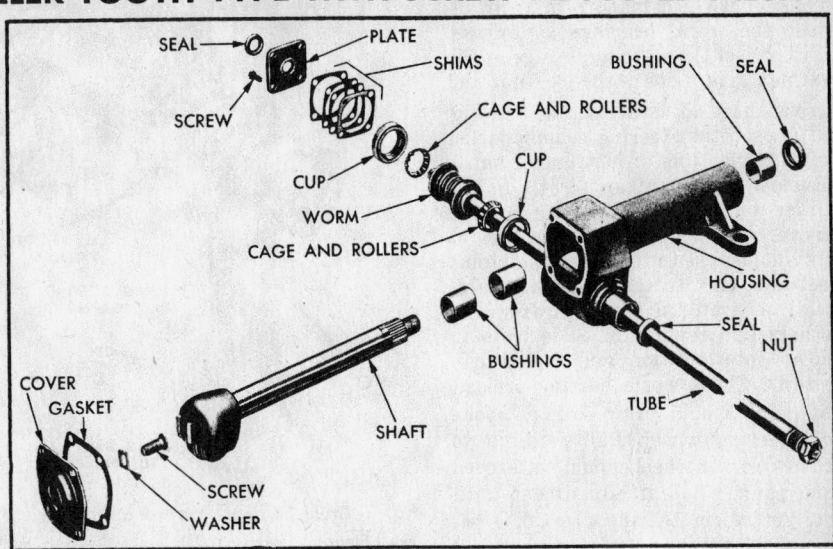

Fig. 2—Exploded view of a Typical Gemmer gear with screw adjusted mesh

time and check pull spring scale until a pull of 1/8 to 3/4 pounds is needed to turn the steering wheel. If the pull required to turn the steering wheel is much more than this it will be necessary to add shims at the lower cover plate. Make a note of the final pull required.

Mesh Adjustment

After a satisfactory worm bearing adjustment has been completed, locate the straight ahead or high spot position of the gear. This is done by first turning the steering wheel to the extreme right, count the number of turns to reach the extreme left, turn wheel back 1/2 the number of turns and gear should be centered. Turn the cross shaft adjusting screw in until all backlash is removed. See Fig. 1. Engage adjusting screw lock plate and install the lock nut. Using the pull spring scale at the steering wheel rim a maximum pull of 1/2 to 1 pound more than was noted to turn the wheel before making this adjustment should be required to turn the steering wheel thru the center position only, slightly less off center pull. The steering wheel should turn freely thru its entire range with no stiffness or binding at any point. When all adjustments have been completed and checked, refill the gear box with lubricant and reconnect the linkage to the pitman arm. Check and reset front wheel toe-in.

Fig. 1—Gear Adjusting Points—Gemmer worm and double Roller Tooth with screw\ adjusted mesh

Steering Gear Adjustments

ADJUSTING SCREW

ADJUSTING SCREW LOCKNUT

Gearshaft Cover Removed

COVER

"O" SEAL RING

NEEDLE BEARING

ADJUSTING SCREW

GEAR HOUSING

GEARSHAFT

STEERING MANUAL

FORD STEERING GEAR—RECIRCULATING BALL TYPE

Section 3

Worm Bearing Adjustment

Refer to section 1 on steering gear alignment. After steering gear has been aligned in car and an inspection of the steering linkage and front suspension has been made, proceed to adjust the worm bearings as follows. Disconnect the steering linkage at the pitman arm. Loosen the lock nut and cross shaft adjusting screw. See Fig. 4. Loosen the steering column jacket clamp at bottom of instrument panel. Remove the four cap screws in top cover on steering column housing, move column and cover upwards to provide access to the adjusting shims between the cap and housing, carefully separate the first shim from the others and remove it. Slide housing down into position and install cap screws. Check worm bearing preload by using a pull spring scale at spoke of steering wheel. Pull required to turn steering wheel should not exceed one pound. Repeat adjustment until correct worm bearing preload is secured. Make a note of the exact pull required when finally adjusted.

Mesh Adjustment

After completing the worm bearing preload adjustment, turn the steering wheel to its mid travel position and adjust gear mesh as follows. Loosen the four cap screws in the cross shaft lower housing. See Fig. 4. It will not be necessary to remove these screws as the housing plate is slotted, rotate the housing in a clockwise or right hand direction enough so that all the backlash or play is just taken out. Check the pounds pull required to

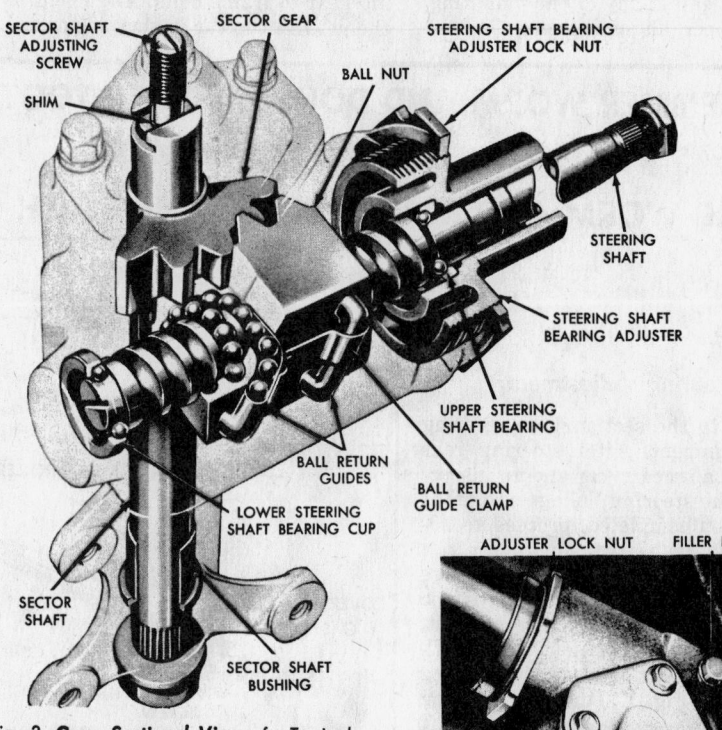

Fig. 3—*Cross Sectional View* of a Typical Ford Steering Gear

turn the steering wheel, using a spring pull scale at the spoke of the steering wheel. This should not exceed one pound more than noted for the worm bearing preload. Repeat adjustment until desired pull is obtained. Tighten all bolts and refill steering gear with lubricant. Check to be sure there is no binding or stiffness when steering wheel is run thru its range.

Cross Shaft End Play Adjustment

Turn the adjusting screw on the top cover of the steering box clockwise until all end play in the cross shaft is

Fig. 4 —*Adjusting Points*

taken out. Tighten lock nut and turn steering wheel to be certain there is no binding or stiffness of the gear. When all adjustments have been completed reconnect steering linkage to pitman arm. Refill gear box with lubricant and reset front wheel toe-in.

SAGINAW RECIRCULATING BALL TYPE

Section 4

Worm Bearing Adjustment

Refer to section 1 in this text on steering gear alignment. After steering gear has been aligned and a complete check of the steering linkage and front end has been made, proceed to adjust the worm bearings as follows. Disconnect the steering linkage from the pitman arm, loosen the pitman shaft adjusting screw lock nut and back off on the adjustment. Turn the steering wheel to the left or right to within one turn of extreme travel. Loosen the lock nut on the bottom end plate of the gear box and turn the

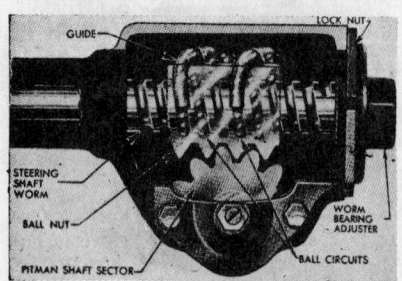

Fig. 6—*Longitudinal cross section of the Saginaw Recirculating Ball Gear*

worm bearing adjuster in until all end play is removed. On some models using this gear the worm bearing adjusting nut is at the top of the gear box (bottom of the mast jacket). Use a pull spring scale at the spoke of the steering wheel and continue to turn the worm bearing adjusting screw in until a pull of approximately one pound is required to turn the steering wheel. Tighten the worm bearing adjuster lock nut. Turn steering wheel from one extreme to the other to be sure there is no stiffness or binding of the gear.

SAGINAW RECIRCULATING BALL TYPE—Continued

Mesh Adjustment

After a satisfactory worm bearing adjustment has been obtained, turn the steering wheel to center or straight ahead position. Tighten pitman shaft adjusting screw in gear box side cover until all end play in pitman shaft has been taken up and

a pull of approximately two pounds is required to turn the steering wheel (using a pull spring scale at spoke of steering wheel). This reading includes worm bearing preload. Tighten pitman shaft adjusting screw lock nut and turn steering wheel from one extreme to the other to check for stiffness or binding of the gear.

Note: This is a push pull adjustment which controls both cross shaft end play and gear mesh, if binding or stiffness is encountered recheck cross shaft and worm bearing adjustments. Fill gear box with lubricant and connect steering linkage to pitman arm. Check and reset front wheel toe-in.

SAGINAW WITH ECCENTRIC CAGE ADJUSTER

Section 5

Worm Bearing Adjustment

Refer to section 1 of this text on steering gear alignment in car. After steering gear has been aligned in car and a thorough check of the steering linkage and front suspension has been completed, proceed to adjust the steering gear worm bearing preload as follows. Disconnect steering linkage from pitman arm. Loosen cross shaft adjusting screw lock nut and back off on adjusting screw. See Fig. 10. Turn steering wheel to the extreme left or right and back up 1/4 turn, this will get the gear off the high spot. Check gear box lower cover plate screws to be sure they are tight. Loosen worm bearing adjuster lock nut and turn adjusting screw in to obtain a 1/2 pound pull at steering wheel rim when measured with a pull spring scale. Hold adjusting screw in this position with a screwdriver and tighten lock nut. Turn steering wheel thru its entire range to be sure no stiffness or binding is present.

Mesh Adjustment

After a satisfactory worm bearing preload adjustment has been made, place the steering gear in the straight ahead position. This is done by first turning the steering wheel to the extreme right, then count the turns to reach the extreme left. Turn wheel back 1/2 the number of turns and the gear will be centered. Loosen lash adjuster plate lock bolt on bottom plate of gear box. Tap lash adjuster plate lightly to turn it in direction of arrow on plate until a pull of about 1 1/2 pounds at the steering wheel rim is required to turn the wheel. See Fig. 10. This is measured with a pull spring scale.

Note: Lash adjuster plate should not be moved more than 1/16 of an inch in relation to the lock bolt at a time and in no case should a pull of

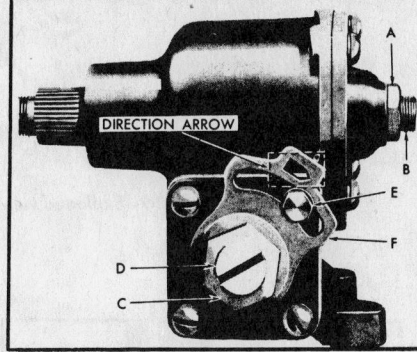

Fig. 7—Adjusting Points.

A–B **Cross Shaft End Play Adjusting Screw and Lock Nut.**
C–D **Worm Thrust Adjusting Screw and Lock Nut.**
  E **Lash Adjuster Lock Bolt.**
  F **Lash Adjuster Plate.**

more than 1 3/4 pounds at the steering wheel rim be permitted to exist as severe damage to the steering gear may result. Tighten lash adjuster plate lock bolt. Turn steering wheel to be sure no stiffness or binding of the gear is present.

Cross Shaft End Play Adjustment

Turn steering wheel to extreme left or right and back up 1/2 turn to get gear off high spot.

Turn cross shaft end play adjusting screw in gear box side cover in until all end play has been removed from the cross shaft. Back adjusting screw out, and turn adjusting screw in again until it just contacts cross shaft. See Fig. 7. Hold adjusting screw in this position with a screwdriver and tighten lock nut. Turn steering wheel thru its entire rotation to be certain there is no stiffness or binding of the gear. If adjustment is satisfactory reconnect the steering linkage to the pitman arm. Check lubricant in gear box and reset front wheel toe-in.

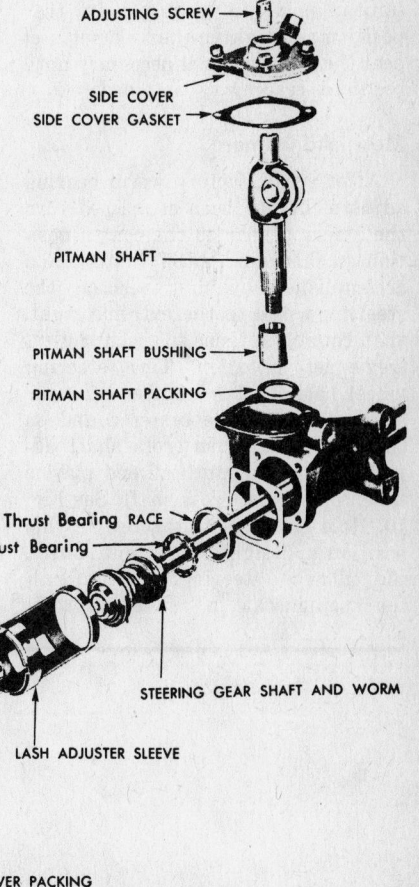

Fig. 8—Exploded view of a typical Saginaw gear with eccentric cage adjuster

STEERING MANUAL

SAGINAW TYPE WITH SCREW ADJUSTED MESH

Worm Bearing Adjustment

Section 6

Refer to section 1 in this text on alignment of steering gear in car. After steering gear has been aligned in car and steering linkage and front suspension have been checked, proceed to adjust steering gear worm bearing as follows. Disconnect the steering linkage from the pitman arm. Loosen the cross shaft adjusting screw lock nut on the gear box side cover and back out the adjusting screw. Turn the steering wheel in either direction until stopped by the gear, then turn back one turn. Attach a pull spring scale to the rim of the steering wheel at one of the spokes, and measure the pull required to turn the steering wheel. The pull spring scale reading should be approximately ½ pound. Proceed to loosen the worm bearing adjuster lock nut on the bottom plate of the gear box. See Fig. 10. Turn the adjuster clockwise to increase the reading, counterclockwise to decrease the reading. When the desired pull at the steering wheel is obtained, hold the adjuster in that position and tighten the lock nut. Repeat the adjustment if necessary until required reading is obtained.

Mesh Adjustment

After a satisfactory worm bearing adjustment has been completed turn the steering gear to the center position on the high spot. This may be a accomplished by first turning the steering wheel to the extreme right, then count the turns to reach the extreme left rotation. Turn steering wheel back ½ the number of turns and gear should be centered and on the high spot. Turn cross shaft adjusting screw in until all end play is taken out of the cross shaft. See Fig. 10. Hold the adjusting screw in this position and tighten lock nut. Check the pull at the steering wheel rim with the spring scale, a pull of approxi-

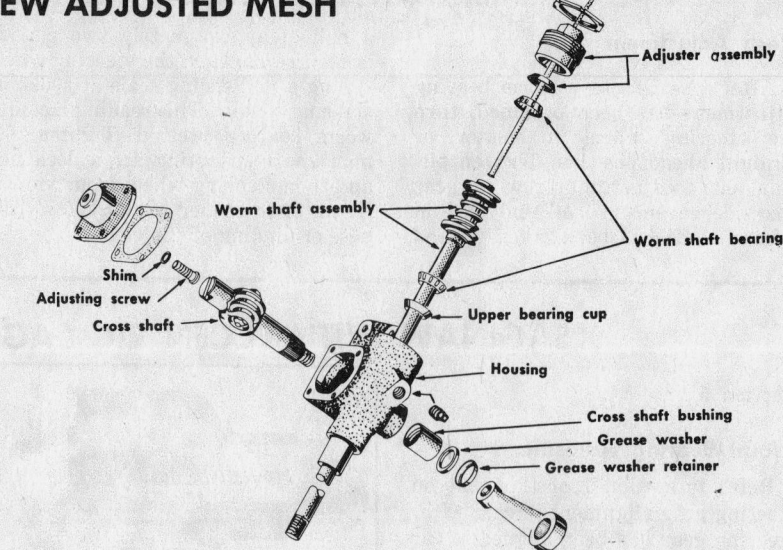

Fig. 9—Exploded view of a typical Saginaw gear with screw adjusted neck

mately one pound to turn the steering wheel should exist. Repeat the adjustment if necessary if necessary until a one pound pull is required to turn the steering wheel and there is no stiffness or binding of the gear. Connect steering linkage to pitman arm. Fill gear box with lubricant and reset front wheel toe-in.

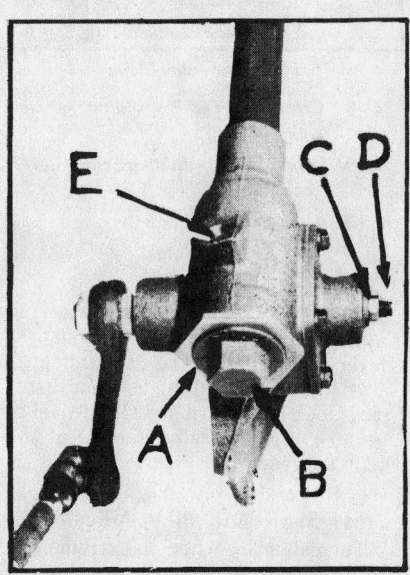

Fig. 10—Adjusting Points

A. Lock nut.
B. Worm bearing adjuster.
C. Lock nut.
D. Mesh adjusting screw.
E. Oil filler hole.

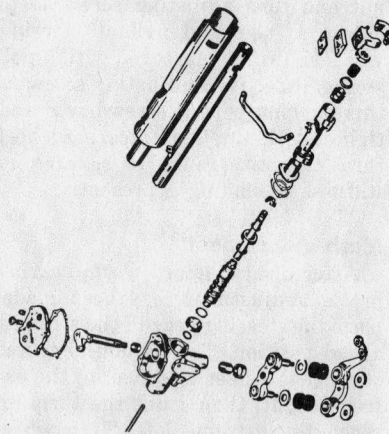

Fig. 11—Exploded view of a typical Ross cam and twin lever gear

ROSS CAM AND TWIN LEVER TYPE

Section 7

Worm Bearing Adjustment

Align steering gear in car as in Section 1 of this text. After alignment and linkage and front end have been checked, proceed to adjust the steering gear worm bearings.

Disconnect linkage from pitman arm. Back off cross shaft adjusting screw. See Fig. 12. Turn steering wheel to the extreme right then back 1/2 turn to be sure gear is off high spot. Loosen column clamp at dash. Loosen screws holding steering box top cover and slide cover up enough to release adjusting shims. Clip and remove one or more shims so that when screws are tightened a slight drag will be noted. Do not remove enough shims to cause stiffness or binding. Retighten column clamp at dash.

Mesh Adjustment

After proper worm bearing adjustment has been made turn the steer-

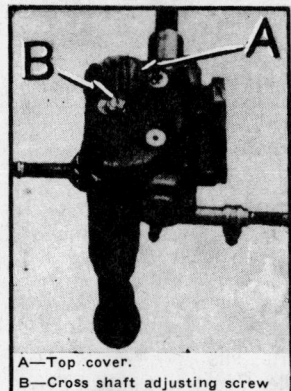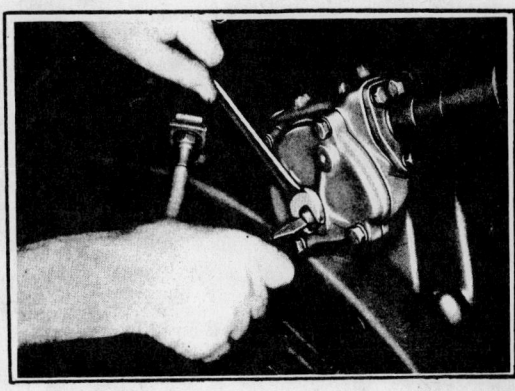

A—Top cover.
B—Cross shaft adjusting screw

Fig. 15—Adjusting Points

ing gear to the high spot or center position. This is done by first turning the steering wheel to extreme right then count the turns to reach extreme left. Turn back 1/2 this number to the center.

Turn the cross shaft adjusting

screw until all end play is removed. Tighten lock nut and test thru entire range to be sure there are no binding or tight spots. Reconnect the linkage to pitman arm. Refill box with lubricant.

CHRYSLER—RECIRCULATING BALL TYPE STEERING GEAR

Section 8

CHRYSLER-BUILT RECIRCULATING BALL TYPE

Worm Bearing Adjustment

A Universal Coupling makes this unit self-aligning.

Disconnect steering linkage at pitman arm. Loosen cross shaft adjusting screw. Adjust the worm screw adjusting nut at top of gear until an approximate one pound pull is obtained at the steering wheel rim. After adjustment is made lock worm adjusting screw in position with the large lock nut at top of housing. Mesh adjustment.

After worm bearing adjustment is completed tighten cross shaft clearance adjusting screw to obtain a mesh that will produce an approximate two pound pull at the steering wheel rim. (This includes the already one pound pull on the worm gear). Lock the nut

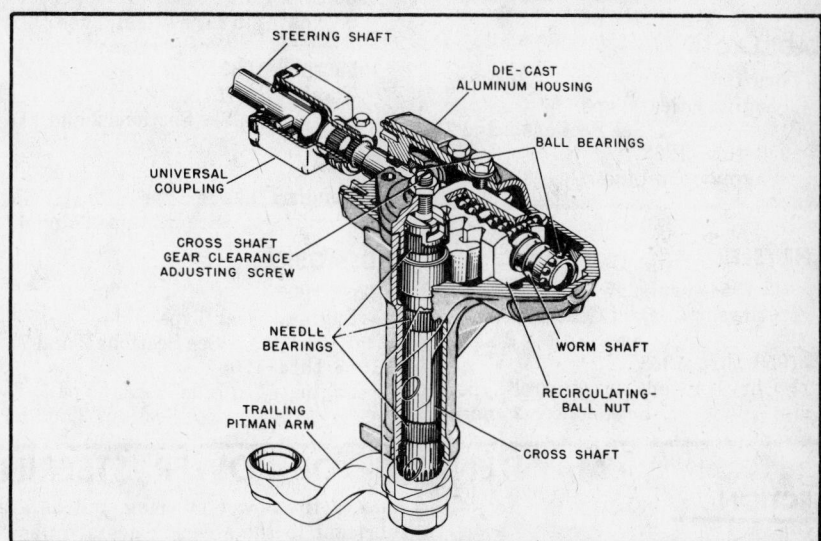

Sectional View of Steering Gear

on the cross shaft screw. Test the pull in all positions to be sure the maximum pull is at the center of the steering wheel travel.

This is a mesh adjustment only as

the cross shaft is carried on roller bearings.

Connect pitman arm, refill box with lubricant.

POWER STEERING

BUICK

Thru 1955
    Saginaw Gear Type
        See Sections 2 and 7
1956 thru 1958
    Saginaw "In Line" Gear Type
        See Sections 2 and 8
1959-63
    Rotary Valve (Torsion
    Bar) Type
        See Sections 2 and 11

BUICK SPECIAL

Rotary Valve (Torsion
Bar) Type
        See Sections 2 and 11

CHEVROLET

Thru 1955
    Saginaw Gear Type
        See Sections 2 and 7
1955 thru 1963
    Saginaw Linkage Type
    See Procedures for
        Bendix Linkage Type
        See Sections 2 and 4

CHEVY II

Saginaw Linkage Type
See Procedure for
    Bendix Linkage Type
        See Sections 2 and 4

CADILLAC

Thru 1955
    Saginaw Gear Type
        See Sections 2 and 7
1956 thru 1963
    Saginaw "In Line" Gear Type
        See Sections 2 and 8

CHRYSLER

Mid-1954 thru 1957
    Chrysler Coaxial Gear Type
        See Sections 2 and 9
1958 thru 1963
    Chrysler Constant Control Type
        See Sections 2 and 10

DE SOTO

1955 thru 1957
    Chrysler Coaxial Gear Type
        See Sections 2 and 9
1958 thru 1961
    Chrysler Constant Control Type
        See Sections 2 and 10

DODGE

1954
    Ross Linkage Type
    See Procedures for
        Bendix Linkage Type
        See Sections 2 and 4
1955 thru 1957
    Chrysler Coaxial Gear Type
        See Sections 2 and 9
1958 thru 1963
    Chrysler Constant Control Type
        See Sections 2 and 10

FORD

Bendix Linkage Type
        See Sections 2 and 4

FAIRLANE-METEOR

Bendix Linkage Type
        See Sections 2 and 4

LINCOLN

Thru 1955
    Saginaw Gear Type
        See Sections 2 and 7
1956 thru 1957
    Saginaw "In Line" Gear Type
        See Sections 2 and 8
1958 thru 1963
    Torsion Bar Type
        See Sections 2 and 11

MERCURY

Bendix Linkage Type
        See Sections 2 and 4

OLDSMOBILE

Thru 1955
    Saginaw Gear Type
        See Sections 2 and 7
1956 thru 1963
    Saginaw "In Line" Gear Type
        See Sections 2 and 8

OLDSMOBILE F-85

Rotary Valve (Torsion
Bar) Type
        See Sections 2 and 11

PLYMOUTH

Thru 1954
    Monroe Linkage Type
        See Sections 2 and 5
1955 thru 1957
    Chrysler Coaxial Gear Type
        See Sections 2 and 9
1958 thru 1963
    Chrysler Constant Control Type
        See Sections 2 and 10

PONTIAC

Thru 1955
    Saginaw Gear Type
        See Sections 2 and 7
1956 thru 1958
    Saginaw "In Line" Gear Type
        See Sections 2 and 8
1959-60-62-63
    Torsion Bar Type
        See Sections 2 and 11
1961
Bendix Linkage Type
        See Sections 2 and 4

RAMBLER

Monroe Linkage Type
        See Sections 2 and 5

VALIANT-LANCER

STARTING WITH 1960
    Chrysler Constant Control Type
        See Sections 2 and 10

STUDEBAKER

Saginaw Gear Type
        See Sections 2 and 7
Bendix Linkage Type
        See Sections 2 and 4

MAINTENANCE OF POWER STEERING SYSTEMS

SECTION 2

Lubrication

Note: Proper lubrication of the steering gear linkage and the front suspension is extremely important on cars equipped with power steering.

Every 1000 miles remove the filler plug from the steering gear box and check the level of the lubricant. Add fluid gear oil SAE 90 if the level is below the filler plug hole. **Caution:** Do not use a pressure gun when adding fluid gear oil as the pressure will force the oil up into the steering column.

Note: The Gemmer unit starting with late 1953 production uses the fluid of the power steering unit as a lubricant in the steering gear box as does also the Chrysler Co-axial starting in 1955, the Chrysler Constant Control starting in 1958, the Saginaw in-line unit starting in 1956 and Torsion Bar starting in 1958.

Oil Level

The oil level in the reservoir of the power steering oil pump should be checked every 30 days or every 1000 miles. Wipe the cover of the reservoir clean so that no dirt can fall into the reservoir. Remove the cover and check that the oil level is at the line stamped into the metal of the reservoir. The line is one inch below the top. Add fluid to bring the level up to the line. If the level is very low, check the system for leaks. **Caution:** Do not disturb the filter element. It is not necessary to change this unit oftener than every 25,000 miles.

BENDIX SAGINAW, CHRYSLER CO-AXIAL, CHRYSLER CONSTANT CONTROL AND TORSION BAR UNITS

These units use Automatic Transmission Fluid Type A. Change the fluid every 25,000 miles.

MAINTENANCE OF POWER STEERING SYSTEMS—Continued

Power Steering Hoses

The hose used to carry fluid from the pump to the unit is smaller than the hose returning the fluid to the pump.

In a majority of cases hoses are equipped with fitting which can only be connected to the correct spot. However, it has been found that, in some cases, the fittings of the two hoses are identical. For this reason it is urged that the fittings of all power steering hoses be match marked to their points of attachment before they are unfastened.

If this is not done and the hoses are reconnected so that pressure is applied into the return side of the unit, the oil seals will be forced out of position which will result in leakage as well as malfunction of the unit.

Draining the System

Clean the fitting which attaches the pressure hose to the control valve assembly and disconnect the hose. Let the oil drain from the hose into a bucket. Start the engine and let it idle. Turn the wheels back and forth from extreme right to left until air begins to sputter out of the hose. Stop the engine, reconnect the hose, and add oil to fill the reservoir to the level mark.

Bleeding the System

When the reservoir has been refilled after draining, it is necessary to bleed the system. Start the engine and let it run. Turn the wheels back and forth between the extreme right and left positions until no more bubbles appear in the oil in the reservoir. Recheck the level and reinstall the cover. On the Gemmer unit there is a bleeder screw at the top center of the cylinder assembly. Remove the screw and proceed as above until oil flows out the hole, then replace the screw.

Checking Steering Effort

To check the steering effort, measure the pull required to turn the wheels on a dry, smooth concrete floor or smooth steel plates. Check that both front tires are properly inflated. Idle the engine at about 475 rpm. Move the wheels back and forth until fluid reaches operating temperature. Attach a spring scale to a spoke near the rim of the steering wheel. Turn the wheel one full turn in each direction from straight ahead by pulling on the scale. If a pull of more than ten pounds is required at any point, check over and grease up the steering linkage and repeat the test. If over ten pounds is still required at any point, check the steering gear adjustment and the trouble chart.

Checking Pump Pressure

If the tires are properly inflated and the steering linkage is well greased and adjusted and the steering gear is not binding, then the lack of proper assistance on turns may be due to poor pump pressure. In order to check the pump pressure:

Connect a pressure gage and a shut-off valve into the pressure line at the pump. (Fig. 1) Turn the shut-off valve to the open position. Start the engine and allow it to idle for several minutes to permit the oil to reach operating temperature. Now turn the wheel one full turn in either direction, reading the pressure gage at the same time. If the pressure reading is equal to or slightly greater than 500 psi on the

Fig. 1—Typical Installation of Oil Pump Test Gage. Cadillac Installation Shown

Gemmer and Monroe units, 300 psi on the Ross unit, 750 psi on the Saginaw unit and 850 psi on the Chrysler Constant Control unit, 975 psi on the Torsion Bar unit, then the pump and power cylinder are OK. In such a case there is no need to check the pressure in the system further. However, if the pressure did not reach the stated figure, then close the shut-off valve on the output side of the gage for not over four seconds and read the pressure shown on the gage. (Do not keep the valve shut for longer than four seconds or the pump may be damaged.) If the pressure shown is equal to or greater than the stated figures, the pump is OK and the trouble is in the power cylinder. If the pressure was below the stated figures, then the trouble is probably in the pump oil flow and pressure relief valve.

Checking the Oil Flow and Pressure Relief Valve in the Pump Assembly

When the wheels are turned hard right, or hard left, against the stops, the oil flow and pressure relief valves come into action so that if these valves are working and are not stuck there should be a slight buzzing noise. Do not hold the wheels in the extreme position for over three or four seconds because, if the pressure relief valve is not working, the pressure could get high enough to damage the system.

Test Driving Car to Check the Power Steering

When test driving to check power steering, drive at a speed between 15 and 20 mph. Make several turns in each direction. When a turn is completed, the front wheels should return to the straight ahead position with very little help from the driver.

If the front wheels fail to return as they should and yet the steering linkage is free, well oiled and properly adjusted, the trouble is probably due to misalignment of the power cylinder or improper adjustment of the spool valve. See the Trouble Chart.

SECTION 3   # POWER STEERING OIL PUMPS

The source of power for all types of power steering is provided by an oil pump. In all installations the oil pump and the reservoir are one unit. The drive for the pump is either by a belt from the engine or by attaching the pump to the rear end of the generator. The fluid used is Automatic Transmission Fluid Type A. (Automatic Transmission Fluid Type A is sold in a can which has stamped into the metal the letters AQTF followed by a number. The number indicates that particular refining company's right to the AQTF designation. The AQTF designation is issued by the Armour Institute of Chicago). The type of fluid to be used in the system is marked on the reservoir. The level of the fluid is important and should be checked every 1,000 miles. Some reservoirs have a measuring stick while others have a line stamped on the side to indicate the correct level. The line is ordinarily one inch below the top. The amount of fluid necessary to fill a system is not a definite amount but seems to approximate three pints. The fluid does not have to be changed oftener than every 25,000 miles. The

POWER STEERING

reservoir is equipped with a filter which does not require replacement in normal service oftener than every 25,000 miles.

In order for the system to have enough power to assist in steering when the engine is idling the volume of fluid delivered by the pump is far too high at driving speeds. Also when the car is going straight and requires no steering the pressure capacity of the pump must be relieved. Therefore on all installations the pumps are equipped with a combination flow control and pressure relief valve. (Fig. 3) The design of this valve is basically the same for all power steering units. The pressure relief valve is located inside the flow control valve. The valve assembly is inside the pump body. When the circulation rises to approximately two gallons per minute the flow control valve is forced to move against the pressure of the return spring. As the valve moves, it opens a passage between the inlet and outlet sides of the pump. Excess oil is thus sent back into the intake and the oil merely circulates in the pump. When the pressure rises above a fixed limit (approx. 600 psi) the relief valve is forced to move against its spring pressure. This movement also uncovers an opening to the inlet side of the pump permitting the oil to circulate within the pump without rise in pressure.

PUMP OVERHAUL

The Gear Type Pump

This type of pump is used with all Chrysler, Bendix, Monroe, Gemmer and Ross units. It is also used in Lincoln and on early Saginaw units. **Note:** Cars using the Gemmer unit employ a pump with two sets of gears. The basic procedure given for

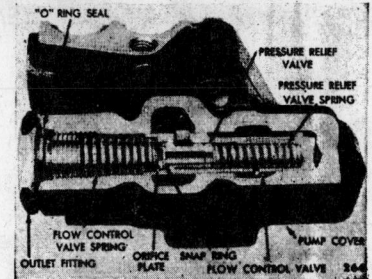

Fig. 3—Typical Oil Flow Control and Pressure Release Valve Assembly. Ford Installation Shown

pumps with only one set of gears will apply to pumps with two sets of gears. (Fig. 4) Note, however, that the two sets are not interchangeable and are not available for service.

REMOVAL

Use a suction gun to empty the reservoir. Unfasten the lines at the pump and fasten them so that the ends point up and the oil does not drip out. Cap the ends, if possible, to keep out dirt. Loosen the bolts holding the pump bracket and remove the drive belt. Remove the attaching bolts with their spacers and washers and remove the pump and bracket as an assembly. In some cases it is only necessary to unbolt the pump from the rear of the generator.

DISASSEMBLY

Clean the exterior of the pump and the reservoir. Remove the filter from inside the reservoir. Remove the orifice body from inside the reservoir. Remove the two cap screws and washers which hold the reservoir reinforcement and reservoir body to the pump body and remove the reservoir. This will permit removal of two "O" ring seals from grooves in the pump body.

Remove the pump pulley screw, lock washer, and the flat washer. Remove the pulley and the pulley key from the pump shaft. Remove two screws and lock washers and the pump cover from the pump housing. Remove three screws and the bracket from the pump housing.

Remove the pump shaft and the gears from the pump body (housing). Remove the outlet fitting and its "O" ring. Lift out the flow control valve spring and tap the cover on a wooden block to remove the combination flow control and relief valve. Using snap ring pliers remove the retaining ring which holds the pressure relief valve and spring in the flow control valve.

CLEANING AND INSPECTION

Wash all the parts in clean solvent. If the pump uses a bearing (Ford) do not put the bearing in the solvent as it is a prelubricated bearing.

Check all the parts for scores and signs of wear. Replace any assemblies that seem to be worn. Check the gears in the pump body. The clear-

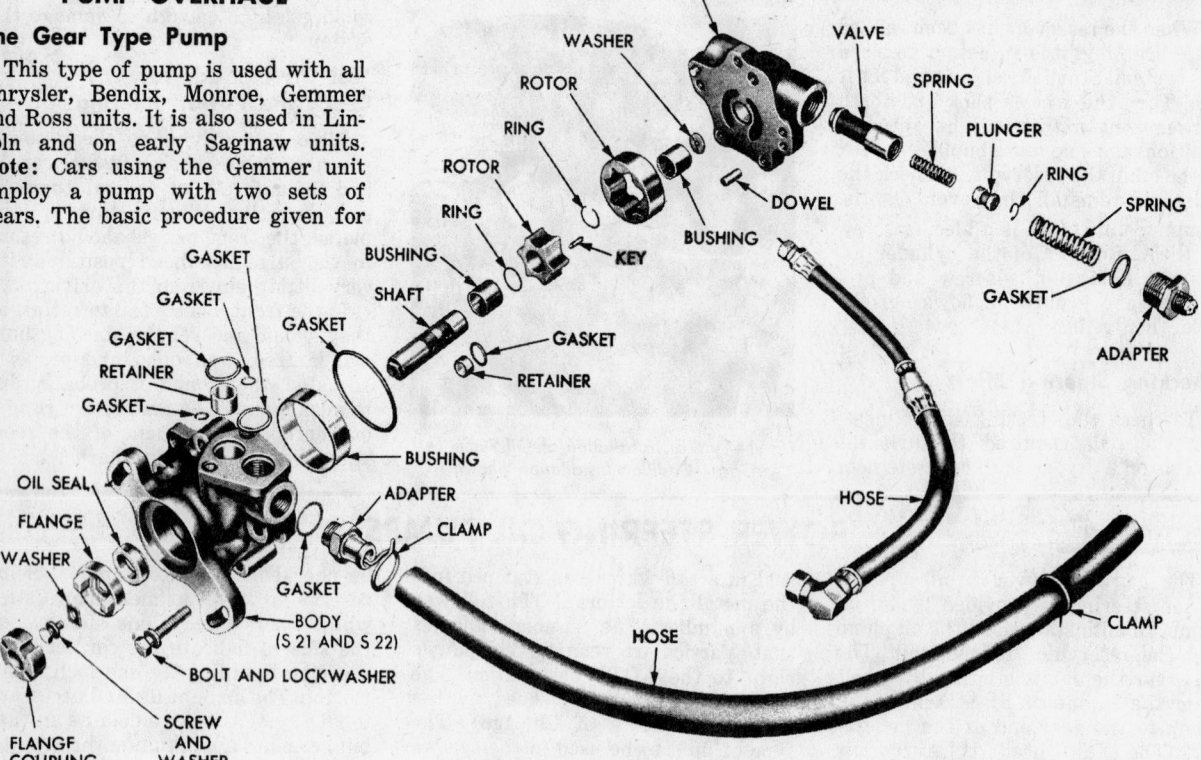

Typical Gear Type Oil Pump

ance between the gears should not exceed .008 in. The clearance between the driven gear and the housing should not exceed .006 in. The end clearance of the gears should not exceed .002 in. Check the flow control valve spring; it should exert 14 lbs. plus or minus 1½ lbs at a length of one and thirteen sixty-fourths in. Check that the relief valve moves freely in the flow control valve.

ASSEMBLY AND INSTALLATION

Coat all the parts with fluid and reverse the procedure to assemble and install. Use new gaskets throughout.

Vane Type Pumps

This type of pump is used on almost all Saginaw units.

REMOVAL

Empty the reservoir and unfasten the lines. The fat line is the return line. Cap the lines to keep out dirt and tie them up out of the way.

Use a 15/16 open end wrench to hold the pump pulley and use a ¾ in. open end wrench to remove the nut and washer holding the pulley to the pump shaft. Loosen the pump to bracket bolts, slide the unit toward the engine, and remove the pulley. Unbolt the pump from the bracket.

DISASSEMBLY

Remove the four bolts holding the reservoir to the pump body. These bolts hold a deflector plate in the bottom of the reservoir. Remove the reservoir and the deflector plate.

Using a 9/16 in. box wrench, remove the four bolts holding the entire pump together. When lifting the pump cover off the pump body be careful not to let the flow control valve drop out. Remove the valve assembly from the pump cover. Remove the snap ring in the end of the valve assembly to release the pressure relief valve.

Lift the pressure plate from the dowel pins which locate the plate

and the cam ring on the pump body. Remove the cam ring assembly which includes the rotor and the vanes. Do not let the rotor and vane assembly fall out of the cam ring.

Turn the pump body over and using snap ring pliers remove the pump shaft front bearing retaining ring. The front bearing is a press fit on the shaft so that the bearing and shaft can be lifted from the housing as an assembly. When doing so be careful of the inner bearing and the lip seal. This seal protects the prelubricated front bearing from contact with the automatic transmission fluid type A which is used in the steering system. Nothing is likely to damage this seal more than careless removal or replacement of the pump shaft. The inner bearing is lubricated by the type A fluid going through the pump.

INSPECTION

Wipe the front bearing and shaft assembly with clean cloths; do not soak in cleaning solvent as the solvent could dilute the lubricant in the sealed bearing.

Inspect the drive shaft for wear and check both ball bearings for roughness or noisy operation. If the large bearing must be replaced, press the new one on the shaft by applying pressure to the inner race only.

Check the fit of the vanes in the rotor, they must be snug yet slide freely in their slots. Tightness may be relieved by thorough cleaning and polishing with crocus cloth or a hard Arkansas stone. If the vanes fit the slots too loosely, replace the vane and rotor assembly. Replace the vanes if they are irregularly worn or scored.

Replace the cam ring if its mating surfaces cannot be polished free of roughness or shows signs of irregular wear. If the inner surface of the ring is scored or worn, replace the ring.

Inspect the flat surfaces of the pressure plate and the pump body for wear and scores. These parts may be repaired by lapping until smooth and

flat. Be careful to remove all traces of compound.

Hair line scratches on the flow control valve and its bore are normal, but heavy scratches must be polished away or the cover must be renewed. Make certain that the valve slides freely in its bore.

There is in use an early type cover in which the rear end of the valve bore is closed by a plug and an "O" ring seal retained by a ring or a pin. If there is an oil leak at the plug, release the retainer and push the plug out of the cover. Remove all burrs from around the countersink and the ring groove with a fine stone. Lubricate the plug with type A fluid, install a new "O" ring seal on the plug and install the assembly in the countersink end of the bore and install the retainer.

ASSEMBLY AND INSTALLATION

Reverse the procedure to reassemble. Be sure all the parts are clean and well covered with Type A fluid. Use new seals and gaskets as this assembly operates at about 760 pounds pressure. If a new lip seal is required, press it into place with force applied at its outer edge. The two 1/16 in. holes in the casing of the seal go to the outside. Install the snap ring which retains the front shaft bearing so that the beveled side is outward.

The cam ring must be installed on the dowel pins so that the arrows on the outer surface of the ring point in the direction of rotation of the pump.

Install the vanes in the slots of the rotor with the rounded edge outward.

When pump cover is installed, turn the cover bolts down to snug but not tight. Install the reservoir with new gaskets, being sure that a spacer is located in each bolt hole. Now tighten the reservoir and pump cover bolts securely. This method is used in order to assure proper alignment of the cover reservoir and body. Check that the pump shaft turns freely.

TROUBLE CHART FOR LINKAGE TYPE POWER GEARS

Note: Always check the fluid level. Excessive turning of the steering wheel with the engine shut off can cause loss of fluid and draw air into the system. Have the fluid in the system at operating temperature. Approx. 170 deg. F.

Hard Steering in Both Directions

This trouble can be caused by a loosen fan belt; low oil level; stiff steering linkage due to lack of lubrication and adjustment; not enough

air in the tires; pitman arm stud too tight on the valve body; power cylinder piston rod bent and binding in the rod guide; low oil pump pressure due to a sticking flow control and relief valve or its springs or non-operation of the pump due to a poor coupling or wear; non-operation of the power cylinder due to leaks; a bind in the steering column; air in the system requires bleeding.

Hard Steering in One Direction

This trouble can be caused by unequal or low tire pressure; a bent power cylinder piston rod; a bind in the steering column; front end out of alignment; improperly adjusted spool valve.

Car Keeps Going to One Side

This trouble can be due to low tire erly inflated tires; pitman arm stud binding in the valve body; spool valve sticking or improperly adjusted.

POWER STEERING

TROUBLE CHART FOR LINKAGE TYPE POWER GEARS

Slow Recovery After Turns

This truble can be due to low tire pressure; pitman arm stud binding on the valve body; a bind in the steering column; steering knuckle bushings too tight; bent power cylinder or rod; wheels not properly aligned; improperly adjusted spool valve; on Dodge V8 the anti-roll pin may be binding in the slot; on Saginaw units the worm thrust bearings may be loose.

Loose Steering

This trouble may show as kickback. It can be due to a maladjusted steering gear, shock absorbers not working, or air in the system.

Oil Leakage

Oil leaks in the hydraulic system are likely at the hose connections, which can be tightened; at the pump body gaskets which necessitates removal of the pump and renewal of the gaskets, and around the piston and seals of the cylinder assembly which can be fixed by replacement of the seals if the rod guide has not been damaged.

Noises

Noises can be caused by a loose fan belt; low oil level; worn bushings in the pump body or cover; dirt and sludge in the pump; pitman arm stud loose on the steering gear or the valve body; reactor link loose on the cylinder (Dodge V8 only); tie rod clamps not in a horizontal position at the bottom of the tie rods; piston rod attachment to the frame loose; kinks or sharp bends in the hoses; air in the system, requires bleeding. On Saginaw units there can be a whistling noise caused by either dirt in the control valve or lack of operational clearance for the spool valve. In either case the unit must be removed and overhauled.

OVERHAUL OF BENDIX LINKAGE TYPE POWER STEERING UNITS

SECTION 4

Control Valve

Drain the system and disconnect the hoses at the valve. Cap the ends of the hoses with masking tape to keep out dirt.

Loosen the clamp bolt which holds the control valve assembly to the steering connecting rod. Drive the anti-roll pin up into the rod just so the end of the pin clears the threads of the clamp. There is no hole on the opposite side of the clamp. This pin is on Ford installations.

Remove the cotter pin from the pitman arm stud and back the nut off flush with the end of the stud. Tap the ball stud out of the pitman arm while supporting the arm with a hammer to absorb the shock. Be careful not to hit the valve assembly. Remove the stud from the pitman arm and turn the wheels to provide room to turn the valve assembly off the rod. Before doing so, measure the distance from the center of the clamp bolt to the center of the nearest steering connecting rod ball stud. This distance must be used at assembly to assure that the steering wheel will be properly located. Remove the grease gun fitting from the valve assembly. Now unscrew the valve assembly from the rod. Remove the anti-roll pin from the rod.

DISASSEMBLY OF THE CONTROL VALVE

Note: Be careful in clamping the valve assembly in a vise as any slight distortion of the body will interfere with the proper action of the spool valve.

Mark or scribe the valve housing, flange, and sleeve, to assure proper reassembly.

Remove the bolts holding the cap and gasket to the end of the valve body and remove it. Remove the nut and washer so exposed from the spool valve bolt. Remove also washers, a spacer, a centering spring, an adapter plate and a bushing if these parts are present.

Remove two bolts and separate the valve sleeve from the valve housing.

Using a small punch, push out the pin that locks the socket tube, the stop screw and the spool valve bolt together at the flange end of the sleeve. Unscrew the stop screw from the socket tube which will also release the spool valve bolt.

Remove the ball seat spring, ball seats and ball stud from the ball socket tube and remove the tube from the sleeve.

The spool valve on Packard installations is held in the body by two push-fit bushigs. Tap lightly on one end of the valve with a brass rod to remove the valve and bushings from either end. The spool valve on Ford installations can be slid out the cap end of the body. In the sleeve end of the body, Ford carries a spacer, a bushing, and a seal.

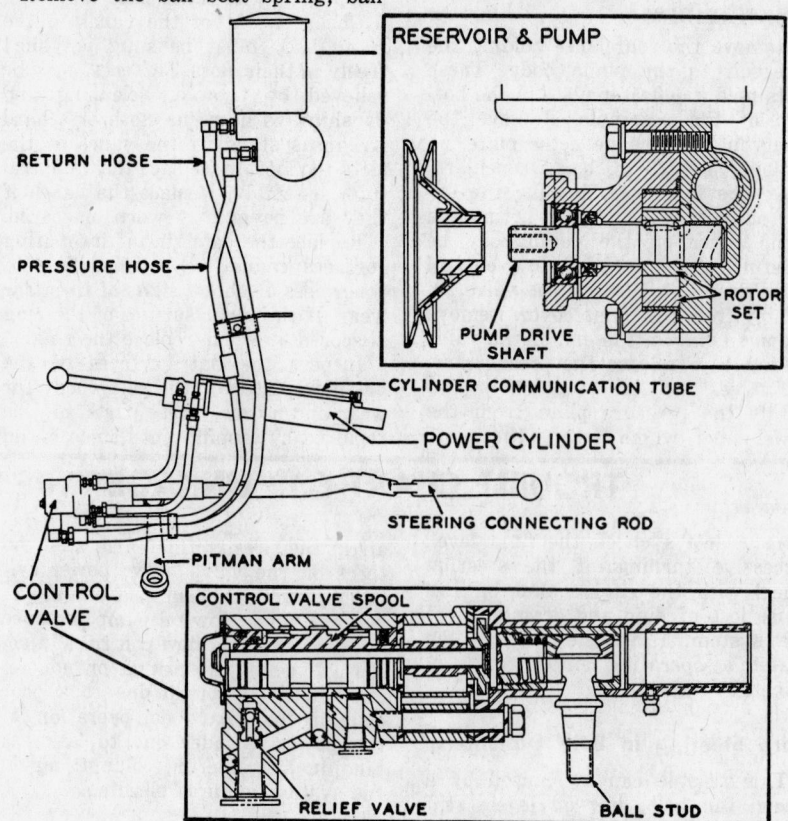

Bendix Unit

INSPECTION OF THE CONTROL VALVE

Clean all the parts thoroughly and inspect them for wear or damage. Examine the lips of the seals most carefully for nicks and scratches that could allow escape of fluid from the valve. Remove any burrs on the spool valve with crocus cloth, being very careful to preserve intact the sharp edges so necessary to proper operation of this type of valve. Check that the spool valve bolt has not been bent and that the bores are not scratched, scored or cracked. Renew any defective parts.

ASSEMBLY AND INSTALLATION OF THE CONTROL VALVE

Reverse the procedure to assemble and install. When installing the spool valve bolt and stop screw, tighten the stop screw in, then back it off enough to allow insertion of the lock pin. The larger diameter end of the spool valve goes away from the sleeve. When installing the nut on the end of the spool valve bolt, tighten the nut securely and then back it off not more than 1/4 turn. Be certain when attaching the sleeve to the body and the adapter that the scribe marks made

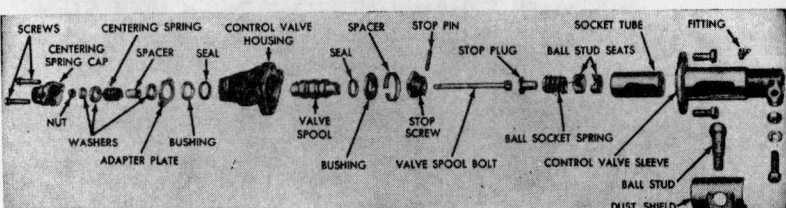

Fig. 13—Bendix Unit. Exploded View of Control Valve. Ford Model Shown

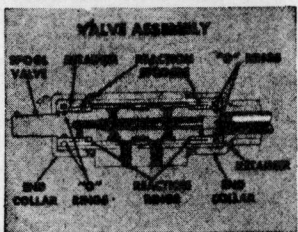

Fig. 12—Ross Unit. Cutaway View of Control Valve. Dodge V8 Installation Shown

at disassembly are aligned. Check that movement of the ball stud results in movement of the spool valve. Total movement of the spool valve is about .060 in.

When installing the valve assembly back onto the steering connecting rod, be sure that the distance from the clamp bolt to the nearest ball stud on

the rod is exactly the same as before removal.

Bendix Power Cylinder
REMOVAL

Disconnect the hoses at the power cylinder, cap them so they do not drip and drain the oil from the cylinder. Move the front wheels to the left and right several times to force all the oil from the cylinder.

Unfasten the piston rod end first and then unfasten the cylinder end. Note that the attachments are rubber mounted.

DISASSEMBLY

Ford recommends that the cylinder assembly be replaced if its operation is defective. Packard cylinder assemblies have replaceable parts.

OVERHAUL OF MONROE LINKAGE TYPE POWER STEERING UNITS

SECTION 5

Removal and Disassembly of the Control Valve

The control valve assembly on these units is a part of the power cylinder assembly.

Remove the right and left tie rod ends from the steering knuckle arms. Place a drain pan under the assembly and remove the hoses. Cap the hose fittings to keep out dirt. Disconnect the assembly from the pitman arm stud by tapping on the arm. (Fig. 18) Do not hammer on the stud or pry between the valve and the steering arm. Support the valve end of the assembly while disconnecting the piston rod from the frame bracket.

Wash the assembly thoroughly, which retains the plug and turn the plug in, counting the number of turns until it bottoms. Record the number of turns and remove the plug.

Remove the retaining ring from the pitman arm stud. Hold the stud with a 3/4 in. open end wrench and remove the retaining nut with a 7/8 in. open end wrench. Remove the washers, cushion and shoes. Pull the stud out of the assembly.

Use a brass rod and the fingers to work the right turn reaction piston and follower out of the assembly. Tap the end of the assembly on a block of

wood to shake out the spool valve and the inner reaction piston.

INSPECTION OF THE CONTROL VALVE

Wash all the parts in solvent and inspect them for scratches and signs of wear. Small burrs and nicks can be removed with crocus cloth. Renew any parts showing signs of excessive wear.

Overhaul of the Piston and Cylinder Assembly

Remove the cylinder cap and pull out the piston rod. (Fig. 20) The piston rod guide, retainer, and seal will come out as an assembly. Remove the tow interlocking oil rings from the piston. Any burrs on the piston should be removed with crocus cloth. Any nicks on the piston rod require

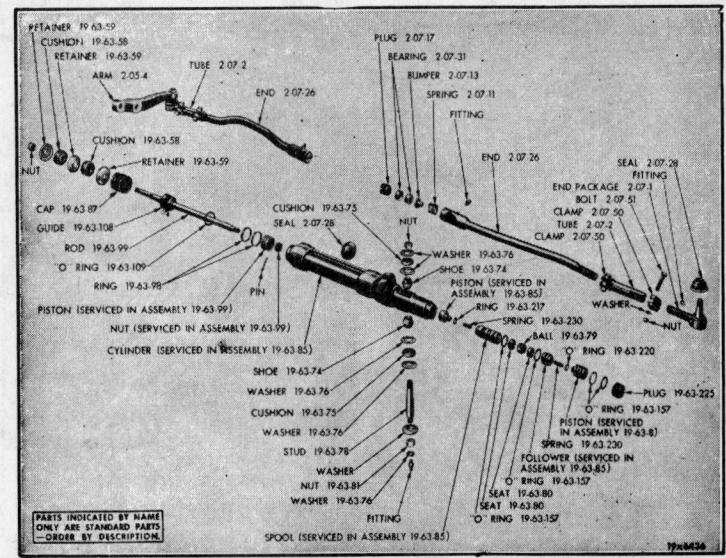

Fig. 16—Exploded View of Monroe Power Steering Unit. Mopar Numbers Plymouth Installation Shown

POWER STEERING

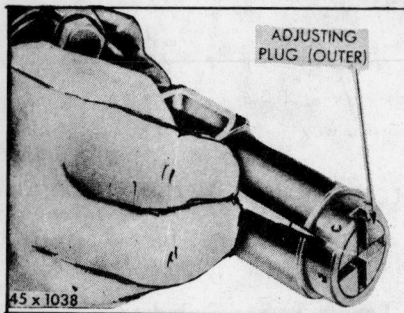

Fig.17—Monroe Unit. Scribing Outer Plug and Housing for Matched Reassembly. Plymouth Installation Shown

that the piston and rod be replaced as an assembly. The piston should not be removed from the rod. When replacing oil rings on the piston be sure that the rings move freely in their grooves.

The piston rod guide and retainer assembly should not be removed from the piston rod unless there is evidence of oil leakage around the neoprene seal or the felt wiping ring. The rod guide and retainer are serviced as an assembly. However, whenever the piston and rod assembly is removed from the cylinder the "O" ring seal on the guide should be replaced. Check the guide for anything that could prevent it from seating squarely on the cylinder. If there is anything, replace the guide as inaccurate seating of the guide will bind the rod and lead to leaks. Coat these parts with Lubriplate to facilitate assembly.

Inspect the cylinder carefully for scoring. The spool valve and the cylinder must be replaced as an assembly since a special lapping operation is required when the two parts are assembled.

Severe damage to the external oil tube will require replacement of the complete power unit. Minor indentations which do not affect the operation of the assembly can be disregarded.

Assembly of the Monroe Unit

PISTON ROD GUIDE AND RETAINER

Coat the parts with Lubriplate. Install the rod guide and retainer over the end of the piston rod. Be very careful as the guide rides over the threads and the milled flats of the rod that the neoprene seal does not get cut. Wrapping the threads and flats in "Scotch" tape will help to prevent damage to the seal.

PISTON ROD ASSEMBLY

Compress the two interlocking oil rings and enter the piston into the cylinder. Keep the rod straight as the piston is pushed into the cylinder.

With the piston installed part way in the cylinder, slide the rod guide and the retainer down until it seats on the end of the cylinder. Install the cylinder cap and move the piston up and down in the cylinder to be sure that all is well. Stake the outer threads on the cylinder through the hole provided in the cap to prevent its shaking loose. Be careful when installing the cap. When it bottoms on the retainer, that is enough. Further tightening is likely to crush the guide.

VALVE ASSEMBLY

Lubricate the new "O" ring seals and install them on the spool valve, reaction pistons and the followers. Assemble the inner reaction piston, spring, and spool valve together, and being careful of the seal rings, slide the assembly into the valve bore. (Fig. 21) Place the inner ball seat and ball on the spool valve. Assemble the outer ball seat, follower, spring and reaction piston with Lubriplate to make them stick. Hold the ball through which the pitman arm stud will pass in place with the finger and install the outer reaction piston assembly into the bore. (Fig. 22)

Install the pitman arm stud and then install the adjusting plug until it bottoms. Back the plug out the same number of turns as found at disassembly and align the scribe marks. Install the cotter key to hold the plug. Check operation of the valve assembly by moving the stud back and forth, then remove the stud.

Install the thin outer cushion washer on the stud followed by the cushion, inner thin washer and shoe. Place the assembly through the pitman arm ball. Place the other shoe on the stud followed by the thin inner washer, the cushion and the thin outer washer. Now install the retaining nut and

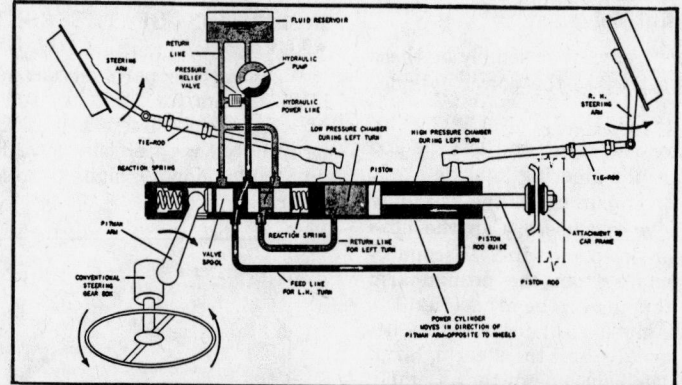

Fig. 19—Fluid Flow in Monroe Power Steering Unit. Left Turn Shown

Fig. 18—Monroe Unit. Cutaway Showing Construction of Attaching Stud. Plymouth Installation Shown

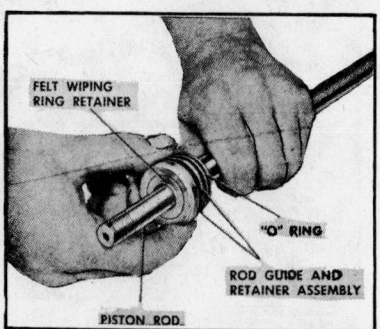

Fig. 20—Monroe Unit. Showing Construction of Piston Rod Guide

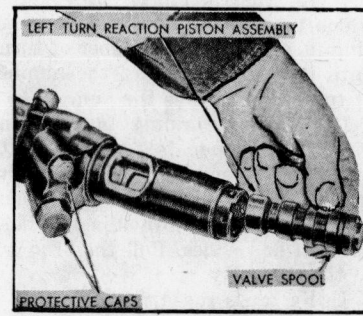

Fig. 21—Monroe Unit Installing Spool Valve Plymouth Installation Shown

OVERHAUL OF MONROE POWER STEERING—Continued

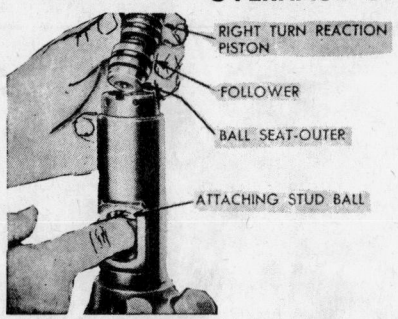

RIGHT TURN REACTION PISTON

FOLLOWER

BALL SEAT-OUTER

ATTACHING STUD BALL

Fig. 22—Monroe Unit. Installing Outer Re-action Piston Assembly. Plymouth Installation Shown

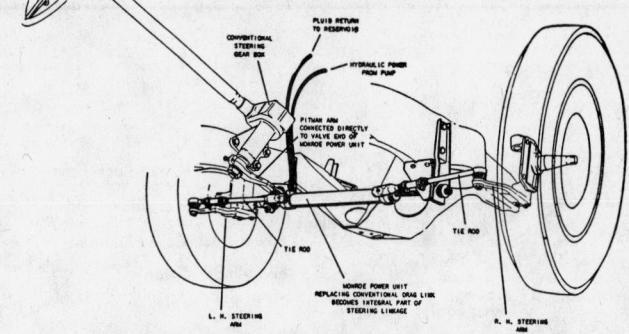

Fig. 23—Typical Installation of Monroe Power Steering Unit

washer, turning the nut until it bottoms on the shoulder. It should not require more than one foot pound of torque to rotate the stud in this assembled condition. If more than one foot pound is required, remove one of the outer thin washers and use a thinner one. If necessary, replace the other thin washer with a thinner one. When the torque is no more than one foot pound, install the retaining ring.

Installation of the Monroe Unit

Reverse the procedure to reinstall the assembly on the car. See the paragraph on Adjustment of the Spool Valve on the Monroe Unit if a road test shows it to be applicable.

CHECKING THE SPOOL VALVE ON THE MONROE UNIT

The attaching nut which holds the pitman arm to the stud should be tightened to 55-65 foot-pounds. This will hold the pitman arm stud properly in the valve assembly and still permit a few thousandths of an inch sideways movement of the stud to

operate the spool valve. If the stud is drawn down too tightly on the valve body, the motion of the spool valve will be interfered with. The result of such is that steering effort is increased and the wheels do not return to a straight ahead position after turns. In order to correct the condition it is necessary to unfasten the stud from the pitman arm and remove one or two of the thin washers which lie on the stud between the rubber cushion and the pitman arm. This will remove the crush from the valve body.

SPOOL VALVE ADJUSTMENT ON THE MONROE UNIT

The spool valve adjustment plug which is at the left end of the power cylinder can be turned in or out, depending upon the action of the cylinder. The plug should be turned one-sixth of a turn at a time and the car road tested after each adjustment.

Turn the plug in: when a left turn is too hard and a right turn is too easy; when there is poor recovery after right turns and good recovery after left turns; when the car wan-

ders to the right.

Turn the plug out: when a right turn is too hard and left turn is too easy; when there is poor recovery after left turns and good recovery after right turns; when the car wanders to the left.

After the correct adjustment has been obtained, install the cotter pin to lock the plug in position.

Steering Gear Adjustment and Adjustment Check
Plymouth and Dodge

Misalignment of the steering column or improper adjustment of the steering gear can cause a bind in the gear that will not allow the power steering system to operate properly.

Correct the column misalignment by adjusting the brackets at the instrument panel and at the frame bracket.

Adjust the steering gear worm shaft bearings and the cross shaft backlash (with the power unit detached) to the minimum limits, that is, a ⅜-pound pull on the steering wheel for the worm shaft bearing adjustment, and a 1-pound pull for the cross shaft backlash adjustment.

OVERHAUL OF SAGINAW GEAR TYPE POWER STEERING UNIT

SECTION 7

Disassembly of the Saginaw Unit

Remove the unit from the car. On almost all models this can be done by sliding the unit out from under the car without disturbing the column jacket.

Starting with '54 production on Cadillac, the gear assembly is connected to the steering shaft by a flexible coupling so that the gear assembly may be removed without disturbing the steering column or steering wheel. Be sure to match mark the coupling flanges and the gear body to properly position the parts at reassembly.

Remove the fluid lines connecting

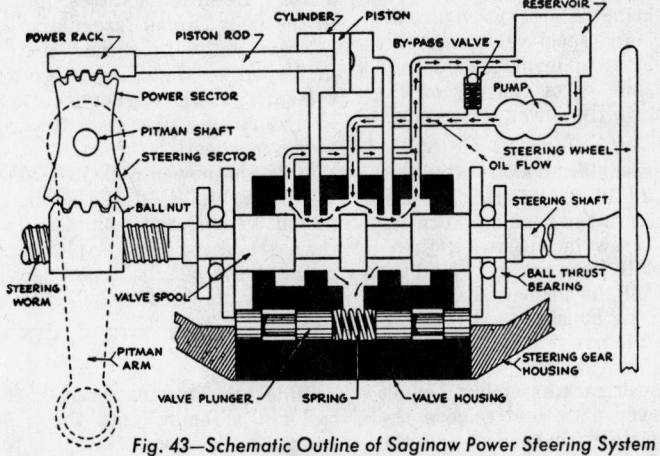

POWER RACK — PISTON ROD — CYLINDER — PISTON — RESERVOIR

BY-PASS VALVE

PUMP

POWER SECTOR

PITMAN SHAFT

STEERING SECTOR

STEERING WHEEL OIL FLOW

BALL NUT

STEERING SHAFT

BALL THRUST BEARING

STEERING WORM

VALVE SPOOL

STEERING GEAR HOUSING

PITMAN ARM

VALVE PLUNGER — SPRING — VALVE HOUSING

Fig. 43—Schematic Outline of Saginaw Power Steering System thru 1955. Straight Ahead Position Shown

POWER STEERING

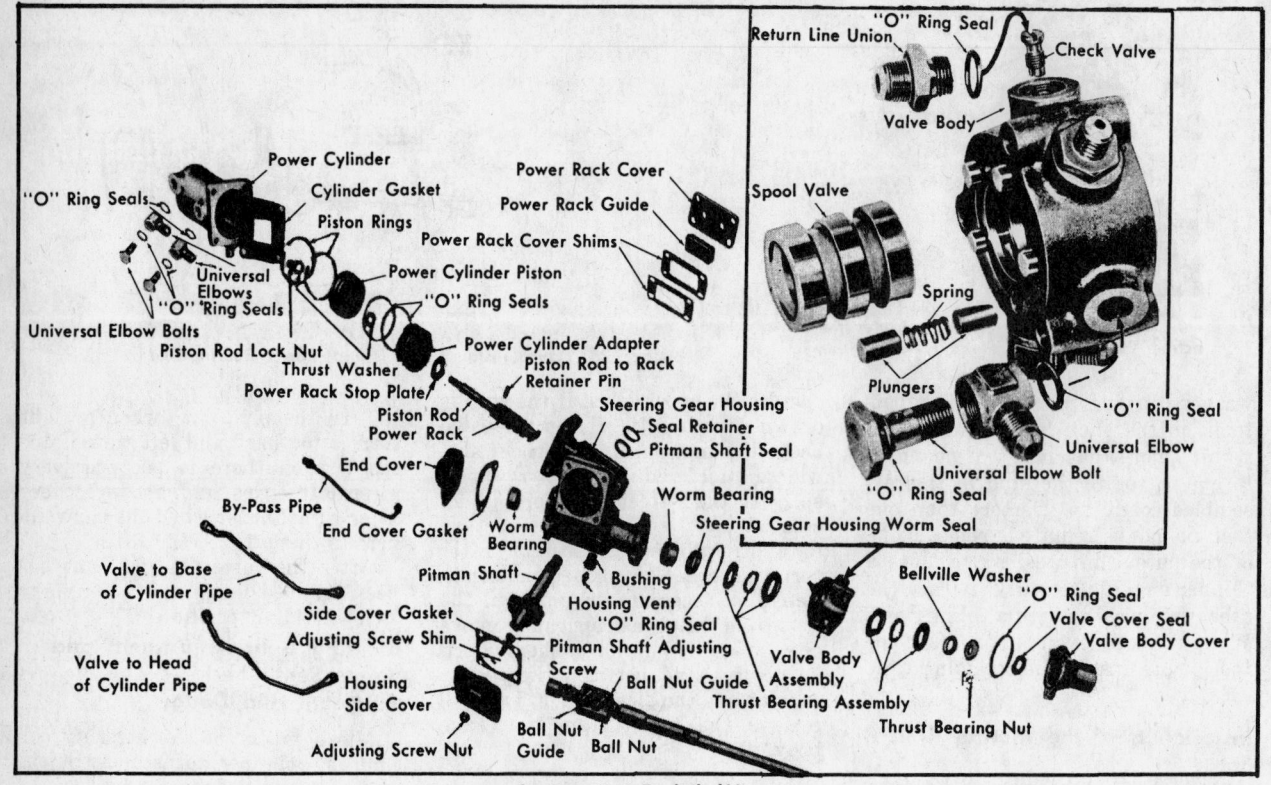

Saginaw Unit. Exploded View.

the valve assembly to the power cylinder. Unless the "O" seal rings require replacement, do not disturb the tube fittings on the cylinder and the valve assemblies. Remove the filler plug on the steering gear box and drain the steering gear oil.

Scribe across the gearbox, the hydraulic valve body, and the valve cover to facilitate alignment at reassembly. Unbolt the cover from the hydraulic valve body and slide it off over the end of the mainshaft. Hold the steering wheel on the end of the mainshaft to keep it from turning and unlock and remove the thrust nut. Remove the washer and the upper thrust bearing. Slide the hydraulic valve body and spool valve assembly off the steering mainshaft. Be careful not to let the parts fall out of the body. Remove the lower thrust bearing assembly.

Remove the pitman shaft adjusting screw lock nut. Remove the bolts holding the plate to the housing. Turn the adjusting screw in, clockwise, to release the plate from the screw and the housing. Pull the pitman shaft from the end of the housing.

Remove the power cylinder to gear box bolts and remove the cylinder and the power rack assembly. Unbolt the end cover plate and remove the plate complete with bearing and the mainshaft assembly.

INSPECTION OF THE PARTS OF THE SAGINAW UNIT

Test the check valve from the valve assembly by blowing through both ends. Ball should seat when blowing through the inner end and should allow air to pass when blowing through the slotted end. The check valve on some models is hidden under the return line union but on most models it is in the lower face of the valve body near the spool valve. The hydraulic valve body and the spool valve are selected fits and are serviced as an assembly. The plunger springs and the check valve are available separately. Be sure the valves slide freely in the body. Small irregularities can be removed with crocus cloth. The drill spots on the plungers go toward the springs. The shallow counterbore in the spool valve goes toward the steering wheel.

Hold the power rack in a vise and tap the cylinder off the adapter and piston with a soft hammer. Inspect the seals on the adapter plate and the rings on the piston. Renew any parts that seem doubtful.

ASSEMBLY OF THE SAGINAW UNIT

Slide the steering mainshaft and ball nut assembly into the housing, being careful not to damage the oil seals. Install a new gasket and the

lower end cover into place and fasten with four bolts and lockwashers.

Install the lower thrust bearing over the mainshaft and into place in the housing (the large race up). Install a new "O" ring seal into place on the upper face of the housing. Carefully slide the valve body assembly over the mainshaft and into place against the lower thrust bearing. Be sure the scratch marks made at disassembly are aligned. Be sure the counterbored end of the spool valve is toward the steering wheel.

Install the upper thrust bearing assembly into place with the large bearing race toward the spool valve. Install the bolts which would hold the valve cover into place together with some spacer washers in the housing in order to hold the valve body down in place and keep it from rotating. Tighten the thrust bearing nut down on the mainshaft. Install the steering wheel on the mainshaft. Turn the steering wheel to the left as far as it will go. This forces the ball nut down against the end bearing and so compress the valve body springs. While holding the steering wheel to the extreme left, tighten the thrust bearing nut firmly to remove all end play of the spool valve. Back off the nut and retighten slightly so that there is .015 in. clearance between the nut and the washer. Although this may not seem

OVERHAUL OF SAGINAW POWER STEERING—Continued

to agree with what follows, it is necessary to prevent overtightening and consequent non-movement of the spool valve when assembly has been completed.

Check that the thrust bearing nut is correctly tightened by using a spring scale to turn the steering wheel. The pull necessary should be between 1/8 and 3/8 of a pound.

On Models using a flexible coupling between the steering shaft and the gear assembly, use a piece of steel bolted to the flange in place of the steering wheel. The spring scale should attach to the piece of steel at a point seven and three-quarters inches from the bolt hole on the flange.

Note that this adjustment seats the thrust bearings against the centering plungers, removes all end play between the bearing races and the spool, and places a slight preload on the thrust bearings. Check that bearing is preloaded by turning outer race. A very heavy drag should be felt.

Stake the nut in place in addition to locking it with the tangs of the washer.

Remove the steering wheel, install a new "O" ring seal in the top face of the valve body and install the valve cover. Be sure the scratches made at disassembly are aligned. Tighten the attaching bolts to 15-20 ft. lbs. This torque tightness is important or else the valve body may be distorted and movement of the spool valve prevented.

Reinstall the cylinder and power rack assembly with a new gasket. Tighten the fluid lines connecting the valve assembly to the cylinder.

Fit the adjusting screw into the slot in the end of the pitman shaft. Check that there is no more than .002 in. clearance between the screw and the end of the shaft. Install shims if need be.

Place the steering wheel on the end of the main shaft and turn the mainshaft until the ball nut has its center groove aligned with the center of the pitman shaft bushing in the case. Adjust the power rack so that the third groove from the piston end is also in line with the center of the bushing.

Install the pitman shaft so that the center tooth in each set of teeth meshes with the center grooves of the ball nut and the power rack.

Turn the pitman shaft adjusting screw out (counterclockwise) while threading the cover plate onto the screw. Using a new gasket, fasten the cover plate into place with four bolts

and lockwashers.

Oil the face of the power rack and guide assembly. Reinstall the assembly with the same number of shims as were removed. Insall but do not tighten the attaching bolts. These must be left loose until the overcenter adjustment has been made.

Saginaw Unit Adjustments
OVERCENTER ADJUSTMENT

Turn the steering wheel through from one side to the other, counting the turns and noting if there is any bind. Turn the wheel back one-half the number of turns to put the ball nut at mid-point. This will be the high point of the pitman arm sector teeth. Turn the pitman arm adjusting screw clockwise to take out all play in the gear teeth. Install and tighten the screw lock nut. Use a spring scale to pull the steering wheel through the center position and note the highest reading. This reading as the wheel is pulled over the high spot should be between one-half and one pound. If the reading is not within the limits, loosen or tighten the adjusting screw until it is.

POWER RACK ADJUSTMENT

Tighten the power rack guide cover bolts evenly. Using a spring scale to pull the steering wheel through the center point, take the highest reading. If this reading as the wheel is pulled through the center point is between one-half and one pound, one .003 in. shim should be removed from between the guide cover and the case. Continue to check and to remove shims until the scale reads more than it did for the plain overcenter adjustment but the increase is less than 1/8 of a pound. If the increase is more than 1/8 of a pound, be sure to add one .003 in. shim. Similarly, if the pull required was greater than that at the plain overcenter adjustment, then shims should be added one at a time until the pull required is decreased to within 1/8 of a pound of that for the overcenter adjustment. Allowing for error, the total pull after all this should not exceed one and one-quarter pounds. Reinstall the unit in the car.

PITMAN SHAFT ADJUSTMENT

This adjustment eliminates backlash between the sector gear and the ball nut.

Disconnect the pitman arm from the steering tie rod. Loosen the pitman shaft adjusting screw lock nut and tighten the adjusting screw to eliminate the backlash.

Check that the reading on a spring scale used to move the steering wheel

through the center or high spot is between one and one and a quarter pounds. Tighten the lock nut and check that the load has not changed.

If elimination of the backlash results in too high a reading of the spring scale, there may be a misalignment of the steering column. Loosen the mounting brackets at the dash and the frame and check the pull required at the center high point. If the reading is now within the limits use shims where needed to hold the column and the steering gear box aligned.

Maintenance of the Saginaw "In Line" Power Steering Unit
FLUID USED

This unit uses Automatic Transmission Fluid Type A. Be sure the can of fluid you use has embossed on its cover the letters AQ-ATF Type A followed by the refiner's identifying number.

MEASURING THE FLUID

The fluid level should be checked every two thousand miles.

The fill plug on the reservoir has a dip stick attached to it. Add sufficient Type A fluid to bring the level to the full mark on the dipstick. Total capacity is approximately one quart.

BLEEDING THE SYSTEM

If the fluid level gets low, or the unit is disassembled, air will get in and cause the wheel to kick back. To bleed the air proceed as follows: Be sure reservoir is full. Loosen the bleed screw, see Fig. 62, on the pitman shaft end cover.

Start the engine and turn the steering wheel from full right to full left and back again several times. The trapped air will escape past the bleed screw. When no more air escapes tighten the screw and recheck the level.

CHECKING STEERING EFFORT

With the engine running and the hand brake holding the car, hook a spring pull scale to the rim of the 18 inch steering wheel and measure the pull required to turn it thru a three inch arc in straight ahead position.

The pull should be between 3½ and 4½ pounds on a dry floor.

CHECKING PUMP OPERATION

Connect a thousand psi gauge into the line running from the pressure side of the pump to the unit. When engine reaches operating temperature turn the wheels full right or full left. The gauge should read between 925 and 950 psi. If it does not, close

POWER STEERING

the valve on the gauge and so shut off the oil delivery to the steering gear. If now the pressure does rise to 925-950 the pump is O.K. and the unit is at fault. If the pressure does not rise the pump is not working correctly. See section on power steering oil pumps.

OIL LEAKS

There is no external piping on this unit other than the two hoses from the pump. Leaks when they occur will be found at the seals, or the hose connections.

If the seals are leaking the unit must be removed from the car and disassembled.

SAGINAW "IN LINE" GEAR TYPE POWER STEERING UNIT.

SECTION 8

Hard Steering in Straight Ahead Position

This trouble is more than likely due to binding steering linkage. To check, disconnect the linkage at the pitman arm and check the pull required to pull the steering wheel thru the mid-point (straight ahead position). If the pull is over 1¾ lbs. loosen the pitman shaft to sector adjusting screw in the pitman shaft cover below the bleed screw shown in Fig. 62.

If the pull required cannot be reduced to between 1¼ and 1¾ lbs. the gear must be disassembled and

Poor Return of Wheels After a Turn

This trouble can be due to: low tire pressure, incorrect steering geometry, tight linkage, or improperly adjusted pitman shaft (see trouble above), or binding of the control valve due to the assembly being improperly mounted, in which case loosening screws holding the valve assembly to the gear will permit the valve to center itself, then retighten the attaching screws to 15-20 ft. lbs.

Sticking Control Valve

The valve can be removed and freed up without disturbing the rest of the mechanism.

Sticking Actuating Lever

The lever is accessible when the valve assembly has been removed, however, the preload on the ball nut or the upper worm thrust bearing may be too great. The gear must be removed and disassembled to check and correct.

Momentary Increase in Effort When Turning Wheels Fast or Excessive Wheel Kick Back

These troubles can be caused by air in the system in which case bleeding the gear and checking the fluid level will correct. If this is not effective, check the steering linkage and the pitman shaft to sector adjustment. When all else fails remove the assembly from the car and check the upper worm thrust bearing for being too

loose.

Hard Steering When Parking

This trouble can be due to a loose pump belt, low fluid level, lack of steering linkage lubrication, low tires, tight adjustment of the pitman shaft, the ball nut of the upper thrust bearing too tight, insufficient oil pressure in which case apply the paragraph on Checking Pump Operation.

Steering Wheel Surges or Jerks

This trouble is due to a loose pump belt. Check by depressing it in the center. It should deflect no more than ¼ inch under a 5 to 7 pound force. There is a slotted hole in the pump support to permit movement of the pump to tighten the belt.

Car Keeps Trying to Go to One Side

This trouble is more than likely due to misalignment of the front end and is not a fault of the power steering unit.

Noises From The Unit

These noises appear as rattles, chuckles or hisses. Aside from adjustment of the pitman shaft sector to the rack there is nothing that can be done

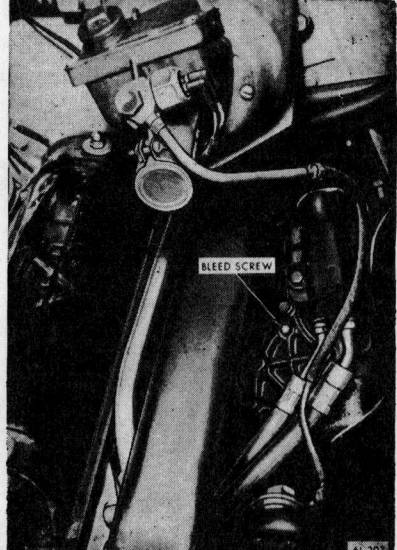

Fig. 62—Location of bleed screw of Saginaw "In Line" unit on Pitman shaft end cover

to obviate the noises. In other words, a slight hissing from the valve while parking is normal and replacement of the valve will not remove the noise. A slight rattle on turns is caused by the increased lash between the ball nut and the worm when off the high point. This lash must not be reduced.

A chuckle-like noise can be due to the high point of the contact between the sector and the worm not coinciding with the straight ahead position of the wheels.

Determine the high point and then rearrange the steering wheel position and the relative lengths of the tie rods to put the high point at the straight ahead position of the wheels.

Removal and installation of this gear varies from car to car and so the procedure for these operations will be found in the section devoted to the make you are working on.

When reinstalling the pitman arm on the pitman shaft do not drive the arm on with a hammer. Use the attaching nut to draw the arm into place, being sure that the large spline of the shaft is aligned with the wide groove in the arm. Tighten the retaining nut to 120-130 ft lbs.

When everything has been reconnected fill the reservoir, loosen the bleed screw and start the engine. Turn steering wheel thru its complete travel several times, thus forcing the trapped air to escape past the bleeder screw. Tighten the screw and check that the pull required to turn the wheel thru mid-point is between 3½ and 4½ lbs. with the wheels on a dry floor.

DISASSEMBLY AND ASSEMBLY OF THE SAGINAW "IN LINE" GEAR TYPE POWER STEERING UNIT

Support the coupling which holds the steering wheel shaft to the unit and drive out the roll pin which will release the shaft. See Fig. 63.

Clean the outside of the unit and drain out the fluid.

Control Valve, Linkage Cover and Actuating Lever

These can be removed from the unit without removing unit from car.

SAGINAW "IN LINE" POWER STEERING—Continued

Remove the control valve retaining screws and lift the valve body and linkage cover from the unit.

Pull the linkage cover from the valve body. Discard all "O" ring seals. New ones must be used at reassembly. body. Slide the spool valve out of the valve body. Hold the spool valve in a vise by the small end. Place a screwdriver in the slot of the valve and turn the actuating link counterclockwise and so out of the spool valve. This will release a spacer, a centering spring and a thrust washer.

Remove the spool valve from the vise and turn it over so that the reaction spool and spring can drop out.

Reverse the procedure to reassem. See Fig. 68 for an exploded view which shows how the parts fit together.

Lubricate the parts with Type A Fluid. The valve and body form a matched assembly and cannot be replaced separately. The centering spring thrust washer is installed with the lip toward the spring. The narrow inner band of the spacer (annular) goes toward the spring.

The actuating lever which enters the slot of the valve is a loose fit in the upper end cover of the gear unit. It can be pulled out at this point, examined and a new "O" ring seal installed. Be sure that it fits over the edge of the center race of the bearing and when reinstalling the link cover and the valve body be sure the slot in the valve fits over the link.

Tighten the valve assembly retaining screws to 15-20 ft lbs. Tighten the lower screw first. Be sure not to force the valve assembly in any direction as this will result in binding of the spool valve or actuating lever.

Pitman Shaft Assembly

The unit need not be removed from the car for this operation if the pitman shaft end cover screws are accessible.

Remove the control valve assembly. Remove the pitman shaft end cover screws and rotate the cover one-half turn. Align the sector gear with opening, have someone tap the lower end of the shaft with a soft hammer and lift the shaft and cover out of the gear housing. See Fig. 69.

Hold the pitman shaft adjusting screw with a screwdriver and remove the adjusting screw lock-nut. Turn the screw out of the cover and then slip the adjusting screw and shim out of the slot in the end of the shaft. Saginaw suggests using a new screw at reassembly.

Use lock ring pliers to remove the pitman shaft oil seal retaining ring. Remove the seal back-up washers and the leather dust seal.

To remove the pitman shaft oil seal, tap an offset screwdriver in between the seal and its supporting shoulder in the housing. Then pry the seal out of the housing being careful not to damage the seal bore. Or use a seal puller.

Check the shaft bearing surfaces on the end cover and in the bushings. The outer bushing is installed and removed from the outside. The inner bushing is driven into the housing to remove and is installed from inside the housing.

When reinstalling the pitman shaft check end play of a new adjusting screw in the slot. Use shims to hold the end play to .002 inch or less. Reinstall oil seals. Use a new "O" ring seal on the end cover. Be sure the middle tooth of the sector enters the middle slot of the rack when reinstalling the shaft.

Tighten the ⅜ inch end cover screws to 24-30 ft. lbs. Tighten the 5/16 screw to 15-20 ft. lbs.

Adjust to get 1¼-1¾ lbs. pull thru center position at the steering wheel.

Rack-Piston and Worm Assembly
DISASSEMBLY

The unit must be removed from the car for this operation.

Remove the control valve assembly and the actuating lever.

Remove the Pitman Shaft assembly.

Remove the cap screws holding the upper end cover to the housing and remove the end cover. See Fig. 74.

Use a small punch or screwdriver to remove the oil seal from the cover. Be careful of the needle bearing. Note that identification number of the bearing is installed to the outside of the cover.

Pull the rack-piston, ball nut and worm assembly from the housing. See Fig. 75 for exploded view of this assembly.

Remove the piston rings from the piston, remove the ball nut retaining screw. Turn the retaining screw hole down so that the balls and their guide do not drop out and slide the ball-nut and worm assembly out of the rack-piston.

Remove the ball guide from the nut and turn the holes down, then turn the worm back and forth until all the balls have been caught on a clean cloth. There are 23 balls. They have a definite size and must be replaced as a set. Their size is stamped on the end of the ball nut. Remove the ball-nut and adapter from the worm.

Remove the retaining ring, washer and seal from the nut side of the adapter.

Check over the ball return guides and clips, the rack-piston, the ball-nut and the worm. The worm and ball-nut are a matched assembly. If one is damaged both must be replaced with a new set.

Do not disturb the end plug in the rack-piston unless it is loose. It can be driven out from the inside of the

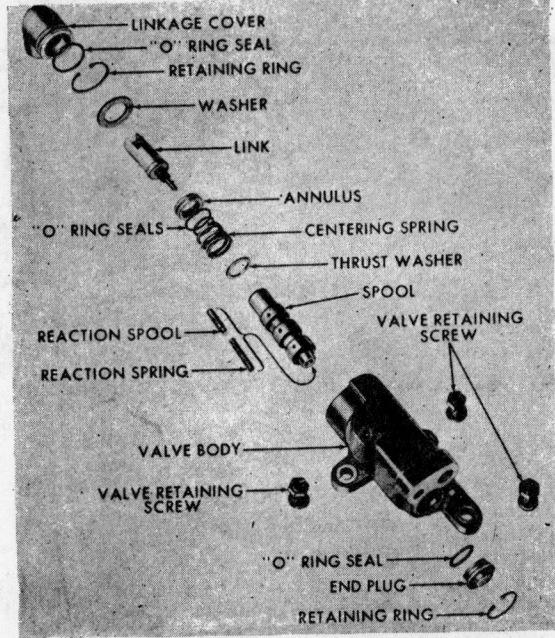

Fig. 68—Exploded view of valve body

LINKAGE COVER
"O" RING SEAL
RETAINING RING
WASHER
LINK
ANNULUS
"O" RING SEALS
CENTERING SPRING
THRUST WASHER
SPOOL
REACTION SPOOL
VALVE RETAINING SCREW
REACTION SPRING
VALVE BODY
VALVE RETAINING SCREW
"O" RING SEAL
END PLUG
RETAINING RING

POWER STEERING

SAGINAW "IN LINE" POWER STEERING—Continued

rack-piston. Stake the new one in place at four points.

The end plug in the housing is driven to the outside but is installed from the inside. It should also be staked at four points.

THRUST BEARING PRELOAD

Check the thrust bearing preload. This preload should be between ¾ and 3 pounds measured at the outer edge of the center of the bearing through an angle of 90°. To measure this preload set the worm up in a vise. Fasten a cord to one of the spring-holding rivets and wrap the cord around the center race several times. Fasten the end of the cord to a spring scale and slowly pull on the scale, noting the pull required. If the preload is not between ¾ and 3 pounds push the staked portion of the thrust bearing nut up out of the threaded groove, and tighten or loosen the nut so that the effort to turn the center race, as shown on the spring scale, is between ¾ and 3 pounds. Restake the nut without turning it and without injuring the thread. Lubricate the bearing with Type A Fluid. If the bearing is rough it should be renewed. If the springs riveted to the bearing are broken, the bearing must be renewed.

ASSEMBLY OF THE RACK-PISTON AND WORM

When reassembling be sure the centering springs are in place in the adapter and align locating pin on adapter with the hole in the bearing. Slide ball nut over worm, with chamfered edge away from the worm shoulder, up to the adapter. Load 17 balls into the hole in the nut farthest

from the adapter. Rotate the nut counterclockwise to feed the balls thru the circuit. Load the two piece guide with the remaining 6 balls and plug in place with grease.

Push the guide into place on the nut. If it does not seat easily, tap it with a soft hammer. Install the guide retaining clips. Use tape to hold the guides in place.

BALL NUT PRELOAD

The worm groove is ground with a high point in the center. When the ball nut passes over this high point it should show a preload of 1 to 6 lbs. To measure the preload set the worm and nut assembly up in a vise.

Fasten a cord to the ball and wind it around the nut. Fasten a spring scale to the cord and check the pull required to rotate the ball over the high point of the worm. The highest

reading obtained after the ball has started to turn should be between 1 and 6 lbs. If preload is too great use size smaller balls.

FINISH INSTALLATION OF WORM SHAFT, BALL NUT AND RACK-PISTON ASSEMBLY

Install washer, new seal, backup washer, retaining washer and ring on the rack-piston end of the worm and lubricate with Type A Fluid.

Install ball nut and worm assembly into the rack-piston being careful of the seals.

Line up retaining screw hole in ball nut with screw hole in the piston and install the retaining screw. Tighten to 30-35 ft. lbs and stake.

Install a new "O" ring seal on the adapter and two rings on the rack-piston.

Fig. 79—Relationship of Saginaw "In Line" Gear Type Steering Unit Assemblies

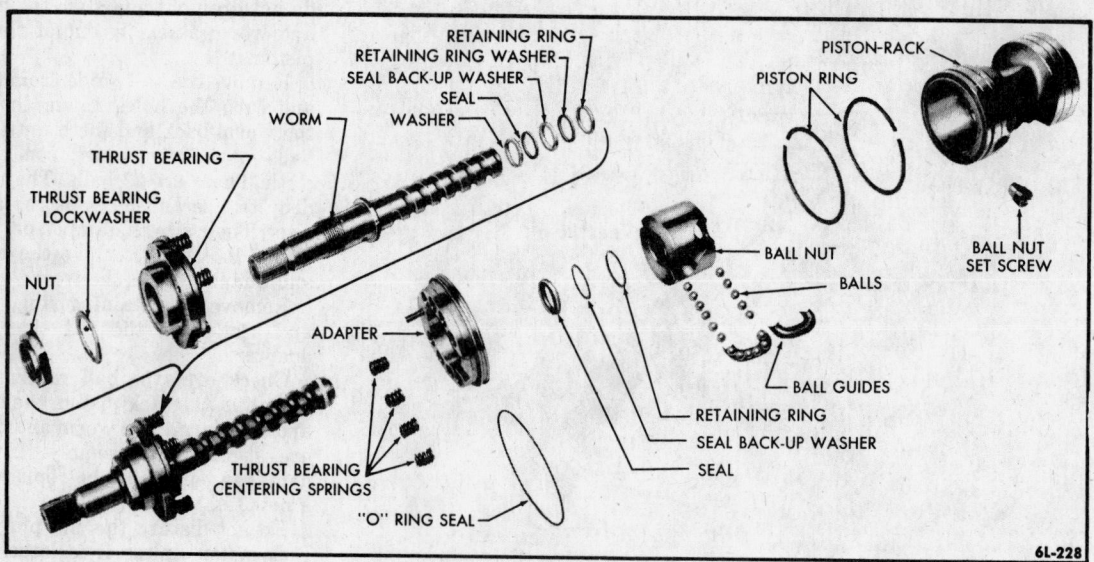

Fig. 75—Exploded view of the rack-piston ball and worm assembly

SAGINAW "IN LINE" POWER STEERING—Continued

Install ring compressor over piston ring and tap the rack-piston assembly into the housing.

Turn the adapter counterclockwise to give clearance or removal of the ring compressor.

Seat the adapter in the housing counterbore aligning the relief in the outer diameter of the adapter with the actuating lever hole. Lubricate the needle bearing in the upper end roller bearing grease of N.L.G.I. No. 1 consistency. Please note that ordinary cup or chassis grease should not be used in this location as they would tend to leak out of the bearing and interfere with the end cover seals.

Install the end cover onto the housing being sure that the adapter locating pin enters the proper hole in the adapter. Tighten the end cover to housing bolts to 25-30 ft. lbs. See Fig. 79 for details of the assemblies.

CHRYSLER FULL TIME POWER STEERING CO-AXIAL TYPE

SECTION 9

The Power Steering Oil Pump is a gear type pump. It is mounted at the rear of the Generator and is driven thru a coupling by the armature.

The overhaul and repair of this Power Steering unit requires special tools, especially in the adjustment of the control valve and the worm bearings. It is recommended, therefore, that no attempt be made to dismantle the assembly in the field. The actual mechanism is not so very complicated but since the control valve in the piston has a total movement of only two and one-half thousandths of an inch, its adjustment requires great care.

While oil pressure on one end of the piston is causing it to move, there is no oil pressure on the opposite end of the piston and any oil trapped there returns freely to the pump.

Should the oil pressure fail, the movement imparted to the Nut by the worm is transferred from the Nut to the upper piston extension or rod thru compression of the rubber seal and so, by the connecting agency of the piston, to the lower piston rod, which carries the rack which moves the sector gear on the pitman shaft.

The movement of the valve in the piston is very small, being only about two and one-half thousandths of an inch. The movement of the Nut before it starts to move the piston is about the same.

The contact between the Nut and the worm is by means of recirculating balls in the worm housing.

Support for the worm shaft is provided by two roller bearings in the upper portion of the steering gear housing assembly.

The steering gear housing assembly has two parts:

MAINTENANCE AND ADJUSTMENT

Lubrication

Proper lubrication of the steering gear and front suspension is very important on vehicles equipped with power steering.

RESERVOIR AND WORM HOUSING

Since there is no connection hydraulically between the Worm Housing and the Gear Housing this power steering system has two separate fluid levels. The level of the oil in the reservoir which is the source of fluid for the gear housing should be checked regularly every thousand miles or thirty days. The reservoir is mounted at the rear of the generator. Make sure the top of the reservoir is absolutely clean. Remove the cover or filler cap and check that the oil level is one-half inch above the filter element at its highest point. Add Type A Fluid as required to bring the level to the proper point.

The level of the oil in the worm housing does not have to be checked unless it shows signs of leakage. The oil should be level with the filler plug opening on the top side of the worm housing. The worm housing takes Type A Fluid.

DRAINING THE SYSTEM

The Worm housing does not require draining, in fact it cannot be drained unless the steering gear assembly is out of the car.

In draining the reservoir which supplies the Gear housing, be very careful that no dirt gets into the system. To avoid damaging the filter element, never insert sharp objects into the reservoir. There is no need to disturb the filter element as periodic changes of this unit are not required.

In draining the reservoir, disconnect the high (small) pressure hose at the gear housing and jack up the car enough so that the front wheels are free. Run the end of the high pressure hose into a container.

Start the engine and while it is idling turn the wheels from full left to full right, back and forth, several times or until fluid coming from the hose shows a large number of bubbles. Unit is now empty. Reconnect the hose to the gear housing and pour in approximately two quarts of Type A Fluid to refill.

BLEEDING THE HYDRAULIC SYSTEM

Start the engine and allow to idle for a short time to circulate the oil.

With the engine running at idle speed turn the wheels from right to left back and forth until no more bubbles are visible in the reservoir. Check that the oil level is one-half inch above the highest point of the filter element, adding oil if necessary to make it so.

Replace the reservoir cover or filler cap.

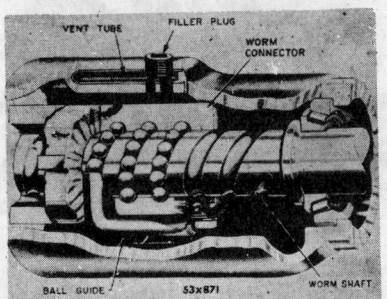

Fig. 86—Worm Connector Assembly (cutaway view)

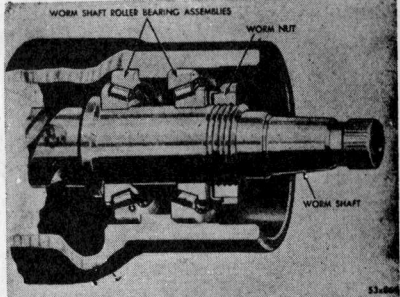

Fig. 87—Worm Shaft Roller Bearings (cutaway view)

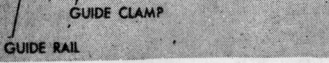

Fig. 85—The Nut (Worm Connector)

POWER STEERING

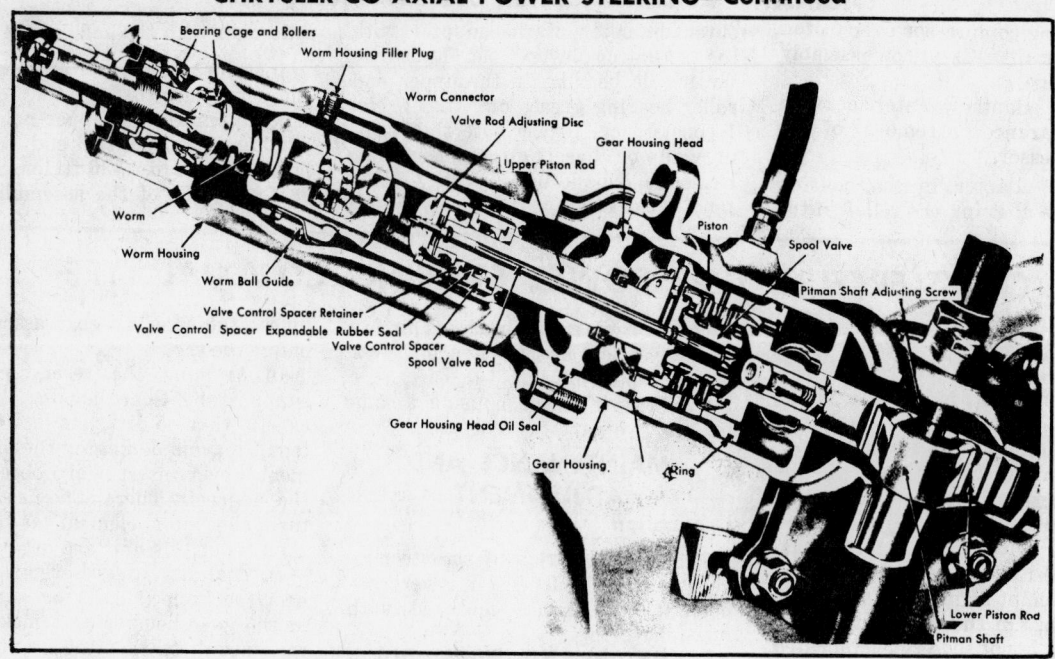

Cutaway view co-axial power steering assembly

SPECIFICATIONS

Fluid Capacity of Hydraulic System (the Gear Housing and Reservoir   2 Quarts

Fluid Capacity of Worm Housing   1 Pint

Type of Fluid Used in Both Housings   Type A Fluid

Maximum Pump Pressure 750-800 PSI

Maximum Pump Rotor Clearances:
Between Rotor Lobes   .800″
Between Outer Rotor and

Bushing   .006″

End Clearance (Between Rotors and Face of Body)   .001″ to .002″

Flow Control Valve Spring:
Free Length   2.13″
Working Length   1.20″
Force at Working Length   12½ to 15½ Lbs.

Pressure Relief Valve Spring:
Free Length   1.51″
Working Length   1.18″

Force at Working Length   30 to 33 Lbs.

Piston Rod Snap Ring Gap (Upper and Lower)   25/64″

Tightening Specifications

Pump Body to Cover Bolts   30-35 Ft. Lbs.

Pump Reservoir to Pump Body Bolts   12-17 Ft. Lbs.

Pump Mounting Bolts   18-23 Ft. Lbs.

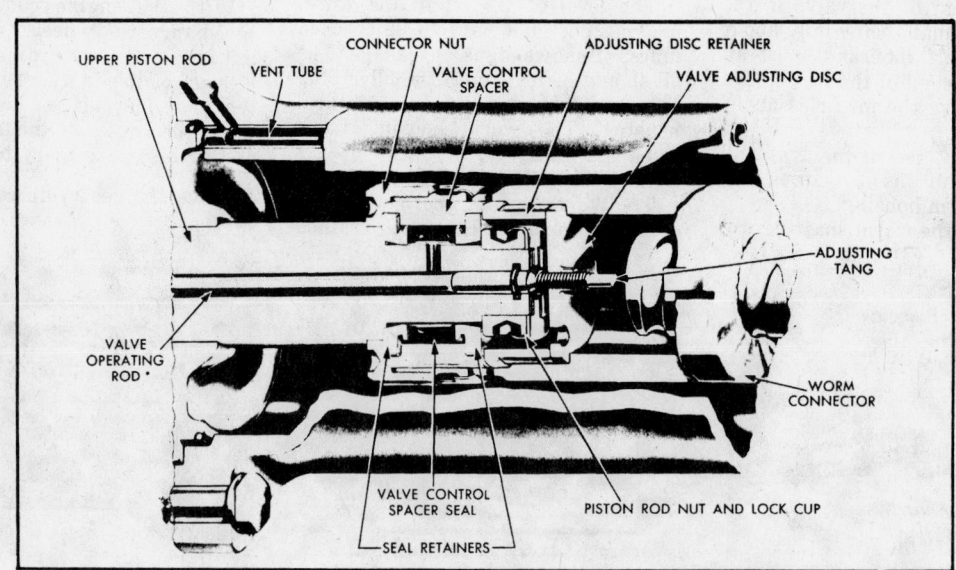

Fig. 90—Cutaway view of lower end of the Nut. Note rubber seal

CHRYSLER CO-AXIAL POWER STEERING—Continued

Pump Reservoir Mounting Stud	30-35 Ft. Lbs.	Frame	50-55 Ft. Lbs.

Pump Reservoir Mounting Stud   30-35 Ft. Lbs.

Steering Knuckle Arm Nuts (Brake Anchor Nuts)   55-75 Ft. Lbs.

Pitman Gear to Pitman Shaft Nut   100-125 Ft. Lbs.

Pitman Arm to Drag Link Nut   55-55 Ft. Lbs.

Steering Gear Assembly to Mounting Bracket   65-70 Ft. Lbs.

Steering Gear Assembly Mounting Bracket to

Frame   50-55 Ft. Lbs.

Steering Wheel to Steering Shaft Nut   35-40 Ft. Lbs.

Shroud to Instrument Panel Screws   15-20 Ft. Lbs.

Tie Rod Clamp Bolts   10-15 Ft. Lbs.

Tie Rod to Steering Knuckle Arm Nuts   45-75 Ft. Lbs.

Pump Coupling Attaching Screw   15-20 Ft. Lbs.

Pump Flow Control and Relief Adapter)

(Retaining)   45-50 Ft. Lbs.

Pump Coupling Flange Attaching Screw   10-12 Ft. Lbs.

Upper Piston Rod Nut   25-30 Ft. Lbs.

Gear Shaft Cover Screws   25-30 Ft. Lbs.

Ball Guide Clamp Screws   10-12 Ft. Lbs.

Worm Housing to Gear Housing Screws   25-30 Ft. Lbs.

Pitman Shaft Adjusting Screw Lock Nut   35-40 Ft. Lbs.

TROUBLE SHOOTING CHRYSLER CO-AXIAL

Hard Steering in Both Directions

MAY BE DUE TO:

1. Leak in steering system.
   Correct leak, fill reservoir to proper level.
2. Pump belt slipping or broken.
   Tighten by moving generator; if still slips install new belt.
3. Fluid level low.
   Check all over for leaks, fill reservoir to proper level.
4. Steering gear linkage not lubricated. Lubricate properly.
5. Tire pressure too low.
   Inflate to proper pressure.
6. Low pump pressure.
   Refer to "Pressure Check."
   (a) Pressure Relief and Flow Control Valve assembly dirty.
   Remove the assembly from the output fitting on the pump and clean all parts.
   (b) Flow Control Valve spring weak or broken.
   Replace spring.
   (c) Relief valve spring weak or broken.
   Replace Pressure Relief and Flow Valve assembly.
   (d) Rotors not turning.
   Check drive coupling flanges, if broken or worn, replace.
   Check generator armature and freeness of rotors.
   (e) Rotors worn.
   Replace both rotors and bushings.
   (f) Pump body or cover worn.
   Replace body or cover.
7. Loss of pressure in power unit.
   Refer to "Pressure Check."
8. Insufficient fluid flow in system.
   Refer to "Pressure Check."
9. Bind in steering column or gear.
   Align steering gear assembly by loosening the screws holding the assembly to the frame and the dash.
10. Improper front end alignment.
    Align front end.

Smaller Turning Radius in One Direction

MAY BE DUE TO:

1. Wheel stops not adjusted properly. Adjust wheel stops.

Hydraulic Fuel Leaks (Locations)

1. At hose adapters.
   Tighten or replace hose adapters and gaskets.
2. At pump body.
   Overhaul pump.
3. Between gear and worm housings.
   Tighten attaching screws. If leak still exists it will be necessary to overhaul the gear assembly.
4. Pitman shaft oil seal.
   Replace oil seal.

Hard Steering in One Direction Only

MAY BE DUE TO:

1. Tire pressure too low.
   Inflate to proper pressure.
2. Steering control valve maladjusted.
   It is necessary to dissassemble the gear assembly to reach the valve.
3. Bind in steering column or gear.
   Align steering gear assembly by loosening the column to chassis and body attaching screws.
4. Improper front end alignment.
   Align front end.

Vehicle Attempts to Turn Unless Force Is Applied to Hold Steering Wheel

MAY BE DUE TO:

1. Tire pressure uneven.
   Inflate to proper pressure.
2. Steering control valve maladjusted.
   With engine running turn wheels from full right to full left and back several times, trouble could be dirt and thus cured by full flow of oil. Steering assembly must be disassembled in order to permit

adjusting this valve. Special tools are required.

Poor Recovery on Turns

MAY BE DUE TO:

1. Tire pressure too low.
   Inflate to proper pressure.
2. Balls in worm connector binding or fitted too tight.
   Unit would have to be disassembled.
3. Bind in steering column or gear.
   Align steering gear assembly by loosening attaching bolts at frame and cowl.
4. Bind in steering knuckles. (Remove wheel and check fit of steering knuckles on king pin.)
   Check king pin and bushings, shim properly.
5. Worm bearing adjustment too tight. Adjust worm bearing.
   Unit would have to be disassembled.
6. Improper front end alignment.
   Align front end.
7. Pitman shaft adjustment too tight.
   Adjust Pitman shaft for mesh of sector and rack by means of adjusting screw at lower left side of gear housing. Steering wheel should turn 150 deg. each way from center position without backlash.

Noise

1. Fan belt tension incorrect.

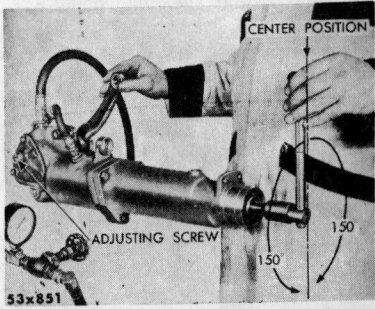

Fig. 95—Checking backlash between steering gear shaft and the Pitman Arm

POWER STEERING

Adjust belt tension. One half inch deflection midway between pulleys.

2. Low fluid level.

Check for leak, fill reservoir to proper level.

3. Pump shaft bearing worn.

Replace pump.

4. Bushings worn in pump body or cover.

Replace pump.

5. Dirt and sludge in pump.

Disassemble pump and clean. Drain system and refill with clean fluid and change filter element.

6. Noise in power unit.

Bleed air from system by swinging wheels from stop to stop with engine running. Watch for bubbles in reservoir. When bubbles cease, air has been eliminated. Check hose clearance. Check Pitman shaft adjustment.

Pressure Check

In cases of malfunction of the Power Steering perform these operations in order to determine if the pump is at fault.

Start the engine and turn the wheels to full right and full left. If the high pressure hose does not flex, pump is in good condition. The high pressure hose is the smaller of the two hoses coming from the pump. If the high pressure hoses flexes, the the pump is not providing enough pressure. Since the minimum pressure setting of the pump is 600 lbs., the pump should be checked as follows:

Remove the reservoir cover and check the flow of oil thru the filter as the wheels are turned from right to left. If there is no oil flow, a stuck flow control valve is indicated. Shut off the engine and unfasten the high pressure hose at the pump. Removal

of the hose permits insertion of a quarter inch blunt probe into the hose fitting on the pump. The probe will come up against the flow valve plunger. If the plunger can be pushed in a quarter inch, it was stuck; the probe has probably freed it, and all will be well. However, if things have not been improved by the probing, then remove the combination relief and flow valve and clean it thoroughly.

If the plunger did not move, a broken coupling is indicated. Remove the pump from the generator.

If either coupling is broken, turn the pump shaft by hand at least ten revolutions. If the shaft turns freely, install new couplings. If the pump shaft binds when turned by hand, replace both the pump and the couplings. If the generator armature has been damaged, replace it and the associated parts.

REMOVAL AND INSTALLATION OF THE CO-AXIAL POWER STEERING UNIT

REMOVAL

Remove horn control ring ornament, cushion and spring. Disconnect the horn wire and remove steering wheel nut and wheel. Remove the jacket bearing, spring and cone shaped spacer. Remove three shroud to toe board cover screws and remove the cover from the shroud. Remove the accelerator and brake pedal pads and the floor mat. Remove the six steering column jacket toe pad screws and slide the toe pad up on the jacket assembly. Remove the pedal opening cover. Disconnect the indicator wires.

Disconnect the pressure and return hoses at the gear housing. Cap the fittings and tie them up above the reservoir to avoid loss of fluid. Disconnect the gearshif control rod at the lever. Turn the wheels full left and disconnect the pitman arm from the pitman shaft.

Remove the access plate in the left front fender shield and remove the front lower steering gear assembly to bracket screw, washer and spacer. Note position of the wedge between the bracket and the gear housing.

Remove the front upper and the rear steering gear assembly to bracket screws, washers and spacers through the toe board opening.

Holding the jacket and shroud assembly in position, remove the two steering column to instrument panel screws. **Note:** The screw retaining plate and anti-squeak pad may fall from behind the instrument panel when these screws are removed.

Lower the jacket and shroud assembly and remove the insulator collar.

Tip the assembly to the right so that the pitman shaft will clear and remove the assembly upward through the toe board opening.

Place the assembly on the bench and loosen the gear shift rod lever nut, then slide lever and oilite spacer off the rod. Loosen the two nuts on the jacket clamp assembly and slide the jacket and shroud assembly from the worm housing. Two spring seats and a spring may fall from the gear shift rod when the jacket and shroud assembly is removed. Remove the steering gear tube insulator pin, then remove the tube and insulator from the coupling.

INSTALLATION

The unit when in good condition has between 150 and 170 degrees of travel either side of the center position with no backlash between the pitman arm and the steerling wheel. (Fig. 95). This no backlash area must be delicately felt for. When in the center of the no backlash travel, the slot in the coupling should be vertical. Should the center of no backlash travel and the vertical position of the coupling not coincide, remove the coupling and reinstall it in the correct position.

Place the steering gear tube insulator on the tube and position the tube onto the coupling so that the master serration at the steering wheel end of the tube is in the up position. Install the steering gear insulator pin.

Install the gear shift rod spring and seats in place on the rod. With the horn contact held out of the way with a piece of wire, and holding the spring and seats on the rod, slide the jacket

and shroud assembly over the steering gear tube, guiding the rod into the bushing on the housing.

Tighten the two nuts on the jacket clamp assembly and remove the piece of wire which was used to hold the horn contact point.

Install steering assembly through the toe board opening.

Install the front upper and the rear steering gear housing to bracket spacers, screws and lockwashers through the opening in the floor pan. Tighten the screws snug, then back off one turn.

Position the insulator collar on the upper shroud and align the jacket and shroud assembly to the instrument panel. Install the two screws and tighten securely. Now tighten the two screws on the brackets (the ones which were backed off one turn) to seventy foot pounds torque.

Install the front lower steering

gear housing to bracket screw complete with spacer but do not tighten. Tap the wedge into position over the front lower bracket screw between the bracket and the frame. The open end of the wedge must point down toward the frame. (Fig. 97.) Be sure that the wedge is properly placed; do not drive it in, just tap it lightly. With the wedge in position, tighten the screw to 70 ft. pounds.

Reinstall the pitman arm on the pitman shaft and tighten the nut to 100-120 ft. lbs. torque. Reconnect the horn and indicator wires. Install the cone shaped steering column bearing spacer and spring. Install the steering wheel and the horn ring and emblem.

REMOVAL AND INSTALLATION OF THE CO-AXIAL POWER STEERING UNIT—Continued

Check the clearance between the steering wheel and the directional signal housing; it must be one-eighth of an inch; to adjust, loosen the jacket to instrument panel screws a mite and loosen the jacket clamp at the top of the gear housing assembly. Now slide the steering column jacket up or down to achieve the required one-eighth inch clearance. Retighten the screws and the clamp. (Fig. 98.)

Slide the oilite gear shift rod lever spacer onto the rod. Position the selector lever in low or reverse, and holding it so, tighten the nut. Connect the gear shift control rod to the lever and install the cotter pin.

Reconnect the hoses to the gear housing. Check the level in the reservoir adding Type A Fluid oil until level is one-half inch above the filter. Start the engine and purge the system by turning the wheels from extreme right to extreme left, back and

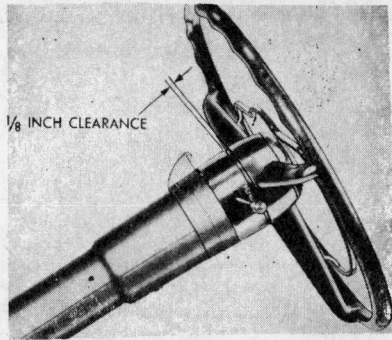

Fig. 98—Steering wheel to signal housing clearance should be ⅛ in.

forth, until no more bubbles appear in the reservoir. Stop the engine and recheck the level.

Place the selector lever pointer at the N on the dial. Disconnect gear shift control rod at the transmission. Position the lever on the transmission

in the neutral position, which is the second detent position from the rear of the vehicle. Now lengthen or shorten the rod so that it is an easy fit onto the lever and fasten.

STEERING CONTROL VALVE ADJUSTMENT

Make a tool as shown in fig. 99. Remove the steering column jacket. Remove the steering coupling screw. Insert the tool thru the screw hole and into the hollow worm shaft so that the slotted end engages the end of the control valve (spool valve) rod. With the engine running and using a torque wrench on the Pitman shaft nut, measure the torque required to turn the Pitman shaft each way from center. Turn the tool to adjust the valve so that the torque is the same in either direction plus or minus 2½ lbs.

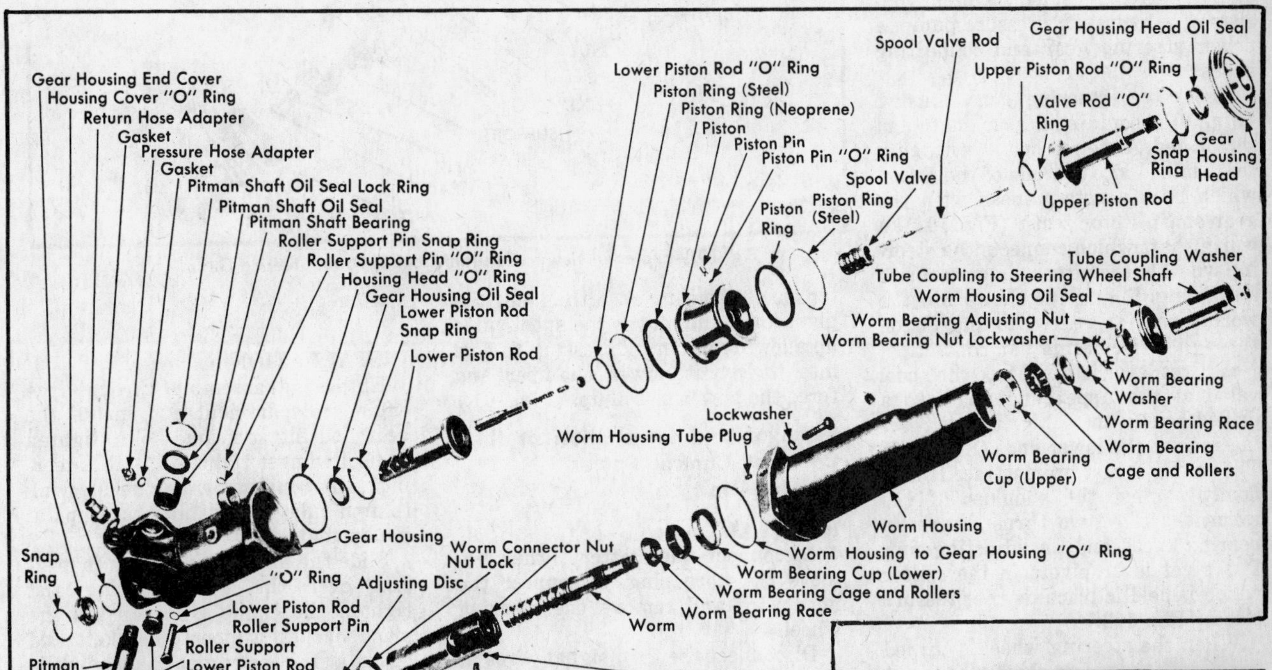

Gear Housing End Cover
Housing Cover "O" Ring
Return Hose Adapter
Gasket
Pressure Hose Adapter
Gasket
Pitman Shaft Oil Seal Lock Ring
Pitman Shaft Oil Seal
Pitman Shaft Bearing
Roller Support Pin Snap Ring
Roller Support Pin "O" Ring
Housing Head "O" Ring
Gear Housing Oil Seal
Lower Piston Rod Snap Ring
Lower Piston Rod

Lower Piston Rod "O" Ring
Piston Ring (Steel)
Piston Ring (Neoprene)
Piston
Piston Pin
Piston Pin "O" Ring
Spool Valve
Piston Ring
Piston Ring (Steel)

Spool Valve Rod
Gear Housing Head Oil Seal
Upper Piston Rod "O" Ring
Valve Rod "O" Ring
Snap Ring
Gear Housing Head
Upper Piston Rod

Tube Coupling to Steering Wheel Shaft
Tube Coupling Washer
Worm Housing Oil Seal
Worm Bearing Adjusting Nut
Worm Bearing Nut Lockwasher
Worm Bearing Washer
Worm Bearing Race
Worm Bearing Cage and Rollers
Worm Bearing Cup (Upper)
Worm Housing
Worm Housing to Gear Housing "O" Ring
Worm Bearing Cup (Lower)
Worm Bearing Cage and Rollers
Worm Bearing Race

Lockwasher
Worm Housing Tube Plug

Snap Ring
Gear Housing
"O" Ring
Adjusting Disc
Lower Piston Rod
Roller Support Pin
Roller Support
Lower Piston Rod
Adjusting Screw Thrust Washer
Pitman Shaft
Adjusting Screw
Adjusting Screw "O"

Worm Connector Nut
Nut Lock
Worm
Worm Ball
Worm Ball Guides
Worm Ball Guide Clamp
Adjusting Disc Retainer
Upper Piston Rod Nut Lock Cup
Upper Piston Rod Nut
Valve Control Spacer Retainer
Valve Control Spacer
Valve Control Spacer Expandable Rubber Seal
Valve Control Spacer Retainer
Worm Connector Nut Retainer

Adjusting Screw Seal
Adjusting Screw Snap Ring
Pitman Shaft Bearing
Pitman Shaft Cover Gasket
Pitman Shaft Cover
SEAL

Power Steering Gear Assembly, (Exploded View)

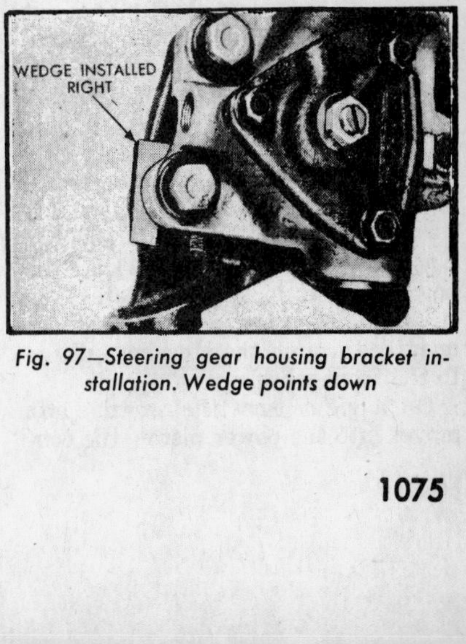

WEDGE INSTALLED RIGHT

Fig. 97—Steering gear housing bracket installation. Wedge points down

POWERSTEERING

CHRYSLER FULL TIME POWER STEERING CONSTANT CONTROL TYPE

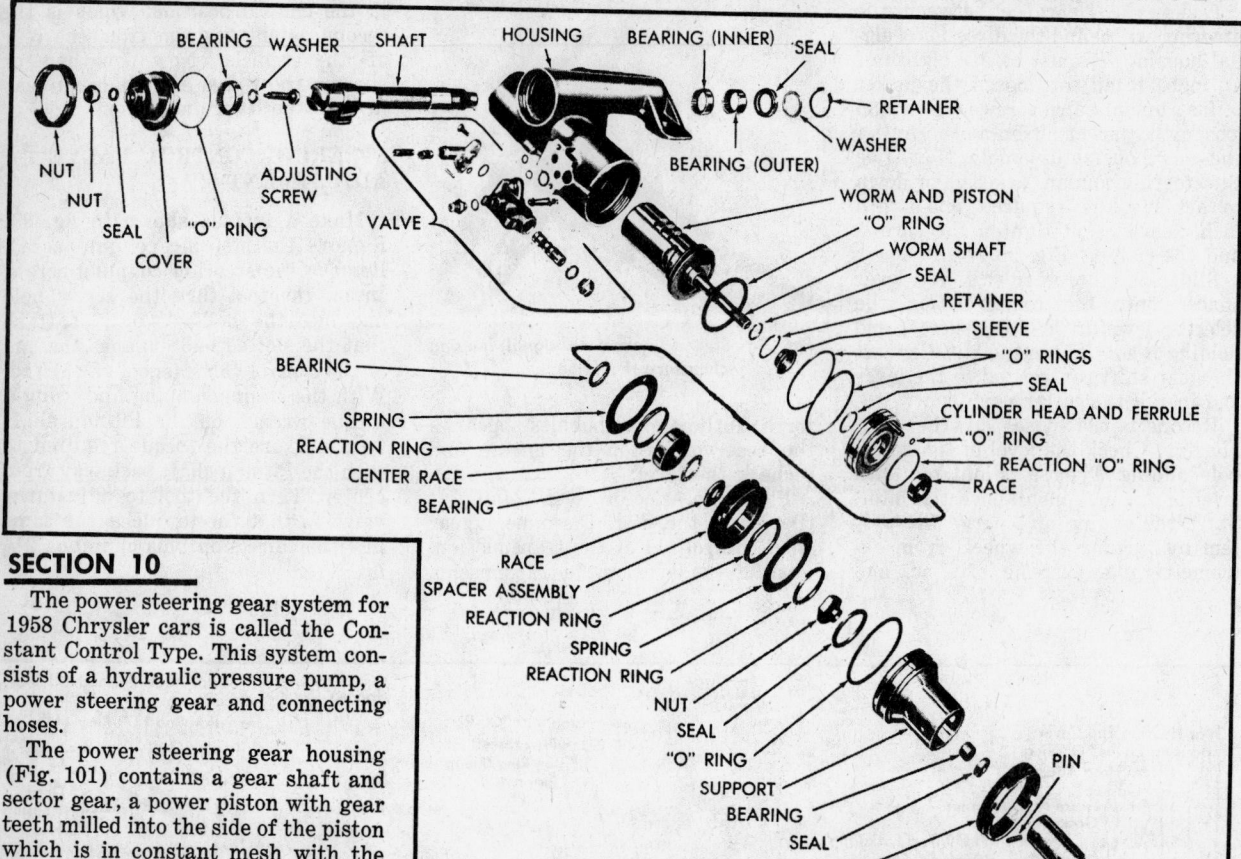

Fig. 101—Exploded view of Constant Control Power Steering Gear

SECTION 10

The power steering gear system for 1958 Chrysler cars is called the Constant Control Type. This system consists of a hydraulic pressure pump, a power steering gear and connecting hoses.

The power steering gear housing (Fig. 101) contains a gear shaft and sector gear, a power piston with gear teeth milled into the side of the piston which is in constant mesh with the gear shaft sector teeth (Fig. 102), a worm shaft which connects the steering wheel to the power piston through a coupling. Figure 101 shows how the worm shaft is geared to the piston through recirculating ball contact.

A pivot lever is fitted into the spool valve at the upper end and into a drilled hole in the center thrust bearing race at the lower end. (Fig. 101.) The center thrust bearing race is held firmly against the shoulder of the worm shaft by two thrust bearings, bearing races and an adjusting nut. The pivot lever pivots in the spacer which is held in place by the pressure plate. (Fig. 103.)

When the steering wheel is turned to the left the worm shaft moves out of the power piston a few thousandths of an inch, the center thrust bearing race moves the same distance since it is clamped to the worm shaft. The race thus tips the pivot lever and moves the spool valve down allowing oil under pressure to flow into the left turn power chamber and force the power piston down. (Fig. 101). As the power piston moves it rotates the cross shaft sector gear and subsequently through the steering linkage to the front wheels.

On a right turn the worm shaft moves into the power piston, the cen-

ter thrust bearing race thus tips the pivot lever and moves the spool valve up allowing oil under pressure to flow into the right power chamber and force the power piston up. (Fig. 101.)

Removal and Installation of the Constant Control Power Steering Unit

REMOVAL

Disconnect the battery, then remove the horn ring, disconnect the horn wire and remove the steering wheel.

Disconnect the turn signal wires at the connectors. Remove the mast jacket support bracket and clamp at the instrument panel. Loosen the two bolts that hold the mast jacket to the gear housing, then push the mast jacket upward to expose the coupling pin and remove the pin.

Remove the drag link from the pitman arm.

Disconnect the pressure and return hoses at the steering gear and cap the ends of the hoses to avoid loss of fluid.

Remove the pitman arm nut and washer, then with a pitman arm puller remove the arm from the cross

shaft.

INSTALLATION

Enter the assembly through the engine compartment and install the gear housing to frame bolts, tighten the bolts finger tight. Align the steering tube coupling with the steering column tube and install the coupling pin, insulator and inserts.

Slide the mast jacket down in position over the gear housing and tighten the clamp bolts. Install the mast jacket support bracket and clamp at the instrument panel, but do not tighten. Connect the turn signal wires, then install the steering wheel, horn wire and horn ring.

Adjust the mast jacket so that there is 1/8" clearance between it and the steering wheel, then tighten the mast jacket clamp.

Now tighten the mast jacket support bracket to the instrument panel, then tighten the gear housing to frame bolts. Install the pitman arm and drag link. Connect the pressure and return hoses, then fill the reservoir to the level mark with Type "A" Automatic Transmission Fluid and bleed the system.

CHRYSLER CONSTANT CONTROL POWER STEERING—Continued

Fig. 103—Power Piston and Cross Shaft Sector Gear

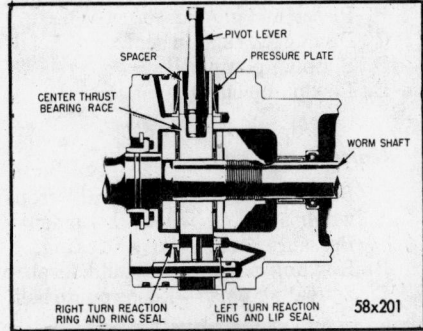

Fig. 104—Pivot Lever

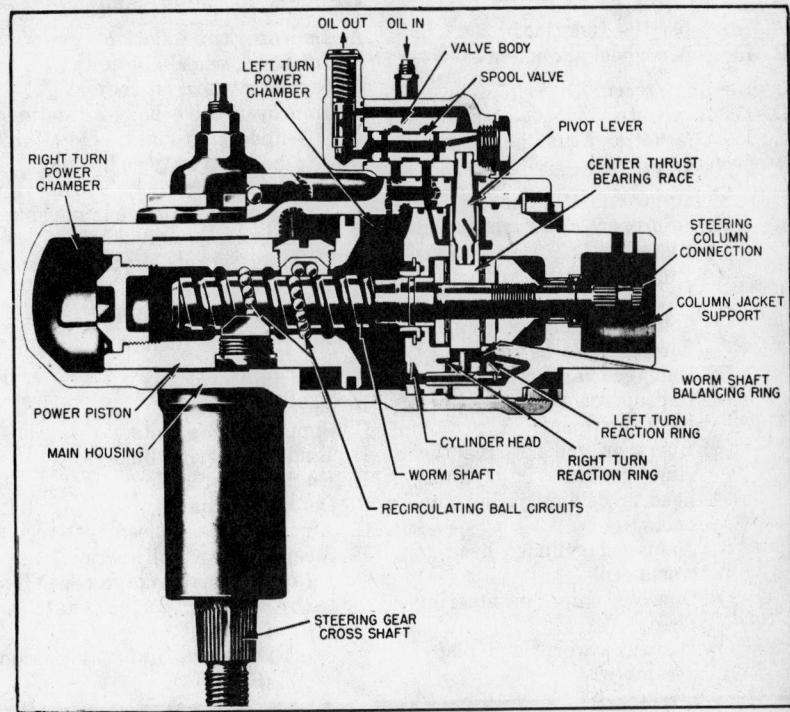

Fig. 102—Cutaway view of Constant Control Power Steering Gear

Maintenance of the Chrysler Constant Control Power Steering Unit

FLUID USED

This unit uses Automatic Transmission Fluid Type A. The fluid capacity for the unit is two quarts.

BLEEDING THE SYSTEM

Fill the reservoir to the level mark with Automatic Transmission Fluid Type A. Start the engine and allow it to idle to come to normal operating temperature. Now turn the steering wheel several times to the right and left to expel air from the system, then recheck the oil level.

CHECKING STEERING EFFORT

Raise the front wheels off the floor. Now start the engine, then hook a spring scale to the spoke of the steering wheel at the outer edge. The effort required to turn the steering wheel should be between five and nine inch pounds.

CROSS SHAFT ADJUSTMENT

Loosen the locknut, then with the cross shaft on center, tighten the cross shaft adjusting screw (See Fig. 100) until the backlash just disappears. From this position, turn the screw in $1\frac{1}{4}$ turns. Hold the screw in place and tighten the locknut.

PRESSURE TEST

Connect the pressure test hoses with the pressure gauge installed between the pump and steering gear.

Now fill the reservoir to the level mark, then start the engine and bleed the system. Allow the engine to idle until the fluid in the reservoir is between 150° F. and 170° F. Now turn the steering wheel to the extreme right and check the pressure reading, then turn the wheel to the extreme left and check the reading again. The gauge reading should be equal in each direction. If not, it indicates excessive internal leakage in the unit.

The pressure should read between 850 to 950 psi for satisfactory power steering operation.

TROUBLE SHOOTING—CONSTANT CONTROL POWER STEERING

Hard Steering

A. Improper tire inflation.
B. Improper wheel alignment.
C. Low fluid level (accompanied by pump noise).
D. Loose pump belt (accompanied by squealing noise).
E. Slipping pump belts (caused by oil on belts).
F. Binding steering leakage.
G. Low pump output.
H. Steering gear malfunction.
   (a) Cross shaft adjusted too tight.

(b) Pressure control valve stuck in closed position.
(c) External fluid leakage at:
   Cross shaft lower oil seal.
   Cross shaft adjusting screw seal.
   Cross shaft cover "O" ring seal.
   Valve body to gear housing "O" rings.
(d) Damaged valve pivot lever.
   If pressure gauge will build up to 850 to 950 psi, check for:
   Damaged cross shaft bearings.

Dirt or chips in steering gear.
Damaged thrust bearings or excessive preload.
Binding worm and piston assembly.

(e) Excessive internal leakage.
   If pressure gauge will not build up to 850 to 950 psi, check for:

   Damaged "O" rings or seals in or between the cylinder head and the column jacket support.

POWER STEERING

Poor Recovery From Turns

A. Improper tire inflation.
B. Improper wheel alignment.
C. Binding steering linkage.
D. Damaged steering tube bearings.
E. Mast jacket and gear housing not properly aligned.
F. Steering gear malfunctions.
    (a) Improper cross shaft adjustment.
    (b) Pressure control valve stuck in open position.
    (c) Column jacket support spanner nut loose.
    (e) Damaged valve pivot lever.
    (f) Improper worm thrust bearing adjustment.
    (g) Burrs or nicks in reaction ring grooves in cylinder head or column jacket support.
    (h) Damaged cylinder head to worm seal.
    (i) Dirt or chips in steering gear.
    (j) Damaged worm and piston assembly.

Wanders to Either Side

A. Improper tire inflation.
B. Improper wheel alignment.
C. Steering wheel off center.
D. Improper valve body adjustment.
    Wanders to right—Move valve body up on gear housing.
    Wanders to left—Move valve body down on gear housing.
E. Damaged valve pivot lever.
F. Column jacket support spanner nut loose.

Temporary Increase in Effort When Making Turn

A. Low fluid level.
B. Loose pump belt.
C. Slipping pump belts.
D. Binding steering linkage.
E. Engine idle too slow.
F. Defective pump.
G. Air in system. (Bleed system).
H. Steering gear malfunction.
    (a) External leakage. (See 1Hc).
    (b) Improper cross shaft adjustment.
    (c) Excessive internal leakage. (See 1He).

Excessive Play in Steering Wheel

A. Improper cross shaft adjustment.
B. Column jacket support spanner nut loose.
C. Improper worm thrust bearing adjustment.

Lack of Assistance

(One Direction)
A. Fluid leaking past worm shaft cast iron seal ring or ferrule "O" ring.

(Both Directions)
A. Broken ring on worm piston.
B. Piston end plug loose.
C. Damaged reaction seal.
D. Slipping pump belt.
E. Low pump output.

Noises

A. Buzzing noise in neutral, stops when steering wheel is turned—Pressure control valve sticking.
B. Howling noise—Low fluid level.
C. Squealing noise—Loose pump belt.

TORSION BAR TYPE POWER STEERING

SECTION 11

The torsion bar type power steering gear is designed with all components in one housing.

The power cylinder is an integral part of the gear housing. A double acting type piston allows oil pressure to be applied to either side of the piston. The one piece piston and power rack is meshed to the sector shaft.

The hydraulic control valve is composed of a sleeve and valve spool. The spool is held in the neutral position by the torsion bar and spool actuator. Twisting of the torsion bar moves the valve spool allowing oil pressure to be directed to either side of the power piston, depending upon the directional rotation of the steering wheel, to give power assist.

Roller Type Pump

This type of pump is used with torsion bar type power steering units (Fig. 105)

Removal and Installation of the Roller Pump

REMOVAL

Remove the reservoir cover and use a suction gun to empty the reservoir. Disconnect the hoses from the pump and tie them in a raised position to prevent oil drainage. Loosen the pump adjusting screw and remove the pump belt, then take out the retaining bolts and remove the pump and reservoir.

NOTE: On cars equipped with air conditioning the pump assembly is removed from underneath the vehicle.

INSTALLATION

Position the pump assembly and install the retaining bolts. Be sure there is clearance between the pump

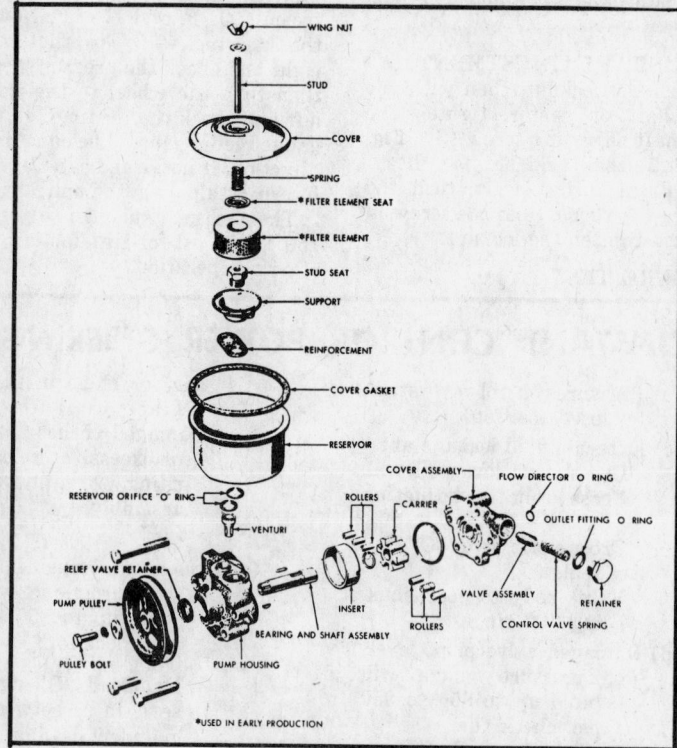

Fig. 105—Torsion Bar Power Steering Pump and Reservoir

TORSION BAR TYPE POWER STEERING—Continued

bracket and the engine front support bracket. Install the hoses and place the pump belt on the pulley. Adjust the belt to ½ inch deflection, then tighten the adjusting screw.

Connect the hoses to the pump assembly.

Fill the reservoir to within ½ inch from the top with Automatic Transmission Fluid Type A.

Start the engine and rotate the steering wheel several times to the right and left to expel air from the system, then recheck the oil level and install the reservoir cover.

Removal and Installation of the Torsion Bar Steering Unit

REMOVAL

Remove the lines from the steering gear and tie them in a raised position to prevent oil drainage.

Remove the power brake assembly.

Using a puller, remove the pitman arm from the sector shaft.

Take out the nuts and bolts that hold the steering shaft coupling to the steering gear.

Remove the bolts that secure the gear assembly to the frame side rail and remove the gear assembly from the vehicle.

INSTALLATION

Position the gear assembly against the frame side rail and install the retaining bolts.

Install the pitman arm, aligning the large spline on the sector shaft with the large groove in the arm.

CAUTION: Do not drive the pitman arm on the sector shaft. Draw the arm in position with the nut.

Replace the power brake assembly.

Assemble the steering shaft coupling to the steering gear.

Install the hoses, then fill and bleed the power steering system.

Fill and bleed the brake system.

Maintenance of the Torsion Bar Power Steering Unit

FLUID USED

This unit uses Automatic Transmission Fluid Type A. The fluid capacity for the unit is 4½ pints.

BLEEDING THE SYSTEM

Fill the pump reservoir to within ½ inch from the top. Start and run the engine to attain normal operating temperatures. Now turn the steering wheel through its entire travel three or four times to expel air from the system, then recheck the fluid level.

CHECKING STEERING EFORT

Run the engine to attain normal operating temperatures. With the wheels on a dry floor, hook a pull scale to the spoke of the steering wheel at the outer edge. The effort required to turn the steering wheel should be 3½ to 5 pounds. If the pull is not within these limits, check the hydraulic pressure.

PRESSURE TEST

To check the hydraulic pressure, disconnect the pressure hose from the gear. Now connect the pressure gauge between the pressure hose from the pump and the steering gear housing. Run the engine to attain normal operating temperatures, then turn the wheel to a full right and a full left turn to the wheel stops.

Hold the wheel in this position only long enough to obtain an accurate reading.

The gauge should read between 975-1100 p.s.i. If the pressure is less than 975 p.s.i., close the valve at the gauge and note the pump pressure. If the pressure is still low the pump is not operating properly. If the pres-

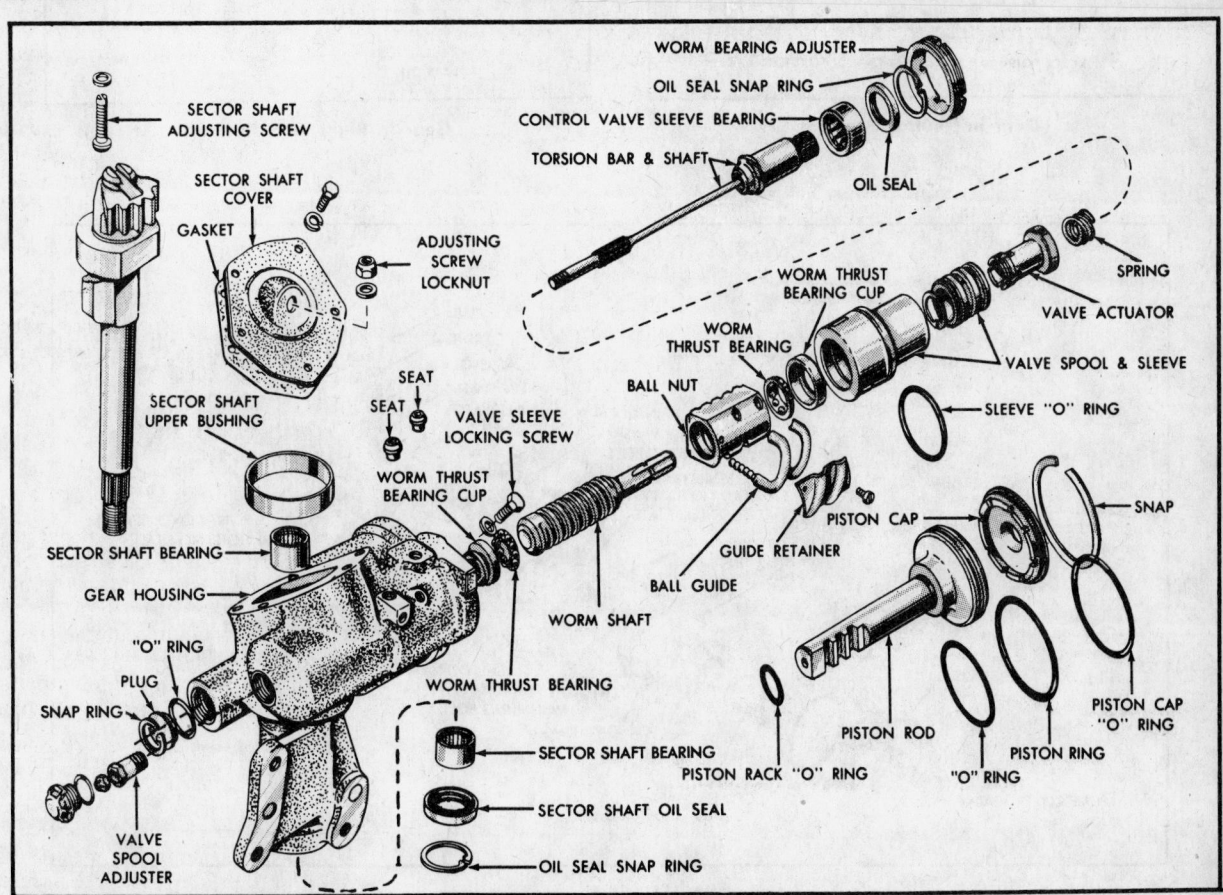

Components of Power Steering Gear

POWER STEERING

TORSION BAR TYPE POWER STEERING—Continued

sure goes up with the valve closed, it indicates internal leakage in the power unit.

WORM BEARING PRELOAD AND SECTOR MESH ADJUSTMENTS

Disconnect the pitman arm from the sector shaft, then back off on the sector shaft adjusting screw which is on the sector shaft cover (Fig. 107).

Center the steering on the high point, then attach a pull scale to the spoke of the steering wheel at the outer edge. The pull required to keep the wheel moving for one complete turn should be ½-⅔ pounds.

If the pull is not within these limits, loosen the thrust bearing locknut and tighten or back off on the valve sleeve adjustor locknut (Fig. 107), to bring the preload within the limits. Tighten the thrust bearing locknut and re-check the preload.

Slowly rotate the steering wheel several times, then center the steering on the high point. Now turn the sector shaft adjusting screw until a steering wheel pull of 1-1½ pounds is required to move the worm through the center point. Tighten the sector shaft adjusting screw locknut and re-check the sector mesh adjustment.

Install the pitman arm and draw the arm in position with the nut.

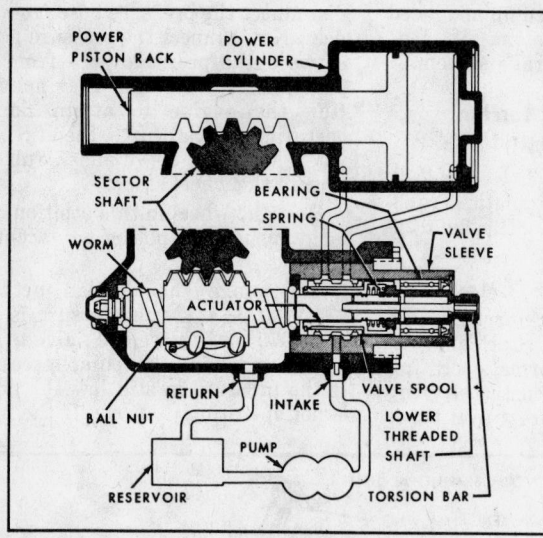

Gear in Neutral Position

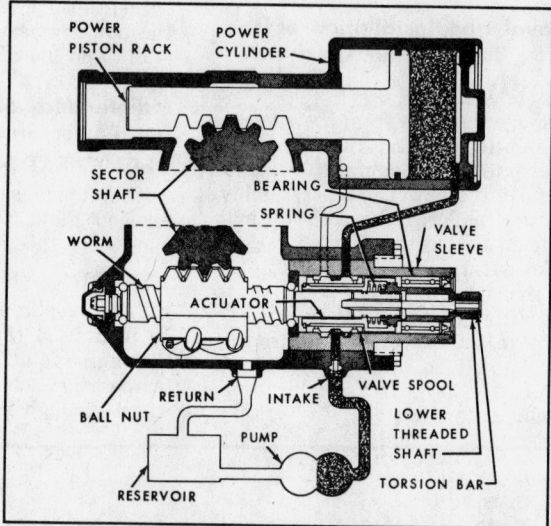

Gear in Right Turn Position

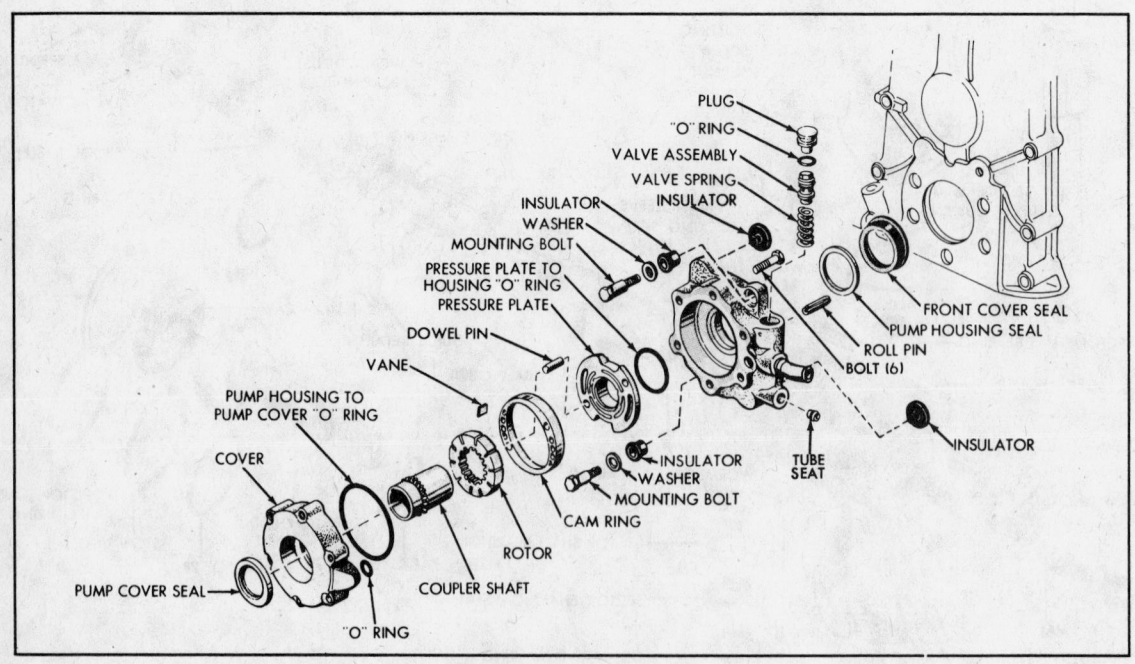

Pump Assembly—Disassembled View

TORSION BAR TYPE POWER STEERING—Continued

TROUBLE SHOOTING CHART

Hard Steering

A. Low or uneven tire pressure.
B. Improper gear adjustment.
C. Improper caster.
D. Improper camber.
E. Insufficient or incorrect hydraulic fluid.
F. Twisted or bent suspension parts, frame, and linkage components.
G. Tight wheel bearings.
H. Steering spindle bent.
I. Pump belt out of adjustment.
J. Pump output low.
K. Air in system.
L. Steering gear out of adjustment.
M. Valve spool out of adjustment.
N. Valve spool sticking.
O. Steering linkage binding.

Hard Steering—straight ahead

A. Steering adjustment too tight.
B. Steering gear shaft binding.

Hard Steering—turning or parking

A. Oil level low.
B. Pump pressure low.
C. Pressure loss in steering gear due to leakage past "O" rings.
D. Pressure loss between valve spool and sleeve.
E. Pressure loss past piston ring or scored housing bore.

Loose Steering

A. Loose wheel bearings.
B. Loose tie rod ends or linkage.
C. Worn ball joints.
D. Worn suspension parts.
E. Fluid level low.
F. Insufficient mesh load.
G. Insufficient worm bearing preload.
H. Valve spool out of adjustment.

Erratic Steering

A. Oil or brake fluid on brake lining.
B. Out of round brake drums.
C. Improperly adjusted brakes.
D. Under-inflated tires.
E. Broken spring or other details in suspension system.
F. Improper caster.

Pull to One Side—(The continuing tendency of the car to veer in one direction only.)

A. Incorrect tire pressure.

B. Wheel bearings improperly adjusted.
C. Dragging brakes.
D. Improper caster or camber.
E. Sagging springs.
F. Incorrect toe-in.
G. Oil or brake fluid on brake linings.
H. Front and rear wheels out of alignment.
I. Bent suspension parts.
J. Worn shock absorbers.

Wandering—(Tendency of car to veer in one direction and, upon correction, to veer in the opposite direction.)

A. Incorrect tire pressure.
B. Incorrect or uneven caster and camber.
C. Ball joints worn.
D. Loose tie rod ends.
E. Improper toe-in.
F. Steering gear adjustments too tight or backlash excessive.
G. Bent suspension parts.

Wheel Tramp—(Excessive vertical motion of wheels.)

A. Improper balance of wheels, tires and brake drums.
B. Loose tie rod ends or steering connections.
C. Incorrect tire pressure.
D. Inoperative or loose shock absorber.

Shimmy—(Oscillation of wheels about spindle ball joints.)

A. Incorrect tire pressure.
B. Worn shock absorbers.
C. Loose wheel bearings.
D. Incorrect steering gear adjustments.
E. Loose tie rod ends.
F. Eccentric or bulged tires.
G. Ball joints worn.
H. Wheel runout.
I. Incorrect toe-in.
J. Worn idler arm bushings.

Road Shocks

A. Worn or damaged shock absorbers.
B. Weak or sagging springs.
C. Improper caster.

D. Improperly adjusted steering gear or linkage.
E. Improperly inflated tires.

Tire Wear

A. Incorrect tire pressure.
B. Incorrect toe-in.
C. Dragging brakes.
D. Improper camber.
E. Bent or broken suspension parts.
F. Excess mileage without rotating tires.
G. Wheel runout.

Binding or Poor Recovery

A. Steering gear shaft binding.
B. Steering gear out of adjustment.
C. Steering linkage binding.
D. Valve spool binding due to dirt, or burred edges.
E. Valve spool out of adjustment.
F. Interference at sector shaft arm and ball stud.
G. Travel regulator stop out of adjustment.

Loss of Power Assist

A. Pump inoperative.
B. Lines damaged.
C. Power cylinder damaged.
D. Valve spool out of adjustment.

Loss of Power Assist—one direction

A. Valve spool out of adjustment.
B. By-pass in control valve inoperative.

Noisy Pump

A. Air being drawn into pump.
B. Lines touching other parts of car.
C. Oil level low.
D. Excessive back pressure caused by obstructions in lines.
E. Excessive wear of internal parts.

Poor Return of Steering Gear to Center

A. Valve spool sticking.
B. Valve spool out of adjustment.

Steering Wheel Surge When Turning

A. Valve spool sticking.
B. Excessive internal leakage.

WHEEL ALIGNMENT

For a car to have safe steering control with a minimum of tire wear, certain established rules must be followed. These rules fix the value of planes, angles and radii relative to each other and to car and tire dimensions. Some factors of this proven plan are built-in, with no provision for adjustment; others are adjustable, within limits. The entire scheme, being a relative one, depends one upon the other, for factor values. It is, therefore, difficult to change some of the established settings without influencing others. This system is called steering goemetry or wheel alignment and requires a complete check of all the factors involved.

Definitions of these factors and explanations of the effect each one has on the car are given in the following paragraphs.

For adjustment data relative to each separate car and year, refer to the car section. Geometry specifications are found under Front Suspension of the car being serviced.

TOE-IN, RELATIVE TO STEERING WHEEL POSITION

Toe-in or straightaway alignment is a value given the negative distance between the front extremes of the two front, or rear, wheels relative to a like measurement taken at the rear extremes of the same wheels.

This factor of alignment is blamed for more steering and tire wear troubles than any other. The careless or inexperienced mechanic will attempt all sorts of corrective measures with a turn of the tie-rod adjustments.

Always check steering wheel alignment in conjunction with and at the same time as toe-in. In fact, the steering wheel spoke location, with the car on a straight piece of highway, may be the first indication of front end

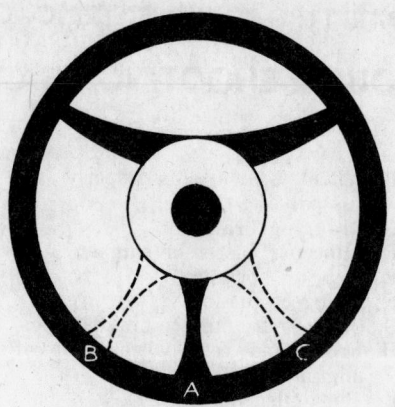

Steering Wheel Position

misalignment.

Check the steering wheel spoke position relative to straight-ahead car travel. If the wheel is not in a normal straight position, the condition may be corrected during toe-in adjustment.

1. Loosen the tie-rod adjusting clamps.

2 (A). If the steering wheel position is satisfactory, shorten or lengthen both tie rods (the same amount) to the required toe-in specifications.

2 (B). If, however, after correcting the toe-in value, the steering wheel position is wrong, shorten the right and lengthen the left tie-rod or shorten the left and lengthen the right tie-rod (the same amount) to obtain the desired steering wheel position, (see steering wheel illustration).

If the car has been wrecked or indicates any evidence of steering gear or linkage disturbance, the pitman arm should be disconnected from the sector shaft. The steering wheel (or gear) should be turned from extreme right to extreme left, to determine the halfway point in its turning scope. This will be the spot on the gear that is in action during straight-ahead driving and in which position

the steering gear should be adjusted.

With the steering wheel in the straight-ahead position and the steering gear adjusted to "no-lash" and "on-the-high-spot" status, reconnect the pitman arm.

To obtain front wheel-to-steering wheel relations refer to steering wheel adjustment illustration.

IF TOE-IN IS CORRECT:

(A) is normal steering wheel position. Adjust both tie-rods an equal amount, to set toe-in and maintain normal steering wheel position.

(B) Shorten the left and lengthen the right rod to obtain an "A" spoke position.

(C) Shorten the right and lengthen the left rod to obtain an "A" spoke position.

IF TOE-IN IS INCORRECT:

(B) Lengthen the left hand rod to increase toe-in and obtain an "A" spoke position.

(B) Shorten the right hand rod to decrease toe-in and obtain an "A" spoke position.

(C) Lengthen the right hand rod to increase toe-in and obtain an "A" spoke position.

(C) Shorten the left hand rod to decrease toe-in and obtain an "A" spoke position.

STEERING GEOMETRY

In order that a car may be steered easily and operate without unnecessary wear on the tires there are certain adjustable angles incorporated into the front suspension. The relation of each of these angles to all of the others is called front end or steering geometry.

Definitions of these angles and explanations of the effect they produce are given in the following paragraphs. For adjustment procedure for each

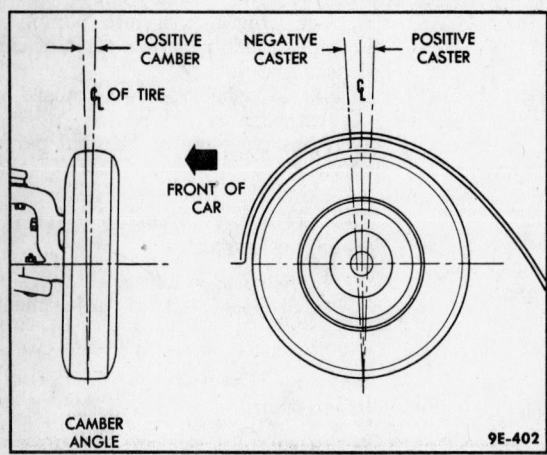

Caster and Camber Angles

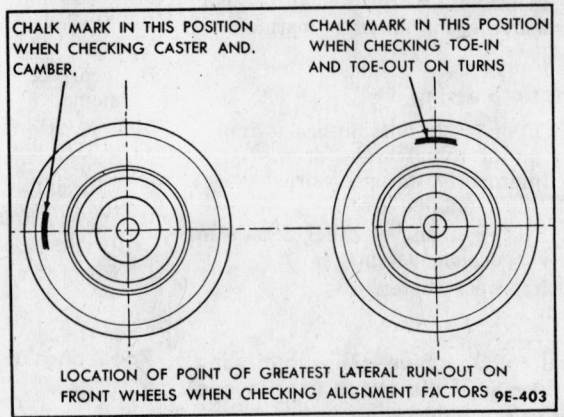

Wheel Position for Checking Alignment

of the angles refer to Front Suspension for the car being served.

Camber Angle

Camber is the amount that the front wheels are inclined outward at the top. Camber is spoken of and measured in degrees from the perpendicular.

The purpose of the camber angle is to take some of the load off the spindle outboard bearing. see Fig. 3.

Caster Angle

Caster is the amount that the king pin (or in the case of cars without king pins, the knuckle support pivots) is tilted towards the back of the car, see Fig. 1. Caster is usually spoken of and measured in degrees. Positive caster means that the top of the king pin is tilted towards the back of the car. Positive caster is indicated by the sign plus (+).

Negative caster is exactly opposite, the top of the king pin is tilted towards the front of the car. This is generally indicated by the minus (−). Negative caster is sometimes referred to as reverse caster.

The effect of positive caster is to cause the car to steer "in the direction in which it tends to go." This is not necessarily a straight line since cars with independently sprung front wheels usually steer easily, positive caster in the front wheels may cause the car to steer down off a crowned road or steer in the direction of a cross wind. For this reason many of our modern cars are arranged with negative caster so that the opposite is true, the car tends to steer up a crowned road and against a cross wind.

Angle of King Pin Slant

In addition to the caster slant the king pins (or in the case of cars without king pins, the knuckle support pivots) are also inclined towards each other at the top. This angle is known as the angle of king pin slant. It is usually spoken of and measured in degrees, see Fig. 3.

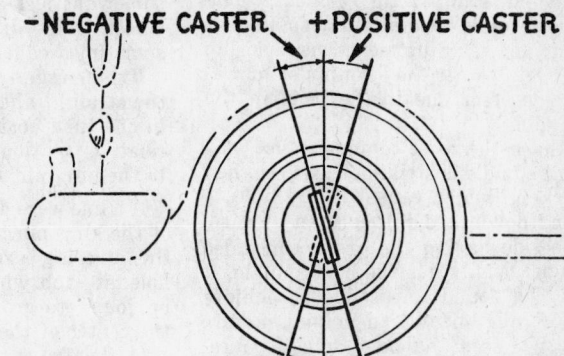

Fig. 1—Caster angle. Note that if the pivot tilts forward caster is negative; Tilted back, caster is positive

The effect of king pin slant is to cause the wheels to steer in a straight line regardless of outside forces such as crowned roads, cross winds, etc., which may tend to make it steer at a tangent. This function of the king pin slant can best be understood by referring to Fig. 2. Notice that as the spindle is moved from extreme right to extreme left it apparently rises and

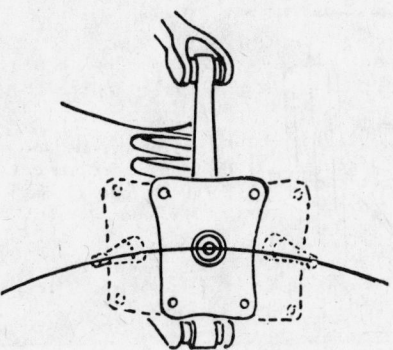

Fig. 2—Spindle arc when wheel turns

falls. Notice that it reaches its extreme high position when the wheels are in the straight ahead position. Now in actual operation the spindle cannot rise and fall because the wheel is in constant contact with the ground. Therefore the car itself will rise at the extreme right turn and come to its lowest position at the

straight ahead point and again rise for an extreme left turn. Therefore, the weight of the car will tend to cause the wheels to come to the straight ahead position which is the lowest position of the car itself.

Before attempting to make corrections to the king pin slant read the paragraph on "Included Angle."

Included Angle

Included angle is the name given to that angle which includes king pin slant and camber, see Fig. 3. It is the relation between the center line of the wheel and the center line of the king pin (or in the case of cars without king pins, the knuckle support pivots). This angle is "built in" to the knuckle (spindle) forging and will remain constant throughout the life of the car unless the spindle itself is damaged.

When checking a car on the front end stand always check king pin slant as well as camber unless some provision is made on the front end stand for checking the condition of the spindle. Where no such provision is made, add the king pin slant to the camber for each side of the car. These totals should be exactly the same regardless of how far from the norm any of the readings are.

For instance: the left side of the car checks 5½ degrees king pin slant and one degree positive camber—total 6½ degrees; the right side of the car is 6½ degrees king pin slant and 0 camber—total 6½ degrees. Since both sides creck exactly the same for the included angle it is unlikely that both spindles are bent exactly the same amount in the same direction, therefore it may be assumed that the spindles in this instance are not bent and adjusting to correct for camber will automatically correct king pin slant.

A bent spindle would show up something like this: left side of the car ¾ degrees positive camber, 5¼ degrees king pin slant—total 6 degrees included angle. Right side of the car 1¼ degrees positive camber, 6 degrees

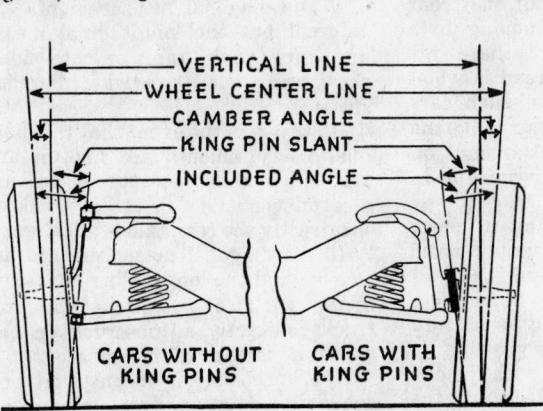

VERTICAL LINE
WHEEL CENTER LINE
CAMBER ANGLE
KING PIN SLANT
INCLUDED ANGLE

CARS WITHOUT KING PINS   CARS WITH KING PINS

Fig. 3—Camber, King Pin Slant and Included Angle

king pin slant—total 7¼ degrees included angle. One of these spindles is bent and if adjustments are made to correct camber the king pin slant will be incorrect due to the bend in the spindle.

Since the most common cause of a bent spindle is striking the curb when parking, which causes the spindle to bend downward rather than upward, the side having the greater included angle usually has the bent spindle. It will be found impossible to achieve good alignment and minimum tire wear unless the bent spindle is replaced.

Toe-In

Toe-in the amount that the front wheels are closer together at the front than they are at the back, see Fig. 5. This dimension is usually spoken of and measured in inches or fractions of inches.

Generally speaking, the wheels are

somewhat less angle than the inside wheel. This difference in angle is sometimes called "toe-out on turns."

The change in angle from toe-in in the straight ahead position to toe-out in the turn position is caused by the relative position of the steering arms to the king pin and to each other.

If a line were drawn from the center of the king pin through the center of the steering arm tie rod attaching hole, at each wheel these lines would be found to cross almost exactly in the center of the rear axle.

If the front end angles, including toe-in are set correctly, and the toe-out is found to be incorrect, one or both of the steering arms are bent.

Tracking

While tracking is more a function of the rear axle and frame than it is the front axle, it is difficult to properly align the front suspension if the car does not track straight.

Therefore, the car must be checked

front wheels and the back wheels, whether or not the wheels are tracking properly. Even a small amount of mistracking will show up to a critical observer. If the car is observed to track incorrectly, the difficulty will be found in either the frame or the rear axle alignment.

Perhaps the easiest way to check tracking is to park the car on a level floor, drop a plumbbob from the extreme outer edge of the front suspension lower A frame, using the same drop point on each side of the car. Make a chalk mark where the plumbbob strikes the floor.

Do the same with the rear axle, selecting a point on the rear axle housing for the plumbbob and being certain that the same point is selected on both sides of the rear axle.

Now measure diagonally from the left rear mark to the right front mark and from the right rear mark to the left front mark. These two diagonal measurements should be exactly the

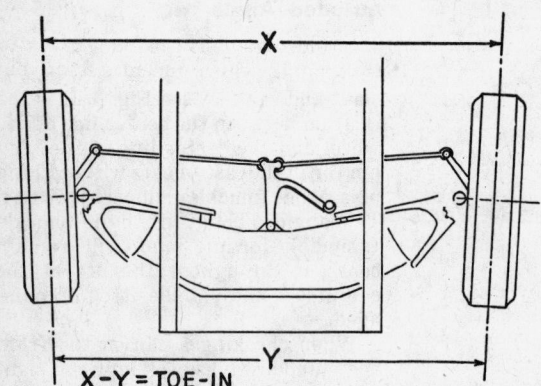

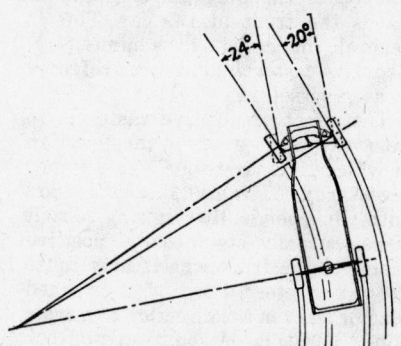

Fig. 5—Toe-in. Note that the wheels are closer at the front than at the rear

X-Y = TOE-IN

Fig. 4—Toe-out. Inside wheel turns a greater number degrees

toed-in because they are cambered. When a car operates with zero camber it will be found to operate with zero toe-in. As the required camber increases, so does the toe-in. The reason for this is that the cambered wheel tends to steer in the direction in which it is cambered. Therefore, it is necessary to overcome this tendency of the wheel by compensating very slightly in the direction opposite to which it tends to roll. Caster and camber both have an effect on toe-in, therefore toe-in is the last angle on the front end which should be corrected. Always set caster, camber and king pin slant (included angle) before setting toe-in.

Procedure for setting toe-in is given for each make of car in the car section.

Toe-Out—Steering Radius

When a car is steered into a turn the outside wheel of the turn describes a much larger circle than the inside wheel, see Fig. 4. Therefore, the outside wheel must be steered to

for tracking before any attempt is made to correct difficulties in the front suspension.

Tracking means that the center line of the rear axle follows exactly the path of the center line of the front axle when the car is moving in a straight line.

With cars which have equal tread, front and rear, the rear tires will follow in exactly the tread of the front tires when the car is moving in a straight line. However, there are many cars whose rear tread is wider than the front tread; on such cars the rear axle tread will straddle the front axle tread an equal amount on both sides when the car is moving in a straight line.

Perhaps the easiest way to check a car for tracking is to simply stand directly in back of it and watch it drive in a straight line down the street. If the observer will stand as near to the center of the car as possible he can observe readily, even with the difference in perspective between the

same. However, a difference of approximately ¼ inch would be acceptable.

If the measurements taken diagonally are not the same for both sides, measure from the right rear to the right front and from the left rear to the left front. These two measurements should also be the same within ¼ inch.

If the diagonal measurements are different but the longitudinal measurements are the same on both sides, the frame is swayed (diamond shaped).

However, in the event that the diagonal measurements are uneven and the longitudinal measurements are also uneven and the car is tracking incorrectly the rear axle is misaligned.

If the diagonal measurements are uneven and the longitudinal measurements are also uneven but the car tracks correctly as observed on the street, a "kneeback" is indicated.

By "kneeback" is meant that one complete side of the front suspension is bent back, thus "the knee is back" or more simply "kneeback."

This is often caused by "crimping" the front wheels against the curb when parking the vehicle and then starting up without straightening out the front wheels. This causes the full power being applied against the wheel which is crimped against the curb, bending the front suspension unit back.

It is possible to have caster, camber, toe-in, king pin slant and included angle exactly correct and, if the car has a kneeback or does not track properly, it will handle very poorly. This in spite of the fact that the front suspension angles are right on the ball.

QUICK CHECKS FOR FRONT WHEEL ALIGNMENT TROUBLES

Spring Sag

Measure from the lower side of the frame to any convenient point on the lower suspension arm on both sides (be sure to measure to the same points on both sides). This measurement should be the same on both sides

Steering Connections

Now place a jack under the lower suspension arm (one side, at about the center of the arm or just under the spring pad.

Jack the car until the wheel is about 4 inches from the floor.

With both hands, work the wheel back and forth around a vertical axis (as though the wheel were being steered) hard enough to take up all play in the steering system but not hard enough to cause the opposite front wheel to move. If the other part of the rim can be moved more than 1/4 inch without moving the opposite wheel, too much play exists in the steering linkage and it will be necessary to have a helper shake the wheel while the operator observes, from under the car, exactly where the play or looseness exists—the tie rod ends, steering arms, intermediate steering arm or bearings, pitman arm, and so forth.

If the brakes are to be examined, jack up both sides of the car and remove both hub and drum assemblies. Examine the brakes as outlined under "Brakes." If the brakes are not to be checked just take off the wheels leaving the drums in place on the car.

Suspension Arm Pivots

Now take a pry bar and pry the inner pins on both the upper and lower arms. A pry bar is required because the weight of the coil spring is partially on the inner pins when the car is jacked up.

Play at the inner bushings should not exceed 1/32 inch.

King Pins and Knuckle Support Pins

Note: On late model cars having the front coil spring on top of the upper arm the jack must be placed under the frame to make the king pin and suspension pin looseness test, otherwise pressure from the spring

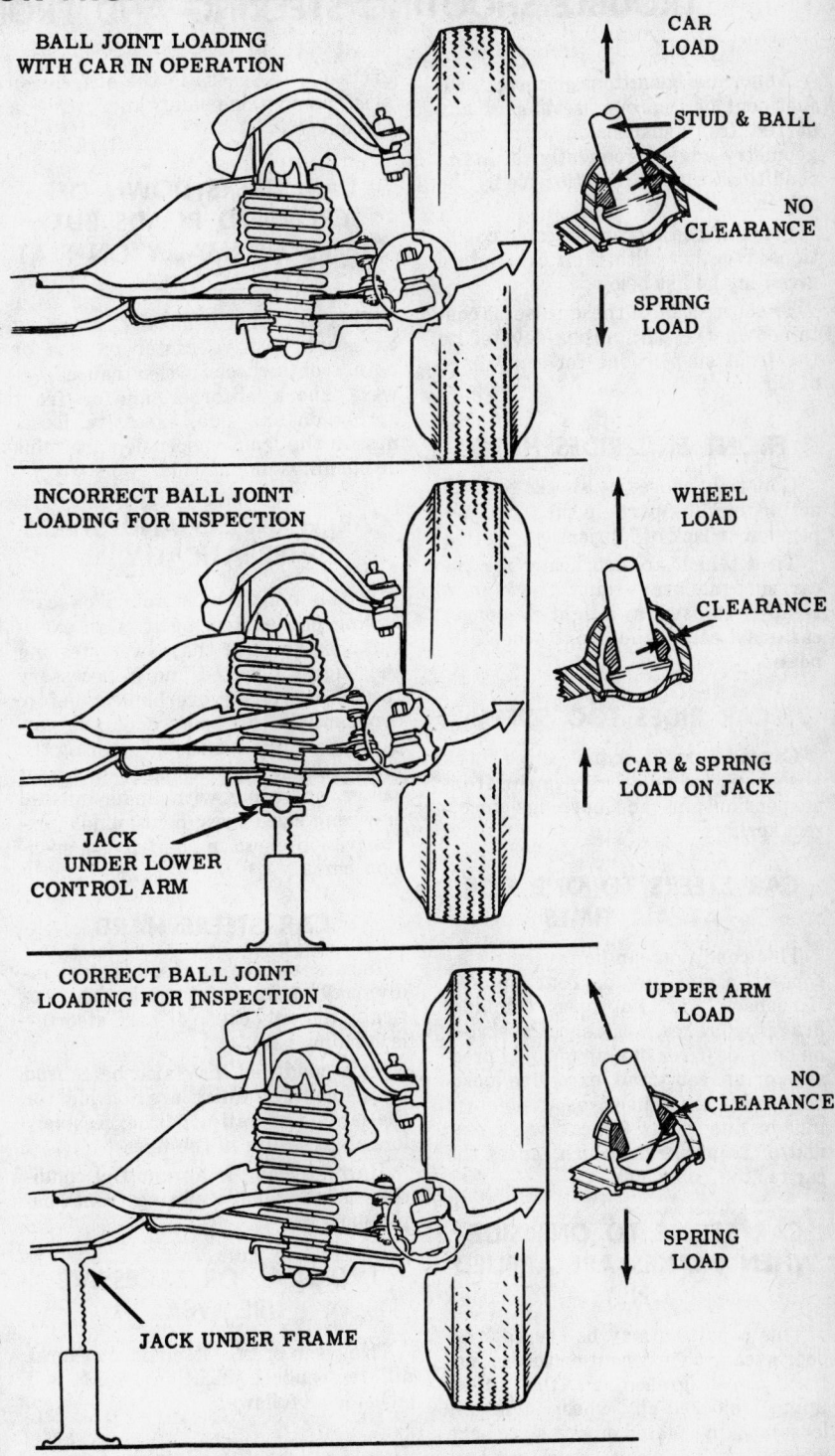

BALL JOINT LOADING WITH CAR IN OPERATION

CAR LOAD

STUD & BALL

NO CLEARANCE

SPRING LOAD

INCORRECT BALL JOINT LOADING FOR INSPECTION

WHEEL LOAD

CLEARANCE

CAR & SPRING LOAD ON JACK

JACK UNDER LOWER CONTROL ARM

CORRECT BALL JOINT LOADING FOR INSPECTION

UPPER ARM LOAD

NO CLEARANCE

SPRING LOAD

JACK UNDER FRAME

Fig. 6— Checking Ball Joints under Different Points of Lift

SUSPENSION, FRONT ALIGN

may "take up" all the play and looseness.

Grasp the wheel at the top and bottom and work the wheel back and forth around a horizontal axis to determine the total play in the king pins, suspension arm pins, (or ball joints) and wheel bearings. If more than 1/4 inch play, measured at the

rim of the wheel exists, have a helper shake the wheel while the operator checks to find the location of the looseness.

Motion (free play) at the king pins should not exceed 1/64 inch, upper pin and bushing assembly should not exceed 1/32 inch, lower pins 1/32 inch.

Any free play at all in the ball

joints (on cars using ball joints instead of king pins) is considered excessive.

Actual free play at the wheel bearing should be too slight to measure. In fact, many shops are now setting up wheel bearings with a slight preload.

TROUBLE SHOOTING STEERING AND FRONT END GEOMETRY

Abnormal conditions, incorrect adjustment or improper setting of any of the front suspension or steering geometry angles frequently results in conditions which are noticeable by the driver.

Some of the more noticeable conditions, together with their causes, are given in the list below.

The correction of these causes is contained in the paragraphs devoted to the front suspensions for each make of car.

FRONT END RIDES HARD

Generally caused by shocks too stiff acting, binding parts in the front suspension or lack of lubrication.

Tires which are too heavy for the car such as heavy duty truck snow tread tires used on a light passenger car may cause the front wheels to pound.

CAR RIDES TOO SOFT

Caused by weak or ineffective shock absorbers, too much play in the front suspension pins and bushings, incorrect springs.

CAR STEERS TO ONE SIDE AT ALL TIMES

This condition can be caused by incorrect caster angle, bent spindle, "kneeback" or improper tracking, dragging brakes, weak shock absorber on one side, tires having unequal pressure or uneven tread, excessive looseness in the king pin or suspension arm pins on one side of the car, weak rear and/or front spring which causes the car to stand unevenly.

CAR STEERS TO ONE SIDE WHEN BRAKES ARE APPLIED ONLY

This condition may be caused by a poor anchor adjustment on the brakes themselves, grease on the brake lining, blocked-up wheel cylinder, loose backing plates on one side, bent wheel spindle, weak spring and/or spring and/or its center bolt weak or

excessive looseness in the suspension arm parts on one side, "kneeback" on one side.

CAR STEERS DOWN OFF CROWNED ROADS BUT STEERS NORMALLY ON FLAT ROADS

This condition is usually caused by excessive positive caster on one or both front wheels. Other causes are weak shock absorber and/or front spring on one side, excessive looseness in the front suspension arm pins or bushings on one side.

CAR WANDERS AND STEERS ERRATICALLY

If this condition is found on cars having power steering it is an excellent idea to have the power steering thoroughly checked and if necessary reconditioned or overhauled before condemning the balance of the car. On cars with conventional steering the most common causes are: incorrect caster, operating with under-inflated or wrong sized tires, bent spindle, excessive looseness in the front suspension parts.

CAR STEERS HARD

In cars with front suspension or individually sprung front wheels, practically the only cause of hard steering is binding pats.

This condition may also be caused by using tires which are too big for the car and operating with excessively low air pressure in the tires.

Hard steering is an unusual condition in individually sprung front suspension cars.

UNEQUAL OR EXCESSIVE TIRE WEAR

Tire wear breaks itself into several different subclassifications which will be listed as follows:

Tires Cup on the Outside Edge Only and Wear in a Ripple

Pattern

Generally caused by incorrect camber-toe-in.

Tires Wear Evenly in the Center Faster than the Outer Edges

This condition is most always caused by operating with too much air pressure in the tires.

Tires Wear and Scuff on both Outer Edges but not in Center

This condition is almost always caused by operating with insufficient tire pressure.

Tires Wear Evenly on the Outer Edge much Faster than the Center or Inner Edge

This condition is frequently caused by the driving habits of the operator. Since many can be taken into turns at excessive high speeds and are driven in such a manner, the outside edge of the tire tends to slip and scuff as it goes around the turns, thus causing an even wear on the outer edge. This is not to be confused with the cupped type wear which is caused by incorrect camber-toe-in.

One Tire Wears much more Quickly than the Tire on the Opposite Wheel

This condition is usually caused by a "kneeback" or the car failing to track properly. However, it may also be caused by different quality tires being used on the front of the car or tires of different size being used on the front of the car.

This condition may also be caused by a bent spindle on that side.

Tire Squeals on Turns

This condition is generally caused by the tires being under-inflated or the driver attempting to take a curve at too high speed.

If the tires squeal badly and the car is moving slowly around a turn it generally indicates that there is a bent steering arm and that "toe-out on turns" is incorrect because of a bent steering arm.

SUSPENSION, FRONT REPAIR

REPLACE WHEEL BEARINGS AND SEALS

Place jack under lower suspension arm. Remove hub cover and grease cap. Remove spindle nut, keyed washer and outer bearing. Slide off hub and drum. In some cases drum wear may require loosening of brake adjustment.

At this point brakes and drums should be inspected for any non-standard condition.

With hub and drum on bench, remove seal and inner bearing. Thoroughly clean all parts. Drive out inner and outer races of roller type. Use care not to mar the bearing surfaces.

Pack bearings thoroughly with approved lubricant. In replacing cups a bearing race driver is best. If a punch is used be sure it is blunt and drive parts in carefully to avoid any cocking of the bearings.

Install new grease seal in hub. Reassemble hub and drum on spindle and replace outer bearing, key washer and nut.

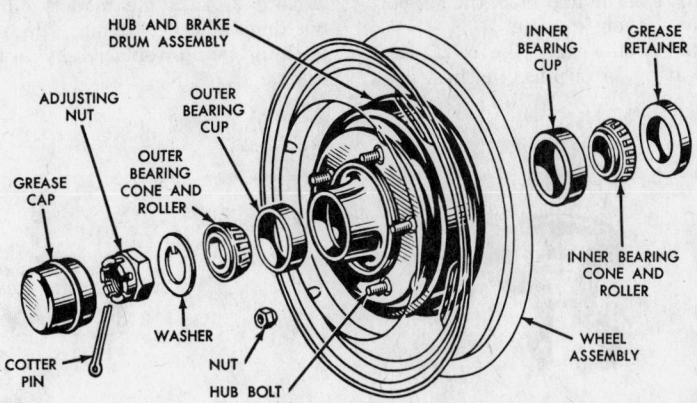

Exploded View of Front Wheel Bearings and Grease Seal

A common method of adjustment is to tighten to zero clearance and back off to first cotter pin castellation. Some manufacturers recommend tightening to an approximate 10 to 12 ft. lb. then back off nut one flat or 1/6 turn. If cotter pin holes do not lineup, loosen slightly more to enter cotter pin.

Readjust brake if necessary and install grease cap and hub cover. Remove jack.

REPLACE KING PINS AND BUSHINGS

King pin and bushings can be placed in two general classes; (A) with bushings in knuckle, (B) with bushings in spindle. Generally the first type will be found in General Motors cars and some Dodges.

In all cases, jack up the car and remove the hub and drum as described under the Wheel Bearing section.

(A) Remove backing plate to knuckle bolts and lift assembly with brakes from knuckle. Suspend it with a piece of wire to prevent damage to brake hose.

Drive out lock pin or bolt. With sharp punch remove top welsh plug. Now drive pin and bottom welsh plug down thru knuckle and support.

Drive bushings from spindle and replace with new. Be sure when driving bushing that grease holes line up with those in knuckle.

Align ream bushings to a snug running fit for the new king pin.

Insert the king pin through the top of spindle, support, thrust bear-ing (with shims to control up-and-down play) and bottom of spindle. Keep king pin in proper rotation so that lock pin can be entered. Replace lock pin or bolt securely. Replace upper and lower welsh plugs.

Reinstall backing plate with steering arms and properly lubricate. Reinstall hubs and drums and wheels and remove jacks.

Alignment should be checked. For cars using the bushed wheel support

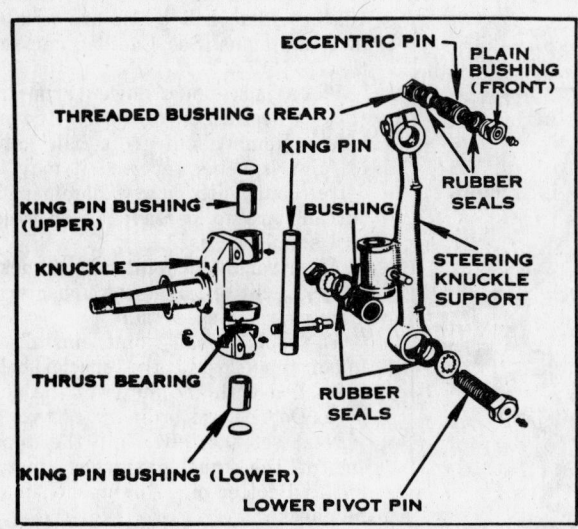

(A)

Exploded View of King Pins and Bushings

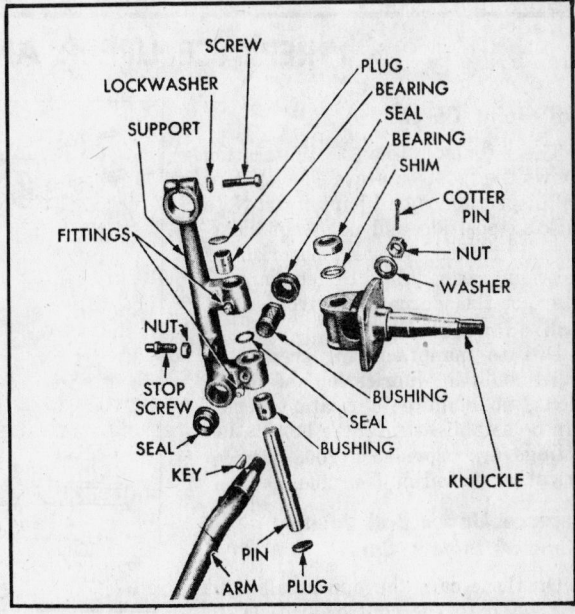

(B)

Exploded View of the King Pin and Bushing

SUSPENSION, FRONT REPAIR

(B), proceed as above. The exception being that the bushings will be removed, replaced and fit in the support instead of the knuckle.

Note 1. Some early Chevrolets have full-floating king pins. In these cars no reaming will be required. Other procedures are the same.

Note 2. In some models only one bushing will be found. The second bushing being replaced by a needle bearing.

Studebaker and Rambler use a modified version of knuckle to support assembly. Service proceedures are similar to the above king pin methods. See illustrations.

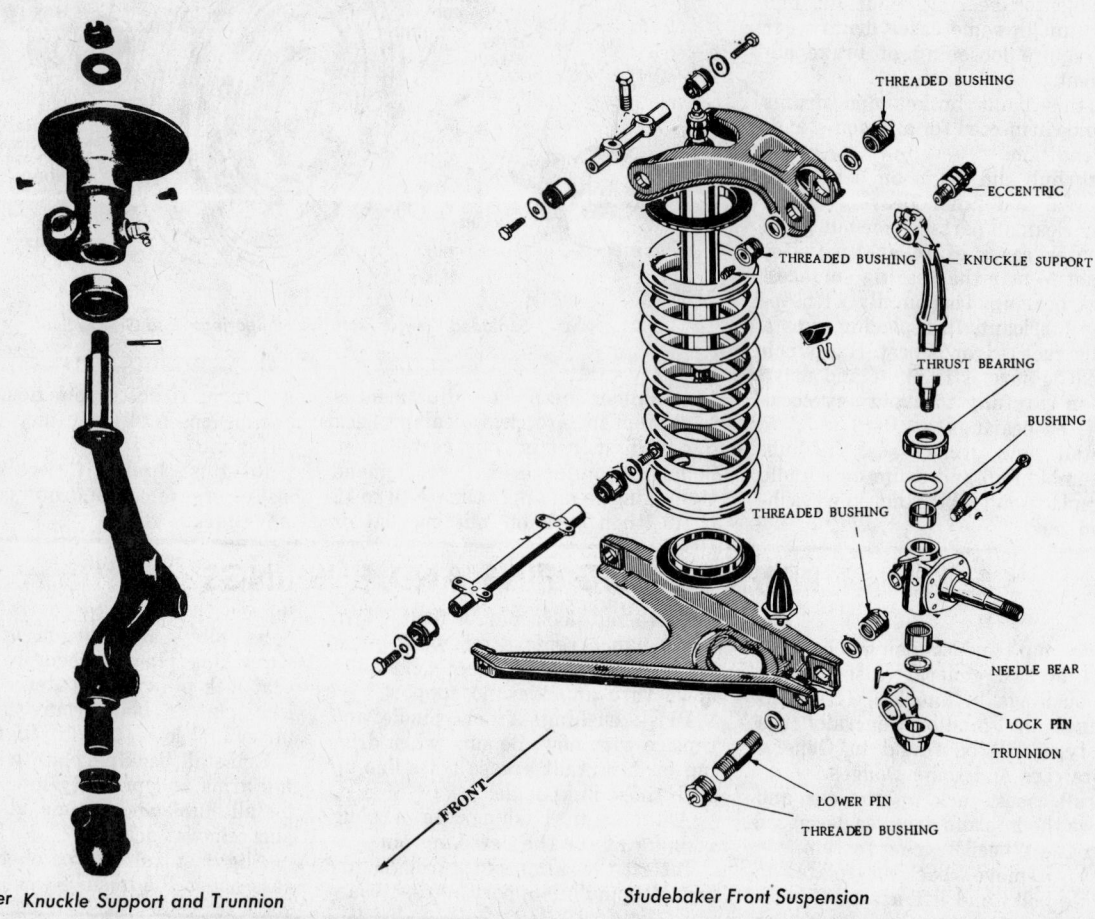

Rambler Knuckle Support and Trunnion

Studebaker Front Suspension

REPLACE UPPER AND LOWER BALL JOINTS

Ball Joint Checks

The former Fig. 6 illustration shows the most accurate way for visual inspection of ball joint wear. Note jacking position and points of clearance indicated, visual inspection of ball joints is required to determine if they are the source of the trouble.

Ball Joint Lubrication

Due to manufacturing trends toward built-in lubrication of these parts, no definite lubrication period can be established. Where lubrication fittings are provided a 2000-mile lubrication period is desirable.

Replace Upper Ball Joint— General Motors Cars

On these cars the upper ball joint is riveted to the control arm, (with the exception of early Buicks and Cadillacs that are bolted in. Starting

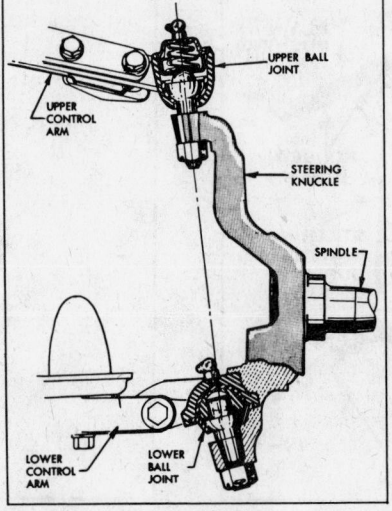

Ball Joint Arrangement on 1957 Buick Typical of most General Motors Cars

1961 Cadillac ball joints are pressed into the arms. See Cadillac car section).

Place jack under lower arm and raise wheel clear of floor. Remove wheel. Remove nut from ball joint. If joint is being renewed it may be driven out with heavy hammer. If threads are to be saved a spreader tool should be used.

After removing joint from knuckle support, cut off rivets at upper arm. Drilling rivet eases this job.

To replace ball joint, install in upper arm, using the special bolts furnished with the joint for the purpose. Do not use ordinary bolts.

Next set the taper into the upper end of the knuckle support, install nut and cotter pin. Alignment should be checked.

Replace Lower Ball Joint— General Motors Cars

This operation is the same as above, except Corvair and Tempest.

The lower ball joint on the Tempest and 1960 Corvair is threaded into the lower arm. The joint has a self-tapping thread. Use 1-9/16" socket for Tempest and 1⅝" for Corvair.

The lower ball joint on the Corvair starting 1961 is pressed in. The Greenbriar models are riveted.

Alignment should be checked after nut and cotter pin.

Replace Upper and/or Lower Ball Joint—Ford Motor Co. Cars

Both upper and lower ball joints are riveted to their respective arms. The replacement operation is the same as that shown above for the upper joints on General Motors cars.

Replace Upper Ball Joint—Chrysler Motor Corp. Cars

On these cars the upper ball joint is threaded into the control arm.

Place jack under lower arm and release load on torsion bar. (See car section). Raise wheel clear of floor. Remove wheel. Remove nut from ball

joint. If joint is being renewed it may be driven with heavy hammer. If threads are to be saved a spreader tool should be used.

After removing joint from knuckle suport, the ball joint can be unscrewed from the suport arm. Tools C-3560, C-3561 or C-3714 are recommended for this operation.

In replacing the ball joint be sure to engage the threads in the control arm squarely. Torque to 125 ft. lbs. If this torque can not be obtained check for bad threads in arm or on joint. Install new balloon seal over joint.

Place joint in knuckle and install nut. Torque to 55 ft. lbs. on Valiant, Lancer, and (Dart models beginning 1963), and 100 ft. lbs. on all others. Reload and adjust torsion bar and reset height.

Replace Lower Ball Joint—Chrysler Motor Corp. Cars

This operation is the same as replacing the upper ball joint described in above section.

Note: Exception: Dodge, Plymouth, Valiant and Lancer starting 1962. On these cars the lower ball joint is integral with the steering arm and is not serviced separately. To service this unit: Remove the upper arm bumper. Raise car so that front suspension is under no load. If jacks are used a support must be placed between jack and "K" member.

Remove the wheel and drum assembly. Remove the two lower bolts holding the steering arm to the backing plate.

Remove tie rod end from the steering arm. Do not damage seal. Remove the ball joint stud from lower control arm. A spreading tool will aid this operation.

To replace, install new seal on ball joint. Bolt the steering arm to the backing plate. Insert the ball joint into control arm and torque nut to 100 ft. lbs.

Reinstall the tie rod end. Install drum and wheel. Reload and adjust torsion bar and reset height. (See car section).

Removing Corvair Ball Joint from Support Arm

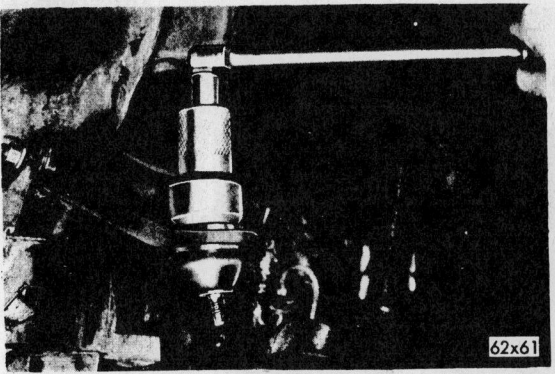

Removing Upper Ball Joint-Chrysler Motor Corporation Cars

CASTER, CAMBER AND TOE-IN ADJUSTMENT

GENERAL MOTORS CARS AND STUDEBAKER USING KING PINS

(EXCEPT CADILLAC AND 1955-56 OLDSMOBILE)

Both caster and camber are adjusted at the eccentric pin in the outer end of the upper support arm.

Set the car up on a front end stand and check caster, camber and toe-in readings.

Make a note of each reading so as to determine which way the eccentric adjuster should be turned.

Remove the grease fitting from the front bushing and, working through the grease fitting with an Allen wrench, engage the eccentric pin at

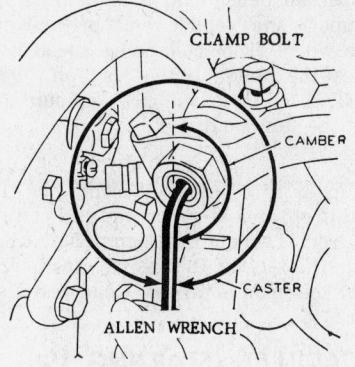

Fig. 27—Caster and camber are adjusted at the same pin. Maximum camber can be obtained in not more than ½ turn from the correct caster setting—Chevrolet shown

the front. Loosen the clamp bolt in the top of the knuckle support which will leave the eccentric pin free to turn.

Now turn the eccentric pin (which has a right hand thread) first in the direction which tends to correct caster, that is, the pin would be turned counterclockwise to increase caster or clockwise to decrease caster. If it is necessary to decrease caster, turn the pin clockwise until the correct caster setting is attained and then rock it back and forth until the correct camber reading is obtained. Since both adjustments are made at the same pin it is sometimes absolutely impossible to get exact readings. However, it will be found that with very little error in caster, the correct camber reading can be obtained.

Recheck the caster and camber readings on the front end stand and, once certain they are correct, secure the clamp bolt and reinstall the lubrication fitting.

Toe-in is adjusted either at the tie rod itself or on some models sleeves at the ends of each of the tie rods.

Where the tie rod itself is turned, simply loosen the clamp bolt which holds the tie rod to the end assembly and turn the rod. In cases where sleeves are used at the end of the tie rods, loosen the clamp bolts which prevent the sleeve from turning and turn the sleeve until the correct toe-in is obtained.

When checking front suspension readings, always be sure to check king pin slant as well as camber in order to determine if the spindle is bent. See Fig. 27.

CADILLAC, 1955-56 OLDSMOBILE AND CHRYSLER CORP. CARS USING KING PINS

On this model caster and camber are both adjusted at the eccentric bushing in the outer end of the upper support arm.

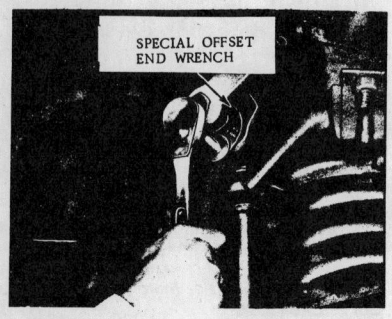

SPECIAL OFFSET END WRENCH

Fig. 28—Special offset end wrench in position on the hex end of the threaded eccentric bushing—Cadillac shown

Set the car up on the front end stand and take caster, camber and toe-in readings.

If adjustments are needed to caster

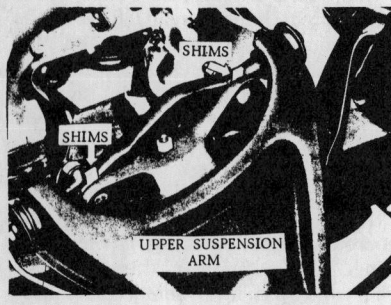

SHIMS

SHIMS

UPPER SUSPENSION ARM

Fig. 29—Location of shims used between the upper suspension arm inner shaft and the frame bracket—Chevrolet shown

and camber, loosen the clamp bolt at the top of the suspension arm and, using a special offset end wrench, such as is shown in Fig. 28, turn the eccentric bushing until the correct caster reading is obtained. From that point a maximum of one-half turn will produce the correct camber setting. If it does not produce the correct camber setting, parts are bent or misaligned or new parts should be installed.

The final thalf turn (maximum) will have very little effect on the caster setting.

Toe-in is adjusted either at the tie rod itself or at sleeves at the end of the tie rod. Loosen the tie rod (or sleeve) clamp screw and turn the tie rod (or sleeve) until the correct toe-in is obtained.

Secure the knuckle support clamp bolt and road test the car.

GENERAL MOTORS CORP. (EXCEPT CADILLAC AND THUNDERBIRD STARTING 1961) AND FORD MOTOR CO. CARS USING BALL JOINTS

On this construction caster and camber are controlled by shims placed between the frame back bracket and the inner shaft of the upper suspension arm. See Fig. 29.

Place the car on a front end stand and check caster, camber and toe-in and record the readings before starting to make corrections.

To increase caster remove shims from the front bolt and place that shim at the back bolt.

When correct caster setting has been obtained recheck camber, and to increase camber remove an equal thickness of shims from both the front and the back bolt.

Keep in mind when loosening the bolts to remove the shims that the upper suspension arm is helping to support the vehicle and preventing the wheel from collapsing so do not back the bolts all the way off, just back them off a sufficient amount to get the shims out.

Toe-in is adjusted at either the tie rod itself or a sleeve at the end of the tie rod. Loosen the clamp bolt and turn the tie rod (or sleeve) until correct toe-in is obtained. Road test the car.

CADILLAC (STARTING 1961)

Caster is adjusted by lengthening or shortening tie-struts at the frame cross member. The splash shield must be removed to get access. Lengthening the struts by loosening the front and tightening the rear nuts produces more negative caster. Reverse this for more positive caster. One turn makes approximately $\frac{1}{2}°$ change.

Camber change is made by turning the camber eccentric at the upper ball joint. This eccentric is between the ball stud and the upper knuckle. Loosen ball stud nut and tap up to free eccentric enough to rotate it in its mounting. Keep the stud to the rear of the eccentric to hold the steering arm angle within limits.

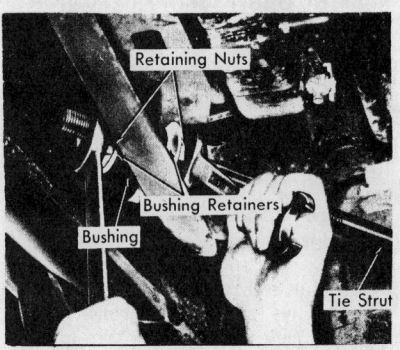

Retaining Nuts

Bushing Retainers

Bushing

Tie Strut

Caster Setting Starting 1961 Cadillac

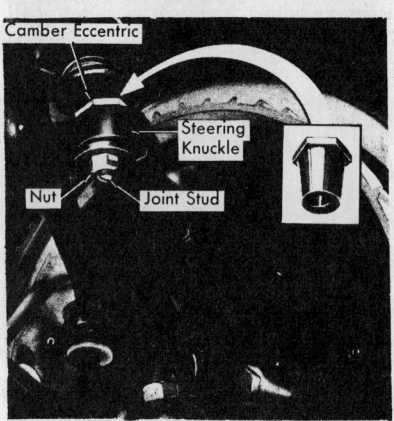

Camber Eccentric

Steering Knuckle

Nut

Joint Stud

Camber Setting Starting 1961 Cadillac

THUNDERBIRD STARTING 1961

Camber

Adjust camber by removing or adding shims between the pivot bracket of the front suspension lower arm and the mounting bracket on the underbody in the engine compartment.

Removal of shims will move the lower ball joint inward, **increasing camber**. **Adding shims** will move the lower ball joint outward, **decreasing camber**. Adjusting shims are available in various thicknesses. A 1/16" change in shim thickness will influence camber angle about $\frac{1}{3}°$. Total shim stack thickness should not exceed 11/16."

Caster

The caster adjustment is made at

the lower control arm strut, front end.

Adjust caster by loosening the retaining washers, nuts and bolts. Lift the strut so that the strut serations will be freed from the serations on the lower arm. **Moving the lower control arm forward** on the strut lengthens the effective length of the strut, **increasing caster.**

Moving the lower control arm rearward on the strut shortens the effective length of the strut, **decreasing caster.**

RAMBLER

Eccentric Type

On these cars caster and camber are controlled by eccentrics at the inner mounting of the lower suspension arm. These eccentrics are actually large washers which fit into a recess in the lower suspension bracket. See Fig. 30.

Put the car on a front end stand and take caster, camber and toe-in readings.

To increase caster, turn the eccentric on the rear suspension arm towards the outside of the car and the eccentric on the front arm towards the middle of the car.

To increase camber, turn both eccentrics an equal amount towards the middle of the car.

Set caster first and then camber.

To turn the eccentric, it is necessary to loosen the lower mounting bolt.

When correct readings are obtained secure the lower mounting bolt.

Adjust toe-in by turning the sleeve at the outer end of each tie rod.

When correct toe-in is obtained secure the sleeve clamp bolts.

Shim Type

On these Nash and Rambler models caster and camber is controlled by shims between the lower suspension arm and the frame mounting. See Fig. 31.

Set the car up on the front end stand and check caster, camber and toe-in.

To increase caster, remove one shim at a time from behind the back mounting bolt at the lower suspension arm and add that shim to the front mounting bolt. To decrease caster, remove the shim from the front mounting bolt and add it to the back mounting bolt. To increase camber, add shims in an equal thickness to both bolts. To decrease camber, remove shims of equal thickness from both bolts.

Set caster first and then camber.

Toe-in is set at the sleeve at the outer end of the tie rod. Loosen the clamp bolts and turn in each tie rod until correct setting is obtained and then secure the clamp bolts at the ends of the sleeve.

CHRYSLER MOTOR CORP. CARS—1957-58

Caster is controlled by shims placed between the frame bracket and the upper suspension arm mounting brackets. See Fig. 32.

Set the car up on a front end stand and set caster, camber and toe-in.

Caster is adjusted first. To increase caster, remove a shim from the front bracket and add that shim to the back bracket, keeping in mind that the upper suspension arm is partially supporting the car. Loosen the bolts just a sufficient amount to get the shims out, no more.

To decrease caster, remove a shim from the rear bolt and add that shim to the front bolt. To increase camber remove an equal thickness of shims from both bolts. To decrease camber, add an equal thickness of shims to both bolts.

Toe-in is adjusted at the sleeves at the outer end of each tie rod. Loosen the clamp bolts and turn the sleeves until correct toe-in is obtained and then secure the clamp bolts.

Road test the car.

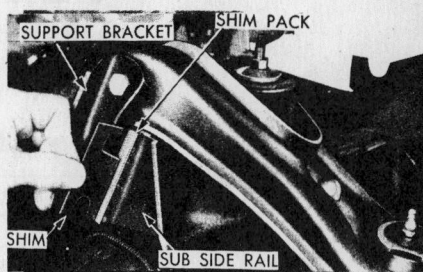

Fig. 32—Shim pack used between the frame bracket and the upper bracket—De Soto 1958 shown

CHRYSLER MOTOR CORP. CARS—STARTING 1959

The upper control arm attaching bolts are fitted thru eccentric washers, one welded to head and one keyed to threaded end.

To set caster or camber, loosen nuts and rotate bolts with washers.

Turning both bolts equal amounts will adjust camber. Turning either front or rear bolt, one more than the other, will adjust caster.

Always recheck caster, camber and toe-in when any one is moved.

Fig. 30—Caster and Camber Eccentrics—
Rambler

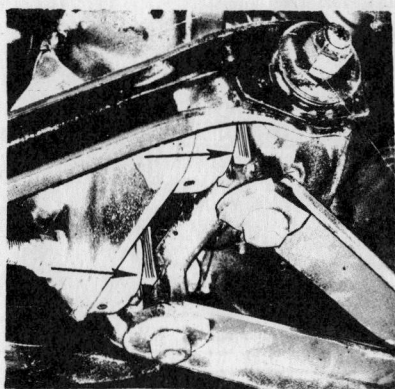

Fig. 31—Shims are used back of the frame bracket at the lower suspension arm—
Rambler shown

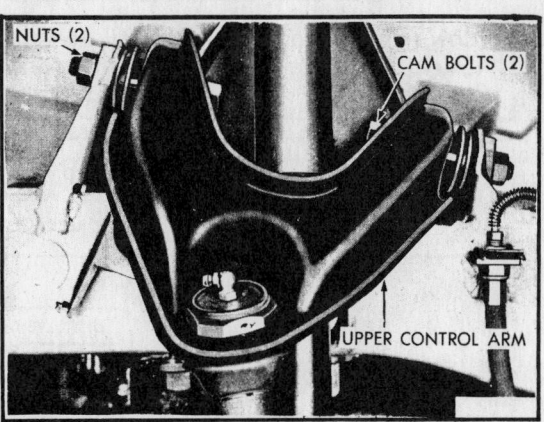

Caster and Camber Adjusting Points —Chrysler

AIR CONDITIONING

FUNDAMENTAL PRINCIPLES OF REFRIGERATION

The principle of operation of the refrigeration system is based on the theory that temperature is a measurement of heat. Heat is a form of energy and when an object cools, it does not absorb cold, but rather it loses heat to a colder object or substance nearby.

When a liquid boils it absorbs heat without changing temperature. For example, when heat is added to water the temperature of the water will rise until it reaches 212° F. If the heat remains the water will boil but the temperature will remain at 212° F. The heat being absorbed by the water is changing the water to steam (vapor) rather than raising the temperature.

Freon, the refrigerant used in air conditioning systems, boils below zero. Thus, if it were exposed to air at normal room temperature, it would absorb heat from the surrounding air and boil, immediately changing to vapor.

When heat is removed from this vapor it will condense back into a liquid.

The temperature at which substances will boil or condense is affected by pressure. If pressure is increased, the liquid will not boil until a higher temperature is reached. Thus we can prevent Freon from boiling if it is kept under high pressure. If this high pressure is suddenly released, Freon will immediately boil.

When the pressure of a vapor is increased, the temperature at which it will condense is also raised.

Operation of Simplified Refrigeration System

Any refrigeration system employs the principles described above. A simple refrigeration system would have five basic parts. They are the compressor, condenser, receiver, expansion valve and evaporator. The refrigeration cycle of this system (Fig. 1) is as follows:

Freon gas under low pressure is drawn into the compressor where it is compressed to a high pressure. The process of compressing also heats the

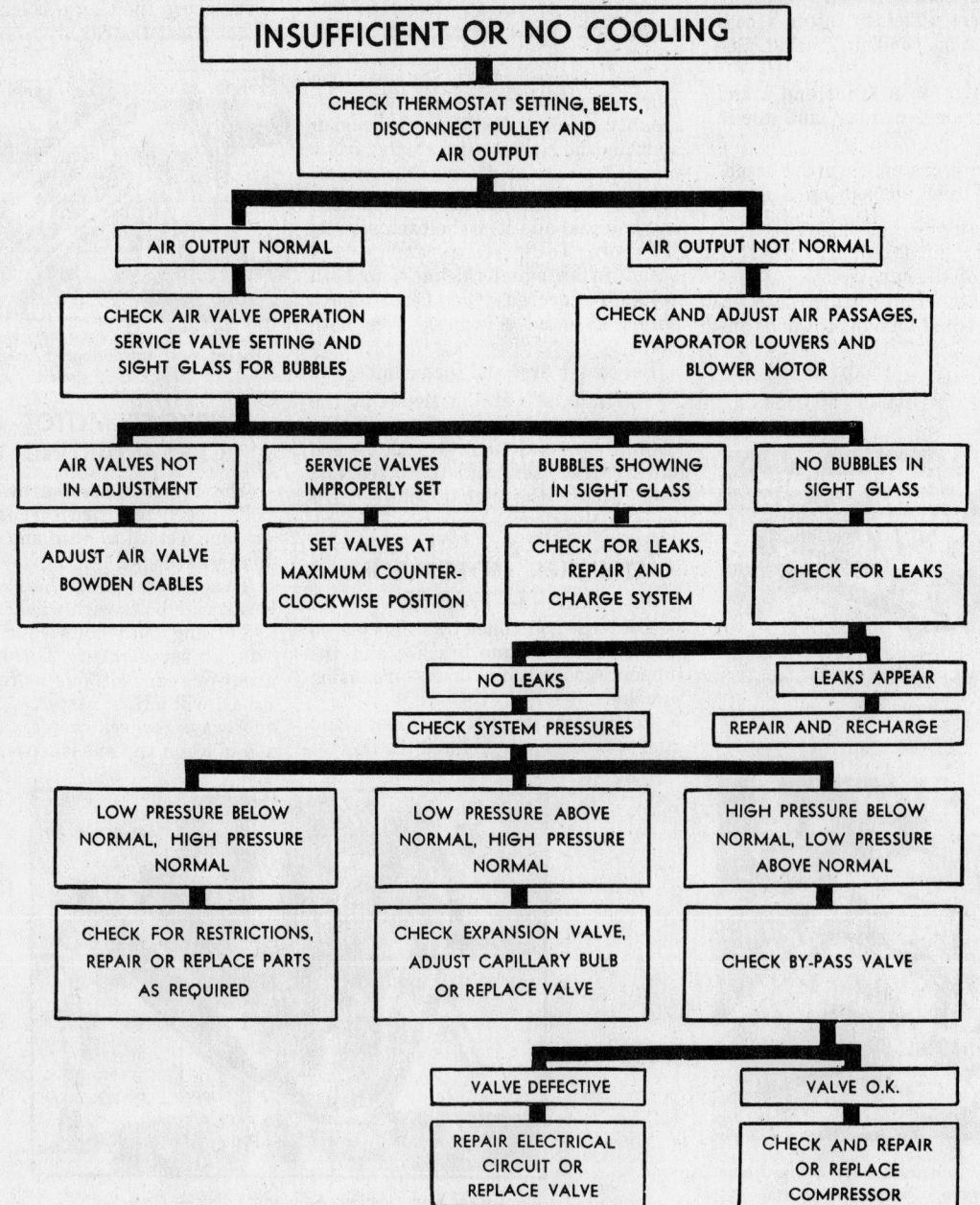

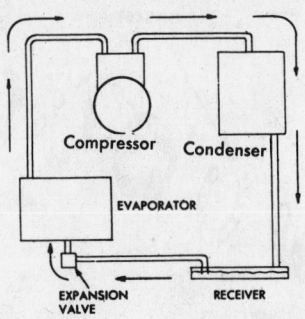

Fig. 1—Simplified Refrigeration Cycle

gas. The hot Freon gas then flows into the condenser where it cools by giving off heat to the metal of the condenser, then to the air passing over the condenser.

As the Freon gas cools while passing through the condenser, it condenses into a liquid under high pressure. From the condenser, the high pressure Freon liquid passes into the receiver. The receiver acts as a reservoir to supply liquid to the expansion valve. Liquid Freon under high pressure passes from the receiver to the expansion valve located at the inlet of the evaporator.

The expansion valve meters Freon into the evaporator where a low pressure is maintained by the suction of the compressor. As the Freon enters this low pressure area it will immedi-

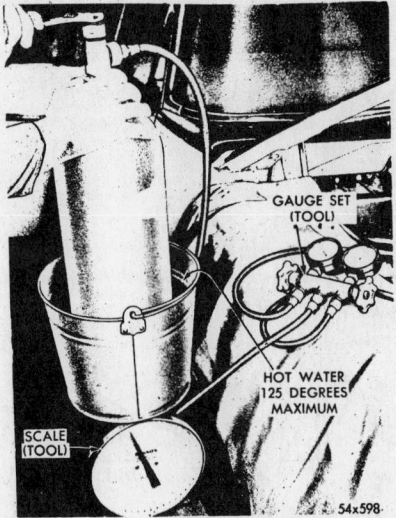

Fig. 8—Charging System

ately begin to boil by absorbing heat from the surrounding area. As the liquid Freon passes through the evaporator it will continue to boil until all the liquid has changed to a vapor at low pressure. The flow of Freon is regulated by the expansion valve so that the Freon will remain in the

evaporator long enough to completely vaporize.

From the evaporator the Freon gas is drawn back into the compressor to repeat the cycle.

Charging the System

With the system completely evacuated of all air and moisture and the manifold gage set installed, make sure the manifold gage valves are closed to the maximum clockwise position, then connect the center line of the gage set to a tank of Freon (Fig. 8). Now crack open the valve on the Freon tank and loosen the center line at the gage set to purge the line of air. Allow Freon to escape for a few seconds, then tighten the center line at the gage and close the Freon tank valve.

Place the Freon tank and bucket on a suitable scale and record the total weight.

Set both service valves to the midway position, start the engine and set at a fast idle, then turn on the air conditioning control to run the compressor. Now open the Freon tank valve, then slowly open the manifold gage low pressure valve. Note the weight of the scale and allow Freon to enter the system until a full charge is taken in (see Freon Capacity Chart), then close the manifold gage low pressure valve. Operate the system for about five minutes at a fast idle with the control lever in the COLD position and the blower at high speed, then observe the sight glass. This check

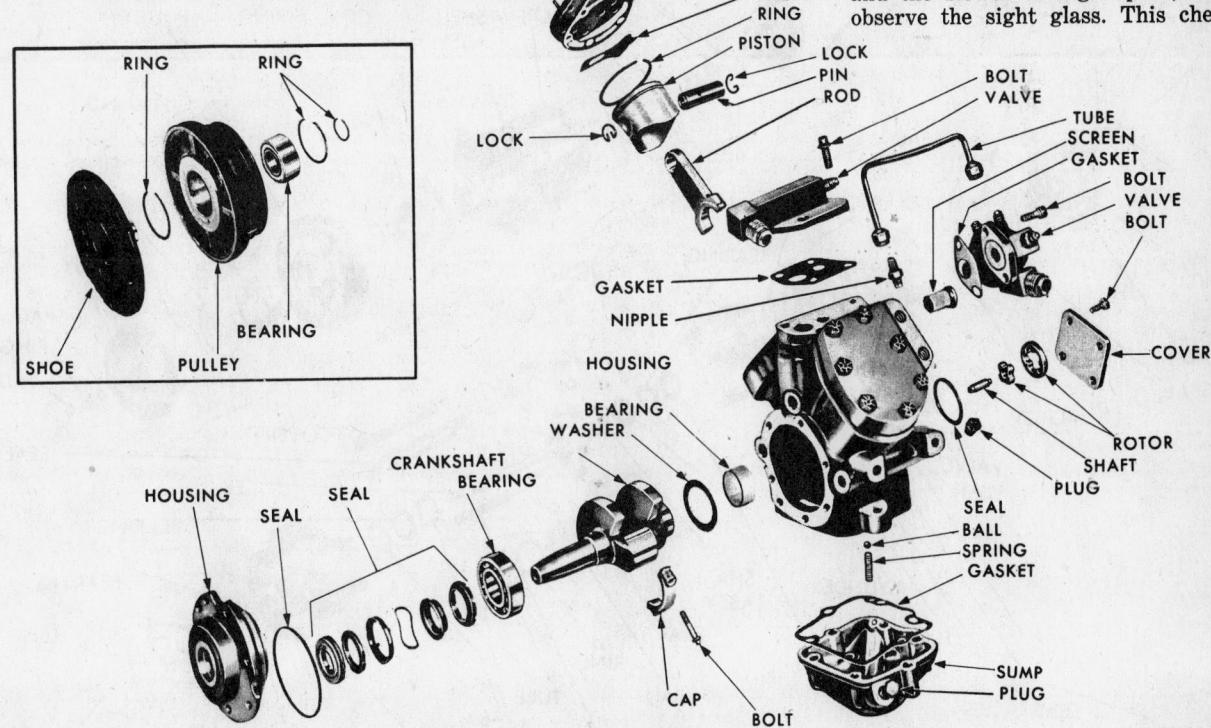

Typical Chrysler Compressor

AIR CONDITIONING —Continued

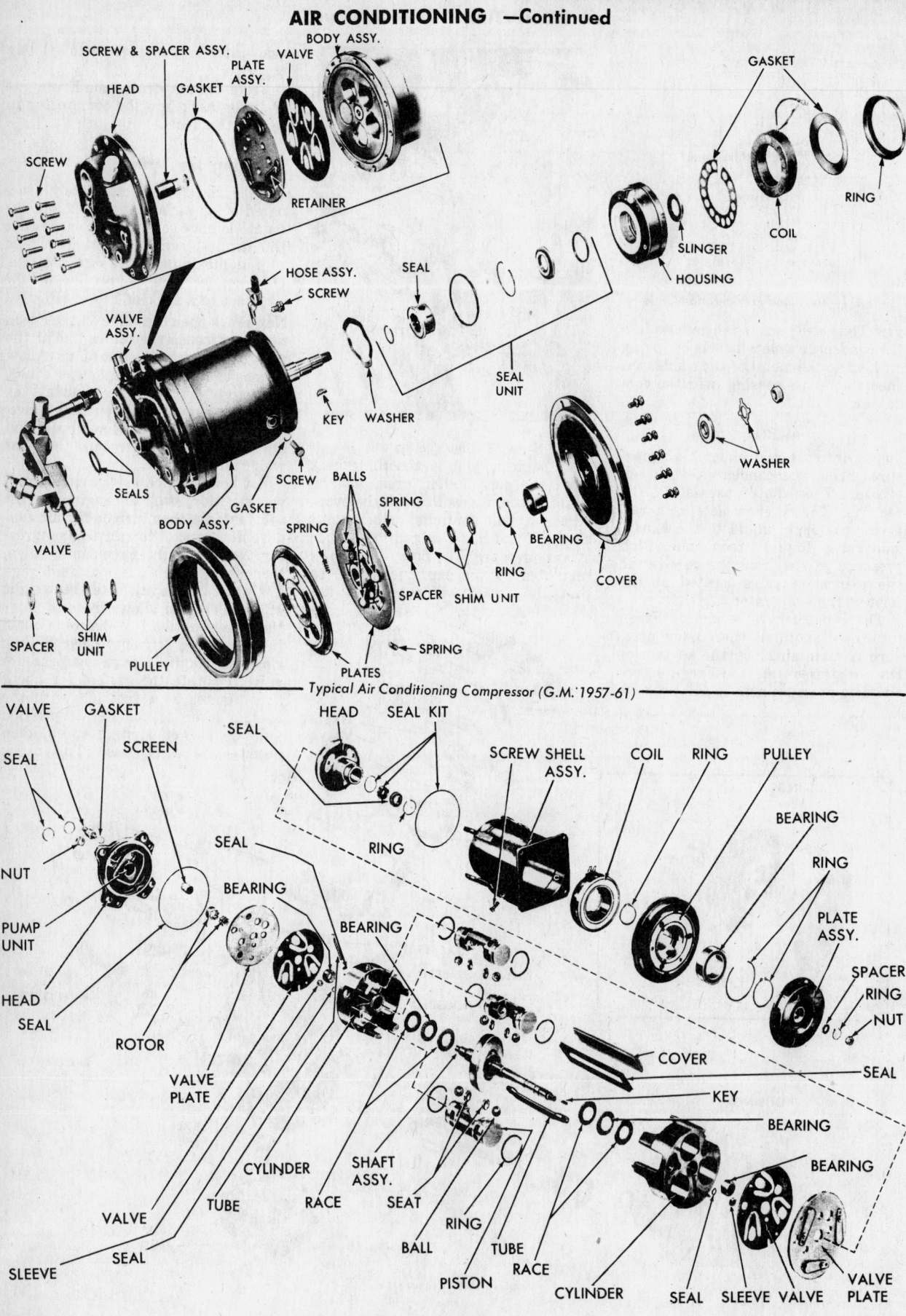

SCREW & SPACER ASSY.

HEAD

GASKET

PLATE ASSY.

VALVE

BODY ASSY.

SCREW

RETAINER

GASKET

RING

COIL

SLINGER

HOUSING

HOSE ASSY.

SCREW

SEAL

VALVE ASSY.

KEY

WASHER

SEAL UNIT

WASHER

SEALS

SCREW

GASKET

BODY ASSY.

BALLS

SPRING

SPRING

SPRING

RING

SPACER

SHIM UNIT

BEARING

COVER

VALVE

SPACER

SHIM UNIT

PULLEY

PLATES

SPRING

Typical Air Conditioning Compressor (G.M. 1957-61)

VALVE

GASKET

SEAL

SCREEN

HEAD

SEAL KIT

SCREW SHELL ASSY.

COIL

RING

PULLEY

BEARING

SEAL

NUT

SEAL

RING

RING

PUMP UNIT

BEARING

PLATE ASSY.

HEAD

SEAL

BEARING

SPACER

RING

NUT

ROTOR

COVER

SEAL

VALVE PLATE

KEY

CYLINDER

BEARING

TUBE

SHAFT ASSY.

BEARING

VALVE

RACE

SEAT

RING

SLEEVE

SEAL

BALL

PISTON

TUBE

RACE

CYLINDER

SEAL

SLEEVE

VALVE

VALVE PLATE

Typical Air Conditioning Compressor (G.M. 1962)

AIR CONDITIONING

AIR CONDITIONING —Continued

should be made with room temperature at 75° F. or better. If bubbles appear in the sight glass, crack open the manifold low pressure valve and slowly allow Freon to enter the system until the bubbles clear up, then close the valve.

When satisfied that the system is operating properly, shut off the air conditioning control and stop the engine. Then turn both service valves counterclockwise to shut off the service ports. Close both gage valves and the Freon tank valve and disconnect the center gage line from the tank.

NOTE: A considerable amount of Freon will collect in the high pressure

line. Since some of this Freon will have condensed into liquid, it will require an appreciable amount of time to allow the pressure to bleed off. Open the high pressure valve slowly and let the Freon out through the center gage line, then remove the gage set and replace the protective caps on the service valve stems and ports.

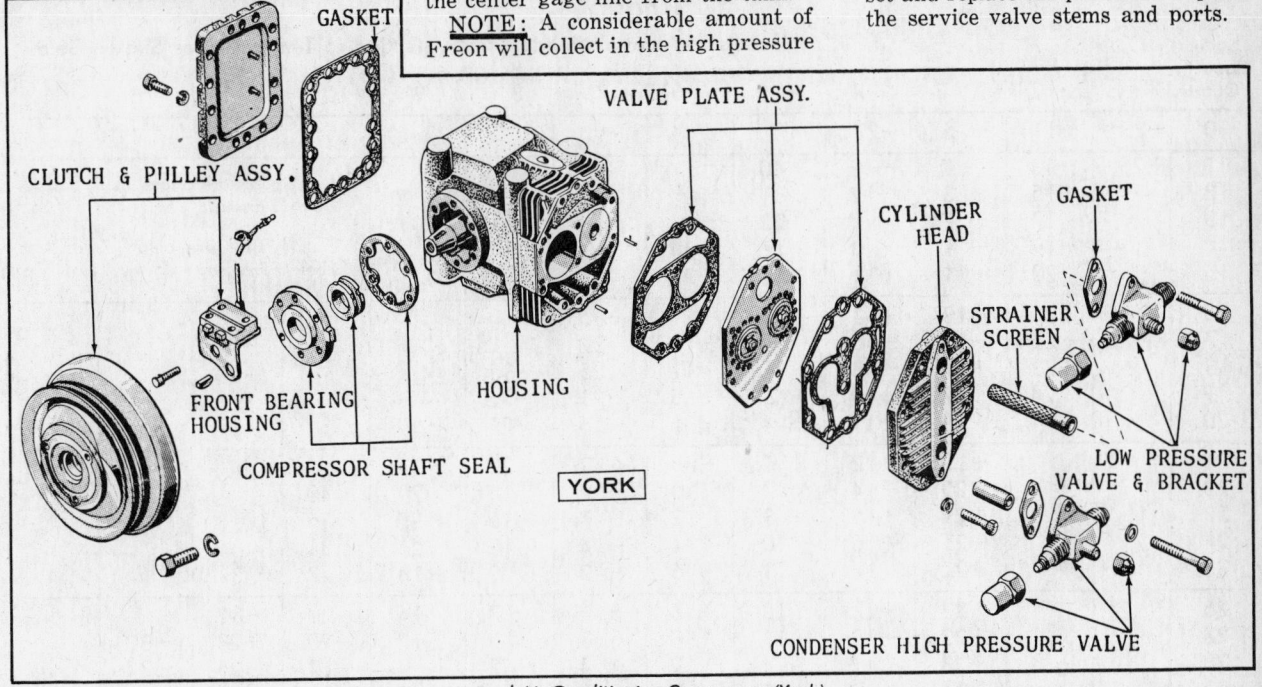

Ford Air Conditioning Compressor (York)

Ford Air Conditioning Compressor (Tecumseh)

ANTI-FREEZE CHART

TEMPERATURES SHOWN IN DEGREES FAHRENHEIT

+32 IS FREEZING

ALCOHOL

Quarts of Alcohol Needed for Protection to Temperatures Shown Below

Cooling System Capacity Quarts	1	2	3	4	5	6	7	8	9	10	11	13	13
10	+23°	+11°	−5°	−27°									
11	+25	+13	0	−18	−40°								
12		+15	+3	−12	−31								
13		+17	+7	−7	−23								
14		+19	+9	−3	−17	−34°							
15		+20	+11	+1	−12	−27							
16		+21	+13	+3	−8	−21	−36°						
17		+22	+16	+6	−4	−16	−29						
18		+23	+17	+8	−1	−12	−25	−38°					
19		+24	+17	+9	+2	−8	−21	−32					
20			+18	+11	+4	−5	−16	−27	−39°				
21			+19	+12	+5	−3	−12	−22	−34				
22			+20	+14	+7	0	−9	−18	−29	−40°			
23			+21	+15	+8	+2	−7	−15	−25	−36			
24			+21	+16	+10	+4	−4	−12	−21	−31			
25			+22	+17	+11	+6	−2	−9	−18	−27	−37°		
26			+22	+17	+12	+7	+1	−7	−14	−23	−32		
27			+23	+18	+13	+8	+3	−5	−12	−20	−28	−39°	
28			+23	+19	+14	+9	+4	−3	−9	−17	−25	−34	
29			+24	+19	+15	+10	+6	−1	−7	−15	−22	−30	−39°
30			+24	+20	+16	+11	+7	+1	−5	−12	−19	−27	−35

+ Figures are above Zero, but below Freezing.

— Figures are below Zero. Also below Freezing.

ETHYLENE GLYCOL

Quarts of Ethylene Glycol Needed for Protection to Temperatures Shown Below

Cooling System Capacity Quarts	1	2	3	4	5	6	7	8	9	10	11	12	13	14
10	+24°	+16°	+4°	−12°	−34°	−62°								
11	+25	+18	+8	−6	−23	−47								
12	+26	+19	+10	0	−15	−34	−57°							
13	+27	+21	+13	+3	−9	−25	−45							
14			+15	+6	−5	−18	−34							
15			+16	+8	0	−12	−26							
16			+17	+10	+2	−8	−19	−34	−52°					
17			+18	+12	+5	−4	−14	−27	−42					
18			+19	−14	+7	0	−10	−21	−34	−50°				
19			+20	+15	+9	+2	−7	−16	−28	−42				
20				+16	+10	+4	−3	−12	−22	−34	−48°			
21				+17	+12	+6	0	−9	−17	−28	−41			
22				+18	+13	+8	+2	−6	−14	−23	−34	−47°		
23				+19	+14	+9	+4	−3	−10	−19	−29	−40		
24				+19	+15	+10	+5	0	−8	−15	−23	−34	−46	
25				+20	+16	+12	+7	+1	−5	−12	−20	−29	−40	−50
26					+17	+13	+8	+3	−3	−9	−16	−25	−34	−44
27					+18	+14	+9	+5	−1	−7	−13	−21	−29	−39
28					+18	+15	+10	+6	+1	−5	−11	−18	−25	−34
29					+19	+16	+12	+7	+2	−3	−8	−15	−22	−29
30					+20	+17	+13	+8	+4	−1	−6	−12	−18	−25

For capacities over 30 Quarts divide true capacity by 3. Find quarts Anti-Freeze for the 1/3 and multiply by 3 for quarts to add.

ANTI-FREEZE INFORMATION

BOILING POINTS OF SOLUTIONS
AND VOLUME PER CENT OF ALCOHOL AND ETHYLENE GLYCOL

Freezing Point of Solution	Alcohol Volume %	Alcohol Boils at	Ethylene Glycol Volume %	Ethylene Glycol Boils at
20°F.	12	196°F.	16	216°F.
10°F.	20	189°F.	25	218°F.
0°F.	27	184°F.	33	220°F.
−10°F.	32	181°F.	39	222°F.
−20°F.	38	178°F.	44	224°F.
−30°F.	42	176°F.	48	225°F.

NOTE: Above boiling points are at sea level. For every 1,000 feet of altitude, boiling points are approximately 2°F. lower than those shown. For every pound of pressure exerted by the pressure cap, the boiling points are approximately 3°F. higher than those shown.

TABLES FOR INCREASING THE FREEZING PROTECTION OF ANTI-FREEZE SOLUTIONS ALREADY INSTALLED

ALCOHOL

Number of Quarts of Alcohol Anti-Freeze Required to Increase Protection

Cooling System Capacity Quarts	From +20°F. to					From +10°F. to					From 0°F. to			
	0°	−10°	−20°	−30°	−40°	0°	−10°	−20°	−30°	−40°	−10°	−20°	−30°	−40°
10	2	2¾	3½	4	4½	1	2	2½	3¼	3¾	1	1¾	2½	3
12	2½	3¼	4	4¾	5¼	1¼	2¼	3	3¾	4½	1¼	2	2¾	3½
14	3	4	4¾	5½	6	1½	2½	3½	4½	5	1¼	2½	3¼	4
16	3¼	4½	5½	6¼	7	1¾	3	4	5	5¾	1½	2¾	3¾	4¾
18	3¾	5	6	7	7¾	2	3¼	4½	5¾	6½	1¾	3	4¼	5¼
20	4	5½	6¾	7¾	8¾	2	3¼	5	6¼	7¼	1¾	3½	4¾	5¾
22	4½	6	7½	8½	9½	2¼	4	5½	6¾	8	2	3¾	5¼	6½
24	5	6¾	8	9¼	10½	2½	4½	6	7½	8¾	2¼	4	5½	7
26	5¼	7¼	8¾	10	11¼	2¾	4¾	6½	8	9½	2½	4½	6	7½
28	5¾	7¾	9½	11	12	3	5¼	7	8¾	10·¼	2½	4¾	6½	8
30	6	8¼	10	11¾	13	3	5½	7½	9¼	10¾	2¾	5	7	8¾

Test radiator solution with proper tester. Determine from the table the number of quarts of solution to be drawn off from a full cooling system and replace with concentrated anti-freeze, to give the desired increased protection. For example, to increase protection of a 22-quart cooling system containing Alcohol anti-freeze, from +10°F. to −20°F. will require the replacement of 5½ quarts of solution with concentrated anti-freeze.

ETHYLENE GLYCOL

Number of Quarts of Ethylene Glycol Anti-Freeze Required to Increase Protection

Cooling System Capacity Quarts	From +20°F. to					From +10°F. to					From 0°F. to			
	0°	−10°	−20°	−30°	−40°	0°	−10°	−20°	−30°	−40°	−10°	−20°	−30°	−40°
10	1¾	2¼	3	3½	3¾	¾	1½	2¼	2¾	3¼	¾	1½	2	2½
12	2	2¾	3½	4	4½	1	1¾	2½	3¼	3¾	1	1¾	2½	3¼
14	2¼	3¼	4	4¾	5½	1¼	2	3	3¾	4½	1	2	3	3½
16	2½	3½	4½	5¼	6	1¼	2½	3½	4¼	5¼	1¼	2¼	3¼	4
18	3	4	5	6	7	1½	2¾	4	5	5¾	1½	2½	3¾	4¾
20	3¼	4½	5¾	6¾	7½	1¾	3	4¼	5½	6½	1½	2¾	4¼	5¼
22	3½	5	6¼	7¼	8¼	1¾	3¼	4¾	6	7¼	1¾	3¼	4½	5½
24	4	5½	7	8	9	2	3½	5	6½	7½	1¾	3½	5	6
26	4¼	6	7½	8¾	10	2	4	5½	7	8¼	2	3¾	5½	6¾
28	4½	6¼	8	9½	10½	2¼	4¼	6	7½	9	2	4	5¾	7¼
30	5	6¾	8½	10	11½	2½	4½	6½	8	9½	2¼	4¼	6¼	7¾

Test radiator solution with proper hydrometer. Determine from the table the number of quarts of solution to be drawn off from a full cooling system and replace with undiluted anti-freeze, to give the desired increased protection. For example, to increase protection of a 22-quart cooling system containing Ethylene Glycol (permanent type) anti-freeze, from +20°F. to −20°F. will require the replacement of 6¼ quarts of solution with undiluted anti-freeze.

FOREIGN CAR TUNE-UP SPECIFICATIONS

MAKE AND MODEL	PLUG	IGNITION SYSTEM						VALVES				CAPACITY		WHEEL ALIGNMENT		
	Gap	Firing Order	Pt. Gap	Cam Angle Deg.	No. 1 Cyl. Location	Ign. Timing Mark Deg.	Mark Location	Tappet Clearance In.	Tappet Clearance Ex.	Mark Location	Inlet Opens	Water U.S.A. Qts.	Oil U.S.A. Qts.	Caster Deg.	Camber (Deg.)	Toe-in in.
A.C.—Britain																
Ace, Aceca	.017	153624	.015	......	......	12½B	......	.020H	.020H	Fly	12½	8½	8.4	5	1P to 2P	1/16
Ace, Aceca	.019	153624	.015	......	......	5B	......	.012H	.012H	FCC	TC	8½	7.2	5	1P to 2P	1/16
Ace, Aceca, 1961-62	.017	153624	.015	......	......	12½B	......	.013H	.013H	Fly	21	8½	......	5	1P to 2P	1/16
ALFA-ROMEO—Italy																
Giulietta	......	1342	.015	......	F	8B	Fly	.016C	.022C	Fly	22	6½	......	......	0	⅛
Giulietta Veloce	......	1342	.015	......	F	8B	Fly	......	......	......	34	6½	......	......	0	⅛
2000, 1959	.017	1243	.015	......	F	10B	Fly	.017C	.019C	Fly	31¼	9¾	5.5	......	2¾ to 4	7/64
Giulietta Berlina & T1	.025	1342	.015	......	F	8B	Fly	.019C	.021C	Fly	25⅓	6½	6.2	......	0	7/64
Giulietta Sprint & Spider	.024	1342	.015	......	F	8B	Fly	.019C	.021C	Fly	25⅓	6½	6.2	......	0	7/64
Giulietta Veloce Sprint & Spider	.024	1342	.015	......	F	8B	Fly	.015C	.021C	Fly	34	6½	6.2	......	0	7/64
Giulietta Sprint Special	.024	1342	.015	......	F	8B	Fly	.011C	.019C	Fly	46	6½	6.2	......	0	7/64
2000 Berlina, 1960	.018	1243	.015	......	F	10B	CP	.017C	.019C	CP	31¾	9¾	5.5	......	1 to 1½	7/64
2000 Spider, 1960	.024	1243	.015	......	F	7B	CP	.017C	.021C	CP	31¾	9¾	5.5	......	1 to 1½	7/64
ALPINE—France																
A108-850	......	1342	......	......	......	7B	......	.020	.030	......	7	4¾	......	......	......	......
A108-904	......	1342	......	......	......	7B	......	.020	.030	......	20	4¾	......	......	......	......
ALVIS—Britain																
TD-21	.025	153624	.014	......	F	5B	Fly	.009H	.012H	Fly	13	12	7.2	1½	1	1/16
TD-21, 1961-62	.025	153624	.014	30	F	5B	VD	.009H	.012H	VD	13	12	7.2	1½	1	1/16
ARMSTRONG-SIDDELEY—Britain																
Sapphire 346	.031	153624	.015	......	F	5B	CP	.016	.014	CCC	8	20	6.0	1	2	3/16
Star Sapphire	.030	153624	.015	......	F	4B	Fly	.008	.008	CCC	12	20	6.0	1½	1	0 to 1/16
Star Sapphire & Limousine	.028	153624	.015	......	F	4B	Fly	.008	.008	CCC	12	20	6.0	¼P to ¾P	¾ to 1¼	0 to 1/16
ASTON-MARTIN—Britain																
DB3	.022	153624	.012	......	F	10B	Fly	.010C	.010C	Fly	17½	17	9.6	2¼	2¾	⅛
DB4	.022	153624	.012	......	F	11B	CD	.011C	.013C	CD	25½	17	9.6	2½	1	⅛
DB4	.022	153624	.015	36	F	11B	CD	.010C	.011C	CD	28	17	9.6	1 to 1¼	½ to 1½	⅛
DB4GT	.016	153624	.015	36	F	7B	CD	.010C	.011C	CD	47½	17	9.6	1 to 1¼	½ to 1½	⅛
AUSTIN—Britain																
A35, A40	.024	1342	.014	......	F	5B	CP	.012C	.012C	Ca	5	5	4.2	3	1	1/16 to ⅛
A95, A105	.024	153624	.014	......	......	TC	CP	.012C	.012C	Ca	5	15	7.2	1¼	¾ to1	0 to ⅛
7	.025	1342	.015	60	......	TC	Fly	.012C	.012C	CC	5	6¼	......	1½	1	⅛
A55	.025	1342	.015	60	F	5B	CP	.015H	.015H	CC	TC	7½	4.2	1½	¾ to 1	1/16 to ⅛
A99	.025	......	.015	35	F	TC	CP	.012H	.012H	CC	5	12½	......	1¼	1	⅛
AUSTIN-HEALEY—Britain																
Sprite	.025	1342	.015	......	......	5B	......	.012C	.012C	CC	5	6	4.2	3	1	1/16 to ⅛
100-6	.025	153624	.015	......	......	6B	FC	.012H	.012H	CC	5	10	6.0	2	1	1/16 to ⅛
3000	.025	153624	.015	35	F	5B	CP	.012H	.012H	CC	5	11½	6.9	2	1	1/16 to ⅛
AUTO UNION—Germany																
1000, 1000S	.025	123	.015	142	R	20½B	......	......	......	......	......	8½	......	¼ to ¾	1 to 2	0 to 5/64
1000Sp	.025	123	.015	142	R	18¾	......	......	......	......	......	8	......	¼ to ¾	1 to 2	0 to 5/64
BENTLEY—Britain																
Continental	.025	142635	.020	44	......	2B	Fly	.006	.012	Fly	TC	16	......	½N to 1P	0	1/16 to 5/32
S	.025	142635	.020	44	......	2B	Fly	.016	.012	Fly	TC	16	19.2	1N to ½P	0	1/16 to 5/32
Continental, S2	.026	A-1	.020	A-3	FR	2B	Fly		......	Fly	20B	12½	......	0	0	1/16 to 5/32
BERKELEY—Britain																
Twosome	......	123	......	......	......	......	......	......	......	......	......	No	......	......	......	......
QB95, QB105	.018	12	.015	......	......	......	CC	......	......	......	30B	No	......	......	2½	......
B95, B105	.022	12	.015	......	......	......	CC	......	......	......	30B	No	......	......	2½	......
Bandit	.023	1243	.015	......	......	10B	TCC	.010	.017	......	10B	......	......	5	½P	1/16
BIANCHINA—Italy																
110B	.022	......	.022	......	......	10B	FP	.018	.015	TG	9B	No	......	9	1	0 to 5/64
110B Special, 110B, 110D	.022	......	.020	......	......	10B	FP	.015	.015	TG	25B	No	......	9	1	0 to 5/64

A-1 —1,5,4,8,6,3,7,2
A-2 —1,12,9,4,5,8,11,2,3,10,7.6.
A —After Top Center
A-3—1960, 44, 1961-62, 34
B —Before Top Center
C —Cold
CAP—Camshaft Pinion
CC —Crankshaft and Camshaft sprockets

CFB—Camshaft and Front Bearing Cap
CP —Crankshaft Pulley
CT —Crankshaft Pulley and Timing Gear Cover
F —Front
FCC—Flywheel and Crankshaft and Camshaft Sprockets
Fly —Flywheel

FP —Fan Drive Pulley
FR —Front Right
H —Hot
N —Negative
No —None
OFC—Crankcase Front Cover
P —Positive

R —Rear
Ri —Right
TC —Top Center
TCC—Timing Chain Cover
TG —Timing Gears
VD —Vibration Damper

FOREIGN CAR TUNE-UP SPECIFICATIONS—Continued

MAKE AND MODEL	PLUG	IGNITION SYSTEM						VALVES				CAPACITY		WHEEL ALIGNMENT		
	Gap	Firing Order	Pt. Gap	Cam Angle Deg.	No. 1 Cyl. Location	Ign. Timing Mark Deg.	Mark Location	Tappet Clearance in.	Tappet Clearance ex.	Mark Location	Inlet Opens	Water U.S.A. qts.	Oil U.S.A. qts.	Caster (Deg.)	Camber Deg.	Toe-in in.
BMW—Germany																
600	.028	12	.016	160	......	9B	......	.006C	.008C	Fa	22	No	2.5	16	1½	5/64 to 7/64
2.6, 2.6 Luxus, 3.2	.035	A-1	.016	30	FR	8B	VD	.010H	.010H	VD	2	9½	7.0	1	1	7/64
3.2 Super	.035	A-1	.016	30	FR	8B	VD	.010H	.010H	VD	10	9½	7.0	1	1	7/64
503	.035	A-1	.016	30	FR	8B	VD	.010H	.010H	VD	10	10½	7.0	3¼	1	7/64
507	.035	A-1	.016	30	FR	8B	VD	.010H	.010H	VD	19½	10	7.0	3¼	1	7/64
700	.028	......	.016	160	......	10B	Fa	.006C	.008C	Fa	35	No	4.2	14	½	5/64 to 7/64
700 Sp. Cpe.	.028	......	.016	160	......	10B	Fa	.006C	.008C	Fa	55B	No	4.2	14	½	5/64 to 7/64
300 Isetta	.024	......	.016	160	......	7½B	Fa	.006	.008	Fa	6B	No	......	12	½	5/64
2.6, 2.6 Lukus, 3.2	.028	A-1	.016	30	FR	5B	VD	.010	.010	VD	2B	9½	7.0	1	1	7/64
3.2 Super	.028	A-1	.016	30	FR	5B	VD	.010	.010	VD	10B	10½	7.0	1	1	7/64
3200 CS	.028	A-1	.016	30	FR	5B	VD	.010	.010	VD	10B	10½	7.0	1	1	7/64
BORGWARD—Germany																
Isabella	.029	1342	.016	90	R	TC	Fly	.008H	.008H	TG	18	6¼	4¾	2½ to 3½	0 to 1	0
Isabella TS	.029	1342	.016	90	R	4A	Fly	.008H	.008H	TG	18	6¼	4¾	2½ to 3½	0 to 1	0
Combi, Isabella	.025	1342	.016	......	R	TC	Fly	.008H	.008H	TG	18	6¼	4¾	2½ to 3½	0 to 1	0
Coupe, Isabella TS	.025	1342	.016	......	R	4A	Fly	.008H	.008H	TG	18	6¼	4¾	2½ to 3½	0 to 1	0
BIG Borgward	.029	153624	.016	90	F	TC	Fly	.008H	.008H	TG	14B	6¼	......	½ to 1	½ to ½	0
BRISTOL—Britain																
406	.020	153624	.015	......	F	5B	Fly	.010	.012	FCC	36B	......	......	2-2½	½N to ½P	⅛ to 3/16
407	.035	A-4	.017	30	FL	10B	CT	.010	.018	CC	13B	18	......	1	0	⅛
CITROEN—Britain																
2CV	.027	12	.015	......	F	12B	Fly	.008H	.008H	Cap	3	No	2.1	¼	1½	5/32 to 3/16
DS19	.026	1342	.011	......	F	8B	Fly	.008C	.010C	CC	3	9¾	4.0	1¾	0 to ¼N	1/32 to 7/64
1D19	.026	1342	.012	......	F	10	Fly	.008C	.010C	CC	3	8⅜	4.0	1¾	0 to ¼N	1/32 to 7/64
CITROEN—France																
1D19P	.021	1342	.016	......	F	12B	......	.008C	.010C	......	½	8¼	4.0	1 to 1½	0 to ½	1/32 to 7/64
DS19	.021	1342	.016	......	F	10B	......	.008C	.010C	......	½	9¾	4.0	1 to 1½	0 to ½	1/32 to 7/64
2CV	.021	1342	.016	......	......	12B	......	.008H	.008H	......	½	No	2.1	3¾	1½	1/32 to 7/64
1D19F	.021	1342	.016	......	F	12B	......	.008C	.010C	......	½	8¼	4.0	1 to 1½	0 to ½	1/32 to 7/64
2CH, AM16	.025	......	.016	......	......	12B	......	.008H	.008H	......	......	No	......	16½	1½	1/32 to 7/64
DAF—Holland																
600	.028	1.2	.015	......	Ri	5B	CP	.004C	.004C	CC	14A	No	2.1	1	1	⅛
600	.028	1.2	.015	......	......	2A	CP	.006C	.006C	CC	14	No	2.1	1	1	⅛
750	.034	1.2	.018	......	......	4B	CP	.006	.006	CP	14	No	2.1	1	1	5/64 to 5/32
DAIMLER—Britain																
Majestic	.025	153624	.014	60	F	10B	VD	.013	.013	TCC	13	11¾	7.5	3	1½	⅛
DK400	.025	153624	.014	60	F	7B	Fly	.015	.015	TCC	13	18	8.2	2	1½	⅛
SP250	.025	......	.016	45	F	10B	VD	.012	.012	CC	13	......	6.0	2	2	⅛
DQ450, DR450	.025	A-4	.015	45	FL	10B	VD	.012	.012	CC	13	15	......	3	1½	⅛
DATSUN—Japan																
PL311-U	.030	......	.020	53	......	15B	CP	.014	.014	TG	14B	4¾	......	1½	1½	3/32 to ⅛
SPL213	.030	......	.020	53	......	15B	CP	.014	.014	TG	14B	6½	......	3	1½	3/32
P312-U, PL312-U	030	......	.020	53	F	15B	CP	.014	.014	CC	15	4¾	......	1½	1½	3/32 to ⅛
DENZEL—Germany																
1300	.027	1,4,3,2	.014	......	......	10B	FP	.008C	.008C	......	32	No	......	½ to ¾	2½	0 to 7/64
DEUTSCH-BONNET—France																
Le Mans, HBR-5	.026	12	.012	60	F	44B	......	.010	.010	No	32	No	......	1	1	7/64 to 5/32
DKW—Germany																
Junior	.020	123	.016	142	R	19¾	......	......	......	......	......	7½	......	¾	¾	0 to 5/64
Junior Deluxe	.020	123	.016	......	......	21½B	......	......	......	......	......	No	......	¼ to ¾	½ to 1	5/64 to ⅛
FACEL VEGA—France																
Facellia	......	1342	......	......	......	......	......	......	......	......	......	12	5.0	......	......	......
FAIRTHORPE—Britain																
Atometa	.020	12	.015	......	F	6B	TCC	.010	.010	......	30	No	......	¾P	2	⅛
Electron Minor	.025	1342	.015	......	F	6½B	CP	.010	.010	CP	10	5	......	¾P	2	⅛
Electron	.018	1342	.015	......	F	5B	......	.006	.006	Fly	20	5	......	0	2	⅛
Atom Major	.025	1342	.015	......	F	6B	CP	.010	.010	CP	10	5	......	¾P	2	⅛

A-1 —1,5,4,8,6,3,7,2
A-2 —1,12,9,4,5,8,11,2,3,10,7,6,
A —After Top Center
B —Before Top Center
C —Cold
CAP —Camshaft Pinion
CC —Crankshaft and Camshaft sprockets

CFB —Camshaft and Front Bearing Cap
CP —Crankshaft Pulley
CT —Crankshaft Pulley and Timing Gear Cover
F —Front
Fly —Flywheel
FP —Fan Drive Pulley

FR —Front Right
H —Hot
N —Negative
No —None
OFC —Crankcase Front Cover
P —Positive
R —Rear

Ri —Right
TC —Top Center
TCC —Timing Chain Cover
TG —Timing Gears
VD —Vibration Damper

FOREIGN CAR TUNE-UP SPECIFICATIONS—Continued

MAKE AND MODEL	PLUG Gap	IGNITION SYSTEM Firing Order	Pt. Gap	Cam Angle (Deg.)	No. 1 Cyl Location	Ign. Timing Mark Deg.	Mark Location	VALVES Tappet Clearance in.	Tappet Clearance ex.	Mark Location	Inlet Opens	CAPACITY Water U.S.A. qts.	Oil U.S.A. qts.	WHEEL ALIGNMENT Caster Deg.	Camber Deg.	Toe-in in.
FAIRTHORPE—Britain																
Zeta	.025	......	.015	......	F	......	......	......	......	......	......	......	......	0	2	⅛
Electrina	.025	1342	.015	......	F	26B	CP	.010	.010	CP	10	5½	......	3	2	⅛
Electron Minor, Electrina	.025	1342	.015	......	F	10B	......	.010	.010	......	10	5½	......	3	3	1/16
Electron	.025	1342	.015	......	F	12B	......	.007	.007	......	20	5½	......	3	3	1/16
FERRARI—Italy																
250 Granturismo	......	A-2	.027	......	FR	26B	Fly	.022	.023	Fly	24	7½	7.4	8	1	7/64
410 Superamerica	......	A-2	.027	......	FR	26B	Fly	.022	.023	Fly	24	7½	......	8	1	7/64
FIAT—Italy																
500	.029	12	.018	......	......	10B	CT	.008C	.008C	CC	9	No	2.0	8 to 10	¾ to 1¼	7/64
600	.029	1342	.018	......	......	10B	CT	.006C	.006C	CC	4	4½	3.1	8 to 10	¾ to 1¼	2½
600 Multipla	.021	1342	.018	......	......	10B	CT	.004C	.004C	CC	10	7	3.1	5½ to 6½	¼ to ¾	0 to 1/32
1100/103D	.029	1342	.018	......	......	TC	CT	.004C	.004C	CC	16	4¾	3.2	1¼	½	3/64 to ⅛
1200, 1200 Granluce	.029	1342	.018	......	......	3A	CT	.004C	.004C	CC	16	4¾	5.7	1¼	½	3/64 to ⅛
1400B	.024	1342	.018	......	......	TC	CT	.006C	.006C	CC	15	4¾	5.7	2 to 2½	½ to 1	5/64 to 5/32
1900B	.024	1342	.018	......	......	TC	CT	.006C	.006C	CC	10	9½	5.7	2 to 2½	½ to 1	5/64 to 5/32
500	.029	12	.020	78	......	10B	CT	.018C	.015C	CC	9	No	2.0	9	1	0 to 5/64
500 Sport	.026	12	.026	78	......	10B	CT	.015C	.015C	CC	25	No	2.0	9	1	0 to 5/64
600 Sedan	.026	1342	.018	50	......	10B	CT	.006C	.006C	CC	4	4½	3.1	9	1	1/32 to ⅛
600 Multipla	.026	1342	.018	50	......	10B	CT	.006C	.006C	CC	4	7	3.1	6	½	0 to 3/64
1100 Family Car, Std. & Del.	.026	1342	.018	58	F	TC	CT	.004C	.004C	CC	16	4¾	3.2	2¼	½	3/64 to ⅛
1200 Granluce & Cabriolet	.026	1342	.018	58	F	3A	CT	.004C	.004C	CC	16	4¾	3.2	2¼	½	3/64 to ⅛
1800 Sedan & Station Wagon	.026	153624	.016	40	F	10B	CT	.008C	.008C	CC	20	2¼	......	1½	1	5/64 to 5/32
1500 Cabriolet	.022	1342	.018	58	F	TC	Cfb	.012C	.014C	CC	20	6¼	......	1	½	3/64 to ⅛
2100 Sedan	.026	153624	.016	40	F	5B	CT	.008C	.008C	Ofc	20	2¼	5.3	1½	1	5/64 to 5/32
1200 Cabriolet	.026	1342	.018	58	F	TC	CT	.004	.004	CC	16	4¾	3.2	2¼	½	3/64 to ¼
1100 Sta. Wag., Exp. Spec.	.026	1342	.018	58	F	TC	CT	.004	.004	CC	16	4¾	......	2¼	½	3/64 to ¼
1300, 1500	.026	1342	.018	51	F	12B	CT	.008	.008	CC	9	7	......	2½ to 2½	¼ to ¾	1/32 to ⅛
1800B, 2300 Familiar & Spec.	.026	153624	.016	40	F	12B	CT	.008	.008	CC	20	9	......	1¼ to 1¾	¾ to 1¼	5/64 to 5/32
2300 S. Coupe	.026	153624	.016	40	F	10B	CT	.008	.010	CC	19	9	......	1¼ to 1¾	¾ to 1¼	5/64 to 5/32
FMR—Germany																
KR200, KR201	......	......	......	......	......	30B	......	......	......	......	......	No	......	5	0 to 1	5/64
TG500						TC						No	......	7	0 to 1	5/64
KR200, Deluxe	.028	......	.017			5B						No	......	5	3	5/64
FORD—Britain																
Popular	.021	1243	.015	60	F	4B	TCC	.013C	.016C	CC	9½	5	2.5	4¼	1½	1/64
Escort, Squire, Anglia, Prefect	.025	1243	.015	60	F	5B	CP	.013C	.013C	CC	3½	5¾	2.8	1 to 2½	¾ to 2¼	1/16 to ⅛
Consul Mk. II	.032	1243	.015	55	F	8B	CP	.014C	.014C	CC	17	9	4.5	½N to ½P	1¼P to 2¼P	1/16 to ⅛
Zephyr, Zodiac	.032	153624	.015	32	F	8B	CP	.014C	.014C	CC	17	11	5.0	½N to ½P	1¼P to 2¼P	1/16 to ⅛
Escort	.025	1243	.015	60	F	5B	CP	.013C	.013C	CC	3½	6	2.8	1 to 2½	¾ to 2¼	1/16 to ⅛
Prefect	.030	1243	.015	55	F	10B	CP	.008C	.018C	CC	10	5¾	2.8	1 to 2½	¾ to 2¼	1/16 to ⅛
Anglia	.030	1243	.015	55	F	10B	CP	.008C	.018C	CC	10	5⅛	2.8	3	1	1/16 to ⅛
Anglia, 1961-62	.026	1243	.015	60	F	10B	CT	.008C	.018C	CC	10	6	2.8	1½ to 3	½ to 2	⅛ to 3/16
375 Consol Mk. II	.032	1243	.015	60	F	8B	CT	.014C	.014C	CC	17	10¾	4.5	½N to ½P	1¼ to 2¼	1/16 to 3/16
Anglia Estate Car, 1962	.026	1234	.015	30	......	10B	CT	.008C	.018C	CC	17	5½	......	¾ to 2½	1 to 2½	⅛ to 3/16
335 Consol Capri, 315	.026	1243	.015	30	......	6B	CT	.008C	.018C	CC	17	5¼	......	¾ to 2½	1 to 2½	⅛ to 3/16
Zephyr, Zodiac Mk. II	.032	153624	.015	35	F	8B	CT	.014C	.014C	CC	17	13¼	5.0	½ to ½	1¼ to 2¼	1/16 to 3/16
FORD—Germany																
Taunus 12M	.029	1243	.018	49	F	11B	CP	.015H	.015H	TG	5	7½	3.2	¾ to 2¼	0 to 1	3/32 to ⅛
Taunus 12M	.030	1243	.018	49	F	8B	CP	.015H	.015H	TG	5	7½	3.2	¾ to 2¼	0 to 1	9/32 to 5/16
Taunus 12M Special	.030	1243	.018	49	F	11B	CP	.012H	.014H	TG	26	8¾	3.2	¾ to 2¼	0 to 1	9/32 to 5/16
Taunus 17M	.030	1243	.018	49	F	22B	CP	.011H	.014H	TG	26	8¾	3.2	0 to ⅔	⅚ to 1⅚	5/64 to 3/16
Taunus 12M, 1961-62	.034	1243	.018	49	F	8B	CP	.015	.015	TG	5	7½	3.2	¾ to 2¼	0 to 1	9/32 to 5/16
Taunus 12M Super	.034	1243	.018	49	F	22B	CP	.017	.014	TG	35	7½	3.2	¾ to 2¼	0 to 1	9/32 to 5/16
Taunus 17M—P3T, P3TS	.034	1243	.018	49	F	21B	CP	.011	.014	TG	35	7½	3.2	¼ to 1¼	1 to 2	1/16 to ⅛
Taunus 17M—TS—P3TC	.034	1243	.018	49	F	TC	CP	.011	.014	TG	35	7½	3.2	¾ to 1¼	1 to 2	1/16 to ⅛
FRAZER—NASH—Britain																
Continental, Grand Turismo, Spyder	.035	A-1	.016	......	FR	......	CP	.010H	.010H	CC	19½	11¼	6.0	3½	1N to 1P	0
FRISKY—Britain																
Convertible, Coupe	.022	12	.020	......	......	......	Fly	......	......	Fly	......	No	......	......	......	......
Sprint	.022	12	.022	......	......	......	......	......	......	......	......	No	......	9	......	⅛

A-1 —1,5,4,8,6,3,7,2
A-2 —1,12,9,4,5,8,11,2,3,10,7,6,
A —After Top Center
B —Before Top Center
C —Cold
CAP —Camshaft Pinion
CC —Crankshaft and Camshaft sprockets
CFB —Camshaft and Front Bearing Cap
CP —Crankshaft Pulley
CT —Crankshaft Pulley and Timing Gear Cover
F —Front
Fly —Flywheel
FP —Fan Drive Pulley
FR —Front Right
H —Hot
N —Negative
No —None
OFC —Crankcase Front Cover
P —Positive
R —Rear
Ri —Right
TC —Top Center
TCC —Timing Chain Cover
TG —Timing Gears
VD —Vibration Damper

FOREIGN CAR TUNE-UP SPECIFICATIONS—Continued

MAKE AND MODEL	PLUG Gap	IGNITION SYSTEM Firing Order	Pt. Gap	Cam Angle Deg.	No. 1 Cyl. Location	Ign. Timing Mark Deg.	Mark Location	VALVES Tappet Clearance in.	Tappet Clearance ex.	Mark Location	Inlet Opens	CAPACITY Water U.S.A. qts.	Oil U.S.A. qts.	WHEEL ALIGNMENT Caster Deg.	Camber Deg.	Toe-In (In.)
GOGGOMOBIL—Germany																
TS-400	.024	....	.014	.....	.....	.....	.....	.....	.....	.....	.....	No	.....	9	5	5/64 to 7/64
T-700	.025	....	.010	.....	.....	5B	Fly	.001C	.001C	Fly	35	No	.....	4	3	5/64 to 7/64
GOLIATH—Germany																
1100, 110B Sedan	.028	1432	.018	45	F	4B	Fly	.008H	.008H	.....	18	8½	3.3	0	1½	0 to 5/64
1100, 1100B Tiger & Empress	.028	1432	.018	45	F	6B	Fly	.008H	.010H	.....	18	8½	3.3	0	1½	0 to 5/64
1100 (40 HP)	.027	1432	.018	.....	.....	4B	.....	.....	.....	.....	.....	8½	3.3	0	1½	0 to 5/64
1100 (55 HP)	.027	1432	.018	.....	.....	6B	.....	.....	.....	.....	.....	8½	3.3	0	1½	0 to 5/64
HEINKEL—Ireland																
T-154	.022	.....	.016	.....	.....	9B	Fly	.006C	.008C	Cap	18½	No	.....	1⅝	2	7/64 to 3/16
T-154	.022	.....	.016	.....	.....	18½A	Fly	.006C	.008C	.....	.....	No	.....	1⅝		7/64 to 3/16
HILLMAN—Britain																
Huskey Ser. I	.025	1342	.015	9	F	6B	CP	.012H	.014H	CC	10	6⅛	4.8	3	¾	¼
Minx Ser. III	.025	1342	.015	9	F	10B	CP	.012H	.014H	CC	10	6⅛	4.8	1¾	¾	⅛ to ¼
Minx Ser. IIIA	.025	1342	.015	.....	F	7B	CP	.012H	.014H	CC	10	6⅛	4.8	1¾	¾	3/16
Minx Ser. IIIB	.025	1342	.015	30	F	7B	CP	.012H	.014H	CC	10	7½	4.8	1¾	¾	¼
Huskey Ser. II	.025	1342	.015	30	F	6B	CP	.012H	.014H	CC	10	7½	4.8	3	¾	3/16
Minx Ser. IIIC	.025	1342	.015	30	F	7B	CP	.012H	.014H	CC	14	7½	4.8	1¾	¾	3/16
Super Minx	.025	1342	.015	30	.....	10B	CP	.012H	.012	.....	14	7	4.8	2	¾	3/16
HINO—Japan																
Contessa PC-10	.024	1342	.016	55	.....	7B	CP	.009	.012	Fly	10	4	.....	10	1⅓	3/16
HOLDEN—Australia																
FC, EK	.031	153624	.014	38	F	2B	Fly	.008	.012	CC	6	9½	.....	1 to 2	0 to 2	1/16 to 3/16
HUMBLER—Britain																
Hawk	.025	1342	.015	9	F	2A	CP	.007	.009	CC	15	12½	6.3	0	¾	⅛
Super Snipe	.025	153624	.015	.....	F	6B	CP	.014	.014	CC	20	15½	9.0	½N	¾	⅛
Hawk	.025	1342	.015	.....	.....	1A	CP	.007	.009	CP	15	12½	6.3	½	¾	⅛
ISETTA—Germany																
300	.024	.....	.016	160	.....	7½B	Fa	.006	.008	Fa	6	No	1.3	12	1½	5/64
JAGUAR—Britain																
2.4 Litre	.030	153624	.015	35	R	6B	Fly	.004C	.006C	Fly	10	12	6.5	½N to 1N	½P to 1P	0 to 1/16
XK150	.025	153624	.015	35	R	6B	VD	.004C	.006C	VD	15	14	7.8	1½P to 2P	½P to 2P	0 to ⅛
3.4 Litre	.025	153624	.015	35	R	2B	Fly	.004C	.006C	Fly	15	13¼	6.5	½N to 1N	½P to 1P	0 to 1/16
Mark VIII	.022	153624	.015	35	R	6B	VD	.004C	.006C	VD	15	13¼	11.5	¼N to ¼P	¾P to 1¼P	⅛ to 3/16
XK150	.025	153624	.015	35	R	9B	VD	.004C	.006C	VD	15	14	7.8	1½P to 2P	½P to 1P	0 to ⅛
Mark IX	.025	153624	.015	35	R	4B	VD	.004C	.006C	VD	15	12	11.5	¼N to ¼P	¾P to 1¼P	⅛ to 3/16
Mark 2 Saloon 2.4 Litre	.025	153624	.015	35	R	8B	Fly	.004C	.006C	Fly	10	12	6.5	0	½P to 1P	0 to 1/16
Mark 2 Saloon 3.4 Litre	.025	153624	.015	35	R	2B	Fly	.004C	.006C	Fly	15	13¼	6.5	0	½P to 1P	0 to 1/16
Mark 2 Saloon 3.8 Litre	.025	153624	.015	35	R	4B	VD	.004C	.006C	VD	15	.....	6.5	0	½P to 1P	0 to 1/16
Mark IX Saloon 3.8 Litre	.025	153624	.015	35	R	4B	VD	.004C	.006C	VD	15	13¼	11.5	½N to ¼P	¾P to 1¼P	⅛ to 3/16
XK150 Roadster 3.4 Litre	.025	153624	.015	35	R	6B	Fly	.004C	.006C	Fly	15	13¼	6.5	1¾P	½P to 1P	0 to ⅛
XK150 Roadster 3.8 Litre	.025	153624	.015	35	R	4B	VD	.004C	.006C	VD	15	13¾	7.8	1¾P	½P to 1P	0 to ⅛
XK150S Roadster 3.4 Litre	.025	153624	.015	35	R	9B	Fly	.004C	.006C	Fly	15	13¾	6.5	1¾P	½P to 1P	0 to ⅛
XK150S Roadster 3.8 Litre	.025	153624	.015	35	R	9B	VD	.004C	.006C	VD	15	13¾	7.8	1¾P	½P to 1P	0 to ⅛
Mk. 2—2.4 Litre	.025	153624	.015	35	R	6B	VD	.004C	.006C	VD	10	12	6.5	¼N to ¼P	½P to 1P	0 to 1/16
Mk. 2—3.4 Litre & 3.8	.025	153624	.015	35	R	TC	VD	.004C	.006C	VD	15	13¼	6.5	¼N to ¼P	½P to 1P	0 to 1/16
Mk. 1X—3.8 Litre	.025	153624	.015	35	R	TC	VD	.004C	.006C	VD	15	13¼	6.5	¼N to ¼P	¾P to 1¼P	⅛ to 3/16
XK150—3.4 Litre	.025	153624	.015	35	R	4B	VD	.004C	.006C	VD	15	.....	7.8	1½P to 2P	½P to 1P	0 to ⅛
XK150, XK150S, 3.8	.025	153624	.015	35	R	.....	VD	.004C	.006C	VD	15	.....	.....	1½P to 2P	½P to 1P	0 to ⅛
XK150S—3.4 Litre	.025	153624	.015	35	R	9B	VD	.004C	.006C	VD	15	.....	.....	1½P to 2P	½P to 1P	0 to ⅛
XK-E, Mk., X	.025	153624	.015	35	R	10B	VD	.004C	.006C	VD	15	19¼	.....	1½P to 2P	0 to ½	1/16 to ⅛
JENSEN—Britain																
541R & Deluxe	.035	153624	.012	.....	F	.....	Fly	.012	.012	Fly	10	15½	9.0	1¼	½	1/16
541S	.035	153624	.012	.....	F	.....	Fly	.012	.012	TG	5	12½	9.0	2	1	0 to 1/16
LAGONDA—Britain																
Rapide	.022	153624	0.15	36	F	20B	VD	.010C	.012C	VD	24	19¼	.....	1 to 1¼	½ to 1½	⅛
LANCIA—Italy																
Appia	.025	1342	.018	.....	FR	15B	Fly	.006C	.008C	.....	15	6	4	0	1	5/32 to ¼
Flaminia Saloon	.022	143652	.018	.....	FL	11B	Fly	.006C	.010C	Fly	11	10	7¼	1	2	5/32 to ¼

A-1 —1,5,4,8,6,3,7,2
A-2 —1,12,9,4,5,8,11,2,3,10,7,6,
A —After Top Center
B —Before Top Center
C —Cold
CAP —Camshaft Pinion
CC —Crankshaft and Camshaft sprockets
CFB —Camshaft and Front Bearing Cap
CP —Crankshaft Pulley
CT —Crankshaft Pulley and Timing Gear Cover
F —Front
Fly —Flywheel
FP —Fan Drive Pulley
FR —Front Right
H —Hot
N —Negative
No —None
OFC —Crankcase Front Cover
P —Positive
R —Rear
Ri —Right
TC —Top Center
TCC —Timing Chain Cover
TG —Timing Gears
VD —Vibration Damper

FOREIGN CAR TUNE-UP SPECIFICATIONS—Continued

MAKE AND MODEL	PLUG Gap	IGNITION SYSTEM Firing Order	Pt. Gap	Cam Angle Deg.	No. 1 Cyl. Location	Ign. Timing Mark Deg.	Mark Location	VALVES Tappet Clearance in.	ex.	Mark Location	Inlet Opens	CAPACITY Water U.S.A. qts.	Oil U.S.A. qts.	WHEEL ALIGNMENT Caster Deg.	Camber Deg.	Toe-in in.
LANCIA—Italy																
Flaminia Coupe	.022	143652	.018	......	FL	11B	Fly	.006C	.010C	Fly	13	10	7¼	1	2	⅛ to ¹⁵⁄₃₂
Flaminia G. T. & Sport	.022	143652	.018	......	FL	11B	Fly	.006C	.010C	Fly	13	10	7¼	3	2	⁵⁄₃₂ to ⅜
Flavia	.022	1324	......			3B		......	......	......		6¾	......	¼ to 1P	2	¹⁄₃₂ to ⁵⁄₆₄
Flaminia Saloon 1962	.022	143652	.018	......	Fly	11B	Fly	.006	.010	Fly	11	10	7¼	¾N to 1¼N	2	⁵⁄₃₂ to ¼
Flaminia Coupe	.022	143652	.018	......	Fly	11B	Fly	.006	.010	Fly	13	10	7¼	¾N to 1¼N	2	⁵⁄₃₂ to ¼
Flaminia G. T. & Sport	.022	143652	.018	......	Fly	11B	Fly	.006	.010	Fly	13	10	7¼	1¾P to 2¼P	2	⁵⁄₃₂ to ⅜
Appia Ser. 111A Sport	.021	1342	.015	......	Fly	......	Fly	.006	.008	Fly	20	6		0	1	⁵⁄₃₂ to ¹⁵⁄₆₄
Flaminia Saloon	.021	143652	.015	......	Fly	......	Fly	.006	.010	Fly	17	10		¾N to 1¼N	2	¹⁄₃₂ to ⅛
LEA-FRANCIS—Britain																
Lynx	.025	153624	.012	......		TC		.014C	.014C	......	85	8	......	2½	1½ to 2	¹⁄₁₆ to ⅛
LLOYD—Germany																
Alexander	.029	12	.016	......		3B	Fly	.006	.008	CS	35	No	2.0	0	2	0 to ¹⁄₁₆
Alexander TS	.029	12	.016	......		TC	Fly	.006	.008	CS	32	No	2.0	0	2	0 to ¹⁄₁₆
Arabella	.029	1432	.018	......		5B	CP	.006	.006	CC	37	6⅜		0	2	¹⁄₃₂ to ⁷⁄₆₄
Arabella 34	.029	1432	.018	......		2B	CP	.006	.006	CC	......			0	2	¹⁄₃₂ to ⁷⁄₆₄
LOTUS—Britain																
Seven	.025	4231	.014	......	F		TG	......	......		5	8	......	5	1P	⅛
Elite (95 HP)	.018	1342	.015	......		2½B	Fly	.006	.008	CC	30	6	4.0	7	1¼ to 1½	⅛ to ³⁄₁₆
Elite (75 HP)	.018	1342	.015	......		2½B	Fly	.006	.008	CC	12	6	4.0	7	1¼ to 1½	⅛ to ³⁄₁₆
MAICO—Germany																
500	.025	12	.016	......	F	30B								3	1½	0 to ¹⁵⁄₆₄
MASERATI—Italy																
3500 GT	.015	153624	.015	......	F	12B		......	......					2	1	¹³⁄₆₄
5000 GT	.015	......	.015	......	FR	12B		......	......			15		2	1	¹³⁄₆₄
MAZAD—Japan																
KRBB, KRBD, KRBC, BRBE	......	12	......	......	LR	10	Fly	......	......		16	No	......	2½	1	
MERCEDES-BENZ—Germany																
180, 190	.037	1342	.018	50	F	8B	VD	.004C	.008C	Cam	12	8	4.0	3 to 4	0 to 1P	0 to ⁵⁄₆₄
180D	......	1342	......		F	......	VD	.007C	.007C	TG	6½	7½	4.0	3 to 4	0 to 1P	0 to ⁵⁄₆₄
190D	......	1342	......		F	......	VD	.006C	.011C	Cam	11	8¼	4.0	3 to 4	0 to 1P	0 to ⁵⁄₆₄
190SL	.029	1342	.018	50	F	9B	VD	.004C	.008C	Cam	17½	8¼	4.3	3 to 4	0 to 1P	0 to ⁵⁄₆₄
219	.029	153624	.014	36	F	1A	VD	.005C	.008C	Cam	10	......	6.3	3 to 4	0 to 1P	0 to ⁵⁄₆₄
220S	.029	153624	.014	36	F	2B	VD	.005C	.008C	Cam	10	10	6.3	3 to 4	0 to 1P	0 to ⁵⁄₆₄
220SE	.023	153624	.014	36	F	2B	VD	.005C	.008C	Cam	29	10	6.3	3 to 4	0 to 1P	0 to ⁵⁄₆₄
300 Automatic	.023	153624	.014	36	F		CV	.004C	.008C	Cam	9	18½		2 to 3	0 to 1P	0 to ⁵⁄₆₄
300 SL	.022	153624	.013		F		CV	.004C	.008C	Cam	20	17½	11.5	3¾ to 4¾	0 to 1P	0 to ⁵⁄₆₄
180, 190	.037	1342	.018		F	4B	VD	.004C	.008C	Cam	12	8	4.3	3½	½	0 to ⁵⁄₆₄
180D	......	1342	......		F	......	VD	.008C	.006C	TG	6½	7½	4.0	3½	½	0 to ⁵⁄₆₄
190D	......	1342	......		F	......	VD	.006C	.012C	Cam	11	7½	4.0	3½	½	0 to ⁵⁄₆₄
190SL	.033	1342	.018		F	8B	VD	.004C	.008C	Cam	17½	8¼	4.3	3½	½	0 to ⁵⁄₆₄
220	.029	153624	.014		F	1A	VD	.003C	.006C	Cam	10	10	6.3	2½	½	0 to ⁵⁄₆₄
220S	.029	153624	.014		F	2B	VD	.003C	.006C	Cam	10	10	6.3	2½	½	0 to ⁵⁄₆₄
220SE	.022	153624	.014		F		VD	.003C	.006C	Cam	10	10	6.3	2½	½	0 to ⁵⁄₆₄
300 Automatic	.023	153624	.014		F	4A	CV	.003C	.008C	Cam	......	18½		2 to 3	½	0 to ⁵⁄₆₄
300SL	.022	153624	0.13		F		CV	.003C	.008C	Cam	......	17½	11.5	4 to 5	½	⁵⁄₆₄ to ⁵⁄₃₂
METROPOLITAN—Britain																
1500	.024	1342	.014	......		5B	CP	.012	.012	Ca	5	7	4.0	......	......	......
MG—Britain																
Magnette	.020	1342	.015	60	F	4B	CC	.012H	.012H	CP	5	5¼	4.3	3	1	0
MGA	.020	1342	.015	60	F	7B	CC	.017H	.017H	CP	16	5	4.3	4	1	0
MGA Twin Cam	.025	1342	.015	60	F	TC	CP	.017C	.017C	CC	20	6¾	6.8	4	1	0
Magnette III	.025	1342	.015	60		TC	FP	.015H	.015H	CC	TC	5¾	4.3	1½	¾ to 1	¹⁄₁₆ to ⅛
MGA 1600	.025	1342	.015	60		TC	TCC	.015H	.015H	CC	5	5	4.3	4	¾ to 1½	0
Magnette MK. IV	.025	1342	.015	60		4B	FP	.015C	.015C	CC	TC	6	4.3	1½	¾ to 1	0 to ⅛
MGA 1600 MK. II	.025	1342	.015	60		10B	FP	.015	.015	CC	16	5	4.3	4	1P	0
Midget	.025	1342	.015	60	F	4B	FP	.012C	.012C	CC	5	5	4.3	3	1	0 to ⅛
MITSUBISHI—Japan																
500 Std. A-10	.027	12	.018	100	......	30B	CT	.016	.016	NO	32	No	......	6	2	⁷⁄₆₄ to ⁹⁄₆₄
Super Del. A-11	.027	12	.018	100	......	30B	CT	.016	.016	NO	15	No	......	6	2	⁷⁄₆₄ to ⁹⁄₆₄

A-1 —1,5,4,8,6,3,7,2
A-2 —1,12,9,4,5,8,11,2,3,10,7,6,
A —After Top Center
B —Before Top Center
C —Cold
CAP —Camshaft Pinion
CC —Crankshaft and Camshaft sprockets
CFB —Camshaft and Front Bearing Cap
CP —Crankshaft Pulley
CT —Crankshaft Pulley and Timing Gear Cover
F —Front
Fly —Flywheel
FP —Fan Drive Pulley
FR —Front Right
H —Hot
N —Negative
No —None
OFC —Crankcase Front Cover
P —Positive
R —Rear
Ri —Right
TC —Top Center
TCC —Timing Chain Cover
TG —Timing Gears
VD —Vibration Damper

FOREIGN CAR TUNE-UP SPECIFICATIONS—Continued

MAKE AND MODEL	PLUG Gap	IGNITION SYSTEM Firing Order	Pt. Gap	Cam Angle Deg.	No. 1 Cyl. Location	Ign. Timing Mark Deg.	Mark Location	VALVES Tappet Clearance in.	Tappet Clearance ex.	Mark Location	Inlet Opens	CAPACITY Water U.S.A. qts.	Oil U.S.A. qts.	WHEEL ALIGNMENT Caster Deg.	Camber Deg.	Toe-in in.
MORGAN—Britain																
4/4 Series II	.025	1243	.014	......	......	5B	......	.012C	.012C	CC	3½	6	3¼	4	2	⅛ to 3/16
Plus 4	.025	1342	.012	......	......	4B	CC	.012H	.012H	CC	15	8	5½	4	2	⅛ to 3/16
4/4 Series III	.030	1243	.015	......	......	10B	CC	.008	.018	CC	10	6	3¼	4	2	⅛ to 3/16
Plus 4, 1962	.018	1342	.015	......	......	45B	CC	.017	.017	CC	16	8	5½	4	2	⅛ to 3/16
4/4 Ser. IV—1962	.025	1243	.015	......	......	17B	CC	.010	.017	CC	6	6	3¼	4	2	⅛ to 3/16
MORRIS—Britain																
Minor 1000	.025	1342	.015	60	F	TC	CC	.012C	.012C	CP	5	2½	4.3	3	1	3/32
Oxford, Cowley	.025	1342	.015	60	F	5B	CC	.015H	.015H	CP	5	5¼	4.3	3	1½	3/32
Mini-Minor	.025	1342	.015	60	......	TC	FP	.012	.012	CC	5	2½	4.5	1½	0	⅛
Oxford Ser. V	.025	1342	.015	60	......	TC	FP	.015	.015	CC	TC	5¾	4.5	1½	¾ to 1	3/16 to ⅛
Mini-Traveller	.025	1342	.015	60	F	TC	F	.012	.012	CC	5	3¼	......	3	1½	⅛
Oxford Traveller Ser. V	.025	1342	.015	60	F	5B	F	.015	.015	CC	TC	7½	......	1½	¾ to 1	1/16 to ⅛
Mini-Minor & Traveller, 1962	.025	1342	.015	60	......	TC	Fly	.012C	.012C	CC	5	3¼	......	3	28	1/16
Oxford Ser. VI-Sal. & Trav	025	1342	.015	60	......	5B	CT	.015C	.015C	CC	TC	7½	......	1½	¾ to 1	1/16 to ⅛
Minor 1000 & Traveller	.025	......	.015	60	......	TC	CT	.012C	.012C	CC	5	6	......	3	1	3/32
Mini-Cooper	......	......	......	......	......	7B	......	......	.014	......	16	3¼	......	......	......	......
NISSEN—Japan																
210-S, L10-S	.026	1342	.020	53	......	17B	CP	.014	.014	CC	13	5½	......	3	1½	7/64
PL-310	.030	1342	.020	53	F	20	CP	.015	.015	CC	10	4¾	......	2½	1½	7/64
P30-U, PL30-U	.030	1342	.020	53	F	5	CP	.017	.017	CC	14	7½	......	14	1½	5/64 to ⅛
NOBLE—Britain																
200	.026	......	.018	......	......	......	......	......	......	......	......	No	......	......	3 to 4	7/64 to 13/64
NSU—Germany																
Prinz II, 30 & Sport	.027	......	.014	......	......	TC	......	.004C	.004C	No	......	No	2.3	6	2	5/32 to 15/64
OPEL—Germany																
Olympia	.037	1342	.018	......	F	TC	Fly	.008H	.012H	Fly	27	8	3.2	1½ to 2	½ to 1½	3/64 to ⅛
Kapitan	.037	153624	.014	......	F	TC	Fly	.008H	.012H	Fly	27	10½	3.2	1 to 2	½N to ¼P	5/64 to 5/32
Olympia	.037	1342	.014	......	F	TC	Fly	.008H	.012H	Fly	27	8	3.2	1 to 2	¼ to 1¾	1/32 to 7/64
Kapitan	.037	153624	.014	......	F	TC	Fly	.008H	.012H	Fly	36	10½	3.2	1 to 2	½N to ½P	3/64 to ⅛
1200	.035	1342	.018	......	F	TC	Fly	.008H	.010H	Fly	27	8½	......	1¼ to 1¾	¼ to 1¾	1/32 to 7/64
PANHARD—France																
PL-17	.024	12	.016	......	......	5B	Fly	.006C	.006C	......	27½	No.	1.5	1¾	1	⅛ to 5/16
Tigre	.027	12	.016	......	......	7½B	Fly	.006C	.006C	Fly	34½	No.	......	1¾	1	⅛ to 5/16
PEERLESS—Britain																
GT2	.025	1342	.015	......	F	4B	CP	.010	.010	Fly	15	7	6.6	4	1½	⅛
PEUGEOT—France																
403	.024	1342	.015	57	R	9½B	Fly	.004C	.008C	......	TC	9½	4.0	2	1	1/16
404	.025	1342	.020	57	R	11B	No	.004C	.008C	Tch	TC	8½	4.0	1 to 3	¼N to ¾P	1/16
PORSCHE—Germany																
356A-1600	.028	1342	.016	......	F	5B	CP	.013	.013	CP	27	No	4.5	4½ to 5½	¼P to 1¼P	3/64 to ⅛
356A-1600S	.028	1342	.016	......	F	5B	CP	.013	.013	CP	44	No	4.5	4½ to 5½	¼P to 1¼P	3/64 to ⅛
356A-1600GS	.016	1342	.014	23½	F	24B	CC	.006C	.006C	CP	38	No	4.5	4½ to 5½	¼P to 1¼P	3/64 to ⅛
356B-1600	.028	1342	.016	50	F	5B	CP	.004	.006	......	5	No	4.5	4½ to 5½	¼P to 1¼P	3/64 to ⅛
356B-1600S	.028	1342	.016	50	F	5B	CP	.006	.004	......	15	No	4.5	4½ to 5½	¼P to 1¼P	3/64 to ⅛
356B-1600S-90	.028	1342	.016	50	F	3B	CP	.006C	.004C	......	15	No	4.5	4½ to 5½	¼P to 1¼P	3/64 to ⅛
PRINCE—Japan																
ALSI-1	.028	1342	.014	61	F	8B	Fly	.010	.010	Fly	19½	10½	3.3	½N	1	0 to 7/64
ALSIEL (A)	.028	1342	.014	61	F	10B	Fly	.010	.010	Fly	19½	10½	3.3	½N	½	1/32 to 7/64
ALSIEL (B)	.028	1342	.014	61	F	5B	Fly	.010	Hyd	Fly	19½	10½	3.3	¼N	½	1/32 to 7/64
BLSI-3, BLSISL-3, BLSIDL-3	.031	1342	.014	58½	......	8B	FC	.010	.010	CC	21½	10½	......	1N	½	1/32 to 7/64
PUBLICA—Japan																
UP10	.032	12	.017	98	CP	8B	FR	Hyd	Hyd	CP	......	No	......	1	1½	1/16
RENAULT—France																
R-1090, 1959	.023	1342	.018	......	F	2B	CP	.008	.012	Cap	6	4¾	2.5	10	1½	⅛ to 13/64
R-1090, 1959	.023	1342	.018	......	F	7B	CP	.008	.012	Cap	6	4¾	2.5	10	1½	⅛ to 13/64
R-1062	.024	1342	.018	......	F	2B	CP	.004	.008	Cap	6	4⅝	2.5	10	1⅓	⅛ to 13/64
R-1090 Dauphine	.024	1342	.018	......	F	TC	CP	.004	.008	Cap	6	4⅞	2.5	10	1N to 1P	⅛ to 13/64
R-1091, 1960	.024	1342	.018	......	F	3B	CP	.006C	.009C	Cap	7	4⅞	2.5	10	1N to 1P	⅛ to 13/64
R-1092	.024	1342	.018	......	F	3B	CP	.006C	.009C	Cap	7	4⅞	2.5	10	1N to 1P	⅛ to 13/64

* —8B 1960-61, 11B 1962
A-1 —1,5,4,8,6,3,7,2
B —Before Top Center
C —Cold
Cap —Camshaft Pinion
CC —Crank and Camshaft Sprockets
CP —Crankshaft Pulley
** —96-11B, 1961 96GT-9B, 1962-2B

F —Front
FCC —Flywheel and Crankshaft and Camshaft Sprockets
Fly —Flywheel
FP —Fan Drive Pulley
FR —Front Right

H —Hot
N —Negative
No —None
P —Positive
R —Rear
TC —Top Center

TCC —Timing Chain Cover
T-F —Timing Case Cover or Flywheel
TG —Timing Gears
TGH —Timing Gear Housing

MAKE AND MODEL	PLUG Gap	Firing Order	Pt. Gap	Cam Angle Deg.	No. 1 Cyl. Location	Ign. Timing Mark Deg.	Mark Location	Tappet Clearance in.	Tappet Clearance ex.	Valve Mark Location	Inlet Opens	Water U.S.A. qts.	Oil U.S.A. qts.	Caster Deg.	Camber Deg.	Toe-in in.
RENAULT—France																
R-1103	.024	1342	.018	.....	R	5B	CP	.005C	.007C	Cap	6	9½	2.5	2 to 4	½ to 1½	5/64 to 5/32
R-1104	.024	1342	.018	.....	R	5B	CP	.005C	.007C	Cap	10	9½	2.5	2 to 4	½ to 1½	5/64 to 5/32
R-1120, R-1122	.024	1342	.018	.....	F	2B	Fly	.006	.008	Cap	6	5¼	2.5	8	2	5/64 to 5/32
RILEY—Britain																
1.5	.025	1342	.015	60	F	TC	CC	.015H	.015H	CP	5	6¼	4.0	3	2 to 5	0
2.6	.025	153624	.015	35	F	4½B	CC	.012H	.012H	CP	5	.....	6.0	3	1	0
4-68	.025	1342	.015	60	.....	TC	FP	.015	.015	TC		6¼	4.0	1½	¾ to 1	1/16 to 1/8
Elf	.025	1342	.015	60	.....	TC	Fly	.012C	.012C	CC	5	2¾	4.0	3	2P	1/16
15 Mk. III	.025	1342	.015	60		6B	CP	.015C	.015C	CC	TC	6½	4.0	3	2P	0
4-72	.025	1342	.015	60		4B	FP	.015C	.015C	CC	TC	6	4.0	1½	¾ to 1	1/16 to 1/8
ROLLS-ROYCE—Britain																
Silver Cloud	.025	142635	.020	44		2B	Fly	.006	.012	Fly	TC	13	9.6	1N to ½P	0	1/16 to 5/32
Silver Wraith	.025	142635	.020	44		2B	Fly	.006	.012	Fly	TC	13	9.6	½N to ½P	0 to 1P	1/16 to 5/32
Silver Cloud II, Phantom V	.026	A-1	.020	44	FR	2B	Fly	.....	.....	Fly	20B	13	.....	0	0	3/32 to 5/32
ROVER—Britain																
60	.031	1342	.015	60	F	10B	Fly	.008	.012	Fly	9	8½	5.5	2	2	0 to 1/8
75, 90	.031	153624	.015	35	F	10B	Fly	.008	.012	Fly	9	10½	9.0	2	2	0 to 1/8
105	.031	153624	.015	35	F	3B	Fly	.008	.012	Fly	9	10½	14.5	2	2	0 to 1/8
80	.031	1342	.015	60	F	6B	Fly	.010	.010	Fly	6	11¼	5.5	2	2	0 to 1/8
100	.031	153624	.015	35	F	3B	Fly	.006	.010	Fly	17½	11¾	.....	2	2	0 to 1/8
3 Litre	.031	153624	.015	35	F	3B	Fly	.006	.010	Fly	17½	11¼	.....	0	2	0 to 1/16
SAAB—Sweden																
93B, 93F	.028	123	.014	.....	R	8B	.....					8		1½ to 2½	½ to 1	1/32 to 1/8
95	.028	123	.014	.....	R	*8B	FP					8		2	¾	3/64 to 1/8
96, 96GT750	.028	123	.014	.....	R	**	FP					8		1½P to 2½P	½P to 1P	1/32 to 1/8
SEAT—Spain																
1400	.022	1342	.016	30	F	10B	.....	.030	.030	.....	15	9¾	.....	2 to 2½	¼ to 1	7/64
600	.022	1342	.016	30	F	10B	CP	.030	.030	CC	10	4½	.....	9	1	5/64
1400C	.022	1342	.016	36	F	TC	CP	.030	.030	CC	15	9¾	.....	2	¾	7/64
SIMCA—France																
Aronde Etoile & Flash	.028	1342	.018	56	F	4B	.....	.004C	.006C	.....	12	5¾	5.6	1½ to 2½	1 to 1½	1/32 to 7/64
Aronde Flash Special	.028	1342	.018	56	F	TC	.....	.004C	.006C	.....	12	5¾	5.6	1½ to 2½	1 to 1½	1/32 to 7/64
Arlane	.027	1342	.016	56	F	4B	.....	.004	.006	.....	12	5¾	4.5	½N to ½P	½ to 1½	1/32 to 7/64
Vedette	.023	A-1	.015	28	FR	2B	.....	.011C	.011C	.....	5	15	4.5	½N to ½P	½ to 1½	1/32 to 7/64
Aronde 6CV, 7CV	.023	1342	.018	56	F	TC	.....	.004	.006	.....	12	5¾	5.6	1½P to 2½P	1 to 1½P	1/32 to 1/8
Aronde Rush	.023	1342	.018	56	F	4B	.....	.004	.006	.....	12	5¾	5.6	1½P to 2½P	1 to 1½P	1/32 to 1/8
Arlane	.023	1342	.018	56	F	4B	.....	.004	.006	.....	12	5¾	4.5	½N to ½P	½P to 1½P	1/32 to 1/8
SINGER—Britain																
Gazelle Ser. III	.025	1342	.015	9	F	10B	CP	.012	.014	CC	10	6⅛	4.8	1¾ to 3	¾	¼
Gazelle Ser. IIIA	.025	1342	.015	.....	F	7B	CP	.012	.014	CC	10	6⅛	4.8	1¾	¾	3/16
Vogur	.025	1342	.015	30	.....	10B	CP	.012	.014	.....	14	7	4.8	2	¾	3/16
Gazelle Ser. IIIC	.025	1342	.015	30	.....	7B	CP	.012	.014	CC	14	7¾	4.8	1¾	¾	3/16
SKODA—Czechoslovakia																
Octavia	.024	1342	.016	16	F	23B	TCC	.006	.008	FCC	13½	6¾	4.5	3¾	1	3/32
Octavia Super	.024	1342	.016	16	F	20B	TCC	.006	.008	FCC	13½	6¾	4.5	3¾	1	3/32
Felicia	.024	1342	.016	4	F	23B	TCC	.006	.008	FCC	29	6¾	4.5	3¾	1	3/32
Touring Sport	.024	1342	.024	225	F	23B	TCC	.006	.008	FCC	9	6¾	4.5	3¾	¾P to 1¼P	5/64 to 1/8
Octavia Combi	.024	1342	.016	45	F	TC	TCC	.004C	.006C	CC	3	6¾	4.5	3¾	¾P to 1¼P	5/64
STANDARD—Britain																
8	.032	1342	.015	110	F	8B	TCC	.010	.010	TCC	10	.....	4.3	1¾	2	0 to 1/16
10, Pennant	.032	1342	.015	110	F	10B	TCC	.010	.010	TCC	10	4½	4.3	1¾	2	0 to 1/16
Ensign	.032	1342	.015	110	F	3B	TCC	.010	.010	TCC	12	8½	.....	1½	2	0 to 1/16
Vanguard IIII, Vignale	.032	1342	.015	110	F	12B	TCC	.010	.010	TCC	12	8½	6.3	1½	2	0 to 1/16
Vanguard Luxury—1961	.025	153624	.015	110	F	15B	TCC	.010	.010	CC	18	8½	6.3	½N to 1½P	0 to 2P	0 to 1/16
Vanguard Luxury—1962	.025	153624	.015	110	F	15B	TCC	.010	.010	CC	18	8½	6.3	1½N	2P	0 to 1/16
STEYR-PUCH—Austria																
2000, 2300 Sport	.035	1342	.016	.....		4B	.....	.008	.008	.....	18	No	.....	2 to 2½	¼ to 1	5/64 to 5/32
500, 700C	.027	12	.016	.....			.....	.006	.006	.....		No	.....	9	¾ to 1¾	0 to 5/64

* —8B 1960-61, 11B 1962
A-1 —1,5,4,8,6,3,7,2
B —Before Top Center
C —Cold
Cap —Camshaft Pinion
CC —Crank and Camshaft Sprockets
CP —Crankshaft Pulley
** —96-11B, 1961 96GT-9B, 1962-2B

F —Front
FCC —Flywheel and Crankshaft and Camshaft Sprockets
Fly —Flywheel
FP —Fan Drive Pulley
FR —Front Right

H —Hot
N —Negative
No —None
P —Positive
R —Rear
TC —Top Center

TCC —Timing Chain Cover
T-F —Timing Case Cover or Flywheel
TG —Timing Gears
TGH —Timing Gear Housing

FOREIGN CAR TUNE-UP SPECIFICATIONS—Continued

MAKE AND MODEL	PLUG	IGNITION SYSTEM						VALVES				CAPACITY		WHEEL ALIGNMENT		
	Gap	Firing Order	Pt. Gap	Cam Angle (Deg.)	No. 1 Cyl Location	Ign. Timing Mark Deg.	Mark Location	Tappet Clearance in.	Tappet Clearance ex.	Mark Location	Inlet Opens	Water U.S.A. qts.	Oil U.S.A. qts.	Caster Deg.	Camber Deg.	Toe-in in.
SUNBEAM—Britain																
Rapier Ser. II	.025	1342	.015	90	F	8B	CP	.012H	.014H	CC	11	6⅛	4.8	1¾	¾	⅛ to ¼
Rapier Ser. III	.025	1342	.015	......	F	6B	CP	.012H	.014H	CC	14	6⅛	4.8	1¾	¾	3/16
Alpine	.025	1342	.015	......	F	6B	CP	.012H	.014H	CC	14	7	4.8	4¾	¾	5/32
TALBOT—France																
Largo	.027	A-1	.020	......	FR	......	......	.028C	.028C	......	......	9¾	......	3	10 to 15	3/64
TATRA—Czechoslovakia																
603—1959	.020	A-3	.020	......	FL	10B	CP	.004	.006	FC	4A	No	......	0	1	7/64
603—1960	.027	A-4	.008	......	FR	13B	CP	.004	.006	CP	15	No	......	0	1½	7/64
TOYOTA—Japan																
Corona ST10	.027	1243	.010	54	F	7B	CP	.008	.010	CP	8	......	......	1	1	5/64
Toyopet Crown RS20	.032	1243	.018	45	F	8B	Fly	.008	.014	Fly	11	8¾	......	1	1	5/64
Crown Custom RS22L	.032	1243	.018	45	F	8B	Fly	.008	.014	Fly	11	8¾	......	1	1	5/64
Toyopet Corona PT20	.032	1342	.018	45	F	10B	CP	.008	.014	CP	11	7	......	2	1	5/64
Toyopet Corona RT20	.032	1243	.018	45	F	8B	CP	.008	.014	Fly	11	8¾	......	2	1	5/64
Toyopet Tiara RT20L	.032	1243	.018	52	......	8B	Fly	.008	.014	Fly	11	8	......	2	1	5/64
Toyopet Cr. Cust. RS32L	.032	1243	.018	52	......	12B	CP	.008	.014	CP	18	8¾	......	1	1	5/64
Toyopet Tiara RT30L	.032	1243	.018	52	F	12B	CP	.008	.014	CP	23	8	......	2	1	5/64
TRIUMPH—Britain																
Sedan	.032	1342	.015	110	F	10B	TCC	.010C	.010C	TCC	10	5	3.9	1¾	2	0 to 1/16
Sports TR3	.025	1342	.015	110	F	4B	TCC	.010C	.010C	TCC	17	8½	6.0	0	1¼	⅛
Sedan & Station Wagon	.025	1342	.015	110	F	10B	TCC	.010C	.010C	TCC	12	4½	3.9	1¾	2	0 to 1/16
Herald Sedan	.025	1342	.015	110	F	10B	TCC	.010C	.010C	TCC	12	5	3.9	4	2	0 to 1/16
Herald Coupe & Convert.	.025	1342	.015	110	F	12B	TCC	.010C	.010C	......	18	5	3.9	4	2	0 to 1/16
TR3	.025	1342	.015	110	F	4B	TCC	.010C	.010C	TCC	17	8½	6.0	0	2	⅛
Herald	.025	1342	.015	......	F	6B	FC	.010C	.010C	FCC	18	5	3.9	0	2	0 to 1/16
TR4	.025	1342	.012	......	F	6B	FC	.010C	.010C	CC	17	8½	6.0	4	2	0 to 1/16
UNICAR—Britain																
T	.018	......	.020	......	......	......	......	......	......	......	......	......	......	0	1	⅛
VANDEN PLAS—Britain																
Princess 3 Litre	.025	153624	.015	......	F	TC	FP	.012H	.012H	FTC	5	10¼	......	0	1	⅛
Princess 4 Litre	.025	153624	.015	......	F	10B	......	.012C	.012C	CC	5	14	......	1¼	¾	⅛
VAUXHALL—Britain																
FD, FW, FBD, FBW	.029	1342	.020	36	F	9B	Fly	.013H	.013H	Fly	19½	7¼	3.6	¼	¼P to 1P	1/16 to ⅛
VOLKSWAGEN—Germany																
11, 14, 1959	.026	1432	.016	42	......	7½B	FP	.004C	.004C	FP	2½	No	2.5	2½	¾	3/32 to 13/16
22	.026	1432	.016	42	......	7½B	FP	.004C	.004C	FP	2½	No	2.5	0	¾	13/16 to 2
11, 14, 1960	.028	1432	.016	42	......	7½B	FP	.004C	.004C	FP	2½	No	2.5	2½	¾	3/64 to ⅛
22	.028	1432	.016	42	......	7½B	FP	.004C	.004C	FP	TC	No	2.5	0	¾	5/64 to 13/64
11, 14, 1961	.028	1432	.016	42	......	10B	FP	.008C	.008C	FP	4	No	2.5	2½	¾	3/64 to ⅛
22	.028	1432	.016	42	......	10B	FP	.008C	.008C	FP	4	No	2.5	0	¾	5/64 to 13/64
11, 14, 1962	.028	1432	.016	42	......	7½B	FP	.008C	.008C	FP	4	No	2.5	2	¾	5/64 to 5/32
22	.028	1432	.016	42	......	7½B	FP	.008C	.008C	FP	4	No	2.5	0	¾	5/64 to 13/64
1500-31, 1500-34	.026	1432	.016	42	......	7½B	FP	.008C	.008C	TE	1	No	......	4½ to 5½	⅓	⅛ to 13/64
VOLVO—Sweden																
P44508, P54408	.030	1342	.018	50	F	4B	Fly	.020H	.020H	Fly	32	9	3.5	¾N to ¼P	¼N to ½P	0 to ⅛
P12208	.030	1342	.018	50	F	4B	Fly	.020H	.020H	Fly	32	9	3.5	0 to 1P	0 to ½P	0 to 5/32
P122S	.028	1342	.018	60	......	23B	CT	.017	.017	CC	13	9	3.5	0 to 1P	0 to ½P	0 to 5/32
P544	.028	1342	.018	60	......	23B	CT	.017	.017	CC	13	9	3.5	¾N to ¼P	¼N to ½P	0 to 3/16
P1800	.028	1342	.018	60	......	18B	CT	.021	.021	CC	24	9	3.5	0 to 1P	0 to ½P	0 to 5/32
WARTBURG—Germany																
Sed., Cpe., Sta. Wag., Roadster	.026	132	.016	No	......	22	CP	......	......	......	......	8	......	0	2	0 to 5/64
WOLSELEY—Britain																
1500	.025	1342	.015	60	F	6B	CC	.015H	.015H	CP	5	6¼	4.3	3	2	0
15-50	.025	1342	.015	60	F	5B	CC	.015H	.015H	CP	5	6¼	4.3	2¾	¾	0
6-90	.025	153624	.015	35	F	3½B	CC	.012H	.012H	CP	5	10½	7.0	3	1¼	0
15-60	.025	1342	.015	60	F	TC	FP	.015H	.015H	CC	TC	6¼	4.3	1½	¾ to 1	1/16 to ⅛
6-99	.025	153624	.015	35	F	7B	FP	.012H	.012H	CC	5	10½	7.0	1¼	1	⅛

* —8B 1960-61, 11B 1962
A-1 —1,5,4,8,6,3,7,2
B —Before Top Center
C —Cold
Cap —Camshaft Pinion
CC —Crank and Camshaft Sprockets
CP —Crankshaft Pulley
** —96-11B, 1961 96GT-9B, 1962-2B

F —Front
FCC —Flywheel and Crankshaft and Camshaft Sprockets
Fly —Flywheel
FP —Fan Drive Pulley
FR —Front Right

H —Hot
N —Negative
No —None
P —Positive
R —Rear
TC —Top Center

TCC —Timing Chain Cover
T-F —Timing Case Cover or Flywheel
TG —Timing Gears
TGH —Timing Gear Housing

TUNE-UP SPECIFICATIONS
1941 to 1953

MAKE AND MODEL	IGNITION SYSTEM							VALVES			CAPACITY		WHEEL ALIGNMENT		
	Plug Gap	Firing Order	Pt. Gap	Cam Angle Deg.	No. 1 Cyl. Location	Ign. Timing Mark Deg.	Mark Location	Tappet Clearance in.	Tappet Clearance ex.	Inlet Opens	Water qts.	Oil qts.	Caster Deg.	Camber Deg.	Toe-in in.
BUICK															
1941-47, Ser. 40-50	.025	16258374	.016	30	F	4B	Fly	.015H	.015H	13B	13¼	6	3/8P	3/8P	1/32
Ser. 60-70-80-90	.025	16258374	.016	30	F	6B	Fly	.015H	.015H	14B	17	7	3/8P	3/8P	1/32
1948-49 Ser. 40-50	.025	16258374	.016	30	F	4B	Fly	.015H	.015H	13B	13	6	3/8P	3/8P	1/32
Ser. 70	.025	16258374	.016	30	F	6B	Fly	Zero	Zero	14B	17	7	3/8P	3/8P	1/32
1950, Ser. 40-50	.025	16258374	.015	31	F	4B	Fly	.015H	.015H	13B	13	6	1/4P to 1 1/2P	5/8N to 7/8P	1/16 to 1/8
1951-53, Ser. 40, W.O./D.	.025	16258374	.015	31	F	4B	Fly	.015H	.015H	13B	13	6	1/4P to 1 1/2P	5/8N to 7/8P□	1/16 to 1/8
1951, Ser. 50	.025	16258374	.015	31	F	4B	Fly	Zero	Zero	13B	13	6	1/4P to 1 1/2P	5/8N to 7/8P	1/16 to 1/8
1951-52, Ser. 70	.025	16258374	.015	31	F	6B	Fly	Zero	Zero	14B	18	7	1/4P to 1 1/2P	5/8N to 7/8P	1/16 to 1/8
1952-53, Ser. 40 W./D.	.025	16258374	.015	31	F	4B	Fly	Zero	Zero	14B	12	6	1/4P to 1 1/2P	5/8N to 7/8P□	1/16 to 1/8
1952, Ser. 50	.025	16258374	.015	31	F	4B	Fly	Zero	Zero	14B	12	6	1/4P to 1 1/2P	5/8N to 7/8P	1/16 to 1/8
1953, 50, 70 V8	.032	16258314	.015	29½	F	5B	Fly	Zero	Zero	25B	12ø	6	1/2N to 3/4P	5/8N to 7/8P	1/16 to 1/8
CADILLAC															
1941-42	.025	18736542	.015	30	LF	5B	V.D.	Zero	Zero	T.C.	25	7	1 3/4N	3/8P	3/32
1946-48	.025	18736542	.015	30	LF	5B	V.D.	Zero	Zero	T.C.	25	7	1/2P	3/8P	8/32
1949	.035	18436572	.015	30	LF	5B	V.D.	Zero	Zero	19B	19	5	1/2N	3/8P	3/32
1950-51	.035	18436572	.015	31	LF	5B	V.D.	Zero	Zero	24B	18	5	1/2N to 1/2P	3/8N to 3/8P	1/32 to 3/32
1952	.035	18436572	.013	31	LF	5B	V.D.	Zero	Zero	14B	19	5	1/2N to 1/2P	3/8N to 3/8P	1/32 to 3/32
1953	.035	18436572	.013	31	LF	2½B	V.D.	Zero	Zero	22B	19¾	5	1/2N to 1/2P	3/8N to 3/8P	1/16 to 1/8
CHEVROLET															
1941-48	.040	153624	.018	34	F	5B	Fly	.006H	.013H	3B	15	5	1/4P	1/4P	1/16
1949	.035	153624	.018	34	F	5B	Fly	.006H	.013H	3B	16	5	1P	1P	1/8
1950-51, W.O./P.G.	.035	153624	.021	34	F	5B	Fly	.006H	.013H	1A	15	5	1P	1P	1/16
1950-51, W./P.G.	.035	153624	.021	34	F	5B	Fly	Zero	Zero	16B	15	5	1P	1P	1/16
1952, W.O./P.G.	.035	153624	.019	39	F	5B	Fly	.006H	.013H	1A	15	5	1P	1P	1/16
1950-52, W./P.G.	.035	153624	.019	39	F	5B	Fly	Zero	Zero	16B	15	5	1P	1P	1/16
1953 W.O./P.G.	.035	153624	.015	42	F	5B	Fly	.006H	.013H	1A	15	5	1P	1P	1/16
1953 W./P.G.	.035	153624	.015	42	F	5B	Fly	Zero	Zero	16B	15	5	1P	1P	1/16
Corvette	.035	153624	.016	44	F	2A	Fly	.010	.020	19½B	17¾	5	1P	1P	1/8
CHRYSLER															
1941-42, Six	.025	153624	.020	35-38	F	T.C.	V.D.	.008H	.010H	12B	18	5	Zero	P3/8	1/16
1941, 8 Cyl.	.025	16258374	.017	27-30	LF	T.C.	V.D.	.008H	.010H	6B	24	6	Zero	P3/8	1/16
1942	.025	16258374	.017	27-30	LF	2A	V.D.	.008H	.010H	6B	26	6	Zero	P3/8	1/32
1946-48, Six	.025	153624	.020	35-38	F	2A	V.D.	.008H	.010H	12B	18	5	Zero	P3/8	1/32
1946-48, 8 Cyl.	.025	16258374	.017	27-30	LF	2A	V.D.	.008H	.010H	12B	26	6	Zero	P3/8	1/32
1949, Six	.035	153624	.020	35-38	F	4A	V.D.	.008H	.010H	12B	17	5	N2	P3/8	1/32
1949, 8 Cyl.	.035	16258374	.017	27-30	LF	2A	V.D.	.008H	.010H	12B	21	6	N2	P3/8	1/32
1950, Six	.030	153624	.020	36½	F	T.C.	V.D.	.008H	.010H	12B	17	5	1N to 3N	P3/4	1/16
1950, 8 Cyl.	.030	16258374	.019	28½	F	T.C.	V.D.	.008H	.010H	12B	21	6	1N to 3N	P3/4	1/16
1951-52, Six	.030	153624	.020	36½	F	2B	V.D.	.008H	.010H	12B	17	5	1N to 3N	P3/4	1/16
1951, V8	.035	18436572	.018	28¾*	F	T.C.	V.D.	Zero	Zero	15B	25	5	1N to 3N	P3/4	1/16
1952-53, V8	.035	18436572	.018	27†	F	4B	V.D.	Zero	Zero	15B	25	5	1N to 3N	3/8N to 3/8P	1/16
1953, Six	.035	153624	.020	39	F	T.C.	V.D.	.008H	.010H	12B	15	5	1N to 3N	3/8N to 3/8P	1/16
DE-SOTO															
1941	.025	153624	.020	35-38	F	T.C.	V.D.	.008H	.010H	12B	18	5	Zero	P3/8	1/16
1942	.025	153624	.020	35-38	F	4A	V.D.	.008H	.010H	12B	18	5	Zero	P3/8	1/32
1946-48	.030	153624	.020	35-38	F	T.C.	V.D.	.008H	.010H	12B	18	5	Zero	P3/8	1/32
1949	.035	153624	.020	35-38	F	2A	V.D.	.008H	.010H	12B	18	5	N2	P3/8	1/32
1950	.030	153624	.020	36	F	T.C.	V.D.	.008H	.010H	12B	17	5	1N to 3N	3/8N to 3/8P	1/16
1951-52, Six	.035	153624	.020	36	F	2B	V.D.	.008H	.010H	12B	15	5	1N to 3N	3/8N to 3/8P	1/16
1952-53, V8	.035	18436572	.018	26-28‡	LF	4B	V.D.	Zero	Zero	12B	22	5	1N to 3N	3/8N to 3/8P	1/16
1953, Six	.035	153624	.020	39	F	2B	V.D.	.008H	.010H	12B	15	5	1N to 3N	3/8N to 3/8P	1/16

□—1953—1/2N to 3/4P
ø—18 Qts.—Series 70
*—35 degrees both sets
†—34 degrees both sets
‡—32-36 degrees both sets

A1—1-4-9-8-5-2-11-10-3-6-7-12
A—After Top Center
B—Before Top Center
C—Cold
CP—Crankshaft Pulley

Dh—Distributor Housing
Fly—Flywheel
F—Front
H—Hot
LF—Left Front

N—Negative
P—Positive
RF—Right Front
TC—Top Center
VD—Vibration Damper

TUNE-UP SPECIFICATIONS
1941 to 1953

MAKE AND MODEL	IGNITION SYSTEM						VALVES				CAPACITY		WHEEL ALIGNMENT		
	Plug Gap	Firing Order	Pt. Gap	Cam Angle Deg.	No. 1 Cyl. Location	Ign. Timing Mark Deg.	Mark Location	Tappet Clearance in.	Tappet Clearance ex.	Inlet Opens	Water qts.	Oil qts.	Caster Deg.	Camber Deg.	Toe-In in.
DODGE															
1941	.025	153624	.020	35-38	F	T.C.	V.D.	.008H	.010H	9B	15	5	Zero	P⅜	1/16
1942	.025	153624	.020	35-38	F	T.C.	V.D.	.008H	.010H	12B	15	5	Zero	P⅜	1/16
1946-48	.025	153624	.020	35-38	F	T.C.	V.D.	.008H	.010H	12B	15	5	Zero	P⅜	1/16
1949	.038	153624	.020	36	F	2B	V.D.	.008H	.010H	8B	15	5	Zero	P⅜	1/32
1950	.035	153624	.020	36	F	T.C.	V.D.	.008H	.010H	8B	15	5	1N to 1P	P¾	1/16
1951-52	.035	153624	.020	36	F	2B	V.D.	.008H	.010H	8B	14	5	1N to 1P	⅜N to ⅜P	1/16
1953, Six	.035	153624	.020	39	F	2B	V.D.	.010H	.010H	8B	14	5	1N to 1P	⅜N to ⅜P	1/16
1953, V8	.035	18436572	.020	26-28‡	LF	4B	V.D.	Zero	Zero	17B	19	5	1N to 1P	⅜N to ⅜P	1/16
EDSEL															
1958 Cor. & Cit.	.034	15426378	.015	27½	RF	3B	C.P.	Zero	Zero	27B	22	5	0 to 1½P	0 to ¾P	1/16 to 3/16
Ran. & Pac.	.034	15426378	.015	27½	RF	3B	C.P.	Zero	Zero	17B	18½	5	½ to 1½P	½P to 1½P	1/32 to ⅛
1959, Six	.034	153624	.025	36½	F	4B	C.P.	.019H	.019H	17B	15	4	0 to 1P	½P to 1½P	1/16 to ⅛
292 cu. in. V8	.034	15486372	.015	27½	RF	3B	C.P.	.018H	.018H	12B	19	5	0 to 1P	½P to 1½P	1/16 to ⅛
332 cu. in. V8	.034	15426378	.015	27½	RF	3B	C.P.	Zero	Zero	22B	19	5	0 to 1P	½P to 1½P	1/16 to ⅛
361 cu. in. V8	.034	15426378	.015	27½	RF	3B	C.P.	Zero	Zero	17B	19	5	0 to 1P	½P to 1½P	1/16 to ⅛
1960, Six	.034	153624	.025	36½	F	4B	C.P.	.019H	.019H	17B	15	4	0 to 1P	½P to 1½P	1/16 to ⅛
292 cu. in. V8	.034	15486372	.015	27½	RF	3B	C.P.	.018H	.018H	12B	19	5	0 to 1P	½P to 1½P	1/16 to ⅛
352 cu. in. V8	.034	15426378	.015	27½	RF	4B	C.P.	Zero	Zero	26B	19	5	0 to 1P	½P to 1½P	1/16 to ⅛
FORD															
1941, 11A	.025	153624	.020	36	F	4B	Dh	.011C	.015C	T.C.	17½	5	5½P to 8P	1P	1/16
1GA	.027	153624	.016	36	F	4B	Dh	.014C	.016C	3B	17½	5	5½P to 8P	1P	1/16
1942, 2GA	.034	153024	.016	38	F	1B	Dh	.011C	.015C	3B	17½	5	5½P to 8P	1P	1/16
21A	.025	15486372	.016	36	LF	4B	Dh	.011C	.015C	T.C.	22	5	5½P to 8P	1P	1/16
1946, 6GA	.034	153624	.016	38	F	1B	Dh	.011C	.015C	3B	14½	5	8P	1P	1/16
69A	.025	15486372	.016	36	LF	4B	Dh	.011C	.015C	T.C.	22	5	8P	1P	1/16
1947-48, 7GA, 87HA	.032	153624	.016	38	F	1B	C.P.	.011C	.015C	5B	14½	5	4½P to 9P	1N	1/16
79A, 89A	.025	15486372	.016	38	LF	4B	Dh	.011C	.015C	T.C.	22	5	4½P to 9P	1N	1/16
1949, 98HA	.032	153624	.025	38	F	T.C.	V.D.	.011C	.015C	11B	15	4	¾N to ¼P	¼N to ¾P	1/16 to ⅛
98BA	.032	15486372	.016	30	LF	2B	C.P.	.011C	.015C	T.C.	22	4	¾N to ¼P	¼N to ¾P	1/16 to ⅛
1950, Six	.030	153624	.025	36	F	T.D.C.	C.P.	.010C	.014C	11B	17	4	1N to ½P	1P	1/16 to ⅛
1950-53, V8	.030	15486372	.015	27	F	2B	C.P.	.014C	.018C	5B	22	4	1N to ½P	1P	1/16 to ⅛
1951, Six	.030	153624	.025	36	F	T.D.C.	C.P.	.014C	.018C	11B	17	4	1N to ½P	1P	1/16 to ⅛
1952, Six	.035	153624	.025	36	F	T.D.C.	C.P.	.015H	.015H	18B	15	4	1N to ½P	1P	1/16 to ⅛
1953, Six	.035	153624	.025	36	F	T.D.C.	C.P.	.015H	.015H	13B	15	4	1N to ½P	1P	⅛ to 5/32
HUDSON															
1941-42, Six	.038	153624	.020	36	F	T.C.	Fly	.006H	.008H	1040′	13	4½	¼P	¾P	1/16
1941-47, 8 Cyl.	.038	16258374	.017	30	LF	T.C.	Fly	.006H	.007H	1040′	18	7	¼P	¾P	1/16
1946-47, Six	.038	153624	.020	34	F	T.C.	Fly	.010H	.012H	2730′	13	4½	¼P	¾P	1/16
1948-49, Six	.038	153624	.020	38	F	T.C.	Fly	.010H	.012H	718′	17	7	1½P	1½P	1/16
8 Cyl.	.038	16258374	.017	27	LF	T.C.	Fly	.006H	.008H	1040′	18	7	1½P	1½P	1/16
1950-51, Six	.032	153624	.020	39	F	T.C.	Fly	.008H	.010H	7⅓B	18½	7	½P to 1½P	½P to 1½P	1/16
1950-52, 8 Cyl.	.032	16258374	.017	27	F	T.C.	Fly	.008H	.010H	10⅔B	18½	7	½P to 1½P	½P to 1½P	1/16
1952, Six	.032	153624	.020	39	F	T.C.	Fly	.008H	.010H	26 7/10B	18½	7	½P to 1½P	½P to 1½P	1/16
1953-54, Jet, 6 Cyl.	.032	153624	.020	39	F	T.C.	C.P.	.010H	.012H	26⅘B	15	5	½P to 1½P	¼P to 1¼P	1/16
Wasp, 6 Cyl.	.032	153624	.020	39	F	T.C.	Fly	.008H	.010H	33 7/10B	18½	5	½P to 1½P	½P to 1½P	1/16
Super Wasp, 6 Cyl.	.032	153624	.020	39	F	T.C.	Fly	.010H	.012H	33 7/10B	18½	5	½P to 1½P	½P to 1½P	1/16
Hornet, 6 Cyl.	.032	153624	.020	39	F	T.C.	Fly	.008H	.010H	33 7/10B	18½	7	½P to 1½P	½P to 1½P	1/16
1955, Wasp, 6 Cyl.	.032	153624	.020	39	F	T.C.	C.P.	.010H	.012H	26⅘B	13	5	0 to ½P	½P to 1½P	1/16 to 3/16
Hornet, 6 Cyl.	.030	153624	.020	39	F	T.C.	Fly	.010H	.012H	33 7/10B	18½	7	0 to ½P	½P to 1½P	1/16 to 3/16
Hornet, V-8	.035	18436572	.017	27*	LF	5B	C.P.	Zero	Zero	14B	27	5	0 to ½P	½P to 1½P	1/16 to 3/16

□—1953—½N to ¾P
ø—18 Qts.—Series 70
*—35 degrees both sets
†—34 degrees both sets
‡—32-36 degrees both sets

A1—1-4-9-8-5-2-11-10-3-6-7-12
A—After Top Center
B—Before Top Center
C—Cold
CP—Crankshaft Pulley

Dh—Distributor Housing
Fly—Flywheel
F—Front
H—Hot
LF—Left Front

N—Negative
P—Positive
RF—Right Front
TC—Top Center
VD—Vibration Damper

TUNE-UP SPECIFICATIONS
1941 to 1953

MAKE AND MODEL	IGNITION SYSTEM							VALVES			CAPACITY		WHEEL ALIGNMENT		
	Plug Gap	Firing Order	Pt. Gap	Cam Angle Deg.	No. 1 Cyl. Location	Ign. Timing Mark Deg.	Mark Location	Tappet Clearance in.	Tappet Clearance ex.	Inlet Opens	Water qts.	Oil qts.	Caster Deg.	Camber Deg.	Toe-In in.
HUDSON (Continued)															
1956, Super Wasp, 6 Cyl.	.032	153624	.020	34	F	T.C.	C.P.	.010H	.012H	26⅛B	13	5	0 to ½P	½P to 1½P	1/16 to 3/16
Hornet, 6 Cyl.	.030	153624	.020	34	F	T.C.	Fly	Zero	Zero	33⁷/₁₀B	18½	7	0 to ½P	½P to 1½P	1/16 to 3/16
Hornet V-8, A.L.	.035	18436572	.017	27	LF	5B	C.P.	Zero	Zero	14B	27	5	0 to ½P	½P to 1½P	1/16 to 3/16
Hornet Spec., V-8 D.R.	.035	18436572	.017	27*	LF	5B	C.P.	Zero	Zero	12½B	21	5	0 to ½P	½P to 1½P	1/16 to 3/16
1957, Hornet Spec., V-8, D.R.	.035	18436572	.017	30	LF	5B	C.P.	Zero	Zero	12½B	19	5	0 to ½P	½P to 1½P	1/16 to 3/16
KAISER & FRAZER															
1947, early	.032	153624	.020	38	F	T.C.	Fly	.014C	.014C	10B	15	5	Zero	P⅜	1/16
1947, late	.032	153624	.020	38	F	T.C.	V.D.	.014C	.014C	10B	15	5	Zero	P⅜	1/16
1948	.032	153624	.020	38	F	4B	V.D.	.014C	.014C	10B	15	5	Zero	P⅜	1/16
1949-50	.032	153624	.020	38	F	4B	V.D.	.014C	.014C	10B	15	5	Zero	P⅜	1/16
1951-52	.032	153624	.020	34	F	4B	V.D.	.014C	.014C	10B	13	5		P⅜	1/16
LINCOLN															
1941-42	.029	A1	.016	36	LF	4B	Dh	Zero	Zero	10½B	27	5	P4	P4	1/16
1946	.029	A1	.016	36	LF	2B	Dh	Zero	Zero	10½B	24	5	P4	P⅞	3/32
1947-48	.029	A1	.016	36	LF	2B	Dh	Zero	Zero	10½B	24½	5	P4	P⅞	3/32
1949	.030	15486372	.018	30	RF	4B	V.D.	Zero	Zero	14B	34½	6	Zero	P⅜	⅛
1950	.025	15486372	.015	27	RF	4B	C.P.	Zero	Zero	5B	34½	6½	1½N to 0	0 to ¾P	3/32 to 5/32
1951	.030	15486372	.015	27	RF	3B	C.P.	Zero	Zero	5B	34½	6½	1½N to 0	0 to ¾P	3/32 to 5/32
1952-53	.030	15486372	.015	27	RF	3B	C.P.	Zero	Zero	18B	22½	5	1½N to 0	0 to ¾P	3/32 to 5/32
MERCURY															
1941	.025	15486372	.016	36	RF	4B	None	.015H	.015H	T.C.	23¾	5	9P	1P	1/16
1942	.025	15486372	.015	36	RF	4B	None	.015H	.015H	T.C.	22	5	9P	1P	1/16
1946-48	.025	15486372	.015	36	RF	4B	None	.011H	.015H	T.C.	22	5	7¼P	1P	1/16
1949	.032	15486372	.015	30	RF	2B	C.P.	.012H	.016H	10B	22	5	½P	¾P	3/32 to 5/32
1950	.030	15486372	.015	27	RF	2B	C.P.	.011H	.015H	10B	22¼	5	1½N to 0	¾P	3/32 to 5/32
1951-53	.030	15486372	.015	27	RF	2B	C.P.	.018H		5B	22	5	3/32 to 5/32	3/32 to 5/32	¾P
NASH									.014H						1½N to 0
1941—"600", Six	.025	153624	.020	35-38	F	T.C.	V.D.	.015H	.015H	6B	14	5	Zero	P¼	1/32
1942	.025	153624	.020	35-38	F	T.C.	V.D.	.015H	.015H	19B	14	5	Zero	P¼	1/32
1946-48	.025	153624	.020	35-38	F	T.C.	V.D.	.015H	.015H	6B	14	5	P½	P½	5/32
1949	.030	153624	.022	31-37	F	T.C.	V.D.	.015H	.015H	6B	14	5	N¼	Zero	⅛
1941—Amb. Six	.025	153624	.020	35-38	F	6B	V.D.	.015H	.015H	24B	17	6	N¼	P½	1/16
1942	.025	153624	.020	35-38	F	4B	V.D.	.015H	.015H	14B	17	6	N¼	P½	1/16
1946	.025	153624	.020	35-38	F	4B	V.D.	.015H	.015H	24B	17	6	N¼	P½	1/16
1947	.025	153624	.020	35-38	F	T.C.	V.D.	.015H	.015H	6B	17	6	N¼	P½	1/16
1948	.025	153624	.020	35-38	F	T.C.	V.D.	.015H	.015H	4B	17	6	N¼	P½	1/16
1949	.025	153624	.022	31-37	F	T.C.	V.D.	.015H	.015H	4B	17	6	N¼	Zero	⅛
1941—Amb. 8	.025	16258374	.017	27-30	F	9B	V.D.	.015H	.015H	20B	16	7	N¼	P½	1/16
1942	.025	16258374	.017	27-30	F	7B	V.D.	.015H	.015H	10½B	16	7	N¼	P½	1/16
1950-52, Ser. 40	.030	153624	.022	35	F	T.C.	C.P.	.015H	.015H	6B	17	5	0 to ½P	¼N to ¼P	1/16 to 3/16
1950-51, Ser. 60	.030	153624	.022	35	F	T.C.	C.P.	.015H	.015H	6B	17	5	0 to ½P	¼N to ¼P	1/16 to 3/16
1952, Ser. 60	.030	153624	.022	35	F	T.C.	C.P.	.015H	.018H	8½B	17	6	0 to ½P	¼N to ¼P	1/16 to 3/16
1953-54, Ser. 40, 6 Cyl.	.030	153624	.022	35	F	4B	C.P.	.015H	.015H	10B	14	4	0 to ½P	¼N to ¼P	1/16 to 3/16
Ser. 60, 6 Cyl.	.030	153624	.022	35	F	T.C.	C.P.	.012H	.016H	12½B	17	6	0 to ½P	¼N to ¼P	1/16 to 3/16
1955, Ser. 40, 6 Cyl.	.030	153624	.022	34	F	4B	C.P.	.015H	.015H	10B	14	4	0 to ½P	¼N to ¼P	1/16 to 3/16
Ser. 60, 6 Cyl.	.030	153624	.022	34	F	4B	C.P.	.012H	.016H	12½B	17	6	0 to ½P	¼N to ¼P	1/16 to 3/16
Ser. 80, V-8	.035	18436572	.017	36	LF	5B	C.P.	Zero	Zero	14B	20	6	0 to ½P	¼N to ¼P	1/16 to 3/16
1956, Ser. 40, 6 Cyl.	.030	153624	.016	31	F	T.C.	C.P.	.012H	.016H	12½B	11	4	0 to ½P	¼N to ¼P	1/16 to 3/16
Ser. 50, V-8	.035	18436572	.016	30	LF	5B	C.P.	Zero	Zero	12½B	27	5	0 to ½P	¼N to ¼P	1/16 to 3/16
Ser. 60, 6 Cyl.	.030	153624	.019	39	F	4B	C.P.	.012H	.016H	12½B	11	4	0 to ½P	¼N to ¼P	1/16 to 3/16
Ser. 80, V-8	.035	18436572	.016	31	LF	5B	C.P.	Zero	Zero	14B	21	5	0 to ½P	¼N to ¼P	1/16 to 3/16
1957, Ser. 80, V-8	.035	18436572	.016	30	LF	5B	C.P.	Zero	Zero	12½B	19	5	0 to ½P	¼N to ¼P	1/16 to 3/16

ø—18 Qts.—Series 70
□—1953—½N to ¾P
*—35 degrees both sets
†—34 degrees both sets
‡—32-36 degrees both sets

A1—1-4-9-8-5-2-11-10-3-6-7-12
A—After Top Center
B—Before Top Center
C—Cold
CP—Crankshaft Pulley

Dh—Distributor Housing
Fly—Flywheel
F—Front
H—Hot
LF—Left Front

N—Negative
P—Positive
RF—Right Front
TC—Top Center
VD—Vibration Damper

TUNE-UP SPECIFICATIONS
1941 to 1953

MAKE AND MODEL	IGNITION SYSTEM							VALVES			CAPACITY		WHEEL ALIGNMENT		
	Plug Gap	Firing Order	Pt. Gap	Cam Angle Deg.	No. 1 Cyl. Location	Ign. Timing Mark Deg.	Mark Location	Tappet Clearance in.	Tappet Clearance ex.	Inlet Opens	Water qts.	Oil qts.	Caster Deg.	Camber Deg.	Toe-in in.
OLDSMOBILE															
1941-48, Six	.040	153624	.020	35	F	T.C.	Fly	.008H	.011H	5B	18	6	¾P	¾P	⅛
1941-48, 8 Cyl.	.030	16258374	.015	31	LF	2B	Fly	.008H	.011H	T.C.	22	5	¾N	¾N	⅛
1949, Six	.040	153624	.020	35	F	T.C.	Fly	.008H	.011H	5B	18½	5	¾N	¾N	⅛
1949, 88	.030	18736542	.015	15	LF	2B	C.P.	Zero	Zero	14B	21½	5	¾N	¾N	⅛
1949, 98	.030	18736542	.015	22	LF	2B	C.P.	Zero	Zero	14B	21½	5	¾N	¾N	⅛
1950, Six	.040	153624	.021	35	F	T.C.	Fly	.008H	.011H	4B	18½	5	¾N	¼P	⅛
1950, 88, 98	.030	18736542	.015	22	LF	2½B	C.P.	Zero	Zero	13½B	21½	5	¾N	¼P	⅛
1951-53, V8	.030	18736542	.016	30	LF	2½B	C.P.	Zero	Zero	13½B	21½	5	¾N	¼P	⅛
PACKARD															
1941, Six	.028	153624	.020	38	F	6B	V.D.	.007H	.010H	1B	15	5	1P	¾P	0
1942, Six	.028	153624	.020	38	F	4B	V.D.	.007H	.010H	1B	15	5	1P	¾P	0
1941-42, 8 Cyl.	.028	16258374	.015	27	F	5B	V.D.	.007H	.010H	1B	17	5½	1⅛P	¾P	0
Super 8	.028	16258374	.015	27	F	4B	V.D.	Zero	Zero	4B	20	7	1½P	0	⅛
1946-47, Six	.028	153624	.020	27	F	7B	V.D.	.007H	.010H	1B	14	5½	2½P	¾P	0
1946-47, 8 Cyl.	.028	16258374	.017	27-30	F	7B	V.D.	.007H	.010H	1B	20	5½	2½P	¾P	0
1948-49, 8 Cyl.	.028	16258374	.017	27-30	F	6B	V.D.	.007H	.010H	10B	20	7	1½P	¾P	0
Super 8	.028	16258374	.017	27-30	F	6B	V.D.	Zero	Zero	4B	20	7	2½P	¾P	0
1950 Std. 8, A.L.	.028	16258374	.017	27	F	6B	V.D.	.007H	.010H	15B	18	7	1½N to ½N	¼N to ¼P	1/16
D.R.	.028	16258374	.017	26	F	6B	V.D.	.007H	.010H	15B	18	7	1½N to ½N	¼N to ¼P	1/16
Super 8, A.L.	.028	16258374	.017	27	F	6B	V.D.	.007H	.010H	15B	18	7	1½N to ½N	¼N to ¼P	1/16
D.R.	.028	16258374	.017	26	F	6B	V.D.	.007H	.010H	15B	18	7	1½N to ½N	¼N to ¼P	1/16
Custom 8, A.L.	.028	16258374	.017	27	F	6B	V.D.	Zero	Zero	4B	20	7	2½N to 1½N	¼N to ¼P	1/16
1951-52, 200, A.L.	.025	16258374	.017	27	F	6B	V.D.	.007H	.010H	15B	20	7	1½N to ½N	¾P	1/16
250, 300, A.L.	.025	16258374	.017	27	F	6B	V.D.	Zero	Zero	15B	20	7	1½N to ½N	¾P	1/16
400, A.L.	.025	16258374	.017	27	F	6B	V.D.	Zero	Zero	15B	20	7	1½N to ½N	¾P	1/16
1953 Clippers St. 8 D.R. De Luxe St. 8 D.R.	.025	16258374	.015	31	F	6B	C.P.	.007H	.010H	15B	20	7	1½N to ½N	¾P	1/16
Mayfair, Caribbean, Cavalier, Convertible St. 8's D.R.	.025	16258374	.015	31	F	6B	C.P.	Zero	Zero	15B	20	7	1½N to ½N	¾P	1/16
Patrician, Cust. St. 8's A-L	.025	16258374	.015	27	F	6B	C.P.	Zero	Zero	15B	20	7	1½N to ½N	¾P	1/16
1954 Clippers Special St. 8 A-L	.025	16258374	.015	27	F	6B	C.P.	.007H	.010H	15B	20	7	1½N to ½N	¼N to ¾P	1/16
De Luxe, Super St. 8's A-L	.025	16258374	.015	27	F	6B	C.P.	.007H	.010H	10B	20	7	1½N to ½N	¼N to ¾P	1/16
1954 Packards Cavalier St. 8 D.R. Pacific, Caribbean, Conv.	.025	16258374	.015	31	F	6B	C.P.	Zero	Zero	10B	20	7	1½N to ½N	¼N to ¾P	1/16
Patrician, Cust. St. 8's D.R.	.025	16258374	.015	31	F	T.C.	C.P.	Zero	Zero	22B	20	7	1½N to ½N	¼N to ¾P	1/16
1955 Clippers De Luxe Super V8 A-L	.035	18436572	.016	27	LF	6B	C.P.	Zero	Zero	15B	26	5	1½N to ½N	¼N to ¾P	1/16
Custom V8 D.R.	.035	18436572	.016	29½	LF	6B	C.P.	Zero	Zero	15B	26	5	1½N to ½N	¼N to ¾P	1/16
1955 Packards Sedan, Hardtop V8 D.R. Caribbean V8 D.R.	.035	18436572	.016	29½	LF	6B	C.P.	Zero	Zero	15B	26	5	1½N to ½N	¼N to ¾P	1/16
1956 Clippers De Luxe, Super V-8 A-L Custom, Executive V8 A-L	.035	18436572	.016	27	LF	5B	C.P.	Zero	Zero	14B	26	5	1½N to ½N	¼N to ¾P	1/16
1956 Packards Sedan, Hardtop V8 D.R. Caribbean V8 D.R.	.035	18436572	.016	29½	LF	10B	C.P.	Zero	Zero	14B	26	5	1½N to ½N	¼N to ¾P	1/16
1957 Clippers Sedan, Sta. Wag. V8 D.R.	.035	18436572	.016	31	LF	4B	C.P.	.024H	.024H	11B	17	5	2½N to 1N	0 to 1 P	⅙ to ⅛
1958 Packards Hawk Hardtop	.035	18436572	.015	31	LF	4B	C.P.	.026H	.026H	11B	17	5	2½N to 1N	0 to 1 P	⅙ to ⅛

*—35 degrees both sets
†—34 degrees both sets
‡—32-36 degrees both sets
A1—1-4-9-8-5-2-11-10-3-6-7-12
A—After Top Center
B—Before Top Center
C—Cold
CP—Crankshaft Pulley
Dh—Distributor Housing
Fly—Flywheel
F—Front
H—Hot
LF—Left Front
N—Neg-tive
P—Positive
RF—Right Front
TC—Top Center
VD—Vibration Damper

TUNE-UP SPECIFICATIONS
1941 to 1953

MAKE AND MODEL	IGNITION SYSTEM							VALVES			CAPACITY		WHEEL ALIGNMENT		
	Plug Gap	Firing Order	Pt. Gap	Cam Angle Deg.	No. 1 Cyl. Location	Ign. Timing Mark Deg.	Mark Location	Tappet Clearance in.	ex.	Inlet Opens	Water qts.	Oil qts.	Caster Deg.	Camber Deg.	Toe-In in.
PLYMOUTH															
1941	.025	153624	.020	38	F	T.C.	V.D.	.008H	.010H	9B	14	5	1P	¾P	¹⁄₁₆
1942	.025	153624	.020	38	F	3B	V.D.	.008H	.010H	12B	15	5	1P	¾P	¹⁄₁₆
1946-48	.025	153624	.020	38	F	T.C.	V.D.	.008H	.010H	12B	15	5	1P	¾P	¹⁄₁₆
1949	.038	153624	.020	38	F	T.C.	V.D.	.008H	.010H	12B	15	5	1P	¾P	¹⁄₁₆
1950	.030	153624	.020	36½	F	T.C.	V.D.	.010H	.010H	12B	15	5	1P	¾P	¹⁄₁₆
1951-52	.030	153624	.020	36½	F	T.C.	V.D.	.010H	.010H	12B	13	5	1P	¾P	¹⁄₁₆
1953	.035	153624	.020	36	F	2B	V.D.	.010H	.010H	12B	13	5	1P	⅜N to ⅜P	¹⁄₁₆
PONTIAC															
1941-48, Six	.025	153624	.020	37	F	4B	Fly	.012H	.012H	5B	18	6	½P	¼P	¹⁄₁₆
1941-48, 8 Cyl.	.025	16258374	.015	31	LF	4B	Fly	.012H	.012H	5B	19½	5	½P	¼P	¹⁄₁₆
1949, Six	.025	153624	.022	31-37	F	6B	V.D.	.012H	.012H	5B	18	5	1N	0	¹⁄₁₆
8 Cyl.	.025	16258374	.016	21-30	LF	6B	V.D.	.012H	.012H	5B	19½	5	1N	0	¹⁄₁₆
1950-51, Six	.025	153624	.022	34	F	6B	V.D.	.012H	.012H	5B	18	5	1¼N to ¼N	½N to ½P	¹⁄₁₆
8 Cyl.	.025	16258374	.016	25½	F	6B	V.D.	.012H	.012H	5B	19½	5	1¼N to ¼N	½N to ½P	¹⁄₁₆
1952, Six	.025	153624	.022	37	F	6B	V.D.	.012H	.012H	5B	18	5	½N to ½P	½N to ½P	¹⁄₁₆
8 Cyl.	.025	16258374	.016	30	F	6B	V.D.	.012H	.012H	5B	19½	5	½N to ½P	½N to ½P	¹⁄₁₆
1953, Six	.025	153624	.022	34	F	3B	V.D.	.012H	.012H	12½B	18	5	½N to ½P	0 to 1P	¹⁄₁₆
8 Cyl.	.025	16258374	.016	25½	F	6B	V.D.	.012H	.012H	5B	18½	5	½N to ½P	0 to 1P	¹⁄₁₆
RAMBLER															
1950	.030	123456	.022	35	F	T.C.	C.P.	.015H	.015H	6B	12	5	¾P to 1¼P	¼P to ¾P	¹⁄₁₆ to ³⁄₁₆
1951-52	.030	123456	.022	35	F	T.C.	C.P.	.015H	.015H	6B	11	5	¾P to 1¼P	¼P to ¾P	⅛ to ¼
STUDEBAKER															
1941, Champ.	.025	153624	.020	35-38	F	2B	Fly	.016C	.016H	15B	10	5	P1½	½P	³⁄₃₂
1942	.025	153624	.020	35-38	F	2B	Fly	.016C	.016C	15B	10½	5	P1½	½P	³⁄₃₂
1941-42, Comm.	.025	153624	.020	35-38	F	2B	V.D.	.016C	.016C	15B	13	6	P¼	½P	³⁄₃₂
1941-42, Pres.	.025	16258374	.017	21-30	F	T.C.	V.D.	.016C	.016C	15B	15	8	P¼	½P	³⁄₃₂
1946, Champ.	.025	153624	.020	35-38	F	2B	V.D.	.016C	.016C	15B	10½	5	P1½	½P	³⁄₃₂
1947-48	.025	153624	.020	35-38	F	2B	V.D.	.016C	.016C	15B	10	5	P1½	½P	³⁄₃₂
1949	.025	153624	.020	35-38	F	2B	V.D.	.016C	.016C	15B	11	5	P1	½P	³⁄₃₂
1947-48, Comm.	.025	153624	.020	35-38	F	2B	V.D.	.016C	.016C	15B	10	5	P½	½P	³⁄₃₂
1949	.025	153624	.020	35-38	F	2B	V.D.	.016C	.016C	15B	13	6	N2½	½P	³⁄₃₂
1950-53, Comm.	.025	153624	.020	39	F	2B	C.P.	0.16H	.016H	15B	10	5	1N to 2½N	1P	¹⁄₁₆ to ⅛
1950, Comm.	.025	153624	.020	34	F	2B	C.P.	0.16H	.016H	11B	13	6	1N to 2½N	1P	¹⁄₁₆ to ⅛
1951-53, Comm.	.035	18436572	.016	26	LF	8B	C.P.	.015H	.016H	11B	17¼	6	1N to 2½N	1P	¹⁄₁₆ to ⅛
WILLYS															
1941-42, 4 Cyl.	.030	1342	.020	41	F	T.C.	Fly	.014C	.014C	9B	11¾	4	3P	2P	⁵⁄₃₂
1946-48, 4 Cyl.	.030	1342	.024	41	F	5B	Fly	.014C	.014C	9B	11	4	3P	2P	³⁄₃₂
1949, 4 Cyl.	.030	1342	.024	50.8	F	5B	Fly	.016C	.016C	9B	11	4	3P	2P	⅛
1950, 4 Cyl.	.030	1342	.020	42	F	5B	Fly	.016C	.016C	9B	11	4	1P	1P	¹⁄₁₆
1951-53, 4 Cyl.	.030	1342	.020	42	F	5B	Fly	.018C	.016C	9B	11	4	1P	1P	¹⁄₁₆
1950-53, 6 Cyl. L. Head	.030	153624	.020	39	F	4B	C.P.	.016C	.016C	5B	13	5	1P	1½	¹⁄₁₆
1950-53, 6 Cyl. F. Head	.030	153624	.020	39	F	5B	C.P.	.018C	.016C	9B	13	5	1P	1½	¹⁄₁₆

TRUCK TUNE-UP SPECIFICATIONS

ENGINE MODEL	Piston Displacment Cubic In.	No. Cyls.	Bore & Stroke	Firing Order	Gap Point	Dwell (deg)	Spark Occurs (deg)	Mark Location	Spark Plug Gap	Compression Pressure	Tappet Clearance (Hot)		Seat Angle (degrees)		Crankcase Qts.
											In	Ex	In	Ex	
CHEVROLET															
153	153	4	3.88x3.25	1342	.019	33°	4°BTDC	Pulley	.035	130	Zero	Zero	45°	45°	4
Turb-Air (Horiz.)	145	6	3-7/16x2-19/32	145236	.019	33°	4°BTDC	Pulley	.035	130	Zero	Zero	45°	45°	4½
230	230	6	3-7/8x3.25	153624	.019	32°	4°BTDC	Damper	.035	135	Zero	Zero	45°	45°	4
235 Thriftmaster	235	6	3-9/16x3-15/16	153624	.019	32°	5°BTDC	Flywhl	.035	130	.006	.018	31°	46°	5
261 Jobmaster	261	6	3-3/4x3-15/16	153624	.019	32°	TDC	Flywhl	.035	130	.006	.020	31°	46°	5
265 Turbofire	265	V8	3-3/4x3	18436572	.019	30°	4°BTDC	Damper	.035	140	Zero	Zero	45°	45°	5
283 Taskmaster	283	8	3-7/8x3	18436572	.019	30°	4°BTDC	Damper	.035	140	Zero	Zero	46°	46°	5
283 Tradmaster	283	8	3-7/8x3	18436572	.019	30°	4°BTDC	Damper	.035	140	Zero	Zero	46°	46°	4
292	292	6	3-7/8x3-1/8	153624	.019	32°	4°BTDC	Damper	.035	130	Zero	Zero	45°	45°	5
322 Loadmaster	322	8	4x3.2	18436572	.019	30°	4°BTDC	Damper	.035	150	Zero	Zero	46°	46°	5
327 Taskmaster	327	V8	4x3.25	18436572	.019	30°	4°BTDC	Damper	.035	150	Zero	Zero	46°	46°	5
348 Workmaster	348	8	4.125x3.25	18436572	.019	30°	8°BTDC	Damper	.035	125	Zero	Zero	46°	46°	6
409 Workmaster	409	V8	4-15/16x3.5	18436572	.019	30°	4°BTDC	Damper	.035	130	Zero	Zero	46°	46°	6
DIVCO															
Divco Super Six	252.6	6	3-1/2x4-3/8	153624	.021	42°	4°ATC	Pulley	.030	120	.012	.016	30°	45°	6
Con. F 4162	162	4	3-7/16x4-3/8	1342	.020	32°	9°BTC	Flywhl	.035	110	.018	.018	30°	45°	3½
Con. F 4162 Super	162	4	3-7/16x4-3/8	1342	.020	30°	9°BTC	Flywhl	.035	110	.018	.018	30°	45°	3½
Her QXD3	229.7	6	3-7/16x4-1/8	153624	.018	31°	4°BTC	Flywhl	.025	120	.008	.010	30°	30°	5
Con F4162 1960	162	4	3-7/16x4-3/8	1342	.022	30°	10°BTDC	Flywhl	.035	120	.014	.014	30°	44°	4
Con G4193	193	4	3-3/4x4-3/8	1342	.022	32°	10°BTDC	Flywhl	.035	120	.014	.014	30°	45°	4
Con FO6226	226	6	3-5/16x4-3/8	153624	.022	35°	5°BTDC	Flywhl	.035	155	.017	.023	30°	45°	5
DODGE															
170	170	6	3-13/32x3-1/8	153624	.020	43°	2.5°BTC	Damper	.035	145	.010	.024	47°	47°	5
218	218	6	3-1/4x4-3/8	153624	.020	39°	1°BTC	Damper	.035	135	.010	.014	45°	45°	5
225	225	6	3-13/32x4-1/8	153624	.020	43°	2.5°BTC	Damper	.035	145	.010	.024	45°	45°	5
230	230.2	6	3.25x4.625	153624	.020	39°	2.5°BTC	Damper	.035	160	.010	.014	45°	45°	5

TRUCK TUNE-UP SPECIFICATIONS

ENGINE MODEL	Piston Displacement Cubic In.	No. Cyls.	Bore & Stroke	Firing Order	Point Gap	Dwell (deg)	Spark Occurs (deg)	Mark Location	Spark Plug Gap	Compression Pressure	Tappet Clearance (Hot) In	Tappet Clearance (Hot) Ex	Seat Angle (degrees) In	Seat Angle (degrees) Ex	Crankcase Qts.
DODGE—continued															
241	241	8	3-7/16x3-1/4	18436572	.035	35°	4°BTC	Damper	.035	135	Zero	Zero	45°	45°	5
250	250.6	6	3.437x4.50	153624	.020	39°	2.5°BTC	Damper	.035	145	.010	.014	45°	45°	5
251	251	6	3-7/16x4-1/2	153624	.020	39°	5°BTC	Damper	.035	138	.010	.016	45°	45°	5
265	265.37	6	3.437x4.766	153624	.020	39°	2.5°BTC	Damper	.035	145	.010	.018	45°	45°	5
265 (a)	265.37	6	3.437x4.766	153624	.020	39°	2.5°BTC	Damper	.035	145	.010	.014	45°	45°	5
270	270	8	3.63x3.259	18436572	.035	35°	4°BTC	Damper	.035	135	Zero	Zero	45°	45°	5
315 HD DR	314.61	V8	3.63x3.80	18436572	.016	31°	6°BTC	Damper	.035	155	Zero	Zero	45°	45°	5
318	318.14	V8	3.91x3.312	18436572	.017	30°	10°BTC	Damper	.035	140	.010	.018	45°	45°	5
318 HD	318.14	V8	3.91x3.312	18436572	.017	30°	10°BTC	Damper	.035	140	Zero	Zero	45°	45°	5
331	331	8	3.81x3.625	18436572			4°BTC	Damper	.035	135			45°	45°	
354 DR	354.06	V8	3.94x3.63	18436572	.016	28°	4°BTC	Damper	.035	140	Zero	Zero	45°	45°	8
354 DR (a)	354.06	V8	3.94x3.63	18436572	.016	30°	4°BTC	Damper	.035	140	Zero	Zero	45°	45°	8
361	361	V8	4-1/8x3-3/8	18436572	.017	30°	10°BTDC	Damper	.035	120	Zero	Zero	45°	45°	8
413	413	8	4.188x3.750	18436572	.017	30°	10°BTC	Damper	.035	120	Zero	Zero	45°	45°	8

(a) Twin 2-barrel carburetors

FORD

ENGINE MODEL	Piston Displacement Cubic In.	No. Cyls.	Bore & Stroke	Firing Order	Point Gap	Dwell (deg)	Spark Occurs (deg)	Mark Location	Spark Plug Gap	Compression Pressure	Tappet Clearance (Hot) In	Tappet Clearance (Hot) Ex	Seat Angle (degrees) In	Seat Angle (degrees) Ex	Crankcase Qts.
144	144	6	3-1/2x2-1/2	153624	.025	36°	2°BTC	Damper	.034	170	.016	.016	45°	45°	3½
170	170	6	3-1/2x2.94	153624	.025	36°	2°BTC	Damper	.034	170	0.16	.016	45°	45°	3½
223 SIX	223	6	3-5/8x3-39/64	153624	.025	36°	4°BTC	Damper	.034	150	.019	.019	45°	45°	5
239	239	V8	3.50x3.10	15486372	.015	27°	10°BTC	Pulley	.030	150	.016	.018	45°	45°	5
256	256	V8	3.62x3.10	15486372	.015	27°	10°BTC	Pulley	.030	150	.016	.018	45°	45°	6
262	262	6	3.718x4.03	153624	.025	36°	4°BTC	Damper	.030	150	.019	.019	45°	45°	6
272	272	V8	3.625x3.30	15486372	.015	27°	10°BTC	Damper	.030	150	.018	.018	45°	45°	5
279	279	V8	3.56x3.50	15486372	.015	27°	10°BTC	Damper	.030	150	.09	.021	45°	45°	8
292 MD	292	V8	3-3/4x3-5/16	15486372	.015	27°	8°BTC	Damper	.034	150	.018	.018	45°	45°	5

ENGINE MODEL	Piston Displacement Cubic In.	No. Cyls.	Bore & Stroke	Firing Order	Gap Point	Dwell (deg)	Spark Occurs (deg)	Mark Location	Spark Plug Gap	Compression Pressure	Tappet Clearance (Hot) In	Tappet Clearance (Hot) Ex	Seat Angle (degrees) In	Seat Angle (degrees) Ex	Crankcase Qts.

FORD—continued

ENGINE MODEL	Piston Displacement Cubic In.	No. Cyls.	Bore & Stroke	Firing Order	Gap Point	Dwell (deg)	Spark Occurs (deg)	Mark Location	Spark Plug Gap	Compression Pressure	In	Ex	In	Ex	Crankcase Qts.
292 HD	292	V8	3-3/4x3-5/16	15486372	.015	27°	8°BTC	Damper	.030	150	.018	.018	45°	45°	6
302 HD	302	V8	3-5/8x3-21/32	15486372	.015	27°	8°BTC	Damper	.030	150	.020	.020	45°	45°	8
317	317	V8	3.80x3.50	15486372	.015	27°	10°BTC	Damper	.030	150	.09	.021	45°	45°	8
332 HD	332	V8	3-51/64x3-21/32	15486372	.015	27°	8°BTC	Damper	.030	150	.020	.020	45°	45°	8
401 SD	401	V8	4-1/8x3-3/4	15486372	.015	27°	8°BTC	Damper	.030	150	.020	.020	45°	45°	9
477 SD	477	V8	4-1/2x3-3/4	15486372	.015	27°	8°BTC	Damper	.030	150	.020	.020	45°	45°	9
534 SD	534	V8	4-1/2x4-13/64	15486372	.015	27°	8°BTC	Damper	.030	150	.020	.020	45°	45°	9

GMC

ENGINE MODEL	Piston Displacement Cubic In.	No. Cyls.	Bore & Stroke	Firing Order	Gap Point	Dwell (deg)	Spark Occurs (deg)	Mark Location	Spark Plug Gap	Compression Pressure	In	Ex	In	Ex	Crankcase Qts.
228	228	6	3-9/16x3-13/16	153624	.016	32°	Ball	Flyhwl	.030	125	.012	.020	.030	.030	8
248	248.5	6	3-23/32x3-13/16	153624	.020	32°	Ball	Flywhl	.030		.012	.020	30°	30°	8
270	269.5	6	3-25/32x4	153624	.016	32°	5°BTC	Flywhl	.030	140	.012	.020	30°	30°	8
288	287.2	8	3-3/4x3-1/4	18436572			TDC	Damper	.035		Zero	Zero	30°	45°	
302	301.6	6	4x4	153624	.016	32°	5°BTC	Flywhl	.030	125	.012	.020	30°	45°	8
316	316.7	8	3-5/16x3-1/4	18436572			5°BTC	Damper	.030		Zero	Zero	30°	45°	
324	324.31	8	3-7/8x3-7/16	18436572	.016	30°	5°BTC	Damper	.030		Zero	Zero	.045	.045	5
336	336.9	8	3-25/32x4	18436572	.016	30°	6°BTC	Damper	.030	125	Zero	Zero	45°	45°	5
347	347	8	3-15/16x3-9/16	18436572				Damper	.030		Zero	Zero	30°	45°	5
360	360.8	6	4-1/8x4-1/2	153624	.020	30°	6°BTC	Flywhl	.030	110	.012	.016	.030	.045	9
370	370.7	8	4x3-11/16	18736542	.016	30°	TC	Damper	.030	125	Zero	Zero	30°	45°	5
503	502.7	6	4-9/16x5-1/8	142635	.016	32°	6°	Flywhl	.030	125	.012	.018	30°	45°	9
305	304.7	V6	4-1/4x3.58	165432	.018	31°	TDC	Damper	.030	125	.012	.018	30°	45°	5
351	351.2	V6	4-9/16x3.58	165432	.018	31°	TDC	Damper	.030	125	.012	.018	30°	45°	8
401	400.9	V6	4-7/8x3.58	165432	.018	31°	TDC	Damper	.030	125	.012	.018	30°	45°	8
426	425.6	6	4-1/4x5	153624			6°BTDC		.030		.012	.020	30°	45°	
478	478	V6	5-1/8x3-55/64	165432	.018	31°	TDC	Damper	.030	125	.012	.018	30°	45°	8
702	702.9	V12	4-9/16x3.58	*	.016	47°	5°BTDC	Damper	.030	125	Zero	Zero	30°	45°	14

*—149852111036712

1113

TRUCK TUNE-UP SPECIFICATIONS

ENGINE MODEL	Piston Displacement Cubic In.	No. Cyls.	Bore & Stroke	Firing Order	Gap Point	Dwell (deg)	Spark Occurs (deg)	Mark Location	Spark Plug Gap	Compression Pressure	Tappet Clearance (Hot)		Seat Angle (degrees)		Crankcase Qts.
											In	Ex	In	Ex	

INTERNATIONAL

ENGINE MODEL	Piston Displacement Cubic In.	No. Cyls.	Bore & Stroke	Firing Order	Gap Point	Dwell (deg)	Spark Occurs (deg)	Mark Location	Spark Plug Gap	Compression Pressure	Tappet Clearance (Hot) In	Tappet Clearance (Hot) Ex	Seat Angle In	Seat Angle Ex	Crankcase Qts.
A55	91	4	2-7/8x3-1/2	1342	.015	....	5°BTC	Pulley	.025	125	0.15	.015	45°	45°	4
BD-220	220	6	3-9/16x3-11/16	153624	.017	32°	4°BTC	Flywhl	.030	125	.025	.025	30°	30°	5
BD-240	240	6	3-9/16x4-1/64	153624	.017	32°	4°BTC	Flywhl	.030	125	.025	.025	30°	30°	5
BD-264	264	6	3-11/16x4-1/8	153624	.017	32°	2°BTC	Pulley	.030	125	.025	.025	30°	30°	7
BD-269	269	6	3-9/16x4-1/2	153624	.019	32°	TDC	Flywhl	.030	125	.021	.021	*45°	45°	7
BD-282	282	6	3-13/16x4-1/8	153624	.017	32°	6°BTC	Pulley	.030	125	.021	.021	*45°	45°	7
BD-308	308	6	3-15/16x4-1/2	153624	.017	32°	3°BTC	Pulley	.030	125	.021	.021	*45°	45°	7
RD-372	372.066	6	4-3/8x4-1/8	153624	.022	34°	5°BTC	Pulley	.030	125	.026	.026	15°	45°	9
RD-406	405.891	6	4-3/8x4-1/2	153624	.022	34°	5°BTC	Pulley	.030	125	.026	.026	15°	45°	9
RD-450	450.990	6	4-3/8x5	153624	.022	34°	5°BTC	Pulley	.030	125	.026	.026	15°	45°	9
RD-501	500.976	6	4-1/2x5-1/4	153624	.022	34°	5°BTC	Pulley	.030	125	.026	.026	15°	45°	9
V-401	401	V8	4-1/8x3-3/4	18736542	.015	30°	5°BTC	Damper	.027	125	Zero	Zero	15°	15°	12
V-461	461	V8	4-1/8x4-5/16	18736542	.015	30°	8°BTC	Damper	.027	125	Zero	Zero	15°	15°	12
V-549	549	V8	4-1/2x4-5/16	18736542	.015	30°	6°BTC	Damper	.027	125	Zero	Zero	15°	45°	5
V-266	266	V8	3-5/8x3-7/32	18736542	.016	30°	4°BTDC	Damper	.028	125	Zero	Zero	45°	45°	5
V-304	304	V8	3-7/8x3-7/32	18736542	.016	30°	TC	Damper	.028	125	Zero	Zero	45°	45°	8
V-345	345	V8	3-7/8x3-21/32	18736542	.016	30°	TC	Damper	.028	125	Zero	Zero	45°	45°	8

* exc. Silichrome 15 degree

STUDEBAKER

ENGINE MODEL	Piston Displacement Cubic In.	No. Cyls.	Bore & Stroke	Firing Order	Gap Point	Dwell (deg)	Spark Occurs (deg)	Mark Location	Spark Plug Gap	Compression Pressure	Tappet Clearance (Hot) In	Tappet Clearance (Hot) Ex	Seat Angle In	Seat Angle Ex	Crankcase Qts.
1E	169.6	6	3x4	153624	.020	39°	2°BTC	Damper	.036	140	.024	.024	45°	45°	5
2E	224	8	3-9/16x2-13/16	18436572	.015	30°	4°BTC	Damper	.030	140	.024	.024	45°	45°	6
3E	259.2	V8	3-9/16x3-1/4	18436572	.015	30°	4°BTC	Damper	.035	140	.024	.024	45°	45°	5
4E	245.6	6	3-5/16x4-3/4	153624	.022	33°	2°BTC	Damper	.030	140	.018	.018	45°	45°	6
5E	289	V8	3-9/16x3-5/8	19436572	.015	30°	4°BTC	Damper	.035	140	.024	.024	45°	45°	5
6E	289	V8	3-9/16x3-5/8	18436572	.015	30°	4°BTC	Damper	.035	140	.024	.024	45°	45°	5
7E	289	8	3-9/16x3-5/8	18436572	.015	30°	4°BTC	Damper	.035	140	.024	.024	45°	45°	5
6-170	170	6	3x4	153624	.022	30°	2°BTC	Damper	.030	140	.018	.018	45°	45°	5
VT	233	8	3-3/8x3-1/4	18436572	.015	30°	4°BTC	Damper	.035	140	.022	.024	45°	45°	5

ENGINE MODEL	Piston Displacement Cubic In.	No. Cyls.	Bore & Stroke	Firing Order	Point Gap	Dwell (deg)	Spark Occurs (deg)	Mark Location	Spark Plug Gap	Tappet Clearance (Hot)		Seat Angle (degrees)		Crankcase Qts.
										In	Ex	In	Ex	

WHITE

ENGINE MODEL	Piston Displacement Cubic In.	No. Cyls.	Bore & Stroke	Firing Order	Point Gap	Dwell (deg)	Spark Occurs (deg)	Mark Location	Spark Plug Gap	Tappet In	Tappet Ex	Seat In	Seat Ex	Crankcase Qts.
55A	245	6	3-1/2x4-1/2	153624	.022	31-37	—	Damper	.028	.09	.012	45°	45°	6
65A	237	6	3-7/16x4-1/4	153624	.020	31-37	—	Flywhl	.025	*	*	45°	45°	—
116A	298	6	3-3/4x4-1/2	153624	.022	31-37	6°BTC	Flywhl	.025	Zero	Zero	45°	45°	12
120A	318	6	3-7/8x4-1/2	153624	.022	31-37	—	Flywhl	.025	Zero	Zero	45°	45°	12
130A	292	6	3-7/8x4-1/8	153624	.022	31-37	4°BTC	Damper	.025	.015	.015	30°	30°	12
140A	362	6	3-7/8x5-1/8	153624	.022	31-37	6°BTC	Flywhl	.025	Zero	Zero	45°	45°	12
145A	331	6	4-1/8x4-1/8	153624	.022	31-37	2°BTC	Damper	.025	.015	.015	30°	30°	12
150A	386	6	4x5-1/8	153624	.022	31-37	3°BTC	Flywhl	.025	Zero	Zero	45°	45°	12
170A	331	6	4-1/8x4-1/8	153624	.016	32	2°BTC	Damper	.025	.022	.022	30°	30°	8
186A	362	6	4-1/4x4-1/4	153624	.016	32	6°BTC	Damper	.025	.022	.022	30°	30°	—
230A	340	6	4x4-1/2	153624	.022	31-37	6°BTC	Flywhl	.025	Zero	Zero	45°	45°	12
235A	440	V8	4-1/8x4-1/8	15486372	.016	30	3°BTC	Damper	.025	.022	.022	30°	30°	9
250A	386	6	4x5-1/8	153624	.022	31-37	3°BTC	Flywhl	.025	Zero	Zero	45°	45°	12
260A	451	6	4-3/8x5	153624	.022	31-37	—	Flywhl	.025	Zero	Zero	45°	45°	15
280A	504	6	4-5/8x5	153624	.022	31-37	—	Flywhl	.025	Zero	Zero	45°	45°	15
290A	504	6	4-5/8x5	153624	.022	31-37	9°BTC	Flywhl	.025	Zero	Zero	45°	45°	15
370A	452	6	4-3/4x4-1/4	153624	.022	31-37	—	Damper	.025	Zero	Zero	30°	30°	—
380A	504	6	4-5/8x5	153624	.022	31-37	9°BTC	Damper	.025	Zero	Zero	30°	30°	15
390A	531	6	4-3/4x5	153624	.022	31-37	9°BTC	Damper	.025	Zero	Zero	30°	30°	15
450A	386	6	4x5-1/8	153624	.022	31-37	3°BTC	Flywhl	.025	Zero	Zero	45°	45°	12
460A	386	6	4x5-1/8	153624	.022	31-37	3°BTC	Flywhl	.025	Zero	Zero	45°	45°	12
462A	386	6	4x5-1/8	153624	.022	31-37	3°BTC	Flywhl	.025	Zero	Zero	45°	45°	—
470A	477	6	4-1/2x5	153624	.022	31-37	6°BTC	Flywhl	.025	Zero	Zero	30°	30°	15
490A	531	6	4-1/2x5	153624	.022	31-37	9°BTC	Flywhl	.025	Zero	Zero	30°	30°	15

* Instructions on engine plate.

TRUCK TRANSMISSIONS

Chevrolet and GMC—3-Speed

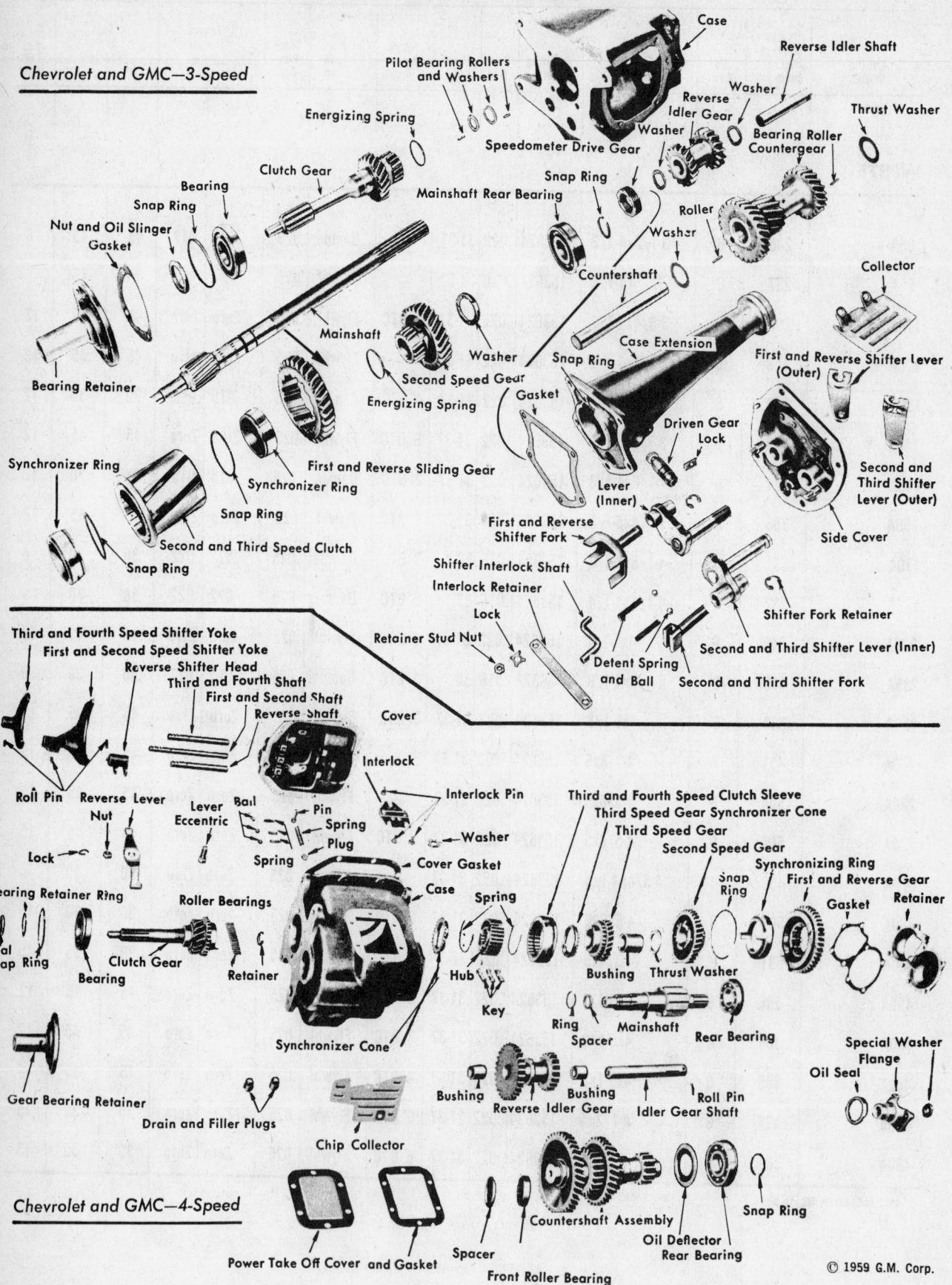

Case
Reverse Idler Shaft
Pilot Bearing Rollers and Washers
Energizing Spring
Reverse Idler Gear
Washer
Thrust Washer
Speedometer Drive Gear
Washer
Bearing Roller Countergear
Clutch Gear
Bearing
Snap Ring
Mainshaft Rear Bearing
Snap Ring
Roller
Nut and Oil Slinger Gasket
Washer
Countershaft
Collector
Mainshaft
Washer
Snap Ring
Case Extension
First and Reverse Shifter Lever (Outer)
Bearing Retainer
Second Speed Gear
Energizing Spring
Gasket
Driven Gear Lock
Second and Third Shifter Lever (Outer)
Synchronizer Ring
First and Reverse Sliding Gear
Lever (Inner)
Synchronizer Ring
Snap Ring
First and Reverse Shifter Fork
Side Cover
Snap Ring
Second and Third Speed Clutch
Shifter Interlock Shaft
Interlock Retainer
Shifter Fork Retainer
Lock
Second and Third Shifter Lever (Inner)
Retainer Stud Nut
Detent Spring and Ball
Second and Third Shifter Fork

Third and Fourth Speed Shifter Yoke
First and Second Speed Shifter Yoke
Reverse Shifter Head
Third and Fourth Shaft
First and Second Shaft
Reverse Shaft
Cover
Interlock
Interlock Pin
Third and Fourth Speed Clutch Sleeve
Third Speed Gear Synchronizer Cone
Third Speed Gear
Second Speed Gear
Synchronizing Ring
First and Reverse Gear
Roll Pin
Reverse Lever Nut
Lever Eccentric
Bail
Pin
Spring
Plug
Washer
Snap Ring
Gasket
Retainer
Lock
Spring
Cover Gasket
Case
Spring
Bushing
Thrust Washer
Bearing Retainer Ring
Roller Bearings
Seal
Snap Ring
Clutch Gear
Retainer
Hub
Bushing
Bearing
Key
Ring Spacer
Mainshaft
Rear Bearing
Synchronizer Cone
Special Washer
Flange
Oil Seal
Gear Bearing Retainer
Drain and Filler Plugs
Bushing
Reverse Idler Gear
Bushing
Idler Gear Shaft
Roll Pin
Chip Collector
Countershaft Assembly
Oil Deflector
Rear Bearing
Snap Ring

Chevrolet and GMC—4-Speed

Power Take Off Cover and Gasket
Spacer
Front Roller Bearing

© 1959 G.M. Corp.

TRUCK TRANSMISSIONS

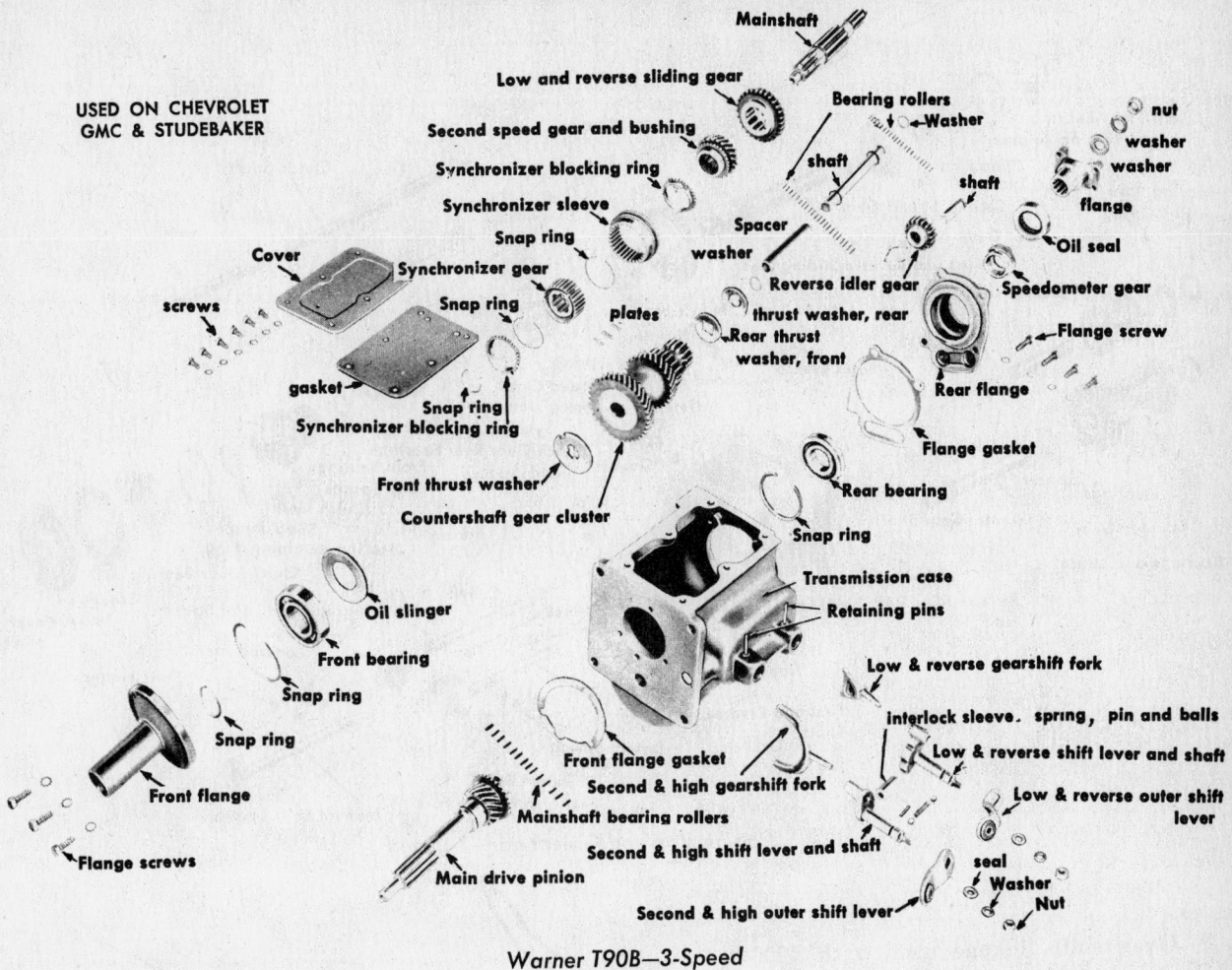

USED ON CHEVROLET
GMC & STUDEBAKER

Mainshaft

Low and reverse sliding gear

Second speed gear and bushing

Synchronizer blocking ring

Synchronizer sleeve

Snap ring

Cover

Synchronizer gear

screws

Snap ring

gasket

Snap ring

Synchronizer blocking ring

Front thrust washer

Countershaft gear cluster

Oil slinger

Front bearing

Snap ring

Snap ring

Front flange

Flange screws

Bearing rollers
Washer

shaft

shaft

Spacer
washer

plates

Reverse idler gear
thrust washer, rear
Rear thrust
washer, front

nut
washer
washer
flange
Oil seal
Speedometer gear
Flange screw
Rear flange
Flange gasket

Rear bearing
Snap ring
Transmission case
Retaining pins

Low & reverse gearshift fork
interlock sleeve, spring, pin and balls
Low & reverse shift lever and shaft
Low & reverse outer shift lever

Front flange gasket
Second & high gearshift fork
Mainshaft bearing rollers
Second & high shift lever and shaft
Main drive pinion

Second & high outer shift lever

seal
Washer
Nut

Warner T90B—3-Speed

bearing retainer
gasket
washer
Clutch gear bearing
Clutch gear
snap rings
oil retaining washer
Mainshaft pilot roller bearing
thrust washer
Countergear
spacer
idler
gear
shaft
Countergear bearings
and retainer washers
gasket

Transmission case
Clutch hub retaining snap ring
Second and third clutch sleeve
Synchronizer
snap ring
Second speed gear
First and reverse gear
Mainshaft
Synchronizing cone
Second and third
clutch hub
Shaft
(bronze) (steel)
Shifter shaft lever
cover

snap rings
bearing

Transmission oil retaining washer

gasket
rear extension
gear spacer
Speedometer
drive gear
flange

Oil Seal

First and reverse shifter shoe
Interlock sleeve
balls
spring

spacer
Shifter shaft
Second and third shifter fork

© 1959 G.M. Corp

Chevrolet—4-Speed H.D.

TRUCK TRANSMISSIONS

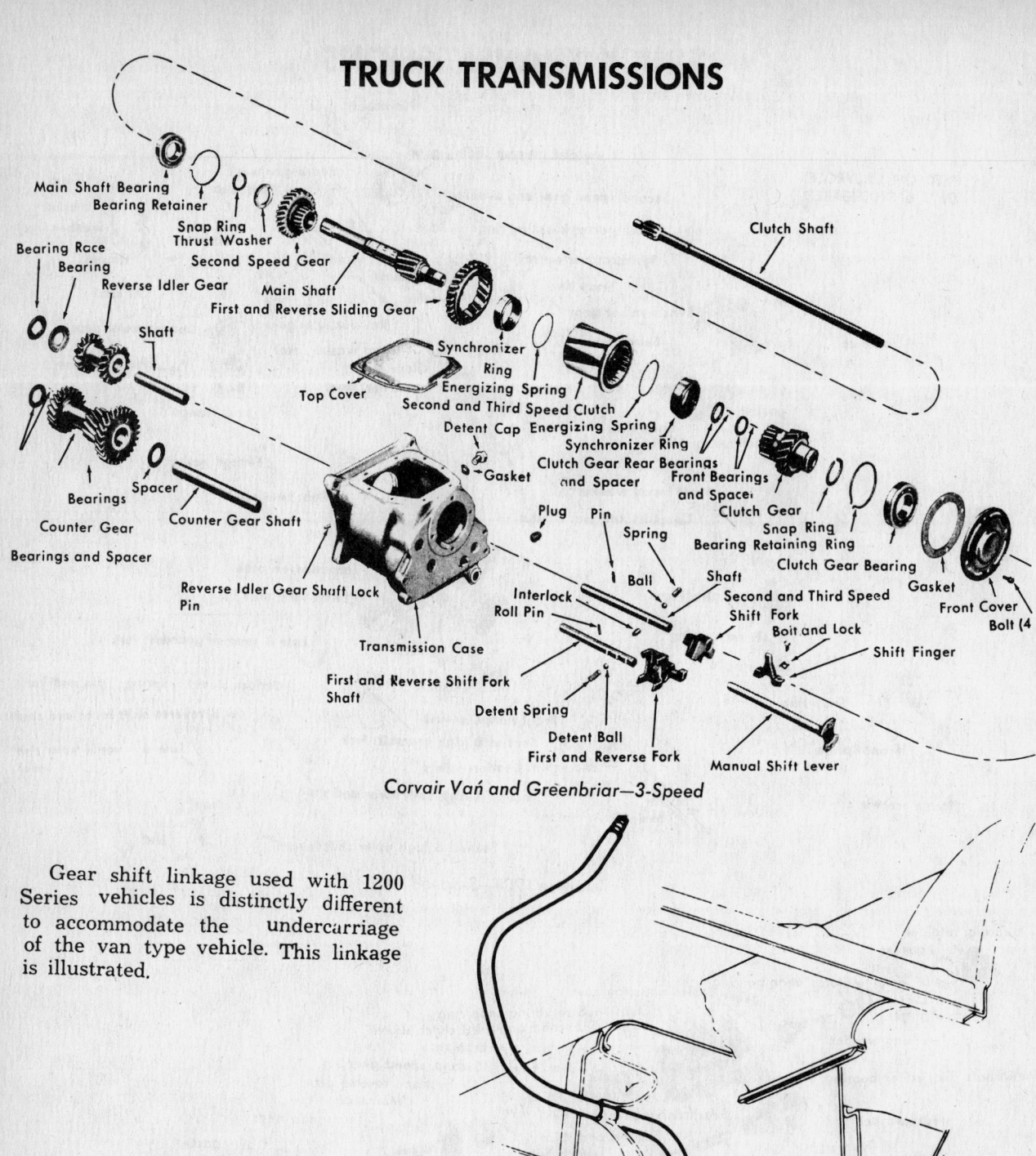

Main Shaft Bearing
Bearing Retainer
Snap Ring
Thrust Washer
Second Speed Gear
Bearing Race
Bearing
Reverse Idler Gear
Shaft
Main Shaft
First and Reverse Sliding Gear
Clutch Shaft
Synchronizer Ring
Energizing Spring
Second and Third Speed Clutch
Top Cover
Detent Cap Energizing Spring
Synchronizer Ring
Clutch Gear Rear Bearings and Spacer
Gasket
Front Bearings and Spacer
Spacer
Bearings
Counter Gear
Counter Gear Shaft
Bearings and Spacer
Plug
Pin
Spring
Clutch Gear
Snap Ring
Bearing Retaining Ring
Clutch Gear Bearing
Gasket
Reverse Idler Gear Shaft Lock Pin
Interlock
Roll Pin
Ball
Shaft
Second and Third Speed Shift Fork
Bolt and Lock
Front Cover
Bolt (4
Transmission Case
Shift Finger
First and Reverse Shift Fork Shaft
Detent Spring
Detent Ball
First and Reverse Fork
Manual Shift Lever

Corvair Van and Greenbriar—3-Speed

Gear shift linkage used with 1200 Series vehicles is distinctly different to accommodate the undercarriage of the van type vehicle. This linkage is illustrated.

Corvair Van and Greenbriar—Control

TRUCK TRANSMISSIONS

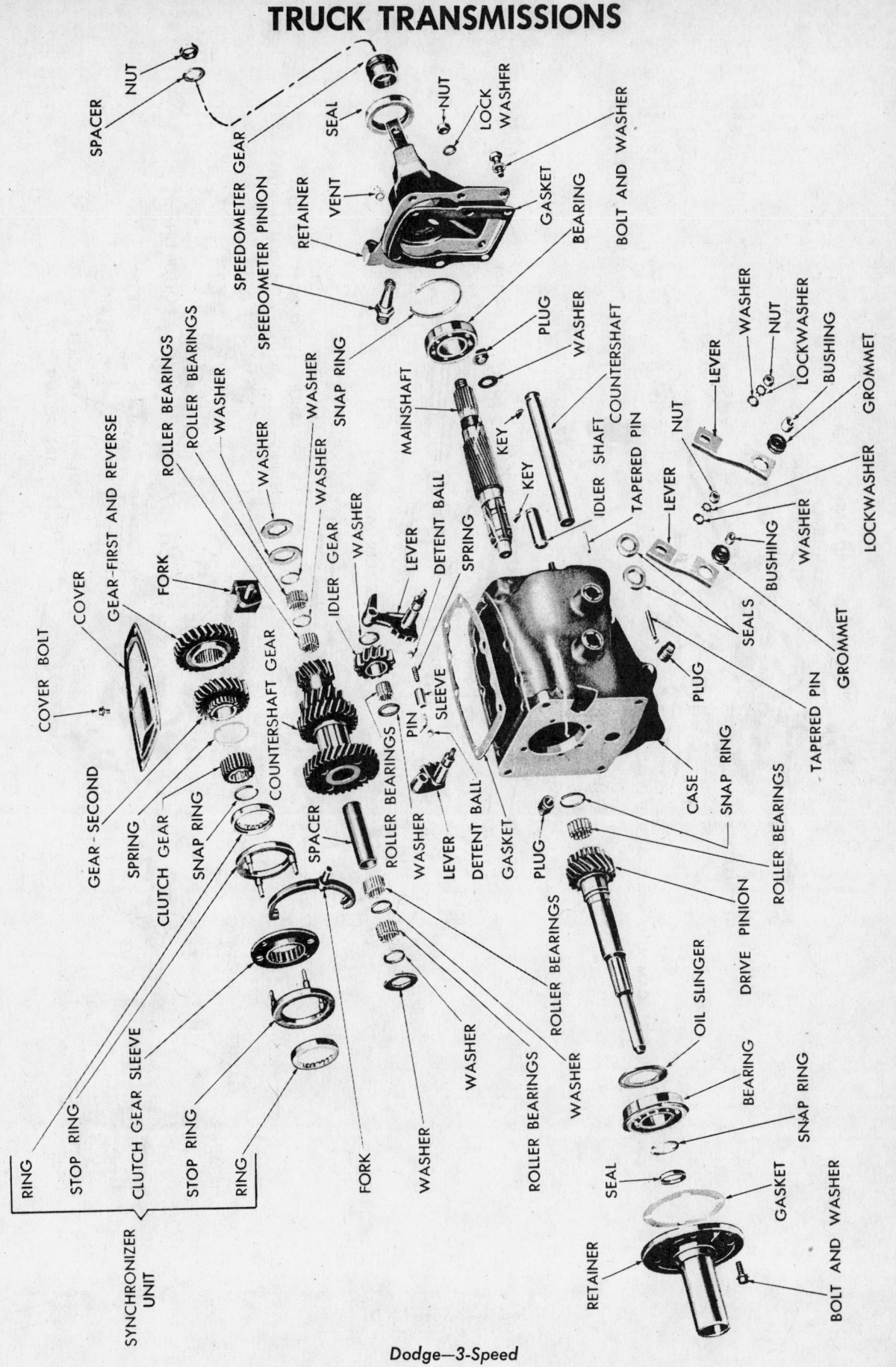

Dodge—3-Speed

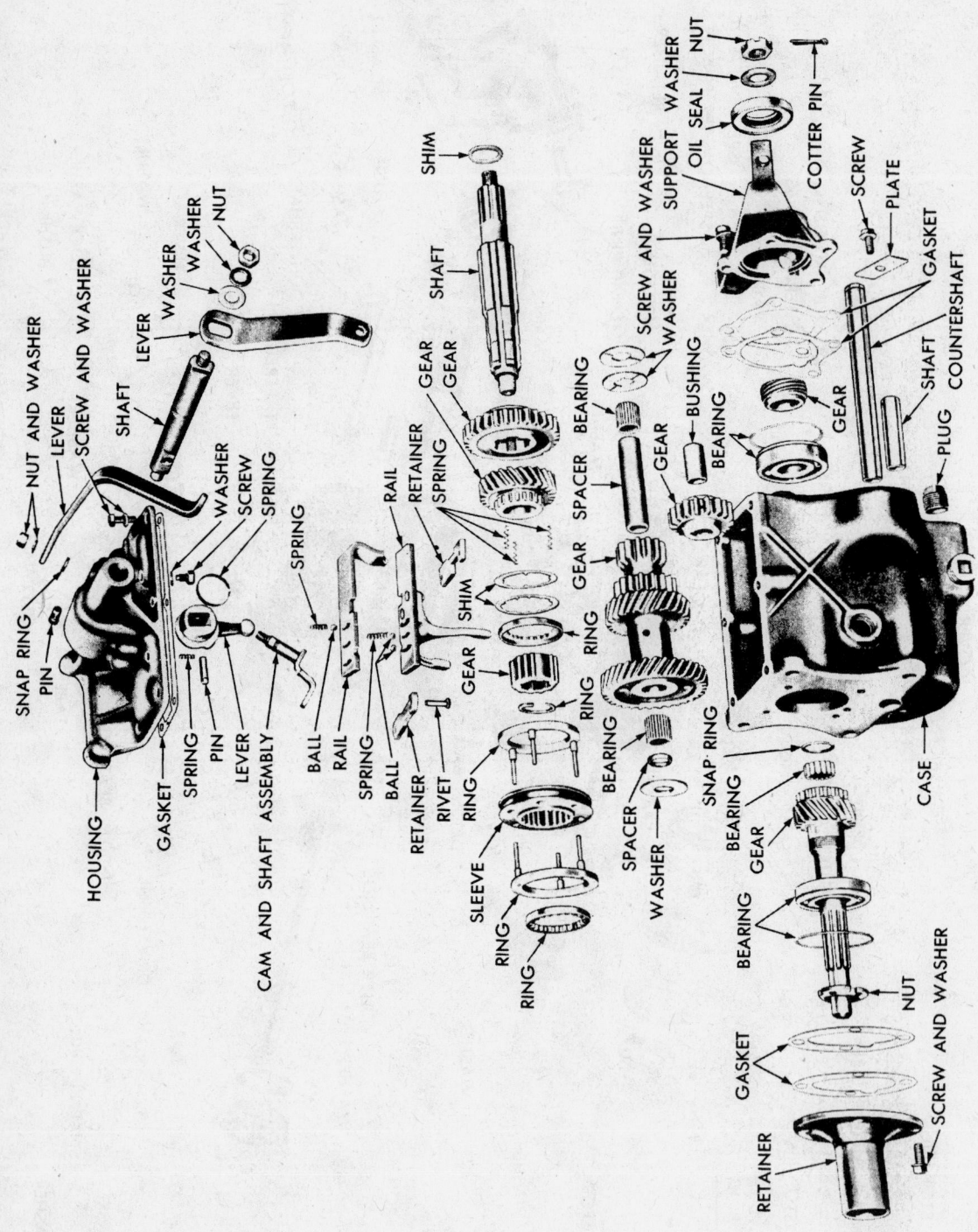

Dodge—3-Speed H.D.

TRUCK TRANSMISSIONS

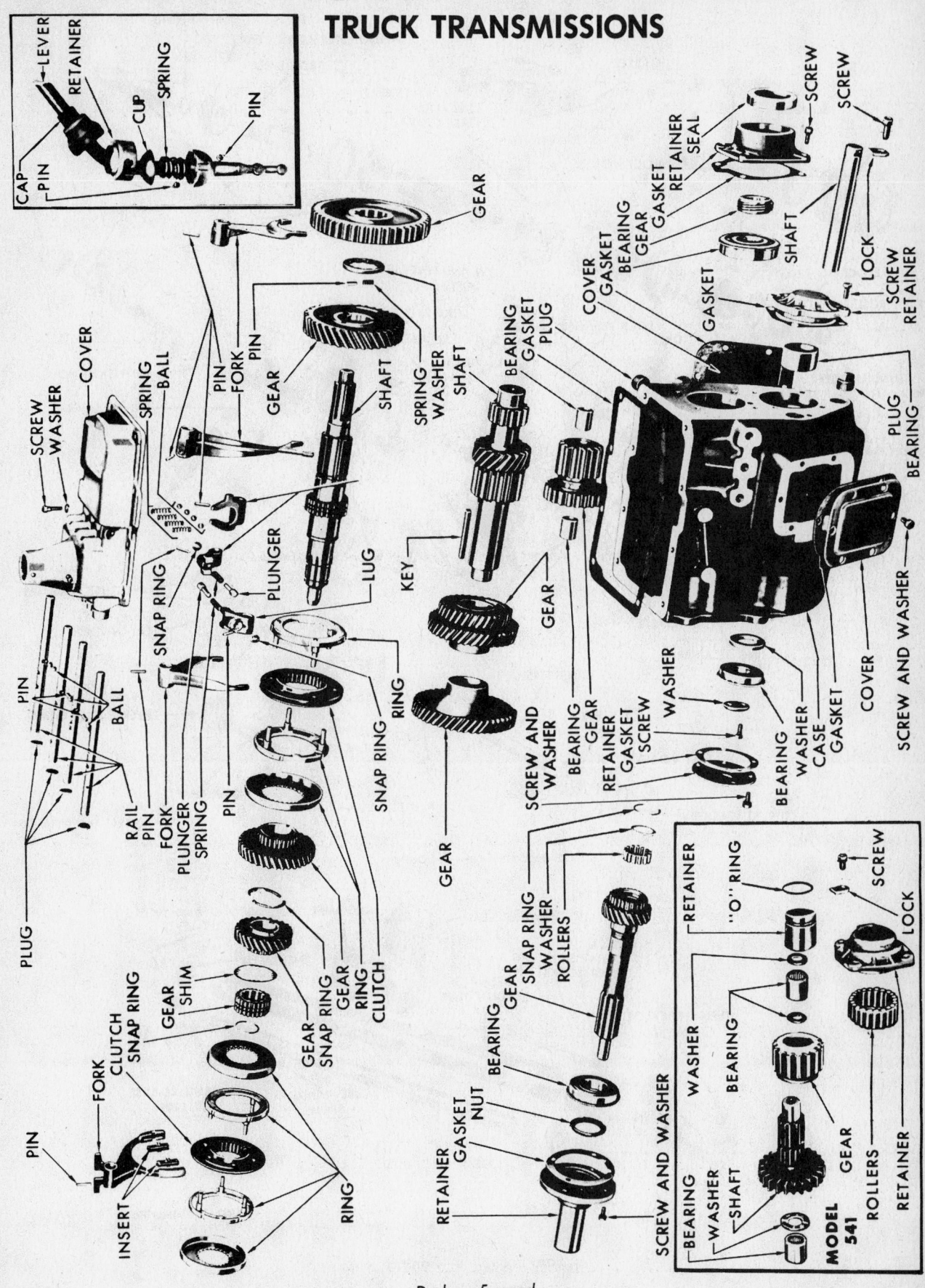

Dodge—5 speed

TRUCK TRANSMISSIONS

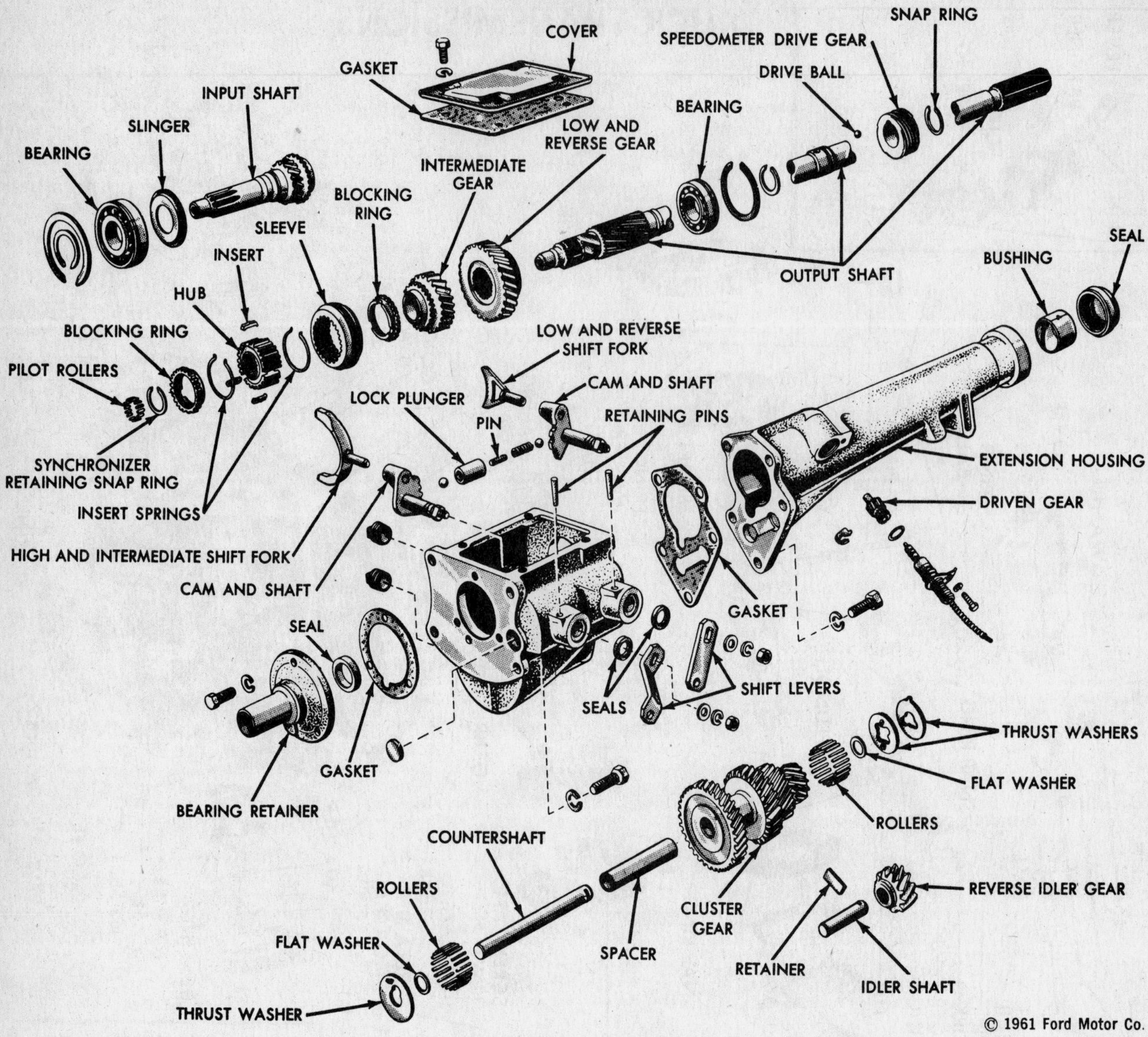

BEARING

SLINGER

INPUT SHAFT

GASKET

COVER

SPEEDOMETER DRIVE GEAR

DRIVE BALL

SNAP RING

BEARING

BLOCKING RING

INTERMEDIATE GEAR

LOW AND REVERSE GEAR

SLEEVE

INSERT

HUB

BLOCKING RING

PILOT ROLLERS

LOW AND REVERSE SHIFT FORK

LOCK PLUNGER

CAM AND SHAFT

PIN

RETAINING PINS

OUTPUT SHAFT

BUSHING

SEAL

SYNCHRONIZER RETAINING SNAP RING

INSERT SPRINGS

HIGH AND INTERMEDIATE SHIFT FORK

CAM AND SHAFT

EXTENSION HOUSING

DRIVEN GEAR

SEAL

GASKET

BEARING RETAINER

GASKET

SEALS

SHIFT LEVERS

THRUST WASHERS

FLAT WASHER

ROLLERS

COUNTERSHAFT

ROLLERS

CLUSTER GEAR

REVERSE IDLER GEAR

FLAT WASHER

SPACER

RETAINER

IDLER SHAFT

THRUST WASHER

© 1961 Ford Motor Co.

Ford Econoline—3-Speed

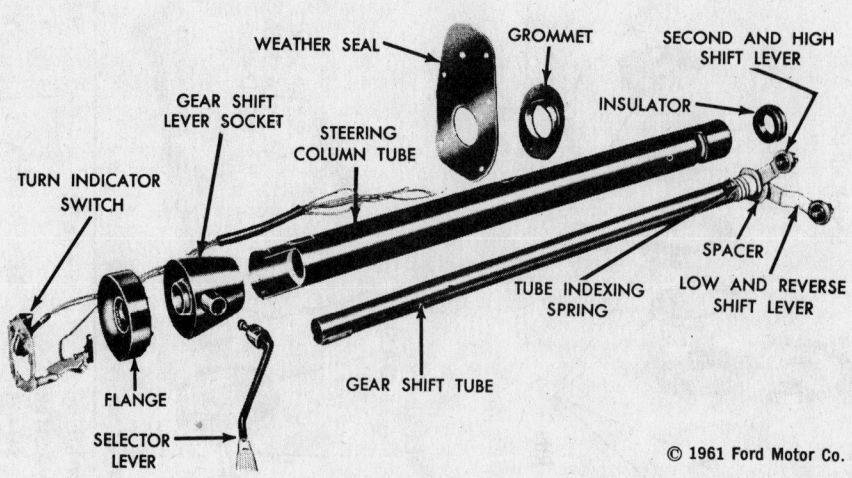

WEATHER SEAL

GROMMET

SECOND AND HIGH SHIFT LEVER

GEAR SHIFT LEVER SOCKET

STEERING COLUMN TUBE

INSULATOR

TURN INDICATOR SWITCH

SPACER

LOW AND REVERSE SHIFT LEVER

TUBE INDEXING SPRING

FLANGE

SELECTOR LEVER

GEAR SHIFT TUBE

© 1961 Ford Motor Co.

Ford Econoline—Control

TRUCK TRANSMISSIONS

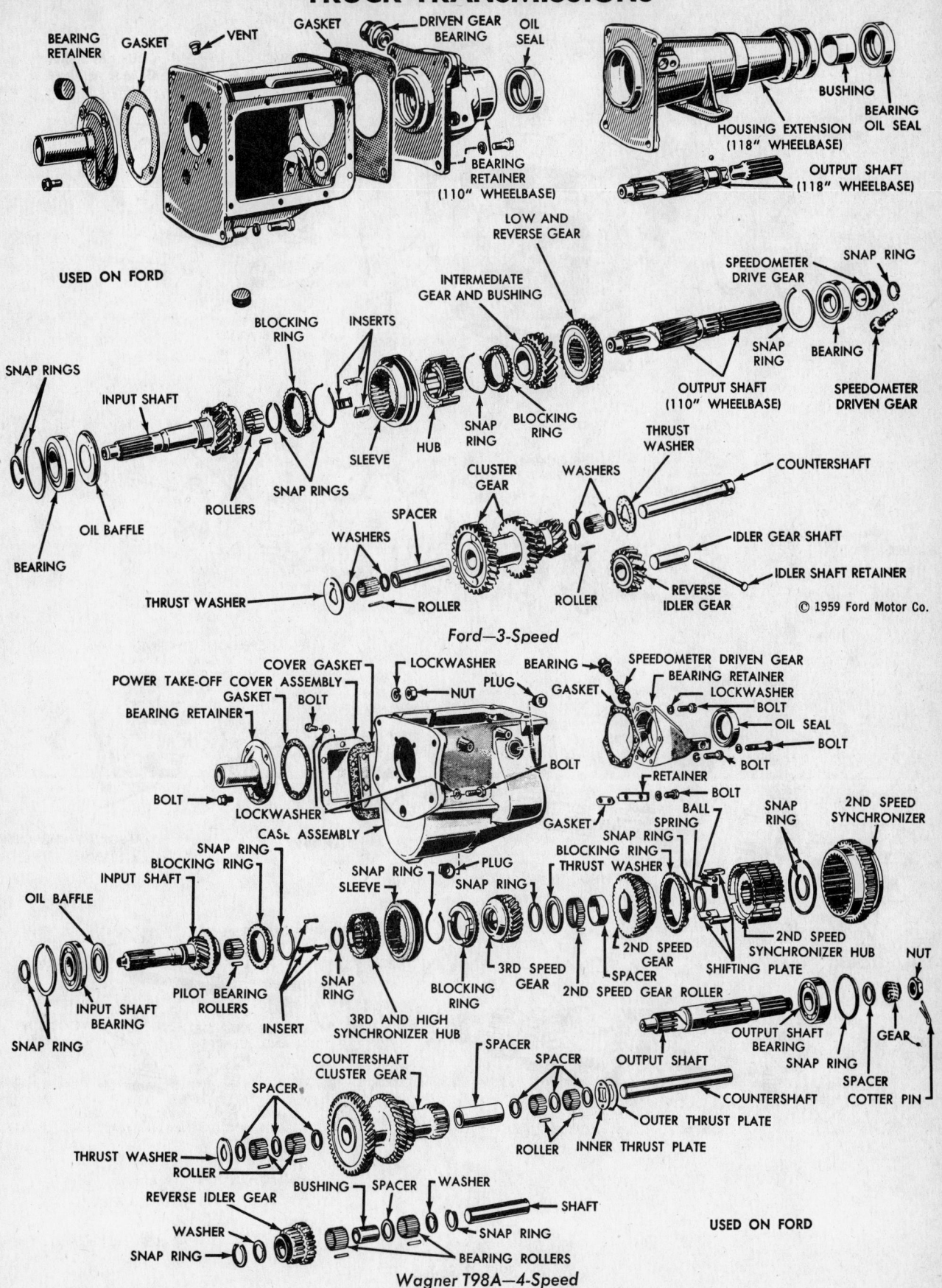

USED ON FORD

Ford—3-Speed

© 1959 Ford Motor Co.

Wagner T98A—4-Speed

USED ON FORD

TRUCK TRANSMISSIONS

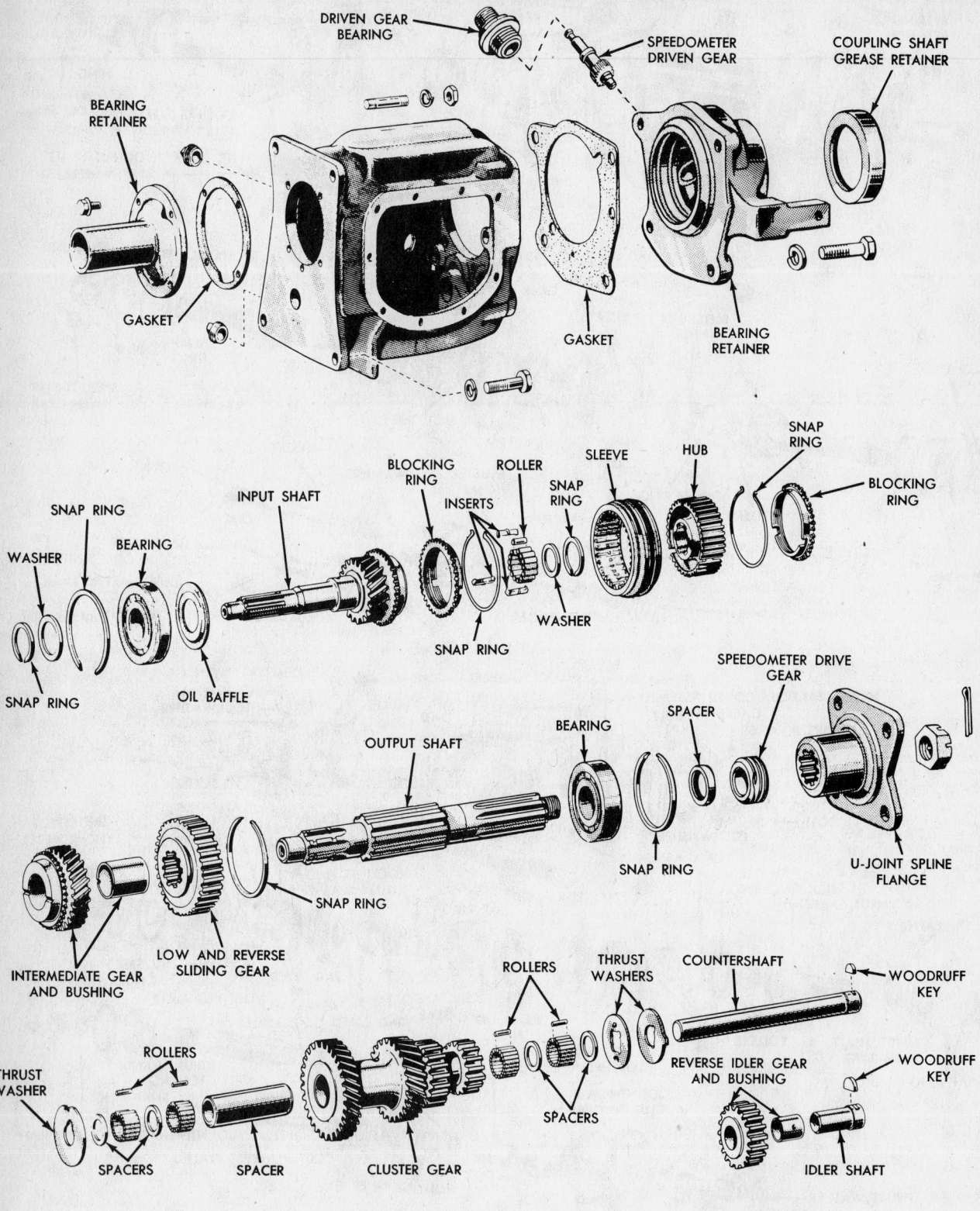

Warner T89C—3-Speed

© 1959 Ford Motor Co.

USED ON FORD

TRUCK TRANSMISSIONS

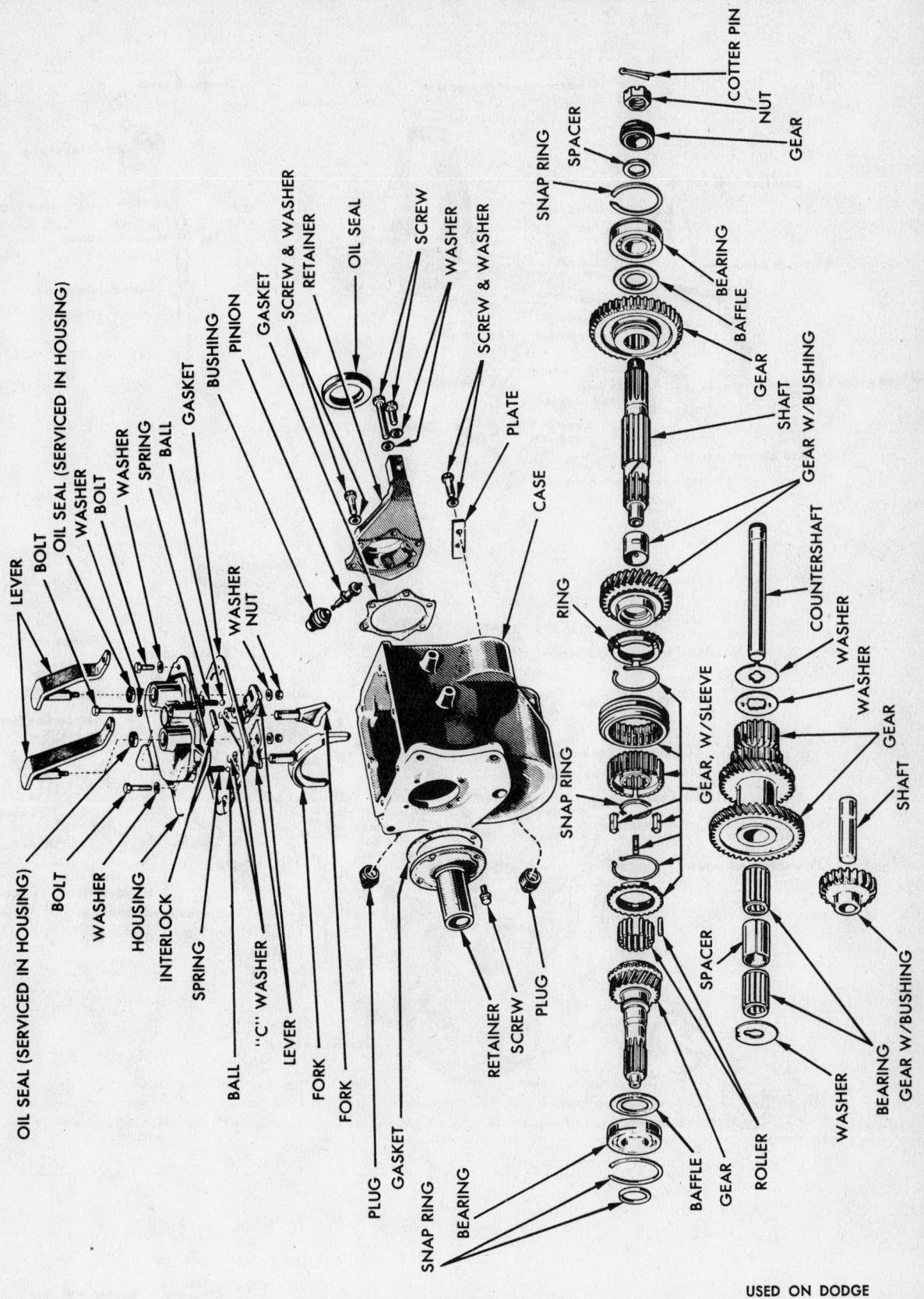

OIL SEAL (SERVICED IN HOUSING)
BOLT
WASHER
HOUSING
INTERLOCK
SPRING
BALL
"C" WASHER
LEVER
FORK
FORK

LEVER
BOLT
OIL SEAL (SERVICED IN HOUSING)
WASHER
BOLT
WASHER
SPRING
BALL
GASKET
GASKET
BUSHING
PINION
GASKET
SCREW & WASHER
RETAINER
OIL SEAL
SCREW
WASHER
SCREW & WASHER

WASHER
NUT

PLATE
CASE

RETAINER
SCREW
PLUG

PLUG
GASKET
SNAP RING
BEARING

BAFFLE
GEAR
ROLLER

SNAP RING
RING

SNAP RING

GEAR, W/SLEEVE

SPACER

WASHER
BEARING
GEAR W/BUSHING

COTTER PIN
NUT
GEAR

SPACER
SNAP RING

BEARING
BAFFLE
GEAR
SHAFT

GEAR W/BUSHING

COUNTERSHAFT
WASHER
WASHER
GEAR
SHAFT

WASHER

Warner T87D—3-Speed

USED ON DODGE

1125

TRUCK TRANSMISSIONS

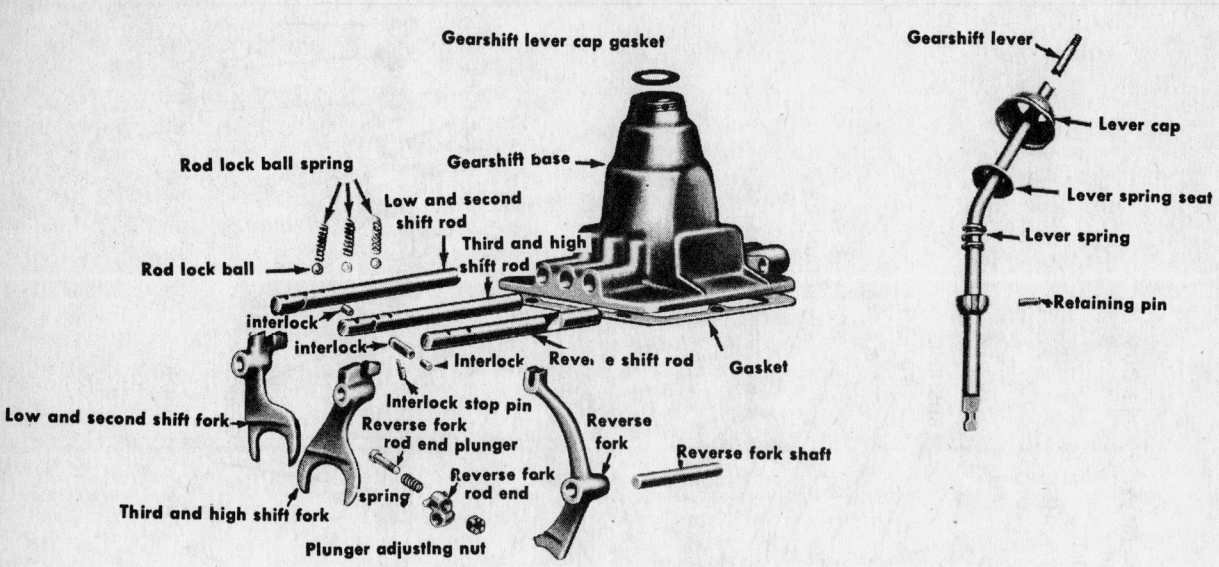

Gearshift lever cap gasket

Gearshift base

Rod lock ball spring

Low and second shift rod

Rod lock ball

Third and high shift rod

interlock

interlock

Interlock

Reverse shift rod

Gasket

Low and second shift fork

Interlock stop pin

Reverse fork rod end plunger

Reverse fork

Reverse fork shaft

spring

Reverse fork rod end

Third and high shift fork

Plunger adjusting nut

Gearshift lever

Lever cap

Lever spring seat

Lever spring

Retaining pin

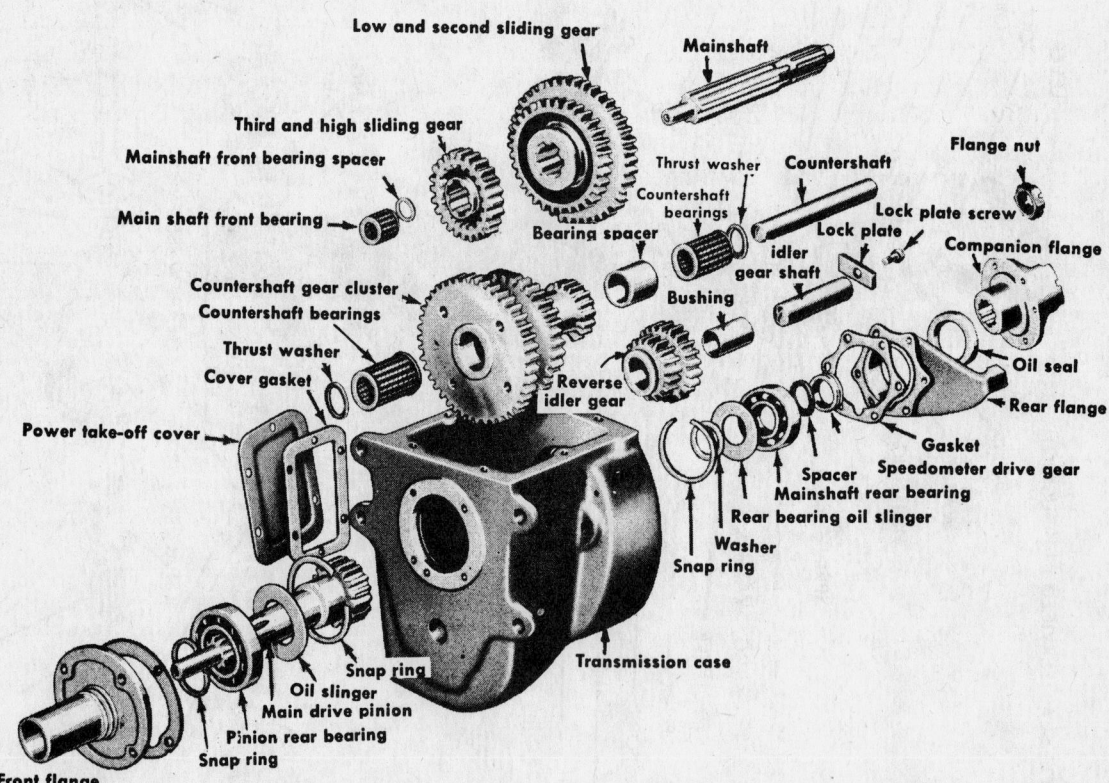

Low and second sliding gear

Mainshaft

Third and high sliding gear

Mainshaft front bearing spacer

Thrust washer

Countershaft

Flange nut

Countershaft bearings

Main shaft front bearing

Bearing spacer

idler gear shaft

Lock plate

Lock plate screw

Companion flange

Countershaft gear cluster

Countershaft bearings

Bushing

Thrust washer

Cover gasket

Reverse idler gear

Oil seal

Power take-off cover

Rear flange

Gasket

Speedometer drive gear

Spacer

Mainshaft rear bearing

Rear bearing oil slinger

Washer

Snap ring

Snap ring

Oil slinger

Main drive pinion

Pinion rear bearing

Snap ring

Transmission case

Front flange

USED ON STUDEBAKER

© 1960 S.P. Corp.

Warner T9A—4-Speed

1126

TRUCK TRANSMISSIONS

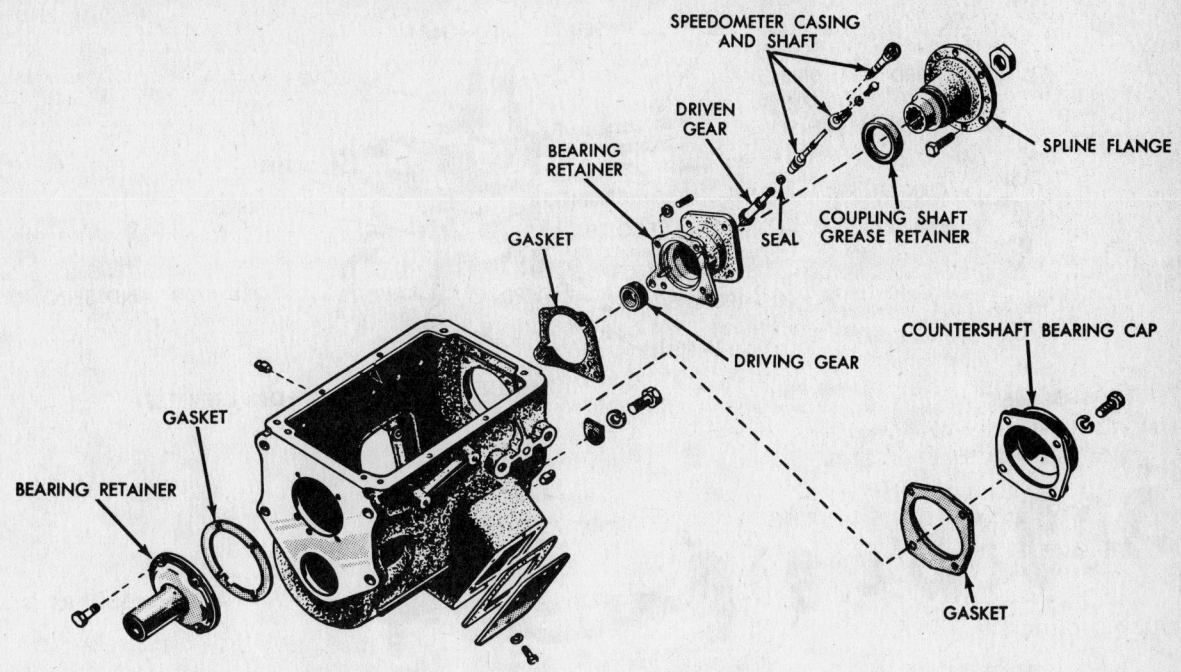

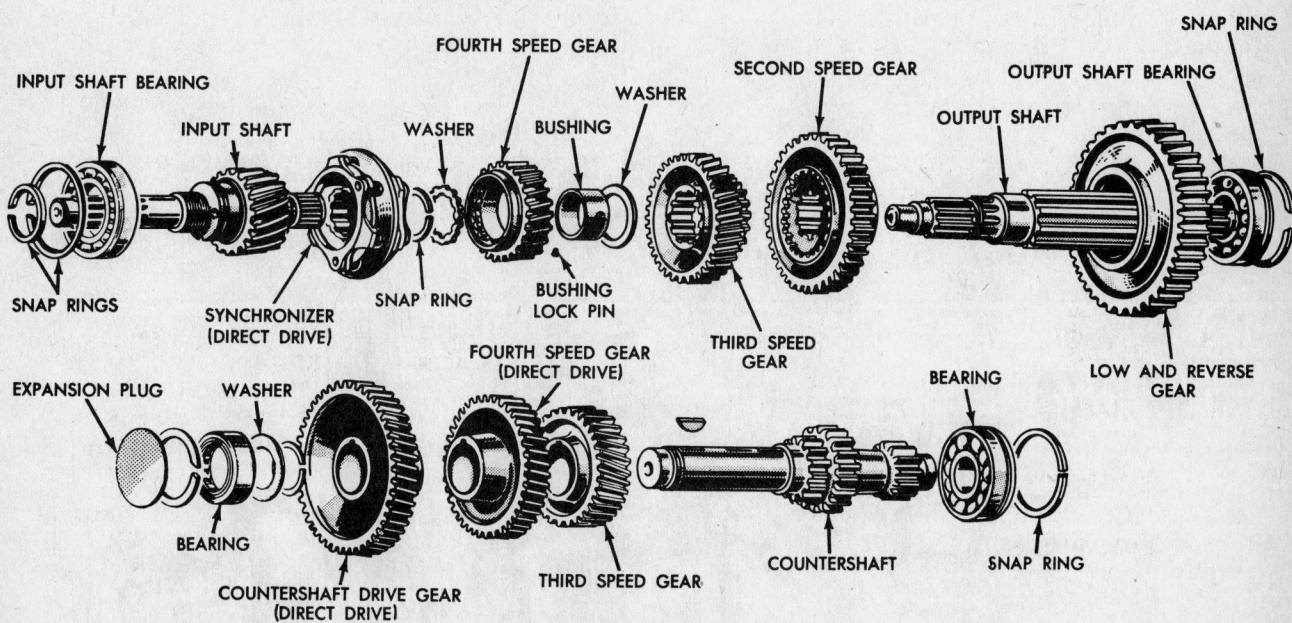

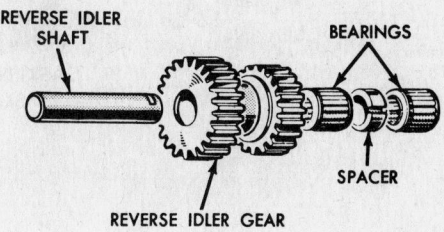

© 1959 Ford Motor Co.

Clark 250—5-Speed Medium Duty

TRUCK TRANSMISSIONS

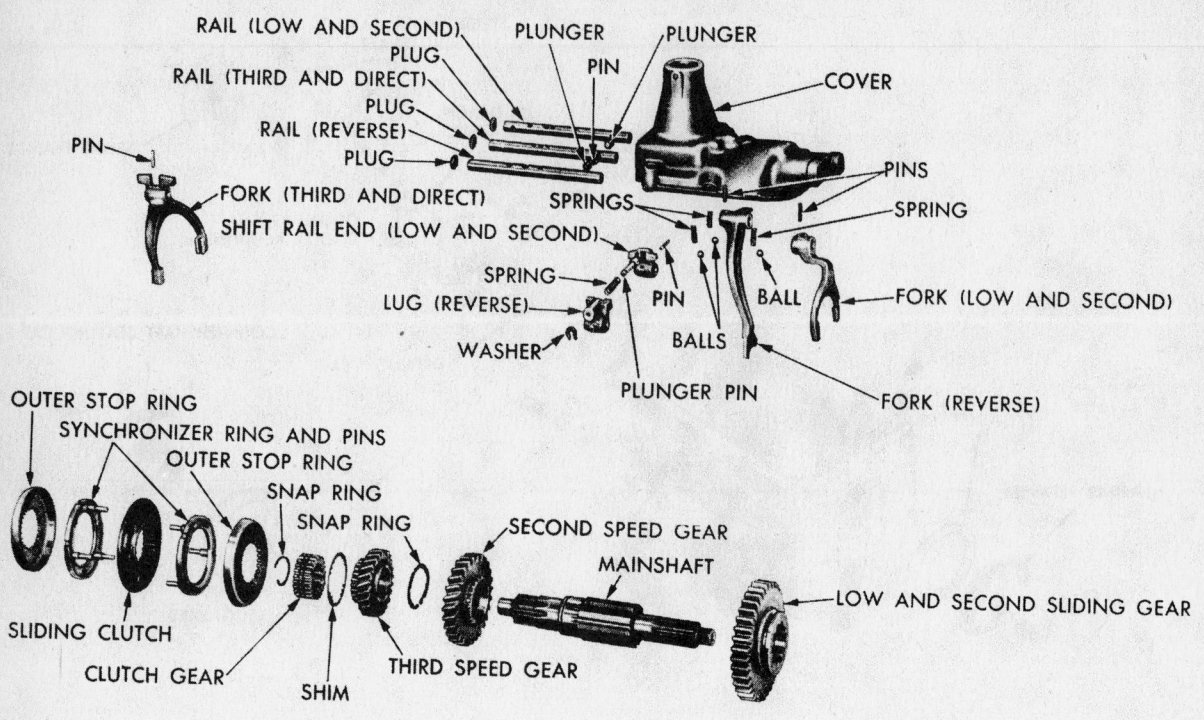

RAIL (LOW AND SECOND)
PLUG
RAIL (THIRD AND DIRECT)
PLUG
RAIL (REVERSE)
PLUG
PIN
FORK (THIRD AND DIRECT)
SHIFT RAIL END (LOW AND SECOND)
SPRING
LUG (REVERSE)
WASHER
PLUNGER
PIN
PLUNGER
COVER
PINS
SPRING
SPRINGS
PIN
BALLS
PLUNGER PIN
BALL
FORK (LOW AND SECOND)
FORK (REVERSE)

OUTER STOP RING
SYNCHRONIZER RING AND PINS
OUTER STOP RING
SNAP RING
SNAP RING
SECOND SPEED GEAR
MAINSHAFT
SLIDING CLUTCH
CLUTCH GEAR
SHIM
THIRD SPEED GEAR
LOW AND SECOND SLIDING GEAR

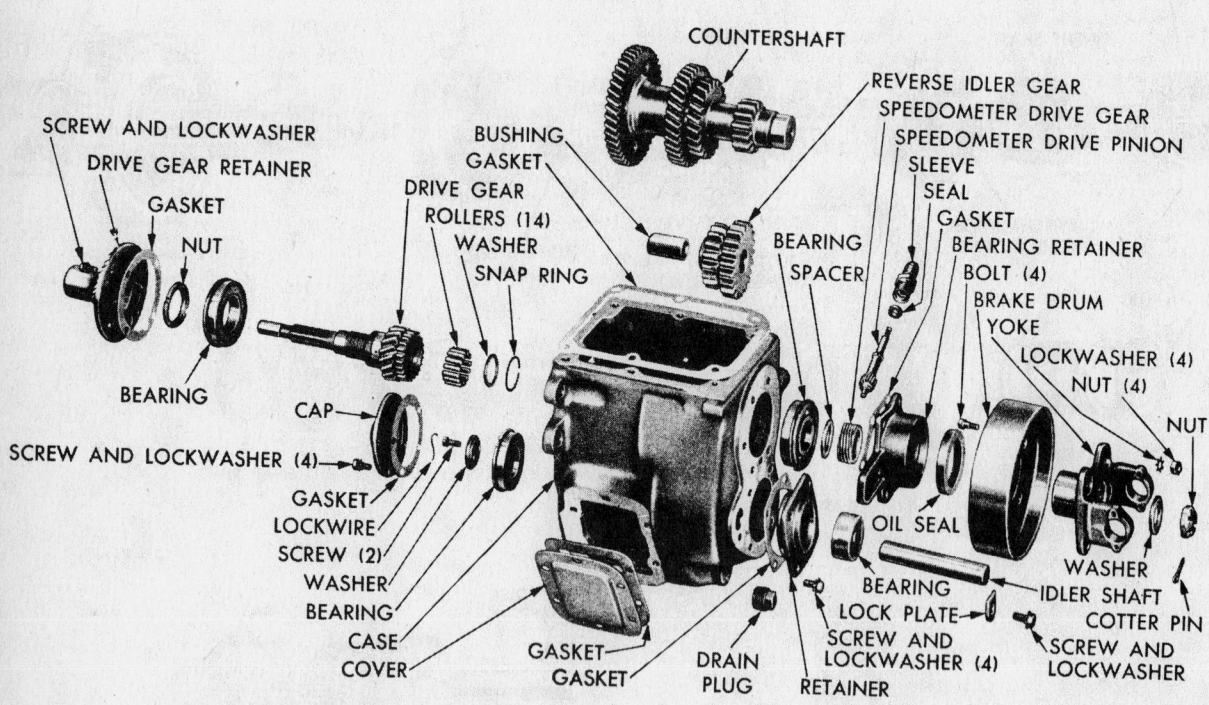

COUNTERSHAFT
SCREW AND LOCKWASHER
DRIVE GEAR RETAINER
GASKET
NUT
BUSHING
GASKET
DRIVE GEAR
ROLLERS (14)
WASHER
SNAP RING
REVERSE IDLER GEAR
SPEEDOMETER DRIVE GEAR
SPEEDOMETER DRIVE PINION
SLEEVE
SEAL
GASKET
BEARING RETAINER
BOLT (4)
BRAKE DRUM
YOKE
LOCKWASHER (4)
NUT (4)
NUT
BEARING
SPACER
BEARING
CAP
SCREW AND LOCKWASHER (4)
GASKET
LOCKWIRE
SCREW (2)
WASHER
BEARING
CASE
COVER
GASKET
GASKET
DRAIN
PLUG
OIL SEAL
BEARING
LOCK PLATE
SCREW AND
LOCKWASHER (4)
RETAINER
WASHER
IDLER SHAFT
COTTER PIN
SCREW AND
LOCKWASHER

USED ON DODGE

New Process—420—4-Speed

TRUCK TRANSMISSIONS

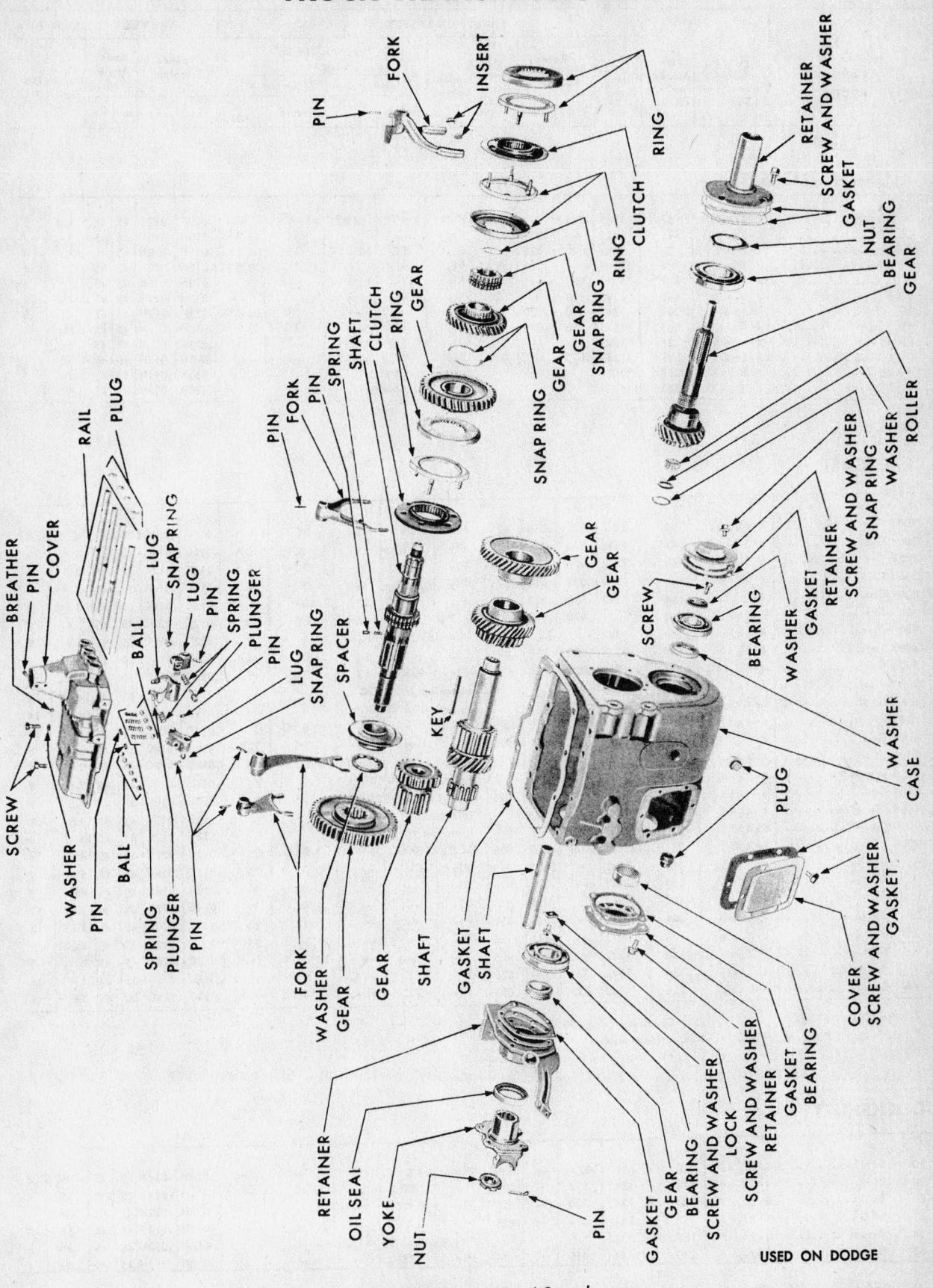

New Process—433D—4-Speed

USED ON DODGE

Tractor Specifications and Tune-Up

ALLIS-CHALMERS

MAKE AND MODEL	No. Cylinder Bore and Stroke	Piston Displacement cu. in.	Firing Order	Ignition System: Point Gap Dist.	Point Gap Mag.	Spark Plug Gap	Ignition Timing Location	Ignition Timing (degrees) Distributor Retard	Distributor Full Adv.	Magneto Retard	Magneto Full Adv.	Valves: Tappet Clearance In	Tappet Clearance Ex	Seat Angle (deg.) In	Seat Angle Ex	Capacities: Water Gal.	Oil Qts.
G	4-2⅜×3½	62	1342	.020	---	.025	Pul	3 BTC	17 BTC	---	---	.012C	.012C	45	45	1.6	3½
BE	4-3¼×3½	116	1243	---	.020	.025	Fly	---	---	TC	30 BTC	.010H	.010H	45	45	2	4
C, CA	4-3⅜×3½	125	1243	.020	.020	.032	Fly	TC	30 BTC	TC	30 BTC	.010H	.010H	45	45	2	4
RC	4-3⅜×3½	125	1243	---	.020	.035	Fly	---	---	TC	30 BTC	.010H	.010H	45	45	2	4
D-10, D-12	4-3⅜×3⅞	139	1243	.022	---	.025	Fly	TC	25 BTC	---	---	.013H	.013H	45	45	2	4½
D-14	4-3½×3⅞	149	1243	.020	---	.030	Fly	TC	30 BTC	---	---	.013H	.013H	45	45	2¼	5
WC, WF	4-4×4	201	1243	---	.020	.035	Fly	---	---	TC	30 BTC	.012H	.012H	45	45	4	6
WD	4-4×4	201	1243	.020	.020	.035	Fly	TC	30 BTC	TC	30 BTC	.012H	.012H	45	45	3½	6
WD-45	4-4×4.5	226	1243	.020	---	.030	Fly	TC	30 BTC	---	---	.012H	.012H	45	45	3½	6
D-17 (Gas.)	4-4×4.5	226	1243	.020	---	.030	Fly	TC	30 BTC	---	---	.013H	.013H	30	45	3½	7
WD-45 Diesel	6-3 7/16×4⅛	230	153624				Injection 21° BTDC					.010H	.019H	45	45	4¼	7
D-17 Diesel	6-3 9/16×4⅜	262	153624				Align Index Marks					.010H	.019H	45	45	4	7

J. I. CASE

MAKE AND MODEL	No. Cylinder Bore and Stroke	Piston Displacement cu. in.	Firing Order	Point Gap Dist.	Point Gap Mag.	Spark Plug Gap	Ignition Timing Location	Distributor Retard	Distributor Full Adv.	Magneto Retard	Magneto Full Adv.	Tappet Clearance In	Tappet Clearance Ex	Seat Angle In	Seat Angle Ex	Water Gal.	Oil Qts.
200B Gas.	4-3⅛×4⅛	126.5	1342	.020	.010	.025	Fly	DC	13	DC	N.A.	.014C	.014C	30	45	3	5
300 Gas.	4-3⅜×4⅛	148	1342	.020	.010	.025	Fly	7/32"B.Ign	13	7/32"B.Ign	N.A.	.014C	.014C	30	45	3	5
300B Gas.	4-3⅜×4⅛	148	1342	.020	.010	.025	Fly	IGN	13	DC	N.A.	.014C	.014C	30	45	3	5
300B LPG	4-3⅜×4⅛	148	1342	.020	.010	.025	Fly	3/32"B.Ign	13	DC	N.A.	.014C	.014C	30	45	3	5
350 Gas.	4-3 9/16×4⅛	164	1342	.020	.010	.025	Fly	IGN	13	IGN	N.A.	.014C	.014C	30	45	3	5
400 Gas.	4-4×5	251	1342	.020	.010	.025	Cr. Pul	TC	26 BTC	TC	25	.012C	.020C	45	45	7.4	9
400 Diesel	4-4×5	251	1342				Injection 26° BTDC					.012C	.012C	45	45	7.4	9
400B Gas.	4-3⅜×4⅛	148	1342	.020	.010	.025	Fly	IGN	13	DC	N.A.	.014C	.014C	30	45	3	5
500B Gas.	4-3 9/16×4⅛	164	1342	.020	.010	.025	Fly	IGN	13	DC	N.A.	.014C	.014C	30	45	3	5
500 Diesel	6-4×5	377	153624				Injection 26° BTDC					.012C	.012C	45	45	14	14
600 Diesel	6-4×5	377	153624				Injection 28° BTDC					.012C	.012C	45	45	14	14
600 LPG	6-4×5	377	153624	---	.010	.025	Cr. Pul	---	---	3 BTC	23	.012C	.020C	45	45	14	14
600B Gas.	4-3 9/16×4⅛	164	1342	.020	.010	.025	Fly	IGN	13	DC	N.A.	.014C	.014C	30	45	3	5
700B Gas.	4-4×5	251	1342	.020	.010	.025	Cr. Pul	TC	26 BTC	TC	25	.012C	.020C	45	45	7.4	9
700B Diesel ◆	4-4⅛×5	267	1342				Injection 27° BTDC					.012C	.012C	45	45	7.4	9
800B Gas. †	4-4×5	251	1342	.020	.010	.025	Cr. Pul	TC	26 BTC	TC	25	.012C	.020C	45	45	7.5	9
800B Diesel ◈	4-4⅛×5	267	1342				Injection 31° BTDC					.012C	.012C	45	45	7.5	9
900B Diesel	6-4×5	377	153624				Injection 28° BTDC					.012C	.012C	45	45	14	14
900B LPG	6-4×5	377	153624	.020	.010	.025	Cr. Pul	2 BTC	26 BTC	3 BTC	23	.012C	.020C	45	45	14	14
C Gas	4-3⅞×5¼	260	1342	---	.015	.025	Fly	---	---	TC	25	.018C	.018C	45	45	5	7
D Gas	4-3⅞×5¼	260	1342	---	.010	.025	Fly	---	---	TC	N.A.	.018C	.018C	45	45	6¾	7
L Gas	4-4⅝×6	404	1342	---	.015	.025	Fly	---	---	TC	30	.018C	.018C	45	45	12½	12
LA Gas	4-4⅝×6	404	1342	---	.015	.030	Fly	---	---	TC	30	.018C	.018C	45	45	15¼	12
R Gas	4-3¼×4	133	1342	---	.015	.030	Fly	---	---	TC	35	.010C	.012C	45	45	4¼	7
S Gas	4-3½×4	154	1342	---	.010	.025	Fly	---	---	½" BTC	N.A.	.010C	.010C	45	45	4	5
V Gas	4-3×4¾	124	1342	.020	.020	.025	Fly	TC	N.A.	TC	15	.014C	.014C	30	45	3	4
VA Gas	4-3¼×3¾	124	1342	.020	.010	.025	Fly	TC	N.A.	3/16"ATC	N.A.	.014C	.014C	30	45	3¼	4

† Wico Dist. 28° BTC
◆ PES. Model Pump, 31° BTDC
◈ PES. Model Pump, 33° BTDC
N.A. - Not available

COCKSHUTT

MAKE AND MODEL	No. Cylinder Bore and Stroke	Piston Displacement cu. in.	Firing Order	Point Gap Dist.	Point Gap Mag.	Spark Plug Gap	Ignition Timing Location	Distributor Retard	Distributor Full Adv.	Magneto Retard	Magneto Full Adv.	Tappet Clearance In	Tappet Clearance Ex	Seat Angle In	Seat Angle Ex	Water Gal.	Oil Qts.
20 Gas.	4-3 3/16×4⅜	140	1342	.020	----	.025	Fly	6 BTC	----	---	---	.014H	.014H	45	45	3¾	4
20 Dist., LPG	4-3 3/16×4⅜	140	1342	.020	---	.025	Fly	TDC	---	---	---	.014H	.014H	45	45	3¾	4
30 Gas.	4-3 7/16×4⅛	153	1342	.020	---	.025	Fly	10 BTC	---	---	---	.012H	.012H	45	45	3½	5
30 LPG	4-3 7/16×4⅛	153	1342	.020	---	.025	Fly	10 BTC	---	---	---	.012H	.012H	45	45	3½	5
30 Diesel	4-3 7/16×4⅛	153	1342				(1) Injection 36° BTC					.012H	.012H	45	45	3½	5
40 Gas.	6-3 7/16×4⅛	230	153624	.020	---	.025	Fly	TDC	---	---	---	.012H	.012H	45	45	4¾	6

(1) – (APE pump 36° BTC, (PSB) pump 26° BTC.

Tractor Specifications and Tune-Up—continued

COCKSHUTT Continued

MAKE AND MODEL	No. Cylinder Bore and Stroke	Piston Displacement cu. in.	Firing Order	Ignition System: Point Gap Dist.	Point Gap Mag.	Spark Plug Gap	Ignition Timing Location	Ignition Timing (degrees) Distributor Retard	Distributor Full Adv.	Magneto Retard	Magneto Full Adv.	Valves: Timing Clearance In	Timing Clearance Ex	Seat Angle (deg.) In	Seat Angle (deg.) Ex	Capacities: Water Gal.	Oil Qts.
40 Diesel	6-3 7/16 × 4⅛	230	153624				(2) Injection 34° BTC					.012H	.012H	45	45	4¾	6
50 Gas.	6-3¾ × 4⅛	273	153624	.020	---	.025	Fly	TDC	---	---	---	.012H	.012H	45	45	4¾	6
50 Diesel	6-3¾ × 4⅛	273	153624				(3) Injection 30° BTC					.012H	.012H	45	45	4¾	6
35 Gas.	4-3¾ × 4½	198	1243	.020	---	.025	Fly	2 BTC	---	---	---	.010H	.010H	45	45	4½	4.8
40 D4 Diesel	4-4¼ × 4¾	269.6	1342				(4) Injection 24° BTC					.010H	.010H	45	45	3⅗	8.4
540 Gas	4-3 7/16 × 4⅜	162	1342	.020	---	.025	Fly	4 DC	---	---	---	.014H	.014H	45	45	3	4
550 Gas.	4-3¾ × 4½	198	1243	.020	---	.025	Fly	4 BTC	---	---	---	.010H	.010H	45	45	4½	4¾
550 Diesel	4-3¾ × 4½	198	1243				(4) Injection 24° BTC					.010H	.010H	45	45	4½	4¾
560 Diesel	4-4¼ × 4¾	269.6	1342				Injection 21° BTC					.010H	.010H	45	45	3½	8.4
570 Gas.	6-3¾ × 4½	298	153624	.020	---	.025	Fly	8 BTC	---	---	---	.010H	.010H	45	45	4¾	8
570 Diesel	6-3¾ × 4½	298	153624				(5) Injection 26° BTC			---	---	.010H	.010H	45	45	4¾	8

(2) – (APE) pump 34° BTC, (PSB) pump 28° BTC.
(3) – (APE) pump 30° BTC, (PSP) pump 25° BTC.
(4) – Bosch 24° BTC, Roosa 26° BTC.
(5) – Bosch 26° BTC, Roosa 32° BTC.

JOHN DEERE

MAKE AND MODEL	No. Cylinder Bore and Stroke	Piston Displacement cu. in.	Firing Order	Ignition System: Point Gap Dist.	Point Gap Mag.	Spark Plug Gap	Ignition Timing Location	Ignition Timing (degrees) Distributor Retard	Distributor Full Adv.	Magneto Retard	Magneto Full Adv.	Valves: Timing Clearance In	Timing Clearance Ex	Seat Angle (deg.) In	Seat Angle (deg.) Ex	Capacities: Water Gal.	Oil Qts.
40 Gas.	2-4 × 4	100.5	1-2	.022	---	.025	Fly	5 ATC	25	---	---	.012C	.012L	30	45	3½	5
50 Gas.	2-4 11/16 × 5½	190	1-2	.022 1	---	.030	Fly	5 ATC	20	---	---	.020H	.020H	30	45	4¾	7
50 All Fuel	2-4 11/16 × 5½	190	1-2	.022 1	---	.030	Fly	TDC	25	---	---	.020H	.020H	30	45	4¾	7
50 LPG	2-4 11/16 × 5½	190	1-2	.022	---	.030	Fly	5 ATC	10	---	---	.020H	.020H	30	45	4¾	7
60 Gas.	2-5½ × 6¾	321	1-2	.022	---	.030	Fly	5 ATC	20	---	---	.020H	.020H	30	45	7½	8
60 All Fuel	2-5½ × 6¾	321	1-2	.022	---	.030	Fly	TDC	25	---	---	.020H	.020H	30	45	7½	8
60 LPG	2-5½ × 6¾	321	1-2	.022	---	.030	Fly	10 ATC	5	---	---	.020H	.020H	30	45	7½	8
70 Gas.	2-5⅞ × 7	379.5	1-2	.022	---	.030	Fly	10 ATC	15	---	---	.020H	.020H	30	45	7¾	11
70 All Fuel	2-6⅛ × 7	412.5	1-2	.022	---	.030	Fly	TDC	25	---	---	.020H	.020H	30	45	7¾	11
70 LPG	2-5⅞ × 7	379.5	1-2	.022	---	.030	Fly	10 ATC	5	---	---	.020H	.020H	30	45	7¾	11
70 Diesel	2-6⅛ × 6⅜	376	1-2				Injection 24° BTC					.020H	.020H	45	45	7	12
320, 330 Gas.	2-4 × 4	100.5	1-2	.022	---	.025	Fly	1 BTC	31	---	---	.012C	.012C	30	45	3½	5
420, 430, 440	2-4¼ × 4	113.3	1-2	.022	---	.025	Fly	2 BTC	28	---	---	.015C	.015C	30	45	2¾	5
435D, 4401 Diesel	2-3⅞ × 4½	106.2	1-2				Use Injector Timing Tool					---	.009H	---	30	2½	9
520, 530	2-4 11/16 × 5½	189.8	1-2	.022	---	.030	Fly	TDC	20	---	---	.020H	.020H	◈	45	2 4½	7
620, 630	2-5½ × 6⅜	302.9	1-2	.022	---	.030	Fly	TDC	20	---	---	.020H	.020H	◈	45	6½	8
720, 730	2-6 × 6⅜	360.5	1-2	.022	---	.030	Fly	TDC	20	---	---	.020H	.020H	◈	45	7⅛	10
720, 730 Diesel	2-6⅛ × 6⅜	376	1-2				Injection 24° BTC					.020H	.020H	45	45	6¼	9
820, 830 Diesel	2-6⅛ × 8	471.5	1-2				Injection 25° BTC					.015H	.020H	45	45	7½	14
A All Fuel	2-5½ × 6¾	321.2	1-2	---	.015	.030	Fly	---	---	TC	30	.020H	.020H	30	45	9¼	9¼
A All Fuel	2-5½ × 6¾	321.2	1-2	.021	.015	.030	Fly	TC	26	TC	25	.020H	.020H	30	45	8½	11
A Gas.	2-5½ × 6¾	321.2	1-2	.021	.015	.030	Fly	TC	26	TC	25	.020H	.020H	30	45	8½	11
B All Fuel	2-4½ × 5½	174.9	1-2	---	.015	.030	Fly	---	---	TC	30	.020H	.020H	30	45	6	7½
B All Fuel	2-4 11/16 × 5½	190.4	1-2	.015	.015	.030	Fly	TC	25	TC	25	.020H	.020H	30	45	7	7
B All Fuel	2-4 11/16 × 5½	190.4	1-2	.015	.015	.030	Fly	TC	25	TC	25	.020H	.020H	30	45	7	7
D All Fuel	2-6¾ × 7	501	1-2	---	.015	.030	Fly	---	---	TC	35	.030H	.030H	30	30	14	13
G All Fuel	2-6⅛ × 7	412.5	1-2	.021	.015	.030	Fly	TC	26	TC	28	.020H	.020H	30	45	13	11
H All Fuel	2-3 9/16 × 5	99.68	1-2	---	.015	.030	Fly	---	---	TC	28	.015H	.015H	30	45	5½	4½
M, MT	2-4 × 4	101	1-2	.020	---	.025	Fly	DC	N.A.	---	---	.012C	.012C	---	45	3½	5

N.A. – Not Available
1 – Wico Distributor .015
2 – 4 Gal. 530
◈ – Intake seat angle. All fuel engines 30°, Gasoline 45°

FERGUSON

MAKE AND MODEL	No. Cylinder Bore and Stroke	Piston Displacement cu. in.	Firing Order	Ignition System: Point Gap Dist.	Point Gap Mag.	Spark Plug Gap	Ignition Timing Location	Ignition Timing (degrees) Distributor Retard	Distributor Full Adv.	Magneto Retard	Magneto Full Adv.	Valves: Timing Clearance In	Timing Clearance Ex	Seat Angle (deg.) In	Seat Angle (deg.) Ex	Capacities: Water Gal.	Oil Qts.
TE 20	4-3 3/16 × 3¾	119.7	1342	.015	---	.025	Fly	TC	29 BTC	---	---	.013H	.013H	45	45	2½	6
TO 20	4-3 3/16 × 3¾	119.7	1342	.022	---	.025	Fly	7 BTC	31 BTC	---	---	.013H	.013H	45	45	2½	6
TO 30	4-3¼ × 3⅞	129	1342	.022	---	.025	Fly	6 BTC	32 BTC	---	---	.013H	.013H	30	45	2½	6

Tractor Specifications and Tune-Up—continued

FORD

MAKE AND MODEL	No. Cylinder Bore and Stroke	Piston Displacement cu. in.	Firing Order	IGNITION SYSTEM								VALVES				Capacities	
				Point Gap		Spark Plug Gap	Ignition Timing Location	Ignition Timing (degrees)				Tappet Clearance		Seat Angle (deg.)		Water Gal.	Oil Qts.
								Distributor		Magneto							
				Dist.	Mag.			Retard	Full Adv.	Retard	Full Adv.	In	Ex	In	Ex		
2N, 9N	4-3 3/16 × 3 3/4	119.7	1243	.015	.015	.025	---	TDC	---	TDC	15 BTC	.011C	.015C	45	45	3	6
8N	4-3 7/16 × 3 3/4	119.7	1243	.025	---	.025	---	(1) TDC	(2) 25B	---	---	.011C	.015C	45	45	3	6
NAA, NAB	4-3.44×3.60	134.0	1243	.025	---	.025	Fly	8 BTC	30 BTC	---	---	.015H	.015H	45	45	3¾	5
600, 700	4-3.44×3.60	134.0	1243	.025	---	.025	Fly	8 BTC	30 BTC	---	---	.015H	.015H	45	45	3¾	5
501, 601, 701 (Gas.)	4-3.44×3.60	134.0	1243	.025	---	.025	Fly	4 BTC	24 BTC	---	---	.015H	.015H	45	45	3¾	5
501, 601, 701 LP-Gas	4-3.44×3.60	134.0	1243	.025	---	.030	Fly	7 BTC	27 BTC	---	---	.015H	.015H	45	45	3¾	5
501D, 601D, 701D	4-3.56×3.60	144.0	1243	Injection 26° BTDC								.015H	.015H	45	45	3¾	5
800, 900 (Gas.)	4-3.9×3.6	172.0	1243	.025	---	.025	Fly	5 BTC	27 BTC	---	---	.015H	.015H	45	45	3¾	5
801, 901, 1801 (Gas.)	4-3.9×3.6	172.0	1243	.025	---	.025	Fly	4 BTC	24 BTC	---	---	.015H	.015H	45	45	3¾	5
801D, 901D, 1801D	4-3.9×3.6	172.0	1243	Injection 18° BTDC								.015H	.015H	45	45	3¾	5
Major-Power Major	4-3 15/16 × 4 17/32	220.0	1243	Injection 19° BTDC								.015H	.012H	30	30	3.6	7.8

(1) – After Engine # 263843 – 4° BTC
(2) – After Engine # 263843 – 17° BTC

INTERNATIONAL-HARVESTER

Cub	4-2 5/8 × 2 3/4	59.5	1342	.020	.013	.025	Pul	TDC	16	TDC	13	.013C	.013C	45	45	2½	3
100, 200, 230, 240	4-3 1/8 × 4	123	1342	.020	.013	.023	Pul	TDC	30	TDC	35	.014H	.014H	45	45	3 3/4	5
130, 140	4-3 1/8 × 4	123	1342	.020	.013	.023	Pul	TDC	26	TDC	35	.014H	.014H	45	45	3¾	5
300 Utility - Gas.	4-3 9/16 × 4 1/4	169	1342	.020	.013	.023	Pul	TDC	(A) 22	TDC	---	.017H	.017H	45	45	4	6
300, 300HC Gas.	4-3 9/16 × 4 1/4	169	1342	.020	---	.023	Pul	TDC	(A) 22	---	---	.017H	.017H	45	45	4 3/8	6
330 Gas.	4-3 1/4 × 4 1/16	135	1342	.020	.013	.023	Pul	TDC	30	TDC	35	.014H	.014H	45	45	3½	6
340 Gas.	4-3 1/4 × 4 1/16	135	1342	.020	.013	.023	Pul	TDC	30	TDC	35	.014H	.014H	45	45	3¾	5
350, 350HC Gas.	4-3 5/8 × 4 1/4	175	1342	.020	---	.023	Pul	TDC	(A) 22	---	---	.017H	.017H	45	45	4 7/8	6
350 Utility	4-3 5/8 × 4 1/4	175	1342	.020	.013	.023	Pul	TDC	(A) 22	TDC	---	.017H	.017H	45	45	4½	6
350, 350HC Diesel	4-3 3/4 × 4 3/8	193	1342	Register with first line on Flywheel								.014H	.014H	45	45	4.3	5
400, 400HC, W400	4-4 × 5 1/4	264	1342	.020	---	.023	Pul	TDC	(B)	---	---	.017H	.017H	45	45	6½	8
450, 450HC, W450	4-4 1/8 × 5 1/4	281	1342	.020	---	.023	Pul	TDC	(B)	---	---	.017H	.017H	45	45	7	8
460 Gas.	6-3 9/16 × 3 11/16	221	153624	.021	---	.025	Pul	2 BTC	30	---	---	.027H	.027H	30	30	* 4 1/8	9
460 LPG	6-3 9/16 × 3 11/16	221	153624	.021	---	.016	Pul	2 BTC	25	---	---	.027H	.027H	30	30	* 4 1/8	9
F460 Diesel	6-3 11/16 × 3 11/16	236	153624	Injection 3° BTC								.027H	.027H	45	45	5¼	9
560 Gas.	6-3 9/16 × 4 3/8	263	153624	.021	----	.025	Pul	2 BTC	30	---	---	.027H	.027H	30	30	4	9
560 Diesel	6-3 11/16 × 4 3/8	282	153624	Injection 3° BTC								.027H	.027H	45	45	5 1/8	9
600, 650 Gas.	4-4 1/2 × 5 1/2	350	1342	.020	.013	.023	Pul	TDC	40	TDC	---	.017H	.017H	45	45	8½	11
650 LPG	4-4 1/2 × 5 1/2	350	1342	.020	---	.023	Pul	TDC	40	---	---	.017H	.017H	45	45	8½	11
660 Gas.	6-3 9/16 × 4 3/8	263	153624	.021	---	.025	Pul	2 BTC	30	---	---	.027H	.027H	45	45	5	9
660 Diesel	6-3 11/16 × 4 3/8	282	153624	Injection 5° BTC								.027H	.027H	45	45	6	9
A, AV, B, BN, C, Sup A, AV	4-3 × 4	113.1	1342	.020	.013	.025	Fly	TDC	40	TDC	35	.014H	.014H	45	45	3¼	5
Super C	4-3 1/8 × 4	122.7	1342	.020	.013	.025	Fly	TDC	30	TDC	35	.014H	.014H	45	45	3¾	5
H, HV, O4, OS4, W4	4-3 3/8 × 4 1/4	152.1	1342	.020	.013	.025	Pul	TDC	40	TDC	35	.017H	.017H	45	45	4¼	6
Super H, HV, W4	4-3 1/2 × 4 1/4	164	1342	.020	.013	.025	Pul	TDC	30	TDC	35	.017H	.017H	45	45	4 1/8	6
M, MV, O6, OS6, W6	4-3 7/8 × 5 1/4	248.7	1342	.020	.013	.025	Pul	TDC	40	TDC	35	.017H	.017H	45	45	6	8
Super MTA, W6TA	4-4 × 5 1/4	264	1342	.020	.013	.025	Pul	TDC	30	TDC	35	.017H	.017H	45	45	6¼	8
W9, WR9	4-4.4 × 5.5	334.5	1342	.020	.013	.025	Pul	TDC	40	TDC	35	.017H	.017H	45	45	10	11
WR9S	4-4.4 × 5.5	334.5	1342	.020	.013	.023	Pul	TDC	40	TDC	35	.017H	.017H	45	45	8½	11

** – International 17½ qts.
(A) – Distilate 30° BTC, LPGas 16° BTC

(B) – Distributor Full Advance – Gas. 25° BTC, Distilate 30° BTC, LPGas 16° BTC

MASSEY-FERGUSON

MASSEY-FERGUSON																	
TO-35 Gas.	4-3 5/16 × 3 7/8	134	1342	.022	---	.025	Fly	6 BTC	30 BTC	---	---	.013H	.013H	30	45	2½	5
TO-35 Diesel	4-3 5/16 × 4	137.8	1342	Injection 17° BTDC								.012C	.008C	45	45	2¼	7
MF-50 Gas.	4-3 5/16 × 3 7/8	134	1342	.022	---	.025	Fly	6 BTC	30 BTC	---	---	.013H	.013H	30	45	2½	5
MF-65 Diesel	4-3.6 × 5.0	203.5	1342	Injection 18° BTDC								.010H	.010H	45	45	2½	6
MF-65 Gas.	4-3.578×4.375	176	1342	.022	---	.026	Fly	6 BTC	28 BTC	---	---	.016H	.018H	30	45	2¾	5
MF-65 LPG	4-3.578×4.375	176	1342	.022	---	.026	Fly	4 BTC	26 BTC	---	---	.016H	.018H	30	45	2¾	5
MF-85 Gas.	4-3 7/8 × 5 1/8	242	1342	.022	---	.025	Fly	5 BTC	21 BTC	---	---	.016H	.018H	30	45	3¾	7
MF-85 LPG	4-3 7/8 × 5 1/8	242	1342	.022	---	.025	Fly	4 BTC	12 BTC	---	---	.016H	.018H	30	45	3¾	7
MF-85 Diesel	4-4 × 5 1/2	276.4	1342	Injection 20° BTDC								.014H	.014H	45	45	5½	7

Tractor Specifications and Tune-Up—continued

MASSEY-FERGUSON Continued

MAKE AND MODEL	No. Cylinder Bore and Stroke	Piston Displacement cu. in.	Firing Order	Point Gap Dist.	Point Gap Mag.	Spark Plug Gap	Ignition Timing Location	Ignition Timing (degrees) Distributor Retard	Distributor Full Adv.	Magneto Retard	Magneto Full Adv.	Tappet Clearance In	Tappet Clearance Ex	Seat Angle (deg.) In	Seat Angle (deg.) Ex	Capacities Water Gal.	Capacities Oil Qts.
MF-88 Gas.	4-3 7/8 × 5 1/8	242	1342	.022	---	.025	Fly	5 BTC	21 BTC	---	---	.016H	.018H	30	45	3 3/4	7
MF-88 Diesel	4-4 × 5 1/2	276.4	1342				Injection 20° BTDC					.014H	.014H	45	45	5 1/2	7
MF-202 Gas.	4-3 5/16 × 3 7/8	134	1342	.022	---	.025	Fly	6 BTC	30 BTC	---	---	.011H	.013H	30	45	2 1/2	5
MF-204 Gas.	4-3 5/16 × 3 7/8	134	1342	.022	---	.025	Fly	6 BTC	30 BTC	---	---	.011H	.013H	30	45	2 1/2	5
MF-303 Gas.	4-3 11/16 × 4 7/8	208	1342	.022	---	.025	Fly	TDC	18 BTC	---	---	.014H	.014H	30	45	4 3/8	7
MF-303 Diesel	4-3 11/16 × 4 7/8	208	1342				Injection 22° BTDC					.014H	.014H	45	45	5 3/4	7
MF-404 Gas.	4-4 × 5 1/2	277	1342	.020	---	.025	Fly	TDC	18 BTC	---	---	.014H	.014H	30	45	5 1/2	7
MF-404 Diesel	4-4 × 5 1/2	277	1342				Injection 25° BTDC *					.014H	.014H	45	45	5 3/4	7
MF-1001 Gas.	4-3 11/16 × 4 7/8	208	1342	.020	---	.025	Fly	TDC	18 BTC	---	---	.014H	.014H	30	45	4 3/8	7
MF-1001 Diesel	4-3 11/16 × 4 7/8	208	1342				Injection 22° BTDC					.014H	.014H	45	45	5 3/4	7

* – APE pump – 32½° BTC

MASSEY-HARRIS

MAKE AND MODEL	No. Cylinder Bore and Stroke	Piston Displacement cu. in.	Firing Order	Point Gap Dist.	Point Gap Mag.	Spark Plug Gap	Ignition Timing Location	Ignition Timing (degrees) Distributor Retard	Distributor Full Adv.	Magneto Retard	Magneto Full Adv.	Tappet Clearance In	Tappet Clearance Ex	Seat Angle (deg.) In	Seat Angle (deg.) Ex	Capacities Water Gal.	Capacities Oil Qts.
MASSEY-HARRIS																	
Pony	4-2 3/8 × 3 1/2	62	1342	.020	---	.025	Fly	TDC	10 BTC	---	---	.012C	.012C	45	45	2	4
Colt (Gas.)	4-3 × 4 3/8	124	1342	.020	---	.025	Fly	TDC	16 BTC	---	---	.014H	.014H	30	45	4	5
Mustang (Gas.)	4-3 3/16 × 4 3/8	140	1342	.020	---	.025	Fly	TDC	16 BTC	---	---	.014H	.014H	30	45	4	5
20 LPG	4-3 × 4 3/8	124	1342	.020	---	.025	Fly	TDC	(D)	---	---	.014H	.014H	30	45	2 3/4	r
20K	4-3 3/16 × 4 3/8	140	1342	.020	---	.025	Fly	TDC	(D)	---	---	.014H	.014H	30	45	2 3/4	4
22	4-3 3/16 × 4 3/8	140	1342	.020	---	.025	Fly	TDC	(D)	---	---	.014H	.014H	30	45	2 3/4	5
22K, 22RT	4-3 3/16 × 4 3/8	140	1342	.020	---	.025	Fly	TDC	(D)	---	---	.014H	.014H	30	45	2 3/4	5
30	4-3 7/16 × 4 3/8	162	1342	.020	---	.025	Fly	TDC	(D)	---	---	.014H	.014H	30	45	3	4
33	4-3 5/8 × 4 7/8	201	1342	.020	---	.025	Fly	TDC	(B)	---	---	.014H	.014H	30	45	5 1/2	7
44 Special	4-3 7/8 × 5 1/2	260	1342	.020	---	.025	Fly	TDC	(A)	---	---	.016H	.016H	30	45	5 3/4	8
44-6 Gas.	6-3 5/16 × 4 3/8	226	153624	.020	---	.025	Fly	TDC	(D)	---	---	.014H	.014H	30	45	4	5
55, 555 Gas.	4-4 1/2 × 6	382	1342	.020	---	.025	Fly	TDC	(C)	---	---	.014H	.014H	30	45	7	9
81	4-3 × 4 3/8	124	1342	.020	---	.025	Fly	TDC	(D)	---	---	.014H	.014H	30	45	2 3/4	4
82	4-3 × 4 3/8	124	1342	.020	---	.025	Fly	TDC	(D)	---	---	.014H	.014H	30	45	2 3/4	4
101 Gas.	6-3 1/8 × 4 3/8	201	153624	.020	---	.025	Fly	.003" ATC	(D)	---	---	.008H	.012H	45	45	4	5
101 Jr, 102G (Gas.)	4-3 × 4 3/8	124	1342	.020	.020	.025	Fly	TDC	(D)	---	---	.014H	.014H	30	45	2 3/4	4
101 Jr	4-3 3/16 × 4 3/8	140	1342	.020	.020	.025	Fly	TDC	(D)	TDC	N.A.	.014H	.014H	30	45	2 3/4	4
101 Jr	4-3 7/16 × 4 3/8	162	1342	.020	.020	.025	Fly	TDC	(D)	TDC	N.A.	.014H	.014H	30	45	2 3/4	4
101 Sr	6-3 5/16 × 4 3/8	226	153624	.020	.020	.025	Fly	TDC	(D)	TDC	N.A.	.014H	.014H	30	45	3 1/2	5
102 Jr	4-3 3/16 × 4 3/8	140	1342	.020	.020	.025	Fly	TDC	(D)	TDC	N.A.	.014H	.014H	30	45	2 3/4	4
102 Sr	4-3 7/16 × 4 3/8	162	1342	.020	.020	.025	Fly	TDC	(D)	TDC	N.A.	.014H	.014H	30	45	2 3/4	4
102 Sr (Low)	6-3 7/16 × 4 3/8	244	153624	.020	.020	.025	Fly	TDC	(D)	TDC	N.A.	.020H	.020H	30	45	4 3/4	6
102G-Sr	6-3 5/16 × 4 3/8	226	153624	.020	.020	.025	Fly	TDC	(D)	TDC	N.A.	.014H	.014H	30	45	4 3/4	6
201 Gas.	6-3 7/16 × 4 1/2	251	153624	.020	---	.025	Fly	TDC	(D)	---	---	.008H	.012H	45	45	4 1/2	5
202 Gas.	6-3 3/8 × 4 3/8	290	153624	.020	---	.025	Fly	TDC	(D)	---	---	.017H	.020H	30	45	4 1/2	7
203	6-4 × 4 3/8	330	153624	.020	---	.025	Fly	TDC	(D)	---	---	.017H	.020H	30	45	5 1/2	7
203G	6-4 × 4 3/8	330	153624	.020	---	.025	Fly	TDC	(D)	---	---	.017H	.020H	30	45	5 1/2	7

(A) – Dist. advanced timing – Gasoline 18° BTDC, Low Grade 24° BTDC, LPG 16° BTDC.

(B) – Dist. advanced timing – Gasoline 16° BTDC, Low Grade 18° BTDC

(C) – Dist. advanced timing – Gasoline 16° BTDC, Low Grade 18° BTDC, LPG 16° BTDC.

(D) – With vacuum gauge attached to manifold and engine at above 1,000 R.P.M., advance distributor to point of highest gauge and R.P.M. reading. Now start to retard distributor until R.P.M. and vacuum reading just starts to drop. Lock up distributor.

N.A. – Not available.

MAKE AND MODEL	No. Cylinder Bore and Stroke	Piston Displacement cu. in.	Firing Order	Point Gap Dist.	Point Gap Mag.	Spark Plug Gap	Ignition Timing Location	Distributor Retard	Distributor Full Adv.	Magneto Retard	Magneto Full Adv.	Tappet Clearance In	Tappet Clearance Ex	Seat Angle In	Seat Angle Ex	Water Gal.	Oil Qts.

MINNEAPOLIS-MOLINE

MINNEAPOLIS - MOLINE																	
BF Gas.	4-3¼×4	133	1243	.021	---	.025	Fly	TC	---	---	---	.006H	.008&	30	30	2¾	5
BG Gas.	4-3¼×4	133	1243	.021	--	.025	Fly	TC	---	---	---	.006H	.008H	30	30	2¾	5
GB Gas.	4-4⅝×6	403.2	1342	.020	---	.025	Fly	♦ 4⅛"	---	---	---	.008H	.010H	45	45	12	9
GB LPG	4-4⅝×6	403.2	1342	.020	---	.025	Fly	♦ 4⅜"	---	---	---	.008H	.010H	45	45	12	9
GB Diesel	6-4¼×5	425.5	153624	Injection 27° BTDC								.008H	.010H	45	45	12	14
GTA Gas.	4-4⅝×6	403	1342	.020	.020	.025	Fly	5° ATC	27	8	27	.008H	.010H	45	45	7	9
GTB Gas.	4-4⅝×6	403	1342	.020	.020	.025	Fly	5° ATC	27	8	27	.008H	.010H	45	45	12	9
G VI Gas.	6-4¼×5	425	153624	.022	---	.024	Fly	◈ 4 1/16"	---	---	---	.008H	.010H	45	45	12½	14
M5 Gas.	4-4⅝×5	336	1342	.020	---	.024	Fly	◈ 3⅛"	999	---	---	.008H	.010H	45	45	5½	9
R Gas.	4-3⅝×4	165	1342	.020	.020	.025	Fly	(1) 8° ATC	(2) 17	(1) 8	(2) 17	.008H	.010H	45	45	3½	7
U Gas.	4-4¼×5	283	1342	.020	.020	.025	Fly	(3) 7° ATC	(4) 25	(5) 10	(4) 25	.008H	.010H	45	45	6	9
UB Gas.	4-4¼×5	283	1342	.020	---	.025	Fly	♦ 3⅞"	---	---	---	.008H	.010H	45	45	6	9
UB LPG	4-4¼×5	283	1342	.020	---	.025	Fly	♦ 4⅛"	---	---	---	.008H	.010H	45	45	6	9
UB Diesel	4-4¼×5	283	1342	Injection 27° BTDC								.008H	.010H	45	45	6	9
V Gas.	4-2⅝×3	65	1243	.021	---	.024	Fly	TC	---	---	---	.006H	.006H	30	30	1½	3
ZA Gas.	4-3⅝×5	206	1342	.020	.020	.025	Fly	7° ATC	18	8	17	.008H	.010H	45	45	6	9
ZB Gas.	4-3⅝×5	206	1342	.020	---	.025	Fly	◈ 2⅛"	---	---	---	.008H	.010H	45	45	3¾	7
ZB LPG	4-3⅝×5	206	1342	.020	---	.025	Fly	◈ 1¾"	---	---	---	.088H	.010H	45	45	3¾	7
ZT	4-3⅝×4½	185.8	1342	.020	.020	.025	Fly	(1) 9° ATC	(2) 16	(1) 9	(2) 16	.008H	.010H	45	45	3½	7
5 Star Gas.	4-4¼×5	283	1342	.022	---	.024	Fly	◈ 3¼	---	---	---	.008H	.010H	45	45	5½	9
335 Gas.	4-3⅝×4	165	1342	.020	---	.024	Fly	**	**	---	---	.008H	.010H	45	45	2¾	8
335 LPG	4-3⅝×4	165	1342	.020	---	.021	Fly	"DC-1"	25	---	---	.008H	.010H	45	45	2¾	8
445 Gas.	4-3⅝×5	206	1342	.020	---	.021	Fly	"DC-1"	25	---	---	.008H	.010H	45	45	3⅜	8
445 LPG	4-3⅝×5	206	1342	.020	---	.021	Fly	†	28	---	---	.008H	.010H	45	45	3⅜	8
Uni-Tractor	4-3⅝×5	206.5	1342	.022	---	.025	Fly	6° ADC	18	---	---	.008H	.010H	45	45	4¾	7

(1) – High Comp. Head, Low Comp. Head 7° ATC
(2) – High Comp. Head, Low Comp. Head 18° BTC
(3) – High Comp. Head, Low Comp. Head 5° ATC
(4) – High Comp. Head, Low Comp. Head 27° BTC
(5) – High Comp. Head, Low Comp. Head 8° ATC

** – Distributor retarded timing 1° before "DC-1" mark
** – Distributor advance timing 24° BTC
† – Distributor advance timing 3° before "DC-1" mark
● – At no load speed of 1430 R.P.M.
◈ – At no load speed of 1500 R.P.M.
♦ – At no load speed of 1650 R.P.M.

OLIVER

OLIVER																	
66HC Gas.	4 × 3 5/16 × 3¾	129	1243	.022	.015	.025	Fly	TDC	22 BTC	5 ATC	15 BTC	.009C	.016C	45	45	3.5	4
66D Diesel	4 – 3 5/16 × 3¾	129	1243	Injection 23° BTDC								.009C	.016C	45	45	3.5	4
66KD	4 – 3½ × 3¾	144	1243	.022	.015	.025	Fly	5 BTC	27 BTC	5 ATC	15 BTC	.009C	.016C	45	45	3.5	4
Super 66HC Gas.	4 – 3½ × 3¾	144	1243	.022	---	.025	Fly	TDC	28 BTC	---	---	.010C	.010C	45	45	3.5	4
Super 66D Diesel	4 – 3½ × 3¾	144	1243	Injection 26° BTDC								.010C	.020C	45	45	3.5	4
550HC Gas.	4 – 3½ × 3¾	144	1243	.022	---	.025	Fly	TDC	28 BTC	---	---	.010C	.016C	45	45	3.5	4
550 Diesel	4 – 3½ × 3¾	144	1243	Injection 26° BTDC								.010C	.020C	45	45	3.5	4
77HC, 77 LPG	6 – 3 5/16 × 3¾	194	153624	.022	.015	.025	Fly	TDC	22 BTC	5 ATC	15 BTC	.009C	.016C	45	45	4.5	5
77D Diesel	6 – 3 5/16 × 3¾	194	153624	Injection 23° BTDC								.009C	.016C	45	45	4.5	5
Super 99GM Diesel	3 – 4¼ × 5	213	132	Injection 1.460" Gauge # J1853 **								---	.009H	---	30	5.5	11
77KD	6 – 3½ × 3¾	216	153624	.022	.015	.025	Fly	5 BTC	27 BTC	5 ATC	15 BTC	.009C	.016C	45	45	4.5	11
Super 77HC, 770HC	6 – 3½ × 3¾	216	153624	.022	---	.025	Fly	TDC	22 BTC	---	---	.010C	.016C	45	45	4.5	5
Super 77D, 770D	6 – 3½ × 3¾	216	153624	Injection 23° BTDC								.010C	.020C	45	45	4.5	5
88HC, 88 LPG	6 – 3½ × 4	231	153624	.022	.015	.025	Fly	TDC	22 BTC	5 ATC	15 BTC	.009C	.016C	45	45	4.5	6
88D	6 – 3½ × 4	231	153624	Injection 23° BTDC								.009C	.016C	45	45	4.5	6
88KD	6 – 3¾ × 4	265	153624	.022	.015	.025	Fly	5 BTC	27 BTC	5 ATC	15 BTC	.009C	.016C	45	45	4.5	6
Super 88HC, 880HC	6 – 3¾ × 4	265	153624	.022	---	.025	Fly	TDC	22 BTC	---	---	.010C	.016C	45	45	4.5	6
Super 88D, 880D	6 – 3¾ × 4	265	153624	Injection 23° BTDC								.010C	.020C	45	45	4.5	6
99HC	6 – 4 × 4	302	153624	.022	.015	.025	Fly	TDC	28 BTC	---	Ign.	.009C	.016C	45	45	5¼	6
99D Diesel	6 – 4 × 4	302	153624	Injection 24½° BTDC								.009C	.016C	45	45	5¼	6
Super 99HC	6 – 4 × 4	302	153624	.022	.015	.025	Fly	TDC	28 BTC	---	Ign.	.009C	.016C	45	45	5½	6
Super 99D Diesel	6 – 4 × 4	302	153624	Injection 24½° BTDC								.009C	.016C	45	45	5½	6

** – 1.484" using Gauge # J1242

THREAD INSERTS

Aluminum is the most abundant metallic element in existence. Science has made great strides in the development of this versatile product of "Bauxite" from the time of its discovery about 100 years ago. In its pure state it is silvery-white, very light in weight and has extremely good heat and electrical conduction qualities. These two properties make it very desirable for use in the automobile industry.

Whether or not it will dominate the ferrous metals in automotive and truck construction is questionable but it is increasing in popularity. Sufficient quantities of aluminum are in use today to warrant field maintenance consideration.

Aluminum, when alloyed to a desirable quality for engine building, transmission case construction and certain other applications, has one outstanding need: the thread strength to hold attaching and mounting bolts.

Published material on the treatment and handling procedures for aluminum products in the field have been sadly neglected. In many cases parts replacement has been the logical choice, over makeshift repairs.

Any of the repair shops or garages having maintenance facilities for automobiles, trucks or power equipment need a method for dealing with aluminum. In some cases, an entire cylinder block, crankcase or transmission case may have to be scrapped because of one hole in which stripped threads can't be repaired. Or a unit may be put out of service for a long time while the threads are repaired by drilling oversize and retapping or by welding and redrilling.

Permanent repairs to stripped spark plug holes, gear cases, cylinder

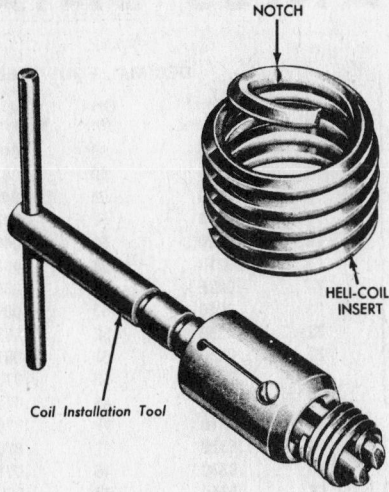

Coil Installation Tool

NOTCH

HELI-COIL INSERT

blocks, intake and exhaust manifolds or virtually any point can now be repaired quickly and on the spot. This is accomplished by the use of stainless steel wire thread inserts.

Wire screw thread inserts are precision formed coils of various sizes. They are tailored to accept a bolt or stud of the original size. When inserted into a hole, the diamond shaped wire forms nominal size internal threads that are stronger and more durable than the original aluminum threads. Greater thread load is possible and wear resistance is improved.

For convenience, inserts are packaged in kits of the most popular sizes. Each kit contains inserts of a given thread size with a tap and inserting tool, a separate "T" handle to drive the inserting tools and a pressure plate for easy starting of inserts. Sizes are available from 8-32 through 5/8"-11.

To repair damaged threads the following procedure should be carefully followed:

1. Drill damaged threads out of the stripped hole. Use the same drill size as the bolt thread O.D. as an example, use a 5/16" drill for a 5/16"-18 thread.

2. Select the correct SPECIAL tap supplied with the kit. The tap is marked for the size and thread desired. As an example, the SPECIAL tap marked 5/16"-18 will not cut the same thread as a standard 5/16"-18 tap. It will, however, form a thread large enough to suit the coiled insert.

AFTER THE INSERT IS INSTALLED, THE ORIGINAL THREAD SIZE IS RESTORED.

3. Select the correct thread inserting tool. These tools are marked for the hole and threat size to be restored. Place the thread insert on the tool and adjust the sleeve to the proper length for the insert being used. Press the insert against the face of the tapped hole while turning the tool clockwise. This will wind the insert into the drilled hole. Continue this action until the isert is ½ turn below the face of the work.

4. Reaching through the thread insert, bend the insert tang straight up and down until it breaks off at the notch.

5. If an error has been made and the results are unsatisfactory, the insert can be removed with the extractor tool. Place the extractor tool in the insert so that the blade contacts the top turn of the coil, ¼ to ½ turn from the end. Tap the tool solidly with a hammer. This will cause the blade to cut into the insert. Press downward on the tool and turn it counterclockwise until the insert is removed.

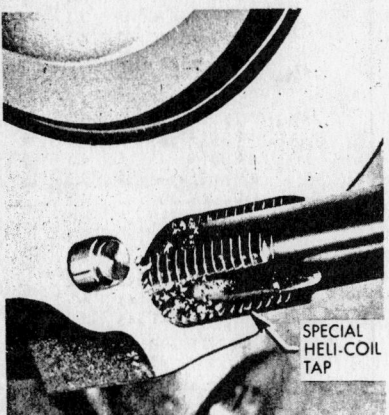

SPECIAL HELI-COIL TAP

Tapping New Thread

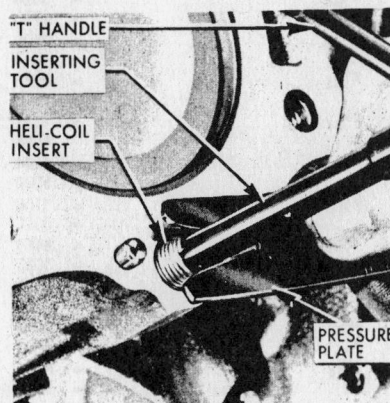

"T" HANDLE

INSERTING TOOL

HELI-COIL INSERT

PRESSURE PLATE

Installing Insert

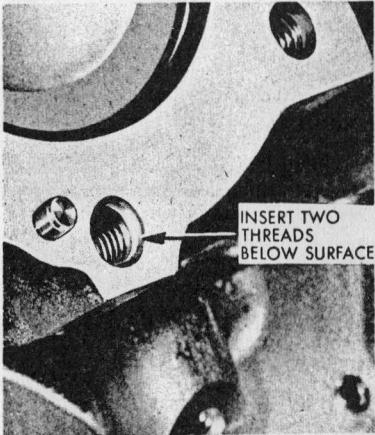

INSERT TWO THREADS BELOW SURFACE

Heli-Coil Insert

MECHANICS DATA PAGE

TABLE OF TAP DRILL SIZES
National Coarse or U.S.S.

Screw & Tap Size	Threads Per Inch	Use Drill Number
No. 5	40	39
No. 6	32	36
No. 8	32	29
No. 10	24	25
No. 12	24	17
1/4	20	8
5/16	18	F
3/8	16	5/16
7/16	14	U
1/2	13	27/64
9/16	12	31/64
5/8	11	17/32
3/4	10	21/32
7/8	9	49/64
1	8	7/8
1 1/8	7	63/64
1 1/4	7	1 7/64
1 1/2	6	1 11/32

National Fine or S.A.E.

Screw & Tap Size	Threads Per Inch	Use Drill Number
No. 5	44	37
No. 6	40	33
No. 8	36	29
No. 10	32	21
No. 12	28	15
1/4	28	3
5/16	24	I
3/8	24	Q
7/16	20	W
1/2	20	29/64
9/16	18	33/64
5/8	18	37/64
3/4	16	11/16
7/8	14	13/16
1 1/8	12	13/64
1 1/4	12	1 11/64
1 1/2	12	1 27/64

DECIMAL EQUIVALENT SIZE OF THE NUMBER DRILLS

Drill No.	Decimal Equivalent	Drill No.	Decimal Equivalent	Drill No.	Decimal Equivalent	Drill No.	Decimal Equivalent
80	.0135	60	.0400	40	.0980	20	.1610
79	.0145	59	.0410	39	.0995	19	.1660
78	.0160	58	.0420	38	.1015	18	.1695
77	.0180	57	.0430	37	.1040	17	.1730
76	.0200	56	.0465	36	.1065	16	.1770
75	.0210	55	.0520	35	.1100	15	.1800
74	.0225	54	.0550	34	.1110	14	.1820
73	.0240	53	.0595	33	.1130	13	.1850
72	.0250	52	.0635	32	.1160	12	.1890
71	.0260	51	.0670	31	.1200	11	.1910
70	.0280	50	.0700	30	.1285	10	.1935
69	.0292	49	.0730	29	.1360	9	.1960
68	.0310	48	.0760	28	.1405	8	.1990
67	.0320	47	.0785	27	.1440	7	.2010
66	.0330	46	.0810	26	.1470	6	.2040
65	.0350	45	.0820	25	.1495	5	.2055
64	.0360	44	.0860	24	.1520	4	.2090
63	.0370	43	.0890	23	.1540	3	.2130
62	.0380	42	.0935	22	.1570	2	.2210
61	.0390	41	.0960	21	.1590	1	.2280

DECIMAL EQUIVALENT SIZE OF THE LETTER DRILLS

Letter Drill	Decimal Equivalent	Letter Drill	Decimal Equivalent
A	.234	N	.302
B	.238	O	.316
C	.242	P	.323
D	.246	Q	.332
E	.250	R	.339
F	.257	S	.348
G	.261	T	.358
H	.266	U	.368
I	.272	V	.377
J	.277	W	.386
K	.281	X	.397
L	.290	Y	.404
M	.295	Z	.413

TABLE OF DECIMAL EQUIVALENTS OF THE COMMON FRACTIONS

1/64			= .0156
	1/32		= .0313
3/64			= .0469
		1/16	= .0625
5/64			= .0781
	3/32		= .0938
7/64			= .1094
		1/8	= .1250
9/64			= .1406
	5/32		= .1563
11/64			= .1719
		3/16	= .1875
13/64			= .2031
	7/32		= .2188
15/64			= .2344
		1/4	= .2500
17/64			= .2656
	9/32		= .2813
19/64			= .2969
		5/16	= .3125

21/64			= .3281
	11/32		= .3438
23/64			= .3594
		3/8	= .3750
25/64			= .3906
	13/32		= .4063
27/64			= .4219
		7/16	= .4375
29/64			= .4531
	15/32		= .4688
31/64			= .4844
		1/2	= .5000
33/64			= .5156
	17/32		= .5313
35/64			= .5469
		9/16	= .5625
37/64			= .5781
	19/32		= .5938
39/64			= .6094
		5/8	= .6250
41/64			= .6406
	21/32		= .6563

43/64			= .6719
		11/16	= .6875
45/64			= .7031
	23/32		= .7188
47/64			= .7344
		3/4	= .7500
49/64			= .7656
	25/32		= .7813
51/64			= .7969
		13/16	= .8125
53/64			= .8281
	27/32		= .8438
55/64			= .8594
		7/8	= .8750
57/64			= .8906
	29/32		= .9063
59/64			= .9219
		15/16	= .9375
61/64			= .9531
	31/32		= .9688
63/64			= .9844

PUSHING OR TOWING AUTO. TRANS.

There are two reasons to push or tow a disabled car. One is to supplement the regular electrical starting system of engine cranking. The other reason is to get the crippled car to some other location. In either case care must be considered to avoid damage to the transmissions of vehicles equipped with automatic units.

If it becomes necessary to push or tow a vehicle so equipped, the following chart should be used for reference.

"Do Not Tow" in the accompanying chart means, do not tow the car with the rear wheels on the ground unless the driveshaft has been disconnected.

For positive transmission-to-car identification, refer to "Transmission Identification Chart," page 704 of this manual.

TRANSMISSION	PUSHING	TOWING	
		MAX. SPEED	MAX. DISTANCE
CHRYSLER PRODUCTS			
POWERFLITE	SHIFT INTO "L" AT 25 M.P.H.	35	100
TORQUEFLITE "A"	SHIFT INTO "L" AT 20 M.P.H.	35	100
TORQUEFLITE "B"	SHIFT INTO "L" AT 15 M.P.H.	35	100
FORD PRODUCTS			
AUTOMATIC	SHIFT INTO "L" AT 30 M.P.H.	15	35
COMET-DRIVE	SHIFT INTO "L" AT 25 M.P.H.	30	15
CRUISE-O-MATIC	SHIFT INTO "L" AT 25 M.P.H.	30	15
FORD-O-MATIC	SHIFT INTO "L" AT 30 M.P.H.	35	15
FORD-O-MATIC 2 SPEED	SHIFT INTO "L" AT 25 M.P.H.	30	15
MERC-O-MATIC	SHIFT INTO "L" AT 25 M.P.H.	35	15
MERC-O-MATIC, 2 SPEED	SHIFT INTO "L" AT 25 M.P.H.	30	15
MILE-O-MATIC	SHIFT INTO "L" AT 30 M.P.H.	35	15
MULTI-DRIVE	SHIFT INTO "L" AT 25 M.P.H.	40	15
TURBO-DRIVE	SHIFT INTO "L" AT 25 M.P.H.	40	15
TWIN RANGE TURBO	SHIFT INTO "L" AT 25 M.P.H.	40	15
GENERAL MOTORS			
CONTROLLED COUPLING	SHIFT INTO "D" AT 30 M.P.H. (NOTE 3)	35	50
DUAL PATH	WILL NOT START BY PUSHING	15	5
DUAL RANGE HYD.	SHIFT INTO "D" AT 25 M.P.H.	DO NOT TOW	
DYNAFLOW	SHIFT INTO "L" AT 15 M.P.H.	15	5
DYNAFLOW FLIGHT P.	SHIFT INTO "G" AT 30 M.P.H. (NOTE 1)	40	UNLIMITED
DYNAFLOW VAR. P.	SHIFT INTO "L" AT 15 M.P.H.	15	5
HYDRAMATIC, 3 SPEED	WILL NOT START BY PUSHING	15	5
JETAWAY HYDRA.	SHIFT INTO "D" AT 35 M.P.H. (NOTE 3)	DO NOT TOW	
POWERGLIDE "A"	SHIFT INTO "L" AT 25 M.P.H.	15	5
POWERGLIDE "B"	SHIFT INTO "L" AT 25 M.P.H. (NOTE 2)	15	5
STRATO-FLIGHT	SHIFT INTO "D" AT 35 M.P.H. (NOTE 3)	DO NOT TOW	
TURBOGLIDE	SHIFT INTO "HR" OR "GR" AT 30 M.P.H.	15	5
AMERICAN MOTORS			
FLASHAWAY	SHIFT INTO "D" AT 25 M.P.H.	DO NOT TOW	
FLASH-O-MATIC	SHIFT INTO "D1" AT 30 M.P.H.	15	5
STUDEBAKER CORP.			
STUDEBAKER AUTO.	SHIFT INTO "D" OR "L" AT 20 M.P.H.	15	5
FLIGHT-O-MATIC	SHIFT INTO "L" AT 20 M.P.H.	15	5

NOTE 1—1959 MODEL HAS NO REAR PUMP, WILL NOT START BY PUSHING
NOTE 2—CORVAIR, TREAT THE SAME AS POWERGLIDE "B"
NOTE 3—BEGINNING 1959, WILL NOT START BY PUSHING